WISDEN

PUBLISHED EVERY
YEAR SINCE 1864

www.wisden.com

138TH YEAR

WISDEN
CRICKETERS' ALMANACK
2001

EDITED BY GRAEME WRIGHT

PUBLISHED BY JOHN WISDEN & CO LTD
25 DOWN ROAD, MERROW
GUILDFORD, SURREY GU1 2PY

Cased edition ISBN 0 947766 63 4	£29.99
Soft cover edition ISBN 0 947766 64 2	£29.99
Leatherbound edition ISBN 0 947766 65 0	£225.00

Published in 2001 by
JOHN WISDEN & CO LTD
25 Down Road, Merrow, Guildford, Surrey GU1 2PY
Tel: 01483 570358   Fax: 01483 533153
E-mail: wisden@ndirect.co.uk
Website: www.wisden.com

Computer typeset by LazerType, Colchester

Printed and bound in Great Britain by Clays Ltd, St Ives plc
Distributed by The Penguin Group
Distributed in Australia by Hardie Grant Books, Melbourne

SIR DONALD BRADMAN
1908–2001

Literally as this *Wisden* was being printed, we received news of the death of Sir Donald Bradman. He was 92 and had been ill for some time. Yet his passing still came as a surprise, for it seemed inconceivable that he would not reach three figures. Only a year ago, in the 2000 Almanack, he was the only one of *Wisden's* Five Cricketers of the Century to receive 100 per cent of the votes. He averaged a hundred every third innings. The words Bradman and century seemed synonymous.

It is a sign of the great esteem in which Sir Donald was held, not only as a cricketer but as a sportsman, that *Wisden's* printers intuitively held back these opening pages, aware that we would want to include this notice, however brief and at the last minute. An obituary, a personal memory by Jim Swanton, and other tributes will appear in *Wisden* 2002.

While cricket followers around the world mourned "The Don", Australians felt his loss most keenly. Through his batting in the 1930s, he had transcended the cricket ground and entered the consciousness of the emerging nation. He was more than the maker of hundreds, the compiler of record-breaking innings, the captain who led his "Invincibles" unbeaten through England in 1948. Sir Donald Bradman was a national icon.

It goes without saying that he was the greatest batsman of all time. His record is unsurpassed, and may remain so. No one comes close to his Test average of 99.94 and first-class career average of 95.14. Crowds flocked to see him bat, but there was more to his innings than the mere accumulation of runs. It was the dynamic way he went about them; the way, as Neville Cardus put it, he knocked "solemnity to smithereens". Those of us who never saw him bat, except perhaps on film, can only study the figures, devour the legends and, closing our eyes, imagine what it must have been like to be there.

Whether as player or administrator, Sir Donald Bradman always encouraged what was best for the development of cricket. He welcomed change, and the articles he wrote for *Wisden* confirm that he was never a reactionary thinker. He had a deep feeling for cricket's welfare and tackled the game's problems fearlessly. Cricket was richer beyond measure for his life; the high standards he set on and off the field, both as a cricketer and a private, humble man, are his legacy.

CONTRIBUTORS

Tanya Aldred
David Rayvern Allen
Andy Arlidge
Chris Aspin
Mike Atherton
Philip Bailey
Jack Bannister
Colin Bateman
Peter Bather
Mike Berry
Scyld Berry
Edward Bevan
J. Watson Blair
Lawrence Booth
Mihir Bose
Stephen Brenkley
Simon Briggs
Robert Brooke
Colin Bryden
Don Cameron
Malcolm Conn
Craig Cozier

Tony Cozier
John Curtis
Geoffrey Dean
Peter Deeley
Ralph Dellor
Norman de Mesquita
Hubert Doggart
Philip Eden
Matthew Engel
Colin Evans
Stephen Fay
Paul Fearn
David Foot
Neville Foulger
Nigel Fuller
Andrew Gidley
David Green
David Hallett
Matthew Hancock
David Hardy
Peter S. Hargreaves
Norman Harris

Samiul Hasan
Les Hatton
Simon Heffer
Richard Hobson
Grenville Holland
David Hopps
Gerald Howat
Martin Johnson
Abid Ali Kazi
Frank Keating
Kate Laven
David Llewellyn
Steven Lynch
John MacKinnon
Neil Manthorp
Vic Marks
Mohandas Menon
Fazeer Mohammed
R. Mohan
Gerald Mortimer
Andy Oldfield
Francis Payne

Gordon Phillips
Derek Pringle
Andrew Radd
Gillian Reynolds
Jonathan Rice
Graham Russell
Dicky Rutnagur
Carol Salmon
Andrew Samson
Derek Scott
Mike Selvey
Utpal Shuvro
Jasmer Singh
Rob Steen
John Stern
Pat Symes
Sa'adi Thawfeeq
Gerry Vaidyasekera
Gordon Vince
John Ward
David Warner
Tim Wellock

Photographers: Briony Allen, Jack Atley, Hamish Blair, Gordon Brooks, John Dawson, Patrick Eagar, Mike Finn-Kelcey, George Herringshaw, Savita Kirloskar, Ross Land, Darren McNamara, Terry Mahoney, Graham Morris, Mueen ud din Hameed, David Munden, Adrian Murrell, Juda Ngwenya, Mike Pollard, Bill Smith and Phil Walter.

Round the World: Anthony Adams, Musaji Banah, Saleh Banah, Ivan Burges, John Cribbin, Geoff Edwards, Haydn Evans, Brian Fell, T. J. Finlayson, Keith Foster, Simone Gambino, Bob Gibb, T. R. Illingworth, Shujaat Ali Khan, John McKillop, Philip Marsdale, Nicoline Palmier, David Parsons, Stanley Perlman, Jai Kumar Shah, Mark Stafford, Derek Thursby, Alan Waters, Bob Wellham, Colin Wolfe and Clive Woodbridge.

Thanks are accorded to the following for checking the scorecards of county and tourist matches: John Blondel, Keith Booth, John Brown, Len Chandler, Byron Denning, Jack Foley, Keith Gerrish, Sam Hale, Neil Harris, Brian Hewes, Brian Hunt, Vic Isaacs, David Kendix, Tony Kingston, Reg May, David Norris, Michael Snook, Gerry Stickley, Gordon Stringfellow, David Wainwright, Alan West, Roy Wilkinson and Graham York.

The editor also acknowledges with gratitude assistance from the following: David Armstrong, Nauman Bader, Eddie Bayton, Brian Bearshaw, Gerry Byrne, David Clark, Lynda Cole, Marion Collin, Brian Croudy, Simon Davie, Nigel Davies, Frank Duckworth, Robert Eastaway, M. L. Fernando, Ric Finlay, Christine Forrest, Bill Frindall, Ghulam Mustafa Khan, Ray Goble, Col. Malcolm Havergal, Kay Hewat, Andrew Hignell, Robin Isherwood, Mohammad Ali Jafri, Frank Kemp, Robin Knight, Rajesh Kumar, David J. Lamming, Stephanie Lawrence, Neil Leitch, Nirav Malavi, Mahendra Mapagunaratne, Pamela Monkhouse, Anthony Morrissey, Don Neely, Em Parkinson, Major R. W. K. Ross-Hurst, Andy Smith, Karen Spink, Mark Stead, Richard Streeton, Jan Traylen, Peter van der Merwe, Charlie Wat, Wendy Wimbush, John Woodcock, Roger Wootton and Peter Wynne-Thomas.

The production of *Wisden* would not be possible without the support and co-operation of many other cricket officials, writers and lovers of the game. To them all, many thanks.

CONTENTS

Part One: Comment

Part Two: The Players

Part Three: Records

Part Four: English Cricket in 2000

Part Five: Overseas Cricket in 1999-2000

Part Six: Administration and Laws

Part Seven: Miscellaneous

PART ONE: COMMENT

NOTES BY THE EDITOR

In Harvard Square in 1896, a man was knocked off his bike by a wagon and subsequently died. The wagon owners claimed that the accident "could not have been helped". "There are some things which must not happen," retorted Josiah Royce, professor of philosophy at Harvard. There are some things which can be avoided.

Royce's reply came back time and again as Hansie Cronje's reputation was peeled away, leaf by leaf, at the King Commission hearings last summer. It wasn't so much the facts themselves: the bribes from bookmakers, the attempts to fix matches and inveigle his team-mates into corrupting cricket's, indeed sport's, very ethos. It was the date when Cronje first crossed the line and accepted money from the Indian bookmaker, M. K. Gupta: 1996. We would learn later, through India's Central Bureau of Investigation, that Mohammad Azharuddin's involvement with Gupta began a year earlier. Still significant. It was in February 1995, you see, that Mark Waugh and Shane Warne admitted to the Australian Cricket Board that they had accepted money from another bookmaker. Admissions that the ACB, with the compliance of the International Cricket Council, whose chief executive was a former ACB employee, chose to keep under wraps. What I kept wondering was whether Azharuddin and Cronje would have become involved with Gupta had those two supposedly responsible organisations gone public immediately, and made an example of Waugh and Warne. As it was, the sound of silence rang out loud and clear both to bookmakers and cricketers. The game's administrators were not going to interfere in their activities. It took the Indian police to throw some light on cricket's darker side.

Cricketers are only cricketers

As Cronje's complicity was revealed, it was remarked that it was fortunate Jim Swanton was not here to witness this latest shame. It would have broken his heart, some said. Yet that misread the man. He would certainly not have condoned Cronje's behaviour; nor Azharuddin's. He would have been deeply saddened at the way cricket's reputation had once again been sullied by those who set their own interests above those of the game. But he would have been one of the first to find understanding and forgiveness, as well as advocating the appropriate punishment. And he wouldn't have been alone. Towards the end of his lengthy inquiry into match-fixing in Pakistan, Justice Malik Mohammad Qayyum was similarly inclined. "To those disappointed with their fallen heroes," he wrote in his report, "it be suggested that humans are fallible. Cricketers are only cricketers."

Cronje's worst crime was not against cricket – accepting the bookies' bribes or trying to fix matches – but against morality and decency. It was in the way he ensnared the two most vulnerable members of his team, Herschelle Gibbs and Henry Williams. Cronje's white team-mates could afford to send him on his joking way with a rejection; he was just the captain, one of the

boys. For Gibbs and Williams, however, even in the rarefied atmosphere of
the new South Africa, Cronje was the white man in charge. It takes more
than a rainbow for generations of social conditioning and economic
deprivation to be washed away.

A system of self-aggrandisement

Of the three government-sponsored inquiries into match-fixing, in India,
Pakistan and South Africa, India's CBI enjoyed much wider scope than the
terms of reference that constricted both Qayyum and Justice Edwin King.
As the title of their report implied, the CBI had freedom to investigate "related
malpractices", allowing them to be wonderfully critical of cricket administrators in a way the other two could not. In spite of much post-Cronje
posturing, the CBI decided, the office-bearers of the Board of Control for
Cricket in India (BCCI) had been negligent by not looking thoroughly into
alleged malpractices in the past, even though there had been clear indications
of the malaise in the game there. The primary reason behind this was "the
lack of accountability of the BCCI to anyone". The BCCI, the report made
clear for anyone who didn't know it, "perpetuates a system of self-
aggrandisement". It is not only in India, either. The men in clover become
so besotted by the opiate of their own importance that they lose the will to
confront problems. The trappings of power become more important than the
judicious exercise of the power.

This might matter less if cricket were still primarily a domestic game,
given a touch of glamour by Tests and one-day tournaments. But it isn't. It
is an international sport, a multi-million-pound enterprise, and the question
of accountability spotlights the dilemma at the heart of the game. Who does
administer it? Well-meaning national representatives with other business and
personal interests, or a coterie of power-players pursuing their own political
or self-serving agendas? The ICC's few years as a governing body – it can
hardly be called independent or autonomous – have not been glorious. It is
still perceived as little more than a talking shop, not always the sum of its
fractious parts and impotent to act without the agreement of its member
countries, with their own vested interests.

The ICC's initial response to Cronje's admission of guilt was to resist calls
for a worldwide inquiry into match-fixing, preferring that each country should
determine its own methods of inquiry. This after India and Pakistan had
already held inconclusive inquiries in recent years. It took a little prodding
from the ECB's more proactive chairman, Lord MacLaurin, to get the nine
Full Members around a table. In due course, the ICC established its own
Anti-Corruption Unit under the former commissioner of London's Metropolitan Police, Sir Paul Condon. Even so, its powers are limited. Although
nominally independent, the unit is none the less financed by the ICC and
its role is to support the ICC's Code of Conduct Commission. By its own
terms of reference, this Commission "recognises and confirms that each
member has sovereign rights over its own players, umpires, team officials
and administrators and… is responsible for all disciplinary matters". In other
words, the countries, not the Anti-Corruption Unit, not the Code of Conduct
Commission, not the ICC, decide what's what.

Take throwing. Cricket balls this time, rather than matches. On December 31, 1999, the ICC banned the Pakistan fast bowler, Shoaib Akhtar, because of a suspect bowling action. Pakistan alleged racial bias, a card that's beginning to fray at the edges, and appealed directly to ICC president Jagmohan Dalmiya and cricket chairman Sir Clyde Walcott. In little more than a week, the Rawalpindi Express was steaming in again, though only in one-day internationals. The thinking behind his reprieve had touches of Alice: Shoaib's bouncer was the delivery that concerned the ICC bowling panel; bouncers are not legitimate deliveries in one-day cricket; ergo, Shoaib won't bowl bouncers and his bowling won't be suspect. Just to be on the safe side, the panel's power to suspend bowlers with suspect actions was revoked, and eventually replaced by a three-stage process that initially puts the issue back in the hands of individual countries.

More recently, there have been discussions about relocating the ICC headquarters to a country with a more favourable tax regime. The United Kingdom, currently at any rate, taxes sporting bodies; the suggested alternatives do not. It explains why the finance men slip away from Lord's to do their deals. In addition to this possible move, the ICC needs a new chief executive to replace David Richards when he has worked through the notice he gave last October. The time must be coming for the member countries to put the ICC on a proper business footing, with full-time executives empowered to take decisive, unilateral action as a centrally functioning administration. Otherwise, it makes no odds whether it's in Singapore or Switzerland, Dublin or Dubai.

Test cricket's ten-year plan...

The ICC's independence might not matter so much if it weren't for its global ambitions and the income cricket now generates through broadcasting rights. Last year, the ICC agreed an eight-year television deal worth a minimum \$US550 million (£355 million), to include the 2003 World Cup in South Africa, 2007 in the Caribbean, and other tournaments. Such is the attraction of one-day internationals, mostly to viewers in the subcontinent. So that Test cricket also has a focus over and above traditional rivalries and piecemeal series, the ICC has agreed a ten-year programme, in which the Test-playing countries meet each other home and away over two five-year periods, and introduced a Test Championship along the lines of the Wisden World Championship. Each series will comprise two or more Tests, accompanied by a one-day series – perhaps as a way of countering the profusion of "offshore" tournaments regarded by some as the feeding-ground of illegal bookmakers and their bribes. A glance at the list on page 28 suggests Test cricket, too, is not beyond suspicion.

Traditional series such as the Ashes will maintain their accustomed timetables within the five-year cycles. While there are bound to be anomalies – cricket revels in them – the ten-year plan prevents Test newcomers like Bangladesh, welcomed last year as the tenth Test-playing nation, from being sidelined in the way Zimbabwe were by Australia, England and West Indies after joining the club in 1992. It also provides a framework into which other countries can be worked; Kenya, who already have one-day international status, have applied to become the 11th Test member. What will be a test for the weak is going to be no more than another outing for the strong.

...brings an official Test Championship

The new ICC Test Championship gets under way this summer with England's series against Pakistan. Wisden is providing data for a league table based on recent series results. Like our own World Championship, introduced in 1996 in the hope that it would stimulate official rankings for Test cricket, the ICC's system will be based on the results of the latest series, home and away, between each of the teams: two points for a win, one for a draw. The interest shown by the media in the Wisden World Championship, not least when England hit bottom, certainly indicated the popularity of a league table. Hardly had a series finished than journalists and broadcasters were phoning or e-mailing to discover their country's new position.

Not that the Australian media have bothered of late. With five straight series victories behind them after hammering West Indies 5–0, giving them a world-record 15 successive Test wins, Steve Waugh's team were impregnably on top. India could stop their winning sequence, if only through drawn games. Reports suggest that pitches will be on the lifeless side to counter Australia's bowling strength. At least the directives are coming from official quarters this time; when Australia lost at Delhi in 1996, bookmaker Gupta claims to have influenced the pitch preparation. The Australians were setting off for India as this Almanack went to press. England, meanwhile, were about to take on Sri Lanka, the last country to beat Australia in a Test and a series.

A series to savour

Whatever the results of those series, they will not diminish interest in this summer's England–Australia Tests. More than a decade has passed since England held the Ashes and, a year ago, the prospect of winning them back was the stuff of fantasy and stand-up comedians. But from the evidence of 2000, England are again starting to take a grip on their game. It is not only the victories over Zimbabwe, West Indies and Pakistan, impressive and encouraging as they were. It is the way the players approached their cricket. After years of managers and coaches who have talked a useful game, it has been a pleasure, not to say relief, to watch a coach who keeps his words to a minimum and lets his team's cricket do the talking. (Lord MacLaurin, who apparently finds himself being misquoted rather regularly, might want to employ a similar tactic.) Duncan Fletcher will be under no illusions when it comes to taking on Australia. Nor will Nasser Hussain. But between them, England's coach and captain will instil the discipline and pragmatism that underpin the most successful sides.

Running parallel with England's resurgence was West Indies' continuing decline. As when Australia were in the doldrums in the 1980s, and England in the 1990s, cricket is the biggest loser. The game needs its star attractions: very few countries are major draws. West Indies were not always pretty to watch in their glory days of high fives and riding high, but they were always good for the box office: they bristled with quality. The background to their demise sounds all too familiar: cricket's diminishing importance in schools, and poor pitches. West Indies' success in winning the Under-15 World Challenge at Lord's last year suggests they are not without young talent. It has to be nurtured, however. The West Indies board have attracted investment through television deals and sponsorship, but cricket in the Caribbean has never been flush. A forward-looking ICC might even look at its own millions and consider whether its global ambitions can afford a weak West Indies.

Planning for the future

Some have said there was an element of good fortune in England's success. Marcus Trescothick, for example, one of the summer's finds, was not a first choice: he came into the side because of injury. It would also be possible to subscribe to the theory, given much currency in England's down time, that success comes in cycles. That depends on how long you're prepared to wait. Good fortune and cycles obscure the planning. Not merely the planning that Hussain and Fletcher put into the team itself, but the planning and strategy that have been set in motion for English cricket's long-term future.

Heaven forbid that these Notes should praise men in suits. But it seems to me that Lord MacLaurin came to the ECB convinced of at least two things. English cricket's future lay with the success of the England team: what MacLaurin, with his businessman's nous, called the shop window. The other was the poor quality of county cricket as a provider of Test cricketers. England Test cricketers, at any rate. That was only four years ago. Not really long enough to drag the game, a way of life for many and something of a sinecure for others, out of the 19th century and into the 21st. But he and the ECB could be getting there.

Much of what they have done and are doing, not only at county level but also in the recreational game, has been viewed with suspicion. Change, let alone radical change, is rarely welcomed. We fear it will destroy what we hold dear. Yet destruction, it has been said, is only the shady side of progress, and the world of cricket is bent on progress.

As Mihir Bose's article on match-fixing explains, multinational companies have seen cricket as a means of furthering their development in Asia, the game's great growth area. But the commercial realities are different for English cricket, which exists in an established economy with more stable growth. The days when sponsors wanted their names associated with cricket for its traditional values and its place in English life have passed. And they passed rather quickly. These days, the money follows football. When England team sponsors Vodafone extended their contract with the ECB until 2005, the new four-year deal was worth £12 million, although "with additional substantial bonuses available for success in Test matches and one-day internationals". When the same company became the principal sponsor of Manchester United for a similar period, the price was £30 million.

This doesn't just put cricket in context. It highlights the problems the board face every time they have to find sponsors, and why a winning national team, attracting good headlines, is essential for English cricket all the way down to the grassroots. Last year the game bade farewell to one of its oldest sponsors, when Cornhill Insurance called it a day. It was sad to see them go. They were as concerned for the game's values as for England's success; those who provided the human face to the corporate body were friendly, warm and generous – as, indeed, cricket's sponsors tend to be. Cornhill benefited commercially from their relationship with cricket since 1978, and deserved to. The game would have been poorer without them, and not only in a financial sense. They came in at a bleak time, during the Packer schism, and remained supportive through less and less thick and lots of thin. It was good they could bow out with England on the rise again.

England claim their cricketers

There are new Test sponsors, npower, presumably providing power if not funding to the nth degree. But financing the county game continues to tax cricket's administrators, and some counties have good reason to be concerned about their futures. So do their members, and 2000 gave them plenty to talk about, with the introduction of the two-division County Championship, a summer of almost continuous international cricket (the blueprint for summers ahead) and the arrival of central contracts for Test cricketers. Some of them, anyway. The system, which essentially put those with central contracts under England's management rather than their county's, was by no means perfect. Counties losing players who were not under contract complained they did not receive the same level of compensation.

However, lessons were learned, and adjustments have been made. In principle, the system worked. At first sight, it appeared more beneficial for bowlers than batsmen to have time off between Tests, though England's 37-year-old wicket-keeper-all-rounder-cum-one-day-opening-batsman-cum-stand-in-captain will have appreciated not having to drive back to The Oval for a county game, as he would in days gone by. County members see central contracts as one more downgrading of the domestic game; the counties themselves recognise who butters their bread and have gone along with them. Meanwhile, that large constituency which follows cricket, without necessarily supporting a particular county, started going around with a smile on its face as England hit their stride. If England get to The Oval with the Ashes still at stake this summer, they'll have to cordon off the Harleyford Road.

The first 12 players given central contracts may be found on page 1517. One can imagine the snorts of derision around some counties when Craig White's name was announced. Then there was the mysterious collapse in the street that put his health, let alone his cricket career, in doubt. So his emergence as a strong candidate to be England's cricketer of the year was worth celebrating. England look all the better for having a fast-bowling all-rounder on board, and always have; the search for one has gone on too long. If White fits the bill, it will also take some pressure off Andrew Flintoff, of whom too much was expected too soon. He was in danger of becoming the Moby Dick of English cricket, forever pursued by his potential.

There's more to it than England, though

After advocating a two-division County Championship in these Notes in 1991, I could hardly turn on it now it has come to pass. Not that I would want to. Three-up three-down may be one too many in a nine-team division, but the third place certainly concentrated some minds last summer. Not all the cricket was noticeably better. And pitches still helped bowlers too much, even allowing for the third-division summer. Batsmen, with five bonus points at their disposal to the bowlers' three, were outscored 576 to 759. No wonder the ECB had their flying squad of pitch inspectors sitting by the phone – if anyone sits by the phone any more. However, if there are fewer meaningless matches, there should be more meaningful cricketers. Not Test cricketers perhaps, but players people will want to watch, and who will stiffen the sinews of those destined for the England team. Even if the county game's role is playing second fiddle to international cricket, it's still a lovely way to spend a day.

There will be, and indeed already are, players who feel they belong in Test cricket, and see Division One competition as essential to the pursuit of their ambition. County contracts increasingly look one-sided affairs: players want the security but not the tie. Yet any trend to pursue advancement through the top counties could have unforeseen consequences. It could offer a rationale for the more radical reformers who advocate a smaller group of first-class counties. After all, if the best players don't want to mix it with the not-so-good, why not have a compact, more competitive first-class structure that brings together only the best? The Professional Cricketers' Association might like to consider this aspect as the players start to come and go.

Life's confusing enough...

The ECB, meanwhile, have been considering slow over-rates in county cricket and decided to call time on loitering with intent. It has been obvious for years now that fines weren't working. Surrey's £8,000 fine last year was a worthwhile investment when they reaped £123,000 in prize money; 12 other counties also incurred financial penalties. Spectators have been short-changed for long enough. From this season, counties will lose Championship points at a quarter-point per over if they fail to average 16 an hour. In one-day games, six runs will be credited to the batting side for each complete over not bowled within the specified playing time.

Someone might also care to consider the county programme in general. Having had a more active interest in following county cricket last summer, I found it anything but consumer conscious. I'm sure this wasn't intentional on the ECB's part, but it struck me that the fixture list took little account of the fact that people like to go to cricket. As for the League, it may be national, but there is only a notional pattern to it: some teams play under lights, others don't; some teams invariably seem to have games in hand. You should be able to read a newspaper in mid-season and know what's going on without a calculator and the back of an envelope. The Championship is not quite so confusing, but two divisions of nine are obviously not ideal when teams have to mark time. Maybe it is an unfair criticism, but I don't think I am alone in finding the county programme irritating.

Still, the domestic season does end. A greater problem, from the viewpoint of editing this Almanack, is the increasingly seamless international season. This edition carries two Test series and a one-day tournament played in Sri Lanka from June to August, and three one-day games between Australia and South Africa in August, played indoors at Melbourne's Colonial Stadium. On the same day as the third Melbourne game, a one-day tournament started in Singapore, but that is for next year's *Wisden*. We had to draw a line somewhere, and the Equator seemed as good a line as any. As for putting the Sri Lankan and Melbourne games into a season, they have been designated 2000 and, when necessary to differentiate them from the English season, the host country's initials appear in brackets: for example, 2000 (SL).

Wisden online

In essence, the old, established rhythms of northern and southern hemisphere seasons have become a thing of the past. Once the ICC's ten-year plan comes into effect, there's every chance of Test cricket being played concurrently in England, northern Australia, Sri Lanka and Zimbabwe. The Almanack will continue to record them for posterity, but Wisden will also be able to capture them immediately, thanks to the expansion of our website, wisden.com. There will be live scores, match reports and rapid analysis, as well as constantly updated records and career figures. Moreover, by incorporating 138 *Wisdens*, the website links the present with the past to provide an interactive reference database. The future has become a reality.

In the eight years since I stepped down as editor of *Wisden*, cricket's growth has been enormous; the issues as well as the games have become manifold. Following the match-fixing story brought that home. *Wisden Cricket Monthly* captured the breaking news through its regular Cronjology feature; the Almanack has had to encapsulate, to provide an overview. A website, journalistically, offers the world. But it also provides a challenge. There is no shortage of websites. Anyone can put up stats and stories. Wisden has to do more than that. It has to maintain its reputation for accuracy, authority and independence. If it doesn't, we know from more than a century's experience that someone will let us know.

A GAME IN SHAME

By MIHIR BOSE

Cricket corruption, like taxes and poverty, may always be with us. But after cricket's *annus horribilis* of 2000 we can, for the first time, understand how a combination of players' greed, dreadful impotence and infighting by cricket administrators, and a radical shift in cricketing power from England to the Indian subcontinent helped create cricket's darkest chapter.

Two incidents illustrate this, and both occurred in India. The first was in 1984, some months after India's unexpected victory in the 1983 World Cup. One evening a Delhi bank clerk, Mukesh Kumar Gupta, was walking near his home in the grimy bylanes of old Delhi when he saw some people betting small amounts on a cricket match. This, as he would later tell the Central Bureau of Investigation, India's top police investigators, caught his imagination. Having ascertained that the betters were neither well educated nor well informed about cricket, Gupta began to hone his cricket knowledge by listening to the BBC. And over the next decade he would travel the world, following cricket and meeting many of the world's top cricketers. Meeting and bribing.

Meanwhile, as Gupta was transforming himself from a lowly bank clerk to cricket's most notorious match-fixer, and enriching himself in the process, cricket was also being reinvented and enriched. By the mid-1990s, even the Ashes Tests, the bedrock of the international game for more than 100 years, had been – away from the insular focus of England – sidelined in favour of one-day internationals.

By 1996, and the heyday of Gupta the match-fixer, there had been an enormous spread of such matches, the greatest expansion in the history of the game, with series in "non-cricketing" venues such as Sharjah, Singapore and Toronto. Sharjah had started by staging benefit matches for Indian and Pakistani cricketers, who had no recourse to an English-style system. Toronto provided a North American haven for India versus Pakistan, not always possible in the subcontinent for political reasons, while Singapore, and similar tournaments, represented the commercial opportunities that limited-overs cricket provided to businessmen seeking to reach the emerging Indian middle-classes.

Companies such as Singer and Pepsi, American but with extensive interests in south Asia, saw the marketing advantages of being associated with subcontinental cricket, and sponsored many of these mini-series. Television companies, in particular Rupert Murdoch's Star, were also keen to reach this new economic group. It is estimated that every second person watching cricket in the world is an Indian, and their insatiable appetite for the one-day game since 1983 has created a market worth cultivating. As Justice Malik Mohammad Qayyum pointed out in his inquiry into match-fixing, submitted to the Pakistan government in 1999, "with the massive influx of money and sheer increase in the number of matches played, cricket has become a business." It was a business, however, that was run like a private members' club.

Not surprisingly, the game's new economic power stimulated the ambitions of Asia's cricket administrators. Our second incident, in the spring of 1996, provided the spur. It happened in the foyer of Taj Bengal, the luxurious Calcutta hotel just opposite the city's zoo, and gathered there were the subcontinent's leading administrators. The World Cup, which was just about to start in the subcontinent, had been thrown into chaos by the refusal of the Australians, for security reasons, to play their group matches in Sri Lanka. The television and sponsorship deals that the Asians had made for the World Cup, which would eventually bring them a profit in excess of $US75 million, were in jeopardy, and the game's governing body, the International Cricket Council, seemed powerless to act. It was against this background that Ana Punchihewa, president of the Sri Lankan board, turned to Jagmohan Dalmiya, the Indian convenor of the World Cup organising committee, and said, "We should have an Asian as the next chairman of the International Cricket Council."

Dalmiya picked up the baton and ran his election campaign as if it was an American presidential race, energetically wooing the ICC Associate Members. But despite winning a simple majority in two ballots, he found the old, established members reluctant to accept him. A bitter power struggle, essentially brown versus white (and black), saw England, Australia, New Zealand and West Indies ranged against the subcontinent. It was so vicious that the scars have never healed. The Asian countries resented the grudging acceptance of them by England and Australia; the old powers felt that the new kids on the block were not following the game's gentlemanly ways.

"There was, is, a power struggle in international cricket," one highly placed ICC source admitted, "and the Asian countries are resentful of England, the old colonial power, but then the subcontinent has not helped matters by being very defensive about match-fixing. We have known for years that match-fixing goes on, helped by the fact that betting is illegal and in the hands of criminals there. But in the past, whenever the matter has been raised, they have said we are cricket administrators, not cops. Then a clean-cut white South African, Hansie Cronje, was caught in the net, the game changed and everyone has had to come clean."

Ironically, it was a Delhi crime-branch detective, Ishwar Singh Redhu, who, on April 7, 2000, forced everyone to come clean. Asked to investigate complaints by Delhi businessmen of extortion with menace, he was listening to telephone taps on two suspects when Cronje's name – and the fixing of one-day games in the current series between India and South Africa – cropped up. Then Cronje himself was heard discussing the fixing of matches with a London-based Indian businessman called Sanjeev (also known as Sanjay) Chawla.

Before that moment, five and a half years after Shane Warne, Mark Waugh and Tim May had made allegations of match-fixing against the Pakistan captain, Salim Malik, there had been inquiries in India, Pakistan and Sri Lanka, as well as media investigations led by the Indian magazine *Outlook*. But apart from the fines on Waugh and Warne for receiving $A6,000 and $A5,000 respectively from an Indian bookmaker in return for information, which the Australian board and ICC had covered up, nothing had been done.

[*Juda Ngwenya, Popperfoto/Reuters*

South African newspapers give their verdict the day after Hansie Cronje admitted receiving $US10,000–15,000 from a bookmaker.

It would subsequently emerge that Justice Qayyum had recommended a life ban on Salim Malik, but his report was still to be published.

The immediate reactions to the Delhi police's charges of match-fixing and betting against Cronje and the team-mates he had mentioned to Chawla – Nicky Boje, Herschelle Gibbs, Pieter Strydom and Henry Williams – were of utter disbelief that a born-again Christian like Cronje could be involved. Cronje denied everything – "Absolute rubbish." Ali Bacher, managing director of South African cricket, backed him – "unquestionable integrity and honesty" – and the South Africans denounced the tactics of the Delhi police. In London, *The Observer* quoted a South African journalist as saying he had heard the tapes and it could not be Cronje as the voice had an Indian accent. It later turned out he had heard Indian actors reading transcripts released by the Delhi police. The tapes themselves had been sealed and placed under the jurisdiction of the Delhi High Court.

Four days after detective Redhu's initial announcement, the cricket world was rocked and shocked. Cronje made the first of many confessions, and the shadowy world of M. K. Gupta and his ilk was about to emerge in the public light. Within two months, all the rumours of match-fixing that had been circulating for years were given substance. The Pakistanis, who had been sitting on Justice Qayyum's report since the previous October, were finally obliged to release it. Qayyum accepted that Waugh, Warne and May had told the truth about Malik seeking to corrupt them. Another cricketer, Ata-ur-Rehman, was found guilty of perjury in relation to evidence about Wasim Akram and a life ban recommended. Fines were also recommended for these two, and for Wasim, Mushtaq Ahmed, Waqar Younis, Inzamam-ul-Haq, Akram Raza and Saeed Anwar. The judge found that the evidence of match-fixing against these others had not come up to the level required, but he concluded none the less that Wasim should never again captain Pakistan. The fines were because, within the terms of the inquiry, these players had either brought the name of the Pakistan team into disrepute or, by "partial amnesia" and withholding evidence, had not co-operated fully.

In June, two weeks after the Qayyum report was published, a South African judicial commission under retired judge Edwin King began to hear devastating evidence from South African players. The entire South African team had considered an offer to throw a one-day match in 1996 and, in yet another confession, Cronje admitted he could have taken as much as $US140,000 from Gupta and other bookmakers between 1996 and 2000. But he asked the world to believe that, while he had lied to the bookies about throwing matches, he was telling the truth in saying he had never tried to fix a match.

At the beginning of November, the Indian government released the CBI's report of their investigation into match-fixing. By interviewing illegal bookmakers as well as players, this added a new dimension to the story. The result was that, for the first time, a cricketer, former Indian captain Mohammad Azharuddin, admitted to being involved in the fixing of one-day internationals. And drawing on the information from Gupta and other bookies, the CBI revealed how international cricketers had been lured and, in some instances, corrupted. What began as a scandal could be seen at last as a conspiracy. Match-fixing could no longer be shrugged off as an occasional isolated instance; there was now a history and a pattern of corruption.

Gupta's first cricket contact was Ajay Sharma, very much a bit-player in international cricket – one Test and 31 one-day internationals for India – but a useful conduit to other cricketers. They first met at a club tournament in Delhi in 1988 when Gupta, impressed by the way Sharma batted, gave him 2,000 rupees (£100 at the current rate of exchange) as a token of his appreciation. Gupta saw this as an investment for the future, and it was to prove a shrewd one. A fortnight later Sharma contacted him and soon the two men had formed a bond which, as the CBI report made clear, "was to prove beneficial to both".

When Sharma toured New Zealand with India in 1990, Gupta claimed he provided him with information about the pitch, weather and the team which he used to make "a good amount of money". Sharma denies he provided any information, but he did later introduce Gupta to Manoj Prabhakar, who was keen to get a new car: "a Maruti Gypsy with wide tyres". On the 1990 tour of England, said Gupta, Prabhakar gave him information about the team and "underperformed" in one of the drawn Tests. Prabhakar got his Maruti Gypsy – he told the CBI he paid for it himself – and Gupta got to know yet more cricketers.

The picture Gupta painted for the CBI, which was often backed in testimony from Sharma, Prabhakar, Azharuddin, Ajay Jadeja and even Cronje,

[Allsport

Hansie Cronje contemplates a life without cricket during the King Commission hearing at Cape Town in June 2000.

shows how frighteningly casual the whole thing was. Gupta goes to Prabhakar's Delhi home for dinner (Prabhakar denies this); Prabhakar rings Gus Logie, who refuses to help (Prabhakar confirms this). When the Sri Lankans tour India in 1990, Prabhakar introduces Gupta to Aravinda de Silva (Prabhakar denies this). He in turn, and over the phone, introduces Gupta to Martin Crowe, and they get on so well that when Gupta visits New Zealand in 1991 – Sri Lanka toured there from January to March – he lunches with Crowe and his wife, Simone, at their home. At a Hong Kong six-a-side tournament, Prabhakar introduces Gupta to Mark Waugh; Gupta flies to Colombo during some festival matches there and, so he claims, meets Dean Jones, Arjuna Ranatunga and Brian Lara. When the winners of the Indian and Pakistani Wills one-day tournaments play in Delhi, Prabhakar introduces him to Salim Malik, and when England tour India in 1993 he introduces him to Alec Stewart. Gupta and Prabhakar agree on this.

Gupta's success with these cricketers varies. During the 1994 Sri Lankan tour of India, he claims, Ranatunga and de Silva agreed to "underperform" – "[they] could manage it since they were the captain and vice-captain," he told the CBI – and he profited when Sri Lanka lost the First Test. For this, he says, he paid de Silva $US15,000. There was talk of fixing other Tests, but the odds were too low.

Gupta claims he paid Crowe $US20,000 for information, but he refused to fix matches. Jones was offered $US40,000, he says, but while Jones promised to think about it, he did nothing. In Hong Kong, says Gupta, Mark Waugh was paid $US20,000 to provide information "whenever Australia played", but on another occasion, in Sharjah in 1994, he refused to help as did Salim Malik. Later that year, however, Gupta recalls making good money on Malik's information that Pakistan would lose to Australia in the Singer World Series in Sri Lanka, a match mentioned in both the CBI and Qayyum reports. When the West Indians toured India in 1994-95, Gupta says he paid Brian Lara $US40,000 to underperform in two one-day games.

After the CBI report was released, de Silva and Ranatunga denied Gupta's allegations. Crowe said he thought he was dealing with a journalist and was duped. Waugh denied accepting Gupta's money and talked of taking legal action. So did Lara. The most robust denial came from Stewart. According to Gupta, Stewart was paid £5,000 for information but refused to fix matches for him. Stewart not only denied receiving any money but claimed he did not remember knowingly meeting Gupta.

It is possible that in the fevered atmosphere of subcontinental cricket Stewart may have met Gupta: for a long time he was identified only as M.K. Confusingly, he was also known as John, although he was not the John who in 1994 paid Waugh and Warne for information, knew Salim Malik and approached Cronje in 1995 with offers to fix the finals of the Mandela Trophy between South Africa and Pakistan. Not yet caught in the web, Cronje turned him down. But as he and Malik walked on to the field before the first final, the Pakistan captain asked him whether he had spoken to John. Cronje told the King Commission that he felt embarrassed and ashamed and merely nodded in response: he did not want to talk about it. South Africa won both games; as far as Qayyum was concerned, Pakistan lost them in controversial circumstances.

> There was an open dispute within the team about the decision of the toss. Since the matches were day/night games and the lights in Johannesburg were not conducive to batting second, Rashid Latif the vice-captain had strongly recommended that if Malik won the toss Pakistan should bat first. Both times Malik won the toss and put the opposition in [and lost]. In cricketing terms the toss in a day/night game is crucial as it is easier to bat first in natural daylight than under the shadows of floodlights. Even *Wisden* notes that [in the first final] Malik made "the puzzling decision to field first". It was also puzzling why, having [fielded] first and lost in the first final, Malik repeated the mistake two days later in the second match as well.

However, whether he was M.K., John or just plain Gupta, there can be no doubt about his intense and close relationship with Azharuddin and Cronje. After Ajay Sharma had introduced Azharuddin to Gupta at the Taj Palace hotel in Delhi in 1995, the two had a relationship that lasted until 1997. During that period, says Gupta, Azhar's wife Sangeeta Bijlani was also involved. He claims he paid Azhar 90 lakh rupees (£150,000: a lakh equals 100,000 rupees) but, finding some of Azhar's predictions "proved incorrect", asked for his money back and was repaid 30 lakh rupees – in instalments from Azharuddin's locker at the Taj Palace.

It was Azhar's unreliability as a forecaster, Gupta told the CBI, that made him seek out Cronje late in 1996. Even so, that Indian season had begun well for him. With Sharma's help, he claims to have had the pitch at Delhi's Feroz Shah Kotla ground doctored for the one-off Test between India and Australia, which India won in three and a half days. He was told that the First Test against South Africa at Ahmedabad would not be a draw – India won and Gupta made money – and that India would lose the Second; again he made money. In Kanpur for the Third Test, he asked Azharuddin to introduce him to Cronje.

The meeting took place on the evening of the third day, with South Africa facing defeat. Azhar introduced him as a diamond merchant, but Gupta quickly told Cronje that he was a match-fixer who wanted to be sure that South Africa would lose. He asked Cronje to obtain the players' co-operation. Cronje would later tell the King Commission, "I led him to believe I would. This seemed an easy way to make money, but I had no intention of doing anything." He accepted $US30,000 from Gupta, hid it in his kit bag and smuggled it out of India, into and out of South Africa, and finally to a bank account in England, so violating the foreign exchange laws of both India and South Africa.

That established the Cronje–Gupta relationship. Cronje says he lied to Gupta about match-fixing but took his money nevertheless. And during the last match of the Indian tour, the entire South African team debated whether to accept Gupta's bribe, variously said to be $US200,000 and $US250,000, to play badly in the one-day international at Mumbai, intended as a benefit match for Mohinder Amarnath. Pat Symcox told the King Commission, "Some guys including myself said it was a lot of money and we should look at it. Some guys were for it, some against." In the end the offer was rejected, but it remains the only known instance of a whole team discussing match-fixing. Cronje met Gupta at three o'clock on the morning of the match to tell him the fix was not on.

Yet when India then went to South Africa for three back-to-back Tests and a one-day tournament, also involving Zimbabwe, the relationship developed. Cronje says he kept lying to Gupta about throwing matches but took his money. Gupta says that when Cronje, like Azharuddin, proved an unreliable forecaster, and he suffered huge losses, Cronje apologised and promised to make amends. Here we have a touch of comic opera.

According to Gupta, Cronje had promised that, during the one-day tournament, South Africa would lose some matches against India. When they didn't, he told Gupta that India had played so badly and missed so many chances that he couldn't do anything about the result. Poor Gupta: he had invested in both camps and still couldn't get the result he wanted. Could it be that other players were in hock to other bookies seeking a different fix?

The age of Gupta the match-fixer ended in May 1998, and there is some evidence to suggest that the high tide of cricket match-fixing ended then, although Majid Khan, former chief executive of the Pakistan board, remains convinced that Pakistan's two World Cup losses to India and Bangladesh

At the King Commission, Marlon Aronstam was revealed as the true instigator of the dramatic
last day of the Centurion Test. Cronje took the plaudits – and pocketed Aronstam's money.

in 1999 were fixed. However, no player or bookie has come forward to
provide any details, and the World Cup did not fall within the compass of
Justice Qayyum's inquiry.

In fact, it is possible that the world at large would never have heard of
Gupta had Cronje not decided he couldn't do without bookies. He would
tell Judge King that his behaviour was like that of an alcoholic, who abstains
only to return when he has one drink. The fateful "drink" was offered by a
South African gambler, Marlon Aronstam. He contacted Cronje on his mobile
phone on the fourth evening of the rain-ruined Fifth Test between England
and South Africa at Centurion Park in January 2000; they agreed to meet at
ten o'clock in Cronje's hotel room. Aronstam wanted Cronje to "make a
game" of the Test by declaring and persuading England to agree to a double
forfeiture, something not only unprecedented in Test history but also not
sanctioned by the Laws.

Aronstam planned to back both sides at long odds. If Cronje agreed,
Aronstam told the King Commission, he was going to give 200,000 rand to
a charity of Cronje's choice. (Cronje remembered the figure as 500,000 rand.)
He claimed that Cronje implied that the only way to make money from
cricket was by fixing matches, and gave the impression that he would be
prepared to throw a one-day international "once South Africa has qualified
for a final". He also offered to throw the first one-day international against
India in Kochi, when South Africa toured there after the triangular series
between South Africa, England and Zimbabwe.

Cronje would later try to qualify his offers, but it remains extraordinary that he had such a discussion with a man he had only just met. As a result, he "made a match" of the Centurion Test, and Aronstam gave him 53,000 rand plus a leather jacket for his wife, even though it had been too late to place his bets by the time the final day was set up. The money for charity never materialised. Cronje denied that the match was fixed. But by his own admission he was hooked again on bookmakers, and a fortnight later, when South Africa were in Durban to play Zimbabwe, he was introduced to Chawla. The intermediary was Hamid "Banjo" Cassim, a South African of Indian origin, who had befriended the South African players by giving them biltong (dried meat). When the Indians toured South Africa in 1996-97, he had provided them with biryani, and one of the sights of the Cape Town Test was "Banjo" hauling biryani up to the Indian dressing-room on a rope.

By the time Cronje left Chawla's room, he was clutching a mobile-phone box filled with perhaps as much as $US15,000. It was to prove a fatal relationship. Cronje felt so invincible he did not seem to care who knew about his match-fixing discussions with Chawla. In India he happily discussed the topic on a mobile phone given to him by Chawla. He asked Pieter Strydom to play badly in the First Test in Mumbai, but Strydom refused. Before the Second Test at Bangalore, he asked Mark Boucher, Jacques Kallis and Lance Klusener – "in passing, jokingly" Klusener remembered – whether they were keen "to throw the game for money". Again, his suggestion was rejected. Then, on the morning of the final one-day match at Nagpur, he lured two non-white players, Herschelle Gibbs and Henry Williams, by offering the former $US15,000 if he scored less than 20 runs and the latter a similar amount if his overs cost more than 50 runs. He had, it transpired, told Chawla he would need $US25,000 each for Gibbs and Williams, and later conceded he might have been "trying to cut something" for himself.

In the event, Gibbs scored 74 and Williams was injured in his second over, but Cronje, who had made the offer with a smile, just laughed it off – part of his strategy, perhaps, to convince his players that it could all be a huge practical joke. What Cronje did not know was that the mobile he had been given by Chawla was being tapped. Two weeks later, when the Delhi police held their press conference, releasing transcripts of taped conversations between Cronje and Chawla, the joke was on Cronje. It would lead to the South African board banning him from cricket for life, just as after the CBI Report the Indian board would issue life bans on Azharuddin and Sharma. Two other Indians, Jadeja and Prabhakar, received five-year bans; South Africans Gibbs and Williams got six-month suspensions.

Yet, in the end, the joke has been played on cricket's administrators. This became evident when in May the ICC, prompted by Lord MacLaurin, held an emergency session to discuss match-fixing. It was the first time in its seven years as an independent organisation that such a meeting had been held. In the weeks beforehand, the various boards manoeuvred to put themselves in the best possible light. Everyone put pressure on Pakistan to release the Qayyum Report, while in an interview with *The Australian* newspaper, Ali Bacher sought to turn the spotlight away from South Africa with allegations that two 1999 World Cup matches were "manipulated" and that an umpire had been paid to "ensure a certain result in a Test match

|Savita Kirloskar, Popperfoto/Reuters

Incensed and incendiary: Indian fans vent their fury at former captain Mohammad Azharuddin's involvement with match-fixers.

in England". Questions were raised in the media about ICC president Dalmiya's own conduct during negotiations for television rights for the 1998 ICC Knockout tournament in Dhaka. This had brought the ICC £12 million, at the time the biggest deal it had transacted.

Just before Dalmiya opened the session, MacLaurin passed round a statement on ECB notepaper, which he asked all the ICC delegates to sign, declaring that they were honest men. Everyone duly complied, but it revealed the curious state of an organisation whose own senior members had to declare they were clean before they could consider corruption among the players. Friends of Dalmiya hinted darkly that this was some English plot. Yet the most persistent questions about the 1998 television deal – whereby Doordarshan, India's state television, had received the rights – were raised in India. Soon, another CBI inquiry would be set up to examine the deal, and also the links between Dalmiya and Mark Mascarenhas, whose media interests include a television company called World-Tel.

CBI officers visited Dalmiya's offices in Calcutta and there was also a raid by income tax officials on his office. The CBI's next report, when it emerges, may reveal the curious ways such television deals are done. Dalmiya, meanwhile, insisted he had done nothing wrong. The ICC, he said, did not lose out, and if Doordarshan paid over the odds that was their responsibility. As for the raids, he claimed they had nothing to do with cricket and were common to all business houses in India.

In a sense, Dalmiya's remarks sum up the problem and the immense cultural divide that the cricket corruption issue raises. In Pakistan, the cricket board is at the mercy of the government; in India, it is autonomous. But in both countries the game is played and administered against a background in which corruption, and police and tax inquiries into prominent persons, are part of life.

In the various countries around the world, the investigations into match-fixing reflect the fact that each country does its own thing. In India, Pakistan and South Africa, the investigations have been either judicial or led by the police but, in all three instances, reporting to the respective governments. In Australia and New Zealand, they are being handled by the cricket bodies and have no legal powers. A strong central cricket administration could have overcome this.

The ICC has taken tentative steps with the setting up of an investigation unit under former London Metropolitan Police commissioner Sir Paul Condon. But, as Sir Paul himself has admitted, he has no legal powers; if he discovers anything, it will be reported to the ICC. He can do nothing to administer justice, he can only react, and what co-ordination he can achieve is through persuasion. It is noteworthy that the very afternoon he held a press conference in London to publicise the work of his new unit, it was overshadowed by the release of the CBI Report. Sir Paul had to delay his press conference to deal with that.

Since its initial report, the CBI has begun looking into links between cricketers, bookmakers and the Indian underworld, and could discover more secrets. The King Commission wants to go back to the beginning of 1992, when South Africa re-emerged into international cricket. It has high hopes of unlocking more secrets, but others in South Africa would prefer to see a line drawn under the whole sorry business. This would be a mistake. The high tide of match-fixing in cricket may have ebbed, but the full story of what happened throughout the 1990s has not yet been told.

Mihir Bose is sports news correspondent of the Daily Telegraph.

A list of matches mentioned in official inquiries can be found on page 28.

MATCHES MENTIONED IN OFFICIAL INQUIRIES

The following matches were mentioned by players, administrators, team officials, journalists or bookmakers during the CBI, Qayyum (Q) and King (K) inquiries in India, Pakistan and South Africa. Inclusion on this list does not necessarily indicate that a match was fixed.

Season	Match	Venue	Type	See Wisden	Inquiry
1979-80	India v Pakistan	Calcutta	Test	1981 p. 1012	CBI, Q
1987-88	Australia v Pakistan	Lahore	one-day	1988 p. 283	Q
1990-91	Delhi v Bombay	Delhi	Ranji	1992 p. 1160	CBI
1991-92	Wills XI v Habib Bank	Delhi	one-day		CBI
	Two India games in B&H World Series in Australia			1993 p. 1047	CBI
1992	England v Pakistan	Nottingham	one-day	1993 p. 303	Q
1992-93	India v England	Calcutta	Test	1994 p. 972	CBI
	India v England	Bangalore	one-day	1994 p. 978	CBI
	India v England	Gwalior	one-day	1994 p. 980	CBI
	India v England	Gwalior	one-day	1994 p. 980	CBI
1993-94	India v Sri Lanka	Lucknow	Test	1995 p. 1091	CBI
	New Zealand v Pakistan	Christchurch	Test	1995 p. 1107	Q
	New Zealand v Pakistan	Christchurch	one-day	1995 p. 1112	Q
	India v Pakistan	Sharjah	one-day	1995 p. 1172	Q
1994-95	Australia v Pakistan	Colombo	one-day	1996 p. 1138	CBI, Q
	Sri Lanka v India	Colombo	one-day	1996 p. 1141	CBI
	Pakistan v Australia	Karachi	Test	1996 p. 1030	Q
	Pakistan v Australia	Rawalpindi	one-day	1996 p. 1147	Q
	India v West Indies	Kanpur	one-day	1996 p. 1152	CBI
	South Africa v Pakistan	Cape Town	one-day	1996 p. 1177	K, Q
	South Africa v Pakistan	Johannesburg	one-day	1996 p. 1178	K, Q
1995-96	India v Pakistan	Bangalore	one-day	1997 p. 1043	Q
	Pakistan v Sri Lanka	Singapore	one-day	1997 p. 1175	Q
1996-97	India v Australia	Delhi	Test	1998 p. 1037	CBI
	India v South Africa	Rajkot	one-day	1998 p. 1156	CBI
	India v South Africa	Mumbai	one-day	1998 p. 1158	CBI
	India v South Africa	Ahmedabad	Test	1998 p. 1049	CBI
	India v South Africa	Calcutta	Test	1998 p. 1050	CBI
	India v South Africa	Mumbai	one-day	1998 p. 1054	CBI, K
	South Africa v India	Durban	Test	1998 p. 1081	K
	South Africa v India	Cape Town	Test	1998 p. 1082	K
	South Africa v India	Johannesburg	Test	1998 p. 1084	CBI, K
	West Indies v India	Bridgetown	Test	1998 p. 1116	CBI
1997-98	Sri Lanka v Pakistan	Colombo	one-day	1999 p. 1171	CBI, Q
	Sahara Cup	Toronto	one-day	1999 p. 1176	CBI, Q
	Pakistan v India	Karachi	one-day	1999 p. 1182	Q
	Pakistan v South Africa	Faisalabad	Test	1999 p. 1083	Q
	Pakistan v Sri Lanka	Lahore	one-day	1999 p. 1194	Q
	England v Pakistan	Sharjah	one-day	1999 p. 1212	Q
	India v New Zealand	Sharjah	one-day	1999 p. 1240	CBI
1998	England v South Africa	Leeds	Test	1999 p. 411	K
1998-99	India v Pakistan	Jaipur	one-day	2000 p. 1281	CBI
	England v Pakistan	Sharjah	one-day	2000 p. 1289	Q
1999	India v Zimbabwe	Leicester	one-day	2000 p. 445	CBI
	Bangladesh v Pakistan	Northampton	one-day	2000 p. 471	K, Q
	India v Pakistan	Manchester	one-day	2000 p. 478	K, Q
1999-2000	Challenger Series between India, India A and India B				CBI
	India v New Zealand	Ahmedabad	Test	2001 p. 1112	CBI
	South Africa v England	Centurion	Test	2001 p. 1075	K
	One-day series between South Africa, England and Zimbabwe				K
	India v South Africa	Mumbai	Test	2001 p. 1196	K
	India v South Africa	Bangalore	Test	2001 p. 1197	K
	India v South Africa	Nagpur	one-day	2001 p. 1202	K

BROTHERS IN ARMS

CURTLY AMBROSE

By MIKE ATHERTON

A cricketer's retirement, in both its timing and manner, can often tell you as much as you need to know about that player's career. In Curtly Ambrose's case, the timing, like his approach to the crease, was near perfect. He was still at the top of his game, as the 2000 series in England showed. Yet, some of his trademark pace and fire was beginning to wane, and in his final spell the aging legs seemed to be sending him a message. Rather than risk a trip too far to Australia, which with its unremitting heat, big grounds and flat wickets is no place for old bones, he decided enough was enough and left us with memories of how great he is, rather than was.

The manner of his retirement, too, was typically Ambrose-like. He announced at the beginning of the summer, with no histrionics, that the series against England would be his last, and, with little or no fuss from the big man himself, he was true to his word. There were precious few titbits for the media to scrap over, although he did give his old pal Michael Holding one interview to ruin that oft-quoted phrase, "Curtly talks to no one." In this modern age of image and spin, with the accent on style rather than substance, he has been a refreshing change. He went, as he came and then conquered, with little to say.

And yet, despite the low-key approach to retirement from Ambrose himself, rarely can a crowd or an opposition team have acknowledged a cricketer's leaving in such a fashion, an indication, if one were needed, of the high esteem in which he is held. It was one of the most touching moments I have seen on a field, when the Oval crowd rose to Ambrose and his great mate, Courtney Walsh, to applaud them off the field for an assumed last time. They left, arm-in-arm, one sensed close to tears, and halfway up the pavilion steps Ambrose symbolically removed his famous white armbands, safe in the knowledge that his legs would have to do no more pounding.

The next day, as he walked to the crease with West Indies on the brink of a famous defeat, the England team lined up and applauded him all the way to the wicket. It was a fitting mark of respect and, no doubt, a private thank you that their tormentor was finally on his way. (A few of us had remembered his wave to the Oval crowd five years before, hoping we wouldn't see him again.) In the middle of the salute he mumbled "Thanks, lads," which is about as much as I've heard him say. In cricket, even when you are losing, you can sometimes be a winner.

In statistical terms, Ambrose's career ranks amongst the very best the modern game has to offer. He took 405 Test wickets at a shade under 21, with a strike-rate of a wicket every 54 balls. Testimony to his parsimony is the 1,000th maiden in Test cricket that he notched up during last summer's series. As someone he dismissed more times than anybody else, I think I am reasonably well qualified to comment and compare him with the other fast bowlers from the last decade of the last millennium.

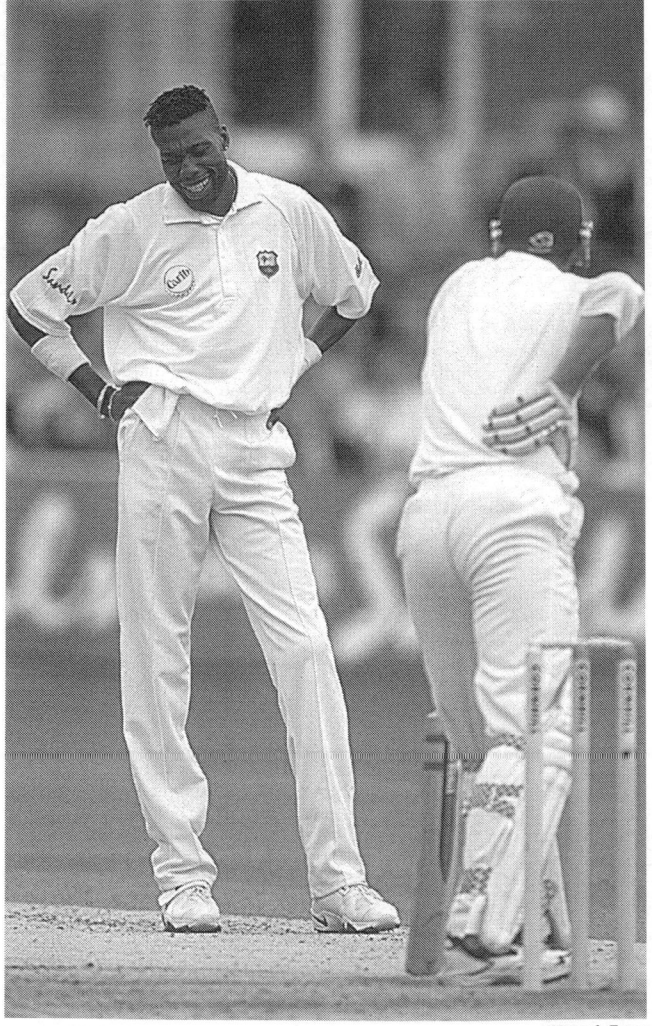

[*Patrick Eagar*

The worthiest of opponents: Curtly Ambrose and Mike Atherton treasure a moment at Lord's.

At his best, there is no doubt he moved beyond the fine line that separates the great from the very good. Quality bowlers essentially need two of three things: pace, movement and accuracy. Ambrose had all three. He was certainly quick, especially in the mid-1990s, and the extra bounce he generated from his beanpole frame made life even more awkward for the batsman. More than anything, though, he was a mean bowler: he hated giving runs away. Twice during last summer's series it took me half an hour to get off the mark, and then it was only a nudge off the inside edge through square leg for one. But each time Ambrose was livid with himself for offering even this measly morsel.

His best spell against England was undoubtedly at Trinidad's Queen's Park Oval in 1994. On a wearing fourth-innings pitch, we needed 194 to win. But from the very first ball, which he nipped back to trap me lbw, it looked a distant target. For the final frenetic hour on the fourth evening Ambrose steamed in, reducing the England innings to tatters (40 for eight) with as good a display of hostile and aggressive fast bowling as you will see. One look at Graham Thorpe's eyes as he walked off that evening told you everything. Ambrose's performance prompted Lord Kitchener to pen a calypso about him and about that extraordinary hour, and for the remainder of the tour the whole of the West Indies could be seen dancing to its beat. Lest you think it was only the English he harassed, his spell in Perth in 1993, when on the first day he took seven wickets for one run in 32 balls on a trampoline of a pitch, was apparently even more devastating. One can only be glad not to have been 22 yards away at the time.

As West Indies became more fragile during the second half of the 1990s, they came to rely on their fast bowlers more and more. So often defeat seemed inevitable, and yet somehow Ambrose and Walsh responded to the call. They always had. Their classic comeback was probably in the inaugural post-apartheid Test against South Africa at Bridgetown, where the West Indians, outplayed for four days, roused themselves through Walsh and Ambrose to an astonishing victory on the last day in front of a deserted Kensington Oval. With South Africa, eight wickets in hand, requiring another 79 runs, Ambrose took four for 16 and Walsh four for eight.

In spite, or maybe because, of the hostility of his bowling, there was never a battle of words with Ambrose. There was no need. In the truest sense, he let his cricket do the talking. The most I ever heard him say was "Morning, skipper," and there were never any verbals during our frequent battles in the middle. Over time, however, there was a little more animation, to add spice to the contest. Before the first ball of the innings, he came to have a habit of walking down the wicket, yards from the batsman, and looking at that area of the pitch he deemed to be the "business area". He would rub his hands with anticipation, and invariably at the end of the day there would be a cluster of ball marks worrying the patch.

This discipline and professionalism typified his bowling throughout his career. With his going, and the imminent departure of Courtney Walsh, West Indies have lost the last link with their great teams of the 1980s and early 1990s. Thankfully, for batsmen, there will no longer be the sight of Ambrose stood in mid-pitch after another wicket, pumping his arms skywards. He has been a magnificent servant to West Indies cricket, playing his part fully in carrying forward the famous fast-bowling legacy. He leaves an enormous hole to fill.

In 2000, Mike Atherton (Cambridge University, Lancashire and England) made his 100th Test appearance in the Third Test against West Indies, having captained England a record 52 times from 1993 to 1998. He writes for Wisden Cricket Monthly *and the* Sunday Telegraph.

COURTNEY WALSH

By VIC MARKS

As Courtney Walsh left the field in the final Test at The Oval, Viv Richards stood up in the BBC commentary box and clapped. He didn't say a word: I daresay that there was a great lump in his throat that prevented speech. For the six others in the box, this was as eloquent a tribute to Walsh as any man could muster. Quite what the millions of listeners made of the ensuing silence, I don't know.

Understand that old cricketers can be an unsentimental, cynical lot, and that clapping in press boxes is as frowned upon as cheering a missed putt at St Andrews. But there was a tear in the Richards eye as his old colleague and friend bade farewell to his English fans after 16 years of devoted international service. Richards knew better than most what a staggering contribution Walsh had made to West Indian cricket. The captor of the most Test wickets in history, he may not have been the greatest fast bowler to emerge from the Caribbean in the modern era. Even so, it is odd that when *Wisden* conducted a poll of 100 cricketers and writers, to establish the Five Cricketers of the Century, Walsh did not receive a single vote. For there has never been a more durable pace man, or a more wholehearted one.

He did not possess the grace of Michael Holding or the swinging guile of Malcolm Marshall, but he just kept going. The gnarled Australian, Dennis Waight, his physio with West Indies for more than a decade, said in 1997: "I've got a feeling that if Courtney stops playing, he'll never get started again." Sometimes he would exasperate Waight. Between Tests, he would pop back to his home club – Melbourne in Kingston, Jamaica – and, discovering they were short, agree to turn out. There, he would at least be fortified by some of the sumptuous Caribbean dishes provided by his mother, Joan, another stalwart of the club.

So he kept playing. When he came out for his final innings of the 2000 Test series, the England players formed a guard of honour. Alec Stewart and Mike Atherton were there, long-time adversaries who had been damned sure they had seen the last of him after the Antigua Test of 1998. They were wrong. But this time they could be certain that he would torment them no more in Test cricket. After all, England were not scheduled to play against West Indies until 2004; Courtney would be 41 by then.

His one regret must be that, when his Test career was coming to a close, West Indies appeared to be in freefall. (When it began, with an innings

[*Patrick Eagar*

Simply the man: Courtney Walsh just kept rolling them over.

COURTNEY WALSH

Season	Opposition	T	O	R	W	BB	5W/i	Avge	Aggregate
1984-85	in Australia	5	146.2	432	13	3-55	0	33.23	13
	v New Zealand	1	25	75	3	2-45	0	25.00	16
1985-86	v England	1	33	103	5	4-74	0	20.60	21
1986-87	v Pakistan	3	97.3	195	11	4-21	0	17.72	32
	in New Zealand	3	120.2	306	13	5-73	1	23.53	45
1987-88	in India	4	137.1	437	26	5-54	2	16.80	71
	v Pakistan	3	86	230	4	3-80	0	57.50	75
1988	in England	5	157.2	412	12	4-46	0	34.33	87
1988-89	in Australia	5	176.5	500	17	4-62	0	29.41	104
	v India	4	123.2	268	18	6-62	1	14.88	122
1989-90	v England	3	93.2	243	12	5-68	1	20.25	134
1990-91	in Pakistan	3	74	222	8	2-27	0	27.75	142
	v Australia	5	179.3	426	17	4-14	0	25.05	159
1991	in England	5	187	493	15	4-64	0	32.86	174
1991-92	v South Africa	1	49	102	4	4-31	0	25.50	178
1992-93	in Australia	5	175.1	467	12	4-91	0	38.91	190
	v Pakistan	3	80	207	12	4-56	0	17.25	202
1993-94	in Sri Lanka	1	30.1	60	1	1-40	0	60.00	203
	v England	5	227.2	646	19	5-94	1	34.00	222
1994-95	in India	3	140.5	361	17	6-79	1	21.23	239
	in New Zealand	2	70	132	16	7-37	2	8.25	255
	v Australia	4	148.3	431	20	6-54	1	21.55	275
1995	in England	6	290	786	26	5-45	1	30.23	301
1995-96	v New Zealand	2	82	204	8	4-72	0	25.50	309
1996-97	in Australia	5	192.3	592	19	5-74	2	31.15	328
	v India	4	119.2	250	4	1-7	0	62.50	332
	v Sri Lanka	2	67	218	7	4-73	0	31.14	339
1997-98	in Pakistan	3	101.1	306	14	5-78	2	21.85	353
	v England	6	261.2	564	22	4-80	0	25.63	375
1998-99	in South Africa	4	158.5	416	22	6-80	1	18.90	397
	v Australia	4	208.1	543	26	5-39	1	20.88	423
1999-2000	in New Zealand	2	78	226	3	2-81	0	75.33	426
	v Zimbabwe	2	80.3	134	9	3-21	0	14.88	435
	v Pakistan	3	123	292	14	5-22	2	20.85	449
2000	in England	5	220.2	436	34	6-74	2	12.82	483
2000-01	in Australia	5	199.4	481	11	2-39	0	43.72	494
Totals		**127**	**4,739.3**	**12,196**	**494**	**7-37**	**21**	**24.68**	

Research: Gordon Vince

victory in Australia in November 1984, they were invincible.) Hence the pleas for Walsh and his great friend and partner, Curtly Ambrose, to keep going beyond their natural lifespan as fast bowlers. Walsh, as ever, succumbed to those pleas and undertook yet another tour to Australia.

In the early days, Walsh was the general dogsbody of the West Indian attack. Bowling with the new ball was denied him; Holding, Marshall or Garner had earned that privilege. If there was a wind, Courtney would bowl into it. If there was a long partnership on a hot afternoon – admittedly a rare occurrence in that era – he would inevitably be tossed the ball, and he would receive it gratefully. So it took him 12 matches to acquire his first five-wicket haul in Test cricket.

However, dispel the notion that facing Walsh was the soft option when

CURTLY AMBROSE

Season	Opposition	T	O	R	W	BB	5W/i	Avge	Aggregate
1987-88	v Pakistan	3	114.2	365	7	2-64	0	52.14	7
1988	in England	5	203.1	445	22	4-53	0	20.22	29
1988-89	in Australia	5	204.3	558	26	5-72	1	21.46	55
	v India	4	93.5	273	5	3-66	0	54.60	60
1989-90	v England	3	132	307	20	8-45	1	15.35	80
1990-91	in Pakistan	3	106.4	239	14	5-35	1	17.07	94
	v Australia	5	205.4	493	18	3-36	0	27.38	112
1991	in England	5	249	560	28	6-52	2	20.00	140
1991-92	v South Africa	1	60.4	81	8	6-34	1	10.12	148
1992-93	in Australia	5	260.3	542	33	7-25	3	16.42	181
	v Pakistan	3	95	208	9	4-34	0	23.11	190
1993-94	in Sri Lanka	1	18.2	27	3	3-14	0	9.00	193
	v England	5	224.2	519	26	6-24	2	19.96	219
1994-95	in New Zealand	2	58.1	113	5	3-57	0	22.60	224
	v Australia	4	100.1	258	13	5-45	1	19.84	237
1995	in England	5	185.1	506	21	5-96	1	24.09	258
1995-96	v New Zealand	2	75	164	8	5-68	1	20.50	266
1996-97	in Australia	4	160.5	444	19	5-43	2	23.36	285
	v India	5	154.4	301	10	5-87	1	30.10	295
	v Sri Lanka	2	46.1	163	11	5-37	1	14.81	306
1997-98	in Pakistan	2	44	139	1	1-63	0	139.00	307
	v England	6	205.5	428	30	5-25	2	14.26	337
1998-99	in South Africa	4	124.5	309	13	6-51	1	23.76	350
	v Australia	4	184.2	423	19	5-94	1	22.26	369
1999-2000	v Zimbabwe	2	77	100	8	4-42	0	12.50	377
	v Pakistan	3	118.3	219	11	4-43	0	19.90	388
2000	in England	5	181.1	317	17	4-30	0	18.64	405
Totals		**98**	**3,683.5**	**8,501**	**405**	**8-45**	**22**	**20.99**	

Research: Gordon Vince

playing against West Indies in the 1980s. His gangling, slightly uncoordinated method of delivery suggested, treacherously, that the ball was coming in to the right-handed batsman. This was not always the case and led to scores of victims in the slip cordon. That distinctive, open-chested action as he glided through the crease – like many West Indian pace men raised on hard grounds, he did not bang his front foot into the turf, which may in part account for his freedom from serious injuries – made the ball hard to pick up. At least Holding had the decency to employ the perfect, classical action, which enabled an early sight of the ball.

Walsh changed his pace devilishly without any discernible change of action. As a result, he hit countless batsmen over the years, far more than Holding or Ambrose. From nowhere a lethal bouncer would appear; in his later days, he developed a brilliant slower ball that could rarely be spotted, either – especially when Graham Thorpe was at the crease. And as he grew older, he grew meaner. The inadequacies of the next generation of West Indian fast bowlers were exaggerated by the fact that Walsh and Ambrose in their final years gave the batsmen nothing to hit.

But it is his stamina and loyalty that single out Walsh, and examples abound of both qualities. In Perth in 1997, when he was leading the West Indian team, he tore a hamstring. "The doctor said he was finished," remembers Dennis Waight. "I iced him down all night and we did some static stretching the following morning. He took the field to give it a try and hobbled in off a short run. I thought he might last four or five overs; in the end he bowled 20 in a row and only stopped when the match was won. He didn't walk properly for another two weeks after that, but for Courtney the pain had all been worthwhile. That's special."

His reaction to his sacking as West Indian captain, when he was replaced by Brian Lara in 1998, is also instructive. In modern times, with the exception of Gerry Alexander and Garry Sobers, no West Indian captain, once removed from the job, had continued to play in the team. Walsh instinctively agreed to keep going and gave the new captain his public backing, which was much-needed as Lara's first match in charge was in Walsh's backyard in Kingston. Mike Atherton has recalled the scene at the start of the shortest Test in history (the match was abandoned because the Sabina Park pitch was dangerous): "As Brian led out his team, he did so with Courtney at his side, arm-in-arm, in an attempt to ease the transition and implore the Jamaicans to back the captain and West Indies. It was a gesture that showed you didn't have to be captain to be a leader of men."

His small ego and big heart dictated that this should be so, which surprised no one in Kingston or his adopted home of Bristol. For Walsh was no less loyal when playing for Gloucestershire. Over a period of 15 years, he was their overseas player. He never shirked, and several times he put the county in contention for the Championship almost single-handedly. In 1986 he took 118 wickets for them; in 1998 he was still at it, taking 106. The only significant spat came at the end, when there was confusion and some bitterness as it was decided later in 1998 that his services should not be retained. He wrote an open letter to his Gloucestershire supporters to explain his side of the dispute, just in case they thought he was deserting them.

Yet before we get too misty-eyed about Courtney, the man with the ever-ready smile off the field and the hilarious pantomime antics when taking guard, we should also bear in mind that, with ball in hand, he remained the most ruthless of operators. There were times when he was prepared to explore the limits of fair play. In 1994 in Jamaica, he launched a madcap assault on England's hopeless No. 11, Devon Malcolm, which could not be justified. Umpire Ian Robinson from Zimbabwe, in a shocking abnegation of his responsibilities, looked on without saying a dicky-bird. Walsh peppered Malcolm with a succession of vicious, needless bouncers. He showed no remorse for that spell.

Equally memorable, though more acceptable, was his assault on Mike Atherton in the same game. Walsh, a keen adherent of the West Indian "cut off the head and the rest will follow" philosophy, targeted Atherton with bouncers from around the wicket and refused to rest until England's captain was removed. He had given the same treatment to David Gower a decade earlier. In this instance, the cricket was awesome; with Malcolm on strike, it was just plain awful.

However, Walsh will be remembered as a gentleman of the game; one who basically kept playing because he loved it. He is also one of its greatest ambassadors. Indeed, he is now an official ambassador for Jamaica and carries a diplomatic passport. He has served West Indies proud. Just occasionally, he had some argument with his cricket board, most notably during the threat of strike action prior to the disastrous tour of South Africa in 1998-99. Then, his seniority demanded that he should be a key spokesman for the players. But once he has rested himself from the rigours of almost two decades of continuous cricket, he could easily re-emerge as a key figure on that board. They could do with his experience and common sense. And, in the knowledge that they no longer have to face him, his smiling face would be greeted without reservation by cricketers in every corner of the globe.

Vic Marks (Oxford University, Somerset, Western Australia and England) is cricket correspondent of The Observer *and author of* The Wisden Illustrated History of Cricket.

NEVER A FAMOUS CRICKETER

By JONATHAN RICE

In the Millennium Edition of *Wisden*, there is a section of photographs under the heading, "Images of the Century". One shows His Majesty King George V at Lord's on July 11, 1919 being introduced to the captains of Eton and Harrow. The captain of Harrow that "relieved yet forlorn summer", as the caption puts it, was W. A. R. Collins, later to gain success and fame as Sir William Collins, the publisher. The photograph prompts the question, how many people are hidden within the pages of *Wisden* who achieved fame in fields other than cricket? How many schoolboy cricketers went on to become publishers, politicians, soldiers or writers? *Wisden* does not only record the cricketers who score centuries at Lord's or take 400 Test wickets. When Sir Edward Lewis, founder and managing director of the Decca Record Company, died in 1980, *Wisden* wryly noted that he was one of those men whose "lifelong devotion to cricket does not stem from personal triumphs on the field". But after all, what do they know of cricket who only cricket know?

We should probably start with royalty. The only member of British royalty to have played first-class cricket is Prince Christian Victor, grandson of Queen Victoria, who had one first-class game, for I Zingari against the Gentlemen of England in August 1887. On page 312 of the 1888 edition, *Wisden* records his scores, stumped 35 and bowled A. E. Stoddart 0, but does not mention how well he played. The *Wisden* obituary of King George VI in 1953 records that he "performed the hat-trick on the private ground on the slopes below Windsor Castle". A left-handed bowler, the future king bowled his grandfather King Edward VII, his father King George V and his elder brother David, later King Edward VIII, with three consecutive balls. The value of this achievement must be qualified by the fact that Edward VII died when the then Prince Albert of Wales was 15, so the hat-trick was by a young boy in the back garden against three people who never showed any aptitude for the game. Still, it made the pages of *Wisden*. And there's a picture of his grandson, Prince Charles, executing a sweep in the 1969 edition. The best recent royal cricketer seems to be the present Duke of York, who features in the 1980 *Wisden* as captain of Gordonstoun's XI. As HRH Prince Andrew, he is credited on page 895 that year with a batting average of 23.55, and a bowling average of 4.54, having taken 11 wickets for just 50 runs. *Wisden* notes sagely that "Gordonstoun had an average team and report a difficulty in obtaining good school fixtures. The batting proved adequate but the bowling lacked penetration."

Many of the soldiers who gain a mention in *Wisden's* despatches do so in the obituary columns, and have only a tenuous link to cricket. Captain the Hon. Fergus Bowes-Lyon, HM the Queen Mother's elder brother, was killed in France on September 24, aged 26, as the 1916 edition reports. "He was a keen cricketer and took part in the autumn fixtures at Glamis Castle." However, Field-Marshal Earl Alexander of Tunis played for Harrow against Eton in 1910, when he was still the Hon. H. R. L. G. Alexander and, several years earlier, another Field-Marshal, Montgomery of Alamein, played for

St Paul's School in 1905 and 1906. He showed his never-say-die attitude at an early stage, as *Wisden* reported in 1906: "When the full team were able to play, they gave a good account of themselves, Cooper and Montgomery against Merton College putting on over 100 for the last wicket when a severe defeat seemed impending." If Waterloo was won on the playing fields of Eton, perhaps El Alamein was won on the playing fields of St Paul's.

A little later on, D. R. S. Bader appears in the St Edmund's, Oxford team of 1928 as captain, "forcing batsman and fast bowler". Three years later, Pilot Officer Bader played for the RAF against the Army and made 65. "Apart from a brilliant display by Bader, whose 65 occupied 40 minutes, the Air Force batting proved very disappointing." An even better rugby player than cricketer, he would probably have been capped by England but for his flying accident.

There are many who have gained greater distinction at other sports who nevertheless found a tiny space in *Wisden*. Geoff Hurst played one game for Essex, against Lancashire at Liverpool in 1962, but scored three fewer than he did in the World Cup final four years later. Mr M. P. Betts, who scored the winning goal in the first FA Cup final in 1872, is listed on page 340 of the 1889 Almanack as seconding a motion at an MCC meeting. England centre-forward Tommy Lawton's obituary in 1997 records that "as a teenager he played Lancashire League cricket for Burnley, and hit Learie Constantine for two consecutive sixes." Other footballers who feature in the pages of *Wisden* include three goalkeepers – Steve Ogrizovic (Shropshire and Coventry City), Andy Goram, a double international for Scotland at cricket and football, and William "Fatty" Foulke, Sheffield United and England's vast but skilful goalkeeper, who played four games for Derbyshire in 1900, making a top score of 53 against Essex.

Gary Lineker's appearance for MCC against Germany in 1992 is not given the full treatment in *Wisden*. The result of the match (a draw) and the team totals are there, and the individual effort of Lineker ("I always score one against Germany") is reported. He crops up again in 1996, on page 1349, where we learn that "In a celebrity match, Bill Wyman of the Rolling Stones took what he claimed was the first televised hat-trick at The Oval. His victims were television newsreader Trevor McDonald, cricket presenter Charles Colvile and Gary Lineker, the retired football star." That's at least as tough a hat-trick as three kings at Windsor.

Billy Williams, the developer of the famous cabbage patch that became Twickenham, played 27 matches for Middlesex between 1885 and 1902, switching from wicket-keeping to leg-breaks halfway through his career. Rugby is indeed a game with many links to cricket: Scotland's 1990 Grand Slam captain, David Sole, topped the Glenalmond batting averages in 1979. The 1980 *Wisden* (page 894) shows D. M. B. Sole with a top score of 73 and an average of 26.15. Rob Andrew first appears in *Wisden* as a schoolboy all-rounder at Barnard Castle – as captain in 1981, his side was neither beaten nor bowled out – and he went on to win his Blue at Cambridge for cricket as well as rugby. W. H. "Dusty" Hare played for Nottinghamshire sporadically from 1971, Simon Halliday played for Oxford University and Dorset, while, across the divide, Great Britain rugby league winger Martin Offiah turned out once for Essex Second Eleven in 1985. Figures of none for 66 in 12 overs, and a duck, suggest "going north" to Widnes, then Wigan, was the right career move. Sir Michael Bonallack, winner of golf's Amateur Championship and a leading administrator in the game, is there on page 286 of the 1952 edition, playing for Haileybury against Cheltenham. He too scored a duck, but took six wickets for 55 in the drawn game.

When H. W. Austin opened the batting for Repton in 1924 and 1925, H. S. Altham noted that "Austin was very sound and correct" yet "may, I fear, transfer his allegiance to another game at Cambridge, whither he has now gone, but he was a good school batsman, sound and imperturbable." The other game was lawn tennis, at which Bunny Austin was twice a Wimbledon singles finalist. He is not the only tennis champion to appear in the pages of *Wisden*, though. Frank Hadow, a 23-year-old tea planter on leave from Ceylon, won the Wimbledon title in 1878 before a crowd of about 500, and then went back to the Orient undefeated. In 1873, at the age of 18, he had played at Lord's for Harrow against Eton in front of 28,000, and scored 54 not out to win the game. The *Wisden* reporter called his innings "one of the ablest displays of true and skilful cricket seen in a Public School match for several seasons."

The connection between cricket and the arts is well known, and rather better catalogued in *Wisden* than one might expect. Joseph Wells, the father of H.G., was a professional cricketer who took four wickets in four balls for Kent against Sussex in 1862. Among his quartet of victims was Spencer Austen-Leigh, the great-nephew of Jane Austen, so providing the only known cricketing connection between *Pride and Prejudice* and *The War of the Worlds*. In 1900, P. G. Wodehouse opened the bowling for Dulwich College with the future England bowler, N. A. Knox. Wodehouse later took the name of his most famous character from the Warwickshire bowler, Percy Jeeves, who was killed in the Great War. Also in 1900, A. A. Milne was playing for Westminster School, but it is not known after which cricketer he named his great character, Eeyore. Another war casualty was R. C. Brooke, whom we find in the 1907 *Wisden* topping the bowling averages at Rugby with 19 wickets at 14.05 each. His obituary in the 1916 edition deals fully with his cricketing career, and also notes that "he gained a reputation as a poet."

Sir Arthur Conan Doyle's obituary in 1931 points out that "although never a famous cricketer, he could hit hard and bowl slows with a puzzling flight. For MCC v Cambridgeshire at Lord's in 1899, he took seven wickets for 61 runs." Alas, the full scorecard is not printed in the 1900 edition. In that game, however, the umpire was Thomas Mycroft, the likely source of the name of Sherlock Holmes's elder brother. Samuel Beckett is the only Nobel literature laureate who played first-class cricket, at least until Dickie Bird is honoured for his writings. Beckett played twice for Dublin University in first-class fixtures, against Northamptonshire in 1925 and 1926. In the latter match he made just four and one, opening the batting with C. M. Deverell, who went on to become Sir Colville Deverell, Governor of the Windward Islands. Beckett's initials in *Wisden* are wrongly given as S. V. (it was S. B. Beckett), but such is fame. Even Bradman was listed as D. J. Bradman when he first came to England.

[Bill Smith]   *[Hulton Getty]*

Left: Shipton Beauty: in *Wisden* as a schools cricketer, Sam Mendes made another entrance when he played in the 1997 National Village final. *Right: Daily Telegraph* cricket correspondent Jim Swanton and Bernard Hollowood, editor of *Punch*, made *Wisden's* pages as cricketers in the 1930s. This opening partnership, for the Authors against the National Book League in 1958, went unrecorded.

Another interesting opening partnership appears in the Eton v Harrow match of 1929, when Harrow's first two were Mr N. M. V. Rothschild and Mr T. M. Rattigan. Terence Rattigan went on to great fame as a writer of plays (and of the screenplay of *The Final Test*, starring Jack Warner, Robert Morley and Len Hutton), while Rothschild played 11 first-class games for Cambridge and Northamptonshire in the early 1930s, before becoming the 3rd Lord Rothschild. More recent captains of industry in *Wisden's* hidden recesses are Steve Russell and the Australian Rod Eddington, appointed in 2000 as chief executive respectively of Boots plc and British Airways.

"S. G. Russell certainly proved an inspiring captain," the 1968 *Wisden* recorded after his third year in the Cambridge eleven, "and... in the University match he was the best and fastest of the quick bowlers on either side". Quick enough, too, to open the bowling for Surrey against Nottinghamshire at the end of the season. Among his charges that summer were freshman Roger Knight, later of Surrey, Gloucestershire and Sussex, and secretary of MCC, and the Essex off-spinner and Olympic fencer, David Acfield. Eddington played eight games for Oxford University as a contemporary of two Test cricketers, Vic Marks and Chris Tavaré, and a sporting parson, Andrew Wingfield Digby. Of his 24 against Middlesex in 1976, batting at No. 11, *Wisden* observed that "Gurr and Eddington contributed a valuable 53 for the last wicket." Sadly, his efforts did not result in a Blue; he was twelfth man at Lord's.

Sam Mendes, the Oscar-winning director of *American Beauty*, did not go to Oxford or Cambridge, but was a brilliant schoolboy cricketer, as *Wisden* records in 1983 and 1984. In those two years for Magdalen College School he scored 1,153 runs at 46, and took 83 wickets at under 16 each. He now plays regularly for Harold Pinter's wandering side, The Gaieties. Bernard Hollowood, cartoonist and editor of *Punch* in its heyday, played for Staffordshire in the 1930s and 1940s. John Fowles, author of *The French Lieutenant's Woman* (for which Pinter wrote the screenplay), appeared for Bedford School from 1942 to 1944 as a swing and "cutting" bowler, and had a trial for Essex: it is possibly not insignificant that he lines up in the 1943 *Wisden* alongside Auden, Bacon and Fletcher. Future academics and critics may be interested in Fowles's belief that "the gate-key to all Pinter's work is his intense and evident love of cricket".

Freddie Grisewood, the broadcaster, played for Radley and once for Worcestershire in 1908. Alec Waugh, C. P. Snow, Edmund Blunden, Andrew Lang and Compton Mackenzie all merit obituaries in *Wisden*. H. L. Aubrey-Fletcher, to be found in the ranks of Buckinghamshire players between 1921 and 1929, wrote detective fiction under the name "Henry Wade". The list goes on and on.

I have not even touched on politicians. Sir Alec Douglas-Home, when Lord Dunglass, is the only prime minister to have played first-class cricket, but plenty of other politicians have featured in *Wisden's* pages. Sam Silkin, attorney-general from 1974 to 1979, played two first-class games in 1938, for Cambridge and Glamorgan. In the 1965 *Wisden*, there is a short Note by the Editor entitled "Prime Ministers at Cricket", which mentions among other odd facts that Ian Smith, then Prime Minister of Rhodesia, watched Mashonaland Country Districts XI play Cross Arrows at Lord's the previous September. The church is as well represented as the state. "It may seem a little strange to include Cardinal Manning's name in a cricket obituary," noted *Wisden* in 1893, "but inasmuch as he played for Harrow against Winchester at Lord's in 1825, in the first match that ever took place between the two schools, his claim cannot be disputed."

And finally, there is Peter the cat. He died in 1964, and Lord's was the lesser for his passing. But *Wisden* in 1965 was all the richer for his obituary.

Jonathan Rice's books on cricket include The Pavilion Book of Pavilions, Curiosities of Cricket *and* One Hundred Lord's Tests. *He features in* Wisden *as a cricketer for the first time in this edition on page 1528.*

COLIN COWDREY – THE SPIRIT OF CRICKET

By HUBERT DOGGART

The initials MCC, given his young son by his cricket-loving father, could well have been a Sword of Damocles over a lesser person. In fact, they proved an inspiration to one who would come to adorn cricket as a batsman and slip-catcher of the highest calibre, a person who displayed those images of clean-cut sportsmanship, even chivalry, to be found in a tale by John Buchan, and an administrator who constantly fought for "The Spirit of Cricket" against shabby behaviour on and off the field. The Preamble with that title to the new code of the Laws of Cricket, published by "MCC the club", owed much to the initiative and inspiration of "MCC the man".

Colin had been making slow but genuine progress after a stroke on July 30, and it came as a considerable shock, almost a reversal of nature, when a friend rang late on the evening of Monday, December 4, to tell us the bleak news about his serious heart attack and subsequent death. It was a death, at the relatively young age of 67, which impinged on a wide circle of friends, in England and overseas, as well as on his immediate family, who meant much to him. The obituaries and other articles that followed Colin's death were understandably warm.

Although I had watched the end of his 116 against Cambridge in 1953, it was not until the 1954 season that I saw at close quarters the effortless strokeplay that became one of the hallmarks of his batting. He really did time the ball "like an angel". We were opposing captains, he for Oxford and I for Sussex, on a grace term from Winchester College. I became immediately aware of his friendly authority and his innate devotion to the game, and we began a partnership and a friendship that lasted until his death. This included playing together in the 1959 and 1960 amateur rackets doubles competition. As you would expect, he was the ideal partner, always skilful, both in anticipation and in striking a rackets ball, always sporting and always unruffled at a time of crisis.

The first chance we had to work together in cricket was 1956, when we went in harness, he as captain and I as vice-captain, on what could fairly be called "E. W. Swanton's First Missionary Journey to the West Indies", the result of Jim's disappointment at the tension that existed between the two Test teams on the MCC tour of 1953-54. Before we left, J. L. Manning, the *Daily Mail* sportswriter, imagined the manager and the players "binding the Commonwealth together with Swantonian cement". I came to recognise, on that tour, the great "binding" gifts displayed by our captain.

This tour took place some 15 months after Colin had played, not many days past his 22nd birthday, what some observers thought his finest innings ever. In the New Year Test at Melbourne, England had lost four wickets quickly to Lindwall and Miller, and Colin's riposte was a wonderful 102, out of a mere 191, with "perfectly timed drives, both straight and to cover" and skilful play off his legs. This remarkable innings helped prepare the way for the great feats of England's bowlers in that Test and the next.

[*Patrick Eagar*

Colin Cowdrey congratulates opposing captain Clive Lloyd after the 1976 West Indians had won their tour-opener at Arundel.

Colin was the first player to appear in 100 Tests, and he captained England in 27, but sadly for him never in Australia, to which he made six tours. The last time, in the winter before he retired, he was summoned as a replacement at the age of 41, almost 42, to face Lillee and Thomson at the height of their ferocity.

Perhaps his happiest memories stemmed from his remarkable partnership at his beloved Kent, he as a successful captain from 1957 to 1971 with Leslie Ames as secretary/manager. In 1970, Kent won the Championship for the first time since 1913. He was, of course, delighted that two of his sons, Chris and Graham, followed him into the Kent side, Chris as captain from 1985 to 1990 – and of England in one Test. Colin was Kent's president at the time of his death and, whenever over the years unable to attend a match, would regularly check the Ceefax in his study to see how they were faring.

A great part of Colin's engaging personality, which included a teasing sense of humour that could transform any exchange, was conditioned by a strict but sympathetic upbringing, his Christian faith, which developed over the years, and his belief that the old-fashioned virtues of the gentleman were of paramount importance. Thus he never spared himself in his service to cricket and to cricketers, and to those other bodies he served.

These included MCC and the ICC, for whom he travelled many thousands of miles on behalf of change, not least for South Africa's return to Test cricket; The Lord's Taverners, for whom, through regular visits to the regions and the evocative power of his speeches, he worked tirelessly as president for three years; the Skinners' Company, of which he was master in 1985-86; the Association of Cricket Umpires, whose president he still was at his death; the Cricket at Arundel Castle, where the indoor cricket school will always be a memorial to him; and, near the end of his life, the House of Lords, to which John Major elevated him as a spokesman on sporting matters, and which he enjoyed to the hilt.

Two brief illustrations reflect his caring and meticulous approach to responsibility. The first concerns the invitation from the headmaster of Caldicott Preparatory School to be the first prize-giver of his tenure. Rare for a prize-giver, Colin insisted on going to Caldicott before the day to "have a net", as cricketers say, and ensure that he would play an innings on prize-giving day as immaculate as that at Melbourne in 1954.

The second is his finding the time and the energy, when he had his own problems near the end of his life, to write to me, on my retirement as president of the English Schools' Cricket Association, a precious note that thanked, applauded and encouraged. Such notes, like his timing of a cricket ball, were very much his hallmark, whether to those in authority or to those who had borne the heat of the day in a more humble role.

In simple truth, Colin Cowdrey was an exceptional person as well as an exceptional player, one who was both inspired by cricket and, through his idealism and his unashamed love for the game, an inspiration to young and old alike.

Hubert Doggart captained Cambridge University and Sussex, and in 1950 played twice for England.

INTO THE DARK, COLD NIGHT

By FRANK KEATING

A radiant era, rich in recollection, seems in a sudden rush to pull down the blinds and shut out its sunlight. In 1997, cavalier nonpareil Compton; two years later, merry gallivant Evans and the rigorous Washbrook. Now, for pity's sake, Statham and Cowdrey.

For those of us of a certain age, when we were wide-eyed Jacks and they were giants, those distant mists through which strode England's cricketers of the 1950s will always be tinged with an auroral sparkle, a golden lustre. For summer after summer when we were young, a civilised, untroubled game rolled amiably along, genially cocooned in its own freemasonry. We in the grey, monochrome crowds, with our single-sheet un-glossy scorecards and unfancy picnics, were illuminated to a rosy glow by these knights in what seemed shining white. I am not absolutely certain about cloudless skies but, golly, the grass really was greener then. And progress was a simple fact, not an order-in-council directive of cockeyed and manic decree.

Those luminaries of England's cricket were household names that tripped off the tongues not only of monarchs and peers and bishops and fathers and sons, but just as readily of wives and mothers, sisters, cousins and aunts. They were praetorian guardsmen of the very culture and lore. Serious poets wrote seriously heroic poems about them. Fore and aft of that mid-century decade, towering figures serenade the memory in a rhapsody of twosomes like love and marriage, horse and carriage: Hutton and Washbrook, Edrich and Compton, May and Cowdrey, Laker and Lock, Statham and Trueman.

Wretched life – or, rather, loss of it. Only a solitary one is left of that resonantly stirring five-brace constellation: only the last is alive still and shining, the man called Fred, good true-to-himself brass tacks 'n' bluster Fred. He was 70 this year, almost two years older than Cowdrey and some half a year younger than Statham. Colin dedicated his whole self to cricket, and in those terms his life of devotion, and achievement, was a mighty long one. He was thinking of the good of cricket on the day he died (and, I daresay, on the day he was born). Brian devoted his life to bowling and so, in comparison, his was a short one. The phrase "he bowled his boots off" was surely minted for, or even because of, him.

Cowdrey and Statham were of the same time, the same land, and both were garlanded for their deeds at the sharpest end of their game's two disciplines. But they had arrived from totally different, and distant, points of ken and culture. In background and outlook they were alpha and omega, sun and moon, or, while we are about it, chalk and cheese.

Did Lord Cowdrey of Tonbridge choose that title because the lovelorn and lonely, but privileged, child had been happiest there at school under the familial canopy of its cloisters? Still in his school cap, the patrician princeling played first for Kent at windswept Derby. Welcome to the hard-graft workaday world, kid. Les Jackson, the former miner, shocked him by bowling a spiteful bouncer. The boy hurried off to enquire of Les Ames and Arthur Fagg the

[*Hulton Getty*

Brian Statham at 20, fresh from national service and ready to do duty for county and country.

correct grip and technique for bouncers. He may have continued forever to fret over the intricacies of his talent, but there was never doubt about his valiance, or the touching gift of his quiet, sheepish, smile at triumph or disappointment alike.

Not many weeks before, in that precise midsummer of the century, the same staunch Arthur Fagg had opened Kent's innings at Old Trafford. He had followed on to that greenest of famed fields a Lancashire team that included for the first time, on his 20th birthday, a stringy uncoached colt who was being warned by his captain, Washbrook: "Don't bowl short to Arthur, lad, else he'll flog you out of sight." The cub, a natural, knew not what an out-swinger was, nor a yorker, let alone which Kent opener answered to Arthur. So he shrugged, and reasoned that if he dropped one short – just one – he would soon find out and take it from there. Arthur went for the hook, but the rearing ball hurried on him: Fagg c Wharton b Statham 4.

Four years later Cowdrey and Statham were England team-mates in Australia. For the next ten summers and winters, there was an aura about their different skills, and an innate pride in us that we possessed such players. Creative invention and authentic artistry. Both Cowdrey and Statham were strong and courageous in their totally different, craft-versed ways. Cowdrey's power was concealed in his timing; his was the gentlest of strengths. As Alan Ross had it, Cowdrey's batsmanship was redolent of both "the richest of ports and the lightest of soufflés". For Statham, invariably up the hill and into the wind, line and length were inseparable companions. Maupassant wrote a tale of a circus knife-thrower who found, when he tried during their act to murder his unfaithful wife, that it was impossible to deviate from his ingrained and grooved pattern of hurling the daggers to miss her by fractions. Or as the bowler's Boswell, Eric Midwinter, bettered: "Brian could no more bowl a bad ball than Paderewski could hit a wrong note."

Even when, in later adult life, I was privileged to meet them, my sense of wonder in their presence never remotely diluted. Almost the sole published testament to his life's work that Statham uttered was, "If they missed, I hit." Enquire about details, and he'd shrug and say, with his unbothered half-grin, "Look it up in the book, it's all in there somewhere." And so it always will be. Indelibly. He lissomly bowled his last first-class delivery – his 100,955th, and the sixth ball of his fifth consecutive maiden – in the 1968 Roses match at Old Trafford, and then loped quietly away from the downstage limelight into more shadows. By happy fluke, all of seven summers on, I saw the very last of Cowdrey's 107 centuries, 119 undefeated against Procter and Graveney and Childs, and nicely at Cheltenham where the mellow, timeless, architecture of his drives, downhill all the way most of them, matched the slumbrous serenity of the College chapel in the golden evening of a heatwave.

In the winter before Colin Cowdrey died, when he was obviously none too well, I helped arrange for the now slippered, ermined eminence to make the journey all the long way westwards from Arundel to open a new technology wing at Hereford Cathedral School. And having done those honours, might he give an evening talk on cricket in Leominster? He would be privileged to do both, he said. Blimey! Squires and farmers' boys (and wives and sisters) packed the Corn Exchange to hear him. We were entranced, tight-squashed and some hanging off the rafters almost, till past 11 o'clock. Surely, he would stay the night? "What a wonderful evening, but no," the morrow was the House of Lords. And off he went, with that soft smile, into the dark, cold, night.

Frank Keating is sports columnist on The Guardian.

[Graham Morris

England captain Nasser Hussain displays the Wisden Trophy at The Oval, after England had won
a West Indies series for the first time since 1969.

OUT OF THE DARKNESS...

[*Graham Morris*

Even fast-fading light could not save Pakistan from a first-ever Test defeat at Karachi. Graham Thorpe and Nasser Hussain head for the pavilion to celebrate England's second series win in Pakistan. Their December victory put the seal on England's triumphant 2000.

[*Darren McNamara, Allsport*

Australia took cricket indoors during their winter when Melbourne's Colonial Stadium staged three one-day internationals against South Africa in August. The pitch was prepared elsewhere, transported by low-loader and dropped into place.

THE LAST TEST

[*Graham Morris*

With almost 900 Test wickets between them, Curtly Ambrose and Courtney Walsh take their leave at The Oval. For Ambrose, it was the end of the line; for Walsh, his last Test in England.

THE FIRST TEST

[PA Photos

November saw Bangladesh become the tenth Test-playing nation when they took on India at Dhaka. Aminul Islam graced the occasion with a century, only the third time a player had reached three figures in his country's debut Test, after Australia's Charles Bannerman in 1877 and Zimbabwe's Dave Houghton in 1992.

TAKE CRICKET TO THE PEOPLE...

[*Mike Finn-Kelcey, Allsport*

More than 10,000 packed Scarborough's North Marine Road ground for the crucial Championship match between Yorkshire and Surrey.

...AND THE PEOPLE WILL COME TO CRICKET

[*Adrian Murrell, Allsport*

The biggest fifth-day crowd in more than a generation swarm across The Oval to acclaim England's victory over West Indies. Thousands more failed to gain entrance when the gates were shut soon after play began.

[*Gordon Brooks*

Since 1986, his vibrant and extravagant costumes had provided a focus for cricket fans at St John's, Antigua. But in May 2000, Labon Kenneth Blackburn Llewelyn Bouchan Benjamin, aka Gravy, decided to call it a day.

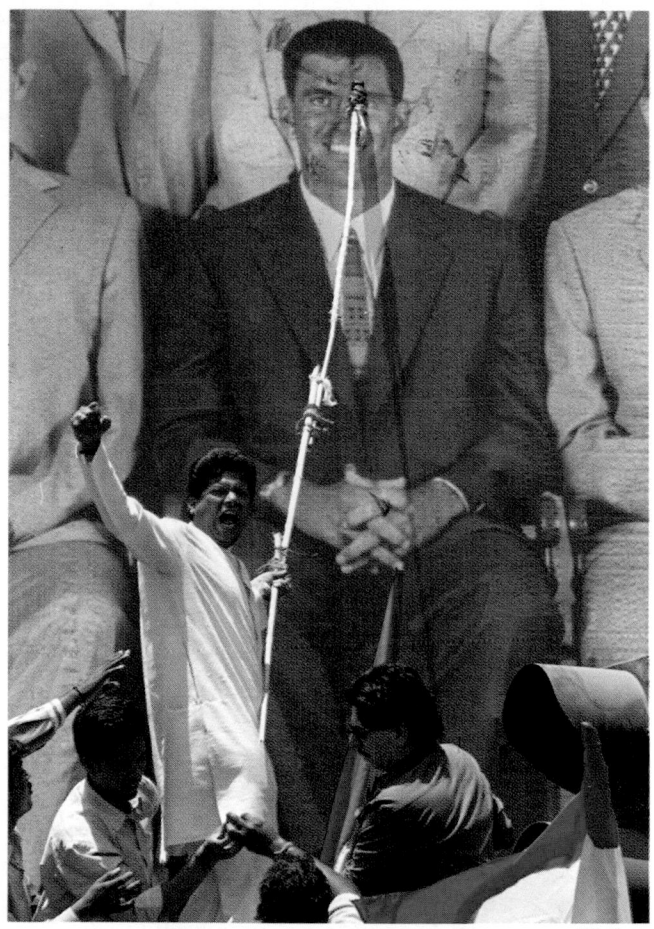

[*PA Photos*

Hansie Cronje's betrayal of cricket excited different reactions around the world. In Mumbai, protesters expressed their anger by defacing a poster of Cronje who, with the South African team, had modelled a range of menswear.

FIVE CRICKETERS OF THE YEAR

[*Graham Morris*

MARK ALLEYNE

FIVE CRICKETERS OF THE YEAR

[*David Munden*

MARTIN BICKNELL

FIVE CRICKETERS OF THE YEAR

[*Graham Morris*

ANDREW CADDICK

[*Graham Morris*

JUSTIN LANGER

[*George Herringshaw, ASP*

DARREN LEHMANN

[Briony Allen

Jim Swanton's cherished 1939 *Wisden*, rebound in remnants of gas cape and glued with rice paste by Foster and Gauld POW Bookbinders, Nakawn Paton, 1944. A fading purple Japanese "not subversive" stamp is discernible top left of the title page; on the left facing page is the inscription, "Major E. W. Swanton, RA, Hut 44 nr Paton." The Almanack now resides in the Lord's Museum.

A WISDEN'S WAR

By DAVID RAYVERN ALLEN

It was a cool evening, but not yet sundown. Sitting on a small but steep concave hill, with straggly bits of cloth their only protection against the early dew, were hundreds of men. On a flat area at the base of the hill was a stage of bamboo, covered with matting. In the centre of the stage, and also made of bamboo and matting, was a structure shaped like a huge radio set. A rectangular section near the top had been cut away, and crude lamps burning peanut oil shone through the aperture to give the effect of a lighted dial. Immediately underneath was a round hole covered with hessian – "a speaker".

Behind the "radio set" was a screen, and behind that Major E. W. Swanton and his assistants were at work. It was time for the weekly "Radio Newsreel" at Tarsao, a grim prisoner-of-war base camp in the jungle on the Burma–Siam Railway. Jim was on the camp entertainment committee, and frequently Tuesday night was devoted to cricket. As he began to speak, the already well-known voice warmed the audience. Although weakened by the loss of some four stone to an unvarying diet of broken rice, watery marrow and infected water, he still could be heard clearly. The geographical lie made a natural amphitheatre. With a large number of Australians in the audience, the topic for the evening, "The Life of Bradman", was a sure success.

On different occasions and on different aspects of cricket, that scene was replicated at camps up and down the line. And fuelling all these talks – lectures, as they were often called – with facts, information and statistics was one book: *Wisden Cricketers' Almanack* 1939, Jim's *Wisden*. Dog-eared and rebound time and again with gas-cape covers, and glued together with rice paste, it was a treasured item, a fundamental source, which had travelled with its owner around various billets in Britain *en route* to Thailand via Nova Scotia, the South Atlantic, South Africa and Singapore. "Thumbed by thousands in 12 different camps," according to E.W.S., it was in such demand that a time limitation of half a day became the condition of "a lend". Fortunately for its long-term preservation and short-term protection there was no shortage of available expertise. At the officers' camp at Kanburi alone, there was a body of professional and amateur bookbinders 20 strong.

Never had the "Cricketer's Bible" more literally suited that description. So many found *Wisden* was the route for escape. For precious moments, harsh reality could be put to one side. The endless days of stamina-sapping humidity and personal discomfort, blasting and drilling rock, digging red clay soil, clearing the jungle itself, the tyrannical regime of their captors and the constant death toll – all of that could be forgotten as the daydream inspired by the Almanack's pages brought back good times in the past and triggered images of better times in the future. In this way, Jim's 1939 *Wisden* was a saviour. We shall never know how many lives were sustained by its being on call to conquer despair.

David Rayvern Allen is the editor of E. W. Swanton, A Celebration of his Life and Work.

FIVE CRICKETERS OF THE YEAR

MARK ALLEYNE

For all that runs and wickets proved elusive, it is eminently possible that no county captain will enjoy a summer quite so thoroughly as Mark Alleyne enjoyed 2000. Winning one-day competitions in England is often a lottery, overly dependent on the vagaries of clouds, dew, pitch and toss. Yet here was this stocky, mild-mannered man leading his club to an unprecedented clean sweep of NatWest Trophy, Benson and Hedges Cup and Norwich Union National League, to go with 1999's NatWest and Benson and Hedges Super Cup triumphs.

That club, improbably, was Gloucestershire – the same sepia-tinted institution boasting alumni such as W.G., Hammond and Parker, Procter, Zaheer and Walsh, yet whom collective glory had shunned with almost sadistic persistence. How instructive, after two pots had turned up all century, that five should arrive in just over a year, due reward for a side whose modest individual talents found ample compensation in an immodest degree of collective spirit and purpose.

One major influence was that perceptive, personable coach, John Bracewell, a rare fusion – in cricket at least – of deft man-manager and proud socialist. New Zealand's greatest off-spinner, appointed at Alleyne's behest, prefers to redirect the plaudits. "Jack [Russell] and Mark were the keys. Jack's the intimidator; Mark's calm, a natural leader. Paternal, extremely tolerant. Has a great way with people, works with them one-on-one, makes them think, 'he thinks I'm important'. They like him, respect him as a man."

Alleyne has scaled personal peaks, notably his 112 off 91 balls that routed Yorkshire in the 1999 Benson and Hedges final at Lord's. He became Gloucestershire's youngest century-maker at 18 and, at 22, their second-youngest Championship double-centurion after Hammond. Composed and inventive in the middle order, canny with seam, elasticated in covers and behind stumps, he was the Championship's most effective all-rounder from 1993 to 1999 (6,409 runs at 32.53, 216 wickets at 31.18). He has also won ten one-day international caps, with power to add. "When we played Surrey in the Super Cup, our first big televised game, Mark came on and nailed them down for ten overs," recalls Bracewell. "It was the defining moment for this side." Nevertheless, memories of Mark Alleyne the player seem destined to be less vivid than those of Mark Alleyne, captain and man.

Mike Procter was still celebrating his maiden county hundred when MARK WAYNE ALLEYNE was born in Tottenham on May 23, 1968. Though he was bred in his parents' native Barbados, the most profound influence was his elder sibling, Stephen. When Stephen's hunger for education brought him back to north London, Mark followed him to the home of a family friend amid the orthodox Jewish enclave of Stamford Hill. "It was very difficult to leave Barbados," reflects Mark, who had just led Harrison College, alma mater to so many Bajan achievers, to the Under-15 Roland Tree Cup, "but I missed Stephen."

Both won places at Haringey Cricket College, a spartan, council-funded enterprise for underprivileged youth. There they came under the keen, avuncular eye of Reg Scarlett, the erstwhile West Indies off-spinner; half a dozen classmates, remarkably, graduated to the first-class lists, including Warwickshire wicket-keeper Keith Piper. For Mark, though, those two years were primarily about moulding character. "There are 13-year-olds who know they're going to get chances because they go to the right school or university. I never had that confidence. We'd *all* had to battle. There was a sense of shared experience, and enormous pleasure when we beat a county Second Eleven, which was often. We inspired each other."

Stephen was captain, but rejection brought disillusionment. When Gloucestershire invited Stephen for a trial, Mark went along in support and found himself playing after others failed to show; he was the brother who impressed. The guilt lingers: "I wouldn't have played cricket if not for Stephen. There was some strain, but he never expressed any jealousy."

Mark soon became "Boo-Boo" – David Lawrence, Gloucestershire's genial giant of a fast bowler, was "Yogi Bear" – but the alias is rarely heard now. "We don't believe in nicknames," asserts Bracewell. "It's a public school thing, and generally derogatory. People at this club used to have a vested interest in mediocrity. Their humour was all about keeping guys down. It needed a clear-out, and Mark oversaw that. The attitude now is 'laugh with, not at'. Mark's also very aware of his social obligations. We don't want to sell him as a black man exclusively, but he won't let those kids down."

The transition from famine to feast, believes Alleyne, began at a team meeting shortly after he assumed the captaincy from Courtney Walsh in 1997, becoming the first Briton of Afro-Caribbean stock to lead a first-class county on a regular basis. "We talked about leaving a legacy at Gloucestershire. I got that commitment. We got rid of anyone who didn't want to be a part of it, no matter how brilliant he might have been. Courtney played a fantastic part in that transition. Unselfish, always gave his all." The baton is in safe hands. – ROB STEEN.

MARTIN BICKNELL

He's tall, six foot four in his cricket boots, and with more physical presence than possibly he imagines. That floppy chocolate fringe is cropped now, and he wears spectacles off the pitch – a hint of the businessman he will become when he retires. But today, aged 32, Martin Bicknell is one of the finest English bowlers of his generation, certainly the best not to have had a decent go at Test cricket. And Surrey have lapped up that selectorial slight.

It's been hard work over the years, but it has reaped its rewards. Even by his standards, though, 2000 was remarkable. He took 60 first-division wickets and won his second Championship medal in a row, as well as promotion for Surrey in the National League. He also made 500, vital, runs for the first time, at an average of 31. Not bad for a man who doesn't enjoy batting that much. Then there were the finest match figures in England since Jim Laker's 19 against Australia at Old Trafford in 1956. Bicknell's came at Guildford, his home club, during Surrey's golden mid-summer run. On a beautiful pitch, after his batsmen had conceded a lead, he annihilated Leicestershire with bowling that was hostile, quick and accurate. His seven for 72 in the first innings, which he considers his best bowling of all, became 16 for 119 by the end of the match. A headline-making sensation.

Bicknell is both a stalwart and a stylist. A classic English new-ball bowler: all short run, high arms and high knees, a natural out-swinger with the knack of cutting the ball back into the right-hander. And, like Alec Bedser in the 1950s, he is the rhythmic heart of Surrey. The metronome to Alex Tudor's scattergun and the Saqlain–Salisbury trickery.

MARTIN PAUL BICKNELL was born in Guildford on January 14, 1969. He was just what his older brother Darren had been waiting for. The pair spent their boyhood tearing around, kicking footballs and imitating the 1976 West Indians. Martin's early loyalty was to Ian Botham's Somerset, but The Oval brought his first experience of Test cricket – England v Australia in 1977: "It rained most of the day and we only saw about an hour's play." The soggy sandwiches worked their magic and Bicknell went to play for local club Normandy when he was ten, opened the batting and bowling at school, and started playing Surrey age-group cricket. However, it wasn't until he shot up – Graham Thorpe, who rose through the ranks with him, was always taller – that he made a real and rapid impact. School was not his strongest suit, and Bicknell left at 16, pocketing some O-levels and climbing straight into his whites. They were to prove more useful than the certificates.

That summer he had a smashing season with Guildford, one excellent, seven-wicket Second Eleven game against Middlesex, and was rewarded with a Surrey contract. He made his debut the following year, 1986, against Derbyshire at The Oval, a year before Darren. *Wisden* tells of the 17-year-old who "swept Derbyshire aside on the final morning by taking three for four in 11 deliveries". From there followed two overseas tours with England Young Cricketers, one with England A (along with Darren) and, in 1989, his county cap. Then, "probably too early", he was picked for England's 1990-91 tour of Australia and New Zealand.

He didn't play a Test – just seven one-day internationals – but he adored it. He loved being part of the set-up, loved the attention and loved the pressure, despite being battered, physically and emotionally, by Dean Jones at Ballarat: none for 94 while Jones struck a savage century for Victoria. All of which made his subsequently brief Test career in the demoralising summer of 1993 – two Tests, 87 overs, four wickets, two ducks and a dodgy knee – so much harder to take.

Bicknell was hampered by the selectorial blind man's buff of the 1990s and plagued by a horrific run of injuries: dislocated shoulder, knee operation, broken bone in his side. But it is a mystery that he has never made the England team-sheet since. He has taken 50 or more first-class wickets in a season nine times and been the spearhead of the most potent attack in the country. Perhaps he's been around so long that he's always been considered older than his years. Maybe he's considered too slow to get players out at Test level. That one rankles: "It doesn't hold much water with me. If you're good enough and you get people out, it doesn't matter at what pace you bowl."

But playing for Surrey brings its own fulfilment. Bicknell has warm respect for his captain, Adam Hollioake, with whom he shares a sixth sense about when he should come on. He enjoys bowling with Alex Tudor more than any of his previous partners. He relishes the mateship of playing with a successful, close-knit side, even if he is different from the young pups who have known nothing but success. He has never been the outgoing sort that a few at Surrey are now. He's rather shy and gentle and not too forthcoming. "I think that has often been perceived as being a bit arrogant at times, but that's the furthest thing from the truth."

Not that he is soft. He is driven by fear, the fear of not being good enough to do it any more. He finds it so hard to switch off that he often wakes in the night, worrying about the next match. His wife, Lorraine, and young daughters Eleanor and Charlotte do their best to distract him. So does the golf course. He plays off a handicap of five and has set up his own business selling clubs and setting up tournaments.

But that's for the future. His more immediate target is 1,000 first-class wickets. He has 174 to go and reckons on pounding another four or five years out of that battered body. While Bicknell is considered superfluous to England's needs, he is living, vigorously appealing proof that county cricket is not yet dead. – TANYA ALDRED.

ANDREW CADDICK

Andrew Caddick's return to favour as a Test bowler was a triumph of resilience and resolve. He defiantly answered those sceptics who made blanket judgments, questioning whether he had the stomach – or, more relevantly, the temperament – for the highest level. He justified the belief of his loyal devotees in the West Country, who had been mystified and then angered by his vulnerability as an England player.

Caddick, sensitive by nature and pained by his omission, had waited impatiently for the overdue call to come again. When it did, against New Zealand in 1999, he demonstrated that he was capable of being one of the most challenging bowlers in the world. Opinions were readjusted; former criticisms, some of which, from his demeanour and less impressive past performances, seemed partially valid, were discreetly forgotten. Often, in South Africa and then last summer against West Indies, he bowled with devastating effect. He had rectified any suggestions of flaw in line and length; his bounce was, for the batsman, more difficult than ever; he genuinely surprised many by the pace and aggression he summoned up.

Never a bowler who relied on speed alone, what Caddick has always possessed is a controlled rhythm. Stamina has not been a problem. Indeed, as successive captains will tell you, it is hard to retrieve the ball from him when the overs are mounting and he senses success. He is a tall, lithe figure who looks like his fellow New Zealander, Richard Hadlee, as he strides purposefully to the wicket, heel distinctively planted first with every step. But to say he is a dead-ringer for Hadlee is not quite true. Dennis Lillee was, he admits, more of an influence.

ANDREW RICHARD CADDICK was born in Christchurch on November 21, 1968, of English parents – from Liverpool and Newcastle – and one would have expected New Zealand to want to hold on to him. He was, after all, in their squad for the 1987-88 Youth World Cup in Australia. Instead, he says, little interest was shown in him and his aspirations. The idea of a cricket career appealed, however, and his instincts and genes beckoned him to England. Wickets for Hampstead in club cricket brought him to the attention of several counties, with Somerset prepared to gamble on a four-year qualification period.

In the West Country his progress was excitedly monitored. He played for Clevedon and was the best for miles; for Somerset's Second Eleven he took 96 wickets in 1991 to win the Rapid Cricketline Player of the Year award, having made his first-class debut earlier that summer against the West Indian tourists. Desmond Haynes and Richie Richardson were his first victims. Against Lancashire at Taunton two years later he took nine for 32 to earn his England debut; in 1998 his marvellous total of first-class wickets was 105. It counted for absolutely nothing when it came to selection for Australia.

Everyone agreed he was not at his best during England's previous winter's tour of the West Indies. On his first visit to the Caribbean, in 1993-94, he had been England's leading wicket-taker. On his second, control of length and line, so often his strength, let him down. He went into his shell, and there were murmurs about his attitude. But his lack of wickets could be attributed to a temporary technical blip with his bowling arm; disappointingly, no one in the England hierarchy pinpointed the problem. Instead, Caddick was marginalised.

Desperately disappointed not to be selected for the Ashes tour, he was hurt by the rumours that he was not a good tour man. Never an extrovert, or an easy communicator, he was apt to alienate some cricket writers when he needed them on his side. And because he cloaked his emotions, he was seen as something of a cold fish. Fellow-players said he did not smile enough.

What the management failed to grasp was that he could still be a match-winner. But the attention and psychology had to be right. As they would be under the new regime of Nasser Hussain and Duncan Fletcher. "I've personally benefited in the way I'm handled and encouraged," he acknowledges. "I'm a quiet person, someone who needs his own space. I don't like hassle. In the past, people were given the wrong impression of me." The evidence of his resurgence has been plain. That brooding persona has disappeared; the cameras have captured hitherto unrevealed smiles.

Caddick's transformation at the highest level was certainly dramatic. In the first two series of his comeback he was England's top wicket-taker, including Test-best figures of seven for 46 against South Africa in Durban. Last summer against West Indies he took 22 wickets at 19.18, with nothing more riveting than his five for 16 off 13 overs at Lord's. "It has to be the highlight," he says. Seven weeks later he bettered that return with five for 14 in 11.2 overs – four wickets in one stupendous over – as West Indies crashed in two days at Headingley.

Back in 1992, Martin Crowe, New Zealand's captain, phoned him. "Why don't you come home and open the bowling for us?" he asked. Even then, however, Caddick was already in spirit a county cricketer, and a future bowler for the country of his parents. He was 32 last November; married to Sarah with a daughter, Ashton. On the circuit, he is considered not only an excellent bowler but also a valued craftsman off the field. He carries a screwdriver in his coffin and has a practical suggestion for anything that needs fixing. It was nearly the family plastering and tiling business for him when he left school. That would have been a real loss to cricket. – DAVID FOOT.

JUSTIN LANGER

Justin Langer feared he was about to lose his place again. He had been in and out of the Australian team over the years, and there had been some heavy speculation in the papers before the Test against Pakistan at Hobart in November 1999. Then, the morning before the game, Steve Waugh sought Langer out and told him to ignore the media: "Just go out and bat," Australia's captain said. Langer did exactly that. In the second innings, he and Adam Gilchrist put on 238 as Australia compiled the third-highest fourth-innings total to win a Test. Langer's 127 was the start of a purple patch that produced 1,003 runs in Australia's 13 Tests in the 1999-2000 season, with four centuries, including 223 against India in Sydney – his highest Test score. After Langer had made 122 not out against New Zealand in April, Steve Waugh called him the best batsman in the world, adding "at the moment – today", as if to remind Langer that nothing is for ever. Langer himself recalls those months as a sweet time: "If I made runs, I'd still be in the side. Destiny was in my hands, and that's a nice feeling." Not many modern cricketers talk about their destiny. But Langer has been conscious of his since he was six.

JUSTIN LEE LANGER was born in Perth, Western Australia, on November 21, 1970, into a Catholic family whose European origins he has never unearthed. His Uncle Robbie played World Series cricket for Australia, and televised games against Viv Richards were an inspiration. His father, a Perth entrepreneur, laid a wicket in the backyard for his three sons, and hired a professional coach to teach Justin the basics. He was still a child when he decided that he must play for Australia. He was spotted early, and joined a boys' team that visited England in 1987. He scored a hundred on the Nursery Ground at Lord's, received a bat contract, and got the first taste of what he wanted to do for a living. He played Under-19 Test cricket, and attended the Academy in Adelaide. Though he never grew taller than 5ft 8in, he regards his size as an advantage, referring to Don Bradman, Sachin Tendulkar and Brian Lara as role models. The point is that small batsmen tend to be nimble, and Langer was rigorously taught as a boy that a short backlift and fast feet are the keys to batting.

To spectators familiar with his range of violent leg-side shots and his fierce cover driving, and who remember that his 122 against New Zealand came off 122 balls, it will seem bizarre that Langer's problem as a young man was that he could not hit the ball off the square. His coach, Rod Marsh, was forced to remind him that batting was about entertaining as well as accumulation, but he had scored enough runs by cutting and glancing to get into the Western Australian team at 21. He proved himself straight away, scoring 149 in the 1991-92 Sheffield Shield final. Langer says this is still his best innings, perhaps because he finally realised he could hit boundaries through the covers.

Langer pulls and drives so well because he sees the ball early – something he had taught himself to do by concentrating on the exact moment of its release from the bowler's hand. Indeed, he believes there is nothing a batsman cannot teach himself. His dedication and his self-conscious striving for excellence seem rooted in Japan rather than in any Anglo-Saxon culture. He studied martial arts as a youth, which gives him physical confidence. (Sledging has never worried him.)

He first played for Australia when they lost to West Indies at Adelaide in January 1993, though in five years after that was selected only seven more times. He toured England in 1997 without playing a Test, but finally became Australia's regular No. 3 during the next Ashes series in 1998-99, scoring 179 not out at Adelaide and averaging 48.44. However, he fits more comfortably into Steve Waugh's team than Mark Taylor's. Langer admires Waugh extravagantly because he has helped him believe in himself, and he returns Waugh's loyalty with energetic displays of togetherness in the field. There is a childlike quality to his pleasure in being in the Australian team; he says it is like playing backyard cricket with ten brothers.

He began to play county cricket for Middlesex, just as their decline set in, in 1998. No blame for this seems to attach to Langer, who was easily their leading run-maker three years in succession. In 2000, he became captain, and relished living in London with his young family. Conscious of the importance of a life outside cricket, he has worked as a stockbroker and a public relations man in Perth, but what he likes best is writing. His diary of an English summer, *From Outback to Outfield*, published in 1999, was a first-rate description of a county cricketer's life, and he wants to go on writing when he retires. A cricket writer? "No," he says surprisingly, "I think I might write novels." – STEPHEN FAY.

DARREN LEHMANN

Domestic first-class cricket in the first year of the new millennium was dominated both in Australia and England by Darren Lehmann, who transferred his phenomenal form in the 1999-2000 Pura Milk Cup to the County Championship with sublime ease. In doing so, he confirmed his peerless ability to adapt to different weather conditions and pitches.

Lehmann returned to Yorkshire for a third season after a break in 1999 because of the World Cup and now felt an even closer part of the family, having married Craig White's sister, Emma, at Christmas. He turned up at Headingley for a practice match in mid-April, after a few days' belated honeymoon in Paris, and the weather could not have been less welcoming for a batsman who, in recent months, had plundered seven centuries in ten first-class matches for South Australia. Yet the shivering rain held off just long enough for Lehmann to stroll out, strike three fours and a six, and play one or two cheeky reverse sweeps. It was, said one team-mate, as if he'd never been away.

And that is how it continued throughout the summer, by the end of which Lehmann emerged as the country's leading run-scorer in first-class matches with 1,477 runs at an average of 67.13. Such was the solidly built left-hander's consistency that he weighed in with four centuries and nine half-centuries in his 23 innings; at one stage he had consecutive scores of 77, 83, 56, 115, 66 and 116 – and this after starting out with knocks of 95, 85 and 133. Without his contribution, Yorkshire would not have finished third in Division One of the Championship or second in Division One of the National League. The rest of their batting was too brittle by far.

As ever, Lehmann was a delight to watch. If sometimes he failed to convert fifties into centuries, owing to a moment's carelessness, that is the price he has to pay for being a Compton or a Miller, rather than a Boycott or a Lawry. He hit it off with players and officials immediately he joined Yorkshire in 1997, and proof that his popularity was not on the wane came late last season when his contract was extended to 2003 and he was appointed vice-captain to David Byas.

DARREN SCOTT LEHMANN was born in Gawler, South Australia, on February 5, 1970, and went on to represent South Australia at all age groups before making his Sheffield Shield debut for them in 1987-88 as a precocious 17-year-old. Two seasons later, at 20 years 32 days, he became the youngest Australian to score 1,000 first-class runs in a domestic season, and has since been in Sheffield Shield-winning sides for both Victoria and South Australia. After three seasons with Victoria in the early 1990s, he returned home to establish himself as one of the most successful Shield batsmen of all time. Having taken over the captaincy of South Australia from Jamie Siddons in 1998-99, he entered the 2000-01 season with a career record of 9,519 Sheffield Shield/Pura Cup runs, a figure exceeded only by Siddons himself with 10,643 and Dean Jones with 9,622. His reward for his phenomenal 1999-2000 season was to be chosen as Pura Milk Cup Player of the Year, and he rounded off his English season with the Walter Lawrence Trophy for the fastest first-class hundred, made off 89 balls against Kent at Canterbury.

Astonishing, therefore, that despite such mastery with the bat, Lehmann should by that time have played only five Tests for Australia, and 60 one-day internationals. Indeed, he holds the dubious distinction of scoring more runs than any other Australian before making his Test debut, and the frequent snubs suggest his face does not quite fit. Perhaps it all dates back to his teens, when he rejected an invitation to join the Australian Cricket Academy because he was already scoring heavily for South Australia. He felt – as did his captain, David Hookes, and others – that he had reached a standard where playing for his state was more beneficial than being at the Academy.

Although not bitter, Lehmann was undoubtedly conscious, when he returned to England for the 2000 season, that a lengthy and distinguished Test career was slipping him by. "If I don't make the Ashes party in 2001, then I'm unlikely to play for Australia again and my future will be in the Sheffield Shield and County Championship." Not that Yorkshire will complain if they have his uninterrupted company over the coming three summers. It is hard to imagine that he was their third choice in 1997 when their previous overseas player, Michael Bevan, was included in Australia's squad for the tour of England, along with Michael Slater. Now, they simply wouldn't dream of being without him. – DAVID WARNER.

[*Patrick Eagar*

Duncan Fletcher and Nasser
Hussain – the partnership
behind England's renaissance.
John Bracewell transformed
Gloucestershire from
underachievers into masters
of the one-day game.

[*Patrick Eagar*

MOTIVATION THROUGH SELF-BELIEF

By SCYLD BERRY

Just as overseas players and coaches are all the rage in English football, overseas coaches have become the fashion in English cricket. The success of Duncan Fletcher with England and John Bracewell with Gloucestershire has fuelled the fad to the point where most counties have looked beyond the White Cliffs of Dover for someone, anyone – no matter how poor his reputation as a coach in his own country. But Fletcher and Bracewell have succeeded because they are excellent coaches, albeit with the advantage of an outsider's perspective.

As coaching is an inexact science, the impact of a coach on a cricket team is impossible to quantify. But it is safe to say that neither England nor Gloucestershire would have come on as they have if they had continued to play as they did before their overseas coaches came along. By the time Fletcher took up his appointment on October 1, 1999, England had failed to get beyond the qualifying round of the World Cup, and just lost the home Test series 2–1 to New Zealand. Gloucestershire, since their unofficial Championships in the years of Grace, had not won anything except two one-day trophies in the 1970s – and did not look like winning anything either – when Bracewell brought over his family from Auckland for the 1998 season.

The two men were vigorous all-rounders in their playing days, but not so talented that they could not understand the difficulties of the game. They also have in common a southern hemisphere enjoyment of fitness, fielding and hard work; the ambition to prove themselves as coaches in the ultimate, international arena; a delight in creating self-belief, and the urge to improve, in cricketers prone to insecurity and complacency; and understanding wives who have let them follow the rainbow to England. But the nature of international cricket is so different from the county game that the challenges facing Fletcher and Bracewell had little in common, beyond the need to convert sceptics and make the most of the English talent at their disposal.

From the moment England's captain, Nasser Hussain, met his future coach in the ECB's offices, they found they were on the same wavelength. Hussain had barely heard of Fletcher: Glamorgan's Championship success in 1997, their first season under Fletcher, had passed him by in the course of the six-Test Ashes series. But he was struck by Fletcher's strength of character and calmness, his never wasting a word or pretending to know what he didn't; he appreciated his manner of suggesting and advising, never dictating. Any Test cricketer is going to be sceptical about the opinions of someone who hasn't played at that level, even if it was through force of circumstance (Fletcher emigrated from Zimbabwe to South Africa in 1984). Soon, though, they evolved the formula whereby the coach would prepare the players to perform and Hussain would add the last ten per cent of mental insight into the forthcoming match.

Through both the way he deports himself and his organisational skills, Fletcher brought calmness and stability to the volatile mass, or rather mess, that was England's cricket. It was not surprising that, while he was serving out the 1999 season with Glamorgan, there was a media outcry that he ought to have been in the England dressing-room when they lost to New Zealand at Lord's – this before he had met most of the players. If anything rammed home the state of cricket education in England, that did. It was typical, too, of English thinking that, for the last Test before Fletcher took over, the outgoing regime brought in Darren Maddy, Ronnie Irani and Ed Giddins for an unbroken run of one whole match, and that England's tail in that match at The Oval consisted of Alan Mullally, Phil Tufnell and Giddins.

Fletcher broke the cycle of chopping and changing and going round in circles. He implemented consistency of selection with an eye on the long term, against the English trend of picking a horse for a course because of the enormous difference between, say, Old Trafford and Headingley. He insisted on selecting bowlers who could bat and, through hard net-practice, made sure they did so. England could not have beaten West Indies at Lord's, or reached parity on first innings against Pakistan in Karachi, if Darren Gough had still been swiping away with both feet together.

Fletcher took his time evaluating the players available to England, often by giving them throw-downs at practice and seeing how they went about their work. Once he made his judgment, the weak started to go out the window. What he looks for is "players who can grow in the game": at Western Province he kept faith with Herschelle Gibbs when he was being written off as an ultra-talented waster. He has found that English cricket – players as well as media – attaches labels to cricketers far too quickly and unsympathetically. The ones branded "too selfish" have often been the ones he is looking for. In 2000, such characters as full of bravura as Gough and empty of it as Craig White, as cocky as Dominic Cork and quiet as Marcus Trescothick, were welded into a team who enjoyed each other's success – not as common as you would suppose among professional sportsmen. With a perception which nobody had brought to the job before, Fletcher identified the cricketers England needed, and had only the experiment of making Mark Ramprakash open to set against it.

Coming from Zimbabwe, where players were if anything fit and loved their fielding, Fletcher was disappointed that English cricketers, with their culture of "getting by", were not the same. But he has come to see that playing too much is the cause, and has set about changing that culture. Whereas his namesake, Keith Fletcher, believed in quantity when it came to fielding practice, with players standing around while one of their number caught (or dropped, it didn't matter which because there was no penalty) a daily ration of skiers – even if he was going to field short-leg – Duncan made it short, sharp and fun. The units in which players practise fielding, simulating match situations, are never larger than four. His speciality is "tens": ten difficult catches that have to be taken in a row, otherwise the player starts again.

Perhaps where it has been most valuable for England to have a foreign coach is that Fletcher was able to come in without any vested interests or suspicions of bias. He was lucky in that central contracts were introduced before his first home summer, but he still had to stand up to carping from the counties whenever he decided that an England player, usually Gough or Andy Caddick, had to be rested. He was lucky again in that, by the time

England had finished beating West Indies in early September, almost all the counties with England Test players had settled their promotion and relegation issues. But even if Yorkshire or Somerset had been fighting to the end of the season, Fletcher would still have stood up for England's interests.

His analysis of opponents has been a cut above what his predecessors managed. The traditional attitude of English cricket, born no doubt when they were the only professional cricketers in the world, has always been, "We'll concentrate on our own game." Without overloading his players, Fletcher watches videotape of forthcoming opponents and their techniques, talks to South African contacts such as Gary Kirsten, and compiles a one-page flip-chart on each of them, which is updated through a series.

He makes sure he is never seen whispering in a corner with his captain, lest the players' insecurity is heightened. He is full of theories but chooses his words carefully, which is why he is heard when he does speak. If it has been a poor fielding practice, he has been known to observe with dry humour: "Well done, England, that's 15 wickets we'll have to take, not ten." He never loses his temper, never dresses a player down in public, and always leaves the final decision to the captain. Although the ECB first targeted Bob Woolmer, they ended up with the best of the five full-time coaches England have had.

Bracewell, a New Zealander by birth but more Australian by nature, is younger and more overtly assertive than Fletcher. He was one of six brothers whose mother died young, so their father – who played first-class rugby for Waikato at 16 and was a good club cricketer – had to look after the boys and fulfil his sporting ambitions through them. Two sons, John and Brendon, played Test cricket, and another two, Doug and Mark, also played first-class cricket. John went on to develop his coaching skills in a range of jobs with Auckland until he found that half-a-dozen first-class games a season were not scope enough.

On his arrival at Bristol, Bracewell found that his chief problem was not something that applied to Fletcher and England, although it might have in the 1980s when Ian Botham was around. The team was over-dependent on one great player. It was no fault of Courtney Walsh that his 80 to 100 wickets every season guaranteed Gloucestershire a place in the upper reaches of the Championship and allowed everyone else to get by. However, the county committee was already thinking that one-day cricket might be the way to go, and Bracewell was pleased when an overseas player of far lower profile, Ian Harvey, took over for 1999.

Even then, no county looked less likely to become the overwhelming force in one-day cricket than the team with Jack Russell as the one player of real note and a tradition of being one of the poorest fielding sides. But at least Gloucestershire's players were ready for the challenge – unlike Middlesex's. They couldn't respond to John Buchanan, who went off to be Australia's coach. Bracewell admits he was lucky to inherit a captain and young first-team squad eager to move forward. "Far better coaches than me have come over here and not found a reception. Our guys are taking control over their own lives and destinies as athletes."

As one small instance, Bracewell asked his players to work out their own code on alcohol and eating. They agreed on a moderate amount of alcohol, because of the social element in cricket; they learned about nutrition from Bracewell, who had done several modules at Level 3 coaching. After Gloucestershire beat Worcestershire in 2000 in their NatWest third-round replay, they had to travel from Worcester to Leicester that same evening to play a fourth-round tie next day. The norm would have been to jump in the car, check in at Leicester, go out for an Indian, slump in front of the telly and feel lethargic next day. When the players decided of their own accord to eat at a motorway service station and digest *en route* before going to bed, Bracewell was as gratified as when they beat Leicestershire by ten runs.

Bracewell had to take a lead, and often be seen to finish first in training, followed by Kim Barnett and Russell, the two oldest players. "It depends where the players are at," he said. "When they're starting out, and aren't sure of the standards they're meant to reach, the captain and coach must set the example. As the team evolves, the coach can stand back." In the same way, Bracewell believes that a democratic structure is ideal for a cricket team, but the autocratic model usually has to precede it.

The first fruits came in 1999, when Gloucestershire won both one-day knockout cups, although they finished bottom in the Championship. In 2000, they won all three one-day trophies, which no county had done before, and missed Championship promotion by two points (only Division Two champions Northamptonshire won more games). Their strength was the defence of almost any one-day total, however small; accurate medium-pacers bowled a full length with plenty of changes of pace, supported by impermeable fielding and Russell standing up to the stumps to keep batsmen inside their crease.

When playing for New Zealand in the latter 1980s, Bracewell was impressed by the way Bobby Simpson took over the Australian team, threw out players who weren't going to "grow", and drilled the team in the basics. He also borrowed the tactic, which Simpson's Australians used in their 1987 World Cup victory, of returning the ball to the keeper on the bounce to soften it. Again, as with Duncan Fletcher, it was not long hours of tedious practice that made Gloucestershire's fielding the best. It was talking individually to each player, starting with what he wanted to achieve in life and narrowing it down to where he wanted to field. Now, Bracewell's players usually practise in pairs, simulating the same angles as match situations. "We'd have won the Championship in the eighties if he'd been around," said second-team coach Tony Wright.

The appalling quality of most one-day pitches in England and the softer white ball have undoubtedly favoured Gloucestershire and their medium-pacers. But the games have still to be won. In 2000, Bracewell was pleased to note how his players continued to win matches after their triumphant cup finals, unlike the year before; and how, when a partnership was broken, the surviving batsman was less likely to follow. "What scares me most about English sportsmen is their fear of success and hard work," said Bracewell. By winning five trophies in two seasons with a team which had won nothing, Bracewell – like England under Fletcher – is beginning to change this culture.

Scyld Berry is cricket correspondent of the Sunday Telegraph.

BACK TO GRASS ROOTS

By DAVID GREEN

Writing as one who first played county cricket 42 seasons ago, and has remained close to the game in one capacity or another, I cannot recall a time when English pitches have caused such dissatisfaction. Despite much-trumpeted advances in knowledge of soils and grasses, and the development of more sophisticated equipment for groundsmen, squares are widely considered unsatisfactory and attract blame when England's Test side performs poorly.

As far back as I can remember, the playing authority – in earlier times, MCC – would keep an eye on pitches. Should a square arouse concern, Bert Lock, the long-serving groundsman at The Oval, would be despatched to offer remedial advice. Now and then, first-class cricket at a particular ground might be suspended while improvements were made – or cease altogether in extreme cases. More recently, harsher measures have been deemed necessary. Championship points have been deducted for poor surfaces; pitch police have been introduced. In 2000, former players such as Tony Brown, David Hughes and Phil Sharpe, operating under the leadership of former England captain Mike Denness, became what were euphemistically called "pitch liaison officers". Their brief was to check that pitches were only lightly grassed, so as not to favour seam bowlers, hard and dry to provide pace and carry for the quicker bowlers, and wearing sufficiently towards the end of the match to help spinners.

PLOs were deemed necessary because two things were happening. First, too many pitches were starting damp. This was one way to ensure that they lasted four days, and that points deductions were avoided. But it also meant that, although seam bowlers received encouragement on the first day, the surface did not wear enough for spinners to gain any purchase. Second, the introduction of substantial prize money for high places in the Championship, along with the presence of high-profile, highly paid coaches, who had to deliver success to keep their jobs, led some counties to produce pitches that were over-helpful to bowlers. And, with the two-division County Championship, promotion and relegation also entered the equation.

It has, of course, been the practice throughout cricket's history for sides to prepare pitches that suit their bowlers. But pitches of regular bounce, which turn or seam, are a different matter from those on which one ball threatens the ribs and the next hits the base of the stumps.

Monitoring should eliminate deliberate "fixing" of pitches. Of more concern to David Bridle, head groundsman at Bristol for 35 years, has been the tendency towards central control of pitches, which he feels has increased over the past 20 years. "There seems to be more and more pressure towards a uniform type of pitch. First Surrey loam was pushed, then Ongar loam. Also, the coarser rye-grasses were recommended ahead of the fine fescue grass favoured in the past." Rye-grass, if not cut close, offers greater movement off the seam. "The problem is that Ongar loam doesn't bond with all soils, and when there's no bond the surface cracks like crazy paving. We have too many different types of soil in this country for standardisation to work." Denness, however, rejected the idea that standardisation was being imposed, insisting that a menu of treatments had been set out from which groundsmen could make their choice.

Bridle, among a good many others, was also worried about the effect on squares of covering by flat-lying tarpaulins for extended periods, often for days at a time. "This appears to me to be hindering the strong, even growth of grass needed for cricket. It has also crossed my mind that covers keep off an awful lot of rain, which would have soaked the squares in pre-covering days. Maybe the cracking that occurs at Headingley and elsewhere is due to squares not getting enough rain."

Such doubts about the long-term value of covering pitches are shared by many who played or watched cricket on fully uncovered pitches. Yet the case for covering is a strong one. Prior to 1970, county pitches remained uncovered after the start of mid-week games, though for matches beginning on Saturday the pitch was covered from Saturday evening to start of play on Monday morning. (This was in that blissful age when county matches were all of three days, started on Wednesday or Saturday, and cricket followers knew where they stood.)

The game, however, was undergoing changes. The need to restore its finances had led to the introduction of the Gillette Cup in 1963 and the John Player League in 1969. Sponsorship was the buzz-word. And so that cricket's new benefactors, along with their corporate guests, would have as much play as possible, it was decided that pitches would be covered overnight, and in addition that covers would be brought on as soon as play had been called off for the day. This, an entirely commercial decision, saved pitches from a good many soakings, but inevitably made life that much harder for spin bowlers.

With Test match pitches in England by now fully covered, and sponsorship increasingly important in balancing the books, the move to full covering in the Championship, made in 1981, was predictable. It was also argued that the other cricketing countries covered their pitches, that covering would mean faster, truer surfaces, which in turn would improve our cricket, and that the leg-spinner – that elusive butterfly of English cricket – would come into his own. In other words, all would be well.

In fact, three-day cricket and covered pitches did not mix. There wasn't time to play out games properly; a plethora of last-day chases ensued, with cheap runs frequently being fed to batsmen to set up a target. It was hardly the way to develop Test cricketers.

The powers that be, realising something was wrong, returned in 1987 to uncovered pitches during the hours of play. Only this time, instead of covering just the bowler's landing area, as had been the case from time immemorial, they covered his run-up and his follow-through as well. Not surprisingly, fast bowlers rather than spinners operated on rain-damaged pitches, and a number of cricketers still in the game today had enough nasty experiences that year to put them off uncovered pitches for good. Covering was resumed and, to obtain more proper finishes, four-day matches were introduced, at first as an experiment, then to the exclusion of three-day.

[*Graham Morris*

Pitch liaison officer Mike Denness discusses the state of the Derby wicket with head groundsman Barry Marsh during the match against Surrey. On the first two days, 33 wickets fell and Derbyshire – despite support from the umpires – were docked eight points for an unsatisfactory pitch.

This seemed a better bet. An extra day's play would, in theory, give pitches more time to wear. But, on the surfaces now being prepared, this has not often happened. Instead, the ball tends to skid off the pitch, albeit at no great pace, rather than causing it to dust. These circumstances have led to a perceptible slackening in batting techniques. With the ball scarcely deviating for the seamers, and spinners finding it hard to relinquish the flat trajectory required in the three limited-overs competitions, it became possible to score reasonably heavily without positive footwork, and without always watching the ball on to the bat.

Those who have not experienced fully uncovered pitches should realise that they were only rarely physically threatening to a batsman. Fast bowlers, because they could not keep their feet, generally could not operate on wet pitches. For slow bowlers, however, and particularly for finger-spinners, such a pitch, as it dried, would form a slight crust from which the ball would "pop" towards the splice of the bat or the glove.

In these circumstances, good footwork and judgment of length were essential for survival. The bowler, meanwhile, needed the strictest control because, with four or more close catchers, there were big spaces to thump the bad ball into. True, a hard pitch might "fly" for a few overs after a shower, but the odd smack in the ribs has always been part of the game. In good weather, there was little difference from today except, vitally, that pitches left open to wind, dew and early sun had a good deal more life in them. Moreover, they generally started as true as the groundsman could make them. There was little point in making "result" pitches when there was a good chance of the elements making them awkward anyway.

However, for all the variety and spice uncovered pitches brought to the English game, they are now among the deader ducks. The compilers of the 1997 MacLaurin report, "Raising the Standard", canvassed old players and umpires about covering. The report acknowledged their overwhelming vote to uncover, but discounted it by saying that, as modern pitches "might be dangerous when wet", covering would remain. Mike Denness has admitted to me that no one actually thought of wetting one to find out what might happen.

English cricket, then, seems likely to remain dominated by bowlers who rely on swing, seam or a combination of both. In fairness, there were signs last year that, on pitches starting absolutely dry, there can be sufficient encouragement for spin on the fourth day. Even so, with England scratching about for one spin bowler of Test quality, it bears recalling that there were times when they picked three in the same side. At Kingston in 1953-54, they won the Fifth Test with an attack comprising Bailey, Trueman, Laker, Lock and Wardle to level the series 2–2. Tony Lock and Johnny Wardle competed for the England slow left-armer's position for a decade, with bowlers of the quality of Sam Cook and Malcolm Hilton hardly getting a look-in. Jim Laker was a great off-spinner, but he had strong challengers and at different times gave way to Roy Tattersall, Bob Appleyard and Jim McConnon. More recently, Derek Underwood, one of the finest bowlers of his time, lost his place, albeit temporarily, to Norman Gifford, then to Phil Edmonds.

Such days are not likely to return under present pitch-covering regulations. Because we miss the contrast and the technical challenge that spin provides, and because batsmen in today's domestic game are plainly missing it, too, this is a matter of regret for many of my generation.

David Green played for Oxford University, Lancashire and Gloucestershire between 1959 and 1971; in 1969, he was one of Wisden's *Five Cricketers of the Year. He writes on cricket for the* Daily Telegraph.

PART TWO: THE PLAYERS

TEST CRICKETERS

Full list from 1877 to September 4, 2000

These lists have been compiled on a home and abroad basis, appearances abroad being printed in *italics*.

Abbreviations. E: England. A: Australia. SA: South Africa. WI: West Indies. NZ: New Zealand. In: India. P: Pakistan. SL: Sri Lanka. Z: Zimbabwe.

All appearances are placed in this order of seniority. Hence, any England cricketer playing against Australia in England has that achievement recorded first and the remainder of his appearances at home (if any) set down before passing to matches abroad. The figures immediately following each name represent the total number of appearances in *all* Tests.

Where the season embraces two different years, the first year is given; i.e. 1876 indicates 1876-77.

ENGLAND

Number of Test cricketers: 603

Abel, R. 13: v A 1888 (3) 1896 (3) 1902 (2); *v A 1891 (3); v SA 1888 (2)*
Absolom, C. A. 1: *v A 1878*
Adams, C. J. 5: *v SA 1999 (5)*
Agnew, J. P. 3: v A 1985 (1); v WI 1984 (1); v SL 1984 (1)
Allen, D. A. 39: v A 1961 (4) 1964 (1); v SA 1960 (2); v WI 1963 (2) 1966 (1); v P 1962 (4); *v A 1962 (1) 1965 (4); v SA 1964 (4); v WI 1959 (5); v NZ 1965 (3); v In 1961 (5); v P 1961 (3)*
Allen, G. O. B. 25: v A 1930 (1) 1934 (2); v WI 1933 (1); v NZ 1931 (3); v In 1936 (3); *v A 1932 (5) 1936 (5); v WI 1947 (3); v NZ 1932 (2)*
Allom, M. J. C. 5: *v SA 1930 (1); v NZ 1929 (4)*
Allott, P. J. W. 13: v A 1981 (1) 1985 (4); v WI 1984 (1); v In 1982 (2); v SL 1984 (1); *v In 1981 (1); v SL 1981 (1)*
Ames, L. E. G. 47: v A 1934 (5) 1938 (2); v SA 1929 (1) 1935 (4); v WI 1933 (3); v NZ 1931 (3) 1937 (3); v In 1932 (1); *v A 1932 (5) 1936 (5); v SA 1938 (5); v WI 1929 (4) 1934 (4); v NZ 1932 (2)*
Amiss, D. L. 50: v A 1968 (1) 1975 (2) 1977 (2); v WI 1966 (1) 1973 (3) 1976 (1); v NZ 1973 (3); v In 1967 (2) 1971 (1) 1974 (3); v P 1967 (1) 1971 (3) 1974 (3); *v A 1974 (5) 1976 (1); v WI 1973 (5); v NZ 1974 (2); v In 1972 (3) 1976 (5); v P 1972 (3)*
Andrew, K. V. 2: v WI 1963 (1); *v A 1954 (1)*
Appleyard, R. 9: v A 1956 (1); v SA 1955 (1); v P 1954 (1); *v A 1954 (4); v NZ 1954 (2)*
Archer, A. G. 1: *v SA 1898*
Armitage, T. 2: *v A 1876 (2)*
Arnold, E. G. 10: v A 1905 (4); v SA 1907 (2); *v A 1903 (4)*
Arnold, G. G. 34: v A 1972 (3) 1975 (1); v WI 1973 (3); v NZ 1969 (1) 1973 (3); v In 1974 (2); v P 1967 (2) 1974 (3); *v A 1974 (4); v WI 1973 (3); v NZ 1974 (2); v In 1972 (4); v P 1972 (3)*
Arnold, J. 1: v NZ 1931
Astill, W. E. 9: *v SA 1927 (5); v WI 1929 (4)*
Atherton, M. A. 102: v A 1989 (2) 1993 (6) 1997 (6); v SA 1994 (3) 1998 (5); v WI 1991 (5) 1995 (6) 2000 (5); v NZ 1990 (3) 1994 (3) 1999 (2); v In 1990 (3) 1996 (3); v P 1992 (3) 1996 (3); v Z 2000 (2); *v A 1990 (5) 1994 (5) 1998 (5); v SA 1995 (5) 1999 (5); v WI 1993 (5) 1997 (6); v NZ 1996 (3); v In 1992 (1); v SL 1992 (1); v Z 1996 (2)*
Athey, C. W. J. 23: v A 1980 (1); v WI 1988 (1); v NZ 1986 (3); v In 1986 (2); v P 1987 (4); *v A 1986 (5) 1987 (1); v WI 1980 (2); v NZ 1987 (1); v P 1987 (3)*
Attewell, W. 10: v A 1890 (1); *v A 1884 (5) 1887 (1) 1891 (3)*

Bailey, R. J. 4: v WI 1988 (1); *v WI 1989 (3)*

Bailey, T. E. 61: v A 1953 (5) 1956 (4); v SA 1951 (2) 1955 (5); v WI 1950 (2) 1957 (4); v NZ 1949 (4) 1958 (4); v P 1954 (3); *v A 1950 (4) 1954 (5) 1958 (5); v SA 1956 (5); v WI 1953 (5); v NZ 1950 (2) 1954 (2)*

Bairstow, D. L. 4: v A 1980 (1); v WI 1980 (1); v In 1979 (1); *v WI 1980 (1)*

Bakewell, A. H. 6: v SA 1935 (2); v WI 1933 (1); v NZ 1931 (2); *v In 1933 (1)*

Balderstone, J. C. 2: v WI 1976 (2)

Barber, R. W. 28: v A 1964 (1) 1968 (1); v SA 1960 (1) 1965 (3); v WI 1966 (2); v NZ 1965 (3); *v A 1965 (5); v SA 1964 (4); v In 1961 (5); v P 1961 (3)*

Barber, W. 2: v SA 1935 (2)

Barlow, G. D. 3: v A 1977 (1); *v In 1976 (2)*

Barlow, R. G. 17: v A 1882 (1) 1884 (3) 1886 (3); *v A 1881 (4) 1882 (4) 1886 (2)*

Barnes, S. F. 27: v A 1902 (1) 1909 (3) 1912 (3); v SA 1912 (3); *v A 1901 (3) 1907 (5) 1911 (5); v SA 1913 (4)*

Barnes, W. 21: v A 1880 (1) 1882 (1) 1884 (2) 1886 (2) 1888 (3) 1890 (2); *v A 1882 (4) 1884 (5) 1886 (1)*

Barnett, C. J. 20: v A 1938 (3) 1948 (1); v SA 1947 (3); v WI 1933 (1); v NZ 1937 (3); v In 1936 (1); *v A 1936 (5); v In 1933 (3)*

Barnett, K. J. 4: v A 1989 (3); v SL 1988 (1)

Barratt, F. 5: v SA 1929 (1); *v NZ 1929 (4)*

Barrington, K. F. 82: v A 1961 (5) 1964 (5) 1968 (3); v SA 1955 (2) 1960 (4) 1965 (3); v WI 1963 (5) 1966 (2); v NZ 1965 (2); v In 1959 (5) 1967 (3); v P 1962 (4) 1967 (3); *v A 1962 (5) 1965 (5); v SA 1964 (5); v WI 1959 (5) 1967 (5); v NZ 1962 (3); v In 1961 (5) 1963 (1); v P 1961 (2)*

Barton, V. A. 1: *v SA 1891*

Bates, W. 15: *v A 1881 (4) 1882 (4) 1884 (5) 1886 (2)*

Bean, G. 3: *v A 1891 (3)*

Bedser, A. V. 51: v A 1948 (5) 1953 (5); v SA 1947 (2) 1951 (5) 1955 (1); v WI 1950 (3); v NZ 1949 (2); v In 1946 (3) 1952 (4); v P 1954 (2); *v A 1946 (5) 1950 (5) 1954 (1); v SA 1948 (5); v NZ 1946 (1) 1950 (2)*

Benjamin, J. E. 1: v SA 1994

Benson, M. R. 1: v In 1986

Berry, R. 2: v WI 1950 (2)

Bicknell, M. P. 2: v A 1993 (2)

Binks, J. G. 2: *v In 1963 (2)*

Bird, M. C. 10: *v SA 1909 (5) 1913 (5)*

Birkenshaw, J. 5: *v WI 1973 (2); v In 1972 (2); v P 1972 (1)*

Blakey, R. J. 2: *v In 1992 (2)*

Bligh, Hon. I. F. W. 4: *v A 1882 (4)*

Blythe, C. 19: v A 1905 (1) 1909 (2); v SA 1907 (3); *v A 1901 (5) 1907 (1); v SA 1905 (5) 1909 (2)*

Board, J. H. 6: *v SA 1898 (2) 1905 (4)*

Bolus, J. B. 7: v WI 1963 (2); *v In 1963 (5)*

Booth, M. W. 2: *v SA 1913 (2)*

Bosanquet, B. J. T. 7: v A 1905 (3); *v A 1903 (4)*

Botham, I. T. 102: v A 1977 (2) 1980 (1) 1981 (6) 1985 (6) 1989 (3); v WI 1980 (5) 1984 (5) 1991 (1); v NZ 1978 (3) 1983 (4) 1986 (1); v In 1979 (4) 1982 (3); v P 1978 (3) 1982 (3) 1987 (5) 1992 (2); v SL 1984 (1) 1991 (1); *v A 1978 (6) 1979 (3) 1982 (5) 1986 (4); v WI 1980 (4) 1985 (5); v NZ 1977 (3) 1983 (3) 1991 (1); v In 1979 (1) 1981 (6); v P 1983 (1); v SL 1981 (1)*

Bowden, M. P. 2: *v SA 1888 (2)*

Bowes, W. E. 15: v A 1934 (3) 1938 (2); v SA 1935 (4); v WI 1939 (2); v In 1932 (1) 1946 (1); *v A 1932 (1); v NZ 1932 (1)*

Bowley, E. H. 5: v SA 1929 (2); *v NZ 1929 (3)*

Boycott, G. 108: v A 1964 (4) 1968 (3) 1972 (2) 1977 (3) 1980 (1) 1981 (6); v SA 1965 (2); v WI 1966 (4) 1969 (3) 1973 (3) 1980 (5); v NZ 1965 (2) 1969 (3) 1973 (3) 1978 (2); v In 1967 (2) 1971 (1) 1974 (1) 1979 (4); v P 1967 (1) 1971 (2); *v A 1965 (5) 1970 (5) 1978 (6) 1979 (3); v SA 1964 (5); v WI 1967 (5) 1973 (5) 1980 (4); v NZ 1965 (2) 1977 (3); v In 1979 (1) 1981 (4); v P 1977 (3)*

Bradley, W. M. 2: v A 1899 (2)

Braund, L. C. 23: v A 1902 (5); v SA 1907 (3); *v A 1901 (5) 1903 (5) 1907 (5)*

Brearley, J. M. 39: v A 1977 (5) 1981 (4); v WI 1976 (2); v NZ 1978 (3); v In 1979 (4); v P 1978 (3); *v A 1976 (1) 1978 (6) 1979 (3); v In 1976 (5) 1979 (1); v P 1977 (3)*

Brearley, W. 4: v A 1905 (2) 1909 (1); v SA 1912 (1)

Brennan, D. V. 2: v SA 1951 (2)

Briggs, John 33: v A 1886 (3) 1888 (3) 1893 (2) 1896 (1) 1899 (1); *v A 1884 (5) 1886 (2) 1887 (1) 1891 (3) 1894 (5) 1897 (5); v SA 1888 (2)*

Broad, B. C. 25: v A 1989 (2); v WI 1984 (4) 1988 (2); v P 1987 (4); v SL 1984 (1); *v A 1986 (5) 1987 (1); v NZ 1987 (3); v P 1987 (3)*

Brockwell, W. 7: v A 1893 (1) 1899 (1); *v A 1894 (5)*

Bromley-Davenport, H. R. 4: *v SA 1895 (3) 1898 (1)*

Brookes, D. 1: *v WI 1947*

Brown, A. 2: *v In 1961 (1); v P 1961 (1)*

Brown, D. J. 26: v A 1968 (4); v SA 1965 (2); v WI 1966 (1) 1969 (3); v NZ 1969 (1); v In 1967 (2): *v A 1965 (4); v WI 1967 (4); v NZ 1965 (2); v P 1968 (3)*

Brown, F. R. 22: v A 1953 (1); v SA 1951 (5); v WI 1950 (1); v NZ 1931 (2) 1937 (1) 1949 (2); v In 1932 (1); *v A 1950 (5); v NZ 1932 (2) 1950 (2)*

Brown, G. 7: v A 1921 (3); *v SA 1922 (4)*

Brown, J. T. 8: v A 1896 (2) 1899 (1); *v A 1894 (5)*

Brown, S. J. E. 1: v P 1996

Buckenham, C. P. 4: *v SA 1909 (4)*

Butcher, A. R. 1: v In 1979

Butcher, M. A. 27: v A 1997 (5); v SA 1998 (3); v NZ 1999 (3); v SL 1998 (1); *v A 1998 (5); v SA 1999 (5); v WI 1997 (5)*

Butcher, R. O. 3: *v WI 1980 (3)*

Butler, H. J. 2: v SA 1947 (1); *v WI 1947 (1)*

Butt, H. R. 3: *v SA 1895 (3)*

Caddick, A. R. 37: v A 1993 (4) 1997 (5); v WI 2000 (5); v NZ 1999 (4); v P 1996 (1); v Z 2000 (2); *v SA 1999 (5); v WI 1993 (4) 1997 (5); v NZ 1996 (2)*

Calthorpe, Hon. F. S. G. 4: *v WI 1929 (4)*

Capel, D. J. 15: v A 1989 (1); v WI 1988 (2); v P 1987 (1); *v A 1987 (1); v WI 1989 (4); v NZ 1987 (3); v P 1987 (3)*

Carr, A. W. 11: v A 1926 (4); v SA 1929 (2); *v SA 1922 (5)*

Carr, D. B. 2: *v In 1951 (2)*

Carr, D. W. 1: v A 1909

Cartwright, T. W. 5: v A 1964 (2); v SA 1965 (1); v NZ 1965 (1); *v SA 1964 (1)*

Chapman, A. P. F. 26: v A 1926 (4) 1930 (4); v SA 1924 (2); v WI 1928 (3); *v A 1924 (4) 1928 (4); v SA 1930 (5)*

Charlwood, H. R. J. 2: *v A 1876 (2)*

Chatterton, W. 1: *v SA 1891*

Childs, J. H. 2: v WI 1988 (2)

Christopherson, S. 1: v A 1884

Clark, E. W. 8: v A 1934 (2); v SA 1929 (1); v WI 1933 (2); *v In 1933 (3)*

Clay, J. C. 1: v SA 1935

Close, D. B. 22: v A 1961 (1); v SA 1955 (1); v WI 1957 (2) 1963 (5) 1966 (1) 1976 (3); v NZ 1949 (1); v In 1959 (1) 1967 (3); v P 1967 (3); *v A 1950 (1)*

Coldwell, L. J. 7: v A 1964 (2); v P 1962 (2); *v A 1962 (2); v NZ 1962 (1)*

Compton, D. C. S. 78: v A 1938 (4) 1948 (5) 1953 (5) 1956 (1); v SA 1947 (5) 1951 (4) 1955 (5); v WI 1939 (3) 1950 (1); v NZ 1937 (1) 1949 (4); v In 1946 (3) 1952 (2); v P 1954 (4); *v A 1946 (5) 1950 (4) 1954 (4); v SA 1948 (5) 1956 (5); v WI 1953 (5); v NZ 1946 (1) 1950 (2)*

Cook, C. 1: v SA 1947

Cook, G. 7: v In 1982 (3); *v A 1982 (3); v SL 1981 (1)*

Cook, N. G. B. 15: v A 1989 (3); v WI 1984 (3); v NZ 1983 (2); *v NZ 1983 (1); v P 1983 (3) 1987 (3)*

Cope, G. A. 3: *v P 1977 (3)*

Copson, W. H. 3: v SA 1947 (1); v WI 1939 (2)

Cork, D. G. 31: v SA 1998 (5); v WI 1995 (5) 2000 (4); v In 1996 (3); v P 1996 (3); v SL 1998 (1); *v A 1998 (2); v SA 1995 (5); v WI 1996 (3)*

Cornford, W. L. 4: *v NZ 1929 (4)*

Cottam, R. M. H. 4: *v In 1972 (2); v P 1968 (2)*

Coventry, Hon. C. J. 2: *v SA 1888 (2)*

Cowans, N. G. 19: v A 1985 (1); v WI 1984 (1); v NZ 1983 (4); *v A 1982 (4); v NZ 1983 (2); v In 1984 (5); v P 1983 (2)*

Cowdrey, C. S. 6: v WI 1988 (1); *v In 1984 (5)*

Cowdrey, M. C. 114: v A 1956 (5) 1961 (4) 1964 (3) 1968 (4); v SA 1955 (1) 1960 (5) 1965 (3); v WI 1957 (5) 1963 (2) 1966 (4); v NZ 1958 (4) 1965 (3); v In 1959 (5); v P 1962 (4) 1967 (2) 1971 (1); *v A 1954 (5) 1958 (5) 1962 (5) 1965 (4) 1970 (3) 1974 (5); v SA 1956 (5); v WI 1959 (5) 1967 (5); v NZ 1954 (2) 1958 (2) 1962 (3) 1965 (3) 1970 (1); v In 1963 (3); v P 1968 (3)*

Coxon, A. 1: v A 1948

Cranston, J. 1: v A 1890

Cranston, K. 8: v A 1948 (1); v SA 1947 (3); *v WI 1947 (4)*

Crapp, J. F. 7: v A 1948 (3); *v SA 1948 (4)*

Crawford, J. N. 12: v SA 1907 (2); *v A 1907 (5); v SA 1905 (5)*

Crawley, J. P. 29: v A 1997 (5); v SA 1994 (3); v WI 1995 (3); v P 1996 (2); v SL 1998 (1); *v A 1994 (3) 1998 (3); v SA 1995 (1); v WI 1997 (3); v NZ 1996 (3); v Z 1996 (2)*

Croft, R. D. B. 17: v A 1997 (5); v SA 1998 (3); v WI 2000 (2); v P 1996 (1); *v A 1998 (1); v WI 1997 (1); v NZ 1996 (2); v Z 1996 (2)*

Curtis, T. S. 5: v A 1989 (3); v WI 1988 (2)

Cuttell, W. R. 2: *v SA 1898 (2)*

Dawson, E. W. 5: *v SA 1927 (1); v NZ 1929 (4)*

Dean, H. 3: v A 1912 (2); v SA 1912 (1)

DeFreitas, P. A. J. 44: v A 1989 (1) 1993 (1); v SA 1994 (3); v WI 1988 (3) 1991 (5) 1995 (1); v NZ 1990 (1) 1994 (3); v P 1987 (1) 1992 (2); v SL 1991 (1); *v A 1986 (4) 1990 (3) 1994 (4); v WI 1989 (2); v NZ 1987 (2) 1991 (3); v In 1992 (1); v P 1987 (2)*

Denness, M. H. 28: v A 1975 (1); v NZ 1969 (1); v In 1974 (3); v P 1974 (3); *v A 1974 (5); v WI 1973 (5); v NZ 1974 (2); v In 1972 (5); v P 1972 (3)*

Denton, D. 11: v A 1905 (1); *v SA 1905 (5) 1909 (5)*

Dewes, J. G. 5: v A 1948 (1); v WI 1950 (2); *v A 1950 (2)*

Dexter, E. R. 62: v A 1961 (5) 1964 (5) 1968 (2); v SA 1960 (5); v WI 1963 (5); v NZ 1958 (1) 1965 (2); v In 1959 (2); v P 1962 (5); *v A 1958 (2) 1962 (5); v SA 1964 (5); v WI 1959 (5); v NZ 1958 (2) 1962 (3); v In 1961 (5); v P 1961 (3)*

Dilley, G. R. 41: v A 1981 (3) 1989 (2); v WI 1980 (3) 1988 (4); v NZ 1983 (1) 1986 (2); v In 1986 (2); v P 1987 (4); *v A 1979 (2) 1986 (4) 1987 (1); v WI 1980 (4); v NZ 1987 (3); v In 1981 (4); v P 1983 (1) 1987 (1)*

Dipper, A. E. 1: v A 1921

Doggart, G. H. G. 2: v WI 1950 (2)

D'Oliveira, B. L. 44: v A 1968 (2) 1972 (5); v WI 1966 (4) 1969 (3); v NZ 1969 (3); v In 1967 (2) 1971 (3); v P 1967 (3) 1971 (3); *v A 1970 (6); v WI 1967 (5); v NZ 1970 (2); v P 1968 (3)*

Dollery, H. E. 4: v A 1948 (2); v SA 1947 (1); v WI 1950 (1)

Dolphin, A. 1: *v A 1920*

Douglas, J. W. H. T. 23: v A 1912 (1) 1921 (5); v SA 1924 (1); *v A 1911 (5) 1920 (5) 1924 (1); v SA 1913 (5)*

Downton, P. R. 30: v A 1981 (1) 1985 (6); v WI 1984 (5) 1988 (3); v In 1986 (1); v SL 1984 (1); *v WI 1980 (3) 1985 (5); v In 1984 (5)*

Druce, N. F. 5: *v A 1897 (5)*

Ducat, A. 1: v A 1921

Duckworth, G. 24: v A 1930 (5); v SA 1924 (1) 1929 (4) 1935 (1); v WI 1928 (1); v In 1936 (3); *v A 1928 (5); v SA 1930 (3); v NZ 1932 (1)*

Duleepsinhji, K. S. 12: v A 1930 (4); v SA 1929 (1); v NZ 1931 (3); *v NZ 1929 (4)*

Durston, F. J. 1: v A 1921

Ealham, M. A. 8: v A 1997 (4); v SA 1998 (2); v In 1996 (1); v P 1996 (1)

Edmonds, P. H. 51: v A 1975 (2) 1985 (5); v NZ 1978 (3) 1983 (2) 1986 (3); v In 1979 (4) 1982 (3) 1986 (2); v P 1978 (3) 1987 (5); *v A 1978 (1) 1986 (5); v WI 1985 (3); v NZ 1977 (3); v In 1984 (5); v P 1977 (2)*

Edrich, J. H. 77: v A 1964 (3) 1968 (5) 1972 (5) 1975 (4); v SA 1965 (1); v WI 1963 (3) 1966 (1) 1969 (3) 1976 (2); v NZ 1965 (1) 1969 (3); v In 1967 (2) 1971 (3) 1974 (3); v P 1971 (3) 1974 (3); *v A 1965 (5) 1970 (6) 1974 (4); v WI 1967 (5); v NZ 1965 (3) 1970 (2) 1974 (2); v In 1963 (2); v P 1968 (3)*

Edrich, W. J. 39: v A 1938 (4) 1948 (5) 1953 (3); v SA 1947 (4); v WI 1950 (2); v NZ 1949 (4); v In 1946 (1); v P 1954 (1); *v A 1946 (5) 1954 (4); v SA 1938 (5); v NZ 1946 (1)*

Elliott, H. 4: v WI 1928 (1); *v SA 1927 (1); v In 1933 (2)*

Ellison, R. M. 11: v A 1985 (2); v WI 1984 (1); v In 1986 (1); v SL 1984 (1); *v WI 1985 (3); v In 1984 (3)*

Emburey, J. E. 64: v A 1980 (1) 1981 (4) 1985 (6) 1989 (3) 1993 (1); v WI 1980 (3) 1988 (3) 1995 (1); v NZ 1978 (1) 1986 (2); v In 1986 (3); v P 1987 (4); v SL 1988 (1); *v A 1978 (4) 1986 (5) 1987 (1); v WI 1980 (4) 1985 (4); v NZ 1987 (3); v In 1979 (1) 1981 (3) 1992 (1); v P 1987 (3); v SL 1981 (1) 1992 (1)*

Emmett, G. M. 1: v A 1948

Emmett, T. 7: *v A 1876 (2) 1878 (1) 1881 (4)*

Evans, A. J. 1: v A 1921

Evans, T. G. 91: v A 1948 (5) 1953 (5) 1956 (5); v SA 1947 (5) 1951 (3) 1955 (3); v WI 1950 (3) 1957 (5); v NZ 1949 (4) 1958 (5); v In 1946 (1) 1952 (4) 1959 (2); v P 1954 (4); *v A 1946 (4) 1950 (5) 1954 (4) 1958 (3); v SA 1948 (3) 1956 (5); v WI 1947 (4) 1953 (4); v NZ 1946 (1) 1950 (2) 1954 (2)*

Fagg, A. E. 5: v WI 1939 (1); v In 1936 (2); *v A 1936 (2)*

Fairbrother, N. H. 10: v NZ 1990 (3); v P 1987 (1); *v NZ 1987 (2); v In 1992 (2); v P 1987 (1); v SL 1992 (1)*

Fane, F. L. 14: *v A 1907 (4); v SA 1905 (5) 1909 (5)*

Farnes, K. 15: v A 1934 (2) 1938 (4); *v A 1936 (2); v SA 1938 (5); v WI 1934 (1)*

Farrimond, W. 4: v SA 1935 (1); *v SA 1930 (2); v WI 1934 (1)*

Fender, P. G. H. 13: v A 1921 (2); v SA 1924 (2) 1929 (1); *v A 1920 (3); v SA 1922 (5)*

Ferris, J. J. 1: *v SA 1891*

Fielder, A. 6: *v A 1903 (2) 1907 (4)*

Fishlock, L. B. 4: v In 1936 (2) 1946 (1); *v A 1946 (1)*

Flavell, J. A. 4: v A 1961 (2) 1964 (2)

Fletcher, K. W. R. 59: v A 1968 (1) 1972 (1) 1975 (2); v WI 1973 (3); v NZ 1969 (2) 1973 (3); v In 1971 (2) 1974 (3); v P 1974 (3); *v A 1970 (5) 1974 (5) 1976 (1); v WI 1973 (4); v NZ 1970 (1) 1974 (2); v In 1972 (5) 1976 (3) 1981 (6); v P 1968 (3) 1972 (3); v SL 1981 (1)*

Flintoff, A. 9: v SA 1998 (2); v WI 2000 (1); v Z 2000 (2); *v SA 1999 (4)*

Flowers, W. 8: v A 1893 (1); *v A 1884 (5) 1886 (2)*

Ford, F. G. J. 5: *v A 1894 (5)*

Foster, F. R. 11: v A 1912 (3); v SA 1912 (3); *v A 1911 (5)*

Foster, N. A. 29: v A 1985 (1) 1989 (3) 1993 (1); v WI 1984 (1) 1988 (2); v NZ 1983 (1) 1986 (1); v In 1986 (1); v P 1987 (5); v SL 1988 (1); *v A 1987 (1); v WI 1985 (3); v NZ 1983 (2); v In 1984 (2); v P 1983 (2) 1987 (2)*

Foster, R. E. 8: v SA 1907 (3); *v A 1903 (5)*

Fothergill, A. J. 2: *v SA 1888 (2)*

Fowler, G. 21: v WI 1984 (5); v NZ 1983 (2); v P 1982 (1); v SL 1984 (1); *v A 1982 (3); v NZ 1983 (2); v In 1984 (5); v P 1983 (2)*

Fraser, A. R. C. 46: v A 1989 (3) 1993 (1); v SA 1994 (2) 1998 (5); v WI 1995 (5); v NZ 1994 (3); v In 1990 (3); v SL 1998 (1); *v A 1990 (3) 1994 (3) 1998 (2); v SA 1995 (3); v WI 1989 (2) 1993 (4) 1997 (6)*

Freeman, A. P. 12: v SA 1929 (3); v WI 1928 (3); *v A 1924 (2); v SA 1927 (4)*

French, B. N. 16: v NZ 1986 (3); v In 1986 (2); v P 1987 (4); *v A 1987 (1); v NZ 1987 (3); v P 1987 (3)*

Fry, C. B. 26: v A 1899 (5) 1902 (3) 1905 (4) 1909 (3) 1912 (3); v SA 1907 (3) 1912 (3); *v SA 1895 (2)*

Gallian, J. E. R. 3: v WI 1995 (2); *v SA 1995 (1)*

Gatting, M. W. 79: v A 1980 (1) 1981 (6) 1985 (6) 1989 (1) 1993 (2); v WI 1980 (4) 1984 (1) 1988 (2); v NZ 1983 (2) 1986 (3); v In 1986 (3); v P 1982 (3) 1987 (5); *v A 1986 (5) 1987 (1) 1994 (5); v WI 1980 (1) 1985 (1); v NZ 1977 (1) 1983 (2) 1987 (3); v In 1981 (5) 1984 (5) 1992 (3); v P 1977 (1) 1983 (3) 1987 (3); v SL 1992 (1)*

Gay, L. H. 1: *v A 1894*

Geary, G. 14: v A 1926 (2) 1930 (1) 1934 (2); v SA 1924 (1) 1929 (2); *v A 1928 (4); v SA 1927(2)*

Gibb, P. A. 8: v In 1946 (2); *v A 1946 (1); v SA 1938 (5)*

Giddins, E. S. H. 4: v WI 2000 (2); v NZ 1999 (1); v Z 2000 (2)

Gifford, N. 15: v A 1964 (2) 1972 (3); v NZ 1973 (2); v In 1971 (2); v P 1971 (2); *v In 1972 (2); v P 1972 (2)*

Giles, A. F. 1: v SA 1998

Gilligan, A. E. R. 11: v SA 1924 (4); *v A 1924 (5); v SA 1922 (2)*

Gilligan, A. H. H. 4: *v NZ 1929 (4)*

Gimblett, H. 3: v WI 1939 (1); v In 1936 (2)

Gladwin, C. 8: v SA 1947 (2); v NZ 1949 (1); *v SA 1948 (5)*

Goddard, T. W. 8: v A 1930 (1); v WI 1939 (2); v NZ 1937 (2); *v SA 1938 (3)*

Gooch, G. A. 118: v A 1975 (2) 1980 (1) 1981 (5) 1985 (6) 1989 (5) 1993 (6); v SA 1994 (3); v WI 1980 (5) 1988 (5) 1991 (5); v NZ 1978 (3) 1986 (3) 1990 (3) 1994 (3); v In 1979 (4) 1986 (3) 1990 (3); v P 1978 (2) 1992 (5); v SL 1988 (1) 1991 (1); *v A 1978 (6) 1979 (2) 1990 (4) 1994 (5); v WI 1980 (4) 1985 (5) 1989 (2); v NZ 1991 (3); v In 1979 (1) 1981 (6) 1992 (2); v P 1987 (3); v SL 1981 (1)*

Gough, D. 43: v A 1997 (4); v SA 1994 (3) 1998 (4); v WI 1995 (3) 2000 (5); v NZ 1994 (1); v SL 1998 (1); v Z 2000 (2); *v A 1994 (3) 1998 (5); v SA 1995 (2) 1999 (5); v NZ 1996 (3); v Z 1996 (2)*

Gover, A. R. 4: v NZ 1937 (2); v In 1936 (1) 1946 (1)

Gower, D. I. 117: v A 1980 (1) 1981 (5) 1985 (6) 1989 (6); v WI 1980 (1) 1984 (5) 1988 (4); v NZ 1978 (3) 1983 (4) 1986 (3); v In 1979 (4) 1982 (3) 1986 (2) 1990 (3); v P 1978 (3) 1982 (3) 1987 (5) 1992 (3); v SL 1984 (1); *v A 1978 (6) 1979 (3) 1982 (5) 1986 (5) 1990 (5); v WI 1980 (4) 1985 (5); v NZ 1983 (3); v In 1979 (1) 1981 (6) 1984 (5); v P 1983 (3); v SL 1981 (1)*

Grace, E. M. 1: v A 1880

Grace, G. F. 1: v A 1880

Grace, W. G. 22: v A 1880 (1) 1882 (1) 1884 (3) 1886 (3) 1888 (3) 1890 (2) 1893 (2) 1896 (3) 1899 (1); *v A 1891 (3)*

Graveney, T. W. 79: v A 1953 (5) 1956 (2) 1968 (5); v SA 1951 (1) 1955 (5); v WI 1957 (4) 1966 (4) 1969 (1); v NZ 1958 (4); v In 1952 (4) 1967 (3); v P 1954 (3) 1962 (4) 1967 (3); *v A 1954 (2) 1958 (5) 1962 (3); v WI 1953 (5) 1967 (5); v NZ 1954 (2) 1958 (2); v In 1951 (4); v P 1968 (3)*

Greenhough, T. 4: v SA 1960 (1); v In 1959 (3)

Greenwood, A. 2: *v A 1876 (2)*

Greig, A. W. 58: v A 1972 (5) 1975 (4) 1977 (5); v WI 1973 (3) 1976 (5); v NZ 1973 (3); v In 1974 (3); v P 1974 (3); *v A 1974 (6) 1976 (1); v WI 1973 (5); v NZ 1974 (2); v In 1972 (5) 1976 (5); v P 1972 (3)*

Greig, I. A. 2: v P 1982 (2)

Grieve, B. A. F. 2: *v SA 1888 (2)*

Griffith, S. C. 3: *v SA 1948 (2); v WI 1947 (1)*

Gunn, G. 15: v A 1909 (1); *v A 1907 (5) 1911 (5); v WI 1929 (4)*

Gunn, J. 6: v A 1905 (1); *v A 1901 (5)*

Gunn, W. 11: v A 1888 (2) 1890 (2) 1893 (3) 1896 (1) 1899 (1); *v A 1886 (2)*

Habib, A. 2: v NZ 1999 (2)

Haig, N. E. 5: v A 1921 (1); *v WI 1929 (4)*

Haigh, S. 11: v A 1905 (2) 1909 (1) 1912 (1); *v SA 1898 (2) 1905 (5)*

Hallows, C. 2: v A 1921 (1); v WI 1928 (1)

Hamilton, G. M. 1: *v SA 1999*

Hammond, W. R. 85: v A 1930 (5) 1934 (5) 1938 (4); v SA 1929 (4) 1935 (5); v WI 1928 (3) 1933 (3) 1939 (3); v NZ 1931 (3) 1937 (3); v In 1932 (1) 1936 (2) 1946 (3); *v A 1928 (5) 1932 (5) 1936 (5) 1946 (4); v SA 1927 (5) 1930 (5) 1938 (5); v WI 1934 (4); v NZ 1932 (2) 1946 (1)*

Hampshire, J. H. 8: v A 1972 (1) 1975 (1); v WI 1969 (2); *v A 1970 (2); v NZ 1970 (2)*

Hardinge, H. T. W. 1: v A 1921

Hardstaff, J. 5: *v A 1907 (5)*

Hardstaff, J. jun. 23: v A 1938 (2) 1948 (1); v SA 1935 (1); v WI 1939 (3); v NZ 1937 (3); v In 1936 (2) 1946 (2); *v A 1936 (5) 1946 (1); v WI 1947 (3)*

Harris, Lord 4: v A 1880 (1) 1884 (2); *v A 1878 (1)*

Hartley, J. C. 2: *v SA 1905 (2)*

Hawke, Lord 5: *v SA 1895 (3) 1898 (2)*

Hayes, E. G. 5: v A 1909 (1); v SA 1912 (1); *v SA 1905 (3)*

Hayes, F. C. 9: v WI 1973 (3) 1976 (2); *v WI 1973 (4)*

Hayward, T. W. 35: v A 1896 (2) 1899 (5) 1902 (1) 1905 (5) 1909 (1); v SA 1907 (3); *v A 1897 (5) 1901 (5) 1903 (5); v SA 1895 (3)*

Headley, D. W. 15: v A 1997 (3); v SA 1998 (1); v NZ 1999 (2); *v A 1998 (3); v WI 1997 (6)*

Hearne, A. 1: *v SA 1891*

Hearne, F. 2: *v SA 1888 (2)*

Hearne, G. G. 1: *v SA 1891*

Hearne, J. T. 12: v A 1896 (3) 1899 (3); *v A 1897 (5); v SA 1891 (1)*

Hearne, J. W. 24: v A 1912 (3) 1921 (1) 1926 (1); v SA 1912 (2) 1924 (3); *v A 1911 (5) 1920 (2) 1924 (4); v SA 1913 (3)*

Hegg, W. K. 2: *v A 1998 (2)*

Hemmings, E. E. 16: v A 1989 (1); v NZ 1990 (3); v In 1990 (3); v P 1982 (2); *v A 1982 (3) 1987 (1) 1990 (1); v NZ 1987 (1); v P 1987 (1)*

Hendren, E. H. 51: v A 1921 (2) 1926 (5) 1930 (2) 1934 (4); v SA 1924 (5) 1929 (5); v WI 1928 (1); *v A 1920 (5) 1924 (5) 1928 (5); v SA 1930 (5); v WI 1929 (4) 1934 (4)*

Hendrick, M. 30: v A 1977 (3) 1980 (1) 1981 (2); v WI 1976 (2) 1980 (2); v NZ 1978 (2); v In 1974 (3) 1979 (4); v P 1974 (3); *v A 1974 (2) 1978 (5); v NZ 1974 (1) 1977 (1)*

Heseltine, C. 2: *v SA 1895 (2)*

Hick, G. A. 60: v A 1993 (3); v SA 1994 (3) 1998 (2); v WI 1991 (4) 1995 (5) 2000 (4); v NZ 1994 (3) 1999 (1); v In 1996 (3); v P 1992 (4) 1996 (1); v SL 1998 (1); v Z 2000 (2); *v A 1994 (3) 1998 (4); v SA 1995 (5); v WI 1993 (5); v NZ 1991 (3); v In 1992 (3); v SL 1992 (1)*

Higgs, K. 15: v A 1968 (1); v WI 1966 (5); v SA 1965 (1); v In 1967 (1); v P 1967 (3); *v A 1965 (1); v NZ 1965 (3)*

Hill, A. 2: *v A 1876 (2)*

Hill, A. J. L. 3: *v SA 1895 (3)*

Hilton, M. J. 4: v SA 1951 (1); v WI 1950 (1); *v In 1951 (2)*

Hirst, G. H. 24: v A 1899 (1) 1902 (4) 1905 (3) 1909 (4); v SA 1907 (3); *v A 1897 (4) 1903 (5)*

Hitch, J. W. 7: v A 1912 (1) 1921 (1); v SA 1912 (1); *v A 1911 (3) 1920 (1)*

Hobbs, J. B. 61: v A 1909 (3) 1912 (3) 1921 (1) 1926 (5) 1930 (5); v SA 1912 (3) 1924 (4) 1929 (1); v WI 1928 (2); *v A 1907 (4) 1911 (5) 1920 (5) 1924 (5) 1928 (5); v SA 1909 (5) 1913 (5)*

Hobbs, R. N. S. 7: v In 1967 (3); v P 1967 (1) 1971 (1); *v WI 1967 (1); v P 1968 (1)*

Hoggard, M. J. 1: v WI 2000

Hollies, W. E. 13: v A 1948 (1); v SA 1947 (3); v WI 1950 (2); v NZ 1949 (4); *v WI 1934 (3)*

Hol-lioake, A. J. 4: v A 1997 (2); *v WI 1997 (2)*

Holioake, B. C. 2: v A 1997 (1); v SL 1998 (1)

Holmes, E. R. T. 5: v SA 1935 (1); *v WI 1934 (4)*

Holmes, P. 7: v A 1921 (1); v In 1932 (1); *v SA 1927 (5)*

Hone, L. 1: *v A 1878*

Hopwood, J. L. 2: v A 1934 (2)

Hornby, A. N. 3: v A 1882 (1) 1884 (1); *v A 1878 (1)*

Horton, M. J. 2: v In 1959 (2)

Howard, N. D. 4: *v In 1951 (4)*

Howell, H. 5: v A 1921 (1); v SA 1924 (1); *v A 1920 (3)*

Howorth, R. 5: v SA 1947 (1); *v WI 1947 (4)*

Humphries, J. 3: *v A 1907 (3)*

Hunter, J. 5: *v A 1884 (5)*

Hussain, N. 53: v A 1993 (4) 1997 (6); v SA 1998 (5); v WI 2000 (4); v NZ 1999 (3); v In 1996 (3); v P 1996 (2); v Z 2000 (2); *v A 1998 (5); v SA 1999 (5); v WI 1989 (3) 1997 (6); v NZ 1996 (3); v Z 1996 (2)*

Hutchings, K. L. 7: v A 1909 (2); *v A 1907 (5)*

Hutton, L. 79: v A 1938 (3) 1948 (4) 1953 (5); v SA 1947 (5) 1951 (5); v WI 1939 (3) 1950 (3); v NZ 1937 (3) 1949 (4); v In 1946 (3) 1952 (4); v P 1954 (2); *v A 1946 (5) 1950 (5) 1954 (5); v SA 1938 (4) 1948 (5); v WI 1947 (2) 1953 (5); v NZ 1950 (2) 1954 (2)*

Hutton, R. A. 5: v In 1971 (3); v P 1971 (2)

Iddon, J. 5: v SA 1935 (1); *v WI 1934 (4)*

Igglesden, A. P. 3: v A 1989 (1); *v WI 1993 (2)*

Ikin, J. T. 18: v SA 1951 (1) 1955 (1); v In 1946 (2) 1952 (2); *v A 1946 (5); v NZ 1946 (1); v WI 1947 (4)*

Illingworth, R. 61: v A 1961 (2) 1968 (3) 1972 (5); v SA 1960 (4); v WI 1966 (2) 1969 (3) 1973 (3); v NZ 1958 (1) 1965 (1) 1969 (3) 1973 (3); v In 1959 (2) 1967 (3) 1971 (3); v P 1962 (1) 1967 (1) 1971 (3); *v A 1962 (2) 1970 (6); v WI 1959 (5); v NZ 1962 (3) 1970 (2)*

Illingworth, R. K. 9: v WI 1991 (2) 1995 (4); *v SA 1995 (3)*

Ilott, M. C. 5: v A 1993 (3); *v SA 1995 (2)*

Insole, D. J. 9: v A 1956 (1); v SA 1955 (1); v WI 1950 (1) 1957 (1); *v SA 1956 (5)*

Irani, R. C. 3: v NZ 1999 (1); v In 1996 (2)

Jackman, R. D. 4: v P 1982 (2); *v WI 1980 (2)*

Jackson, F. S. 20: v A 1893 (2) 1896 (3) 1899 (5) 1902 (5) 1905 (5)
Jackson, H. L. 2: v A 1961 (1); v NZ 1949 (1)
James, S. P. 2: v SA 1998 (1); v SL 1998 (1)
Jameson, J. A. 4: v In 1971 (2); *v WI 1973 (2)*
Jardine, D. R. 22: v WI 1928 (2) 1933 (2); v NZ 1931 (3); v In 1932 (1); *v A 1928 (5) 1932 (5);*
    v NZ 1932 (1); v In 1933 (3)
Jarvis, P. W. 9: v A 1989 (2); v WI 1988 (2); *v NZ 1987 (2); v In 1992 (2); v SL 1992 (1)*
Jenkins, R. O. 9: v WI 1950 (2); v In 1952 (2); *v SA 1948 (5)*
Jessop, G. L. 18: v A 1899 (1) 1902 (4) 1905 (1) 1909 (2); v SA 1907 (3) 1912 (2); *v A 1901 (5)*
Jones, A. O. 12: v A 1899 (1) 1905 (2) 1909 (2); *v A 1901 (5) 1907 (2)*
Jones, I. J. 15: v WI 1966 (2); *v A 1965 (4); v WI 1967 (5); v NZ 1965 (3); v In 1963 (1)*
Jupp, H. 2: *v A 1876 (2)*
Jupp, V. W. C. 8: v A 1921 (2); v WI 1928 (2); *v SA 1922 (4)*

Keeton, W. W. 2: v A 1934 (1); v WI 1939 (1)
Kennedy, A. S. 5: *v SA 1922 (5)*
Kenyon, D. 8: v A 1953 (2); v SA 1955 (3); *v In 1951 (3)*
Killick, E. T. 2: v SA 1929 (2)
Kilner, R. 9: v A 1926 (4); v SA 1924 (2); *v A 1924 (3)*
King, J. H. 1: v A 1909
Kinneir, S. P. 1: *v A 1911*
Knight, A. E. 3: *v A 1903 (3)*
Knight, B. R. 29: v A 1968 (2); v WI 1966 (1) 1969 (3); v NZ 1969 (2); v P 1962 (2); *v A 1962 (1)*
    1965 (2); v NZ 1962 (3) 1965 (2); v In 1961 (4) 1963 (5); v P 1961 (2)
Knight, D. J. 2: v A 1921 (2)
Knight, N. V. 16: v SA 1998 (1); v WI 1995 (2) 2000 (2); v In 1996 (1); v P 1996 (3); v Z 2000 (2);
    v NZ 1996 (3); v Z 1996 (2)
Knott, A. P. E. 95: v A 1968 (5) 1972 (5) 1975 (4) 1977 (5) 1981 (2); v WI 1969 (3) 1973 (3)
    1976 (5) 1980 (4); v NZ 1969 (3) 1973 (3); v In 1971 (3) 1974 (3); v P 1967 (2) 1971 (3)
    1974 (3); *v A 1970 (6) 1974 (6) 1976 (1); v WI 1967 (2) 1973 (5); v NZ 1970 (1) 1974 (2); v In*
    1972 (5) 1976 (5); v P 1968 (3) 1972 (3)
Knox, N. A. 2: v SA 1907 (2)

Laker, J. C. 46: v A 1948 (3) 1953 (3) 1956 (5); v SA 1951 (2) 1955 (1); v WI 1950 (1) 1957 (4);
    v NZ 1949 (1) 1958 (4); v In 1952 (4); v P 1954 (1); *v A 1958 (4); v SA 1956 (5); v WI 1947 (4)*
    1953 (4)
Lamb, A. J. 79: v A 1985 (6) 1989 (1); v WI 1984 (5) 1988 (4) 1991 (4); v NZ 1983 (4) 1986 (1)
    1990 (3); v In 1982 (3) 1986 (2) 1990 (3); v P 1982 (3) 1992 (2); v SL 1984 (1) 1988 (1); *v A*
    1982 (3) 1986 (5) 1990 (3); v WI 1985 (5) 1989 (4); v NZ 1983 (3) 1991 (3); v In 1984 (5);
    v P 1983 (3)
Langridge, James 8: v SA 1935 (1); v WI 1933 (2), v In 1936 (1) 1946 (1); *v In 1933 (3)*
Larkins, W. 13: v A 1981 (1); v WI 1980 (3); *v A 1979 (1) 1990 (3); v WI 1989 (4); v In 1979 (1)*
Larter, J. D. F. 10: v SA 1965 (2); v NZ 1965 (1); v P 1962 (1); *v NZ 1962 (3); v In 1963 (3)*
Larwood, H. 21: v A 1926 (2) 1930 (3); v SA 1929 (3); v WI 1928 (2); v NZ 1931 (1); *v A 1928 (5)*
    1932 (5)
Lathwell, M. N. 2: v A 1993 (2)
Lawrence, D. V. 5: v WI 1991 (2); v SL 1988 (1) 1991 (1); *v NZ 1991 (1)*
Leadbeater, E. 2: *v In 1951 (2)*
Lee, H. W. 1: *v SA 1930*
Lees, W. S. 5: *v SA 1905 (5)*
Legge, G. B. 5: *v SA 1927 (1); v NZ 1929 (4)*
Leslie, C. F. H. 4: *v A 1882 (4)*
Lever, J. K. 21: v A 1977 (3); v WI 1980 (1); v In 1979 (1) 1986 (1); *v A 1976 (1) 1978 (1) 1979 (1);*
    v NZ 1977 (1); v In 1976 (5) 1979 (1) 1981 (2); v P 1977 (3)
Lever, P. 17: v A 1972 (1) 1975 (1); v In 1971 (1); v P 1971 (3); *v A 1970 (5) 1974 (2); v NZ*
    1970 (2) 1974 (2)
Leveson Gower, H. D. G. 3: *v SA 1909 (3)*
Levett, W. H. V. 1: *v In 1933*
Lewis, A. R. 9: v NZ 1973 (1); *v In 1972 (5); v P 1972 (3)*

Lewis, C. C. 32: v A 1993 (2); v WI 1991 (2); v NZ 1990 (1); v In 1990 (2) 1996 (3); v P 1992 (5) 1996 (2); v SL 1991 (1); *v A 1990 (1) 1994 (2); v WI 1993 (5); v NZ 1991 (2); v In 1992 (3); v SL 1992 (1)*

Leyland, M. 41: v A 1930 (3) 1934 (5) 1938 (1); v SA 1929 (5) 1935 (4); v WI 1928 (1) 1933 (1); v In 1936 (2); *v A 1928 (1) 1932 (5) 1936 (5); v SA 1930 (5); v WI 1934 (3)*

Lilley, A. A. 35: v A 1896 (3) 1899 (4) 1902 (5) 1905 (5) 1909 (5); v SA 1907 (3); *v A 1901 (5) 1903 (5)*

Lillywhite, James jun. 2: *v A 1876 (2)*

Lloyd, D. 9: v In 1974 (2); v P 1974 (3); *v A 1974 (4)*

Lloyd, T. A. 1: v WI 1984

Loader, P. J. 13: v SA 1955 (1); v WI 1957 (2); v NZ 1958 (3); v P 1954 (1); *v A 1958 (2); v SA 1956 (4)*

Lock, G. A. R. 49: v A 1953 (2) 1956 (4) 1961 (3); v SA 1955 (3); v WI 1957 (3) 1963 (3); v NZ 1958 (5); v In 1952 (2); v P 1962 (3); *v A 1958 (4); v SA 1956 (1); v WI 1953 (5) 1967 (2); v NZ 1958 (2); v In 1961 (5); v P 1961 (2)*

Lockwood, W. H. 12: v A 1893 (2) 1899 (1) 1902 (4); *v A 1894 (5)*

Lohmann, G. A. 18: v A 1886 (3) 1888 (3) 1890 (2) 1896 (1); *v A 1886 (2) 1887 (1) 1891 (3); v SA 1895 (3)*

Lowson, F. A. 7: v SA 1951 (2) 1955 (1); *v In 1951 (4)*

Lucas, A. P. 5: v A 1880 (1) 1882 (1) 1884 (2); *v A 1878 (1)*

Luckhurst, B. W. 21: v A 1972 (4); v WI 1973 (2); v In 1971 (3); v P 1971 (3); *v A 1970 (5) 1974 (2); v NZ 1970 (2)*

Lyttelton, Hon. A. 4: v A 1880 (1) 1882 (1) 1884 (2)

Macaulay, G. G. 8: v A 1926 (1); v SA 1924 (1); v WI 1933 (2); *v SA 1922 (4)*

MacBryan, J. C. W. 1: v SA 1924

McCague, M. J. 3: v A 1993 (2); *v A 1994 (1)*

McConnon, J. E. 2: v P 1954 (2)

McGahey, C. P. 2: *v A 1901 (2)*

MacGregor, G. 8: v A 1890 (2) 1893 (3); *v A 1891 (3)*

McIntyre, A. J. W. 3: v SA 1955 (1); v WI 1950 (1); *v A 1950 (1)*

MacKinnon, F. A. 1: *v A 1878*

MacLaren, A. C. 35: v A 1896 (2) 1899 (4) 1902 (5) 1905 (4) 1909 (5); *v A 1894 (5) 1897 (5) 1901 (5)*

McMaster, J. E. P. 1: *v SA 1888*

Maddy, D. L. 3: v NZ 1999 (1); *v SA 1999 (2)*

Makepeace, J. W. H. 4: *v A 1920 (4)*

Malcolm, D. E. 40: v A 1989 (1) 1993 (1) 1997 (4); v SA 1994 (1); v WI 1991 (2) 1995 (2); v NZ 1990 (3) 1994 (1); v In 1990 (3); v P 1992 (3); *v A 1990 (5) 1994 (4); v SA 1995 (2); v WI 1989 (4) 1993 (1); v In 1992 (2); v SL 1992 (1)*

Mallender, N. A. 2: v P 1992 (2)

Mann, F. G. 7: v NZ 1949 (2); *v SA 1948 (5)*

Mann, F. T. 5: *v SA 1922 (5)*

Marks, V. J. 6: v NZ 1983 (1); v P 1982 (1); *v NZ 1983 (1); v P 1983 (3)*

Marriott, C. S. 1: v WI 1933

Martin, F. 2: v A 1890 (1); *v SA 1891 (1)*

Martin, J. W. 1: v SA 1947

Martin, P. J. 8: v A 1997 (1); v WI 1995 (3); v In 1996 (1); *v SA 1995 (3)*

Mason, J. R. 5: *v A 1897 (5)*

Matthews, A. D. G. 1: v NZ 1937

May, P. B. H. 66: v A 1953 (2) 1956 (5) 1961 (4); v SA 1951 (2) 1955 (5); v WI 1957 (5); v NZ 1958 (5); v In 1952 (4) 1959 (3); v P 1954 (4); *v A 1954 (5) 1958 (5); v SA 1956 (5); v WI 1953 (5) 1959 (3); v NZ 1954 (2) 1958 (2)*

Maynard, M. P. 4: v A 1993 (2); v WI 1988 (1); *v WI 1993 (1)*

Mead, C. P. 17: v A 1921 (2); *v A 1911 (4) 1928 (1); v SA 1913 (5) 1922 (5)*

Mead, W. 1: v A 1899

Midwinter, W. E. 4: *v A 1881 (4)*

Milburn, C. 9: v A 1968 (2); v WI 1966 (4); v In 1967 (1); v P 1967 (1); *v P 1968 (1)*

Miller, A. M. 1: *v SA 1895*

Miller, G. 34: v A 1977 (2); v WI 1976 (1) 1984 (2); v NZ 1978 (2); v In 1979 (3) 1982 (1); v P 1978 (3) 1982 (1); *v A 1978 (6) 1979 (1) 1982 (5); v WI 1980 (1); v NZ 1977 (3); v P 1977 (3)*

Milligan, F. W. 2: *v SA 1898 (2)*
Millman, G. 6: v P 1962 (2); *v In 1961 (2); v P 1961 (2)*
Milton, C. A. 6: v NZ 1958 (2); v In 1959 (2); *v A 1958 (2)*
Mitchell, A. 6: v SA 1935 (2); v In 1936 (1); *v In 1933 (3)*
Mitchell, F. 2: *v SA 1898 (2)*
Mitchell, T. B. 5: v A 1934 (1); v SA 1935 (1); *v A 1932 (1); v NZ 1932 (1)*
Mitchell-Innes, N. S. 1: v SA 1935
Mold, A. W. 3: v A 1893 (3)
Moon, L. J. 4: *v SA 1905 (4)*
Morley, F. 4: v A 1880 (1); *v A 1882 (3)*
Morris, H. 3: v WI 1991 (2); v SL 1991 (1)
Morris, J. E. 3: v In 1990 (3)
Mortimore, J. B. 9: v A 1964 (1); v In 1959 (2); *v A 1958 (1); v NZ 1958 (2); v In 1963 (3)*
Moss, A. E. 9: v A 1956 (1); v SA 1960 (2); v In 1959 (3); *v WI 1953 (1) 1959 (2)*
Moxon, M. D. 10: v A 1989 (1); v WI 1988 (2); v NZ 1986 (2); v P 1987 (1); *v A 1987 (1); v NZ 1987 (3)*
Mullally, A. D. 18: v NZ 1999 (3); v In 1996 (3); v P 1996 (3); *v A 1998 (4); v SA 1999 (2); v NZ 1996 (1); v Z 1996 (2)*
Munton, T. A. 2: v P 1992 (2)
Murdoch, W. L. 1: *v SA 1891*
Murray, J. T. 21: v A 1961 (5); v WI 1966 (1); v In 1967 (3); v P 1962 (3) 1967 (1); *v A 1962 (1); v SA 1964 (1); v NZ 1962 (1) 1965 (1); v In 1961 (3); v P 1961 (1)*

Newham, W. 1: *v A 1887*
Newport, P. J. 3: v A 1989 (1); v SL 1988 (1); *v A 1990 (1)*
Nichols, M. S. 14: v A 1930 (1); v SA 1935 (4); v WI 1933 (1) 1939 (1); *v NZ 1929 (4); v In 1933 (3)*

Oakman, A. S. M. 2: v A 1956 (2)
O'Brien, Sir T. C. 5: v A 1884 (1) 1888 (1); *v SA 1895 (3)*
O'Connor, J. 4: v SA 1929 (1); *v WI 1929 (3)*
Old, C. M. 46: v A 1975 (3) 1977 (2) 1980 (1) 1981 (2); v WI 1973 (1) 1976 (2) 1980 (1); v NZ 1973 (2) 1978 (1); v In 1974 (3); v P 1974 (3) 1978 (3); *v A 1974 (2) 1976 (1) 1978 (1); v WI 1973 (4) 1980 (1); v NZ 1974 (1) 1977 (2); v In 1972 (4) 1976 (4); v P 1972 (4) 1977 (1)*
Oldfield, N. 1: v WI 1939

Padgett, D. E. V. 2: v SA 1960 (2)
Paine, G. A. E. 4: *v WI 1934 (4)*
Palairet, L. C. H. 2: v A 1902 (2)
Palmer, C. H. 1: *v WI 1953*
Palmer, K. E. 1. *v SA 1964*
Parfitt, P. H. 37: v A 1964 (4) 1972 (3); v SA 1965 (2); v WI 1969 (1); v NZ 1965 (2), v P 1962 (5); *v A 1962 (2); v SA 1964 (5); v NZ 1962 (3) 1965 (3); v In 1961 (2) 1963 (3); v P 1961 (2)*
Parker, C. W. L. 1: v A 1921
Parker, P. W. G. 1: v A 1981
Parkhouse, W. G. A. 7: v WI 1950 (2); v In 1959 (2); *v A 1950 (2); v NZ 1950 (1)*
Parkin, C. H. 10: v A 1921 (4); v SA 1924 (1); *v A 1920 (5)*
Parks, J. H. 1: v NZ 1937
Parks, J. M. 46: v A 1964 (5); v SA 1960 (5) 1965 (3); v WI 1963 (4) 1966 (4); v NZ 1965 (3); v P 1954 (1); *v A 1965 (5); v SA 1964 (5); v WI 1959 (1) 1967 (3); v NZ 1965 (2); v In 1963 (5)*
Pataudi sen., Nawab of, 3: v A 1934 (1); *v A 1932 (2)*
Patel, M. M. 2: v In 1996 (2)
Paynter, E. 20: v A 1938 (4); v WI 1939 (2); v NZ 1931 (1) 1937 (2); v In 1932 (1); *v A 1932 (3); v SA 1938 (5); v NZ 1932 (2)*
Peate, E. 9: v A 1882 (1) 1884 (3) 1886 (1); *v A 1881 (4)*
Peebles, I. A. R. 13: v A 1930 (2); v NZ 1931 (3); *v SA 1927 (4) 1930 (4)*
Peel, R. 20: v A 1888 (3) 1890 (1) 1893 (1) 1896 (1); *v A 1884 (5) 1887 (1) 1891 (3) 1894 (5)*
Penn, F. 1: v A 1880
Perks, R. T. D. 2: v WI 1939 (1); *v SA 1938 (1)*
Philipson, H. 5: *v A 1891 (1) 1894 (4)*

Pigott, A. C. S. 1: *v NZ 1983*

Pilling, R. 8: v A 1884 (1) 1886 (1) 1888 (1); *v A 1881 (4) 1887 (1)*

Place, W. 3: *v WI 1947 (3)*

Pocock, P. I. 25: v A 1968 (1); v WI 1976 (2) 1984 (2); v SL 1984 (1); *v WI 1967 (2) 1973 (4); v In 1972 (4) 1984 (5); v P 1968 (1) 1972 (3)*

Pollard, R. 4: v A 1948 (2); v In 1946 (1); *v NZ 1946 (1)*

Poole, C. J. 3: *v In 1951 (3)*

Pope, G. H. 1: v SA 1947

Pougher, A. D. 1: *v SA 1891*

Price, J. S. E. 15: v A 1964 (2) 1972 (1); v In 1971 (3); v P 1971 (1); *v SA 1964 (4); v In 1963 (4)*

Price, W. F. F. 1: v A 1938

Prideaux, R. M. 3: v A 1968 (1); *v P 1968 (2)*

Pringle, D. R. 30: v A 1989 (2); v WI 1984 (3) 1988 (4) 1991 (4); v NZ 1986 (1); v In 1982 (3) 1986 (3); v P 1982 (1) 1992 (3); v SL 1988 (1); *v A 1982 (3); v NZ 1991 (2)*

Pullar, G. 28: v A 1961 (5); v SA 1960 (3); v In 1959 (3); v P 1962 (2); *v A 1962 (4); v WI 1959 (5); v In 1961 (3); v P 1961 (3)*

Quaife, W. G. 7: v A 1899 (2); *v A 1901 (5)*

Radford, N. V. 3: v NZ 1986 (1); v In 1986 (1); *v NZ 1987 (1)*

Radley, C. T. 8: v NZ 1978 (3); v P 1978 (3); *v NZ 1977 (2)*

Ramprakash, M. R. 42: v A 1993 (1) 1997 (1); v SA 1998 (5); v WI 1991 (5) 1995 (2) 2000 (2); v NZ 1999 (4); v P 1992 (3); v SL 1991 (1) 1998 (1); v Z 2000 (2); *v A 1994 (1) 1998 (5); v WI 1993 (4) 1997 (3); v SA 1995 (2)*

Randall, D. W. 47: v A 1977 (5); v WI 1984 (1); v NZ 1983 (3); v In 1979 (3) 1982 (3); v P 1982 (3); *v A 1976 (1) 1978 (6) 1979 (2) 1982 (4); v NZ 1977 (3) 1983 (3); v In 1976 (4); v P 1977 (3) 1983 (3)*

Ranjitsinhji, K. S. 15: v A 1896 (2) 1899 (5) 1902 (3); *v A 1897 (5)*

Read, C. M. W. 3: v NZ 1999 (3)

Read, H. D. 1: v SA 1935

Read, J. M. 17: v A 1882 (1) 1890 (2) 1893 (1); *v A 1884 (5) 1886 (2) 1887 (1) 1891 (3); v SA 1888 (2)*

Read, W. W. 18: v A 1884 (2) 1886 (3) 1888 (3) 1890 (2) 1893 (2); *v A 1882 (4) 1887 (1); v SA 1891 (1)*

Reeve, D. A. 3: *v NZ 1991 (3)*

Relf, A. E. 13: v A 1909 (1); *v A 1903 (2); v SA 1905 (5) 1913 (5)*

Rhodes, H. J. 2: v In 1959 (2)

Rhodes, S. J. 11: v SA 1994 (3); v NZ 1994 (3); *v A 1994 (5)*

Rhodes, W. 58: v A 1899 (3) 1902 (5) 1905 (4) 1909 (4) 1912 (3) 1921 (1) 1926 (1); v SA 1912 (3); *v A 1903 (5) 1907 (5) 1911 (5) 1920 (5); v SA 1909 (5) 1913 (5); v WI 1929 (4)*

Richards, C. J. 8: v WI 1988 (2); v P 1987 (1); *v A 1986 (5)*

Richardson, D. W. 1: v WI 1957

Richardson, P. E. 34: v A 1956 (5); v WI 1957 (5) 1963 (1); v NZ 1958 (4); *v A 1958 (4); v SA 1956 (5); v NZ 1958 (2); v In 1961 (5); v P 1961 (3)*

Richardson, T. 14: v A 1893 (1) 1896 (3); *v A 1894 (5) 1897 (5)*

Richmond, T. L. 1: v A 1921

Ridgway, F. 5: *v In 1951 (5)*

Robertson, J. D. 11: v SA 1947 (1); v NZ 1949 (1); *v WI 1947 (4); v In 1951 (5)*

Robins, R. W. V. 19: v A 1930 (2); v SA 1929 (1) 1935 (3); v WI 1933 (2); v NZ 1931 (1) 1937 (3); v In 1932 (1) 1936 (2); *v A 1936 (4)*

Robinson, R. T. 29: v A 1985 (6) 1989 (1); v In 1986 (1); v P 1987 (5); v SL 1988 (1); *v A 1987 (1); v WI 1985 (4); v NZ 1987 (3); v In 1984 (5); v P 1987 (2)*

Roope, G. R. J. 21: v A 1975 (1) 1977 (2); v WI 1973 (1); v NZ 1973 (3) 1978 (3); v P 1978 (3); *v NZ 1977 (3); v In 1972 (2); v P 1972 (2) 1977 (3)*

Root, C. F. 3: v A 1926 (3)

Rose, B. C. 9: v WI 1980 (3); *v WI 1980 (1); v NZ 1977 (2); v P 1977 (3)*

Royle, V. P. F. A. 1: *v A 1878*

Rumsey, F. E. 5: v A 1964 (1); v SA 1965 (1); v NZ 1965 (3)

Russell, A. C. 10: v A 1921 (2); *v A 1920 (4); v SA 1922 (4)*

Russell, R. C. 54: v A 1989 (6); v WI 1991 (4) 1995 (3); v NZ 1990 (3); v In 1990 (3) 1996 (3); v P 1992 (3) 1996 (2); v SL 1988 (1) 1991 (1); *v A 1990 (3); v SA 1995 (5); v WI 1989 (4) 1993 (5) 1997 (5); v NZ 1991 (3)*

Russell, W. E. 10: v SA 1965 (1); v WI 1966 (2); v P 1967 (1); *v A 1965 (1); v NZ 1965 (3); v In 1961 (1); v P 1961 (1)*

Salisbury, I. D. K. 12: v SA 1994 (1) 1998 (2); v P 1992 (2) 1996 (2); v SL 1998 (1); *v WI 1993 (2); v In 1992 (2)*

Sandham, A. 14: v A 1921 (1); v SA 1924 (1); *v A 1924 (2); v SA 1922 (5); v WI 1929 (4)*

Schofield, C. P. 2: v Z 2000 (2)

Schultz, S. S. 1: *v A 1878*

Scotton, W. H. 15: v A 1884 (1) 1886 (3); *v A 1881 (4) 1884 (5) 1886 (2)*

Selby, J. 6: *v A 1876 (2) 1881 (4)*

Selvey, M. W. W. 3: v WI 1976 (2); *v In 1976 (1)*

Shackleton, D. 7: v SA 1951 (1); v WI 1950 (1) 1963 (4); *v In 1951 (1)*

Sharp, J. 3: v A 1909 (3)

Sharpe, J. W. 3: v A 1890 (1); *v A 1891 (2)*

Sharpe, P. J. 12: v A 1964 (2); v WI 1963 (3) 1969 (3); v NZ 1969 (3); *v In 1963 (1)*

Shaw, A. 7: v A 1880 (1); *v A 1876 (2) 1881 (4)*

Sheppard, Rev. D. S. 22: v A 1956 (2); v WI 1950 (1) 1957 (2); v In 1952 (2); v P 1954 (2) 1962 (2); *v A 1950 (2) 1962 (5); v NZ 1950 (1) 1962 (3)*

Sherwin, M. 3: v A 1888 (1); *v A 1886 (2)*

Shrewsbury, A. 23: v A 1884 (3) 1886 (3) 1890 (2) 1893 (3); *v A 1881 (4) 1884 (5) 1886 (2) 1887 (1)*

Shuter, J. 1: v A 1888

Shuttleworth, K. 5: v P 1971 (1); *v A 1970 (2); v NZ 1970 (2)*

Sidebottom, A. 1: v A 1985

Silverwood, C. E. W. 5: *v SA 1999 (4); v Z 1996 (1)*

Simpson, R. T. 27: v A 1953 (3); v SA 1951 (3); v WI 1950 (3); v NZ 1949 (2); v In 1952 (2); v P 1954 (2); *v A 1950 (5) 1954 (1); v SA 1948 (1); v NZ 1950 (2) 1954 (2)*

Simpson-Hayward, G. H. 5: *v SA 1909 (5)*

Sims, J. M. 4: v SA 1935 (1); v In 1936 (1); *v A 1936 (2)*

Sinfield, R. A. 1: v A 1938

Slack, W. N. 3: v In 1986 (1); *v WI 1985 (2)*

Smailes, T. F. 1: v In 1946

Small, G. C. 17: v A 1989 (1); v WI 1988 (1); v NZ 1986 (2) 1990 (3); *v A 1986 (2) 1990 (4); v WI 1989 (4)*

Smith, A. C. 6: *v A 1962 (4); v NZ 1962 (2)*

Smith, A. M. 1: v A 1997

Smith, C. A. 1: *v SA 1888*

Smith, C. I. J. 5: v NZ 1937 (1); *v WI 1934 (4)*

Smith, C. L. 8: v NZ 1983 (2); v In 1986 (1); *v NZ 1983 (2); v P 1983 (3)*

Smith, D. 2: v SA 1935 (2)

Smith, D. M. 2: *v WI 1985 (2)*

Smith, D. R. 5: *v In 1961 (5)*

Smith, D. V. 3: v WI 1957 (3)

Smith, E. J. 11: v A 1912 (3); v SA 1912 (3); *v A 1911 (4); v SA 1913 (1)*

Smith, H. 1: v WI 1928

Smith, M. J. K. 50: v A 1961 (1) 1972 (3); v SA 1960 (4) 1965 (3); v WI 1966 (1); v NZ 1958 (3) 1965 (3); v In 1959 (2); *v A 1965 (5); v SA 1964 (5); v WI 1959 (5); v NZ 1965 (3); v In 1961 (4) 1963 (5); v P 1961 (3)*

Smith, R. A. 62: v A 1989 (5) 1993 (5); v WI 1988 (2) 1991 (4) 1995 (4); v NZ 1990 (3) 1994 (3); v In 1990 (3); v P 1992 (5); v SL 1988 (1) 1991 (1); *v A 1990 (5); v SA 1995 (5); v WI 1989 (4) 1993 (5); v NZ 1991 (3); v In 1992 (3); v SL 1992 (1)*

Smith, T. P. B. 4: v In 1946 (1); *v A 1946 (2); v NZ 1946 (1)*

Smithson, G. A. 2: *v WI 1947 (2)*

Snow, J. A. 49: v A 1968 (5) 1972 (5) 1975 (4); v SA 1965 (1); v WI 1966 (3) 1969 (3) 1973 (1) 1976 (3); v NZ 1965 (1) 1969 (2) 1973 (3); v In 1967 (3) 1971 (2); v P 1967 (1); *v A 1970 (6); v WI 1967 (4); v P 1968 (2)*

Southerton, J. 2: *v A 1876 (2)*

Spooner, R. H. 10: v A 1905 (2) 1909 (2) 1912 (3); v SA 1912 (3)

Spooner, R. T. 7: v SA 1955 (1); *v In 1951 (5); v WI 1953 (1)*

Stanyforth, R. T. 4: *v SA 1927 (4)*

Staples, S. J. 3: *v SA 1927 (3)*

Statham, J. B. 70: v A 1953 (1) 1956 (3) 1961 (4); v SA 1951 (2) 1955 (4) 1960 (5) 1965 (1); v WI 1957 (3) 1963 (2); v NZ 1958 (2); v In 1959 (3); v P 1954 (4) 1962 (3); *v A 1954 (5) 1958 (4) 1962 (5); v SA 1956 (4); v WI 1953 (4) 1959 (3); v NZ 1950 (1) 1954 (2); v In 1951 (5)*

Steel, A. G. 13: v A 1880 (1) 1882 (1) 1884 (3) 1886 (3) 1888 (1); *v A 1882 (4)*

Steele, D. S. 8: v A 1975 (3); v WI 1976 (5)

Stephenson, J. P. 1: v A 1989

Stevens, G. T. S. 10: v A 1926 (2); *v SA 1922 (1) 1927 (5); v WI 1929 (2)*

Stevenson, G. B. 2: *v WI 1980 (1); v In 1979 (1)*

Stewart, A. J. 102: v A 1993 (6) 1997 (6); v SA 1994 (3) 1998 (5); v WI 1991 (1) 1995 (3) 2000 (5); v NZ 1990 (3) 1994 (3) 1999 (4); v In 1996 (2); v P 1992 (5) 1996 (3); v SL 1991 (1) 1998 (1); v Z 2000 (2); *v A 1990 (5) 1994 (2) 1998 (5); v SA 1995 (5) 1999 (5); v WI 1989 (4) 1993 (5) 1997 (6); v NZ 1991 (3) 1996 (3); v In 1992 (3); v SL 1992 (1); v Z 1996 (2)*

Stewart, M. J. 8: v WI 1963 (4); v P 1962 (2); *v In 1963 (2)*

Stoddart, A. E. 16: v A 1893 (3) 1896 (2); *v A 1887 (1) 1891 (3) 1894 (5) 1897 (2)*

Storer, W. 6: v A 1899 (1); *v A 1897 (5)*

Street, G. B. 1: *v SA 1922*

Strudwick, H. 28: v A 1921 (2) 1926 (5); v SA 1924 (1); *v A 1911 (1) 1920 (4) 1924 (5); v SA 1909 (5) 1913 (5)*

Studd, C. T. 5: v A 1882 (1); *v A 1882 (4)*

Studd, G. B. 4: *v A 1882 (4)*

Subba Row, R. 13: v A 1961 (5); v SA 1960 (4); v NZ 1958 (1); v In 1959 (1); *v WI 1959 (2)*

Such, P. M. 11: v A 1993 (5); v NZ 1994 (3) 1999 (1); *v A 1998 (2)*

Sugg, F. H. 2: v A 1888 (2)

Sutcliffe, H. 54: v A 1926 (5) 1930 (4) 1934 (4); v SA 1924 (5) 1929 (5) 1935 (2); v WI 1928 (3) 1933 (2); v NZ 1931 (2); v In 1932 (1); *v A 1924 (5) 1928 (4) 1932 (5); v SA 1927 (5); v NZ 1932 (2)*

Swetman, R. 11: v In 1959 (3); *v A 1958 (2); v WI 1959 (4); v NZ 1958 (2)*

Tate, F. W. 1: v A 1902

Tate, M. W. 39: v A 1926 (5) 1930 (5); v SA 1924 (5) 1929 (3) 1935 (1); v WI 1928 (3); v NZ 1931 (1); *v A 1924 (5) 1928 (5); v SA 1930 (5); v NZ 1932 (1)*

Tattersall, R. 16: v A 1953 (1); v SA 1951 (5); v P 1954 (1); *v A 1950 (2); v NZ 1950 (2); v In 1951 (5)*

Tavaré, C. J. 31: v A 1981 (2) 1989 (1); v WI 1980 (2) 1984 (1); v NZ 1983 (4); v In 1982 (3); v P 1982 (3); v SL 1984 (1); *v A 1982 (5); v NZ 1983 (2); v In 1981 (6); v SL 1981 (1)*

Taylor, J. P. 2: v NZ 1994 (1); *v In 1992 (1)*

Taylor, K. 3: v A 1964 (1); v In 1959 (2)

Taylor, L. B. 2: v A 1985 (2)

Taylor, R. W. 57: v A 1981 (3); v NZ 1978 (3) 1983 (4); v In 1979 (3) 1982 (3); v P 1978 (3) 1982 (3); *v A 1978 (6) 1979 (3) 1982 (5); v NZ 1970 (1) 1977 (3) 1983 (3); v In 1979 (1) 1981 (6); v P 1977 (3) 1983 (3); v SL 1981 (1)*

Tennyson, Hon. L. H. 9: v A 1921 (4); *v SA 1913 (5)*

Terry, V. P. 2: v WI 1984 (2)

Thomas, J. G. 5: v NZ 1986 (1); *v WI 1985 (4)*

Thompson, G. J. 6: v A 1909 (1); *v SA 1909 (5)*

Thomson, N. I. 5: *v SA 1964 (5)*

Thorpe, G. P. 60: v A 1993 (4) 1997 (6); v SA 1994 (2) 1998 (5); v WI 1995 (6) 2000 (3); v NZ 1999 (4); v In 1996 (3); v P 1996 (3); *v A 1994 (5) 1998 (1); v SA 1995 (5); v WI 1993 (5) 1997 (6); v NZ 1996 (2); v Z 1996 (2)*

Titmus, F. J. 53: v A 1964 (5); v SA 1955 (2) 1965 (3); v WI 1963 (4) 1966 (3); v NZ 1965 (3); v P 1962 (2) 1967 (2); *v A 1962 (5) 1965 (5) 1974 (4); v SA 1964 (5); v WI 1967 (2); v NZ 1962 (3); v In 1963 (5)*

Tolchard, R. W. 4: *v In 1976 (4)*

Townsend, C. L. 2: v A 1899 (2)

Townsend, D. C. H. 3: *v WI 1934 (3)*

Townsend, L. F. 4: *v WI 1929 (1); v In 1933 (3)*

Tremlett, M. F. 3: *v WI 1947 (3)*

Trescothick, M. E. 3: v WI 2000 (3)

Trott, A. E. 2: *v SA 1898 (2)*

Trueman, F. S. 67: v A 1953 (1) 1956 (2) 1961 (4) 1964 (4); v SA 1955 (1) 1960 (5); v WI 1957 (5) 1963 (5); v NZ 1958 (5) 1965 (2); v In 1952 (4) 1959 (5); v P 1962 (4); *v A 1958 (3) 1962 (5); v WI 1953 (3) 1959 (5); v NZ 1958 (2) 1962 (2)*

Tudor, A. J. 3: v NZ 1999 (1); *v A 1998 (2)*

Tufnell, N. C. 1: *v SA 1909*

Tufnell, P. C. R. 41: v A 1993 (2) 1997 (1); v SA 1994 (1); v WI 1991 (1); v NZ 1999 (4); v P 1992 (1); v SL 1991 (1); *v A 1990 (4) 1994 (4); v SA 1999 (3); v WI 1993 (2) 1997 (6); v NZ 1991 (3) 1996 (3); v In 1992 (2); v SL 1992 (1); v Z 1996 (2)*

Turnbull, M. J. 9: v WI 1933 (2); v In 1936 (1); *v SA 1930 (5); v NZ 1929 (1)*

Tyldesley, E. 14: v A 1921 (3) 1926 (1); v SA 1924 (1); v WI 1928 (3); *v A 1928 (1): v SA 1927 (5)*

Tyldesley, J. T. 31: v A 1899 (2) 1902 (5) 1905 (5) 1909 (4); v SA 1907 (3); *v A 1901 (5) 1903 (5); v SA 1898 (2)*

Tyldesley, R. K. 7: v A 1930 (2); v SA 1924 (4); *v A 1924 (1)*

Tylecote, E. F. S. 6: v A 1886 (2); *v A 1882 (4)*

Tyler, E. J. 1: *v SA 1895*

Tyson, F. H. 17: v A 1956 (1); v SA 1955 (2); v P 1954 (1); *v A 1954 (5) 1958 (2); v SA 1956 (2); v NZ 1954 (2) 1958 (2)*

Ulyett, G. 25: v A 1882 (1) 1884 (3) 1886 (3) 1888 (2) 1890 (1); *v A 1876 (2) 1878 (1) 1881 (4) 1884 (5) 1887 (1); v SA 1888 (2)*

Underwood, D. L. 86: v A 1968 (4) 1972 (2) 1975 (4) 1977 (5); v WI 1966 (2) 1969 (2) 1973 (3) 1976 (5) 1980 (1); v NZ 1969 (3) 1973 (1); v In 1971 (1) 1974 (3); v P 1967 (2) 1971 (1) 1974 (3); *v A 1970 (5) 1974 (5) 1976 (1) 1979 (3); v WI 1973 (4); v NZ 1970 (2) 1974 (2); v In 1972 (4) 1976 (5) 1979 (1) 1981 (6); v P 1968 (3) 1972 (2); v SL 1981 (1)*

Valentine, B. H. 7: *v SA 1938 (5); v In 1933 (2)*

Vaughan, M. P. 8: v WI 2000 (4); *v SA 1999 (4)*

Verity, H. 40: v A 1934 (5) 1938 (4); v SA 1935 (4); v WI 1933 (2) 1939 (1); v NZ 1931 (2) 1937 (1); v In 1936 (3); *v A 1932 (4) 1936 (5); v SA 1938 (5); v NZ 1932 (1); v In 1933 (3)*

Vernon, G. F. 1: *v A 1882*

Vine, J. 2: *v A 1911 (2)*

Voce, W. 27: v NZ 1931 (1) 1937 (1); v In 1932 (1) 1936 (1) 1946 (1); *v A 1932 (4) 1936 (5) 1946 (2); v SA 1930 (5); v WI 1929 (4); v NZ 1932 (2)*

Waddington, A. 2: *v A 1920 (2)*

Wainwright, E. 5: v A 1893 (1); *v A 1897 (4)*

Walker, P. M. 3: v SA 1960 (3)

Walters, C. F. 11: v A 1934 (5); v WI 1933 (3); *v In 1933 (3)*

Ward, A. 5: v WI 1976 (1); v NZ 1969 (3); v P 1971 (1)

Ward, A. 7: v A 1893 (2); *v A 1894 (5)*

Wardle, J. H. 28: v A 1953 (3) 1956 (1); v SA 1951 (2) 1955 (3); v WI 1950 (1) 1957 (1); v P 1954 (4); *v A 1954 (4); v SA 1956 (4); v WI 1947 (1) 1953 (2); v NZ 1954 (2)*

Warner, P. F. 15: v A 1909 (1) 1912 (1); v SA 1912 (1); *v A 1903 (5); v SA 1898 (2) 1905 (5)*

Warr, J. J. 2: *v A 1950 (2)*

Warren, A. R. 1: v A 1905

Washbrook, C. 37: v A 1948 (4) 1956 (3); v SA 1947 (5); v WI 1950 (2); v NZ 1937 (1) 1949 (2); v In 1946 (3); *v A 1946 (5) 1950 (5); v SA 1948 (5); v NZ 1946 (1) 1950 (1)*

Watkin, S. L. 3: v A 1993 (1); v WI 1991 (1)

Watkins, A. J. 15: v A 1948 (1); v NZ 1949 (1); v In 1952 (3); *v SA 1948 (5); v In 1951 (5)*

Watkinson, M. 4: v WI 1995 (3); *v SA 1995 (1)*

Watson, W. 23: v A 1953 (3) 1956 (2); v SA 1951 (5) 1955 (1); v NZ 1958 (2); v In 1952 (1); *v A 1958 (2); v WI 1953 (5); v NZ 1958 (2)*

Webbe, A. J. 1: *v A 1878*

Wellard, A. W. 2: v A 1938 (1); v NZ 1937 (1)

Wells, A. P. 1: v WI 1995

Wharton, A. 1: v NZ 1949

Whitaker, J. J. 1: *v A 1986*

White, C. 12: v SA 1994 (1); v WI 1995 (2) 2000 (4); v NZ 1994 (3); *v NZ 1996 (1); v Z 1996 (1)*

White, D. W. 2: v P 1961 (2)

White, J. C. 15: v A 1921 (1) 1930 (1); v SA 1929 (3); v WI 1928 (1); *v A 1928 (5); v SA 1930 (4)*

Whysall, W. W. 4: v A 1930 (1); *v A 1924 (3)*

Wilkinson, L. L. 3: *v SA 1938 (3)*

Willey, P. 26: v A 1980 (1) 1981 (4) 1985 (1); v WI 1976 (2) 1980 (5); v NZ 1986 (1); v In 1979 (1); *v A 1979 (3); v WI 1980 (4) 1985 (4)*

Williams, N. F. 1: v In 1990

Willis, R. G. D. 90: v A 1977 (5) 1981 (6); v WI 1973 (1) 1976 (2) 1980 (4) 1984 (3); v NZ 1978 (3) 1983 (4); v In 1974 (1) 1979 (3) 1982 (3); v P 1974 (1) 1978 (3) 1982 (2); *v A 1970 (4) 1974 (5) 1976 (1) 1978 (6) 1979 (3) 1982 (5); v WI 1973 (3); v NZ 1970 (1) 1977 (3) 1983 (3); v In 1976 (5) 1981 (5); v P 1977 (3) 1983 (1); v SL 1981 (1)*

Wilson, C. E. M. 2: *v SA 1898 (2)*

Wilson, D. 6: *v NZ 1970 (1); v In 1963 (5)*

Wilson, E. R. 1: *v A 1920*

Wood, A. 4: v A 1938 (1); v WI 1939 (3)

Wood, B. 12: v A 1972 (1) 1975 (3); v WI 1976 (1); v P 1978 (1); *v NZ 1974 (2); v In 1972 (3); v P 1972 (1)*

Wood, G. E. C. 3: v SA 1924 (3)

Wood, H. 4: v A 1888 (1); *v SA 1888 (2) 1891 (1)*

Wood, R. 1: *v A 1886*

Woods S. M. J. 3: *v SA 1895 (3)*

Woolley, F. E. 64: v A 1909 (1) 1912 (3) 1921 (5) 1926 (5) 1930 (2) 1934 (1); v SA 1912 (3) 1924 (5) 1929 (3); v NZ 1931 (1); v In 1932 (1); *v A 1911 (5) 1920 (5) 1924 (5); v SA 1909 (5) 1913 (5) 1922 (5); v NZ 1929 (4)*

Woolmer, R. A. 19: v A 1975 (2) 1977 (5) 1981 (2); v WI 1976 (5) 1980 (2); *v A 1976 (1); v In 1976 (2)*

Worthington, T. S. 9: v In 1936 (2); *v A 1936 (3); v NZ 1929 (4)*

Wright, C. W. 3: *v SA 1895 (3)*

Wright, D. V. P. 34: v A 1938 (3) 1948 (1); v SA 1947 (4); v WI 1939 (3) 1950 (1); v NZ 1949 (1); v In 1946 (2); *v A 1946 (5) 1950 (5); v SA 1938 (3) 1948 (3); v NZ 1946 (1) 1950 (2)*

Wyatt, R. E. S. 40: v A 1930 (1) 1934 (4); v SA 1929 (2) 1935 (5); v WI 1933 (2); v In 1936 (1); *v A 1932 (5) 1936 (2); v SA 1927 (5) 1930 (5); v WI 1929 (2) 1934 (4); v NZ 1932 (2)*

Wynyard, E. G. 3: v A 1896 (1); *v SA 1905 (2)*

Yardley, N. W. D. 20: v A 1948 (5); v SA 1947 (5); v WI 1950 (3); *v A 1946 (5); v SA 1938 (1); v NZ 1946 (1)*

Young, H. I. 2: v A 1899 (2)

Young, J. A. 8: v A 1948 (3); v SA 1947 (1); v NZ 1949 (2); *v SA 1948 (2)*

Young, R. A. 2: *v A 1907 (2)*

AUSTRALIA

Number of Test cricketers: 383

a'Beckett, E. L. 4: v E 1928 (2); v SA 1931 (1); *v E 1930 (1)*

Alderman, T. M. 41: v E 1982 (1) 1990 (4); v WI 1981 (2) 1984 (3) 1988 (2); v NZ 1989 (1); v P 1981 (3) 1989 (2); v SL 1989 (2); *v E 1981 (6) 1989 (6); v WI 1983 (3) 1990 (1); v NZ 1981 (3) 1989 (1); v P 1982 (1)*

Alexander, G. 2: v E 1884 (1); *v E 1880 (1)*

Alexander, H. H. 1: v E 1932

Allan, F. E. 1: v E 1878

Allan, P. J. 1: v E 1965

Allen, R. C. 1: v E 1886

Andrews, T. J. E. 16: v E 1924 (3); *v E 1921 (5) 1926 (5); v SA 1921 (3)*

Angel, J. 4: v E 1994 (1); v WI 1992 (1); *v P 1994 (2)*

Archer, K. A. 5: v E 1950 (3); v WI 1951 (2)
Archer, R. G. 19: v E 1954 (4); v SA 1952 (1); *v E 1953 (3) 1956 (5); v WI 1954 (5); v P 1956 (1)*
Armstrong, W. W. 50: v E 1901 (4) 1903 (3) 1907 (5) 1911 (5) 1920 (5); v SA 1910 (5); *v E 1902 (5) 1905 (5) 1909 (5) 1921 (5); v SA 1902 (3)*

Badcock, C. L. 7: v E 1936 (3); *v E 1938 (4)*
Bannerman, A. C. 28: v E 1878 (1) 1881 (3) 1882 (4) 1884 (4) 1886 (1) 1887 (1) 1891 (3); *v E 1880 (1) 1882 (1) 1884 (3) 1888 (3) 1893 (3)*
Bannerman, C. 3: v E 1876 (2) 1878 (1)
Bardsley, W. 41: v E 1911 (4) 1920 (5) 1924 (3); v SA 1910 (5); *v E 1909 (5) 1912 (3) 1921 (5) 1926 (5); v SA 1912 (3) 1921 (3)*
Barnes, S. G. 13: v E 1946 (4); v In 1947 (3); *v E 1938 (1) 1948 (4); v NZ 1945 (1)*
Barnett, B. A. 4: *v E 1938 (4)*
Barrett, J. E. 2: *v E 1890 (2)*
Beard, G. R. 3: *v P 1979 (3)*
Benaud, J. 3: v P 1972 (2); *v WI 1972 (1)*
Benaud, R. 63: v E 1954 (5) 1958 (5) 1962 (5); v SA 1952 (4) 1963 (4); v WI 1951 (1) 1960 (5); *v E 1953 (3) 1956 (5) 1961 (4); v SA 1957 (5); v WI 1954 (5); v In 1956 (3) 1959 (5); v P 1956 (1) 1959 (3)*
Bennett, M. J. 3: v WI 1984 (2); *v E 1985 (1)*
Bevan, M. G. 18: v E 1994 (3); v SA 1997 (1); v WI 1996 (4); *v E 1997 (3); v SA 1996 (3); v In 1996 (1); v P 1994 (3)*
Bichel, A. J. 3: v SA 1997 (1); v WI 1996 (2)
Blackham, J. McC. 35: v E 1876 (2) 1878 (1) 1881 (4) 1882 (4) 1884 (2) 1886 (1) 1887 (1) 1891 (3) 1894 (1); *v E 1880 (1) 1882 (1) 1884 (3) 1886 (3) 1888 (3) 1890 (2) 1893 (3)*
Blackie, D. D. 3: v E 1928 (3)
Blewett, G. S. 46: v E 1994 (2); v SA 1997 (3); v WI 1996 (4); v NZ 1997 (3); v In 1999 (3); v P 1995 (3) 1999 (3); *v E 1997 (6); v SA 1996 (3); v WI 1994 (4) 1998 (3); v NZ 1999 (2); v In 1997 (3); v SL 1999 (3); v Z 1999 (1)*
Bonnor, G. J. 17: v E 1882 (4) 1884 (3); *v E 1880 (1) 1882 (1) 1884 (3) 1886 (2) 1888 (3)*
Boon, D. C. 107: v E 1986 (4) 1987 (1) 1990 (5) 1994 (5); v SA 1993 (3); v WI 1984 (3) 1988 (5) 1992 (5); v NZ 1985 (3) 1987 (3) 1993 (3); v In 1985 (3) 1991 (5); v P 1989 (2) 1995 (3); v SL 1987 (1) 1989 (2) 1995 (3); *v E 1985 (4) 1989 (6) 1993 (6); v SA 1993 (3); v WI 1990 (5) 1994 (4); v NZ 1985 (3) 1989 (1) 1992 (3); v In 1986 (3); v P 1988 (3) 1994 (3); v SL 1992 (3)*
Booth, B. C. 29: v E 1962 (5) 1965 (3); v SA 1963 (4); v P 1964 (1); *v E 1961 (2) 1964 (5); v WI 1964 (3); v In 1964 (3); v P 1964 (1)*
Border, A. R. 156: v E 1978 (3) 1979 (3) 1982 (5) 1986 (5) 1987 (1) 1990 (5); v SA 1993 (3); v WI 1979 (3) 1981 (3) 1984 (5) 1988 (5) 1992 (5); v NZ 1980 (3) 1985 (3) 1987 (3) 1989 (1) 1993 (3); v In 1980 (3) 1985 (3) 1991 (5); v P 1978 (2) 1981 (3) 1983 (5) 1989 (3); v SL 1987 (1) 1989 (2); *v E 1980 (1) 1981 (6) 1985 (6) 1989 (6) 1993 (6); v SA 1993 (3); v WI 1983 (5) 1990 (5); v NZ 1981 (3) 1985 (3) 1989 (1) 1992 (3), v In 1979 (6) 1986 (3); v P 1979 (3) 1982 (3) 1988 (3); v SL 1982 (1) 1992 (3)*
Boyle, H. F. 12: v E 1878 (1) 1881 (4) 1882 (1) 1884 (1); *v E 1880 (1) 1882 (1) 1884 (3)*
Bradman, D. G. 52: v E 1928 (4) 1932 (4) 1936 (5) 1946 (5); v SA 1931 (5); v WI 1930 (5); v In 1947 (5); *v E 1930 (5) 1934 (5) 1938 (4) 1948 (5)*
Bright, R. J. 25: v E 1979 (1); v WI 1979 (1); v NZ 1985 (1); v In 1985 (3); *v E 1977 (3) 1980 (1) 1981 (2); v NZ 1985 (2); v In 1986 (3); v P 1979 (3) 1982 (2)*
Bromley, E. H. 2: v E 1932 (1); *v E 1934 (1)*
Brown, W. A. 22: v E 1936 (2); v In 1947 (3); *v E 1934 (5) 1938 (4) 1948 (2); v SA 1935 (5); v NZ 1945 (1)*
Bruce, W. 14: v E 1884 (2) 1891 (3) 1894 (4); *v E 1886 (2) 1893 (3)*
Burge, P. J. 42: v E 1954 (1) 1958 (1) 1962 (3) 1965 (4); v SA 1963 (5); v WI 1960 (2); *v E 1956 (3) 1961 (5) 1964 (5); v SA 1957 (1); v WI 1954 (1); v In 1956 (3) 1959 (2) 1964 (3); v P 1959 (2) 1964 (1)*
Burke, J. W. 24: v E 1950 (2) 1954 (2) 1958 (5); v WI 1951 (1); *v E 1956 (5); v SA 1957 (5); v In 1956 (3); v P 1956 (1)*
Burn, K. E. 2: *v E 1890 (2)*
Burton, F. J. 2: v E 1886 (1) 1887 (1)

Callaway, S. T. 3: v E 1891 (2) 1894 (1)

Callen, I. W. 1: v In 1977
Campbell, G. D. 4: v P 1989 (1); v SL 1989 (1); *v E 1989 (1); v NZ 1989 (1)*
Carkeek, W. 6: *v E 1912 (3); v SA 1912 (3)*
Carlson, P. H. 2: v E 1978 (2)
Carter, H. 28: v E 1907 (5) 1911 (5) 1920 (2); v SA 1910 (5); *v E 1909 (5) 1921 (4); v SA 1921 (2)*
Chappell, G. S. 87: v E 1970 (5) 1974 (6) 1976 (1) 1979 (3) 1982 (5); v WI 1975 (6) 1979 (3)
    1981 (3); v NZ 1973 (3) 1980 (3); v In 1980 (3); v P 1972 (3) 1976 (3) 1981 (3) 1983 (5);
    *v E 1972 (5) 1975 (4) 1977 (5) 1980 (1); v WI 1972 (5); v NZ 1973 (3) 1976 (2) 1981 (3);
    v P 1979 (3); v SL 1982 (1)*
Chappell, I. M. 75: v E 1965 (2) 1970 (6) 1974 (6) 1979 (2); v WI 1968 (5) 1975 (6) 1979 (1); v NZ
    1973 (3); v In 1967 (4); v P 1964 (1) 1972 (3); *v E 1968 (5) 1972 (5) 1975 (4); v SA 1966 (5)
    1969 (4); v WI 1972 (5); v NZ 1973 (3); v In 1969 (5)*
Chappell, T. M. 3: *v E 1981 (3)*
Charlton, P. C. 2: *v E 1890 (2)*
Chipperfield, A. G. 14: v E 1936 (3); *v E 1934 (5) 1938 (1); v SA 1935 (5)*
Clark, W. M. 10: v In 1977 (5); v P 1978 (1); *v WI 1977 (4)*
Colley, D. J. 3: *v E 1972 (3)*
Collins, H. L. 19: v E 1920 (5) 1924 (5); *v E 1921 (3) 1926 (3); v SA 1921 (3)*
Coningham, A. 1: v E 1894
Connolly, A. N. 29: v E 1965 (1) 1970 (1); v SA 1963 (1); v WI 1968 (5); v In 1967 (3); *v E
    1968 (5); v SA 1969 (4); v In 1964 (2) 1969 (5)*
Cook, S. H. 2: v NZ 1997 (2)
Cooper, B. B. 1: v E 1876
Cooper, W. H. 2: v E 1881 (1) 1884 (1)
Corling, G. E. 5: *v E 1964 (5)*
Cosier, G. J. 18: v E 1976 (1) 1978 (2); v WI 1975 (3); v In 1977 (4); v P 1976 (3); *v WI 1977 (3);
    v NZ 1976 (2)*
Cottam, J. T. 1: v E 1886
Cotter, A. 21: v E 1903 (2) 1907 (2) 1911 (4); v SA 1910 (5); *v E 1905 (3) 1909 (5)*
Coulthard, G. 1: v E 1881
Cowper, R. M. 27: v E 1965 (4); v In 1967 (4); v P 1964 (1); *v E 1964 (1) 1968 (4); v SA 1966 (5);
    v WI 1964 (5); v In 1964 (2); v P 1964 (1)*
Craig, I. D. 11: v SA 1952 (1); *v E 1956 (2); v SA 1957 (5); v In 1956 (2); v P 1956 (1)*
Crawford, P. 4: *v E 1956 (1); v In 1956 (3)*

Dale, A. C. 2: *v WI 1998 (1); v In 1997 (1)*
Darling, J. 34: v E 1894 (5) 1897 (5) 1901 (3); *v E 1896 (3) 1899 (5) 1902 (5) 1905 (5); v SA
    1902 (3)*
Darling, L. S. 12: v E 1932 (2) 1936 (1); *v E 1934 (4); v SA 1935 (5)*
Darling, W. M. 14: v E 1978 (4); v In 1977 (1); v P 1978 (1); *v WI 1977 (3); v In 1979 (5)*
Davidson, A. K. 44: v E 1954 (3) 1958 (5) 1962 (5); v WI 1960 (4); *v E 1953 (5) 1956 (2) 1961 (5);
    v SA 1957 (5); v In 1956 (1) 1959 (5); v P 1956 (1) 1959 (3)*
Davis, I. C. 15: v E 1976 (1); v NZ 1973 (3); v P 1976 (3); *v E 1977 (3); v NZ 1973 (3) 1976 (2)*
Davis, S. P. 1: *v NZ 1985*
De Courcy, J. H. 3: *v E 1953 (3)*
Dell, A. R. 2: v E 1970 (1); v NZ 1973 (1)
Dodemaide, A. I. C. 10: v E 1987 (1); v WI 1988 (2); v NZ 1987 (1); v SL 1987 (1); *v P 1988 (3);
    v SL 1992 (1)*
Donnan, H. 5: v E 1891 (2); *v E 1896 (3)*
Dooland, B. 3: v E 1946 (2); v In 1947 (1)
Duff, R. A. 22: v E 1901 (4) 1903 (5); *v E 1902 (5) 1905 (5); v SA 1902 (3)*
Duncan, J. R. F. 1: v E 1970
Dyer, G. C. 6: v E 1986 (1) 1987 (1); v NZ 1987 (3); v SL 1987 (1)
Dymock, G. 21: v E 1974 (1) 1978 (3) 1979 (3); v WI 1979 (2); v NZ 1973 (1); v P 1978 (1); *v NZ
    1973 (2); v In 1979 (5); v P 1979 (3)*
Dyson, J. 30: v E 1982 (5); v WI 1981 (2) 1984 (3); v NZ 1980 (3); v In 1977 (3) 1980 (3); *v E
    1981 (3); v NZ 1981 (3); v P 1982 (3)*

Eady, C. J. 2: v E 1901 (1); *v E 1896 (1)*
Eastwood, K. H. 1: v E 1970

Ebeling, H. I. 1: *v E 1934*

Edwards, J. D. 3: *v E 1888 (3)*

Edwards, R. 20: v E 1974 (5); v P 1972 (2); *v E 1972 (4) 1975 (4); v WI 1972 (5)*

Edwards, W. J. 3: v E 1974 (3)

Elliott, M. T. G. 20: v SA 1997 (3); v WI 1996 (2); v NZ 1997 (3); *v E 1997 (6); v SA 1996 (3); v WI 1998 (3)*

Emery, P. A. 1: *v P 1994*

Emery, S. H. 4: *v E 1912 (2); v SA 1912 (2)*

Evans, E. 6: v E 1881 (2) 1882 (1) 1884 (1); *v E 1886 (2)*

Fairfax, A. G. 10: v E 1928 (1); v WI 1930 (5); *v E 1930 (4)*

Favell, L. E. 19: v E 1954 (4) 1958 (2); v WI 1960 (4); *v WI 1954 (2); v In 1959 (4); v P 1959 (3)*

Ferris, J. J. 8: v E 1886 (2) 1887 (1); *v E 1888 (3) 1890 (2)*

Fingleton, J. H. 18: v E 1932 (3) 1936 (5); v SA 1931 (1); *v E 1938 (4); v SA 1935 (5)*

Fleetwood-Smith, L. O'B. 10: v E 1936 (3); *v E 1938 (4); v SA 1935 (3)*

Fleming, D. W. 19: v E 1994 (3) 1998 (4); v In 1999 (3); v P 1999 (3); *v P 1994 (1) 1998 (2); v SL 1999 (2); v Z 1999 (1)*

Francis, B. C. 3: *v E 1972 (3)*

Freeman, E. W. 11: v WI 1968 (4); v In 1967 (2); *v E 1968 (2); v SA 1969 (2); v In 1969 (1)*

Freer, F. W. 1: v E 1946

Gannon, J. B. 3: v In 1977 (3)

Garrett, T. W. 19: v E 1876 (2) 1878 (1) 1881 (3) 1882 (3) 1884 (3) 1886 (3) 1887 (1); *v E 1882 (1) 1886 (3)*

Gaunt, R. A. 3: v SA 1963 (1); *v E 1961 (1); v SA 1957 (1)*

Gehrs, D. R. A. 6: v E 1903 (1); v SA 1910 (4); *v E 1905 (1)*

Giffen, G. 31: v E 1881 (3) 1882 (4) 1884 (3) 1891 (3) 1894 (5); *v E 1882 (1) 1884 (3) 1886 (3) 1893 (3) 1896 (3)*

Giffen, W. F. 3: v E 1886 (1) 1891 (2)

Gilbert, D. R. 9: v NZ 1985 (3); v In 1985 (2); *v E 1985 (1); v NZ 1985 (1); v In 1986 (2)*

Gilchrist, A. C. 9: v In 1999 (3); v P 1999 (3); *v NZ 1999 (3)*

Gillespie, J. N. 14: v E 1998 (1); v WI 1996 (2); *v E 1997 (4); v SA 1996 (3); v WI 1998 (3); v SL 1999 (1)*

Gilmour, G. J. 15: v E 1976 (1); v WI 1975 (5); v NZ 1973 (2); v P 1976 (3); *v E 1975 (1); v NZ 1973 (1) 1976 (2)*

Gleeson, J. W. 29: v E 1970 (5); v WI 1968 (5); v In 1967 (4); *v E 1968 (5) 1972 (3); v SA 1969 (4); v In 1969 (3)*

Graham, H. 6: v E 1894 (2); *v E 1893 (3) 1896 (1)*

Gregory, D. W. 3: v E 1876 (2) 1878 (1)

Gregory, E. J. 1: v E 1876

Gregory, J. M. 24: v F 1920 (5) 1924 (5) 1928 (1); *v E 1921 (5) 1926 (5); v SA 1921 (3)*

Gregory, R. G. 2: v E 1936 (2)

Gregory, S. E. 58: v E 1891 (1) 1894 (5) 1897 (5) 1901 (5) 1903 (4) 1907 (2) 1911 (5); *v E 1890 (2) 1893 (3) 1896 (3) 1899 (5) 1902 (5) 1905 (3) 1909 (5) 1912 (3); v SA 1902 (3) 1912 (3)*

Grimmett, C. V. 37: v E 1924 (1) 1928 (5) 1932 (3); v SA 1931 (5); v WI 1930 (5); *v E 1926 (3) 1930 (5) 1934 (5); v SA 1935 (5)*

Groube, T. U. 1: *v E 1880*

Grout, A. T. W. 51: v E 1958 (5) 1962 (2) 1965 (5); v SA 1963 (5); v WI 1960 (5); *v E 1961 (5) 1964 (5); v SA 1957 (5); v WI 1964 (5); v In 1959 (4) 1964 (1); v P 1959 (3) 1964 (1)*

Guest, C. E. J. 1: v E 1962

Hamence, R. A. 3: v E 1946 (1); v In 1947 (2)

Hammond, J. R. 5: *v WI 1972 (5)*

Harry, J. 1: v E 1894

Hartigan, R. J. 2: v E 1907 (2)

Hartkopf, A. E. V. 1: v E 1924

Harvey, M. R. 1: v E 1946

Harvey, R. N. 79: v E 1950 (5) 1954 (5) 1958 (5) 1962 (5); v SA 1952 (5); v WI 1951 (5) 1960 (4); v In 1947 (2); *v E 1948 (2) 1953 (5) 1956 (5) 1961 (5); v SA 1949 (5) 1957 (4); v WI 1954 (5); v In 1956 (3) 1959 (5); v P 1956 (1) 1959 (3)*

Hassett, A. L. 43: v E 1946 (5) 1950 (5); v SA 1952 (5); v WI 1951 (4); v In 1947 (4); *v E 1938 (4) 1948 (5) 1953 (5); v SA 1949 (5); v NZ 1945 (1)*

Hawke, N. J. N. 27: v E 1962 (1) 1965 (4); v SA 1963 (4); v In 1967 (1); v P 1964 (1); *v E 1964 (5) 1968 (2); v SA 1966 (2); v WI 1964 (5); v In 1964 (1); v P 1964 (1)*

Hayden, M. L. 8: v WI 1996 (3); *v SA 1993 (1) 1996 (3); v NZ 1999 (1)*

Hazlitt, G. R. 9: v E 1907 (2) 1911 (1); *v E 1912 (3); v SA 1912 (3)*

Healy, I. A. 119: v E 1990 (5) 1994 (5) 1998 (5); v SA 1993 (3) 1997 (3); v WI 1988 (5) 1992 (5) 1996 (5); v NZ 1989 (1) 1993 (3) 1997 (3); v In 1991 (5); v P 1989 (3) 1995 (3); v SL 1989 (2) 1995 (3); *v E 1989 (6) 1993 (6) 1997 (6); v SA 1993 (3) 1996 (3); v WI 1990 (5) 1994 (4) 1998 (4); v NZ 1989 (1) 1992 (3); v In 1996 (1) 1997 (3); v P 1988 (3) 1994 (2) 1998 (3); v SL 1992 (3) 1999 (3); v Z 1999 (1)*

Hendry, H. L. 11: v E 1924 (1) 1928 (4); *v E 1921 (4); v SA 1921 (2)*

Hibbert, P. A. 1: v In 1977

Higgs, J. D. 22: v E 1978 (5) 1979 (1); v WI 1979 (1); v NZ 1980 (3); v In 1980 (2); *v WI 1977 (4); v In 1979 (6)*

Hilditch, A. M. J. 18: v E 1978 (1); v WI 1984 (2); v NZ 1985 (1); v P 1978 (2); *v E 1985 (6); v In 1979 (6)*

Hill, C. 49: v E 1897 (5) 1901 (5) 1903 (5) 1907 (5) 1911 (5); v SA 1910 (5); *v E 1896 (3) 1899 (3) 1902 (5) 1905 (5); v SA 1902 (3)*

Hill, J. C. 3: *v E 1953 (2); v WI 1954 (1)*

Hoare, D. E. 1: v WI 1960

Hodges, J. 2: v E 1876 (2)

Hogan, T. G. 7: v P 1983 (1); *v WI 1983 (5); v SL 1982 (1)*

Hogg, G. B. 1: *v In 1996*

Hogg, R. M. 38: v E 1978 (6) 1982 (3); v WI 1979 (2) 1984 (4); v NZ 1980 (2); v In 1980 (2); v P 1978 (2) 1983 (4); *v E 1981 (2); v WI 1983 (4); v In 1979 (6); v SL 1982 (1)*

Hohns, T. V. 7: v WI 1988 (2); *v E 1989 (5)*

Hole, G. B. 18: v E 1950 (1) 1954 (3); v SA 1952 (4); v WI 1951 (5); *v E 1953 (5)*

Holland, R. G. 11: v WI 1984 (3); v NZ 1985 (3); v In 1985 (1); *v E 1985 (4)*

Hookes, D. W. 23: v E 1976 (1) 1982 (5); v WI 1979 (1); v NZ 1985 (2); v In 1985 (2); *v E 1977 (5); v WI 1983 (5); v P 1979 (1); v SL 1982 (1)*

Hopkins, A. J. 20: v E 1901 (2) 1903 (5); *v E 1902 (5) 1905 (3) 1909 (2); v SA 1902 (3)*

Horan, T. P. 15: v E 1876 (1) 1878 (1) 1881 (4) 1882 (4) 1884 (4); *v E 1882 (1)*

Hordern, H. V. 7: v E 1911 (5); v SA 1910 (2)

Hornibrook, P. M. 6: v E 1928 (1); *v E 1930 (5)*

Howell, W. P. 18: v E 1897 (3) 1901 (4) 1903 (3); *v E 1899 (5) 1902 (1); v SA 1902 (2)*

Hughes, K. J. 70: v E 1978 (6) 1979 (3) 1982 (5); v WI 1979 (3) 1981 (3) 1984 (4); v NZ 1980 (3); v In 1977 (2) 1980 (3); v P 1978 (2) 1981 (3) 1983 (5); *v E 1977 (1) 1980 (1) 1981 (6); v WI 1983 (5); v NZ 1981 (3); v In 1979 (6); v P 1979 (3) 1982 (3)*

Hughes, M. G. 53: v E 1986 (4) 1990 (4); v WI 1988 (4) 1992 (5); v NZ 1987 (1) 1989 (1); v In 1985 (1) 1991 (5); v P 1989 (3); v SL 1987 (1) 1989 (2); *v E 1989 (6) 1993 (6); v SA 1993 (2); v WI 1990 (5); v NZ 1992 (3)*

Hunt, W. A. 1: v SA 1931

Hurst, A. G. 12: v E 1978 (6); v NZ 1973 (1); v In 1977 (1); v P 1978 (2); *v In 1979 (2)*

Hurwood, A. 2: v WI 1930 (2)

Inverarity, R. J. 6: v WI 1968 (1); *v E 1968 (2) 1972 (3)*

Iredale, F. A. 14: v E 1894 (5) 1897 (4); *v E 1896 (2) 1899 (3)*

Ironmonger, H. 14: v E 1928 (2) 1932 (4); v SA 1931 (4); v WI 1930 (4)

Iverson, J. B. 5: v E 1950 (5)

Jackson, A. A. 8: v E 1928 (2); v WI 1930 (4); *v E 1930 (2)*

Jarman, B. N. 19: v E 1962 (3); v WI 1968 (4); v In 1967 (1); v P 1964 (1); *v E 1968 (4); v In 1959 (1) 1964 (2)*

Jarvis, A. H. 11: v E 1884 (3) 1894 (4); *v E 1886 (2) 1888 (2)*

Jenner, T. J. 9: v E 1970 (2) 1974 (2); v WI 1975 (1); *v WI 1972 (4)*

Jennings, C. B. 6: *v E 1912 (3); v SA 1912 (3)*

Johnson I. W. 45: v E 1946 (4) 1950 (5) 1954 (4); v SA 1952 (1); v WI 1951 (4); v In 1947 (4); *v E 1948 (4) 1956 (5); v SA 1949 (5); v WI 1954 (5); v NZ 1945 (1); v In 1956 (2); v P 1956 (1)*

Johnson, L. J. 1: v In 1947

Johnston, W. A. 40: v E 1950 (5) 1954 (4); v SA 1952 (5); v WI 1951 (5); v In 1947 (4); *v E 1948 (5) 1953 (3); v SA 1949 (5); v WI 1954 (4)*

Jones, D. M. 52: v E 1986 (5) 1987 (1) 1990 (5); v WI 1988 (3); v NZ 1987 (3) 1989 (1); v In 1991 (5); v P 1989 (3); v SL 1987 (1) 1989 (2); *v E 1989 (6); v WI 1983 (2) 1990 (5); v NZ 1989 (1); v In 1986 (3); v P 1988 (3); v SL 1992 (3)*

Jones, E. 19: v E 1894 (1) 1897 (5) 1901 (2); *v E 1896 (3) 1899 (5) 1902 (2); v SA 1902 (1)*

Jones, S. P. 12: v E 1881 (2) 1884 (4) 1886 (1) 1887 (1); *v E 1882 (1) 1886 (3)*

Joslin, L. R. 1: v In 1967

Julian, B. P. 7: v SL 1995 (1); *v E 1993 (2); v WI 1994 (4)*

Kasprowicz, M. S. 16: v E 1998 (1); v SA 1997 (2); v WI 1996 (2); v NZ 1997 (3); v In 1999 (1); v P 1999 (1); *v E 1997 (3); v In 1997 (3)*

Kelleway, C. 26: v E 1911 (4) 1920 (5) 1924 (5) 1928 (1); v SA 1910 (5); *v E 1912 (3); v SA 1912 (3)*

Kelly, J. J. 36: v E 1897 (5) 1901 (5) 1903 (5); *v E 1896 (3) 1899 (5) 1902 (5) 1905 (5); v SA 1902 (3)*

Kelly, T. J. D. 2: v E 1876 (1) 1878 (1)

Kendall, T. 2: v E 1876 (2)

Kent, M. F. 3: *v E 1981 (3)*

Kerr, R. B. 2: v NZ 1985 (2)

Kippax, A. F. 22: v E 1924 (1) 1928 (5) 1932 (1); v SA 1931 (4); v WI 1930 (5); *v E 1930 (5) 1934 (1)*

Kline L. F. 13: v E 1958 (2); v WI 1960 (2); *v SA 1957 (5); v In 1959 (3); v P 1959 (1)*

Laird, B. M. 21: v E 1979 (2); v WI 1979 (3) 1981 (3); v P 1981 (3); *v E 1980 (1); v NZ 1981 (3); v P 1979 (3) 1982 (3)*

Langer, J. L. 33: v E 1998 (5); v WI 1992 (2) 1996 (2); v In 1999 (3); v P 1999 (3); *v WI 1998 (4); v NZ 1992 (3) 1999 (3); v P 1994 (1) 1998 (3); v SL 1999 (3); v Z 1999 (1)*

Langley, G. R. A. 26: v E 1954 (2); v SA 1952 (5); v WI 1951 (5); *v E 1953 (4) 1956 (3); v WI 1954 (4); v In 1956 (2); v P 1956 (1)*

Laughlin, T. J. 3: v E 1978 (1); *v WI 1977 (2)*

Laver, F. 15: v E 1901 (1) 1903 (1); *v E 1899 (4) 1905 (5) 1909 (4)*

Law, S. G. 1: v SL 1995

Lawry, W. M. 67: v E 1962 (5) 1965 (5) 1970 (5); v SA 1963 (5); v WI 1968 (5); v In 1967 (4); v P 1964 (1); *v E 1961 (5) 1964 (5) 1968 (4); v SA 1966 (5) 1969 (4); v WI 1964 (5); v In 1964 (3) 1969 (5); v P 1964 (1)*

Lawson, G. F. 46: v E 1982 (5) 1986 (1); v WI 1981 (1) 1984 (5) 1988 (1); v NZ 1980 (1) 1985 (2) 1989 (1); v P 1983 (5); v SL 1989 (1); *v E 1981 (3) 1985 (6) 1989 (6); v WI 1983 (5); v P 1982 (3)*

Lee, B. 5: v In 1999 (5); *v NZ 1999 (3)*

Lee, P. K. 2: v E 1932 (1); v SA 1931 (1)

Lehmann, D. S. 5: v E 1998 (2); *v In 1997 (1); v P 1998 (2)*

Lillee, D. K. 70: v E 1970 (2) 1974 (6) 1976 (1) 1979 (3) 1982 (1); v WI 1975 (5) 1979 (3) 1981 (3); v NZ 1980 (3); v In 1980 (3); v P 1972 (3) 1976 (3) 1981 (3) 1983 (5); *v E 1972 (5) 1975 (4) 1980 (1) 1981 (6); v WI 1972 (1); v NZ 1976 (2) 1981 (3); v P 1979 (3); v SL 1982 (1)*

Lindwall, R. R. 61: v E 1946 (4) 1950 (5) 1954 (4) 1958 (2); v SA 1952 (5); v WI 1951 (5); v In 1947 (5); *v E 1948 (5) 1953 (5) 1956 (4); v SA 1949 (4); v WI 1954 (5); v NZ 1945 (1); v In 1956 (3) 1959 (2); v P 1956 (1) 1959 (2)*

Love, H. S. B. 1: v E 1932

Loxton, S. J. E. 12: v E 1950 (3); v In 1947 (1); *v E 1948 (3); v SA 1949 (5)*

Lyons, J. J. 14: v E 1886 (1) 1891 (3) 1894 (3) 1897 (1); *v E 1888 (1) 1890 (2) 1893 (3)*

McAlister, P. A. 8: v E 1903 (2) 1907 (4); *v E 1909 (2)*

Macartney, C. G. 35: v E 1907 (5) 1911 (5) 1920 (2); v SA 1910 (4); *v E 1909 (5) 1912 (3) 1921 (5) 1926 (5); v SA 1912 (3) 1921 (2)*

McCabe, S. J. 39: v E 1932 (5) 1936 (5); v SA 1931 (5); v WI 1930 (5); *v E 1930 (5) 1934 (5) 1938 (4); v SA 1935 (5)*

McCool, C. L. 14: v E 1946 (5); v In 1947 (3); *v SA 1949 (5); v NZ 1945 (1)*

McCormick, E. L. 12: v E 1936 (4); *v E 1938 (3); v SA 1935 (5)*

McCosker, R. B. 25: v E 1974 (3) 1976 (1) 1979 (2); v WI 1975 (4) 1979 (1); v P 1976 (3); *v E 1975 (4) 1977 (5); v NZ 1976 (2)*

McDermott, C. J. 71: v E 1986 (1) 1987 (1) 1990 (2) 1994 (5); v SA 1993 (3); v WI 1984 (2) 1988 (2) 1992 (5); v NZ 1985 (2) 1987 (3) 1993 (3); v In 1985 (2) 1991 (5); v P 1995 (3); v SL 1987 (1) 1995 (3); *v E 1985 (6) 1993 (2); v SA 1993 (3); v WI 1990 (5); v NZ 1985 (2) 1992 (3); v In 1986 (2); v P 1994 (2); v SL 1992 (3)*

McDonald, C. C. 47: v E 1954 (2) 1958 (5); v SA 1952 (5); v WI 1951 (1) 1960 (5); *v E 1956 (5) 1961 (3); v SA 1957 (5); v WI 1954 (5); v In 1956 (2) 1959 (5); v P 1956 (1) 1959 (3)*

McDonald, E. A. 11: v E 1920 (3); *v E 1921 (5); v SA 1921 (3)*

McDonnell, P. S. 19: v E 1881 (4) 1882 (3) 1884 (2) 1886 (2) 1887 (1); *v E 1880 (1) 1884 (3) 1888 (3)*

MacGill, S. C. G. 12: v E 1998 (4); v SA 1997 (1); *v WI 1998 (4); v P 1998 (3)*

McGrath, G. D. 62: v E 1994 (2) 1998 (5); v SA 1993 (1) 1997 (2); v WI 1996 (5); v NZ 1993 (2) 1997 (1); v In 1999 (3); v P 1995 (3) 1999 (3); v SL 1995 (3); *v E 1997 (6); v SA 1993 (2) 1996 (3); v WI 1994 (4) 1998 (4); v NZ 1999 (3); v In 1996 (1); v P 1994 (2) 1998 (3); v SL 1999 (3); v Z 1999 (1)*

McIlwraith, J. 1: *v E 1886*

McIntyre, P. E. 2: v E 1994 (1); *v In 1996 (1)*

Mackay, K. D. 37: v E 1958 (5) 1962 (3); v WI 1960 (5); *v E 1956 (3) 1961 (5); v SA 1957 (5); v In 1956 (3) 1959 (5); v P 1959 (3)*

McKenzie, G. D. 60: v E 1962 (5) 1965 (4) 1970 (3); v SA 1963 (5); v WI 1968 (5); v In 1967 (2); v P 1964 (1); *v E 1961 (3) 1964 (5) 1968 (5); v SA 1966 (5) 1969 (3); v WI 1964 (5); v In 1964 (3) 1969 (5); v P 1964 (1)*

McKibbin, T. R. 5: v E 1894 (1) 1897 (2); *v E 1896 (2)*

McLaren, J. W. 1: v E 1911

Maclean, J. A. 4: v E 1978 (4)

McLeod, C. E. 17: v E 1894 (1) 1897 (5) 1901 (2) 1903 (3); *v E 1899 (1) 1905 (5)*

McLeod, R. W. 6: v E 1891 (3); *v E 1893 (3)*

McShane, P. G. 3: v E 1884 (1) 1886 (1) 1887 (1)

Maddocks, L. V. 7: v E 1954 (3); *v E 1956 (2); v WI 1954 (1); v In 1956 (1)*

Maguire, J. N. 3: v P 1983 (1); *v WI 1983 (2)*

Mailey, A. A. 21: v E 1920 (5) 1924 (5); *v E 1921 (3) 1926 (5); v SA 1921 (3)*

Mallett, A. A. 38: v E 1970 (2) 1974 (5) 1979 (1); v WI 1968 (1) 1975 (6) 1979 (1); v NZ 1973 (3); v P 1972 (2); *v E 1968 (1) 1972 (2) 1975 (4) 1980 (1); v SA 1969 (1); v NZ 1973 (3); v In 1969 (5)*

Malone, M. F. 1: *v E 1977*

Mann, A. L. 4: v In 1977 (4)

Marr, A. P. 1: v E 1884

Marsh, G. R. 50: v E 1986 (5) 1987 (1) 1990 (5); v WI 1988 (5), v NZ 1987 (3); v In 1985 (3) 1991 (4), v P 1989 (2); v SL 1987 (1); *v E 1989 (6); v WI 1990 (5); v NZ 1985 (3) 1989 (1); v In 1986 (3); v P 1988 (3)*

Marsh, R. W. 96: v E 1970 (6) 1974 (6) 1976 (1) 1979 (3) 1982 (5); v WI 1975 (6) 1979 (3) 1981 (3); v NZ 1973 (3) 1980 (3); v In 1980 (3); v P 1972 (3) 1976 (3) 1981 (3) 1983 (5); *v E 1972 (5) 1975 (4) 1977 (5) 1980 (1) 1981 (6); v WI 1972 (5); v NZ 1973 (3) 1976 (2) 1981 (3); v P 1979 (3) 1982 (3)*

Martin, J. W. 8: v SA 1963 (1); v WI 1960 (3); *v SA 1966 (1); v In 1964 (2); v P 1964 (1)*

Martyn, D. R. 10: v SA 1993 (2); v WI 1992 (4); *v NZ 1992 (1) 1999 (3)*

Massie, H. H. 9: v E 1881 (4) 1882 (3) 1884 (1); *v E 1882 (1)*

Massie, R. A. L. 6: v P 1972 (2); *v E 1972 (4)*

Matthews, C. D. 3: v E 1986 (2); v WI 1988 (1)

Matthews, G. R. J. 33: v E 1986 (4) 1990 (5); v WI 1984 (1) 1992 (2); v NZ 1985 (3); v In 1985 (3); v P 1983 (2); *v E 1985 (1); v WI 1983 (1) 1990 (2); v NZ 1985 (3); v In 1986 (3); v SL 1992 (3)*

Matthews, T. J. 8: v E 1911 (2); *v E 1912 (3); v SA 1912 (3)*

May, T. B. A. 24: v E 1994 (3); v SA 1993 (3); v WI 1988 (3) 1992 (1); v NZ 1987 (1) 1993 (2); *v E 1993 (5); v SA 1993 (1); v P 1988 (3) 1994 (2)*

Mayne, E. R. 4: *v E 1912 (1); v SA 1912 (1) 1921 (2)*

Mayne, L. C. 6: *v SA 1969 (2); v WI 1964 (3); v In 1969 (1)*

Meckiff, I. 18: v E 1958 (4); v SA 1963 (1); v WI 1960 (2); *v SA 1957 (4); v In 1959 (5); v P 1959 (2)*

Meuleman, K. D. 1: *v NZ 1945*

Midwinter, W. E. 8: v E 1876 (2) 1882 (1) 1886 (2); *v E 1884 (3)*

Miller, C. R. 14: v E 1998 (3); *v WI 1998 (1); v NZ 1999 (3); v P 1998 (3); v SL 1999 (3); v Z 1999 (1)*

Miller, K. R. 55: v E 1946 (5) 1950 (5) 1954 (4); v SA 1952 (4); v WI 1951 (5); v In 1947 (5);
   v E 1948 (5) 1953 (5) 1956 (5); v SA 1949 (5); v WI 1954 (5); v NZ 1945 (1); v P 1956 (1)
Minnett, R. B. 9: v E 1911 (5); *v E 1912 (1); v SA 1912 (3)*
Misson, F. M. 5: v WI 1960 (3); *v E 1961 (2)*
Moody, T. M. 8: v NZ 1989 (1); v In 1991 (1); v P 1989 (1); v SL 1989 (2); *v SL 1992 (3)*
Moroney, J. 7: v E 1950 (1); v WI 1951 (1); *v SA 1949 (5)*
Morris, A. R. 46: v E 1946 (5) 1950 (5) 1954 (4); v SA 1952 (5); v WI 1951 (5); v In 1947 (4);
   v E 1948 (5) 1953 (5); v SA 1949 (5); v WI 1954 (4)
Morris, S. 1: v E 1884
Moses, H. 6: v E 1886 (2) 1887 (1) 1891 (2) 1894 (1)
Moss, J. K. 1: v P 1978
Moule, W. H. 1: *v E 1880*
Muller, S. A. 2: v P 1999 (2)
Murdoch, W. L. 18: v E 1876 (1) 1878 (1) 1881 (4) 1882 (4) 1884 (1); *v E 1880 (1) 1882 (1) 1884 (3)
   1890 (2)*
Musgrove, H. 1: v E 1884

Nagel, L. E. 1: v E 1932
Nash, L. J. 2: v E 1936 (1); v SA 1931 (1)
Nicholson, M. J. 1: v E 1998
Nitschke, H. C. 2: v SA 1931 (2)
Noble, M. A. 42: v E 1897 (4) 1901 (5) 1903 (5) 1907 (5); *v E 1899 (5) 1902 (5) 1905 (5) 1909 (5);
   v SA 1902 (3)*
Noblet, G. 3: v SA 1952 (1); v WI 1951 (1); *v SA 1949 (1)*
Nothling, O. E. 1: v E 1928

O'Brien, L. P. J. 5: v E 1932 (2) 1936 (1); *v SA 1935 (2)*
O'Connor, J. D. A. 4: v E 1907 (3); *v E 1909 (1)*
O'Donnell, S. P. 6: v NZ 1985 (1); *v E 1985 (5)*
Ogilvie, A. D. 5: v In 1977 (3); *v WI 1977 (2)*
O'Keeffe, K. J. 24: v E 1970 (2) 1976 (1); v NZ 1973 (3); v P 1972 (2) 1976 (3); *v E 1977 (3); v WI
   1972 (5); v NZ 1973 (3) 1976 (2)*
Oldfield, W. A. 54: v E 1920 (3) 1924 (5) 1928 (5) 1932 (4) 1936 (5); v SA 1931 (5); v WI 1930 (5);
   v E 1921 (1) 1926 (5) 1930 (5) 1934 (5); v SA 1921 (1) 1935 (5)
O'Neill, N. C. 42: v E 1958 (5) 1962 (5); v SA 1963 (4); v WI 1960 (5); *v E 1961 (5) 1964 (4);
   v WI 1964 (4); v In 1959 (5) 1964 (2); v P 1959 (3)*
O'Reilly, W. J. 27: v E 1932 (5) 1936 (5); v SA 1931 (2); *v E 1934 (5) 1938 (4); v SA 1935 (5);
   v NZ 1945 (1)*
Oxenham, R. K. 7: v E 1928 (3); v SA 1931 (1); v WI 1930 (3)

Palmer, G. E. 17: v E 1881 (4) 1882 (4) 1884 (2); *v E 1880 (1) 1884 (3) 1886 (3)*
Park, R. L. 1: v E 1920
Pascoe, L. S. 14: v E 1979 (2); v WI 1979 (1) 1981 (1); v NZ 1980 (3); v In 1980 (3); *v E 1977 (3)
   1980 (1)*
Pellew, C. E. 10: v E 1920 (4); *v E 1921 (5); v SA 1921 (1)*
Phillips, W. B. 27: v WI 1984 (2); v NZ 1985 (3); v In 1985 (3); v P 1983 (5); *v E 1985 (6); v WI
   1983 (5); v NZ 1985 (3)*
Phillips, W. N. 1: v In 1991
Philpott, P. I. 8: v E 1965 (3); *v WI 1964 (5)*
Ponsford, W. H. 29: v E 1924 (5) 1928 (2) 1932 (3); v SA 1931 (4); v WI 1930 (5); *v E 1926 (2) 1930
   (4) 1934 (4)*
Ponting, R. T. 34: v E 1998 (3); v SA 1997 (3); v WI 1996 (2); v NZ 1997 (3); v In 1999 (3); v P
   1999 (3); v SL 1995 (3); *v E 1997 (3); v WI 1998 (2); v In 1996 (1) 1997 (3); v P 1998 (1); v SL
   1999 (3); v Z 1999 (1)*
Pope, R. J. 1: v E 1884

Rackemann, C. G. 12: v E 1982 (1) 1990 (1); v WI 1984 (1); v NZ 1989 (1); v P 1983 (2) 1989 (3);
   v SL 1989 (1); *v WI 1983 (1); v NZ 1989 (1)*
Ransford, V. S. 20: v E 1907 (5) 1911 (5); v SA 1910 (5); *v E 1909 (5)*
Redpath, I. R. 66: v E 1965 (1) 1970 (6) 1974 (6); v SA 1963 (1); v WI 1968 (5) 1975 (6); v In
   1967 (3); v P 1972 (3); *v E 1964 (5) 1968 (5); v SA 1966 (5) 1969 (4); v WI 1972 (5); v NZ
   1973 (3); v In 1964 (2) 1969 (5); v P 1964 (1)*

Reedman, J. C. 1: v E 1894

Reid, B. A. 27: v E 1986 (5) 1990 (4); v WI 1992 (1); v NZ 1987 (2); v In 1985 (3) 1991 (2); *v WI 1990 (2); v NZ 1985 (3); v In 1986 (2); v P 1988 (3)*

Reiffel, P. R. 35: v SA 1993 (2) 1997 (2); v WI 1996 (3); v NZ 1993 (2) 1997 (3); v In 1991 (1); v P 1995 (3); v SL 1995 (2); *v E 1993 (3) 1997 (4); v SA 1993 (1); v WI 1994 (4); v NZ 1992 (3); v In 1996 (1) 1997 (1)*

Renneberg, D. A. 8: v In 1967 (3); *v SA 1966 (5)*

Richardson, A. J. 9: v E 1924 (4); *v E 1926 (5)*

Richardson, V. Y. 19: v E 1924 (3) 1928 (2) 1932 (5); *v E 1930 (4); v SA 1935 (5)*

Rigg, K. E. 8: v E 1936 (3); v SA 1931 (4); v WI 1930 (1)

Ring, D. T. 13: v SA 1952 (5); v WI 1951 (5); v In 1947 (1); *v E 1948 (1) 1953 (1)*

Ritchie, G. M. 30: v E 1986 (4); v WI 1984 (1); v NZ 1985 (3); v In 1985 (2); *v E 1985 (6); v WI 1983 (5); v NZ 1985 (3); v In 1986 (3); v P 1982 (3)*

Rixon, S. J. 13: v WI 1984 (3); v In 1977 (5); *v WI 1977 (5)*

Robertson, G. R. 4: *v In 1997 (3); v P 1998 (1)*

Robertson, W. R. 1: v E 1884

Robinson, R. D. 3: *v E 1977 (3)*

Robinson, R. H. 1: v E 1936

Rorke, G. F. 4: v E 1958 (2); *v In 1959 (2)*

Rutherford, J. W. 1: *v In 1956*

Ryder, J. 20: v E 1920 (5) 1924 (3) 1928 (5); *v E 1926 (4); v SA 1921 (3)*

Saggers, R. A. 6: *v E 1948 (1); v SA 1949 (5)*

Saunders, J. V. 14: v E 1901 (1) 1903 (2) 1907 (5); *v E 1902 (4); v SA 1902 (2)*

Scott, H. J. H. 8: v E 1884 (2); *v E 1884 (3) 1886 (3)*

Sellers, R. H. D. 1: *v In 1964*

Serjeant, C. S. 12: v In 1977 (4); *v E 1977 (3); v WI 1977 (5)*

Sheahan, A. P. 31: v E 1970 (2); v WI 1968 (5); v NZ 1973 (2); v In 1967 (4); v P 1972 (2); *v E 1968 (5) 1972 (2); v SA 1969 (4); v In 1969 (5)*

Shepherd, B. K. 9: v E 1962 (2); v SA 1963 (4); v P 1964 (1); *v WI 1964 (2)*

Sievers, M. W. 3: v E 1936 (3)

Simpson, R. B. 62: v E 1958 (1) 1962 (5) 1965 (3); v SA 1963 (5); v WI 1960 (5); v In 1967 (3) 1977 (5); v P 1964 (1); *v E 1961 (5) 1964 (5); v SA 1957 (5) 1966 (5); v WI 1964 (5) 1977 (5); v In 1964 (3); v P 1964 (1)*

Sincock, D. J. 3: v E 1965 (1); v P 1964 (1); *v WI 1964 (1)*

Slater, K. N. 1: v E 1958

Slater, M. J. 62: v E 1994 (5) 1998 (5); v SA 1993 (3); v NZ 1993 (3); v In 1999 (3); v P 1995 (3) 1999 (3); v SL 1995 (3); *v E 1993 (6); v SA 1993 (3); v WI 1994 (4) 1998 (4); v NZ 1999 (3); v In 1996 (1) 1997 (3); v P 1994 (3) 1998 (3); SL 1999 (3); v Z 1999 (1)*

Sleep, P. R. 14: v E 1986 (3) 1987 (1); v NZ 1987 (3); v P 1978 (1) 1989 (1); v SL 1989 (1); *v In 1979 (2); v P 1982 (1) 1988 (1)*

Slight, J. 1: *v E 1880*

Smith, D. B. M. 2: *v E 1912 (2)*

Smith, S. B. 3: *v WI 1983 (3)*

Spofforth, F. R. 18: v E 1876 (1) 1878 (1) 1881 (1) 1882 (4) 1884 (3) 1886 (1); *v E 1882 (1) 1884 (3) 1886 (3)*

Stackpole, K. R. 43: v E 1965 (2) 1970 (6); v WI 1968 (5); v NZ 1973 (3); v P 1972 (1); *v E 1972 (5); v SA 1966 (5) 1969 (4); v WI 1972 (4); v NZ 1973 (3); v In 1969 (5)*

Stevens, G. B. 4: *v In 1959 (2); v P 1959 (2)*

Taber, H. B. 16: v WI 1968 (1); *v E 1968 (1); v SA 1966 (5) 1969 (4); v In 1969 (5)*

Tallon, D. 21: v E 1946 (5) 1950 (5); v In 1947 (5); *v E 1948 (4) 1953 (1); v NZ 1945 (1)*

Taylor, J. M. 20: v E 1920 (5) 1924 (5); *v E 1921 (5) 1926 (3); v SA 1921 (2)*

Taylor, M. A. 104: v E 1990 (5) 1994 (5) 1998 (5); v SA 1993 (3) 1997 (3); v WI 1988 (2) 1992 (4) 1996 (5); v NZ 1989 (3) 1993 (3) 1997 (3); v In 1989 (3) 1991 (5); v P 1989 (3) 1995 (3); v SL 1989 (2) 1995 (3); *v E 1989 (6) 1993 (6) 1997 (6); v SA 1993 (2) 1996 (3); v WI 1990 (5) 1994 (4); v NZ 1989 (1) 1992 (3); v In 1996 (1) 1997 (3); v P 1994 (3) 1998 (3); v SL 1992 (3)*

Taylor, P. L. 13: v E 1986 (1) 1987 (1); v WI 1988 (2); v In 1991 (2); v P 1989 (2); v SL 1987 (1); *v WI 1990 (1); v NZ 1989 (1); v P 1988 (2)*

Thomas, G. 8: v E 1965 (3); *v WI 1964 (5)*

Thoms, G. R. 1: v WI 1951

Thomson, A. L. 4: v E 1970 (4)
Thomson, J. R. 51: v E 1974 (5) 1979 (1) 1982 (4); v WI 1975 (6) 1979 (1) 1981 (2); v In 1977 (5); v P 1972 (1) 1976 (1) 1981 (3); *v E 1975 (4) 1977 (5) 1985 (2); v WI 1977 (5); v NZ 1981 (3); v P 1982 (3)*
Thomson, N. F. D. 2: v E 1876 (2)
Thurlow, H. M. 1: v SA 1931
Toohey, P. M. 15: v E 1978 (5) 1979 (1); v WI 1979 (1); v In 1977 (5); *v WI 1977 (3)*
Toshack, E. R. H. 12: v E 1946 (5); v In 1947 (2); *v E 1948 (4); v NZ 1945 (1)*
Travers, J. P. F. 1: v E 1901
Tribe, G. E. 3: v E 1946 (3)
Trott, A. E. 3: v E 1894 (3)
Trott, G. H. S. 24: v E 1891 (3) 1894 (5) 1897 (5); *v E 1888 (3) 1890 (2) 1893 (3) 1896 (3)*
Trumble, H. 32: v E 1894 (1) 1897 (5) 1901 (5) 1903 (4); *v E 1890 (2) 1893 (3) 1896 (3) 1899 (5) 1902 (3); v SA 1902 (1)*
Trumble, J. W. 7: v E 1884 (4); *v E 1886 (3)*
Trumper, V. T. 48: v E 1901 (5) 1903 (5) 1907 (5) 1911 (5); v SA 1910 (5); *v E 1899 (5) 1902 (5) 1905 (5) 1909 (5); v SA 1902 (3)*
Turner, A. 14: v WI 1975 (6); v P 1976 (3); *v E 1975 (3); v NZ 1976 (2)*
Turner, C. T. B. 17: v E 1886 (2) 1887 (1) 1891 (3) 1894 (3); *v E 1888 (3) 1890 (2) 1893 (3)*

Veivers, T. R. 21: v E 1965 (4); v SA 1963 (3); v P 1964 (1); *v E 1964 (5); v SA 1966 (4); v In 1964 (3); v P 1964 (1)*
Veletta, M. R. J. 8: v E 1987 (1); v WI 1988 (2); v NZ 1987 (3); v P 1989 (1); v SL 1987 (1)

Waite, M. G. 2: *v E 1938 (2)*
Walker, M. H. N. 34: v E 1974 (6) 1976 (1); v WI 1975 (3); v NZ 1973 (1); v P 1972 (2) 1976 (2); *v E 1975 (4) 1977 (5); v WI 1972 (5); v NZ 1973 (3) 1976 (2)*
Wall, T. W. 18: v E 1928 (1) 1932 (4); v SA 1931 (3); v WI 1930 (1); *v E 1930 (5) 1934 (4)*
Walters, F. H. 1: v E 1884
Walters, K. D. 74: v E 1965 (5) 1970 (6) 1974 (6) 1976 (1); v WI 1968 (4); v NZ 1973 (3) 1980 (3); v In 1967 (2) 1980 (3); v P 1972 (1) 1976 (3); *v E 1968 (5) 1972 (4) 1975 (4) 1977 (5); v SA 1969 (4); v WI 1972 (5); v NZ 1973 (3) 1976 (2); v In 1969 (5)*
Ward, F. A. 4: v E 1936 (3); *v E 1938 (1)*
Warne, S. K. 84: v E 1994 (5) 1998 (1); v SA 1993 (3) 1997 (3); v WI 1992 (4) 1996 (5); v NZ 1993 (3) 1997 (3); v In 1991 (2) 1999 (3); v P 1995 (3) 1999 (3); v SL 1995 (3); *v E 1993 (6) 1997 (6); v SA 1993 (3) 1996 (3); v WI 1994 (4) 1998 (3); v NZ 1992 (3) 1999 (3); v In 1997 (3); v P 1994 (3); v SL 1992 (2) 1999 (3); v Z 1999 (1)*
Watkins, J. R. 1: v P 1972
Watson, G. D. 5: *v E 1972 (2); v SA 1966 (3)*
Watson, W. 1 4: v E 1954 (1); *v WI 1954 (3)*
Waugh, M. E. 103: v E 1990 (2) 1994 (5) 1998 (5), v SA 1993 (3) 1997 (3); v WI 1992 (5) 1996 (5); v NZ 1993 (3) 1997 (3); v In 1991 (4) 1999 (3); v P 1995 (3) 1999 (3); v SL 1995 (3); *v E 1993 (6) 1997 (6); v SA 1993 (3) 1996 (3); v WI 1990 (5) 1994 (4) 1998 (4); v NZ 1992 (2) 1999 (3); v In 1996 (1) 1997 (3); v P 1994 (3) 1998 (3); v SL 1992 (3) 1999 (3); v Z 1999 (1)*
Waugh, S. R. 128: v E 1986 (5) 1987 (1) 1990 (3) 1994 (5) 1998 (5); v SA 1993 (1) 1997 (3); v WI 1988 (5) 1992 (5) 1996 (5); v NZ 1987 (3) 1989 (1) 1993 (3) 1997 (3); v In 1985 (2) 1999 (3); v P 1989 (3) 1995 (3) 1999 (3); v SL 1987 (1) 1989 (2) 1995 (2); *v E 1989 (6) 1993 (6) 1997 (6); v SA 1993 (3) 1996 (3); v WI 1990 (5) 1994 (4) 1998 (4); v NZ 1985 (3) 1989 (1) 1992 (3) 1999 (3); v In 1986 (3) 1996 (1) 1997 (2); v P 1988 (3) 1994 (2) 1998 (3); SL 1992 (3); v Z 1999 (1)*
Wellham, D. M. 6: v E 1986 (1); v WI 1981 (1); v P 1981 (2); *v E 1981 (1) 1985 (1)*
Wessels, K. C. 24: v E 1982 (4); v WI 1984 (5); v NZ 1985 (1); v P 1983 (5); *v E 1985 (6); v WI 1983 (2); v SL 1982 (1)*
Whatmore, D. F. 7: v P 1978 (2); *v In 1979 (5)*
Whitney, M. R. 12: v WI 1988 (1) 1992 (1); v NZ 1987 (1); v In 1991 (3); *v E 1981 (2); v WI 1990 (2); v SL 1992 (2)*
Whitty, W. J. 14: v E 1911 (2); v SA 1910 (5); *v E 1909 (1) 1912 (3); v SA 1912 (3)*
Wiener, J. M. 6: v E 1979 (2); v WI 1979 (2); *v P 1979 (2)*
Wilson, J. W. 1: *v In 1956*
Wilson, P. 1: *v In 1997*

Wood, G. M. 59: v E 1978 (6) 1982 (1); v WI 1981 (3) 1984 (5) 1988 (3); v NZ 1980 (3); v In 1977 (1) 1980 (3); v P 1978 (1) 1981 (3); *v E 1980 (1) 1981 (6) 1985 (5); v WI 1977 (5) 1983 (1); v NZ 1981 (3); v In 1979 (2); v P 1982 (3) 1988 (3); v SL 1982 (1)*
Woodcock, A. J. 1: v NZ 1973
Woodfull, W. M. 35: v E 1928 (5) 1932 (5); v SA 1931 (5); v WI 1930 (5); *v E 1926 (5) 1930 (5) 1934 (5)*
Woods, S. M. J. 3: *v E 1888 (3)*
Woolley, R. D. 2: *v WI 1983 (1); v SL 1982 (1)*
Worrall, J. 11: v E 1884 (1) 1887 (1) 1894 (1) 1897 (1); *v E 1888 (3) 1899 (4)*
Wright, K. J. 10: v E 1978 (2); v P 1978 (2); *v In 1979 (6)*

Yallop, G. N. 39: v E 1978 (6); v WI 1975 (3) 1984 (1); v In 1977 (1); v P 1978 (1) 1981 (1) 1983 (5); *v E 1980 (1) 1981 (6); v WI 1977 (4); v In 1979 (6); v P 1979 (3); v SL 1982 (1)*
Yardley, B. 33: v E 1978 (4) 1982 (5); v WI 1981 (3); v In 1977 (1) 1980 (2); v P 1978 (1) 1981 (3); *v WI 1977 (5); v NZ 1981 (3); v In 1979 (3); v P 1982 (2); v SL 1982 (1)*
Young, S. 1: *v E 1997*

Zoehrer, T. J. 10: v E 1986 (4); *v NZ 1985 (3); v In 1986 (3)*

SOUTH AFRICA

Number of Test cricketers: 277

Ackerman, H. D. 4: v P 1997 (2); v SL 1997 (2)
Adams, P. R. 33: v E 1995 (2) 1999 (4); v A 1996 (2); v WI 1998 (2); v In 1996 (2); v P 1997 (1); v SL 1997 (2); v Z 1999 (1); *v E 1998 (4); v A 1997 (1); v NZ 1998 (3); v In 1996 (3); v P 1997 (2); v SL 2000 (3); v Z 1999 (1)*
Adcock, N. A. T. 26: v E 1956 (5); v A 1957 (5); v NZ 1953 (5) 1961 (2); *v E 1955 (4) 1960 (5)*
Anderson, J. H. 1: v A 1902
Ashley, W. H. 1: v E 1888

Bacher, A. 12: v A 1966 (5) 1969 (4); *v E 1965 (3)*
Bacher, A. M. 19: v A 1996 (2); v WI 1998 (1); v In 1996 (3); v P 1997 (3); v SL 1997 (1); v Z 1999 (1); *v E 1998 (1); v A 1997 (3); v P 1997 (3); v Z 1999 (1)*
Balaskas, X. C. 9: v E 1930 (2) 1938 (1); v A 1935 (3); *v E 1935 (1); v NZ 1931 (2)*
Barlow, E. J. 30: v E 1964 (5); v A 1966 (5) 1969 (4); v NZ 1961 (5); *v E 1965 (3); v A 1963 (5); v NZ 1963 (3)*
Baumgartner, H. V. 1: v E 1913
Beaumont, R. 5: v E 1913 (2); *v E 1912 (1); v A 1912 (2)*
Begbie, D. W. 5: v E 1948 (3); v A 1949 (2)
Bell, A. J. 16: v E 1930 (3); *v E 1929 (3) 1935 (3); v A 1931 (5); v NZ 1931 (2)*
Bisset, M. 3: v E 1898 (2) 1909 (1)
Bissett, G. F. 4: v E 1927 (4)
Blanckenberg, J. M. 18: v E 1913 (5) 1922 (5); v A 1921 (3); *v E 1924 (5)*
Bland, K. C. 21: v E 1964 (5); v A 1966 (1); v NZ 1961 (5); *v E 1965 (3); v A 1963 (4); v NZ 1963 (3)*
Bock, E. G. 1: v A 1935
Boje, N. 5: *v In 1999 (2); v SL 2000 (3)*
Bond, G. E. 1: v E 1938
Bosch, T. 1: *v WI 1991*
Botten, J. T. 3: *v E 1965 (3)*
Boucher, M. V. 31: v E 1999 (5); v WI 1998 (5); v P 1997 (3); v SL 1997 (2); v Z 1999 (1); *v E 1998 (5); v NZ 1998 (3); v In 1999 (2); v P 1997 (1); v SL 2000 (3); v Z 1999 (1)*
Brann, W. H. 3: v E 1922 (3)
Briscoe, A. W. 2: v E 1938 (1); v A 1935 (1)
Bromfield, H. D. 9: v E 1964 (3); v NZ 1961 (5); *v E 1965 (1)*
Brown, L. S. 2: *v A 1931 (1); v NZ 1931 (1)*

Burger, C. G. de V. 2: v A 1957 (2)
Burke, S. F. 2: v E 1964 (1); v NZ 1961 (1)
Buys, I. D. 1: v E 1922

Cameron, H. B. 26: v E 1927 (5) 1930 (5); *v E 1929 (4) 1935 (5); v A 1931 (5); v NZ 1931 (2)*
Campbell, T. 5: v E 1909 (4); *v E 1912 (1)*
Carlstein, P. R. 8: v A 1957 (1); *v E 1960 (5); v A 1963 (2)*
Carter, C. P. 10: v E 1913 (2); v A 1921 (3); *v E 1912 (2) 1924 (3)*
Catterall, R. H. 24: v E 1922 (5) 1927 (5) 1930 (4); *v E 1924 (5) 1929 (5)*
Chapman, H. W. 2: v E 1913 (1); v A 1921 (1)
Cheetham, J. E. 24: v E 1948 (1); v A 1949 (3); v NZ 1953 (5); *v E 1951 (5) 1955 (3); v A 1952 (5); v NZ 1952 (2)*
Chevalier, G. A. 1: v A 1969
Christy, J. A. J. 10: v E 1930 (1); *v E 1929 (2); v A 1931 (5); v NZ 1931 (2)*
Chubb, G. W. A. 5: *v E 1951 (5)*
Cochran, J. A. K. 1: v E 1930
Coen, S. K. 2: v E 1927 (2)
Commaille, J. M. M. 12: v E 1909 (5) 1927 (2); *v E 1924 (5)*
Commins, J. B. 3: v NZ 1994 (2); v P 1994 (1)
Conyngham, D. P. 1: v E 1922
Cook, F. J. 1: v E 1895
Cook, S. J. 3: v In 1992 (2); *v SL 1993 (1)*
Cooper, A. H. C. 1: v E 1913
Cox, J. L. 3: v E 1913 (3)
Cripps, G. 1: v E 1891
Crisp, R. J. 9: v A 1935 (4); *v E 1935 (5)*
Cronje, W. J. 68: v E 1995 (5) 1999 (5); v A 1993 (3) 1996 (3); v WI 1998 (5); v NZ 1994 (3); v In 1992 (3) 1996 (3); v P 1994 (1) 1997 (2); v SL 1997 (2); v Z 1999 (1); *v E 1994 (3) 1998 (5); v A 1993 (3) 1997 (3); v WI 1991 (1); v NZ 1994 (1) 1998 (3); v In 1996 (3) 1999 (2); v P 1997 (3); v SL 1993 (3); v Z 1995 (1) 1999 (1)*
Cullinan, D. J. 59: v E 1995 (5) 1999 (5); v A 1996 (3); v WI 1998 (5); v NZ 1994 (3); v In 1992 (1) 1996 (3); v P 1994 (1) 1997 (1); v SL 1997 (2); v Z 1999 (1); *v E 1994 (1) 1998 (5); v A 1993 (3) 1997 (1); v NZ 1994 (1) 1998 (3); v In 1996 (3) 1999 (1); v P 1997 (3); v SL 1993 (3) 2000 (3); v Z 1995 (1) 1999 (1)*
Curnow, S. H. 7: v E 1930 (3); *v A 1931 (4)*

Dalton, E. L. 15: v E 1930 (1) 1938 (4); v A 1935 (1); *v E 1929 (1) 1935 (4); v A 1931 (2); v NZ 1931 (2)*
Davies, E. Q. 5: v E 1938 (3); v A 1935 (2)
Dawson, O. C. 9: v E 1948 (4); *v E 1947 (5)*
Deane, H. G. 17: v E 1927 (5) 1930 (2); *v E 1924 (5) 1929 (5)*
de Villiers, P. S. 18: v A 1993 (3); v NZ 1994 (3); v P 1994 (1) 1997 (2); *v E 1994 (3); v A 1993 (3); v NZ 1994 (1); v In 1996 (2)*
Dippenaar, H. H. 2: v Z 1999 (1); *v Z 1999 (1)*
Dixon, C. D. 1: v E 1913
Donald, A. A. 62: v E 1995 (5) 1999 (4); v A 1993 (3) 1996 (3); v WI 1998 (5); v In 1992 (4) 1996 (3); v P 1994 (1) 1997 (3); v SL 1997 (2); v Z 1999 (1); *v E 1994 (3) 1998 (5); v A 1993 (3) 1997 (2); v WI 1991 (1); v NZ 1994 (1) 1998 (2); v In 1996 (2) 1999 (2); v P 1997 (2); v SL 1993 (3); v Z 1995 (1) 1999 (1)*
Dower, R. R. 1: v E 1898
Draper, R. G. 2: v A 1949 (2)
Duckworth, C. A. R. 2: v E 1956 (2)
Dumbrill, R. 5: v A 1966 (2); *v E 1965 (3)*
Duminy, J. P. 3: v E 1927 (2); *v E 1929 (1)*
Dunell, O. R. 2: v E 1888 (2)
Du Preez, J. H. 2: v A 1966 (2)
Du Toit, J. F. 1: v E 1891
Dyer, D. V. 3: *v E 1947 (3)*

Eksteen, C. E. 7: v E 1995 (1); v NZ 1994 (2); v P 1994 (1); *v NZ 1994 (1); v In 1999 (1); v SL 1993 (1)*
Elgie, M. K. 3: v NZ 1961 (3)
Elworthy, S. 2: *v E 1998 (1); v NZ 1998 (1)*
Endean, W. R. 28: v E 1956 (5); v A 1957 (5); v NZ 1953 (5); *v E 1951 (1) 1955 (5); v A 1952 (5); v NZ 1952 (2)*

Farrer, W. S. 6: v NZ 1961 (3); *v NZ 1963 (3)*
Faulkner, G. A. 25: v E 1905 (5) 1909 (5); *v E 1907 (3) 1912 (3) 1924 (1); v A 1910 (5) 1912 (3)*
Fellows-Smith, J. P. 4: *v E 1960 (4)*
Fichardt, C. G. 2: v E 1891 (1) 1895 (1)
Finlason, C. E. 1: v E 1888
Floquet, C. E. 1: v E 1909
Francis, H. H. 2: v E 1898 (2)
Francois, C. M. 5: v E 1922 (5)
Frank, C. N. 3: v A 1921 (3)
Frank, W. H. B. 1: v E 1895
Fuller, E. R. H. 7: v A 1957 (1); *v E 1955 (2); v A 1952 (2); v NZ 1952 (2)*
Fullerton, G. M. 7: v A 1949 (2); *v E 1947 (2) 1951 (3)*
Funston, K. J. 18: v E 1956 (3); v A 1957 (5); v NZ 1953 (3); *v A 1952 (5); v NZ 1952 (2)*

Gamsy, D. 2: v A 1969 (2)
Gibbs, H. H. 21: v E 1999 (5); v A 1996 (1); v WI 1998 (4); v In 1996 (1); v P 1997 (1); *v A 1997 (2); v NZ 1998 (3); v In 1996 (2) 1999 (2)*
Gleeson, R. A. 1: v E 1895
Glover, G. K. 1: v E 1895
Goddard, T. L. 41: v E 1956 (5) 1964 (5); v A 1957 (5) 1966 (5) 1969 (3); *v E 1955 (5) 1960 (5); v A 1963 (5); v NZ 1963 (3)*
Gordon, N. 5: v E 1938 (5)
Graham, R. 2: v E 1898 (2)
Grieveson, R. E. 2: v E 1938 (2)
Griffin, G. M. 2: *v E 1960 (2)*

Hall, A. E. 7: v E 1922 (4) 1927 (2) 1930 (1)
Hall, G. G. 1: v E 1964
Halliwell, E. A. 8: v E 1891 (1) 1895 (3) 1898 (1); v A 1902 (3)
Halse, C. G. 3: *v A 1963 (3)*
Hands, P. A. M. 7: v E 1913 (5), v A 1921 (1); *v E 1924 (1)*
Hands, R. H. M. 1: v E 1913
Hanley, M. A. 1: v E 1948
Harris, T. A. 3: v E 1948 (1); *v E 1947 (2)*
Hartigan, G. P. D. 5: v E 1913 (3); *v E 1912 (1); v A 1912 (1)*
Harvey, R. L. 2: v A 1935 (2)
Hathorn, C. M. H. 12: v E 1905 (5); v A 1902 (3); *v E 1907 (3); v A 1910 (1)*
Hayward, M. 6: v E 1999 (3); *v In 1999 (1); v SL 2000 (2)*
Hearne, F. 4: v E 1891 (1) 1895 (3)
Hearne, G. A. L. 3: v E 1922 (2); *v E 1924 (1)*
Heine, P. S. 14: v E 1956 (5); v A 1957 (4); v NZ 1961 (1); *v E 1955 (4)*
Henry, O. 3: v In 1992 (3)
Hime, C. F. W. 1: v E 1895
Hudson, A. C. 35: v E 1995 (5); v A 1993 (3) 1996 (1); v NZ 1994 (2); v In 1992 (4) 1996 (3); v P 1997 (3); *v E 1994 (2); v A 1993 (3); v WI 1991 (1); v NZ 1994 (1); v In 1996 (3); v SL 1993 (3); v Z 1995 (1)*
Hutchinson, P. 2: v E 1888 (2)

Ironside, D. E. J. 3: v NZ 1953 (3)
Irvine, B. L. 4: v A 1969 (4)

Jack, S. D. 2: v NZ 1994 (2)
Johnson, C. L. 1: v E 1895

Kallis, J. H. 39: v E 1995 (2) 1999 (5); v A 1996 (3); v WI 1998 (5); v P 1997 (3); v SL 1997 (2); v Z 1999 (1); *v E 1998 (5); v A 1997 (3); v NZ 1998 (3); v In 1999 (2); v P 1997 (1); v SL 2000 (3); v Z 1999 (1)*

Keith, H. J. 8: v E 1956 (3); *v E 1955 (4); v A 1952 (1)*

Kempis, G. A. 1: v E 1888

Kirsten, G. 63: v E 1995 (5) 1999 (5); v A 1993 (3) 1996 (3); v WI 1998 (5); v NZ 1994 (3); v In 1996 (3); v P 1994 (1) 1997 (3); v SL 1997 (2); *v E 1994 (3) 1998 (5); v A 1993 (3) 1997 (3); v NZ 1994 (1) 1998 (3); v In 1996 (3) 1999 (2); v P 1997 (3); v SL 2000 (3); v Z 1995 (1)*

Kirsten, P. N. 12: v A 1993 (3); v In 1992 (4); *v E 1994 (3); v A 1993 (1); v WI 1991 (1)*

Klusener, L. 32: v E 1999 (5); v A 1996 (2); v WI 1998 (5); v In 1996 (3); v P 1997 (2); v Z 1999 (1); *v E 1998 (3); v A 1997 (2); v NZ 1998 (3); v In 1996 (2) 1999 (2); v P 1997 (2); v SL 2000 (3); v Z 1999 (1)*

Kotze, J. J. 3: v A 1902 (2); *v E 1907 (1)*

Kuiper, A. P. 1: *v WI 1991*

Kuys, F. 1: v E 1898

Lance, H. R. 13: v A 1966 (5) 1969 (3); v NZ 1961 (2); *v E 1965 (3)*

Langton, A. B. C. 15: v E 1938 (5); v A 1935 (5); *v E 1935 (5)*

Lawrence, G. B. 5: v NZ 1961 (5)

le Roux, F. L. 1: v E 1913

Lewis, P. T. 1: v E 1913

Liebenberg, G. F. J. 5: v SL 1997 (1); *v E 1998 (4)*

Lindsay, D. T. 19: v E 1964 (3); v A 1966 (5) 1969 (2); *v E 1965 (3); v A 1963 (3); v NZ 1963 (3)*

Lindsay, J. D. 3: *v E 1947 (3)*

Lindsay, N. V. 1: v A 1921

Ling, W. V. S. 6: v E 1922 (3); v A 1921 (3)

Llewellyn, C. B. 15: v E 1895 (1) 1898 (1); v A 1902 (3); *v E 1912 (3); v A 1910 (5) 1912 (2)*

Lundie, E. B. 1: v E 1913

Macaulay, M. J. 1: v E 1964

McCarthy, C. N. 15: v E 1948 (5); v A 1949 (5); *v E 1951 (5)*

McGlew, D. J. 34: v E 1956 (1); v A 1957 (5); v NZ 1953 (5) 1961 (5); *v E 1951 (2) 1955 (5) 1960 (5); v A 1952 (4); v NZ 1952 (2)*

McKenzie, N. D. 3: *v SL 2000 (3)*

McKinnon, A. H. 8: v E 1964 (2); v A 1966 (2); v NZ 1961 (1); *v E 1960 (1) 1965 (2)*

McLean, R. A. 40: v E 1956 (5) 1964 (2); v A 1957 (4); v NZ 1953 (4) 1961 (5); *v E 1951 (3) 1955 (5) 1960 (5); v A 1952 (5); v NZ 1952 (2)*

McMillan, B. M. 38: v E 1995 (5); v A 1993 (3) 1996 (3); v NZ 1994 (3); v In 1992 (4) 1996 (3); v P 1994 (1); *v E 1994 (3) 1998 (1); v A 1993 (1) 1997 (3); v In 1996 (3); v P 1997 (3); v SL 1993 (2); v Z 1995 (1)*

McMillan, Q. 13: v E 1930 (5); *v E 1929 (2); v A 1931 (4); v NZ 1931 (2)*

Mann, N. B. F. 19: v E 1948 (5); v A 1949 (5); *v E 1947 (5) 1951 (4)*

Mansell, P. N. F. 13: *v E 1951 (2) 1955 (4); v A 1952 (5); v NZ 1952 (2)*

Markham, L. A. 1: v E 1948

Marx, W. F. E. 3: v A 1921 (3)

Matthews, C. R. 18: v E 1995 (3); v A 1993 (3); v NZ 1994 (2); v In 1992 (3); *v E 1994 (3); v A 1993 (2); v NZ 1994 (1); v Z 1995 (1)*

Meintjes, D. J. 2: v E 1922 (2)

Melle, M. G. 7: v A 1949 (2); *v E 1951 (1); v A 1952 (4)*

Melville, A. 11: v E 1938 (5) 1948 (1); *v E 1947 (5)*

Middleton, J. 6: v E 1895 (2) 1898 (2); v A 1902 (2)

Mills, C. 1: v E 1891

Milton, W. H. 3: v E 1888 (2) 1891 (1)

Mitchell, B. 42: v E 1930 (5) 1938 (5) 1948 (5); v A 1935 (5); *v E 1929 (5) 1935 (5) 1947 (5); v A 1931 (5); v NZ 1931 (2)*

Mitchell, F. 3: *v E 1912 (1); v A 1912 (2)*

Morkel, D. P. B. 16: v E 1927 (5); *v E 1929 (5); v A 1931 (5); v NZ 1931 (1)*

Murray, A. R. A. 10: v NZ 1953 (4); *v A 1952 (4); v NZ 1952 (2)*

Nel, J. D. 6: v A 1949 (5) 1957 (1)

Newberry, C. 4: v E 1913 (4)

Newson, E. S. 3: v E 1930 (1) 1938 (2)
Nicholson, F. 4: v A 1935 (4)
Nicolson, J. F. W. 3: v E 1927 (3)
Norton, N. O. 1: v E 1909
Nourse, A. D. 34: v E 1938 (5) 1948 (5); v A 1935 (5) 1949 (5); *v E 1935 (4) 1947 (5) 1951 (5)*
Nourse, A. W. 45: v E 1905 (5) 1909 (5) 1913 (5) 1922 (5); v A 1902 (3) 1921 (3); *v E 1907 (3) 1912 (3) 1924 (5); v A 1910 (5) 1912 (3)*
Ntini, M. 5: v SL 1997 (2); *v E 1998 (2); v SL 2000 (1)*
Nupen, E. P. 17: v E 1922 (4) 1927 (5) 1930 (3); v A 1921 (2) 1935 (1); *v E 1924 (2)*

Ochse, A. E. 2: v E 1888 (2)
Ochse, A. L. 3: v E 1927 (1); *v E 1929 (2)*
O'Linn, S. 7: v NZ 1961 (2); *v E 1960 (5)*
Owen-Smith, H. G. 5: *v E 1929 (5)*

Palm, A. W. 1: v E 1927
Parker, G. M. 2: *v E 1924 (2)*
Parkin, D. C. 1: v E 1891
Partridge, J. T. 11: v E 1964 (3); *v A 1963 (5); v NZ 1963 (3)*
Pearse, O. C. 3: *v A 1910 (3)*
Pegler, S. J. 16: v E 1909 (1); *v E 1912 (3) 1924 (5); v A 1910 (4) 1912 (3)*
Pithey, A. J. 17: v E 1956 (1) 1964 (5); *v E 1960 (2); v A 1963 (4); v NZ 1963 (3)*
Pithey, D. B. 8: v A 1966 (2); *v A 1963 (3); v NZ 1963 (3)*
Plimsoll, J. B. 1: *v E 1947*
Pollock, P. M. 28: v E 1964 (5); v A 1966 (5) 1969 (4); v NZ 1961 (3); *v E 1965 (3); v A 1963 (5); v NZ 1963 (3)*
Pollock, R. G. 23: v E 1964 (5); v A 1966 (5) 1969 (4); *v E 1965 (3); v A 1963 (5); v NZ 1963 (1)*
Pollock, S. M. 45: v E 1995 (5) 1999 (5); v A 1996 (2); v WI 1998 (5); v In 1996 (3); v P 1997 (3); v SL 1997 (2); v Z 1999 (1); *v E 1998 (4); v A 1997 (3); v NZ 1998 (3); v In 1999 (2); v P 1997 (3); v SL 2000 (3); v Z 1999 (1)*
Poore, R. M. 3: v E 1895 (3)
Pothecary, J. E. 3: *v E 1960 (3)*
Powell, A. W. 1: v E 1898
Prince, C. F. H. 1: v E 1898
Pringle, M. W. 4: v E 1995 (1); v In 1992 (2); *v WI 1991 (1)*
Procter, M. J. 7: v A 1966 (3) 1969 (4)
Promnitz, H. L. E. 2: v E 1927 (2)

Quinn, N. A. 12: v E 1930 (1); *v E 1929 (4), v A 1931 (5); v NZ 1931 (2)*

Reid, N. 1: v A 1921
Rhodes, J. N. 52: v E 1995 (5) 1999 (3); v A 1993 (3) 1996 (1); v WI 1998 (5); v NZ 1994 (3); v In 1992 (4); v P 1994 (2); v Z 1999 (1); *v E 1994 (3) 1998 (5); v A 1993 (3) 1997 (1); v NZ 1994 (1) 1998 (3); v In 1996 (1); v P 1997 (1); v SL 1993 (3) 2000 (3); v Z 1995 (1) 1999 (1)*
Richards, A. R. 1: v E 1895
Richards, B. A. 4: v A 1969 (4)
Richards, W. H. 1: v E 1888
Richardson, D. J. 42: v E 1995 (5); v A 1993 (3) 1996 (3); v NZ 1994 (3); v In 1992 (4) 1996 (3); v P 1994 (1); *v E 1994 (3); v A 1993 (3) 1997 (3); v WI 1991 (1); v NZ 1994 (1); v In 1996 (3); v P 1997 (2); v SL 1993 (3); v Z 1995 (1)*
Robertson, J. B. 3: v A 1935 (3)
Rose-Innes, A. 2: v E 1888 (2)
Routledge, T. W. 4: v E 1891 (1) 1895 (3)
Rowan, A. M. B. 15: v E 1948 (5); *v E 1947 (5) 1951 (5)*
Rowan, E. A. B. 26: v E 1938 (4) 1948 (4); v A 1935 (3) 1949 (5); *v E 1935 (5) 1951 (5)*
Rowe, G. A. 5: v E 1895 (2) 1898 (2); v A 1902 (1)
Rushmere, M. W. 1: *v WI 1991*

Samuelson, S. V. 1: v E 1909
Schultz, B. N. 9: v E 1995 (1); v A 1996 (1); v In 1992 (2); *v P 1997 (1); v SL 1993 (3); v Z 1995 (1)*
Schwarz, R. O. 20: v E 1905 (5) 1909 (4); *v E 1907 (3) 1912 (1); v A 1910 (5) 1912 (2)*
Seccull, A. W. 1: v E 1895

Seymour, M. A. 7: v E 1964 (2); v A 1969 (1); *v A 1963 (4)*
Shalders, W. A. 12: v E 1898 (1) 1905 (5); v A 1902 (3); *v E 1907 (3)*
Shepstone, G. H. 2: v E 1895 (1) 1898 (1)
Sherwell, P. W. 13: v E 1905 (5); *v E 1907 (3); v A 1910 (5)*
Siedle, I. J. 18: v E 1927 (1) 1930 (5); v A 1935 (5); *v E 1929 (3) 1935 (4)*
Sinclair, J. H. 25: v E 1895 (3) 1898 (2) 1905 (5) 1909 (4); v A 1902 (3); *v E 1907 (3); v A 1910 (5)*
Smith, C. J. E. 3: v A 1902 (3)
Smith, F. W. 3: v E 1888 (2) 1895 (1)
Smith, V. I. 9: v A 1949 (3) 1957 (1); *v E 1947 (4) 1955 (1)*
Snell, R. P. 5: v NZ 1994 (1); *v A 1993 (1); v WI 1991 (1); v SL 1993 (2)*
Snooke, S. D. 1: *v E 1907*
Snooke, S. J. 26: v E 1905 (5) 1909 (5) 1922 (3); *v E 1907 (3) 1912 (3); v A 1910 (5) 1912 (2)*
Solomon, W. R. 1: v E 1898
Stewart, R. B. 1: v E 1888
Steyn, P. J. R. 3: v NZ 1994 (1); v P 1994 (1); *v NZ 1994 (1)*
Stricker, L. A. 13: v E 1909 (4); *v E 1912 (2); v A 1910 (5) 1912 (2)*
Strydom, P. C. 2: v E 1999 (1); *v In 1999 (1)*
Susskind, M. J. 5: *v E 1924 (5)*
Symcox, P. L. 20: v A 1996 (1); v WI 1998 (3); v P 1997 (1); *v A 1993 (2) 1997 (3); v In 1996 (3);
    v P 1997 (3); v SL 1993 (3); v Z 1995 (1)*

Taberer, H. M. 1: v A 1902
Tancred, A. B. 2: v E 1888 (2)
Tancred, L. J. 14: v E 1905 (5) 1913 (1); v A 1902 (3); *v E 1907 (1) 1912 (2); v A 1912 (2)*
Tancred, V. M. 1: v E 1898
Tapscott, G. L. 1: v E 1913
Tapscott, L. E. 2: v E 1922 (2)
Tayfield, H. J. 37: v E 1956 (5); v A 1949 (5) 1957 (5); v NZ 1953 (5); *v E 1955 (5) 1960 (5); v A
    1952 (5); v NZ 1952 (2)*
Taylor, A. I. 1: v E 1956
Taylor, D. 2: v E 1913 (2)
Taylor, H. W. 42: v E 1913 (5) 1922 (5) 1927 (5) 1930 (4); v A 1921 (3); *v E 1912 (3) 1924 (5)
    1929 (3); v A 1912 (3) 1931 (5); v NZ 1931 (1)*
Terbrugge, D. J. 4: v WI 1998 (4)
Theunissen, N. H. 1: v E 1888
Thornton, P. G. 1: v A 1902
Tomlinson, D. S. 1: *v E 1935*
Traicos, A. J. 3: v A 1969 (3)
Trimborn, P. H. J. 4: v A 1966 (3) 1969 (1)
Tuckett, L. 9: v E 1948 (4); *v E 1947 (5)*
Tuckett, L. R. 1: v E 1913
Twentyman Jones, P. S. 1: v A 1902

van der Bijl, P. G. V. 5: v E 1938 (5)
Van der Merwe, E. A. 2: v A 1935 (1); *v E 1929 (1)*
Van der Merwe, P. L. 15: v E 1964 (2); v A 1966 (5); *v E 1965 (3); v A 1963 (3); v NZ 1963 (2)*
Van Ryneveld, C. B. 19: v E 1956 (5); v A 1957 (4); v NZ 1953 (5); *v E 1951 (5)*
Varnals, G. D. 3: v E 1964 (3)
Viljoen, K. G. 27: v E 1930 (3) 1938 (4) 1948 (2); v A 1935 (4); *v E 1935 (4) 1947 (5); v A
    1931 (4); v NZ 1931 (1)*
Vincent, C. L. 25: v E 1927 (5) 1930 (5); *v E 1929 (4) 1935 (4); v A 1931 (5); v NZ 1931 (2)*
Vintcent, C. H. 3: v E 1888 (2) 1891 (1)
Vogler, A. E. E. 15: v E 1905 (5) 1909 (5); *v E 1907 (3); v A 1910 (2)*

Wade, H. F. 10: v A 1935 (5); *v E 1935 (5)*
Wade, W. W. 11: v E 1938 (3) 1948 (5); v A 1949 (3)
Waite, J. H. B. 50: v E 1956 (5) 1964 (2); v A 1957 (5); v NZ 1953 (5) 1961 (5); *v E 1951 (4)
    1955 (5) 1960 (5); v A 1952 (5) 1963 (4); v NZ 1952 (2) 1963 (3)*
Walter, K. A. 2: v NZ 1961 (2)
Ward, T. A. 23: v E 1913 (5) 1922 (5); v A 1921 (3); *v E 1912 (2) 1924 (5); v A 1912 (3)*
Watkins, J. C. 15: v E 1956 (2); v A 1949 (3); v NZ 1953 (3); *v A 1952 (5); v NZ 1952 (2)*

Wesley, C. 3: *v E 1960 (3)*
Wessels, K. C. 16: v A 1993 (3); v In 1992 (4); *v E 1994 (3); v A 1993 (2); v WI 1991 (1); SL 1993 (3)*
Westcott, R. J. 5: v A 1957 (2); v NZ 1953 (3)
White, G. C. 17: v E 1905 (5) 1909 (4); *v E 1907 (3) 1912 (2); v A 1912 (3)*
Willoughby, J. T. 2: v E 1895 (2)
Wimble, C. S. 1: v E 1891
Winslow, P. L. 5: v A 1949 (2); *v E 1955 (3)*
Wynne, O. E. 6: v E 1948 (3); v A 1949 (3)

Zulch, J. W. 16: v E 1909 (5) 1913 (3); v A 1921 (3); *v A 1910 (5)*

WEST INDIES

Number of Test cricketers: 235

Achong, E. 6: v E 1929 (1) 1934 (2); *v E 1933 (3)*
Adams, J. C. 49: v E 1993 (5) 1997 (4); v A 1994 (4) 1998 (4); v SA 1991 (1); v NZ 1995 (2); v P 1999 (3); v Z 1999 (2); *v E 1995 (4) 2000 (5); v A 1992 (3) 1996 (5); v NZ 1994 (2) 1999 (2); v In 1994 (3)*
Alexander, F. C. M. 25: v E 1959 (5); v P 1957 (5); *v E 1957 (2); v A 1960 (5); v In 1958 (5); v P 1958 (3)*
Ali, Imtiaz 1: v In 1975
Ali, Inshan 12: v E 1973 (2); v A 1972 (3); v In 1970 (1); v P 1976 (1); v NZ 1971 (3); *v E 1973 (1); v A 1975 (1)*
Allan, D. W. 5: v A 1964 (1); v In 1961 (2); *v E 1966 (2)*
Allen, I. B. A. 2: *v E 1991 (2)*
Ambrose, C. E. L. 98: v E 1989 (3) 1993 (5) 1997 (6); v A 1990 (5) 1994 (4) 1998 (4); v SA 1991 (1); v NZ 1995 (2); v In 1988 (4) 1996 (5); v P 1987 (3) 1992 (3) 1999 (3); v SL 1996 (2); v Z 1999 (2); *v E 1988 (5) 1991 (5) 1995 (5) 2000 (5); v A 1988 (5) 1992 (5) 1996 (4); v SA 1998 (4); v NZ 1994 (2) 1999 (2); v P 1990 (3) 1997 (2); v SL 1993 (1)*
Arthurton, K. L. T. 33: v E 1993 (5); v A 1994 (3); v SA 1991 (1); v In 1988 (4); v P 1992 (3); *v E 1988 (1) 1995 (5); v A 1992 (5); v NZ 1994 (2); v In 1994 (3); v SL 1993 (1)*
Asgarali, N. 2: *v E 1957 (2)*
Atkinson, D. St E. 22: v E 1953 (4); v A 1954 (4); v P 1957 (1); *v E 1957 (2); v A 1951 (2); v NZ 1951 (1) 1955 (4); v In 1948 (4)*
Atkinson, E. St E. 8: v P 1957 (3); *v In 1958 (3); v P 1958 (2)*
Austin, R. A. 2: v A 1977 (2)

Bacchus, S. F. A. F. 19: v A 1977 (2); *v E 1980 (5); v A 1981 (2); v In 1978 (6); v P 1980 (4)*
Baichan, L. 3: *v A 1975 (1); v P 1974 (2)*
Baptiste, E. A. E. 10: v E 1989 (1); v A 1983 (3); *v E 1984 (5); v In 1983 (1)*
Barrett, A. G. 6: v E 1973 (2); v In 1970 (2); *v In 1974 (2)*
Barrow, I. 11: v E 1929 (1) 1934 (1); *v E 1933 (3) 1939 (1); v A 1930 (5)*
Bartlett, E. L. 5: *v E 1928 (1); v A 1930 (4)*
Benjamin, K. C. G. 26: v E 1993 (5) 1997 (2); v A 1994 (4); v SA 1991 (1); *v E 1995 (5); v A 1992 (1) 1996 (3); v NZ 1994 (2); v In 1994 (3)*
Benjamin, W. K. M. 21: v E 1993 (5); v A 1994 (4); v In 1988 (1); v P 1987 (3) 1992 (2); *v E 1988 (3); v NZ 1994 (1); v In 1987 (1); v SL 1993 (1)*
Best, C. A. 8: v E 1985 (3) 1989 (3); *v P 1990 (2)*
Betancourt, N. 1: v E 1929
Binns, A. P. 5: v A 1954 (1); v In 1952 (1); *v NZ 1955 (3)*
Birkett, L. S. 4: *v A 1930 (4)*
Bishop, I. R. 43: v E 1989 (4) 1997 (3); v NZ 1995 (2); v In 1988 (4) 1996 (4); v P 1992 (2); v SL 1996 (2); *v E 1995 (6); v A 1992 (5) 1996 (3); v P 1990 (3) 1997 (3)*
Boyce, K. D. 21: v E 1973 (4); v A 1972 (3); v In 1970 (1); *v E 1973 (3); v A 1975 (4); v In 1974 (3); v P 1974 (2)*
Browne, C. O. 13: v A 1994 (1); v NZ 1995 (2); v In 1996 (3); v SL 1996 (2); *v E 1995 (2); v A 1996 (3)*

Browne, C. R. 4: v E 1929 (2); *v E 1928 (2)*

Butcher, B. F. 44: v E 1959 (2) 1967 (5); v A 1964 (5); *v E 1963 (5) 1966 (5) 1969 (3); v A 1968 (5); v NZ 1968 (3); v In 1958 (5) 1966 (3); v P 1958 (3)*

Butler, L. 1: v A 1954

Butts, C. G. 7: v NZ 1984 (1); *v NZ 1986 (1); v In 1987 (3); v P 1986 (2)*

Bynoe, M. R. 4: *v In 1966 (3); v P 1958 (1)*

Camacho, G. S. 11: v E 1967 (5); v In 1970 (2); *v E 1969 (2); v A 1968 (2)*

Cameron, F. J. 5: *v In 1948 (5)*

Cameron, J. H. 2: *v E 1939 (2)*

Campbell, S. L. 46: v E 1997 (4); v A 1994 (1) 1998 (4); v NZ 1995 (2); v In 1996 (5); v P 1999 (3); v SL 1996 (2); v Z 1999 (2); *v E 1995 (6) 2000 (5); v A 1996 (5); v NZ 1994 (2) 1999 (2); v P 1997 (3)*

Carew, G. M. 4: v E 1934 (1) 1947 (2); *v In 1948 (1)*

Carew, M. C. 19: v E 1967 (1); v NZ 1971 (3); v In 1970 (3); *v E 1963 (2) 1966 (1) 1969 (1); v A 1968 (5); v NZ 1968 (3)*

Challenor, G. 3: *v E 1928 (3)*

Chanderpaul, S. 44: v E 1993 (4) 1997 (6); v NZ 1995 (2); v In 1996 (5); v P 1999 (3); v Z 1999 (2); *v E 1995 (2) 2000 (2); v A 1996 (5); v SA 1998 (5); v NZ 1994 (2) 1999 (2); v In 1994 (1); v P 1997 (3)*

Chang, H. S. 1: *v In 1978*

Christiani, C. M. 4: v E 1934 (4)

Christiani, R. J. 22: v E 1947 (4) 1953 (1); v In 1952 (2); *v E 1950 (4); v A 1951 (5); v NZ 1951 (1); v In 1948 (5)*

Clarke, C. B. 3: *v E 1939 (3)*

Clarke, S. T. 11: v A 1977 (1); *v A 1981 (1); v In 1978 (5); v P 1980 (4)*

Collins, P. T. 3: v A 1998 (3)

Collymore, C. D. 1: v A 1998

Constantine, L. N. 18: v E 1929 (3) 1934 (3); *v E 1928 (3) 1933 (1) 1939 (3); v A 1930 (5)*

Croft, C. E. H. 27: v E 1980 (4); v A 1977 (2); v P 1976 (5); *v E 1980 (3); v A 1979 (3) 1981 (3); v NZ 1979 (3); v P 1980 (4)*

Cuffy, C. E. 3: *v A 1996 (1); v In 1994 (2)*

Cummins, A. C. 5: v P 1992 (2); *v A 1992 (1); v In 1994 (2)*

Da Costa, O. C. 5: v E 1929 (1) 1934 (1); *v E 1933 (3)*

Daniel, W. W. 10: v A 1983 (2); v In 1975 (1); *v E 1976 (4); v In 1983 (3)*

Davis, B. A. 4: v A 1964 (4)

Davis, C. A. 15: v A 1972 (2); v NZ 1971 (5); v In 1970 (4); *v E 1969 (3); v A 1968 (1)*

Davis, W. W. 15: v A 1983 (1); v NZ 1984 (2); v In 1982 (1); *v E 1984 (1); v In 1983 (6) 1987 (4)*

De Caires, F. I. 3: v E 1929 (3)

Depeiza, C. C. 5: v A 1954 (3); *v NZ 1955 (2)*

Dewdney, T. 9: v A 1954 (2); v P 1957 (3); *v E 1957 (1); v NZ 1955 (3)*

Dhanraj, R. 4: v NZ 1995 (1); *v E 1995 (1); v NZ 1994 (1); v In 1994 (1)*

Dillon, M. 7: v A 1998 (1); v In 1996 (2); *v SA 1998 (3); v P 1997 (1)*

Dowe, U. G. 4: v A 1972 (1); v NZ 1971 (1); v In 1970 (2)

Dujon, P. J. L. 81: v E 1985 (4) 1989 (4); v A 1983 (5) 1990 (5); v NZ 1984 (4); v In 1982 (5) 1988 (4); v P 1987 (3); *v E 1984 (5) 1988 (5) 1991 (5); v A 1981 (3) 1984 (5) 1988 (5); v NZ 1986 (3); v In 1983 (6) 1987 (4); v P 1986 (3) 1990 (3)*

Edwards, R. M. 5: *v A 1968 (2); v NZ 1968 (3)*

Ferguson, W. 8: v E 1947 (4) 1953 (1); *v In 1948 (3)*

Fernandes, M. P. 2: v E 1929 (1); *v E 1928 (1)*

Findlay, T. M. 10: v A 1972 (1); v NZ 1971 (5); v In 1970 (2); *v E 1969 (2)*

Foster, M. L. C. 14: v E 1973 (1); v A 1972 (4) 1977 (1); v NZ 1971 (3); v In 1970 (2); v P 1976 (1); *v E 1969 (1) 1973 (1)*

Francis, G. N. 10: v E 1929 (1); *v E 1928 (3) 1933 (1); v A 1930 (5)*

Frederick, M. 1: v E 1953

Fredericks, R. C. 59: v E 1973 (5); v A 1972 (5); v NZ 1971 (5); v In 1970 (4) 1975 (4); v P 1976 (5); *v E 1969 (3) 1973 (3) 1976 (5); v A 1968 (4) 1975 (6); v NZ 1968 (3); v In 1974 (5); v P 1974 (2)*

Fuller, R. L. 1: v E 1934

Furlonge, H. A. 3: v A 1954 (1); *v NZ 1955 (2)*

Ganga, D. 4: *v SA 1998 (3); v NZ 1999 (1)*

Ganteaume, A. G. 1: v E 1947

Garner, J. 58: v E 1980 (4) 1985 (5); v A 1977 (2) 1983 (5); v NZ 1984 (4); v In 1982 (4); v P 1976 (5); *v E 1980 (5) 1984 (5); v A 1979 (3) 1981 (3) 1984 (5); v NZ 1979 (3) 1986 (2); v P 1980 (3)*

Gaskin, B. B. M. 2: v E 1947 (2)

Gayle, C. H. 4: v P 1999 (1); v Z 1999 (2); *v E 2000 (1)*

Gibbs, G. L. 1: v A 1954

Gibbs, L. R. 79: v E 1967 (5) 1973 (5); v A 1964 (5) 1972 (5); v NZ 1971 (2); v In 1961 (5) 1970 (1); v P 1957 (4); *v E 1963 (5) 1966 (5) 1969 (3) 1973 (3); v A 1960 (3) 1968 (5) 1975 (6); v NZ 1968 (3); v In 1958 (1) 1966 (3) 1974 (5); v P 1958 (3) 1974 (2)*

Gibson, O. D. 2: *v E 1995 (1); v SA 1998 (1)*

Gilchrist, R. 13: *v P 1957 (5); v E 1957 (4); v In 1958 (4)*

Gladstone, G. 1: v E 1929

Goddard, J. D. C. 27: v E 1947 (4); *v E 1950 (4) 1957 (5); v A 1951 (4); v NZ 1951 (2) 1955 (3); v In 1948 (5)*

Gomes, H. A. 60: v E 1980 (4) 1985 (5); v A 1977 (2) 1983 (2); v NZ 1984 (4); v In 1982 (5); *v E 1976 (2) 1984 (5); v A 1981 (3) 1984 (5); v NZ 1986 (3); v In 1978 (6) 1983 (6); v P 1980 (4) 1986 (3)*

Gomez, G. E. 29: v E 1947 (4) 1953 (4); v In 1952 (4); *v E 1939 (2) 1950 (4); v A 1951 (5); v NZ 1951 (1); v In 1948 (5)*

Grant, G. C. 12: v E 1934 (4); *v E 1933 (3); v A 1930 (5)*

Grant, R. S. 7: v E 1934 (4); *v E 1939 (3)*

Gray, A. H. 5: *v NZ 1986 (2); v P 1986 (3)*

Greenidge, A. E. 6: v A 1977 (2); *v In 1978 (4)*

Greenidge, C. G. 108: v E 1980 (4) 1985 (5) 1989 (4); v A 1977 (2) 1983 (5) 1990 (5); v NZ 1984 (4); v In 1982 (5) 1988 (4); v P 1976 (5) 1987 (3); *v E 1976 (5) 1980 (5) 1984 (5) 1988 (4); v A 1975 (2) 1979 (3) 1981 (2) 1984 (5) 1988 (5); v NZ 1979 (3) 1986 (3); v In 1974 (5) 1983 (6) 1987 (3); v P 1986 (3) 1990 (3)*

Greenidge, G. A. 5: v A 1972 (3); v NZ 1971 (2)

Grell, M. G. 1: v E 1929

Griffith, A. F. G. 14: v A 1998 (2); v P 1999 (3); v Z 1999 (2); *v E 2000 (4); v A 1996 (1); v NZ 1999 (2)*

Griffith, C. C. 28: v E 1959 (1) 1967 (4); v A 1964 (5); *v E 1963 (5) 1966 (5); v A 1968 (3); v NZ 1968 (2); v In 1966 (3)*

Griffith, H. C. 13: v E 1929 (3); *v E 1928 (3) 1933 (2); v A 1930 (5)*

Guillen, S. C. 5: *v A 1951 (3); v NZ 1951 (2)*

Hall, W. W. 48: v E 1959 (5) 1967 (4); v A 1964 (5); v In 1961 (5); *v E 1963 (5) 1966 (5); v A 1960 (5) 1968 (2); v NZ 1968 (1); v In 1958 (5) 1966 (3); v P 1958 (3)*

Harper, R. A. 25: v E 1985 (2); v A 1983 (4); v NZ 1984 (1); *v E 1984 (5) 1988 (5); v A 1984 (2) 1988 (1); v In 1983 (2) 1987 (1); v P 1986 (3); v SL 1993 (1)*

Haynes, D. L. 116: v E 1980 (4) 1985 (5) 1989 (4) 1993 (4); v A 1977 (2) 1983 (5) 1990 (5); v SA 1991 (1); v NZ 1984 (4); v In 1982 (5) 1988 (4); v P 1987 (3) 1992 (3); *v E 1980 (5) 1984 (5) 1988 (4) 1991 (5); v A 1979 (3) 1981 (3) 1984 (5) 1988 (5) 1992 (5); v NZ 1979 (3) 1986 (3); v In 1983 (6) 1987 (4); v P 1980 (4) 1986 (3) 1990 (3); v SL 1993 (1)*

Headley, G. A. 22: v E 1929 (4) 1934 (4) 1947 (1) 1953 (1); *v E 1933 (3) 1939 (3); v A 1930 (5); v In 1948 (1)*

Headley, R. G. A. 2: *v E 1973 (2)*

Hendriks, J. L. 20: v A 1964 (4); v In 1961 (1); *v E 1966 (3) 1969 (1); v A 1968 (5); v NZ 1968 (3); v In 1966 (3)*

Hinds, W. W. 10: v P 1999 (3); v Z 1999 (2); *v E 2000 (5)*

Hoad, E. L. G. 4: v E 1929 (1); *v E 1928 (1) 1933 (2)*

Holder, R. I. C. 11: v E 1997 (2); v A 1998 (1); v In 1996 (5); v SL 1996 (2); *v P 1997 (1)*

Holder, V. A. 40: v E 1973 (1); v A 1972 (3) 1977 (3); v NZ 1971 (4); v In 1970 (3) 1975 (1); v P 1976 (1); *v E 1969 (3) 1973 (2) 1976 (4); v A 1975 (3); v In 1974 (4) 1978 (6); v P 1974 (2)*

Holding, M. A. 60: v E 1980 (4) 1985 (4); v A 1983 (3); v NZ 1984 (3); v In 1975 (4) 1982 (5); *v E 1976 (4) 1980 (5) 1984 (4); v A 1975 (5) 1979 (3) 1981 (3) 1984 (3); v NZ 1979 (3) 1986 (1); v In 1983 (6)*

Holford, D. A. J. 24: v E 1967 (4); v NZ 1971 (5); v In 1970 (1) 1975 (2); v P 1976 (1); *v E 1966 (5); v A 1968 (2); v NZ 1968 (3); v In 1966 (1)*

Holt, J. K. 17: v E 1953 (5); v A 1954 (5); *v In 1958 (5); v P 1958 (2)*

Hooper, C. L. 80: v E 1989 (3) 1997 (6); v A 1990 (5) 1994 (4) 1998 (2); v In 1996 (5); v P 1987 (3) 1992 (3); v SL 1996 (2); *v E 1988 (5) 1991 (5) 1995 (5); v A 1988 (5) 1992 (4) 1996 (5); v SA 1998 (5); v In 1987 (3) 1994 (3); v P 1990 (3) 1997 (3); v SL 1993 (1)*

Howard, A. B. 1: v NZ 1971

Hunte, C. C. 44: v E 1959 (5); v A 1964 (5); v In 1961 (5); v P 1957 (5); *v E 1963 (5) 1966 (5); v A 1960 (5); v In 1958 (5) 1966 (3); v P 1958 (1)*

Hunte, E. A. C. 3: v E 1929 (3)

Hylton, L. G. 6: v E 1934 (4); *v E 1939 (2)*

Jacobs, R. D. 21: v A 1998 (4); v P 1999 (3); v Z 1999 (2); *v E 2000 (5); v SA 1998 (5); v NZ 1999 (2)*

Johnson, H. H. H. 3: v E 1947 (1); *v E 1950 (2)*

Johnson, T. F. 1: *v E 1939*

Jones, C. M. 4: v E 1929 (1) 1934 (3)

Jones, P. E. 9: v E 1947 (1); *v E 1950 (2); v A 1951 (1); v In 1948 (5)*

Joseph, D. R. E. 4: v A 1998 (4)

Julien, B. D. 24: v E 1973 (5); v In 1975 (4); v P 1976 (1); *v E 1973 (3) 1976 (2); v A 1975 (3); v In 1974 (4); v P 1974 (2)*

Jumadeen, R. R. 12: v A 1972 (1) 1977 (2); v NZ 1971 (1); v In 1975 (4); v P 1976 (1); *v E 1976 (1); v In 1978 (2)*

Kallicharran, A. I. 66: v E 1973 (5); v A 1972 (5) 1977 (5); v NZ 1971 (2); v In 1975 (4); v P 1976 (5); *v E 1973 (3) 1976 (3) 1980 (5); v A 1975 (6) 1979 (3); v NZ 1979 (3); v In 1974 (5) 1978 (6); v P 1974 (2) 1980 (4)*

Kanhai, R. B. 79: v E 1959 (5) 1967 (5) 1973 (5); v A 1964 (5) 1972 (5); v In 1961 (5) 1970 (5); v P 1957 (5); *v E 1957 (5) 1963 (5) 1966 (5) 1973 (3); v A 1960 (5) 1968 (5); v In 1958 (5) 1966 (3); v P 1958 (3)*

Kentish, E. S. M. 2: v E 1947 (1) 1953 (1)

King, C. L. 9: v P 1976 (1); *v E 1976 (3) 1980 (1); v A 1979 (1); v NZ 1979 (3)*

King, F. M. 14: v E 1953 (3); v A 1954 (4); v In 1952 (5); *v NZ 1955 (2)*

King, L. A. 2: v E 1967 (1); v In 1961 (1)

King, R. D. 12: v P 1999 (3); v Z 1999 (2); *v E 2000 (4); v SA 1998 (1); v NZ 1999 (2)*

Lambert, C. B. 5: v E 1997 (2); *v E 1991 (1); v SA 1998 (2)*

Lara, B. C. 70: v E 1993 (5) 1997 (6); v A 1994 (4) 1998 (4); v SA 1991 (1); v NZ 1995 (2); v In 1996 (5); v P 1992 (3); v SL 1996 (2); *v E 1995 (6) 2000 (5); v A 1992 (5) 1996 (5); v SA 1998 (5); v NZ 1994 (2) 1999 (2); v In 1994 (3); v P 1990 (1) 1997 (3); v SL 1993 (1)*

Lashley, P. D. 4: *v E 1966 (2); v A 1960 (2)*

Legall, R. 4: v In 1952 (4)

Lewis, D. M. 3: v In 1970 (3)

Lewis, R. N. 3: *v SA 1998 (2); v P 1997 (1)*

Lloyd, C. H. 110: v E 1967 (5) 1973 (5) 1980 (4); v A 1972 (3) 1977 (2) 1983 (4); v NZ 1971 (2); v In 1970 (5) 1975 (4) 1982 (5); v P 1976 (5); *v E 1969 (3) 1973 (3) 1976 (5) 1980 (4) 1984 (5); v A 1968 (4) 1975 (6) 1979 (2) 1981 (3) 1984 (5); v NZ 1968 (3) 1979 (3); v In 1966 (3) 1974 (5) 1983 (6); v P 1974 (2) 1980 (4)*

Logie, A. L. 52: v E 1989 (3); v A 1983 (1) 1990 (5); v NZ 1984 (4); v In 1982 (5) 1988 (4); v P 1987 (3); *v E 1988 (5) 1991 (4); v A 1988 (5); v NZ 1986 (4); v In 1983 (3) 1987 (4); v P 1990 (3)*

McLean, N. A. M. 12: v E 1997 (4); v P 1999 (2); *v E 2000 (2); v SA 1998 (4)*

McMorris, E. D. A. St J. 13: v E 1959 (4); v In 1961 (4); v P 1957 (1); *v E 1963 (2) 1966 (2)*

McWatt, C. A. 6: v E 1953 (5); v A 1954 (1)

Madray, I. S. 2: v P 1957 (2)

Marshall, M. D. 81: v E 1980 (1) 1985 (5) 1989 (2); v A 1983 (4) 1990 (5); v NZ 1984 (4); v In 1982 (5) 1988 (3); v P 1987 (2); *v E 1980 (4) 1984 (4) 1988 (5) 1991 (5); v A 1984 (5) 1988 (5); v NZ 1986 (3); v In 1978 (3) 1983 (6); v P 1980 (4) 1986 (3) 1990 (3)*

Marshall, N. E. 1: v A 1954

Marshall, R. E. 4: *v A 1951 (2); v NZ 1951 (2)*

Martin, F. R. 9: v E 1929 (1); *v E 1928 (3); v A 1930 (5)*

Martindale, E. A. 10: v E 1934 (4); *v E 1933 (3) 1939 (3)*

Mattis, E. H. 4: v E 1980 (4)

Mendonca, I. L. 2: v In 1961 (2)

Merry, C. A. 2: *v E 1933 (2)*

Miller, R. 1: v In 1952

Moodie, G. H. 1: v E 1934

Moseley, E. A. 2: v E 1989 (2)

Murray, D. A. 19: v E 1980 (4); v A 1977 (3); *v A 1981 (2); v In 1978 (6); v P 1980 (4)*

Murray, D. L. 62: v E 1967 (5) 1973 (5); v A 1972 (4) 1977 (2); v In 1975 (4); v P 1976 (5); *v E 1963 (5) 1973 (3) 1976 (5) 1980 (5); v A 1975 (6) 1979 (3); v NZ 1979 (3); v In 1974 (5); v P 1974 (2)*

Murray, J. R. 31: v E 1993 (5) 1997 (1); v A 1994 (3); v In 1996 (2); v P 1992 (3); *v E 1995 (4); v A 1992 (3) 1996 (2); v SA 1998 (2); v NZ 1994 (2); v In 1994 (3); v SL 1993 (1)*

Nagamootoo, M. V. 1: *v E 2000*

Nanan, R. 1: *v P 1980*

Neblett, J. M. 1: v E 1934

Noreiga, J. M. 4: v In 1970 (4)

Nunes, R. K. 4: v E 1929 (1); *v E 1928 (3)*

Nurse, S. M. 29: v E 1959 (1) 1967 (5); v A 1964 (4); v In 1961 (1); *v E 1966 (5); v A 1960 (3) 1968 (5); v NZ 1968 (3); v In 1966 (2)*

Padmore, A. L. 2: v In 1975 (1); *v E 1976 (1)*

Pairaudeau, B. H. 13: v E 1953 (2); v In 1952 (5): *v E 1957 (2); v NZ 1955 (4)*

Parry, D. R. 12: v A 1977 (5); *v NZ 1979 (1); v In 1978 (6)*

Passailaigue, C. C. 1: v E 1929

Patterson, B. P. 28: v E 1985 (5) 1989 (1); v A 1990 (5); v SA 1991 (1); v P 1987 (1); *v E 1988 (2) 1991 (3); v A 1988 (4) 1992 (1); v In 1987 (4); v P 1986 (1)*

Payne, T. R. O. 1: v E 1985

Perry, N. O. 4: v A 1998 (3); *v NZ 1999 (1)*

Phillip, N. 9: v A 1977 (3); *v In 1978 (6)*

Pierre, L. R. 1: v E 1947

Powell, R. L. 1: *v NZ 1999*

Rae, A. F. 15: v In 1952 (2); *v E 1950 (4); v A 1951 (3); v NZ 1951 (1); v In 1948 (5)*

Ragoonath, S. 2: v A 1998 (2)

Ramadhin, S. 43: v E 1953 (5) 1959 (4); v A 1954 (4); v In 1952 (4); *v E 1950 (4) 1957 (5); v A 1951 (5) 1960 (2); v NZ 1951 (2) 1955 (4); v In 1958 (2); v P 1958 (2)*

Ramnarine, D. 3: v E 1997 (2); *v NZ 1999 (1)*

Reifer, F. L. 4: v SL 1996 (2); *v SA 1998 (2)*

Richards, I. V. A. 121: v E 1980 (4) 1985 (5) 1989 (3); v A 1977 (2) 1983 (5) 1990 (5); v NZ 1984 (4); v In 1975 (4) 1982 (5) 1988 (4); v P 1976 (5) 1987 (2); *v E 1976 (4) 1980 (5) 1984 (5) 1988 (5) 1991 (5); v A 1975 (6) 1979 (3) 1981 (3) 1984 (5) 1988 (5); v NZ 1986 (3); v In 1974 (5) 1983 (6) 1987 (4); v P 1974 (2) 1980 (4) 1986 (3)*

Richardson, R. B. 86: v E 1985 (5) 1989 (5) 1993 (4); v A 1983 (5) 1990 (5) 1994 (4); v SA 1991 (1); v NZ 1984 (4); v In 1988 (4); v P 1987 (3) 1992 (3); *v E 1988 (3) 1991 (5) 1995 (6); v A 1984 (5) 1988 (5) 1992 (5); v NZ 1986 (3); v In 1983 (1) 1987 (4); v P 1986 (3) 1990 (3); v SL 1993 (1)*

Rickards, K. R. 2: v E 1947 (1); *v A 1951 (1)*

Roach, C. A. 16: v E 1929 (4) 1934 (1); *v E 1928 (3) 1933 (3); v A 1930 (5)*

Roberts, A. M. E. 47: v E 1973 (1) 1980 (3); v A 1977 (2); v In 1975 (2) 1982 (5); v P 1976 (5); *v E 1976 (5) 1980 (3); v A 1975 (5) 1979 (3) 1981 (2); v NZ 1979 (2); v In 1974 (5) 1983 (2); v P 1974 (2)*

Roberts, A. T. 1: v NZ 1955
Roberts, L. A. 1: v A 1998
Rodriguez, W. V. 5: v E 1967 (1); v A 1964 (1); v In 1961 (2); *v E 1963 (1)*
Rose, F. A. 19: v E 1997 (1); v In 1996 (5); v P 1999 (1); v SL 1996 (2); v Z 1999 (2); *v E 2000 (3); v SA 1998 (1); v NZ 1999 (2); v P 1997 (2)*
Rowe, L. G. 30: v E 1973 (5); v A 1972 (3); v NZ 1971 (4); v In 1975 (4); *v E 1976 (2); v A 1975 (6) 1979 (3); v NZ 1979 (3)*

St Hill, E. L. 2: v E 1929 (2)
St Hill, W. H. 3: v E 1929 (1); *v E 1928 (2)*
Samuels, R. G. 6: v NZ 1995 (2); *v A 1996 (4)*
Sarwan, R. R. 5: v P 1999 (2); *v E 2000 (3)*
Scarlett, R. O. 3: v E 1959 (3)
Scott, A. P. H. 1: v In 1952
Scott, O. C. 8: v E 1929 (1); *v E 1928 (2); v A 1930 (5)*
Sealey, B. J. 1: *v E 1933*
Sealy, J. E. D. 11: v E 1929 (2) 1934 (4); *v E 1939 (3); v A 1930 (2)*
Shepherd, J. N. 5: v In 1970 (2); *v E 1969 (3)*
Shillingford, G. C. 7: v NZ 1971 (2); v In 1970 (3); *v E 1969 (2)*
Shillingford, I. T. 4: v A 1977 (1); v P 1976 (3)
Shivnarine, S. 8: v A 1977 (3); *v In 1978 (5)*
Simmons, P. V. 26: v E 1993 (2); v SA 1991 (1); v NZ 1995 (2); v P 1987 (1) 1992 (3); *v E 1991 (5); v A 1992 (5) 1996 (1); v In 1987 (1) 1994 (3); v P 1997 (1); v SL 1993 (1)*
Singh, C. K. 2: v E 1959 (2)
Small, J. A. 3: v E 1929 (1); *v E 1928 (2)*
Small, M. A. 2: v A 1983 (1); *v E 1984 (1)*
Smith, C. W. 5: v In 1961 (1); *v A 1960 (4)*
Smith, O. G. 26: v A 1954 (4); v P 1957 (5); *v E 1957 (5); v NZ 1955 (4); v In 1958 (5); v P 1958 (3)*
Sobers, G. S. 93: v E 1953 (1) 1959 (5) 1967 (5) 1973 (4); v A 1954 (4) 1964 (5); v NZ 1971 (5); v In 1961 (5) 1970 (5); v P 1957 (5); *v E 1957 (5) 1963 (5) 1966 (5) 1969 (3) 1973 (3); v A 1960 (5) 1968 (5); v NZ 1955 (4) 1968 (3); v In 1958 (5) 1966 (3); v P 1958 (3)*
Solomon, J. S. 27: v E 1959 (2); v A 1964 (4); v In 1961 (4); *v E 1963 (5); v A 1960 (5); v In 1958 (4); v P 1958 (3)*
Stayers, S. C. 4: v In 1961 (4)
Stollmeyer, J. B. 32: v E 1947 (2) 1953 (5); v A 1954 (2); v In 1952 (5); *v E 1939 (3) 1950 (4); v A 1951 (5); v NZ 1951 (2); v In 1948 (4)*
Stollmeyer, V. H. 1: *v E 1939*

Taylor, J. 3: v P 1957 (1); *v In 1958 (1); v P 1958 (1)*
Thompson, P. I. C. 2: v NZ 1995 (1); *v A 1996 (1)*
Trim, J. 4: v E 1947 (1), *v A 1951 (1); v In 1948 (2)*

Valentine, A. L. 36: v E 1953 (3); v A 1954 (3); v In 1952 (5) 1961 (2); v P 1957 (1), *v E 1950 (4) 1957 (2); v A 1951 (5) 1960 (5); v NZ 1951 (2) 1955 (4)*
Valentine, V. A. 2: *v E 1933 (2)*

Walcott, C. L. 44: v E 1947 (4) 1953 (5) 1959 (2); v A 1954 (5); v In 1952 (5); v P 1957 (4); *v E 1950 (4) 1957 (5); v A 1951 (3); v NZ 1951 (2); v In 1948 (5)*
Walcott, L. A. 1: v E 1929
Wallace, P. A. 7: v E 1997 (2); *v SA 1998 (4); v P 1997 (1)*
Walsh, C. A. 122: v E 1985 (1) 1989 (3) 1993 (5) 1997 (6); v A 1990 (5) 1994 (4) 1998 (4); v SA 1991 (1); v NZ 1984 (1) 1995 (2); v In 1988 (4) 1996 (4); v P 1987 (3) 1992 (3) 1999 (3); v SL 1996 (2); v Z 1999 (2); *v E 1988 (5) 1991 (5) 1995 (6) 2000 (5); v A 1984 (5) 1988 (5) 1992 (5) 1996 (5); v SA 1998 (4); v NZ 1986 (3) 1994 (2) 1999 (2); v In 1987 (4) 1994 (3); v P 1986 (3) 1990 (3) 1997 (3); v SL 1993 (1)*
Watson, C. 7: v E 1959 (5); v In 1961 (1); *v A 1960 (1)*
Weekes, E. D. 48: v E 1947 (4) 1953 (4); v A 1954 (5); v In 1952 (5); v P 1957 (5); *v E 1950 (4) 1957 (5); v A 1951 (5); v NZ 1951 (2) 1955 (4); v In 1948 (5)*
Weekes, K. H. 2: *v E 1939 (2)*

White, W. A. 2: v A 1964 (2)
Wight, C. V. 2: v E 1929 (1); *v E 1928 (1)*
Wight, G. L. 1: v In 1952
Wiles, C. A. 1: *v E 1933*
Willett, E. T. 5: v A 1972 (3); *v In 1974 (2)*
Williams, A. B. 7: v A 1977 (3); *v In 1978 (4)*
Williams, D. 11: v E 1997 (5); v SA 1991 (1); *v A 1992 (2); v P 1997 (3)*
Williams, E. A. V. 4: v E 1947 (3); *v E 1939 (1)*
Williams, S. C. 28: v E 1993 (1) 1997 (4); v A 1994 (4); v In 1996 (5); v SL 1996 (2); *v E 1995 (2); v SA 1998 (2); v NZ 1994 (2); v In 1994 (3); v P 1997 (3)*
Wishart, K. L. 1: v E 1934
Worrell, F. M. M. 51: v E 1947 (3) 1953 (4) 1959 (4); v A 1954 (4); v In 1952 (5) 1961 (5); *v E 1950 (4) 1957 (5) 1963 (5); v A 1951 (5) 1960 (5); v NZ 1951 (2)*

NEW ZEALAND

Number of Test cricketers: 209

Alabaster, J. C. 21: v E 1962 (2); v WI 1955 (1); v In 1967 (4); *v E 1958 (2); v SA 1961 (5); v WI 1971 (2); v In 1955 (4); v P 1955 (1)*
Allcott, C. F. W. 6: v E 1929 (2); v SA 1931 (1); *v E 1931 (3)*
Allott, G. I. 10: v E 1996 (2); v SA 1998 (2); v Z 1995 (2); *v E 1999 (2); v A 1997 (2)*
Anderson, R. W. 9: v E 1977 (3); *v E 1978 (3); v P 1976 (3)*
Anderson, W. M. 1: v A 1945
Andrews, B. 2: *v A 1973 (2)*
Astle, N. J. 37: v E 1996 (3); v A 1999 (3); v SA 1998 (3); v WI 1999 (2); v In 1998 (1); v SL 1996 (2); v Z 1995 (2) 1997 (2); *v E 1999 (4); v A 1997 (3); v WI 1995 (3); v In 1999 (3); v P 1996 (2); v SL 1997 (3); v Z 1997 (2)*

Badcock, F. T. 7: v E 1929 (3) 1932 (2); v SA 1931 (2)
Barber, R. T. 1: v WI 1955
Bartlett, G. A. 10: v E 1965 (2); v In 1967 (2); v P 1964 (1); *v SA 1961 (5)*
Barton, P. T. 7: v E 1962 (3); *v SA 1961 (4)*
Beard, D. D. 4: v WI 1951 (2) 1955 (2)
Beck, J. E. F. 8: v WI 1955 (4); *v SA 1953 (4)*
Bell, M. D. 8: v SA 1998 (1); v In 1998 (2); *v E 1999 (3); In 1999 (2)*
Bell, W. 2: *v SA 1953 (2)*
Bilby, G. P. 2: v E 1965 (2)
Blain, T. E. 11: v A 1992 (2); v P 1993 (3); *v E 1986 (1); v A 1993 (3); v In 1988 (2)*
Blair, R. W. 19: v E 1954 (1) 1958 (2) 1962 (2); v SA 1952 (2) 1963 (3); v WI 1955 (2); *v E 1958 (3); v SA 1953 (4)*
Blunt, R. C. 9: v E 1929 (4); v SA 1931 (2); *v E 1931 (3)*
Bolton, B. A. 2: v E 1958 (2)
Boock, S. L. 30: v E 1977 (3) 1983 (2) 1987 (1); v WI 1979 (3) 1986 (2); v P 1978 (3) 1984 (2) 1988 (1); *v E 1978 (3); v A 1985 (1); v WI 1984 (3); v P 1984 (3); v SL 1983 (3)*
Bracewell, B. P. 6: v P 1978 (1) 1984 (1); *v E 1978 (3); v A 1980 (1)*
Bracewell, J. G. 41: v E 1987 (3); v A 1985 (2) 1989 (1); v WI 1986 (3); v In 1980 (1) 1989 (2); v P 1988 (2); *v E 1983 (4) 1986 (3) 1990 (3); v A 1980 (3) 1985 (2) 1987 (3); v WI 1984 (1); v In 1988 (3); v P 1984 (2); v SL 1983 (2) 1986 (1)*
Bradburn, G. E. 5: v SL 1990 (1); *v P 1990 (3); v SL 1992 (1)*
Bradburn, W. P. 2: v SA 1963 (2)
Brown, V. R. 2: *v A 1985 (2)*
Burgess, M. G. 50: v E 1970 (1) 1977 (3); v A 1973 (1) 1976 (2); v WI 1968 (2); v In 1967 (4) 1975 (3); v P 1972 (3) 1978 (3); *v E 1969 (2) 1973 (3) 1978 (3); v A 1980 (3); v WI 1971 (5); v In 1969 (3) 1976 (3); v P 1969 (3) 1976 (3)*
Burke, C. 1: v A 1945
Burtt, T. B. 10: v E 1946 (1) 1950 (2); v SA 1952 (1); v WI 1951 (2); *v E 1949 (4)*
Butterfield, L. A. 1: v A 1945

Cairns, B. L. 43: v E 1974 (1) 1977 (1) 1983 (3); v A 1976 (1) 1981 (3); v WI 1979 (3); v In 1975 (1) 1980 (3); v P 1978 (3) 1984 (3); v SL 1982 (2); *v E 1978 (2) 1983 (4); v A 1973 (1) 1980 (3) 1985 (1); v WI 1984 (2); v In 1976 (2); v P 1976 (2); v SL 1983 (2)*

Cairns, C. L. 47: v E 1991 (3) 1996 (3); v A 1992 (2) 1999 (3); v WI 1999 (3); v In 1998 (2); v P 1993 (1) 1995 (1); v SL 1990 (1) 1996 (2); v Z 1995 (2) 1997 (2); *v E 1999 (4); v A 1989 (1) 1993 (2) 1997 (3); v In 1995 (3) 1999 (3); v P 1996 (2); v SL 1997 (3); v Z 1997 (2)*

Cameron, F. J. 19: v E 1962 (3); v SA 1963 (3); v P 1964 (3); *v E 1965 (3); v SA 1961 (5); v In 1964 (1); v P 1964 (2)*

Cave, H. B. 19: v E 1954 (2); v WI 1955 (3); *v E 1949 (4) 1958 (2); v In 1955 (5); v P 1955 (3)*

Chapple, M. E. 14: v E 1954 (1) 1965 (1); v SA 1952 (1) 1963 (3); v WI 1955 (1); *v SA 1953 (5) 1961 (2)*

Chatfield, E. J. 43: v E 1974 (1) 1977 (1) 1983 (3) 1987 (3); v A 1976 (2) 1981 (1) 1985 (3); v WI 1986 (3); v P 1984 (3) 1988 (2); v SL 1982 (2); *v E 1983 (3) 1986 (1); v A 1985 (2) 1987 (2); v WI 1984 (3); v In 1988 (3); v P 1984 (1); v SL 1983 (2) 1986 (1)*

Cleverley, D. C. 2: v SA 1931 (1); v A 1945 (1)

Collinge, R. O. 35: v E 1970 (2) 1974 (2) 1977 (3); v A 1973 (3); v In 1967 (2) 1975 (2); v P 1964 (3) 1972 (2); *v E 1965 (3) 1969 (1) 1973 (3) 1978 (1); v In 1964 (2) 1976 (1); v P 1964 (2) 1976 (2)*

Colquhoun, I. A. 2: v E 1954 (2)

Coney, J. V. 52: v E 1983 (3); v A 1973 (3) 1981 (3) 1985 (3); v WI 1979 (3) 1986 (3); v In 1980 (3); v P 1978 (3) 1984 (3); v SL 1982 (2); *v E 1983 (4) 1986 (3); v A 1973 (2) 1980 (2) 1985 (3); v WI 1984 (4); v In 1976 (2); v P 1984 (3); v SL 1983 (3)*

Congdon, B. E. 61: v E 1965 (3) 1970 (2) 1974 (2) 1977 (3); v A 1973 (3) 1976 (2); v WI 1968 (3); v In 1967 (4) 1975 (3); v P 1964 (3) 1972 (2); *v E 1965 (3) 1969 (3) 1973 (3) 1978 (3); v A 1973 (3); v WI 1971 (5); v In 1964 (3) 1969 (3); v P 1964 (1) 1969 (3)*

Cowie, J. 9: v E 1946 (1); v A 1945 (1); *v E 1937 (3) 1949 (4)*

Cresswell G. F. 3: v E 1950 (2); *v E 1949 (1)*

Cromb, I. B. 5: v SA 1931 (2); *v E 1931 (3)*

Crowe, J. J. 39: v E 1983 (3) 1987 (2); v A 1989 (1); v WI 1986 (3); v P 1984 (3) 1988 (2); v SL 1982 (2); *v E 1983 (2) 1986 (3); v A 1985 (3) 1987 (3) 1989 (1); v WI 1984 (4); v P 1984 (3); v SL 1983 (3) 1986 (1)*

Crowe, M. D. 77: v E 1983 (3) 1987 (3) 1991 (3); v A 1981 (3) 1985 (3) 1992 (3); v SA 1994 (1); v WI 1986 (3); v In 1989 (3); v P 1984 (3) 1988 (2); v SL 1990 (2); *v E 1983 (4) 1986 (3) 1990 (3) 1994 (3); v A 1985 (3) 1987 (3) 1989 (1) 1993 (1); v SA 1994 (3); v WI 1984 (4); v In 1995 (3); v P 1984 (3) 1990 (3); v SL 1983 (3) 1986 (1) 1992 (2); v Z 1992 (2)*

Cunis, R. S. 20: v E 1965 (3) 1970 (2); v SA 1963 (1); v WI 1968 (3); *v E 1969 (1); v WI 1971 (5); v In 1969 (3); v P 1969 (2)*

D'Arcy, J. W. 5: *v E 1958 (5)*

Davis, H. T. 5: v E 1996 (1); v SL 1996 (2); *v E 1994 (1); v Z 1997 (1)*

de Groen, R. P. 5: v P 1993 (2); *v A 1993 (2); v SA 1994 (1)*

Dempster, C. S. 10: v E 1929 (4) 1932 (2); v SA 1931 (2); *v E 1931 (2)*

Dempster, E. W. 5: v SA 1952 (1); *v SA 1953 (4)*

Dick, A. E. 17: v E 1962 (3); v SA 1963 (3); v P 1964 (2); *v E 1965 (2); v SA 1961 (5); v P 1964 (3)*

Dickinson, G. R. 3: v E 1929 (1); v SA 1931 (1)

Donnelly, M. P. 7: *v E 1937 (3) 1949 (4)*

Doull, S. B. 32: v E 1996 (3); v A 1999 (2); v SA 1998 (3); v WI 1994 (2); v In 1998 (3); v P 1993 (1); v SL 1996 (2); v Z 1997 (2); *v E 1999 (1); v A 1993 (2) 1997 (3); v SA 1994 (3); v P 1996 (2); v SL 1997 (1); v Z 1992 (1)*

Dowling, G. T. 39: v E 1962 (3) 1970 (2); v SA 1963 (3); v WI 1968 (3); v In 1967 (4); v P 1964 (2); *v E 1965 (3) 1969 (3); v SA 1961 (4); v WI 1971 (2); v In 1964 (4) 1969 (3); v P 1964 (2) 1969 (3)*

Dunning, J. A. 4: v E 1932 (1); *v E 1937 (3)*

Edgar, B. A. 39: v E 1983 (3); v A 1981 (3) 1985 (3); v WI 1979 (3); v In 1980 (3); v P 1978 (3); v SL 1982 (2); *v E 1978 (3) 1983 (4) 1986 (3); v A 1980 (3) 1985 (3); v P 1984 (3)*

Edwards, G. N. 8: v E 1977 (1); v A 1976 (2); v In 1980 (2); *v E 1978 (2)*

Emery, R. W. G. 2: v WI 1951 (2)

Fisher, F. E. 1: v SA 1952

Fleming, S. P. 51: v E 1996 (3); v A 1999 (3); v SA 1994 (1); v WI 1994 (2) 1999 (2); v In 1993 (1) 1998 (2); v P 1995 (1); v SL 1994 (2) 1996 (2); v Z 1995 (2) 1997 (2); *v E 1994 (3) 1999 (4); v A 1997 (3); SA 1994 (3); v WI 1995 (2); v In 1995 (3) 1999 (3); v P 1996 (2); v SL 1997 (3); v Z 1997 (2)*

Foley, H. 1: v E 1929

Franklin, T. J. 21: v E 1987 (3); v A 1985 (1) 1989 (1); v In 1989 (3); v SL 1990 (3); *v E 1983 (1) 1990 (3); v In 1988 (3); v P 1990 (3)*

Freeman, D. L. 2: v E 1932 (2)

Gallichan, N. 1: *v E 1937*

Gedye, S. G. 4: v SA 1963 (3); v P 1964 (1)

Germon, L. K. 12: v E 1996 (2); v P 1995 (1); v Z 1995 (2); *v WI 1995 (2); v In 1995 (3); v P 1996 (2)*

Gillespie, S. R. 1: v A 1985

Gray, E. J. 10: *v E 1983 (2) 1986 (3); v A 1987 (1); v In 1988 (1); v P 1984 (2); v SL 1986 (1)*

Greatbatch, M. J. 41: v E 1987 (2) 1991 (1); v A 1989 (1) 1992 (3); v In 1989 (3) 1993 (1); v P 1988 (1) 1992 (1) 1993 (3); v SL 1990 (2) 1994 (2); *v E 1990 (3) 1994 (1); v A 1989 (1) 1993 (3); v In 1988 (3) 1995 (3); v P 1990 (3) 1996 (2); v Z 1992 (2)*

Guillen, S. C. 3: v WI 1955 (3)

Guy, J. W. 12: v E 1958 (2); v WI 1955 (2); *v SA 1961 (2); v In 1955 (5); v P 1955 (1)*

Hadlee, D. R. 26: v E 1974 (2) 1977 (1); v A 1973 (3) 1976 (1); v In 1975 (3); v P 1972 (2); *v E 1969 (2) 1973 (3); v A 1973 (3); v In 1969 (3); v P 1969 (3)*

Hadlee, R. J. 86: v E 1977 (3) 1983 (3) 1987 (1); v A 1973 (3) 1976 (2) 1981 (3) 1985 (3) 1989 (1); v WI 1979 (3) 1986 (3); v In 1975 (2) 1980 (3) 1989 (3); v P 1972 (1) 1978 (3) 1984 (3) 1988 (2); v SL 1982 (2); *v E 1973 (1) 1978 (3) 1983 (4) 1986 (3) 1990 (3); v A 1973 (3) 1980 (3) 1985 (3) 1987 (3); v WI 1984 (4); v In 1976 (3) 1988 (3); v P 1976 (3); v SL 1983 (3) 1986 (1)*

Hadlee, W. A. 11: v E 1946 (1) 1950 (2); v A 1945 (1); *v E 1937 (3) 1949 (4)*

Harford, N. S. 8: *v E 1958 (4); v In 1955 (2); v P 1955 (2)*

Harford, R. I. 3: v In 1967 (3)

Harris, C. Z. 19: v A 1992 (1); v SA 1998 (3); v P 1992 (2); *v E 1999 (1); v A 1993 (1) 1997 (1); v WI 1995 (2); v In 1999 (1); v P 1996 (2); v SL 1992 (2) 1997 (2); v Z 1997 (2)*

Harris, P. G. Z. 9: v P 1964 (1); *v SA 1961 (5); v In 1955 (1); v P 1955 (2)*

Harris, R. M. 2: v E 1958 (2)

Hart, M. N. 14: v SA 1994 (1); v WI 1994 (2); v In 1993 (1); v P 1993 (2); *v E 1994 (3); v SA 1994 (3); v In 1995 (2)*

Hartland, B. R. 9: v E 1991 (3); v In 1993 (1); v P 1992 (1) 1993 (1), *v E 1994 (1); v SL 1992 (2)*

Haslam, M. J. 4: *v In 1995 (2); v Z 1992 (2)*

Hastings, B. F. 31: v E 1974 (2); v A 1973 (3); v WI 1968 (3); v In 1975 (1); v P 1972 (3); *v E 1969 (3) 1973 (3); v A 1973 (3); v WI 1971 (5); v In 1969 (2); v P 1969 (3)*

Hayes, J. A. 15: v E 1950 (2) 1954 (1); v WI 1951 (2); *v E 1958 (4); v In 1955 (5); v P 1955 (1)*

Henderson, M. 1: v E 1929

Horne, M. J. 27: v E 1996 (1); v A 1999 (3); v SA 1998 (3); v WI 1999 (1); v In 1998 (2); v SL 1996 (2); v Z 1997 (2); *v E 1999 (4); v A 1997 (1); v In 1999 (3); v SL 1997 (3); v Z 1997 (2)*

Horne, P. A. 4: v WI 1986 (1); *v A 1987 (1); v P 1990 (1); v SL 1986 (1)*

Hough, K. W. 2: v E 1958 (2)

Howarth, G. P. 47: v E 1974 (2) 1977 (3) 1983 (3); v A 1976 (2) 1981 (3); v WI 1979 (3); v In 1980 (3); v P 1978 (3) 1984 (3); v SL 1982 (2); *v E 1978 (3) 1983 (4); v A 1980 (2); v WI 1984 (4); v In 1976 (2); v P 1976 (2); v SL 1983 (3)*

Howarth, H. J. 30: v E 1970 (2) 1974 (2); v A 1973 (3) 1976 (2); v In 1975 (2); v P 1972 (3); *v E 1969 (3) 1973 (2); v WI 1971 (5); v In 1969 (3); v P 1969 (3)*

James, K. C. 11: v E 1929 (4) 1932 (2); v SA 1931 (2); *v E 1931 (3)*

Jarvis, T. W. 13: v E 1965 (1); v P 1972 (3); *v WI 1971 (4); v In 1964 (2); v P 1964 (3)*

Jones, A. H. 39: v E 1987 (1) 1991 (3); v A 1989 (1) 1992 (3); v WI 1994 (2); v In 1989 (3); v P 1988 (2) 1992 (1) 1993 (3); v SL 1990 (3); *v E 1990 (3); v A 1987 (3) 1993 (3); v In 1988 (3); v SL 1986 (1) 1992 (1); v Z 1992 (2)*

Kennedy, R. J. 4: v Z 1995 (2); *v WI 1995 (2)*

Kerr, J. L. 7: v E 1932 (2); v SA 1931 (1); *v E 1931 (2) 1937 (2)*

Kuggeleijn, C. M. 2: v In 1988 (2)

Larsen, G. R. 8: v SA 1994 (1); v P 1995 (1); v SL 1994 (2); v Z 1995 (1); *v E 1994 (1); v WI 1995 (2)*
Latham, R. T. 4: v E 1991 (1); v P 1992 (1); *v Z 1992 (2)*
Lees, W. K. 21: v E 1977 (2); v A 1976 (1); v WI 1979 (3); v P 1978 (3); v SL 1982 (2); *v E 1983 (2); v A 1980 (2); v In 1976 (3); v P 1976 (3)*
Leggat, I. B. 1: *v SA 1953*
Leggat, J. G. 9: v E 1954 (1); v SA 1952 (1); v WI 1951 (1) 1955 (1); *v In 1955 (3); v P 1955 (2)*
Lissette, A. F. 2: v WI 1955 (2)
Loveridge, G. R. 1: v Z 1995
Lowry, T. C. 7: v E 1929 (4); *v E 1931 (3)*

McEwan, P. E. 4: v WI 1979 (1); *v A 1980 (2); v P 1984 (1)*
MacGibbon, A. R. 26: v E 1950 (2) 1954 (2); v SA 1952 (1); v WI 1955 (3); *v E 1958 (5); v SA 1953 (5); v In 1955 (5); v P 1955 (3)*
McGirr, H. M. 2: v E 1929 (2)
McGregor, S. N. 25: v E 1954 (2) 1958 (2); v SA 1963 (3); v WI 1955 (4); v P 1964 (2); *v SA 1961 (2); v In 1955 (4); v P 1955 (3)*
McLeod, E. G. 1: v E 1929
McMahon, T. G. 5: v WI 1955 (1); *v In 1955 (3); v P 1955 (1)*
McMillan, C. D. 22: v A 1999 (3); v SA 1998 (1); v WI 1999 (2); v In 1998 (2); v Z 1997 (2); *v E 1999 (4); v A 1997 (3); v In 1999 (2); v SL 1997 (3)*
McRae, D. A. N. 1: v A 1945
Matheson, A. M. 2: v E 1929 (1); *v E 1931 (1)*
Meale, T. 2: *v E 1958 (2)*
Merritt, W. E. 6: v E 1929 (4); *v E 1931 (2)*
Meuli, E. M. 1: v SA 1952
Milburn, B. D. 3: v WI 1968 (3)
Miller, L. S. M. 13: v SA 1952 (2); v WI 1955 (3); *v E 1958 (4); v SA 1953 (4)*
Mills, J. E. 7: v E 1929 (3) 1932 (1); *v E 1931 (3)*
Moir, A. M. 17: v E 1950 (2) 1954 (2) 1958 (2); v SA 1952 (1); v WI 1951 (2) 1955 (1); *v E 1958 (2); v In 1955 (2); v P 1955 (3)*
Moloney D. A. R. 3: *v E 1937 (3)*
Mooney, F. L. H. 14: v E 1950 (2); v SA 1952 (2); v WI 1951 (2); *v E 1949 (3); v SA 1953 (5)*
Morgan, R. W. 20: v E 1965 (2) 1970 (2); v WI 1968 (1); v P 1964 (2); *v E 1965 (3); v WI 1971 (3); v In 1964 (4); v P 1964 (3)*
Morrison, B. D. 1: v E 1962
Morrison, D. K. 48: v E 1987 (3) 1991 (3) 1996 (1); v A 1989 (1) 1992 (3); v SA 1994 (1); v WI 1994 (2); v In 1989 (3) 1993 (1); v P 1988 (1) 1992 (1) 1993 (2) 1995 (1); v SL 1990 (3) 1994 (1), *v E 1990 (3); v A 1987 (3) 1989 (1) 1993 (3); v SA 1994 (2); v WI 1995 (2); v In 1988 (1) 1995 (3); v P 1990 (3)*
Morrison, J. F. M. 17: v E 1974 (2); v A 1973 (3) 1981 (3); v In 1975 (3); *v A 1973 (3); v In 1976 (1); v P 1976 (2)*
Motz, R. C. 32: v E 1962 (2) 1965 (3); v SA 1963 (2); v WI 1968 (3); v In 1967 (4); v P 1964 (3); *v E 1965 (3) 1969 (3); v SA 1961 (5); v In 1964 (3); v P 1964 (1)*
Murray, B. A. G. 13: v E 1970 (1); v In 1967 (4); *v E 1969 (2); v In 1969 (3); v P 1969 (3)*
Murray, D. J. 8: v SA 1994 (1); v WI 1994 (2); v SL 1994 (2); *v SA 1994 (3)*

Nash, D. J. 30: v SA 1994 (1) 1998 (3); v WI 1994 (1) 1999 (2); v In 1993 (1) 1998 (2); v P 1995 (1); v SL 1994 (1); v Z 1997 (2); *v E 1994 (3) 1999 (4); v SA 1994 (1); v In 1995 (3) 1999 (3); v SL 1992 (1); v Z 1992 (1)*
Newman J. 3: v E 1932 (2); v SA 1931 (1)

O'Connor, S. B. 12: v A 1999 (2); v SA 1998 (1); v WI 1999 (1); v Z 1997 (1); *v E 1999 (1); v A 1997 (2); v In 1999 (1); v SL 1997 (1); v Z 1997 (2)*
O'Sullivan, D. R. 11: v In 1975 (1); v P 1972 (1); *v A 1973 (3); v In 1976 (3); v P 1976 (3)*
Overton, G. W. F. 3: *v SA 1953 (3)*
Owens, M. B. 8: v A 1992 (2); v P 1992 (1) 1993 (1); *v E 1994 (2); v SL 1992 (2)*

Page, M. L. 14: v E 1929 (4) 1932 (2); v SA 1931 (2); *v E 1931 (3) 1937 (3)*

Parker, J. M. 36: v E 1974 (2) 1977 (3); v A 1973 (3) 1976 (2); v WI 1979 (3); v In 1975 (3); v P 1972 (1) 1978 (2); *v E 1973 (3) 1978 (2); v A 1973 (3) 1980 (3); v In 1976 (3); v P 1976 (3)*

Parker, N. M. 3: *v In 1976 (2); v P 1976 (1)*

Parore, A. C. 61: v E 1991 (1) 1996 (3); v A 1992 (1) 1999 (3); v SA 1994 (1) 1998 (3); v WI 1994 (2) 1999 (2); v In 1993 (1) 1998 (2); v P 1992 (1) 1995 (1); v SL 1994 (2) 1996 (2); v Z 1995 (2) 1997 (2); *v E 1990 (1) 1994 (3) 1999 (4); v A 1997 (3); v SA 1994 (3); v WI 1995 (1); v In 1995 (3) 1999 (3); v P 1996 (2); v SL 1992 (2) 1997 (3); v Z 1992 (2) 1997 (2)*

Patel, D. N. 37: v E 1991 (3) 1996 (2); v A 1992 (3); v SA 1994 (1); v WI 1986 (3); v P 1988 (1) 1992 (1) 1995 (1); v SL 1990 (2) 1994 (1) 1996 (2); v Z 1995 (2); *v A 1987 (3) 1989 (1) 1993 (3); v WI 1995 (1); v P 1990 (3) 1996 (2); v Z 1992 (2)*

Petherick, P. J. 6: v A 1976 (1); *v In 1976 (3); v P 1976 (2)*

Petrie, E. C. 14: v E 1958 (2) 1965 (3); *v E 1958 (5); v In 1955 (2); v P 1955 (2)*

Playle, W. R. 8: v E 1962 (3); *v E 1958 (5)*

Pocock, B. A. 15: v E 1996 (3); v P 1993 (3); v SL 1996 (2); *v E 1994 (1); v A 1993 (3) 1997 (2); v Z 1997 (2)*

Pollard, V. 32: v E 1965 (3) 1970 (1); v WI 1968 (3); v In 1967 (4); v P 1972 (1); *v E 1965 (3) 1969 (3) 1973 (3); v In 1964 (4) 1969 (1); v P 1964 (3) 1969 (3)*

Poore, M. B. 14: v E 1954 (1); v SA 1952 (1); *v SA 1953 (5); v In 1955 (4); v P 1955 (3)*

Priest, M. W. 3: v Z 1997 (1); *v E 1990 (1); v SL 1997 (1)*

Pringle, C. 14: v E 1991 (1); v In 1993 (1); v P 1993 (1); v SL 1990 (2) 1994 (1); *v E 1994 (2); v SA 1994 (1); v P 1990 (3); v SL 1992 (1)*

Puna, N. 3: v E 1965 (3)

Rabone, G. O. 12: v E 1954 (2); v SA 1952 (1); v WI 1951 (2); *v E 1949 (4); v SA 1953 (3)*

Redmond, R. E. 1: v P 1972

Reid, J. F. 19: v A 1985 (3); v In 1980 (3); v P 1978 (1) 1984 (3); *v A 1985 (3); v P 1984 (3); v SL 1983 (3)*

Reid, J. R. 58: v E 1950 (2) 1954 (2) 1958 (2) 1962 (3); v SA 1952 (2) 1963 (3); v WI 1951 (2) 1955 (4); v P 1964 (3); *v E 1949 (2) 1958 (5) 1965 (3); v SA 1953 (5) 1961 (5); v In 1955 (5) 1964 (4); v P 1955 (3) 1964 (3)*

Roberts, A. D. G. 7: v In 1975 (2); *v In 1976 (3); v P 1976 (2)*

Roberts, A. W. 5: v E 1929 (1); v SA 1931 (2); *v E 1937 (2)*

Robertson, G. K. 1: v A 1985

Rowe, C. G. 1: v A 1945

Rutherford, K. R. 56: v E 1987 (2) 1991 (2); v A 1985 (3) 1989 (1) 1992 (3); v SA 1994 (1); v WI 1986 (2) 1994 (2); v In 1989 (3) 1993 (1); v P 1992 (1) 1993 (3); v SL 1990 (3) 1994 (2); *v E 1986 (1) 1990 (2) 1994 (3); v A 1987 (1) 1993 (3); v SA 1994 (3); v WI 1984 (4); v In 1988 (2); v P 1990 (3); v SL 1986 (1) 1992 (2); v Z 1992 (2)*

Scott, R. H. 1: v E 1946

Scott, V. J. 10: v E 1946 (1) 1950 (2); v A 1945 (1); v WI 1951 (2); *v E 1949 (4)*

Sewell, D. G. 1: *v Z 1997*

Shrimpton, M. J. F. 10: v E 1962 (2) 1965 (3) 1970 (2); v SA 1963 (1); *v A 1973 (2)*

Sinclair, B. W. 21: v E 1962 (3) 1965 (3); v SA 1963 (3); v In 1967 (2); v P 1964 (2); *v E 1965 (3); v In 1964 (2); v P 1964 (3)*

Sinclair, I. M. 2: v WI 1955 (2)

Sinclair, M. S. 4: v A 1999 (3); v WI 1999 (1)

Smith, F. B. 4: v E 1946 (1); v WI 1951 (1); *v E 1949 (2)*

Smith, H. D. 1: v E 1932

Smith, I. D. S. 63: v E 1983 (3) 1987 (3) 1991 (2); v A 1981 (3) 1985 (3) 1989 (1); v WI 1986 (3); v In 1980 (3) 1989 (3); v P 1984 (3) 1988 (2); v SL 1990 (3); *v E 1983 (3) 1986 (2) 1990 (2); v A 1980 (1) 1985 (3) 1987 (3) 1989 (1); v WI 1984 (4); v In 1988 (3); v P 1984 (3) 1990 (3); v SL 1983 (3) 1986 (1)*

Snedden, C. A. 1: v E 1946

Snedden, M. C. 25: v E 1983 (1) 1987 (2); v A 1981 (3) 1989 (1); v WI 1986 (1); v In 1980 (3) 1989 (3); v SL 1982 (2); *v E 1983 (1) 1990 (3); v A 1985 (1) 1987 (1) 1989 (1); v In 1988 (1); v SL 1986 (1)*

Sparling, J. T. 11: v E 1958 (2) 1962 (1); v SA 1963 (2); *v E 1958 (3); v SA 1961 (3)*

Spearman, C. M. 16: v A 1999 (3); v WI 1999 (2); v P 1995 (1); v Z 1995 (2); *v WI 1995 (2); v In 1999 (3); v SL 1997 (1); v Z 1997 (2)*

Stead, G. R. 5: v SA 1998 (2); v WI 1999 (2); *v In 1999 (1)*

Stirling, D. A. 6: *v E 1986 (2); v WI 1984 (1); v P 1984 (3)*

Su'a, M. L. 13: v E 1991 (2); v A 1992 (2); v WI 1994 (1); v P 1992 (1); v SL 1994 (1); *v A 1993 (2) 1994 (2); v Z 1992 (2)*

Sutcliffe, B. 42: v E 1946 (1) 1950 (2) 1954 (2) 1958 (2); v SA 1952 (2); v WI 1951 (2) 1955 (2); *v E 1949 (4) 1958 (4) 1965 (1); v SA 1953 (5); v In 1955 (5) 1964 (4); v P 1955 (3) 1964 (3)*

Taylor, B. R. 30: v E 1965 (1); v WI 1968 (3); v In 1967 (3); v P 1972 (3); *v E 1965 (2) 1969 (2) 1973 (3); v WI 1971 (4); v In 1964 (3) 1969 (2); v P 1964 (3) 1969 (1)*

Taylor, D. D. 3: v E 1946 (1); v WI 1955 (2)

Thomson, K. 2: v In 1967 (2)

Thomson, S. A. 19: v E 1991 (1); v WI 1994 (2); v In 1989 (1) 1993 (1); v P 1993 (3); v SL 1990 (2) 1994 (1); *v E 1994 (3); v SA 1994 (3); v In 1995 (2)*

Tindill, E. W. T. 5: v E 1946 (1); v A 1945 (1); *v E 1937 (3)*

Troup, G. B. 15: v A 1981 (2) 1985 (2); v WI 1979 (3); v In 1980 (2); v P 1978 (2); *v A 1980 (2); v WI 1984 (1); v In 1976 (1)*

Truscott, P. B. 1: v P 1964

Tuffey, D. R. 1: v A 1999

Turner, G. M. 41: v E 1970 (2) 1974 (2); v A 1973 (3) 1976 (2); v WI 1968 (3); v In 1975 (3); v P 1972 (3); v SL 1982 (2); *v E 1969 (2) 1973 (3); v A 1973 (2); v WI 1971 (5); v In 1969 (3) 1976 (3); v P 1969 (1) 1976 (2)*

Twose, R. G. 16: v SA 1998 (3); v In 1998 (1); v P 1995 (1); v Z 1995 (2); *v E 1999 (4); v A 1997 (1); v WI 1995 (2); v In 1995 (2)*

Vance, R. H. 4: v E 1987 (1); v P 1988 (2); *v A 1989 (1)*

Vaughan, J. T. C. 6: v E 1996 (1); *v WI 1995 (2); v P 1996 (2); v SL 1992 (1)*

Vettori, D. L. 30: v E 1996 (2); v A 1999 (2); v SA 1998 (3); v WI 1999 (2); v In 1998 (2); v SL 1996 (2); v Z 1997 (2); *v E 1999 (4); v A 1997 (3); v In 1999 (3); v SL 1997 (3); v Z 1997 (2)*

Vivian, G. E. 5: *v WI 1971 (4); v In 1964 (1)*

Vivian, H. G. 7: v E 1932 (1); v SA 1931 (1); *v E 1931 (2) 1937 (3)*

Wadsworth, K. J. 33: v E 1970 (2) 1974 (2); v A 1973 (3); v In 1975 (3); v P 1972 (3); *v E 1969 (3) 1973 (3); v A 1973 (3); v WI 1971 (5); v In 1969 (3); v P 1969 (3)*

Wallace, W. M. 13: v E 1946 (1) 1950 (2); v A 1945 (1); v SA 1952 (2); *v E 1937 (3) 1949 (4)*

Walmsley, K. P. 2: v SL 1994 (2)

Ward, J. T. 8: v SA 1963 (1); v In 1967 (1); v P 1964 (1); *v E 1965 (1); v In 1964 (4)*

Watson, W. 15: v E 1991 (1); v A 1992 (2); v SL 1990 (3); *v E 1986 (2); v A 1989 (1) 1993 (1); v P 1990 (3); v Z 1992 (2)*

Watt, L. 1: v E 1954

Webb, M. G. 3: v E 1970 (1); v A 1973 (1); *v WI 1971 (1)*

Webb, P. N. 2: v WI 1979 (2)

Weir, G. L. 11: v E 1929 (3) 1932 (2); v SA 1931 (2); *v E 1931 (3) 1937 (3)*

White, D. J. 2: *v P 1990 (2)*

Whitelaw, P. E. 2: v E 1932 (2)

Wiseman, P. J. 10: v A 1999 (2); v WI 1999 (1); v In 1998 (2); *v In 1999 (2); v SL 1997 (3)*

Wright, J. G. 82: v E 1977 (3) 1983 (3) 1987 (3) 1991 (3); v A 1981 (3) 1985 (2) 1989 (1) 1992 (3); v WI 1979 (3) 1986 (3); v In 1980 (3) 1989 (3); v P 1978 (3) 1984 (3)1988 (2); v SL 1982 (2) 1990 (3); *v E 1978 (2) 1983 (3) 1986 (3) 1990 (3); v A 1980 (3) 1985 (3) 1987 (3) 1989 (1); v WI 1984 (4); v In 1988 (3); v P 1984 (3); v SL 1983 (3) 1992 (2)*

Young, B. A. 35: v E 1996 (3); v SA 1994 (1) 1998 (2); v WI 1994 (2); v In 1993 (1); v P 1993 (3) 1995 (1); v SL 1994 (2) 1996 (2); v Z 1997 (2); *v E 1994 (3); v A 1993 (1) 1997 (3); v SA 1994 (3); v In 1995 (1); v P 1996 (2); v SL 1997 (3)*

Yuile, B. W. 17: v E 1962 (2); v WI 1968 (3); v In 1967 (3); v P 1964 (3); *v E 1965 (1); v In 1964 (3) 1969 (1); v P 1964 (1) 1969 (2)*

INDIA

Number of Test cricketers: 228

Abid Ali, S. 29: v E 1972 (4); v A 1969 (1); v WI 1974 (2); v NZ 1969 (3); *v E 1971 (3) 1974 (3); v A 1967 (4); v WI 1970 (5); v NZ 1967 (4)*

Adhikari, H. R. 21: v E 1951 (3); v A 1956 (2); v WI 1948 (5) 1958 (1); v P 1952 (2); *v E 1952 (3); v A 1947 (5)*

Agarkar, A. B. 5: v SA 1999 (1); *v A 1999 (3); v Z 1998 (1)*

Amarnath, L. 24: v E 1933 (3) 1951 (3); v WI 1948 (5); v P 1952 (5); *v E 1946 (3); v A 1947 (5)*

Amarnath, M. 69: v E 1976 (2) 1984 (5); v A 1969 (1) 1979 (1) 1986 (3); v WI 1978 (2) 1983 (3) 1987 (3); v NZ 1976 (3); v P 1983 (2) 1986 (5); v SL 1986 (2); *v E 1979 (2) 1986 (2); v A 1977 (5) 1985 (3); v WI 1975 (4) 1982 (5); v NZ 1975 (3); v P 1978 (3) 1982 (6) 1984 (2); v SL 1985 (2)*

Amarnath, S. 10: v E 1976 (2): *v WI 1975 (2); v NZ 1975 (3); v P 1978 (3)*

Amar Singh 7: v E 1933 (3); *v E 1932 (1) 1936 (3)*

Amir Elahi 1: *v A 1947*

Amre, P. K. 11: v E 1992 (3); v Z 1992 (1); *v SA 1992 (4); v SL 1993 (3)*

Ankola, S. A. 1: *v P 1989*

Apte, A. L. 1: *v E 1959*

Apte, M. L. 7: v P 1952 (2); *v WI 1952 (5)*

Arshad Ayub 13: v WI 1987 (4); v NZ 1988 (3); *v WI 1988 (4); v P 1989 (2)*

Arun, B. 2: v SL 1986 (2)

Arun Lal 16: v WI 1987 (4); v NZ 1988 (3); v P 1986 (1); v SL 1982 (1); *v WI 1988 (4); v P 1982 (3)*

Azad, K. 7: v E 1981 (3); v WI 1983 (2); v P 1983 (1); *v NZ 1980 (1)*

Azharuddin, M. 99: v E 1984 (3) 1992 (3); v A 1986 (3) 1996 (1) 1997 (3); v SA 1996 (3) 1999 (1); v WI 1987 (3) 1994 (3); v NZ 1988 (3) 1995 (3); v P 1986 (5) 1998 (3); v SL 1986 (1) 1990 (1) 1993 (3) 1997 (3); v Z 1992 (1); *v E 1986 (3) 1990 (3) 1996 (3); v A 1985 (3) 1991 (5); v SA 1992 (4) 1996 (3); v WI 1988 (3) 1996 (5); v NZ 1989 (3) 1993 (1) 1998 (2); v P 1989 (4); v SL 1985 (3) 1993 (3) 1997 (2) 1998 (1); v Z 1992 (1) 1998 (1)*

Baig, A. A. 10: v A 1959 (3); v WI 1966 (2); v P 1960 (3); *v E 1959 (2)*

Banerjee, S. A. 1: v WI 1948

Banerjee, S. N. 1: v WI 1948

Banerjee, S. T. 1: *v A 1991*

Baqa Jılanı, M. 1: *v E 1936*

Bedi, B. S. 67: v E 1972 (5) 1976 (5); v A 1969 (5); v WI 1966 (2) 1974 (4) 1978 (3); v NZ 1969 (3) 1976 (3); *v E 1967 (3) 1971 (3) 1974 (3) 1979 (3); v A 1967 (2) 1977 (5); v WI 1970 (5) 1975 (4); v NZ 1967 (4) 1975 (2); v P 1978 (3)*

Bhandari, P. 3: v A 1956 (1); v NZ 1955 (1); *v P 1954 (1)*

Bharadwaj, R. V. 3: v NZ 1999 (2); *v A 1999 (1)*

Bhat, A. R. 2: v WI 1983 (1); v P 1983 (1)

Binny, R. M. H. 27: v E 1979 (1); v WI 1983 (6); v P 1979 (6) 1983 (2) 1986 (3); *v E 1986 (3); v A 1980 (1) 1985 (2); v NZ 1980 (1); v P 1984 (1); v SL 1985 (1)*

Borde, C. G. 55: v E 1961 (5) 1963 (5); v A 1959 (5) 1964 (3) 1969 (1); v WI 1958 (4) 1966 (3); v NZ 1964 (4); v P 1960 (5); *v E 1959 (4) 1967 (3); v A 1967 (4); v WI 1961 (5); v NZ 1967 (4)*

Chandrasekhar, B. S. 58: v E 1963 (4) 1972 (5) 1976 (5); v A 1964 (2); v WI 1966 (3) 1974 (4) 1978 (4); v NZ 1964 (2) 1976 (3); *v E 1967 (3) 1971 (3) 1974 (2) 1979 (1); v A 1967 (2) 1977(5); v WI 1975 (4); v P 1978 (3)*

Chauhan, C. P. S. 40: v E 1972 (2); v A 1969 (1) 1979 (6); v WI 1978 (6); v NZ 1969 (2); v P 1979 (6); *v E 1979 (4); v A 1977 (4) 1980 (3); v NZ 1980 (3); v P 1978 (3)*

Chauhan, R. K. 21: v E 1992 (3); v A 1997 (2); v WI 1994 (2); v NZ 1995 (2); v SL 1993 (3) 1997 (3); v Z 1992 (1); *v NZ 1993 (1); v SL 1993 (3) 1997 (1)*

Chopra, N. 1: v SA 1999

Chowdhury, N. R. 2: v E 1951 (1); v WI 1948 (1)

Colah, S. H. M. 2: v E 1933 (1); *v E 1932 (1)*

Contractor, N. J. 31: v E 1961 (5); v A 1956 (1) 1959 (5); v WI 1958 (5); v NZ 1955 (4); v P 1960 (5); *v E 1959 (4); v WI 1961 (2)*

Dani, H. T. 1: v P 1952

Desai, R. B. 28: v E 1961 (4) 1963 (2); v A 1959 (3); v WI 1958 (1); v NZ 1964 (3); v P 1960 (5); *v E 1959 (5); v A 1967 (1); v WI 1961 (3); v NZ 1967 (1)*

Dilawar Hussain 3: v E 1933 (2); *v E 1936 (1)*

Divecha, R. V. 5: v E 1951 (2); v P 1952 (1); *v E 1952 (2)*

Doshi, D. R. 33: v E 1979 (1) 1981 (6); v A 1979 (6); v P 1979 (6) 1983 (1); v SL 1982 (1); *v E 1982 (3); v A 1980 (3); v NZ 1980 (2); v P 1982 (4)*

Dravid, R. 37: v A 1996 (1) 1997 (3); v SA 1996 (3) 1999 (2); v NZ 1999 (3); v P 1998 (3); v SL 1997 (3); *v E 1996 (2); v A 1999 (3); v SA 1996 (3); v WI 1996 (5); v NZ 1998 (2); v SL 1997 (2) 1998 (1); v Z 1998 (1)*

Durani, S. A. 29: v E 1961 (5) 1963 (5) 1972 (3); v A 1959 (1) 1964 (3); v WI 1966 (1); v NZ 1964 (3); *v WI 1961 (5) 1970 (3)*

Engineer, F. M. 46: v E 1961 (4) 1972 (5); v A 1969 (5); v WI 1966 (1) 1974 (5); v NZ 1964 (4) 1969 (2); *v E 1967 (3) 1971 (3) 1974 (3); v A 1967 (4); v WI 1961 (3); v NZ 1967 (4)*

Gadkari, C. V. 6: *v WI 1952 (3); v P 1954 (3)*

Gaekwad, A. D. 40: v E 1976 (4) 1984 (3); v WI 1974 (3) 1978 (5) 1983 (6); v NZ 1976 (3); v P 1983 (3); *v E 1979 (2); v A 1977 (1); v WI 1975 (3) 1982 (5); v P 1984 (2)*

Gaekwad, D. K. 11: v WI 1958 (1); v P 1952 (2) 1960 (1); *v E 1952 (1) 1959 (4); v WI 1952 (2)*

Gaekwad, H. G. 1: v P 1952

Gandhi, D. J. 4: v NZ 1999 (3); *v A 1999 (1)*

Gandotra, A. 2: v A 1969 (1); v NZ 1969 (1)

Ganesh, D. 4: *v SA 1996 (2); v WI 1996 (2)*

Ganguly, S. C. 35: v A 1996 (1) 1997 (3); v SA 1996 (2) 1999 (2); v NZ 1999 (3); v P 1998 (3); v SL 1997 (3); *v E 1996 (2); v A 1999 (3); v SA 1996 (3); v WI 1996 (4); v NZ 1998 (2); v SL 1997 (2) 1998 (1); v Z 1998 (1)*

Gavaskar, S. M. 125: v E 1972 (5) 1976 (5) 1979 (1) 1981 (6) 1984 (5); v A 1979 (6) 1986 (3); v WI 1974 (2) 1978 (6) 1983 (6); v NZ 1976 (3); v P 1979 (6) 1983 (3) 1986 (4); v SL 1982 (1) 1986 (3); *v E 1971 (3) 1974 (3) 1979 (4) 1982 (3) 1986 (3); v A 1977 (5) 1980 (3) 1985 (3); v WI 1970 (4) 1975 (4) 1982 (5); v NZ 1975 (3) 1980 (3); v P 1978 (3) 1982 (6) 1984 (2); v SL 1985 (3)*

Ghavri, K. D. 39: v E 1976 (3) 1979 (1); v A 1979 (6); v WI 1974 (3) 1978 (6); v NZ 1976 (2); v P 1979 (6); *v E 1979 (4); v A 1977 (3) 1980 (3); v NZ 1980 (1); v P 1978 (1)*

Ghorpade, J. M. 8: v A 1956 (1); v WI 1958 (1); v NZ 1955 (1); *v E 1959 (3); v WI 1952 (2)*

Ghulam Ahmed 22: v E 1951 (2); v A 1956 (2); v WI 1948 (3) 1958 (2); v NZ 1955 (1); v P 1952 (4); *v E 1952 (4); v P 1954 (4)*

Gopalan, M. J. 1: v E 1933

Gopinath, C. D. 8: v E 1951 (3); v A 1959 (1); v P 1952 (1); *v E 1952 (1); v P 1954 (2)*

Guard, G. M. 2: v A 1959 (1); v WI 1958 (1)

Guha, S. 4: v A 1969 (3); *v E 1967 (1)*

Gul Mahomed 8: v P 1952 (2); *v E 1946 (1); v A 1947 (5)*

Gupte, B. P. 3: v E 1963 (1); v NZ 1964 (1); v P 1960 (1)

Gupte, S. P. 36: v E 1951 (1) 1961 (2); v A 1956 (3); v WI 1958 (5); v NZ 1955 (5); v P 1952 (2) 1960 (3); *v E 1959 (5); v WI 1952 (5); v P 1954 (5)*

Gursharan Singh 1: *v NZ 1989*

Hafeez, A. 3: *v E 1946 (3)*

Hanumant Singh 14: v E 1963 (2); v A 1964 (3); v WI 1966 (2); v NZ 1964 (4) 1969 (1); *v E 1967 (2)*

Harbhajan Singh 8: v A 1997 (1); v NZ 1999 (2); v P 1998 (2); *v NZ 1998 (1); v SL 1998 (1); v Z 1998 (1)*

Hardikar, M. S. 2: v WI 1958 (2)

Harvinder Singh 2: v A 1997 (2)

Hazare, V. S. 30: v E 1951 (5); v WI 1948 (5); v P 1952 (3); *v E 1946 (3) 1952 (4); v A 1947 (5); v WI 1952 (5)*

Hindlekar, D. D. 4: *v E 1936 (1) 1946 (3)*

Hirwani, N. D. 17: v SA 1996 (2); v WI 1987 (1); v NZ 1988 (3) 1995 (1); v SL 1990 (1); *v E 1990 (3); v WI 1988 (3); v NZ 1989 (3)*

Ibrahim, K. C. 4: v WI 1948 (4)

Indrajitsinhji, K. S. 4: v A 1964 (3); v NZ 1969 (1)

Irani, J. K. 2: *v A 1947 (2)*

Jadeja, A. 15: v SA 1999 (1); v NZ 1995 (3) 1999 (1); *v E 1996 (2); v SA 1992 (3); v WI 1996 (2); v NZ 1998 (2); v SL 1997 (1)*

Jahangir Khan, M. 4: *v E 1932 (1) 1936 (3)*

Jai, L. P. 1: v E 1933

Jaisimha, M. L. 39: v E 1961 (5) 1963 (5); v A 1959 (1) 1964 (3); v WI 1966 (2); v NZ 1964 (4) 1969 (1); *v E 1959 (1); v A 1967 (2); v WI 1961 (4) 1970 (3); v NZ 1967 (4)*

Jamshedji, R. J. 1: v E 1933

Jayantilal, K. 1: *v WI 1970*

Johnson, D. J. 2: v A 1996 (1); *v SA 1996 (1)*

Joshi, P. G. 12: v E 1951 (2); v A 1959 (1); v WI 1958 (1); v P 1952 (1) 1960 (1); *v E 1959 (3); v WI 1952 (3)*

Joshi, S. B. 12: v A 1996 (1); v SA 1996 (3); v NZ 1999 (2); v P 1998 (1); *v E 1996 (1); v WI 1996 (4)*

Kaif, M. 1: v SA 1999

Kambli, V. G. 17: v E 1992 (3); v WI 1994 (3); v NZ 1995 (3); v SL 1993 (3); v Z 1992 (1); *v NZ 1993 (1); v SL 1993 (3)*

Kanitkar, H. H. 2: *v A 1999 (2)*

Kanitkar, H. S. 2: v WI 1974 (2)

Kapil Dev 131: v E 1979 (1) 1981 (6) 1984 (4) 1992 (3); v A 1979 (6) 1986 (3); v WI 1978 (6) 1983 (6) 1987 (4); v NZ 1988 (3); v P 1979 (6) 1983 (3) 1986 (5); v SL 1982 (1) 1986 (3) 1990 (1) 1993 (3); v Z 1992 (1); *v E 1979 (4) 1982 (3) 1986 (3) 1990 (3); v A 1980 (3) 1985 (3) 1991 (5); v SA 1992 (4); v WI 1982 (5) 1988 (4); v NZ 1980 (3) 1989 (3) 1993 (1); v P 1978 (3) 1982 (6) 1984 (2) 1989 (4); v SL 1985 (3) 1993 (3); v Z 1992 (1)*

Kapoor, A. R. 4: v A 1996 (1); v SA 1996 (1); v WI 1994 (1); v NZ 1995 (1)

Kardar, A. H. (*see* Hafeez)

Kartik, M. 2: v SA 1999 (2)

Kenny, R. B. 5: v A 1959 (4); v WI 1958 (1)

Kirmani, S. M. H. 88: v E 1976 (5) 1979 (1) 1981 (6) 1984 (5); v A 1979 (6); v WI 1978 (6) 1983 (6); v NZ 1976 (3); v P 1979 (6) 1983 (3); v SL 1982 (1); *v E 1982 (3); v A 1977 (5) 1980 (3) 1985 (3); v WI 1975 (4) 1982 (5); v NZ 1975 (3) 1980 (3); v P 1978 (3) 1982 (6) 1984 (2)*

Kischenchand, G. 5: v P 1952 (1); *v A 1947 (4)*

Kripal Singh, A. G. 14: v E 1961 (3) 1963 (2); v A 1956 (2) 1964 (1); v WI 1958 (1); v NZ 1955 (4); *v E 1959 (1)*

Krishnamurthy, P. 5: *v WI 1970 (5)*

Kulkarni, N. M. 2: v SL 1997 (1); *v SL 1997 (1)*

Kulkarni, R. R. 3: v A 1986 (1); v P 1986 (2)

Kulkarni, U. N. 4: *v A 1967 (3); v NZ 1967 (1)*

Kumar, V. V. 2: v E 1961 (1); v P 1960 (1)

Kumble, A. 61: v E 1992 (3); v A 1996 (1) 1997 (3); v SA 1996 (3) 1999 (2); v WI 1994 (3); v NZ 1995 (3) 1999 (3); v P 1998 (3); v SL 1993 (3) 1997 (3); v Z 1992 (1); *v E 1990 (1) 1996 (3); v A 1999 (3); v SA 1992 (4) 1996 (3); v WI 1996 (5); v NZ 1993 (1) 1998 (2); v SL 1993 (3) 1997 (2) 1998 (1); v Z 1992 (1) 1998 (1)*

Kunderan, B. K. 18: v E 1961 (1) 1963 (5); v A 1959 (3); v WI 1966 (2); v NZ 1964 (1); v P 1960 (2); *v E 1967 (2); v WI 1961 (2)*

Kuruvilla, A. 10: v SL 1997 (3); *v WI 1996 (5); v SL 1997 (2)*

Lall Singh 1: *v E 1932*

Lamba, R. 4: v WI 1987 (1); v SL 1986 (3)

Laxman, V. V. S. 18: v A 1997 (2); v SA 1996 (2) 1999 (1); v P 1998 (3); *v A 1999 (3); v SA 1996 (2); v WI 1996 (4); v SL 1998 (1)*

Madan Lal 39: v E 1976 (2) 1981 (6); v WI 1974 (2) 1983 (3); v NZ 1976 (1); v P 1983 (3); v SL 1982 (1); *v E 1974 (2) 1982 (3) 1986 (1); v A 1977 (2); v WI 1975 (4) 1982 (2); v NZ 1975 (3); v P 1982 (3) 1984 (1)*

Maka, E. S. 2: v P 1952 (1); *v WI 1952 (1)*

Malhotra, A. 7: v E 1981 (2) 1984 (1); v WI 1983 (3); *v E 1982 (1)*

Maninder Singh 35: v A 1986 (3); v WI 1983 (4) 1987 (3); v P 1986 (4); v SL 1986 (3); v Z 1992 (1); *v E 1986 (3); v WI 1982 (3); v P 1982 (5) 1984 (1) 1989 (3); v SL 1985 (2)*

Manjrekar, S. V. 37: v SA 1996 (1); v WI 1987 (1) 1994 (3); v NZ 1995 (1); v SL 1990 (1) 1993 (3); *v E 1990 (3) 1996 (2); v A 1991 (5); v SA 1992 (4); v WI 1988 (4); v NZ 1989 (3) 1993 (1); v P 1989 (4); v Z 1992 (1)*

Manjrekar, V. L. 55: v E 1951 (2) 1961 (5) 1963 (4); v A 1956 (3) 1964 (3); v WI 1958 (4); v NZ 1955 (5) 1964 (1); v P 1952 (3) 1960 (5); *v E 1952 (4) 1959 (2); v WI 1952 (4) 1961 (5); v P 1954 (5)*

Mankad, A. V. 22: v E 1976 (1); v A 1969 (5); v WI 1974 (1); v NZ 1969 (2) 1976 (3); *v E 1971 (3) 1974 (1); v A 1977 (3); v WI 1970 (3)*

Mankad, V. M. 44: v E 1951 (5); v A 1956 (3); v WI 1948 (5) 1958 (2); v NZ 1955 (4); v P 1952 (4); *v E 1946 (3) 1952 (3); v A 1947 (5); v WI 1952 (5); v P 1954 (5)*

Mansur Ali Khan (*see* Pataudi)

Mantri, M. K. 4: v E 1951 (1); *v E 1952 (2); v P 1954 (1)*

Meherhomji, K. R. 1: *v E 1936*

Mehra, V. L. 8: v E 1961 (1) 1963 (2); v NZ 1955 (2); *v WI 1961 (3)*

Merchant, V. M. 10: v E 1933 (3) 1951 (1); *v E 1936 (3) 1946 (3)*

Mhambrey, P. L. 2: *v E 1996 (2)*

Milkha Singh, A. G. 4: v E 1961 (1); v A 1959 (1); v P 1960 (2)

Modi, R. S. 10: v E 1951 (1); v WI 1948 (5); v P 1952 (1); *v E 1946 (3)*

Mohanty, D. S. 2: v SL 1997 (1); *v SL 1997 (1)*

Mongia, N. R. 42: v A 1996 (1) 1997 (3); v SA 1996 (3) 1999 (2); v WI 1994 (3); v NZ 1995 (3); v P 1998 (3); v SL 1993 (3) 1997 (3); *v E 1996 (3); v SA 1996 (3); v WI 1996 (5); v NZ 1993 (1) 1998 (2); v SL 1997 (2) 1998 (1); v Z 1998 (1)*

More, K. S. 49: v E 1992 (3); v A 1986 (2); v WI 1987 (4); v NZ 1988 (3); v P 1986 (5); v SL 1986 (3) 1990 (1); *v E 1986 (3) 1990 (3); v A 1991 (3); v SA 1992 (4); v WI 1988 (4); v NZ 1989 (3); v P 1989 (4); v SL 1993 (3); v Z 1992 (1)*

Muddiah, V. M. 2: v A 1959 (1); v P 1960 (1)

Mushtaq Ali, S. 11: v E 1933 (2) 1951 (1); v WI 1948 (3); *v E 1936 (3) 1946 (2)*

Nadkarni, R. G. 41: v E 1961 (1) 1963 (5); v A 1959 (5) 1964 (3); v WI 1958 (1) 1966 (1); v NZ 1955 (1) 1964 (4); v P 1960 (4); *v E 1959 (4); v A 1967 (3); v WI 1961 (5); v NZ 1967 (4)*

Naik, S. S. 3: v WI 1974 (2); *v E 1974 (1)*

Naoomal Jeoomal 3: v E 1933 (2); *v E 1932 (1)*

Narasimha Rao, M. V. 4: v A 1979 (2); v WI 1978 (2)

Navle, J. G. 2: v E 1933 (1); *v E 1932 (1)*

Nayak, S. V. 2: *v E 1982 (2)*

Nayudu, C. K. 7: v E 1933 (3); *v E 1932 (1) 1936 (3)*

Nayudu, C. S. 11: v E 1933 (2) 1951 (1); *v E 1936 (2) 1946 (2); v A 1947 (4)*

Nazir Ali, S. 2: v E 1933 (1); *v E 1932 (1)*

Nehra, A. 1: *v SL 1998*

Nissar, Mahomed 6: v E 1933 (2); *v E 1932 (1) 1936 (3)*

Nyalchand, S. 1: v P 1952

Pai, A. M. 1: v NZ 1969

Palia, P. E. 2: *v E 1932 (1) 1936 (1)*

Pandit, C. S. 5: v A 1986 (2); *v E 1986 (1); v A 1991 (2)*

Parkar, G. A. 1: *v E 1982*

Parkar, R. D. 2: v E 1972 (2)

Parsana, D. D. 2: v WI 1978 (2)

Patankar, C. T. 1: v NZ 1955

Pataudi sen., Nawab of, 3: *v E 1946 (3)*

Pataudi jun., Nawab of (now Mansur Ali Khan) 46: v E 1961 (3) 1963 (5) 1972 (3); v A 1964 (3) 1969 (5); v WI 1966 (3) 1974 (4); v NZ 1964 (4) 1969 (3); *v E 1967 (3); v A 1967 (3); v WI 1961 (3); v NZ 1967 (4)*

Patel, B. P. 21: v E 1976 (5); v WI 1974 (3); v NZ 1976 (3); *v E 1974 (2); v A 1977 (2); v WI 1975 (3); v NZ 1975 (3)*

Patel, J. M. 7: v A 1956 (2) 1959 (3); v NZ 1955 (1); *v P 1954 (1)*

Patel, R. 1: v NZ 1988

Patiala, Yuvraj of, 1: v E 1933

Patil, S. M. 29: v E 1979 (1) 1981 (4) 1984 (2); v WI 1983 (2); v P 1979 (2) 1983 (3); v SL 1982 (1); *v E 1982 (2); v A 1980 (3); v NZ 1980 (3); v P 1982 (4) 1984 (2)*

Patil, S. R. 1: v NZ 1955

Phadkar, D. G. 31: v E 1951 (4); v A 1956 (1); v WI 1948 (4) 1958 (1); v NZ 1955 (4); v P 1952 (2); *v E 1952 (4); v A 1947 (4); v WI 1952 (4); v P 1954 (3)*

Prabhakar, M. 39: v E 1984 (2) 1992 (3); v WI 1994 (3); v NZ 1995 (3); v SL 1990 (1) 1993 (3); v Z 1992 (1); *v E 1990 (3); v A 1991 (5); v SA 1992 (4); v NZ 1989 (3); v P 1989 (4); v SL 1993 (3); v Z 1992 (1)*

Prasad, B. K. V. 29: v A 1996 (1); v SA 1996 (3); v NZ 1999 (2); v P 1998 (3); v SL 1997 (1); *v E 1996 (3); v A 1999 (3); v SA 1996 (3); v WI 1996 (5); v NZ 1998 (2); v SL 1997 (2) 1998 (1)*

Prasad, M. S. K. 6: v NZ 1999 (3); *v A 1999 (3)*

Prasanna, E. A. S. 49: v E 1961 (1) 1972 (3) 1976 (4); v A 1969 (5); v WI 1966 (1) 1974 (5); v NZ 1969 (3); *v E 1967 (3) 1974 (2); v A 1967 (4) 1977 (4); v WI 1961 (1) 1970 (3) 1975 (1); v NZ 1967 (4) 1975 (3); v P 1978 (2)*

Punjabi, P. H. 5: *v P 1954 (5)*

Rai Singh, K. 1: *v A 1947*

Rajinder Pal 1: v E 1963

Rajindernath, V. 1: v P 1952

Rajput, L. S. 2: *v SL 1985 (2)*

Raju, S. L. V. 27: v E 1992 (3); v A 1997 (3); v WI 1994 (3); v NZ 1995 (2); v SL 1990 (1) 1993 (3); *v E 1996 (1); v A 1991 (4); v SA 1992 (2); v NZ 1989 (2) 1993 (1); v SL 1993 (1); v Z 1992 (1)*

Raman, W. V. 11: v SA 1996 (1); v WI 1987 (1); v NZ 1988 (1); *v SA 1992 (1) 1996 (2); v WI 1988 (1); v NZ 1989 (3); v Z 1992 (1)*

Ramaswami, C. 2: *v E 1936 (2)*

Ramchand, G. S. 33: v A 1956 (3) 1959 (5); v WI 1958 (3); v NZ 1955 (5); v P 1952 (3); *v E 1952 (4); v WI 1952 (5); v P 1954 (5)*

Ramesh, S. 9: v NZ 1999 (3); v P 1998 (3); *v A 1999 (2); v SL 1998 (1)*

Ramji, L. 1: v E 1933

Rangachari, C. R. 4: v WI 1948 (2); *v A 1947 (2)*

Rangnekar, K. M. 3: *v A 1947 (3)*

Ranjane, V. B. 7: v E 1961 (3) 1963 (1); v A 1964 (1); v WI 1958 (1); *v WI 1961 (1)*

Rathore, V. 6: v A 1996 (1); *v E 1996 (3); v SA 1996 (2)*

Razdan, V. 2: *v P 1989 (2)*

Reddy, B. 4: *v E 1979 (4)*

Rege, M. R. 1: v WI 1948

Roy, A. 4: v A 1969 (2); v NZ 1969 (2)

Roy, Pankaj 43: v E 1951 (5); v A 1956 (3) 1959 (5); v WI 1958 (5); v NZ 1955 (3); v P 1952 (3) 1960 (1); *v E 1952 (4) 1959 (5); v WI 1952 (4); v P 1954 (5)*

Roy, Pranab 2: v E 1981 (2)

Sandhu, B. S. 8: v WI 1983 (1); *v WI 1982 (4); v P 1982 (3)*

Sardesai, D N. 30: v E 1961 (1) 1963 (5) 1972 (1); v A 1964 (3) 1969 (1); v WI 1966 (2); v NZ 1964 (3); *v E 1967 (1) 1971 (3); v A 1967 (2); v WI 1961 (3) 1970 (5)*

Sarwate, C. T. 9: v E 1951 (1); v WI 1948 (2); *v E 1946 (1); v A 1947 (5)*

Saxena, R. C. 1: *v E 1967*

Sekar, T. A. P. 2: *v P 1982 (2)*

Sen, P. 14: v E 1951 (2); v WI 1948 (5); v P 1952 (2); *v E 1952 (2); v A 1947 (3)*

Sen Gupta, A. K. 1: v WI 1958

Sharma, Ajay 1: v WI 1987

Sharma, Chetan 23: v E 1984 (3); v A 1986 (2); v WI 1987 (3); v SL 1986 (2); *v E 1986 (2); v A 1985 (2); v WI 1988 (4); v P 1984 (2); v SL 1985 (3)*

Sharma, Gopal 5: v E 1984 (1); v P 1986 (2); v SL 1990 (1); *v SL 1985 (1)*

Sharma, P. 5: v E 1976 (2); v WI 1974 (2); *v WI 1975 (1)*

Sharma, Sanjeev 2: v NZ 1988 (1); *v E 1990 (1)*

Shastri, R. J. 80: v E 1981 (6) 1984 (5); v A 1986 (3); v WI 1983 (6) 1987 (4); v NZ 1988 (3); v P 1983 (2) 1986 (5); v SL 1986 (3) 1990 (1); *v E 1982 (3) 1986 (3) 1990 (3); v A 1985 (3) 1991 (3); v SA 1992 (3); v WI 1982 (5) 1988 (4); v NZ 1980 (3); v P 1982 (2) 1984 (2) 1989 (4); v SL 1985 (3); v Z 1992 (1)*

Shinde, S. G. 7: v E 1951 (3); v WI 1948 (1); *v E 1946 (1) 1952 (2)*

Shodhan, R. H. 3: v P 1952 (1); *v WI 1952 (2)*

Shukla, R. C. 1: v SL 1982

Sidhu, N. S. 51: v E 1992 (3); v A 1997 (3); v WI 1983 (2) 1994 (3); v NZ 1988 (3) 1995 (2); v SL 1993 (3) 1997 (3); v Z 1992 (1); *v E 1990 (3); v A 1991 (3); v WI 1988 (4) 1996 (4); v NZ 1989 (1) 1993 (1) 1998 (2); v P 1989 (4); v SL 1993 (1) 1997 (2); v Z 1998 (1)*

Singh, R. 1: *v NZ 1998*
Singh, R. R. 1: *v Z 1998*
Sivaramakrishnan, L. 9: v E 1984 (5); *v A 1985 (2); v WI 1982 (1); v SL 1985 (1)*
Sohoni, S. W. 4: v E 1951 (1); *v E 1946 (2); v A 1947 (1)*
Solkar, E. D. 27: v E 1972 (5) 1976 (1); v A 1969 (4); v WI 1974 (4); v NZ 1969 (1); *v E 1971 (3) 1974 (3); v WI 1970 (5) 1975 (1)*
Sood, M. M. 1: v A 1959
Srikkanth, K. 43: v E 1981 (4) 1984 (2); v A 1986 (3); v WI 1987 (4); v NZ 1988 (3); v P 1986 (5); v SL 1986 (3); *v E 1986 (3); v A 1985 (3) 1991 (4); v P 1982 (2) 1989 (4); v SL 1985 (3)*
Srinath, J. 46: v E 1996 (3) 1999 (2); v SA 1996 (3) 1999 (2); v WI 1994 (3); v NZ 1995 (3) 1999 (3); v P 1998 (3); v SL 1997 (3); *v E 1996 (3); v A 1991 (5) 1999 (3); v SA 1992 (3) 1996 (3); v NZ 1993 (1) 1998 (2); v SL 1997 (3); v Z 1992 (1) 1998 (1)*
Srinivasan, T. E. 1: *v NZ 1980*
Subramanya, V. 9: v WI 1966 (2); v NZ 1964 (1); *v E 1967 (2); v A 1967 (3); v NZ 1967 (2)*
Sunderram, G. 2: v NZ 1955 (2)
Surendranath, R. 11: v A 1959 (2); v WI 1958 (2); v P 1960 (2); *v E 1959 (5)*
Surti, R. F. 26: v E 1963 (1); v A 1964 (2) 1969 (1); v WI 1966 (2); v NZ 1964 (1) 1969 (2); v P 1960 (2); *v E 1967 (2); v A 1967 (4); v WI 1961 (5); v NZ 1967 (4)*
Swamy, V. N. 1: v NZ 1955

Tamhane, N. S. 21: v A 1956 (3) 1959 (1); v WI 1958 (4); v NZ 1955 (4); v P 1960 (2); *v E 1959 (2); v P 1954 (5)*
Tarapore, K. K. 1: v WI 1948
Tendulkar, S. R. 76: v E 1992 (3); v A 1996 (1) 1997 (3); v SA 1996 (3) 1999 (2); v WI 1994 (3); v NZ 1995 (3) 1999 (3); v P 1998 (3); v SL 1990 (1) 1993 (3) 1997 (3); v Z 1992 (1); *v E 1990 (3) 1996 (3); v A 1991 (5) 1999 (3); v SA 1992 (4) 1996 (3); v WI 1996 (5); v NZ 1989 (3) 1993 (1) 1998 (2); v P 1989 (4); v SL 1993 (3) 1997 (2) 1998 (1); v Z 1992 (1) 1998 (1)*

Umrigar, P. R. 59: v E 1951 (5) 1961 (4); v A 1956 (3) 1959 (3); v WI 1948 (1) 1958 (5); v NZ 1955 (5); v P 1952 (5) 1960 (5); *v E 1952 (4) 1959 (4); v WI 1952 (5) 1961 (5); v P 1954 (5)*

Vengsarkar, D. B. 116: v E 1976 (1) 1979 (1) 1981 (6) 1984 (5); v A 1979 (6) 1986 (2); v WI 1978 (6) 1983 (5) 1987 (3); v NZ 1988 (3); v P 1979 (5) 1983 (1) 1986 (5); v SL 1982 (1) 1986 (3) 1990 (1); *v E 1979 (4) 1982 (3) 1986 (3) 1990 (3); v A 1977 (5) 1980 (3) 1985 (3) 1991 (5); v WI 1975 (2) 1982 (5) 1988 (4); v NZ 1975 (3) 1980 (3) 1989 (2); v P 1978 (3) 1982 (6) 1984 (2); v SL 1985 (3)*
Venkataraghavan, S. 57: v E 1972 (2) 1976 (1); v A 1969 (5) 1979 (3); v WI 1966 (2) 1974 (2) 1978 (6); v NZ 1964 (4) 1969 (2) 1976 (3); v P 1983 (2); *v E 1967 (1) 1971 (3) 1974 (2) 1979 (4); v A 1977 (1); v WI 1970 (5) 1975 (3) 1982 (5); v NZ 1975 (1)*
Venkataramana, M. 1: *v WI 1988*
Viswanath, G. R. 91: v E 1972 (5) 1976 (5) 1979 (1) 1981 (6); v A 1969 (4) 1979 (6); v WI 1974 (5) 1978 (6); v NZ 1976 (3); v P 1979 (6); v SL 1982 (1); *v E 1971 (3) 1974 (3) 1979 (4) 1982 (3); v A 1977 (5) 1980 (3); v WI 1970 (5) 1975 (4); v NZ 1975 (3) 1980 (3); v P 1978 (3) 1982 (6)*
Viswanath, S. 3: *v SL 1985 (3)*
Vizianagram, Maharaj Kumar of, Sir Vijay A. 3: *v E 1936 (3)*

Wadekar, A. L. 37: v E 1972 (5); v A 1969 (3); v WI 1966 (2); v NZ 1969 (3); *v E 1967 (3) 1971 (3) 1974 (3); v A 1967 (4); v WI 1970 (5); v NZ 1967 (4)*
Wasim Jaffer 2: v SA 1999 (2)
Wassan, A. S. 4: *v E 1990 (1); v NZ 1989 (3)*
Wazir Ali, S. 7: v E 1933 (3); *v E 1932 (1) 1936 (3)*

Yadav, N. S. 35: v E 1979 (1) 1981 (1) 1984 (4); v A 1979 (5) 1986 (3); v WI 1983 (3); v P 1979 (5) 1986 (4); v SL 1986 (2); *v A 1980 (2) 1985 (3); v NZ 1980 (1); v P 1984 (1)*
Yadav, V. S. 1: v Z 1992
Yajurvindra Singh 4: v E 1976 (2); v A 1979 (1); *v E 1979 (1)*
Yashpal Sharma 37: v E 1979 (1) 1981 (2); v A 1979 (6); v WI 1983 (1); v P 1979 (6) 1983 (3); v SL 1982 (1); *v E 1979 (3) 1982 (3); v A 1980 (3); v WI 1982 (5); v NZ 1980 (1); v P 1982 (2)*
Yograj Singh 1: *v NZ 1980*

Note: Hafeez, on going later to Oxford University, took his correct name, Kardar.

PAKISTAN

Number of Test cricketers: 161

Aamer Malik 14: v E 1987 (2); v A 1988 (1) 1994 (1); v WI 1990 (1); v In 1989 (4); *v A 1989 (2); v WI 1987 (1); v NZ 1988 (2)*

Aamir Nazir 6: v SL 1995 (1); *v SA 1994 (1); v WI 1992 (1); v NZ 1993 (1); v Z 1994 (2)*

Aamir Sohail 47: v A 1994 (3) 1998 (3); v SA 1997 (1); v WI 1997 (3); v SL 1995 (3) 1999 (2); v Z 1993 (3) 1996 (2) 1998 (1); *v E 1992 (5) 1996 (2); v A 1995 (3); v SA 1994 (1) 1997 (3); v WI 1992 (2); v NZ 1992 (1) 1993 (3) 1995 (1); v SL 1994 (2); v Z 1994 (3)*

Abdul Kadir 4: v A 1964 (1); *v A 1964 (1); v NZ 1964 (2)*

Abdul Qadir 67: v E 1977 (3) 1983 (1) 1987 (3); v A 1982 (3) 1988 (3); v WI 1980 (2) 1986 (3) 1990 (2); v NZ 1984 (3) 1990 (2); v In 1982 (5) 1984 (1) 1989 (4); v SL 1985 (3); *v E 1982 (3) 1987 (4); v A 1983 (5); v WI 1987 (3); v NZ 1984 (2) 1988 (2); v In 1979 (3) 1986 (3); v SL 1985 (2)*

Abdur Razzaq 9: v SL 1999 (2); *v A 1999 (1); v WI 1999 (3); v SL 2000 (3)*

Afaq Hussain 2: v E 1961 (1); *v A 1964 (1)*

Aftab Baloch 2: v WI 1974 (1); v NZ 1969 (1)

Aftab Gul 6: v E 1968 (2); v NZ 1969 (1); *v E 1971 (3)*

Agha Saadat Ali 1: v NZ 1955

Agha Zahid 1: v WI 1974

Akram Raza 9: v A 1994 (2); v WI 1990 (1); v In 1989 (1); v SL 1991 (1); *v NZ 1993 (2); v SL 1994 (1); v Z 1994 (1)*

Ali Hussain Rizvi 1: v SA 1997

Alim-ud-Din 25: v E 1961 (2); v A 1956 (1) 1959 (1); v WI 1958 (1); v NZ 1955 (3); v In 1954 (5); *v E 1954 (3) 1962 (3); v WI 1957 (5); v In 1960 (1)*

Ali Naqvi 5: v SA 1997 (3); *v Z 1997 (2)*

Amir Elahi 5: *v In 1952 (5)*

Anil Dalpat 9: v E 1983 (3); v NZ 1984 (3); *v NZ 1984 (3)*

Anwar Hussain 4: *v In 1952 (4)*

Anwar Khan 1: *v NZ 1978*

Aqib Javed 22: v A 1994 (1); v NZ 1990 (3); v SL 1991 (3) 1995 (3); v Z 1998 (1); *v E 1992 (5); v A 1989 (1); v SA 1994 (1); v NZ 1988 (1) 1992 (1); v Z 1994 (2)*

Arif Butt 3: *v A 1964 (1); v NZ 1964 (2)*

Arshad Khan 7: v A 1998 (1); v WI 1997 (1); v SL 1999 (1); *v SL 1998 (1) 2000 (3)*

Ashfaq Ahmed 1: v Z 1993

Ashraf Ali 8: v E 1987 (3); v In 1984 (2), v SL 1981 (2) 1985 (1)

Asif Iqbal 58: v E 1968 (3) 1972 (3); v A 1964 (1); v WI 1974 (1); v NZ 1964 (3) 1969 (3) 1976 (3); v In 1978 (3); *v E 1967 (3) 1971 (3) 1974 (3); v A 1964 (1) 1972 (3) 1976 (3) 1978 (2); v WI 1976 (5); v NZ 1964 (3) 1972 (3) 1978 (2); v In 1979 (6)*

Asif Masood 16: v E 1968 (2) 1972 (1); v WI 1974 (2); v NZ 1969 (1); *v E 1971 (3) 1974 (3); v A 1972 (3) 1976 (1)*

Asif Mujtaba 25: v E 1987 (1); v WI 1986 (2); v Z 1993 (3); *v E 1992 (5) 1996 (2); v SA 1994 (1); v WI 1992 (3); v NZ 1992 (1) 1993 (2); v SL 1994 (2) 1996 (2); v Z 1994 (1)*

Ata-ur-Rehman 13: v SL 1995 (1); v Z 1993 (3); *v E 1992 (1) 1996 (2); v WI 1992 (3); v NZ 1993 (2) 1995 (1)*

Atif Rauf 1: *v NZ 1993*

Atiq-uz-Zaman 1: v SL 1999

Azam Khan 1: v Z 1996

Azeem Hafeez 18: v E 1983 (2); v NZ 1984 (3); v In 1984 (2); *v A 1983 (5); v NZ 1984 (3); v In 1983 (3)*

Azhar Khan 1: v A 1979

Azhar Mahmood 19: v A 1998 (2); v SA 1997 (3); v WI 1997 (3); v Z 1998 (1); *v A 1999 (3); v SA 1997 (3); v In 1998 (1); v SL 2000 (1); v Z 1997 (2)*

Azmat Rana 1: v A 1979

Basit Ali 19: v A 1994 (2); v SL 1995 (1); v Z 1993 (3); *v A 1995 (3); v WI 1992 (3); v NZ 1993 (3) 1995 (1); v SL 1994 (2); v Z 1994 (1)*

Burki, J. 25: v E 1961 (3); v A 1964 (1); v NZ 1964 (3) 1969 (1); *v E 1962 (5) 1967 (3); v A 1964 (1); v NZ 1964 (3); v In 1960 (5)*

D'Souza, A. 6: v E 1961 (2); v WI 1958 (1); *v E 1962 (3)*

Ehtesham-ud-Din 5: v A 1979 (1); *v E 1982 (1); v In 1979 (3)*

Farooq Hamid 1: *v A 1964*
Farrukh Zaman 1: v NZ 1976
Fazal Mahmood 34: v E 1961 (1); v A 1956 (1) 1959 (2); v WI 1958 (3); v NZ 1955 (2); v In 1954 (4); *v E 1954 (4) 1962 (2); v WI 1957 (5); v In 1952 (5) 1960 (5)*
Fazl-e-Akbar 2: v SL 1998 (1); *v SA 1997 (1)*

Ghazali, M. E. Z. 2: *v E 1954 (2)*
Ghulam Abbas 1: *v E 1967*
Gul Mahomed 1: v A 1956

Hanif Mohammad 55: v E 1961 (3) 1968 (3); v A 1956 (1) 1959 (3) 1964 (1); v WI 1958 (1); v NZ 1955 (3) 1964 (3) 1969 (1); v In 1954 (5); *v E 1954 (4) 1962 (5) 1967 (3); v A 1964 (1); v WI 1958 (1); v NZ 1964 (3) 1969 (1); v In 1952 (5) 1960 (5)*
Haroon Rashid 23: v E 1977 (3); v A 1979 (2) 1982 (3); v In 1982 (1); v SL 1981 (2); *v E 1978 (3) 1982 (1); v A 1976 (1) 1978 (1); v WI 1976 (5); v NZ 1978 (1)*
Hasan Raza 2: v Z 1996 (1) 1998 (1)
Haseeb Ahsan 12: v E 1961 (2); v A 1959 (1); v WI 1958 (1); *v WI 1957 (3); v In 1960 (5)*

Ibadulla, K. 4: v A 1964 (1); *v E 1967 (2); v NZ 1964 (1)*
Ijaz Ahmed, sen. 58: v E 1987 (3); v A 1988 (3) 1994 (1) 1998 (2); v SA 1997 (3); v WI 1990 (3) 1997 (3); v NZ 1996 (2); v SL 1999 (1); v Z 1996 (2) 1998 (2); *v E 1987 (4) 1996 (3); v A 1989(3) 1995 (2) 1999 (3); v SA 1994 (1) 1997 (3); v WI 1987 (2); v NZ 1995 (1); v In 1986 (1) 1998 (3); v SL 1996 (2) 1998 (1); v Z 1994 (3) 1997 (1)*
Ijaz Ahmed, jun. 2: v SL 1995 (2)
Ijaz Butt 8: v A 1959 (2); v WI 1958 (3); *v E 1962 (3)*
Ijaz Faqih 5: v WI 1980 (1); *v A 1981 (1); v WI 1987 (2); v In 1986 (1)*
Imran Khan 88: v A 1979 (2) 1982 (3); v WI 1980 (4) 1986 (3) 1990 (3); v NZ 1976 (3); v In 1978 (3) 1982 (6) 1989 (4); v SL 1981 (1) 1985 (3) 1991 (3); *v E 1971 (1) 1974 (3) 1982 (3) 1987 (5); v A 1976 (3) 1978 (2) 1981 (3) 1983 (2) 1989 (3); v WI 1976 (5) 1987 (3); v NZ 1978 (2) 1988 (2); v In 1979 (5) 1986 (5); v SL 1985 (3)*
Imran Nazir 4: v SL 1998 (1); *v WI 1999 (2); v SL 2000 (1)*
Imtiaz Ahmed 41: v E 1961 (3); v A 1956 (1) 1959 (3); v WI 1958 (3); v NZ 1955 (3); v In 1954 (3); *v E 1954 (4) 1962 (4); v WI 1957 (5); v In 1952 (5) 1960 (5)*
Intikhab Alam 47: v E 1961 (2) 1968 (3) 1972 (3); v A 1959 (1) 1964 (1); v WI 1974 (2); v NZ 1964 (3) 1969 (3) 1976 (3); *v E 1962 (3) 1967 (3) 1971 (3) 1974 (3); v A 1964 (1) 1972 (3); v WI 1976 (1); v NZ 1964 (3) 1972 (3); v In 1960 (3)*
Inzamam-ul-Haq 67: v A 1994 (3) 1998 (3); v SA 1997 (3); v WI 1997 (3); v NZ 1996 (2); v SL 1995 (3) 1998 (1) 1999 (3); v Z 1993 (3) 1998 (1); *v E 1992 (4) 1996 (3); v A 1995 (3) 1999 (3); v SA 1994 (1) 1997 (2); v WI 1992 (3) 1999 (3); v NZ 1992 (1) 1993 (3) 1995 (1); v In 1998 (2); v SL 1994 (2) 1996 (2) 1998 (1) 2000 (3); v Z 1994 (3) 1997 (2)*
Iqbal Qasim 50: v E 1977 (3) 1987 (3); v A 1979 (3) 1982 (2) 1988 (3); v WI 1980 (4); v NZ 1984 (3); v In 1978 (3) 1982 (2); v SL 1981 (3); *v E 1978 (3); v A 1976 (3) 1981 (2); v WI 1976 (2); v NZ 1984 (1); v In 1979 (6) 1983 (1) 1986 (3)*
Irfan Fazil 1: v SL 1999
Israr Ali 4: v A 1959 (2); *v In 1952 (2)*

Jalal-ud-Din 6: v A 1982 (1); v In 1982 (2) 1984 (2); v SL 1985 (1)
Javed Akhtar 1: *v E 1962*
Javed Miandad 124: v E 1977 (3) 1987 (3); v A 1979 (3) 1982 (3) 1988 (3); v WI 1980 (4) 1986 (3) 1990 (2); v NZ 1976 (3) 1984 (3) 1990 (3); v In 1978 (3) 1982 (6) 1984 (2) 1989 (4); v SL 1981 (3) 1985 (3) 1991 (3); v Z 1993 (3); *v E 1978 (3) 1982 (3) 1987 (5) 1992 (5); v A 1976 (3) 1978 (2) 1981 (3) 1983 (5) 1989 (3); v WI 1976 (1) 1987 (3) 1992 (3); v NZ 1978 (3) 1984 (3) 1988 (2) 1992 (1); v In 1979 (6) 1983 (3) 1986 (4); v SL 1985 (3)*

Kabir Khan 4: *v SA 1994 (1); v SL 1994 (1); v Z 1994 (2)*
Kardar, A. H. 23: v A 1956 (1); v NZ 1955 (3); v In 1954 (5); *v E 1954 (4); v WI 1957 (5); v In 1952 (5)*

Khalid Hassan 1: *v E 1954*
Khalid Wazir 2: *v E 1954 (2)*
Khan Mohammad 13: v A 1956 (1); v NZ 1955 (3); v In 1954 (4); *v E 1954 (2); v WI 1957 (2); v In 1952 (1)*

Liaqat Ali 5: v E 1977 (2); v WI 1974 (1); *v E 1978 (2)*

Mahmood Hussain 27: v E 1961 (1); v WI 1958 (3); v NZ 1955 (1); v In 1954 (5); *v E 1954 (2) 1962 (3); v WI 1957 (3); v In 1952 (4) 1960 (5)*
Majid Khan 63: v E 1968 (3) 1972 (3); v A 1964 (1) 1979 (3); v WI 1974 (2) 1980 (4); v NZ 1964 (3) 1976 (3); v In 1978 (3) 1982 (1); v SL 1981 (1); *v E 1967 (3) 1971 (2) 1974 (3) 1982 (1); v A 1972 (3) 1976 (3) 1978 (2) 1981 (3); v WI 1976 (5); v NZ 1972 (3) 1978 (2); v In 1979 (6)*
Mansoor Akhtar 19: v A 1982 (3); v WI 1980 (2); v In 1982 (3); v SL 1981 (1); *v E 1982 (3) 1987 (5); v A 1981 (1) 1989 (1)*
Manzoor Elahi 6: v NZ 1984 (1); v In 1984 (1); *v In 1986 (2); v Z 1994 (2)*
Maqsood Ahmed 16: v NZ 1955 (2); v In 1954 (5); *v E 1954 (4); v In 1952 (5)*
Masood Anwar 1: v WI 1990
Mathias, Wallis 21: v E 1961 (1); v A 1956 (1) 1959 (2); v WI 1958 (3); v NZ 1955 (1); *v E 1962 (3); v WI 1957 (5); v In 1960 (5)*
Miran Bux 2: v In 1954 (2)
Mohammad Akram 8: v NZ 1996 (1); v SL 1995 (2) 1999 (1); *v E 1996 (1); v A 1995 (2) 1999 (1)*
Mohammad Aslam 1: *v E 1954*
Mohammad Farooq 7: v NZ 1964 (3); *v E 1962 (2); v In 1960 (2)*
Mohammad Hussain 2: v A 1998 (1); v Z 1996 (1)
Mohammad Ilyas 10: v E 1968 (2); v NZ 1964 (3); *v E 1967 (1); v A 1964 (1); v NZ 1964 (3)*
Mohammad Munaf 4: v E 1961 (2); v A 1959 (2)
Mohammad Nazir 14: v E 1972 (1); v WI 1980 (4); v NZ 1969 (3); *v A 1983 (3); v In 1983 (3)*
Mohammad Ramzan 1: v SA 1997
Mohammad Wasim 18: v A 1998 (1); v SA 1997 (2); v WI 1997 (3); v NZ 1996 (2); *v A 1999 (2); v SA 1997 (2); v WI 1999 (3); v SL 2000 (2); v Z 1997 (1)*
Mohammad Zahid 4: v A 1998 (1); v NZ 1996 (1); *v SL 1996 (2)*
Mohsin Kamal 9: v E 1983 (1); v A 1994 (2); v SL 1985 (1); *v E 1987 (4); v SL 1985 (1)*
Mohsin Khan 48: v E 1977 (1) 1983 (3); v A 1982 (3); v WI 1986 (3); v NZ 1984 (2); v In 1982 (6) 1984 (2); v SL 1981 (2) 1985 (2); *v E 1978 (3) 1982 (3); v A 1978 (1) 1981 (2) 1983 (5); v NZ 1978 (1) 1984 (3); v In 1983 (3); v SL 1985 (3)*
Moin Khan 58: v A 1994 (1) 1998 (3); v SA 1997 (3); v WI 1990 (?) 1997 (3); v NZ 1996 (2); v SL 1991 (3) 1995 (3) 1998 (1) 1999 (2); v Z 1996 (2) 1998 (2); *v E 1992 (4) 1996 (2); v A 1995 (2) 1999 (3); v SA 1994 (1) 1997 (3); v WI 1992 (2) 1999 (3); v In 1998 (3); v SL 1996 (2) 1998 (1) 2000 (3); v Z 1997 (2)*
Mudassar Nazar 76: v E 1977 (3) 1983 (1) 1987 (3); v A 1979 (3) 1982 (3) 1988 (3); v WI 1986 (2); v NZ 1984 (3); v In 1978 (2) 1982 (6) 1984 (2); v SL 1981 (1) 1985 (3) ; *v E 1978 (3) 1982 (3) 1987 (5); v A 1976 (1) 1978 (1) 1981 (3) 1983 (5); v WI 1987 (3); v NZ 1978 (1) 1984 (3) 1988 (2); v In 1979 (5) 1983 (3); v SL 1985 (3)*
Mufasir-ul-Haq 1: *v NZ 1964*
Munir Malik 3: v A 1959 (1); *v E 1962 (2)*
Mushtaq Ahmed 48: v A 1994 (3) 1998 (2); v SA 1997 (3); v WI 1990 (2) 1997 (3); v NZ 1996 (2); v Z 1993 (2) 1998 (1); *v E 1992 (5) 1996 (3); v A 1989 (1) 1995 (2) 1999 (1); v SA 1997 (3); v WI 1992 (1) 1999 (3); v NZ 1992 (1) 1993 (1) 1995 (1); v In 1998 (1); v SL 1994 (2) 1996 (2) 2000 (2); v Z 1997 (1)*
Mushtaq Mohammad 57: v E 1961 (3) 1968 (3) 1972 (3); v WI 1958 (1) 1974 (2); v NZ 1969 (2) 1976 (3); v In 1978 (3); *v E 1962 (5) 1967 (3) 1971 (3) 1974 (3); v A 1972 (3) 1976 (3) 1978 (2); v WI 1976 (5); v NZ 1972 (2) 1978 (3); v In 1960 (5)*

Nadeem Abbasi 3: v In 1989 (3)
Nadeem Ghauri 1: *v A 1989*
Nadeem Khan 2: *v WI 1992 (1); v In 1998 (1)*
Nasim-ul-Ghani 29: v E 1961 (2); v A 1959 (2) 1964 (1); v WI 1958 (3); *v E 1962 (5) 1967 (2); v A 1964 (1) 1972 (1); v WI 1957 (5); v NZ 1964 (3); v In 1960 (4)*
Naushad Ali 6: v NZ 1964 (3); *v NZ 1964 (3)*

Naved Anjum 2: v NZ 1990 (1); v In 1989 (1)
Naved Ashraf 2: v SL 1999 (1); v Z 1998 (1)
Nazar Mohammad 5: *v In 1952 (5)*
Nazir Junior (*see* Mohammad Nazir)
Niaz Ahmed 2: v E 1968 (1); *v E 1967 (1)*

Pervez Sajjad 19: v E 1968 (1) 1972 (2); v A 1964 (1); v NZ 1964 (3) 1969 (3); *v E 1971 (3); v NZ 1964 (3) 1972 (3)*

Qasim Omar 26: v E 1983 (3); v WI 1986 (3); v NZ 1984 (3); v In 1984 (2); v SL 1985 (3); *v A 1983 (5); v NZ 1984 (3); v In 1983 (1); v SL 1985 (3)*

Ramiz Raja 57: v E 1983 (2) 1987 (3); v A 1988 (3); v WI 1986 (3) 1990 (2); v NZ 1990 (3); v In 1989 (4); v SL 1985 (1) 1991 (3) 1995 (3); *v E 1987 (2) 1992 (5); v A 1989 (2) 1995 (3); v WI 1987 (3) 1992 (3); v NZ 1992 (1) 1995 (1); v In 1986 (5); v SL 1985 (3) 1996 (2)*
Rashid Khan 4: v SL 1981 (2); *v A 1983 (1); v NZ 1984 (1)*
Rashid Latif 22: v A 1994 (2); v Z 1993 (3); *v E 1992 (1) 1996 (1); v A 1995 (1); v SA 1997 (1); v WI 1992 (1); v NZ 1992 (1) 1993 (3) 1995 (1); v SL 1994 (2); v Z 1994 (3) 1997 (2)*
Rehman, S. F. 1: *v WI 1957*
Rizwan-uz-Zaman 11: v WI 1986 (1); v SL 1981 (2); *v A 1981 (1); v NZ 1988 (2); v In 1986 (5)*

Sadiq Mohammad 41: v E 1972 (3) 1977 (2); v WI 1974 (1) 1980 (3); v NZ 1969 (3) 1976 (3); v In 1978 (1); *v E 1971 (3) 1974 (3) 1978 (3); v A 1972 (3) 1976 (2); v WI 1976 (5); v NZ 1972 (3); v In 1979 (3)*
Saeed Ahmed 41: v E 1961 (3) 1968 (3); v A 1959 (3) 1964 (1); v WI 1958 (3); v NZ 1964 (3); *v E 1962 (5) 1967 (3) 1971 (1); v A 1964 (1) 1972 (2); v WI 1957 (5); v NZ 1964 (3); v In 1960 (5)*
Saeed Anwar 49: v A 1994 (3) 1998 (2); v SA 1997 (3); v WI 1990 (1) 1997 (3); v NZ 1996 (2); v SL 1995 (2) 1998 (1) 1999 (2); v Z 1996 (2) 1998 (2); *v E 1996 (3); v A 1999 (3); v SA 1994 (1) 1997 (3); v NZ 1993 (3); v In 1998 (3); v SL 1994 (2) 1998 (1) 2000 (3); v Z 1994 (2) 1997 (2)*
Salah-ud-Din 5: v E 1968 (1); v NZ 1964 (3) 1969 (1)
Saleem Jaffer 14: v E 1987 (1); v A 1988 (2); v WI 1986 (1); v NZ 1990 (2); v In 1989 (1); v SL 1991 (2); *v WI 1987 (1); v NZ 1988 (2); v In 1986 (2)*
Salim Altaf 21: v E 1972 (3); v NZ 1969 (2); v In 1978 (1); *v E 1967 (2) 1971 (2); v A 1972 (3) 1976 (2); v WI 1976 (3); v NZ 1972 (3)*
Salim Elahi 4: *v A 1995 (2); v SL 1996 (2)*
Salim Malik 103: v E 1983 (3) 1987 (3); v A 1988 (3) 1994 (3) 1998 (3); v WI 1986 (1) 1990 (3); v NZ 1984 (3) 1990 (3) 1996 (2); v In 1982 (6) 1984 (2) 1989 (4); v SL 1981 (2) 1985 (3) 1991 (3); v Z 1996 (2) 1998 (1); *v E 1987 (5) 1992 (5) 1996 (3); v A 1983 (3) 1989 (1) 1995 (2); v SA 1994 (1); v WI 1987 (3); v NZ 1984 (3) 1988 (2) 1992 (1) 1993 (3) 1995 (1); v In 1983 (2) 1986 (3) 1998 (3); v SL 1985 (3) 1994 (2) 1996 (2); v Z 1994 (3)*
Salim Yousuf 32: v A 1988 (3); v WI 1986 (3) 1990 (1); v NZ 1990 (3); v In 1989 (1); v SL 1981 (1) 1985 (2); *v E 1987 (5); v A 1989 (3); v WI 1987 (3); v NZ 1988 (3); v In 1986 (5)*
Saqlain Mushtaq 28: v A 1998 (1); v SA 1997 (3); v WI 1997 (1); v NZ 1996 (2); v SL 1995 (2) 1998 (1) 1999 (1); v Z 1996 (2) 1998 (1); *v A 1995 (2) 1999 (2); v SA 1997 (1); v WI 1999 (3); v In 1998 (3); v SL 1996 (2) 1998 (1); v Z 1997 (1)*
Sarfraz Nawaz 55: v E 1968 (1) 1972 (2) 1977 (2) 1983 (3); v A 1979 (3); v WI 1974 (2) 1980 (2); v NZ 1976 (3); v In 1978 (3) 1982 (6); *v E 1974 (3) 1978 (2) 1982 (1); v A 1972 (2) 1976 (2) 1978 (2) 1981 (3) 1983 (3); v WI 1976 (4); v NZ 1972 (3) 1978 (3)*
Shadab Kabir 3: v Z 1996 (1); *v E 1996 (2)*
Shafiq Ahmed 6: v E 1977 (3); v WI 1980 (2); *v E 1974 (1)*
Shafqat Rana 5: v E 1968 (2); v A 1964 (1); v NZ 1969 (2)
Shahid Afridi 8: v A 1998 (1); v SL 1998 (1) 1999 (2); *v In 1998 (3); v SL 1998 (1)*
Shahid Israr 1: v NZ 1976
Shahid Mahboob 1: v In 1989
Shahid Mahmood 1: *v E 1962*
Shahid Nazir 8: v WI 1997 (1); v NZ 1996 (2); v SL 1998 (1); v Z 1996 (2); *v SL 1996 (2)*
Shahid Saeed 1: v In 1989
Shakeel Ahmed, sen. 1: v A 1998

Shakeel Ahmed, jun. 3: *v WI 1992 (1); v Z 1994 (2)*

Sharpe, D. 3: v A 1959 (3)

Shoaib Akhtar 15: v A 1998 (2); v WI 1997 (1); v SL 1999 (2); v Z 1998 (1); *v A 1999 (3); v SA 1997 (3); v In 1998 (1); v SL 1998 (1); v Z 1997 (1)*

Shoaib Mohammad 45: v E 1983 (1) 1987 (1); v A 1988 (3); v WI 1990 (3); v NZ 1984 (1) 1990 (3); v In 1989 (4); v SL 1985 (1) 1991 (3) 1995 (3); v Z 1993 (3); *v E 1987 (4) 1992 (1); v A 1989 (3); v WI 1987 (3); v NZ 1984 (1) 1988 (2); v In 1983 (2) 1986 (3)*

Shuja-ud-Din 19: v E 1961 (2); v A 1959 (3); v WI 1958 (3); v NZ 1955 (3); v In 1954 (5); *v E 1954 (3)*

Sikander Bakht 26: v E 1977 (2); v WI 1980 (1); v NZ 1976 (1); v In 1978 (2) 1982 (1); *v E 1978 (3) 1982 (2); v A 1978 (2) 1981 (3); v WI 1976 (1); v NZ 1978 (3); v In 1979 (5)*

Tahir Naqqash 15: v A 1982 (3); v In 1982 (2); v SL 1981 (3); *v E 1982 (2); v A 1983 (1); v NZ 1984 (1); v In 1983 (3)*

Talat Ali 10: v E 1972 (3); *v E 1978 (2); v A 1972 (1); v NZ 1972 (1) 1978 (3)*

Taslim Arif 6: v A 1979 (3); v WI 1980 (2); *v In 1979 (1)*

Tauseef Ahmed 34: v E 1983 (2) 1987 (2); v A 1979 (3) 1988 (3); v WI 1986 (3); v NZ 1984 (1) 1990 (2); v In 1984 (1); v SL 1981 (3) 1985 (1); v Z 1993 (1); *v E 1987 (2); v A 1989 (3); v NZ 1988 (1); v In 1986 (4); v SL 1985 (2)*

Wajahatullah Wasti 6: v SL 1998 (1) 1999 (1); *v A 1999 (1); v WI 1999 (1); v In 1998 (1); v SL 1998 (1)*

Waqar Hassan 21: v A 1956 (1) 1959 (1); v WI 1958 (1); v NZ 1955 (3); v In 1954 (5); *v E 1954 (4); v WI 1957 (1); v In 1952 (5)*

Waqar Younis 67: v A 1994 (2); v SA 1997 (2); v WI 1990 (3) 1997 (2); v NZ 1990 (3) 1996 (1); v In 1989 (2); v SL 1991 (3) 1995 (1) 1999 (3); v Z 1993 (3) 1996 (2) 1998 (2); *v E 1992 (5) 1996 (3); v A 1989 (3) 1995 (3) 1999 (1); v SA 1997 (3); v WI 1992 (3) 1999 (3); v NZ 1992 (1) 1993 (3) 1995 (1); v In 1998 (3); v SL 1994 (2) 2000 (3); v Z 1997 (2)*

Wasim Akram 98: v E 1987 (2); v A 1994 (2) 1998 (2); v SA 1997 (2); v WI 1986 (2) 1990 (3) 1997 (3); v NZ 1990 (2); v In 1989 (4); v SL 1985 (3) 1991 (3) 1995 (2) 1998 (1) 1999 (1); v Z 1993 (2) 1996 (2) 1998 (2); *v E 1987 (5) 1992 (4) 1996 (3); v A 1989 (3) 1995 (3) 1999 (3); v SA 1994 (1) 1997 (1); v WI 1987 (3) 1992 (3) 1999 (3); v NZ 1984 (2) 1992 (1) 1993 (3) 1995 (1); v In 1986 (5) 1998 (3); v SL 1985 (3) 1994 (2) 1998 (1) 2000 (3); v Z 1994 (3) 1997 (1)*

Wasim Bari 81: v E 1968 (3) 1972 (3) 1977 (3); v A 1982 (3); v WI 1974 (2) 1980 (2); v NZ 1969 (3) 1976 (2); v In 1978 (3) 1982 (6); *v E 1967 (3) 1971 (3) 1974 (3) 1978 (3) 1982 (3); v A 1972 (3) 1976 (3) 1978 (2) 1981 (3) 1983 (5); v WI 1976 (5); v NZ 1972 (3) 1978 (3); v In 1979 (6) 1983 (3)*

Wasim Raja 57: v E 1972 (1) 1977 (3) 1983 (3); v A 1979 (3); v WI 1974 (2) 1980 (4); v NZ 1976 (1) 1984 (1); v In 1982 (1) 1984 (1); v SL 1981 (3); *v E 1974 (2) 1978 (3) 1982 (1); v A 1978 (1) 1981 (3) 1983 (2); v WI 1976 (5); v NZ 1972 (3) 1978 (3) 1984 (2); v In 1979 (6) 1983 (3)*

Wazir Mohammad 20: v A 1956 (1) 1959 (1); v WI 1958 (3); v NZ 1955 (2); v In 1954 (5); *v E 1954 (2); v WI 1957 (5); v In 1952 (1)*

Younis Ahmed 4: v NZ 1969 (2); *v In 1986 (2)*

Younis Khan 9: v SL 1999 (3); *v WI 1999 (3); v SL 2000 (3)*

Yousuf Youhana 24: v A 1998 (2); v SL 1998 (1) 1999 (3); v Z 1998 (2); *v A 1999 (3); v SA 1997 (1); v WI 1999 (3); v In 1998 (3); v SL 1998 (1) 2000 (3); v Z 1997 (2)*

Zaheer Abbas 78: v E 1972 (2) 1983 (3); v A 1979 (2) 1982 (3); v WI 1974 (2) 1980 (3); v NZ 1969 (1) 1976 (3) 1984 (3); v In 1978 (3) 1982 (6) 1984 (2); v SL 1981 (1) 1985 (2); *v E 1971 (3) 1974 (3) 1982 (3); v A 1972 (3) 1976 (3) 1978 (2) 1981 (2) 1983 (5); v WI 1976 (3); v NZ 1972 (3) 1978 (2) 1984 (2); v In 1979 (5) 1983 (3)*

Zahid Fazal 9: v A 1994 (2); v WI 1990 (3); v SL 1991 (3) 1995 (1)

Zahoor Elahi 2: v NZ 1996 (2)

Zakir Khan 2: v In 1989 (1); *v SL 1985 (1)*

Zulfiqar Ahmed 9: v A 1956 (1); v NZ 1955 (3); *v E 1954 (2); v In 1952 (3)*

Zulqarnain 3: v SL 1985 (3)

SRI LANKA

Number of Test cricketers: 84

Ahangama, F. S. 3: v In 1985 (3)
Amalean, K. N. 2: v P 1985 (1); *v A 1987 (1)*
Amerasinghe, A. M. J. G. 2: v NZ 1983 (2)
Anurasiri, S. D. 18: v A 1992 (3); v WI 1993 (1); v NZ 1986 (1) 1992 (2); v P 1985 (2); v Z 1997 (1); *v E 1991 (1); v In 1986 (1) 1993 (3); v P 1991 (3)*
Arnold, R. P. 21: v A 1999 (3); v SA 2000 (3); v In 1998 (1); v P 1996 (2) 2000 (3); *v WI 1996 (1); v P 1998 (2) 1999 (3); v Z 1999 (3)*
Atapattu, M. S. 38: v A 1992 (1) 1999 (3); v SA 2000 (3); v NZ 1997 (3); v In 1997 (2) 1998 (1); v P 1996 (2) 2000 (3); v Z 1997 (2); *v E 1998 (1); v SA 1997 (2); v WI 1996 (1); v NZ 1996 (1); v In 1990 (1) 1993 (1) 1997 (3); v P 1998 (2) 1999 (3); v Z 1999 (3)*

Bandara, C. M. 1: v NZ 1997
Bandaratilleke, M. R. C. N. 4: v NZ 1997 (3); *v P 1998 (1)*

Chandana, U. D. U. 5: v A 1999 (1); v SA 2000 (3); *v P 1998 (1)*

Dassanayake, P. B. 11: v SA 1993 (3); v WI 1993 (1); v P 1994 (2); *v In 1993 (3); v Z 1994 (2)*
de Alwis, R. G. 11: v A 1982 (1); v NZ 1983 (3); v P 1985 (2); *v A 1987 (1); v NZ 1982 (1); v In 1986 (1)*
de Mel, A. L. F. 17: v E 1981 (1); v A 1982 (1); v In 1985 (3); v P 1985 (3); *v E 1984 (1); v In 1982 (1) 1986 (1); v P 1981 (3) 1985 (3)*
de Saram, S. I. 4: *v P 1999 (1); v Z 1999 (3)*
de Silva, A. M. 3: v E 1992 (1); v In 1993 (2)
de Silva, D. S. 12: v E 1981 (1); v A 1982 (1); v NZ 1983 (3); *v E 1984 (1); v NZ 1982 (2); v In 1982 (1); v P 1981 (3)*
de Silva, E. A. R. 10: v In 1985 (1); v P 1985 (1); *v A 1989 (2); v NZ 1990 (3); v In 1986 (3)*
de Silva, G. R. A. 4: v E 1981 (1); *v In 1982 (1); v P 1981 (2)*
de Silva, K. S. C. 8: v In 1997 (1); v P 1996 (1); *v WI 1996 (2); v NZ 1996 (1); v In 1997 (1); v P 1998 (2)*
de Silva, P. A. 85: v E 1992 (1); v A 1992 (3) 1999 (3); v SA 1993 (3) 2000 (1); v WI 1993 (1); v NZ 1992 (2) 1997 (3); v In 1985 (3) 1993 (3) 1997 (2) 1998 (1); v P 1985 (3) 1994 (2) 1996 (2) 2000 (3); v Z 1996 (2) 1997 (2); *v E 1984 (1) 1988 (1) 1991 (1) 1998 (1); v A 1987 (1) 1989 (2) 1995 (3); v SA 1997 (2); v WI 1996 (2); v NZ 1990 (3) 1994 (2) 1996 (2); v In 1986 (3) 1990 (1) 1993 (3) 1997 (3); v P 1985 (3) 1991 (3) 1995 (2) 1998 (1) 1999 (2); v Z 1994 (3)*
de Silva, S. K. L. 3: *v In 1997 (3)*
Dharmasena, H. D. P. K. 23: v SA 1993 (2) 2000 (2); v NZ 1997 (2); v P 1994 (2) 1996 (1) 2000 (1); v Z 1996 (1); *v E 1998 (1); v A 1995 (2); v WI 1996 (2); v NZ 1996 (1); v In 1997 (2); v P 1995 (2); v Z 1994 (2)*
Dias, R. L. 20: v E 1981 (1); v A 1982 (1); v NZ 1983 (2) 1986 (1); v In 1985 (3); v P 1985 (1); *v E 1984 (1); v In 1982 (1) 1986 (3); v P 1981 (3) 1985 (3)*
Dilshan, T. M. 5: *v P 1999 (2); v Z 1999 (3)*
Dunusinghe, C. I. 5: *v NZ 1994 (2); v P 1995 (3)*

Fernando, E. R. N. S. 5: v A 1982 (1); v NZ 1983 (2); *v NZ 1982 (2)*
Fernando, C. R. D. 1: v P 2000

Gallage, I. S. 1: *v Z 1999*
Goonatillake, H. M. 5: v E 1981 (1); *v In 1982 (1); v P 1981 (3)*
Gunasekera, Y. 2: *v NZ 1982 (2)*
Gunawardene, D. A. 2: *v P 1998 (2)*
Guneratne, R. P. W. 1: v A 1982
Gurusinha, A. P. 41: v E 1992 (1); v A 1992 (3); v SA 1993 (1); v NZ 1986 (1) 1992 (2); v In 1993 (3); v P 1985 (2) 1994 (1); v Z 1996 (2); *v E 1991 (1); v A 1989 (2) 1995 (3); v NZ 1990 (3) 1994 (2); v In 1986 (3) 1990 (1); v P 1985 (1) 1991 (3) 1995 (3); v Z 1994 (3)*

Hathurusinghe, U. C. 26: v E 1992 (1); v A 1992 (3); v SA 1993 (3); v NZ 1992 (2); v In 1993 (3) 1998 (1); *v E 1991 (1); v A 1995 (3); v NZ 1990 (2); v P 1991 (3) 1995 (3) 1998 (1)*
Herath, R. 3: v A 1999 (2); v P 2000 (1)

Jayasekera, R. S. A. 1: *v P 1981*
Jayasuriya S. T. 53: v E 1992 (1); v A 1992 (2) 1999 (3); v SA 1993 (2) 2000 (3); v WI 1993 (1); v NZ 1997 (3); v In 1993 (1) 1997 (2); v P 1994 (1) 1996 (2) 2000 (3); v Z 1996 (2) 1997 (2); *v E 1991 (1) 1998 (1); v A 1995 (1); v SA 1997 (2); v WI 1996 (2); v NZ 1990 (2) 1996 (2); v In 1993 (1) 1997 (3); v P 1991 (3) 1999 (3); v Z 1994 (1) 1999 (3)*
Jayawardene, D. P. M. D. 24: v A 1999 (3); v SA 2000 (3); v NZ 1997 (3); v In 1997 (2) 1998 (1); v P 2000 (3); *v E 1998 (1); v P 1998 (2) 1999 (3); v Z 1999 (3)*
Jayawardene, H. A. P. W. 1: v P 2000
Jeganathan, S. 2: *v NZ 1982 (2)*
John, V. B. 6: v NZ 1983 (3); *v E 1984 (1); v NZ 1982 (2)*
Jurangpathy, B. R. 2: v In 1985 (1); *v In 1986 (1)*

Kalpage, R. S. 11: v SA 1993 (1); v WI 1993 (1); v NZ 1997 (1); v In 1993 (1); v P 1994 (1) 1996 (1); *v In 1993 (3); v P 1998 (1); v Z 1994 (1)*
Kaluperuma, L. W. 2: v E 1981 (1); *v P 1981 (1)*
Kaluperuma, S. M. S. 4: v NZ 1983 (3); *v A 1987 (1)*
Kaluwitharana, R. S. 38: v A 1992 (2) 1999 (3); v NZ 1997 (3); v In 1993 (1) 1997 (2) 1998 (1); v P 1996 (2) 2000 (2); v Z 1996 (2) 1997 (2); *v E 1998 (1); A 1995 (3); v SA 1997 (2); v WI 1996 (2); v NZ 1996 (2); v P 1998 (2) 1999 (3); v Z 1999 (3)*
Kuruppu, D. S. B. P. 4: v NZ 1986 (1); *v E 1988 (1) 1991 (1); v A 1987 (1)*
Kuruppuarachchi, A. K. 2: v NZ 1986 (1); v P 1985 (1)

Labrooy, G. F. 9: *v E 1988 (1); v A 1987 (1) 1989 (2); v NZ 1990 (3); v In 1986 (1) 1990 (1)*
Liyanage, D. K. 8: v A 1992 (2); v SA 1993 (1); v NZ 1992 (2); v In 1993 (2); *v In 1993 (1)*

Madugalle, R. S. 21: v E 1981 (1); v A 1982 (1); v NZ 1983 (3) 1986 (1); v In 1985 (3); *v E 1984 (1) 1988 (1); v A 1987 (1); v NZ 1982 (2); v In 1982 (1); v P 1981 (3) 1985 (3)*
Madurasinghe, A. W. R. 3: v A 1992 (1); *v E 1988 (1); v In 1990 (1)*
Mahanama, R. S. 52: v E 1992 (1); v A 1992 (3); v SA 1993 (3); v WI 1993 (1); v NZ 1986 (1) 1992 (2); v In 1993 (3) 1997 (2); v P 1985 (2) 1994 (2); v Z 1996 (2) 1997 (2); *v E 1991 (1); v A 1987 (1) 1989 (2) 1995 (2); v SA 1997 (2); v WI 1996 (2); v NZ 1990 (1) 1996 (2); v In 1990 (1) 1993 (3) 1997 (3); v P 1991 (2) 1995 (3); v Z 1994 (3)*
Mendis, L. R. D. 24: v E 1981 (1); v A 1982 (1); v NZ 1983 (3) 1986 (1); v In 1985 (3); v P 1985 (3); *v E 1984 (1) 1988 (1); v In 1982 (1) 1986 (3); v P 1981 (3) 1985 (3)*
Muralitharan, M. 57: v E 1992 (1); v A 1992 (2) 1999 (3); v SA 1993 (3) 2000 (3); v WI 1993 (1); v NZ 1992 (1) 1997 (3); v In 1993 (2) 1997 (2); v P 1994 (1) 1996 (1) 2000 (3); v Z 1996 (2) 1997 (2); *v E 1998 (1); v A 1995 (2); v SA 1997 (2); v WI 1996 (2); v NZ 1994 (2) 1996 (2); v In 1993 (3) 1997 (2); v P 1995 (3) 1999 (3); v Z 1994 (2) 1999 (3)*

Perera, A. S. A. 1: *v E 1998*
Perera, P. D. R. L. 2: v SA 2000 (1); v In 1998 (1)
Pushpakumara, K. R. 22: v In 1997 (2); v P 1994 (1) 2000 (1); v Z 1996 (1) 1997 (2); *v A 1995 (1); v SA 1997 (2); v WI 1996 (2); v NZ 1994 (2); v In 1997 (2); v P 1995 (1) 1999 (2); v Z 1994 (2) 1999 (1)*

Ramanayake, C. P. H. 18: v E 1992 (1); v A 1992 (3); v SA 1993 (2); v NZ 1992 (1); v In 1993 (1); *v E 1988 (1) 1991 (1); v A 1987 (1) 1989 (2); v NZ 1990 (3); v P 1991 (2)*
Ranasinghe, A. N. 2: *v In 1982 (1); v P 1981 (1)*
Ranatunga, A. 93: v E 1981 (1) 1992 (1); v A 1982 (1) 1992 (3) 1999 (3) ; v SA 1993 (3) 2000 (3); v WI 1993 (1); v NZ 1983 (3) 1986 (1) 1992 (2) 1997 (3); v In 1985 (3) 1993 (3) 1997 (2) 1998 (1); v P 1985 (3) 1994 (2) 1996 (2) 2000 (3); v Z 1996 (2) 1997 (2); *v E 1984 (1) 1988 (1) 1998 (1); v A 1987 (1) 1989 (2) 1995 (2); v SA 1997 (2); v WI 1996 (2); v NZ 1990 (3) 1994 (2) 1996 (2); v In 1982 (1) 1986 (3) 1990 (1) 1993 (3) 1997 (3); v P 1981 (2) 1985 (3) 1991 (3) 1995 (3) 1999 (1); v Z 1994 (3)*
Ranatunga, D. 2: *v A 1989 (2)*

Ranatunga, S. 9: v P 1994 (1); *v A 1995 (1); v WI 1996 (1); v NZ 1994 (2); v P 1995 (1); v Z 1994 (3)*

Ratnayake, R. J. 23: v A 1982 (1); v NZ 1983 (1) 1986 (1); v In 1985 (3); v P 1985 (1); *v E 1991 (1); v A 1989 (1); v NZ 1982 (2) 1990 (3); v In 1986 (2) 1990 (1); v P 1985 (3) 1991 (3)*

Ratnayeke, J. R. 22: v NZ 1983 (2) 1986 (1); v P 1985 (3); *v E 1984 (1) 1988 (1); v A 1987 (1) 1989 (2); v NZ 1982 (2); v In 1982 (1) 1986 (3); v P 1981 (2) 1985 (3)*

Samarasekera, M. A. R. 4: *v E 1988 (1); v A 1989 (1); v In 1990 (1); v P 1991 (1)*

Samaraweera, D. P. 7: v WI 1993 (1); v P 1994 (1); *v NZ 1994 (2); v In 1993 (3)*

Sangakkara, K. 3: v SA 2000 (3)

Senanayake, C. P. 3: *v NZ 1990 (3)*

Silva, K. J. 7: v In 1997 (1); v P 1996 (1); v Z 1996 (2) 1997 (1); *v A 1995 (1); v In 1997 (1)*

Silva, S. A. R. 9: v In 1985 (3); v P 1985 (1); *v E 1984 (1) 1988 (1); v NZ 1982 (1); v P 1985 (2)*

Tillekeratne, H. P. 56: v E 1992 (1); v A 1992 (1); v SA 1993 (3); v WI 1993 (1); v NZ 1992 (2) 1997 (2); v In 1993 (3) 1998 (1); v P 1994 (2) 1996 (2); v Z 1996 (2) 1997 (2); *v E 1991 (1) 1998 (1); v A 1989 (1) 1995 (3); v SA 1997 (2); v WI 1996 (1); v NZ 1990 (3) 1994 (2) 1996 (2); v In 1990 (1) 1993 (3) 1997 (3); v P 1991 (3) 1995 (3) 1998 (2); v Z 1994 (3)*

Upashantha, K. E. A. 1: v In 1998

Vaas, W. P. U. J. C. 43: v A 1999 (3); v SA 2000 (3); v In 1997 (2) 1998 (1); v P 1994 (1) 1996 (2) 2000 (3); v Z 1996 (2) 1997 (2); *v A 1995 (3); v SA 1997 (1); v NZ 1994 (2) 1996 (2); v In 1997 (3); v P 1995 (3) 1998 (1) 1999 (3); v Z 1994 (3) 1999 (3)*

Warnapura, B. 4: v E 1981 (1); *v In 1982 (1); v P 1981 (2)*

Warnaweera, K. P. J. 10: v E 1992 (1); v NZ 1992 (2); v In 1993 (3); v P 1985 (1) 1994 (1); *v NZ 1990 (1); v In 1990 (1)*

Weerasinghe, C. D. U. S. 1: v In 1985

Wettimuny, M. D. 2: *v NZ 1982 (2)*

Wettimuny, S. 23: v E 1981 (1); v A 1982 (1); v NZ 1983 (3); v In 1985 (3); v P 1985 (3); *v E 1984 (1); v NZ 1982 (2); v In 1986 (3); v P 1981 (3) 1985 (3)*

Wickremasinghe, A. G. D. 3: v NZ 1992 (2); *v A 1989 (1)*

Wickremasinghe, G. P. 39: v A 1992 (1); v SA 1993 (2); v WI 1993 (1); v NZ 1997 (3); v In 1993 (2); v P 1994 (1); *v E 1998 (1); v A 1995 (3); v SA 1997 (2); v NZ 1994 (2) 1996 (1); v In 1993 (3) 1997 (3); v P 1991 (3) 1995 (3) 1998 (2) 1999 (3); v Z 1994 (2) 1999 (3)*

Wijegunawardene, K. I. W. 2: *v E 1991 (1); v P 1991 (1)*

Wijesuriya, R. G. C. E. 4: *v P 1981 (1) 1985 (3)*

Wijetunge, P. K. 1: v SA 1993

Zoysa, D. N. T. 13: v A 1999 (3); v SA 2000 (2); v P 1996 (1) 2000 (2); *v SA 1997 (1); v NZ 1996 (2); v P 1999 (1); v Z 1999 (1)*

ZIMBABWE

Number of Test cricketers: 45

Arnott, K. J. 4: v NZ 1992 (2); v In 1992 (1); *v In 1992 (1)*

Brain, D. H. 9: v NZ 1992 (1); v P 1994 (3); v SL 1994 (2); *v In 1992 (1); v P 1993 (2)*

Brandes, E. A. 10: v E 1996 (1); v NZ 1992 (1); v In 1992 (1); v SL 1999 (1); *v NZ 1995 (2); v In 1992 (1); v P 1993 (3)*

Brent, G. B. 2: v SL 1999 (2)

Briant, G. A. 1: *v In 1992*

Bruk-Jackson, G. K. 2: *v P 1993 (2)*

Burmester, M. G. 3: v NZ 1992 (2); v In 1992 (1)

Butchart, I. P. 1: v P 1994

Campbell, A. D. R. 43: v E 1996 (2); v A 1999 (1); v SA 1995 (1) 1999 (1); v NZ 1992 (2) 1997 (2); v In 1992 (1) 1998 (1); v P 1994 (3) 1997 (2); v SL 1994 (3) 1999 (3); *v E 2000 (2); v SA 1999 (1); v WI 1999 (2); v NZ 1995 (2) 1997 (2); v In 1992 (1); v P 1993 (3) 1996 (2) 1998 (2); v SL 1996 (2) 1997 (2)*

Carlisle, S. V. 9: v E 1996 (1); v P 1994 (3); *v E 2000 (1); v WI 1999 (2); v NZ 1995 (2)*

Crocker, G. J. 3: v NZ 1992 (2); v In 1992 (1)

Dekker, M. H. 14: v E 1996 (1); v SA 1995 (1); v P 1994 (2); v SL 1994 (3); *v P 1993 (3) 1996 (2); v SL 1996 (2)*

Evans, C. N. 2: v In 1998 (1); *v SL 1996 (1)*

Flower, A. 43: v E 1996 (2); v A 1999 (1); v SA 1995 (1) 1999 (1); v NZ 1992 (2) 1997 (2); v In 1992 (1) 1998 (1); v P 1994 (3) 1997 (2); v SL 1994 (3) 1999 (3); *v E 2000 (2); v SA 1999 (1); v WI 1999 (2); v NZ 1995 (2) 1997 (2); v In 1992 (1); v P 1993 (3) 1996 (2) 1998 (2); v SL 1996 (2) 1997 (2)*

Flower, G. W. 42: v E 1996 (2); v A 1999 (1); v SA 1995 (1) 1999 (1); v NZ 1992 (2) 1997 (2); v In 1992 (1); v P 1994 (3) 1997 (2); v SL 1994 (3) 1999 (3); *v E 2000 (2); v SA 1999 (1); v WI 1999 (2); v NZ 1995 (2) 1997 (2); v In 1992 (1); v P 1993 (3) 1996 (2) 1998 (2); v SL 1996 (2) 1997 (2)*

Goodwin, M. W. 19: v A 1999 (1); v SA 1999 (1); v In 1998 (1); v P 1997 (2); v SL 1999 (3); *v E 2000 (2); v SA 1999 (1); v WI 1999 (2); v NZ 1997 (2); v P 1998 (2); v SL 1997 (2)*

Gripper, T. R. 7: v A 1999 (1); v SA 1999 (1); v SL 1999 (1); *v E 2000 (1); v SA 1999 (1); v WI 1999 (2)*

Houghton, D. L. 22: v E 1996 (2); v SA 1995 (1); v NZ 1992 (2) 1997 (2); v In 1992 (1); v P 1994 (3); v SL 1994 (3); *v NZ 1995 (2); v In 1992 (1); v P 1993 (3) 1996 (2)*

Huckle, A. G. 8: v NZ 1997 (2); v In 1998 (1); v P 1997 (1); *v NZ 1997 (2); v P 1998 (1); v SL 1997 (1)*

James, W. R. 4: v SL 1994 (3); *v P 1993 (1)*

Jarvis, M. P. 5: v NZ 1992 (1); v In 1992 (1); v SL 1994 (3)

Johnson, N. C. 13: v A 1999 (1); v SA 1999 (1); v In 1998 (1); v SL 1999 (3); *v E 2000 (2); v SA 1999 (1); v WI 1999 (2); v P 1998 (2)*

Lock, A. C. I. 1: v SA 1995

Madondo, T. N. 2: v P 1997 (2)

Matambanadzo, E. Z. 3: v NZ 1997 (1); v SL 1999 (1); *v P 1996 (1)*

Mbangwa, M. 14: v SA 1999 (1); v In 1998 (1); v P 1997 (2); *v E 2000 (2); v SA 1999 (1); v WI 1999 (1); v NZ 1997 (2); v P 1996 (1) 1998 (2); v SL 1997 (1)*

Murphy, B. A. 4: *v E 2000 (2); v WI 1999 (2)*

Nkala, M. L. 1: *v E 2000*

Olonga, H. K. 18: v E 1996 (2); v A 1999 (1); v SA 1999 (1); v In 1998 (1); v P 1994 (1); v SL 1999 (3); *v SA 1999 (1); v WI 1999 (2); v NZ 1995 (1); v P 1996 (1) 1998 (2); v SL 1996 (2)*

Peall, S. G. 4: v SL 1994 (2); *v P 1993 (2)*

Price, R. W. 1: v SL 1999

Pycroft, A. J. 3: v NZ 1992 (2); v In 1992 (1)

Ranchod, U. 1: *v In 1992*

Rennie, G. J. 14: v A 1999 (1); v SA 1999 (1); v NZ 1997 (2); v In 1998 (1); v P 1997 (1); v SL 1999 (1); *v SA 1999 (1); v NZ 1997 (2); v P 1998 (2); v SL 1997 (2)*

Rennie, J. A. 4: v NZ 1997 (1); v SL 1994 (1); *v P 1993 (2)*

Shah, A. H. 3: v NZ 1992 (1); *v In 1992 (1); v SL 1996 (1)*

Strang, B. C. 21: v E 1996 (1); v A 1999 (1); v SA 1995 (1) 1999 (1); v NZ 1997 (2); v P 1994 (2) 1997 (1); v SL 1999 (3); *v E 2000 (1); v SA 1999 (1); v WI 1999 (1); v NZ 1995 (2); v P 1996 (2); v SL 1996 (1) 1997 (1)*

Strang, P. A. 20: v E 1996 (2); v SA 1995 (1); v NZ 1997 (2); v P 1994 (3) 1997 (1); v SL 1994 (1);
v NZ 1995 (2) 1997 (2); v P 1996 (2); v SL 1996 (2) 1997 (2)
Streak, H. H. 31: v E 1996 (2); v A 1999 (1); v SA 1995 (1); v NZ 1997 (2); v In 1998 (1); v P
1994 (3) 1997 (2); v SL 1994 (3); *v E 2000 (2); v WI 1999 (2); v NZ 1995 (2) 1997 (2); v P
1993 (3) 1998 (2); v SL 1996 (1) 1997 (2)*

Traicos, A. J. 4: v NZ 1992 (2); v In 1992 (1); *v In 1992 (1)*

Viljoen, D. P. 1: v P 1997

Waller, A. C. 2: v E 1996 (2)
Whittall, A. R. 10: v P 1997 (1); v SL 1999 (1); *v NZ 1997 (2); v P 1996 (1) 1998 (1); v SL 1996 (2)
1997 (2)*
Whittall, G. J. 33: v E 1996 (2); v A 1999 (1); v SA 1995 (1) 1999 (1); v NZ 1997 (2); v P 1994 (3)
1997 (2); v SL 1994 (3) 1999 (3); *v E 2000 (2); v SA 1999 (1); v NZ 1995 (2) 1997 (2); v P
1993 (3) 1996 (2); v SL 1996 (2) 1997 (1)*
Wishart, C. B. 12: v SA 1995 (1); v In 1998 (1); v SL 1999 (1); *v NZ 1995 (1); v P 1996 (2)
1998 (2); v SL 1996 (2) 1997 (2)*

TWO COUNTRIES

Fourteen cricketers have appeared for two countries in Test matches, namely:

Amir Elahi, *India and Pakistan.*
J. J. Ferris, *Australia and England.*
S. C. Guillen, *West Indies and NZ.*
Gul Mahomed, *India and Pakistan.*
F. Hearne, *England and South Africa.*
A. H. Kardar, *India and Pakistan.*
W. E. Midwinter, *England and Australia.*

F. Mitchell, *England and South Africa.*
W. L. Murdoch, *Australia and England.*
Nawab of Pataudi, sen., *England and India.*
A. J. Traicos, *South Africa and Zimbabwe.*
A. E. Trott, *Australia and England.*
K. C. Wessels, *Australia and South Africa.*
S. M. J. Woods, *Australia and England.*

ENGLAND v REST OF THE WORLD

In 1970, owing to the cancellation of the South African tour to England, a series of matches was arranged, with the trappings of a full Test series, between England and the Rest of the World. It was played for the Guinness Trophy.

The following were awarded England caps for playing against the Rest of the World in that series, although the five matches played are now generally considered not to have rated as full Tests: D. L. Amiss (1), G. Boycott (2), D. J. Brown (2), M. C. Cowdrey (4), M. H. Denness (1), B. L. D'Oliveira (4), J. H. Edrich (2), K. W. R. Fletcher (4), A. W. Greig (3), R. Illingworth (5), A. Jones (1), A. P. E. Knott (5), P. Lever (1), B. W. Luckhurst (5), C. M. Old (2), P. J. Sharpe (1), K. Shuttleworth (1), J. A. Snow (5), D. L. Underwood (3), A. Ward (1), D. Wilson (2).

The following players represented the Rest of the World: E. J. Barlow (5), F. M. Engineer (2), L. R. Gibbs (4), Intikhab Alam (5), R. B. Kanhai (5), C. H. Lloyd (5), G. D. McKenzie (3), D. L. Murray (3), Mushtaq Mohammad (2), P. M. Pollock (1), R. G. Pollock (5), M. J. Procter (5), B. A. Richards (5), G. S. Sobers (5).

LIMITED-OVERS INTERNATIONAL CRICKETERS

The following players have appeared for Test-playing countries in limited-overs internationals but had not represented their countries in Test matches by August 20, 2000:

England M. W. Alleyne, I. D. Austin, A. D. Brown, D. R. Brown, M. V. Fleming, P. J. Franks, I. J. Gould, G. W. Humpage, T. E. Jesty, G. D. Lloyd, J. D. Love, M. A. Lynch, M. J. Smith, N. M. K. Smith, V. S. Solanki, G. P. Swann, S. D. Udal, C. M. Wells, V. J. Wells.

Australia G. A. Bishop, M. J. Di Venuto, S. F. Graf, I. J. Harvey, S. Lee, R. J. McCurdy, K. H. MacLeay, J. P. Maher, G. D. Porter, J. D. Siddons, A. M. Stuart, A. Symonds, G. S. Trimble, B. E. Young, A. K. Zesers.

South Africa D. M. Benkenstein, R. E. Bryson, D. J. Callaghan, D. N. Crookes, A. C. Dawson, A. J. Hall, L. J. Koen, P. V. Mpitsang, S. J. Palframan, C. E. B. Rice, M. J. R. Rindel, D. B. Rundle, T. G. Shaw, E. O. Simons, E. L. R. Stewart, R. Telemachus, C. J. P. G. van Zyl, H. S. Williams, C. M. Willoughby, M. Yachad.

West Indies H. A. G. Anthony, B. St A. Browne, H. R. Bryan, V. C. Drakes, R. S. Gabriel, R. C. Haynes, S. C. Joseph, N. C. McGarrell, M. R. Pydanna, K. F. Semple, C. M. Tuckett, L. R. Williams.

New Zealand M. D. Bailey, B. R. Blair, C. E. Bulfin, P. G. Coman, M. W. Douglas, C. J. Drum, B. G. Hadlee, R. T. Hart, R. L. Hayes, L. G. Howell, B. J. McKechnie, E. B. McSweeney, J. P. Millmow, C. J. Nevin, A. J. Penn, R. G. Petrie, R. B. Reid, S. J. Roberts, L. W. Stott, S. B. Styris, A. R. Tait, R. J. Webb, J. W. Wilson, W. A. Wisneski.

India H. K. Badani, S. V. Bahutule, A. C. Bedade, A. Bhandari, Bhupinder Singh, sen., G. Bose, V. B. Chandrasekhar, U. Chatterjee, N. A. David, P. Dharmani, S. S. Dighe, R. S. Ghai, S. S. Karim, S. C. Khanna, G. K. Khoda, A. R. Khurasiya, T. Kumaran, J. J. Martin, S. P. Mukherjee, G. K. Pandey, J. V. Paranjpe, A. K. Patel, Randhir Singh, S. S. Raul, R. Sanghvi, V. Shewag, L. R. Shukla, R. P. Singh, S. Somasunder, S. Sriram, Sudhakar Rao, P. S. Vaidya.

Pakistan Aamer Hameed, Aamer Hanif, Akhtar Sarfraz, Arshad Pervez, Asif Mahmood, Faisal Iqbal, Ghulam Ali, Haafiz Shahid, Hasan Jamil, Imran Abbas, Iqbal Sikandar, Irfan Bhatti, Javed Qadir, Mahmood Hamid, Mansoor Rana, Manzoor Akhtar, Maqsood Rana, Masood Iqbal, Moin-ul-Atiq, Mujahid Jamshed, Naeem Ahmed, Naeem Ashraf, Naseer Malik, Parvez Mir, Saadat Ali, Saeed Azad, Sajid Ali, Sajjad Akbar, Salim Pervez, Shabbir Ahmed, Shahid Anwar, Shakil Khan, Shoaib Malik, Sohail Fazal, Tanvir Mehdi, Wasim Haider, Yasir Arafat, Zafar Iqbal, Zahid Ahmed.

Sri Lanka J. W. H. D. Boteju, D. L. S. de Silva, G. N. de Silva, E. R. Fernando, T. L. Fernando, U. N. K. Fernando, J. C. Gamage, F. R. M. Goonatillake, A. A. W. Gunawardene, P. D. Heyn, S. A. Jayasinghe, S. H. U. Karnain, C. Mendis, A. M. N. Munasinghe, M. N. Nawaz, A. R. M. Opatha, S. P. Pasqual, K. G. Perera, H. S. M. Pieris, S. K. Ranasinghe, N. Ranatunga, N. L. K. Ratnayake, T. T. Samaraweera, L. P. C. Silva, A. P. B. Tennekoon, M. H. Tissera, D. M. Vonhagt, A. P. Weerakkody, K. Weeraratne, S. R. de S. Wettimuny, R. P. A. H. Wickremaratne.

Zimbabwe A. M. Blignaut, R. D. Brown, K. M. Curran, S. G. Davies, K. G. Duers, E. A. Essop-Adam, D. A. G. Fletcher, J. G. Heron, V. R. Hogg, G. C. Martin, M. A. Meman, D. T. Mutendera, G. A. Paterson, G. E. Peckover, P. W. E. Rawson.

Shahid Afridi appeared for Pakistan in 66 limited-overs internationals before making his Test debut.

BIRTHS AND DEATHS OF PAST CRICKETERS

Details of current first-class players are no longer listed in this section but may be found in the Register of Players on pages 170–189.

The qualifications for inclusion are as follows:

1. All players who have appeared in a Test match and are no longer playing first-class cricket.

2. All players who have appeared in a one-day international for a Test-match playing country and are no longer playing first-class cricket.

3. County players who appeared in 200 or more first-class matches during their careers, or 100 after the Second World War, and are no longer playing first-class cricket.

4. English county captains who captained their county in three seasons or more since 1890 and are no longer playing first-class cricket.

5. All *Wisden* Cricketers of the Year who are no longer playing first-class cricket, including the Public Schoolboys chosen for the 1918 and 1919 Almanacks. Cricketers of the Year are identified by the italic notation *CY* and year of appearance. A list of the Cricketers of the Year from 1889 to 2001 appears on pages 190–192.

6. Players or personalities not otherwise qualified who are thought to be of sufficient interest to merit inclusion.

Key to abbreviations and symbols

CU – Cambridge University, OU – Oxford University.

Australian states: NSW – New South Wales, Qld – Queensland, S. Aust. – South Australia, Tas. – Tasmania, Vic. – Victoria, W. Aust. – Western Australia.

Indian teams: Eur. – Europeans, Guj. – Gujarat, H'bad – Hyderabad, H. Pradesh – Himachal Pradesh, Ind. Rlwys – Indian Railways, Ind. Serv. – Indian Services, J/K – Jammu and Kashmir, Karn. – Karnataka (Mysore to 1972-73), M. Pradesh – Madhya Pradesh (Central India [C. Ind.] to 1939-40, Holkar to 1954-55, Madhya Bharat to 1956-57), M'tra – Maharashtra, Naw. – Nawanagar, Raja. – Rajasthan, S'tra – Saurashtra (West India [W. Ind.] to 1945-46, Kathiawar to 1949-50), S. Punjab – Southern Punjab (Patiala to 1958-59, Punjab since 1968-69), TC – Travancore-Cochin (Kerala since 1956-57), TN – Tamil Nadu (Madras to 1959-60), U. Pradesh – Uttar Pradesh (United Provinces [U. Prov.] to 1948-49), Vidarbha (CP & Berar to 1949-50, Madhya Pradesh to 1956-57).

New Zealand provinces: Auck. – Auckland, Cant. – Canterbury, C. Dist. – Central Districts, N. Dist. – Northern Districts, Wgtn – Wellington.

Pakistani teams: ADBP – Agricultural Development Bank of Pakistan, B'pur – Bahawalpur, Customs – Pakistan Customs, F'bad – Faisalabad, HBFC – House Building Finance Corporation, HBL – Habib Bank Ltd, I'bad – Islamabad, IDBP – Industrial Development Bank of Pakistan, Kar. – Karachi, KRL – Khan Research Laboratories, MCB – Muslim Commercial Bank, NBP – National Bank of Pakistan, NWFP – North-West Frontier Province, PACO – Pakistan Automobile Corporation, Pak. Rlwys – Pakistan Railways, Pak. Us – Pakistan Universities, PIA – Pakistan International Airlines, PNSC – Pakistan National Shipping Corporation, PWD – Public Works Department, R'pindi – Rawalpindi, UBL – United Bank Ltd, WAPDA – Water and Power Development Authority.

South African provinces: E. Prov. – Eastern Province, E. Tvl – Eastern Transvaal (Easterns since 1995-96), Griq. W. – Griqualand West, N. Tvl – Northern Transvaal (Northerns since 1997-98), NE Tvl – North-Eastern Transvaal, OFS – Orange Free State (Free State [FS] since 1995-96), Rhod. – Rhodesia, Tvl – Transvaal (Gauteng since 1997-98), W. Prov. – Western Province, W. Tvl – Western Transvaal (North West since 1996-97).

Sri Lankan teams: Ant. – Antonians, Bloom. – Bloomfield Cricket and Athletic Club, BRC – Burgher Recreation Club, CCC – Colombo Cricket Club, Mor. – Moratuwa Sports Club, NCC – Nondescripts Cricket Club, Pan. – Panadura Sports Club, Seb. – Sebastianites, SLAF – Air Force, SSC – Sinhalese Sports Club, TU – Tamil Union Cricket and Athletic Club, Under-23 – Board Under-23 XI, WPC – Western Province (City), WPN – Western Province (North), WPS – Western Province (South).

West Indies islands: B'dos – Barbados, BG – British Guiana (Guyana since 1966), Comb. Is. – Combined Islands, Jam. – Jamaica, T/T – Trinidad & Tobago.

Zimbabwean teams: Mash. – Mashonaland, Mat. – Matabeleland, MCD – Mashonaland Country Districts, Under-24 – Mashonaland Under-24, Zimb. – Zimbabwe.

* *Denotes Test player.* ** *Denotes appeared for two countries. There is a list of Test players country by country from page 67.*
† *Denotes also played for team under its previous name.*

Aamer Hameed (Pak. Us, Lahore, Punjab & OU) b Oct. 18, 1954
*Aamer Malik (ADBP, PIA, Multan & Lahore) b Jan. 3, 1963
Abberley, R. N. (Warwicks) b April 22, 1944
*a'Beckett, E. L. (Vic.) b Aug. 11, 1907, d June 2, 1989
*Abdul Kadir (Kar. & NBP) b May 10, 1944
*Abdul Qadir (HBL, Lahore & Punjab) b Sept. 15, 1955
*Abel, R. (Surrey; *CY 1890*) b Nov. 30, 1857, d Dec. 10, 1936
*Abid Ali, S. (H'bad) b Sept. 9, 1941
Abrahams, J. (Lancs) b July 21, 1952
*Absolom, C. A. (CU & Kent) b June 7, 1846, d July 30, 1889
Acfield, D. L. (CU & Essex) b July 24, 1947
*Achong, E. (T/T) b Feb. 16, 1904, d Aug. 29, 1986
Ackerman, H. M. (Border, NE Tvl, Northants, Natal & W. Prov.) b April 28, 1947
Adams, P. W. (Cheltenham & Sussex; *CY 1919*) b Sept. 5, 1900, d Sept. 28, 1962
*Adcock, N. A. T. (Tvl & Natal; *CY 1961*) b March 8, 1931
*Adhikari, H. R. (Guj., Baroda & Ind. Serv.) b July 31, 1919
*Afaq Hussain (Kar., Pak Us, PIA & PWD) b Dec. 31, 1939
Afford, J. A. (Notts) b May 12, 1964
*Aftab Baloch (PWD, Kar., Sind, NBP & PIA) b April 1, 1953
*Aftab Gul (Punjab U., Pak. Us & Lahore) b March 31, 1946
*Agha Saadat Ali (Pak. Us, Punjab, B'pur & Lahore) b June 21, 1929, d Oct. 26, 1995
*Agha Zahid (Pak Us, Punjab, Lahore & HBL) b Jan. 7, 1953
*Agnew, J. P. (Leics; *CY 1988;* broadcaster) b April 4, 1960
*Ahangama, F. S. (SSC) b Sept. 14, 1959
Aird, R. (CU & Hants; Sec. MCC 1953-62, Pres. MCC 1968-69) b May 4, 1902, d Aug. 16, 1986

Aislabie, B. (Surrey, Hants, Kent & Sussex; Sec. MCC 1822-42) b Jan. 14, 1774, d June 2, 1842
Aitchison, Rev. J. K. (Scotland) b May 26, 1920, d Feb. 13, 1994
*Alabaster, J. C. (Otago) b July 11, 1930
Alcock, C. W. (Sec. Surrey CCC 1872-1907; Editor *Cricket* 1882-1907) b Dec. 2, 1842, d Feb. 26, 1907
Alderman, A. E. (Derbys) b Oct. 30, 1907, d June 4, 1990
*Alderman, T. M. (W. Aust., Kent & Glos; *CY 1982*) b June 12, 1956
*Alexander, F. C. M. (CU & Jam.) b Nov. 2, 1928
*Alexander, G. (Vic.) b April 22, 1851, d Nov. 6, 1930
*Alexander, H. H. (Vic.) b June 9, 1905, d April 15, 1993
Alexander, Lord (Pres. MCC 2000-01) b Sept. 5, 1936
Alikhan, R. I. (Sussex, PIA, Surrey & PNSC) b Dec. 28, 1962
*Alim-ud-Din (Rajputana, Guj., Sind, B'pur, Kar. & PWD) b Dec. 15, 1930
*Allan, D. W. (B'dos) b Nov. 5, 1937
*Allan, F. E. (Vic.) b Dec. 2, 1849, d Feb. 9, 1917
Allan, J. M. (OU, Kent, Warwicks & Scotland) b April 2, 1932
*Allan, P. J. (Qld) b Dec. 31, 1935
*Allcott, C. F. W. (Auck.) b Oct. 7, 1896, d Nov. 19, 1973
Allen, B. O. (CU & Glos) b Oct. 13, 1911, d May 1, 1981
*Allen, D. A. (Glos) b Oct. 29, 1935
*Allen, Sir George O. B. (CU & Middx; Pres. MCC 1963-64) b July 31, 1902, d Nov. 29, 1989
*Allen, I. B. A. (Windwards) b Oct. 6, 1965
Allen, M. H. J. (Northants & Derbys) b Jan. 7, 1933, d Oct. 6, 1999
*Allen, R. C. (NSW) b July 2, 1858, d May 2, 1952
Alletson, E. B. (Notts) b March 6, 1884, d July 5, 1963

Alley, W. E. (NSW & Som; Test umpire; *CY 1962*) b Feb. 3, 1919

*Allom, M. J. C. (CU & Surrey; Pres. MCC 1969-70) b March 23, 1906, d April 8, 1995

*Allott, P. J. W. (Lancs & Wgtn) b Sept. 14, 1956

Altham, H. S. CBE (OU, Surrey & Hants; historian; Pres. MCC 1959-60) b Nov. 30, 1888, d March 11, 1965

*Amalean, K. N. (SL) b April 7, 1965

*Amarnath, Lala (N. B.) (N. Ind., S. Punjab, Guj., Patiala, U. Pradesh & Ind. Rlwys) b Sept. 11, 1911, d Aug. 5, 2000

*Amarnath, M. (Punjab & Delhi; *CY 1984*) b Sept. 24, 1950

*Amarnath, S. (Punjab & Delhi) b Dec. 30, 1948

*Amar Singh, L. (Patiala, W. Ind. & Naw.) b Dec. 4, 1910, d May 20, 1940

*Amerasinghe, A. M. J. G. (Nomads & Ant.) b Feb. 2, 1954

*Ames, L. E. G. CBE (Kent; *CY 1929*) b Dec. 3, 1905, d Feb. 26, 1990

**Amir Elahi (Baroda, N. Ind., S. Punjab & B'pur) b Sept. 1, 1908, d Dec. 28, 1980

*Amiss, D. L. MBE (Warwicks; *CY 1975*) b April 7, 1943

Anderson, I. S. (Derbys & Boland) b April 24, 1960

*Anderson, J. H. (W. Prov.) b April 26, 1874, d March 11, 1926

*Anderson, R. W. (Cant., N. Dist., Otago & C. Dist.) b Oct. 2, 1948

*Anderson, W. M. (Cant.) b Oct. 8, 1919, d Dec. 21, 1979

Andrew, K. V. (Northants) b Dec. 15, 1929

Andrew, S. J. W. (Hants & Essex) b Jan. 27, 1966

*Andrews, B. (Cant., C. Dist. & Otago) b April 4, 1945

*Andrews, T. J. E. (NSW) b Aug. 26, 1890, d Jan. 28, 1970

Andrews, W. H. R. (Som) b April 14, 1908, d Jan. 9, 1989

Angell, F. L. (Som) b June 29, 1922

*Anil Dalpat (Kar. & PIA) b Sept. 20, 1963

Anisur Rehman (Bangladesh) b March 1, 1971

*Ankola, S. A. (M'tra & †Mumbai) b March 1, 1968

Anthony, H. A. G. (Leewards & Glam) b Jan 16, 1971

*Anurasiri, S. D. (Pan. & WPS) b Feb. 25, 1966

*Anwar Hussain (N. Ind., Bombay, Sind & Kar.) b July 16, 1920

*Anwar Khan (Kar., Sind & NBP) b Dec. 24, 1955

*Appleyard, R. (Yorks; *CY 1952*) b June 27, 1924

*Apte, A. L. (Ind. Us, Bombay & Raja.) b Oct. 24, 1934

*Apte, M. L. (Bombay & Bengal) b Oct. 5, 1932

*Archer, A. G. (Worcs) b Dec. 6, 1871, d July 15, 1935

Archer, G. F. (Notts) b Sept. 26, 1970

*Archer, K. A. (Qld) b Jan. 17, 1928

*Archer, R. G. (Qld) b Oct. 25, 1933

*Arif Butt (Lahore & Pak. Rlwys) b May 17, 1944

Arlott, John OBE (Writer & broadcaster) b Feb. 25, 1914, d Dec. 14, 1991

*Armitage, T. (Yorks) b April 25, 1848, d Sept. 21, 1922

Armstrong, N. F. (Leics) b Dec. 22, 1892, d Jan. 19, 1990

*Armstrong, W. W. (Vic.; *CY 1903*) b May 22, 1879, d July 13, 1947

Arnold, A. P. (Cant. & Northants) b Oct. 16, 1926

*Arnold, E. G. (Worcs) b Nov. 7, 1876, d Oct. 25, 1942

*Arnold, G. G. (Surrey & Sussex; *CY 1972*) b Sept. 3, 1944

*Arnold, J. (Hants) b Nov. 30, 1907, d April 4, 1984

*Arnott, K. J. (MCD) b March 8, 1961

Arnott, T. (Glam) b Feb. 16, 1902, d Feb. 2, 1975

*Arshad Ayub (H'bad) b Aug. 2, 1958

Arshad Pervez (Sargodha, Lahore, Pak. Us, Servis Ind., HBL & Punjab) b Oct. 1, 1952

*Arun, B. (TN) b Dec. 14, 1962

*Arun Lal (Delhi & Bengal) b Aug. 1, 1955

*Asgarali, N. (T/T) b Dec. 28, 1920

Ashdown, W. H. (Kent) b Dec. 27, 1898, d Sept. 15, 1979

*Ashley, W. H. (W. Prov.) b Feb. 10, 1862, d July 14, 1930

*Ashraf Ali (Lahore, Income Tax, Pak. Us, Pak. Rlways & UBL) b April 22, 1958

Ashton, C. T. (CU & Essex) b Feb. 19, 1901, d Oct. 31, 1942

Ashton, G. (CU & Worcs) b Sept. 27, 1896, d Feb. 6, 1981

Ashton, Sir Hubert (CU & Essex; *CY 1922*; Pres. MCC 1960-61) b Feb. 13, 1898, d June 17, 1979

Asif Din, M. (Warwicks) b Sept. 21, 1960

*Asif Iqbal (H'bad, Kar., Kent, PIA & NBP; *CY 1968*) b June 6, 1943

*Asif Masood (Lahore, Punjab U. & PIA) b Jan. 23, 1946

Aslett, D. G. (Kent) b Feb. 12, 1958

*Astill, W. E. (Leics; *CY 1933*) b March 1, 1888, d Feb. 10, 1948

Athar Zaidi (Test umpire) b Nov. 12, 1946

Ather Ali Khan (Bangladesh) b Feb. 10, 1962

*Athey, C. W. J. (Yorks, Glos & Sussex) b Sept. 27, 1957

*Atif Rauf (Lahore, I'bad & ADBP) b March 3, 1964

Atkinson, C. R. M. CBE (Som) b July 23, 1931, d June 25, 1991

*Atkinson, D. St E. (B'dos & T/T) b Aug. 9, 1926

*Atkinson, E. St E. (B'dos) b Nov. 6, 1927, d May 29, 1998

Atkinson, G. (Som & Lancs) b March 29, 1938

*Attewell, W. (Notts; *CY 1892*) b June 12, 1861, d June 11, 1927

Austin, Sir Harold B. G. (B'dos) b July 15, 1877, d July 27, 1943

*Austin, R. A. (Jam.) b Sept. 5, 1954

Avery, A. V. (Essex) b Dec. 19, 1914, d May 10, 1997

Aylward, James (Hants & All-England) b 1741, *buried* Dec. 27, 1827

*Azad, K. (Delhi) b Jan. 2, 1959

*Azeem Hafeez (Kar., Allied Bank & PIA) b July 29, 1963

*Azhar Khan (Lahore, Punjab, Pak. Us, PIA & HBL) b Sept. 7, 1955

*Azmat Rana (B'pur, PIA, Punjab, Lahore & MCB) b Nov. 3, 1951

*Bacchus, S. F. A. F. (Guyana, W. Prov. & Border) b Jan. 31, 1954

*Bacher, Dr A. (Tvl; Managing Director UCBSA) b May 24, 1942

*Badcock, C. L. (Tas. & S. Aust.) b April 10, 1914, d Dec. 13, 1982

*Badcock, F. T. (Wgtn & Otago) b Aug. 9, 1897, d Sept. 19, 1982

Baggallay, R. R. C. (Derbys) b May 4, 1884, d Dec. 12, 1975

*Baichan, L. (Guyana) b May 12, 1946

*Baig, A. A. (H'bad, OU & Som) b March 19, 1939

Bailcy, J. (Hants) b April 6, 1908, d Feb. 9, 1988

Bailey, J. A. (Essex & OU; Sec. MCC 1974-87) b June 22, 1930

*Bailey, T. E. CBE (Essex & CU; *CY 1950*) b Dec. 3, 1923

Baillie, A. W. (Sec. MCC 1858-63) b June 22, 1830, d May 10, 1867

Bainbridge, H. W. (Surrey, CU & Warwicks) b Oct. 29, 1862, d March 3, 1940

Bainbridge, P. (Glos & Durham; *CY 1986*) b April 16, 1958

*Bairstow, D. L. (Yorks & Griq. W.) b Sept. 1, 1951, d Jan. 5, 1998

Baker, C. S. (Warwicks) b Jan. 5, 1883, d Dec. 16, 1976

Baker, G. R. (Yorks & Lancs) b April 18, 1862, d Dec. 6, 1938

*Bakewell, A. H. (Northants; *CY 1934*) b Nov. 2, 1908, d Jan. 23, 1983

*Balaskas, X. C. (Griq. W., Border, W. Prov., Tvl & NE Tvl) b Oct. 15, 1910, d May 12, 1994

*Balderstone, J. C. (Yorks & Leics) b Nov. 16, 1940, d March 6, 2000

Baldry, D. O. (Middx & Hants) b Dec. 26, 1931

*Banerjee, S. A. (Bengal & Bihar) b Nov. 1, 1919, d Sept. 14, 1992

*Banerjee, S. N. (Bengal, Naw., Bihar & M. Pradesh) b Oct. 3, 1911, d Oct. 14, 1980

*Banerjee, S. T. (Bihar & Bengal) b Feb. 13, 1969

*Bannerman, A. C. (NSW) b March 22, 1854, d Sept. 19, 1924

*Bannerman, Charles (NSW) b July 23, 1851, d Aug. 20, 1930

Bannister, J. D. (Warwicks) b Aug. 23, 1930

*Baqa Jilani, M. (N. Ind.) b July 20, 1911, d July 2, 1941

*Barber, R. T. (Wgton & C. Dist.) b June 3, 1925

*Barber, R. W. (Lancs, CU & Warwicks; *CY 1967*) b Sept. 26, 1935

*Barber, W. (Yorks) b April 18, 1901, d Sept. 10, 1968

Barclay, J. R. T. (Sussex & OFS) b Jan. 22, 1954

*Bardsley, W. (NSW; *CY 1910*) b Dec. 6, 1882, d Jan. 20, 1954

Barker, G. (Essex) b July 6, 1931

Barling, T. H. (Surrey) b Sept. 1, 1906, d Jan. 2, 1993

*Barlow, E. J. (Tvl, E. Prov., W. Prov., Derbys & Boland) b Aug. 12, 1940

*Barlow, G. D. (Middx) b March 26, 1950

*Barlow, R. G. (Lancs) b May 28, 1851, d July 31, 1919

Barnard, H. M. (Hants) b July 18, 1933

*Barnes, S. F. (Warwicks & Lancs; *CY 1910*) b April 19, 1873, d Dec. 26, 1967

*Barnes, S. G. (NSW) b June 5, 1916, d Dec. 16, 1973

*Barnes, W. (Notts; *CY 1890*) b May 27, 1852, d March 24, 1899

*Barnett, B. A. (Vic.) b March 23, 1908, d June 29, 1979

*Barnett, C. J. (Glos; *CY 1937*) b July 3, 1910, d May 28, 1993

Baroda, Maharaja of (Manager, Ind. in Eng. 1959) b April 2, 1930, d Sept. 1, 1988

*Barratt, F. (Notts) b April 12, 1894, d Jan. 29, 1947

*Barrett, A. G. (Jam.) b April 5, 1942

*Barrett, Dr J. E. (Vic.) b Oct. 15, 1866, d Feb. 6, 1916

Barrick, D. W. (Northants) b April 28, 1926

*Barrington, K. F. (Surrey; *CY 1960*) b Nov. 24, 1930, d March 14, 1981

Barron, W. (Lancs & Northants) b Oct. 26, 1917

*Barrow, I. (Jam.) b Jan. 6, 1911, d April 2, 1979

*Bartlett, E. L. (B'dos) b March 10, 1906, d Dec. 21, 1976

*Bartlett, G. A. (C. Dist. & Cant.) b Feb. 3, 1941

Bartlett, H. T. (CU, Surrey & Sussex; *CY 1939*) b Oct. 7, 1914, d June 26, 1988

Bartley, T. J. (Test umpire) b March 19, 1908, d April 2, 1964

Barton, M. R. (OU & Surrey) b Oct. 14, 1914

*Barton, P. T. (Wgtn) b Oct. 9, 1935

*Barton, V. A. (Kent & Hants) b Oct. 6, 1867, d March 23, 1906

Barwick, S. R. (Glam) b Sept. 6, 1960

Base, S. J. (W. Prov., Glam, Boland, Derbys & Border) b Jan. 2, 1960

*Basit Ali (Kar. & UBL) b Dec. 13, 1970

Bates, D. L. (Sussex) b May 10, 1933

Bates, L. A. (Warwicks) b March 20, 1895, d March 11, 1971

*Bates, W. (Yorks) b Nov. 19, 1855, d Jan. 8, 1900

Bates, W. E. (Yorks & Glam) b March 5, 1884, d Jan. 17, 1957

*Baumgartner, H. V. (OFS & Tvl) b Nov. 17, 1883, d April 8, 1938

*Bean, G. (Notts & Sussex) b March 7, 1864, d March 16, 1923

Bear, M. J. (Essex & Cant.) b Feb. 23, 1934, d April 7, 2000

*Beard, D. D. (C. Dist. & N. Dist.) b Jan. 14, 1920, d July 15, 1982

*Beard, G. R. (NSW) b Aug. 19, 1950

Beauclerk, Lord Frederick (Middx, Surrey & MCC) b May 8, 1773, d April 22, 1850

*Beaumont, R. (Tvl) b Feb. 4, 1884, d May 25, 1958

*Beck, J. E. F. (Wgtn) b Aug. 1, 1934, d April 23, 2000

*Bedi, B. S. (N. Punjab, Delhi & Northants) b Sept. 25, 1946

*Bedser, Sir Alec V. (Surrey; *CY 1947*) b July 4, 1918

Bedser, E. A. (Surrey) b July 4, 1918

Beet, G. (Derbys; Test umpire) b April 24, 1886, d Dec. 13, 1946

*Begbie, D. W. (Tvl) b Dec. 12, 1914

Beldam, W. (Hambledon & Surrey) b Feb. 5, 1766, d Feb. 20, 1862

*Bell, A. J. (W. Prov. & Rhod.) b April 15, 1906, d Aug. 1, 1985

Bell, R. V. (Middx & Sussex) b Jan. 7, 1931, d Oct. 26, 1989

*Bell, W. (Cant.) b Sept. 5, 1931

Bellamy, B. W. (Northants) b April 22, 1891, d Dec. 22, 1985

*Benaud, J. (NSW) b May 11, 1944

*Benaud, R. OBE (NSW; *CY 1962*; broadcaster) b Oct. 6, 1930

*Benjamin, J. E. (Warwicks & Surrey) b Feb. 2, 1961

*Benjamin, W. K. M. (Leewards, Leics & Hants) b Dec. 31, 1964

Bencraft, Sir H. W. Russell (Hants) b March 4, 1858, d Dec. 25, 1943

Bennett, D. (Middx) b Dec. 18, 1933

*Bennett, M. J. (NSW) b Oct. 6, 1956

*Benson, M. R. (Kent) b July 6, 1958

Berry, L. G. (Leics) b April 28, 1906, d Feb. 5, 1985

*Berry, R. (Lancs, Worcs & Derbys) b Jan. 29, 1926

Berry, Scyld (Writer) b April 28, 1954

*Best, C. A. (B'dos & W. Prov.) b May 14, 1959

Bestwick, W. (Derbys) b Feb. 24, 1875, d May 2, 1938

*Betancourt, N. (T/T) b June 4, 1887, d Oct. 12, 1947

Bhalekar, R. B. (M'tra) b Feb. 17, 1952

*Bhandari, P. (Delhi & Bengal) b Nov. 27, 1935

*Bhat, A. R. (Karn.) b April 16, 1958

Bhupinder Singh (Punjab) b April 1, 1965

Bick, D. A. (Middx) b Feb. 22, 1936, d Jan. 13, 1992

Bicknell, D. J. (Surrey) b June 24, 1967

*Bilby, G. P. (Wgtn) b May 7, 1941

*Binks, J. G. (Yorks; *CY 1969*) b Oct. 5, 1935

*Binns, A. P. (Jam.) b July 24, 1929

*Binny, R. M. H. (Karn.) b July 19, 1955

Birch, J. D. (Notts) b June 18, 1955

Bird, H. D. MBE (Yorks & Leics; Test umpire) b April 19, 1933

*Bird, M. C. (Lancs & Surrey) b March 25, 1888, d Dec. 9, 1933

Bird, R. E. (Worcs) b April 4, 1915, d Feb. 20, 1985

Birkenshaw, J. (Yorks, Leics & Worcs) b Nov. 13, 1940

*Birkett, L. S. (B'dos, BG & T/T) b April 14, 1904, d Jan. 16, 1998

Bishop, G. A. (S. Aust.) b Feb. 25, 1960

*Bishop, I. R. (T/T & Derbys) b Oct. 24, 1967

*Bisset, Sir Murray (M.) (W. Prov.) b April 14, 1876, d Oct. 24, 1931

*Bissett, G. F. (Griq. W., W. Prov. & Tvl) b Nov. 5, 1905, d Nov. 14, 1965

Bissex, M. (Glos) b Sept. 28, 1944

*Blackham, J. McC. (Vic; *CY 1891*) b May 11, 1854, d Dec. 28, 1932

*Blackie, D. D. (Vic.) b April 5, 1882, d April 18, 1955

Blain, T. E. (C. Dist.) b Feb. 17, 1962

Blair, B. R. (Otago) b Dec. 27, 1957

*Blair, R. W. (Wgtn & C. Dist.) b June 23, 1932

*Blanckenberg, J. M. (W. Prov. & Natal) b Dec. 31, 1892, dead

*Bland, K. C. (Rhod., E. Prov. & OFS; *CY 1966*) b April 5, 1938

Blenkiron, W. (Warwicks) b July 21, 1942

*Bligh, Hon. Ivo (I. F. W.) (8th Earl of Darnley) (CU & Kent; Pres. MCC 1900) b March 13, 1859, d April 10, 1927

Blofeld, H. C. (CU; writer & broadcaster) b Sept. 23, 1939

*Blunt, R. C. MBE (Cant. & Otago; *CY 1928*) b Nov. 3, 1900, d June 22, 1966

*Blythe, C. (Kent; *CY 1904*) b May 30, 1879, d Nov. 8, 1917

*Board, J. H. (Glos) b Feb. 23, 1867, d April 15, 1924

*Bock, E. G. (Griq. W., Tvl & W. Prov.) b Sept. 17, 1908, d Sept. 5, 1961

*Bolton, B. A. (Cant. & Wgtn) b May 31, 1935

*Bolus, J. B. (Yorks, Notts & Derbys) b Jan. 31, 1934

*Bond, G. E. (W. Prov.) b April 5, 1909, d Aug. 27, 1965

Bond, J. D. (Lancs & Notts; *CY 1971*) b May 6, 1932

*Bonnor, G. J. (Vic. & NSW) b Feb. 25, 1855, d June 27, 1912

*Boock, S. L. (Otago & Cant.) b Sept. 20, 1951

*Boon, D. C. MBE (Tas. & Durham; *CY 1994*) b Dec. 29, 1960

Boon, T. J. (Leics) b Nov. 1, 1961

*Booth, B. C. MBE (NSW) b Oct. 19, 1933

Booth, B. J. (Lancs & Leics) b Dec. 3, 1935

Booth, C. (CU & Hants) b May 11, 1842, d July 14, 1926

*Booth, M. W. (Yorks; *CY 1914*) b Dec. 10, 1886, d July 1, 1916

Booth, R. (Yorks & Worcs) b Oct. 1, 1926

*Borde, C. G. (Baroda & M'tra) b July 21, 1933

*Border, A. R. (NSW, Glos, Qld & Essex; *CY 1982*) b July 27, 1955

Bore, M. K. (Yorks & Notts) b June 2, 1947

Borrington, A. J. (Derbys) b Dec. 8, 1948

*Bosanquet, B. J. T. (OU & Middx; *CY 1905*) b Oct. 13, 1877, d Oct. 12, 1936

*Bosch, T. (N. Tvl & Natal) b March 14, 1966, d Feb. 13, 2000

Bose, G. (Bengal) b May 20, 1947

Boshier, B. S. (Leics) b March 6, 1932

*Botham, I. T. OBE (Som, Worcs, Durham & Qld; *CY 1978*) b Nov. 24, 1955

*Botten, J. T. (NE Tvl & N. Tvl) b June 21, 1938

Boucher, J. C. (Ireland) b Dec. 22, 1910, d Dec. 25, 1995

Bowden, J. (Derbys) b Oct. 8, 1884, d March 1, 1958

*Bowden, M. P. (Surrey & Tvl) b Nov. 1, 1865, d Feb. 19, 1892

Bowell, A. (Hants) b April 27, 1880, d Aug. 28, 1957

*Bowes, W. E. (Yorks; *CY 1932*) b July 25, 1908, d Sept. 5, 1987

*Bowley, F. H. (Sussex & Auck.; *CY 1930*) b June 6, 1890, d July 9, 1974

Bowley, F. L. (Worcs) b Nov. 9 1873, d May 31, 1943

Box, T. (Sussex) b Feb. 7, 1808, d July 12, 1876

*Boyce, K. D. (B'dos & Essex; *CY 1974*) b Oct. 11, 1943, d Oct. 11, 1996

*Boycott, G. OBE (Yorks & N. Tvl; *CY 1965*) b Oct. 21, 1940

Boyd-Moss, R. J. (CU & Northants) b Dec. 16, 1959

Boyes, G. S. (Hants) b March 31, 1899, d Feb. 11, 1973

*Boyle, H. F. (Vic.) b Dec. 10, 1847, d Nov. 21, 1907

*Bracewell, B. P. (C. Dist., Otago & N. Dist.) b Sept. 14, 1959

*Bracewell, J. G. (Otago & Auck.) b April 15, 1958

*Bradburn, W. P. (N. Dist.) b Nov. 24, 1938

*Bradley, W. M. (Kent) b Jan. 2, 1875, d June 19, 1944

*Bradman, Sir Donald G. (NSW & S. Aust.; *CY 1931*) b Aug. 27, 1908

Brain, B. M. (Worcs & Glos) b Sept. 13, 1940

*Brain, D. H. (Mash.) b Oct. 4, 1964

Brann, G. (Sussex) b April 23, 1865, d June 14, 1954

*Brann, W. H. (E. Prov.) b April 4, 1899, d Sept. 22, 1953

Brassington, A. J. (Glos) b Aug. 9, 1954

*Braund, L. C. (Surrey & Som; *CY 1902*) b Oct. 18, 1875, d Dec. 23, 1955

Bray, C. (Essex) b April 6, 1898, d Sept. 12, 1993

Brayshaw, I. J. (W. Aust.) b Jan. 14, 1942

Breakwell, D. (Northants & Som) b July 2, 1948

*Brearley, J. M. OBE (CU & Middx; *CY 1977*) b April 28, 1942

*Brearley, W. (Lancs; *CY 1909*) b March 11, 1876, d Jan. 13, 1937

Brennan, D. V. (Yorks) b Feb. 10, 1920, d Jan. 9, 1985

*Briant, G. A. (Mash.) b April 11, 1969

Bridges, J. J. (Som) b June 28, 1887, d Sept. 26, 1966

Brierley, T. L. (Glam, Lancs & Canada) b June 15, 1910, d Jan. 7, 1989

Briers, N. E. (Leics; *CY 1993*) b Jan. 15, 1955

*Briggs, John (Lancs; *CY 1889*) b Oct. 3, 1862, d Jan. 11, 1902

*Bright, R. J. (Vic.) b July 13, 1954

*Briscoe, A. W. (Tvl) b Feb. 6, 1911, d April 22, 1941

*Broad, B. C. (Glos & Notts) b Sept. 29, 1957

Broadbent, R. G. (Worcs) b June 21, 1924, d April 26, 1993

*Brockwell, W. (Surrey & Kimberley; *CY 1895*) b Jan. 21, 1865, d June 30, 1935

Broderick, V. (Northants) b Aug. 17, 1920

*Bromfield, H. D. (W. Prov.) b June 26, 1932

*Bromley, E. H. (W. Aust. & Vic.) b Sept. 2, 1912, d Feb. 1, 1967

*Bromley-Davenport, H. R. (CU, Eur., & Middx) b Aug. 18, 1870, d May 23, 1954

*Brookes, D. (Northants; *CY 1957*) b Oct. 29, 1915

Brookes, Wilfrid H. (Editor of *Wisden* 1936-39) b Dec. 5, 1894, d May 28, 1955

*Brown, A. (Kent) b Oct. 17, 1935

Brown, A. D. (Surrey) b Feb. 11, 1970

Brown, A. S. (Glos) b June 24, 1936

*Brown, D. J. (Warwicks) b Jan. 30, 1942

*Brown, F. R. MBE (CU, Surrey & Northants; *CY 1933;* Pres. MCC 1971-72) b Dec. 16, 1910, d July 24, 1991

*Brown, G. (Hants) b Oct. 6, 1887, d Dec. 3, 1964

Brown, J. MBE (Scotland) b Sept. 24, 1931

*Brown, J. T. (Yorks; *CY 1895*) b Aug. 20, 1869, d Nov. 4, 1904

Brown, K. R. (Middx) b March 18, 1963

*Brown, L. S. (Tvl, NE Tvl & Rhod.) b Nov. 24, 1910, d Sept. 1, 1983

Brown, R. D. (Mash.) b March 11, 1951

Brown, S. M. (Middx) b Dec. 8, 1917, d Dec. 28, 1987

*Brown, V. R. (Cant. & Auck.) b Nov. 3, 1959

*Brown, W. A. (NSW & Qld; *CY 1939*) b July 31, 1912

Brown, W. C. (Northants) b Nov. 13, 1900, d Jan. 20, 1986

Browne, B. St A. (Guyana) b Sept. 16, 1967

*Browne, C. R. (B'dos & BG) b Oct. 8, 1890, d Jan. 12, 1964

*Bruce, W. (Vic.) b May 22, 1864, d Aug. 3, 1925

*Bruk-Jackson, G. K. (MCD & Mash.) b April 25, 1969

Bryan, G. J. CBE (Kent) b Dec. 29, 1902, d April 4, 1991

Bryan, J. L. (CU & Kent; *CY 1922*) b May 26, 1896, d April 23, 1985

Bryan, R. T. (Kent) b July 30, 1898, d July 27, 1970

Bryson, R. E. (†Northerns, E. Prov. & Surrey) b July 25, 1968

*Buckenham, C. P. (Essex) b Jan. 16, 1876, d Feb. 23, 1937

Bucknor, S. A. (Test umpire) b May 31, 1946

Buckston, R. H. R. (Derbys) b Oct. 10, 1908, d May 16, 1967

Budd, E. H. (Middx & All-England) b Feb. 23, 1785, d March 29, 1875

Budd, W. L. (Hants; Test umpire) b Oct. 25, 1913, d Aug. 23, 1986

Bull, F. G. (Essex; *CY 1898*) b April 2, 1875, d Sept. 16, 1910

Buller, J. S. MBE (Yorks & Worcs; Test umpire) b Aug. 23, 1909, d Aug. 7, 1970

Burden, M. D. (Hants) b Oct. 4, 1930, d Nov. 9, 1987

*Burge, P. J. (Qld; *CY 1965;* ICC referee) b May 17, 1932

*Burger, C. G. de V. (Natal) b July 12, 1935

Burgess, G. I. (Som) b May 5, 1943

*Burgess, M. G. (Auck.) b July 17, 1944

*Burke, C. (Auck.) b March 22, 1914, d Aug. 4, 1997

*Burke, J. W. (NSW; *CY 1957*) b June 12, 1930, d Feb. 2, 1979

*Burke, S. F. (NE Tvl & OFS) b March 11, 1934

*Burki, Javed (Pak. Us, OU, Punjab, Lahore, Kar., R'pindi & NWFP; ICC referee) b May 8, 1938

*Burn, K. E. (Tas.) b Sept. 17, 1862, d July 20, 1956

Burns, N. D. (Essex, W. Prov., Som) b Sept. 19, 1965

Burns, W. B. (Worcs) b Aug. 29, 1883, d July 7, 1916

Burnup, C. J. (CU & Kent; *CY 1903*) b Nov. 21, 1875, d April 5, 1960

Burrough, H. D. (Som) b Feb. 6, 1909, d April 9, 1994

Burrows, R. D. (Worcs) b June 6, 1871, d Feb. 12, 1943

Burton, D. C. F. (Yorks) b Sept. 13, 1887, d Sept. 24, 1971

*Burton, F. J. (Vic. & NSW) b Nov. 2, 1865, d Aug. 25, 1929

*Burtt, T. B. (Cant.) b Jan. 22, 1915, d May 24, 1988

Buse, H. T. F. (Som) b Aug. 5, 1910, d Feb. 23, 1992

Buss, A. (Sussex) b Sept. 1, 1939

Buss, M. A. (Sussex & OFS) b Jan. 24, 1944

*Butchart, I. P. (MCD) b May 9, 1960

*Butcher, A. R. (Surrey & Glam; *CY 1991*) b Jan. 7, 1954

*Butcher, B. F. (Guyana; *CY 1970*) b Sept. 3, 1933

Butcher, I. P. (Leics & Glos) b July 1, 1962

*Butcher, R. O. (Middx, B'dos & Tas.) b Oct. 14, 1953

*Butler, H. J. (Notts) b March 12, 1913, d July 17, 1991

*Butler, L. (T/T) b Feb. 9, 1929

*Butt, H. R. (Sussex) b Dec. 27, 1865, d Dec. 21, 1928

*Butterfield, L. A. (Cant.) b Aug. 29, 1913, d July 7, 1999

*Butts, C. G. (Guyana) b July 8, 1957

Buxton, I. R. (Derbys) b April 17, 1938

*Buys, I. D. (W. Prov.) b Feb. 3, 1895, dead

*Bynoe, M. R. (B'dos) b Feb. 23, 1941

Byrne, J. F. (Warwicks) b June 19, 1871, d May 10, 1954

Cadman, S. (Derbys) b Jan. 29, 1877, d May 6, 1952

Caesar, Julius (Surrey & All-England) b March 25, 1830, d March 6, 1878

Caffyn, W. (Surrey & NSW) b Feb. 2, 1828, d Aug. 28, 1919

Caine, C. Stewart (Editor of *Wisden* 1926-33) b Oct. 28, 1861, d April 15, 1933

*Cairns, B. L. (C. Dist., Otago & N. Dist.) b Oct. 10, 1949

Calder, H. L. (Cranleigh; *CY 1918*) b Jan. 24, 1901, d Sept. 15, 1995

*Callaway, S. T. (NSW & Cant.) b Feb. 6, 1868, d Nov. 25, 1923

*Callen, I. W. (Vic. & Boland) b May 2, 1955

*Calthorpe, Hon. F. S. Gough- (CU, Sussex & Warwicks) b May 27, 1892, d Nov. 19, 1935

*Camacho, G. S. (Guyana; Chief Exec. WICB) b Oct. 15, 1945

*Cameron, F. J. (Jam.) b June 22, 1923, d Feb. 1995

*Cameron, F. J. MBE (Otago) b June 1, 1932

*Cameron, H. B. (Tvl, E. Prov. & W. Prov.; *CY 1936*) b July 5, 1905, d Nov. 2, 1935

*Cameron, J. H. (CU, Jam. & Som) b April 8, 1914, d Feb. 13, 2000

*Campbell, G. D. (Tas.) b March 10, 1964

*Campbell, T. (Tvl) b Feb. 9, 1882, d Oct. 5, 1924

Cannings, V. H. D. (Warwicks & Hants) b April 3, 1919

*Capel, D. J. (Northants & E. Prov.) b Feb. 6, 1963

Cardus, Sir Neville (Writer) b April 3, 1888, d Feb. 27, 1975

*Carew, G. M. (B'dos) b June 4, 1910, d Dec. 9, 1974

*Carew, M. C. (T/T) b Sept. 15, 1937

*Carkeek, W. (Vic.) b Oct. 17, 1878, d Feb. 20, 1937

*Carlisle, S. V. (Zimb. U-24) b May 10, 1972

*Carlson, P. H. (Qld) b Aug. 8, 1951

*Carlstein, P. R. (OFS, Tvl, Natal & Rhod.) b Oct. 28, 1938

Carpenter, D. (Glos) b Sept. 12, 1935

Carpenter, H. A. (Essex) b July 12, 1869, d Dec. 12, 1933

Carpenter, R. (Cambs & Utd England XI) b Nov. 18, 1830, d July 13, 1901

*Carr, A. W. (Notts; *CY 1923*) b May 21, 1893, d Feb. 7, 1963

*Carr, D. B. OBE (OU & Derbys; *CY 1960*; Sec. TCCB 1974-86) b Dec. 28, 1926

*Carr, D. W. (Kent; *CY 1910*) b March 17, 1872, d March 23, 1950

Carr, J. D. (OU & Middx) b June 15, 1963

Carrick, P. (Yorks & E. Prov.) b July 16, 1952, d Jan. 11, 2000

*Carter, C. P. (Natal & Tvl) b April 23, 1881, d Nov. 8, 1952

*Carter, H. (NSW) b March 15, 1878, d June 8, 1948

Carter, R. G. M. (Worcs) b July 11, 1937

*Cartwright, T. W. (Warwicks, Som & Glam) b July 22, 1935

Case, C. C. C. (Som) b Sept. 7, 1895, d Nov. 11, 1969

Cass, G. R. (Essex, Worcs & Tas.) b April 23, 1940

Catt, A. W. (Kent & W. Prov.) b Oct. 2, 1933

*Catterall, R. H. (Tvl, Rhod., Natal & OFS; *CY 1925*) b July 10, 1900, d Jan. 3, 1961

*Cave, H. B. (Wgtn & C. Dist.) b Oct. 10, 1922, d Sept. 15, 1989

Chalk, F. G. H. (OU & Kent) b Sept. 7, 1910, d Feb. 17, 1943

*Challenor, G. (B'dos) b June 28, 1888, d July 30, 1947

Chamberlain, W. R. F. (Northants; Chairman TCCB 1990-94) b April 13, 1925

*Chandrasekhar, B. S. (†Karn.; *CY 1972*) b May 17, 1945

Chandrasekhar, V. B. (Goa) b Aug. 21, 1961

*Chang, H. S. (Jam.) b July 22, 1952

Chaplin, H. P. (Sussex & Eur.) b March 1, 1883, d March 6, 1970

*Chapman, A. P. F. (Uppingham, CU & Kent; *CY 1919*) b Sept. 3, 1900, d Sept. 16, 1961

*Chapman, H. W. (Natal) b June 30, 1890, d Dec. 1, 1941

Chapman, J. (Derbys) b March 11, 1877, d Aug. 12, 1956

*Chappell, G. S. MBE (S. Aust., Som & Qld; *CY 1973*) b Aug. 7, 1948

*Chappell, I. M. (S. Aust. & Lancs; *CY 1976*; broadcaster) b Sept. 26, 1943

*Chappell, T. M. (S. Aust., W. Aust. & NSW) b Oct. 21, 1952

*Chapple, M. E. (Cant. & C. Dist.) b July 25, 1930, d July 31, 1985

Charlesworth, C. (Warwicks) b Feb. 12, 1875, d June 15, 1953

*Charlton, P. C. (NSW) b April 9, 1867, d Sept. 30, 1954

*Charlwood, H. R. J. (Sussex) b Dec. 19, 1846, d June 6, 1888

*Chatfield, E. J. MBE (Wgtn) b July 3, 1950

*Chatterton, W. (Derbys) b Dec. 27, 1861, d March 19, 1913

*Chauhan, C. P. S. (M'tra & Delhi) b July 21, 1947

*Cheetham, J. E. (W. Prov.) b May 26, 1920, d Aug. 21, 1980

Chester, F. (Worcs; Test umpire) b Jan. 20, 1895, d April 8, 1957

*Chevalier, G. A. (W. Prov.) b March 9, 1937

*Childs, J. H. (Glos & Essex; *CY 1987*) b Aug. 15, 1951

*Chipperfield, A. G. (NSW) b Nov. 17, 1905, d July 29, 1987

Chisholm, R. H. E. (Scotland) b May 22, 1927

*Chowdhury, N. R. (Bihar & Bengal) b May 23, 1923, d Dec. 14, 1979

*Christiani, C. M. (BG) b Oct. 28, 1913, d April 4, 1938

*Christiani, R. J. (BG) b July 19, 1920

*Christopherson, S. (Kent; Pres. MCC 1939-45) b Nov. 11, 1861, d April 6, 1949

*Christy, J. A. J. (Tvl & Qld) b Dec. 12, 1904, d Feb. 1, 1971

*Chubb, G. W. A. (Border & Tvl) b April 12, 1911, d Aug. 28, 1982

Clark, D. G. (Kent; Pres. MCC 1977-78) b Jan. 27, 1919

Clark, E. A. (Middx) b April 15, 1937

*Clark, E. W. (Northants) b Aug. 9, 1902, d April 28, 1982

Clark, T. H. (Surrey) b Oct. 5, 1924, d June 14, 1981

*Clark, W. M. (W. Aust.) b Sept. 19, 1953

*Clarke, Dr C. B. OBE (B'dos, Northants & Essex) b April 7, 1918, d Oct. 14, 1993

Clarke, R. W. (Northants) b April 22, 1924, d Aug. 3, 1981

*Clarke, S. T. (B'dos, Surrey, Tvl, OFS & N. Tvl) b Dec. 11, 1954, d Dec. 4, 1999

Clarke, William (Notts; founded All-England XI & Trent Bridge ground) b Dec. 24, 1798, d Aug. 25, 1856

Clarkson, A. (Yorks & Som) b Sept. 5, 1939

*Clay, J. C. (Glam) b March 18, 1898, d Aug. 12, 1973

Clay, J. D. (Notts) b Oct. 15, 1924

Clayton, G. (Lancs & Som) b Feb. 3, 1938

*Cleverley, D. C. (Auck.) b Dec. 23, 1909

Clift, Patrick B. (Rhod., Leics & Natal) b July 14, 1953, d Sept. 3, 1996

Clift, Phil B. (Glam) b Sept. 3, 1918

Clinton, G. S. (Kent, Surrey & Zimb.-Rhod.) b May 5, 1953

*Close, D. B. CBE (Yorks & Som; *CY 1964*) b Feb. 24, 1931

Cobb, R. A. (Leics & N. Tvl) b May 18, 1961

Cobham, 10th Visct (Hon. C. J. Lyttelton) (Worcs; Pres. MCC 1954) b Aug. 8, 1909, d March 20, 1977

*Cochrane, J. A. K. (Tvl & Griq. W.) b July 15, 1909, d June 15, 1987

Coe, S. (Leics) b June 3, 1873, d Nov. 4, 1955

*Coen, S. K. (OFS, W. Prov., Tvl & Border) b Oct. 14, 1902, d Jan. 28, 1967

*Colah, S. M. H. (Bombay, W. Ind. & Naw.) b Sept. 22, 1902, d Sept. 11, 1950

Colchin, Robert ("Long Robin") (Kent & All-England) b Nov. 1713, d April 1750

*Coldwell, L. J. (Worcs) b Jan. 10, 1933, d Aug. 6, 1996

*Colley, D. J. (NSW) b March 15, 1947

*Collinge, R. O. (C. Dist., Wgtn & N. Dist.) b April 2, 1946

Collins, A. E. J. (Clifton Coll. & Royal Engineers) b Aug. 18, 1885, d Nov. 11, 1914

Collins, G. C. (Kent) b Sept. 21, 1889, d Jan. 23, 1949

*Collins, H. L. (NSW) b Jan. 21, 1888, d May 28, 1959

Collins, R. (Lancs) b March 10, 1934

*Colquhoun, I. A. (C. Dist.) b June 8, 1924

Coman, P. G. (Cant.) b April 13, 1943

*Commaille, J. M. M. (W. Prov., Natal, OFS & Griq. W.) b Feb. 21, 1883, d July 28, 1956

*Compton, D. C. S. CBE (Middx & Holkar; *CY 1939*) b May 23, 1918, d April 23, 1997

Compton, L. H. (Middx) b Sept. 12, 1912, d Dec. 27, 1984

*Coney, J. V. MBE (Wgtn; *CY 1984*) b June 21, 1952

*Congdon, B. E. OBE (C. Dist., Wgtn, Otago & Cant.; *CY 1974*) b Feb. 11, 1938

*Coningham, A. (NSW & Qld) b July 14, 1863, d June 13, 1939

*Connolly, A. N. (Vic. & Middx) b June 29, 1939

Connor, C. A. (Hants) b March 24, 1961

Constable, B. (Surrey) b Feb. 19, 1921, d May 15, 1997

Constant, D. J. (Kent & Leics; Test umpire) b Nov. 9, 1941

*Constantine, L. N. (later Baron Constantine of Maraval and Nelson) (T/T & B'dos; *CY 1940*) b Sept. 21, 1902, d July 1, 1971

Constantine, L. S. (T/T) b May 25, 1874, d Jan. 5, 1942

*Contractor, N. J. (Guj. & Ind. Rlwys) b March 7, 1934

*Conyngham, D. P. (Natal, Tvl & W. Prov.) b May 10, 1897, d July 7, 1979

*Cook, C. (Glos) b Aug. 23, 1921, d Sept. 4, 1996

*Cook, F. J. (E. Prov.) b 1870, d Nov. 30, 1914

*Cook, G. (Northants & E. Prov.) b Oct. 9, 1951

Cook, L. W. (Lancs) b March 28, 1885, d Dec. 2, 1933

*Cook, N. G. B. (Leics & Northants) b June 17, 1956

*Cook, S. H. (NSW) b Jan. 29, 1972

*Cook, S. J. (Tvl & Som; *CY 1990*) b July 31, 1953

Cook, T. E. R. (Sussex) b Jan. 5, 1901, d Jan. 15, 1950

*Cooper, A. H. C. (Tvl) b Sept. 2, 1893, d July 18, 1963

*Cooper, B. B. (Middx, Kent & Vic.) b March 15, 1844, d Aug. 7, 1914

Cooper, E. (Worcs) b Nov. 30, 1915, d Oct. 29, 1968

Cooper, F. S. Ashley- (Historian) b March 22, 1877, d Jan. 31, 1932

Cooper, G. C. (Sussex) b Sept. 2, 1936

Cooper, K. E. (Notts & Glos) b Dec. 27, 1957

*Cooper, W. H. (Vic.) b Sept. 11, 1849, d April 5, 1939

Cooray, B. C. (Test umpire) b May 15, 1941

*Cope, G. A. (Yorks) b Feb. 23, 1947

*Copson, W. H. (Derbys; *CY 1937*) b April 27, 1908, d Sept. 14, 1971

Cordle, A. E. (Glam) b Sept. 21, 1940

*Corling, G. E. (NSW) b July 13, 1941

Cornford, J. H. (Sussex) b Dec. 9, 1911, d June 17, 1985

*Cornford, W. L. (Sussex) b Dec. 25, 1900, d Feb. 6, 1964

Cornwallis, W. S. (later 2nd Baron) (Kent) b March 14, 1892, d Jan. 4, 1982

Corrall, P. (Leics) b July 16, 1906, d Feb. 1994

Corran, A. J. (OU & Notts) b Nov. 25, 1936

*Cosier, G. J. (Vic., S. Aust. & Qld) b April 25, 1953

*Cottam, J. T. (NSW) b Sept. 5, 1867, d Jan. 30, 1897

*Cottam, R. M. H. (Hants & Northants) b Oct. 16, 1944

*Cotter, A. (NSW) b Dec. 3, 1884, d Oct. 31, 1917

Cotton, J. (Notts & Leics) b Nov. 7, 1940

*Coulthard, G. (Vic.; Test umpire) b Aug. 1, 1856, d Oct. 22, 1883

*Coventry, Hon. C. J. (Worcs) b Feb. 26, 1867, d June 2, 1929

*Cowans, N. G. (Middx & Hants) b April 17, 1961

*Cowdrey, C. S. (Kent & Glam) b Oct. 20, 1957

Cowdrey, G. R. (Kent) b June 27, 1964

*Cowdrey, M. C. (later Baron Cowdrey of Tonbridge) (OU & Kent; *CY 1956;* Pres. MCC 1986-87) b Dec. 24, 1932, d Dec. 4, 2000

Cowie, D. B. (Test umpire) b Dec. 2, 1946

*Cowie, J. OBE (Auck.) b March 30, 1912, d June 3, 1994

Cowley, N. G. (Hants & Glam) b March 1, 1953

*Cowper, R. M. (Vic. & W. Aust.) b Oct. 5, 1940

Cox, A. L. (Northants) b July 22, 1907, d Nov. 13, 1986

Cox, G., jun. (Sussex) b Aug. 23, 1911, d March 30, 1985

Cox, G., sen. (Sussex) b Nov. 29, 1873, d March 24, 1949

*Cox, J. L. (Natal) b June 28, 1886, d July 4, 1971

*Coxon, A. (Yorks) b Jan. 18, 1916

Cozier, Tony (Writer & broadcaster) b July 10, 1940

*Craig, I. D. (NSW) b June 12, 1935

Cranfield, L. M. (Glos) b Aug. 29, 1909, d Nov. 18, 1993

Cranmer, P. (Warwicks & Eur.) b Sept. 10, 1914, d May 29, 1994

*Cranston, J. (Glos) b Jan. 9, 1859, d Dec. 10, 1904

*Cranston, K. (Lancs) b Oct. 20, 1917

*Crapp, J. F. (Glos; Test umpire) b Oct. 14, 1912, d Feb. 15, 1981

*Crawford, J. N. (Surrey, S. Aust., Wgtn & Otago; *CY 1907*) b Dec. 1, 1886, d May 2, 1963

*Crawford, P. (NSW) b Mar. 3, 1933

Crawford, V. F. S. (Surrey & Leics) b April 11, 1879, d Aug. 21, 1922

Crawley, A. M. MBE (OU & Kent; Pres. MCC 1972-73) b April 10, 1908, d Nov. 3, 1993

Cray, S. J. (Essex) b May 29, 1921

Creese, W. L. (Hants) b Dec. 27, 1907, d March 9, 1974

*Cresswell, G. F. (Wgtn & C. Dist.) b March 22, 1915, d Jan. 10, 1966

*Cripps, G. (W. Prov.) b Oct. 19, 1865, d Oct. 27, 1943

*Crisp, R. J. (Rhod., W. Prov. & Worcs) b May 28, 1911, d March 3, 1994

*Crocker, G. J. (MCD) b May 16, 1962

*Croft, C. E. H. (Guyana & Lancs) b March 15, 1953

*Cromb, I. B. (Cant.) b June 25, 1905, d March 6, 1984

Croom, A. J. (Warwicks) b May 23, 1896, d Aug. 16, 1947

*Crowe, J. J. (S. Aust. & Auck.) b Sept. 14, 1958

*Crowe, M. D. MBE (Auck., C. Dist., Som & Wgtn; *CY 1985*) b Sept. 22, 1962

Crump, B. S. (Northants) b April 25, 1938

Cuffe, J. A. (NSW & Worcs) b June 26, 1880, d May 16, 1931

Cumbes, J. (Lancs, Surrey, Worcs & Warwicks) b May 4, 1944

*Cummins, A. C. (B'dos & Durham) b May 7, 1966

*Cunis, R. S. (Auck. & N. Dist.) b Jan. 5, 1941

*Curnow, S. H. (Tvl) b Dec. 16, 1907, d July 28, 1986

Curran, K. M. (Zimb., Glos, Natal, Northants, Boland) b Sept. 7, 1959

*Curtis, T. S. (Worcs & CU) b Jan. 15, 1960

Cutmore, J. A. (Essex) b Dec. 28, 1898, d Nov. 30, 1985

*Cuttell, W. R. (Lancs; *CY 1898*) b Sept. 13, 1864, d Dec. 9, 1929

*Da Costa, O. C. (Jam.) b Sept. 11, 1907, d Oct. 1, 1936

Dacre, C. C. (Auck. & Glos) b May 15, 1899, d Nov. 2, 1975

Daft, H. B. (Notts) b April 5, 1866, d Jan. 12, 1945

Daft, Richard (Notts & All-England) b Nov. 2, 1835, d July 18, 1900

Dalmeny, Lord (later 6th Earl of Rosebery) (Middx, Surrey & Scotland) b Jan. 8, 1882, d May 30, 1974

Dalmiya, J. (President ICC 1997-2000) b May 30, 1940

*Dalton, E. L. (Natal) b Dec. 2, 1906, d June 3, 1981

*Dani, H. T. (M'tra & Ind. Serv.) b May 24, 1933, d Dec. 19, 1999

*Daniel, W. W. (B'dos, Middx & W. Aust.) b Jan. 16, 1956

*D'Arcy, J. W. (Cant., Wgtn & Otago) b April 23, 1936

Dare, R. (Hants) b Nov. 26, 1921

*Darling, J. (S. Aust.; *CY 1900*) b Nov. 21, 1870, d Jan. 2, 1946

*Darling, L. S. (Vic.) b Aug. 14, 1909, d June 24, 1992

*Darling, W. M. (S. Aust.) b May 1, 1957

Davey, J. (Glos) b Sept. 4, 1944

David, N. A. (H'bad) b Feb. 26, 1971

*Davidson, A. K. OBE (NSW; *CY 1962*) b June 14, 1929

Davidson, G. (Derbys) b June 29, 1866, d Feb. 8, 1899

Davies, Dai (Glam; Test umpire) b Aug. 26, 1896, d July 16, 1976

Davies, Emrys (Glam; Test umpire) b June 27, 1904, d Nov. 10, 1975

*Davies, E. Q. (E. Prov., Tvl & NE Tvl) b Aug. 26, 1909, d Nov. 11, 1976

Davies, H. G. (Glam) b April 23, 1912, d Sept. 4, 1993

Davies, J. G. W. OBE (CU & Kent; Pres. MCC 1985-86) b Sept. 10, 1911, d Nov. 5, 1992

Davies, S. G. (Mat.) b May 12, 1977

Davies, T. (Glam) b Oct. 25, 1960

*Davis, B. A. (T/T & Glam) b May 2, 1940

*Davis, C. A. (T/T) b Jan. 1, 1944

Davis, E. (Northants) b March 8, 1922

*Davis, H. T. (Wgtn) b Nov. 30, 1971

*Davis, I. C. (NSW & Qld) b June 25, 1953

Davis, P. (Northants) b May 24, 1915

Davis, R. C. (Glam) b Jan. 15, 1946

Davis, R. P. (Kent, Warwicks & Glos) b March 18, 1966

*Davis, S. P. (Vic.) b Nov. 8, 1959

*Davis, W. W. (Windwards, Glam, Tas., Northants & Wgtn) b Sept. 18, 1958

Davison, B. F. (Rhod., Leics, Tas. & Glos) b Dec. 21, 1946

Davison, I. J. (Notts) b Oct. 4, 1937

Dawkes, G. O. (Leics & Derbys) b July 19, 1920

*Dawson, E. W. (CU & Leics) b Feb. 13, 1904, d June 4, 1979

*Dawson, O. C. (Natal & Border) b Sept. 1, 1919

Day, A. P. (Kent; *CY 1910*) b April 10, 1885, d Jan. 22, 1969

*de Alwis, R. G. (SSC) b Feb. 15, 1959

*Dean, H. (Lancs) b Aug. 13, 1884, d March 12, 1957

Dean, J., sen. (Sussex) b Jan. 4, 1816, d Dec. 25, 1881

*Deane, H. G. (Natal & Tvl) b July 21, 1895, d Oct. 21, 1939

*De Caires, F. I. (BG) b May 12, 1909, d Feb. 2, 1959

*De Courcy, J. H. (NSW) b April 18, 1927, d June 20, 2000

*de Groen, R. P. (Auck. & N. Dist.) b Aug. 5, 1962

*Dekker, M. H. (Mat.) b Dec. 5, 1969

*Dell, A. R. (Qld) b Aug. 6, 1947

*de Mel, A. L. F. (SL) b May 9, 1959

*Dempster, C. S. (Wgtn, Leics, Scotland & Warwicks; *CY 1932*) b Nov. 15, 1903, d Feb. 14, 1974

*Dempster, E. W. (Wgtn) b Jan. 25, 1925

*Denness, M. H. (Scotland, Kent & Essex; *CY 1975*; ICC referee) b Dec. 1, 1940

Dennett, G. (Glos) b April 27, 1880, d Sept. 14, 1937

Denning, P. W. (Som) b Dec. 16, 1949

Dennis, F. (Yorks) b June 11, 1907, d Dec. 21, 2000

Dennis, S. J. (Yorks, OFS & Glam) b Oct. 18, 1960

*Denton, D. (Yorks; *CY 1906*) b July 4, 1874, d Feb. 16, 1950

*Deodhar, D. B. (M'tra) b Jan. 14, 1892, d Aug. 24, 1993

*Depeiza, C. C. (B'dos) b Oct. 10, 1928, d Nov. 10, 1995

*Desai, R. B. (Bombay) b June 20, 1939, d April 27, 1998

*de Silva, A. M. (CCC) b Dec. 3, 1963

de Silva, D. L. S. (SL) b Nov. 17, 1956, d April 12, 1980

*de Silva, D. S. (Bloom.) b June 11, 1942

*de Silva, E. A. R. (NCC & Galle) b March 28, 1956

de Silva, G. N. (SL) b March 12, 1955

*de Silva, G. R. A. (SL) b Dec. 12, 1952

de Smidt, R. W. (W. Prov.) b Nov. 24, 1883, d Aug. 3, 1986

De Trafford, C. E. (Lancs & Leics) b May 21, 1864, d Nov. 11, 1951

Devereux, L. N. (Middx, Worcs & Glam) b Oct. 20, 1931

*de Villiers, P. S. (Northerns, N. Tvl & Kent) b Oct. 13, 1964

*Dewdney, C. T. (Jam.) b Oct. 23, 1933

Dewes, J. G. (CU & Middx) b Oct. 11, 1926

Dews, G. (Worcs) b June 5, 1921

*Dexter, E. R. (CU & Sussex; *CY 1961*) b May 15, 1935

*Dhanraj, R. (T/T) b Feb. 6, 1969

*Dias, R. L. (CCC) b Oct. 18, 1952

*Dick, A. E. (Otago & Wgtn) b Oct. 10, 1936

*Dickinson, G. R. (Otago) b March 11, 1903, d March 17, 1978

*Dilawar Hussain (C. Ind. and U. Prov.) b March 19, 1907, d Aug. 26, 1967

*Dilley, G. R. (Kent, Natal & Worcs) b May 18, 1959

Dillon, E. W. (Kent & OU) b Feb. 15, 1881, d April 20, 1941

*Dipper, A. E. (Glos) b Nov. 9, 1885, d Nov. 7, 1945

*Divecha, R. V. (Bombay, OU, Northants, Vidarbha & S'tra) b Oct. 18, 1927

Diver, A. J. D. (Cambs., Middx, Notts & All-England) b June 6, 1824, d March 25, 1876

Diver, E. J. (Surrey & Warwicks) b March 20, 1861, d Dec. 27, 1924

Dixon, A. L. (Kent) b Nov. 27, 1933

*Dixon, C. D. (Tvl) b Feb. 12, 1891, d Sept. 9, 1969

Dixon, J. A. (Notts) b May 27, 1861, d June 8, 1931

Dodds, T. C. (Essex) b May 29, 1919

*Dodemaide, A. I. C. (Vic. & Sussex) b Oct. 5, 1963

*Doggart, G. H. G. OBE (CU & Sussex; Pres. MCC 1981-82) b July 18, 1925

*D'Oliveira, B. L. OBE (Worcs; *CY 1967*) b Oct. 4, 1931

D'Oliveira, D. B. (Worcs) b Oct. 19, 1960

*Dollery, H. E. (Warwicks & Wgtn; *CY 1952*) b Oct. 14, 1914, d Jan. 20, 1987

*Dolphin, A. (Yorks) b Dec. 24, 1885, d Oct. 23, 1942

*Donnan, H. (NSW) b Nov. 12, 1864, d Aug. 13, 1956

*Donnelly, M. P. (Wgtn, Cant., OU, Middx & Warwicks; *CY 1948*) b Oct. 17, 1917, d Oct. 22, 1999

*Dooland, B. (S. Aust. & Notts; *CY 1955*) b Nov. 1, 1923, d Sept. 8, 1980

Dorrinton, W. (Kent & All-England) b April 29, 1809, d Nov. 8, 1848

Dorset, 3rd Duke of (Kent) b March 24, 1745, d July 19, 1799

*Doshi, D. R. (Bengal, Notts, Warwicks & S'tra) b Dec. 22, 1947

*Douglas, J. W. H. T. (Essex; *CY 1915*) b Sept. 3, 1882, d Dec. 19, 1930

Dovey, R. R. (Kent) b July 18, 1920, d Dec. 27, 1974

Dowe, U. G. (Jam.) b March 29, 1949

*Dower, R. R. (E. Prov.) b June 4, 1876, d Sept. 15, 1964

*Dowling, G. T. OBE (Cant.; ICC referee) b March 4, 1937

*Downton, P. R. (Kent & Middx) b April 4, 1957

*Draper, R. G. (E. Prov. & Griq. W.) b Dec. 24, 1926

Dredge, C. H. (Som) b Aug. 4, 1954

*Druce, N. F. (CU & Surrey; *CY 1898*) b Jan. 1, 1875, d Oct. 27, 1954

Drybrough, C. D. (OU & Middx) b Aug. 31, 1938

*D'Souza, A. (Kar., Peshawar & PIA) b Jan. 17, 1939

*Ducat, A. (Surrey; *CY 1920*) b Feb. 16, 1886, d July 23, 1942

*Duckworth, C. A. R. (Natal & Rhod.) b March 22, 1933

*Duckworth, G. (Lancs; *CY 1929*) b May 9, 1901, d Jan. 5, 1966

Dudleston, B. (Leics, Glos & Rhod.; Test umpire) b July 16, 1945

Duers, K. G. (Mash.) b June 30, 1960

*Duff, R. A. (NSW) b Aug. 17, 1878, d Dec. 13, 1911

*Dujon, P. J. L. (Jam.; *CY 1989*) b May 28, 1956

*Duleepsinhji, K. S. (CU & Sussex; *CY 1930*) b June 13, 1905, d Dec. 5, 1959

*Dumbrill, R. (Natal & Tvl) b Nov. 19, 1938

*Duminy, J. P. (OU, W. Prov. & Tvl) b Dec. 16, 1897, d Jan. 31, 1980

*Duncan, J. R. F. (Qld & Vic.) b March 25, 1944

*Dunell, O. R. (E. Prov.) b July 15, 1856, d Oct. 21, 1929

Dunne, R. S. (Otago; Test umpire) b April 22, 1943

*Dunning, J. A. (Otago & OU) b Feb. 6, 1903, d June 24, 1971

*Dunusinghe, C. I. (Ant. & NCC) b Oct. 19, 1970

*Du Preez, J. H. (Rhod. & Zimb.) b Nov. 14, 1942

*Durani, S. A. (S'tra, Guj. & Raja.) b Dec. 11, 1934

*Durston, F. J. (Middx) b July 11, 1893, d April 8, 1965

*Du Toit, J. F. (SA) b April 5, 1868, d July 10, 1909

Dye, J. C. J. (Kent, Northants & E. Prov.) b July 24, 1942

*Dyer, D. V. (Natal) b May 2, 1914, d June 18, 1990

*Dyer, G. C. (NSW) b March 16, 1959

*Dymock, G. (Qld) b July 21, 1945

Dyson, A. H. (Glam) b July 10, 1905, d June 7, 1978

Dyson, Jack (Lancs) b July 8, 1934, d Nov. 16, 2000

*Dyson, John (NSW) b June 11, 1954

*Eady, C. J. (Tas.) b Oct. 29, 1870, d Dec. 20, 1945

Eagar, E. D. R. (OU, Glos & Hants) b Dec. 8, 1917, d Sept. 13, 1977

Ealham, A. G. E. (Kent) b Aug. 30, 1944

East, D. E. (Essex) b July 27, 1959

East, R. E. (Essex) b June 20, 1947

Eastman, L. C (Essex & Otago) b June 3, 1897, d April 17, 1941

*Eastwood, K. H. (Vic.) b Nov. 23, 1935

*Ebeling, H. I. MBE (Vic.) b Jan. 1, 1905, d Jan. 12, 1980

Ebrahim, Ahmed (ICC referee) b Dec. 2, 1937

Eckersley, P. T. (Lancs) b July 2, 1904, d Aug. 13, 1940

*Edgar, B. A. (Wgtn) b Nov. 23, 1956

Edinburgh, HRH Duke of (Pres. MCC 1948-49, 1974-75) b June 10, 1921

Edmeades, B. E. A. (Essex) b Sept. 17, 1941

*Edmonds, P. H. (CU, Middx & E. Prov.) b March 8, 1951

Edrich, B. R. (Kent & Glam) b Aug. 18, 1922

Edrich, E. H. (Lancs) b March 27, 1914, d July 9, 1993

Edrich, G. A. (Lancs) b July 13, 1918

*Edrich, J. H. MBE (Surrey; *CY 1966*) b June 21, 1937

*Edrich, W. J. (Middx; *CY 1940*) b March 26, 1916, d April 24, 1986

*Edwards, G. N. (C. Dist.) b May 27, 1955

*Edwards, J. D. (Vic.) b June 12, 1862, d July 31, 1911

Edwards, M. J. (CU & Surrey) b March 1, 1940

*Edwards, R. (W. Aust. & NSW) b Dec. 1, 1942

*Edwards, R. M. (B'dos) b June 3, 1940

*Edwards, W. J. (W. Aust.) b Dec. 23, 1949

*Ehtesham-ud-Din (Lahore, Punjab, PIA, NBP & UBL) b Sept. 4, 1950

*Elgie, M. K. (Natal) b March 6, 1933

Elliott, C. S. MBE (Derbys; Test umpire) b April 24, 1912

Elliott, Harold (Lancs; Test umpire) b June 15, 1904, d April 15, 1969

Elliott, Harry (Derbys) b Nov. 2, 1891, d Feb. 2, 1976

*Ellison, R. M. (Kent & Tas.; *CY 1986*) b Sept. 21, 1959

*Emburey, J. E. (Middx, W. Prov. & Northants; *CY 1984*) b Aug. 20, 1952

*Emery, P. A. (NSW) b June 25, 1964

*Emery, R. W. G. (Auck. & Cant.) b March 28, 1915, d Dec. 18, 1982

*Emery, S. H. (NSW) b Oct. 16, 1885, d Jan. 7, 1967

*Emmett, G. M. (Glos) b Dec. 2, 1912, d Dec. 18, 1976

*Emmett, T. (Yorks) b Sept. 3, 1841, d June 30, 1904

*Endean, W. R. (Tvl) b May 31, 1924

Engel, Matthew L. (Editor of *Wisden* 1993-2000) b June 11, 1951

*Engineer, F. M. (Bombay & Lancs) b Feb. 25, 1938

Enthoven, H. J. (CU & Middx) b June 4, 1903, d June 29, 1975

Essop-Adam, E. A. (Mash.) b Nov. 16, 1968

*Evans, A. J. (OU, Hants & Kent) b May 1, 1889, d Sept. 18, 1960

Evans, D. G. L. (Glam; Test umpire) b July 27, 1933, d March 25, 1990

*Evans, E. (NSW) b March 26, 1849, d July 2, 1921

*Evans, K. P. (Notts) b Sept. 10, 1963

*Evans, T. G. CBE (Kent; *CY 1951*) b Aug. 18, 1920, d May 3, 1999

Evershed, Sir Sydney H. (Derbys) b Jan. 13, 1861, d March 7, 1937

Every, T. (Glam) b Dec. 19, 1909, d Jan. 20, 1990

Eyre, T. J. P. (Derbys) b Oct. 17, 1939

*Fagg, A. E. (Kent; Test umpire) b June 18, 1915, d Sept. 13, 1977

*Fairfax, A. G. (NSW) b June 16, 1906, d May 17, 1955

Fairservice, W. J. (Kent) b May 16, 1881, d June 26, 1971

*Fane, F. L. (OU & Essex) b April 27, 1875, d Nov. 27, 1960

*Farnes, K. (CU & Essex; *CY 1939*) b July 8, 1911, d Oct. 20, 1941

*Farooq Hamid (Lahore & PIA) b March 3, 1945

*Farrer, W. S. (Border) b Dec. 8, 1936

*Farrimond, W. (Lancs) b May 23, 1903, d Nov. 14, 1979

*Farrukh Zaman (Peshawar, NWFP, Punjab & MCB) b April 2, 1956

*Faulkner, G. A. (Tvl) b Dec. 17, 1881, d Sept. 10, 1930

*Favell, L. E. MBE (S. Aust.) b Oct. 6, 1929, d June 14, 1987

*Fazal Mahmood (N. Ind., Punjab & Lahore; *CY 1955*) b Feb. 18, 1927

Fearnley, C. D. (Worcs; bat-maker) b April 12, 1940

Featherstone, N. G. (Tvl, N. Tvl, Middx & Glam) b Aug. 20, 1949

'Felix', N. (Wanostrocht) (Kent, Surrey & All-England) b Oct. 4, 1804, d Sept. 3, 1876

*Fellows-Smith, J. P. (OU, Tvl & Northants) b Feb. 3, 1932

Feltham, M. A. (Surrey & Middx) b June 26, 1963

Felton, N. A. (Som & Northants) b Oct. 24, 1960

*Fender, P. G. H. (Sussex & Surrey; *CY 1915*) b Aug. 22, 1892, d June 15, 1985

*Ferguson, W. (T/T) b Dec. 14, 1917, d Feb. 23, 1961

Ferguson, W. H. BEM (Scorer) b June 6, 1880, d Sept. 22, 1957

*Fernandes, M. P. (BG) b Aug. 12, 1897, d May 8, 1981

Fernando, E. A. (SL) b Feb. 22, 1944

*Fernando, E. R. N. S. (SLAF) b Dec. 19, 1955

*Fernando, T. L. (Colts & BRC) b Dec. 27, 1962

Ferreira, A. M. (N. Tvl & Warwicks) b April 13, 1955

**Ferris, J. J. (NSW, Glos & S. Aust.; *CY 1889*) b May 21, 1867, d Nov. 21, 1900

*Fichardt, C. G. (OFS) b March 20, 1870, d May 30, 1923

Fiddling, K. (Yorks & Northants) b Oct. 13, 1917, d June 19, 1992

Field, F. E. (Warwicks) b Sept. 23, 1874, d Aug. 25, 1934

*Fielder, A. (Kent; *CY 1907*) b July 19, 1877, d Aug. 30, 1949

*Findlay, T. M. MBE (Comb. Is. & Windwards) b Oct. 19, 1943

Findlay, W. (OU & Lancs; Sec. Surrey CCC 1907-19; Sec. MCC 1926-36) b June 22, 1880, d June 19, 1953

*Fingleton, J. H. OBE (NSW; writer) b April 28, 1908, d Nov. 22, 1981

*Finlason, C. E. (Tvl & Griq. W.) b Feb. 19, 1860, d July 31, 1917

Finney, R. J. (Derbys) b Aug. 2, 1960

Firth, Canon J. D'E. E. (Winchester, OU & Notts; *CY 1918*) b Jan. 21, 1900, d Sept. 21, 1957

Firth, J. (Yorks & Leics) b June 27, 1917, d Sept. 7, 1981

*Fisher, F. E. (Wgtn & C. Dist.) b July 28, 1924, d June 19, 1996

*Fishlock, L. B. (Surrey; *CY 1947*) b Jan. 2, 1907, d June 26, 1986

Fishwick, T. S. (Warwicks) b July 24, 1876, d Feb. 21, 1950

Fitzgerald, R. A. (CU & Middx; Sec. MCC 1863-76) b Oct. 1, 1834, d Oct. 28, 1881

Fitzroy-Newdegate, Hon. J. M. (Northants) b March 20, 1897, d May 7, 1976

*Flavell, J. A. (Worcs; *CY 1965*) b May 15, 1929

*Fleetwood-Smith, L. O'B. (Vic.) b March 30, 1908, d March 16, 1971

Fletcher, D. A. G. (Rhod. & Zimb.) b Sept. 27, 1948

Fletcher, D. G. W. (Surrey) b July 6, 1924

*Fletcher, K. W. R. OBE (Essex; *CY 1974*) b May 20, 1944

Fletcher, S. D. (Yorks & Lancs) b June 8, 1964

*Floquet, C. E. (Tvl) b Nov. 3, 1884, d Nov. 22, 1963

*Flowers, W. (Notts) b Dec. 7, 1856, d Nov. 1, 1926

*Foley, H. (Wgtn) b Jan. 28, 1906, d Oct. 16, 1948

Folley, I. (Lancs & Derbys) b Jan. 9, 1963, d Aug. 30, 1993

Forbes, C. (Notts) b Aug. 9, 1936

*Ford, F. G. J. (CU & Middx) b Dec. 14, 1866, d Feb. 7, 1940

Fordham, A. (Northants) b Nov. 9, 1964

Foreman, D. J. (W. Prov. & Sussex) b Feb. 1, 1933

*Foster, F. R. (Warwicks; *CY 1912*) b Jan. 31, 1889, d May 3, 1958

Foster, G. N. (OU, Worcs & Kent) b Oct. 16, 1884, d Aug. 11, 1971

Foster, H. K. (OU & Worcs; *CY 1911*) b Oct. 30, 1873, d June 23, 1950

Foster, M. K. (Worcs) b Jan. 1, 1889, d Dec. 3, 1940

*Foster, M. L. C. (Jam.) b May 9, 1943

*Foster, N. A. (Essex & Tvl; *CY 1988*) b May 6, 1962

*Foster, R. E. (OU & Worcs; *CY 1901*) b April 16, 1878, d May 13, 1914

*Fothergill, A. J. (Som) b Aug. 26, 1854, d Aug. 1, 1932

Fowke, G. H. S. (Leics) b Oct. 14, 1880, d June 24, 1946

*Fowler, G. (Lancs & Durham) b April 20, 1957

*Francis, B. C. (NSW & Essex) b Feb. 18, 1948

Francis, D. A. (Glam) b Nov. 29, 1953

*Francis, G. N. (B'dos) b Dec. 11, 1897, d Jan. 7, 1942

*Francis, H. H. (Glos & W. Prov.) b May 26, 1868, d Jan. 7, 1936

Francis, K. T. (Test umpire) b Oct. 15, 1949

Francke, F. M. (SL & Qld) b March 29, 1941

*Francois, C. M. (Griq. W.) b June 20, 1897, d May 26, 1944

*Frank, C. N. (Tvl) b Jan. 27, 1891, d Dec. 25, 1961

*Frank, W. H. B. (SA) b Nov. 23, 1872, d Feb. 16, 1945

*Franklin, T. J. (Auck.) b March 18, 1962

*Frederick, M. (B'dos, Derbys & Jam.) b May 6, 1927

*Fredericks, R. C. (†Guyana & Glam; *CY 1974*) b Nov. 11, 1942, d Sept. 5, 2000

*Freeman, A. P. (Kent; *CY 1923*) b May 17, 1888, d Jan. 28, 1965

*Freeman, D. L. (Wgtn) b Sept. 8, 1914, d May 31, 1994

*Freeman, E. W. (S. Aust.) b July 13, 1944

Freeman, J. R. (Essex) b Sept. 3, 1883, d Aug. 8, 1958

*Freer, F. W. (Vic.) b Dec. 4, 1915, d Nov. 2 1998

*French, B. N. (Notts) b Aug. 13, 1959

Frost, G. (Notts) b Jan. 15, 1947

*Fry, C. B. (OU, Sussex & Hants; *CY 1895*) b April 25, 1872, d Sept. 7, 1956

*Fuller, E. R. H. (W. Prov.) b Aug. 2, 1931

*Fuller, R. L. (Jam.) b Jan. 30, 1913, d May 3, 1987

*Fullerton, G. M. (Tvl) b Dec. 8, 1922

*Funston, K. J. (NE Tvl, OFS & Tvl) b Dec. 3, 1925

*Furlonge, H. A. (T/T) b June 19, 1934

Gabriel, R. S. (T/T) b June 5, 1952

*Gadkari, C. V. (M'tra & Ind. Serv.) b Feb. 3, 1928, d Jan. 11, 1998

*Gaekwad, A. D. (Baroda) b Sept. 23, 1952

*Gaekwad, D. K. (Baroda) b Oct. 27, 1928

*Gaekwad, H. G. (†M. Pradesh) b Aug. 29, 1923

Gale, R. A. (Middx) b Dec. 10, 1933

*Gallichan, N. (Wgtn) b June 3, 1906, d March 25, 1969

Gamage, J. C. (Colts & Galle) b April 17, 1964

*Gamsy, D. (Natal) b Feb. 17, 1940

*Gandotra, A. (Delhi & Bengal) b Nov. 24, 1948

*Gannon, J. B. (W. Aust.) b Feb. 8, 1947

*Ganteaume, A. G. (T/T) b Jan. 22, 1921

Gard, T. (Som) b June 2, 1957

Gardiner, Howard (ICC referee) b Jan. 1, 1944

Gardner, F. C. (Warwicks) b June 4, 1922, d Jan. 12, 1979

Gardner, L. R. (Leics) b Feb. 23, 1934

Garland-Wells, H. M. (OU & Surrey) b Nov. 14, 1907, d May 28, 1993

Garlick, R. G. (Lancs & Northants) b April 11, 1917, d May 16, 1988

*Garner, J. MBE (B'dos, Som & S. Aust.; *CY 1980*) b Dec. 16, 1952

Garnham, M. A. (Glos, Leics & Essex) b Aug. 20, 1960

*Garrett, T. W. (NSW) b July 26, 1858, d Aug. 6, 1943

*Gaskin, B. B. M. (BG) b March 21, 1908, d May 1, 1979

*Gatting, M. W. OBE (Middx; *CY 1984*) b June 6, 1957

*Gaunt, R. A. (W. Aust. & Vic.) b Feb. 26, 1934

*Gavaskar, S. M. (Bombay & Som; *CY 1980*) b July 10, 1949

*Gay, L. H. (CU, Hants & Som) b March 24, 1871, d Nov. 1, 1949

*Geary, G. (Leics; *CY 1927*) b July 9, 1893, d March 6, 1981

Gedye, S. G. (Auck.) b May 2, 1929

*Gehrs, D. R. A. (S. Aust.) b Nov. 29, 1880, d June 25, 1953

*Germon, L. K. (Cant.) b Nov. 4, 1968

Ghai, R. S. (Punjab) b June 12, 1960

*Ghavri, K. D. (S'tra & Bombay) b Feb. 28, 1951

*Ghazali, M. E. Z. (M'tra & Pak. Serv.) b June 15, 1924

*Ghorpade, J. M. (Baroda) b Oct. 2, 1930, d March 29, 1978

*Ghulam Abbas (Kar., NBP & PIA) b May 1, 1947

*Ghulam Ahmed (H'bad) b July 4, 1922, d Oct. 28, 1998

*Gibb, P. A. (CU, Scotland, Yorks & Essex) b July 11, 1913, d Dec. 7, 1977

Gibbons, H. H. (Worcs) b Oct. 10, 1904, d Feb. 16, 1973

Gibbs, G. L. (BG) b Dec. 27, 1925, d Feb. 21, 1979

*Gibbs, L. R. (†Guyana, S. Aust. & Warwicks; *CY 1972*) b Sept. 29, 1934

Gibbs, P. J. K. (OU & Derbys) b Aug. 17, 1944

Gibson, C. H. (Eton, CU & Sussex; *CY 1918*) b Aug. 23, 1900, d Dec. 31, 1976

Gibson, D. (Surrey) b May 1, 1936

*Giffen, G. (S. Aust.; *CY 1894*) b March 27, 1859, d Nov. 29, 1927

*Giffen, W. F. (S. Aust.) b Sept. 20, 1861, d June 29, 1949

*Gifford, N. MBE (Worcs & Warwicks; *CY 1975*) b March 30, 1940

*Gilbert, D. R. (NSW, Tas. & Glos) b Dec. 29, 1960

*Gilchrist, R. (Jam. & H'bad) b June 28, 1934

Giles, R. J. (Notts) b Oct. 17, 1919

Gilhouley, K. (Yorks & Notts) b Aug. 8, 1934

*Gillespie, S. R. (Auck.) b March 2, 1957

Gilliat, R. M. C. (OU & Hants) b May 20, 1944

*Gilligan, A. E. R. (CU, Surrey & Sussex; *CY 1924*; Pres. MCC 1967-68) b Dec. 23, 1894, d Sept. 5, 1976

*Gilligan, A. H. H. (Sussex) b June 29, 1896, d May 5, 1978

Gilligan, F. W. (OU & Essex) b Sept. 20, 1893, d May 4, 1960

Gillingham, Canon F. H. (Essex) b Sept. 6, 1875, d April 1, 1953

*Gilmour, G. J. (NSW) b June 26, 1951

*Gimblett, H. (Som; *CY 1953*) b Oct. 19, 1914, d March 30, 1978

*Gladstone, G. (*see* Marais, G. G.)

*Gladwin, Cliff (Derbys) b April 3, 1916, d April 10, 1988

*Gleeson, J. W. (NSW & E. Prov.) b March 14, 1938

*Gleeson, R. A. (E. Prov.) b Dec. 6, 1873, d Sept. 27, 1919

Glover, A. C. S. (Warwicks) b April 19, 1872, d May 22, 1949

*Glover, G. K. (Kimberley & Griq. W.) b May 13, 1870, d Nov. 15, 1938

*Goddard, J. D. C. OBE (B'dos) b April 21, 1919, d Aug. 26, 1987

*Goddard, T. L. (Natal & NE Tvl) b Aug. 1, 1931

*Goddard, T. W. (Glos; *CY 1938*) b Oct. 1, 1900, d May 22, 1966

Goel, R. (Patiala & Haryana) b Sept. 29, 1942

*Gomes, H. A. (T/T & Middx; *CY 1985*) b July 13, 1953

*Gomez, G. E. (T/T) b Oct. 10, 1919, d Aug. 6, 1996

*Gooch, G. A. OBE (Essex & W. Prov.; *CY 1980*) b July 23, 1953

Goodwin, K. (Lancs) b June 25, 1938

Goodwin, T. J. (Leics) b Jan. 22, 1929

Goonatillake, F. R. M. de S. (SL) b Aug. 15, 1951

*Goonatillake, H. M. (SL) b Aug. 16, 1952

Goonesena, G. (Ceylon, Notts, CU & NSW) b Feb. 16, 1931

*Gopalan, M. J. (Madras) b June 6, 1909

*Gopinath, C. D. (Madras) b March 1, 1930

*Gordon, N. (Tvl) b Aug. 6, 1911

Gore, A. C. (Eton & Army, *CY 1919*) b May 14, 1900, d June 7, 1990

Gould, I. J. (Middx, Auck. & Sussex) b Aug. 19, 1957

*Gover, A. R. MBE (Surrey; *CY 1937; oldest surviving CY and oldest living Test cricketer at end of 2000*) b Feb. 29, 1908

*Gower, D. I. OBE (Leics & Hants; *CY 1979*) b April 1, 1957

Grace, C. B. (London County; son of W. G.) b March 1882, d June 6, 1938

*Grace, Dr E. M. (Glos; brother of W. G.) b Nov. 28, 1841, d May 20, 1911

*Grace, G. F. (Glos; brother of W. G.) b Dec. 13, 1850, d Sept. 22, 1880

Grace, Dr Henry (Glos; brother of W. G.) b Jan. 31, 1833, d Nov. 15, 1895

Grace, Dr H. M. (father of W. G.) b Feb. 21, 1808, d Dec. 23, 1871

Grace, Mrs H. M. (mother of W. G.) b July 18, 1812, d July 25, 1884

*Grace, Dr W. G. (Glos; *CY 1896*) b July 18, 1848, d Oct. 23, 1915

Grace, W. G., jun. (CU & Glos; son of W. G.) b July 6, 1874, d March 2, 1905

Graf, S. F. (Vic., W. Aust. & Hants) b May 19, 1957

*Graham, H. (Vic. & Otago) b Nov. 22, 1870, d Feb. 7, 1911

Graham, J. N. (Kent) b May 8, 1943

*Graham, R. (W. Prov.) b Sept. 16, 1877, d April 21, 1946

*Grant, G. C. (CU, T/T & Rhod.) b May 9, 1907, d Oct. 26, 1978

*Grant, R. S. (CU & T/T) b Dec. 15, 1909, d Oct. 18, 1977

Graveney, D. A. (Glos, Som & Durham) b Jan. 2, 1953

Graveney, J. K. (Glos) b Dec. 16, 1924

*Graveney, T. W. OBE (Glos, Worcs & Qld; *CY 1953*) b June 16, 1927

Graves, P. J. (Sussex & OFS) b May 19, 1946

*Gray, A. H. (T/T, Surrey & W. Tvl) b May 23, 1963

*Gray, E. J. (Wgtn) b Nov. 18, 1954

Gray, J. R. (Hants) b May 19, 1926

Gray, L. H. (Middx) b Dec. 15, 1915, d Jan. 3, 1983

Gray, M. A. (President ICC 2000-) b May 30, 1940

*Greatbatch, M. J. (C. Dist.) b Dec. 11, 1963

Green, A. M. (Sussex & OFS) b May 28, 1960

Green, D. M. (OU, Lancs & Glos; *CY 1969*) b Nov. 10, 1939

Green, Major L. (Lancs) b Feb. 1, 1890, d March 2, 1963

*Greenhough, T. (Lancs) b Nov. 9, 1931

*Greenidge, A. E. (B'dos) b Aug. 20, 1956

*Greenidge, C. G. MBE (Hants & B'dos; *CY 1977*) b May 1, 1951

*Greenidge, G. A. (B'dos & Sussex) b May 26, 1948

Greensmith, W. T. (Essex) b Aug. 16, 1930

*Greenwood, A. (Yorks) b Aug. 20, 1847, d Feb. 12, 1889

Greetham, C. (Som) b Aug. 28, 1936

*Gregory, D. W. (NSW; first Australian captain) b April 15, 1845, d Aug. 4, 1919

*Gregory, E. J. (NSW) b May 29, 1839, d April 22, 1899

*Gregory, J. M. (NSW; *CY 1922*) b Aug. 14, 1895, d Aug. 7, 1973

*Gregory, R. G. (Vic.) b Feb. 28, 1916, d June 10, 1942

Gregory, R. J. (Surrey) b Aug. 26, 1902, d Oct. 6, 1973

*Gregory, S. E. (NSW; *CY 1897*) b April 14, 1870, d Aug. 1, 1929

*Greig, A. W. (Border, E. Prov. & Sussex; *CY 1975*) b Oct. 6, 1946

*Greig, I. A. (CU, Border, Sussex & Surrey) b Dec. 8, 1955

*Grell, M. G. (T/T) b Dec. 18, 1899, d Jan. 11, 1976

*Grieve, B. A. F. (Eng.) b May 28, 1864, d Nov. 19, 1917

Grieves, K. J. (NSW & Lancs) b Aug. 27, 1925, d Jan. 3, 1992

*Grieveson, R. E. OBE (Tvl) b Aug. 24, 1909, d July 24, 1998

*Griffin, G. M. (Natal & Rhod.) b June 12, 1939

*Griffith, C. C. (B'dos; *CY 1964*) b Dec. 14, 1938

Griffith, G. ("Ben") (Surrey & Utd England XI) b Dec. 20, 1833, d May 3, 1879

*Griffith, H. C. (B'dos) b Dec. 1, 1893, d March 18, 1980

Griffith, M. G. (CU & Sussex) b Nov. 25, 1943

*Griffith, S. C. CBE (CU, Surrey & Sussex; Sec. MCC 1962-74; Pres. MCC 1979-80) b June 16, 1914, d April 7, 1993

Griffiths, B. J. (Northants) b June 13, 1949

*Grimmett, C. V. (Wgtn, Vic., & S. Aust.; *CY 1931*) b Dec. 25, 1891, d May 2, 1980

*Groube, T. U. (Vic.) b Sept. 2, 1857, d Aug. 5, 1927

*Grout, A. T. W. (Qld) b March 30, 1927, d Nov. 9, 1968

Grove, C. W. (Warwicks & Worcs) b Dec. 16, 1912, d Feb. 15, 1982

Grundy, James (Notts & Utd England XI) b March 5, 1824, d Nov. 24, 1873

*Guard, G. M. (Bombay & Guj.) b Dec. 12, 1925, d March 13, 1978

*Guest, C. E. J. (Vic. & W. Aust.) b Oct. 7, 1937

*Guha, S. (Bengal) b Jan. 31, 1946

*Guillen, S. C. (T/T & Cant.) b Sept. 24, 1924

**Gul Mahomed (N. Ind., Baroda, H'bad, Punjab & Lahore) b Oct. 15, 1921, d May 8, 1992

*Gunasekera, Y. (SL) b Nov. 8, 1957

*Guneratne, R. P. W. (Nomads) b Jan. 26, 1962

*Gunn, G. (Notts; *CY 1914*) b June 13, 1879, d June 29, 1958

Gunn, G. V. (Notts) b June 21, 1905, d Oct. 14, 1957

*Gunn, J. (Notts; *CY 1904*) b July 19, 1876, d Aug. 21, 1963

*Gunn, W. (Notts; *CY 1890*) b Dec. 4, 1858, d Jan. 29, 1921

*Gupte, B. P. (Bombay, Bengal & Ind. Rlwys) b Aug. 30, 1934

*Gupte, S. P. (Bombay, Bengal, Raja. & T/T) b Dec. 11, 1929

*Gursharan Singh (Punjab) b March 8, 1963

*Gurusinha, A. P. (SSC & NCC) b Sept. 16, 1966

*Guy, J. W. (C. Dist., Wgtn, Northants, Cant., Otago & N. Dist.) b Aug. 29, 1934

Haafiz Shahid (WAPDA) b May 10, 1963

Hadlee, B. G. (Cant.) b Dec. 14, 1941

*Hadlee, D. R. (Cant.) b Jan. 6, 1948

*Hadlee, Sir Richard J. (Cant., Notts & Tas.; *CY 1982*) b July 3, 1951

*Hadlee, W. A. CBE (Cant. & Otago) b June 4, 1915

*Hafeez, A. (*see* Kardar)

*Haig, N. E. (Middx) b Dec. 12, 1887, d Oct. 27, 1966

*Haigh, S. (Yorks; *CY 1901*) b March 19, 1871, d Feb. 27, 1921

Hair, D. B. (Test umpire) b Sept. 30, 1952

Halfyard, D. J. (Kent & Notts) b April 3, 1931, d Aug. 23, 1996

*Hall, A. E. (Tvl & Lancs) b Jan. 23, 1896, d Jan. 1, 1964

*Hall, G. G. (NE Tvl & E. Prov.) b May 24, 1938, d June 26, 1987

Hall, I. W. (Derbys) b Dec. 27, 1939

Hall, L. (Yorks; *CY 1890*) b Nov. 1, 1852, d Nov. 19, 1915

*Hall, W. W. (B'dos, T/T & Qld) b Sept. 12, 1937

Hallam, A. W. (Lancs & Notts; *CY 1908*) b Nov. 12, 1869, d July 24, 1940

Hallam, M. R. (Leics) b Sept. 10, 1931, d Jan. 1, 2000

Halliday, H. (Yorks) b Feb. 9, 1920, d Aug. 27, 1967

*Halliwell, E. A. (Tvl & Middx; *CY 1905*) b Sept. 7, 1864, d Oct. 2, 1919

*Hallows, C. (Lancs; *CY 1928*) b April 4, 1895, d Nov. 10, 1972

Hallows, J. (Lancs; *CY 1905*) b Nov. 14, 1873, d May 20, 1910

*Halse, C. G. (Natal) b Feb. 28, 1935

*Hamence, R. A. (S. Aust.) b Nov. 25, 1915

Hamer, A. (Yorks & Derbys) b Dec. 8, 1916, d Nov. 3, 1993

Hammond, H. E. (Sussex) b Nov. 7, 1907, d June 16, 1985

*Hammond, J. R. (S. Aust.) b April 19, 1950

*Hammond, W. R. (Glos; *CY 1928*) b June 19, 1903, d July 1, 1965

*Hampshire, J. H. (Yorks, Derbys & Tas.; Test umpire) b Feb. 10, 1941

Hampton, G. S. (Auck.; *believed to be oldest living first-class cricketer at end of 2000*) b Aug. 31, 1905

*Hands, P. A. M. (W. Prov.) b March 18, 1890, d April 27, 1951

*Hands, R. H. M. (W. Prov.) b July 26, 1888, d April 20, 1918

*Hanif Mohammad (B'pur, Kar. & PIA; *CY 1968*) b Dec. 21, 1934

*Hanley, M. A. (Border & W. Prov.) b Nov. 10, 1918, d June 2, 2000

*Hanumant Singh (M. Pradesh & Raja.; ICC referee) b March 29, 1939

Hardie, B. R. (Scotland & Essex) b Jan. 14, 1950

*Hardikar, M. S. (Bombay) b Feb. 8, 1936, d Feb. 4, 1995

*Hardinge, H. T. W. (Kent; *CY 1915*) b Feb. 25, 1886, d May 8, 1965

*Hardstaff, J. (Notts; Test umpire) b Nov. 9, 1882, d April 2, 1947

*Hardstaff, J., jun. (Notts & Auck.; *CY 1938*) b July 3, 1911, d Jan. 1, 1990

Hardy, J. J. E. (Hants, Som, W. Prov. & Glos) b Oct. 2, 1960

*Harford, N. S. (C. Dist. & Auck.) b Aug. 30, 1930, d March 30, 1981

*Harford, R. I. (Auck.) b May 30, 1936

Hargreave, S. (Warwicks) b Sept. 22, 1875, d Jan. 1, 1929

Harman, R. (Surrey) b Dec. 28, 1941

Haroon Rashid (Kar., Sind, NBP, PIA & UBL) b March 25, 1953

*Harper, D. J. (Test umpire) b Oct. 23, 1951

*Harper, R. A. (Guyana & Northants) b March 17, 1963

*Harris, 4th Lord (OU & Kent; Pres. MCC 1895) b Feb. 3, 1851, d March 24, 1932

Harris, C. B. (Notts) b Dec. 6, 1907, d Aug. 8, 1954

Harris, David (Hants & All-England) b 1755, d May 19, 1803

Harris, J. H. (Som; umpire) b Feb. 13, 1936

Harris, M. J. (Middx, Notts, E. Prov. & Wgtn) b May 25, 1944

*Harris, P. G. Z. (Cant.) b July 18, 1927, d Dec. 1, 1991

*Harris, R. M. (Auck.) b July 27, 1933

*Harris, T. A. (Griq. W. & Tvl) b Aug. 27, 1916, d March 7, 1993

Harrison, L. (Hants) b June 8, 1922

*Harry, J. (Vic.) b Aug. 1, 1857, d Oct. 27, 1919

*Hart, M. N. (N. Dist.) b May 16, 1972

Hart, R. T. (C. Dist. & Wgtn) b Nov. 7, 1961

*Hartigan, G. P. D. (Border) b Dec. 30, 1884, d Jan. 7, 1955

*Hartigan, R. J. (NSW & Qld) b Dec. 12, 1879, d June 7, 1958

*Hartkopf, A. E. V. (Vic.) b Dec. 28, 1889, d May 20, 1968

*Hartland, B. R. (Cant.) b Oct. 22, 1966

Hartley, A. (Lancs; *CY 1911*) b April 11, 1879, d Oct. 9, 1918

*Hartley, J. C. (OU & Sussex) b Nov. 15, 1874, d March 8, 1963

Hartley, S. N. (Yorks & OFS) b March 18, 1956

Harvey, J. F. (Derbys) b Sept. 27, 1939

*Harvey, M. R. (Vic.) b April 29, 1918, d March 20, 1995

Harvey, P. F. (Notts) b Jan. 15, 1923

*Harvey, R. L. (Natal) b Sept. 14, 1911, d July 20, 2000

*Harvey, R. N. MBE (Vic. & NSW; *CY 1954*) b Oct. 8, 1928

Hasan Jamil (Kalat, Kar., Pak. Us & PIA) b July 25, 1952

*Haseeb Ahsan (Peshawar, Pak. Us, Kar. & PIA) b July 15, 1939

*Haslam, M. J. (Auck.) b Sept. 26, 1972

Hassan, B. (Notts) b March 24, 1944

*Hassett, A. L. MBE (Vic.; *CY 1949*) b Aug. 28, 1913, d June 16, 1993

*Hastings, B. F. (Wgtn, C. Dist. & Cant.; ICC referee) b March 23, 1940

*Hathorn, C. M. H. (Tvl) b April 7, 1878, d May 17, 1920

*Hawke, 7th Lord (CU & Yorks; *CY 1909; Pres. MCC 1914-18) b Aug. 16, 1860, d Oct. 10, 1938

*Hawke, N. J. N. (W. Aust., S. Aust. & Tas.) b June 27, 1939, d Dec. 25, 2000

Hawkins, D. G. (Glos) b May 18, 1935

*Hayes, E. G. (Surrey & Leics; *CY 1907*) b Nov. 6, 1876, d Dec. 2, 1953

*Hayes, F. C. (Lancs) b Dec. 6, 1946

*Hayes, J. A. (Auck. & Cant.) b Jan. 11, 1927

Hayes, R. L. (N. Dist.) b May 9, 1971

*Haygarth, A. (Sussex; Historian) b Aug. 4, 1825, d May 1, 1903

Hayhurst, A. N. (Lancs, Som & Derbys) b Nov. 23, 1962

*Haynes, D. L. (B'dos, Middx & W. Prov.; *CY 1991*) b Feb. 15, 1956

Haynes, G. R. (Worcs) b Sept. 29, 1969

Haynes, R. C. (Jam.) b Nov. 11, 1964

Hayward, T. (Cambs. & All-England) b March 21, 1835, d July 21, 1876

*Hayward, T. W. (Surrey; *CY 1895*) b March 29, 1871, d July 19, 1939

*Hazare, V. S. (M'tra, C. Ind. & Baroda) b March 11, 1915

Hazell, H. L. (Som) b Sept. 30, 1909, d March 31, 1990

Hazlerigg, Sir A. G. Bt (later 1st Lord) (Leics) b Nov. 17, 1878, d May 25, 1949

Hazlitt, G. R. (Vic. & NSW) b Sept. 4, 1888, d Oct. 30, 1915

*Headley, G. A. MBE (Jam.; *CY 1934*) b May 30, 1909, d Nov. 30, 1983

*Headley, R. G. A. (Worcs & Jam.) b June 29, 1939

Heane, G. F. H. (Notts) b Jan. 2, 1904, d Oct. 24, 1969

Heap, J. S. (Lancs) b Aug. 12, 1882, d Jan. 30, 1951

Hearn, P. (Kent) b Nov. 18, 1925

*Hearne, A. (Kent; *CY 1894*) b July 22, 1863, d May 16, 1952

**Hearne, F. (Kent & W. Prov.) b Nov. 23, 1858, d July 14, 1949

*Hearne, G. A. L. (W. Prov.) b March 27, 1888, d Nov. 13, 1978

*Hearne, G. G. (Kent) b July 7, 1856, d Feb. 13, 1932

*Hearne, J. T. (Middx; *CY 1892*) b May 3, 1867, d April 17, 1944

*Hearne, J. W. (Middx; *CY 1912*) b Feb. 11, 1891, d Sept. 14, 1965

Hearne, T. (Middx) b Sept. 4, 1826, d May 13, 1900

Heath, G. E. M. (Hants) b Feb. 20, 1913

Heath, M. (Hants) b March 9, 1934

Hedges, B. (Glam) b Nov. 10, 1927

Hedges, L. P. (Tonbridge, OU, Kent & Glos; *CY 1919*) b July 13, 1900, d Jan. 12, 1933

*Heine, P. S. (NE Tvl, OFS & Tvl) b June 28, 1928

*Hemmings, E. E. (Warwicks, Notts & Sussex) b Feb. 20, 1949

Hemsley, E. J. O. (Worcs) b Sept. 1, 1943

*Henderson, M. (Wgtn) b Aug. 2, 1895, d June 17, 1970

Henderson, R. (Surrey; *CY 1890*) b March 30, 1865, d Jan. 29, 1931

*Hendren, E. H. (Middx; *CY 1920*) b Feb. 5, 1889, d Oct. 4, 1962

*Hendrick, M. (Derbys & Notts; *CY 1978*) b Oct. 22, 1948

*Hendriks, J. L. (Jam.; ICC referee) b Dec. 21, 1933

*Hendry, H. L. (NSW & Vic.) b May 24, 1895, d Dec. 16, 1988

*Henry, O. (W. Prov., Boland, OFS & Scotland) b Jan. 23, 1952

Herman, O. W. (Hants) b Sept. 18, 1907, d June 24, 1987

Herman, R. S. (Middx, Border, Griq. W. & Hants) b Nov. 30, 1946

Heron, J. G. (Zimb.) b Nov. 8, 1948

*Heseltine, C. (Hants) b Nov. 26, 1869, d June 13, 1944

Hever, N. G. (Middx & Glam) b Dec. 17, 1924, d Sept. 11, 1987

Hewett, H. T. (OU & Som; *CY 1893*) b May 25, 1864, d March 4, 1921.

Heyhoe-Flint, Rachael (England Women) b June 11, 1939

Heyn, P. D. (SL) b June 26, 1945

*Hibbert, P. A. (Vic.) b July 23, 1952

Hide, M. E. (Molly) (England Women) b Oct. 24, 1913, d Sept. 10, 1995

*Higgs, J. D. (Vic.) b July 11, 1950

*Higgs, K. (Lancs & Leics; *CY 1968*) b Jan. 14, 1937

Hignell, A. J. (CU & Glos) b Sept. 4, 1955

*Hilditch, A. M. J. (NSW & S. Aust.) b May 20, 1956

Hill, Alan (Derbys & OFS) b June 29, 1950

*Hill, Allen (Yorks) b Nov. 14, 1843, d Aug. 29, 1910

*Hill, A. J. L. (CU & Hants) b July 26, 1871, d Sept. 6, 1950

*Hill, C. (S. Aust.; *CY 1900*) b March 18, 1877, d Sept. 5, 1945

Hill, E. (Som) b July 9, 1923

Hill, G. (Hants) b April 15, 1913

*Hill, J. C. (Vic.) b June 25, 1923, d Aug. 11, 1974

Hill, M. (Notts, Derbys & Som) b Sept. 14, 1935

Hill, N. W. (Notts) b Aug. 22, 1935

Hill, W. A. (Warwicks) b April 27, 1910, d Aug. 11, 1995

Hill-Wood, Sir Samuel H. (Derbys) b March 21, 1872, d Jan. 4, 1949

Hillyer, W. R. (Kent & Surrey) b March 5, 1813, d Jan. 8, 1861

Hilton, C. (Lancs & Essex) b Sept. 26, 1937

*Hilton, M. J. (Lancs; *CY 1957*) b Aug. 2, 1928, d July 8, 1990

*Hime, C. F. W. (Natal) b Oct. 24, 1869, d Dec. 6, 1940

*Hindlekar, D. D. (Bombay) b Jan. 1, 1909, d March 30, 1949

Hinks, S. G. (Kent & Glos) b Oct. 12, 1960

Hipkin, A. B. (Essex) b Aug. 8, 1900, d Feb. 11, 1957

*Hirst, G. H. (Yorks; *CY 1901*) b Sept. 7, 1871, d May 10, 1954

*Hitch, J. W. (Surrey; *CY 1914*) b May 7, 1886, d July 7, 1965

Hitchcock, R. E. (Cant. & Warwicks) b Nov. 28, 1929

*Hoad, E. L. G. (B'dos) b Jan. 29, 1896, d March 5, 1986

*Hoare, D. E. (W. Aust.) b Oct. 19, 1934

*Hobbs, Sir John B. "Jack" (Surrey; *CY 1909, special portrait 1926*) b Dec. 16, 1882, d Dec. 21, 1963

*Hobbs, R. N. S. (Essex & Glam) b May 8, 1942

*Hodges, J. (Vic.) b Aug. 11, 1855, death unknown

Hodgson, A. (Northants) b Oct. 27, 1951

Hodgson, D. (Glos) b Oct. 22, 1966

*Hogan, T. G. (W. Aust.) b Sept. 23, 1956

*Hogg, R. M. (S. Aust.) b March 5, 1951

Hogg, V. R. (Zimb.) b July 3, 1952

*Hohns, T. V. (Qld) b Jan. 23, 1954

Holder, J. W. (Hants; Test umpire) b March 19, 1945

*Holder, V. A. (B'dos, Worcs & OFS) b Oct. 8, 1945

*Holding, M. A. (Jam., Lancs, Derbys, Tas. & Cant.; *CY 1977*) b Feb. 16, 1954

*Hole, G. B. (NSW & S. Aust.) b Jan. 6, 1931, d Feb. 14, 1990

*Holford, D. A. J. (B'dos & T/T) b April 16, 1940

Holland, F. C. (Surrey) b Feb. 10, 1876, d Feb. 5, 1957

*Holland, R. G. (NSW & Wgtn) b Oct. 19, 1946

*Hollies, W. E. (Warwicks; *CY 1955*) b June 5, 1912, d April 16, 1981

Holmes, Gp Capt. A. J. (Sussex) b June 30, 1899, d May 21, 1950

*Holmes, E. R. T. (OU & Surrey; *CY 1936*) b Aug. 21, 1905, d Aug. 16, 1960

Holmes, G. C. (Glam) b Sept. 16, 1958

*Holmes, P. (Yorks; *CY 1920*) b Nov. 25, 1886, d Sept. 3, 1971

Holt, A. G. (Hants) b April 8, 1911, d July 28, 1994

*Holt, J. K., jun. (Jam.) b Aug. 12, 1923, d July 2, 1997

Home of the Hirsel, Lord (Middx; Pres. MCC 1966-67) b July 2, 1903, d Oct. 9, 1995

*Hone, L. (MCC) b Jan. 30, 1853, d Dec. 31, 1896

Hooker, R. W. (Middx) b Feb. 22, 1935

*Hookes, D. W. (S. Aust.) b May 3, 1955

*Hooper, C. L. (Guyana & Kent) b Dec. 15, 1966

Hopkins, A. J. (NSW) b May 3, 1874, d April 25, 1931

Hopkins, J. A. (Glam & E. Prov.) b June 16, 1953

Hopkins, V. (Glos) b Jan. 21, 1911, d Aug. 6, 1984

*Hopwood, J. L. (Lancs) b Oct. 30, 1903, d June 15, 1985

*Horan, T. P. (Vic.) b March 8, 1854, d April 16, 1916

*Hordern, Dr H. V. (NSW & Philadelphia) b Feb. 10, 1884, d June 17, 1938

Hornby, A. H. (CU & Lancs) b July 29, 1877, d Sept. 6, 1952

*Hornby, A. N. (Lancs) b Feb. 10, 1847, d Dec. 17, 1925

*Horne, P. A. (Auck.) b Jan. 21, 1960

Horner, N. F. (Yorks & Warwicks) b May 10, 1926

*Hornibrook, P. M. (Qld) b July 27, 1899, d Aug. 25, 1976

Horsfall, R. (Essex & Glam) b June 26, 1920, d Aug. 25, 1981

Horton, H. (Worcs & Hants) b April 18, 1923, d Nov. 2, 1998

*Horton, M. J. (Worcs & N. Dist.) b April 21, 1934

*Hough, K. W. (Auck.) b Oct. 24, 1928

*Houghton, D. L. (Mash.) b June 23, 1957

*Howard, A. D. (B'dos) b Aug. 27, 1946

*Howard, N. D. (Lancs) b May 18, 1925, d May 31, 1979

Howard, Major R. (Lancs; MCC Team Manager) b April 17, 1890, d Sept. 10, 1967

*Howarth, G. P. OBE (Auck., Surrey & N. Dist.) b March 29, 1951

*Howarth, H. J. (Auck.) b Dec. 25, 1943

*Howell, H. (Warwicks) b Nov. 29, 1890, d July 9, 1932

*Howell, W. P. (NSW) b Dec. 29, 1869, d July 14, 1940

*Howorth, R. (Worcs) b April 26, 1909, d April 2, 1980

Hubble, J. C. (Kent) b Feb. 10, 1881, d Feb. 26, 1965

*Huckle, A. G. (Mat.) b Sept. 21, 1971

Huggins, H. J. (Glos) b March 15, 1877, d Nov. 20, 1942

Hughes, D. P. (Lancs & Tas.; *CY 1988*) b May 13, 1947

*Hughes, K. J. (W. Aust. & Natal; *CY 1981*) b Jan. 26, 1954

*Hughes, M. G. (Vic. & Essex; *CY 1994*) b Nov. 23, 1961

Hughes, S. P. (Middx, N. Tvl & Durham) b Dec. 20, 1959

Huish, F. H. (Kent) b Nov. 15, 1869, d March 16, 1957

Hulme, J. H. A. (Middx) b Aug. 26, 1904, d Sept. 26, 1991

Humpage, G. W. (Warwicks & OFS; *CY 1985*) b April 24, 1954

Humphrey, T. (Surrey) b Jan. 16, 1839, d Sept. 3, 1878

Humphreys, E. (Kent & Cant.) b Aug. 24, 1881, d Nov. 6, 1949

Humphreys, W. A. (Sussex & Hants) b Oct. 28, 1849, d March 23, 1924

Humphries, D. J. (Leics & Worcs) b Aug. 6, 1953

*Humphries, J. (Derbys) b May 19, 1876, d May 7, 1946

Hunt, A. V. (Scotland & Bermuda) b Oct. 1, 1910, d March 3, 1999

Hunt, G. E. (Som) b Sept. 30, 1896, d Jan. 22, 1959

*Hunt, W. A. (NSW) b Aug. 26, 1908, d Dec. 30, 1983

*Hunte, Sir Conrad C. (B'dos; *CY 1964*) b May 9, 1932, d Dec. 3, 1999

*Hunte, E. A. C. (T/T) b Oct. 3, 1905, d June 26, 1967

Hunter, D. (Yorks) b Feb. 23, 1860, d Jan. 11, 1927

*Hunter, J. (Yorks) b Aug. 3, 1855, d Jan. 4, 1891

*Hurst, A. G. (Vic.) b July 15, 1950

Hurst, R. J. (Middx) b Dec. 29, 1933, d Feb. 10, 1996

*Hurwood, A. (Qld) b June 17, 1902, d Sept. 26, 1982

*Hutchings, K. L. (Kent; *CY 1907*) b Dec. 7, 1882, d Sept. 3, 1916

Hutchinson, J. M. (Derbys; *believed to be longest-lived first-class cricketer at 103 years 344 days*) b Nov. 29, 1896, d Nov. 7, 2000

*Hutchinson, P. (SA) b Jan. 26, 1862, d Sept. 30, 1925

*Hutton, Sir Leonard (Yorks; *CY 1938*) b June 23, 1916, d Sept. 6, 1990

*Hutton, R. A. (CU, Yorks & Tvl) b Sept. 6, 1942

*Hylton, L. G. (Jam.) b March 29, 1905, d May 17, 1955

*Ibadulla, K. (Punjab, Warwicks, Tas. & Otago) b Dec. 20, 1935

*Ibrahim, K. C. (Bombay) b Jan. 26, 1919

Iddison, R. (Yorks & Lancs) b Sept. 15, 1834, d March 19, 1890

*Iddon, J. (Lancs) b Jan. 8, 1902, d April 17, 1946

*Igglesden, A. P. (Kent & W. Prov.) b Oct. 8, 1964

*Ijaz Butt (Pak. Us, Punjab, Lahore, R'pindi & Multan) b March 10, 1938

*Ijaz Faqih (Kar., Sind, PWD & MCB) b March 24, 1956

*Ikin, J. T. (Lancs) b March 7, 1918, d Sept. 15, 1984

*Illingworth, R. CBE (Yorks & Leics; *CY 1960*) b June 8, 1932

*Imran Khan (Lahore, Dawood, Worcs, OU, PIA, Sussex & NSW; *CY 1983*) b Nov. 25, 1952

*Imtiaz Ahmed (N. Ind., Comb. Us, NWFP, Pak. Servs, Peshawar & PAF) b Jan. 5, 1928

*Imtiaz Ali (T/T) b July 28, 1954

Inchmore, J. D. (Worcs & N. Tvl) b Feb. 22, 1949

*Indrajitsinhji, K. S. (S'tra & Delhi) b June 15, 1937

Ingle, R. A. (Som) b Nov. 5, 1903, d Dec. 19, 1992

Ingleby-Mackenzie, A. C. D. (Hants; Pres. MCC 1996-98) b Sept. 15, 1933

Inman, C. C. (Ceylon & Leics) b Jan. 29, 1936

*Inshan Ali (T/T) b Sept. 25, 1949, d June 24, 1995

*Insole, D. J. CBE (CU & Essex; *CY 1956*; Chairman TCCB 1975-78) b April 18, 1926

*Intikhab Alam (Kar., PIA, Surrey, PWD, Sind, Punjab; ICC referee) b Dec. 28, 1941

*Inverarity, R. J. (W. Aust. & S. Aust.) b Jan. 31, 1944

*Iqbal Qasim (Kar., Sind & NBP) b Aug. 6, 1953

*Irani, J. K. (Sind) b Aug. 18, 1923, d Feb. 25, 1982

Iredale, F. A. (NSW) b June 19, 1867, d April 15, 1926

Iremonger, J. (Notts; *CY 1903*) b March 5, 1876, d March 25, 1956

*Ironmonger, H. (Qld & Vic.) b April 7, 1882, d June 1, 1971

*Ironside, D. E. J. (Tvl) b May 2, 1925

*Irvine, B. L. (W. Prov., Natal, Essex & Tvl) b March 9, 1944

Isaacs, E. (ICC referee) b Jan. 26, 1945

*Israr Ali (S. Punjab, B'pur & Multan) b May 1, 1927

*Iverson, J. B. (Vic.) b July 27, 1915, d Oct. 24, 1973

*Jack, S. D. (Tvl) b Aug. 4, 1970

*Jackman, R. D. (Surrey, W. Prov. & Rhod.; *CY 1981*) b Aug. 13, 1945

*Jackson, A. A. (NSW) b Sept. 5, 1909, d Feb. 16, 1933

Jackson, A. B. (Derbys) b Aug. 21, 1933

*Jackson, Rt Hon. Sir F. Stanley (CU & Yorks; CY 1894; Pres. MCC 1921) b Nov. 21, 1870, d March 9, 1947

Jackson, G. R. (Derbys) b June 23, 1896, d Feb. 21, 1966

*Jackson, H. L. (Derbys; CY 1959) b April 5, 1921

Jackson, J. (Notts & All-England) b May 21, 1833, d Nov. 4, 1901

Jackson, P. F. (Worcs) b May 11, 1911, d April 27, 1999

Jackson, V. E. (NSW & Leics) b Oct. 25, 1916, d Jan. 30, 1965

*Jahangir Khan (N. Ind. & CU) b Feb. 1, 1910, d July 23, 1988

*Jai, L. P. (Bombay) b April 1, 1902, d Jan. 29, 1968

*Jaisimha, M. L. (H'bad) b March 3, 1939, d July 6, 1999

Jakeman, F. (Yorks & Northants) b Jan. 10, 1920, d May 18, 1986

*Jalal-ud-Din (PWD, Kar., IDBP & Allied Bank) b June 12, 1959

James, A. E. (Sussex) b Aug. 7, 1924

James, C. L. R. (Writer) b Jan. 4, 1901, d May 31, 1989

*James, K. C. (Wgtn & Northants) b March 12, 1904, d Aug. 21, 1976

James, K. D. (Middx, Wgtn & Hants) b March 18, 1961

*James, W. R. (Mat.) b Aug. 27, 1965

*Jameson, J. A. (Warwicks) b June 30, 1941

*Jamshedji, R. J. (Bombay) b Nov. 18, 1892, d April 5, 1976

*Jardine, D. R. (OU & Surrey; CY 1928) b Oct. 23, 1900, d June 18, 1958

*Jarman, B. N. (S. Aust.; ICC referee) b Feb. 17, 1936

*Jarvis, A. H. (S. Aust.) b Oct. 19, 1860, d Nov. 15, 1933

Jarvis, K. B. S. (Kent & Glos) b April 23, 1953

*Jarvis, M. P. (Mash.) b Dec. 6, 1955

*Jarvis, T. W. (Auck. & Cant.) b July 29, 1944

*Javed Akhtar (R'pindi & Pak. Serv.; Test umpire) b Nov. 21, 1940

*Javed Miandad (Kar., Sind, Sussex, HBL & Glam; CY 1982) b June 12, 1957

*Jayantilal, K. (H'bad) b Jan. 13, 1948

Jayaprakash, A. V. (Test umpire) b March 14, 1950

*Jayasekera, R. S. A. (SL) b Dec. 7, 1957

Jayasinghe, S. (Ceylon & Leics) b Jan. 19, 1931

Jayasinghe, S. A. (SL) b July 15, 1955, d April 20, 1995

Jeeves, P. (Warwicks) b March 5, 1888, d July 22, 1916

Jefferies, S. T. (W. Prov., Derbys, Lancs, Hants & Boland) b Dec. 8, 1959

*Jeganathan, S. (SL) b July 11, 1951, d May 14, 1996

*Jenkins, R. O. (Worcs; CY 1950) b Nov. 24, 1918, d July 21, 1995

*Jenner, T. J. (W. Aust. & S. Aust.) b Sept. 8, 1944

*Jennings, C. B. (S. Aust. & Qld) b June 5, 1884, d June 20, 1950

Jennings, R. V. (Tvl & N. Tvl) b Aug. 9, 1954

Jephson, D. L. A. (CU & Surrey) b Feb. 23, 1871, d Jan. 19, 1926

Jepson, A. (Notts; Test umpire) b July 12, 1915, d July 17, 1997

*Jessop, G. L. (CU & Glos; CY 1898) b May 19, 1874, d May 11, 1955

Jesty, T. E. (Hants, Border, Griq. W., Cant., Surrey & Lancs; CY 1983) b June 2, 1948

Jewell, Major M. F. S. (Worcs & Sussex) b Sept. 15, 1885, d May 28, 1978

*John, V. B. (SL) b May 27, 1960

*Johnson, C. L. (Tvl) b 1871, d May 31, 1908

*Johnson, D. J. (Karn.) b Oct. 16, 1971

Johnson, G. W. (Kent & Tvl) b Nov. 8, 1946

*Johnson, H. H. H. (Jam.) b July 17, 1910, d June 24, 1987

Johnson, H. L. (Derbys) b Nov. 8, 1927

*Johnson, I. W. OBE (Vic.) b Dec. 8, 1917, d Oct. 9, 1998

Johnson, L. A. (Northants) b Aug. 12, 1936

*Johnson, L. J. (Qld) b March 18, 1919, d April 20, 1977

Johnson, P. R. (CU & Som) b Aug. 5, 1880, d July 1, 1959

*Johnson, T. F. (T/T) b Jan. 10, 1917, d April 5, 1985

Johnston, Brian A. CBE (Broadcaster) b June 24, 1912, d Jan. 5, 1994

*Johnston, W. A. (Vic.; CY 1949) b Feb. 26, 1922

Jones, A. MBE (Glam, W. Aust., N. Tvl & Natal; CY 1978) b Nov. 4, 1938

Jones, A. A. (Sussex, Som, Middx, Glam, N. Tvl & OFS) b Dec. 9, 1947

*Jones, A. H. (Wgtn & C. Dist.) b May 9, 1959

Jones, A. L. (Glam) b June 1, 1957

Jones, A. N. (Sussex, Border & Som) b July 22, 1961

*Jones, A. O. (Notts & CU; CY 1900) b Aug. 16, 1872, d Dec. 21, 1914

*Jones, C. M. (BG) b Nov. 3, 1902, d Dec. 10, 1959

*Jones, D. M. (Vic., Durham & Derbys; CY 1990) b March 24, 1961

*Jones, Ernest (S. Aust. & W. Aust.) b Sept. 30, 1869, d Nov. 23, 1943

Jones, E. C. (Glam) b Dec. 14, 1911, d April 14, 1989

Jones, E. W. (Glam) b June 25, 1942

*Jones, I. J. (Glam) b Dec. 10, 1941

Jones, K. V. (Middx) b March 28, 1942

*Jones, P. E. (T/T) b June 6, 1917, d Nov. 21, 1991

Jones, P. H. (Kent) b June 19, 1935

*Jones, S. P. (NSW, Qld & Auck.) b Aug. 1, 1861, d July 14, 1951

Jones, W. E. (Glam) b Oct. 31, 1916, d July 25, 1996

Jordon, R. C. (Vic.) b Feb. 17, 1937

*Joshi, P. G. (M'tra) b Oct. 27, 1926, d Jan. 8, 1987

Joshi, U. C. (S'tra, Ind. Rlwys, Guj. & Sussex) b Dec. 23, 1944

*Joslin, L. R. (Vic.) b Dec. 13, 1947

Julian, R. (Leics) b Aug. 23, 1936

*Julien, B. D. (T/T & Kent) b March 13, 1950

*Jumadeen, R. R. (T/T) b April 12, 1948

*Jupp, H. (Surrey) b Nov. 19, 1841, d April 8, 1889

*Jupp, V. W. C. (Sussex & Northants; *CY 1928*) b March 27, 1891, d July 9, 1960

*Jurangpathy, B. R. (CCC) b June 25, 1967

*Kallicharran, A. I. (Guyana, Warwicks, Qld, Tvl & OFS; *CY 1983*) b March 21, 1949

*Kaluperuma, L. W. (SL) b May 25, 1949

*Kaluperuma, S. M. S. (SL) b Oct. 22, 1961

*Kanhai, R. B. (†Guyana, T/T, W. Aust., Warwicks & Tas.; *CY 1964*) b Dec. 26, 1935

*Kanitkar, H. S. (M'tra) b Dec. 8, 1942

*Kapil Dev (Haryana, Northants & Worcs; *CY 1983*) b Jan. 6, 1959

**Kardar, A. H. (formerly Abdul Hafeez) (N. Ind., OU, Warwicks & Pak. Serv.) b Jan. 17, 1925, d April 21, 1996

Karnain, S. H. U. (NCC & Moors) b Aug. 11, 1962

*Keeton, W. W. (Notts; *CY 1940*) b April 30, 1905, d Oct. 10, 1980

*Keith, H. J. (Natal) b Oct. 25, 1927, d Nov. 17, 1997

*Kelleway, C. (NSW) b April 25, 1886, d Nov. 16, 1944

*Kelly, J. J. (NSW; *CY 1903*) b May 10, 1867, d Aug. 14, 1938

Kelly, J. M. (Lancs & Derbys) b March 19, 1922, d Nov. 13, 1979

*Kelly, T. J. D. (Vic.) b May 3, 1844, d July 20, 1893

*Kempis, G. A. (Natal) b Aug. 4, 1865, d May 19, 1890

*Kendall, T. (Vic. & Tas.) b Aug. 24, 1851, d Aug. 17, 1924

Kennedy, A. (Lancs) b Nov. 4, 1949

*Kennedy, A. S. (Hants; *CY 1933*) b Jan. 24, 1891, d Nov. 15, 1959

*Kenny, R. B. (Bombay & Bengal) b Sept. 29, 1930, d Nov. 21, 1985

*Kent, M. F. (Qld) b Nov. 23, 1953

*Kentish, E. S. M. (Jam. & OU) b Nov. 21, 1916

*Kenyon, D. (Worcs; *CY 1963*) b May 15, 1924, d Nov. 12, 1996

Kenyon, M. N. (Lancs) b Dec. 25, 1886, d Nov. 21, 1960

*Kerr, J. L. (Cant.) b Dec. 28, 1910

*Kerr, R. B. (Qld) b June 16, 1961

Key, Sir Kingsmill J. (Surrey & OU) b Oct. 11, 1864, d Aug. 9, 1932

*Khalid Hassan (Punjab & Lahore) b July 14, 1937

*Khalid Wazir (Pak.) b April 27, 1936

*Khan Mohammad (N. Ind., Pak. Us, Som, B'pur, Sind, Kar. & Lahore) b Jan. 1, 1928

Khanna, S. C. (Delhi) b June 3, 1956

Killick, E. H. (Sussex) b Jan. 17, 1875, d Sept. 29, 1948

*Killick, Rev. E. T. (CU & Middx) b May 9, 1907, d May 18, 1953

Kilner, N. (Yorks & Warwicks) b July 21, 1895, d April 28, 1979

*Kilner, R. (Yorks; *CY 1924*) b Oct. 17, 1890, d April 5, 1928

King, B. P. (Worcs & Lancs) b April 22, 1915, d March 31, 1970

*King, C. L. (B'dos, Glam, Worcs & Natal) b June 11, 1951

*King, F. M. (B'dos) b Dec. 14, 1926, d Dec. 23, 1990

King, J. B. (Philadelphia) b Oct. 19, 1873, d Oct. 17, 1965

*King, J. H. (Leics) b April 16, 1871, d Nov. 18, 1946

*King, L. A. (Jam. & Bengal) b Feb. 27, 1939, d July 9, 1998

*Kinneir, S. P. (Warwicks; *CY 1912*) b May 13, 1871, d Oct. 16, 1928

*Kippax, A. F. (NSW) b May 25, 1897, d Sept. 4, 1972

Kirby, D. (CU & Leics) b Jan. 18, 1939

*Kirmani, S. M. H. (†Karn.) b Dec. 29, 1949

*Kirsten, P. N. (W. Prov., Sussex, Derbys & Border) b May 14, 1955

*Kischenchand, G. (W. Ind., Guj. & Baroda) b April 14, 1925, d April 16, 1997

Kitchen, M. J. (Som; Test umpire) b Aug. 1, 1940

*Kline, L. F. (Vic.) b Sept. 29, 1934

*Knight, A. E. (Leics; *CY 1904*) b Oct. 8, 1872, d April 25, 1946

*Knight, B. R. (Essex & Leics) b Feb. 18, 1938

*Knight, D. J. (OU & Surrey; *CY 1915*) b May 12, 1894, d Jan. 5, 1960

Knight, R. D. V. (CU, Surrey, Glos & Sussex; Sec. MCC 1994-) b Sept. 6, 1946

Knight, W. H. (Editor of *Wisden* 1870-79) b Nov. 29, 1812, d Aug. 16, 1879

*Knott, A. P. E. (Kent & Tas.; *CY 1970*) b April 9, 1946

Knott, C. J. (Hants) b Nov. 26, 1914

Knowles, J. (Notts) b March 25, 1910

*Knox, N. A. (Surrey; *CY 1907*) b Oct. 10, 1884, d March 3, 1935

Koertzen, R. E. (Test umpire) b March 26, 1949

Kortright, C. J. (Essex) b Jan. 9, 1871, d Dec. 12, 1952
*Kotze, J. J. (Tvl & W. Prov.) b Aug. 7, 1879, d July 7, 1931
*Kripal Singh, A. G. (Madras & H'bad) b Aug. 6, 1933, d July 23, 1987
*Krishnamurthy, P. (H'bad) b July 12, 1947, d Jan. 28, 1999
*Kuggeleijn, C. M. (N. Dist.) b May 10, 1956
*Kuiper, A. P. (W. Prov., Derbys & Boland) b Aug. 24, 1959
*Kulkarni, R. R. (Bombay) b Sept. 25, 1962
*Kulkarni, U. N. (Bombay) b March 7, 1942
*Kumar, V. V. (†TN) b June 22, 1935
*Kunderan, B. K. (Ind. Rlwys & Mysore) b Oct. 2, 1939
*Kuruppu, D. S. B. P. (BRC) b Jan. 5, 1962
*Kuruppuarachchi, A. K. (NCC) b Nov. 1, 1964
*Kuys, F. (W. Prov.) b March 21, 1870, d Sept. 12, 1953
Kynaston, R. (Middx; Sec. MCC 1846-58) b Nov. 5, 1805, d June 21, 1874

*Labrooy, G. F. (CCC) b June 7, 1964
Lacey, Sir Francis E. (CU & Hants; Sec. MCC 1898-1926) b Oct. 19, 1859, d May 26, 1946
*Laird, B. M. (W. Aust.) b Nov. 21, 1950
*Laker, J. C. (Surrey, Auck. & Essex; *CY 1952*) b Feb. 9, 1922, d April 23, 1986
*Lall Singh (S. Punjab) b Dec. 16, 1909, d Nov. 19, 1985
*Lamb, A. J. (W. Prov., Northants & OFS; *CY 1981*) b June 20, 1954
Lamb, Hon. T. M. (OU, Middx & Northants; Chief Exec. ECB, 1997-) b March 24, 1953
*Lamba, R. (Delhi) b Jan. 2, 1960, d Feb. 23, 1998
*Lambert, C. B. (Guyana & N. Tvl) b Feb. 10, 1962
Lambert, G. E. (Glos & Som) b May 11, 1918, d Oct. 31, 1991
Lambert, R. H. (Ireland) b July 18, 1874, d March 24, 1956
Lambert, Wm (Surrey) b 1779, d April 19, 1851
*Lance, H. R. (NE Tvl & Tvl) b June 6, 1940
Langdon, T. (Glos) b Jan. 8, 1879, d Nov. 30, 1944
Langford, B. A. (Som) b Dec. 17, 1935
*Langley, G. R. A. (S. Aust.; *CY 1957*) b Sept. 14, 1919
*Langridge, James (Sussex; *CY 1932*) b July 10, 1906, d Sept. 10, 1966
Langridge, John G. MBE (Sussex; Test umpire; *CY 1950*) b Feb. 10, 1910, d June 27, 1999
Langridge, R. J. (Sussex) b April 13, 1939
*Langton, A. B. C. (Tvl) b March 2, 1912, d Nov. 27, 1942

*Larkins, W. (Northants, E. Prov. & Durham) b Nov. 22, 1953
*Larsen, G. R. (Wgtn) b Sept. 27, 1962
*Larter, J. D. F. (Northants) b April 24, 1940
*Larwood, H. MBE (Notts; *CY 1927*) b Nov. 14, 1904, d July 22, 1995
*Lashley, P. D. (B'dos) b Feb. 11, 1937
Latchman, H. C. (Middx & Notts) b July 26, 1943
*Latham, R. T. (Cant.) b June 12, 1961
*Laughlin, T. J. (Vic.) b Jan. 30, 1951
*Laver, F. (Vic.) b Dec. 7, 1869, d Sept. 24, 1919
Lavis, G. (Glam) b Aug. 17, 1908, d July 29, 1956
*Lawrence, D. V. (Glos) b Jan. 28, 1964
*Lawrence, G. B. (Rhod. & Natal) b March 31, 1932
Lawrence, J. (Som) b March 29, 1914, d Dec. 10, 1988
*Lawry, W. M. (Vic.; *CY 1962*) b Feb. 11, 1937
*Lawson, G. F. (NSW & Lancs) b Dec. 7, 1957
Lawton, A. E. (Derbys & Lancs) b March 31, 1879, d Dec. 25, 1955
Leach, G. (Sussex) b July 18, 1881, d Jan. 10, 1945
Leadbeater, B. (Yorks) b Aug. 14, 1943
*Leadbeater, E. (Yorks & Warwicks) b Aug. 15, 1927
Leary, S. E. (Kent) b April 30, 1933, d Aug. 21, 1988
Lee, C. (Yorks & Derbys) b March 17, 1924, d Sept. 3, 1999
Lee, F. S. (Middx & Som; Test umpire) b July 24, 1905, d March 30, 1982
Lee, G. M. (Notts & Derbys) b June 7, 1887, d Feb. 29, 1976
*Lee, H. W. (Middx) b Oct. 26, 1890, d April 21, 1981
Lee, J. W. (Middx & Som) b Feb. 1, 1904, d June 20, 1944
Lee, P. G. (Northants & Lancs; *CY 1976*) b Aug. 27, 1945
*Lee, P. K. (S. Aust.) b Sept. 15, 1904, d Aug 9, 1980
*Lees, W. K. MBE (Otago) b March 19, 1952
*Lees, W. S. (Surrey; *CY 1906*) b Dec. 25, 1875, d Sept. 10, 1924
Lefebvre, R. P. (Holland, Som, Cant. & Glam) b Feb. 7, 1963
*Legall, R. (B'dos & T/T) b Dec. 1, 1925
*Leggat, I. B. (C. Dist.) b June 7, 1930
*Leggat, J. G. (Cant.) b May 27, 1926, d March 9, 1973
*Legge, G. B. (OU & Kent) b Jan. 26, 1903, d Nov. 21, 1940
Lenham, L. J. (Sussex) b May 24, 1936
Lenham, N. J. (Sussex) b Dec. 17, 1965
*le Roux, F. L. (Tvl & E. Prov.) b Feb. 5, 1882, d Sept. 22, 1963
le Roux, G. S. (W. Prov. & Sussex) b Sept. 4, 1955

Lynch, M. A. (Surrey, Glos & Guyana) b May 21, 1958

Lyon, B. H. (OU & Glos; *CY 1931*) b Jan. 19, 1902, d June 22, 1970

Lyon, M. D. (CU & Som) b April 22, 1898, d Feb. 17, 1964

*Lyons, J. J. (S. Aust.) b May 21, 1863, d July 21, 1927

*Lyttelton, Hon. Alfred (CU & Middx; Pres. MCC 1898) b Feb. 7, 1857, d July 5, 1913

Lyttelton, Rev. Hon. C. F. (CU & Worcs) b Jan. 26, 1887, d Oct. 3, 1931

Lyttelton, Hon. C. G. (CU) b Oct. 27, 1842, d June 9, 1922

Lyttelton, Hon. C. J. (*see* 10th Visct Cobham)

*McAlister, P. A. (Vic.) b July 11, 1869, d May 10, 1938

*Macartney, C. G. (NSW & Otago; *CY 1922*) b June 27, 1886, d Sept. 9, 1958

*Macaulay, G. G. (Yorks; *CY 1924*) b Dec. 7, 1897, d Dec. 13, 1940

*Macaulay, M. J. (Tvl, W. Prov., OFS, NE Tvl & E. Prov.) b April 1939

*MacBryan, J. C. W. (CU & Som; *CY 1925*) b July 22, 1892, d July 14, 1983

*McCabe, S. J. (NSW; *CY 1935*) b July 16, 1910, d Aug. 25, 1968

*McCarthy, C. N. (Natal & CU) b March 24, 1929, d Aug. 14, 2000

*McConnon, J. E. (Glam) b June 21, 1922

*McCool, C. L. (NSW, Qld & Som) b Dec. 9, 1916, d April 5, 1986

McCorkell, N. (Hants) b March 23, 1912

*McCormick, E. L. (Vic.) b May 16, 1906, d June 28, 1991

*McCosker, R. B. (NSW; *CY 1976*) b Dec. 11, 1946

McCurdy, R. J. (Vic., Derbys, S. Aust., E. Prov. & Natal) b Dec. 30, 1959

*McDermott, C. J. (Qld; *CY 1986*) b April 14, 1965

*McDonald, C. C. (Vic.) b Nov. 17, 1928

*McDonald, E. A. (Tas., Vic. & Lancs; *CY 1922*) b Jan. 6, 1891, d July 22, 1937

*McDonnell, P. S. (Vic., NSW & Qld) b Nov. 13, 1858, d Sept. 24, 1896

McEwan, K. S. (E. Prov., W. Prov., Essex & W. Aust.; *CY 1978*) b July 16, 1952

*McEwan, P. E. (Cant.) b Dec. 19, 1953

*McGahey, C. P. (Essex; *CY 1902*) b Feb. 12, 1871, d Jan. 10, 1935

*MacGibbon, A. R. (Cant.) b Aug. 28, 1924

McGilvray, A. D. (NSW; broadcaster) b Dec. 6, 1909, d July 16, 1996

*McGirr, H. M. (Wgtn) b Nov. 5, 1891, d April 14, 1964

*McGlew, D. J. (Natal; *CY 1956*) b March 11, 1929, d June 9, 1998

*MacGregor, G. (CU & Middx; *CY 1891*) b Aug. 31, 1869, d Aug. 20, 1919

*McGregor, S. N. (Otago) b Dec. 18, 1931

*McIlwraith, J. (Vic.) b Sept. 7, 1857, d July 5, 1938

*McIntyre, A. J. (Surrey; *CY 1958*) b May 14, 1918

*Mackay, K. D. MBE (Qld) b Oct. 24, 1925, d June 13, 1982

McKechnie, B. J. (Otago) b Nov. 6, 1953

*McKenzie, G. D. (W. Aust. & Leics; *CY 1965*) b June 24, 1941

*McKibbin, T. R. (NSW) b Dec. 10, 1870, d Dec. 15, 1939

*McKinnon, A. H. (E. Prov. & Tvl) b Aug. 20, 1932, d Dec. 1, 1983

*MacKinnon, F. A. (CU & Kent; *believed to be longest-lived Test cricketer*) b April 9, 1848, d Feb. 27, 1947

*MacLaren, A. C. (Lancs; *CY 1895*) b Dec. 1, 1871, d Nov. 17, 1944

*McLaren, J. W. (Qld) b Dec. 24, 1887, d Nov. 17, 1921

MacLaurin of Knebworth, Lord (Chairman ECB 1997-) b March 30, 1937

*Maclean, J. A. (Qld) b April 27, 1946

*McLean, R. A. (Natal; *CY 1961*) b July 9, 1930

MacLeay, K. H. (W. Aust. & Som) b April 2, 1959

*McLeod, C. E. (Vic.) b Oct. 24, 1869, d Nov. 26, 1918

*McLeod, E. G. (Auck. & Wgtn) b Oct. 14, 1900, d Sept. 14, 1989

*McLeod, R. W. (Vic.) b Jan. 19, 1868, d June 14, 1907

McMahon, J. W. (Surrey & Som) b Dec. 28, 1919

*McMahon, T. G. (Wgtn) b Nov. 8, 1929

*McMaster, J. E. P. (Eng.) b March 16, 1861, d June 7, 1929

*McMillan, Q. (Tvl) b June 23, 1904, d July 3, 1948

*McMorris, E. D. A. (Jam.) b April 4, 1935

*McRae, D. A. N. (Cant.) b Dec. 25, 1912, d Aug. 10, 1986

McShane, P. G. (Vic.) b 1857, d Dec. 11, 1903

McSweeney, E. B. (C. Dist & Wgtn) b March 8, 1957

McVicker, N. M. (Warwicks & Leics) b Nov. 4, 1940

*McWatt, C. A. (BG) b Feb. 1, 1922, d July 12, 1997

*Madan Lal (Punjab & Delhi) b March 20, 1951

*Maddocks, L. V. (Vic. & Tas.) b May 24, 1926

*Madray, I. S. (BG) b July 2, 1934

*Madugalle, R. S. (NCC; ICC referee) b April 22, 1959

Mafizur Rehman (Bangladesh) b Nov. 10, 1978

*Maguire, J. N. (Qld, E. Prov. & Leics) b Sept. 15, 1956

*Mahanama, R. S. (CCC & Bloom.) b May 31, 1966

Maher, B. J. M. (Derbys) b Feb. 11, 1958

Mahmood Hamid (UBL, PNSC, Kar. & PIA) b Jan. 19, 1969

*Mahmood Hussain (Pak. Us, Punjab, Kar., E. Pak. & NTB) b April 2, 1932, d Dec. 25, 1991

*Mailey, A. A. (NSW; writer) b Jan. 3, 1886, d Dec. 31, 1967

*Majid Khan (Lahore, Pak. Us, CU, Glam, PIA, Qld, Punjab; *CY 1970*) b Sept. 28, 1946

*Maka, E. S. (Bombay) b March 5, 1922, dead

*Makepeace, H. (Lancs) b Aug. 22, 1881, d Dec. 19, 1952

Malhotra, A. (Haryana, Bengal & Delhi) b Jan. 26, 1957

*Mallender, N. A. (Northants, Otago & Som) b Aug. 13, 1961

*Mallett, A. A. (S. Aust.) b July 13, 1945

*Malone, M. F. (W. Aust. & Lancs) b Oct. 9, 1950

*Maninder Singh (Delhi) b June 13, 1965

*Manjrekar, V. L. (Bombay, Bengal, Andhra, U. Pradesh, Raja. & M'tra) b Sept. 26, 1931, d Oct. 18, 1983

*Manjrekar, S. V. (†Mumbai) b July 12, 1965

*Mankad, A. V. (Bombay) b Oct. 12, 1946

*Mankad, V. (M. H.) (W. Ind., Naw., M'tra, Guj., Bengal, Bombay & Raja.; *CY 1947*) b April 12, 1917, d Aug. 21, 1978

*Mann, A. L. (W. Aust.) b Nov. 8, 1945

*Mann, F. G. CBE (CU & Middx; Chairman TCCB 1978-83; Pres. MCC 1984-85) b Sept. 6, 1917

*Mann, F. T. (CU & Middx) b March 3, 1888, d Oct. 6, 1964

*Mann, N. B. F. (Natal & E. Prov.) b Dec. 28, 1920, d July 31, 1952

Manning, J. S. (S. Aust. & Northants) b June 11, 1924, d May 5, 1988

Manning, T. E. (Northants) b Sept. 2, 1884, d Nov. 22, 1975

*Mansell, P. N. F. MBE (Rhod.) b March 16, 1920, d May 9, 1995

*Mansoor Akhtar (Kar., UBL & Sind) b Dec. 25, 1957

Mansur Ali Khan (*see* Pataudi, Mansur Ali, Nawab of)

*Mantri, M. K. (Bombay & M'tra) b Sept. 1, 1921

Manuel, P. (Test umpire) b Nov. 18, 1950

*Maqsood Ahmed (S. Punjab, R'pindi, B'pur & Kar.) b March 26, 1925, d Jan. 4, 1999

Maqsood Rana (Lahore, R'pindi & NBP) b Aug. 1, 1972

*Marais, G. G. ("G. Gladstone") (Jam.) b Jan. 14, 1901, d May 19, 1978

Marchant, H. (Kent & CU) b May 22, 1864, d April 13, 1946

*Markham, L. A. (Natal) b Sept. 12, 1924, d Aug. 5, 2000

*Marks, V. J. (OU, Som & W. Aust.; writer) b June 25, 1955

Marlar, R. G. (CU & Sussex; writer) b Jan. 2, 1931

Marlow, F. W. (Sussex) b Oct. 8, 1867, d Aug. 7, 1952

Marner, P. T. (Lancs & Leics) b March 31, 1936

*Marr, A. P. (NSW) b March 28, 1862, d March 15, 1940

*Marriott, C. S. (CU, Lancs & Kent) b Sept. 14, 1895, d Oct. 13, 1966

Marsden, Tom (Eng.) b 1805, d Feb. 27, 1843

*Marsh, G. R. (W. Aust.) b Dec. 31, 1958

*Marsh, R. W. MBE (W. Aust.; *CY 1982*) b Nov. 4, 1947

Marsh, S. A. (Kent) b Jan. 27, 1961

Marshal, Alan (Qld & Surrey; *CY 1909*) b June 12, 1883, d July 23, 1915

*Marshall, M. D. (B'dos, Hants & Natal; *CY 1983*) b April 18, 1958, d Nov. 4, 1999

*Marshall, N. E. (B'dos & T/T) b Feb. 27, 1924

*Marshall, R. E. (B'dos & Hants; *CY 1959*) b April 25, 1930, d Oct. 27, 1992

Marsham, C. H. B. (OU & Kent) b Feb. 10, 1879, d July 19, 1928

Martin, E. J. (Notts) b Aug. 17, 1925

*Martin, F. (Kent; *CY 1892*) b Oct. 12, 1861, d Dec. 13, 1921

*Martin, F. R. (Jam.) b Oct. 12, 1893, d Nov. 23, 1967

Martin, G. C. (Mash.) b May 30, 1966

*Martin, J. W. (NSW & S. Aust.) b July 28, 1931, d July 16, 1992

*Martin, J. W. (Kent) b Feb. 16, 1917, d Jan. 4, 1987

Martin, S. H. (Worcs, Natal & Rhod.) b Jan. 11, 1909, d Feb. 17, 1988

*Martindale, E. A. (B'dos) b Nov. 25, 1909, d March 17, 1972

Martin-Jenkins, Christopher (Writer & broadcaster) b Jan. 20, 1945

Maru, R. J. (Middx & Hants) b Oct. 28, 1962

*Marx, W. F. E. (Tvl) b July 4, 1895, d June 2, 1974

*Mason, J. R. (Kent; *CY 1898*) b March 26, 1874, d Oct. 15, 1958

*Masood Anwar (UBL, Multan, F'bad & Lahore) b Dec. 12, 1967

Masood Iqbal (Lahore, Punjab U., Pak. Us & HBL) b April 17, 1952

*Massie, H. H. (NSW) b April 11, 1854, d Oct. 12, 1938

*Massie, R. A. L. (W. Aust.; *CY 1973*) b April 14, 1947

*Matheson, A. M. (Auck.) b Feb. 27, 1906, d Dec. 31, 1985

*Mathias, Wallis (Sind, Kar. & NBP) b Feb. 4, 1935, d Sept. 1, 1994

*Matthews, A. D. G. (Northants & Glam) b May 3, 1904, d July 29, 1977

*Matthews, C. D. (W. Aust. & Lancs) b Sept. 22, 1962

*Matthews, G. R. J. (NSW) b Dec. 15, 1959

*Matthews, T. J. (Vic.) b April 3, 1884, d Oct. 14, 1943

*Mattis, E. H. (Jam.) b April 11, 1957

*May, P. B. H. CBE (CU & Surrey; *CY 1952*; Pres. MCC 1980-81) b Dec. 31, 1929, d Dec. 27, 1994

*May, T. B. A. (S. Aust.) b Jan. 26, 1962

Mayer, J. H. (Warwicks) b March 2, 1902, d Sept. 6, 1981

Maynard, C. (Warwicks & Lancs) b April 8, 1958

*Mayne, E. R. (S. Aust. & Vict.) b July 2, 1882, d Oct. 26, 1961

*Mayne, L. C. (W. Aust.) b Jan. 23, 1942

*Mead, C. P. (Hants; *CY 1912*) b March 9, 1887, d March 26, 1958

*Mead, W. (Essex; *CY 1904*) b March 25, 1868, d March 18, 1954

Meads, E. A. (Notts) b Aug. 17, 1916

*Meale, T. (Wgtn) b Nov. 11, 1928

*Meckiff, I. (Vic.) b Jan. 6, 1935

Medlycott, K. T. (Surrey & N. Tvl) b May 12, 1965

*Meherhomji, K. R. (W. Ind. & Bombay) b Aug. 9, 1911, d Feb. 10, 1982

*Mehra, V. L. (E. Punjab, Ind. Rlwys & Delhi) b March 12, 1938

*Meintjes, D. J. (Tvl) b June 9, 1890, d July 17, 1979

*Melle, M. G. (Tvl & W. Prov.) b June 3, 1930

*Melville, A. (OU, Sussex, Natal & Tvl; *CY 1948*) b May 19, 1910, d April 18, 1983

Meman, M. A. (Zimb.) b June 26, 1952

Mendis, G. D. (Sussex & Lancs) b April 20, 1955

*Mendis, L. R. D. (SSC) b Aug. 25, 1952

Mendis, M. C. (Colts) b Dec. 28, 1968

*Mendonca, I. L. (BG) b July 13, 1934

Mercer, J. (Sussex, Glam & Northants; *CY 1927*) b April 22, 1893, d Aug. 31, 1987

*Merchant, V. M. (Bombay; *CY 1937*) b Oct. 12, 1911, d Oct. 27, 1987

*Merritt, W. E. (Cant. & Northants) b Aug. 18, 1908, d June 9, 1977

*Merry, C. A. (T/T) b Jan. 20, 1911, d April 19, 1964

Metcalfe, A. A. (Yorks & Notts) b Dec. 25, 1963

Metson, C. P. (Middx & Glam) b July 2, 1963

*Meuleman, K. D. (Vic. & W. Aust.) b Sept. 5, 1923

*Meuli, E. M. (C. Dist.) b Feb. 20, 1926

Meyer, B. J. (Glos; Test umpire) b Aug. 21, 1932

Meyer, R. J. O. OBE (CU, Som & W. Ind.) b March 15, 1905, d March 9, 1991

Mian Mohammad Aslam (Test umpire) b April 1, 1949

Mian Mohammed Saeed (N. India, Patiala & S. Punjab) b Aug. 31, 1910, d Aug. 23, 1979

*Middleton, J. (W. Prov.) b Sept. 30, 1865, d Dec. 23, 1913

Middleton, T. C. (Hants) b Feb. 1, 1964

**Midwinter, W. E. (Vic. & Glos) b June 19, 1851, d Dec. 3, 1890

*Milburn, B. D. (Otago) b Nov. 24, 1943

*Milburn, C. (Northants & W. Aust.; *CY 1967*) b Oct. 23, 1941, d Feb. 28, 1990

*Milkha Singh, A. G. (Madras) b Dec. 31, 1941

*Miller, A. M. (Eng.) b Oct. 19, 1869, d June 26, 1959

Miller, F. P. (Surrey) b July 29, 1828, d Nov. 22, 1875

*Miller, G. (Derbys, Natal & Essex) b Sept. 8, 1952

*Miller, K. R. MBE (Vic., NSW & Notts; *CY 1954*) b Nov. 28, 1919

*Miller, L. S. M. (C. Dist. & Wgtn) b March 31, 1923, d Dec. 17, 1996

Miller, R. (Warwicks) b Jan. 6, 1941, d May 7, 1996

*Miller, R. C. (Jam.) b Dec. 24, 1924

*Milligan, F. W. (Yorks) b March 19, 1870, d March 31, 1900

*Millman, G. (Notts) b Oct. 2, 1934

Millmow, J. P. (Wgtn) b Sept. 22, 1967

*Mills, C. H. (Surrey, Kimberley & W. Prov.) b Nov. 26, 1867, d July 26, 1948

*Mills, J. E. (Auck.) b Sept. 3, 1905, d Dec. 11, 1972

Mills, P. T. (Glos) b May 7, 1879, d Dec. 8, 1950

*Milton, C. A. (Glos; *CY 1959*) b March 10, 1928

*Milton, Sir William H. (W. Prov.) b Dec. 3, 1854, d March 6, 1930

*Minnett, R. B. (NSW) b June 13, 1888, d Oct. 21, 1955

Minshull, John (scorer of first recorded century) b *circa* 1741, d Oct. 1793

*Miran Bux (Pak. Serv., Punjab & R'pindi) b April 20, 1907, d Feb. 8, 1991

*Misson, F. M. (NSW) b Nov. 19, 1938

*Mitchell, A. (Yorks) b Sept. 13, 1902, d Dec. 25, 1976

*Mitchell, B. (Tvl; *CY 1936*) b Jan. 8, 1909, d July 2, 1995

**Mitchell, F. (CU, Yorks & Tvl; *CY 1902*) b Aug. 13, 1872, d Oct. 11, 1935

*Mitchell, T. B. (Derbys) b Sept. 4, 1902, d Jan. 27, 1996

*Mitchell-Innes, N. S. (OU & Som) b Sept. 7, 1914

Mitchley, C. J. (Tvl; Test umpire) b July 4, 1938

*Modi, R. S. (Bombay) b Nov. 11, 1924, d May 17, 1996

*Mohammad Aslam (N. Ind. & Pak. Rlwys) b Jan. 5, 1920

*Mohammad Farooq (Kar.) b April 8, 1938
*Mohammad Ilyas (Lahore & PIA) b March 19, 1946
*Mohammad Munaf (Sind, E. Pak., Kar. & PIA) b Nov. 2, 1935
*Mohammad Nazir (Pak. Rlwys) b March 8, 1946
*Mohammad Zahid (PIA) b Aug. 2, 1976
*Mohsin Kamal (Lahore, Allied Bank & PNSC) b June 16, 1963
*Mohsin Khan (Pak. Rlwys, Kar., Sind, Pak. Us & HBL) b March 15, 1955
*Moir, A. M. (Otago) b July 17, 1919, d June 17, 2000
*Mold, A. (Lancs; *CY 1892*) b May 27, 1863, d April 29, 1921
Moles, A. J. (Warwicks & Griq. W.) b Feb. 12, 1961
*Moloney, D. A. R. (Wgtn, Otago & Cant.) b Aug. 11, 1910, d July 15, 1942
*Moodie, G. H. (Jam.) b Nov. 25, 1915
*Moon, L. J. (CU & Middx) b Feb. 9, 1878, d Nov. 23, 1916
*Mooney, F. L. H. (Wgtn) b May 26, 1921
Moore, H. I. (Notts) b Feb. 28, 1941
Moore, R. H. (Hants) b Nov. 14, 1913
Moores (Worcs & Sussex) b Dec. 18, 1962
Moorhouse, R. (Yorks) b Sept. 7, 1866, d Jan. 7, 1921
*More, K. S. (Baroda) b Sept. 4, 1962
Morgan, D. C. (Derbys) b Feb. 26, 1929
*Morgan, R. W. (Auck.) b Feb. 12, 1941
*Morkel, D. P. B. (W. Prov.) b Jan. 25, 1906, d Oct. 6, 1980
*Morley, F. (Notts) b Dec. 16, 1850, d Sept. 28, 1884
*Moroney, J. (NSW) b July 24, 1917, d July 1, 1999
*Morris, A. R. MBE (NSW; *CY 1949*) b Jan. 19, 1922
*Morris, H. (Glam) b Oct. 5, 1963
Morris, H. M. (Essex & CU) b April 16, 1898, d Nov. 18, 1984
*Morris, S. (Vic.) b June 22, 1855, d Sept. 20, 1931
*Morrison, B. D. (Wgtn) b Dec. 17, 1933
*Morrison, D. K. (Auck. & Lancs) b Feb. 3, 1966
*Morrison, J. F. M. (C. Dist. & Wgtn) b Aug. 27, 1947
Morshed Ali Khan (Bangladesh) b May 14, 1972
Mortensen, O. H. (Denmark & Derbys) b Jan. 29, 1958
*Mortimore, J. B. (Glos) b May 14, 1933
Mortlock, W. (Surrey & Utd Eng. XI) b July 18, 1832, d Jan. 23, 1884
Morton, A., jun. (Derbys) b May 7, 1883, d Dec. 19, 1935
*Moseley, E. A. (B'dos, Glam, E. Prov. & N. Tvl) b Jan. 5, 1958

Moseley, H. R. (B'dos & Som) b May 28, 1948
*Moses, H. (NSW) b Feb. 13, 1858, d Dec. 7, 1938
*Moss, A. E. (Middx) b Nov. 14, 1930
*Moss, J. K. (Vic.) b June 29, 1947
*Motz, R. C. (Cant.; *CY 1966*) b Jan. 12, 1940
*Moule, W. H. (Vic.) b Jan. 31, 1858, d Aug. 24, 1939
*Moxon, M. D. (Yorks & Griq. W.; *CY 1993*) b May 4, 1960
*Mudassar Nazar (Lahore, Punjab, Pak. Us, HBL, PIA & UBL) b April 6, 1956
*Muddiah, V. M. (Mysore & Ind. Servs) b June 8, 1929
*Mufasir-ul-Haq (Kar., Dacca, PWD, E. Pak. & NBP) b Aug. 16, 1944, d July 27, 1983
Mukherjee, S. P. (Bengal) b Oct. 5, 1964
Munasinghe, A. M. N. (SSC) b Dec. 10, 1971
Muncer, B. L. (Glam & Middx) b Oct. 23, 1913, d Jan. 18, 1982
Munden, V. S. (Leics) b Jan. 2, 1928
*Munir Malik (Punjab, R'pindi, Pak. Serv. & Kar.) b July 10, 1934
**Murdoch, W. L. (NSW & Sussex) b Oct. 18, 1854, d Feb. 18, 1911
*Murray, A. R. A. (E. Prov.) b April 30, 1922, d April 17, 1995
*Murray, B. A. G. (Wgtn) b Sept. 18, 1940
*Murray, D. A. (B'dos) b Sept. 29, 1950
*Murray, D. J. (Cant.) b Sept. 4, 1967
*Murray, D. L. (T/T, CU, Notts & Warwicks) b May 20, 1943
*Murray, J. T. MBE (Middx; *CY 1967*) b April 1, 1935
Murray-Wood, W. (OU & Kent) b June 30, 1917, d Dec. 21, 1968
Murrell, H. R. (Kent & Middx) b Nov. 19, 1879, d Aug. 15, 1952
*Musgrove, H. (Vic.) b Nov. 27, 1860, d Nov. 2, 1931
*Mushtaq Ali, S. (C. Ind., Guj., †M. Pradesh & U. Pradesh) b Dec. 17, 1914
*Mushtaq Mohammad (Kar., Northants & PIA; *CY 1963*) b Nov. 22, 1943
Mynn, Alfred (Kent & All-Eng.) b Jan. 19, 1807, d Nov. 1, 1861

*Nadeem Ghauri (Lahore, Pak. Rlwys & HBL) b Oct. 12, 1962
*Nadkarni, R. G. (M'tra & Bombay) b April 4, 1932
Naeem Ahmed (Kar., Pak Us, NBP, UBL & PIA) b Sept. 20, 1952
*Nagel, L. E. (Vic.) b March 6, 1905, d Nov. 23, 1971
*Naik, S. S. (Bombay) b Feb. 21, 1945
*Nanan, R. (T/T) b May 29, 1953
*Naoomal Jeoomal, M. (N. Ind. & Sind) b April 17, 1904, d July 18, 1980
*Narasimha Rao, M. V. (H'bad) b Aug. 11, 1954

Naseer Malik (Khairpair & NBP) b Feb. 1, 1950, d Aug. 1, 1999

*Nash, L. J. (Tas. & Vic.) b May 2, 1910, d July 24, 1986

Nash, M. A. (Glam) b May 9, 1945

*Nasim-ul-Ghani (Kar., Pak. Us, Dacca, E. Pak., PWD & NBP) b May 14, 1941

*Naushad Ali (Kar., E. Pak., R'pindi, Peshawar, NWFP, Punjab & Pak. Serv.; ICC referee) b Oct. 1, 1943

*Naved Anjum (Railways, Lahore, UBL & HBL) b July 27, 1963

*Navle, J. G. (Rajputana, C. Ind., Holkar & Gwalior) b Dec. 7, 1902, d Sept. 7, 1979

*Nayak, S. V. (Bombay) b Oct. 20, 1954

*Nayudu, Col. C. K. (C. Ind., Andhra, U. Pradesh & Holkar; *CY 1933*) b Oct. 31, 1895, d Nov. 14, 1967

*Nayudu, C. S. (C. Ind., Holkar, Baroda, Bengal, Andhra & U. Pradesh) b April 18, 1914

*Nazar Mohammad (N. Ind. & Punjab) b March 5, 1921, d July 12, 1996

*Nazir Ali, S. (S. Punjab & Sussex) b June 8, 1906, d Feb. 18, 1975

Neale, P. A. (Worcs; *CY 1989*) b June 5, 1954

Neale, W. L. (Glos) b March 3, 1904, d Oct. 26, 1955

*Neblett, J. M. (B'dos & BG) b Nov. 13, 1901, d March 28, 1959

Needham, A. (Surrey & Middx) b March 23, 1957

*Nel, J. D. (W. Prov.) b July 10, 1928

Nelson, R. P. (Middx, CU & Northants) b Aug. 7, 1912, d Oct. 29, 1940

*Newberry, C. (Tvl) b 1889, d Aug. 1, 1916

Newell, M. (Notts) b Feb. 25, 1965

*Newham, W. (Sussex) b Dec. 12, 1860, d June 26, 1944

Newland, Richard (Sussex) b *circa* 1718, d May 29, 1791

*Newman, Sir Jack (Wgtn & Cant.) b July 3, 1902, d Sept. 23, 1996

Newman, J. A. (Hants & Cant.) b Nov. 12, 1884, d Dec. 21, 1973

Newman, P. G. (Derbys) b Jan. 10, 1959

*Newport, P. J. (Worcs. Boland & N. Tvl) b Oct. 11, 1962

*Newson, E. S. OBE (Tvl & Rhod.) b Dec. 2, 1910, d April 24, 1988

Newstead, J. T. (Yorks; *CY 1909*) b Sept. 8, 1877, d March 25, 1952

Newton, A. E. (OU & Som) b Sept. 12, 1862, d Sept. 15, 1952

*Niaz Ahmed (Dacca, E. Pak., PWD & Pak. Rlwys) b Nov. 11, 1945

Nicholas, M. C. J. (Hants) b Sept. 29, 1957

Nicholls, D. (Kent) b Dec. 8, 1943

Nicholls, E. A. (Test umpire) b Dec. 10, 1947

Nicholls, R. B. (Glos) b Dec. 4, 1933, d July 21, 1994

*Nichols, M. S. (Essex; *CY 1934*) b Oct. 6, 1900, d Jan. 26, 1961

Nicholson, A. G. (Yorks) b June 25, 1938, d Nov. 4, 1985

*Nicholson, F. (Griq. W.) b Sept. 17, 1909, d July 30, 1982

*Nicolson, J. F. W. (Natal & OU) b July 19, 1899, d Dec. 13, 1935

*Nissar, Mahomed (Patiala, S. Punjab & U. Pradesh) b Aug. 1, 1910, d March 11, 1963

*Nitschke, H. C. (S. Aust.) b April 14, 1905, d Sept. 29, 1982

*Noble, M. A. (NSW; *CY 1900*) b Jan. 28, 1873, d June 22, 1940

*Noblet, G. (S. Aust.) b Sept. 14, 1916

*Noreiga, J. M. (T/T) b April 15, 1936

Norman, M. E. J. C. (Northants & Leics) b Jan. 19, 1933

*Norton, N. O. (W. Prov. & Border) b May 11, 1881, d June 27, 1968

*Nothling, O. E. (NSW & Qld) b Aug. 1, 1900, d Sept. 26, 1965

*Nourse, A. D. ("Dudley") (Natal; *CY 1948*) b Nov. 12, 1910, d Aug. 14, 1981

*Nourse, A. W. ("Dave") (Natal, Tvl & W. Prov.) b Jan. 26, 1878, d July 8, 1948

*Nunes, R. K. (Jam.) b June 7, 1894, d July 22, 1958

*Nupen, E. P. (Tvl) b Jan. 1, 1902, d Jan. 29, 1977

*Nurse, S. M. (B'dos; *CY 1967*) b Nov. 10, 1933

Nutter, A. E. (Lancs & Northants) b June 28, 1913, d June 3, 1996

*Nyalchand, S. (W. Ind., Kathiawar, Guj., & S'tra) b Sept. 14, 1919, d Jan. 3, 1997

Nyren, John (Hants) b Dec. 15, 1764, d June 28, 1837

Nyren, Richard (Hants & Sussex; Proprietor Bat & Ball Inn, Broadhalfpenny Down) b 1734, d April 25, 1797

Oakes, C. (Sussex) b Aug. 10, 1912

Oakes, J. (Sussex) b March 3, 1916, d July 4, 1997

*Oakman, A. S. M. (Sussex) b April 20, 1930

Oates, T. W. (Notts) b Aug. 9, 1875, d June 18, 1949

Oates, W. F. (Yorks & Derbys) b June 11, 1929

*O'Brien, L. P. J. (Vic.) b July 2, 1907, d March 13, 1997

*O'Brien, Sir Timothy C. (OU & Middx) b Nov. 5, 1861, d Dec. 9, 1948

*Ochse, A. E. (Tvl) b March 11, 1870, d April 11, 1918

*Ochse, A. L. (E. Prov.) b Oct. 11, 1899, d May 5, 1949

*O'Connor, J. (Essex) b Nov. 6, 1897, d Feb. 22, 1977

*O'Connor, J. D. A. (NSW & S. Aust.) b Sept. 9, 1875, d Aug. 23, 1941

*O'Donnell, S. P. (Vic.) b Jan. 26, 1963

*Ogilvie, A. D. (Qld) b June 3, 1951

O'Gorman, T. J. G. (Derbys) b May 15, 1967

*O'Keeffe, K. J. (NSW & Som) b Nov. 25, 1949

*Old, C. M. (Yorks, Warwicks & N. Tvl; *CY 1979*) b Dec. 22, 1948

*Oldfield, N. (Lancs & Northants; Test umpire) b May 5, 1911, d April 19, 1996

Oldfield, W. A. MBE (NSW; *CY 1927*) b Sept. 9, 1894, d Aug. 10, 1976

Oldham, S. (Yorks & Derbys) b July 26, 1948

Oldroyd, E. (Yorks) b Oct. 1, 1888, d Dec. 27, 1964

*O'Linn, S. (Kent, W. Prov. & Tvl) b May 5, 1927

Oliver, L. (Derbys) b Oct. 18, 1886, d Jan. 22, 1948

*O'Neill, N. C. (NSW; *CY 1962*) b Feb. 19, 1937

Ontong, R. C. (Border, Tvl, N. Tvl & Glam) b Sept. 9, 1955

Onyango, L. (Kenya) b Sept. 22, 1973

Opatha, A. R. M. (SL) b Aug. 5, 1947

Orchard, D. L. (Natal; Test umpire) b June 24, 1948

Ord, J. S. (Warwicks) b July 12, 1912, d Jan. 14, 2001

*O'Reilly, W. J. OBE (NSW; *CY 1935*) b Dec. 20, 1905, d Oct. 6, 1992

Ormrod, J. A. (Worcs & Lancs) b Dec. 22, 1942

Oscroft, W. (Notts) b Dec. 16, 1843, d Oct. 10, 1905

O'Shaughnessy, S. J. (Lancs & Worcs) b Sept. 9, 1961

Oslear, D. O. (Test umpire) b March 3, 1929

*O'Sullivan, D. R. (C. Dist. & Hants) b Nov. 16, 1944

Outschoorn, L. (Worcs) b Sept. 26, 1918, d Jan. 9, 1994

*Overton, G. W. F. (Otago) b June 8, 1919, d Sept. 7, 1993

Owen, H. G. P. (CU & Essex) b May 19, 1859, d Oct. 20, 1912

*Owens, M. B. (Cant.) b Nov. 11, 1969

Owen-Smith, H. G. (W. Prov., OU & Middx; *CY 1930*) b Feb. 18, 1909, d Feb. 28, 1990

Owen-Thomas, D. R. (CU & Surrey) b Sept. 20, 1948

*Oxenham, R. K. (Qld) b July 28, 1891, d Aug. 16, 1939

*Padgett, D. E. V. (Yorks) b July 20, 1934

*Padmore, A. L. (B'dos) b Dec. 17, 1946

Page, J. C. T. (Kent) b May 20, 1930, d Dec. 14, 1990

Page, M. H. (Derbys) b June 17, 1941

*Page, M. L. (Cant.) b May 8, 1902, d Feb. 13, 1987

*Pai, A. M. (Bombay) b April 28, 1945

*Paine, G. A. E. (Middx & Warwicks; *CY 1935*) b June 11, 1908, d March 30, 1978

*Pairaudeau, B. H. (BG & N. Dist.) b April 14, 1931

*Palairet, L. C. H. (OU & Som; *CY 1893*) b May 27, 1870, d March 27, 1933

Palairet, R. C. N. (OU & Som) b June 25, 1871, d Feb. 11, 1955

*Palia, P. E. (Parsis, Madras, U. Prov., Bombay, Mysore & Bengal) b Sept. 5, 1910, d Sept. 9, 1981

*Palm, A. W. (W. Prov.) b June 8, 1901, d Aug. 17, 1966

*Palmer, C. H. CBE (Worcs & Leics; Pres. MCC 1978-79; Chairman TCCB 1983-85) b May 15, 1919

*Palmer, G. E. (Vic. & Tas.) b Feb. 22, 1859, d Aug. 22, 1910

*Palmer, K. E. (Som; Test umpire) b April 22, 1937

Palmer, R. (Som; Test umpire) b July 12, 1942

*Pandit, C. S. (Bombay, M. Pradesh & Assam) b Sept. 30, 1961

Paranjpe, J. V. (†Mumbai) b April 17, 1972

Pardon, Charles F. (Editor of *Wisden* 1887-90) b March 28, 1850, d April 18, 1890

Pardon, Sydney H. (Editor of *Wisden* 1891-1925) b Sept. 23, 1855, d Nov. 20, 1925

*Parfitt, P. H. (Middx; *CY 1963*) b Dec. 8, 1936

Paris, C. G. A. (Hants; Chairman TCCB 1968-75; Pres. MCC 1975-76) b Aug. 20, 1911, d April 4, 1998

Parish, R. J. (Aust. Administrator) b May 7, 1916

*Park, Dr R. L. (Vic.) b July 30, 1892, d Jan. 23, 1947

*Parkar, G. A. (Bombay) b Oct. 24, 1955

*Parkar, R. D. (Bombay) b Oct. 31, 1946, d Aug. 11, 1999

Parkar, Z. (Bombay) b Nov. 22, 1957

*Parker, C. W. L. (Glos; *CY 1923*) b Oct. 14, 1882, d July 11, 1959

*Parker, G. M. (SA) b May 27, 1899, d May 1, 1969

Parker, J. F. (Surrey) b April 23, 1913, d Jan. 27, 1983

*Parker, J. M. (N. Dist. & Worcs) b Feb. 21, 1951

*Parker, N. M. (Otago & Cant.) b Aug. 28, 1948

*Parker, P. W. G. (CU, Sussex, Natal & Durham) b Jan. 15, 1956

*Parkhouse, W. G. A. (Glam) b Oct. 12, 1925, d Aug. 10, 2000

*Parkin, C. H. (Yorks & Lancs; *CY 1924*) b Feb. 18, 1886, d June 15, 1943

*Parkin, D. C. (E. Prov., Tvl & Griq. W.) b Feb. 20, 1873, d March 20, 1936

Parks, H. W. (Sussex) b July 18, 1906, d May 7, 1984

*Parks, J. H. (Sussex & Cant.; *CY 1938*) b May 12, 1903, d Nov. 21, 1980

*Parks, J. M. (Sussex & Som; *CY 1968*) b Oct. 21, 1931

Parks, R. J. (Hants & Kent) b June 15, 1959

Parr, George (Notts & All-England) b May 22, 1826, d June 23, 1891

*Parry, D. R. (Comb. Is. & Leewards) b Dec. 22, 1954

*Parsana, D. D. (S'tra, Ind. Rlwys & Guj.) b Dec. 2, 1947

Parsons, A. B. D. (CU & Surrey) b Sept. 20, 1933, d Feb. 11, 1999

Parsons, G. J. (Leics, Warwicks, Boland, Griq. W. & OFS) b Oct. 17, 1959

Parsons, Canon J. H. (Warwicks) b May 30, 1890, d Feb. 2, 1981

*Partridge, J. T. (Rhod.) b Dec. 9, 1932, d June 7, 1988

Partridge, N. E. (Malvern, CU & Warwicks; *CY 1919*) b Aug. 10, 1900, d March 10, 1982

Partridge, R. J. (Northants) b Feb. 11, 1912, d Feb. 1, 1997

Parvez Mir (R'pindi, Lahore, Punjab, Pak. Us, Derbys, HBL & Glam) b Sept. 24, 1953

*Pascoe, L. S. (NSW) b Feb. 13, 1950

Pasqual, S. P. (SL) b Oct. 15, 1961

*Passailaigue, C. C. (Jam.) b Aug. 1902, d Jan. 7, 1972

Patankar, C. T. (Bombay) b Nov. 24, 1930

**Pataudi, Iftiqar Ali, Nawab of (OU, Worcs, Patiala, N. Ind. & S. Punjab; *CY 1932*) b March 16, 1910, d Jan. 5, 1952

*Pataudi, Mansur Ali, Nawab of (Sussex, OU, Delhi & H'bad; *CY 1968*) b Jan. 5, 1941

Patel, A. K. (S'tra) b March 6, 1957

*Patel, B. P. (Karn.) b Nov. 24, 1952

*Patel, D. N. (Worcs & Auck.) b Oct. 25, 1958

*Patel, J. M. (Guj.) b Nov. 26, 1924, d Dec. 12, 1992

*Patel, R. G. M. (Baroda) b June 1, 1964

Paterson, G. A. (Zimb.) b June 9, 1960

*Patiala, Maharaja of (N. Ind., Patiala & S. Punjab) b Jan. 17, 1913, d June 17, 1974

*Patil, S. M. (Bombay & M. Pradesh) b Aug. 18, 1956

*Patil, S. R. (M'tra) b Oct. 10, 1933

*Patterson, B. P. (Jam., Tas. & Lancs) b Sept. 15, 1961

Patterson, W. H. (OU & Kent) b March 11, 1859, d May 3, 1946

*Payne, T. R. O. (B'dos) b Feb. 13, 1957

*Paynter, E. (Lancs; *CY 1938*) b Nov. 5, 1901, d Feb. 5, 1979

Payton, W. R. D. (Notts) b Feb. 13, 1882, d May 2, 1943

Peach, H. A. (Surrey) b Oct. 6, 1890, d Oct. 8, 1961

*Peall, S. G. (MCD) b Sept. 2, 1969

Pearce, T. N. (Essex) b Nov. 3, 1905, d April 10, 1994

*Pearse, O. C. (Natal) b Oct. 10, 1884, d May 7, 1953

Pearson, F. (Worcs & Auck.) b Sept. 23, 1880, d Nov. 10, 1963

*Peate, E. (Yorks) b March 2, 1855, d March 11, 1900

Peckover, G. E. (Zimb.) b June 2, 1955

*Peebles, I. A. R. (OU, Middx & Scotland; writer; *CY 1931*) b Jan. 20, 1908, d Feb. 28, 1980

*Peel, R. (Yorks; *CY 1889*) b Feb. 12, 1857, d Aug. 12, 1941

*Pegler, S. J. (Tvl) b July 28, 1888, d Sept. 10, 1972

*Pellew, C. E. (S. Aust.) b Sept. 21, 1893, d May 9, 1981

Penn, C. (Kent) b June 19, 1963

*Penn, F. (Kent) b March 7, 1851, d Dec. 26, 1916

Pepper, C. G. (NSW & Aust. Serv.; umpire) b Sept. 15, 1916, d March 24, 1993

Perkins, H. (CU & Cambs; Sec. MCC 1876-97) b Dec. 10, 1832, d May 6, 1916

*Perks, R. T. D. (Worcs) b Oct. 4, 1911, d Nov. 22, 1977

Perrin, P. A. (Essex; *CY 1905*) b May 26, 1876, d Nov. 20, 1945

Perryman, S. P. (Warwicks & Worcs) b Oct. 22, 1955

*Pervez Sajjad (Lahore, PIA & Kar.) b Aug. 30, 1942

Petherick, P. J. (Otago & Wgtn) b Sept. 25, 1942

Petrie, E. C. (Auck. & N. Dist.) b May 22, 1927

Pettiford, J. (NSW & Kent) b Nov. 29, 1919, d Oct. 11, 1964

*Phadkar, D. G. (M'tra, Bombay, Bengal & Ind. Rlwys) b Dec. 10, 1925, d March 17, 1985

Phebey, A. H. (Kent) b Oct. 1, 1924, d June 28, 1998

Phelan, P. J. (Essex) b Feb. 9, 1938

*Philipson, H. (OU & Middx) b June 8, 1866, d Dec. 4, 1935

*Phillip, N. (Comb. Is., Windwards & Essex) b June 12, 1948

Phillips, H. (Sussex) b Oct. 14, 1844, d July 3, 1919

Phillips, R. B. (NSW & Qld) b May 23, 1954

*Phillips, W. B. (S. Aust.) b March 1, 1958

*Phillips, W. N. (Vic.) b Nov. 7, 1962

Phillipson, C. P. (Sussex) b Feb. 10, 1952

Phillipson, W. E. (Lancs; Test umpire) b Dec. 3, 1910, d Aug. 24, 1991

*Philpott, P. I. (NSW) b Nov. 21, 1934

Pick, R. A. (Notts & Wgtn) b Nov. 19, 1963

Pienaar, R. F. (Tvl, †Northerns, W. Prov & Kent) b July 17, 1961

Pieris, H. S. M. (SL) b Feb. 16, 1946

*Pierre, L. R. (T/T) b June 5, 1921, d April 14, 1989

*Pigott, A. C. S. (Sussex, Wgtn & Surrey) b June 4, 1958

Pilch, Fuller (Norfolk & Kent) b March 17, 1804, d May 1, 1870

Pilling, H. (Lancs) b Feb. 23, 1943

*Pilling, R. (Lancs; *CY 1891*) b July 5, 1855, d March 28, 1891

*Pithey, A. J. (Rhod. & W. Prov.) b July 17, 1933

*Pithey, D. B. (Rhod., OU, Northants, W. Prov., Natal & Tvl) b Oct. 4, 1936

*Place, W. (Lancs) b Dec. 7, 1914

Platt, R. K. (Yorks & Northants) b Dec. 21, 1932

*Playle, W. R. (Auck. & W. Aust.) b Dec. 1, 1938

Pleass, J. E. (Glam) b May 21, 1923

Plews, N. T. (Test umpire) b Sept. 5, 1934

*Plimsoll, J. B. (W. Prov. & Natal) b Oct. 27, 1917, d Nov. 11, 1999

Pocock, N. E. J. (Hants) b Dec. 15, 1951

*Pocock, P. I. (Surrey & N. Tvl) b Sept. 24, 1946

*Pollard, R. (Lancs) b June 19, 1912, d Dec. 16, 1985

*Pollard, V. (C. Dist. & Cant.) b Sept. 7, 1945

*Pollock, P. M. (E. Prov.; *CY 1966*) b June 30, 1941

*Pollock, R. G. (E. Prov. & Tvl; *CY 1966*) b Feb. 27, 1944

*Ponsford, W. H. MBE (Vic.; *CY 1935*) b Oct. 19, 1900, d April 6, 1991

Pont, K. R. (Essex) b Jan. 16, 1953

*Poole, C. J. (Notts) b March 13, 1921, d Feb. 11, 1996

Pooley, E. (Surrey & first England tour) b Feb. 13, 1842, d July 18, 1907

*Poore, M. B. (Cant.) b June 1, 1930

*Poore, Brig-Gen. R. M. (Hants & SA; *CY 1900*) b March 20, 1866, d July 14, 1938

Pope, A. V. (Derbys) b Aug. 15, 1909, d May 11, 1996

*Pope, G. H. (Derbys) b Jan. 27, 1911, d Oct. 29, 1993

*Pope, Dr R. J. (NSW) b Feb. 18, 1864, d July 27, 1952

Popplewell, N. F. M. (CU & Som) b Aug. 8, 1957

Popplewell, Hon. Sir Oliver B. (CU; Pres. MCC 1994-96) b Aug. 15, 1927

Porter, G. D. (W. Aust.) b March 18, 1955

Pothecary, A. E. (Hants) b March 1, 1906, d May 21, 1991

Pothecary, J. E. (W. Prov.) b Dec. 6, 1933

Potter, L. (Kent, Griq. W., Leics & OFS) b Nov. 7, 1962

*Pougher, A. D. (Leics) b April 19, 1865, d May 20, 1926

*Powell, A. W. (Griq. W.) b July 18, 1873, d Sept. 11, 1948

*Prabhakar, M. (Delhi & Durham) b April 15, 1963

*Prasanna, E. A. S. (†Karn.) b May 22, 1940

Prentice, F. T. (Leics) b April 22, 1912, d July 10, 1978

Pressdee, J. S. (Glam & NE Tvl) b June 19, 1933

Preston, Hubert (Editor of *Wisden* 1944-51) b Dec. 16, 1868, d Aug. 6, 1960

Preston, K. C. (Essex) b Aug. 22, 1925

Preston, Norman MBE (Editor of *Wisden* 1952-80) b March 18, 1903, d March 6, 1980

Pretlove, J. F. (CU & Kent) b Nov. 23, 1932

*Price, J. S. E. (Middx) b July 22, 1937

*Price, W. F. (Middx; Test umpire) b April 25, 1902, d Jan. 13, 1969

*Prideaux, R. M. (CU, Kent, Northants, Sussex & OFS) b July 31, 1939

Pridgeon, A. P. (Worcs) b Feb. 22, 1954

*Priest, M. W. (Cant.) b Aug. 12, 1961

*Prince, C. F. H. (W. Prov., Border & E. Prov.) b Sept. 11, 1874, d Feb. 2, 1949

*Pringle, C. (Auck.) b Jan. 26, 1968

*Pringle, D. R. (CU & Essex) b Sept. 18, 1958

Pritchard, T. L. (Wgtn, Warwicks & Kent) b March 10, 1917

*Procter, M. J. (Glos, Natal, W. Prov., Rhod. & OFS; *CY 1970*) b Sept. 15, 1946

Prodger, J. M. (Kent) b Sept. 1, 1935

*Promnitz, H. L. E. (Border, Griq. W. & OFS) b Feb. 23, 1904, d Sept. 7, 1983

*Pullar, G. (Lancs & Glos; *CY 1960*) b Aug. 1, 1935

*Puna, N. (N. Dist.) b Oct. 28, 1929, d June 7, 1996

*Punjabi, P. H. (Sind & Guj.) b Sept. 20, 1921

*Pycroft, A. J. (Zimb.) b June 6, 1956

Pydanna, M. R. (Guyana) b Jan. 27, 1950

*Qasim Omar (Kar. & MCB) b Feb. 9, 1957

Quaife, B. W. (Warwicks & Worcs) b Nov. 24, 1899, d Nov. 28, 1984

Quaife, Walter (Sussex & Warwicks) b April 1, 1864, d Jan. 18, 1943

*Quaife, William (W. G.) (Warwicks & Griq. W.; *CY 1902*) b March 17, 1872, d Oct. 13, 1951

*Quinn, N. A. (Griq. W. & Tvl) b Feb. 21, 1908, d Aug. 5, 1934

*Rabone, G. O. (Wgtn & Auck.) b Nov. 6, 1921

*Rackemann, C. G. (Qld & Surrey) b June 3, 1960

Radcliffe, Sir Everard J. Bt (Yorks) b Jan. 27, 1884, d Nov. 23, 1969

*Radford, N. V. (Lancs, Tvl & Worcs; *CY 1986*) b June 7, 1957

*Radley, C. T. (Middx; *CY 1979*) b May 13, 1944

*Rae, A. F. (Jam.) b Sept. 30, 1922

Raees Mohammad (Kar.) b Dec. 24, 1932

*Rai Singh, K. (S. Punjab & Ind. Serv.) b Feb. 24, 1922

Rait Kerr, Col. R. S. (Eur.; Sec. MCC 1936-52) b April 13, 1891, d April 2, 1961

Rajab Ali (Kenya) b Nov. 19, 1965

Rajadurai, B. E. A. (SSC) b Aug. 24, 1965

*Rajindernath, V. (N. Ind., U. Prov., S. Punjab, Bihar & E. Punjab) b Jan. 7, 1928, d Nov. 22, 1989

*Rajinder Pal (Delhi, S. Punjab & Punjab) b Nov. 18, 1937

*Rajput, L. S. (Bombay & Vidarbha) b Dec. 18, 1961

Ralph, L. H. R. (Essex) b May 22, 1920

*Ramadhin, S. (T/T & Lancs; *CY 1951*) b May 1, 1929

*Raman, W. V. (TN) b May 23, 1965

*Ramaswami, C. (Madras) b June 18, 1896, presumed dead.

Ramaswamy, V. K. (Test umpire) b April 26, 1946

*Ramchand, G. S. (Sind, Bombay & Raja.) b July 26, 1927

*Ramiz Raja (Lahore, Allied Bank, PNSC & I'bad) b Aug. 14, 1962

*Ramji, L. (W. Ind.) b Oct. 2, 1902, d Dec. 20, 1948

*Ranasinghe, A. N. (BRC) b Oct. 13, 1956, d Nov. 9, 1998

Ranasinghe, S. K. (SL) b July 4, 1962

*Ranatunga, D. (SSC) b Oct. 12, 1962

Ranatunga, N. (Colts & WPN) b Jan. 22, 1966

*Ranchod, U. (Mash.) b May 17, 1969

*Randall, D. W. (Notts; *CY 1980*) b Feb. 24, 1951

Randhir Singh (Orissa & Bihar) b Aug. 16, 1957

*Rangachari, C. R. (Madras) b April 14, 1916, d Oct. 9, 1993

*Rangnekar, K. M. (M'tra, Bombay & †M. Pradesh) b June 27, 1917, d Oct. 11, 1984

*Ranjane, V. B. (M'tra & Ind. Rlwys) b July 22, 1937

*Ranjitsinhji, K. S., (later H. H. the Jam Sahib of Nawanagar) (CU & Sussex; *CY 1897*) b Sept. 10, 1872, d April 2, 1933

*Ransford, V. S. (Vic.; *CY 1910*) b March 20, 1885, d March 19, 1958

*Rashid Khan (PWD, Kar. & PIA) b Dec. 15, 1959

Ratnayake, N. L. K. (SSC) b Nov. 22, 1968

*Ratnayeke, J. R. (NCC) b May 2, 1960

Rawlin, J. T. (Yorks & Middx) b Nov. 10, 1856, d Jan. 19, 1924

Rawson, P. W. E. (Zimb. & Natal) b May 25, 1957

Rayment, A. W. H. (Hants) b May 29, 1928

*Razdan, V. (Delhi) b Aug. 25, 1969

*Read, H. D. (Surrey & Essex) b Jan. 28, 1910, d Jan. 5, 2000

*Read, J. M. (Surrey; *CY 1890*) b Feb. 9, 1859, d Feb. 17, 1929

*Read, W. W. (Surrey; *CY 1893*) b Nov. 23, 1855, d Jan. 6, 1907

*Reddy, B. (TN) b Nov. 12, 1954

*Redmond, R. E. (Wgtn & Auck.) b Dec. 29, 1944

*Redpath, I. R. MBE (Vic.) b May 11, 1941

Reed, B. L. (Hants) b Sept. 17, 1937

*Reedman, J. C. (S. Aust.) b Oct. 9, 1865, d March 25, 1924

Rees, A. (Glam) b Feb. 17, 1938

*Reeve, D. A. OBE (Sussex & Warwicks; *CY 1996*) b April 2, 1963

Reeves, W. (Essex; Test umpire) b Jan. 22, 1875, d March 22, 1944

*Rege, M. R. (M'tra) b March 18, 1924

*Rehman, S. F. (Punjab, Pak. Us & Lahore) b June 11, 1935

*Reid, B. A. (W. Aust.) b March 14, 1963

*Reid, J. F. (Auck.) b March 3, 1956

*Reid, J. R. OBE (Wgtn & Otago; *CY 1959;* ICC referee) b June 3, 1928

*Reid, N. (W. Prov.) b Dec. 26, 1890, d June 6, 1947

Reid, R. B. (Wgtn & Auck.) b Dec. 3, 1958

Reidy, B. W. (Lancs) b Sept. 18, 1953

*Relf, A. E. (Sussex & Auck.; *CY 1914*) b June 26, 1874, d March 26, 1937

Relf, R. R. (Sussex) b Sept. 1, 1883, d April 28, 1965

*Renneberg, D. A. (NSW) b Sept. 23, 1942

Revill, A. C. (Derbys & Leics) b March 27, 1923, d July 6, 1998

Reynolds, B. L. (Northants) b June 10, 1932

Rhodes, A. E. G. (Derbys; Test umpire) b Oct. 10, 1916, d Oct. 18, 1983

*Rhodes, H. J. (Derbys) b July 22, 1936

*Rhodes, W. (Yorks; *CY 1899*) b Oct. 29, 1877, d July 8, 1973

Riazuddin (Test umpire) b Dec. 15, 1958

Rice, C. E. B. (Tvl & Notts; *CY 1981*) b July 23, 1949

Rice, J. M. (Hants) b Oct. 23, 1949

Richards, A. R. (W. Prov.) b Dec. 14, 1867, d Jan. 9, 1904

*Richards, B. A. (Natal, Glos, Hants & S. Aust.; *CY 1969*) b July 21, 1945

*Richards, C. J. (Surrey & OFS) b Aug. 10, 1958

Richards, D. L. (Chief Exec. ICC 1993-) b July 28, 1946

Richards, G. (Glam) b Nov. 29, 1951

*Richards, Sir Vivian (I. V. A.) OBE (Comb. Is., Leewards, Som, Qld & Glam; *CY 1977*) b March 7, 1952

*Richards, W. H. (SA) b March 26, 1862, d Jan. 4, 1903

*Richardson, A. J. (S. Aust.) b July 24, 1888, d Dec. 23, 1973

Richardson, A. W. (Derbys) b March 4, 1907, d July 29, 1983

*Richardson, D. J. (E. Prov & N. Tvl) b Sept. 16, 1959

*Richardson, D. W. (Worcs) b Nov. 3, 1934

*Richardson, P. E. (Worcs & Kent; *CY 1957*) b July 4, 1931

*Richardson, R. B. (Leewards, Yorks, N. Tvl & Windwards; *CY 1992*) b Jan. 12, 1962

*Richardson, T. (Surrey & Som; *CY 1897*) b Aug. 11, 1870, d July 2, 1912

*Richardson, V. Y. (S. Aust.) b Sept. 7, 1894, d Oct. 29, 1969

Riches, N. V. H. (Glam) b June 9, 1883, d Nov. 6, 1975

*Richmond, T. L. (Notts) b June 23, 1890, d Dec. 29, 1957

*Rickards, K. R. (Jam. & Essex) b Aug. 23, 1923, d Aug. 21, 1995

Riddington, A. (Leics) b Dec. 22, 1911, d Feb. 25, 1998

*Ridgway, F. (Kent) b Aug. 10, 1923

*Rigg, K. E. (Vic.) b May 21, 1906, d Feb. 28, 1995

Rindel, M. J. R. (Tvl & †Northerns) b Feb. 9, 1963

*Ring, D. T. (Vic.) b Oct. 14, 1918

*Ritchie, G. M. (Qld) b Jan. 23, 1960

*Rixon, S. J. (NSW) b Feb. 25, 1954

*Roach, C. A. (T/T) b March 13, 1904, d April 16, 1988

*Roberts, A. D. G. (N. Dist.) b May 6, 1947, d Oct. 26, 1989

*Roberts, A. M. E. CBE (Comb. Is., Leewards, Hants, NSW & Leics; *CY 1975*) b Jan. 29, 1951

*Roberts, A. T. (Windwards & T/T) b Sept. 18, 1937, d July 24, 1996

*Roberts, A. W. (Cant. & Otago) b Aug. 20, 1909, d May 13, 1978

Roberts, B. (Tvl & Derbys) b May 30, 1962

Roberts, F. G. (Glos) b April 1, 1862, d April 7, 1936

Roberts, S. J. (Cant.) b March 22, 1965

Roberts, W. B. (Lancs & Victory Tests) b Sept. 27, 1914, d Aug. 24, 1951

*Robertson, G. K. (C. Dist.) b July 15, 1960

*Robertson, J. B. (W. Prov.) b June 5, 1906, d July 5, 1985

*Robertson, J. D. (Middx; *CY 1948*) b Feb. 22, 1917, d Oct. 12, 1996

*Robertson, W. R. (Vic.) b Oct. 6, 1861, d June 24, 1938

Robertson-Glasgow, R. C. (OU & Som; writer) b July 15, 1901, d March 4, 1965

Robins, D. H. (Warwicks) b June 26, 1914

*Robins, R. W. V. (CU & Middx; *CY 1930*) b June 3, 1906, d Dec. 12, 1968

Robinson, D. C. (Glos & Essex) b April 20, 1884, d July 29, 1963

Robinson, E. (Yorks) b Nov. 16, 1883, d Nov. 17, 1969

Robinson, E. P. (Yorks & Som) b Aug. 10, 1911, d Nov. 10, 1998

Robinson, Sir Foster G. (Glos) b Sept. 19, 1880, d Oct. 31, 1967

Robinson, I. D. (Test umpire) b March 11, 1947

Robinson, P. E. (Yorks & Leics) b Aug. 3, 1963

Robinson, P. J. (Worcs & Som) b Feb. 9, 1943

*Robinson, R. D. (Vic.) b June 8, 1946

*Robinson, R. H. (NSW, S. Aust. & Otago) b March 26, 1914, d Aug. 10, 1965

*Robinson, R. T. (Notts; *CY 1986*) b Nov. 21, 1958

Robson, C. (Hants) b June 20, 1859, d Sept. 27, 1943

Robson, E. (Som) b May 1, 1870, d May 23, 1924

*Rodriguez, W. V. (T/T) b June 25, 1934

Roe, B. (Som) b Jan. 27, 1939

Roebuck, P. M. (CU & Som; *CY 1988*) b March 6, 1956

Rogers, N. H. (Hants) b March 9, 1918

Rogers, S. S. (Eur. & Som) b March 18, 1923, d Nov. 6, 1969

Romaines, P. W. (Northants, Glos & Griq. W.) b Dec. 25, 1955

*Roope, G. R. J. (Surrey & Griq. W.) b July 12, 1946

*Root, C. F. (Derbys & Worcs) b April 16, 1890, d Jan. 20, 1954

*Rorke, G. F. (NSW) b June 27, 1938

*Rose, B. C. (Som; *CY 1980*) b June 4, 1950

*Rose-Innes, A. (Kimberley & Tvl) b Feb. 16, 1868, d Nov. 22, 1946

Rotherham, G. A. (Rugby, CU, Warwicks & Wgtn.; *CY 1918*) b May 28, 1899, d Jan. 31, 1985

Rouse, S. J. (Warwicks) b Jan. 20, 1949

*Routledge, T. W. (W. Prov. & Tvl) b April 18, 1867, d May 9, 1927

*Rowan, A. M. B. (Tvl) b Feb. 7, 1921, d Feb. 21, 1998

*Rowan, E. A. B. (Tvl; *CY 1952*) b July 20, 1909, d April 30, 1993

Rowbotham, J. (Yorks; Test umpire) b July 8, 1831, d Dec. 22, 1899

*Rowe, C. G. (Wgtn & C. Dist.) b June 30, 1915, d June 9, 1995

Rowe, C. J. C. (Kent & Glam) b Nov. 11, 1951

Rowe, E. J. (Notts) b July 21, 1920, d Dec. 17, 1989

*Rowe, G. A. (W. Prov.) b June 15, 1874, d Jan. 8, 1950

*Rowe, L. G. (Jam. & Derbys) b Jan. 8, 1949

*Roy, A. (Bengal) b June 5, 1945, d Sept. 19, 1997

*Roy, Pankaj (Bengal) b May 31, 1928

*Roy, Pranab (Bengal) b Feb. 10, 1957

*Royle, Rev. V. P. F. A. (OU & Lancs) b Jan. 29, 1854, d May 21, 1929

*Rumsey, F. E. (Worcs, Som & Derbys) b Dec. 4, 1935

Rundle, D. B. (W. Prov.) b Sept. 25, 1965

Rushby, T. (Surrey) b Sept. 6, 1880, d July 13, 1962

*Russell, A. C. (Essex; *CY 1923*) b Oct. 7, 1887, d March 23, 1961

Russell, P. E. (Derbys) b May 9, 1944

Russell, S. E. J. (Middx & Glos) b Oct. 4, 1937, d June 18, 1994

*Russell, W. E. (Middx) b July 3, 1936

*Rutherford, J. W. (W. Aust.) b Sept. 25, 1929

Ryan, F. (Hants & Glam) b Nov. 14, 1888, d Jan. 5, 1954

Ryan, M. (Yorks) b June 23, 1933

*Ryder, J. (Vic.) b Aug. 8, 1889, d April 3, 1977

Saadat Ali (Lahore, UBL & HBFC) b Feb. 6, 1955

*Sadiq Mohammad (Kar., PIA, Tas., Essex, Glos & UBL) b May 3, 1945

*Saeed Ahmed (Punjab, Pak. Us, Lahore, PIA, Kar., PWD & Sind) b Oct. 1, 1937

*Saggers, R. A. (NSW) b May 15, 1917, d March 17, 1987

Saiful Islam (Bangladesh) b April 14, 1969

Sainsbury, P. J. (Hants; *CY 1974*) b June 13, 1934

*St Hill, E. L. (T/T) b March 9, 1904, d May 21, 1957

*St Hill, W. H. (T/T) b July 6, 1893, d *circa* 1957

*Salah-ud-Din (Kar., PIA & Pak. Us) b Feb. 14, 1947

*Saleem Altaf (Lahore & PIA) b April 19, 1944

*Saleem Jaffer (Kar. & UBL) b Nov. 19, 1962

Salim Badar (Test umpire) b May 16, 1953

Salim Pervez (NBP) b Sept. 9, 1947

*Salim Yousuf (Sind, Kar., IDBP, Allied Bank & Customs) b Dec. 7, 1959

Samaranayake, A. D. A. (SL) b Feb. 25, 1962

*Samarasekera, M. A. R. (CCC) b Aug. 5, 1961

Sampson, H. (Yorks & All-England) b March 13, 1813, d March 29, 1885

*Samuelson, S. V. (Natal) b Nov. 21, 1883, d Nov. 18, 1958

*Sandham, A. (Surrey; *CY 1923*) b July 6, 1890, d April 20, 1982

Sandhu, B. S. (Bombay) b Aug. 3, 1956

Santall, F. R. (Warwicks) b July 12, 1903, d Nov. 3, 1950

Santall, S. (Warwicks) b June 10, 1873, d March 19, 1957

Sanuar Hossain (Bangladesh) b Aug. 5, 1973

*Sardesai, D. N. (Bombay) b Aug. 8, 1940

*Sarfraz Nawaz (Lahore, Punjab, Northants, Pak. Rlwys & UBL) b Dec. 1, 1948

*Sarwate, C. T. (CP & B, M'tra, Bombay & †M. Pradesh) b June 22, 1920

*Saunders, J. V. (Vic. & Wgtn) b March 21, 1876, d Dec. 21, 1927

Savage, J. S. (Leics & Lancs) b March 3, 1929

Savill, L. A. (Essex) b June 30, 1935

Saville, G. J. (Essex) b Feb. 5, 1944

Saxelby, K. (Notts) b Feb. 23, 1959

*Saxena, R. C. (Delhi & Bihar) b Sept. 20, 1944

Sayer, D. M. (OU & Kent) b Sept. 19, 1936

*Scarlett, R. O. (Jam.) b Aug. 15, 1934

*Schultz, B. N. (E. Prov. & W. Prov) b Aug. 26, 1970

*Schultz, S. S. (CU & Lancs) b Aug. 29, 1857, d Dec. 18, 1937

*Schwarz, R. O. (Middx & Natal; *CY 1908*) b May 4, 1875, d Nov. 18, 1918

*Scott, A. P. H. (Jam.) b July 29, 1934

Scott, C. J. (Glos) b May 1, 1919, d Nov. 22, 1992

Scott, C. W. (Notts & Durham) b Jan. 23, 1964

*Scott, H. J. H. (Vic.) b Dec. 26, 1858, d Sept. 23, 1910

Scott, M. E. (Northants) b May 8, 1936

*Scott, O. C. (Jam.) b Aug. 14, 1893, d June 15, 1961

*Scott, R. H. (Cant.) b March 6, 1917

Scott, S. W. (Middx; *CY 1893*) b March 24, 1854, d Dec. 8, 1933

*Scott, V. J. (Auck.) b July 31, 1916, d Aug. 2, 1980

*Scotton, W. H. (Notts) b Jan. 15, 1856, d July 9, 1893

*Sealey, B. J. (T/T) b Aug. 12, 1899, d Sept. 12, 1963

*Sealy, J. E. D. (B'dos & T/T) b Sept. 11, 1912, d Jan. 3, 1982

*Seccull, A. W. (Kimberley, W. Prov. & Tvl) b Sept. 14, 1868, d July 20, 1945

*Sekar, T. A. P. (TN) b March 28, 1955

*Selby, J. (Notts) b July 1, 1849, d March 11, 1894

Sellers, A. B. MBE (Yorks; *CY 1940*) b March 5, 1907, d Feb. 20, 1981

*Sellers, R. H. D. (S. Aust.) b Aug. 20, 1940

*Selvey, M. W. W. (CU, Surrey, Middx, Glam & OFS; writer) b April 25, 1948

*Sen, P. (Bengal) b May 31, 1926, d Jan. 27, 1970

*Sen Gupta, A. K. (Ind. Serv.) b Aug. 3, 1939

Senanayake, C. P. (CCC) b Dec. 19, 1962

*Serjeant, C. S. (W. Aust.) b Nov. 1, 1951

Seymour, James (Kent) b Oct. 25, 1879, d Sept. 30, 1930

Seymour, M. A. (W. Prov.) b June 5, 1936

*Shackleton, D. (Hants; *CY 1959*) b Aug. 12, 1924

*Shafiq Ahmed (Lahore, Punjab, NBP & UBL) b March 28, 1949

*Shafqat Rana (Lahore & PIA) b Aug. 10, 1943

*Shah, A. H. (Mash.) b Aug. 7, 1959

*Shahid Israr (Kar. & Sind) b March 1, 1950

*Shahid Mahboob (Kar., Quetta, R'pindi, I'bad, PACO & Allied Bank) b Aug. 25, 1962

*Shahid Mahmoud (Kar., Pak. Us & PWD) b March 17, 1939

*Shahid Saeed (HBFC, Lahore & PACO) b Jan. 6, 1966

*Shalders, W. A. (Griq. W. & Tvl) b Feb. 12, 1880, d March 18, 1917

Shariful Haq (Bangladesh) b Jan. 15, 1976

*Sharma, Chetan (Haryana & Bengal) b Jan. 3, 1966

*Sharma, Gopal (U. Pradesh) b Aug. 3, 1960

*Sharma, P. (Raja.) b Jan. 5, 1948

Sharp, G. (Northants; Test umpire) b March 12, 1950

Sharp, H. P. (Middx) b Oct. 6, 1917, d Jan. 15, 1995

*Sharp, J. (Lancs) b Feb. 15, 1878, d Jan. 28, 1938

Sharp, K. (Yorks & Griq. W.) b April 6, 1959

*Sharpe, D. (Punjab, Pak. Rlwys, Lahore & S. Aust.) b Aug. 3, 1937

*Sharpe, J. W. (Surrey & Notts; *CY 1892*) b Dec. 9, 1866, d June 19, 1936

*Sharpe, P. J. (Yorks & Derbys; *CY 1963*) b Dec. 27, 1936

*Shastri, R. J. (Bombay & Glam) b May 27, 1962

*Shaw, Alfred (Notts & Sussex) b Aug. 29, 1842, d Jan. 16, 1907

Shaw, T. G. (E. Prov.) b July 5, 1959

*Sheahan, A. P. (Vic.) b Sept. 30, 1946

Sheffield, J. R. (Essex & Wgtn) b Nov. 19, 1906, d Nov. 16, 1997

Sheikh Salahuddin (Bangladesh) b Feb. 10, 1969

*Shepherd, B. K. (W. Aust.) b April 23, 1937

Shepherd, D. J. (Glam; *CY 1970*) b Aug. 12, 1927

Shepherd, D. R. MBE (Glos; Test umpire) b Dec. 27, 1940

*Shepherd, J. N. (B'dos, Kent, Rhod. & Glos; *CY 1979*) b Nov. 9, 1943

Shepherd, T. F. (Surrey) b Dec. 5, 1889, d Feb. 13, 1957

*Sheppard, Rt Rev. D. S. (Bishop of Liverpool; later Baron Sheppard) (CU & Sussex; *CY 1953*) b March 6, 1929

*Shepstone, G. H. (Tvl) b April 9, 1876, d July 3, 1940

*Sherwell, P. W. (Tvl) b Aug. 17, 1880, d April 17, 1948

*Sherwin, M. (Notts; *CY 1891*) b Feb. 26, 1851, d July 3, 1910

Shields, J. (Leics) b Feb. 1, 1882, d May 11, 1960

*Shillingford, G. C. (Comb. Is. & Windwards) b Sept. 25, 1944

*Shillingford, I. T. (Comb. Is. & Windwards) b April 18, 1944

*Shinde, S. G. (Baroda, M'tra & Bombay) b Aug. 18, 1923, d June 22, 1955

Shine, K. J. (Hants, Middx & Somerset) b Feb. 22, 1969

Shipman, A. W. (Leics) b March 7, 1901, d Dec. 12, 1979

Shirreff, A. C. (CU, Hants, Kent & Som) b Feb. 12, 1919

*Shivnarine, S. (Guyana) b May 13, 1952

*Shodhan, R. H. (Guj. & Baroda) b Oct. 18, 1928

*Shrewsbury, A. (Notts; *CY 1890*) b April 11, 1856, d May 19, 1903

*Shrimpton, M. J. F. (C. Dist. & N. Dist.) b June 23, 1940

*Shuja-ud-Din, Col. (N. Ind., Pak. Us, Pak. Serv., B'pur & R'pindi) b April 10, 1930

*Shukla, R. C. (Bihar & Delhi) b Feb. 4, 1948

*Shuter, J. (Kent & Surrey) b Feb. 9, 1855, d July 5, 1920

*Shuttleworth, K. (Lancs & Leics) b Nov. 13, 1944

Sibbles, F. M. (Lancs) b March 15, 1904, d July 20, 1973

*Sidebottom, A. (Yorks & OFS) b April 1, 1954

Sidwell, T. E. (Leics) b Jan. 30, 1888, d Dec. 8, 1958

*Siedle, I. J. (Natal) b Jan. 11, 1903, d Aug. 24, 1982

*Sievers, M. W. (Vic.) b April 13, 1912, d May 10, 1968

*Sikander Bakht (PWD, PIA, Sind, Kar. & UBL) b Aug. 25, 1957

Silk, D. R. W. CBE (CU & Som; Pres. MCC 1992-94; Chairman TCCB 1994-96) b Oct. 8, 1931

*Silva, K. J. (Bloom. & SSC) b June 2, 1973

*Silva, S. A. R. (NCC) b Dec. 12, 1960

Sime, W. A. MBE (OU & Notts) b Feb. 8, 1909, d May 5, 1983

Simmons, J. MBE (Lancs & Tas.; *CY 1985*) b March 28, 1941

Simons, E. O. (W. Prov. & N. Tvl) b March 9, 1962

*Simpson, R. B. (NSW & W. Aust.; *CY 1965*) b Feb. 3, 1936

*Simpson, R. T. (Sind & Notts; *CY 1950*) b Feb. 27, 1920

*Simpson-Hayward, G. H. (Worcs) b June 7, 1875, d Oct. 2, 1936

Sims, Sir Arthur (Cant.) b July 22, 1877, d April 27, 1969

*Sims, J. M. (Middx) b May 13, 1903, d April 27, 1973

*Sinclair, B. W. (Wgtn) b Oct. 23, 1936

*Sinclair, I. M. (Cant.) b June 1, 1933

*Sinclair, J. H. (Tvl) b Oct. 16, 1876, d Feb. 23, 1913

*Sincock, D. J. (S. Aust.) b Feb. 1, 1942

*Sinfield, R. A. (Glos) b Dec. 24, 1900, d March 17, 1988

*Singh, Charan K. (T/T) b Nov. 27, 1935

Singh, R. P. (U. Pradesh) b Jan. 6, 1963

Singleton, A. P. (OU, Worcs & Rhod.) b Aug. 5, 1914, d March 22, 1999

*Sivaramakrishnan, L. (TN & Baroda) b Dec. 31, 1965

Skelding, A. (Leics; umpire) b Sept. 5, 1886, d April 17, 1960

*Slack, W. N. (Middx & Windwards) b Dec. 12, 1954, d Jan. 15, 1989

Slade, D. N. F. (Worcs) b Aug. 24, 1940

Slater, A. G. (Derbys) b Nov. 22, 1890, d July 22, 1949

*Slater, K. N. (W. Aust.) b March 12, 1935

*Sleep, P. R. (S. Aust.) b May 4, 1957

*Slight, J. (Vic.) b Oct. 20, 1855, d Dec. 9, 1930

Slocombe, P. A. (Som) b Sept. 6, 1954

*Smailes, T. F. (Yorks) b March 27, 1910, d Dec. 1, 1970

Smales, K. (Yorks & Notts) b Sept. 15, 1927

*Small, G. C. (Warwicks & S. Aust.) b Oct. 18, 1961

Small, John, sen. (Hants & All-England) b April 19, 1737, d Dec. 31, 1826

*Small, J. A. (T/T) b Nov. 3, 1892, d April 26, 1958

*Small, M. A. (B'dos) b Feb. 12, 1964

Smart, C. C. (Warwicks & Glam) b July 23, 1898, d May 21, 1975

Smart, J. A. (Warwicks) b April 12, 1891, d Oct. 3, 1979

Smedley, M. J. (Notts) b Oct. 28, 1941

*Smith, A. C. CBE (OU & Warwicks; Chief Exec. TCCB 1987-96; ICC referee) b Oct. 25, 1936

*Smith, Sir C. Aubrey (CU, Sussex & Tvl) b July 21, 1863, d Dec. 20, 1948

*Smith, C. I. J. (Middx; *CY 1935*) b Aug. 25, 1906, d Feb. 9, 1979

*Smith, C. J. E. (Tvl) b Dec. 25, 1872, d March 27, 1947

*Smith, C. L. (Natal, Glam & Hants; *CY 1984*) b Oct. 15, 1958

Smith, C. L. A. (Sussex) b Jan. 1, 1879, d Nov. 22, 1949

Smith, C. S. (later Sir Colin Stansfield-) (CU & Lancs) b Oct. 1, 1932

*Smith, C. W. (B'dos; ICC referee) b July 29, 1933

*Smith, Denis (Derbys; *CY 1936*) b Jan. 24, 1907, d Sept. 12, 1979

*Smith, D. B. M. (Vic.) b Sept. 14, 1884, d July 29, 1963

Smith, D. H. K. (Derbys & OFS) b June 29, 1940

*Smith, D. M. (Surrey, Worcs & Sussex) b Jan. 9, 1956

*Smith, D. R. (Glos) b Oct. 5, 1934

*Smith, D. V. (Sussex) b June 14, 1923

Smith, Edwin (Derbys) b Jan. 2, 1934

Smith, Ernest (OU & Yorks) b Oct. 19, 1869, d April 9, 1945

*Smith, E. J. (Warwicks) b Feb. 6, 1886, d Aug. 31, 1979

*Smith, F. B. (Cant.) b March 13, 1922, d July 6, 1997

*Smith, F. W. (Tvl) b unknown, d April 17, 1914, aged 53

Smith, G. J. (Essex) b April 2, 1935

*Smith, Harry (Glos) b May 21, 1890, d Nov. 12, 1937

Smith, H. A. (Leics) b March 29, 1901, d Aug. 7, 1948

*Smith, H. D. (Otago & Cant.) b Jan. 8, 1913, d Jan. 25, 1986

*Smith, I. D. S. MBE (C. Dist. & Auck.) b Feb. 28, 1957

Smith, K. D. (Warwicks) b July 9, 1956

Smith, M. J. (Middx) b Jan. 4, 1942

*Smith, M. J. K. OBE (Leics, OU & Warwicks; *CY 1960*) b June 30, 1933

Smith, N. (Yorks & Essex) b April 1, 1949

*Smith, O. G. ("Collie") (Jam.; *CY 1958*) b May 5, 1933, d Sept. 9, 1959

Smith, P. A. (Warwicks) b April 5, 1964

Smith, Ray (Essex) b Aug. 10, 1914, d Feb. 21, 1996

Smith, Roy (Som) b April 14, 1930

Smith, R. C. (Leics) b Aug. 3, 1935

*Smith, S. B. (NSW & Tvl) b Oct. 18, 1961

*Smith, S. G. (T/T, Northants & Auck.; *CY 1915*) b Jan. 15, 1881, d Oct. 25, 1963

*Smith, T. P. B. (Essex; *CY 1947*) b Oct. 30, 1908, d Aug. 4, 1967

*Smith, V. I. (Natal) b Feb. 23, 1925

Smith, W. A. (Surrey) b Sept. 15, 1937

Smith, W. C. (Surrey; *CY 1911*) b Oct. 4, 1877, d July 16, 1946

*Smithson, G. A. (Yorks & Leics) b Nov. 1, 1926, d Sept. 6, 1970

*Snedden, C. A. (Auck.) b Jan. 7, 1918

*Snedden, M. C. (Auck.) b Nov. 23, 1958

*Snell, R. P. (Natal, Tvl, Somerset & Gauteng) b Sept. 12, 1968

Snellgrove, K. L. (Lancs) b Nov. 12, 1941

*Snooke, S. D. (W. Prov. & Tvl) b Nov. 11, 1878, d April 6, 1959

*Snooke, S. J. (Border, W. Prov. & Tvl) b Feb. 1, 1881, d Aug. 14, 1966

*Snow, J. A. (Sussex; *CY 1973*) b Oct. 13, 1941

*Sobers, Sir Garfield S. (B'dos, S. Aust. & Notts; *CY 1964*) b July 28, 1936

Sohail Fazal (HBL) b Nov. 11, 1967

*Sohoni, S. W. (M'tra, Baroda & Bombay) b March 5, 1918, d May 19, 1993

*Solkar, E. D. (Bombay & Sussex) b March 18, 1948

*Solomon, J. S. (BG) b Aug. 26, 1930

*Solomon, W. R. (Tvl & E. Prov.) b April 23, 1872, d July 12, 1964

*Sood, M. M. (Delhi) b July 6, 1939

Southern, J. W. (Hants) b Sept. 2, 1952

*Southerton, James (Surrey, Hants & Sussex) b Nov. 16, 1827, d June 16, 1880

Southerton, S. J. (Editor of *Wisden* 1934-35) b July 7, 1874, d March 12, 1935

*Sparling, J. T. (Auck.) b July 24, 1938

Spencer, C. T. (Leics) b Aug. 18, 1931

Spencer, J. (CU & Sussex) b Oct. 6, 1949

Spencer, T. W. OBE (Kent; Test umpire) b March 22, 1914

Sperry, J. (Leics) b March 19, 1910, d April 21, 1997

*Spofforth, F. R. (NSW & Vic.) b Sept. 9, 1853, d June 4, 1926

*Spooner, R. H. (Lancs; *CY 1905*) b Oct. 21, 1880, d Oct. 2, 1961

*Spooner, R. T. (Warwicks) b Dec. 30, 1919, d Dec. 20, 1997

Springall, J. D. (Notts) b Sept. 19, 1932

Sprot, E. M. (Hants) b Feb. 4, 1872, d Oct. 8, 1945

Squires, H. S. (Surrey) b Feb. 22, 1909, d Jan. 24, 1950

*Srikkanth, K. (TN) b Dec. 21, 1959

*Srinivasan, T. E. (TN) b Oct. 26, 1950

*Stackpole, K. R. MBE (Vic.; *CY 1973*) b July 10, 1940

Standen, J. A. (Worcs) b May 30, 1935

*Stanyforth, Lt.-Col. R. T. (Yorks) b May 30, 1892, d Feb. 20, 1964

Staples, A. (Notts) b Feb. 4, 1899, d Sept. 9, 1965

*Staples, S. J. (Notts; *CY 1929*) b Sept. 18, 1892, d June 4, 1950

*Statham, J. B. CBE (Lancs; *CY 1955*) b June 17, 1930, d June 10, 2000

*Stayers, S. C. (†Guyana & Bombay) b June 9, 1937

Stead, B. (Yorks, Essex, Notts & N. Tvl) b June 21, 1939, d April 15, 1980

*Steel, A. G. (CU & Lancs; Pres. MCC 1902) b Sept. 24, 1858, d June 15, 1914

*Steele, D. S. OBE (Northants & Derbys; *CY 1976*) b Sept. 29, 1941

Steele, J. F. (Leics, Natal & Glam) b July 23, 1946

Stephens, E. J. (Glos) b March 23, 1909, d April 3, 1983

Stephenson, F. D. (B'dos, Glos, Tas., Notts, Sussex & †FS; *CY 1989*) b April 8, 1959

Stephenson, G. R. (Derbys & Hants) b Nov. 19, 1942

Stephenson, H. H. (Surrey & All-England) b May 3, 1832, d Dec. 17, 1896

Stephenson, H. W. (Som) b July 18, 1920

Stephenson, Lt.-Col. J. R. CBE (Sec. MCC 1987-93) b Feb. 25, 1931

Stephenson, Lt.-Col. J. W. A. (Essex, Worcs, Army, Europeans & Victory Tests) b Aug. 1, 1907, d May 20, 1982

Stevens, Edward ("Lumpy") (Hants) b circa 1735, d Sept. 7, 1819

*Stevens, G. B. (S. Aust.) b Feb. 29, 1932

*Stevens, G. T. S. (UCS, OU & Middx; *CY 1918*) b Jan. 7, 1901, d Sept. 19, 1970

*Stevenson, G. B. (Yorks & Northants) b Dec. 16, 1955

Stevenson, K. (Derbys & Hants) b Oct. 6, 1950

*Stewart, M. J. OBE (Surrey; *CY 1958*) b Sept. 16, 1932

*Stewart, R. B. (SA) b Sept. 3, 1856, d Sept. 12, 1913

Stewart, W. J. (Warwicks & Northants) b Oct. 31, 1934

*Stirling, D. A. (C. Dist.) b Oct. 5, 1961

Stocks, F. W. (Notts) b Nov. 6, 1918, d Feb. 23, 1996

*Stoddart, A. E. (Middx; *CY 1893*) b March 11, 1863, d April 3, 1915

*Stollmeyer, J. B. (T/T) b April 11, 1921, d Sept. 10, 1989

*Stollmeyer, V. H. (T/T) b Jan. 24, 1916, d Sept. 21, 1999

Stone, J. (Hants & Glam) b Nov. 29, 1876, d Nov. 15, 1942

Storer, H. jun. (Derbys) b Feb. 2, 1898, d Sept. 1, 1967

*Storer, W. (Derbys; *CY 1899*) b Jan. 25, 1867, d Feb. 28, 1912

Storey, S. J. (Surrey & Sussex) b Jan. 6, 1941

Stott, L. W. (Auck.) b Dec. 8, 1946

Stott, W. B. (Yorks) b July 18, 1934

Stovold, A. W. (Glos & OFS) b March 19, 1953

*Street, G. B. (Sussex) b Dec. 6, 1889, d April 24, 1924

*Stricker, L. A. (Tvl) b May 26, 1884, d Feb. 5, 1960

*Strudwick, H. (Surrey; *CY 1912*) b Jan. 28, 1880, d Feb. 14, 1970

Stuart, A. M. (NSW) b Jan. 2, 1970

*Studd, C. T. (CU & Middx) b Dec. 2, 1860, d July 16, 1931

*Studd, G. B. (CU & Middx) b Oct. 20, 1859, d Feb. 13, 1945

Studd, Sir J. E. Kynaston (Middx & CU; Pres. MCC 1930) b July 26, 1858, d Jan. 14, 1944

*Su'a, M. L. (N. Dist. & Auck.) b Nov. 7, 1966

*Subba Row, R. CBE (CU, Surrey & Northants; *CY 1961*; Chairman TCCB 1985-90; ICC referee) b Jan. 29, 1932

*Subramanya, V. (Mysore) b July 16, 1936

Sudhakar Rao, R. (Karn.) b Aug. 8, 1952

Sueter, T. (Hants & Surrey) b circa 1749, d Feb. 17, 1827

*Sugg, F. H. (Yorks, Derbys & Lancs; *CY 1890*) b Jan. 11, 1862, d May 29, 1933

Sullivan, J. (Lancs) b Feb. 5, 1945

Sully, H. (Som & Northants) b Nov. 1, 1939

*Sunderram, G. (Bombay & Raja.) b March 29, 1930

*Surendranath, R. (Ind. Serv.) b Jan. 4, 1937

Surridge, W. S. (Surrey; *CY 1953*) b Sept. 3, 1917, d April 13, 1992

*Surti, R. F. (Guj., Raja., & Qld) b May 25, 1936

*Susskind, M. J. (CU, Middx & Tvl) b June 8, 1891, d July 9, 1957

*Sutcliffe, B. MBE (Auck., Otago & N. Dist.; *CY 1950*) b Nov. 17, 1923

*Sutcliffe, H. (Yorks; *CY 1920*) b Nov. 24, 1894, d Jan. 22, 1978

Sutcliffe, W. H. H. (Yorks) b Oct. 10, 1926, d Sept. 16, 1998

Suttle, K. G. (Sussex) b Aug. 25, 1928

Swanton, E. W. CBE (Middx; writer & broadcaster) b Feb. 11, 1907, d Jan. 22, 2000

Swarbrook, F. W. (Derbys, Griq. W. & OFS) b Dec. 17, 1950

Swart, P. D. (Rhod., W. Prov., Glam & Boland) b April 27, 1946, d March 13, 2000

*Swetman, R. (Surrey, Notts & Glos) b Oct. 25, 1933

Sydenham, D. A. D. (Surrey) b April 6, 1934

*Taber, H. B. (NSW) b April 29, 1940

*Taberer, H. M. (OU & Natal) b Oct. 7, 1870, d June 5, 1932

*Tahir Naqqash (Servis Ind., MCB, Punjab & Lahore) b July 6, 1959

*Talat Ali (Lahore, PIA & UBL; ICC referee) b May 29, 1950

*Tallon, D. (Qld; *CY 1949*) b Feb. 17, 1916, d Sept. 7, 1984

*Tamhane, N. S. (Bombay) b Aug. 4, 1931

*Tancred, A. B. (Kimberley, Griq. W. & Tvl) b Aug. 20, 1865, d Nov. 23, 1911

*Tancred, L. J. (Tvl) b Oct. 7, 1876, d July 28, 1934

*Tancred, V. M. (Tvl) b July 7, 1875, d June 3, 1904

Tanvir Mehdi (Lahore & UBL) b Nov. 7, 1972

*Tapscott, G. L. (Griq. W.) b Nov. 7, 1889, d Dec. 13, 1940

*Tapscott, L. E. (Griq. W.) b March 18, 1894, d July 7, 1934

*Tarapore, K. K. (Bombay) b Dec. 17, 1910, d June 15, 1986

Tarbox, C. V. (Worcs) b July 2, 1891, d June 15, 1978

Tarrant, F. A. (Vic., Middx & Patiala; *CY 1908*) b Dec. 11, 1880, d Jan. 29, 1951

Tarrant, G. F. (Cambs & All-England) b Dec. 7, 1838, d July 2, 1870

*Taslim Arif (Kar., Sind & NBP) b May 1, 1954

*Tate, F. W. (Sussex) b July 24, 1867, d Feb. 24, 1943

*Tate, M. W. (Sussex; *CY 1924*) b May 30, 1895, d May 18, 1956

*Tattersall, R. (Lancs) b Aug. 17, 1922

*Tauseef Ahmed (PWD, UBL, Kar. & Customs) b May 10, 1958

*Tavaré, C. J. (OU, Kent & Som) b Oct. 27, 1954

*Tayfield, H. J. (Natal, Rhod. & Tvl; *CY 1956*) b Jan. 30, 1929, d Feb. 25, 1994

*Taylor, A. I. (Tvl) b July 25, 1925

Taylor, B. (Essex; *CY 1972*) b June 19, 1932

*Taylor, B. R. (Cant. & Wgtn) b July 12, 1943

Taylor, C. G. (CU & Sussex) b Nov. 21, 1816, d Sept. 10, 1869

*Taylor, Daniel (Natal) b Jan. 9, 1887, d Jan. 24, 1957

*Taylor, D. D. (Auck. & Warwicks) b March 2, 1923, d Dec. 5, 1980

Taylor, D. J. S. (Surrey, Som & Griq. W.) b Nov. 12, 1942

*Taylor, H. W. (Natal, Tvl & W. Prov.; *CY 1925*) b May 5, 1889, d Feb. 8, 1973

*Taylor, J. (T/T) b Jan. 3, 1932, d Nov. 13, 1999

*Taylor, J. M. (NSW) b Oct. 10, 1895, d May 12, 1971

*Taylor, K. (Yorks & Auck.) b Aug. 21, 1935

*Taylor, L. B. (Leics & Natal) b Oct. 25, 1953

*Taylor, M. A. (NSW; *CY 1990*) b Oct. 27, 1964

Taylor, M. N. S. (Notts & Hants) b Nov. 12, 1942

Taylor, N. R. (Kent & Sussex) b July 21, 1959

*Taylor, P. L. (NSW & Qld) b Aug. 22, 1956

Taylor, R. M. (Essex) b Nov. 30, 1909, d Jan. 7, 1984

*Taylor, R. W. MBE (Derbys; *CY 1977*) b July 17, 1941

Taylor, T. L. (CU & Yorks; *CY 1901*) b May 25, 1878, d March 16, 1960

Tennekoon, A. P. B. (SL) b Oct. 29, 1946

*Tennyson, 3rd Lord (Hon. L. H.) (Hants; *CY 1914*) b Nov. 7, 1889, d June 6, 1951

Terry, V. P. (Hants) b Jan. 14, 1959

*Theunissen, N. H. (W. Prov.) b May 4, 1867, d Nov. 9, 1929

Thomas, A. E. (Northants) b June 7, 1893, d March 21, 1965

Thomas, D. J. (Surrey, N. Tvl, Natal & Glos) b June 30, 1959

*Thomas, G. (NSW) b March 21, 1938

*Thomas, J. G. (Glam, Border, E. Prov. & Northants) b Aug. 12, 1960

Thompson, A. (Middx) b April 17, 1916

*Thompson, G. J. (Northants; Test umpire; *CY 1906*) b Oct. 27, 1877, d March 3, 1943

*Thompson, P. I. C. (B'dos) b Sept. 26, 1971

Thompson, R. G. (Warwicks) b Sept. 26, 1932

*Thoms, G. R. (Vic.) b March 22, 1927

*Thomson, A. L. (Vic.) b Dec. 2, 1945

*Thomson, J. R. (NSW, Qld & Middx) b Aug. 16, 1950

*Thomson, K. (Cant.) b Feb. 26, 1941

*Thomson, N. F. D. (NSW) b May 29, 1839, d Sept. 2, 1896

*Thomson, N. I. (Sussex) b Jan. 23, 1929

*Thomson, S. A. (N. Dist.) b Jan. 27, 1969

Thornton, C. I. (CU, Kent & Middx) b March 20, 1850, d Dec. 10, 1929

*Thornton, Dr P. G. (Yorks, Middx & SA) b Dec. 24, 1867, d Jan. 31, 1939
*Thurlow, H. M. (Qld) b Jan. 10, 1903, d Dec. 3, 1975
Tiffin, R. B. (Test umpire) b June 4, 1959
Timms, B. S. V. (Hants & Warwicks) b Dec. 17, 1940
Timms, J. E. (Northants) b Nov. 3, 1906, d May 18, 1980
Tindall, R. A. E. (Surrey) b Sept. 23, 1935
*Tindill, E. W. T. (Wgtn) b Dec. 18, 1910
Tissera, M. H. (SL) b March 23, 1939
*Titmus, F. J. MBE (Middx, Surrey & OFS; *CY 1963*) b Nov. 24, 1932
Todd, L. J. (Kent) b June 19, 1907, d Aug. 20, 1967
Todd, P. A. (Notts & Glam) b March 12, 1953
*Tolchard, R. W. (Leics) b June 15, 1946
Tomlins, K. P. (Middx & Glos) b Oct. 23, 1957
*Tomlinson, D. S. (Rhod. & Border) b Sept. 4, 1910, d July 11, 1993
Tompkin, M. (Leics) b Feb. 17, 1919, d Sept. 27, 1956
*Toohey, P. M. (NSW) b April 20, 1954
Topley, T. D. (Surrey, Essex & Griq. W.) b Feb. 25, 1964
*Toshack, E. R. H. (NSW) b Dec. 15, 1914
Townsend, A. (Warwicks) b Aug. 26, 1921
Townsend, A. F. (Derbys) b March 29, 1912, d Feb. 25, 1994
*Townsend, C. L. (Glos; *CY 1899*) b Nov. 7, 1876, d Oct. 17, 1958
*Townsend, D. C. H. (OU) b April 20, 1912, d Jan. 27, 1997
*Townsend, L. F. (Derbys & Auck.; *CY 1934*) b June 8, 1903, d Feb. 17, 1993
**Traicos, A. J. (Rhod. & Mash.) b May 17, 1947
*Travers, J. P. F. (S. Aust.) b Jan. 10, 1871, d Sept. 15, 1942
*Tremlett, M. F. (Som & C. Dist.) b July 5, 1923, d July 30, 1984
Tremlett, T. M. (Hants) b July 26, 1956
*Tribe, G. E. (Vic. & Northants; *CY 1955*) b Oct. 4, 1920
*Trim, J. (BG) b Jan. 25, 1915, d Nov. 12, 1960
Trimble, G. S. (Qld) b Jan. 1, 1963
*Trimborn, P. H. J. (Natal) b May 18, 1940
**Trott, A. E. (Vic., Middx & Hawkes Bay; *CY 1899*) b Feb. 6, 1873, d July 30, 1914
*Trott, G. H. S. (Vic.; *CY 1894*) b Aug. 5, 1866, d Nov. 10, 1917
Troughton, L. H. W. (Kent) b May 17, 1879, d Aug. 31, 1933
*Troup, G. B. (Auck.) b Oct. 3, 1952
*Trueman, F. S. OBE (Yorks; *CY 1953*) b Feb. 6, 1931
*Trumble, H. (Vic.; *CY 1897*) b May 12, 1867, d Aug. 14, 1938
*Trumble, J. W. (Vic.) b Sept. 16, 1863, d Aug. 17, 1944

*Trumper, V. T. (NSW; *CY 1903*) b Nov. 2, 1877, d June 28, 1915
*Truscott, P. B. (Wgtn) b Aug. 14, 1941
*Tuckett, L. (OFS) b Feb. 6, 1919
*Tuckett, L. R. (Natal & OFS) b April 19, 1885, d April 8, 1963
*Tufnell, N. C. (CU & Surrey) b June 13, 1887, d Aug. 3, 1951
Tunnicliffe, C. J. (Derbys) b Aug. 11, 1951
Tunnicliffe, J. (Yorks; *CY 1901*) b Aug. 26, 1866, d July 11, 1948
*Turnbull, M. J. (CU & Glam; *CY 1931*) b March 16, 1906, d Aug. 5, 1944
*Turner, A. (NSW) b July 23, 1950
Turner, C. (Yorks) b Jan. 11, 1902, d Nov. 19, 1968
*Turner, C. T. B. (NSW; *CY 1889*) b Nov. 16, 1862, d Jan. 1, 1944
Turner, D. R. (Hants & W. Prov.) b Feb. 5, 1949
Turner, F. M. MBE (Leics) b Aug. 8, 1934
*Turner, G. M. (Otago, N. Dist. & Worcs; *CY 1971*) b May 26, 1947
Turner, S. (Essex & Natal) b July 18, 1943
*Twentyman-Jones, Sir Percy S. (W. Prov.) b Sept. 13, 1876, d March 8, 1954
*Tyldesley, E. (Lancs; *CY 1920*) b Feb. 5, 1889, d May 5, 1962
*Tyldesley, J. T. (Lancs; *CY 1902*) b Nov. 22, 1873, d Nov. 27, 1930
*Tyldesley, R. K. (Lancs; *CY 1925*) b March 11, 1897, d Sept. 17, 1943
*Tylecote, E. F. S. (OU & Kent) b June 23, 1849, d March 15, 1938
*Tyler, E. J. (Som) b Oct. 13, 1864, d Jan. 25, 1917
*Tyson, F. H. (Northants; *CY 1956*) b June 6, 1930

Ufton, D. G. (Kent) b May 31, 1928
*Ulyett, G. (Yorks) b Oct. 21, 1851, d June 18, 1898
*Umrigar, P. R. (Bombay & Guj.) b March 28, 1926
*Underwood, D. L. MBE (Kent; *CY 1969*) b June 8, 1945

Vaidya, P. S. (Bengal) b Sept. 23, 1967
*Valentine, A. L. (Jam.; *CY 1951*) b April 29, 1930
*Valentine, B. H. (CU & Kent) b Jan. 17, 1908, d Feb. 2, 1983
*Valentine, V. A. (Jam.) b April 4, 1908, d July 6, 1972
*Vance, R. H. (Wgtn) b March 31, 1955
*van der Bijl, P. G. (W. Prov. & OU) b Oct. 21, 1907, d Feb. 16, 1973
van der Bijl, V. A. P. (Natal, Middx & Tvl; *CY 1981*) b March 19, 1948
*Van der Merwe, E. A. (Tvl) b Nov. 9, 1904, d Feb. 26, 1971

*Van der Merwe, P. L. (W. Prov. & E. Prov.; ICC referee) b March 14, 1937

van Geloven, J. (Yorks & Leics) b Jan. 4, 1934

*Van Ryneveld, C. B. (W. Prov. & OU) b March 19, 1928

van Zyl, C. J. P. G. (OFS & Glam) b Oct. 1, 1961

*Varnals, G. D. (E. Prov., Tvl & Natal) b July 24, 1935

*Vaughan, J. T. C. (Auck.) b Aug. 30, 1967

*Veivers, T. R. (Qld) b April 6, 1937

*Veletta, M. R. J. (W. Aust.) b Oct. 30, 1963

*Vengsarkar, D. B. (Bombay; *CY 1987*) b April 6, 1956

*Venkataraghavan, S. (†TN & Derbys; Test umpire) b April 21, 1946

*Venkataramana, M. (TN) b April 24, 1966

*Verity, H. (Yorks; *CY 1932*) b May 18, 1905, d July 31, 1943

*Vernon, G. F. (Middx) b June 20, 1856, d Aug. 10, 1902

Vials, G. A. T. (Northants) b March 18, 1887, d April 26, 1974

Vigar, F. H. (Essex) b July 7, 1917

*Viljoen, K. G. (Griq. W., OFS & Tvl) b May 14, 1910, d Jan. 21, 1974

*Vincent, C. L. (Tvl) b Feb. 16, 1902, d Aug. 24, 1968

*Vine, J. (Sussex; *CY 1906*) b May 15, 1875, d April 25, 1946

*Vintcent, C. H. (Tvl & Griq. W.) b Sept. 2, 1866, d Sept. 28, 1943

Virgin, R. T. (Som, Northants & W. Prov.; *CY 1971*) b Aug. 26, 1939

*Viswanath, G. R. (†Karn.; ICC referee) b Feb. 12, 1949

*Viswanath, S. (Karn.) b Nov. 29, 1962

*Vivian, G. E. (Auck.) b Feb. 28, 1946

*Vivian, H. G. (Auck.) b Nov. 4, 1912, d Aug. 12, 1983

*Vizianagram, Maharaj Kumar of, Sir Vijay A., (U. Prov.) b Dec. 28, 1905, d Dec. 2, 1965

*Voce, W (Notts; *CY 1933*) b Aug. 8, 1909, d June 6, 1984

*Vogler, A. E. E. (Middx, Natal, Tvl & E. Prov.; *CY 1908*) b Nov. 28, 1876, d Aug. 9, 1946

Vonhagt, D. M. (Moors) b March 31, 1965

*Waddington, A. (Yorks) b Feb. 4, 1893, d Oct. 28, 1959

*Wade, H. F. (Natal) b Sept. 14, 1905, d Nov. 23, 1980

Wade, T. H. (Essex) b Nov. 24, 1910, d July 25, 1987

*Wade, W. W. (Natal) b June 18, 1914

*Wadekar, A. L. (Bombay) b April 1, 1941

*Wadsworth, K. J. (C. Dist. & Cant.) b Nov. 30, 1946, d Aug. 19, 1976

*Wainwright, E. (Yorks; *CY 1894*) b April 8, 1865, d Oct. 28, 1919

*Waite, J. H. B. (E. Prov. & Tvl) b Jan. 19, 1930

*Waite, M. G. (S. Aust.) b Jan. 7, 1911, d Dec. 16, 1985

*Walcott, Sir Clyde L. (B'dos & BG; *CY 1958*; Chairman ICC 1993-97) b Jan. 17, 1926

*Walcott, L. A. (B'dos) b Jan. 18, 1894, d Feb. 27, 1984

Walden, F. (Northants; Test umpire) b March 1, 1888, d May 3, 1949

Walker, A. (Northants & Durham) b July 7, 1962

Walker, C. (Yorks & Hants) b June 27, 1919, d Dec. 3, 1992

Walker, I. D. (Middx) b Jan. 8, 1844, d July 6, 1898

*Walker, M. H. N. (Vic.) b Sept. 12, 1948

*Walker, P. M. (Glam, Tvl & W. Prov.) b Feb. 17, 1936

Walker, V. E. (Middx) b April 20, 1837, d Jan. 3, 1906

Walker, W. (Notts) b Nov. 24, 1892, d Dec. 3, 1991

*Wall, T. W. (S. Aust.) b May 13, 1904, d March 25, 1981

*Wallace, W. M. (Auck.) b Dec. 19, 1916

*Waller, A. C. (Mash.) b Sept. 25, 1959

Waller, C. E. (Surrey & Sussex) b Oct. 3, 1948

Walsh, J. E. (NSW & Leics) b Dec. 4, 1912, d May 20, 1980

*Walter, K. A. (Tvl) b Nov. 5, 1939

*Walters, C. F. (Glam & Worcs; *CY 1934*) b Aug. 28, 1905, d Dec. 23, 1992

*Walters, F. H. (Vic. & NSW) b Feb. 9, 1860, d June 1, 1922

*Walters, K. D. MBE (NSW) b Dec. 21, 1945

*Waqar Hassan (Pak. Us, Punjab, Pak. Serv. & Kar.) b Sept. 12, 1932

*Ward, Alan (Derbys, Leics & Border) b Aug. 10, 1947

*Ward, Albert (Yorks & Lancs; *CY 1890*) b Nov. 21, 1865, d Jan. 6, 1939

Ward, B. (Essex) b Feb. 28, 1944

Ward, D. (Glam) b Aug. 30, 1934

Ward, D. M. (Surrey) b Feb. 10, 1961

*Ward, F. A. (S. Aust.) b Feb. 23, 1906, d March 25, 1974

*Ward, J. T. (Cant.) b March 11, 1937

*Ward, T. A. (Tvl) b Aug. 2, 1887, d Feb. 16, 1936

Ward, William (MCC & Hants) b July 24, 1787, d June 30, 1849

*Wardle, J. H. (Yorks; *CY 1954*) b Jan. 8, 1923, d July 23, 1985

*Warnapura, B. (SL; ICC referee) b March 1, 1953

*Warnaweera, K. P. J. (Galle & Singha) b Nov. 23, 1960

Warner, A. E. (Worcs & Derbys) b May 12, 1959

*Warner, Sir Pelham F. (OU & Middx; *CY 1904, special portrait 1921*; Pres. MCC 1950-51) b Oct. 2, 1873, d Jan. 30, 1963

*Warr, J. J. (CU & Middx; Pres. MCC 1987-88) b July 16, 1927

*Warren, A. R. (Derbys) b April 2, 1875, d Sept. 3, 1951

*Washbrook, C. CBE (Lancs; *CY 1947*) b Dec. 6, 1914, d April 27, 1999

*Wasim Bari (Kar., PIA & Sind) b March 23, 1948

Wasim Haider (PIA & F'bad) b June 6, 1967

*Wasim Raja (Lahore, Sargodha, Pak. Us, PIA, Punjab & NBP) b July 3, 1952

Wass, T. G. (Notts; *CY 1908*) b Dec. 26, 1873, d Oct. 27, 1953

*Wassan, A. S. (Delhi) b March 23, 1968

Wassell, A. (Hants) b April 15, 1940

*Watkins, A. J. (Glam) b April 21, 1922

*Watkins, J. C. (Natal) b April 10, 1923

*Watkins, J. R. (NSW) b April 16, 1943

*Watkinson, M. (Lancs) b Aug. 1, 1961

Watson, A. (Lancs) b Nov. 4, 1844, d Oct. 26, 1920

*Watson, C. (Jam. & Delhi) b July 1, 1938

Watson, F. (Lancs) b Sept. 17, 1898, d Feb. 1, 1976

*Watson, G. D. (Vic., W. Aust. & NSW) b March 8, 1945

Watson, G. S. (Kent & Leics) b April 10, 1907, d April 1, 1974

*Watson, W. (Yorks & Leics; *CY 1954*) b March 7, 1920

*Watson, W. (Auck.) b Aug. 31, 1965

*Watson, W. J. (NSW) b Jan. 31, 1931

Watt, A. E. (Kent) b June 19, 1907, d Feb. 3, 1974

*Watt, L. (Otago) b Sept. 17, 1924, d Nov. 15, 1996

Watts, E. A. (Surrey) b Aug. 1, 1911, d May 2, 1982

Watts, P. D. (Northants & Notts) b March 31, 1938

Watts, P. J. (Northants) b June 16, 1940

*Wazir, Ali, S. (C. Ind., S. Punjab & Patiala) b Sept. 15, 1903, d June 17, 1950

*Wazir Mohammad (B'pur & Kar.) b Dec. 22, 1929

*Webb, M. G. (Otago & Cant.) b June 22, 1947

*Webb, P. N. (Auck.) b July 14, 1957

Webb, R. J. (Otago) b Sept. 15, 1952

Webb, R. T. (Sussex) b July 11, 1922

*Webbe, A. J. (OU & Middx) b Jan. 16, 1855, d Feb. 19, 1941

Webber, Roy (Statistician) b July 23, 1914, d Nov. 14, 1962

*Weekes, Sir Everton D. (B'dos; *CY 1951*) b Feb. 26, 1925

*Weekes, K. H. (Jam.) b Jan. 24, 1912, d Feb. 9, 1998

Weeks, R. T. (Warwicks) b April 30, 1930

Weerakkody, A. P. (NCC) b Oct. 1, 1970

*Weerasinghe, C. D. U. S. (TU & NCC) b March 1, 1968

Weigall, G. J. V. (CU & Kent) b Oct. 19, 1870, d May 17, 1944

*Weir, G. L. (Auck.) b June 2, 1908

*Wellard, A. W. (Som; *CY 1936*) b April 8, 1902, d Dec. 31, 1980

*Wellham, D. M. (NSW, Tas. & Qld) b March 13, 1959

Wells, B. D. (Glos & Notts) b July 27, 1930

Wells, C. M. (Sussex, Border, W. Prov. & Derbys) b March 3, 1960

Wells, W. (Northants) b March 14, 1881, d March 18, 1939

Wenman, E. G. (Kent & England) b Aug. 18, 1803, d Dec. 31, 1879

Wensley, A. F. (Sussex, Auck., Naw. & Eur.) b May 23, 1898, d June 17, 1970

*Wesley, C. (Natal) b Sept. 5, 1937

West, G. H. (Editor of *Wisden* 1880-86) b 1851, d Oct. 6, 1896

*Westcott, R. J. (W. Prov.) b Sept. 19, 1927

Weston, M. J. (Worcs) b April 8, 1959

*Wettimuny, M. D. (SL) b June 11, 1951

*Wettimuny, S. (SL; *CY 1985;* ICC referee) b Aug. 12, 1956

Wettimuny, S. R. de S. (SL) b Feb. 7, 1949

*Wharton, A. (Lancs & Leics) b April 30, 1923, d Aug. 26, 1993

*Whatmore, D. F. (Vic.) b March 16, 1954

Wheatley, O. S. CBE (CU, Warwicks & Glam; *CY 1969*) b May 28, 1935

Whitaker, Haddon OBE (Editor of *Wisden* 1940-43) b Aug. 30, 1908, d Jan. 5, 1982

*Whitaker, J. J. (Leics; *CY 1987*) b May 5, 1962

White, A. F. T. (CU, Warwicks & Worcs) b Sept. 5, 1915, d March 16, 1993

White, Sir Archibald W. 4th Bt (Yorks) b Oct. 14, 1877, d Dec. 16, 1945

*White, D. J. (N. Dist.) b June 26, 1961

*White, D. W. (Hants & Glam) b Dec. 14, 1935

*White, G. C. (Tvl) b Feb. 5, 1882, d Oct. 17, 1918

*White, J. C. (Som; *CY 1929*) b Feb. 19, 1891, d May 2, 1961

White, Hon. L. R. (5th Lord Annaly) (Middx & Victory Test) b March 15, 1927, d Sept. 30, 1990

White, R. A. (Middx & Notts) b Oct. 6, 1936

White, R. C. (CU, Glos & Tvl) b Jan. 29, 1941

*White, W. A. (B'dos) b Nov. 20, 1938

Whitehead, A. G. T. (Som; Test umpire) b Oct. 28, 1940

Whitehead, H. (Leics) b Sept. 19, 1874, d Sept. 14, 1944

Whitehouse, J. (Warwicks) b April 8, 1949

*Whitelaw, P. E. (Auck.) b Feb. 10, 1910, d Aug. 28, 1988

Whiteside, J. P. (Lancs & Leics) b June 11, 1861, d March 8, 1946

Whitfield, E. W. (Surrey & Northants) b May 31, 1911, d Aug. 10, 1996

Whitington, R. S. (S. Aust. & Victory Tests; writer) b June 30, 1912, d March 13, 1984

*Whitney, M. R. (NSW & Glos) b Feb. 24, 1959

Whittaker, G. J. (Surrey) b May 29, 1916, d April 20, 1997

Whitticase, P. (Leics) b March 15, 1965

Whittingham, N. B. (Notts) b Oct. 22, 1940

*Whitty, W. J. (S. Aust.) b Aug. 15, 1886, d Jan. 30, 1974

*Whysall, W. W. (Notts; *CY 1925*) b Oct. 31, 1887, d Nov. 11, 1930

*Wickremasinghe, A. G. D. (NCC) b Dec. 27, 1965

*Wiener, J. M. (Vic.) b May 1, 1955

*Wight, C. V. (BG) b July 28, 1902, d Oct. 4, 1969

*Wight, G. L. (BG) b May 28, 1929

Wight, P. B. (BG, Som & Cant.) b June 25, 1930

*Wijegunawardene, K. I. W. (CCC) b Nov. 23, 1964

*Wijesuriya, R. G. C. E. (Mor. & Colts) b Feb. 18, 1960

*Wijetunge, P. K. (SSC & Moors) b Aug. 6, 1971

Wilcox, D. R. (Essex & CU) b June 4, 1910, d Feb. 6, 1953

Wild, D. J. (Northants) b Nov. 28, 1962

*Wiles, C. A. (B'dos & T/T) b Aug. 11, 1892, d Nov. 4, 1957

Wilkins, C. P. (Derbys, Border, E. Prov. & Natal) b July 31, 1944

Wilkinson, C. T. A. (Surrey) b Oct. 4, 1884, d Dec. 16, 1970

*Wilkinson, L. L. (Lancs) b Nov. 5, 1916

Willatt, G. L. (CU, Notts & Derbys) b May 7, 1918

*Willett, E. T. (Comb. Is. & Leewards) b May 1, 1953

Willett, M. D. (Surrey) b April 21, 1933

*Willey, P. (Northants, E. Prov. & Leics; Test umpire) b Dec. 6, 1949

*Williams, A. B. (Jam.) b Nov. 21, 1949

*Williams, D. (T/T) b Nov. 4, 1963

Williams, D. L. (Glam) b Nov. 20, 1946

*Williams, E. A. V. (B'dos) b April 10, 1914, d April 13, 1997

*Williams, N. F. (Middx, Essex, Windwards & Tas.) b July 2, 1962

Williams, R. G. (Northants) b Aug. 10, 1957

*Willis, R. G. D. MBE (Surrey, Warwicks & N. Tvl; *CY 1978*) b May 30, 1949

*Willoughby, J. T. (SA) b Nov. 7, 1874, d March 11, 1952

Willsher, E. (Kent & All-England) b Nov. 22, 1828, d Oct. 7, 1885

Wilson, A. (Lancs) b April 24, 1921

Wilson, A. E. (Middx & Glos) b May 18, 1910

*Wilson, Rev. C. E. M. (CU & Yorks) b May 15, 1875, d Feb. 8, 1944

*Wilson, D. (Yorks) b Aug. 7, 1937

Wilson, E. R. (Betty) (Australia Women) b Nov. 21, 1921

*Wilson, E. R. (CU & Yorks) b March 25, 1879, d July 21, 1957

Wilson, G. (CU & Yorks) b Aug. 21, 1895, d Nov. 29, 1960

Wilson, H. L. (Sussex) b June 27, 1881, d March 15, 1937

*Wilson, J. V. (Yorks; *CY 1961*) b Jan. 17, 1921

Wilson, J. W. (Otago) b Oct. 24, 1973

*Wilson, J. W. (Vic. & S. Aust.) b Aug. 20, 1921, d Oct. 13, 1985

Wilson, M. R. (E. Prov.; ICC referee) b Sept. 8, 1944

Wilson, R. C. (Kent) b Feb. 18, 1928

*Wimble, C. S. (Tvl) b April 22, 1861, d Jan. 28, 1930

Windows, A. R. (Glos & CU) b Sept. 25, 1942

Winfield, H. M. (Notts) b June 13, 1933

Winrow, H. F. (Notts) b Jan. 17, 1916, d Aug. 19, 1973

*Winslow, P. L. (Sussex, Tvl & Rhod.) b May 21, 1929

Wisden, John (Sussex; founder John Wisden & Co and *Wisden's Cricketers' Almanack; special portrait 1913*) b Sept. 5, 1826, d April 5, 1884

*Wishart, K. L. (BG) b Nov. 28, 1908, d Oct. 18, 1972

Wolton, A. V. (Warwicks) b June 12, 1919, d Sept. 9, 1990

*Wood, A. (Yorks; *CY 1939*) b Aug. 25, 1898, d April 1, 1973

*Wood, B. (Yorks, Lancs, Derbys & E. Prov.) b Dec. 26, 1942

Wood, C. J. B. (Leics) b Nov. 21, 1875, d June 5, 1960

Wood, D. J. (Sussex) b May 19, 1914, d March 12, 1989

*Wood, G. E. C. (CU & Kent) b Aug. 22, 1893, d March 18, 1971

*Wood, G. M. (W. Aust.) b Nov. 6, 1956

*Wood, H. (Kent & Surrey; *CY 1891*) b Dec. 14, 1854, d April 30, 1919

*Wood, R. (Lancs & Vic.) b March 7, 1860, d Jan. 6, 1915

*Woodcock, A. J. (S. Aust.) b Feb. 27, 1948

Woodcock, John C. OBE (Writer; Editor of *Wisden* 1981-86) b Aug. 7, 1926

*Woodfull, W. M. OBE (Vic.; *CY 1927*) b Aug. 22, 1897, d Aug. 11, 1965

Woodhead, F. G. (Notts) b Oct. 30, 1912, d May 24, 1991

**Woods, S. M. J. (CU & Som; *CY 1889*) b April 13, 1867, d April 30, 1931

Wooler, W. (CU & Glam) b Nov. 20, 1912, d March 10, 1997

Woolley, C. N. (Glos & Northants) b May 5, 1886, d Nov. 3, 1962

*Woolley, F. E. (Kent; *CY 1911*) b May 27, 1887, d Oct. 18, 1978

*Woolley, R. D. (Tas.) b Sept. 16, 1954

*Woolmer, R. A. (Kent, Natal & W. Prov.; *CY 1976*) b May 14, 1948

*Worrall, J. (Vic.) b June 21, 1861, d Nov. 17, 1937

*Worrell, Sir Frank M. M. (B'dos & Jam.; *CY 1951*) b Aug. 1, 1924, d March 13, 1967

Worsley, D. R. (OU & Lancs) b July 18, 1941

*Worthington, T. S. (Derbys; *CY 1937*) b Aug. 21, 1905, d Aug. 31, 1973

Wrathall, H. (Glos) b Feb. 1, 1869, d June 1, 1944

Wright, A. C. (Kent) b April 4, 1895, d May 26, 1959

Wright, A. J. (Glos) b June 27, 1962

*Wright, C. W. (CU & Notts) b May 27, 1863, d Jan. 10, 1936

*Wright, D. V. P. (Kent; *CY 1940*) b Aug. 21, 1914, d Nov. 13, 1998

Wright, Graeme A. (Editor of *Wisden* 1987-92 & 2001) b April 23, 1943

*Wright, J. G. MBE (N. Dist., Derbys, Cant. & Auck.) b July 5, 1954

*Wright, K. J. (W. Aust. & S. Aust.) b Dec. 27, 1953

Wright, L. G. (Derbys; *CY 1906*) b June 15, 1862, d Jan. 11, 1953

Wright, W. (Notts & Kent) b Feb. 29, 1856, d March 22, 1940

*Wyatt, R. E. S. (Warwicks & Worcs; *CY 1930*) b May 2, 1901, d April 20, 1995

*Wynne, O. E. (Tvl & W. Prov.) b June 1, 1919, d July 13, 1975

*Wynyard, E. G. (Hants) b April 1, 1861, d Oct. 30, 1936

Yachad, M. (Tvl) b Nov. 17, 1960

*Yadav, N. S. (H'bad) b Jan. 26, 1957

*Yadav, V. S. (Haryana) b March 14, 1967

*Yajurvindra Singh (M'tra & S'tra) b Aug. 1, 1952

*Yallop, G. N. (Vic.) b Oct. 7, 1952

*Yardley, B. (W. Aust.) b Sept. 5, 1947

*Yardley, N. W. D. (CU & Yorks; *CY 1948*) b March 19, 1915, d Oct. 4, 1989

Yardley, T. J. (Worcs & Northants) b Oct. 27, 1946

Yarnold, H. (Worcs) b July 6, 1917, d Aug. 13, 1974

*Yashpal Sharma (Punjab) b Aug. 11, 1954

Yawar Saeed (Som & Punjab) b Jan. 22, 1935

*Yograj Singh (Haryana & Punjab) b March 25, 1958

Young, A. (Som) b Nov. 6, 1890, d April 2, 1936

*Young, B. A. (N. Dist. & Auck.) b Nov. 3, 1964

Young, D. M. (Worcs & Glos) b April 15, 1924, d June 18, 1993

Young, H. I. (Essex) b Feb. 5, 1876, d Dec. 12, 1964

*Young, J. A. (Middx) b Oct. 14, 1912, d Feb. 5, 1993

*Young, R. A. (CU & Sussex) b Sept. 16, 1885, d July 1, 1968

*Younis Ahmed (Lahore, Kar., Surrey, PIA, S. Aust., Worcs & Glam) b Oct. 20, 1947

*Yuile, B. W. (C. Dist.) b Oct. 29, 1941

*Zaheer Abbas (Kar., Glos, PWD, Dawood Ind., Sind & PIA; *CY 1972*) b July 24, 1947

Zakir Hassan (Bangladesh) b Dec. 1, 1972

*Zakir Khan (Sind, Peshawar & ADBP) b April 3, 1963

Zesers, A. K. (S. Aust.) b March 11, 1967

*Zoehrer, T. J. (W. Aust.) b Sept. 25, 1961

*Zulch, J. W. (Tvl) b Jan. 2, 1886, d May 19, 1924

*Zulfiqar Ahmed (B'pur & PIA) b Nov. 22, 1926

*Zulqarnain (Pak. Rlwys, Lahore, HBFC & PACO) b May 25, 1962

REGISTER OF CURRENT PLAYERS

The qualifications for inclusion are as follows:

1. All players who appeared in Tests or one-day internationals for a Test-playing country in 1999-2000 or 2000.

2. All players who appeared in the County Championship in 2000.

3. All players who appeared in the Pura Milk Cup, Supersport Series, Busta Cup, Shell Conference and Duleep Trophy in 1999-2000.

4. All players who appeared in first-class domestic cricket in 1999-2000 or 2000, who have also played in Tests or one-day international cricket.

5. All players who appeared in one-day internationals for Bangladesh and Kenya in 1999-2000.

6. All players who appeared in first-class cricket for their national A-team in 1999-2000.

Notes: The forename by which the player is known is underlined if it is not his first name.

Teams are those played for in 1999-2000 and/or 2000, or the last domestic team for which that player appeared.

Countries are those for which players are qualified.

The country of birth is given if it is not the one for which a player is qualified. It is also given to differentiate between nations in the Leeward and Windward Islands, and where it is essential for clarity.

* *Denotes Test player.*

	Team	Country	Born	Birthplace
Aamer Hanif	Allied Bank	P	4.10.71	*Karachi*
* **Aamir Nazir**	Allied Bank	P	2.1.71	*Lahore*
* **Aamir Sohail**	Allied Bank	P	14.9.66	*Lahore*
Ababu Josephat	Kenya	K	15.4.80	*Kenya*
Abbas Ali Syed	Madhya Pradesh	I	20.2.76	*Indore*
* **Abdur Razzaq**	PIA	P	2.12.79	*Lahore*
Abrahams Andre Peter	Free State	SA	25.1.81	*Springbok*
Abrahams Shafiek	Eastern Province	SA	4.3.68	*Port Elizabeth*
Abrahim Zahir Ahmed	Griqualand West	SA	5.6.72	*Robertson*
* **Ackerman** Hylton Deon	Western Province	SA	14.2.73	*Cape Town*
Ackermann Sean	Western Province	SA	6.6.77	*Cape Town*
* **Adams** Christopher John	Sussex	E	6.5.70	*Whitwell*
Adams Fabian <u>Alex</u>	Leeward Islands	WI	7.1.75	*The Valley, Anguilla*
* **Adams** James <u>Clive</u>	Jamaica	WI	9.1.68	*Port Maria*
Adams Kristian	Kent	E	26.11.76	*Cleethorpes*
* **Adams** Paul Regan	Western Province	SA	20.1.77	*Cape Town*
Afzaal Usman	Nottinghamshire	E	9.6.77	*Rawalpindi, Pakistan*
* **Agarkar** Ajit Bhalchandra	Mumbai	I	4.12.77	*Bombay*
Ahmed Kamal	Bangladesh	B	28.12.77	*Court Para*
Akhtar Sarfraz	National Bank	P	20.2.76	*Peshawar*
Akram Khan	Bangladesh	B	1.11.68	*Chittagong*
* **Akram Raza**	Habib Bank	P	22.11.64	*Lahore*
Aldred Paul	Derbyshire	E	4.2.69	*Chellaston*
Ali Kabir	Worcestershire	E	24.11.80	*Moseley*
Ali Kadeer	Worcestershire	E	7.3.83	*Moseley*
Ali Syed <u>Muazam</u>	Durham	E	23.10.79	*Whipps Cross*
* **Ali Hussain Rizvi**	Karachi	P	6.1.74	*Karachi*
* **Ali Naqvi**	Customs	P	19.3.77	*Lahore*
Alleyne Mark Wayne	Gloucestershire	E	23.5.68	*Tottenham*
* †**Allott** Geoffrey Ian	Canterbury	NZ	24.12.71	*Christchurch*
Al-Shahriar Rokon	Bangladesh	B	23.4.78	*Dhaka*
Altree Darren Anthony	Warwickshire	E	30.9.74	*Rugby*
* **Ambrose** Curtly Elconn Lynwall	Leeward Islands	WI	21.9.63	*Swetes Village, Antigua*
Amin Rupesh Mahesh	Surrey	E	20.8.77	*Clapham*
Aminul Islam, sen.	Bangladesh	B	2.2.68	*Dhaka*

† *Allott did not play in 1999-2000, but returned in 2000-01.*

	Team	Country	Born	Birthplace
Amla Ahmed Mahomed	KwaZulu-Natal	SA	15.9.79	*Durban*
* **Amre** Pravin Kalyan	Boland	I	14.8.68	*Bombay*
Anderson Matthew Allan	Queensland	A	10.11.76	*Darwin*
Anderson Ricaldo Sherman Glenroy	Essex	E	22.9.76	*Hammersmith*
Andrews Sean Edward	Eastern Province	SA	20.1.78	*Cape Town*
* **Angel** Jo	Western Australia	A	22.4.68	*Mount Lawley*
* **Aqib** Javed	Allied Bank	P	5.8.72	*Sheikhupura*
Arnberger Jason Lee	Victoria	A	18.11.72	*Penrith*
* **Arnold** Russel Premakumaran	Nondescripts	SL	25.10.73	*Colombo*
* **Arshad** Khan	Allied Bank	P	22.3.71	*Peshawar*
Arthur John <u>Michael</u>	Griqualand West	SA	17.5.68	*Johannesburg*
* **Arthurton** Keith Lloyd Thomas	Leeward Islands	WI	21.2.65	*Charlestown, Nevis*
Arun Kumar Jagdish	Karnataka	I	18.1.75	*Bangalore*
* **Ashfaq** Ahmed	Lahore City	P	6.6.73	*Lahore*
Asif Mahmood	Pakistan Reserves	P	18.12.75	*Rawalpindi*
* **Asif** Mujtaba	PIA	P	4.11.67	*Karachi*
* **Astle** Nathan John	Canterbury	NZ	15.9.71	*Christchurch*
* **Atapattu** Marvan Samson	Sinhalese	SL	22.11.70	*Kalutara*
* **Ata-ur-Rehman**	Allied Bank	P	28.3.75	*Lahore*
* **Atherton** Michael Andrew	Lancashire	E	23.3.68	*Manchester*
* **Atiq-uz-Zaman**	Pakistan Reserves	P	20.7.75	*Karachi*
Atkinson Mark Neville	Tasmania	A	11.2.69	*Sydney*
Austin Ian David	Lancashire	E	30.5.66	*Haslingden*
Averis James Maxwell Michael	Gloucestershire	E	28.5.74	*Bristol*
Ayer Razeen Steve	Easterns	SA	10.11.79	*Benoni*
Aymes Adrian Nigel	Hampshire	E	4.6.64	*Southampton*
* **Azam** Khan	Customs	P	1.3.69	*Karachi*
* **Azhar** Mahmood	PIA	P	28.2.75	*Rawalpindi*
* **Azharuddin** Mohammad	Hyderabad	I	8.2.63	*Hyderabad*
* **Bacher** Adam Marc	Gauteng	SA	29.10.73	*Johannesburg*
Badani Hemang Kamal	Tamil Nadu	I	14.11.76	*Madras*
Bahutule Sairaj Vasant	Mumbai	I	6.1.73	*Bombay*
Bailey Mark David	Northern Districts	NZ	26.11.70	*Hamilton*
* **Bailey** Robert John	Derbyshire	E	28.10.63	*Biddulph*
Bailey Tobin Michael Barnaby	Northamptonshire	E	28.8.76	*Kettering*
Baker Robert Michael	Western Australia	A	24.7.75	*Osborne Park*
Bakker Jason Richard	Victoria	A	12.11.67	*Geelong*
Bakkes Herman Charles	Free State	SA	24.12.69	*Port Elizabeth*
Ball Martyn Charles John	Gloucestershire	E	26.4.70	*Bristol*
Balliram Anil	Trinidad & Tobago	WI	27.2.74	*Trinidad*
* **Bandara** Charitha <u>Malinga</u>	Nondescripts	SL	31.12.79	*Kalutara*
* **Bandaratilleke** Mapa Rallage Chandima <u>Niroshan</u>	Tamil Union	SL	16.5.75	*Colombo*
Bangar Sanjay Bapusaheb	Railways	I	11.10.72	*Beed*
* **Baptiste** Eldine Ashworth Elderfield	KwaZulu-Natal	WI	12.3.60	*Liberta, Antigua*
Barik Ajay	Orissa	I	10.1.76	*Cuttack*
Barnard Pieter Hendrik	Griqualand West	SA	8.5.70	*Nelspruit*
Barnes Aaron Craig	Auckland	NZ	21.12.71	*Turangi*
* **Barnett** Kim John	Gloucestershire	E	17.7.60	*Stoke-on-Trent*
Bates Justin Jonathan	Sussex	E	9.4.76	*Farnborough, Hants*
Batt Christopher James	Middlesex	E	22.9.76	*Taplow*
Batty Jonathan Neil	Surrey	E	18.4.74	*Chesterfield*
Bedade Atul Chandrakant	Baroda	I	24.9.66	*Bombay*
* **Bell** Matthew David	Wellington	NZ	25.2.77	*Dunedin*
Benfield Mark Rowland	Eastern Province	SA	3.12.76	*Potgietersrus*
* **Benjamin** Kenneth Charlie Griffith	Gauteng	WI	8.4.67	*St John's, Antigua*
Benkenstein Dale Martin	KwaZulu-Natal	SA	9.6.74	*Salisbury, Rhodesia*
Benn Sulieman Jamaal	Barbados	WI	22.7.81	*Haynesville*
Berry Darren Shane	Victoria	A	10.12.69	*Melbourne*

	Team	Country	Born	Birthplace
Betts Melvyn Morris	Durham	E	26.3.75	Sacriston
Beukes Jonathan Alan	Free State	SA	15.3.79	Kimberley
*** Bevan** Michael Gwyl	New South Wales/Sussex	A	8.5.70	Belconnen
Bhandari Amit	Delhi	I	1.10.78	Delhi
*** Bharadwaj** Raghvendrarao Vijay	Karnataka	I	15.8.75	Bangalore
*** Bichel** Andrew John	Queensland	A	27.8.70	Laidley
Bicknell Darren John	Nottinghamshire	E	24.6.67	Guildford
*** Bicknell** Martin Paul	Surrey	E	14.1.69	Guildford
Bishop Ian Emlyn	Surrey	E	26.8.77	Taunton
Black Marlon Ian	Trinidad & Tobago	WI	7.6.75	Trinidad
Blackman Wayne Ricardo	Barbados	WI	25.12.75	Waterhall
Blackwell Ian David	Somerset	E	10.6.78	Chesterfield
Blain John Angus Rae	Northamptonshire	S	4.1.79	Edinburgh
*** Blakey** Richard John	Yorkshire	E	15.1.67	Huddersfield
Blewett Gregory Scott	South Australia	A	29.10.71	Adelaide
Blignaut Arnoldus Mauritius	Mashonaland	Z	1.8.78	Salisbury
Bloomfield Timothy Francis	Middlesex	E	31.5.73	Ashford, Middlesex
Bodi Ghulam Hussain	KwaZulu-Natal	SA	4.1.79	Hathuran, India
*** Boje** Nico	Free State	SA	20.3.73	Bloemfontein
Bosman Lungile Loots	Griqualand West	SA	14.4.77	Kimberley
Bossenger Wendell	Griqualand West	SA	23.10.76	Cape Town
Boswell Scott Antony John	Leicestershire	E	11.9.74	Fulford
Boteju Jayawardene Welathanthrige Hemantha Devapriya	Colombo	SL	3.11.77	Colombo
Botha Andre Cornelius	Griqualand West	SA	12.9.75	Johannesburg
Botha Anthony Greyvensteyn	Easterns	SA	17.11.76	Pretoria
Botha Peterus Johannes	Border	SA	28.9.66	Vereeniging
*** Boucher** Mark Verdon	Border	SA	3.12.76	East London
Bowen Mark Nicholas	Nottinghamshire	E	6.12.67	Redcar
Bowler Peter Duncan	Somerset	E	30.7.63	Plymouth
Bracken Nathan Wade	New South Wales	A	12.9.77	Penrith
*** Bradburn** Grant Eric	Northern Districts	NZ	26.5.66	Hamilton
Bradfield Carl Crispin	Eastern Province	SA	18.1.75	Grahamstown
Bradshaw Ian David Russell	Barbados	WI	9.7.74	Hopewell
Bradstreet Shawn David	New South Wales	A	28.2.72	Wollongong
Brand Derek	Easterns	SA	29.5.75	Bellville
Brandes Eddo Andre	Mashonaland	Z	5.3.63	Port Shepstone, SA
Breese Gareth Rohan	Jamaica	WI	9.1.76	Montego Bay
*** Brent** Gary Bazil	Manicaland	Z	13.1.76	Sinoia
Bressington Alastair Nigel	Gloucestershire	E	28.11.79	Bristol
Brooker Finley Clint	Griqualand West	SA	26.12.72	Kimberley
Brophy Gerard Louis	Free State	SA	26.11.75	Welkom
Brown Alistair Duncan	Surrey	E	11.2.70	Beckenham
Brown Darryl	Trinidad & Tobago	WI	18.12.73	McBean
Brown Douglas Robert	Warwickshire	E	29.10.69	Stirling, Scotland
Brown Jason Fred	Northamptonshire	E	10.10.74	Newcastle-under-Lyme
*** Brown** Simon John Emmerson	Durham	E	29.6.69	Cleadon
*** Browne** Courtney Oswald	Barbados	WI	7.12.70	Lambeth, England
Bruyns Mark Lloyd	KwaZulu-Natal	SA	8.11.73	Pietermaritzburg
Bryan Henderson Ricardo	Barbados	WI	21.3.70	Barbados
Bryant James Douglas Campbell	Eastern Province	SA	4.2.76	Durban
Bulbeck Matthew Paul Leonard	Somerset	E	8.11.79	Taunton
Bulfin Carl Edwin	Central Districts	NZ	19.8.73	Blenheim
Bundela Devendra Singh	Madhya Pradesh	I	22.2.77	Indore
*** Burmester** Mark Greville	Manicaland	Z	24.1.68	Durban, South Africa
Burns Michael	Somerset	E	2.6.69	Barrow-in-Furness
Burns Neil David	Leicestershire	E	19.9.65	Chelmsford
Butcher Gary Paul	Surrey	E	11.3.75	Clapham
*** Butcher** Mark Alan	Surrey	E	23.8.72	Croydon
Byas David	Yorkshire	E	26.8.63	Kilham

	Team	Country	Born	Birthplace
* **Caddick** Andrew Richard	Somerset	E	21.11.68	*Christchurch, NZ*
* **Cairns** Christopher Lance	Canterbury	NZ	13.6.70	*Picton*
Callaghan David John	Eastern Province	SA	1.2.65	*Queenstown*
* **Campbell** Alistair Douglas Ross	Mashonaland	Z	23.9.72	*Salisbury*
Campbell Donald James Ross	Mashonaland	Z	24.6.74	*Salisbury*
Campbell Ryan John	Western Australia	A	7.2.72	*Osborne Park*
* **Campbell** Sherwin Legay	Barbados	WI	1.11.70	*Bridgetown*
Canning Tamahau Karangatukituki	Auckland	NZ	7.4.77	*Rose Park, Australia*
Cannonier Colin Darren	Leeward Islands	WI	22.5.73	*Antigua*
* **Carlisle** Stuart Vance	Mashonaland	Z	10.5.72	*Salisbury*
Carter Neil Miller	Boland	SA	29.1.75	*Cape Town*
Cary Sean Ross	Western Australia	A	10.3.71	*Subiaco*
Cassar Matthew Edward	Derbyshire	E	16.10.72	*Sydney, Australia*
Cawdron Michael John	Gloucestershire	E	7.10.74	*Luton*
Chan Navin Indaraj	Trinidad & Tobago	WI	29.12.78	*Port of Spain*
* **Chandana** Umagiliya Durage Upul	Tamil Union	SL	7.5.72	*Galle*
* **Chanderpaul** Shivnarine	Guyana	WI	18.8.74	*Unity Village*
Chapple Glen	Lancashire	E	23.1.74	*Skipton*
Chatterjee Utpal	Bengal	I	13.7.64	*Calcutta*
* **Chauhan** Rajesh Kumar	Madhya Pradesh	I	19.12.66	*Ranchi*
Chilton Mark James	Lancashire	E	2.10.76	*Sheffield*
Chopra Nikhil	Delhi	I	26.12.73	*Allahabad*
Christopher Ricky Joseph	Leeward Islands	WI		*Antigua*
Cilliers Sarel Arnold	Free State	SA	6.6.71	*Klerksdorp*
Clarke Vincent John	New South Wales	A	2.4.81	*Liverpool*
Coetzee Ralph Terence	Easterns	SA	1.10.71	*Pinelands*
Collingwood Paul David	Durham	E	26.5.76	*Shotley Bridge*
* **Collins** Pedro Tyrone	Barbados	WI	12.8.76	*Boscobelle*
* **Collymore** Corey Dalanelo	Barbados	WI	21.12.77	*Boscobelle*
* **Commins** John Brian	Western Province	SA	19.2.65	*East London*
Conyers Mark Andrew	Easterns	SA	23.9.77	*Oranjemund, SW Africa*
Cook Jeffrey William	Northamptonshire	E	2.2.72	*Sydney, Australia*
Cook Simon James	Middlesex	E	15.1.77	*Oxford*
Copeland Craig Anthony	Griqualand West	SA	2.1.77	*Cape Town*
* **Cork** Dominic Gerald	Derbyshire	E	7.8.71	*Newcastle-under-Lyme*
Cornwall Wilden Winston	Leeward Islands	WI	29.4.73	*Antigua*
Cosker Dean Andrew	Glamorgan	E	7.1.78	*Weymouth*
Cotterell Thomas Paul	Gloucestershire	E	9.3.77	*Hounslow*
Cottey Phillip Anthony	Sussex	E	2.6.66	*Swansea*
Cousins Darren Mark	Northamptonshire	E	24.9.71	*Cambridge*
Cowan Ashley Preston	Essex	E	7.5.75	*Hitchin*
Cox Jamie	Tasmania/Somerset	A	15.10.69	*Burnie*
Craig Shawn Andrew Jacob	Victoria	A	23.6.73	*Carlton*
Craven Victor John	Yorkshire	E	31.7.80	*Harrogate*
* **Crawley** John Paul	Lancashire	E	21.9.71	*Maldon*
Creed Murray Wayne	Eastern Province	SA	5.3.79	*Port Elizabeth*
* **Croft** Robert Damien Bale	Glamorgan	E	25.5.70	*Morriston*
* **Cronje** Wessel Johannes (Hansie)	Free State	SA	25.9.69	*Bloemfontein*
Crookes Derek Norman	Gauteng	SA	5.3.69	*Mariannhill*
Crowe Carl Daniel	Leicestershire	E	25.11.75	*Leicester*
Croy Martyn Gilbert	Otago	NZ	23.1.74	*Hamilton*
* **Cuffy** Cameron Eustace	Windward Islands	WI	8.2.70	*South Rivers, St Vincent*
* **Cullinan** Daryll John	Gauteng	SA	4.3.67	*Kimberley*
Cumming Craig Derek	Canterbury	NZ	31.8.75	*Timaru*
Cunliffe Robert John	Gloucestershire	E	8.11.73	*Oxford*
Dagnall Charles Edward	Warwickshire	E	10.7.76	*Bury*
Dahiya Vijay	Delhi	I	10.5.73	*Delhi*
Dakin Jonathan Michael	Leicestershire	E	28.2.73	*Hitchin*

	Team	Country	Born	Birthplace
* **Dale** Adam Craig	Queensland	A	30.12.68	*Ivanhoe*
Dale Adrian	Glamorgan	E	24.10.68	*Germiston, South Africa*
Daley James Arthur	Durham	E	24.9.73	*Sunderland*
Dani Ashu	Delhi	I	3.10.74	*Delhi*
Danish Kaneria	Pakistan Reserves	P	16.12.80	*Karachi*
Darlington Kevin Godfrey	Guyana	WI	26.4.72	*Guyana*
Das Shiv Sunder	Orissa	I	5.11.77	*Bhubaneshwar*
* **Dassanayake** Pubudu Bathiya	Bloomfield	SL	11.7.70	*Kandy*
Davies Christopher James	South Australia	A	15.11.78	*Adelaide*
Davies Michael Kenton	Northamptonshire	E	17.7.76	*Ashby-de-la-Zouch*
Davis Mark Jeffrey Gronow	Northerns	SA	10.10.71	*Port Elizabeth*
Davison John Michael	Victoria	A	9.5.70	*Campbell River, Canada*
Davison Rodney John	New South Wales	A	26.6.69	*Kogarah*
Dawes Joseph Henry	Queensland	A	29.8.70	*Herston*
Dawson Alan Charles	Western Province	SA	27.11.69	*Cape Town*
Dean Kevin James	Derbyshire	E	16.10.75	*Derby*
de Bruyn Pierre	Easterns	SA	31.3.77	*Pretoria*
de Bruyn Zander	Gauteng	SA	5.7.75	*Johannesburg*
* **DeFreitas** Phillip Anthony Jason	Leicestershire	E	18.2.66	*Scotts Head, Dominica*
De Groot Nicholas Alexander	Guyana	WI	22.10.75	*Guyana*
Deitz Shane Andrew	South Australia	A	4.5.75	*Bankstown*
Denton Gerard John	Tasmania	A	7.8.75	*Mount Isa*
* **de Saram** Samantha Indika	Tamil Union	SL	2.9.73	*Matara*
* **de Silva** Karunakalage Sajeewa Chanaka	Burgher	SL	11.1.71	*Kalutara*
* **de Silva** Pinnaduwage Aravinda	Nondescripts	SL	17.10.65	*Colombo*
* **de Silva** Sanjeewa Kumara Lanka	Colombo	SL	29.7.75	*Kurunegala*
de Vos Dirk Johannes Jacobus	Northerns	SA	15.6.75	*Pretoria*
de Vos Hendrik Moller	North West	SA	5.10.69	*Klerksdorp*
Dharmani Pankaj	Punjab	I	27.9.74	*Delhi*
* **Dharmasena** Handunnettige Deepthi Priyantha Kumar	Bloomfield	SL	24.4.71	*Colombo*
Dighe Samir Sudhakar	Mumbai	I	8.10.68	*Bombay*
Dighton Michael Gray	Western Australia	A	24.7.76	*Toowoomba*
* **Dillon** Mervyn	Trinidad & Tobago	WI	5.6.74	*Toco*
* **Dilshan** Tillekeratne Mudiyanselage	Sebastianites	SL	14.10.76	*Kalutara*
* **Dippenaar** Hendrik Human	Free State	SA	14.6.77	*Kimberley*
Di Venuto Michael James	Tasmania/Derbyshire	A	12.12.73	*Hobart*
Dixon Troy James	Queensland	A	22.12.69	*Geelong*
Dobson Derrick Kevin	Griqualand West	SA	23.9.78	*Kimberley*
* **Donald** Allan Anthony	Free State/Warwickshire	SA	20.10.66	*Bloemfontein*
Douglas Mark William	Central Districts	NZ	20.10.68	*Nelson*
* **Doull** Simon Blair	Northern Districts	NZ	6.8.69	*Pukekohe*
Dowlin Travis Montague	Guyana	WI	24.2.77	*Georgetown*
Dowman Mathew Peter	Derbyshire	E	10.5.74	*Grantham*
Downton Andrew Graham	Tasmania	A	17.7.77	*Auburn*
Drakes Vasbert Conniel	Border	WI	5.8.69	*St James*
* **Dravid** Rahul	Karnataka/Kent	I	11.1.73	*Indore*
Dreyer Jan Nicolaas	North West	SA	9.9.76	*Amanzimtoti*
Driver Ryan Craig	Worcestershire	E	30.4.79	*Truro*
Dros Gerald	Northerns	SA	2.4.73	*Pretoria*
Drum Christopher James	Auckland	NZ	10.7.74	*Auckland*
Dry Willem Moolman	Griqualand West	SA	9.1.71	*Vryburg*
Dutch Keith Philip	Middlesex	E	21.3.73	*Harrow*
Dykes James Andrew	Tasmania	A	15.11.71	*Hobart*
* **Ealham** Mark Alan	Kent	E	27.8.69	*Willesborough*
Ebrahim Dion Digby	Matabeleland	Z	7.8.80	*Bulawayo*
* **Eksteen** Clive Edward	Gauteng	SA	2.12.66	*Johannesburg*
Elliott Grant David	Griqualand West	SA	21.3.79	*Johannesburg*
* **Elliott** Matthew Thomas Gray	Victoria/Glamorgan	A	28.9.71	*Chelsea*

	Team	Country	Born	Birthplace
Elstub Christopher John	Yorkshire	E	3.2.81	Dewsbury
* **Elworthy** Steven	Northerns	SA	23.2.65	Bulawayo, Rhodesia
Enamul Haque	Bangladesh	B	27.2.67	Comilla
Englefield Jarrod Ian	Central Districts	NZ	18.12.79	Blenheim
Enslin Christian Thinus	North West	SA	16.9.75	Klerksdorp
Erasmus Frikkie	Easterns	SA	17.5.74	Boksburg
Evans Alun Wyn	Glamorgan	E	20.8.75	Glanamman
* **Evans** Craig Neil	Mashonaland	Z	29.11.69	Salisbury
* **Fairbrother** Neil Harvey	Lancashire	E	9.9.63	Warrington
Faisal Iqbal	Pakistan Reserves	P	30.12.81	Karachi
* **Fazl-e-Akbar**	Pakistan Reserves	P	20.10.80	Peshawar
Fellows Gary Matthew	Yorkshire	E	30.7.78	Halifax
Fernando Upekha Ashantha	Sinhalese	SL	17.12.79	Colombo
Fernando Kandana Aratchchige Dinusha Manoj	Sebastianites	SL	10.8.79	Panadura
* **Fernando** Conganige Randhi Dilhara	Sinhalese	SL	19.7.79	Colombo
Fernando Sajith Ian	Colts	SL	27.9.72	Kandy
Fernando Ungamandalige Nisal Kumudusiri	Burgher	SL	10.3.70	Colombo
Ferreira Lloyd Douglas	Western Province	SA	6.5.74	Johannesburg
Ferreira Neil Robert	Manicaland	Z	3.6.79	Salisbury
Fisher Ian Douglas	Yorkshire	E	31.5.76	Bradford
Fitzgerald David Andrew	South Australia	A	30.11.72	Osborne Park
Flanagan Ian Nicholas	Essex	E	5.6.80	Colchester
* **Fleming** Damien William	Victoria	A	24.4.70	Bentley
Fleming Matthew Valentine	Kent	E	12.12.64	Macclesfield
* **Fleming** Stephen Paul	Canterbury	NZ	1.4.73	Christchurch
* **Flintoff** Andrew	Lancashire	E	6.12.77	Preston
* **Flower** Andrew	Mashonaland	Z	28.4.68	Cape Town, SA
* **Flower** Grant William	Mashonaland	Z	20.12.70	Salisbury
Flusk Gareth Edward	Easterns	SA	8.11.74	Johannesburg
Foley Geoffrey Ian	Queensland	A	11.10.67	Jandowae
Foster James Savin	Essex	E	15.4.80	Whipps Cross
Fourie Gerald	Free State	SA	29.1.76	Virginia
Francis Simon Richard George	Hampshire	E	15.8.78	Bromley
Franks Paul John	Nottinghamshire	E	3.2.79	Mansfield
* **Fraser** Angus Robert Charles	Middlesex	E	8.8.65	Billinge
Fulton David Paul	Kent	E	15.11.71	Lewisham
Gaffaney Christopher Blair	Otago	NZ	30.11.75	Dunedin
Gain Douglas Robert	Boland	SA	29.12.76	Johannesburg
Gait Andrew Ian	Free State	SA	19.12.78	Bulawayo, Rhodesia
* **Gallage** Indika Sanjeewa	Colombo	SL	22.11.75	Panadura
* **Gallian** Jason Edward Riche	Nottinghamshire	E	25.6.71	Sydney, Australia
Gamiet Laden Liep	Border	SA	23.1.78	East London
Gandhe Pritam Vithal	Vidarbha	I	6.8.71	Nagpur
* **Gandhi** Devang Jayant	Bengal	I	6.9.71	Bhavnagar
* **Ganesh** Doddanarasiah	Karnataka	I	30.6.73	Bangalore
* **Ganga** Daren	Trinidad & Tobago	WI	14.1.79	Barrackpore
* **Ganguly** Sourav Chandidas	Bengal/Lancashire	I	8.7.72	Calcutta
Gannon Benjamin Ward	Gloucestershire	E	5.9.75	Oxford
Gavaskar Rohan Sunil	Bengal	I	20.2.76	Kanpur
* **Gayle** Christopher Henry	Jamaica	WI	21.9.79	Kingston
Ghulam Ali	PIA	P	8.9.66	Karachi
* **Gibbs** Herschelle Herman	Western Province	SA	23.2.74	Cape Town
Gibson Ottis Delroy	Griqualand West	WI	16.3.69	Sion Hill, Barbados
* **Giddins** Edward Simon Hunter	Warwickshire	E	20.7.71	Eastbourne
Gidley Martyn Ian	Griqualand West	SA	30.9.68	Leicester, England
* **Gilchrist** Adam Craig	Western Australia	A	14.11.71	Bellingen
Gilder Gary Michael	KwaZulu-Natal	SA	6.7.74	Salisbury, Rhodesia

	Team	Country	Born	Birthplace
* **Giles** Ashley Fraser	Warwickshire	E	19.3.73	*Chertsey*
* **Gillespie** Jason Neil	South Australia	A	19.4.75	*Darlinghurst*
* **Gonsalves** Andrew	Guyana	WI	31.5.78	*Suddie*
* **Gooch** Graham Alan	MCC	E	23.7.53	*Leytonstone*
* **Goodwin** Murray William	Mashonaland	Z	11.12.72	*Salisbury, Rhodesia*
* **Gough** Darren	Yorkshire	E	18.9.70	*Barnsley*
Gough Michael Andrew	Durham	E	18.12.79	*Hartlepool*
Grace Graham Vernon	Eastern Province	SA	16.8.75	*Salisbury, Rhodesia*
Grayson Adrian Paul	Essex	E	31.3.71	*Ripon*
Greatbatch Mark John	Central Districts	NZ	11.12.63	*Auckland*
Green Richard James	Lancashire	E	13.3.76	*Warrington*
Greenidge Carl Gary	Surrey	E	20.4.78	*Basingstoke*
Griffith Adrian Frank Gordon	Barbados	WI	19.11.71	*Barbados*
* **Gripper** Trevor Raymond	Mashonaland	Z	28.12.75	*Salisbury*
Grove Jamie Oliver	Somerset	E	3.7.79	*Bury St Edmunds*
Gunawardene Aruna Alwis Wijesiri	Moors	SL	31.3.69	*Colombo*
* **Gunawardene** Dihan Avishka	Sinhalese	SL	26.5.77	*Colombo*
Guy Simon Mark	Yorkshire	E	17.11.78	*Rotherham*
* **Habib** Aftab	Leicestershire	E	7.2.72	*Reading*
Habibul Bashar	Bangladesh	B	17.8.72	*Kushtia*
Haddin Bradley James	New South Wales	A	23.10.77	*Cowra*
Haldipur Nikhil	Bengal	I	19.12.77	*Calcutta*
Hall Andrew James	Gauteng	SA	31.7.75	*Johannesburg*
* **Hamilton** Gavin Mark	Yorkshire	E	16.9.74	*Broxburn*
Hamilton Lance John	Central Districts	NZ	5.4.73	*Papakura*
Hancock Timothy Harold Coulter	Gloucestershire	E	20.4.72	*Reading*
Haniff Azeemul	Guyana	WI	24.10.77	*Guyana*
Haniff Zaheer Abbas	Guyana	WI	13.4.74	*Guyana*
* **Harbhajan Singh**	Punjab	I	3.7.80	*Jullundur*
Harden Richard John	Yorkshire	E	16.8.65	*Bridgwater*
Hardinges Mark Andrew	Gloucestershire	E	5.2.78	*Gloucester*
Harmison Stephen James	Durham	E	23.10.78	*Ashington*
Harper Laurence Damien	Victoria	A	10.12.70	*Deniliquin*
Harris Andrew James	Nottinghamshire	E	26.6.73	*Ashton-under-Lyne*
* **Harris** Chris Zinzan	Canterbury	NZ	20.11.69	*Christchurch*
Harris Danny	Windward Islands	WI		*St Lucia*
Harris Daniel Joseph	South Australia	A	31.12.79	*North Adelaide*
Harrison David Stuart	Glamorgan	E	30.7.81	*Newport*
Harrity Mark Andrew	South Australia	A	9.3.74	*Semaphore*
Hartley Peter John	Hampshire	E	18.4.60	*Keighley*
Harvey Ian Joseph	Victoria/Gloucestershire	A	10.4.72	*Wonthaggi*
* **Harvinder Singh**	Railways	I	23.12.77	*Amritsar*
* **Hasan Raza**	Habib Bank	P	11.3.82	*Karachi*
Hasibul Hussain	Bangladesh	B	3.6.77	*Dhaka*
* **Hathurusinghe** Upul Chandika	Moors	SL	13.9.68	*Colombo*
* **Hayden** Matthew Lawrence	Queensland/Northants	A	29.10.71	*Kingaroy*
Hayne Gregory John	New South Wales	A	2.10.71	*Moree*
* **Hayward** Mornantau	Eastern Province	SA	6.3.77	*Uitenhage*
Hazel Kenneth Clayton	Trinidad & Tobago	WI	6.8.71	*Santa Cruz*
* †**Headley** Dean Warren	Kent	E	27.1.70	*Stourbridge*
* **Healy** Ian Andrew	Queensland	A	30.4.64	*Spring Hill*
Hearle Philip Kenyon	Easterns	SA	31.5.78	*Johannesburg*
Heath Jamie Matthew	New South Wales	A	25.4.77	*Belmont*
* **Hegg** Warren Kevin	Lancashire	E	23.2.68	*Whitefield*
Hemp David Lloyd	Warwickshire	E	8.11.70	*Hamilton, Bermuda*
Henderson Claude William	Western Province	SA	14.6.72	*Worcester*
Henderson James Michael	Boland	SA	6.8.75	*Worcester*

† *Headley did not play in 2000, but was expected to return in 2001.*

	Team	Country	Born	Birthplace
Henderson Tyron	Border	SA	1.8.74	*Durban*
* **Herath** Rangana	Moors	SL	19.3.78	*Kurunegala*
Hewage Randy Pradeep	Nondescripts	SL	7.12.78	*Colombo*
Hewison Christopher Jon	Nottinghamshire	E	6.10.79	*Gateshead*
Hewitt Glen Michael	North West	SA	16.4.73	*Johannesburg*
Hewson Dominic Robert	Gloucestershire	E	3.10.74	*Cheltenham*
* **Hick** Graeme Ashley	Worcestershire	E	23.5.66	*Salisbury, Rhodesia*
Higgs Mark Anthony	New South Wales	A	30.6.76	*Queanbeyan*
Hills Dene Fleetwood	Tasmania	A	27.8.70	*Wynyard*
Hinds Ryan O'Neal	Barbados	WI	17.2.81	*Holders Hill*
* **Hinds** Wavell Wayne	Jamaica	WI	7.9.76	*Kingston*
* **Hirwani** Narendra Deepchand	Madhya Pradesh	I	18.10.68	*Gorakhpur*
Hockley James Bernard	Kent	E	16.4.79	*Beckenham*
Hodge Bradley John	Victoria	A	29.12.74	*Sandringham*
* **Hogg** George Bradley	Western Australia	A	6.2.71	*Narrogin*
* **Hoggard** Matthew James	Yorkshire/Free State	E	31.12.76	*Leeds*
* **Holder** Roland Irwin Christopher	Barbados	WI	22.12.67	*Port-of-Spain, Trinidad*
* **Hollioake** Adam John	Surrey	E	5.9.71	*Melbourne, Australia*
* **Hollioake** Benjamin Caine	Surrey	E	11.11.77	*Melbourne, Australia*
Holloway Piran Charles Laity	Somerset	E	1.10.70	*Helston*
Hopkins Gareth James	Canterbury	NZ	24.11.76	*Lower Hutt*
* **Horne** Matthew Jeffery	Otago	NZ	5.12.70	*Takapuna*
House William John	Sussex	E	16.3.76	*Sheffield*
Howell Llorne Gregory	Auckland	NZ	8.7.72	*Napier*
* **Hudson** Andrew Charles	KwaZulu-Natal	SA	17.3.65	*Eshowe*
Humphries Shaun	Sussex	E	11.1.73	*Horsham*
Hunter Ian David	Durham	E	11.9.79	*Durham*
Hurley Ryan Neal	Barbados	WI	13.9.75	*Barbados*
* **Hussain** Nasser	Essex	E	28.3.68	*Madras, India*
Hussey Michael Edward	Western Australia	A	27.5.75	*Morley*
Hutchison Paul Michael	Yorkshire	E	9.6.77	*Leeds*
Hutton Benjamin Leonard	Middlesex	E	29.1.77	*Johannesburg, S. Africa*
Hyam Barry James	Essex	E	9.9.75	*Romford*
* **Ijaz Ahmed**, sen.	Habib Bank	P	20.9.68	*Sialkot*
* **Ijaz Ahmed**, jun.	Allied Bank	P	2.2.69	*Lyallpur*
* **Illingworth** Richard Keith	Worcestershire	E	23.8.63	*Bradford*
* **Ilott** Mark Christopher	Essex	E	27.8.70	*Watford*
Imran Abbas	ADBP	P	25.3.78	*Gujranwala*
Imran Farhat	Pakistan Reserves	P	20.5.82	*Lahore*
* **Imran Nazir**	Pakistan Reserves	P	16.12.81	*Gujranwala*
Innes Kevin John	Northamptonshire	E	24.9.75	*Wellingborough*
Inness Mathew William Hunter	Victoria	A	13.1.78	*East Melbourne*
* **Inzamam-ul-Haq**	Faisalabad	P	3.3.70	*Multan*
Iqbal Sikandar	Karachi	P	19.12.58	*Karachi*
* **Irani** Ronald Charles	Essex	E	26.10.71	*Leigh, Lancashire*
Irfan Bhatti	Rawalpindi	P	28.9.64	*Peshawar*
* **Irfan Fazil**	Habib Bank	P	2.11.81	*Lahore*
Jackson Kenneth Charles	Boland	SA	16.8.64	*Kitwe, Zambia*
Jacobs Arno	North West	SA	13.3.77	*Potchefstroom*
* **Jacobs** Ridley Detamore	Leeward Islands	WI	26.11.67	*Swetes Village, Antigua*
* **Jadeja** Ajaysinhji	Haryana	I	1.2.71	*Jamnagar*
* **James** Stephen Peter	Glamorgan	E	7.9.67	*Lydney*
Jan Asif Iqbal	Trinidad & Tobago	WI	11.2.79	*Mafeking Village*
Jan Imran Haniff	Trinidad & Tobago	WI	11.2.79	*Mafeking Village*
* **Jarvis** Paul William	Somerset	E	29.6.65	*Redcar*
Javed Omar	Bangladesh	B	25.11.76	*Dhaka*
Javed Qadir	PIA	P	25.8.76	*Karachi*
Javed Zaman	Assam	I	8.8.76	*Dhubri*
* **Jayasuriya** Sanath Teran	Bloomfield	SL	30.6.69	*Matara*

	Team	Country	Born	Birthplace
* **Jayawardene** Denagamage Proboth Mahela De Silva	Sinhalese	SL	27.5.77	*Colombo*
* **Jayawardene** Hewasadatchige Asiri Prasanna Wishwanath	Sebastianites	SL	10.9.79	*Colombo*
Jefferson Mark Robin	Wellington	NZ	28.6.76	*Oamaru*
Jefferson William Ingleby	Essex	E	25.10.79	*Derby*
Jennings Dylan	Gauteng	SA	14.9.79	*Johannesburg*
Jeremy Kerry Clifford Bryan	Leeward Islands	WI	6.2.80	*Antigua*
Jitender Singh	Haryana	I	10.1.76	*Rohtak*
Joffe Ryan	Western Province	SA	19.4.75	*Cape Town*
Johnson Benjamin Andrew	South Australia	A	1.8.73	*Naracoorte*
* **Johnson** David Jude	Karnataka	I	16.10.71	*Arasikere*
* **Johnson** Neil Clarkson	Matabeleland	Z	24.1.70	*Salisbury*
Johnson Paul	Nottinghamshire	E	24.4.65	*Newark*
Johnson Richard Leonard	Middlesex	E	29.12.74	*Chertsey*
Johnston David Trent	New South Wales	A	29.4.74	*Wollongong*
Jones Philip Steffan	Somerset	E	9.2.74	*Llanelli*
Jones Simon Philip	Glamorgan	E	25.12.78	*Swansea*
Jordaan Deon	Easterns	SA	3.12.70	*Bloemfontein*
Jordaan Lucas Cornelius Rudolph	North West	SA	20.7.63	*Johannesburg*
* **Joseph** David Rolston Emmanuel	Leeward Islands	WI	15.11.69	*Antigua*
Joseph Sylvester Cleofoster	Leeward Islands	WI	5.9.78	*New Winthorpes, Antigua*
* **Joshi** Sunil Bandacharya	Karnataka	I	6.6.69	*Gadag*
Joubert Pierre	Northerns	SA	2.5.78	*Pretoria*
Joyce Edmund Christopher	Middlesex	E	22.9.78	*Dublin, Ireland*
* **Julian** Brendon Paul	Western Australia	A	10.8.70	*Hamilton, New Zealand*
* **Kabir Khan**	Habib Bank	P	12.4.74	*Peshawar*
* **Kaif** Mohammad	Uttar Pradesh	I	1.12.80	*Allahabad*
Kalawithigoda Shantha	Sinhalese	SL	23.12.77	*Colombo*
Kale Abhijit Vasant	Maharashtra	I	3.7.73	*Ahmednagar*
* **Kallis** Jacques Henry	Western Province	SA	16.10.75	*Cape Town*
* **Kalpage** Ruwan Senani	Nondescripts	SL	19.2.70	*Kandy*
* **Kaluwitharana** Romesh Shantha	Colts	SL	24.11.69	*Colombo*
Kamande James Kabatha	Kenya	K	12.12.78	*Muranga*
* **Kambli** Vinod Ganpat	Mumbai	I	18.1.72	*Bombay*
* **Kanitkar** Hrishikesh Hemant	Maharashtra	I	14.11.74	*Poona*
* **Kapoor** Aashish Rakesh	Rajasthan	I	25.3.71	*Madras*
Karim Syed Saba	Bengal	I	14.11.67	*Patna*
* **Kartik** Murali	Railways	I	11.9.76	*Madras*
Kasprowicz Michael Scott	Queensland	A	10.2.72	*South Brisbane*
Katich Simon Mathew	Western Australia/Durham	A	21.8.75	*Middle Swan*
Keedy Gary	Lancashire	E	27.11.74	*Wakefield*
Kemp Justin Miles	Eastern Province	SA	2.10.77	*Queenstown*
Kendall William Salwey	Hampshire	E	18.12.73	*Wimbledon*
* **Kennedy** Robert John	Wellington	NZ	3.6.72	*Dunedin*
Kent John Carter	KwaZulu-Natal	SA	7.5.79	*Cape Town*
Kenway Derek Anthony	Hampshire	E	12.6.78	*Fareham*
Kerr Jason Ian Douglas	Somerset	E	7.4.74	*Bolton*
Key Robert William Trevor	Kent	E	12.5.79	*East Dulwich*
Khaled Mahmud	Bangladesh	B	26.7.71	*Dhaka*
Khaled Masud	Bangladesh	B	8.2.76	*Rajshahi*
Khan Mansoor Ali	Karnataka	I	22.5.71	*Bangalore*
Khan Wasim Gulzar	Sussex	E	26.2.71	*Birmingham*
Khoda Gagan Kishanlal	Rajasthan	I	24.10.74	*Barmer*
Khurasiya Amay Ramsevak	Madhya Pradesh	I	18.5.72	*Jabalpur*
Kidwell Errol Wayne	Griqualand West	SA	6.6.75	*Vereeniging*
Killeen Neil	Durham	E	17.10.75	*Shotley Bridge*
* **King** Reon Dane	Guyana	WI	6.10.75	*Berbice*

	Team	Country	Born	Birthplace
* **Kirsten** Gary	Western Province	SA	23.11.67	*Cape Town*
Kirsten Paul	Western Province	SA	30.10.69	*Cape Town*
Kirtley Robert James	Sussex	E	10.1.75	*Eastbourne*
Klinger Michael	Victoria	A	4.7.80	*Kew*
* **Klusener** Lance	KwaZulu-Natal	SA	4.9.71	*Durban*
* **Knight** Nicholas Verity	Warwickshire	E	28.11.69	*Watford*
Koch Donovan Marius	Boland	SA	11.10.76	*Somerset West*
Koen Louis Johannes	Boland	SA	28.3.67	*Paarl*
Koenig Sven Gaetan	Gauteng	SA	9.12.73	*Durban*
Koortzen Pieter Petrus Johannes	Griqualand West	SA	24.9.79	*Kimberley*
Kremerskothen Scott Paul	Tasmania	A	5.1.79	*Launceston*
Kreusch Justin Peter	Border	SA	27.9.79	*East London*
Krikken Karl Matthew	Derbyshire	E	9.4.69	*Bolton*
Kruger Garnett John-Peter	Eastern Province	SA	5.1.77	*Port Elizabeth*
Kruis Gideon Jacobus	Griqualand West	SA	9.5.74	*Pretoria*
Kuiler Ian Radcliffe	Gauteng	SA	2.1.75	*Malmesbury*
* **Kulkarni** Nilesh Moreshwar	Mumbai	I	3.4.73	*Dombivili*
Kumaran Thirunavukkarasu	Tamil Nadu	I	30.12.75	*Madras*
* **Kumble** Anil	Karnataka/Leicestershire	I	17.10.70	*Bangalore*
* **Kuruvilla** Abey	Mumbai	I	8.8.68	*Mannar*
Lacey Simon James	Derbyshire	E	9.3.75	*Nottingham*
Lake Anthony Jermaine Alphonso	Leeward Islands	WI	22.3.74	*Antigua*
Lamb Gregory Arthur	Zimbabwe Academy	Z	4.3.80	*Harare*
Lambert Greg Andrew	Yorkshire	E	4.1.80	*Stoke-on-Trent*
Lampitt Stuart Richard	Worcestershire	E	29.7.66	*Wolverhampton*
Laney Jason Scott	Hampshire	E	27.4.73	*Winchester*
* **Langer** Justin Lee	W. Australia/Middlesex	A	21.11.70	*Perth*
Langeveldt Charl Kenneth	Boland	SA	17.12.74	*Stellenbosch*
* **Lara** Brian Charles	Trinidad & Tobago	WI	2.5.69	*Santa Cruz*
* **Lathwell** Mark Nicholas	Somerset	E	26.12.71	*Bletchley*
Lavine Mark John	North West	SA	4.3.73	*Black Bess, Barbados*
Law Danny Richard	Essex	E	15.7.75	*Lambeth*
* **Law** Stuart Grant	Queensland/Essex	A	18.10.68	*Herston*
Law Wayne Lincoln	Glamorgan	E	4.9.78	*Swansea*
Lawson Andrew Grant	North West	SA	4.3.67	*Durban*
Lawson Robert Arthur	Otago	NZ	14.9.74	*Dunedin*
* **Laxman** Vangipurappu Venkata Sai	Hyderabad	I	1.11.74	*Hyderabad*
Leatherdale David Antony	Worcestershire	E	26.11.67	*Bradford*
* **Lee** Brett	New South Wales	A	8.11.76	*Wollongong*
Lee Shane	New South Wales	A	8.8.73	*Wollongong*
* **Lehmann** Darren Scott	South Australia/Yorkshire	A	5.2.70	*Gawler*
* **Lewis** Clairmonte Christopher	Leicestershire	E	14.2.68	*Georgetown, Guyana*
Lewis Jonathan	Gloucestershire	E	26.8.75	*Aylesbury*
Lewis Jonathan James Benjamin	Durham	E	21.5.70	*Isleworth*
Lewis Michael Llewellyn	Victoria	A	29.6.74	*Greensborough*
* **Lewis** Rawl Nicholas	Windward Islands	WI	5.9.74	*Union Village, Grenada*
Lewry Jason David	Sussex	E	2.4.71	*Worthing*
* **Liebenberg** Gerhardus Frederick Johannes	Free State	SA	7.4.72	*Upington*
Light Craig	North West	SA	23.9.72	*Randburg*
Liptrot Christopher George	Worcestershire	E	13.2.80	*Wigan*
* **Liyanage** Dulip Kapila	Colts	SL	6.6.72	*Kalutara*
Lloyd Graham David	Lancashire	E	1.7.69	*Accrington*
Logan Richard James	Northamptonshire	E	28.1.80	*Stone*
Love Geoff Terry	Border	SA	19.9.76	*Port Elizabeth*
Love Martin Lloyd	Queensland	A	30.3.74	*Mundubbera*
Loye Malachy Bernard	Northamptonshire	E	27.9.72	*Northampton*
Lucas David Scott	Nottinghamshire	E	19.8.78	*Nottingham*

	Team	Country	Born	Birthplace
*McCague Martin John	Kent	E	24.5.69	Larne, N. Ireland
McGarrell Neil Christopher	Guyana	WI	12.7.72	Guyana
McGarry Andrew Charles	Essex	E	8.11.81	Basildon
*MacGill Stuart Charles Glyndwr	New South Wales	A	25.2.71	Mount Lawley
McGrath Anthony	Yorkshire	E	6.10.75	Bradford
*McGrath Glenn Donald	NSW/Worcestershire	A	9.2.70	Dubbo
*McIntyre Peter Edward	South Australia	A	27.4.66	Gisborne
Mackay Angus James	Mashonaland	Z	13.6.67	Salisbury
*McKenzie Neil Douglas	Northerns	SA	24.11.75	Johannesburg
McKeown Patrick Christopher	Lancashire	E	1.6.76	Liverpool
McLaren Adrian Peter	Griqualand West	SA	21.4.80	Kimberley
*McLean Nixon Alexei McNamara	Windward Islands	WI	20.7.73	Stubbs, St Vincent
McLean Reynold Julius Jefferson	Windward Islands	WI	9.4.73	Stubbs, St Vincent
*McMillan Brian Mervin	Western Province	SA	22.12.63	Welkom
*McMillan Craig Douglas	Canterbury	NZ	13.9.76	Christchurch
MacQueen Robert Bruce	KwaZulu-Natal	SA	6.9.77	Durban
Madanagopal Jayaraman	Tamil Nadu	I	7.11.74	Madras
Maddy Darren Lee	Leicestershire	E	23.5.74	Leicester
*Madondo Trevor Nyasha	Mashonaland	Z	22.11.76	Mount Darwin
*Madurasinghe Arachchige Wijaysiri Raniith	Kurunegala Youth	SL	30.1.61	Kurunegala
Mafa Johnson Tumelo	Gauteng	SA	5.2.78	Johannesburg
Magiet Rashaad	Western Province	SA	30.5.79	Cape Town
Maher James Patrick	Queensland	A	27.2.74	Innistail
Mahesh Sadagoppan	Tamil Nadu	I	2.4.73	Madras
Mail Gregory John	New South Wales	A	29.4.78	Penrith
Mais Dwight Hugh	Jamaica	WI	27.10.77	St Catherine
*Malcolm Devon Eugene	Northamptonshire	E	22.2.63	Kingston, Jamaica
Manack Hussein Ahmed	Easterns	SA	10.4.68	Pretoria
Manjurul Islam	Bangladesh	B	7.11.79	Khulna
Manou Graham Allan	South Australia	A	23.4.79	Modbury
Mansoor Rana	ADBP	P	27.12.62	Lahore
Manzoor Akhtar	Allied Bank	P	16.4.68	Karachi
*Manzoor Elahi	ADBP	P	15.4.63	Sahiwal
Maregwede Alester	Zimbabwe Academy	Z	5.8.81	Harare
Marillier Douglas Anthony	Midlands	Z	24.6.78	Salisbury
Marsh Daniel James	Tasmania	A	14.6.73	Subiaco
Marshall Dave Kerwin	Barbados	WI	24.5.72	Barbados
Marshall James Andrew Hamilton	Northern Districts	NZ	15.2.79	Warkworth
Marshall Roy Ashworth	Windward Islands	WI	1.4.65	St Joseph, Dominica
Martin Bruce Philip	Northern Districts	NZ	25.4.80	Whangarei
Martin Christopher Stewart	Canterbury	NZ	10.12.74	Christchurch
Martin Jacob Joseph	Baroda	I	11.5.72	Baroda
*Martin Peter James	Lancashire	E	15.11.68	Accrington
Martin-Jenkins Robin Simon Christopher	Sussex	E	28.10.75	Guildford
*Martyn Damien Richard	Western Australia	A	21.10.71	Darwin
*Mascarenhas Adrian Dimitri	Hampshire	E	30.10.77	Chiswick
Masimula Walter Bafana	Gauteng	SA	23.10.75	Johannesburg
Mason Keno	Trinidad & Tobago	WI	13.11.72	Trinidad
Mason Michael James	Central Districts	NZ	27.8.74	Carterton
Mason Scott Robert	Tasmania	A	27.7.76	Launceston
Mason Timothy James	Essex	E	12.4.75	Leicester
Masters David Daniel	Kent	E	22.4.78	Chatham
*Matambanadzo Everton Zvikomborero	Mashonaland	Z	13.4.76	Salisbury
*Matthews Craig Russell	Western Province	SA	15.2.65	Cape Town
Mayers Antonio Nigel	Barbados	WI	23.10.79	Horse Hill
Maynard Dayne Romano	Barbados	WI	1.4.69	Barbados
*Maynard Matthew Peter	Glamorgan	E	21.3.66	Oldham
*Mbangwa Mpumelelo	Matabeleland	Z	26.6.76	Plumtree

	Team	Country	Born	Birthplace
Mehrab Hossain	Bangladesh	B	22.9.78	*Dhaka*
Mehta Bhavin Niranjan	Gujarat	I	17.1.69	*Ahmedabad*
Mendis Chaminda	Colts	SL	28.12.68	*Galle*
* **Mhambrey** Paras Laxmikant	Mumbai	I	20.6.72	*Bombay*
Middlebrook James Daniel	Yorkshire	E	13.5.77	*Leeds*
* **Miller** Colin Reid	Tasmania	A	6.2.64	*Footscray*
Millns David James	Nottinghamshire	E	27.2.65	*Clipstone*
Mitchell Ian	Border	SA	14.12.77	*Johannesburg*
Modi Hitesh Subhash	Kenya	K	13.10.71	*Kisumu*
* **Mohammad Akram**	Allied Bank	P	10.9.74	*Islamabad*
* **Mohammad Hussain**	Lahore City	P	8.10.76	*Lahore*
Mohammad Rafiq	Bangladesh	B	15.5.70	*Dhaka*
* **Mohammad Ramzan**	PNSC	P	25.12.70	*Lyallpur*
Mohammad Sheikh	Kenya	K	29.8.80	*Nairobi*
* **Mohammad Wasim**	KRL	P	8.8.77	*Rawalpindi*
* **Mohammad Zahid**	PIA	P	2.8.76	*Gaggu Mandi*
Mohammed Imraan	Customs/Gloucestershire	E	31.12.76	*Solihull*
* **Mohanty** Debasis Sarbeswar	Orissa	I	20.7.76	*Bhubaneshwar*
* **Moin Khan**	PIA	P	23.9.71	*Rawalpindi*
Moin-ul-Atiq	Habib Bank	P	5.8.64	*Karachi*
Mokopanele Mokete David	Free State	SA	30.6.76	*Bloemfontein*
Mongia Dinesh	Punjab	I	17.4.77	*Chandigarh*
* **Mongia** Nayan Ramlal	Baroda	I	19.12.69	*Baroda*
Montgomerie Richard Robert	Sussex	E	3.7.71	*Rugby*
* **Moody** Thomas Masson	Western Australia	A	2.10.65	*Adelaide*
Moore Tibbles Isaac	Windward Islands	WI	14.9.74	*Grenada*
Morgan Delroy Simeon	Jamaica	WI	4.3.67	*Rollington Town*
Morgan Grant	Northerns	SA	19.5.71	*Port Elizabeth*
Morgan McNeil Junior	Windward Islands	WI	18.10.70	*St Vincent*
Morkel Johannes Albertus	Easterns	SA	10.6.81	*Vereeniging*
Morris Alexander Corfield	Hampshire	E	4.10.76	*Barnsley*
* **Morris** John Edward	Nottinghamshire	E	1.4.64	*Crewe*
Morton Runako Shaku	Leeward Islands	WI	22.7.68	*Nevis*
Mostert Marius Jacobus	Easterns	SA	17.2.76	*Pretoria*
Mott Matthew Peter	Victoria	A	3.10.73	*Charleville*
Mpitsang Phenyo Victor	Free State	SA	28.3.80	*Kimberley*
Mudgal Manoj Sitaram	Uttar Pradesh	I	18.10.72	*Meerut*
Mujahid Jamshed	Habib Bank	P	1.12.71	*Muredke*
* **Mullally** Alan David	Hampshire	E	12.7.69	*Southend-on-Sea*
* **Muller** Scott Andrew	Queensland	A	11.7.71	*Herston*
Mullick Pravanjan Madhabnanda	Orissa	I	12.9.76	*Bhubaneshwar*
Munnik Renier	Western Province	SA	7.1.78	*Cape Town*
* **Munton** Timothy Alan	Derbyshire	E	30.7.65	*Melton Mowbray*
* **Muralitharan** Muttiah	Tamil Union	SL	17.4.72	*Kandy*
* **Murphy** Brian Andrew	Mashonaland	Z	1.12.76	*Salisbury, Rhodesia*
Murphy Brian Samuel	Jamaica	WI	7.4.73	*Jamaica*
Murray Denys Wayne	Eastern Province	SA	29.7.77	*Graaff-Reinet*
* **Murray** Junior Randalph	Windward Islands	WI	20.1.68	*St Georges, Grenada*
Mushfiqur Rehman	Bangladesh	B	1.1.80	*Rajshahi*
* **Mushtaq Ahmed**	National Bank	P	28.6.70	*Sahiwal*
Mutendera David Travolta	Midlands	Z	25.1.79	*Salisbury*
Muzumdar Amol Anil	Mumbai	I	11.11.74	*Bombay*
Myburgh Johannes Gerhardus	Northerns	SA	22.10.80	*Pretoria*
* **Nadeem Abbasi**	KRL	P	15.4.64	*Rawalpindi*
* **Nadeem Khan**	PIA	P	10.12.69	*Rawalpindi*
Naeem Ashraf	National Bank	P	10.11.72	*Lahore*
* **Nagamootoo** Mahendra Veeren	Guyana	WI	9.10.75	*Guyana*
Nagamootoo Vishal	Guyana	WI	7.1.77	*Guyana*
Naidu Venatswamy Suryaprakash Thilak	Karnataka	I	27.1.78	*Bangalore*

	Team	Country	Born	Birthplace
Naimur Rahman	Bangladesh	B	19.9.74	*Dhaka*
Nandakishore Ammanabrole	Hyderabad	I	10.7.70	*Warangal*
Napier Graham Richard	Essex	E	6.1.80	*Colchester*
Nash Donald Anthony	New South Wales	A	29.3.78	*Dubbo*
Nash David Charles	Middlesex	E	19.1.78	*Chertsey*
* **Nash** Dion Joseph	Auckland	NZ	20.11.71	*Auckland*
Navdeep Singh	Punjab	I	24.1.74	*Chandigarh*
* **Naved Ashraf**	Redco	P	4.9.74	*Rawalpindi*
Nawaz Mohamed Naveed	Nondescripts	SL	20.9.73	*Colombo*
Nayyar Rajiv	Himachal Pradesh	I	28.3.70	*Delhi*
Ndima Solomzi Solomon	Gauteng	SA	16.5.77	*Johannesburg*
Nedd Gavin Hilton	Guyana	WI	21.7.72	*Guyana*
* **Nehra** Ashish	Delhi	I	29.4.79	*Delhi*
Nel Andre	Easterns	SA	15.7.77	*Germiston*
Nevin Christopher John	Wellington	NZ	3.8.75	*Dunedin*
Newell Keith	Glamorgan	E	25.3.72	*Crawley*
Ngam Mfuneko	Eastern Province	SA	29.1.79	*Middledrift*
* **Nicholson** Matthew James	Western Australia	A	2.10.74	*St Leonards*
Nissanka Ratnayake Arachchige Prabath	Matara	SL	25.10.80	*Ambalantota*
Nixon Paul Andrew	Kent	E	21.10.70	*Carlisle*
* **Nkala** Mluleki Luke	Matabeleland	Z	1.4.81	*Bulawayo*
Noffke Ashley Allan	Queensland	A	30.4.77	*Nambour*
Noon Wayne Michael	Nottinghamshire	E	5.2.71	*Grimsby*
North Marcus James	Western Australia	A	28.7.79	*Pakenham*
* **Ntini** Makhaya	Border	SA	6.7.77	*Zwelitsha*
Ochieng Peter	Kenya	K	2.2.77	*Kenya*
* **O'Connor** Shayne Barry	Otago	NZ	15.11.73	*Hastings*
Odoyo Thomas Migai	Kenya	K	12.5.78	*Nairobi*
Odumbe Maurice Omondi	Kenya	K	15.6.69	*Nairobi*
Oldroyd Bradley John	Western Australia	A	5.11.73	*Bentley*
* **Olonga** Henry Khaaba	Matabeleland	Z	3.7.76	*Lusaka, Zambia*
Ontong Justin Lee	Boland	SA	4.1.80	*Paarl*
Oosthuizen Riaan Carel	Western Province	SA	3.5.72	*Cape Town*
Oram Jacob David Philip	Central Districts	NZ	28.7.78	*Palmerston North*
Ormond James	Leicestershire	E	20.8.77	*Walsgrave*
Ostler Dominic Piers	Warwickshire	E	15.7.70	*Solihull*
Otieno Kennedy Obhya	Kenya	K	11.3.72	*Nairobi*
Palframan Steven John	Boland	SA	12.5.70	*East London*
Pandey Gyanendrakumar Kedarnath	Uttar Pradesh	I	12.8.72	*Lucknow*
Pangarker Hassan	Western Province	SA	31.8.68	*Cape Town*
Papps Michael Hugh William	Canterbury	NZ	2.7.79	*Christchurch*
Parchment Brenton Anthony	Jamaica	WI	24.6.82	*St Elizabeth*
Parida Rashmi Ranjan	Orissa	I	7.9.74	*Bhubaneswar*
Parkin Owen Thomas	Glamorgan	E	24.9.72	*Coventry*
* **Parore** Adam Craig	Auckland	NZ	23.1.71	*Auckland*
Parsons Keith Alan	Somerset	E	2.5.73	*Taunton*
* **Patel** Minal Mahesh	Kent	E	7.7.70	*Bombay, India*
Patel Pathik Hasmukhbhai	Gujarat	I	10.9.72	*Ahmedabad*
Patterson Andrew David	Ireland/Sussex	E	4.9.75	*Belfast*
Peacock Daniel James	Mashonaland	Z	26.4.75	*Reading, England*
Peake Clinton John	Victoria	A	25.3.77	*Geelong*
Pedi Mpho Lionel Gift	Northerns	SA	14.9.76	*Bloemfontein*
Peirce Michael Toby Edward	Sussex	E	14.6.73	*Maidenhead*
Penberthy Anthony Leonard	Northamptonshire	E	1.9.69	*Troon, Cornwall*
Peng Nicky	Durham	E	18.9.82	*Newcastle upon Tyne*
Penn Andrew Jonathan	Central Districts	NZ	27.7.74	*Wanganui*
Penney Trevor Lionel	Warwicks/Mashonaland	E	12.6.68	*Salisbury, Rhodesia*
* **Perera** Anhettige Suresh Asanka	Sinhalese	SL	16.2.78	*Colombo*

	Team	Country	Born	Birthplace
Perera Kahawelage <u>Gamini</u>	Galle	SL	22.5.64	*Colombo*
Perera Modara Muthugalage Don <u>Nimesh Randika Gayan</u>	Sebastianites	SL	5.9.77	*Colombo*
* **Perera** Panagodage Don <u>Ruchira</u> Laksiri	Sinhalese	SL	6.4.77	*Colombo*
Perera Wagawattage Maithree Bathiya	Colombo	SL	28.4.77	*Colombo*
Perren Clinton Terrence	Queensland	A	22.2.75	*Herston*
* **Perry** Nehemiah Odolphus	Jamaica	WI	16.6.68	*Jamaica*
Persad Mukesh	Trinidad & Tobago	WI	1.5.70	*Trinidad*
Peters Stephen David	Essex	E	10.12.78	*Harold Wood*
Peterson Robin John	Eastern Province	SA	4.8.79	*Port Elizabeth*
Petrie Richard George	Wellington	NZ	23.8.67	*Christchurch*
Phelps Matthew James	New South Wales	A	1.9.72	*Lismore*
Phillip Wayne	Windward Islands	WI	25.11.77	*Dominica*
Phillip Warrington Dexter	Leeward Islands	WI	23.7.68	*Nevis*
Phillips Nicholas Charles	Durham	E	10.5.74	*Pembury*
Pierson Adrian Roger Kirshaw	Somerset	E	21.7.63	*Enfield, Middlesex*
Pietersen Kevin Peter	KwaZulu-Natal	SA	27.6.80	*Pietermaritzburg*
Pipe David James	Worcestershire	E	16.12.77	*Bradford*
Piper Keith John	Warwickshire	E	18.12.69	*Leicester*
Player Bradley Thomas	Boland	SA	18.1.67	*Benoni*
* **Pocock** Blair Andrew	Auckland	NZ	18.6.71	*Papakura*
Pollard Paul Raymond	Worcestershire	E	24.9.68	*Nottingham*
Pollock Graeme Anthony	Easterns	SA	7.4.73	*Port Elizabeth*
* **Pollock** Shaun Maclean	KwaZulu-Natal	SA	16.7.73	*Port Elizabeth*
* **Ponting** Ricky Thomas	Tasmania	A	19.12.74	*Launceston*
Poole Ezra Glynn	North West	SA	10.2.75	*Cape Town*
Pope Steven Charles	Border	SA	15.11.72	*East London*
Pothas Nic	Gauteng	SA	18.11.73	*Johannesburg*
Powell Mark John	Northamptonshire	E	4.11.80	*Northampton*
Powell Michael James	Warwickshire	E	5.4.75	*Bolton*
Powell Michael John	Glamorgan	E	3.2.77	*Abergavenny*
* **Powell** Ricardo Lloyd	Jamaica	WI	16.12.78	*St Elizabeth*
Powell Tony Orlando	Jamaica	WI	22.12.72	*Jamaica*
* **Prasad** Bapu Krishnarao <u>Venkatesh</u>	Karnataka	I	5.8.69	*Bangalore*
* **Prasad** Mannava Sri Kanth	Andhra	I	24.4.75	*Guntur*
Pratt Andrew	Durham	E	4.3.75	*Helmington Row*
Pratt Gary Joseph	Durham	E	22.12.81	*Bishop Auckland*
Pretorius Dewald	Free State	SA	6.12.77	*Pretoria*
* **Price** Raymond William	Midlands	Z	12.6.76	*Salisbury*
Prichard Paul John	Essex	E	7.1.65	*Billericay*
Prince Ashwell Gavin	Western Province	SA	28.5.77	*Port Elizabeth*
Prince Goldwyn Terrence	Leeward Islands	WI	18.6.74	*Antigua*
* **Pringle** Meyrick Wayne	Eastern Province	SA	22.6.66	*Adelaide*
Prittipaul Lawrence Roland	Hampshire	E	19.10.79	*Portsmouth*
Pryke David John	North West	SA	26.11.70	*Welkom*
* **Pushpakumara** Karuppiahyage <u>Ravindra</u>	Nondescripts	SL	21.7.75	*Panadura*
Pyemont James Patrick	Derbyshire/Camb. U.	E	10.4.78	*Eastbourne*
* **Ragoonath** Suruj	Trinidad & Tobago	WI	22.3.68	*Trinidad*
Raja Ali	Madhya Pradesh	I	5.7.76	*Bhopal*
* **Raju** Sagi Lakshmi Venkatapathy	Hyderabad	I	9.7.69	*Hyderabad*
* **Ramanayake** Champaka Priyadarshana Hewage	Galle	SL	8.1.65	*Colombo*
* **Ramesh** Sadagoppan	Tamil Nadu	I	16.10.75	*Madras*
* **Ramnarine** Dinanath	Trinidad & Tobago	WI	4.6.75	*Trinidad*
Rampersad Denis	Trinidad & Tobago	WI	22.9.74	*Trinidad*
* **Ramprakash** Mark Ravin	Middlesex	E	5.9.69	*Bushey*

	Team	Country	Born	Birthplace
Ramsden Gary	Yorkshire	E	2.3.83	*Dewsbury*
* **Ranatunga** Arjuna	Sinhalese	SL	1.12.63	*Colombo*
* **Ranatunga** Sanjeeva	Sinhalese	SL	25.4.69	*Colombo*
Randall Stephen John	Nottinghamshire	E	9.6.80	*Nottingham*
* **Rashid** Latif	Allied Bank	P	14.10.68	*Karachi*
Rashid Umar Bin Abdul	Sussex	E	6.2.76	*Southampton*
Ratcliffe Jason David	Surrey	E	19.6.69	*Solihull*
Rathore Vikram	Punjab	I	26.3.69	*Jullundur*
* **Ratnayake** Rumesh Joseph	Nondescripts	SL	2.1.64	*Colombo*
Raul Sanjay Susanta	Orissa	I	6.10.76	*Cuttack*
Rawnsley Matthew James	Worcestershire	E	8.6.76	*Birmingham*
* **Read** Christopher Mark Wells	Nottinghamshire	E	10.8.78	*Paignton*
Redmond Aaron James	Canterbury	NZ	23.9.79	*Perth, Australia*
* **Reifer** Floyd Lamonte	Barbados	WI	23.7.72	*Parish Land*
* **Reiffel** Paul Ronald	Victoria/Nottinghamshire	A	19.4.66	*Box Hill*
* **Rennie** Gavin James	Mashonaland	Z	12.1.76	*Fort Victoria*
* **Rennie** John Alexander	Matabeleland	Z	29.7.70	*Fort Victoria*
Renshaw Simon John	Hampshire	E	6.3.74	*Bebington*
* **Rhodes** Jonathan Neil	KwaZulu-Natal	SA	27.7.69	*Pietermaritzburg*
* **Rhodes** Steven John	Worcestershire	E	17.6.64	*Bradford*
Richards Corey John	New South Wales	A	25.8.75	*Camden*
Richardson Alan	Warwickshire	E	6.5.75	*Newcastle-under-Lyme*
Richardson Mark Hunter	Otago	NZ	11.6.71	*Hastings*
Ridgway Mark William	Tasmania	A	21.5.63	*Warragul*
Ripley David	Northamptonshire	E	13.9.66	*Leeds*
Rizwan-uz-Zaman	PIA	P	4.9.61	*Karachi*
* **Roberts** Lincoln Abraham	Trinidad & Tobago	WI	4.9.74	*Accord, Antigua*
* **Robertson** Gavin Ron	New South Wales	A	28.5.66	*Sydney*
Robinson Darren David John	Essex	E	2.3.73	*Braintree*
Robinson Mark Andrew	Sussex	E	23.11.66	*Hull*
Roe Garth Anthony	Griqualand West	SA	9.7.73	*Port Elizabeth*
Rogers Christopher John Llewellyn	Western Australia	A	31.8.77	*Sydney*
Rollins Adrian Stewart	Northamptonshire	E	8.2.72	*Barking*
Romero Leon Constantine	Trinidad & Tobago	WI	29.12.74	*Trinidad*
* **Rose** Franklyn Albert	Jamaica	WI	1.2.72	*St Ann's Bay*
Rose Graham David	Somerset	E	12.4.64	*Tottenham*
Roseberry Michael Anthony	Middlesex	E	28.11.66	*Sunderland*
Rossouw Daniel	North West	SA	30.4.70	*Port Elizabeth*
Rudolph Jacobus Andries	Northerns	SA	4.5.81	*Springs*
Rummans Graeme Clifford	New South Wales	A	13.12.76	*Camperdown*
* **Rushmere** Mark Weir	Eastern Province	SA	7.1.65	*Port Elizabeth*
* **Russell** Robert Charles	Gloucestershire	E	15.8.63	*Stroud*
* **Rutherford** Kenneth Robert	Gauteng	NZ	26.10.65	*Dunedin*
* **Saeed** Anwar	ADBP	P	6.9.68	*Karachi*
Saeed Azad	National Bank	P	14.8.66	*Karachi*
Saggers Martin John	Kent	E	23.5.72	*King's Lynn*
Saif Mohammad	Uttar Pradesh	I	21.7.76	*Allahabad*
Sajid Ali	National Bank	P	1.7.63	*Karachi*
Sajid Shah	Habib Bank	P	19.10.74	*Mardan*
Sajjad Akbar	PNSC	P	1.3.61	*Lahore*
Saker David James	Victoria	A	29.5.66	*Oakleigh*
Sales David John	Northamptonshire	E	3.12.77	*Carshalton*
* **Salim** Elahi	Habib Bank	P	21.11.76	*Sahiwal*
* **Salim** Malik	Habib Bank	P	16.4.63	*Lahore*
* **Salisbury** Ian David Kenneth	Surrey	E	21.1.70	*Northampton*
* **Samaraweera** Dulip Prasanna	Colts	SL	12.2.72	*Colombo*
Samaraweera Thilan Thusara	Sinhalese	SL	22.9.76	*Colombo*
Samaroo Avidesh	Trinidad & Tobago	WI	22.1.78	*Trinidad*
Samuels Marlon Nathaniel	Jamaica	WI	5.1.81	*Kingston*

	Team	Country	Born	Birthplace
* **Samuels** Robert George	Jamaica	WI	13.3.71	*Jamaica*
* **Sangakkara** Kumar	Nondescripts	SL	27.10.77	*Colombo*
Sanghvi Rahul Laxman	Delhi	I	3.9.74	*Surat*
Sanson Audley Algan	Jamaica	WI	5.11.74	*Clarendon*
* **Saqlain** Mushtaq	PIA/Surrey	P	29.12.76	*Lahore*
* **Sarwan** Ramnaresh Ronnie	Guyana	WI	23.6.80	*Wakeanam*
Satpathy Sanjay Kumar	Orissa	I	15.4.79	*Bhubaneshwar*
Saxelby Mark	Derbyshire	E	4.1.69	*Worksop*
Died October 11, 2000.				
* **Schofield** Christopher Paul	Lancashire	E	6.10.78	*Rochdale*
Scott Darren Anthony	Kent	E	26.8.72	*Canterbury*
Scuderi Joseph Charles	Lancashire	E	24.12.68	*Ingham, Australia*
Seccombe Wade Anthony	Queensland	A	30.10.71	*Murgon*
Semple Keith Fitzpatrick	Guyana	WI	21.8.70	*Georgetown*
* **Sewell** David Graham	Otago	NZ	20.10.77	*Christchurch*
Sexton Andrew John	Hampshire	E	23.7.79	*Southampton*
Seymore Andre Johan	Gauteng	SA	16.2.75	*Rustenburg*
Shabbir Ahmed	Pakistan Reserves	P	21.4.76	*Khanewal*
* **Shadab** Kabir	Redco	P	12.11.77	*Karachi*
Shafiuddin Ahmed	Bangladesh	B	1.6.73	*Dhaka*
Shah Kasir Zamir	Derbyshire	E	15.6.78	*Jhelum, Pakistan*
Shah Owais Alam	Middlesex	E	22.10.78	*Karachi, Pakistan*
Shah Ravindu Dhirajlac	Kenya	K	28.8.72	*Nairobi*
Shahid Nadeem	Surrey	E	23.4.69	*Karachi, Pakistan*
* **Shahid** Afridi	Habib Bank	P	1.3.80	*Khyber Agency*
Shahid Anwar	National Bank	P	5.7.68	*Multan*
* **Shahid** Nazir	Habib Bank	P	4.12.77	*Faisalabad*
Shahriar Hossain	Bangladesh	B	1.6.76	*Narayangonj*
* **Shakeel** Ahmed, jun	Easterns	P	12.11.71	*Daska*
* **Shakeel** Ahmed, sen.	KRL	P	12.2.66	*Kuwait City, Kuwait*
Shakeel Khan	Habib Bank	P	28.5.68	*Lahore*
Shakti Singh	Himachal Pradesh	I	19.5.68	*Mandi*
Sharath Sridharan	Tamil Nadu	I	31.10.72	*Madras*
* **Sharma** Ajay	Delhi	I	3.4.64	*Delhi*
* **Sharma** Sanjeev	Rajasthan	I	25.8.65	*Delhi*
Shaw Adrian David	Glamorgan	E	17.2.72	*Neath*
Sheikh Mohamed Avez	Warwickshire	E	2.7.73	*Birmingham*
Sheriyar Alamgir	Worcestershire	E	15.11.73	*Birmingham*
Shewag Virender	Delhi	I	20.10.78	*Delhi*
* **Shoaib** Akhtar	KRL	P	13.8.75	*Rawalpindi*
Shoaib Malik	Pakistan Reserves	P	1.2.82	*Sialkot*
* **Shoaib** Mohammad	PIA	P	8.1.61	*Karachi*
Shukla Laxmi Ratan	Bengal	I	6.5.81	*Howrah*
Shukla Saurabh Anand	Uttar Pradesh	I	24.11.67	*Lucknow*
Siddiqui Iqbal	Maharashtra	I	26.12.74	*Aurangabad*
Siddons James Darren	South Australia	A	25.4.64	*Robinvale*
Sidebottom Ryan Jay	Yorkshire	E	15.6.78	*Huddersfield*
* **Sidhu** Navjot Singh	Punjab	I	20.10.63	*Patiala*
Silva Lindamlilage Prageeth Chamara	Panadura	SL	14.12.79	*Panadura*
* **Silverwood** Christopher Eric Wilfred	Yorkshire	E	5.3.75	*Pontefract*
Simmonds Joel McKenzie	Leeward Islands	WI	27.1.76	*Nevis*
* **Simmons** Philip Verant	Easterns	WI	18.4.63	*Arima*
Sinclair Matthew George	Jamaica	WI	26.1.80	*St Elizabeth*
* **Sinclair** Mathew Stuart	Central Districts	NZ	9.11.75	*Katherine, Australia*
Singh Anurag	Warwickshire	E	9.9.75	*Kanpur, India*
* **Singh** Rabindra Ramanarayan (Robin)	Tamil Nadu	I	14.9.63	*Princes Town, Trinidad*
* **Singh** Robin	Delhi	I	1.1.70	*Delhi*
* **Slater** Michael Jonathon	New South Wales	A	21.2.70	*Wagga Wagga*

Register of Current Players

	Team	Country	Born	Birthplace
Smethurst Michael Paul	Lancashire	E	11.10.76	*Oldham*
* **Smith** Andrew Michael	Gloucestershire	E	1.10.67	*Dewsbury*
Smith Aldin Neuratin	Northerns	SA	11.3.79	*Middelburg*
Smith Benjamin Francis	Leicestershire	E	3.4.72	*Corby*
Smith Dennis James	Easterns	SA	26.11.71	*Durban*
Smith Devon Sheldon	Windward Islands	WI	21.10.81	*Grenada*
Smith Edward Thomas	Kent	E	19.7.77	*Pembury*
Smith Graeme Craig	Western Province	SA	1.2.81	*Johannesburg*
Smith Gregory James	Northerns	SA	30.10.71	*Pretoria*
Smith Michael John	South Australia	A	17.7.73	*Rose Park*
Smith Neil Michael Knight	Warwickshire	E	27.7.67	*Birmingham*
Smith Richard Andrew Mortimer	Trinidad & Tobago	WI	17.7.71	*Trinidad*
* **Smith** Robin Arnold	Hampshire	E	13.9.63	*Durban, South Africa*
Smith Trevor Mark	Derbyshire	E	18.1.77	*Derby*
Snape Jeremy Nicholas	Gloucestershire	E	27.4.73	*Stoke-on-Trent*
Sodhi Harvinder Singh	Madhya Pradesh	I	17.10.71	*Agra*
Sodhi Reetinder Singh	Punjab	I	18.10.80	*Patiala*
Solanki Vikram Singh	Worcestershire	E	1.4.76	*Udaipur, India*
Somasekhar Shiraguppi	Karnataka	I	14.6.74	*Dharwad*
Somasunder Sujith	Karnataka	I	2.12.72	*Bangalore*
Sooklal Rodney Ian	Trinidad & Tobago	WI	21.12.80	*Freeport*
Speak Nicholas Jason	Durham	E	21.11.66	*Manchester*
* **Spearman** Craig Murray	Central Districts	NZ	4.7.72	*Auckland*
Speight Martin Peter	Durham	E	24.10.67	*Walsall*
Spiring Karl Reuben	Worcestershire	E	13.11.74	*Southport*
* **Srinath** Javagal	Karnataka	I	31.8.69	*Mysore*
Sriram Sridharan	Tamil Nadu	I	21.2.76	*Madras*
Stapleton Bertram Bennett	Windward Islands	WI	19.10.70	*St Vincent*
* **Stead** Gary Raymond	Canterbury	NZ	9.1.72	*Christchurch*
Stelling William Frederick	Leicestershire	E	30.6.69	*Johannesburg, South Africa*
Stemp Richard David	Nottinghamshire	E	11.12.67	*Birmingham*
* **Stephenson** John Patrick	Hampshire	E	14.3.65	*Stebbing*
Stevens Darren Ian	Leicestershire	E	30.4.76	*Leicester*
* **Stewart** Alec James	Surrey	E	8.4.63	*Merton*
Stewart Errol Leslie Rae	KwaZulu-Natal	SA	30.7.69	*Durban*
Stewart James	New South Wales	A	22.8.70	*East Fremantle*
* **Steyn** Philippus Jeremia Rudolf	Northerns	SA	30.6.67	*Kimberley*
Still Quentin Raxham	Northerns	SA	8.8.74	*Pietermaritzburg*
* **Strang** Bryan Colin	Mashonaland	Z	9.6.72	*Bulawayo*
* **Strang** Paul Andrew	Zimbabwe Academy	Z	28.7.70	*Bulawayo*
Strauss Andrew John	Middlesex	E	2.3.77	*Johannesburg, SA*
* **Streak** Heath Hilton	Matabeleland	Z	16.3.74	*Bulawayo*
Street Matthew Russell	Gauteng	SA	17.12.78	*Johannesburg*
Strong Michael Richard	Northamptonshire	E	28.6.74	*Cuckfield*
Strydom Morne	North West	SA	20.2.74	*Port Elizabeth*
* **Strydom** Pieter Coenraad	Border	SA	10.6.69	*Somerset East*
Stuart Colin Ellsworth Laurie	Guyana	WI	28.9.73	*Guyana*
Stubbings Stephen David	Derbyshire	E	31.3.78	*Huddersfield*
Styris Scott Bernard	Northern Districts	NZ	10.7.75	*Brisbane, Australia*
* **Such** Peter Mark	Essex	E	12.6.64	*Helensburgh, Scotland*
Sugden Craig Brian	KwaZulu-Natal	SA	7.3.74	*Durban*
Suji Anthony Ondik	Kenya	K	5.2.76	*Nairobi*
Suji Martin Armon	Kenya	K	2.6.71	*Nairobi*
Sukhbinder Singh	Assam	I	23.2.67	*Jullundur*
Sulzberger Glen Paul	Central Districts	NZ	14.3.73	*Kaponga*
Sutcliffe Iain John	Leicestershire	E	20.12.74	*Leeds*

	Team	Country	Born	Birthplace
Sutton Luke David	Derbyshire	E	4.10.76	*Keynsham*
Swain Brett Andrew	South Australia	A	14.2.74	*Stirling*
Swan Gavin Graham	Western Australia	A	30.10.70	*Subiaco*
Swanepoel Adriaan Johannes	Griqualand West	SA	19.3.72	*Kimberley*
Swann Alec James	Northamptonshire	E	26.10.76	*Northampton*
Swann Graeme Peter	Northamptonshire	E	24.3.79	*Northampton*
Sylvester Kester Kenneth	Windward Islands	WI	5.12.73	*Grenada*
* **Symcox** Patrick Leonard	Griqualand West	SA	14.4.60	*Kimberley*
Symington Marc Joseph	Durham	E	10.1.80	*Newcastle upon Tyne*
Symonds Andrew	Queensland	A	9.6.75	*Birmingham, England*
Taibu Tatenda	Mashonaland	Z	14.5.83	*Harare*
Tait Alex Ross	Northern Districts	NZ	13.6.72	*Paparoa*
Taljard Dion	Border	SA	7.1.70	*East London*
Tariq-ur-Rehman	Assam	I	22.2.74	*Darbanga*
Taylor Billy Victor	Sussex	E	11.1.77	*Southampton*
Taylor Christopher Glyn	Gloucestershire	E	27.9.76	*Bristol*
* **Taylor** Jonathan Paul	Northamptonshire	E	8.8.64	*Ashby-de-la-Zouch*
Telemachus Roger	Western Province	SA	27.3.73	*Stellenbosch*
* **Tendulkar** Sachin Ramesh	Mumbai	I	24.4.73	*Bombay*
* **Terbrugge** David John	Gauteng	SA	31.1.77	*Ladysmith*
Thomas Dennison	Windward Islands	WI	3.3.68	*Grenada*
Thomas Ian James	Glamorgan	E	9.5.79	*Newport*
Thomas Stuart Darren	Glamorgan	E	25.1.75	*Morriston*
* **Thorpe** Graham Paul	Surrey	E	1.8.69	*Farnham*
Tikolo Stephen Ogomji	Kenya	K	25.6.71	*Nairobi*
Tillekeratne Hashan Prasantha	Nondescripts	SL	14.7.67	*Colombo*
Titchard Stephen Paul	Derbyshire	E	17.12.67	*Warrington*
Tolley Christopher Mark	Nottinghamshire	E	30.12.67	*Kidderminster*
Townsend David Hume	Northerns	SA	22.12.77	*Port Elizabeth*
Toyana Geoffrey	Gauteng	SA	27.2.74	*Soweto*
Trego Peter David	Somerset	E	12.6.81	*Weston-super-Mare*
* **Trescothick** Marcus Edward	Somerset	E	25.12.75	*Keynsham*
Trott Benjamin James	Kent	E	14.3.75	*Wellington*
Tsolekile Thami Lungisa	Western Province	SA	9.10.80	*Cape Town*
Tubb Shannon Ben	Tasmania	A	11.5.80	*Launceston*
Tuckett Carl McArthur	Leeward Islands	WI	18.5.70	*Nevis*
* **Tudor** Alex Jeremy	Surrey	E	23.10.77	*Kensington*
Tuffey Daryl Raymond	Northern Districts	NZ	11.6.78	*Milton*
* **Tufnell** Philip Charles Roderick	Middlesex	E	29.4.66	*Barnet*
Turner Robert Julian	Somerset	E	25.11.67	*Malvern*
* **Twose** Roger Graham	Wellington	NZ	17.4.68	*Torquay, England*
Udal Shaun David	Hampshire	E	18.3.69	*Farnborough, Hants*
* **Upashantha** Kalutarage Eric Amila	Colts	SL	10.6.72	*Kurunegala*
* **Vaas** Warnakulasuriya Patabendige				
Ushantha Joseph Chaminda	Colts	SL	27.1.74	*Mattumagala*
Vadher Alpesh Vallabhdas	Kenya	K	7.9.74	*Nairobi*
van Deinsen Brett Paul	New South Wales	A	28.12.77	*Camperdown*
van den Berg Adolf Matthys	Easterns	SA	9.3.78	*Randfontein*
van der Merwe Francois	North West	SA	5.7.76	*Kempton Park*
van der Wath Johannes Jacobus	Free State	SA	10.1.78	*Newcastle*
van Jaarsveld Martin	Northerns	SA	18.6.74	*Klerksdorp*
van Wyk Morne Nico	Free State	SA	20.3.79	*Bloemfontein*
Vaughan Jeffrey Mark	South Australia	A	26.3.74	*Blacktown*
* **Vaughan** Michael Paul	Yorkshire	E	29.10.74	*Manchester*

	Team	Country	Born	Birthplace
Veenstra Ross Edward	KwaZulu-Natal	SA	22.4.72	*Estcourt*
Venter Jacobus Francois	Free State	SA	1.10.69	*Bloemfontein*
Venter Martin Colin	North West	SA	12.12.68	*East London*
Vermeulen Mark Andrew	Matabeleland	Z	2.3.79	*Salisbury*
* **Vettori** Daniel Luca	Northern Districts	NZ	27.1.79	*Auckland*
* **Viljoen** Dirk Peter	Mashonaland	Z	11.3.77	*Salisbury*
Vimpani Graeme Ronald	Victoria	A	27.1.72	*Herston*
Vincent Lou	Auckland	NZ	12.11.78	*Auckland*
Wagh Mark Anant	Warwickshire	E	20.10.76	*Birmingham*
* **Wajahatullah Wasti**	Allied Bank	P	11.11.74	*Peshawar*
Walker Brooke Graeme Keith	Auckland	NZ	25.3.77	*Auckland*
Walker Matthew Jonathan	Kent	E	2.1.74	*Gravesend*
Wallace Mark Alexander	Glamorgan	E	19.11.81	*Abergavenny*
* **Wallace** Philo Alphonso	Barbados	WI	2.8.70	*Haynesville*
Walmsley Kerry Peter	Auckland	NZ	23.8.73	*Dunedin*
* **Walsh** Courtney Andrew	Jamaica	WI	30.10.62	*Kingston*
Walsh Mark Jason	Western Australia	A	28.4.72	*Townsville*
* **Waqar Younis**	Redco	P	16.11.71	*Vehari*
Ward Ian James	Surrey	E	30.9.72	*Plymouth*
Ward Trevor Robert	Leicestershire	E	18.1.68	*Farningham*
* **Warne** Shane Keith	Victoria/Hampshire	A	13.9.69	*Ferntree Gully*
Warren Russell John	Northamptonshire	E	10.9.71	*Northampton*
* **Wasim Akram**	PIA	P	3.6.66	*Lahore*
Wasim Haider	Faisalabad	P	6.6.67	*Lyallpur*
* **Wasim Jaffer**	Mumbai	I	16.2.78	*Bombay*
Wates Darren Jude	Western Australia	A	2.7.77	*Subiaco*
* **Watkin** Steven Llewellyn	Glamorgan	E	15.9.64	*Maesteg*
Watson Douglas James	KwaZulu-Natal	SA	15.5.73	*Pietermaritzburg*
Watt Balthazar Michael	Windward Islands	WI	12.4.75	*Dominica*
* **Waugh** Mark Edward	New South Wales	A	2.6.65	*Sydney*
* **Waugh** Stephen Rodger	New South Wales	A	2.6.65	*Sydney*
Weekes Paul Nicholas	Middlesex	E	8.7.69	*Hackney*
Weeraratne Kaushalya	Nondescripts	SL	29.1.81	*Gampola*
Welch Graeme	Warwickshire	E	21.3.72	*Durham*
* **Wells** Alan Peter	Kent	E	2.10.61	*Newhaven*
Wells Vincent John	Leicestershire	E	6.8.65	*Dartford*
Welton Guy Edward	Nottinghamshire	E	4.5.78	*Grimsby*
* **Wessels** Kepler Christoffel	Griqualand West	SA	14.9.57	*Bloemfontein*
Weston Robin Michael Swann	Middlesex	E	7.6.75	*Durham*
Weston William Philip Christopher	Worcestershire	E	16.6.73	*Durham*
Wharf Alexander George	Glamorgan	E	4.6.75	*Bradford*
Wharton Lian James	Derbyshire	E	21.2.77	*Holbrook*
Whiley Matthew Jeffrey Allen	Nottinghamshire	E	6.5.80	*Nottingham*
White Brad Middleton	Border	SA	15.5.70	*Johannesburg*
* **White** Craig	Yorkshire	E	16.12.69	*Morley*
White Giles William	Hampshire	E	23.3.72	*Barnstaple*
* **Whittall** Andrew Richard	Manicaland	Z	28.3.73	*Mutare*
* **Whittall** Guy James	Manicaland	Z	5.9.72	*Chipinga*
Wiblin Wayne	Border	SA	13.2.69	*Grahamstown*
Wickremaratne Ranasinghe Pattikirikoralalage Aruna Hemantha	Sinhalese	SL	21.2.71	*Colombo*
* **Wickremasinghe** Gallage Pramodya	Sinhalese	SL	14.8.71	*Matara*
Widdup Simon	Yorkshire	E	10.11.77	*Doncaster*
Wilkinson Louis Johannes	Free State	SA	19.11.66	*Vereeniging*
Williams Brad Andrew	Western Australia	A	20.11.74	*Frankston*
Williams Connor Cecil	Baroda	I	7.8.73	*Baroda*
Williams Henry Smith	Boland	SA	11.6.67	*Stellenbosch*
Williams Laurie Rohan	Jamaica	WI	12.12.68	*Jamaica*
Williams Richard Charles James	Gloucestershire	E	8.8.69	*Southmead*

	Team	Country	Born	Birthplace
* **Williams** Stuart Clayton	Leeward Islands	WI	12.8.69	*Government Road, Nevis*
Williamson Dominic	Leicestershire	E	15.11.75	*Durham*
Willoughby Charl Myles	Boland	SA	3.12.74	*Cape Town*
Wilson Craig Rhys	Boland	SA	24.3.74	*Cradock*
Wilson Elliott James	Worcestershire	E	3.11.76	*St Pancras*
* **Wilson** Paul	South Australia	A	12.1.72	*Newcastle*
Wilton Nicholas James	Sussex	E	23.9.78	*Pembury*
Windows Matthew Guy Norman	Gloucestershire	E	5.4.73	*Bristol*
* **Wiseman** Paul John	Otago	NZ	4.5.70	*Auckland*
* **Wishart** Craig Brian	Mashonaland	Z	9.1.74	*Salisbury*
Wisneski Warren Anthony	Canterbury	NZ	19.2.69	*New Plymouth*
Wood John	Durham	E	22.7.70	*Crofton*
Wood Matthew James	Yorkshire	E	6.4.77	*Huddersfield*
Wood Nathan Theodore	Lancashire	E	4.10.74	*Thornhill Edge*
Wright Carl DaCosta	Jamaica	WI	17.9.77	*St Elizabeth*
Wright Damien Geoffrey	Tasmania	A	25.7.75	*Casino*
Yadav Jai Prakash	Madhya Pradesh	I	7.8.74	*Bhopal*
Yadav Jyoti Prasad	Uttar Pradesh	I	26.9.77	*Allahabad*
Yardy Michael Howard	Sussex	E	27.11.80	*Pembury*
Yasir Arafat	Pakistan Reserves	P	12.3.82	*Rawalpindi*
Yasir Hameed	Peshawar	P	28.2.78	*Peshawar*
Yates Gary	Lancashire	E	20.9.67	*Ashton-under-Lyne*
Young Bradley Evan	South Australia	A	23.2.73	*Semaphore*
* **Young** Shaun	Tasmania	A	13.6.70	*Burnie*
* **Younis Khan**	Habib Bank	P	29.11.77	*Mardan*
* **Yousuf Youhana**	PIA	P	27.8.74	*Lahore*
Zafar Iqbal	National Bank	P	6.3.69	*Karachi*
Zaheer Khan	Baroda	I	7.10.78	*Shrirampur*
Zahid Ahmed	PIA	P	15.11.61	*Karachi*
* **Zahid Fazal**	PIA	P	10.11.73	*Sialkot*
Zahid Saeed	Pakistan Reserves	P	5.7.81	*Aalomahar*
* **Zahoor Elahi**	ADBP	P	1.3.71	*Sahiwal*
Zaidi Ashish Winston	Uttar Pradesh	I	16.9.71	*Allahabad*
* **Zoysa** Demuni <u>Nuwan</u> Tharanga	Sinhalese	SL	13.5.78	*Colombo*

WISDEN'S CRICKETERS OF THE YEAR, 1889–2001

1889	*Six Great Bowlers of the Year:* J. Briggs, J. J. Ferris, G. A. Lohmann, R. Peel, C. T. B. Turner, S. M. J. Woods.
1890	*Nine Great Batsmen of the Year:* R. Abel, W. Barnes, W. Gunn, L. Hall, R. Henderson, J. M. Read, A. Shrewsbury, F. H. Sugg, A. Ward.
1891	*Five Great Wicket-Keepers:* J. McC. Blackham, G. MacGregor, R. Pilling, M. Sherwin, H. Wood.
1892	*Five Great Bowlers:* W. Attewell, J. T. Hearne, F. Martin, A. W. Mold, J. W. Sharpe.
1893	*Five Batsmen of the Year:* H. T. Hewett, L. C. H. Palairet, W. W. Read, S. W. Scott, A. E. Stoddart.
1894	*Five All-Round Cricketers:* G. Giffen, A. Hearne, F. S. Jackson, G. H. S. Trott, E. Wainwright.
1895	*Five Young Batsmen of the Season:* W. Brockwell, J. T. Brown, C. B. Fry, T. W. Hayward, A. C. MacLaren.
1896	W. G. Grace.
1897	*Five Cricketers of the Season:* S. E. Gregory, A. A. Lilley, K. S. Ranjitsinhji, T. Richardson, H. Trumble.
1898	*Five Cricketers of the Year:* F. G. Bull, W. R. Cuttell, N. F. Druce, G. L. Jessop, J. R. Mason.
1899	*Five Great Players of the Season:* W. H. Lockwood, W. Rhodes, W. Storer, C. L. Townsend, A. E. Trott.
1900	*Five Cricketers of the Season:* J. Darling, C. Hill, A. O. Jones, M. A. Noble, Major R. M. Poore.
1901	*Mr R. E. Foster and Four Yorkshiremen:* R. E. Foster, S. Haigh, G. H. Hirst, T. L. Taylor, J. Tunnicliffe.
1902	L. C. Braund, C. P. McGahey, F. Mitchell, W. G. Quaife, J. T. Tyldesley.
1903	W. W. Armstrong, C. J. Burnup, J. Iremonger, J. J. Kelly, V. T. Trumper.
1904	C. Blythe, J. Gunn, A. E. Knight, W. Mead, P. F. Warner.
1905	B. J. T. Bosanquet, E. A. Halliwell, J. Hallows, P. A. Perrin, R. H. Spooner.
1906	D. Denton, W. S. Lees, G. J. Thompson, J. Vine, L. G. Wright.
1907	J. N. Crawford, A. Fielder, E. G. Hayes, K. L. Hutchings, N. A. Knox.
1908	A. W. Hallam, R. O. Schwarz, F. A. Tarrant, A. E. E. Vogler, T. G. Wass.
1909	*Lord Hawke and Four Cricketers of the Year:* W. Brearley, Lord Hawke, J. B. Hobbs, A. Marshal, J. T. Newstead.
1910	W. Bardsley, S. F. Barnes, D. W. Carr, A. P. Day, V. S. Ransford.
1911	H. K. Foster, A. Hartley, C. B. Llewellyn, W. C. Smith, F. E. Woolley.
1912	*Five Members of the MCC's Team in Australia:* F. R. Foster, J. W. Hearne, S. P. Kinneir, C. P. Mead, H. Strudwick.
1913	John Wisden: Personal Recollections.
1914	M. W. Booth, G. Gunn, J. W. Hitch, A. E. Relf, Hon. L. H. Tennyson.
1915	J. W. H. T. Douglas, P. G. H. Fender, H. T. W. Hardinge, D. J. Knight, S. G. Smith.
1916-17	No portraits appeared.
1918	*School Bowlers of the Year:* H. L. Calder, J. E. D'E. Firth, C. H. Gibson, G. A. Rotherham, G. T. S. Stevens.
1919	*Five Public School Cricketers of the Year:* P. W. Adams, A. P. F. Chapman, A. C. Gore, L. P. Hedges, N. E. Partridge.
1920	*Five Batsmen of the Year:* A. Ducat, E. H. Hendren, P. Holmes, H. Sutcliffe, E. Tyldesley.
1921	P. F. Warner.
1922	H. Ashton, J. L. Bryan, J. M. Gregory, C. G. Macartney, E. A. McDonald.
1923	A. W. Carr, A. P. Freeman, C. W. L. Parker, A. C. Russell, A. Sandham.
1924	*Five Bowlers of the Year:* A. E. R. Gilligan, R. Kilner, G. G. Macaulay, C. H. Parkin, M. W. Tate.
1925	R. H. Catterall, J. C. W. MacBryan, H. W. Taylor, R. K. Tyldesley, W. W. Whysall.
1926	J. B. Hobbs.

1927	G. Geary, H. Larwood, J. Mercer, W. A. Oldfield, W. M. Woodfull.
1928	R. C. Blunt, C. Hallows, W. R. Hammond, D. R. Jardine, V. W. C. Jupp.
1929	L. E. G. Ames, G. Duckworth, M. Leyland, S. J. Staples, J. C. White.
1930	E. H. Bowley, K. S. Duleepsinhji, H. G. Owen-Smith, R. W. V. Robins, R. E. S. Wyatt.
1931	D. G. Bradman, C. V. Grimmett, B. H. Lyon, I. A. R. Peebles, M. J. Turnbull.
1932	W. E. Bowes, C. S. Dempster, James Langridge, Nawab of Pataudi sen., H. Verity.
1933	W. E. Astill, F. R. Brown, A. S. Kennedy, C. K. Nayudu, W. Voce.
1934	A. H. Bakewell, G. A. Headley, M. S. Nichols, L. F. Townsend, C. F. Walters.
1935	S. J. McCabe, W. J. O'Reilly, G. A. E. Paine, W. H. Ponsford, C. I. J. Smith.
1936	H. B. Cameron, E. R. T. Holmes, B. Mitchell, D. Smith, A. W. Wellard.
1937	C. J. Barnett, W. H. Copson, A. R. Gover, V. M. Merchant, T. S. Worthington.
1938	T. W. J. Goddard, J. Hardstaff jun., L. Hutton, J. H. Parks, E. Paynter.
1939	H. T. Bartlett, W. A. Brown, D. C. S. Compton, K. Farnes, A. Wood.
1940	L. N. Constantine, W. J. Edrich, W. W. Keeton, A. B. Sellers, D. V. P. Wright.
1941-46	No portraits appeared.
1947	A. V. Bedser, L. B. Fishlock, V. (M. H.) Mankad, T. P. B. Smith, C. Washbrook.
1948	M. P. Donnelly, A. Melville, A. D. Nourse, J. D. Robertson, N. W. D. Yardley.
1949	A. L. Hassett, W. A. Johnston, R. R. Lindwall, A. R. Morris, D. Tallon.
1950	T. E. Bailey, R. O. Jenkins, John Langridge, R. T. Simpson, B. Sutcliffe.
1951	T. G. Evans, S. Ramadhin, A. L. Valentine, E. D. Weekes, F. M. M. Worrell.
1952	R. Appleyard, H. E. Dollery, J. C. Laker, P. B. H. May, E. A. B. Rowan.
1953	H. Gimblett, T. W. Graveney, D. S. Sheppard, W. S. Surridge, F. S. Trueman.
1954	R. N. Harvey, G. A. R. Lock, K. R. Miller, J. H. Wardle, W. Watson.
1955	B. Dooland, Fazal Mahmood, W. E. Hollies, J. B. Statham, G. E. Tribe.
1956	M. C. Cowdrey, D. J. Insole, D. J. McGlew, H. J. Tayfield, F. H. Tyson.
1957	D. Brookes, J. W. Burke, M. J. Hilton, G. R. A. Langley, P. E. Richardson.
1958	P. J. Loader, A. J. McIntyre, O. G. Smith, M. J. Stewart, C. L. Walcott.
1959	H. L. Jackson, R. E. Marshall, C. A. Milton, J. R. Reid, D. Shackleton.
1960	K. F. Barrington, D. B. Carr, R. Illingworth, G. Pullar, M. J. K. Smith.
1961	N. A. T. Adcock, E. R. Dexter, R. A. McLean, R. Subba Row, J. V. Wilson.
1962	W. E. Alley, R. Benaud, A. K. Davidson, W. M. Lawry, N. C. O'Neill.
1963	D. Kenyon, Mushtaq Mohammad, P. H. Parfitt, P. J. Sharpe, F. J. Titmus.
1964	D. B. Close, C. C. Griffith, C. C. Hunte, R. B. Kanhai, G. S. Sobers.
1965	G. Boycott, P. J. Burge, J. A. Flavell, G. D. McKenzie, R. B. Simpson.
1966	K. C. Bland, J. H. Edrich, R. C. Motz, P. M. Pollock, R. G. Pollock.
1967	R. W. Barber, B. L. D'Oliveira, C. Milburn, J. T. Murray, S. M. Nurse.
1968	Asif Iqbal, Hanif Mohammad, K. Higgs, J. M. Parks, Nawab of Pataudi jun.
1969	J. G. Binks, D. M. Green, B. A. Richards, D. L. Underwood, O. S. Wheatley.
1970	B. F. Butcher, A. P. E. Knott, Majid Khan, M. J. Procter, D. J. Shepherd.
1971	J. D. Bond, C. H. Lloyd, B. W. Luckhurst, G. M. Turner, R. T. Virgin.
1972	G. G. Arnold, B. S. Chandrasekhar, L. R. Gibbs, B. Taylor, Zaheer Abbas.
1973	G. S. Chappell, D. K. Lillee, R. A. L. Massie, J. A. Snow, K. R. Stackpole.
1974	K. D. Boyce, B. E. Congdon, K. W. R. Fletcher, R. C. Fredericks, P. J. Sainsbury.
1975	D. L. Amiss, M. H. Denness, N. Gifford, A. W. Greig, A. M. E. Roberts.
1976	I. M. Chappell, P. G. Lee, R. B. McCosker, D. S. Steele, R. A. Woolmer.
1977	J. M. Brearley, C. G. Greenidge, M. A. Holding, I. V. A. Richards, R. W. Taylor.
1978	I. T. Botham, M. Hendrick, A. Jones, K. S. McEwan, R. G. D. Willis.
1979	D. I. Gower, J. K. Lever, C. M. Old, C. T. Radley, J. N. Shepherd.
1980	J. Garner, S. M. Gavaskar, G. A. Gooch, D. W. Randall, B. C. Rose.
1981	K. J. Hughes, R. D. Jackman, A. J. Lamb, C. E. B. Rice, V. A. P. van der Bijl.
1982	T. M. Alderman, A. R. Border, R. J. Hadlee, Javed Miandad, R. W. Marsh.
1983	Imran Khan, T. E. Jesty, A. I. Kallicharran, Kapil Dev, M. D. Marshall.
1984	M. Amarnath, J. V. Coney, J. E. Emburey, M. W. Gatting, C. L. Smith.
1985	M. D. Crowe, H. A. Gomes, G. W. Humpage, J. Simmons, S. Wettimuny.
1986	P. Bainbridge, R. M. Ellison, C. J. McDermott, N. V. Radford, R. T. Robinson.
1987	J. H. Childs, G. A. Hick, D. B. Vengsarkar, C. A. Walsh, J. J. Whitaker.
1988	J. P. Agnew, N. A. Foster, D. P. Hughes, P. M. Roebuck, Salim Malik.
1989	K. J. Barnett, P. J. L. Dujon, P. A. Neale, F. D. Stephenson, S. R. Waugh.

1990 S. J. Cook, D. M. Jones, R. C. Russell, R. A. Smith, M. A. Taylor.
1991 M. A. Atherton, M. Azharuddin, A. R. Butcher, D. L. Haynes, M. E. Waugh.
1992 C. E. L. Ambrose, P. A. J. DeFreitas, A. A. Donald, R. B. Richardson, Waqar Younis.
1993 N. E. Briers, M. D. Moxon, I. D. K. Salisbury, A. J. Stewart, Wasim Akram.
1994 D. C. Boon, I. A. Healy, M. G. Hughes, S. K. Warne, S. L. Watkin.
1995 B. C. Lara, D. E. Malcolm, T. A. Munton, S. J. Rhodes, K. C. Wessels.
1996 D. G. Cork, P. A. de Silva, A. R. C. Fraser, A. Kumble, D. A. Reeve.
1997 S. T. Jayasuriya, Mushtaq Ahmed, Saeed Anwar, P. V. Simmons, S. R. Tendulkar.
1998 M. T. G. Elliott, S. G. Law, G. D. McGrath, M. P. Maynard, G. P. Thorpe.
1999 I. D. Austin, D. Gough, M. Muralitharan, A. Ranatunga, J. N. Rhodes.
2000 C. L. Cairns, R. Dravid, L. Klusener, T. M. Moody, Saqlain Mushtaq.
Cricketers of the Century D. G. Bradman, G. S. Sobers, J. B. Hobbs, S. K. Warne, I. V. A. Richards.
2001 M. W. Alleyne, M. P. Bicknell, A. R. Caddick, J. L. Langer, D. S. Lehmann.

CRICKETERS OF THE YEAR: AN ANALYSIS

The five players selected to be Cricketers of the Year for 2001 bring the number chosen since selection began in 1889 to 512. They have been chosen from 36 different teams as follows:

Derbyshire	13	Northants	13	Cambridge Univ.	10	Cheltenham College	1
Essex	22	Nottinghamshire	25	Australians	63	Cranleigh School	1
Glamorgan	10	Somerset	17	South Africans	21	Eton College	2
Gloucestershire	16	Surrey	47	West Indians	23	Malvern College	1
Hampshire	14	Sussex	20	New Zealanders	8	Rugby School	1
Kent	25	Warwickshire	19	Indians	12	Tonbridge School	1
Lancashire	31	Worcestershire	15	Pakistanis	11	Univ. Coll. School	1
Leicestershire	8	Yorkshire	40	Sri Lankans	4	Uppingham School	1
Middlesex	26	Oxford Univ.	6	Staffordshire	1	Winchester College	1

Durham and the Zimbabweans have as yet had no team members chosen as Cricketers of the Year.

Notes: Schoolboys were chosen in 1918 and 1919 when first-class cricket was suspended due to war. The total of sides comes to 530 because 18 players played regularly for two teams (England excluded) in the year for which they were chosen. John Wisden, listed as a Sussex player, retired 50 years before his posthumous selection.

Types of Players

Of the 512 Cricketers of the Year, 258 are best classified as batsmen, 147 as bowlers, 75 as all-rounders and 32 as wicket-keepers.

Nationalities

At the time they were chosen, 326 players (63.67 per cent) were qualified to play for England, 74 for Australia, 36 West Indies, 31 South Africa, 14 Pakistan, 13 India, 12 New Zealand, 5 Sri Lanka and 1 Zimbabwe.

Note: Nationalities and teams are not necessarily identical.

Ages

On April 1 in the year of selection

Youngest: 17 years 67 days H. L. Calder, 1918. The youngest first-class cricketer was Mushtaq Mohammad, 19 years 130 days in 1963.

Oldest: 48 years 228 days Lord Hawke, 1909. (This excludes John Wisden, whose portrait appeared 87 years after his birth and 29 years after his death.)

An analysis of post-war Cricketers of the Year may be found in Wisden *1998, page 174.*

Research: Robert Brooke

PART THREE: RECORDS

CRICKET RECORDS

First-class and limited-overs records by PHILIP BAILEY
Test match records by PHILIP BAILEY and GORDON VINCE

All records are amended to the end of the 2000 season in England, including those matches played in Sri Lanka and Australia after their 1999-2000 seasons. These are designated 2000 (SL) and 2000 (A).

Updated Test records can be found on the Wisden website, www.wisden.com.

Unless otherwise stated, all records apply only to first-class cricket. This is considered to have started in 1815, after the Napoleonic War.
   * Denotes not out or an unbroken partnership.
   (A), (SA), (WI), (NZ), (I), (P), (SL) or (Z) indicates either the nationality of the player, or the country in which the record was made.

FIRST-CLASS RECORDS

BATTING RECORDS

BOWLING RECORDS

ALL-ROUND RECORDS

WICKET-KEEPING RECORDS

FIELDING RECORDS

TEAM RECORDS

TEST MATCH RECORDS

BATTING RECORDS

BOWLING RECORDS

ALL-ROUND RECORDS

WICKET-KEEPING RECORDS

FIELDING RECORDS

TEAM RECORDS

PLAYERS

CAPTAINCY

UMPIRING

TEST SERIES

LIMITED-OVERS INTERNATIONAL RECORDS

MISCELLANEOUS

FIRST-CLASS RECORDS

BATTING RECORDS

HIGHEST INDIVIDUAL SCORES

501*	B. C. Lara	Warwickshire v Durham at Birmingham	1994
499	Hanif Mohammad	Karachi v Bahawalpur at Karachi	1958-59
452*	D. G. Bradman	NSW v Queensland at Sydney	1929-30
443*	B. B. Nimbalkar	Maharashtra v Kathiawar at Poona	1948-49
437	W. H. Ponsford	Victoria v Queensland at Melbourne	1927-28
429	W. H. Ponsford	Victoria v Tasmania at Melbourne	1922-23
428	Aftab Baloch	Sind v Baluchistan at Karachi	1973-74
424	A. C. MacLaren	Lancashire v Somerset at Taunton	1895
405*	G. A. Hick	Worcestershire v Somerset at Taunton	1988
385	B. Sutcliffe	Otago v Canterbury at Christchurch	1952-53
383	C. W. Gregory	NSW v Queensland at Brisbane	1906-07
377	S. V. Manjrekar	Bombay v Hyderabad at Bombay	1990-91
375	B. C. Lara	West Indies v England at St John's	1993-94
369	D. G. Bradman	South Australia v Tasmania at Adelaide	1935-36
366	N. H. Fairbrother	Lancashire v Surrey at The Oval	1990
366	M. V. Sridhar	Hyderabad v Andhra at Secunderabad	1993-94
365*	C. Hill	South Australia v NSW at Adelaide	1900-01
365*	G. S. Sobers	West Indies v Pakistan at Kingston	1957-58
364	L. Hutton	England v Australia at The Oval	1938
359*	V. M. Merchant	Bombay v Maharashtra at Bombay	1943-44
359	R. B. Simpson	NSW v Queensland at Brisbane	1963-64
357*	R. Abel	Surrey v Somerset at The Oval	1899
357	D. G. Bradman	South Australia v Victoria at Melbourne	1935-36
356	B. A. Richards	South Australia v Western Australia at Perth	1970-71
355*	G. R. Marsh	Western Australia v South Australia at Perth	1989-90
355	B. Sutcliffe	Otago v Auckland at Dunedin	1949-50
353	V. V. S. Laxman	Hyderabad v Karnataka at Bangalore	1999-2000
352	W. H. Ponsford	Victoria v NSW at Melbourne	1926-27
350	Rashid Israr	Habib Bank v National Bank at Lahore	1976-77
345	C. G. Macartney	Australians v Nottinghamshire at Nottingham	1921
344*	G. A. Headley	Jamaica v Lord Tennyson's XI at Kingston	1931-32
344	W. G. Grace	MCC v Kent at Canterbury	1876
343*	P. A. Perrin	Essex v Derbyshire at Chesterfield	1904
341	G. H. Hirst	Yorkshire v Leicestershire at Leicester	1905
340*	D. G. Bradman	NSW v Victoria at Sydney	1928-29
340	S. M. Gavaskar	Bombay v Bengal at Bombay	1981-82
340	S. T. Jayasuriya	Sri Lanka v India at Colombo	1997-98
338*	R. C. Blunt	Otago v Canterbury at Christchurch	1931-32
338	W. W. Read	Surrey v Oxford University at The Oval	1888
337*	Pervez Akhtar	Railways v Dera Ismail Khan at Lahore	1964-65
337*	D. J. Cullinan	Transvaal v Northern Transvaal at Johannesburg	1993-94
337	Hanif Mohammad	Pakistan v West Indies at Bridgetown	1957-58
336*	W. R. Hammond	England v New Zealand at Auckland	1932-33
336	W. H. Ponsford	Victoria v South Australia at Melbourne	1927-28
334*	M. A. Taylor	Australia v Pakistan at Peshawar	1998-99
334	D. G. Bradman	Australia v England at Leeds	1930
333	K. S. Duleepsinhji	Sussex v Northamptonshire at Hove	1930
333	G. A. Gooch	England v India at Lord's	1990
332	W. H. Ashdown	Kent v Essex at Brentwood	1934
331*	J. D. Robertson	Middlesex v Worcestershire at Worcester	1949
325*	H. L. Hendry	Victoria v New Zealanders at Melbourne	1925-26
325	A. Sandham	England v West Indies at Kingston	1929-30
325	C. L. Badcock	South Australia v Victoria at Adelaide	1935-36

324*	D. M. Jones	Victoria v South Australia at Melbourne	1994-95
324	J. B. Stollmeyer	Trinidad v British Guiana at Port-of-Spain	1946-47
324	Waheed Mirza	Karachi Whites v Quetta at Karachi	1976-77
323	A. L. Wadekar	Bombay v Mysore at Bombay	1966-67
323	D. Gandhi	Bengal v Assam at Gauhati	1998-99
322*	M. B. Loye	Northamptonshire v Glamorgan at Northampton	1998
322	E. Paynter	Lancashire v Sussex at Hove	1937
322	I. V. A. Richards	Somerset v Warwickshire at Taunton	1985
321	W. L. Murdoch	NSW v Victoria at Sydney	1881-82
320	R. Lamba	North Zone v West Zone at Bhilai	1987-88
319	Gul Mahomed	Baroda v Holkar at Baroda	1946-47
318*	W. G. Grace	Gloucestershire v Yorkshire at Cheltenham	1876
317	W. R. Hammond	Gloucestershire v Nottinghamshire at Gloucester	1936
317	K. R. Rutherford	New Zealanders v D. B. Close's XI at Scarborough	1986
316*	J. B. Hobbs	Surrey v Middlesex at Lord's	1926
316*	V. S. Hazare	Maharashtra v Baroda at Poona	1939-40
316	R. H. Moore	Hampshire v Warwickshire at Bournemouth	1937
315*	T. W. Hayward	Surrey v Lancashire at The Oval	1898
315*	P. Holmes	Yorkshire v Middlesex at Lord's	1925
315*	A. F. Kippax	NSW v Queensland at Sydney	1927-28
314*	C. L. Walcott	Barbados v Trinidad at Port-of-Spain	1945-46
314*	Wasim Jaffer	Mumbai v Saurashtra at Rajkot	1996-97
313*	S. J. Cook	Somerset v Glamorgan at Cardiff	1990
313	H. Sutcliffe	Yorkshire v Essex at Leyton	1932
313	W. V. Raman‡	Tamil Nadu v Goa at Panjim	1988-89
312*	W. W. Keeton	Nottinghamshire v Middlesex at The Oval†	1939
312*	J. M. Brearley	MCC Under-25 v North Zone at Peshawar	1966-67
312	R. Lamba	Delhi v Himachal Pradesh at Delhi	1994-95
312	J. E. R. Gallian	Lancashire v Derbyshire at Manchester	1996
311*	G. M. Turner	Worcestershire v Warwickshire at Worcester	1982
311	J. T. Brown	Yorkshire v Sussex at Sheffield	1897
311	R. B. Simpson	Australia v England at Manchester	1964
311	Javed Miandad	Karachi Whites v National Bank at Karachi	1974-75
310*	J. H. Edrich	England v New Zealand at Leeds	1965
310	H. Gimblett	Somerset v Sussex at Eastbourne	1948
309*	S. P. James	Glamorgan v Sussex at Colwyn Bay	2000
309	V. S. Hazare	The Rest v Hindus at Bombay	1943-44
308*	F. M. M. Worrell	Barbados v Trinidad at Bridgetown	1943-44
307*	T. N. Lazard	Boland v W. Province at Worcester, Cape Province	1993-94
307	M. C. Cowdrey	MCC v South Australia at Adelaide	1962-63
307	R. M. Cowper	Australia v England at Melbourne	1965-66
306*	A. Ducat	Surrey v Oxford University at The Oval	1919
306*	E. A. B. Rowan	Transvaal v Natal at Johannesburg	1939-40
306*	D. W. Hookes	South Australia v Tasmania at Adelaide	1986-87
305*	F. E. Woolley	MCC v Tasmania at Hobart	1911-12
305*	F. R. Foster	Warwickshire v Worcestershire at Dudley	1914
305*	W. H. Ashdown	Kent v Derbyshire at Dover	1935
305*	P. Dharmani	Punjab v Jammu and Kashmir at Ludhiana	1999-2000
304*	A. W. Nourse	Natal v Transvaal at Johannesburg	1919-20
304*	P. H. Tarilton	Barbados v Trinidad at Bridgetown	1919-20
304*	E. D. Weekes	West Indians v Cambridge University at Cambridge	1950
304	R. M. Poore	Hampshire v Somerset at Taunton	1899
304	D. G. Bradman	Australia v England at Leeds	1934
303*	W. W. Armstrong	Australians v Somerset at Bath	1905
303*	Mushtaq Mohammad	Karachi Blues v Karachi University at Karachi	1967-68
303*	Abdul Azeem	Hyderabad v Tamil Nadu at Hyderabad	1986-87
303*	S. Chanderpaul	Guyana v Jamaica at Kingston	1995-96
303*	G. A. Hick	Worcestershire v Hampshire at Southampton	1997
303*	D. J. Sales	Northamptonshire v Essex at Northampton	1999
302*	P. Holmes	Yorkshire v Hampshire at Portsmouth	1920
302*	W. R. Hammond	Gloucestershire v Glamorgan at Bristol	1934

302*	Arjan Kripal Singh‡	Tamil Nadu v Goa at Panjim	1988-89
302	W. R. Hammond	Gloucestershire v Glamorgan at Newport..........	1939
302	L. G. Rowe	West Indies v England at Bridgetown	1973-74
301*	E. H. Hendren	Middlesex v Worcestershire at Dudley	1933
301*	V. V. S. Laxman	Hyderabad v Bihar at Jamshedpur	1997-98
301	W. G. Grace	Gloucestershire v Sussex at Bristol..............	1896
300*	V. T. Trumper	Australians v Sussex at Hove	1899
300*	F. B. Watson	Lancashire v Surrey at Manchester.............	1928
300*	Imtiaz Ahmed	PM's XI v Commonwealth XI at Bombay	1950-51
300	J. T. Brown	Yorkshire v Derbyshire at Chesterfield..........	1898
300	D. C. S. Compton	MCC v N. E. Transvaal at Benoni	1948-49
300	R. Subba Row	Northamptonshire v Surrey at The Oval	1958
300	Ramiz Raja	Allied Bank v Habib Bank at Lahore	1994-95

† *Played at The Oval because Lord's was required for Eton v Harrow.*

‡ *In the same innings, a unique occurrence.*

DOUBLE-HUNDRED ON DEBUT

227	T. Marsden	Sheffield & Leicester v Nottingham at Sheffield	1826
207	N. F. Callaway†	New South Wales v Queensland at Sydney	1914-15
240	W. F. E. Marx	Transvaal v Griqualand West at Johannesburg	1920-21
200*	A. Maynard	Trinidad v MCC at Port-of-Spain	1934-35
232*	S. J. E. Loxton	Victoria v Queensland at Melbourne.............	1946-47
215*	G. H. G. Doggart	Cambridge University v Lancashire at Cambridge	1948
202	J. Hallebone	Victoria v Tasmania at Melbourne	1951-52
230	G. R. Viswanath	Mysore v Andhra at Vijayawada...............	1967-68
260	A. A. Muzumdar	Bombay v Haryana at Faridabad	1993-94
209*	A. Pandey	Madhya Pradesh v Uttar Pradesh at Bhilai.........	1995-96
210*	D. J. Sales	Northants v Worcestershire at Kidderminster	1996
200*	M. J. Powell	Glamorgan v Oxford University at Oxford	1997

† *In his only first-class innings. He was killed in action in France in 1917.*

TWO SEPARATE HUNDREDS ON DEBUT

148 and 111	A. R. Morris	New South Wales v Queensland at Sydney.....	1940-41
152 and 102*	N. J. Contractor	Gujarat v Baroda at Baroda	1952-53
132* and 110	Aamer Malik	Lahore A v Railways at Lahore	1979-80

HUNDRED ON DEBUT IN ENGLAND

This does not include players who have previously appeared in first-class cricket outside the British Isles. The following have achieved the feat since 1990. For fuller lists please see earlier *Wisdens*.

116*	J. J. B. Lewis	Essex v Surrey at The Oval	1990
117	J. D. Glendenen	Durham v Oxford University at Oxford	1992
109	J. R. Wileman	Nottinghamshire v Cambridge University at Nottingham..	1992
123	A. J. Holliaoke†	Surrey v Derbyshire at Ilkeston	1993
101	E. T. Smith	Cambridge University v Glamorgan at Cambridge......	1996
110	S. D. Peters	Essex v Cambridge University at Cambridge	1996
210*	D. J. Sales†	Northamptonshire v Worcestershire at Kidderminster	1996
200*	M. J. Powell	Glamorgan v Oxford University at Oxford	1997
104	C. G. Taylor	Gloucestershire v Middlesex at Lord's.............	2000

† *In his second innings.*

TWO DOUBLE-HUNDREDS IN A MATCH

A. E. Fagg   244   202*   Kent v Essex at Colchester 1938

TRIPLE-HUNDRED AND HUNDRED IN A MATCH

G. A. Gooch 333   123   England v India at Lord's   1990

DOUBLE-HUNDRED AND HUNDRED IN A MATCH

C. B. Fry	125	229	Sussex v Surrey at Hove	1900
W. W. Armstrong	157*	245	Victoria v South Australia at Melbourne. . .	1920-21
H. T. W. Hardinge . . .	207	102*	Kent v Surrey at Blackheath	1921
C. P. Mead	113	224	Hampshire v Sussex at Horsham	1921
K. S. Duleepsinhji . . .	115	246	Sussex v Kent at Hastings	1929
D. G. Bradman	124	225	Woodfull's XI v Ryder's XI at Sydney	1929-30
B. Sutcliffe	243	100*	New Zealanders v Essex at Southend.	1949
M. R. Hallam	210*	157	Leicestershire v Glamorgan at Leicester . . .	1959
M. R. Hallam	203*	143*	Leicestershire v Sussex at Worthing	1961
Hanumant Singh	109	213*	Rajasthan v Bombay at Bombay	1966-67
Salah-ud-Din	256	102*	Karachi v East Pakistan at Karachi	1968-69
K. D. Walters	242	103	Australia v West Indies at Sydney	1968-69
S. M. Gavaskar	124	220	India v West Indies at Port-of-Spain.	1970-71
L. G. Rowe.	214	100*	West Indies v New Zealand at Kingston . . .	1971-72
G. S. Chappell.	247*	133	Australia v New Zealand at Wellington. . . .	1973-74
L. Baichan	216*	102	Berbice v Demerara at Georgetown	1973-74
Zaheer Abbas	216*	156*	Gloucestershire v Surrey at The Oval.	1976
Zaheer Abbas	230*	104*	Gloucestershire v Kent at Canterbury.	1976
Zaheer Abbas	205*	108*	Gloucestershire v Sussex at Cheltenham . . .	1977
Saadat Ali.	141	222	Income Tax v Multan at Multan	1977-78
Talat Ali.	214*	104	PIA v Punjab at Lahore.	1978-79
Shafiq Ahmad	129	217*	National Bank v MCB at Karachi	1978-79
D. W. Randall	209	146	Nottinghamshire v Middlesex at Nottingham	1979
Zaheer Abbas	215*	150*	Gloucestershire v Somerset at Bath	1981
Qasim Omar	210*	110	MCB v Lahore at Lahore	1982-83
A. I. Kallicharran . . .	200*	117*	Warwickshire v Northants at Birmingham. .	1984
Rizwan-uz-Zaman . . .	139	217*	PIA v PACO at Lahore	1989-90
G. A. Hick	252*	100*	Worcestershire v Glamorgan at Abergavenny	1990
N. R. Taylor	204	142	Kent v Surrey at Canterbury	1990
N. R. Taylor	111	203*	Kent v Sussex at Hove	1991
W. V. Raman	226	120	Tamil Nadu v Haryana at Faridabad	1991-92
A. J. Lamb	209	107	Northants v Warwicks at Northampton . . .	1992
G. A. Gooch	101	205	Essex v Worcestershire at Worcester.	1994
P. A. de Silva	255	116	Kent v Derbyshire at Maidstone	1995
M. C. Mendis	111	200*	Colts CC v Singha SC at Colombo	1995-96
A. M. Bacher	210	112*	Transvaal v Griqualand West at Kimberley .	1996-97
H. H. Gibbs	200*	171	South Africans v India A at Nagpur.	1996-97
M. L. Hayden	235*	119	Hampshire v Warwickshire at Southampton.	1997
G. S. Blewett.	169*	213*	Australian XI v England XI at Hobart	1998-99
A. Jadeja	136	202*	Haryana v Saurashtra at Rajkot.	1998-99
J. Cox	216	129*	Somerset v Hampshire at Southampton. . . .	1999

TWO SEPARATE HUNDREDS IN A MATCH

Eight times: Zaheer Abbas.
Seven times: W. R. Hammond.
Six times: J. B. Hobbs, G. M. Turner.
Five times: C. B. Fry, G. A. Gooch.
Four times: D. G. Bradman, G. S. Chappell, J. H. Edrich, L. B. Fishlock, T. W. Graveney, C. G. Greenidge, H. T. W. Hardinge, E. H. Hendren, G. A. Hick, Javed Miandad, G. L. Jessop, H. Morris, P. A. Perrin, M. R. Ramprakash, B. Sutcliffe, H. Sutcliffe.

Three times: Agha Zahid, L. E. G. Ames, Basit Ali, G. Boycott, I. M. Chappell, D. C. S. Compton, S. J. Cook, M. C. Cowdrey, D. Denton, P. A. de Silva, K. S. Duleepsinhji, R. E. Foster, R. C. Fredericks, S. M. Gavaskar, W. G. Grace, G. Gunn, M. R. Hallam, Hanif Mohammad, M. J. Harris, M. L. Hayden, T. W. Hayward, V. S. Hazare, D. W. Hookes, L. Hutton, A. Jones, D. M. Jones, P. N. Kirsten, R. B. McCosker, P. B. H. May, C. P. Mead, T. M. Moody, M. H. Parmar, R. T. Ponting, Rizwan-uz-Zaman, R. T. Robinson, A. C. Russell, Sadiq Mohammad, J. T. Tyldesley, K. C. Wessels.

Notes: W. Lambert scored 107 and 157 for Sussex v Epsom at Lord's in 1817, and it was not until W. G. Grace made 130 and 102* for South of the Thames v North of the Thames at Canterbury in 1868 that the feat was repeated.

C. J. B. Wood, 107* and 117* for Leicestershire v Yorkshire at Bradford in 1911, and S. J. Cook, 120* and 131* for Somerset v Nottinghamshire at Nottingham in 1989, are alone in carrying their bats and scoring hundreds in each innings.

FOUR HUNDREDS OR MORE IN SUCCESSION

Six in succession: D. G. Bradman 1938-39; C. B. Fry 1901; M. J. Procter 1970-71.

Five in succession: B. C. Lara 1993-94/1994; E. D. Weekes 1955-56.

Four in succession: C. W. J. Athey 1987; M. Azharuddin 1984-85; M. G. Bevan 1990-91; G. S. Blewett 1998-99; A. R. Border 1985; D. G. Bradman 1931-32, 1948/1948-49; D. C. S. Compton 1946-47; N. J. Contractor 1957-58; S. J. Cook 1989; K. S. Duleepsinhji 1931; C. B. Fry 1911; C. G. Greenidge 1986; W. R. Hammond 1936-37, 1945/1946; H. T. W. Harding 1913; T. W. Hayward 1906; G. A. Hick 1998; J. B. Hobbs 1920, 1925; D. W. Hookes 1976-77; Ijaz Ahmed, jun. 1994-95; R. S. Kaluwitharana 1996-97; P. N. Kirsten 1976-77; J. G. Langridge 1949; C. G. Macartney 1921; K. S. McEwan 1977; P. B. H. May 1956-57; V. M. Merchant 1941-42; A. Mitchell 1933; Nawab of Pataudi sen. 1931; Rizwan-uz-Zaman 1989-90; L. G. Rowe 1971-72; Pankaj Roy 1962-63; Sadiq Mohammad 1976; Saeed Ahmed 1961-62; M. V. Sridhar 1990-91/1991-92; H. Sutcliffe 1931, 1939; S. R. Tendulkar 1994-95; E. Tyldesley 1926; W. W. Whysall 1930; F. E. Woolley 1929; Younis Khan 1999-2000; Zaheer Abbas 1970-71, 1982-83.

Notes: T. W. Hayward (Surrey v Nottinghamshire and Leicestershire) and D. W. Hookes (South Australia v Queensland and New South Wales) are the only players listed above to score two hundreds in two successive matches. Hayward scored his in six days, June 4-9, 1906.

The most fifties in consecutive innings is ten – by E. Tyldesley in 1926, by D. G. Bradman in the 1947-48 and 1948 seasons and by R. S. Kaluwitharana in 1994-95.

MOST HUNDREDS IN A SEASON

Eighteen: D. C. S. Compton 1947.

Sixteen: J. B. Hobbs 1925.

Fifteen: W. R. Hammond 1938.

Fourteen: H. Sutcliffe 1932.

Thirteen: G. Boycott 1971, D. G. Bradman 1938, C. B. Fry 1901, W. R. Hammond 1933 and 1937, T. W. Hayward 1906, E. H. Hendren 1923, 1927 and 1928, C. P. Mead 1928, H. Sutcliffe 1928 and 1931.

Since 1969 (excluding G. Boycott – above)

Twelve: G. A. Gooch 1990.

Eleven: S. J. Cook 1991, Zaheer Abbas 1976.

Ten: G. A. Hick 1988, H. Morris 1990, M. R. Ramprakash 1995, G. M. Turner 1970, Zaheer Abbas 1981.

Note: The most achieved outside England is eight by D. G. Bradman in Australia (1947-48), D. C. S. Compton (1948-49), R. N. Harvey and A. R. Morris (both 1949-50) in South Africa, M. D. Crowe in New Zealand (1986-87), Asif Mujtaba in Pakistan (1995-96) and V. V. S. Laxman in India (1999-2000).

MOST DOUBLE-HUNDREDS IN A SEASON

Six: D. G. Bradman 1930.

Five: K. S. Ranjitsinhji 1900; E. D. Weekes 1950.

Four: Arun Lal 1986-87; C. B. Fry 1901; W. R. Hammond 1933, 1934; E. H. Hendren 1929-30; V. M. Merchant 1944-45; G. M. Turner 1971-72.

Three: L. E. G. Ames 1933; Arshad Pervez 1977-78; D. G. Bradman 1930-31, 1931-32, 1934, 1935-36, 1936-37, 1938, 1939-40; W. J. Edrich 1947; C. B. Fry 1903, 1904; M. W. Gatting 1994; G. A. Gooch 1994; W. R. Hammond 1928, 1928-29, 1932-33, 1938; J. Hardstaff jun. 1937, 1947; V. S. Hazare 1943-44; E. H. Hendren 1925; J. B. Hobbs 1914, 1926; L. Hutton 1949; D. M. Jones 1991-92; A. I. Kallicharran 1982; V. G. Kambli 1992-93; P. N. Kirsten 1980; R. S. Modi 1944-45; Nawab of Pataudi sen. 1933; W. H. Ponsford 1927-28, 1934; W. V. Raman 1988-89; M. R. Ramprakash 1995; K. S. Ranjitsinhji 1901; I. V. A. Richards 1977; R. B. Simpson 1963-64; P. R. Umrigar 1952, 1959; F. B. Watson 1928.

MOST HUNDREDS IN A CAREER

(35 or more)

		Total	Total Inns	100th 100 Season	Inns	400s	300s	200s
1	J. B. Hobbs	197	1,315	1923	821	0	1	15
2	E. H. Hendren	170	1,300	1928-29	740	0	1	21
3	W. R. Hammond	167	1,005	1935	679	0	4	32
4	C. P. Mead	153	1,340	1927	892	0	0	13
5	G. Boycott	151	1,014	1977	645	0	0	10
6	H. Sutcliffe	149	1,088	1932	700	0	1	16
7	F. E. Woolley	145	1,532	1929	1,031	0	1	8
8	L. Hutton	129	814	1951	619	0	1	10
9	**G. A. Gooch**	**128**	**990**	**1992-93**	**820**	**0**	**1**	**12**
10	W. G. Grace	126	1,493	1895	1,113	0	3	10
11	D. C. S. Compton	123	839	1952	552	0	1	8
12	T. W. Graveney	122	1,223	1964	940	0	0	7
13	D. G. Bradman	117	338	1947-48	295	1	5	31
14	I. V. A. Richards	114	796	1988-89	658	0	1	9
15	**G. A. Hick**	**111**	**653**	**1998**	**574**	**1**	**1**	**9**
16	Zaheer Abbas	108	768	1982-83	658	0	0	10
17	A. Sandham	107	1,000	1935	871	0	1	10
	M. C. Cowdrey	107	1,130	1973	1,035	0	1	2
19	T. W. Hayward	104	1,138	1913	1,076	0	1	7
20	G. M. Turner	103	792	1982	779	0	1	9
	J. H. Edrich	103	979	1977	945	0	1	3
22	L. E. G. Ames	102	951	1950	915	0	0	9
	E. Tyldesley	102	961	1934	919	0	0	7
	D. L. Amiss	102	1,139	1986	1,081	0	0	3

E. H. Hendren, D. G. Bradman and I. V. A. Richards scored their 100th hundreds in Australia; G. A. Gooch scored his in India. His record includes his century in South Africa in 1981-82, which is no longer accepted by ICC. Zaheer Abbas scored his 100th in Pakistan. Zaheer Abbas and G. Boycott did so in Test matches.

Most double-hundreds scored by batsmen not included in the above list:

Sixteen: C. B. Fry. **Fourteen:** C. G. Greenidge, K. S. Ranjitsinhji. **Thirteen:** W. H. Ponsford (including two 400s and two 300s), J. T. Tyldesley. **Twelve:** P. Holmes, Javed Miandad, R. B. Simpson. **Eleven:** J. W. Hearne, V. M. Merchant. **Ten:** S. M. Gavaskar, J. Hardstaff, jun., V. S. Hazare, A. Shrewsbury, R. T. Simpson.

J. W. Hearne 96	P. H. Parfitt 58	A. C. MacLaren 47
C. B. Fry 94	W. Rhodes 58	**M. P. Maynard** **47**
M. W. Gatting 94	**S. R. Waugh** **58**	P. W. G. Parker 47
C. G. Greenidge 92	**K. J. Barnett** **57**	W. H. Ponsford 47
A. J. Lamb 89	P. N. Kirsten 57	C. L. Smith 47
A. I. Kallicharran 87	L. B. Fishlock 56	**R. J. Bailey** **46**
W. J. Edrich 86	A. Jones 56	A. R. Butcher 46
G. S. Sobers 86	C. A. Milton 56	J. Iddon 46
J. T. Tyldesley 86	**R. A. Smith** **56**	**J. L. Langer** **46**
P. B. H. May 85	C. W. J. Athey 55	A. R. Morris 46
R. E. S. Wyatt 85	C. Hallows 55	C. T. Radley 46
J. Hardstaff, jun. 83	Hanif Mohammad 55	**A. J. Stewart** **46**
R. B. Kanhai 83	D. M. Jones 55	**A. P. Wells** **46**
S. M. Gavaskar 81	D. B. Vengsarkar 55	Younis Ahmed 46
Javed Miandad 80	W. Watson 55	W. W. Armstrong 45
M. Leyland 80	**M. Azharuddin** **54**	Asif Iqbal 45
B. A. Richards 80	D. J. Insole 54	L. G. Berry 45
C. H. Lloyd 79	W. W. Keeton 54	J. M. Brearley 45
K. F. Barrington 76	W. Bardsley 53	A. W. Carr 45
J. G. Langridge 76	B. F. Davison 53	C. Hill 45
C. Washbrook 76	A. E. Dipper 53	M. D. Moxon 45
H. T. W. Hardinge 75	D. I. Gower 53	N. C. O'Neill 45
R. Abel 74	G. L. Jessop 53	E. Paynter 45
G. S. Chappell 74	H. Morris 53	Rev. D. S. Sheppard . . . 45
D. Kenyon 74	James Seymour 53	N. R. Taylor 45
K. S. McEwan 74	Shafiq Ahmad 53	K. D. Walters 45
Majid Khan 73	**M. A. Atherton** **52**	H. H. Gibbons 44
M. E. Waugh **73**	E. H. Bowley 52	**M. L. Hayden** **44**
Mushtaq Mohammad . . . 72	D. B. Close 52	V. M. Merchant 44
J. O'Connor 72	A. Ducat 52	A. Mitchell 44
W. G. Quaife 72	D. W. Randall 52	P. E. Richardson 44
K. S. Ranjitsinhji 72	E. R. Dexter 51	B. Sutcliffe 44
D. Brookes 71	J. M. Parks 51	G. R. Viswanath 44
M. D. Crowe 71	**M. R. Ramprakash** **51**	P. Willey 44
A. C. Russell 71	W. W. Whysall 51	E. J. Barlow 43
A. R. Border 70	B. C. Broad 50	T. S. Curtis 43
D. Denton 69	G. Cox, jun. 50	B. L. D'Oliveira 43
M. J. K. Smith 69	H. E. Dollery 50	J. H. Hampshire 43
D. C. Boon 68	K. S. Duleepsinhji 50	**N. Hussain** **43**
R. E. Marshall 68	H. Gimblett 50	A. F. Kippax 43
R. N. Harvey 67	W. M. Lawry 50	J. W. H. Makepeace 43
P. Holmes 67	**J. E. Morris** **50**	**Rizwan-uz-Zaman** **43**
J. D. Robertson 67	Sadiq Mohammad 50	**Salim Malik** **43**
P. A. Perrin 66	F. B. Watson 50	**S. R. Tendulkar** **43**
K. C. Wessels **66**	C. L. Hooper 49	**N. H. Fairbrother** **42**
S. J. Cook 64	C. G. Macartney 49	**S. P. James** **42**
T. M. Moody 64	M. J. Stewart 49	James Langridge 42
R. G. Pollock 64	K. G. Suttle 49	Mudassar Nazar 42
R. T. Simpson 64	P. R. Umrigar 49	H. W. Parks 42
K. W. R. Fletcher 63	W. M. Woodfull 49	T. F. Shepherd 42
R. T. Robinson 63	C. J. Barnett 48	V. T. Trumper 42
G. Gunn 62	M. R. Benson 48	M. J. Harris 41
D. L. Haynes 61	W. Gunn 48	G. D. Mendis 41
V. S. Hazare 60	E. G. Hayes 48	K. R. Miller 41
G. H. Hirst 60	**S. G. Law** **48**	A. D. Nourse 41
R. B. Simpson 60	**D. S. Lehmann** **48**	J. H. Parks 41
P. F. Warner 60	B. W. Luckhurst 48	R. M. Prideaux 41
I. M. Chappell 59	M. J. Procter 48	G. Pullar 41
A. L. Hassett 59	C. E. B. Rice 48	W. E. Russell 41
W. Larkins 59	C. J. Tavaré 48	M. A. Taylor 41
A. Shrewsbury 59	**M. G. Bevan** **47**	**Asif Mujtaba** **40**
J. G. Wright 59		
A. E. Fagg 58		

P. D. Bowler **40**	D. Lloyd 38	R. T. Virgin 37
R. C. Fredericks 40	V. L. Manjrekar 38	C. J. B. Wood 37
J. Gunn 40	A. W. Nourse 38	N. F. Armstrong 36
B. C. Lara **40**	N. Oldfield 38	G. Fowler 36
M. J. Smith 40	Rev. J. H. Parsons 38	M. C. J. Nicholas 36
C. L. Walcott 40	W. W. Read 38	E. Oldroyd 36
D. M. Young 40	**Ajay Sharma** **38**	W. Place 36
Arshad Pervez 39	J. Sharp 38	**G. P. Thorpe** **36**
W. H. Ashdown 39	V. P. Terry 38	A. L. Wadekar 36
J. B. Bolus 39	L. J. Todd 38	E. D. Weekes 36
W. A. Brown 39	J. J. Whitaker 38	**J. Cox** **35**
P. A. de Silva **39**	J. Arnold 37	**D. J. Cullinan** **35**
R. J. Gregory 39	G. Brown 37	C. S. Dempster 35
M. A. Lynch 39	G. Cook 37	D. R. Jardine 35
W. R. D. Payton 39	**J. P. Crawley** **37**	T. E. Jesty 35
J. R. Reid 39	G. M. Emmett 37	**K. R. Rutherford** **35**
F. M. M. Worrell 39	H. W. Lee 37	**Sajid Ali** **35**
I. T. Botham 38	M. A. Noble 37	**J. D. Siddons** **35**
F. L. Bowley 38	B. P. Patel 37	B. H. Valentine 35
P. J. Burge 38	R. B. Richardson 37	G. M. Wood 35
J. F. Crapp 38	**Shoaib Mohammad** . . . **37**	
P. Johnson **38**	H. S. Squires 37	

Bold type denotes those who played in 1999-2000 and 2000 seasons.

MOST RUNS IN A SEASON

	Season	I	NO	R	HS	100s	Avge
D. C. S. Compton	1947	50	8	3,816	246	18	90.85
W. J. Edrich	1947	52	8	3,539	267*	12	80.43
T. W. Hayward	1906	61	8	3,518	219	13	66.37
L. Hutton	1949	56	6	3,429	269*	12	68.58
F. E. Woolley	1928	59	4	3,352	198	12	60.94
H. Sutcliffe	1932	52	7	3,336	313	14	74.13
W. R. Hammond	1933	54	5	3,323	264	13	67.81
E. H. Hendren	1928	54	7	3,311	209*	13	70.44
R. Abel	1901	68	8	3,309	247	7	55.15

Notes: 3,000 in a season has been surpassed on 19 other occasions (a full list can be found in *Wisden* 1999 and earlier editions). W. R. Hammond, E. H. Hendren and H. Sutcliffe are the only players to achieve the feat three times. M. J. K. Smith (3,245 in 1959) and W. E. Alley (3,019 in 1961) are the only players except those listed above to have reached 3,000 since World War II.

2,000 RUNS IN A SEASON

Since Reduction of Championship Matches in 1969

Five times: G. A. Gooch 2,746 (1990), 2,559 (1984), 2,324 (1988), 2,208 (1985), 2,023 (1993).

Three times: D. L. Amiss 2,239 (1984), 2,110 (1976), 2,030 (1978); S. J. Cook 2,755† (1991), 2,608 (1990), 2,241 (1989); M. W. Gatting 2,257 (1984), 2,057 (1991), 2,000 (1992); G. A. Hick 2,713 (1988), 2,347 (1990), 2,004 (1986); G. M. Turner 2,416 (1973), 2,379 (1970), 2,101 (1981).

Twice: G. Boycott 2,503 (1971), 2,051 (1970); J. H. Edrich 2,238 (1969), 2,031 (1971); A. I. Kallicharran 2,301 (1984), 2,120 (1982); Zaheer Abbas 2,554 (1976), 2,306 (1981).

Once: M. Azharuddin 2,016 (1991); J. B. Bolus 2,143 (1970); P. D. Bowler 2,044 (1992); B. C. Broad 2,226 (1990); A. R. Butcher 2,116 (1990); C. G. Greenidge 2,035 (1986); M. J. Harris 2,238 (1971); D. L. Haynes 2,346 (1990); Javed Miandad 2,083 (1981); A. J. Lamb 2,049 (1981); B. C. Lara 2,066 (1994); K. S. McEwan 2,176 (1983); Majid Khan 2,074 (1972); A. A. Metcalfe 2,047 (1990); H. Morris 2,276 (1990); M. R. Ramprakash 2,258 (1995); D. W. Randall 2,151 (1985); I. V. A. Richards 2,161 (1977); R. T. Robinson 2,032 (1984); M. A. Roseberry 2,044 (1992); C. L. Smith 2,000 (1985); R. T. Virgin 2,223 (1970); D. M. Ward 2,072 (1990); M. E. Waugh 2,072 (1990).

Notes: W. G. Grace scored 2,739 runs in 1871 – the first batsman to reach 2,000 runs in a season. He made ten hundreds and twice exceeded 200, with an average of 78.25 in all first-class matches.
† *Highest since the reduction of Championship matches in 1969.*

1,000 RUNS IN A SEASON MOST TIMES

(Includes Overseas Tours and Seasons)

28 times: W. G. Grace 2,000 (6); F. E. Woolley 3,000 (1), 2,000 (12).
27 times: M. C. Cowdrey 2,000 (2); C. P. Mead 3,000 (2), 2,000 (9).
26 times: G. Boycott 2,000 (3); J. B. Hobbs 3,000 (1), 2,000 (16).
25 times: E. H. Hendren 3,000 (3), 2,000 (12).
24 times: D. L. Amiss 2,000 (3); W. G. Quaife 2,000 (1); H. Sutcliffe 3,000 (3), 2,000 (12).
23 times: A. Jones.
22 times: T. W. Graveney 2,000 (7); W. R. Hammond 3,000 (3), 2,000 (9).
21 times: D. Denton 2,000 (5); J. H. Edrich 2,000 (6); G. A. Gooch 2,000 (5); W. Rhodes 2,000 (2).
20 times: D. B. Close; K. W. R. Fletcher; M. W. Gatting 2,000 (3); G. Gunn; T. W. Hayward 3,000 (2), 2,000 (8); James Langridge 2,000 (1); J. M. Parks 2,000 (3); A. Sandham 2,000 (8); M. J. K. Smith 3,000 (1), 2,000 (5); C. Washbrook 2,000 (2).
19 times: J. W. Hearne 2,000 (4); G. H. Hirst 2,000 (3); D. Kenyon 2,000 (7); E. Tyldesley 3,000 (1), 2,000 (5); J. T. Tyldesley 3,000 (1), 2,000 (4).
18 times: L. G. Berry 2,000 (1); H. T. W. Hardinge 2,000 (5); R. E. Marshall 2,000 (6); P. A. Perrin 2,000 (1); G. M. Turner 2,000 (3); R. E. S. Wyatt 2,000 (5).
17 times: L. E. G. Ames 3,000 (1), 2,000 (5); T. E. Bailey 2,000 (1); D. Brookes 2,000 (6); D. C. S. Compton 3,000 (1), 2,000 (5); C. G. Greenidge 2,000 (1); L. Hutton 3,000 (1), 2,000 (8); J. G. Langridge 2,000 (11); M. Leyland 2,000 (1); I. V. A. Richards 2,000 (1); K. G. Suttle 2,000 (1); Zaheer Abbas 2,000 (1).
16 times: D. G. Bradman 2,000 (4); D. E. Davies 2,000 (1); E. G. Hayes 2,000 (2); G. A. Hick 2,000 (3); C. A. Milton 2,000 (1); J. O'Connor 2,000 (4); C. T. Radley; James Seymour 2,000 (1); C. J. Tavaré.
15 times: G. Barker; K. J. Barnett; K. F. Barrington 2,000 (3); E. H. Bowley 2,000 (4); M. H. Denness; A. E. Dipper 2,000 (5); H. E. Dollery 2,000 (2); W. J. Edrich 3,000 (1), 2,000 (8); J. H. Hampshire; P. Holmes 2,000 (7); Mushtaq Mohammad; R. B. Nicholls 2,000 (1); P. H. Parfitt 2,000 (3); W. G. A. Parkhouse 2,000 (1); B. A. Richards 2,000 (1); J. D. Robertson 2,000 (9); G. S. Sobers; M. J. Stewart 2,000 (1).

Notes: F. E. Woolley reached 1,000 runs in 28 consecutive seasons (1907-1938), C. P. Mead in 27 (1906-1936).

Outside England, 1,000 runs in a season has been reached most times by D. G. Bradman (in 12 seasons in Australia).

Three batsmen have scored 1,000 runs in a season in each of four different countries: G. S. Sobers in West Indies, England, India and Australia; M. C. Cowdrey and G. Boycott in England, South Africa, West Indies and Australia.

HIGHEST AGGREGATES OUTSIDE ENGLAND

	Season	I	NO	R	HS	100s	Avge
In Australia							
D. G. Bradman	1928-29	24	6	1,690	340*	7	93.88
In South Africa							
J. R. Reid	1961-62	30	2	1,915	203	7	68.39
In West Indies							
E. H. Hendren	1929-30	18	5	1,765	254*	6	135.76
In New Zealand							
M. D. Crowe	1986-87	21	3	1,676	175*	8	93.11
In India							
C. G. Borde	1964-65	28	3	1,604	168	6	64.16
In Pakistan							
Saadat Ali	1983-84	27	1	1,649	208	4	63.42

In Sri Lanka	Season	I	NO	R	HS	100s	Avge
R. P. Arnold	1995-96	24	3	1,475	217*	5	70.23

In Zimbabwe							
G. W. Flower	1994-95	20	3	983	201*	4	57.82

Note: In more than one country, the following aggregates of over 2,000 runs have been recorded:

M. Amarnath (P/I/WI)	1982-83	34	6	2,234	207	9	79.78
J. R. Reid (SA/A/NZ)	1961-62	40	2	2,188	203	7	57.57
S. M. Gavaskar (I/P)	1978-79	30	6	2,121	205	10	88.37
R. B. Simpson (I/P/A/WI)....	1964-65	34	4	2,063	201	8	68.76

LEADING BATSMEN IN AN ENGLISH SEASON

(Qualification: 8 completed innings)

Season	Leading scorer	Runs	Avge	Top of averages	Runs	Avge
1946	D. C. S. Compton ...	2,403	61.61	W. R. Hammond	1,783	84.90
1947	D. C. S. Compton ...	3,816	90.85	D. C. S. Compton ...	3,816	90.85
1948	L. Hutton	2,654	64.73	D. G. Bradman	2,428	89.92
1949	L. Hutton	3,429	68.58	J. Hardstaff........	2,251	72.61
1950	R. T. Simpson	2,576	62.82	E. Weekes..........	2,310	79.65
1951	J. D. Robertson.....	2,917	56.09	P. B. H. May......	2,339	68.79
1952	L. Hutton	2,567	61.11	D. S. Sheppard	2,262	64.62
1953	W. J. Edrich	2,557	47.35	R. N. Harvey	2,040	65.80
1954	D. Kenyon	2,636	51.68	D. C. S. Compton ...	1,524	58.61
1955	D. J. Insole	2,427	42.57	D. J. McGlew	1,871	58.46
1956	T. W. Graveney.....	2,397	49.93	K. Mackay	1,103	52.52
1957	T. W. Graveney.....	2,361	49.18	P. B. H. May......	2,347	61.76
1958	P. B. H. May	2,231	63.74	P. B. H. May......	2,231	63.74
1959	M. J. K. Smith	3,245	57.94	V. L. Manjrekar....	755	68.63
1960	M. J. K. Smith	2,551	45.55	R. Subba Row.....	1,503	55.66
1961	W. E. Alley	3,019	56.96	W. M. Lawry	2,019	61.18
1962	J. H. Edrich	2,482	51.70	R. T. Simpson	867	54.18
1963	J. B. Bolus	2,190	41.32	G. S. Sobers	1,333	47.60
1964	T. W. Graveney.....	2,385	54.20	K. F. Barrington.....	1,872	62.40
1965	J. H. Edrich	2,319	62.67	M. C. Cowdrey	2,093	63.42
1966	A. R. Lewis	2,198	41.47	G. S. Sobers	1,349	61.31
1967	C. A. Milton	2,089	46.42	K. F. Barrington....	2,059	68.63
1968	B. A. Richards	2,395	47.90	G. Boycott	1,487	64.65
1969	J. H. Edrich	2,238	69.93	J. H. Edrich	2,238	69.93
1970	G. M. Turner	2,379	61.00	G. S. Sobers	1,742	75.73
1971	G. Boycott	2,503	100.12	G. Boycott	2,503	100.12
1972	Majid Khan	2,074	61.00	G. Boycott	1,230	72.35
1973	G. M. Turner	2,416	67.11	G. M. Turner......	2,416	67.11
1974	R. T. Virgin	1,936	56.94	C. H. Lloyd	1,458	63.39
1975	G. Boycott	1,915	73.65	R. B. Kanhai	1,073	82.53
1976	Zaheer Abbas......	2,554	75.11	Zaheer Abbas	2,554	75.11
1977	I. V. A. Richards ...	2,161	65.48	G. Boycott	1,701	68.04
1978	D. L. Amiss.......	2,030	53.42	C. E. B. Rice	1,871	66.82
1979	K. C. Wessels......	1,800	52.94	G. Boycott	1,538	102.53
1980	P. N. Kirsten	1,895	63.16	A. J. Lamb	1,797	66.55
1981	Zaheer Abbas......	2,306	88.69	Zaheer Abbas	2,306	88.69
1982	A. I. Kallicharran ...	2,120	66.25	G. M. Turner......	1,171	90.07
1983	K. S. McEwan	2,176	64.00	I. V. A. Richards ...	1,204	75.25
1984	G. A. Gooch	2,559	67.34	C. G. Greenidge	1,069	82.23
1985	G. A. Gooch	2,208	71.22	I. V. A. Richards ...	1,836	76.50
1986	C. G. Greenidge	2,035	67.83	C. G. Greenidge	2,035	67.83

Season	Leading scorer	Runs	Avge	Top of averages	Runs	Avge
1987	G. A. Hick	1,879	52.19	M. D. Crowe	1,627	67.79
1988	G. A. Hick	2,713	77.51	R. A. Harper	622	77.75
1989	S. J. Cook	2,241	60.56	D. M. Jones	1,510	88.82
1990	G. A. Gooch	2,746	101.70	G. A. Gooch	2,746	101.70
1991	S. J. Cook	2,755	81.02	C. L. Hooper	1,501	93.81
1992	⎰ P. D. Bowler	2,044	65.93			
	⎱ M. A. Roseberry	2,044	56.77	Salim Malik	1,184	78.93
1993	G. A. Gooch	2,023	63.21	D. C. Boon	1,437	75.63
1994	B. C. Lara	2,066	89.82	J. D. Carr	1,543	90.76
1995	M. R. Ramprakash . .	2,258	77.86	M. R. Ramprakash . . .	2,258	77.86
1996	G. A. Gooch	1,944	67.03	S. C. Ganguly	762	95.25
1997	S. P. James	1,775	68.26	G. A. Hick	1,524	69.27
1998	J. P. Crawley	1,851	74.04	J. P. Crawley	1,851	74.04
1999	S. G. Law	1,833	73.32	S. G. Law	1,833	73.32
2000	D. S. Lehmann	1,477	67.13	M. G. Bevan	1,124	74.93

Notes: The highest average recorded in an English season was 115.66 (2,429 runs, 26 innings) by D. G. Bradman in 1938.

In 1953, W. A. Johnston averaged 102.00 from 17 innings, 16 not out.

25,000 RUNS IN A CAREER

Dates in italics denote the first half of an overseas season; i.e. *1945* denotes the 1945-46 season.

		Career	R	I	NO	HS	100s	Avge
1	J. B. Hobbs	1905-34	61,237	1,315	106	316*	197	50.65
2	F. E. Woolley	1906-38	58,969	1,532	85	305*	145	40.75
3	E. H. Hendren	1907-38	57,611	1,300	166	301*	170	50.80
4	C. P. Mead	1905-36	55,061	1,340	185	280*	153	47.67
5	W. G. Grace	1865-1908	54,896	1,493	105	344	126	39.55
6	W. R. Hammond	1920-51	50,551	1,005	104	336*	167	56.10
7	H. Sutcliffe	1919-45	50,138	1,088	123	313	149	51.95
8	G. Boycott	1962-86	48,426	1,014	162	261*	151	56.83
9	T. W. Graveney	1948-*71*	47,793	1,223	159	258	122	44.91
10	**G. A. Gooch**	**1973-2000**	**44,846**	**990**	**75**	**333**	**128**	**49.01**
11	T. W. Hayward	1893-1914	43,551	1,138	96	315*	104	41.79
12	D. L. Amiss	1960-87	43,423	1,139	126	262*	102	42.86
13	M. C. Cowdrey	1950-76	42,719	1,130	134	307	107	42.89
14	A. Sandham	1911-*37*	41,284	1,000	79	325	107	44.82
15	L. Hutton	1934-60	40,140	814	91	364	129	55.51
16	M. J. K. Smith	1951-75	39,832	1,091	139	204	69	41.84
17	W. Rhodes	1898-1930	39,802	1,528	237	267*	58	30.83
18	J. H. Edrich	1956-78	39,790	979	104	310*	103	45.47
19	R. E. S. Wyatt	1923-57	39,405	1,141	157	232	85	40.04
20	D. C. S. Compton . . .	1936-64	38,942	839	88	300	123	51.85
21	E. Tyldesley	1909-36	38,874	961	106	256*	102	45.46
22	J. T. Tyldesley	1895-1923	37,897	994	62	295*	86	40.66
23	K. W. R. Fletcher	1962-88	37,665	1,167	170	228*	63	37.77
24	C. G. Greenidge	1970-92	37,354	889	75	273*	92	45.88
25	J. W. Hearne	1909-36	37,252	1,025	116	285*	96	40.98
26	L. E. G. Ames	1926-51	37,248	951	95	295	102	43.51
27	D. Kenyon	1946-67	37,002	1,159	59	259	74	33.63
28	W. J. Edrich	1934-58	36,965	964	92	267*	86	42.39
29	J. M. Parks	1949-76	36,673	1,227	172	205*	51	34.76
30	M. W. Gatting	1975-98	36,549	861	123	258	94	49.52
31	D. Denton	1894-1920	36,479	1,163	70	221	69	33.37
32	G. H. Hirst	1891-1929	36,323	1,215	151	341	60	34.13
33	I. V. A. Richards	*1971*-93	36,212	796	63	322	114	49.40
34	A. Jones	1957-83	36,049	1,168	72	204*	56	32.89
35	W. G. Quaife	1894-1928	36,012	1,203	185	255*	72	35.37
36	R. E. Marshall	*1945*-72	35,725	1,053	59	228*	68	35.94

		Career	R	I	NO	HS	100s	Avge
37	G. Gunn	1902-32	35,208	1,061	82	220	62	35.96
38	D. B. Close	1949-86	34,994	1,225	173	198	52	33.26
39	Zaheer Abbas	1965-86	34,843	768	92	274	108	51.54
40	J. G. Langridge	1928-55	34,380	984	66	250*	76	37.45
41	G. M. Turner	1964-82	34,346	792	101	311*	103	49.70
42	C. Washbrook	1933-64	34,101	906	107	251*	76	42.67
43	M. Leyland	1920-48	33,660	932	101	263	80	40.50
44	H. T. W. Hardinge. . .	1902-33	33,519	1,021	103	263*	75	36.51
45	R. Abel	1881-1904	33,124	1,007	73	357*	74	35.46
46	A. I. Kallicharran . . .	1966-90	32,650	834	86	243*	87	43.64
47	A. J. Lamb	1972-95	32,502	772	108	294	89	48.94
48	C. A. Milton	1948-74	32,150	1,078	125	170	56	33.73
49	**G. A. Hick**	**1983-2000**	**32,082**	**653**	**62**	**405***	**111**	**54.28**
50	J. D. Robertson.	1937-59	31,914	897	46	331*	67	37.50
51	J. Hardstaff, jun. . . .	1930-55	31,847	812	94	266	83	44.35
52	James Langridge	1924-53	31,716	1,058	157	167	42	35.20
53	K. F. Barrington	1953-68	31,714	831	136	256	76	45.63
54	C. H. Lloyd	1963-86	31,232	730	96	242*	79	49.26
55	Mushtaq Mohammad . .	1956-85	31,091	843	104	303*	72	42.07
56	C. B. Fry	1892-1921	30,886	658	43	258*	94	50.22
57	D. Brookes	1934-59	30,874	925	70	257	71	36.10
58	P. Holmes	1913-35	30,573	810	84	315*	67	42.11
59	R. T. Simpson	1944-63	30,546	852	55	259	64	38.32
60	{L. G. Berry	1924-51	30,225	1,056	57	232	45	30.25
	{K. G. Suttle.	1949-71	30,225	1,064	92	204*	49	31.09
62	P. A. Perrin	1896-1928	29,709	918	91	343*	66	35.92
63	P. F. Warner	1894-1929	29,028	875	75	244	60	36.28
64	R. B. Kanhai	1954-81	28,774	669	82	256	83	49.01
65	J. O'Connor	1921-39	28,764	903	79	248	72	34.90
66	Javed Miandad	1973-93	28,647	631	95	311	80	53.44
67	T. E. Bailey	1945-67	28,641	1,072	215	205	28	33.42
68	D. W. Randall	1972-93	28,456	827	81	237	52	38.14
69	E. H. Bowley	1912-34	28,378	859	47	283	52	34.94
70	B. A. Richards	1964-82	28,358	576	58	356	80	54.74
71	G. S. Sobers	1952-74	28,315	609	93	365*	86	54.87
72	A. E. Dipper	1908-32	28,075	865	69	252*	53	35.27
73	D. G. Bradman	1927-48	28,067	338	43	452*	117	95.14
74	J. H. Hampshire	1961-84	28,059	924	112	183*	43	34.55
75	P. B. H. May	1948-63	27,592	618	77	285*	85	51.00
76	R. T. Robinson	1978-99	27,571	739	85	220*	63	42.15
77	B. F. Davison	1967-87	27,453	766	79	189	53	39.96
78	Majid Khan	1961-84	27,444	700	62	241	73	43.01
79	A. C. Russell	1908-30	27,358	717	59	273	71	41.57
80	E. G. Hayes	1896-1926	27,318	896	48	276	48	32.21
81	A. E. Fagg	1932-57	27,291	803	46	269*	58	36.05
82	James Seymour	1900-26	27,237	911	62	218*	53	32.08
83	W. Larkins.	1972-95	27,142	842	54	252	59	34.44
84	A. R. Border	1976-95	27,131	625	97	205	70	51.38
85	P. H. Parfitt	1956-73	26,924	845	104	200*	58	36.33
86	**K. J. Barnett . . . . . .**	**1979-2000**	**26,923**	**744**	**71**	**239***	**57**	**40.00**
87	G. L. Jessop	1894-1914	26,698	855	37	286	53	32.63
88	K. S. McEwan	1972-91	26,628	705	67	218	74	41.73
89	D. E. Davies	1924-54	26,564	1,032	80	287*	32	27.90
90	A. Shrewsbury	1875-1902	26,505	813	90	267	59	36.65
91	M. J. Stewart	1954-72	26,492	898	93	227*	49	32.90
92	C. T. Radley	1964-87	26,441	880	134	200	46	35.44
93	D. I. Gower	1975-93	26,339	727	70	228	53	40.08
94	C. E. B. Rice.	1969-93	26,331	766	123	246	48	40.95
95	Younis Ahmed	1961-86	26,073	762	118	221*	46	40.48
96	P. E. Richardson	1949-65	26,055	794	41	185	44	34.60
97	D. L. Haynes	1976-96	26,030	639	72	255*	61	45.90

		Career	R	I	NO	HS	100s	Avge
98	M. H. Denness.	1959-80	25,886	838	65	195	33	33.48
99	S. M. Gavaskar	*1966-87*	25,834	563	61	340	81	51.46
100	J. W. H. Makepeace. .	1906-30	25,799	778	66	203	43	36.23
101	W. Gunn	1880-1904	25,691	850	72	273	48	33.02
102	W. Watson	1939-64	25,670	753	109	257	55	39.86
103	G. Brown	1908-33	25,649	1,012	52	232*	37	26.71
104	G. M. Emmett	1936-59	25,602	865	50	188	37	31.41
105	J. B. Bolus	1956-75	25,598	833	81	202*	39	34.03
106	W. E. Russell.	1956-72	25,525	796	64	193	41	34.87
107	C. W. J. Athey	1976-97	25,453	784	71	184	55	35.69
108	C. J. Barnett	1927-*53*	25,389	821	45	259	48	32.71
109	L. B. Fishlock	1931-52	25,376	699	54	253	56	39.34
110	D. J. Insole	1947-63	25,241	743	72	219*	54	37.61
111	J. M. Brearley	1961-83	25,185	768	102	312*	45	37.81
112	J. Vine	1896-1922	25,171	920	79	202	34	29.92
113	R. M. Prideaux	1958-*74*	25,136	808	75	202*	41	34.29
114	J. H. King	1895-1925	25,122	988	69	227*	34	27.33
115	J. G. Wright.	*1975-92*	25,073	636	44	192	59	42.35

Bold type denotes those who played in 1999-2000 and 2000 seasons.

Note: Some works of reference provide career figures which differ from those in this list, owing to the exclusion or inclusion of matches recognised or not recognised as first-class by *Wisden*.

Current Players with 20,000 Runs

	Career	R	I	NO	HS	100s	Avge
K. C. Wessels	*1973-99*	24,738	539	50	254	66	50.58
R. A. Smith.	*1980-2000*	24,203	651	83	209*	56	42.61
A. J. Stewart	1981-2000	23,357	654	70	271*	46	39.99
M. E. Waugh.	*1985-99*	23,023	499	63	229*	73	52.80
R. J. Bailey	1982-2000	21,329	603	88	224*	46	41.41
A. P. Wells	1981-2000	21,099	628	81	253*	46	38.57
J. E. Morris.	1982-2000	20,899	596	33	229	50	37.12
M. P. Maynard	1985-2000	20,897	549	56	243	47	42.38
M. A. Atherton.	1987-2000	20,598	545	45	268*	52	41.19

CAREER AVERAGE OVER 50

(Qualification: 10,000 runs)

Avge		Career	I	NO	R	HS	100s
95.14	D. G. Bradman	*1927-48*	338	43	28,067	452*	117
71.22	V. M. Merchant	*1929-51*	229	43	13,248	359*	44
67.80	**Ajay Sharma**	*1984-99*	164	15	10,103	**259***	**38**
65.18	W. H. Ponsford	*1920-34*	235	23	13,819	437	47
64.99	W. M. Woodfull	*1921-34*	245	39	13,388	284	49
61.20	**S. R. Tendulkar**	*1988-2000*	246	26	13,466	**233***	**43**
58.24	A. L. Hassett	*1932-53*	322	32	16,890	232	59
58.19	V. S. Hazare	*1934-66*	365	45	18,621	316*	60
57.22	A. F. Kippax	*1918-35*	256	33	12,762	315*	43
56.83	G. Boycott	1962-86	1,014	162	48,426	261*	151
56.55	C. L. Walcott	*1941-63*	238	29	11,820	314*	40
56.37	K. S. Ranjitsinhji	1893-1920	500	62	24,692	285*	72
56.22	R. B. Simpson	*1952-77*	436	62	21,029	359	60
56.10	W. R. Hammond	1920-51	1,005	104	50,551	336*	167
56.02	M. D. Crowe	*1979-95*	412	62	19,608	299	71
55.85	**M. G. Bevan**	*1989-2000*	**301**	**54**	**13,796**	**203***	**47**
55.51	L. Hutton	1934-60	814	91	40,140	364	129
55.34	E. D. Weekes	*1944-64*	241	24	12,010	304*	36

Avge		Career	I	NO	R	HS	100s
55.11	S. V. Manjrekar	*1984-97*	217	31	10,252	377	31
54.92	**D. S. Lehmann**	***1987-2000***	**288**	**18**	**14,829**	**255**	**48**
54.87	G. S. Sobers	*1952-74*	609	93	28,315	365*	86
54.74	B. A. Richards	*1964-82*	576	58	28,358	356	80
54.72	**R. Dravid**	***1990-2000***	**221**	**30**	**10,453**	**215**	**28**
54.67	R. G. Pollock	*1960-86*	437	54	20,940	274	64
54.28	**G. A. Hick**	***1983-2000***	**653**	**62**	**32,082**	**405***	**111**
54.24	F. M. M. Worrell	*1941-64*	326	49	15,025	308*	39
53.78	R. M. Cowper	*1959-69*	228	31	10,595	307	26
53.67	A. R. Morris	*1940-63*	250	15	12,614	290	46
53.44	Javed Miandad	*1973-93*	631	95	28,647	311	80
53.14	**J. L. Langer**	***1991-2000***	**311**	**35**	**14,668**	**274***	**46**
52.86	D. B. Vengsarkar	*1975-91*	390	52	17,868	284	55
52.80	**M. E. Waugh**	***1985-99***	**499**	**63**	**23,023**	**229***	**73**
52.37	**S. R. Waugh**	***1984-99***	**441**	**74**	**19,221**	**216***	**58**
52.33	**M. L. Hayden**	***1991-2000***	**296**	**31**	**13,870**	**235***	**44**
52.32	Hanif Mohammad	*1951-75*	371	45	17,059	499	55
52.27	P. R. Umrigar	*1944-67*	350	41	16,154	252*	49
52.20	G. S. Chappell	*1966-83*	542	72	24,535	247*	74
51.98	**M. Azharuddin**	***1981-99***	**343**	**38**	**15,855**	**226**	**54**
51.95	H. Sutcliffe	*1919-45*	1,088	123	50,138	313	149
51.85	D. M. Jones	*1981-97*	415	45	19,188	324*	55
51.85	D. C. S. Compton	*1936-64*	839	88	38,942	300	123
51.54	Zaheer Abbas	*1965-86*	768	92	34,843	274	108
51.53	A. D. Nourse	*1931-52*	269	27	12,472	260*	41
51.46	S. M. Gavaskar	*1966-87*	563	61	25,834	340	81
51.44	W. A. Brown	*1932-49*	284	15	13,838	265*	39
51.38	A. R. Border	*1976-95*	625	97	27,131	205	70
51.00	P. B. H. May	*1948-63*	618	77	27,592	285*	85
50.95	N. C. O'Neill	*1955-67*	306	34	13,859	284	45
50.93	R. N. Harvey	*1946-62*	461	35	21,699	231*	67
50.90	W. M. Lawry	*1955-71*	417	49	18,734	266	50
50.90	A. V. Mankad	*1963-82*	326	71	12,980	265	31
50.80	E. H. Hendren	*1907-38*	1,300	166	57,611	301*	170
50.65	J. B. Hobbs	*1905-34*	1,315	106	61,237	316*	197
50.58	**K. C. Wessels**	***1973-99***	**539**	**50**	**24,738**	**254**	**66**
50.58	S. J. Cook	*1972-94*	475	57	21,143	313*	64
50.49	**Asif Mujtaba**	***1984-2000***	**368**	**72**	**14,947**	**208**	**40**
50.32	**Inzamam-ul-Haq**	***1985-2000 (SL)***	**279**	**45**	**11,777**	**201***	**31**
50.22	C. B. Fry	*1892-1921*	658	43	30,886	258*	94
50.01	Shafiq Ahmad	*1967-90*	449	58	19,555	217*	53

Note: G. A. Headley (*1927*-1954) scored 9,921 runs, average 69.86.

Bold type denotes those who played in 1999-2000 and 2000 seasons.

FASTEST FIFTIES

Minutes			
11	C. I. J. Smith (66)	Middlesex v Gloucestershire at Bristol	1938
14	S. J. Pegler (50)	South Africans v Tasmania at Launceston	1910-11
14	F. T. Mann (53)	Middlesex v Nottinghamshire at Lord's	1921
14	H. B. Cameron (56)	Transvaal v Orange Free State at Johannesburg . . .	1934-35
14	C. I. J. Smith (52)	Middlesex v Kent at Maidstone	1935

Note: The following fast fifties were scored in contrived circumstances when runs were given from full tosses and long hops to expedite a declaration: C. C. Inman (8 minutes), Leicestershire v Nottinghamshire at Nottingham, 1965; G. Chapple (10 minutes), Lancashire v Glamorgan at Manchester, 1993; T. M. Moody (11 minutes), Warwickshire v Glamorgan at Swansea, 1990; A. J. Stewart (14 minutes), Surrey v Kent at Dartford, 1986; M. P. Maynard (14 minutes), Glamorgan v Yorkshire at Cardiff, 1987.

FASTEST HUNDREDS

Minutes

35	P. G. H. Fender (113*)	Surrey v Northamptonshire at Northampton	1920
40	G. L. Jessop (101)	Gloucestershire v Yorkshire at Harrogate.	1897
40	Ahsan-ul-Haq (100*)	Muslims v Sikhs at Lahore	1923-24
42	G. L. Jessop (191)	Gentlemen of South v Players of South at Hastings	1907
43	A. H. Hornby (106)	Lancashire v Somerset at Manchester.	1905
43	D. W. Hookes (107)	South Australia v Victoria at Adelaide	1982-83
44	R. N. S. Hobbs (100)	Essex v Australians at Chelmsford.	1975

Notes: The fastest recorded authentic hundred in terms of balls received was scored off 34 balls by D. W. Hookes (above).

Research of the scorebook has shown that P. G. H. Fender scored his hundred from between 40 and 46 balls. He contributed 113 to an unfinished sixth-wicket partnership of 171 in 42 minutes with H. A. Peach.

E. B. Alletson (Nottinghamshire) scored 189 out of 227 runs in 90 minutes against Sussex at Hove in 1911. It has been estimated that his last 139 runs took 37 minutes.

The following fast hundreds were scored in contrived circumstances when runs were given from full tosses and long hops to expedite a declaration: G. Chapple (21 minutes), Lancashire v Glamorgan at Manchester, 1993; T. M. Moody (26 minutes), Warwickshire v Glamorgan at Swansea, 1990; S. J. O'Shaughnessy (35 minutes), Lancashire v Leicestershire at Manchester, 1983; C. M. Old (37 minutes), Yorkshire v Warwickshire at Birmingham, 1977; N. F. M. Popplewell (41 minutes), Somerset v Gloucestershire at Bath, 1983.

FASTEST DOUBLE-HUNDREDS

Minutes

113	R. J. Shastri (200*)	Bombay v Baroda at Bombay	1984-85
120	G. L. Jessop (286)	Gloucestershire v Sussex at Hove	1903
120	C. H. Lloyd (201*)	West Indians v Glamorgan at Swansea	1976
130	G. L. Jessop (234)	Gloucestershire v Somerset at Bristol	1905
131	V. T. Trumper (293)	Australians v Canterbury at Christchurch	1913-14

FASTEST TRIPLE-HUNDREDS

Minutes

181	D. C. S. Compton (300)	MCC v N. E. Transvaal at Benoni	1948-49
205	F. E. Woolley (305*)	MCC v Tasmania at Hobart	1911-12
205	C. G. Macartney (345)	Australians v Nottinghamshire at Nottingham.	1921
213	D. G. Bradman (369)	South Australia v Tasmania at Adelaide	1935-36

300 RUNS IN ONE DAY

390*	B. C. Lara	Warwickshire v Durham at Birmingham	1994
345	C. G. Macartney	Australians v Nottinghamshire at Nottingham.	1921
334	W. H. Ponsford	Victoria v New South Wales at Melbourne	1926-27
333	K. S. Duleepsinhji	Sussex v Northamptonshire at Hove	1930
331*	J. D. Robertson	Middlesex v Worcestershire at Worcester	1949
325*	B. A. Richards	S. Australia v W. Australia at Perth	1970-71
322†	E. Paynter	Lancashire v Sussex at Hove.	1937
322	I. V. A. Richards	Somerset v Warwickshire at Taunton	1985
318	C. W. Gregory	New South Wales v Queensland at Brisbane	1906-07
317	K. R. Rutherford	New Zealanders v D. B. Close's XI at Scarborough.	1986

316†	R. H. Moore	Hampshire v Warwickshire at Bournemouth	1937
315*	R. C. Blunt	Otago v Canterbury at Christchurch	1931-32
312*	J. M. Brearley	MCC Under-25 v North Zone at Peshawar.	1966-67
311*	G. M. Turner	Worcestershire v Warwickshire at Worcester	1982
311*	N. H. Fairbrother	Lancashire v Surrey at The Oval	1990
309*	D. G. Bradman	Australia v England at Leeds.	1930
307*	W. H. Ashdown	Kent v Essex at Brentwood.	1934
306*	A. Ducat	Surrey v Oxford University at The Oval	1919
305*	F. R. Foster	Warwickshire v Worcestershire at Dudley.	1914

† *E. Paynter's 322 and R. H. Moore's 316 were scored on the same day: July 28, 1937.*

These scores do not necessarily represent the complete innings. See pages 198–200.

LONGEST INNINGS

Mins

1,015	R. Nayyar (271)	Himachal Pradesh v Jammu and Kashmir at Chamba	1999-2000
970	Hanif Mohammad (337)	Pakistan v West Indies at Bridgetown	1957-58
	Hanif believes he batted 999 minutes.		
878	G. Kirsten (275)	South Africa v England at Durban	1999-2000
799	S. T. Jayasuriya (340)	Sri Lanka v India at Colombo	1997-98
797	L. Hutton (364)	England v Australia at The Oval	1938

1,000 RUNS IN MAY

	Runs	*Avge*
W. G. Grace, May 9 to May 30, 1895 (22 days):		
13, 103, 18, 25, 288, 52, 257, 73*, 18, 169	1,016	112.88
Grace was within two months of completing his 47th year.		
W. R. Hammond, May 7 to May 31, 1927 (25 days):		
27, 135, 108, 128, 17, 11, 99, 187, 4, 30, 83, 7, 192, 14	1,042	74.42
Hammond scored his 1,000th run on May 28, thus equalling		
Grace's record of 22 days.		
C. Hallows, May 5 to May 31, 1928 (27 days):		
100, 101, 51*, 123, 101*, 22, 74, 104, 58, 34*, 232	1,000	125.00

1,000 RUNS IN APRIL AND MAY

	Runs	*Avge*
T. W. Hayward, April 16 to May 31, 1900:		
120*, 55, 108, 131*, 55, 193, 120, 5, 6, 3, 40, 146, 92	1,074	97.63
D. G. Bradman, April 30 to May 31, 1930:		
236, 185*, 78, 9, 48*, 66, 4, 44, 252*, 32, 47*	1,001	143.00
On April 30 Bradman was 75 not out.		
D. G. Bradman, April 30 to May 31, 1938:		
258, 58, 137, 278, 2, 143, 145*, 5, 30*	1,056	150.85
Bradman scored 258 on April 30, and his 1,000th run on May 27.		
W. J. Edrich, April 30 to May 31, 1938:		
104, 37, 115, 63, 20*, 182, 71, 31, 53*, 45, 15, 245, 0, 9, 20*	1,010	84.16
Edrich was 21 not out on April 30. All his runs were scored at Lord's.		
G. M. Turner, April 24 to May 31, 1973:		
41, 151*, 143, 85, 7, 8, 17*, 81, 13, 53, 44, 153*, 3, 2, 66*, 30, 10*, 111	1,018	78.30
G. A. Hick, April 17 to May 29, 1988:		
61, 37, 212, 86, 14, 405*, 8, 11, 6, 7, 172	1,019	101.90
Hick scored a record 410 runs in April, and his 1,000th run on May 28.		

1,000 RUNS IN TWO SEPARATE MONTHS

Only four batsmen, C. B. Fry, K. S. Ranjitsinhji, H. Sutcliffe and L. Hutton, have scored over 1,000 runs in each of two months in the same season. L. Hutton, by scoring 1,294 in June 1949, made more runs in a single month than anyone else. He also made 1,050 in August 1949.

MOST RUNS SCORED OFF ONE OVER

(All instances refer to six-ball overs)

36	G. S. Sobers	off M. A. Nash, Nottinghamshire v Glamorgan at Swansea (six sixes)	1968
36	R. J. Shastri	off Tilak Raj, Bombay v Baroda at Bombay (six sixes)	1984-85
34	E. B. Alletson	off E. H. Killick, Nottinghamshire v Sussex at Hove (46604446; including two no-balls)	1911
34	F. C. Hayes	off M. A. Nash, Lancashire v Glamorgan at Swansea (646666)	1977
34†	A. Flintoff	off A. J. Tudor, Lancashire v Surrey at Manchester (64444660; including two no-balls)	1998
32	I. T. Botham	off I. R. Snook, England XI v Central Districts at Palmerston North (466466)	1983-84
32	P. W. G. Parker	off A. I. Kallicharran, Sussex v Warwickshire at Birmingham (466664)	1982
32	I. R. Redpath	off N. Rosendorff, Australians v Orange Free State at Bloemfontein (666644)	1969-70
32	C. C. Smart	off G. Hill, Glamorgan v Hampshire at Cardiff (664664)	1935

† *Altogether 38 runs were scored off this over, the two no-balls counting for two extra runs each under ECB regulations.*

Notes: The following instances have been excluded from the above table because of the bowlers' compliance: 34 – M. P. Maynard off S. A. Marsh, Glamorgan v Kent at Swansea, 1992; 34 – G. Chapple off P. A. Cottey, Lancashire v Glamorgan at Manchester, 1993; 34 – F. B. Touzel off F. J. J. Viljoen, Western Province B v Griqualand West at Kimberley, 1993-94; 32 – C. C. Inman off N. W. Hill, Leicestershire v Nottinghamshire at Nottingham, 1965; 32 – T. E. Jesty off R. J. Boyd-Moss, Hampshire v Northamptonshire at Southampton, 1984; 32 – M. A. Ealham off G. D. Hodgson, Kent v Gloucestershire at Bristol, 1992; 32 – G. Chapple off P. A. Cottey, Lancashire v Glamorgan at Manchester, 1993. Chapple's 34 and 32 came off successive overs from Cottey.

There were 35 runs off an over received by A. T. Reinholds off H. T. Davis, Auckland v Wellington at Auckland 1995-96, but this included six no-balls (counting as two runs each), four byes and only 19 off the bat.

The greatest number of runs scored off an eight-ball over was 34 (40446664) by R. M. Edwards off M. C. Carew, Governor-General's XI v West Indians at Auckland, 1968-69.

In a Shell Trophy match against Canterbury at Christchurch in 1989-90, R. H. Vance (Wellington), acting on the instructions of his captain, deliberately conceded 77 runs in an over of full tosses which contained 17 no-balls and, owing to the umpire's understandable miscalculation, only five legitimate deliveries.

MOST SIXES IN AN INNINGS

16	A. Symonds (254*)	Gloucestershire v Glamorgan at Abergavenny	1995
15	J. R. Reid (296)	Wellington v Northern Districts at Wellington	1962-63
14	Shakti Singh (128)	Himachal Pradesh v Haryana at Dharmsala	1990-91
13	Majid Khan (147*)	Pakistanis v Glamorgan at Swansea	1967
13	C. G. Greenidge (273*)	D. H. Robins' XI v Pakistanis at Eastbourne	1974
13	C. G. Greenidge (259)	Hampshire v Sussex at Southampton	1975
13	G. W. Humpage (254)	Warwickshire v Lancashire at Southport	1982
13	R. J. Shastri (200*)	Bombay v Baroda at Bombay	1984-85
12	Gulfraz Khan (207)	Railways v Universities at Lahore	1976-77
12	I. T. Botham (138*)	Somerset v Warwickshire at Birmingham	1985

12	R. A. Harper (234)	Northamptonshire v Gloucestershire at Northampton .	1986
12	D. M. Jones (248)	Australians v Warwickshire at Birmingham.	1989
12	U. N. K. Fernando (160)	Sinhalese SC v Sebastianites C and AC at Colombo. .	1990-91
12	D. N. Patel (204)	Auckland v Northern Districts at Auckland.	1991-92
12	W. V. Raman (206)	Tamil Nadu v Kerala at Madras	1991-92
12	G. D. Lloyd (241)	Lancashire v Essex at Chelmsford	1996
12	Wasim Akram (257*)	Pakistan v Zimbabwe at Sheikhupura.	1996-97
11	C. K. Nayudu (153)	Hindus v MCC at Bombay	1926-27
11	C. J. Barnett (194)	Gloucestershire v Somerset at Bath	1934
11	R. Benaud (135)	Australians v T. N. Pearce's XI at Scarborough	1953
11	R. Bora (126)	Assam v Tripura at Gauhati.	1987-88
11	G. A. Hick (405*)	Worcestershire v Somerset at Taunton	1988
11	A. S. Jayasinghe (183)	Tamil Union v Burgher RC at Colombo	1996-97

Note: F. B. Touzel (128*) hit 13 sixes for Western Province B v Griqualand West in contrived circumstances at Kimberley in 1993-94.

MOST SIXES IN A MATCH

| 20 | A. Symonds (254*, 76) | Gloucestershire v Glamorgan at Abergavenny . . . . . . | 1995 |
| 17 | W. J. Stewart (155, 125) | Warwickshire v Lancashire at Blackpool . . . . | 1959 |

MOST SIXES IN A SEASON

80	I. T. Botham	1985		49	I. V. A. Richards.	1985
66	A. W. Wellard.	1935		48	A. W. Carr.	1925
57	A. W. Wellard.	1936		48	J. H. Edrich	1965
57	A. W. Wellard.	1938		48	A. Symonds.	1995
51	A. W. Wellard.	1933				

MOST BOUNDARIES IN AN INNINGS

	4s/6s			
72	62/10	B. C. Lara (501*)	Warwickshire v Durham at Birmingham.	1994
68	68/–	P. A Perrin (343*)	Essex v Derbyshire at Chesterfield	1904
65	64/1	A. C. MacLaren (424)	Lancashire v Somerset at Taunton.	1895
64	64/–	Hanif Mohammad (499)	Karachi v Bahawalpur at Karachi	1958-59
57	52/5	J. H. Edrich (310*)	England v New Zealand at Leeds	1965
55	55/–	C. W. Gregory (383)	NSW v Queensland at Brisbane	1906-07
55	51/3†	S. V. Manjrekar (377)	Bombay v Hyderabad at Bombay	1990-91
55	53/2	G. R. Marsh (355*)	W. Australia v S. Australia at Perth. . . .	1989-90
54	53/1	G. H. Hirst (341)	Yorkshire v Leicestershire at Leicester . .	1905
53	51/2	V. V. S. Laxman (353)	Hyderabad v Karnataka at Bangalore. . .	1999-2000
53	53/–	A. W. Nourse (304*)	Natal v Transvaal at Johannesburg.	1919-20
53	45/8	K. R. Rutherford (317)	New Zealanders v D. B. Close's XI at Scarborough	1986
52	47/5	N. H. Fairbrother (366)	Lancashire v Surrey at The Oval	1990
51	51/–	W. G. Grace (344)	MCC v Kent at Canterbury	1876
51	47/4	C. G. Macartney (345)	Australians v Notts at Nottingham	1921
51	50/1	B. B. Nimbalkar (443*)	Maharashtra v Kathiawar at Poona	1948-49
50	46/4	D. G. Bradman (369)	S. Australia v Tasmania at Adelaide. . . .	1935-36
50	47/–‡	A. Ducat (306*)	Surrey v Oxford U. at The Oval	1919
50	35/15	J. R. Reid (296)	Wellington v N. Districts at Wellington .	1962-63
50	42/8	I. V. A. Richards (322)	Somerset v Warwickshire at Taunton . . .	1985

† *Plus one five.*
‡ *Plus three fives.*

PARTNERSHIPS OVER 500

577	V. S. Hazare (288) and Gul Mahomed (319), fourth wicket, Baroda v Holkar at Baroda 1946-47
576	S. T. Jayasuriya (340) and R. S. Mahanama (225), second wicket, Sri Lanka v India at Colombo 1997-98
574*	F. M. M. Worrell (255*) and C. L. Walcott (314*), fourth wicket, Barbados v Trinidad at Port-of-Spain 1945-46
561	Waheed Mirza (324) and Mansoor Akhtar (224*), first wicket, Karachi Whites v Quetta at Karachi 1976-77
555	P. Holmes (224*) and H. Sutcliffe (313), first wicket, Yorkshire v Essex at Leyton 1932
554	J. T. Brown (300) and J. Tunnicliffe (243), first wicket, Yorkshire v Derbyshire at Chesterfield 1898
502*	F. M. M. Worrell (308*) and J. D. C. Goddard (218*), fourth wicket, Barbados v Trinidad at Bridgetown 1943-44

HIGHEST PARTNERSHIPS FOR EACH WICKET

The following lists include all stands above 400; otherwise the top ten for each wicket.

First Wicket

561	Waheed Mirza and Mansoor Akhtar, Karachi Whites v Quetta at Karachi . . .	1976-77
555	P. Holmes and H. Sutcliffe, Yorkshire v Essex at Leyton	1932
554	J. T. Brown and J. Tunnicliffe, Yorkshire v Derbyshire at Chesterfield	1898
490	E. H. Bowley and J. G. Langridge, Sussex v Middlesex at Hove	1933
464	R. Sehgal and R. Lamba, Delhi v Himachal Pradesh at Delhi	1994-95
459	Wasim Jaffer and S. K. Kulkarni, Mumbai v Saurashtra at Rajkot	1996-97
456	E. R. Mayne and W. H. Ponsford, Victoria v Queensland at Melbourne.	1923-24
451*	S. Desai and R. M. H. Binny, Karnataka v Kerala at Chikmagalur.	1977-78
431	M. R. J. Veletta and G. R. Marsh, Western Australia v South Australia at Perth	1989-90
428	J. B. Hobbs and A. Sandham, Surrey v Oxford University at The Oval.	1926
424	I. J. Siedle and J. F. W. Nicolson, Natal v Orange Free State at Bloemfontein	1926-27
421	S. M. Gavaskar and G. A. Parkar, Bombay v Bengal at Bombay	1981-82
418	Kamal Najamuddin and Khalid Alvi, Karachi v Railways at Karachi	1980-81
413	V. Mankad and Pankaj Roy, India v New Zealand at Madras	1955-56
406*†	D. J. Bicknell and G. E. Welton, Notts v Warwickshire at Birmingham.	2000
405	C. P. S. Chauhan and M. S. Gupte, Maharashtra v Vidarbha at Poona	1972-73
403	Rizwan-uz-Zaman and Shoaib Mohammad, PIA v Hyderabad at Hyderabad .	1999-2000

Second Wicket

576	S. T. Jayasuriya and R. S. Mahanama, Sri Lanka v India at Colombo.	1997-98
475	Zahir Alam and L. S. Rajput, Assam v Tripura at Gauhati	1991-92
465*	J. A. Jameson and R. B. Kanhai, Warwicks v Gloucestershire at Birmingham	1974
455	K. V. Bhandarkar and B. B. Nimbalkar, Maharashtra v Kathiawar at Poona . .	1948-49
451	W. H. Ponsford and D. G. Bradman, Australia v England at The Oval	1934
446	C. C. Hunte and G. S. Sobers, West Indies v Pakistan at Kingston	1957-58
429*	J. G. Dewes and G. H. G. Doggart, Cambridge U. v Essex at Cambridge . . .	1949
426	Arshad Pervez and Mohsin Khan, Habib Bank v Income Tax at Lahore	1977-78
417†	K. J. Barnett and T. A. Tweats, Derbyshire v Yorkshire at Derby	1997
415	A. Jadeja and S. V. Manjrekar, Indians v Bowl XI at Springs	1992-93
403	G. A. Gooch and P. J. Prichard, Essex v Leicestershire at Chelmsford	1990

Third Wicket

467	A. H. Jones and M. D. Crowe, New Zealand v Sri Lanka at Wellington	1990-91
456	Khalid Irtiza and Aslam Ali, United Bank v Multan at Karachi	1975-76
451	Mudassar Nazar and Javed Miandad, Pakistan v India at Hyderabad	1982-83
445	P. E. Whitelaw and W. N. Carson, Auckland v Otago at Dunedin	1936-37
438*†	G. A. Hick and T. M. Moody, Worcestershire v Hampshire at Southampton . .	1997
434	J. B. Stollmeyer and G. E. Gomez, Trinidad v British Guiana at Port-of-Spain	1946-47
424*	W. J. Edrich and D. C. S. Compton, Middlesex v Somerset at Lord's	1948
413	D. J. Bicknell and D. M. Ward, Surrey v Kent at Canterbury	1990
410*	R. S. Modi and L. Amarnath, India in England v The Rest at Calcutta	1946-47
406*	R. S. Gavaskar and S. J. Kalyani, Bengal v Tripura at Agartala	1999-2000
405	A. Jadeja and A. S. Kaypee, Haryana v Services at Faridabad	1991-92

Fourth Wicket

577	V. S. Hazare and Gul Mahomed, Baroda v Holkar at Baroda	1946-47
574*	C. L. Walcott and F. M. M. Worrell, Barbados v Trinidad at Port-of-Spain . . .	1945-46
502*	F. M. M. Worrell and J. D. C. Goddard, Barbados v Trinidad at Bridgetown . .	1943-44
470	A. I. Kallicharran and G. W. Humpage, Warwicks v Lancs at Southport	1982
462*	D. W. Hookes and W. B. Phillips, South Australia v Tasmania at Adelaide . . .	1986-87
448	R. Abel and T. W. Hayward, Surrey v Yorkshire at The Oval	1899
436	S. Abbas Ali and P. K. Dwevedi, Madhya Pradesh v Railways at Indore	1997-98
425*†	A. Dale and I. V. A. Richards, Glamorgan v Middlesex at Cardiff	1993
424	I. S. Lee and S. O. Quin, Victoria v Tasmania at Melbourne	1933-34
411	P. B. H. May and M. C. Cowdrey, England v West Indies at Birmingham . . .	1957
410	G. Abraham and P. Balan Pandit, Kerala v Andhra at Palghat	1959-60
402	W. Watson and T. W. Graveney, MCC v British Guiana at Georgetown	1953-54
402	R. B. Kanhai and K. Ibadulla, Warwicks v Notts at Nottingham.	1968

Fifth Wicket

464*†	M. E. Waugh and S. R. Waugh, New South Wales v Western Australia at Perth	1990-91
405	S. G. Barnes and D. G. Bradman, Australia v England at Sydney.	1946-47
401†	M. B. Loye and D. Ripley, Northamptonshire v Glamorgan at Northampton . .	1998
397	W. Bardsley and C. Kelleway, New South Wales v South Australia at Sydney.	1920-21
393	E. G. Arnold and W. B. Burns, Worcestershire v Warwickshire at Birmingham.	1909
391	A. Malhotra and S. Dogra, Delhi v Services at Delhi.	1995-96
385	S. R. Waugh and G. S. Blewett, Australia v South Africa at Johannesburg . . .	1996-97
381	R. Nayyar and V. Shewag, North Zone v South Zone at Agartala	1999-2000
377*	G. P. Thorpe and M. R. Ramprakash, England XI v South Australia at Adelaide	1998-99
360	U. M. Merchant and M. N. Raiji, Bombay v Hyderabad at Bombay	1947-48

Sixth Wicket

487*	G. A. Headley and C. C. Passailaigue, Jamaica v Lord Tennyson's XI at Kingston	1931-32
428	W. W. Armstrong and M. A. Noble, Australians v Sussex at Hove	1902
411	R. M. Poore and E. G. Wynyard, Hampshire v Somerset at Taunton	1899
376	R. Subba Row and A. Lightfoot, Northamptonshire v Surrey at The Oval . . .	1958
371	V. M. Merchant and R. S. Modi, Bombay v Maharashtra at Bombay.	1943-44
356	W. V. Raman and A. Kripal Singh, Tamil Nadu v Goa at Panjim	1988-89
353	Salah-ud-Din and Zaheer Abbas, Karachi v East Pakistan at Karachi.	1968-69
346	J. H. W. Fingleton and D. G. Bradman, Australia v England at Melbourne . . .	1936-37
337†	R. R. Montgomerie and D. J. Capel, Northamptonshire v Kent at Canterbury .	1995
332	N. G. Marks and G. Thomas, New South Wales v South Australia at Sydney .	1958-59

Seventh Wicket

460	Bhupinder Singh, jun. and P. Dharmani, Punjab v Delhi at Delhi	1994-95
347	D. St E. Atkinson and C. C. Depeiza, West Indies v Australia at Bridgetown .	1954-55
344	K. S. Ranjitsinhji and W. Newham, Sussex v Essex at Leyton	1902
340	K. J. Key and H. Philipson, Oxford University v Middlesex at Chiswick Park	1887
336	F. C. W. Newman and C. R. N. Maxwell, Sir J. Cahn's XI v Leicestershire at Nottingham.	1935
335	C. W. Andrews and E. C. Bensted, Queensland v New South Wales at Sydney	1934-35
325	G. Brown and C. H. Abercrombie, Hampshire v Essex at Leyton	1913
323	E. H. Hendren and L. F. Townsend, MCC v Barbados at Bridgetown	1929-30
308	Waqar Hassan and Imtiaz Ahmed, Pakistan v New Zealand at Lahore	1955-56
301	C. C. Lewis and B. N. French, Nottinghamshire v Durham at Chester-le-Street	1993

Eighth Wicket

433	V. T. Trumper and A. Sims, A. Sims' Aust. XI v Canterbury at Christchurch	1913-14
313	Wasim Akram and Saqlain Mushtaq, Pakistan v Zimbabwe at Sheikhupura . .	1996-97
292	R. Peel and Lord Hawke, Yorkshire v Warwickshire at Birmingham	1896
270	V. T. Trumper and E. P. Barbour, New South Wales v Victoria at Sydney. . . .	1912-13
263	D. R. Wilcox and R. M. Taylor, Essex v Warwickshire at Southend	1946
255	E. A. V. Williams and E. A. Martindale, Barbados v Trinidad at Bridgetown. .	1935-36
249*	Shaukat Mirza and Akram Raza, Habib Bank v PNSC at Lahore	1993-94
246	L. E. G. Ames and G. O. B. Allen, England v New Zealand at Lord's	1931
243	R. J. Hartigan and C. Hill, Australia v England at Adelaide.	1907-08
242*	T. J. Zoehrer and K. H. MacLeay, W. Australia v New South Wales at Perth .	1990-91

Ninth Wicket

283	J. Chapman and A. Warren, Derbyshire v Warwickshire at Blackwell	1910
268	J. B. Commins and N. Boje, South Africa A v Mashonaland at Harare	1994-95
251	J. W. H. T. Douglas and S. N. Hare, Essex v Derbyshire at Leyton.	1921
245	V. S. Hazare and N. D. Nagarwalla, Maharashtra v Baroda at Poona	1939-40
244*	Arshad Ayub and M. V. Ramanamurthy, Hyderabad v Bihar at Hyderabad . . .	1986-87
239	H. B. Cave and I. B. Leggat, Central Districts v Otago at Dunedin.	1952-53
232	C. Hill and E. Walkley, South Australia v New South Wales at Adelaide	1900-01
231	P Sen and J. Mitter, Bengal v Bihar at Jamshedpur	1950-51
230	D. A. Livingstone and A. T. Castell, Hampshire v Surrey at Southampton . . .	1962
226	C. Kelleway and W. A. Oldfield, New South Wales v Victoria at Melbourne. .	1925-26

Tenth Wicket

307	A. F. Kippax and J. E. H. Hooker, New South Wales v Victoria at Melbourne	1928-29
249	C. T. Sarwate and S. N. Banerjee, Indians v Surrey at The Oval	1946
235	F. E. Woolley and A. Fielder, Kent v Worcestershire at Stourbridge.	1909
233	Ajay Sharma and Maninder Singh, Delhi v Bombay at Bombay.	1991-92
230	R. W. Nicholls and W. Roche, Middlesex v Kent at Lord's	1899
228	R. Illingworth and K. Higgs, Leicestershire v Northamptonshire at Leicester .	1977
218	F. H. Vigar and T. P. B. Smith, Essex v Derbyshire at Chesterfield	1947
211	M. Ellis and T. J. Hastings, Victoria v South Australia at Melbourne.	1902-03
196*	Nadim Yousuf and Maqsood Kundi, MCB v National Bank at Lahore	1981-82
192	H. A. W. Bowell and W. H. Livsey, Hampshire v Worcs at Bournemouth	1921

† *Partnerships affected by ECB or ACB regulations governing no-balls and wides.*

UNUSUAL DISMISSALS

Handled the Ball

J. Grundy	MCC v Kent at Lord's	1857
G. Bennett	Kent v Sussex at Hove	1872
W. H. Scotton	Smokers v Non-Smokers at East Melbourne	1886-87
C. W. Wright	Nottinghamshire v Gloucestershire at Bristol	1893
E. Jones	South Australia v Victoria at Melbourne	1894-95
A. W. Nourse	South Africans v Sussex at Hove	1907
E. T. Benson	MCC v Auckland at Auckland	1929-30
A. W. Gilbertson	Otago v Auckland at Auckland	1952-53
W. R. Endean	South Africa v England at Cape Town	1956-57
P. J. Burge	Queensland v New South Wales at Sydney	1958-59
Dildar Awan	Services v Lahore at Lahore	1959-60
M. Mehra	Railways v Delhi at Delhi	1959-60
Mahmood-ul-Hasan	Karachi University v Railways-Quetta at Karachi	1960-61
Ali Raza	Karachi Greens v Hyderabad at Karachi	1961-62
Mohammad Yusuf	Rawalpindi v Peshawar at Peshawar	1962-63
A. Rees	Glamorgan v Middlesex at Lord's	1965
Pervez Akhtar	Multan v Karachi Greens at Sahiwal	1971-72
Javed Mirza	Railways v Punjab at Lahore	1972-73
R. G. Pollock	Eastern Province v Western Province at Cape Town	1973-74
C. I. Dey	Northern Transvaal v Orange Free State at Bloemfontein	1973-74
Nasir Valika	Karachi Whites v National Bank at Karachi	1974-75
Haji Yousuf	National Bank v Railways at Lahore	1974-75
Masood-ul-Hasan	PIA v National Bank B at Lyallpur	1975-76
Hanif Solangi	Hyderabad v Karachi B at Hyderabad	1977-78
D. K. Pearse	Natal v Western Province at Cape Town	1978-79
A. M. J. Hilditch	Australia v Pakistan at Perth	1978-79
Musleh-ud-Din	Railways v Lahore at Lahore	1979-80
Jalal-ud-Din	IDBP v Habib Bank at Bahawalpur	1981-82
Mohsin Khan	Pakistan v Australia at Karachi	1982-83
D. L. Haynes	West Indies v India at Bombay	1983-84
K. Azad	Delhi v Punjab at Amritsar	1983-84
Athar A. Khan	Allied Bank v HBFC at Sialkot	1983-84
A. N. Pandya	Saurashtra v Baroda at Baroda	1984-85
G. L. Linton	Barbados v Windward Islands at Bridgetown	1985-86
R. B. Gartrell	Tasmania v Victoria at Melbourne	1986-87
R. Nayyar	Himachal Pradesh v Punjab at Una	1988-89
R. Weerawardene	Moratuwa v Nomads SC at Colombo	1988-89
A. M. Kane	Vidarbha v Railways at Nagpur	1989-90
P. Bali	Jammu and Kashmir v Services at Delhi	1991-92
M. J. G. Davis	Northern Transvaal B v OFS B at Bloemfontein	1991-92
J. T. C. Vaughan	Emerging Players v England XI at Hamilton	1991-92
G. A. Gooch	England v Australia at Manchester	1993
A. C. Waller	Mashonaland CD v Mashonaland Under-24 at Harare	1994-95
K. M. Krikken	Derbyshire v Indians at Derby	1996
A. Badenhorst	Eastern Province B v North West at Fochville	1998-99

Obstructing the Field

C. A. Absolom	Cambridge University v Surrey at The Oval	1868
T. Straw	Worcestershire v Warwickshire at Worcester	1899
T. Straw	Worcestershire v Warwickshire at Birmingham	1901
J. P. Whiteside	Leicestershire v Lancashire at Leicester	1901
L. Hutton	England v South Africa at The Oval	1951
J. A. Hayes	Canterbury v Central Districts at Christchurch	1954-55
D. D. Deshpande	Madhya Pradesh v Uttar Pradesh at Benares	1956-57
K. Ibadulla	Warwickshire v Hampshire at Coventry	1963
Qaiser Khan	Dera Ismail Khan v Railways at Lahore	1964-65

Ijaz Ahmed	Lahore Greens v Lahore Blues at Lahore	1973-74
Qasim Feroze	Bahawalpur v Universities at Lahore	1974-75
T. Quirk	Northern Transvaal v Border at East London	1978-79
Mahmood Rashid	United Bank v Muslim Commercial Bank at Bahawalpur	1981-82
Arshad Ali	Sukkur v Quetta at Quetta	1983-84
H. R. Wasu	Vidarbha v Rajasthan at Akola	1984-85
Khalid Javed	Railways v Lahore at Lahore	1985-86
C. Binduhewa	Singha SC v Sinhalese SC at Colombo	1990-91
S. J. Kalyani	Bengal v Orissa at Calcutta	1994-95

Hit the Ball Twice

G. Rawlins	Sheffield v Nottingham at Nottingham	1827
H. E. Bull	MCC v Oxford University at Lord's	1864
H. R. J. Charlwood	Sussex v Surrey at Hove	1872
R. G. Barlow	North v South at Lord's	1878
P. S. Wimble	Transvaal v Griqualand West at Kimberley	1892-93
G. B. Nicholls	Somerset v Gloucestershire at Bristol	1896
A. A. Lilley	Warwickshire v Yorkshire at Birmingham	1897
J. H. King	Leicestershire v Surrey at The Oval	1906
A. P. Binns	Jamaica v British Guiana at Georgetown	1956-57
K. Bhavanna	Andhra v Mysore at Guntur	1963-64
Zaheer Abbas	PIA A v Karachi Blues at Karachi	1969-70
Anwar Miandad	IDBP v United Bank at Lahore	1979-80
Anwar Iqbal	Hyderabad v Sukkur at Hyderabad	1983-84
Iqtidar Ali	Allied Bank v Muslim Commercial Bank at Lahore	1983-84
Aziz Malik	Lahore Division v Faisalabad at Sialkot	1984-85
Javed Mohammad	Multan v Karachi Whites at Sahiwal	1986-87
Shahid Pervez	Jammu and Kashmir v Punjab at Srinagar	1986-87
Ali Naqvi	PNSC v National Bank at Faisalabad	1998-99
A. George	Tamil Nadu v Maharashtra at Pune	1998-99
Maqsood Raza	Lahore Division v PNSC at Sheikhupura	1999-2000

Timed Out

H. Yadav	Tripura v Orissa at Cuttack	1997-98

BOWLING RECORDS

TEN WICKETS IN AN INNINGS

	O	M	R		
E. Hinkly (Kent)				v England at Lord's	1848
*J. Wisden (North)				v South at Lord's	1850
V. E. Walker (England)	43	17	74	v Surrey at The Oval	1859
V. E. Walker (Middlesex)	44.2	5	104	v Lancashire at Manchester	1865
G. Wootton (All England)	31.3	9	54	v Yorkshire at Sheffield	1865
W. Hickton (Lancashire)	36.2	19	46	v Hampshire at Manchester	1870
S. E. Butler (Oxford)	24.1	11	38	v Cambridge at Lord's	1871
James Lillywhite (South)	60.2	22	129	v North at Canterbury	1872
A. Shaw (MCC)	36.2	8	73	v North at Lord's	1874
E. Barratt (Players)	29	11	43	v Australians at The Oval	1878
G. Giffen (Australian XI)	26	10	66	v The Rest at Sydney	1883-84
W. G. Grace (MCC)	36.2	17	49	v Oxford University at Oxford	1886
G. Burton (Middlesex)	52.3	25	59	v Surrey at The Oval	1888
†A. E. Moss (Canterbury)	21.3	10	28	v Wellington at Christchurch	1889-90
S. M. J. Woods (Cambridge U.)	31	6	69	v Thornton's XI at Cambridge	1890
T. Richardson (Surrey)	15.3	3	45	v Essex at The Oval	1894
H. Pickett (Essex)	27	11	32	v Leicestershire at Leyton	1895

	O	M	R		
E. J. Tyler (Somerset)	34.3	15	49	v Surrey at Taunton	1895
W. P. Howell (Australians)	23.2	14	28	v Surrey at The Oval	1899
C. H. G. Bland (Sussex)	25.2	10	48	v Kent at Tonbridge	1899
J. Briggs (Lancashire)	28.5	7	55	v Worcestershire at Manchester	1900
A. E. Trott (Middlesex)	14.2	5	42	v Somerset at Taunton	1900
A. Fielder (Players)	24.5	1	90	v Gentlemen at Lord's	1906
E. G. Dennett (Gloucestershire)	19.4	7	40	v Essex at Bristol	1906
A. E. E. Vogler (E. Province)	12	2	26	v Griqualand W. at Johannesburg	1906-07
C. Blythe (Kent)	16	7	30	v Northants at Northampton	1907
J. B. King (Philadelphia)	18.1	7	53	v Ireland at Haverford‡	1909
A. Drake (Yorkshire)	8.5	0	35	v Somerset at Weston-s-Mare	1914
W. Bestwick (Derbyshire)	19	2	40	v Glamorgan at Cardiff	1921
A. A. Mailey (Australians)	28.4	5	66	v Gloucestershire at Cheltenham	1921
C. W. L. Parker (Glos.)	40.3	13	79	v Somerset at Bristol	1921
T. Rushby (Surrey)	17.5	4	43	v Somerset at Taunton	1921
J. C. White (Somerset)	42.2	11	76	v Worcestershire at Worcester	1921
G. C. Collins (Kent)	19.3	4	65	v Nottinghamshire at Dover	1922
H. Howell (Warwickshire)	25.1	5	51	v Yorkshire at Birmingham	1923
A. S. Kennedy (Players)	22.4	10	37	v Gentlemen at The Oval	1927
G. O. B. Allen (Middlesex)	25.3	10	40	v Lancashire at Lord's	1929
A. P. Freeman (Kent)	42	9	131	v Lancashire at Maidstone	1929
G. Geary (Leicestershire)	16.2	8	18	v Glamorgan at Pontypridd	1929
C. V. Grimmett (Australians)	22.3	8	37	v Yorkshire at Sheffield	1930
A. P. Freeman (Kent)	30.4	8	53	v Essex at Southend	1930
H. Verity (Yorkshire)	18.4	6	36	v Warwickshire at Leeds	1931
A. P. Freeman (Kent)	36.1	9	79	v Lancashire at Manchester	1931
V. W. C. Jupp (Northants)	39	6	127	v Kent at Tunbridge Wells	1932
H. Verity (Yorkshire)	19.4	16	10	v Nottinghamshire at Leeds	1932
T. W. Wall (South Australia)	12.4	2	36	v New South Wales at Sydney	1932-33
T. B. Mitchell (Derbyshire)	19.1	4	64	v Leicestershire at Leicester	1935
J. Mercer (Glamorgan)	26	10	51	v Worcestershire at Worcester	1936
T. W. J. Goddard (Glos.)	28.4	4	113	v Worcestershire at Cheltenham	1937
T. F. Smailes (Yorkshire)	17.1	5	47	v Derbyshire at Sheffield	1939
E. A. Watts (Surrey)	24.1	8	67	v Warwickshire at Birmingham	1939
*W. E. Hollies (Warwickshire)	20.4	4	49	v Notts at Birmingham	1946
J. M. Sims (East)	18.4	2	90	v West at Kingston	1948
T. E. Bailey (Essex)	39.4	9	90	v Lancashire at Clacton	1949
J. K. Graveney (Glos.)	18.4	2	66	v Derbyshire at Chesterfield	1949
R. Berry (Lancashire)	36.2	9	102	v Worcestershire at Blackpool	1953
S. P. Gupte (President's XI)	24.2	7	78	v Combined XI at Bombay	1954-55
J. C. Laker (Surrey)	46	18	88	v Australians at The Oval	1956
J. C. Laker (England)	51.2	23	53	v Australia at Manchester	1956
G. A. R. Lock (Surrey)	29.1	18	54	v Kent at Blackheath	1956
K. Smales (Nottinghamshire)	41.3	20	66	v Gloucestershire at Stroud	1956
P. M. Chatterjee (Bengal)	19	11	20	v Assam at Jorhat	1956-57
J. D. Bannister (Warwickshire)	23.3	11	41	v Comb. Services at Birmingham§	1959
A. J. G. Pearson (Cambridge U.)	30.3	8	78	v Leics at Loughborough	1961
N. I. Thomson (Sussex)	34.2	19	49	v Warwickshire at Worthing	1964
P. J. Allan (Queensland)	15.6	3	61	v Victoria at Melbourne	1965-66
I. J. Brayshaw (W. Australia)	17.6	4	44	v Victoria at Perth	1967-68
Shahid Mahmood (Karachi Whites)	25	5	58	v Khairpur at Karachi	1969-70
E. E. Hemmings (International XI)	49.3	14	175	v West Indies XI at Kingston	1982-83
P. Sunderam (Rajasthan)	22	5	78	v Vidarbha at Jodhpur	1985-86
S. T. Jefferies (W. Province)	22.5	7	59	v Orange Free State at Cape Town	1987-88
Imran Adil (Bahawalpur)	22.5	3	92	v Faisalabad at Faisalabad	1989-90
G. P. Wickremasinghe (Sinhalese)	19.2	5	41	v Kalutara at Colombo	1991-92
R. L. Johnson (Middlesex)	18.5	6	45	v Derbyshire at Derby	1994
Naeem Akhtar (Rawalpindi B)	21.3	10	28	v Peshawar at Peshawar	1995-96
A. Kumble (India)	26.3	9	74	v Pakistan at Delhi	1998-99

Notes: D. S. Mohanty returned figures of 19–5–46–10 for East Zone v South Zone at Agartala in 2000-01, after the deadline for this section.

The following instances were achieved in 12-a-side matches:

	O	M	R		
E. M. Grace (MCC).............	32.2	7	69	v Gents of Kent at Canterbury..	1862
W. G. Grace (MCC).............	46.1	15	92	v Kent at Canterbury.........	1873
†D. C. S. Hinds (A. B. St Hill's XII)	19.1	6	36	v Trinidad at Port-of-Spain ...	1900-01

* *J. Wisden and W. E. Hollies achieved the feat without the direct assistance of a fielder. Wisden's ten were all bowled; Hollies bowled seven and had three lbw.*

† *On debut in first-class cricket.* ‡ *Pennsylvania.* § *Mitchells & Butlers Ground.*

OUTSTANDING ANALYSES

	O	M	R	W		
H. Verity (Yorkshire)	19.4	16	10	10	v Nottinghamshire at Leeds ..	1932
G. Elliott (Victoria)	19	17	2	9	v Tasmania at Launceston ...	1857-58
Ahad Khan (Railways)	6.3	4	7	9	v Dera Ismail Khan at Lahore	1964-65
J. C. Laker (England).......	14	12	2	8	v The Rest at Bradford	1950
D. Shackleton (Hampshire) ...	11.1	7	4	8	v Somerset at Weston-s-Mare .	1955
E. Peate (Yorkshire)	16	11	5	8	v Surrey at Holbeck	1883
F. R. Spofforth (Australians) ..	8.3	6	3	7	v England XI at Birmingham .	1884
W. A. Henderson (North-Eastern Transvaal)	9.3	7	4	7	v Orange Free State at Bloem-fontein	1937-38
Rajinder Goel (Haryana)	7	4	4	7	v Jammu and Kashmir at Chandigarh...........	1977-78
V. I. Smith (South Africans)...	4.5	3	1	6	v Derbyshire at Derby......	1947
S. Cosstick (Victoria)	21.1	20	1	6	v Tasmania at Melbourne....	1868-69
Israr Ali (Bahawalpur).......	11	10	1	6	v Dacca U. at Bahawalpur ...	1957-58
A. D. Pougher (MCC).......	3	3	0	5	v Australians at Lord's	1896
G. R. Cox (Sussex)	6	6	0	5	v Somerset at Weston-s-Mare .	1921
R. K. Tyldesley (Lancashire) ..	5	5	0	5	v Leicestershire at Manchester	1924
P. T. Mills (Gloucestershire)...	6.4	6	0	5	v Somerset at Bristol	1928

MOST WICKETS IN A MATCH

19-90	J. C. Laker	England v Australia at Manchester	1956
17-48†	C. Blythe	Kent v Northamptonshire at Northampton.........	1907
17-50	C. T. B. Turner	Australians v England XI at Hastings	1888
17-54	W. P. Howell	Australians v Western Province at Cape Town	1902-03
17-56	C. W. L. Parker	Gloucestershire v Essex at Gloucester	1925
17-67	A. P. Freeman	Kent v Sussex at Hove	1922
17-89	W. G. Grace	Gloucestershire v Nottinghamshire at Cheltenham ...	1877
17-89	F. C. L. Matthews	Nottinghamshire v Northants at Nottingham	1923
17-91	H. Dean	Lancashire v Yorkshire at Liverpool	1913
17-91†	H. Verity	Yorkshire v Essex at Leyton	1933
17-92	A. P. Freeman	Kent v Warwickshire at Folkestone	1932
17-103	W. Mycroft	Derbyshire v Hampshire at Southampton.........	1876
17-106	G. R. Cox	Sussex v Warwickshire at Horsham	1926
17-106†	T. W. J. Goddard	Gloucestershire v Kent at Bristol	1939
17-119	W. Mead	Essex v Hampshire at Southampton............	1895
17-137	W. Brearley	Lancashire v Somerset at Manchester...........	1905
17-159	S. F. Barnes	England v South Africa at Johannesburg.........	1913-14
17-201	G. Giffen	South Australia v Victoria at Adelaide	1885-86
17-212	J. C. Clay	Glamorgan v Worcestershire at Swansea..........	1937

† *Achieved in a single day.*

FOUR WICKETS WITH CONSECUTIVE BALLS

J. Wells	Kent v Sussex at Brighton	1862
G. Ulyett	Lord Harris's XI v New South Wales at Sydney	1878-79
G. Nash	Lancashire v Somerset at Manchester	1882
J. B. Hide	Sussex v MCC and Ground at Lord's	1890
F. J. Shacklock	Nottinghamshire v Somerset at Nottingham	1893
A. D. Downes	Otago v Auckland at Dunedin	1893-94
F. Martin	MCC and Ground v Derbyshire at Lord's	1895
A. W. Mold	Lancashire v Nottinghamshire at Nottingham	1895
W. Brearley†	Lancashire v Somerset at Manchester	1905
S. Haigh	MCC v Army XI at Pretoria	1905-06
A. E. Trott‡	Middlesex v Somerset at Lord's	1907
F. A. Tarrant	Middlesex v Gloucestershire at Bristol.	1907
A. Drake	Yorkshire v Derbyshire at Chesterfield	1914
S. G. Smith	Northamptonshire v Warwickshire at Birmingham	1914
H. A. Peach	Surrey v Sussex at The Oval	1924
A. F. Borland	Natal v Griqualand West at Kimberley.	1926-27
J. E. H. Hooker†	New South Wales v Victoria at Sydney	1928-29
R. K. Tyldesley†	Lancashire v Derbyshire at Derby.	1929
R. J. Crisp	Western Province v Griqualand West at Johannesburg.	1931-32
R. J. Crisp	Western Province v Natal at Durban	1933-34
A. R. Gover	Surrey v Worcestershire at Worcester.	1935
W. H. Copson	Derbyshire v Warwickshire at Derby	1937
W. A. Henderson	N.E. Transvaal v Orange Free State at Bloemfontein	1937-38
F. Ridgway	Kent v Derbyshire at Folkestone	1951
A. K. Walker§	Nottinghamshire v Leicestershire at Leicester	1956
D. Robins	South Australia v New South Wales at Adelaide	1965-66
S. N. Mohol	President's XI v Combined XI at Poona.	1965-66
P. I. Pocock	Surrey v Sussex at Eastbourne	1972
S. S. Saini†	Delhi v Himachal Pradesh at Delhi.	1988-89
D. Dias	W. Province (Suburbs) v Central Province at Colombo	1990-91
Ali Gauhar	Karachi Blues v United Bank at Peshawar	1994-95
K. D. James**	Hampshire v Indians at Southampton	1996
G. P. Butcher	Surrey v Derbyshire at The Oval	2000

† *Not all in the same innings.*

‡ *Trott achieved another hat-trick in the same innings of this, his benefit match.*

§ *Having bowled Firth with the last ball of the first innings, Walker achieved a unique feat by dismissing Lester, Tompkin and Smithson with the first three balls of the second.*

** *James also scored a century, a unique double.*

Notes: In their match with England at The Oval in 1863, Surrey lost four wickets in the course of a four-ball over from G. Bennett.

Sussex lost five wickets in the course of the final (six-ball) over of their match with Surrey at Eastbourne in 1972. P. I. Pocock, who had taken three wickets in his previous over, captured four more, taking in all seven wickets with 11 balls, a feat unique in first-class matches. (The eighth wicket fell to a run-out.)

HAT-TRICKS

Double Hat-Trick

Besides Trott's performance, which is given in the preceding section, the following instances are recorded of players having performed the hat-trick twice in the same match, Rao doing so in the same innings.

A. Shaw	Nottinghamshire v Gloucestershire at Nottingham	1884
T. J. Matthews	Australia v South Africa at Manchester	1912
C. W. L. Parker	Gloucestershire v Middlesex at Bristol.	1924
R. O. Jenkins	Worcestershire v Surrey at Worcester.	1949
J. S. Rao	Services v Northern Punjab at Amritsar	1963-64
Amin Lakhani	Combined XI v Indians at Multan	1978-79

Five Wickets in Six Balls

W. H. Copson	Derbyshire v Warwickshire at Derby	1937
W. A. Henderson	N.E. Transvaal v Orange Free State at Bloemfontein	1937-38
P. I. Pocock	Surrey v Sussex at Eastbourne	1972

Most Hat-Tricks

Seven times: D. V. P. Wright.

Six times: T. W. J. Goddard, C. W. L. Parker.

Five times: S. Haigh, V. W. C. Jupp, A. E. G. Rhodes, F. A. Tarrant.

Four times: R. G. Barlow, A. P. Freeman, J. T. Hearne, J. C. Laker, G. A. R. Lock, G. G. Macaulay, T. J. Matthews, M. J. Procter, T. Richardson, F. R. Spofforth, F. S. Trueman.

Three times: W. M. Bradley, H. J. Butler, S. T. Clarke, W. H. Copson, R. J. Crisp, J. W. H. T. Douglas, J. A. Flavell, G. Giffen, D. W. Headley, K. Higgs, A. Hill, W. A. Humphreys, R. D. Jackman, R. O. Jenkins, A. S. Kennedy, W. H. Lockwood, E. A. McDonald, T. L. Pritchard, J. S. Rao, A. Shaw, J. B. Statham, M. W. Tate, H. Trumble, Wasim Akram, D. Wilson, G. A. Wilson.

Twice (current players only): D. G. Cork, D. Gough, A. Kumble, A. Sheriyar.

Hat-Trick on Debut

H. Hay	South Australia v Lord Hawke's XI at Unley, Adelaide	1902-03
H. A. Sedgwick . . .	Yorkshire v Worcestershire at Hull	1906
R. Wooster.	Northamptonshire v Dublin University at Northampton	1925
J. C. Treanor	New South Wales v Queensland at Brisbane	1954-55
V. B. Ranjane	Maharashtra v Saurashtra at Poona	1956-57
N. Frederick	Ceylon v Madras at Colombo	1963-64
J. S. Rao	Services v Jammu and Kashmir at Delhi	1963-64
Mehboodullah	Uttar Pradesh v Madhya Pradesh at Lucknow	1971-72
R. O. Estwick	Barbados v Guyana at Bridgetown	1982-83
S. A. Ankola	Maharashtra v Gujarat at Poona	1988-89
J. Srinath	Karnataka v Hyderabad at Secunderabad	1989-90
S. P. Mukherjee . . .	Bengal v Hyderabad at Secunderabad	1989-90

Notes: R. R. Phillips (Border) took a hat-trick in his first over in first-class cricket (v Eastern Province at Port Elizabeth, 1939-40) having previously played in four matches without bowling.

J. S. Rao took two more hat-tricks in his next match.

250 WICKETS IN A SEASON

	Season	O	M	R	W	Avge
A. P. Freeman . . . . , ...	1928	1,976.1	423	5,489	304	18.05
A. P. Freeman	1933	2,039	651	4,549	298	15.26
T. Richardson	1895‡	1,690.1	463	4,170	290	14.37
C. T. B. Turner	1888†	2,427.2	1,127	3,307	283	11.68
A. P. Freeman	1931	1,618	360	4,307	276	15.60
A. P. Freeman	1930	1,914.3	472	4,632	275	16.84
T. Richardson	1897‡	1,603.4	495	3,945	273	14.45
A. P. Freeman	1929	1,670.5	381	4,879	267	18.27
W. Rhodes	1900	1,553	455	3,606	261	13.81
J. T. Hearne	1896	2,003.1	818	3,670	257	14.28
A. P. Freeman	1932	1,565.5	404	4,149	253	16.39
W. Rhodes	1901	1,565	505	3,797	251	15.12

† *Indicates 4-ball overs;* ‡ *5-ball overs.*

Notes: In four consecutive seasons (1928-31), A. P. Freeman took 1,122 wickets, and in eight consecutive seasons (1928-35), 2,090 wickets. In each of these eight seasons he took over 200 wickets.

T. Richardson took 1,005 wickets in four consecutive seasons (1894-97).

In 1896, J. T. Hearne took his 100th wicket as early as June 12. In 1931, C. W. L. Parker did the same and A. P. Freeman obtained his 100th wicket a day later.

LEADING BOWLERS IN AN ENGLISH SEASON

(Qualification: 10 wickets in 10 innings)

Season	Leading wicket-taker	Wkts	Avge	Top of averages	Wkts	Avge
1946	W. E. Hollies	184	15.60	A. Booth	111	11.61
1947	T. W. J. Goddard	238	17.30	J. C. Clay	65	16.44
1948	J. E. Walsh	174	19.56	J. C. Clay	41	14.17
1949	R. O. Jenkins	183	21.19	T. W. J. Goddard	160	19.18
1950	R. Tattersall	193	13.59	R. Tattersall	193	13.59
1951	R. Appleyard	200	14.14	R. Appleyard	200	14.14
1952	J. H. Wardle	177	19.54	F. S. Trueman	61	13.78
1953	B. Dooland	172	16.58	C. J. Knott	38	13.71
1954	B. Dooland	196	15.48	J. B. Statham	92	14.13
1955	G. A. R. Lock	216	14.49	R. Appleyard	85	13.01
1956	D. J. Shepherd	177	15.36	G. A. R. Lock	155	12.46
1957	G. A. R. Lock	212	12.02	G. A. R. Lock	212	12.02
1958	G. A. R. Lock	170	12.08	H. L. Jackson	143	10.99
1959	D. Shackleton	148	21.55	J. B. Statham	139	15.01
1960	F. S. Trueman	175	13.98	J. B. Statham	135	12.31
1961	J. A. Flavell	171	17.79	J. A. Flavell	171	17.79
1962	D. Shackleton	172	20.15	C. Cook	58	17.13
1963	D. Shackleton	146	16.75	C. C. Griffith	119	12.83
1964	D. Shackleton	142	20.40	J. A. Standen	64	13.00
1965	D. Shackleton	144	16.08	H. J. Rhodes	119	11.04
1966	D. L. Underwood	157	13.80	D. L. Underwood	157	13.80
1967	T. W. Cartwright	147	15.52	D. L. Underwood	136	12.39
1968	R. Illingworth	131	14.36	O. S. Wheatley	82	12.95
1969	R. M. H. Cottam	109	21.04	A. Ward	69	14.82
1970	D. J. Shepherd	106	19.16	Majid Khan	11	18.81
1971	L. R. Gibbs	131	18.89	G. G. Arnold	83	17.12
1972	T. W. Cartwright	98	18.64	I. M. Chappell	10	10.60
	B. Stead	98	20.38			
1973	B. S. Bedi	105	17.94	T. W. Cartwright	89	15.84
1974	A. M. E. Roberts	119	13.62	A. M. E. Roberts	119	13.62
1975	P. G. Lee	112	18.45	A. M. E. Roberts	57	15.80
1976	G. A. Cope	93	24.13	M. A. Holding	55	14.38
1977	M. J. Procter	109	18.04	R. A. Woolmer	19	15.21
1978	D. L. Underwood	110	14.49	D. L. Underwood	110	14.49
1979	D. L. Underwood	106	14.85	J. Garner	55	13.83
	J. K. Lever	106	17.30			
1980	R. D. Jackman	121	15.40	J. Garner	49	13.93
1981	R. J. Hadlee	105	14.89	R. J. Hadlee	105	14.89
1982	M. D. Marshall	134	15.73	R. J. Hadlee	61	14.57
1983	J. K. Lever	106	16.28	Imran Khan	12	7.16
	D. L. Underwood	106	19.28			
1984	R. J. Hadlee	117	14.05	R. J. Hadlee	117	14.05
1985	N. V. Radford	101	24.68	R. M. Ellison	65	17.20
1986	C. A. Walsh	118	18.17	M. D. Marshall	100	15.08
1987	N. V. Radford	109	20.81	R. J. Hadlee	97	12.64
1988	F. D. Stephenson	125	18.31	M. D. Marshall	42	13.16
1989	D. R. Pringle	94	18.64	T. M. Alderman	70	15.64
	S. L. Watkin	94	25.09			
1990	N. A. Foster	94	26.61	I. R. Bishop	59	19.05
1991	Waqar Younis	113	14.65	Waqar Younis	113	14.65
1992	C. A. Walsh	92	15.96	C. A. Walsh	92	15.96
1993	S. L. Watkin	92	22.80	Wasim Akram	59	19.27
1994	M. M. Patel	90	22.86	C. E. L. Ambrose	77	14.45
1995	A. Kumble	105	20.40	A. A. Donald	89	16.07

Season	Leading wicket-taker	Wkts	Avge	Top of averages	Wkts	Avge
1996	C. A. Walsh	85	16.84	C. E. L. Ambrose	43	16.67
1997	A. M. Smith	83	17.63	A. A. Donald	60	15.63
1998	C. A. Walsh	106	17.31	V. J. Wells	36	14.27
1999	A. Sheriyar	92	24.70	Saqlain Mushtaq	58	11.37
2000	G. D. McGrath	80	13.21	C. A. Walsh	40	11.42

100 WICKETS IN A SEASON

Since Reduction of Championship Matches in 1969

Five times: D. L. Underwood 110 (1978), 106 (1979), 106 (1983), 102 (1971), 101 (1969).
Four times: J. K. Lever 116 (1984), 106 (1978), 106 (1979), 106 (1983).
Twice: B. S. Bedi 112 (1974), 105 (1973); T. W. Cartwright 108 (1969), 104 (1971); N. A. Foster 105 (1986), 102 (1991); N. Gifford 105 (1970), 104 (1983); R. J. Hadlee 117 (1984), 105 (1981); P. G. Lee 112 (1975), 101 (1973); M. D. Marshall 134 (1982), 100 (1986); M. J. Procter 109 (1977), 108 (1969); N. V. Radford 109 (1987), 101 (1985); F. J. Titmus 105 (1970), 104 (1971); C. A. Walsh 118 (1986), 106 (1998).
Once: J. P. Agnew 101 (1987); I. T. Botham 100 (1978); A. R. Caddick 105 (1998); K. E. Cooper 101 (1988); R. M. H. Cottam 109 (1969); D. R. Doshi 101 (1980); J. E. Emburey 103 (1983); L. R. Gibbs 131 (1971); R. N. S. Hobbs 102 (1970); Intikhab Alam 104 (1971); R. D. Jackman 121 (1980); A. Kumble 105 (1995); A. M. E. Roberts 119 (1974); P. J. Sainsbury 107 (1971); Sarfraz Nawaz 101 (1975); M. W. W. Selvey 101 (1978); D. J. Shepherd 106 (1970); F. D. Stephenson 125 (1988); Waqar Younis 113 (1991); D. Wilson 102 (1969).

100 WICKETS IN A SEASON MOST TIMES

(Includes Overseas Tours and Seasons)

23 times: W. Rhodes 200 wkts (3).
20 times: D. Shackleton (In successive seasons – 1949 to 1968 inclusive).
17 times: A. P. Freeman 300 wkts (1), 200 wkts (7).
16 times: T. W. J. Goddard 200 wkts (4), C. W. L. Parker 200 wkts (5), R. T. D. Perks, F. J. Titmus.
15 times: J. T. Hearne 200 wkts (3), G. H. Hirst 200 wkts (1), A. S. Kennedy 200 wkts (1).
14 times: C. Blythe 200 wkts (1), W. E. Hollies, G. A. R. Lock 200 wkts (2), M. W. Tate 200 wkts (3), J. C. White.
13 times: J. B. Statham.
12 times: J. Briggs, E. G. Dennett 200 wkts (1), C. Gladwin, D. J. Shepherd, N. I. Thomson, F. S. Trueman.
11 times: A. V. Bedser, G. Geary, S. Haigh, J. C. Laker, M. S. Nichols, A. E. Relf.
10 times: W. Attewell, W. G. Grace, R. Illingworth, H. L. Jackson, V. W. C. Jupp, G. G. Macaulay 200 wkts (1), W. Mead, T. B. Mitchell, T. Richardson 200 wkts (3), J. Southerton 200 wkts (1), R. K. Tyldesley, D. L. Underwood, J. H. Wardle, T. G. Wass, D. V. P. Wright.

100 WICKETS IN A SEASON OUTSIDE ENGLAND

W		Season	Country	R	Avge
116	M. W. Tate	1926-27	India/Ceylon	1,599	13.78
113	Kabir Khan	1998-99	Pakistan	1,706	15.09
107	Ijaz Faqih	1985-86	Pakistan	1,719	16.06
106	C. T. B. Turner	1887-88	Australia	1,441	13.59
106	R. Benaud	1957-58	South Africa	2,056	19.39
105	Murtaza Hussain	1995-96	Pakistan	1,882	17.92
104	S. F. Barnes	1913-14	South Africa	1,117	10.74
104	Sajjad Akbar	1989-90	Pakistan	2,328	22.38
103	Abdul Qadir	1982-83	Pakistan	2,367	22.98

1,500 WICKETS IN A CAREER

Dates in italics denote the first half of an overseas season; i.e. *1970* denotes the 1970-71 season.

		Career	W	R	Avge
1	W. Rhodes	1898-1930	4,187	69,993	16.71
2	A. P. Freeman	1914-36	3,776	69,577	18.42
3	C. W. L. Parker	1903-35	3,278	63,817	19.46
4	J. T. Hearne	1888-1923	3,061	54,352	17.75
5	T. W. J. Goddard	1922-52	2,979	59,116	19.84
6	W. G. Grace	1865-1908	2,876	51,545	17.92
7	A. S. Kennedy	1907-36	2,874	61,034	21.23
8	D. Shackleton	1948-69	2,857	53,303	18.65
9	G. A. R. Lock	1946-*70*	2,844	54,709	19.23
10	F. J. Titmus	1949-82	2,830	63,313	22.37
11	M. W. Tate	1912-37	2,784	50,571	18.16
12	G. H. Hirst	1891-1929	2,739	51,282	18.72
13	C. Blythe	1899-1914	2,506	42,136	16.81
14	D. L. Underwood	1963-87	2,465	49,993	20.28
15	W. E. Astill	1906-39	2,431	57,783	23.76
16	J. C. White	1909-37	2,356	43,759	18.57
17	W. E. Hollies	1932-57	2,323	48,656	20.94
18	F. S. Trueman	1949-69	2,304	42,154	18.29
19	J. B. Statham	1950-68	2,260	36,999	16.37
20	R. T. D. Perks	1930-55	2,233	53,770	24.07
21	J. Briggs	1879-1900	2,221	35,431	15.95
22	D. J. Shepherd	1950-72	2,218	47,302	21.32
23	E. G. Dennett	1903-26	2,147	42,571	19.82
24	T. Richardson	1892-1905	2,104	38,794	18.43
25	T. E. Bailey	1945-67	2,082	48,170	23.13
26	R. Illingworth	1951-83	2,072	42,023	20.28
27	{ N. Gifford	1960-88	2,068	48,731	23.56
	{ F. E. Woolley	1906-38	2,068	41,066	19.85
29	G. Geary	1912-38	2,063	41,339	20.03
30	D. V. P. Wright	1932-57	2,056	49,307	23.98
31	J. A. Newman	1906-30	2,032	51,111	25.15
32	†A. Shaw	1864-97	2,027	24,580	12.12
33	S. Haigh	1895-1913	2,012	32,091	15.94
34	H. Verity	1930-39	1,956	29,146	14.90
35	W. Attewell	1881-1900	1,951	29,896	15.32
36	J. C. Laker	1946-*64*	1,944	35,791	18.41
37	A. V. Bedser	1939-60	1,924	39,279	20.41
38	W. Mead	1892-1913	1,916	36,388	18.99
39	A. E. Relf	1900-21	1,897	39,724	20.94
40	P. G. H. Fender	1910-36	1,894	47,458	25.05
41	J. W. H. T. Douglas	1901-30	1,893	44,159	23.32
42	J. H. Wardle	1946-*67*	1,846	35,027	18.97
43	G. R. Cox	1895-1928	1,843	42,136	22.86
44	G. A. Lohmann	1884-*97*	1,841	25,295	13.73
45	J. W. Hearne	1909-36	1,839	44,926	24.42
46	G. G. Macaulay	1920-35	1,837	32,440	17.65
47	M. S. Nichols	1924-39	1,833	39,666	21.63
48	J. B. Mortimore	1950-75	1,807	41,904	23.18
49	C. Cook	1946-64	1,782	36,578	20.52
50	**C. A. Walsh**	***1981*-2000**	**1,755**	**37,995**	**21.64**
51	R. Peel	1882-99	1,752	28,442	16.23
52	H. L. Jackson	1947-63	1,733	30,101	17.36
53	J. K. Lever	1967-89	1,722	41,772	24.25
54	T. P. B. Smith	1929-52	1,697	45,059	26.55
55	J. Southerton	1854-79	1,681	24,290	14.44
56	A. E. Trott	*1892*-1911	1,674	35,317	21.09

		Career	W	R	Avge
57	A. W. Mold	1889-1901	1,673	26,010	15.54
58	T. G. Wass..........	1896-1920	1,666	34,092	20.46
59	V. W. C. Jupp	1909-38	1,658	38,166	23.01
60	C. Gladwin..........	1939-58	1,653	30,265	18.30
61	M. D. Marshall.......	*1977-95*	1,651	31,548	19.10
62	W. E. Bowes.........	1928-47	1,639	27,470	16.76
63	A. W. Wellard.......	1927-50	1,614	39,302	24.35
64	J. E. Emburey........	1973-97	1,608	41,958	26.09
65	P. I. Pocock	1964-86	1,607	42,648	26.53
66	N. I. Thomson	1952-72	1,597	32,867	20.58
67	{ J. Mercer..........	1919-47	1,591	37,210	23.38
	{ G. J. Thompson	1897-1922	1,591	30,058	18.89
69	J. M. Sims	1929-53	1,581	39,401	24.92
70	{ T. Emmett	1866-88	1,571	21,314	13.56
	{ Intikhab Alam........	*1957-82*	1,571	43,474	27.67
72	B. S. Bedi	*1961-81*	1,560	33,843	21.69
73	W. Voce.............	1927-52	1,558	35,961	23.08
74	A. R. Gover	1928-48	1,555	36,753	23.63
75	{ T. W. Cartwright	1952-77	1,536	29,357	19.11
	{ K. Higgs	1958-86	1,536	36,267	23.61
77	James Langridge	1924-53	1,530	34,524	22.56
78	J. A. Flavell	1949-67	1,529	32,847	21.48
79	E. E. Hemmings	1966-95	1,515	44,403	29.30
80	{ C. F. Root	1910-33	1,512	31,933	21.11
	{ F. A. Tarrant........	*1898-1936*	1,512	26,450	17.49
82	R. K. Tyldesley......	1919-35	1,509	25,980	17.21

Bold type denotes those who played in 1998-99 and 1999 seasons.

  † *The figures for A. Shaw exclude one wicket for which no analysis is available.*

Note: Some works of reference provide career figures which differ from those in this list, owing to the exclusion or inclusion of matches recognised or not recognised as first-class by *Wisden*.

Current Players with 1,000 Wickets

	Career	W	R	Avge
A. A. Donald	*1985-2000*	1,136	25,394	22.35
P. A. J. DeFreitas......	1985-2000	1,060	29,368	27.70

ALL-ROUND RECORDS

HUNDRED RUNS AND TEN WICKETS IN AN INNINGS

V. E. Walker, England v Surrey at The Oval; 20*, 108, ten for 74, and four for 17 . .   1859
W. G. Grace, MCC v Oxford University at Oxford; 104, two for 60, and ten for 49 . .   1886

Note: E. M. Grace, for MCC v Gentlemen of Kent in a 12-a-side match at Canterbury in 1862, scored 192* and took five for 77 and ten for 69.

TWO HUNDRED RUNS AND SIXTEEN WICKETS

G. Giffen, South Australia v Victoria at Adelaide; 271, nine for 96, and seven for 70 . .   1891-92

HUNDRED IN EACH INNINGS AND FIVE WICKETS TWICE

G. H. Hirst, Yorkshire v Somerset at Bath; 111, 117*, six for 70, and five for 45 . . .   1906

HUNDRED IN EACH INNINGS AND TEN WICKETS

B. J. T. Bosanquet, Middlesex v Sussex at Lord's; 103, 100*, three for 75, and eight for 53. 1905

F. D. Stephenson, Nottinghamshire v Yorkshire at Nottingham; 111, 117, four for 105, and seven for 117 1988

HUNDRED AND FOUR WICKETS WITH CONSECUTIVE BALLS

K. D. James, Hampshire v Indians at Southampton; 103 and five for 74 including four wickets with consecutive balls. 1996

HUNDRED AND HAT-TRICK

G. Giffen, Australians v Lancashire at Manchester 1884
W. E. Roller, Surrey v Sussex at The Oval. *Unique instance of 200 and hat-trick*. . . 1885
W. B. Burns, Worcestershire v Gloucestershire at Worcester. 1913
V. W. C. Jupp, Sussex v Essex at Colchester. 1921
R. E. S. Wyatt, MCC v Ceylon at Colombo 1926-27
L. N. Constantine, West Indians v Northamptonshire at Northampton. 1928
D. E. Davies, Glamorgan v Leicestershire at Leicester. 1937
V. M. Merchant, Dr C. R. Pereira's XI v Sir Homi Mehta's XI at Bombay 1946-47
M. J. Procter, Gloucestershire v Essex at Westcliff-on-Sea. 1972
M. J. Procter, Gloucestershire v Leicestershire at Bristol. 1979

SEASON DOUBLES

2,000 Runs and 200 Wickets

| 1906 | G. H. Hirst | 2,385 runs and 208 wickets |

3,000 Runs and 100 Wickets

| 1937 | J. H. Parks | 3,003 runs and 101 wickets |

2,000 Runs and 100 Wickets

	Season	R	W		Season	R	W
W. G. Grace.	1873	2,139	106	F. E. Woolley.	1914	2,272	125
W. G. Grace.	1876	2,622	130	J. W. Hearne	1920	2,148	142
C. L. Townsend	1899	2,440	101	V. W. C. Jupp	1921	2,169	121
G. L. Jessop	1900	2,210	104	F. E. Woolley.	1921	2,101	167
G. H. Hirst	1904	2,501	132	F. E. Woolley.	1922	2,022	163
G. H. Hirst	1905	2,266	110	F. E. Woolley.	1923	2,091	101
W. Rhodes	1909	2,094	141	L. F. Townsend	1933	2,268	100
W. Rhodes	1911	2,261	117	D. E. Davies	1937	2,012	103
F. A. Tarrant	1911	2,030	111	James Langridge	1937	2,082	101
J. W. Hearne	1913	2,036	124	T. E. Bailey.	1959	2,011	100
J. W. Hearne	1914	2,116	123				

1,000 Runs and 200 Wickets

	Season	R	W		Season	R	W
A. E. Trott	1899	1,175	239	M. W. Tate	1923	1,168	219
A. E. Trott	1900	1,337	211	M. W. Tate	1924	1,419	205
A. S. Kennedy	1922	1,129	205	M. W. Tate	1925	1,290	228

1,000 Runs and 100 Wickets

Sixteen times: W. Rhodes.
Fourteen times: G. H. Hirst.
Ten times: V. W. C. Jupp.
Nine times: W. E. Astill.
Eight times: T. E. Bailey, W. G. Grace, M. S. Nichols, A. E. Relf, F. A. Tarrant, M. W. Tate†, F. J. Titmus, F. E. Woolley.
Seven times: G. E. Tribe.

† *M. W. Tate also scored 1,193 runs and took 116 wickets for MCC in first-class matches on the 1926-27 MCC tour of India and Ceylon.*

Note: R. J. Hadlee (1984) and F. D. Stephenson (1988) are the only players to perform the feat since the reduction of County Championship matches. A complete list of those performing the feat before then will be found on page 202 of the 1982 *Wisden*.

Wicket-Keeper's Double

	Season	R	D
L. E. G. Ames.....................	1928	1,919	122
L. E. G. Ames.....................	1929	1,795	128
L. E. G. Ames.....................	1932	2,482	104
J. T. Murray	1957	1,025	104

20,000 RUNS AND 2,000 WICKETS IN A CAREER

	Career	R	Avge	W	Avge	Doubles
W. E. Astill	1906-39	22,731	22.55	2,431	23.76	9
T. E. Bailey	1945-67	28,641	33.42	2,082	23.13	8
W. G. Grace	1865-1908	54,896	39.55	2,876	17.92	8
G. H. Hirst	1891-1929	36,323	34.13	2,739	18.72	14
R. Illingworth	1951-83	24,134	28.06	2,072	20.28	6
W. Rhodes	1898-1930	39,802	30.83	4,187	16.71	16
M. W. Tate	1912-37	21,717	25.01	2,784	18.16	8†
F. J. Titmus	1949-82	21,588	23.11	2,830	22.37	8
F. E. Woolley	1906-38	58,969	40.75	2,068	19.85	8

† *Plus one double overseas (see above).*

WICKET-KEEPING RECORDS

MOST DISMISSALS IN AN INNINGS

9 (8ct, 1st)	Tahir Rashid	Habib Bank v PACO at Gujranwala	1992-93
9 (7ct, 2st)	W. R. James*	Matabeleland v Mashonaland CD at Bulawayo	1995-96
8 (all ct)	A. T. W. Grout	Queensland v Western Australia at Brisbane	1959-60
8 (all ct)†	D. E. East	Essex v Somerset at Taunton	1985
8 (all ct)	S. A. Marsh‡	Kent v Middlesex at Lord's	1991

8 (6ct, 2st)	T. J. Zoehrer	Australians v Surrey at The Oval	1993
8 (7ct, 1st)	D. S. Berry	Victoria v South Australia at Melbourne	1996-97
7 (4ct, 3st)	E. J. Smith	Warwickshire v Derbyshire at Birmingham	1926
7 (6ct, 1st)	W. Farrimond	Lancashire v Kent at Manchester	1930
7 (all ct)	W. F. F. Price	Middlesex v Yorkshire at Lord's	1937
7 (3ct, 4st)	D. Tallon	Queensland v Victoria at Brisbane	1938-39
7 (all ct)	R. A. Saggers	New South Wales v Combined XI at Brisbane	1940-41
7 (1ct, 6st)	H. Yarnold	Worcestershire v Scotland at Dundee	1951
7 (4ct, 3st)	J. Brown	Scotland v Ireland at Dublin	1957
7 (6ct, 1st)	N. Kirsten	Border v Rhodesia at East London	1959-60
7 (all ct)	M. S. Smith	Natal v Border at East London	1959-60
7 (all ct)	K. V. Andrew	Northamptonshire v Lancashire at Manchester	1962
7 (all ct)	A. Long	Surrey v Sussex at Hove	1964
7 (all ct)	R. M. Schofield	Central Districts v Wellington at Wellington	1964-65
7 (all ct)	R. W. Taylor	Derbyshire v Glamorgan at Derby	1966
7 (6ct, 1st)	H. B. Taber	New South Wales v South Australia at Adelaide	1968-69
7 (6ct, 1st)	E. W. Jones	Glamorgan v Cambridge University at Cambridge	1970
7 (6ct, 1st)	S. Benjamin	Central Zone v North Zone at Bombay	1973-74
7 (all ct)	R. W. Taylor	Derbyshire v Yorkshire at Chesterfield	1975
7 (6ct, 1st)	Shahid Israr	Karachi Whites v Quetta at Karachi	1976-77
7 (4ct, 3st)	Wasim Bari	PIA v Sind at Lahore	1977-78
7 (all ct)	J. A. Maclean	Queensland v Victoria at Melbourne	1977-78
7 (5ct, 2st)	Taslim Arif	National Bank v Punjab at Lahore	1978-79
7 (all ct)	Wasim Bari	Pakistan v New Zealand at Auckland	1978-79
7 (all ct)	R. W. Taylor	England v India at Bombay	1979-80
7 (all ct)	D. L. Bairstow	Yorkshire v Derbyshire at Scarborough	1982
7 (6ct, 1st)	R. B. Phillips	Queensland v New Zealanders at Bundaberg	1982-83
7 (3ct, 4st)	Masood Iqbal	Habib Bank v Lahore at Lahore	1982-83
7 (3ct, 4st)	Arif-ud-Din	United Bank v PACO at Sahiwal	1983-84
7 (6ct, 1st)	R. J. East	OFS v Western Province B at Cape Town	1984-85
7 (all ct)	B. A. Young	Northern Districts v Canterbury at Christchurch	1986-87
7 (all ct)	D. J. Richardson	Eastern Province v OFS at Bloemfontein	1988-89
7 (6ct, 1st)	Dildar Malik	Multan v Faisalabad at Sahiwal	1988-89
7 (all ct)	W. K. Hegg	Lancashire v Derbyshire at Chesterfield	1989
7 (all ct)	Imran Zia	Bahawalpur v Faisalabad at Faisalabad	1989-90
7 (all ct)	I. D. S. Smith	New Zealand v Sri Lanka at Hamilton	1990-91
7 (all ct)	J. F. Holyman	Tasmania v Western Australia at Hobart	1990-91
7 (all ct)	P. J. L. Radley	OFS v Western Province at Cape Town	1990-91
7 (all ct)	C. P. Metson	Glamorgan v Derbyshire at Chesterfield	1991
7 (all ct)	H. M. de Vos	W. Transvaal v E. Transvaal at Potchefstroom	1993-94
7 (all ct)	P. Kirsten	Griqualand West v W. Transvaal at Potchefstroom	1993-94
7 (6ct, 1st)	S. A. Marsh	Kent v Durham at Canterbury	1994
7 (all ct)	K. J. Piper	Warwickshire v Essex at Birmingham	1994
7 (6ct, 1st)	K. J. Piper	Warwickshire v Derbyshire at Chesterfield	1994
7 (all ct)	H. H. Devapriya	Colts v Sinhalese at Colombo	1995-96
7 (all ct)	D. J. R. Campbell	Mashonaland CD v Matabeleland at Bulawayo	1995-96
7 (all ct)	A. C. Gilchrist	Western Australia v South Australia at Perth	1995-96
7 (all ct)	C. W. Scott	Durham v Yorkshire at Chester-le-Street	1996
7 (all ct)	Zahid Umar	WAPDA v Habib Bank at Sheikhupura	1997-98
7 (all ct)	K. S. M. Iyer	Vidarbha v Uttar Pradesh at Allahabad	1997-98
7 (all ct)	W. M. Noon	Nottinghamshire v Kent at Nottingham	1999
7 (all ct)	Aamer Iqbal	Pakistan Customs v Karachi Whites at Karachi	1999-2000
7 (all ct)	H. A. P. W. Jayawardene	Sebastianites v Sinhalese at Colombo	1999-2000

* *W. R. James also scored 99 and 99 not out.*

† *The first eight wickets to fall.*

‡ *S. A. Marsh also scored 108 not out.*

Note: R. D. Jacobs made seven dismissals (all ct) for West Indies v Australia at Melbourne in 2000-01, after the deadline for this section.

WICKET-KEEPERS' HAT-TRICKS

W. H. Brain, Gloucestershire v Somerset at Cheltenham, 1893 – three stumpings off successive balls from C. L. Townsend.

G. O. Dawkes, Derbyshire v Worcestershire at Kidderminster, 1958 – three catches off successive balls from H. L. Jackson.

R. C. Russell, Gloucestershire v Surrey at The Oval, 1986 – three catches off successive balls from C. A. Walsh and D. V. Lawrence (2).

MOST DISMISSALS IN A MATCH

13 (11ct, 2st)	W. R. James*	Matabeleland v Mashonaland CD at Bulawayo ..	1995-96
12 (8ct, 4st)	E. Pooley	Surrey v Sussex at The Oval	1868
12 (9ct, 3st)	D. Tallon	Queensland v New South Wales at Sydney	1938-39
12 (9ct, 3st)	H. B. Taber	New South Wales v South Australia at Adelaide .	1968-69
11 (all ct)	A. Long	Surrey v Sussex at Hove	1964
11 (all ct)	R. W. Marsh	Western Australia v Victoria at Perth	1975-76
11 (all ct)	D. L. Bairstow	Yorkshire v Derbyshire at Scarborough.	1982
11 (all ct)	W. K. Hegg	Lancashire v Derbyshire at Chesterfield	1989
11 (all ct)	A. J. Stewart	Surrey v Leicestershire at Leicester..........	1989
11 (all ct)	T. J. Nielsen	South Australia v Western Australia at Perth	1990-91
11 (10ct, 1st)	I. A. Healy	Australians v N. Transvaal at Verwoerdburg	1993-94
11 (10ct, 1st)	K. J. Piper	Warwickshire v Derbyshire at Chesterfield	1994
11 (all ct)	D. S. Berry	Victoria v Pakistanis at Melbourne	1995-96
11 (10ct, 1st)	W. A. Seccombe	Queensland v Western Australia at Brisbane	1995-96
11 (all ct)	R. C. Russell	England v South Africa (2nd Test) at Johannesburg	1995-96
11 (10ct, 1st)	D. S. Berry	Victoria v South Australia at Melbourne.......	1996-97
11 (all ct)	Wasim Yousufi	Peshawar v Bahawalpur at Peshawar	1997-98
11 (all ct)	Aamer Iqbal	Pakistan Customs v Karachi Whites at Karachi ..	1999-2000

* W. R. James also scored 99 and 99 not out.

MOST DISMISSALS IN A SEASON

128 (79ct, 49st)	L. E. G. Ames	1929	104 (82ct, 22st)	J. T. Murray	1957
122 (70ct, 52st)	L. E. G. Ames	1928	102 (69ct, 33st)	F. H. Huish	1913
110 (63ct, 47st)	H. Yarnold	1949	102 (95ct, 7st)	J. T. Murray	1960
107 (77ct, 30st)	G. Duckworth	1928	101 (62ct, 39st)	F. H. Huish	1911
107 (96ct, 11st)	J. G. Binks	1960	101 (85ct, 16st)	R. Booth	1960
104 (40ct, 64st)	L. E. G. Ames	1932	100 (91ct, 9st)	R. Booth	1964

MOST DISMISSALS IN A CAREER

Dates in italics denote the first half of an overseas season; i.e. *1914* denotes the 1914-15 season.

		Career	M	Ct	St	Total
1	R. W. Taylor	1960-88	639	1,473	176	1,649
2	J. T. Murray	1952-75	635	1,270	257	1,527
3	H. Strudwick........	1902-27	675	1,242	255	1,497
4	A. P. E. Knott	1964-85	511	1,211	133	1,344
5	F. H. Huish	1895-1914.	497	933	377	1,310
6	B. Taylor	1949-73	572	1,083	211	1,294
7	D. Hunter...........	1889-1909.	548	906	347	1,253
8	H. R. Butt	1890-1912	550	953	275	1,228

		Career	M	Ct	St	Total
9	J. H. Board	1891-*1914*	525	852	355	1,207
10	H. Elliott	1920-47	532	904	302	1,206
11	**R. C. Russell**	**1981-2000**	**425**	**1,077**	**120**	**1,197**
12	J. M. Parks	1949-76	739	1,088	93	1,181
13	R. Booth	1951-70	468	948	178	1,126
14	L. E. G. Ames	1926-51	593	703	418†	1,121
15	D. L. Bairstow	1970-90	459	961	138	1,099
16	G. Duckworth	1923-47	504	753	343	1,096
17	**S. J. Rhodes**	**1981-2000**	**382**	**969**	**113**	**1,082**
18	H. W. Stephenson	1948-64	462	748	334	1,082
19	J. G. Binks	1955-75	502	895	176	1,071
20	T. G. Evans	1939-69	465	816	250	1,066
21	A. Long	1960-80	452	922	124	1,046
22	G. O. Dawkes	1937-61	482	895	148	1,043
23	R. W. Tolchard	1965-83	483	912	125	1,037
24	W. L. Cornford	1921-47	496	675	342	1,017

Bold type denotes those who played in 1999-2000 and 2000 seasons.

  † *Record.*

Current Players with 500 Dismissals

	Career	M	Ct	St	Total
I. A. Healy	*1986-99*	231	698	69	767
W. K. Hegg	1986-2000	275	663	76	739
R. J. Blakey	1985-2000	304	668	50	718
D. Ripley	1984-2000	292	633	82	715
P. A. Nixon	1989-2000	200	515	42	557
Tahir Rashid	*1979-99*	176	488	61	549

Note: In 395 matches since 1981, A. J. Stewart has achieved 581 catches and 21 stumpings, but 213 of his catches were taken as a fielder.

FIELDING RECORDS

(Excluding wicket-keepers)

MOST CATCHES IN AN INNINGS

7	M. J. Stewart	Surrey v Northamptonshire at Northampton	1957
7	A. S. Brown	Gloucestershire v Nottinghamshire at Nottingham	1966

MOST CATCHES IN A MATCH

10	W. R. Hammond†	Gloucestershire v Surrey at Cheltenham	1928
8	W. B. Burns	Worcestershire v Yorkshire at Bradford	1907
8	F. G. Travers	Europeans v Parsees at Bombay	1923-24
8	A. H. Bakewell	Northamptonshire v Essex at Leyton	1928
8	W. R. Hammond	Gloucestershire v Worcestershire at Cheltenham	1932
8	K. J. Grieves	Lancashire v Sussex at Manchester	1951
8	C. A. Milton	Gloucestershire v Sussex at Hove	1952
8	G. A. R. Lock	Surrey v Warwickshire at The Oval	1957
8	J. M. Prodger	Kent v Gloucestershire at Cheltenham	1961
8	P. M. Walker	Glamorgan v Derbyshire at Swansea	1970
8	Masood Anwar	Rawalpindi v Lahore Division at Rawalpindi	1983-84
8	M. C. J. Ball	Gloucestershire v Yorkshire at Cheltenham	1994
8	J. D. Carr	Middlesex v Warwickshire at Birmingham	1995

  † *Hammond also scored a hundred in each innings.*

First-Class Records – Teams

MOST CATCHES IN A SEASON

78	W. R. Hammond	1928		69	P. M. Walker.	1960
77	M. J. Stewart.	1957		66	J. Tunnicliffe.	1895
73	P. M. Walker.	1961		65	W. R. Hammond	1925
71	P. J. Sharpe.	1962		65	P. M. Walker.	1959
70	J. Tunnicliffe.	1901		65	D. W. Richardson.	1961
69	J. G. Langridge	1955				

Note: The most catches by a fielder since the reduction of County Championship matches in 1969 is 49 by C. J. Tavaré in 1978.

MOST CATCHES IN A CAREER

Dates in italics denote the first half of an overseas season; i.e. *1970* denotes the 1970-71 season.

1,018	F. E. Woolley (1906-38)		784	J. G. Langridge (1928-55)
887	W. G. Grace (1865-1908)		764	W. Rhodes (1898-1930)
830	G. A. R. Lock (1946-*70*)		758	C. A. Milton (1948-74)
819	W. R. Hammond (1920-51)		754	E. H. Hendren (1907-38)
813	D. B. Close (1949-86)			

Most Catches by Current Players

555	G. A. Gooch (1973-2000)	491	G. A. Hick (*1983*-2000)

TEAM RECORDS

HIGHEST INNINGS TOTALS

1,107	Victoria v New South Wales at Melbourne	1926-27
1,059	Victoria v Tasmania at Melbourne	1922-23
952-6 dec.	Sri Lanka v India at Colombo	1997-98
951-7 dec.	Sind v Baluchistan at Karachi	1973-74
944-6 dec.	Hyderabad v Andhra at Secunderabad	1993-94
918	New South Wales v South Australia at Sydney	1900-01
912-8 dec.	Holkar v Mysore at Indore	1945-46
912-6 dec.†	Tamil Nadu v Goa at Panjim	1988-89
910-6 dec.	Railways v Dera Ismail Khan at Lahore	1964-65
903-7 dec.	England v Australia at The Oval	1938
887	Yorkshire v Warwickshire at Birmingham	1896
868†	North Zone v West Zone at Bhilai	1987-88
863	Lancashire v Surrey at The Oval.	1990
855-6 dec.†	Bombay v Hyderabad at Bombay	1990-91
849	England v West Indies at Kingston	1929-30
843	Australians v Oxford & Cambridge U P & P at Portsmouth	1893
839	New South Wales v Tasmania at Sydney	1898-99
826-4	Maharashtra v Kathiawar at Poona	1948-49
824	Lahore Greens v Bahawalpur at Lahore	1965-66

821-7 dec.	South Australia v Queensland at Adelaide	1939-40
815	New South Wales v Victoria at Sydney	1908-09
811	Surrey v Somerset at The Oval	1899
810-4 dec.	Warwickshire v Durham at Birmingham	1994
807	New South Wales v South Australia at Adelaide	1899-1900
805	New South Wales v Victoria at Melbourne	1905-06
803-4 dec.	Kent v Essex at Brentwood	1934
803	Non-Smokers v Smokers at East Melbourne	1886-87
802-8 dec.	Karachi Blues v Lahore City at Peshawar	1994-95
802	New South Wales v South Australia at Sydney	1920-21
801	Lancashire v Somerset at Taunton	1895
798	Maharashtra v Northern India at Poona	1940-41
793	Victoria v Queensland at Melbourne	1927-28
791-6 dec.	Karnataka v Bengal at Calcutta	1990-91
790-3 dec.	West Indies v Pakistan at Kingston	1957-58
786	New South Wales v South Australia at Adelaide	1922-23
784	Baroda v Holkar at Baroda	1946-47
783-8 dec.	Hyderabad v Bihar at Secunderabad	1986-87
781-7 dec.	Northamptonshire v Nottinghamshire at Northampton	1995
780-8	Punjab v Delhi at Delhi	1994-95
777	Canterbury v Otago at Christchurch	1996-97
775	New South Wales v Victoria at Sydney	1881-82

† *Tamil Nadu's total of 912-6 dec. included 52 penalty runs from their opponents' failure to meet the required bowling rate. North Zone's total of 868 included 68, and Bombay's total of 855-6 dec. included 48.*

HIGHEST FOURTH-INNINGS TOTALS

(Unless otherwise stated, the side making the runs won the match.)

654-5	England v South Africa at Durban	1938-39
	After being set 696 to win. The match was left drawn on the tenth day.	
604	Maharashtra (*set 959 to win*) v Bombay at Poona	1948-49
576-8	Trinidad (*set 672 to win*) v Barbados at Port-of-Spain	1945-46
572	New South Wales (*set 593 to win*) v South Australia at Sydney	1907-08
529-9	Combined XI (*set 579 to win*) v South Africans at Perth	1963-64
518	Victoria (*set 753 to win*) v Queensland at Brisbane	1926-27
507-7	Cambridge University v MCC and Ground at Lord's	1896
506-6	South Australia v Queensland at Adelaide	1991-92
502-6	Middlesex v Nottinghamshire at Nottingham	1925
502-8	Players v Gentlemen at Lord's	1900
500-7	South African Universities v Western Province at Stellenbosch	1978-79

HIGHEST MATCH AGGREGATES

Runs	Wkts		
2,376	37	Maharashtra v Bombay at Poona	1948-49
2,078	40	Bombay v Holkar at Bombay	1944-45
1,981	35	England v South Africa at Durban	1938-39
1,945	18	Canterbury v Wellington at Christchurch	1994-95
1,929	39	New South Wales v South Australia at Sydney	1925-26
1,911	34	New South Wales v Victoria at Sydney	1908-09
1,905	40	Otago v Wellington at Dunedin	1923-24

In Britain

Runs	Wkts		
1,808	20	Sussex v Essex at Hove............................	1993
1,723	31	England v Australia at Leeds	1948
1,706	23	Hampshire v Warwickshire at Southampton	1997
1,650	19	Surrey v Lancashire at The Oval	1990
1,642	29	Nottinghamshire v Kent at Nottingham	1995
1,641	16	Glamorgan v Worcestershire at Abergavenny	1990
1,614	30	England v India at Manchester	1990
1,606	34	Somerset v Derbyshire at Taunton	1996
1,603	28	England v India at Lord's	1990
1,601	29	England v Australia at Lord's	1930
1,601	35	Kent v Surrey at Canterbury.......................	1995

LOWEST INNINGS TOTALS

12	Oxford University v MCC and Ground at Oxford	†1877
12	Northamptonshire v Gloucestershire at Gloucester.................	1907
13	Auckland v Canterbury at Auckland	1877-78
13	Nottinghamshire v Yorkshire at Nottingham	1901
14	Surrey v Essex at Chelmsford	1983
15	MCC v Surrey at Lord's	1839
15	Victoria v MCC at Melbourne..............................	†1903-04
15	Northamptonshire v Yorkshire at Northampton	†1908
15	Hampshire v Warwickshire at Birmingham	1922

Following on, Hampshire scored 521 and won by 155 runs.

16	MCC and Ground v Surrey at Lord's	1872
16	Derbyshire v Nottinghamshire at Nottingham	1879
16	Surrey v Nottinghamshire at The Oval	1880
16	Warwickshire v Kent at Tonbridge	1913
16	Trinidad v Barbados at Bridgetown............................	1942-43
16	Border v Natal at East London (first innings)....................	1959-60
17	Gentlemen of Kent v Gentlemen of England at Lord's	1850
17	Gloucestershire v Australians at Cheltenham	1896
18	The Bs v England at Lord's	1831
18	Kent v Sussex at Gravesend	†1867
18	Tasmania v Victoria at Melbourne	1868-69
18	Australians v MCC and Ground at Lord's	†1896
18	Border v Natal at East London (second innings).................	1959-60
19	Sussex v Surrey at Godalming...............................	1830
19	Sussex v Nottinghamshire at Hove...........................	†1873
19	MCC and Ground v Australians at Lord's	1878
19	Wellington v Nelson at Nelson	1885-86

† *Signifies that one man was absent.*

Note: At Lord's in 1810, The Bs, with one man absent, were dismissed by England for 6.

LOWEST TOTAL IN A MATCH

34	(16 and 18) Border v Natal at East London	1959-60
42	(27 and 15) Northamptonshire v Yorkshire at Northampton	1908

Note: Northamptonshire batted one man short in each innings.

LOWEST AGGREGATE IN A COMPLETED MATCH

Runs	Wkts		
105	31	MCC v Australians at Lord's.......................	1878

Note: The lowest aggregate since 1900 is 157 for 22 wickets, Surrey v Worcestershire at The Oval, 1954.

LARGEST VICTORIES

Largest Innings Victories

Inns and 851 runs:	Railways (910-6 dec.) v Dera Ismail Khan at Lahore	1964-65
Inns and 666 runs:	Victoria (1,059) v Tasmania at Melbourne	1922-23
Inns and 656 runs:	Victoria (1,107) v New South Wales at Melbourne	1926-27
Inns and 605 runs:	New South Wales (918) v South Australia at Sydney	1900-01
Inns and 579 runs:	England (903-7 dec.) v Australia at The Oval	1938
Inns and 575 runs:	Sind (951-7 dec.) v Baluchistan at Karachi	1973-74
Inns and 527 runs:	New South Wales (713) v South Australia at Adelaide	1908-09
Inns and 517 runs:	Australians (675) v Nottinghamshire at Nottingham	1921

Largest Victories by Runs Margin

685 runs:	New South Wales (235 and 761-8 dec.) v Queensland at Sydney	1929-30
675 runs:	England (521 and 342-8 dec.) v Australia at Brisbane	1928-29
638 runs:	New South Wales (304 and 770) v South Australia at Adelaide	1920-21
609 runs:	Muslim Commercial Bank (575 and 282-0 dec.) v WAPDA at Lahore . . .	1977-78
585 runs:	Sargodha (336 and 416) v Lahore Municipal Corporation at Faisalabad . .	1978-79
573 runs:	Sinhalese SC (395-7 dec. and 350-2 dec.) v Sebastianites C and AC at Colombo	1990-91
571 runs:	Victoria (304 and 649) v South Australia at Adelaide	1926-27
562 runs:	Australia (701 and 327) v England at The Oval	1934
556 runs:	Nondescripts (397-8 dec. and 313-6 dec.) v Matara at Colombo	1998-99

Victory Without Losing a Wicket

Lancashire (166-0 dec. and 66-0) beat Leicestershire by ten wickets at Manchester . .	1956
Karachi A (277-0 dec.) beat Sind A by an innings and 77 runs at Karachi	1957-58
Railways (236-0 dec. and 16-0) beat Jammu and Kashmir by ten wickets at Srinagar .	1960-61
Karnataka (451-0 dec.) beat Kerala by an innings and 186 runs at Chikmagalur	1977-78

TIED MATCHES

Since 1948 a tie has been recognised only when the scores are level with all the wickets down in the fourth innings.

The following are the instances since then:

Hampshire v Kent at Southampton	1950
Sussex v Warwickshire at Hove	1952
Essex v Lancashire at Brentwood	1952
Northamptonshire v Middlesex at Peterborough	1953
Yorkshire v Leicestershire at Huddersfield	1954
Sussex v Hampshire at Eastbourne	1955
Victoria v New South Wales at Melbourne	1956-57
T. N. Pearce's XI v New Zealanders at Scarborough	1958
Essex v Gloucestershire at Leyton	1959
Australia v West Indies (First Test) at Brisbane	1960-61
Bahawalpur v Lahore B at Bahawalpur	1961-62
Hampshire v Middlesex at Portsmouth	1967
England XI v England Under-25 XI at Scarborough	1968
Yorkshire v Middlesex at Bradford	1973
Sussex v Essex at Hove	1974
South Australia v Queensland at Adelaide	1976-77
Central Districts v England XI at New Plymouth	1977-78
Victoria v New Zealanders at Melbourne	1982-83

Muslim Commercial Bank v Railways at Sialkot 1983-84
Sussex v Kent at Hastings. 1984
Northamptonshire v Kent at Northampton 1984
Eastern Province B v Boland at Albany SC, Grahamstown 1985-86
Natal B v Eastern Province B at Pietermaritzburg 1985-86
India v Australia (First Test) at Madras 1986-87
Gloucestershire v Derbyshire at Bristol 1987
Bahawalpur v Peshawar at Bahawalpur. 1988-89
Wellington v Canterbury at Wellington 1988-89
Sussex v Kent at Hove . . . . †1991
Nottinghamshire v Worcestershire at Nottingham 1993

† *Sussex (436) scored the highest total to tie a first-class match.*

MATCHES BEGUN AND FINISHED ON FIRST DAY

Since World War II.

Derbyshire v Somerset at Chesterfield, June 11 1947
Lancashire v Sussex at Manchester, July 12 1950
Surrey v Warwickshire at The Oval, May 16. 1953
Somerset v Lancashire at Bath, June 6 (H. F. T. Buse's benefit) 1953
Kent v Worcestershire at Tunbridge Wells, June 15 1960

THE ASHES

"In affectionate remembrance of English cricket which died at The Oval, 29th August, 1882. Deeply lamented by a large circle of sorrowing friends and acquaintances, R.I.P.
N.B. The body will be cremated and the Ashes taken to Australia."

Australia's first victory on English soil over the full strength of England, on August 29, 1882, inspired a young London journalist, Reginald Shirley Brooks, to write this mock "obituary". It appeared in the *Sporting Times*.

Before England's defeat at The Oval, by seven runs, arrangements had already been made for the Hon. Ivo Bligh, afterwards Lord Darnley, to lead a team to Australia. Three weeks later they set out, now with the popular objective of recovering the Ashes. In the event, Australia won the First Test by nine wickets, but with England winning the next two it became generally accepted that they brought back the Ashes.

It was long believed that the real Ashes – a small urn thought to contain the ashes of a bail used in the third match – were presented to Bligh by a group of Melbourne women. In 1998, Lord Darnley's 82-year-old daughter-in-law said they were the remains of her mother-in-law's veil, not a bail. Other evidence suggests a ball. The certain origin of the Ashes, therefore, is the subject of some dispute.

After Lord Darnley's death in 1927, the urn was given to MCC by Lord Darnley's Australian-born widow, Florence. It can be seen in the cricket museum at Lord's, together with a red and gold velvet bag, made specially for it, and the scorecard of the 1882 match.

TEST MATCH RECORDS

Note: This section covers all Tests up to September 11, 2000.

BATTING RECORDS

HIGHEST INDIVIDUAL INNINGS

375	B. C. Lara	West Indies v England at St John's	1993-94
365*	G. S. Sobers	West Indies v Pakistan at Kingston	1957-58
364	L. Hutton	England v Australia at The Oval	1938
340	S. T. Jayasuriya	Sri Lanka v India at Colombo (RPS)	1997-98
337	Hanif Mohammad	Pakistan v West Indies at Bridgetown	1957-58
336*	W. R. Hammond	England v New Zealand at Auckland	1932-33
334*	M. A. Taylor	Australia v Pakistan at Peshawar	1998-99
334	D. G. Bradman	Australia v England at Leeds	1930
333	G. A. Gooch	England v India at Lord's	1990
325	A. Sandham	England v West Indies at Kingston	1929-30
311	R. B. Simpson	Australia v England at Manchester	1964
310*	J. H. Edrich	England v New Zealand at Leeds	1965
307	R. M. Cowper	Australia v England at Melbourne	1965-66
304	D. G. Bradman	Australia v England at Leeds	1934
302	L. G. Rowe	West Indies v England at Bridgetown	1973-74
299*	D. G. Bradman	Australia v South Africa at Adelaide	1931-32
299	M. D. Crowe	New Zealand v Sri Lanka at Wellington	1990-91
291	I. V. A. Richards	West Indies v England at The Oval	1976
287	R. E. Foster	England v Australia at Sydney	1903-04
285*	P. B. H. May	England v West Indies at Birmingham	1957
280*	Javed Miandad	Pakistan v India at Hyderabad	1982-83
278	D. C. S. Compton	England v Pakistan at Nottingham	1954
277	B. C. Lara	West Indies v Australia at Sydney	1992-93
275*	D. J. Cullinan	South Africa v New Zealand at Auckland	1998-99
275	G. Kirsten	South Africa v England at Durban	1999-2000
274	R. G. Pollock	South Africa v Australia at Durban	1969-70
274	Zaheer Abbas	Pakistan v England at Birmingham	1971
271	Javed Miandad	Pakistan v New Zealand at Auckland	1988-89
270*	G. A. Headley	West Indies v England at Kingston	1934-35
270	D. G. Bradman	Australia v England at Melbourne	1936-37
268	G. N. Yallop	Australia v Pakistan at Melbourne	1983-84
267*	B. A. Young	New Zealand v Sri Lanka at Dunedin	1996-97
267	P. A. de Silva	Sri Lanka v New Zealand at Wellington	1990-91
266	W. H. Ponsford	Australia v England at The Oval	1934
266	D. L. Houghton	Zimbabwe v Sri Lanka at Bulawayo	1994-95
262*	D. L. Amiss	England v West Indies at Kingston	1973-74
261	F. M. M. Worrell	West Indies v England at Nottingham	1950
260	C. C. Hunte	West Indies v Pakistan at Kingston	1957-58
260	Javed Miandad	Pakistan v England at The Oval	1987
259	G. M. Turner	New Zealand v West Indies at Georgetown	1971-72
258	T. W. Graveney	England v West Indies at Nottingham	1957
258	S. M. Nurse	West Indies v New Zealand at Christchurch	1968-69
257*	Wasim Akram	Pakistan v Zimbabwe at Sheikhupura	1996-97
256	R. B. Kanhai	West Indies v India at Calcutta	1958-59
256	K. F. Barrington	England v Australia at Manchester	1964
255*	D. J. McGlew	South Africa v New Zealand at Wellington	1952-53
254	D. G. Bradman	Australia v England at Lord's	1930
251	W. R. Hammond	England v Australia at Sydney	1928-29
250	K. D. Walters	Australia v New Zealand at Christchurch	1976-77
250	S. F. A. F. Bacchus . . .	West Indies v India at Kanpur	1978-79

The highest individual innings for India is:

236*	S. M. Gavaskar	India v West Indies at Madras	1983-84

HUNDRED ON TEST DEBUT

C. Bannerman (165*)	Australia v England at Melbourne	1876-77
W. G. Grace (152)	England v Australia at The Oval	1880
H. Graham (107)	Australia v England at Lord's	1893
†K. S. Ranjitsinhji (154*) . . .	England v Australia at Manchester	1896
†P. F. Warner (132*)	England v South Africa at Johannesburg	1898-99
†R. A. Duff (104)	Australia v England at Melbourne	1901-02
R. E. Foster (287)	England v Australia at Sydney	1903-04
G. Gunn (119)	England v Australia at Sydney	1907-08
†R. J. Hartigan (116)	Australia v England at Adelaide	1907-08
†H. L. Collins (104)	Australia v England at Sydney	1920-21
W. H. Ponsford (110)	Australia v England at Sydney	1924-25
A. A. Jackson (164)	Australia v England at Adelaide	1928-29
†G. A. Headley (176)	West Indies v England at Bridgetown	1929-30
J. E. Mills (117)	New Zealand v England at Wellington	1929-30
Nawab of Pataudi sen. (102) .	England v Australia at Sydney	1932-33
B. H. Valentine (136)	England v India at Bombay	1933-34
†L. Amarnath (118)	India v England at Bombay	1933-34
†P. A. Gibb (106)	England v South Africa at Johannesburg	1938-39
S. C. Griffith (140)	England v West Indies at Port-of-Spain	1947-48
A. G. Ganteaume (112)	West Indies v England at Port-of-Spain	1947-48
†J. W. Burke (101*)	Australia v England at Adelaide	1950-51
P. B. H. May (138)	England v South Africa at Leeds	1951
R. H. Shodhan (110)	India v Pakistan at Calcutta	1952-53
B. H. Pairaudeau (115)	West Indies v India at Port-of-Spain	1952-53
†O. G. Smith (104)	West Indies v Australia at Kingston	1954-55
A. G. Kripal Singh (100*) . .	India v New Zealand at Hyderabad	1955-56
C. C. Hunte (142)	West Indies v Pakistan at Bridgetown	1957-58
C. A. Milton (104*)	England v New Zealand at Leeds	1958
†A. A. Baig (112)	India v England at Manchester	1959
Hanumant Singh (105)	India v England at Delhi	1963-64
Khalid Ibadulla (166)	Pakistan v Australia at Karachi	1964-65
B. R. Taylor (105)	New Zealand v India at Calcutta	1964-65
K. D. Walters (155)	Australia v England at Brisbane	1965-66
J. H. Hampshire (107)	England v West Indies at Lord's	1969
†G. R. Viswanath (137)	India v Australia at Kanpur	1969-70
G. S. Chappell (108)	Australia v England at Perth	1970-71
‡L. G. Rowe (214, 100*) . . .	West Indies v New Zealand at Kingston	1971-72
A. I. Kallicharran (100*) . . .	West Indies v New Zealand at Georgetown	1971-72
R F. Redmond (107)	New Zealand v Pakistan at Auckland	1972-73
†F. C. Hayes (106*)	England v West Indies at The Oval	1973
†C. G. Greenidge (107)	West Indies v India at Bangalore	1974-75
†L. Baichan (105*)	West Indies v Pakistan at Lahore	1974-75
G. J. Cosier (109)	Australia v West Indies at Melbourne	1975-76
S. Amarnath (124)	India v New Zealand at Auckland	1975-76
Javed Miandad (163)	Pakistan v New Zealand at Lahore	1976-77
†A. B. Williams (100)	West Indies v Australia at Georgetown	1977-78
†D. M. Wellham (103)	Australia v England at The Oval	1981
†Salim Malik (100*)	Pakistan v Sri Lanka at Karachi	1981-82
K. C. Wessels (162)	Australia v England at Brisbane	1982-83
W. B. Phillips (159)	Australia v Pakistan at Perth	1983-84
§M. Azharuddin (110)	India v England at Calcutta	1984-85
D. S. B. P. Kuruppu (201*) . .	Sri Lanka v New Zealand at Colombo (CCC) . .	1986-87
†M. J. Greatbatch (107*) . . .	New Zealand v England at Auckland	1987-88
M. E. Waugh (138)	Australia v England at Adelaide	1990-91
A. C. Hudson (163)	South Africa v West Indies at Bridgetown	1991-92
R. S. Kaluwitharana (132*) . .	Sri Lanka v Australia at Colombo (SSC)	1992-93
D. L. Houghton (121)	Zimbabwe v India at Harare	1992-93
P. K. Amre (103)	India v South Africa at Durban	1992-93

†G. P. Thorpe (114*)	England v Australia at Nottingham	1993
G. S. Blewett (102*).	Australia v England at Adelaide	1994-95
S. C. Ganguly (131).	India v England at Lord's	1996
†Mohammad Wasim (109*). .	Pakistan v New Zealand at Lahore	1996-97
Ali Naqvi (115).	Pakistan v South Africa at Rawalpindi.	1997-98
Azhar Mahmood (128*). . . .	Pakistan v South Africa at Rawalpindi.	1997-98
M. S. Sinclair (214)	New Zealand v West Indies at Wellington	1999-2000
†Younis Khan (107)	Pakistan v Sri Lanka at Rawalpindi.	1999-2000

† *In his second innings of the match.*

‡ *L. G. Rowe is the only batsman to score a hundred in each innings on debut.*

§ *M. Azharuddin is the only batsman to score hundreds in each of his first three Tests.*

Notes: L. Amarnath and S. Amarnath were father and son.

Ali Naqvi and Azhar Mahmood achieved the feat in the same innings.

Aminul Islam scored 145 for Bangladesh v India at Dhaka in 2000-01, after the deadline for this section. He was the third player after Bannerman and Houghton to score a hundred in his country's first Test.

300 RUNS IN FIRST TEST

314	L. G. Rowe (214, 100*)	West Indies v New Zealand at Kingston	1971-72
306	R. E. Foster (287, 19)	England v Australia at Sydney	1903-04

TWO SEPARATE HUNDREDS IN A TEST

Three times: S. M. Gavaskar.

Twice in one series: C. L. Walcott v Australia (1954-55).

Twice: †A. R. Border; G. S. Chappell; ‡P. A. de Silva; G. A. Headley; H. Sutcliffe.

Once: W. Bardsley; D. G. Bradman; I. M. Chappell; D. C. S. Compton; R. Dravid; G. W. Flower; G. A. Gooch; C. G. Greenidge; A. P. Gurusinha; W. R. Hammond; Hanif Mohammad; V. S. Hazare; G. P. Howarth; Javed Miandad; A. H. Jones; D. M. Jones; R. B. Kanhai; G. Kirsten; A. Melville; L. R. D. Mendis; B. Mitchell; J. Moroney; A. R. Morris; E. Paynter; §L. G. Rowe; A. C. Russell; R. B. Simpson; G. S. Sobers; A. J. Stewart; G. M. Turner; Wajahatullah Wasti; K. D. Walters; S. R. Waugh; E. D. Weekes.

† *A. R. Border scored 150* and 153 against Pakistan in 1979-80 to become the first to score 150 in each innings of a Test match.*

‡ *P. A. de Silva scored 138* and 103* against Pakistan in 1996-97 to become the first to score two not out hundreds in a Test match.*

§ *L. G. Rowe's two hundreds were on his Test debut.*

TRIPLE-HUNDRED AND HUNDRED IN SAME TEST

G. A. Gooch (England)	333 and 123 v India at Lord's	1990

The only instance in first-class cricket. M. A. Taylor (Australia) scored 334 and 92 v Pakistan at Peshawar in 1998-99.*

DOUBLE-HUNDRED AND HUNDRED IN SAME TEST

K. D. Walters (Australia)	242 and 103 v West Indies at Sydney	1968-69
S. M. Gavaskar (India)	124 and 220 v West Indies at Port-of-Spain	1970-71
†L. G. Rowe (West Indies)	214 and 100* v New Zealand at Kingston	1971-72
G. S. Chappell (Australia)	247* and 133 v New Zealand at Wellington	1973-74

† *On Test debut.*

MOST RUNS IN A SERIES

	T	I	NO	R	HS	100s	Avge		
D. G. Bradman. . . .	5	7	0	974	334	4	139.14	A v E	1930
W. R. Hammond. . . .	5	9	1	905	251	4	113.12	E v A	1928-29
M. A. Taylor	6	11	1	839	219	2	83.90	A v E	1989
R. N. Harvey.	5	9	0	834	205	4	92.66	A v SA	1952-53
I. V. A. Richards. . .	4	7	0	829	291	3	118.42	WI v E	1976
C. L. Walcott.	5	10	0	827	155	5	82.70	WI v A	1954-55
G. S. Sobers	5	8	2	824	365*	3	137.33	WI v P	1957-58
D. G. Bradman. . . .	5	9	0	810	270	3	90.00	A v E	1936-37
D. G. Bradman. . . .	5	5	1	806	299*	4	201.50	A v SA	1931-32
B. C. Lara.	5	8	0	798	375	2	99.75	WI v E	1993-94
E. D. Weekes.	5	7	0	779	194	4	111.28	WI v I	1948-49
†S. M. Gavaskar. . . .	4	8	3	774	220	4	154.80	I v WI	1970-71
B. C. Lara.	6	10	1	765	179	3	85.00	WI v E	1995
Mudassar Nazar	6	8	2	761	231	4	126.83	P v I	1982-83
D. G. Bradman. . . .	5	8	0	758	304	2	94.75	A v E	1934
D. C. S. Compton. . .	5	8	0	753	208	4	94.12	E v SA	1947
‡G. A. Gooch	3	6	0	752	333	3	125.33	E v I	1990

† *Gavaskar's aggregate was achieved in his first Test series.*
‡ *G. A. Gooch is alone in scoring 1,000 runs in Test cricket during an English season with 1,058 runs in 11 innings against New Zealand and India in 1990.*

MOST RUNS IN A CALENDAR YEAR

	T	I	NO	R	HS	100s	Avge	Year
I. V. A. Richards (WI)	11	19	0	1,710	291	7	90.00	1976
S. M. Gavaskar (I)	18	27	1	1,555	221	5	59.80	1979
G. R. Viswanath (I)	17	26	3	1,388	179	5	60.34	1979
R. B. Simpson (A)	14	26	3	1,381	311	3	60.04	1964
D. L. Amiss (E)	13	22	2	1,379	262*	5	68.95	1974
S. M. Gavaskar (I)	18	32	4	1,310	236*	5	46.78	1983
S. T. Jayasuriya (SL)	11	19	0	1,271	340	3	66.89	1997
G. A. Gooch (E).	9	17	1	1,264	333	4	79.00	1990
D. C. Boon (A)	16	25	5	1,241	164*	4	62.05	1993
B. C. Lara (WI)	12	20	2	1,222	179	4	67.88	1995
A. J. Stewart (E).	16	31	3	1,222	164	2	43.64	1998
P. A. de Silva (SL)	11	19	3	1,220	168	7	76.25	1997
M. A Taylor (A).	11	20	1	1,219	219	4	64.15	1989†

† *The year of his debut.*

Notes: M. Amarnath reached 1,000 runs in 1983 on May 3.
The only batsman to score 1,000 runs in a year before World War II was C. Hill of Australia: 1,061 in 1902.

MOST RUNS IN A CAREER

(Qualification: 2,500 runs)

ENGLAND

		T	I	NO	R	HS	100s	Avge
1	G. A. Gooch	118	215	6	8,900	333	20	42.58
2	D. I. Gower	117	204	18	8,231	215	18	44.25
3	G. Boycott.	108	193	23	8,114	246*	22	47.72
4	M. C. Cowdrey	114	188	15	7,624	182	22	44.06
5	W. R. Hammond.	85	140	16	7,249	336*	22	58.45
6	L. Hutton	79	138	15	6,971	364	19	56.67

		T	I	NO	R	HS	100s	Avge
7	**M. A. Atherton**	**102**	**187**	**6**	**6,939**	**185***	**15**	**38.33**
8	**A. J. Stewart**	**102**	**183**	**13**	**6,868**	**190**	**14**	**40.40**
9	K. F. Barrington	82	131	15	6,806	256	20	58.67
10	D. C. S. Compton	78	131	15	5,807	278	17	50.06
11	J. B. Hobbs	61	102	7	5,410	211	15	56.94
12	I. T. Botham	102	161	6	5,200	208	14	33.54
13	J. H. Edrich	77	127	9	5,138	310*	12	43.54
14	T. W. Graveney	79	123	13	4,882	258	11	44.38
15	A. J. Lamb	79	139	10	4,656	142	14	36.09
16	H. Sutcliffe	54	84	9	4,555	194	16	60.73
17	P. B. H. May	66	106	9	4,537	285*	13	46.77
18	E. R. Dexter	62	102	8	4,502	205	9	47.89
19	M. W. Gatting	79	138	14	4,409	207	10	35.55
20	A. P. E. Knott	95	149	15	4,389	135	5	32.75
21	R. A. Smith	62	112	15	4,236	175	9	43.67
22	**G. P. Thorpe**	**60**	**109**	**13**	**3,695**	**138**	**6**	**38.48**
23	D. L. Amiss	50	88	10	3,612	262*	11	46.30
24	A. W. Greig	58	93	4	3,599	148	8	40.43
25	E. H. Hendren	51	83	9	3,525	205*	7	47.63
26	F. E. Woolley	64	98	7	3,283	154	5	36.07
27	K. W. R. Fletcher	59	96	14	3,272	216	7	39.90
28	**G. A. Hick**	**60**	**104**	**6**	**3,257**	**178**	**6**	**33.23**
29	**N. Hussain**	**53**	**94**	**9**	**3,066**	**207**	**8**	**36.07**
30	M. Leyland	41	65	5	2,764	187	9	46.06
31	C. Washbrook	37	66	6	2,569	195	6	42.81

AUSTRALIA

		T	I	NO	R	HS	100s	Avge
1	A. R. Border	156	265	44	11,174	205	27	50.56
2	**S. R. Waugh**	**128**	**204**	**38**	**8,373**	**200**	**22**	**50.43**
3	M. A. Taylor	104	186	13	7,525	334*	19	43.49
4	D. C. Boon	107	190	20	7,422	200	21	43.65
5	G. S. Chappell	87	151	19	7,110	247*	24	53.86
6	D. G. Bradman	52	80	10	6,996	334	29	99.94
7	**M. E. Waugh**	**103**	**171**	**13**	**6,593**	**153***	**17**	**41.72**
8	R. N. Harvey	79	137	10	6,149	205	21	48.41
9	K. D. Walters	74	125	14	5,357	250	15	48.26
10	I. M. Chappell	75	136	10	5,345	196	14	42.42
11	W. M. Lawry	67	123	12	5,234	210	13	47.15
12	R. B. Simpson	62	111	7	4,869	311	10	46.81
13	I. R. Redpath	66	120	11	4,737	171	8	43.45
14	**M. J. Slater**	**62**	**110**	**5**	**4,603**	**219**	**14**	**43.83**
15	K. J. Hughes	70	124	6	4,415	213	9	37.41
16	**I. A. Healy**	**119**	**182**	**23**	**4,356**	**161***	**4**	**27.39**
17	R. W. Marsh	96	150	13	3,633	132	3	26.51
18	D. M. Jones	52	89	11	3,631	216	11	46.55
19	A. R. Morris	46	79	3	3,533	206	12	46.48
20	C. Hill	49	89	2	3,412	191	7	39.21
21	G. M. Wood	59	112	6	3,374	172	9	31.83
22	V. T. Trumper	48	89	8	3,163	214*	8	39.04
23	C. C. McDonald	47	83	4	3,107	170	5	39.32
24	A. L. Hassett	43	69	3	3,073	198*	10	46.56
25	K. R. Miller	55	87	7	2,958	147	7	36.97
26	W. W. Armstrong	50	84	10	2,863	159*	6	38.68
27	G. R. Marsh	50	93	7	2,854	138	4	33.18
28	K. R. Stackpole	43	80	5	2,807	207	7	37.42
29	N. C. O'Neill	42	69	8	2,779	181	6	45.55
30	G. N. Yallop	39	70	3	2,756	268	8	41.13
31	S. J. McCabe	39	62	5	2,748	232	6	48.21
32	**G. S. Blewett**	**46**	**79**	**4**	**2,552**	**214**	**4**	**34.02**

SOUTH AFRICA

		T	I	NO	R	HS	100s	Avge
1	**G. Kirsten**	63	111	9	4,152	275	10	40.70
2	**D. J. Cullinan**	59	96	9	3,748	275*	11	43.08
3	**W. J. Cronje**	68	111	9	3,714	135	6	36.41
4	B. Mitchell	42	80	9	3,471	189*	8	48.88
5	A. D. Nourse	34	62	7	2,960	231	9	53.81
6	H. W. Taylor	42	76	4	2,936	176	7	40.77
7	**J. N. Rhodes**	52	80	9	2,532	117	3	35.66
8 {	E. J. Barlow	30	57	2	2,516	201	6	45.74
	T. L. Goddard	41	78	5	2,516	112	1	34.46

K. C. Wessels scored 2,788 runs in 40 Tests: 1,761 (average 42.95) in 24 Tests for Australia, and 1,027 (average 38.03) in 16 Tests for South Africa.

WEST INDIES

		T	I	NO	R	HS	100s	Avge
1	I. V. A. Richards	121	182	12	8,540	291	24	50.23
2	G. S. Sobers	93	160	21	8,032	365*	26	57.78
3	C. G. Greenidge	108	185	16	7,558	226	19	44.72
4	C. H. Lloyd	110	175	14	7,515	242*	19	46.67
5	D. L. Haynes	116	202	25	7,487	184	18	42.29
6	R. B. Kanhai	79	137	6	6,227	256	15	47.53
7	R. B. Richardson	86	146	12	5,949	194	16	44.39
8	**B. C. Lara**	70	121	4	5,812	375	14	49.67
9	E. D. Weekes	48	81	5	4,455	207	15	58.61
10	A. I. Kallicharran	66	109	10	4,399	187	12	44.43
11	R. C. Fredericks	59	109	7	4,334	169	8	42.49
12	C. L. Hooper	80	136	13	4,153	178*	9	33.76
13	F. M. M. Worrell	51	87	9	3,860	261	9	49.48
14	C. L. Walcott	44	74	7	3,798	220	15	56.68
15	P. J. L. Dujon	81	115	11	3,322	139	5	31.94
16	C. C. Hunte	44	78	6	3,245	260	8	45.06
17	H. A. Gomes	60	91	11	3,171	143	9	39.63
18	B. F. Butcher	44	78	6	3,104	209*	7	43.11
19	**J. C. Adams**	49	80	15	2,861	208*	6	44.01
20	**S. L. Campbell**	46	81	4	2,669	208	4	34.66
21	**S. Chanderpaul**	44	73	8	2,602	137*	2	40.03
22	S. M. Nurse	29	54	1	2,523	258	6	47.60

NEW ZEALAND

		T	I	NO	R	HS	100s	Avge
1	M. D. Crowe	77	131	11	5,444	299	17	45.36
2	J. G. Wright	82	148	7	5,334	185	12	37.82
3	B. E. Congdon	61	114	7	3,448	176	7	32.22
4	J. R. Reid	58	108	5	3,428	142	6	33.28
5	R. J. Hadlee	86	134	19	3,124	151*	2	27.16
6	**S. P. Fleming**	51	90	6	3,121	174*	2	37.15
7	G. M. Turner	41	73	6	2,991	259	7	44.64
8	A. H. Jones	39	74	8	2,922	186	7	44.27
9	B. Sutcliffe	42	76	8	2,727	230*	5	40.10
10	M. G. Burgess	50	92	6	2,684	119*	5	31.20
11	J. V. Coney	52	85	14	2,668	174*	3	37.57
12	G. P. Howarth	47	83	5	2,531	147	6	32.44

INDIA

		T	I	NO	R	HS	100s	Avge
1	S. M. Gavaskar	125	214	16	10,122	236*	34	51.12
2	D. B. Vengsarkar	116	185	22	6,868	166	17	42.13
3	**M. Azharuddin**	**99**	**147**	**9**	**6,215**	**199**	**22**	**45.03**
4	G. R. Viswanath	91	155	10	6,080	222	14	41.93
5	**S. R. Tendulkar**	**76**	**121**	**12**	**6,036**	**217**	**22**	**55.37**
6	Kapil Dev	131	184	15	5,248	163	8	31.05
7	M. Amarnath	69	113	10	4,378	138	11	42.50
8	R. J. Shastri	80	121	14	3,830	206	11	35.79
9	P. R. Umrigar	59	94	8	3,631	223	12	42.22
10	V. L. Manjrekar	55	92	10	3,208	189*	7	39.12
11	N. S. Sidhu	51	78	2	3,202	201	9	42.13
12	C. G. Borde	55	97	11	3,061	177*	5	35.59
13	**R. Dravid**	**37**	**64**	**4**	**2,821**	**190**	**6**	**47.01**
14	Nawab of Pataudi jun.	46	83	3	2,793	203*	6	34.91
15	S. M. H. Kirmani	88	124	22	2,759	102	2	27.04
16	F. M. Engineer	46	87	3	2,611	121	2	31.08
17	**S. C. Ganguly**	**35**	**60**	**5**	**2,505**	**173**	**7**	**45.54**

PAKISTAN

		T	I	NO	R	HS	100s	Avge
1	Javed Miandad	124	189	21	8,832	280*	23	52.57
2	Salim Malik	103	154	22	5,768	237	15	43.69
3	Zaheer Abbas	78	124	11	5,062	274	12	44.79
4	**Inzamam-ul-Haq**	**67**	**111**	**12**	**4,504**	**200***	**11**	**45.49**
5	Mudassar Nazar	76	116	8	4,114	231	10	38.09
6	Majid Khan	63	106	5	3,931	167	8	38.92
7	Hanif Mohammad	55	97	8	3,915	337	12	43.98
8	Imran Khan	88	126	25	3,807	136	6	37.69
9	**Saeed Anwar**	**49**	**82**	**2**	**3,768**	**188***	**10**	**47.10**
10	Mushtaq Mohammad	57	100	7	3,643	201	10	39.17
11	Asif Iqbal	58	99	7	3,575	175	11	38.85
12	**Ijaz Ahmed, sen.**	**58**	**89**	**4**	**3,282**	**211**	**12**	**38.61**
13	Saeed Ahmed	41	78	4	2,991	172	5	40.41
14	Ramiz Raja	57	94	5	2,833	122	2	31.83
15	**Aamir Sohail**	**47**	**83**	**3**	**2,823**	**205**	**5**	**35.28**
16	Wasim Raja	57	92	14	2,821	125	4	36.16
17	**Wasim Akram**	**98**	**140**	**17**	**2,809**	**257***	**3**	**22.83**
18	Mohsin Khan	48	79	6	2,709	200	7	37.10
19	Shoaib Mohammad	45	68	7	2,705	203*	7	44.34
20	Sadiq Mohammad	41	74	2	2,579	166	5	35.81

SRI LANKA

		T	I	NO	R	HS	100s	Avge
1	**P. A. de Silva**	**85**	**146**	**11**	**5,728**	**267**	**18**	**42.42**
2	**A. Ranatunga**	**93**	**155**	**12**	**5,105**	**135***	**4**	**35.69**
3	**S. T. Jayasuriya**	**53**	**90**	**9**	**3,447**	**340**	**7**	**42.55**
4	H. P. Tillekeratne	56	91	14	2,972	126*	6	38.59
5	R. S. Mahanama	52	89	1	2,576	225	4	29.27

ZIMBABWE

		T	I	NO	R	HS	100s	Avge
1	**A. Flower**	**43**	**77**	**13**	**2,842**	**156**	**7**	**44.40**

Bold type denotes those who played Test cricket in 1999-2000 and 2000 seasons.

HIGHEST CAREER AVERAGES

(Qualification: 20 innings)

Avge		*T*	*I*	*NO*	*R*	*HS*	*100s*
99.94	D. G. Bradman (A).......	52	80	10	6,996	334	29
60.97	R. G. Pollock (SA)........	23	41	4	2,256	274	7
60.83	G. A. Headley (WI).......	22	40	4	2,190	270*	10
60.73	H. Sutcliffe (E)	54	84	9	4,555	194	16
59.23	E. Paynter (E)	20	31	5	1,540	243	4
58.67	K. F. Barrington (E).......	82	131	15	6,806	256	20
58.61	E. D. Weekes (WI)........	48	81	5	4,455	207	15
58.45	W. R. Hammond (E).......	85	140	16	7,249	336*	22
57.78	G. S. Sobers (WI)	93	160	21	8,032	365*	26
56.94	J. B. Hobbs (E)	61	102	7	5,410	211	15
56.68	C. L. Walcott (WI)........	44	74	7	3,798	220	15
56.67	L. Hutton (E)	79	138	15	6,971	364	19
55.37	**S. R. Tendulkar (I)**	**76**	**121**	**12**	**6,036**	**217**	**22**
55.00	E. Tyldesley (E)..........	14	20	2	990	122	3
54.20	C. A. Davis (WI)..........	15	29	5	1,301	183	4
54.20	V. G. Kambli (I)...........	17	21	1	1,084	227	4
53.86	G. S. Chappell (A)........	87	151	19	7,110	247*	24
53.81	A. D. Nourse (SA)........	34	62	7	2,960	231	9
52.57	Javed Miandad (P)	124	189	21	8,832	280*	23
51.62	J. Ryder (A)	20	32	5	1,394	201*	3
51.12	S. M. Gavaskar (I)	125	214	16	10,122	236*	34
50.56	A. R. Border (A)	156	265	44	11,174	205	27
50.43	**S. R. Waugh (A)**	**128**	**204**	**38**	**8,373**	**200**	**22**
50.23	I. V. A. Richards (WI)......	121	182	12	8,540	291	24
50.06	D. C. S. Compton (E)......	78	131	15	5,807	278	17

Bold type denotes those who played Test cricket in 1999-2000 and 2000 seasons.

MOST HUNDREDS

	Total	*200+*	*Inns*	*E*	*A*	*SA*	*WI*	*NZ*	*I*	*P*	*SL*	*Z*
S. M. Gavaskar (I) ..	34	4	214	4	8	–	13	2	–	5	2	–
D. G. Bradman (A)..	29	12	80	19	–	4	2	–	4	–	–	–
A. R. Border (A)...	27	2	265	8	–	0	3	5	4	6	1	–
G. S. Sobers (WI)...	26	2	160	10	4	–	–	1	8	3	–	–
G. S. Chappell (A) ..	24	4	151	9	–	–	5	3	1	6	0	–
I. V. A. Richards (WI)	24	3	182	8	5	–	–	1	8	2	–	–
Javed Miandad (P) ..	23	6	189	2	6	–	2	7	5	–	1	–
M. Azharuddin (I)..	**22**	**0**	**147**	**6**	**2**	**4**	**0**	**2**	**–**	**3**	**5**	**0**
G. Boycott (E).....	22	1	193	–	7	1	5	2	4	3	–	–
M. C. Cowdrey (E)..	22	0	188	–	5	3	6	2	3	3	–	–
W. R. Hammond (E).	22	7	140	–	9	6	1	4	2	–	–	–
S. R. Tendulkar (I) .	**22**	**1**	**121**	**4**	**5**	**2**	**1**	**3**	**–**	**1**	**6**	**0**
S. R. Waugh (A) ..	**22**	**1**	**204**	**7**	**–**	**2**	**4**	**2**	**1**	**2**	**3**	**1**
D. C. Boon (A)	21	1	190	7	–	–	3	3	6	1	1	–
R. N. Harvey (A)...	21	2	137	6	–	8	3	–	4	0	–	–
K. F. Barrington (E) .	20	1	131	–	5	2	3	3	3	4	–	–
G. A. Gooch (E)....	20	2	215	–	4	–	5	4	5	1	1	–

Notes: The most hundreds for Sri Lanka is 18 by **P. A. de Silva** in 146 innings, for New Zealand 17 by M. D. Crowe in 131 innings, for South Africa 11 by **D. J. Cullinan** in 96 innings, and for Zimbabwe 7 by **A. Flower** in 77 innings.

The most double-hundreds by batsmen not qualifying for the above list is four by C. G. Greenidge (West Indies), L. Hutton (England) and Zaheer Abbas (Pakistan).

Bold type denotes those who played Test cricket in 1999-2000 and 2000 seasons. Dashes indicate that a player did not play against the country concerned.

CARRYING BAT THROUGH TEST INNINGS

(Figures in brackets show side's total)

A. B. Tancred	26* (47)	South Africa v England at Cape Town	1888-89
J. E. Barrett.	67* (176)	Australia v England at Lord's.	1890
R. Abel	132* (307)	England v Australia at Sydney	1891-92
P. F. Warner	132* (237)	England v South Africa at Johannesburg . . .	1898-99
W. W. Armstrong . .	159* (309)	Australia v South Africa at Johannesburg . . .	1902-03
J. W. Zulch	43* (103)	South Africa v England at Cape Town	1909-10
W. Bardsley.	193* (383)	Australia v England at Lord's.	1926
W. M. Woodfull . . .	30* (66)‡	Australia v England at Brisbane	1928-29
W. M. Woodfull . . .	73* (193)†	Australia v England at Adelaide	1932-33
W. A. Brown	206* (422)	Australia v England at Lord's.	1938
L. Hutton	202* (344)	England v West Indies at The Oval	1950
L. Hutton	156* (272)	England v Australia at Adelaide	1950-51
Nazar Mohammad§.	124* (331)	Pakistan v India at Lucknow	1952-53
F. M. M. Worrell . .	191* (372)	West Indies v England at Nottingham	1957
T. L. Goddard	56* (99)	South Africa v Australia at Cape Town	1957-58
D. J. McGlew	127* (292)	South Africa v New Zealand at Durban	1961-62
C. C. Hunte	60* (131)	West Indies v Australia at Port-of-Spain. . . .	1964-65
G. M. Turner	43* (131)	New Zealand v England at Lord's.	1969
W. M. Lawry.	49* (107)	Australia v India at Delhi	1969-70
W. M. Lawry.	60* (116)†	Australia v England at Sydney	1970-71
G. M. Turner	223* (386)	New Zealand v West Indies at Kingston. . . .	1971-72
I. R. Redpath.	159* (346)	Australia v New Zealand at Auckland	1973-74
G. Boycott	99* (215)	England v Australia at Perth	1979-80
S. M. Gavaskar . . .	127* (286)	India v Pakistan at Faisalabad	1982-83
Mudassar Nazar§ . .	152* (323)	Pakistan v India at Lahore.	1982-83
S. Wettimuny	63* (144)	Sri Lanka v New Zealand at Christchurch . .	1982-83
D. C. Boon	58* (103)	Australia v New Zealand at Auckland	1985-86
D. L. Haynes	88* (211)	West Indies v Pakistan at Karachi	1986-87
G. A. Gooch	154* (252)	England v West Indies at Leeds	1991
D. L. Haynes	75* (176)	West Indies v England at The Oval	1991
A. J. Stewart	69* (175)	England v Pakistan at Lord's	1992
D. L. Haynes	143* (382)	West Indies v Pakistan at Port-of-Spain	1992-93
M. H. Dekker	68* (187)	Zimbabwe v Pakistan at Rawalpindi	1993-94
M. A. Atherton . . .	94* (228)	England v New Zealand at Christchurch . . .	1996-97
G. Kirsten.	100* (239)	South Africa v Pakistan at Faisalabad	1997-98
M. A. Taylor	169* (350)	Australia v South Africa at Adelaide	1997-98
G. W. Flower	156* (321)	Zimbabwe v Pakistan at Bulawayo	1997-98
Saeed Anwar	188* (316)	Pakistan v India at Calcutta	1998-99
M. S. Atapattu	216* (428)	Sri Lanka v Zimbabwe at Bulawayo	1999-2000
R. P. Arnold	104* (231)	Sri Lanka v Zimbabwe at Harare	1999-2000

† *One man absent.* ‡ *Two men absent.* § *Father and son.*

Notes: G. M. Turner (223*) holds the record for the highest score by a player carrying his bat through a Test innings. He is also the youngest player to do so, being 22 years 63 days old when he first achieved the feat (1969).

D. L. Haynes, who is alone in achieving this feat on three occasions, also opened the batting and was last man out in each innings for West Indies v New Zealand at Dunedin, 1979-80.

FASTEST FIFTIES

Minutes

28	J. T. Brown	England v Australia at Melbourne	1894-95
29	S. A. Durani	India v England at Kanpur.	1963-64
30	E. A. V. Williams . . .	West Indies v England at Bridgetown.	1947-48
30	B. R. Taylor.	New Zealand v West Indies at Auckland.	1968-69
33	C. A. Roach	West Indies v England at The Oval	1933
34	C. R. Browne.	West Indies v England at Georgetown	1929-30

The fastest fifties in terms of balls received (where recorded) are:

Balls

30	Kapil Dev	India v Pakistan at Karachi (2nd Test)	1982-83
31	W. J. Cronje	South Africa v Sri Lanka at Centurion	1997-98
32	I. V. A. Richards. . . .	West Indies v India at Kingston	1982-83
32	I. T. Botham	England v New Zealand at The Oval	1986
33	R. C. Fredericks. . . .	West Indies v Australia at Perth	1975-76
33	Kapil Dev	India v Pakistan at Karachi	1978-79
33	Kapil Dev	India v England at Manchester	1982
33	A. J. Lamb	England v New Zealand at Auckland	1991-92

FASTEST HUNDREDS

Minutes

70	J. M. Gregory	Australia v South Africa at Johannesburg	1921-22
75	G. L. Jessop	England v Australia at The Oval.	1902
78	R. Benaud	Australia v West Indies at Kingston.	1954-55
80	J. H. Sinclair	South Africa v Australia at Cape Town.	1902-03
81	I. V. A. Richards. . . .	West Indies v England at St John's	1985-86
86	B. R. Taylor.	New Zealand v West Indies at Auckland.	1968-69

The fastest hundreds in terms of balls received (where recorded) are:

Balls

56	I. V. A. Richards. . . .	West Indies v England at St John's	1985-86
67	J. M. Gregory	Australia v South Africa at Johannesburg	1921-22
71	R. C. Fredericks. . . .	West Indies v Australia at Perth	1975-76
74	Majid Khan	Pakistan v New Zealand at Karachi	1976-77
74	Kapil Dev	India v Sri Lanka at Kanpur	1986-87
74	M. Azharuddin.	India v South Africa at Calcutta	1996-97
76	G. L. Jessop	England v Australia at The Oval	1902

FASTEST DOUBLE-HUNDREDS

Minutes

214	D. G. Bradman.	Australia v England at Leeds	1930
223	S. J. McCabe	Australia v England at Nottingham	1938
226	V. T. Trumper.	Australia v South Africa at Adelaide	1910-11
234	D. G. Bradman.	Australia v England at Lord's.	1930
240	W. R. Hammond. . . .	England v New Zealand at Auckland	1932-33
241	S. E. Gregory	Australia v England at Sydney	1894-95
245	D. C. S. Compton. . .	England v Pakistan at Nottingham.	1954

The fastest double-hundreds in terms of balls received (where recorded) are:

Balls

220	I. T. Botham	England v India at The Oval	1982
232	C. G. Greenidge. . . .	West Indies v England at Lord's.	1984
240	C. H. Lloyd	West Indies v India at Bombay.	1974-75
241	Zaheer Abbas	Pakistan v India at Lahore.	1982-83
242	D. G. Bradman.	Australia v England at The Oval.	1934
242	I. V. A. Richards. . . .	West Indies v Australia at Melbourne	1984-85

FASTEST TRIPLE-HUNDREDS

Minutes

288	W. R. Hammond. . . .	England v New Zealand at Auckland	1932-33
336	D. G. Bradman.	Australia v England at Leeds	1930

MOST RUNS IN A DAY BY A BATSMAN

309	D. G. Bradman.	Australia v England at Leeds	1930
295	W. R. Hammond. . . .	England v New Zealand at Auckland	1932-33
273	D. C. S. Compton . .	England v Pakistan at Nottingham	1954
271	D. G. Bradman.	Australia v England at Leeds	1934

SLOWEST INDIVIDUAL BATTING

0	in 101 minutes	G. I. Allott, New Zealand v South Africa at Auckland. . . .	1998-99
5	in 102 minutes	Nawab of Pataudi jun., India v England at Bombay	1972-73
6	in 106 minutes	D. R. Martyn, Australia v South Africa at Sydney	1993-94
7	in 123 minutes	G. Miller, England v Australia at Melbourne	1978-79
9	in 132 minutes	R. K. Chauhan, India v Sri Lanka at Ahmedabad	1993-94
10*	in 133 minutes	T. G. Evans, England v Australia at Adelaide	1946-47
14*	in 165 minutes	D. K. Morrison, New Zealand v England at Auckland. . . .	1996-97
18	in 194 minutes	W. R. Playle, New Zealand v England at Leeds	1958
19	in 217 minutes	M. D. Crowe, New Zealand v Sri Lanka at Colombo (SSC)	1983-84
25	in 242 minutes	D. K. Morrison, New Zealand v Pakistan at Faisalabad . . .	1990-91
29*	in 277 minutes	R. C. Russell, England v South Africa at Johannesburg . . .	1995-96
35	in 332 minutes	C. J. Tavaré, England v India at Madras	1981-82
60	in 390 minutes	D. N. Sardesai, India v West Indies at Bridgetown	1961-62
62	in 408 minutes	Ramiz Raja, Pakistan v West Indies at Karachi	1986-87
68	in 458 minutes	T. E. Bailey, England v Australia at Brisbane	1958-59
99	in 505 minutes	M. L. Jaisimha, India v Pakistan at Kanpur.	1960-61
105	in 575 minutes	D. J. McGlew, South Africa v Australia at Durban	1957-58
114	in 591 minutes	Mudassar Nazar, Pakistan v England at Lahore	1977-78
146*	in 635 minutes	N. Hussain, England v South Africa at Durban	1999-2000
163	in 720 minutes	Shoaib Mohammad, Pakistan v New Zealand at Wellington	1988-89
201*	in 777 minutes	D. S. B. P. Kuruppu, Sri Lanka v New Zealand at Colombo (CCC)	1986-87
275	in 878 minutes	G. Kirsten, South Africa v England at Durban	1999-2000
337	in 970 minutes	Hanif Mohammad, Pakistan v West Indies at Bridgetown. .	1957-58

SLOWEST HUNDREDS

557 minutes	Mudassar Nazar, Pakistan v England at Lahore.	1977-78
545 minutes	D. J. McGlew, South Africa v Australia at Durban.	1957-58
535 minutes	A. P. Gurusinha, Sri Lanka v Zimbabwe at Harare	1994-95
516 minutes	J. J. Crowe, New Zealand v Sri Lanka at Colombo (CCC)	1986-87
500 minutes	S. V. Manjrekar, India v Zimbabwe at Harare.	1992-93
488 minutes	P. E. Richardson, England v South Africa at Johannesburg	1956-57

Notes: The slowest hundred for any Test in England is 458 minutes (329 balls) by K. W. R. Fletcher, England v Pakistan, The Oval, 1974.

The slowest double-hundred in a Test was scored in 777 minutes (548 balls) by D. S. B. P. Kuruppu for Sri Lanka v New Zealand at Colombo (CCC), 1986-87, on his debut. It is also the slowest-ever first-class double-hundred.

MOST DUCKS

C. A. Walsh (West Indies) 37; C. E. L. Ambrose (West Indies) 26; D. K. Morrison (New Zealand) 24; B. S. Chandrasekhar (India) 23.

PARTNERSHIPS OVER 400

576	for 2nd	S. T. Jayasuriya (340)/R. S. Mahanama (225) .	SL v I	Colombo (RPS)	1997-98
467	for 3rd	A. H. Jones (186)/M. D. Crowe (299)	NZ v SL	Wellington	1990-91
451	for 2nd	W. H. Ponsford (266)/D. G. Bradman (244) . .	A v E	The Oval	1934
451	for 3rd	Mudassar Nazar (231)/Javed Miandad (280*) .	P v I	Hyderabad	1982-83
446	for 2nd	C. C. Hunte (260)/G. S. Sobers (365*)	WI v P	Kingston	1957-58
413	for 1st	V. Mankad (231)/Pankaj Roy (173)	I v NZ	Madras	1955-56
411	for 4th	P. B. H. May (285*)/M. C. Cowdrey (154) . . .	E v WI	Birmingham	1957
405	for 5th	S. G. Barnes (234)/D. G. Bradman (234)	A v E	Sydney	1946-47

Note: 415 runs were scored for the third wicket for India v England at Madras in 1981-82 between D. B. Vengsarkar (retired hurt), G. R. Viswanath and Yashpal Sharma.

HIGHEST PARTNERSHIPS FOR EACH WICKET

The following lists include all stands above 300; otherwise the top ten for each wicket.

First Wicket

413	V. Mankad (231)/Pankaj Roy (173)	I v NZ	Madras	1955-56
387	G. M. Turner (259)/T. W. Jarvis (182)	NZ v WI	Georgetown	1971-72
382	W. M. Lawry (210)/R. B. Simpson (201)	A v WI	Bridgetown	1964-65
359	L. Hutton (158)/C. Washbrook (195)	E v SA	Johannesburg	1948-49
335	M. S. Atapattu (207*)/S. T. Jayasuriya (188)	SL v P	Kandy	2000 (SL)
329	G. R. Marsh (138)/M. A. Taylor (219)	A v E	Nottingham	1989
323	J. B. Hobbs (178)/W. Rhodes (179)	E v A	Melbourne	1911-12
298	C. G. Greenidge (149)/D. L. Haynes (167)	WI v E	St John's	1989-90
298	Aamir Sohail (160)/Ijaz Ahmed, sen. (151)	P v WI	Karachi	1997-98
296	C. G. Greenidge (154*)/D. L. Haynes (136)	WI v I	St John's	1982-83

Second Wicket

576	S. T. Jayasuriya (340)/R. S. Mahanama (225)	SL v I	Colombo (RPS)	1997-98
451	W. H. Ponsford (266)/D. G. Bradman (244)	A v E	The Oval	1934
446	C. C. Hunte (260)/G. S. Sobers (365*)	WI v P	Kingston	1957-58
382	L. Hutton (364)/M. Leyland (187)	E v A	The Oval	1938
369	J. H. Edrich (310*)/K. F. Barrington (163)	E v NZ	Leeds	1965
351	G. A. Gooch (196)/D. I. Gower (157)	E v A	The Oval	1985
344*	S. M. Gavaskar (182*)/D. B. Vengsarkar (157*) . . .	I v WI	Calcutta	1978-79
331	R. T. Robinson (148)/D. I. Gower (215)	E v A	Birmingham	1985
315*	H. H. Gibbs (211*)/J. H. Kallis (148*)	SA v NZ	Christchurch	1998-99
301	A. R. Morris (182)/D. G. Bradman (173*)	A v E	Leeds	1948

Third Wicket

467	A. H. Jones (186)/M. D. Crowe (299)	NZ v SL	Wellington	1990-91
451	Mudassar Nazar (231)/Javed Miandad (280*)	P v I	Hyderabad	1982-83
397	Qasim Omar (206)/Javed Miandad (203*)	P v SL	Faisalabad	1985-86
370	W. J. Edrich (189)/D. C. S. Compton (208)	E v SA	Lord's	1947
352*‡	Ijaz Ahmed, sen. (211)/Inzamam-ul-Haq (200*) . . .	P v SL	Dhaka	1998-99
341	E. J. Barlow (201)/R. G. Pollock (175)	SA v A	Adelaide	1963-64
338	E. D. Weekes (206)/F. M. M. Worrell (167)	WI v E	Port-of-Spain	1953-54
323	Aamir Sohail (160)/Inzamam-ul-Haq (177)	P v WI	Rawalpindi	1997-98
319	A. Melville (189)/A. D. Nourse (149)	SA v E	Nottingham	1947
316†	G. R. Viswanath (222)/Yashpal Sharma (140)	I v E	Madras	1981-82
308	R. B. Richardson (154)/I. V. A. Richards (178)	WI v A	St John's	1983-84

308	G. A. Gooch (333)/A. J. Lamb (139)	E v I	Lord's	1990
303	I. V. A. Richards (232)/A. I. Kallicharran (97) . .	WI v E	Nottingham	1976
303	M. A. Atherton (135)/R. A. Smith (175)	E v WI	St John's	1993-94

† *415 runs were scored for this wicket in two separate partnerships; D. B. Vengsarkar retired hurt when he and Viswanath had added 99 runs.*

‡ *366 runs were scored for this wicket in two separate partnerships; Inzamam retired ill when he and Ijaz had added 352 runs.*

Fourth Wicket

411	P. B. H. May (285*)/M. C. Cowdrey (154)	E v WI	Birmingham	1957
399	G. S. Sobers (226)/F. M. M. Worrell (197*). . . .	WI v E	Bridgetown	1959-60
388	W. H. Ponsford (181)/D. G. Bradman (304). . . .	A v E	Leeds	1934
350	Mushtaq Mohammad (201)/Asif Iqbal (175). . . .	P v NZ	Dunedin	1972-73
336	W. M. Lawry (151)/K. D. Walters (242)	A v WI	Sydney	1968-69
322	Javed Miandad (153*)/Salim Malik (165)	P v E	Birmingham	1992
288	N. Hussain (207)/G. P. Thorpe (138).	E v A	Birmingham	1997
287	Javed Miandad (126)/Zaheer Abbas (168)	P v I	Faisalabad	1982-83
283	F. M. M. Worrell (261)/E. D. Weekes (129). . . .	WI v E	Nottingham	1950
281	S. R. Tendulkar (217)/S. C. Ganguly (125)	I v NZ	Ahmedabad	1999-2000

Fifth Wicket

405	S. G. Barnes (234)/D. G. Bradman (234).	A v E	Sydney	1946-47
385	S. R. Waugh (160)/G. S. Blewett (214).	A v SA	Johannesburg	1996-97
332*	A. R. Border (200*)/S. R. Waugh (157*).	A v E	Leeds	1993
327	J. L. Langer (144)/R. T. Ponting (197)	A v P	Perth	1999-2000
322†	B. C. Lara (213)/J. C. Adams (94).	WI v A	Kingston	1998-99
281	Javed Miandad (163)/Asif Iqbal (166).	P v NZ	Lahore	1976-77
281	S. R. Waugh (199)/R. T. Ponting (104)	A v WI	Bridgetown	1998-99
277*	M. W. Goodwin (166*)/A. Flower (100*)	Z v P	Bulawayo	1997-98
268	M. T. G. Elliott (199)/R. T. Ponting (127)	A v E	Leeds	1997
265	S. M. Nurse (137)/G. S. Sobers (174).	WI v E	Leeds	1966

† *344 runs were scored for this wicket in two separate partnerships; P. T. Collins retired hurt when he and Lara had added 22 runs.*

Sixth Wicket

346	J. H. Fingleton (136)/D. G. Bradman (270)	A v E	Melbourne	1936-37
298*	D. B. Vengsarkar (164*)/R. J. Shastri (121*) . . .	I v A	Bombay	1986-87
274*	G. S. Sobers (163*)/D. A. J. Holford (105*) . . .	WI v E	Lord's	1966
272	M. Azharuddin (199)/Kapil Dev (163)	I v SL	Kanpur	1986-87
260*	D. M. Jones (118*)/S. R. Waugh (134*)	A v SL	Hobart	1989-90
254	C. A. Davis (183)/G. S. Sobers (142)	WI v NZ	Bridgetown	1971-72
250	C. H. Lloyd (242*)/D. L. Murray (91)	WI v I	Bombay	1974-75
246*	J. J. Crowe (120*)/R. J. Hadlee (151*)	NZ v SL	Colombo (CCC)	1986-87
240	P. H. Parfitt (131*)/B. R. Knight (125)	E v NZ	Auckland	1962-63
238	J. L. Langer (127)/A. C. Gilchrist (149*).	A v P	Hobart	1999-2000

Seventh Wicket

347	D. St E. Atkinson (219)/C. C. Depeiza (122) . . .	WI v A	Bridgetown	1954-55
308	Waqar Hassan (189)/Imtiaz Ahmed (209).	P v NZ	Lahore	1955-56
246	D. J. McGlew (255*)/A. R. A. Murray (109) . . .	SA v NZ	Wellington	1952-53
235	R. J. Shastri (142)/S. M. H. Kirmani (102) . . .	I v E	Bombay	1984-85
221	D. T. Lindsay (182)/P. L. van der Merwe (76) . .	SA v A	Johannesburg	1966-67
217	K. D. Walters (250)/G. J. Gilmour (101)	A v NZ	Christchurch	1976-77
197	M. J. K. Smith (96)/J. M. Parks (101*).	E v WI	Port-of-Spain	1959-60
186	D. N. Sardesai (150)/E. D. Solkar (65)	I v WI	Bridgetown	1970-71
186	W. K. Lees (152)/R. J. Hadlee (87)	NZ v P	Karachi	1976-77
185	G. N. Yallop (268)/G. R. J. Matthews (75). . . .	A v P	Melbourne	1983-84

Eighth Wicket

313	Wasim Akram (257*)/Saqlain Mushtaq (79).	P v Z	Sheikhupura	1996-97
246	L. E. G. Ames (137)/G. O. B. Allen (122)	E v NZ	Lord's	1931
243	R. J. Hartigan (116)/C. Hill (160)	A v E	Adelaide	1907-08
217	T. W. Graveney (165)/J. T. Murray (112).	E v WI	The Oval	1966
173	C. E. Pellew (116)/J. M. Gregory (100)	A v E	Melbourne	1920-21
168	R. Illingworth (107)/P. Lever (88*)	E v I	Manchester	1971
161	M. Azharuddin (109)/A. Kumble (88).	I v SA	Calcutta	1996-97
154	G. J. Bonnor (128)/S. P. Jones (40)	A v E	Sydney	1884-85
154	C. W. Wright (71)/H. R. Bromley-Davenport (84)..	E v SA	Johannesburg	1895-96
154	D. Tallon (92)/R. R. Lindwall (100).	A v E	Melbourne	1946-47

Ninth Wicket

195	M. V. Boucher (78)/P. L. Symcox (108)	SA v P	Johannesburg	1997-98
190	Asif Iqbal (146)/Intikhab Alam (51).	P v E	The Oval	1967
163*	M. C. Cowdrey (128*)/A. C. Smith (69*).	E v NZ	Wellington	1962-63
161	C. H. Lloyd (161*)/A. M. E. Roberts (68)	WI v I	Calcutta	1983-84
161	Zaheer Abbas (82*)/Sarfraz Nawaz (90)	P v E	Lahore	1983-84
154	S. E. Gregory (201)/J. McC. Blackham (74)	A v E	Sydney	1894-95
151	W. H. Scotton (90)/W. W. Read (117).	E v A	The Oval	1884
150	E. A. E. Baptiste (87*)/M. A. Holding (69).	WI v E	Birmingham	1984
149	P. G. Joshi (52*)/R. B. Desai (85).	I v P	Bombay	1960-61
147	Mohammad Wasim (192)/Mushtaq Ahmed (57) . . .	P v Z	Harare	1997-98

Tenth Wicket

151	B. F. Hastings (110)/R. O. Collinge (68*)	NZ v P	Auckland	1972-73
151	Azhar Mahmood (128*)/Mushtaq Ahmed (59)	P v SA	Rawalpindi	1997-98
133	Wasim Raja (71)/Wasim Bari (60*).	P v WI	Bridgetown	1976-77
130	R. E. Foster (287)/W. Rhodes (40*).	E v A	Sydney	1903-04
128	K. Higgs (63)/J. A. Snow (59*).	E v WI	The Oval	1966
127	J. M. Taylor (108)/A. A. Mailey (46*)	A v E	Sydney	1924-25
124	J. G. Bracewell (83*)/S. L. Boock (37).	NZ v A	Sydney	1985-86
120	R. A. Duff (104)/W. W. Armstrong (45*)	A v E	Melbourne	1901-02
117*	P. Willey (100*)/R. G. D. Willis (24*)	E v WI	The Oval	1980
109	H. R. Adhikari (81*)/Ghulam Ahmed (50).	I v P	Delhi	1952-53

BOWLING RECORDS

MOST WICKETS IN AN INNINGS

10-53	J. C. Laker	England v Australia at Manchester	1956
10-74	A. Kumble	India v Pakistan at Delhi	1998-99
9-28	G. A. Lohmann	England v South Africa at Johannesburg	1895-96
9-37	J. C. Laker	England v Australia at Manchester	1956
9-52	R. J. Hadlee	New Zealand v Australia at Brisbane	1985-86
9-56	Abdul Qadir	Pakistan v England at Lahore	1987-88
9-57	D. E. Malcolm	England v South Africa at The Oval	1994
9-65	M. Muralitharan . . .	Sri Lanka v England at The Oval	1998
9-69	J. M. Patel	India v Australia at Kanpur	1959-60
9-83	Kapil Dev	India v West Indies at Ahmedabad	1983-84
9-86	Sarfraz Nawaz.	Pakistan v Australia at Melbourne	1978-79
9-95	J. M. Noreiga	West Indies v India at Port-of-Spain	1970-71
9-102	S. P. Gupte	India v West Indies at Kanpur	1958-59
9-103	S. F. Barnes	England v South Africa at Johannesburg	1913-14
9-113	H. J. Tayfield	South Africa v England at Johannesburg	1956-57
9-121	A. A. Mailey	Australia v England at Melbourne	1920-21
8-7	G. A. Lohmann. . . .	England v South Africa at Port Elizabeth	1895-96
8-11	J. Briggs	England v South Africa at Cape Town.	1888-89

8-29	S. F. Barnes	England v South Africa at The Oval	1912
8-29	C. E. H. Croft	West Indies v Pakistan at Port-of-Spain	1976-77
8-31	F. Laver	Australia v England at Manchester	1909
8-31	F. S. Trueman	England v India at Manchester.	1952
8-34	I. T. Botham	England v Pakistan at Lord's	1978
8-35	G. A. Lohmann	England v Australia at Sydney	1886-87
8-38	L. R. Gibbs	West Indies v India at Bridgetown	1961-62
8-38	G. D. McGrath	Australia v England at Lord's	1997
8-43†	A. E. Trott	Australia v England at Adelaide	1894-95
8-43	H. Verity	England v Australia at Lord's.	1934
8-43	R. G. D. Willis	England v Australia at Leeds	1981
8-45	C. E. L. Ambrose . .	West Indies v England at Bridgetown	1989-90
8-51	D. L. Underwood. . .	England v Pakistan at Lord's	1974
8-52	V. Mankad	India v Pakistan at Delhi	1952-53
8-53	G. B. Lawrence . . .	South Africa v New Zealand at Johannesburg	1961-62
8-53†	R. A. L. Massie . . .	Australia v England at Lord's	1972
8-53	A. R. C. Fraser	England v West Indies at Port-of-Spain	1997-98
8-55	V. Mankad	India v England at Madras	1951-52
8-56	S. F. Barnes	England v South Africa at Johannesburg	1913-14
8-58	G. A. Lohmann	England v Australia at Sydney	1891-92
8-58	Imran Khan	Pakistan v Sri Lanka at Lahore	1981-82
8-59	C. Blythe	England v South Africa at Leeds	1907
8-59	A. A. Mallett	Australia v Pakistan at Adelaide	1972-73
8-60	Imran Khan	Pakistan v India at Karachi	1982-83
8-61†	N. D. Hirwani	India v West Indies at Madras	1987-88
8-64†	L. Klusener	South Africa v India at Calcutta	1996-97
8-65	H. Trumble.	Australia v England at The Oval	1902
8-68	W. Rhodes	England v Australia at Melbourne	1903-04
8-69	H. J. Tayfield	South Africa v England at Durban	1956-57
8-69	Sikander Bakht	Pakistan v India at Delhi	1979-80
8-70	S. J. Snooke	South Africa v England at Johannesburg	1905-06
8-71	G. D. McKenzie . . .	Australia v West Indies at Melbourne	1968-69
8-71	S. K. Warne	Australia v England at Brisbane	1994-95
8-71	A. A. Donald	South Africa v Zimbabwe at Harare	1995-96
8-72	S. Venkataraghavan .	India v New Zealand at Delhi	1964-65
8-75†	N. D. Hirwani	India v West Indies at Madras	1987-88
8-75	A. R. C. Fraser	England v West Indies at Bridgetown	1993-94
8-76	E. A. S. Prasanna . .	India v New Zealand at Auckland	1975-76
8-79	B. S. Chandrasekhar.	India v England at Delhi	1972-73
8-81	L. C. Braund	England v Australia at Melbourne	1903-04
8-83	J. R. Ratnayeke	Sri Lanka v Pakistan at Sialkot	1985-86
8-84†	R. A. L. Massie . . .	Australia v England at Lord's	1972
8-85	Kapil Dev	India v Pakistan at Lahore	1982-83
8-86	A. W. Greig	England v West Indies at Port-of-Spain	1973-74
8-86	J. Srinath	India v Pakistan at Calcutta	1998-99
8-87	M. G. Hughes	Australia v West Indies at Perth	1988-89
8-92	M. A. Holding	West Indies v England at The Oval	1976
8-94	T. Richardson	England v Australia at Sydney	1897-98
8-97	C. J. McDermott . . .	Australia v England at Perth	1990-91
8-103	I. T. Botham	England v West Indies at Lord's.	1984
8-104†	A. L. Valentine	West Indies v England at Manchester	1950
8-106	Kapil Dev	India v Australia at Adelaide	1985-86
8-107	B. J. T. Bosanquet .	England v Australia at Nottingham	1905
8-107	N. A. Foster	England v Pakistan at Leeds	1987
8-112	G. F. Lawson	Australia v West Indies at Adelaide	1984-85
8-126	J. C. White.	England v Australia at Adelaide	1928-29
8-141	C. J. McDermott . . .	Australia v England at Manchester	1985
8-143	M. H. N. Walker . . .	Australia v England at Melbourne	1974-75

† *On Test debut.*

Note: The best for Zimbabwe within the deadline for this section was 6-87 by H. H. Streak against England at Lord's in May 2000; in September 2000, P. A. Strang took 8-109 against New Zealand at Bulawayo.

OUTSTANDING ANALYSES

	O	M	R	W		
J. C. Laker (E)	51.2	23	53	10	v Australia at Manchester........	1956
A. Kumble (I)	26.3	9	74	10	v Pakistan at Delhi.............	1998-99
G. A. Lohmann (E)	14.2	6	28	9	v South Africa at Johannesburg....	1895-96
J. C. Laker (E)	16.4	4	37	9	v Australia at Manchester........	1956
G. A. Lohmann (E)	9.4	5	7	8	v South Africa at Port Elizabeth ...	1895-96
J. Briggs (E)	14.2	5	11	8	v South Africa at Cape Town	1888-89
J. Briggs (E)	19.1	11	17	7	v South Africa at Cape Town	1888-89
M. A. Noble (A)	7.4	2	17	7	v England at Melbourne	1901-02
W. Rhodes (E)	11	3	17	7	v Australia at Birmingham	1902
A. E. R. Gilligan (E)	6.3	4	7	6	v South Africa at Birmingham	1924
S. Haigh (E)	11.4	6	11	6	v South Africa at Cape Town	1898-99
D. L. Underwood (E)	11.6	7	12	6	v New Zealand at Christchurch....	1970-71
S. L. V. Raju (I)	17.5	13	12	6	v Sri Lanka at Chandigarh	1990-91
H. J. Tayfield (SA)	14	7	13	6	v New Zealand at Johannesburg ...	1953-54
C. T. B. Turner (A)	18	11	15	6	v England at Sydney...........	1886-87
M. H. N. Walker (A)	16	8	15	6	v Pakistan at Sydney..........	1972-73
E. R. H. Toshack (A)	2.3	1	2	5	v India at Brisbane...........	1947-48
H. Ironmonger (A)	7.2	5	6	5	v South Africa at Melbourne	1931-32
T. B. A. May (A)	6.5	3	9	5	v West Indies at Adelaide	1992-93
Pervez Sajjad (P)	12	8	5	4	v New Zealand at Rawalpindi	1964-65
K. Higgs (E)	9	7	5	4	v New Zealand at Christchurch ...	1965-66
P. H. Edmonds (E)	8	6	6	4	v Pakistan at Lord's	1978
J. C. White (E)	6.3	2	7	4	v Australia at Brisbane	1928-29
J. H. Wardle (E)	5	2	7	4	v Australia at Manchester	1953
R. Appleyard (E)	6	3	7	4	v New Zealand at Auckland	1954-55
R. Benaud (A)	3.4	3	0	3	v India at Delhi.............	1959-60

MOST WICKETS IN A MATCH

19-90	J. C. Laker......	England v Australia at Manchester	1956
17-159	S. F. Barnes......	England v South Africa at Johannesburg	1913-14
16-136†	N. D. Hirwani....	India v West Indies at Madras	1987-88
16-137†	R. A. L. Massie....	Australia v England at Lord's	1972
16-220	M. Muralitharan...	Sri Lanka v England at The Oval	1998
15-28	J. Briggs........	England v South Africa at Cape Town......	1888-89
15-45	G. A. Lohmann	England v South Africa at Port Elizabeth ...	1895-96
15-99	C. Blythe	England v South Africa at Leeds	1907
15-104	H. Verity........	England v Australia at Lord's.............	1934
15-123	R. J. Hadlee.....	New Zealand v Australia at Brisbane	1985-86
15-124	W. Rhodes.......	England v Australia at Melbourne.........	1903-04
14-90	F. R. Spofforth	Australia v England at The Oval	1882
14-99	A. V. Bedser.....	England v Australia at Nottingham	1953
14-102	W. Bates	England v Australia at Melbourne.........	1882-83
14-116	Imran Khan	Pakistan v Sri Lanka at Lahore	1981-82
14-124	J. M. Patel......	India v Australia at Kanpur	1959-60
14-144	S. F. Barnes.....	England v South Africa at Durban	1913-14
14-149	M. A. Holding	West Indies v England at The Oval	1976
14-149	A. Kumble......	India v Pakistan at Delhi...............	1998-99
14-199	C. V. Grimmett	Australia v South Africa at Adelaide	1931-32

† *On Test debut.*

Note: The best for South Africa is 13-165 by H. J. Tayfield against Australia at Melbourne, 1952-53, and for Zimbabwe 11-255 by A. G. Huckle v New Zealand at Bulawayo, 1997-98.

MOST WICKETS IN A SERIES

	T	R	W	Avge		
S. F. Barnes	4	536	49	10.93	England v South Africa . . .	1913-14
J. C. Laker	5	442	46	9.60	England v Australia	1956
C. V. Grimmett	5	642	44	14.59	Australia v South Africa . .	1935-36
T. M. Alderman	6	893	42	21.26	Australia v England	1981
R. M. Hogg	6	527	41	12.85	Australia v England	1978-79
T. M. Alderman	6	712	41	17.36	Australia v England	1989
Imran Khan.	6	558	40	13.95	Pakistan v India	1982-83
A. V. Bedser	5	682	39	17.48	England v Australia	1953
D. K. Lillee	6	870	39	22.30	Australia v England	1981
M. W. Tate	5	881	38	23.18	England v Australia	1924-25
W. J. Whitty	5	632	37	17.08	Australia v South Africa . .	1910-11
H. J. Tayfield.	5	636	37	17.18	South Africa v England . . .	1956-57
A. E. E. Vogler	5	783	36	21.75	South Africa v England . . .	1909-10
A. A. Mailey	5	946	36	26.27	Australia v England	1920-21
G. D. McGrath	6	701	36	19.47	Australia v England	1997
G. A. Lohmann	3	203	35	5.80	England v South Africa . . .	1895-96
B. S. Chandrasekhar	5	662	35	18.91	India v England	1972-73
M. D. Marshall	5	443	35	12.65	West Indies v England . . .	1988

Notes: The most for New Zealand is 33 by R. J. Hadlee against Australia in 1985-86, for Sri Lanka 20 by R. J. Ratnayake against India in 1985-86, and for Zimbabwe 22 by H. H. Streak against Pakistan in 1994-95.

MOST WICKETS IN A CALENDAR YEAR

	T	R	W	Avge	5W/i	10W/m	Year
D. K. Lillee (A).	13	1,781	85	20.95	5	2	1981
A. A. Donald (SA).	14	1,571	80	19.63	7	–	1998
J. Garner (WI).	15	1,604	77	20.83	4	–	1984
Kapil Dev (I)	18	1,739	75	23.18	5	1	1983
Kapil Dev (I)	18	1,720	74	23.24	5	–	1979
M. D. Marshall (WI). . . .	13	1,471	73	20.15	9	1	1984
S. K. Warne (A)	16	1,697	72	23.56	2	–	1993
G. D. McKenzie (A) . . .	14	1,737	71	24.46	4	–	1964
S. K. Warne (A)	10	1,274	70	18.20	6	2	1994

MOST WICKETS IN A CAREER

(Qualification: 100 wickets)

ENGLAND

		T	Balls	R	W	Avge	5W/i	10W/m
1	I. T. Botham.	102	21,815	10,878	383	28.40	27	4
2	R. G. D. Willis	90	17,357	8,190	325	25.20	16	—
3	F. S. Trueman.	67	15,178	6,625	307	21.57	17	3
4	D. L. Underwood . . .	86	21,862	7,674	297	25.83	17	6
5	J. B. Statham	70	16,056	6,261	252	24.84	9	1
6	A. V. Bedser.	51	15,918	5,876	236	24.89	15	5
7	J. A. Snow.	49	12,021	5,387	202	26.66	8	1
8	J. C. Laker	46	12,027	4,101	193	21.24	9	3
9	S. F. Barnes	27	7,873	3,106	189	16.43	24	7
10	A. R. C. Fraser.	46	10,876	4,836	177	27.32	13	2
11	G. A. R. Lock	49	13,147	4,451	174	25.58	9	3

		T	Balls	R	W	Avge	5W/i	10W/m
12	**D. Gough**	**43**	**9,062**	**4,809**	**173**	**27.79**	**7**	—
13	M. W. Tate	39	12,523	4,055	155	26.16	7	1
14	F. J. Titmus	53	15,118	4,931	153	32.22	7	—
15	J. E. Emburey.	64	15,391	5,646	147	38.40	6	—
16	H. Verity	40	11,173	3,510	144	24.37	5	2
17	C. M. Old	46	8,858	4,020	143	28.11	4	—
18	A. W. Greig	58	9,802	4,541	141	32.20	6	2
19	{ P. A. J. DeFreitas. . . .	44	9,838	4,700	140	33.57	4	—
	A. R. Caddick	**37**	**8,059**	**3,828**	**140**	**27.34**	**9**	—
21	G. R. Dilley.	41	8,192	4,107	138	29.76	6	—
22	T. E. Bailey	61	9,712	3,856	132	29.21	5	1
23	D. E. Malcolm	40	8,480	4,748	128	37.09	5	2
24	W. Rhodes	58	8,231	3,425	127	26.96	6	1
25	P. H. Edmonds	51	12,028	4,273	125	34.18	2	—
26	{ D. A. Allen	39	11,297	3,779	122	30.97	4	—
	{ R. Illingworth	61	11,934	3,807	122	31.20	3	—
28	**P. C. R. Tufnell**	**41**	**11,054**	**4,386**	**120**	**36.55**	**5**	**2**
29	{ J. Briggs	33	5,332	2,095	118	17.75	9	4
	D. G. Cork	**31**	**6,622**	**3,363**	**118**	**28.50**	**5**	—
31	G. G. Arnold	34	7,650	3,254	115	28.29	6	—
32	G. A. Lohmann	18	3,821	1,205	112	10.75	9	5
33	D. V. P. Wright	34	8,135	4,224	108	39.11	6	1
34	J. H. Wardle	28	6,597	2,080	102	20.39	5	1
35	R. Peel	20	5,216	1,715	101	16.98	5	1
36	C. Blythe.	19	4,546	1,863	100	18.63	9	4

AUSTRALIA

		T	Balls	R	W	Avge	5W/i	10W/m
1	**S. K. Warne**.	**84**	**23,502**	**9,505**	**366**	**25.96**	**16**	**4**
2	D. K. Lillee	70	18,467	8,493	355	23.92	23	7
3	C. J. McDermott	71	16,586	8,332	291	28.63	14	2
4	**G. D. McGrath**	**62**	**14,863**	**6,458**	**288**	**22.42**	**17**	**2**
5	R. Benaud	63	19,108	6,704	248	27.03	16	1
6	G. D. McKenzie	60	17,681	7,328	246	29.78	16	3
7	R. R. Lindwall	61	13,650	5,251	228	23.03	12	—
8	C. V. Grimmett	37	14,513	5,231	216	24.21	21	7
9	M. G. Hughes	53	12,285	6,017	212	28.38	7	1
10	J. R. Thomson	51	10,535	5,601	200	28.00	8	—
11	A. K. Davidson	44	11,587	3,819	186	20.53	14	2
12	G. F. Lawson	46	11,118	5,501	180	30.56	11	2
13	{ K. R. Miller.	55	10,461	3,906	170	22.97	7	1
	{ T. M. Alderman	41	10,181	4,616	170	27.15	14	1
15	W. A. Johnston	40	11,048	3,826	160	23.91	7	—
16	W. J. O'Reilly.	27	10,024	3,254	144	22.59	11	3
17	H. Trumble	32	8,099	3,072	141	21.78	9	3
18	M. H. N. Walker. . . .	34	10,094	3,792	138	27.47	6	—
19	A. A. Mallett	38	9,990	3,940	132	29.84	6	1
20	B. Yardley	33	8,909	3,986	126	31.63	6	1
21	R. M. Hogg	38	7,633	3,503	123	28.47	6	2
22	M. A. Noble	42	7,159	3,025	121	25.00	9	2
23	B. A. Reid.	27	6,244	2,784	113	24.63	5	2
24	I. W. Johnson	45	8,780	3,182	109	29.19	3	—
25	P. R. Reiffel	35	6,403	2,804	104	26.96	5	—
26	G. Giffen.	31	6,457	2,791	103	27.09	7	1
27	A. N. Connolly	29	7,818	2,981	102	29.22	4	—
28	C. T. B. Turner	17	5,179	1,670	101	16.53	11	2

SOUTH AFRICA

		T	Balls	R	W	Avge	5W/i	10W/m
1	**A. A. Donald**	62	13,564	6,415	297	21.59	20	3
2	**S. M. Pollock**	45	9,839	3,805	186	20.45	10	—
3	H. J. Tayfield	37	13,568	4,405	170	25.91	14	2
4	T. L. Goddard	41	11,736	3,226	123	26.22	5	—
5	P. M. Pollock	28	6,522	2,806	116	24.18	9	1
6	N. A. T. Adcock	26	6,391	2,195	104	21.10	5	—

Note: Donald became the first South African to take 300 Test wickets in November 2000, after the deadline for this section.

WEST INDIES

		T	Balls	R	W	Avge	5W/i	10W/m
1	**C. A. Walsh**	122	27,239	11,715	483	24.25	21	3
2	**C. E. L. Ambrose** . .	98	22,103	8,501	405	20.99	22	3
3	M. D. Marshall	81	17,584	7,876	376	20.94	22	4
4	L. R. Gibbs	79	27,115	8,989	309	29.09	18	2
5	J. Garner	58	13,169	5,433	259	20.97	7	—
6	M. A. Holding	60	12,680	5,898	249	23.68	13	2
7	G. S. Sobers	93	21,599	7,999	235	34.03	6	—
8	A. M. E. Roberts . . .	47	11,136	5,174	202	25.61	11	2
9	W. W. Hall	48	10,421	5,066	192	26.38	9	1
10	I. R. Bishop	43	8,407	3,909	161	24.27	6	—
11	S. Ramadhin	43	13,939	4,579	158	28.98	10	1
12	A. L. Valentine	36	12,953	4,215	139	30.32	8	2
13	C. E. H. Croft	27	6,165	2,913	125	23.30	3	—
14	V. A. Holder	40	9,095	3,627	109	33.27	3	—

NEW ZEALAND

		T	Balls	R	W	Avge	5W/i	10W/m
1	R. J. Hadlee	86	21,918	9,612	431	22.29	36	9
2	D. K. Morrison	48	10,064	5,549	160	34.68	10	—
	C. L. Cairns	**47**	**8,821**	**4,774**	**160**	**29.83**	**9**	**1**
4	B. L. Cairns	43	10,628	4,280	130	32.92	6	1
5	F. J. Chatfield	43	10,360	3,958	123	32.17	3	1
6	R. O. Collinge	35	7,689	3,392	116	29.24	3	—
7	B. R. Taylor	30	6,334	2,953	111	26.60	4	—
8	**D. L. Vettori**	30	7,983	3,379	105	32.18	5	1
9	J. G. Bracewell	41	8,403	3,653	102	35.81	4	1
10	R. C. Motz	32	7,034	3,148	100	31.48	5	—

INDIA

		T	Balls	R	W	Avge	5W/i	10W/m
1	Kapil Dev	131	27,740	12,867	434	29.64	23	2
2	**A. Kumble**	61	19,115	7,728	276	28.00	16	3
3	B. S. Bedi	67	21,364	7,637	266	28.71	14	1
4	B. S. Chandrasekhar .	58	15,963	7,199	242	29.74	16	2
5	E. A. S. Prasanna . . .	49	14,353	5,742	189	30.38	10	2
6	**J. Srinath**	46	10,664	5,121	168	30.48	6	1
7	V. Mankad	44	14,686	5,236	162	32.32	8	2
8	S. Venkataraghavan . .	57	14,877	5,634	156	36.11	3	1
9	R. J. Shastri	80	15,751	6,185	151	40.96	2	—
10	S. P. Gupte	36	11,284	4,403	149	29.55	12	1
11	D. R. Doshi	33	9,322	3,502	114	30.71	6	—
12	K. D. Ghavri	39	7,042	3,656	109	33.54	4	—
13	N. S. Yadav	35	8,349	3,580	102	35.09	3	—

PAKISTAN

		T	Balls	R	W	Avge	5W/i	10W/m
1	**Wasim Akram**	98	21,621	9,355	407	22.98	25	5
2	Imran Khan	88	19,458	8,258	362	22.81	23	6
3	**Waqar Younis**	67	12,967	6,930	308	22.50	21	5
4	Abdul Qadir	67	17,126	7,742	236	32.80	15	5
5	**Mushtaq Ahmed** . . .	48	11,728	5,654	181	31.23	10	3
6	Sarfraz Nawaz	55	13,927	5,798	177	32.75	4	1
7	Iqbal Qasim	50	13,019	4,807	171	28.11	8	2
8	Fazal Mahmood	34	9,834	3,434	139	24.70	13	4
9	Intikhab Alam	47	10,474	4,494	125	35.95	5	2
10	**Saqlain Mushtaq** . . .	28	8,122	3,530	116	30.43	10	2

SRI LANKA

		T	Balls	R	W	Avge	5W/i	10W/m
1	M. Muralitharan . . .	57	18,211	7,442	291	25.57	22	4
2	W. P. U. J. C. Vaas . .	43	9,175	3,897	127	30.68	4	1

Note: Muralitharan became the first Sri Lankan to take 300 Test wickets in December 2000, after the deadline for this section.

ZIMBABWE

		T	Balls	R	W	Avge	5W/i	10W/m
1	**H. H. Streak**	31	6,920	2,980	129	23.10	6	—

Bold type denotes those who played Test cricket in 1999-2000 and 2000 seasons.

WICKET WITH FIRST BALL IN TEST CRICKET

	Batsman dismissed			
A. Coningham	A. C. MacLaren	A v E	Melbourne	1894-95
W. M. Bradley	F. Laver	E v A	Manchester	1899
E. G. Arnold	V. T. Trumper	E v A	Sydney	1903-04
G. G. Macaulay	G. A. L. Hearne	E v SA	Cape Town	1922-23
M. W. Tate	M. J. Susskind	E v SA	Birmingham	1924
M. Henderson	E. W. Dawson	NZ v E	Christchurch	1929-30
H. D. Smith	E. Paynter	NZ v E	Christchurch	1932-33
T. F. Johnson	W. W. Keeton	WI v E	The Oval	1939
R. Howorth	D. V. Dyer	E v SA	The Oval	1947
Intikhab Alam	C. C. McDonald	P v A	Karachi	1959-60
R. K. Illingworth	P. V. Simmons	E v WI	Nottingham	1991
N. M. Kulkarni	M. S. Atapattu	I v SL	Colombo (RPS) . .	1997-98

HAT-TRICKS

F. R. Spofforth	Australia v England at Melbourne	1878-79
W. Bates	England v Australia at Melbourne	1882-83
J. Briggs	England v Australia at Sydney	1891-92
G. A. Lohmann	England v South Africa at Port Elizabeth	1895-96
J. T. Hearne	England v Australia at Leeds	1899
H. Trumble	Australia v England at Melbourne	1901-02
H. Trumble	Australia v England at Melbourne	1903-04
T. J. Matthews† . . . . . } Australia v South Africa at Manchester	1912
T. J. Matthews		
M. J. C. Allom‡	England v New Zealand at Christchurch	1929-30
T. W. J. Goddard	England v South Africa at Johannesburg	1938-39

P. J. Loader	England v West Indies at Leeds	1957
L. F. Kline	Australia v South Africa at Cape Town.	1957-58
W. W. Hall	West Indies v Pakistan at Lahore.	1958-59
G. M. Griffin	South Africa v England at Lord's	1960
L. R. Gibbs.	West Indies v Australia at Adelaide	1960-61
P. J. Petherick‡.	New Zealand v Pakistan at Lahore	1976-77
C. A. Walsh§.	West Indies v Australia at Brisbane	1988-89
M. G. Hughes§	Australia v West Indies at Perth	1988-89
D. W. Fleming‡	Australia v Pakistan at Rawalpindi.	1994-95
S. K. Warne	Australia v England at Melbourne	1994-95
D. G. Cork	England v West Indies at Manchester.	1995
D. Gough	England v Australia at Sydney	1998-99
Wasim Akram**	Pakistan v Sri Lanka at Lahore.	1998-99
Wasim Akram**	Pakistan v Sri Lanka at Dhaka	1998-99
D. N. T. Zoysa	Sri Lanka v Zimbabwe at Harare	1999-2000
Abdur Razzaq	Pakistan v Sri Lanka at Galle.	2000 (SL)

    † *T. J. Matthews did the hat-trick in each innings of the same match.*
    ‡ *On Test debut.*
    § *Not all in the same innings.*
    ** *Wasim Akram did the hat-trick in successive matches.*

FOUR WICKETS IN FIVE BALLS

M. J. C. Allom	England v New Zealand at Christchurch.	1929-30
	On debut, in his eighth over: W-WWW	
C. M. Old	England v Pakistan at Birmingham	1978
	Sequence interrupted by a no-ball: WW-WW	
Wasim Akram	Pakistan v West Indies at Lahore (*WW-WW*)	1990-91

MOST BALLS BOWLED IN A TEST

S. Ramadhin (West Indies) sent down 774 balls in 129 overs against England at Birmingham, 1957. It was the most delivered by any bowler in a Test, beating H. Verity's 766 for England against South Africa at Durban, 1938-39. In this match Ramadhin also bowled the most balls (588) in any single first-class innings, including Tests.

ALL-ROUND RECORDS

100 RUNS AND FIVE WICKETS IN AN INNINGS

England

A. W. Greig	148	6-164	v West Indies	Bridgetown	1973-74
I. T. Botham	103	5-73	v New Zealand	Christchurch	1977-78
I. T. Botham	108	8-34	v Pakistan	Lord's	1978
I. T. Botham	114	6-58 } 7-48 }	v India	Bombay	1979-80
I. T. Botham	149*	6-95	v Australia	Leeds	1981
I. T. Botham	138	5-59	v New Zealand	Wellington	1983-84

Australia

C. Kelleway	114	5-33	v South Africa	Manchester	1912
J. M. Gregory	100	7-69	v England	Melbourne	1920-21
K. R. Miller	109	6-107	v West Indies	Kingston	1954-55
R. Benaud	100	5-84	v South Africa	Johannesburg	1957-58

South Africa

J. H. Sinclair	106	6-26	v England	Cape Town	1898-99
G. A. Faulkner	123	5-120	v England	Johannesburg	1909-10
J. H. Kallis	110	5-90	v West Indies	Cape Town	1998-99

West Indies

D. St E. Atkinson	219	5-56	v Australia	Bridgetown	1954-55
O. G. Smith	100	5-90	v India	Delhi	1958-59
G. S. Sobers	104	5-63	v India	Kingston	1961-62
G. S. Sobers	174	5-41	v England	Leeds	1966

New Zealand

B. R. Taylor†	105	5-86	v India	Calcutta	1964-65

India

V. Mankad	184	5-196	v England	Lord's	1952
P. R. Umrigar	172*	5-107	v West Indies	Port-of-Spain	1961-62

Pakistan

Mushtaq Mohammad	201	5-49	v New Zealand	Dunedin	1972-73
Mushtaq Mohammad	121	5-28	v West Indies	Port-of-Spain	1976-77
Imran Khan	117	6-98 } 5-82 }	v India	Faisalabad	1982-83
Wasim Akram	123	5-100	v Australia	Adelaide	1989-90

Zimbabwe

P. A. Strang	106*	5-212	v Pakistan	Sheikhupura	1996-97

† *On debut.*

100 RUNS AND FIVE DISMISSALS IN AN INNINGS

D. T. Lindsay	182	6ct	SA v A......	Johannesburg	1966-67
I. D. S. Smith	113*	4ct, 1st	NZ v E......	Auckland..........	1983-84
S. A. R. Silva	111	5ct	SL v I	Colombo (PSS)......	1985-86

100 RUNS AND TEN WICKETS IN A TEST

A. K. Davidson	44 80	5-135 } 6-87 }	A v WI.......	Brisbane	1960-61
I. T. Botham	114	6-58 } 7-48 }	E v I........	Bombay	1979-80
Imran Khan	117	6-98 } 5-82 }	P v I	Faisalabad	1982-83

1,000 RUNS AND 100 WICKETS IN A CAREER

	Tests	Runs	Wkts	Tests for Double
England				
T. E. Bailey..................	61	2,290	132	47
†I. T. Botham..................	102	5,200	383	21
J. E. Emburey	64	1,713	147	46
A. W. Greig	58	3,599	141	37
R. Illingworth	61	1,836	122	47
W. Rhodes	58	2,325	127	44
M. W. Tate	39	1,198	155	33
F. J. Titmus	53	1,449	153	40

	Tests	Runs	Wkts	Tests for Double
Australia				
R. Benaud	63	2,201	248	32
A. K. Davidson	44	1,328	186	34
G. Giffen	31	1,238	103	30
M. G. Hughes	53	1,032	212	52
I. W. Johnson	45	1,000	109	45
R. R. Lindwall	61	1,502	228	38
K. R. Miller	55	2,958	170	33
M. A. Noble	42	1,997	121	27
S. K. Warne	**84**	**1,613**	**366**	**58**
South Africa				
T. L. Goddard	41	2,516	123	36
S. M. Pollock	**45**	**1,531**	**186**	**26**
West Indies				
C. E. L. Ambrose	**98**	**1,439**	**405**	**69**
M. D. Marshall	81	1,810	376	49
†G. S. Sobers	93	8,032	235	48
New Zealand				
J. G. Bracewell	41	1,001	102	41
C. L. Cairns	**47**	**2,396**	**160**	**33**
R. J. Hadlee	86	3,124	431	28
India				
Kapil Dev	131	5,248	434	25
A. Kumble	**61**	**1,192**	**276**	**56**
V. Mankad	44	2,109	162	23
R. J. Shastri	80	3,830	151	44
Pakistan				
Abdul Qadir	67	1,029	236	62
Imran Khan	88	3,807	362	30
Intikhab Alam	47	1,493	125	41
Sarfraz Nawaz	55	1,045	177	55
Wasim Akram	**98**	**2,809**	**407**	**45**

Bold type denotes those who played Test cricket in 1999-2000 and 2000 seasons.

† I. T. Botham (120 catches) and G. S. Sobers (109) are the only players to have achieved the treble of 1,000 runs, 100 wickets and 100 catches.

WICKET-KEEPING RECORDS

MOST DISMISSALS IN AN INNINGS

7 (all ct)	Wasim Bari	Pakistan v New Zealand at Auckland	1978-79
7 (all ct)	R. W. Taylor	England v India at Bombay	1979-80
7 (all ct)	I. D. S. Smith	New Zealand v Sri Lanka at Hamilton	1990-91
6 (all ct)	A. T. W. Grout	Australia v South Africa at Johannesburg	1957-58
6 (all ct)	D. T. Lindsay	South Africa v Australia at Johannesburg	1966-67
6 (all ct)	J. T. Murray	England v India at Lord's	1967
6 (5ct, 1st)	S. M. H. Kirmani	India v New Zealand at Christchurch	1975-76
6 (all ct)	R. W. Marsh	Australia v England at Brisbane	1982-83
6 (all ct)	S. A. R. Silva	Sri Lanka v India at Colombo (SSC)	1985-86
6 (all ct)	R. C. Russell	England v Australia at Melbourne	1990-91
6 (all ct)	R. C. Russell	England v South Africa at Johannesburg	1995-96
6 (all ct)	I. A. Healy	Australia v England at Birmingham	1997
6 (all ct)	A. J. Stewart	England v Australia at Manchester	1997

6 (all ct)	M. V. Boucher	South Africa v Pakistan at Port Elizabeth .	1997-98
6 (all ct)	Rashid Latif	Pakistan v Zimbabwe at Bulawayo	1997-98
6 (all ct)	M. V. Boucher	South Africa v Sri Lanka at Cape Town . .	1997-98
6 (5ct, 1st)	†C. M. W. Read	England v New Zealand at Birmingham . .	1999

† *On debut.*

Notes: The most stumpings in an innings is 5 by K. S. More for India v West Indies at Madras in 1987-88.

R. D. Jacobs made seven dismissals (all ct) for West Indies v Australia at Melbourne in 2000-01, after the deadline for this section.

MOST DISMISSALS IN A TEST

11 (all ct)	R. C. Russell	England v South Africa at Johannesburg . .	1995-96
10 (all ct)	R. W. Taylor	England v India at Bombay	1979-80
10 (all ct)	A. C. Gilchrist	Australia v New Zealand at Hamilton. . . .	1999-2000
9 (8ct, 1st)	G. R. A. Langley . . .	Australia v England at Lord's	1956
9 (all ct)	D. A. Murray	West Indies v Australia at Melbourne. . . .	1981-82
9 (all ct)	R. W. Marsh	Australia v England at Brisbane	1982-83
9 (all ct)	S. A. R. Silva	Sri Lanka v India at Colombo (SSC)	1985-86
9 (8ct, 1st)	S. A. R. Silva	Sri Lanka v India at Colombo (PSS)	1985-86
9 (all ct)	D. J. Richardson	South Africa v India at Port Elizabeth . . .	1992-93
9 (all ct)	Rashid Latif	Pakistan v New Zealand at Auckland	1993-94
9 (all ct)	I. A. Healy	Australia v England at Brisbane	1994-95
9 (all ct)	C. O. Browne	West Indies v England at Nottingham. . . .	1995
9 (7ct, 2st)	R. C. Russell	England v South Africa at Port Elizabeth .	1995-96
9 (8ct, 1st)	M. V. Boucher	South Africa v Pakistan at Port Elizabeth .	1997-98

Notes: S. A. R. Silva made 18 dismissals in two successive Tests.

The most stumpings in a match is 6 by K. S. More for India v West Indies at Madras in 1987-88.

J. J. Kelly (8ct) for Australia v England in 1901-02 and L. E. G. Ames (6ct, 2st) for England v West Indies in 1933 were the only wicket-keepers to make eight dismissals in a Test before World War II.

MOST DISMISSALS IN A SERIES

(Played in 5 Tests unless otherwise stated)

28 (all ct)	R. W. Marsh	Australia v England	1982-83
27 (25ct, 2st)	R. C. Russell	England v South Africa	1995-96
27 (25ct, 2st)	I. A. Healy	Australia v England (6 Tests)	1997
26 (23ct, 3st)	J. H. B. Waite	South Africa v New Zealand.	1961-62
26 (all ct)	R. W. Marsh	Australia v West Indies (6 Tests)	1975-76
26 (21ct, 5st)	I. A. Healy	Australia v England (6 Tests)	1993
26 (25ct, 1st)	M. V. Boucher	South Africa v England	1998
25 (23ct, 2st)	I. A. Healy	Australia v England	1994-95

Notes: S. A. R. Silva made 22 dismissals (21ct, 1st) in three Tests for Sri Lanka v India in 1985-86.

H. Strudwick, with 21 (15ct, 6st) for England v South Africa in 1913-14, was the only wicket-keeper to make as many as 20 dismissals in a series before World War II.

MOST DISMISSALS IN A CAREER

		T	Ct	St	Total
1	**I. A. Healy (Australia)**.	119	366	29	**395**
2	R. W. Marsh (Australia)	96	343	12	355
3	P. J. L. Dujon (West Indies).	81	267	5	272
4	A. P. E. Knott (England).	95	250	19	269
5	Wasim Bari (Pakistan)	81	201	27	228

		T	Ct	St	Total
6	T. G. Evans (England)	91	173	46	219
7	{ S. M. H. Kirmani (India)	88	160	38	198
	A. J. Stewart (England)	**102**	**189**	**9**	**198**
9	D. L. Murray (West Indies)	62	181	8	189
10	A. T. W. Grout (Australia)	51	163	24	187
11	I. D. S. Smith (New Zealand)	63	168	8	176
12	R. W. Taylor (England)	57	167	7	174
13	R. C. Russell (England)	54	153	12	165
14	D. J. Richardson (South Africa)	42	150	2	152
15	**A. C. Parore (New Zealand)**	**61**	**138**	**7**	**145**
16	J. H. B. Waite (South Africa)	50	124	17	141
17	{ K. S. More (India)	49	110	20	130
	W. A. S. Oldfield (Australia)	54	78	52	130
19	**M. V. Boucher (South Africa)**	**31**	**123**	**3**	**126**
20	**Moin Khan (Pakistan)**	**58**	**106**	**18**	**124**
21	**A. Flower (Zimbabwe)**	**43**	**113**	**5**	**118**
22	J. M. Parks (England)	46	103	11	114
23	Salim Yousuf (Pakistan)	32	91	13	104
24	**N. R. Mongia (India)**	**42**	**94**	**7**	**101**

Notes: The records for P. J. L. Dujon and J. M. Parks each include two catches taken when not keeping wicket in two and three Tests respectively. A. J. Stewart's record includes 36 catches taken in 51 Tests when not keeping wicket and A. C. Parore's includes three in 11 Tests when not keeping wicket.

The most wicket-keeping dismissals for Sri Lanka is 86 (**R. S. Kaluwitharana** 66ct, 20st in 38 Tests).

Bold type denotes those who played Test cricket in 1999-2000 and 2000 seasons.

FIELDING RECORDS

(Excluding wicket-keepers)

MOST CATCHES IN AN INNINGS

5	V. Y. Richardson	Australia v South Africa at Durban	1935-36
5	Yajurvindra Singh	India v England at Bangalore	1976-77
5	M. Azharuddin	India v Pakistan at Karachi	1989-90
5	K. Srikkanth	India v Australia at Perth	1991-92
5	S. P. Fleming	New Zealand v Zimbabwe at Harare	1997-98

MOST CATCHES IN A TEST

7	G. S. Chappell	Australia v England at Perth	1974-75
7	Yajurvindra Singh	India v England at Bangalore	1976-77
7	H. P. Tillekeratne	Sri Lanka v New Zealand at Colombo (SSC)	1992-93
7	S. P. Fleming	New Zealand v Zimbabwe at Harare	1997-98
6	A. Shrewsbury	England v Australia at Sydney	1887-88
6	A. E. E. Vogler	South Africa v England at Durban	1909-10
6	F. E. Woolley	England v Australia at Sydney	1911-12
6	J. M. Gregory	Australia v England at Sydney	1920-21
6	B. Mitchell	South Africa v Australia at Melbourne	1931-32
6	V. Y. Richardson	Australia v South Africa at Durban	1935-36
6	R. N. Harvey	Australia v England at Sydney	1962-63
6	M. C. Cowdrey	England v West Indies at Lord's	1963
6	E. D. Solkar	India v West Indies at Port-of-Spain	1970-71
6	G. S. Sobers	West Indies v England at Lord's	1973
6	I. M. Chappell	Australia v New Zealand at Adelaide	1973-74
6	A. W. Greig	England v Pakistan at Leeds	1974
6	D. F. Whatmore	Australia v India at Kanpur	1979-80

6	A. J. Lamb	England v New Zealand at Lord's	. .	1983
6	G. A. Hick	England v Pakistan at Leeds	. .	1992
6	B. A. Young	New Zealand v Pakistan at Auckland	. .	1993-94
6	J. C. Adams	West Indies v England at Kingston	. .	1993-94
6	S. P. Fleming	New Zealand v Australia at Brisbane	. .	1997-98
6	D. P. M. D. Jayawardene .	Sri Lanka v Pakistan at Peshawar	.	1999-2000

MOST CATCHES IN A SERIES

15	J. M. Gregory	Australia v England	1920-21
14	G. S. Chappell	Australia v England (6 Tests)	1974-75
13	R. B. Simpson	Australia v South Africa	1957-58
13	R. B. Simpson	Australia v West Indies	1960-61
13	B. C. Lara	West Indies v England (6 Tests)	1997-98

MOST CATCHES IN A CAREER

	T	*Ct*		*T*	*Ct*
M. A. Taylor (Australia)	104	157	W. R. Hammond (England)	85	110
A. R. Border (Australia)	156	156	R. B. Simpson (Australia)	62	110
M. E. Waugh (Australia)	**103**	**133**	G. S. Sobers (West Indies)	93	109
G. S. Chappell (Australia)	87	122	S. M. Gavaskar (India)	125	108
I. V. A. Richards (West Indies)	121	122	**M. Azharuddin (India)**	**99**	**105**
I. T. Botham (England)	102	120	I. M. Chappell (Australia)	75	105
M. C. Cowdrey (England)	114	120	G. A. Gooch (England)	118	103

The most catches in the field for other countries are South Africa 56 in 42 Tests (B. Mitchell); New Zealand **84** in 51 Tests (**S. P. Fleming**); Pakistan 93 in 124 Tests (Javed Miandad); Sri Lanka 56 in 52 Tests (R. S. Mahanama); Zimbabwe **44** in 43 Tests (**A. D. R. Campbell**).

Bold type denotes those who played Test cricket in 1999-2000 and 2000 seasons.

TEAM RECORDS

HIGHEST INNINGS TOTALS

952-6 dec.	Sri Lanka v India at Colombo (RPS)	1997-98
903-7 dec.	England v Australia at The Oval	1938
849	England v West Indies at Kingston	1929-30
790-3 dec.	West Indies v Pakistan at Kingston	1957-58
758-8 dec.	Australia v West Indies at Kingston	1954-55
729-6 dec.	Australia v England at Lord's	1930
708	Pakistan v England at The Oval	1987
701	Australia v England at The Oval	1934
699-5	Pakistan v India at Lahore	1989-90
695	Australia v England at The Oval	1930
692-8 dec.	West Indies v England at The Oval	1995
687-8 dec.	West Indies v England at The Oval	1976
681-8 dec.	West Indies v England at Port-of-Spain	1953-54
676-7	India v Sri Lanka at Kanpur	1986-87
674-6	Pakistan v India at Faisalabad	1984-85
674	Australia v India at Adelaide	1947-48
671-4	New Zealand v Sri Lanka at Wellington	1990-91
668	Australia v West Indies at Bridgetown	1954-55
660-5 dec.	West Indies v New Zealand at Wellington	1994-95

The highest innings for the countries not mentioned above are:

622-9 dec.	South Africa v Australia at Durban	1969-70
544-4 dec.	Zimbabwe v Pakistan at Harare	1994-95

HIGHEST FOURTH-INNINGS TOTALS

To win

406-4	India (needing 403) v West Indies at Port-of-Spain	1975-76
404-3	Australia (needing 404) v England at Leeds	1948
369-6	Australia (needing 369) v Pakistan at Hobart	1999-2000
362-7	Australia (needing 359) v West Indies at Georgetown	1977-78
348-5	West Indies (needing 345) v New Zealand at Auckland	1968-69
344-1	West Indies (needing 342) v England at Lord's	1984

To tie

347	India v Australia at Madras	1986-87

To draw

654-5	England (needing 696 to win) v South Africa at Durban	1938-39
429-8	India (needing 438 to win) v England at The Oval	1979
423-7	South Africa (needing 451 to win) v England at The Oval	1947
408-5	West Indies (needing 836 to win) v England at Kingston	1929-30

To lose

445	India (lost by 47 runs) v Australia at Adelaide	1977-78
440	New Zealand (lost by 38 runs) v England at Nottingham	1973
417	England (lost by 45 runs) v Australia at Melbourne	1976-77
411	England (lost by 193 runs) v Australia at Sydney	1924-25
402	Australia (lost by 103 runs) v England at Manchester	1981

MOST RUNS IN A DAY (BOTH SIDES)

588	England (398-6), India (190-0) at Manchester (2nd day)	1936
522	England (503-2), South Africa (19-0) at Lord's (2nd day)	1924
508	England (221-2), South Africa (287-6) at The Oval (3rd day)	1935

MOST RUNS IN A DAY (ONE SIDE)

503	England (503-2) v South Africa at Lord's (2nd day)	1924
494	Australia (494-6) v South Africa at Sydney (1st day)	1910-11
475	Australia (475-2) v England at The Oval (1st day)	1934
471	England (471-8) v India at The Oval (1st day)	1936
458	Australia (458-3) v England at Leeds (1st day)	1930
455	Australia (455-1) v England at Leeds (2nd day)	1934

MOST WICKETS IN A DAY

27	England (18-3 to 53 all out and 62) v Australia (60) at Lord's (2nd day)	1888
25	Australia (112 and 48-5) v England (61) at Melbourne (1st day)	1901-02

HIGHEST MATCH AGGREGATES

Runs	Wkts			Days played
1,981	35	South Africa v England at Durban	1938-39	10†
1,815	34	West Indies v England at Kingston	1929-30	9‡
1,764	39	Australia v West Indies at Adelaide	1968-69	5
1,753	40	Australia v England at Adelaide	1920-21	6
1,723	31	England v Australia at Leeds	1948	5
1,661	36	West Indies v Australia at Bridgetown	1954-55	6

† *No play on one day.*   ‡ *No play on two days.*

LOWEST INNINGS TOTALS

26	New Zealand v England at Auckland	1954-55
30	South Africa v England at Port Elizabeth	1895-96
30	South Africa v England at Birmingham	1924
35	South Africa v England at Cape Town	1898-99
36	Australia v England at Birmingham	1902
36	South Africa v Australia at Melbourne	1931-32
42	Australia v England at Sydney	1887-88
42	New Zealand v Australia at Wellington	1945-46
42†	India v England at Lord's	1974
43	South Africa v England at Cape Town	1888-89
44	Australia v England at The Oval	1896
45	England v Australia at Sydney	1886-87
45	South Africa v Australia at Melbourne	1931-32
46	England v West Indies at Port-of-Spain	1993-94
47	South Africa v England at Cape Town	1888-89
47	New Zealand v England at Lord's	1958

The lowest innings for the countries not mentioned above are:

51	West Indies v Australia at Port-of-Spain	1998-99
62	Pakistan v Australia at Perth	1981-82
63	Zimbabwe v West Indies at Port-of-Spain	1999-2000
71	Sri Lanka v Pakistan at Kandy	1994-95

† *Batted one man short.*

FEWEST RUNS IN A FULL DAY'S PLAY

95   At Karachi, October 11, 1956. Australia 80 all out; Pakistan 15 for two (first day, 5½ hours).

104   At Karachi, December 8, 1959. Pakistan 0 for no wicket to 104 for five v Australia (fourth day, 5½ hours).

106   At Brisbane, December 9, 1958. England 92 for two to 198 all out v Australia (fourth day, 5 hours). *England were dismissed five minutes before the close of play, leaving no time for Australia to start their second innings.*

112   At Karachi, October 15, 1956. Australia 138 for six to 187 all out; Pakistan 63 for one (fourth day, 5½ hours).

115   At Karachi, September 19, 1988. Australia 116 for seven to 165 all out and 66 for five following on v Pakistan (fourth day, 5½ hours).

117   At Madras, October 19, 1956. India 117 for five v Australia (first day, 5½ hours).

117   At Colombo (SSC), March 21, 1984. New Zealand 6 for no wicket to 123 for four (fifth day, 5 hours 47 minutes).

In England

151   At Lord's, August 26, 1978. England 175 for two to 289 all out; New Zealand 37 for seven (third day, 6 hours).

158   At Manchester, July 6, 1998. England 211 for two to 369 for nine v South Africa (fifth day, 6 hours).

159   At Leeds, July 10, 1971. Pakistan 208 for four to 350 all out; England 17 for one (third day, 6 hours).

LOWEST MATCH AGGREGATES

(For a completed match)

Runs	Wkts			Days played
234	29	Australia v South Africa at Melbourne	1931-32	3†
291	40	England v Australia at Lord's	1888	2
295	28	New Zealand v Australia at Wellington	1945-46	2
309	29	West Indies v England at Bridgetown	1934-35	3
323	30	England v Australia at Manchester	1888	2

† *No play on one day.*

PLAYERS

YOUNGEST TEST PLAYERS

Years	Days			
14	227†	Hasan Raza	Pakistan v Zimbabwe at Faisalabad	1996-97
15	124	Mushtaq Mohammad	Pakistan v West Indies at Lahore.	1958-59
16	189	Aqib Javed	Pakistan v New Zealand at Wellington . .	1988-89
16	205	S. R. Tendulkar	India v Pakistan at Karachi	1989-90
16	221	Aftab Baloch	Pakistan v New Zealand at Dacca	1969-70
16	248	Nasim-ul-Ghani	Pakistan v West Indies at Bridgetown. . . .	1957-58
16	352	Khalid Hassan	Pakistan v England at Nottingham.	1954
17	5	Zahid Fazal	Pakistan v West Indies at Karachi	1990-91
17	69	Ata-ur-Rehman	Pakistan v England at Birmingham	1992
17	78	Imran Nazir.	Pakistan v Sri Lanka at Lahore.	1998-99
17	118	L. Sivaramakrishnan	India v West Indies at St John's	1982-83
17	122	J. E. D. Sealy.	West Indies v England at Bridgetown . .	1929-30
17	129	Fazl-e-Akbar	Pakistan v South Africa at Durban.	1997-98
17	189	C. D. U. S. Weerasinghe. . .	Sri Lanka v India at Colombo (PSS) . . .	1985-86
17	193	Maninder Singh	India v Pakistan at Karachi	1982-83
17	239	I. D. Craig.	Australia v South Africa at Melbourne. .	1952-53
17	245	G. S. Sobers	West Indies v England at Kingston	1953-54
17	265	V. L. Mehra	India v New Zealand at Bombay	1955-56
17	265	Harbhajan Singh.	India v Australia at Bangalore	1997-98
17	300	Hanif Mohammad	Pakistan v India at Delhi.	1952-53
17	341	Intikhab Alam	Pakistan v Australia at Karachi	1959-60
17	364	Waqar Younis	Pakistan v India at Karachi	1989-90

† *Hasan Raza's age is in dispute and has been rejected by the Pakistan Cricket Board.*

Note: The youngest Test players for countries not mentioned above are: England – D. B. Close, 18 years 149 days, v New Zealand at Manchester, 1949; New Zealand – D. L. Vettori, 18 years 10 days, v England at Wellington, 1996-97; South Africa – P. R. Adams, 18 years 340 days v England at Port Elizabeth, 1995-96; Zimbabwe – H. K. Olonga, 18 years 212 days, v Pakistan at Harare, 1994-95.

OLDEST PLAYERS ON TEST DEBUT

Years	Days			
49	119	J. Southerton	England v Australia at Melbourne	1876-77
47	284	Miran Bux	Pakistan v India at Lahore	1954-55
46	253	D. D. Blackie	Australia v England at Sydney	1928-29
46	237	H. Ironmonger	Australia v England at Brisbane	1928-29
42	242	N. Betancourt	West Indies v England at Port-of-Spain .	1929-30
41	337	E. R. Wilson	England v Australia at Sydney	1920-21
41	27	R. J. D. Jamshedji.	India v England at Bombay	1933-34
40	345	C. A. Wiles	West Indies v England at Manchester. . .	1933
40	295	O. Henry.	South Africa v India at Durban.	1992-93
40	216	S. P. Kinneir	England v Australia at Sydney	1911-12
40	110	H. W. Lee	England v South Africa at Johannesburg.	1930-31
40	56	G. W. A. Chubb	South Africa v England at Nottingham. .	1951
40	37	C. Ramaswami.	India v England at Manchester	1936

Note: The oldest Test player on debut for New Zealand was H. M. McGirr, 38 years 101 days, v England at Auckland, 1929-30; for Sri Lanka, D. S. de Silva, 39 years 251 days, v England at Colombo (PSS), 1981-82; for Zimbabwe, A. C. Waller, 37 years 84 days, v England at Bulawayo, 1996-97. A. J. Traicos was 45 years 154 days old when he made his debut for Zimbabwe (v India at Harare, 1992-93) having played three Tests for South Africa in 1969-70.

OLDEST TEST PLAYERS

(Age on final day of their last Test match)

Years	Days			
52	165	W. Rhodes	England v West Indies at Kingston	1929-30
50	327	H. Ironmonger	Australia v England at Sydney	1932-33
50	320	W. G. Grace	England v Australia at Nottingham	1899
50	303	G. Gunn	England v West Indies at Kingston ...	1929-30
49	139	J. Southerton	England v Australia at Melbourne	1876-77
47	302	Miran Bux	Pakistan v India at Peshawar	1954-55
47	249	J. B. Hobbs	England v Australia at The Oval	1930
47	87	F. E. Woolley	England v Australia at The Oval	1934
46	309	D. D. Blackie	Australia v England at Adelaide	1928-29
46	206	A. W. Nourse	South Africa v England at The Oval ...	1924
46	202	H. Strudwick	England v Australia at The Oval	1926
46	41	E. H. Hendren	England v Australia at Kingston	1934-35
45	304	A. J. Traicos	Zimbabwe v India at Delhi	1992-93
45	245	G. O. B. Allen	England v West Indies at Kingston ...	1947-48
45	215	P. Holmes	England v India at Lord's	1932
45	140	D. B. Close	England v West Indies at Manchester...	1976

MOST TEST APPEARANCES

156	A. R. Border (Australia)		114	M. C. Cowdrey (England)
131	Kapil Dev (India)		110	C. H. Lloyd (West Indies)
128	**S. R. Waugh (Australia)**		108	G. Boycott (England)
125	S. M. Gavaskar (India)		108	C. G. Greenidge (West Indies)
124	Javed Miandad (Pakistan)		107	D. C. Boon (Australia)
122	**C. A. Walsh (West Indies)**		104	M. A. Taylor (Australia)
121	I. V. A. Richards (West Indies)		103	Salim Malik (Pakistan)
119	**I. A. Healy (Australia)**		**103**	**M. E. Waugh (Australia)**
118	G. A. Gooch (England)		**102**	**M. A. Atherton (England)**
117	D. I. Gower (England)		102	I. T. Botham (England)
116	D. L. Haynes (West Indies)		**102**	**A. J. Stewart (England)**
116	D. B. Vengsarkar (India)			

The most appearances for Sri Lanka is 93 by **A. Ranatunga**, for New Zealand 86 by R. J. Hadlee, for South Africa 68 by **W. J. Cronje** and for Zimbabwe 43 by **A. D. R. Campbell** and **A. Flower**.

Bold type denotes those who played Test cricket in 1999-2000 and 2000 seasons.

MOST CONSECUTIVE TEST APPEARANCES

153	A. R. Border (Australia)..........	March 1979 to March 1994
106	S. M. Gavaskar (India)...........	January 1975 to February 1987
87	G. R. Viswanath (India)	March 1971 to February 1983
85	G. S. Sobers (West Indies)	April 1955 to April 1972
82	M. E. Waugh (Australia)..........	June 1993 to April 2000
76†	S. R. Tendulkar (India)...........	November 1989 to March 2000
72	D. L. Haynes (West Indies)........	December 1979 to June 1988
71	I. M. Chappell (Australia).........	January 1966 to February 1976
69	M. Azharuddin (India)	April 1989 to February 1999
66	Kapil Dev (India)	October 1978 to December 1984
65	I. T. Botham (England)...........	February 1978 to March 1984
65	Kapil Dev (India)	January 1985 to March 1994
65	A. P. E. Knott (England).........	March 1971 to August 1977

The most consecutive Test appearances for the countries not mentioned on the previous page are:

58†	J. R. Reid (New Zealand)	July 1949 to July 1965
53	Javed Miandad (Pakistan)	December 1977 to January 1984
53	G. Kirsten (South Africa)	December 1993 to March 1999
43	{ A. D. R. Campbell (Zimbabwe) . . . . . } { A. Flower (Zimbabwe) . . . . }	October 1992 to June 2000
35	P. A. de Silva (Sri Lanka)	February 1988 to March 1995

Note: By February 26, 2001, after the deadline for this section, M. E. Waugh and S. R. Tendulkar had extended their sequence of consecutive Test appearances to 87 and 79 respectively. A. D. R. Campbell and A. Flower had taken their sequence to 48.

† *Indicates complete Test career.*

CAPTAINCY

MOST TESTS AS CAPTAIN

	P	W	L	D		P	W	L	D
A. R. Border (A)	93	32	22	38*	R. B. Simpson (A)	39	12	12	15
C. H. Lloyd (WI)	74	36	12	26	G. S. Sobers (WI)	39	9	10	20
A. Ranatunga (SL)	56	12	19	25	G. A. Gooch (E)	34	10	12	12
W. J. Cronje (SA)	**53**	**27**	**11**	**15**	Javed Miandad (P)	34	14	6	14
M. A. Atherton (E)	52	13	19	20	Kapil Dev (I)	34	4	7	22*
I. V. A. Richards (WI)	50	27	8	15	J. R. Reid (NZ)	34	3	18	13
M. A. Taylor (A)	50	26	13	11	D. I. Gower (E)	32	5	18	9
G. S. Chappell (A)	48	21	13	14	J. M. Brearley (E)	31	18	4	9
Imran Khan (P)	48	14	8	26	R. Illingworth (E)	31	12	5	14
M. Azharuddin (I)	47	14	14	19	I. M. Chappell (A)	30	15	5	10
S. M. Gavaskar (I)	47	9	8	30	E. R. Dexter (E)	30	9	7	14
P. B. H. May (E)	41	20	10	11	G. P. Howarth (NZ)	30	11	7	12
Nawab of Pataudi jun. (I)	40	9	19	12					

* *One match tied.*

Most Tests as captain of Zimbabwe:

	P	W	L	D
A. Flower	20	1	10	9

Notes: A. R. Border captained Australia in 93 consecutive Tests.

W. W. Armstrong (Australia) captained his country in the most Tests without being defeated: ten matches with eight wins and two draws.

I. T. Botham (England) captained his country in the most Tests without ever winning: 12 matches with eight draws and four defeats.

Bold type denotes those who were captains in 1999-2000 and 2000 seasons.

UMPIRING

MOST TEST MATCHES

		First Test	Last Test
66	H. D. Bird (England)	1973	1996
52	**D. R. Shepherd (England)**	**1985**	**2000**
51	**S. A. Bucknor (West Indies)**	**1988-89**	**2000 (SL)**
48	F. Chester (England)	1924	1955
42	C. S. Elliott (England)	1957	1974
39	**S. Venkataraghavan (India)**	**1992-93**	**2000**
36	D. J. Constant (England)	1971	1988
36	S. G. Randell (Australia)	1984-85	1997-98
35	**R. S. Dunne (New Zealand)**	**1988-89**	**1999-2000**

		First Test	*Last Test*
34	Khizar Hayat (Pakistan)	1979-80	1996-97
33	J. S. Buller (England)	1956	1969
33	A. R. Crafter (Australia)	1978-79	1991-92
32	R. W. Crockett (Australia)	1901-02	1924-25
32	**D. B. Hair (Australia)**	**1991-92**	**1999-2000**
31	D. Sang Hue (West Indies)	1961-62	1980-81

Bold type indicates umpires who stood in 1999-2000 or 2000 seasons.

SUMMARY OF ALL TEST MATCHES

To September 4, 2000

	Opponents	Tests	E	A	SA	WI	NZ	I	P	SL	Z	Tied	Drawn
England	Australia	296	93	117	–	–	–	–	–	–	–	–	86
	South Africa	120	50	–	23	–	–	–	–	–	–	–	47
	West Indies	126	31	–	–	52	–	–	–	–	–	–	43
	New Zealand	82	37	–	–	–	6	–	–	–	–	–	39
	India	84	32	–	–	–	–	14	–	–	–	–	38
	Pakistan	55	14	–	–	–	–	–	9	–	–	–	32
	Sri Lanka	6	3	–	–	–	–	–	–	2	–	–	1
	Zimbabwe	4	1	–	–	–	–	–	–	–	0	–	3
Australia	South Africa	65	–	34	14	–	–	–	–	–	–	–	17
	West Indies	90	–	37	–	31	–	–	–	–	–	1	21
	New Zealand	38	–	18	–	–	7	–	–	–	–	–	13
	India	57	–	28	–	–	–	11	–	–	–	1	17
	Pakistan	46	–	18	–	–	–	–	11	–	–	–	17
	Sri Lanka	13	–	7	–	–	–	–	–	1	–	–	5
	Zimbabwe	1	–	1	–	–	–	–	–	–	0	–	0
South Africa	West Indies	6	–	–	5	1	–	–	–	–	–	–	0
	New Zealand	24	–	–	13	–	3	–	–	–	–	–	8
	India	12	–	–	6	–	–	2	–	–	–	–	4
	Pakistan	7	–	–	3	–	–	–	1	–	–	–	3
	Sri Lanka	8	–	–	4	–	–	–	–	1	–	–	3
	Zimbabwe	3	–	–	3	–	–	–	–	–	0	–	0
West Indies	New Zealand	30	–	–	–	10	6	–	–	–	–	–	14
	India	70	–	–	–	28	–	7	–	–	–	–	35
	Pakistan	37	–	–	–	13	–	–	10	–	–	–	14
	Sri Lanka	3	–	–	–	1	–	–	–	0	–	–	2
	Zimbabwe	2	–	–	–	2	–	–	–	–	0	–	0
New Zealand	India	40	–	–	–	–	7	14	–	–	–	–	19
	Pakistan	39	–	–	–	–	5	–	18	–	–	–	16
	Sri Lanka	18	–	–	–	–	7	–	–	4	–	–	7
	Zimbabwe	8	–	–	–	–	3	–	–	–	0	–	5
India	Pakistan	47	–	–	–	–	–	5	9	–	–	–	33
	Sri Lanka	20	–	–	–	–	–	7	–	1	–	–	12
	Zimbabwe	3	–	–	–	–	–	1	–	–	1	–	1
Pakistan	Sri Lanka	27	–	–	–	–	–	–	13	5	–	–	9
	Zimbabwe	12	–	–	–	–	–	–	6	–	2	–	4
Sri Lanka	Zimbabwe	10	–	–	–	–	–	–	–	5	0	–	5
		1,509	261	260	71	138	44	61	77	19	3	2	573

	Tests	Won	Lost	Drawn	Tied	Toss Won
England	773	261	223	289	–	377
Australia	606	260	168	176	2	307
South Africa	245	71	92	82	–	114
West Indies	364	138	96	129	1	190
New Zealand	279	44	114	121	–	140
India	333	61	112	159	1	173
Pakistan	270	77	65	128	–	128
Sri Lanka	105	19	42	44	–	56
Zimbabwe	43	3	22	18	–	24

ENGLAND v AUSTRALIA

		Captains				
Season	*England*	*Australia*	*T*	*E*	*A*	*D*
1876-77	James Lillywhite	D. W. Gregory	2	1	1	0
1878-79	Lord Harris	D. W. Gregory	1	0	1	0
1880	Lord Harris	W. L. Murdoch	1	1	0	0
1881-82	A. Shaw	W. L. Murdoch	4	0	2	2
1882	A. N. Hornby	W. L. Murdoch	1	0	1	0

THE ASHES

		Captains					
Season	*England*	*Australia*	*T*	*E*	*A*	*D*	*Held by*
1882-83	Hon. Ivo Bligh	W. L. Murdoch	4*	2	2	0	E
1884	Lord Harris[1]	W. L. Murdoch	3	1	0	2	E
1884-85	A. Shrewsbury	T. P. Horan[2]	5	3	2	0	E
1886	A. G. Steel	H. J. H. Scott	3	3	0	0	E
1886-87	A. Shrewsbury	P. S. McDonnell	2	2	0	0	E
1887-88	W. W. Read	P. S. McDonnell	1	1	0	0	E
1888	W. G. Grace[3]	P. S. McDonnell	3	2	1	0	E
1890†	W. G. Grace	W. L. Murdoch	2	2	0	0	E
1891-92	W. G. Grace	J. McC. Blackham	3	1	2	0	A
1893	W. G. Grace[4]	J. McC. Blackham	3	1	0	2	E
1894-95	A. E. Stoddart	G. Giffen[5]	5	3	2	0	E
1896	W. G. Grace	G. H. S. Trott	3	2	1	0	E
1897-98	A. E. Stoddart[6]	G. H. S. Trott	5	1	4	0	A
1899	A. C. MacLaren[7]	J. Darling	5	0	1	4	A
1901-02	A. C. MacLaren	J. Darling[8]	5	1	4	0	A
1902	A. C. MacLaren	J. Darling	5	1	2	2	A
1903-04	P. F. Warner	M. A. Noble	5	3	2	0	E
1905	Hon. F. S. Jackson	J. Darling	5	2	0	3	E
1907-08	A. O. Jones[9]	M. A. Noble	5	1	4	0	A
1909	A. C. MacLaren	M. A. Noble	5	1	2	2	A
1911-12	J. W. H. T. Douglas	C. Hill	5	4	1	0	E
1912	C. B. Fry	S. E. Gregory	3	1	0	2	E
1920-21	J. W. H. T. Douglas	W. W. Armstrong	5	0	5	0	A
1921	Hon. L. H. Tennyson[10]	W. W. Armstrong	5	0	3	2	A
1924-25	A. E. R. Gilligan	H. L. Collins	5	1	4	0	A
1926	A. W. Carr[11]	H. L. Collins[12]	5	1	0	4	E
1928-29	A. P. F. Chapman[13]	J. Ryder	5	4	1	0	E
1930	A. P. F. Chapman[14]	W. M. Woodfull	5	1	2	2	A
1932-33	D. R. Jardine	W. M. Woodfull	5	4	1	0	E
1934	R. E. S. Wyatt[15]	W. M. Woodfull	5	1	2	2	A
1936-37	G. O. B. Allen	D. G. Bradman	5	2	3	0	A
1938†	W. R. Hammond	D. G. Bradman	4	1	1	2	A
1946-47	W. R. Hammond[16]	D. G. Bradman	5	0	3	2	A
1948	N. W. D. Yardley	D. G. Bradman	5	0	4	1	A
1950-51	F. R. Brown	A. L. Hassett	5	1	4	0	A
1953	L. Hutton	A. L. Hassett	5	1	0	4	E
1954-55	L. Hutton	I. W. Johnson[17]	5	3	1	1	E
1956	P. B. H. May	I. W. Johnson	5	2	1	2	E
1958-59	P. B. H. May	R. Benaud	5	0	4	1	A
1961	P. B. H. May[18]	R. Benaud[19]	5	1	2	2	A
1962-63	E. R. Dexter	R. Benaud	5	1	1	3	A
1964	E. R. Dexter	R. B. Simpson	5	0	1	4	A
1965-66	M. J. K. Smith	R. B. Simpson[20]	5	1	1	3	A
1968	M. C. Cowdrey[21]	W. M. Lawry[22]	5	1	1	3	A
1970-71†	R. Illingworth	W. M. Lawry[23]	6	2	0	4	E
1972	R. Illingworth	I. M. Chappell	5	2	2	1	E
1974-75	M. H. Denness[24]	I. M. Chappell	6	1	4	1	A

Captains

Season	England	Australia	T	E	A	D	Held by
1975	A. W. Greig[25]	I. M. Chappell	4	0	1	3	A
1976-77‡	A. W. Greig	G. S. Chappell	1	0	1	0	—
1977	J. M. Brearley	G. S. Chappell	5	3	0	2	E
1978-79	J. M. Brearley	G. N. Yallop	6	5	1	0	E
1979-80‡	J. M. Brearley	G. S. Chappell	3	0	3	0	—
1980‡	I. T. Botham	G. S. Chappell	1	0	0	1	—
1981	J. M. Brearley[26]	K. J. Hughes	6	3	1	2	E
1982-83	R. G. D. Willis	G. S. Chappell	5	1	2	2	A
1985	D. I. Gower	A. R. Border	6	3	1	2	E
1986-87	M. W. Gatting	A. R. Border	5	2	1	2	E
1987-88‡	M. W. Gatting	A. R. Border	1	0	0	1	—
1989	D. I. Gower	A. R. Border	6	0	4	2	A
1990-91	G. A. Gooch[27]	A. R. Border	5	0	3	2	A
1993	G. A. Gooch[28]	A. R. Border	6	1	4	1	A
1994-95	M. A. Atherton	M. A. Taylor	5	1	3	1	A
1997	M. A. Atherton	M. A. Taylor	6	2	3	1	A
1998-99	A. J. Stewart	M. A. Taylor	5	1	3	1	A

In Australia		155	53	76	26	
In England.		141	40	41	60	

| Totals | . . . . | 296 | 93 | 117 | 86 |

* *The Ashes were awarded in 1882-83 after a series of three matches which England won 2–1. A fourth match was played and this was won by Australia.*

† *The matches at Manchester in 1890 and 1938 and at Melbourne (Third Test) in 1970-71 were abandoned without a ball being bowled and are excluded.*

‡ *The Ashes were not at stake in these series.*

Notes: The following deputised for the official touring captain or were appointed by the home authority for only a minor proportion of the series:

[1]A. N. Hornby (First). [2]W. L. Murdoch (First), H. H. Massie (Third), J. McC. Blackham (Fourth). [3]A. G. Steel (First). [4]A. E. Stoddart (First). [5]J. McC. Blackham (First). [6]A. C. MacLaren (First, Second and Fifth). [7]W. G. Grace (First). [8]H. Trumble (Fourth and Fifth). [9]F. L. Fane (First, Second and Third). [10]J. W. H. T. Douglas (First and Second). [11]A. P. F. Chapman (Fifth). [12]W. Bardsley (Third and Fourth). [13]J. C. White (Fifth). [14]R. E. S. Wyatt (Fifth). [15]C. F. Walters (First). [16]N. W. D. Yardley (Fifth). [17]A. R. Morris (Second). [18]M. C. Cowdrey (First and Second). [19]R. N. Harvey (Second). [20]B. C. Booth (First and Third). [21]T. W. Graveney (Fourth). [22]B. N. Jarman (Fourth). [23]I. M. Chappell (Seventh). [24]J. H. Edrich (Fourth). [25]M. H. Denness (First). [26]I. T. Botham (First and Second). [27]A. J. Lamb (First). [28]M. A. Atherton (Fifth and Sixth).

HIGHEST INNINGS TOTALS

| For England in England: 903-7 dec. at The Oval . . . . | 1938 |
| in Australia: 636 at Sydney . . . . | 1928-29 |

| For Australia in England: 729-6 dec. at Lord's . . . . | 1930 |
| in Australia: 659-8 dec. at Sydney . . . . | 1946-47 |

LOWEST INNINGS TOTALS

| For England in England: 52 at The Oval . . . . | 1948 |
| in Australia: 45 at Sydney . . . . | 1886-87 |

| For Australia in England: 36 at Birmingham . . . . | 1902 |
| in Australia: 42 at Sydney . . . . | 1887-88 |

INDIVIDUAL HUNDREDS
For England (206)

R. Abel (1)
132*‡ Sydney 1891-92
L. E. G. Ames (1)
120 Lord's 1934
M. A. Atherton (1)
105 Sydney 1990-91
R. W. Barber (1)
185 Sydney 1965-66
W. Barnes (1)
134 Adelaide ... 1884-85
C. J. Barnett (2)
129 Adelaide ... 1936-37
126 Nottingham . 1938
K. F. Barrington (5)
132* Adelaide ... 1962-63
101 Sydney 1962-63
256 Manchester.. 1964
102 Adelaide ... 1965-66
115 Melbourne .. 1965-66
I. T. Botham (4)
119* Melbourne .. 1979-80
149* Leeds 1981
118 Manchester.. 1981
138 Brisbane ... 1986-87
G. Boycott (7)
113 The Oval... 1964
142* Sydney 1970-71
119* Adelaide ... 1970-71
107 Nottingham . 1977
191 Leeds 1977
128* Lord's 1980
137 The Oval... 1981
L. C. Braund (2)
103* Adelaide ... 1901-02
102 Sydney 1903-04
J. Briggs (1)
121 Melbourne .. 1884-85
B. C. Broad (4)
162 Perth...... 1986-87
116 Adelaide ... 1986-87
112 Melbourne .. 1986-87
139 Sydney 1987-88
J. T. Brown (1)
140 Melbourne .. 1894-95
M. A. Butcher (1)
116 Brisbane ... 1998-99
A. P. F. Chapman (1)
121 Lord's 1930
D. C. S. Compton (5)
102† Nottingham 1938
147 }
103* } Adelaide ... 1946-47
184 Nottingham . 1948
145* Manchester.. 1948
M. C. Cowdrey (5)
102 Melbourne .. 1954-55
100* Sydney 1958-59

113 Melbourne .. 1962-63
104 Melbourne .. 1965-66
104 Birmingham . 1968
M. H. Denness (1)
188 Melbourne .. 1974-75
E. R. Dexter (2)
180 Birmingham . 1961
174 Manchester.. 1964
B. L. D'Oliveira (2)
158 The Oval... 1968
117 Melbourne .. 1970-71
K. S. Duleepsinhji (1)
173† Lord's 1930
J. H. Edrich (7)
120† Lord's 1964
109 Melbourne .. 1965-66
103 Sydney 1965-66
164 The Oval... 1968
115* Perth...... 1970-71
130 Adelaide ... 1970-71
175 Lord's 1975
W. J. Edrich (2)
119 Sydney 1946-47
111 Leeds 1948
K. W. R. Fletcher (1)
146 Melbourne .. 1974-75
R. E. Foster (1)
287† Sydney 1903-04
C. B. Fry (1)
144 The Oval... 1905
M. W. Gatting (4)
160 Manchester.. 1985
100* Birmingham . 1985
100 Adelaide ... 1986-87
117 Adelaide ... 1994-95
G. A. Gooch (4)
196 The Oval... 1985
117 Adelaide ... 1990-91
133 Manchester.. 1993
120 Nottingham . 1993
D. I. Gower (9)
102 Perth...... 1978-79
114 Adelaide ... 1982-83
166 Nottingham . 1985
215 Birmingham . 1985
157 The Oval... 1985
136 Perth...... 1986-87
106 Lord's 1989
100 Melbourne .. 1990-91
123 Sydney 1990-91
W. G. Grace (2)
152† The Oval... 1880
170 The Oval... 1886
T. W. Graveney (1)
111 Sydney 1954-55
A. W. Greig (1)
110 Brisbane ... 1974-75

G. Gunn (2)
119† Sydney 1907-08
122* Sydney 1907-08
W. Gunn (1)
102* Manchester.. 1893
W. R. Hammond (9)
251 Sydney 1928-29
200 Melbourne .. 1928-29
119* }
177 } Adelaide ... 1928-29
113 Leeds 1930
112 Sydney 1932-33
101 Sydney 1932-33
231* Sydney 1936-37
240 Lord's 1938
J. Hardstaff jun. (1)
169* The Oval... 1938
T. W. Hayward (2)
130 Manchester.. 1899
137 The Oval... 1899
J. W. Hearne (1)
114 Melbourne .. 1911-12
E. H. Hendren (3)
127* Lord's 1926
169 Brisbane ... 1928-29
132 Manchester.. 1934
J. B. Hobbs (12)
126* Melbourne .. 1911-12
187 Adelaide ... 1911-12
178 Melbourne .. 1911-12
107 Lord's 1912
122 Melbourne .. 1920-21
123 Adelaide ... 1920-21
115 Sydney 1924-25
154 Melbourne .. 1924-25
119 Adelaide ... 1924-25
119 Lord's 1926
100 The Oval... 1926
142 Melbourne .. 1928-29
N. Hussain (2)
207 Birmingham . 1997
105 Leeds 1997
K. L. Hutchings (1)
126 Melbourne .. 1907-08
L. Hutton (5)
100† Nottingham 1938
364 The Oval... 1938
122* Sydney 1946-47
156*‡ Adelaide ... 1950-51
145 Lord's 1953
Hon. F. S. Jackson (5)
103 The Oval... 1893
118 The Oval... 1899
128 Manchester.. 1902
144* Leeds 1905
113 Manchester.. 1905

G. L. Jessop (1)
104   The Oval...   1902

A. P. E. Knott (2)
106* Adelaide ...   1974-75
135   Nottingham .   1977

A. J. Lamb (1)
125   Leeds   1989

M. Leyland (7)
137† Melbourne .   1928-29
109   Lord's   1934
153   Manchester. .   1934
110   The Oval...   1934
126   Brisbane ...   1936-37
111* Melbourne . .   1936-37
187   The Oval...   1938

B. W. Luckhurst (2)
131   Perth......   1970-71
109   Melbourne . .   1970-71

A. C. MacLaren (5)
120   Melbourne . .   1894-95
109   Sydney   1897-98
124   Adelaide ...   1897-98
116   Sydney   1901-02
140   Nottingham .   1905

J. W. H. Makepeace (1)
117   Melbourne . .   1920-21

P. B. H. May (3)
104   Sydney   1954-55
101   Leeds   1956
113   Melbourne . .   1958-59

C. P. Mead (1)
182* The Oval...   1921

Nawab of Pataudi sen. (1)
102† Sydney   1932-33

E. Paynter (1)
216* Nottingham .   1938

D. W. Randall (3)
174† Melbourne . .   1976-77
150   Sydney   1978-79
115   Perth......   1982-83

K. S. Ranjitsinhji (2)
154*† Manchester. .   1896
175   Sydney   1897-98

W. W. Read (1)
117   The Oval...   1884

W. Rhodes (1)
179   Melbourne . .   1911-12

C. J. Richards (1)
133   Perth......   1986-87

P. E. Richardson (1)
104   Manchester. .   1956

R. T. Robinson (2)
175† Leeds   1985
148   Birmingham .   1985

A. C. Russell (3)
135* Adelaide ...   1920-21
101   Manchester. .   1921
102* The Oval...   1921

R. C. Russell (1)
128* Manchester. .   1989

J. Sharp (1)
105   The Oval...   1909

Rev. D. S. Sheppard (2)
113   Manchester. .   1956
113   Melbourne . .   1962-63

A. Shrewsbury (3)
105* Melbourne . .   1884-85
164   Lord's   1886
106   Lord's   1893

R. T. Simpson (1)
156* Melbourne . .   1950-51

R. A. Smith (2)
143   Manchester. .   1989
101   Nottingham .   1989

A. G. Steel (2)
135* Sydney   1882-83
148   Lord's   1884

A. J. Stewart (1)
107   Melbourne . .   1998-99

A. E. Stoddart (2)
134   Adelaide ...   1891-92
173   Melbourne . .   1894-95

R. Subba Row (2)
112† Birmingham .   1961
137   The Oval...   1961

H. Sutcliffe (8)
115† Sydney   1924-25
176 }   1924-25
127 } Melbourne . .
143   Melbourne . .   1924-25
161   The Oval...   1926
135   Melbourne . .   1928-29
161   The Oval...   1928-29
194   Sydney   1932-33

G. P. Thorpe (3)
114*† Nottingham .   1993
123   Perth......   1994-95
138   Birmingham .   1997

J. T. Tyldesley (3)
138   Birmingham .   1902
100   Leeds   1905
112* The Oval...   1905

G. Ulyett (1)
149   Melbourne . .   1881-82

A. Ward (1)
117   Sydney   1894-95

C. Washbrook (2)
112   Melbourne . .   1946-47
143   Leeds   1948

W. Watson (1)
109† Lord's   1953

F. E. Woolley (2)
133* Sydney   1911-12
123   Sydney   1924-25

R. A. Woolmer (3)
149   The Oval...   1975
120   Lord's   1977
137   Manchester. .   1977

† *Signifies hundred on first appearance in England–Australia Tests.*
‡ *Carried his bat.*

For Australia (247)

W. W. Armstrong (4)
133* Melbourne . .   1907-08
158   Sydney   1920-21
121   Adelaide ...   1920-21
123* Melbourne . .   1920-21

C. L. Badcock (1)
118   Melbourne . .   1936-37

C. Bannerman (1)
165*† Melbourne . .   1876-77

W. Bardsley (3)
136 }
130 } The Oval...   1909
193*‡ Lord's   1926

S. G. Barnes (2)
234   Sydney   1946-47
141   Lord's   1948

G. S. Blewett (3)
102*† Adelaide ...   1994-95
115   Perth......   1994-95
125   Birmingham .   1997

G. J. Bonnor (1)
128   Sydney   1884-85

D. C. Boon (7)
103   Adelaide ...   1986-87
184* Sydney   1987-88
121   Adelaide ...   1990-91
164* Lord's   1993
101   Nottingham .   1993
107   Leeds   1993
131   Melbourne . .   1994-95

B. C. Booth (2)
112   Brisbane ...   1962-63
103   Melbourne . .   1962-63

A. R. Border (8)
115   Perth......   1979-80
123* Manchester. .   1981
106* The Oval...   1981
196   Lord's   1985
146* Manchester. .   1985
125   Perth......   1986-87
100* Adelaide ...   1986-87
200* Leeds   1993

D. G. Bradman (19)
112   Melbourne . .   1928-29
123   Melbourne . .   1928-29

131	Nottingham .	1930
254	Lord's	1930
334	Leeds	1930
232	The Oval . . .	1930
103*	Melbourne . .	1932-33
304	Leeds	1934
244	The Oval . . .	1934
270	Melbourne . .	1936-37
212	Adelaide . . .	1936-37
169	Melbourne . .	1936-37
144*	Nottingham .	1938
102*	Lord's	1938
103	Leeds	1938
187	Brisbane . . .	1946-47
234	Sydney	1946-47
138	Nottingham .	1948
173*	Leeds	1948

W. A. Brown (3)

105	Lord's	1934
133	Nottingham .	1938
206*‡	Lord's	1938

P. J. Burge (4)

181	The Oval . . .	1961
103	Sydney	1962-63
160	Leeds	1964
120	Melbourne . .	1965-66

J. W. Burke (1)

101*†	Adelaide . . .	1950-51

G. S. Chappell (9)

108†	Perth.	1970-71
131	Lord's	1972
113	The Oval . . .	1972
144	Sydney	1974-75
102	Melbourne . .	1974-75
112	Manchester. .	1977
114	Melbourne . .	1979-80
117	Perth.	1982-83
115	Adelaide . . .	1982-83

I. M. Chappell (4)

111	Melbourne . .	1970-71
104	Adelaide . . .	1970-71
118	The Oval . . .	1972
192	The Oval . . .	1975

H. L. Collins (3)

104†	Sydney	1920-21
162	Adelaide . . .	1920-21
114	Sydney	1924-25

R. M. Cowper (1)

307	Melbourne . .	1965-66

J. Darling (3)

101	Sydney	1897-98
178	Adelaide . . .	1897-98
160	Sydney	1897-98

R. A. Duff (2)

104†	Melbourne . .	1901-02
146	The Oval . . .	1905

J. Dyson (1)

102	Leeds	1981

R. Edwards (2)

170*	Nottingham .	1972
115	Perth.	1974-75

M. T. G. Elliott (2)

112	Lord's	1997
199	Leeds	1997

J. H. Fingleton (2)

100	Brisbane . . .	1936-37
136	Melbourne . .	1936-37

G. Giffen (1)

161	Sydney	1894-95

H. Graham (2)

107†	Lord's	1893
105	Sydney	1894-95

J. M. Gregory (1)

100	Melbourne . .	1920-21

S. E. Gregory (4)

201	Sydney	1894-95
103	Lord's	1896
117	The Oval . . .	1899
112	Adelaide . . .	1903-04

R. J. Hartigan (1)

116†	Adelaide . . .	1907-08

R. N. Harvey (6)

112†	Leeds	1948
122	Manchester. .	1953
162	Brisbane . . .	1954-55
167	Melbourne . .	1958-59
114	Birmingham .	1961
154	Adelaide . . .	1962-63

A. L. Hassett (4)

128	Brisbane . . .	1946-47
137	Nottingham .	1948
115	Nottingham .	1953
104	Lord's	1953

I. A. Healy (2)

102*	Manchester. .	1993
134	Brisbane . . .	1998-99

H. L. Hendry (1)

112	Sydney	1928-29

A. M. J. Hilditch (1)

119	Leeds	1985

C. Hill (4)

188	Melbourne . .	1897-98
135	Lord's	1899
119	Sheffield . . .	1902
160	Adelaide . . .	1907-08

T. P. Horan (1)

124	Melbourne . .	1881-82

K. J. Hughes (3)

129	Brisbane . . .	1978-79
117	Lord's	1980
137	Sydney	1982-83

F. A. Iredale (2)

140	Adelaide . . .	1894-95
108	Manchester. .	1896

A. A. Jackson (1)

164†	Adelaide . . .	1928-29

D. M. Jones (3)

184*	Sydney	1986-87
157	Birmingham .	1989
122	The Oval . . .	1989

C. Kelleway (1)

147	Adelaide . . .	1920-21

A. F. Kippax (1)

100	Melbourne . .	1928-29

J. L. Langer (1)

179*	Adelaide . . .	1998-99

W. M. Lawry (7)

130	Lord's	1961
102	Manchester. .	1961
106	Manchester. .	1964
166	Brisbane . . .	1965-66
119	Adelaide . . .	1965-66
108	Melbourne . .	1965-66
135	The Oval . . .	1968

R. R. Lindwall (1)

100	Melbourne . .	1946-47

J. J. Lyons (1)

134	Sydney	1891-92

C. G. Macartney (5)

170	Sydney	1920-21
115	Leeds	1921
133*	Lord's	1926
151	Leeds	1926
109	Manchester. .	1926

S. J. McCabe (4)

187*	Sydney	1932-33
137	Manchester. .	1934
112	Melbourne . .	1936-37
232	Nottingham .	1938

C. L. McCool (1)

104*	Melbourne . .	1946-47

R. B. McCosker (2)

127	The Oval . . .	1975
107	Nottingham .	1977

C. C. McDonald (2)

170	Adelaide . . .	1958-59
133	Melbourne . .	1958-59

P. S. McDonnell (3)

147	Sydney	1881-82
103	The Oval . . .	1884
124	Adelaide . . .	1884-85

C. E. McLeod (1)

112	Melbourne . .	1897-98

G. R. Marsh (2)

110†	Brisbane . . .	1986-87
138	Nottingham .	1989

R. W. Marsh (1)

110*	Melbourne . .	1976-77

G. R. J. Matthews (1)

128	Sydney	1990-91

K. R. Miller (3)

141*	Adelaide . . .	1946-47
145*	Sydney	1950-51
109	Lord's	1953

A. R. Morris (8)

155	Melbourne . .	1946-47
122 } 124*}	Adelaide . . .	1946-47
105	Lord's	1948
182	Leeds	1948
196	The Oval . . .	1948
206	Adelaide . . .	1950-51
153	Brisbane . . .	1954-55

W. L. Murdoch (2)		
153*	The Oval . . .	1880
211	The Oval . . .	1884
M. A. Noble (1)		
133	Sydney	1903-04
N. C. O'Neill (2)		
117	The Oval . . .	1961
100	Adelaide . . .	1962-63
C. E. Pellew (2)		
116	Melbourne . .	1920-21
104	Adelaide . . .	1920-21
W. H. Ponsford (5)		
110†	Sydney	1924-25
128	Melbourne . .	1924-25
110	The Oval . . .	1930
181	Leeds	1934
266	The Oval . . .	1934
R. T. Ponting (1)		
127†	Leeds	1997
V. S. Ransford (1)		
143*	Lord's	1909
I. R. Redpath (2)		
171	Perth	1970-71
105	Sydney	1974-75
A. J. Richardson (1)		
100	Leeds	1926
V. Y. Richardson (1)		
138	Melbourne . .	1924-25
G. M. Ritchie (1)		
146	Nottingham .	1985
J. Ryder (2)		
201*	Adelaide . . .	1924-25
112	Melbourne . .	1928-29
H. J. H. Scott (1)		
102	The Oval . . .	1884

R. B. Simpson (2)		
311	Manchester . .	1964
225	Adelaide . . .	1965-66
M. J. Slater (7)		
152	Lord's	1993
176	Brisbane . . .	1994-95
103	Sydney	1994-95
124	Perth	1994-95
113	Brisbane . . .	1998-99
103	Adelaide . . .	1998-99
123	Sydney	1998-99
K. R. Stackpole (3)		
207	Brisbane . . .	1970-71
136	Adelaide . . .	1970-71
114	Nottingham .	1972
J. M. Taylor (1)		
108	Sydney	1924-25
M. A. Taylor (6)		
136†	Leeds	1989
219	Nottingham .	1989
124	Manchester . .	1993
111	Lord's	1993
113	Sydney	1994-95
129	Birmingham .	1997
G. H. S. Trott (1)		
143	Lord's	1896
V. T. Trumper (6)		
135*	Lord's	1899
104	Manchester . .	1902
185*	Sydney	1903-04
113	Adelaide . . .	1903-04
166	Sydney	1907-08
113	Sydney	1911-12
K. D. Walters (4)		
155†	Brisbane . . .	1965-66

115	Melbourne . .	1965-66
112	Brisbane . . .	1970-71
103	Perth	1974-75
M. E. Waugh (4)		
138†	Adelaide . . .	1990-91
137	Birmingham .	1993
140	Brisbane . . .	1994-95
121	Sydney	1998-99
S. R. Waugh (7)		
177*	Leeds	1989
152*	Lord's	1989
157*	Leeds	1993
108 }	Manchester . .	1997
116 }		
112	Brisbane . . .	1998-99
122*	Melbourne . .	1998-99
D. M. Wellham (1)		
103†	The Oval . . .	1981
K. C. Wessels (1)		
162†	Brisbane . . .	1982-83
G. M. Wood (3)		
100	Melbourne . .	1978-79
112	Lord's	1980
172	Nottingham .	1985
W. M. Woodfull (6)		
141	Leeds	1926
117	Manchester . .	1926
111	Sydney	1928-29
107	Melbourne . .	1928-29
102	Melbourne . .	1928-29
155	Lord's	1930
G. N. Yallop (3)		
102†	Brisbane . . .	1978-79
121	Sydney	1978-79
114	Manchester . .	1981

† *Signifies hundred on first appearance in England–Australia Tests.*
‡ *Carried his bat.*

RECORD PARTNERSHIPS FOR EACH WICKET

For England

323 for 1st	J. B. Hobbs and W. Rhodes at Melbourne		1911-12
382 for 2nd†	L. Hutton and M. Leyland at The Oval		1938
262 for 3rd	W. R. Hammond and D. R. Jardine at Adelaide		1928-29
288 for 4th	N. Hussain and G. P. Thorpe at Birmingham		1997
206 for 5th	E. Paynter and D. C. S. Compton at Nottingham		1938
215 for 6th	{ L. Hutton and J. Hardstaff jun. at The Oval		1938
	{ G. Boycott and A. P. E. Knott at Nottingham		1977
143 for 7th	F. E. Woolley and J. Vine at Sydney		1911-12
124 for 8th	E. H. Hendren and H. Larwood at Brisbane		1928-29
151 for 9th	W. H. Scotton and W. W. Read at The Oval		1884
130 for 10th†	R. E. Foster and W. Rhodes at Sydney		1903-04

For Australia

329 for 1st	G. R. Marsh and M. A. Taylor at Nottingham.	1989
451 for 2nd†	W. H. Ponsford and D. G. Bradman at The Oval.	1934
276 for 3rd	D. G. Bradman and A. L. Hassett at Brisbane.	1946-47
388 for 4th†	W. H. Ponsford and D. G. Bradman at Leeds	1934
405 for 5th†	S. G. Barnes and D. G. Bradman at Sydney.	1946-47
346 for 6th†	J. H. Fingleton and D. G. Bradman at Melbourne	1936-37
165 for 7th	C. Hill and H. Trumble at Melbourne	1897-98
243 for 8th†	R. J. Hartigan and C. Hill at Adelaide	1907-08
154 for 9th†	S. E. Gregory and J. McC. Blackham at Sydney	1894-95
127 for 10th†	J. M. Taylor and A. A. Mailey at Sydney.	1924-25

† *Denotes record partnership against all countries.*

MOST RUNS IN A SERIES

England in England.	732 (average 81.33)	D. I. Gower	1985
England in Australia	905 (average 113.12)	W. R. Hammond	1928-29
Australia in England	974 (average 139.14)	D. G. Bradman	1930
Australia in Australia	810 (average 90.00)	D. G. Bradman	1936-37

TEN WICKETS OR MORE IN A MATCH

For England (37)

13-163 (6-42, 7-121)	S. F. Barnes, Melbourne.	1901-02
14-102 (7-28, 7-74)	W. Bates, Melbourne.	1882-83
10-105 (5-46, 5-59)	A. V. Bedser, Melbourne.	1950-51
14-99 (7-55, 7-44)	A. V. Bedser, Nottingham.	1953
11-102 (6-44, 5-58)	C. Blythe, Birmingham	1909
11-176 (6-78, 5-98)	I. T. Botham, Perth	1979-80
10-253 (6-125, 4-128)	I. T. Botham, The Oval	1981
11-74 (5-29, 6-45)	J. Briggs, Lord's	1886
12-136 (6-49, 6-87)	J. Briggs, Adelaide	1891-92
10-148 (5-34, 5-114)	J. Briggs, The Oval	1893
10-104 (6-77, 4-27)†	R. M. Ellison, Birmingham	1985
10-179 (5-102, 5-77)†	K. Farnes, Nottingham.	1934
10-60 (6-41, 4-19)	J. T. Hearne, The Oval	1896
11-113 (5-58, 6-55)	J. C. Laker, Leeds	1956
19-90 (9-37, 10-53)	J. C. Laker, Manchester	1956
10-124 (5-96, 5-28)	H. Larwood, Sydney	1932-33
11-76 (6-48, 5-28)	W. H. Lockwood, Manchester	1902
12-104 (7-36, 5-68)	G. A. Lohmann, The Oval	1886
10-87 (8-35, 2-52)	G. A. Lohmann, Sydney.	1886-87
10-142 (8-58, 2-84)	G. A. Lohmann, Sydney.	1891-92
12-102 (6-50, 6-52)†	F. Martin, The Oval.	1890
11-68 (7-31, 4-37)	R. Peel, Manchester	1888
15-124 (7-56, 8-68)	W. Rhodes, Melbourne	1903-04
10-156 (5-49, 5-107)†	T. Richardson, Manchester	1893
11-173 (6-39, 5-134)	T. Richardson, Lord's.	1896
13-244 (7-168, 6-76)	T. Richardson, Manchester	1896
10-204 (8-94, 2-110)	T. Richardson, Sydney	1897-98

11-228 (6-130, 5-98)†	M. W. Tate, Sydney....................................	1924-25
11-88 (5-58, 6-30)	F. S. Trueman, Leeds	1961
11-93 (7-66, 4-27)	P. C. R. Tufnell, The Oval	1997
10-130 (4-45, 6-85)	F. H. Tyson, Sydney.................................	1954-55
10-82 (4-37, 6-45)	D. L. Underwood, Leeds	1972
11-215 (7-113, 4-102)	D. L. Underwood, Adelaide.......................	1974-75
15-104 (7-61, 8-43)	H. Verity, Lord's	1934
10-57 (6-41, 4-16)	W. Voce, Brisbane	1936-37
13-256 (5-130, 8-126)	J. C. White, Adelaide..............................	1928-29
10-49 (5-29, 5-20)	F. E. Woolley, The Oval	1912

For Australia (40)

10-151 (5-107, 5-44)	T. M. Alderman, Leeds	1989
10-239 (4-129, 6-110)	L. O'B. Fleetwood-Smith, Adelaide................	1936-37
10-160 (4-88, 6-72)	G. Giffen, Sydney...................................	1891-92
11-82 (5-45, 6-37)†	C. V. Grimmett, Sydney............................	1924-25
10-201 (5-107, 5-94)	C. V. Grimmett, Nottingham	1930
10-122 (5-65, 5-57)	R. M. Hogg, Perth	1978-79
10-66 (5-30, 5-36)	R. M. Hogg, Melbourne............................	1978-79
12-175 (5-85, 7-90)†	H. V. Hordern, Sydney.............................	1911-12
10-161 (5-95, 5-66)	H. V. Hordern, Sydney.............................	1911-12
10-164 (7-88, 3-76)	E. Jones, Lord's	1899
11-134 (6-47, 5-87)	G. F. Lawson, Brisbane	1982-83
10-181 (5-58, 5-123)	D. K. Lillee, The Oval	1972
11-165 (6-26, 5-139)	D. K. Lillee, Melbourne............................	1976-77
11-138 (6-60, 5-78)	D. K. Lillee, Melbourne............................	1979-80
11-159 (7-89, 4-70)	D. K. Lillee, The Oval	1981
11-85 (7-58, 4-27)	C. G. Macartney, Leeds	1909
11-157 (5-97, 3-60)	C. J. McDermott, Perth	1990-91
12-107 (5-57, 7-50)	S. C. G. MacGill, Sydney	1998-99
10-302 (5-160, 5-142)	A. A. Mailey, Adelaide............................	1920-21
13-236 (4-115, 9-121)	A. A. Mailey, Melbourne..........................	1920-21
16-137 (8-84, 8-53)†	R. A. L. Massie, Lord's............................	1972
10-152 (5-72, 5-80)	K. R. Miller, Lord's.................................	1956
13-77 (7-17, 6-60)	M. A. Noble, Melbourne	1901-02
11-103 (5-51, 6-52)	M. A. Noble, Sheffield.............................	1902
10-129 (5-63, 5-66)	W. J. O'Reilly, Melbourne	1932-33
11-129 (4-75, 7-54)	W. J. O'Reilly, Nottingham	1934
10-122 (5-66, 5-56)	W. J. O'Reilly, Leeds	1938
11-165 (7-68, 4-97)	G. E. Palmer, Sydney	1881-82
10-126 (7-65, 3-61)	G. E. Palmer, Melbourne	1882-83
13-148 (6-97, 7-51)	B. A. Reid, Melbourne	1990-91
13-110 (6-48, 7-62)	F. R. Spofforth, Melbourne........................	1878-79
14-90 (7-46, 7-44)	F. R. Spofforth, The Oval	1882
11-117 (4-73, 7-44)	F. R. Spofforth, Sydney	1882-83
10-144 (4-54, 6-90)	F. R. Spofforth, Sydney	1884-85
12-89 (6-59, 6-30)	H. Trumble, The Oval	1896
10-128 (4-75, 6-53)	H. Trumble, Manchester............................	1902
12-173 (8-65, 4-108)	H. Trumble, The Oval	1902
12-87 (5-44, 7-43)	C. T. B. Turner, Sydney............................	1887-88
10-63 (5-27, 5-36)	C. T. B. Turner, Lord's.............................	1888
11-110 (3-39, 8-71)	S. K. Warne, Brisbane	1994-95

† *Signifies ten wickets or more on first appearance in England–Australia Tests.*

Note: J. Briggs, J. C. Laker, T. Richardson in 1896, R. M. Hogg, A. A. Mailey, H. Trumble and C. T. B. Turner took ten wickets or more in successive Tests. J. Briggs was omitted, however, from the England team for the first Test match in 1893.

MOST WICKETS IN A SERIES

England in England	46 (average 9.60)	J. C. Laker	1956
England in Australia	38 (average 23.18)	M. W. Tate	1924-25
Australia in England	42 (average 21.26)	T. M. Alderman (6 Tests). .	1981
Australia in Australia	41 (average 12.85)	R. M. Hogg (6 Tests)	1978-79

WICKET-KEEPING – MOST DISMISSALS

	M	Ct	St	Total
†R. W. Marsh (Australia)	42	141	7	148
I. A. Healy (Australia)	33	123	12	135
A. P. E. Knott (England)	34	97	8	105
†W. A. Oldfield (Australia)	38	59	31	90
A. A. Lilley (England)	32	65	19	84
A. T. W. Grout (Australia).	22	69	7	76
T. G. Evans (England)	31	64	12	76

† *The number of catches by R. W. Marsh (141) and stumpings by W. A. Oldfield (31) are respective records in England–Australia Tests.*

SCORERS OF OVER 2,000 RUNS

	T		I		NO		R		HS		Avge
D. G. Bradman	37	..	63	..	7	..	5,028	..	334	..	89.78
J. B. Hobbs.	41	..	71	..	4	..	3,636	..	187	..	54.26
A. R. Border.	47	..	82	..	19	..	3,548	..	200*	..	56.31
D. I. Gower	42	..	77	..	4	..	3,269	..	215	..	44.78
G. Boycott	38	..	71	..	9	..	2,945	..	191	..	47.50
W. R. Hammond	33	..	58	..	3	..	2,852	..	251	..	51.85
H. Sutcliffe.	27	..	46	..	5	..	2,741	..	194	..	66.85
C. Hill.	41	..	76	..	1	..	2,660	..	188	..	35.46
J. H. Edrich	32	..	57	..	3	..	2,644	..	175	..	48.96
G. A. Gooch	42	..	79	..	0	..	2,632	..	196	..	33.31
G. S. Chappell	35	..	65	..	8	..	2,619	..	144	..	45.94
S. R. Waugh	37	..	60	..	16	..	2,574	..	177*	..	58.50
M. A. Taylor.	33	..	61	..	2	..	2,496	..	219	..	42.30
M. C. Cowdrey	43	..	75	..	4	..	2,433	..	113	..	34.26
L. Hutton	27	..	49	..	6	..	2,428	..	364	..	56.46
R. N. Harvey	37	..	68	..	5	..	2,416	..	167	..	38.34
V. T. Trumper	40	..	74	..	5	..	2,263	..	185*	..	32.79
D. C. Boon	31	..	57	..	8	..	2,237	..	184	..	45.65
W. M. Lawry	29	..	51	..	5	..	2,233	..	166	..	48.54
S. E. Gregory	52	..	92	..	7	..	2,193	..	201	..	25.80
W. W. Armstrong	42	..	71	..	9	..	2,172	..	158	..	35.03
I. M. Chappell	30	..	56	..	4	..	2,138	..	192	..	41.11
K. F. Barrington	23	..	39	..	6	..	2,111	..	256	..	63.96
A. R. Morris.	24	..	43	..	2	..	2,080	..	206	..	50.73

BOWLERS WITH 100 WICKETS

	T		Balls		R		W		5W/i		Avge
D. K. Lillee	29	..	8,516	..	3,507	..	167	..	11	..	21.00
I. T. Botham	36	..	8,479	..	4,093	..	148	..	9	..	27.65
H. Trumble	31	..	7,895	..	2,945	..	141	..	9	..	20.88
R. G. D. Willis	35	..	7,294	..	3,346	..	128	..	7	..	26.14
M. A. Noble	39	..	6,845	..	2,860	..	115	..	9	..	24.86
R. R. Lindwall	29	..	6,728	..	2,559	..	114	..	6	..	22.44
W. Rhodes	41	..	5,791	..	2,616	..	109	..	6	..	24.00
S. F. Barnes	20	..	5,749	..	2,288	..	106	..	12	..	21.58
C. V. Grimmett	22	..	9,224	..	3,439	..	106	..	11	..	32.44
D. L. Underwood	29	..	8,000	..	2,770	..	105	..	4	..	26.38
A. V. Bedser	21	..	7,065	..	2,859	..	104	..	7	..	27.49
G. Giffen	31	..	6,457	..	2,791	..	103	..	7	..	27.09
W. J. O'Reilly	19	..	7,864	..	2,587	..	102	..	8	..	25.36
R. Peel	20	..	5,216	..	1,715	..	101	..	5	..	16.98
C. T. B. Turner	17	..	5,195	..	1,670	..	101	..	11	..	16.53
T. M. Alderman	17	..	4,717	..	2,117	..	100	..	11	..	21.17
J. R. Thomson	21	..	4,951	..	2,418	..	100	..	5	..	24.18

RESULTS ON EACH GROUND

In England

THE OVAL (32)

England (15)	1880, 1886, 1888, 1890, 1893, 1896, 1902, 1912, 1926, 1938, 1953, 1968, 1985, 1993, 1997.
Australia (5)	1882, 1930, 1934, 1948, 1972.
Drawn (12)	1884, 1899, 1905, 1909, 1921, 1956, 1961, 1964, 1975, 1977, 1981, 1989.

MANCHESTER (27)

England (7)	1886, 1888, 1905, 1956, 1972, 1977, 1981.
Australia (7)	1896, 1902, 1961, 1968, 1989, 1993, 1997.
Drawn (13)	1884, 1893, 1899, 1909, 1912, 1921, 1926, 1930, 1934, 1948, 1953, 1964, 1985.

The scheduled matches in 1890 and 1938 were abandoned without a ball bowled and are excluded.

LORD'S (31)

England (5)	1884, 1886, 1890, 1896, 1934.
Australia (12)	1888, 1899, 1909, 1921, 1930, 1948, 1956, 1961, 1972, 1985, 1989, 1993.
Drawn (14)	1893, 1902, 1905, 1912, 1926, 1938, 1953, 1964, 1968, 1975, 1977, 1980, 1981, 1997.

NOTTINGHAM (18)

England (3)	1905, 1930, 1977.
Australia (6)	1921, 1934, 1948, 1981, 1989, 1997.
Drawn (9)	1899, 1926, 1938, 1953, 1956, 1964, 1972, 1985, 1993.

LEEDS (22)

England (6)	1956, 1961, 1972, 1977, 1981, 1985.
Australia (8)	1909, 1921, 1938, 1948, 1964, 1989, 1993, 1997.
Drawn (8)	1899, 1905, 1926, 1930, 1934, 1953, 1968, 1975.

BIRMINGHAM (10)

England (4)	1909, 1981, 1985, 1997.
Australia (2)	1975, 1993.
Drawn (4)	1902, 1961, 1968, 1989.

SHEFFIELD (1)

Australia (1)	1902.

In Australia

MELBOURNE (51)

England (19)	*1876, 1882, 1884*(2), *1894*(2), *1903, 1907, 1911*(2), *1924, 1928, 1950, 1954, 1962, 1974, 1982, 1986, 1998.*
Australia (25)	*1876, 1878, 1882, 1891, 1897*(2), *1901*(2), *1903, 1907, 1920*(2), *1924, 1928, 1932, 1936*(2), *1950, 1958*(2), *1976, 1978, 1979, 1990, 1994.*
Drawn (7)	*1881*(2), *1946, 1965*(2), *1970, 1974.*

One scheduled match in 1970-71 was abandoned without a ball bowled and is excluded.

SYDNEY (51)

England (20)	*1882, 1886*(2), *1887, 1894, 1897, 1901, 1903*(2), *1911, 1928, 1932*(2), *1936, 1954, 1965, 1970*(2), *1978*(2).
Australia (24)	*1881*(2), *1882, 1884*(2), *1891, 1894, 1897, 1901, 1907*(2), *1911, 1920*(2), *1924*(2), *1946*(2), *1950, 1962, 1974, 1979, 1986, 1998.*
Drawn (7)	*1954, 1958, 1962, 1982, 1987, 1990, 1994.*

ADELAIDE (27)

England (8)	*1884, 1891, 1911, 1928, 1932, 1954, 1978, 1994.*
Australia (14)	*1894, 1897, 1901, 1903, 1907, 1920, 1924, 1936, 1950, 1958, 1965, 1974, 1982, 1998.*
Drawn (5)	*1946, 1962, 1970, 1986, 1990.*

BRISBANE Exhibition Ground (1)

England (1)	*1928.*

BRISBANE Woolloongabba (16)

England (4)	*1932, 1936, 1978, 1986.*
Australia (8)	*1946, 1950, 1954, 1958, 1974, 1982, 1990, 1994.*
Drawn (4)	*1962, 1965, 1970, 1998.*

PERTH (9)

England (1)	*1978.*
Australia (5)	*1974, 1979, 1990, 1994, 1998.*
Drawn (3)	*1970, 1982, 1986.*

For Tests in Australia the first year of the season is given in italics; i.e. *1876* denotes the 1876-77 season.

ENGLAND v SOUTH AFRICA

Season	England	South Africa	T	E	SA	D
	Captains					
1888-89	C. A. Smith[1]	O. R. Dunell[2]	2	2	0	0
1891-92	W. W. Read	W. H. Milton	1	1	0	0
1895-96	Lord Hawke[3]	E. A. Halliwell[4]	3	3	0	0
1898-99	Lord Hawke	M. Bisset	2	2	0	0
1905-06	P. F. Warner	P. W. Sherwell	5	1	4	0
1907	R. E. Foster	P. W. Sherwell	3	1	0	2
1909-10	H. D. G. Leveson Gower[5]	S. J. Snooke	5	2	3	0
1912	C. B. Fry	F. Mitchell[6]	3	3	0	0
1913-14	J. W. H. T. Douglas	H. W. Taylor	5	4	0	1
1922-23	F. T. Mann	H. W. Taylor	5	2	1	2
1924	A. E. R. Gilligan[7]	H. W. Taylor	5	3	0	2
1927-28	R. T. Stanyforth[8]	H. G. Deane	5	2	2	1
1929	J. C. White[9]	H. G. Deane	5	2	0	3
1930-31	A. P. F. Chapman	H. G. Deane[10]	5	0	1	4
1935	R. E. S. Wyatt	H. F. Wade	5	0	1	4
1938-39	W. R. Hammond	A. Melville	5	1	0	4
1947	N. W. D. Yardley	A. Melville	5	3	0	2
1948-49	F. G. Mann	A. D. Nourse	5	2	0	3
1951	F. R. Brown	A. D. Nourse	5	3	1	1
1955	P. B. H. May	J. E. Cheetham[11]	5	3	2	0
1956-57	P. B. H. May	C. B. van Ryneveld[12]	5	2	2	1
1960	M. C. Cowdrey	D. J. McGlew	5	3	0	2
1964-65	M. J. K. Smith	T. L. Goddard	5	1	0	4
1965	M. J. K. Smith	P. L. van der Merwe	3	0	1	2
1994	M. A. Atherton	K. C. Wessels	3	1	1	1
1995-96	M. A. Atherton	W. J. Cronje	5	0	1	4
1998	A. J. Stewart	W. J. Cronje	5	2	1	2
1999-2000	N. Hussain	W. J. Cronje	5	1	2	2
	In South Africa.................		68	26	16	26
	In England.....................		52	24	7	21
	Totals		120	50	23	47

Notes: The following deputised for the official touring captain or were appointed by the home authority for only a minor proportion of the series:

[1]M. P. Bowden (Second). [2]W. H. Milton (Second). [3]Sir T. C. O'Brien (First). [4]A. R. Richards (Third). [5]F. L. Fane (Fourth and Fifth). [6]L. J. Tancred (Second and Third). [7]J. W. H. T. Douglas (Fourth). [8]G. T. S. Stevens (Fifth). [9]A. W. Carr (Fourth and Fifth). [10]E. P. Nupen (First), H. B. Cameron (Fourth and Fifth). [11]D. J. McGlew (Third and Fourth). [12]D. J. McGlew (Second).

HIGHEST INNINGS TOTALS

For England in England: 554-8 dec. at Lord's	1947
in South Africa: 654-5 at Durban........................	1938-39
For South Africa in England: 552-5 dec. at Manchester...................	1998
in South Africa: 572-7 at Durban	1999-2000

LOWEST INNINGS TOTALS

For England in England: 76 at Leeds		1907
in South Africa: 92 at Cape Town		1898-99
For South Africa in England: 30 at Birmingham		1924
in South Africa: 30 at Port Elizabeth		1895-96

INDIVIDUAL HUNDREDS

For England (96)

R. Abel (1)
120   Cape Town. .   1888-89
L. E. G. Ames (2)
148*   The Oval. . .   1935
115   Cape Town. .   1938-39
M. A. Atherton (3)
185*   Johannesburg   1995-96
103   Birmingham .   1998
108   Port Elizabeth   1999-00
K. F. Barrington (2)
148*   Durban   1964-65
121   Johannesburg   1964-65
G. Boycott (1)
117   Port Elizabeth   1964-65
L. C. Braund (1)
104†   Lord's   1907
M. A. Butcher (1)
116   Leeds   1998
D. C. S. Compton (7)
163†   Nottingham .   1947
208   Lord's   1947
115   Manchester. .   1947
113   The Oval . . .   1947
114   Johannesburg   1948-49
112   Nottingham .   1951
158   Manchester. .   1955
M. C. Cowdrey (3)
101   Cape Town. .   1956-57
155   The Oval. . .   1960
105   Nottingham .   1965
D. Denton (1)
104   Johannesburg   1909-10
E. R. Dexter (1)
172   Johannesburg   1964-65
J. W. H. T. Douglas (1)
119†   Durban   1913-14
W. J. Edrich (3)
219   Durban   1938-39
189   Lord's   1947
191   Manchester. .   1947
F. L. Fane (1)
143   Johannesburg   1905-06
C. B. Fry (1)
129   The Oval. . .   1907
P. A. Gibb (2)
106†   Johannesburg   1938-39
120   Durban   1938-39
W. R. Hammond (6)
138*   Birmingham .   1929
101*   The Oval. . .   1929

136*   Durban   1930-31
181   Cape Town. .   1938-39
120   Durban   1938-39
140   Durban   1938-39
T. W. Hayward (1)
122   Johannesburg   1895-96
E. H. Hendren (2)
132   Leeds   1924
142   The Oval. . .   1924
G. A. Hick (2)
110   Leeds   1994
141   Centurion. . .   1995-96
A. J. L. Hill (1)
124   Cape Town. .   1895-96
J. B. Hobbs (2)
187   Cape Town. .   1909-10
211   Lord's   1924
N. Hussain (2)
105   Lord's   1998
146*   Durban   1999-00
L. Hutton (4)
100   Leeds   1947
158   Johannesburg   1948-49
123   Johannesburg   1948-49
100   Leeds   1951
D. J. Insole (1)
110*   Durban   1956-57
M. Leyland (2)
102   Lord's   1929
161   The Oval. . .   1935
F. G. Mann (1)
136*   Port Elizabeth   1948-49
P. B. H. May (3)
138†   Leeds   1951
112   Lord's   1955
117   Manchester. .   1955
C. P. Mead (3)
102   Johannesburg   1913-14
117   Port Elizabeth   1913-14
181   Durban   1922-23
P. H. Parfitt (1)
122*   Johannesburg   1964-65
J. M. Parks (1)
108*   Durban   1964-65
E. Paynter (3)
117* } †Johannesburg   1938-39
100
243   Durban   1938-39
G. Pullar (1)
175   The Oval. . .   1960

W. Rhodes (1)
152   Johannesburg   1913-14
P. E. Richardson (1)
117†   Johannesburg   1956-57
R. W. V. Robins (1)
108   Manchester. .   1935
A. C. Russell (2)
140 } Durban   1922-23
111
R. T. Simpson (1)
137   Nottingham .   1951
M. J. K. Smith (1)
121   Cape Town. .   1964-65
R. H. Spooner (1)
119†   Lord's   1912
A. J. Stewart (1)
164   Manchester. .   1998
H. Sutcliffe (6)
122   Lord's   1924
102   Johannesburg   1927-28
114   Birmingham .   1929
100   Lord's   1929
104 } The Oval . . .   1929
109*
M. W. Tate (1)
100*   Lord's   1929
E. Tyldesley (2)
122   Johannesburg   1927-28
100   Durban   1927-28
J. T. Tyldesley (1)
112   Cape Town. .   1898-99
B. H. Valentine (1)
112   Cape Town. .   1938-39
P. F. Warner (1)
132*†‡Johannesburg   1898-99
C. Washbrook (1)
195   Johannesburg   1948-49
A. J. Watkins (1)
111   Johannesburg   1948-49
H. Wood (1)
134*   Cape Town. .   1891-92
F. E. Woolley (3)
115*   Johannesburg   1922-23
134*   Lord's   1924
154   Manchester. .   1929
R. E. S. Wyatt (2)
113   Manchester. .   1929
149   Nottingham .   1935

For South Africa (72)

E. J. Barlow (1)			
138	Cape Town. .	1964-65	
K. C. Bland (2)			
144*	Johannesburg	1964-65	
127	The Oval . . .	1965	
M. V. Boucher (1)			
108	Durban	1999-00	
R. H. Catterall (3)			
120	Birmingham .	1924	
120	Lord's	1924	
119	Durban	1927-28	
W. J. Cronje (1)			
126	Nottingham .	1998	
D. J. Cullinan (2)			
108	Johannesburg	1999-00	
120	Cape Town. .	1999-00	
E. L. Dalton (2)			
117	The Oval . . .	1935	
102	Johannesburg	1938-39	
W. R. Endean (1)			
116*	Leeds	1955	
G. A. Faulkner (1)			
123	Johannesburg	1909-10	
T. L. Goddard (1)			
112	Johannesburg	1964-65	
C. M. H. Hathorn (1)			
102	Johannesburg	1905-06	
J. H. Kallis (2)			
132	Manchester. .	1998	
105	Cape Town. .	1999-00	
G. Kirsten (3)			
110	Johannesburg	1995-96	
210	Manchester. .	1998	
275	Durban	1999-00	
P. N. Kirsten (1)			
104	Leeds	1994	

L. Klusener (1)			
174	Port Elizabeth	1999-00	
D. J. McGlew (2)			
104*	Manchester. .	1955	
133	Leeds	1955	
R. A. McLean (3)			
142	Lord's	1955	
100	Durban	1956-57	
109	Manchester. .	1960	
B. M. McMillan (1)			
100*	Johannesburg	1995-96	
A. Melville (4)			
103	Durban	1938-39	
189 }	Nottingham .	1947	
104* }			
117	Lord's	1947	
B. Mitchell (7)			
123	Cape Town. .	1930-31	
164*	Lord's	1935	
128	The Oval . . .	1935	
109	Durban	1938-39	
120 }	The Oval . . .	1947	
189* }			
120	Cape Town. .	1948-49	
A. D. Nourse (7)			
120	Cape Town. .	1938-39	
103	Durban	1938-39	
149	Nottingham .	1947	
115	Manchester. .	1947	
112	Cape Town. .	1948-49	
129*	Johannesburg	1948-49	
208	Nottingham .	1951	
H. G. Owen-Smith (1)			
129	Leeds	1929	
A. J. Pithey (1)			
154	Cape Town. .	1964-65	
R. G. Pollock (2)			
137	Port Elizabeth	1964-65	

125	Nottingham .	1965	
J. N. Rhodes (1)			
117	Lord's	1998	
E. A. B. Rowan (2)			
156*	Johannesburg	1948-49	
236	Leeds	1951	
P. W. Sherwell (1)			
115	Lord's	1907	
I. J. Siedle (1)			
141	Cape Town. .	1930-31	
J. H. Sinclair (1)			
106	Cape Town. .	1898-99	
H. W. Taylor (7)			
109	Durban	1913-14	
176	Johannesburg	1922-23	
101	Johannesburg	1922-23	
102	Durban	1922-23	
101	Johannesburg	1927-28	
121	The Oval . . .	1929	
117	Cape Town. .	1930-31	
P. G. V. van der Bijl (1)			
125	Durban	1938-39	
K. G. Viljoen (1)			
124	Manchester. .	1935	
W. W. Wade (1)			
125	Port Elizabeth	1948-49	
J. H. B. Waite (1)			
113	Manchester. .	1955	
K. C. Wessels (1)			
105†	Lord's	1994	
G. C. White (2)			
147	Johannesburg	1905-06	
118	Durban	1909-10	
P. L. Winslow (1)			
108	Manchester. .	1955	

† *Signifies hundred on first appearance in England–South Africa Tests. K. C. Wessels had earlier scored 162 on his Test debut for Australia against England at Brisbane in 1982-83.*

‡ *P. F. Warner carried his bat through the second innings.*

Notes: A. Melville's four hundreds were made in successive Test innings.

H. Wood scored the only hundred of his career in a Test match.

RECORD PARTNERSHIPS FOR EACH WICKET

For England

359	for 1st†	L. Hutton and C. Washbrook at Johannesburg	1948-49
280	for 2nd	P. A. Gibb and W. J. Edrich at Durban	1938-39
370	for 3rd†	W. J. Edrich and D. C. S. Compton at Lord's	1947
197	for 4th	W. R. Hammond and L. E. G. Ames at Cape Town	1938-39
237	for 5th	D. C. S. Compton and N. W. D. Yardley at Nottingham	1947
206*	for 6th	K. F. Barrington and J. M. Parks at Durban	1964-65
115	for 7th	J. W. H. T. Douglas and M. C. Bird at Durban	1913-14
154	for 8th	C. W. Wright and H. R. Bromley-Davenport at Johannesburg	1895-96
71	for 9th	H. Wood and J. T. Hearne at Cape Town	1891-92
92	for 10th	A. C. Russell and A. E. R. Gilligan at Durban	1922-23

For South Africa

260	for 1st†	B. Mitchell and I. J. Siedle at Cape Town.	1930-31
238	for 2nd	G. Kirsten and J. H. Kallis at Manchester.	1998
319	for 3rd	A. Melville and A. D. Nourse at Nottingham	1947
214	for 4th†	H. W. Taylor and H. G. Deane at The Oval.	1929
192	for 5th†	G. Kirsten and M. V. Boucher at Durban	1999-2000
171	for 6th	J. H. B. Waite and P. L. Winslow at Manchester	1955
123	for 7th	H. G. Deane and E. P. Nupen at Durban	1927-28
119	for 8th	L. Klusener and M. V. Boucher at Port Elizabeth	1999-2000
137	for 9th	E. L. Dalton and A. B. C. Langton at The Oval.	1935
103	for 10th†	H. G. Owen-Smith and A. J. Bell at Leeds	1929

† *Denotes record partnership against all countries.*

MOST RUNS IN A SERIES

England in England	753 (average 94.12)	D. C. S. Compton .	1947
England in South Africa	653 (average 81.62)	E. Paynter.	1938-39
South Africa in England	621 (average 69.00)	A. D. Nourse.	1947
South Africa in South Africa . . .	582 (average 64.66)	H. W. Taylor	1922-23

TEN WICKETS OR MORE IN A MATCH

For England (25)

11-110 (5-25, 6-85)†	S. F. Barnes, Lord's	1912
10-115 (6-52, 4-63)	S. F. Barnes, Leeds	1912
13-57 (5-28, 8-29)	S. F. Barnes, The Oval	1912
10-105 (5-57, 5-48)	S. F. Barnes, Durban	1913-14
17-159 (8-56, 9-103)	S. F. Barnes, Johannesburg	1913-14
14-144 (7-56, 7-88)	S. F. Barnes, Durban	1913-14
12-112 (7-58, 5-54)	A. V. Bedser, Manchester	1951
11-118 (6-68, 5-50)	C. Blythe, Cape Town	1905-06
15-99 (8-59, 7-40)	C. Blythe, Leeds	1907
10-104 (7-46, 3-58)	C. Blythe, Cape Town	1909-10
15-28 (7-17, 8-11)	J. Briggs, Cape Town	1888-89
13-91 (6-54, 7-37)†	J. J. Ferris, Cape Town	1891-92
10-122 (5-60, 5-62)	A. R. C. Fraser, Nottingham	1998
10-207 (7-115, 3-92)	A. P. Freeman, Leeds	1929
12-171 (7-71, 5-100)	A. P. Freeman, Manchester	1929
12-130 (7-70, 5-60)	G. Geary, Johannesburg	1927-28
11-90 (6-7, 5-83)	A. E. R. Gilligan, Birmingham.	1924
10-119 (4-64, 6-55)	J. C. Laker, The Oval	1951
15-45 (7-38, 8-7)†	G. A. Lohmann, Port Elizabeth	1895-96
12-71 (9-28, 3-43)	G. A. Lohmann, Johannesburg	1895-96
10-138 (1-81, 9-57)	D. E. Malcolm, The Oval	1994
11-97 (6-63, 5-34)	J. B. Statham, Lord's	1960
12-101 (7-52, 5-49)	R. Tattersall, Lord's	1951
12-89 (5-53, 7-36)	J. H. Wardle, Cape Town.	1956-57
10-175 (5-95, 5-80)	D. V. P. Wright, Lord's	1947

For South Africa (7)

11-127 (6-53, 5-74)	A. A. Donald, Johannesburg.	1999-2000
11-112 (4-49, 7-63)†	A. E. Hall, Cape Town	1922-23
11-150 (5-63, 6-87)	E. P. Nupen, Johannesburg	1930-31
10-87 (5-53, 5-34)	P. M. Pollock, Nottingham.	1965
12-127 (4-57, 8-70)	S. J. Snooke, Johannesburg.	1905-06

| 13-192 (4-79, 9-113) | H. J. Tayfield, Johannesburg .... | 1956-57 |
| 12-181 (5-87, 7-94) | A. E. E. Vogler, Johannesburg .... | 1909-10 |

† *Signifies ten wickets or more on first appearance in England–South Africa Tests.*

Note: S. F. Barnes took ten wickets or more in his first five Tests v South Africa and in six of his seven Tests v South Africa. A. P. Freeman and G. A. Lohmann took ten wickets or more in successive matches.

MOST WICKETS IN A SERIES

England in England	34 (average 8.29)	S. F. Barnes	1912
England in South Africa	49 (average 10.93)	S. F. Barnes	1913-14
South Africa in England	33 (average 19.78)	A. A. Donald	1998
South Africa in South Africa ..	37 (average 17.18)	H. J. Tayfield	1956-57

ENGLAND v WEST INDIES

		Captains				
Season	*England*	*West Indies*	*T*	*E*	*WI*	*D*
1928	A. P. F. Chapman	R. K. Nunes	3	3	0	0
1929-30	Hon. F. S. G. Calthorpe	E. L. G. Hoad[1]	4	1	1	2
1933	D. R. Jardine[2]	G. C. Grant	3	2	0	1
1934-35	R. E. S. Wyatt	G. C. Grant	4	1	2	1
1939	W. R. Hammond	R. S. Grant	3	1	0	2
1947-48	G. O. B. Allen[3]	J. D. C. Goddard[4]	4	0	2	2
1950	N. W. D. Yardley[5]	J. D. C. Goddard	4	1	3	0
1953-54	L. Hutton	J. B. Stollmeyer	5	2	2	1
1957	P. B. H. May	J. D. C. Goddard	5	3	0	2
1959-60	P. B. H. May[6]	F. C. M. Alexander	5	1	0	4

THE WISDEN TROPHY

		Captains					
Season	*England*	*West Indies*	*T*	*E*	*WI*	*D*	*Held by*
1963	E. R. Dexter	F. M. M. Worrell	5	1	3	1	WI
1966	M. C. Cowdrey[7]	G. S. Sobers	5	1	3	1	WI
1967-68	M. C. Cowdrey	G. S. Sobers	5	1	0	4	E
1969	R. Illingworth	G. S. Sobers	3	2	0	1	E
1973	R. Illingworth	R. B. Kanhai	3	0	2	1	WI
1973-74	M. H. Denness	R. B. Kanhai	5	1	1	3	WI
1976	A. W. Greig	C. H. Lloyd	5	0	3	2	WI
1980	I. T. Botham	C. H. Lloyd	5	0	1	4	WI
1980-81†	I. T. Botham	C. H. Lloyd	4	0	2	2	WI
1984	D. I. Gower	C. H. Lloyd	5	0	5	0	WI
1985-86	D. I. Gower	I. V. A. Richards	5	0	5	0	WI
1988	J. E. Emburey[9]	I. V. A. Richards	5	0	4	1	WI
1989-90‡	G. A. Gooch[10]	I. V. A. Richards[11]	4	1	2	1	WI
1991	G. A. Gooch	I. V. A. Richards	5	2	2	1	WI
1993-94	M. A. Atherton	R. B. Richardson[12]	5	1	3	1	WI
1995	M. A. Atherton	R. B. Richardson	6	2	2	2	WI
1997-98	M. A. Atherton	B. C. Lara	6	1	3	2	WI
2000	N. Hussain[13]	J. C. Adams	5	3	1	1	E

In England	70	21	29	20
In West Indies	56	10	23	23
Totals........................	126	31	52	43

† *The Second Test, at Georgetown, was cancelled owing to political pressure and is excluded.*
‡ *The Second Test, at Georgetown, was abandoned without a ball being bowled and is excluded.*

Notes: The following deputised for the official touring captain or were appointed by the home authority for only a minor proportion of the series:

[1]N. Betancourt (Second), M. P. Fernandes (Third), R. K. Nunes (Fourth). [2]R. E. S. Wyatt (Third). [3]K. Cranston (First). [4]G. A. Headley (First), G. E. Gomez (Second). •[5]F. R. Brown (Fourth). [6]M. C. Cowdrey (Fourth and Fifth). [7]M. J. K. Smith (First), D. B. Close (Fifth). [8]I. V. A. Richards (Fifth). [9]M. W. Gatting (First), C. S. Cowdrey (Fourth), G. A. Gooch (Fifth). [10]A. J. Lamb (Fourth and Fifth). [11]D. L. Haynes (Third). [12]C. A. Walsh (Fifth). [13]A. J. Stewart (Second).

HIGHEST INNINGS TOTALS

For England in England: 619-6 dec. at Nottingham 1957
      in West Indies: 849 at Kingston 1929-30

For West Indies in England: 692-8 dec. at The Oval. 1995
      in West Indies: 681-8 dec. at Port-of-Spain. 1953-54

LOWEST INNINGS TOTALS

For England in England: 71 at Manchester. 1976
      in West Indies: 46 at Port-of-Spain 1993-94

For West Indies in England: 54 at Lord's 2000
      in West Indies: 102 at Bridgetown 1934-35

INDIVIDUAL HUNDREDS

For England (100)

L. E. G. Ames (3)
105   Port-of-Spain 1929-30
149   Kingston . . . 1929-30
126   Kingston . . . 1934-35
D. L. Amiss (4)
174   Port-of-Spain 1973-74
262* Kingston . . . 1973-74
118   Georgetown . 1973-74
203   The Oval . . . 1976
M. A. Atherton (4)
144   Georgetown . 1993-94
135   St John's . . . 1993-94
113   Nottingham . 1995
108   The Oval . . . 2000
A. H. Bakewell (1)
107† The Oval . . . 1933
K. F. Barrington (3)
128† Bridgetown . 1959-60
121   Port-of-Spain 1959-60
143   Port-of-Spain 1967-68
G. Boycott (5)
116   Georgetown . 1967-68
128   Manchester. . 1969
106   Lord's 1969
112   Port-of-Spain 1973-74
104* St John's . . . 1980-81
D. C. S. Compton (2)
120† Lord's 1939
133   Port-of-Spain 1953-54

M. C. Cowdrey (6)
154† Birmingham . 1957
152   Lord's 1957
114   Kingston . . . 1959-60
119   Port-of-Spain 1959-60
101   Kingston . . . 1967-68
148   Port-of-Spain 1967-68
E. R. Dexter (2)
136*† Bridgetown . 1959-60
110   Georgetown . 1959-60
J. H. Edrich (1)
146   Bridgetown . 1967-68
T. G. Evans (1)
104   Manchester. . 1950
K. W. R. Fletcher (1)
129* Bridgetown . 1973-74
G. Fowler (1)
106   Lord's 1984
G. A. Gooch (5)
123   Lord's 1980
116   Bridgetown . 1980-81
153   Kingston . . . 1980-81
146   Nottingham . 1988
154*‡ Leeds 1991
D. I. Gower (1)
154* Kingston . . . 1980-81
T. W. Graveney (5)
258   Nottingham . 1957
164   The Oval . . . 1957
109   Nottingham . 1966

165   The Oval . . . 1966
118   Port-of-Spain 1967-68
A. W. Greig (3)
148   Bridgetown . 1973-74
121   Georgetown . 1973-74
116   Leeds 1976
S. C. Griffith (1)
140† Port-of-Spain 1947-48
W. R. Hammond (1)
138   The Oval . . . 1939
J. H. Hampshire (1)
107† Lord's 1969
F. C. Hayes (1)
106*† The Oval . . . 1973
E. H. Hendren (2)
205* Port-of-Spain 1929-30
123   Georgetown . 1929-30
G. A. Hick (1)
118* Nottingham . 1995
J. B. Hobbs (1)
159   The Oval . . . 1928
N. Hussain (1)
106   St John's . . . 1997-98
L. Hutton (5)
196† Lord's 1939
165* The Oval . . . 1939
202*‡ The Oval . . . 1950
169   Georgetown . 1953-54
205   Kingston . . . 1953-54

R. Illingworth (1)
113   Lord's   1969
D. R. Jardine (1)
127   Manchester . .   1933
A. P. E. Knott (1)
116   Leeds   1976
A. J. Lamb (6)
110   Lord's   1984
100   Leeds   1984
100* Manchester. .   1984
113   Lord's   1988
132   Kingston . . .   1989-90
119   Bridgetown .   1989-90
P. B. H. May (3)
135   Port-of-Spain   1953-54
285* Birmingham .   1957
104   Nottingham .   1957
C. Milburn (1)
126* Lord's   1966
J. T. Murray (1)
112† The Oval . . .   1966

J. M. Parks (1)
101*† Port-of-Spain   1959-60
W. Place (1)
107   Kingston . . .   1947-48
M. R. Ramprakash (1)
154   Bridgetown .   1997-98
P. E. Richardson (2)
126   Nottingham .   1957
107   The Oval . . .   1957
J. D. Robertson (1)
133   Port-of-Spain   1947-48
A. Sandham (2)
152† Bridgetown .   1929-30
325   Kingston . . .   1929-30
M. J. K. Smith (1)
108   Port-of-Spain   1959-60
R. A. Smith (3)
148* Lord's   1991
109   The Oval . . .   1991
175   St John's . . .   1993-94

D. S. Steele (1)
106† Nottingham .   1976
A. J. Stewart (3)
118 ⎫
143 ⎬ Bridgetown .   1993-94
105   Manchester. .   2000
R. Subba Row (1)
100† Georgetown .   1959-60
G. P. Thorpe (1)
103   Bridgetown .   1997-98
E. Tyldesley (1)
122† Lord's   1928
C. Washbrook (2)
114† Lord's   1950
102   Nottingham .   1950
W. Watson (1)
116† Kingston . . .   1953-54
P. Willey (2)
100* The Oval . . .   1980
102* St John's . . .   1980-81

For West Indies (111)

J. C. Adams (1)
137   Georgetown .   1993-94
K. L. T. Arthurton (1)
126   Kingston . . .   1993-94
I. Barrow (1)
105   Manchester. .   1933
C. A. Best (1)
164   Bridgetown .   1989-90
B. F. Butcher (2)
133   Lord's   1963
209* Nottingham .   1966
G. M. Carew (1)
107   Port-of-Spain   1947-48
S. Chanderpaul (1)
118   Georgetown .   1997-98
C. A. Davis (1)
103   Lord's   1969
P. J. L. Dujon (1)
101   Manchester. .   1984
R. C. Fredericks (3)
150   Birmingham .   1973
138   Lord's   1976
109   Leeds   1976
A. G. Ganteaume (1)
112† Port-of-Spain   1947-48
H. A. Gomes (2)
143   Birmingham .   1984
104* Leeds   1984
C. G. Greenidge (7)
134 ⎫
101 ⎬ Manchester. .   1976
115   Leeds   1976
214* Lord's   1984
223   Manchester. .   1984
103   Lord's   1988
149   St John's . . .   1989-90

D. L. Haynes (5)
184   Lord's   1980
125   The Oval . . .   1984
131   St John's . . .   1985-86
109   Bridgetown .   1989-90
167   St John's . . .   1989-90
G. A. Headley (8)
176† Bridgetown .   1929-30
114 ⎫
112 ⎬ Georgetown .   1929-30
223   Kingston . . .   1929-30
169* Manchester. .   1933
270* Kingston . . .   1934-35
106 ⎫
107 ⎬ Lord's   1939
D. A. J. Holford (1)
105* Lord's   1966
J. K. Holt (1)
166   Bridgetown .   1953-54
C. L. Hooper (3)
111   Lord's   1991
127   The Oval . . .   1995
108* St John's . . .   1997-98
C. C. Hunte (3)
182   Manchester. .   1963
108* The Oval . . .   1963
135   Manchester. .   1966
B. D. Julien (1)
121   Lord's   1973
A. I. Kallicharran (2)
158   Port-of-Spain   1973-74
119   Bridgetown .   1973-74
R. B. Kanhai (5)
110   Port-of-Spain   1959-60
104   The Oval . . .   1966
153   Port-of-Spain   1967-68

150   Georgetown .   1967-68
157   Lord's   1973
C. B. Lambert (1)
104   St John's . . .   1997-98
B. C. Lara (6)
167   Georgetown .   1993-94
375   St John's . . .   1993-94
145   Manchester. .   1995
152   Nottingham .   1995
179   The Oval . . .   1995
112   Manchester. .   2000
C. H. Lloyd (5)
118† Port-of-Spain   1967-68
113* Bridgetown .   1967-68
132   The Oval . . .   1973
101   Manchester. .   1980
100   Bridgetown .   1980-81
S. M. Nurse (2)
137   Leeds   1966
136   Port-of-Spain   1967-68
A. F. Rae (2)
106   Lord's   1950
109   The Oval . . .   1950
I. V. A. Richards (8)
232† Nottingham .   1976
135   Manchester. .   1976
291   The Oval . . .   1976
145   Lord's   1980
182* Bridgetown .   1980-81
114   St John's . . .   1980-81
117   Birmingham .   1984
110* St John's . . .   1985-86
R. B. Richardson (4)
102   Port-of-Spain   1985-86
160   Bridgetown .   1985-86
104   Birmingham .   1991
121   The Oval . . .   1991

C. A. Roach (2)			145	Georgetown .	1959-60	**E. D. Weekes** (3)		
122	Bridgetown .	1929-30	102	Leeds	1963	141	Kingston . . .	1947-48
209	Georgetown .	1929-30	161	Manchester. .	1966	129	Nottingham .	1950
L. G. Rowe (3)			163*	Lord's	1966	206	Port-of-Spain	1953-54
120	Kingston . . .	1973-74	174	Leeds	1966	**K. H. Weekes** (1)		
302	Bridgetown .	1973-74	113*	Kingston . . .	1967-68	137	The Oval . . .	1939
123	Port-of-Spain	1973-74	152	Georgetown .	1967-68	**F. M. M. Worrell** (6)		
O. G. Smith (2)			150*	Lord's	1973	131*	Georgetown .	1947-48
161†	Birmingham .	1957	**C. L. Walcott** (4)			261	Nottingham .	1950
168	Nottingham .	1957	168*	Lord's	1950	138	The Oval . . .	1950
G. S. Sobers (10)			220	Bridgetown .	1953-54	167	Port-of-Spain	1953-54
226	Bridgetown .	1959-60	124	Port-of-Spain	1953-54	191*‡	Nottingham .	1957
147	Kingston . . .	1959-60	116	Kingston . . .	1953-54	197*	Bridgetown .	1959-60

† *Signifies hundred on first appearance in England–West Indies Tests. S. C. Griffith provides the only instance for England of a player hitting his maiden century in first-class cricket in his first Test.*

‡ *Carried his bat.*

RECORD PARTNERSHIPS FOR EACH WICKET

For England

212	for 1st	C. Washbrook and R. T. Simpson at Nottingham	1950
266	for 2nd	P. E. Richardson and T. W. Graveney at Nottingham	1957
303	for 3rd	M. A. Atherton and R. A. Smith at St John's	1993-94
411	for 4th†	P. B. H. May and M. C. Cowdrey at Birmingham	1957
150	for 5th	A. J. Stewart and G. P. Thorpe at Bridgetown	1993-94
205	for 6th	M. R. Ramprakash and G. P. Thorpe at Bridgetown	1997-98
197	for 7th†	M. J. K. Smith and J. M. Parks at Port-of-Spain	1959-60
217	for 8th	T. W. Graveney and J. T. Murray at The Oval	1966
109	for 9th	G. A. R. Lock and P. I. Pocock at Georgetown	1967-68
128	for 10th	K. Higgs and J. A. Snow at The Oval	1966

For West Indies

298	for 1st†	C. G. Greenidge and D. L. Haynes at St John's	1989-90
287*	for 2nd	C. G. Greenidge and H. A. Gomes at Lord's	1984
338	for 3rd†	E. D. Weekes and F. M. M. Worrell at Port-of-Spain	1953-54
399	for 4th†	G. S. Sobers and F. M. M. Worrell at Bridgetown	1959-60
265	for 5th	S. M. Nurse and G. S. Sobers at Leeds	1966
274*	for 6th†	G. S. Sobers and D. A. J. Holford at Lord's	1966
155*	for 7th‡	G. S. Sobers and B. D. Julien at Lord's	1973
99	for 8th	C. A. McWatt and J. K. Holt at Georgetown	1953-54
150	for 9th	E. A. E. Baptiste and M. A. Holding at Birmingham	1984
70	for 10th	I. R. Bishop and D. Ramnarine at Georgetown	1997-98

† *Denotes record partnership against all countries.*

‡ *231 runs were added for this wicket in two separate partnerships: G. S. Sobers retired ill and was replaced by K. D. Boyce when 155 had been added.*

TEN WICKETS OR MORE IN A MATCH

For England (12)

11-98 (7-44, 4-54)	T. E. Bailey, Lord's	1957
11-110 (8-53, 3-57)	A. R. C. Fraser, Port-of-Spain	1997-98
10-93 (5-54, 5-39)	A. P. Freeman, Manchester	1928
13-156 (8-86, 5-70)	A. W. Greig, Port-of-Spain	1973-74

11-48 (5-28, 6-20)	G. A. R. Lock, The Oval	1957
10-137 (4-60, 6-77)	D. E. Malcolm, Port-of-Spain	1989-90
11-96 (5-37, 6-59)†	C. S. Marriott, The Oval	1933
10-142 (4-82, 6-60)	J. A. Snow, Georgetown	1967-68
10-195 (5-105, 5-90)†	G. T. S. Stevens, Bridgetown.	1929-30
11-152 (6-100, 5-52)	F. S. Trueman, Lord's	1963
12-119 (5-75, 7-44)	F. S. Trueman, Birmingham	1963
11-149 (4-79, 7-70)	W. Voce, Port-of-Spain	1929-30

For West Indies (15)

10-127 (2-82, 8-45)	C. E. L. Ambrose, Bridgetown	1989-90
11-84 (5-60, 6-24)	C. E. L. Ambrose, Port-of-Spain	1993-94
10-174 (5-105, 5-69)	K. C. G. Benjamin, Nottingham	1995
11-147 (5-70, 6-77)†	K. D. Boyce, The Oval	1973
11-229 (5-137, 6-92)	W. Ferguson, Port-of-Spain	1947-48
11-157 (5-59, 6-98)†	L. R. Gibbs, Manchester	1963
10-106 (5-37, 5-69)	L. R. Gibbs, Manchester	1966
14-149 (8-92, 6-57)	M. A. Holding, The Oval	1976
10-96 (5-41, 5-55)†	H. H. H. Johnson, Kingston	1947-48
10-92 (6-32, 4-60)	M. D. Marshall, Lord's.	1988
11-152 (5-66, 6-86)	S. Ramadhin, Lord's	1950
10-123 (5-60, 5-63)	A. M. E. Roberts, Lord's	1976
11-204 (8-104, 3-100)†	A. L. Valentine, Manchester	1950
10-160 (4-121, 6-39)	A. L. Valentine, The Oval.	1950
10-117 (4-43, 6-74)	C. A. Walsh, Lord's.	2000

† *Signifies ten wickets or more on first appearance in England–West Indies Tests.*

Note: F. S. Trueman took ten wickets or more in successive matches.

ENGLAND v NEW ZEALAND

Captains

Season	England	New Zealand	T	E	NZ	D
1929-30	A. H. H. Gilligan	T. C. Lowry	4	1	0	3
1931	D. R. Jardine	T. C. Lowry	3	1	0	2
1932-33	D. R. Jardine[1]	M. L. Page	2	0	0	2
1937	R. W. V. Robins	M. L. Page	3	1	0	2
1946-47	W. R. Hammond	W. A. Hadlee	1	0	0	1
1949	F. G. Mann[2]	W. A. Hadlee	4	0	0	4
1950-51	F. R. Brown	W. A. Hadlee	2	1	0	1
1954-55	L. Hutton	G. O. Rabone	2	2	0	0
1958	P. B. H. May	J. R. Reid	5	4	0	1
1958-59	P. B. H. May	J. R. Reid	2	1	0	1
1962-63	E. R. Dexter	J. R. Reid	3	3	0	0
1965	M. J. K. Smith	J. R. Reid	3	3	0	0
1965-66	M. J. K. Smith	B. W. Sinclair[3]	3	0	0	3
1969	R. Illingworth	G. T. Dowling	3	2	0	1
1970-71	R. Illingworth	G. T. Dowling	2	1	0	1
1973	R. Illingworth	B. E. Congdon	3	2	0	1
1974-75	M. H. Denness	B. E. Congdon	2	1	0	1
1977-78	G. Boycott	M. G. Burgess	3	1	1	1
1978	J. M. Brearley	M. G. Burgess	3	3	0	0
1983	R. G. D. Willis	G. P. Howarth	4	3	1	0
1983-84	R. G. D. Willis	G. P. Howarth	3	0	1	2
1986	M. W. Gatting	J. V. Coney	3	0	1	2
1987-88	M. W. Gatting	J. J. Crowe[4]	3	0	0	3
1990	G. A. Gooch	J. G. Wright	3	1	0	2

Season	England	New Zealand	T	E	NZ	D
1991-92	G. A. Gooch	M. D. Crowe	3	2	0	1
1994	M. A. Atherton	K. R. Rutherford	3	1	0	2
1996-97	M. A. Atherton	L. K. Germon[5]	3	2	0	1
1999	N. Hussain[6]	S. P. Fleming	4	1	2	1
	In New Zealand		38	15	2	21
	In England		44	22	4	18
	Totals		82	37	6	39

Notes: The following deputised for the official touring captain or were appointed by the home authority for only a minor proportion of the series:
[1]R. E. S. Wyatt (Second). [2]F. R. Brown (Third and Fourth). [3]M. E. Chapple (First). [4]J. G. Wright (Third). [5]S. P. Fleming (Third). [6]M. A. Butcher (Third).

HIGHEST INNINGS TOTALS

For England in England: 567-8 dec. at Nottingham	1994
in New Zealand: 593-6 dec. at Auckland	1974-75
For New Zealand in England: 551-9 dec. at Lord's	1973
in New Zealand: 537 at Wellington.	1983-84

LOWEST INNINGS TOTALS

For England in England: 126 at Birmingham	1999
in New Zealand: 64 at Wellington.	1977-78
For New Zealand in England: 47 at Lord's.	1958
in New Zealand: 26 at Auckland	1954-55

INDIVIDUAL HUNDREDS

For England (83)

G. O. B. Allen (1)
122† Lord's 1931

L. E. G. Ames (2)
137† Lord's 1931
103 Christchurch . 1932-33

D. L. Amiss (2)
138*† Nottingham . 1973
164* Christchurch . 1974-75

M. A. Atherton (4)
151† Nottingham . 1990
101 Nottingham . 1994
111 Manchester . 1994
118 Christchurch . 1996-97

T. E. Bailey (1)
134* Christchurch . 1950-51

K. F. Barrington (3)
126† Auckland . . . 1962-63
137 Birmingham . 1965
163 Leeds 1965

I. T. Botham (3)
103 Christchurch . 1977-78
103 Nottingham . 1983
138 Wellington . . 1983-84

E. H. Bowley (1)
109 Auckland . . . 1929-30

G. Boycott (2)
115 Leeds 1973
131 Nottingham . 1978

B. C. Broad (1)
114† Christchurch . 1987-88

D. C. S. Compton (2)
114 Leeds 1949
116 Lord's 1949

M. C. Cowdrey (2)
128* Wellington . . 1962-63
119 Lord's 1965

M. H. Denness (1)
181 Auckland . . . 1974-75

E. R. Dexter (1)
141   Christchurch. 1958-59
B. L. D'Oliveira (1)
100   Christchurch. 1970-71
K. S. Duleepsinhji (2)
117   Auckland. . . 1929-30
109   The Oval . . .   1931
J. H. Edrich (3)
310*† Leeds   1965
115   Lord's   1969
155   Nottingham .   1969
W. J. Edrich (1)
100   The Oval . . .   1949
K. W. R. Fletcher (2)
178   Lord's   1973
216   Auckland. . . 1974-75
G. Fowler (1)
105† The Oval . . .   1983
M. W. Gatting (1)
121   The Oval . . .   1986
G. A. Gooch (4)
183   Lord's   1986
154   Birmingham .   1990
114   Auckland. . . 1991-92
210   Nottingham .   1994
D. I. Gower (4)
111† The Oval . . .   1978
112* Leeds   1983
108   Lord's   1983
131   The Oval . . .   1986

A. W. Greig (1)
139† Nottingham . .   1973
W. R. Hammond (4)
100* The Oval . . .   1931
227   Christchurch. 1932-33
336* Auckland. . . 1932-33
140   Lord's   1937
J. Hardstaff jun. (2)
114† Lord's   1937
103   The Oval . . .   1937
L. Hutton (3)
100   Manchester. .   1937
101   Leeds   1949
206   The Oval . . .   1949
B. R. Knight (1)
125† Auckland. . . 1962-63
A. P. E. Knott (1)
101   Auckland. . . 1970-71
A. J. Lamb (3)
102*† The Oval . . .   1983
137† Nottingham .   1983
142   Wellington . . 1991-92
G. B. Legge (1)
196   Auckland. . . 1929-30
P. B. H. May (3)
113* Leeds   1958
101   Manchester. .   1958
124* Auckland. . . 1958-59
C. A. Milton (1)
104*† Leeds   1958

P. H. Parfitt (1)
131*† Auckland. . . 1962-63
C. T. Radley (1)
158   Auckland. . . 1977-78
D. W. Randall (2)
164   Wellington . . 1983-84
104   Auckland. . . 1983-84
P. E. Richardson (1)
100† Birmingham .   1958
J. D. Robertson (1)
121† Lord's   1949
P. J. Sharpe (1)
111   Nottingham .   1969
R. T. Simpson (1)
103† Manchester. .   1949
A. J. Stewart (4)
148   Christchurch. 1991-92
107   Wellington . . 1991-92
119   Lord's   1994
173   Auckland. . . 1996-97
H. Sutcliffe (2)
117† The Oval . . .   1931
109* Manchester. .   1931
C. J. Tavaré (1)
109† The Oval . . .   1983
G. P. Thorpe (2)
119† Auckland. . . 1996-97
108   Wellington . . 1996-97
C. Washbrook (1)
103* Leeds   1949

For New Zealand (43)

N. J. Astle (2)
102*† Auckland. . . 1996-97
101   Manchester. .   1999
J. G. Bracewell (1)
110   Nottingham .   1986
M. G. Burgess (2)
104   Auckland. . . 1970-71
105   Lord's   1973
J. V. Coney (1)
174* Wellington . . 1983-84
B. E. Congdon (3)
104   Christchurch. 1965-66
176   Nottingham .   1973
175   Lord's   1973
J. J. Crowe (1)
128   Auckland. . . 1983-84
M. D. Crowe (5)
100   Wellington . . 1983-84
106   Lord's   1986
143   Wellington . . 1987-88
142   Lord's   1994
115   Nottingham .   1994
C. S. Dempster (2)
136   Wellington . . 1929-30

120   Lord's   1931
M. P. Donnelly (1)
206   Lord's   1949
S. P. Fleming (1)
129   Auckland. . . 1996-97
T. J. Franklin (1)
101   Lord's   1990
M. J. Greatbatch (1)
107*† Auckland. . . 1987-88
W. A. Hadlee (1)
116   Christchurch. 1946-47
M. J. Horne (1)
100   Lord's   1999
G. P. Howarth (3)
122 }
102 } Auckland. . . 1977-78
123   Lord's   1978
A. H. Jones (1)
143   Wellington . . 1991-92
C. D. McMillan (1)
107* Manchester. .   1999
J. E. Mills (1)
117† Wellington . . 1929-30

M. L. Page (1)
104   Lord's   1931
J. M. Parker (1)
121   Auckland. . . 1974-75
V. Pollard (2)
116   Nottingham .   1973
105* Lord's   1973
J. R. Reid (1)
100   Christchurch. 1962-63
K. R. Rutherford (1)
107* Wellington . . 1987-88
B. W. Sinclair (1)
114   Auckland. . . 1965-66
I. D. S. Smith (1)
113* Auckland. . . 1983-84
B. Sutcliffe (2)
101   Manchester. .   1949
116   Christchurch. 1950-51
J. G. Wright (4)
130   Auckland. . . 1983-84
119   The Oval . . .   1986
103   Auckland. . . 1987-88
116   Wellington . . 1991-92

† *Signifies hundred on first appearance in England–New Zealand Tests.*

RECORD PARTNERSHIPS FOR EACH WICKET

For England

223	for 1st	G. Fowler and C. J. Tavaré at The Oval	1983
369	for 2nd	J. H. Edrich and K. F. Barrington at Leeds	1965
245	for 3rd	J. Hardstaff jun. and W. R. Hammond at Lord's	1937
266	for 4th	M. H. Denness and K. W. R. Fletcher at Auckland	1974-75
242	for 5th	W. R. Hammond and L. E. G. Ames at Christchurch	1932-33
240	for 6th†	P. H. Parfitt and B. R. Knight at Auckland	1962-63
149	for 7th	A. P. E. Knott and P. Lever at Auckland	1970-71
246	for 8th†	L. E. G. Ames and G. O. B. Allen at Lord's	1931
163*	for 9th†	M. C. Cowdrey and A. C. Smith at Wellington	1962-63
59	for 10th	A. P. E. Knott and N. Gifford at Nottingham	1973

For New Zealand

276	for 1st	C. S. Dempster and J. E. Mills at Wellington	1929-30
241	for 2nd†	J. G. Wright and A. H. Jones at Wellington	1991-92
210	for 3rd	B. A. Edgar and M. D. Crowe at Lord's	1986
155	for 4th	M. D. Crowe and M. J. Greatbatch at Wellington	1987-88
180	for 5th	M. D. Crowe and S. A. Thomson at Lord's	1994
141	for 6th	M. D. Crowe and A. C. Parore at Manchester	1994
117	for 7th	D. N. Patel and C. L. Cairns at Christchurch	1991-92
104	for 8th	D. A. R. Moloney and A. W. Roberts at Lord's	1937
118	for 9th	J. V. Coney and B. L. Cairns at Wellington	1983-84
106*	for 10th	N. J. Astle and D. K. Morrison at Auckland	1996-97

† *Denotes record partnership against all countries.*

TEN WICKETS OR MORE IN A MATCH

For England (8)

11-140 (6-101, 5-39)	I. T. Botham, Lord's	1978
10-149 (5-98, 5-51)	A. W. Greig, Auckland	1974-75
11-65 (4-14, 7-51)	G. A. R. Lock, Leeds	1958
11-84 (5-31, 6-53)	G. A. R. Lock, Christchurch	1958-59
11-147 (4-100, 7-47)†	P. C. R. Tufnell, Christchurch	1991-92
11-70 (4-38, 7-32)†	D. L. Underwood, Lord's	1969
12-101 (6-41, 6-60)	D. L. Underwood, The Oval	1969
12-97 (6-12, 6-85)	D. L. Underwood, Christchurch	1970-71

For New Zealand (5)

10-144 (7-74, 3-70)	B. L. Cairns, Leeds	1983
10-140 (4-73, 6-67)	J. Cowie, Manchester	1937
10-100 (4-74, 6-26)	R. J. Hadlee, Wellington	1977-78
10-140 (6-80, 4-60)	R. J. Hadlee, Nottingham	1986
11-169 (6-76, 5-93)	D. J. Nash, Lord's	1994

† *Signifies ten wickets or more on first appearance in England–New Zealand Tests.*

Note: D. L. Underwood took 12 wickets in successive matches against New Zealand in 1969 and 1970-71.

ENGLAND v INDIA

Captains

Season	England	India	T	E	I	D
1932	D. R. Jardine	C. K. Nayudu	1	1	0	0
1933-34	D. R. Jardine	C. K. Nayudu	3	2	0	1
1936	G. O. B. Allen	Maharaj of Vizianagram	3	2	0	1
1946	W. R. Hammond	Nawab of Pataudi sen.	3	1	0	2
1951-52	N. D. Howard[1]	V. S. Hazare	5	1	1	3
1952	L. Hutton	V. S. Hazare	4	3	0	1
1959	P. B. H. May[2]	D. K. Gaekwad[3]	5	5	0	0
1961-62	E. R. Dexter	N. J. Contractor	5	0	2	3
1963-64	M. J. K. Smith	Nawab of Pataudi jun.	5	0	0	5
1967	D. B. Close	Nawab of Pataudi jun.	3	3	0	0
1971	R. Illingworth	A. L. Wadekar	3	0	1	2
1972-73	A. R. Lewis	A. L. Wadekar	5	1	2	2
1974	M. H. Denness	A. L. Wadekar	3	3	0	0
1976-77	A. W. Greig	B. S. Bedi	5	3	1	1
1979	J. M. Brearley	S. Venkataraghavan	4	1	0	3
1979-80	J. M. Brearley	G. R. Viswanath	1	1	0	0
1981-82	K. W. R. Fletcher	S. M. Gavaskar	6	0	1	5
1982	R. G. D. Willis	S. M. Gavaskar	3	1	0	2
1984-85	D. I. Gower	S. M. Gavaskar	5	2	1	2
1986	M. W. Gatting[4]	Kapil Dev	3	0	2	1
1990	G. A. Gooch	M. Azharuddin	3	1	0	2
1992-93	G. A. Gooch[5]	M. Azharuddin	3	0	3	0
1996	M. A. Atherton	M. Azharuddin	3	1	0	2
	In England		41	22	3	16
	In India		43	10	11	22
	Totals.		84	32	14	38

Notes: The 1932 Indian touring team was captained by the Maharaj of Porbandar but he did not play in the Test match.

The following deputised for the official touring captain or were appointed by the home authority for only a minor proportion of the series:

[1]D. B. Carr (Fifth). [2]M. C. Cowdrey (Fourth and Fifth). [3]Pankaj Roy (Second). [4]D. I. Gower (First). [5]A. J. Stewart (Second).

HIGHEST INNINGS TOTALS

For England in England: 653-4 dec. at Lord's	1990
in India: 652-7 dec. at Madras	1984-85
For India in England: 606-9 dec. at The Oval	1990
in India: 591 at Bombay	1992-93

LOWEST INNINGS TOTALS

For England in England: 101 at The Oval	1971
in India: 102 at Bombay	1981-82
For India in England: 42 at Lord's	1974
in India: 83 at Madras	1976-77

INDIVIDUAL HUNDREDS

For England (76)

D. L. Amiss (2)
188 Lord's 1974
179 Delhi 1976-77
M. A. Atherton (2)
131 Manchester. . 1990
160 Nottingham . 1996
K. F. Barrington (3)
151* Bombay. . . . 1961-62
172 Kanpur 1961-62
113* Delhi 1961-62
I. T. Botham (5)
137 Leeds 1979
114 Bombay. . . . 1979-80
142 Kanpur 1981-82
128 Manchester. . 1982
208 The Oval . . . 1982
G. Boycott (4)
246*† Leeds 1967
155 Birmingham . 1979
125 The Oval . . . 1979
105 Delhi 1981-82
M. C. Cowdrey (3)
160 Leeds 1959
107 Calcutta. . . . 1963-64
151 Delhi 1963-64
M. H. Denness (2)
118 Lord's 1974
100 Birmingham . 1974
E. R. Dexter (1)
126* Kanpur 1961-62
B. L. D'Oliveira (1)
109† Leeds 1967
J. H. Edrich (1)
100* Manchester. . 1974
T. G. Evans (1)
104 Lord's 1952
K. W. R. Fletcher (2)
113 Bombay. . . . 1972-73
123* Manchester. . 1974

G. Fowler (1)
201 Madras 1984-85
M. W. Gatting (3)
136 Bombay. . . . 1984-85
207 Madras 1984-85
183* Birmingham . 1986
G. A. Gooch (5)
127 Madras 1981-82
114 Lord's 1986
333 } Lord's 1990
123 }
116 Manchester. . 1990
D. I. Gower (2)
200*† Birmingham . 1979
157* The Oval . . . 1990
T. W. Graveney (2)
175† Bombay. . . . 1951-52
151 Lord's 1967
A. W. Greig (3)
148 Bombay. . . . 1972-73
106 Lord's 1974
103 Calcutta. . . . 1976-77
W. R. Hammond (2)
167 Manchester. . 1936
217 The Oval . . . 1936
J. Hardstaff jun. (1)
205* Lord's 1946
G. A. Hick (1)
178 Bombay. . . . 1992-93
N. Hussain (2)
128† Birmingham . 1996
107* Nottingham . 1996
L. Hutton (2)
150 Lord's 1952
104 Manchester. . 1952
R. Illingworth (1)
107 Manchester. . 1971
B. R. Knight (1)
127 Kanpur 1963-64
A. J. Lamb (3)
107 The Oval . . . 1982

139 Lord's 1990
109 Manchester. . 1990
A. R. Lewis (1)
125 Kanpur 1972-73
C. C. Lewis (1)
117 Madras 1992-93
D. Lloyd (1)
214* Birmingham . 1974
B. W. Luckhurst (1)
101 Manchester. . 1971
P. B. H. May (1)
106 Nottingham . 1959
P. H. Parfitt (1)
121 Kanpur 1963-64
G. Pullar (2)
131 Manchester. . 1959
119 Kanpur 1961-62
D. W. Randall (1)
126 Lord's 1982
R. T. Robinson (1)
160 Delhi 1984-85
R. C. Russell (1)
124 Lord's 1996
D. S. Sheppard (1)
119 The Oval . . . 1952
M. J. K. Smith (1)
100† Manchester. . 1959
R. A. Smith (2)
100*† Lord's 1990
121* Lord's 1990
C. J. Tavaré (1)
149 Delhi 1981-82
B. H. Valentine (1)
136† Bombay. . . . 1933-34
C. F. Walters (1)
102 Madras 1933-34
A. J. Watkins (1)
137*† Delhi 1951-52
T. S. Worthington (1)
128 The Oval . . . 1936

For India (64)

L. Amarnath (1)
118† Bombay. . . . 1933-34
M. Azharuddin (6)
110† Calcutta. . . . 1984-85
105 Madras 1984-85
122 Kanpur 1984-85
121 Lord's 1990
179 Manchester. . 1990
182 Calcutta. . . . 1992-93
A. A. Baig (1)
112† Manchester. . 1959
F. M. Engineer (1)
121 Bombay. . . . 1972-73

S. C. Ganguly (2)
131† Lord's 1996
136 Nottingham . 1996
S. M. Gavaskar (4)
101 Manchester. . 1974
108 Bombay. . . . 1976-77
221 The Oval . . . 1979
172 Bangalore . . 1981-82
Hanumant Singh (1)
105† Delhi 1963-64
V. S. Hazare (2)
164* Delhi 1951-52
155 Bombay. . . . 1951-52

M. L. Jaisimha (2)
127 Delhi 1961-62
129 Calcutta. . . . 1963-64
V. G. Kambli (1)
224 Bombay. . . . 1992-93
Kapil Dev (2)
116 Kanpur 1981-82
110 The Oval . . . 1990
S. M. H. Kirmani (1)
102 Bombay. . . . 1984-85
B. K. Kunderan (2)
192 Madras 1963-64
100 Delhi 1963-64

V. L. Manjrekar (3)	**S. M. Patil** (1)	**P. R. Umrigar** (3)
133 Leeds 1952	129* Manchester. . 1982	130* Madras 1951-52
189* Delhi 1961-62	**D. G. Phadkar** (1)	118 Manchester. . 1959
108 Madras 1963-64	115 Calcutta. . . . 1951-52	147* Kanpur 1961-62
V. Mankad (1)	**Pankaj Roy** (2)	**D. B. Vengsarkar** (5)
184 Lord's 1952	140 Bombay. . . . 1951-52	103 Lord's 1979
V. M. Merchant (3)	111 Madras 1951-52	157 Lord's 1982
114 Manchester. . 1936	**R. J. Shastri** (4)	137 Kanpur 1984-85
128 The Oval . . . 1946	142 Bombay. . . . 1984-85	126* Lord's 1986
154 Delhi 1951-52	111 Calcutta. . . . 1984-85	102* Leeds 1986
Mushtaq Ali (1)	100 Lord's 1990	**G. R. Viswanath** (4)
112 Manchester. . 1936	187 The Oval . . . 1990	113 Bombay. . . . 1972-73
R. G. Nadkarni (1)	**N. S. Sidhu** (1)	113 Lord's 1979
122* Kanpur 1963-64	106 Madras 1992-93	107 Delhi 1981-82
Nawab of Pataudi jun. (3)	**S. R. Tendulkar** (4)	222 Madras 1981-82
103 Madras 1961-62	119* Manchester. . 1990	**Yashpal Sharma** (1)
203* Delhi 1963-64	165 Madras 1992-93	140 Madras 1981-82
148 Leeds 1967	122 Birmingham . 1996	
	177 Nottingham . 1996	

† *Signifies hundred on first appearance in England–India Tests.*

Notes: G. A. Gooch's match aggregate of 456 (333 and 123) for England at Lord's in 1990 is the record in Test matches and provides the only instance of a batsman scoring a triple-hundred and a hundred in the same first-class match. His 333 is the highest innings in any match at Lord's.

M. Azharuddin scored hundreds in each of his first three Tests.

RECORD PARTNERSHIPS FOR EACH WICKET

For England

225 for 1st	G. A. Gooch and M. A. Atherton at Manchester	1990
241 for 2nd	G. Fowler and M. W. Gatting at Madras	1984-85
308 for 3rd	G. A. Gooch and A. J. Lamb at Lord's	1990
266 for 4th	W. R. Hammond and T. S. Worthington at The Oval	1936
254 for 5th†	K. W. R. Fletcher and A. W. Greig at Bombay	1972-73
171 for 6th	I. T. Botham and R. W. Taylor at Bombay	1979-80
125 for 7th	D. W. Randall and P. H. Edmonds at Lord's	1982
168 for 8th	R. Illingworth and P. Lever at Manchester	1971
83 for 9th	K. W. R. Fletcher and N. Gifford at Madras	1972-73
70 for 10th	P. J. W. Allott and R. G. D. Willis at Lord's	1982

For India

213 for 1st	S. M. Gavaskar and C. P. S. Chauhan at The Oval	1979
192 for 2nd	F. M. Engineer and A. L. Wadekar at Bombay	1972-73
316 for 3rd†‡	G. R. Viswanath and Yashpal Sharma at Madras	1981-82
222 for 4th	V. S. Hazare and V. L. Manjrekar at Leeds	1952
214 for 5th†	M. Azharuddin and R. J. Shastri at Calcutta	1984-85
130 for 6th	S. M. H. Kirmani and Kapil Dev at The Oval	1982
235 for 7th†	R. J. Shastri and S. M. H. Kirmani at Bombay	1984-85
128 for 8th	R. J. Shastri and S. M. H. Kirmani at Delhi	1981-82
104 for 9th	R. J. Shastri and Madan Lal at Delhi	1981-82
51 for 10th	{ R. G. Nadkarni and B. S. Chandrasekhar at Calcutta	1963-64
	{ S. M. H. Kirmani and Chetan Sharma at Madras	1984-85

† *Denotes record partnership against all countries.*

‡ *415 runs were added between the fall of the 2nd and 3rd wickets: D. B. Vengsarkar retired hurt when he and Viswanath had added 99 runs.*

TEN WICKETS OR MORE IN A MATCH

For England (7)

10-78 (5-35, 5-43)†	G. O. B. Allen, Lord's	1936
11-145 (7-49, 4-96)†	A. V. Bedser, Lord's	1946
11-93 (4-41, 7-52)	A. V. Bedser, Manchester	1946
13-106 (6-58, 7-48)	I. T. Botham, Bombay	1979-80
11-163 (6-104, 5-59)†	N. A. Foster, Madras	1984-85
10-70 (7-46, 3-24)†	J. K. Lever, Delhi	1976-77
11-153 (7-49, 4-104)	H. Verity, Madras	1933-34

For India (4)

10-177 (6-105, 4-72)	S. A. Durani, Madras	1961-62
12-108 (8-55, 4-53)	V. Mankad, Madras	1951-52
10-188 (4-130, 6-58)	Chetan Sharma, Birmingham	1986
12-181 (6-64, 6-117)†	L. Sivaramakrishnan, Bombay	1984-85

† *Signifies ten wickets or more on first appearance in England–India Tests.*

Note: A. V. Bedser took 11 wickets in a match in each of the first two Tests of his career.

ENGLAND v PAKISTAN

		Captains				
Season	England	Pakistan	T	E	P	D
1954	L. Hutton[1]	A. H. Kardar	4	1	1	2
1961-62	E. R. Dexter	Imtiaz Ahmed	3	1	0	2
1962	E. R. Dexter[2]	Javed Burki	5	4	0	1
1967	D. B. Close	Hanif Mohammad	3	2	0	1
1968-69	M. C. Cowdrey	Saeed Ahmed	3	0	0	3
1971	R. Illingworth	Intikhab Alam	3	1	0	2
1972-73	A. R. Lewis	Majid Khan	3	0	0	3
1974	M. H. Denness	Intikhab Alam	3	0	0	3
1977-78	J. M. Brearley[3]	Wasim Bari	3	0	0	3
1978	J. M. Brearley	Wasim Bari	3	2	0	1
1982	R. G. D. Willis[4]	Imran Khan	3	2	1	0
1983-84	R. G. D. Willis[5]	Zaheer Abbas	3	0	1	2
1987	M. W. Gatting	Imran Khan	5	0	1	4
1987-88	M. W. Gatting	Javed Miandad	3	0	1	2
1992	G. A. Gooch	Javed Miandad	5	1	2	2
1996	M. A. Atherton	Wasim Akram	3	0	2	1
	In England		37	13	7	17
	In Pakistan		18	1	2	15
	Totals.		55	14	9	32

Notes: The following deputised for the official touring captain or were appointed by the home authority for only a minor proportion of the series:

[1]D. S. Sheppard (Second and Third). [2]M. C. Cowdrey (Third). [3]G. Boycott (Third). [4]D. I. Gower (Second). [5]D. I. Gower (Second and Third).

HIGHEST INNINGS TOTALS

For England in England: 558-6 dec. at Nottingham	1954
in Pakistan: 546-8 dec. at Faisalabad	1983-84
For Pakistan in England: 708 at The Oval	1987
in Pakistan: 569-9 dec. at Hyderabad.	1972-73

LOWEST INNINGS TOTALS

For England in England: 130 at The Oval 1954
           in Pakistan: 130 at Lahore 1987-88

For Pakistan in England: 87 at Lord's 1954
           in Pakistan: 191 at Faisalabad 1987-88

INDIVIDUAL HUNDREDS

For England (47)

D. L. Amiss (3)
112   Lahore   1972-73
158   Hyderabad . .   1972-73
183   The Oval . . .   1974
C. W. J. Athey (1)
123   Lord's   1987
K. F. Barrington (4)
139†   Lahore   1961-62
148   Lord's   1967
109*   Nottingham .   1967
142   The Oval . . .   1967
I. T. Botham (2)
100†   Birmingham .   1978
108   Lord's   1978
G. Boycott (3)
121*   Lord's   1971
112   Leeds   1971
100*   Hyderabad . .   1977-78
B. C. Broad (1)
116   Faisalabad . .   1987-88
D. C. S. Compton (1)
278   Nottingham . .   1954
M. C. Cowdrey (3)
159†   Birmingham .   1962
182   The Oval . . .   1962
100   Lahore   1968-69

J. P. Crawley (1)
106   The Oval . . .   1996
E. R. Dexter (2)
205   Karachi   1961-62
172   The Oval . . .   1962
B. L. D'Oliveira (1)
114*   Dacca   1968-69
K. W. R. Fletcher (1)
122   The Oval . . .   1974
M. W. Gatting (2)
124   Birmingham .   1987
150*   The Oval . . .   1987
G. A. Gooch (1)
135   Leeds   1992
D. I. Gower (2)
152   Faisalabad . .   1983-84
173*   Lahore   1983-84
T. W. Graveney (3)
153   Lord's   1962
114   Nottingham .   1962
105   Karachi   1968-69
N. V. Knight (1)
113   Leeds   1996
A. P. E. Knott (1)
116   Birmingham .   1971

B. W. Luckhurst (1)
108*†   Birmingham .   1971
C. Milburn (1)
139   Karachi   1968-69
P. H. Parfitt (4)
111   Karachi   1961-62
101*   Birmingham .   1962
119   Leeds   1962
101*   Nottingham .   1962
G. Pullar (1)
165   Dacca   1961-62
C. T. Radley (1)
106†   Birmingham .   1978
D. W. Randall (1)
105   Birmingham .   1982
R. T. Robinson (1)
166†   Manchester . .   1987
R. T. Simpson (1)
101   Nottingham .   1954
R. A. Smith (1)
127†   Birmingham .   1992
A. J. Stewart (2)
190†   Birmingham .   1992
170   Leeds   1996

For Pakistan (38)

Aamir Sohail (1)
205   Manchester . .   1992
Alim-ud-Din (1)
109   Karachi   1961-62
Asif Iqbal (3)
146   The Oval . . .   1967
104*   Birmingham .   1971
102   Lahore   1972-73
Hanif Mohammad (3)
111 ⎫
104 ⎬ Dacca   1961-62
187*   Lord's   1967
Haroon Rashid (2)
122†   Lahore   1977-78
108   Hyderabad . .   1977-78

Ijaz Ahmed, sen. (1)
141   Leeds   1996
Imran Khan (1)
118   The Oval . . .   1987
Intikhab Alam (1)
138   Hyderabad . .   1972-73
Inzamam-ul-Haq (1)
148   Lord's   1996
Javed Burki (3)
138†   Lahore   1961-62
140   Dacca   1961-62
101   Lord's   1962
Javed Miandad (2)
260   The Oval . . .   1987
153*   Birmingham .   1992

Mohsin Khan (2)
200   Lord's   1982
104   Lahore   1983-84
Moin Khan (1)
105   Leeds   1996
Mudassar Nazar (3)
114†   Lahore   1977-78
124   Birmingham .   1987
120   Lahore   1987-88
Mushtaq Mohammad (3)
100*   Nottingham .   1962
100   Birmingham .   1971
157   Hyderabad . .   1972-73
Nasim-ul-Ghani (1)
101   Lord's   1962

Sadiq Mohammad (1)		102	The Oval...	1987	**Zaheer Abbas** (2)	
119 Lahore	1972-73	165	Birmingham.	1992	274† Birmingham.	1971
Saeed Anwar (1)		100*	The Oval...	1996	240 The Oval...	1974
176 The Oval...	1996	**Wasim Raja** (1)				
Salim Malik (4)		112	Faisalabad .. 1983-84			
116 Faisalabad .. 1983-84						

    † *Signifies hundred on first appearance in England–Pakistan Tests.*

Note: Three batsmen – Majid Khan, Mushtaq Mohammad and D. L. Amiss – were dismissed for 99 at Karachi, 1972-73: the only instance in Test matches.

RECORD PARTNERSHIPS FOR EACH WICKET

For England

198	for 1st	G. Pullar and R. W. Barber at Dacca	1961-62
248	for 2nd	M. C. Cowdrey and E. R. Dexter at The Oval	1962
227	for 3rd	A. J. Stewart and R. A. Smith at Birmingham	1992
188	for 4th	E. R. Dexter and P. H. Parfitt at Karachi	1961-62
192	for 5th	D. C. S. Compton and T. E. Bailey at Nottingham.	1954
153*	for 6th	P. H. Parfitt and D. A. Allen at Birmingham.	1962
167	for 7th	D. I. Gower and V. J. Marks at Faisalabad	1983-84
99	for 8th	P. H. Parfitt and D. A. Allen at Leeds	1962
76	for 9th	T. W. Graveney and F. S. Trueman at Lord's.	1962
79	for 10th	R. W. Taylor and R. G. D. Willis at Birmingham.	1982

For Pakistan

173	for 1st	Mohsin Khan and Shoaib Mohammad at Lahore.	1983-84
291	for 2nd†	Zaheer Abbas and Mushtaq Mohammad at Birmingham	1971
180	for 3rd	Mudassar Nazar and Haroon Rashid at Lahore	1977-78
322	for 4th	Javed Miandad and Salim Malik at Birmingham	1992
197	for 5th	Javed Burki and Nasim-ul-Ghani at Lord's.	1962
145	for 6th	Mushtaq Mohammad and Intikhab Alam at Hyderabad.	1972-73
112	for 7th	Asif Mujtaba and Moin Khan at Leeds	1996
130	for 8th	Hanif Mohammad and Asif Iqbal at Lord's	1967
190	for 9th†	Asif Iqbal and Intikhab Alam at The Oval	1967
62	for 10th	Sarfraz Nawaz and Asif Masood at Leeds	1974

    † *Denotes record partnership against all countries.*

TEN WICKETS OR MORE IN A MATCH

For England (2)

11-83 (6-65, 5-18)†	N. G. B. Cook, Karachi.......................	1983-84
13-71 (5-20, 8-51)	D. L. Underwood, Lord's	1974

For Pakistan (6)

10-194 (5-84, 5-110)	Abdul Qadir, Lahore	1983-84
10-211 (7-96, 3-115)	Abdul Qadir, The Oval	1987
13-101 (9-56, 4-45)	Abdul Qadir, Lahore	1987-88
10-186 (5-88, 5-98)	Abdul Qadir, Karachi	1987-88
12-99 (6-53, 6-46)	Fazal Mahmood, The Oval	1954
10-77 (3-37, 7-40)	Imran Khan, Leeds	1987

    † *Signifies ten wickets or more on first appearance in England–Pakistan Tests.*

ENGLAND v SRI LANKA

	Captains					
Season	*England*	*Sri Lanka*	*T*	*E*	*SL*	*D*
1981-82	K. W. R. Fletcher	B. Warnapura	1	1	0	0
1984	D. I. Gower	L. R. D. Mendis	1	0	0	1
1988	G. A. Gooch	R. S. Madugalle	1	1	0	0
1991	G. A. Gooch	P. A. de Silva	1	1	0	0
1992-93	A. J. Stewart	A. Ranatunga	1	0	1	0
1998	A. J. Stewart	A. Ranatunga	1	0	1	0
	In England		4	2	1	1
	In Sri Lanka		2	1	1	0
	Totals.		6	3	2	1

HIGHEST INNINGS TOTALS

For England in England: 445 at The Oval		1998
in Sri Lanka: 380 at Colombo (SSC).		1992-93
For Sri Lanka in England: 591 at The Oval		1998
in Sri Lanka: 469 at Colombo (SSC).		1992-93

LOWEST INNINGS TOTALS

For England in England: 181 at The Oval		1998
in Sri Lanka: 223 at Colombo (PSS).		1981-82
For Sri Lanka in England: 194 at Lord's		1988
in Sri Lanka: 175 at Colombo (PSS).		1981-82

INDIVIDUAL HUNDREDS

For England (6)

J. P. Crawley (1)	**G. A. Hick** (1)	**R. A. Smith** (1)
156*† The Oval . . . 1998	107 The Oval . . . 1998	128 Colombo (SSC) 1992-93
G. A. Gooch (1)	**A. J. Lamb** (1)	**A. J. Stewart** (1)
174 Lord's 1991	107† Lord's 1984	113*† Lord's 1991

For Sri Lanka (5)

P. A. de Silva (1)	**L. R. D. Mendis** (1)	**S. Wettimuny** (1)
152 The Oval . . . 1998	111 Lord's 1984	190 Lord's 1984
S. T. Jayasuriya (1)	**S. A. R. Silva** (1)	
213 The Oval . . . 1998	102*† Lord's 1984	

† *Signifies hundred on first appearance in England–Sri Lanka Tests.*

RECORD PARTNERSHIPS FOR EACH WICKET

For England

78 for 1st	G. A. Gooch and H. Morris at Lord's	1991
139 for 2nd	G. A. Gooch and A. J. Stewart at Lord's	1991
112 for 3rd	R. A. Smith and G. A. Hick at Colombo (SSC)	1992-93
128 for 4th	G. A. Hick and M. R. Ramprakash at The Oval	1998
40 for 5th	A. J. Stewart and I. T. Botham at Lord's	1991
87 for 6th	A. J. Lamb and R. M. Ellison at Lord's.	1984
63 for 7th	A. J. Stewart and R. C. Russell at Lord's	1991
20 for 8th	J. E. Emburey and P. W. Jarvis at Colombo (SSC).	1992-93
37 for 9th	P. J. Newport and N. A. Foster at Lord's	1988
89 for 10th	J. P. Crawley and A. R. C. Fraser at The Oval	1998

For Sri Lanka

99 for 1st	R. S. Mahanama and U. C. Hathurusinghe at Colombo (SSC)	1992-93
83 for 2nd	B. Warnapura and R. L. Dias at Colombo (PSS).	1981-82
243 for 3rd†	S. T. Jayasuriya and P. A. de Silva at The Oval.	1998
148 for 4th	S. Wettimuny and A. Ranatunga at Lord's	1984
150 for 5th†	S. Wettimuny and L. R. D. Mendis at Lord's	1984
138 for 6th	S. A. R. Silva and L. R. D. Mendis at Lord's	1984
74 for 7th	U. C. Hathurusinghe and R. J. Ratnayake at Lord's	1991
29 for 8th	R. J. Ratnayake and C. P. H. Ramanayake at Lord's.	1991
83 for 9th†	H. P. Tillekeratne and M. Muralitharan at Colombo (SSC)	1992-93
64 for 10th	J. R. Ratnayeke and G. F. Labrooy at Lord's.	1988

† *Denotes record partnership against all countries.*

TEN WICKETS OR MORE IN A MATCH

For Sri Lanka (1)

16-220 (7-155, 9-65)	M. Muralitharan at The Oval	1998

Note: The best match figures by an England bowler are 8-95 (5-28, 3-67) by D. L. Underwood at Colombo (PSS), 1981-82.

ENGLAND v ZIMBABWE

	Captains					
Season	England	Zimbabwe	T	E	Z	D
1996-97	M. A. Atherton	A. D. R. Campbell	2	0	0	2
2000	N. Hussain	A. Flower	2	1	0	1
	In England		2	1	0	1
	In Zimbabwe.		2	0	0	2
	Totals.		4	1	0	3

HIGHEST INNINGS TOTALS

For England in England: 415 at Lord's	2000
in Zimbabwe: 406 at Bulawayo.	1996-97
For Zimbabwe in England: 285-4 dec. at Nottingham	2000
in Zimbabwe: 376 at Bulawayo	1996-97

LOWEST INNINGS TOTALS

For England in England: 147 at Nottingham   2000
          in Zimbabwe 156 at Harare   1996-97

For Zimbabwe in England: 83 at Lord's   2000
          in Zimbabwe: 215 at Harare   1996-97

INDIVIDUAL HUNDREDS

For England (6)

M. A. Atherton (1)
136   Nottingham .   2000

J. P. Crawley (1)
112†   Bulawayo. . .   1996-97

G. Hick (1)
101†   Lord's   2000

N. Hussain (1)
113†   Bulawayo. . .   1996-97

A. J. Stewart (2)
101*   Harare.   1996-97
124*   Lord's   2000

For Zimbabwe (2)

A. Flower (1)
112†   Bulawayo. . .   1996-97

M. W. Goodwin (1)
148*   Nottingham .   2000

   † *Signifies hundred on first appearance in England–Zimbabwe Tests.*

HUNDRED PARTNERSHIPS

For England

121	for 1st	M. A. Atherton and M. R. Ramprakash at Nottingham	2000
137	for 2nd	N. V. Knight and A. J. Stewart at Bulawayo	1996-97
149	for 4th	G. A. Hick and A. J. Stewart at Lord's	2000
106*	for 4th	A. J. Stewart and G. P. Thorpe at Harare	1996-97
148	for 5th	N. Hussain and J. P. Crawley at Bulawayo	1996-97
114	for 5th	A. J. Stewart and N. V. Knight at Lord's	2000

For Zimbabwe

127	for 2nd	G. W. Flower and A. D. R. Campbell at Bulawayo.	1996-97
129	for 3rd	M. W. Goodwin and N. C. Johnson at Nottingham	2000
122	for 4th	M. W. Goodwin and A. Flower at Nottingham	2000

BEST MATCH BOWLING ANALYSES

For England

7-42 (5-15, 2-27)†   E. S. H. Giddins, Lord's   2000

For Zimbabwe

7-186 (5-123, 2-63)†   P. A. Strang, Bulawayo.   1996-97

   † *Signifies on first appearance in England–Zimbabwe Tests.*

AUSTRALIA v SOUTH AFRICA

	Captains					
Season	*Australia*	*South Africa*	*T*	*A*	*SA*	*D*
1902-03*S*	J. Darling	H. M. Taberer[1]	3	2	0	1
1910-11*A*	C. Hill	P. W. Sherwell	5	4	1	0
1912*E*	S. E. Gregory	F. Mitchell[2]	3	2	0	1
1921-22*S*	H. L. Collins	H. W. Taylor	3	1	0	2
1931-32*A*	W. M. Woodfull	H. B. Cameron	5	5	0	0
1935-36*S*	V. Y. Richardson	H. F. Wade	5	4	0	1
1949-50*S*	A. L. Hassett	A. D. Nourse	5	4	0	1
1952-53*A*	A. L. Hassett	J. E. Cheetham	5	2	2	1
1957-58*S*	I. D. Craig	C. B. van Ryneveld[3]	5	3	0	2
1963-64*A*	R. B. Simpson[4]	T. L. Goddard	5	1	1	3
1966-67*S*	R. B. Simpson	P. L. van der Merwe	5	1	3	1
1969-70*S*	W. M. Lawry	A. Bacher	4	0	4	0
1993-94*A*	A. R. Border	K. C. Wessels[5]	3	1	1	1
1993-94*S*	A. R. Border	K. C. Wessels	3	1	1	1
1996-97*S*	M. A. Taylor	W. J. Cronje	3	2	1	0
1997-98*A*	M. A. Taylor	W. J. Cronje	3	1	0	2
	In South Africa		36	18	9	9
	In Australia		26	14	5	7
	In England		3	2	0	1
	Totals		65	34	14	17

S Played in South Africa.   A Played in Australia.   E Played in England.

Notes: The following deputised for the official touring captain or were appointed by the home authority for only a minor proportion of the series:
[1]J. H. Anderson (Second), E. A. Halliwell (Third). [2]L. J. Tancred (Third). [3]D. J. McGlew (First). [4]R. Benaud (First). [5]W. J. Cronje (Third).

HIGHEST INNINGS TOTALS

For Australia in Australia: 578 at Melbourne		1910-11
in South Africa: 628-8 dec. at Johannesburg		1996-97
For South Africa in Australia: 595 at Adelaide		1963-64
in South Africa: 622-9 dec. at Durban		1969-70

LOWEST INNINGS TOTALS

For Australia in Australia: 111 at Sydney		1993-94
in South Africa: 75 at Durban		1949-50
For South Africa in Australia: 36† at Melbourne		1931-32
in South Africa: 85‡ at Johannesburg		1902-03
85‡ at Cape Town		1902-03

† *Scored 45 in the second innings giving the smallest aggregate of 81 (12 extras) in Test cricket.*
‡ *In successive innings.*

INDIVIDUAL HUNDREDS

For Australia (65)

W. W. Armstrong (2)
159*‡ Johannesburg 1902-03
132 Melbourne . . 1910-11

W. Bardsley (3)
132† Sydney 1910-11
121 Manchester. . 1912
164 Lord's 1912

R. Benaud (2)
122 Johannesburg 1957-58
100 Johannesburg 1957-58

G. S. Blewett (1)
214† Johannesburg 1996-97

B. C. Booth (2)
169† Brisbane . . . 1963-64
102* Sydney 1963-64

D. G. Bradman (4)
226† Brisbane . . . 1931-32
112 Sydney 1931-32
167 Melbourne . . 1931-32
299* Adelaide . . . 1931-32

W. A. Brown (1)
121 Cape Town. . 1935-36

J. W. Burke (1)
189 Cape Town. . 1957-58

A. G. Chipperfield (1)
109† Durban 1935-36

H. L. Collins (1)
203 Johannesburg 1921-22

J. H. Fingleton (3)
112 Cape Town. . 1935-36
108 Johannesburg 1935-36
118 Durban 1935-36

J. M. Gregory (1)
119 Johannesburg 1921-22

R. N. Harvey (8)
178 Cape Town. . 1949-50
151* Durban 1949-50
100 Johannesburg 1949-50
116 Port Elizabeth 1949-50
109 Brisbane . . . 1952-53
190 Sydney 1952-53
116 Adelaide . . . 1952-53
205 Melbourne . . 1952-53

A. L. Hassett (3)
112† Johannesburg 1949-50
167 Port Elizabeth 1949-50
163 Adelaide . . . 1952-53

C. Hill (3)
142† Johannesburg 1902-03
191 Sydney 1910-11
100 Melbourne . . 1910-11

C. Kelleway (2)
114 Manchester. . 1912
102 Lord's 1912

W. M. Lawry (1)
157 Melbourne . . 1963-64

S. J. E. Loxton (1)
101† Johannesburg 1949-50

C. G. Macartney (2)
137 Sydney 1910-11
116 Durban 1921-22

S. J. McCabe (2)
149 Durban 1935-36
189* Johannesburg 1935-36

C. C. McDonald (1)
154 Adelaide . . . 1952-53

J. Moroney (2)
118 ⎫
101*⎭ Johannesburg 1949-50

A. R. Morris (2)
111 Johannesburg 1949-50
157 Port Elizabeth 1949-50

R. T. Ponting (1)
105† Melbourne . . 1997-98

K. E. Rigg (1)
127† Sydney 1931-32

J. Ryder (1)
142 Cape Town. . 1921-22

R. B. Simpson (1)
153 Cape Town. . 1966-67

K. R. Stackpole (1)
134 Cape Town. . 1966-67

M. A. Taylor (2)
170† Melbourne . . 1993-94
169*‡ Adelaide . . . 1997-98

V. T. Trumper (2)
159 Melbourne . . 1910-11
214* Adelaide . . . 1910-11

M. E. Waugh (4)
113* Durban 1993-94
116 Port Elizabeth 1996-97
100 Sydney 1997-98
115* Adelaide . . . 1997-98

S. R. Waugh (2)
164† Adelaide . . . 1993-94
160 Johannesburg 1996-97

W. M. Woodfull (1)
161 Melbourne . . 1931-32

For South Africa (40)

E. J. Barlow (5)
114† Brisbane . . . 1963-64
109 Melbourne . . 1963-64
201 Adelaide . . . 1963-64
127 Cape Town. . 1969-70
110 Johannesburg 1969-70

K. C. Bland (1)
126 Sydney 1963-64

W. J. Cronje (1)
122 Johannesburg 1993-94

W. R. Endean (1)
162* Melbourne . . 1952-53

G. A. Faulkner (3)
204 Melbourne . . 1910-11
115 Adelaide . . . 1910-11
122* Manchester. . 1912

C. N. Frank (1)
152 Johannesburg 1921-22

A. C. Hudson (1)
102 Cape Town. . 1993-94

B. L. Irvine (1)
102 Port Elizabeth 1969-70

J. H. Kallis (1)
101 Melbourne . . 1997-98

G. Kirsten (1)
108* Adelaide . . . 1997-98

D. T. Lindsay (3)
182 Johannesburg 1966-67
137 Durban 1966-67
131 Johannesburg 1966-67

D. J. McGlew (2)
108 Johannesburg 1957-58

105 Durban 1957-58

A. D. Nourse (2)
231 Johannesburg 1935-36
114 Cape Town. . 1949-50

A. W. Nourse (1)
111 Johannesburg 1921-22

R. G. Pollock (5)
122 Sydney 1963-64
175 Adelaide . . . 1963-64
209 Cape Town. . 1966-67
105 Port Elizabeth 1966-67
274 Durban 1969-70

B. A. Richards (2)
140 Durban 1969-70
126 Port Elizabeth 1969-70

E. A. B. Rowan (1)		**S. J. Snooke** (1)		134	Durban 1957-58
143	Durban 1949-50	103	Adelaide . . . 1910-11	**J. W. Zulch** (2)	
J. H. Sinclair (2)		**K. G. Viljoen** (1)		105	Adelaide . . . 1910-11
101	Johannesburg 1902-03	111	Melbourne . . 1931-32	150	Sydney 1910-11
104	Cape Town. . 1902-03	**J. H. B. Waite** (1)			
		115	Johannesburg 1957-58		

† *Signifies hundred on first appearance in Australia–South Africa Tests.*
‡ *Carried his bat.*

RECORD PARTNERSHIPS FOR EACH WICKET

For Australia

233 for 1st	J. H. Fingleton and W. A. Brown at Cape Town	1935-36
275 for 2nd	C. C. McDonald and A. L. Hassett at Adelaide.	1952-53
242 for 3rd	C. Kelleway and W. Bardsley at Lord's	1912
169 for 4th	M. A. Taylor and M. E. Waugh at Melbourne	1993-94
385 for 5th	S. R. Waugh and G. S. Blewett at Johannesburg	1996-97
108 for 6th	S. R. Waugh and I. A. Healy at Cape Town	1993-94
160 for 7th	R. Benaud and G. D. McKenzie at Sydney	1963-64
83 for 8th	A. G. Chipperfield and C. V. Grimmett at Durban	1935-36
78 for 9th	{ D. G. Bradman and W. J. O'Reilly at Adelaide	1931-32
	{ K. D. Mackay and I. Meckiff at Johannesburg	1957-58
82 for 10th	V. S. Ransford and W. J. Whitty at Melbourne	1910-11

For South Africa

176 for 1st	D. J. McGlew and T. L. Goddard at Johannesburg	1957-58
173 for 2nd	L. J. Tancred and C. B. Llewellyn at Johannesburg	1902-03
341 for 3rd†	E. J. Barlow and R. G. Pollock at Adelaide	1963-64
206 for 4th	C. N. Frank and A. W. Nourse at Johannesburg	1921-22
129 for 5th	J. H. B. Waite and W. R. Endean at Johannesburg	1957-58
200 for 6th†	R. G. Pollock and H. R. Lance at Durban	1969-70
221 for 7th	D. T. Lindsay and P. L. van der Merwe at Johannesburg	1966-67
124 for 8th	A. W. Nourse and E. A. Halliwell at Johannesburg	1902-03
85 for 9th	R. G. Pollock and P. M. Pollock at Cape Town	1966-67
74 for 10th	B. M. McMillan and P. L. Symcox at Adelaide	1997-98

† *Denotes record partnership against all countries.*

TEN WICKETS OR MORE IN A MATCH

For Australia (7)

14-199 (7-116, 7-83)	C. V. Grimmett, Adelaide	1931-32
10-88 (5-32, 5-56)	C. V. Grimmett, Cape Town	1935-36
10-110 (3-70, 7-40)	C. V. Grimmett, Johannesburg	1935-36
13-173 (7-100, 6-73)	C. V. Grimmett, Durban	1935-36
11-24 (5-6, 6-18)	H. Ironmonger, Melbourne	1931-32
12-128 (7-56, 5-72)	S. K. Warne, Sydney	1993-94
11-109 (5-75, 6-34)	S. K. Warne, Sydney	1997-98

For South Africa (3)

10-123 (4-80, 6-43)	P. S. de Villiers, Sydney.	1993-94
10-116 (5-43, 5-73)	C. B. Llewellyn, Johannesburg.	1902-03
13-165 (6-84, 7-81)	H. J. Tayfield, Melbourne	1952-53

Note: C. V. Grimmett took ten wickets or more in three consecutive matches in 1935-36.

AUSTRALIA v WEST INDIES

Captains

Season	Australia	West Indies	T	A	WI	T	D
1930-31*A*	W. M. Woodfull	G. C. Grant	5	4	1	0	0
1951-52*A*	A. L. Hassett[1]	J. D. C. Goddard[2]	5	4	1	0	0
1954-55*W*	I. W. Johnson	D. St E. Atkinson[3]	5	3	0	0	2

THE FRANK WORRELL TROPHY

Captains

Season	Australia	West Indies	T	A	WI	T	D	Held by
1960-61*A*	R. Benaud	F. M. M. Worrell	5	2	1	1	1	A
1964-65*W*	R. B. Simpson	G. S. Sobers	5	1	2	0	2	WI
1968-69*A*	W. M. Lawry	G. S. Sobers	5	3	1	0	1	A
1972-73*W*	I. M. Chappell	R. B. Kanhai	5	2	0	0	3	A
1975-76*A*	G. S. Chappell	C. H. Lloyd	6	5	1	0	0	A
1977-78*W*	R. B. Simpson	A. I. Kallicharran[4]	5	1	3	0	1	WI
1979-80*A*	G. S. Chappell	C. H. Lloyd[5]	3	0	2	0	1	WI
1981-82*A*	G. S. Chappell	C. H. Lloyd	3	1	1	0	1	WI
1983-84*W*	K. J. Hughes	C. H. Lloyd[6]	5	0	3	0	2	WI
1984-85*A*	A. R. Border[7]	C. H. Lloyd	5	1	3	0	1	WI
1988-89*A*	A. R. Border	I. V. A. Richards	5	1	3	0	1	WI
1990-91*W*	A. R. Border	I. V. A. Richards	5	1	2	0	2	WI
1992-93*A*	A. R. Border	R. B. Richardson	5	1	2	0	2	WI
1994-95*W*	M. A. Taylor	R. B. Richardson	4	2	1	0	1	A
1996-97*A*	M. A. Taylor	C. A. Walsh	5	3	2	0	0	A
1998-99*W*	S. R. Waugh	B. C. Lara	4	2	2	0	0	A

			T	A	WI	T	D
In Australia...................			52	25	18	1	8
In West Indies...............			38	12	13	0	13
Totals			90	37	31	1	21

A Played in Australia.   W Played in West Indies.

Notes: The following deputised for the official touring captain or were appointed by the home authority for only a minor proportion of the series:
[1]A. R. Morris (Third). [2]J. B. Stollmeyer (Fifth). [3]J. B. Stollmeyer (Second and Third). [4]C. H. Lloyd (First and Second). [5]D. L. Murray (First). [6]I. V. A. Richards (Second). [7]K. J. Hughes (First and Second).

HIGHEST INNINGS TOTALS

For Australia in Australia: 619 at Sydney............................... 1968-69
                in West Indies: 758-8 dec. at Kingston 1954-55

For West Indies in Australia: 616 at Adelaide 1968-69
                in West Indies: 573 at Bridgetown 1964-65

LOWEST INNINGS TOTALS

For Australia in Australia: 76 at Perth.................................. 1984-85
                in West Indies: 90 at Port-of-Spain......................... 1977-78

For West Indies in Australia: 78 at Sydney.............................. 1951-52
                in West Indies: 51 at Port-of-Spain 1998-99

INDIVIDUAL HUNDREDS

For Australia (83)

R. G. Archer (1)
128 Kingston . . . 1954-55
R. Benaud (1)
121 Kingston . . . 1954-55
D. C. Boon (3)
149 Sydney 1988-89
109* Kingston . . 1990-91
111 Brisbane . . . 1992-93
B. C. Booth (1)
117 Port-of-Spain 1964-65
A. R. Border (3)
126 Adelaide . . . 1981-82
100* Port-of-Spain 1983-84
110 Melbourne . . 1992-93
D. G. Bradman (2)
223 Brisbane . . . 1930-31
152 Melbourne . . 1930-31
G. S. Chappell (5)
106 Bridgetown . 1972-73
123 ⎱‡Brisbane . . . 1975-76
109* ⎰
182* Sydney 1975-76
124 Brisbane . . . 1979-80
I. M. Chappell (5)
117† Brisbane . . 1968-69
165 Melbourne . . 1968-69
106* Bridgetown . 1972-73
109 Georgetown . 1972-73
156 Perth. 1975-76
G. J. Cosier (1)
109† Melbourne . . 1975-76
R. M. Cowper (2)
143 Port-of-Spain 1964-65
102 Bridgetown . 1964-65
J. Dyson (1)
127*† Sydney 1981-82
R. N. Harvey (3)
133 Kingston . . . 1954-55
133 Port-of-Spain 1954-55
204 Kingston . . . 1954-55
A. L. Hassett (2)
132 Sydney 1951-52

102 Melbourne . . 1951-52
M. L. Hayden (1)
125 Adelaide . . . 1996-97
I. A. Healy (1)
161* Brisbane . . . 1996-97
A. M. J. Hilditch (1)
113† Melbourne . . 1984-85
K. J. Hughes (2)
130*† Brisbane . . . 1979-80
100* Melbourne . . 1981-82
D. M. Jones (1)
216 Adelaide . . . 1988-89
A. F. Kippax (1)
146† Adelaide . . . 1930-31
J. L. Langer (1)
127 St John's . . . 1998-99
W. M. Lawry (4)
210 Bridgetown . 1964-65
105 Brisbane . . . 1968-69
205 Melbourne . . 1968-69
151 Sydney 1968-69
R. R. Lindwall (1)
118 Bridgetown . 1954-55
R. B. McCosker (1)
109* Melbourne . . 1975-76
C. C. McDonald (2)
110 Port-of-Spain 1954-55
127 Kingston . . . 1954-55
K. R. Miller (4)
129 Sydney 1951-52
147 Kingston . . . 1954-55
137 Bridgetown . 1954-55
109 Kingston . . . 1954-55
A. R. Morris (1)
111 Port-of-Spain 1954-55
N. C. O'Neill (1)
181† Brisbane . . . 1960-61
W. B. Phillips (1)
120 Bridgetown . 1983-84
W. H. Ponsford (2)
183 Sydney 1930-31
109 Brisbane . . . 1930-31

R. T. Ponting (1)
104 Bridgetown . 1998-99
I. R. Redpath (4)
132 Sydney 1968-69
102 Melbourne . . 1975-76
103 Adelaide . . . 1975-76
101 Melbourne . . 1975-76
C. S. Serjeant (1)
124 Georgetown . 1977-78
R. B. Simpson (1)
201 Bridgetown . 1964-65
M. J. Slater (1)
106 Port-of-Spain 1998-99
K. R. Stackpole (1)
142 Kingston . . . 1972-73
M. A. Taylor (1)
144 St John's . . . 1990-91
P. M. Toohey (1)
122 Kingston . . . 1977-78
A. Turner (1)
136 Adelaide . . . 1975-76
K. D. Walters (6)
118 Sydney 1968-69
110 Adelaide . . . 1968-69
242 ⎱ Sydney . . . 1968-69
103 ⎰
102* Bridgetown . 1972-73
112 Port-of-Spain 1972-73
M. E. Waugh (3)
139* St John's . . . 1990-91
112 Melbourne . . 1992-93
126 Kingston . . . 1994-95
S. R. Waugh (4)
100 Sydney 1992-93
200 Kingston . . . 1994-95
100 Kingston . . . 1998-99
199 Bridgetown . 1998-99
K. C. Wessels (1)
173 Sydney 1984-85
G. M. Wood (2)
126 Georgetown . 1977-78
111 Perth. 1988-89

For West Indies (85)

F. C. M. Alexander (1)
108 Sydney 1960-61
K. L. T. Arthurton (1)
157*† Brisbane . . . 1992-93
D. St E. Atkinson (1)
219 Bridgetown . 1954-55
B. F. Butcher (3)
117 Port-of-Spain 1964-65
101 Sydney 1968-69
118 Adelaide . . . 1968-69

S. L. Campbell (2)
113 Brisbane . . . 1996-97
105 Bridgetown . 1998-99
C. C. Depeiza (1)
122 Bridgetown . 1954-55
P. J. L. Dujon (2)
130 Port-of-Spain 1983-84
139 Perth. 1984-85
M. L. C. Foster (1)
125† Kingston . . . 1972-73

R. C. Fredericks (1)
169 Perth. 1975-76
H. A. Gomes (6)
101† Georgetown . 1977-78
115 Kingston . . . 1977-78
126 Sydney 1981-82
124* Adelaide . . . 1981-82
127 Perth. 1984-85
120* Adelaide . . . 1984-85

C. G. Greenidge (4)

120*	Georgetown .	1983-84
127	Kingston . . .	1983-84
104	Adelaide . . .	1988-89
226	Bridgetown .	1990-91

D. L. Haynes (5)

103*	Georgetown .	1983-84
145	Bridgetown .	1983-84
100	Perth.	1988-89
143	Sydney	1988-89
111	Georgetown .	1990-91

G. A. Headley (2)

102*	Brisbane . . .	1930-31
105	Sydney	1930-31

C. L. Hooper (1)

102	Brisbane . . .	1996-97

C. C. Hunte (1)

110	Melbourne . .	1960-61

A. I. Kallicharran (4)

101	Brisbane . . .	1975-76
127	Port-of-Spain	1977-78
126	Kingston . . .	1977-78
106	Adelaide . . .	1979-80

R. B. Kanhai (5)

117	} Adelaide . . .	1960-61
115		
129	Bridgetown .	1964-65
121	Port-of-Spain	1964-65
105	Bridgetown .	1972-73

B. C. Lara (5)

277	Sydney	1992-93
132	Perth.	1996-97
213	Kingston . . .	1998-99
100	St John's . . .	1998-99
153*	Bridgetown .	1998-99

C. H. Lloyd (6)

129†	Brisbane . . .	1968-69
178	Georgetown .	1972-73
149	Perth.	1975-76
102	Melbourne . .	1975-76
121	Adelaide . . .	1979-80
114	Brisbane . . .	1984-85

F. R. Martin (1)

123*	Sydney	1930-31

S. M. Nurse (2)

201	Bridgetown .	1964-65
137	Sydney	1968-69

I. V. A. Richards (5)

101	Adelaide . . .	1975-76
140	Brisbane . . .	1979-80
178	St John's . . .	1983-84
208	Melbourne . .	1984-85
146	Perth.	1988-89

R. B. Richardson (9)

131*	Bridgetown .	1983-84
154	St John's . . .	1983-84
138	Brisbane . . .	1984-85
122	Melbourne . .	1988-89
106	Adelaide . . .	1988-89

104*	Kingston . . .	1990-91
182	Georgetown .	1990-91
109	Sydney	1992-93
100	Kingston . . .	1994-95

L. G. Rowe (1)

107	Brisbane . . .	1975-76

P. V. Simmons (1)

110	Melbourne . .	1992-93

O. G. Smith (1)

104†	Kingston . . .	1954-55

G. S. Sobers (4)

132	Brisbane . . .	1960-61
168	Sydney	1960-61
110	Adelaide . . .	1968-69
113	Sydney	1968-69

J. B. Stollmeyer (1)

104	Sydney	1951-52

C. L. Walcott (5)

108	Kingston . . .	1954-55
126	} Port-of-Spain	1954-55
110		
155	} Kingston . . .	1954-55
110		

E. D. Weekes (1)

139	Port-of-Spain	1954-55

A. B. Williams (1)

100†	Georgetown .	1977-78

F. M. M. Worrell (1)

108	Melbourne . .	1951-52

† *Signifies hundred on first appearance in Australia–West Indies Tests.*
‡ *G. S. Chappell is the only player to score hundreds in both innings of his first Test as captain.*

Note: F. C. M. Alexander and C. C. Depeiza scored the only hundreds of their first-class careers in a Test match.

RECORD PARTNERSHIPS FOR EACH WICKET

For Australia

382 for 1st†	W. M. Lawry and R. B. Simpson at Bridgetown	1964-65
298 for 2nd	W. M. Lawry and I. M. Chappell at Melbourne	1968-69
295 for 3rd†	C. C. McDonald and R. N. Harvey at Kingston	1954-55
336 for 4th	W. M. Lawry and K. D. Walters at Sydney	1968-69
281 for 5th	S. R. Waugh and R. T. Ponting at Bridgetown	1998-99
206 for 6th	K. R. Miller and R. G. Archer at Bridgetown.	1954-55
134 for 7th	A. K. Davidson and R. Benaud at Brisbane	1960-61
137 for 8th	R. Benaud and I. W. Johnson at Kingston	1954-55
114 for 9th	D. M. Jones and M. G. Hughes at Adelaide	1988-89
97 for 10th	T. G. Hogan and R. M. Hogg at Georgetown	1983-84

For West Indies

250*	for 1st	C. G. Greenidge and D. L. Haynes at Georgetown.	1983-84
297	for 2nd	D. L. Haynes and R. B. Richardson at Georgetown	1990-91
308	for 3rd	R. B. Richardson and I. V. A. Richards at St John's.	1983-84
198	for 4th	L. G. Rowe and A. I. Kallicharran at Brisbane	1975-76
322	for 5th†‡	B. C. Lara and J. C. Adams at Kingston	1998-99
165	for 6th	R. B. Kanhai and D. L. Murray at Bridgetown	1972-73
347	for 7th†	D. St E. Atkinson and C. C. Depeiza at Bridgetown	1954-55
87	for 8th	P. J. L. Dujon and C. E. L. Ambrose at Port-of-Spain	1990-91
122	for 9th	D. A. J. Holford and J. L. Hendriks at Adelaide	1968-69
56	for 10th	J. Garner and C. E. H. Croft at Brisbane.	1979-80

† *Denotes record partnership against all countries.*

‡ *344 runs were added between the fall of the 4th and 5th wickets: P. T. Collins retired hurt when he and Lara had added 22 runs.*

TEN WICKETS OR MORE IN A MATCH

For Australia (13)

10-113 (4-31, 6-82)	M. G. Bevan, Adelaide	1996-97
11-96 (7-46, 4-50)	A. R. Border, Sydney	1988-89
11-222 (5-135, 6-87)†	A. K. Davidson, Brisbane	1960-61
11-183 (7-87, 4-96)†	C. V. Grimmett, Adelaide	1930-31
10-115 (6-72, 4-43)	N. J. N. Hawke, Georgetown	1964-65
10-144 (6-54, 4-90)	R. G. Holland, Sydney.	1984-85
13-217 (5-130, 8-87)	M. G. Hughes, Perth	1988-89
11-79 (7-23, 4-56)	H. Ironmonger, Melbourne	1930-31
11-181 (8-112, 3-69)	G. F. Lawson, Adelaide	1984-85
10-127 (7-83, 3-44)	D. K. Lillee, Melbourne	1981-82
10-78 (5-50, 5-28)	G. D. McGrath, Port-of-Spain	1998-99
10-159 (8-71, 2-88)	G. D. McKenzie, Melbourne	1968-69
10-185 (3-87, 7-98)	B. Yardley, Sydney	1981 82

For West Indies (4)

10-120 (6-74, 4-46)	C. E. L. Ambrose, Adelaide	1992-93
10-113 (7-55, 3-58)	G. E. Gomez, Sydney	1951-52
11-107 (5-45, 6-62)	M. A. Holding, Melbourne	1981-82
10-107 (5-69, 5-38)	M. D. Marshall, Adelaide	1984-85

† *Signifies ten wickets or more on first appearance in Australia–West Indies Tests.*

AUSTRALIA v NEW ZEALAND

Captains

Season	Australia	New Zealand	T	A	NZ	D
1945-46*N*	W. A. Brown	W. A. Hadlee	1	1	0	0
1973-74*A*	I. M. Chappell	B. E. Congdon	3	2	0	1
1973-74*N*	I. M. Chappell	B. E. Congdon	3	1	1	1
1976-77*N*	G. S. Chappell	G. M. Turner	2	1	0	1
1980-81*A*	G. S. Chappell	G. P. Howarth[1]	3	2	0	1
1981-82*N*	G. S. Chappell	G. P. Howarth	3	1	1	1

TRANS-TASMAN TROPHY

Season	Australia	Captains	New Zealand	T	A	NZ	D	Held by
1985-86*A*	A. R. Border		J. V. Coney	3	1	2	0	NZ
1985-86*N*	A. R. Border		J. V. Coney	3	0	1	2	NZ
1987-88*A*	A. R. Border		J. J. Crowe	3	1	0	2	A
1989-90*A*	A. R. Border		J. G. Wright	1	0	0	1	A
1989-90*N*	A. R. Border		J. G. Wright	1	0	1	0	NZ
1992-93*N*	A. R. Border		M. D. Crowe	3	1	1	1	NZ
1993-94*A*	A. R. Border		M. D. Crowe[2]	3	2	0	1	A
1997-98*A*	M. A. Taylor		S. P. Fleming	3	2	0	1	A
1999-2000*N*	S. R. Waugh		S. P. Fleming	3	3	0	0	A
	In Australia			19	10	2	7	
	In New Zealand			19	8	5	6	
	Totals			38	18	7	13	

A Played in Australia.   N Played in New Zealand.

Note: The following deputised for the official touring captain: [1]M. G. Burgess (Second). [2]K. R. Rutherford (Second and Third).

HIGHEST INNINGS TOTALS

For Australia in Australia: 607-6 dec. at Brisbane	....	1993-94
in New Zealand: 552 at Christchurch	....	1976-77
For New Zealand in Australia: 553-7 dec. at Brisbane	....	1985-86
in New Zealand: 484 at Wellington	....	1973-74

LOWEST INNINGS TOTALS

For Australia in Australia: 162 at Sydney	....	1973-74
in New Zealand: 103 at Auckland	....	1985-86
For New Zealand in Australia: 121 at Perth	....	1980-81
in New Zealand: 42 at Wellington	....	1945-46

INDIVIDUAL HUNDREDS

For Australia (35)

D. C. Boon (3)
143   Brisbane . . .   1987-88
200   Perth.   1989-90
106   Hobart   1993-94

A. R. Border (5)
152*   Brisbane . .   1985-86
140 }
114*} Christchurch.   1985-86
205   Adelaide . . .   1987-88
105   Brisbane . . .   1993-94

G. S. Chappell (3)
247*}
133 } Wellington . .   1973-74
176   Christchurch.   1981-82

I. M. Chappell (2)
145 }
121 } Wellington . .   1973-74

M. T. G. Elliott (1)
114   Hobart   1997-98

G. J. Gilmour (1)
101   Christchurch.   1976-77

I. A. Healy (1)
113*   Perth.   1993-94

J. L. Langer (1)
122*   Hamilton . . .   1999-00

G. R. Marsh (1)
118   Auckland . . .   1985-86

R. W. Marsh (1)
132   Adelaide . . .   1973-74

G. R. J. Matthews (2)
115†   Brisbane . . .   1985-86
130   Wellington . .   1985-86

I. R. Redpath (1)
159*‡   Auckland. . .   1973-74

M. J. Slater (2)
168   Hobart   1993-94

143   Wellington .   1999-00

K. R. Stackpole (1)
122†   Melbourne . .   1973-74

M. A. Taylor (2)
142*   Perth.   1993-94
112   Brisbane . . .   1997-98

K. D. Walters (3)
104*   Auckland. . .   1973-74
250   Christchurch.   1976-77
107   Melbourne . .   1980-81

M. E. Waugh (1)
111   Hobart   1993-94

S. R. Waugh (2)
147*   Brisbane . . .   1993-94
151*   Wellington . .   1999-00

G. M. Wood (2)
111†   Brisbane . . .   1980-81
100   Auckland. . .   1981-82

For New Zealand (21)

C. L. Cairns (1)	**M. J. Greatbatch** (1)	**J. F. Reid** (1)
109 Wellington . . 1999-00	146*† Perth. 1989-90	108† Brisbane . . . 1985-86
J. V. Coney (1)	**B. F. Hastings** (1)	**K. R. Rutherford** (1)
101* Wellington . . 1985-86	101 Wellington . . 1973-74	102 Christchurch . 1992-93
B. E. Congdon (2)	**M. J. Horne** (1)	**G. M. Turner** (2)
132 Wellington . . 1973-74	133† Hobart 1997-98	101 ⎫
107* Christchurch . 1976-77	**A. H. Jones** (2)	110*⎭ Christchurch . 1973-74
M. D. Crowe (3)	150 Adelaide . . . 1987-88	**J. G. Wright** (2)
188 Brisbane . . . 1985-86	143 Perth. 1993-94	141 Christchurch . 1981-82
137 Christchurch . 1985-86	**J. F. M. Morrison** (1)	117* Wellington . . 1989-90
137 Adelaide . . . 1987-88	117 Sydney 1973-74	
B. A. Edgar (1)	**J. M. Parker** (1)	
161 Auckland. . . 1981-82	108 Sydney 1973-74	

   † *Signifies hundred on first appearance in Australia–New Zealand Tests.*
   ‡ *Carried his bat.*

Notes: G. S. and I. M. Chappell at Wellington in 1973-74 provide the only instance in Test matches of brothers both scoring a hundred in each innings and in the same Test.

RECORD PARTNERSHIPS FOR EACH WICKET

For Australia

198 for 1st	M. J. Slater and M. A. Taylor at Perth.	1993-94
235 for 2nd	M. J. Slater and D. C. Boon at Hobart.	1993-94
264 for 3rd	I. M. Chappell and G. S. Chappell at Wellington	1973-74
153 for 4th	M. E. Waugh and S. R. Waugh at Perth.	1997-98
213 for 5th	G. M. Ritchie and G. R. J. Matthews at Wellington	1985-86
197 for 6th	A. R. Border and G. R. J. Matthews at Brisbane	1985-86
217 for 7th†	K. D. Walters and G. J. Gilmour at Christchurch	1976-77
93 for 8th	G. J. Gilmour and K. J. O'Keeffe at Auckland	1976-77
69 for 9th	I. A. Healy and C. J. McDermott at Perth.	1993-94
60 for 10th	K. D. Walters and J. D. Higgs at Melbourne	1980-81

For New Zealand

111 for 1st	M. J. Greatbatch and J. G. Wright at Wellington	1992-93
132 for 2nd	M. J. Horne and A. C. Parore at Hobart.	1997-98
224 for 3rd	J. F. Reid and M. D. Crowe at Brisbane	1985-86
229 for 4th	B. E. Congdon and B. F. Hastings at Wellington	1973-74
88 for 5th	J. V. Coney and M. G. Burgess at Perth	1980-81
110 for 6th	S. P. Fleming and C. L. Cairns at Wellington	1999-2000
132* for 7th	J. V. Coney and R. J. Hadlee at Wellington	1985-86
88* for 8th	M. J. Greatbatch and M. C. Snedden at Perth	1989-90
73 for 9th	H. J. Howarth and D. R. Hadlee at Christchurch	1976-77
124 for 10th	J. G. Bracewell and S. L. Boock at Sydney	1985-86

   † *Denotes record partnership against all countries.*

TEN WICKETS OR MORE IN A MATCH

For Australia (2)

10-174 (6-106, 4-68)	R. G. Holland, Sydney	1985-86
11-123 (5-51, 6-72)	D. K. Lillee, Auckland	1976-77

For New Zealand (5)

10-106 (4-74, 6-32)	J. G. Bracewell, Auckland	1985-86
15-123 (9-52, 6-71)	R. J. Hadlee, Brisbane	1985-86
11-155 (5-65, 6-90)	R. J. Hadlee, Perth	1985-86
10-176 (5-109, 5-67)	R. J. Hadlee, Melbourne	1987-88
12-149 (5-62, 7-87)	D. L. Vettori, Auckland	1999-2000

AUSTRALIA v INDIA

Captains

Season	Australia	India	T	A	I	T	D
1947-48*A*	D. G. Bradman	L. Amarnath	5	4	0	0	1
1956-57*I*	I. W. Johnson[1]	P. R. Umrigar	3	2	0	0	1
1959-60*I*	R. Benaud	G. S. Ramchand	5	2	1	0	2
1964-65*I*	R. B. Simpson	Nawab of Pataudi jun.	3	1	1	0	1
1967-68*A*	R. B. Simpson[2]	Nawab of Pataudi jun.[3]	4	4	0	0	0
1969-70*I*	W. M. Lawry	Nawab of Pataudi jun.	5	3	1	0	1
1977-78*A*	R. B. Simpson	B. S. Bedi	5	3	2	0	0
1979-80*I*	K. J. Hughes	S. M. Gavaskar	6	0	2	0	4
1980-81*A*	G. S. Chappell	S. M. Gavaskar	3	1	1	0	1
1985-86*A*	A. R. Border	Kapil Dev	3	0	0	0	3
1986-87*I*	A. R. Border	Kapil Dev	3	0	0	1	2
1991-92*A*	A. R. Border	M. Azharuddin	5	4	0	0	1
1996-97*I*	M. A. Taylor	S. R. Tendulkar	1	0	1	0	0
1997-98*I*	M. A. Taylor	M. Azharuddin	3	1	2	0	0
1999-2000*A*	S. R. Waugh	S. R. Tendulkar	3	3	0	0	0
	In Australia		28	19	3	0	6
	In India		29	9	8	1	11
	Totals		57	28	11	1	17

A Played in Australia. I Played in India.

Notes: The following deputised for the official touring captain or were appointed by the home authority for only a minor proportion of the series:

[1]R. R. Lindwall (Second). [2]W. M. Lawry (Third and Fourth). [3]C. G. Borde (First).

HIGHEST INNINGS TOTALS

For Australia in Australia: 674 at Adelaide	1947-48
in India: 574-7 dec. at Madras	1986-87
For India in Australia: 600-4 dec. at Sydney	1985-86
in India: 633-5 dec. at Calcutta	1997-98

LOWEST INNINGS TOTALS

For Australia in Australia: 83 at Melbourne	1980-81
in India: 105 at Kanpur	1959-60
For India in Australia: 58 at Brisbane	1947-48
in India: 135 at Delhi	1959-60

INDIVIDUAL HUNDREDS

For Australia (57)

S. G. Barnes (1)
112   Adelaide . . . 1947-48

D. C. Boon (6)
123† Adelaide . . . 1985-86
131   Sydney 1985-86
122   Madras . . . 1986-87
129* Sydney 1991-92
135   Adelaide . . . 1991-92
107   Perth. 1991-92

A. R. Border (4)
162† Madras . . . 1979-80
124   Melbourne . . 1980-81
163   Adelaide . . . 1985-86
106   Madras . . . 1986-87

D. G. Bradman (4)
185† Brisbane . . . 1947-48
132   ⎫
127* ⎬ Melbourne . . 1947-48
201   Adelaide . . . 1947-48

J. W. Burke (1)
161   Bombay. . . . 1956-57

G. S. Chappell (1)
204† Sydney 1980-81

I. M. Chappell (2)
151   Melbourne . . 1967-68
138   Delhi 1969-70

R. M. Cowper (2)
108   Adelaide . . . 1967-68
165   Sydney 1967-68

L. E. Favell (1)
101   Madras 1959-60

R. N. Harvey (4)
153   Melbourne . . 1947-48
140   Bombay. . . . 1956-57
114   Delhi 1959-60
102   Bombay. . . . 1959-60

A. L. Hassett (1)
198* Adelaide . . . 1947-48

K. J. Hughes (2)
100   Madras . . . 1979-80
213   Adelaide . . . 1980-81

D. M. Jones (2)
210† Madras . . . 1986-87
150* Perth. 1991-92

J. L. Langer (1)
223   Sydney 1999-00

W. M. Lawry (1)
100   Melbourne . . 1967-68

A. L. Mann (1)
105   Perth. 1977-78

G. R. Marsh (1)
101   Bombay. . . . 1986-87

G. R. J. Matthews (1)
100* Melbourne . . 1985-86

T. M. Moody (1)
101† Perth. 1991-92

A. R. Morris (1)
100* Melbourne . . 1947-48

N. C. O'Neill (2)
163   Bombay. . . . 1959-60
113   Calcutta. . . . 1959-60

R. T. Ponting (2)
125   Adelaide . . . 1999-00
141* Sydney 1999-00

G. M. Ritchie (1)
128† Adelaide . . . 1985-86

A. P. Sheahan (1)
114   Kanpur . . . 1969-70

R. B. Simpson (4)
103   Adelaide . . . 1967-68
109   Melbourne . . 1967-68
176   Perth. 1977-78
100   Adelaide . . . 1977-78

K. R. Stackpole (1)
103† Bombay. . . . 1969-70

M. A. Taylor (2)
100   Adelaide . . . 1991-92
102* Bangalore . . 1997-98

K. D. Walters (1)
102   Madras . . . 1969-70

M. E. Waugh (1)
153* Bangalore . . 1997-98

S. R. Waugh (1)
150   Adelaide . . . 1999-00

G. M. Wood (1)
125   Adelaide . . . 1980-81

G. N. Yallop (1)
121† Adelaide . . . 1977-78
167   Calcutta. . . . 1979-80

For India (41)

M. Amarnath (2)
100   Perth. 1977-78
138   Sydney 1985-86

M. Azharuddin (2)
106   Adelaide . . . 1991-92
163* Calcutta. . . . 1997-98

N. J. Contractor (1)
108   Bombay. . . . 1959-60

S. M. Gavaskar (8)
113† Brisbane . . . 1977-78
127   Perth. 1977-78
118   Melbourne . . 1977-78
115   Delhi 1979-80
123   Bombay. . . . 1979-80
166* Adelaide . . . 1985-86
172   Sydney 1985-86
103   Bombay. . . . 1986-87

V. S. Hazare (2)
116 ⎫
145 ⎬ Adelaide . . . 1947-48

M. L. Jaisimha (1)
101   Brisbane . . . 1967-68

Kapil Dev (1)
119   Madras . . . 1986-87

S. M. H. Kirmani (1)
101* Bombay. . . . 1979-80

V. V. S. Laxman (1)
167   Sydney 1999-00

V. Mankad (2)
116   Melbourne . . 1947-48
111   Melbourne . . 1947-48

N. R. Mongia (1)
152† Delhi 1996-97

Nawab of Pataudi jun. (1)
128*† Madras . . . 1964-65

S. M. Patil (1)
174   Adelaide . . . 1980-81

D. G. Phadkar (1)
123   Adelaide . . . 1947-48

G. S. Ramchand (1)
109   Bombay. . . . 1956-57

R. J. Shastri (2)
121* Bombay. . . . 1986-87
206   Sydney 1991-92

K. Srikkanth (1)
116   Sydney 1985-86

S. R. Tendulkar (5)
148* Sydney 1991-92
114   Perth. 1991-92
155* Chennai. . . . 1997-98
177   Bangalore . . 1997-98
116   Melbourne . . 1999-00

D. B. Vengsarkar (2)
112   Bangalore . . 1979-80
164* Bombay. . . . 1986-87

G. R. Viswanath (4)
137† Kanpur 1969-70
161* Bangalore . . 1979-80
131   Delhi 1979-80
114   Melbourne . . 1980-81

Yashpal Sharma (1)
100* Delhi 1979-80

† *Signifies hundred on first appearance in Australia–India Tests.*

RECORD PARTNERSHIPS FOR EACH WICKET

For Australia

217	for 1st	D. C. Boon and G. R. Marsh at Sydney.................	1985-86
236	for 2nd	S. G. Barnes and D. G. Bradman at Adelaide	1947-48
222	for 3rd	A. R. Border and K. J. Hughes at Madras	1979-80
178	for 4th	D. M. Jones and A. R. Border at Madras	1986-87
239	for 5th	S. R. Waugh and R. T. Ponting at Adelaide.............	1999-2000
151	for 6th	T. R. Veivers and B. N. Jarman at Bombay.............	1964-65
108	for 7th	S. R. Waugh and S. K. Warne at Adelaide.............	1999-2000
73	for 8th	T. R. Veivers and G. D. McKenzie at Madras	1964-65
96	for 9th	I. A. Healy and G. R. Robertson at Chennai.............	1997-98
77	for 10th	A. R. Border and D. R. Gilbert at Melbourne	1985-86

For India

192	for 1st	S. M. Gavaskar and C. P. S. Chauhan at Bombay............	1979-80
224	for 2nd	S. M. Gavaskar and M. Amarnath at Sydney.............	1985-86
159	for 3rd	S. M. Gavaskar and G. R. Viswanath at Delhi.............	1979-80
159	for 4th	D. B. Vengsarkar and G. R. Viswanath at Bangalore.........	1979-80
196	for 5th	R. J. Shastri and S. R. Tendulkar at Sydney	1991-92
298*	for 6th†	D. B. Vengsarkar and R. J. Shastri at Bombay.............	1986-87
132	for 7th	V. S. Hazare and H. R. Adhikari at Adelaide.............	1947-48
127	for 8th	S. M. H. Kirmani and K. D. Ghavri at Bombay.............	1979-80
81	for 9th	S. R. Tendulkar and K. S. More at Perth	1991-92
94	for 10th	S. M. Gavaskar and N. S. Yadav at Adelaide.............	1985-86

† *Denotes record partnership against all countries.*

TEN WICKETS OR MORE IN A MATCH

For Australia (12)

11-105 (6-52, 5-53)	R. Benaud, Calcutta.....................	1956-57
12-124 (5-31, 7-93)	A. K. Davidson, Kanpur.....................	1959-60
12-166 (5-99, 7-67)	G. Dymock, Kanpur.....................	1979-80
10-168 (5-76, 5-92)	C. J. McDermott, Adelaide.....................	1991-92
10-103 (5-48, 5-55)	G. D. McGrath, Sydney	1999-2000
10-91 (6-58, 4-33)†	G. D. McKenzie, Madras	1964-65
10-151 (7-66, 3-85)	G. D. McKenzie, Melbourne	1967-68
10-144 (5-91, 5-53)	A. A. Mallett, Madras	1969-70
10-249 (5-103, 5-146)	G. R. J. Matthews, Madras	1986-87
12-126 (6-66, 6-60)	B. A. Reid, Melbourne	1991-92
11-31 (5-2, 6-29)†	E. R. H. Toshack, Brisbane	1947-48
11-95 (4-68, 7-27)	M. R. Whitney, Perth	1991-92

For India (6)

10-194 (5-89, 5-105)	B. S. Bedi, Perth.....................	1977-78
12-104 (6-52, 6-52)	B. S. Chandrasekhar, Melbourne.................	1977-78
10-130 (7-49, 3-81)	Ghulam Ahmed, Calcutta.....................	1956-57
11-122 (5-31, 6-91)	R. G. Nadkarni, Madras	1964-65
14-124 (9-69, 5-55)	J. M. Patel, Kanpur	1959-60
10-174 (4-100, 6-74)	E. A. S. Prasanna, Madras.....................	1969-70

† *Signifies ten wickets or more on first appearance in Australia–India Tests.*

AUSTRALIA v PAKISTAN

Season	Australia	Pakistan	T	A	P	D
		Captains				
1956-57P	I. W. Johnson	A. H. Kardar	1	0	1	0
1959-60P	R. Benaud	Fazal Mahmood[1]	3	2	0	1
1964-65P	R. B. Simpson	Hanif Mohammad	1	0	0	1
1964-65A	R. B. Simpson	Hanif Mohammad	1	0	0	1
1972-73A	I. M. Chappell	Intikhab Alam	3	3	0	0
1976-77A	G. S. Chappell	Mushtaq Mohammad	3	1	1	1
1978-79A	G. N. Yallop[2]	Mushtaq Mohammad	2	1	1	0
1979-80P	G. S. Chappell	Javed Miandad	3	0	1	2
1981-82A	G. S. Chappell	Javed Miandad	3	2	1	0
1982-83P	K. J. Hughes	Imran Khan	3	0	3	0
1983-84A	K. J. Hughes	Imran Khan[3]	5	2	0	3
1988-89P	A. R. Border	Javed Miandad	3	0	1	2
1989-90A	A. R. Border	Imran Khan	3	1	0	2
1994-95P	M. A. Taylor	Salim Malik	3	0	1	2
1995-96A	M. A. Taylor	Wasim Akram	3	2	1	0
1998-99P	M. A. Taylor	Aamir Sohail	3	1	0	2
1999-2000A	S. R. Waugh	Wasim Akram	3	3	0	0
	In Pakistan		20	3	7	10
	In Australia		26	15	4	7
	Totals		46	18	11	17

A Played in Australia. P Played in Pakistan.

Notes: The following deputised for the official touring captain or were appointed by the home authority for only a minor proportion of the series:
[1]Imtiaz Ahmed (Second). [2]K. J. Hughes (Second). [3]Zaheer Abbas (First, Second and Third).

HIGHEST INNINGS TOTALS

For Australia in Australia: 585 at Adelaide 1972-73
in Pakistan: 617 at Faisalabad 1979-80

For Pakistan in Australia: 624 at Adelaide 1983-84
in Pakistan: 580-9 dec. at Peshawar. 1998-99

LOWEST INNINGS TOTALS

For Australia in Australia: 125 at Melbourne. 1981-82
in Pakistan: 80 at Karachi. 1956-57

For Pakistan in Australia: 62 at Perth 1981-82
in Pakistan: 134 at Dacca 1959-60

INDIVIDUAL HUNDREDS

For Australia (53)

J. Benaud (1)
142   Melbourne . . 1972-73

D. C. Boon (1)
114* Karachi 1994-95

A. R. Border (6)
105† Melbourne . . 1978-79
150* } Lahore 1979-80
153 }
118   Brisbane . . . 1983-84
117* Adelaide . . . 1983-84
113* Faisalabad . . 1988-89

G. S. Chappell (6)
116* Melbourne . . 1972-73
121   Melbourne . . 1976-77
235   Faisalabad . . 1979-80
201   Brisbane . . . 1981-82
150* Brisbane . . . 1983-84
182   Sydney 1983-84

I. M. Chappell (1)
196   Adelaide . . . 1972-73

G. J. Cosier (1)
168   Melbourne . . 1976-77

I. C. Davis (1)
105† Adelaide . . . 1976-77

A. C. Gilchrist (1)
149* Hobart 1999-00

K. J. Hughes (2)
106   Perth. 1981-82

106   Adelaide . . . 1983-84

D. M. Jones (2)
116 }
121* } Adelaide . . . 1989-90

J. L. Langer (3)
116   Peshawar . . . 1998-99
127   Hobart 1999-00
144   Perth. 1999-00

R. B. McCosker (1)
105   Melbourne . . 1976-77

R. W. Marsh (1)
118† Adelaide . . . 1972-73

N. C. O'Neill (1)
134   Lahore 1959-60

W. B. Phillips (1)
159† Perth. 1983-84

R. T. Ponting (1)
197   Perth. 1999-00

I. R. Redpath (1)
135   Melbourne . . 1972-73

G. M. Ritchie (1)
106* Faisalabad . . 1982-83

A. P. Sheahan (1)
127   Melbourne . . 1972-73

R. B. Simpson (2)
153 }
115 }†Karachi 1964-65

M. J. Slater (3)
110   Rawalpindi . . 1994-95
108   Rawalpindi . . 1998-99
169   Brisbane . . . 1999-00

M. A. Taylor (4)
101† Melbourne . . 1989-90
101* Sydney 1989-90
123   Hobart 1995-96
334* Peshawar . . . 1998-99

K. D. Walters (1)
107   Adelaide . . . 1976-77

M. E. Waugh (3)
116   Sydney 1995-96
117   Karachi 1998-99
100   Brisbane . . . 1999-00

S. R. Waugh (2)
112* Brisbane . . . 1995-96
157   Rawalpindi . . 1998-99

K. C. Wessels (1)
179   Adelaide . . . 1983-84

G. M. Wood (1)
100   Melbourne . . 1981-82

G. N. Yallop (3)
172   Faisalabad . . 1979-80
141   Perth. 1983-84
268   Melbourne . . 1983-84

For Pakistan (44)

Aamir Sohail (2)
105   Lahore 1994-95
133   Karachi 1998-99

Asif Iqbal (3)
152* Adelaide . . . 1976-77
120   Sydney 1976-77
134* Perth. 1978-79

Hanif Mohammad (2)
101* Karachi 1959-60
104   Melbourne . . 1964-65

Ijaz Ahmed, sen. (6)
122   Faisalabad . . 1988-89
121   Melbourne . . 1989-90
137   Sydney 1995-96
155   Peshawar . . . 1998-99
120* Karachi 1998-99
115   Perth. 1999-00

Imran Khan (1)
136   Adelaide . . . 1989-90

Inzamam-ul-Haq (1)
118   Hobart 1999-00

Javed Miandad (6)
129* Perth. 1978-79

106* Faisalabad . . 1979-80
138   Lahore 1982-83
131   Adelaide . . . 1983-84
211   Karachi 1988-89
107   Faisalabad . . 1988-89

Khalid Ibadulla (1)
166† Karachi 1964-65

Majid Khan (3)
158   Melbourne . . 1972-73
108   Melbourne . . 1978-79
110* Lahore 1979-80

Mansoor Akhtar (1)
111   Faisalabad . . 1982-83

Mohsin Khan (3)
135   Lahore 1982-83
149   Adelaide . . . 1983-84
152   Melbourne . . 1983-84

Moin Khan (1)
115*† Lahore 1994-95

Mushtaq Mohammad (1)
121   Sydney 1972-73

Qasim Omar (1)
113   Adelaide . . . 1983-84

Sadiq Mohammad (2)
137   Melbourne . . 1972-73
105   Melbourne . . 1976-77

Saeed Ahmed (1)
166   Lahore 1959-60

Saeed Anwar (3)
145   Rawalpindi . . 1998-99
126   Peshawar . . . 1998-99
119   Brisbane . . . 1999-00

Salim Malik (2)
237   Rawalpindi . . 1994-95
143   Lahore 1994-95

Taslim Arif (1)
210* Faisalabad . . 1979-80

Wasim Akram (1)
123   Adelaide . . . 1989-90

Zaheer Abbas (2)
101   Adelaide . . . 1976-77
126   Faisalabad . . 1982-83

† *Signifies hundred on first appearance in Australia–Pakistan Tests.*

RECORD PARTNERSHIPS FOR EACH WICKET

For Australia

269 for 1st	M. J. Slater and G. S. Blewett at Brisbane	1999-2000
279 for 2nd	M. A. Taylor and J. L. Langer at Peshawar	1998-99
203 for 3rd	G. N. Yallop and K. J. Hughes at Melbourne.	1983-84
217 for 4th	G. S. Chappell and G. N. Yallop at Faisalabad.	1979-80
327 for 5th	J. L. Langer and R. T. Ponting at Perth	1999-2000
238 for 6th	J. L. Langer and A. C. Gilchrist at Hobart.	1999-2000
185 for 7th	G. N. Yallop and G. R. J. Matthews at Melbourne	1983-84
117 for 8th	G. J. Cosier and K. J. O'Keeffe at Melbourne	1976-77
83 for 9th	J. R. Watkins and R. A. L. Massie at Sydney	1972-73
86 for 10th	S. K. Warne and S. A. Muller at Brisbane	1999-2000

For Pakistan

249 for 1st	Khalid Ibadulla and Abdul Kadir at Karachi	1964-65
233 for 2nd	Mohsin Khan and Qasim Omar at Adelaide	1983-84
223* for 3rd	Taslim Arif and Javed Miandad at Faisalabad	1979-80
177 for 4th	Saeed Anwar and Yousuf Youhana at Brisbane.	1999-2000
186 for 5th	Javed Miandad and Salim Malik at Adelaide.	1983-84
196 for 6th	Salim Malik and Aamir Sohail at Lahore	1994-95
104 for 7th	Intikhab Alam and Wasim Bari at Adelaide	1972-73
111 for 8th	Majid Khan and Imran Khan at Lahore	1979-80
120 for 9th	Saeed Anwar and Mushtaq Ahmed at Rawalpindi.	1998-99
87 for 10th	Asif Iqbal and Iqbal Qasim at Adelaide	1976-77

TEN WICKETS OR MORE IN A MATCH

For Australia (4)

10-111 (7-87, 3-24)†	R. J. Bright, Karachi	1979-80
10-135 (6-82, 4-53)	D. K. Lillee, Melbourne	1976-77
11-118 (5-32, 6-86)†	C. G. Rackemann, Perth	1983-84
11-77 (7-23, 4-54)	S. K. Warne, Brisbane	1995-96

For Pakistan (6)

11-218 (4-76, 7-142)	Abdul Qadir, Faisalabad	1982-83
13-114 (6-34, 7-80)†	Fazal Mahmood, Karachi.	1956-57
12-165 (6-102, 6-63)	Imran Khan, Sydney	1976-77
11-118 (4-69, 7-49)	Iqbal Qasim, Karachi	1979-80
11-125 (2-39, 9-86)	Sarfraz Nawaz, Melbourne.	1978-79
11-160 (6-62, 5-98)†	Wasim Akram, Melbourne.	1989-90

† *Signifies ten wickets or more on first appearance in Australia–Pakistan Tests.*

AUSTRALIA v SRI LANKA

	Captains		T	A	SL	D
Season	*Australia*	*Sri Lanka*				
1982-83*S*	G. S. Chappell	L. R. D. Mendis	1	1	0	0
1987-88*A*	A. R. Border	R. S. Madugalle	1	1	0	0
1989-90*A*	A. R. Border	A. Ranatunga	2	1	0	1
1992-93*S*	A. R. Border	A. Ranatunga	3	1	0	2
1995-96*A*	M. A. Taylor	A. Ranatunga[1]	3	3	0	0
1999-2000*S*	S. R. Waugh	S. T. Jayasuriya	3	0	1	2
	In Australia		6	5	0	1
	In Sri Lanka		7	2	1	4
	Totals		13	7	1	5

A Played in Australia. S Played in Sri Lanka.

Note: The following deputised for the official touring captain:
[1]P. A. de Silva (Third).

HIGHEST INNINGS TOTALS

For Australia in Australia: 617-5 dec. at Perth	1995-96
in Sri Lanka: 514-4 dec. at Kandy	1982-83
For Sri Lanka in Australia: 418 in Brisbane	1989-90
in Sri Lanka: 547-8 dec. at Colombo (SSC).	1992-93

LOWEST INNINGS TOTALS

For Australia in Australia: 224 at Hobart	1989-90
in Sri Lanka: 140 at Kandy	1999-2000
For Sri Lanka in Australia: 153 at Perth	1987-88
in Sri Lanka: 164 at Colombo (SSC)	1992-93

INDIVIDUAL HUNDREDS

For Australia (16)

D. C. Boon (1)	100* Colombo (KS) 1992-93	108 Hobart 1989-90
110 Melbourne . . 1995-96	**T. M. Moody** (1)	**M. E. Waugh** (1)
A. R. Border (1)	106† Brisbane . . . 1989-90	111 Perth. 1995-96
106 Moratuwa . . 1992-93	**R. T. Ponting** (1)	**S. R. Waugh** (3)
D. W. Hookes (1)	105* Colombo (SSC) 1999-00	134* Hobart 1989-90
143*† Kandy. 1982-83	**M. J. Slater** (1)	131* Melbourne . . 1995-96
D. M. Jones (3)	219† Perth. 1995-96	170 Adelaide . . . 1995-96
102† Perth. 1987-88	**M. A. Taylor** (2)	**K. C. Wessels** (1)
118* Hobart 1989-90	164† Brisbane . . . 1989-90	141† Kandy. 1982-83

For Sri Lanka (7)

P. A. de Silva (1)	**S. T. Jayasuriya** (1)	**A. Ranatunga** (1)
167 Brisbane ... 1989-90	112 Adelaide ... 1995-96	127 Colombo (SSC) 1992-93
A. P. Gurusinha (2)	**R. S. Kaluwitharana** (1)	**H. P. Tillekeratne** (1)
137 Colombo (SSC) 1992-93	132*† Colombo (SSC) 1992-93	119 Perth...... 1995-96
143 Melbourne .. 1995-96		

† *Signifies hundred on first appearance in Australia–Sri Lanka Tests.*

RECORD PARTNERSHIPS FOR EACH WICKET

For Australia

228	for 1st	M. J. Slater and M. A. Taylor at Perth....................	1995-96
170	for 2nd	K. C. Wessels and G. N. Yallop at Kandy...............	1982-83
158	for 3rd	T. M. Moody and A. R. Border at Brisbane	1989-90
163	for 4th	M. A. Taylor and A. R. Border at Hobart...............	1989-90
155*	for 5th	D. W. Hookes and A. R. Border at Kandy	1982-83
260*	for 6th	D. M. Jones and S. R. Waugh at Hobart................	1989-90
129	for 7th	G. R. J. Matthews and I. A. Healy at Moratuwa..........	1992-93
107	for 8th	R. T. Ponting and J. N. Gillespie at Kandy	1999-2000
45	for 9th	I. A. Healy and S. K. Warne at Colombo (SSC)	1992-93
49	for 10th	I. A. Healy and M. R. Whitney at Colombo (SSC)........	1992-93

For Sri Lanka

110	for 1st	R. S. Mahanama and U. C. Hathurusinghe at Colombo (KS)	1992-93
92	for 2nd	R. S. Mahanama and A. P. Gurusinha at Colombo (SSC).......	1992-93
125	for 3rd	S. T. Jayasuriya and S. Ranatunga at Adelaide..............	1995-96
230	for 4th	A. P. Gurusinha and A. Ranatunga at Colombo (SSC)........	1992-93
116	for 5th	H. P. Tillekeratne and A. Ranatunga at Moratuwa..........	1992-93
96	for 6th	A. P. Gurusinha and R. S. Kaluwitharana at Colombo (SSC) ...	1992-93
144	for 7th†	P. A. de Silva and J. R. Ratnayeke at Brisbane	1989-90
33	for 8th	A. Ranatunga and C. P. H. Ramanayake at Perth	1987-88
46	for 9th	H. D. P. K. Dharmasena and G. P. Wickremasinghe at Perth.....	1995-96
27	for 10th	P. A. de Silva and C. P. H. Ramanayake at Brisbane..........	1989-90

† *Denotes record partnership against all countries.*

BEST MATCH BOWLING ANALYSES

For Australia

8-156 (3-68, 5-88)	M. G. Hughes, Hobart	1989-90

For Sri Lanka

8-157 (5-82, 3-75)	C. P. H. Ramanayake, Moratuwa.................	1992-93

AUSTRALIA v ZIMBABWE

		Captains				
Season	*Australia*	*Zimbabwe*	*T*	*A*	*Z*	*D*
1999-2000Z	S. R. Waugh	A. D. R. Campbell	1	1	0	0

Z Played in Zimbabwe.

HIGHEST INNINGS TOTALS

For Australia: 422 at Harare 1999-2000

For Zimbabwe: 232 at Harare 1999-2000

INDIVIDUAL HUNDRED

For Australia (1)

S. R. Waugh (1)
151*† Harare 1999-00

Highest score for Zimbabwe: 91 by M. W. Goodwin at Harare 1999-2000.

† *Signifies hundred on first appearance in Australia–Zimbabwe Tests.*

HIGHEST PARTNERSHIPS

For Australia

114 for 8th   S. R. Waugh and D. W. Fleming at Harare 1999-2000

For Zimbabwe

98 for 2nd   T. R. Gripper and M. W. Goodwin at Harare 1999-2000

BEST MATCH BOWLING ANALYSES

For Australia

6-90 (3-44, 3-46)   G. D. McGrath, Harare 1999-2000

For Zimbabwe

5-93 (5-93)   H. H. Streak, Harare 1999-2000

SOUTH AFRICA v WEST INDIES

Season	South Africa	Captains West Indies	T	SA	WI	D
1991-92*W*	K. C. Wessels	R. B. Richardson	1	0	1	0
1998-99*S*	W. J. Cronje	B. C. Lara	5	5	0	0
	In South Africa		5	5	0	0
	In West Indies		1	0	1	0
	Totals		6	5	1	0

S Played in South Africa.   W Played in West Indies.

HIGHEST INNINGS TOTALS

For South Africa in South Africa: 406-8 dec. at Cape Town	1998-99
in West Indies: 345 at Bridgetown	1991-92
For West Indies in South Africa: 271 at Cape Town	1998-99
in West Indies: 283 at Bridgetown	1991-92

LOWEST INNINGS TOTALS

For South Africa in South Africa: 195 at Port Elizabeth	1998-99
in West Indies: 148 at Bridgetown	1991-92
For West Indies in South Africa: 121 at Port Elizabeth	1998-99
in West Indies: 262 at Bridgetown	1991-92

INDIVIDUAL HUNDREDS

For South Africa (6)

M. V. Boucher (1)	**A. C. Hudson** (1)	**G. Kirsten** (1)
100 Centurion. . . 1998-99	163† Bridgetown . 1991-92	134 Centurion . . 1998-99
D. J. Cullinan (1)	**J. H. Kallis** (1)	**J. N. Rhodes** (1)
168 Cape Town. . 1998-99	110 Cape Town. . 1998-99	103* Centurion . . 1998-99

Highest score for West Indies: 86 at Cape Town 1998-99 by C. L. Hooper.

† *Signifies hundred on first appearance in South Africa–West Indies Tests.*

RECORD PARTNERSHIPS FOR EACH WICKET

For South Africa

97 for 1st	G. Kirsten and H. H. Gibbs at Durban	1998-99
125 for 2nd	A. C. Hudson and K. C. Wessels at Bridgetown	1991-92
235 for 3rd	J. H. Kallis and D. J. Cullinan at Cape Town	1998-99
107 for 4th	G. Kirsten and W. J. Cronje at Centurion	1998-99
115 for 5th	G. Kirsten and J. N. Rhodes at Centurion	1998-99
92 for 6th	J. N. Rhodes and S. M. Pollock at Port Elizabeth	1998-99
92 for 7th	J. H. Kallis and M. V. Boucher at Centurion	1998-99
55 for 8th	M. V. Boucher and L. Klusener at Centurion	1998-99
66 for 9th	P. L. Symcox and A. A. Donald at Port Elizabeth	1998-99
25 for 10th	P. L. Symcox and D. J. Terbrugge at Johannesburg	1998-99

For West Indies

99 for 1st	D. L. Haynes and P. V. Simmons at Bridgetown	1991-92
56 for 2nd	D. L. Haynes and B. C. Lara at Bridgetown	1991-92
160 for 3rd	S. Chanderpaul and B. C. Lara at Durban	1998-99
91 for 4th	S. Chanderpaul and C. L. Hooper at Johannesburg	1998-99
74 for 5th	C. L. Hooper and D. Ganga at Cape Town	1998-99
68 for 6th	R. D. Jacobs and C. L. Hooper at Johannesburg	1998-99
81 for 7th	R. D. Jacobs and N. A. M. McLean at Centurion	1998-99
65 for 8th	R. D. Jacobs and N. A. M. McLean at Cape Town	1998-99
34 for 9th	R. D. Jacobs and C. E. L. Ambrose at Cape Town	1998-99
64 for 10th	R. D. Jacobs and M. Dillon at Cape Town	1998-99

BEST MATCH BOWLING ANALYSES

For South Africa

9-103 (5-54, 4-49)   S. M. Pollock, Johannesburg.....................   1998-99

For West Indies

8-79 (2-28, 6-51)   C. E. L. Ambrose, Port Elizabeth.................   1998-99

SOUTH AFRICA v NEW ZEALAND

Season	South Africa	*Captains* New Zealand	T	SA	NZ	D
1931-32*N*	H. B. Cameron	M. L. Page	2	2	0	0
1952-53*N*	J. E. Cheetham	W. M. Wallace	2	1	0	1
1953-54*S*	J. E. Cheetham	G. O. Rabone[1]	5	4	0	1
1961-62*S*	D. J. McGlew	J. R. Reid	5	2	2	1
1963-64*N*	T. L. Goddard	J. R. Reid	3	0	0	3
1994-95*S*	W. J. Cronje	K. R. Rutherford	3	2	1	0
1994-95*N*	W. J. Cronje	K. R. Rutherford	1	1	0	0
1998-99*N*	W. J. Cronje	D. J. Nash	3	1	0	2
	In New Zealand...............		11	5	0	6
	In South Africa		13	8	3	2
	Totals.....................		24	13	3	8

N Played in New Zealand. S Played in South Africa.

Note: The following deputised for the official touring captain:
[1]B. Sutcliffe (Fourth and Fifth).

HIGHEST INNINGS TOTALS

For South Africa in South Africa: 464 at Johannesburg   1961-62
in New Zealand: 621-5 dec. at Auckland   1998-99

For New Zealand in South Africa: 505 at Cape Town...................   1953-54
in New Zealand: 364 at Wellington.......................   1931-32

LOWEST INNINGS TOTALS

For South Africa in South Africa: 148 at Johannesburg   1953-54
in New Zealand: 223 at Dunedin   1963-64

For New Zealand in South Africa: 79 at Johannesburg...................   1953-54
in New Zealand: 138 at Dunedin   1963-64

INDIVIDUAL HUNDREDS

For South Africa (20)

X. C. Balaskas (1)
122* Wellington . . 1931-32
J. A. J. Christy (1)
103† Christchurch. 1931-32
W. J. Cronje (2)
112 Cape Town. . 1994-95
101 Auckland. . . 1994-95
D. J. Cullinan (2)
275* Auckland. . . 1998-99
152 Wellington . . 1998-99
W. R. Endean (1)
116 Auckland. . . 1952-53

H. H. Gibbs (2)
211* Christchurch. 1998-99
120 Wellington . . 1998-99
J. H. Kallis (1)
148* Christchurch. 1998-99
G. Kirsten (1)
128 Auckland. . . 1998-99
D. J. McGlew (3)
255*† Wellington . . 1952-53
127*‡ Durban 1961-62
120 Johannesburg 1961-62

R. A. McLean (2)
101 Durban 1953-54
113 Cape Town. . 1961-62
B. Mitchell (1)
113† Christchurch. 1931-32
A. R. A. Murray (1)
109† Wellington . . 1952-53
D. J. Richardson (1)
109 Cape Town. . 1994-95
J. H. B. Waite (1)
101 Johannesburg 1961-62

For New Zealand (7)

P. T. Barton (1)
109 Port Elizabeth 1961-62
P. G. Z. Harris (1)
101 Cape Town. . 1961-62

G. O. Rabone (1)
107 Durban 1953-54
J. R. Reid (2)
135 Cape Town. . 1953-54
142 Johannesburg 1961-62

B. W. Sinclair (1)
138 Auckland. . . 1963-64
H. G. Vivian (1)
100† Wellington . . 1931-32

† *Signifies hundred on first appearance in South Africa–New Zealand Tests.*
‡ *Carried his bat.*

RECORD PARTNERSHIPS FOR EACH WICKET

For South Africa

196	for 1st	J. A. J. Christy and B. Mitchell at Christchurch.	1931-32
315*	for 2nd†	H. H. Gibbs and J. H. Kallis at Christchurch	1998-99
183	for 3rd	G. Kirsten and D. J. Cullinan at Auckland	1998-99
145	for 4th	D. J. Cullinan and W. J. Cronje at Wellington	1998-99
141	for 5th	D. J. Cullinan and J. N. Rhodes at Auckland	1998-99
126*	for 6th	D. J. Cullinan and S. M. Pollock at Auckland	1998-99
246	for 7th†	D. J. McGlew and A. R. A. Murray at Wellington	1952-53
95	for 8th	J. E. Cheetham and H. J. Tayfield at Cape Town	1953-54
60	for 9th	P. M. Pollock and N. A. T. Adcock at Port Elizabeth	1961-62
47	for 10th	D. J. McGlew and H. D. Bromfield at Port Elizabeth	1961-62

For New Zealand

126	for 1st	G. O. Rabone and M. E. Chapple at Cape Town	1953-54
90	for 2nd	M. J. Horne and N. J. Astle at Auckland	1998-99
94	for 3rd	M. B. Poore and B. Sutcliffe at Cape Town	1953-54
171	for 4th	B. W. Sinclair and S. N. McGregor at Auckland	1963-64
174	for 5th	J. R. Reid and J. E. F. Beck at Cape Town.	1953-54
100	for 6th	H. G. Vivian and F. T. Badcock at Wellington.	1931-32
84	for 7th	J. R. Reid and G. A. Bartlett at Johannesburg	1961-62
74	for 8th	S. A. Thomson and D. J. Nash at Johannesburg	1994-95
69	for 9th	C. F. W. Allcott and I. B. Cromb at Wellington.	1931-32
57	for 10th	S. B. Doull and R. P. de Groen at Johannesburg	1994-95

† *Denotes record partnership against all countries.*

TEN WICKETS OR MORE IN A MATCH

For South Africa (1)

11-196 (6-128, 5-68)†   S. F. Burke, Cape Town   1961-62

   † *Signifies ten wickets or more on first appearance in South Africa–New Zealand Tests.*

Note: The best match figures by a New Zealand bowler are 8-134 (3-57, 5-77), M. N. Hart at Johannesburg, 1994-95.

SOUTH AFRICA v INDIA

		Captains				
Season	South Africa	India	T	SA	I	D
1992-93S	K. C. Wessels	M. Azharuddin	4	1	0	3
1996-97I	W. J. Cronje	S. R. Tendulkar	3	1	2	0
1996-97S	W. J. Cronje	S. R. Tendulkar	3	2	0	1
1999-2000I	W. J. Cronje	S. R. Tendulkar	2	2	0	0
	In South Africa		7	3	0	4
	In India		5	3	2	0
	Totals.		12	6	2	4

S Played in South Africa.   I Played in India.

HIGHEST INNINGS TOTALS

For South Africa in South Africa: 529-7 dec. at Cape Town   1996-97
            in India: 479 at Bangalore   1999-2000

For India in South Africa: 410 at Johannesburg   1996-97
          in India: 400-7 dec. at Kanpur.   1996-97

LOWEST INNINGS TOTALS

For South Africa in South Africa: 235 at Durban   1996-97
            in India: 105 at Ahmedabad   1996-97

For India in South Africa: 66 at Durban   1996-97
          in India: 113 at Mumbai.   1999-2000

INDIVIDUAL HUNDREDS

For South Africa (10)

W. J. Cronje (1)
135   Port Elizabeth 1992-93

D. J. Cullinan (2)
153*   Calcutta. . . .   1996-97
122*   Johannesburg 1996-97

A. C. Hudson (1)
146   Calcutta. . . .   1996-97

G. Kirsten (3)
102 }
133 } Calcutta. . . .   1996-97
103   Cape Town. .   1996-97

L. Klusener (1)
102*   Cape Town. .   1996-97

B. M. McMillan (1)
103*   Cape Town. .   1996-97

K. C. Wessels (1)
118†   Durban   1992-93

For India (9)

P. K. Amre (1)

103†   Durban   1992-93

M. Azharuddin (4)

109   Calcutta. . . .   1996-97

163*   Kanpur   1996-97

115   Cape Town. .   1996-97

102   Bangalore . .   1999-00

R. Dravid (1)

148   Johannesburg   1996-97

Kapil Dev (1)

129   Port Elizabeth   1992-93

S. R. Tendulkar (2)

111   Johannesburg   1992-93

169   Cape Town. .   1996-97

    † *Signifies hundred on first appearance in South Africa–India Tests.*

RECORD PARTNERSHIPS FOR EACH WICKET

For South Africa

236	for 1st	A. C. Hudson and G. Kirsten at Calcutta	1996-97
212	for 2nd	G. Kirsten and D. J. Cullinan at Calcutta	1996-97
114	for 3rd	G. Kirsten and D. J. Cullinan at Cape Town	1996-97
94	for 4th	A. C. Hudson and D. J. Cullinan at Cape Town	1996-97
164	for 5th	J. H. Kallis and L. Klusener at Bangalore.	1999-2000
112	for 6th	B. M. McMillan and S. M. Pollock at Johannesburg.	1996-97
101*	for 7th	B. M. McMillan and S. M. Pollock at Cape Town	1996-97
147*	for 8th	B. M. McMillan and L. Klusener at Cape Town	1996-97
60	for 9th	P. S. de Villiers and A. A. Donald at Ahmedabad.	1996-97
74	for 10th	B. M. McMillan and A. A. Donald at Durban	1996-97

For India

90	for 1st	V. Rathore and N. R. Mongia at Johannesburg.	1996-97
85	for 2nd	M. Prabhakar and S. V. Manjrekar at Cape Town	1992-93
54	for 3rd	R. Dravid and S. R. Tendulkar at Johannesburg	1996-97
145	for 4th	R. Dravid and S. C. Ganguly at Johannesburg	1996-97
87	for 5th	M. Azharuddin and P. K. Amre at Durban	1992-93
222	for 6th	S. R. Tendulkar and M. Azharuddin at Cape Town	1996-97
76	for 7th	R. Dravid and J. Srinath at Johannesburg	1996-97
161	for 8th†	M. Azharuddin and A. Kumble at Calcutta	1996-97
77	for 9th	Kapil Dev and A. Kumble at Port Elizabeth	1992-93
52	for 10th	A. B. Agarkar and M. Kartik at Mumbai	1999-2000

    † *Denotes record partnership against all countries.*

TEN WICKETS OR MORE IN A MATCH

For South Africa (1)

12-139 (5-55, 7-84)	A. A. Donald, Port Elizabeth	1992-93

For India (1)

10-153 (5-60, 5-93)	B. K. V. Prasad, Durban	1996-97

SOUTH AFRICA v PAKISTAN

		Captains				
Season	South Africa	Pakistan	T	SA	P	D
1994-95S	W. J. Cronje	Salim Malik	1	1	0	0
1997-98P	W. J. Cronje	Saeed Anwar	3	1	0	2
1997-98S	W. J. Cronje[1]	Rashid Latif[2]	3	1	1	1
	In South Africa		4	2	1	1
	In Pakistan		3	1	0	2
	Totals.....................		7	3	1	3

S Played in South Africa. P Played in Pakistan.

Notes: The following deputised for the official touring captain or were appointed by the home authority for only a minor proportion of the series:
[1]G. Kirsten (First). [2]Aamir Sohail (First and Second).

HIGHEST INNINGS TOTALS

For South Africa: 460 at Johannesburg 1994-95

For Pakistan: 456 at Rawalpindi................................. 1997-98

LOWEST INNINGS TOTALS

For South Africa: 214 at Faisalabad 1997-98

For Pakistan: 92 at Faisalabad................................. 1997-98

INDIVIDUAL HUNDREDS

For South Africa (3)

G. Kirsten (1)	**B. M. McMillan** (1)	**P. L. Symcox** (1)
100*‡ Faisalabad .. 1997-98	113† Johannesburg 1994-95	108 Johannesburg 1997-98

For Pakistan (5)

Ali Naqvi (1)	**Azhar Mahmood** (3)	**Saeed Anwar** (1)
115† Rawalpindi.. 1997-98	128*† Rawalpindi.. 1997-98	118 Durban 1997-98
	136 Johannesburg 1997-98	
	132 Durban 1997-98	

† *Signifies hundred on first appearance in South Africa–Pakistan Tests.*
‡ *Carried his bat.*

RECORD PARTNERSHIPS FOR EACH WICKET

For South Africa

135 for 1st	G. Kirsten and A. M. Bacher at Sheikhupura	1997-98
114 for 2nd	G. Kirsten and J. H. Kallis at Rawalpindi	1997-98
83 for 3rd	J. H. Kallis and H. D. Ackerman at Durban	1997-98
79 for 4th	G. Kirsten and W. J. Cronje at Johannesburg	1994-95
43 for 5th	P. L. Symcox and W. J. Cronje at Faisalabad	1997-98

157 for 6th	J. N. Rhodes and B. M. McMillan at Johannesburg	1994-95
106 for 7th	S. M. Pollock and D. J. Richardson at Rawalpindi.	1997-98
124 for 8th	G. Kirsten and P. L. Symcox at Faisalabad.	1997-98
195 for 9th†	M. V. Boucher and P. L. Symcox at Johannesburg	1997-98
71 for 10th	P. S. de Villiers and A. A. Donald at Johannesburg	1994-95

For Pakistan

101 for 1st	Saeed Anwar and Aamir Sohail at Durban	1997-98
69 for 2nd	Ali Naqvi and Mohammad Ramzan at Rawalpindi.	1997-98
72 for 3rd	Ijaz Ahmed, sen. and Mohammad Wasim at Johannesburg.	1997-98
93 for 4th	Asif Mujtaba and Inzamam-ul-Haq at Johannesburg.	1994-95
44 for 5th	Ali Naqvi and Mohammad Wasim at Rawalpindi.	1997-98
144 for 6th	Inzamam-ul-Haq and Moin Khan at Faisalabad	1997-98
35 for 7th	Salim Malik and Wasim Akram at Johannesburg.	1994-95
40 for 8th	Inzamam-ul-Haq and Kabir Khan at Johannesburg.	1994-95
80 for 9th	Azhar Mahmood and Shoaib Akhtar at Durban	1997-98
151 for 10th†	Azhar Mahmood and Mushtaq Ahmed at Rawalpindi	1997-98

† *Denotes record partnership against all countries.*

TEN WICKETS OR MORE IN A MATCH

For South Africa (1)

10-108 (6-81, 4-27)†	P. S. de Villiers, Johannesburg.	1994-95

For Pakistan (1)

10-133 (6-78, 4-55)	Waqar Younis, Port Elizabeth	1997-98

† *Signifies ten wickets or more on first appearance in South Africa–Pakistan Tests.*

SOUTH AFRICA v SRI LANKA

Season	South Africa	*Captains* Sri Lanka	T	SA	SL	D
1993-94*SL*	K. C. Wessels	A. Ranatunga	3	1	0	2
1997-98*SA*	W. J. Cronje	A. Ranatunga	2	2	0	0
2000*SL*	S. M. Pollock	S. T. Jayasuriya	3	1	1	1
	In South Africa		2	2	0	0
	In Sri Lanka		6	2	1	3
	Totals.		8	4	1	3

SA Played in South Africa. SL Played in Sri Lanka.

HIGHEST INNINGS TOTALS

For South Africa in South Africa: 418 at Cape Town	1997-98
in Sri Lanka: 495 at Colombo (SSC).	1993-94
For Sri Lanka in South Africa: 306 at Cape Town (in each innings)	1997-98
in Sri Lanka: 522 at Galle	2000

LOWEST INNINGS TOTALS

For South Africa in South Africa: 200 at Centurion 1997-98
                in Sri Lanka: 231 at Kandy 2000

For Sri Lanka in South Africa: 122 at Centurion 1997-98
              in Sri Lanka: 119 at Colombo (SSC) 1993-94

INDIVIDUAL HUNDREDS

For South Africa (7)

W. J. Cronje (1)
122   Colombo (SSC) 1993-94
D. J. Cullinan (4)
102   Colombo (PSS) 1993-94
113   Cape Town . . 1997-98

103   Centurion. . . 1997-98
114*   Galle.   2000
L. Klusener (1)
118*   Kandy   2000

J. N. Rhodes (1)
101*† Moratuwa . . 1993-94

For Sri Lanka (5)

M. S. Atapattu (1)
120   Kandy.   2000
S. T. Jayasuriya (1)
148   Galle.   2000

D. P. M. D. Jayawardene (2)
167†   Galle.   2000
101*   Colombo (SSC)   2000

A. Ranatunga (1)
131†   Moratuwa . . 1993-94

† *Signifies hundred on first appearance in South Africa–Sri Lanka Tests.*

RECORD PARTNERSHIPS FOR EACH WICKET

For South Africa

137 for 1st	K. C. Wessels and A. C. Hudson at Colombo (SSC)	1993-94
54 for 2nd	G. Kirsten and J. H. Kallis at Galle	2000
116 for 3rd	J. H. Kallis and D. J. Cullinan at Cape Town	1997-98
116 for 4th	G. Kirsten and W. J. Cronje at Centurion.	1997-98
45 for 5th	J. N. Rhodes and L. Klusener at Colombo (SSC)	2000
124 for 6th	L. Klusener and M. V. Boucher at Kandy , , ...	2000
95 for 7th	S. M. Pollock and M. V. Boucher at Cape Town	1997-98
79 for 8th	P. L. Symcox and R. P. Snell at Colombo (SSC).	1993-94
45 for 9th	N. Boje and P. R. Adams at Kandy	2000
43 for 10th	L. Klusener and M. Hayward at Kandy.	2000

For Sri Lanka

193 for 1st	M. S. Atapattu and S. T. Jayasuriya at Galle.	2000
103 for 2nd	S. T. Jayasuriya and R. P. Arnold at Colombo (SSC)	2000
129 for 3rd	M. S. Atapattu and P. A. de Silva at Cape Town	1997-98
118 for 4th	R. S. Mahanama and A. Ranatunga at Centurion.	1997-98
121 for 5th	P. A. de Silva and A. Ranatunga at Moratuwa.	1993-94
103 for 6th	A. Ranatunga and H. P. Tillekeratne at Moratuwa	1993-94
43 for 7th	P. A. de Silva and G. P. Wickremasinghe at Centurion	1997-98
117 for 8th†	D. P. M. D. Jayawardene and W. P. U. J. C. Vaas at Galle	2000
48 for 9th	G. P. Wickremasinghe and M. Muralitharan at Cape Town	1997-98
22 for 10th	W. P. U. J. C. Vaas and M. Muralitharan at Galle	2000

† *Denotes record partnership against all countries.*

TEN WICKETS OR MORE IN A MATCH

For Sri Lanka (1)

13-171 (6-87, 7-84)   M. Muralitharan at Galle   2000

Note: The best match figures for South Africa are 9-106 (5-48, 4-58) by B. N. Schultz at Colombo (SSC), 1993-94.

SOUTH AFRICA v ZIMBABWE

		Captains				
Season	*South Africa*	*Zimbabwe*	*T*	*SA*	*Z*	*D*
1995-96Z	W. J. Cronje	A. Flower	1	1	0	0
1999-2000S	W. J. Cronje	A. D. R. Campbell	1	1	0	0
1999-2000Z	W. J. Cronje	A. Flower	1	1	0	0
	In Zimbabwe		2	2	0	0
	In South Africa		1	1	0	0
	Totals		3	3	0	0

S Played in South Africa.   Z Played in Zimbabwe.

HIGHEST INNINGS TOTALS

For South Africa: 462-9 dec. at Harare   1999-2000

For Zimbabwe: 283 at Harare   1995-96

LOWEST INNINGS TOTALS

For South Africa: 346 at Harare   1995-96

For Zimbabwe: 102 at Harare   1999-2000

INDIVIDUAL HUNDREDS

For South Africa (3)

M. V. Boucher (1)	**A. C. Hudson** (1)	**J. H. Kallis** (1)
125 Harare 1999-00	135† Harare 1995-96	115 Harare 1999-00

Highest score for Zimbabwe: 85 by G. J. Whittall at Bloemfontein 1999-2000.

† *Signifies hundred on first appearance in South Africa–Zimbabwe Tests.*

HUNDRED PARTNERSHIPS

For South Africa

100 for 4th	J. H. Kallis and W. J. Cronje at Harare	1999-2000
101 for 6th	A. C. Hudson and B. M. McMillan at Harare	1995-96
148 for 8th†	M. V. Boucher and S. M. Pollock at Harare	1999-2000

† *Denotes record partnership against all countries.*

Note: The highest partnership for Zimbabwe is 97 for the 5th wicket between A. Flower and G. J. Whittall at Harare, 1995-96.

TEN WICKETS OR MORE IN A MATCH

For South Africa (1)

11-113 (3-42, 8-71)†   A. A. Donald, Harare   1995-96

Note: The best match figures for Zimbabwe are 5-105 (3-68, 2-37) by A. C. I. Lock at Harare, 1995-96.

　† *Signifies ten wickets or more on first appearance in South Africa–Zimbabwe Tests.*

WEST INDIES v NEW ZEALAND

		Captains				
Season	*West Indies*	*New Zealand*	*T*	*WI*	*NZ*	*D*
1951-52*N*	J. D. C. Goddard	B. Sutcliffe	2	1	0	1
1955-56*N*	D. St E. Atkinson	J. R. Reid[1]	4	3	1	0
1968-69*N*	G. S. Sobers	G. T. Dowling	3	1	1	1
1971-72*W*	G. S. Sobers	G. T. Dowling[2]	5	0	0	5
1979-80*N*	C. H. Lloyd	G. P. Howarth	3	0	1	2
1984-85*W*	I. V. A. Richards	G. P. Howarth	4	2	0	2
1986-87*N*	I. V. A. Richards	J. V. Coney	3	1	1	1
1994-95*N*	C. A. Walsh	K. R. Rutherford	2	1	0	1
1995-96*W*	C. A. Walsh	L. K. Germon	2	1	0	1
1999-2000*N*	B. C. Lara	S. P. Fleming	2	0	2	0
	In New Zealand		19	7	6	6
	In West Indies		11	3	0	8
	Totals		30	10	6	14

N Played in New Zealand.   W Played in West Indies.

Notes: The following deputised for the official touring captain or were appointed by the home authority for only a minor proportion of the series:
[1]H. B. Cave (First). [2]B. E. Congdon (Third, Fourth and Fifth).

HIGHEST INNINGS TOTALS

For West Indies in West Indies: 564-8 at Bridgetown   1971-72
　　　　　　　　in New Zealand: 660-5 dec. at Wellington   1994-95

For New Zealand in West Indies: 543-3 dec. at Georgetown   1971-72
　　　　　　　　in New Zealand: 518-9 dec. at Wellington   1999-2000

LOWEST INNINGS TOTALS

For West Indies in West Indies: 133 at Bridgetown   1971-72
　　　　　　　　in New Zealand: 77 at Auckland   1955-56

For New Zealand in West Indies: 94 at Bridgetown   1984-85
　　　　　　　　in New Zealand: 74 at Dunedin   1955-56

INDIVIDUAL HUNDREDS

By West Indies (33)

J. C. Adams (2)
151 Wellington . . 1994-95
208* St John's . . . 1995-96
S. L. Campbell (2)
208 Bridgetown . 1995-96
170 Hamilton . . . 1999-00
M. C. Carew (1)
109† Auckland. . . 1968-69
C. A. Davis (1)
183 Bridgetown . 1971-72
R. C. Fredericks (1)
163 Kingston . . . 1971-72
C. G. Greenidge (2)
100 Port-of-Spain 1984-85
213 Auckland . . . 1986-87
A. F. G. Griffith (1)
114† Hamilton . . . 1999-00
D. L. Haynes (3)
105† Dunedin . . . 1979-80

122 Christchurch . 1979-80
121 Wellington . . 1986-87
A. I. Kallicharran (2)
100*† Georgetown . 1971-72
101 Port-of-Spain 1971-72
C. L. King (1)
100* Christchurch . 1979-80
B. C. Lara (1)
147 Wellington . . 1994-95
J. R. Murray (1)
101* Wellington . . 1994-95
S. M. Nurse (2)
168† Auckland. . . 1968-69
258 Christchurch . 1968-69
I. V. A. Richards (1)
105 Bridgetown . 1984-85
R. B. Richardson (1)
185 Georgetown . 1984-85

L. G. Rowe (3)
214 }
100*} †Kingston . . . 1971-72
100 Christchurch . 1979-80
R. G. Samuels (1)
125 St John's . . . 1995-96
G. S. Sobers (1)
142 Bridgetown . 1971-72
J. B. Stollmeyer (1)
152 Auckland . . . 1951-52
C. L. Walcott (1)
115 Auckland . . . 1951-52
E. D. Weekes (3)
123 Dunedin . . . 1955-56
103 Christchurch . 1955-56
156 Wellington . . 1955-56
F. M. M. Worrell (1)
100 Auckland. . . 1951-52

By New Zealand (21)

N. J. Astle (2)
125† Bridgetown . 1995-96
103 St John's . . . 1995-96
M. G. Burgess (1)
101 Kingston . . . 1971-72
B. E. Congdon (2)
166* Port-of-Spain 1971-72
126 Bridgetown . 1971-72
J. J. Crowe (1)
112 Kingston . . . 1984-85
M. D. Crowe (3)
188 Georgetown . 1984-85
119 Wellington . . 1986-87

104 Auckland. . . 1986-87
B. A. Edgar (1)
127 Auckland . . . 1979-80
R. J. Hadlee (1)
103 Christchurch . 1979-80
B. F. Hastings (2)
117* Christchurch . 1968-69
105 Bridgetown . 1971-72
G. P. Howarth (1)
147 Christchurch . 1979-80
T. W. Jarvis (1)
182 Georgetown . 1971-72

A. C. Parore (1)
100*† Christchurch . 1994-95
M. S. Sinclair (1)
214† Wellington . . 1999-00
B. R. Taylor (1)
124† Auckland . . . 1968-69
G. M. Turner (2)
223*‡ Kingston . . . 1971-72
259 Georgetown . 1971-72
J. G. Wright (1)
138 Wellington . . 1986-87

  † *Signifies hundred on first appearance in West Indies–New Zealand Tests.*
  ‡ *Carried his bat.*

Notes: E. D. Weekes in 1955-56 made three hundreds in consecutive innings.
  L. G. Rowe and A. I. Kallicharran each scored hundreds in their first two innings in Test cricket, Rowe being the only batsman to do so in his first match.

RECORD PARTNERSHIPS FOR EACH WICKET

For West Indies

276 for 1st	A. F. G. Griffith and S. L. Campbell at Hamilton.	1999-2000
269 for 2nd	R. C. Fredericks and L. G. Rowe at Kingston	1971-72
221 for 3rd	B. C. Lara and J. C. Adams at Wellington	1994-95
162 for 4th	{ E. D. Weekes and O. G. Smith at Dunedin	1955-56
	{ C. G. Greenidge and A. I. Kallicharran at Christchurch.	1979-80
189 for 5th	F. M. M. Worrell and C. L. Walcott at Auckland	1951-52
254 for 6th	C. A. Davis and G. S. Sobers at Bridgetown.	1971-72
143 for 7th	D. St E. Atkinson and J. D. C. Goddard at Christchurch	1955-56
83 for 8th	I. V. A. Richards and M. D. Marshall at Bridgetown	1984-85
70 for 9th	M. D. Marshall and J. Garner at Bridgetown.	1984-85
31 for 10th	T. M. Findlay and G. C. Shillingford at Bridgetown	1971-72

For New Zealand

387	for 1st†	G. M. Turner and T. W. Jarvis at Georgetown	1971-72
210	for 2nd	G. P. Howarth and J. J. Crowe at Kingston	1984-85
241	for 3rd	J. G. Wright and M. D. Crowe at Wellington...............	1986-87
189	for 4th	M. S. Sinclair and N. J. Astle at Wellington	1999-2000
144	for 5th	N. J. Astle and J. T. C. Vaughan at Bridgetown	1995-96
220	for 6th	G. M. Turner and K. J. Wadsworth at Kingston	1971-72
143	for 7th	M. D. Crowe and I. D. S. Smith at Georgetown............	1984-85
136	for 8th	B. E. Congdon and R. S. Cunis at Port-of-Spain	1971-72
62*	for 9th	V. Pollard and R. S. Cunis at Auckland	1968-69
45	for 10th	D. K. Morrison and R. J. Kennedy at Bridgetown	1995-96

† *Denotes record partnership against all countries.*

TEN WICKETS OR MORE IN A MATCH

For West Indies (2)

11-120 (4-40, 7-80)	M. D. Marshall, Bridgetown	1984-85
13-55 (7-37, 6-18)	C. A. Walsh, Wellington	1994-95

For New Zealand (4)

10-100 (3-73, 7-27)†	C. L. Cairns, Hamilton.......................	1999-2000
10-124 (4-51, 6-73)†	E. J. Chatfield, Port-of-Spain	1984-85
11-102 (5-34, 6-68)†	R. J. Hadlee, Dunedin	1979-80
10-166 (4-71, 6-95)	G. B. Troup, Auckland	1979-80

† *Signifies ten wickets or more on first appearance in West Indies–New Zealand Tests.*

WEST INDIES v INDIA

Captains

Season	West Indies	India	T	WI	I	D
1948-49*I*	J. D. C. Goddard	L. Amarnath	5	1	0	4
1952-53*W*	J. B. Stollmeyer	V. S. Hazare	5	1	0	4
1958-59*I*	F. C. M. Alexander	Ghulam Ahmed[1]	5	3	0	2
1961-62*W*	F. M. M. Worrell	N. J. Contractor[2]	5	5	0	0
1966-67*I*	G. S. Sobers	Nawab of Pataudi jun.	3	2	0	1
1970-71*W*	G. S. Sobers	A. L. Wadekar	5	0	1	4
1974-75*I*	C. H. Lloyd	Nawab of Pataudi jun.[3]	5	3	2	0
1975-76*W*	C. H. Lloyd	B. S. Bedi	4	2	1	1
1978-79*I*	A. I. Kallicharran	S. M. Gavaskar	6	0	1	5
1982-83*W*	C. H. Lloyd	Kapil Dev	5	2	0	3
1983-84*I*	C. H. Lloyd	Kapil Dev	6	3	0	3
1987-88*I*	I. V. A. Richards	D. B. Vengsarkar[4]	4	1	1	2
1988-89*W*	I. V. A. Richards	D. B. Vengsarkar	4	3	0	1
1994-95*I*	C. A. Walsh	M. Azharuddin	3	1	1	1
1996-97*W*	C. A. Walsh[5]	S. R. Tendulkar	5	1	0	4
	In India		37	14	5	18
	In West Indies		33	14	2	17
	Totals....................		70	28	7	35

I Played in India.   W Played in West Indies.

Notes: The following deputised for the official touring captain or were appointed by the home authority for only a minor proportion of the series:

[1]P. R. Umrigar (First), V. Mankad (Fourth), H. R. Adhikari (Fifth). [2]Nawab of Pataudi jun. (Third, Fourth and Fifth). [3]S. Venkataraghavan (Second). [4]R. J. Shastri (Fourth). [5]B. C. Lara (Third).

HIGHEST INNINGS TOTALS

For West Indies in West Indies: 631-8 dec. at Kingston. 1961-62
in India: 644-8 dec. at Delhi 1958-59

For India in West Indies: 469-7 at Port-of-Spain 1982-83
in India: 644-7 dec. at Kanpur 1978-79

LOWEST INNINGS TOTALS

For West Indies in West Indies: 140 at Bridgetown 1996-97
in India: 127 at Delhi. 1987-88

For India in West Indies: 81 at Bridgetown. 1996-97
in India: 75 at Delhi. 1987-88

INDIVIDUAL HUNDREDS

For West Indies (82)

J. C. Adams (2)
125*   Nagpur   1994-95
174*   Mohali   1994-95
S. F. A. F. Bacchus (1)
250   Kanpur   1978-79
B. F. Butcher (2)
103   Calcutta. . . . 1958-59
142   Madras   1958-59
S. Chanderpaul (1)
137*   Bridgetown .   1996-97
R. J. Christiani (1)
107†   Delhi 1948-49
C. A. Davis (2)
125*   Georgetown .   1970-71
105   Port-of-Spain   1970-71
P. J. L. Dujon (1)
110   St John's . . . 1982-83
R. C. Fredericks (2)
100   Calcutta. . . . 1974-75
104   Bombay. . . .   1974-75
H. A. Gomes (1)
123   Port-of-Spain   1982-83
G. E. Gomez (1)
101†   Delhi 1948-49
C. G. Greenidge (5)
107†   Bangalore . .   1974-75
154*   St John's . . . 1982-83
194   Kanpur   1983-84
141   Calcutta. . . . 1987-88
117   Bridgetown .   1988-89
D. L. Haynes (2)
136   St John's . . . 1982-83
112*   Bridgetown .   1988-89
J. K. Holt (1)
123   Delhi 1958-59
C. L. Hooper (2)
100*   Calcutta. . . . 1987-88
129   Kingston . . .   1996-97
C. C. Hunte (1)
101   Bombay. . . .   1966-67

A. I. Kallicharran (3)
124†   Bangalore . .   1974-75
103*   Port-of-Spain   1975-76
187   Bombay. . . .   1978-79
R. B. Kanhai (4)
256   Calcutta. . . . 1958-59
138   Kingston . .   1961-62
139   Port-of-Spain   1961-62
158*   Kingston . . .   1970-71
B. C. Lara (1)
103   St John's . . . 1996-97
C. H. Lloyd (7)
163   Bangalore . .   1974-75
242*   Bombay. . . .   1974-75
102   Bridgetown .   1975-76
143   Port-of-Spain   1982-83
106   St John's . . . 1982-83
103   Delhi 1983-84
161*   Calcutta. . . . 1983-84
A. L. Logie (2)
130   Bridgetown .   1982-83
101   Calcutta. . . . 1987-88
E. D. A. McMorris (1)
125†   Kingston . . .   1961-62
B. H. Pairaudeau (1)
115†   Port-of-Spain   1952-53
A. F. Rae (2)
104   Bombay. . . .   1948-49
109   Madras   1948-49
I. V. A. Richards (8)
192*   Delhi 1974-75
142   Bridgetown .   1975-76
130   Port-of-Spain   1975-76
177   Port-of-Spain   1975-76
109   Georgetown .   1982-83
120   Bombay. . . .   1983-84
109*   Delhi 1987-88
110   Kingston . . .   1988-89

R. B. Richardson (2)
194   Georgetown .   1988-89
156   Kingston . . .   1988-89
O. G. Smith (1)
100   Delhi 1958-59
G. S. Sobers (8)
142*† Bombay. . . .   1958-59
198   Kanpur   1958-59
106*   Calcutta. . . . 1958-59
153   Kingston . . .   1961-62
104   Kingston . . .   1961-62
108*   Georgetown .   1970-71
178*   Bridgetown .   1970-71
132   Port-of-Spain   1970-71
J. S. Solomon (1)
100*   Delhi 1958-59
J. B. Stollmeyer (2)
160   Madras   1948-49
104*   Port-of-Spain   1952-53
C. L. Walcott (4)
152†   Delhi 1948-49
108   Calcutta. . . . 1948-49
125   Georgetown .   1952-53
118   Kingston . . .   1952-53
E. D. Weekes (7)
128†   Delhi 1948-49
194   Bombay. . . .   1948-49
162 }
101 } Calcutta. . . . 1948-49
207   Port-of-Spain   1952-53
161   Port-of-Spain   1952-53
109   Kingston . . .   1952-53
A. B. Williams (1)
111   Calcutta. . . . 1978-79
S. C. Williams (1)
128   Port-of-Spain   1996-97
F. M. M. Worrell (1)
237   Kingston . . .   1952-53

For India (59)

H. R. Adhikari (1)
114*† Delhi 1948-49

M. Amarnath (3)
101* Kanpur 1978-79
117 Port-of-Spain 1982-83
116 St John's . . . 1982-83

M. L. Apte (1)
163* Port-of-Spain 1952-53

C. G. Borde (3)
109 Delhi 1958-59
121 Bombay. . . . 1966-67
125 Madras 1966-67

S. A. Durani (1)
104 Port-of-Spain 1961-62

F. M. Engineer (1)
109 Madras 1966-67

A. D. Gaekwad (1)
102 Kanpur 1978-79

S. M. Gavaskar (13)
116 Georgetown . 1970-71
117* Bridgetown . 1970-71
124 } Port-of-Spain 1970-71
220 }
156 Port-of-Spain 1975-76
102 Port-of-Spain 1975-76
205 Bombay. . . . 1978-79
107 } Calcutta. . . . 1978-79
182* }

120 Delhi 1978-79
147* Georgetown . 1982-83
121 Delhi 1983-84
236* Madras 1983-84

V. S. Hazare (2)
134* Bombay. . . . 1948-49
122 Bombay. . . . 1948-49

Kapil Dev (3)
126* Delhi 1978-79
100* Port-of-Spain 1982-83
109 Madras 1987-88

S. V. Manjrekar (1)
108 Bridgetown . 1988-89

V. L. Manjrekar (1)
118 Kingston . . . 1952-53

R. S. Modi (1)
112 Bombay. . . . 1948-49

Mushtaq Ali (1)
106† Calcutta. . . . 1948-49

B. P. Patel (1)
115* Port-of-Spain 1975-76

M. Prabhakar (1)
120 Mohali 1994-95

Pankaj Roy (1)
150 Kingston . . . 1952-53

D. N. Sardesai (3)
212 Kingston . . . 1970-71
112 Port-of-Spain 1970-71

150 Bridgetown . 1970-71

R. J. Shastri (2)
102 St John's . . . 1982-83
107 Bridgetown . 1988-89

N. S. Sidhu (3)
116 Kingston . . . 1988-89
107 Nagpur 1994-95
201 Port-of-Spain 1996-97

E. D. Solkar (1)
102 Bombay. . . . 1974-75

S. R. Tendulkar (1)
179 Nagpur 1994-95

P. R. Umrigar (3)
130 Port-of-Spain 1952-53
117 Kingston . . . 1952-53
172* Port-of-Spain 1961-62

D. B. Vengsarkar (6)
157* Calcutta. . . . 1978-79
109 Delhi 1978-79
159 Delhi 1983-84
100 Bombay. . . . 1983-84
102 Delhi 1987-88
102* Calcutta. . . . 1987-88

G. R. Viswanath (4)
139 Calcutta. . . . 1974-75
112 Port-of-Spain 1975-76
124 Madras 1978-79
179 Kanpur 1978-79

† *Signifies hundred on first appearance in West Indies–India Tests.*

RECORD PARTNERSHIPS FOR EACH WICKET

For West Indies

296	for 1st	C. G. Greenidge and D. L. Haynes at St John's	1982-83
255	for 2nd	E. D. A. McMorris and R. B. Kanhai at Kingston	1961-62
220	for 3rd	I. V. A. Richards and A. I. Kallicharran at Bridgetown	1975-76
267	for 4th	C. L. Walcott and G. E. Gomez at Delhi	1948-49
219	for 5th	F. D. Weekes and B. H. Pairaudeau at Port-of-Spain	1952-53
250	for 6th	C. H. Lloyd and D. L. Murray at Bombay	1974-75
130	for 7th	C. G. Greenidge and M. D. Marshall at Kanpur	1983-84
124	for 8th	I. V. A. Richards and K. D. Boyce at Delhi	1974-75
161	for 9th†	C. H. Lloyd and A. M. E. Roberts at Calcutta	1983-84
98*	for 10th	F. M. M. Worrell and W. W. Hall at Port-of-Spain	1961-62

For India

153	for 1st	S. M. Gavaskar and C. P. S. Chauhan at Bombay	1978-79
344*	for 2nd†	S. M. Gavaskar and D. B. Vengsarkar at Calcutta	1978-79
177	for 3rd	N. S. Sidhu and S. R. Tendulkar at Nagpur	1994-95
172	for 4th	G. R. Viswanath and A. D. Gaekwad at Kanpur	1978-79
204	for 5th	S. M. Gavaskar and B. P. Patel at Port-of-Spain	1975-76
170	for 6th	S. M. Gavaskar and R. J. Shastri at Madras	1983-84
186	for 7th	D. N. Sardesai and E. D. Solkar at Bridgetown	1970-71
107	for 8th	Yashpal Sharma and B. S. Sandhu at Kingston	1982-83
143*	for 9th	S. M. Gavaskar and S. M. H. Kirmani at Madras	1983-84
64	for 10th	J. Srinath and S. L. V. Raju at Mohali.	1994-95

† *Denotes record partnership against all countries.*

TEN WICKETS OR MORE IN A MATCH

For West Indies (4)

11-126 (6-50, 5-76)	W. W. Hall, Kanpur..................................	1958-59
11-89 (5-34, 6-55)	M. D. Marshall, Port-of-Spain..................	1988-89
12-121 (7-64, 5-57)	A. M. E. Roberts, Madras......................	1974-75
10-101 (6-62, 4-39)	C. A. Walsh, Kingston..........................	1988-89

For India (4)

11-235 (7-157, 4-78)†	B. S. Chandrasekhar, Bombay...................	1966-67
10-223 (9-102, 1-121)	S. P. Gupte, Kanpur...........................	1958-59
16-136 (8-61, 8-75)†	N. D. Hirwani, Madras........................	1987-88
10-135 (1-52, 9-83)	Kapil Dev, Ahmedabad	1983-84

† *Signifies ten wickets or more on first appearance in West Indies–India Tests.*

WEST INDIES v PAKISTAN

Captains

Season	West Indies	Pakistan	T	WI	P	D
1957-58*W*	F. C. M. Alexander	A. H. Kardar	5	3	1	1
1958-59*P*	F. C. M. Alexander	Fazal Mahmood	3	1	2	0
1974-75*W*	C. H. Lloyd	Intikhab Alam	2	0	0	2
1976-77*W*	C. H. Lloyd	Mushtaq Mohammad	5	2	1	2
1980-81*P*	C. H. Lloyd	Javed Miandad	4	1	0	3
1986-87*P*	I. V. A. Richards	Imran Khan	3	1	1	1
1987-88*W*	I. V. A. Richards[1]	Imran Khan	3	1	1	1
1990-91*P*	D. L. Haynes	Imran Khan	3	1	1	1
1992-93*W*	R. B. Richardson	Wasim Akram	3	2	0	1
1997-98*P*	C. A. Walsh	Wasim Akram	3	0	3	0
1999-2000*W*	J. C. Adams	Moin Khan	3	1	0	2
	In West Indies		19	9	3	7
	In Pakistan		18	4	7	7
	Totals		37	13	10	14

P Played in Pakistan.   W Played in West Indies.

Note: The following was appointed by the home authority for only a minor proportion of the series:

[1]C. G. Greenidge (First).

HIGHEST INNINGS TOTALS

For West Indies in West Indies: 790-3 dec. at Kingston..................... 1957-58
              in Pakistan: 493 at Karachi............................ 1974-75

For Pakistan in West Indies: 657-8 dec. at Bridgetown................. 1957-58
            in Pakistan: 471 at Rawalpindi....................... 1997-98

LOWEST INNINGS TOTALS

For West Indies in West Indies: 127 at Port-of-Spain..................... 1992-93
              in Pakistan: 53 at Faisalabad........................ 1986-87

For Pakistan in West Indies: 106 at Bridgetown....................... 1957-58
            in Pakistan: 77 at Lahore............................ 1986-87

INDIVIDUAL HUNDREDS

For West Indies (26)

L. Baichan (1)
105*† Lahore 1974-75

P. J. L. Dujon (1)
106* Port-of-Spain 1987-88

R. C. Fredericks (1)
120 Port-of-Spain 1976-77

C. G. Greenidge (1)
100 Kingston . . . 1976-77

D. L. Haynes (3)
117 Karachi 1990-91
143*‡ Port-of-Spain 1992-93
125 Bridgetown . 1992-93

W. W. Hinds (1)
165 Bridgetown . 1999-00

C. L. Hooper (3)
134 Lahore 1990-91
178* St John's . . . 1992-93
106 Karachi 1997-98

C. C. Hunte (3)
142† Bridgetown . 1957-58
260 Kingston . . . 1957-58
114 Georgetown . 1957-58

B. D. Julien (1)
101 Karachi 1974-75

A. I. Kallicharran (1)
115 Karachi 1974-75

R. B. Kanhai (1)
217 Lahore 1958-59

C. H. Lloyd (1)
157 Bridgetown . 1976-77

I. V. A. Richards (2)
120* Multan 1980-81
123 Port-of-Spain 1987-88

I. T. Shillingford (1)
120 Georgetown . 1976-77

G. S. Sobers (3)
365* Kingston . . . 1957-58
125
109* } Georgetown . 1957-58

C. L. Walcott (1)
145 Georgetown . 1957-58

E. D. Weekes (1)
197† Bridgetown . 1957-58

For Pakistan (26)

Aamir Sohail (2)
160 Rawalpindi . . 1997-98
160 Karachi 1997-98

Asif Iqbal (1)
135 Kingston . . . 1976-77

Hanif Mohammad (2)
337† Bridgetown . 1957-58
103 Karachi 1958-59

Ijaz Ahmed, sen. (1)
151 Karachi 1997-98

Imtiaz Ahmed (1)
122 Kingston . . . 1957-58

Imran Khan (1)
123 Lahore 1980-81

Imran Nazir (1)
131† Bridgetown . 1999-00

Inzamam-ul-Haq (3)
123 St John's . . . 1992-93
177 Rawalpindi . . 1997-98
135 Georgetown . 1999-00

Javed Miandad (2)
114 Georgetown . 1987-88
102 Port-of-Spain 1987-88

Majid Khan (2)
100 Karachi 1974-75
167 Georgetown . 1976-77

Mushtaq Mohammad (2)
123 Lahore 1974-75

121 Port-of-Spain 1976-77

Saeed Ahmed (1)
150 Georgetown . 1957-58

Salim Malik (1)
102 Karachi 1990-91

Wasim Raja (2)
107* Karachi 1974-75
117* Bridgetown . 1976-77

Wazir Mohammad (2)
106 Kingston . . . 1957-58
189 Port-of-Spain 1957-58

Yousuf Youhana (2)
115 Bridgetown . 1999-00
103* St John's . . . 1999-00

† *Signifies hundred on first appearance in West Indies–Pakistan Tests.*
‡ *Carried his bat.*

RECORD PARTNERSHIPS FOR EACH WICKET

For West Indies

182	for 1st	R. C. Fredericks and C. G. Greenidge at Kingston	1976-77
446	for 2nd†	C. C. Hunte and G. S. Sobers at Kingston	1957-58
169	for 3rd	D. L. Haynes and B. C. Lara at Port-of-Spain	1992-93
188*	for 4th	G. S. Sobers and C. L. Walcott at Kingston	1957-58
185	for 5th	E. D. Weekes and O. G. Smith at Bridgetown	1957-58
151	for 6th	C. H. Lloyd and D. L. Murray at Bridgetown	1976-77
74	for 7th	S. Chanderpaul and N. A. M. McLean at Georgetown	1999-2000
60	for 8th	C. L. Hooper and A. C. Cummins at St John's	1992-93
61*	for 9th	P. J. L. Dujon and W. K. M. Benjamin at Bridgetown	1987-88
106	for 10th†	C. L. Hooper and C. A. Walsh at St John's	1992-93

For Pakistan

298	for 1st†	Aamir Sohail and Ijaz Ahmed, sen. at Karachi	1997-98
178	for 2nd	Hanif Mohammad and Saeed Ahmed at Karachi	1958-59
323	for 3rd	Aamir Sohail and Inzamam-ul-Haq at Rawalpindi	1997-98
174	for 4th	Shoaib Mohammad and Salim Malik at Karachi	1990-91

88	for 5th	Basit Ali and Inzamam-ul-Haq at St John's................	1992-93
206	for 6th	Inzamam-ul-Haq and Abdur Razzaq at Georgetown	1999-2000
128	for 7th[1]	Wasim Raja and Wasim Bari at Karachi..................	1974-75
94	for 8th	Salim Malik and Salim Yousuf at Port-of-Spain	1987-88
96	for 9th	Inzamam-ul-Haq and Nadeem Khan at St John's	1992-93
133	for 10th	Wasim Raja and Wasim Bari at Bridgetown	1976-77

† *Denotes record partnership against all countries.*
[1]*Although the seventh wicket added 168 runs against West Indies at Lahore in 1980-81, this comprised two partnerships with Imran Khan adding 72* with Abdul Qadir (retired hurt) and a further 96 with Sarfraz Nawaz.*

TEN WICKETS OR MORE IN A MATCH

For Pakistan (4)

12-100 (6-34, 6-66)	Fazal Mahmood, Dacca......................	1958-59
11-121 (7-80, 4-41)	Imran Khan, Georgetown	1987-88
10-106 (5-35, 5-71)	Mushtaq Ahmed, Peshawar	1997-98
11-110 (6-61, 5-49)	Wasim Akram, St John's.....................	1999-2000

Note: The best match figures for West Indies are 9-95 (8-29, 1-66) by C. E. H. Croft at Port-of-Spain, 1976-77.

WEST INDIES v SRI LANKA

	Captains					
Season	*West Indies*	*Sri Lanka*	*T*	*WI*	*SL*	*D*
1993-94*S*	R. B. Richardson	A. Ranatunga	1	0	0	1
1996-97*W*	C. A. Walsh	A. Ranatunga	2	1	0	1
	In West Indies		2	1	0	1
	In Sri Lanka		1	0	0	1
	Totals......................		3	1	0	2

W Played in West Indies. S Played in Sri Lanka.

HIGHEST INNINGS TOTALS

For West Indies: 343 at St Vincent		1996-97
For Sri Lanka: 233-8 at St Vincent................................		1996-97

LOWEST INNINGS TOTALS

For West Indies: 147 at St Vincent		1996-97
For Sri Lanka: 152 at St John's.................................		1996-97

INDIVIDUAL HUNDREDS
For West Indies (1)

B. C. Lara (1)
115   St Vincent . . 1996-97

Highest score for Sri Lanka: 90 by S. T. Jayasuriya at St Vincent   1996-97

HUNDRED PARTNERSHIPS
For West Indies
160 for 1st   S. L. Campbell and S. C. Williams at St John's   1996-97

For Sri Lanka
110 for 4th   S. T. Jayasuriya and A. Ranatunga at St John's   1996-97

BEST MATCH BOWLING ANALYSES
For West Indies
8-78 (5-37, 3-41)   C. E. L. Ambrose, St John's   1996-97

For Sri Lanka
8-106 (5-34, 3-72)   M. Muralitharan, St John's   1996-97

WEST INDIES v ZIMBABWE

Season	West Indies	Captains	Zimbabwe	T	WI	Z	D
1999-2000*W*	J. C. Adams		A. Flower	2	2	0	0

W Played in West Indies.

HIGHEST INNINGS TOTALS

For West Indies: 339 at Kingston.   1999-2000

For Zimbabwe: 308 at Kingston   1999-2000

LOWEST INNINGS TOTALS

For West Indies: 147 at Port-of-Spain.   1999-2000

For Zimbabwe: 63 at Port-of-Spain   1999-2000

INDIVIDUAL HUNDREDS
For West Indies (1)

J. C. Adams (1)
101*   Kingston . . . 1999-00

For Zimbabwe (2)

A. Flower (1)	**M. W. Goodwin** (1)
113*† Port-of-Spain 1999-00	113 Kingston . . . 1999-00

† *Signifies hundred on first appearance in West Indies–Zimbabwe Tests.*

HUNDRED PARTNERSHIPS

For West Indies

147 for 8th†   J. C. Adams and F. A. Rose at Kingston.   1999-2000

For Zimbabwe

176 for 4th   M. W. Goodwin and A. Flower at Kingston.   1999-2000
117 for 4th   T. R. Gripper and A. Flower at Port-of-Spain.   1999-2000

† *Denotes record partnership against all countries. S. V. Carlisle and H. K. Olonga added 54 for Zimbabwe's 10th wicket at Kingston in 1999-2000, also a record against all countries.*

BEST MATCH BOWLING ANALYSES

For West Indies

7-50 (4-42, 3-8)   C. E. L. Ambrose, Port-of-Spain   1999-2000

For Zimbabwe

9-72 (4-45, 5-27)   H. H. Streak, Port-of-Spain   1999-2000

NEW ZEALAND v INDIA

		Captains				
Season	*New Zealand*	*India*	*T*	*NZ*	*I*	*D*
1955-56*I*	H. B. Cave	P. R. Umrigar[1]	5	0	2	3
1964-65*I*	J. R. Reid	Nawab of Pataudi jun.	4	0	1	3
1967-68*N*	G. T. Dowling[2]	Nawab of Pataudi jun.	4	1	3	0
1969-70*I*	G. T. Dowling	Nawab of Pataudi jun.	3	1	1	1
1975-76*N*	G. M. Turner	B. S. Bedi[3]	3	1	1	1
1976-77*I*	G. M. Turner	B. S. Bedi	3	0	2	1
1980-81*N*	G. P. Howarth	S. M. Gavaskar	3	1	0	2
1988-89*I*	J. G. Wright	D. B. Vengsarkar	3	1	2	0
1989-90*N*	J. G. Wright	M. Azharuddin	3	1	0	2
1993-94*N*	K. R. Rutherford	M. Azharuddin	1	0	0	1
1995-96*I*	L. K. Germon	M. Azharuddin	3	0	1	2
1998-99*N*†	S. P. Fleming	M. Azharuddin	2	1	0	1
1999-2000*I*	S. P. Fleming	S. R. Tendulkar	3	0	1	2
	In India		24	2	10	12
	In New Zealand		16	5	4	7
	Totals		40	7	14	19

I Played in India. N Played in New Zealand.

† *The First Test at Dunedin was abandoned without a ball being bowled and is excluded.*

Notes: The following deputised for the official touring captain or were appointed by the home authority for a minor proportion of the series:
[1]Ghulam Ahmed (First). [2]B. W. Sinclair (First). [3]S. M. Gavaskar (First).

HIGHEST INNINGS TOTALS

For New Zealand in New Zealand: 502 at Christchurch   1967-68
        in India: 462-9 dec. at Calcutta   1964-65

For India in New Zealand: 482 at Auckland   1989-90
       in India: 583-7 dec. at Ahmedabad   1999-2000

LOWEST INNINGS TOTALS

For New Zealand in New Zealand: 100 at Wellington   1980-81
        in India: 124 at Hyderabad   1988-89

For India in New Zealand: 81 at Wellington   1975-76
       in India: 83 at Mohali   1999-2000

INDIVIDUAL HUNDREDS

For New Zealand (22)

C. L. Cairns (1)
126   Hamilton . . . 1998-99
M. D. Crowe (1)
113   Auckland . . . 1989-90
G. T. Dowling (3)
129   Bombay. . . . 1964-65
143   Dunedin . . . 1967-68
239   Christchurch . 1967-68
J. W. Guy (1)
102† Hyderabad . . 1955-56
G. P. Howarth (1)
137* Wellington . . 1980-81

A. H. Jones (1)
170* Auckland . . . 1989-90
J. M. Parker (1)
104   Bombay. . . . 1976-77
J. F. Reid (1)
123* Christchurch . 1980-81
J. R. Reid (2)
119* Delhi 1955-56
120   Calcutta. . . . 1955-56
I. D. S. Smith (1)
173   Auckland . . . 1989-90

B. Sutcliffe (3)
137*† Hyderabad . . 1955-56
230* Delhi 1955-56
151* Calcutta. . . . 1964-65
B. R. Taylor (1)
105† Calcutta. . . . 1964-65
G. M. Turner (2)
117   Christchurch . 1975-76
113   Kanpur 1976-77
J. G. Wright (3)
110   Auckland . . . 1980-81
185   Christchurch . 1989-90
113* Napier. 1989-90

For India (32)

S. Amarnath (1)
124† Auckland . . . 1975-76
M. Azharuddin (2)
192   Auckland . . . 1989-90
103* Wellington . . 1998-99
C. G. Borde (1)
109   Bombay. . . . 1964-65
R. Dravid (3)
190 }
103*} Hamilton . . . 1998-99
144   Mohali 1999-00
S. C. Ganguly (2)
101* Hamilton . . . 1998-99
125   Ahmedabad . 1999-00
S. M. Gavaskar (2)
116† Auckland . . . 1975-76
119   Bombay. . . . 1976-77

A. G. Kripal Singh (1)
100*† Hyderabad . . 1955-56
V. L. Manjrekar (3)
118† Hyderabad . . 1955-56
177   Delhi 1955-56
102* Madras 1964-65
V. Mankad (2)
223   Bombay. . . . 1955-56
231   Madras 1955-56
Nawab of Pataudi jun. (2)
153   Calcutta. . . . 1964-65
113   Delhi 1964-65
G. S. Ramchand (1)
106* Calcutta. . . . 1955-56
S. Ramesh (1)
110   Ahmedabad . 1999-00
Pankaj Roy (2)
100   Calcutta. . . . 1955-56

173   Madras 1955-56
D. N. Sardesai (2)
200* Bombay. . . . 1964-65
106   Delhi 1964-65
N. S. Sidhu (1)
116† Bangalore . . 1988-89
S. R. Tendulkar (3)
113   Wellington . . 1998-99
126* Mohali 1999-00
217   Ahmedabad . 1999-00
P. R. Umrigar (1)
223† Hyderabad . . 1955-56
G. R. Viswanath (1)
103* Kanpur 1976-77
A. L. Wadekar (1)
143   Wellington . . 1967-68

† *Signifies hundred on first appearance in New Zealand–India Tests. B. R. Taylor provides the only instance for New Zealand of a player scoring his maiden hundred in first-class cricket in his first Test.*

RECORD PARTNERSHIPS FOR EACH WICKET

For New Zealand

149	for 1st	T. J. Franklin and J. G. Wright at Napier	1989-90
155	for 2nd	G. T. Dowling and B. E. Congdon at Dunedin.	1967-68
222*	for 3rd	B. Sutcliffe and J. R. Reid at Delhi.	1955-56
160	for 4th	R. G. Twose and C. D. McMillan at Hamilton.	1998-99
140	for 5th	C. D. McMillan and A. C. Parore at Hamilton.	1998-99
137	for 6th	C. D. McMillan and C. L. Cairns at Wellington	1998-99
163	for 7th	B. Sutcliffe and B. R. Taylor at Calcutta.	1964-65
137	for 8th†	D. J. Nash and D. L. Vettori at Wellington	1998-99
136	for 9th†	I. D. S. Smith and M. C. Snedden at Auckland	1989-90
61	for 10th	J. T. Ward and R. O. Collinge at Madras	1964-65

For India

413	for 1st†	V. Mankad and Pankaj Roy at Madras	1955-56
204	for 2nd	S. M. Gavaskar and S. Amarnath at Auckland.	1975-76
238	for 3rd	P. R. Umrigar and V. L. Manjrekar at Hyderabad	1955-56
281	for 4th†	S. R. Tendulkar and S. C. Ganguly at Ahmedabad	1999-2000
127	for 5th	V. L. Manjrekar and G. S. Ramchand at Delhi.	1955-56
193*	for 6th	D. N. Sardesai and Hanumant Singh at Bombay	1964-65
128	for 7th	S. R. Tendulkar and K. S. More at Napier	1989-90
144	for 8th	R. Dravid and J. Srinath at Hamilton.	1998-99
105	for 9th	{ S. M. H. Kirmani and B. S. Bedi at Bombay	1976-77
		{ S. M. H. Kirmani and N. S. Yadav at Auckland.	1980-81
57	for 10th	R. B. Desai and B. S. Bedi at Dunedin	1967-68

† *Denotes record partnership against all countries.*

TEN WICKETS OR MORE IN A MATCH

For New Zealand (2)

11-58 (4-35, 7-23)	R. J. Hadlee, Wellington	1975-76
10-88 (6-49, 4-39)	R. J. Hadlee, Bombay.	1988-89

For India (3)

10-134 (4-67, 6-67)	A. Kumble, Kanpur	1999-2000
11-140 (3-64, 8-76)	E. A. S. Prasanna, Auckland	1975-76
12-152 (8-72, 4-80)	S. Venkataraghavan, Delhi.	1964-65

NEW ZEALAND v PAKISTAN

		Captains				
Season	New Zealand	Pakistan	T	NZ	P	D
1955-56*P*	H. B. Cave	A. H. Kardar	3	0	2	1
1964-65*N*	J. R. Reid	Hanif Mohammad	3	0	0	3
1964-65*P*	J. R. Reid	Hanif Mohammad	3	0	2	1
1969-70*P*	G. T. Dowling	Intikhab Alam	3	1	0	2
1972-73*N*	B. E. Congdon	Intikhab Alam	3	0	1	2
1976-77*P*	G. M. Turner[i]	Mushtaq Mohammad	3	0	2	1
1978-79*N*	M. G. Burgess	Mushtaq Mohammad	3	0	1	2
1984-85*P*	J. V. Coney	Zaheer Abbas	3	0	2	1

Captains

Season	New Zealand	Pakistan	T	NZ	P	D
1984-85*N*	G. P. Howarth	Javed Miandad	3	2	0	1
1988-89*N†*	J. G. Wright	Imran Khan	2	0	0	2
1990-91*P*	M. D. Crowe	Javed Miandad	3	0	3	0
1992-93*N*	K. R. Rutherford	Javed Miandad	1	0	1	0
1993-94*N*	K. R. Rutherford	Salim Malik	3	1	2	0
1995-96*N*	L. K. Germon	Wasim Akram	1	0	1	0
1996-97*P*	L. K. Germon	Saeed Anwar	2	1	1	0
	In Pakistan		20	2	12	6
	In New Zealand		19	3	6	10
	Totals		39	5	18	16

N Played in New Zealand. P Played in Pakistan.

　† *The First Test at Dunedin was abandoned without a ball being bowled and is excluded.*

Note: The following deputised for the official touring captain:
¹J. M. Parker (Third).

HIGHEST INNINGS TOTALS

For New Zealand in New Zealand: 492 at Wellington . . . . 　1984-85
　　　　　　　　　　in Pakistan: 482-6 dec. at Lahore . . . . 　1964-65

For Pakistan in New Zealand: 616-5 dec. at Auckland . . . . 　1988-89
　　　　　　　　　　in Pakistan: 565-9 dec. at Karachi . . . . 　1976-77

LOWEST INNINGS TOTALS

For New Zealand in New Zealand: 93 at Hamilton . . . . 　1992-93
　　　　　　　　　　in Pakistan: 70 at Dacca . . . . 　1955-56

For Pakistan in New Zealand: 169 at Auckland . . . . 　1984-85
　　　　　　　　　　in Pakistan: 102 at Faisalabad . . . . 　1990-91

INDIVIDUAL HUNDREDS

For New Zealand (21)

M. G. Burgess (2)
119*　Dacca . . . . . 　1969-70
111　Lahore . . . . 　1976-77
J. V. Coney (1)
111*　Dunedin . . . 　1984-85
M. D. Crowe (2)
174　Wellington . . 　1988-89
108*　Lahore . . . . 　1990-91
B. A. Edgar (1)
129†　Christchurch . 　1978-79
M. J. Greatbatch (1)
133　Hamilton . . . 　1992-93
B. F. Hastings (1)
110　Auckland . . . 　1972-73

G. P. Howarth (1)
114　Napier . . . . 　1978-79
W. K. Lees (1)
152　Karachi . . . . 　1976-77
S. N. McGregor (1)
111　Lahore . . . . 　1955-56
R. E. Redmond (1)
107†　Auckland . . . 　1972-73
J. F. Reid (3)
106　Hyderabad . . 　1984-85
148　Wellington . . 　1984-85
158*　Auckland . . . 　1984-85
J. R. Reid (1)
128　Karachi . . . . 　1964-65

B. W. Sinclair (1)
130　Lahore . . . . 　1964-65
S. A. Thomson (1)
120*　Christchurch . 　1993-94
G. M. Turner (1)
110†　Dacca . . . . . 　1969-70
J. G. Wright (1)
107　Karachi . . . . 　1984-85
B. A. Young (1)
120　Christchurch . 　1993-94

For Pakistan (41)

Asif Iqbal (3)
175 Dunedin . . . 1972-73
166 Lahore 1976-77
104 Napier. 1978-79
Basit Ali (1)
103 Christchurch . 1993-94
Hanif Mohammad (3)
103 Dacca 1955-56
100* Christchurch . 1964-65
203* Lahore 1964-65
Ijaz Ahmed, sen. (2)
103 Christchurch . 1995-96
125 Rawalpindi . . 1996-97
Imtiaz Ahmed (1)
209 Lahore 1955-56
Inzamam-ul-Haq (1)
135* Wellington . . 1993-94
Javed Miandad (7)
163† Lahore 1976-77
206 Karachi 1976-77

160* Christchurch . 1978-79
104 } Hyderabad . . 1984-85
103*}
118 Wellington . . 1988-89
271 Auckland . . . 1988-89
Majid Khan (3)
110 Auckland . . . 1972-73
112 Karachi 1976-77
119* Napier. 1978-79
Mohammad Ilyas (1)
126 Karachi 1964-65
Mohammad Wasim (1)
109*† Lahore 1996-97
Mudassar Nazar (1)
106 Hyderabad . . 1984-85
Mushtaq Mohammad (3)
201 Dunedin . . . 1972-73
101 Hyderabad . . 1976-77
107 Karachi 1976-77
Sadiq Mohammad (2)
166 Wellington . . 1972-73

103* Hyderabad . . 1976-77
Saeed Ahmed (1)
172 Karachi 1964-65
Saeed Anwar (2)
169 Wellington . . 1993-94
149 Rawalpindi . . 1996-97
Salim Malik (2)
119* Karachi 1984-85
140 Wellington . . 1993-94
Shoaib Mohammad (5)
163 Wellington . . 1988-89
112 Auckland . . . 1988-89
203* Karachi 1990-91
105 Lahore 1990-91
142 Faisalabad . . 1990-91
Waqar Hassan (1)
189 Lahore 1955-56
Zaheer Abbas (1)
135 Auckland . . . 1978-79

† *Signifies hundred on first appearance in New Zealand–Pakistan Tests.*

Notes: Mushtaq and Sadiq Mohammad, at Hyderabad in 1976-77, provide the fourth instance in Test matches, after the Chappells (thrice), of brothers each scoring hundreds in the same innings.

RECORD PARTNERSHIPS FOR EACH WICKET

For New Zealand

159 for 1st	R. E. Redmond and G. M. Turner at Auckland	1972-73
195 for 2nd	J. G. Wright and G. P. Howarth at Napier	1978-79
178 for 3rd	B. W. Sinclair and J. R. Reid at Lahore	1964-65
128 for 4th	B. F. Hastings and M. G. Burgess at Wellington	1972-73
183 for 5th†	M. G. Burgess and R. W. Anderson at Lahore	1976-77
145 for 6th	J. F. Reid and R. J. Hadlee at Wellington	1984-85
186 for 7th†	W. K. Lees and R. J. Hadlee at Karachi	1976-77
100 for 8th	B. W. Yuile and D. R. Hadlee at Karachi	1969-70
96 for 9th	M. G. Burgess and R. S. Cunis at Dacca	1969-70
151 for 10th†	B. F. Hastings and R. O. Collinge at Auckland	1972-73

For Pakistan

172 for 1st	Ramiz Raja and Shoaib Mohammad at Karachi	1990-91
262 for 2nd	Saeed Anwar and Ijaz Ahmed, sen. at Rawalpindi	1996-97
248 for 3rd	Shoaib Mohammad and Javed Miandad at Auckland	1988-89
350 for 4th†	Mushtaq Mohammad and Asif Iqbal at Dunedin	1972-73
281 for 5th†	Javed Miandad and Asif Iqbal at Lahore	1976-77
217 for 6th†	Hanif Mohammad and Majid Khan at Lahore.	1964-65
308 for 7th†	Waqar Hassan and Imtiaz Ahmed at Lahore	1955-56
89 for 8th	Anil Dalpat and Iqbal Qasim at Karachi	1984-85
52 for 9th	Intikhab Alam and Arif Butt at Auckland	1964-65
65 for 10th	Salah-ud-Din and Mohammad Farooq at Rawalpindi	1964-65

† *Denotes record partnership against all countries.*

TEN WICKETS OR MORE IN A MATCH

For New Zealand (1)

11-152 (7-52, 4-100)   C. Pringle, Faisalabad   1990-91

For Pakistan (10)

10-182 (5-91, 5-91)	Intikhab Alam, Dacca	1969-70
11-130 (7-52, 4-78)	Intikhab Alam, Dunedin	1972-73
11-130 (4-64, 7-66)†	Mohammad Zahid, Rawalpindi	1996-97
10-171 (3-115, 7-56)	Mushtaq Ahmed, Christchurch	1995-96
10-143 (4-59, 6-84)	Mushtaq Ahmed, Lahore	1996-97
10-106 (3-20, 7-86)	Waqar Younis, Lahore	1990-91
12-130 (7-76, 5-54)	Waqar Younis, Faisalabad	1990-91
10-128 (5-56, 5-72)	Wasim Akram, Dunedin	1984-85
11-179 (4-60, 7-119)	Wasim Akram, Wellington	1993-94
11-79 (5-37, 6-42)†	Zulfiqar Ahmed, Karachi	1955-56

† *Signifies ten wickets or more on first appearance in New Zealand–Pakistan Tests.*

Note: Waqar Younis's performances were in successive matches.

NEW ZEALAND v SRI LANKA

	Captains					
Season	*New Zealand*	*Sri Lanka*	*T*	*NZ*	*SL*	*D*
1982-83*N*	G. P. Howarth	D. S. de Silva	2	2	0	0
1983-84*S*	G. P. Howarth	L. R. D. Mendis	3	2	0	1
1986-87*S*†	J. J. Crowe	L. R. D. Mendis	1	0	0	1
1990-91*N*	M. D. Crowe[1]	A. Ranatunga	3	0	0	3
1992-93*S*	M. D. Crowe	A. Ranatunga	2	0	1	1
1994-95*N*	K. R. Rutherford	A. Ranatunga	2	0	1	1
1996-97*N*	S. P. Fleming	A. Ranatunga	2	2	0	0
1997-98*S*	S. P. Fleming	A. Ranatunga	3	1	2	0
	In New Zealand		9	4	1	4
	In Sri Lanka		9	3	3	3
	Totals		18	7	4	7

N Played in New Zealand.   S Played in Sri Lanka.

† *The Second and Third Tests were cancelled owing to civil disturbances.*

Note: The following was appointed by the home authority for only a minor proportion of the series:
[1] I. D. S. Smith (Third).

HIGHEST INNINGS TOTALS

For New Zealand in New Zealand: 671-4 at Wellington		1990-91
in Sri Lanka: 459 at Colombo (CCC)		1983-84
For Sri Lanka in New Zealand: 497 at Wellington		1990-91
in Sri Lanka: 397-9 dec. at Colombo (CCC)		1986-87

LOWEST INNINGS TOTALS

For New Zealand in New Zealand: 109 at Napier		1994-95
in Sri Lanka: 102 at Colombo (SSC)		1992-93
For Sri Lanka in New Zealand: 93 at Wellington		1982-83
in Sri Lanka: 97 at Kandy		1986-87

INDIVIDUAL HUNDREDS

For New Zealand (13)

J. J. Crowe (1)
120* Colombo (CCC) 1986-87
M. D. Crowe (2)
299 Wellington . . 1990-91
107 Colombo (SSC) 1992-93
S. P. Fleming (1)
174* Colombo (RPS) 1997-98
R. J. Hadlee (1)
151* Colombo (CCC) 1986-87

A. H. Jones (3)
186 Wellington . . 1990-91
122 } Hamilton . . . 1990-91
100* }
C. D. McMillan (1)
142† Colombo (RPS) 1997-98
J. F. Reid (1)
180 Colombo (CCC) 1983-84

K. R. Rutherford (1)
105 Moratuwa . . 1992-93
J. G. Wright (1)
101 Hamilton . . . 1990-91
B. A. Young (1)
267* Dunedin . . . 1996-97

For Sri Lanka (12)

P. A. de Silva (2)
267† Wellington . . 1990-91
123 Auckland . . . 1990-91
R. L. Dias (1)
108† Colombo (SSC) 1983-84
A. P. Gurusinha (3)
119 } Hamilton . . . 1990-91
102 }

127 Dunedin . . . 1994-95
D. P. M. D. Jayawardene (1)
167 Galle 1997-98
R. S. Kaluwitharana (1)
103† Dunedin . . . 1996-97
D. S. B. P. Kuruppu (1)
201*† Colombo (CCC) 1986-87

R. S. Mahanama (2)
153 Moratuwa . . 1992-93
109 Colombo (SSC) 1992-93
H. P. Tillekeratne (1)
108 Dunedin . . . 1994-95

† *Signifies hundred on first appearance in New Zealand–Sri Lanka Tests.*

Note: A. P. Gurusinha and A. H. Jones at Hamilton in 1990-91 provided the second instance of a player on each side hitting two separate hundreds in a Test match.

RECORD PARTNERSHIPS FOR EACH WICKET

For New Zealand

161	for 1st	T. J. Franklin and J. G. Wright at Hamilton	1990-91
140	for 2nd	B. A. Young and M. J. Horne at Dunedin	1996-97
467	for 3rd†‡	A. H. Jones and M. D. Crowe at Wellington	1990-91
240	for 4th	S. P. Fleming and C. D. McMillan at Colombo (RPS)	1997-98
151	for 5th	K. R. Rutherford and C. Z. Harris at Moratuwa	1992-93
246*	for 6th†	I. J. Crowe and R. J. Hadlee at Colombo (CCC)	1986-87
47	for 7th	D. N. Patel and M. L. Su'a at Dunedin	1994-95
79	for 8th	J. V. Coney and W. K. Lees at Christchurch	1982-83
43	for 9th	A. C. Parore and P. J. Wiseman at Galle	1997-98
52	for 10th	W. K. Lees and E. J. Chatfield at Christchurch	1982-83

For Sri Lanka

102	for 1st	R. S. Mahanama and U. C. Hathurusinghe at Colombo (SSC)	1992-93
138	for 2nd	R. S. Mahanama and A. P. Gurusinha at Moratuwa	1992-93
159*	for 3rd[1]	S. Wettimuny and R. L. Dias at Colombo (SSC)	1983-84
192	for 4th	A. P. Gurusinha and H. P. Tillekeratne at Dunedin	1994-95
130	for 5th	R. S. Madugalle and D. S. de Silva at Wellington	1982-83
109*	for 6th[2]	R. S. Madugalle and A. Ranatunga at Colombo (CCC)	1983-84
137	for 7th	R. S. Kaluwitharana and W. P. U. J. C. Vaas at Dunedin	1996-97
73	for 8th	H. P. Tillekeratne and G. P. Wickremasinghe at Dunedin	1996-97
31	for 9th	{ G. F. Labrooy and R. J. Ratnayake at Auckland	1990-91
		{ S. T. Jayasuriya and R. J. Ratnayake at Auckland	1990-91
71	for 10th	R. S. Kaluwitharana and M. Muralitharan at Colombo (SSC)	1997-98

† *Denotes record partnership against all countries.*

‡ *Record third-wicket partnership in first-class cricket.*

[1] *163 runs were added for this wicket in two separate partnerships: S. Wettimuny retired hurt and was replaced by J. R. Ratnayeke when 159 had been added.*

[2] *119 runs were added for this wicket in two separate partnerships: R. S. Madugalle retired hurt and was replaced by D. S. de Silva when 109 had been added.*

TEN WICKETS OR MORE IN A MATCH

For New Zealand (1)

10-102 (5-73, 5-29)   R. J. Hadlee, Colombo (CCC)...................   1983-84

For Sri Lanka (1)

10-90 (5-47, 5-43)†   W. P. U. J. C. Vaas, Napier.....................   1994-95

† *Signifies ten wickets or more on first appearance in New Zealand–Sri Lanka Tests.*

NEW ZEALAND v ZIMBABWE

Season	New Zealand	*Captains* Zimbabwe	T	NZ	Z	D
1992-93Z	M. D. Crowe	D. L. Houghton	2	1	0	1
1995-96N	L. K. Germon	A. Flower	2	0	0	2
1997-98Z	S. P. Fleming	A. D. R. Campbell	2	0	0	2
1997-98N	S. P. Fleming	A. D. R. Campbell	2	2	0	0
	In New Zealand...............		4	2	0	2
	In Zimbabwe.................		4	1	0	3
	Totals......................		8	3	0	5

N Played in New Zealand.   Z Played in Zimbabwe.

HIGHEST INNINGS TOTALS

For New Zealand in New Zealand: 460 at Auckland......................   1997-98
in Zimbabwe: 403 at Bulawayo   1997-98

For Zimbabwe in New Zealand: 326 at Auckland   1995-96
in Zimbabwe: 461 at Bulawayo   1997-98

LOWEST INNINGS TOTALS

For New Zealand in New Zealand: 251 at Auckland......................   1995-96
in Zimbabwe: 207 at Harare   1997-98

For Zimbabwe in New Zealand: 170 at Auckland   1997-98
in Zimbabwe: 137 at Harare......................   1992-93

INDIVIDUAL HUNDREDS

For New Zealand (7)

N. J. Astle (1)
114   Auckland... 1997-98

M. J. Horne (1)
157   Auckland... 1997-98

C. M. Spearman (1)
112   Auckland... 1995-96

C. L. Cairns (1)
120   Auckland... 1995-96

R. T. Latham (1)
119†   Bulawayo... 1992-93

M. D. Crowe (1)
140   Harare..... 1992-93

C. D. McMillan (1)
139†   Wellington .. 1997-98

For Zimbabwe (5)

K. J. Arnott (1)
101*† Bulawayo... 1992-93

D. L. Houghton (1)
104*   Auckland... 1995-96

G. W. Flower (2)
104 }
151 } Harare..... 1997-98

G. J. Whittall (1)
203*   Bulawayo... 1997-98

† *Signifies hundred on first appearance in New Zealand–Zimbabwe Tests.*

RECORD PARTNERSHIPS FOR EACH WICKET

For New Zealand

214	for 1st	C. M. Spearman and R. G. Twose at Auckland...............	1995-96
127	for 2nd	R. T. Latham and A. H. Jones at Bulawayo	1992-93
71	for 3rd	A. H. Jones and M. D. Crowe at Bulawayo	1992-93
243	for 4th†	M. J. Horne and N. J. Astle at Auckland..................	1997-98
166	for 5th	A. C. Parore and C. L. Cairns at Auckland	1995-96
82*	for 6th	A. C. Parore and L. K. Germon at Hamilton	1995-96
108	for 7th	C. D. McMillan and D. J. Nash at Wellington..............	1997-98
112	for 8th	C. Z. Harris and D. L. Vettori at Bulawayo	1997-98
18	for 9th	D. L. Vettori and S. B. O'Connor at Bulawayo	1997-98
27	for 10th	C. D. McMillan and S. B. Doull at Auckland..............	1997-98

For Zimbabwe

156	for 1st†	G. J. Rennie and G. W. Flower at Harare..................	1997-98
107	for 2nd	K. J. Arnott and A. D. R. Campbell at Harare	1992-93
70	for 3rd	A. Flower and G. J. Whittall at Bulawayo	1997-98
88	for 4th	D. L. Houghton and A. Flower at Auckland	1995-96
78	for 5th	G. J. Whittall and D. L. Houghton at Bulawayo	1997-98
70	for 6th	D. L. Houghton and A. Flower at Bulawayo	1992-93
91	for 7th	G. J. Whittall and P. A. Strang at Hamilton	1995-96
94	for 8th	A. D. R. Campbell and H. H. Streak at Wellington	1997-98
46	for 9th	G. J. Crocker and M. G. Burmester at Harare.............	1992-93
40	for 10th	G. J. Whittall and E. Matambanadzo at Bulawayo	1997-98

† *Denotes record partnership against all countries.*

TEN WICKETS OR MORE IN A MATCH

For Zimbabwe (1)

11-255 (6-109, 5-146) A. G. Huckle, Bulawayo 1997-98

Note: The best match figures for New Zealand are 8-85 (4-35, 4-50) by S. B. Doull at Auckland, 1997-98.

INDIA v PAKISTAN

		Captains				
Season	India	Pakistan	T	I	P	D
1952-53*I*	L. Amarnath	A. H. Kardar	5	2	1	2
1954-55*P*	V. Mankad	A. H. Kardar	5	0	0	5
1960-61*I*	N. J. Contractor	Fazal Mahmood	5	0	0	5
1978-79*P*	B. S. Bedi	Mushtaq Mohammad	3	0	2	1
1979-80*I*	S. M. Gavaskar[1]	Asif Iqbal	6	2	0	4
1982-83*P*	S. M. Gavaskar	Imran Khan	6	0	3	3
1983-84*I*	Kapil Dev	Zaheer Abbas	3	0	0	3
1984-85*P*	S. M. Gavaskar	Zaheer Abbas	2	0	0	2
1986-87*I*	Kapil Dev	Imran Khan	5	0	1	4
1989-90*P*	K. Srikkanth	Imran Khan	4	0	0	4
1998-99*I*	M. Azharuddin	Wasim Akram	2	1	1	0
1998-99*I*†	M. Azharuddin	Wasim Akram	1	0	1	0
	In India		27	5	4	18
	In Pakistan		20	0	5	15
	Totals......................		47	5	9	33

I Played in India. P Played in Pakistan.

 † *This Test was part of the Asian Test Championship and was not counted as part of the preceding bilateral series.*

Note: The following was appointed by the home authority for only a minor proportion of the series:
 [1]G. R. Viswanath (Sixth).

HIGHEST INNINGS TOTALS

For India in India: 539-9 dec. at Madras   1960-61
     in Pakistan: 509 at Lahore   1989-90

For Pakistan in India: 487-9 dec. at Madras   1986-87
     in Pakistan: 699-5 at Lahore   1989-90

LOWEST INNINGS TOTALS

For India in India: 106 at Lucknow.   1952-53
     in Pakistan: 145 at Karachi   1954-55

For Pakistan in India: 116 at Bangalore   1986-87
     in Pakistan: 158 at Dacca   1954-55

INDIVIDUAL HUNDREDS

For India (32)

M. Amarnath (4)
109*	Lahore	1982-83
120	Lahore	1982-83
103*	Karachi	1982-83
101*	Lahore	1984-85

M. Azharuddin (3)
141	Calcutta	1986-87
110	Jaipur	1986-87
109	Faisalabad	1989-90

C. G. Borde (1)
177*	Madras	1960-61

A. D. Gaekwad (1)
201	Jullundur	1983-84

S. M. Gavaskar (5)
111 / 137 }	Karachi	1978-79
166	Madras	1979-80
127*‡	Faisalabad	1982-83
103*	Bangalore	1983-84

V. S. Hazare (1)
146*	Bombay	1952-53

S. V. Manjrekar (2)
113*†	Karachi	1989-90
218	Lahore	1989-90

S. M. Patil (1)
127	Faisalabad	1984-85

R. J. Shastri (3)
128	Karachi	1982-83
139	Faisalabad	1984-85
125	Jaipur	1986-87

R. H. Shodhan (1)
110†	Calcutta	1952-53

K. Srikkanth (1)
123	Madras	1986-87

S. R. Tendulkar (1)
136	Chennai	1998-99

P. R. Umrigar (5)
102	Bombay	1952-53
108	Peshawar	1954-55
115	Kanpur	1960-61
117	Madras	1960-61
112	Delhi	1960-61

D. B. Vengsarkar (2)
146*	Delhi	1979-80
109	Ahmedabad	1986-87

G. R. Viswanath (1)
145†	Faisalabad	1978-79

For Pakistan (43)

Aamer Malik (2)
117	Faisalabad	1989-90
113	Lahore	1989-90

Alim ud-Din (1)
103*	Karachi	1954-55

Asif Iqbal (1)
104†	Faisalabad	1978-79

Hanif Mohammad (2)
142	Bahawalpur	1954-55
160	Bombay	1960-61

Ijaz Faqih (1)
105†	Ahmedabad	1986-87

Imtiaz Ahmed (1)
135	Madras	1960-61

Imran Khan (3)
117	Faisalabad	1982-83
135*	Madras	1986-87
109*	Karachi	1989-90

Javed Miandad (5)
154*†	Faisalabad	1978-79
100	Karachi	1978-79
126	Faisalabad	1982-83
280*	Hyderabad	1982-83
145	Lahore	1989-90

Mohsin Khan (1)
101*†	Lahore	1982-83

Mudassar Nazar (6)
126	Bangalore	1979-80
119	Karachi	1982-83
231	Hyderabad	1982-83
152*‡	Lahore	1982-83
152	Karachi	1982-83
199	Faisalabad	1984-85

Mushtaq Mohammad (1)
101	Delhi	1960-61

Nazar Mohammad (1)
124*‡	Lucknow	1952-53

Qasim Omar (1)
210	Faisalabad	1984-85

Ramiz Raja (1)
114	Jaipur	1986-87

Saeed Ahmed (2)
121†	Bombay	1960-61
103	Madras	1960-61

Saeed Anwar (1)
188*‡	Calcutta	1998-99

Salim Malik (3)
107	Faisalabad	1982-83
102*	Faisalabad	1984-85
102*	Karachi	1989-90

Shahid Afridi (1)
141†	Chennai	1998-99

Shoaib Mohammad (2)
101	Madras	1986-87
203*	Lahore	1989-90

Wasim Raja (1)
125	Jullundur	1983-84

Zaheer Abbas (6)
176†	Faisalabad	1978-79
235*	Lahore	1978-79
215	Lahore	1982-83
186	Karachi	1982-83
168	Faisalabad	1982-83
168*	Lahore	1984-85

† *Signifies hundred on first appearance in India–Pakistan Tests.*
‡ *Carried his bat.*

RECORD PARTNERSHIPS FOR EACH WICKET

For India

200 for 1st	S. M. Gavaskar and K. Srikkanth at Madras	1986-87
135 for 2nd	N. S. Sidhu and S. V. Manjrekar at Karachi	1989-90
190 for 3rd	M. Amarnath and Yashpal Sharma at Lahore	1982-83
186 for 4th	S. V. Manjrekar and R. J. Shastri at Lahore	1989-90
200 for 5th	S. M. Patil and R. J. Shastri at Faisalabad	1984-85
143 for 6th	M. Azharuddin and Kapil Dev at Calcutta	1986-87
155 for 7th	R. M. H. Binny and Madan Lal at Bangalore	1983-84
122 for 8th	S. M. H. Kirmani and Madan Lal at Faisalabad	1982-83
149 for 9th†	P. G. Joshi and R. B. Desai at Bombay	1960-61
109 for 10th†	H. R. Adhikari and Ghulam Ahmed at Delhi	1952-53

For Pakistan

162 for 1st	Hanif Mohammad and Imtiaz Ahmed at Madras	1960-61
250 for 2nd	Mudassar Nazar and Qasim Omar at Faisalabad	1984-85
451 for 3rd†	Mudassar Nazar and Javed Miandad at Hyderabad	1982-83
287 for 4th	Javed Miandad and Zaheer Abbas at Faisalabad	1982-83
213 for 5th	Zaheer Abbas and Mudassar Nazar at Karachi	1982-83
207 for 6th	Salim Malik and Imran Khan at Faisalabad	1982-83
154 for 7th	Imran Khan and Ijaz Faqih at Ahmedabad	1986-87
112 for 8th	Imran Khan and Wasim Akram at Madras	1986-87
60 for 9th	Wasim Bari and Iqbal Qasim at Bangalore	1979-80
104 for 10th	Zulfiqar Ahmed and Amir Elahi at Madras	1952-53

† *Denotes record partnership against all countries.*

TEN WICKETS OR MORE IN A MATCH

For India (5)

11-146 (4-90, 7-56)	Kapil Dev, Madras	1979-80
14-149 (4-75, 10-74)	A. Kumble, Delhi	1998-99
10-126 (7-27, 3-99)	Maninder Singh, Bangalore	1986-87
13-131 (8-52, 5-79)†	V. Mankad, Delhi	1952-53
13-132 (5-46, 8-86)	J. Srinath, Calcutta	1998-99

For Pakistan (7)

12-94 (5-52, 7-42)	Fazal Mahmood, Lucknow	1952-53
11-79 (3-19, 8-60)	Imran Khan, Karachi	1982-83
11-180 (6-98, 5-82)	Imran Khan, Faisalabad	1982-83
10-175 (4-135, 6-40)	Iqbal Qasim, Bombay	1979-80
10-187 (5-94, 5-93)†	Saqlain Mushtaq, Chennai	1998-99
10-216 (5-94, 5-122)	Saqlain Mushtaq, Delhi	1998-99
11-190 (8-69, 3-121)	Sikander Bakht, Delhi	1979-80

† *Signifies ten wickets or more on first appearance in India–Pakistan Tests.*

INDIA v SRI LANKA

	Captains					
Season	*India*	*Sri Lanka*	*T*	*I*	*SL*	*D*
1982-83*I*	S. M. Gavaskar	B. Warnapura	1	0	0	1
1985-86*S*	Kapil Dev	L. R. D. Mendis	3	0	1	2
1986-87*I*	Kapil Dev	L. R. D. Mendis	3	2	0	1
1990-91*I*	M. Azharuddin	A. Ranatunga	1	1	0	0
1993-94*S*	M. Azharuddin	A. Ranatunga	3	1	0	2
1993-94*I*	M. Azharuddin	A. Ranatunga	3	3	0	0
1997-98*S*	S. R. Tendulkar	A. Ranatunga	2	0	0	2
1997-98*I*	S. R. Tendulkar	A. Ranatunga	3	0	0	3
1998-99*S*†	M. Azharuddin	A. Ranatunga	1	0	0	1
	In India		11	6	0	5
	In Sri Lanka		9	1	1	7
	Totals		20	7	1	12

I Played in India.   S Played in Sri Lanka.

† *This Test was part of the Asian Test Championship.*

HIGHEST INNINGS TOTALS

For India in India: 676-7 at Kanpur 1986-87
        in Sri Lanka: 537-8 dec. at Colombo (RPS) 1997-98

For Sri Lanka in India: 420 at Kanpur 1986-87
        in Sri Lanka: 952-6 dec. at Colombo (RPS) 1997-98

LOWEST INNINGS TOTALS

For India in India: 288 at Chandigarh 1990-91
        in Sri Lanka: 198 at Colombo (PSS) 1985-86

For Sri Lanka in India: 82 at Chandigarh 1990-91
        in Sri Lanka: 198 at Kandy 1985-86

INDIVIDUAL HUNDREDS

For India (30)

M. Amarnath (2)
116*   Kandy   1985-86
131   Nagpur   1986-87
M. Azharuddin (5)
199   Kanpur   1986-87
108   Bangalore . .   1993-94
152   Ahmedabad .   1993-94
126   Colombo (RPS)   1997-98
108*   Colombo (SSC)   1997-98
R. Dravid (1)
107   Colombo (SSC)   1998-99
S. C. Ganguly (3)
147   Colombo (SSC)   1997-98
109   Mohali   1997-98
173   Mumbai   1997-98

S. M. Gavaskar (2)
155†   Madras   1982-83
176   Kanpur   1986-87
V. G. Kambli (2)
125   Colombo (SSC)   1993-94
120   Colombo (PSS)   1993-94
Kapil Dev (1)
163   Kanpur   1986-87
S. M. Patil (1)
114*†   Madras   1982-83
S. Ramesh (1)
143†   Colombo (SSC)   1998-99
N. S. Sidhu (4)
104   Colombo (SSC)   1993-94

124   Lucknow . . .   1993-94
111   Colombo (RPS)   1997-98
131   Mohali   1997-98
S. R. Tendulkar (6)
104*   Colombo (SSC)   1993-94
142   Lucknow . . .   1993-94
143   Colombo (RPS)   1997-98
139   Colombo (SSC)   1997-98
148   Mumbai   1997-98
124*   Colombo (SSC)   1998-99
D. B. Vengsarkar (2)
153   Nagpur   1986-87
166   Cuttack   1986-87

Look to the Future
and win a free Almanack for life

Wisden will launch its new Internet service this summer.
Register now at www.wisden.com and you could win
a free Almanack for life.

WISDEN
www.wisden.com

For Sri Lanka (18)

M. S. Atapattu (1)		**S. T. Jayasuriya** (2)		225	Colombo (RPS) 1997-98
108	Mohali 1997-98	340	Colombo (RPS) 1997-98	**L. R. D. Mendis** (3)	
P. A. de Silva (5)		199	Colombo (SSC) 1997-98	105	
148	Colombo (PSS) 1993-94	**D. P. M. D. Jayawardene** (1)		105	†Madras 1982-83
126	Colombo (RPS) 1997-98	242	Colombo (SSC) 1998-99	124	Kandy..... 1985-86
146	Colombo (SSC) 1997-98	**R. S. Madugalle** (1)		**A. Ranatunga** (1)	
120		103	Colombo (SSC) 1985-86	111	Colombo (SSC) 1985-86
110*	Mohali 1997-98	**R. S. Mahanama** (2)		**S. A. R. Silva** (1)	
R. L. Dias (1)		151	Colombo (PSS) 1993-94	111	Colombo (PSS) 1985-86
106	Kandy..... 1985-86				

† *Signifies hundred on first appearance in India–Sri Lanka Tests.*

RECORD PARTNERSHIPS FOR EACH WICKET

For India

171	for 1st	M. Prabhakar and N. S. Sidhu at Colombo (SSC)	1993-94
232	for 2nd	S. Ramesh and R. Dravid at Colombo (SSC)	1998-99
173	for 3rd	M. Amarnath and D. B. Vengsarkar at Nagpur	1986-87
256	for 4th	S. C. Ganguly and S. R. Tendulkar at Mumbai	1997-98
150	for 5th	S. R. Tendulkar and S. C. Ganguly at Colombo (SSC)	1997-98
272	for 6th	M. Azharuddin and Kapil Dev at Kanpur.	1986-87
78*	for 7th	S. M. Patil and Madan Lal at Madras	1982-83
70	for 8th	Kapil Dev and L. Sivaramakrishnan at Colombo (PSS).	1985-86
89	for 9th	S. C. Ganguly and A. Kuruvilla at Mohali	1997-98
29	for 10th	Kapil Dev and Chetan Sharma at Colombo (PSS)	1985-86

For Sri Lanka

159	for 1st	S. Wettimuny and J. R. Ratnayeke at Kanpur	1986-87
576	for 2nd†	S. T. Jayasuriya and R. S. Mahanama at Colombo (RPS)	1997-98
218	for 3rd	S. T. Jayasuriya and P. A. de Silva at Colombo (SSC)	1997-98
216	for 4th	R. L. Dias and L. R. D. Mendis at Kandy.	1985-86
144	for 5th[1]	R. S. Madugalle and A. Ranatunga at Colombo (SSC)	1985-86
103	for 6th	P. A. de Silva and H. D. P. K. Dharmasena at Mohali	1997-98
77	for 7th	R. S. Madugalle and D. S. de Silva at Madras	1982-83
48	for 8th	P. A. de Silva and M. Muralitharan at Colombo (SSC).	1997-98
60	for 9th	H. P. Tillekeratne and A. W. R. Madurasinghe at Chandigarh.	1990-91
44	for 10th	R. J. Ratnayake and E. A. R. de Silva at Nagpur	1986-87

† *Denotes record partnership against all countries.*

[1] *Although the fifth wicket added 176 runs against India at Colombo (SSC) in 1998-99, this comprised two partnerships with D. P. M. D. Jayawardene adding 115* with A. Ranatunga (retired hurt) and a further 61 with H. P. Tillekeratne.*

TEN WICKETS OR MORE IN A MATCH

For India (3)

11-128 (4-69, 7-59)	A. Kumble, Lucknow.	1993-94
10-107 (3-56, 7-51)	Maninder Singh, Nagpur	1986-87
11-125 (5-38, 6-87)	S. L. V. Raju, Ahmedabad	1993-94

Note: The best match figures for Sri Lanka are 9-125 (4-76, 5-49) by R. J. Ratnayake at Colombo (PSS), 1985-86.

INDIA v ZIMBABWE

Season	India	*Captains* Zimbabwe	T	I	Z	D
1992-93*Z*	M. Azharuddin	D. L. Houghton	1	0	0	1
1992-93*I*	M. Azharuddin	D. L. Houghton	1	1	0	0
1998-99*Z*	M. Azharuddin	A. D. R. Campbell	1	0	1	0
	In India		1	1	0	0
	In Zimbabwe		2	0	1	1
	Totals		3	1	1	1

I Played in India.   Z Played in Zimbabwe.

HIGHEST INNINGS TOTALS

For India: 536-7 dec. at Delhi   1992-93

For Zimbabwe: 456 at Harare   1992-93

INDIVIDUAL HUNDREDS

For India (3)

R. Dravid (1)	**V. G. Kambli** (1)	**S. V. Manjrekar** (1)
118† Harare. 1998-99	227† Delhi 1992-93	104† Harare. 1992-93

For Zimbabwe (2)

A. Flower (1)	**D. L. Houghton** (1)
115 Delhi 1992-93	121† Harare. 1992-93

† *Signifies hundred on first appearance in India–Zimbabwe Tests.*

HUNDRED PARTNERSHIPS

For India

107 for 2nd	N. S. Sidhu and V. G. Kambli at Delhi	1992-93
137 for 3rd	V. G. Kambli and S. R. Tendulkar at Delhi	1992-93
107 for 4th	V. G. Kambli and M. Azharuddin at Delhi	1992-93

For Zimbabwe

138 for 1st	G. J. Rennie and C. B. Wishart at Harare	1998-99
100 for 1st	K. J. Arnott and G. W. Flower at Harare	1992-93
192 for 4th	G. W. Flower and A. Flower at Delhi	1992-93
165 for 6th†	D. L. Houghton and A. Flower at Harare	1992-93

† *Denotes record partnership against all countries.*

BEST MATCH BOWLING ANALYSES

For India

8-160 (3-90, 5-70)	A. Kumble, Delhi	1992-93

For Zimbabwe

6-110 (5-70, 1-40)	H. K. Olonga, Harare	1998-99

PAKISTAN v SRI LANKA

Captains

Season	Pakistan	Sri Lanka	T	P	SL	D
1981-82*P*	Javed Miandad	B. Warnapura[1]	3	2	0	1
1985-86*P*	Javed Miandad	L. R. D. Mendis	3	2	0	1
1985-86*S*	Imran Khan	L. R. D. Mendis	3	1	1	1
1991-92*P*	Imran Khan	P. A. de Silva	3	1	0	2
1994-95*S*†	Salim Malik	A. Ranatunga	2	2	0	0
1995-96*P*	Ramiz Raja	A. Ranatunga	3	1	2	0
1996-97*S*	Ramiz Raja	A. Ranatunga	2	0	0	2
1998-99*P*‡	Wasim Akram	H. P. Tillekeratne	1	0	0	1
1998-99*B*‡	Wasim Akram	P. A. de Silva	1	1	0	0
1999-2000*P*	Saeed Anwar[2]	S. T. Jayasuriya	3	1	2	0
2000*S*	Moin Khan	S. T. Jayasuriya	3	2	0	1
	In Pakistan		16	7	4	5
	In Sri Lanka		10	5	1	4
	In Bangladesh		1	1	0	0
	Totals......................		27	13	5	9

P Played in Pakistan. S Played in Sri Lanka. B Played in Bangladesh.

† One Test was cancelled owing to the threat of civil disturbances following a general election.
‡ These two Tests were part of the Asian Test Championship.

Note: The following deputised for the official touring captain or were appointed by the home authority for only a minor proportion of the series:
[1]L. R. D. Mendis (Second). [2]Moin Khan (Third).

HIGHEST INNINGS TOTALS

For Pakistan in Pakistan: 555-3 at Faisalabad...........................	1985-86
in Sri Lanka: 600-8 dec. at Galle.......................	2000
in Bangladesh: 594 at Dhaka	1998-99
For Sri Lanka in Pakistan: 479 at Faisalabad	1985-86
in Sri Lanka: 467-5 at Kandy	2000

LOWEST INNINGS TOTALS

For Pakistan in Pakistan: 182 at Rawalpindi	1999-2000
in Sri Lanka: 132 at Colombo (CCC)...................	1985-86
For Sri Lanka in Pakistan: 149 at Karachi.......................	1981-82
in Sri Lanka: 71 at Kandy	1994-95

INDIVIDUAL HUNDREDS

For Pakistan (23)

Haroon Rashid (1)
153† Karachi 1981-82
Ijaz Ahmed, sen. (2)
113† Colombo (RPS) 1996-97
211 Dhaka..... 1998-99
Inzamam-ul-Haq (4)
100* Kandy 1994-95
200* Dhaka 1998-99
138 Karachi.... 1999-00
112 Galle...... 2000

Javed Miandad (1)
203* Faisalabad .. 1985-86
Mohsin Khan (1)
129 Lahore 1981-82
Moin Khan (1)
117* Sialkot 1995-96
Qasim Omar (1)
206† Faisalabad .. 1985-86
Ramiz Raja (1)
122 Colombo (PSS) 1985-86

Saeed Anwar (2)
136† Colombo (PSS) 1994-95
123 Galle...... 2000
Salim Malik (3)
100*† Karachi 1981-82
101 Sialkot 1991-92
155 Colombo (SSC) 1996-97
Wajahatullah Wasti (2)
133†} Lahore 1998-99
121*}

Wasim Akram (1)	**Younis Khan** (2)		**Zaheer Abbas** (1)
100 Galle 2000	107† Rawalpindi.. 1999-00		134† Lahore 1981-82
	116 Galle...... 2000		

For Sri Lanka (19)

R. P. Arnold (1)	138*⎫ Colombo (SSC) 1996-97		188 Kandy..... 2000
123 Lahore 1998-99	103*⎭		**R. S. Kaluwitharana** (1)
M. S. Atapattu (1)	112 Rawalpindi.. 1999-00		100 Lahore 1998-99
207* Kandy..... 2000	**R. L. Dias** (1)		**A. Ranatunga** (1)
P. A. de Silva (8)	109 Lahore 1981-82		135* Colombo (PSS) 1985-86
122† Faisalabad .. 1985-86	**A. P. Gurusinha** (1)		**H. P. Tillekeratne** (2)
105 Karachi.... 1985-86	116* Colombo (PSS) 1985-86		115 Faisalabad .. 1995-96
127 Colombo (PSS) 1994-95	**S. T. Jayasuriya** (2)		103 Colombo (RPS) 1996-97
105 Faisalabad .. 1995-96	113 Colombo (SSC) 1996-97		**S. Wettimuny** (1)
168 Colombo (RPS) 1996-97			157 Faisalabad .. 1981-82

† *Signifies hundred on first appearance in Pakistan–Sri Lanka Tests.*

RECORD PARTNERSHIPS FOR EACH WICKET

For Pakistan

156 for 1st	Wajahatullah Wasti and Shahid Afridi at Lahore	1998-99
151 for 2nd	Mohsin Khan and Majid Khan at Lahore	1981-82
397 for 3rd	Qasim Omar and Javed Miandad at Faisalabad	1985-86
178 for 4th	Wajahatullah Wasti and Yousuf Youhana at Lahore	1998-99
132 for 5th	Salim Malik and Imran Khan at Sialkot.................	1991-92
124 for 6th	Inzamam-ul-Haq and Younis Khan at Karachi..............	1999-2000
120 for 7th	Younis Khan and Wasim Akram at Galle	2000
88 for 8th	Moin Khan and Waqar Younis at Karachi................	1999-2000
145 for 9th	Younis Khan and Wasim Akram at Rawalpindi	1999-2000
90 for 10th	Wasim Akram and Arshad Khan at Colombo (SSC)	2000

For Sri Lanka

335 for 1st†	M. S. Atapattu and S. T. Jayasuriya at Kandy	2000
217 for 2nd	S. Wettimuny and R. L. Dias at Faisalabad	1981-82
176 for 3rd	U. C. Hathurusinghe and P. A. de Silva at Faisalabad	1995-96
240* for 4th†	A. P. Gurusinha and A. Ranatunga at Colombo (PSS)........	1985-86
143 for 5th	R. P. Arnold and R. S. Kaluwitharana at Lahore	1998-99
121 for 6th	A. Ranatunga and P. A. de Silva at Faisalabad.............	1985-86
131 for 7th	H. P. Tillekeratne and R. S. Kalpage at Kandy.............	1994-95
76 for 8th	P. A. de Silva and W. P. U. J. C. Vaas at Colombo (SSC)	1996-97
52 for 9th	P. A. de Silva and R. J. Ratnayake at Faisalabad	1985-86
73 for 10th†	H. P. Tillekeratne and K. S. C. de Silva at Dhaka	1998-99

† *Denotes record partnership against all countries.*

TEN WICKETS OR MORE IN A MATCH

For Pakistan (2)

14-116 (8-58, 6-58)	Imran Khan, Lahore.........................	1981-82
11-119 (6-34, 5-85)	Waqar Younis, Kandy........................	1994-95

For Sri Lanka (1)

10-148 (4-77, 6-71)	M. Muralitharan, Peshawar	1999-2000

PAKISTAN v ZIMBABWE

Season	Pakistan	Captains Zimbabwe	T	P	Z	D
1993-94P	Wasim Akram[1]	A. Flower	3	2	0	1
1994-95Z	Salim Malik	A. Flower	3	2	1	0
1996-97P	Wasim Akram	A. D. R. Campbell	2	1	0	1
1997-98Z	Rashid Latif	A. D. R. Campbell	2	1	0	1
1998-99P†	Aamir Sohail[2]	A. D. R. Campbell	2	0	1	1
	In Pakistan		7	3	1	3
	In Zimbabwe		5	3	1	1
	Totals		12	6	2	4

P Played in Pakistan. Z Played in Zimbabwe.

† *The Third Test at Faisalabad was abandoned without a ball being bowled and is excluded.*

Note: The following were appointed by the home authority for only a minor proportion of the series:

[1]Waqar Younis (First). [2]Moin Khan (Second).

HIGHEST INNINGS TOTALS

For Pakistan in Pakistan: 553 at Sheikhupura 1996-97
                in Zimbabwe: 354 at Harare 1997-98

For Zimbabwe in Pakistan: 375 at Sheikhupura 1996-97
                in Zimbabwe: 544-4 dec. at Harare 1994-95

LOWEST INNINGS TOTALS

For Pakistan in Pakistan: 103 at Peshawar 1998-99
                in Zimbabwe: 158 at Harare 1994-95

For Zimbabwe in Pakistan: 133 at Faisalabad 1996-97
                in Zimbabwe: 139 at Harare 1994-95

INDIVIDUAL HUNDREDS

For Pakistan (4)

Inzamam-ul-Haq (1)
101   Harare 1994-95
Mohammad Wasim (1)
192†   Harare 1997-98

Wasim Akram (1)
257* Sheikhupura . 1996-97
Yousuf Youhana (1)
120* Lahore 1998-99

For Zimbabwe (9)

A. Flower (2)
156   Harare 1994-95
100* Bulawayo . . . 1997-98
G. W. Flower (3)
201* Harare 1994-95
110   Sheikhupura . 1996-97

156*‡ Bulawayo . . . 1997-98
M. W. Goodwin (1)
166*† Bulawayo . . . 1997-98
N. C. Johnson (1)
107† Peshawar . . . 1998-99

P. A. Strang (1)
106* Sheikhupura . 1996-97
G. J. Whittall (1)
113* Harare 1994-95

† *Signifies hundred on first appearance in Pakistan–Zimbabwe Tests.*
‡ *Carried his bat.*

RECORD PARTNERSHIPS FOR EACH WICKET

For Pakistan

95	for 1st	Aamir Sohail and Shoaib Mohammad at Karachi (DS)	1993-94
118*	for 2nd	Shoaib Mohammad and Asif Mujtaba at Lahore.	1993-94
83	for 3rd	Shoaib Mohammad and Javed Miandad at Karachi (DS)	1993-94
118	for 4th	Ijaz Ahmed, sen. and Yousuf Youhana at Peshawar	1998-99
110	for 5th	Yousuf Youhana and Moin Khan at Bulawayo	1997-98
96	for 6th	Inzamam-ul-Haq and Rashid Latif at Harare	1994-95
120	for 7th	Ijaz Ahmed, sen. and Inzamam-ul-Haq at Harare	1994-95
313	for 8th†	Wasim Akram and Saqlain Mushtaq at Sheikhupura	1996-97
147	for 9th	Mohammad Wasim and Mushtaq Ahmed at Harare.	1997-98
50*	for 10th	Yousuf Youhana and Waqar Younis at Lahore.	1998-99

For Zimbabwe

48*	for 1st	G. J. Rennie and G. W. Flower at Lahore	1998-99
135	for 2nd†	M. H. Dekker and A. D. R. Campbell at Rawalpindi	1993-94
84	for 3rd	G. W. Flower and D. L. Houghton at Sheikhupura	1996-97
269	for 4th†	G. W. Flower and A. Flower at Harare	1994-95
277*	for 5th†	M. W. Goodwin and A. Flower at Bulawayo	1997-98
72	for 6th	M. H. Dekker and G. J. Whittall at Rawalpindi	1993-94
131	for 7th†	G. W. Flower and P. A. Strang at Sheikhupura	1996-97
110	for 8th†	G. J. Whittall and B. C. Strang at Harare	1997-98
87	for 9th†	P. A. Strang and B. C. Strang at Sheikhupura	1996-97
29	for 10th	E. A. Brandes and S. G. Peall at Rawalpindi	1993-94

† *Denotes record partnership against all countries.*

TEN WICKETS OR MORE IN A MATCH

For Pakistan (2)

13-135 (7-91, 6-44)†	Waqar Younis, Karachi (DS)	1993-94
10-106 (6-48, 4-58)	Wasim Akram, Faisalabad	1996-97

Note: The best match figures for Zimbabwe are 9-105 (6-90, 3-15) by H. H. Streak at Harare, 1994-95.

† *Signifies ten wickets or more on first appearance in Pakistan–Zimbabwe Tests.*

SRI LANKA v ZIMBABWE

		Captains				
Season	*Sri Lanka*	*Zimbabwe*	T	SL	Z	D
1994-95Z	A. Ranatunga	A. Flower	3	0	0	3
1996-97S	A. Ranatunga	A. D. R. Campbell	2	2	0	0
1997-98S	A. Ranatunga	A. D. R. Campbell	2	2	0	0
1999-2000Z	S. T. Jayasuriya	A. Flower	3	1	0	2
	In Sri Lanka		4	4	0	0
	In Zimbabwe		6	1	0	5
	Totals.		10	5	0	5

S Played in Sri Lanka.   Z Played in Zimbabwe.

HIGHEST INNINGS TOTALS

For Sri Lanka in Sri Lanka: 469-9 dec. at Kandy 1997-98
in Zimbabwe: 432 at Harare 1999-2000

For Zimbabwe in Sri Lanka: 338 at Kandy 1997-98
in Zimbabwe: 462-9 dec. at Bulawayo 1994-95

LOWEST INNINGS TOTALS

For Sri Lanka in Sri Lanka: 225 at Colombo (SSC) 1997-98
in Zimbabwe: 218 at Bulawayo 1994-95

For Zimbabwe in Sri Lanka: 127 at Colombo (RPS) 1996-97
in Zimbabwe: 174 at Harare 1999-2000

INDIVIDUAL HUNDREDS

For Sri Lanka (10)

R. P. Arnold (1)
104*‡ Harare 1999-00

M. S. Atapattu (2)
223† Kandy 1997-98
216*‡ Bulawayo . . . 1999-00

P. A. de Silva (1)
143* Colombo (SSC) 1997-98

T. M. Dilshan (1)
163* Harare 1999-00

A. P. Gurusinha (1)
128† Harare 1994-95

S. Ranatunga (2)
118† Harare 1994-95
100* Bulawayo . . . 1994-95

H. P. Tillekeratne (2)
116 Harare 1994-95
126* Colombo (SSC) 1996-97

For Zimbabwe (4)

A. Flower (2)
105* Colombo (SSC) 1997-98
129 Harare 1999-00

D. L. Houghton (2)
266 Bulawayo . . . 1994-95
142 Harare 1994-95

† *Signifies hundred on first appearance in Sri Lanka–Zimbabwe Tests.*
‡ *Carried his bat.*

RECORD PARTNERSHIPS FOR EACH WICKET

For Sri Lanka

85	for 1st	M. S. Atapattu and S. T. Jayasuriya at Bulawayo.	1999-2000
217	for 2nd	A. P. Gurusinha and S. Ranatunga at Harare	1994-95
140	for 3rd	M. S. Atapattu and P. A. de Silva at Kandy	1997-98
178	for 4th	D. P. M. D. Jayawardene and T. M. Dilshan at Harare	1999-2000
114	for 5th	A. P. Gurusinha and H. P. Tillekeratne at Colombo (SSC)	1996-97
189*	for 6th†	P. A. de Silva and A. Ranatunga at Colombo (SSC).	1997-98
57	for 7th	M. S. Atapattu and W. P. U. J. C. Vaas at Kandy.	1997-98
73	for 8th	H. D. P. K. Dharmasena and W. P. U. J. C. Vaas at Colombo (RPS)	1996-97
30	for 9th	R. P. Arnold and G. P. Wickremasinghe at Harare	1999-2000
25	for 10th	H. D. P. K. Dharmasena and M. Muralitharan at Bulawayo	1994-95

For Zimbabwe

113 for 1st	G. W. Flower and M. H. Dekker at Harare.		1994-95
40 for 2nd	G. J. Rennie and M. W. Goodwin at Colombo (SSC).		1997-98
194 for 3rd†	A. D. R. Campbell and D. L. Houghton at Harare		1994-95
121 for 4th	D. L. Houghton and A. Flower at Bulawayo.		1994-95
101 for 5th	M. W. Goodwin and A. Flower at Harare.		1999-2000
100 for 6th	D. L. Houghton and W. R. James at Bulawayo		1994-95
125 for 7th	A. Flower and G. J. Whittall at Harare		1999-2000
84 for 8th	D. L. Houghton and J. A. Rennie at Bulawayo		1994-95
43 for 9th	J. A. Rennie and S. G. Peall at Bulawayo		1994-95
34 for 10th	P. A. Strang and H. K. Olonga at Colombo (SSC).		1996-97

† *Denotes record partnership against all countries.*

TEN WICKETS OR MORE IN A MATCH

For Sri Lanka (1)

12-117 (5-23, 7-94)	M. Muralitharan, Kandy.	1997-98

Note: The best match figures for Zimbabwe are 6-112 (2-28, 4-84) by H. H. Streak at Colombo (SSC), 1997-98.

TEST MATCH GROUNDS

In Chronological Sequence

City and Ground	First Test Match		Tests
1 Melbourne, Melbourne Cricket Ground	March 15, 1877	A v E	92
2 London, Kennington Oval	September 6, 1880	E v A	83
3 Sydney, Sydney Cricket Ground (No. 1)	February 17, 1882	A v E	86
4 Manchester, Old Trafford	July 11, 1884	E v A	66
5 London, Lord's	July 21, 1884	E v A	100
6 Adelaide, Adelaide Oval	December 12, 1884	A v E	58
7 Port Elizabeth, St George's Park	March 12, 1889	SA v E	18
8 Cape Town, Newlands	March 25, 1889	SA v E	32
9 Johannesburg, Old Wanderers	March 2, 1896	SA v E	22
Now the site of Johannesburg Railway Station.			
10 Nottingham, Trent Bridge	June 1, 1899	E v A	47
11 Leeds, Headingley	June 29, 1899	E v A	61
12 Birmingham, Edgbaston	May 29, 1902	E v A	36
13 Sheffield, Bramall Lane	July 3, 1902	E v A	1
Sheffield United Football Club have built a stand over the cricket pitch.			
14 Durban, Lord's	January 21, 1910	SA v E	4
Ground destroyed and built on.			
15 Durban, Kingsmead	January 18, 1923	SA v E	27
16 Brisbane, Exhibition Ground	November 30, 1928	A v E	2
No longer used for cricket.			
17 Christchurch, Lancaster Park	January 10, 1930	NZ v E	36
Ground also known under sponsors' names.			
18 Bridgetown, Kensington Oval	January 11, 1930	WI v E	36
19 Wellington, Basin Reserve	January 24, 1930	NZ v E	36
20 Port-of-Spain, Queen's Park Oval	February 1, 1930	WI v E	49
21 Auckland, Eden Park	February 17, 1930	NZ v E	42
22 Georgetown, Bourda	February 21, 1930	WI v E	26
23 Kingston, Sabina Park	April 3, 1930	WI v E	35
24 Brisbane, Woolloongabba	November 27, 1931	A v SA	42
25 Bombay, Gymkhana Ground	December 15, 1933	I v E	1
No longer used for first-class cricket.			
26 Calcutta, Eden Gardens	January 5, 1934	I v E	30

	City and Ground	*First Test Match*		*Tests*
27	Madras (*now Chennai*),			
	Chepauk (Chidambaram Stadium)	February 10, 1934	I v E	24
28	Delhi, Feroz Shah Kotla	November 10, 1948	I v WI	25
29	Bombay, Brabourne Stadium	December 9, 1948	I v WI	17
	Rarely used for first-class cricket.			
30	Johannesburg, Ellis Park	December 27, 1948	SA v E	6
	Mainly a rugby stadium, no longer used for cricket.			
31	Kanpur, Green Park (Modi Stadium)	January 12, 1952	I v E	18
32	Lucknow, University Ground	October 25, 1952	I v P	1
	Ground destroyed, now partly under a river bed.			
33	Dacca (*now Dhaka*),			
	Dacca (now Bangabandhu) Stadium	January 1, 1955	P v I	8
	Originally in East Pakistan, now Bangladesh.			
34	Bahawalpur, Dring (now Bahawal) Stadium	January 15, 1955	P v I	1
	Still used for first-class cricket.			
35	Lahore, Lawrence Gardens (Bagh-i-Jinnah)	January 29, 1955	P v I	3
	Still used for club and occasional first-class matches.			
36	Peshawar, Services Ground	February 13, 1955	P v I	1
	Superseded by new stadium.			
37	Karachi, National Stadium	February 26, 1955	P v I	34
38	Dunedin, Carisbrook	March 11, 1955	NZ v E	10
39	Hyderabad, Fateh Maidan			
	(Lal Bahadur Stadium)	November 19, 1955	I v NZ	3
40	Madras, Corporation Stadium	January 6, 1956	I v NZ	9
	Superseded by rebuilt Chepauk Stadium.			
41	Johannesburg, Wanderers	December 24, 1956	SA v E	21
42	Lahore, Gaddafi Stadium	November 21, 1959	P v A	30
43	Rawalpindi, Pindi Club Ground	March 27, 1965	P v NZ	1
	Superseded by new stadium.			
44	Nagpur, Vidarbha C.A. Ground	October 3, 1969	I v NZ	5
45	Perth, Western Australian C.A. Ground	December 11, 1970	A v E	27
46	Hyderabad, Niaz Stadium	March 16, 1973	P v E	5
47	Bangalore, Karnataka State C.A. Ground			
	(Chinnaswamy Stadium)	November 22, 1974	I v WI	13
48	Bombay (*now Mumbai*), Wankhede Stadium	January 23, 1975	I v WI	17
49	Faisalabad, Iqbal Stadium	October 16, 1978	P v I	19
50	Napier, McLean Park	February 16, 1979	NZ v P	3
51	Multan, Ibn-e-Qasim Bagh Stadium	December 30, 1980	P v WI	1
52	St John's (Antigua), Recreation Ground	March 27, 1981	WI v E	15
53	Colombo, P. Saravanamuttu Stadium	February 17, 1982	SL v E	6
54	Kandy, Asgiriya Stadium	April 22, 1983	SL v A	10
55	Jullundur, Burlton Park	September 24, 1983	I v P	1
56	Ahmedabad, Gujarat Stadium	November 12, 1983	I v WI	5
57	Colombo, Sinhalese Sports Club Ground	March 16, 1984	SL v NZ	16
58	Colombo, Colombo Cricket Club Ground	March 24, 1984	SL v NZ	3
59	Sialkot, Jinnah Stadium	October 27, 1985	P v SL	4
60	Cuttack, Barabati Stadium	January 4, 1987	I v SL	2
61	Jaipur, Sawai Mansingh Stadium	February 21, 1987	I v P	1
62	Hobart, Bellerive Oval	December 16, 1989	A v SL	5
63	Chandigarh, Sector 16 Stadium	November 23, 1990	I v SL	1
	Superseded by Mohali ground.			
64	Hamilton, Seddon Park	February 22, 1991	NZ v SL	8
	Ground also known under various sponsors' names.			
65	Gujranwala, Municipal Stadium	December 20, 1991	P v SL	1
66	Colombo, R. Premadasa (Khettarama) Stadium	August 28, 1992	SL v A	5
67	Moratuwa, Tyronne Fernando Stadium	September 8, 1992	SL v A	4
68	Harare, Harare Sports Club	October 18, 1992	Z v I	15
69	Bulawayo, Bulawayo Athletic Club	November 1, 1992	Z v NZ	1
	Superseded by Queens Sports Club ground.			
70	Karachi, Defence Stadium	December 1, 1993	P v Z	1

	City and Ground	*First Test Match*		*Tests*
71	Rawalpindi, Rawalpindi Cricket Stadium	December 9, 1993	P v Z	7
72	Lucknow, K. D. "Babu" Singh Stadium	January 18, 1994	I v SL	1
73	Bulawayo, Queens Sports Club	October 20, 1994	Z v SL	6
74	Mohali, Punjab Cricket Association Stadium	December 10, 1994	I v WI	3
75	Peshawar, Arbab Niaz Stadium	September 8, 1995	P v SL	5
76	Centurion (*formerly Verwoerdburg*), Centurion Park	November 16, 1995	SA v E	5
77	Sheikhupura, Municipal Stadium	October 17, 1996	P v Z	2
78	St Vincent, Arnos Vale	June 20, 1997	WI v SL	1
79	Galle, International Stadium	June 3, 1998	SL v NZ	4
80	Springbok Park, Bloemfontein	October 29, 1999	SA v Z	1

FAMILIES IN TEST CRICKET

GRANDFATHER, FATHER AND SON

G. A. Headley (West Indies, 22 Tests, 1929-30–1953-54), R. G. A. Headley (West Indies, 2 Tests, 1973) and D. W. Headley (England, 15 Tests, 1997–1999).

FATHERS AND SONS

England

A. R. Butcher (1 Test, 1979) and M. A. Butcher (27 Tests, 1997–1999-2000).
M. C. Cowdrey (114 Tests, 1954-55–1974-75) and C. S. Cowdrey (6 Tests, 1984-85–1988).
J. Hardstaff (5 Tests, 1907-08) and J. Hardstaff jun. (23 Tests, 1935–1948).
L. Hutton (79 Tests, 1937–1954-55) and R. A. Hutton (5 Tests, 1971).
F. T. Mann (5 Tests, 1922-23) and F. G. Mann (7 Tests, 1948-49–1949).
J. H. Parks (1 Test, 1937) and J. M. Parks (46 Tests, 1954–1967-68).
M. J. Stewart (8 Tests, 1962–1963-64) and A. J. Stewart (102 Tests, 1989-90–2000).
F. W. Tate (1 Test, 1902) and M. W. Tate (39 Tests, 1924–1935).
C. L. Townsend (2 Tests, 1899) and D. C. H. Townsend (3 Tests, 1934-35).

Australia

E. J. Gregory (1 Test, 1876-77) and S. E. Gregory (58 Tests, 1890–1912).

South Africa

F. Hearne (4 Tests, 1891-92–1895-96) and G. A. L. Hearne (3 Tests, 1922-23–1924).
  F. Hearne also played 2 Tests for England in 1888-89.
J. D. Lindsay (3 Tests, 1947) and D. T. Lindsay (19 Tests, 1963-64–1969-70).
A. W. Nourse (45 Tests, 1902-03–1924) and A. D. Nourse (34 Tests, 1935–1951).
P. M. Pollock (28 Tests, 1961-62–1969-70) and S. M. Pollock (45 Tests, 1995-96–2000 (SL)).
L. R. Tuckett (1 Test, 1913-14) and L. Tuckett (9 Tests, 1947–1948-49).

West Indies

O. C. Scott (8 Tests, 1928–1930-31) and A. P. H. Scott (1 Test, 1952-53).

New Zealand

W. M. Anderson (1 Test, 1945-46) and R. W. Anderson (9 Tests, 1976-77–1978).
W. P. Bradburn (2 Tests, 1963-64) and G. E. Bradburn (4 Tests, 1990-91).
B. L. Cairns (43 Tests, 1973-74–1985-86) and C. L. Cairns (47 Tests, 1989-90–1999-2000).
W. A. Hadlee (11 Tests, 1937–1950-51) and D. R. Hadlee (26 Tests, 1969–1977-78); R. J. Hadlee (86 Tests, 1972-73–1990).
P. G. Z. Harris (9 Tests, 1955-56–1964-65) and C. Z. Harris (19 Tests, 1993-94–1999-2000).
H. G. Vivian (7 Tests, 1931–1937) and G. E. Vivian (5 Tests, 1964-65–1971-72).

India
L. Amarnath (24 Tests, 1933-34–1952-53) and M. Amarnath (69 Tests, 1969-70–1987-88); S. Amarnath (10 Tests, 1975-76–1978-79).
D. K. Gaekwad (11 Tests, 1952–1960-61) and A. D. Gaekwad (40 Tests, 1974-75–1984-85).
H. S. Kanitkar (2 Tests, 1974-75) and H. H. Kanitkar (2 Tests, 1999-2000).
Nawab of Pataudi (Iftikhar Ali Khan) (3 Tests, 1946) and Nawab of Pataudi (Mansur Ali Khan) (46 Tests, 1961-62–1974-75).
Nawab of Pataudi sen. also played 3 Tests for England, 1932-33–1934.
V. L. Manjrekar (55 Tests, 1951-52–1964-65) and S. V. Manjrekar (37 Tests, 1987-88–1996-97).
V. Mankad (44 Tests, 1946–1958-59) and A. V. Mankad (22 Tests, 1969-70–1977-78).
Pankaj Roy (43 Tests, 1951-52–1960-61) and Pranab Roy (2 Tests, 1981-82).

India and Pakistan
M. Jahangir Khan (4 Tests, 1932–1936) and Majid Khan (63 Tests, 1964-65–1982-83).
S. Wazir Ali (7 Tests, 1932–1936) and Khalid Wazir (2 Tests, 1954).

Pakistan
Hanif Mohammad (55 Tests, 1952-53–1969-70) and Shoaib Mohammad (45 Tests, 1983-84–1995-96).
Nazar Mohammad (5 Tests, 1952-53) and Mudassar Nazar (76 Tests, 1976-77–1988-89).

GRANDFATHER AND GRANDSONS

Australia
V. Y. Richardson (19 Tests, 1924-25–1935-36) and G. S. Chappell (87 Tests, 1970-71–1983-84); I. M. Chappell (75 Tests, 1964-65–1979-80); T. M. Chappell (3 Tests, 1981).

GREAT-GRANDFATHER AND GREAT-GRANDSON

Australia
W. H. Cooper (2 Tests, 1881-82 and 1884-85) and A. P. Sheahan (31 Tests, 1967-68–1973-74).

BROTHERS IN SAME TEST TEAM

England
E. M., G. F. and W. G. Grace: 1 Test, 1880; C. T. and G. B. Studd: 4 Tests, 1882-83; A. and G. G. Hearne: 1 Test, 1891-92. *F. Hearne, their brother, played in this match for South Africa*; D. W. and P. E. Richardson: 1 Test, 1957; A. J. and B. C. Hollioake: 1 Test, 1997.

Australia
E. J. and D. W. Gregory: 1 Test, 1876-77; C. and A. C. Bannerman: 1 Test, 1878-79; G. and W. F. Giffen: 2 Tests, 1891-92; G. H. S. and A. E. Trott: 3 Tests, 1894-95; I. M. and G. S. Chappell: 43 Tests, 1970-71–1979-80; S. R. and M. E. Waugh: 85 Tests, 1990-91–1999-2000 – the only instance of twins appearing together.

South Africa
S. J. and S. D. Snooke: 1 Test, 1907; D. and H. W. Taylor: 2 Tests, 1913-14; R. H. M. and P. A. M. Hands: 1 Test, 1913-14; E. A. B. and A. M. B. Rowan: 9 Tests, 1948-49–1951; P. M. and R. G. Pollock: 23 Tests, 1963-64–1969-70; A. J. and D. B. Pithey: 5 Tests, 1963-64; P. N. and G. Kirsten (half-brothers): 7 Tests, 1993-94–1994.

West Indies
G. C. and R. S. Grant: 4 Tests, 1934-35; J. B. and V. H. Stollmeyer: 1 Test, 1939; D. St E. and E. St E. Atkinson: 1 Test, 1957-58.

New Zealand
D. R. and R. J. Hadlee: 10 Tests, 1973–1977-78; H. J. and G. P. Howarth: 4 Tests, 1974-75–1976-77; J. M. and N. M. Parker: 3 Tests, 1976-77; B. P. and J. G. Bracewell: 1 Test, 1980-81; J. J. and M. D. Crowe: 34 Tests, 1983–1989-90.

India

S. Wazir Ali and S. Nazir Ali: 2 Tests, 1932–1933-34; L. Ramji and Amar Singh: 1 Test, 1933-34; C. K. and C. S. Nayudu: 4 Tests, 1933-34–1936; A. G. Kripal Singh and A. G. Milkha Singh: 1 Test, 1961-62; S. and M. Amarnath: 8 Tests, 1975-76–1978-79.

Pakistan

Wazir and Hanif Mohammad: 18 Tests, 1952-53–1959-60; Wazir and Mushtaq Mohammad: 1 Test, 1958-59; Hanif and Mushtaq Mohammad: 19 Tests, 1960-61–1969-70; Hanif, Mushtaq and Sadiq Mohammad: 1 Test, 1969-70; Mushtaq and Sadiq Mohammad: 26 Tests, 1969-70–1978–79; Wasim and Ramiz Raja: 2 Tests, 1983-84; Moin and Nadeem Khan: 1 Test, 1998-99.

Sri Lanka

M. D. and S. Wettimuny: 2 Tests, 1982-83; A. and D. Ranatunga: 2 Tests, 1989-90; A. and S. Ranatunga: 8 Tests, 1994-95–1996-97.

Zimbabwe

A. and G. W. Flower: 42 Tests, 1992-93–2000; J. A. and G. J. Rennie: 1 Test, 1997-98; P. A. and B. C. Strang: 12 Tests, 1994-95–1997-98.

THE DUCKWORTH/LEWIS METHOD

In 1997, the ECB's limited-overs competitions adopted a new method to revise targets in interrupted games, devised by Frank Duckworth of the Royal Statistical Society and Tony Lewis of the University of the West of England. The method was gradually taken up by other countries and, in 1999, ICC decided to incorporate it into the standard playing conditions for limited-overs internationals for an experimental period of two years to August 2001.

The system aims to preserve any advantage that one team has established before the interruption. It uses the idea that teams have two resources from which they make runs – an allocated number of overs and ten wickets. It also takes into account when the interruption occurs, because of the different scoring-rates typical of different stages of an innings. Traditional run-rate calculations relied only on the overs available, and ignored wickets lost.

After modifications, the system now uses one table with 50 rows, covering matches of any length up to 50 overs, and ten columns, from nought to nine wickets down. Each figure in the table gives the percentage of the total runs in an innings that would, on average, be scored with a certain number of overs left and wickets lost.

If overs are lost, the table is used to calculate the percentage of runs the team would be expected to score in those missing overs. This is obtained by reading off the figure for the number of overs left and wickets down when play stops and subtracting from it the corresponding figure for the number of overs remaining when it resumes.

If the first innings is complete and the second innings is interrupted, the target to be beaten is reduced by the percentage of the innings lost. If the suspension occurs between innings, as in the ICC Trophy final between Bangladesh and Kenya at Kuala Lumpur in April 1997, only one figure is required: the percentage of the innings remaining for the reduced number of overs with no wicket lost. Kenya scored 241 from 50 overs, but rain restricted Bangladesh to 25 overs. On the traditional average run-rate, losing half their overs would have halved the target to 121. But they had all ten wickets, so had more than half their run-scoring resources. The table showed that, on average, 25 overs should yield 68.7 per cent of a 50-over total. Bangladesh's target was set at 166 (68.7 per cent of 241 = 165.56), which they reached off the final ball.

The system also covers interruptions to the first innings, multiple interruptions and innings terminated by rain.

LIMITED-OVERS INTERNATIONAL RECORDS

Note: This section covers all limited-overs internationals up to and including the Australia v South Africa series at Melbourne which ended on August 20, 2000, but not the tournament in Singapore which began that day.

Limited-overs international matches do not have first-class status.

SUMMARY OF ALL LIMITED-OVERS INTERNATIONALS

1970-71 to 2000

	Opponents	Matches	E	A	SA	WI	NZ	I	P	SL	Z	Ass	Tied	NR
England	Australia	67	31	34	–	–	–	–	–	–	–	–	1	1
	South Africa	22	7		15	–	–	–	–	–	–	–	–	–
	West Indies	61	26	–	–	32	–	–	–	–	–	–	–	3
	New Zealand	47	23	–	–	–	20	–	–	–	–	–	1	3
	India	36	19	–	–	–	–	16	–	–	–	–	–	1
	Pakistan	43	27	–	–	–	–	–	15	–	–	–	–	1
	Sri Lanka	20	13	–	–	–	–	–	–	7	–	–	–	–
	Zimbabwe	16	9	–	–	–	–	–	–	–	7	–	–	–
	Associates	5	5	–	–	–	–	–	–	–	–	0	–	–
Australia	South Africa	45	–	21	22	–	–	–	–	–	–	–	2	–
	West Indies	92	–	37	–	52	–	–	–	–	–	–	2	1
	New Zealand	80	–	55	–	–	22	–	–	–	–	–	–	3
	India	61	–	36	–	–	–	22	–	–	–	–	–	3
	Pakistan	57	–	31	–	–	–	–	23	–	–	–	1	2
	Sri Lanka	43	–	28	–	–	–	–	–	13	–	–	–	2
	Zimbabwe	15	–	14	–	–	–	–	–	–	1	–	–	–
	Associates	5	–	5	–	–	–	–	–	–	–	0	–	–
South Africa	West Indies	18	–	–	12	6	–	–	–	–	–	–	–	–
	New Zealand	20	–	–	11	–	7	–	–	–	–	–	–	2
	India	37	–	–	24	–	–	12	–	–	–	–	–	1
	Pakistan	27	–	–	18	–	–	–	9	–	–	–	–	–
	Sri Lanka	19	–	–	9	–	–	–	–	9	–	–	–	1
	Zimbabwe	12	–	–	9	–	–	–	–	–	2	–	–	1
	Associates	5	–	–	5	–	–	–	–	–	–	0	–	–
West Indies	New Zealand	30	–	–	–	19	9	–	–	–	–	–	–	2
	India	63	–	–	–	40	–	21	–	–	–	–	1	1
	Pakistan	95	–	–	–	59	–	–	34	–	–	–	2	–
	Sri Lanka	31	–	–	–	21	–	–	–	9	–	–	–	1
	Zimbabwe	11	–	–	–	8	–	–	–	–	3	–	–	–
	Associates	5	–	–	–	4	–	–	–	–	–	1*	–	–
New Zealand	India	57	–	–	–	–	24	30	–	–	–	–	–	3
	Pakistan	50	–	–	–	–	18	–	30	–	–	–	1	1
	Sri Lanka	40	–	–	–	–	24	–	–	13	–	–	1	2
	Zimbabwe	18	–	–	–	–	13	–	–	–	3	–	1	1
	Associates	6	–	–	–	–	6	–	–	–	–	0	–	–
India	Pakistan	85	–	–	–	–	–	29	52	–	–	–	–	4
	Sri Lanka	63	–	–	–	–	–	34	–	24	–	–	–	5
	Zimbabwe	27	–	–	–	–	–	20	–	–	5	–	2	–
	Associates	16	–	–	–	–	–	15	–	–	–	1†	–	–
Pakistan	Sri Lanka	83	–	–	–	–	–	–	51	29	–	–	1	2
	Zimbabwe	22	–	–	–	–	–	–	19	–	2	–	1	–
	Associates	14	–	–	–	–	–	–	13	–	–	1‡	–	–
Sri Lanka	Zimbabwe	21	–	–	–	–	–	–	–	15	5	–	–	1
	Associates	9	–	–	–	–	–	–	–	9	–	0	–	–
Zimbabwe	Associates	15	–	–	–	–	–	–	–	–	14	0	–	1
Associates	Associates	8	–	–	–	–	–	–	–	–	–	8§	–	–
		1,622	160	261	125	241	143	199	246	128	42	11	17	49

* *Kenya beat West Indies in the 1996 World Cup.*
† *Kenya beat India at Gwalior, 1997-98.*
‡ *Bangladesh beat Pakistan in the 1999 World Cup.*
§ *United Arab Emirates beat Holland in the 1996 World Cup. Bangladesh met Kenya six times in 1997-99: Bangladesh won 1, Kenya won 5. Bangladesh beat Scotland in the 1999 World Cup.*

Note: Current Associate Members of ICC who have played one-day internationals are Bangladesh, Canada, East Africa, Holland, Kenya and United Arab Emirates. Sri Lanka and Zimbabwe also played one-day internationals before being given Test status; these are not included among the Associates' results.

RESULTS SUMMARY OF ALL LIMITED-OVERS INTERNATIONALS

1970-71 to 2000 (1,622 matches)

	Matches	Won	Lost	Tied	No Result	% Won (excl. NR)
South Africa	205	125	73	2	5	62.50
West Indies.	406	241	152	5	8	60.55
Australia	465	261	186	6	12	57.61
Pakistan	476	246	214	6	10	52.78
England	317	160	146	2	9	51.94
India	445	199	225	3	18	46.60
New Zealand	348	143	184	4	17	43.20
Sri Lanka	329	128	185	2	14	40.63
Zimbabwe.	157	42	107	4	4	27.45
Kenya	33	7	25	–	1	21.87
United Arab Emirates . .	7	1	6	–	–	14.28
Bangladesh	40	3	37	–	–	7.50
Canada	3	–	3	–	–	–
East Africa	3	–	3	–	–	–
Holland	5	–	5	–	–	–
Scotland	5	–	5	–	–	–

Note: Matches abandoned without a ball bowled are not included. Those called off after play began are counted as official internationals in their own right, even when replayed, according to the ICC's ruling.

MOST RUNS

	M	I	NO	R	HS	100s	Avge
M. Azharuddin (India)	334	308	54	9,378	153*	7	36.92
S. R. Tendulkar (India).	249	242	22	9,262	186*	25	42.10
D. L. Haynes (West Indies)	238	237	28	8,648	152*	17	41.37
P. A. de Silva (Sri Lanka).	268	260	26	8,334	145	11	35.61
M. E. Waugh (Australia).	220	215	16	7,558	130	14	37.97
A. Ranatunga (Sri Lanka).	269	255	47	7,456	131*	4	35.84
Inzamam-ul-Haq (Pakistan)	229	218	31	7,417	137*	7	39.66
Javed Miandad (Pakistan)	233	218	41	7,381	119*	8	41.70
Saeed Anwar (Pakistan)	207	204	15	7,318	194	17	38.71
Salim Malik (Pakistan).	283	256	38	7,170	102	5	32.88
S. R. Waugh (Australia)	298	267	54	6,874	120*	3	32.27
I. V. A. Richards (West Indies). .	187	167	24	6,721	189*	11	47.00
A. R. Border (Australia).	273	252	39	6,524	127*	3	30.62
B. C. Lara (West Indies)	172	168	15	6,520	169	13	42.61
Ijaz Ahmed, sen. (Pakistan). . . .	245	228	29	6,425	139*	10	32.28
R. B. Richardson (West Indies) .	224	217	30	6,249	122	5	33.41
D. M. Jones (Australia)	164	161	25	6,068	145	7	44.61
D. C. Boon (Australia)	181	177	16	5,964	122	5	37.04
Ramiz Raja (Pakistan)	198	197	15	5,841	119*	9	32.09
S. T. Jayasuriya (Sri Lanka) . . .	210	202	8	5,569	151*	8	28.70
S. C. Ganguly (India).	145	140	12	5,567	183	13	43.49
W. J. Cronje (South Africa). . . .	188	175	31	5,565	112	2	38.64
A. Jadeja (India).	196	179	36	5,359	119	6	37.47
R. S. Mahanama (Sri Lanka). . .	213	198	23	5,162	119*	4	29.49
C. G. Greenidge (West Indies). .	128	127	13	5,134	133*	11	45.03
G. Kirsten (South Africa)	135	135	13	4,919	188*	9	40.31
Aamir Sohail (Pakistan)	156	155	5	4,780	134	5	31.86

	M	I	NO	R	HS	100s	Avge
M. G. Bevan (Australia)	144	128	44	4,761	108*	5	56.67
M. D. Crowe (New Zealand)	143	140	18	4,704	107*	4	38.55
C. L. Hooper (West Indies)	182	166	36	4,612	113*	6	35.47
N. S. Sidhu (India)	136	127	8	4,413	134*	6	37.08
G. R. Marsh (Australia)	117	115	6	4,357	126*	9	39.97
G. A. Gooch (England)	125	122	6	4,290	142	8	36.98
A. Flower (Zimbabwe)	145	142	10	4,270	115*	1	32.34
K. Srikkanth (India)	146	145	4	4,092	123	4	29.02
R. Dravid (India)	128	120	9	4,085	153	7	36.80
G. W. Flower (Zimbabwe)	132	130	10	4,075	140	3	33.95
J. N. Rhodes (South Africa)	179	163	32	4,057	121	1	30.96
A. J. Lamb (England)	122	118	16	4,010	118	4	39.31

HIGHEST INDIVIDUAL SCORES

194	Saeed Anwar	Pakistan v India at Chennai	1996-97
189*	I. V. A. Richards	West Indies v England at Manchester	1984
188*	G. Kirsten	South Africa v UAE at Rawalpindi	1995-96
186*	S. R. Tendulkar	India v New Zealand at Hyderabad	1999-2000
183	S. C. Ganguly	India v Sri Lanka at Taunton	1999
181	I. V. A. Richards	West Indies v Sri Lanka at Karachi	1987-88
175*	Kapil Dev	India v Zimbabwe at Tunbridge Wells	1983
171*	G. M. Turner	New Zealand v East Africa at Birmingham	1975
169*	D. J. Callaghan	South Africa v New Zealand at Verwoerdburg	1994-95
169	B. C. Lara	West Indies v Sri Lanka at Sharjah	1995-96
167*	R. A. Smith	England v Australia at Birmingham	1993
161	A. C. Hudson	South Africa v Holland at Rawalpindi	1995-96
158	D. I. Gower	England v New Zealand at Brisbane	1982-83
154	A. C. Gilchrist	Australia v Sri Lanka at Melbourne	1998-99
153*	I. V. A. Richards	West Indies v Australia at Melbourne	1979-80
153*	M. Azharuddin	India v Zimbabwe at Cuttack	1997-98
153*	S. C. Ganguly	India v New Zealand at Gwalior	1999-2000
153	B. C. Lara	West Indies v Pakistan at Sharjah	1993-94
153	R. Dravid	India v New Zealand at Hyderabad	1999-2000
152*	D. L. Haynes	West Indies v India at Georgetown	1988-89
151*	S. T. Jayasuriya	Sri Lanka v India at Mumbai	1996-97
150	S. Chanderpaul	West Indies v South Africa at East London	1998-99

Highest individual score for Zimbabwe:

142	D. L. Houghton	Zimbabwe v New Zealand at Hyderabad, India	1987-88

MOST HUNDREDS

Total		E	A	SA	WI	NZ	I	P	SL	Z	Ass
25	S. R. Tendulkar (India)	0	5	2	1	3	–	2	5	4	3
17	D. L. Haynes (West Indies)	2	6	0	–	2	2	4	1	0	–
17	Saeed Anwar (Pakistan)	0	1	0	2	3	3	–	6	2	0
14	M. E. Waugh (Australia)	1	–	2	1	3	2	1	1	2	1
13	S. C. Ganguly (India)	0	1	1	0	2	–	2	4	2	1
13	B. C. Lara (West Indies)	1	2	2	–	2	0	4	1	0	1
11	P. A. de Silva (Sri Lanka)	2	2	0	0	0	3	3	–	2	1
11	C. G. Greenidge (West Indies)	0	1	–	–	3	3	2	1	1	–
11	I. V. A. Richards (West Indies)	3	3	–	–	1	3	0	1	0	–
10	Ijaz Ahmed, sen. (Pakistan)	1	1	2	0	0	2	–	1	2	1

Note: Ass = Associate Members.

HIGHEST PARTNERSHIP FOR EACH WICKET

252	for 1st	S. C. Ganguly and S. R. Tendulkar	I v SL	Colombo (RPS)	1997-98
331	for 2nd	S. R. Tendulkar and R. Dravid	I v NZ	Hyderabad	1999-2000
237*	for 3rd	R. Dravid and S. R. Tendulkar	I v K	Bristol	1999
275*	for 4th	M. Azharuddin and A. Jadeja	I v Z	Cuttack	1997-98
223	for 5th	M. Azharuddin and A. Jadeja	I v SL	Colombo (RPS)	1997-98
161	for 6th	M. O. Odumbe and A. V. Vadher	K v SL	Southampton	1999
119	for 7th	T. M. Odoyo and A. O. Suji	K v Z	Nairobi (Aga Khan)	1997-98
119	for 8th	P. R. Reiffel and S. K. Warne	A v SA	Port Elizabeth	1993-94
126*	for 9th	Kapil Dev and S. M. H. Kirmani	I v Z	Tunbridge Wells	1983
106*	for 10th	I. V. A. Richards and M. A. Holding	WI v E	Manchester	1984

MOST WICKETS

	M	Balls	R	W	BB	4W/i	Avge
Wasim Akram (Pakistan)	306	15,727	10,084	427	5-15	21	23.61
Waqar Younis (Pakistan)	195	9,640	7,342	311	6-26	22	23.60
A. Kumble (India)	203	10,891	7,630	267	6-12	9	28.57
Kapil Dev (India)	225	11,202	6,945	253	5-43	4	27.45
J. Srinath (India)	187	9,775	7,223	252	5-23	7	28.66
S. K. Warne (Australia)	149	8,230	5,710	230	5-33	12	24.82
Saqlain Mushtaq (Pakistan)	124	6,491	4,613	227	5-29	14	20.32
C. A. Walsh (West Indies)	205	10,822	6,918	227	5-1	7	30.47
C. E. L. Ambrose (West Indies) . .	176	9,353	5,429	225	5-17	10	24.12
A. A. Donald (South Africa).	121	6,438	4,336	206	6-23	11	21.04
C. J. McDermott (Australia).	138	7,461	5,018	203	5-44	5	24.71
M. Muralitharan (Sri Lanka).	141	7,675	5,267	194	5-23	7	27.14
S. R. Waugh (Australia)	298	8,763	6,645	191	4-33	3	34.79
S. T. Jayasuriya (Sri Lanka)	210	7,799	6,315	184	6-29	8	34.32
G. D. McGrath (Australia).	121	6,473	4,266	183	5-14	10	23.31
Imran Khan (Pakistan)	175	7,461	4,845	182	6-14	4	26.62
Aqib Javed (Pakistan)	163	8,012	5,721	182	7-37	6	31.43
B. K. V. Prasad (India)	146	7,391	5,683	174	5-27	4	32.66
W. P. U. J. C. Vaas (Sri Lanka) . . .	137	6,630	4,700	163	4-20	3	28.83
C. L. Hooper (West Indies)	182	7,597	5,548	163	4-34	3	34.03
Mushtaq Ahmed (Pakistan).	140	7,303	5,168	159	5-36	4	32.50
R. J. Hadlee (New Zealand)	115	6,182	3,407	158	5-25	6	21.56
M. D. Marshall (West Indies)	136	7,175	4,233	157	4-18	6	26.96
M. Prabhakar (India).	130	6,360	4,535	157	5-33	6	28.88
S. M. Pollock (South Africa)	108	5,695	3,681	155	6-35	8	23.74
J. Garner (West Indies)	98	5,330	2,752	146	5-31	5	18.84
I. T. Botham (England)	116	6,271	4,139	145	4-31	3	28.54
C. Z. Harris (New Zealand)	152	6,878	4,914	144	5-42	3	34.12
M. A. Holding (West Indies)	102	5,473	3,034	142	5-26	6	21.36
E. J. Chatfield (New Zealand). . . .	114	6,065	3,618	140	5-34	4	25.84
D. Gough (England)	81	4,476	3,083	133	5-44	8	23.18
Abdul Qadir (Pakistan)	104	5,100	3,453	132	5-44	6	26.15
R. J. Shastri (India).	150	6,613	4,650	129	5-15	3	36.04
L. Klusener (South Africa).	94	4,252	3,325	127	6-49	6	26.18
D. K. Morrison (New Zealand) . . .	96	4,586	3,470	126	5-34	3	27.53
C. L. Cairns (New Zealand)	126	5,169	4,008	124	5-42	3	32.32
H. H. Streak (Zimbabwe).	98	4,924	3,614	121	5-32	4	29.86
D. W. Fleming (Australia)	76	3,971	2,904	118	5-36	5	24.61
I. R. Bishop (West Indies)	84	4,332	3,127	118	5-25	9	26.50
I. V. A. Richards (West Indies) . . .	187	5,644	4,228	118	6-41	3	35.83
P. A. J. DeFreitas (England)	103	5,712	3,775	115	4-35	1	32.82
M. C. Snedden (New Zealand) . . .	93	4,525	3,237	114	4-34	1	28.39

	M	Balls	R	W	BB	4W/i	Avge
W. J. Cronje (South Africa)	188	5,354	3,966	114	5-32	2	34.78
G. R. Larsen (New Zealand).	121	6,368	4,000	113	4-24	1	35.39
Mudassar Nazar (Pakistan).	122	4,855	3,432	111	5-28	2	30.91
S. P. O'Donnell (Australia).	87	4,350	3,102	108	5-13	6	28.72
P. R. Reiffel (Australia).	92	4,732	3,095	106	4-13	5	29.20
G. P. Wickremasinghe (Sri Lanka).	127	5,490	4,090	104	4-48	1	39.32
D. K. Lillee (Australia)	63	3,593	2,145	103	5-34	6	20.82
C. Pringle (New Zealand)	64	3,314	2,455	103	5-45	3	23.83
W. K. M. Benjamin (West Indies) .	85	4,442	3,079	100	5-22	1	30.79
R. A. Harper (West Indies).	105	5,175	3,431	100	4-40	3	34.31

BEST ANALYSES

7-37	Aqib Javed	Pakistan v India at Sharjah	1991-92
7-51	W. W. Davis	West Indies v Australia at Leeds	1983
6-12	A. Kumble	India v West Indies at Calcutta	1993-94
6-14	G. J. Gilmour	Australia v England at Leeds.	1975
6-14	Imran Khan	Pakistan v India at Sharjah	1984-85
6-15	C. E. H. Croft	West Indies v England at St Vincent.	1980-81
6-18	Azhar Mahmood	Pakistan v West Indies at Sharjah.	1999-2000
6-19	H. K. Olonga	Zimbabwe v England at Cape Town	1999-2000
6-20	B. C. Strang	Zimbabwe v Bangladesh at Nairobi (Aga Khan) . .	1997-98
6-23	A. A. Donald	South Africa v Kenya at Nairobi (Gymkhana). . . .	1996-97
6-26	Waqar Younis	Pakistan v Sri Lanka at Moratuwa	1989-90
6-29	B. P. Patterson	West Indies v India at Nagpur.	1987-88
6-29	S. T. Jayasuriya	Sri Lanka v England at Moratuwa	1992-93
6-30	Waqar Younis	Pakistan v New Zealand at Auckland	1993-94
6-35	S. M. Pollock	South Africa v West Indies at East London	1998-99
6-39	K. H. MacLeay	Australia v India at Nottingham.	1983
6-41	I. V. A. Richards	West Indies v India at Delhi	1989-90
6-44	Waqar Younis	Pakistan v New Zealand at Sharjah.	1996-97
6-49	L. Klusener	South Africa v Sri Lanka at Lahore	1997-98
6-50	A. H. Gray	West Indies v Australia at Port-of-Spain	1990-91

Best analyses for other Test-playing countries:

5-15	M. A. Ealham	England v Zimbabwe at Kimberley.	1999-2000
5-22	M. N. Hart	New Zealand v West Indies at Margao	1994-95

Note: M. Muralitharan took 7-30 for Sri Lanka against India at Sharjah in 2000-01, after the deadline for this section.

HAT-TRICKS

Jalal-ud-Din	Pakistan v Australia at Hyderabad	1982-83
B. A. Reid	Australia v New Zealand at Sydney.	1985-86
Chetan Sharma	India v New Zealand at Nagpur.	1987-88
Wasim Akram	Pakistan v West Indies at Sharjah	1989-90
Wasim Akram	Pakistan v Australia at Sharjah	1989-90
Kapil Dev	India v Sri Lanka at Calcutta	1990-91
Aqib Javed	Pakistan v India at Sharjah.	1991-92
D. K. Morrison	New Zealand v India at Napier.	1993-94
Waqar Younis	Pakistan v New Zealand at East London.	1994-95
Saqlain Mushtaq†	Pakistan v Zimbabwe at Peshawar	1996-97
E. A. Brandes	Zimbabwe v England at Harare.	1996-97
A. M. Stuart	Australia v Pakistan at Melbourne.	1996-97
Saqlain Mushtaq	Pakistan v Zimbabwe at The Oval	1999

† *Four wickets in five balls.*

MOST DISMISSALS IN AN INNINGS

6 (all ct)	A. C. Gilchrist	Australia v South Africa at Cape Town	1999-2000
6 (all ct)	A. J. Stewart	England v Zimbabwe at Manchester	2000

MOST DISMISSALS IN A CAREER

		M	Ct	St	Total
1	Moin Khan (Pakistan)	180	178	61	239
2	I. A. Healy (Australia)	168	195	39	234
3	P. J. L. Dujon (West Indies)	169	183	21	204
4	D. J. Richardson (South Africa)	122	148	17	165
5	R. S. Kaluwitharana (Sri Lanka)	139	96	62	158
6	N. R. Mongia (India)	140	110	44	154
7	A. C. Gilchrist (Australia)	98	127	19	146
8	A. J. Stewart (England)	132	123	11	134
9	A. Flower (Zimbabwe)	145	102	28	130
10	R. W. Marsh (Australia)	92	120	4	124
11	Rashid Latif (Pakistan)	101	94	28	122
12	M. V. Boucher (South Africa)	70	103	4	107
13	R. D. Jacobs (West Indies)	62	86	17	103
14	Salim Yousuf (Pakistan)	86	81	22	103
15	A. C. Parore (New Zealand)	137	79	21	100

Note: A. J. Stewart's record includes 11 catches taken in 32 limited-overs internationals when not keeping wicket; A. C. Parore's includes 5 in 29 when not keeping wicket.

MOST CATCHES IN AN INNINGS

(Excluding wicket-keepers)

5	J. N. Rhodes	South Africa v West Indies at Bombay	1993-94
4	Salim Malik	Pakistan v New Zealand at Sialkot	1984-85
4	S. M. Gavaskar	India v Pakistan at Sharjah	1984-85
4	R. B. Richardson	West Indies v England at Birmingham	1991
4	K. C. Wessels	South Africa v West Indies at Kingston	1991-92
4	M. A. Taylor	Australia v West Indies at Sydney	1992-93
4	C. L. Hooper	West Indies v Pakistan at Durban	1992-93
4	K. R. Rutherford	New Zealand v India at Napier	1994-95
4	P. V. Simmons	West Indies v Sri Lanka at Sharjah	1995-96
4	M. Azharuddin	India v Pakistan at Toronto	1997-98
4	S. R. Tendulkar	India v Pakistan at Dhaka	1997-98
4	R. Dravid	India v West Indies at Toronto	1999-2000
4	G. J. Whittall	Zimbabwe v England at The Oval	2000

Note: While fielding as substitute, J. G. Bracewell held 4 catches for New Zealand v Australia at Adelaide, 1980-81.

MOST CATCHES IN A CAREER

	M	Ct		M	Ct
M. Azharuddin (India)	334	156	S. R. Tendulkar (India)	249	84
A. R. Border (Australia)	273	127	Wasim Akram (Pakistan)	306	82
R. S. Mahanama (Sri Lanka)	213	109	Salim Malik (Pakistan)	283	81
S. R. Waugh (Australia)	298	102	B. C. Lara (West Indies)	172	75
I. V. A. Richards (West Indies)	187	101	R. B. Richardson (West Indies)	224	75
M. E. Waugh (Australia)	220	95			
Ijaz Ahmed, sen. (Pakistan)	245	89	*Most catches for other countries:*		
C. L. Hooper (West Indies)	182	87	G. A. Hick (England)	112	59
P. A. de Silva (Sri Lanka)	268	84	S. P. Fleming (New Zealand)	125	56
J. N. Rhodes (South Africa)	179	84	A. D. R. Campbell (Zimbabwe)	134	50

1,000 RUNS AND 100 WICKETS

	M	*R*	*W*
I. T. Botham (England)	116	2,113	145
C. L. Cairns (New Zealand)	126	2,892	124
W. J. Cronje (South Africa).	188	5,565	114
R. J. Hadlee (New Zealand)	115	1,751	158
C. Z. Harris (New Zealand)	152	2,696	144
C. L. Hooper (West Indies)	182	4,612	163
Imran Khan (Pakistan)	175	3,709	182
S. T. Jayasuriya (Sri Lanka)	210	5,569	184
Kapil Dev (India)	225	3,783	253
L. Klusener (South Africa)	94	2,311	127
Mudassar Nazar (Pakistan)	122	2,653	111
S. P. O'Donnell (Australia)	87	1,242	108
S. M. Pollock (South Africa).	108	1,336	155
M. Prabhakar (India)	130	1,858	157
I. V. A. Richards (West Indies)	187	6,721	118
R. J. Shastri (India)	150	3,108	129
H. H. Streak (Zimbabwe)	98	1,083	121
Wasim Akram (Pakistan)	306	3,222	427
S. R. Waugh (Australia)	298	6,874	191

1,000 RUNS AND 100 DISMISSALS

	M	*R*	*W*
P. J. L. Dujon (West Indies)	169	1,945	204
A. Flower (Zimbabwe).	145	4,270	130
A. C. Gilchrist (Australia)	98	3,069	146
I. A. Healy (Australia)	168	1,764	234
R. S. Kaluwitharana (Sri Lanka)	139	2,609	158
R. W. Marsh (Australia)	92	1,225	124
Moin Khan (Pakistan)	180	2,731	239
N. R. Mongia (India).	140	1,272	154
A. C. Parore (New Zealand)	137	2,842	100
A. J. Stewart (England)	132	3,786	134

HIGHEST INNINGS TOTALS

398-5	(50 overs)	Sri Lanka v Kenya at Kandy.	1995-96
376-2	(50 overs)	India v New Zealand at Hyderabad.	1999-2000
373-6	(50 overs)	India v Sri Lanka at Taunton.	1999
371-9	(50 overs)	Pakistan v Sri Lanka at Nairobi (Gymkhana)	1996-97
363-7	(55 overs)	England v Pakistan at Nottingham	1992
360-4	(50 overs)	West Indies v Sri Lanka at Karachi	1987-88
349-6	(50 overs)	Australia v New Zealand at Auckland	1999-2000
349-9	(50 overs)	Sri Lanka v Pakistan at Singapore	1995-96
349-9	(50 overs)	New Zealand v India at Rajkot	1999-2000
348-8	(50 overs)	New Zealand v India at Nagpur.	1995-96
347-3	(50 overs)	Kenya v Bangladesh at Nairobi (Gymkhana)	1997-98
339-4	(50 overs)	Sri Lanka v Pakistan at Mohali	1996-97
338-4	(50 overs)	New Zealand v Bangladesh at Sharjah	1989-90
338-5	(60 overs)	Pakistan v Sri Lanka at Swansea	1983
337-7	(50 overs)	Australia v Pakistan at Sydney.	1999-2000

Highest totals by other Test-playing countries:

328-3	(50 overs)	South Africa v Holland at Rawalpindi.	1995-96
325-6	(50 overs)	Zimbabwe v Kenya at Dhaka	1998-99

HIGHEST TOTALS BATTING SECOND

329	(49.3 overs)	Sri Lanka v West Indies at Sharjah.	1995-96
		(*Lost by 4 runs*)	
316-7	(47.5 overs)	India v Pakistan at Dhaka.	1997-98
		(*Won by 3 wickets*)	
316-4	(48.5 overs)	Australia v Pakistan at Lahore.	1998-99
		(*Won by 6 wickets*)	
315	(49.4 overs)	Pakistan v Sri Lanka at Singapore	1995-96
		(*Lost by 34 runs*)	
313-7	(49.2 overs)	Sri Lanka v Zimbabwe at New Plymouth.	1991-92
		(*Won by 3 wickets*)	
310	(48.5 overs)	India v South Africa at Nagpur	1999-2000
		(*Lost by 10 runs*)	

HIGHEST MATCH AGGREGATES

664-19	(99.4 overs)	Pakistan v Sri Lanka at Singapore	1995-96
662-17	(99.3 overs)	Sri Lanka v West Indies at Sharjah.	1995-96
660-19	(99.5 overs)	Pakistan v Sri Lanka at Nairobi (Gymkhana)	1996-97
655-19	(97 overs)	India v New Zealand at Rajkot	1999-2000
652-12	(100 overs)	Sri Lanka v Kenya at Kandy.	1995-96
650-15	(100 overs)	New Zealand v Australia at Auckland	1999-2000

LOWEST INNINGS TOTALS

43	(19.5 overs)	Pakistan v West Indies at Cape Town	1992-93
45	(40.3 overs)	Canada v England at Manchester	1979
55	(28.3 overs)	Sri Lanka v West Indies at Sharjah.	1986-87
63	(25.5 overs)	India v Australia at Sydney.	1980-81
64	(35.5 overs)	New Zealand v Pakistan at Sharjah.	1985-86
68	(31.3 overs)	Scotland v West Indies at Leicester	1999
69	(28 overs)	South Africa v Australia at Sydney.	1993-94
70	(25.2 overs)	Australia v England at Birmingham	1977
70	(26.3 overs)	Australia v New Zealand at Adelaide	1985-86

Note: This section does not take into account those matches in which the number of overs was reduced.

Lowest totals by other Test-playing countries:

87	(29.3 overs)	West Indies v Australia at Sydney	1992-93
93	(36.2 overs)	England v Australia at Leeds.	1975
94	(31.4 overs)	Zimbabwe v Pakistan at Sharjah	1996-97

LARGEST VICTORIES

233 runs Pakistan (320-3 in 50 overs) v Bangladesh (87 in 34.2 overs) at Dhaka .	1999-2000
232 runs Australia (323-2 in 50 overs) v Sri Lanka (91 in 35.5 overs) at Adelaide	1984-85
206 runs New Zealand (276-7 in 50 overs) v Australia (70 in 26.3 overs)	
at Adelaide	1985-86
202 runs England (334-4 in 60 overs) v India (132-3 in 60 overs) at Lord's	1975
202 runs South Africa (305-8 in 50 overs) v Kenya (103 in 25.1 overs) at Nairobi	1996-97

By ten wickets: there have been 13 instances of victory by ten wickets.

Note: Sri Lanka (299-5 in 50 overs) beat India (54 in 26.3 overs) by 245 runs at Sharjah in 2000-01, after the deadline for this section.

TIED MATCHES

West Indies 222-5 (50 overs) v Australia 222-9 (50 overs) at Melbourne........	1983-84
England 226-5 (55 overs) v Australia 226-8 (55 overs) at Nottingham	1989
West Indies 186-5 (39 overs) v Pakistan 186-9 (39 overs) at Lahore	1991-92
India 126 (47.4 overs) v West Indies 126 (41 overs) at Perth	1991-92
Australia 228-7 (50 overs) v Pakistan 228-9 (50 overs) at Hobart	1992-93
Pakistan 244-6 (50 overs) v West Indies 244-5 (50 overs) at Georgetown	1992-93
India 248-5 (50 overs) v Zimbabwe 248 (50 overs) at Indore	1993-94
Pakistan 161-9 (50 overs) v New Zealand 161 (49.4 overs) at Auckland........	1993-94
Zimbabwe 219-9 (50 overs) v Pakistan 219 (49.5 overs) at Harare...........	1994-95
New Zealand 169-8 (50 overs) v Sri Lanka 169 (48 overs) at Sharjah	1996-97
Zimbabwe 236-8 (50 overs) v India 236 (49.5 overs) at Paarl	1996-97
New Zealand 237 (49.4 overs) v England 237-8 (50 overs) at Napier..........	1996-97
Zimbabwe 233-8 (50 overs) v New Zealand 233-9 (50 overs) at Bulawayo	1997-98
West Indies 173-5 (30 overs) v Australia 173-7 (30 overs) at Georgetown.......	1998-99
Australia 213 (49.2 overs) v South Africa 213 (49.4 overs) at Birmingham	1999
Pakistan 196 (49.4 overs) v Sri Lanka 196 (49.1 overs) at Sharjah............	1999-2000
South Africa 226 (50 overs) v Australia 226-9 (50 overs) at Melbourne (CS).....	2000 (A)

MOST APPEARANCES

(200 or more)

	Total	E	A	SA	WI	NZ	I	P	SL	Z	Ass
M. Azharuddin (I).....	334	24	43	33	43	40	–	64	53	22	12
Wasim Akram (P).....	306	27	41	19	63	28	47	–	50	21	10
S. R. Waugh (A)......	298	27	–	43	46	56	47	40	24	11	4
Salim Malik (P)......	283	26	26	16	46	43	52	–	53	13	8
A. R. Border (A)	273	43	–	15	61	52	38	34	23	5	2
A. Ranatunga (SL)	269	18	33	16	22	35	56	67	–	15	7
P. A. de Silva (SL)	268	13	30	16	27	31	55	72	–	15	9
S. R. Tendulkar (I)	249	14	27	35	26	30	–	43	42	21	11
Ijaz Ahmed, sen. (P) ...	245	19	34	18	38	25	53	–	38	13	7
D. L. Haynes (WI)	238	35	64	8	–	13	36	65	14	3	–
Javed Miandad (P).....	233	27	35	3	64	24	35	–	35	6	4
Inzamam-ul-Haq (P) ...	229	12	20	22	35	24	44	–	45	17	10
Kapil Dev (I)........	225	23	41	13	42	29	–	32	34	9	2
R. B. Richardson (WI)..	224	35	51	9	–	11	32	61	21	3	1
M. E. Waugh (A)	220	19	–	39	41	35	24	26	23	10	3
R. S. Mahanama (SL) ..	213	11	26	15	22	22	45	52	–	14	6
S. T. Jayasuriya (SL) ..	210	11	25	18	19	20	39	52	–	19	7
Saeed Anwar (P)......	207	6	22	22	17	23	49	–	44	13	11
C. A. Walsh (WI)	205	31	36	5	–	38	16	52	22	2	3
A. Kumble (I)	203	15	20	31	21	25	–	30	35	18	8

Most appearances for other Test-playing countries:

W. J. Cronje (SA).....	188	22	39	–	17	20	34	24	15	12	5
C. Z. Harris (NZ).....	152	17	27	17	14	–	23	20	18	13	3
A. Flower (Z)........	145	16	11	12	9	16	23	22	21	–	15
A. J. Stewart (E)......	132	–	20	14	25	19	14	15	12	10	3

LIMITED-OVERS INTERNATIONAL CAPTAINS

England (317 matches; 21 captains)

G. A. Gooch 50; M. A. Atherton 43; M. W. Gatting 37; A. J. Stewart 34; R. G. D. Willis 29; J. M. Brearley 25; D. I. Gower 24; A. J. Hollioake 14; N. Hussain 13; M. H. Denness 12; I. T. Botham 9; K. W. R. Fletcher 5; J. E. Emburey 4; A. J. Lamb 4; D. B. Close 3; R. Illingworth 3; G. Boycott 2; N. Gifford 2; A. W. Greig 2; J. H. Edrich 1; A. P. E. Knott 1.

Australia (465 matches; 14 captains)

A. R. Border 178; S. R. Waugh 79; M. A. Taylor 67; G. S. Chappell 49; K. J. Hughes 49; I. M. Chappell 11; S. K. Warne 11; I. A. Healy 8; G. R. Marsh 4; G. N. Yallop 4; R. B. Simpson 2; R. J. Bright 1; D. W. Hookes 1; W. M. Lawry 1.

South Africa (205 matches; 4 captains)

W. J. Cronje 138; K. C. Wessels 52; S. M. Pollock 12; C. E. B. Rice 3.

West Indies (406 matches; 14 captains)

I. V. A. Richards 108; R. B. Richardson 87; C. H. Lloyd 81; B. C. Lara 44; C. A. Walsh 43; J. C. Adams 16; C. G. Greenidge 8; D. L. Haynes 7; C. L. Hooper 4; M. A. Holding 2; R. B. Kanhai 2; D. L. Murray 2; P. J. L. Dujon 1; A. I. Kallicharran 1.

New Zealand (348 matches; 14 captains)

S. P. Fleming 65; G. P. Howarth 60; M. D. Crowe 44; K. R. Rutherford 37; L. K. Germon 36; J. G. Wright 31; J. V. Coney 25; J. J. Crowe 16; M. G. Burgess 8; G. M. Turner 8; D. J. Nash 7; B. E. Congdon 6; G. R. Larsen 3; A. H. Jones 2.

India (445 matches; 15 captains)

M. Azharuddin 174; Kapil Dev 74; S. R. Tendulkar 73; S. M. Gavaskar 37; D. B. Vengsarkar 18; S. C. Ganguly 16; A. Jadeja 13; K. Srikkanth 13; R. J. Shastri 11; S. Venkataraghavan 7; B. S. Bedi 4; A. L. Wadekar 2; M. Amarnath 1; S. M. H. Kirmani 1; G. R. Viswanath 1.

Pakistan (476 matches; 18 captains)

Imran Khan 139; Wasim Akram 110; Javed Miandad 62; Salim Malik 34; Moin Khan 24; Aamir Sohail 22; Ramiz Raja 22; Rashid Latif 13; Zaheer Abbas 13; Saeed Anwar 10; Asif Iqbal 6; Abdul Qadir 5; Wasim Bari 5; Mushtaq Mohammad 4; Intikhab Alam 3; Majid Khan 2; Sarfraz Nawaz 1; Waqar Younis 1.

Sri Lanka (329 matches; 10 captains)

A. Ranatunga 193; L. R. D. Mendis 61; S. T. Jayasuriya 28; P. A. de Silva 18; R. S. Madugalle 13; B. Warnapura 8; A. P. B. Tennekoon 4; R. S. Mahanama 2; D. S. de Silva 1; J. R. Ratnayeke 1.

Zimbabwe (157 matches; 5 captains)

A. D. R. Campbell 76; A. Flower 52; D. L. Houghton 17; D. A. G. Fletcher 6; A. J. Traicos 6.

Associate Members (96 matches; 12 captains)

A. Y. Karim (Kenya) 21; Akram Khan (Bangladesh) 15; Aminul Islam (Bangladesh) 16; M. O. Odumbe (Kenya) 12; Gazi Ashraf (Bangladesh) 7; Sultan M. Zarawani (UAE) 7; G. Salmond (Scotland) 5; S. W. Lubbers (Holland) 4; B. M. Mauricette (Canada) 3; Harilal R. Shah (East Africa) 3; Minhaz-ul-Abedin (Bangladesh) 2; R. P. Lefebvre (Holland) 1.

WORLD CUP FINALS

1975	WEST INDIES (291-8) beat Australia (274) by 17 runs	Lord's
1979	WEST INDIES (286-9) beat England (194) by 92 runs	Lord's
1983	INDIA (183) beat West Indies (140) by 43 runs	Lord's
1987-88	AUSTRALIA (253-5) beat England (246-8) by seven runs	Calcutta
1991-92	PAKISTAN (249-6) beat England (227) by 22 runs	Melbourne
1995-96	SRI LANKA (245-3) beat Australia (241-7) by seven wickets	Lahore
1999	AUSTRALIA (133-2) beat Pakistan (132) by eight wickets	Lord's

MISCELLANEOUS

LARGE ATTENDANCES

Test Series

943,000	Australia v England (5 Tests)	1936-37
In England		
549,650	England v Australia (5 Tests)	1953

Test Matches

†‡465,000	India v Pakistan, Calcutta	1998-99
350,534	Australia v England, Melbourne (Third Test)	1936-37

Note: Attendance at India v England at Calcutta in 1981-82 may have exceeded 350,000.

In England		
158,000+	England v Australia, Leeds	1948
137,915	England v Australia, Lord's	1953

Test Match Day

‡100,000	India v Pakistan, Calcutta (first four days)	1998-99
90,800	Australia v West Indies, Melbourne (Fifth Test, second day)	1960-61

Other First-Class Matches in England

93,000	England v Australia, Lord's (Fourth Victory Match, 3 days)	1945
80,000+	Surrey v Yorkshire, The Oval (3 days)	1906
78,792	Yorkshire v Lancashire, Leeds (3 days)	1904
76,617	Lancashire v Yorkshire, Manchester (3 days)	1926

Limited-Overs Internationals

‡100,000	India v South Africa, Calcutta	1993-94
‡100,000	India v West Indies, Calcutta	1993-94
‡100,000	India v West Indies, Calcutta	1994-95
‡100,000	India v Sri Lanka, Calcutta (World Cup semi-final)	1995-96
‡90,000	India v Pakistan, Calcutta	1986-87
‡90,000	India v South Africa, Calcutta	1991-92
87,182	England v Pakistan, Melbourne (World Cup final)	1991-92
86,133	Australia v West Indies, Melbourne	1983-84

† *Estimated.*
‡ *No official attendance figures were issued for these games, but capacity is believed to have reached 100,000 following rebuilding in 1993.*

LORD'S CRICKET GROUND

Lord's and the Marylebone Cricket Club were founded in 1787. The Club has enjoyed an uninterrupted career since that date, but there have been three grounds known as Lord's. The first (1787–1810) was situated where Dorset Square now is; the second (1809–13), at North Bank, had to be abandoned owing to the cutting of the Regent's Canal; and the third, opened in 1814, is the present one at St John's Wood. It was not until 1866 that the freehold of Lord's was secured by MCC. The present pavilion was erected in 1890 at a cost of £21,000.

HIGHEST INDIVIDUAL SCORES MADE AT LORD'S

333	G. A. Gooch	England v India	1990
316*	J. B. Hobbs	Surrey v Middlesex	1926
315*	P. Holmes	Yorkshire v Middlesex	1925

Note: The longest innings in a first-class match at Lord's was played by S. Wettimuny (636 minutes, 190 runs) for Sri Lanka v England, 1984.

HIGHEST TOTALS AT LORD'S

First-Class Matches

729-6 dec.	Australia v England	1930
665	West Indians v Middlesex	1939
653-4 dec.	England v India	1990
652-8 dec.	West Indies v England	1973

Minor Match

735-9 dec.	MCC and Ground v Wiltshire	1888

BIGGEST HIT AT LORD'S

The only known instance of a batsman hitting a ball over the present pavilion at Lord's occurred when A. E. Trott, appearing for MCC against Australians on July 31, August 1, 2, 1899, drove M. A. Noble so far and high that the ball struck a chimney pot and fell behind the building.

MINOR CRICKET

HIGHEST INDIVIDUAL SCORES

628*	A. E. J. Collins, Clark's House v North Town at Clifton College. (A Junior House match. His innings of 6 hours 50 minutes was spread over four afternoons.)	1899
566	C. J. Eady, Break-o'-Day v Wellington at Hobart	1901-02
515	D. R. Havewalla, B.B. and C.I. Rly v St Xavier's at Bombay	1933-34
506*	J. C. Sharp, Melbourne GS v Geelong College at Melbourne	1914-15
502*	Chaman Lal, Mehandra Coll., Patiala v Government Coll., Rupar at Patiala . . .	1956-57
485	A. E. Stoddart, Hampstead v Stoics at Hampstead	1886
475*	Mohammad Iqbal, Muslim Model HS v Islamia HS, Sialkot at Lahore	1958-59
466*	G. T. S. Stevens, Beta v Lambda (University College School House match) at Neasden	1919
459	J. A. Prout, Wesley College v Geelong College at Geelong	1908-09

Note: The highest score in a Minor County match is 323* by F. E. Lacey for Hampshire v Norfolk at Southampton in 1887; the highest in the Minor Counties Championship is 282 by E. Garnett for Berkshire v Wiltshire at Reading in 1908.

HIGHEST PARTNERSHIP

664* for 3rd   V. G. Kambli and S. R. Tendulkar, Sharadashram Vidyamandir School
v St Xavier's High School at Bombay   1987-88

RECORD HIT

The Rev. W. Fellows, while at practice on the Christ Church ground at Oxford in 1856, drove a ball bowled by Charles Rogers 175 yards from hit to pitch.

THROWING THE CRICKET BALL

140 yards 2 feet, Robert Percival, on the Durham Sands racecourse, Co. Durham . . .   c1882
140 yards 9 inches, Ross Mackenzie, at Toronto   1872
140 yards, "King Billy" the Aborigine, at Clermont, Queensland   1872

Note: Extensive research by David Rayvern Allen has shown that these traditional records are probably authentic, if not necessarily wholly accurate. Modern competitions have failed to produce similar distances although Ian Pont, the Essex all-rounder who also played baseball, was reported to have thrown 138 yards in Cape Town in 1981. There have been speculative reports attributing throws of 150 yards or more to figures as diverse as the South African Test player Colin Bland, the Latvian javelin thrower Janis Lusis, who won a gold medal for the Soviet Union in the 1968 Olympics, and the British sprinter Charley Ransome. The definitive record is still awaited.

COUNTY CHAMPIONSHIP

MOST APPEARANCES

762	W. Rhodes	Yorkshire	1898-1930
707	F. E. Woolley. . .	Kent	1906-38
668	C. P. Mead	Hampshire	1906-36
617	N. Gifford.	Worcestershire (484), Warwickshire (133)	1960-88
611	W. G. Quaife . . .	Warwickshire	1895-1928
601	G. H. Hirst	Yorkshire	1891-1921

MOST CONSECUTIVE APPEARANCES

423	K. G. Suttle	Sussex	1954-69
412	J. G. Binks	Yorkshire	1955-69

Notes: J. Vine made 417 consecutive appearances for Sussex in all first-class matches (399 of them in the Championship) between July 1900 and September 1914.

J. G. Binks did not miss a Championship match for Yorkshire between making his debut in June 1955 and retiring at the end of the 1969 season.

UMPIRES

MOST COUNTY CHAMPIONSHIP APPEARANCES

569	T. W. Spencer	1950-1980
533	F. Chester	1922-1955
516	H. G. Baldwin	1932-1962
481	P. B. Wight	1966-1995
462	J. Moss	1899-1929
457	A. Skelding	1931-1958

MOST SEASONS ON FIRST-CLASS LIST

32	**D. J. Constant**	**1969-2000**
31	T. W. Spencer	1950-1980
31	**A. G. T. Whitehead**	**1970-2000**
30	P. B. Wight	1966-1995
29	H. D. Bird	1970-1998
29	**R. Julian**	**1972-2000**
29	**K. E. Palmer**	**1972-2000**
28	F. Chester	1922-1955
27	J. Moss	1899-1929
26	W. A. J. West	1896-1925
25	H. G. Baldwin	1932-1962
25	A. Jepson	1960-1984
25	J. G. Langridge	1956-1980
25	B. J. Meyer	1973-1997

Bold type denotes umpires who stood in the 2000 season.

WOMEN'S TEST MATCH RECORDS

Amended by MARION COLLIN to the end of the 2000 season in England

HIGHEST INDIVIDUAL SCORES

204	K. E. Flavell	New Zealand v England at Scarborough	1996
200	J. Broadbent	Australia v England at Guildford	1998
193	D. A. Annetts	Australia v England at Collingham	1987
190	S. Agarwal	India v England at Worcester	1986
189	E. A. Snowball	England v New Zealand at Christchurch	1934-35
179	R. Heyhoe-Flint . . .	England v Australia at The Oval	1976
176*	K. L. Rolton	Australia v England at Worcester	1998

MOST RUNS IN A CAREER

1,935	J. A. Brittin (England)		1,110	S. Agarwal (India)
1,594	R. Heyhoe Flint (England)		1,078	F. Bakewell (England)
1,301	D. A. Hockley (New Zealand)		1,007	M. E. Maclagan (England)
1,164	C. A. Hodges (England)			

BEST ANALYSES

8-53	N. David	India v England at Jamshedpur	1995-96
7-6	M. B. Duggan .	England v Australia at Melbourne	1957-58
7-7	E. R. Wilson . .	Australia v England at Melbourne	1957-58
7-10	M. E. Maclagan	England v Australia at Brisbane	1934-35
7-18	A. Palmer	Australia v England at Brisbane	1934-35

MOST WICKETS IN A MATCH

11-16	E. R. Wilson	Australia v England at Melbourne	1957-58
11-63	J. Greenwood . . .	England v West Indies at Canterbury	1979

MOST WICKETS IN A CAREER

77	M. B. Duggan (England)		57	R. H. Thompson (Australia)
68	E. R. Wilson (Australia)		55	J. Lord (New Zealand)
60	M. E. Maclagan (England)		50	E. Bakewell (England)

MOST DISMISSALS IN AN INNINGS

8 (6ct, 2st)	L. Nye	England v New Zealand at New Plymouth	1991-92
6 (2ct, 4st)	B. Brentnall . . .	New Zealand v South Africa at Johannesburg . . .	1971-72

MOST DISMISSALS IN A MATCH

9 (8ct, 1st)	C. Matthews . .	Australia v India at Adelaide	1990-91
8 (6ct, 2st)	L. Nye	England v New Zealand at New Plymouth	1991-92

MOST DISMISSALS IN A CAREER

C. Matthews (Australia)	58	(46ct, 12st)
S. A. Hodges (England)	36	(19ct, 17st)
B. Brentnall (New Zealand)	28	(16ct, 12st)

HIGHEST INNINGS TOTALS

569-6 dec.	Australia v England at Guildford	1998
525	Australia v India at Ahmedabad	1983-84
517-8	New Zealand v England at Scarborough	1996
503-5 dec.	England v New Zealand at Christchurch	1934-35

LOWEST INNINGS TOTALS

35	England v Australia at Melbourne	1957-58
38	Australia v England at Melbourne	1957-58
44	New Zealand v England at Christchurch	1934-35
47	Australia v England at Brisbane	1934-35

PART FOUR: ENGLISH CRICKET IN 2000

FEATURES OF 2000

Double-Hundreds (9)

309*†	S. P. James	Glamorgan v Sussex at Colwyn Bay.
295*	A. D. Brown	Surrey v Leicestershire at Oakham School.
276	D. J. Sales	Northamptonshire v Nottinghamshire at Northampton.
233	N. V. Knight	Warwickshire v Glamorgan at Birmingham.
213*	J. L. Langer	Middlesex v Glamorgan at Cardiff.
212*	M. H. Richardson	New Zealand A v Sussex at Hove.
203	D. R. Brown	Warwickshire v Sussex at Hove.
200*	D. G. Cork	Derbyshire v Durham at Derby.
200*	G. E. Welton	Nottinghamshire v Warwickshire at Birmingham.

† *County record.*

Hundred on First-Class Debut

104	C. G. Taylor	Gloucestershire v Middlesex at Lord's.

Three or More Hundreds in Successive Innings

M. G. Bevan (Sussex)	151* v Essex at Arundel
	166 and 174 v Nottinghamshire at Hove.

Hundred in Each Innings of a Match

M. G. Bevan	166	174	Sussex v Nottinghamshire at Hove.
M. R. Ramprakash	110*	112	Middlesex v Sussex at Southgate.

Fastest Hundred

D. S. Lehmann	89 balls	Yorkshire v Kent at Canterbury.

Hundred Before Lunch

G. D. Lloyd	17* to 126*	Lancashire v Somerset at Manchester (2nd day).

Carrying Bat Through Completed Innings

G. W. White	78*	Hampshire (126) v Somerset at Southampton.
G. W. White	80*	Hampshire (136) v Kent at Portsmouth.
E. J. Wilson	104*	Worcestershire (182) v Middlesex at Worcester.

First to 1,000 Runs

M. G. Bevan (Sussex) on July 31.

No batsman scored 2,000 runs. The highest aggregate was 1,477 by D. S. Lehmann (Yorkshire).

Highest Partnerships

First Wicket

406*† D. J. Bicknell/G. E. Welton, Nottinghamshire v Warwickshire at Birmingham.
374† M. T. G. Elliott/S. P. James, Glamorgan v Sussex at Colwyn Bay.
359 M. A. Butcher/I. J. Ward, Surrey v Durham at The Oval.
293* S. D. Stubbings/S. P. Titchard, Derbyshire v Kent at Canterbury.

Second Wicket

306 M. J. Powell/D. P. Ostler, Warwickshire v Northamptonshire at Northampton.
292 R. R. Montgomerie/M. G. Bevan, Sussex v Nottinghamshire at Hove (1st innings).
265 R. R. Montgomerie/M. G. Bevan, Sussex v Nottinghamshire at Hove (2nd innings).

Third Wicket

276 S. L. Campbell/B. C. Lara, West Indians v Zimbabweans at Arundel.
248 A. P. Grayson/S. G. Law, Essex v Nottinghamshire at Nottingham.

Fourth Wicket

305 P. D. Bowler/M. Burns, Somerset v Oxford Universities at Taunton.

Fifth Wicket

275 A. Habib/J. M. Dakin, Leicestershire v Somerset at Leicester.

Sixth Wicket

232 C. J. Adams/U. B. A. Rashid, Sussex v Glamorgan at Colwyn Bay.

Seventh Wicket

289† D. R. Brown/A. F. Giles, Warwickshire v Sussex at Hove.
258† M. P. Dowman/D. G. Cork, Derbyshire v Durham at Derby.

Tenth Wicket

152† U. Afzaal/A. J. Harris, Nottinghamshire v Worcestershire at Nottingham.
141 A. D. Brown/Saqlain Mushtaq, Surrey v Leicestershire at Oakham School.
134 A. F. Gofton/Salman Khan, Oxford Universities v Northamptonshire at Oxford.
125 P. A. Nixon/D. D. Masters, Kent v Hampshire at Canterbury.
116 M. P. Bicknell/Saqlain Mushtaq, Surrey v Lancashire at Manchester.
103 Kabir Ali/G. D. McGrath, Worcestershire v Nottinghamshire at Worcester.

† *County record. Afzaal and Harris equalled Nottinghamshire's existing tenth-wicket record.*

Eight or More Wickets in an Innings (8)

9-47	M. P. Bicknell	Surrey v Leicestershire at Guildford.
9-93	A. D. Mullally	Hampshire v Derbyshire at Derby.
8-41	G. D. McGrath	Worcestershire v Northamptonshire at Worcester.
8-52	K. J. Dean	Derbyshire v Kent at Canterbury.
8-60	I. D. K. Salisbury	Surrey v Somerset at The Oval.
8-86	G. D. McGrath	Worcestershire v Nottinghamshire at Nottingham.
8-90	A. F. Giles	Warwickshire v Northamptonshire at Northampton.
8-95	J. Lewis	Gloucestershire v Zimbabweans at Gloucester.

Twelve or More Wickets in a Match (7)

16-119	M. P. Bicknell	Surrey v Leicestershire at Guildford.
14-188	A. D. Mullally	Hampshire v Derbyshire at Derby.
12-91	I. D. K. Salisbury	Surrey v Somerset at The Oval.
12-116	G. D. McGrath	Worcestershire v Northamptonshire at Worcester.
12-126	A. R. Caddick	Somerset v Hampshire at Southampton.
12-135	A. F. Giles	Warwickshire v Northamptonshire at Northampton.
12-218	P. M. Such	Essex v Middlesex at Chelmsford.

Hat-Tricks (4)

G. P. Butcher. . . . . .   Surrey v Derbyshire at The Oval.
  Butcher took four wickets in four balls.
K. J. Dean . . . .   Derbyshire v Leicestershire at Leicester.
J. I. D. Kerr . . . .   Somerset v West Indians at Taunton.
J. Lewis . . . .   Gloucestershire v Nottinghamshire at Nottingham.

Four Wickets in Five Balls

J. D. Middlebrook. . . .   Yorkshire v Hampshire at Southampton.

Wicket with First Ball in First-Class Cricket

C. T. Tremlett . . . . . .   Hampshire v New Zealand A at Portsmouth.
J. P. Tucker . . . .   Somerset v West Indians at Taunton (*first legitimate ball, after a wide*).

Outstanding Innings Analysis

9.3–5–11–7   Saqlain Mushtaq   Surrey v Derbyshire at The Oval.

100 Wickets

No bowler took 100 wickets. The highest aggregate was 80 by G. D. McGrath (Worcestershire).

Six Wicket-Keeping Dismissals in an Innings

6 ct. . . . . . .   S. J. Rhodes   Worcestershire v Nottinghamshire at Nottingham.

Eight or More Wicket-Keeping Dismissals in a Match

8 ct, 1 st . . .   A. N. Aymes   Hampshire v Leicestershire at Southampton.
9 ct. . . . . . .   S. J. Rhodes   Worcestershire v Gloucestershire at Worcester.
8 ct. . . . . . .   N. D. Burns   Leicestershire v Somerset at Leicester.
8 ct. . . . . . .   S. J. Rhodes   Worcestershire v Nottinghamshire at Nottingham.

Five Catches in an Innings in the Field

K. P. Dutch . . . .   Middlesex v Cambridge University at Cambridge.

Six Catches in a Match in the Field

D. Byas. . . . .   Yorkshire v Derbyshire at Leeds.
I. N. Flanagan . . . .   Essex v Middlesex at Chelmsford.
D. P. Fulton . . . .   Kent v Hampshire at Canterbury.

No Byes Conceded in a Total of 500 or More

J. S. Foster . . . .   Essex v Glamorgan (507-9 dec.) at Southend.
W. K. Hegg . . . .   Lancashire v Somerset (565) at Taunton.

Highest Innings Total

718-3 dec.† . . . . . .   Glamorgan v Sussex at Colwyn Bay.

   † *County record.*

Lowest Innings Totals

54 . . . .   West Indies v England (Second Test) at Lord's.
61 . . . .   West Indies v England (Fourth Test) at Leeds.
65 . . . .   Sussex v Northamptonshire at Eastbourne.
68 . . . .   Zimbabweans v Yorkshire at Leeds.
71 . . . .   Sussex v Gloucestershire at Hove.
74† . . . .   Oxford Universities v Somerset at Taunton.

   † *One batsman short.*

Largest Margins of Victory

524 runs . . .   Zimbabweans (568 and 258-2 dec.) beat Gloucestershire (167 and 135) at
                 Gloucester.
404 runs . . .   Somerset (362-4 dec. and 260-2 dec.) beat Oxford Universities (144 and 74) at
                 Taunton.

Match Aggregate of 1,450 Runs

1,473 for 31 . . . . . .   Sussex v Nottinghamshire at Hove.

Most Extras in an Innings

	b	l-b	w	n-b	
76	27	15	34	0	Warwickshire (568-9 dec.) v Northamptonshire at Northampton.
76	5	11	8	52	Essex (462) v Worcestershire at Kidderminster.
68	15	16	12	25	Yorkshire (399) v Hampshire at Leeds.
64	1	15	2	46	Somerset (411-7 dec.) v Leicestershire at Taunton.
63	19	16	18	10	Nottinghamshire (368) v Warwickshire at Nottingham.
61	1	26	4	30	Middlesex (412) v Nottinghamshire at Nottingham.

There were 16 further instances of 50 extras in an innings.

Career Aggregate Milestones

20,000 runs . . . .   M. A. Atherton.
10,000 runs . . . .   J. C. Adams, R. Dravid.
500 wickets . . . .   S. J. E. Brown, G. D. McGrath, P. R. Reiffel.

FIRST-CLASS AVERAGES, 2000

BATTING

(Qualification: 8 completed innings)

Signifies not out.   † *Denotes a left-handed batsman.*

		M	I	NO	R	HS	100s	50s	Avge	Ct/St
1	†M. G. Bevan (*Sussex*)	12	18	3	1,124	174	5	1	74.93	2
2	†M. H. Richardson (*New Zealand A*)	6	11	2	642	212*	1	4	71.33	1
3	†D. S. Lehmann (*Yorks*)	16	23	1	1,477	136	4	9	67.13	8
4	M. W. Goodwin (*Zimbabweans*)	8	12	2	651	194	3	1	65.10	3
5	P. D. Bowler (*Somerset*)	18	26	5	1,305	157*	5	4	62.14	8
6	†J. L. Langer (*Middx*)	16	27	3	1,472	213*	5	7	61.33	25
7	†M. L. Hayden (*Northants*)	15	22	0	1,270	164	4	6	57.72	21
8	R. Dravid (*Kent*)	16	25	3	1,221	182	2	8	55.50	15
9	S. G. Law (*Essex*)	16	27	2	1,385	189	5	6	55.40	19
10	R. C. Irani (*Essex*)	17	29	7	1,196	168*	1	9	54.36	2
11	A. D. Brown (*Surrey*)	16	23	5	935	295*	2	4	51.94	16
12	†M. T. G. Elliott (*Glam*)	13	21	0	1,076	177	4	4	51.23	19
13	D. P. Ostler (*Warwicks*)	16	24	2	1,096	145	2	7	49.81	19
14	M. R. Ramprakash (*Middx*)	17	28	4	1,183	120*	4	7	49.29	15
15	R. J. Bailey (*Derbys*)	13	19	4	728	118	2	5	48.53	4
16	A. Habib (*Leics*)	17	23	1	1,038	172*	2	8	47.18	8
17	†N. H. Fairbrother (*Lancs*)	15	23	5	823	138	2	3	45.72	16
18	K. J. Barnett (*Glos*)	11	16	2	640	118*	2	3	45.71	8
19	M. A. Wagh (*Warwicks*)	9	16	3	592	137	2	3	45.53	4
20	J. P. Crawley (*Lancs*)	15	22	1	951	156	5	0	45.28	6
21	P. A. J. DeFreitas (*Leics*)	14	18	3	677	123*	1	4	45.13	1
22	†U. Afzaal (*Notts*)	16	26	3	1,018	151*	3	4	44.26	9
23	V. S. Solanki (*Worcs*)	16	28	2	1,138	161*	2	8	43.76	23
24	M. J. Powell (*Warwicks*)	17	26	2	1,046	145	2	8	43.58	10
25	†S. M. Katich (*Durham*)	16	28	3	1,089	137*	3	5	43.56	21
26	†M. E. Trescothick (*Somerset*)	12	19	2	738	105	1	5	43.41	11
27	M. P. Vaughan (*Yorks*)	13	21	1	866	155*	2	4	43.30	2
28	†M. A. Butcher (*Surrey*)	16	25	4	891	191	2	3	42.42	13
29	D. G. Cork (*Derbys*)	14	17	4	542	200*	1	2	41.69	10
30	†J. M. Dakin (*Leics*)	9	12	1	458	135	1	3	41.63	2
31	†A. Penberthy (*Northants*)	15	21	2	785	116	1	5	41.31	10
32	W. S. Kendall (*Hants*)	18	31	3	1,156	161	3	6	41.28	17
33	S. P. James (*Glam*)	17	28	2	1,070	309*	3	2	41.15	5
34	M. Burns (*Somerset*)	15	20	1	775	160	2	5	40.78	3
35	T. L. Penney (*Warwicks*)	13	18	4	569	100*	1	2	40.64	8
36	†I. J. Ward (*Surrey*)	16	25	3	894	158*	3	3	40.63	4
37	A. F. Giles (*Warwicks*)	13	14	3	444	128*	1	1	40.36	4
38	C. J. Adams (*Sussex*)	16	26	3	913	156	1	7	39.69	15
39	†N. V. Knight (*Warwicks*)	10	15	0	593	233	1	1	39.53	7
40	J. Cox (*Somerset*)	17	26	1	983	171	3	3	39.32	6
41	G. D. Rose (*Somerset*)	15	18	5	510	124	2	1	39.23	4
42	D. A. Leatherdale (*Worcs*)	17	30	5	975	132*	2	7	39.00	9
43	D. R. Brown (*Warwicks*)	16	22	6	622	203	1	2	38.87	11
44	M. A. Atherton (*Lancs*)	18	29	1	1,068	136	3	6	38.14	15
45	†D. L. Hemp (*Warwicks*)	17	24	2	834	129	1	5	37.90	9
46	K. A. Parsons (*Somerset*)	15	22	2	745	193*	2	1	37.25	17
47	M. G. N. Windows (*Glos*)	19	31	3	1,042	166	2	6	37.21	5
48	†W. W. Hinds (*West Indians*)	11	19	1	669	150	3	3	37.16	11
49	†A. D. R. Campbell (*Zimbabweans*)	8	10	2	292	150*	1	1	36.50	11

		M	I	NO	R	HS	100s	50s	Avge	Ct/St
50	N. Shahid (*Surrey*)	9	12	0	434	80	0	3	36.16	13
51	D. J. Sales (*Northants*)	13	20	0	713	276	1	5	35.65	9
52	A. D. Shaw (*Glam*)	12	18	5	462	88*	0	3	35.53	29/4
53	W. K. Hegg (*Lancs*)	17	23	5	639	128	1	4	35.50	39/6
54	J. N. Snape (*Glos*)	15	20	3	598	69	0	4	35.17	8
55	G. A. Hick (*Worcs*)	14	24	2	773	122	3	3	35.13	16
56	D. D. J. Robinson (*Essex*)	12	19	3	561	93*	0	4	35.06	5
57	A. Flintoff (*Lancs*)	13	19	1	631	119	1	4	35.05	12
58	A. Dale (*Glam*)	17	27	3	837	81	0	5	34.87	8
59	R. J. Warren (*Northants*)	9	13	1	417	151	1	2	34.75	3
60	J. E. R. Gallian (*Notts*)	16	26	3	796	150	3	0	34.60	23
61	†D. J. Bicknell (*Notts*)	16	28	3	858	180*	2	2	34.32	3
62	†R. W. J. Howitt (*CU*)	6	10	2	274	118*	1	1	34.25	0
63	M. P. Maynard (*Glam*)	15	22	1	716	119*	2	5	34.09	17/2
64	†A. Flower (*Zimbabweans*)	7	10	1	300	116*	1	0	33.33	16/1
65	†N. C. Johnson (*Zimbabweans*) . . .	7	8	0	266	83	0	3	33.25	6
66	†A. J. Strauss (*Middx*)	17	28	2	862	111*	1	3	33.15	6
67	†M. J. Di Venuto (*Derbys*)	16	25	3	725	92*	0	6	32.95	12
68	B. F. Smith (*Leics*)	17	23	2	686	111*	2	2	32.66	10
69	M. A. Roseberry (*Middx*)	11	20	3	549	139*	1	2	32.29	3
70	A. J. Stewart (*Surrey*)	10	15	1	451	124*	2	0	32.21	24/1
71	P. A. Cottey (*Sussex*)	16	23	0	740	154	2	2	32.17	8
72	†P. A. Nixon (*Kent*)	18	25	7	578	134*	1	3	32.11	46/2
73	R. R. Montgomerie (*Sussex*)	17	30	2	899	133	2	4	32.10	17
74	G. E. Welton (*Notts*)	13	23	2	674	200*	1	3	32.09	8
75	†M. P. Dowman (*Derbys*)	17	29	3	833	140	2	4	32.03	11
76	†S. C. Ganguly (*Lancs*)	14	21	0	671	99	0	6	31.95	10
77	†S. D. Stubbings (*Derbys*)	18	32	4	889	135*	1	4	31.75	4
78	D. Ripley (*Northants*)	13	18	3	475	56	0	3	31.66	38/4
79	S. L. Campbell (*West Indians*) . . .	12	20	0	629	146	1	4	31.45	13
80	†J. W. Cook (*Northants*)	11	17	1	502	137	2	1	31.37	4
81	M. P. Bicknell (*Surrey*)	15	18	2	500	79*	0	4	31.25	5
82	S. P. Titchard (*Derbys*)	11	19	2	530	141*	1	3	31.17	0
83	†S. B. Styris (*New Zealand A*)	5	9	1	247	72	0	1	30.87	4
84	†U. B. A. Rashid (*Sussex*)	15	22	3	585	110	1	4	30.78	6
85	G. J. Whittall (*Zimbabweans*)	7	11	1	304	89	0	2	30.40	2
86	I. J. Harvey (*Glos*)	10	14	1	395	79	0	4	30.38	10
87	†R. G. Smalley (*OU*)	6	10	1	272	83	0	1	30.22	6/4
88	R. R. Sarwan (*West Indians*)	9	16	2	423	59*	0	3	30.21	2
89	†C. H. Gayle (*West Indians*)	8	14	1	392	128	1	2	30.15	5
90	M. J. Powell (*Glam*)	18	28	0	843	128	2	4	30.10	11
91	J. E. Morris (*Notts*)	13	20	0	601	115	1	3	30.05	7
92	A. J. Hollioake (*Surrey*)	16	23	0	689	80	0	3	29.95	27
93	†J. J. Porter (*OU & British Us.*) . . .	6	10	0	297	93	0	4	29.70	0
94	†R. C. Russell (*Glos*)	16	23	3	593	110*	1	2	29.65	50/4
95	M. B. Loye (*Northants*)	12	18	1	504	93	0	3	29.64	1
96	M. V. Fleming (*Kent*)	14	18	2	471	47	0	0	29.43	4
97	N. J. Speak (*Durham*)	14	24	5	552	89*	0	4	29.05	3
98	G. D. Lloyd (*Lancs*)	16	22	1	608	126	1	2	28.95	20
99	V. J. Wells (*Leics*)	15	19	0	549	98	0	4	28.89	8
100	A. McGrath (*Yorks*)	10	14	1	375	133	1	1	28.84	8
101	†B. C. Lara (*West Indians*)	10	18	0	519	176	2	1	28.83	15
102	†G. M. Hamilton (*Yorks*)	13	16	2	402	125	1	2	28.71	7
103	T. R. Gripper (*Zimbabweans*)	6	11	2	258	66*	0	2	28.66	5
104	G. W. White (*Hants*)	18	32	4	797	96	0	5	28.46	14
105	†P. R. Pollard (*Worcs*)	14	24	1	652	123*	1	5	28.34	3
106	A. J. Tudor (*Surrey*)	14	16	6	283	64*	0	2	28.30	5
107	C. M. Tolley (*Notts*)	6	9	1	223	60	0	2	27.87	2

		M	I	NO	R	HS	100s	50s	Avge	Ct/St
108	A. P. Grayson (*Essex*)	17	31	2	807	144	1	5	27.82	10
109	†I. D. Blackwell (*Somerset*)	18	23	2	582	109	1	2	27.71	6
110	P. J. Prichard (*Essex*)	17	31	3	775	96	0	5	27.67	10
111	M. H. W. Papps (*New Zealand A*) .	5	10	2	220	63	0	1	27.50	2/1
112	S. D. Peters (*Essex*)	16	28	6	602	77*	0	4	27.36	12
113	†M. V. Nagamootoo (*West Indians*) .	9	16	2	381	100	1	0	27.21	2
114	L. D. Sutton (*Derbys*)	10	16	1	407	79	0	2	27.13	20/1
115	S. J. Rhodes (*Worcs*)	18	28	6	591	103	1	1	26.86	54/1
116	E. J. Wilson (*Worcs*)	17	31	2	779	104*	2	4	26.86	9
117	A. S. Rollins (*Northants*)	16	24	0	636	100	1	4	26.50	19
118	†C. P. Schofield (*Lancs*)	17	22	2	528	70*	0	4	26.40	6
119	D. A. Kenway (*Hants*)	15	27	1	685	136	1	3	26.34	13/1
120	†P. J. Franks (*Notts*)	13	18	1	447	60	0	3	26.29	5
121	D. L. Maddy (*Leics*)	17	25	1	630	102	1	4	26.25	16
122	†N. D. Burns (*Leics*)	16	21	4	445	67*	0	3	26.17	36/1
123	C. G. Taylor (*Glos*)	12	22	3	492	104	1	0	25.89	6
124	†S. D. Thomas (*Glam*)	17	20	7	336	52	0	1	25.84	2
125	N. M. K. Smith (*Warwicks*)	17	20	2	464	87	0	4	25.77	8
126	†M. J. Walker (*Kent*)	15	25	4	536	61	0	1	25.52	12
127	P. D. Collingwood (*Durham*)	16	27	0	681	111	1	4	25.22	19
128	†V. J. Craven (*Yorks*)	8	11	1	251	58	0	2	25.10	6
129	G. P. Swann (*Northants*)	16	24	0	597	72	0	3	24.87	8
130	†D. Byas (*Yorks*)	17	26	2	596	84	0	2	24.83	22
131	J. J. B. Lewis (*Durham*)	16	28	2	645	115	1	4	24.80	8
132	J. I. Englefield (*New Zealand A*) . .	6	11	1	248	90	0	1	24.80	3
133	O. A. Shah (*Middx*)	12	20	0	489	76	0	3	24.45	7
134	†A. F. G. Griffith (*West Indians*) . . .	11	21	1	486	130	1	2	24.30	5
135	I. D. K. Salisbury (*Surrey*)	16	19	6	313	57*	0	2	24.07	6
136	C. M. W. Read (*Notts*)	16	23	3	479	56*	0	3	23.95	40
137	J. C. Scuderi (*Lancs*)	9	13	2	261	51	0	1	23.72	0
138	†G. P. Thorpe (*Surrey*)	11	16	0	376	115	1	1	23.50	9
139	†R. D. Jacobs (*West Indians*)	8	14	2	281	78	0	1	23.41	23/2
140	A. N. Aymes (*Hants*)	13	22	5	398	74*	0	3	23.41	32/6
141	†R. C. Driver (*Worcs*)	11	20	4	372	64	0	1	23.25	2
142	E. T. Smith (*Kent*)	11	18	0	415	175	1	0	23.05	7
143	R. S. C. Martin-Jenkins (*Sussex*) . .	15	23	1	499	86	0	2	22.68	4
144	†I. D. Fisher (*Yorks*)	6	10	2	181	68*	0	1	22.62	1
145	†G. P. Sulzberger (*New Zealand A*) .	6	11	0	248	60	0	1	22.54	8
146	M. A. Ealham (*Kent*)	11	14	1	293	83	0	2	22.53	3
147	D. R. Hewson (*Glos*)	11	21	1	448	67	0	3	22.40	5
148	I. P. Pyemont (*CU, British Us. & Derbys*)	11	15	1	313	124	1	0	22.35	5
149	D. P. Fulton (*Kent*)	14	24	1	512	115	1	1	22.26	29
150	M. J. Chilton (*Lancs*)	10	14	1	286	46	0	0	22.00	10
151	A. G. Wharf (*Glam*)	10	15	2	285	101*	2	0	21.92	5
152	R. D. B. Croft (*Glam*)	14	17	4	282	56	0	2	21.69	4
153	S. K. Warne (*Hants*)	15	22	2	431	69	0	3	21.55	14
154	G. M. Fellows (*Yorks*)	14	20	4	341	46	0	0	21.31	8
155	†A. Pratt (*Durham*)	7	10	1	191	38	0	0	21.22	7
156	R. W. T. Key (*Kent*)	17	29	1	584	83	0	5	20.85	4
157	M. P. Speight (*Durham*)	11	18	1	354	55	0	1	20.82	29
158	D. I. Stevens (*Leics*)	15	22	0	457	78	0	2	20.77	6
159	P. Johnson (*Notts*)	12	19	2	353	100	1	0	20.76	9
160	R. L. Johnson (*Middx*)	15	23	3	414	69	0	2	20.70	13
161	A. D. Mascarenhas (*Hants*)	16	24	1	473	100	1	2	20.56	3
162	R. A. Smith (*Hants*)	17	29	0	595	61	0	3	20.51	3
163	R. J. Turner (*Somerset*)	18	26	2	492	75	0	2	20.50	39
164	J. S. Laney (*Hants*)	14	25	1	489	81	0	2	20.37	12
165	†P. N. Weekes (*Middx*)	8	13	1	244	39	0	0	20.33	8
165	M. C. J. Ball (*Glos*)	9	14	2	244	53	0	1	20.33	13

		M	I	NO	R	HS	100s	50s	Avge	Ct/St
167	D. C. Nash (*Middx*)	17	24	2	445	75*	0	1	20.22	32/4
168	†I. J. Sutcliffe (*Leics*)	12	17	1	319	53	0	2	19.93	11
169	†P. C. L. Holloway (*Somerset*)	13	20	1	377	113	1	1	19.84	9
170	M. N. Lathwell (*Somerset*)	9	14	1	257	54*	0	1	19.76	4
171	J. N. Batty (*Surrey*)	13	16	2	276	100*	1	0	19.71	29/7
172	†M. T. E. Peirce (*Sussex*)	14	24	1	446	86	0	1	19.39	3
173	T. H. C. Hancock (*Glos*)	15	22	1	407	85	0	1	19.38	7
174	†W. Phillip (*West Indians*)	6	11	3	155	67*	0	1	19.37	22/1
175	S. D. Udal (*Hants*)	12	21	3	346	85	0	1	19.22	8
176	M. E. Cassar (*Derbys*)	14	20	2	341	77*	0	1	18.94	1
177	R. M. S. Weston (*Middx*)	6	10	1	170	39	0	0	18.88	3
178	S. J. Lacey (*Derbys*)	11	17	4	242	55*	0	1	18.61	1
179	†J. C. Adams (*West Indians*)	10	17	0	313	98	0	2	18.41	6
180	M. J. Wood (*Yorks*)	11	17	3	256	100*	1	0	18.28	5
181	Saqlain Mushtaq (*Surrey*)	12	14	2	217	66	0	2	18.08	8
182	D. R. Law (*Essex*)	15	23	3	360	68*	0	2	18.00	6
183	M. M. Patel (*Kent*)	14	16	1	269	60	0	1	17.93	13
184	M. P. Smethurst (*Lancs*)	16	19	10	161	66	0	1	17.88	3
185	K. Newell (*Glam*)	13	21	1	356	64	0	1	17.80	5
186	Kabir Ali (*Worcs*)	10	15	3	213	50*	0	1	17.75	5
187	A. P. Cowan (*Essex*)	14	20	6	245	67	0	1	17.50	4
188	A. P. Wells (*Kent*)	12	19	2	297	60*	0	2	17.47	5
189	S. R. Lampitt (*Worcs*)	18	27	8	331	56*	0	1	17.42	12
190	M. J. McCague (*Kent*)	7	11	0	191	72	0	1	17.36	2
191	K. J. Piper (*Warwicks*)	16	18	3	260	69	0	1	17.33	28/3
192	C. E. W. Silverwood (*Yorks*)	9	11	1	173	48	0	0	17.30	1
193	M. W. Alleyne (*Glos*)	16	24	0	410	126	1	0	17.08	14
194	K. M. Krikken (*Derbys*)	10	13	0	221	51	0	1	17.00	18/2
195	P. J. Martin (*Lancs*)	9	11	3	134	40	0	0	16.75	2
196	N. J. Wilton (*Sussex*)	8	11	2	150	46	0	0	16.66	19
197	N. Peng (*Durham*)	8	14	0	231	98	0	1	16.50	1
198	G. W. Flower (*Zimbabweans*)	7	13	2	180	76*	0	1	16.36	10
199	R. J. Cunliffe (*Glos*)	9	14	0	229	74	0	1	16.35	10
200	F. A. Rose (*West Indians*)	8	11	1	162	48	0	0	16.20	0
201	W. L. Law (*Glam*)	8	11	1	161	85	0	1	16.10	4
202	†W. P. C. Weston (*Worcs*)	10	19	2	269	58*	0	2	15.82	1
203	†M. J. Cawdron (*Glos*)	6	8	0	125	32	0	0	15.62	1
204	R. J. Blakey (*Yorks*)	12	18	1	264	56	0	1	15.52	41/2
205	S. Widdup (*Yorks*)	9	14	1	201	44	0	0	15.46	6
206	R. K. Illingworth (*Worcs*)	10	12	2	154	44*	0	0	15.40	5
207	A. J. Harris (*Notts*)	11	14	4	153	39	0	0	15.30	4
208	J. A. H. Marshall (*New Zealand A*)	5	9	0	133	69	0	1	14.77	11
209	M. A. Gough (*Durham*)	7	12	0	176	33	0	0	14.66	3
210	†C. E. L. Ambrose (*West Indians*) .	6	10	2	117	36*	0	0	14.62	1
211	J. A. Daley (*Durham*)	10	17	0	247	50	0	1	14.52	4
212	S. J. Cook (*Middx*)	7	10	0	145	43	0	0	14.50	2
213	†B. L. Hutton (*Middx*)	10	15	2	188	55	0	1	14.46	8
214	A. R. C. Fraser (*Middx*)	15	22	6	227	30	0	0	14.18	4
215	†A. C. Morris (*Hants*)	8	12	1	154	60	0	1	14.00	4
216	†T. M. Smith (*Derbys*)	10	13	2	152	53*	0	1	13.81	4
217	M. M. Betts (*Durham*)	11	18	4	192	55	0	1	13.71	4
218	J. D. Middlebrook (*Yorks*)	11	15	0	201	45	0	0	13.40	5
219	†M. C. Ilott (*Essex*)	10	13	4	119	25	0	0	13.22	4
220	D. M. Cousins (*Northants*)	16	23	7	210	29*	0	0	13.12	3
221	D. Gough (*Yorks*)	10	13	3	131	23*	0	0	13.10	3
222	T. A. Munton (*Derbys*)	16	22	7	191	52	0	1	12.73	7
223	C. White (*Yorks*)	7	9	1	100	27	0	0	12.50	1
224	†W. J. House (*Sussex*)	6	10	1	112	35	0	0	12.44	3
225	T. R. Ward (*Leics*)	7	10	1	110	39	0	0	12.22	8
226	G. Chapple (*Lancs*)	16	19	1	218	41	0	0	12.11	4

		M	I	NO	R	HS	100s	50s	Avge	Ct/St
227	J. Wood (*Durham*)	10	15	0	181	44	0	0	12.06	2
228	†G. Keedy (*Lancs*)	13	15	3	144	34	0	0	12.00	2
229	J. Ormond (*Leics*)	12	15	7	95	30*	0	0	11.87	1
230	T. J. Mason (*Essex*)	10	14	2	140	52*	0	1	11.66	4
231	P. Aldred (*Derbys*)	11	14	1	149	38	0	0	11.46	4
232	A. Kumble (*Leics*)	12	16	0	181	56	0	1	11.31	3
233	†I. N. Flanagan (*Essex*)	4	8	0	89	23	0	0	11.12	7
234	N. Hussain (*Essex*)	10	16	1	166	33	0	0	11.06	7
235	B. C. Hollioake (*Surrey*)	10	14	1	142	29	0	0	10.92	8
236	S. J. W. Lewis (*CU*)	6	10	1	98	26	0	0	10.88	2
237	A. R. Caddick (*Somerset*)	10	15	2	141	21*	0	0	10.84	3
238	B. J. Hyam (*Essex*)	15	24	0	256	53	0	1	10.66	49/6
238	†J. P. Taylor (*Northants*)	7	10	1	96	27	0	0	10.66	3
240	N. Killeen (*Durham*)	10	15	1	144	38*	0	0	10.28	1
241	P. S. Jones (*Somerset*)	15	16	4	122	56*	0	1	10.16	4
242	M. K. Davies (*Northants*)	5	8	0	79	25	0	0	9.87	2
243	G. D. McGrath (*Worcs*)	14	15	3	112	55	0	0	9.33	3
244	S. J. E. Brown (*Durham*)	14	21	12	82	19	0	0	9.11	2
245	S. J. Harmison (*Durham*)	11	15	3	104	33*	0	0	8.66	2
246	A. Sheriyar (*Worcs*)	11	11	3	69	17	0	0	8.62	0
247	N. C. Phillips (*Durham*)	5	9	0	76	29	0	0	8.44	3
248	P. C. R. Tufnell (*Middx*)	16	21	9	100	19	0	0	8.33	4
249	†N. A. M. McLean (*West Indians*) .	9	17	2	122	29	0	0	8.13	0
250	R. J. Kirtley (*Sussex*)	16	22	4	146	26*	0	0	8.11	5
251	J. Lewis (*Glos*)	17	23	2	169	38	0	0	8.04	4
252	D. A. Cosker (*Glam*)	12	15	4	88	14*	0	0	8.00	9
253	M. J. Rawnsley (*Worcs*)	9	13	0	102	18	0	0	7.84	5
254	†J. D. Lewry (*Sussex*)	17	24	5	149	39	0	0	7.84	5
255	R. D. King (*West Indians*)	9	12	4	62	21	0	0	7.75	0
256	M. J. Saggers (*Kent*)	14	17	5	91	24	0	0	7.58	3
257	M. J. Hoggard (*Yorks*)	16	18	4	103	20*	0	0	7.35	3
258	J. P. Stephenson (*Hants*)	10	15	0	96	19	0	0	6.40	7
259	A. D. Mullally (*Hants*)	8	12	2	60	12	0	0	6.00	0
260	P. M. Such (*Essex*)	12	13	4	53	14	0	0	5.88	3
261	D. D. Masters (*Kent*)	16	20	7	71	21	0	0	5.46	4
262	A. D. Patterson (*Sussex*)	7	9	0	37	8	0	0	4.11	15
263	†K. J. Dean (*Derbys*)	12	15	3	49	22	0	0	4.08	0
264	J. F. Brown (*Northants*)	10	14	5	30	11	0	0	3.33	3
265	E. S. H. Giddins (*Warwicks*)	12	11	3	25	14	0	0	3.12	1
266	D. E. Malcolm (*Northants*)	7	10	1	24	8	0	0	2.66	0

BOWLING

(Qualification: 10 wickets in 10 innings)

		Style	O	M	R	W	BB	5W/i	Avge
1	C. A. Walsh (*West Indians*)	RFM	242.2	106	457	40	6-74	3	11.42
2	R. J. Sidebottom (*Yorks*)	LFM	134.2	46	300	24	6-16	4	12.50
3	G. D. McGrath (*Worcs*)	RFM	415.4	132	1,057	80	8-41	6	13.21
4	M. Mbangwa (*Zimbabweans*)	RFM	211.5	86	428	30	6-14	2	14.26
5	Saqlain Mushtaq (*Surrey*)	OB/LB	451.2	127	1,016	66	7-11	6	15.39
6	A. R. Caddick (*Somerset*)	RFM	329.4	88	848	55	7-64	5	15.41
7	P. J. Martin (*Lancs*)	RFM	236.2	83	464	30	7-67	3	15.46
8	G. P. Sulzberger (*New Zealand A*) .	OB	189.3	61	458	28	5-55	1	16.35
9	I. J. Harvey (*Glos*)	RM	254.2	79	658	40	6-19	3	16.45
10	A. D. Mullally (*Hants*)	LFM	343.5	105	832	49	9-93	5	16.97

		Style	O	M	R	W	BB	5W/i	Avge
11	C. White (*Yorks*)	RF	157.3	32	430	25	5-32	2	17.20
12	M. P. Bicknell (*Surrey*)	RFM	413.2	115	1,052	60	9-47	3	17.53
13	K. J. Dean (*Derbys*)	LFM	246	57	785	44	8-52	4	17.84
14	M. M. Betts (*Durham*)	RFM	354	91	832	44	7-30	1	18.90
15	I. D. K. Salisbury (*Surrey*)	LBG	380.3	101	984	52	8-60	3	18.92
16	D. Gough (*Yorks*)	RF	324.1	62	949	50	6-63	2	18.98
17	A. Flintoff (*Lancs*)	RFM	135.2	49	290	15	4-18	0	19.33
18	D. M. Cousins (*Northants*)	RFM	510.4	142	1,318	67	5-123	1	19.67
19	M. J. Saggers (*Kent*)	RFM	425.2	99	1,148	57	7-79	2	20.14
20	J. F. Brown (*Northants*)	OB	517.5	142	1,258	61	7-78	4	20.62
21	M. P. Smethurst (*Lancs*)	RFM	378.1	90	1,161	56	7-37	3	20.73
22	A. M. Smith (*Glos*)	LFM	250.4	70	623	30	5-52	1	20.76
23	J. Lewis (*Glos*)	RFM	562.3	169	1,506	72	8-95	4	20.91
24	S. R. Lampitt (*Worcs*)	RM	412.5	108	1,173	56	7-45	2	20.94
25	D. G. Cork (*Derbys*)	RFM	356.4	94	886	42	6-41	1	21.09
26	M. J. Cawdron (*Glos*)	RM	199.5	64	534	25	6-25	2	21.36
27	K. P. Dutch (*Middx*)	OB	143.4	45	366	17	6-62	1	21.52
28	S. J. E. Brown (*Durham*)	LFM	442.2	110	1,208	56	7-51	4	21.57
29	G. M. Hamilton (*Yorks*)	RFM	313.4	80	866	40	5-22	1	21.65
30	S. L. Watkin (*Glam*)	RFM	389.4	108	1,067	48	6-26	2	22.22
31	A. L. Penberthy (*Northants*)	RM	131	30	358	16	5-54	1	22.37
32	C. E. L. Ambrose (*West Indians*)	RFM	207.1	65	403	18	4-30	0	22.38
33	J. P. Taylor (*Northants*)	LFM	212.3	50	540	24	6-27	1	22.50
34	A. J. Tudor (*Surrey*)	RF	304.3	71	1,071	47	7-48	3	22.78
35	N. A. M. McLean (*West Indians*)	RFM	271.3	68	803	35	5-30	2	22.94
36	{ P. C. R. Tufnell (*Middx*)	SLA	738.3	255	1,500	65	6-48	3	23.07
	{ A. F. Giles (*Warwicks*)	SLA	526.4	163	1,200	52	8-90	5	23.07
38	S. K. Warne (*Hants*)	LBG	639.4	183	1,620	70	6-34	5	23.14
39	A. R. C. Fraser (*Middx*)	RFM	474.3	150	1,111	48	6-64	1	23.14
40	M. E. Cassar (*Derbys*)	RM	212.2	54	702	30	6-76	1	23.40
41	J. C. Scuderi (*Lancs*)	RM	120	28	333	14	4-58	0	23.78
42	J. N. Snape (*Glos*)	OB	113.3	44	239	10	3-70	0	23.90
43	G. Chapple (*Lancs*)	RFM	431.5	101	1,175	49	6-42	1	23.97
44	R. C. Irani (*Essex*)	RFM	407.3	120	1,008	42	5-79	1	24.00
45	D. D. Masters (*Kent*)	RFM	435.2	104	1,161	48	6-27	3	24.18
46	C. D. Collymore (*West Indians*)	RFM	126.4	40	369	15	3-18	0	24.60
47	R. D. King (*West Indians*)	RFM	195.1	45	618	25	3-28	0	24.72
48	R. J. Kirtley (*Sussex*)	RFM	521.4	138	1,559	63	6-41	4	24.74
49	J. D. Middlebrook (*Yorks*)	OB	281.1	68	771	31	6-82	1	24.87
50	A. P. Cowan (*Essex*)	RFM	398.5	98	1,175	47	5-54	2	25.00
51	B. C. Strang (*Zimbabweans*)	LFM	187.3	59	452	18	5-68	1	25.11
52	M. M. Patel (*Kent*)	SLA	570.3	202	1,157	46	6-77	2	25.15
53	A. Kumble (*Leics*)	LBG	498.3	139	1,133	45	6-44	2	25.17
54	B. W. Gannon (*Glos*)	RFM	201.5	38	732	29	5-58	1	25.24
55	J. Ormond (*Leics*)	RFM	380.3	75	1,116	44	6-50	3	25.36
56	A. G. Wharf (*Glam*)	RM	256.3	51	940	37	5-68	1	25.40
57	P. M. Hutchison (*Yorks*)	LFM	129.3	32	420	16	3-62	0	26.25
58	M. J. Hoggard (*Yorks*)	RFM	501.4	134	1,323	50	5-50	2	26.46
59	A. A. Donald (*Warwicks*)	RF	205.3	60	530	20	4-59	0	26.50
60	D. A. Leatherdale (*Worcs*)	RM	154	34	508	19	3-17	0	26.73
61	M. V. Fleming (*Kent*)	RM	278.1	72	753	28	4-77	0	26.89
62	S. B. Styris (*New Zealand A*)	RFM	115.4	27	325	12	3-45	0	27.08
63	G. Keedy (*Lancs*)	SLA	478	142	1,005	37	6-56	1	27.16
64	S. D. Udal (*Hants*)	OB	350.3	104	818	30	5-58	1	27.26
65	M. W. Alleyne (*Glos*)	RM	254.5	72	684	25	6-49	1	27.36
66	M. Burns (*Somerset*)	RM	132.2	33	387	14	3-11	0	27.64
67	J. Wood (*Durham*)	RFM	319.4	66	918	33	5-36	3	27.81
68	M. C. Ilott (*Essex*)	LFM	283.2	85	724	26	3-37	0	27.84
69	P. R. Reiffel (*Notts*)	RFM	233.3	60	586	21	5-62	1	27.90
70	E. S. H. Giddins (*Warwicks*)	RFM	285.5	92	813	29	5-15	1	28.03

	Style	O	M	R	W	BB	5W/i	Avge
71 A. Dale (*Glam*).............	RM	240.4	54	645	23	5-25	2	28.04
72 V. J. Wells (*Leics*)...........	RM	222.3	48	648	23	4-54	0	28.17
73 C. P. Schofield (*Lancs*).......	LBG	374	80	1,102	39	5-48	1	28.25
74 A. D. Mascarenhas (*Hants*)......	RM	313.5	88	796	28	4-52	0	28.42
75 D. E. Malcolm (*Northants*).....	RFM	184.1	46	541	19	5-45	1	28.47
76 R. L. Johnson (*Middx*)........	RFM	473	129	1,429	50	6-71	2	28.58
77 R. D. Stemp (*Notts*)..........	SLA	398.2	140	946	33	5-123	1	28.66
78 S. D. Thomas (*Glam*)..........	RFM	488	93	1,612	56	5-43	2	28.78
79 M. A. Ealham (*Kent*)..........	RM	271.5	67	703	24	5-35	1	29.29
80 P. M. Such (*Essex*)...........	OB	422.4	101	1,055	36	7-167	3	29.30
81 C. E. W. Silverwood (*Yorks*).....	RF	292.3	80	762	26	4-60	0	29.30
82 D. J. Millns (*Notts*)..........	RFM	226.1	42	880	30	5-58	1	29.33
83 M. J. McCague (*Kent*).........	RFM	129.4	20	412	14	5-52	1	29.42
84 J. D. Lewry (*Sussex*)..........	LFM	524.4	137	1,569	53	6-66	3	29.60
85 P. J. Franks (*Notts*)..........	RFM	393.4	81	1,247	42	7-56	2	29.69
86 C. D. Crowe (*Leics*)..........	OB	185.3	50	453	15	4-55	0	30.20
87 R. S. G. Anderson (*Essex*)......	RFM	234.4	56	729	24	6-34	3	30.37
88 S. J. Cook (*Middx*)..........	RFM	137	41	335	11	4-13	0	30.45
89 A. J. Harris (*Notts*)..........	RFM	384.3	62	1,358	44	6-110	4	30.86
90 F. A. Rose (*West Indians*)......	RFM	153	32	527	17	4-63	0	31.00
91 A. C. Morris (*Hants*)..........	RM	183.1	43	562	18	3-48	0	31.22
92 T. A. Munton (*Derbys*)........	RFM	439.3	122	1,093	35	7-34	2	31.22
93 N. M. K. Smith (*Warwicks*).....	OB	310.4	70	875	28	5-66	1	31.25
94 G. D. Rose (*Somerset*)........	RFM	332.3	79	908	29	5-74	1	31.31
95 S. J. Harmison (*Durham*)......	RF	304.1	69	822	26	4-74	0	31.61
96 N. Killeen (*Durham*)..........	RFM	288.3	84	697	22	3-14	0	31.68
97 P. S. Jones (*Somerset*)........	RFM	403.4	88	1,294	40	5-41	1	32.35
98 D. A. Cosker (*Glam*)..........	SLA	429.5	141	944	29	4-82	0	32.55
99 D. S. Lucas (*Notts*)..........	LFM	271.5	57	888	27	4-61	0	32.88
100 G. P. Swann (*Northants*)......	OB	467.3	122	1,366	41	6-118	2	33.31
101 P. A. J. DeFreitas (*Leics*).....	RM/OB	459.2	122	1,105	33	4-41	0	33.48
102 P. D. Trego (*Somerset*).......	RFM	165.1	34	603	18	4-84	0	33.50
103 M. A. Robinson (*Sussex*)......	RM	228	77	537	16	3-88	0	33.56
104 D. R. Law (*Essex*)..........	RFM	291.4	50	1,042	30	5-78	1	34.73
105 J. O. Grove (*Somerset*).......	RFM	192.5	27	733	21	5-90	1	34.90
106 R. D. B. Croft (*Glam*)........	OB	586.1	153	1,432	40	5-26	2	35.80
107 T. F. Bloomfield (*Middx*).....	RFM	222.3	35	834	23	4-46	0	36.26
108 R. S. C. Martin-Jenkins (*Sussex*)..	RFM	360.1	75	1,202	33	5-94	1	36.42
109 P. Aldred (*Derbys*)..........	RM	203.3	44	624	17	4-97	0	36.70
110 I. D. Fisher (*Yorks*).........	SLA	211.1	48	588	16	3-40	0	36.75
111 B. C. Hollioake (*Surrey*)......	RFM	117.5	25	407	11	4-41	0	37.00
112 R. K. Illingworth (*Worcs*).....	SLA	221.5	72	483	13	3-34	0	37.15
113 A. Sheriyar (*Worcs*).........	LFM	278.2	59	1,048	28	4-51	0	37.42
114 M. V. Nagamootoo (*West Indians*)..	LBG	328.4	93	801	21	4-12	0	38.14
115 D. R. Brown (*Warwicks*)......	RFM	268.2	49	917	24	5-87	1	38.20
116 A. Richardson (*Warwicks*).....	RFM	368.2	96	1,040	27	4-69	0	38.51
117 S. J. Lacey (*Derbys*)........	OB	241.5	68	626	16	4-84	0	39.12
118 P. D. Collingwood (*Durham*)....	RM	214.2	61	474	12	2-21	0	39.50
119 S. R. G. Francis (*Hants*)......	RFM	170.2	37	602	15	4-95	0	40.13
120 K. A. Parsons (*Somerset*)......	RM	150.4	41	443	11	5-13	1	40.27
121 Kabir Ali (*Worcs*)..........	RFM	219	41	811	20	4-114	0	40.55
122 U. B. A. Rashid (*Sussex*)......	SLA	343.5	84	994	23	5-103	1	43.21
123 J. P. Stephenson (*Hants*)......	RM	172.1	33	566	13	4-68	0	43.53
124 M. C. J. Ball (*Glos*)........	OB	243.1	58	658	15	3-31	0	43.86
125 I. D. Blackwell (*Somerset*).....	SLA	411.3	123	1,010	23	4-18	0	43.91
126 A. P. Grayson (*Essex*).......	SLA	178	39	443	10	3-55	0	44.30
127 J. M. Dakin (*Leics*).........	RM	211.4	39	641	14	2-20	0	45.78
128 P. J. Hartley (*Hants*)........	RM	204.2	33	697	15	3-91	0	46.46
129 T. J. Mason (*Essex*)........	OB	239.3	55	710	14	3-38	0	50.71

The following bowlers took ten wickets but bowled in fewer than ten innings:

	Style	O	M	R	W	BB	5W/i	Avge
O. T. Parkin (*Glam*)	RFM	108	30	291	17	4-14	0	17.11
G. J. Whittall (*Zimbabweans*)	RM	106	31	290	16	3-14	0	18.12
H. H. Streak (*Zimbabweans*)	RFM	156.1	50	346	18	6-87	2	19.22
L. J. Hamilton (*New Zealand A*)	LFM	94	22	287	14	5-55	1	20.50
M. R. Strong (*Northants*)	RFM	84.2	15	269	12	4-46	0	22.41
D. R. Tuffey (*New Zealand A*)	RFM	116	23	373	16	5-74	1	23.31
C. R. Pimlott (*CU & British Us.*)	RFM	93	31	303	12	3-42	0	25.25
S. P. Jones (*Glam*)	RF	104	12	374	10	4-47	0	37.40
B. P. Martin (*New Zealand A*)	SLA	133	35	378	10	3-43	0	37.80
N. C. Johnson (*Zimbabweans*)	RFM	158.5	44	500	13	4-28	0	38.46
L. J. Wharton (*Derbys*)	SLA	164	42	464	12	5-96	1	38.66
T. C. Hicks (*OU*)	OB	147	29	570	14	5-54	1	40.71
R. J. Logan (*Northants*)	RFM	133.1	33	453	11	5-61	1	41.18

BOWLING STYLES

LB	Leg-breaks (1)	**RF**	Right-arm fast (7)
LBG	Leg-breaks and googlies (5)	**RFM**	Right-arm fast-medium (63)
LFM	Left-arm fast-medium (13)	**RM**	Right-arm medium (25)
OB	Off-breaks (17)	**SLA**	Slow left-arm (13)

Note: The total comes to 144, because Saqlain Mushtaq and P. A. J. DeFreitas have two styles of bowling.

COUNTY CAPS AWARDED IN 2000

Derbyshire	R. J. Bailey, M. J. Di Venuto, M. P. Dowman, T. A. Munton.
Durham	S. M. Katich.
Glamorgan	D. A. Cosker, M. T. G. Elliott, M. J. Powell, A. G. Wharf.
Hampshire	A. D. Mullally, S. K. Warne.
Kent	R. Dravid, P. A. Nixon, M. J. Walker.
Lancashire	G. Keedy.
Leicestershire	J. M. Dakin, A. Kumble.
Middlesex	D. C. Nash, O. A. Shah.
Northamptonshire	J. F. Brown, D. M. Cousins.
Nottinghamshire	U. Afzaal, D. J. Bicknell, A. J. Harris, D. J. Millns, J. E. Morris, P. R. Reiffel, R. D. Stemp.
Surrey	I. J. Ward.
Sussex	R. S. C. Martin-Jenkins.
Warwickshire	M. A. Wagh.
Worcestershire	G. D. McGrath.
Yorkshire	M. J. Hoggard, R. J. Sidebottom.

No caps were awarded by Essex, Gloucestershire or Somerset.

INDIVIDUAL SCORES OF 100 AND OVER

There were 196 three-figure innings in 182 first-class matches in 2000, 25 fewer than in 1999 when 187 matches were played. Of these, nine were double-hundreds, compared with 13 in 1999. The list includes 154 hundreds hit in the County Championship, compared with 176 in 1999.

Signifies not out.

M. G. Bevan (5)
107   Sussex v Glam, Hove
151*   Sussex v Essex, Arundel
166 }
174 } Sussex v Notts, Hove
173*   Sussex v Middx, Southgate

P. D. Bowler (5)
157*   Somerset v Oxford Us., Taunton
108   Somerset v Kent, Maidstone
107   Somerset v Durham, Chester-le-Street
139*   Somerset v Yorks, Taunton
117*   Somerset v Derbys, Derby

J. P. Crawley (5)
126   Lancs v Cambridge U., Cambridge
156   Lancs v New Zealand A, Liverpool
120   Lancs v Somerset, Taunton
117   Lancs v Durham, Manchester
139   Lancs v Leics, Leicester

J. L. Langer (5)
120   Middx v Northants, Lord's
104   Middx v Notts, Lord's
108   Middx v Notts, Nottingham
109   Middx v Warwicks, Birmingham
213*   Middx v Glam, Cardiff

S. G. Law (5)
120   Essex v Notts, Chelmsford
165   Essex v Notts, Nottingham
133*   Essex v Worcs, Chelmsford
189   Essex v Worcs, Kidderminster
119*   Essex v Northants, Northampton

M. T. G. Elliott (4)
117   Glam v Warwicks, Birmingham
127   Glam v Middx, Southgate
117   Glam v Northants, Cardiff
177   Glam v Sussex, Colwyn Bay

M. L. Hayden (4)
101   Northants v Notts, Northampton
122   Northants v Warwicks, Birmingham
147   Northants v Worcs, Northampton
164   Northants v Essex, Northampton

D. S. Lehmann (4)
133   Yorks v Derbys, Derby
136   Yorks v Durham, Leeds
115   Yorks v Leics, Leicester
116   Yorks v Kent, Canterbury

M. R. Ramprakash (4)
101   Middx v Worcs, Southgate
110* }
112 } Middx v Sussex, Southgate
120*   Middx v Warwicks, Birmingham

U. Afzaal (3)
151*   Notts v Worcs, Nottingham
127   Notts v Middx, Lord's
103   Notts v Glam, Cardiff

M. A. Atherton (3)
136   England v Zimbabwe, Nottingham
113   Lancs v Somerset, Taunton
108   England v West Indies, The Oval

J. Cox (3)
100   Somerset v Oxford Us., Taunton
153   Somerset v Hants, Southampton
171   Somerset v Lancs, Taunton

J. E. R. Gallian (3)
120   Notts v Sussex, Hove
110*   Notts v Sussex, Nottingham
150   Notts v Glam, Nottingham

M. W. Goodwin (3)
148*   Zimbabwe v England, Nottingham
126   Zimbabweans v West Indians, Arundel
194   Zimbabweans v Glos, Gloucester

G. A. Hick (3)
115*   Worcs v Middx, Worcester
101   England v Zimbabwe, Lord's
122   Worcs v Notts, Nottingham

W. W. Hinds (3)
105*   West Indians v Glam, Cardiff
150   West Indians v Leics, Leicester
104   West Indians v Derbys, Derby

S. P. James (3)
166   Glam v Warwicks, Birmingham
109   Glam v Glos, Cardiff
309*   Glam v Sussex, Colwyn Bay

S. M. Katich (3)
137*   Durham v Leics, Chester-le-Street
114   Durham v Derbys, Darlington
129   Durham v Lancs, Manchester

W. S. Kendall (3)
161   Hants v Somerset, Taunton
119* Hants v Durham, Chester-le-Street
143   Hants v Derbys, Southampton

I. J. Ward (3)
158* Surrey v Kent, Canterbury
107   Surrey v Leics, Guildford
144   Surrey v Durham, The Oval

R. J. Bailey (2)
118   Derbys v Leics, Derby
112* Derbys v West Indians, Derby

K. J. Barnett (2)
118* Glos v Oxford Us., Bristol
106   Glos v Warwicks, Birmingham

D. J. Bicknell (2)
180* Notts v Warwicks, Birmingham
144   Notts v Sussex, Nottingham

A. D. Brown (2)
295* Surrey v Leics, Oakham School
140* Surrey v Yorks, The Oval

M. Burns (2)
160   Somerset v Oxford Us., Taunton
108   Somerset v Lancs, Taunton

M. A. Butcher (2)
116* Surrey v Hants, Southampton
191   Surrey v Durham, The Oval

S. Chanderpaul (2)
161* West Indians v Worcs, Worcester
103* West Indians v Zimbabweans, Arundel

J. W. Cook (2)
137   Northants v Glos, Cheltenham
116   Northants v Sussex, Eastbourne

P. A. Cottey (2)
154   Sussex v Essex, Chelmsford
112   Sussex v Northants, Northampton

M. P. Dowman (2)
110   Derbys v Hants, Derby
140   Derbys v Durham, Derby

R. Dravid (2)
182   Kent v Zimbabweans, Canterbury
137   Kent v Hants, Portsmouth

N. H. Fairbrother (2)
138   Lancs v Leics, Manchester
100* Lancs v Leics, Leicester

A. Habib (2)
172* Leics v Somerset, Leicester
164   Leics v Derbys, Leicester

B. C. Lara (2)
176   West Indians v Zimbabweans, Arundel
112   West Indies v England, Manchester

D. A. Leatherdale (2)
117   Worcs v Notts, Nottingham
132* Worcs v Northants, Northampton

M. P. Maynard (2)
119* Glam v Glos, Cardiff
102   Glam v Essex, Southend

R. R. Montgomerie (2)
133   Sussex v Notts, Hove
129   Sussex v Notts, Nottingham

D. P. Ostler (2)
144   Warwicks v Essex, Birmingham
145   Warwicks v Northants, Northampton

K. A. Parsons (2)
108* Somerset v Yorks, Taunton
193* Somerset v West Indians, Taunton

M. J. Powell (2)
145   Warwicks v Northants, Northampton
106   Warwicks v Essex, Chelmsford

M. J. Powell (2)
128   Glam v Essex, Southend
114   Glam v Middx, Cardiff

G. D. Rose (2)
124   Somerset v Yorks, Taunton
102   Somerset v Durham, Taunton

B. F. Smith (2)
111* Leics v Durham, Leicester
102   Leics v Surrey, Guildford

V. S. Solanki (2)
161* Worcs v Glos, Bristol
160   Worcs v Warwicks, Worcester

A. J. Stewart (2)
124* England v Zimbabwe, Lord's
105   England v West Indies, Manchester

M. P. Vaughan (2)
155* Yorks v Derbys, Leeds
118   Yorks v Durham, Leeds

M. A. Wagh (2)
130   Warwicks v Worcs, Birmingham
137   Warwicks v Essex, Chelmsford

A. G. Wharf (2)
100* Glam v Oxford Us., Oxford
101* Glam v Northants, Northampton

E. J. Wilson (2)
104*   Worcs v Middx, Worcester
102   Worcs v Notts, Worcester

M. G. N. Windows (2)
166   Glos v Oxford Us., Bristol
107   Glos v Essex, Bristol

The following each played one three-figure innings:

C. J. Adams, 156, Sussex v Glam, Colwyn Bay; M. W. Alleyne, 126, Glos v Notts, Nottingham.
J. N. Batty, 100*, Surrey v Somerset, The Oval; I. D. Blackwell, 109, Somerset v Leics, Taunton; D. R. Brown, 203, Warwicks v Sussex, Hove.
A. D. R. Campbell, 150*, Zimbabweans v Hants, Southampton; S. L. Campbell, 146, West Indians v Zimbabweans, Arundel; P. D. Collingwood, 111, Durham v Derbys, Darlington; D. G. Cork, 200*, Derbys v Durham, Derby.
J. M. Dakin, 135, Leics v Somerset, Leicester; A. R. Danson, 117*, Cambridge U. v Derbys, Cambridge; P. A. J. DeFreitas, 123*, Leics v Lancs, Leicester; A. R. Dunlop, 150, Ireland v Scotland, Ayr.
A. Flintoff, 119, Lancs v Leics, Manchester; A. Flower, 116*, Zimbabweans v Glos, Gloucester; D. P. Fulton, 115, Kent v Somerset, Maidstone.
C. H. Gayle, 128, West Indians v Derbys, Derby; A. F. Giles, 128*, Warwicks v Sussex, Hove; A. P. Grayson, 124, Essex v Notts, Nottingham; A. F. G. Griffith, 130, West Indians v New Zealand A, Chelmsford.
G. M. Hamilton, 125, Yorks v Hants, Leeds; W. K. Hegg, 128, Lancs v Somerset, Manchester; D. L. Hemp, 129, Warwicks v Middx, Lord's; P. C. L. Holloway, 113, Somerset v Hants, Taunton; R. W. J. Howitt, 118*, Cambridge U. v Middx, Cambridge; Q. J. Hughes, 119, Cambridge U. v Oxford U., Lord's.
R. C. Irani, 168*, Essex v Glam, Cardiff.
P. Johnson, 100, Notts v Essex, Chelmsford.
D. A. Kenway, 136, Hants v Derbys, Derby; N. V. Knight, 233, Warwicks v Glam, Birmingham.
J. J. B. Lewis, 115, Durham v Somerset, Chester-le-Street; G. D. Lloyd, 126, Lancs v Somerset, Manchester.
A. McGrath, 133, Yorks v Kent, Canterbury; D. L. Maddy, 102, Leics v Somerset, Taunton; A. D. Mascarenhas, 100, Hants v Derbys, Derby; J. E. Morris, 115, Notts v Sussex, Hove.
M. V. Nagamootoo, 100, West Indians v Somerset, Taunton; P. A. Nixon, 134*, Kent v Hants, Canterbury.
A. L. Penberthy, 116, Northants v Glos, Northampton; T. L. Penney, 100*, Warwicks v Oxford Us., Oxford; P. R. Pollard, 123*, Worcs v Essex, Kidderminster; L. R. Prittipaul, 152, Hants v Derbys, Southampton; J. P. Pyemont, 124, Cambridge U. v Oxford U., Lord's.
U. B. A. Rashid, 110, Sussex v Glam, Colwyn Bay; S. J. Rhodes, 103, Worcs v Notts, Worcester; M. H. Richardson, 212*, New Zealand A v Sussex, Hove; A. S. Rollins, 100, Northants v Middx, Lord's; M. A. Roseberry, 139*, Middx v Cambridge U., Cambridge; R. C. Russell, 110*, Glos v Northants, Cheltenham.
D. J. Sales, 276, Northants v Notts, Northampton; E. T. Smith, 175, Kent v Durham, Chester-le-Street; A. J. Strauss, 111*, Middx v Northants, Lord's; S. D. Stubbings, 135*, Derbys v Kent, Canterbury; A. J. Swann, 108, Northants v Oxford Us., Oxford.
C. G. Taylor, 104, Glos v Middx, Lord's; G. P. Thorpe, 115, Surrey v Somerset, The Oval; S. P. Titchard, 141*, Derbys v Kent, Canterbury; M. E. Trescothick, 105, Somerset v Leics, Leicester.
R. J. Warren, 151, Northants v Sussex, Northampton; G. E. Welton, 200*, Notts v Warwicks, Birmingham; C. B. Wishart, 116, Zimbabweans v British Universities, Cambridge; M. J. Wood, 100*, Yorks v Derbys, Leeds.

TEN WICKETS IN A MATCH

There were 27 instances of bowlers taking ten or more wickets in a match in first-class cricket in 2000, two more than in 1999. The list includes 24 in the County Championship. There was one instance of two bowlers achieving the feat in the same match: A. F. Giles took 11 wickets for Warwickshire and J. F. Brown 11 for Northamptonshire at Birmingham.

G. D. McGrath (3)
10-143, Worcs v Notts, Nottingham; 10-69, Worcs v Glos, Worcester; 12-116, Worcs v Northants, Worcester.

J. F. Brown (2)
11-178, Northants v Warwicks, Birmingham; 11-131, Northants v Sussex, Northampton.

A. R. Caddick (2)
12-126, Somerset v Hants, Southampton; 10-97, Somerset v Kent, Bath.

A. F. Giles (2)
12-135, Warwicks v Northants, Northampton; 11-196, Warwicks v Northants, Birmingham.

I. D. K. Salisbury (2)
12-91, Surrey v Somerset, The Oval; 11-154, Surrey v Durham, The Oval.

Saqlain Mushtaq (2)
10-135, Surrey v Hants, Southampton; 11-104, Surrey v Yorks, The Oval.

The following each took ten wickets in a match on one occasion:

R. S. G. Anderson, 11-111, Essex v Northants, Ilford.
M. M. Betts, 10-88, Durham v Derbys, Darlington; M. P. Bicknell, 16-119, Surrey v Leics, Guildford.
M. J. Cawdron, 10-74, First-Class Counties Select XI v New Zealand A, Milton Keynes.
I. J. Harvey, 10-32, Glos v Sussex, Hove.
G. Keedy, 10-155, Lancs v Durham, Manchester; A. Kumble, 10-105, Leics v Kent, Canterbury.
M. Mbangwa, 10-53, Zimbabweans v Yorks, Leeds; J. D. Middlebrook, 10-170, Yorks v Hants, Southampton; A. D. Mullally, 14-188, Hants v Derbys, Derby.
R. J. Sidebottom, 11-43, Yorks v Kent, Leeds; P. M. Such, 12-218, Essex v Middx, Chelmsford.
J. P. Taylor, 10-69, Northants v Sussex, Eastbourne.
C. A. Walsh, 10-117, West Indies v England, Lord's.

PROFESSIONAL CRICKETERS' ASSOCIATION AWARDS

At the Professional Cricketers' Association annual dinner in September 2000, Marcus Trescothick was named Player of the Year for 2000; he was also voted SFL Net Player of the Year by amateur clubs throughout England. Matthew Hoggard of Yorkshire was the Young Player of the Year. Jimmy Adams received the MCC Spirit of Cricket award. Alec Stewart won the Slazenger Sheer Instinct Award, for his performances in the NatWest Series and the Tests against West Indies, and was also Channel 4 Personality of the Year. The Walter Lawrence Trophy, sponsored by EDS, for the fastest first-class century in 2000 was won by Darren Lehmann of Yorkshire, who reached 100 in 89 balls against Kent at Canterbury. Darren Gough received the Freeserve Award for the fastest delivery of the season – 93.1mph at Lord's on May 20 – and was also voted Sports.com Cricketer of the Year via the Internet. The Vodafone Lady Cricketer of the Year Award was won by Lucy Pearson. Ravi Rampaul of West Indies Under-15 was Costcutter Under-15 Player of the Year. Ray Julian received the Andersen Umpire of the Year award for the third year running. The Jardine Lloyd Thompson Special Merit Award went to the Primary Club. Mike Newnham, general manager of Cornhill Insurance, received a special ECB award to commemorate their 23 years of sponsoring Test cricket.

THE ZIMBABWEANS IN ENGLAND, 2000

Review by STEPHEN BRENKLEY

All the elements were in place for Zimbabwe's first full tour of England to end in tears and acrimony. Civil disorder at home was at its zenith, and several players' immediate families, living on isolated farms, were in danger. The long-standing pay dispute between the team and the Zimbabwe Cricket Union festered. When they were humiliated by England in the First Test, it seemed likely that disarray and defeat would accompany the rest of the visit. In the event, Zimbabwe doggedly regrouped and demonstrated again that they are usually greater than the sum of their parts. If the tour did not culminate in resounding triumph, it was testimony to the Zimbabweans' spirit that they gave England a fright in the Second Test of the two-match series and then reached the final of the triangular one-day tournament, having embarrassed both the hosts and West Indies along the way.

Zimbabwe had been waiting a long time for this trip. Eight years had passed since their elevation to Test status, opposed at the time by England, who had subsequently been reluctant to invite them to tour. Thus, Zimbabwe arrived bearing well-concealed grievances, and with points to make. Perhaps it was this, allied to other distractions, which led to their crash at Lord's in mid-May, the earliest Test played in an English summer. Almost to a man, they froze, and the outcome was in little doubt from the first morning when they lost the toss and found themselves at eight for three in the first half-hour of the match. So much for the theory that overseas visitors save their best for Lord's.

Somehow, they put it behind them. The news from Zimbabwe was invariably grim. Farms were being occupied daily as the government insisted that land must be redistributed. The players declared that it was their duty to give those at home something to cheer, although they may have excluded their administrators from such thoughts. They had been frustrated and embittered at the ZCU's refusal to offer more money. The captain, Andy Flower, was one of the more vociferous proponents of a better deal for his team and was unafraid to voice an opinion. The players did not seek riches, but could not understand why they should be worse off than before they turned professional. Flower's articulate stance was eventually to cost him his job. While giving the captaincy his all, he might not have been too unhappy to shed the responsibility. His other roles as front-line batsman and wicket-keeper already presented him with a full plate. During the Lord's Test his wicket-keeping was constantly poor, presumably because he had too much else to think about.

Flower usually led the side positively, and if Zimbabwe's lack of flair precluded risks, his declaration at Trent Bridge in the Second Test confirmed a sense of adventure. There was a brief period, alarming to English eyes, when they might have sneaked victory. They came to command respect and Murray Goodwin's century revealed him as a batsman of high class.

Goodwin and Neil Johnson, two of the few players in the squad who rose above the rank of journeyman, added to Zimbabwe's travails by announcing

THE ZIMBABWEAN TOURING PARTY

[*Graham Morris*]

Standing: J. R. Thomson (*bowling coach*), A. Machikicho (*physiotherapist*), D. P. Viljoen, G. J. Whittall, S. V. Carlisle, G. B. Brent, T. R. Gripper, M. Mbangwa, M. L. Nkala, B. A. Murphy, H. K. Olonga, T. Taibu, J. Bryceland (*fitness trainer*), M. Snook (*scorer*). *Seated:* A. J. Pycroft (*coach*), N. C. Johnson, G. W. Flower, M. W. Goodwin, A. Flower (*captain*), H. H. Streak (*vice-captain*), A. D. R. Campbell, B. C. Strang, D. D. Stannard (*manager*).

their retirement from Test cricket. Both were born in Zimbabwe and had moved elsewhere with their families before returning to establish international careers. Goodwin went back to Australia, Johnson set up home again in South Africa. However, suggestions that Goodwin might have been persuaded to stay, had the right offer been forthcoming, again reflected badly on the ZCU. Life without both would inevitably expose shortcomings in the upper order. Neither Flower, a proven international batsman, nor his brother, Grant, made the runs that might have been expected of them, and Alistair Campbell's Test form seemed to be in a permanent rut. For the peripheral players, coping with English pitches early in the season was always likely to be a struggle.

Heath Streak, the vice-captain who was to succeed Andy Flower as skipper, was easily the best bowler. He struggled with fitness, but managed both Tests. His movement and deceptive pace lent them a cutting edge, and without his six wickets in England's only innings at Lord's their plight might have been even sorrier. Streak was not, however, the leading first-class wicket-taker on the tour. That honour (and fourth place in the first-class bowling averages) belonged to Pommie Mbangwa, said to lack pace and penetration but whose ability to swing the ball brought him ten wickets against Yorkshire, and 30 in all. Generally, though, Streak needed more support. The prolonged absence of Henry Olonga, whose troublesome ankle eventually ended his tour, deprived the squad not only of extra speed, but of charisma. Olonga is one of those players who has a tendency to make things happen.

If the majority of the squad were workmanlike players and recognised it, there were signs that the further development of cricket amongst the black population would pay future dividends. Tatenda Taibu, a wicket-keeper/batsman aged 16 at the beginning of the tour, was selected solely to gain experience. Yet Andy Flower's poor form at Lord's prompted serious consideration of Taibu keeping wicket in the Second Test. If it was wise to keep him waiting, he demonstrated enough with the gloves and his elegant batting to suggest that more will be heard of him. Another teenager to suggest Zimbabwean cricket might have a bright future was Mluleki Nkala. The transition to Test level appeared not to faze him at all, and his controlled in-swing bowling accounted for Nasser Hussain twice in the Nottingham Test.

It was surprising to reflect that Zimbabwe used 19 players in all, because they invariably conveyed the impression of being constant with selection. There were undoubtedly less pressure for places, which was simultaneously a drawback and a benefit; while it might encourage complacency, it also made for a greater sense of community in the dressing-room. Flower and his team made much of being friends as well as team-mates. When they were down, they closed ranks.

Their spirited performance at Trent Bridge set them up for the triangular tournament. Campbell, whose attacking style was better suited to the one-day game, rediscovered his form, and Zimbabwe inflicted an embarrassing defeat on England at The Oval. Three wins against West Indies, whom they had never beaten before, ensured qualification for the final, where they were victims of England's renewed efficiency.

It was not lost on Zimbabwe that one of the chief plotters of their downfall was their countryman, Duncan Fletcher, who had once been their captain

[*Patrick Eagar*

Heath Streak ended Mike Atherton's hopes of his first first-class hundred at Lord's when he had
him lbw for 55. Few of the Zimbabweans did themselves justice in that match, their first Test in
England. Streak, whose six for 87 included England's top four, was a magnificent exception.
He went on to share the series' bowling honours with Darren Gough.

but was now England's coach. Perhaps it was inevitable that Graeme Hick,
also born and bred in Salisbury but long since qualified for England, should
score his first Test century at Lord's against them.

England were unquestionably slicker than they had been for years. Hussain
embodied Fletcher's inclusive management style on the field, and for the first
time the notion of "Team England" seemed more than simply jargon. Despite
the distraction of sorry form with the bat, Hussain's captaincy was generally
praised. Less of a success was the choice of Mike Atherton's umpteenth
opening partner. The new pair managed a convincing century partnership at
Trent Bridge – and Atherton enjoyed himself at Lord's, too – but Mark
Ramprakash never seemed comfortable in the role. Critics claimed they were
too similar and, after failures in the first two Tests against West Indies,
Ramprakash returned to the wilderness. In his place, England wanted
someone more aggressively minded, and a left-hander for preference. Nick
Knight might have liked the sound of that job description, but, as others had
discovered, getting noticed from No. 6 was not easy. He had mixed fortunes,
squandering his opportunity as a stand-in opener at Trent Bridge. Alec Stewart
and Hick helped themselves to hundreds against an out-of-sorts attack in the
First Test, but reflected the prevailing mood and struggled in the next.

Andrew Flintoff's batting continued to exasperate; his bowling was little used, though the speed gun showed he could generate remarkable pace from his powerful frame. Ed Giddins had a dream game at Lord's, but did nothing else to indicate he could be relied on to provide regular support for the established new-ball bowlers. These two, Darren Gough and Andrew Caddick, gave an awesome display of exploiting a greenish spring wicket in the First Test, and typified the most noticeable improvement in England's game: a new-found determination to press home the advantage. The undoubted disappointment was Chris Schofield. Denied a bowl at Lord's, he was ineffectual when given his chance at Trent Bridge. Conditions were not in his favour, but nor was his inability to control line or length. He was one of five players, so rampant in May, no longer in the team by August.

ZIMBABWEAN TOURING PARTY

A. Flower (Mashonaland) (*captain*), H. H. Streak (Matabeleland) (*vice-captain*), G. B. Brent (Manicaland), A. D. R. Campbell (Mashonaland), S. V. Carlisle (Mashonaland), G. W. Flower (Mashonaland), M. W. Goodwin (Mashonaland), T. R. Gripper (Mashonaland), N. C. Johnson (Matabeleland), M. Mbangwa (Matabeleland), M. L. Nkala (Matabeleland), H. K. Olonga (Matabeleland), B. C. Strang (Mashonaland), T. Taibu (Mashonaland), D. P. Viljoen (Mashonaland), G. J. Whittall (Manicaland).

B. A. Murphy (Mashonaland) reinforced the party before the Tests, after which Olonga flew home injured, accompanied by Taibu, who was returning to school. C. B. Wishart (Mashonaland) and P. A. Strang (Mashonaland) joined the party after the Tests.

Manager: D. D. Stannard.　　　*Coach:* A. J. Pycroft.
Bowling coaches: J. R. Thomson and C. G. Rackemann.　　　*Physiotherapist:* A. Machikicho.

ZIMBABWEAN TOUR RESULTS

Test matches – Played 2: Lost 1, Drawn 1.
First-class matches – Played 9: Won 2, Lost 2, Drawn 5.
Wins – Yorkshire, Gloucestershire.
Losses – England, Kent.
Draws – England, Hampshire, Essex, West Indians, British Universities.
One-day internationals – Played 7: Won 4, Lost 3. *Wins* – England, West Indies (3). *Losses* – England (3).
Other non-first-class matches – Played 11: Won 9, Lost 1, No result 1. *Wins* – Sussex, Essex, MCC, Ireland (2), England Board XI, Somerset, Durham, Nottinghamshire. *Loss* – Northamptonshire. *No result* – New Zealand A.

TEST MATCH AVERAGES

ENGLAND – BATTING

	T	I	NO	R	HS	100s	50s	Avge	Ct
M. A. Atherton	2	3	0	225	136	1	1	75.00	2
A. J. Stewart	2	3	1	148	124*	1	0	74.00	4
G. A. Hick	2	3	0	136	101	1	0	45.33	3
M. R. Ramprakash	2	3	0	75	56	0	1	25.00	2
C. P. Schofield	2	3	0	67	57	0	1	22.33	0
N. V. Knight	2	3	0	51	44	0	0	17.00	3
A. R. Caddick	2	3	0	38	13	0	0	12.66	0
A. Flintoff	2	3	0	33	16	0	0	11.00	0
N. Hussain	2	3	0	31	21	0	0	10.33	0
E. S. H. Giddins	2	3	2	10	7	0	0	10.00	0
D. Gough	2	3	0	17	9	0	0	5.66	1

* Signifies not out.

BOWLING

	O	M	R	W	BB	5W/i	Avge
E. S. H. Giddins.	30	10	88	8	5-15	1	11.00
A. R. Caddick	44.5	13	132	8	4-38	0	16.50
D. Gough	49.3	6	174	9	4-57	0	19.33

Also bowled: A. Flintoff 13–5–35–0; M. R. Ramprakash 1–0–1–0; C. P. Schofield 18–2–73–0.

ZIMBABWE – BATTING

	T	I	NO	R	HS	100s	50s	Avge	Ct
M. W. Goodwin	2	4	2	178	148*	1	0	89.00	0
G. J. Whittall	2	4	1	78	28	0	0	26.00	0
N. C. Johnson	2	3	0	74	51	0	1	24.66	2
A. Flower	2	3	0	68	42	0	0	22.66	6
B. A. Murphy	2	3	1	14	14	0	0	7.00	3
G. W. Flower	2	4	0	18	12	0	0	4.50	4

Played in two Tests: A. D. R. Campbell 0, 4 (3 ct); M. Mbangwa 1*, 8; H. H. Streak 4, 0 (2 ct). Played in one Test: T. R. Gripper 1, 5; B. C. Strang 0, 37* (1 ct); S. V. Carlisle and M. L. Nkala did not bat.

* *Signifies not out.*

BOWLING

	O	M	R	W	BB	5W/i	Avge
G. J. Whittall	34	10	88	8	3-14	0	11.00
H. H. Streak	84.5	27	182	9	6-87	1	20.22
M. L. Nkala	42	12	104	5	3-82	0	20.80
B. A. Murphy	49.2	13	112	3	1-19	0	37.33
N. C. Johnson	54	14	159	3	2-41	0	53.00

Also bowled: G. W. Flower 1–0–2–0; M. Mbangwa 54–19–134–2; B. C. Strang 27–4–86–0.

ZIMBABWEAN TOUR AVERAGES – FIRST-CLASS MATCHES

BATTING

	M	I	NO	R	HS	100s	50s	Avge	Ct/St
M. W. Goodwin	8	12	2	651	194	3	1	65.10	3
C. B. Wishart.	3	5	0	198	116	1	0	39.60	0
A. D. R. Campbell	8	10	2	292	150*	1	1	36.50	11
B. C. Strang	6	7	3	134	73	0	1	33.50	2
A. Flower	7	10	1	300	116*	1	0	33.33	16/1
N. C. Johnson	7	8	0	266	83	0	3	33.25	6
D. P. Viljoen	5	6	1	155	72*	0	1	31.00	3
G. J. Whittall	7	11	1	304	89	0	2	30.40	2
T. R. Gripper.	6	11	2	258	66*	0	2	28.66	5
H. H. Streak	5	5	1	109	71*	0	1	27.25	2
M. L. Nkala	4	6	1	92	40	0	0	18.40	1
G. W. Flower	7	13	2	180	76*	0	1	16.36	10
S. V. Carlisle	6	7	0	112	65	0	1	16.00	6
T. Taibu	3	5	1	53	36	0	0	13.25	7
M. Mbangwa	8	8	5	30	9*	0	0	10.00	0

Played in three matches: P. A. Strang 12, 36 (1 ct). Played in two matches: G. B. Brent 21*, 0 (1 ct); B. A. Murphy 0, 14, 0* (3 ct); H. K. Olonga 45 (1 ct).

* *Signifies not out.*

BOWLING

	O	M	R	W	BB	5W/i	Avge
M. Mbangwa	211.5	86	428	30	6-14	2	14.26
G. J. Whittall	106	31	290	16	3-14	0	18.12
H. H. Streak	156.1	50	346	18	6-87	2	19.22
B. C. Strang	187.3	59	452	18	5-68	1	25.11
M. L. Nkala	91	19	308	9	3-82	0	34.22
P. A. Strang	67	17	184	5	1-11	0	36.80
N. C. Johnson	158.5	44	500	13	4-28	0	38.46
D. P. Viljoen	66	17	228	5	2-33	0	45.60

Also bowled: G. B. Brent 36.3–14–97–2; A. D. R. Campbell 5–2–8–0; G. W. Flower 41–10–93–1; M. W. Goodwin 4–1–19–0; T. R. Gripper 7–1–36–0; B. A. Murphy 49.2–13–112–3; H. K. Olonga 47.3–9–164–2.

Note: Matches in this section which were not first-class are signified by a dagger.

HAMPSHIRE v ZIMBABWEANS

At Southampton, April 27, 28, 29, 30. Drawn. Toss: Zimbabweans. First-class debut: C. G. van der Gucht.

Five wet sessions and an easy-paced pitch prevented the Zimbabweans from opening their tour with a win. There were compensations: Mbangwa and Johnson bowled well as Hampshire's experienced batting subsided under overcast skies on the opening day, and 16-year-old wicket-keeper Taibu gave a tidy display in front of and behind the stumps. After a second-day washout, the Zimbabweans built a lead of 233, thanks largely to an unbeaten four-and-a-half-hour 150 from Campbell, who had ended the Caribbean tour in wretched form. Several others also gained useful batting practice against an attack missing five senior bowlers, including Warne and Mullally, and Hampshire's batsmen were less troubled second time round as they easily avoided defeat. After lunch on the last day, the scorers briefly found themselves shut out of the scorebox and had to resort to making notes.

Close of play: First day, Zimbabweans 19-1 (Gripper 5*, Goodwin 13*); Second day, No play; Third day, Zimbabweans 281-6 (Campbell 108*, Taibu 5*).

Hampshire

G. W. White c Taibu b Mbangwa	10	– b Mbangwa	28
J. S. Laney c Johnson b Mbangwa	4	– c Gripper b Whittall	44
W. S. Kendall c Carlisle b Johnson	27	– not out	56
*R. A. Smith b Strang	6	– c Campbell b Johnson	60
†D. A. Kenway b Whittall	48	– c Taibu b Whittall	2
J. P. Stephenson c Taibu b Johnson	0		
L. Savident c Taibu b Mbangwa	7	– (6) not out	10
A. C. Morris c Flower b Mbangwa	1		
S. J. Renshaw c Campbell b Johnson	12		
S. R. G. Francis c Flower b Johnson	1		
C. G. van der Gucht not out	0		
B 8, l-b 1, n-b 6	15	B 1, l-b 7, w 2, n-b 24 . . .	34

1/14 2/15 3/26 4/72 5/76   131   1/86 2/86 3/209 4/214   (4 wkts) 234
6/108 7/109 8/110 9/124

Bowling: *First Innings*—Olonga 13–3–31–0; Strang 9–2–19–1; Mbangwa 16–9–19–4; Johnson 8.5–3–28–4; Whittall 7–1–25–1. *Second Innings*—Olonga 12–0–60–0; Strang 14–3–29–0; Johnson 14–2–63–1; Whittall 16–7–31–2; Mbangwa 7–2–18–1; Flower 6–0–25–0.

Zimbabweans

G. W. Flower c Kenway b Francis	0	G. J. Whittall c Kenway b Renshaw	24
T. R. Gripper c Savident b van der Gucht	24	†T. Taibu lbw b Francis	36
M. W. Goodwin c Morris		B. C. Strang not out	5
b van der Gucht	70	L-b 8, w 10, n-b 36	54
*A. D. R. Campbell not out	150		
S. V. Carlisle c Renshaw		1/1 2/104 3/127 (7 wkts dec.)	364
b van der Gucht	1	4/139 5/139	
N. C. Johnson c Laney b Renshaw	0	6/255 7/349	

H. K. Olonga and M. Mbangwa did not bat.

Bowling: Morris 24–9–56–0; Francis 15–2–62–2; Renshaw 25–5–86–2; Stephenson 9–1–27–0; van der Gucht 22–7–75–3; Savident 8–0–39–0; White 3–0–11–0.

Umpires: M. J. Kitchen and P. Willey.

KENT v ZIMBABWEANS

At Canterbury, May 3, 4, 5. Kent won by an innings and 163 runs. Toss: Zimbabweans. First-class debut: D. D. Masters.

Kent picked up £11,000 for demolishing the Zimbabweans with a day to spare. The tourists arrived late on the opening day after a meeting to discuss the pay dispute with their board; rain delayed the start anyway, but the distraction probably contributed to their collapsing twice against an inexperienced attack. David Masters, a 22-year-old seamer, claimed five wickets in the second innings – not since Ted Witherden in 1951 had a Kent player done so on debut – and ended with nine in the match. Kent's other hero was Dravid, who hit 27 fours in a high-class 182, his maiden county century. He shared partnerships worth 104 with Wells and 208 with Hockley, who made 74 in his fourth first-class innings. Nixon joined in with his first fifty since leaving Leicestershire. Johnson, another former Leicestershire player, and Nkala gave Zimbabwe's second innings a modicum of substance but it was never enough to prevent an innings defeat. To make matters worse, Streak injured his troublesome left knee and was unable to play on the third day.

Close of play: First day, Kent 10-1 (Key 4*, Masters 0*); Second day, Kent 380-5 (Dravid 182*, Nixon 27*).

Zimbabweans

G. W. Flower c Dravid b Masters	10	– c Nixon b Masters	0
T. R. Gripper lbw b Masters	13	– c Nixon b Patel	13
M. W. Goodwin c Smith b Golding	21	– lbw b Masters	7
G. J. Whittall lbw b Masters	15	– c Patel b Masters	4
N. C. Johnson c Fleming b Masters	0	– c and b Masters	70
S. V. Carlisle c Fleming b Scott	14	– b Masters	1
D. P. Viljoen lbw b Patel	10	– c Dravid b Scott	16
*H. H. Streak c and b Patel	23	– absent hurt	
†T. Taibu not out	9	– (8) c Smith b Scott	3
M. L. Nkala c Scott b Patel	24	– (9) c Wells b Patel	40
M. Mbangwa b Patel	0	– (10) not out	3
B 12, l-b 8	20	B 2, l-b 4, n-b 2	8

1/15 2/32 3/56 4/60 5/67	159	1/4 2/18 3/24 4/32 5/34	165
6/86 7/115 8/129 9/159		6/64 7/88 8/139 9/165	

Bowling: *First Innings*—Golding 17–7–38–1; Masters 18–3–44–4; Patel 30.4–14–44–4; Fleming 11–4–10–0; Scott 2–1–3–1. *Second Innings*—Masters 17–8–37–5; Patel 25.4–10–82–2; Scott 9–1–40–2.

Kent

E. T. Smith lbw b Streak	4		*M. V. Fleming c Johnson b Nkala	38
R. W. T. Key lbw b Streak	4		J. M. Golding not out	18
D. D. Masters c Carlisle b Mbangwa	0			
R. Dravid c Carlisle b Whittall	182		B 16, l-b 13, w 8, n-b 18	55
A. P. Wells c Johnson b Viljoen	58			
J. B. Hockley c sub (G. B. Brent)			1/6 2/11 3/11	(8 wkts dec.) 487
b Whittall	74		4/115 5/323 6/384	
†P. A. Nixon b Flower	54		7/458 8/487	

M. M. Patel and D. A. Scott did not bat.

Bowling: Streak 22–7–49–2; Mbangwa 9–3–14–1; Johnson 23–4–95–0; Nkala 18–0–82–1; Whittall 26–3–99–2; Viljoen 9–0–48–1; Flower 29–7–62–1; Gripper 2–0–9–0.

Umpires: M. J. Harris and J. W. Lloyds.

†SUSSEX v ZIMBABWEANS

At Hastings, May 7. Zimbabweans won by eight wickets. Toss: Sussex. First-team debut: M. H. Yardy.

Sussex returned to Hastings for the first time since developers bulldozed Priory Meadow after the 1989 season. The new venue, Horntye Park, proved an instant hit with the batsmen, and between them the teams managed 531 runs for six wickets from 97 overs. Sussex recovered easily from the early loss of Adams: by the time the second wicket fell, Montgomerie and Cottey had added 176. Montgomerie finished on a one-day career-best 129 not out from 154 balls, only to be upstaged by Johnson, whose sparkling century eased Zimbabwe home with three overs to spare. There was more good news for the tourists: their pay dispute with the ZCU had been settled.

Sussex

R. R. Montgomerie not out	129		W. J. House not out	8
*C. J. Adams b Strang	1		B 1, l-b 5, w 6, n-b 8	20
P. A. Cottey lbw b Goodwin	85			
U. B. A. Rashid run out	11		1/19 2/195	(4 wkts, 50 overs) 264
J. R. Carpenter st A. Flower b Viljoen	10		3/233 4/253	

R. S. C. Martin-Jenkins, M. H. Yardy, J. D. Lewry, †S. Humphries and R. J. Kirtley did not bat.

Bowling: Olonga 8–1–52–0; Strang 10–1–30–1; Brent 10–0–52–0; Viljoen 8–0–37–1; Johnson 3–0–23–0; G. W. Flower 5–0–33–0; Whittall 2–0–13–0; Goodwin 4–0–18–1.

Zimbabweans

N. C. Johnson not out	107	
G. W. Flower run out	53	
M. W. Goodwin c Adams b Yardy	63	
A. D. R. Campbell not out	26	
B 1, l-b 5, w 8, n-b 4	18	

1/104 2/219   (2 wkts, 47 overs) 267

*†A. Flower, S. V. Carlisle, G. J. Whittall, D. P. Viljoen, H. K. Olonga, G. B. Brent and B. C. Strang did not bat.

Bowling: Lewry 8–1–37–0; Kirtley 8–0–37–0; Martin-Jenkins 8–0–47–0; Yardy 10–0–47–1; Rashid 5–0–39–0; House 3–0–25–0; Adams 5–0–29–0.

Umpires: N. L. Bainton and J. F. Steele.

†ESSEX v ZIMBABWEANS

At Chelmsford, May 9. Zimbabweans won by seven wickets. Toss: Essex.

Andy Flower said afterwards he would have preferred a three-day match to the two limited-overs games against Sussex and Essex. The Zimbabweans did at least win both handsomely, though whether they gained anything from this victory was debatable. On a straightforward pitch, Olonga and Strang had Essex 20 for four, then 48 for five, a feeble display of batting. Danny Law initiated a fightback, but the target was always within the tourists' range. The only surprise was that they lost as many as three wickets. Johnson and Goodwin continued their recent good form, but Grant Flower missed out again. His brother Andy, despite a blow to the thumb while keeping, struck the winning runs with 15 overs to spare.

Essex

P. J. Prichard c Campbell b Olonga	0	†B. J. Hyam not out	22
A. P. Grayson b Olonga.	5	A. P. Cowan c Carlisle b Strang	2
D. D. J. Robinson lbw b Strang.	0	R. S. G. Anderson c and b Viljoen	2
*S. G. Law c and b Strang	2	B 1, l-b 5, w 17, n-b 12	35
S. D. Peters run out	6		
D. R. Law st A. Flower b Viljoen	41	1/9 2/12 3/18 (47.2 overs) 172
G. R. Napier c Brent b Viljoen	35	4/20 5/48 6/99
T. J. Mason c G. W. Flower b Strang . . .	22	7/121 8/162 9/167

Bowling: Olonga 8–0–31–2; Strang 10–3–22–4; Johnson 7–0–26–0; Brent 6–0–24–0; Viljoen 9.2–3–36–3; Nkala 3–0–15–0; G. W. Flower 4–0–12–0.

Zimbabweans

N. C. Johnson b Napier.	41	S. V. Carlisle not out.	1
G. W. Flower c S. G. Law b Anderson . .	4	L-b 10, w 18, n-b 10	38
M. W. Goodwin run out	50		
*†A. Flower not out	41	1/9 2/99 3/159 (3 wkts, 34.4 overs) 175

A. D. R. Campbell, D. P. Viljoen, M. L. Nkala, B. C. Strang, G. B. Brent and H. K. Olonga did not bat.

Bowling: Cowan 6–1–18–0; Anderson 6–0–35–1; D. R. Law 3–0–24–0; Napier 4–0–23–1; Mason 9–0–38–0; Grayson 6.4–0–27–0.

Umpires: M. R. Benson and G. Sharp.

ESSEX v ZIMBABWEANS

At Chelmsford, May 11, 12, 13, 14. Drawn. Toss: Essex.

After the first day and much of the second were lost to rain, this match was destined for a draw. Entertainment was at a premium even when the sun shone: on the final morning, Essex scored just 34. Hussain, as intent upon denying the Zimbabweans time at the crease as on playing himself into shape for the Lord's Test, spent almost three hours over his 33; Danny Law (a natural strokeplayer) and Mason each took two hours to score 22. Earlier, Johnson had played the most fluent innings of the game, hitting 50 of his 83 in boundaries to rescue the Zimbabweans from an unhealthy 69 for four. Whittall contributed a solid 54 and Olonga a career-best 45 as the last two wickets added 98, countering the damage inflicted by Anderson, who bowled well for his five for 69. There was time enough at the end for the Zimbabwean openers to improve on their poor first-class record – a best of 15 in four previous attempts – but the ankle injury that Olonga suffered in this game would rule him out of the First Test.

Close of play: First day, No play; Second day, Zimbabweans 143-4 (A. Flower 23*, Johnson 45*); Third day, Essex 117-3 (Hussain 17*, Irani 13*).

Zimbabweans

G. W. Flower c Hyam b D. R. Law	10	– not out	28
T. R. Gripper c Hyam b Thompson	0	– not out	32
M. W. Goodwin c Such b Anderson	34		
A. D. R. Campbell b Anderson	13		
*†A. Flower c Hyam b Anderson	30		
N. C. Johnson lbw b Such	83		
S. V. Carlisle b Anderson	0		
G. J. Whittall c S. G. Law b Anderson	54		
D. P. Viljoen lbw b Such	0		
H. K. Olonga lbw b Thompson	45		
M. Mbangwa not out	9		
B 1, l-b 12, w 12, n-b 12	37	B 5, l-b 3, w 5, n-b 2	15

1/2 2/51 3/68 4/69 5/168   315   (no wkt dec.) 75
6/168 7/217 8/217 9/289

Bowling: *First Innings*—Anderson 26–5–69–5; Thompson 26.3–8–76–2; D. R. Law 25–8–66–1; Mason 14–2–54–0; Such 14–5–37–2. *Second Innings*—Anderson 5–2–7–0; Thompson 4–1–20–0; Such 4–1–14–0; Mason 4–0–26–0.

Essex

P. J. Prichard c Gripper b Johnson	28	R. S. G. Anderson b Mbangwa	19
A. P. Grayson c A. Flower b Whittall	15	D. J. Thompson c and b Viljoen	15
N. Hussain c A. Flower b Whittall	33	P. M. Such not out	6
S. G. Law c G. W. Flower b Mbangwa	33		
*R. C. Irani c Olonga b Johnson	21	L-b 10, w 2, n-b 16	28
D. R. Law c A. Flower b Johnson	22		
†B. J. Hyam b Olonga	7	1/42 2/52 3/104 4/137 5/146	249
T. J. Mason lbw b Olonga	22	6/166 7/182 8/212 9/240	

Bowling: Olonga 22.3–6–73–2; Mbangwa 30–13–47–2; Johnson 22–7–55–3; Whittall 14–6–24–2; Viljoen 8–1–38–1; G. W. Flower 3–2–2–0.

Umpires: J. H. Evans and R. A. White.

ENGLAND v ZIMBABWE

First Cornhill Test

At Lord's, May 18, 19, 20, 21. England won by an innings and 209 runs. Toss: England. Test debut: C. P. Schofield.

Another Lord's Test, another humiliating defeat characterised by two abject batting displays. Only this time it was different. England – excepting an ugly passage on the third afternoon – dominated from start to finish. It was Zimbabwe, in their first Test here, who were the whipping boys, giving England their biggest win since they crushed India by an innings and 285, also on this ground, in 1974. England outplayed their opponents in every respect. Even their fielding was faultless: not a catch dropped, not a run given away.

THE ENGLAND TEAM FOR THE LORD'S TEST

[*Graham Morris*]

Standing: G. A. Hick, S. J. Harmison, A. R. Caddick, A. Flintoff, E. S. H. Giddins, N. V. Knight. *Seated:* C. White, D. Gough, A. J. Stewart, N. Hussain (*captain*), M. A. Atherton, M. R. Ramprakash, C. P. Schofield.

[*Patrick Eagar*

Darren Gough gets Zimbabwe's second-innings demolition under way by trapping Grant Flower
lbw for two. He claimed four wickets as their first five went for 36 on the third evening.

No visiting team had won their first Test at Lord's, and circumstances conspired
against Zimbabwe. They had just toured the West Indies, and this, the earliest Test
staged in England, was played in distinctly un-Caribbean conditions. The damp and
chill of an English spring were meat and drink to the English seamers. There was also
a more disturbing backdrop: in Zimbabwe, violence was being directed towards the
farming community from which several players came.

In March, the ECB had contracted 12 players to form the core of the Test squad,
but injuries ruled out two. Vaughan had a broken finger and Headley a long-term back
problem. From Warwickshire came Knight and Giddins, while Chris Schofield, a 21-
year-old leg-spinner, made his Test debut in his 23rd first-class game. He got a third-
ball duck and did not bowl. Zimbabwe were forced to leave out Olonga, whose ankle
injury had deteriorated.

A greenish pitch, thick cloud cover and the forecast of showers all persuaded Hussain,
winning his fifth consecutive Test toss, to field. Within half an hour, Caddick had ripped
out three batsmen with a testing spell of hostile fast bowling. It would have been 14
for four if umpire Orchard had seen Andy Flower tickling a ball to Stewart. Seven
overs before lunch, Giddins came on and, in conditions ideal for medium-pace bowling,
he got the ball to swing both ways, and late. His fourth delivery had Flower caught
at first slip, and he went on to finish with five wickets in his second Test. Zimbabwe
were skittled for just 83; in their first 39 Tests they had never been bowled out for
under 100, but now they had succumbed twice in three games, here and in Trinidad.

After years shepherding England's friable tail from No. 6, Ramprakash became
Atherton's 12th opening partner. But he did nothing to disabuse those who felt Atherton
required a more attacking foil; his solitary boundary was an inside edge, he was dropped
behind the stumps on seven and departed for 15 to the last ball of the first day, half-

forward to one that nipped back. Nine Test innings on his home ground had brought 79 runs. Atherton, who had never scored a first-class hundred at Lord's, cruised to fifty, then was gone, playing back to Streak. Replays showed the ball had hit bat first, but umpire Willey did not hesitate. Having beaten the bat time and again, Streak deserved his luck.

At 113 for three, England were not yet in control. Hick had started uncertainly, frustrated by an inability to pierce the field, but despite rain interruptions he grew in self-assurance. By stumps on day two, he and Stewart had taken the score to 175 and the game, in all likelihood, was beyond Zimbabwe's reach. Runs came quickly next morning until Hick spent 22 minutes hovering nervously on 99. A push to mid-wicket brought him his sixth Test century – in his first Test against his native country – but Streak ended the celebrations next ball. Hick and Stewart had added 149, the highest stand yet in England–Zimbabwe Tests.

In afternoon sunshine, England should have forged ahead, for rain was forecast for the last two days. Instead, Stewart went into his shell. As he and Knight put on 114 at around three an over, there was a danger of England letting the match drift. Knight's departure for a dour 44 was the belated signal to increase the tempo. But it was the fall of wickets rather than the gathering of runs that picked up speed. England nose-dived from 376 for four to 415 all out, in which time Stewart contributed just nine. Streak, who had bowled magnificently with patchy support, took six for 87, the best by a Zimbabwean in Tests.

England had spent most of the day batting in good conditions; their collapse allowed their bowlers at least 50 minutes at Zimbabwe's batsmen in worsening light. Gough was irresistible. He swung the ball at pace and removed three batsmen in his first four overs. The Zimbabweans were furious at Gripper's wicket. There was genuine doubt whether the ball carried to third slip, just as there had been when Stewart, on 24, had gloved it to the keeper earlier in the day. John Holder, the third umpire, reprieved Stewart but condemned Gripper. Worse was to follow. First Caddick removed Goodwin, and then Murphy, the night-watchman facing the last scheduled over of the day, called Andy Flower for a single. It was against all common sense, and two balls later it cost the captain his wicket. Cock-a-hoop, England claimed the extra half-hour, but bad light closed in after 16 balls. When Sunday's rain relented, Giddins and Caddick, briefly detained by the entertaining antics of Strang, finished the job. – HUGH CHEVALLIER.

Man of the Match: E. S. H. Giddins.   *Attendance:* 46,309; *receipts* £823,601.

Close of play: First day, England 29-1 (Atherton 13*); Second day, England 175-3 (Hick 62*, Stewart 14*); Third day, Zimbabwe 39-5 (Murphy 11*, Johnson 1*).

Zimbabwe

G. W. Flower b Caddick	4	– lbw b Gough	2
T. R. Gripper c Stewart b Caddick	1	– c Knight b Gough	5
M. W. Goodwin c Knight b Gough	18	– lbw b Caddick	11
A. D. R. Campbell c Stewart b Caddick	0	– lbw b Gough	4
*†A. Flower c Atherton b Giddins	24	– (6) lbw b Gough	2
N. C. Johnson c Gough b Giddins	14	– (7) c Hick b Caddick	9
G. J. Whittall b Giddins	15	– (8) c Hick b Caddick	23
H. H. Streak c Atherton b Giddins	4	– (9) c Knight b Giddins	0
B. C. Strang c Ramprakash b Giddins	0	– (10) not out	37
B. A. Murphy c Stewart b Gough	0	– (5) lbw b Giddins	14
M. Mbangwa not out	1	– b Caddick	8
L-b 2	2	L-b 1, n-b 7	8

1/5 (1) 2/8 (2) 3/8 (4) 4/46 (5)   83   1/2 (1) 2/7 (2) 3/18 (4) 4/33 (3)   123
5/48 (3) 6/67 (7) 7/77 (8)   5/36 (6) 6/49 (7) 7/74 (5)
8/79 (9) 9/82 (6) 10/83 (10)   8/74 (9) 9/92 (8) 10/123 (11)

Bowling: *First Innings*—Gough 12.3–1–36–2; Caddick 8–3–28–3; Flintoff 3–2–2–0; Giddins 7–2–15–5. *Second Innings*—Gough 15–3–57–4; Caddick 16.2–5–38–4; Giddins 7–3–27–2.

England

M. A. Atherton lbw b Streak	55	D. Gough c Campbell b Murphy	5
M. R. Ramprakash lbw b Streak	15	E. S. H. Giddins c Strang b Streak	7
*N. Hussain c Murphy b Streak	10		
G. A. Hick lbw b Streak	101	B 5, l-b 29, w 1, n-b 5	40
†A. J. Stewart not out	124		—
N. V. Knight c Johnson b Whittall	44	1/29 (2) 2/49 (3) 3/113 (1)	415
A. Flintoff c Streak b Whittall	1	4/262 (4) 5/376 (6) 6/378 (7)	
C. P. Schofield c Johnson b Whittall	0	7/378 (8) 8/398 (9)	
A. R. Caddick c A. Flower b Streak	13	9/407 (10) 10/415 (11)	

Bowling: Streak 35.5–12–87–6; Strang 27–4–86–0; Mbangwa 21–5–69–0; Johnson 20–5–55–0; Whittall 7–0–27–3; Murphy 25–6–57–1.

Umpires: D. L. Orchard (South Africa) and P. Willey.
Referee: G. T. Dowling (New Zealand).

YORKSHIRE v ZIMBABWEANS

At Leeds, May 24, 25, 26, 27. Zimbabweans won by 32 runs. Toss: Yorkshire. First-class debuts: S. M. Guy, M. J. Lumb.

The Zimbabweans shrugged aside the inclement weather and put their unhappy Lord's experience behind them in the best possible way by registering their first first-class victory in England. Mbangwa provided the spur with match figures of ten for 53 on a pitch whose lateral movement and slow bounce favoured seam bowling. His first-innings six for 14, from 18 boundaryless overs, was the best return for a touring side against Yorkshire since 1935, when South African leg-spinner Xenophon Balaskas took eight for 99. Zimbabwe's batting, however, was still getting over being shot to pieces in the First Test. Only Whittall looked convincing on the first day – until the reverse sweep at Middlebrook that dismissed him – and on the third day they crumbled for 68, even lower than their Test catastrophe. A target of 180 looked attainable, even for a Yorkshire side without seven first-choice players, either resting or injured, but 13 for four was an inadequate platform. Michael Lumb, son of former Yorkshire opening bat Richard, played splendidly for an unbeaten 66 on debut.

Close of play: First day, Zimbabweans 235; Second day, Yorkshire 119-9 (Guy 24*, Hoggard 1*); Third day, Zimbabweans 68.

Zimbabweans

G. W. Flower c Fellows b Hoggard	0	– b Hoggard	3
G. J. Whittall lbw b Middlebrook	89	– b Hamilton	15
M. W. Goodwin lbw b Hamilton	17	– c Guy b Hutchison	4
†T. Taibu b Fellows	1	– c Hamilton b Hoggard	4
*A. Flower b Middlebrook	47	– c Guy b Hamilton	15
A. D. R. Campbell lbw b Middlebrook	0	– (7) c Guy b Hamilton	0
S. V. Carlisle run out	31	– (6) lbw b Fellows	0
M. L. Nkala lbw b Middlebrook	0	– lbw b Hamilton	11
B. C. Strang c Guy b Hutchison	0	– c Hutchison b Hamilton	14
G. B. Brent not out	0	– b Hoggard	0
M. Mbangwa lbw b Hamilton	9	– not out	0
B 1, l-b 19	20	B 1, l-b 1	2

1/0 2/54 3/59 4/165 5/165	235	1/4 2/11 3/20 4/39 5/42	68
6/176 7/182 8/182 9/216		6/43 7/46 8/67 9/68	

Bowling: *First Innings*—Hoggard 21–9–40–1; Hutchison 15–5–38–1; Middlebrook 29–5–89–4; Hamilton 20.1–11–24–2; Fellows 13–4–24–1. *Second Innings*—Hoggard 11–1–18–3; Hutchison 7–4–8–1; Fellows 5–0–18–1; Hamilton 7.3–1–22–5.

Yorkshire

*D. Byas c Whittall b Mbangwa	1	– c Goodwin b Mbangwa	1
V. J. Craven lbw b Mbangwa	21	– c G. W. Flower b Strang	3
R. J. Harden c Taibu b Mbangwa	0	– c Nkala b Mbangwa	1
M. J. Wood c Carlisle b Nkala	32	– c Brent b Mbangwa	0
G. M. Fellows lbw b Mbangwa	14	– c A. Flower b Strang	22
M. J. Lumb c Taibu b Mbangwa	2	– not out	66
G. M. Hamilton c Carlisle b Strang	12	– c A. Flower b Nkala	15
J. D. Middlebrook lbw b Mbangwa	0	– c G. W. Flower b Nkala	7
†S. M. Guy not out	29	– c A. Flower b Strang	10
P. M. Hutchison c Goodwin b Whittall	0	– c Carlisle b Strang	0
M. J. Hoggard c Taibu b Strang	1	– lbw b Mbangwa	10
B 8, l-b 1, w 1, n-b 2	12	B 8, w 4	12

1/3 2/3 3/50 4/72 5/79   124   1/2 2/6 3/11 4/13 5/54   147
6/80 7/84 8/97 9/117   6/94 7/110 8/128 9/128

Bowling: *First Innings*—Strang 21.4–7–60–2; Mbangwa 18–10–14–6; Brent 6–1–14–0; G. W. Flower 2–1–2–0; Nkala 8–3–25–1; Whittall 3–3–0–1. *Second Innings*—Strang 16–4–41–4; Mbangwa 14–2–39–4; Nkala 10–2–24–2; Brent 8–5–12–0; Whittall 6–1–23–0.

Umpires: R. Palmer and K. Shuttleworth.

†MCC v ZIMBABWEANS

At Castleford, May 28. Zimbabweans won by 22 runs (D/L method). Toss: MCC.

This match helped launch the Regional Centres Initiative to promote cricket in towns and cities where the game's stock has fallen. In Castleford – home of Chris Silverwood's old club – cricket is no longer taught in any schools, so the coaching element of MCC's visit was especially valuable. The scheme had also contributed to the renovation of Savile Park's pavilion. On the field, the Zimbabweans, buoyed by their Headingley victory the day before, won with ease, though neither Grant Flower nor Campbell, two batsmen desperate for runs, profited. Johnson hit a sound 40, but top score came from Extras, swollen by 23 wides. For MCC, Yorkshire's McGrath hung on doggedly for 46 in what was always a losing cause. Although Duckworth/Lewis was brought into play after an interruption in Zimbabwe's 13th over, no one noticed as, for once, the target happened to be identical.

Zimbabweans

N. C. Johnson c Ward b de Bruyn	40	D. P. Viljoen not out	25
G. W. Flower lbw b Pryke	1	H. H. Streak not out	5
M. W. Goodwin lbw b Brown	2	B 3, l-b 9, w 23, n-b 12	47
A. D. R. Campbell c Berry b de Bruyn	7		
*†A. Flower b Dodemaide	9	1/1 2/27 3/71 (7 wkts, 46 overs) 164
S. V. Carlisle lbw b Brown	28	4/86 5/105
G. J. Whittall c Brown b Dodemaide	0	6/106 7/144

G. B. Brent and M. L. Nkala did not bat.

Bowling: Pryke 8–1–22–1; Brown 9–1–31–2; de Bruyn 9–1–41–2; Dodemaide 9–1–25–2; Dutch 6–1–16–0; Wileman 5–0–17–0.

MCC

M. A. Roseberry c Goodwin b Johnson	2	†D. S. Berry b Nkala	13
A. McGrath b Nkala	46	A. I. C. Dodemaide run out	1
M. J. Wood lbw b Streak	1	D. J. Pryke not out	0
*D. M. Ward c Carlisle b Viljoen	12	L-b 5, w 17	22
Z. de Bruyn c A. Flower b Nkala	24		
J. R. Wileman b G. W. Flower	5	1/16 2/22 3/67 (45.1 overs) 142
K. P. Dutch run out	11	4/97 5/106 6/110
D. R. Brown b G. W. Flower	5	7/115 8/138 9/142

Bowling: Streak 10–2–32–1; Johnson 9–3–19–1; Whittall 5–1–13–0; Viljoen 7–0–18–1; Brent 5–0–19–0; Nkala 6.1–0–28–3; G. W. Flower 3–1–8–2.

Umpires: G. I. Burgess and C. S. Kelly.

ENGLAND v ZIMBABWE

Second Cornhill Test

At Nottingham, June 1, 2, 3, 4, 5. Drawn. Toss: Zimbabwe. Test debut: M. L. Nkala.
   The Zimbabwean worm turned here. After the obloquy of Lord's – which Andy Flower described as their worst showing since gaining Test status – they produced a sparky performance that finally kick-started their tour. But while Flower's imaginative last-morning declaration may have embarrassed England, rain had already washed away any real chance of a result. Given the loss of four of the first six sessions, Zimbabwe needed to take control much earlier than they did.

MOST TEST RUNS AT TRENT BRIDGE

	Runs	Tests	Innings	NO	100s	Avge	Dates
M. A. Atherton	**1,032**	**10**	**17**	**1**	**5**	**64.50**	**1989-2000**
D. C. S. Compton	955	7	10	0	5	95.50	1938-1955
G. A. Gooch	936	10	17	0	3	55.05	1978-1994
T. W. Graveney	735	8	11	2	3	81.66	1953-1967
G. Boycott	663	10	17	2	2	44.20	1964-1981
D. I. Gower	628	8	15	1	1	44.85	1978-1989
M. C. Cowdrey	594	8	14	1	1	45.69	1956-1967
I. V. A. Richards	567	4	6	0	1	94.50	1976-1991
D. G. Bradman	526	4	8	1	3	75.14	1930-1948

Research: Gordon Vince

England kept the same team and, on the first day, the same position of ascendancy. Flower eagerly inserted them when play began after lunch. But in damp, swinging conditions, his bowlers' line went awry, allowing Atherton and Ramprakash to capitalise with an opening stand of 121. An eye-popping lifter removed Ramprakash, but Atherton reached the close on 96; as rain turned Friday into the first blank day at a Nottingham Test for 33 years, he could not complete the job until the weekend. But his fifth Test hundred at Trent Bridge, and 50th in all first-class cricket, was rarely in doubt. He was the one Englishman to deal appropriately with Zimbabwe's gentle out-swing bowlers, despatching them through the cover ring off the front foot with a technical neatness many thought he had lost. He batted nearly eight hours, faced 330 balls, and hit 19 fours as well as a hooked six off Streak.

Apart from the openers, the only batsman to make an impact was Schofield, who carved out an enterprising 57 in his second Test. However, his style was so unorthodox, with his back foot wandering towards square leg and his penchant for the reverse sweep, that his innings may have aroused as much anxiety as approbation in the selectors' minds.

It was soon clear that England would need every run they had scraped out. After Grant Flower had fallen in Gough's opening over – another failure in the dying moments of the game took his first-class total on tour to 69 from 11 innings – the Zimbabweans revelled in a rich diet of long-hops, a particular boon for Goodwin, who cashed in

[*Patrick Eagar*

Short of a length was given short shrift by Zimbabwe's Murray Goodwin during his Trent Bridge 148. Lord's Man of the Match Ed Giddins was not the only England bowler to feed Goodwin's strength square of the wicket.

with a chanceless unbeaten 148, his third Test century. Raised on the trampoline pitches of Perth, Western Australia, he was lethal on the back foot, though vulnerable when drawn forward, and hit 20 fours in his stay of five and a half hours. He added 129 with Johnson – both were playing in their last Test for Zimbabwe – and another 122 with Andy Flower.

England's bowling had shown none of the sharpness of Lord's. Observing Caddick's sluggish display, Hussain wondered whether it had been right to pull him out of the preceding round of county matches. But the biggest disappointment was Schofield, who bowled with near-complete disregard for the niceties of line and length. England's latest slow-bowling prospect failed to take a wicket from 18 overs that cost just over four apiece.

Resuming 89 ahead, England had to wait for Atherton, who had missed most of Sunday with a gastric bug, to become available. The reshuffled top six soon lost their own appetite in the face of two early strikes from debutant Mluleki Nkala, a 19-year-old in-swing bowler from Falcon College in Matabeleland. First, Ramprakash edged a drive at the variation straight one, then Hussain opted to leave alone and was beaten by a boomeranging break-back. When Knight fell across his stumps, his technique evaporating, and was bowled by Streak's yorker, England were an undignified 12 for three.

Flintoff, as is his wont, tried to hit his way out of trouble, launching Mbangwa over long-off with a ballistic drive. But Streak made him look oafish with one superb, remote-controlled over. Flintoff played and missed four times before finally nicking a catch behind. It was a rapid decline, but never rapid enough for Zimbabwe. A rare filibuster of an innings from Hick, batting almost three hours for 30, held them up until the arrival of Atherton, who settled England's stomach by top-scoring again. In the first innings, he had passed Denis Compton's record 955 Test runs at Nottingham;

now he was into his second thousand. Zimbabwe were left just five overs to bat, and lost Grant Flower before the hand-shaking began.

So England had still not shrugged off the inconsistency that dogged their performances throughout the 1990s. Most worryingly, their two young Lancastrians, Flintoff and Schofield, appeared to lack the nous required at the highest level. But Trent Bridge proved to be a Rubicon for Zimbabwe, whose domestic troubles were placing them under increasing strain. On Thursday, the players wore black armbands in honour of Tony Oates, a farmer and friend of several of the team, who had been shot dead on his farm the day before the match. – SIMON BRIGGS.

Man of the Match: M. W. Goodwin.　　　　*Attendance:* 23,273; *receipts* £358,379.

Men of the Series: England – M. A. Atherton; Zimbabwe – H. H. Streak.

Close of play: First day, England 203-3 (Atherton 96*, Stewart 8*); Second day, No play; Third day, Zimbabwe 51-2 (Goodwin 11*, Johnson 9*); Fourth day, Zimbabwe 285-4 (Goodwin 148*, Murphy 0*).

England

M. A. Atherton c G. W. Flower b Mbangwa . . .	136	– (7) c G. W. Flower b Whittall 34
M. R. Ramprakash c G. W. Flower b Johnson . .	56	– c A. Flower b Nkala 4
*N. Hussain c Streak b Nkala	21	– lbw b Nkala 0
G. A. Hick c Murphy b Nkala	9	– c A. Flower b Johnson 30
†A. J. Stewart lbw b Whittall	9	– c A. Flower b Johnson 15
N. V. Knight lbw b Whittall	1	– (1) b Streak 6
A. Flintoff lbw b Mbangwa	16	– (6) c A. Flower b Streak 16
C. P. Schofield b Murphy	57	– c Campbell b Murphy 10
A. R. Caddick c G. W. Flower b Nkala	13	– c A. Flower b Whittall 12
D. Gough c Campbell b Streak	9	– c Murphy b Whittall 3
E. S. H. Giddins not out	3	– not out 0
B 9, l-b 13, w 16, n-b 10	48	B 5, l-b 8, w 1, n-b 3 17

1/121 (2) 2/182 (3) 3/188 (4) 4/209 (5) 　　　374　　1/6 (2) 2/6 (3) 3/12 (1) 　　　147
5/221 (6) 6/264 (7) 7/303 (1) 　　　　　　　　　　　4/44 (5) 5/73 (6) 6/95 (4)
8/335 (9) 9/358 (10) 10/374 (8) 　　　　　　　　　7/110 (8) 8/139 (9)
　　　　　　　　　　　　　　　　　　　　　　　　　　9/140 (7) 10/147 (10)

Bowling: *First Innings*—Streak 32–7–82–1; Nkala 31–7–82–3; Johnson 22–7–63–1; Mbangwa 18–6–40–2; Murphy 12.2–1–36–1; Whittall 19–7–47–2; G. W. Flower 1–0–2–0. *Second Innings*—Streak 17–8–13–2; Nkala 11–5–22–2; Johnson 12–2–41–2; Mbangwa 15–8–25–0; Whittall 8–3–14–3; Murphy 12–6–19–1.

Zimbabwe

G. W. Flower c Ramprakash b Gough	0	– c Hick b Caddick 12
G. J. Whittall lbw b Giddins	28	– not out 12
M. W. Goodwin not out	148	– not out 1
N. C. Johnson c Stewart b Gough	51	
*†A. Flower b Gough	42	
B. A. Murphy not out	0	
B 5, l-b 5, n-b 6	16	

1/1 (1) 2/33 (2) 　　　　　　(4 wkts dec.) 285　　1/17 (1) 　　　　　　(1 wkt) 25
3/162 (4) 4/284 (5)

S. V. Carlisle, A. D. R. Campbell, M. L. Nkala, H. H. Streak and M. Mbangwa did not bat.

Bowling: *First Innings*—Gough 20–2–66–3; Caddick 18.3–4–57–0; Giddins 16–5–46–1; Schofield 18–2–73–0; Flintoff 10–3–33–0. *Second Innings*—Gough 2–0–15–0; Caddick 2–1–9–1; Ramprakash 1–0–1–0.

Umpires: D. L. Orchard (South Africa) and M. J. Kitchen.
Referee: G. T. Dowling (New Zealand).

†IRELAND v ZIMBABWEANS

At Castle Avenue, Dublin, June 7. Zimbabweans won by 49 runs. Toss: Zimbabweans.

Both sides made a nervous start, Butler opening with four successive wides and Johnson falling to Mooney for a duck. But Wishart, one of two reinforcements for the touring party along with leg-spinner Paul Strang, put the innings on track, and there were fifties for the out-of-form Campbell and Grant Flower, who got off the mark with a six. Later, Dunlop emulated him as he embarked on a stand of 64 with Ireland's guest star, Australian Mark Waugh, their top-scorer with a steady 38. When Flower made the breakthrough, Ireland still needed 97 from 11 overs; Viljoen's three wickets put that out of the question.

Zimbabweans

N. C. Johnson b Mooney	0	D. P. Viljoen not out		30
C. B. Wishart c Waugh b Dwyer	35	B 1, l-b 5, w 23, n-b 4		33
†M. W. Goodwin b Cooke	13			
A. D. R. Campbell c Waugh b McCallan	52	1/8 2/59	(4 wkts, 50 overs)	227
G. W. Flower not out	64	3/88 4/185		

T. R. Gripper, P. A. Strang, *H. H. Streak, B. C. Strang and M. Mbangwa did not bat.

Bowling: Butler 9–0–56–0; Mooney 9–0–42–1; Cooke 8–2–24–1; Dwyer 10–3–28–1; McCallan 9–0–47–1; Waugh 5–0–24–0.

Ireland

B. J. Archer b Streak	13	G. Cooke st Campbell b Viljoen		5
P. J. Davy c Goodwin b Johnson	1	†J. A. Bushe not out		5
P. G. Gillespie c Streak b P. A. Strang	23			
M. E. Waugh b Flower	38	B 5, l-b 8, w 17		30
*A. R. Dunlop c Johnson b Viljoen	35			
W. K. McCallan c sub (G. J. Whittall)		1/14 2/45 3/67	(7 wkts, 50 overs)	178
b Viljoen	3	4/131 5/136		
P. J. K. Mooney not out	25	6/146 7/159		

O. F. X. Butler and M. D. Dwyer did not bat.

Bowling: Johnson 6–1–19–1; B. C. Strang 9–4–20–0; Streak 5–1–7–1; Mbangwa 6–0–26–0; P. A. Strang 9–0–29–1; Viljoen 10–0–51–3; Flower 5–1–13–1.

Umpires: S. Daultrey and T. Henry.

†IRELAND v ZIMBABWEANS

At Castle Avenue, Dublin, June 8. Zimbabweans won by five wickets. Toss: Zimbabweans.

Ireland's best effort came not from Test batsman Mark Waugh but home player Kyle McCallan. His 65 included three fours and a six, when no one else could hit a boundary; the next highest score was Waugh's 17. The Zimbabweans' seven bowlers dismissed their hosts so quickly that their own batsmen had time for 11 overs before lunch. But they were in for a nasty shock. Mooney seized four for nine in five overs, leaving Viljoen, promoted to open, to stage a recovery in the afternoon. Hitting nine fours in his 55, he added 67 with Streak, and there were 14 overs to spare when Streak and Bryan Strang secured victory.

Ireland

W. K. McCallan c and b Viljoen	65	G. Cooke c A. Flower b Viljoen		1
B. J. Archer b Johnson	4	†J. A. Bushe c and b P. A. Strang		0
P. G. Gillespie c A. Flower b Mbangwa	14	M. D. Dwyer c Streak b G. W. Flower		0
M. E. Waugh c Johnson b Streak	17	L-b 3, w 12		15
*A. R. Dunlop c Campbell b Streak	0			
N. G. Doak b B. C. Strang	0	1/7 2/44 3/82	(44 overs)	121
D. Heasley b P. A. Strang	3	4/86 5/90 6/113		
P. J. K. Mooney not out	2	7/113 8/119 9/120		

Bowling: Johnson 4–0–16–1; B. C. Strang 8–1–20–1; Mbangwa 6–0–18–1; P. A. Strang 10–1–30–2; Streak 5–1–6–2; Viljoen 10–2–27–2; G. W. Flower 1–0–1–1.

Zimbabweans

T. R. Gripper lbw b Mooney	0	B. C. Strang not out		11
D. P. Viljoen c Dwyer b McCallan	55			
*A. Flower c Gillespie b Mooney	0	B 4, l-b 4, w 7		15
G. W. Flower b Mooney	0			
P. A. Strang b Mooney	7	1/1 2/8 3/14	(5 wkts, 35.5 overs)	125
H. H. Streak not out	37	4/30 5/97		

N. C. Johnson, M. W. Goodwin, †A. D. R. Campbell and M. Mbangwa did not bat.

Bowling: Cooke 6–0–24–0; Mooney 10–1–24–4; Doak 7–2–16–0; Heasley 4.5–0–26–0; Dwyer 5–2–6–0; McCallan 3–0–21–1.

Umpires: W. B. Arlow and L. P. Hogan.

At Arundel, June 10, 11, 12. ZIMBABWEANS drew with WEST INDIANS (See West Indian tour section).

†ENGLAND BOARD XI v ZIMBABWEANS

At Beaconsfield, June 14. Zimbabweans won by 74 runs. Toss: England Board XI.

Despite some slipshod batting, the Zimbabweans had sufficient fire-power to run out easy winners. Gripper and Goodwin put on 64 for the second wicket, after which the tourists were undone by the leg-spin of Vyv Pike, long the mainstay of the Dorset attack, and captain Steve Foster's medium-pace. Pike's guile and accuracy brought him four for 29 as Zimbabwe were dismissed with four overs unused. In reply, the Board XI never found the necessary momentum: Andy Pugh of Devon hit 30 but, once he was out, the innings fell away in the face of fine swing bowling from Streak and Bryan Strang, who shared six wickets at negligible cost.

Zimbabweans

T. R. Gripper st Mole b Pike	43	P. A. Strang c Mole b Carruthers		0
C. B. Wishart c Pugh b Pennett	0	B. C. Strang c and b Pike		9
M. W. Goodwin c Mole b Foster	34	M. Mbangwa c Pugh b Pennett		6
*†A. Flower c Pugh b Foster	1	B 4, l-b 12, w 23, n-b 2		41
A. D. R. Campbell b Foster	14			
G. W. Flower c Clarke b Pike	4	1/4 2/68 3/72	(45.4 overs)	175
D. P. Viljoen not out	23	4/114 5/120 6/135		
H. H. Streak b Pike	0	7/136 8/138 9/154		

Bowling: Carruthers 10–1–36–1; Pennett 7.4–0–29–2; Stoneman 8–0–26–0; Foster 10–0–39–3; Pike 10–2–29–4.

England Board XI

*S. J. Foster c A. Flower b Mbangwa	17		D. B. Pennett c P. A. Strang b Streak	0	
R. G. Halsall run out	9		V. J. Pike c P. A. Strang b B. C. Strang	2	
P. E. Wellings lbw b Mbangwa	2		J. R. Carruthers b B. C. Strang	0	
R. G. Hignett lbw b B. C. Strang	3		L-b 6, w 8	14	
A. J. Pugh b Viljoen	30				
D. R. Clarke not out	22		1/17 2/22 3/27	(42.5 overs)	101
†C. M. Mole lbw b Streak	0		4/37 5/84 6/85		
S. A. Stoneman c A. Flower b Streak	2		7/94 8/94 9/98		

Bowling: Streak 8–2–14–3; B. C. Strang 9.5–3–9–3; Mbangwa 8–2–23–2; P. A. Strang 7–1–24–0; Viljoen 8–0–23–1; G. W. Flower 2–1–2–0.

Umpires: J. H. Harris and V. A. Holder.

GLOUCESTERSHIRE v ZIMBABWEANS

At Gloucester, June 16, 17, 18, 19. Zimbabweans won by 524 runs. Toss: Zimbabweans.

Gloucestershire paid for fielding a substandard side with the biggest run-thrashing in their history, surpassing their 470-run defeat by Sussex at Hove in 1913. It was the second-highest margin of victory by runs in England after Australia's win over England by 562 at The Oval in 1934. The loss of acting-captain Hancock, who broke a knuckle in the second-morning warm-up, did not help, but nor did restricting themselves to one established pace bowler. While his colleagues rarely threatened Zimbabwe's batsmen on a good surface, Lewis returned a career-best eight for 95 in the first innings. As they rattled along, Goodwin hit his third first-class century in consecutive matches, a personal-best 194 that included five fours from one under-pitched Cawdron over. In all, Goodwin struck 30 fours, plus a mid-wicket six, in 238 balls. Despite a lead of 401 – no home batsman reached 50 – Andy Flower preferred batting practice to enforcing the follow-on in hot, clammy conditions. He and his brother put on 170 in 27 overs, and the eventual declaration gave his bowlers four sessions in which to complete Gloucestershire's humiliation. Mbangwa claimed five wickets, as Streak had in the first innings.

Close of play: First day, Zimbabweans 405-4 (A. Flower 24*, G. W. Flower 32*); Second day, Gloucestershire 146-7 (Ball 17*, Gannon 1*); Third day, Gloucestershire 98-4 (Russell 19*, Cawdron 12*).

Zimbabweans

T. R. Gripper c Russell b Gannon	54	– c Russell b Lewis	8	
C. B. Wishart c Russell b Lewis	12	– c Russell b Gannon	40	
M. W. Goodwin lbw b Lewis	194			
A. D. R. Campbell c Russell b Lewis	59	– (5) not out	9	
*†A. Flower c Russell b Lewis	24	– (4) not out	116	
G. W. Flower b Lewis	35	– (3) retired hurt	76	
D. P. Viljoen lbw b Cawdron	24			
H. H. Streak lbw b Lewis	11			
P. A. Strang c Taylor b Lewis	36			
B. C. Strang c Windows b Lewis	73			
M. Mbangwa not out	0			
B 4, l-b 25, w 7, n-b 10	46	B 4, l-b 4, w 1	9	

1/27 2/154 3/345 4/346 5/405　　　568　　1/48 2/50　　(2 wkts dec.) 258
6/414 7/430 8/469 9/549

In the second innings G. W. Flower retired hurt at 220.

Bowling: *First Innings*—Lewis 34.2–11–95–8; Gannon 28–3–107–1; Cawdron 23–6–94–1; Hancock 13–2–50–0; Ball 22–3–89–0; Cotterell 17–4–74–0; Hewson 5–1–30–0. *Second Innings*—Lewis 10–2–33–1; Gannon 9–4–36–1; Cawdron 16–2–66–0; Cotterell 19–0–86–0; Ball 3–0–29–0.

Gloucestershire

D. R. Hewson c A. Flower b Mbangwa	27	– c Viljoen b Streak	11
I. Mohammed c Campbell b Streak	0	– lbw b Mbangwa	4
M. G. N. Windows c P. A. Strang b Streak	47	– b Streak	25
C. G. Taylor c Gripper b B. C. Strang	14	– lbw b P. A. Strang	3
†R. C. Russell c A. Flower b Streak	27	– c Campbell b Mbangwa	28
M. J. Cawdron c G. W. Flower b Streak	0	– lbw b Mbangwa	19
M. C. J. Ball c A. Flower b Streak	25	– c Gripper b B. C. Strang	7
J. Lewis c Viljoen b P. A. Strang	4	– c Campbell b Mbangwa	0
B. W. Gannon c A. Flower b B. C. Strang	9	– not out	1
T. P. Cotterell not out	0	– c Campbell b Mbangwa	1
*T. H. C. Hancock absent hurt		– absent hurt	
B 1, l-b 6, w 1, n-b 6	14	B 28, l-b 7, w 1	36

1/13 2/48 3/78 4/97 5/97   167   1/20 2/54 3/61 4/69 5/116   135
6/135 7/140 8/167 9/167   6/128 7/128 8/128 9/135

Bowling: *First Innings*—Streak 18.2–4–72–5; B. C. Strang 19–9–32–2; P. A. Strang 11–2–27–1; Mbangwa 12–7–11–1; Viljoen 9–3–18–0. *Second Innings*—Streak 11–3–22–2; B. C. Strang 17–9–30–1; Viljoen 7–6–6–0; Mbangwa 15.5–10–23–5; P. A. Strang 5–2–11–1; Gripper 2–1–8–0.

Umpires: V. A. Holder and A. A. Jones.

BRITISH UNIVERSITIES v ZIMBABWEANS

At Cambridge, June 21, 22, 23. Drawn. Toss: British Universities. First-class debuts: R. K. J. Dawson, J. S. Foster, G. D. Franklin, W. I. Jefferson, T. J. Murtagh, M. A. Tournier.

The Zimbabweans concluded the first-class section of their tour with a rain-affected draw. The first day belonged to the students, despite a mid-innings wobble in which three wickets – all to Bryan Strang – tumbled for eight runs. Watching from the other end was left-hander Joe Porter, whose eventual dismissal seven short of a maiden first-class century prompted an immediate declaration. The weather deteriorated, but not the recent improvement in the Zimbabwean batting. On a shortened second day, Carlisle compiled a steady fifty, and Wishart advanced next day to his fourth first-class hundred. He eventually became the first of three victims for Mark Tournier, a 29-year-old Australian seamer. As the students' bowling tired, Viljoen and Streak helped themselves to easy runs, though the game had long since lost any meaning.

Close of play: First day, British Universities 247-7 (Porter 90*, Murtagh 6*); Second day, Zimbabweans 196-2 (Carlisle 60*, Wishart 58*).

British Universities

W. I. Jefferson (*Durham*) c Whittall b P. A. Strang	41	M. A. Hardinges (*Bath*) c Johnson b B. C. Strang — 3
M. J. Banes (*Durham*) c Campbell b B. C. Strang	51	†J. S. Foster (*Durham*) lbw b Brent — 16
J. P. Pyemont (*Cambridge*) lbw b Viljoen	4	G. D. Franklin (*Durham*) lbw b Viljoen — 12
J. J. Porter (*Oxford Brookes*) c B. C. Strang b Brent	93	T. J. Murtagh (*St Mary's UC*) not out — 12
*R. K. J. Dawson (*Exeter*) lbw b B. C. Strang	1	B 9, l-b 12, w 3, n-b 4 — 28

1/64 2/73 3/117   (8 wkts dec.) 261
4/121 5/125 6/182
7/230 8/261

C. R. Pimlott (*Cambridge*) and M. A. Tournier (*Loughborough*) did not bat.

Bowling: Streak 20–9–21–0; B. C. Strang 22–9–42–3; Johnson 15–5–42–0; Brent 22.3–8–71–2; P. A. Strang 19–8–31–1; Viljoen 15–5–33–2.

Zimbabweans

N. C. Johnson c Foster b Dawson	39		D. P. Viljoen not out		72
G. J. Whittall c Foster b Murtagh	25		H. H. Streak not out		71
S. V. Carlisle c Pyemont b Pimlott	65		B 6, l-b 11, w 2, n-b 8		27
C. B. Wishart lbw b Tournier	116				
†A. D. R. Campbell b Tournier	26		1/71 2/97 3/205	(6 wkts dec.)	441
*A. Flower c Pimlott b Tournier	0		4/283 5/289 6/293		

P. A. Strang, G. B. Brent and B. C. Strang did not bat.

Bowling: Tournier 34–6–117–3; Pimlott 15–5–38–1; Hardinges 27–8–63–0; Dawson 34–7–115–1; Murtagh 2–0–6–1; Porter 2–0–7–0; Franklin 10–0–78–0.

Umpires: B. Dudleston and N. J. Llong.

†SOMERSET v ZIMBABWEANS

At Taunton, June 25. Zimbabweans won by 21 runs. Toss: Zimbabweans.

Johnson's century – he began in belligerent mood, slowed and survived a difficult return catch on 99 – made things difficult for Somerset. They had rested their captain, Cox, and were without several other regulars. Kennis, recovered from a long-term back injury, returned for his first senior match since scoring 175 against the New Zealanders precisely a year earlier. On his own comeback after a hamstring injury, Rose bowled economically, but Grove struggled for control. Carlisle and Campbell gave Johnson sound support and, in reply, there were fifties from Holloway and Burns. Just when a Somerset victory seemed a possibility, however, the last four wickets disappeared for seven runs.

Zimbabweans

N. C. Johnson c Lathwell b Trego	101		G. J. Whittall not out		6
C. B. Wishart c Parsons b Blackwell	18		L-b 13, w 14, n-b 6		33
S. V. Carlisle c Blackwell b Parsons	40				
†A. D. R. Campbell not out	45		1/81 2/154	(4 wkts, 50 overs)	248
M. W. Goodwin b Trescothick	5		3/222 4/232		

D. P. Viljoen, *H. H. Streak, P. A. Strang, M. L. Nkala and G. B. Brent did not bat.

Bowling: Rose 8–1–22–0; Grove 6–1–41–0; Trego 5–0–36–1; Blackwell 10–0–40–1; Parsons 10–0–39–1; Pierson 6–0–29–0; Trescothick 5–0–28–1.

Somerset

*M. E. Trescothick lbw b Nkala	25		P. D. Trego lbw b Brent		1
G. J. Kennis lbw b Streak	27		A. R. K. Pierson not out		4
P. C. L. Holloway c Johnson b Viljoen	55		J. O. Grove b Streak		0
M. N. Lathwell c Strang b Brent	13		L-b 14, w 8, n-b 2		24
K. A. Parsons lbw b Brent	1				
†M. Burns b Brent	68		1/44 2/78 3/104	(48.4 overs)	227
I. D. Blackwell c and b Strang	8		4/106 5/177 6/203		
G. D. Rose b Streak	1		7/220 8/220 9/224		

Bowling: Johnson 3–0–22–0; Nkala 7–1–25–1; Streak 9.4–0–27–3; Viljoen 8–0–41–1; Brent 10–2–36–4; Strang 8–0–49–1; Whittall 3–0–13–0.

Umpires: J. H. Hampshire and K. E. Palmer.

†DURHAM v ZIMBABWEANS

At Chester-le-Street, June 27. Zimbabweans won by eight wickets. Toss: Durham.

The tourists brushed aside the half-hearted challenge of Durham, a poor one-day county further weakened by the absence of Katich. Six batsmen made double figures, but only Lewis tiptoed beyond the twenties. He was despatched after an hour and a half by Viljoen, whose ten overs of slow left-arm cost just 20. Johnson was the brightest star of the Zimbabwean batting firmament, striking 11 fours in an unbeaten 81 to guide his side home with almost ten overs unused.

Durham

J. J. B. Lewis c Johnson b Viljoen	37	I. D. Hunter run out	1
S. M. Ali c Goodwin b Strang	9	N. Killeen c Carlisle b Nkala	6
P. D. Collingwood c Carlisle b Strang	4	S. J. E. Brown c Brent b Nkala	0
†M. P. Speight c Johnson b Viljoen	23	L-b 5, w 9, n-b 8	22
*N. J. Speak c Nkala b Brent	10		
N. Peng c Flower b Strang	10	1/30 2/45 3/79	(50 overs) 168
N. C. Phillips b Mbangwa	26	4/89 5/103 6/112	
J. Wood not out	20	7/152 8/154 9/167	

Bowling: Johnson 3–0–16–0; Nkala 8–2–34–2; Strang 10–0–37–3; Mbangwa 10–1–25–1; Viljoen 10–1–20–2; Brent 9–1–31–1.

Zimbabweans

N. C. Johnson not out	81
C. B. Wishart b Hunter	34
M. W. Goodwin c Collingwood b Killeen	5
S. V. Carlisle not out	35
B 1, l-b 4, w 9	14

1/74 2/79   (2 wkts, 40.2 overs) 169

*†A. Flower, G. J. Whittall, D. P. Viljoen, M. L. Nkala, B. C. Strang, G. B. Brent and M. Mbangwa did not bat.

Bowling: Brown 8–0–43–0; Wood 6–0–31–0; Hunter 8–1–17–1; Killeen 9–0–36–1; Phillips 6–0–27–0; Collingwood 3.2–0–10–0.

Umpires: D. J. Constant and K. J. Lyons.

†NOTTINGHAMSHIRE v ZIMBABWEANS

At Nottingham, June 29. Zimbabweans won by five wickets. Toss: Zimbabweans.

The Zimbabweans continued their slick preparations for the NatWest triangular tournament with an unflustered win. Nottinghamshire began perkily, with Welton, who batted throughout their innings, sharing fifty partnerships with Afzaal and then Read. But the innings fell away against the slower bowlers, with five middle-order wickets going for 55 as Grant Flower and Trent Bridge old boy Paul Strang obtained some turn. Nottinghamshire would still have rated their chances when the Zimbabweans were 149 for five, but Johnson promptly put paid to them with a whirlwind 26-ball 40 bristling with eight fours. His last three innings had brought 222 runs for one dismissal.

Nottinghamshire

G. E. Welton c Goodwin b Nkala	94	M. N. Bowen run out	9
U. Afzaal c P. A. Strang b Johnson	21	A. J. Harris b Olonga	5
*J. E. R. Gallian c Johnson b B. C. Strang	1	R. D. Stemp not out	1
†C. M. W. Read c and b G. W. Flower	39	L-b 8, w 3, n-b 4	15
C. M. Tolley c and b G. W. Flower	10		
D. J. Bicknell c Olonga b P. A. Strang	6	1/52 2/53 3/108	(49.3 overs) 207
G. R. Haywood c and b P. A. Strang	3	4/124 5/143 6/151	
D. S. Lucas lbw b P. A. Strang	3	7/163 8/197 9/205	

Bowling: Johnson 8–1–26–1; Olonga 7–0–38–1; B. C. Strang 8–1–39–1; Nkala 7.3–0–24–1; P. A. Strang 10–0–31–3; G. W. Flower 9–1–41–2.

Zimbabweans

G. J. Whittall c Read b Harris	44	N. C. Johnson not out		40
C. B. Wishart b Lucas	16			
M. W. Goodwin c Afzaal b Tolley	3	L-b 3, w 23, n-b 4		30
A. D. R. Campbell not out	39			
*†A. Flower lbw b Stemp	26	1/31 2/69 3/79	(5 wkts, 41.3 overs)	211
G. W. Flower c Stemp b Haywood	13	4/114 5/149		

P. A. Strang, B. C. Strang, M. L. Nkala and H. K. Olonga did not bat.

Bowling: Lucas 8–0–62–1; Bowen 10–0–42–0; Tolley 8–2–22–1; Harris 7–1–30–1; Stemp 5–0–34–1; Haywood 2–0–10–1; Afzaal 1.3–0–8–0.

Umpires: J. H. Evans and B. Leadbeater.

†NORTHAMPTONSHIRE v ZIMBABWEANS

At Northampton, July 1. Northamptonshire won by 42 runs (D/L method). Toss: Zimbabweans.

Sped on their way by a magnificent opening stand of 218 in 39 overs, Northamptonshire inflicted the first one-day defeat on the Zimbabweans in ten matches since their arrival in April. Rollins went for a combative 75, though he played second fiddle to Loye, whose 112 contained ten fours and three sixes and came from 130 balls. When rain interrupted Northamptonshire's innings, the game became a 45-over contest, and Zimbabwe's Duckworth/Lewis target was a daunting 287. They were dealt a blow when Johnson fell third ball, caught by Cook off Strong, who combined twice more, Strong going on to one-day best figures of five for 39. Carlisle and Grant Flower hit fifties, but to no avail.

Northamptonshire

A. S. Rollins b Streak	75	G. P. Swann not out		13
M. B. Loye run out	112	L-b 11, w 16, n-b 8		35
*M. L. Hayden c G. W. Flower b Brent	16			
R. J. Warren not out	13	1/218 2/220 3/243	(3 wkts, 45 overs)	264

J. W. Cook, A. L. Penberthy, †D. Ripley, J. F. Brown, M. R. Strong and J. A. R. Blain did not bat.

Bowling: Johnson 10–2–49–0; Olonga 8–0–52–0; Mbangwa 5–0–34–0; Streak 9–1–37–1; Viljoen 6–0–32–0; Brent 5–0–35–1; G. W. Flower 2–0–14–0.

Zimbabweans

N. C. Johnson c Cook b Strong	0	G. B. Brent c Cook b Strong		5
G. J. Whittall c Cook b Strong	11	H. K. Olonga b Penberthy		4
M. W. Goodwin b Strong	22	M. Mbangwa not out		0
S. V. Carlisle c Ripley b Hayden	58	B 1, l-b 7, w 14, n-b 2		24
*†A. Flower lbw b Hayden	20			
G. W. Flower c and b Strong	84	1/0 2/18 3/45	(42.1 overs)	244
D. P. Viljoen c Brown b Swann	5	4/75 5/199 6/204		
H. H. Streak c and b Penberthy	11	7/229 8/235 9/244		

Bowling: Strong 8.1–1–39–5; Blain 7–0–30–0; Hayden 5–0–46–2; Penberthy 8–0–43–2; Brown 9–0–50–0; Swann 5–0–28–1.

Umpires: A. Clarkson and N. A. Mallender.

†ZIMBABWEANS v NEW ZEALAND A

At Bristol, July 3. No result (D/L method). Toss: New Zealand A.

June had been kind to the Zimbabweans – seven wins, three draws, no losses – but July began ominously. First, they lost to Northamptonshire; then, in fielding practice, they lost their two most potent bowlers, Streak and Mbangwa, both of whom missed several games in the triangular tournament. Now they lost the co-operation of the weather. Had there been time for three more overs, the Zimbabweans would have won handsomely under Duckworth/Lewis rules, having already made a revised target of 194 from 41 overs look inadequate. As it was, they could take comfort from another aggressive innings from Goodwin, who was 61 off 65 balls when the rain came. For New Zealand A, Marshall hit 76 in an opening stand of 122, but no one matched his fluency.

New Zealand A

J. A. H. Marshall c B. C. Strang b Nkala	76		*S. B. Styris not out.............	9
†M. H. W. Papps c P. A. Strang b Brent.	40		L-b 3, w 19, n-b 2........	24
J. D. P. Oram not out	21			
J. I. Englefield c A. Flower b Whittall ..	3		1/122 2/145 3/155 (3 wkts, 41 overs)	173

G. P. Sulzberger, A. J. Redmond, T. K. Canning, B. G. K. Walker, D. R. Tuffey and L. J. Hamilton did not bat.

Bowling: B. C. Strang 8–3–21–0; Nkala 6–1–33–1; Brent 8–0–35–1; P. A. Strang 4–0–22–0; G. W. Flower 8–0–25–0; Whittall 7–0–34–1.

Zimbabweans

G. J. Whittall c Marshall b Tuffey	9
C. B. Wishart b Tuffey	26
M. W. Goodwin not out............	61
A. D. R. Campbell not out..........	9
L-b 4, w 7, n-b 12.........	23
1/18 2/80 (2 wkts, 22 overs)	128

S. V. Carlisle, *†A. Flower, G. W. Flower, P. A. Strang, B. C. Strang, G. B. Brent and M. L. Nkala did not bat.

Bowling: Tuffey 5–0–28–2; Hamilton 5–0–23–0; Canning 3–0–15–0; Styris 5–0–23–0; Oram 3–0–32–0; Walker 1–0–3–0.

Umpires: G. I. Burgess and A. Clarkson.

Zimbabwe's matches v West Indies and England in the NatWest Series (July 6–22) may be found in that section.

THE WEST INDIANS IN ENGLAND, 2000

Review by TONY COZIER

The extraordinary scenes on a sunlit, early September afternoon at The Oval aptly and vividly illustrated the contrasting states of English and West Indian cricket at the start of the 21st century. England had convincingly won the final Test to secure the series 3–1 and regain the Wisden Trophy that had been in West Indies' assured possession for 27 years. As captain Nasser Hussain and his triumphant players stood on the balcony, showering themselves with champagne, their achievement was hailed by thousands of joyful fans below, many of whom had not been born when Ray Illingworth was the last England captain to claim the Trophy on July 1, 1969.

Confident that this last day of the international summer would bring to an end the prolonged and painful period of Caribbean dominance, so many spectators streamed into the ground that the gates had to be closed within half an hour of the first ball, leaving an estimated 5,000 latecomers outside. Lord's, where England had drawn level with an unimaginable victory in the Second Test, and Headingley, where they had gone one up with their first two-day win since 1912, had witnessed similar public outpourings. This was the climax.

It was a stark contrast to events a year earlier. That summer had seen England eliminated from the World Cup at the group stage and beaten in the subsequent Test series by the unfancied New Zealanders. Hussain, new to the captaincy, was booed and heckled from the same Oval outfield that now cheered him. In 1999, *The Sun*, parodying the *Sporting Times*' famous notice that in 1882 gave rise to the Ashes, had devoted its entire front page to another mock obituary of English cricket. Now headlines and editorials were gushing in their praise. For a fleeting moment, football, the sporting obsession of the British media, was kicked off the front page. There were a few cautionary voices amid the tumult, but the elation was understandable.

For West Indies, it was the passing of an era in more ways than one. Even as they were folding to inevitable defeat, their 13th in 15 overseas Tests, the Oval crowd – and the England team with their guards of honour – bade a warm and generous farewell to the two survivors from the glory years of the 1980s, the great fast bowlers Curtly Ambrose and Courtney Walsh. Their team had gone under despite their yeoman efforts and, as Ambrose walked off a Test ground for the last time, 405 wickets to his account (and with Walsh, on 483, declaring that he would soon follow), it was clear such an enduring and successful partnership was unlikely to emerge in the foreseeable future.

It was obvious, too, that West Indies were in disarray. While England rejoiced, the West Indian players returned home to biting criticism from both their passionate public and former champion players, embarrassed at the loss of their legacy. Sir Viv Richards and Michael Holding, commentators on radio and television throughout the series, railed at the lack of commitment and discipline shown on the field – and reportedly off it. It was all the more painful since West Indies had arrived with expectations raised by victorious home series against Zimbabwe and Pakistan, achieved without Brian Lara

THE WEST INDIAN TOURING PARTY

[*Graham Morris*]

Standing: R. Rogers (*physiotherapist*), R. R. Sarwan, C. D. Collymore, W. W. Hinds, A. F. G. Griffith, C. H. Gayle, N. A. M. McLean, F. D. Rose, R. D. King, M. V. Nagamootoo, P. J. L. Dujon (*assistant coach*). *Seated:* R. O. Skerritt (*manager*), C. E. L. Ambrose, S. Chanderpaul, S. L. Campbell (*vice-captain*), J. C. Adams (*captain*), B. C. Lara, R. D. Jacobs, C. A. Walsh, R. A. Harper (*coach*).

and under a brand new regime: captain Jimmy Adams, coach Roger Harper and manager Ricky Skerritt. New young players such as Wavell Hinds, Ramnaresh Sarwan and Reon King had quickly asserted themselves at the highest level. Prospects seemed bright.

The optimism was heightened first by the return of Lara, back after his resignation as captain and self-imposed four-month break from the game, and then by a clinically efficient win in the First Test. Victory by an innings inside three days of Caribbean-like sunshine suggested West Indian supremacy was not diminished. That impression was seemingly confirmed when they claimed a first-innings lead of 133 after tea on the second day of the Second Test.

It should have enabled them to mark the 100th Test at Lord's – and the 50th anniversary of their first victory there – with the triumph that would surely have clinched the series. Instead, complacency and inspired England fast bowling got the better of them and, in a couple of mad, breathtaking hours, before packed stands, West Indies were routed for 54, their lowest total against England. Among those watching in disbelief were five of their countrymen who played in that historic 1950 victory, in London specially for the occasion. It was the turning-point of the series. In spite of typically heroic efforts next day, Ambrose and Walsh could not prevent an astounding England win, a psychological blow from which West Indies did not recover.

They managed only one, last-over victory in the triangular NatWest limited-overs tournament that interrupted the Tests, losing all three matches to Zimbabwe and failing to qualify for the final. It took a masterful century by Lara, their only three-figure innings of the series, to convert a deficit of 146 into a draw in the rain-affected Third Test at Old Trafford, but it was a brief, deceptive revival. Their tour ended in ignominious fashion: the Fourth Test at Headingley brought another disastrous second-innings collapse to 61 all out and their first two-day defeat in almost 70 years; a below-strength Somerset trounced them by 269 runs at Taunton; and, finally, came the inevitable surrender of the Wisden Trophy at The Oval where, at least, they managed to carry the match into a fifth day. Even before The Oval, Harper was acknowledging that his players were "very low" and "just waiting for it to end". His predecessors had said much the same on successive overseas reversals in Pakistan, South Africa and New Zealand. Once more the team's fragile spirit, as much as fragile techniques, had buckled, and they were at a loss to know how to turn things round.

Only Walsh and Ambrose came out of the *débâcle* with their reputations intact. Indeed, Walsh enhanced his by taking 34 wickets, his best in a series in 16 years of international cricket. At the age of 37, he even added a new trick to his repertoire, a bamboozling slower ball that twice accounted for Graham Thorpe. Yet those expected to take their place – King, Franklyn Rose and Nixon McLean – were so disappointing that Ambrose was moved to comment publicly on their lack of support.

The experienced batsmen – Lara, Adams and vice-captain Sherwin Campbell – produced only one significant innings each, and failed to give the expected lead to the younger brigade, of whom none made any real advance, and several seemed rather to regress. Sarwan, who turned 20 in June, did best, though his chance did not come until tendonitis of the right

[*Patrick Eagar*

Dominic Cork and Darren Gough, complete with souvenirs, set off for the Oval pavilion to celebrate England's first victorious Wisden Trophy series since 1969.

elbow ended Shivnarine Chanderpaul's tour. As he had on his debut against Pakistan in May, Sarwan displayed both class and temperament, and batted with level-headed, technically correct assurance, while his senior team-mates were being embarrassed by fast, full-length swing bowling. Yet his highest score on tour was his unbeaten 59 at Headingley.

Hinds, the tall, fortnight left-hander, could not maintain an encouraging start that included three hundreds against the counties. He could at least claim to have been unlucky: when in his best form, he, more than anyone, was victim of a few dodgy decisions. Chris Gayle failed in West Indies' sole triumph, at Edgbaston, and was promptly replaced as Campbell's opening partner by Adrian Griffith, with limited success. Griffith's eight Test innings included one fifty, when West Indies temporarily found their batting feet in the second innings at Manchester. Among the bowlers, King's control and confidence deserted him and he was replaced at The Oval by leg-spinner Mahendra Nagamootoo, for his first Test. Fast bowler Corey Collymore did not appear in the Tests or one-day internationals. Such was the selectors' disaffection that, two months after the England tour, five were dropped from the winter party to Australia.

England's revival could be attributed to several factors, quite apart from West Indian weakness. It coincided with the recall of Dominic Cork and Craig White, two all-rounders who had been in the Test wilderness for some time, and the discovery, by default, of the left-handed Marcus Trescothick as a reliable and complementary opening partner for the durable Mike Atherton. The effect of the leadership provided by the partnership of Hussain and Duncan Fletcher, the former Zimbabwe captain who had taken over as coach before the South African tour the previous winter, was also significant. It was, indeed, to Hussain's credit that he never allowed either his own horrid form – 61 runs at an average of 10.16, culminating in a pair at The Oval – or the broken thumb that sidelined him for the Lord's Test to affect his captaincy.

Fletcher's insistence that, for centrally contracted players, England requirements (including enforced rest) should take precedence over county claims met with some resistance, but it was not coincidence that there was barely a pulled muscle or a strained back to send selectors scurrying for replacements. Critically, it allowed continuity: England used 17 players, the fewest for a home series of five or more Tests since 1987, when 16 took on Pakistan. So it was more for reasons of strategy than injury that England, after the heavy loss at Edgbaston, needed to rebuild. Cork and White were summoned, the latter only five weeks after collapsing with a mystery blackout; Michael Vaughan, the dependable young Yorkshire batsman who had slotted easily into Test cricket in South Africa, returned after breaking a finger.

Cork, overtly aggressive, was at the heart of the Lord's victory with ball and bat. He provided telling support for the hostile pace of Darren Gough and Andrew Caddick in West Indies' collapse, and withstood the tension of the closing stages to hit a match-winning, unbeaten 33. He had had a similar effect the last time West Indies played Test cricket in England, in his debut series in 1995, and they wondered what had happened to him in the interim. White was a revelation, consistently generating more pace than anyone from a strong body action and creating mayhem with his reverse swing. While Gough, for once strong and fit throughout, and Caddick caused the early damage in the frequent West Indian breakdowns, White and Cork repeatedly exploited the openings. They shared 33 wickets between them, at an average of less than 15; the West Indian second string – King, McLean and Rose – managed only 19 at almost 40.

The bowlers' job was made easier by both pitch and ball favouring fast swing and seam bowling. In five Tests there were just three individual centuries – one each for the most experienced batsmen – while only three of the 16 completed innings stretched beyond 300. The most equitable conditions were at Old Trafford, which Hussain described as "a proper Test match on a proper Test-match pitch". Here Alec Stewart marked his 100th Test with a century of high, attacking quality, and Lara, for the only time in the series, approached his best in scoring 112. It was at Old Trafford, too, that Trescothick made his Test debut. His break had come in the limited-overs series when, as a replacement for the injured Nick Knight, he had shown an unflappable temperament and sound judgment. His arrival also spelled the end of the experiment of opening the innings with Mark Ramprakash. Quite possibly, it spelled the end of Ramprakash's unhappy Test career, too. In Trescothick's first three Tests, facing Walsh and Ambrose on challenging pitches, he averaged 47.50, more than anyone on either side, and shared partnerships of 179 with Stewart and 159 with Atherton. He looked the part.

Like Stewart, Atherton also played his 100th Test at Manchester, but all he could muster on his home patch were scores of one and 28. By the final Test, when he was averaging a little over 17 in the series, there was even media speculation he could lose his place. His response was emphatic: 83 and 108 in a match in which Trescothick's 78 was the only other half-century. There were still gaps in the England team, notably the absence of a genuine spin bowler – Robert Croft had been especially ineffectual at Old Trafford – and Hussain warned that there were difficult times ahead on the winter tours to Pakistan and Sri Lanka. Yet it was a time for English cricket to celebrate, just as, for West Indies, so far from their previous lofty standards, it was a time for introspection.

For the ECB, however, the euphoria was tempered by financial reality. The First and Second Tests were over in three days, the Fourth in two, while poor weather limited attendances at the Third. All told, it amounted to a shortfall on estimated revenue of around £2 million, a considerable setback, even offset by the elation of defeating West Indies. It was not a consideration that would have worried those merry fans at The Oval. Their view would have been echoed in the *Times* editorial that noted: "The passage of time has made the yearned for victory all the sweeter."

WEST INDIAN TOURING PARTY

J. C. Adams (Jamaica) (*captain*), S. L. Campbell (Barbados) (*vice-captain*), C. E. L. Ambrose (Leeward Islands), S. Chanderpaul (Guyana), C. D. Collymore (Barbados), C. H. Gayle (Jamaica), A. F. G. Griffith (Barbados), W. W. Hinds (Jamaica), R. D. Jacobs (Leeward Islands), R. D. King (Guyana), B. C. Lara (Trinidad & Tobago), N. A. M. McLean (Windward Islands), M. V. Nagamootoo (Guyana), W. Phillip (Windward Islands), F. A. Rose (Jamaica), R. R. Sarwan (Guyana), C. A. Walsh (Jamaica).

Phillip was not in the party originally named, but was drafted from MCC on the team's arrival. M. Dillon (Trinidad & Tobago) and R. L. Powell (Jamaica) joined the party for the NatWest Series.

Manager: R. O. Skerritt. *Coach:* R. A. Harper. *Assistant coach:* P. J. L. Dujon.
Physiotherapist: R. Rogers.

WEST INDIAN TOUR RESULTS

Test matches – Played 5: Won 1, Lost 3, Drawn 1.
First-class matches – Played 13: Won 4, Lost 4, Drawn 5.
Wins – England, Glamorgan, Yorkshire, Derbyshire.
Losses – England (3), Somerset.
Draws – England, Worcestershire, Zimbabweans, New Zealand A, Leicestershire.
One-day internationals – Played 6: Won 1, Lost 5. *Win* – England. *Losses* – Zimbabwe (3), England (2).
Other non-first-class matches – Played 2: Won 2. Abandoned 1. *Wins* – Hampshire, Scotland.
  Abandoned – New Zealand A.

TEST MATCH AVERAGES

ENGLAND – BATTING

	T	I	NO	R	HS	100s	50s	Avge	Ct/St
M. E. Trescothick	3	5	1	190	78	0	2	47.50	3
M. A. Atherton.	5	9	0	311	108	1	1	34.55	2
M. P. Vaughan	4	6	0	169	76	0	1	28.16	0
A. J. Stewart	5	8	0	195	105	1	0	24.37	13/1
G. P. Thorpe	3	4	0	96	46	0	0	24.00	3
D. G. Cork	4	6	2	90	33*	0	0	22.50	3
D. Gough	5	8	3	86	23*	0	0	17.20	1
N. V. Knight	2	4	0	68	34	0	0	17.00	0
G. A. Hick	4	7	0	116	59	0	1	16.57	5
C. White.	4	6	1	62	27	0	0	12.40	1
N. Hussain	4	7	1	61	22	0	0	10.16	2
A. R. Caddick	5	8	1	51	21*	0	0	7.28	2
M. R. Ramprakash	2	4	0	20	18	0	0	5.00	4

Played in two Tests: R. D. B. Croft 18, 1, 27*. Played in one Test: A. Flintoff 16, 12 (1 ct);
E. S. H. Giddins 0, 0; M. J. Hoggard 12* (1 ct).

* Signifies not out.

BOWLING

	O	M	R	W	BB	5W/i	Avge
D. G. Cork	109.5	31	245	20	4-23	0	12.25
C. White.	81.3	14	236	13	5-32	2	18.15
A. R. Caddick	170.5	53	422	22	5-14	2	19.18
D. Gough	173.5	34	530	25	5-109	1	21.20

Also bowled: R. D. B. Croft 76–17–177–3; A. Flintoff 23–10–48–1; E. S. H. Giddins
18–4–73–0; M. J. Hoggard 13–3–49–0; M. E. Trescothick 1–0–2–0; M. P. Vaughan 8–3–25–0.

WEST INDIES – BATTING

	T	I	NO	R	HS	100s	50s	Avge	Ct/St
R. R. Sarwan	3	6	2	163	59*	0	1	40.75	0
S. L. Campbell.	5	9	0	270	82	0	3	30.00	8
B. C. Lara	5	9	0	239	112	1	1	26.55	10
J. C. Adams	5	9	0	220	98	0	2	24.44	1
F. A. Rose	3	5	0	104	48	0	0	20.80	0
N. A. M. McLean	2	4	1	59	29	0	0	19.66	0
R. D. Jacobs	5	9	2	137	42*	0	0	19.57	20/1
A. F. G. Griffith	4	8	0	132	54	0	1	16.50	2
W. W. Hinds	5	9	0	147	59	0	1	16.33	5
C. E. L. Ambrose	5	9	1	95	36*	0	0	11.87	1
R. D. King	4	6	2	29	12*	0	0	7.25	0
C. A. Walsh	5	8	2	23	7	0	0	3.83	0

Played in two Tests: S. Chanderpaul 73, 22, 9. Played in one Test: C. H. Gayle 0; M. V.
Nagamootoo 18, 13.

* Signifies not out.

BOWLING

	O	M	R	W	BB	5W/i	Avge
C. A. Walsh...........	220.2	92	436	34	6-74	2	12.82
C. E. L. Ambrose.......	181.1	63	317	17	4-30	0	18.64
R. D. King	67.1	16	244	8	3-28	0	30.50
N. A. M. McLean.......	73	16	233	7	3-60	0	33.28

Also bowled: J. C. Adams 36–10–92–3; C. H. Gayle 3–0–4–0; M. V. Nagamootoo 43–14–92–3; F. A. Rose 66–12–270–4.

WEST INDIAN TOUR AVERAGES – FIRST-CLASS MATCHES

BATTING

	M	I	NO	R	HS	100s	50s	Avge	Ct/St
S. Chanderpaul........	5	9	3	418	161*	2	1	69.66	3
W. W. Hinds	11	19	1	669	150	3	3	37.16	11
S. L. Campbell........	12	20	0	629	146	1	4	31.45	13
R. R. Sarwan.........	9	16	2	423	59*	0	3	30.21	2
C. H. Gayle..........	8	14	1	392	128	1	2	30.15	5
B. C. Lara...........	10	18	0	519	176	2	1	28.83	15
M. V. Nagamootoo	9	16	2	381	100	1	0	27.21	2
A. F. G. Griffith	11	21	1	486	130	1	2	24.30	5
R. D. Jacobs.........	8	14	2	281	78	0	1	23.41	23/2
W. Phillip	6	11	3	155	67*	0	1	19.37	22/1
J. C. Adams..........	10	17	0	313	98	0	2	18.41	6
F. A. Rose...........	8	11	1	162	48	0	0	16.20	0
C. E. L. Ambrose.......	6	10	2	117	36*	0	0	14.62	1
N. A. M. McLean.......	9	17	2	122	29	0	0	8.13	0
R. D. King	9	12	4	62	21	0	0	7.75	0
C. D. Collymore.......	6	9	3	29	14	0	0	4.83	1
C. A. Walsh..........	6	9	3	26	7	0	0	4.33	0

* *Signifies not out.*

BOWLING

	O	M	R	W	BB	5W/i	Avge
C. A. Walsh...........	242.2	106	457	40	6-74	3	11.42
C. E. L. Ambrose.......	207.1	65	403	18	4-30	0	22.38
N. A. M. McLean.......	271.3	68	803	35	5-30	2	22.94
C. D. Collymore........	126.4	40	369	15	3-18	0	24.60
R. D. King	195.1	45	618	25	3-28	0	24.72
F. A. Rose	153	32	527	17	4-63	0	31.00
C. H. Gayle...........	61	8	188	5	4-86	0	37.60
M. V. Nagamootoo	328.4	93	801	21	4-12	0	38.14
J. C. Adams..........	90	26	212	5	2-5	0	42.40

Also bowled: S. L. Campbell 17–5–50–0; A. F. G. Griffith 1–0–7–0; W. W. Hinds 23.5–5–62–3; R. R. Sarwan 6–5–1–1.

Note: Matches in this section which were not first-class are signified by a dagger.

WORCESTERSHIRE v WEST INDIES

At Worcester, June 2, 3, 4. Drawn. Toss: West Indians.

The West Indians, on the back foot for most of the match, were saved from looming defeat by a solid hundred from Chanderpaul. Worcestershire rested McGrath and Sheriyar but, on a rain-hit first day, their young replacements, Catterall and Kabir Ali, helped rout the tourists for 164. After a sapping last-gasp victory over Pakistan in Antigua four days earlier, the West Indians could plead exhaustion. But for Lara, returning after a four-month sabbatical from international cricket, rustiness was the problem: he was caught, fourth ball, down the leg side off Ali for a single. Solanki rescued Worcestershire from 24 for three with an impressive fifty, and added 91 with Driver. Then Lampitt and Catterall coaxed the lead towards 68 before Catterall removed both openers, leaving the West Indians an uneasy 45 for two at the second-day close. Next morning, when Lara's second ball produced a carbon copy of his first dismissal, they were effectively 25 for four. But the Guyanese pair of Chanderpaul and 19-year-old Sarwan averted disaster with a partnership of 78.

Close of play: First day, Worcestershire 4-0 (Weston 1*, Wilson 1*); Second day, West Indians 45-2 (Gayle 1*, Chanderpaul 14*).

West Indians

*S. L. Campbell b Ali	0	– c Lampitt b Catterall	5
A. F. G. Griffith lbw b Catterall	13	– b Catterall	13
C. H. Gayle b Illingworth	38	– c Liptrot b Illingworth	15
B. C. Lara c Rhodes b Ali	1	– (5) c Rhodes b Lampitt	1
S. Chanderpaul lbw b Lampitt	19	– (4) not out	161
R. R. Sarwan c Solanki b Catterall	27	– c and b Illingworth	30
M. V. Nagamootoo b Catterall	37	– c Rhodes b Lampitt	22
N. A. M. McLean c and b Catterall	8	– c Rhodes b Solanki	11
F. A. Rose c Liptrot b Illingworth	3	– c Liptrot b Ali	0
†W. Phillip not out	2	– c Solanki b Lampitt	11
C. D. Collymore run out	0	– not out	1
L-b 3, w 5, n-b 8	16	L-b 2, w 9, n-b 20	31

1/0 2/14 3/15 4/59 5/91   164   1/19 2/24 3/92   (9 wkts dec.) 301
6/150 7/153 8/162 9/162   4/93 5/171 6/216
                                               7/252 8/253 9/291

Bowling: *First Innings*—Ali 13–2–50–2; Catterall 14.2–2–50–4; Lampitt 13–4–24–1; Illingworth 18–8–24–2; Liptrot 4–0–13–0. *Second Innings*—Ali 26–5–100–1; Catterall 11–3–42–2; Lampitt 16–6–39–3; Illingworth 31–12–55–2; Liptrot 7–1–30–0; Solanki 7–0–33–1.

Worcestershire

W. P. C. Weston c Griffith b McLean	5	R. K. Illingworth run out	14
E. J. Wilson c Phillip b Collymore	5	Kabir Ali c Nagamootoo b Rose	12
V. S. Solanki c Griffith b Rose	51	C. G. Liptrot not out	0
P. R. Pollard c Phillip b McLean	0	B 4, l-b 9, n-b 30	43
R. C. Driver c Gayle b Rose	47		
*†S. J. Rhodes b Rose	4	1/11 2/21 3/24	232
S. R. Lampitt c Phillip b Collymore	26	4/115 5/132 6/141	
D. N. Catterall lbw b Collymore	25	7/203 8/204 9/220	

Bowling: Rose 16–2–63–4; McLean 14–4–40–2; Collymore 16.4–4–59–3; Gayle 4–1–18–0; Nagamootoo 14–4–39–0.

Umpires: J. H. Evans and J. H. Hampshire.

GLAMORGAN v WEST INDIES

At Cardiff, June 6, 7, 8. West Indians won by 20 runs. Toss: West Indians.

In a low-scoring match, Glamorgan came tantalisingly close to repeating their victories over the 1923 and 1939 West Indians. Hinds struck an excellent first-innings century – contributing 105 to the 153 added while he was batting – but all eyes were on Lara and Croft. Lara desperately needed time in the middle; Croft, meanwhile, was in the running for an England recall if his off-spin troubled the legion West Indian left-handers. It did: he continued Lara's miserable start by twice dismissing him cheaply, and returned match figures of eight for 70 from 56 overs, enough to be picked for the Edgbaston Test. However, Nagamootoo's wrist-spin proved as potent, and Glamorgan trailed by 36. After crumbling again, for a dismal 97, the tourists left a target of only 134. That appeared attainable while Elliott and James shared 49 in 15 overs. But once James was run out, McLean's pace destroyed Glamorgan, and West Indian pride was restored. A swarm of bees interrupted the second day, causing many of the West Indian fielders to sprint for cover.

Close of play: First day, Glamorgan 44-2 (James 31*, Cosker 1*); Second day, West Indians 97.

West Indians

S. L. Campbell lbw b Wharf	18	– c and b Wharf		2
C. H. Gayle lbw b Wharf	17	– lbw b Wharf		1
W. W. Hinds not out	105	– c Dale b Parkin		0
B. C. Lara st Shaw b Croft	0	– lbw b Croft		11
*J. C. Adams lbw b Croft	1	– c Shaw b Wharf		13
R. D. Jacobs c Elliott b Croft	1	– c Newell b Parkin		43
M. V. Nagamootoo lbw b Wharf	22	– lbw b Wharf		0
N. A. M. McLean c Elliott b Croft	0	– c Shaw b Parkin		20
†W. Phillip c Powell b Croft	7	– c Powell b Croft		0
R. D. King lbw b Cosker	2	– lbw b Croft		1
C. D. Collymore lbw b Cosker	0	– not out		0
B 3	3	B 4, l-b 2		6

1/23 2/40 3/51 4/61 5/63   176   1/3 2/4 3/8 4/20 5/70   97
6/126 7/127 8/163 9/176   6/70 7/89 8/89 9/97

Bowling: *First Innings*—Parkin 8–2–23–0; Wharf 13–4–57–3; Croft 34–19–26–5; Cosker 16.1–3–51–2; Dale 4–0–16–0. *Second Innings*—Parkin 11–5–23–3; Wharf 10–4–9–4; Croft 22.1–8–44–3; Cosker 7–1–15–0.

Glamorgan

M. T. G. Elliott c Phillip b King	9	– (2) c Adams b McLean		25
*S. P. James b King	39	– (1) run out		27
M. J. Powell c Lara b Nagamootoo	2	– c Campbell b Collymore		11
D. A. Cosker b McLean	1	– (10) not out		0
W. L. Law lbw b McLean	0	– (4) lbw b McLean		2
A. Dale lbw b McLean	15	– (5) lbw b King		17
K. Newell lbw b Nagamootoo	27	– (6) c Phillip b Nagamootoo		12
†A. D. Shaw c Gayle b Nagamootoo	23	– (7) lbw b King		2
R. D. B. Croft not out	1	– (8) b McLean		8
A. G. Wharf c Lara b Nagamootoo	1	– (9) lbw b McLean		0
O. T. Parkin b King	0	– b McLean		0
L-b 14, n-b 8	22	L-b 7, n-b 2		9

1/34 2/39 3/45 4/45 5/67   140   1/49 2/53 3/57 4/70 5/91   113
6/82 7/125 8/130 9/136   6/95 7/113 8/113 9/113

Bowling: *First Innings*—King 20.4–3–45–3; McLean 14–3–36–3; Nagamootoo 19–11–12–4; Collymore 15–5–33–0. *Second Innings*—King 12–4–34–2; McLean 13.3–2–30–5; Nagamootoo 24–9–27–1; Collymore 8–3–11–1; Adams 1–0–4–0.

Umpires: D. R. Shepherd and J. F. Steele.

WEST INDIANS v ZIMBABWEANS

At Arundel, June 10, 11, 12. Drawn. Toss: Zimbabweans.

To the delight of the 3,000 spectators drinking in the first-day Sussex sun, Lara at last came good – very good. And with the First Test against England following just three days after this game, his timing was impeccable. He was quickly into his stride, reaching his first fifty from 43 balls, his second in another 50. A magnificent 176 came from 163 deliveries and included 130 in boundaries: 25 fours and five sixes. This from a man whose four previous innings on tour had totalled 13. Lara and Sherwin Campbell shared a third-wicket partnership of 276 before Bryan Strang's medium-pace induced a mid-innings collapse. Goodwin then exploited the absence of West Indies' front-line bowlers to raise his second century of the week. Flower declared 132 behind, but Adams plumped for batting practice, setting Zimbabwe a meaningless 333 in 39 overs only after Chanderpaul had reached the game's fourth hundred. The last time two senior international touring teams had contested a first-class match in England was in 1912, when Australia took on South Africa in Test cricket's first triangular tournament.

Close of play: First day, West Indians 364-6 (Campbell 141*, Nagamootoo 7*); Second day, West Indians 12-0 (Griffith 12*, Sarwan 0*).

West Indians

S. L. Campbell run out	146			
A. F. G. Griffith lbw b Johnson	6	– (1) lbw b Mbangwa	17
S. Chanderpaul c Campbell b Johnson	17	– not out	103
B. C. Lara b B. C. Strang	176			
*J. C. Adams c Goodwin b B. C. Strang	0	– (4) st Flower b Viljoen.	21
R. R. Sarwan lbw b B. C. Strang	1	– (2) lbw b Mbangwa	19
†R. D. Jacobs lbw b Mbangwa	0	– (5) lbw b Mbangwa	22
M. V. Nagamootoo c Gripper b B. C. Strang . . .	28	– (6) c sub (G. W. Flower) b P. A. Strang .	10
N. A. M. McLean lbw b P. A. Strang.	2	– (7) not out.	4
F. A. Rose not out	13			
C. D. Collymore b B. C. Strang	0			
B 2, l-b 2, w 4, n-b 10	18	B 1, l-b 3	4

1/9 2/55 3/331 4/331 5/333   407   1/33 2/38 3/101   (5 wkts dec.) 200
6/338 7/378 8/383 9/407   4/130 5/185

Bowling: *First Innings*—Nkala 13–2–73–0; Johnson 22–9–58–2; B. C. Strang 26.5–8–68–5; Mbangwa 21–4–73–1; P. A. Strang 22–3–77–1; Viljoen 10–1–54–0. *Second Innings*—B. C. Strang 15–4–45–0; Mbangwa 15–7–36–3; Goodwin 4–1–19–0; Campbell 5–2–8–0; P. A. Strang 10–2–38–1; Viljoen 8–1–31–1; Gripper 3–0–19–0.

Zimbabweans

T. R. Gripper c Griffith b Collymore	42	– not out	66
C. B. Wishart c Campbell b Rose	9	– c Jacobs b Nagamootoo	21
M. W. Goodwin c Chanderpaul b McLean	126		
A. D. R. Campbell c Campbell b McLean	31		
*†A. Flower c Campbell b McLean.	0		
D. P. Viljoen lbw b Rose	33		
M. L. Nkala lbw b Rose	0	– (3) not out	17
P. A. Strang c Jacobs b McLean	12		
B. C. Strang not out	5		
B 2, l-b 11, n-b 4	17	B 1, w 1, n-b 2	4

1/23 2/83 3/153 4/155   (8 wkts dec.) 275   1/63   (1 wkt) 108
5/258 6/258 7/258 8/275

N. C. Johnson and M. Mbangwa did not bat.

Bowling: *First Innings*—Rose 21–5–62–3; McLean 17.5–2–64–4; Collymore 13–4–34–1; Nagamootoo 14–1–52–0; Adams 15–3–38–0; Campbell 3–0–12–0. *Second Innings*—Rose 5–2–8–0; McLean 5–1–31–0; Campbell 10–5–18–0; Nagamootoo 12–2–42–1; Sarwan 3–2–1–0; Griffith 1–0–7–0.

Umpires: N. G. Cowley and T. E. Jesty.

ENGLAND v WEST INDIES

First Cornhill Test

At Birmingham, June 15, 16, 17. West Indies won by an innings and 93 runs. Toss: West Indies.

West Indies, having failed to win a Test outside the Caribbean since February 1997 – since when they had suffered ten consecutive overseas defeats – won this opening match by an innings inside three days, just as they had on their previous visit here in 1995. It was the 1,500th Test to be played.

The major factors in England's defeat were the undiminished powers of Walsh and Ambrose, despite a combined age of 74, and the virtue – rarely associated with West Indian batsmen, for all their brilliance – of discipline. Conditions throughout the three days did not favour batting, with the ball moving both off the seam and through the air, but the difference between the two attacks was glaring. While Walsh and Ambrose regularly honed in on a spot the size of a dinner-plate, England's spread was more of tablecloth dimensions, and the disparity in pressure on the respective batting line-ups was vast.

Put in under overcast skies, England were as much to blame for their disappointing first-innings total as Walsh's five for 36, his best return against them. It was the 20th time he had taken five or more in a Test innings, and included his 450th Test wicket, a landmark no other bowler had reached. England's batting problems were typified by their captain, Hussain, who began the match with 95 first-class runs to his name. The days of a thousand runs before the end of May belonged to a different century and more friendly weather patterns. Hussain, despite spending more than two and a half hours at the crease, emerged from this game with only 23 more.

Five years earlier, Ambrose's first ball in the Edgbaston Test had reared from just short of a length and shot over Atherton's head to the boundary. Batsmen's lives were not in such peril this time, though Atherton could manage no more than three runs from Ambrose's first seven overs, confirming he had lost none of his legendary accuracy. All great fast bowlers have a mean streak, but Walsh and Ambrose are mean in the skinflint sense as well; when Atherton looked up at the scoreboard after a battling, grafting first hour, he had just those three to his name. The most misleading statistic from the whole game, given how well he bowled, was Ambrose taking only one wicket.

That came when he induced Stewart to defend down the wrong line, the ball ricocheting off an inside edge on to leg stump, leaving England a troubled 57 for four. Knight then scrabbled uncomfortably for 26, the highest point of a sombre card. When he and Flintoff both fell at 112, there remained only the tail, but it wagged unaccustomedly to realise 67.

England were probably grateful to pick up Lara's wicket for only 50, but Gough's wonderful battle with him was the only uplifting part of their bowling. Two rather more prosaic left-handers provided the cement for the visitors' imposing total. Despite the widespread belief that all West Indian batsmen are brought up playing on beaches, joyously launching tennis balls into the surf, Adams and Chanderpaul give the impression they learned their craft inside a telephone box. Their self-restraint in waiting for the right delivery was an object lesson to some of the home batsmen.

[*Patrick Eagar*

A tuck here, a turn there – nothing too extravagant for West Indies captain Jimmy Adams. He even went without the century his Edgbaston innings warranted.

They came together at 136 for four, when England briefly saw a way back into the match. Adams's range of strokes did not stretch much further than from A to B, but he reaffirmed his reputation as a doughty opponent who gives nothing away, as did Chanderpaul, who on the second afternoon was especially harsh on Caddick. The off-spin of Croft, specifically identified by the selectors as likely to trouble a predominantly left-handed batting line-up, proved hopelessly inadequate. He did pick up two wickets, though both came in what had been misdiagnosed as a sickly West Indian lower order. Adams eked 105 from the last three partnerships before he was caught two runs short of his century, leaving Walsh not out for the 56th time in Tests, which beat Bob Willis's record. It made certain that England would not recover. Their first-innings 179 was around 80 runs below par for the conditions, and West Indies' lead of 218 was psychologically crushing.

The experiment of Ramprakash opening failed again – he continued to look too anxious and diffident at Test level – while Hick had a reminder of his unhappy debut series against West Indies in 1991, bagging his first pair in first-class cricket. He was unlucky to be given out caught behind in his second innings, when he seemed to have withdrawn his bat, and both he and Ramprakash ended the game with their places under threat from Vaughan, making his county comeback after breaking a finger. Knight resisted for three hours to top-score again and, for the second time in the game, England's final three wickets contributed more than their first four. – MARTIN JOHNSON.

Man of the Match: C. A. Walsh.   *Attendance:* 51,331; *receipts* £1,198,336.

Close of play: First day, West Indies 50-2 (Campbell 28*, Lara 6*); Second day, West Indies 336-7 (Adams 66*, Rose 33*).

England

M. A. Atherton c Jacobs b Walsh	20	– b King	19
M. R. Ramprakash c Hinds b Walsh	18	– lbw b Walsh	0
*N. Hussain c Jacobs b Rose	15	– c Jacobs b Walsh	8
G. A. Hick c Campbell b Walsh	0	– c Jacobs b Walsh	0
†A. J. Stewart b Ambrose	6	– b Rose	8
N. V. Knight c Lara b King	26	– c Hinds b Adams	34
A. Flintoff c Lara b Walsh	16	– b King	12
R. D. B. Croft c Jacobs b Walsh	18	– c Hinds b King	1
A. R. Caddick not out	21	– c Hinds b Rose	4
D. Gough run out	23	– not out	23
E. S. H. Giddins c Jacobs b King	0	– b Adams	0
L-b 6, w 1, n-b 9	16	L-b 7, w 1, n-b 8	16
	179		**125**

1/26 (2) 2/44 (1) 3/45 (4) 4/57 (5)
5/82 (3) 6/112 (6) 7/112 (7)
8/134 (8) 9/173 (10) 10/179 (11)

1/0 (2) 2/14 (3) 3/14 (4)
4/24 (5) 5/60 (1) 6/78 (7)
7/83 (8) 8/94 (9)
9/117 (6) 10/125 (11)

Bowling: *First Innings*—Ambrose 20.5–10–32–1; Walsh 21–9–36–5; King 14.1–2–60–2; Rose 13–3–45–1. *Second Innings*—Ambrose 14–8–16–0; Walsh 19–10–22–3; Rose 10–1–43–2; King 9–4–28–3; Gayle 3–0–4–0; Adams 3–1–5–2.

West Indies

S. L. Campbell b Gough	59	F. A. Rose lbw b Gough	48
C. H. Gayle lbw b Gough	0	R. D. King st Stewart b Croft	1
W. W. Hinds c Hussain b Caddick	12	C. A. Walsh not out	3
B. C. Lara c Stewart b Gough	50	B 6, l-b 14, n-b 6	26
S. Chanderpaul c Stewart b Flintoff	73		
*J. C. Adams c Flintoff b Gough	98	1/5 (2) 2/24 (3) 3/123 (1) 4/136 (4)	397
†R. D. Jacobs c Stewart b Caddick	5	5/230 (5) 6/237 (7) 7/292 (8)	
C. E. L. Ambrose lbw b Croft	22	8/354 (9) 9/385 (10) 10/397 (6)	

Bowling: Gough 36.5–7–109–5; Caddick 30–6–94–2; Giddins 18–4–73–0; Croft 29–9–53–2; Flintoff 23–10–48–1.

Umpires: S. Venkataraghavan (India) and D. R. Shepherd.
Referee: G. T. Dowling (New Zealand).

WEST INDIANS v NEW ZEALAND A

At Chelmsford, June 21, 22, 23, 24. Drawn. Toss: West Indians.

A determined four-and-a-quarter-hour 74 from Richardson, bad light which ended the last day early and a hamstring injury to Rose all helped New Zealand A to emerge with a creditable draw. A series of rash strokes explained the West Indians' modest first-innings total, but a testing line from McLean ensured them a slender lead. Five New Zealanders played themselves in, but none reached a half-century. It was altogether easier for the West Indians in their second innings: Griffith, completing his first century for six months, Hinds, with his second fluent fifty of the match, and Sarwan, with 53 on his 20th birthday, allowed Adams to declare, 420 ahead, first thing on the fourth morning. As New Zealand A battled to survive, Englefield, in a fit of pique at being run out, flung his bat 20 yards. His petulance earned him a reprimand and an undisclosed fine.

Close of play: First day, New Zealand A 90-2 (Richardson 38*, B. P. Martin 0*); Second day, West Indians 50-0 (Griffith 26*, Gayle 23*); Third day, West Indians 381-7 (Nagamootoo 7*, Phillip 0*).

West Indians

A. F. G. Griffith c Croy b Styris	22	– st Croy b Sulzberger	130
C. H. Gayle b Sulzberger	43	– b B. P. Martin	65
W. W. Hinds c Croy b Tuffey	61	– c Styris b B. P. Martin	74
B. C. Lara st Croy b Sulzberger	33	– c Croy b Tuffey	16
R. R. Sarwan run out	24	– c Papps b Sulzberger	53
*J. C. Adams c Croy b Tuffey	2	– c C. S. Martin b Sulzberger	8
M. V. Nagamootoo c Marshall b B. P. Martin	25	– not out	7
F. A. Rose lbw b B. P. Martin	1		
N. A. M. McLean c Croy b Styris	4	– (8) c Tuffey b Sulzberger	0
†W. Phillip c B. P. Martin b Styris	2	– (9) not out	0
R. D. King not out	0		
L-b 10, w 1, n-b 4	15	B 2, l-b 8, n-b 18	28

1/73 2/73 3/129 4/181 5/183   232   1/132 2/242 3/286   (7 wkts dec.) 381
6/219 7/225 8/230 9/230   4/335 5/353
                                          6/380 7/380

Bowling: *First Innings*—C. S. Martin 11–2–47–0; Tuffey 16–3–52–2; Styris 15.4–3–45–3; Sulzberger 19–7–56–2; B. P. Martin 9–2–22–2. *Second Innings*—C. S. Martin 19–6–55–0; Tuffey 15–4–56–1; Sulzberger 34–10–102–4; B. P. Martin 21–4–79–2; Styris 15–4–51–0; Oram 11–1–28–0.

New Zealand A

J. A. H. Marshall lbw b King	0	– lbw b King	4
M. H. Richardson c Lara b King	39	– c sub (S. L. Campbell) b Sarwan	74
M. H. W. Papps c Gayle b Nagamootoo	42	– c Phillip b King	0
B. P. Martin c sub (S. Chanderpaul) b McLean	1		
G. P. Sulzberger c Phillip b Adams	37	– (4) c and b Adams	32
J. D. P. Oram run out	0	– (5) lbw b Nagamootoo	20
J. I. Englefield b Nagamootoo	30	– (6) run out	5
*S. B. Styris b McLean	22	– (7) not out	31
†M. G. Croy not out	6	– (8) not out	18
D. R. Tuffey c Phillip b McLean	0		
C. S. Martin run out	1		
B 4, l-b 5, n-b 6	15	B 5, l-b 8, w 1, n-b 8	22

1/0 2/85 3/92 4/92 5/95   193   1/4 2/8 3/68   (6 wkts) 206
6/158 7/176 8/192 9/192   4/111 5/130 6/159

Bowling: *First Innings*—King 19–8–28–2; Rose 9–2–33–0; McLean 21.2–7–37–3; Nagamootoo 34–11–68–2; Adams 9–5–18–1. *Second Innings*—King 14–4–39–2; McLean 15–4–49–0; Hinds 4–2–8–0; Nagamootoo 33–13–61–1; Adams 21–8–36–1; Sarwan 3–3–0–1.

Umpires: N. L. Bainton and M. R. Benson.

†HAMPSHIRE v WEST INDIANS

At Southampton, June 25. West Indians won by four wickets. Toss: West Indians.

The West Indians completed their preparations for the Second Test with a finely judged win over a full-strength Hampshire, albeit only in a one-day game. Jacobs pulled a delivery from Francis to the mid-wicket boundary with four balls remaining. Mascarenhas underpinned the Hampshire innings with 52 from 71 balls – and later proved their most successful bowler – but Ambrose, conceding 11 runs from nine overs, and Walsh prevented any acceleration. Gayle and Adams gave the West Indian reply substance with a stand of 66 for the fourth wicket. A capacity crowd of 3,750 brought in receipts of more than £24,000, a club record for a limited-overs match.

Hampshire

G. W. White c Jacobs b Walsh	6	†A. N. Aymes not out	10
J. P. Stephenson run out	14	A. D. Mullally c Jacobs b Collymore	4
A. D. Mascarenhas c Jacobs b Ambrose	52	S. R. G. Francis b Ambrose	7
*R. A. Smith c Adams b Walsh	30	L-b 5, w 7, n-b 12	24
W. S. Kendall c Adams b Walsh	18		
J. S. Laney b Adams	10	1/18 2/65 3/92 (49.1 overs) 189	
S. K. Warne c Gayle b Collymore	13	4/134 5/143 6/149	
S. D. Udal c Hinds b Adams	1	7/159 8/165 9/173	

Bowling: Ambrose 9.1–6–11–2; Walsh 10–2–36–3; Collymore 10–0–41–2; Hinds 2–0–21–0; Nagamootoo 10–1–41–0; Adams 8–0–34–2.

West Indians

S. L. Campbell b Mascarenhas	7	†R. D. Jacobs not out	7
A. F. G. Griffith lbw b Warne	26	M. V. Nagamootoo not out	5
W. W. Hinds c Warne b Udal	36	B 4, l-b 3, w 7	14
C. H. Gayle c Mascarenhas b Mullally	47		
*J. C. Adams c Udal b Mascarenhas	32	1/9 2/71 3/83 (6 wkts, 49.2 overs) 190	
R. R. Sarwan b Mascarenhas	16	4/149 5/177 6/180	

C. E. L. Ambrose, C. D. Collymore and C. A. Walsh did not bat.

Bowling: Francis 9.2–0–42–0; Mascarenhas 10–1–49–3; Mullally 10–2–31–1; Udal 10–2–34–1; Warne 10–0–27–1.

Umpires: N. G. Cowley and A. A. Jones.

ENGLAND v WEST INDIES

Second Cornhill Test

At Lord's, June 29, 30, July 1. England won by two wickets. Toss: England. Test debut: M. J. Hoggard.

The 100th Test match played at Lord's also proved to be one of the most exciting, with England winning a low-scoring encounter by two wickets to level the series. Many talk about the Lord's Test of 1963 as being the apogee between these two sides: for sheer drama and sustained excitement, this one may have usurped it.

The uncertainty was contagious and, right up until Cork struck the winning boundary just after 7 p.m. on Saturday, it was a match that defied prediction. Momentum in Test cricket is usually a gradual, shifting force, but here it changed hands quicker than a spare ticket among the touts, who, sensing something special, thronged the pavements surrounding the ground. Whether or not the innovation of live music during the lunch break played a part – on the first day it was Third World and the Jools Holland Big Band – business was brisk. On Friday, when 21 wickets fell in 75 overs, including West Indies' second innings for just 54, value for money was given ten times over. In fact, the day saw at least one ball of all four innings, an instance unique in more than 1,500 Tests.

After losing heavily at Edgbaston, England turned up at Lord's – not somewhere recently associated with home victories – without the services of their captain, Hussain, who had cracked a thumb playing for Essex the previous weekend. It created an irony in which English cricket seems to specialise: Stewart, almost a year to the day after being sacked as captain, was once more asked to lead the side. In the event, it proved something of a masterstroke: Stewart's terse dressing-room speech – following England's first-innings collapse – was later cited as a contributory factor to West Indies' capitulation immediately afterwards.

It was probably not planned that way. Under leaden skies, Stewart won the toss and asked West Indies to bat – something no England captain had done in a home Test. No doubt expecting swing, the England bowlers found little movement. Caddick, so lethal at Lord's in the Test against Zimbabwe six weeks earlier, was insipid, and his opening spell simply fed Campbell's two favourite shots: the cut and the square drive. Together, he and his less fluent partner, Griffith, batted through the morning session. They had put on 80 when Griffith, coming back for a risky second run, was run out by Caddick's accurate throw from long leg.

The breach, two balls after lunch, might have spared Stewart a few blushes, but Hinds soon revealed his talent with a spree of three off-side boundaries in one over from White. At tea, West Indies were 170 for two and, with Lara at the crease, England's prospects were not good. But a wild swish from him and an unfortunate umpiring decision against Hinds suddenly saw Gough and Cork – in his first Test for more than 18 months and now with his 100th Test victim – back among the wickets. West Indies closed on 267 for nine.

LOWEST COMPLETED TOTALS AGAINST ENGLAND SINCE 1960

42† India at Lord's (second innings)	1974
54 West Indies at Lord's (second innings)	**2000**
61 West Indies at Leeds (second innings)	**2000**
65 New Zealand at Christchurch (first innings)	1970-71
67 New Zealand at Lord's (second innings)	1978
78 ‡Australia at Lord's (first innings)	1968
83 India at Madras (second innings)	1976-77
83 Zimbabwe at Lord's (first innings)	**2000**
88 South Africa at Nottingham (first innings)	1960
89 New Zealand at Auckland (second innings)	1962-63

† One man absent. ‡ Drawn. All other Tests won by England.

Next morning, Caddick removed Walsh first ball, his only wicket of the innings. It was a harbinger of the chaos to come, for in their opening two overs England lost both Ramprakash and Atherton to poor shots. Once Ambrose, whose 150th wicket against England accounted for Vaughan, had settled, it became obvious that the pitch had more pace, bounce and movement than the previous day. Only a brief cameo by Hick, who took four fours off Rose's first over, and two gritty efforts by Stewart and White prevented complete humiliation. West Indies' heroes, inevitably, were Ambrose and Walsh, who both finished with four wickets to give them a lead of 133. Victory, if not as familiar to this as to past sides, was recognisably close at hand.

At this point, as the British public prepared their "here we go again" routine, Stewart read his team the riot act. Their response was emphatic, bold and, given the evidence of the first day, entirely unexpected. It also required some early fortune to start the process, which happened in the fourth over when Campbell was caught, cutting Caddick to third man.

The wicket turned Caddick, with his curious tendency to be more effective in the second innings, into an assassin. Eschewing the theory that West Indies batsmen are vulnerable to the ball of full length, he banged it in short and literally went for the jugular. Less familiar with throat balls than their predecessors – most Caribbean pitches have become slow, with low bounce – they fell in rapid succession, three to catches by Ramprakash at short leg. Even Lara, failing for the second time in the match, had no riposte, while only Jacobs, with a couple of fortuitous boundaries, made double figures. West Indies' 54 was their third-lowest total, their lowest-ever against England.

[*Patrick Eagar*

All fall down: Shivnarine Chanderpaul was not the only West Indian batsman brought to his knees as Andy Caddick's hostile fast bowling turned the Lord's Test on its head.

Just over two hours of incredible drama had transformed a match with only one conceivable outcome into an endgame where both teams had a chance of victory.

Chasing 188 did not sound much, but on a bouncy seaming pitch, against two of the world's best new-ball bowlers, the task was stern. If most realists made West Indies favourites, they hadn't reckoned on Atherton and his heir apparent, Vaughan (playing only because of Hussain's injury) Coming together in the sixth over, after Ramprakash had played on to Walsh, they added 92 painstaking runs, each one cheered to the echo by a full house now reaching the point of emotional saturation – itself a rarity at Lord's.

Taking 29 balls to get off the mark – two more than his partner – Vaughan showed will-power to match that of Atherton, who simply relishes such situations. Perhaps most impressive, particularly with Ambrose beating the bat time and again, was the way neither became frustrated enough to abandon their game plan. With the job only half done, both fell in the forties to Walsh, who took the first six wickets to fall and improved his best figures against England for the second Test running, completing ten in the match for the first time against them. At 140 for six the pendulum, having creaked England's way, was back in West Indies' territory. When Knight, nursing a cracked finger, fell to Rose for a two that had spanned a courageous hour, their second victory looked assured.

However, Cork, dripping adrenalin and with a decisive glint in his eye, had entered the fray at the fall of the sixth wicket. Unfazed by the tension, he set about getting the runs. A lofted drive for four off the tiring Walsh, a pull for six off Rose and sundry stolen singles were all executed with his usual sense of theatre. As Gough kept him company with an admirably straight bat, Cork chipped away at both the total and the heartstrings of the public. Only when he had forced Walsh through the covers for the winning runs was the tension finally released, amid euphoria and ecstasy. – DEREK PRINGLE.

Man of the Match: D. G. Cork.   *Attendance:* 81,539; receipts £2,425,283.

Close of play: First day, West Indies 267-9 (King 12*, Walsh 1*); Second day, England 0-0 (Atherton 0*, Ramprakash 0*).

West Indies

S. L. Campbell c Hoggard b Cork	82	– c Gough b Caddick	4
A. F. G. Griffith run out	27	– c Stewart b Gough	1
W. W. Hinds c Stewart b Cork	59	– c Ramprakash b Caddick	0
B. C. Lara c Stewart b Gough	6	– c Cork b Caddick	5
S. Chanderpaul b Gough	22	– c Ramprakash b Gough	9
*J. C. Adams lbw b Gough	1	– lbw b Cork	3
†R. D. Jacobs c Stewart b Cork	10	– c Atherton b Caddick	12
C. E. L. Ambrose c Ramprakash b Cork	5	– c Ramprakash b Caddick	0
F. A. Rose lbw b Gough	29	– c and b Cork	1
R. D. King not out	12	– lbw b Cork	7
C. A. Walsh lbw b Caddick	1	– not out	3
B 1, l-b 8, w 2, n-b 2	13	L-b 8, n-b 1	9

1/80 (2) 2/162 (1) 3/175 (4) 4/185 (3)   267   1/6 (1) 2/6 (3) 3/10 (2) 4/24 (4)   54
5/186 (6) 6/207 (7) 7/216 (8)   5/24 (5) 6/39 (7) 7/39 (6)
8/253 (9) 9/258 (5) 10/267 (11)   8/39 (8) 9/41 (9) 10/54 (10)

Bowling: *First Innings*—Gough 21–5–72–4; Caddick 20.3–3–58–1; Hoggard 13–3–49–0; Cork 24–8–39–4; White 8–1–30–0; Vaughan 3–1–10–0. *Second Innings*—Gough 8–3–17–2; Caddick 13–8–16–5; Cork 5.4–2–13–3.

England

M. A. Atherton c Lara b Walsh	1	– lbw b Walsh	45
M. R. Ramprakash c Lara b Ambrose	0	– b Walsh	2
M. P. Vaughan b Ambrose	4	– c Jacobs b Walsh	41
G. A. Hick b Ambrose	25	– c Lara b Walsh	15
*†A. J. Stewart c Jacobs b Walsh	28	– lbw b Walsh	18
N. V. Knight c Campbell b King	6	– c Jacobs b Rose	2
C. White run out	27	– c Jacobs b Walsh	0
D. G. Cork c Jacobs b Walsh	4	– not out	33
A. R. Caddick c Jacobs b Walsh	6	– lbw b Ambrose	7
D. Gough c Lara b Ambrose	13	– not out	4
M. J. Hoggard not out	12		
L-b 5, n-b 3	8	B 3, l-b 8, w 1, n-b 12	24

1/1 (2) 2/1 (1) 3/9 (3) 4/37 (4)   134   1/3 (2) 2/95 (3)   (8 wkts) 191
5/50 (6) 6/85 (5) 7/100 (7)   3/119 (4) 4/120 (1)
8/100 (8) 9/118 (9) 10/134 (10)   5/140 (5) 6/140 (7)
                                                          7/149 (6) 8/160 (9)

Bowling: *First Innings*—Ambrose 14.2–6–30–4; Walsh 17–6–43–4; Rose 7–2–32–0; King 10–3–24–1. *Second Innings*—Ambrose 22–11–22–1; Walsh 23.5–5–74–6; Rose 16–3–67–1; King 8–2–17–0.

Umpires: S. Venkataraghavan (India) and J. H. Hampshire.
Referee: G. T. Dowling (New Zealand).

†WEST INDIANS v NEW ZEALAND A

At Bristol, July 4 (day/night). No result (abandoned).

West Indies' matches v Zimbabwe and England in the NatWest Series (July 6–20) may be found in that section.

YORKSHIRE v WEST INDIANS

At Leeds, July 24, 25. West Indians won by ten wickets. Toss: Yorkshire. First-class debuts: J. W. Inglis, S. A. Richardson.

Yorkshire, including just three capped players, were sunk by Walsh in the first innings and McLean in the second. Craven managed a well-constructed fifty and Byas twice batted solidly from No. 6, but they lost inside two days. On a helpful pitch, Walsh took five for 19 without ever exerting himself. But it wasn't only Yorkshire who struggled against Caribbean fast bowling. Working up a brisk pace, Montserrat-born Lesroy Weekes – plucked from the Huddersfield League to make his first Yorkshire appearance for six years – helped reduce the West Indians to a precarious 38 for four. Weekes, who once played with Ambrose for the Leeward Islands and joined Northamptonshire, Ambrose's former county, for the 2001 season, ended with six for 56. He was well supported by 19-year-old seamer Elstub when Hutchison tore a shoulder muscle, but the West Indians' tail ensured a recovery. McLean then sliced through Yorkshire's second innings to make it a forgettable game for their two young top-order debutants.

Close of play: First day, West Indians 83-4 (Adams 14*, Sarwan 31*).

Yorkshire

S. Widdup lbw b McLean	4	– c Adams b Walsh	2
S. A. Richardson c Hinds b Walsh	3	– c Gayle b McLean	11
J. W. Inglis lbw b McLean	2	– c Phillip b Collymore	2
†R. J. Blakey c Phillip b Collymore	2	– c Phillip b Collymore	0
V. J. Craven c Hinds b Collymore	53	– c Adams b McLean	10
*D. Byas not out	41	– c Adams b McLean	30
J. D. Middlebrook b Walsh	2	– b McLean	8
I. D. Fisher c Hinds b Nagamootoo	1	– b McLean	13
L. C. Weekes b Walsh	10	– st Phillip b Nagamootoo	10
P. M. Hutchison c Phillip b Walsh	0	– absent hurt	
C. J. Elstub c Phillip b Walsh	0	– (10) not out	0
B 2, l-b 4, n-b 2	8	L-b 3, w 1, n-b 4	8

1/7 2/7 3/9 4/26 5/96　　　　　126　　1/7 2/16 3/16 4/16 5/30　　　　　94
6/104 7/113 8/126 9/126　　　　　　　　6/52 7/71 8/90 9/94

Bowling: *First Innings*—Walsh 16–10–19–5; McLean 18–8–33–2; Collymore 13–5–29–2; Nagamootoo 16–6–39–1. *Second Innings*—Walsh 6–4–2–1; McLean 16.5–5–49–5; Collymore 8–6–14–2; Nagamootoo 6–1–26–1.

West Indians

A. F. G. Griffith lbw b Weekes	5	– not out	3
C. H. Gayle b Weekes	1	– not out	7
W. W. Hinds c Blakey b Elstub	15		
S. L. Campbell b Weekes	7		
*J. C. Adams c Middlebrook b Elstub	27		
R. R. Sarwan c Middlebrook b Weekes	32		
M. V. Nagamootoo c Blakey b Weekes	40		
N. A. M. McLean c Blakey b Fisher	6		
†W. Phillip lbw b Elstub	38		
C. D. Collymore lbw b Weekes	14		
C. A. Walsh not out	3		
B 2, l-b 13, n-b 6	21	L-b 2	2

1/7 2/12 3/38 4/38 5/85　　　　　209　　(no wkt) 12
6/114 7/127 8/157 9/185

Bowling: *First Innings*—Weekes 23–10–56–6; Hutchison 6.5–1–24–0; Elstub 20.1–3–37–3; Byas 4.1–0–8–0; Fisher 21–4–44–1; Middlebrook 12–4–25–0. *Second Innings*—Fisher 3–1–3–0; Middlebrook 2.2–1–7–0.

Umpires: K. J. Lyons and K. E. Palmer.

LEICESTERSHIRE v WEST INDIANS

At Leicester, July 28, 29, 30. Drawn. Toss: Leicestershire. First-class debuts: S. J. Adshead, P. Griffiths.

The West Indians fielded a powerful side in preparation for the Old Trafford Test, though Lara dropped out at the last minute with a hamstring niggle. Ambrose, given leave of absence from the NatWest Series, was back from Antigua and brushed off any rust with 26 overs in Leicestershire's first innings. Smith and Wells were the mainstays for the home team, adding 152 together, while leg-spinner Nagamootoo bowled tidily to take three for 68. Without Ormond, Kumble and DeFreitas, Leicestershire's attack was effectively their second string. Paul Griffiths, a 24-year-old medium-pacer playing for Wolverhampton in the Birmingham League, claimed the wicket of his near-namesake with his third ball in first-class cricket, and another newcomer, 20-year-old Stephen Adshead, caught the eye by smartly stumping Sarwan. Hinds hit 150, with 24 fours, as the West Indians helped themselves to some welcome batting practice.

Close of play: First day, Leicestershire 210-5 (Smith 40*, Wells 38*); Second day, West Indians 131-3 (Hinds 57*, Adams 19*).

Leicestershire

D. L. Maddy c Hinds b Rose	48	– b King	1
I. J. Sutcliffe lbw b Rose	34	– not out	2
D. I. Stevens c Hinds b King	12	– lbw b Rose	11
J. M. Dakin b Nagamootoo	11		
B. F. Smith c Jacobs b Ambrose	76		
A. Habib lbw b Nagamootoo	0		
*V. J. Wells st Jacobs b Nagamootoo	84		
D. Williamson not out	21		
C. D. Crowe not out	3		
†S. J. Adshead (did not bat)		– (4) lbw b Rose	0
B 10, l-b 4, n-b 30	44	L-b 4, n-b 8	12

1/90 2/113 3/117 4/129   (7 wkts dec.) 333   1/3 2/24 3/26   (3 wkts) 26
5/133 6/285 7/321

P. Griffiths did not bat.

Bowling: *First Innings*—Ambrose 26–2–86–1; King 18–1–89–1; Rose 18–3–50–2; Nagamootoo 23–3–68–3; Adams 8–0–24–0; Gayle 1–0–2–0. *Second Innings*—Rose 4–1–8–2; King 3–0–14–1.

West Indians

S. L. Campbell lbw b Williamson	17	F. A. Rose c Stevens b Crowe	41
A. F. G. Griffith c Smith b Griffiths	10	C. E. L. Ambrose not out	22
W. W. Hinds b Maddy	150	R. D. King b Williamson	4
C. H. Gayle c and b Crowe	16		
*J. C. Adams c Crowe b Dakin	21	B 8, l-b 8, w 1, n-b 6	23
R. R. Sarwan st Adshead b Crowe	22		
†R. D. Jacobs b Williamson	78	1/33 2/45 3/80 4/157 5/193	414
M. V. Nagamootoo c Sutcliffe b Dakin	10	6/284 7/337 8/382 9/398	

Bowling: Dakin 25–3–90–2; Wells 11–2–32–0; Williamson 18–3–65–3; Griffiths 21–3–65–1; Crowe 37–14–89–3; Maddy 10–1–57–1; Smith 1–1–0–0.

Umpires: J. H. Harris and B. Leadbeater.

ENGLAND v WEST INDIES

Third Cornhill Test

At Manchester, August 3, 4, 5, 6, 7. Drawn. Toss: West Indies. Test debut: M. E. Trescothick.

A sporadically exhilarating match ended the time-honoured Mancunian way when the last day vanished into the drizzle, leaving behind the memory of two sensational centuries and a contest of exceptional fluctuations. On the second day, Stewart led England to the commanding heights. But this produced the one thing his team most dreaded: it awoke Lara, the sleeping dragon. And by the time the match dribbled away, it was West Indies who were striving for victory.

Lara's hundred was not his greatest, though it made England fearful of what might lie ahead. Stewart's innings was simply sprinkled with stardust. Like Atherton, he was playing his 100th Test match. But while Atherton had an indifferent game, Stewart unleashed a parade of dazzling and nonchalant-looking strokes: the sort of batting that used to be regarded as specifically West Indian.

England's batsmen provided few reminders of the team who had not managed a fifty between them in the two previous Tests. Indeed, three of the Lord's top six were changed. When the 13-man squad was announced (unusually, ten days in advance), Ramprakash and Knight had already been swept away. Then Hick was sent home, allowing the return of Hussain and Thorpe and a first cap for Marcus Trescothick of Somerset, who had won golden opinions in the one-day series. The Lord's debutant, Hoggard, was omitted from the final eleven, leaving room for off-spinner Croft. West Indies brought in Sarwan for the injured Chanderpaul.

Adams unexpectedly chose to bat in overcast conditions and quickly lost the initiative, despite a truncated first day. Thorpe began his return with a marvellous low slip catch to dismiss Campbell, and later caught Lara for an out-of-sorts 13. Poor Hinds appeared to get an unfortunate decision (from umpire Cowie) for the third successive Test innings. But there was little ill luck about most of the dismissals, and next day West Indies were whipped out for 157. Cork took four for 23, but the bonus for England was the bowling of the fourth seamer, White, who surprised the batsmen (and most spectators) with 90mph pace and aggression from an unpretentious run-up.

England's start was extraordinary. Atherton was caught at third slip for one, and the out-of-form Hussain at gully for ten, a score mainly built on a hook caught on the boundary by Walsh, who then saw to his horror that he had stepped back on to the rope: six rather than out. Walsh made amends himself, and then immediately produced a perfect slower ball for Thorpe, who lost sight of it and ducked instinctively. Next thing he knew, he was plumb lbw – 17 for three.

This, however, was the day Britain was celebrating the Queen Mother's 100th birthday. In came a revered cricketing survivor, Stewart, to reach his own regal century and so emulate Colin Cowdrey, Javed Miandad and Gordon Greenidge by scoring a hundred in his 100th Test. Continuing his top form of the one-day series, he struck the ball square of the wickets with monumental assurance; anything off line (and there was plenty from King and Rose) was clattered away with utter assurance. The innings of a man without a smidgin of doubt about his cricket or his life, it lasted three hours, spanned 153 balls, included 13 fours – and took the breath away.

Stewart was helped by the stiff wind blowing from the Stretford End. Neither Walsh nor Ambrose seemed anxious to bowl into it, and thus hardly bowled in tandem on the second afternoon. With West Indies' support bowling so weak, this took the pressure off. But his main help came from Trescothick, who confirmed the impression that he was a player with enough robustness in both his technique and his temperament to become England's regular opener.

However, next day (the only sunny one of the five), England fell away. Stewart was out second ball; Trescothick added only one to his overnight 65, and England had to

[*Patrick Eagar*

Mike Atherton and Alec Stewart model the caps that marked their 100th Test match: Stewart
graced the occasion with a hundred; Atherton could afford to wait.

settle for a lead of 146, still handy, but well short of their hopes. By the time the West
Indian openers had put on 96, those hopes were starting to become fears. With the
pitch now taking slow turn, here at last was an opportunity for Croft. He had some
bad luck and showed some imagination, but the more he bowled, the less likely he
looked to dismiss competent batsmen.

And West Indies were now looking competent again – even before Lara, who used
the second innings of the Old Trafford Test, just as he had in 1995, to make his
intentions belatedly clear. His strokeplay was not as clear-cut as it once was, but it
still made the fielders quail. Meanwhile, his determination was stronger than ever: he
spent Sunday lunchtime (when he was 49 not out) having a net. He was finally run
out – his damaged hamstring inhibiting a quick turn – for 112. His runs came at a
similar pace to Stewart's; in all, he faced 158 balls, striking 13 fours and a six, and
batted three and a quarter hours. On the final morning, England's last hopes of bowling
out West Indies and getting a chaseable target disappeared. Adams was able to declare
and set England a theoretical 293 in 71 overs before everything disappeared into the
damp. The England players were relieved; the fifth-day crowd felt cheated.

This Monday turnout was surprisingly large. On Friday and Saturday, the ground
was almost full, but on Thursday and Sunday more than half-empty, all of which left
officials a little baffled. Five of the Saturday crowd (and another on Friday) chose an
early exit by running on to the field in varying degrees of nakedness. This led to calls
for stronger punishments. The streakers faced only expulsion from the ground, and
maybe some regrets when they sobered up. – MATTHEW ENGEL.

Man of the Match: A. J. Stewart.   *Attendance:* 54,228; *receipts* £964,045.

Close of play: First day, West Indies 87-4 (Adams 16*, Sarwan 17*); Second day, England
196-3 (Trescothick 65*, Stewart 105*); Third day, West Indies 131-1 (Griffith 41*, Hinds 20*);
Fourth day, West Indies 381-6 (Jacobs 25*, Rose 8*).

West Indies

S. L. Campbell c Thorpe b Gough	2	– c Cork b White	55
A. F. G. Griffith lbw b Caddick	2	– lbw b Croft	54
W. W. Hinds c Stewart b Cork	26	– c Stewart b Gough	25
B. C. Lara c Thorpe b Gough	13	– run out	112
*J. C. Adams c Thorpe b White	24	– lbw b Cork	53
R. R. Sarwan c Thorpe b Cork	36	– lbw b Caddick	19
†R. D. Jacobs b Caddick	5	– not out	42
F. A. Rose lbw b Cork	16	– lbw b White	10
C. E. L. Ambrose c Hussain b Caddick	3	– not out	36
R. D. King not out	3		
C. A. Walsh lbw b Cork	7		
B 1, l-b 12, n-b 7	20	B 14, l-b 4, w 2, n-b 12	32

1/3 (1) 2/12 (2) 3/49 (3) 4/49 (4)   157 1/96 (1) 2/145 (3) (7 wkts dec.) 438
5/118 (6) 6/126 (7) 7/130 (5)   3/164 (2) 4/302 (4)
8/135 (9) 9/148 (8) 10/157 (11)   5/335 (6) 6/373 (5) 7/384 (8)

Bowling: *First Innings*—Gough 21–3–58–2; Caddick 24–10–45–3; Cork 17.1–8–23–4; White 9–1–18–1. *Second Innings*—Gough 27–5–96–1; Caddick 23–4–64–1; Cork 28–9–64–1; Croft 47–8–124–1; White 27–5–67–2; Trescothick 1–0–2–0; Vaughan 2–1–3–0.

England

M. A. Atherton c Campbell b Walsh	1	– c Jacobs b Walsh	28
M. E. Trescothick b Walsh	66	– not out	38
*N. Hussain c Adams b Walsh	10	– not out	6
G. P. Thorpe lbw b Walsh	0		
†A. J. Stewart c Jacobs b Ambrose	105		
M. P. Vaughan c Lara b Ambrose	29		
C. White b King	6		
D. G. Cork c Jacobs b Ambrose	16		
R. D. B. Croft not out	27		
A. R. Caddick lbw b Ambrose	3		
D. Gough c Ambrose b King	12		
B 10, l-b 6, n-b 12	28	B 4, l-b 1, n-b 3	8

1/1 (1) 2/17 (3) 3/17 (4) 4/196 (5)   303 1/61 (1)   (1 wkt) 80
5/198 (2) 6/210 (7) 7/251 (8)
8/275 (6) 9/283 (10) 10/303 (11)

Bowling: *First Innings*—Ambrose 27–7–70–4; Walsh 27–14–50–4; Rose 20–3–83–0; King 12.2–3–32–2; Adams 11–4–32–0. *Second Innings*—Ambrose 12–2–31–0; Walsh 14–6–19–1; King 2.4–0–15–0; Adams 5–1–10–0.

Umpires: D. B. Cowie (New Zealand) and P. Willey.
Referee: R. S. Madugalle (Sri Lanka).

DERBYSHIRE v WEST INDIANS

At Derby, August 9, 10, 11. West Indians won by 224 runs. Toss: West Indians.

Already without Cork (omitted on England orders), three other first-choice seamers and Di Venuto, Derbyshire soon lost Smith to an ankle injury that ended his season. Wharton, a 23-year-old slow left-armer playing his fourth first-class match, came in for heavy punishment as Hinds and Gayle cashed in on a benign pitch with hundreds, putting on 202 in 47 overs, but his perseverance was rewarded with five for six in a 47-ball spell. On the second day, Bailey took advantage of the visitors' own patchy attack to hit the first century for Derbyshire in their 15 games against the West Indians, stretching back to 1906. His 13 boundaries included a six off Nagamootoo which struck a spectator on the full, sending him to hospital. Bailey's sporting declaration kept the game alive and, though they pottered aimlessly on the last morning, the tourists eventually sauntered to victory. Rose was unable to bowl after spraining his ankle in a warm-down game of football, but McLean and Collymore showed more urgency than in the first innings. Only Bailey, with an unbeaten fifty, stood in their way.

Close of play: First day, West Indians 390-9 (King 5*, Collymore 2*); Second day, West Indians 110-3 (Gayle 19*, Phillip 0*).

West Indians

A. F. G. Griffith run out	22	– b Dowman	36
*S. L. Campbell c Sutton b Cassar	47	– c sub (I. J. Darlington) b Wharton	52
W. W. Hinds c Dowman b Shah	104	– (6) b Wharton	3
C. H. Gayle b Wharton	128	– b Wharton	57
R. R. Sarwan c Sutton b Shah	52	– (3) b Cassar	0
M. V. Nagamootoo lbw b Wharton	2	– (7) not out	38
F. A. Rose lbw b Wharton	0		
N. A. M. McLean c Bailey b Wharton	1	– run out	0
†W. Phillip c Smith b Wharton	9	– (5) c Sutton b Wharton	2
R. D. King not out	5	– (9) lbw b Lacey	21
C. D. Collymore not out	2		
B 5, l-b 2, w 1, n-b 10	18	B 3, l-b 1, n-b 8	12

1/46 2/80 3/282 4/331 5/337   (9 wkts dec.) 390
6/338 7/340 8/358 9/388

1/64 2/65 3/105   (8 wkts dec.) 221
4/121 5/156 6/179
7/180 8/221

Bowling: *First Innings*—Smith 5.3–1–28–0; Shah 17–1–112–2; Cassar 15.3–5–39–1; Lacey 22–12–47–0; Wharton 31–7–96–5; Dowman 10–0–41–0; Pyemont 4–0–20–0; Bailey 1–1–0–0. *Second Innings*—Shah 11–3–51–0; Cassar 5–0–37–1; Dowman 2–0–16–1; Wharton 22–8–83–4; Bailey 4–2–5–0; Lacey 8–2–25–1.

Derbyshire

S. D. Stubbings c Phillip b Rose	7	– c Phillip b McLean	23
S. P. Titchard lbw b King	5	– lbw b King	0
J. P. Pyemont c Phillip b Collymore	4	– b McLean	11
*R. J. Bailey not out	112	– (7) not out	65
M. P. Dowman c Collymore b Rose	39	– (4) b Collymore	1
†L. D. Sutton c and b Nagamootoo	34	– c Phillip b Collymore	0
M. E. Cassar not out	21	– (5) c Sarwan b King	9
S. J. Lacey (did not bat)		– c Sarwan b Collymore	0
K. Z. Shah (did not bat)		– c Phillip b Nagamootoo	14
T. M. Smith (did not bat)		– lbw b Gayle	4
L. J. Wharton (did not bat)		– b King	7
B 4, l-b 7, w 1, n-b 8	20	B 1, l-b 7, w 1, n-b 2	11

1/12 2/12 3/32   (5 wkts dec.) 242
4/115 5/210

1/11 2/24 3/37 4/48 5/48   145
6/63 7/73 8/112 9/129

Bowling: *First Innings*—Rose 14–5–33–2; King 16–6–27–1; McLean 10–2–32–0; Collymore 7–0–39–1; Nagamootoo 23.4–4–83–1; Gayle 9–1–17–0. *Second Innings*—King 11.2–2–28–3; McLean 14–1–49–2; Collymore 10–3–18–3; Gayle 6–3–10–1; Nagamootoo 13–6–32–1.

Umpires: P. Adams and D. J. Constant.

†SCOTLAND v WEST INDIANS

At Uddingston, Glasgow, August 13. West Indians won by 21 runs. Toss: Scotland.

The West Indian slow bowlers had too many options for the Scots on a wet day at Bothwell Castle. Patterson and Lockhart opened with 85 before leg-spinner Nagamootoo made the breakthrough, and Gayle's off-breaks claimed the next three wickets with only seven runs added.

Adams checked Salmond's recovery with a return catch off his left-arm spin, and King finally struck a blow for pace with the last ball of the match. Earlier, in a West Indian innings interrupted by rain, Gayle and Adams, who hit two sixes, had added 94 after Hinds fell for a duck. The fixture was originally scheduled for Titwood, but was moved when the umpires ruled that pitch dangerous.

West Indians

A. F. G. Griffith c Lockhart b Wright	31	N. A. M. McLean b Asim Butt	18
S. L. Campbell c Patterson b Asim Butt	11		
W. W. Hinds c Smith b Brinkley	0	L-b 6, w 17, n-b 4	27
C. H. Gayle b Cox	45		
*J. C. Adams lbw b Brinkley	48	1/38 2/49 3/57 (7 wkts, 43 overs)	204
R. R. Sarwan c Wright b Williamson	3	4/151 5/154	
M. V. Nagamootoo not out	21	6/165 7/204	

†W. Phillip, R. D. King and C. D. Collymore did not bat.

Bowling: Brinkley 9–1–32–2; Asim Butt 9–0–36–2; Cox 8–1–34–1; Wright 9–1–45–1; Maiden 3–0–26–0; Williamson 5–0–25–1.

Scotland

B. M. W. Patterson c Adams b Nagamootoo	36	C. M. Wright not out	26
D. R. Lockhart b Gayle	48	J. E. Brinkley b King	3
†C. J. O. Smith lbw b Gayle	1	B 1, l-b 3, w 3, n-b 6	13
R. A. Parsons b Gayle	0		
*G. Salmond c and b Adams	26	1/85 2/86 3/86 (7 wkts, 43 overs)	183
J. G. Williamson run out	30	4/92 5/136	
		6/173 7/183	

G. I. Maiden, D. J. Cox and Asim Butt did not bat.

Bowling: King 8–2–17–1; McLean 8–0–31–0; Collymore 4–1–17–0; Nagamootoo 8–2–31–1; Gayle 9–1–37–3; Campbell 2–0–17–0; Adams 4–0–29–1.

Umpires: B. Anderson and L. A. Redford.

ENGLAND v WEST INDIES

Fourth Cornhill Test

At Leeds, August 17, 18. England won by an innings and 39 runs. Toss: West Indies.

The first two-day Test win for 54 years – and England's first since crushing South Africa at Old Trafford in 1912 – ensured the 2000 Headingley Test would claim a prominent place in cricket folklore. Inspirational English pace bowling, a mediocre surface and West Indies' continued fallibility against the seaming or swinging ball combined to bring England victory with astonishing haste. It was their first innings win over West Indies since 1966.

The worldwide trend for shorter Test matches – out of kilter with the game's reputation as an imperceptible battle for supremacy over five long and contemplative days – had already been noted with some disquiet. But nowhere had the pace been so unremittingly frenetic as at Headingley. West Indies were routed just as they had been at Lord's, dismissed in their second innings for only 61 in 26.2 overs, in seven minutes over two hours. The Leeds crowd, beside itself with excitement, could even crow that, at almost every stage, Yorkshire players led the way. Rarely has a Test bowler spectacularly rounded things off with five for five in 15 balls – including four wickets in an over – and still imagined himself a support act. That, though, was the fate to befall Caddick, of Somerset.

White's England career had attracted more than a few dismissive comments over the previous six years, and not three months had passed since he fell unconscious in a Scarborough side street and feared for his long-term health. At 30, his hair was beginning to thin, but his upper body was stronger and the 90mph delivery, once an occasional shock weapon, was now produced with regularity. His reverse swing, delivered from around the wicket to West Indies' procession of left-handers, also proved devastating. On the opening day, he took five in a Test innings for the first time as the tourists were bundled out for 172 inside 49 overs on a damp and uneven surface.

White and his Yorkshire team-mate, Gough, took all five pre-lunch wickets. Fifty was raised with misleading ease – only Campbell had departed, caught at the squarer of two gullies – but then four wickets fell for ten runs, three in 17 balls to White. Hinds was caught behind off an inside edge, Lara offered no stroke and Adams dragged on. With Griffith cutting feebly at Gough, only Sarwan, with a fluent and unbeaten half-century, countered a capricious pitch with *élan*.

TESTS COMPLETED WITHIN TWO DAYS SINCE 1900

Australia (448) beat South Africa (265 and 95) by an innings and 88 runs at
   Manchester* 1912
South Africa (95 and 93) lost to England (176 and 14-0) by ten wickets at The Oval*‡ 1912
England (112 and 147) lost to Australia (232 and 30-0) by ten wickets at Nottingham* 1921
West Indies (99 and 107) lost to Australia (328-8 dec.) by an innings and 122 runs at
   Melbourne† 1930-31
South Africa (157 and 98) lost to Australia (439) by an innings and 184 runs at
   Johannesburg† 1935-36
New Zealand (42 and 54) lost to Australia (199-8 dec.) by an innings and 103 runs
   at Wellington† 1945-46
West Indies (172 and 61) lost to England (272) by an innings and 39 runs at Leeds   **2000**

  * *Scheduled for three days.*
  † *Scheduled for four days.*
  ‡ *Play ended before lunch on the second day.*

By the close of a breathless first day, England too were in disarray and, at 105 for five, could have had no confidence of even the slenderest lead. Ambrose stalked England's top order with silent and deadly efficiency, both openers going in his first three overs. Atherton's nibble to slip brought him his 400th Test wicket, a feat greeted by the highest of high-fives and a melon smile. With Walsh already well past the mark, two 400-wicket men bowled in tandem for the first time in history. Walsh claimed three victims of his own by the close, two nip-backers ending the partial recovery engineered by Hussain and Thorpe, who added 70 for the third wicket. Hussain's 22 in almost two hours was his highest Test score of a tormented batting summer.

On the second morning, the match swung England's way. Vaughan, on his home midden and batting in the scholarly, slightly formal manner of a country parson, made a Test-best 76. Hick, at No. 8 thanks to Caddick's night-watchman duties, hit a half-century just as composed, especially while cutting. Vaughan's strokeplay was judicious – watchful in defence, stylish in the drive and strikingly dominant on the pull shot – his running between the wickets set a positive tone, and West Indies' fielding became slipshod. After three and a quarter hours, he succumbed to Ambrose and the second new ball, but not before he had added 45 useful runs with Cork, who was comically missed on nought as Hinds misjudged a skier. When Walsh claimed Gough's wicket, the unimagined bounty of another 167 runs, at four an over, had put England exactly 100 ahead.

[Patrick Eagar

Out of sorts and without a wicket, Andrew Caddick finally got to bowl from the end he wanted after tea on Friday. So much for Saturday's play: in his third over from Headingley's Rugby Stand End, Caddick sent West Indies crashing from 52 for five to 53 for nine. His first ball removed (1) Ridley Jacobs, lbw; the third, fourth and sixth legitimate deliveries bowled (2) Nixon McLean, (3) Curtly Ambrose and (4) Reon King.

What followed rivalled even the drama of Headingley 1981, when Ian Botham banished the Australians. The bounce had been awkward for batsmen facing bowling from the Rugby Stand End, but West Indies' collapse was primarily brought about by high-quality swing bowling at speed. Gough, twice overshadowed by Yorkshire colleagues, now delivered for the faithful, dismissing a trio of left-handers with in-duckers in his first three overs. Griffith and Hinds both fell first ball, with Griffith's stumps splayed and Hinds struck on the back leg. Lara barely jammed down on the hat-trick ball, but he fell in Gough's next over, lbw without playing a shot for the second time in the match. Cork, eager to join the fray, then struck Jimmy Adams on the hand and, after treatment, caused him to drag on next ball.

FOUR WICKETS IN AN OVER IN A TEST

		Innings analysis	
M. J. C. Allom	England v New Zealand at Christchurch*†...	19–4–38–5	1929-30
K. Cranston	England v South Africa at Leeds	7–3–12–4	1947
F. J. Titmus	England v New Zealand at Leeds.........	26–17–19–5	1965
C. M. Old	England v Pakistan at Birmingham†	22.4–6–50–7	1978
Wasim Akram	Pakistan v West Indies at Lahore†	9–0–28–5	1990-91
A. R. Caddick	**England v West Indies at Leeds**.........	**11.2–5–14–5**	**2000**

* *Includes hat-trick.*
† *Four wickets in five balls.*

Note: In each instance, except the drawn match at Lahore, the bowler ended on the winning side.

After tea, Caddick was finally allowed to switch to the Rugby Stand End, where he produced the most devastating over of his Test career. Jacobs was lbw to the first ball, then the stumps were shattered three times – dismissing McLean, Ambrose and King – in four legitimate deliveries to leave this impassive cricketer wheeling around the outfield in disbelief. It took him another eight balls to complete the job. Five batsmen had departed for ducks in the lowest Test total recorded at Headingley. England took a 2–1 lead and Saturday's sell-out crowd had to make other arrangements. – DAVID HOPPS.

Man of the Match: M. P. Vaughan.   *Attendance:* 25,563; *receipts* £867,104.
Close of play: First day, England 105-5 (Vaughan 6*, Caddick 3*).

West Indies

S. L. Campbell c Trescothick b Gough......	8	– c Hick b Gough	12
A. F. G. Griffith c Stewart b Gough.........	22	– b Gough	0
W. W. Hinds c Stewart b White	16	– lbw b Gough	0
B. C. Lara lbw b White..................	4	– lbw b Gough	2
*J. C. Adams b White...................	2	– b Cork	19
R. R. Sarwan not out	59	– not out	17
†R. D. Jacobs c Caddick b Cork..........	35	– lbw b Caddick	1
N. A. M. McLean c Stewart b White........	7	– b Caddick	0
C. E. L. Ambrose b Cork	1	– b Caddick	0
R. D. King lbw b Gough	6	– b Caddick	0
C. A. Walsh c Caddick b White	1	– b Caddick	3
L-b 2, n-b 9.................	11	L-b 3, n-b 4	7

1/11 (1) 2/50 (3) 3/54 (4) 4/56 (2)   172
5/60 (5) 6/128 (7) 7/143 (8)
8/148 (9) 9/168 (10) 10/172 (11)

1/3 (2) 2/3 (3) 3/11 (4)   61
4/21 (1) 5/49 (5) 6/52 (7)
7/52 (8) 8/52 (9)
9/53 (10) 10/61 (11)

Bowling: *First Innings*—Gough 17–2–59–3; Caddick 10–3–35–0; White 14.4–4–57–5; Cork 7–0–19–2. *Second Innings*—Gough 10–3–30–4; Caddick 11.2–5–14–5; Cork 5–0–14–1.

England

M. A. Atherton c Lara b Ambrose	6	C. White c Jacobs b McLean	0
M. E. Trescothick c Lara b Ambrose	1	D. G. Cork not out	11
*N. Hussain lbw b Walsh	22	D. Gough c Griffith b Walsh	2
G. P. Thorpe lbw b Walsh	46	B 4, l-b 13, w 3, n-b 18	38
†A. J. Stewart c Campbell b Walsh	5		
M. P. Vaughan c Jacobs b Ambrose	76		272
A. R. Caddick c Jacobs b Ambrose	6	1/7 (2) 2/10 (1) 3/80 (3) 4/93 (4)	
G. A. Hick st Jacobs b Adams	59	5/96 (5) 6/124 (7) 7/222 (8)	
		8/224 (9) 9/269 (6) 10/272 (11)	

Bowling: Ambrose 18–3–42–4; Walsh 24.5–9–51–4; King 11–2–48–0; McLean 22–5–93–1; Adams 6–1–21–1.

Umpires: D. B. Cowie (New Zealand) and G. Sharp.
Referee: R. S. Madugalle (Sri Lanka).

SOMERSET v WEST INDIANS

At Taunton, August 23, 24, 25, 26. Somerset won by 269 runs. Toss: Somerset. First-class debut: J. Tucker.

This was a demoralising result for the West Indians. If they had hoped for batting practice before the final Test, they failed miserably against what was in effect a reserve attack. Moreover, the instep injury that King incurred in Somerset's first innings ruled him out for The Oval. Apart from a maiden hundred by Nagamootoo, a first fifty by Phillip, and some optimistic runs from Griffith, everything of merit came from Somerset, the only county to pocket £11,000 for beating these tourists. On a track made for runs, Parsons hit a career-best 193, Somerset's best against the West Indians, before running out of partners; Bowler passed 1,000 runs for the ninth time, and Burns made two fifties. Joe Tucker, a graduate of the Taunton academy, took a memorable wicket with his second ball in first-class cricket – Lara, caught hooking at fine leg – and Kerr, making his first first-class appearance of the season, won the match with a hat-trick as the West Indians caved in for 169 in 55 overs. Sarwan, meanwhile, had flown home for the funeral of his childhood sweetheart.

Close of play: First day, Somerset 390-6 (Parsons 151*, Kerr 13*); Second day, West Indians 238-7 (Nagamootoo 97*, Phillip 35*); Third day, West Indians 5-1 (Griffith 4*, Phillip 0*).

Somerset

*J. Cox b King	41			
†R. J. Turner c Gayle b King	6	– lbw b Gayle	43
P. C. L. Holloway lbw b Collymore	1	– c Chanderpaul b Gayle	0
P. D. Bowler c Lara b Nagamootoo	47	– c Phillip b Nagamootoo	11
K. A. Parsons not out	193	– run out	2
M. Burns lbw b Collymore	55	– not out	78
I. D. Blackwell c Campbell b Hinds	25	– c Hinds b Gayle	39
J. I. D. Kerr c Lara b McLean	32		
A. R. K. Pierson c Phillip b McLean	1	– (1) c Chanderpaul b Gayle	48
J. Tucker c Phillip b Hinds	14		
J. O. Grove b Hinds	17		
B 8, l-b 8, w 6, n-b 34	56	B 9, l-b 10	19

1/33 2/61 3/67 4/159 5/297   488   1/77 2/81 3/96   (6 wkts dec.) 240
6/349 7/422 8/430 9/458   4/98 5/142 6/240

Bowling: *First Innings*—King 14–1–70–2; McLean 30–10–99–2; Collymore 19–7–74–2; Nagamootoo 41–6–126–1; Gayle 15–0–51–0; Campbell 4–0–20–0; Hinds 12.5–3–32–3. *Second Innings*—McLean 9–3–21–0; Collymore 17–3–58–0; Hinds 7–0–22–0; Gayle 23–3–86–4; Nagamootoo 13–2–34–1.

West Indians

A. F. G. Griffith c Turner b Grove	0	– c Turner b Grove	77
C. H. Gayle c Parsons b Kerr	4	– b Kerr	0
*S. L. Campbell c Parsons b Pierson	36	– (4) c Tucker b Burns	29
B. C. Lara c Cox b Tucker	18	– (5) b Kerr	24
S. Chanderpaul lbw b Parsons	10	– (8) not out	4
W. W. Hinds lbw b Grove	10	– c Turner b Grove	0
M. V. Nagamootoo c Parsons b Blackwell	100	– lbw b Grove	9
N. A. M. McLean c sub (G. D. Rose) b Blackwell	7	– (9) c Turner b Kerr	0
†W. Phillip not out	67	– (3) c Burns b Blackwell	17
C. D. Collymore b Grove	12	– lbw b Kerr	0
R. D. King absent hurt		– absent hurt	
B 5, l-b 3, w 4, n-b 14	26	L-b 1, w 2, n-b 6	9
	290		**169**

1/2 2/15 3/40 4/78 5/82 6/118 7/141 8/255 9/290

1/0 2/45 3/124 4/149 5/149 6/159 7/169 8/169 9/169

Bowling: *First Innings*—Grove 17.2–0–64–3; Kerr 13–3–40–1; Tucker 8–3–28–1; Parsons 11–3–45–1; Pierson 18–10–45–1; Blackwell 23–3–60–2. *Second Innings*—Grove 17–3–59–3; Kerr 11–6–18–4; Tucker 3–0–19–0; Blackwell 10–3–20–1; Pierson 8–2–24–0; Burns 6–1–28–1.

Umpires: N. A. Mallender and R. Palmer.

†At Wormsley, August 28. Drawn. Toss: West Indians. West Indians 246 for three dec. (A. F. G. Griffith 60, S. L. Campbell 40, B. C. Lara 103 not out, J. C. Adams 36 not out); Sir Paul Getty's XII 126 for nine.

Not part of the official tour programme. Each side fielded 12 players, of whom 11 could bat and 11 field.

ENGLAND v WEST INDIES

Fifth Cornhill Test

At The Oval, August 31, September 1, 2, 3, 4. England won by 158 runs. Toss: West Indies. Test debut: M. V. Nagamootoo.

Earlier in the season, a critic of the sport had described cricket as "a grey game played by grey people". The misguided journalist should have been at The Oval on the final day to see the conclusion of a momentous contest, itself the culmination of a memorable series. This was sport at its vibrant, colourful best, and it rekindled the public's love affair with cricket. Some 18,500 spectators crammed into the ground; thousands more were turned away, left to wander the Harleyford Road, hearing the roar that urged England on to triumph. In a show of admirable common sense, the Surrey club – who also admitted children at no cost – gave several hundred luckier fans access to the executive boxes.

Consensus suggested it was the first sell-out on a final day in England since Hutton, Compton, *et al.* recovered the Ashes here in 1953. Now, as then, England needed merely to hold their nerve. A victory would complete a summer that had already seen Zimbabwe beaten in a Test series, and both West Indies and Zimbabwe overcome in the one-day NatWest Series.

When Cork trapped Walsh 12 minutes after tea to complete the 3–1 win, the jubilant crowd packed in front of the pavilion and stretched back as far as the square to witness the presentation ceremony. Some of them, a year previously, had booed Hussain, the England captain, after a miserable defeat by New Zealand, but such churlishness was long forgotten as England celebrated a first series win against West Indies in 31 years. There could be no doubting the choice of Man of the Match. Atherton, who hinted during the game at retirement after the 2001 Ashes series, top-scored in both innings,

Left: A moment that defined the series: Craig White's dramatic removal of Brian Lara's leg stump left no doubt whose star was in the ascendant by the time the teams reached The Oval. *Below:* The England players form a guard of honour for Courtney Walsh.

[Patrick Eagar

in all batting for more than 12 hours on a pitch that showed enough life to keep the bowlers interested throughout.

Even so, Adams's decision to bowl was surprising, and once Atherton and Trescothick had put on 159 in 62 overs for the first wicket, England never ceded the initiative. Mahendra Nagamootoo, the debutant wrist-spinner from Guyana, and McLean at least gave Ambrose and Walsh better support than their colleagues had earlier in the series. Indeed, Nagamootoo, flat but accurate, ended the opening stand when Trescothick cut to slip on the stroke of tea; he then forced a thin edge from Hussain two balls after the resumption. Atherton remained ever vigilant but, next day, after Thorpe had succumbed to Walsh's slower ball for the second time in three Tests, the lower order offered only flimsy resistance between showers.

MOST LBWS IN A TEST

17	West Indies v Pakistan at Port-of-Spain	1992-93
15	Pakistan v New Zealand at Lahore	1996-97
15	West Indies v Australia at Port-of-Spain...........................	1998-99
14	Pakistan v Sri Lanka at Faisalabad	1991-92
14	West Indies v Australia at Bridgetown	1998-99
14	**England v West Indies at The Oval**	**2000**
13	New Zealand v England at Auckland...............................	1991-92
13	India v South Africa at Ahmedabad	1996-97

Research: M. L. Fernando

For almost an hour on a gloomy evening, Campbell and Griffith remained resolute under a searching examination of bounce and swing from Gough and Caddick. However, the frailties of the tourists' top order, which had become increasingly evident through the summer, resurfaced spectacularly on Saturday morning. Eight wickets fell for 73 runs before lunch, including five batsmen for seven runs in 22 balls, the collapse begun when Campbell dragged one that kept low on to his stumps.

For a moment, it looked as if they might not get past the follow-on target of 82, but some lusty hitting by McLean saw them over that hurdle. White, who had shared the first six wickets with Cork, was rewarded for bowling fast and straight with the last two wickets, giving him figures of five for 32, the best of a Test career rejuvenated under Fletcher's tutelage. His victims included Lara, bowled leg stump going too far across the crease, for his first golden duck at Test level. Trescothick's stunning catch at gully to remove Sarwan typified the general improvement in England's fielding.

Not even the dismissal of Hussain for a pair, completing his woeful series with the bat, could dampen home optimism. Atherton, largely eschewing the drive, again dug in courageously against the pace attack, as though roused by the challenge of the indefatigable Walsh, who on the fourth morning conceded just four runs in a magnificent 11-over spell. Regularly he would narrowly miss the edge. But Atherton, beaten three times in one perfect over, would smile ruefully, and then concentrate on the next ball rather than worry about the last.

Stewart, White and Cork all chipped in, but Atherton's 108, chiselled out in 444 minutes from 331 balls, was more than four times greater than the second-highest contribution. His century, modestly acknowledged, prompted a standing ovation to match that given Stewart at Old Trafford. It seemed he would carry his bat until he gave a thin edge to Jacobs, and became Walsh's 34th victim of the series, one short of Malcolm Marshall's record for England–West Indies series. As the leading wicket-taker in this rubber, though, Walsh became the first winner of the Malcolm Marshall award.

West Indies needed 374, their highest-ever winning fourth-innings total, to level the series, but wickets fell steadily once Hick held Campbell at second slip. Gough and Caddick managed to pin down Lara, as well as making further inroads, and an underarm throw by Thorpe accounted for Sarwan. Then as Lara began to expand his range, he was unfortunate to be given lbw to Gough. England formed guards of honour for Ambrose, playing his final Test, and Walsh, his last in England, as they strode to the crease, but there was nothing either man could do to reverse the result. – RICHARD HOBSON.

Man of the Match: M. A. Atherton.   *Attendance:* 86,825; *receipts* £1,649,897.
Men of the Series: England – D. Gough; West Indies – C. A. Walsh.

Close of play: First day, England 221-5 (Thorpe 31*, Hick 2*); Second day, West Indies 13-0 (Campbell 6*, Griffith 4*); Third day, England 56-2 (Atherton 36*, Thorpe 10*); Fourth day, West Indies 33-0 (Campbell 15*, Griffith 17*).

England

M. A. Atherton b McLean	83	– c Jacobs b Walsh 108
M. E. Trescothick c Campbell b Nagamootoo	78	– c Lara b Ambrose............ 7
*N. Hussain c Jacobs b Nagamootoo	0	– lbw b McLean 0
G. P. Thorpe lbw b Walsh	40	– c Griffith b Walsh.......... 10
†A. J. Stewart lbw b McLean	0	– c Campbell b Nagamootoo 25
M. P. Vaughan lbw b Ambrose	10	– lbw b Walsh 9
G. A. Hick lbw b Ambrose	17	– c Campbell b Walsh 0
C. White not out	11	– run out 18
D. G. Cork lbw b McLean	0	– lbw b McLean 26
A. R. Caddick c Hinds b Walsh	4	– c Jacobs b McLean........... 0
D. Gough b Walsh	8	– not out 1
B 4, l-b 15, w 1, n-b 10.........	30	B 1, l-b 7, n-b 5........ 13

1/159 (2) 2/159 (3) 3/184 (1) 4/184 (5)   281   1/21 (2) 2/29 (3) 3/56 (4)   217
5/214 (6) 6/254 (7) 7/254 (4)   4/121 (5) 5/139 (6) 6/139 (7)
8/255 (9) 9/264 (10) 10/281 (11)   7/163 (8) 8/207 (9)
     9/207 (10) 10/217 (1)

Bowling: *First Innings*—Ambrose 31–8–38–2; Walsh 35.4–16–68–3; McLean 29–6–80–3; Nagamootoo 24–7–63–2; Adams 4–0–13–0. *Second Innings*—Ambrose 22–8–36–1; Walsh 38–17–73–4; McLean 22–5–60–3; Nagamootoo 19–7–29–1; Adams 7–3–11–0.

West Indies

S. L. Campbell b Cork	20	– c Hick b Gough 28
A. F. G. Griffith c Hick b White	6	– c Stewart b Caddick 20
W. W. Hinds lbw b Cork	2	– (4) lbw b Caddick........... 7
B. C. Lara b White	0	– (3) lbw b Gough 47
*J. C. Adams c Hick b Cork	3	– c White b Caddick 15
R. R. Sarwan c Trescothick b White	5	– run out 27
†R. D. Jacobs not out	26	– c Hick b Caddick 1
M. V. Nagamootoo c Trescothick b Gough	18	– lbw b Gough 13
C. E. L. Ambrose lbw b Caddick	0	– (10) c Atherton b Cork 28
N. A. M. McLean b White	29	– (9) not out................. 23
C. A. Walsh b White	5	– lbw b Cork 0
L-b 3, n-b 6	9	L-b 3, w 1, n-b 2........ 6

1/32 (1) 2/32 (2) 3/32 (4) 4/34 (3)   125   1/50 (1) 2/50 (2) 3/58 (4)   215
5/39 (6) 6/51 (5) 7/74 (8)   4/94 (5) 5/140 (6) 6/142 (7)
8/75 (9) 9/119 (10) 10/125 (11)   7/150 (3) 8/167 (8)
     9/215 (10) 10/215 (11)

Bowling: *First Innings*—Gough 13–3–25–1; Caddick 18–7–42–1; White 11.5–1–32–5; Cork 8–3–23–3. *Second Innings*—Gough 20–3–64–3; Caddick 21–7–54–4; White 11–2–32–0; Cork 15–1–50–2; Vaughan 3–1–12–0.

Umpires: D. J. Harper (Australia) and D. R. Shepherd.
Referee: R. S. Madugalle (Sri Lanka).

THE NATWEST SERIES, 2000

By KATE LAVEN

The inaugural NatWest Series was a resounding success for England, who claimed a one-day tournament for the first time since Adam Hollioake lifted the Champions Trophy at Sharjah in December 1997. Since then, England had not looked like winning anything, the nadir coming when they crashed out of the 1999 World Cup at the first hurdle. They were now pitted against West Indies – fallers at that same first fence – and Zimbabwe, who in 2000 had already lost limited-overs series against England at home and in the West Indies. This was not a contest between the titans of the one-day game. For all three sides, failure would signal crisis.

England would not have been thrilled with the scheduling: the tournament was timetabled to avoid a clash with Euro 2000, a soccer championship that dominated sports headlines in June. It made sense, but it meant interrupting the Test series against West Indies for a month after Lord's, where England had found their feet following a couple of poor matches. And selection was not straightforward: both Nasser Hussain and Nick Knight, who had forged a successful opening combination the previous winter, were out with hand injuries. In came Somerset left-hander Marcus Trescothick, while Alec Stewart was given the chance to revive a one-day career apparently ended by his sacking as captain after the World Cup fiasco. These two turned out to be the stars of the show, Stewart's abrupt change in fortune underlined by his being chosen to lead England in place of Hussain.

Initial signs were not good for England. They lost abjectly to Zimbabwe in their first game, would probably have suffered the same fate against West Indies in the next had rain not intervened, and Stewart seemed stuck on 12. At least by the third of his dozens, he was leading a winning team. Buoyed by the success of Trescothick – who hit 244 in his first four innings – England came back strongly and humbled both opponents, skittling Zimbabwe for 114 and crushing West Indies by ten wickets. The seamers formed a settled, efficient unit, profligate in nothing but dot balls, though it was Stewart who lorded it over the tournament's second half. He hit 408 at 81.60, following his 12s with 74 not out, 101, 100 not out and 97. For good measure, he equalled the record of six dismissals in a limited-overs international.

The pace-setters, however, were Zimbabwe, who coped admirably despite starting without front-line bowlers Heath Streak, Henry Olonga and Pommie Mbangwa, and qualified for the final halfway through the preliminaries. Their established batsmen did them proud, four – the Flowers, Neil Johnson and Alistair Campbell – passing 200 runs. Murray Goodwin was not far behind. Streak, once fit, took ten wickets at less than 20, while Grant Flower turned in a useful all-round performance. Zimbabwe steam-rollered England when they first met, but thereafter prospered only against West Indies.

West Indies were in a sorry state. The policy of resting Curtly Ambrose and Courtney Walsh for alternate one-day tournaments came unstuck when Walsh injured his foot. With Ambrose back in the Caribbean, the West Indian attack was weak and ill-disciplined. All five main English bowlers cost less

[Graham Morris

Two captains, one triumph: Nasser Hussain and Alec Stewart hold the NatWest Series trophy at Lord's.

than four an over; by contrast, just one West Indian, part-time spinner Chris Gayle, squeezed under at 3.99. The batting was arguably even worse: Brian Lara hit three fifties without cutting loose, Sherwin Campbell managed a century, but in essence, that was it. They did win the last, dead preliminary match, largely by virtue of suicidal English batsmanship. It all confirmed that West Indian cricket was in deep crisis.

The competition was also memorable for the arrival of floodlit internationals in England and the use of three non-Test grounds for their first internationals outside the World Cup. Both ventures proved popular with spectators and NatWest, who continue their sponsorship of this tournament in 2001, when England, taking on Pakistan and Australia, face a stiffer test.

Note: Matches in this section were not first-class.

WEST INDIES v ZIMBABWE

At Bristol, July 6 (day/night). Zimbabwe won by six wickets. Toss: West Indies.

The curtain went up on the NatWest Series to reveal a sea of light: some 7,000 spectators watched the first official day/night international in England, initially under afternoon sun, then under evening floodlights. With England themselves held back to attract the weekend crowds, the occasion marked Zimbabwe's first victory over West Indies after losing eight one-day internationals and two Tests. Jamaican left-handers Hinds and Gayle gave West Indies early impetus, built on by Lara and Powell, who blasted 36 from 23 balls, including five fours and a six. But a Zimbabwe attack without three first-choice bowlers worked tirelessly on a slow pitch and, helped by two excellent run-outs, restricted West Indies to a catchable 232. With Ambrose putting his feet up in the Caribbean and Walsh his on the physio's table, the Zimbabwean batsmen eagerly exploited the subsequent vacuum. Johnson was there throughout, his style determined by his partners – aggressive with Goodwin, who hit a run-a-ball 23, restrained with the Flowers – as they cruised home with five overs to spare. Among the varied interval distractions was a game of giant rollerball, similar in concept to the exercise bubble used by hamsters.

Man of the Match: N. C. Johnson.   *Attendance:* 7,405; *receipts* £98,912.

West Indies

A. F. G. Griffith c Brent b Nkala	10	
C. H. Gayle run out	41	
W. W. Hinds c Wishart b G. W. Flower	51	
B. C. Lara c Johnson b G. W. Flower	60	
R. L. Powell c G. W. Flower b Brent	36	
†R. D. Jacobs not out	16	
F. A. Rose lbw b Brent	0	
N. A. M. McLean run out	2	

*J. C. Adams not out	2	
L-b 4, w 7, n-b 3	14	
1/33 (1) 2/101 (2)	(7 wkts, 50 overs) 232	
3/135 (3) 4/191 (5)		
5/222 (4) 6/223 (7)		
7/225 (8)	Score at 15 overs: 50-1	

M. Dillon and R. D. King did not bat.

Bowling: Strang 10–2–32–0; Nkala 8–2–40–1; Johnson 3–0–14–0; Brent 10–1–59–2; Viljoen 10–0–41–0; Whittall 3–0–15–0; G. W. Flower 6–0–27–2.

Zimbabwe

N. C. Johnson not out	95	
C. B. Wishart c Powell b Rose	7	
M. W. Goodwin c Hinds b Rose	23	
A. D. R. Campbell c Jacobs b Dillon	17	
*†A. Flower c Gayle b King	42	

G. W. Flower not out	26	
L-b 6, w 8, n-b 9	23	
1/24 (2) 2/57 (3)	(4 wkts, 45 overs) 233
3/90 (4) 4/160 (5)	Score at 15 overs: 83-2

G. J. Whittall, D. P. Viljoen, M. L. Nkala, B. C. Strang and G. B. Brent did not bat.

Bowling: King 9–0–43–1; Rose 10–0–50–2; McLean 9–0–63–0; Dillon 9–0–35–1; Gayle 8–1–35–0; Adams 0–0–1–0.

Umpires: J. W. Lloyds and P. Willey.

ENGLAND v ZIMBABWE

At The Oval, July 8. Zimbabwe won by five wickets. Toss: England. International debut: M. E. Trescothick.

Any momentum England gained from their heart-stopping defeat of West Indies in the Lord's Test seemed abruptly lost when the fall of the second English wicket sparked an all-too-familiar collapse. It had started so well: on debut, Marcus Trescothick – drafted in because Knight had broken a finger – hit an unflappable 79. Critics carped at a lack of foot movement, but his century partnership with Hick saved England from humiliation. The rest of the team batted with the conviction of rabbits dazzled by headlights, so mesmerised were they by Paul Strang's leg-spin. At one stage, he took three for five, and only a spirited 32 from Ealham helped England past 200. Zimbabwe's reply faltered as Caddick worked up early pace and aggression. But Campbell's return to form, hitting his first fifty for 14 one-day internationals, together with sterling work from the Flowers and errors in the outfield, saw Zimbabwe home with ten balls to spare. Stewart, captain in place of the injured Hussain, had nothing to celebrate other than surpassing Graham Gooch's England record of 125 limited-overs international appearances.

Man of the Match: A. D. R. Campbell.   *Attendance:* 17,182; *receipts* £422,011.

England

M. E. Trescothick c Campbell b P. A. Strang .	79	
*†A. J. Stewart lbw b Johnson	12	
G. A. Hick c G. W. Flower b P. A. Strang .	50	
M. P. Maynard b P. A. Strang	3	
G. P. Thorpe c and b Viljoen	12	
A. Flintoff c Whittall b B. C. Strang . .	2	
M. A. Ealham c Whittall b G. W. Flower.	32	
R. D. B. Croft c Whittall b Viljoen	5	

A. R. Caddick b G. W. Flower	2
D. Gough not out	3
A. D. Mullally c Whittall b G. W. Flower	0
L-b 2, w 5	7

1/30 (2) 2/136 (3) 3/150 (1)   (50 overs) 207
4/150 (4) 5/153 (6)
6/183 (5) 7/191 (8)
8/197 (9) 9/206 (7)
10/207 (11)   Score at 15 overs: 60-1

Bowling: Johnson 8–1–25–1; B. C. Strang 10–1–39–1; Brent 7–0–42–0; Viljoen 10–0–45–2; P. A. Strang 10–0–36–3; Whittall 2–0–9–0; G. W. Flower 3–0–9–3.

Zimbabwe

N. C. Johnson c Maynard b Caddick . . .	0
C. B. Wishart lbw b Caddick	2
M. W. Goodwin lbw b Ealham	11
A. D. R. Campbell lbw b Croft.	80
*†A. Flower b Mullally	61
G. W. Flower not out	33

G. J. Whittall not out	4
B 4, l-b 5, w 4, n-b 6	19

1/0 (1) 2/9 (2)   (5 wkts, 48.2 overs) 210
3/35 (3) 4/158 (4)
5/206 (5)   Score at 15 overs: 42-3

D. P. Viljoen, P. A. Strang, B. C. Strang and G. B. Brent did not bat.

Bowling: Caddick 10–2–27–2; Gough 10–0–47–0; Ealham 10–0–44–1; Mullally 9.2–2–33–1; Croft 5–0–30–1; Flintoff 4–0–20–0.

Umpires: K. E. Palmer and D. R. Shepherd.

ENGLAND v WEST INDIES

At Lord's, July 9. No result. Toss: West Indies.

On a dank morning, England made another miserable stab at run-making against an inexperienced attack. Stewart was taken at slip, Hick at the wicket – and England were caught unawares by the lateral movement generated by McLean and Collymore. Flintoff's troublesome back kept him out, though Trescothick, his former England Under-19 team-mate, provided more evidence of a sound temperament. He remained calm as his more senior partners came and went until, on 49, he gave a soft return catch to an off-break from Gayle. Thorpe, back in international cricket after taking the winter off, made 42 before miscuing Rose; no one else contributed more than 17. Torrential rain intervened in the 44th over with England a shoddy 158 for eight.

Attendance: 25,374; receipts £768,888.

England

M. E. Trescothick c and b Gayle.	49
*†A. J. Stewart c Gayle b McLean	12
G. A. Hick c Jacobs b McLean.	12
M. P. Maynard b Collymore	0
G. P. Thorpe c Dillon b Rose	42
C. White c Jacobs b Rose	10
M. A. Ealham b Gayle	17
R. D. B. Croft not out.	5

A. R. Caddick c Gayle b Rose	0
D. Gough not out	2
L-b 4, w 3, n-b 2	9

1/23 (2) 2/41 (3)   (8 wkts, 43.5 overs) 158
3/47 (4) 4/99 (1)
5/120 (6) 6/148 (5)
7/152 (7) 8/153 (9)   Score at 15 overs: 51-3

A. D. Mullally did not bat.

Bowling: McLean 8–2–25–2; Collymore 10–0–46–1; Rose 9–1–42–3; Gayle 10–1–28–2; Dillon 6.5–3–13–0.

West Indies

S. L. Campbell, C. H. Gayle, W. W. Hinds, B. C. Lara, R. L. Powell, *J. C. Adams, †R. D. Jacobs, F. A. Rose, N. A. M. McLean, M. Dillon and C. D. Collymore.

Umpires: R. Julian and K. E. Palmer.

WEST INDIES v ZIMBABWE

At Canterbury, July 11. Zimbabwe won by 70 runs. Toss: West Indies.

Zimbabwe's third straight win meant that, with more than half the tournament still to play, they had already secured their place in the final. Their resounding success here was due more to West Indian failings than their own performance, though Whittall, whose 83 matched his highest one-day international score, and the blossoming Alistair Campbell found the going easy against some toothless bowling. Whittall was dropped three times, while Jacobs missed a clear chance to stump Campbell. Zimbabwe's keen eye for the quick single – only 50 runs came from boundaries – exposed countless deficiencies in the field. The West Indian batsmen looked no better organised when they set off in pursuit of 257: the first five went for 40, leaving the lower order to salvage some pride. Jacobs made 37 and McLean a 70-ball half-century, but it was much too little much too late.

Man of the Match: G. J. Whittall. *Attendance:* 5,200; *receipts* £83,003.

Zimbabwe

N. C. Johnson run out	51	*†A. Flower not out		7
G. J. Whittall c Hinds b Rose	83	B 2, l-b 7, w 7		16
M. W. Goodwin b Gayle	16			
A. D. R. Campbell not out	77	1/89 (1) 2/118 (3)	(4 wkts, 50 overs)	256
G. W. Flower c Campbell b Rose	6	3/214 (2) 4/229 (5)	Score at 15 overs: 73-0	

S. V. Carlisle, D. P. Viljoen, H. H. Streak, P. A. Strang and B. C. Strang did not bat.

Bowling: McLean 8–0–46–0; Collymore 7–0–40–0; Dillon 10–1–44–0; Rose 10–0–47–2; Gayle 10–0–42–1; Adams 5–0–28–0.

West Indies

C. H. Gayle c Streak b Johnson	6	N. A. M. McLean not out		50
S. L. Campbell c G. W. Flower b Johnson	2	M. Dillon not out		6
W. W. Hinds c and b B. C. Strang	9			
B. C. Lara b Streak	3	L-b 4, w 15		19
*J. C. Adams run out	10	1/7 (2) 2/18 (1)	(8 wkts, 50 overs)	186
R. L. Powell b Viljoen	14	3/23 (3) 4/40 (5)		
†R. D. Jacobs lbw b G. W. Flower	37	5/40 (4) 6/57 (6)		
F. A. Rose lbw b P. A. Strang	30	7/103 (8) 8/157 (7)	Score at 15 overs: 45-5	

C. D. Collymore did not bat.

Bowling: Johnson 6–0–16–2; B. C. Strang 10–2–35–1; Streak 8–0–23–1; Viljoen 9–1–26–1; P. A. Strang 10–0–58–1; G. W. Flower 5–0–18–1; Whittall 2–0–6–0.

Umpires: B. Dudleston and R. Julian.

ENGLAND v ZIMBABWE

At Manchester, July 13 (day/night). England won by eight wickets. Toss: Zimbabwe.

England's victory was as ruthless as their previous defeat had been gutless. And it showed the potential value of net run-rate had clearly sunk in. Andy Flower chose to bat on a lively pitch, only for wickets to fall like autumnal leaves as Zimbabwe were bowled out for 114 in the 39th over. Stewart equalled Adam Gilchrist's record of six one-day dismissals in an innings, while all

England's bowlers finished with something in the bag, even Trescothick, who netted two wickets from ten balls. Zimbabwe's last four batsmen departed at the same score. In theory, this was England's first home game under lights – though with a 7.30 p.m. finish as England won inside 21 overs, they were barely noticeable. Flintoff helped ensure a rapid conclusion, wielding his bat as Thor did his hammer, bludgeoning 42 off 45 balls, the smartest riposte to questions concerning his weight and fitness. He greeted his match award with the comment: "All right for a fat lad." Trescothick added another 29 to his tournament tally, while Stewart's 12 was his third in succession.

Man of the Match: A. Flintoff.   *Attendance:* 11,388; *receipts* £260,434.

Zimbabwe

N. C. Johnson c Stewart b Caddick	7	H. H. Streak not out	0
G. J. Whittall c Stewart b Gough	15	P. A. Strang lbw b Trescothick	0
M. W. Goodwin b Ealham	21	B 1, l-b 4, n-b 8	13
A. D. R. Campbell run out	10		—
*†A. Flower c Stewart b White	28	1/14 (1) 2/38 (2) 3/55 (4) (38.4 overs)	114
B. C. Strang b Mullally	1	4/64 (3) 5/65 (6)	
G. W. Flower c Stewart b Mullally	0	6/65 (7) 7/114 (5)	
S. V. Carlisle c Stewart b Trescothick	19	8/114 (9) 9/114 (8)	
D. P. Viljoen c Stewart b White	0	10/114 (11) Score at 15 overs: 52-2	

Bowling: Caddick 8–2–26–1; Gough 8–1–31–1; Mullally 8–2–13–2; Ealham 10–4–19–1; White 3–0–13–2; Trescothick 1.4–0–7–2.

England

M. E. Trescothick lbw b Streak	29
*†A. J. Stewart lbw b Streak	12
A. Flintoff not out	42
G. A. Hick not out	23
L-b 1, w 3, n-b 5	9

1/28 (2) 2/57 (1)   (2 wkts, 20.3 overs) 115
Score at 15 overs: 66-2

M. P. Maynard, G. P. Thorpe, C. White, M. A. Ealham, A. R. Caddick, D. Gough and A. D. Mullally did not bat.

Bowling: Johnson 3–0–12–0; B. C. Strang 6–1–22–0; Streak 6–0–32–2; Whittall 2–1–15–0; P. A. Strang 2.3–0–28–0; Viljoen 1–0–5–0.

Umpires: J. W. Holder and G. Sharp.

ENGLAND v WEST INDIES

At Chester-le-Street, July 15. England won by ten wickets. Toss: England.

Though England's opening batsmen grabbed the headlines, the bowlers had already tilted the match firmly their way. Mullally, in particular, bowled a miserly line and length, and his three top-order wickets crushed West Indies' spirit; even Lara was sluggish, making 54 from 101 balls and hitting just three fours. England fielded out of their skins, conceded only 65 in the last 17 overs and restricted West Indies to an inadequate 169. When England batted, Trescothick's dream start to his international career showed no sign of abating. More than Stewart even, he dominated an increasingly demoralised attack. His strokeplay was uncomplicated and effective, and together they made serene progress to their modest target. In 313 previous one-day internationals England had never won by ten wickets. Nor had West Indies, in 403 games, lost so heavily.

Man of the Match: M. E. Trescothick.   *Attendance:* 14,825; *receipts* £389,442.

VICTORY BY TEN WICKETS IN ONE-DAY INTERNATIONALS

India (123-0) beat East Africa (120) at Leeds 1975
New Zealand (113-0) beat India (112-9) at Melbourne 1980-81
West Indies (172-0) beat Zimbabwe (171) at Birmingham 1983
India (97-0) beat Sri Lanka (96) at Sharjah 1983-84
West Indies (117-0) beat New Zealand (116) at Port-of-Spain 1984-85
Pakistan (66-0) beat New Zealand (64) at Sharjah 1985-86
West Indies (192-0) beat New Zealand (191-9) at Christchurch 1986-87
West Indies (221-0) beat Pakistan (220-2) at Melbourne 1991-92
West Indies (154-0) beat South Africa (152) at Port-of-Spain 1991-92
West Indies (200-0) beat India (199-7) at Bridgetown 1996-97
India (197-0) beat Zimbabwe (196-9) at Sharjah 1998-99
South Africa (168-0) beat India (164) at Sharjah 1999-2000
England (171-0) beat West Indies (169-8) at Chester-le-Street **2000**

West Indies

S. L. Campbell c White b Mullally	14	N. A. M. McLean not out	3
W. W. Hinds lbw b Gough	1	M. Dillon not out.	0
B. C. Lara c Flintoff b Ealham	54	B 1, l-b 6, n-b 6	13
*J. C. Adams b Mullally	0		
C. H. Gayle c Thorpe b Caddick	26	1/6 (2) 2/41 (1) (8 wkts, 50 overs) 169	
R. L. Powell c Trescothick b Mullally . .	15	3/43 (4) 4/104 (3)	
†R. D. Jacobs c Stewart b White	25	5/104 (5) 6/134 (6)	
F. A. Rose c Flintoff b Gough	18	7/162 (7) 8/168 (8) Score at 15 overs: 42-2	

R. D. King did not bat.

Bowling: Caddick 10–1–30–1; Gough 10–1–38–2; Mullally 10–1–27–3; Ealham 10–2–31–1; Trescothick 2–0–13–0; White 8–1–23–1.

England

M. E. Trescothick not out 87
*†A. J. Stewart not out 74
      L-b 4, w 1, n-b 5 10

          (no wkt, 35.2 overs) 171
          Score at 15 overs: 64-0

A. Flintoff, G. A. Hick, M. P. Maynard, G. P. Thorpe, C. White, M. A. Ealham, A. R. Caddick, D. Gough and A. D. Mullally did not bat.

Bowling: King 6–0–30–0; McLean 6–1–22–0; Dillon 6–0–24–0; Rose 5–0–31–0; Gayle 8–0–34–0; Adams 4–0–20–0; Powell 0.2–0–6–0.

Umpires: J. H. Hampshire and G. Sharp.

WEST INDIES v ZIMBABWE

At Chester-le-Street, July 16. Zimbabwe won by six wickets. Toss: West Indies.

A beauty of a pitch – even-paced yet offering encouragement to the bowlers – helped create the most exciting game of the tournament thus far. Sherwin Campbell made a stylish century, while Lara was his familiar pugnacious self, hitting three sixes and six fours in a 76-ball 87. West Indies must have believed 287, comfortably the highest total of the competition to date, would bring their first victory, but Zimbabwe were not going to keel over without a struggle. Grant

Flower and Goodwin came together in the 23rd over at a precarious 104 for four, and just kept going, disturbing the bowlers' rhythm with finely crafted and powerful strokeplay. Ten overs out, they needed 90; with five left, it was 47. Aided by lavish helpings of no-balls and wides, they got home at the beginning of the last over. Goodwin made a magnificent 112 from 139 balls with seven fours, Flower a strongarm 96 from 86 (eight fours and a six). It was Zimbabwe's highest score batting second, and ruled West Indies out of the final.

Man of the Match: M. W. Goodwin.   *Attendance:* 5,006; *receipts* £73,772.

West Indies

S. L. Campbell c Campbell b Viljoen . . . 105		M. V. Nagamootoo not out		2
W. W. Hinds c Carlisle b Viljoen 42		B 2, l-b 8, w 14, n-b 5		29
B. C. Lara b Viljoen 87				—
R. L. Powell run out 12		1/86 (2) 2/259 (3) (5 wkts, 50 overs) 287		
C. H. Gayle c Campbell b Streak 3		3/260 (1) 4/265 (5)		
†R. D. Jacobs not out 7		5/284 (4) Score at 15 overs: 60-0		

*J. C. Adams, N. A. M. McLean, M. Dillon and R. D. King did not bat.

Bowling: Strang 10–1–50–0; Rennie 10–1–48–0; Streak 10–0–47–1; Viljoen 10–0–75–3; Whittall 6–0–33–0; G. W. Flower 3–0–16–0; Campbell 1–0–8–0.

Zimbabwe

N. C. Johnson c Jacobs b Dillon 4		G. W. Flower not out 96		
G. J. Whittall c Powell b Dillon 23		L-b 12, w 14, n-b 6 32		
M. W. Goodwin not out 112				—
A. D. R. Campbell run out 12		1/18 (1) 2/55 (2) (4 wkts, 49.1 overs) 290		
*†A. Flower run out 11		3/79 (4) 4/104 (5) Score at 15 overs: 65-2		

S. V. Carlisle, D. P. Viljoen, H. H. Streak, J. A. Rennie and B. C. Strang did not bat.

Bowling: King 9.1–1–42–0; Dillon 10–1–52–2; McLean 10–0–63–0; Nagamootoo 9–0–49–0; Gayle 4–0–27–0; Adams 7–0–45–0.

Umpires: J. H. Hampshire and J. W. Holder.

ENGLAND v ZIMBABWE

At Birmingham, July 18 (day/night). England won by 52 runs. Toss: England.

With Hussain deemed fit for action, Stewart stepped aside as captain, though not out of the limelight. As in their last game, England put on a confident, energetic and organised show. And there was none more organised, confident or energetic than Stewart who, at 37, remained as youthful as a butcher's pup. He stayed until four overs from the end for a 144-ball 101, scampering enthusiastically between the wickets. Hussain, whose form had faded before injuring his finger, was one of several to provide support, and England set a target of 263. Zimbabwe began purposefully and had reached 87 for one when Hick struck twice in successive balls in the 23rd over, which also saw Goodwin run out. That was it, really. Campbell aside, none of the middle order managed double figures under lighting rightly criticised as inadequate. A late dart from Streak, 45 from 52 balls, merely limited the margin of defeat; England could look ahead to Lord's with the psychological advantage. Johnson's announcement that he was leaving Zimbabwe for South Africa added to the tourists' gloom.

Man of the Match: A. J. Stewart.   *Attendance:* 12,927; *receipts* £315,671.

[*Patrick Eagar*

Stepping up to international cricket held no fear for England newcomer Marcus Trescothick. Only his opening partner, Alec Stewart, scored more runs in the NatWest Series.

England

M. E. Trescothick b Streak	20	A. R. Caddick b Streak	1
†A. J. Stewart b Viljoen	101	D. Gough not out	2
A. Flintoff c A. Flower b Johnson	24	L-b 5, w 11, n-b 1	17
G. A. Hick lbw b Johnson	0		
G. P. Thorpe b G. W. Flower	33	1/41 (1) 2/85 (3) (8 wkts, 50 overs)	262
*N. Hussain c Viljoen b Whittall	34	3/85 (4) 4/166 (5)	
C. White c Johnson b Streak	21	5/218 (2) 6/246 (7)	
M. A. Ealham not out	9	7/251 (6) 8/259 (9) Score at 15 overs: 82-1	

A. D. Mullally did not bat.

Bowling: Streak 10–0–59–3; Johnson 7–0–37–2; Mbangwa 10–0–43–0; Viljoen 7–0–27–1; Strang 4–0–20–0; Whittall 7–0–31–1; G. W. Flower 5–0–40–1.

Zimbabwe

N. C. Johnson c Stewart b Hick	52	P. A. Strang not out	7
G. J. Whittall c White b Caddick	3	M. Mbangwa not out	5
A. D. R. Campbell c Hussain b White	60	B 1, l-b 5, w 4, n-b 6	16
S. V. Carlisle c Stewart b Hick	0		
M. W. Goodwin run out	3	1/25 (2) 2/87 (1) (9 wkts, 50 overs)	210
G. W. Flower run out	9	3/87 (4) 4/90 (5)	
*†A. Flower c Stewart b White	4	5/110 (6) 6/123 (7)	
D. P. Viljoen c Stewart b White	6	7/133 (8) 8/172 (3)	
H. H. Streak c Flintoff b Gough	45	9/203 (9) Score at 15 overs: 48-1	

Bowling: Caddick 8–3–22–1; Gough 8–1–43–1; Mullally 9–1–37–0; Hick 7–0–37–2; Ealham 10–1–31–0; White 8–0–34–3.

Umpires: D. J. Constant and M. J. Kitchen.

ENGLAND v WEST INDIES

At Nottingham, July 20. West Indies won by three runs. Toss: England. International debut: P. J. Franks.

The finalists long since decided, England rested Caddick and gave a cap to 21-year-old Paul Franks on his home ground. It was hardly an ideal debut: his wayward nine overs went wicketless and he was run out for four by Stewart in the last over of the game. That last over – England began it needing five runs with three wickets remaining – brought out familiar failings of hesitancy and lack of confidence as Gayle's off-spin picked off the last two wickets. For once, it happened in a meaningless match. Not that the West Indians stinted on celebrating their sole tournament

CARRYING BAT THROUGH ONE-DAY INTERNATIONAL INNINGS

G. W. Flower . .	84*	Zimbabwe (205, 49.3 overs) v England at Sydney	1994-95
Saeed Anwar . .	103*	Pakistan (219, 49.5 overs) v Zimbabwe at Harare	1994-95
N. V. Knight. . .	125*	England (246, 50 overs) v Pakistan at Nottingham	1996
R. D. Jacobs. . .	49*	West Indies (110, 46.4 overs) v Australia at Manchester .	1999
D. R. Martyn . .	116*	Australia (191, 46.2 overs) v New Zealand at Auckland. .	1999-2000
H. H. Gibbs . . .	59*	South Africa (101†, 26.5 overs) v Pakistan at Sharjah . . .	1999-2000
A. J. Stewart . .	**100***	**England (192, 49.5 overs) v West Indies at Nottingham**	**2000**

† *One man retired hurt. In 1994-95, Zimbabwe beat England and Pakistan tied with Zimbabwe; in all other cases, the batsman was on the losing side.*

victory. Stewart's contribution had been immense: he hit his second hundred in three days and carried his bat. No one else passed 37. Without Lara, nursing a hamstring injury, West Indies were underdogs and, at 139 for seven, in a muddle until a brisk 29 from Rose took them to 195. At 46 without loss, England had been coasting, but three wickets in nine balls from King wreaked significant damage.

Man of the Match: C. H. Gayle.   *Attendance:* 13,592; *receipts* £348,874.

West Indies

S. L. Campbell b Gough	12	
C. H. Gayle c White b Ealham	37	
W. W. Hinds c Hussain b Ealham	10	
*J. C. Adams b Mullally	36	
R. R. Sarwan b White	20	
R. L. Powell b White	1	
†R. D. Jacobs run out	5	
M. V. Nagamootoo c Ealham b Gough . .	11	
F. A. Rose c Franks b White	29	

M. Dillon not out	14
R. D. King not out	1
B 2, l-b 4, w 5, n-b 8	19

1/34 (1) 2/63 (3)   (9 wkts, 50 overs) 195
3/70 (2) 4/101 (5)
5/107 (6) 6/132 (7)
7/139 (4) 8/170 (8)
9/189 (9)   Score at 15 overs: 46-1

Bowling: Franks 9–0–48–0; Gough 10–0–34–2; Mullally 10–0–29–1; Ealham 10–0–37–2; White 10–0–35–3; Hick 1–0–6–0.

England

M. E. Trescothick c Jacobs b King	23	D. Gough b Gayle		0
†A. J. Stewart not out	100	A. D. Mullally lbw b Gayle		0
A. Flintoff c Jacobs b King	2	L-b 6, w 7, n-b 7		20
G. A. Hick b King	0			
G. P. Thorpe run out	5	1/46 (1) 2/49 (3) 3/49 (4)	(49.5 overs)	192
*N. Hussain c Jacobs b Nagamootoo	3	4/56 (5) 5/75 (6)		
C. White run out	19	6/138 (7) 7/170 (8)		
M. A. Ealham c Gayle b Rose	16	8/191 (9) 9/192 (10)		
P. J. Franks run out	4	10/192 (11)	Score at 15 overs: 52-3	

Bowling: King 10–1–30–3; Dillon 10–1–52–0; Rose 10–0–31–1; Nagamootoo 10–1–41–1; Gayle 6.5–0–21–2; Adams 3–0–11–0.

Umpires: M. J. Kitchen and B. Leadbeater.

QUALIFYING TABLE

	Played	Won	Lost	No result	Points	Net run-rate
Zimbabwe	6	4	2	0	8	−0.27
England	6	3	2	1	7	0.98
West Indies	6	1	4	1	3	−0.70

Net run-rate is calculated by subtracting runs conceded per over from runs scored per over.

FINAL

ENGLAND v ZIMBABWE

At Lord's, July 22. England beat Zimbabwe by six wickets. Toss: England.

Caddick, Gough and Mullally exploited the cloudy conditions to make early dents in the Zimbabwe innings: after 15 overs they were 31 for four. Although a stand of 89 from the Flower brothers kept Zimbabwean hopes alive, outstanding fielding, combined with Gough's intelligently varied attack, restricted them to an unprepossessing 169. Yet had Stewart not been enjoying the purplest of patches, there might have been a tense conclusion, for England stuttered in the opening overs. Trescothick experienced his first failure in his seventh international innings and, with Flintoff departing four balls later, there was palpable optimism in Zimbabwe's camp. However, Stewart and Hick put on 134 in 34 overs, both producing some dreamy shots in the summer sun, and Stewart was three short of becoming the first Englishman to hit three successive one-day international hundreds when he flashed impulsively at Streak. He faced 123 balls and hit 14 fours. By then, though, the job was all but done, and soon afterwards England had won their first one-day trophy for two and a half years.

Man of the Match: A. J. Stewart.   *Attendance:* 25,038; *receipts* £750,814.
Man of the Series: A. J. Stewart.

Zimbabwe

N. C. Johnson b Caddick	21	B. C. Strang not out		0
G. J. Whittall c Hick b Gough	0			
M. W. Goodwin b Gough	3	B 1, l-b 6, w 2, n-b 2		11
A. D. R. Campbell c White b Mullally	1			
*†A. Flower b Stewart b White	48	1/4 (2) 2/12 (3)	(7 wkts, 50 overs)	169
G. W. Flower not out	53	3/21 (4) 4/31 (1)		
S. V. Carlisle c Caddick b White	14	5/120 (5) 6/143 (7)		
H. H. Streak lbw b Gough	18	7/169 (8)	Score at 15 overs: 31-4	

D. P. Viljoen and M. L. Nkala did not bat.

Bowling: Caddick 10–2–23–1; Gough 10–2–20–3; Mullally 10–1–32–1; White 10–2–46–2; Ealham 10–0–41–0.

[*Patrick Eagar*

Coming together at 31 for four in the final, Andy and Grant Flower added 89 to save Zimbabwean blushes, though not the match: Graeme Hick, here unable to prevent a run, had the last laugh.

England

M. E. Trescothick c Campbell b Streak	1	*N. Hussain not out		9
†A. J. Stewart c A. Flower b Streak	97	L-b 5, w 5, n-b 2		12
A. Flintoff b Streak	0			
G. A. Hick c and b Viljoen	41	1/9 (1) 2/9 (3)	(4 wkts, 45.2 overs)	170
G. P. Thorpe not out	10	3/143 (2) 4/149 (4)	Score at 15 overs 48-2	

C. White, M. A. Ealham, A. R. Caddick, D. Gough and A. D. Mullally did not bat.

Bowling: Streak 10–3–30–3; Nkala 5–0–30–0; Strang 10–3–26–0; Johnson 6–0–22–0; Viljoen 10–0–35–1; Whittall 4–0–20–0; Campbell 0.2–0–2–0.

Umpires: D. R. Shepherd and P. Willey.   Series referee: R. S. Madugalle (Sri Lanka).

NEW ZEALAND A IN ENGLAND, 2000

The importance New Zealand placed on their first A tour overseas could be gauged from the decision to send the senior side's manager and coach, Jeff Crowe and Dave Trist, with the team. Add the presence of Sir Richard Hadlee, the recently appointed chairman of selectors, and the message to the players was clear: this was a tour for potential to be converted into performance.

Given their small cadre of first-class cricketers capable of making the transition from provincial to international cricket, New Zealand viewed the tour as a means of exploring options – both for Test cricket and one-day internationals. For example, after the two warm-up games against Holland, left-handed opener Mark Richardson played in only the first-class matches by way of grooming him for Test cricket; captain Scott Styris, already a New Zealand one-day player, batted higher up the order so his value would be as a batsman who bowled rather than the other way round. In fact, the tour had been planned, with help from the ECB, to provide a judicious mix of first-class and one-day games. It was, in Trist's words, "a learning tour". He wasn't primarily concerned with the results; he was looking for good points that could be worked on if the players were to take their opportunities to develop in the coming years.

Just how much they learned, and in particular how they had learned to think about their cricket, was seen in the final game, against an MCC team led by former England captain Graham Gooch. Having grown accustomed to letting the ball do the work on damp, seaming pitches, their bowlers suddenly found themselves shown scant courtesy on a dry Oxford pitch offering little lateral movement. The batsmen, after a steady diet of playing low and forward to English seam bowling, found themselves under fire from Australian and South African bowlers who banged the ball in short and gave no quarter. Second time round, the New Zealand bowlers bent their backs while the batsmen straightened theirs, stood taller and played later. Defeat by three runs, chasing a target of 331, cost them their unbeaten record in first-class games but left them better cricketers.

Two of the team, wicket-keeper Martyn Croy and leg-spinner Brooke Walker, had toured England with the senior team in 1999, while opening bowler Daryl Tuffey had played one Test against Australia in the recent home series. Before the year was out, fellow-tourists Richardson and seam-bowler Chris Martin would be playing Test cricket in South Africa with Tuffey and Walker.

By heading New Zealand's averages against South Africa in November and December, Richardson confirmed the impression he made in England in June and July as a cricketer possessing concentration and an appetite for batting. At 29 he was the oldest member of the tour party, and had made his first-class debut ten years earlier as a left-arm spinner and tailender. Glen Sulzberger, also left-handed, Jarrod Englefield and Styris all progressed as batsmen, but it was Sulzberger's advance as an off-spinner, allied to his slip fielding, that really marked his tour. He was easily the leading wicket-taker in the first-class games with 28 at 16.35. Bruce Martin, a slow left-armer who had taken 37 wickets at 17.72 in 1999-2000, his debut season, and who was in the New Zealand squad for the last Test against Australia, showed he still had a lot to learn. His ten first-class wickets on tour cost more than 37 each.

If there was one area of concern, it was in the opening bowling. With injuries putting question marks over the careers of Geoff Allott, Chris Cairns, Simon Doull and Dion Nash, New Zealand desperately needed to find alternative pace men. Tuffey came on; others failed to make an impact, although at the end of the tour left-armer Lance Hamilton struck rich form with 14 wickets against Hampshire and MCC. When, several months later, another fast bowler was needed to strengthen the senior team in South Africa, Chris Martin was the one to whom the selectors successfully turned.

NEW ZEALAND A TOURING PARTY

S. B. Styris (Northern Districts) (*captain*), T. K. Canning (Auckland), M. G. Croy (Otago), J. I. Englefield (Canterbury), L. J. Hamilton (Central Districts), J. A. H. Marshall (Northern Districts), B. P. Martin (Northern Districts), C. S. Martin (Canterbury), J. D. P. Oram (Central Districts), M. H. W. Papps (Canterbury), A. J. Redmond (Canterbury), M. H. Richardson (Otago), G. P. Sulzberger (Central Districts), D. R. Tuffey (Northern Districts), B. G. K. Walker (Auckland).

M. J. Mason (Central Districts) and C. J. Nevin (Wellington) were originally selected but withdrew and were replaced by Hamilton and Croy.

Manager: J. J. Crowe.　　　*Coach:* D. G. Trist.

NEW ZEALAND A TOUR RESULTS

First-class matches – Played 6: Won 2, Lost 1, Drawn 3.
Wins – Sussex, Hampshire.
Loss – MCC.
Draws – Lancashire, West Indians, First-Class Counties Select XI.
Non-first-class matches – Played 8: Won 5, Lost 2, No result 1. Abandoned 1. *Wins* – Holland (2), British Universities, Worcestershire, Gloucestershire. *Losses* – Leicestershire, Surrey. *No result* – Zimbabweans. *Abandoned* – West Indians.

NEW ZEALAND A TOUR AVERAGES – FIRST-CLASS MATCHES

BATTING

	M	I	NO	R	HS	100s	50s	Avge	Ct/St
M. H. Richardson	6	11	2	642	212*	0	4	71.33	1
S. B. Styris	5	9	1	247	72	0	1	30.87	4
A. J. Redmond	3	5	0	142	92	0	1	28.40	4
M. H. W. Papps	5	10	2	220	63	0	1	27.50	2/1
J. I. Englefield	6	11	1	248	90	0	1	24.80	3
G. P. Sulzberger	6	11	0	248	60	0	1	22.54	8
D. R. Tuffey	4	6	2	90	51	0	1	22.50	1
M. G. Croy	5	8	3	88	28	0	0	17.60	14/3
J. A. H. Marshall	5	9	0	133	69	0	1	14.77	11
B. P. Martin	4	4	0	55	29	0	0	13.75	2
J. D. P. Oram	4	7	0	93	27	0	0	13.28	1
B. G. K. Walker	4	5	1	48	22*	0	0	12.00	1
L. J. Hamilton	3	4	2	8	4	0	0	4.00	2
C. S. Martin	4	4	1	8	6*	0	0	2.66	2

Played in two matches: T. K. Canning 0, 3, 2 (1 ct).

* Signifies not out.

BOWLING

	O	M	R	W	BB	5W/i	Avge
G. P. Sulzberger	189.3	61	458	28	5-55	1	16.35
L. J. Hamilton	94	22	287	14	5-55	1	20.50
D. R. Tuffey	116	23	373	16	5-74	1	23.31
S. B. Styris	115.4	27	325	12	3-45	0	27.08
B. G. K. Walker	97.2	34	222	8	4-32	0	27.75
B. P. Martin	133	35	378	10	3-43	0	37.80
C. S. Martin	118	38	321	5	2-28	0	64.20

Also bowled: T. K. Canning 31–6–102–3; J. D. P. Oram 52–12–123–2; A. J. Redmond 7–1–32–0.

Note: Matches in this section which were not first-class are signified by a dagger.

†At Amstelveen, June 7. New Zealand A won by 108 runs. Toss: Holland. New Zealand A 216 (48 overs) (J. A. H. Marshall 35, G. P. Sulzberger 33, A. J. Redmond 32, S. B. Styris 44; T. B. M. de Leede four for 46, R. Singh three for 36); Holland 108 (41.1 overs) (B. G. K. Walker three for two).

Walker's complete figures were 5–3–2–3.

†At Amstelveen, June 8. New Zealand A won by 112 runs. Toss: Holland. New Zealand A 233 for five (50 overs) (G. P. Sulzberger 80, S. B. Styris 34, M. G. Croy 41 not out); Holland 121 (44.2 overs) (B. G. K. Walker three for 15, B. P. Martin four for 40).

†At Oxford, June 11. New Zealand A won by 85 runs. Toss: British Universities. New Zealand A 249 for six (50 overs) (J. A. H. Marshall 37, J. I. Englefield 35, S. B. Styris 46, M. H. W. Papps 31, T. K. Canning 46 not out); British Universities 164 (46.5 overs) (J. P. Pyemont 62; B. P. Martin three for 30, B. G. K. Walker four for 31).

LANCASHIRE v NEW ZEALAND A

At Liverpool, June 13, 14, 15, 16. Drawn. Toss: Lancashire.

New Zealand A opened their first-class account with a damp draw. Lancashire captain Crawley, out of form of late, used the first day profitably to make his second hundred of the season. His first had come two months earlier, against Cambridge University, and in between he had eked out just 91 runs in six Championship innings. Now he batted for five hours and hit 20 fours and a six in a fine 156. When four sessions were stolen by the weather on the second and third days, Lancashire declared. Confident batting by Richardson and Sulzberger helped the New Zealanders to 154 for three by the close, but ten wickets on the final morning turned the game on its head. As Smethurst claimed five wickets to finish with a career-best seven for 37, the tourists lost seven for 40 in 16.2 overs; Lancashire, not imposing the follow-on, then lurched to three for three. Lunch disposed of such madness. Crawley's second declaration left the New Zealanders with two and a half hours' batting, and stumps were drawn soon after Richardson completed a measured fifty.

Close of play: First day, Lancashire 352-5 (Scuderi 12*, Haynes 7*); Second day, No play; Third day, New Zealand A 154-3 (Sulzberger 60*, Englefield 8*).

Lancashire

M. J. Chilton b Styris	16	– (2) c Canning b Tuffey	0
*J. P. Crawley st Croy b Walker	156		
P. C. McKeown lbw b Styris	33	– (1) c Croy b Canning	2
S. C. Ganguly c Sulzberger b Tuffey	21	– c Styris b Sulzberger	6
G. D. Lloyd c Marshall b Tuffey	83	– (8) not out	37
J. C. Scuderi not out	12	– (3) c Croy b Tuffey	0
†J. J. Haynes not out	7	– (6) not out	27
C. P. Schofield (did not bat)		– (5) c Marshall b Tuffey	26
R. J. Green (did not bat)		– (7) c Englefield b Canning	0
B 16, l-b 5, w 1, n-b 2	24	W 1, n-b 2	3

1/58 2/126 3/180 4/303 5/333   (5 wkts dec.) 352   1/1 2/2 3/2   (6 wkts dec.) 101
                                                            4/30 5/42 6/45

G. Keedy and M. P. Smethurst did not bat.

Bowling: *First Innings*—Tuffey 18–5–41–2; Canning 16–4–54–0; Styris 22–8–59–2; Martin 20–5–73–0; Sulzberger 14–2–44–0; Walker 18–3–60–1. *Second Innings*—Tuffey 11–2–41–3; Canning 7–1–19–2; Sulzberger 1–0–6–1; Martin 3–0–16–0; Styris 3–1–8–0; Walker 3–1–11–0.

New Zealand A

J. A. H. Marshall lbw b Smethurst	0	– c McKeown b Smethurst 0
M. H. Richardson b Schofield	47	– not out 57
M. H. W. Papps c Chilton b Smethurst	18	– b Scuderi 5
G. P. Sulzberger c Lloyd b Smethurst	60	– c Green b Schofield 29
J. I. Englefield c and b Keedy	10	– not out 15
*S. B. Styris b Smethurst	13	
†M. G. Croy c Green b Smethurst.	13	
T. K. Canning b Smethurst.	0	
B. G. K. Walker c Haynes b Smethurst	4	
D. R. Tuffey not out	4	
B. P. Martin c Lloyd b Schofield.	2	
L-b 8, w 1, n-b 14	23	L-b 2, n-b 6 8

1/0 2/39 3/127 4/156 5/168   194   1/0 2/26 3/77   (3 wkts) 114
6/172 7/172 8/188 9/191

Bowling: *First Innings*—Smethurst 16–6–37–7; Green 11–2–42–0; Scuderi 4–0–17–0; Schofield 22.2–8–41–2; Keedy 22–6–47–1; Chilton 2–1–2–0. *Second Innings*—Smethurst 6–3–10–1; Green 3–0–13–0; Keedy 11–4–8–0; Scuderi 5–1–17–1; Schofield 10–0–49–1; Chilton 2–0–15–0.

Umpires: N. L. Bainton and J. F. Steele.

†At Leicester, June 18. Leicestershire won by five wickets. Toss: New Zealand A. New Zealand A 152 (43.4 overs) (J. A. H. Marshall 31, G. P. Sulzberger 44; D. Williamson three for 27); Leicestershire 153 for five (45 overs) (D. L. Maddy 37, B. F. Smith 65 not out).

†At The Oval, June 19. Surrey won by 24 runs. Toss: Surrey. Surrey 249 for eight (50 overs) (M. A. Butcher 89, I. J. Ward 53); New Zealand A 225 for nine (50 overs) (J. A. H. Marshall 78; I. D. K. Salisbury four for 17).

At Chelmsford, June 21, 22, 23, 24. NEW ZEALAND A drew with WEST INDIANS (See West Indian tour section).

†At Worcester, June 26. New Zealand A won by four wickets. Toss: New Zealand A. Worcestershire 194 for nine (50 overs) (S. J. Rhodes 39, D. J. Pipe 56; D. R. Tuffey five for 21); New Zealand A 196 for six (47.3 overs) (J. I. Englefield 72, M. G. Croy 49 not out, Extras 38).
Worcestershire recovered from 17 for four (all to Tuffey), while New Zealand A lost their first three batsmen for ducks.

SUSSEX v NEW ZEALAND A

At Hove, June 28, 29, 30, July 1. New Zealand A won by an innings and 57 runs. Toss: New Zealand A. First-class debut: M. H. Yardy.

Captaining Sussex for the first time, Lewry lost the toss and condemned his side to five sessions in the field while the New Zealanders built an impregnable position on a flat pitch. Richardson's formidable concentration – he batted 669 minutes, faced 561 balls and hit 22 fours in his maiden double-century – came as no surprise to Sussex Second Eleven coach Keith Greenfield, who had spotted the left-hander's potential when he played two seasons with Brighton and Hove in the

Sussex League in the early 1990s. Englefield and Redmond, son of one-time Test batsman Rodney, missed out on maiden hundreds after sharing major century partnerships with Richardson. Sussex in reply began well, but it was a different story when the ball began to turn on the third day. Their batting failed miserably against a medley of off-breaks, leg-spin and slow left-arm from Sulzberger, Walker and Bruce Martin respectively. Sulzberger had match figures of nine for 111 and every Sussex wicket bar the second-last fell to spin. Montgomerie, top-scorer in both innings, resisted for more than six hours in the second until he was last out for 89.

Close of play: First day, New Zealand A 238-2 (Richardson 110*, Sulzberger 19*); Second day, Sussex 51-0 (Montgomerie 28*, Peirce 13*); Third day, Sussex 81-3 (Montgomerie 37*, Humphries 0*).

New Zealand A

J. A. H. Marshall lbw b Lewry	7	†M. G. Croy not out	3
M. H. Richardson not out	212		
J. I. Englefield lbw b Martin-Jenkins	90	B 13, l-b 9, n-b 8	30
G. P. Sulzberger c Martin-Jenkins b Bates	30		
*J. D. P. Oram c Humphries b Bates	27	1/22 2/198 3/267 (5 wkts dec.) 491	
A. J. Redmond b Lewry	92	4/298 5/476	

B. G. K. Walker, B. P. Martin, L. J. Hamilton and C. S. Martin did not bat.

Bowling: Lewry 30–15–62–2; Martin-Jenkins 25–4–67–1; Yardy 24–7–67–0; Bates 47–21–120–2; Rashid 46–11–102–0; House 16–5–42–0; Khan 3–0–9–0.

Sussex

R. R. Montgomerie c Sulzberger b B. P. Martin	41	– c Marshall b Walker	89
M. T. E. Peirce c Croy b Sulzberger	34	– b Walker	11
W. G. Khan c Marshall b Walker	38	– lbw b Sulzberger	20
J. R. Carpenter b Sulzberger	0	– c Hamilton b Sulzberger	8
W. J. House c Croy b B. P. Martin	15	– (6) lbw b B. P. Martin	7
R. S. C. Martin-Jenkins c Redmond b Walker	14	– (7) c Redmond b Sulzberger	20
U. B. A. Rashid c Oram b Sulzberger	6	– (8) lbw b Walker	19
M. H. Yardy b B. P. Martin	25	– (9) b Walker	0
J. J. Bates c Marshall b Sulzberger	12	– (10) b C. S. Martin	9
†S. Humphries not out	14	– (5) c Marshall b Sulzberger	5
*J. D. Lewry c Marshall b Sulzberger	0	– not out	0
B 5, l-b 5, n-b 20	30	B 1, l-b 2, n-b 14	17

1/86 2/86 3/86 4/113 5/161   229   1/24 2/65 3/81 4/105 5/124   205
6/178 7/178 8/215 9/215   6/153 7/176 8/176 9/205

Bowling: *First Innings*—C. S. Martin 13–5–30–0; Hamilton 12–4–27–0; Walker 22–9–46–2; B. P. Martin 26–10–43–3; Sulzberger 26–9–55–5; Redmond 5–1–18–0. *Second Innings*—C. S. Martin 18–6–33–1; Hamilton 8–1–23–0; Walker 26.2–13–32–4; Sulzberger 38–15–56–4; B. P. Martin 21–4–58–1.

Umpires: M. J. Harris and N. J. Llong.

At Bristol, July 3 (day/night). NEW ZEALAND A v ZIMBABWEANS. No result (See Zimbabwean tour section).

At Bristol, July 4 (day/night). NEW ZEALAND A v WEST INDIANS. No result (abandoned).

FIRST-CLASS COUNTIES SELECT XI v NEW ZEALAND A

At Milton Keynes, July 7, 8, 9, 10. Drawn. Toss: First-Class Counties Select XI. First-class debut: R. H. Joseph.

More rain on the last afternoon saved the New Zealanders from probable defeat, though there was still enough movement and uneven bounce in the pitch to make 102 a stiff target for the Select XI. The side comprised Gloucestershire and Kent players as the other counties were involved in Championship games. There was moisture beneath the surface when Nixon inserted the tourists, and Cawdron took full advantage to claim a career-best six for 25. Another four in the second innings brought his first ten-wicket return. Robert Joseph, a brisk 18-year-old seam bowler qualified for both England and West Indies and at school in Kent, captured his maiden first-class wicket. Among the New Zealanders, only Papps displayed the technique and judgment to counter the seaming conditions. Batting was less of a struggle on the second day, and the Select XI established a 97-run lead. The tourists looked to be well beaten when, on the shower-beset third day, they lost their eighth wicket with the scores level. But Tuffey, first with Croy (who batted with a runner after being injured in the first innings) and then Martin, put on 101 for the last two wickets.

Close of play: First day, First-Class Counties Select XI 96-4 (Walker 30*); Second day, New Zealand A 44-2 (Richardson 21*, Walker 3*); Third day, New Zealand A 198.

New Zealand A

M. H. W. Papps lbw b Cawdron	63	– lbw b Cawdron	13
M. H. Richardson run out	1	– lbw b Walker	29
J. I. Englefield b Cawdron	8	– b Cawdron	0
*S. B. Styris lbw b Cawdron	0	– (5) b Lewis	1
G. P. Sulzberger c Nixon b Patel	11	– (6) b Cawdron	17
J. D. P. Oram b Joseph	7	– (7) c Lewis b Patel	20
T. K. Canning lbw b Cawdron	3	– (8) c Nixon b Cawdron	2
†M. G. Croy b Cawdron	1	– (9) c Taylor b Patel	28
B. G. K. Walker c Windows b Walker	7	– (4) lbw b Lewis	3
D. R. Tuffey not out	13	– c Nixon b Lewis	51
C. S. Martin lbw b Cawdron	0	– not out	6
B 9, l-b 6, w 1, n-b 2	18	B 5, l-b 10, w 1, n-b 12	28
	132		**198**

1/7 2/33 3/33 4/54 5/72
6/80 7/88 8/113 9/126

1/40 2/40 3/50 4/52 5/54
6/87 7/91 8/97 9/156

Bowling: First Innings—Lewis 13–6–18–0; Joseph 12–6–23–1; Cawdron 19.4–8–25–6; Patel 21–6–37–1; Snape 5–3–11–0; Walker 3–1–3–1. *Second Innings*—Lewis 23.3–11–41–3; Joseph 13–2–33–0; Cawdron 21–7–49–4; Patel 12–3–34–2; Walker 9–3–18–1; Snape 2–1–8–0.

First-Class Counties Select XI

R. J. Cunliffe c Croy b Oram	28		
R. W. T. Key b Tuffey	0	– lbw b Styris	22
M. G. N. Windows c Croy b Tuffey	1	– (1) lbw b Styris	13
M. J. Walker c Sulzberger b Martin	45	– (3) not out	1
C. G. Taylor lbw b Sulzberger	16	– (4) not out	0
*†P. A. Nixon c Styris b Canning	11		
J. N. Snape c Richardson b Sulzberger	38		
M. J. Cawdron lbw b Walker	32		
M. M. Patel c Englefield b Sulzberger	11		
J. H. Lewis b Martin	9		
R. H. Joseph not out	0		
B 12, l-b 6, n-b 20	38	N-b 4	4
	229	(2 wkts)	**40**

1/20 2/24 3/59 4/96 5/126
6/127 7/176 8/202 9/227

1/39 2/40

Bowling: First Innings—Martin 19–8–28–2; Tuffey 17–3–58–2; Styris 12–0–31–0; Canning 8–1–29–1; Oram 8–0–38–1; Walker 11–4–15–1; Sulzberger 5.4–2–12–3. *Second Innings*—Martin 3–0–23–0; Tuffey 5.1–2–9–0; Styris 3–1–8–2.

Umpires: N. L. Bainton and K. Shuttleworth.

HAMPSHIRE v NEW ZEALAND A

At Portsmouth, July 12, 13, 14, 15. New Zealand A won by two wickets. Toss: New Zealand A. First-class debuts: I. Brunnschweiler, C. T. Tremlett.

New Zealand's young tourists hardly proved a profitable draw. There were 52 paying customers on the first day, 33 on the second, while on the third thieves stole £70 from a turnstile. To counter both problems, no charge was made for entry on the fourth, and a small crowd witnessed an exciting finish. New Zealand A successfully chased 337 – the second-highest fourth-innings total to win in 118 years of first-class cricket at the United Services Ground. Moisture in the wicket caused low scoring in the first two innings, but careful batting from Kendall and Udal in a century stand effected Hampshire's second-innings recovery from 98 for six and ensured the challenging target. Marshall and Richardson began the chase with 141, and New Zealand A reached 301 for five before wobbling. Papps, again compact against the moving ball, and Hamilton kept their nerve, however, and Hampshire were left to rue seven dropped catches. Chris Tremlett, 18-year-old son of club coach Tim and grandson of England all-rounder Maurice, made an auspicious debut, taking four for 16 including the in-form Richardson with his first ball in first-class cricket.

Close of play: First day, New Zealand A 87-3 (Marshall 39*, Oram 8*); Second day, Hampshire 189-6 (Kendall 88*, Udal 35*); Third day, New Zealand A 193-2 (Englefield 28*, B. P. Martin 1*).

Hampshire

G. W. White lbw b Hamilton	14	– lbw b Hamilton	3
A. J. Sexton b C. S. Martin	3	– c Sulzberger b Hamilton	16
W. S. Kendall b Hamilton	2	– b C. S. Martin	92
J. S. Laney lbw b Hamilton	49	– c Redmond b Sulzberger	28
D. A. Kenway c and b B. P. Martin	20	– b Sulzberger	0
J. P. Stephenson b Sulzberger	8	– lbw b Hamilton	4
A. D. Mascarenhas b Hamilton	25	– c Marshall b Hamilton	0
*S. D. Udal lbw b Oram	31	– c C. S. Martin b Styris	85
†I. Brunnschweiler c Marshall b Styris	3	– lbw b Styris	19
S. R. G. Francis not out	15	– not out	5
C. T. Tremlett c Englefield b Sulzberger	16	– st Papps b B. P. Martin	17
B 1, l-b 7, w 2, n-b 8	18	B 3, l-b 11, n-b 2	16
	204		**285**

1/13 2/21 3/29 4/95 5/104   204   1/5 2/26 3/89 4/89 5/94   285
6/116 7/147 8/155 9/171   6/98 7/214 8/259 9/264

Bowling: *First Innings*—C. S. Martin 14–4–36–1; Hamilton 17–3–49–4; Styris 6–0–33–1; Oram 18–5–26–1; B. P. Martin 10–3–28–1; Sulzberger 6.4–1–24–2. *Second Innings*—C. S. Martin 21–7–69–1; Hamilton 17–3–58–4; Styris 7–3–14–2; Oram 15–6–31–0; B. P. Martin 23–7–59–1; Sulzberger 20–5–38–2; Redmond 1–0–2–0.

New Zealand A

J. A. H. Marshall b Tremlett	49	– lbw b Stephenson	69
M. H. Richardson c Stephenson b Tremlett	0	– b Francis	85
J. I. Englefield b Tremlett	9	– lbw b Mascarenhas	48
*S. B. Styris b Francis	26	– (5) c Kendall b Stephenson	43
J. D. P. Oram c Udal b Mascarenhas	19	– (6) c Brunnschweiler b Tremlett	0
G. P. Sulzberger c Brunnschweiler b Mascarenhas	0	– (7) lbw b Stephenson	17
A. J. Redmond c Brunnschweiler b Tremlett	0	– (8) c Brunnschweiler b Stephenson	0
†M. H. W. Papps not out	15	– (9) not out	19
B. P. Martin lbw b Udal	23	– (4) c White b Tremlett	29
L. J. Hamilton b Udal	0	– not out	2
C. S. Martin b Francis	1		
B 6, l-b 4, w 1	11	B 2, l-b 11, w 2, n-b 12	27
	153	(8 wkts)	**339**

1/0 2/22 3/74 4/103 5/104   153   1/141 2/192 3/230   (8 wkts) 339
6/105 7/116 8/148 9/152   4/274 5/278 6/301
                                7/303 8/324

Bowling: First Innings—Francis 15.1–3–53–2; Tremlett 13–6–16–4; Stephenson 5–1–19–0; Mascarenhas 16–3–47–2; Udal 10–5–8–2. *Second Innings*—Tremlett 24–8–75–2; Francis 20–6–53–1; Mascarenhas 20–5–51–1; Udal 40–15–65–0; Stephenson 21.1–5–68–4; Kendall 1–0–1–0; White 2–0–13–0.

Umpires: K. J. Lyons and R. A. White.

†At Cheltenham, July 17. New Zealand A won by 134 runs. Toss: New Zealand A. New Zealand A 279 for nine (50 overs) (M. H. W. Papps 66, J. D. P. Oram 51, S. B. Styris 57, Extras 36; I. J. Harvey three for 22); Gloucestershire 145 (37.2 overs) (I. J. Harvey 50; S. B. Styris three for 34).

MCC v NEW ZEALAND A

At Oxford, July 18, 19, 20, 21. MCC won by three runs. Toss: MCC.

Photographers and camera crews descended on The Parks for Graham Gooch's return to first-class cricket, a week short of his 47th birthday. Three years out of county cricket, he said he had accepted MCC's invitation thinking it was for a one-day game. His dismissal, lbw on the back foot to Tuffey to the second ball of the match, made it a wasted journey for the media latecomers. Gooch's colleagues fared better, with half-centuries from Callaghan of Eastern Province, Pakistan's Asif Mujtaba and Victorian left-hander Wrigglesworth, who hit a career-best 85. Nineteen wickets fell on the second day. Some uncertain bounce, encouraged by hard-wicket bowlers used to digging the ball in, found the New Zealanders' technique wanting. However, their own fast bowlers proved quick learners, as they showed after Gooch, wary of how the pitch might deteriorate, had waived the follow-on. Caught at slip off his eighth delivery, though the ball might have brushed thigh pad rather than bat, he probably wished he hadn't. The New Zealanders' fightback left them to make 331 to win, eight fewer than they achieved against Hampshire. By the last morning, they needed 46 with four wickets left. The overnight pair soon went, but Croy and Tuffey took their side ever closer. Mujtaba's left-arm spin finally got them both, and with them went New Zealand A's unbeaten first-class record on tour.

Close of play: First day, MCC 341-8 (Kruis 24*, Townsend 10*); Second day, MCC 110-7 (Wrigglesworth 9*); Third day, New Zealand A 285-6 (Redmond 25*, Walker 9*).

MCC

*G. A. Gooch lbw b Tuffey	0	– c Sulzberger b Hamilton	5
S. J. Dean c Croy b Tuffey	12	– absent hurt	
D. J. Callaghan b Sulzberger	54	– c Sulzberger b Hamilton	0
Asif Mujtaba b Hamilton	76	– c Redmond b Hamilton	6
Z. de Bruyn c Marshall b Sulzberger	5	– b Styris	9
J. D. Robinson c Hamilton b Sulzberger	10	– (2) c Walker b Tuffey	35
I. A. Wrigglesworth c and b Styris	85	– (6) c Papps b Hamilton	9
M. J. G. Davis c Croy b Tuffey	9	– (7) c Sulzberger b Hamilton	19
G. J. Kruis c Croy b Tuffey	24	– b Sulzberger	25
†C. J. Townsend not out	15	– (8) b Sulzberger	3
D. J. Pryke c Sulzberger b Tuffey	2	– (10) not out	5
B 13, l-b 10, w 13, n-b 22	58	B 10, l-b 4, w 6, n-b 8	28

1/0 2/49 3/139 4/148 5/169   350   1/5 2/5 3/28 4/46 5/66   144
6/285 7/307 8/307 9/346   6/103 7/110 8/120 9/144

Bowling: First Innings—Tuffey 26.5–4–74–5; Hamilton 23–6–75–1; Styris 22–5–54–1; Walker 17–4–58–0; Sulzberger 21–9–54–3; Redmond 1–0–12–0. *Second Innings*—Tuffey 7–0–42–1; Hamilton 17–5–55–5; Styris 10–2–22–1; Sulzberger 4.1–1–11–2.

New Zealand A

J. A. H. Marshall c sub (J. Newell) b Kruis....	1	– c Wrigglesworth b Kruis	3
M. H. Richardson run out	32	– b Kruis...................	66
M. H. W. Papps b Pryke	9	– c Townsend b Kruis	36
G. P. Sulzberger c Wrigglesworth b Pryke.....	0	– b Asif Mujtaba..............	15
*S. B. Styris c Callaghan b Kruis..........	39	– c and b Davis	72
J. I. Englefield c Asif Mujtaba b Wrigglesworth.	0	– lbw b Kruis................	33
A. J. Redmond c and b Asif Mujtaba........	21	– c Callaghan b Kruis	29
†M. G. Croy c Callaghan b Pryke..........	5	– (9) c Callaghan b Asif Mujtaba...	14
B. G. K. Walker not out	22	– (8) lbw b Callaghan	12
D. R. Tuffey run out..................	8	– b Asif Mujtaba..............	14
L. J. Hamilton b Asif Mujtaba	4	– not out	2
B 2, l-b 9, w 2, n-b 10	23	B 9, l-b 5, w 1, n-b 16 ...	31

1/8 2/23 3/23 4/85 5/85   164   1/6 2/71 3/106 4/171 5/233   327
6/95 7/105 8/143 9/158   6/258 7/288 8/292 9/322

Bowling: *First Innings*—Kruis 20–7–49–2; Pryke 10–0–32–3; Wrigglesworth 11–4–31–1; de Bruyn 7–1–17–0; Asif Mujtaba 11.2–4–19–2; Davis 6–4–5–0. *Second Innings*—Kruis 32–6–100–5; Wrigglesworth 13–4–49–0; Asif Mujtaba 27.2–12–48–3; Davis 25–12–39–1; de Bruyn 11–2–58–0; Callaghan 10–6–19–1.

Umpires: C. S. Kelly and G. Sharp.

GROUNDSMEN OF THE YEAR

Paul Brind of Surrey was named the ECB's Groundsman of the Year for his work at The Oval, with last year's winner, Phil Frost of Somerset, runner-up for Taunton. Colin Dick of Arundel won the award for county outgrounds.

PPP HEALTHCARE
COUNTY CHAMPIONSHIP, 2000

SURREY
COUNTY CRICKET CLUB

Adam Hollioake

It took some time, but the 20th century finally caught up with the County Championship. Over the years, as spectators fell away, there had been attempts to make it more attractive, and, as England's Test fortunes plumbed new depths, more competitive and more meaningful. But in recent years, its critics had come to view the Championship, the premier competition, as little more than a comfort zone for a nucleus of journeyman cricketers, rather than the finishing school for Test players (unless from overseas). They argued that it was a Victorian framework out of its time, and they won the day.

For 2000, the Championship was split into two divisions of nine, according to the counties' final placings in 1999. At the end of the season, three would be relegated from Division One and three promoted from Division Two. This, the argument ran, would produce tougher, more competitive cricket and cricketers. As if by appointment, England then won three successive Test series. It had to be a coincidence, if for no other reason than that the England players, most of whom were centrally contracted to the ECB, had restricted Championship seasons. Cricket and irony have often gone hand in hand.

The first year of two divisions quickly revealed the new system's pros and cons. Playing fewer teams on a home and away basis meant fewer easy games: and indeed there was some good county cricket in 2000. With the Championship divided into two groups of nine, however, at least one team from each division was uninvolved in each round, with the result that positions could fluctuate appreciably from week to week. Throw in unseasonal weather and bonus points, and dreamy, deckchair Championship cricket suddenly became as volatile as the Stock Exchange.

Surrey's first win in defence of their title, for example, lifted them three places; when they lost their next game, at Derby, they dropped from fourth to sixth. In Division Two, Northamptonshire's first two wins of a five-game winning streak rocketed them from seventh to top by early August, and they remained there, clinching both promotion and the divisional title in their penultimate game. By way of contrast, it had required every one of Glamorgan's four consecutive mid-season wins to get them from last to equal first – and two games later they were down at seventh. Second-division Sussex went from bottom to top and back to bottom; it was hardly surprising their season ended in confusion.

The weather, not content with the nationwide washout of the opening day of Championship cricket for the first time since 1966, had a significant impact on the distribution of bonus points. Conditions generally favoured bowlers ahead of batsmen. Available batting points had been increased to five and bowling points reduced to three, partly as an incentive for batsmen to build big innings, partly as a disincentive to

COUNTY CHAMPIONSHIP TABLE

Divsion One	Played	Won	Lost	Drawn	Bonus Points Batting	Bonus Points Bowling	Points
1 – Surrey (1)	16	9	2	5	44	41	213
2 – Lancashire (2)	16	7	1	8	35	42	193
3 – Yorkshire (6)	16	7	2	7	36	48	188*
4 – Leicestershire (3)	16	4	3	9	42	39	165
5 – Somerset (4)	16	2	4	10	41	40	145
6 – Kent (5)	16	4	4	8	18	42	140
7 – Hampshire (7)	16	3	9	4	20	48	112*†
8 – Durham (8)	16	2	9	5	27	41	112
9 – Derbyshire (9)	16	2	6	8	19	44	111*

Division Two	Played	Won	Lost	Drawn	Bonus Points Batting	Bonus Points Bowling	Points
1 – Northamptonshire (13)	16	7	4	5	39	45	188
2 – Essex (12)	16	5	2	9	28	41	165
3 – Glamorgan (14)	16	5	3	8	27	41	160
4 – Gloucestershire (18)	16	6	4	6	20	42	158
5 – Worcestershire (15)	16	5	5	6	25	42	151
6 – Warwickshire (10)	16	2	3	11	47	35	150
7 – Nottinghamshire (17)	16	2	4	10	41	43	148
8 – Middlesex (16)	16	2	6	8	36	46	138
9 – Sussex (11)	16	3	6	7	31	39	134

1999 positions in the single-division Championship are shown in brackets.

Win = 12 pts Draw = 4 pts.

* *Yorkshire, Hampshire and Derbyshire each had eight points deducted because of a poor pitch.*
† *Hampshire finished above Durham by virtue of winning one more match.*

The bottom three teams in Division One are relegated for 2001, the top three teams in Division Two are promoted.

counties tempted to prepare bowlers' pitches. But only five counties managed more than half the 80 batting points on offer. Warwickshire, sixth in Division Two, had most with 47. On the other hand, Yorkshire and Hampshire took the maximum 48 bowling points and only three counties had less than 40. Even in the absence of Darren Gough and Craig White for most of their season, Yorkshire could call on three international fast bowlers. Hampshire looked principally to their expensive imports, leg-spinner Shane Warne and pace man Alan Mullally, though much good it did them: relegation hung like a pall over their last season at Northlands Road.

As it should be, Surrey and Northamptonshire, the division winners, had the most wins as well as most bonus points. Both deserved their titles, and showed that Championship cricket still has a place in English sport. Unlike 1999, when they stormed to the Championship, Surrey were slow to start, but once in gear there was no stopping them. Seven straight wins burned off most of the opposition. They still needed a point from their final game, at Old Trafford, but well before then Yorkshire, who had led the field through June, and Lancashire were essentially fighting for second-place prize money. There was nothing for third, which was Yorkshire's fate after an eight-point deduction for a Scarborough pitch that failed to meet the pitch panel's approval. Derbyshire and Hampshire, both of whom were relegated, suffered similar pitch penalties. Durham, who sprang the surprise of the season by beating Surrey first time out, also went down.

As the ECB were hoping, promotion and relegation kept the Championship alive until the end of the season. Kent's survival in Division One was not guaranteed until their last game. Six second-division counties – Essex, Glamorgan, Gloucestershire, Nottinghamshire, Warwickshire and Worcestershire – went into the final round with a chance of finishing second and third to join Northamptonshire in Division One. The rain's interference merely heightened the drama. When it relented, Glamorgan calculated that two more bowling points and a draw against lowly Middlesex would see them through. Essex and Warwickshire, Gloucestershire and Nottinghamshire resorted to negotiating targets to determine their futures. When Essex captain Ronnie Irani hit the winning runs against Warwickshire, Gloucestershire's sixth victory of the season – only winners Northamptonshire won more games in that division – had little consequence other than fourth place. Promotion would have crowned Gloucestershire's already remarkable season, but the lowest total of bonus points in the division told against them in the end. It was a lesson they, and every other county, would take into 2001. There was no allowance for coasting in the new-style Championship.

Pre-season betting (William Hill): *Division One* – 15–8 Surrey; 100–30 Lancashire; 5–1 Yorkshire; 7–1 Leicestershire; 8–1 Hampshire; 9–1 Kent; 14–1 Somerset; 33–1 Derbyshire; 80–1 Durham.
Division Two – 9–4 Warwickshire; 4–1 Worcestershire; 11–2 Middlesex; 6–1 Essex; 8–1 Sussex; 10–1 Glamorgan; 12–1 Nottinghamshire; 14–1 Northamptonshire; 16–1 Gloucestershire.

Leaders: *Division One* – from May 14 Lancashire; May 21 Yorkshire; May 27 Leicestershire; June 10 Yorkshire; July 10 Surrey. Surrey became champions on September 13.
Division Two – from May 14 Northamptonshire; May 21 Warwickshire; May 27 Warwickshire and Worcestershire; June 5 Warwickshire; June 10 Worcestershire; June 18 Warwickshire and Worcestershire; July 2 Warwickshire; July 15 Worcestershire; July 22 Essex and Glamorgan; July 31 Sussex; August 7 Northamptonshire. Northamptonshire became champions on September 9.

Bottom place: *Division One* – from May 14 Hampshire; May 21 Kent; June 5 Hampshire; June 18 Durham; July 2 Derbyshire; July 10 Kent; July 15 Hampshire; July 22 Derbyshire; July 31 Hampshire; September 10 Derbyshire.
Division Two – from May 14 Sussex; June 5 Middlesex; June 10 Glamorgan; July 2 Northamptonshire; July 15 Middlesex; August 12 Gloucestershire; August 25 Middlesex; September 16 Sussex.

Prize money

Division One
£105,000 for winners: SURREY.
£50,000 for runners-up: LANCASHIRE.

Division Two
£40,000 for winners: NORTHAMPTONSHIRE.
£25,000 for runners-up: ESSEX.

Winners of each match (both divisions): £2,000.

Scoring of Points

(*a*) For a win, 12 points plus any points scored in the first innings.

(*b*) In a tie, each side scores six points, plus any points scored in the first innings.

(*c*) In a drawn match, each side scores four points, plus any points scored in the first innings (see paragraph (*f*)).

(*d*) If the scores are equal in a drawn match, the side batting in the fourth innings scores six points, plus any points scored in the first innings, and the opposing side scores four points plus any points scored in the first innings.

(*e*) First-innings points (awarded only for performances in the first 130 overs of each first innings and retained whatever the result of the match).

(i) A maximum of five batting points to be available: 200 to 249 runs – 1 point; 250 to 299 runs – 2 points; 300 to 349 runs – 3 points; 350 to 399 runs – 4 points; 400 runs or over – 5 points.

(ii) A maximum of three bowling points to be available: 3 to 5 wickets taken – 1 point; 6 to 8 wickets taken – 2 points; 9 to 10 wickets taken – 3 points.

(*f*) If play starts when less than eight hours' playing time remains and a one-innings match is played, the first-innings points shall be scored. The side winning on the one innings scores 12 points. In a tie, each side scores six points. In a drawn match, each side scores four points. If the scores are equal in a drawn match, the side batting in the second innings scores six points and the opposing side scores four points.

(*g*) If a match is abandoned without a ball being bowled, each side scores four points.

(*h*) The side which has the highest aggregate of points shall be the Champion County of their respective Division. Should any sides in the Championship table be equal on points, the following tie-breakers will be applied in the order stated: most wins, fewest losses, team achieving most points in head-to-head contests between teams level on points, most wickets taken, most runs scored. At the end of the season, the top three teams from the second division will be promoted and the bottom three teams from the first division will be relegated.

(*i*) A county which is adjudged to have prepared a pitch unfit for four-day first-class cricket will have 20 points deducted. A county adjudged to have prepared a poor pitch will have eight points deducted. This penalty will rise to 12 points if the county has prepared a poor or unfit pitch within the previous 12 months.

Under ECB playing conditions, two extras were scored for every no-ball and wide bowled whether scored off or not. Any runs scored off the bat were credited to the batsman, while byes and leg-byes were counted as no-balls or wides, as appropriate, in accordance with Law 24.9, in addition to the initial penalty.

CONSTITUTION OF COUNTY CHAMPIONSHIP

At least four possible dates have been given for the start of county cricket in England. The first, patchy, references began in 1825. The earliest mention in any cricket publication is in 1864 and eight counties have come to be regarded as first-class from that date, including Cambridgeshire, who dropped out after 1871. For many years, the County Championship was considered to have started in 1873, when regulations governing qualification first applied; indeed, a special commemorative stamp was issued by the Post Office in 1973. However, the Championship was not formally organised until 1890 and before then champions were proclaimed by the press; sometimes publications differed in their views and no definitive list of champions can start before that date. Eight teams contested the 1890 competition – Gloucestershire, Kent, Lancashire, Middlesex, Nottinghamshire, Surrey, Sussex and Yorkshire. Somerset joined in the following year, and in 1895 the Championship began to acquire something of its modern shape when Derbyshire, Essex, Hampshire, Leicestershire and Warwickshire were added. At that point MCC officially recognised the competition's existence. Worcestershire, Northamptonshire and Glamorgan were admitted to the Championship in 1899, 1905 and 1921 respectively and are regarded as first-class from these dates. An invitation in 1921 to Buckinghamshire to enter the Championship was declined, owing to the lack of necessary playing facilities, and an application by Devon in 1948 was unsuccessful. Durham were admitted to the Championship in 1992 and were granted first-class status prior to their pre-season tour of Zimbabwe.

In 2000, the Championship was split for the first time into two divisions, on the basis of counties' standings in the 1999 competition.

COUNTY CHAMPIONS

The title of champion county is unreliable before 1890. In 1963, *Wisden* formally accepted the list of champions "most generally selected" by contemporaries, as researched by the late Rowland Bowen (See *Wisden* 1959, pp 91-98). This appears to be the most accurate available list but has no official status. The county champions from 1864 to 1890 were, according to Bowen:

1864 Surrey; 1865 Nottinghamshire; 1866 Middlesex; 1867 Yorkshire; 1868 Nottinghamshire; 1869 Nottinghamshire and Yorkshire; 1870 Yorkshire; 1871 Nottinghamshire; 1872 Nottinghamshire; 1873 Gloucestershire and Nottinghamshire; 1874 Gloucestershire; 1875 Nottinghamshire; 1876 Gloucestershire; 1877 Gloucestershire; 1878 undecided; 1879 Lancashire and Nottinghamshire; 1880 Nottinghamshire; 1881 Lancashire; 1882 Lancashire and Nottinghamshire; 1883 Nottinghamshire; 1884 Nottinghamshire; 1885 Nottinghamshire; 1886 Nottinghamshire; 1887 Surrey; 1888 Surrey; 1889 Lancashire, Nottinghamshire and Surrey.

Official champions					
1890	Surrey	1928	Lancashire	1967	Yorkshire
1891	Surrey	1929	Nottinghamshire	1968	Yorkshire
1892	Surrey	1930	Lancashire	1969	Glamorgan
1893	Yorkshire	1931	Yorkshire	1970	Kent
1894	Surrey	1932	Yorkshire	1971	Surrey
1895	Surrey	1933	Yorkshire	1972	Warwickshire
1896	Yorkshire	1934	Lancashire	1973	Hampshire
1897	Lancashire	1935	Yorkshire	1974	Worcestershire
1898	Yorkshire	1936	Derbyshire	1975	Leicestershire
1899	Surrey	1937	Yorkshire	1976	Middlesex
1900	Yorkshire	1938	Yorkshire	1977 {	Middlesex
1901	Yorkshire	1939	Yorkshire		Kent
1902	Yorkshire	1946	Yorkshire	1978	Kent
1903	Middlesex	1947	Middlesex	1979	Essex
1904	Lancashire	1948	Glamorgan	1980	Middlesex
1905	Yorkshire	1949 {	Middlesex	1981	Nottinghamshire
1906	Kent		Yorkshire	1982	Middlesex
1907	Nottinghamshire	1950 {	Lancashire	1983	Essex
1908	Yorkshire		Surrey	1984	Essex
1909	Kent	1951	Warwickshire	1985	Middlesex
1910	Kent	1952	Surrey	1986	Essex
1911	Warwickshire	1953	Surrey	1987	Nottinghamshire
1912	Yorkshire	1954	Surrey	1988	Worcestershire
1913	Kent	1955	Surrey	1989	Worcestershire
1914	Surrey	1956	Surrey	1990	Middlesex
1919	Yorkshire	1957	Surrey	1991	Essex
1920	Middlesex	1958	Surrey	1992	Essex
1921	Middlesex	1959	Yorkshire	1993	Middlesex
1922	Yorkshire	1960	Yorkshire	1994	Warwickshire
1923	Yorkshire	1961	Hampshire	1995	Warwickshire
1924	Yorkshire	1962	Yorkshire	1996	Leicestershire
1925	Yorkshire	1963	Yorkshire	1997	Glamorgan
1926	Lancashire	1964	Worcestershire	1998	Leicestershire
1927	Lancashire	1965	Worcestershire	1999	Surrey
		1966	Yorkshire	2000	Surrey

Notes: Since the championship was constituted in 1890 it has been won outright as follows: Yorkshire 29 times, Surrey 17, Middlesex 10, Lancashire 7, Essex and Kent 6, Warwickshire and Worcestershire 5, Nottinghamshire 4, Glamorgan and Leicestershire 3, Hampshire 2, Derbyshire 1.

The title has been shared three times since 1890, involving Middlesex twice, Kent, Lancashire, Surrey and Yorkshire.

Wooden Spoons: since the major expansion of the Championship from nine teams to 14 in 1895, the counties have finished outright bottom as follows: Derbyshire, Northamptonshire and Somerset 11; Glamorgan 9; Nottinghamshire and Sussex 8; Gloucestershire and Leicestershire 7; Worcestershire 6; Hampshire 5; Durham and Warwickshire 3; Essex and Kent 2; Yorkshire 1. Lancashire, Middlesex and Surrey have never finished bottom. Leicestershire have also shared bottom place twice, once with Hampshire and once with Somerset.

From 1977 to 1983 the Championship was sponsored by Schweppes, from 1984 to 1998 by Britannic Assurance, and from 1999 to 2000 by PPP Healthcare.

COUNTY CHAMPIONSHIP – FINAL POSITIONS, 1890-2000

	Derbyshire	Essex	Glamorgan	Gloucestershire	Hampshire	Kent	Lancashire	Leicestershire	Middlesex	Northamptonshire	Nottinghamshire	Somerset	Surrey	Sussex	Warwickshire	Worcestershire	Yorkshire
1890	—	—	—	6	—	3	2	—	7	—	5	—	1	8	—	—	3
1891	—	—	—	9	—	5	2	—	3	—	4	5	1	7	—	—	8
1892	—	—	—	7	—	7	4	—	5	—	2	3	1	9	—	—	6
1893	—	—	—	9	—	4	2	—	3	—	6	8	5	7	—	—	1
1894	—	—	—	9	—	4	4	—	3	—	7	6	1	8	—	—	2
1895	5	9	—	4	10	14	2	12	6	—	12	8	1	11	6	—	3
1896	7	5	—	10	8	9	2	13	3	—	6	11	4	14	12	—	1
1897	14	3	—	5	9	12	1	13	8	—	10	11	2	6	7	—	4
1898	9	5	—	3	12	7	6	13	2	—	8	13	4	9	9	—	1
1899	15	6	—	9	10	8	4	13	2	—	10	13	1	5	7	12	3
1900	13	10	—	7	15	3	2	14	7	—	5	11	7	3	6	12	1
1901	15	10	—	14	7	7	3	12	2	—	9	12	6	4	5	11	1
1902	10	13	—	14	15	7	5	11	12	—	3	7	4	2	6	9	1
1903	12	8	—	13	14	8	4	14	1	—	5	10	11	2	7	6	3
1904	10	14	—	9	15	3	1	7	4	—	5	12	11	6	7	13	2
1905	14	12	—	8	16	6	2	5	11	13	10	15	4	3	7	8	1
1906	16	7	—	9	8	1	4	15	11	11	5	11	3	10	6	14	2
1907	16	7	—	10	12	8	6	11	5	15	1	14	4	13	9	2	2
1908	14	11	—	10	9	2	7	13	4	15	8	16	3	5	12	6	1
1909	15	14	—	16	8	1	2	13	6	7	10	11	5	4	12	8	3
1910	15	11	—	12	6	1	4	10	3	9	5	16	2	7	14	13	8
1911	14	6	—	12	11	2	4	15	3	10	8	16	5	13	1	9	7
1912	12	15	—	11	6	3	4	13	5	2	8	14	7	10	9	16	1
1913	13	15	—	9	10	1	8	14	6	4	5	16	3	7	11	12	2
1914	12	8	—	16	5	3	11	13	2	9	10	15	1	6	7	14	4
1919	9	14	—	8	7	2	5	9	13	12	3	5	4	11	15	—	1
1920	16	9	—	8	11	5	2	13	1	14	7	10	3	6	12	15	4
1921	12	15	17	7	6	4	5	11	1	13	8	10	2	9	16	14	3
1922	11	8	16	13	6	4	5	14	7	15	2	10	3	9	12	17	1
1923	10	13	16	11	7	5	3	14	8	17	2	9	4	6	12	15	1
1924	17	15	13	6	12	5	4	11	2	16	6	8	3	10	9	14	1
1925	14	7	17	10	9	5	3	12	6	11	4	15	2	13	8	16	1
1926	11	9	8	15	7	3	1	13	6	16	4	14	5	10	12	17	2
1927	5	8	15	12	13	4	1	7	9	16	2	14	6	10	11	17	3
1928	10	16	15	5	12	2	1	9	8	13	3	14	6	7	11	17	4
1929	7	12	17	4	11	8	2	9	6	13	1	15	10	4	14	16	2
1930	9	6	11	2	13	5	1	12	16	17	4	13	8	7	15	10	3
1931	7	10	15	2	12	3	6	16	11	17	5	13	8	4	9	14	1
1932	10	14	15	13	8	3	6	12	10	16	4	7	5	2	9	17	1
1933	6	4	16	10	14	3	5	17	12	13	8	11	9	2	7	15	1
1934	3	8	13	7	14	5	1	12	10	17	9	15	11	2	4	16	5
1935	2	9	13	15	16	10	4	6	3	17	5	14	11	7	8	12	1
1936	1	9	16	4	10	8	11	15	2	17	5	7	6	14	13	12	3
1937	3	6	7	4	14	12	9	16	2	17	10	13	8	5	11	15	1
1938	5	6	16	10	14	9	4	15	2	17	12	7	3	8	13	11	1
1939	9	4	13	3	15	5	6	17	2	16	12	14	8	10	11	7	1
1946	15	8	6	5	10	6	3	11	2	16	13	4	11	17	14	8	1
1947	5	11	9	2	16	4	3	14	1	17	11	11	6	9	15	7	7
1948	6	13	1	8	9	15	5	11	3	17	14	12	2	16	7	10	4
1949	15	9	8	7	16	13	11	17	1	6	11	9	5	13	4	3	1
1950	5	17	11	7	12	9	1	16	14	10	15	7	1	13	4	6	3

	Derbyshire	Durham	Essex	Glamorgan	Gloucestershire	Hampshire	Kent	Lancashire	Leicestershire	Middlesex	Northamptonshire	Nottinghamshire	Somerset	Surrey	Sussex	Warwickshire	Worcestershire	Yorkshire
1951	11	—	8	5	12	9	16	3	15	7	13	17	14	6	10	1	4	2
1952	4	—	10	7	9	12	15	3	6	5	8	16	17	1	13	10	14	2
1953	6	—	12	10	6	14	16	3	5	11	8	17	1	2	9	15	12	2
1954	3	—	15	4	13	14	11	10	16	7	7	5	17	1	9	6	11	2
1955	8	—	14	16	12	3	13	9	6	5	7	11	17	1	4	9	15	2
1956	12	—	11	13	3	6	16	2	17	5	4	8	15	1	9	14	9	7
1957	4	—	5	9	12	13	14	6	17	7	2	15	8	1	9	11	16	3
1958	5	—	6	15	14	2	8	7	12	10	4	17	3	1	13	16	9	11
1959	7	—	9	6	2	8	13	5	16	10	11	17	12	3	15	4	14	1
1960	5	—	6	11	8	12	10	2	17	3	9	16	14	7	4	15	13	1
1961	7	—	6	14	5	1	11	13	9	3	16	17	10	15	8	12	4	2
1962	7	—	9	14	4	10	11	16	17	13	8	15	6	5	12	3	2	1
1963	17	—	12	2	8	10	13	15	16	6	7	9	3	11	4	4	14	1
1964	12	—	10	11	17	12	7	14	16	6	3	15	8	4	9	2	1	5
1965	9	—	15	3	10	12	5	13	14	6	2	17	7	8	16	11	1	4
1966	9	—	16	14	15	11	4	12	8	12	5	17	3	7	10	6	2	1
1967	6	—	15	14	17	12	2	11	2	7	9	15	8	4	13	10	5	1
1968	8	—	14	3	16	5	2	6	9	10	13	4	12	15	17	11	7	1
1969	16	—	6	1	2	5	10	15	14	11	9	8	17	3	7	4	12	13
1970	7	—	12	2	17	10	1	3	15	16	14	11	13	5	9	7	6	4
1971	17	—	10	16	8	9	4	3	5	6	14	12	7	1	11	2	15	13
1972	17	—	5	13	3	9	2	15	6	8	4	14	11	12	16	1	7	10
1973	16	—	8	11	5	1	4	12	9	13	3	17	10	2	15	7	6	14
1974	17	—	12	16	14	2	10	8	4	6	3	15	5	7	13	9	1	11
1975	15	—	7	9	16	3	5	4	1	11	8	13	12	6	17	14	10	2
1976	15	—	6	17	3	12	14	16	4	1	2	13	7	9	10	5	11	8
1977	7	—	6	14	3	11	1	16	5	1	9	17	4	14	8	10	13	12
1978	14	—	2	13	10	8	1	12	6	3	17	7	5	16	9	11	15	4
1979	16	—	1	17	10	12	5	13	6	14	11	9	8	3	4	15	2	7
1980	9	—	8	13	7	17	16	15	10	1	12	3	5	2	4	14	11	6
1981	12	—	5	14	13	7	9	16	8	4	15	1	3	6	2	17	11	10
1982	11	—	7	16	15	3	13	12	2	1	9	4	6	5	8	17	14	10
1983	9	—	1	15	12	3	7	12	4	2	6	14	10	8	11	5	16	17
1984	12	—	1	13	17	15	5	16	4	3	11	2	7	8	6	9	10	14
1985	13	—	4	12	3	2	9	14	16	1	10	8	17	6	7	15	5	11
1986	11	—	1	17	2	6	8	15	7	12	9	4	16	3	14	12	5	10
1987	6	—	12	13	10	5	14	2	3	16	7	1	11	4	17	15	9	8
1988	14	—	3	17	10	15	2	9	8	7	12	5	11	4	16	6	1	13
1989	6	—	2	17	9	6	15	4	13	3	5	11	14	12	10	8	1	16
1990	12	—	2	8	13	3	16	6	7	1	11	13	15	9	17	5	4	10
1991	3	—	1	12	13	9	6	8	16	15	10	4	17	5	11	2	6	14
1992	5	18	1	14	10	15	2	12	8	11	3	4	9	13	7	6	17	16
1993	15	18	11	3	17	13	8	13	9	1	4	7	5	6	10	16	2	12
1994	17	16	6	18	12	13	9	10	2	4	5	3	11	7	8	1	15	13
1995	14	17	5	16	6	13	18	4	7	2	3	11	9	12	15	1	10	8
1996	2	18	5	10	13	14	4	15	1	9	16	17	11	3	12	8	7	6
1997	16	17	8	1	7	14	2	11	10	4	15	13	12	8	18	4	3	6
1998	10	14	18	12	4	6	11	2	1	17	15	16	9	5	7	8	13	3
1999	9	8	12	14	18	7	5	2	3	16	13	17	4	1	11	10	15	6
2000	9	8	2	3	4	7	6	2	4	8	1	7	5	1	9	6	5	3

Note: For the 2000 Championship, Division One placings are shown in **bold**, Division Two in *italic*.

MATCH RESULTS, 1864-2000

County	Years of Play	Played	Won	Lost	Tied	Drawn
Derbyshire	1871-87; 1895-2000	2,291	571	839	1	880
Durham	1992-2000	156	25	88	0	43
Essex	1895-2000	2,253	651	658	5	939
Glamorgan	1921-2000	1,788	398	607	0	783
Gloucestershire . . .	1870-2000	2,527	751	936	2	838
Hampshire	1864-85; 1895-2000	2,362	614	816	4	928
Kent	1864-2000	2,651	957	797	5	892
Lancashire	1865-2000	2,728	1,016	568	3	1,141
Leicestershire . . .	1895-2000	2,220	506	804	1	909
Middlesex	1864-2000	2,430	902	618	5	905
Northamptonshire .	1905-2000	1,988	491	692	3	802
Nottinghamshire . .	1864-2000	2,560	770	690	1	1,099
Somerset	1882-85; 1891-2000	2,261	536	903	3	819
Surrey	1864-2000	2,808	1,117	622	4	1,065
Sussex	1864-2000	2,700	750	936	6	1,008
Warwickshire	1895-2000	2,233	609	650	1	973
Worcestershire . . .	1899-2000	2,175	546	752	2	875
Yorkshire	1864-2000	2,828	1,256	490	2	1,080
Cambridgeshire . . .	1864-69; 1871	19	8	8	0	3
		20,489	12,474	12,474	24	7,991

Notes: Matches abandoned without a ball bowled are wholly excluded.

Counties participated in the years shown, except that there were no matches in the years 1915-18 and 1940-45; Hampshire did not play inter-county matches in 1868-69, 1871-74 and 1879; Worcestershire did not take part in the Championship in 1919.

COUNTY CHAMPIONSHIP STATISTICS FOR 2000

	For			Against		
County	Runs	Wickets	Avge	Runs	Wickets	Avge
Derbyshire	6,100	224	27.23	5,583	173	32.27
Durham	5,679	252	22.53	6,663	221	30.14
Essex	7,106	234	30.36	7,086	233	30.41
Glamorgan	6,913	214	32.30	7,074	224	31.58
Gloucestershire . . .	5,681	232	24.48	6,131	247	24.82
Hampshire	6,161	251	24.54	6,492	239	27.16
Kent	5,669	220	25.76	6,034	223	27.05
Lancashire	6,247	208	30.03	5,880	231	25.45
Leicestershire	6,256	210	29.79	6,165	199	30.97
Middlesex	7,105	239	29.72	6,551	227	28.85
Northamptonshire .	7,041	233	30.21	6,548	256	25.57
Nottinghamshire . .	7,015	220	31.88	7,360	224	32.85
Somerset	6,569	206	31.88	6,306	182	34.64
Surrey	6,631	203	32.66	5,516	260	21.21
Sussex	6,328	226	28.00	7,303	208	35.11
Warwickshire	7,107	187	38.00	6,723	185	36.34
Worcestershire	6,530	244	26.76	6,050	225	26.88
Yorkshire	5,888	200	29.44	6,561	246	26.67
	116,026	4,003	28.98	116,026	4,003	28.98

OVERS BOWLED AND RUNS SCORED IN THE COUNTY CHAMPIONSHIP, 2000

County	Over-rate per hour	Run-rate/ 100 balls
Derbyshire (**9**)	15.58*	46.81
Durham (**8**)	15.81*	44.51
Essex (*2*)	15.82*	47.25
Glamorgan (*3*)	16.45	49.23
Gloucestershire (*4*)	15.62*	44.10
Hampshire (**7**)	15.57*	47.08
Kent (**6**)	15.76*	41.44
Lancashire (**2**)	16.24	52.74
Leicestershire (*4*)	15.82*	49.44
Middlesex (*8*)	16.03	52.86
Northamptonshire (*1*)	16.23	50.14
Nottinghamshire (*7*)	15.93*	51.97
Somerset (**5**)	15.83*	49.40
Surrey (**1**)	14.89‡	52.94
Sussex (*9*)	15.56*	52.68
Warwickshire (**6**)	16.47	52.22
Worcestershire (**5**)	15.08†	48.77
Yorkshire (*3*)	15.85*	49.11
2000 average rate	15.80	48.99

2000 Championship positions are shown in brackets: Division One in bold, Division Two in italic.

* £4,000 fine.   † £6,000 fine.   ‡ £8,000 fine.

ECB COUNTY PITCHES TABLE OF MERIT

First-Class Matches and Under-19 Tests

		Points	Matches	Average in 2000	Average in 1999
1	Surrey (3)	94	9	5.22	4.95
2	Somerset (1)	104	10	5.20	5.39
3	Cambridge University (7=)	60	6	5.00	4.75
4	Oxford University (12=)	39	4	4.88	4.67
5	Kent (6)	85	9	4.72	4.78
6	Essex (4)	94	10	4.70	4.88
7	Lancashire (19)	92	10	4.60	4.05
7	Nottinghamshire (20)	92	10	4.60	3.83
9	Durham (18)	73	8	4.56	4.10
10	Northamptonshire (15)	82	9	4.56	4.45
10	Warwickshire (17)	82	9	4.56	4.18
12	Middlesex (10)	100	11	4.55	4.70
13	Hampshire (5)	88	10	4.40	4.83
14	Derbyshire (11)	79	9	4.39	4.69
15	Leicestershire (2)	78	9	4.33	5.11
16	Sussex (7=)	86	10	4.30	4.75
17	Gloucestershire (12=)	84	10	4.20	4.67
17	Worcestershire (14)	84	10	4.20	4.56
19	Glamorgan (9)	75	9	4.17	4.72
20	Yorkshire (16)	85	11	3.86	4.19

One-Day Matches

		Points	Matches	Average in 2000	Average in 1999
1	Oxford University (–)........	12	1	6.00	—
2	Sussex (3)	136	13	5.23	5.06
3	Somerset (1)	112	11	5.09	5.25
4	Surrey (14)	108	11	4.91	4.29
5	Nottinghamshire (6).........	137	14	4.89	4.83
6	Northamptonshire (7=).......	105	11	4.77	4.75
7	Essex (9=)..............	114	12	4.75	4.56
8	Hampshire (4)	85	9	4.72	5.05
9	Durham (12)	141	15	4.70	4.41
10	Kent (16)...............	101	11	4.59	4.06
11	Yorkshire (18)	100	11	4.55	3.85
12	Middlesex (2).............	136	15	4.53	5.14
13	Warwickshire (9=)..........	125	14	4.46	4.56
14	Glamorgan (11)	114	13	4.38	4.50
15	Gloucestershire (13)........	139	16	4.34	4.31
16	Worcestershire (15)........	121	14	4.32	4.25
17	Leicestershire (7=).........	94	11	4.27	4.75
18	Lancashire (19)...........	111	13	4.27	3.45
19	Derbyshire (5)	91	11	4.14	4.94
	Cambridge University (17)	—	—	—	4.00

In both tables 1999 positions are shown in brackets. Each umpire in a game marks the pitch on the following scale of merit: 6 – very good; 5 – good; 4 – above average; 3 – below average; 2 – poor; 1 – unfit.

The tables, provided by the ECB, cover all major matches, including Tests, Under-19 internationals and women's internationals, played on grounds under the county's jurisdiction. Middlesex pitches at Lord's are the responsibility of MCC.

The ECB points out that the tables of merit are not a direct assessment of the groundsmen's ability. Marks may be affected by many factors including weather, soil conditions and the resources available.

FIFTY YEARS AGO

From WISDEN CRICKETERS' ALMANACK 1951

THE COUNTY CHAMPIONSHIP IN 1950 – "The County Championship, for the second year running, resulted in a tie, Lancashire and Surrey sharing first place. Considering that prior to 1949 the previous instance of a tie occurred in 1889 such an outcome twice in succession was remarkable. Lancashire, eleventh the summer before, went to the top of the table on July 18 and were never deposed. They looked to have the Championship within their grasp until the last two matches. Rain interfered with their game against Warwickshire and restricted Lancashire to four points, and in the last vital match at The Oval Surrey took four points and Lancashire none... At one period Surrey looked too far behind to make a serious challenge to Lancashire, but they finished in great form with seven successive victories, a first innings lead and another win in their last nine Championship matches."

THE PUBLIC SCHOOLS IN 1950, by E. M. Wellings – "M. C. Cowdrey of Tonbridge was... a stroke player of exceptional skill among schoolboys. It is usually a risky proceeding to take a youngster straight from Schools cricket and push him into his county side. That Kent could do this with Cowdrey without apparent risk to his future development fixes his status among boy cricketers. We have now seen two unusually gifted schoolboy batsmen in the five post-war years. The other was P. B. H. May of Charterhouse... I would not attempt to say who of May and Cowdrey was the better as a schoolboy batsman. They both had the makings of top-class players, and Cowdrey has the chance to go just as far as May."

DERBYSHIRE

Dominic Cork

President: 2000 – H. L. Jackson
             2001 – Sir Nigel Rudd
Chairman: G. T. Bowring
Chief Executive: J. T. Smedley
Chairman, Cricket Committee: L. C. Elliott
Captain: D. G. Cork
Cricket Manager: C. M. Wells
Head Groundsman: B. Marsh
Scorer: J. M. Brown

There was always a suspicion in Derbyshire that, sooner rather than later, Dominic Cork would be recalled to the England team. He made an immediate impact against West Indies at Lord's but, while there was pleasure in their captain's success, it clearly reduced Derbyshire's chance of staying in Division One of the County Championship. With Cork not only leading them but also batting and bowling, they might have been able to survive. Without him, they were overstretched, and it was one of Derbyshire's disputes with the ECB that they received compensation only when he was playing in a Test match. The new system of centrally contracted players was exposed as flawed when, prior to the Old Trafford Test, the England management asked that Cork, who was not contracted, be rested from the Championship match at Canterbury. Derbyshire complied and received nothing, while Kent had Dean Headley sitting on the treatment table with a central contract.

Derbyshire's other gripe came when pitch liaison officers deducted eight points for an unsatisfactory pitch after they beat Surrey in June. In a period of heavy rain, it was felt that the groundsman, Barry Marsh, and his staff did well to get the game started on time. The umpires, Barry Dudleston and Vanburn Holder, were satisfied with conditions but were overruled by the pitch panel. Despite the fact that the ECB's criteria relate to the start of play, judgment was reached later, and the attitude of several Surrey players helped to point the decision in one direction. Derbyshire's appeal was rejected, but the larger issue was a further diminution of umpires' authority.

In the end, Derbyshire were not good enough to compete, as a wretched National League season, with only two victories, confirmed. This was the more disappointing after impressive displays in the first three Benson and Hedges Cup matches. Never again could they recapture that efficiency. Derbyshire had done well to finish in the top half of the Championship in 1999, to go into Division One, but they then lost five players who would certainly have figured in 2000: Ian Blackwell, Phillip DeFreitas, Andrew Harris, Adrian Rollins and Robin Weston. Not all found success elsewhere, but Derbyshire's best performers have hurried to the exit for a decade and more. In 2000, seven of their former players scored centuries. If that annoyed members, so did the sight of Australians elsewhere passing 1,000 runs. After two unproductive seasons from Michael Slater, Derbyshire found Michael

Di Venuto equally fallible. His only hundred was against the Derbyshire Board in the NatWest Trophy.

Hopes of prosperity were based around the seam bowling but were not realised. Kevin Dean, an unknown quantity after major back surgery in the winter, proved the most successful. Despite a remodelled action, his ability to swing the ball was undiminished and he produced some outstanding performances, notably a career-best eight for 52 at Canterbury. Tim Munton, who had moved from Warwickshire, was reliable after a slow start, during which he collected every injury going, but Paul Aldred, hampered by a broken finger, never recaptured his 1999 magic. Trevor Smith finally gave way to a spur in his left ankle that required an operation. The most improved bowler was Matthew Cassar, who discovered extra pace until a groin injury reduced his effectiveness, but his Championship batting again fell short of expectations. His departure to Northamptonshire in the winter provided an opening for the Warwickshire all-rounder, Graeme Welch. Lian Wharton, a left-arm spinner from local club Ockbrook and Borrowash, showed promise and should benefit from the presence of the former England and Worcestershire spinner, Richard Illingworth.

The batting, always prone to collapse, was Derbyshire's gravest problem. Only Kent gathered fewer batting points and, for the second successive season, no batsman reached 1,000 runs. Steve Stubbings, who scored a maiden century when he and Steve Titchard batted through the final day at Canterbury, came closest and showed determination. It was particularly unfortunate that Rob Bailey, who hit the season's first Championship hundred, was out for six weeks after straining a calf muscle at the end of June in the first floodlit game at the County Ground. Derbyshire were hoping that his ability to construct an innings would have its effect on others. Mathew Dowman began as an opener but proved more comfortable in the middle order. If his first century after moving from Nottinghamshire owed much to Hampshire's fielding lapses, he often batted with style, never more so than in a county seventh-wicket record partnership of 258 with Cork against Durham. Cork went on to an unbeaten 200 with a thrilling display, and Derbyshire's substantial victory, one of only two in the Championship, offered a brief hope of avoiding relegation. This was rapidly extinguished by an innings defeat at Southampton in their next game. Karl Krikken suffered a broken finger in a National League game at Chelmsford in July, allowing Luke Sutton a run in the team. After only limited experience with Somerset, Sutton quickly gained confidence, keeping wicket competently and batting well enough to be an effective opener. He is one of a limited number able to feel he advanced in 2000.

Derbyshire were not the only club to be worried about the future of Championship cricket, but they continued to look ahead. During the season, the Virgin Health Centre rose on land behind the pavilion, and there were plans to sell a second plot. The aim is to construct an indoor school but Derbyshire are unsure about the site. It could be incorporated into the existing grandstand, which became increasingly forlorn when its distinctive dome was removed. There is much to be done, on and off the field, and Derbyshire took steps to compensate for the possible absence of Cork in 2001 by appointing Munton as vice-captain. He took over from Krikken, who wished to concentrate on his wicket-keeping. – GERALD MORTIMER.

DERBYSHIRE 2000

[*Bill Smith*]

Back row: R. M. Khan, L. D. Sutton, T. Lungley, R. L. Eagleson, S. D. Stubbings, Z. M. Khan, K. Z. Shah, L. J. Wharton. *Middle row:* S. J. Lacey, M. P. Dowman, B. L. Spendlove, T. M. Smith, S. P. Titchard, M. E. Cassar, C. Ranson (*physiotherapist*). *Front row:* A. M. Brown, R. J. Bailey, M. J. Di Venuto, C. M. Wells (*cricket manager*), D. G. Cork (*captain*), K. M. Krikken, T. A. Munton, K. J. Dean, P. Aldred, J. T. Smedley (*chief executive*).

DERBYSHIRE RESULTS

All first-class matches – Played 18: Won 2, Lost 7, Drawn 9.

County Championship matches – Played 16: Won 2, Lost 6, Drawn 8.

PPP Healthcare County Championship, 9th in Division 1; NatWest Trophy, 4th round; Benson and Hedges Cup, 4th in North Group; Norwich Union National League, 9th in Division 2.

COUNTY CHAMPIONSHIP AVERAGES

BATTING

Cap		M	I	NO	R	HS	100s	50s	Avge	Ct/St
1993	D. G. Cork	10	11	2	452	200*	1	2	50.22	7
	S. P. Titchard	9	16	2	517	141*	1	3	36.92	0
2000	R. J. Bailey	12	17	2	551	118	1	4	36.73	3
2000	M. J. Di Venuto§ . . .	16	25	3	725	92*	0	6	32.95	12
	S. D. Stubbings	16	29	4	767	135*	1	3	30.68	4
2000	M. P. Dowman	15	26	3	699	140	2	3	30.39	9
	L. D. Sutton	8	13	1	355	79	0	2	29.58	14/1
	K. Z. Shah	3	5	2	88	38*	0	0	29.33	0
	S. J. Lacey	9	15	3	240	55*	0	1	20.00	0
1992	K. M. Krikken	10	13	0	221	51	0	1	17.00	18/2
	T. M. Smith†	9	12	2	148	53*	0	1	14.80	3
	M. E. Cassar	12	17	0	234	47	0	0	13.76	1
2000	T. A. Munton	16	22	7	191	52	0	1	12.73	7
1999	P. Aldred†	11	14	1	149	38	0	0	11.46	4
1998	K. J. Dean†	11	15	3	49	22	0	0	4.08	0
	L. J. Wharton†	5	8	4	8	6*	0	0	2.00	7

Also batted: J. P. Pyemont (3 matches) 4, 40, 20; M. Saxelby (1 match) 17, 6.

* Signifies not out. † *Born in Derbyshire.* § *Overseas player.*

BOWLING

	O	M	R	W	BB	5W/i	Avge
K. J. Dean	223	45	754	38	8-52	3	19.84
M. E. Cassar	174.5	43	599	26	6-76	1	23.03
D. G. Cork	246.5	63	641	22	6-41	1	29.13
T. A. Munton	439.3	122	1,093	35	7-34	2	31.22
S. J. Lacey	182.5	40	512	14	4-84	0	36.57
P. Aldred	203.3	44	624	17	4-97	0	36.70

Also bowled: R. J. Bailey 41–7–104–2; M. J. Di Venuto 8.3–3–19–0; M. P. Dowman 17–2–53–2; J. P. Pyemont 4–0–15–0; K. Z. Shah 28–4–97–2; T. M. Smith 143.3–23–543–9; S. P. Titchard 2–0–4–0; L. J. Wharton 86–17–248–3.

COUNTY RECORDS

Highest score for:	274	G. Davidson v Lancashire at Manchester	1896
Highest score against:	343*	P. A. Perrin (Essex) at Chesterfield	1904
Best bowling for:	10-40	W. Bestwick v Glamorgan at Cardiff	1921
Best bowling against:	10-45	R. L. Johnson (Middlesex) at Derby	1994
Highest total for:	645	v Hampshire at Derby	1898
Highest total against:	662	by Yorkshire at Chesterfield	1898
Lowest total for:	16	v Nottinghamshire at Nottingham	1879
Lowest total against:	23	by Hampshire at Burton upon Trent	1958

DERBYSHIRE v LEICESTERSHIRE

At Derby, April 26, 27, 28, 29. Drawn. Derbyshire 10 pts, Leicestershire 9 pts. Toss: Leicestershire.

After a nationwide washout on the opening day – and later starts elsewhere – the first ball of the new two-division Championship was bowled by Ormond. The first hundred was scored here, too: Bailey, on his first-class debut for Derbyshire after 18 seasons at Northampton, made a painstaking 118. It was just the mature, binding performance Derbyshire had had in mind when they engaged him, and it helped them bat 140.3 overs, more than in any innings the previous year. Fewer runs but more sparkle came from the Tasmanian Di Venuto, recruited from Sussex. He made a crisp 70, despite being declared out before starting his innings – the Tannoy announcer had confused him with Dowman, yet another new arrival, who was first to fall. Cork and Smith had Leicestershire in trouble at 87 for five, but Stevens began a recovery. Burns, the former Somerset keeper who had left the first-class game for five years, and DeFreitas, back with his original employers after 11 seasons away, first at Lancashire then Derbyshire, kept it going with a fine eighth-wicket stand of 108.

Close of play: First day, No play; Second day, Derbyshire 227-6 (Bailey 64*, Krikken 22*); Third day, Leicestershire 100-5 (Stevens 10*, Lewis 2*).

Derbyshire

M. P. Dowman b Ormond	8	– (2) not out	0
S. D. Stubbings c Stevens b DeFreitas	21	– (1) not out	2
M. J. Di Venuto b Lewis	70		
S. P. Titchard lbw b Kumble	8		
R. J. Bailey b Wells	118		
*D. G. Cork b Ormond	8		
M. E. Cassar c Ward b Wells	11		
†K. M. Krikken lbw b DeFreitas	51		
P. Aldred b Kumble	36		
T. A. Munton b Kumble	4		
T. M. Smith not out	2		
L-b 10, w 2, n-b 10	22		

1/16 2/43 3/102 4/129 5/156   359   (no wkt dec.) 2
6/175 7/272 8/335 9/343

Bonus points – Derbyshire 3, Leicestershire 2 (Score at 130 overs: 341-8).

Bowling: *First Innings*—Ormond 23–4–94–2; Lewis 21–4–44–1; DeFreitas 34–7–85–2; Kumble 42–13–86–3; Wells 20.3–5–40–2. *Second Innings*—Maddy 2–1–2–0; Stevens 2–2–0–0.

Leicestershire

*V. J. Wells c Aldred b Cork	0	P. A. J. DeFreitas st Krikken b Bailey	79
D. L. Maddy lbw b Cork	4	A. Kumble hit wkt b Cassar	1
T. R. Ward run out	1	J. Ormond not out	1
B. F. Smith lbw b Smith	38		
A. Habib lbw b Smith	33	B 5, l-b 13, n-b 4	22
D. I. Stevens b Aldred	78		
C. C. Lewis c Smith b Cork	15	1/4 2/5 3/9 4/78 5/87	309
†N. D. Burns c Cork b Cassar	37	6/144 7/198 8/306 9/306	

Bonus points – Leicestershire 3, Derbyshire 3.

Bowling: Cork 26–8–60–3; Munton 18–2–83–0; Smith 15–2–54–2; Aldred 17–2–60–1; Cassar 9.5–5–16–2; Bailey 9–2–18–1.

Umpires: K. E. Palmer and J. F. Steele.

At Leeds, May 3, 4, 5. DERBYSHIRE lost to YORKSHIRE by an innings and 79 runs.

At Cambridge, May 12, 13, 14. DERBYSHIRE drew with CAMBRIDGE UNIVERSITY.

DERBYSHIRE v YORKSHIRE

At Derby, May 17, 18, 19, 20. Drawn. Derbyshire 10 pts, Yorkshire 10 pts. Toss: Derbyshire. First-class debut: G. Ramsden.

The loss of more than 130 overs rendered a result impossible on a good pitch. Derbyshire might have made more of it in the first innings, as eight batsmen reached double figures, yet none went on to a half-century: 303 was their highest total without an individual 50, surpassing 272 against Somerset in 1985. In reply, Craven, in his second Championship match, scored a maiden first-class fifty in an opening stand of 112 before Cassar struck three times in nine balls. Significantly quicker after a winter of club cricket in Australia, Cassar finished with a career-best six for 76, spread across three interrupted days. Lehmann's century occupied a similar span and, after good support from Middlebrook, he was last out with Yorkshire 46 ahead. Derbyshire were an untroubled 209 for one when the rain returned. Before play on the second day, Munton was hit above the eye when receiving throw-downs, needed 40 stitches and took no further part in the game, which gave Cassar his opportunity to impress.

Close of play: First day, Derbyshire 285-8 (Smith 9*, Munton 2*); Second day, Yorkshire 171-6 (Lehmann 38*, Hamilton 8*); Third day, Yorkshire 216-7 (Lehmann 59*, Middlebrook 15*).

Derbyshire

S. D. Stubbings c Byas b Hutchison	49	– not out	84
M. P. Dowman c Wood b Hutchison	16	– c Wood b Middlebrook	20
M. J. Di Venuto b Hamilton	30	– not out	81
M. E. Cassar c and b Hutchison	47		
R. J. Bailey c Blakey b Ramsden	29		
†K. M. Krikken b Hoggard	9		
*D. G. Cork c Craven b Lehmann	43		
S. J. Lacey b Lehmann	25		
T. M. Smith b Hamilton	19		
T. A. Munton retired hurt	2		
K. J. Dean not out	6		
B 1, l-b 4, w 3, n-b 20	28	B 8, l-b 4, n-b 12	24

1/28 2/85 3/137 4/166 5/183   303   1/56   (1 wkt) 209
6/198 7/268 8/283 9/303

Bonus points – Derbyshire 3, Yorkshire 3.

In the first innings Munton retired hurt at 285.

Bowling: *First Innings*—Hoggard 23–4–72–1; Hutchison 18–1–74–3; Ramsden 8–1–32–1; Hamilton 18.1–5–42–2; Middlebrook 23–4–61–0; Lehmann 10–3–17–2. *Second Innings*—Hoggard 6–0–35–0; Hutchison 7–0–37–0; Middlebrook 12–3–35–1; Hamilton 5–1–24–0; Ramsden 4–0–36–0; Lehmann 6–0–30–0.

Yorkshire

*D. Byas c Krikken b Cassar	49	J. D. Middlebrook lbw b Bailey	45
V. J. Craven c Krikken b Lacey	58	M. J. Hoggard c Krikken b Cassar	11
†R. J. Blakey c sub b Cassar	0	G. Ramsden not out	0
D. S. Lehmann c Cork b Cassar	133		
R. J. Harden c Krikken b Cassar	0	B 3, l-b 14, w 4, n-b 8	29
M. J. Wood c Krikken b Cork	9		
P. M. Hutchison lbw b Cork	0	1/112 2/112 3/112 4/116 5/154	349
G. M. Hamilton c sub b Cassar	15	6/160 7/180 8/294 9/328	

Bonus points – Yorkshire 3, Derbyshire 3.

Bowling: Cork 23–4–52–2; Dean 15–4–42–0; Cassar 29.1–8–76–6; Smith 15–3–45–0; Lacey 43–12–110–1; Bailey 3–1–7–1.

Umpires: R. Julian and J. F. Steele.

At Taunton, May 24, 25, 26, 27. DERBYSHIRE drew with SOMERSET.

At Manchester, May 31, June 1, 2, 3. DERBYSHIRE drew with LANCASHIRE.

DERBYSHIRE v SURREY

At Derby, June 7, 8, 9. Derbyshire won by seven wickets. Derbyshire 15 pts, Surrey 3 pts. Toss: Surrey.

Derbyshire were outraged by the deduction of eight points for what pitch liaison officers Mike Denness, Chris Wood and David Hughes condemned as a poor pitch. The county contended that groundsman Barry Marsh and his staff did well to have the surface dry at the start, given recent storms and the requisition of their water-hog by Trent Bridge for the Zimbabwe Test. It was returned, damaged, on the day before the game, Derbyshire claimed, and so the pitch was not dry to the required depth. Umpires Dudleston and Holder supported Derbyshire at the appeal hearing, which nevertheless upheld the penalty. While there was certainly movement to help quality bowlers – 33 wickets fell on the first two days, nine of them to Munton – Ward for Surrey and Dowman for Derbyshire showed it was possible to graft substantial innings, and Stewart and Brown played well when Surrey batted again. On the third morning, after Di Venuto and Bailey had hurried Derbyshire to their first Championship victory of the season, some of the Surrey players became involved in shouted exchanges with members angered by the pitch penalty.

Close of play: First day, Derbyshire 181-9 (Cork 35*, Munton 0*); Second day, Derbyshire 119-3 (Di Venuto 57*, Bailey 27*).

Surrey

M. A. Butcher b Munton	3	– c Bailey b Cork	6
I. J. Ward c Di Venuto b Cork	41	– c Aldred b Munton	10
G. P. Thorpe lbw b Munton	0	– b Munton	8
†A. J. Stewart b Munton	14	– c and b Cork	42
A. D. Brown b Aldred	12	– c Krikken b Cassar	75
*A. J. Hollioake c Dowman b Munton	16	– c Cork b Cassar	21
J. D. Ratcliffe b Munton	0	– c Krikken b Cassar	2
M. P. Bicknell c Krikken b Munton	7	– run out	4
A. J. Tudor b Munton	16	– b Cork	7
I. D. K. Salisbury lbw b Cork	4	– not out	20
Saqlain Mushtaq not out	8	– c Munton b Aldred	12
B 5, l-b 2, n-b 10	17	B 1, l-b 8, n-b 2	11

1/9 2/9 3/31 4/51 5/93   138   1/12 2/24 3/28 4/108 5/160   218
6/93 7/109 8/109 9/118   6/164 7/171 8/179 9/183

Bonus points – Derbyshire 3.

Bowling: *First Innings*—Cork 22–4–62–2; Munton 19.5–7–34–7; Aldred 4–2–13–1; Cassar 4–0–11–0; Smith 2–0–11–0. *Second Innings*—Cork 25–8–62–3; Munton 15–2–53–2; Aldred 8.4–1–25–1; Smith 2–0–23–0; Cassar 12–0–46–3.

Derbyshire

M. P. Dowman b Tudor	69	– b Bicknell	10
S. D. Stubbings c Stewart b Bicknell	3	– c Stewart b Tudor	0
M. J. Di Venuto c Ward b Bicknell	16	– not out	92
M. E. Cassar lbw b Tudor	5	– lbw b Saqlain Mushtaq	4
R. J. Bailey c Stewart b Tudor	0	– not out	40
S. P. Titchard c Salisbury b Tudor	3		
†K. M. Krikken lbw b Tudor	17		
*D. G. Cork not out	44		
P. Aldred c Ratcliffe b Tudor	0		
T. M. Smith lbw b Ratcliffe	0		
T. A. Munton c Stewart b Bicknell	1		
L-b 5, w 4, n-b 24	33	B 3, l-b 4, w 2, n-b 12	21
	191	(3 wkts)	**167**

1/13 2/41 3/62 4/62 5/65   1/8 2/26 3/65
6/94 7/181 8/181 9/181

Bonus points – Surrey 3.

Bowling: *First Innings*—Bicknell 19.1–1–75–4; Tudor 17–3–64–5; Ratcliffe 7–2–21–1; Hollioake 4–1–13–0; Saqlain Mushtaq 3–0–13–0. *Second Innings*—Bicknell 18–5–52–1; Tudor 11–0–59–1; Ratcliffe 2.5–0–25–0; Saqlain Mushtaq 13–5–24–1.

Umpires: B. Dudleston and V. A. Holder.

At Leicester, June 14, 15, 16, 17. DERBYSHIRE lost to LEICESTERSHIRE by ten wickets.

At Darlington, June 28, 29, 30. DERBYSHIRE lost to DURHAM by an innings and 79 runs.

DERBYSHIRE v LANCASHIRE

At Derby, July 7, 8, 9, 10. Drawn. Derbyshire 10 pts, Lancashire 7 pts. Toss: Derbyshire. First-class debut: K. Z. Shah. County debut: M. Saxelby.

Cork, still in overdrive after the Lord's Test victory over West Indies, returned his best figures since September 1995, also against Lancashire, to give Derbyshire a first-innings lead of 135. But they were denied further success by the weather. Only 17.3 overs were bowled on the third day and none on the fourth. After five Championship matches without a batting point, Derbyshire had applied themselves more resolutely on the opening day, helped by Lancashire fielders either dropping or ignoring chances. Stubbings emerged from a lean spell, Cork batted with authority and, on the second morning, Smith completed a maiden fifty. Cork promptly removed Atherton, and Kasir Shah yorked Crawley with his second ball in first-class cricket, adding Fairbrother in his next over. Lancashire lost their last seven wickets for 37. When Dowman withdrew through injury, Derbyshire had rushed to register Mark Saxelby, the former Nottinghamshire and Durham batsman, doing so with seven minutes to spare, then having to wait as he drove from a Second Eleven match in Saffron Walden.

Close of play: First day, Derbyshire 300-9 (Smith 48*, Shah 10*); Second day, Derbyshire 40-2 (Stubbings 13*); Third day, Derbyshire 80-4 (Sutton 15*, Lacey 9*).

Derbyshire

S. D. Stubbings c Hegg b Keedy	64	– c Lloyd b Chapple	27
S. P. Titchard b Ganguly	32	– (4) c Hegg b Chapple	0
M. J. Di Venuto c Fairbrother b Keedy	1	– b Keedy	17
L. D. Sutton run out	8	– (5) not out	15
†K. M. Krikken c Fairbrother b Ganguly	25		
M. Saxelby c Fairbrother b Keedy	17	– (2) lbw b Chapple	6
*D. G. Cork c Lloyd b Chapple	52		
S. J. Lacey run out	12	– (6) not out	9
T. M. Smith not out	53		
T. A. Munton b Smethurst	12		
K. Z. Shah b Chapple	10		
B 5, l-b 4, w 2, n-b 10	21	B 2, l-b 2, w 2	6
	307	**(4 wkts)**	**80**

1/53 2/60 3/81 4/129 5/143   307   1/19 2/40 3/43 4/64   (4 wkts) 80
6/171 7/202 8/236 9/258

Bonus points – Derbyshire 3, Lancashire 3.

Bowling: *First Innings*—Chapple 22.4–5–58–2; Smethurst 25–4–87–1; Green 16–3–52–0; Ganguly 11–3–39–2; Keedy 32–9–62–3. *Second Innings*—Chapple 16–1–43–3; Smethurst 4–1–10–0; Keedy 13–4–23–1.

Lancashire

M. A. Atherton c Di Venuto b Cork	0	R. J. Green c Sutton b Lacey		0
*J. P. Crawley b Shah	37	G. Keedy lbw b Cork		4
N. H. Fairbrother c Munton b Shah	28	M. P. Smethurst c Krikken b Cork		0
S. C. Ganguly lbw b Cork	36			
G. D. Lloyd run out	28	L-b 6, n-b 2		8
P. C. McKeown lbw b Cork	4			
†W. K. Hegg not out	26	1/6 2/65 3/74 4/135 5/136		172
G. Chapple b Cork	1	6/156 7/162 8/167 9/172		

Bonus points – Derbyshire 3.

Bowling: Cork 22–8–41–6; Munton 11–1–36–0; Smith 12–3–29–0; Shah 6–0–24–2; Lacey 10–0–36–1.

Umpires: M. J. Harris and T. E. Jesty.

DERBYSHIRE v KENT

At Derby, July 12, 13, 14, 15. Kent won by eight wickets. Kent 17 pts, Derbyshire 3 pts. Toss: Derbyshire. County debut: B. J. Trott.

Raman Subba Row, an ECB pitch liaison officer, saw Derbyshire's early collapse, but blamed technique, not the surface. Bailey's continuing absence, with a torn calf muscle, made their batting even more vulnerable and, although Stubbings and Cork hit fifties for the second successive match, a total of 181 conceded the advantage. Key, dropped twice off Smith, and Dravid replied with a stand of 140 before Kent, another brittle batting side, wobbled. Then Fleming, with an attacking 47, and the tail rode to the rescue, adding 100 for the last four wickets. Munton took six for 54 and bowled magnificently. Second time round, Derbyshire's batsmen let them down again: only Titchard and Lacey resisted as Patel worked through the innings, bowling more than 60 overs for match figures of eight for 108. Munton and Shah, a lively young cricketer, added 78 for the last wicket, which at least made Kent work for their win. Even so, Dravid, nursing a dislocated finger, could happily watch from the pavilion as they moved off the bottom of the table.

Close of play: First day, Kent 27-1 (Key 9*, Dravid 9*); Second day, Kent 257-8 (Masters 7*, Saggers 6*); Third day, Derbyshire 239-9 (Munton 24*, Shah 21*).

Derbyshire

S. D. Stubbings c Key b Masters	72	– c Walker b Fleming	16
S. P. Titchard c Patel b Saggers	4	– c Nixon b Fleming	74
M. J. Di Venuto c Nixon b Trott	0	– c Nixon b Masters	3
L. D. Sutton c Dravid b Saggers	10	– c Dravid b Patel	14
S. J. Lacey c Nixon b Saggers	0	– c Fulton b Patel	37
M. P. Dowman c Fulton b Saggers	21	– lbw b Patel	9
*D. G. Cork c Dravid b Patel	58	– (8) c Nixon b Patel	0
†K. M. Krikken c Nixon b Masters	0	– (7) lbw b Fleming	17
T. M. Smith b Masters	1	– c Trott b Patel	0
T. A. Munton c Walker b Patel	11	– c Fulton b Patel	37
K. Z. Shah not out	0	– not out	38
L-b 2, n-b 2	4	B 15, l-b 7, w 2	24

1/5 2/8 3/33 4/41 5/93	181	1/30 2/39 3/65 4/153 5/164	269
6/140 7/140 8/142 9/173		6/175 7/175 8/177 9/191	

Bonus points – Kent 3.

Bowling: *First Innings*—Saggers 21–3–62–4; Trott 14–3–45–1; Masters 14–4–24–3; Fleming 6–0–17–0; Patel 26.5–13–31–2. *Second Innings*—Saggers 14–4–35–0; Trott 11–2–29–0; Fleming 23–4–71–3; Masters 14–3–24–1; Patel 34.3–11–77–6; Walker 5–0–11–0.

Kent

D. P. Fulton c Krikken b Munton	9	– not out	66
R. W. T. Key b Munton	83	– c Sutton b Lacey	38
R. Dravid c Krikken b Cork	55		
A. P. Wells lbw b Munton	4	– (3) c Di Venuto b Munton	1
M. J. Walker c Krikken b Munton	5	– (4) not out	41
†P. A. Nixon b Lacey	4		
*M. V. Fleming lbw b Smith	47		
M. M. Patel b Smith	13		
D. D. Masters lbw b Munton	12		
M. J. Saggers c Dowman b Munton	24		
B. J. Trott not out	0		
B 9, l-b 5, n-b 10	24	B 15, l-b 6, w 2, n-b 2	25

1/9 2/149 3/164 4/171 5/178	280	1/55 2/62	(2 wkts) 171
6/180 7/244 8/245 9/271			

Bonus points – Kent 2, Derbyshire 3.

Bowling: *First Innings*—Cork 32–11–77–1; Munton 35–14–54–6; Shah 10–1–32–0; Smith 23–5–63–2; Lacey 16–4–40–1. *Second Innings*—Cork 11–2–33–0; Munton 17–5–44–1; Smith 2–0–14–0; Lacey 18–3–34–1; Shah 4–2–6–0; Di Venuto 8.3–3–19–0.

Umpires: M. J. Kitchen and J. W. Lloyds.

At Canterbury, July 28, 29, 30, 31. DERBYSHIRE drew with KENT.

DERBYSHIRE v HAMPSHIRE

At Derby, August 2, 3, 4, 5. Drawn. Derbyshire 10 pts, Hampshire 11 pts. Toss: Derbyshire.

Mullally took a career-best nine for 93 in Derbyshire's first innings and 14 for 188 in all, but Hampshire paid heavily for their fielding, especially poor on the first day. Dowman lived a charmed life: as well as being dropped on five occasions – four times off Mullally and three by Stephenson – he survived when a ball from Mascarenhas clipped his off stump without dislodging a bail, and advanced to his first century since leaving Nottinghamshire. His wicket was the only one to elude

Mullally. After wasting one opportunity, Hampshire created another. A partnership of 187 between centurions Kenway and Mascarenhas – scoring the first hundred of his career – ensured a useful lead, and Mullally then had Derbyshire 66 for four on the third evening. Next morning, however, Kenway, keeping wicket in place of the injured Aymes, dropped a straightforward chance from night-watchman Dean before the deficit had been erased. Di Venuto, batting down the order because of back trouble and aided by a maiden fifty from Sutton, earned a draw. Mullally deserved better.

Close of play: First day, Derbyshire 241-5 (Dowman 102*, Lacey 29*); Second day, Hampshire 141-5 (Kenway 50*, Mascarenhas 4*); Third day, Derbyshire 66-4 (Sutton 28*, Dean 0*).

Derbyshire

S. D. Stubbings c Udal b Mullally	0	– c Kenway b Mullally	20
S. P. Titchard b Mullally	18	– b Mullally	6
M. J. Di Venuto c Kenway b Mullally	14	– (7) not out	78
R. J. Bailey c Stephenson b Mullally	20	– (3) c Kenway b Mullally	0
M. P. Dowman b Hartley	110	– (4) c Kenway b Mullally	4
†L. D. Sutton c Laney b Mullally	36	– (5) c sub b Udal	79
S. J. Lacey not out	55	– (8) c Kenway b Warne	5
P. Aldred b Mullally	10	– (9) b Warne	0
K. Z. Shah c Smith b Mullally	7	– (10) lbw b Udal	33
*T. A. Munton b Mullally	4	– (11) not out	6
K. J. Dean b Mullally	0	– (6) b Mullally	22
B 10, l-b 20, n-b 6	36	B 8, l-b 16, n-b 16	40

1/0 2/20 3/39 4/74 5/165		310	1/7 2/7 3/15		(9 wkts dec.) 293
6/271 7/286 8/294 9/300			4/60 5/132 6/188
					7/203 8/203 9/282

Bonus points – Derbyshire 3, Hampshire 3.

Bowling: *First Innings*—Mullally 37.3–12–93–9; Hartley 24–5–81–1; Warne 23–8–42–0; Mascarenhas 10–1–37–0; Udal 14–6–11–0; Stephenson 7–3–16–0. *Second Innings*—Mullally 33–8–95–5; Hartley 4–0–16–0; Udal 27–8–60–2; Warne 36–9–63–2; Mascarenhas 3–1–6–0; Stephenson 9–2–29–0.

Hampshire

G. W. White lbw b Dean	0	S. D. Udal not out	28
J. P. Stephenson lbw b Dean	16	P. J. Hartley b Lacey	14
W. S. Kendall c Sutton b Munton	8	A. D. Mullally c Bailey b Lacey	6
*R. A. Smith lbw b Aldred	50		
J. S. Laney c Munton b Dean	2	B 6, l-b 10, w 4, n-b 2	22
†D. A. Kenway b Lacey	136		
A. D. Mascarenhas c Sutton b Munton	100	1/0 2/19 3/47 4/53 5/131	394
S. K. Warne b Lacey	12	6/318 7/333 8/364 9/384	

Bonus points – Hampshire 4, Derbyshire 3 (Score at 130 overs: 385-9).

Bowling: Dean 29–4–98–3; Munton 35–8–86–2; Aldred 23–5–61–1; Shah 8–1–35–0; Lacey 30.2–8–84–4; Bailey 6–1–14–0.

Umpires: N. A. Mallender and D. R. Shepherd.

At Derby, August 9, 10, 11. DERBYSHIRE lost to WEST INDIANS by 224 runs (See West Indian tour section).

At The Oval, August 16, 17. DERBYSHIRE lost to SURREY by an innings and 45 runs.

DERBYSHIRE v DURHAM

At Derby, August 22, 23, 24, 25. Derbyshire won by 232 runs. Derbyshire 15 pts, Durham 3 pts. Toss: Durham.

Derbyshire's convincing win maintained their notional chance of avoiding relegation, though on the second day – 144 ahead with four second-innings wickets remaining – defeat seemed as likely. Then Cork joined Dowman and they added 258, a Derbyshire seventh-wicket record, passing the unbroken 241 scored by George Pope and Bert Rhodes at Portsmouth in 1948. Dowman hit 140, his Derbyshire best, but was eclipsed by his captain. Resuming at a career-best 105 on the third morning, Cork surged to an unbeaten 200 in 63 balls with a wonderful display of clean striking. He batted five hours 24 minutes, with three sixes and 32 fours from 264 balls, before setting Durham 500 in five sessions – and dismissing Lewis first ball. Katich and Collingwood shared a hundred partnership, but on the final morning the last four batsmen departed in five overs. Pitch liaison officer A. C. Smith, called in after 20 wickets fell on the opening day, diagnosed nothing more than the batsmen's inability to counter swing. Dean took the honours with six for 52. Durham's defeat spelled the end of the captaincy for Speak.

Close of play: First day, Derbyshire 0-0 (Aldred 0*, Stubbings 0*); Second day, Derbyshire 346-6 (Dowman 129*, Cork 105*); Third day, Durham 257-6 (Pratt 17*, Wood 10*).

Derbyshire

S. D. Stubbings lbw b Brown	9	– (2) lbw b Brown	5
†L. D. Sutton lbw b Brown	2	– (3) c Pratt b Harmison	15
M. J. Di Venuto b Brown	0	– (4) c Speak b Harmison	31
R. J. Bailey lbw b Collingwood	54	– (5) b Betts	23
M. P. Dowman c Lewis b Betts	2	– (6) b Harmison	140
M. E. Cassar c Gough b Harmison	28	– (7) c Pratt b Brown	1
*D. G. Cork c Katich b Betts	45	– (8) not out	200
P. Aldred b Betts	3	– (1) lbw b Betts	14
T. A. Munton c and b Harmison	2	– not out	21
K. J. Dean c Katich b Harmison	3		
L. J. Wharton not out	1		
L-b 8, n-b 10	18	B 2, l-b 20, w 4	26

1/10 2/10 3/17 4/20 5/57   167   1/9 2/23 3/53 4/72   (7 wkts dec.) 476
6/138 7/152 8/157 9/165   5/116 6/121 7/379

Bonus points Durham 3.

Bowling: First Innings—Brown 10–3–31–3; Betts 14–3–41–3; Wood 10–1–33–0; Harmison 10.3–1–42–3; Collingwood 5–0–8–1; Katich 1–0–4–0. *Second Innings*—Brown 24–6–88–2; Betts 22–5–82–2; Harmison 23.1–5–81–3; Wood 20–4–94–0; Collingwood 14–4–30–0; Gough 18–6–55–0; Katich 2–0–15–0; Daley 3–0–9–0.

Durham

J. J. B. Lewis lbw b Dean	11	– lbw b Cork	0
M. A. Gough b Dean	9	– b Aldred	25
S. M. Katich c Sutton b Munton	38	– c Di Venuto b Munton	70
P. D. Collingwood lbw b Dean	0	– c Munton b Wharton	66
*N. J. Speak lbw b Munton	23	– b Aldred	39
J. A. Daley c Munton b Cassar	27	– lbw b Dean	14
†A. Pratt c Dowman b Cassar	0	– c Sutton b Munton	21
J. Wood c Sutton b Dean	30	– lbw b Dean	10
M. M. Betts not out	3	– lbw b Dean	2
S. J. Harmison c Sutton b Dean	0	– b Munton	1
S. J. E. Brown c Di Venuto b Dean	1	– not out	3
L-b 2	2	B 11, l-b 3, n-b 2	16

1/15 2/20 3/20 4/54 5/92   144   1/0 2/43 3/152 4/186 5/228   267
6/92 7/116 8/142 9/142   6/228 7/257 8/261 9/263

Bonus points – Derbyshire 3.

Bowling: *First Innings*—Cork 11–2–28–0; Dean 14.5–4–52–6; Munton 13–4–27–2; Cassar 9–2–35–2. *Second Innings*—Cork 7–0–35–1; Dean 14–3–49–3; Munton 20–10–44–3; Wharton 21–4–46–1; Aldred 12–3–47–2; Cassar 5–2–15–0; Bailey 7–1–17–0.

Umpires: M. J. Harris and P. Willey.

At Southampton, September 6, 7, 8, 9. DERBYSHIRE lost to HAMPSHIRE by an innings and three runs.

DERBYSHIRE v SOMERSET

At Derby, September 13, 14, 15, 16. Drawn. Derbyshire 7 pts, Somerset 7 pts. Toss: Derbyshire.
    A meaningless match – Derbyshire were already relegated and Somerset safe – was destroyed by rain, which limited play to the first day. That was time enough for a hundred, inevitably from Bowler. His fifth of the summer and third in three visits to the County Ground since his acrimonious departure in 1994 took his Championship average for Somerset against Derbyshire to 78.37. Bowler had some work to do after Aldred, with three wickets in an over, reduced Somerset to 58 for four. Taking few risks, he had 15 fours when bad light ended proceedings ten overs early. Dowman, who took a catch behind the stumps after Sutton was hit in the mouth, was capped during the lunch interval. Members were unimpressed as the sun shone on a blank final day of the Championship season, which denied Derbyshire the chance to avoid the extra humiliation of finishing bottom of the division.
    Close of play: First day, Somerset 311-9 (Bowler 117*, Grove 0*); Second day, No play; Third day, No play.

Somerset

M. N. Lathwell b Dean	4		J. I. D. Kerr c Sutton b Cassar	34
A. R. K. Pierson c Stubbings b Aldred	14		P. S. Jones b Dean	28
M. Burns c Munton b Aldred	30		J. O. Grove not out	0
*P. D. Bowler not out	117			
K. A. Parsons c Dowman b Aldred	0		B 9, l-b 5, n-b 4	18
†R. J. Turner lbw b Dean	13			—
G. D. Rose c Sutton b Cork	37		1/7 2/57 3/58 4/58 5/90 (9 wkts) 311
I. D. Blackwell c Cork b Dean	16		6/143 7/182 8/265 9/310	

Bonus points – Somerset 3, Derbyshire 3.

Bowling: Cork 13–1–40–1; Dean 19–7–47–4; Munton 19.3 5–64–0; Aldred 23–2–72–3; Cassar 16 2–64–1, Bailey 4–0–10–0.

Derbyshire

S. D. Stubbings, †L. D. Sutton, M. J. Di Venuto, R. J. Bailey, M. P. Dowman, J. P. Pyemont, *D. G. Cork, M. E. Cassar, P. Aldred, T. A. Munton and K. J. Dean.

Umpires: J. H. Harris and N. A. Mallender.

DURHAM

Simon Katich

President: J. D. Robson
Chairman: D. W. Midgley
Chief Executive: D. Harker
Chairman, Cricket Committee: R. Jackson
Director of Cricket: G. Cook
Captain: 2000 – N. J. Speak
             2001 – J. J. B. Lewis
First-Team Coach: 2000 – N. Gifford
Head Coach: 2001 – M. D. Moxon
Head Groundsman: D. Measor
Scorer: B. Hunt

Division One was always going to be a tall order for Durham. But in the wake of the expectations created by their opening Championship win against Surrey, relegation came as a bitter disappointment. Similar high hopes were engendered by the Benson and Hedges win over Yorkshire in the first game of the season, with captain Nick Speak taking the Gold Award. Five months later, those early triumphs were a distant memory: Speak was relieved of the captaincy and the side's fortunes continued to plummet.

It was a familiar story. Only in David Boon's final season had Durham been able to reverse their customary slide, rising from the depths to clinch that Division One place. From mid-July 2000, it seemed they would finish seventh, their best position in nine years in the County Championship – though not enough to keep them up. But acting-captain Jon Lewis was forced to gamble in the rain-ruined home match against Hampshire. They lost, then lost again to Surrey in their last fixture, and avoided bottom place only because Derbyshire had eight points deducted.

There had been much talk about improving one-day performances, and three wins out of five in the Benson and Hedges group stages held much promise. Lancashire nipped that in the bud and, despite the prolific scoring of Simon Katich, the Western Australian left-hander, and Paul Collingwood, the National League again proved a struggle. Only Dean Jones, with 656 runs in 1992, had made more than Collingwood's 607 and Katich's 598 in a League season. Eventually Durham sneaked into seventh place in Division Two by winning their last two games. There was brief hope that Ryan Robinson might be the kind of one-day player Durham needed. But his blistering 68 against Derbyshire in the Benson and Hedges Cup proved to be a one-off and he was released at the end of the season, as was Muazam Ali.

That others did not go with them could reflect the renewed influence of Geoff Cook, who was reinstated as director of cricket, a role from which he was removed during Boon's three-year captaincy. Less was seen of Graham Gooch, the batting coach, and at the end of the season Norman Gifford retired as coach. In his place comes the highly regarded Yorkshireman, Martyn Moxon. Two other departures were seamers Melvyn Betts and John Wood. Betts, among those who felt the cricket management needed an overhaul, rejected a new contract and went to Warwickshire, while Wood, after an initial refusal, was released from the final year of his contract following an approach by Lancashire. To help fill this gap, Durham signed the Essex all-rounder, Danny Law. Their spin bowling continued to decline, producing only 17 Championship wickets, and this imbalance contributed heavily to several defeats away from home, where pitches inevitably militated against them.

The new chairman, Bill Midgley, concentrated on the vital task of sorting out the finances, and the club made a huge success of staging two one-day internationals. Meanwhile, the team was on the slide. A big turning-point came at Headingley in early July, when Yorkshire were dismissed for 129, only to make 386 for four when asked to follow on. Questions are bound to be asked about the captain in such situations, and Speak, who had averaged only 8.18 in his first 11 Championship innings, began to lose the faith of some players. Unlike others, however, he was always prepared to battle and he went on to finish second in the batting averages, admittedly a long way behind Katich but ahead of several whose failure to average 30 was a cause for concern. Speak lost the toss in eight of the first nine Championship matches, most crucially in a game he had hoped to win on a difficult surface at Basingstoke. But what cooked his goose was the defeat at Derby that wrecked Durham's survival hopes. This provoked a huge row, after which the captain's position was felt to be untenable. It was a sad end for the likeable Lancastrian, who would have stood a better chance given stronger management.

Simon Brown topped 50 Championship wickets for the seventh time in nine seasons, and Betts was back to his best in mid-season, yet once more failed to last the distance. Not that the seam attack always produced the goods. They conceded 1,075 runs while taking six wickets between Dominic Cork's arrival at the crease at Derby and Ian Ward's dismissal at The Oval, ending his stand of 359 with Mark Butcher. Neil Killeen suffered an early-season side injury and lost the previous year's knack of taking Championship wickets. He was, however, the foremost one-day bowler, returning the club's best League analysis, six for 31, at Derby to equal Anderson Cummins's county record of 29 League wickets in a season. The biggest disappointment was Steve Harmison's increasing lack of control. After being included in the season's first three England squads, he suffered from sore shins, and his form on his return was dreadful.

Katich, on the other hand, was superb. Aged 24 and on his first visit to England, he adapted remarkably well after a sketchy start and was head and shoulders above the rest of the Durham batsmen. He also proved very polite and cheerful. Collingwood matched his runs in the one-day stakes, and the members voted him Player of the Year, but his Championship average of 25.22 was below par. The season's highlight was 17-year-old Nicky Peng's 98 on debut against Surrey, while at Old Trafford Durham fielded their first pair of brothers in first-class cricket, Gary and Andrew Pratt, the latter keeping wicket admirably after replacing Martin Speight. It was announced at the end of the season that Lewis would be captain in 2001. – TIM WELLOCK.

DURHAM 2000

[*Bill Smith*]

Standing: B. Hunt (*scorer*), N. Gifford (*first-team coach*), I. D. Hunter, A. Pratt, N. C. Phillips, N. G. Hatch, M. A. Gough, R. Robinson, M. J. Symington, S. M. Ali, G. D. Bridge, A. Walker, N. A. Kent (*physiotherapist*). *Seated:* N. Killeen, P. D. Collingwood, M. M. Betts, M. P. Speight, S. M. Katich, N. J. Speak (*captain*), J. I. B. Lewis, S. J. E. Brown, J. Wood, S. J. Harmison, J. A. Daley.

DURHAM RESULTS

All first-class matches – Played 16: Won 2, Lost 9, Drawn 5.

County Championship matches – Played 16: Won 2, Lost 9, Drawn 5.

PPP Healthcare County Championship, 8th in Division 1; NatWest Trophy, 4th round;
Benson and Hedges Cup, q-f; Norwich Union National League, 7th in Division 2.

COUNTY CHAMPIONSHIP AVERAGES

BATTING

Cap		M	I	NO	R	HS	100s	50s	Avge	Ct
2000	S. M. Katich§	16	28	3	1,089	137*	3	5	43.56	21
1998	N. J. Speak	14	24	5	552	89*	0	4	29.05	3
1998	P. D. Collingwood† . .	16	27	0	681	111	1	4	25.22	19
1998	J. J. B. Lewis.	16	28	2	645	115	1	4	24.80	8
	A. Pratt†.	7	10	1	191	38	0	0	21.22	7
1998	M. P. Speight.	11	18	1	354	55	0	1	20.82	29
	I. D. Hunter†.	3	4	0	83	63	0	1	20.75	0
	N. Peng	8	14	0	231	98	0	1	16.50	1
	M. A. Gough†	7	12	0	176	33	0	0	14.66	3
1999	J. A. Daley†	10	17	0	247	50	0	1	14.52	4
1998	M. M. Betts†.	11	18	4	192	55	0	1	13.71	7
1998	J. Wood	10	15	0	181	44	0	0	12.06	2
1999	N. Killeen†	10	15	1	144	38*	0	0	10.28	1
1998	S. J. E. Brown†	14	21	12	82	19	0	0	9.11	2
1999	S. J. Harmison.	11	15	3	104	33*	0	0	8.66	2
	N. C. Phillips	5	9	0	76	29	0	0	8.44	3
	S. M. Ali	4	5	0	25	18	0	0	5.00	1

Also batted: G. J. Pratt† (2 matches) 5, 11, 23 (1 ct); M. J. Symington (1 match) 8*, 36.

* Signifies not out.   † Born in Durham.   § Overseas player.

BOWLING

	O	M	R	W	BB	5W/i	Avge
M. M. Betts	354	91	832	44	7-30	1	18.90
S. J. E. Brown	442.2	110	1,208	56	7-51	4	21.57
J. Wood	319.4	66	918	33	5-36	3	27.81
S. J. Harmison.	304.1	69	822	26	4-74	0	31.61
N. Killeen.	288.3	84	697	22	3-14	0	31.68
P. D. Collingwood. . . .	214.2	61	474	12	2-21	0	39.50

Also bowled: S. M. Ali 3–0–9–0; J. A. Daley 7–0–20–0; M. A. Gough 76.1–14–280–5;
I. D. Hunter 69.3–12–228–6; S. M. Katich 117.4–14–342–5; N. C. Phillips 156.5–36–415–7;
M. J. Symington 17–2–67–1.

COUNTY RECORDS

Highest score for:	210*	J. J. B. Lewis v Oxford University at Oxford. . . .	1997
Highest score against:	501*	B. C. Lara (Warwickshire) at Birmingham	1994
Best bowling for:	9-64	M. M. Betts v Northamptonshire at Northampton .	1997
Best bowling against:	8-22	D. Follett (Middlesex) at Lord's.	1996
Highest total for:	625-6 dec.	v Derbyshire at Chesterfield	1994
Highest total against:	810-4 dec.	by Warwickshire at Birmingham	1994
Lowest total for:	67	v Middlesex at Lord's	1996
Lowest total against:	73	by Oxford University at Oxford.	1994

DURHAM v SURREY

At Chester-le-Street, May 2, 3, 4. Durham won by 231 runs. Durham 16 pts, Surrey 3 pts. Toss: Surrey. First-class debut: N. Peng. Championship debut: S. M. Katich.

Since entering the first-class game in 1992, Durham had played Surrey 18 times in all competitions and lost every match. This first win in nine Championship meetings – and with a day to spare – was achieved on the back of a quite magnificent 98 by Peng, aged 17 years 227 days, the highest score for Durham on Championship debut. He went in at 48 for four, took 15 balls to get off the mark, reached 50 off 104 balls and made his remaining 48 runs off only 41 before being last out. He hit 17 fours. His decision to concentrate on cricket, rather than continue with his A-level studies at Newcastle Royal Grammar School, looked fully justified, and Surrey's captain, Adam Hollioake, described him as "the best young player I've ever seen". Though his birth certificate records him as Nicky Peng Gillender, combining the surnames of his parents (both of whom watched this debut), he asked to be known simply by his mother's name. With moisture just below the surface after the wet April, Durham's seam attack proved better suited to the conditions than Surrey's, and the reigning champions, unbeaten the previous season, twice recorded the lowest Championship total made against Durham. On the second day, they avoided the follow-on figure of 84 through their last pair; on the third, they collapsed from 41 without loss to 85 all out inside the afternoon session.

Close of play: First day, Surrey 47-2 (Butcher 10*, Tudor 0*); Second day, Durham 121-7 (Katich 43*, Betts 2*).

Durham

J. J. B. Lewis b Tudor	10	– c Batty b Tudor	5
J. A. Daley b Bicknell	1	– lbw b Bicknell	4
S. M. Katich c Thorpe b Bicknell	8	– lbw b B. C. Hollioake	65
P. D. Collingwood c Batty b Tudor	66	– c Butcher b Tudor	0
*N. J. Speak c Batty b B. C. Hollioake	3	– c Batty b Bicknell	1
N. Peng c Batty b B. C. Hollioake	98	– c Batty b Bicknell	23
†M. P. Speight lbw b Bicknell	9	– c Batty b Tudor	36
N. Killeen c Brown b B. C. Hollioake	7	– b Bicknell	0
M. M. Betts b Bishop	0	– lbw b Bicknell	23
S. J. Harmison lbw b B. C. Hollioake	15	– b B. C. Hollioake	0
S. J. E. Brown not out	4	– not out	4
B 3, l-b 6, n-b 4	13	L-b 8, n-b 17	25

1/5 2/21 3/25 4/48 5/119   234   1/11 2/11 3/13 4/14 5/61   186
6/143 7/175 8/176 9/219   6/113 7/118 8/168 9/173

Bonus points – Durham 1, Surrey 3.

Bowling: *First Innings*—Bicknell 20–5–52–3; Tudor 17–5–39–2; Bishop 13–1–54–1; B. C. Hollioake 13.4–3–41–4; Salisbury 12–2–39–0. *Second Innings*—Bicknell 27–6–85–5; Tudor 19–4–45–3; B. C. Hollioake 13.1–6–27–2; Bishop 4–2–20–0; A. J. Hollioake 2–1–1–0.

Surrey

M. A. Butcher c Katich b Brown	15	– b Brown	24
I. J. Ward run out	12	– c Collingwood b Killeen	17
G. P. Thorpe c Speight b Harmison	18	– c Daley b Harmison	1
A. J. Tudor c Brown b Betts	5	– (10) not out	17
B. C. Hollioake c Speight b Brown	2	– (4) lbw b Brown	0
A. D. Brown c Speight b Killeen	9	– (5) lbw b Killeen	4
*A. J. Hollioake c Collingwood b Killeen	7	– (6) lbw b Killeen	0
†J. N. Batty lbw b Killeen	0	– (7) c Katich b Betts	7
M. P. Bicknell c Betts b Brown	1	– (8) b Betts	7
I. D. K. Salisbury not out	11	– (9) b Harmison	0
I. E. Bishop c Betts b Collingwood	12	– b Brown	2
L-b 10, w 2	12	B 2, w 2, n-b 2	6

1/13 2/46 3/57 4/57 5/62   104   1/41 2/45 3/45 4/50 5/50   85
6/68 7/70 8/73 9/81   6/50 7/57 8/58 9/66

Bonus points – Durham 3.

Bowling: *First Innings*—Brown 18–7–29–3; Betts 15–7–19–1; Killeen 13–4–19–3; Collingwood 2.5–1–3–1; Harmison 7–0–24–1. *Second Innings*—Betts 10–1–36–2; Harmison 12–4–19–2; Brown 8.4–6–8–3; Collingwood 1–0–6–0; Killeen 10–5–14–3.

Umpires: G. I. Burgess and T. E. Jesty.

DURHAM v LANCASHIRE

At Chester-le-Street, May 11, 12, 13. Lancashire won by 141 runs. Lancashire 17 pts, Durham 3 pts. Toss: Durham.

This was the only toss Speak won in his first nine Championship matches after succeeding to Durham's captaincy, and his decision to insert his former team-mates proved flawed. In chilly, cloudy conditions, Lancashire recovered from 123 for six to 263. But as the temperature rose, and the ball swung on a damp surface also offering movement off the seam, batting was always a trial. There were career-best returns from Durham's Brown, in the second innings, and by Lancashire's Chapple and Smethurst. The first two produced lavish swing, while the 6ft 5in Smethurst hit the pitch to good effect and sent Durham crashing to defeat on the third afternoon. But the turning-point was Chapple's three wickets in the over before lunch on the second day. They confirmed the value of Ganguly's carefully constructed 73 the previous day, when the enterprising Schofield scored a second successive Championship half-century. On the third and final morning, Schofield, who bowled the only two overs of spin in the seam-friendly conditions, and Harmison learned they would join Atherton and Flintoff in England's 13 for the Lord's Test against Zimbabwe.

Close of play: First day, Durham 60-2 (Katich 18*, Collingwood 18*); Second day, Lancashire 128-7 (Fairbrother 39*, Chapple 4*).

Lancashire

M. A. Atherton lbw b Killeen	25	– c Speight b Brown	4
*J. P. Crawley b Harmison	5	– lbw b Brown	7
A. Flintoff b Harmison	10	– c Speight b Betts	18
S. C. Ganguly b Killeen	73	– lbw b Brown	5
N. H. Fairbrother c Speight b Betts	2	– c Speight b Brown	41
G. D. Lloyd b Betts	31	– c Speight b Brown	1
†W. K. Hegg c Katich b Betts	3	– c Speight b Collingwood	26
C. P. Schofield run out	50	– b Betts	18
G. Chapple b Harmison	0	– lbw b Brown	7
P. J. Martin c Lewis b Harmison	40	– c sub b Brown	0
M. P. Smethurst not out	2	– not out	1
B 4, l-b 4, w 8, n-b 6	22	L-b 2, w 2, n-b 2	6

1/8 2/28 3/52 4/59 5/117	**263**	1/11 2/16 3/38 4/38 5/41	**134**
6/123 7/201 8/212 9/235		6/80 7/112 8/131 9/131

Bonus points – Lancashire 2, Durham 3.

Bowling: *First Innings*—Brown 18–3–43–0; Harmison 18–3–74–4; Killeen 20–4–54–2; Betts 16–4–52–3; Collingwood 8–1–32–0. *Second Innings*—Brown 17.3–6–51–7; Harmison 14–3–23–0; Betts 21–6–47–2; Killeen 1.5–0–6–0; Collingwood 4–2–5–1.

Durham

J. J. B. Lewis run out	2	– lbw b Chapple	2
J. A. Daley c Hegg b Chapple	7	– lbw b Smethurst	15
S. M. Katich c Hegg b Martin	45	– c Hegg b Smethurst	13
P. D. Collingwood c Hegg b Chapple	37	– lbw b Martin	8
*N. J. Speak lbw b Ganguly	4	– c Lloyd b Smethurst	2
N. Peng b Chapple	0	– c Atherton b Smethurst	12
†M. P. Speight lbw b Chapple	0	– c Fairbrother b Smethurst	18
M. M. Betts c Lloyd b Martin	10	– c Atherton b Smethurst	5
N. Killeen c and b Chapple	11	– b Smethurst	0
S. J. Harmison c Atherton b Chapple	3	– b Chapple	1
S. J. E. Brown not out	0	– not out	0
B 9, l-b 11, n-b 25	45	L-b 6, n-b 10	16

1/8 2/13 3/108 4/121 5/121   164   1/3 2/31 3/32 4/46 5/48   92
6/121 7/139 8/156 9/164   6/74 7/86 8/91 9/92

Bonus points – Lancashire 3.

Bowling: *First Innings*—Martin 22.4–14–27–2; Chapple 20–7–42–6; Smethurst 9–2–31–0; Schofield 2–0–2–0; Flintoff 5–2–10–0; Ganguly 10–2–32–1. *Second Innings*—Martin 9–4–12–1; Chapple 12–7–14–2; Ganguly 2–1–7–0; Smethurst 15.3–3–50–7; Flintoff 4–1–3–0.

Umpires: J. H. Hampshire and J. W. Holder.

DURHAM v LEICESTERSHIRE

At Chester-le-Street, May 24, 25, 26, 27. Drawn. Durham 10 pts, Leicestershire 9 pts. Toss: Leicestershire. First-class debut: I. D. Hunter.

Katich's first century for Durham spanned three rain-interrupted days and overshadowed the earlier efforts of DeFreitas. Batting at No. 10 for Leicestershire, DeFreitas shared stands of 85 with Dakin and 84 with Crowe, reaching 81 not out; then, after a lengthy break for rain, he took three wickets in consecutive overs, reducing Durham to 52 for three. That became 82 for five, but Katich put on 148 with night-watchman Ian Hunter, who played some bold strokes in his debut 63. Play began at 3.20 p.m. on the final day, with only bonus points at stake; Leicestershire were not best pleased when Durham denied them the chance of a third bowling point by declaring with 6.4 overs still available. As Leicestershire were drifting to 167 for eight on the opening day, the ball dominated as in the two previous Championship games here. But suddenly the pitch became benign: only one wicket fell in each of the third and fourth sessions. Katich faced few problems from a Leicestershire attack that lacked support for DeFreitas. His first 50 came off 126 balls, the second off 75, but on the final day he ground the bowlers down by adding 35 in 37 overs.

Close of play: First day, Leicestershire 256-9 (DeFreitas 31*, Crowe 3*); Second day, Durham 82-5 (Katich 28*, Hunter 0*); Third day, Durham 222-5 (Katich 102*, Hunter 59*).

Leicestershire

D. I. Stevens c Collingwood b Betts	10	†N. D. Burns lbw b Betts	1
D. L. Maddy b Betts	50	P. A. J. DeFreitas not out	81
T. R. Ward b Harmison	0	C. D. Crowe lbw b Harmison	21
B. F. Smith c Collingwood b Wood	14	B 6, l-b 9, n-b 18	33
A. Habib lbw b Wood	11		
*V. J. Wells c Betts b Harmison	17	1/27 2/28 3/58	336
J. M. Dakin b Wood	89	4/92 5/98 6/128	
C. C. Lewis b Katich	9	7/164 8/167 9/252	

Bonus points – Leicestershire 3, Durham 3.

Bowling: Harmison 30.3–9–61–3; Betts 33–4–73–2; Hunter 22–4–66–0; Wood 30–2–89–3; Collingwood 4–0–7–0; Katich 10–1–25–1.

Durham

J. J. B. Lewis b DeFreitas	25	J. Wood lbw b Crowe	26
J. A. Daley c Maddy b DeFreitas	16	M. M. Betts not out	0
S. M. Katich not out	137		
P. D. Collingwood b DeFreitas	2	B 2, l-b 10, n-b 4	16
*N. J. Speak b Lewis	1		
N. Peng b Crowe	4	1/43 2/46 3/52	(8 wkts dec.) 302
I. D. Hunter st Burns b Crowe	63	4/63 5/82 6/230	
†M. P. Speight c Maddy b Dakin	12	7/253 8/302	

S. J. Harmison did not bat.

Bonus points – Durham 3, Leicestershire 2.

Bowling: DeFreitas 38–9–99–3; Lewis 20–2–50–1; Dakin 20–4–55–1; Wells 12–2–42–0; Maddy 8–5–11–0; Crowe 19.2–8–33–3.

Umpires: M. R. Benson and N. A. Mallender.

At Tunbridge Wells, May 31, June 1, 2, 3. DURHAM lost to KENT by 190 runs.

DURHAM v YORKSHIRE

At Chester-le-Street, June 7, 8, 9. Yorkshire won by six wickets. Yorkshire 17 pts, Durham 3 pts. Toss: Yorkshire.

Gough's excellent bowling was decisive, twice removing Katich cheaply and, in the second innings, bringing him his first six-wicket return in the Championship for nearly four years. But it was Hoggard who sent the wickets tumbling on the opening day, when eight batsmen succumbed between lunch and tea. Without three injured seamers in Brown, Killeen and Wood, Durham's attack lacked such depth. Vaughan celebrated his first-class return after a five-week lay-off with a cultured 94, and Lehmann made 79 before Hunter claimed three wickets in five balls. The game looked like ending in two days when Durham slid to 35 for four in their second innings, still 70 behind, but Speak made a resilient 32 and, after a delayed start next day, night-watchman Symington added 72 in 30 overs with Speight. Speight ruffled a few feathers as his sweeping – orthodox and reverse – carried him to 44, and the words spoken on his dismissal prompted umpire Burgess to admonish Lehmann. Yorkshire claimed the extra half-hour, preferring to chase runs in poor light rather than chance the weather on the final day.

Close of play: First day, Yorkshire 105-1 (Vaughan 52*, Blakey 16*); Second day, Durham 94-5 (Peng 12*, Symington 5*).

Durham

J. J. B. Lewis c and b Hoggard	52	– c Blakey b Gough	0
J. A. Daley lbw b Hutchison	16	– c Vaughan b Hamilton	10
S. M. Katich c Blakey b Gough	4	– b Gough	5
P. D. Collingwood c Byas b Hoggard	20	– lbw b Hamilton	16
*N. J. Speak c Byas b Middlebrook	11	– lbw b Gough	32
N. Peng c Blakey b Hamilton	9	– c Blakey b Gough	12
†M. P. Speight c Vaughan b Hoggard	37	– (8) st Blakey b Middlebrook	44
I. D. Hunter c Hamilton b Hoggard	1	– (9) c Blakey b Hutchison	3
M. M. Betts c Gough b Hamilton	1	– (10) lbw b Gough	5
M. J. Symington not out	8	– (7) c sub b Gough	36
S. J. Harmison c Blakey b Hoggard	9	– not out	0
B 4, l-b 5, w 8, n-b 4	21	B 8, l-b 8, w 2, n-b 20	38

1/34 2/51 3/98 4/103 5/119	189	1/0 2/14 3/24 4/35 5/79	201
6/137 7/158 8/168 9/168		6/96 7/168 8/190 9/201	

Bonus points – Yorkshire 3.

Bowling: *First Innings*—Gough 14–2–28–1; Hoggard 21.5–5–67–5; Hamilton 14–2–33–2; Hutchison 13–6–19–1; Middlebrook 11–0–33–1. *Second Innings*—Gough 26.2–5–63–6; Hoggard 20–7–37–0; Hamilton 12–4–33–2; Hutchison 7–3–20–1; Middlebrook 16–4–32–1.

Yorkshire

*D. Byas lbw b Symington	29	– lbw b Betts	6
M. P. Vaughan b Hunter	94	– b Betts	7
†R. J. Blakey c Collingwood b Betts	21	– not out	34
D. S. Lehmann c Speight b Hunter	79	– c Katich b Hunter	20
M. J. Wood c Daley b Harmison	9	– b Collingwood	12
G. M. Fellows c Betts b Harmison	3	– not out	7
G. M. Hamilton lbw b Betts	6		
J. D. Middlebrook c Katich b Collingwood	22		
D. Gough c Katich b Hunter	5		
M. J. Hoggard not out	1		
P. M. Hutchison lbw b Hunter	0		
L-b 17, w 4, n-b 4	25	B 5, l-b 6	11

1/59 2/138 3/172 4/191 5/203   294   1/11 2/22 3/53 4/84   (4 wkts) 97
6/233 7/276 8/291 9/294

Bonus points – Yorkshire 2, Durham 3.

Bowling: *First Innings*—Harmison 26–7–58–2; Betts 23–4–42–2; Symington 13–1–61–1; Hunter 22.3–4–73–4; Collingwood 14–3–43–1. *Second Innings*—Harmison 14–4–27–0; Betts 13–3–30–2; Hunter 7–2–11–1; Collingwood 7.3–1–12–1; Symington 4–1–6–0.

Umpires: G. I. Burgess and J. H. Harris.

At Basingstoke, June 14, 15, 16. DURHAM lost to HAMPSHIRE by an innings and 164 runs.

At Chester-le-Street, June 27. DURHAM lost to ZIMBABWEANS by eight wickets (See Zimbabwean tour section).

DURHAM v DERBYSHIRE

At Darlington, June 28, 29, 30. Durham won by an innings and 79 runs. Durham 20 pts, Derbyshire 2 pts. Toss: Derbyshire. First-class debut: S. M. Ali. Championship debut: L. J. Wharton.

Betts underlined that he was back to his 1998 form with seven for 30 in 12 overs, his pace and accuracy proving too much for a fragile Derbyshire line-up missing Cork and Bailey. He was on a hat-trick twice, and the return gave him three of Durham's four best first-class analyses, including seven for 29 here against Kent in 1997. No blame can be attached to the pitch, for Durham proceeded to their second-highest Championship total on a home ground. There were flawless centuries from Katich and Collingwood (a career-best); Speak, averaging 8.18 from his first six Championship games in charge, made a fluent 78, and Betts continued his vendetta with a quickfire fifty as 391 runs were scored on the second day. From the third ball of the third morning, which brought his 500th first-class wicket, the final day belonged to Brown. Dowman hit 12 fours in a classy 61, and Titchard survived five and a half hours for 87 not out, but Brown's six-wicket haul secured Durham's second Championship win of the season, with maximum points.

Close of play: First day, Durham 88-2 (Katich 34*, Collingwood 15*); Second day, Durham 479-9 (Brown 10*, Harmison 33*).

Derbyshire

M. P. Dowman b Brown	12	– c Harmison b Betts	61
S. D. Stubbings c Speight b Harmison	6	– c Speight b Brown	0
M. J. Di Venuto c Speight b Killeen	49	– lbw b Betts	11
S. P. Titchard b Betts	23	– not out	87
M. E. Cassar lbw b Betts	0	– c Collingwood b Harmison	7
*†K. M. Krikken c Collingwood b Betts	0	– c Speight b Brown	6
S. J. Lacey lbw b Betts	10	– lbw b Brown	7
T. M. Smith b Betts	22	– b Brown	0
T. A. Munton b Betts	0	– c Betts b Brown	52
K. J. Dean not out	3	– c Katich b Betts	0
L. J. Wharton b Betts	0	– b Brown	1
B 8, l-b 2, n-b 16	26	L-b 9, w 2, n-b 6	17

1/10 2/20 3/84 4/84 5/90   151   1/1 2/12 3/113 4/129 5/153   249
6/106 7/134 8/134 9/149   6/161 7/161 8/241 9/244

Bonus points – Durham 3.

Bowling: First Innings—Brown 11–0–37–1; Harmison 12–2–40–1; Killeen 14–3–34–1; Betts 12–4–30–7. *Second Innings*—Brown 16.4–5–40–6; Betts 19–3–58–3; Harmison 17–6–43–1; Killeen 15–4–38–0; Katich 9–1–39–0; Collingwood 13–6–22–0.

Durham

J. J. B. Lewis lbw b Munton	36	N. Killeen lbw b Wharton	14
S. M. Ali lbw b Munton	0	S. J. E. Brown not out	10
S. M. Katich c Di Venuto b Smith	114	S. J. Harmison not out	33
P. D. Collingwood c Di Venuto b Dowman	111		
*N. J. Speak c Dowman b Munton	78	L-b 5	5
N. Peng lbw b Dean	23	1/1 2/62 3/219	(9 wkts dec.) 479
†M. P. Speight lbw b Dean	0	4/303 5/345 6/345	
M. M. Betts st Krikken b Dowman	55	7/381 8/435 9/435	

Bonus points – Durham 5, Derbyshire 2 (Score at 130 overs: 435-8).

Bowling: Munton 41–13–84–3; Dean 19–2–83–2; Smith 22–2–108–1; Lacey 19–3–65–0; Wharton 24–4–88–1; Dowman 15–1–46–2.

Umpires: G. Sharp and P. Willey.

At Leeds, July 7, 8, 9, 10. DURHAM drew with YORKSHIRE.

At Leicester, July 12, 13, 14. DURHAM lost to LEICESTERSHIRE by 217 runs.

At Manchester, July 19, 20, 21, 22. DURHAM lost to LANCASHIRE by six wickets.

DURHAM v SOMERSET

At Chester-le-Street, July 28, 29, 30, 31. Drawn. Durham 9 pts, Somerset 9 pts. Toss: Durham.
Lewis's first century for just over a year and Bowler's 38th first-class, on his 37th birthday, were the features of a match ruined by rain. On a lifeless pitch, the sides were already struggling to make up for the loss of 31 overs on the first day by the time 21 more were lost on the third; the final day was washed out. Hit by injuries and England's needs, Somerset brought back Jarvis and, from 33 for two after 15 overs, Durham's total doubled in 13 balls when he and Grove came on. Lewis, punishing anything short outside off stump, hit 16 fours in 261 balls. Bowler's innings was more sedate, extending over six and a half hours as he dug Somerset out of trouble at 88 for six. He and Rose added 157 in 70 overs, and the general lack of enterprise suggested a draw was always likely, even without the final rain.
Close of play: First day, Durham 215-5 (Lewis 113*); Second day, Somerset 144-6 (Bowler 62*, Rose 15*); Third day, Durham 73-3 (Katich 36*, Speak 1*).

Durham

J. J. B. Lewis c Turner b Jones	115	– b Rose	12
M. A. Gough c Parsons b Rose	9	– c Parsons b Rose	5
S. M. Katich b Rose	0	– not out	36
P. D. Collingwood c Turner b Parsons	34	– lbw b Jarvis	17
*N. J. Speak lbw b Jarvis	7	– not out	1
S. M. Ali c Jarvis b Grove	18		
†A. Pratt lbw b Grove	3		
J. Wood c Turner b Grove	4		
M. M. Betts not out	33		
N. Killeen c Turner b Jarvis	15		
S. J. E. Brown b Grove	10		
B 1, l-b 11, w 12, n-b 20	44	L-b 2	2

1/17 2/17 3/122 4/158 5/215   292   1/12 2/29 3/58   (3 wkts) 73
6/218 7/226 8/234 9/259

Bonus points – Durham 2, Somerset 3.

Bowling: *First Innings*—Rose 24–7–50–2; Jones 24–8–60–1; Grove 16–3–58–4; Jarvis 18–1–80–2; Parsons 15–7–21–1; Trescothick 3–0–10–0; Blackwell 5–4–1–0. *Second Innings*—Jones 7–1–16–0; Rose 9–1–21–2; Jarvis 5.2–2–23–1; Grove 3–0–11–0.

Somerset

*J. Cox b Betts	5	P. W. Jarvis c Katich b Wood	1
M. E. Trescothick b Brown	17	P. S. Jones b Brown	3
P. C. L. Holloway lbw b Wood	14	J. O. Grove b Wood	8
P. D. Bowler b Brown	107		
K. A. Parsons c Pratt b Killeen	1	B 1, l-b 14, w 4, n-b 10	29
†R. J. Turner c Lewis b Wood	3		
I. D. Blackwell c Pratt b Wood	10	1/9 2/31 3/50 4/51 5/62	280
G. D. Rose not out	82	6/88 7/245 8/252 9/263	

Bonus points – Somerset 2, Durham 3.

Bowling: Brown 35–8–69–3; Betts 12–5–22–1; Killeen 32–9–52–1; Wood 28–4–88–5; Collingwood 9–0–17–0; Gough 10–3–17–0.

Umpires: J. H. Hampshire and M. J. Kitchen.

DURHAM v KENT

At Chester-le-Street, August 9, 10, 11, 12. Drawn. Durham 8 pts, Kent 7 pts. Toss: Durham.

Durham's hopes of closing the gap on relegation rivals Kent were thwarted by Smith's second-innings 175 in 302 balls, his first Championship century for almost three years. He survived two half-chances in his first fifty, then gave a flawless display of glorious strokes, hitting 22 fours in all, on a pitch that had eased as it dried. Fifteen wickets had fallen in the first two sessions on the second day (three to Brown in the first over), but only 12 after that. McCague's 44-ball 45 and Speak's diligently crafted 89 off 228 balls provided contrasting substance to the respective first innings. Kent finally set Durham a target of 302 in 69 overs, which became 196 off 36 overs by tea with nine wickets left. But when Katich edged the first ball after the interval to the wicket-keeper, Durham opted for safety. Saggers, playing against his old county, savoured a career-best seven for 79 in Durham's first innings, and nine in the match; Kent's other bowlers took only three wickets between them.

Close of play: First day, Kent 71-3 (Smith 19*, Walker 6*); Second day, Durham 209-8 (Speak 79*, Killeen 31*); Third day, Kent 260-4 (Smith 139*, Hockley 12*).

Kent

D. P. Fulton c Collingwood b Killeen	27	– c Collingwood b Wood	17
R. W. T. Key run out	4	– b Wood	11
R. Dravid lbw b Killeen	7	– c and b Katich	47
E. T. Smith c Collingwood b Brown	19	– c Katich b Brown	175
M. J. Walker b Brown	15	– lbw b Killeen	19
J. B. Hockley lbw b Brown	0	– lbw b Brown	33
†P. A. Nixon c Lewis b Brown	0	– (8) not out	11
*M. V. Fleming c Peng b Killeen	35	– (9) not out	22
M. J. McCague b Hunter	45	– (7) b Wood	4
M. J. Saggers not out	6		
D. D. Masters lbw b Brown	1		
B 1, l-b 10	11	B 5, l-b 4, w 4, n-b 2	15

1/4 2/42 3/51 4/71 5/71   170   1/28 2/29 3/128   (7 wkts dec.) 354
6/71 7/88 8/147 9/167   4/213 5/303
          6/312 7/324

Bonus points – Durham 3.

Bowling: *First Innings*—Brown 16.4–3–59–5; Wood 16–4–32–0; Killeen 19–4–53–3; Hunter 5–1–15–1. *Second Innings*—Brown 29–3–96–2; Wood 28.2–8–81–3; Hunter 13–1–63–0; Killeen 20–7–46–1; Collingwood 12–6–29–0; Katich 16–5–30–1.

Durham

J. J. B. Lewis b Saggers	0	– not out	59
N. Peng run out	2	– lbw b Saggers	18
S. M. Katich lbw b Saggers	6	– c Nixon b Fleming	36
P. D. Collingwood lbw b Saggers	28	– c Dravid b Saggers	21
*N. J. Speak not out	89	– not out	11
G. J. Pratt c Hockley b Fleming	23		
†A. Pratt b Saggers	6		
J. Wood c Fulton b Saggers	0		
I. D. Hunter c Fulton b McCague	16		
N. Killeen b Saggers	34		
S. J. E. Brown lbw b Saggers	0		
B 4, l-b 9, w 6	19	L-b 12	12

1/0 2/10 3/16 4/41 5/96   223   1/44 2/106 3/138   (3 wkts) 157
6/107 7/107 8/130 9/223

Bonus points – Durham 1, Kent 3.

Bowling: *First Innings*—Saggers 26.5–5–79–7; McCague 22–4–56–1; Masters 17–5–34–0; Fleming 12–3–25–1; Walker 7–1–16–0. *Second Innings*—Saggers 17–3–44–2; McCague 8–1–22–0; Masters 13–2–37–0; Fleming 10–2–26–1; Dravid 7–1–16–0; Hockley 3–3–0–0.

Umpires: V. A. Holder and D. R. Shepherd.

At Taunton, August 16, 17, 18, 19. DURHAM drew with SOMERSET.

At Derby, August 22, 23, 24, 25. DURHAM lost to DERBYSHIRE by 232 runs.

DURHAM v HAMPSHIRE

At Chester-le-Street, August 31, September 1, 2, 3. Hampshire won by six wickets. Hampshire 15 pts, Durham 3 pts. Toss: Durham.

With both relegation-threatened sides desperate to win a rain-ruined game, two last-day declarations set up a target of 291 in 91 overs for Hampshire. They lost White to the first ball, but Kendall, showing the same composure as when he made 105 here the previous year, hit 119 not out (16 fours) to see them home with 13.5 overs to spare. He put on 98 with Laney, 100 with Smith and 77 with Prittipaul. Durham, having lost by an innings on what they felt was a substandard pitch at Basingstoke, could only reflect on the injustice of handing Hampshire victory on such a featherbed. There were first Championship half-centuries of the season for Daley and Speight, while Katich passed 1,000 Championship runs during the three overs of declaration bowling in their second innings. Lewis led Durham after Speak was relieved of the captaincy.

Close of play: First day, Durham 104-1 (Lewis 34*, Katich 50*); Second day, Durham 246-4 (Daley 31*, Speight 36*); Third day, Hampshire 69-0 (White 23*, Laney 26*).

Durham

*J. J. B. Lewis b Warne	70	– not out	12
M. A. Gough lbw b Mullally	0	– c Smith b Aymes	7
S. M. Katich c Warne b Mascarenhas	60	– not out	16
P. D. Collingwood c Laney b Hartley	12		
J. A. Daley lbw b Warne	50		
M. P. Speight c Laney b Morris	55		
†A. Pratt not out	27		
J. Wood run out	0		
N. Killeen lbw b Morris	1		
S. J. Harmison b Morris	8		
B 3, l-b 3, w 11, n-b 20	37	W 4	4

1/9 2/134 3/162 4/172 5/284 (9 wkts dec.) 320   1/20 (1 wkt dec.) 39
6/286 7/286 8/298 9/320

S. J. E. Brown did not bat.

Bonus points – Durham 3, Hampshire 3.

Bowling: *First Innings*—Mullally 24–4–74–1; Morris 21.3–6–68–3; Mascarenhas 9–2–39–1; Warne 27–10–76–2; Hartley 10–0–54–1; White 1–0–3–0. *Second Innings*—Smith 2–0–26–0; Aymes 1–0–13–1.

Hampshire

G. W. White not out	23	– c Speight b Brown	0
J. S. Laney not out	26	– lbw b Brown	52
W. S. Kendall (did not bat)		– not out	119
*R. A. Smith (did not bat)		– lbw b Killeen	41
L. R. Prittipaul (did not bat)		– c Speight b Katich	35
†A. N. Aymes (did not bat)		– not out	4
L-b 11, w 5, n-b 4	20	B 5, l-b 13, w 6, n-b 17	41

(no wkt dec.) 69   1/0 2/98 3/198 4/275 (4 wkts) 292

A. D. Mascarenhas, S. K. Warne, A. C. Morris, P. J. Hartley and A. D. Mullally did not bat.

Bowling: *First Innings*—Brown 4–0–16–0; Killeen 8–1–27–0; Harmison 4–0–10–0; Wood 4–2–5–0. *Second Innings*—Brown 18–2–80–2; Killeen 21–6–47–1; Wood 14–2–61–0; Harmison 14–0–42–0; Collingwood 2–0–4–0; Gough 5.1–0–30–0; Katich 3–1–10–1.

Umpires: M. R. Benson and J. F. Steele.

At The Oval, September 6, 7, 8, 9. DURHAM lost to SURREY by an innings and 68 runs.

ESSEX

Ashley Cowan

President: D. J. Insole
Chairman: D. L. Acfield
Chief Executive: D. E. East
Chairman, Cricket Committee: G. J. Saville
Club Secretary: M. C. Field
Club Captain: N. Hussain
Team Captain: R. C. Irani
First-Team Coach: K. W. R. Fletcher
Head Groundsman: S. Kerrison
Scorer: D. J. Norris

It was fitting that Ronnie Irani's straight-driven four sealed Essex's promotion on the final day of the Championship season. The burden of captaincy can prove an insurmountable handicap, but Irani thrived on it with an enthusiasm and consistency that was to signal his most successful season. In that final match, against Warwickshire at Chelmsford, he made two unbeaten half-centuries to finish with just under 1,200 first-class runs at an average of 54.36. Including a controversial hundred at Cardiff, he went past 50 ten times, usually when his side were in trouble, and he also confirmed his all-round qualities with 42 wickets at 24 apiece, a return which would have been greater had a back problem not sometimes prevented him bowling.

Stuart Law was another discomforted by back trouble, for most of the summer in fact, but that did not stop him scoring 1,385 first-class runs at 55.40. There is no finer sight on the circuit than Law in full flow, but the failures of others required him to curb his attacking instinct on several occasions to anchor the innings. Among his five centuries, two stood out: his unbeaten 119 at Northampton in the penultimate match of the season, which earned a draw, and the unbeaten 133 against Worcestershire, at Chelmsford in July, that turned a potential defeat into a four-wicket victory.

It was just as well that Irani and Law delivered fluency and form at the crease. Their colleagues were frustratingly inconsistent. Paul Prichard, Paul Grayson and Stephen Peters each finished with a first-class average of around 27, while Nasser Hussain's contribution in three Championship games was a miserable 41 from five innings. Peters's first-class aggregate of 602 was a particular disappointment from a young batsman with such obvious talent. Too often he got himself out after looking well set, a failing which suggests a lack of concentration, but no one who saw his performance against Warwickshire on the last day would doubt his ability. His unbeaten 77, including 13 boundaries, confirmed that, so far, Peters has underachieved. He is still without a Championship hundred after playing nearly 40 games but, at the age of 22, he has time on his side.

Few of the bowlers stood out, although injuries did not help. Much was expected of seamer Ricky Anderson, who was starting to fulfil expectations when he collected career-best figures of 11 for 111 in the Ilford victory over Northamptonshire in June. But a broken toe during that match kept him out until the last three games of the campaign. Mark Ilott was also sidelined by injury for a lengthy spell, which left Ashley Cowan to make the decisive inroads with the new ball. He emerged as the county's leading wicket-taker with 47, while Irani and the willing if wayward Danny Law provided solid back-up.

The omission of Peter Such for the opening weeks of the summer was the subject of heated debate: Essex opted instead for Tim Mason, their acquisition from Leicestershire, which struck supporters as strange and looked stranger still as Mason struggled to make an impression. When Such did come in for his first Championship match, against Middlesex towards the end of June, he announced his return with figures of 12 for 218. If he was never able to impose himself in the same vein after that, he did go on to finish with 36 first-class wickets for an average of 29.30. Mason's 14 arrived at 50.71 each.

Championship promotion more than compensated for the county's early elimination in the Benson and Hedges Cup and NatWest Trophy, as well as their middle-of-the-table showing in the National League second division. There was also immense satisfaction in the emergence of their youngsters as the club began to reap the harvest of an aggressive youth development policy. Andrew McGarry, a lively fast bowler, opening batsman Will Jefferson, and wicket-keeper Jamie Foster all made Championship debuts, while others such as left-arm seamer Justin Bishop seem set to follow. Foster, who replaced Barry Hyam in mid-August, crowned a remarkable final few weeks with selection for England A's tour to the West Indies. McGarry and Bishop went to India with England Under-19, but will be only too aware of the tremendous leap to be made before they establish themselves on the county circuit. Indeed, they need look no further than their own county. Of the five Essex players who helped England win the Under-19 World Cup in 1998, only two remain on the staff – Peters and Graham Napier. Jonathan Powell was forced to abandon his career because of injury, Jamie Grove was deemed surplus to requirements in 1999 and moved to Somerset, while Ian Flanagan was released, along with David Thompson, at the end of 2000. However, Danny Law's move to Durham after four seasons at Essex offers some younger players an opportunity to advance.

A season that ended on a joyful note was tinged with great sadness at the start because of the death, earlier in the year, of Peter Edwards. He died at the age of 63 after suffering a heart attack while in charge of a supporters tour of South Africa. His arrival as secretary/general manager in 1979 coincided with Essex winning the Championship for the first time. In the years that followed, he commanded tremendous respect from a wide circle of friends in all walks of life. David East, who played for the county between 1981 and 1991, and had filled the role of commercial manager since 1998, took over Peter's chair with the title of chief executive. – NIGEL FULLER.

ESSEX 2000

[Bill Smith]

Back row: S. D. Peters, R. S. G. Anderson, T. J. Mason, G. R. Napier, J. G. Foster, T. J. Phillips, J. E. Bishop. Middle row: J. Davis (physiotherapist), B. J. Hyam, I. N. Flanagan, D. R. Law, W. I. Jefferson, A. P. Cowan, D. J. Thompson, A. P. Grayson. Front row: D. D. J. Robinson, P. M. Such, N. Hussain (club captain), F. C. Irani (team captain), S. G. Law, P. J. Prichard, M. C. Ilott.

ESSEX RESULTS

All first-class matches – Played 18: Won 5, Lost 2, Drawn 11.

County Championship matches – Played 16: Won 5, Lost 2, Drawn 9.

*PPP Healthcare County Championship, 2nd in Division 2; NatWest Trophy, 4th round;
Benson and Hedges Cup, 5th in South Group; Norwich Union National League, 5th in Division 2.*

COUNTY CHAMPIONSHIP AVERAGES

BATTING

Cap		M	I	NO	R	HS	100s	50s	Avge	Ct/St
1996	S. G. Law§.	15	26	2	1,352	189	5	6	56.33	18
1994	R. C. Irani	16	28	7	1,175	168*	1	9	55.95	2
	J. S. Foster†	3	4	2	109	52	0	1	54.50	4
	R. S. G. Anderson . .	7	7	3	151	67*	0	1	37.75	0
1997	D. D. J. Robinson† . .	11	17	2	519	93*	0	4	34.60	5
1996	A. P. Grayson	15	28	2	772	144	1	5	29.69	10
	S. D. Peters†	15	26	6	576	77*	0	4	28.80	12
1986	P. J. Prichard†	16	30	3	747	96	0	5	27.66	10
1997	A. P. Cowan	13	18	5	236	67	0	1	18.15	4
	D. R. Law	13	20	2	275	68*	0	1	15.27	6
1993	M. C. Ilott	10	13	4	119	25	0	0	13.22	4
	T. J. Mason	8	11	2	108	52*	0	1	12.00	4
1999	B. J. Hyam†	13	21	0	219	53	0	1	10.42	45/6
	I. N. Flanagan†	3	6	0	61	21	0	0	10.16	7
1989	N. Hussain‡	3	5	0	41	24	0	0	8.20	5
1991	P. M. Such	10	11	2	44	14	0	0	4.88	2

Also batted: W. I. Jefferson (1 match) 1, 4 (1 ct); A. C. McGarry† (3 matches) 1, 0*, 0*;
G. R. Napier† (1 match) 21, 5 (4 ct).

* Signifies not out.   † Born in Essex.   ‡ ECB contract.   § Overseas player.

BOWLING

	O	M	R	W	BB	5W/i	Avge
R. C. Irani	407.3	120	1,008	42	5-79	1	24.00
A. P. Cowan	392.5	96	1,164	47	5-54	2	24.76
M. C. Ilott	283.2	85	724	26	3-37	0	27.84
P. M. Such	398.4	92	999	34	7-167	3	29.38
R. S. G. Anderson . . .	198.4	47	647	19	6-34	2	34.05
D. R. Law.	261.4	40	968	28	5-78	1	34.57
A. P. Grayson	176	38	441	10	3-55	0	44.10
T. J. Mason	217.3	51	626	14	3-38	0	44.71

Also bowled: S. G. Law 1–0–11–0; A. C. McGarry 57–10–227–6; G. R. Napier 8–2–28–0;
D. D. J. Robinson 0.3–0–8–0.

COUNTY RECORDS

Highest score for:	343*	P. A. Perrin v Derbyshire at Chesterfield	1904
Highest score against:	332	W. H. Ashdown (Kent) at Brentwood	1934
Best bowling for:	10-32	H. Pickett v Leicestershire at Leyton	1895
Best bowling against:	10-40	E. G. Dennett (Gloucestershire) at Bristol	1906
Highest total for:	761-6 dec.	v Leicestershire at Chelmsford	1990
Highest total against:	803-4 dec.	by Kent at Brentwood	1934
Lowest total for:	30	v Yorkshire at Leyton	1901
Lowest total against:	14	by Surrey at Chelmsford	1983

At Cambridge, April 26, 27, 28. ESSEX drew with CAMBRIDGE UNIVERSITY.

ESSEX v NOTTINGHAMSHIRE

At Chelmsford, May 3, 4, 5, 6. Drawn. Essex 9 pts, Nottinghamshire 10 pts. Toss: Nottinghamshire.

Stuart Law lit up a gloomy, rain-restricted opening day with a magnificent century, hitting 17 fours, but he departed to the fourth ball of the second morning without addition. Grayson, with a solid half-century, had provided the only meaningful support, helping him add 126 in 29 overs in conditions that helped the seam bowlers. Lucas brought Nottinghamshire back into the game with four wickets in 13 balls, and Johnson's pugnacious century, in 160 balls and containing 15 fours, plus fifties from Bicknell, Tolley and Franks, guided them to a lead of 66. Essex stumbled in their second innings, after Law's dismissal for a more restrained 55, but a last-wicket stand of 62 between Cowan and Anderson frustrated Nottinghamshire's hopes by taking up 28 vital overs. It left them only 51 in which to score 198, and at 66 for four the game could have gone either way. Tolley and Franks again batted with composure to ensure honours finished even.

Close of play: First day, Essex 216-6 (Law 120*, Cowan 2*); Second day, Nottinghamshire 240-6 (Tolley 29*, Franks 13*); Third day, Essex 184-7 (Mason 4*, Cowan 4*).

Essex

P. J. Prichard retired hurt	7	– (7) hit wkt b Franks		29
A. P. Grayson lbw b Millns	58	– b Millns		28
N. Hussain c Johnson b Franks	24	– lbw b Millns		24
S. G. Law lbw b Franks	120	– b Stemp		55
*R. C. Irani c Read b Lucas	16	– c Tolley b Franks		20
S. D. Peters lbw b Lucas	0	– c Read b Millns		0
T. J. Mason lbw b Lucas	1	– (8) c Gallian b Lucas		5
†B. J. Hyam b Lucas	0	– (1) c Read b Franks		8
A. P. Cowan c Bicknell b Franks	15	– not out		39
M. C. Ilott not out	11	– c Stemp b Lucas		4
R. S. G. Anderson c Read b Millns	31	– c Gallian b Stemp		30
L-b 5, w 6	11	B 4, l-b 9, w 4, n-b 4		21

1/12 2/138 3/202 4/204 5/206   274   1/10 2/47 3/125 4/131 5/131   263
6/208 7/216 8/235 9/274   6/173 7/176 8/193 9/201

Bonus points – Essex 2, Nottinghamshire 3.

In the first innings Prichard retired hurt at 8.

Bowling: *First Innings*—Franks 24–4–91–3; Millns 17.2–5–64–2; Lucas 19–3–61–4; Stemp 14–3–37–0; Tolley 5–1–16–0. *Second Innings*—Franks 30–11–60–3; Millns 16–3–58–3; Tolley 7–5–7–0; Lucas 21–5–53–2; Stemp 35.4–14–66–2; Afzaal 2–1–6–0.

Nottinghamshire

D. J. Bicknell c and b Cowan	59	– c Hyam b Irani		5
U. Afzaal lbw b Irani	0	– c Law b Ilott		3
*J. E. R. Gallian c Hyam b Irani	11	– c Hussain b Anderson		12
P. Johnson c Grayson b Mason	100	– b Cowan		13
J. E. Morris c Hussain b Mason	1	– c Hyam b Ilott		44
†C. M. W. Read c Law b Irani	19	– c Hussain b Mason		17
C. M. Tolley st Hyam b Mason	51	– not out		25
P. J. Franks c Hyam b Irani	53	– not out		22
D. J. Millns not out	20			
D. S. Lucas c Law b Ilott	6			
R. D. Stemp run out	4			
B 5, l-b 3, w 2, n-b 6	16	L-b 3, n-b 6		9

1/6 2/26 3/148 4/159 5/185   340   1/5 2/9 3/27   (6 wkts) 150
6/210 7/285 8/316 9/329   4/66 5/91 6/116

Bonus points – Nottinghamshire 3, Essex 3.

Bowling: *First Innings*—Ilott 28–8–82–1; Irani 22–5–57–4; Anderson 25–10–68–0; Cowan 17.1–3–56–1; Mason 24–6–60–3; Grayson 3–0–9–0. *Second Innings*—Ilott 12–3–24–2; Irani 6–2–5–1; Cowan 6–0–17–1; Anderson 9–2–41–1; Mason 16–3–54–1; Grayson 2–0–6–0.

Umpires: M. R. Benson and B. Leadbeater.

At Chelmsford, May 9. ESSEX lost to ZIMBABWEANS by seven wickets (See Zimbabwean tour section).

At Chelmsford, May 11, 12, 13, 14. ESSEX drew with ZIMBABWEANS (See Zimbabwean tour section).

At Birmingham, May 17, 18, 19, 20. ESSEX drew with WARWICKSHIRE.

ESSEX v SUSSEX

At Chelmsford, May 23, 24, 25, 26. Drawn. Essex 8 pts, Sussex 11 pts. Toss: Essex.

Most of the first day and all but 12.4 overs of the last were washed out by rain. Following early damage inflicted by Kirtley's lively pace, Essex eventually owed their recovery to a maiden half-century from Anderson, who struck 67 in 87 deliveries as the last two wickets put on 115. Sussex lost Bevan and Adams in the first two overs on the third morning, but Cottey produced an innings of real authority, his driving off the front foot and nimbleness against the spinners being particularly impressive. His century was Sussex's first in the Championship in 12 matches since July 1999; by the time he departed to a top-edged sweep for 154, he had hit 19 fours and a six. With Peirce, whose typically stolid 86 spanned nearly four and a half hours, Cottey added 198 in 59 overs.

Close of play: First day, Essex 59-3 (Grayson 26*, Irani 4*); Second day, Sussex 21-1 (Peirce 4*, Bevan 10*); Third day, Sussex 360-7 (Rashid 55*, Lewry 1*).

Essex

P. J. Prichard b Kirtley	7	– not out	13
A. P. Grayson b Lewry	31	– not out	4
D. D. J. Robinson b Kirtley	9		
S. G. Law c Patterson b Kirtley	6		
*R. C. Irani c Bevan b Robinson	46		
S. D. Peters lbw b Martin-Jenkins	22		
D. R. Law c Lewry b Martin-Jenkins	1		
†B. J. Hyam b Rashid	34		
T. J. Mason b Robinson	0		
R. S. G. Anderson not out	67		
M. C. Ilott b Martin-Jenkins	10		
B 1, l-b 5, n-b 16	22	B 1, l-b 4	5

1/11 2/31 3/47 4/67 5/132   255   (no wkt) 22
6/132 7/133 8/140 9/226

Bonus points – Essex 2, Sussex 3.

Bowling: *First Innings*—Lewry 20–2–82–1; Kirtley 23–6–69–3; Martin-Jenkins 12–4–38–3; Robinson 17–6–39–2; Rashid 7–2–21–1. *Second Innings*—Lewry 3.2–0–11–0; Kirtley 3–0–6–0.

Sussex

R. R. Montgomerie c Peters b Ilott	5	R. S. C. Martin-Jenkins c Hyam b Ilott	17
M. T. E. Peirce b Mason	86	J. D. Lewry not out	7
M. G. Bevan c Peters b Anderson	10	B 7, l-b 3, w 4, n-b 20	34
*C. J. Adams c Grayson b Irani	0		
P. A. Cottey c Ilott b Grayson	154	1/8 2/21 3/24 (7 wkts dec.)	374
†A. D. Patterson c and b Grayson	0	4/222 5/223	
U. B. A. Rashid not out	61	6/298 7/353	

R. J. Kirtley and M. A. Robinson did not bat.

Bonus points – Sussex 4, Essex 2.

Bowling: Ilott 24.2–6–64–2; Irani 16–2–62–1; Anderson 18–3–59–1; D. R. Law 13–2–38–0; Mason 25–5–93–1; Grayson 21–6–48–2.

Umpires: G. I. Burgess and M. J. Kitchen.

ESSEX v NORTHAMPTONSHIRE

At Ilford, May 31, June 1, 2, 3. Essex won by five wickets. Essex 16 pts, Northamptonshire 3 pts. Toss: Northamptonshire. First-class debut: J. W. Cook.

Robinson's disciplined 93 not out guided Essex to their first Championship victory against Northamptonshire since 1991, well before lunch on the final day. It was also Irani's first Championship success as captain in 11 attempts. The visitors were soon regretting their decision to bat on a sluggish pitch when Anderson's nagging accuracy and career-best return sent them tumbling from 53 without loss to 114 all out. His last five wickets came in 14 balls for two runs, to which Malcolm later responded with four in 11 deliveries for a single as Essex lost their last six wickets for 12. They were already well ahead, however, and finished with a lead of 102. Hayden and Loye led a fighting recovery, adding 118 in 31 overs before Anderson made a timely breakthrough. He struck again on the third day, when Northamptonshire extended their lead to 225, and was rewarded with match figures of 11 for 111. Malcolm's opening burst of 7–1–9–3 had Essex 47 for three, but Irani, with his second fifty of the match, and Robinson put on 121 to ease them towards their first Championship win of the summer.

Close of play: First day, Essex 147-3 (S. G. Law 32*, Irani 16*); Second day, Northamptonshire 203-4 (Cook 16*, Swann 20*); Third day, Essex 170-4 (Robinson 70*, Hyam 0*).

Northamptonshire

A. S. Rollins c Grayson b D. R. Law	9	– (2) lbw b Ilott	9
*M. L. Hayden lbw b Anderson	28	– (1) c Hyam b Anderson	73
M. B. Loye lbw b Ilott	23	– c Hyam b Irani	62
D. J. Sales lbw b Irani	2	– b D. R. Law	18
J. W. Cook not out	13	– b Irani	39
G. P. Swann c D. R. Law b Irani	3	– c Prichard b Anderson	47
†D. Ripley c Hyam b Anderson	6	– lbw b Irani	0
R. J. Logan c Robinson b Anderson	0	– c Hyam b Anderson	24
M. K. Davies c Robinson b Anderson	2	– c S. G. Law b Anderson	25
D. M. Cousins c S. G. Law b Anderson	0	– not out	2
D. E. Malcolm b Anderson	0	– b Anderson	4
B 2, l-b 8, w 4, n-b 14	28	B 4, l-b 6, w 2, n-b 12	24

1/53 2/53 3/85 4/85 5/95	114	1/29 2/147 3/149 4/175 5/254	327
6/110 7/112 8/114 9/114		6/256 7/261 8/320 9/321	

Bonus points – Essex 3.

Bowling: *First Innings*—Ilott 9–4–16–1; Irani 15–5–36–2; Anderson 15–3–34–6; D. R. Law 8–2–18–1. *Second Innings*—Ilott 23–4–82–1; Irani 27–13–40–3; D. R. Law 20–8–59–1; Anderson 33.2–12–77–5; Mason 15–3–49–0; Grayson 2–0–10–0.

Essex

P. J. Prichard lbw b Cousins	9	– c Ripley b Malcolm	20
A. P. Grayson lbw b Cousins	47	– b Malcolm	4
D. D. J. Robinson c Hayden b Cousins	31	– not out	93
S. G. Law c Hayden b Cousins	37	– c Swann b Malcolm	9
*R. C. Irani run out	53	– c Davies b Swann	55
S. D. Peters c Sales b Malcolm	22	– (7) not out	17
D. R. Law c Logan b Davies	0		
†B. J. Hyam c Ripley b Malcolm	1	– (6) c Ripley b Cousins	18
T. J. Mason c Sales b Malcolm	0		
R. S. G. Anderson not out	2		
M. C. Ilott c Cook b Malcolm	0		
B 6, l-b 2, w 6	14	L-b 10, w 2	12

1/21 2/90 3/103 4/162 5/204   216   1/30 2/33 3/47   (5 wkts) 228
6/208 7/209 8/209 9/216   4/168 5/203

Bonus points – Essex 1, Northamptonshire 3.

Bowling: *First Innings*—Malcolm 16.5–5–53–4; Cousins 25–9–44–4; Logan 14–5–50–0; Hayden 7–1–22–0; Davies 16–4–33–1; Swann 4–0–6–0. *Second Innings*—Malcolm 18–4–40–3; Cousins 19.2–4–71–1; Logan 5–0–26–0; Davies 8–1–30–0; Swann 22–4–51–1.

Umpires: N. G. Cowley and J. F. Steele.

At Bristol, June 6, 7, 8. ESSEX beat GLOUCESTERSHIRE by 109 runs.

At Cardiff, June 15, 16, 17, 18. ESSEX drew with GLAMORGAN.

ESSEX v MIDDLESEX

At Chelmsford, June 28, 29, 30. Middlesex won by 237 runs. Middlesex 16 pts, Essex 3 pts. Toss: Middlesex.

Two neglected off-spinners made an immediate impression on their first Championship appearance of the season. Dutch marked his with two career-bests and Middlesex's first Championship win, while his opposite number, Such, emerged with 12 for 218, although he proved expensive in the second innings. Beginning with Strauss and Langer – dismissed with successive balls – Such had figures of five for 27 on the opening afternoon before Dutch saved Middlesex with his first half-century of the game, adding 73 with Fraser. Peters apart, Essex showed little heart against Fraser and Tufnell and, on a dry pitch, Middlesex were well placed at the second-day close, 186 ahead with six wickets in hand. The third, and final, day belonged to Dutch. First came his highest score, 91 with three sixes in 12 boundaries; he and Johnson, whose maiden Championship fifty included two sixes and ten fours, added 108 in 16 overs. Then, as Essex faced a target of 380, Dutch spun them to a humiliating defeat in 41 overs, returning best figures of six for 62.

Close of play: First day, Essex 40-3 (Flanagan 15*, Irani 1*); Second day, Middlesex 100-4 (Weekes 26*, Nash 20*).

Middlesex

A. J. Strauss b Such	35	– c Hyam b Ilott	10
M. A. Roseberry c Hyam b Irani	47	– b Ilott	5
*J. L. Langer c Flanagan b Such	0	– lbw b Cowan	15
O. A. Shah c Flanagan b Irani	21	– c Hyam b Such	13
P. N. Weekes c Flanagan b Such	2	– c S. G. Law b Such	26
†D. C. Nash c Hyam b Such	4	– c Flanagan b Such	25
K. P. Dutch c Flanagan b Cowan	55	– st Hyam b Such	91
S. J. Cook c Robinson b Such	10	– c D. R. Law b Such	5
R. L. Johnson b Cowan	0	– (10) c Hyam b Such	69
A. R. C. Fraser c and b Cowan	19	– (9) c Flanagan b Such	15
P. C. R. Tufnell not out	1	– not out	0
B 2, l-b 12, w 10, n-b 4	28	B 11, l-b 8	19

1/84 2/84 3/114 4/121 5/123	222	1/13 2/20 3/39 4/57 5/101	293
6/128 7/142 8/148 9/221		6/116 7/140 8/172 9/280	

Bonus points – Middlesex 1, Essex 3.

Bowling: *First Innings*—Ilott 12–4–26–0; Irani 15–3–50–2; Cowan 15–3–40–3; D. R. Law 12–0–41–0; Such 24–4–51–5. *Second Innings*—Ilott 17–7–38–2; Irani 10–6–11–0; Such 41.2–7–167–7; Cowan 20–2–39–1; D. R. Law 4–0–8–0; S. G. Law 1–0–11–0.

Essex

P. J. Prichard lbw b Fraser	7	– b Dutch	25
I. N. Flanagan b Fraser	18	– lbw b Dutch	3
D. D. J. Robinson c Strauss b Fraser	9	– c Weekes b Dutch	5
S. G. Law c Weekes b Tufnell	5	– c Langer b Tufnell	6
*R. C. Irani b Fraser	3	– c Shah b Dutch	12
S. D. Peters not out	54	– c Weekes b Tufnell	9
†B. J. Hyam lbw b Johnson	7	– c Dutch b Tufnell	25
D. R. Law lbw b Tufnell	1	– c Shah b Dutch	12
A. P. Cowan c Langer b Tufnell	1	– c and b Dutch	8
M. C. Ilott lbw b Dutch	24	– not out	14
P. M. Such c sub b Tufnell	0	– c Johnson b Weekes	14
B 4, l-b 1, n-b 2	7	B 5, l-b 4	9

1/7 2/30 3/35 4/42 5/47	136	1/24 2/33 3/40 4/40 5/61	142
6/67 7/68 8/78 9/136		6/74 7/99 8/113 9/115	

Bonus points – Middlesex 3.

Bowling: *First Innings*—Johnson 14–5–33–1; Fraser 20–7–31–4; Tufnell 34–15–39–4; Dutch 16–6–28–1. *Second Innings*—Fraser 4–0–6–0; Johnson 3–0–17–0; Dutch 16–5–62–6; Tufnell 16–4–46–3; Weekes 1.1–0–2–1.

Umpires: J. W. Holder and D. R. Shepherd.

At Nottingham, July 7, 8, 9, 10. ESSEX drew with NOTTINGHAMSHIRE.

At Arundel, July 12, 13, 14, 15. ESSEX drew with SUSSEX.

ESSEX v WORCESTERSHIRE

At Chelmsford, July 19, 20, 21. Essex won by four wickets. Essex 15 pts, Worcestershire 4 pts.
Toss: Worcestershire. Championship debut: A. C. McGarry.

Stuart Law's century carried Essex to their first win in five games and, briefly, leadership of
Division Two. Patient while moving to fifty in 123 balls, he then exploited wayward bowling to
reach 133 off another 97, hitting a six and 19 fours in all. He shared century partnerships with
Grayson, whose fifty arrived with a six off McGrath, and the obdurate Irani. Pollard, with his
highest first-class score yet for Worcestershire, and Leatherdale had provided the backbone to the
visitors' first innings, with 117 in 49 overs. McGrath's hostile accuracy, and some rash strokes,
undermined the ten-man Essex reply – Robinson broke a thumb fielding – and left Worcestershire
109 ahead. They increased this to 233 by the end of the second day, on which 19 wickets fell.
Andrew McGarry, an 18-year-old seamer, took his match return to five wickets on Championship
debut, but it was Such's nagging accuracy, on a pitch offering only slow turn, that kept
Worcestershire in check. Even so, Essex's target of 286, the highest total of the match, looked
notional until Law imposed himself.

Close of play: First day, Worcestershire 232-7 (Lampitt 2*, Ali 13*); Second day, Worcestershire
124-7 (Lampitt 7*, Ali 11*).

Worcestershire

W. P. C. Weston c Peters b McGarry	27	– (2) c Hyam b Ilott	0
E. J. Wilson c S. G. Law b Irani	12	– (1) c Hyam b McGarry	6
P. R. Pollard lbw b McGarry	77	– lbw b McGarry	10
V. S. Solanki c Peters b Such	2	– c Peters b Such	53
D. A. Leatherdale c Grayson b D. R. Law	62	– c Hyam b D. R. Law	7
R. C. Driver b McGarry	1	– st Hyam b Such	0
*†S. J. Rhodes lbw b Irani	13	– c Prichard b Such	13
S. R. Lampitt b Irani	4	– c D. R. Law b Such	10
Kabir Ali c Hyam b Ilott	13	– c Hyam b D. R. Law	43
M. J. Rawnsley c Hyam b Ilott	5	– c S. G. Law b Such	7
G. D. McGrath not out	1	– not out	1
B 4, l-b 5, w 8, n-b 6	23	B 8, l-b 4, w 8, n-b 6	26
	240		**176**

1/28 2/66 3/75 4/192 5/198   240
6/209 7/219 8/232 9/238

1/11 2/19 3/40 4/61 5/80   176
6/89 7/106 8/137 9/175

Bonus points – Worcestershire 1, Essex 3.

Bowling: *First Innings*—Ilott 19–4–47–2; Irani 18.4–4–47–3; D. R. Law 15–5–37–1;
McGarry 16–6–29–3; Such 36–11–61–1; Grayson 5–2–10–0. *Second Innings*—Ilott 4–1–12–1;
Irani 2–0–5–0; McGarry 13–1–62–2; D. R. Law 9–3–42–2; Such 22.3–8–39–5; Grayson
7–4–4–0.

Essex

P. J. Prichard st Rhodes b Rawnsley	45	– c McGrath b Ali	20
A. P. Grayson c Solanki b McGrath	0	– c Lampitt b Leatherdale	69
†B. J. Hyam c Rhodes b Ali	0	– (6) c Rhodes b McGrath	0
S. G. Law c Wilson b McGrath	19	– (3) not out	133
*R. C. Irani c Ali b McGrath	0	– (4) c Driver b Solanki	35
S. D. Peters c Leatherdale b McGrath	23	– (5) c Rhodes b McGrath	0
D. R. Law c Solanki b Rawnsley	2	– lbw b McGrath	4
M. C. Ilott c Solanki b McGrath	25	– not out	14
P. M. Such not out	6		
A. C. McGarry c and b Solanki	1		
D. D. J. Robinson absent hurt			
B 4, n-b 6	10	B 2, w 2, n-b 8	12
	131		**(6 wkts) 287**

1/3 2/4 3/35 4/35 5/79   131
6/85 7/121 8/130 9/131

1/35 2/153 3/258   (6 wkts) 287
4/259 5/259 6/265

Bonus points – Worcestershire 3.

Bowling: *First Innings*—McGrath 18–7–40–5; Ali 7–2–29–1; Rawnsley 18–7–35–2; Solanki 3.3–0–7–1; Lampitt 7–2–16–0. *Second Innings*—McGrath 18.5–4–75–3; Ali 11–3–38–1; Rawnsley 26–7–64–0; Lampitt 4–0–23–0; Solanki 18–0–75–1; Leatherdale 3–1–10–1.

Umpires: A. Clarkson and A. A. Jones.

At Lord's, August 2, 3, 4, 5. ESSEX drew with MIDDLESEX.

At Kidderminster, August 9, 10, 11, 12. ESSEX beat WORCESTERSHIRE by ten wickets.

ESSEX v GLOUCESTERSHIRE

At Colchester, August 16, 17, 18, 19. Gloucestershire won by 104 runs. Gloucestershire 18 pts, Essex 2 pts. Toss: Gloucestershire.

Team-work rather than individual brilliance underwrote bottom-placed Gloucestershire's second straight win. A last-wicket partnership of 58 between the pugnacious Snape and Gannon, Gloucestershire's best in their first innings, followed by three important wickets from Gannon in a substandard Essex response, had its reward in the eventual lead of 150. Having noted the influence of spinners Such and Ball, and fearing the pitch might deteriorate, Alleyne did not enforce the follow-on. At 17 for four, with Cowan getting lift and movement, that decision looked debatable. But Barnett dug in, Snape hit 39 in 35 balls, and ultimately Essex needed 348 to win. They were mounting a serious challenge as Grayson and Stuart Law advanced to 123. Once they were out late on the third day, Gloucestershire had victory in hand. Irani resisted for almost two and three-quarter hours on the last day, but Alleyne wrapped up the match soon after lunch with three wickets.

Close of play: First day, Gloucestershire 278-9 (Snape 33*, Gannon 8*); Second day, Gloucestershire 11-2 (Hancock 0*, Barnett 0*); Third day, Essex 141-4 (Irani 5*, Peters 4*).

Gloucestershire

T. H. C. Hancock c Napier b Irani	43	– (2) b Cowan		2
D. R. Hewson c S. G. Law b Irani	12	– (1) c S. G. Law b Cowan		10
M. G. N. Windows c Peters b Such	25	– c Hyam b Irani		1
K. J. Barnett c Grayson b Cowan	24	– c Mason b Cowan		57
*M. W. Alleyne b Cowan	43	– c Peters b Cowan		2
C. G. Taylor c Napier b Mason	35	– c Prichard b Mason		37
†R. C. Russell c D. R. Law b Such	16	– lbw b Cowan		1
J. N. Snape not out	54	– c Napier b Mason		39
M. C. J. Ball b Such	6	– st Hyam b Mason		33
J. Lewis c Peters b Such	0	– c Napier b Irani		2
B. W. Gannon b Irani	28	– not out		4
B 7, l-b 5, w 8, n-b 18	38	L-b 1, n-b 8		9

1/30 2/85 3/105 4/135 5/184	324	1/10 2/11 3/13 4/17 5/112	197
6/215 7/258 8/266 9/266		6/115 7/128 8/173 9/179	

Bonus points – Gloucestershire 3, Essex 3.

Bowling: *First Innings*—Cowan 25–5–83–2; Irani 24.2–7–56–3; D. R. Law 9–1–41–0; Napier 8–2–28–0; Such 32–10–60–4; Mason 11–3–27–1; Grayson 12–3–17–0. *Second Innings*—Cowan 15–0–66–5; Irani 18–2–53–2; Such 11–5–22–0; D. R. Law 4–0–17–0; Mason 15.1–3–38–3.

Essex

P. J. Prichard c Taylor b Gannon	0	– c Ball b Lewis	12
A. P. Grayson c Windows b Lewis	56	– lbw b Ball	47
S. G. Law c Russell b Gannon	7	– c Ball b Gannon	58
*R. C. Irani c Barnett b Hancock	21	– (5) not out	33
S. D. Peters b Gannon	18	– (6) c Barnett b Gannon	16
G. R. Napier c Gannon b Ball	21	– (7) c Alleyne b Lewis	5
†B. J. Hyam b Alleyne	7	– (8) c Ball b Snape	2
D. R. Law c and b Ball	15	– (9) c Taylor b Alleyne	29
T. J. Mason not out	24	– (10) b Alleyne	3
A. P. Cowan c Russell b Ball	1	– (11) c Taylor b Alleyne	6
P. M. Such c Snape b Lewis	0	– (4) c Alleyne b Gannon	2
L-b 2, n-b 2	4	B 7, l-b 9, w 10, n-b 4	30
	174		**243**

1/1 2/15 3/48 4/75 5/110   1/30 2/123 3/128 4/137 5/163
6/128 7/141 8/155 9/171   6/171 7/188 8/227 9/237

Bonus points – Gloucestershire 3.

Bowling: *First Innings*—Lewis 16.3–7–37–2; Gannon 14–0–61–3; Hancock 10–3–18–1; Alleyne 10–3–24–1; Ball 17–4–32–3. *Second Innings*—Lewis 18–9–40–2; Gannon 14–0–66–3; Ball 29–10–52–1; Hancock 4–3–4–0; Alleyne 14–4–44–3; Snape 5–0–21–1.

Umpires: G. I. Burgess and N. G. Cowley.

ESSEX v GLAMORGAN

At Southend, August 30, 31, September 1, 2. Drawn. Essex 8 pts, Glamorgan 12 pts. Toss: Essex. Championship debuts: J. S. Foster, W. I. Jefferson; I. J. Thomas.

Essex began the final day requiring 140 from their remaining seven wickets to avoid an innings defeat by fellow promotion contenders Glamorgan. But Stuart Law and night-watchman Cowan completed a century stand in the morning, after which the steadfast Irani guided his team to safety. Like Law, he had been a major contributor to Essex's first innings, along with debutant Jamie Foster, who followed up his fifty by helping Irani add 77 in the second innings. In between, Glamorgan's batsmen, fresh from scoring 718 against Sussex, went past 500 against Essex for only the second time (previously 1948) and took a lead of 215. Maynard – captain, stand-in wicket-keeper and century-maker – was dropped behind on ten and went on to add 227 with Powell (15 fours), a county fourth-wicket record against Essex, before Such got them both in successive overs. A third hundred was in the offing until Ian Thomas was caught at long-off for 82, just when it seemed he could become the first Glamorgan player to hit one on Championship debut since Maynard in 1985.

Close of play: First day, Glamorgan 40-1 (Evans 2*, Cosker 0*); Second day, Glamorgan 360-6 (Dale 33*, I. J. Thomas 0*); Third day, Essex 75-3 (S. G. Law 18*, Cowan 7*).

Essex

P. J. Prichard b Watkin	8	– c Maynard b Cosker	32
A. P. Grayson lbw b S. D. Thomas	0	– c Maynard b Watkin	9
W. I. Jefferson lbw b Watkin	1	– b Croft	4
S. G. Law c Cosker b Croft	70	– c Newell b Croft	82
*R. C. Irani lbw b Cosker	95	– (6) not out	83
S. D. Peters c Maynard b S. D. Thomas	27	– (7) lbw b Cosker	8
†J. S. Foster lbw b Watkin	52	– (8) b Croft	34
D. R. Law c Maynard b Croft	3	– (9) c Powell b S. D. Thomas	1
R. S. G. Anderson c I. J. Thomas b Croft	0	– (10) not out	17
A. P. Cowan not out	30	– (5) st Maynard b Cosker	67
P. M. Such b S. D. Thomas	0		
L-b 6	6	B 6, l-b 5, n-b 2	13
	292		**(8 wkts dec.) 350**

1/4 2/8 3/13 4/124 5/166   1/27 2/49 3/53   (8 wkts dec.) 350
6/225 7/230 8/230 9/283   4/199 5/213 6/223
                     7/300 8/311

Bonus points – Essex 2, Glamorgan 3.

Bowling: *First Innings*—Watkin 18–5–46–3; S. D. Thomas 14.2–1–70–3; Newell 7–1–23–0; Dale 4–0–19–0; Croft 33–5–83–3; Cosker 27–6–45–1. *Second Innings*—Watkin 22–7–67–1; S. D. Thomas 23–4–71–1; Dale 9–1–19–0; Croft 48–13–114–3; Cosker 26–6–68–3.

Glamorgan

S. P. James b Cowan	30	R. D. B. Croft b Anderson		22
A. W. Evans c Peters b Cowan	8	S. D. Thomas not out		12
D. A. Cosker c Foster b Irani	5	S. L. Watkin not out		1
M. J. Powell c Prichard b Such	128	L-b 6, w 16, n-b 34		56
*†M. P. Maynard b Such	102			—
A. Dale c Grayson b Anderson	48	1/36 2/53 3/82	(9 wkts dec.)	507
K. Newell lbw b D. R. Law	13	4/309 5/312 6/349		
I. J. Thomas c Jefferson b Such	82	7/392 8/461 9/502		

Bonus points – Glamorgan 5, Essex 2 (Score at 130 overs: 401-7).

Bowling: Cowan 31–9–83–2; Irani 17–3–60–1; Anderson 29–8–109–2; D. R. Law 19–0–82–1; Such 41.5–8–95–3; Grayson 25–3–72–0.

Umpires: M. J. Harris and K. E. Palmer.

At Northampton, September 6, 7, 8, 9. ESSEX drew with NORTHAMPTONSHIRE.

ESSEX v WARWICKSHIRE

At Chelmsford, September 13, 14, 15, 16. Essex won by six wickets. Essex 15 pts, Warwickshire 6 pts. Toss: Essex.

On the last day of the season, both teams needed a win to ensure promotion. But after the washout of the third day, and the loss of the final morning, only contrivance could create a result. Despite having had the better of the first two days, Warwickshire were forced to agree a generous target for Essex – 201 in 56 overs – and gamble on bowling them out. It looked like paying off at 64 for four, but Irani and Peters snuffed out their hopes with an unbroken stand of 138 in 24 overs. Peters's 77 from 84 balls (13 fours) was his season's best. On the opening day, Wagh and Powell had taken toll of indifferent Essex bowling while running up 230, the highest opening stand in matches between these counties. Wagh's Championship-best 137 included 100 in boundaries and won him his county cap; next day, his suspect bowling action prompted the umpires to request he be taken off after one over. Robinson and Irani batted Essex out of trouble against an attack lacking Donald, Giddins and Giles – and on the final day Irani crowned his first year as captain by negotiating excellent terms, then getting Essex home in 39 overs to seal promotion.

Close of play: First day, Warwickshire 348-5 (Penney 5*, Brown 15*); Second day, Essex 208-5 (Irani 72*, Foster 7*); Third day, No play.

Warwickshire

M. J. Powell run out	106	– (2) not out	0
M. A. Wagh c Prichard b Such	137	– (1) not out	8
D. P. Ostler b Such	32		
D. L. Hemp c Foster b Anderson	11		
A. Singh c and b Such	7		
T. L. Penney not out	28		
D. R. Brown b Ilott	15		
*N. M. K. Smith b Ilott	13		
†K. J. Piper c Prichard b Cowan	0		
C. E. Dagnall not out	6		
B 4, l-b 9, w 2, n-b 30	45		

1/230 2/306 3/315 4/321   (8 wkts dec.) 400   (no wkt dec.) 8
5/329 6/348 7/370 8/379

A. Richardson did not bat.

Bonus points – Warwickshire 5, Essex 2.

Bowling: *First Innings*—Cowan 29–6–115–1; Ilott 25–10–64–2; Irani 13–5–18–0; Anderson 30.2–6–107–1; Such 28–7–83–3. *Second Innings*—Robinson 0.3–0–8–0.

Essex

P. J. Prichard lbw b Dagnall	0	– c Singh b Brown	19
A. P. Grayson lbw b Brown	17	– c Piper b Dagnall	7
D. D. J. Robinson c Ostler b Smith	92	– c Hemp b Dagnall	5
S. G. Law c Penney b Richardson	10	– lbw b Richardson	8
*R. C. Irani not out	72	– not out	64
S. D. Peters c Brown b Smith	1	– not out	77
†J. S. Foster not out	7		
L-b 1, n-b 8	9	B 8, l-b 4, w 8, n-b 2	22

1/0 2/38 3/63 4/179 5/183   (5 wkts dec.) 208   1/36 2/46 3/51 4/64   (4 wkts) 202

A. P. Cowan, R. S. G. Anderson, M. C. Ilott and P. M. Such did not bat.

Bonus points – Essex 1, Warwickshire 1.

Bowling: *First Innings*—Dagnall 19–8–48–1; Richardson 20–4–57–1; Brown 17–3–49–1; Smith 20–3–49–2; Wagh 1–0–4–0. *Second Innings*—Richardson 10–1–57–1; Dagnall 11.4–2–57–2; Brown 11–1–51–1; Smith 5–0–21–0; Hemp 1–0–4–0.

Umpires: B. Dudleston and J. H. Hampshire.

GLAMORGAN

Matthew Elliott

President: A. R. Lewis
Chairman: G. Elias
Chief Executive: M. J. Fatkin
Chairman, Cricket Committee: R. Needham
Cricket Secretary: C. L. Watkin
Captain: 2000 – M. P. Maynard
        2001 – S. P. James
First-Team Coach: J. R. Hammond
Head Groundsman: L. A. Smith
Scorer: B. T. Denning

At the start of his final season as captain, Matthew Maynard would have settled for an appearance at Lord's in a one-day final and Championship promotion to Division One. Not that promotion looked a possibility at the time of Glamorgan's Benson and Hedges Cup final against Gloucestershire – a joyful occasion for the club and their supporters, in spite of defeat. That was on June 10. They did not register their first Championship win for another three weeks, when Worcestershire were beaten at Swansea, the first of four successive victories that lifted Glamorgan from bottom to the head of the division. From then on, they remained in contention for a place in the top three.

Yet throughout that winning sequence, they were seldom able to field their best side. Robert Croft missed three of the four games and Maynard the middle two because of England calls, while injury prevented Steve Watkin from playing in the win against Middlesex at Southgate. There, and in the following game against Northamptonshire, they successfully chased targets in excess of 300 thanks to hundreds from Matthew Elliott, their Australian opening batsman. The left-handed Victorian topped the county batting averages with 1,076 first-class runs, even though he missed the last three Championship games because of a knee injury.

The club's commercial decision to allow a giant marquee at Sophia Gardens during the previous autumn's rugby union World Cup, covering the entire square and most of the playing area, gave head groundsman Len Smith enormous problems when it came to preparing for the 2000 season. He deserved much credit for getting pitches ready for the start, but for the first half of the season they lacked pace and bounce, with no team exceeding 300 in the first innings until Essex totalled 410 for seven in mid-June. The conditions were certainly a factor in Glamorgan acquiring as few as 27 batting points all season; only Gloucestershire and Worcestershire gained fewer in Division Two.

The annual game at Colwyn Bay, however, again created new batting records, with Glamorgan declaring at 718 for three after being inserted by Sussex. Steve James broke the club's individual record with 309 not out, Glamorgan's first triple-hundred, and with Elliott he shared a record opening partnership of 374. James, too, reached his 1,000 runs, although he was not as prolific as in previous seasons. Having led the side competently in Maynard's absence, he succeeds him in 2001.

Maynard's five years at the helm were marked by Glamorgan's Championship success in 1997 and imaginative leadership throughout. If his Championship runs fell short of expectations in 2000, hundreds in the Benson and Hedges semi-final and final reminded everyone, including the England selectors, of his batting talent. Michael Powell batted superbly at times and was awarded his cap after scoring a century against Essex at Southend. He ended the season with a blazing hundred against Middlesex to confirm that he is at his best playing shots. He strikes the ball as hard as anyone in the game and, once he eliminates the odd rash stroke and tightens his defence, has enough natural ability to play at the highest level.

After the euphoria of reaching a one-day final for the first time since 1977, Glamorgan made a promising start in the NatWest Trophy, beating Kent at Canterbury in the fourth round, but were outplayed by Warwickshire in the next. A six-match unbeaten run early on gave rise to promotion hopes in the National League, but they dropped to sixth after losing their final three games.

Darren Thomas was the only bowler to take 50 first-class wickets, although Watkin, with 48, would have but for missing three games through injury. Alex Wharf proved a useful acquisition from Nottinghamshire: as well as strengthening the seam attack, he hit his maiden Championship century after Glamorgan had been 77 for six at Northampton. The dependable Adrian Dale once more made his customary all-round contribution, but the county must be concerned that their younger players failed to progress. Alun Evans and Wayne Law suffered lean seasons, and Law, an exciting strokeplayer who in 1998 scored a century in his second Championship game, was released.

Simon Jones exhibited raw pace but was seldom fit, and Owen Parkin, although finishing high in the national averages, played only five first-class games. Croft and Dean Cosker rarely bowled in tandem; whenever a bowler was omitted from the chosen twelve, Cosker was generally the unlucky one, as pitches yet again encouraged counties to play only one spinner. He had been encouraged to adjust his action at the start of the season, but there was little evidence of any significant improvement. Adrian Shaw had his best season behind the stumps, until injury sidelined him in July, while his batting blossomed with three Championship fifties. Mark Wallace deputised and, when he was required for England's Under-19 Test side, Maynard took the gloves for Championship games and missed nothing.

Glamorgan have the talent to hold their own in Division One, but their prospects took a knock when they heard South Africa would not allow Jacques Kallis, their contracted overseas player, to return after a season's absence. Hopes that Elliott might agree to another year came to nothing, and left Glamorgan to find a replacement with a lot to live up to. – EDWARD BEVAN.

GLAMORGAN 2000

[*Bill Smith*]

Back row: A. W. Evans, W. L. Law, A. J. Davies, S. P. Jones, D. S. Harrison, A. P. Davies, I. J. Thomas, J. Hughes, M. A. Wallace. *Middle row*: G. N. Lewis (*Second Eleven scorer*), J. Derrick (*assistant coach*), K. Newell, A. G. Wharf, O. T. Parkin, M. J. Powell, D. A. Cosker, E. Mustafa (*physiotherapist*), B. T. Denning (*First Eleven scorer*). *Front row*: A. D. Shaw, M. T. G. Elliott, S. L. Watkin, J. R. Hammond (*first-team coach*), M. P. Maynard (*captain*), S. P. James, R. D. B. Croft, A. Dale, S. D. Thomas. *Inset*: D. D. Cherry.

GLAMORGAN RESULTS

All first-class matches – Played 18: Won 6, Lost 4, Drawn 8.

County Championship matches – Played 16: Won 5, Lost 3, Drawn 8.

PPP Healthcare County Championship, 3rd in Division 2; NatWest Trophy, q-f;
Benson and Hedges Cup, finalists; Norwich Union National League, 6th in Division 2.

COUNTY CHAMPIONSHIP AVERAGES

BATTING

Cap		M	I	NO	R	HS	100s	50s	Avge	Ct/St
2000	M. T. G. Elliott§ . . .	12	19	0	1,042	177	4	4	54.84	17
	I. J. Thomas†	3	5	1	177	82	0	1	44.25	3
1999	A. D. Shaw†	10	15	5	423	88*	0	3	42.30	24/3
1992	S. P. James	16	26	2	1,004	309*	3	2	41.83	5
1992	A. Dale	16	25	3	805	81	0	5	36.59	7
1987	M. P. Maynard	14	21	1	645	119*	2	4	32.25	17/2
2000	M. J. Powell†	16	25	0	784	128	2	4	31.36	9
	O. T. Parkin	3	4	3	30	13*	0	0	30.00	0
	M. A. Wallace†	3	5	1	116	59*	0	1	29.00	10
1997	S. D. Thomas†	16	19	6	318	52	0	1	24.46	2
1992	R. D. B. Croft†	11	12	2	227	56	0	2	22.70	4
1989	S. L. Watkin†	13	13	6	125	51	0	1	17.85	1
2000	A. G. Wharf	8	12	1	184	101*	1	0	16.72	4
	K. Newell	11	18	1	253	38*	0	0	14.88	4
	A. W. Evans†	3	5	0	56	19	0	0	11.20	0
	W. L. Law†	6	8	1	74	27	0	0	10.57	3
2000	D. A. Cosker.	10	13	3	87	14*	0	0	8.70	6

Also batted: D. S. Harrison† (1 match) 0, 27; S. P. Jones† (4 matches) 0, 0, 13.

* *Signifies not out.* † *Born in Wales.* § *Overseas player.*

BOWLING

	O	M	R	W	BB	5W/i	Avge
S. L. Watkin	389.4	108	1,067	48	6-26	2	22.22
A. G. Wharf	214.3	41	815	30	5-68	1	27.16
A. Dale	236.4	54	629	23	5-25	2	27.34
S. D. Thomas	468.4	88	1,579	51	5-43	2	30.96
D. A. Cosker	384.5	129	831	24	4-82	0	34.62
R. D. B. Croft	454	109	1,185	29	5-108	1	40.86

Also bowled: M. T. G. Elliott 20–5–43–0; D. S. Harrison 10–2–45–0; S. P. Jones 81–6–319–7;
M. P. Maynard 15.3–5–32–0; K. Newell 40–17–82–3; O. T. Parkin 69–17–197–7.

COUNTY RECORDS

Highest score for:	309*	S. P. James v Sussex at Colwyn Bay	2000
Highest score against:	322*	M. B. Loye (Northamptonshire) at Northampton. .	1998
Best bowling for:	10-51	J. Mercer v Worcestershire at Worcester	1936
Best bowling against:	10-18	G. Geary (Leicestershire) at Pontypridd	1929
Highest total for:	718-3 dec.	v Sussex at Colwyn Bay	2000
Highest total against:	712	by Northamptonshire at Northampton	1998
Lowest total for:	22	v Lancashire at Liverpool	1924
Lowest total against:	33	by Leicestershire at Ebbw Vale	1965

At Worcester, April 26, 27, 28, 29. GLAMORGAN drew with WORCESTERSHIRE.

At Birmingham, May 3, 4, 5, 6. GLAMORGAN drew with WARWICKSHIRE.

GLAMORGAN v GLOUCESTERSHIRE

At Cardiff, May 11, 12, 13, 14. Drawn. Glamorgan 9 pts, Gloucestershire 8 pts. Toss: Glamorgan.

Glamorgan's hopes of victory were thwarted by Russell and the Gloucestershire tailenders, who resisted for more than two hours after seven wickets had fallen between lunch and tea. Russell and Averis defended throughout 28 overs, and although Averis eventually lost Russell, then Lewis, Gloucestershire's last pair survived the final nine balls. On the opening day, Glamorgan had recovered from 13 for four, principally through Elliott's sound technique, and went on to gain two batting points, thanks to a last-wicket stand of 84 between Shaw and Watkin. Both achieved Championship-best scores, with Watkin's first half-century in 14 years of county cricket warmly applauded. That same day his wife, Caryl, was appointed Glamorgan's cricket secretary. They gained a slender lead when Gloucestershire lost their last five wickets for eight runs on the third morning, and they built on it with centuries from James and Maynard. A target of 309 in a minimum of 85 overs was always out of the visitors' reach. A. C. Smith, one of the ECB's pitch liaison officers, was at the ground on the first day but exonerated the Sophia Gardens strip, criticised after the Benson and Hedges quarter-final two days earlier.

Close of play: First day, Glamorgan 169-9 (Shaw 64*, Watkin 1*); Second day, Gloucestershire 161-4 (Barnett 41*, Harvey 54*); Third day, Glamorgan 258-4 (Maynard 97*).

Glamorgan

M. T. G. Elliott run out	49	– (2) run out		17
S. P. James c Russell b Lewis	0	– (1) st Russell b Ball		109
A. Dale b Lewis	6	– lbw b Cotterell		1
*M. P. Maynard b Harvey	1	– not out		119
M. J. Powell c Russell b Lewis	1	– c Hancock b Cotterell		19
W. L. Law b Harvey	1	– not out		17
†A. D. Shaw not out	88			
R. D. B. Croft lbw b Lewis	0			
S. D. Thomas st Russell b Cotterell	26			
D. A. Cosker lbw b Lewis	7			
S. L. Watkin c Alleyne b Lewis	51			
B 8, l-b 10, n-b 2	20	B 3, l-b 5, n-b 10		18

1/5 2/11 3/12 4/13 5/40	250	1/66 2/88	(4 wkts dec.) 300
6/83 7/94 8/147 9/166		3/175 4/258	

Bonus points – Glamorgan 2, Gloucestershire 3.

Bowling: *First Innings*—Lewis 28.4–6–73–6; Harvey 21–9–38–2; Averis 11–1–37–0; Cotterell 31–13–54–1; Ball 9–1–25–0; Alleyne 2–1–5–0. *Second Innings*—Lewis 12–2–38–0; Averis 11–5–31–0; Alleyne 11–2–38–0; Ball 21–1–113–1; Cotterell 23–2–72–2.

Gloucestershire

R. J. Cunliffe c Shaw b Watkin	19	–	(2) c Maynard b Cosker		22
T. H. C. Hancock b Croft	29	–	(1) c Law b Croft		30
M. G. N. Windows c Elliott b Watkin	4	–	c Law b Croft		0
K. J. Barnett lbw b Cosker	76	–	run out		5
*M. W. Alleyne b Croft	7	–	b Thomas		7
I. J. Harvey c Croft b Cosker	79	–	c Shaw b Croft		11
†R. C. Russell not out	14	–	lbw b Croft		46
M. C. J. Ball lbw b Croft	0	–	lbw b Cosker		5
J. M. M. Averis c Elliott b Watkin	4	–	not out		25
J. Lewis c Elliott b Thomas	0	–	c Dale b Watkin		20
T. P. Cotterell b Thomas	0	–	not out		0
B 2, l-b 4, w 2, n-b 2	10		L-b 3		3

1/34 2/42 3/72 4/90 5/198   242   1/53 2/55 3/55   (9 wkts) 174
6/234 7/235 8/241 9/242   4/61 5/75 6/79
                                      7/90 8/141 9/174

Bonus points – Gloucestershire 1, Glamorgan 3.

Bowling: *First Innings*—Watkin 16–4–48–3; Thomas 15.5–2–59–2; Croft 35–10–61–3; Dale 4–0–9–0; Cosker 30–12–58–2; Elliott 1–0–1–0. *Second Innings*—Thomas 14–3–28–1; Watkin 13–5–34–1; Cosker 38–23–40–2; Croft 41–16–65–4; Maynard 1–0–4–0.

Umpires: R. Palmer and P. Willey.

At Oxford, May 16, 17, 18. GLAMORGAN beat OXFORD UNIVERSITIES by an innings and 203 runs.

GLAMORGAN v WARWICKSHIRE

At Cardiff, May 23, 24, 25, 26. Drawn. Glamorgan 5 pts, Warwickshire 6 pts. Toss: Warwickshire.
Only 92 overs were possible in a game giving second-best to the weather. After the first day was washed out, Knight and Powell shared their second century opening partnership against Glamorgan in three weeks. Knight, who scored 233 in the game at Edgbaston, was in sight of another hundred when he became the second day's only casualty. It was a different story next day, once play eventually resumed at 4.30 p.m. With the fourth delivery, Jones began a collapse in which he took four wickets for one run in 12 balls. Watched by his father Jeff, the former Test bowler, who was attending a Glamorgan players' reunion, Jones uprooted Smith's leg stump with such pace that the groundstaff had to repair the wicket area. However, Glamorgan were denied further inroads: Penney and Brown added an unbroken 94 to earn Warwickshire two batting points. There was no play on the final day.
Close of play: First day, No play; Second day, Warwickshire 184-1 (Powell 73*, Ostler 26*); Third day, Warwickshire 280-5 (Penney 39*, Brown 54*).

Warwickshire

M. J. Powell b Jones	73	D. R. Brown not out		54
N. V. Knight lbw b Thomas	80			
D. P. Ostler b Jones	26	B 1, l-b 5, w 2		8
D. L. Hemp c Elliott b Jones	0			
T. L. Penney not out	39	1/135 2/185 3/185	(5 wkts)	280
*N. M. K. Smith b Jones	0	4/186 5/186		

A. Richardson, A. F. Giles, †K. J. Piper and E. S. H. Giddins did not bat.

Bonus points – Warwickshire 2, Glamorgan 1.

Bowling: Watkin 16–6–32–0; Thomas 20–3–76–1; Croft 34–6–85–0; Jones 14–1–47–4; Dale 7–0–27–0; Elliott 1–0–7–0.

Glamorgan

M. T. G. Elliott, S. P. James, M. J. Powell, *M. P. Maynard, A. Dale, W. L. Law, †A. D. Shaw, R. D. B. Croft, S. D. Thomas, S. P. Jones and S. L. Watkin.

Umpires: N. G. Cowley and B. Dudleston.

At Hove, May 31, June 1, 2, 3. GLAMORGAN lost to SUSSEX by ten wickets.

At Cardiff, June 6, 7, 8. GLAMORGAN lost to WEST INDIANS by 20 runs (See West Indian tour section).

GLAMORGAN v ESSEX

At Cardiff, June 15, 16, 17, 18. Drawn. Glamorgan 8 pts, Essex 8 pts. Toss: Essex.

More than 70 people walked out on the second day as Essex continued their first innings until 55 minutes before the close. The spectators became impatient with Irani's tactics when he spent nine hours 13 minutes over his career-best 168 not out. Mason, his cohort for the last four hours, compiled a maiden fifty. For all that they had to contend with a slow pitch, there was no excuse for scoring just 34 runs in 25 overs off Elliott and Maynard. As if the run-rate, just under two an over, hardly taxed the attention, only two wickets fell all day. Next morning, Glamorgan slumped to 72 for six. They were rescued by Maynard and Shaw, who put on 135, and as soon as the follow-on was avoided, Maynard declared. Watkin struck quickly, snatching three wickets in 11 balls, and with Thomas was chiefly responsible for Essex sliding to 92 for nine on the final morning. However, their last pair robbed Glamorgan of another half-hour, leaving 68 overs in which to chase 250. Because Irani deployed defensive fields, and employed a four-man seam attack until the final 15 minutes, they were seldom in contention. Fletcher, the Essex coach, blamed the pitch for his team's slow scoring, but Irani appeared over-preoccupied with not losing.

Close of play: First day, Essex 223-6 (Irani 69*, Law 21*); Second day, Glamorgan 47-1 (Elliott 32*, Cosker 0*); Third day, Essex 63-3 (Robinson 22*, Irani 14*).

Essex

P. J. Prichard b Cosker	59	– b Watkin	6
A. P. Grayson lbw b Watkin	5	– lbw b Watkin	13
D. D. J. Robinson c Elliott b Thomas	0	– c Shaw b Watkin	28
S. D. Peters b Watkin	39	– b Watkin	0
*R. C. Irani not out	168	– c Wharf b Thomas	19
I. N. Flanagan lbw b Newell	6	– lbw b Watkin	0
†B. J. Hyam lbw b Wharf	6	– c Cosker b Thomas	10
D. R. Law b Thomas	36	– lbw b Thomas	2
T. J. Mason not out	52	– c Shaw b Wharf	2
A. P. Cowan (did not bat)		– not out	3
M. C. Ilott (did not bat)		– lbw b Watkin	5
B 6, l-b 21, w 8, n-b 4	39	B 5, l-b 9	14

1/13 2/16 3/90 4/129   (7 wkts dec.) 410   1/16 2/23 3/23 4/70 5/76   102
5/155 6/190 7/263   6/77 7/89 8/92 9/92

Bonus points – Essex 2, Glamorgan 2 (Score at 130 overs: 265-7).

Bowling: *First Innings*—Watkin 31–12–65–2; Thomas 36–8–94–2; Dale 13–5–23–0; Wharf 28–7–79–1; Newell 21–14–21–1; Cosker 49–20–67–1; Elliott 13–4–20–0; Maynard 12–5–14–0. *Second Innings*—Watkin 14.2–6–26–6; Wharf 14–4–44–1; Thomas 16–9–14–3; Cosker 3–1–4–0.

Glamorgan

M. T. G. Elliott c Hyam b Ilott	32	– (2)	b Irani	52
S. P. James b Mason	6	– (1)	c Irani b Ilott	5
D. A. Cosker c Flanagan b Ilott	0			
M. J. Powell b Ilott	2	– (3)	b Cowan	34
*M. P. Maynard c Peters b Law	98	– (4)	c and b Law	44
A. Dale c Ilott b Cowan	10	– (5)	not out	24
K. Newell lbw b Cowan	0	– (6)	c Peters b Law	6
†A. D. Shaw not out	80	– (7)	not out	3
A. G. Wharf lbw b Cowan	1			
S. D. Thomas not out	15			
B 6, l-b 9, n-b 4	19		L-b 3, w 4, n-b 2	9

1/47 2/47 3/49 4/54   (8 wkts dec.) 263   1/12 2/86 3/110   (5 wkts) 177
5/72 6/72 7/207 8/233   4/162 5/172

S. L. Watkin did not bat.

Bonus points – Glamorgan 2, Essex 2.

Bowling: *First Innings*—Ilott 20–7–37–3; Cowan 21–6–56–3; Mason 25.2–9–65–1; Irani 15–5–34–0; Law 7–0–35–1; Grayson 6–0–21–0. *Second Innings*—Ilott 14–5–34–1; Irani 17–4–33–1; Cowan 16–3–57–1; Law 12–0–44–2; Mason 4–2–4–0; Grayson 3–2–2–0.

Umpires: M. J. Harris and N. A. Mallender.

GLAMORGAN v WORCESTERSHIRE

At Swansea, June 28, 29, 30, July 1. Glamorgan won by 81 runs. Glamorgan 16 pts, Worcestershire 3 pts. Toss: Glamorgan. Championship debut: Kadeer Ali.

The St Helen's Balconiers, whose fund-raising helps Glamorgan make a profit from their annual visit to Swansea, were delighted with the weather, the pitch – described by McGrath as the best he had seen all season – and the support from west Wales cricket followers. To crown it all, Glamorgan won their first Championship victory since visiting Headingley in September 1999. When McGrath had James caught behind in the first over of Glamorgan's second innings, the match was evenly poised. The home team's lead had been kept down to 22, thanks to a prolonged half-century from Leatherdale. Still, Elliott and Powell counter-attacked with relish for the next 24 overs to put on 102 and, with Dale adding a third half-century, Worcestershire's eventual target was 334 at two and a half runs an over. They were 147 for six on the final morning, but the sensible batting of Lampitt and Illingworth kept them in touch. Glamorgan's relief was audible when Lampitt was caught at bat-pad from Cosker's first ball after lunch, and from then on they retained control. Defeat cost Worcestershire the leadership of Division Two, while on the third day they learned that they would have to replay their NatWest tie with Gloucestershire.

Close of play: First day, Worcestershire 51-1 (Driver 12*, Rawnsley 18*); Second day, Glamorgan 156-3 (Powell 60*, Dale 19*); Third day, Worcestershire 134-4 (Leatherdale 47*, Rhodes 35*).

Glamorgan

M. T. G. Elliott lbw b McGrath	62	– (2) b Rawnsley	57
S. P. James c Rhodes b McGrath	28	– (1) c Rhodes b McGrath	0
M. J. Powell c Rhodes b Kabir Ali	20	– c Rhodes b Kabir Ali	70
*M. P. Maynard c Illingworth b Kabir Ali	6	– lbw b Lampitt	14
A. Dale run out	34	– b Lampitt	66
K. Newell c and b Lampitt	5	– lbw b Leatherdale	38
†A. D. Shaw c Wilson b McGrath	1	– c Solanki b Leatherdale	21
A. G. Wharf c Rawnsley b Leatherdale	20	– c Kabir Ali b McGrath	3
S. D. Thomas c Wilson b McGrath	6	– b Leatherdale	17
D. A. Cosker not out	12	– c Rhodes b McGrath	8
S. L. Watkin c Lampitt b Illingworth	0	– not out	2
L-b 8, n-b 16	24	L-b 7, n-b 8	15

1/74 2/126 3/133 4/134 5/172   218   1/0 2/102 3/123 4/186 5/229   311
6/179 7/188 8/194 9/217   6/271 7/276 8/287 9/301

Bonus points – Glamorgan 1, Worcestershire 3.

Bowling: *First Innings*—McGrath 20–3–72–3; Kabir Ali 13–5–39–2; Lampitt 12–4–31–1; Leatherdale 9–2–23–2; Illingworth 18.5–6–23–1; Rawnsley 14–4–21–0; Solanki 1–0–1–0. *Second Innings*—McGrath 24.1–8–70–3; Kabir Ali 14–1–42–1; Illingworth 22–9–51–0; Lampitt 19–7–40–2; Rawnsley 19–2–71–1; Solanki 3–0–13–0; Leatherdale 7–3–17–3.

Worcestershire

E. J. Wilson lbw b Thomas	18	– (2) c Maynard b Wharf	7
R. C. Driver lbw b Watkin	18	– (1) b Cosker	35
M. J. Rawnsley b Wharf	18	– (9) b Thomas	16
V. S. Solanki c Shaw b Thomas	40	– (3) lbw b Watkin	8
D. A. Leatherdale not out	59	– (4) lbw b Watkin	50
Kadeer Ali lbw b Thomas	0	– (5) c Elliott b Thomas	0
*†S. J. Rhodes c James b Wharf	4	– (6) c Dale b Cosker	37
S. R. Lampitt c Dale b Cosker	1	– (7) c Powell b Cosker	43
R. K. Illingworth b Wharf	15	– (8) c Shaw b Thomas	44
Kabir Ali c Cosker b Thomas	9	– c James b Cosker	5
G. D. McGrath c Shaw b Thomas	2	– not out	0
B 1, l-b 5, w 6	12	L-b 5, n-b 2	7

1/25 2/51 3/59 4/118 5/118   196   1/18 2/27 3/71 4/74 5/137   252
6/126 7/127 8/152 9/176   6/147 7/217 8/247 9/252

Bonus points – Glamorgan 3.

Bowling: *First Innings*—Watkin 18–4–48–1; Thomas 19.5–4–72–5; Wharf 14–3–41–3; Dale 7–1–14–0; Cosker 12–5–15–1. *Second Innings*—Watkin 19–5–49–2; Wharf 17–3–63–1; Cosker 37–10–82–4; Thomas 14.2–1–50–3; Elliott 2–1–2–0; Newell 1–0–1–0.

Umpires: M. R. Benson and R. A. White.

At Northampton, July 7, 8, 9. GLAMORGAN beat NORTHAMPTONSHIRE by 144 runs.

At Southgate, July 12, 13, 14, 15. GLAMORGAN beat MIDDLESEX by two wickets.

GLAMORGAN v NORTHAMPTONSHIRE

At Cardiff, July 19, 20, 21, 22. Glamorgan won by five wickets. Glamorgan 15 pts, Northamptonshire 4 pts. Toss: Northamptonshire.

Glamorgan's fourth consecutive win capped a run of form which lifted them from the bottom to the head of Division Two. For the second successive Saturday, they successfully chased more than 300, thanks again to a century from Elliott, who laid the foundation by batting for five and a quarter hours; with Powell, he added 129 for the second wicket. Although Glamorgan still needed 100 when he was fourth out, their middle order led them to victory with 16 overs remaining. After both sides had moderate first innings, Northamptonshire were better placed at the end of the second day, 141 ahead with eight wickets in hand and Glamorgan weakened by Watkin's groin strain. However, Croft's five wickets in an unchanged spell of 34 overs on the third day, and three more for Thomas after his first-innings five, undermined Northamptonshire. They lost their last four wickets without a run. Croft's success suggested Northamptonshire's off-spinners, Brown and Swann, would dictate the course of the final day; instead, Elliott held sway.

Close of play: First day, Glamorgan 39-2 (Elliott 19*, Maynard 6*); Second day, Northamptonshire 110-2 (Loye 42*, Sales 17*); Third day, Glamorgan 125-1 (Elliott 66*, Powell 37*).

Northamptonshire

A. S. Rollins lbw b Watkin	0	– (2) c Elliott b Dale	0
*M. L. Hayden st Shaw b Dale	40	– (1) c Shaw b Cosker	51
M. B. Loye c Shaw b Thomas	0	– c Elliott b Croft	42
D. J. Sales c Shaw b Thomas	2	– c Thomas b Croft	51
J. W. Cook b Thomas	53	– lbw b Croft	11
A. L. Penberthy c Shaw b Croft	26	– c sub b Thomas	57
G. P. Swann c Elliott b Croft	48	– lbw b Thomas	19
†D. Ripley c Maynard b Thomas	27	– c Dale b Thomas	33
M. R. Strong b Croft	18	– c Powell b Croft	0
D. M. Cousins c Elliott b Thomas	1	– st Shaw b Croft	0
J. F. Brown not out	8	– not out	0
L-b 2, w 4	6	B 5, l-b 8	13

1/0 2/3 3/13 4/62 5/107	229	1/6 2/72 3/110 4/140 5/177	277
6/172 7/175 8/207 9/215		6/213 7/277 8/277 9/277	

Bonus points – Northamptonshire 1, Glamorgan 3.

Bowling: *First Innings*—Watkin 7.3–4–15–1; Thomas 21–6–43–5; Croft 28.2–8–77–3; Dale 16–4–50–1; Cosker 14–3–40–0; Maynard 0.3–0–2–0. *Second Innings*—Thomas 20.3–9–47–3; Dale 14–4–27–1; Croft 46–10–108–5; Cosker 22–2–82–1.

Glamorgan

M. T. G. Elliott c Ripley b Brown	76	– (2) c Ripley b Brown	117
S. P. James c Ripley b Cousins	8	– (1) lbw b Cousins	15
M. J. Powell lbw b Strong	2	– lbw b Cousins	53
*M. P. Maynard c Cook b Strong	6	– c and b Swann	1
A. Dale c and b Strong	6	– c Rollins b Brown	35
K. Newell c Ripley b Brown	27	– not out	38
†A. D. Shaw st Ripley b Brown	36	– not out	37
R. D. B. Croft c Cousins b Brown	19		
S. D. Thomas c Hayden b Strong	6		
D. A. Cosker lbw b Cousins	2		
S. L. Watkin not out	2		
W 4, n-b 4	8	B 7, l-b 3, w 2, n-b 2	14

1/21 2/32 3/42 4/50 5/104	198	1/36 2/165 3/166	(5 wkts)	310
6/145 7/171 8/178 9/190		4/209 5/242		

Bonus points – Northamptonshire 3.

Bowling: *First Innings*—Cousins 21–8–45–2; Strong 17–4–50–4; Brown 31.2–13–56–4; Penberthy 9–0–26–0; Swann 7–2–21–0. *Second Innings*—Cousins 18–4–35–2; Strong 9–0–35–0; Swann 28.3–6–95–1; Penberthy 21–7–42–0; Brown 41–7–93–2.

Umpires: J. W. Holder and R. Palmer.

At Bristol, August 2, 3, 4, 5. GLAMORGAN lost to GLOUCESTERSHIRE by ten wickets.

GLAMORGAN v NOTTINGHAMSHIRE

At Cardiff, August 16, 17, 18, 19. Drawn. Glamorgan 9 pts, Nottinghamshire 10 pts. Toss: Glamorgan.
Nottinghamshire had Glamorgan 88 for six on the final afternoon, just 33 ahead, but Dale and Croft blocked out the last ten overs, leaving the visitors to rue the rain that wiped out the third day and cost them the first hour of the final morning. There was appreciable turn for their slow left-armers, Stemp – who had opened the bowling – and Afzaal, but even so Glamorgan displayed a lack of application, just as they had in the latter part of their first innings. On the opening day, seven wickets tumbled for 59 after James, Maynard and Dale had seen them to 229 for three. Nottinghamshire's top order also batted profitably. Afzaal took three hours to reach the nineties but another hour for his hundred, getting there in the last over of the second day. But for the weather, he might then have proved a match-winner with the ball.
Close of play: First day, Nottinghamshire 10-0 (Bicknell 1*, Welton 9*); Second day, Nottinghamshire 316-6 (Afzaal 100*, Franks 22*); Third day, No play.

Glamorgan

S. P. James c and b Franks	77	– c Gallian b Stemp	30
W. L. Law c Johnson b Stemp	27	– c Gallian b Stemp	0
M. J. Powell c Read b Franks	2	– c Franks b Stemp	33
*M. P. Maynard b Harris	77	– c Johnson b Afzaal	0
A. Dale lbw b Harris	36	– not out	20
K. Newell b Stemp	3	– b Afzaal	2
†M. A. Wallace lbw b Stemp	11	– c Welton b Afzaal	2
R. D. B. Croft c Gallian b Harris	13	– not out	1
A. G. Wharf b Harris	1		
S. D. Thomas b Stemp	5		
D. A. Cosker not out	14		
B 4, l-b 8, w 2, n-b 8	22	B 6, l-b 5	11

1/52 2/65 3/166 4/229 5/232   **288**   1/3 2/67 3/67   (6 wkts) 99
6/252 7/252 8/253 9/262   4/69 5/78 6/88

Bonus points – Glamorgan 2, Nottinghamshire 3.

Bowling: *First Innings*—Reiffel 13–1–49–0; Harris 28.5–6–101–4; Franks 13–0–40–2; Stemp 33–12–67–4; Afzaal 9–2–19–0. *Second Innings*—Stemp 33–21–34–3; Reiffel 5–4–4–0; Franks 3–1–6–0; Afzaal 21–11–26–3; Harris 5–0–18–0; Bicknell 1–1–0–0.

Nottinghamshire

D. J. Bicknell lbw b Croft	20	P. R. Reiffel c and b Wharf	4
G. E. Welton c Wallace b Thomas	74	A. J. Harris lbw b Thomas	3
*J. E. R. Gallian c Maynard b Croft	13	R. D. Stemp not out	4
U. Afzaal c Maynard b Wharf	103		
J. E. Morris c Newell b Cosker	28	B 6, l-b 2, n-b 9	17
P. Johnson b Cosker	43		
†C. M. W. Read lbw b Croft	1	1/55 2/97 3/127 4/184 5/279	343
P. J. Franks c Wallace b Wharf	33	6/288 7/332 8/336 9/337	

Bonus points – Nottinghamshire 3, Glamorgan 3.

Bowling: Wharf 16–3–47–3; Thomas 22–3–69–2; Croft 45–14–108–3; Cosker 36–8–96–2; Dale 5–1–15–0.

Umpires: M. J. Kitchen and P. Willey.

GLAMORGAN v SUSSEX

At Colwyn Bay, August 22, 23, 24, 25. Glamorgan won by an innings and 60 runs. Glamorgan 20 pts, Sussex 3 pts. Toss: Sussex. Championship debut: M. H. Yardy.

For the second year in succession, a trip to the Rhos ground brought Glamorgan's biggest total. Their 718 for three, exceeding their previous best of 648 for four here against Nottinghamshire a year earlier, was the highest Championship score for fewer than four wickets, and the 12th highest ever. Again, James paved the way, passing Emrys Davies's 61-year-old record of 287 not out, against Gloucestershire at Newport, to become the first batsman to score a triple-hundred for Glamorgan. Put in by Adams on a green pitch, he and Elliott opened with 374 in five hours, eclipsing the county's previous first-wicket record. Elliott's fourth and biggest Championship

---

PARTNERSHIPS OF 300 OR MORE FOR GLAMORGAN

425* for 4th	A. Dale and I. V. A. Richards v Middlesex at Cardiff	1993
374 for 1st	**M. T. G. Elliott and S. P. James v Sussex at Colwyn Bay**	**2000**
330 for 1st	A. Jones and R. C. Fredericks v Northamptonshire at Swansea	1972
313 for 3rd	D. E. Davies and W. E. Jones v Essex at Brentwood	1948
306* for 4th	Javed Miandad and Younis Ahmed v Australians at Neath	1985
306 for 3rd	D. L. Hemp and M. P. Maynard v Gloucestershire at Abergavenny . .	1995

Research: Andrew Hignell

HIGHEST TOTALS IN THE COUNTY CHAMPIONSHIP

887	Yorkshire v Warwickshire at Birmingham	1896
863	Lancashire v Surrey at The Oval	1990
811	Surrey v Somerset at The Oval	1899
810-4 dec.	Warwickshire v Durham at Birmingham	1994
803-4 dec.	Kent v Essex at Brentwood	1934
801	Lancashire v Somerset at Taunton	1895
781-7 dec.	Northamptonshire v Nottinghamshire at Northampton	1995
761-6 dec.	Essex v Leicestershire at Chelmsford	1990
742	Surrey v Hampshire at The Oval	1909
739-7 dec.	Nottinghamshire v Leicestershire at Nottingham	1903
726	Nottinghamshire v Sussex at Nottingham	1895
718-3 dec.	**Glamorgan v Sussex at Colwyn Bay**	**2000**

---

hundred contained seven sixes and 15 fours; James's fifth double-century for the club beat the record he had shared with Javed Miandad. He had further century stands with Powell and Maynard, and had batted a minute over ten hours, hitting 41 fours – the most by a Glamorgan batsman in an innings – from 491 balls when Maynard declared on the second afternoon. Five Sussex bowlers had conceded more than 100 and, not surprisingly, their early batsmen were swamped by the prospect of making 569 to avoid the follow-on. However, Adams and Rashid, scoring his maiden hundred, put on 232 before the last five wickets fell for 24 to Wharf, Watkin and the second new ball. Wharf returned five in an innings for the first time and received his cap. Despite valiant half-centuries from Adams, Martin-Jenkins and Rashid on Sussex's second attempt, Glamorgan banked maximum points just after lunch and jumped from seventh to third in the table.

Close of play: First day, Glamorgan 457-1 (James 193*, Powell 48*); Second day, Sussex 112-5 (Adams 55*, Rashid 13*); Third day, Sussex 168-4 (Adams 68*, Martin-Jenkins 40*).

Glamorgan

M. T. G. Elliott b Kirtley	177	A. Dale not out	48
S. P. James not out	309	B 12, l-b 13, w 8, n-b 20	53
M. J. Powell b Kirtley	64		
*†M. P. Maynard b House	67	1/374 2/497 3/631 (3 wkts dec.)	718

K. Newell, R. D. B. Croft, S. D. Thomas, A. G. Wharf, D. A. Cosker and S. L. Watkin did not bat.

Bonus points – Glamorgan 5 (Score at 130 overs: 584-2).

Bowling: Lewry 29–3–131–0; Kirtley 40–5–169–2; Martin-Jenkins 22–2–117–0; Robinson 30–4–111–0; Rashid 24–3–111–0; Yardy 5–0–17–0; House 10–0–34–1; Adams 2–0–3–0.

Sussex

R. R. Montgomerie c Maynard b Cosker	23	– c Powell b Watkin	6
M. H. Yardy b Wharf	4	– b Wharf	9
P. A. Cottey c Maynard b Wharf	2	– c sub b Watkin	2
*C. J. Adams c Cosker b Wharf	156	– lbw b Wharf	68
W. J. House c Croft b Watkin	0	– lbw b Dale	13
R. S. C. Martin-Jenkins c sub b Watkin	8	– b Dale	77
U. B. A. Rashid c Croft b Watkin	110	– c Wharf b Dale	54
†N. J. Wilton c James b Wharf	15	– not out	32
R. J. Kirtley c Maynard b Watkin	4	– b Dale	12
J. D. Lewry not out	1	– b Dale	4
M. A. Robinson b Wharf	0	– b Croft	2
L-b 5, n-b 14	19	B 4, l-b 15, n-b 18	37

1/9 2/11 3/77 4/78 5/86   342   1/19 2/21 3/26 4/50 5/176   316
6/318 7/322 8/336 9/342   6/260 7/267 8/293 9/305

Bonus points – Sussex 3, Glamorgan 3.

Bowling: *First Innings*—Wharf 16.5–3–68–5; Watkin 26–7–76–4; Thomas 21–5–69–0; Croft 25–5–77–0; Cosker 18–9–43–1; Dale 2–1–4–0. *Second Innings*—Wharf 9–0–65–2; Watkin 15–4–45–2; Croft 14.5–2–42–1; Thomas 15–2–72–0; Dale 16–4–46–5; Cosker 7–0–27–0.

Umpires: J. W. Holder and J. W. Lloyds.

At Southend, August 30, 31, September 1, 2. GLAMORGAN drew with ESSEX.

At Nottingham, September 6, 7, 8. GLAMORGAN lost to NOTTINGHAMSHIRE by seven wickets.

GLAMORGAN v MIDDLESEX

At Cardiff, September 13, 14, 15, 16. Drawn. Glamorgan 10 pts, Middlesex 11 pts. Toss: Middlesex.
    Two bowling points on the final day, plus the eventual draw, were enough to secure Glamorgan promotion, a satisfying conclusion to Maynard's captaincy. Five other teams began the day in contention but, because rain played havoc with the round, results rather than bonus points were the priority elsewhere. As the drama unfolded, Glamorgan knew that six more points would guarantee at least third place. However, Middlesex, anxious not to finish last for the first time in their history, made Glamorgan fight for their wickets after Parkin's early strikes had them 40 for four in the brief spells of play on the previous two days. Langer, dropped behind on eight, ended his season with an unbeaten double-century, hitting a six and 22 fours in five hours nine minutes and 250 balls. Thomas made the breakthrough by dismissing Ramprakash and ensured promotion by taking the ninth wicket. Powell lit up the opening day with 114, featuring 18 fours in 135 balls, an innings resplendent with drives and among the best by a Glamorgan batsman all season.
    Close of play: First day, Glamorgan 325; Second day, Middlesex 38-3 (Shah 15*, Ramprakash 8*); Third day, Middlesex 101-4 (Ramprakash 40*, Langer 29*).

Glamorgan

S. P. James c Nash b Fraser	0	– not out	35
I. J. Thomas c Fraser b Johnson	5	– not out	45
M. J. Powell c Shah b Tufnell	114		
*M. P. Maynard c Nash b Johnson	11		
A. Dale c Langer b Tufnell	57		
K. Newell c Nash b Johnson	1		
†M. A. Wallace c Hutton b Bloomfield	34		
R. D. B. Croft c Joyce b Johnson	50		
S. D. Thomas c Joyce b Tufnell	3		
S. L. Watkin lbw b Tufnell	7		
O. T. Parkin not out	13		
B 4, l-b 12, n-b 14	30	B 4, l-b 1, n-b 8	13

1/0 2/26 3/65 4/176 5/183	325	(no wkt) 93
6/217 7/270 8/289 9/305		

Bonus points – Glamorgan 3, Middlesex 3.

Bowling: *First Innings*—Fraser 15–4–47–1; Bloomfield 13–2–65–0; Johnson 26–8–76–4; Tufnell 36.1–11–74–4; Hutton 5–0–22–0; Shah 1–0–8–0; Ramprakash 7–1–17–0. *Second Innings*—Fraser 5–0–28–0; Bloomfield 4–0–17–0; Tufnell 5–0–15–0; Joyce 4–1–15–0; Strauss 1–0–13–0.

Middlesex

A. J. Strauss c Dale b Parkin	9	A. R. C. Fraser c Dale b Croft	0
B. L. Hutton c Wallace b Parkin	6	T. F. Bloomfield c Wallace	
O. A. Shah lbw b Parkin	15	b S. D. Thomas	2
E. C. Joyce lbw b Parkin	0	P. C. R. Tufnell c and b Croft	0
M. R. Ramprakash c Maynard			
b S. D. Thomas	51	L-b 7, n-b 2	9
*J. L. Langer not out	213		
†D. C. Nash c Powell b Newell	41	1/12 2/19 3/19 4/40 5/134	387
R. L. Johnson c Powell b S. D. Thomas	41	6/221 7/302 8/323 9/331	

Bonus points – Middlesex 4, Glamorgan 3.

Bowling: Watkin 20–3–78–0; Parkin 24–5–74–4; Croft 25.5–2–109–2; S. D. Thomas 19–1–88–3; Dale 5–1–16–0; Newell 4–1–12–1; Maynard 1–0–3–0.

Umpires: G. I. Burgess and D. J. Constant.

540

GLOUCESTERSHIRE

President: N. P. Walters
Chairman: J. C. Higson
Chief Executive: C. L. Sexstone
Chairman, Cricket Committee: A. S. Brown
Captain: M. W. Alleyne
Director of Development: A. W. Stovold
Director of Cricket: J. G. Bracewell
Head Groundsman: D. Bridle
Scorer: K. T. Gerrish

Jon Lewis

A "Trophy" was once a beer that Gloucestershire sold in the club bars, not something they put in the committee-room cabinet. But times have changed at Nevil Road. Two cups in 1999 seemed a feast, but they were simply the *hors d'oeuvre* for 2000 when, in their best summer ever, the county made a unique clean sweep of the three limited-overs competitions, and missed Championship promotion by two points. Yet even such heady success had a down side. Prize money came to £176,400 but, with the players banking record bonuses and revenue affected by the wretched weather, Gloucestershire faced a financial loss. In the circumstances, the club had every reason to be critical of ticket allocation for the showpiece Lord's games, feeling that the participating counties received less than their due.

Getting there was not without scares. They scrambled through the Benson and Hedges Cup qualifying stage after losing the opening tie to Glamorgan, their eventual opponents at Lord's. Eleven days after retaining that title, they looked to have lost their hold on the NatWest Trophy when Worcestershire beat them by three wickets. But a journalist spotted an ineligible player in their neighbours' ranks, the ECB decreed a replay, and Gloucestershire lived again, winning by five runs. Next day, they won against all the odds at Leicester and marched on to Lord's with home victories over Northamptonshire and Lancashire. Deciding the final on Duckworth/Lewis calculations might have been unsatisfactory for Warwickshire and the neutrals in the crowd; Gloucestershire supporters, brandishing their frozen chicken talisman, were happy to settle for any method.

The League title came their way ten days later in a hotel lounge in Brighton, where the Gloucestershire players watched Somerset, the only side who could deny them, lose a televised floodlit match at Old Trafford. By way of celebrating, they demolished Sussex in the Championship inside two days, with Ian Harvey returning match figures of ten for 32. This gave them an outside chance of promotion, a considerable turnaround for a side whose early performances had produced a stream of critical letters to chief executive Colin Sexstone. In mid-August, they were propping up Division Two.

Yet even at that low point, the one-day spirit was surging through their Championship veins, and they won five of their last six matches to finish with six wins in all. Only divisional champions Northamptonshire won more. What let them down in the promotion stakes was their batting, which managed just 20 points, the lowest tally in the division. By late summer the search was on for a batsman, preferably a left-hander, to help rectify this weakness in 2001.

A troika of coach John Bracewell, captain Mark Alleyne and veteran Jack Russell moulded the side so that it was always more than the sum of its parts. For the coach, the vital thing was that his team at last stepped out of the shadow of Courtney Walsh. Their success, particularly in the one-day game, derived from their ability to group around an individual success with bat or ball and build upon it. This gave them a collective mental toughness, reflected in catches held and runs saved, which they latterly carried through into their Championship cricket.

Bracewell was rewarded with an extended contract and the title of director of cricket, while Alleyne's leadership qualities were again recognised by the England A selectors. It was not an easy season for the captain. Persistent back pain put him on pain-killers, and he missed his first county match in ten summers. At one point, with his batting average around 17, he had to be dissuaded from dropping himself. A hand injury in the Zimbabwean game interrupted Tim Hancock's season, but he came back with a first one-day hundred to set up the NatWest quarter-final win, and his bowling was Alleyne's trump card in the final.

There was irritation, bordering on indignation, when no one apart from Alleyne won a tour place. Jon Lewis was certainly unlucky, until Steve Harmison's withdrawal from the A side gave him his chance. With a grip more over the top of the ball, so that he hit the pitch much harder, and bowling a shorter length, Lewis took more first-class wickets, 72 at 20.91, than any bowler except Worcestershire's Glenn McGrath. Matt Windows came through a poor patch to reach his 1,000 runs for a second time, but like Lewis he was not immediately apparent in the national averages. Both have a case to prove if they are to step up into international cricket. Mike Smith, though his wicket haul was down, remained a pillar of the shorter game, bowling straight through at the start of an innings with mean economy, and Kim Barnett, who turned 40 mid-season, set aside both his years and tendonitis in a knee as he harnessed his experience to the hunt for trophies.

This is the time for younger players to come through. Chris Taylor, who made 300 not out for the Second Eleven at Taunton in 1999, marked his first-class debut with a century at Lord's, rallying Gloucestershire with classical cuts and pulls after they had been 29 for four. James Averis, stronger for a winter abroad, emerged as a staunch member of the one-day attack, while Ben Gannon was given the freedom to bowl as fast as he liked and encouraged to experiment with his grip and run. When he develops rhythm, he has the potential to take the new ball in the Championship. Certainly, the talent available makes the future exciting; no one is taking Gloucestershire lightly now. – GRAHAM RUSSELL.

GLOUCESTERSHIRE 2000

[*Bill Smith*]

Back row: P. White (*physiotherapist*), I. Mohammad, T. P. Cotterell, D. J. Forder, M. J. Cawdron, B. W. Gannon, C. G. Taylor. *Middle row:* K. T. Gerrish (*scorer*), J. G. Bracewell (*first-team coach*), A. J. Wright (*Second Eleven coach*), D. R. Hewson, J. N. Snape, M. A. Hardinges, J. M. M. Averis, R. J. Cunliffe, K. J. Barnett, A. W. Stovold (*director of development*). *Front row:* J. Lewis, M. G. N. Windows, T. H. C. Hancock, M. W. Alleyne (*captain*), J. C. Higson (*chairman*), R. C. Russell, A. M. Smith, M. C. J. Ball, R. C. J. Williams. *Inset:* I. J. Harvey.

GLOUCESTERSHIRE RESULTS

All first-class matches – Played 18: Won 6, Lost 5, Drawn 7.

County Championship matches – Played 16: Won 6, Lost 4, Drawn 6.

PPP Healthcare County Championship, 4th in Division 2; NatWest Trophy, winners; Benson and Hedges Cup, winners; Norwich Union National League, winners in Division 1.

COUNTY CHAMPIONSHIP AVERAGES

BATTING

Cap		M	I	NO	R	HS	100s	50s	Avge	Ct/St
1999	K. J. Barnett	10	15	1	522	106	1	3	37.28	8
1998	M. G. N. Windows† . .	16	26	3	790	107	1	6	34.34	3
1999	J. N. Snape.	13	18	3	491	54*	0	3	32.73	7
1985	R. C. Russell†	14	20	3	522	110*	1	2	30.70	39/3
1999	I. J. Harvey§	10	14	1	395	79	0	4	30.38	10
	C. G. Taylor†	10	18	2	459	104	1	0	28.68	6
	D. R. Hewson†	10	19	1	410	67	0	3	22.77	5
1996	M. C. J. Ball†	8	12	2	212	53	0	1	21.20	13
1990	M. W. Alleyne.	15	23	0	409	126	1	0	17.78	13
	I. Mohammed	3	4	0	67	24	0	0	16.75	1
1998	T. H. C. Hancock . .	13	21	1	322	46	0	0	16.10	7
	M. J. Cawdron	3	5	0	74	27	0	0	14.80	1
1995	A. M. Smith	9	10	6	54	14	0	0	13.50	1
	B. W. Gannon	7	8	3	64	28	0	0	12.80	3
	R. J. Cunliffe	7	12	0	127	36	0	0	10.58	10
	J. M. M. Averis† . . .	4	7	1	60	25*	0	0	10.00	1
1998	J. Lewis	14	20	2	156	38	0	0	8.66	3
	T. P. Cotterell	6	8	3	6	5*	0	0	1.20	1

Also batted: A. N. Bressington† (1 match) 2* (1 ct); M. A. Hardinges† (1 match) 0, 0; R. C. J. Williams† (cap 1996) (2 matches) 28*, 5, 43 (11 ct, 1 st).

* Signifies not out.   † Born in Gloucestershire.   § Overseas player.

BOWLING

	O	M	R	W	BB	5W/i	Avge
I. J. Harvey	254.2	79	658	40	6-19	3	16.45
A. M. Smith	250.4	70	623	30	5-52	1	20.76
M. J. Cawdron	98.1	32	258	12	5-45	1	21.50
B. W. Gannon	164.5	31	589	27	5-58	1	21.81
J. Lewis	463.4	131	1,285	56	6-47	3	22.94
M. W. Alleyne	241.5	68	665	24	6-49	1	27.70
M. C. J. Ball	218.1	55	540	15	3-31	0	36.00

Also bowled: J. M. M. Averis 118.2–29–388–5; A. N. Bressington 20–6–49–5; T. P. Cotterell 121–31–329–6; T. H. C. Hancock 65–20–143–8; M. A. Hardinges 23–9–36–3; J. N. Snape 77.3–20–202–6; C. G. Taylor 27.3–5–136–3.

COUNTY RECORDS

Highest score for:	318*	W. G. Grace v Yorkshire at Cheltenham	1876
Highest score against:	296	A. O. Jones (Nottinghamshire) at Nottingham	1903
Best bowling for:	10-40	E. G. Dennett v Essex at Bristol	1906
Best bowling against:	{ 10-66	A. A. Mailey (Australians) at Cheltenham	1921
	{ 10-66	K. Smales (Nottinghamshire) at Stroud	1956
Highest total for:	653-6 dec.	v Glamorgan at Bristol	1928
Highest total against:	774-7 dec.	by Australians at Bristol	1948
Lowest total for:	17	v Australians at Cheltenham	1896
Lowest total against:	12	by Northamptonshire at Gloucester	1907

GLOUCESTERSHIRE v SUSSEX

At Bristol, April 26, 27, 28, 29. Drawn. Gloucestershire 5 pts, Sussex 4 pts. County debut: I. Mohammed. Toss: Sussex.

The water-hog pumped 10,000 gallons from Bristol's big ground during April, twice as much as in an average season, but it could not save Gloucestershire's first match of the new-style Championship from being washed out. Only 39 overs were bowled, all of them on the third day. Bevan scored a comfortable 46, before fellow-Australian Harvey had him caught at the wicket, flicking at a long-hop. Smith skilfully exploited the conditions to snare three wickets in his ten overs.

Close of play: First day, No play; Second day, No play; Third day, Sussex 110-5 (House 0*, Martin-Jenkins 4*).

Sussex

R. R. Montgomerie lbw b Smith	0	R. S. C. Martin-Jenkins not out	4
M. T. E. Peirce c Alleyne b Smith	2		
M. G. Bevan c Russell b Harvey	46	B 10, l-b 3, w 2, n-b 6	21
*C. J. Adams b Lewis	16		
P. A. Cottey lbw b Smith	21	1/4 2/11 3/53 (5 wkts) 110	
W. J. House not out	0	4/87 5/101	

†N. J. Wilton, J. D. Lewry, R. J. Kirtley and M. A. Robinson did not bat.

Bonus point – Gloucestershire 1.

Bowling: Smith 10–5–13–3; Lewis 10–3–21–1; Harvey 10–2–38–1; Cotterell 5–1–9–0; Alleyne 4–1–16–0.

Gloucestershire

T. H. C. Hancock, I. Mohammed, M. G. N. Windows, K. J. Barnett, *M. W. Alleyne, I. J. Harvey, †R. C. Russell, J. N. Snape, J. Lewis, A. M. Smith and T. P. Cotterell.

Umpires: J. H. Hampshire and N. A. Mallender.

GLOUCESTERSHIRE v OXFORD UNIVERSITIES

At Bristol, May 3, 4, 5. Drawn. Toss: Oxford Universities. First-class debuts: R. W. S. Carroll, J. R. S. Redmayne.

Centuries from Windows and Barnett revealed the Universities' attack as anything but first-class, despite some accurate off-spin from the New Zealander, Weenink. Batting virtually throughout without a helmet, Windows reached his hundred in 145 balls before, hitting powerfully off the back foot on both sides of the wicket, he hammered on to 166 in another 34. One of his half-dozen sixes travelled 110 yards, but the day's biggest hit came from Hancock, 140 yards on to the sports hall roof. Wanting batting practice, Gloucestershire waited until lunch on the second day to declare; a stylish 83 from wicket-keeper Smalley suggested this was a miscalculation. Although Oxford followed on 298 behind on the final afternoon, the county bowlers, with Lewis unwell, lacked the penetration to dismiss them a second time.

Close of play: First day, Gloucestershire 425-4 (Barnett 74*, Snape 20*); Second day, Oxford Universities 153-4 (Porter 18*, Redmayne 6*).

Gloucestershire

R. J. Cunliffe c Smalley b Salman Khan	74	†R. C. Russell b Garland	16
*T. H. C. Hancock lbw b Weenink	85		
M. G. N. Windows st Smalley b Weenink	166	B 4, l-b 6, n-b 2	12
K. J. Barnett not out	118		
M. W. Alleyne c Garland b Weenink	1	1/148 2/178 3/384 (6 wkts dec.) 541	
J. N. Snape c Smalley b Garland	69	4/388 5/517 6/541	

M. J. Cawdron, J. Lewis, J. M. M. Averis and T. P. Cotterell did not bat.

Bowling: Salman Khan 33–8–99–1; Garland 17.3–1–103–2; Gofton 21–2–85–0; Hicks 19–5–71–0; Weenink 31–4–121–3; Carroll 7–0–52–0.

Oxford Universities

A. S. Bones lbw b Lewis	7	– lbw b Averis 2
†R. G. Smalley b Snape	83	– run out 19
A. F. Gofton c Russell b Snape	25	– c Snape b Lewis 0
S. W. Weenink lbw b Cawdron	7	– lbw b Snape 14
J. J. Porter b Averis	67	– c Alleyne b Cawdron 5
J. R. S. Redmayne c Russell b Alleyne	6	– c Russell b Snape 7
R. Garland st Russell b Cotterell	15	– not out 6
A. M. T. Janmohamed c and b Cotterell	5	– not out 5
*T. C. Hicks c Russell b Lewis	2	
Salman Khan c Russell b Lewis	13	
R. W. S. Carroll not out	0	
B 2, l-b 7, n-b 4	13	B 2, l-b 2, w 2, n-b 6 12

1/14 2/112 3/121 4/125 5/153   243   1/2 2/5 3/37   (6 wkts) 70
6/202 7/216 8/221 9/243   4/42 5/49 6/56

Bowling: *First Innings*—Lewis 16–6–34–3; Averis 20.4–6–65–1; Cawdron 16–8–30–1; Cotterell 27–4–69–2; Hancock 5–1–16–0; Snape 15–11–7–2; Alleyne 8–3–13–1. *Second Innings*—Averis 6–1–13–1; Lewis 2–2–0–1; Alleyne 5–1–6–0; Cawdron 6–1–12–1; Cotterell 18–9–24–0; Snape 14–9–11–2.

Umpires: D. J. Constant and N. G. Cowley.

At Cardiff, May 11, 12, 13, 14. GLOUCESTERSHIRE drew with GLAMORGAN.

At Nottingham, May 17, 18, 19, 20. GLOUCESTERSHIRE drew with NOTTINGHAMSHIRE.

GLOUCESTERSHIRE v WORCESTERSHIRE

At Bristol, May 23, 24, 25, 26. Drawn. Gloucestershire 6 pts, Worcestershire 10 pts. Toss: Worcestershire.

Although the first and last days were lost to the weather, and the middle two rain-affected, there was time for two excellent innings from Harvey and Solanki. Gloucestershire had collapsed to 19 for four when Harvey arrived, and were soon 31 for five. But, hitting 11 fours and a six, he picked them up with a counter-attack that added 98 with Snape. Both fell to Illingworth's left-arm spin, Harvey cutting to point, Snape top-edging to long leg, and Gloucestershire failed to secure a batting point. Next day, fielding at third slip because of a tweaked hamstring, Harvey took three brilliant catches that had Worcestershire 56 for three. Then Solanki took over. Impressive and controlled, he mastered the attack to reach 161 off 207 balls, with 112 coming in boundaries. He needed 11 more runs to pass his Championship-best, made at Cheltenham the year before, but the rain put paid to that.

Close of play: First day, No play; Second day, Gloucestershire 176-8 (Lewis 2*, Smith 0*); Third day, Worcestershire 310-6 (Solanki 161*, Lampitt 0*).

Gloucestershire

R. J. Cunliffe b Sheriyar	7	J. Lewis c Lampitt b Sheriyar	12
T. H. C. Hancock b Sheriyar	0	A. M. Smith not out	12
M. G. N. Windows c Rhodes b McGrath	0	T. P. Cotterell c Wilson b McGrath	1
K. J. Barnett b Lampitt	16		
*M. W. Alleyne lbw b Sheriyar	0	B 2, l-b 8, n-b 12	22
I. J. Harvey c Lampitt b Illingworth	70		
†R. C. Russell lbw b Lampitt	16	1/2 2/9 3/19 4/19 5/31	199
J. N. Snape c McGrath b Illingworth	43	6/69 7/167 8/176 9/198	

Bonus points – Worcestershire 3.

Bowling: McGrath 18.1–7–50–2; Sheriyar 21–8–51–4; Lampitt 12–5–41–2; Illingworth 7–1–19–2; Leatherdale 4–0–28–0.

Worcestershire

P. R. Pollard c Harvey b Lewis	7	†S. J. Rhodes st Russell b Cotterell	16
E. J. Wilson c Harvey b Lewis	4	S. R. Lampitt not out	0
*G. A. Hick c Harvey b Smith	14	B 4, l-b 3, w 2, n-b 6	15
V. S. Solanki not out	161		
K. R. Spiring c and b Alleyne	28	1/12 2/13 3/56	(6 wkts) 310
D. A. Leatherdale c Russell b Alleyne	65	4/134 5/246 6/295	

R. K. Illingworth, G. D. McGrath and A. Sheriyar did not bat.

Bonus points – Worcestershire 3, Gloucestershire 2.

Bowling: Lewis 18–5–64–2; Smith 16–3–46–1; Harvey 5–0–22–0; Alleyne 16–3–68–2; Cotterell 15–4–49–1; Snape 7–1–33–0; Hancock 4–0–21–0.

Umpires: T. E. Jesty and G. Sharp.

At Lord's, May 31, June 1, 2, 3. GLOUCESTERSHIRE beat MIDDLESEX by 85 runs.

GLOUCESTERSHIRE v ESSEX

At Bristol, June 6, 7, 8. Essex won by 109 runs. Essex 17 pts, Gloucestershire 5 pts. Toss: Gloucestershire.

England's captain Hussain, looking to play himself into form before the First Test against West Indies, was lbw for three off his ninth ball in the first innings and caught behind off his fifth without scoring in the second. Headed by Prichard's 96, with fifties from Irani and wicket-keeper Hyam, Essex batted competently after being put in. But Gloucestershire would pay a heavy price for resting four senior players, Harvey, Barnett, Russell and Smith, ahead of Saturday's Benson and Hedges Cup final. On a pitch becoming increasingly dry, they failed to build a proper lead around Windows's century – his third in successive Championship innings against Essex – and poor technique was exposed when they batted a second time. The bounce was variable and, needing 195 for their first home Championship win in almost a year, they were skittled out in just over two hours for 85. Earlier in the day, Lewis had set up this chance of victory by keeping Essex in check with six for 47.

Close of play: First day, Gloucestershire 5-0 (Cunliffe 1*, Hancock 4*); Second day, Essex 22-2 (Grayson 19*, Hussain 0*).

Essex

P. J. Prichard run out	96	– c Alleyne b Lewis	1
A. P. Grayson c Snape b Cawdron	19	– b Hardinges	52
N. Hussain lbw b Cawdron	3	– (4) c Williams b Lewis	0
S. G. Law c Williams b Cawdron	4	– (5) b Lewis	28
*R. C. Irani b Alleyne	52	– (6) c Cunliffe b Hardinges	42
D. D. J. Robinson c Williams b Averis	0	– (7) not out	32
†B. J. Hyam c Cunliffe b Averis	53	– (3) c Alleyne b Lewis	0
D. R. Law c Cawdron b Hardinges	6	– c Williams b Lewis	0
T. J. Mason c Williams b Alleyne	12	– c Alleyne b Snape	9
A. P. Cowan b Alleyne	0	– b Lewis	21
M. C. Ilott not out	4	– b Snape	3
B 4, l-b 4, n-b 6	14	B 4, l-b 3, n-b 4	11

1/52 2/58 3/74 4/160 5/161   263
6/186 7/197 8/250 9/250

1/8 2/22 3/22 4/54 5/127   199
6/127 7/134 8/157 9/184

Bonus points – Essex 2, Gloucestershire 3.

Bowling: *First Innings*—Lewis 17–4–64–0; Averis 17.2–3–50–2; Cawdron 23–5–65–3; Alleyne 18–5–32–3; Hardinges 10–3–20–1; Hancock 4–0–6–0; Snape 13–6–18–0. *Second Innings*—Lewis 22–10–47–6; Averis 16–5–58–0; Cawdron 10–5–24–0; Alleyne 12–4–29–0; Hardinges 13–6–16–2; Snape 6.3–2–18–2.

Gloucestershire

R. J. Cunliffe c Hussain b Ilott	2	– (2) c S. G. Law b Irani	3
T. H. C. Hancock lbw b Irani	4	– (1) lbw b Cowan	26
M. G. N. Windows c Robinson b Mason	107	– c Hyam b Ilott	0
*M. W. Alleyne c and b Ilott	8	– b Cowan	4
C. G. Taylor c S. G. Law b Cowan	18	– b Irani	0
J. N. Snape c Robinson b Cowan	54	– b D. R. Law	16
M. A. Hardinges lbw b D. R. Law	0	– b Irani	0
†R. C. J. Williams not out	28	– c S. G. Law b D. R. Law	5
M. J. Cawdron c Hyam b D. R. Law	27	– c Mason b D. R. Law	15
J. M. M. Averis c Hussain b Ilott	7	– c Grayson b D. R. Law	3
J. Lewis c Hyam b D. R. Law	1	– not out	0
L-b 6, w 2, n-b 4	12	B 1, l-b 1, w 3, n-b 8	13

1/6 2/8 3/46 4/122 5/170   268
6/173 7/220 8/254 9/265

1/12 2/19 3/26 4/37 5/39   85
6/46 7/67 8/74 9/85

Bonus points – Gloucestershire 2, Essex 3.

Bowling: *First Innings*—Ilott 19–6–67–3; Irani 16–5–47–1; D. R. Law 20.3–1–70–3; Cowan 18–8–36–2; Mason 21–7–42–1. *Second Innings*—Ilott 7–2–17–1; Irani 11–5–30–3; Cowan 7–3–15–2; D. R. Law 4.4–0–15–4; Mason 2–0–6–0.

Umpires: A. Clarkson and R. A. White.

At Gloucester, June 16, 17, 18, 19. GLOUCESTERSHIRE lost to ZIMBABWEANS by 524 runs (See Zimbabwean tour section).

At Birmingham, June 28, 29, 30, July 1. GLOUCESTERSHIRE drew with WARWICKSHIRE.

GLOUCESTERSHIRE v NORTHAMPTONSHIRE

At Cheltenham, July 12, 13, 14, 15. Northamptonshire won by an innings and 99 runs. Northamptonshire 20 pts, Gloucestershire 2 pts. Toss: Northamptonshire.

Groundsman Geoff Swift had despaired 48 hours before the start when the College Ground was under water. By tea on the second day, Gloucestershire shared his feelings. Northamptonshire had run up their highest total against them, bettering 516 at Bristol in 1913; Cook, Sydney-born but England-qualified, had hit a maiden century in his second Championship game, batting four and a half hours for a memorable 137, with 23 fours. Gloucestershire's only excuse was an early injury to left-arm spinner Cotterell. On a pitch beginning to help spin, they were 77 for four by the close, and heading for the follow-on. An accomplished 57 by Hewson rallied their second innings, Taylor again batted well, and Harvey raised spirits with three sixes and six fours. But it was Russell who ensured a fourth day, digging in for four and three-quarter hours for his first hundred in three years. No. 10 Smith helped him by staying two hours, but nothing could stop the win that lifted Northamptonshire off the bottom of the ladder. Off-spinner Swann returned his best figures of the season.

Close of play: First day, Northamptonshire 387-4 (Cook 113*, Penberthy 18*); Second day, Gloucestershire 77-4 (Taylor 27*, Russell 10*); Third day, Gloucestershire 275-8 (Russell 72*, Smith 0*).

Northamptonshire

A. S. Rollins b Smith	63	M. R. Strong c Windows b Cawdron	3
*M. L. Hayden lbw b Smith	75	D. M. Cousins c Russell b Taylor	15
J. W. Cook b Harvey	137	J. F. Brown c Hewson b Taylor	11
D. J. Sales c and b Taylor	76		
M. B. Loye c Harvey b Cawdron	39	B 1, l-b 7, n-b 2	10
A. L. Penberthy c sub b Harvey	26		
G. P. Swann c Russell b Cawdron	40	1/131 2/144 3/264 4/362 5/416	543
†D. Ripley not out	48	6/427 7/471 8/475 9/517	

Bonus points – Northamptonshire 5, Gloucestershire 2 (Score at 130 overs: 460-6).

Bowling: Smith 32–6–94–2; Lewis 31–5–111–0; Cawdron 28–9–70–3; Cotterell 3–1–10–0; Harvey 29–4–101–2; Alleyne 10–2–23–0; Taylor 21.3–1–126–3.

Gloucestershire

R. J. Cunliffe c Hayden b Cousins	13	– (2) lbw b Cousins	2
D. R. Hewson b Cousins	3	– (1) c Sales b Swann	57
M. G. N. Windows c Brown b Penberthy	15	– c Hayden b Brown	24
*M. W. Alleyne lbw b Penberthy	6	– b Brown	8
C. G. Taylor b Brown	42	– c and b Swann	41
†R. C. Russell c Ripley b Cousins	15	– not out	110
I. J. Harvey c and b Cousins	0	– lbw b Swann	52
M. J. Cawdron b Swann	18	– lbw b Swann	2
J. Lewis b Brown	0	– c Penberthy b Swann	4
A. M. Smith not out	0	– c Penberthy b Brown	14
T. P. Cotterell c Rollins b Swann	0	– c Penberthy b Swann	0
L-b 2, w 2	4	B 4, l-b 8, w 2	14

1/9 2/18 3/27 4/40 5/91	116	1/3 2/59 3/85 4/103 5/174	328
6/91 7/108 8/108 9/116		6/245 7/249 8/269 9/327	

Bonus points – Northamptonshire 3.

Bowling: *First Innings*—Cousins 15–5–28–4; Strong 5–0–17–0; Penberthy 15–5–41–2; Brown 15–8–15–2; Swann 9.1–6–13–2. *Second Innings*—Cousins 14–3–27–1; Strong 8–1–18–0; Penberthy 5–0–17–0; Brown 55–18–136–3; Swann 49.5–12–118–6.

Umpires: D. J. Constant and M. J. Harris.

At Cheltenham, July 17. GLOUCESTERSHIRE lost to NEW ZEALAND A by 134 runs (See New Zealand A tour section).

GLOUCESTERSHIRE v WARWICKSHIRE

At Cheltenham, July 19, 20, 21, 22. Drawn. Gloucestershire 9 pts, Warwickshire 9 pts. Toss: Warwickshire.

Warwickshire fancied their chances on the final day, having left Gloucestershire to make 323 or bat out the game. But, confronted by the home side's defiance, they lacked the imagination to force a win; both teams had settled for a draw long before the final curtain. To return to the top of the table, Warwickshire had needed a better first-innings platform: 260 was moderate on a firm pitch. Harvey's variation of pace and length, bringing him five for 29, commanded undue respect, but then Gloucestershire also batted circumspectly. Piper, sent in as night-watchman with two stumpings and two catches already to his credit, put the visitors in control as he saw them to 177, aided by Powell and Ostler. His 69 was his best for four years. By the time Harvey ended their innings with three wickets in four balls, Warwickshire had set the terms. Donald pinned Gloucestershire down, but Giles, whirling through 45 overs, never lured them into attempting the assault that might have put them under pressure.

Close of play: First day, Warwickshire 260; Second day, Warwickshire 38-1 (Powell 9*, Piper 8*); Third day, Warwickshire 316.

Warwickshire

M. J. Powell lbw b Harvey		25	– c Hancock b Gannon	28
M. A. Wagh c Ball b Gannon		59	– lbw b Lewis	18
D. P. Ostler c Ball b Harvey		28	– (4) lbw b Lewis	54
D. L. Hemp c Taylor b Gannon		58	– (5) b Gannon	35
T. L. Penney c Alleyne b Harvey		11	– (6) c Russell b Gannon	42
D. R. Brown c Hancock b Harvey		0	– (7) b Harvey	25
A. F. Giles lbw b Harvey		37	– (8) c and b Harvey	6
*N. M. K. Smith c Taylor b Ball		9	– (9) c and b Harvey	19
†K. J. Piper c Russell b Gannon		12	– (3) c Russell b Lewis	69
A. A. Donald c Hancock b Ball		2	– not out	1
E. S. H. Giddins not out		1	– b Harvey	0
B 2, l-b 4, w 4, n-b 8		18	B 4, l-b 11, w 2, n-b 2	19
		260		**316**

1/50 2/107 3/132 4/164 5/164
6/223 7/245 8/246 9/250

1/29 2/87 3/177 4/190 5/252
6/273 7/282 8/309 9/316

Bonus points – Warwickshire 2, Gloucestershire 3.

Bowling: *First Innings*—Lewis 22–6–53–0; Gannon 20.5–1–62–3; Harvey 23–12–29–5; Alleyne 15–3–57–0; Ball 22–7–53–2. *Second Innings*—Lewis 25–6–50–3; Gannon 22–4–66–3; Harvey 23.2–5–71–4; Ball 29–7–67–0; Alleyne 11–2–41–0; Taylor 3–2–6–0.

Gloucestershire

T. H. C. Hancock st Piper b Giles		46	– (2) lbw b Giles	25
D. R. Hewson c Penney b Giddins		1	– (1) c Smith b Giles	67
I. Mohammed c Giles b Giddins		24	– lbw b Donald	14
M. G. N. Windows c Piper b Donald		79	– not out	62
*M. W. Alleyne c Ostler b Giles		16	– c Penney b Giles	37
C. G. Taylor c Powell b Smith		22	– c Penney b Giles	9
I. J. Harvey st Piper b Smith		25	– not out	5
†R. C. Russell c Piper b Brown		2		
M. C. J. Ball c Smith b Brown		21		
J. Lewis lbw b Giddins		1		
B. W. Gannon not out		1		
B 4, l-b 4, w 4, n-b 4		16	B 4, l-b 11, w 3	18
		254	(5 wkts)	**237**

1/2 2/59 3/79 4/119 5/183
6/199 7/224 8/233 9/244

1/60 2/99 3/123
4/189 5/225

Bonus points – Gloucestershire 2, Warwickshire 3.

Bowling: *First Innings*—Donald 17–3–39–1; Giddins 26–7–77–3; Brown 18.2–5–52–2; Giles 21–10–49–2; Smith 7–2–29–2. *Second Innings*—Donald 19–11–22–1; Giddins 10–4–24–0; Brown 12–2–38–0; Giles 45–14–74–4; Smith 19–6–54–0; Wagh 3–1–10–0.

Umpires: R. Julian and R. A. White.

At Worcester, July 28, 29, 30. GLOUCESTERSHIRE lost to WORCESTERSHIRE by 52 runs.

GLOUCESTERSHIRE v GLAMORGAN

At Bristol, August 2, 3, 4, 5. Gloucestershire won by ten wickets. Gloucestershire 18 pts, Glamorgan 3 pts. Toss: Glamorgan. First-class debut: A. N. Bressington.

Registered half an hour before play began, 20-year-old Alastair Bressington took a wicket with his third ball, another with his first in the second innings, and finished with a match analysis of five for 49 as Gloucestershire's second Championship victory ended Glamorgan's four-win streak. Glamorgan misjudged the pitch by electing to bat, and alerted pitch liaison officer A. C. Smith when they were put out inside 41 overs by a quartet of almost-novice seamers, with nine Championship wickets between them all season. After the second day was lost to rain, Gloucestershire defended the pitch's reputation by accumulating a careful 308. Windows, refusing to be drawn into any rashness, batted four and a half hours for 82, and then Ball struck a breezy 53, including ten fours. Glamorgan just managed to make Gloucestershire bat again.

Close of play: First day, Gloucestershire 99-4 (Windows 26*, Averis 4*); Second day, No play; Third day, Glamorgan 115-5 (Powell 57*, Wharf 21*).

Glamorgan

M. T. G. Elliott c Hewson b Cawdron	6	– (2) b Cawdron	16
S. P. James c Russell b Averis	8	– (1) c Hancock b Averis	1
M. J. Powell c and b Bressington	9	– c Russell b Bressington	61
*†M. P. Maynard lbw b Cawdron	0	– c Snape b Bressington	1
A. Dale c Ball b Cawdron	2	– c Barnett b Bressington	0
K. Newell c Russell b Hancock	4	– c Ball b Hancock	3
A. G. Wharf c Russell b Averis	16	– c Ball b Bressington	31
D. S. Harrison lbw b Hancock	0	– lbw b Hancock	27
S. D. Thomas c Barnett b Cawdron	52	– not out	48
D. A. Cosker lbw b Cawdron	4	– b Hancock	0
O. T. Parkin not out	10	– run out	2
L-b 5, w 2, n-b 4	11	B 4, l-b 4, n-b 12	20
	122		**210**

1/13 2/17 3/17 4/19 5/31
6/37 7/45 8/59 9/93

1/2 2/36 3/47 4/53 5/66
6/131 7/134 8/202 9/202

Bonus points – Gloucestershire 3.

Bowling: *First Innings*—Averis 13–4–40–2; Cawdron 13.3–5–45–5; Bressington 5–3–13–1; Hancock 9–4–19–2. *Second Innings*—Averis 20–5–72–1; Cawdron 23.4–8–54–1; Bressington 15–3–36–4; Hancock 12–2–24–3; Alleyne 3–1–4–0; Ball 5–2–12–0.

Gloucestershire

T. H. C. Hancock c Elliott b Wharf	1	– (2) not out	4
D. R. Hewson c Maynard b Wharf	1	– (1) not out	13
M. G. N. Windows c Maynard b Cosker	82		
K. J. Barnett c Maynard b Parkin	11		
*M. W. Alleyne c Maynard b Dale	38		
J. M. M. Averis c Cosker b Parkin	7		
J. N. Snape b Parkin	40		
†R. C. Russell lbw b Wharf	10		
M. C. J. Ball c and b Thomas	53		
M. J. Cawdron st Maynard b Cosker	12		
A. N. Bressington not out	2		
B 9, l-b 16, w 4, n-b 22	51	W 6, n-b 4	10

1/6 2/13 3/26 4/90 5/120   308   (no wkt) 27
6/214 7/226 8/247 9/304

Bonus points – Gloucestershire 3, Glamorgan 3.

Bowling: *First Innings*—Wharf 23–5–102–3; Parkin 20–7–29–3; Thomas 14–2–52–1; Harrison 10–2–45–0; Dale 9–3–21–1; Cosker 19.1–8–34–2. *Second Innings*—Wharf 2.3–0–23–0; Parkin 2–1–4–0.

Umpires: M. R. Benson and V. A. Holder.

At Colchester, August 16, 17, 18, 19. GLOUCESTERSHIRE beat ESSEX by 104 runs.

GLOUCESTERSHIRE v MIDDLESEX

At Bristol, August 21, 22, 23, 24. Gloucestershire won by seven wickets. Gloucestershire 15 pts, Middlesex 4 pts. Toss: Middlesex.

Contrasting alternatives were on offer to both sides: the likelihood of the wooden spoon or an outside chance of promotion. After the inevitable rain on the first day, the prize went to Gloucestershire, with their third Championship win in a row lifting them four places to fifth, while Middlesex sank to the bottom of the table. Langer, batting between the showers, took seven fours off 14 balls from Lewis, who next morning had him caught down the leg side with only one added to his overnight 76. Tufnell's demanding spin brought Middlesex five wickets, and cost 0.63 an over, but they could not sustain their first-innings advantage. Lewis again dismissed Langer and Ramprakash and, but for Joyce's stubborn 49, Gloucestershire would have required less than 144 to win. As it was, they started the final day needing 100, with only one wicket down. Taking no chances, they scored just 66 in the two hours to lunch, then rattled off the rest in even time.

Close of play: First day, Middlesex 151-5 (Langer 76*, Nash 1*); Second day, Gloucestershire 157-7 (Williams 30*, Gannon 2*); Third day, Gloucestershire 44-1 (Hancock 19*, Windows 20*).

Middlesex

A. J. Strauss c Williams b Smith	4	– lbw b Ball	10
M. A. Roseberry c Williams b Lewis	4	– (7) b Gannon	3
*J. L. Langer c Williams b Lewis	77	– c Williams b Lewis	20
M. R. Ramprakash b Lewis	5	– b Lewis	3
E. C. Joyce lbw b Hancock	31	– not out	49
B. L. Hutton c Williams b Lewis	22	– (2) c Williams b Lewis	0
†D. C. Nash lbw b Smith	11	– (6) run out	10
S. J. Cook b Ball	5	– b Smith	16
R. L. Johnson st Williams b Ball	31	– b Smith	6
A. R. C. Fraser c Lewis b Ball	7	– lbw b Ball	1
P. C. R. Tufnell not out	0	– c Alleyne b Lewis	4
L-b 4, w 4, n-b 2	10	L-b 2	2
	207		**124**

1/6 2/14 3/24 4/96 5/150   1/4 2/28 3/32 4/34 5/45
6/153 7/169 8/169 9/187   6/56 7/84 8/92 9/105

Bonus points – Middlesex 1, Gloucestershire 3.

Bowling: *First Innings*—Smith 18–5–47–2; Lewis 22–6–72–4; Gannon 9–2–19–0; Hancock 6–2–19–1; Ball 14.1–5–31–3; Alleyne 4–0–15–0. *Second Innings*—Smith 12–6–32–2; Lewis 15.1–6–36–4; Ball 19–4–35–2; Gannon 5–1–19–1.

Gloucestershire

T. H. C. Hancock lbw b Fraser	0	– (2) b Johnson	35
D. R. Hewson c Langer b Tufnell	43	– (1) lbw b Fraser	0
M. G. N. Windows lbw b Tufnell	10	– not out	70
*M. W. Alleyne c Strauss b Tufnell	22	– c Hutton b Johnson	0
C. G. Taylor lbw b Fraser	2	– not out	32
J. N. Snape c Nash b Cook	27		
†R. C. J. Williams b Johnson	43		
M. C. J. Ball c Cook b Johnson	16		
B. W. Gannon c Hutton b Tufnell	13		
J. Lewis c Hutton b Tufnell	0		
A. M. Smith not out	2		
B 4, l-b 4, n-b 2	10	B 3, l-b 5, n-b 2	10
	188	**(3 wkts)**	**147**

1/8 2/49 3/58 4/67 5/83   1/0 2/75 3/75
6/127 7/147 8/186 9/186

Bonus points – Middlesex 3.

Bowling: *First Innings*—Fraser 24–7–47–2; Johnson 22–6–58–2; Cook 14–5–36–1; Tufnell 36.3–21–23–5; Ramprakash 5–1–16–0. *Second Innings*—Fraser 19.3–12–23–1; Johnson 12–4–22–2; Tufnell 27–12–53–0; Cook 6–1–20–0; Ramprakash 5–1–6–0; Hutton 3–0–9–0; Langer 1–0–6–0.

Umpires: A. Clarkson and K. E. Palmer.

At Northampton, August 30, 31, September 1, 2. GLOUCESTERSHIRE lost to NORTHAMPTONSHIRE by an innings and 74 runs.

At Hove, September 7, 8. GLOUCESTERSHIRE beat SUSSEX by an innings and 18 runs.

GLOUCESTERSHIRE v NOTTINGHAMSHIRE

At Bristol, September 13, 14, 15, 16. Gloucestershire won by three wickets. Gloucestershire 15 pts, Nottinghamshire 1 pt. Toss: Nottinghamshire.

An old-fashioned negotiated finish saw Gloucestershire defy the weather to snatch a sixth Championship win, but it was not quite enough to gain promotion. They had to settle for fourth place. The ball swung considerably on the first day, when Franks and Bowen added 70 for Nottinghamshire's seventh wicket and Lucas got them to 216 with some adventurous hitting. Only 16.4 overs were possible on the second day – time enough for Windows to achieve his first-class 1,000 for the season – and, following a third-day washout and a delayed start to the fourth, Gloucestershire declared without batting on. With promotion hopes of their own – despite having only two wins, they started the game four points ahead – Nottinghamshire chased runs and eventually set a target of 248 in 59 overs. The cricket was lively, highlighted by Bowen's brilliant diving catch at mid-on to separate Windows and Russell. However, Russell went on to fifty, and Taylor eased Gloucestershire to their bittersweet win with nine balls to spare.

Close of play: First day, Gloucestershire 13-0 (Hewson 3*, Barnett 5*); Second day, Gloucestershire 73-1 (Barnett 41*, Windows 18*); Third day, No play.

Nottinghamshire

D. J. Bicknell b Harvey	19	– (6) not out		4
G. E. Welton b Alleyne	23	– (1) b Lewis		21
*J. E. R. Gallian c Harvey b Lewis	19	– (5) not out		0
U. Afzaal c Barnett b Gannon	7	– (2) c Gannon b Lewis		36
P. Johnson c Harvey b Lewis	21	– (3) retired hurt		23
†C. M. W. Read b Smith	0			
P. J. Franks c Snape b Alleyne	41			
M. N. Bowen c Snape b Alleyne	22	– (4) c Alleyne b Lewis		13
D. S. Lucas not out	21			
A. J. Harris b Smith	4			
R. D. Stemp c Russell b Lewis	11			
L-b 8, w 8, n-b 12	28	L-b 3, w 2, n-b 2		7

1/31 2/60 3/74 4/74 5/75   216   1/42 2/93 3/100   (3 wkts dec.) 104
6/101 7/171 8/180 9/191

Bonus points – Nottinghamshire 1, Gloucestershire 3.

In the second innings Johnson retired hurt at 82.

Bowling: *First Innings*—Smith 21–5–52–2; Lewis 23.1–8–45–3; Harvey 13–5–23–1; Gannon 15–6–47–1; Alleyne 13–3–26–3; Snape 11–4–15–0. *Second Innings*—Lewis 9.5–1–50–3; Smith 5–0–30–0; Gannon 4–0–21–0.

Gloucestershire

D. R. Hewson c Welton b Lucas	3	– b Bowen		15
K. J. Barnett not out	41	– c Read b Bowen		28
M. G. N. Windows not out	18	– c Bowen b Harris		38
I. J. Harvey (did not bat)	–	c Read b Lucas		10
†R. C. Russell (did not bat)	–	c Read b Franks		53
J. N. Snape (did not bat)	–	c and b Stemp		10
*M. W. Alleyne (did not bat)	–	c Read b Stemp		8
C. G. Taylor (did not bat)	–	not out		38
J. Lewis (did not bat)	–	not out		16
L-b 3, w 4, n-b 4	11	B 1, l-b 11, w 10, n-b 10		32

1/13   (1 wkt dec.) 73   1/42 2/73 3/90 4/134   (7 wkts) 248
5/151 6/167 7/212

B. W. Gannon and A. M. Smith did not bat.

Bowling: *First Innings*—Franks 6.4–2–12–0; Lucas 9–3–22–1; Harris 5–1–36–0; Bowen 1–1–0–0. *Second Innings*—Franks 14.3–0–67–1; Lucas 12–1–58–1; Bowen 13–2–47–2; Harris 8–1–29–1; Stemp 10–1–35–2.

Umpires: M. R. Benson and K. E. Palmer.

HAMPSHIRE

President: W. J. Weld
Chairman: 2000 – B. G. Ford
            2001 – R. G. Bransgrove
Chief Executive: A. F. Baker
Chairman, Cricket Committee: D. J. Robinson
Captain: R. A. Smith
Director of Cricket: T. M. Tremlett
First-Team Coach: S. J. Cook
Head Groundsman: N. Gray
Scorer: V. H Isaacs

Shane Warne

Hampshire had not had many seasons, if any, quite as revolutionary or extraordinary as the one they experienced in 2000. From the moment Shane Warne touched down in the dawn of a wet April morning – to unprecedented publicity as the club's overseas player – through to the emotion-charged last day at Northlands Road in the gloom of a September evening, this was a summer never to be forgotten.

On the field, little went right, in spite of Warne's presence and the international-calibre bowling of Alan Mullally, who between them cost Hampshire more than £200,000 in salaries. Off the field, it was a case of bidding farewell to the comfort of three familiar old grounds as Hampshire prepared to move to the new £17 million stadium taking shape, somewhat slowly, on farmland at West End on the eastern outskirts of Southampton.

But as bulldozers waited at the gates of Northlands Road in autumn, ready to turn the ground into housing, there was little outward evidence that the new Hampshire Rose Bowl would be able to sustain the trappings of first-class cricket, although the pitch itself had been used successfully in Second Eleven fixtures. Funding was still £5 million short, and the collapse of a structure within the pavilion had delayed construction work. The last thing Hampshire needed was the atrocious winter weather that followed.

With Dean Park in Bournemouth having gone from the fixture list in 1992, leaving Northlands Road (first match 1885) signalled the completion of a decade of major change for Hampshire. But while there was sadness that they would never play there again – or, it seemed, at the United Services Ground at Portsmouth (first match 1882) or Basingstoke's May's Bounty (1906), where the annual festival was so eagerly awaited in the northern part of the county – there was also optimism at the prospect of moving to a ground which, when completed, will be the envy of the County Championship. Meanwhile, a determined band of supporters remained hopeful of reviving county cricket at May's Bounty at a later date.

It would have been helpful if the playing side had prospered while the difficulties and upheaval of the move were being negotiated. Instead, Hampshire were relegated from Division One, with only three wins to offset nine defeats, and finished second-last in Division Two of the National League.

It was somehow typical of their season that, while artefacts were being packed for transportation to the Rose Bowl, and award-winning groundsman Nigel Gray was preparing pitches there, the club should be docked eight points because of a below-standard pitch for their 565th and last first-class match at Northlands Road.

Warne got them to the quarter-finals of the Benson and Hedges Cup with arguably his most decisive spell of bowling – two for six off two overs in a ten-over slog – but a crushing defeat at Cardiff was pitiful reward. After that, the NatWest Trophy offered the most realistic chance of silverware. Easy wins over the Kent Board XI, Durham and Middlesex secured them a semi-final against Warwickshire: just the occasion to produce the best of Warne. But there was a clause in his six-figure contract (rumoured but not confirmed to be the biggest-ever for a county player) which allowed him to be recalled by Australia. So, as Hampshire were going down by 19 runs, Warne was at home in Melbourne for three indoor games against South Africa, keeping in touch with Edgbaston by a series of anxious phone calls.

Warne enjoyed his county season, taking 109 wickets in all cricket, and said he would like to return in 2002. In the meantime, Hampshire signed the former Zimbabwean all-rounder, Neil Johnson, to fill the overseas spot. Warne responded to the sympathetic handling of Robin Smith with a willingness to bowl beyond the call of duty. The other Hampshire players, once they overcame being star-struck, responded positively to him, and the fielding was better than for some years.

Warne and Mullally accounted for half the club's Championship wickets, and with only Yorkshire matching Hampshire's achievement of maximum bowling bonus points in every match, the bowling was not the problem. The batting was. There was no doubting the talent available to new coach Jimmy Cook, but the application left much to be desired. Only once, and then not until September, did they collect a full hand of batting points; seven times before then, they failed to manage one. Some of their performances were abject, devoid of confidence and resolution, and the trail of supine collapses left the bowlers little scope to force a winning position.

Only Will Kendall, who scored three of Hampshire's six first-class centuries, passed 1,000 runs and emerged with his reputation enhanced. Derek Kenway, Chris Tremlett, who announced himself against New Zealand A with a wicket with his first ball in first-class cricket, and Lawrence Prittipaul, a cousin of West Indies Test batsman Shivnarine Chanderpaul, all hinted at better things to come. Giles White twice carried his bat, though he failed to hit a hundred, while Dimitri Mascarenhas, who did, revealed undeniable all-round talent for one-day cricket but has still to consolidate in the longer game.

Adding to the end-of-season nostalgia was the retirement of Peter Hartley. County cricket's oldest player at 40, he had taken 683 first-class wickets, 102 in a three-year Indian summer at Hampshire. Later, Brian Ford resigned as chairman, citing business reasons, the week after a mix-up in which the job of chief executive Tony Baker was advertised, then withdrawn. Ford was replaced by multi-millionaire Rod Bransgrove. – PAT SYMES.

HAMPSHIRE 2000

[Bill Smith]

Back row: C. G. van der Gucht, W. S. Kendall, J. H. K. Adams, L. R. Prittipaul, I. Brunnschweiler, J. R. C. Hamblin. *Middle row:* T. C. Middleton (*Second Eleven coach*), S. J. Cook (*first-team coach*), G. W. White, S. R. G. Francis, S. J. Renshaw, L. Savident, A. C. Morris, Z. C. Morris, D. A. Kenway, T. M. Tremlett (*director of cricket*). *Front row:* A. D. Mullally, A. N. Aymes, S. D. Udal, R. A. Smith (*captain*), J. P. Stephenson, P. J. Hartley, J. S. Laney. *Absent:* S. K. Warne.

HAMPSHIRE RESULTS

All first-class matches – Played 18: Won 3, Lost 10, Drawn 5. Abandoned 1.

County Championship matches – Played 16: Won 3, Lost 9, Drawn 4.

PPP Healthcare County Championship, 7th in Division 1; NatWest Trophy, s-f;
Benson and Hedges Cup, q-f; Norwich Union National League, 8th in Division 2.

COUNTY CHAMPIONSHIP AVERAGES

BATTING

Cap		M	I	NO	R	HS	100s	50s	Avge	Ct/St
	L. R. Prittipault† ...	4	6	0	298	152	1	1	49.66	1
1999	W. S. Kendall	16	27	2	979	161	3	3	39.16	16
1998	G. W. White	16	28	4	742	96	0	5	30.91	13
	D. A. Kenway†	13	23	1	615	136	1	3	27.95	11/1
1991	A. N. Aymes†	13	22	5	398	74*	0	3	23.41	32/6
2000	S. K. Warne§	15	22	2	431	69	0	3	21.55	14
1998	A. D. Mascarenhas..	15	22	1	448	100	1	2	21.33	3
1985	R. A. Smith	16	27	0	529	61	0	2	19.59	3
1996	J. S. Laney†	12	21	1	364	81	0	2	18.20	11
1998	P. J. Hartley	9	11	5	103	23*	0	0	17.16	0
	A. C. Morris......	7	11	1	153	60	0	1	15.30	3
1992	S. D. Udal†	11	19	3	230	35	0	0	14.37	7
	S. J. Renshaw	3	6	1	57	26	0	0	11.40	0
	A. J. Sexton†	3	5	0	52	36	0	0	10.40	3
	S. R. G. Francis ...	7	10	5	43	30*	0	0	8.60	1
1995	J. P. Stephenson ...	8	12	0	84	19	0	0	7.00	6
2000	A. D. Mullally	8	12	2	60	12	0	0	6.00	0

* Signifies not out.   † Born in Hampshire.   § Overseas player.

BOWLING

	O	M	R	W	BB	5W/i	Avge
A. D. Mullally	343.5	105	832	49	9-93	5	16.97
S. K. Warne	639.4	183	1,620	70	6-34	5	23.14
S. D. Udal	300.3	84	745	28	5-58	1	26.60
A. D. Mascarenhas ...	277.5	80	698	25	4-52	0	27.92
A. C. Morris	159.1	34	506	18	3-48	0	28.11
S. R. G. Francis	120.1	26	434	10	4-95	0	43.40
P. J. Hartley	204.2	33	697	15	3-91	0	46.46

Also bowled: A. N. Aymes 1–0–13–1; S. J. Renshaw 57.1–17–133–5; R. A. Smith 2–0–26–0;
J. P. Stephenson 137–26–452–9; G. W. White 8.1–1–34–2.

COUNTY RECORDS

Highest score for:	316	R. H. Moore v Warwickshire at Bournemouth ...	1937
Highest score against:	303*	G. A. Hick (Worcestershire) at Southampton ...	1997
Best bowling for:	9-25	R. M. H. Cottam v Lancashire at Manchester ...	1965
Best bowling against:	10-46	W. Hickton (Lancashire) at Manchester	1870
Highest total for:	672-7 dec.	v Somerset at Taunton	1899
Highest total against:	742	by Surrey at The Oval	1909
Lowest total for:	15	v Warwickshire at Birmingham.............	1922
Lowest total against:	23	by Yorkshire at Middlesbrough	1965

At Oxford, April 11, 12, 13. OXFORD UNIVERSITIES v HAMPSHIRE. Abandoned.

At Southampton, April 27, 28, 29, 30. HAMPSHIRE drew with ZIMBABWEANS. (See Zimbabwean tour section).

HAMPSHIRE v SOMERSET

At Southampton, May 3, 4, 5. Somerset won by nine wickets. Somerset 18 pts, Hampshire 4 pts. Toss: Hampshire. Championship debut: S. K. Warne.

Shane Warne recorded the first pair of his career, out third ball in each innings. His contribution to a match Hampshire lost before tea on the third day was a solitary wicket – and even then replays suggested Holloway had not touched the ball. Cox, the Somerset captain, will miss Northlands Road. He followed scores of 216 and 129 not out there in 1999 with a six-and-a-half-hour 153, sharing century partnerships with Bowler and Turner, to emphasise the inadequacy of Hampshire's batting on a blameless pitch. Caddick vied with Cox for man of the match, shepherding a Somerset attack that lost Bulbeck and Jones through injury to finish with 12 for 126. Hampshire were redeemed only by Kenway's diligent four-hour 93 in the first innings, and by a patient 78 in the second from White, the first to carry his bat for Hampshire since Paul Terry against Yorkshire in 1994.

Close of play: First day, Somerset 14-2 (Cox 11*, Holloway 0*); Second day, Hampshire 10-0 (Laney 4*, White 3*).

Hampshire

J. S. Laney c Holloway b Caddick	14	– c Trescothick b Rose	6
G. W. White c Turner b Jones	34	– not out	78
W. S. Kendall c Trescothick b Jones	11	– b Caddick	0
*R. A. Smith c Bowler b Rose	6	– c Holloway b Caddick	1
†D. A. Kenway not out	93	– c Holloway b Blackwell	1
J. P. Stephenson lbw b Caddick	19	– c sub b Trescothick	4
A. D. Mascarenhas lbw b Caddick	2	– lbw b Caddick	17
S. K. Warne lbw b Caddick	0	– c Turner b Caddick	0
S. D. Udal lbw b Rose	5	– lbw b Caddick	0
A. C. Morris c Trescothick b Blackwell	31	– c Turner b Caddick	10
S. J. Renshaw c Holloway b Caddick	4	– c and b Caddick	2
B 1, l-b 12	13	L-b 7	7

1/32 2/58 3/69 4/75 5/99	232	1/23 2/28 3/38 4/48 5/55	126
6/107 7/107 8/123 9/198		6/82 7/88 8/88 9/116	

Bonus points – Hampshire 1, Somerset 3.

Bowling: *First Innings*—Caddick 24.5–7–62–5; Bulbeck 4–1–11–0; Jones 19–6–47–2; Rose 16–7–50–2; Blackwell 22–12–26–1; Trescothick 6–1–23–0. *Second Innings*—Caddick 23.1–5–64–7; Rose 9–5–8–1; Blackwell 16–5–29–1; Trescothick 9–4–18–1.

Somerset

M. E. Trescothick b Udal	3	– (2) not out	15
*J. Cox c Kenway b Renshaw	153	– (1) c White b Renshaw	4
A. R. Caddick c and b Udal	0		
P. C. L. Holloway c Kenway b Warne	0	– (3) not out	13
P. D. Bowler lbw b Morris	56		
†M. Burns b Morris	1		
R. J. Turner c Morris b Renshaw	56		
I. D. Blackwell c Laney b Morris	15		
G. D. Rose not out	13		
P. S. Jones run out	0		
M. P. L. Bulbeck lbw b Renshaw	3		
B 6, l-b 11, w 2	19	L-b 6, w 2	8
	319	**(1 wkt)**	**40**

1/14 2/14 3/23 4/142 5/152
6/283 7/291 8/303 9/307

1/18

Bonus points – Somerset 3, Hampshire 3.

Bowling: *First Innings*—Morris 20–2–80–3; Warne 33–10–83–1; Udal 23–6–51–2; Renshaw 14.1–6–23–3; Mascarenhas 13–2–41–0; Stephenson 8–2–24–0. *Second Innings*—Renshaw 5–0–13–1; Morris 5–1–17–0; White 0.1–0–4–0.

Umpires: R. Palmer and J. F. Steele.

At Leeds, May 12, 13, 14. HAMPSHIRE lost to YORKSHIRE by an innings and 100 runs.

At Leicester, May 17, 18, 19, 20. HAMPSHIRE drew with LEICESTERSHIRE.

HAMPSHIRE v LANCASHIRE

At Southampton, May 23, 24, 25, 26. Drawn. Hampshire 7 pts, Lancashire 6 pts. Toss: Hampshire.
Rain washed out the first and last days and cut heavily into the other two. After their poor start to the season, Hampshire showed signs of recovery in reducing Lancashire to 119 for seven, but the lower order added another 96 to give them an unlikely batting point. Schofield's application with the bat served his side well; as a bowler he was less successful, finding length and line elusive. His only wicket in Hampshire's truncated reply came when Kendall pulled a long-hop to mid-wicket. Smith hit ten boundaries in his 61, and White batted freely until rain denied Hampshire the chance to build their first substantial total of a troubled summer.

Close of play: First day, No play; Second day, Lancashire 125-7 (Schofield 2*, Chapple 5*); Third day, Hampshire 175-4 (White 45*, Aymes 7*).

Lancashire

M. J. Chilton c Laney b Francis	18	G. Chapple b Warne	20
*J. P. Crawley c Aymes b Mascarenhas	33	P. J. Martin c sub b Mascarenhas	21
A. Flintoff c Laney b Francis	5	G. Keedy c Stephenson b Mascarenhas	13
N. H. Fairbrother b Mascarenhas	7	L-b 2, n-b 6	8
G. D. Lloyd c Aymes b Hartley	28		
J. C. Scuderi c Aymes b Warne	17	1/41 2/53 3/60	215
†W. K. Hegg c Aymes b Hartley	6	4/71 5/104 6/116	
C. P. Schofield not out	39	7/119 8/154 9/197	

Bonus points – Lancashire 1, Hampshire 3.

Bowling: Hartley 10.5–2–33–2; Francis 12.1–2–63–2; Stephenson 5–0–14–0; Mascarenhas 14.5–3–52–4; Warne 21–4–51–2.

Hampshire

J. S. Laney lbw b Martin	14	†A. N. Aymes not out	7
D. A. Kenway b Martin	5		
W. S. Kendall c Chilton b Schofield	36	L-b 1, n-b 6	7
*R. A. Smith c Flintoff b Keedy	61		
G. W. White not out	45	1/7 2/34 3/116 4/136 (4 wkts) 175	

J. P. Stephenson, A. D. Mascarenhas, S. K. Warne, P. J. Hartley and S. R. G. Francis did not bat.

Bonus point – Lancashire 1.

Bowling: Martin 15–5–22–2; Chapple 10–3–26–0; Scuderi 8–4–23–0; Flintoff 5–1–20–0; Schofield 17–4–42–1; Keedy 14–3–41–1.

Umpires: M. J. Harris and D. R. Shepherd.

At The Oval, June 1, 2, 3, 4. HAMPSHIRE lost to SURREY by two runs.

At Liverpool, June 6, 7, 8. HAMPSHIRE lost to LANCASHIRE by an innings and 35 runs.

HAMPSHIRE v DURHAM

At Basingstoke, June 14, 15, 16. Hampshire won by an innings and 164 runs. Hampshire 18 pts, Durham 3 pts. Toss: Hampshire. First-class debut: A. J. Sexton.

Hampshire's final first-class match at Basingstoke, before moving all fixtures to their new Southampton headquarters, brought their first Championship win of the summer. Yet it could easily have been a disaster. Tony Brown led an ECB panel of experts to investigate the May's Bounty pitch when 17 wickets fell on the second day; by lunch on the third, Durham were already beaten. After categorising the strip as "below average", however, the panel decided Hampshire were not culpable and let them retain their precious points. All the same, the toss had been vital, for there were early signs of wear as Hampshire compiled 340, their biggest total of the season so far, despite no one reaching 50. Andrew Sexton, 20, made an important contribution on his debut. Warne, though never at his best, took four wickets in each innings as Durham were bowled out twice in less than three sessions. What undoubtedly saved Hampshire from a pitch penalty was the umpires' opinion that their opponents' batting was below average, too.

Close of play: First day, Hampshire 255-4 (Kenway 39*, Aymes 31*); Second day, Durham 12-1 (Lewis 3*, Betts 9*).

Hampshire

G. W. White c Collingwood b Harmison	29	S. D. Udal c Speight b Brown	35
A. J. Sexton lbw b Betts	36	A. D. Mullally lbw b Betts	0
W. S. Kendall c Phillips b Collingwood	42	S. R. G. Francis not out	5
*R. A. Smith c Speight b Collingwood	43		
D. A. Kenway lbw b Brown	47	L-b 16, w 2, n-b 18	36
†A. N. Aymes lbw b Brown	40		
A. D. Mascarenhas c Speight b Wood	27	1/62 2/104 3/171 4/176 5/271 340	
S. K. Warne c Speight b Brown	0	6/272 7/274 8/315 9/324	

Bonus points – Hampshire 3, Durham 3.

Bowling: Brown 22.1–3–62–4; Harmison 19–6–33–1; Betts 32–9–76–2; Wood 24–4–94–1; Phillips 13–4–23–0; Collingwood 15–5–34–2; Katich 3–1–2–0.

Durham

J. J. B. Lewis c White b Mullally	0	– c Kendall b Mullally	3
N. Peng c Kendall b Mascarenhas	9	– lbw b Udal	0
S. M. Katich lbw b Mascarenhas	2	– (4) c Kendall b Warne	26
P. D. Collingwood c Warne b Mascarenhas	6	– (5) c White b Udal	13
*N. J. Speak c Sexton b Warne	22	– (6) c Aymes b Warne	6
†M. P. Speight c Kendall b Mullally	12	– (7) b Warne	17
N. C. Phillips lbw b Mullally	1	– (8) c Kendall b Warne	2
J. Wood c Aymes b Warne	11	– (9) c Mascarenhas b Udal	1
M. M. Betts b Warne	12	– (3) lbw b Mullally	23
S. J. E. Brown c Mascarenhas b Warne	1	– not out	2
S. J. Harmison not out	0	– absent hurt	
B 1, l-b 4, w 2	7		

1/0 2/7 3/13 4/22 5/51   83   1/1 2/12 3/31 4/59 5/66   93
6/52 7/67 8/71 9/82   6/77 7/90 8/91 9/93

Bonus points – Hampshire 3.

Bowling: *First Innings*—Mullally 17–9–18–3; Francis 4–2–6–0; Mascarenhas 8–3–17–3; Warne 18.4–7–34–4; Udal 2–1–3–0. *Second Innings*—Mullally 7–3–12–2; Francis 4–2–10–0; Udal 14.3–2–35–3; Warne 11–2–22–4; Mascarenhas 6–1–14–0.

Umpires: A. Clarkson and T. E. Jesty.

At Southampton, June 25. HAMPSHIRE lost to WEST INDIANS by four wickets (See West Indian tour section).

HAMPSHIRE v SURREY

At Southampton, June 29, 30, July 1, 2. Surrey won by 120 runs. Surrey 18 pts, Hampshire 3 pts. Toss: Surrey.

Surrey needed only 14 balls on the final day to complete a victory as comprehensive as it was inevitable once they had set Hampshire a daunting 393 in five sessions. Adam Hollioake had elected not to enforce the follow-on, but did claim the extra half-hour on the third evening. Aymes, his face bruised by a blow from the ball while keeping on the first day, batted 140 minutes for a typically cussed fifty against the odds, and at least ensured nine minutes' action on the fourth morning. Both sides bowled well on an uncooperative pitch, but none better than Saqlain Mushtaq, whose match figures of ten for 135 reflected Surrey's dominance. Warne took seven wickets, but was not as consistent, while Mullally claimed six for 75 on the opening day. The real difference lay in the batting, frail Hampshire having no one to match Butcher's patience. His 116 off 221 balls was his third century at Southampton, and enabled Hollioake to choose the timing of his declaration without pressure.

Close of play: First day, Hampshire 6-0 (White 3*, Sexton 3*); Second day, Surrey 134-3 (Butcher 60*, A. J. Hollioake 0*); Third day, Hampshire 265-9 (Aymes 43*, Francis 0*).

Surrey

M. A. Butcher lbw b Mullally	34	– not out	116
I. J. Ward c Kendall b Mullally	15	– c Aymes b Warne	42
G. P. Thorpe b Mullally	44	– c Sexton b Udal	9
*A. J. Hollioake c Kendall b Mascarenhas	47	– (5) st Kenway b Warne	24
A. D. Brown st Aymes b Mascarenhas	71	– (6) c White b Warne	0
B. C. Hollioake c Smith b Mullally	1	– (7) lbw b Warne	10
†J. N. Batty b Warne	26	– (8) not out	1
M. P. Bicknell not out	56		
A. J. Tudor b Warne	5		
I. D. K. Salisbury c Kenway b Mullally	7		
Saqlain Mushtaq c Warne b Mullally	0	– (4) lbw b Warne	17
B 4, l-b 7, w 8, n-b 6	25	L-b 5, w 2, n-b 2	9

1/37 2/100 3/107 4/216 5/217   331   1/92 2/113 3/134   (6 wkts dec.) 228
6/231 7/270 8/284 9/331   4/180 5/182 6/218

Bonus points – Surrey 3, Hampshire 3.

Bowling: *First Innings*—Mullally 24.2–6–75–6; Francis 14–2–58–0; Mascarenhas 14–4–34–2; Udal 16–2–63–0; Warne 31–12–90–2. *Second Innings*—Mullally 15–4–48–0; Francis 6–0–22–0; Warne 29.1–3–90–5; Udal 13–3–40–1; Mascarenhas 8–1–23–0.

Hampshire

G. W. White lbw b Bicknell	6	– b Salisbury	73
A. J. Sexton c Batty b Bicknell	5	– lbw b Bicknell	5
W. S. Kendall c Thorpe b Salisbury	23	– run out	15
*R. A. Smith lbw b Saqlain Mushtaq	36	– lbw b Salisbury	3
D. A. Kenway lbw b Saqlain Mushtaq	30	– lbw b Salisbury	23
†A. N. Aymes lbw b Saqlain Mushtaq	2	– (8) lbw b Saqlain Mushtaq	50
A. D. Mascarenhas c Butcher b Saqlain Mushtaq	12	– (6) c and b Saqlain Mushtaq	2
S. K. Warne st Batty b Saqlain Mushtaq	17	– (7) c B. C. Hollioake b Salisbury	23
S. D. Udal not out	3	– lbw b Saqlain Mushtaq	24
A. D. Mullally b Saqlain Mushtaq	12	– c and b Saqlain Mushtaq	10
S. R. G. Francis c A. J. Hollioake b Salisbury	4	– not out	0
L-b 1, n-b 16	17	B 13, l-b 17, w 6, n-b 8	44

1/10 2/17 3/84 4/84 5/87   167   1/25 2/56 3/63 4/101 5/110   272
6/113 7/147 8/150 9/162   6/161 7/187 8/230 9/265

Bonus points – Surrey 3.

Bowling: *First Innings*—Tudor 9–1–26–0; Bicknell 10–2–25–2; B. C. Hollioake 3–0–24–0; Saqlain Mushtaq 22–4–51–6; Salisbury 19.3–7–40–2. *Second Innings*—Bicknell 10–2–27–1; Tudor 14–1–46–0; Saqlain Mushtaq 23.2–1–84–4; Salisbury 32–4–84–4; Brown 1–0–1–0.

Umpires: K. E. Palmer and A. G. T. Whitehead.

At Taunton, July 7, 8, 9, 10. HAMPSHIRE drew with SOMERSET.

At Portsmouth, July 12, 13, 14, 15. HAMPSHIRE lost to NEW ZEALAND A by two wickets (See New Zealand A tour section).

HAMPSHIRE v KENT

At Portsmouth, July 19, 20, 21, 22. Kent won by six wickets. Kent 17 pts, Hampshire 6 pts. Toss: Hampshire.

After 112 years of visiting Portsmouth, Hampshire bade their Championship farewell to the United Services Ground with a defeat. The slow, dry pitch had clearly been prepared with Warne in mind, and his battle with Dravid proved crucial: Dravid's mastery in both innings tipped the balance. Playing Warne in soft-handed defence or effortless, wristy attack, he hit his first Championship century, batting almost six hours for 137. With negligible help, he limited Kent's deficit to 68, after Laney and Warne had contributed fifties to Hampshire's second-highest total of the season thus far. Dravid was equally authoritative on the last day as Kent reached a target of 205 – and Warne went wicketless. Most effective of the spinners was Patel, the Kent left-armer, who took nine wickets in the match. For Hampshire, Udal claimed six, Warne just four. What cost them the game, though, was a supine second-innings performance mitigated only by White, who carried his bat for the second time in 2000. First-class cricket had been played at Portsmouth ever since Cambridge University Past and Present beat the Australians by 20 runs in 1882; Hampshire arrived six years later when they lost to Sussex by an innings. Norman Olden, 90, who saw Portsmouth's first Cricket Week in 1920, was here to witness the last.

Close of play: First day, Kent 31-2 (Fulton 17*, Dravid 12*); Second day, Hampshire 16-1 (White 9*, Kendall 0*); Third day, Kent 117-1 (Key 41*, Dravid 25*).

Hampshire

G. W. White lbw b Saggers	9	– not out 80
D. A. Kenway c Nixon b Patel	35	– c Fulton b Trott 1
W. S. Kendall c Nixon b Masters	21	– run out 0
*R. A. Smith c Nixon b Patel	13	– b Patel 4
J. S. Laney b Key b Trott	81	– b Patel 9
†A. N. Aymes b Walker b Patel	13	– lbw b Saggers 1
A. D. Mascarenhas lbw b Trott	7	– c Fulton b Patel 17
S. K. Warne b Patel	69	– c Walker b Fleming......... 4
S. D. Udal c Fulton b Saggers	31	– c Fulton b Patel 1
P. J. Hartley not out	23	– c Walker b Patel........... 4
S. R. G. Francis run out	1	– c Patel b Fleming 0
L-b 13, n-b 4	17	B 10, l-b 3, w 2 15

1/32 2/60 3/84 4/84 5/162   **320**   1/8 2/26 3/35 4/45 5/54   **136**
6/189 7/218 8/289 9/301   6/97 7/112 8/125 9/135

Bonus points – Hampshire 3, Kent 3.

Bowling: *First Innings*—Saggers 22–4–63–2; Trott 9–1–44–2; Masters 17–5–60–1; Patel 39.3–10–118–4; Fleming 6–0–22–0. *Second Innings*—Saggers 12–3–25–1; Trott 8–3–15–1; Patel 26–6–46–5; Dravid 1–0–2–0; Masters 3–0–18–0; Fleming 6.2–2–17–2.

Kent

D. P. Fulton c Kendall b Francis	33	– lbw b Udal 42
R. W. T. Key c White b Warne	0	– c Warne b Udal 60
D. D. Masters lbw b Warne	0	
R. Dravid b White	137	– (3) not out............. 73
A. P. Wells b Warne	7	– (4) lbw b Udal............ 0
M. J. Walker c Warne b Mascarenhas	0	– (5) c Warne b Udal......... 4
†P. A. Nixon lbw b Udal	17	– (6) not out............. 5
*M. V. Fleming lbw b Warne	15	
M. M. Patel c Warne b White	15	
M. J. Saggers c White b Udal	0	
B. J. Trott not out	0	
B 4, l-b 6, w 4, n-b 14	28	B 2, l-b 7, n-b 12 21

1/15 2/15 3/81 4/98 5/99   **252**   1/67 2/182 3/182 4/194   (4 wkts) **205**
6/153 7/210 8/249 9/252

Bonus points – Kent 2, Hampshire 3.

Bowling: *First Innings*—Hartley 13–2–54–0; Francis 11–5–27–1; Warne 37–11–81–4; Udal 20.2–5–52–2; Mascarenhas 17–8–26–1; White 2–1–2–2. *Second Innings*—Hartley 18–5–56–0; Francis 4–1–14–0; Warne 31.4–13–69–0; Mascarenhas 10–5–11–0; Udal 20–8–42–4; White 1–0–4–0.

Umpires: J. H. Hampshire and J. H. Harris.

At Derby, August 2, 3, 4, 5. HAMPSHIRE drew with DERBYSHIRE.

HAMPSHIRE v LEICESTERSHIRE

At Southampton, August 8, 9, 10, 11. Leicestershire won by 61 runs. Leicestershire 17 pts, Hampshire 4 pts. Toss: Hampshire.

Hampshire were left rooted to the bottom of the table after a demoralising defeat by an understrength Leicestershire: four front-line bowlers were out injured and a fifth, Dakin, limped off after one over on the final morning. Hampshire were minus one expensive acquisition – Warne was in Melbourne for international cricket's first indoor match – and relied heavily on another. Mullally, in his first game against his old club, took nine wickets from a rigorous match total of 65 overs – including an uninterrupted spell of 29 stretching from the second evening to the third afternoon – but it was not enough. After Leicestershire had consolidated a modest first-innings lead to set a target of 279, the largest score of the match, Wells skilfully manipulated his depleted attack. With Hampshire halfway there for the loss of two wickets, and night-watchman Morris making a comfortable, Championship-best 60, it looked as if Leicestershire had run out of ideas and bowlers. But Crowe and Wells bowled with tenacity and purpose, and Hampshire inexplicably lost their last eight batsmen for 73.

Close of play: First day, Leicestershire 265-9 (Crowe 26*, Boswell 4*); Second day, Leicestershire 42-0 (Maddy 18*, Sutcliffe 22*); Third day, Hampshire 54-2 (White 22*, Morris 5*).

Leicestershire

D. L. Maddy c Kendall b Mullally	8	– lbw b Mascarenhas	18
I. J. Sutcliffe c sub b Morris	53	– c Aymes b Mascarenhas	37
B. F. Smith c Aymes b Mullally	5	– b Mullally	15
A. Habib c Aymes b Mascarenhas	61	– c Udal b Mullally	13
D. I. Stevens c Aymes b Mascarenhas	12	– c Aymes b Mullally	24
*V. J. Wells lbw b Mullally	22	– c Aymes b Mullally	20
J. M. Dakin c Laney b Stephenson	60	– run out	8
D. Williamson lbw b Mullally	4	– (9) not out	43
†N. D. Burns c Aymes b Mullally	0	– (8) st Aymes b Udal	23
C. D. Crowe c Aymes b Morris	26	– b Stephenson	2
S. A. J. Boswell not out	5	– c Kendall b Udal	20
L-b 4, w 2, n-b 4	10	B 1, l-b 6, w 2, n-b 8	17

1/18 2/28 3/120 4/142 5/167   266   1/43 2/72 3/72 4/104 5/111   240
6/169 7/189 8/189 9/260   6/129 7/150 8/164 9/175

Bonus points – Leicestershire 2, Hampshire 3.

Bowling: *First Innings*—Mullally 28–6–84–5; Morris 18.3–2–54–2; Stephenson 13–1–49–1; Mascarenhas 20–4–59–2; Udal 4–0–16–0. *Second Innings*—Mullally 37–15–59–4; Morris 11–3–22–0; Stephenson 10–0–51–1; Udal 15.3–5–36–2; Mascarenhas 23–5–65–2.

Hampshire

G. W. White b Dakin	2	– b Williamson	50
D. A. Kenway lbw b Dakin	8	– c Crowe b Dakin	7
W. S. Kendall b Boswell	20	– lbw b Wells	16
*R. A. Smith c Wells b Williamson	15	– (5) c Burns b Crowe	20
J. S. Laney c Wells b Boswell	15	– (6) c and b Crowe	6
†A. N. Aymes c Burns b Wells	71	– (7) c Maddy b Crowe	6
A. D. Mascarenhas b Wells	34	– (8) not out	27
J. P. Stephenson c Wells b Crowe	14	– (9) c Burns b Wells	5
S. D. Udal c Burns b Boswell	12	– (10) lbw b Wells	1
A. C. Morris c Smith b Wells	19	– (4) c Smith b Crowe	60
A. D. Mullally not out	1	– c Sutcliffe b Wells	0
L-b 3, n-b 14	17	L-b 7, n-b 12	19
	228		**217**

1/4 2/19 3/46 4/64 5/72   228   1/13 2/45 3/144 4/144 5/166   217
6/124 7/149 8/173 9/227   6/179 7/190 8/211 9/217

Bonus points – Hampshire 1, Leicestershire 3.

Bowling: *First Innings*—Dakin 21–3–70–2; Boswell 15–4–39–3; Wells 20–6–39–3; Williamson 7–0–37–1; Crowe 14–3–28–1; Maddy 4–0–12–0. *Second Innings*—Dakin 7–1–29–1; Boswell 12–3–30–0; Wells 20.4–4–54–4; Crowe 27–7–55–4; Williamson 13–2–42–1.

Umpires: M. J. Kitchen and R. A. White.

At Canterbury, August 22, 23, 24, 25. HAMPSHIRE lost to KENT by 15 runs.

At Chester-le-Street, August 31, September 1, 2, 3. HAMPSHIRE beat DURHAM by six wickets.

HAMPSHIRE v DERBYSHIRE

At Southampton, September 6, 7, 8, 9. Hampshire won by an innings and three runs. Hampshire 20 pts, Derbyshire 6 pts. Toss: Hampshire.

Lawrence Prittipaul, a 20-year-old right-hand batsman from Portsmouth, hit 152, the highest score by a Hampshire player on home Championship debut, beating Dennis Baldry's 151 against Glamorgan in 1959. Prittipaul's scintillating innings lasted four hours, and he stroked 25 fours from 225 balls. He and Kendall, who compiled his third hundred of the summer, put on 248 for the fourth wicket and helped Hampshire to 522, their highest total of the season and their best against Derbyshire in 138 Championship meetings. At 346 for four, Derbyshire were 27 short of saving the follow-on and, in all likelihood, the match. Then Morris and Warne demolished their brittle lower order: the last six wickets fell for six runs. Batting again 170 behind, they disintegrated a second time, despite another half-century from Bailey. This time, Udal, emerging from Warne's shadow to take his only five-wicket haul of the season, undermined the resistance. Maximum points gave Hampshire the faintest of chances of survival in the top division; Derbyshire's fate was now sealed.

Close of play: First day, Hampshire 368-4 (Prittipaul 149*, Aymes 2*); Second day, Derbyshire 188-2 (Sutton 65*, Bailey 7*); Third day, Derbyshire 32-2 (Sutton 13*).

Hampshire

J. S. Laney c Cassar b Munton	10	S. D. Udal b Lacey	1
G. W. White c Sutton b Dean	10	A. C. Morris st Sutton b Lacey	8
W. S. Kendall c Bailey b Lacey	143	P. J. Hartley not out	17
*R. A. Smith c Di Venuto b Cassar	33		
L. R. Prittipaul lbw b Munton	152	B 6, l-b 18, n-b 8	32
†A. N. Aymes b Cassar	20		
A. D. Mascarenhas c Sutton b Wharton	62	1/21 2/21 3/107 4/355 5/379	522
S. K. Warne c Stubbings b Lacey	34	6/412 7/495 8/497 9/497	

Bonus points – Hampshire 5, Derbyshire 2 (Score at 130 overs: 497-8).

Bowling: Dean 28–3–134–1; Munton 29–8–76–2; Cassar 21–6–76–2; Wharton 24–6–81–1; Lacey 25.3–2–98–4; Pyemont 4–0–15–0; Bailey 3–0–18–0.

Derbyshire

S. D. Stubbings b Warne	36	– c Morris b Udal	19
†L. D. Sutton c White b Udal	77	– c Warne b Hartley	37
M. J. Di Venuto c White b Mascarenhas	52	– c Aymes b Udal	0
R. J. Bailey b Morris	90	– lbw b Morris	53
M. P. Dowman c Kendall b Udal	1	– c Aymes b Udal	4
J. P. Pyemont c Laney b Morris	40	– c White b Udal	20
M. E. Cassar c Aymes b Warne	0	– run out	5
S. J. Lacey c Udal b Morris	2	– c Warne b Udal	10
*T. A. Munton c Aymes b Warne	1	– c Morris b Warne	0
K. J. Dean b Warne	0	– not out	0
L. J. Wharton not out	0	– c White b Warne	0
B 15, l-b 18, n-b 20	53	B 13, l-b 6	19

1/85 2/157 3/217 4/223 5/346	352	1/30 2/32 3/116 4/120 5/120	167
6/349 7/349 8/352 9/352		6/126 7/166 8/167 9/167	

Bonus points – Derbyshire 4, Hampshire 3.

Bowling: *First Innings*—Hartley 10–0–44–0; Morris 13.2–3–48–3; Warne 41–14–103–4; Udal 31–8–81–2; Mascarenhas 15–6–28–1; White 3–0–15–0. *Second Innings*—Morris 13–5–23–1; Hartley 9–2–25–1; Warne 24.2–13–36–2; Udal 26–9–58–5; Mascarenhas 2–1–6–0.

Umpires: V. A. Holder and A. A. Jones.

HAMPSHIRE v YORKSHIRE

At Southampton, September 13, 14, 15, 16. Yorkshire won by 72 runs. Yorkshire 16 pts, Hampshire 4 pts. Toss: Yorkshire.

Hampshire took their first-class leave of Northlands Road, after 565 games, on a sad note. They lost the match, eight points for preparing a poor pitch, and their first-division status. Avoiding relegation was theoretically possible at the outset, but a point for Kent at Leicester soon ruled that out. Hampshire still went all out for victory, but in the eyes of the ECB pitches panel – convened after 16 wickets fell on the opening day – they used foul means as well as fair. Just 30 minutes after the start, Warne was bowling on a dry pitch already taking an abnormal amount of spin. Not that it bothered Lehmann, top scorer in both Yorkshire innings. He hit an aggressive 46 from 34 balls in the first and a polished 92, punctuated by a third-day washout, in the second. Hampshire needed 258 for victory, but Middlebrook checked their advance. In Hampshire's first innings he had spun his way to a career-best six wickets, including four in five balls; now he took another four to finish with ten for 170. In a tense conclusion, Hartley, playing his last first-class innings before retiring, watched as Morris (like his partner a former Yorkshire player) survived five balls of the final over. The sixth he edged to second slip. This was Yorkshire's 11th Championship victory at Northlands Road since their first visit in 1895; they had also drawn ten matches there and never lost.

Close of play: First day, Hampshire 151-6 (Kendall 56*, Warne 48*); Second day, Yorkshire 181-6 (Lehmann 72*, Hamilton 28*); Third day, No play.

Yorkshire

S. Widdup c Aymes b Hartley	9	– c Warne b Hartley	1
M. P. Vaughan c Kendall b Warne	30	– c Aymes b Hartley	16
A. McGrath lbw b Warne	4	– c Kendall b Udal	17
D. S. Lehmann c Aymes b Mascarenhas	46	– c Mascarenhas b Udal	92
*D. Byas lbw b Warne	26	– (7) c Udal b Warne	16
G. M. Fellows lbw b Warne	28	– c Kendall b Warne	17
G. M. Hamilton c Aymes b Mascarenhas	3	– (8) run out	61
J. D. Middlebrook run out	22	– (9) c and b Udal	5
I. D. Fisher c White b Warne	4	– (10) not out	19
†S. M. Guy not out	21	– (5) c Kendall b Udal	0
M. J. Hoggard c White b Udal	0	– b Mascarenhas	6
B 1, l-b 3, w 6, n-b 2	12	B 10, l-b 1, w 2, n-b 2	15

1/26 2/40 3/59 4/109 5/121	205	1/6 2/19 3/62 4/62 5/93	265
6/126 7/164 8/180 9/201		6/129 7/228 8/234 9/256

Bonus points – Yorkshire 1, Hampshire 3.

Bowling: *First Innings*—Hartley 13–3–42–1; Morris 6–0–39–0; Warne 27–6–92–5; Mascarenhas 7–5–13–2; Udal 7.1–2–15–1. *Second Innings*—Hartley 16–3–30–2; Morris 5–2–11–0; Warne 21–0–116–2; Udal 23–6–76–4; Mascarenhas 10–3–21–1.

Hampshire

D. A. Kenway c Guy b Hoggard	13	– run out	58
G. W. White lbw b Hamilton	11	– c Hoggard b Middlebrook	37
W. S. Kendall c Guy b Middlebrook	73	– c Widdup b Middlebrook	13
*R. A. Smith lbw b Middlebrook	20	– c Lehmann b Middlebrook	6
L. R. Prittipaul c Lehmann b Middlebrook	0	– (6) c Guy b Fisher	24
†A. N. Aymes c Lehmann b Middlebrook	0	– (7) lbw b Lehmann	1
A. D. Mascarenhas c Guy b Middlebrook	0	– (8) c Byas b Fisher	17
S. K. Warne c McGrath b Hoggard	65	– (5) st Guy b Middlebrook	4
S. D. Udal not out	14	– c McGrath b Lehmann	12
A. C. Morris c Widdup b Fisher	13	– c Hamilton b Fisher	4
P. J. Hartley lbw b Middlebrook	0	– not out	0
B 1, l-b 1, n-b 2	4	B 2, l-b 3, w 2, n-b 2	9

1/22 2/24 3/76 4/76 5/78	213	1/65 2/113 3/114 4/123 5/132	185
6/78 7/173 8/187 9/210		6/133 7/158 8/177 9/185

Bonus points – Hampshire 1, Yorkshire 3.

Bowling: *First Innings*—Hoggard 13–3–44–2; Hamilton 9–3–27–1; Middlebrook 28.5–11–82–6; Fisher 16–1–58–1. *Second Innings*—Hoggard 5–0–16–0; Hamilton 3–1–20–0; Fisher 21–7–40–3; Middlebrook 30–4–88–4; Lehmann 13–5–16–2.

Umpires: J. W. Holder and T. E. Jesty.

HAMPSHIRE IN 1900

"Never can a county have had to labour under greater disadvantages than beset Hampshire during the season of 1900. The [Boer] War meant more to them than to any other team. Several counties had representatives at the front, but none suffered to the same extent as Hampshire. Major R. M. Poore and Mr. C. Heseltine, to mention only the most famous of many men, were in the Transvaal; and the necessarily increased military duties prevented Captain Wynyard and Captain Quinton from playing in more than very few matches. So it cannot be wondered that Hampshire should have had a disastrous summer in the field."

KENT

Martin Saggers

President: 2000 – Lord Cowdrey
2001 – D. G. Ufton
Chairman: C. F. Openshaw
Chief Executive: P. E. Millman
Chairman, Cricket Committee: 2000 – D. G. Ufton
Director of Cricket Development: W. G. Dover
Captain: M. V. Fleming
First-Team Coach: 2000 – J. G. Wright
2001 – R. J. Inverarity
Cricket Administration Manager: S. C. Willis
Head Groundsman: M. Grantham
Scorer: J. C. Foley

It was close-run at times, but by the end of 2000 Kent remained one of only three counties, along with Yorkshire and Leicestershire, to enjoy continuous first-division status in both the County Championship and National League. Handicapped by bad weather and a horrendous injury list, they had flirted with relegation on both fronts for much of the season until an eight-wicket victory over Worcestershire on the last day of the season – their fifth win in six games – guaranteed they would make the National League cut. An exhilarating 15-run win over Hampshire towards the end of August, their sole Championship win at Canterbury, had already proved crucial to their survival in that competition.

Few of Kent's games went unaffected by the weather. Even pre-season practice was badly hit, and there was an early taste of the summer to come when three of their Benson and Hedges Cup group matches were washed out. That essentially put paid to Kent making the quarter-finals, while defeat by Glamorgan in yet another rain-affected game ended progress in the NatWest Trophy after two rounds. The Championship season, already a stop–start affair owing to fixture planning, suffered badly with more than 1,500 overs lost, and two League games were abandoned without a ball bowled.

Kent's ill fortune with injuries began with the news that Dean Headley would miss the entire season with a back injury. Weeks later, Julian Thompson's knee trouble was diagnosed as serious, and his long-term absence was a great disappointment for player and county. Having decided to put cricket before medicine, he found himself in the role of frustrated spectator and in the winter announced his retirement. Ben Phillips was another player sidelined – in his case for the second successive season. After missing the previous summer with a broken collarbone, he managed only three early limited-overs games – claiming one-day best figures of four for 25 against Northamptonshire in the League – before incurring a back injury that required an operation similar to Headley's. Mark Ealham (broken finger), Matthew Fleming (calf), Alan Wells (septicaemia) and Min Patel (shoulder) all missed games as Kent's injury woes continued.

However, a silver lining emerged in the seam bowling of Martin Saggers and David Masters, neither of whom could have imagined playing a major role at the start of the season. Both took their chances admirably, stayed fit and, by the end of the summer, were able to reflect on impressive statistics. Between them, they sent down more than 800 overs in the Championship, taking 96 wickets, and Saggers, who had missed half the previous season with a stress fracture of the back, was tipped for a possible England A call-up. Career-best figures of seven for 79 against his former county, Durham, at Chester-le-Street, as he hit a rich vein of wicket-taking in the second half of the campaign, contributed to 57 wickets at 20.14 each. Masters burst upon the scene with a nine-wicket match return against the Zimbabweans, followed four weeks later by six for 27 against Durham at Tunbridge Wells, and finished with 48 first-class wickets at 24.18. Saggers and Masters were deservedly named joint players of the season. Min Patel bowled more overs than anyone, at a cost of little more than two an over, and claimed 46 first-class wickets before his season, too, ended early.

Once again, Kent's batting proved a major problem. It lacked any real consistency, particularly among the top five, and they relied heavily on their Indian overseas player, Rahul Dravid. One of only four century-makers in the side – Ed Smith, Paul Nixon, and David Fulton were the others – Dravid was the only player to score 1,000 runs in a summer that saw Kent muster just 18 batting bonus points – the lowest total in either division. They were hampered by a sequence of poor starts, but benefited from Nixon's experience further down the order: he added 131 with Patel for the eighth wicket against Derbyshire, and 125 with Masters for the tenth against Hampshire. Nixon's first season after moving from Leicestershire was crowned by selection for England's winter tours.

Matthew Walker's ability to develop into an all-rounder, especially in one-day games, was recognised by a county cap, while left-arm swing bowler Kristian Adams made an exciting impression by claiming six for 24 against Cumberland in the NatWest Trophy. He also bowled encouragingly at Leicester on his first League outing, but his Championship opportunities were limited.

Former captain Steve Marsh announced his retirement from first-class cricket, ending a distinguished career with Kent, and received a standing ovation when he made his final appearance at Canterbury, against Yorkshire in the county's first home floodlit fixture. Having started a successful business venture in sports hospitality, Marsh has plans to coach – he has not ruled out the prospect of playing again – but 2001 would have been too soon for him to step into the vacancy left by John Wright's appointment as India's coach. The county turned instead to the former Australian Test cricketer, John Inverarity, who had filled the role of cricket adviser in 1988 with some success. England Under-19 winter tourist Rob Ferley, reserve wicket-keeper Geraint Jones and Ben Trott were all offered contracts, but Richard Clinton and James Watson were released at the end of the season. Darren Scott retired from first-class cricket after two years on the staff. – ANDREW GIDLEY.

KENT 2000

[Terry Mahoney]

Back row: M. Sigley (first-team physiotherapist), M. J. Banes, M. J. Saggers, D. A. Scott, J. B. Hockley, K. Adams, M. J. Walker, N. Reid (second-team physiotherapist). Middle row: C. Stone (second-team coach), J. M. Golding, J. B. D. Thompson, B. J. Phillips, J. D. Watson, D. D. Masters, E. T. Smith, R. W. T. Key, R. S. Clinton, J. G. Wright (first-team coach), J. C. Foley (scorer). Front row: D. P. Fulton, R. Dravid, M. M. Patel, M. A. Ealham, M. V. Fleming (captain), S. A. Marsh, M. J. McCague, A. P. Wells, P. A. Nixon. Inset: D. W. Headley.

KENT RESULTS

All first-class matches – Played 17: Won 5, Lost 4, Drawn 8.

County Championship matches – Played 16: Won 4, Lost 4, Drawn 8.

PPP Healthcare County Championship, 6th in Division 1; NatWest Trophy, 4th round; Benson and Hedges Cup, 4th in South Group; Norwich Union National League, 5th in Division 1.

COUNTY CHAMPIONSHIP AVERAGES

BATTING

Cap		M	I	NO	R	HS	100s	50s	Avge	Ct/St
2000	R. Dravid§	15	24	3	1,039	137	1	8	49.47	13
2000	P. A. Nixon	16	23	7	513	134*	1	2	32.06	41/2
1990	M. V. Fleming	13	17	2	433	47	0	0	28.86	2
2000	M. J. Walker†	14	23	3	490	61	0	1	24.50	12
	E. T. Smith†	10	17	0	411	175	1	0	24.17	5
1992	M. A. Ealham†	11	14	1	293	83	0	2	22.53	3
	R. W. T. Key	15	26	1	558	83	0	5	22.32	4
1998	D. P. Fulton	14	24	1	512	115	1	1	22.26	29
1994	M. M. Patel	12	15	1	258	60	0	1	18.42	11
1992	M. J. McCague	7	11	0	191	72	0	1	17.36	2
1997	A. P. Wells	11	18	2	239	60*	0	1	14.93	2
	J. B. Hockley†	4	4	0	37	33	0	0	9.25	2
	M. J. Saggers	14	17	5	91	24	0	0	7.58	3
	D. D. Masters†	15	19	7	71	21	0	0	5.91	3

Also batted: D. A. Scott† (2 matches) 2, 4*, 2* (1 ct); B. J. Trott (2 matches) 0*, 0* (1 ct). K. Adams (1 match) did not bat.

* Signifies not out.   † Born in Kent.   § Overseas player.

BOWLING

	O	M	R	W	BB	5W/i	Avge
M. J. Saggers	425.2	99	1,148	57	7-79	2	20.14
M. M. Patel	471.1	159	960	37	6-77	2	25.94
M. V. Fleming	267.1	68	743	28	4-77	0	26.53
D. D. Masters	400.2	93	1,080	39	6-27	2	27.69
M. A. Ealham	271.5	67	703	24	5-35	1	29.29
M. J. McCague	129.4	20	412	14	5-52	1	29.42

Also bowled: K. Adams 22–4–58–2; R. Dravid 53.5–11–128–4; D. P. Fulton 17–5–45–0; J. B. Hockley 3–3–0–0; R. W. T. Key 9.4–1–34–0; P. A. Nixon 3–1–10–0; D. A. Scott 46–16–114–1; E. T. Smith 6–0–20–0; B. J. Trott 42–9–133–4; M. J. Walker 62–8–166–4.

COUNTY RECORDS

Highest score for:	332	W. H. Ashdown v Essex at Brentwood	1934
Highest score against:	344	W. G. Grace (MCC) at Canterbury	1876
Best bowling for:	10-30	C. Blythe v Northamptonshire at Northampton . . .	1907
Best bowling against:	10-48	C. H. G. Bland (Sussex) at Tonbridge	1899
Highest total for:	803-4 dec.	v Essex at Brentwood	1934
Highest total against:	676	by Australians at Canterbury.	1921
Lowest total for:	18	v Sussex at Gravesend	1867
Lowest total against:	16	by Warwickshire at Tonbridge.	1913

KENT v LANCASHIRE

At Canterbury, April 26, 27, 28, 29. Drawn. Kent 7 pts, Lancashire 4 pts. Toss: Kent. Championship debuts: R. Dravid; S. C. Ganguly, J. C. Scuderi.

When the umpires abandoned this rain-ruined contest shortly after lunch on the final day, the weather had allowed just 66 soggy overs. Ironically, the game was called off under blue skies and in warm sunshine, but an overnight downpour had saturated the outfield and left the bowlers' run-ups unfit. After an opening-day washout and a delayed start on the second, Lancashire stuttered to 38 for three – Ealham removing Scuderi and Ganguly in two balls – before Flintoff and Chilton added 77. Flintoff's pugnacious 77 in 82 balls, with 13 fours, was the cornerstone of the innings.

Close of play: First day, No play; Second day, Lancashire 95-3 (Chilton 33*, Flintoff 34*); Third day, Kent 29-1 (Key 10*, Dravid 17*).

Lancashire

M. A. Atherton c Hockley b McCague	17	G. Chapple c Nixon b Fleming		4
M. J. Chilton c Nixon b Ealham	38	P. J. Martin c Nixon b Patel		2
J. C. Scuderi lbw b Ealham	9	M. P. Smethurst not out		1
S. C. Ganguly lbw b Ealham	0			
A. Flintoff c Dravid b Saggers	77	L-b 2		2
G. D. Lloyd c Dravid b Ealham	0			—
*†W. K. Hegg c Fleming b Saggers	2	1/29 2/38 3/38 4/115 5/123		186
C. P. Schofield st Nixon b Patel	34	6/128 7/159 8/183 9/183		

Bonus points – Kent 3.

Bowling: Ealham 20–6–53–4; Saggers 15–2–53–2; McCague 5–1–15–1; Fleming 13–4–56–1; Patel 3.5–1–7–2.

Kent

E. T. Smith lbw b Chapple	0
R. W. T. Key not out	10
R. Dravid not out	17
L-b 2	2
	—
1/3 (1 wkt)	29

A. P. Wells, M. A. Ealham, †P. A. Nixon, *M. V. Fleming, J. B. Hockley, M. M. Patel, M. J. Saggers and M. J. McCague did not bat.

Bowling: Martin 5–3–10–0; Chapple 4–0–17–1.

Umpires: B. Leadbeater and R. A. White.

At Canterbury, May 3, 4, 5. KENT beat ZIMBABWEANS by an innings and 163 runs (See Zimbabwean tour section).

At The Oval, May 11, 12, 13, 14. KENT drew with SURREY.

KENT v SURREY

At Canterbury, May 23, 24, 25, 26. Drawn. Kent 6 pts, Surrey 7 pts. Toss: Surrey. First-class debut: K. Adams.

Ward spent every moment of this truncated, stop-start match at the crease. Rain, which washed out the third day, limited play to just 118 overs and a single, uncompleted innings – but Ward's immense concentration saw him to the second and highest century of his career. His unbeaten 158 spanned 365 balls and included 18 fours. He had no major ally, though Tudor hit a rollicking 33 not out from 32 balls before rain returned for the last time. Kent gave a first-class debut to left-arm seamer Kristian Adams, who claimed the notable scalp of Thorpe as his first wicket. This was the second of back-to-back Championship fixtures between these counties; both were hit by the weather.

Close of play: First day, Surrey 135-2 (Ward 73*, B. C. Hollioake 24*); Second day, Surrey 283-7 (Ward 127*, Salisbury 4*); Third day, No play.

Surrey

M. A. Butcher c Nixon b Ealham	32	I. D. K. Salisbury c Fulton b Ealham . . . 5
I. J. Ward not out	158	A. J. Tudor not out 33
G. P. Thorpe c Nixon b Adams	3	
B. C. Hollioake c Dravid b Fleming	29	B 1, l-b 5 6
A. D. Brown c Patel b Masters	28	
*A. J. Hollioake c Nixon b Dravid	17	1/66 2/69 3/143 (8 wkts) 348
†J. N. Batty lbw b Adams	10	4/176 5/211 6/225
M. P. Bicknell c Nixon b Masters	27	7/275 8/284

C. G. Greenidge did not bat.

Bonus points – Surrey 3, Kent 2.

Bowling: Ealham 29–8–91–2; Adams 22–4–58–2; Masters 23–8–74–2; Fleming 22–5–60–1; Patel 20–4–49–0; Dravid 2–0–10–1.

Kent

D. P. Fulton, R. W. T. Key, R. Dravid, A. P. Wells, M. A. Ealham, M. J. Walker, †P. A. Nixon, *M. V. Fleming, M. M. Patel, D. D. Masters and K. Adams.

Umpires: A. Clarkson and J. F. Steele.

KENT v DURHAM

At Tunbridge Wells, May 31, June 1, 2, 3. Kent won by 190 runs. Kent 15 pts, Durham 3 pts. Toss: Kent.

Kent moved off the bottom of Division One with their only Championship win of a damp spring. Durham's last pair, Speight and Brown, delayed the victory by putting on 40, but escape was never likely once Katich was out just after lunch on the final day, starting a collapse of five for eight in 11 overs. Fleming, believing that the pitch – under water three days before the start – was unlikely to get better, had chosen to bat first. Sure enough, it played low and slow, and Kent struggled. Fleming's 169-ball 39 was the best of some drear batting, but that was plain sailing by comparison with Durham's dire reply: 81 was their third-lowest first-class total. Masters continued his promising arrival in county cricket with six for 27, in his third Championship match, earning Kent a 96-run advantage. But they plummeted to 76 for seven before Ealham, batting positively, shared stands of 95 with Fleming and 66 with Patel, allowing Kent to declare after tea on the third day and leave Durham to chase 334.

Close of play: First day, Kent 171-8 (Fleming 37*); Second day, Kent 45-4 (Wells 16*, Masters 0*); Third day, Durham 44-2 (Katich 18*, Phillips 0*).

Kent

D. P. Fulton c Lewis b Betts	13	– lbw b Brown	5
R. W. T. Key b Wood	6	– b Betts	1
E. T. Smith lbw b Brown	8	– lbw b Brown	0
A. P. Wells c Speight b Wood	7	– c Wood b Betts	24
M. J. Walker lbw b Wood	20	– lbw b Collingwood	21
M. A. Ealham run out	9	– (7) not out	72
†P. A. Nixon c Speight b Katich	19	– (8) lbw b Collingwood	8
*M. V. Fleming c Lewis b Wood	39	– (9) c and b Phillips	40
M. M. Patel c Speight b Betts	26	– (10) c Collingwood b Wood	40
D. D. Masters not out	1	– (6) c Katich b Wood	9
M. J. Saggers lbw b Wood	2		
B 13, l-b 12, w 2	27	B 4, l-b 11, w 2	17

1/23 2/27 3/41 4/41 5/74	177	1/4 2/6 3/7	(9 wkts dec.) 237
6/80 7/127 8/171 9/173		4/41 5/60 6/63	
		7/76 8/171 9/237	

Bonus points – Durham 3.

Bowling: *First Innings*—Brown 15–4–36–1; Betts 25–10–28–2; Wood 30.2–12–36–5; Collingwood 15–7–15–0; Phillips 17–5–25–0; Katich 8–2–12–1. *Second Innings*—Brown 23–10–37–2; Betts 16–7–33–2; Wood 19.3–6–46–2; Collingwood 15–3–21–2; Phillips 17–4–47–1; Katich 12–2–27–0; Daley 4–0–11–0.

Durham

J. J. B. Lewis b Saggers	12	– lbw b Saggers	3
J. A. Daley lbw b Saggers	12	– c Fulton b Patel	14
S. M. Katich lbw b Ealham	2	– c Wells b Patel	41
P. D. Collingwood c Walker b Ealham	14	– (5) c and b Walker	12
*N. J. Speak lbw b Masters	4	– (6) c Smith b Patel	4
N. Peng lbw b Masters	21	– (7) lbw b Fleming	0
†M. P. Speight c Fleming b Masters	8	– (8) not out	22
J. Wood lbw b Masters	1	– (9) lbw b Patel	0
M. M. Betts not out	4	– (10) lbw b Fleming	2
N. C. Phillips b Masters	0	– (4) c Walker b Fleming	8
S. J. E. Brown c Nixon b Masters	0	– b Ealham	12
L-b 3	3	B 9, l-b 16	25
	81		**143**

1/16 2/23 3/29 4/34 5/55   81   1/22 2/38 3/57 4/78 5/95   143
6/69 7/76 8/81 9/81   6/96 7/100 8/100 9/103

Bonus points – Kent 3.

Bowling: *First Innings*—Masters 19.2–6–27–6; Ealham 15–4–24–2; Saggers 12–4–18–2; Fleming 7–3–6–0; Patel 11–8–3–0. *Second Innings*—Saggers 15–5–32–1; Ealham 11.4–6–9–1; Patel 30–15–38–4; Masters 12–4–21–0; Fleming 15–9–14–3; Walker 1–0–4–1.

Umpires: D. J. Constant and R. Julian.

At Bath, June 6, 7, 8, 9. KENT lost to SOMERSET by two wickets.

At Leeds, June 14, 15, 16. KENT lost to YORKSHIRE by six wickets.

KENT v SOMERSET

At Maidstone, June 28, 29, 30, July 1. Drawn. Kent 8 pts, Somerset 11 pts. Toss: Somerset.

Following on, Kent at last found the batting form that had eluded them, and staved off what would have been a third successive Championship defeat. Fulton, who had also saved them on this ground in 1998, when he batted more than ten hours against Yorkshire, hit 115 in almost four and a half hours. It was Kent's first Championship hundred of the season. Crucially, Fulton, whose seven previous Championship innings had brought 35 runs, was dropped at square leg when four. In addition, Somerset were convinced he was caught behind on the third evening, and subjected him to prolonged sledging. Fulton's opening partnership of 130 with Key was matched by Dravid and Wells for the third wicket – with Dravid taking his aggregate against Somerset to 290 from four innings before Trego dismissed him, five short of his first Championship century. Earlier, Somerset, led by Trescothick and Bowler, had batted consistently well for a commanding total. Despite missing several front-line bowlers, they made intelligent use of humid conditions on the third day to set up a chance of victory. Then the Mote reverted to type, and the game was drawn.

Close of play: First day, Somerset 290-5 (Bowler 102*, Blackwell 1*); Second day, Kent 128-1 (Key 42*, Dravid 73*); Third day, Kent 124-0 (Fulton 65*, Key 53*).

Somerset

*J. Cox lbw b Saggers	17	P. D. Trego run out	35
M. E. Trescothick c Saggers b Patel	90	A. R. K. Pierson c Patel b Saggers	18
P. C. L. Holloway c Nixon b Patel	31	P. S. Jones not out	8
P. D. Bowler c Patel b Masters	108		
K. A. Parsons b Patel	25	B 2, l-b 15, n-b 2	19
M. Burns b Fleming	20		—
I. D. Blackwell c Nixon b Patel	69	1/36 2/129 3/146 4/206 5/285	475
†R. J. Turner c Nixon b Fleming	35	6/313 7/372 8/440 9/455	

Bonus points – Somerset 4, Kent 2 (Score at 130 overs: 372-6).

Bowling: Ealham 12–1–43–0; Saggers 29.4–3–112–2; Masters 26–6–88–1; Fleming 23–5–68–2; Patel 54–16–118–4; Walker 10–1–29–0.

Kent

D. P. Fulton c Parsons b Jones	5	– c Parsons b Trego	115
R. W. T. Key b Jones	51	– c Pierson b Burns	54
R. Dravid c Bowler b Burns	88	– c and b Trego	95
A. P. Wells lbw b Burns	0	– not out	60
M. J. Walker c Turner b Trego	15		
†P. A. Nixon c Bowler b Trego	1		
M. A. Ealham c Blackwell b Jones	11		
*M. V. Fleming b Pierson	40		
M. M. Patel c Parsons b Blackwell	30		
D. D. Masters not out	2		
M. J. Saggers run out	1	– (5) not out	0
B 1, l-b 4, w 2, n-b 10	17	L-b 4, w 2, n-b 8	14
1/16 2/145 3/146 4/169 5/170	261	1/130 2/208 3/338 (3 wkts dec.)	338
6/171 7/202 8/254 9/258			

Bonus points – Kent 2, Somerset 3.

Bowling: *First Innings*—Jones 26–3–74–3; Trego 19–7–58–2; Burns 17–9–20–2; Parsons 12–4–34–0; Blackwell 22–5–54–1; Pierson 9.4–4–9–1; Trescothick 1–0–7–0. *Second Innings*—Jones 14–3–22–0; Trego 16–2–69–2; Pierson 26–2–77–0; Burns 11–3–32–1; Blackwell 23–5–77–0; Parsons 16–6–36–0; Trescothick 6–2–17–0; Holloway 2–0–4–0.

Umpires: B. Dudleston and J. F. Steele.

At Derby, July 12, 13, 14, 15. KENT beat DERBYSHIRE by eight wickets.

At Portsmouth, July 19, 20, 21, 22. KENT beat HAMPSHIRE by six wickets.

KENT v DERBYSHIRE

At Canterbury, July 28, 29, 30, 31. Drawn. Kent 9 pts, Derbyshire 9 pts. Toss: Derbyshire.

Spectators jeered and slow hand-clapped as the final day degenerated into farce. The captains – Munton standing in for Cork, resting at the ECB's request – were desperate to deny their relegation rivals a victory and could not agree a target. Fleming effectively resorted to declaration bowling, with all 11 players trying at least three overs, but none could separate the Derbyshire openers. Titchard, making his highest score since leaving Lancashire, and Stubbings, with a maiden hundred, became the first Derbyshire pair to bat through an entire day. They meandered to 293, the county's highest first-wicket stand since 1929. Rain had shortened the first two days, and Kent, responding to 279, struggled against the left-arm swing of Dean, who reduced them to 76 for six.

Nixon and Patel added 131 to turn the situation around, though Dean went on to a career-best eight for 52, taking his tally to 22 wickets in his last three matches against Kent. Fleming declared after gaining a second batting point. The news that Kent president Lord Cowdrey had suffered a stroke cast a pall over the festival week.

Close of play: First day, Derbyshire 167-5 (Dowman 30*, Dean 0*); Second day, Kent 63-4 (Key 26*, Ealham 4*); Third day, Derbyshire 54-0 (Stubbings 17*, Titchard 37*).

Derbyshire

S. D. Stubbings c Fulton b Saggers	41	– not out	135
S. P. Titchard lbw b Masters	52	– not out	141
M. J. Di Venuto b Saggers	13		
J. P. Pyemont run out	4		
M. P. Dowman c Fulton b Patel	77		
†L. D. Sutton b Fleming	13		
K. J. Dean c Fulton b Saggers	0		
S. J. Lacey c Nixon b Fleming	48		
P. Aldred c Ealham b Saggers	1		
*T. A. Munton b Ealham	3		
L. J. Wharton not out	6		
B 1, l-b 16, w 4	21	B 7, w 4, n-b 6	17
	——		——
	279	(no wkt dec.)	293

1/85 2/111 3/117 4/121 5/163
6/167 7/235 8/250 9/255

Bonus points – Derbyshire 2, Kent 3.

Bowling: *First Innings*—Saggers 25–6–72–4; Fleming 15.5–4–41–2; Ealham 28–8–55–1; Masters 12–1–35–1; Patel 26–10–44–1; Dravid 5–2–5–0; Walker 4–0–10–0. *Second Innings*—Saggers 10–2–32–0; Ealham 10–1–36–0; Patel 17–4–45–0; Masters 15–3–30–0; Dravid 10–1–18–0; Fulton 17–5–45–0; Walker 7–1–18–0; Smith 6–0–20–0; Key 9–1–17–0; Fleming 4–1–15–0; Nixon 3–1–10–0.

Kent

D. P. Fulton c Sutton b Dean	16	M. M. Patel c Wharton b Dean	60
R. W. T. Key c Sutton b Dean	37	D. D. Masters b Dean	0
R. Dravid c Dowman b Dean	2	M. J. Saggers not out	0
E. T. Smith c Di Venuto b Dean	2	B 16, l-b 11	27
M. J. Walker b Dean	0		——
M. A. Ealham lbw b Dean	4	1/27 2/31 3/33	(9 wkts dec.) 251
†P. A. Nixon not out	80	4/37 5/69 6/76	
*M. V. Fleming c Munton b Aldred	23	7/111 8/242 9/243	

Bonus points – Kent 2, Derbyshire 3.

Bowling: Munton 38.1–11–56–0; Dean 28–7–52–8; Aldred 26–6–69–1; Lacey 15–6–27–0; Wharton 9–2–20–0.

Umpires: G. I. Burgess and R. Palmer.

KENT v LEICESTERSHIRE

At Canterbury, August 2, 3, 4, 5. Drawn. Kent 8 pts, Leicestershire 11 pts. Toss: Leicestershire.
Another rain-affected game – almost 100 overs were lost, all told – made it a disappointing Canterbury festival. Not that Kumble minded: he recorded a maiden Championship fifty and then bowled Leicestershire to the brink of victory with match figures of ten for 105, including a county-best six for 44. The visitors had had a shaky start but, helped by a century stand between Habib and Wells, the last six wickets added an impressive 277. Kumble was last out for 56, from 124

balls, having frustrated Kent's hopes of polishing off the tail. When Kent replied, Walker did his best to avert the follow-on, but was left stranded after batting in determined fashion for 131 balls. Kent, 174 behind, again struggled to combat Kumble, and the prospect of an innings defeat was only avoided with four wickets remaining. Leicestershire, though, ran out of time and had to make do with no more than a moral victory.

Close of play: First day, Leicestershire 263-6 (Habib 78*, Kumble 2*); Second day, Leicestershire 324-8 (Kumble 32*, Crowe 4*); Third day, Kent 184-8 (Walker 36*, Masters 0*).

Leicestershire

D. L. Maddy lbw b Fleming	22	†N. D. Burns c and b Patel	23
I. J. Sutcliffe lbw b Fleming	15	C. D. Crowe c Nixon b Saggers	12
B. F. Smith c Nixon b Walker	27	J. Ormond not out	9
A. Habib c Nixon b Saggers	78		
J. M. Dakin c Nixon b Saggers	10	B 2, l-b 17, w 10, n-b 6	35
*V. J. Wells lbw b Ealham	72		
P. A. J. DeFreitas lbw b Masters	16	1/39 2/48 3/79 4/98 5/226	375
A. Kumble c Ealham b Saggers	56	6/253 7/263 8/319 9/352	

Bonus points – Leicestershire 4, Kent 3 (Score at 130 overs: 356-9).

Bowling: Saggers 33.5–10–70–4; Masters 32–7–92–1; Ealham 22–6–56–1; Fleming 13–1–54–2; Walker 10–3–18–1; Patel 20–6–65–1; Dravid 3–2–1–0.

Kent

D. P. Fulton lbw b Kumble	11	– c Smith b Kumble	21
R. W. T. Key b Kumble	14	– b Kumble	53
R. Dravid lbw b Dakin	32	– c Smith b Kumble	24
E. T. Smith c Burns b Dakin	40	– c Smith b Kumble	13
M. J. Walker not out	48	– not out	24
M. A. Ealham c Sutcliffe b Crowe	6	– b Kumble	3
†P. A. Nixon c Sutcliffe b Kumble	2	– b Crowe	1
*M. V. Fleming c Sutcliffe b Ormond	18	– lbw b Kumble	5
M. M. Patel c Maddy b Ormond	8	– not out	5
D. D. Masters c Smith b Kumble	0		
M. J. Saggers lbw b Ormond	1		
B 5, l-b 4, n-b 12	21	B 12, l-b 6, w 6, n-b 14	38
1/21 2/36 3/93 4/108 5/123	201	1/59 2/115 3/134 4/141 (7 wkts)	187
6/128 7/155 8/179 9/184		5/163 6/168 7/175	

Bonus points – Kent 1, Leicestershire 3.

Bowling: *First Innings*—Ormond 22.2–10–57–3; DeFreitas 10–5–13–0; Kumble 32–9–61–4; Wells 4–0–15–0; Dakin 7–1–20–2; Crowe 13–5–26–1. *Second Innings*—Ormond 10–3–28–0; DeFreitas 10–3–34–0; Dakin 7–4–7–0; Kumble 33–13–44–6; Crowe 25–6–56–1.

Umpires: B. Dudleston and J. W. Holder.

At Chester-le-Street, August 9, 10, 11, 12. KENT drew with DURHAM.

At Manchester, August 17, 18, 19. KENT lost to LANCASHIRE by 154 runs.

KENT v HAMPSHIRE

At Canterbury, August 22, 23, 24, 25. Kent won by 15 runs. Kent 18 pts, Hampshire 3 pts. Toss: Kent. First-class debut: L. R. Prittipaul.

With Hampshire inching towards victory, McCague took two wickets in three balls to snatch a vital win, Kent's only Championship success at Canterbury in 2000. The result effectively relegated Hampshire, while sparing Kent. Set 314, the visitors began the last day needing 63 with four wickets intact. Mascarenhas and Warne went in McCague's first spell, but acting-captain Wells preferred to throw the new ball to first-innings heroes Saggers and Masters; Aymes and Udal added 31 before McCague's devastating return. On the first morning, Warne touched down at 6 a.m. after a 26-hour flight from Melbourne, then removed Ed Smith with his fifth ball. Kent were 102 for five when Nixon began a recovery with Walker, and he ended it with Masters in a last-wicket stand that brought all three batting points; Nixon hit a career-best 134 not out. Wells waived the follow-on after Hampshire had relied almost entirely on debutant Lawrence Prittipaul and the indefatigable Warne. Kent then fared even worse, as Warne claimed a Championship-best six for 34, including his 50th wicket of the season. As the tension grew on the third evening, Fulton flung down his helmet after a bat-pad appeal was rejected. He was reported to Lord's and fined £250 by Kent.

Close of play: First day, Kent 268-9 (Nixon 92*, Masters 10*); Second day, Kent 83-5 (Fulton 40*, Wells 0*); Third day, Hampshire 251-6 (Aymes 6*, Mascarenhas 11*).

Kent

D. P. Fulton lbw b Mullally	20	– lbw b Warne	48
R. W. T. Key c Aymes b Mullally	4	– lbw b Morris	0
R. Dravid b Mullally	20	– lbw b Morris	10
E. T. Smith lbw b Warne	0	– lbw b Mascarenhas	21
M. J. Walker c and b Warne	47	– c Aymes b Warne	2
*A. P. Wells c Warne b Morris	26	– (7) c Prittipaul b Warne	9
†P. A. Nixon not out	134	– (8) b Warne	8
M. J. McCague b Warne	8	– (9) c Udal b Warne	24
D. A. Scott lbw b Mullally	2	– (10) not out	4
M. J. Saggers lbw b Mullally	18	– (6) b Mullally	0
D. D. Masters b Morris	21	– st Aymes b Warne	5
B 1, l-b 8, w 4, n-b 10	23	B 10, l-b 5	15
	323		**146**

1/13 2/30 3/31 4/63 5/102
6/137 7/149 8/170 9/198

1/4 2/22 3/53 4/70 5/81
6/99 7/109 8/126 9/137

Bonus points – Kent 3, Hampshire 3.

Bowling: *First Innings*—Mullally 39–10–90–5; Morris 17.5–7–51–2; Warne 32–4–107–3; Mascarenhas 16–6–32–0; Udal 16–4–34–0. *Second Innings*—Mullally 16–5–46–1; Morris 7–0–21–2, Warne 20.2 10 34–6; Mascarenhas 5–2–13–1; Udal 3–0–17–0.

Hampshire

G. W. White b Masters	4	– lbw b Dravid	29
*R. A. Smith c Fulton b Saggers	5	– (4) lbw b Saggers	14
W. S. Kendall lbw b Saggers	4	– c Fulton b Saggers	72
J. S. Laney b Saggers	9	– (5) c Dravid b McCague	43
L. R. Prittipaul lbw b Saggers	52	– (6) lbw b Scott	35
†A. N. Aymes c Scott b Masters	1	– (7) not out	18
A. D. Mascarenhas c Fulton b Saggers	0	– (8) c Nixon b McCague	12
S. K. Warne c Masters b McCague	45	– (9) c Fulton b McCague	4
S. D. Udal c Fulton b Masters	21	– (10) lbw b McCague	28
A. C. Morris not out	4	– (2) b Saggers	0
A. D. Mullally c Fulton b Masters	3	– b McCague	0
L-b 6, w 2	8	B 20, l-b 7, w 6, n-b 10	43
	156		**298**

1/9 2/9 3/22 4/25 5/30
6/43 7/101 8/140 9/149

1/1 2/109 3/135 4/154 5/220
6/226 7/252 8/260 9/298

Bonus points – Kent 3.

Bowling: *First Innings*—Saggers 17–3–47–5; Masters 12.1–3–31–4; Scott 12–4–28–0; Walker 4–1–25–0; McCague 6–1–19–1. *Second Innings*—Saggers 30–11–53–3; Masters 27–5–69–0; McCague 19–4–52–5; Scott 34–12–86–1; Dravid 2–0–5–1; Walker 3–0–6–0.

Umpires: G. I. Burgess and R. Julian.

KENT v YORKSHIRE

At Canterbury, September 7, 8, 9, 10. Yorkshire won by 32 runs. Yorkshire 20 pts, Kent 6 pts. Toss: Yorkshire.

Shortly before tea on the final day, Yorkshire completed their first Championship victory at Canterbury since 1987. Fisher's left-arm spin took the last three wickets, after Hamilton, with three in five balls, had threatened to end the match before lunch. However, McCague and Fleming launched a spirited counter-attack, adding 102 for the eighth wicket. McCague's career-best 72 came from 80 balls, with 12 fours and a six, while Fleming battled on bravely after being struck a painful blow on the right thumb by Hoggard. On the opening day, Lehmann continued his good record against Kent – his 89-ball hundred was the fastest of the first-class season – and he shared a pugnacious partnership of 195 with McGrath, who hit his sole century of a difficult summer. Ealham bowled Kent back into contention on the penultimate afternoon, only for their top order to implode next morning. Defeat left them needing one point from their final game to make certain of avoiding relegation, while Yorkshire moved up one place to third.

Close of play: First day, Yorkshire 365-7 (Hamilton 8*, Fisher 7*); Second day, Kent 194-4 (Walker 9*, Ealham 4*); Third day, Kent 2-0 (Fulton 2*, Key 0*).

Yorkshire

S. Widdup c Dravid b Masters	3	– lbw b Saggers	6
M. P. Vaughan c Dravid b Fleming	69	– c Fulton b Ealham	14
A. McGrath c Nixon b Fleming	133	– lbw b Ealham	21
D. S. Lehmann c Nixon b Fleming	116	– c Nixon b Saggers	42
*D. Byas c Dravid b Saggers	7	– c McCague b Fleming	7
G. M. Fellows c Nixon b Fleming	4	– b Saggers	12
G. M. Hamilton run out	28	– c Nixon b Saggers	0
†S. M. Guy b Masters	7	– b Ealham	10
I. D. Fisher c Ealham b Saggers	16	– c Smith b Ealham	28
M. J. Hoggard c Walker b Masters	2	– c Dravid b Ealham	1
G. A. Lambert not out	3	– not out	2
B 1, l-b 8, w 4	13	L-b 2	2
	401		**145**

1/9 2/132 3/327 4/330 5/336 6/344 7/355 8/384 9/391   401

1/10 2/41 3/42 4/65 5/103 6/104 7/105 8/136 9/138   145

Bonus points – Yorkshire 5, Kent 3.

Bowling: *First Innings*—Saggers 26–6–78–2; Masters 25–3–74–3; Ealham 19–5–41–0; Fleming 23–3–77–4; McCague 13–0–74–0; Dravid 6–0–35–0; Walker 3–0–13–0. *Second Innings*—Saggers 14–3–45–4; Masters 4–0–13–0; Ealham 12.2–0–35–5; Fleming 7–2–22–1; McCague 9–1–28–0.

Kent

D. P. Fulton b Hamilton	25	– c Widdup b Hoggard	8
R. W. T. Key c Lehmann b Lambert	18	– b Hamilton	3
R. Dravid lbw b Hoggard	72	– lbw b Hamilton	2
E. T. Smith c McGrath b Hoggard	46	– b Hamilton	3
M. J. Walker b Fisher	42	– lbw b Lambert	6
M. A. Ealham c and b Lambert	7	– lbw b Hamilton	0
†P. A. Nixon c Byas b Vaughan	23	– b Hoggard	19
*M. V. Fleming lbw b Hoggard	23	– c Hamilton b Fisher	42
M. J. McCague c Fellows b Vaughan	14	– b Fisher	72
M. J. Saggers b Hoggard	12	– b Fisher	13
D. D. Masters not out	2	– not out	5
B 9, l-b 8, w 2, n-b 14	33	B 8, l-b 7, n-b 9	24

1/34 2/56 3/173 4/180 5/205   317   1/14 2/14 3/20 4/21 5/21   197
6/261 7/261 8/281 9/314   6/33 7/59 8/161 9/181

Bonus points – Kent 3, Yorkshire 3.

Bowling: *First Innings*—Hoggard 22.1–8–46–4; Lambert 20–5–62–2; Hamilton 22–8–49–1; Fellows 16–5–40–0; Fisher 28–11–71–1; Vaughan 15–1–32–2. *Second Innings*—Hoggard 20–4–48–2; Hamilton 15–5–34–4; Lambert 8–0–25–1; Fisher 16.4–4–45–3; Fellows 2–0–9–0; Vaughan 7–1–21–0.

Umpires: A. Clarkson and D. J. Constant.

At Leicester, September 13, 14, 15, 16. KENT drew with LEICESTERSHIRE.

DATES OF FORMATION OF FIRST-CLASS COUNTIES

County	First known organisation	Original date	Present Club Reorganisation, if substantial	First-class status from
Derbyshire	1870	1870	—	1871
Durham	1874	1882	1991	1992
Essex	By 1790	1876	—	1895
Glamorgan	1861	1888	—	1921
Gloucestershire	1863	1871	—	1870
Hampshire	1849	1863	1879	1864
Kent	1842	1859	1870	1864
Lancashire	1864	1864	—	1865
Leicestershire	By 1820	1879	—	1895
Middlesex	1863	1864	—	1864
Northamptonshire	1820†	1878	—	1905
Nottinghamshire	1841	1841	1866	1864
Somerset	1864	1875	—	1882
Surrey	1845	1845	—	1864
Sussex	1836	1839	1857	1864
Warwickshire	1826	1882	—	1895
Worcestershire	1844	1865	—	1899
Yorkshire	1861	1863	1891	1864

Note: Derbyshire lost first-class status from 1888 to 1894, Hampshire between 1886 and 1894 and Somerset between 1886 and 1890.

† *Town club.*

Gary Keedy

LANCASHIRE

President: 2000 – Sir Patrick Russell
2001 – J. F. Blackledge
Chairman: J. Simmons
Chief Executive: J. Cumbes
Chairman, Cricket Committee: G. Ogden
Cricket Secretary: D. M. R. Edmundson
Captain: J. P. Crawley
First-Team Coach: R. B. Simpson
Head Groundsman: P. Marron
Scorer: A. West

Lancashire are accustomed to not winning the County Championship, so finishing runners-up for the third year in succession was greeted with a degree of satisfaction. After all, it was their best positional sequence since their domination of the competition between 1926 and 1930. But their fall from grace in one-day cricket was difficult to accept. They reached two semi-finals, only to be outclassed each time by Gloucestershire at Bristol – and by their own admission they were lucky to get beyond the qualifying stage of the Benson and Hedges Cup. As for the League champions of 1998 and 1999 being dumped into Division Two: well, how could it happen?

One conclusion was clear. The clock has been running down for an aging squad, even if the oldest of the lot, 37-year-old Neil Fairbrother, did top their Championship batting averages. Fresh blood is needed, and not just from the anticipated return of the Sri Lankan spinner, Muttiah Muralitharan. Coach Bob Simpson talked of reorganisation and a new era.

An encouraging feature was the progress of left-arm spinner Gary Keedy and seam bowler Mike Smethurst. Keedy emerged as the first-choice spinner, ahead of Chris Schofield and Gary Yates, and Smethurst marked his second full year by taking 56 first-class wickets at 20.73 each. With Andrew Flintoff and Schofield, they formed a youthful quartet on whom Lancashire can pin their hopes for another decade.

Flintoff and Schofield epitomised Lancashire's topsy-turvy season. The young guns experienced the highs and lows, linking up in the two Tests against Zimbabwe but then finding themselves under fire from all directions when things did not go according to expectations. Flintoff had fitness problems – a chronic back complaint, not helped, in England's view, by his being overweight. Schofield bowled poorly in his second Test. Both were dropped. Simpson, and others at Old Trafford, had publicly warned about the dangers of promoting Schofield too early to Test cricket, and the damage it could wreak on his confidence. They were proved right. It took the novice leg-spinner a long time to recover, during which he needed a brief spell in the Second Eleven, and it was to his credit that he came back forcefully in the last third of the season to earn a second England A tour. Flintoff tried to shrug off the headlines and knuckled down to a new fitness regime. Any doubts over his natural ability were demolished, along with Surrey, during his NatWest Trophy century at The Oval, described by many as one of the greatest innings in domestic one-day cricket.

Indian captain Sourav Ganguly provided some outstanding one-day performances, including three centuries, though he was less than prolific in the Championship and failed to endear himself to some team-mates for a variety of reasons. This became manifest after he was involved in two run-outs in a floodlit match at Old Trafford. On reaching his half-century, he raised his bat in a salute to the home balcony – and found there was no one there to take it.

Popularity has never worried Mike Atherton, and he lost some friends among the Old Trafford faithful at the start of the year when, in a radio interview, he questioned the value of county cricket. But his sterling performances for England and the fact that he worked hard for Lancashire, appearing in ten Championship games, quelled the mutterings. Whether 2001 will be his swan-song remains to be seen, but his contract finishes at the end of the year and he will have a decision to make.

Lancashire's Championship bid faltered with a heavy defeat at The Oval early in August – their first loss since being beaten at the same venue in June 1999 – and their inability to beat Leicestershire three weeks later, after scoring 574 for five declared, prevented them making up lost ground. Yet they were generally competitive throughout, despite constantly having to switch the side around and having Peter Martin on the sidelines for nine weeks with a broken right thumb. Later, in the warm-up for that vital Grace Road match, he fractured his left thumb. "I hadn't had two injuries of any kind in ten years," he said. "Now I've had two broken thumbs in ten weeks." What with injuries, international calls and lack of consistency, Lancashire used 21 players in 2000.

Captain John Crawley overcame a nightmarish first half to the season to record five first-class centuries, three in the Championship, and deservedly earned a place on the England A tour of the West Indies as vice-captain. He missed the last week of the season because of an appendix operation, otherwise he might have become the only batsman to reach 1,000 runs for Lancashire. Vice-captain Warren Hegg finished third in the batting averages and established a Lancashire record when he went past George Duckworth's mark of 634 catches.

Lancashire face a major challenge. The cracks are showing in a squad which achieved so much in the 1990s, and careful reconstruction is essential over the next two or three years. This was recognised by contracts for three young players, James Anderson, Kyle Hogg, and Tim Roberts, after the release of Nathan Wood, Paddy McKeown and Mark Harvey, and the signing of Ryan Driver, a forceful left-handed batsman from Worcestershire. A more experienced acquisition was Durham seamer John Wood. – COLIN EVANS.

LANCASHIRE 2000

[*John Dawson, Cricket Images*

Back row: N. T. Wood, M. J. Chilton, M. P. Smethurst, P. M. Ridgway, P. C. McKeown, J. J. Haynes, M. E. Harvey, J. C. Scuderi. *Middle row:* A. West (*First Eleven scorer*), R. B. Simpson (*first-team coach*), G. Keedy, R. J. Green, C. P. Schofield, M. Watkinson, L. G. Brown (*physiotherapist*), D. White (*Second Eleven scorer*). *Front row:* G. Chapple, A. Flintoff, N. H. Fairbrother, M. A. Atherton, J. P. Crawley (*captain*), W. K. Hegg, P. J. Martin, I. D. Austin, G. Yates, G. D. Lloyd. *Inset:* S. C. Ganguly.

LANCASHIRE RESULTS

All first-class matches – Played 18: Won 8, Lost 1, Drawn 9.

County Championship matches – Played 16: Won 7, Lost 1, Drawn 8.

PPP Healthcare County Championship, 2nd in Division 1; NatWest Trophy, s-f;
Benson and Hedges Cup, s-f; Norwich Union National League, 8th in Division 1.

COUNTY CHAMPIONSHIP AVERAGES
BATTING

Cap		M	I	NO	R	HS	100s	50s	Avge	Ct/St
1985	N. H. Fairbrother† ..	14	22	4	754	138	2	3	41.88	12
1998	A. Flintoff†‡......	9	13	0	490	119	1	3	37.69	10
1989	W. K. Hegg†......	16	22	5	631	128	1	4	37.11	36/5
1989	M. A. Atherton†‡ ..	10	15	1	505	113	1	4	36.07	10
1994	J. P. Crawley......	13	20	1	669	139	3	0	35.21	4
	S. C. Ganguly§....	13	19	0	644	99	0	6	33.89	10
	C. P. Schofield†‡...	13	17	2	399	70*	0	3	26.60	6
1992	G. D. Lloyd†	14	19	0	475	126	1	1	25.00	18
	M. J. Chilton	9	12	1	270	46	0	0	24.54	9
	J. C. Scuderi......	7	10	1	198	46	0	0	22.00	0
	M. P. Smethurst†..	14	18	9	158	66	0	1	17.55	3
1994	P. J. Martin†......	8	10	2	120	40	0	0	15.00	2
1994	G. Chapple.......	15	18	1	218	41	0	0	12.82	4
2000	G. Keedy........	12	15	3	144	34	0	0	12.00	1

Also batted: I. D. Austin† (cap 1990) (1 match) 0; R. J. Green† (2 matches) 0, 29*; P. C. McKeown† (2 matches) 30, 4; N. T. Wood (1 match) 27; G. Yates† (cap 1994) (3 matches) 0, 3, 7 (3 ct).

* Signifies not out.   † Born in Lancashire.   ‡ ECB contract.   § Overseas player.

BOWLING

	O	M	R	W	BB	5W/i	Avge
A. Flintoff	92.2	30	199	14	4-18	0	14.21
P. J. Martin	203.2	65	417	28	7-67	3	14.89
J. C. Scuderi	96	25	251	11	4-58	0	22.81
M. P. Smethurst ...	324	69	1,057	43	7-50	2	24.58
G. Chapple	398.5	89	1,126	44	6-42	1	25.59
G. Keedy	445	132	950	36	6-56	1	26.38
C. P. Schofield......	291.5	62	877	30	4-25	0	29.23

Also bowled: I. D. Austin 24–14–32–2; M. J. Chilton 1–0–3–0; J. P. Crawley 1–0–19–0; N. H. Fairbrother 6.2–2–11–1; S. C. Ganguly 83.4–11–311–4; R. J. Green 34–7–120–1; G. Yates 85.4–28–192–9.

COUNTY RECORDS

Highest score for:	424	A. C. MacLaren v Somerset at Taunton	1895
Highest score against:	315*	T. W. Hayward (Surrey) at The Oval	1898
Best bowling for:	10-46	W. Hickton v Hampshire at Manchester	1870
Best bowling against:	10-40	G. O. B. Allen (Middlesex) at Lord's	1929
Highest total for:	863	v Surrey at The Oval	1990
Highest total against:	707-9 dec.	by Surrey at The Oval	1990
Lowest total for:	25	v Derbyshire at Manchester	1871
Lowest total against:	22	by Glamorgan at Liverpool	1924

At Cambridge, April 7, 8, 9. LANCASHIRE beat CAMBRIDGE UNIVERSITY by 170 runs.

At Canterbury, April 26, 27, 28, 29. LANCASHIRE drew with KENT.

LANCASHIRE v LEICESTERSHIRE

At Manchester, May 3, 4, 5, 6. Lancashire won by an innings and 25 runs. Lancashire 20 pts, Leicestershire 4 pts. Toss: Leicestershire.

Lancashire made a fine start to the home Championship season, winning 75 minutes into the final day. Three players in particular caught the eye. Martin undermined Leicestershire with seven for 67, only his 12th analysis of five wickets or more in 12 seasons, and easily his best at Old Trafford. He started with nought for 41 from his first ten overs, but "I suddenly realised I wasn't running in straight enough," he explained. Lancashire's response highlighted their batting depth. Four of the top six contributed only 56 between them, but sparkling centuries from Flintoff and Fairbrother, and solid support from the lower order, earned a lead of 223. Flintoff had remodelled his stance, now more upright with his feet closer together, and showed greater restraint, taking four and a half hours over his 119, although he hit 19 fours and a six, and was dropped twice. Lancashire's new coach, Bob Simpson, argued that Flintoff should bat at No. 4 or 5 for England. Schofield followed up with his maiden Championship fifty, and then another encouraging display of leg-spin as Leicestershire stumbled to defeat.

Close of play: First day, Leicestershire 263-9 (Kumble 14*, Ormond 29*); Second day, Lancashire 342-5 (Fairbrother 112*, Hegg 29*); Third day, Leicestershire 155-6 (Wells 45*, Burns 3*).

Leicestershire

D. L. Maddy b Chapple	6	– c Ganguly b Schofield	18
D. I. Stevens c Schofield b Flintoff	41	– c Lloyd b Chapple	7
T. R. Ward b Martin	39	– c Lloyd b Chapple	4
B. F. Smith c Hegg b Flintoff	4	– c Flintoff b Chapple	19
A. Habib lbw b Martin	4	– c Martin b Smethurst	37
*V. J. Wells c Hegg b Martin	56	– c Ganguly b Schofield	45
C. C. Lewis lbw b Martin	24	– c Schofield b Flintoff	5
†N. D. Burns c Hegg b Martin	6	– st Hegg b Schofield	28
P. A. J. DeFreitas c Atherton b Martin	1	– b Martin	13
A. Kumble c Atherton b Martin	15	– b Schofield	0
J. Ormond not out	30	– not out	0
B 2, l-b 4, w 12, n-b 20	39	B 4, l-b 4, w 6, n-b 8	22

1/29 2/56 3/64 4/103 5/134   265   1/10 2/18 3/45 4/79 5/130   198
6/204 7/212 8/217 9/218   6/137 7/155 8/188 9/193

Bonus points – Leicestershire 2, Lancashire 3.

Bowling: *First Innings*—Martin 31.5–9–67–7; Chapple 16–4–39–1; Flintoff 18–7–31–2; Smethurst 10–1–50–0; Ganguly 7–2–24–0; Schofield 22–6–47–0. *Second Innings*—Martin 26–9–44–1; Chapple 12–1–43–3; Schofield 27.1–6–82–4; Smethurst 6–2–13–1; Flintoff 8–4–8–1.

Lancashire

M. A. Atherton c Kumble b Lewis	1	G. Chapple c Maddy b Ormond	25
*J. P. Crawley c Ward b Ormond	1	P. J. Martin c Burns b Ormond	16
A. Flintoff c Lewis b DeFreitas	119	M. P. Smethurst not out	0
S. C. Ganguly c Burns b Lewis	30		
N. H. Fairbrother c Burns b DeFreitas	138	B 5, l-b 8, w 8, n-b 18	39
G. D. Lloyd c Burns b Ormond	24		
†W. K. Hegg b Kumble	29	1/3 2/15 3/94 4/233 5/288	488
C. P. Schofield b Kumble	66	6/343 7/415 8/459 9/488	

Bonus points – Lancashire 5, Leicestershire 2 (Score at 130 overs: 440-7).

Bowling: Ormond 34–6–122–4; Lewis 20–0–108–2; DeFreitas 34–13–84–2; Kumble 36.1–11–93–2; Wells 17–3–59–0; Maddy 2–0–9–0.

Umpires: A. Clarkson and R. Julian.

At Chester-le-Street, May 11, 12, 13. LANCASHIRE beat DURHAM by 141 runs.

At Southampton, May 23, 24, 25, 26. LANCASHIRE drew with HAMPSHIRE.

LANCASHIRE v DERBYSHIRE

At Manchester, May 31, June 1, 2, 3. Drawn. Lancashire 8 pts, Derbyshire 7 pts. Toss: Derbyshire.
Lancashire suffered a serious blow in a rain-ruined match when Martin's thumb was struck by a ball from Cork. An X-ray revealed a dislocated fracture needing a two-hour operation and he did not return until August. The 31-year-old Martin had been on course for perhaps his best season; five wickets for 44, against some careless Derbyshire batting on the opening day, had given him 18 in five Championship matches. His only consolation was that he was free to continue his hobby of painting: while he bats and bowls with his right hand, he writes and paints with the left. Before the injury, Martin helped Scuderi, who hit a Championship-best 41 in 51 balls, secure a batting point and steer Lancashire to a useful first-innings lead, but the last two days were washed out.
Close of play: First day, Lancashire 36-1 (Chilton 8*, Keedy 0*); Second day, Derbyshire 24-2 (Dowman 5*); Third day, No play.

Derbyshire

S. D. Stubbings b Chapple	42	– c Hegg b Keedy	11
M. P. Dowman lbw b Martin	4	– not out	5
M. J. Di Venuto b Martin	15		
M. E. Cassar c Crawley b Keedy	22		
R. J. Bailey run out	12		
†K. M. Krikken c Lloyd b Martin	7		
*D. G. Cork c Yates b Martin	1		
S. J. Lacey b Chapple	13		
P. Aldred not out	22		
T. M. Smith b Keedy	13	– (3) b Yates	2
T. A. Munton lbw b Martin	2		
L-b 11, n-b 6	17	B 2, l-b 2, n-b 2	6

1/7 2/37 3/76 4/98 5/112	170	1/21 2/24	(2 wkts) 24
6/112 7/115 8/132 9/157			

Bonus points – Lancashire 3.

Bowling: *First Innings*—Martin 20.5–5–44–5; Chapple 20–3–53–2; Keedy 27–13–30–2; Scuderi 12–2–29–0; Yates 1–0–3–0. *Second Innings*—Chapple 5–2–8–0; Scuderi 4–0–9–0; Keedy 6–3–3–1; Yates 1.4–1–0–1.

Lancashire

N. T. Wood b Cassar	27	G. Chapple c Krikken b Lacey	8
M. J. Chilton c Smith b Cassar	13	G. Yates b Lacey	0
G. Keedy lbw b Aldred	29	P. J. Martin retired hurt	5
*J. P. Crawley c Smith b Munton	22		
P. C. McKeown lbw b Cork	30	B 5, l-b 9, w 2	16
G. D. Lloyd lbw b Cork	22		
J. C. Scuderi not out	41	1/36 2/47 3/89 4/101 5/140	213
†W. K. Hegg c Dowman b Cork	0	6/171 7/171 8/184 9/188	

Bonus points – Lancashire 1, Derbyshire 3.

Bowling: Cork 17.5–6–52–3; Munton 16–4–41–1; Smith 11–3–43–0; Cassar 11–6–25–2; Aldred 9–2–20–1; Lacey 6–2–18–2.

Umpires: J. H. Harris and N. A. Mallender.

LANCASHIRE v HAMPSHIRE

At Liverpool, June 6, 7, 8. Lancashire won by an innings and 35 runs. Lancashire 17 pts, Hampshire 3 pts. Toss: Lancashire.

After failing to impress in England's Tests against Zimbabwe, Flintoff had something to prove. His excellent all-round performance – 73 runs and seven wickets – helped Lancashire demolish a fragile Hampshire in the equivalent of two days, and briefly made them Championship leaders. But the early honours went to Smethurst. Left out for two matches, despite a career-best seven for 50 at Chester-le-Street, he seized his chance as cover for the injured Martin, bowling with pace and bounce to earn four for 15 as Hampshire scraped to 95. Lancashire had problems batting against Warne and Mullally, but a stand of 129 between Flintoff and Fairbrother, limping from a calf strain, looked like paving the way to a substantial total. Though the last six fell for 34, a lead of 174 was quite enough: Hampshire slumped again, with Flintoff bowling a venomous spell to mop up the final four wickets. Lancashire physio Lawrie Brown played the most important role, however, helping to save a spectator who collapsed with a heart attack. Brown rushed out of the pavilion to assist a paramedic with resuscitation – the patient later recovered in hospital.

Close of play: First day, Lancashire 54-3 (Flintoff 1*, Fairbrother 5*); Second day, Hampshire 45-3 (Kendall 16*, Kenway 7*).

Hampshire

G. W. White c Hegg b Smethurst	12	– c Lloyd b Chapple	9
J. S. Laney c Hegg b Scuderi	17	– lbw b Austin	6
W. S. Kendall lbw b Smethurst	14	– c Lloyd b Austin	18
*R. A. Smith c Chilton b Smethurst	4	– lbw b Smethurst	6
D. A. Kenway c Hegg b Smethurst	0	– b Scuderi	35
†A. N. Aymes c Lloyd b Flintoff	10	– c Flintoff b Scuderi	7
J. P. Stephenson c Crawley b Flintoff	7	– lbw b Flintoff	0
S. K. Warne not out	18	– c Chapple b Flintoff	11
S. J. Renshaw b Flintoff	0	– b Flintoff	23
A. D. Mullally c Fairbrother b Scuderi	8	– c Lloyd b Flintoff	8
S. R. G. Francis c Fairbrother b Scuderi	0	– not out	1
L-b 3, n-b 2	5	B 4, l-b 5, w 2, n-b 4	15
1/26 2/30 3/35 4/43 5/48	95	1/12 2/18 3/34 4/48 5/80	139
6/63 7/66 8/74 9/95		6/89 7/91 8/108 9/118	

Bonus points – Lancashire 3.

Bowling: *First Innings*—Chapple 15–4–36–0; Austin 5–1–9–0; Scuderi 8–4–20–3; Smethurst 11–3–15–4; Flintoff 5–2–12–3. *Second Innings*—Chapple 17–5–44–1; Austin 19–13–23–2; Scuderi 10–3–25–2; Smethurst 8–1–20–1; Flintoff 10.4–5–18–4.

Lancashire

M. J. Chilton lbw b Stephenson	18	C. P. Schofield b Mullally	0
*J. P. Crawley c Laney b Francis	23	I. D. Austin b Warne	0
G. Chapple lbw b Stephenson	0	M. P. Smethurst b Warne	18
A. Flintoff lbw b Mullally	73		
N. H. Fairbrother not out	77	B 1, l-b 5, w 4, n-b 16	26
G. D. Lloyd lbw b Warne	29		
J. C. Scuderi lbw b Warne	0	1/43 2/43 3/43 4/172 5/235	269
†W. K. Hegg b Mullally	5	6/237 7/246 8/246 9/247	

Bonus points – Lancashire 2, Hampshire 3.

Bowling: Mullally 26–10–64–3; Renshaw 15–4–50–0; Stephenson 18–4–52–2; Francis 16–4–30–1; Warne 16.4–4–61–4; White 1–0–6–0.

Umpires: D. J. Constant and N. A. Mallender.

At Liverpool, June 13, 14, 15, 16. LANCASHIRE drew with NEW ZEALAND A (See New Zealand A tour section).

LANCASHIRE v YORKSHIRE

At Manchester, June 29, 30, July 1. Lancashire won by nine wickets. Lancashire 17 pts, Yorkshire 3 pts. Toss: Yorkshire. First-class debut: S. Widdup.

Lancashire completed a hat-trick of Roses victories for the first time since 1893, and cut Yorkshire's Championship lead to two points, when Fairbrother struck the winning six on the third afternoon. Eight senior players were missing from the two sides, either at the Lord's Test or through injury, and leg-spinner Schofield, in England's line-up a month earlier, bowled only ten overs in all. Two spin team-mates took precedence, with left-armer Keedy the most potent, claiming match figures of seven for 88 against his former club. Since joining Lancashire in 1995, Keedy had learned to wait for his opportunities, but this performance made him their No. 1 spinner. Bowlers, both spin and seam, held sway throughout, but Yorkshire's first-day collapse, from 126 for two at lunch to 164 all out, took some explaining. Lancashire had to work for their runs but the tail, marshalled by Hegg, established a lead of 105. Then, their slow bowlers came into their own; helped by a run-out, Keedy and off-spinner Yates combined to send back the first six batsmen for 84. After that, Yorkshire did well to make Lancashire bat again.

Close of play: First day, Lancashire 149-5 (Keedy 0*, Hegg 2*); Second day, Yorkshire 130-7 (Middlebrook 22*, Silverwood 18*).

Yorkshire

*D. Byas c Lloyd b Chapple	2	– lbw b Keedy	30
S. Widdup c Ganguly b Keedy	26	– b Keedy	9
†R. J. Blakey c Hegg b Keedy	56	– c Hegg b Yates	32
D. S. Lehmann lbw b Chapple	38	– c Hegg b Yates	2
M. J. Wood c Hegg b Chapple	6	– lbw b Keedy	0
A. McGrath c Hegg b Chapple	4	– run out	0
J. D. Middlebrook c Ganguly b Smethurst	6	– c Lloyd b Chapple	31
I. D. Fisher c Lloyd b Keedy	3	– c Ganguly b Keedy	5
C. E. W. Silverwood b Smethurst	1	– c Yates b Smethurst	18
R. J. Sidebottom lbw b Smethurst	0	– c Ganguly b Smethurst	0
P. M. Hutchison not out	0	– not out	3
B 5, l-b 7, n-b 10	22	B 4, l-b 5, n-b 12	21

1/12 2/67 3/126 4/134 5/140	164	1/32 2/65 3/72 4/83 5/84	151
6/160 7/162 8/164 9/164		6/84 7/101 8/130 9/130	

Bonus points – Lancashire 3.

Bowling: *First Innings*—Chapple 13–2–27–4; Smethurst 13.2–3–40–3; Ganguly 8–0–28–0; Keedy 20–7–41–3; Schofield 5–1–16–0. *Second Innings*—Chapple 10.2–4–24–1; Smethurst 13–5–29–2; Keedy 27–8–47–4; Schofield 5–1–11–0; Yates 17–4–31–2.

Lancashire

M. J. Chilton c Blakey b Hutchison	35	– not out	22
*J. P. Crawley b Silverwood	0	– b Hutchison	6
N. H. Fairbrother lbw b Middlebrook	18	– not out	19
S. C. Ganguly c Fisher b Middlebrook	44		
G. D. Lloyd b Fisher	35		
G. Keedy c Blakey b Silverwood	2		
†W. K. Hegg c Hutchison b Silverwood	58		
C. P. Schofield c Byas b Fisher	23		
G. Chapple c Sidebottom b Middlebrook	24		
G. Yates c Blakey b Silverwood	3		
M. P. Smethurst not out	4		
B 1, l-b 8, n-b 14	23		

1/1 2/51 3/78 4/147 5/147   269   1/10   (1 wkt) 47
6/166 7/201 8/248 9/258

Bonus points – Lancashire 2, Yorkshire 3.

Bowling: *First Innings*—Silverwood 23.4–9–67–4; Hutchison 6–0–34–1; Sidebottom 13–3–30–0; Middlebrook 23–8–63–3; Fisher 17–4–56–2; Lehmann 3–0–10–0. *Second Innings*—Silverwood 5–1–13–0; Hutchison 5–1–18–1; Fisher 1.3–0–11–0; Sidebottom 1–0–5–0.

Umpires: V. A. Holder and J. W. Lloyds.

At Derby, July 7, 8, 9, 10. LANCASHIRE drew with DERBYSHIRE.

At Taunton, July 12, 13, 14, 15. LANCASHIRE drew with SOMERSET.

LANCASHIRE v DURHAM

At Manchester, July 19, 20, 21, 22. Lancashire won by six wickets. Lancashire 20 pts, Durham 6 pts. Toss: Durham. First-class debut: G. J. Pratt.

Katich's superb opening-day century briefly prompted thoughts of Durham breaking Lancashire's stranglehold over them. Of nine Championship encounters, Lancashire had won eight, with one rain-affected draw. But left-armer Keedy, leading a three-man spin attack, removed him on his way to match figures of ten for 155, including a career-best six for 56 from 50 overs in the second innings, which set up a ninth victory. Brought into the attack half an hour into the game, he dismissed three of Durham's top five in each innings. Crawley also played a key role, with his second successive hundred and century partnerships with Atherton and Ganguly, which helped establish a lead of 75. Durham lost one wicket clearing the arrears, then crumbled to Keedy; Atherton led Lancashire home with his fourth half-century in two matches, completing victory with an hour to spare.

Close of play: First day, Durham 355-9 (Killeen 28*, Brown 8*); Second day, Lancashire 299-4 (Lloyd 17*, Hegg 16*); Third day, Durham 123-6 (Speak 12*, Wood 1*).

Durham

J. J. B. Lewis c Atherton b Keedy	25	– c Chapple b Keedy	47
M. A. Gough b Chapple	4	– c Crawley b Keedy	12
S. M. Katich c Crawley b Keedy	129	– c Hegg b Yates	23
P. D. Collingwood lbw b Smethurst	60	– c Lloyd b Keedy	3
*N. J. Speak st Hegg b Keedy	10	– not out	38
G. J. Pratt lbw b Yates	5	– b Hegg b Yates	11
†A. Pratt c sub b Schofield	28	– b Yates	1
J. Wood c Hegg b Keedy	3	– c Fairbrother b Keedy	44
N. C. Phillips c Schofield b Yates	25	– c Yates b Keedy	1
N. Killeen not out	38	– lbw b Yates	0
S. J. E. Brown c Hegg b Chapple	12	– c Atherton b Keedy	2
B 5, l-b 12, w 10, n-b 4	31	B 4, l-b 8, w 2, n-b 10	24

1/13 2/88 3/234 4/251 5/256   370   1/47 2/86 3/90 4/97 5/116   206
6/262 7/268 8/305 9/325   6/118 7/186 8/200 9/201

Bonus points – Durham 4, Lancashire 3.

Bowling: *First Innings*—Chapple 13.5–1–59–2; Smethurst 15–3–62–1; Keedy 46–15–99–4; Ganguly 2–0–7–0; Schofield 13–1–59–1; Yates 22–7–67–2. *Second Innings*—Chapple 5–1–19–0; Smethurst 5–1–9–0; Keedy 50–22–56–6; Yates 44–16–91–4; Schofield 10–3–19–0.

Lancashire

M. A. Atherton c Lewis b Gough	64	– not out	64
*J. P. Crawley c and b Gough	117	– c G. J. Pratt b Phillips	17
N. H. Fairbrother lbw b Gough	8	– c Killeen b Phillips	12
S. C. Ganguly b Gough	65	– c sub b Gough	4
G. D. Lloyd c Katich b Phillips	86	– c and b Phillips	32
†W. K. Hegg b Wood	38	– not out	1
C. P. Schofield c Gough b Wood	2		
G. Chapple c Collingwood b Wood	12		
G. Yates c A. Pratt b Killeen	7		
G. Keedy not out	6		
M. P. Smethurst c Collingwood b Wood	13		
B 5, l-b 18, w 2, n-b 2	27	L-b 2	2

1/135 2/157 3/265 4/270 5/346   445   1/46 2/59 3/77 4/130   (4 wkts) 132
6/348 7/372 8/385 9/432

Bonus points – Lancashire 5, Durham 2 (Score at 130 overs: 404-8).

Bowling: *First Innings*—Brown 17–7–31–0; Wood 28.1–4–81–4; Killeen 14–4–46–1; Collingwood 2–0–5–0; Phillips 36–10–95–1; Gough 28–4–106–4; Katich 15–0–58–0. *Second Innings*—Brown 3–1–9–0; Wood 4–1–9–0; Killeen 3–0–10–0; Gough 7–1–39–1; Phillips 11–1–53–3; Katich 4.4–0–10–0.

Umpires: K. E. Palmer and A. G. T. Whitehead.

At Leeds, July 28, 29, 30, 31. LANCASHIRE drew with YORKSHIRE.

At The Oval, August 2, 3, 4, 5. LANCASHIRE lost to SURREY by 272 runs.

LANCASHIRE v KENT

At Manchester, August 17, 18, 19. Lancashire won by 154 runs. Lancashire 16 pts, Kent 3 pts. Toss: Lancashire.

Schofield had endured a difficult period since being dropped by England, but this was his most telling all-round performance for Lancashire. In the second innings, he arrived at the crease when Lancashire had stumbled to 43 for six, and displayed his exciting, if unorthodox, technique in his fourth and highest half-century of the season; no one else reached 50 in a low-scoring match. First with Fairbrother, then with the tail, he added vital runs, and finally broke Kent hearts in a last-wicket stand of 54 with Martin. Chasing 280, Kent were already on the slide when Schofield was introduced at 70 for four; he promptly grabbed three wickets in four balls. Patel denied him a hat-trick, and continued to resist, forcing Lancashire to claim the extra half-hour to complete victory on the third evening. Schofield had the last say, having him caught at mid-off. Lancashire had batted carelessly on the opening day, but Martin took five wickets in his first Championship outing for 11 weeks to gain them first-innings advantage.

Close of play: First day, Kent 41-4 (Walker 16*, Wells 10*); Second day, Lancashire 110-7 (Schofield 22*, Keedy 12*).

Lancashire

M. J. Chilton	c Smith b Masters	23	– c Walker b Masters	1
*J. P. Crawley	c Key b Patel	42	– b Masters	3
A. Flintoff	c Fulton b Saggers	29	– lbw b Saggers	5
S. C. Ganguly	c and b Patel	0	– c McCague b Masters	5
N. H. Fairbrother	c Fulton b Saggers	48	– lbw b Walker	43
J. C. Scuderi	c Masters b McCague	23	– b McCague	11
†W. K. Hegg	lbw b Saggers	22	– lbw b McCague	0
C. P. Schofield	c Fulton b McCague	16	– not out	70
P. J. Martin	c Wells b Saggers	0	– (11) c Saggers b McCague	27
G. Keedy	not out	17	– (9) c Fulton b Patel	17
M. P. Smethurst	c and b Patel	5	– (10) b Saggers	2
	L-b 1, w 2, n-b 8	11	B 4, l-b 2, w 8	14

1/59 2/94 3/95 4/102 5/141   236   1/6 2/11 3/17 4/24 5/43   198
6/195 7/202 8/202 9/231   6/43 7/96 8/119 9/144

Bonus points – Lancashire 1, Kent 3

Bowling: *First Innings*—Saggers 22–6–54–4; McCague 14–3–40–2; Masters 15–1–60–1; Patel 32.3–9–72–3; Dravid 4–1–9–0. *Second Innings*—Saggers 14–3–47–2; Masters 15–3–49–3; McCague 12.4–2–29–3; Patel 25–7–47–1; Dravid 6–1–11–0; Walker 4–0–9–1.

Kent

D. P. Fulton	c Flintoff b Martin	2	– c Fairbrother b Smethurst	1
R. W. T. Key	lbw b Martin	6	– run out	15
R. Dravid	lbw b Smethurst	1	– lbw b Martin	6
E. T. Smith	c Hegg b Smethurst	0	– lbw b Keedy	15
M. J. Walker	c Ganguly b Martin	46	– st Hegg b Schofield	16
*A. P. Wells	c Flintoff b Keedy	45	– b Schofield	8
†P. A. Nixon	lbw b Schofield	14	– lbw b Keedy	10
M. J. McCague	lbw b Martin	11	– c Hegg b Schofield	0
M. M. Patel	b Schofield	17	– c Martin b Schofield	35
M. J. Saggers	hit wkt b Martin	0	– lbw b Keedy	2
D. D. Masters	not out	0	– not out	0
	B 10, l-b 3	13	B 4, l-b 9, n-b 4	17

1/7 2/14 3/14 4/14 5/89   155   1/1 2/20 3/39 4/41 5/71   125
6/127 7/127 8/155 9/155   6/72 7/72 8/90 9/123

Bonus points – Lancashire 3.

Bowling: *First Innings*—Martin 19–5–42–5; Smethurst 11–2–27–2; Keedy 12–2–36–1; Flintoff 4–2–6–0; Schofield 9–3–31–2. *Second Innings*—Martin 11–3–18–1; Smethurst 11–2–36–1; Keedy 16–9–13–3; Flintoff 9–0–20–0; Schofield 11.4–4–25–4.

Umpires: J. H. Hampshire and K. E. Palmer.

At Leicester, August 22, 23, 24, 25. LANCASHIRE drew with LEICESTERSHIRE.

LANCASHIRE v SOMERSET

At Manchester, September 8, 9, 10. Lancashire won by an innings and 109 runs. Lancashire 20 pts, Somerset 3 pts. Toss: Lancashire.

Lancashire collected maximum points just after lunch on the third day, but Surrey's own innings victory over Durham meant that the Championship was effectively settled. However, Lancashire's place as runners-up was threatened when the ECB's pitch assessors congregated on the second day, after an initial inspection by Mike Denness, who had scuppered Yorkshire's ambitions with an eight-point penalty the previous week. Somerset had been routed inside 50 overs, but the panel eventually agreed that their downfall was simply due to fine swing bowling from Chapple and Smethurst. Lloyd underlined Lancashire's case with a glorious morning session, plundering 100 runs before lunch for the third time. Hegg, acting-captain after Crawley went down with appendicitis, also batted magnificently for the fifth century of his 14-year career, which he rated the best. Together, they added 152, hauling Lancashire into a commanding position after left-arm spinner Blackwell had caused problems. Hegg reached another landmark by beating George Duckworth's record of 634 catches for Lancashire between 1923 and 1938 – though his 76 stumpings lagged far behind Duckworth's 288.

Close of play: First day, Lancashire 142-3 (Atherton 54*, Lloyd 17*); Second day, Somerset 65-4 (Bowler 22*, Burns 2*).

Somerset

M. N. Lathwell b Martin	16	– (2) b Martin	5
*J. Cox c Chilton b Smethurst	53	(1) lbw b Smethurst	20
†R. J. Turner lbw b Smethurst	0	– c Chilton b Smethurst	2
P. D. Bowler b Smethurst	14	– c Chilton b Keedy	75
K. A. Parsons b Chapple	0	– b Chapple	10
M. Burns c Atherton b Chapple	20	– c Hegg b Martin	9
G. D. Rose c and b Schofield	8	– c Hegg b Smethurst	2
I. D. Blackwell c Fairbrother b Chapple	0	– c Hegg b Chapple	36
J. I. D. Kerr c Chilton b Chapple	4	– c Smethurst b Schofield	27
A. R. K. Pierson lbw b Schofield	1	– not out	12
P. S. Jones not out	1	– run out	1
B 6, l-b 9	15	B 19, w 2, n-b 2	23

1/38 2/45 3/67 4/72 5/94   132   1/11 2/30 3/31 4/52 5/74   222
6/122 7/122 8/126 9/131   6/101 7/152 8/207 9/211

Bonus points – Lancashire 3.

Bowling: *First Innings*—Martin 14–1–41–1; Chapple 15–6–34–4; Smethurst 13–3–29–3; Ganguly 2–0–9–0; Schofield 5.4–4–4–2. *Second Innings*—Martin 17–6–39–2; Chapple 12–2–56–2; Smethurst 13–3–58–3; Schofield 11.3–4–36–1; Keedy 2–0–14–1.

Lancashire

M. A. Atherton c Lathwell b Jones	....	57
M. J. Chilton b Blackwell	....	46
S. C. Ganguly c Cox b Blackwell	.....	1
N. H. Fairbrother b Blackwell	....	17
G. D. Lloyd lbw b Burns	....	126
C. P. Schofield c Turner b Jones	......	6
*†W. K. Hegg c Jones b Pierson	......	128
G. Chapple b Jones	....	41

G. Keedy c Pierson b Burns	....	0
M. P. Smethurst not out	....	15
B 5, l-b 11, w 10	....	26
	(9 wkts. dec.)	463

P. J. Martin did not bat.

1/88 2/94 3/118
4/150 5/160 6/312
7/379 8/396 9/463

Bonus points – Lancashire 5, Somerset 3.

Bowling: Jones 28–8–97–3; Rose 26–6–74–0; Kerr 15–1–93–0; Burns 11–3–28–2; Blackwell 25–7–72–3; Parsons 8–1–24–0; Pierson 14.2–3–59–1.

Umpires: R. A. White and P. Willey.

LANCASHIRE v SURREY

At Manchester, September 13, 14, 15, 16. Drawn. Lancashire 10 pts, Surrey 11 pts. Toss: Lancashire.

Surrey retained the Championship when their captain, Hollioake, flung himself to his left at third slip to hold the catch that earned their first bonus point, the only one needed to clinch the title. Theoretically, Lancashire could have overhauled them by scoring 400 for fewer than three wickets, dismissing them for under 200 in their first innings, and going on to win; cynics pointed out that Surrey could simply declare to deny them full bowling points. Lancashire made certain of second place, for the third year running, when Schofield sent back Batty with a classic leg-break on the second day. This was interrupted twice by the now familiar end-of-season problem of the sun reflecting off the roof of the Stretford End media centre into the batsmen's eyes. Lancashire, who had pledged to remedy this, might have been severely embarrassed if the title had been undecided; as it was, the public announcer apologised to the crowd, adding: "Hopefully we will soon get some cloud cover." The Manchester climate duly obliged, and the next day was washed out. On the final day, Bicknell and Saqlain Mushtaq added 116 for Surrey's last wicket, but later Hollioake ignored the chance to press for victory when Lancashire led by only 126, with three wickets standing and 50 overs left. He used nine bowlers, excluding star spinners Saqlain and Salisbury, to end the season on a joky, unsatisfactory note.

Close of play: First day, Surrey 28-2 (Ward 18*, Hollioake 6*); Second day, Surrey 297-9 (Bicknell 46*, Saqlain Mushtaq 33*); Third day, No play.

Lancashire

M. A. Atherton lbw b Bicknell	....	5	– b Tudor	11
M. J. Chilton run out	....	30	– c Batty b Bicknell	5
S. C. Ganguly c Hollioake b Tudor	....	54	– c Salisbury b M. A. Butcher	65
N. H. Fairbrother b Saqlain Mushtaq	....	10	– lbw b Brown	90
G. D. Lloyd b Tudor	....	1	– c Brown b M. A. Butcher.	1
C. P. Schofield b Saqlain Mushtaq	....	24	– b M. A. Butcher	9
*†W. K. Hegg not out	....	93	– (11) not out	21
G. Chapple lbw b Saqlain Mushtaq	....	0	– (7) c Tudor b M. A. Butcher.	5
G. Keedy c Shahid b Hollioake	....	34	– (8) lbw b M. A. Butcher	1
M. P. Smethurst lbw b Saqlain Mushtaq	......	17	– (9) c Bicknell b Batty	66
P. J. Martin c Ward b Salisbury	....	4	– (10) not out.	5
B 19, l-b 7, w 6, n-b 20	....	52	B 18, l-b 3, n-b 4	25

1/10 2/99 3/121 4/123 5/125   324
6/154 7/154 8/261 9/315

1/17 2/17 3/125   (9 wkts. dec.) 304
4/127 5/147 6/159
7/161 8/274 9/274

Bonus points – Lancashire 3, Surrey 3.

Bowling: *First Innings*—Bicknell 14–2–49–1; Tudor 19–2–98–2; G. P. Butcher 4–0–11–0; Saqlain Mushtaq 34–8–81–4; Salisbury 10.5–1–38–1; Hollioake 6–0–21–1. *Second Innings*—Bicknell 6–1–22–1; Tudor 5–1–41–1; M. A. Butcher 27–7–86–5; Brown 24–9–56–1; Hollioake 9–1–31–0; Shahid 1–0–6–0; Batty 6–0–21–1; Ward 5–2–10–0; G. P. Butcher 2–0–10–0.

Surrey

M. A. Butcher lbw b Martin	0	A. J. Tudor lbw b Schofield	5
I. J. Ward c Hegg b Chapple	28	M. P. Bicknell not out	79
N. Shahid lbw b Chapple	2	Saqlain Mushtaq b Smethurst	54
*A. J. Hollioake b Smethurst	49		
A. D. Brown c Lloyd b Schofield	23	B 8, l-b 14, w 4	26
G. P. Butcher c Smethurst b Chapple	66		
†J. N. Batty c Lloyd b Schofield	24	1/2 2/13 3/79 4/95 5/111	359
I. D. K. Salisbury c Hegg b Schofield	3	6/161 7/179 8/193 9/243	

Bonus points – Surrey 4, Lancashire 3.

Bowling: Martin 12–1–51–1; Chapple 26–4–79–3; Smethurst 17.1–4–53–2; Schofield 30–5–94–4; Keedy 21–4–60–0.

Umpires: R. Julian and G. Sharp.

COUNTY MEMBERSHIP

	1990	1999	2000	Variation
Derbyshire	1,693	2,486	3,444	+958
Durham	—	6,575	8,901	+2,326
Essex	9,124	6,850	6,173	−677
Glamorgan	3,393	10,863	8,280	−2,583
Gloucestershire	4,420	5,623	6,382	+759
Hampshire	5,004	4,409	4,757	+348
Kent	5,011	5,797	8,051	+2,254
Lancashire	13,272	13,248	12,979	−269
Leicestershire	3,200	5,631	4,775	−856
Middlesex	8,861	9,010	8,585	−425
Northamptonshire	2,094	3,880	3,295	−585
Nottinghamshire	4,500	5,379	6,191	+812
Somerset	5,185	5,859	6,741	+882
Surrey	5,071	7,854	8,541	+687
Sussex	4,531	6,062	5,720	−342
Warwickshire	10,152	14,329	12,378	−1,951
Worcestershire	6,094	4,949	4,954	+5
Yorkshire	8,439	9,027	16,695	+7,668
MCC	19,237	19,831	19,825	−6
	119,281	147,662	156,667	+9,005

Note: All the first-class counties now quote their membership in terms of the total number of individuals affiliated to their clubs. Until 2000, Derbyshire, Kent and Yorkshire registered corporate or joint membership as representing one person.

LEICESTERSHIRE

Phillip DeFreitas

President: B. A. F. Smith
Chairman: R. Goadby
Secretary/General Manager: J. J. Whitaker
Chairman, Cricket Committee: P. R. Haywood
Administrative Secretary: K. P. Hill
Captain: V. J. Wells
Cricket Manager: J. Birkenshaw
Head Groundsman: 2000 – S. Wright
Scorer: G. A. York

Like the summer itself, Leicestershire's season left a lot to be desired. There were some bright spells, but not enough to lift the air of gloom and disappointment that hung over Grace Road for much of the time. It was a far remove from the Championship-winning summers of 1996 and 1998, when Leicestershire appeared to have put down their marker for years to come. In 2000, they too often looked to be in a muddle rather than the huddle that became synonymous with their success.

They won only four games in the Championship, failed miserably again in the two knockout competitions, and had to haul themselves up by their bootstraps to avoid relegation in the National League. In football parlance, they were staring relegation in the face when they lost four League games in a row in August. But they responded by rediscovering qualities that were their hallmark in previous seasons. Winning their last three games took them back to their mid-season fourth. That was where they finished in the Championship as well.

Leicestershire aspire to higher than that, however. "For many counties, fourth place in both competitions would be acceptable," said manager Jack Birkenshaw. "But not for us. Only in the last month of the season did we play consistently good cricket, and some of our players will look back on a season that never was."

In truth, with so many changes on and off the field, it was always going to be a year of rebuilding and stabilising for Leicestershire and their new captain, Vince Wells. Former captain James Whitaker replaced chief executive David Collier, who left to join Nottinghamshire, and there were new faces inside the dressing-room. Fast bowlers Alan Mullally and David Millns, along with wicket-keeper Paul Nixon, had gone to new counties, and overseas player Michael Kasprowicz had been released.

Five new players were signed, with Indian wrist-spinner Anil Kumble the star arrival. Birkenshaw had decided on a shift in emphasis and was gambling on Kumble reproducing the form he showed for Northamptonshire in 1995, when he took 105 wickets. Sadly, the combination of slow, low pitches and a niggling shoulder injury restricted Kumble's effectiveness and, although he was Leicestershire's leading wicket-taker, he claimed only 45 in the Championship. For 2001, the club signed Daniel Marsh, son of former

Australian wicket-keeper Rod. A hard-hitting right-handed batsman and slow left-arm spinner, he has represented Australia A and was Tasmania's Player of the Year in 1999-2000.

The other newcomers in 2000 were wicket-keeper Neil Burns, returning to county cricket after a six-year absence, opening batsman Trevor Ward from Kent, South African all-rounder Billy Stelling and veteran Phillip DeFreitas, who had first played for Leicestershire in 1985 and later moved to Lancashire and Derbyshire. They enjoyed mixed fortunes. Burns kept beautifully, and his batting improved as the season progressed. But Ward and Stelling made little impact, the latter suffering a series of injuries. DeFreitas proved to be the consummate professional, bowled better than his figures suggest, and batted well. Innings of 97 and 123 against Lancashire at the end of August hinted at scores being settled as well as made.

More often than not, though, the batsmen were frustrating, and only Aftab Habib reached 1,000 runs. He produced the consistency and confidence that others lacked, hit two big centuries, and ended the season with scores of 59, 93, 73 and 72. A second successive England A tour confirmed that an international career remains a possibility.

Leicestershire's bowling problems are reflected in their bonus points, the least obtained by any attack in the first division. There were times when even Birkenshaw must have wondered about the wisdom of allowing both Mullally and Millns to leave. The problem was compounded by Chris Lewis's degenerative hip condition. He sent down fewer than 100 overs in the Championship, claiming only seven wickets – he scored just 80 runs in seven innings as well – and it came as no surprise when his contract was terminated during the winter by mutual agreement. Controversy off the field did not help, either, with Lewis making front-page headlines following his allegations to the ECB that three England players had been involved in match-fixing.

It meant that a huge burden was placed on the broad but young shoulders of James Ormond, who at times looked genuinely hostile and a fast bowler of real quality. He provided the central thrust for Leicestershire's ten-wicket win over Derbyshire in June with six for 50, claiming his last four wickets for six runs in 22 balls. He also took six against Surrey at Guildford, but was unable to prevent the eventual champions winning by ten wickets. That was Surrey's second big victory over Leicestershire. Two weeks earlier, on a superb pitch at Oakham School, they had triumphed by an innings and 178 runs. Lancashire were the only other side to beat Leicestershire in the Championship.

Leicestershire's summer, and their penchant for shooting themselves in the foot, was encapsulated in their NatWest Trophy fourth-round match against holders Gloucestershire at Grace Road. Chasing a modest 211, they needed 20 off the last five overs with five wickets in hand. All five wickets fell for nine runs in 18 balls. "We will improve," Birkenshaw promised. There is certainly room for it. – NEVILLE FOULGER.

LEICESTERSHIRE 2000

[*Bill Smith*]

Back row: A. A. Khan, S. J. Adshead, C. D. Crowe, A. S. Wright, A. Sachdeva, D. Williamson. *Middle row:* H. Eaton (*physiotherapist*), N. D. Burns, T. R. Ward, S. A. J. Boswell, J. M. Dakin, J. Ormond, W. F. Stelling, I. J. Sutcliffe, M. T. Brimson, D. I. Stevens, P. E. Robinson, C. Eaton (*physiotherapist*). *Front row:* A. Habib, C. C. Lewis, B. F. Smith, R. Goadby (*chairman*), J. Birkenshaw (*cricket manager*), B. A. F. Smith (*president*), V. J. Wells (*captain*), J. J. Whitaker (*secretary/general manager*), D. L. Maddy, A. Kumble, P. A. J. DeFreitas.

LEICESTERSHIRE RESULTS

All first-class matches – Played 17: Won 4, Lost 3, Drawn 10.

County Championship matches – Played 16: Won 4, Lost 3, Drawn 9.

PPP Healthcare County Championship, 4th in Division 1; NatWest Trophy, 4th round;
Benson and Hedges Cup, 5th in North Group; Norwich Union National League, 4th in Division 1.

COUNTY CHAMPIONSHIP AVERAGES

BATTING

Cap		M	I	NO	R	HS	100s	50s	Avge	Ct/St
1998	A. Habib	16	22	1	1,038	172*	2	8	49.42	8
	D. Williamson	2	4	2	95	47	0	0	47.50	0
1986	P. A. J. DeFreitas . . .	14	18	3	677	123*	1	4	45.13	1
2000	J. M. Dakin	8	11	1	447	135	1	3	44.70	2
1995	B. F. Smith	16	22	2	610	111*	2	1	30.50	9
1996	D. L. Maddy†	16	23	1	581	102	1	4	26.40	16
	N. D. Burns	16	21	4	445	67*	0	3	26.17	36/1
1994	V. J. Wells	14	18	0	465	98	0	3	25.83	8
	D. I. Stevens†	14	20	0	434	78	0	2	21.70	5
1997	I. J. Sutcliffe	11	15	0	283	53	0	2	18.86	10
	C. D. Crowe†	7	7	1	100	30	0	0	16.66	2
	S. A. J. Boswell	5	7	3	63	20	0	0	15.75	0
	T. R. Ward	7	10	1	110	39	0	0	12.22	8
1999	J. Ormond	12	15	7	95	30*	0	0	11.87	1
1990	C. C. Lewis	5	7	0	80	24	0	0	11.42	6
2000	A. Kumble§	12	16	0	181	56	0	1	11.31	3

W. F. Stelling (1 match) did not bat.

* *Signifies not out.*   † *Born in Leicestershire.*   § *Overseas player.*

BOWLING

	O	M	R	W	BB	5W/i	Avge
A. Kumble	498.3	139	1,133	45	6-44	2	25.17
J. Ormond	380.3	75	1,116	44	6-50	3	25.36
V. J. Wells	211.3	46	616	23	4-54	0	26.78
C. D. Crowe	148.3	36	364	12	4-55	0	30.33
P. A. J. DeFreitas	459.2	122	1,105	33	4-41	0	33.48
J. M. Dakin	186.4	36	551	12	2-20	0	45.91

Also bowled: S. A. J. Boswell 93.4–21–278–9; C. C. Lewis 98.1–12–302–7; D. L. Maddy 75–16–220–6; B. F. Smith 2–0–6–0; W. F. Stelling 25–8–49–5; D. I. Stevens 6–2–14–0; I. J. Sutcliffe 1.3–0–12–0; D. Williamson 33–4–113–2.

COUNTY RECORDS

Highest score for:	261	P. V. Simmons v Northamptonshire at Leicester . .	1994
Highest score against:	341	G. H. Hirst (Yorkshire) at Leicester	1905
Best bowling for:	10-18	G. Geary v Glamorgan at Pontypridd	1929
Best bowling against:	10-32	H. Pickett (Essex) at Leyton	1895
Highest total for:	701-4 dec.	v Worcestershire at Worcester	1906
Highest total against:	761-6 dec.	by Essex at Chelmsford	1990
Lowest total for:	25	v Kent at Leicester	1912
Lowest total against: {	24	by Glamorgan at Leicester	1971
	24	by Oxford University at Oxford.	1985

At Derby, April 26, 27, 28, 29. LEICESTERSHIRE drew with DERBYSHIRE.

At Manchester, May 3, 4, 5, 6. LEICESTERSHIRE lost to LANCASHIRE by an innings and 25 runs.

LEICESTERSHIRE v SOMERSET

At Leicester, May 11, 12, 13, 14. Leicestershire won by six wickets. Leicestershire 19 pts, Somerset 4 pts. Toss: Somerset. County debut: J. O. Grove.

A match illuminated by three splendid centuries went Leicestershire's way with six overs to spare. Despite losing the toss, they quickly had Somerset in crisis at 88 for five, Ormond taking three for three in 21 balls, but a century stand between Trescothick and Blackwell revived them. Trescothick hit a near-faultless 105 in almost six hours. In reply, Leicestershire were hauled out of their own trouble by hundreds from Habib and Dakin. They shared a fifth-wicket partnership of 275, a county record against Somerset, who badly missed Caddick (able to play, but rested with a blistered toe ahead of the Lord's Test). Habib finished undefeated on 172, facing 380 balls and hitting 21 fours; Dakin, rewarded with his cap, made 135, striking 20 fours and a six in 298 balls. Stevens and Extras contributed the only other double-figure scores. Rose and Jamie Grove, the former Essex seamer, each took five wickets, as did Kumble in Somerset's second innings, which left Leicestershire to chase 122 in 36 overs. Smith, captain because of injury to Wells and Lewis, saw them home.

Close of play: First day, Leicestershire 3-0 (Stevens 1*, Maddy 2*); Second day, Leicestershire 275-4 (Habib 120*, Dakin 110*); Third day, Somerset 124-2 (Holloway 27*, Bowler 10*).

Somerset

M. E. Trescothick c Maddy b Kumble	105	– (2) c Maddy b Kumble	43
*J. Cox c Burns b DeFreitas	8	– (1) c Burns b Kumble	24
P. C. L. Holloway lbw b Dakin	17	– c Burns b DeFreitas	27
P. D. Bowler lbw b Ormond	8	– lbw b Maddy	48
M. Burns c Burns b Ormond	4	– b DeFreitas	6
†R. J. Turner b Ormond	0	– lbw b Kumble	15
K. A. Parsons c Burns b Dakin	20	– b Maddy	25
G. D. Rose c Stevens b DeFreitas	1	– lbw b Kumble	2
I. D. Blackwell c Burns b Kumble	58	– c Burns b DeFreitas	19
A. R. K. Pierson c Burns b DeFreitas	16	– not out	1
J. O. Grove not out	8	– lbw b Kumble	0
B 4, l-b 5, w 4, n-b 4	17	B 14, l-b 16, w 2, n-b 4	36

1/10 2/65 3/78 4/88 5/88   262   1/66 2/97 3/124 4/130 5/170   246
6/120 7/138 8/238 9/239   6/213 7/220 8/230 9/243

Bonus points – Somerset 2, Leicestershire 3.

Bowling: *First Innings*—Ormond 25–4–79–3; DeFreitas 24.5–10–49–3; Kumble 26–9–62–2; Dakin 22–6–44–2; Crowe 4–0–19–0. *Second Innings*—Ormond 21–4–58–0; DeFreitas 27–11–48–3; Kumble 38.2–12–61–5; Crowe 5–1–12–0; Dakin 18–7–27–0; Maddy 4–2–10–2.

Leicestershire

D. I. Stevens lbw b Rose	13	– lbw b Rose	3
D. L. Maddy b Grove	5	– b Pierson	39
T. R. Ward lbw b Rose	2	– lbw b Rose	0
*B. F. Smith c Parsons b Rose	3	– not out	45
A. Habib not out	172	– lbw b Parsons	9
J. M. Dakin c Cox b Grove	135	– not out	19
†N. D. Burns c Turner b Grove	6		
P. A. J. DeFreitas c Burns b Grove	0		
A. Kumble c Turner b Rose	4		
C. D. Crowe c Turner b Rose	9		
J. Ormond lbw b Grove	8		
B 4, l-b 10, w 4, n-b 12	30	B 4, l-b 5	9

1/20 2/24 3/29 4/34 5/309   387   1/8 2/8 3/71 4/94   (4 wkts) 124
6/323 7/323 8/336 9/368

Bonus points – Leicestershire 4, Somerset 2 (Score at 130 overs: 360-8).

Bowling: *First Innings*—Rose 34–11–74–5; Grove 30.5–7–90–5; Parsons 12–3–41–0; Trescothick 8–0–50–0; Blackwell 29–9–78–0; Pierson 26–8–40–0. *Second Innings*—Rose 9–1–28–2; Grove 7–0–26–0; Blackwell 2–0–15–0; Pierson 6–0–18–1; Parsons 5.5–0–28–1.

Umpires: M. J. Harris and T. E. Jesty.

LEICESTERSHIRE v HAMPSHIRE

At Leicester, May 17, 18, 19, 20. Drawn. Leicestershire 9 pts, Hampshire 8 pts. Toss: Hampshire.
This clash between the world's best wrist-spinners – Warne and Kumble – never lived up to expectations, mainly because of the weather. Rain and bad light chopped 66 overs from the second day and 42 from the third, when there were six stoppages. Neither side could gain much momentum, though Warne was nearer his best after a disappointing start to his Hampshire career, and was clearly delighted to end a run of four consecutive ducks. Aymes, in his first Championship innings of the season, made a solid unbeaten 74, but, against an attack blunted by the absence of Ormond and Lewis, 229 was a poor total. Kumble claimed two wickets in two balls, but was upstaged later by Warne, who went through his entire repertoire, blowing on his chilly fingers as he returned five for 86 from 43 overs. Sixties from Habib and Burns steered Leicestershire to a lead of 60. Had it not been for the rain, they would surely have won: Hampshire finished 63 ahead with two wickets left.
Close of play: First day, Hampshire 227-9 (Aymes 74*, Hartley 5*); Second day, Leicestershire 89-3 (Smith 24*, Habib 19*); Third day, Leicestershire 212-6 (Habib 63*, Burns 18*).

Hampshire

J. S. Laney b DeFreitas	8	– c Ward b Boswell	14
D. A. Kenway c Maddy b Kumble	30	– b DeFreitas	5
W. S. Kendall lbw b DeFreitas	4	– c Burns b Kumble	8
*R. A. Smith c Burns b Boswell	26	– c Ward b Kumble	31
G. W. White lbw b Kumble	0	– lbw b Wells	6
†A. N. Aymes not out	74	– lbw b DeFreitas	13
A. D. Mascarenhas c Burns b DeFreitas	8	– c Wells b DeFreitas	10
S. K. Warne b Maddy	16	– not out	11
S. D. Udal c Burns b Maddy	7	– c Dakin b DeFreitas	1
S. J. Renshaw c Maddy b Wells	26	– not out	2
P. J. Hartley c Stevens b Dakin	7		
B 1, l-b 8, w 4, n-b 10	23	B 10, l-b 4, w 2, n-b 6	22

1/10 2/28 3/61 4/61 5/91   229   1/21 2/21 3/60 4/67   (8 wkts) 123
6/116 7/135 8/149 9/213   5/91 6/107 7/109 8/117

Bonus points – Hampshire 1, Leicestershire 3.

Bowling: *First Innings*—DeFreitas 20.3–6–36–3; Dakin 18.4–4–49–1; Wells 11.3–3–30–1; Kumble 27–4–53–2; Boswell 12–3–40–1; Maddy 6–1–12–2. *Second Innings*—DeFreitas 21–7–41–4; Boswell 7–2–23–1; Dakin 3–1–8–0; Kumble 22–7–27–2; Wells 5–2–8–1; Maddy 2–1–2–0.

Leicestershire

D. L. Maddy lbw b Hartley	22	P. A. J. DeFreitas b Warne	0
D. I. Stevens lbw b Warne	19	A. Kumble c Aymes b Mascarenhas	2
T. R. Ward st Aymes b Warne	1	S. A. J. Boswell c Aymes b Renshaw	14
B. F. Smith lbw b Mascarenhas	32		
A. Habib st Aymes b Warne	66	B 6, l-b 12, w 4, n-b 6	28
*V. J. Wells c Aymes b Hartley	2		
J. M. Dakin lbw b Warne	36	1/40 2/41 3/56 4/104 5/111	289
†N. D. Burns not out	67	6/165 7/230 8/232 9/237	

Bonus points – Leicestershire 2, Hampshire 3.

Bowling: Hartley 29–5–70–2; Renshaw 23–7–47–1; Warne 43–13–86–5; Mascarenhas 19–4–33–2; Udal 15–5–35–0.

Umpires: D. J. Constant and G. Sharp.

At Chester-le-Street, May 24, 25, 26, 27. LEICESTERSHIRE drew with DURHAM.

At Leeds, May 31, June 1, 2, 3. LEICESTERSHIRE drew with YORKSHIRE.

LEICESTERSHIRE v DERBYSHIRE

At Leicester, June 14, 15, 16, 17. Leicestershire won by ten wickets. Leicestershire 18 pts, Derbyshire 3 pts. Toss: Leicestershire.

Dean ended Leicestershire's first innings with a hat-trick, completing a spell of four in eight balls, but not before an imperious 164 from Habib on a slow, difficult pitch had tilted matters their way. No one else could manage so much as a fifty. After the first day had been lost to rain, it was Derbyshire who began more promisingly, reducing the home side to 57 for four. But then Habib, who hit 21 fours and two sixes from 225 balls, shared century partnerships with Sutcliffe and DeFreitas before becoming the first victim of Dean's hat-trick. Replying, Derbyshire were unable to cope with Ormond, whose pace and accuracy brought him six for 50, including four for six from his last 22 balls. They were dismissed for 133, with the last five wickets falling for 11 in six overs, and followed on 177 behind. Despite batting with greater purpose, Derbyshire did not hold out long enough; Leicestershire had knocked off the winning runs by mid-afternoon.

Close of play: First day, No play; Second day, Derbyshire 17-2 (Di Venuto 8*, Titchard 4*); Third day, Derbyshire 116-5 (Titchard 26*, Cassar 0*).

Leicestershire

T. R. Ward lbw b Munton	5	– not out	34
D. L. Maddy c Di Venuto b Munton	22	– not out	11
*V. J. Wells lbw b Cassar	11		
B. F. Smith c Dowman b Cassar	3		
A. Habib b Dean	164		
I. J. Sutcliffe c Krikken b Cassar	43		
C. C. Lewis c Krikken b Cassar	0		
P. A. J. DeFreitas b Dean	37		
†N. D. Burns not out	0		
A. Kumble lbw b Dean	0		
J. Ormond lbw b Dean	0		
B 1, l-b 8, w 14, n-b 2	25	L-b 2	2

1/5 2/36 3/40 4/57 5/186   310   (no wkt) 47
6/186 7/307 8/310 9/310

Bonus points – Leicestershire 3, Derbyshire 3.

Bowling: *First Innings*—Cork 23–5–61–0; Munton 25–9–69–2; Cassar 15–2–62–4; Aldred 12.5–2–53–0; Dean 8.4–1–47–4; Bailey 6–2–9–0. *Second Innings*—Cork 3–0–13–0; Munton 5–3–13–0; Cassar 3–0–19–0.

Derbyshire

S. D. Stubbings c Ward b Ormond	0	– b Ormond	8
M. P. Dowman b Ormond	1	– c Sutcliffe b Wells	28
M. J. Di Venuto b Kumble	26	– c Lewis b Wells	13
S. P. Titchard c Kumble b DeFreitas	16	– c Kumble b Ormond	38
R. J. Bailey b Kumble	11	– lbw b Kumble	24
M. E. Cassar c Ward b Ormond	30	– (7) c Habib b Wells	40
†K. M. Krikken c Lewis b Ormond	24	– (8) b Lewis	27
*D. G. Cork lbw b Ormond	1	– (9) lbw b Wells	0
P. Aldred c Ward b DeFreitas	5	– (10) c Wells b Lewis	10
T. A. Munton not out	0	– (11) not out	0
K. J. Dean c Lewis b Ormond	0	– (6) c Ward b Kumble	0
B 7, l-b 4, w 2, n-b 6	19	L-b 7, w 6, n-b 22	35

1/0 2/9 3/46 4/56 5/63   133   1/20 2/46 3/65 4/113 5/115   223
6/122 7/126 8/133 9/133   6/149 7/194 8/194 9/222

Bonus points – Leicestershire 3.

Bowling: *First Innings*—Ormond 14.5–2–50–6; DeFreitas 23–8–39–2; Kumble 12–5–21–2; Lewis 4–1–7–0; Wells 2–1–4–0; Maddy 1–0–1–0. *Second Innings*—Ormond 24–7–58–2; DeFreitas 2–0–3–0; Wells 21–6–58–4; Lewis 15.1–3–33–2; Kumble 40–17–58–2; Maddy 3–0–6–0.

Umpires: D. J. Constant and N. G. Cowley.

At Leicester, June 18. LEICESTERSHIRE beat NEW ZEALAND A by five wickets (See New Zealand A tour section).

LEICESTERSHIRE v SURREY

At Oakham School, July 7, 8, 9. Surrey won by an innings and 178 runs. Surrey 20 pts, Leicestershire 3 pts. Toss: Surrey.

First-class cricket made a triumphant return to Oakham School after 62 years. Attendances were excellent, the pitch played fast and true, and much of the cricket – at least from Surrey – matched the delightful setting. But for Leicestershire, there was an unwelcome symmetry with their last Championship game here, in 1938. They followed on and crashed to a heavy defeat. Then, Bryan Valentine made 242 for Kent; now, Brown scored a career-best 295 not out for Surrey. Though he gave four chances, it was a splendid innings. He batted eight hours and 37 minutes, faced 392 balls, and hit 32 fours and a six. Leicestershire did let their opponents wriggle off the hook: with the rest of the top order contributing little, Surrey had been 190 for seven. But Brown found stauncher allies in the tail and shared two partnerships of 141, first with Tudor and then, for the tenth wicket, with Saqlain Mushtaq, who hit his maiden Championship fifty. Completely demoralised, Leicestershire slumped to 51 for seven on the second afternoon and followed on, 362 behind, next morning. Stevens's aggressive 68 from 80 balls was the one bright spot as Saqlain took five wickets, including the last three in ten balls, in failing light and drizzle. Surrey's third successive victory lifted them to the top of the table – where they would stay.

Close of play: First day, Surrey 334-8 (Brown 211*, Salisbury 0*); Second day, Leicestershire 134-9 (Burns 24*, Ormond 2*).

Surrey

M. A. Butcher c Wells b Ormond	0	A. J. Tudor c Maddy b Wells	22
I. J. Ward lbw b Ormond	6	I. D. K. Salisbury c Maddy b DeFreitas	12
N. Shahid c Burns b DeFreitas	37	Saqlain Mushtaq b Wells	66
*A. J. Hollioake c Lewis b Ormond	4		
A. D. Brown not out	295	B 3, l-b 10, w 2, n-b 22	37
B. C. Hollioake c Habib b DeFreitas	2		
†J. N. Batty c Lewis b Maddy	19		505
M. P. Bicknell c Burns b Lewis	5		

1/0 2/11 3/25 4/113 5/125
6/181 7/190 8/331 9/364

Bonus points – Surrey 5, Leicestershire 3 (Score at 130 overs: 431-9).

Bowling: Ormond 34–4–92–3; DeFreitas 29–6–115–3; Kumble 35–5–101–0; Lewis 18–2–60–1; Wells 17.5–1–65–2; Maddy 15–2–59–1.

Leicestershire

D. L. Maddy c A. J. Hol, bke b Bicknell	10	– c Batty b Bicknell	0
I. J. Sutcliffe c Brown b Tudor	1	– c Batty b B. C. Hollioake	14
*V. J. Wells c Saqlain Mushtaq b Tudor	13	– b Bicknell	9
B. F. Smith run out	3	– c Brown b Bicknell	20
A. Habib c Brown b Bicknell	0	– st Batty b Saqlain Mushtaq	4
D. I. Stevens lbw b Tudor	6	– b Saqlain Mushtaq	68
C. C. Lewis lbw b Bicknell	3	– c Batty b B. C. Hollioake	24
P. A. J. DeFreitas c A. J. Hollioake b Saqlain Mushtaq	38	– not out	25
†N. D. Burns c A. J. Hollioake b Saqlain Mushtaq	30	– c Batty b Saqlain Mushtaq	8
A. Kumble b Salisbury	10	– c A. J. Hollioake b Saqlain Mushtaq	0
J. Ormond not out	5	– lbw b Saqlain Mushtaq	0
B 2, l-b 12, n-b 10	24	B 5, l-b 3, n-b 4	12

1/12 2/16 3/27 4/27 5/44   143   1/0 2/22 3/26 4/40 5/56   184
6/49 7/51 8/106 9/131   6/118 7/149 8/182 9/184

Bonus points – Surrey 3.

Bowling: *First Innings*—Bicknell 11–3–41–3; Tudor 11–6–34–3; Salisbury 18–8–29–1; Saqlain Mushtaq 17.2–8–25–2. *Second Innings*—Bicknell 15–4–44–3; B. C. Hollioake 15–4–48–2; Salisbury 14–4–41–0; Saqlain Mushtaq 15–4–35–5; Brown 1–0–8–0.

Umpires: A. Clarkson and J. W. Holder.

LEICESTERSHIRE v DURHAM

At Leicester, July 12, 13, 14. Leicestershire won by 217 runs. Leicestershire 16 pts, Durham 3 pts. Toss: Leicestershire.

A century from Smith and some excellent bowling saw Leicestershire to a comfortable three-day win. But much discussion centred on the relaid pitch – badly cracked even before play started: many balls kept low, while the occasional one bucked. Pitch liaison officer Phil Sharpe was present, but took no action. Smith, struck on the forearm early in his innings by one that flew off a length, reached 50 for the first time in the Championship season. His watchful unbeaten 111 – exactly half Leicestershire's total – lasted over six hours and contained ten fours. Wood, with five for 60, was the pick of the bowlers. In reply, Durham worked their way to 107 for two, then lost eight wickets, split between Ormond and Kumble, for 64. Despite another five-wicket return for Durham, this time by Brown, half-centuries from Maddy and Habib helped Leicestershire set them an improbable target of 311. They were bowled out for 93 as Ormond (completing match figures of nine for 78) and Kumble (eight for 55) again dismantled the innings.

Close of play: First day, Durham 8-0 (Lewis 1*, Daley 2*); Second day, Leicestershire 98-3 (Maddy 39*, Habib 36*).

Leicestershire

D. L. Maddy c Speight b Brown	0	– c Lewis b Killeen		77
I. J. Sutcliffe b Betts	0	– lbw b Betts		0
*V. J. Wells lbw b Betts	12	– c Speight b Brown		10
B. F. Smith not out	111	– c Betts b Brown		8
A. Habib c Speight b Wood	9	– c Wood b Brown		52
D. I. Stevens c Daley b Wood	40	– c Speight b Wood		19
P. A. J. DeFreitas c Katich b Killeen	10	– c Speak b Katich		36
†N. D. Burns c Katich b Wood	10	– not out		36
A. Kumble c Daley b Collingwood	3	– c Collingwood b Brown		1
J. Ormond b Wood	14	– c Katich b Brown		0
S. A. J. Boswell c Speight b Wood	0	– b Killeen		12
L-b 9, w 2, n-b 2	13	L-b 8		8

1/0 2/0 3/19 4/37 5/98   222   1/0 2/15 3/25 4/125 5/167   259
6/110 7/162 8/173 9/222   6/181 7/224 8/234 9/234

Bonus points – Leicestershire 1, Durham 3.

Bowling: *First Innings*—Brown 21–7–41–1; Betts 23–7–40–2; Killeen 15–7–34–1; Wood 21.4–4–60–5; Collingwood 10–2–24–1; Katich 4–0–14–0. *Second Innings*—Brown 21–2–70–5; Betts 11–4–20–1; Wood 21–4–59–1; Killeen 12.4–3–51–2; Collingwood 6–2–15–0; Katich 14–1–36–1.

Durham

J. J. B. Lewis b Wells	33	– b Ormond		5
J. A. Daley lbw b DeFreitas	4	– (3) c Sutcliffe b DeFreitas		7
S. M. Katich c Wells b Ormond	43	– (4) c Sutcliffe b Kumble		18
P. D. Collingwood lbw b Ormond	22	– (5) b Ormond		8
*N. J. Speak b Kumble	18	– (6) b Kumble		9
S. M. Ali lbw b Ormond	0	– (2) lbw b Ormond		7
†M. P. Speight b Kumble	18	– c Maddy b Kumble		0
M. M. Betts lbw b Kumble	0	– c Maddy b Kumble		9
J. Wood b Ormond	15	– b Ormond		10
N. Killeen lbw b Kumble	0	– b Ormond		0
S. J. E. Brown not out	0	– not out		0
L-b 6, w 8, n-b 4	18	L-b 4, w 2, n-b 14		20

1/11 2/52 3/107 4/120 5/120   171   1/6 2/19 3/19 4/39 5/55   93
6/144 7/146 8/171 9/171   6/55 7/60 8/93 9/93

Bonus points – Leicestershire 3.

Bowling: *First Innings*—Ormond 22.1–5–44–4; Boswell 10–3–28–0; Kumble 14–4–32–4; Wells 7–0–21–1; DeFreitas 17–6–36–1; Maddy 1–0–4–0. *Second Innings*—Ormond 11.1–0–34–5; DeFreitas 6–0–14–1; Kumble 10–5–23–4; Boswell 5–0–18–0.

Umpires: J. H. Harris and D. R. Shepherd.

At Guildford, July 19, 20, 21. LEICESTERSHIRE lost to SURREY by ten wickets.

At Leicester, July 28, 29, 30. LEICESTERSHIRE drew with WEST INDIANS (See West Indian tour section).

At Canterbury, August 2, 3, 4, 5. LEICESTERSHIRE drew with KENT.

At Southampton, August 8, 9, 10, 11. LEICESTERSHIRE beat HAMPSHIRE by 61 runs.

LEICESTERSHIRE v YORKSHIRE

At Leicester, August 16, 17, 18, 19. Drawn. Leicestershire 11 pts, Yorkshire 10 pts. Toss: Leicestershire.

Yorkshire needed a win to keep the pressure on Surrey at the top of the table, but rain – all the third day and the fourth morning were lost – had the last laugh. The first two days promised an interesting contest, despite Yorkshire being without seven key players, four of whom were on international duty at Headingley. Leicestershire, themselves missing DeFreitas, batted down the order to reach a fourth batting point; Silverwood, swinging the ball considerably and gathering four for 60, was the pick of the bowlers. Yorkshire looked in trouble at 123 for five on the second evening. When play eventually resumed on the last afternoon, acting-captain Lehmann, batting at No. 7 because of a painful back, went on to his third hundred of the season, his second in successive innings – separated by three years – at Leicester. It was enough to make him the country's leading run-scorer, but Yorkshire still lost ground.

Close of play: First day, Leicestershire 286-8 (Burns 26*, Crowe 3*); Second day, Yorkshire 194-5 (Hamilton 58*, Lehmann 51*); Third day, No play.

Leicestershire

D. L. Maddy c Guy b Silverwood	66	†N. D. Burns b Silverwood	58
I. J. Sutcliffe c Guy b Elstub	2	C. D. Crowe b Silverwood	30
B. F. Smith c McGrath b Fellows	0	J. Ormond not out	6
A. Habib c Widdup b Silverwood	59		
D. I. Stevens lbw b Hamilton	49	B 2, l-b 6, w 8, n-b 13	29
*V. J. Wells b Hamilton	27		
J. M. Dakin c Elstub b Fisher	6	1/25 2/28 3/136 4/151 5/221	351
A. Kumble st Guy b Fisher	19	6/222 7/244 8/271 9/332	

Bonus points – Leicestershire 4, Yorkshire 3.

Bowling: Silverwood 25.3–4–60–4; Hamilton 24–2–82–2; Elstub 17–3–44–1; Fellows 17–5–49–1; Fisher 26–2–103–2; Lehmann 1–0–5–0.

Yorkshire

S. Widdup c Stevens b Kumble	38	I. D. Fisher c Habib b Crowe	24
V. J. Craven c Smith b Wells	15	C. E. W. Silverwood c Ormond b Crowe.	17
A. McGrath c Smith b Wells	1	C. J. Elstub not out	2
M. J. Wood lbw b Wells	0		
G. M. Fellows c Burns b Ormond	16	B 6, l-b 9, w 2, n-b 12	29
G. M. Hamilton b Ormond	66		
*D. S. Lehmann c and b Dakin	115	1/22 2/24 3/24 4/61 5/123	340
†S. M. Guy c Habib b Dakin	17	6/207 7/265 8/312 9/335	

Bonus points – Yorkshire 3, Leicestershire 3.

Bowling: Ormond 27–3–82–2; Dakin 19–1–71–2; Wells 12–5–30–3; Kumble 32–9–81–1; Crowe 21.1–4–61–2.

Umpires: M. R. Benson and M. J. Harris.

LEICESTERSHIRE v LANCASHIRE

At Leicester, August 22, 23, 24, 25. Drawn. Leicestershire 9 pts, Lancashire 12 pts. Toss: Leicestershire.

DeFreitas exploited a benign pitch – the three innings averaged over 450 – for a personal triumph against former employers. After falling three short in Leicestershire's first innings, he made certain of a century next time, finishing on a career-best unbeaten 123; twice he shared hundred partnerships with Habib. It was a pitch on which any batsman worth his salt would expect to dip his bread. The Lancastrians certainly did: Crawley hit 139, Flintoff smashed 55 off 64 balls, Ganguly played beautifully, and Fairbrother scored his second hundred of the season against Leicestershire – enabling Lancashire to declare 202 ahead. On this pitch, however, it was not enough, despite the efforts of spinners Keedy and Schofield, who between them bowled 77 overs and took all six wickets. Maximum points would have put Lancashire level with leaders Surrey. It was a bad game for injuries and illness: in warm-up fielding before the start, Peter Martin, having just recovered from breaking his right thumb, fractured his left; on the third day, Crowe felt too sick to field and umpire Whitehead, suffering from gout, had to swap places with John Steele, the third umpire for a satellite broadcast.

Close of play: First day, Leicestershire 362-7 (DeFreitas 90*, Kumble 25*); Second day, Lancashire 334-3 (Crawley 129*, Ganguly 42*); Third day, Leicestershire 75-1 (Sutcliffe 44*, Smith 17*).

Leicestershire

D. L. Maddy c Chilton b Flintoff	26	– c Hegg b Schofield			9
I. J. Sutcliffe lbw b Chapple	7	– c Chapple b Keedy			52
*B. F. Smith c Chilton b Smethurst	10	– c Ganguly b Schofield			44
A. Habib c Atherton b Schofield	93	– c Ganguly b Keedy			73
D. I. Stevens c Fairbrother b Flintoff	0	– c Chilton b Keedy			16
J. M. Dakin c Ganguly b Schofield	50	– c Flintoff b Schofield			18
P. A. J. DeFreitas b Smethurst	97	– not out			123
†N. D. Burns b Schofield	15	– not out			30
A. Kumble b Chapple	28				
C. D. Crowe not out	0				
J. Ormond b Chapple	0				
B 13, l-b 9, w 4, n-b 20	46	B 11, l-b 14, w 16, n-b 2			43
1/21 2/36 3/70 4/70 5/167	372	1/37 2/89 3/131	(6 wkts)		408
6/280 7/297 8/372 9/372		4/168 5/195 6/306			

Bonus points – Leicestershire 4, Lancashire 3.

Bowling: *First Innings*—Chapple 19–4–54–3; Smethurst 21–3–72–2; Flintoff 13–3–43–2; Ganguly 9–1–45–0; Keedy 16–3–49–0; Schofield 27–3–78–3; Chilton 1–0–3–0; Fairbrother 3–1–6–0. *Second Innings*—Chapple 20–1–89–0; Smethurst 9–2–32–0; Schofield 43–8–149–3; Keedy 34–7–77–3; Flintoff 2–0–9–0; Ganguly 3–0–8–0; Crawley 1–0–19–0.

Lancashire

M. A. Atherton lbw b DeFreitas	48	†W. K. Hegg not out	65
M. J. Chilton b DeFreitas	21		
*J. P. Crawley c Stevens b Dakin	139	B 18, l-b 21, w 6, n-b 14	59
A. Flintoff c Sutcliffe b Kumble	55		
S. C. Ganguly lbw b Ormond	87	1/59 2/156 3/245	(5 wkts dec.) 574
N. H. Fairbrother not out	100	4/352 5/436	

C. P. Schofield, G. Chapple, G. Keedy and M. P. Smethurst did not bat.

Bonus points – Lancashire 5, Leicestershire 1 (Score at 130 overs: 414-4).

Bowling: Ormond 29–3–76–1; Dakin 30–2–112–1; DeFreitas 47–7–112–2; Kumble 45–9–140–1; Crowe 20–2–74–0; Maddy 6–1–21–0.

Umpires: N. G. Cowley and A. G. T. Whitehead
(J. F. Steele deputised for Whitehead on the 3rd day).

At Taunton, September 1, 2, 3, 4. LEICESTERSHIRE drew with SOMERSET.

LEICESTERSHIRE v KENT

At Leicester, September 13, 14, 15, 16. Drawn. Leicestershire 6 pts, Kent 5 pts. Toss: Kent. Championship debut: W. F. Stelling.

With Leicestershire assured of fourth place, all eyes were on Kent as they sought the bonus point that would guarantee survival in Division One. It eventually arrived in the 84th over of the first – and only – day. Former Leicestershire wicket-keeper Nixon pulled South African all-rounder (and Dutch-passport holder) Billy Stelling to the mid-wicket boundary and took Kent to 200. Essentially, that was it, for the next three days were washed out. Stelling, though, had spent his single day of Championship cricket in 2000 to good effect. After a succession of injuries and indifferent form, the 31-year-old had been advised to look for another club for 2001. But his splendid away-swing bowling brought him a career-best five for 49 in 25 overs, and an invitation from Leicestershire manager Jack Birkenshaw to remain.

Close of play: First day, Kent 228-8 (Nixon 29*, Scott 2*); Second day, No play; Third day, No play.

Kent

D. P. Fulton c Wells b Ormond	16	M. J. Saggers c Burns b Stelling	6
J. B. Hockley c Burns b Ormond	2	D. A. Scott not out	2
R. Dravid c Burns b Stelling	77		
E. T. Smith c Maddy b Stelling	40	B 4, l-b 3, w 2, n-b 6	15
M. J. Walker c Burns b Wells	19		
*M. A. Ealham c Maddy b Stelling	19	1/13 2/42 3/114	(8 wkts) 228
†P. A. Nixon not out	29	4/156 5/181 6/188	
M. J. McCague c Burns b Stelling	3	7/194 8/210	

D. D. Masters did not bat.

Bonus points – Kent 1, Leicestershire 2.

Bowling: Ormond 27–2–91–2; DeFreitas 20–4–46–0; Wells 16–5–28–1; Stelling 25–8–49–5; Maddy 4–1–7–0.

Leicestershire

*V. J. Wells, D. L. Maddy, I. J. Sutcliffe, B. F. Smith, A. Habib, D. I. Stevens, W. F. Stelling, P. A. J. DeFreitas, †N. D. Burns, C. D. Crowe and J. Ormond.

Umpires: R. Palmer and A. G. T. Whitehead.

MIDDLESEX

Andy Strauss

President: R. Gerard
Chairman: P. H. Edmonds
Chairman, Cricket Committee: A. J. T. Miller
Secretary: V. J. Codrington
Captain: 2000 – J. L. Langer
          2001 – A. R. C. Fraser
Director of Coaching: 2000 – M. W. Gatting
Club Coach: 2000 – I. J. Gould
          2001 – J. E. Emburey
Scorer: M. J. Smith

The harsh realities of modern county cricket finally caught up with Middlesex after difficulties on and off the field in 2000. It was a sorry enough time when the end of August brought the unexpected departure of two icons, Mike Gatting and Ian Gould. But the loss of Mark Ramprakash in the New Year, to join traditional rivals Surrey, cut much deeper. He was a recent captain, had just enjoyed a benefit year and, in its hour of need, was turning his back on the club to pursue his ambition for England honours. This, he claimed, required first-division cricket – something he had not experienced with Middlesex in either the Championship or the League. Gatting and Gould, as director of coaching and club coach respectively, had paid the price for the county winning nothing since the 1993 Championship, and for never looking as if they would end that barren run over the past three seasons. Both first played for Middlesex in 1975 and were so strongly identified with the county that it was hard to imagine either having a role there any more.

Yet the main reason for Middlesex's failings – lack of experience resulting from short-sighted selection policies – dates back to long before Gatting and Gould became responsible for coaching and selection. Think of players who have been let go over the years: Graham Rose, Aftab Habib, Umer Rashid, Colin Metson, Rajesh Maru, Kevan James, Dean Headley and now, both to Somerset, Keith Dutch and Richard Johnson. Dutch made his debut as John Emburey's understudy in 1993, but since Emburey's departure in 1995 he had played in only 19 Championship games – hardly a reasonable chance to show what he could do. Richard Johnson, fit again after his struggles with injury, bowled as well in 2000 as in 1998 and picked up 50 Championship wickets. Others released were Chris Batt and David Goodchild, whose appearances were limited by injury, and Alex Edwards, signed from Sussex less than a year earlier. It was no secret that more players would have gone had their contracts not had another year to run.

Justin Langer's first full year as captain was something of a curate's egg, and not helped by the weather. The Benson and Hedges Cup was into its final qualifying round before Middlesex could take the field. There was no lack of enthusiasm – at times there was an excess, and too many overthrows were given away. But there were occasions when the batting seemed to lack guidance. In a match that had to be won if Middlesex were to have any chance of promotion in the National League, David Alleyne played two injudicious shots in one over. He was out to the second, yet his captain, at the other end, had apparently said nothing to curb him. Langer batted too low in the order sometimes, as in the NatWest Trophy quarter-final defeat by Hampshire when four wickets were down before he faced a ball.

Andy Strauss, one of the few successes of the season, had eight different opening partners in first-class and limited-overs matches, and there were four other opening pairs not involving Strauss. Ben Hutton, who many thought might form a permanent partnership with him, as they had at school and university, was criticised by some committee members for not scoring enough runs. But it was hardly Hutton's fault: he never knew from one match to the next whether he would be selected, let alone where he would be in the order. He batted anywhere from Nos 1 to 7.

Only twice did the batting earn maximum bonus points; eight times it failed to manage more than one. There was too much reliance on Langer and Ramprakash, both of whom passed 1,000 runs, and it needed a double-hundred by the captain in the final game to prevent Middlesex finishing last in the Championship for the first time. Had they not salvaged the eight points deducted for a poor pitch at Southgate in July, that humiliation would have been a certainty. Langer was the country's second-highest scorer and set a demanding standard for his replacement, New Zealand captain Stephen Fleming, also a left-hander, to follow. Angus Fraser was appointed captain for 2001, while Emburey was given a second chance to establish his coaching career after an unsuccessful spell at Northamptonshire.

Though awarded his cap, Owais Shah was again a bitter disappointment. He passed 50 only three times, but not after early June, and was left out of the side for five of the last six matches, a terrible waste of what should be a marvellous talent. By contrast, the 21-year-old Irish international, Ed Joyce, seemed less likely to squander his talents. He played six games in August and September, appearing to have the right temperament and very much looking the part. Mike Roseberry rediscovered some form in mid-season, but too many players batted far below expectations.

Fraser was his usual, reliable, workhorse self, while Simon Cook and Aaron Laraman, of the younger bowlers, made most progress; with experience they should develop the consistency required. Philip Tufnell, voted Player of the Year, was leading wicket-taker, but Dutch's departure left the spin department thin. David Nash, another to be capped, had a goodish year behind the stumps, although Alleyne seemed to gain favour towards the end of the season and replaced him in limited-overs matches. As he demonstrated more than once, Alleyne has much to learn about the technique of wicket-keeping.

It was also a difficult year for the club financially after their landlord, MCC, unexpectedly ended the arrangement by which Middlesex traditionally derived income from gate receipts and advertising. This left them close to £200,000 light on income and resulted in acrimonious exchanges before cooler heads sat down to plan a more businesslike partnership. Middlesex are fortunate: they can count on a hard core of loyal support. But improvement on the field is essential. Even the staunchest of members were losing patience in 2000. – NORMAN de MESQUITA.

MIDDLESEX 2000

[*Bill Smith*]

Back row: K. P. Dutch, D. Alleyne, S. J. Cook. C. J. Batt, A. W. Laraman, R. B. Bryan, A. J. Strauss, J. W. M. Dalrymple. *Middle row:* M. W. Gatting (*director of coaching*), S. G. M. Shepard (*physiotherapist*), M. J. Smith (*first-team scorer*), T. A. Hunt, T. F. Bloomfield, B. L. Hutton, D. J. Goodchild, A. D. Edwards, M. J. Brown, J. K. Maunders, A. Jones (*Second Eleven scorer*), I. J. Gould (*club coach*), C. H. G. St George (*fitness adviser*). *Front row:* O. A. Shah, D. C. Nash, J. P. Hewitt, P. C. R. Tufnell, A. R. C. Fraser, J. L. Langer (*captain*), M. R. Ramprakash, M. A. Roseberry, R. L. Johnson, P. N. Weekes. *Insets:* E. C. Joyce, R. M. S. Weston.

MIDDLESEX RESULTS

All first-class matches – Played 17: Won 2, Lost 6, Drawn 9.

County Championship matches – Played 16: Won 2, Lost 6, Drawn 8.

PPP Healthcare County Championship, 8th in Division 2; NatWest Trophy, q-f;
Benson and Hedges Cup, 6th in South Group; Norwich Union National League, 4th in Division 2.

COUNTY CHAMPIONSHIP AVERAGES

BATTING

Cap		M	I	NO	R	HS	100s	50s	Avge	Ct/St
1990	M. R. Ramprakash‡.	13	21	4	1,088	120*	4	6	64.00	9
1998	J. L. Langer§	16	27	3	1,472	213*	5	7	61.33	25
	A. J. Strauss	16	28	2	862	111*	1	3	33.15	6
	E. C. Joyce	6	8	1	195	51	0	1	27.85	7
1990	M. A. Roseberry . . .	10	19	2	410	87	0	2	24.11	3
2000	O. A. Shah	11	19	0	446	76	0	3	23.47	7
	K. P. Dutch†	4	7	0	160	91	0	2	22.85	4
1995	R. L. Johnson	15	23	3	414	69	0	2	20.70	13
2000	D. C. Nash	16	24	2	445	75*	0	1	20.22	32/4
1993	P. N. Weekes	7	12	0	239	39	0	0	19.91	7
	R. M. S. Weston . . .	5	9	0	138	39	0	0	15.33	2
	S. J. Cook	6	10	0	145	43	0	0	14.50	2
1988	A. R. C. Fraser	15	22	6	227	30	0	0	14.18	4
	B. L. Hutton	9	14	2	157	55	0	1	13.08	8
1990	P. C. R. Tufnell	16	21	9	100	19	0	0	8.33	4
	T. F. Bloomfield . . .	9	8	2	16	4*	0	0	2.66	1

Also batted: C. J. Batt (2 matches) 21, 0, 6 (1 ct).

* *Signifies not out.* † *Born in Middlesex.* ‡ *ECB contract.* § *Overseas player.*

BOWLING

	O	M	R	W	BB	5W/i	Avge
K. P. Dutch	121.4	38	323	15	6-62	1	21.53
P. C. R. Tufnell	738.3	255	1,500	65	6-48	3	23.07
A. R. C. Fraser	474.3	150	1,111	48	6-64	1	23.14
S. J. Cook	115	36	281	10	4-13	0	28.10
R. L. Johnson	473	129	1,429	50	6-71	2	28.58
T. F. Bloomfield	192.3	31	751	18	4-46	0	41.72

Also bowled: C. J. Batt 41–11–146–4; B. L. Hutton 56.2–14–200–5; E. C. Joyce 5–1–24–0; J. L. Langer 6–1–35–1; M. R. Ramprakash 67–18–147–1; O. A. Shah 35–8–126–4; A. J. Strauss 1–0–13–0; P. N. Weekes 64.5–16–190–4.

COUNTY RECORDS

Highest score for:	331*	J. D. Robertson v Worcestershire at Worcester . . .	1949
Highest score against:	316*	J. B. Hobbs (Surrey) at Lord's	1926
Best bowling for:	10-40	G. O. B. Allen v Lancashire at Lord's	1929
Best bowling against:	9-38	R. C. Robertson-Glasgow (Somerset) at Lord's. . .	1924
Highest total for:	642-3 dec.	v Hampshire at Southampton	1923
Highest total against:	665	by West Indians at Lord's.	1939
Lowest total for:	20	v MCC at Lord's	1864
Lowest total against: {	31	by Gloucestershire at Bristol	1924
	31	by Glamorgan at Cardiff	1997

MIDDLESEX v NORTHAMPTONSHIRE

At Lord's, May 3, 4, 5, 6. Drawn. Middlesex 12 pts, Northamptonshire 8 pts. Toss: Northamptonshire.

Although unable to bowl Northamptonshire out a second time, Middlesex made an encouraging start to their Championship season by gaining maximum batting points, something that happened only twice in 1999. Ramprakash, accustoming himself to his new role as opener, hit three sixes and nine fours in his 93, adding 196 in 45 overs with Langer, his successor as captain. Langer, too, found the short Tavern boundary inviting, hit 17 fours in scoring 120, and was able to declare an hour after lunch on the second day. At 129 for five, Northamptonshire had much to do to avoid the follow-on: they managed it only with their last pair at the crease. Rollins, who reached 100 with a six off Fraser, tried to edge him to slip next ball, provided the bulk of their resistance in a century stand with Penberthy. A maiden hundred from Strauss enabled Langer to set a target of 391 in 83 overs. Despite Rollins and Hayden sending Northamptonshire off with 152 in 42, it always appeared beyond them. By the time Rollins was caught at mid-off, trying to raise his second century of the match, both sides were ready to settle for the draw.

Close of play: First day, Middlesex 282-3 (Shah 18*, Weston 9*); Second day, Northamptonshire 132-5 (Rollins 57*, Penberthy 0*); Third day, Middlesex 168-2 (Strauss 84*, Weston 33*).

Middlesex

A. J. Strauss c Cousins	28	– not out	111
M. R. Ramprakash b Logan	93	– c Ripley b Swann	38
*J. L. Langer b Cousins	120	– (5) not out	37
O. A. Shah b Logan	76	– (3) st Ripley b Swann	7
R. M. S. Weston lbw b Cousins	12	– (4) lbw b Penberthy	39
P. N. Weekes c Ripley b Cousins	39		
†D. C. Nash c Hayden b Cousins	17		
R. L. Johnson st Ripley b Swann	8		
A. R. C. Fraser not out	3		
L-b 4, w 21, n-b 6	31	B 2, l-b 7, w 2	11

1/41 2/237 3/261 4/297   (8 wkts dec.) 427   1/102 2/122 3/178   (3 wkts dec.) 243
5/373 6/407 7/423 8/427

T. F. Bloomfield and P. C. R. Tufnell did not bat.

Bonus points – Middlesex 5, Northamptonshire 2.

Bowling: First Innings—Malcolm 30–8–73–0; Cousins 36–8–123–5; Logan 27.3–6–100–2; Penberthy 7–2–25–0; Hayden 6–1–26–0; Swann 20–1–76–1. *Second Innings*—Malcolm 7–2–31–0; Cousins 13–4–41–0; Logan 15–2–65–0; Swann 12–0–72–2; Penberthy 5–1–25–1.

Northamptonshire

*M. L. Hayden lbw b Fraser	20	– (2) b Johnson	93
A. S. Rollins c Langer b Fraser	100	– (1) c Johnson b Bloomfield	96
M. B. Loye lbw b Bloomfield	13	– retired hurt	0
D. J. Sales c Weekes b Johnson	25	– lbw b Tufnell	3
R. J. Warren b Tufnell	13	– not out	32
D. M. Cousins lbw b Tufnell	0		
A. L. Penberthy c Weekes b Tufnell	59		
G. P. Swann c Weston b Fraser	19		
†D. Ripley c Nash b Fraser	6		
R. J. Logan not out	2		
D. E. Malcolm c Bloomfield b Johnson	3		
B 4, l-b 6, w 2, n-b 8	20	B 1, l-b 8, n-b 4	13

1/28 2/49 3/101 4/129 5/129   280   1/152 2/164 3/237   (3 wkts) 237
6/237 7/250 8/273 9/274

Bonus points – Northamptonshire 2, Middlesex 3.

In the second innings Loye retired hurt at 152.

Bowling: *First Innings*—Fraser 28–13–49–4; Johnson 23.2–4–75–2; Bloomfield 17–2–62–1; Tufnell 27–10–49–3; Shah 2–0–7–0; Weekes 12–1–19–0; Ramprakash 4–1–9–0. *Second Innings*—Fraser 10–3–23–0; Johnson 9–2–23–1; Bloomfield 11.1–3–42–1; Weekes 18–5–60–0; Tufnell 24–4–67–1; Ramprakash 5–0–13–0.

Umpires: M. J. Kitchen and R. A. White.

At Worcester, May 11, 12, 13. MIDDLESEX lost to WORCESTERSHIRE by seven wickets.

At Cambridge, May 16, 17, 18. MIDDLESEX drew with CAMBRIDGE UNIVERSITY.

At Northampton, May 24, 25, 26, 27. MIDDLESEX drew with NORTHAMPTONSHIRE.

MIDDLESEX v GLOUCESTERSHIRE

At Lord's, May 31, June 1, 2, 3. Gloucestershire won by 85 runs. Gloucestershire 17 pts, Middlesex 4 pts. Toss: Middlesex. First-class debut: C. G. Taylor.

Chris Taylor became the first batsman to hit a Championship hundred at Lord's on his first-class debut. The only two debutants who had scored centuries at Lord's previously were both playing for MCC, before the First World War: Cecil Payne against Derbyshire in 1905 and the Hon. Lionel Tennyson against Oxford in 1913. Coming to the wicket in the 12th over, with Gloucestershire already 29 for four, Taylor demonstrated sound technique and mature temperament in his 184-ball 104, out of 191 runs added in 59 overs. He hit 14 boundaries, as well as two all-run fours, and in his second innings, when Gloucestershire strengthened their position, he swept Tufnell for six. As for Middlesex, all the old failings returned. Catches were dropped and, when they batted, only Langer reached 40 in either innings. Needing 298 for their first Championship win of the season, they subsided from a promising 133 for two to 212 all out, the last six wickets falling for 39 in 13 overs. Alleyne led his side off the field with his career-best return of six for 49 and Gloucestershire's first Championship win to celebrate.

Close of play: First day, Middlesex 45-1 (Hutton 11*, Langer 25*); Second day, Gloucestershire 20-0 (Hancock 12*, Cunliffe 7*); Third day, Middlesex 39-0 (Strauss 29*, Hutton 9*).

Gloucestershire

R. J. Cunliffe b Fraser	5	– (2) b Fraser	7
T. H. C. Hancock b Fraser	0	– (1) b Johnson	23
M. G. N. Windows c Nash b Johnson	3	– c Strauss b Shah	54
K. J. Barnett c Nash b Johnson	18	– c Strauss b Fraser	82
*M. W. Alleyne c Langer b Tufnell	33	– c Nash b Johnson	4
C. G. Taylor b Shah	104	– b Bloomfield	25
†R. C. Russell lbw b Johnson	15	– c Langer b Fraser	1
J. N. Snape c and b Johnson	52	– c Shah b Johnson	12
J. M. M. Averis c Roseberry b Tufnell	4	– c Langer b Johnson	10
J. Lewis b Johnson	5	– c Langer b Bloomfield	16
A. M. Smith not out	0	– not out	1
L-b 6, w 6, n-b 8	20	L-b 5, n-b 2	7

1/3 2/8 3/8 4/29 5/112   259   1/20 2/46 3/112 4/132 5/195   242
6/161 7/220 8/250 9/256   6/197 7/209 8/217 9/236

Bonus points – Gloucestershire 2, Middlesex 3.

Bowling: *First Innings*—Fraser 17–2–50–2; Johnson 23.4–9–83–5; Bloomfield 13–4–47–0; Hutton 3–0–17–0; Tufnell 23–9–35–2; Shah 6–1–21–1. *Second Innings*—Johnson 24–5–66–4; Fraser 21–10–49–3; Bloomfield 9.4–1–61–2; Tufnell 24–8–50–0; Shah 2–0–11–1.

Middlesex

A. J. Strauss c Russell b Smith	0	– c Cunliffe b Lewis	36
B. L. Hutton lbw b Smith	11	– c Russell b Smith	13
*J. L. Langer c Alleyne b Smith	41	– c Russell b Alleyne	49
O. A. Shah c Cunliffe b Alleyne	30	– run out	33
R. M. S. Weston c Cunliffe b Hancock	32	– b Alleyne	19
M. A. Roseberry c Russell b Smith	26	– b Smith	13
†D. C. Nash lbw b Lewis	14	– lbw b Alleyne	2
R. L. Johnson b Smith	13	– c Barnett b Alleyne	2
A. R. C. Fraser c Barnett b Lewis	8	– c Barnett b Alleyne	9
P. C. R. Tufnell not out	8	– c Averis b Alleyne	10
T. F. Bloomfield (did not bat)	–	– not out	4
L-b 5, w 2, n-b 14	21	L-b 6, n-b 16	22

1/0 2/57 3/62 4/116 5/131   (9 wkts dec.) 204   1/51 2/57 3/133 4/154 5/173   212
6/173 7/173 8/186 9/204   6/178 7/186 8/187 9/203

Bonus points – Middlesex 1, Gloucestershire 3.

Bowling: *First Innings*—Smith 21–7–52–5; Lewis 22.2–7–51–2; Averis 16–5–33–0; Alleyne 13–1–51–1; Hancock 7–4–12–1. *Second Innings*—Smith 15–2–40–2; Lewis 22–6–45–1; Averis 14–1–67–0; Snape 2–0–5–0; Alleyne 20.5–6–49–6.

Umpires: B. Leadbeater and A. G. T. Whitehead.

At Horsham, June 7, 8, 9, 10. MIDDLESEX drew with SUSSEX.

MIDDLESEX v NOTTINGHAMSHIRE

At Lord's, June 14, 15, 16, 17. Nottinghamshire won by 169 runs. Nottinghamshire 17 pts, Middlesex 3 pts. Toss: Nottinghamshire.

Without a Championship win since beating Middlesex the previous August, Nottinghamshire were rewarded for playing the more purposeful cricket. The loss of 22 overs to bad light on the first day – when Tufnell took his 900th first-class wicket – meant their first innings extended until an hour before lunch on the second, but all-too-familiar, inadequate Middlesex batting helped them make up lost time. Franks took three wickets in 15 balls, reducing Middlesex to 21 for three by the seventh over; as usual, Langer was the one bright spot. When four short of his century, he was caught at slip as Franks captured four of the last five wickets to register career-best figures of seven for 56. Afzaal's second hundred in successive games occupied five and a half hours, and allowed Gallian to declare and set Middlesex an unlikely target of 393 in four sessions. It looked even more unlikely when Shah's lack of discretion had him caught at long leg in the third over of the final morning. Langer did reach three figures this time, hitting 13 fours and two sixes, but once again his was a lone hand.

Close of play: First day, Nottinghamshire 218-6 (Gallian 28*, Read 13*); Second day, Nottinghamshire 67-3 (Afzaal 13*, Gallian 7*); Third day, Middlesex 67-2 (Shah 31*, Weekes 16*).

Nottinghamshire

D. J. Bicknell b Johnson	11	– c Weekes b Batt	34
G. E. Welton c Johnson b Tufnell	36	– run out	6
J. E. Morris lbw b Batt	67	– b Fraser	5
U. Afzaal c Nash b Tufnell	28	– b Johnson	127
*J. E. R. Gallian b Langer b Tufnell	28	– c Langer b Tufnell	16
C. M. Tolley c Weston b Tufnell	12	– c and b Batt	34
P. J. Franks lbw b Fraser	5		
†C. M. W. Read c Strauss b Johnson	45	– (7) not out	56
A. J. Harris b Fraser	6		
M. N. Bowen c Weekes b Fraser	7		
R. D. Stemp not out	2		
B 5, l-b 7, n-b 6	18	L-b 15	15

1/35 2/74 3/134 4/158 5/177   265   1/25 2/30 3/56   (6 wkts dec.) 293
6/202 7/222 8/247 9/263   4/87 5/182 6/293

Bonus points – Nottinghamshire 2, Middlesex 3.

Bowling: *First Innings*—Fraser 22.2–6–51–3; Johnson 26–6–89–2; Batt 13–5–53–1; Tufnell 36–12–56–4; Shah 4–3–4–0; Weekes 1–1–0–0. *Second Innings*—Johnson 22–6–63–1; Fraser 18–3–65–1; Batt 16–3–49–2; Tufnell 31–12–52–1; Weekes 8–1–28–0; Shah 6–2–21–0.

Middlesex

R. M. S. Weston lbw b Franks	4	– (2) c Gallian b Harris	0
A. J. Strauss c Read b Franks	6	– (1) c Tolley b Stemp	10
*J. L. Langer c Gallian b Franks	96	– (5) c Read b Harris	104
O. A. Shah lbw b Franks	0	– (3) c Harris b Franks	31
P. N. Weekes c Read b Stemp	27	– (4) c and b Stemp	36
M. A. Roseberry c Welton b Stemp	0	– b Stemp	3
†D. C. Nash c Gallian b Franks	4	– c Gallian b Bowen	9
R. L. Johnson b Franks	0	– b Harris	9
A. R. C. Fraser c Morris b Stemp	16	– not out	0
C. J. Batt c Read b Franks	0	– c Bowen b Harris	6
P. C. R. Tufnell not out	0	– c Morris b Harris	0
L-b 1, w 2, n-b 10	13	L-b 3, n-b 12	15

1/4 2/21 3/21 4/108 5/108   166   1/0 2/25 3/69 4/131 5/147   223
6/123 7/133 8/152 9/154   6/186 7/206 8/217 9/223

Bonus points – Nottinghamshire 3.

Bowling: *First Innings*—Franks 17–3–56–7; Harris 9–2–36–0; Tolley 2–1–3–0; Stemp 20.4–5–58–3; Bowen 5–1–12–0. *Second Innings*—Franks 18–5–45–1; Harris 20.4–8–34–5; Stemp 39–10–103–3; Bowen 7–2–11–1; Afzaal 7–2–24–0; Tolley 3–1–3–0.

Umpires: J. W. Lloyds and R. A. White.

At Chelmsford, June 28, 29, 30. MIDDLESEX beat ESSEX by 237 runs.

MIDDLESEX v WORCESTERSHIRE

At Southgate, July 7, 8, 9, 10. Drawn. Middlesex 10 pts, Worcestershire 7 pts. Toss: Middlesex.
With ten stoppages for rain or bad light, the hardest-worked men were the groundstaff, and it was no surprise when rain had the last word soon after lunch on the last day. The only uninterrupted day was the first, during which Middlesex, buoyed by their first win of the season at Chelmsford, gained more than one batting point for only the third time in eight matches. Strauss, frustrated

by defensive bowling and field placing, gave away a deserved century when he swept needlessly at Rawnsley's left-arm spin, which claimed five Championship wickets for the first time. However, Ramprakash, abandoning the opening experiment, had Rawnsley's measure when he raced from 86 to 99 in the last over of the first day; he duly completed his first hundred of the season next morning. It was then a question of whether Worcestershire would avoid the follow-on between the stoppages. They did not quite manage it, but there was too little time spared by the weather for Middlesex to force a win.

Close of play: First day, Middlesex 288-8 (Ramprakash 99*, Tufnell 9*); Second day, Worcestershire 111-8 (Rhodes 22*, McGrath 2*); Third day, Worcestershire 15-1 (Wilson 5*, Pollard 8*).

Middlesex

A. J. Strauss c Lampitt b Rawnsley	90
†D. C. Nash lbw b Lampitt	18
*J. L. Langer c Kadeer Ali b Rawnsley .	23
M. R. Ramprakash b Lampitt	101
O. A. Shah lbw b Kabir Ali	8
P. N. Weekes b Rawnsley	3
K. P. Dutch b Rawnsley	1
A. R. C. Fraser lbw b McGrath	9

R. L. Johnson c Wilson b Rawnsley	4
P. C. R. Tufnell c Leatherdale b McGrath	19
T. F. Bloomfield not out	0
B 1, l-b 2, n-b 24	27

1/36 2/96 3/181 4/222 5/227　　　　303
6/229 7/250 8/261 9/303

Bonus points – Middlesex 3, Worcestershire 3.

Bowling: McGrath 23.2–8–43–2; Kabir Ali 21–5–52–1; Lampitt 19–5–58–2; Rawnsley 39–8–125–5; Leatherdale 6–0–22–0.

Worcestershire

W. P. C. Weston c Shah b Fraser	0	– (2) lbw b Bloomfield	0
E. J. Wilson lbw b Johnson	0	– (1) c and b Tufnell	11
P. R. Pollard c Shah b Dutch	12	– c Johnson b Dutch	22
D. A. Leatherdale c Ramprakash b Tufnell	20	– b Tufnell	12
R. C. Driver c and b Johnson	12	– not out	22
Kadeer Ali b Johnson	8	– c Ramprakash b Tufnell	0
*†S. J. Rhodes not out	33	– not out	16
S. R. Lampitt lbw b Tufnell	4		
M. J. Rawnsley b Tufnell	18		
G. D. McGrath c and b Tufnell	5		
Kabir Ali c Shah b Dutch	12		
B 3, l-b 4, n-b 10	17	L-b 4, n-b 8	12

1/0 2/0 3/33 4/37 5/54　　　　　　141　　1/0 2/34 3/48　　　　(5 wkts) 95
6/59 7/84 8/108 9/120　　　　　　　　　　4/61 5/66

Bonus points – Middlesex 3.

Bowling: *First Innings*—Fraser 9–6–8–1; Johnson 21–10–39–3; Bloomfield 3–0–15–0; Tufnell 33–9–48–4; Dutch 17.1–8–24–2. *Second Innings*—Fraser 4–2–5–0; Bloomfield 3–0–7–1; Tufnell 15–3–39–3; Dutch 10–5–15–1; Johnson 9–6–8–0; Weekes 8–4–17–0.

Umpires: N. G. Cowley and A. G. T. Whitehead.

MIDDLESEX v GLAMORGAN

At Southgate, July 12, 13, 14, 15. Glamorgan won by two wickets. Glamorgan 16 pts, Middlesex 3 pts. Toss: Middlesex.

The presence of pitch liaison officer Mike Denness was a notable distraction on the first day. Once 17 wickets had fallen, it was inevitable that the pitch would be deemed "poor" and Middlesex have eight points deducted. Yet, as Glamorgan scored 307 in the fourth innings to win, it seemed a hasty decision. When the ECB's appeal panel took into account six days' rain-affected play at

Southgate in the previous week, which had hampered preparation and covering, Middlesex's appeal was upheld. They had expressed reservations about the pitch before the match and, in all fairness, the groundsman could not be held responsible for much of the batting. Only Ramprakash and Dale revealed the patience and technique to stay longer than an hour on the opening day. When Glamorgan resumed next afternoon, overnight rain having ruled out the morning, the pitch played much more easily and they took a lead of 68. Although Dale's spell of three for one in 28 balls exposed the Middlesex middle order, they made a better fist of their second innings to set a testing target. That Glamorgan achieved it, in the last hour of an enthralling fourth day, owed much to Elliott, who scored 127 out of 231, with 13 fours and three sixes – one off Dutch and two in the Tufnell over that raised his second Championship century.

Close of play: First day, Glamorgan 144-7 (Dale 42*, Thomas 12*); Second day, Middlesex 130-1 (Strauss 56*, Langer 56*); Third day, Glamorgan 69-0 (James 27*, Elliott 38*).

Middlesex

A. J. Strauss lbw b Wharf	3	– lbw b Dale	73
†D. C. Nash run out	13	– (5) b Dale	1
*J. L. Langer b Thomas	7	– lbw b Thomas	61
M. R. Ramprakash lbw b Wharf	83	– b Dale	40
O. A. Shah lbw b Dale	23	– (6) c James b Cosker	40
P. N. Weekes c Shaw b Dale	2	– (7) c Cosker b Wharf	32
B. L. Hutton lbw b Thomas	11	– (2) b Thomas	4
K. P. Dutch lbw b Thomas	1	– lbw b Cosker	8
A. R. C. Fraser c Shaw b Thomas	1	– c Shaw b Dale	30
R. L. Johnson c Powell b Wharf	10	– not out	46
P. C. R. Tufnell not out	0	– c Elliott b Dale	9
B 2, l-b 2, w 2, n-b 4	10	B 5, l-b 9, n-b 16	30

1/5 2/23 3/25 4/55 5/67   164   1/37 2/136 3/182 4/198 5/209   374
6/99 7/114 8/134 9/159   6/250 7/270 8/284 9/358

Bonus points – Glamorgan 3.

Bowling: *First Innings*—Thomas 19–3–55–4; Wharf 17.1–7–36–3; Dale 14–2–37–2; Cosker 2–1–10–0; Parkin 5–1–22–0. *Second Innings*—Thomas 23–3–99–2; Parkin 18–3–68–0; Wharf 21–3–80–1; Dale 22.4–12–25–5; Cosker 27–8–83–2; Newell 1–0–5–0.

Glamorgan

M. T. G. Elliott c Nash b Fraser	17	– (2) st Nash b Weekes	127
*S. P. James lbw b Johnson	3	– (1) c Langer b Tufnell	31
M. J. Powell b Johnson	0	– lbw b Weekes	26
A. W. Evans lbw b Johnson	10	– lbw b Shah	17
A. Dale lbw b Hutton	81	– c and b Dutch	23
K. Newell lbw b Fraser	28	– lbw b Fraser	26
†A. D. Shaw lbw b Dutch	23	– c Ramprakash b Fraser	14
A. G. Wharf lbw b Tufnell	1	– c Johnson b Fraser	5
S. D. Thomas c Hutton b Weekes	30	– not out	11
D. A. Cosker c Nash b Hutton	13	– not out	1
O. T. Parkin not out	5		
B 4, l-b 9, w 2, n-b 6	21	B 10, l-b 8, n-b 8	26

1/6 2/14 3/30 4/30 5/73   232   1/73 2/147 3/209   (8 wkts) 307
6/110 7/111 8/173 9/218   4/231 5/257 6/276
                                                7/286 8/306

Bonus points – Glamorgan 1, Middlesex 3.

Bowling: *First Innings*—Fraser 19–3–46–2; Johnson 21–3–83–3; Dutch 14–3–31–1; Tufnell 16–5–40–1; Hutton 5.2–3–9–2; Weekes 2–1–10–1. *Second Innings*—Johnson 17–5–50–0; Fraser 22–4–47–3; Tufnell 32–10–69–1; Dutch 16–5–48–1; Hutton 10–5–27–0; Weekes 12–3–32–2; Shah 4–1–16–1.

Umpires: B. Dudleston and R. Julian.

MIDDLESEX v SUSSEX

At Southgate, July 28, 29, 30, 31. Sussex won by seven wickets. Sussex 16 pts, Middlesex 4 pts. Toss: Middlesex.

Ramprakash hit two hundreds in a match for the fourth time, his 49th and 50th in first-class cricket, and took his aggregate in five innings at Southgate to 446. In the end, though, he was outshone by Bevan, whose magnificent 173 not out carried his side to victory; it also made him the first batsman to 1,000 first-class runs for the season, including 694, with four centuries, in his last five innings. He faced 193 balls and hit three sixes and 21 fours. With four sessions to get 268, and the pitch offering minimum help to a Middlesex attack weakened by Johnson's knee injury (Langer ran for him as he helped Ramprakash add 104 for the eighth wicket), Sussex had no need to hurry. Bevan and night-watchman Kirtley tipped the scales on the final morning to reach their target shortly after lunch. They put on 166 together, of which Kirtley's share was 26. With match figures of nine for 115, including his third "five" in three games, he had already played his part in Sussex's third Championship win, which briefly made them divisional leaders; Middlesex remained bottom.

Close of play: First day, Sussex 84-2 (Bevan 17*, Kirtley 5*); Second day, Middlesex 125-3 (Ramprakash 27*, Shah 5*); Third day, Sussex 118-3 (Bevan 57*, Kirtley 1*).

Middlesex

A. J. Strauss c Wilton b Martin-Jenkins	39	– lbw b Kirtley		3
M. A. Roseberry c Wilton b Kirtley	4	– c Bates b Rashid		28
*J. L. Langer lbw b Kirtley	0	– c Lewry b Rashid		48
M. R. Ramprakash not out	110	– c Cottey b Kirtley		112
O. A. Shah b Martin-Jenkins	2	– c and b Kirtley		11
†D. C. Nash c Montgomerie b Adams	15	– c Wilton b Kirtley		5
K. P. Dutch c Wilton b Martin-Jenkins	3	– c Wilton b Rashid		1
S. J. Cook lbw b Kirtley	1	– c Montgomerie b Rashid		4
A. R. C. Fraser c Montgomerie b Kirtley	1	– (10) not out		2
R. L. Johnson b Lewry	14	– (9) c Wilton b Lewry		52
P. C. R. Tufnell c Montgomerie b Kirtley	8	– c Montgomerie b Lewry		1
B 14, l-b 2, n-b 14	30	L-b 12, n-b 4		16

1/12 2/26 3/74 4/78 5/127   227   1/5 2/65 3/98 4/145 5/161   283
6/150 7/155 8/169 9/202   6/164 7/176 8/280 9/282

Bonus points – Middlesex 1, Sussex 3.

Bowling: *First Innings*—Lewry 13–1–59–1; Kirtley 15.5–5–50–5; Martin-Jenkins 16–2–55–3; Adams 5–1–17–1; Rashid 3–1–7–0; Bevan 5–0–23–0. *Second Innings*—Lewry 23.1–6–45–2; Kirtley 29–10–65–4; Rashid 35–8–80–4; Martin-Jenkins 2–0–14–0; Bates 7–1–28–0; Adams 1–0–6–0; Bevan 7–0–33–0.

Sussex

R. R. Montgomerie c Langer b Tufnell	30	– c Nash b Cook		7
M. T. E. Peirce c Dutch b Cook	22	– c Ramprakash b Tufnell		25
M. G. Bevan st Nash b Tufnell	30	– not out		173
R. J. Kirtley c Langer b Tufnell	21	– (5) not out		26
*C. J. Adams st Nash b Tufnell	0	– (4) c Nash b Tufnell		20
P. A. Cottey c sub b Dutch	42			
R. S. C. Martin-Jenkins lbw b Fraser	44			
U. B. A. Rashid c Fraser b Dutch	6			
J. J. Bates lbw b Dutch	15			
†N. J. Wilton not out	2			
J. D. Lewry b Cook	1			
L-b 8, w 2, n-b 20	30	B 4, l-b 3, n-b 12		19

1/42 2/76 3/99 4/103 5/152   243   1/11 2/53 3/104   (3 wkts) 270
6/176 7/192 8/234 9/240

Bonus points – Sussex 1, Middlesex 3.

Bowling: *First Innings*—Fraser 13–6–39–1; Johnson 12–2–37–0; Tufnell 40–16–88–4; Cook 13.1–7–16–2; Dutch 18–3–40–3; Shah 5–1–15–0. *Second Innings*—Fraser 19–5–58–0; Cook 12–1–39–1; Tufnell 29–8–75–2; Dutch 14.3–3–75–0; Ramprakash 3–0–16–0.

Umpires: M. R. Benson and V. A. Holder.

MIDDLESEX v ESSEX

At Lord's, August 2, 3, 4, 5. Drawn. Middlesex 9 pts, Essex 8 pts. Toss: Essex.

Another rain-affected match and, on the second day, another instance of the Lord's groundstaff failing to appear when the rain stopped – until the umpires roused them out of their hut to prepare for a resumption. In all, 71 overs were lost during the first two days and, even in a relatively low-scoring game, there was not enough time to achieve a positive result. Essex, left what became 74 overs in which to score 262, were way off the pace long before Irani and Cowan batted through the last hour and a half to secure the draw. Cook's three wickets in 11 balls, the basis for career-best figures, had opened up the game for Middlesex after Tufnell, with nine for 93 in the match, prised out the top three. With the exception of Ramprakash, in a class of his own, Hutton and Irani, the batting was never particularly distinguished.

Close of play: First day, Middlesex 214-5 (Nash 22*, Hutton 21*); Second day, Essex 64-1 (Grayson 34*, Flanagan 7*); Third day, Middlesex 93-3 (Ramprakash 39*, Cook 17*)

Middlesex

A. J. Strauss b McGarry	45	– c Irani b Such	29
M. A. Roseberry c D. R. Law b Cowan	0	– (10) lbw b D. R. Law	13
*J. L. Langer b Cowan	5	– lbw b Cowan	0
M. R. Ramprakash c Hyam b Cowan	84	– b Cowan	49
E. C. Joyce run out	10	– (6) st Hyam b Grayson	9
†D. C. Nash b Grayson	22	– (2) lbw b Irani	1
B. L. Hutton b D. R. Law	55	– run out	8
S. J. Cook c Hyam b Cowan	14	– (5) b Grayson	24
A. R. C. Fraser run out	4	– (8) not out	22
T. F. Bloomfield c Cowan b Irani	2		
P. C. R. Tufnell not out	17	– (9) run out	3
B 3, l-b 5, n-b 21	29	L-b 8, w 4, n-b 4	16

1/1 2/21 3/116 4/157 5/166 287   1/2 2/9 3/59 (9 wkts dec.) 174
6/224 7/260 8/267 9/268   4/111 5/119 6/134
                              7/135 8/140 9/174

Bonus points – Middlesex 2, Essex 3.

Bowling: *First Innings*—Cowan 28–7–70–4; Irani 17–1–59–1; D. R. Law 16–5–50–1; McGarry 12–2–48–1; Such 22–10–24–0; Grayson 13–3–28–1. *Second Innings*—Cowan 18–5–55–2; Irani 5–3–5–1; Such 9–1–29–1; D. R. Law 10.3–1–39–1; Grayson 14–1–38–2.

Essex

P. J. Prichard c Ramprakash b Fraser	14	– lbw b Tufnell	26
A. P. Grayson c Langer b Tufnell	36	– c Cook b Tufnell	23
I. N. Flanagan c Nash b Tufnell	21	– (4) c Nash b Cook	13
S. G. Law c Fraser b Tufnell	2	– (3) c Ramprakash b Tufnell	26
*R. C. Irani c Nash b Tufnell	76	– not out	25
S. D. Peters c Hutton b Fraser	9	– c Joyce b Cook	4
†B. J. Hyam c Nash b Fraser	0	– lbw b Cook	0
D. R. Law b Hutton	13	– lbw b Cook	0
A. P. Cowan c and b Tufnell	1	– not out	5
P. M. Such c Hutton b Tufnell	1		
A. C. McGarry not out	0		
L-b 5, w 2, n-b 20	27	B 5, l-b 1, n-b 2	8

1/22 2/68 3/80 4/97 5/138   200   1/43 2/64 3/94   (7 wkts) 130
6/138 7/180 8/181 9/191   4/94 5/108 6/110 7/110

Bonus points – Essex 1, Middlesex 3.

Bowling: *First Innings*—Fraser 24–11–45–3; Bloomfield 18–4–56–0; Tufnell 35.2–19–48–6; Cook 10–2–25–0; Ramprakash 4–2–5–0; Hutton 6–0–16–1. *Second Innings*—Fraser 13–3–28–0; Bloomfield 11.4–1–37–0; Tufnell 31–14–45–3; Cook 14–9–13–4; Ramprakash 4–3–1–0.

Umpires: J. H. Hampshire and G. Sharp.

At Nottingham, August 9, 10, 11. MIDDLESEX beat NOTTINGHAMSHIRE by ten wickets.

At Birmingham, August 17, 18, 19, 20. MIDDLESEX drew with WARWICKSHIRE.

At Bristol, August 21, 22, 23, 24. MIDDLESEX lost to GLOUCESTERSHIRE by seven wickets.

MIDDLESEX v WARWICKSHIRE

At Lord's, September 5, 6, 7, 8. Drawn. Middlesex 11 pts, Warwickshire 10 pts. Toss: Warwickshire. Championship debut: C. E. Dagnall.

Almost predictably in a summer bedevilled by rain, the final day of Middlesex's home Championship season was washed out. On the first day, 43 overs were lost. Warwickshire, needful of bonus points to sustain their promotion prospects, took full advantage of some poor bowling, Fraser apart, to run up the highest total conceded by Middlesex in 2000. Powell established the innings with a stylish 92, then Hemp made his first hundred of the year, hitting 18 fours in 216 balls. Middlesex began their reply after tea on the second day, but the fun came on the third, when Langer struck Donald for seven of the ten fours in his 27-ball fifty. Once he played on to Brown for 70, the entertainment was over. Joyce confirmed previous favourable impressions with a solid 45, and Ramprakash was 12 short of a century when Langer declared with a fourth batting point in the bag. That set the game up for a good finish; the weather ruled it out.

Close of play: First day, Warwickshire 228-4 (Hemp 16*, Brown 28*); Second day, Middlesex 82-0 (Strauss 40*, Roseberry 23*); Third day, Warwickshire 109-1 (Wagh 74*, Ostler 9*).

Warwickshire

M. J. Powell c Joyce b Hutton	92		
M. A. Wagh c Ramprakash b Bloomfield	14	– not out	74
D. P. Ostler c Nash b Johnson	52	– not out	9
D. L. Hemp c Joyce b Fraser	129		
A. Singh c Langer b Johnson	0		
D. R. Brown c Hutton b Fraser	36		
*N. M. K. Smith c Langer b Ramprakash	22		
†K. J. Piper c Johnson b Bloomfield	20	– (1) lbw b Langer	17
A. A. Donald c Nash b Tufnell	8		
C. E. Dagnall not out	5		
A. Richardson c Joyce b Tufnell	0		
B 4, l-b 12, w 10, n-b 12	38	L-b 5, w 2, n-b 2	9

1/48 2/162 3/184 4/185 5/240   416   1/90   (1 wkt) 109
6/324 7/379 8/409 9/411

Bonus points – Warwickshire 5, Middlesex 3.

Bowling: *First Innings*—Fraser 32–13–48–2; Johnson 24–1–107–2; Bloomfield 21–0–117–2; Tufnell 22.3–3–71–2; Hutton 11–3–37–1; Joyce 1–0–9–0; Ramprakash 6–2–11–1. *Second Innings*—Fraser 5–0–31–0; Bloomfield 5–1–15–0; Johnson 2–0–11–0; Tufnell 6–1–18–0; Langer 5–1–29–1.

Middlesex

A. J. Strauss c Piper b Brown	75	B. L. Hutton not out	7
M. A. Roseberry c Wagh b Dagnall	23		
*J. L. Langer b Brown	70	B 1, l-b 12, w 13, n-b 11	37
M. R. Ramprakash not out	88		
R. L. Johnson b Dagnall	5	1/82 2/188 3/197 (5 wkts dec.) 350
E. C. Joyce c Wagh b Brown	45	4/219 5/339

†D. C. Nash, A. R. C. Fraser, P. C. R. Tufnell and T. F. Bloomfield did not bat.

Bonus points – Middlesex 4, Warwickshire 1.

Bowling: Donald 16–6–65–0; Richardson 25–7–69–0; Dagnall 24–6–76–2; Brown 18.4–4–55–3; Smith 19–5–44–0; Wagh 5–0–11–0; Hemp 4–1–17–0.

Umpires: J. W. Holder and K. E. Palmer.

At Cardiff, September 13, 14, 15, 16. MIDDLESEX drew with GLAMORGAN.

NORTHAMPTONSHIRE

Darren Cousins

President: L. A. Wilson
Chairman: S. G. Schanschieff
Chief Executive: S. P. Coverdale
Chairman, Cricket Committee: R. T. Virgin
Captain: 2000 – M. L. Hayden
　　　　　2001 – D. Ripley
Director of Cricket: R. M. Carter
Director of Excellence: D. J. Capel
Head Groundsman: D. Bates
Scorer: A. C. Kingston

When Northamptonshire celebrated their considerable achievements in 2000 with an end-of-season presentation dinner, the County Championship's Division Two trophy was illuminated throughout the evening by a single spotlight. It could have been the Holy Grail, for it represented the club's first league title since Tom Horton's men were Minor Counties champions in 1904, paving the way for elevation to first-class status the following year.

Under the firm and intelligent guidance of their director of cricket, Bob Carter, Northamptonshire made progress on all fronts. Bottom of the Championship after an abject batting performance condemned them to a home defeat by Glamorgan on July 9, they then put together a run of six victories in seven games, five in succession. Both promotion and the trophy were secured in their penultimate fixture, against Essex. Northamptonshire also recovered from an appalling start in Division One of the National League to finish third, just two points behind winners Gloucestershire, who earlier in the summer had ended Northamptonshire's interest in the NatWest Trophy at the quarter-final stage. The establishment of the club's cricket academy, with the initial intake of seven young cricketers selected and announced in October, further enhanced the optimistic mood.

The side's Championship revival owed much to two crucial decisions: bringing in off-spinner Jason Brown for the sadly out-of-sorts slow left-armer Michael Davies, who was released at the end of the season, and opting for an additional batsman at the expense of Devon Malcolm. The veteran fast bowler, a high-profile signing in 1998, was dropped after seven matches and spent a brief period in the Second Eleven before moving to Leicestershire with the club's consent. In Malcolm's absence, Darren Cousins – granted the opportunity to relaunch his career after six injury-plagued years with Essex – produced a string of outstanding performances that fully justified Northamptonshire's faith in him. His wholehearted approach was rewarded with 67 Championship wickets and the club's Player of the Year award.

That accolade might just as easily have gone to Brown. Long regarded as the most accomplished slow bowler on the staff, but denied regular first-team cricket by his lack of batting ability, he made such an immediate and substantial impact that the England selectors named him in their A team to the West Indies, then later drafted him into the senior team for Sri Lanka.

Outwardly easy-going but quietly determined, Brown captured 57 wickets in only nine games, including match-winning hauls of 11 for 178 and 11 for 131 against Warwickshire and Sussex respectively.

Matthew Hayden and Tony Penberthy completed Northamptonshire's quartet of key players. Hayden's success with the bat was entirely predictable; his thoughtful, tactically aware captaincy rather less so. Focus, rather than flair, was still his watchword, but there was a greater willingness to experiment, and the close working relationship between Hayden and Carter imbued Northamptonshire's cricket with a sense of purpose and professionalism rarely seen since the retirement of Allan Lamb in 1995.

Hayden's unavailability for 2001 prompted the appointment of long-serving wicket-keeper David Ripley in his place, with Penberthy as vice-captain. Penberthy shone in both first-class and limited-overs cricket in 2000, scoring runs consistently and picking up useful wickets. He missed only one Championship match, against Essex at Ilford following the death of his father, and had the satisfaction of leading Northamptonshire to an emphatic victory over Worcestershire in the first – hugely successful – floodlit League game at Wantage Road. Hayden's replacement as overseas player was another left-hander, Western Australia's Michael Hussey.

Jeff Cook, another Australian-born left-hander, obliged to complete a seven-year residential qualification before becoming available for first-team cricket, recorded two centuries in his debut season. The second, on a difficult pitch at Eastbourne, was rivalled only by Hayden's magnificent 164 in the title-clinching game against Essex in terms of importance to the campaign. David Sales threatened another productive season, punishing Nottinghamshire's attack to the tune of 276 in eight hours during the first home Championship match, but thereafter his most telling contributions were made in the League. Sales's prospects for 2001 were thrown into doubt when he injured his knee playing beach volleyball on England A's tour of the West Indies.

Following on from a frustrating, underemployed winter with the England team in South Africa, Graeme Swann failed to make the hoped-for advance with either bat or ball. A lingering sense of grievance at his treatment by those in charge of the national team seemed, on occasions, to distract him from the job in hand. Paul Taylor, the linchpin of Northamptonshire's seam bowling over the previous decade, missed the first part of the season through injury, only to make his mark with two vital wickets in the win over Gloucestershire – as a left-arm spinner. The final match of the summer, at New Road, saw him become only the 16th bowler, and the first since Sarfraz Nawaz in 1982, to take 500 first-class wickets for the county.

Maintaining Northamptonshire's dual first-division status, particularly without Hayden's runs, presents Carter and his team with their biggest challenge yet. To provide depth in seam bowling, contracts were offered to Matthew Cassar, the Derbyshire all-rounder, and Montserrat-born Lesroy Weekes, who in 2000 turned out for Yorkshire for the first time in six years and took six for 56 against the West Indian tourists. The club will also look for signs of continuing improvement from the likes of Northampton-born batsman Mark Powell and England Under-19 slow left-armer Mudhsuden Singh "Monty" Panesar, available full-time in 2001. – ANDREW RADD.

NORTHAMPTONSHIRE 2000

[Bill Smith]

Back row: M. R. Strong, M. S. Panesar, J. A. R Blain, D. M. Cousins, R. J. Logan, M. C. Dobson, T. M. B. Bailey, R. A. White. *Middle row:* K. A. Russell (*physiotherapist*), J. F. Brown, D. J. Sales, A. J. Swann, J. W. Cook, R. V. Sutcliffe, G. P. Swann, M. K. Davies, D. J. Roberts, K. J. Innes. *Front row:* R. M. Carter (*director of cricket*), D. E. Malcolm, M. B. Loye, A. L. Penberthy, D. Ripley, J. P. Taylor, R. J. Warren, A. S. Rollins, N. G. B. Cook (*Second Eleven coach*). *Inset:* M. L. Hayden (*captain*).

NORTHAMPTONSHIRE RESULTS

All first-class matches – Played 17: Won 7, Lost 5, Drawn 5.

County Championship matches – Played 16: Won 7, Lost 4, Drawn 5.

PPP Healthcare County Championship, winners in Division 2; NatWest Trophy, q-f;
Benson and Hedges Cup, 4th in Midlands/Wales/West Group;
Norwich Union National League, 3rd in Division 1.

COUNTY CHAMPIONSHIP AVERAGES

BATTING

Cap		M	I	NO	R	HS	100s	50s	Avge	Ct/St
1999	M. L. Hayden§	15	22	0	1,270	164	4	6	57.72	21
1994	A. L. Penberthy	15	21	2	785	116	1	5	41.31	10
1995	R. J. Warren†	8	11	1	384	151	1	2	38.40	1
	T. M. B. Bailey† . . .	3	5	1	149	96*	0	1	37.25	8/1
1999	D. J. Sales	13	20	0	713	276	1	5	35.65	9
	J. W. Cook	10	15	1	465	137	2	1	33.21	4
1987	D. Ripley	13	18	3	475	56	0	3	31.66	38/4
1994	M. B. Loye†	12	18	1	504	93	0	3	29.64	1
	A. S. Rollins	16	24	0	636	100	1	4	26.50	19
1999	G. P. Swann†	15	22	0	524	72	0	2	23.81	7
2000	D. M. Cousins.	16	23	7	210	29*	0	0	13.12	3
	M. R. Strong	3	5	1	48	27*	0	0	12.00	1
	M. K. Davies	4	6	0	65	25	0	0	10.83	2
1992	J. P. Taylor	7	10	1	96	27	0	0	10.66	3
	R. J. Logan.	6	8	1	51	24	0	0	7.28	1
2000	J. F. Brown	9	13	4	29	11	0	0	3.22	3
1999	D. E. Malcolm	7	10	1	24	8	0	0	2.66	0

Also batted: K. J. Innes† (1 match) 5, 25; M. J. Powell† (1 match) 1, 1; A. J. Swann† (2 matches) 61*, 19, 13 (1 ct).

* Signifies not out.   † Born in Northamptonshire.   § Overseas player.

BOWLING

	O	M	R	W	BB	5W/i	Avge
D. M. Cousins	510.4	142	1,318	67	5-123	1	19.67
J. F. Brown	485	138	1,149	57	7-78	4	20.15
A. L. Penberthy	131	30	358	16	5-54	1	22.37
J. P. Taylor	212.3	50	540	24	6-27	1	22.50
D. E. Malcolm	184.1	46	541	19	5-45	1	28.47
G. P. Swann	445.3	89	1,293	41	6-118	2	31.53
R. J. Logan	133.1	33	453	11	5-61	1	41.18

Also bowled: J. W. Cook 1–0–7–0; M. K. Davies 109–37–273–8; M. L. Hayden 15–2–56–1; K. J. Innes 4.3–0–28–1; M. R. Strong 57.2–7–192–6; A. J. Swann 28–13–42–3.

COUNTY RECORDS

Highest score for:	322*	M. B. Loye v Glamorgan at Northampton	1998
Highest score against:	333	K. S. Duleepsinhji (Sussex) at Hove	1930
Best bowling for:	10-127	V. W. C. Jupp v Kent at Tunbridge Wells	1932
Best bowling against:	10-30	C. Blythe (Kent) at Northampton	1907
Highest total for:	781-7 dec.	v Nottinghamshire at Northampton	1995
Highest total against:	670-9 dec.	by Sussex at Hove	1921
Lowest total for:	12	v Gloucestershire at Gloucester.	1907
Lowest total against:	33	by Lancashire at Northampton	1977

At Nottingham, April 26, 27, 28, 29. NORTHAMPTONSHIRE drew with NOTTINGHAMSHIRE.

At Lord's, May 3, 4, 5, 6. NORTHAMPTONSHIRE drew with MIDDLESEX.

NORTHAMPTONSHIRE v NOTTINGHAMSHIRE

At Northampton, May 11, 12, 13, 14. Northamptonshire won by an innings and 124 runs. Toss: Northamptonshire. Northamptonshire 20 pts, Nottinghamshire 5 pts.

Sales, still only 22, passed 200 for the fourth time, setting up an emphatic victory and establishing more batting records. His 276, off 375 balls in eight hours five minutes, with three sixes and 33 fours, surpassed Fred Bakewell's 246 in 1933 as Northamptonshire's highest score against Nottinghamshire. And his sixth-wicket partnership of 197 in 47 overs with Hayden, batting down the order because of a sore back, was also a county record against them. Sales had his career-best 303 not out in his sights when he was run out, attempting a sharp single with Davies. Initially, the visitors replied strongly, Gallian and Morris adding 132 for the third wicket, but the remaining batsmen – Millns excepted – made scant contribution. Malcolm took his 900th first-class wicket when Read was caught behind by Ripley. Following on, Nottinghamshire's second innings was a disaster: only Morris, again, and Johnson, struggling with a shoulder injury, came to terms with Cousins's pace and Davies's accuracy.

Close of play: First day, Northamptonshire 402-5 (Sales 199*, Hayden 44*); Second day, Nottinghamshire 72-2 (Gallian 1*, Morris 1*); Third day, Nottinghamshire 44-2 (Afzaal 15*, Morris 17*).

Northamptonshire

A. S. Rollins lbw b Lucas	8	M. K. Davies c Lucas b Stemp	10
M. B. Loye lbw b Lucas	9	D. M. Cousins not out	19
A. L. Penberthy c Read b Stemp	62	D. E. Malcolm c Franks b Millns	6
D. J. Sales run out	276	B 3, l-b 11, w 10, n-b 2	26
G. P. Swann c Gallian b Afzaal	25		
†D. Ripley lbw b Millns	39	1/20 2/23 3/117	585
*M. L. Hayden c Lucas b Stemp	101	4/219 5/298 6/495	
R. J. Logan c and b Stemp	4	7/517 8/556 9/558	

Bonus points – Northamptonshire 5, Nottinghamshire 2 (Score at 130 overs: 519-7).

Bowling: Franks 23–2–111–0; Millns 23.3–5–102–2; Lucas 26–5–115–2; Bowen 24–4–80–0; Stemp 36–7–127–4; Afzaal 12–2–36–1.

Nottinghamshire

D. J. Bicknell c Ripley b Logan	33	– lbw b Cousins	3
U. Afzaal c Hayden b Davies	33	– c Rollins b Davies	15
*J. E. R. Gallian c Rollins b Malcolm	45	– lbw b Malcolm	1
J. E. Morris c Ripley b Davies	88	– lbw b Cousins	46
†C. M. W. Read c Ripley b Malcolm	9	– lbw b Cousins	8
P. J. Franks lbw b Davies	9	– c Rollins b Davies	2
D. J. Millns not out	50	– b Cousins	1
P. Johnson c Ripley b Logan	12	– b Davies	26
D. S. Lucas lbw b Logan	0	– c Ripley b Swann	10
M. N. Bowen b Cousins	24	– b Swann	4
R. D. Stemp b Cousins	5	– not out	0
B 11, l-b 7, w 4, n-b 3	25	B 6, l-b 6	12
1/69 2/69 3/201 4/219 5/227	333	1/17 2/22 3/45 4/72 5/83	128
6/235 7/261 8/263 9/305		6/85 7/85 8/124 9/128	

Bonus points – Nottinghamshire 3, Northamptonshire 3.

Bowling: *First Innings*—Malcolm 18–5–39–2; Cousins 23–6–78–2; Logan 31–13–68–3; Davies 31–9–83–3; Swann 17–3–47–0. *Second Innings*—Malcolm 6–1–13–1; Cousins 16–4–41–4; Logan 5–1–26–0; Davies 19–11–25–3; Swann 8.1–3–11–2.

Umpires: B. Dudleston and R. Julian.

NORTHAMPTONSHIRE v MIDDLESEX

At Northampton, May 24, 25, 26, 27. Drawn. Toss: Middlesex. Northamptonshire 10 pts, Middlesex 8 pts.

Rain prevented any possibility of a result, washing out the third day and ending play soon after lunch on the fourth. Ramprakash, in need of time at the crease ahead of the Nottingham Test, completed a stylish fifty, including two sixes off Swann, but fellow-opener Strauss had a less fortunate start. He required seven stitches after a short ball from Malcolm squeezed between helmet peak and grille. In a 27-ball spell, Logan took four wickets – including Ramprakash – for five runs to undermine the Middlesex middle order, and he finished with his first five-wicket haul. On the second day, a century partnership between Hayden and Loye put Northamptonshire on course for a useful lead of 102, despite Tufnell's six for 92, his best Championship return since 1996. Middlesex had hardly begun their second innings when a hailstorm broke.

Close of play: First day, Middlesex 217; Second day, Northamptonshire 265-7 (Ripley 28*, Davies 5*); Third day, No play.

Middlesex

A. J. Strauss b Malcolm	18		
M. R. Ramprakash lbw b Logan	54	– not out	16
*J. L. Langer b Malcolm	17		
O. A. Shah lbw b Logan	15		
R. M. S. Weston lbw b Logan	1		
†D. C. Nash c Penberthy b Davies	35		
B. L. Hutton c Sales b Logan	4	– (1) not out	4
R. L. Johnson c Sales b Cousins	20		
A. R. C. Fraser not out	22		
T. F. Bloomfield c Hayden b Malcolm	4		
P. C. R. Tufnell c Loye b Logan	16		
L-b 9, w 2	11	B 4	4
1/28 2/69 3/75 4/94 5/98	217	(no wkt)	24
6/148 7/160 8/180 9/194			

Bonus points – Middlesex 1, Northamptonshire 3.

In the first innings Strauss, when 0, retired hurt at 2 and resumed at 148.

Bowling: *First Innings*—Malcolm 24–8–62–3; Cousins 17–5–39–1; Davies 10–0–32–1; Logan 17.4–2–61–5; Swann 1–0–14–0. *Second Innings*—Malcolm 4.2–2–9–0; Cousins 4–1–11–0.

Northamptonshire

A. S. Rollins c Nash b Bloomfield	21	
*M. L. Hayden st Nash b Tufnell	69	
M. B. Loye c Johnson b Tufnell	47	
D. J. Sales lbw b Tufnell	1	
A. L. Penberthy c Nash b Bloomfield	23	
G. P. Swann c Nash b Bloomfield	43	
†D. Ripley c Langer b Bloomfield	55	
R. J. Logan b Tufnell	2	
M. K. Davies c Nash b Tufnell	25	
D. M. Cousins not out	7	
D. E. Malcolm c Langer b Tufnell	0	
B 9, l-b 11, n-b 6	26	
1/37 2/142 3/142 4/151 5/219	319	
6/236 7/239 8/299 9/319		

Bonus points – Northamptonshire 3, Middlesex 3.

Bowling: Fraser 25–8–56–0; Johnson 25–7–70–0; Bloomfield 16–4–46–4; Tufnell 38–13–92–6; Hutton 2–1–9–0; Ramprakash 9–2–26–0.

Umpires: J. H. Hampshire and A. A. Jones.

At Ilford, May 31, June 1, 2, 3. NORTHAMPTONSHIRE lost to ESSEX by five wickets.

At Oxford, June 6, 7, 8. NORTHAMPTONSHIRE lost to OXFORD UNIVERSITIES by three wickets.

NORTHAMPTONSHIRE v WARWICKSHIRE

At Northampton, June 14, 15, 16, 17. Warwickshire won by an innings and 53 runs. Toss: Warwickshire. Warwickshire 20 pts, Northamptonshire 4 pts.

Warwickshire won their fourth consecutive victory at Wantage Road with two sessions to spare. Powell and Ostler confirmed Smith's decision to bat by both hitting 145 – Powell's best score – and sharing a partnership of 306 in 92 overs, an all-wicket record in Warwickshire–Northamptonshire fixtures. Penberthy briefly struck back, with a burst of five for five in 35 balls as Warwickshire crashed from 420 for two to 442 for eight; then they kicked on again. The tail, plus 76 extras, carried them to their highest total against Northamptonshire. The home side had an outside chance of saving the follow-on while Loye was there. But he fell immediately after the umpires asked Smith to tone down his close fielders' aggressive appealing, and the last six wickets went for 30 as Giles began to have an impact. On a pitch taking increasing turn, he took eight for 90 in the second innings to claim 12 for 135 in the match, both career-bests.

Close of play: First day, Warwickshire 289-1 (Powell 100*, Ostler 93*); Second day, Northamptonshire 147-3 (Loye 54*, Davies 0*); Third day, Northamptonshire 160-4 (Rollins 71*, Swann 9*).

Warwickshire

M. J. Powell c Ripley b Penberthy 145	†K. J. Piper b Penberthy 0
G. Welch b Cousins 55	M. A. Sheikh not out 58
D. P. Ostler c Hayden b Logan 145	A. Richardson not out 17
D. L. Hemp c Rollins b Penberthy 14	B 27, l-b 15, w 34. 76
T. L. Penney b Penberthy 2	
D. R. Brown c Davies b Cousins 5	1/87 2/393 3/420 (9 wkts dec.) 568
*N. M. K. Smith lbw b Penberthy 7	4/423 5/428 6/428
A. F. Giles c Ripley b Hayden 44	7/442 8/442 9/514

Bonus points – Warwickshire 5, Northamptonshire 2 (Score at 130 overs: 442-6).

Bowling: Malcolm 25–4–89–0; Cousins 41–8–132–2; Logan 17–3–57–1; Penberthy 23–5–54–5; Davies 25–12–70–0; Swann 28–2–116–0; Hayden 2–0–8–1.

Northamptonshire

*M. L. Hayden c Piper b Richardson	30	– (2) lbw b Smith 47
A. S. Rollins c Powell b Sheikh	42	– (1) b Giles 76
M. B. Loye c Hemp b Richardson	93	– c Powell b Giles 1
D. J. Sales c Brown b Smith	9	– lbw b Giles 4
M. K. Davies c Piper b Smith	1	– (9) c Ostler b Smith 2
A. L. Penberthy c Hemp b Giles	46	– (5) lbw b Giles 21
G. P. Swann lbw b Giles	0	– (6) c Piper b Giles 72
†D. Ripley not out	15	– (7) c Brown b Giles 12
R. J. Logan c Powell b Giles	1	– (8) b Giles 3
D. M. Cousins c Brown b Giles	7	– c Smith b Giles 4
D. E. Malcolm c Giles b Smith	0	– not out 0
B 4, l-b 16, n-b 2	22	B 3, l-b 2, n-b 2. 7

1/68 2/88 3/147 4/155 5/236	266	1/73 2/80 3/94 4/144 5/185 249
6/238 7/240 8/245 9/265		6/223 7/240 8/243 9/247

Bonus points – Northamptonshire 2, Warwickshire 3.

Bowling: *First Innings*—Welch 12–0–60–0; Richardson 20–5–63–2; Sheikh 8–1–36–1; Giles 29–16–45–4; Smith 14.5–6–42–3. *Second Innings*—Welch 8–2–19–0; Richardson 13–5–23–0; Sheikh 15–6–32–0; Giles 44–17–90–8; Smith 25–4–80–2.

Umpires: J. W. Holder and A. G. T. Whitehead.

At Northampton, July 1. NORTHAMPTONSHIRE beat ZIMBABWEANS by 42 runs (D/L method) (See Zimbabwean tour section).

NORTHAMPTONSHIRE v GLAMORGAN

At Northampton, July 7, 8, 9. Glamorgan won by 144 runs. Toss: Glamorgan. Glamorgan 16 pts, Northamptonshire 3 pts.

Already bottom of Division Two, Northamptonshire slumped to a fourth successive first-class defeat shortly after tea on the third day. They had not beaten Glamorgan on this ground since 1981, but looked well-placed on reducing them to 77 for six. The visitors were rescued by Wharf, whose maiden Championship century included 16 fours and secured an improbable batting point. Northamptonshire's reply quickly ran into even worse trouble, and only Loye and Ripley applied themselves. Loye was given out lbw by umpire Burgess for 43, but was recalled after the umpire realised he had played the ball with his bat. Wharf would have fancied his chances of emulating Emrys Davies – who combined a century with a hat-trick for Glamorgan against Leicestershire in 1937 – when, having removed Ripley and Brown with successive balls, he saw who was coming out. But Malcolm denied him. Glamorgan built on their lead with fifties from James and Dale, leaving a target of 323, whereupon the home side subsided again. Careless shot selection did not help: even Sales's stout resistance ended with a miscued hook.

Close of play: First day, Northamptonshire 85-7 (Ripley 3*); Second day, Glamorgan 223-9 (Thomas 13*, Watkin 0*).

Glamorgan

M. T. G. Elliott lbw b Malcolm	1	– (2) c Ripley b Penberthy	26
*S. P. James c Ripley b Cousins	14	– (1) lbw b Penberthy	62
M. J. Powell b Strong	23	– c Ripley b Penberthy	6
A. W. Evans lbw b Cousins	2	– c Rollins b Swann	19
A. Dale b Swann	47	– b Brown	53
K. Newell b Penberthy	4	– b Brown	17
†A. D. Shaw c Hayden b Swann	3	– st Ripley b Brown	0
A. G. Wharf not out	101	– b Swann	5
S. D. Thomas b Penberthy	8	– not out	34
D. A. Cosker b Brown	7	– c Ripley b Swann	14
S. L. Watkin b Strong	6	– b Swann	11
B 4, l-b 10, w 2, n-b 2	18	B 1, l-b 5, n-b 2	8

1/2 2/30 3/36 4/42 5/72   234   1/72 2/81 3/102 4/121 5/172   255
6/77 7/136 8/161 9/215   6/178 7/187 8/191 9/215

Bonus points – Glamorgan 1, Northamptonshire 3.

Bowling: *First Innings*—Malcolm 12–1–47–1; Cousins 19–5–51–2; Strong 12.2–2–37–2; Penberthy 13–4–34–2; Swann 11–4–41–2; Brown 6–2–10–1. *Second Innings*—Malcolm 11–4–40–0; Cousins 8–0–35–0; Strong 6–0–35–0; Penberthy 9–1–26–3; Brown 21–2–58–3; Swann 16.3–1–55–4.

Northamptonshire

A. S. Rollins c Shaw b Thomas	6	– (2) lbw b Wharf	0
*M. L. Hayden lbw b Wharf	4	– (1) lbw b Dale	41
M. B. Loye lbw b Watkin	47	– lbw b Watkin	10
D. J. Sales b Dale	15	– c Dale b Wharf	61
A. L. Penberthy b Dale	0	– lbw b Thomas	2
G. P. Swann st Shaw b Dale	1	– b Cosker	19
†D. Ripley c Shaw b Wharf	44	– b Watkin	5
M. R. Strong b Watkin	0	– not out	27
D. M. Cousins not out	29	– c Powell b Watkin	7
J. F. Brown lbw b Wharf	0	– c Elliott b Thomas	0
D. E. Malcolm c Wharf b Cosker	3	– b Thomas	0
B 4, l-b 4, w 8, n-b 2	18	B 1, l-b 1, n-b 4	6

1/6 2/35 3/66 4/66 5/75   167   1/0 2/49 3/78 4/101 5/132   178
6/85 7/85 8/164 9/164   6/138 7/152 8/162 9/168

Bonus points – Glamorgan 3.

Bowling: *First Innings*—Watkin 17–5–45–2; Wharf 11–3–37–3; Thomas 18–7–35–1; Dale 11–3–29–3; Cosker 5.4–2–13–1. *Second Innings*—Watkin 11.4–2–31–3; Wharf 11–0–64–2; Thomas 9.5–0–48–3; Dale 7–3–9–1; Cosker 12–5–24–1.

Umpires: G. I. Burgess and J. H. Hampshire.

At Cheltenham, July 12, 13, 14, 15. NORTHAMPTONSHIRE beat GLOUCESTERSHIRE by an innings and 99 runs.

At Cardiff, July 19, 20, 21, 22. NORTHAMPTONSHIRE lost to GLAMORGAN by five wickets.

At Birmingham, July 28, 29, 30. NORTHAMPTONSHIRE beat WARWICKSHIRE by 54 runs.

NORTHAMPTONSHIRE v WORCESTERSHIRE

At Northampton, August 4, 5, 6, 7. Northamptonshire won by an innings and 72 runs. Northamptonshire 19 pts, Worcestershire 2 pts. Toss: Northamptonshire.

Northamptonshire jumped from sixth to the top of Division Two after securing a comfortable victory with two sessions to spare. Worcestershire may have been bolstered by the unexpected arrival of Hick, discarded by England for the Old Trafford Test, but they badly missed McGrath, on international duty in Melbourne. Six Northamptonshire batsmen passed 50 in an innings, as they had only twice before, against Sussex in 1914 and Nottinghamshire in 1995. Hayden converted his fifty into a big hundred, and became the third – after fellow-Australians Michael Bevan and Darren Lehmann – to 1,000 first-class runs for the season. He hit two sixes and 19 fours, putting on 195 for the first wicket with Rollins; another century partnership, between Penberthy and Ripley, pressed home the advantage. Apart from Leatherdale's third-day defiance, Worcestershire's batting was dismal, and epitomised by Hick's dismissals: bowled off his pad, the ball looping back on to the stumps, and then caught at mid-wicket off a full toss. Northamptonshire off-spinners Brown and Swann captured 16 wickets.

Close of play: First day, Northamptonshire 340-4 (Warren 33*, Penberthy 10*); Second day, Worcestershire 97-4 (Pollard 9*, Leatherdale 26*); Third day, Worcestershire 102-6 (Pollard 5*, Rhodes 3*).

Northamptonshire

A. S. Rollins c Wilson b Lampitt	. . . . .	63	J. P. Taylor not out		3
*M. L. Hayden c Ali b Solanki	. . . .	147	D. M. Cousins lbw b Lampitt		2
M. B. Loye b Illingworth	. . . .	52	J. F. Brown lbw b Lampitt		0
R. J. Warren b Lampitt	. . . .	60			
J. W. Cook c Hick b Solanki	. . . .	1	B 10, l-b 10, w 10, n-b 18	. . .	48
A. L. Penberthy c Hick b Lampitt	. . . . .	83			
G. P. Swann c and b Solanki	. . . .	4	1/195 2/267 3/301 4/314 5/391		519
†D. Ripley c Leatherdale b Illingworth	. .	56	6/406 7/514 8/514 9/519		

Bonus points – Northamptonshire 4, Worcestershire 1 (Score at 130 overs: 399-5).

Bowling: Sheriyar 21–5–83–0; Ali 12–3–50–0; Lampitt 25–6–63–5; Illingworth 45–9–118–2; Hick 27–6–72–0; Solanki 29–6–80–3; Leatherdale 11–1–33–0.

Worcestershire

W. P. C. Weston c Ripley b Taylor	3	– (2) lbw b Swann	40
E. J. Wilson lbw b Cousins	3	– (1) c Ripley b Cousins	2
*G. A. Hick b Brown	15	– c Warren b Swann	46
V. S. Solanki c Ripley b Cousins	32	– b Swann	0
P. R. Pollard lbw b Swann	32	– c Ripley b Brown	9
D. A. Leatherdale not out	132	– c Hayden b Brown	1
†S. J. Rhodes c Rollins b Brown	4	– (8) b Brown	4
S. R. Lampitt lbw b Brown	7	– (9) not out	56
R. K. Illingworth c Penberthy b Brown	3	– (7) c Hayden b Swann	0
Kabir Ali c Hayden b Brown	1	– c Penberthy b Swann	12
A. Sheriyar c Penberthy b Swann	4	– c sub b Brown	17
B 5, l-b 8	13	L-b 9, n-b 2	11

1/7 2/7 3/60 4/62 5/177   249   1/2 2/83 3/85 4/94 5/97   198
6/188 7/210 8/230 9/234   6/98 7/103 8/140 9/171

Bonus points – Worcestershire 1, Northamptonshire 3.

Bowling: *First Innings*—Cousins 12–6–13–2; Taylor 22–6–51–1; Brown 42–9–100–5; Swann 33–7–72–2. *Second Innings*—Cousins 13–6–19–1; Taylor 11–4–27–0; Brown 33–13–88–4; Swann 24–7–55–5.

Umpires: D. J. Constant and J. W. Lloyds.

NORTHAMPTONSHIRE v SUSSEX

At Northampton, August 9, 10, 11, 12. Northamptonshire won by an innings and 17 runs. Northamptonshire 19 pts, Sussex 3 pts. Toss: Sussex.

Brown maintained his remarkable form, returning a career-best seven for 78 in Sussex's second innings and 11 for 131 in the match. In three games, he had claimed 31 first-class wickets, taking him past 100 in his 23rd game. Brown finished off Sussex with the 20th ball of the final morning, though the end would have come the night before had Cook not dropped Lewry at slip in the last over of the extra half-hour. Despite a dogged 74 from Khan, in their first Championship outing of the summer, Sussex could not capitalise on first use of a pitch that grew increasingly helpful to the spinners. The inadequacy of their total was emphasised by Warren and Penberthy, who added 204 – a Northamptonshire fifth-wicket record against Sussex. Warren, in for the injured Sales, went on to his highest score for three years, striking a six and 21 fours in his painstaking eight-hour 151. Then Brown undid the Sussex innings, although he met his match in Cottey who, unlike his crease-bound team-mates, used his feet superbly during a fighting 112.

Close of play: First day, Northamptonshire 23-0 (Rollins 9*, Hayden 14*); Second day, Northamptonshire 327-4 (Warren 113*, Penberthy 92*); Third day, Sussex 202-9 (Cottey 104*, Lewry 1*).

Sussex

R. R. Montgomerie lbw b Cousins	10	– lbw b Cousins	10
M. T. E. Peirce b Swann	21	– c Ripley b Brown	14
W. G. Khan c Rollins b Brown	74	– c Hayden b Brown	10
*C. J. Adams b Swann	11	– lbw b Brown	16
P. A. Cottey c Ripley b Cousins	22	– b Brown	112
R. S. C. Martin-Jenkins b Brown	27	– c Rollins b Brown	0
U. B. A. Rashid b Brown	27	– c Ripley b Brown	33
J. J. Bates b Cousins	17	– c Swann b Brown	0
†N. J. Wilton lbw b Cousins	2	– c and b Swann	2
J. D. Lewry c Cousins b Brown	7	– (11) not out	2
R. J. Kirtley not out	0	– (10) lbw b Brown	2
B 8, l-b 4, n-b 2	14	B 10	10

1/12 2/53 3/91 4/124 5/175   232   1/14 2/32 3/42 4/69 5/69   211
6/182 7/223 8/225 9/232   6/160 7/164 8/175 9/194

Bonus points – Sussex 1, Northamptonshire 3.

Bowling: *First Innings*—Cousins 22–7–36–4; Taylor 15–1–41–0; Penberthy 4–1–16–0; Brown 32.3–12–53–4; Swann 29–8–74–2. *Second Innings*—Cousins 13–3–25–1; Taylor 9–2–26–0; Swann 26–7–72–2; Brown 22.2–1–78–7.

Northamptonshire

A. S. Rollins c Wilton b Rashid	30	J. P. Taylor c Lewry b Rashid	13	
*M. L. Hayden c Cottey b Kirtley	18	D. M. Cousins c Martin-Jenkins b Rashid	17	
M. B. Loye lbw b Kirtley	18	J. F. Brown not out	1	
R. J. Warren c Bates b Rashid	151	B 8, l-b 10, w 2, n-b 22	42	
J. W. Cook c Adams b Bates	23			
A. L. Penberthy lbw b Kirtley	96	1/44 2/66 3/76	460	
G. P. Swann run out	30	4/139 5/343 6/391		
†D. Ripley c Montgomerie b Rashid	21	7/424 8/433 9/446		

Bonus points – Northamptonshire 4, Sussex 2 (Score at 130 overs: 395-6).

Bowling: Lewry 17–3–50–0; Kirtley 31–8–94–3; Rashid 43.5–13–103–5; Martin-Jenkins 23–6–64–0; Bates 28–6–90–1; Adams 5–0–19–0; Khan 7–0–22–0.

Umpires: N. G. Cowley and R. Palmer.

At Eastbourne, August 16, 17, 18. NORTHAMPTONSHIRE beat SUSSEX by 162 runs.

NORTHAMPTONSHIRE v GLOUCESTERSHIRE

At Northampton, August 30, 31, September 1, 2. Northamptonshire won by an innings and 74 runs. Northamptonshire 18 pts, Gloucestershire 1 pt. Toss: Northamptonshire.

In a breathless finish, Northamptonshire recorded a fifth successive Championship win, and their fifth innings victory of the season. When Cousins, armed with the second new ball, captured the last three wickets in nine deliveries, Gloucestershire were sunk ten balls from safety. From a precarious 110 for five, Alleyne and Russell had added 59 in 30 overs. But then Paul Taylor, switching from his usual seam to slow left-arm, removed both, paving the way for Cousins's dramatic finale. Northamptonshire had batted solidly, underpinned by Penberthy's first Championship hundred for more than a year, and by three fifties from the middle order. Against Cousins and Brown, Northamptonshire's outstanding bowlers of the season, Gloucestershire could not avert the follow-on. Hewson and Russell twice offered spirited resistance, and the presence of rain – there were three brief stoppages on the final day – also threatened to frustrate Northamptonshire. On the second afternoon, Stephen Coverdale, their chief executive, deputised at square leg for umpire Burgess.

Close of play: First day, Northamptonshire 282-5 (Penberthy 42*, Taylor 0*); Second day, Gloucestershire 65-3 (Hewson 36*, Ball 0*); Third day, Gloucestershire 15-0 (Hewson 9*, Hancock 6*).

Northamptonshire

A. S. Rollins lbw b Lewis	49	†D. Ripley c Russell b Snape	10	
*M. L. Hayden c Russell b Ball	41	D. M. Cousins b Snape	15	
J. W. Cook b Cotterell	4	J. F. Brown c Hewson b Ball	2	
D. J. Sales b Ball	55			
R. J. Warren c Snape b Lewis	61	B 14, l-b 13, w 2, n-b 6	35	
A. L. Penberthy b Snape	116			
J. P. Taylor b Alleyne	20	1/82 2/91 3/123 4/185 5/280	469	
A. J. Swann not out	61	6/314 7/420 8/442 9/464		

Bonus points – Northamptonshire 3, Gloucestershire 1 (Score at 130 overs: 314-5).

Bowling: Lewis 32–11–96–2; Alleyne 26–12–51–1; Hancock 8–2–15–0; Ball 53–14–120–3; Cotterell 33–8–90–1; Snape 27–4–70–3.

Gloucestershire

T. H. C. Hancock lbw b Brown	22	– (2) c Ripley b Brown	9
D. R. Hewson c Hayden b Brown	45	– (1) c and b Swann	39
M. G. N. Windows lbw b Brown	2	– c Cook b Brown	36
K. J. Barnett lbw b Cousins	5	– c Rollins b Swann	13
M. C. J. Ball b Taylor	15	– (9) c Sales b Cousins	12
*M. W. Alleyne lbw b Cousins	4	– (5) c Hayden b Taylor	18
C. G. Taylor c Rollins b Brown	8	– (6) b Brown	6
†R. C. Russell c Ripley b Cousins	40	– (7) b Taylor	41
J. N. Snape c Hayden b Swann	15	– (8) not out	23
J. Lewis c Rollins b Cousins	22	– c Ripley b Cousins	0
T. P. Cotterell not out	0	– c Sales b Cousins	0
L-b 6, n-b 2	8	B 7, l-b 5	12

1/44 2/60 3/65 4/75 5/84   186   1/21 2/60 3/104 4/104 5/110   209
6/97 7/119 8/151 9/183   6/169 7/176 8/202 9/207

Bonus points – Northamptonshire 3.

Bowling: *First Innings*—Cousins 20–10–41–4; Taylor 20–4–59–1; Brown 34–12–68–4; Swann 6–2–12–1. *Second Innings*—Cousins 24.2–9–38–3; Taylor 20–6–45–2; Brown 43–17–84–3; Swann 22–11–30–2.

Umpires: G. I. Burgess and P. Willey.

NORTHAMPTONSHIRE v ESSEX

At Northampton, September 6, 7, 8, 9. Drawn. Northamptonshire 12 pts, Essex 8 pts. Toss: Essex.
    A game of ups and downs ended with Hayden receiving the Division Two trophy, but not before Northamptonshire hearts had missed a beat. After a delayed start, Essex reached 172 for three, only for Irani's dismissal to trigger a collapse of seven for 61. When Law was sixth out at 4.40 p.m. on the first afternoon, a second bonus point apparently guaranteed Northamptonshire promotion. But pitch liaison officer Phil Sharpe had misgivings about the turn obtained by Brown and Swann so early on, and convened an inspection panel. The prospect of a points penalty spurred Hayden to shift the blame from the pitch to the Essex batsmen. Hitting with power and precision, he used his feet skilfully to strike a six and 17 fours in his 341-minute 164, and pointedly acknowledged the ECB delegation on reaching his fifty and hundred. The strategy worked: Hayden's eloquent riposte was enough for the pitch to be exonerated at tea on the second afternoon; Northamptonshire breathed again. Rain allowed only 70 minutes' play on the third day and, thanks to Law's fifth hundred of the summer, Essex easily secured a draw, moving up a place to third.
    Close of play: First day, Northamptonshire 25-0 (Rollins 7*, Hayden 9*); Second day, Northamptonshire 337-7 (Ripley 23*, Taylor 12*); Third day, Northamptonshire 397-9 (Cousins 7*, Brown 3*).

Essex

P. J. Prichard c Rollins b Cousins	31	– lbw b Cousins	0
A. P. Grayson c Ripley b Penberthy	20	– c Ripley b Cousins	8
D. D. J. Robinson b Taylor	6	– b Cousins	42
S. G. Law c Ripley b Brown	59	– not out	119
*R. C. Irani run out	27	– lbw b Cousins	2
S. D. Peters c Rollins b Swann	11	– not out	50
†J. S. Foster not out	16		
A. P. Cowan c Ripley b Brown	0		
T. J. Mason lbw b Brown	0		
R. S. G. Anderson lbw b Swann	4		
P. M. Such b Brown	14		
B 9, l-b 18, w 8, n-b 10	45	L-b 1, w 3	4

1/52 2/63 3/94 4/172 5/193   233   1/0 2/25 3/108 4/110   (4 wkts) 225
6/193 7/193 8/197 9/206

Bonus points – Essex 1, Northamptonshire 3.

Bowling: *First Innings*—Cousins 15–0–51–1; Taylor 14–3–39–1; Penberthy 5–0–15–1; Swann 20–1–67–2; Brown 14.4–4–34–4. *Second Innings*—Cousins 21–7–50–4; Taylor 14–1–35–0; Brown 20–3–62–0; Swann 24–3–70–0; Cook 1–0–7–0.

Northamptonshire

A. S. Rollins lbw b Mason	20	J. P. Taylor c Grayson b Anderson	27
*M. L. Hayden c and b Such	164	D. M. Cousins not out	16
J. W. Cook c Prichard b Mason	4	J. F. Brown c Foster b Cowan	7
D. J. Sales c Prichard b Such	61		
R. J. Warren c Prichard b Mason	10	B 7, l-b 15, n-b 4	26
A. L. Penberthy lbw b Such	15		—
G. P. Swann c Foster b Grayson	6		410
†D. Ripley c Law b Anderson	54		

1/48 2/56 3/178 4/215 5/262
6/271 7/315 8/384 9/389

Bonus points – Northamptonshire 5, Essex 3.

Bowling: Cowan 13.3–2–51–1; Irani 7–2–18–0; Such 45–5–127–3; Mason 28–3–106–3; Grayson 13–1–39–1; Anderson 14–0–47–2.

Umpires: G. I. Burgess and B. Leadbeater.

At Worcester, September 13, 14, 15, 16. NORTHAMPTONSHIRE drew with WORCESTERSHIRE.

COUNTY BENEFITS AWARDED FOR 2001

Derbyshire	D. G. Cork.	Leicestershire	V. J. Wells.
Durham	S. J. E. Brown.	Middlesex	Crusade for Kids' Cricket.
Essex	P. M. Such.	Somerset	Somerset CCC.
Glamorgan	S. P. James.	Surrey	Surrey CCC.
Gloucestershire	A. M. Smith.	Warwickshire	K. J. Piper.
Hampshire	J. P. Stephenson.	Worcestershire	Worcestershire CCC.
Kent	M. V. Fleming.	Yorkshire	D. Gough.
Lancashire	G. D. Lloyd.		

No benefit was awarded by Northamptonshire, Nottinghamshire or Sussex.

NOTTINGHAMSHIRE

Usman Afzaal

President: J. R. Cope
Chairman: A. Bocking
Chief Executive: D. G. Collier
Chairman, Cricket Committee: S. E. Foster
Secretary: 2000 – B. Robson
Captain: J. E. R. Gallian
Director of Cricket: C. E. B. Rice
Head Groundsman: S. Birks
Scorer: G. Stringfellow

Nottinghamshire developed the backbone and belief during 2000 that had been conspicuously absent the previous year. Pre-season predictions, by players and management, of promotion in both the Championship and the League appeared fanciful for a county that had slumped to ten defeats in their last 11 four-day games in 1999. To Nottinghamshire's credit, however, the fighting talk was backed by action on the pitch. Going into the last week of the season, they had already booked a place in Division One of the National League and still had a chance of joining the top flight of the County Championship, despite a record of only two wins.

Had the weather played fair, they might easily have won more often, for they were frustrated by rain a number of times. They had remained in contention thanks to their lower-order batsmen's stubborn streak when it came to rebuilding an innings, and to an uncanny knack of picking up bonus points. Only Division One champions Surrey bettered their total of 84.

The unavailability of an overseas player, until the Victorian captain, Paul Reiffel, took up residence in mid-June, cost Nottinghamshire dear. An increased membership had been eagerly awaiting the arrival of their original choice, the exciting Pakistani fast bowler Shoaib Akhtar, but, sadly for the Trent Bridge faithful and for Shoaib himself, his only appearance was as twelfth man before a rib injury ruled him out for the season. Reiffel, who answered a similar SOS when the Australians toured England in 1997, went about his business with little fuss, showing steady improvement to sneak almost unnoticed to the top of both the bowling and batting averages. Had he been in the dressing-room from April, those fanciful predictions of dual promotion might well have come true.

Inconsistency with bat and ball ultimately prevented Nottinghamshire from achieving their aims. Too often, too many players performed below par; as a team they rarely fired at the same time. Even Usman Afzaal, the one Nottinghamshire batsman to reach the 1,000-run mark, doing so for the first time, had a somewhat seesaw season. After five Championship matches, he had only 65 runs to his name, but on the eve of his 23rd birthday the left-hander rediscovered his form; he finished with 1,018 runs and selection for the England A tour, alongside team-mates Paul Franks and Chris Read. The turning-point came against a Worcestershire attack led by Glenn McGrath. While the Australian Test bowler took eight for 86, Afzaal remained unbeaten on 151. He could have made more, but turned down runs as he and Andrew Harris put on 152 for the last wicket to equal the county record set in 1911 by Ted Alletson and William Riley.

At Edgbaston a week earlier, former Surrey opener Darren Bicknell and Guy Welton had passed the 110-year-old record for any Nottinghamshire wicket with an unbroken opening partnership of 406. The compact Welton turned his maiden century into an unbeaten 200, but he struggled to recapture that form as the season progressed. His more experienced partner enjoyed a solid first year with his new county but, Afzaal aside, others at the top of the order provided runs in sporadic bursts.

The bowlers, too, had a mixed season. Spinner Richard Stemp bowled tidily whenever called upon, while Andrew Harris, a signing from Derbyshire, missed the opening weeks with a broken finger but came back to finish top wicket-taker with 44. His aggressive, whole-hearted approach quickly won him new admirers. David Millns celebrated his return to his home county by taking wickets regularly before his season was ended prematurely by injury, and Franks showed touches of real class until he lost his edge after being picked, then largely ignored, by England for the triangular series.

Nottinghamshire reserved their best cricket for the League, racking up 11 wins to finish second, two points behind Surrey. Bizarrely, however, they lost all five of their knockout games; another was washed out. Bicknell shone in the promotion run, passing 500 runs, and with Jason Gallian shared a county-record opening stand for the competition when they put on 196 against Surrey. Gallian and John Morris also scored good runs, Franks enjoyed a fine League season with the ball, and wicket-keeper Read set a county record with 27 League dismissals. Promotion was clinched with a dramatic home win over Glamorgan and, after a lean 1999, the pitch invasion and joyous scenes that followed were understandable. The overdue success sent players and supporters away with renewed optimism.

Nottinghamshire, who signed six new players the previous winter, had seamers Andy Oram and Mark Bowen retire in 2000, while Giles Haywood was released. As a result, director of cricket Clive Rice immediately set about searching for new talent, and signed up youngsters Chris Hewison and Gareth Clough, effectively on trial, for 2001. There were also acquisitions, perhaps not surprisingly, from South Africa in the Northerns left-arm pace man, Greg Smith, and Kevin Pietersen, a young off-spinning all-rounder from KwaZulu-Natal. By having a British parent, neither filled the overseas slot, which went to Greg Blewett. The Australian batsman was an interesting choice for Rice: having suffered by going without an overseas star for the first months of 2000, he was gambling on his new man not being required by the touring Ashes party. – PAUL FEARN.

637

NOTTINGHAMSHIRE 2000

[Bill Smith]

Back row: S. J. Randall, D. S. Lucas, M. J. A. Whiley, A. R. Oram, G. E. Welton, G. R. Haywood. Middle row: W. M. Noon, J. E. Morris, A. J. Harris, D. J. Bicknell, D. J. Millns, U. Afzaal, R. D. Stemp. Front row: C. M. W. Read, P. J. Franks, M. N. Bowen, C. E. B. Rice (director of cricket), J. E. R. Gallian (captain), P. Johnson, C. M. Tolley, M. Newell. Inset: P. R. Reiffel.

NOTTINGHAMSHIRE RESULTS

All first-class matches – Played 16: Won 2, Lost 4, Drawn 10. Abandoned 1.

County Championship matches – Played 16: Won 2, Lost 4, Drawn 10.

PPP Healthcare County Championship, 7th in Division 2; NatWest Trophy, 3rd round; Benson and Hedges Cup, 6th in North Group; Norwich Union National League, 2nd in Division 2.

COUNTY CHAMPIONSHIP AVERAGES

BATTING

Cap		M	I	NO	R	HS	100s	50s	Avge	Ct
2000	P. R. Reiffel§	7	8	4	275	74	0	3	68.75	0
2000	U. Afzaal	16	26	3	1,018	151*	3	4	44.26	9
1998	J. E. R. Gallian	16	26	3	796	150	3	0	34.60	23
2000	D. J. Bicknell.	16	28	3	858	180*	2	2	34.32	3
	G. E. Welton	13	23	2	674	200*	1	3	32.09	8
2000	J. E. Morris.	13	20	0	601	115	1	3	30.05	7
1997	C. M. Tolley	6	9	1	223	60	0	2	27.87	0
2000	D. J. Millns†	8	11	4	195	50*	0	1	27.85	2
1999	P. J. Franks†	13	18	1	447	60	0	3	26.29	5
	D. S. Lucas†	10	12	5	184	46*	0	0	26.28	3
1999	C. M. W. Read.	16	23	3	479	56*	0	3	23.95	40
1986	P. Johnson†	12	19	2	353	100	1	0	20.76	9
2000	A. J. Harris.	11	14	4	153	39	0	0	15.30	4
	M. N. Bowen.	4	6	0	83	24	0	0	13.83	2
2000	R. D. Stemp	11	11	5	45	11	0	0	7.50	7

Also batted: C. J. Hewison (1 match) 24, 6 (5 ct); W. M. Noon (cap 1995) (1 match) 0, 7 (1 ct); M. J. A. Whiley† (1 match) 0, 0 (1 ct). S. J. Randall† (1 match) did not bat.

* Signifies not out.   *† Born in Nottinghamshire.*   *§ Overseas player.*

BOWLING

	O	M	R	W	BB	5W/i	Avge
P. R. Reiffel	233.3	60	586	21	5-62	1	27.90
R. D. Stemp	398.2	140	946	33	5-123	1	28.66
D. J. Millns	226.1	42	880	30	5-58	1	29.33
P. J. Franks	393.4	81	1,247	42	7-56	2	29.69
A. J. Harris	384.3	62	1,358	44	6-110	4	30.86
D. S. Lucas	271.5	57	888	27	4-61	0	32.88

Also bowled: U. Afzaal 149.2–46–379–9; D. J. Bicknell 1–1–0–0; M. N. Bowen 68–14–208–4; J. E. R. Gallian 92–24–278–5; J. E. Morris 2.4–0–26–1; S. J. Randall 22–2–109–1; C. M. Tolley 52–22–107–4; G. E. Welton 1–0–1–0; M. J. A. Whiley 13.3–2–76–0.

COUNTY RECORDS

Highest score for:	312*	W. W. Keeton v Middlesex at The Oval	1939
Highest score against:	345	C. G. Macartney (Australians) at Nottingham . . .	1921
Best bowling for:	10-66	K. Smales v Gloucestershire at Stroud	1956
Best bowling against:	10-10	H. Verity (Yorkshire) at Leeds.	1932
Highest total for:	739-7 dec.	v Leicestershire at Nottingham	1903
Highest total against:	781-7 dec.	by Northamptonshire at Northampton	1995
Lowest total for:	13	v Yorkshire at Nottingham	1901
Lowest total against:	{ 16	by Derbyshire at Nottingham	1879
	16	by Surrey at The Oval	1880

NOTTINGHAMSHIRE v CAMBRIDGE UNIVERSITY

At Nottingham, April 11, 12, 13. Abandoned.

NOTTINGHAMSHIRE v NORTHAMPTONSHIRE

At Nottingham, April 26, 27, 28, 29. Drawn. Nottinghamshire 7 pts, Northamptonshire 7 pts. Toss: Nottinghamshire.

Day three saw the only play possible, but that was enough time for 19 wickets to fall, causing the ECB to despatch a pitch liaison officer to check on a lively surface that was never uncovered on the fourth day. Millns, back home at Trent Bridge after a decade at Leicester, was the chief beneficiary of some poor Northamptonshire batting, his five for 58 bettering anything he had managed in 15 first-class games in his initial two seasons with Nottinghamshire. Only Penberthy offered resistance and, aided by dropped catches, coaxed 64 from the last three wickets. Nottinghamshire's batsmen fared even worse against Malcolm and Cousins, the latter also making an early impression after a change of county and returning Championship-best figures. They were 40 for eight before No. 10 Lucas got to grips with the conditions and held firm until the light deteriorated.

Close of play: First day, No play; Second day, No play; Third day, Nottinghamshire 79-9 (Lucas 25*, Stemp 6*).

Northamptonshire

A. S. Rollins c Read b Millns	0	R. J. Logan c Morris b Millns	15
*M. L. Hayden c Read b Franks	7	D. M. Cousins c Read b Millns	4
M. B. Loye c Read b Millns	21	D. E. Malcolm c Lucas b Franks	8
D. J. Sales lbw b Lucas	5		
R. J. Warren b Millns	2	L-b 7, w 6, n-b 2	15
A. L. Penberthy not out	47		——
G. P. Swann c Johnson b Lucas	25	1/3 2/19 3/29 4/31 5/41	153
†T. M. B. Bailey c Read b Lucas	4	6/83 7/89 8/114 9/128	

Bonus points – Nottinghamshire 3.

Bowling: Franks 19.4–8–32–2; Millns 20–6–58–5; Lucas 12–4–44–3; Tolley 3–1–12–0.

Nottinghamshire

D. J. Bicknell c Penberthy b Malcolm	11	D. J. Millns lbw b Malcolm	9
U. Afzaal lbw b Malcolm	0	D. S. Lucas not out	25
*J. E. R. Gallian c Bailey b Cousins	2	R. D. Stemp not out	6
P. Johnson c Bailey b Cousins	0		
J. E. Morris c Sales b Cousins	5	L-b 3, w 4, n-b 4	11
†C. M. W. Read lbw b Cousins	7		——
C. M. Tolley c Bailey b Malcolm	2	1/1 2/8 3/8 4/26 5/26	(9 wkts) 79
P. J. Franks b Malcolm	1	6/33 7/35 8/40 9/63	

Bonus points – Northamptonshire 3.

Bowling: Malcolm 12–2–45–5; Cousins 13–4–31–4; Logan 1–1–0–0.

Umpires: A. Clarkson and D. R. Shepherd.

At Chelmsford, May 3, 4, 5, 6. NOTTINGHAMSHIRE drew with ESSEX.

At Northampton, May 11, 12, 13, 14. NOTTINGHAMSHIRE lost to NORTHAMPTONSHIRE by an innings and 124 runs.

NOTTINGHAMSHIRE v GLOUCESTERSHIRE

At Nottingham, May 17, 18, 19, 20. Drawn. Nottinghamshire 8 pts, Gloucestershire 9 pts. Toss: Nottinghamshire.

With 15 wickets on the opening day, and the pitch producing occasional low bounce, the game looked unlikely to last even three days. But rain shortened the next two and made a draw inevitable. Lewis, having already run out Bicknell with a direct hit, had Nottinghamshire in deep trouble in his seventh over with his first hat-trick: two lbw and Morris caught at mid-on off a leading edge. When Noon followed, they were 40 for five. However, recalled opener Welton rallied the lower order and the last five added 175. Gloucestershire mirrored Nottinghamshire's poor start: Franks took three wickets for just two singles in his first nine overs, and two from Lucas had them 29 for five. Though the pitch attracted further ECB attention, Alleyne and Russell found it to their liking whenever the weather relented, eventually adding 135. Alleyne reached his first Championship century since August 1998 and had batted every day when he was out early on the fourth morning. Harvey upset Nottinghamshire's batting practice with an aggressive spell before the game petered out.

Close of play: First day, Gloucestershire 47-5 (Alleyne 12*, Russell 6*); Second day, Gloucestershire 144-5 (Alleyne 68*, Russell 32*); Third day, Gloucestershire 212-6 (Alleyne 122*, Snape 4*).

Nottinghamshire

D. J. Bicknell run out	2	– c Russell b Smith	2
G. E. Welton c Russell b Alleyne	74	– b Harvey	42
*J. E. R. Gallian lbw b Lewis	11	– lbw b Harvey	42
U. Afzaal lbw b Lewis	0	– b Cotterell	14
J. E. Morris c Cotterell b Lewis	0	– c Hancock b Harvey	19
W. M. Noon lbw b Smith	0	– lbw b Harvey	7
†C. M. W. Read lbw b Smith	20	– b Lewis	25
P. J. Franks c Cunliffe b Lewis	26	– b Lewis	14
D. J. Millns not out	36	– not out	14
D. S. Lucas c Cunliffe b Lewis	25	– not out	10
R. D. Stemp c Russell b Smith	1		
B 2, l-b 12, n-b 6	20	B 1, l-b 4, w 2, n-b 11	18

1/7 2/35 3/35 4/35 5/40   215   1/4 2/94 3/111 4/113   (8 wkts) 207
6/92 7/131 8/165 9/214   5/133 6/144 7/177 8/192

Bonus points – Nottinghamshire 1, Gloucestershire 3.

Bowling: *First Innings*—Smith 18.2–6–50–3; Lewis 20–4–55–5; Harvey 15–5–47–0; Alleyne 11–5–31–1; Cotterell 6–2–18–0. *Second Innings*—Smith 15–3–36–1; Lewis 18–4–53–2; Snape 2–0–18–0; Harvey 19–6–63–4; Cotterell 5–0–27–1; Hancock 1–0–5–0.

Gloucestershire

R. J. Cunliffe lbw b Franks	4		J. Lewis b Franks	38
T. H. C. Hancock c Noon b Franks	4		A. M. Smith b Millns	11
M. G. N. Windows lbw b Franks	9		T. P. Cotterell not out	5
K. J. Barnett lbw b Lucas	3			
*M. W. Alleyne b Stemp	126		B 4, l-b 16, w 10, n-b 4	34
I. J. Harvey lbw b Lucas	0			
†R. C. Russell c Gallian b Millns	38		1/9 2/10 3/21 4/29 5/29	290
J. N. Snape lbw b Lucas	18		6/164 7/216 8/241 9/274	

Bonus points – Gloucestershire 2, Nottinghamshire 3.

Bowling: Franks 31.2–15–43–4; Lucas 40–11–92–3; Millns 23–3–90–2; Stemp 14–6–29–1; Gallian 9–6–16–0.

Umpires: A. A. Jones and M. J. Kitchen.

At Birmingham, June 2, 3, 4, 5. NOTTINGHAMSHIRE drew with WARWICKSHIRE.

NOTTINGHAMSHIRE v WORCESTERSHIRE

At Nottingham, June 7, 8, 9, 10. Worcestershire won by 106 runs. Worcestershire 20 pts, Nottinghamshire 6 pts. Toss: Worcestershire.

Worcestershire went ten points clear at the top of Division Two after four days of thrilling cricket. Under clear skies, Hick and Leatherdale used the favourable conditions to gain maximum batting points. Hick's 122 contained a six and 18 fours, and Leatherdale lost nothing in comparison, hitting 19 fours in his 117. McGrath's high-class pace then put the previously placid pitch into context: he had Nottinghamshire nine down, with 92 still needed to avoid the follow-on. But from that hopeless position, Afzaal, given two lives, and Harris hit career-bests as they added 152, equalling the county's tenth-wicket record, by Ted Alletson and William Riley at Hove in 1911. Their lead cut to 89, Worcestershire went for quick runs against an attack that lost Millns and then Lucas through injuries; Solanki's classy 80 in 100 balls allowed Hick to declare late on the third day. Nottinghamshire survived McGrath's four-over evening onslaught, but Leatherdale's less demanding medium-pace had them four down before lunch. Lampitt exploited the breach, and McGrath sealed victory with his tenth wicket of the match. The previous day, Nottinghamshire suffered a devastating blow when they had to release their own overseas player, Shoaib Akhtar, whose recurring side strain had prevented him bowling a ball.

Close of play: First day, Worcestershire 354-7 (Leatherdale 96*, Illingworth 15*); Second day, Nottinghamshire 300-9 (Afzaal 146*, Harris 35*); Third day, Nottinghamshire 13-0 (Bicknell 11*, Welton 2*).

Worcestershire

E. J. Wilson lbw b Harris	23	– (2) c Bicknell b Harris	54
W. P. C. Weston c Read b Millns	1	– (1) lbw b Millns	13
*G. A. Hick lbw b Gallian	122	– c and b Harris	26
V. S. Solanki b Millns	27	– c sub b Afzaal	80
R. C. Driver c Gallian b Lucas	16	– c Read b Harris	0
D. A. Leatherdale b Lucas	117	– b Harris	11
†S. J. Rhodes c Franks b Millns	16	– c Read b Franks	7
S. R. Lampitt b Afzaal	6	– not out	34
R. K. Illingworth c Gallian b Millns	15	– not out	44
G. D. McGrath b Lucas	8		
A. Sheriyar not out	15		
B 2, l-b 16, w 4, n-b 14	36	B 1, l-b 14, w 2, n-b 6	23

1/6 2/68 3/136 4/163 5/248   **402**   1/19 2/66 3/138   (7 wkts dec.) **292**
6/304 7/315 8/362 9/379   4/148 5/186
                                             6/212 7/218

Bonus points – Worcestershire 5, Nottinghamshire 3.

Bowling: First Innings—Franks 25–4–85–0; Millns 24–6–92–4; Lucas 25.5–5–86–3; Harris 18–2–58–1; Afzaal 15–3–45–1; Gallian 5–1–18–1. *Second Innings*—Franks 23.4–5–81–1; Millns 5.2–2–17–1; Lucas 3–1–12–0; Harris 25–3–85–4; Gallian 11–0–49–0; Afzaal 16–6–33–1.

Nottinghamshire

D. J. Bicknell lbw b McGrath	12	– c Rhodes b McGrath	43
G. E. Welton b McGrath	3	– c Rhodes b Illingworth	60
*J. E. R. Gallian lbw b McGrath	23	– (5) c Hick b Lampitt	0
P. Johnson lbw b Lampitt	10	– c Hick b Leatherdale	6
J. E. Morris lbw b McGrath	4	– (3) lbw b Leatherdale	26
U. Afzaal not out	151	– c Rhodes b Lampitt	13
†C. M. W. Read b Lampitt	0	– b Leatherdale	13
P. J. Franks c Rhodes b McGrath	27	– c Rhodes b Lampitt	60
D. J. Millns c Rhodes b McGrath	4	– c Rhodes b Lampitt	25
D. S. Lucas b McGrath	6	– c Rhodes b McGrath	7
A. J. Harris hit wkt b McGrath	39	– not out	0
B 2, l-b 2, n-b 30	34	B 8, l-b 8, n-b 6	22

1/7 2/36 3/51 4/56 5/69   **313**   1/50 2/106 3/112 4/113 5/151   **275**
6/82 7/143 8/149 9/161   6/166 7/212 8/250 9/275

Bonus points – Nottinghamshire 3, Worcestershire 3.

Bowling: *First Innings*—McGrath 28.1–8–86–8; Sheriyar 19–5–77–0; Lampitt 21–3–69–2; Illingworth 20–4–53–0; Leatherdale 3–0–10–0; Hick 4–0–14–0; Solanki 1–1–0–0. *Second Innings*—McGrath 20.4–6–57–2; Sheriyar 16–2–71–0; Illingworth 11–5–32–1; Lampitt 19–7–42–4; Leatherdale 11–3–52–3; Hick 1–0–5–0.

Umpires: M. J. Harris and P. Willey.

At Lord's, June 14, 15, 16, 17. NOTTINGHAMSHIRE beat MIDDLESEX by 169 runs.

At Nottingham, June 29. NOTTINGHAMSHIRE lost to ZIMBABWEANS by five wickets (See Zimbabwean tour section).

NOTTINGHAMSHIRE v ESSEX

At Nottingham, July 7, 8, 9, 10. Drawn. Nottinghamshire 6 pts, Essex 10 pts. Toss: Essex. Championship debut: P. R. Reiffel.

On an excellent pitch, against some mediocre bowling, Essex grabbed an early initiative when Grayson and Stuart Law added 248 in 65 overs. Harris removed them both on his way to five wickets, but Danny Law's entertaining 68, with three sixes and seven fours, allowed Irani to call his men in late on the second day with 500 on the board. Nottinghamshire, after fighting back well with the second new ball, desperately missed Franks, with England's one-day squad, and Stemp, who had torn knee ligaments. They were, however, finally able to field an overseas player, Paul Reiffel, in their eighth Championship game. The Essex bowlers then strengthened their position further by removing five top-order batsmen before rain swept in for a second time on the third day, and washed out the fourth.

Close of play: First day, Essex 348-3 (S. G. Law 152*, Irani 13*), Second day, Nottinghamshire 45-1 (Bicknell 29*, Gallian 1*); Third day, Nottinghamshire 180-5 (Afzaal 65*, Read 0*).

Essex

P. J. Prichard lbw b Reiffel	19	A. P. Cowan lbw b Randall		30
A. P. Grayson c Johnson b Harris	144	M. C. Ilott c Welton b Harris		4
D. D. J. Robinson b Harris	9	P. M. Such not out		3
S. G. Law c Read b Harris	165	B 8, l-b 12, w 3, n-b 10		33
*R. C. Irani c Afzaal b Reiffel	26			
S. D. Peters lbw b Harris	0	1/42 2/65 3/313	(9 wkts dec.)	505
†B. J. Hyam b Reiffel	4	4/369 5/375 6/375		
D. R. Law not out	68	7/394 8/458 9/475		

Bonus points – Essex 5, Nottinghamshire 2 (Score at 130 overs: 431-7).

Bowling: Reiffel 32–11–74–3; Lucas 28–5–94–0; Harris 43–7–139–5; Randall 22–2–109–1; Gallian 10–1–33–0; Afzaal 11–1–36–0.

Nottinghamshire

D. J. Bicknell c Hyam b Ilott	64	†C. M. W. Read not out		0
G. E. Welton c Cowan b Irani	13			
*J. E. R. Gallian lbw b Irani	3	L-b 1, w 6, n-b 8		15
J. E. Morris c Peters b Cowan	11			
U. Afzaal not out	65	1/39 2/51 3/72	(5 wkts)	180
P. Johnson c Hyam b Cowan	9	4/125 5/173		

P. R. Reiffel, D. S. Lucas, S. J. Randall and A. J. Harris did not bat.

Bonus point – Essex 1.

Bowling: Ilott 17–6–34–1; Irani 17–5–52–2; Cowan 15.3–5–44–2; Such 4–2–15–0; D. R. Law 6–0–34–0.

Umpires: M. R. Benson and D. J. Constant.

At Worcester, July 12, 13, 14, 15. NOTTINGHAMSHIRE drew with WORCESTERSHIRE.

At Hove, July 19, 20, 21, 22. NOTTINGHAMSHIRE drew with SUSSEX.

NOTTINGHAMSHIRE v WARWICKSHIRE

At Nottingham, August 3, 4, 5, 6. Drawn. Nottinghamshire 11 pts, Warwickshire 10 pts. Toss: Warwickshire.

Twice, Warwickshire's bowlers allowed Nottinghamshire's lower order to rescue their side from difficult positions. Wicket-keeper Read led the first-innings recovery, adding 91 with Franks so that Afzaal's latest half-century was not wasted. For all that, the visitors looked to be batting towards a lead until Reiffel, with the second new ball, dismissed their last four batsmen in 27 deliveries to record his first five-wicket haul in county cricket. Giddins followed this with four of his own to have Nottinghamshire 55 for five, but Reiffel's first Championship fifty, and other handy scores down the line, made the game safe. A back spasm prevented Reiffel from bowling in the last innings. Gallian's far-from-generous target, 277 from 49 overs, meant a disappointing end to an excellent match, robbed of a more fitting finish by the loss of half the first day to rain.

Close of play: First day, Nottinghamshire 149-3 (Afzaal 58*, Johnson 12*); Second day, Warwickshire 121-3 (Hemp 26*, Piper 0*); Third day, Nottinghamshire 85-5 (Read 14*, Bicknell 15*).

Nottinghamshire

D. J. Bicknell lbw b Donald	10	–	(7) c Giles b Donald	25
G. E. Welton b Donald	10	–	(1) lbw b Giddins	9
*J. E. R. Gallian c Brown b Giddins	31	–	(2) lbw b Giddins	2
U. Afzaal c Ostler b Giles	82	–	(3) b Giddins	0
P. Johnson c Penney b Donald	22	–	(4) c Penney b Brown	19
C. M. Tolley c Hemp b Brown	23	–	(5) c Piper b Giddins	14
†C. M. W. Read c Piper b Brown	52	–	(6) c Piper b Donald	45
P. J. Franks c Piper b Brown	26	–	c Ostler b Brown	20
P. R. Reiffel not out	26	–	not out	60
D. S. Lucas lbw b Brown	9			
A. J. Harris lbw b Brown	14	–	(10) not out	12
B 19, l-b 16, w 18, n-b 10	63		B 9, l-b 11, w 6	26

1/20 2/33 3/122 4/159 5/216	**368**	1/8 2/10 3/33	(8 wkts dec.) **232**
6/220 7/311 8/312 9/322		4/49 5/55 6/104	
		7/135 8/183	

Bonus points – Nottinghamshire 4, Warwickshire 3.

Bowling: *First Innings*—Donald 31.3–6–100–3; Giddins 32–10–90–1; Brown 26–5–87–5; Hemp 2–0–13–0; Giles 21.3–5–43–1. *Second Innings*—Donald 27–6–60–2; Giddins 28–9–70–4; Brown 16–3–74–2; Giles 8–4–8–0.

Warwickshire

M. J. Powell lbw b Franks	11	– c Read b Harris	5
N. V. Knight c Read b Harris	29	– b Tolley	37
D. P. Ostler lbw b Tolley	41	– c Johnson b Lucas	9
D. L. Hemp c Harris b Reiffel	70	– c Read b Lucas	8
†K. J. Piper c Read b Tolley	28		
T. L. Penney c Johnson b Tolley	6	– (5) not out	38
D. R. Brown lbw b Reiffel	37	– (6) not out	19
A. F. Giles c Gallian b Reiffel	37		
*N. M. K. Smith c Gallian b Reiffel	0		
A. A. Donald not out	10		
E. S. H. Giddins b Reiffel	14		
B 2, l-b 8, w 2, n-b 29	41	L-b 6, n-b 10	16

1/25 2/67 3/119 4/185 5/203   324   1/13 2/32 3/48 4/83   (4 wkts) 132
6/227 7/290 8/297 9/308

Bonus points – Warwickshire 3, Nottinghamshire 3.

Bowling: *First Innings*—Reiffel 26.3–8–62–5; Franks 24–1–102–1; Harris 21–1–76–1; Lucas 19–4–52–0; Tolley 16–10–22–3; Afzaal 2–2–0–0. *Second Innings*—Franks 11–2–41–0; Harris 13–2–35–1; Lucas 9–1–33–2; Tolley 5–2–9–1; Afzaal 2–0–7–0; Welton 1–0–1–0.

Umpires: T. E. Jesty and B. Leadbeater.

NOTTINGHAMSHIRE v MIDDLESEX

At Nottingham, August 9, 10, 11. Middlesex won by ten wickets. Middlesex 20 pts, Nottinghamshire 4 pts. Toss: Nottinghamshire.

Exquisite batting by Langer and textbook seam bowling from Fraser earned Middlesex maximum points for a crushing three-day victory. Gallian's decision to bowl was undermined by his indisciplined attack, who dished up a generous selection of short and wide deliveries. Langer, so strong on the back foot, found them much to his taste, crashing 108 in 123 balls (17 fours), while Joyce, who shared a century stand with Nash, notched his maiden fifty. Having helped Cook guide Middlesex to full batting points, Fraser then removed three top-order batsmen before going off with a sore knee. Though Tolley made a gritty 60, and Middlesex put down six catches, Nottinghamshire were following on late on the second day. The next morning was disastrous: eight wickets fell in the first session as Fraser and Johnson rarely strayed in line or length. Fraser, twice taking wickets with successive balls, recorded season's best figures – six for 46 on the day – and it took staunch batting by Franks and the tail to make Middlesex bat again. As it was, they needed only 21 balls to reach their second win of the season.

Close of play: First day, Middlesex 377-8 (Cook 32*, Fraser 2*); Second day, Nottinghamshire 29-0 (Bicknell 8*, Welton 16*).

Middlesex

A. J. Strauss c Afzaal b Franks	43	– not out	13
M. A. Roseberry lbw b Harris	8	– not out	2
*J. L. Langer c Read b Lucas	108		
M. R. Ramprakash c Read b Lucas	1		
E. C. Joyce c Whiley b Franks	51		
†D. C. Nash lbw b Franks	48		
B. L. Hutton c Morris b Lucas	7		
S. J. Cook c Afzaal b Harris	43		
R. L. Johnson b Gallian	23		
A. R. C. Fraser c Afzaal b Lucas	19		
P. C. R. Tufnell not out	0		
B 1, l-b 26, w 4, n-b 30	61	B 1, l-b 1, w 10	12

1/16 2/129 3/146 4/185 5/286   412   (no wkt) 27
6/297 7/318 8/361 9/410

Bonus points – Middlesex 5, Nottinghamshire 3.

Bowling: *First Innings*—Franks 28–4–90–3; Harris 23.4–4–87–2; Lucas 22–5–73–4; Whiley 13–2–71–0; Tolley 11–1–35–0; Afzaal 4–0–12–0; Gallian 8–4–17–1. *Second Innings*—Lucas 2–0–9–0; Franks 1–0–11–0; Whiley 0.3–0–5–0.

Nottinghamshire

D. J. Bicknell b Fraser	4	– c Langer b Johnson	20
G. E. Welton c Nash b Johnson	8	– b Fraser	18
*J. E. R. Gallian b Fraser	44	– c Langer b Fraser	0
U. Afzaal lbw b Fraser	37	– c Nash b Johnson	11
J. E. Morris c Nash b Johnson	6	– lbw b Fraser	4
C. M. Tolley lbw b Tufnell	60	– lbw b Fraser	2
†C. M. W. Read c Langer b Tufnell	28	– lbw b Johnson	17
P. J. Franks c Johnson b Tufnell	20	– c Joyce b Fraser	50
A. J. Harris c Ramprakash b Johnson	6	– lbw b Tufnell	15
D. S. Lucas not out	19	– not out	46
M. J. A. Whiley c Roseberry b Cook	0	– c Nash b Fraser	0
L-b 3, w 2, n-b 8	13	B 5, l-b 4	9

1/16 2/16 3/94 4/103 5/109   245   1/37 2/37 3/53 4/62 5/62   192
6/161 7/186 8/211 9/236   6/68 7/82 8/124 9/192

Bonus points – Nottinghamshire 1, Middlesex 3.

Bowling: *First Innings*—Fraser 14–4–39–3; Johnson 24–4–90–3; Cook 15.5–2–48–1; Tufnell 22–7–41–3; Hutton 4–0–24–0. *Second Innings*—Fraser 19.4–3–64–6; Johnson 22–7–76–3; Tufnell 13–2–28–1; Cook 6–2–15–0.

Umpires: M. J. Harris and A. A. Jones.

At Cardiff, August 16, 17, 18, 19. NOTTINGHAMSHIRE drew with GLAMORGAN.

NOTTINGHAMSHIRE v SUSSEX

At Nottingham, August 30, 31, September 1, 2. Drawn. Nottinghamshire 11 pts, Sussex 9 pts. Toss: Nottinghamshire.

Having manoeuvred themselves into a commanding position, Nottinghamshire were denied any chance of victory by the weather. Bicknell, missed at gully when 27, batted throughout the first day, getting Nottinghamshire away from trouble at 163 for seven by adding 143 in 35 overs with Reiffel. Montgomerie responded in kind with a chanceless century to ease Sussex past the follow-on. Although the bat was dominant, and the bowling at times ordinary, Lewry and then Harris grafted away for their respective sides and were rewarded with six wickets apiece. Gallian wasted no time building on Nottinghamshire's 64-run lead, hitting 110 from 115 balls with two sixes and 17 fours; like Montgomerie, he had also made a century when the counties met at Hove in July. Sussex were set 303 to win in 88 overs, but less than five were possible before the rain, having cut short the previous day, returned in earnest to leave Nottinghamshire still looking for their first home win of the season.

Close of play: First day, Nottinghamshire 336-8 (Bicknell 139*, Harris 16*); Second day, Sussex 235-6 (Montgomerie 116*, Wilton 20*); Third day, Nottinghamshire 177-3 (Gallian 82*, Morris 30*).

Nottinghamshire

D. J. Bicknell c Cottey b Lewry	144	– lbw b Martin-Jenkins	35
G. E. Welton lbw b Lewry	2	– c Wilton b Lewry	11
*J. E. R. Gallian c Montgomerie b Kirtley	9	– not out	110
U. Afzaal c Montgomerie b Kirtley	45	– b Taylor	0
J. E. Morris c Wilton b Lewry	18	– b Adams	30
P. Johnson c Wilton b Kirtley	0	– not out	33
†C. M. W. Read c Montgomerie b Lewry	0		
P. J. Franks c Wilton b Lewry	6		
P. R. Reiffel c Wilton b Rashid	74		
A. J. Harris c Adams b Lewry	19		
R. D. Stemp not out	5		
B 5, l-b 4, w 12, n-b 8	29	B 1, l-b 4, w 2, n-b 12	19

1/9 2/30 3/102 4/141 5/142   351   1/29 2/106   (4 wkts dec.) 238
6/143 7/163 8/306 9/342   3/107 4/181

Bonus points – Nottinghamshire 4, Sussex 3.

Bowling: *First Innings*—Lewry 34.4–12–89–6; Kirtley 31–11–71–3; Martin-Jenkins 16–4–59–0; Taylor 17–4–79–0; Rashid 11–6–26–1; Bevan 3–0–18–0. *Second Innings*—Lewry 13–2–50–1; Kirtley 11–2–23–0; Taylor 9–1–45–1; Martin-Jenkins 7–0–42–1; Adams 6–0–39–1; Rashid 2–0–5–0; Bevan 2.4–0–29–0.

Sussex

R. R. Montgomerie c Afzaal b Franks	129	– not out	2
M. H. Yardy c Gallian b Reiffel	0	– not out	0
M. G. Bevan b Harris	26		
*C. J. Adams c Johnson b Harris	9		
P. A. Cottey b Harris	3		
R. S. C. Martin-Jenkins c Read b Reiffel	14		
U. B. A. Rashid c Stemp b Franks	25		
†N. J. Wilton c Afzaal b Harris	46		
R. J. Kirtley c Read b Harris	5		
J. D. Lewry b Harris	8		
B. V. Taylor not out	0		
L-b 6, w 14, n-b 2	22	B 1, l-b 1	2

1/3 2/70 3/84 4/112 5/139   287   (no wkt) 4
6/199 7/274 8/274 9/286

Bonus points – Sussex 2, Nottinghamshire 3.

Bowling· *First Innings*—Reiffel 27 7 69 2; Franks 20–3–74–2; Harris 29.1–4–110–6; Stemp 3–1–16–0; Gallian 6–2–12–0. *Second Innings*—Reiffel 2.5–2–1–0; Harris 2–1–1–0.

Umpires: D. J. Constant and R. A. White.

NOTTINGHAMSHIRE v GLAMORGAN

At Nottingham, September 6, 7, 8. Nottinghamshire won by seven wickets. Nottinghamshire 19 pts, Glamorgan 3 pts. Toss: Nottinghamshire. First-class debut: C. J. Hewison.

Nottinghamshire wrapped up a three-day victory over second-placed Glamorgan with such ease that it was hard to believe this was their first home Championship win since May 1999. Though it was only their second win anywhere this season, an impressive hoard of bonus points meant that they entered the final round in fourth place, with their own hopes of promotion revived. Resurgent skipper Gallian, fresh from an unbeaten century in his previous Championship innings, led the way again with 150, his highest for Nottinghamshire, hitting one six and 22 fours. Not for the first time, the lower order contributed significantly, too: Reiffel's fifty was his third in four innings. Hewison had come out of a Second Eleven game at Boots, where he made a second-ball duck, to replace the injured Morris. Glamorgan, who had scored 1,225 in their last two Championship innings, got off to a flying start next morning. They were 84 for one from 14 overs, with stand-in opener Croft racing to a 41-ball half-century – James had broken a thumb, fielding. Nottinghamshire's bowlers tightened their line and length after lunch and took out the nine remaining wickets for 103 in one session. Harris claimed five for the fourth time in 2000. When Glamorgan followed on, Franks took three wickets before bad light halted play, and three more next day as the seamers methodically worked through the batting.

Close of play: First day, Nottinghamshire 309-7 (Gallian 127*, Franks 14*); Second day, Glamorgan 22-3 (I. J. Thomas 11*, Dale 0*).

Nottinghamshire

D. J. Bicknell c Newell b Wharf	20	–	c Wallace b Watkin		3
G. E. Welton lbw b Watkin	4	–	c Wallace b Watkin		4
*J. E. R. Gallian c sub b Watkin	150	–	(5) not out		15
U. Afzaal b Watkin	29	–	(3) not out		36
P. Johnson c Newell b Watkin	6				
C. J. Hewison c Wallace b S. D. Thomas	24	–	(4) c Wallace b Watkin		6
†C. M. W. Read c Wallace b Newell	20				
P. R. Reiffel c I. J. Thomas b Watkin	50				
P. J. Franks c Wallace b Dale	32				
M. N. Bowen c I. J. Thomas b Wharf	13				
A. J. Harris not out	2				
B 8, l-b 9, w 4	21		N-b 2		2

1/11 2/41 3/89 4/95 5/159   371   1/7 2/12 3/28   (3 wkts) 66
6/191 7/269 8/353 9/359

Bonus points – Nottinghamshire 4, Glamorgan 3.

Bowling: *First Innings*—Watkin 25–2–99–5; Wharf 14–0–66–2; S. D. Thomas 22–1–87–1; Dale 16–3–47–1; Croft 10–1–35–0; Newell 6–1–20–1. *Second Innings*—Watkin 10.1–2–31–3; Dale 9–0–26–0; Maynard 1–0–9–0.

Glamorgan

R. D. B. Croft c Hewison b Franks	56	–	c Hewison b Franks		7
I. J. Thomas b Harris	10	–	c Hewison b Reiffel		35
M. J. Powell c Gallian b Reiffel	13	–	b Franks		4
*M. P. Maynard lbw b Bowen	37	–	b Franks		0
A. Dale c Afzaal b Franks	14	–	c Hewison b Harris		41
K. Newell c Afzaal b Harris	3	–	(7) lbw b Franks		35
†M. A. Wallace c Hewison b Harris	10	–	(8) not out		59
S. P. James c Read b Reiffel	3	–	(6) b Franks		24
A. G. Wharf lbw b Harris	0	–	lbw b Harris		0
S. D. Thomas not out	26	–	c Bicknell b Franks		4
S. L. Watkin b Harris	6	–	c Welton b Reiffel		28
L-b 7, w 2	9		L-b 3, w 2, n-b 4		9

1/34 2/86 3/86 4/125 5/134   187   1/12 2/16 3/20 4/71 5/111   246
6/152 7/154 8/154 9/166   6/131 7/177 8/182 9/195

Bonus points – Nottinghamshire 3.

Bowling: *First Innings*—Reiffel 13–2–42–2; Harris 15.3–0–69–5; Bowen 8–2–27–1; Franks 10–2–42–2; Afzaal 1–1–0–0. *Second Innings*—Franks 20–5–59–6; Reiffel 21.1–4–57–2; Harris 24–2–96–2; Bowen 10–2–31–0; Afzaal 1–1–0–0.

Umpires: N. G. Cowley and A. G. T. Whitehead.

At Bristol, September 13, 14, 15, 16. NOTTINGHAMSHIRE lost to GLOUCESTERSHIRE by three wickets.

SOMERSET

Peter Bowler

President: M. F. Hill
Chairman: R. Parsons
Chief Executive: P. W. Anderson
Chairman, Cricket Committee: V. J. Marks
Cricket Secretary: P. J. Robinson
Captain: J. Cox
First-Team Coach: 2000 – D. A. Reeve
2001 – K. J. Shine
Head Groundsman: P. Frost
Scorer: G. A. Stickley

It is too easy, and deceptive, to point out that Somerset did enough to retain their position in the first division of both the County Championship and the National League. In the same way, the fact that Peter Bowler came fifth in the national batting averages and Andrew Caddick sixth in the bowling hardly reflects either the frustrations among members or an honest acceptance within the Taunton dressing-room that the county should have done better.

There were some valid excuses. Caddick and Marcus Trescothick, two genuine match-winners, were often missing when their varying skills were badly needed, their obligations to England's cause leaving Somerset at times looking worryingly bereft. Once, Test elevation reflected glowingly on the counties concerned. Now, with cricket existing in a more pragmatic context, such county depletions – certainly not unique to Somerset – are grudgingly borne by many of the regional faithful. When their best players were lost at crucial stages of the summer, there was perplexed talk at Taunton, and in other parts of the country, of a disturbing disincentive to county cricket and its membership.

The problems of Somerset attempting to field their most balanced and strongest team were compounded by the serious back injury that kept their other new-ball bowler, the promising Matthew Bulbeck, out of action for most of the season. The county's Tasmanian captain, Jamie Cox, was no longer spoilt for choice. He was continually forced to compromise, shuffling his available resources and aware no doubt that he was short of the kind of well-structured side that could challenge for trophies. He would have benefited from another seam bowler – and from a genuine spinner. Too many matches were affected by bad weather; but too many also drifted away through a lack of sparkle, resolve and penetration.

It did not help that several batsmen seemed to go into decline. Cox himself was seldom the batsman of the previous season, when he made such an attractive and profitable entry to England's domestic scene. This time he failed to reach 1,000 runs, though in truth only just. There were still three hundreds from him and still a generous array of off-side strokes. It was just that they did not come so frequently; the consistency that characterised his 1999 innings was less apparent.

He continued to lead Somerset with encouraging enthusiasm, although results slipped away under the clouds. On occasions, fibre, historically an elusive quality at Somerset, was inclined to let them down when they were most tested. The county won only two Championship matches, the same number as the bottom two teams in Division One, and failed to win at all in the Benson and Hedges Cup. Their exit from the NatWest Trophy would be easily forgotten were it not in the record books as equalling their lowest one-day total. Yet early on they gave the impression that they were capable of running away with the National League title. They restored some necessary parochial pride, after the miscalculations in the previous season's NatWest final, by beating Gloucestershire; against Kent, Trescothick and Cox charged away with an opening stand of 145 to set up their fourth straight win. But the sequence was not sustained.

Bowler, at least, was back to some of his best form, which meant orthodox, controlled batting, watchful and never frenetic. There were five first-class centuries from him and 1,305 runs, but he was the only Somerset player to reach his thousand. Graham Rose, always thought of primarily as a swing bowler, could take pleasure from his two hundreds, as could Keith Parsons, who gave enough hints of what he might – and needs to – achieve as a regular middle-order batsman. He also surprised any detractors of his bowling by taking five for 13 against Lancashire.

But what happened to Rob Turner? Twelve months earlier he had impressed everyone by demonstrating that he could score good-looking runs as well as keep wicket. He never remotely approached that form in 2000. His batting was tentative and beset by technical hazards; he ended with fewer than 500 runs. Piran Holloway laboriously totalled under 400 from five games fewer. At last, though, there seemed to be an opportunity for Mark Lathwell to re-establish his credentials. Injuries out of the way, he came in for Trescothick, but there was not much evidence that he had rediscovered that old zest. Among the bowlers, Steffan Jones accepted his added responsibilities and took 40 wickets, although at a cost. What Somerset lacked too often were different options in attack. The return of Bulbeck, with his left-arm in-swing, should help. So would better results at Taunton: all seven Championship matches there were drawn.

There were highlights, however – like the 565 against Lancashire, when Cox and that valued journeyman, Michael Burns, scored centuries. There was a maiden hundred by the beefy Ian Blackwell, nominally recruited from Derbyshire as a slow left-arm bowler. There were precocious moments from Peter Trego, and the 269-run victory over the touring West Indians, initiated by Parsons's unbeaten 193 and completed by Jason Kerr's hat-trick. Then, of course, there was Trescothick, the likeable left-hander who was suddenly and rightly, heralded as England's new opener.

The season marked the end of Paul Jarvis's career as a county cricketer. Also on his way was Dermot Reeve, the innovative and outspoken coach taken on by Somerset to lift them, so it was said, from a surfeit of unfulfilment. He introduced ideas but led the county to no trophies, despite one Lord's final. In future, it appears, his opinions will be reserved for a television audience. – DAVID FOOT.

SOMERSET 2000

[*Bill Smith*]

Back row: J. G. Wyatt (*Second Eleven coach*), D. Veness (*physiotherapist*), P. C. L. Holloway, M. J. Wood, J. O. Grove, P. S. Jones, P. D. Trego, I. D. Blackwell, C. M. Gazzard, K. J. Shine (*assistant coach*). *Middle row:* M. N. Lathwell, M. Burns, G. J. Kennis, I. Jones, J. I. D. Kerr, J. P. Tucker, M. P. Bulbeck, K. A. Parsons, P. W. Jarvis. *Front row:* G. D. Rose, A. R. Caddick, R. Parsons (*chairman*), M. E. Trescothick, J. Cox (*captain*), D. A. Reeve (*first-team coach*), M. F. Hill (*president*), R. J. Turner, P. D. Bowler. *Inset:* A. R. K. Pierson.

SOMERSET RESULTS

All first-class matches – Played 18: Won 4, Lost 4, Drawn 10.

County Championship matches – Played 16: Won 2, Lost 4, Drawn 10.

*PPP Healthcare County Championship, 5th in Division 1; NatWest Trophy, 4th round;
Benson and Hedges Cup, 6th in Midlands/Wales/West Group;
Norwich Union National League, 6th in Division 1.*

COUNTY CHAMPIONSHIP AVERAGES

BATTING

Cap		M	I	NO	R	HS	100s	50s	Avge	Ct
1995	P. D. Bowler	16	23	4	1,090	139*	4	4	57.36	7
1999	M. E. Trescothick† . . .	8	12	1	470	105	1	2	42.72	8
1988	G. D. Rose	14	18	5	510	124	2	1	39.23	4
1999	J. Cox§.	15	23	1	835	171	2	3	37.95	5
1999	K. A. Parsons†	14	20	1	550	108*	1	1	28.94	14
1999	M. Burns	13	17	0	482	108	1	3	28.35	2
	J. I. D. Kerr	3	4	1	84	34	0	0	28.00	0
	I. D. Blackwell.	16	21	2	518	109	1	2	27.26	5
1997	P. C. L. Holloway. . .	12	18	1	376	113	1	1	22.11	9
	A. R. K. Pierson . . .	5	7	3	77	18	0	0	19.25	1
	P. D. Trego†	6	8	1	134	62	0	1	19.14	3
1994	R. J. Turner	16	22	0	410	75	0	2	18.63	33
1992	A. R. Caddick‡	3	4	1	52	21*	0	0	17.33	1
1992	M. N. Lathwell	8	12	0	199	47	0	0	16.58	4
	P. S. Jones	15	16	4	122	56*	0	1	10.16	4
	J. O. Grove	9	9	5	39	12*	0	0	9.75	0

Also batted: M. P. L. Bulbeck† (2 matches) 3*, 3; P. W. Jarvis (1 match) 1 (1 ct).

* Signifies not out.   *† Born in Somerset.*   *‡ ECB contract.*   *§ Overseas player.*

BOWLING

	O	M	R	W	BB	5W/i	Avge
A. R. Caddick	114	32	294	25	7-64	3	11.76
M. Burns	119.2	29	354	13	3-11	0	27.23
P. S. Jones	403.4	88	1,294	40	5-41	1	32.35
G. D. Rose	317.3	76	886	27	5-74	1	32.81
P. D. Trego	146.1	28	556	16	4-84	0	34.75
K. A. Parsons	139.4	38	398	10	5-13	1	39.80
J. O. Grove	158.3	24	610	15	5-90	1	40.66
I. D. Blackwell	364.3	109	912	16	3-72	0	57.00

Also bowled: M. P. L. Bulbeck 16–4–55–2; J. Cox 14–3–35–0; P. C. L. Holloway 2–0–4–0;
P. W. Jarvis 23.2–3–103–3; J. I. D. Kerr 38–4–190–4; A. R. K. Pierson 103–25–244–6;
M. E. Trescothick 53–10–182–2.

COUNTY RECORDS

Highest score for:	322	I. V. A. Richards v Warwickshire at Taunton	1985
Highest score against:	424	A. C. MacLaren (Lancashire) at Taunton	1895
Best bowling for:	10-49	E. J. Tyler v Surrey at Taunton	1895
Best bowling against:	10-35	A. Drake (Yorkshire) at Weston-super-Mare	1914
Highest total for:	675-9 dec.	v Hampshire at Bath.	1924
Highest total against:	811	by Surrey at The Oval	1899
Lowest total for:	25	v Gloucestershire at Bristol	1947
Lowest total against:	22	by Gloucestershire at Bristol	1920

SOMERSET v OXFORD UNIVERSITIES

At Taunton, April 7, 8, 9. Somerset won by 404 runs. Toss: Somerset. First-class debuts: P. D. Trego; A. S. Bones, A. M. T. Janmohamed, J. J. Porter, B. M. Vonwiller, C. C. M. Warren, S. W. Weenink. County debut: I. D. Blackwell.

This was hardly an uplifting start to Oxford's first outing as a plural entity – they included three players from Oxford Brookes University alongside eight from the older institution. Three cheap Somerset wickets offered a deceptive prelude, but the county went on to score almost at will. Bowler and, more forcefully, Burns hit big hundreds in the first innings, adding 305 in 229 minutes, and it was Cox's turn in the second. Batting practice was especially useful for Lathwell, making his return after missing the previous season with knee problems. For the students, New Zealander Scott Weenink alone resisted, scoring half of their fragile 144. It was even worse the second time: they collapsed against the swing of Jarvis and Bulbeck for 74 in 30 overs. Left-hander Smalley could only delay the inevitable. Gofton was unable to bat after earlier being struck on the head by a return shot from Cox.

Close of play: First day, Oxford Universities 23-3 (Weenink 3*); Second day, Somerset 260-2 (Lathwell 54*, Turner 18*).

Somerset

*J. Cox b Mather	17	– (2) c Vonwiller b Mather	100
M. E. Trescothick c Hicks b Vonwiller	0	– (1) st Smalley b Hicks	78
P. D. Bowler not out	157		
M. N. Lathwell c Vonwiller b Mather	4	– (3) not out	54
M. Burns b Gofton	160		
†R. J. Turner not out	15	– (4) not out	18
L-b 5, w 14	19	B 2, l-b 4, w 4	10

1/10 2/14 3/28 4/333   (4 wkts dec.) 362   1/116 2/231   (2 wkts dec.) 260

I. D. Blackwell, G. D. Rose, M. P. L. Bulbeck, P. W. Jarvis and P. D. Trego did not bat.

Bowling: *First Innings*—Mather 20–6–73–2; Vonwiller 13–2–55–1; Gofton 15–1–61–1; Hicks 21–3–96–0; Weenink 13–1–54–0; Janmohamed 3–0–18–0. *Second Innings*—Mather 9–0–43–1; Vonwiller 3–0–23–0; Gofton 4.2–0–22–0; Hicks 11–0–83–1; Porter 4–0–43–0; Weenink 5.4–0–29–0; Janmohamed 3–0–11–0.

Oxford Universities

A. S. Bones lbw b Bulbeck	6	– b Bulbeck	5
J. A. Claughton b Rose	3	– c Turner b Bulbeck	1
J. J. Porter b Bulbeck	10	– c Blackwell b Rose	2
S. W. Weenink not out	72	– (7) b Jarvis	2
A. F. Gofton lbw b Trego	19	– absent hurt	
C. C. M. Warren c Bowler b Blackwell	3	– (5) lbw b Bulbeck	9
A. M. T. Janmohamed b Trescothick	0	– (6) lbw b Jarvis	6
*T. C. Hicks run out	2	– b Jarvis	1
†R. G. Smalley b Blackwell	4	– (4) b Trego	37
D. P. Mather c Jarvis b Blackwell	13	– (9) c Turner b Jarvis	5
B. M. Vonwiller b Blackwell	0	– (10) not out	1
B 4, l-b 6, n-b 2	12	L-b 1, n-b 4	5

1/9 2/9 3/23 4/56 5/81   144   1/8 2/9 3/17 4/30 5/45   74
6/86 7/92 8/112 9/140   6/67 7/67 8/73 9/74

Bowling: *First Innings*—Rose 7–1–12–1; Bulbeck 13–3–31–2; Trego 12–2–28–1; Burns 7–3–5–0; Jarvis 7–2–17–0; Blackwell 14–8–18–4; Trescothick 8–3–23–1. *Second Innings*—Rose 8–2–10–1; Bulbeck 8–2–23–3; Jarvis 7.1–2–21–4; Trego 7–4–19–1.

Umpires: K. J. Lyons and D. R. Shepherd.

SOMERSET v SURREY

At Taunton, April 26, 27, 28, 29. Drawn. Somerset 10 pts, Surrey 6 pts. Toss: Somerset.

Bad weather restricted play to 54 overs on the first three days, lending the cricket little meaning on the last. After an opening-day washout, Brown and Adam Hollioake played some sturdy shots to shore up Surrey after three top-order batsmen went for virtually nothing. Then Jones brushed off a shaky opening over to take five of the last six wickets, a Championship-best, bowling with the resolve of a seamer eager for greater responsibility in Caddick's absence. Somerset's reply was not immediately reassuring: Bicknell accounted for Cox and Holloway in his first over of the third morning. Trescothick took a long time to offset his unease, but on the last afternoon he cast out the technical demons and rediscovered the skills and poise that had intermittently surfaced so encouragingly. He and Burns were deceived by Salisbury in the eighties. Somerset, having eased to a third batting point, astutely declared an over before the close, denying Surrey the chance of a final bowling point.

Close of play: First day, No play; Second day, Somerset 4-0 (Cox 2*, Trescothick 0*); Third day, Somerset 15-2 (Trescothick 0*, Bowler 6*).

Surrey

M. A. Butcher lbw b Bulbeck	4	I. D. K. Salisbury c Turner b Jones	2
I. J. Ward c Burns b Caddick	1	A. J. Tudor not out	16
G. P. Thorpe c Turner b Caddick	0	I. E. Bishop b Jones	0
†A. J. Stewart lbw b Bulbeck	16		
A. D. Brown c Trescothick b Jones	47	W 2	2
*A. J. Hollioake c Turner b Jones	59		
B. C. Hollioake c Jones b Caddick	20		185
M. P. Bicknell b Jones	18	1/3 2/3 3/11 4/38 5/112	
		6/129 7/151 8/167 9/173	

Bonus points – Somerset 3.

Bowling: Caddick 16–2–71–3; Bulbeck 12–3–44–2; Rose 7–1–29–0; Jones 10–2–41–5.

Somerset

*J. Cox lbw b Bicknell	2	A. R. Caddick b A. J. Hollioake	19
M. E. Trescothick c Brown b Salisbury	85	M. P. L. Bulbeck not out	3
P. C. L. Holloway c Stewart b Bicknell	0		
P. D. Bowler lbw b Bishop	37	B 1, l-b 3, w 10, n-b 22	36
M. Burns lbw b Salisbury	81		
†R. J. Turner c Tudor b Salisbury	0		(8 wkts dec.) 302
I. D. Blackwell c Thorpe b Tudor	2	1/4 2/4 3/90	
G. D. Rose not out	37	4/218 5/222 6/225	
		7/249 8/294	

P. S. Jones did not bat.

Bonus points – Somerset 3, Surrey 2.

Bowling: Bicknell 19–5–48–2; Tudor 21–5–81–1; B. C. Hollioake 15–3–66–0; Bishop 12–5–24–1; Salisbury 24–6–56–3; A. J. Hollioake 4.2–1–23–1.

Umpires: J. W. Lloyds and A. G. T. Whitehead.

At Southampton, May 3, 4, 5. SOMERSET beat HAMPSHIRE by nine wickets.

At Leicester, May 11, 12, 13, 14. SOMERSET lost to LEICESTERSHIRE by six wickets.

SOMERSET v DERBYSHIRE

At Taunton, May 24, 25, 26, 27. Drawn. Somerset 5 pts, Derbyshire 7 pts. Toss: Derbyshire.

A match badly truncated by rain left home supporters reflecting on how modest Somerset's attack can look without Caddick – rested on England's instructions – and the injured Bulbeck. By way of compensation, Bowler scored a stylish fifty against his former county, and Parsons looked to be batting better than at any time in an uncertain eight-year career, hitting eight fours. But Cassar removed both, plus Blackwell, who tried to go after him, in five eventful overs, and Somerset's first-innings total was a disappointing one. The weather allowed Derbyshire a mere 26 overs; Dowman and Stubbings scored 101 without being parted before the last two days were wiped out. On his home debut, former Essex bowler Grove revealed pace and aggression, offset by no-balls and waywardness. As a tonsorial diversion amid the stoppages, five Somerset players, including the captain, opted for drastically shaven heads, with the adept co-operation of the club's physiotherapist.

Close of play: First day, Somerset 117-4 (Bowler 18*, Turner 0*); Second day, Derbyshire 101-0 (Dowman 41*, Stubbings 41*); Third day, No play.

Somerset

M. E. Trescothick c Cork b Smith	30	I. D. Blackwell c Aldred b Cassar	16
*J. Cox c Krikken b Dean	16	P. S. Jones c Cork b Smith	0
P. C. L. Holloway c Di Venuto b Aldred	23	J. O. Grove not out	0
P. D. Bowler c Krikken b Cassar	57		
M. Burns c Krikken b Munton	1	B 4, l-b 15, w 2, n-b 13	34
†R. J. Turner c Dowman b Munton	14		
K. A. Parsons lbw b Cassar	47	1/69 2/77 3/109 4/116 5/156	240
G. D. Rose b Smith	2	6/207 7/222 8/230 9/232	

Bonus points – Somerset 1, Derbyshire 3.

Bowling: Cork 11–4–25–0; Munton 19–7–43–2; Dean 9–3–25–1; Smith 13–1–51–3; Aldred 14–4–39–1; Cassar 4.5–0–38–3.

Derbyshire

M. P. Dowman not out	41
S. D. Stubbings not out	41
L-b 1, n-b 18	19

(no wkt) 101

M. J. Di Venuto, M. E. Cassar, R. J. Bailey, †K. M. Krikken, *D. G. Cork, P. Aldred, T. M. Smith, T. A. Munton and K. J. Dean did not bat.

Bowling: Rose 10–1–28–0; Grove 6–0–45–0; Jones 8 1 21 0; Blackwell 2–0–6–0.

Umpires: J. W. Lloyds and K. E. Palmer.

SOMERSET v KENT

At Bath, June 6, 7, 8, 9. Somerset won by two wickets. Somerset 17 pts, Kent 5 pts. Toss: Kent.

Caddick, home after his frustrations in the Trent Bridge Test, excelled with bat as well as ball. His match figures of ten for 97 were evidence of sustained accuracy and bounce, but he also figured in the crucial ninth-wicket partnership with Blackwell that swayed the match Somerset's way in an absorbing finish. They selectively added 41 runs, and Caddick was named Player of the Bath Festival. There were other aspects to admire: the handsome first-innings performance of Dravid, just back from the Asia Cup, for Kent, and the defiance and recovery made possible by Walker, who added 99 with Ealham, in the second. Kent had looked pleased at the end of the third day when Trescothick went first ball, Holloway was stumped impulsively charging Patel, and the night-watchman, Jones, was oddly run out after leaving his ground, only to be surprised by Ealham's throw from mid-off. Friday's story has a different tale.

Close of play: First day, Somerset 47-0 (Cox 23*, Trescothick 21*); Second day, Kent 4-1 (Key 0*); Third day, Somerset 50-3 (Cox 27*, Bowler 4*).

Kent

D. P. Fulton c Parsons b Caddick	4	– c Holloway b Caddick	4
R. W. T. Key c Rose b Grove	27	– c Trescothick b Caddick	22
R. Dravid c Turner b Rose	90	– c Turner b Jones	17
A. P. Wells c Cox b Caddick	10	– c Parsons b Caddick	7
M. J. Walker c Turner b Jones	25	– c Trescothick b Blackwell	61
M. A. Ealham c Trescothick b Caddick	28	– c Turner b Caddick	43
†P. A. Nixon c Holloway b Caddick	16	– not out	28
*M. V. Fleming not out	25	– c Parsons b Blackwell	23
M. M. Patel c Turner b Caddick	0	– run out	1
M. J. McCague b Caddick	10	– b Jones	0
D. D. Masters c Trescothick b Jones	0	– lbw b Jones	1
B 4, l-b 4, w 2, n-b 16	26	L-b 8, n-b 8	16

1/12 2/74 3/109 4/170 5/176   261   1/4 2/48 3/59 4/60 5/159   223
6/221 7/232 8/232 9/260   6/183 7/215 8/216 9/217

Bonus points – Kent 2, Somerset 3.

Bowling: *First Innings*—Caddick 25–6–57–6; Jones 18.5–3–63–2; Grove 13–3–53–1; Rose 14–2–39–1; Blackwell 7–2–27–0; Parsons 4–1–14–0. *Second Innings*—Caddick 25–12–40–4; Jones 23–4–74–3; Rose 0.2–0–2–0; Grove 6.4–0–35–0; Trescothick 7–2–17–0; Blackwell 20–7–33–2; Cox 7–2–14–0.

Somerset

*J. Cox lbw b Patel	52	– (2) b Patel	43
M. E. Trescothick c Nixon b Ealham	24	– (1) c Nixon b McCague	0
P. C. L. Holloway c Fulton b Masters	50	– st Nixon b Patel	19
P. D. Bowler b Fleming	5	– (5) c Fulton b Ealham	11
K. A. Parsons b Walker	62	– (6) c Nixon b Ealham	18
†R. J. Turner c Key b Masters	0	– (7) c Fulton b Patel	17
G. D. Rose not out	45	– (8) lbw b Masters	18
I. D. Blackwell c Patel b Masters	16	– (9) not out	27
A. R. Caddick c Walker b Ealham	12	– (10) not out	21
P. S. Jones c Walker b Masters	10	– (4) run out	0
J. O. Grove c Nixon b Masters	5		
L-b 8, w 2, n-b 4	14	B 10, l-b 7, w 2	19

1/50 2/99 3/112 4/173 5/173   295   1/0 2/41 3/43 4/68   (8 wkts) 193
6/227 7/256 8/270 9/283   5/78 6/97 7/127 8/152

Bonus points – Somerset 2, Kent 3.

Bowling: *First Innings*—Ealham 26–8–68–2; Masters 23.5–9–55–5; McCague 17–3–56–0; Fleming 18–6–42–1; Patel 30–9–59–1; Walker 4–1–7–1. *Second Innings*—McCague 4–0–21–1; Ealham 19.4–3–61–2; Patel 36–20–43–3; Masters 15–2–37–1; Fleming 4–0–14–0.

Umpires: A. A. Jones and B. Leadbeater.

At The Oval, June 14, 15, 16. SOMERSET lost to SURREY by an innings and 213 runs.

At Taunton, June 25. SOMERSET lost to ZIMBABWEANS by 21 runs (See Zimbabwean tour section).

At Maidstone, June 28, 29, 30, July 1. SOMERSET drew with KENT.

SOMERSET v HAMPSHIRE

At Taunton, July 7, 8, 9, 10. Drawn. Somerset 11 pts, Hampshire 7 pts. Toss: Somerset.

At one stage, Somerset looked to be heading for an innings win. But when Hampshire batted again, they improved on their dismal form, and Somerset lacked the bowling strength and variety to curb a resolute stand of 160 between Kendall and Kenway. It was Hampshire's first century stand in the 2000 Championship, while Kendall's assured 161 was their first hundred in any cricket all season. Eventually, bad weather ruled out any chance of a result, allowing only 44 overs on the third day and none on the last. Hampshire had initially been as fragile as ever when Jones and Rose both took four wickets. In reply, Holloway regained confidence by reaching a dogged century – his first for almost 12 months – but the loudest cheer was reserved for relayed news of Trescothick's fifty on his England debut in the one-day international series. In his absence, Lathwell was welcomed back for his first Championship match since 1998.

Close of play: First day, Somerset 208-4 (Holloway 53*, Trego 6*); Second day, Hampshire 140-2 (Kendall 74*, Smith 35*); Third day, Hampshire 319-5 (Aymes 3*, Hartley 9*).

Hampshire

G. W. White c Turner b Rose	44	– lbw b Jones	18
A. J. Sexton lbw b Jones	2	– c Turner b Jones	4
W. S. Kendall lbw b Rose	29	– c Holloway b Burns	161
*R. A. Smith c Parsons b Trego	6	– b Jones	36
D. A. Kenway c Bowler b Trego	11	– lbw b Burns	54
†A. N. Aymes lbw b Jones	11	– not out	3
J. P. Stephenson lbw b Jones	0		
A. D. Mascarenhas lbw b Rose	5		
S. K. Warne c and b Rose	29		
P. J. Hartley b Jones	2	– (7) not out	9
S. R. G. Francis not out	0		
L-b 8, n-b 6	14	B 6, l-b 6, n-b 22	34

1/4 2/62 3/73 4/77 5/95   142   1/4 2/64 3/144   (5 wkts) 319
6/95 7/104 8/121 9/142   4/304 5/309

Bonus points – Somerset 3.

Bowling: *First Innings*—Rose 17.1 3 47 4; Jones 15–3–43–4; Trego 9–0–42–2. *Second Innings*—Rose 21–8–61–0; Jones 22–3–92–3; Trego 9–1–56–0; Blackwell 17–5–35–0; Parsons 15–4–38–0; Burns 11–2–25–2.

Somerset

M. N. Lathwell c Sexton b Stephenson	25	I. D. Blackwell c Aymes b Hartley	18
*J. Cox b Stephenson	26	G. D. Rose lbw b Hartley	4
P. C. L. Holloway c Aymes b Warne	113	P. S. Jones not out	0
P. D. Bowler lbw b Francis	16		
K. A. Parsons c Francis b Warne	46	L-b 4, w 4, n-b 36	44
P. D. Trego lbw b Warne	6		
M. Burns st Aymes b Mascarenhas	56	1/58 2/67 3/106 4/196 5/210	368
†R. J. Turner lbw b Warne	14	6/320 7/335 8/364 9/364	

Bonus points – Somerset 4, Hampshire 3.

Bowling: Hartley 21.3–1–101–2; Francis 16–3–51–1; Mascarenhas 14–4–47–1; Warne 38–11–91–4; Stephenson 21–3–74–2.

Umpires: V. A. Holder and G. Sharp.

SOMERSET v LANCASHIRE

At Taunton, July 12, 13, 14, 15. Drawn. Somerset 11 pts, Lancashire 7 pts. Toss: Somerset.

Without Caddick and the injured Bulbeck, Somerset failed to convert a dominant position into victory. Their 565 – with centuries from Cox and Burns, and a near-miss from Bowler – was their highest against Lancashire, but ultimately they were frustrated by some determined tail-end batting. At 324 for eight in their second innings, Lancashire were still two behind with 59 overs left. Then Chapple and Schofield took charge, with valuable backing from Smethurst. It was a notable fightback, though the pitch generally favoured batsmen. Lancashire, however, had been unable to build on Atherton's composed first-day hundred, and lost their last six for 23, all bar one to Parsons's medium-pace. His career-best five for 13 came out of the blue: until now, his season's return had been one for 214. Second time round, it was Crawley's turn for a good-looking hundred, while Ganguly fell one short to Burns, another unlikely bowling hero, before Lancashire's late batsmen ensured the absorbing finish.

Close of play: First day, Somerset 48-0 (Cox 25*, Lathwell 19*); Second day, Somerset 370-6 (Burns 10*, Turner 0*); Third day, Lancashire 133-2 (Crawley 68*, Keedy 0*).

Lancashire

M. A. Atherton lbw b Parsons	113	– b Trego		58
*J. P. Crawley b Jones	6	– lbw b Burns		120
N. H. Fairbrother lbw b Rose	2	– c Turner b Blackwell		1
S. C. Ganguly c Turner b Trego	21	– (5) c Holloway b Burns		99
G. D. Lloyd b Trego	17	– (6) c Turner b Jones		1
J. C. Scuderi c Lathwell b Parsons	46	– (7) c Bowler b Jones		5
†W. K. Hegg lbw b Parsons	13	– (8) b Burns		4
C. P. Schofield c Bowler b Jones	2	– (9) b Rose		35
G. Chapple c Lathwell b Parsons	2	– (10) not out		39
G. Keedy c and b Parsons	0	– (4) b Parsons		12
M. P. Smethurst not out	1	– not out		13
L-b 6, n-b 10	16	L-b 10, w 2, n-b 18		30

1/21 2/24 3/62 4/104 5/216   239   1/124 2/131 3/163   (9 wkts) 417
6/223 7/236 8/238 9/238   4/314 5/315 6/315
                                                    7/324 8/324 9/380

Bonus points – Lancashire 1, Somerset 3.

Bowling: *First Innings*—Jones 19–3–77–2; Rose 14–3–47–1; Trego 11–3–39–2; Burns 8–2–36–0; Blackwell 6–1–21–0; Parsons 7.5–2–13–5. *Second Innings*—Rose 17–3–64–1; Jones 35–9–111–2; Blackwell 53–19–105–1; Trego 23–4–86–1; Parsons 7–2–30–1; Burns 5–1–11–3.

Somerset

*J. Cox lbw b Scuderi	171	I. D. Blackwell c and b Schofield		8
M. N. Lathwell lbw b Scuderi	43	G. D. Rose not out		6
P. C. L. Holloway run out	1	P. S. Jones c sub b Schofield		0
P. D. Bowler c Hegg b Smethurst	95			
K. A. Parsons c Lloyd b Scuderi	25	L-b 15, w 4, n-b 14		33
P. D. Trego c Hegg b Scuderi	0			
M. Burns st Hegg b Schofield	108	1/104 2/106 3/305 4/358 5/358		565
†R. J. Turner lbw b Ganguly	75	6/361 7/537 8/548 9/563		

Bonus points – Somerset 4, Lancashire 2 (Score at 130 overs: 399-6).

Bowling: Chapple 29–8–91–0; Smethurst 27–2–131–1; Scuderi 27–7–58–4; Keedy 47–14–109–0; Ganguly 17–0–79–1; Schofield 29–6–82–3; Fairbrother 1–1–0–0.

Umpires: A. Clarkson and B. Leadbeater.

At Scarborough, July 19, 20, 21. SOMERSET lost to YORKSHIRE by an innings and six runs.

At Chester-le-Street, July 28, 29, 30, 31. SOMERSET drew with DURHAM.

SOMERSET v YORKSHIRE

At Taunton, August 2, 3, 4, 5. Drawn. Somerset 11 pts, Yorkshire 10 pts. Toss: Somerset.
Championship debut: S. M. Guy.

Test calls and injuries depleted both counties' attacks and, on an easy pitch, the game ground
wearily to a draw. Somerset staged a marked recovery after losing early wickets: Rose, at No. 7,
scored his tenth first-class hundred with a minimum of trouble, and his late stand of 132 with
Trego, who reached a maiden fifty, helped to secure an unlikely fourth batting point. In reply,
Lehmann became the second player to 1,000 first-class runs for the summer, after Michael Bevan;
he later assumed the captaincy when Byas tore his knee cartilage. McGrath hit a tidy half-century,
while left-arm spinner Fisher, with a career-best, proved he could bat too. There was also an
encouraging debut for 21-year-old wicket-keeper Simon Guy – Blakey was dropped for the first
time in his 15-year career – who made five catches and a fighting 42. On the final day, with no
attempt at a result, the correct Bowler and Parsons simply kept going in an unbeaten stand of
227. Both hit centuries, Parsons's a Championship-first.

Close of play: First day, Somerset 73-3 (Bowler 29*, Parsons 11*); Second day, Yorkshire 5-0
(Widdup 3*, Craven 2*); Third day, Somerset 33-0 (Lathwell 12*, Cox 11*).

Somerset

*J. Cox c Guy b Silverwood	4	– (2) c Guy b Silverwood	27
M. N. Lathwell b Hoggard	8	– (1) c Guy b Fellows	47
P. C. L. Holloway c Fellows b Hamilton	15	– b Hoggard	0
P. D. Bowler c Guy b Hoggard	34	– not out	139
K. A. Parsons lbw b Hamilton	32	– not out	108
†R. J. Turner c Guy b Fellows	36		
G. D. Rose c McGrath b Fisher	124		
I. D. Blackwell c Byas b Hamilton	11		
P. D. Trego lbw b Fisher	62		
P. S. Jones c Hamilton b Fisher	6		
J. O. Grove not out	5		
B 2, l-b 6, w 4, n-b 10	22	B 18, l-b 9, w 6, n-b 14	47

1/12 2/16 3/51 4/96 5/115   359   1/55 2/56 3/141   (3 wkts) 368
6/183 7/212 8/344 9/352

Bonus points – Somerset 4, Yorkshire 3.

Bowling: *First Innings*—Silverwood 28–7–62–1; Hoggard 29–7–82–2; Hamilton 22–2–73–3;
Fisher 28–8–66–3; Fellows 13–4–32–1; Lehmann 8–0–36–0. *Second Innings*—Silverwood
9–1–27–1; Hoggard 9–3–38–1; Fisher 33–6–91–0; Hamilton 13–1–45–0; Fellows 13–1–54–1;
Lehmann 19–0–63–0; Craven 8–1–15–0; Guy 4–1–8–0.

Yorkshire

S. Widdup c Trego b Jones	5	I. D. Fisher not out	68
V. J. Craven c Trego b Blackwell	42	C. E. W. Silverwood c Lathwell	
A. McGrath c and b Blackwell	74	b Parsons	4
D. S. Lehmann b Trego	56	M. J. Hoggard c Rose b Jones	6
*D. Byas retired hurt	2	B 4, l-b 4, w 2, n-b 4	14
G. M. Fellows lbw b Rose	11		
G. M. Hamilton c Turner b Rose	3	1/19 2/74 3/165 4/201 5/201	327
†S. M. Guy lbw b Parsons	42	6/208 7/300 8/304 9/327	

Bonus points – Yorkshire 3, Somerset 3.

Byas retired hurt at 175.

Bowling: Jones 18.4–6–56–2; Trego 11–1–43–1; Blackwell 32–7–77–2; Rose 16–2–47–2;
Grove 15–1–54–0; Parsons 4–0–29–2; Cox 2–0–13–0.

Umpires: G. I. Burgess and N. G. Cowley.

SOMERSET v DURHAM

At Taunton, August 16, 17, 18, 19. Drawn. Somerset 11 pts, Durham 10 pts. Toss: Durham.

Rain accounted for most of the second and third days, ruling out the result needed by two counties in or near the relegation zone. On an easy pitch, Durham took advantage of the gaps in Somerset's attack, which now included Trego, playing for England Under-19. A middle-order stand of 128 between Collingwood and Speak ensured a useful total; off-spinner Pierson and right-arm seamer Grove took three wickets each. When Somerset batted, the openers, both in search of the reassurance of runs, met with modest success, but interruptions ultimately denied the fixture meaning. Rose reminded spectators of his all-round credentials by scoring a stylish second successive century, and with Burns shared an assertive sixth-wicket partnership of 170. Cox, believing the next bonus point was likelier to be won by Durham, declared before the close. Harmison, returning after injury, looked rusty, but Wood was more convincing as he claimed four for 50.

Close of play: First day, Durham 324-6 (Pratt 15*, Wood 21*); Second day, Somerset 58-0 (Cox 22*, Lathwell 25*); Third day, Somerset 92-2 (Turner 9*, Bowler 6*).

Durham

J. J. B. Lewis c Parsons b Rose	31	N. C. Phillips c Blackwell b Pierson		9
M. A. Gough c Turner b Grove	33	S. J. Harmison c Blackwell b Jones		15
S. M. Katich lbw b Grove	20	S. J. E. Brown not out		2
P. D. Collingwood c Rose b Blackwell	74			
*N. J. Speak c Pierson b Grove	78	L-b 10, w 2, n-b 6		18
J. A. Daley run out	34			
†A. Pratt b Pierson	38	1/52 2/85 3/88 4/216 5/281		378
J. Wood lbw b Pierson	26	6/287 7/341 8/356 9/365		

Bonus points – Durham 4, Somerset 3.

Bowling: Rose 22–8–58–1; Jones 27.1–4–112–1; Burns 9–1–29–0; Grove 19–4–53–3; Parsons 8–1–25–0; Blackwell 21–7–50–1; Pierson 21–8–41–3.

Somerset

*J. Cox lbw b Wood	25	I. D. Blackwell c Katich b Brown		0
M. N. Lathwell lbw b Collingwood	39	A. R. K. Pierson not out		15
†R. J. Turner b Wood	18	B 8, l-b 9, w 2, n-b 12		31
P. D. Bowler c Pratt b Harmison	31			
K. A. Parsons b Phillips	12	1/63 2/82 3/114	(8 wkts dec.)	362
M. Burns c Pratt b Wood	89	4/129 5/153 6/323		
G. D. Rose b Wood	102	7/324 8/362		

P. S. Jones and J. O. Grove did not bat.

Bonus points – Somerset 4, Durham 2.

Bowling: Brown 25–6–85–1; Harmison 20–4–69–1; Phillips 23–5–62–1; Wood 20.4–4–50–4; Collingwood 11–2–26–1; Gough 6–0–24–0; Katich 6–0–29–0.

Umpires: B. Dudleston and R. A. White.

At Taunton, August 23, 24, 25, 26. SOMERSET beat WEST INDIANS by 269 runs (See West Indian tour section).

SOMERSET v LEICESTERSHIRE

At Taunton, September 1, 2, 3, 4. Drawn. Somerset 12 pts, Leicestershire 11 pts. Toss: Leicestershire.

All seven Championship matches at batsman-friendly Taunton in 2000 were drawn, and Leicestershire's 470 was the ninth total in succession over 300. With the weather contributing too, no team so much as started a fourth innings. Somerset's survival in Division One was effectively guaranteed by avoiding defeat, so they had little incentive to concoct a competitive final day. Leicestershire's overtures – they had prize money to chase – came to nothing and the game, after several fine individual performances, petered out. Blackwell, who had joined Somerset primarily as a slow left-armer, scored a maiden hundred, full of bold strokes that earned him 14 fours and a six. Two Leicestershire batsmen in indeterminate form also did well: Maddy reached his first century of the summer, while Wells fell two short. Their wicket-keeper, Neil Burns, had an impressive game against his former county, taking four catches and hitting 57. Only three balls were possible on the opening day, still enough to dismiss Lathwell, whose season, after he missed all of 1999, had been disappointing. Cox managed an overdue fifty, but it was Blackwell who lifted a tepid match.

Close of play: First day, Somerset 0-1 (Cox 0*); Second day, Somerset 273-6 (Blackwell 40*, Bowler 1*); Third day, Leicestershire 233-4 (Habib 34*, Wells 19*).

Somerset

M. N. Lathwell c Burns b DeFreitas	0	– (2) c Maddy b Boswell	7
*J. Cox lbw b DeFreitas	58	– (1) not out	40
†R. J. Turner lbw b Kumble	47	– c Burns b DeFreitas	3
K. A. Parsons c Sutcliffe b Kumble	48		
M. Burns c Burns b Boswell	23		
G. D. Rose c Burns b Boswell	5		
I. D. Blackwell c Habib b Maddy	109		
P. D. Bowler not out	38	– (4) not out	27
J. I. D. Kerr not out	19		
B 1, l-b 15, w 2, n-b 46	64	L-b 1, n-b 12	13

1/0 2/123 3/139 4/191 (7 wkts dec.) 411   1/14 2/21 (2 wkts) 90
5/205 6/259 7/383

P. S. Jones and J. O. Grove did not bat.

Bonus points – Somerset 5, Leicestershire 2.

Bowling: *First Innings*—DeFreitas 25–4–81–2; Boswell 17–3–64–2; Dakin 14–2–59–0; Kumble 34–5–117–2; Wells 7–0–40–0; Maddy 6–0–34–1. *Second Innings*—DeFreitas 8–1–24–1; Boswell 6–0–18–1; Maddy 6–1–15–0; Wells 4–1–20–0; Smith 2–0–6–0; Stevens 1–0–6–0.

Leicestershire

D. L. Maddy lbw b Grove	102	†N. D. Burns c Turner b Jones	57
I. J. Sutcliffe lbw b Jones	1	A. Kumble c Bowler b Burns	35
B. F. Smith c Cox b Rose	69	S. A. J. Boswell not out	0
A. Habib lbw b Kerr	72		
D. I. Stevens c Turner b Kerr	0	B 4, l-b 6, n-b 10	20
*V. J. Wells c Jones b Kerr	98		
J. M. Dakin b Blackwell	16	1/6 2/154 3/196 4/199 5/340	470
P. A. J. DeFreitas c Turner b Kerr	0	6/361 7/362 8/386 9/470	

Bonus points – Leicestershire 5, Somerset 3.

Bowling: Rose 25–4–69–1; Jones 28–5–116–2; Kerr 23–3–97–4; Grove 18–3–72–1; Blackwell 21–4–78–1; Burns 7.2–0–28–1.

Umpires: V. A. Holder and T. E. Jesty.

At Manchester, September 8, 9, 10. SOMERSET lost to LANCASHIRE by an innings and 109 runs.

At Derby, September 13, 14, 15, 16. SOMERSET drew with DERBYSHIRE.

SURREY

Ian Ward

President: The Rt Hon. J. Major
Chairman: M. J. Soper
Chief Executive: P. C. J. Sheldon
Director of Cricket Development: M. J. Edwards
Cricket Secretary: A. Gibson
Captain: A. J. Hollioake
Cricket Manager: K. T. Medlycott
Head Groundsman: P. D. Brind
Scorer: K. R. Booth

While there will always be someone proclaiming that Surrey's Championship-winning side of 2000 had to beat only eight other counties – that it was half a Championship – the teams in Division One were the best, and had to be played twice. In that this represented a truer test, it could be argued that there was more merit in lifting this second successive Championship – Surrey's 17th title since 1890 – than there was in winning it the previous year. Surrey were unbeaten then; in 2000, there were defeats by Durham and Derbyshire before Adam Holloake's men asserted themselves with seven consecutive wins. Even so, the trophy was not theirs until the final game.

In contrast, Surrey had the National League Division Two title parcelled up by the end of August and could use their remaining matches to blood some younger players. After their unbeaten run of 13 League games from the start of the season, the losses they subsequently suffered raised a few eyebrows, but did not spoil the supporters' enjoyment. Promotion was their compensation for the disappointment that followed earlier Benson and Hedges Cup semi-final and NatWest Trophy quarter-final defeats.

The first year of two-division Championship cricket was certainly a proving-ground. For only the third time in more than a century, no Surrey batsman reached 1,000 runs, but determination and experience gave them depth down the order. No other team in the first division collected as many batting bonus points; only second-division Warwickshire picked up more. Ally Brown emerged as the top run-maker for the fourth successive season with 935. His career-best 295 not out at Oakham School against Leicestershire marked him out not merely as a destructive force to be feared but also a high-class batsman to be respected. There was not a false stroke; every boundary was as earthbound as the innings was heavenly.

Ian Ward's 894 runs merited as much praise, and earned him his second England A tour in a row. He added three hundreds to his maiden one the previous season and forged a formidable left-handed opening partnership with Mark Butcher. Butcher struggled to find his touch until mid-season, when his unbeaten hundred at Southampton launched a more consistent run. Alec Stewart's Championship season was restricted to just three games early on, and Graham Thorpe followed him into the England team at the end of

June after signalling he was returning to his old self with 115 against Somerset. Wicket-keeper Jonathan Batty hit his maiden hundred in the same match. Thanks to runs from Adam Hollioake, Nadeem Shahid and Martin Bicknell, Stewart and Thorpe's absence was hardly an issue. Mark Ramprakash's winter move south of the river should ensure it won't be one in 2001, either.

Bicknell scored 500 runs for the first time, giving him credence as an all-rounder, and while his 60 wickets at 17.53 were apparently not enough to catch the eye of the England selectors, they went a long way to securing the Championship for Surrey. He had a memorable game against Leicestershire on his home ground, Woodbridge Road, Guildford, claiming the best match return by an England bowler – 16 for 119 – since Jim Laker's 19 for 90 against Australia in 1956. In recent years, his flawless seam bowling has been singularly neglected by his country. Instead, the selectors returned their attention to Ian Salisbury's leg-spin for England's winter tours to Pakistan and Sri Lanka, attracted by his 52 Championship wickets at 18.92. As a foil to Saqlain Mushtaq's masterful off-spin and bewitching variations, which brought 66 wickets at 15.39, Salisbury enjoyed an impressive domestic season, but he was found wanting in Pakistan, doing neither himself nor his county figures justice in the three Tests. He was not taken to Sri Lanka.

Alex Tudor went close to 50 Championship wickets, enough to win a place in the England A team and an upgrade to the senior side when Andrew Flintoff was unfit to bowl. The Butcher brothers did their bit with the ball as well, but the decision to sign Ed Giddins for 2001 confirmed the need for an experienced bowler in an attack that had been heavily dependent on four men. Not called on to bowl until the final Championship match of the season, against Lancashire at Old Trafford, Mark Butcher claimed five in an innings for the first time in his career. But it was younger brother Gary who made the headlines, taking four wickets in four balls against Derbyshire at The Oval. He later hit a half-century at Old Trafford to remind everyone of his all-round ability, and unintentionally underlined the sorry situation of the man he replaced, Ben Hollioake.

Hollioake in 2000 was but a shadow of the exciting, naturally gifted cricketer who had captured the country's imagination three years earlier with two audacious one-day innings at Lord's: a debut 63 against Australia and 98 in the Benson and Hedges Cup final. His 285 runs and 24 wickets in 24 first-team games in 2000 were inadequate returns for someone of his talent, and yet it was difficult to pinpoint what had gone wrong. It might just have been one of those seasons; most players have one at some time. The sensible thing would have been to let him sort out his game in the Second Eleven. Instead, no doubt working on the principle that bad trots have to end some time, the selectors persisted with him, which may have exacerbated the problem. The 2001 season must be regarded with some concern if the same outlook prevails. – DAVID LLEWELLYN.

663

SURREY 2000

[Bill Smith]

Back row: C. G. Greenidge, G. J. Batty, M. W. Patterson, P. J. Sampson, K. A. O. Barrett, M. A. Carberry. Middle row: K. R. Booth (scorer), J. Gloster (physiotherapist), D. Naylor (physiotherapist), G. P. Butcher, R. M. Amin, I. E. Bishop, R. N. Batty, I. J. Ward, K. T. Medlycott (cricket manager), A. R. Butcher (Second Eleven coach). Front row: A. J. Tudor, J. D. Ratcliffe, A. D. Brown, Saqlain Mushtaq, G. P. Thorpe, A. J. Stewart, A. J. Hollioake (captain), M. P. Bicknell, M. A. Butcher, I. D. K. Salisbury, N. Shahid, B. C. Hollioake.

SURREY RESULTS

All first-class matches – Played 16: Won 9, Lost 2, Drawn 5.

County Championship matches – Played 16: Won 9, Lost 2, Drawn 5.

PPP Healthcare County Championship, winners in Division 1; NatWest Trophy, q-f; Benson and Hedges Cup, s-f; Norwich Union National League, winners in Division 2.

COUNTY CHAMPIONSHIP AVERAGES

BATTING

Cap		M	I	NO	R	HS	100s	50s	Avge	Ct/St
1994	A. D. Brown......	16	23	5	935	295*	2	4	51.94	16
1996	M. A. Butcher†....	16	25	4	891	191	2	3	42.42	13
2000	I. J. Ward........	16	25	3	894	158*	3	3	40.63	4
	G. P. Butcher†.....	4	4	1	110	66	0	1	36.66	0
1998	N. Shahid........	9	12	0	434	80	0	3	36.16	13
1989	M. P. Bicknell†....	15	18	2	500	79*	0	4	31.25	5
1995	A. J. Hollioake	16	23	0	689	80	0	3	29.95	27
1999	A. J. Tudor.......	14	16	6	283	64*	0	1	28.30	5
1985	A. J. Stewart†‡....	3	4	0	108	42	0	0	27.00	7
1998	I. D. K. Salisbury ..	16	19	6	313	57*	0	2	24.07	6
1991	G. P. Thorpe†.....	8	12	0	280	115	1	1	23.33	6
	J. N. Batty.......	13	16	2	276	100*	1	0	19.71	29/7
1998	Saqlain Mushtaq§..	12	14	2	217	66	0	2	18.08	8
1999	B. C. Hollioake....	10	14	1	142	29	0	0	10.92	8
1998	J. D. Ratcliffe	2	4	0	28	26	0	0	7.00	2

Also batted: R. M. Amin† (1 match) 3 (1 ct); I. E. Bishop (2 matches) 0, 12, 2; C. G. Greenidge (3 matches) 3, 6.

* Signifies not out.   † Born in Surrey.   ‡ ECB contract.   § Overseas player.

BOWLING

	O	M	R	W	BB	5W/i	Avge
Saqlain Mushtaq.....	451.2	127	1,016	66	7-11	6	15.39
M. P. Bicknell	413.2	115	1,052	60	9-47	3	17.53
I. D. K. Salisbury....	380.3	101	984	52	8-60	3	18.92
A. J. Tudor	304.3	71	1,071	47	7-48	3	22.78
B. C. Hollioake	117.5	25	407	11	4-41	0	37.00

Also bowled: R. M. Amin 21–4–67–0; J. N. Batty 6–0–21–1; I. E. Bishop 29–8–98–2; A. D. Brown 28–9–70–1; G. P. Butcher 21.3–4–65–5; M. A. Butcher 27–7–86–5; C. G. Greenidge 35–13–106–1; A. J. Hollioake 42.2–12–119–3; J. D. Ratcliffe 9.5–2–46–1; N. Shahid 1–0–6–0; I. J. Ward 5–2–10–0.

COUNTY RECORDS

Highest score for:	357*	R. Abel v Somerset at The Oval...............	1899
Highest score against:	366	N. H. Fairbrother (Lancashire) at The Oval........	1990
Best bowling for:	10-43	T. Rushby v Somerset at Taunton	1921
Best bowling against:	10-28	W. P. Howell (Australians) at The Oval	1899
Highest total for:	811	v Somerset at The Oval	1899
Highest total against:	863	by Lancashire at The Oval.................	1990
Lowest total for:	14	v Essex at Chelmsford	1983
Lowest total against:	16	by MCC at Lord's	1872

At Taunton, April 26, 27, 28, 29. SURREY drew with SOMERSET.

At Chester-le-Street, May 2, 3, 4. SURREY lost to DURHAM by 231 runs.

SURREY v KENT

At The Oval, May 11, 12, 13, 14. Drawn. Surrey 8 pts, Kent 6 pts. Toss: Kent. Championship debut: D. D. Masters.

Rain claimed the first day, and on the last morning the captains, to foster a result, agreed that Kent would declare at their overnight total, 302 runs behind, and chase 320 off 93 overs. The umpires looked a little surprised to see Kent walking out to proffer Surrey their make-weight 17, and the serious business had barely begun when umpire Harris retired with a migraine. In his absence, coaches Medlycott and Wright took it in turns to stand at square leg. For a while, as Dravid batted for three and a half hours making 71, the target looked attainable; when he skied Bicknell to cover, Kent's chances receded. Ealham, having put on 102 with Dravid, added 52 more with Nixon but, once he and Fleming went, Nixon concentrated on the draw, reaching his first Championship fifty for Kent. Though Thorpe went cheaply again, Surrey had batted solidly on an attritional second day, then more freely next morning as Bicknell and Salisbury earned two more batting points.

Close of play: First day, No play; Second day, Surrey 278-6 (A. J. Hollioake 46*, Bicknell 10*); Third day, Kent 115-2 (Dravid 44*, Wells 22*).

Surrey

M. A. Butcher c Patel b Fleming	47	– not out	17
I. J. Ward c Smith b Masters	38	– not out	0
G. P. Thorpe lbw b Saggers	11		
†A. J. Stewart c Nixon b Dravid	36		
A. D. Brown lbw b Masters	60		
*A. J. Hollioake b Ealham	51		
B. C. Hollioake c Smith b Masters	6		
M. P. Bicknell c Masters b Dravid	73		
I. D. K. Salisbury lbw b Saggers	50		
A. J. Tudor not out	7		
R. M. Amin run out	3		
B 10, l-b 17, w 8	35		

1/78 2/101 3/105 4/181 5/234   417   (no wkt dec.) 17
6/244 7/288 8/401 9/409

Bonus points – Surrey 4, Kent 2 (Score at 130 overs: 375-7).

Bowling: *First Innings*—Ealham 25–5–76–1; Saggers 23–6–66–2; Masters 28–8–75–3; Fleming 23–8–59–1; Patel 36–7–98–0; Dravid 7.5–3–16–2. *Second Innings*—Key 0.4–0–17–0.

Kent

E. T. Smith c Salisbury b Bicknell	24	– c Brown b Tudor	5
R. W. T. Key c B. C. Hollieake b Salisbury	19	– c Stewart b Bicknell	7
R. Dravid not out	44	– c A. J. Hollieake b Bicknell	71
A. P. Wells not out	22	– c Stewart b Tudor	0
J. B. Hockley (did not bat)		– lbw b Bicknell	2
M. A. Ealham (did not bat)		– b Salisbury	83
†P. A. Nixon (did not bat)		– not out	50
*M. V. Fleming (did not bat)		– c Amin b Tudor	7
M. M. Patel (did not bat)		– lbw b Salisbury	7
D. D. Masters (did not bat)		– not out	0
W 2, n-b 4	6	L-b 5, w 4, n-b 14	23

1/34 2/63   (2 wkts dec.) 115   1/7 2/31 3/40 4/45   (8 wkts) 255
                                                   5/147 6/199 7/224 8/244

M. J. Saggers did not bat.

Bowling: *First Innings*—Bicknell 9–3–19–1; Tudor 8–4–18–0; B. C. Hollieake 6–2–14–0; A. J. Hollieake 3–2–4–0; Amin 9–2–27–0; Salisbury 10–3–33–1. *Second Innings*—Bicknell 25–7–53–3; Tudor 18.5–2–67–3; B. C. Hollieake 2–0–9–0; Salisbury 35–10–81–2; Amin 12–2–40–0.

Umpires: J. H. Harris and A. A. Jones.
(K. T. Medlycott and J. G. Wright deputised for Harris on the fourth day).

At Canterbury, May 23, 24, 25, 26. SURREY drew with KENT.

SURREY v HAMPSHIRE

At The Oval, June 1, 2, 3, 4. Surrey won by two runs. Surrey 18 pts, Hampshire 4 pts. Toss: Surrey.

Title-holders Surrey recorded their first Championship win – but only just. That Hampshire came so tantalisingly close to reaching 266 in four sessions owed much to a remarkable last-wicket partnership of 90 between Mascarenhas, batting with a runner because of a hamstring strain, and the inexperienced Francis. Three more runs and they would have established a new world-record tenth-wicket stand to win a first-class match, beating 77 by Ron Oxenham and Tom Leather for an Australian XI v Madras President's XI at Madras in 1935-36. (The highest tenth-wicket stand to win a County Championship match is 66 by Ian Bedford and Michael Sturt, Middlesex v Gloucestershire at Gloucester, 1961.) Instead Mascarenhas, his concentration interrupted by the tea interval, top-edged an attempted pull and was caught by Tudor off his own bowling. Several other bowlers took the eye with the bat, beginning with Bicknell and Tudor, whose county-best 64 in 68 balls and match return of eight for 109 underlined his potential as an all-rounder. On the last day, Warne's 60-ball fifty, his first for Hampshire, revived them from 87 for six and launched their brave attempt on what then seemed an impossible target. The chase was only possible at all because Warne, with five for 31, and Mullally, swinging the ball late, quickly wound up Surrey's second innings.

Close of play: First day, Surrey 268-8 (Bicknell 53*, Tudor 29*); Second day, Hampshire 207-8 (Mascarenhas 2*, Mullally 8*); Third day, Hampshire 58-2 (Kendall 22*, Smith 3*).

Surrey

M. A. Butcher run out	32	– c Warne b Mullally	2
I. J. Ward c Warne b Francis	5	– c Aymes b Francis	0
G. P. Thorpe lbw b Stephenson	58	– lbw b Mullally	13
*A. J. Hollioake lbw b Stephenson	37	– b Warne	41
A. D. Brown c sub b Mullally	24	– b Mullally	7
J. D. Ratcliffe b Warne	0	– b Warne	26
†J. N. Batty c Kendall b Francis	16	– c Stephenson b Warne	9
M. P. Bicknell b Francis	59	– lbw b Mullally	14
I. D. K. Salisbury c Kenway b Francis	1	– (10) not out	8
A. J. Tudor not out	64	– (9) c Laney b Warne	0
Saqlain Mushtaq lbw b Warne	21	– c Aymes b Warne	10
B 1, l-b 9, w 4, n-b 2	16	B 2, l-b 4, w 4, n-b 2	12
	333		**142**

1/6 2/79 3/124 4/153 5/156 **333**   1/4 2/4 3/24 4/44 5/90 **142**
6/166 7/207 8/215 9/278   6/106 7/109 8/121 9/131

Bonus points – Surrey 3, Hampshire 3.

Bowling: *First Innings*—Mullally 23–8–43–1; Francis 23–5–95–4; Mascarenhas 14–6–30–0; Stephenson 20–4–74–2; Warne 30.1–9–81–2. *Second Innings*—Mullally 17–5–31–4; Francis 10–0–58–1; Warne 21.1–7–31–5; Stephenson 9–4–16–0.

Hampshire

G. W. White c Ward b Saqlain Mushtaq	96	– st Batty b Salisbury	23
J. S. Laney c Brown b Bicknell	0	– c Hollioake b Tudor	0
W. S. Kendall c Thorpe b Bicknell	7	– c Thorpe b Tudor	41
*R. A. Smith c Batty b Bicknell	0	– c Butcher b Bicknell	12
D. A. Kenway c Brown b Tudor	12	– c Hollioake b Tudor	1
†A. N. Aymes c Hollioake b Tudor	44	– c Batty b Tudor	2
J. P. Stephenson c Thorpe b Saqlain Mushtaq	6	– c Hollioake b Saqlain Mushtaq	1
S. K. Warne b Tudor	19	– c and b Saqlain Mushtaq	50
A. D. Mascarenhas c Brown b Bicknell	2	– c and b Tudor	59
A. D. Mullally not out	8	– c Ratcliffe b Saqlain Mushtaq	4
S. R. G. Francis c Hollioake b Saqlain Mushtaq	2	– not out	30
B 6, l-b 2, w 2, n-b 4	14	B 7, l-b 19, n-b 14	40
	210		**263**

1/9 2/33 3/33 4/73 5/151 **210**   1/4 2/40 3/74 4/84 5/86 **263**
6/161 7/193 8/198 9/207   6/87 7/125 8/161 9/173

Bonus points – Hampshire 1, Surrey 3.

Bowling: *First Innings*—Bicknell 29–12–52–4; Tudor 16–5–52–3; Saqlain Mushtaq 34–10–65–3; Salisbury 13–4–33–0. *Second Innings*—Bicknell 26–8–60–1; Tudor 19.3–8–57–5; Saqlain Mushtaq 44–15–89–3; Salisbury 16–7–31–1.

Umpires: J. W. Holder and R. Palmer.

At Derby, June 7, 8, 9, 10. SURREY lost to DERBYSHIRE by seven wickets.

SURREY v SOMERSET

At The Oval, June 14, 15, 16. Surrey won by an innings and 213 runs. Surrey 20 pts, Somerset 2 pts. Toss: Surrey. Championship debut: P. D. Trego.

When these teams last met at The Oval, a year earlier, Surrey enjoyed an unbeaten maiden hundred from Salisbury, a first innings over 500 and a dramatic win. This time, they won handsomely in three days, having put on 548, while Batty reached a maiden century after Thorpe had hit his first hundred for 11 months. When 20, Thorpe completed 10,000 runs for Surrey. Butcher, with whom he added 190, a record for the county's second wicket against Somerset, also lifted himself out of a lean trot, and Shahid marked his first game of the summer with a sparkling half-century. Batty's 100 not out, in 173 balls with 12 fours, set the match up for Surrey's spinners on a slow but hard pitch, already turning by the second day. Saqlain Mushtaq claimed six in Somerset's first innings and Salisbury, who took the other four, spun them to defeat with eight for 60 and match figures of 12 for 91, both career-bests. Of Somerset there was precious little sign. Their bowling was hard hit by Caddick's absence with England and injuries to Bulbeck and Rose; the batsmen seemed incapable of playing high-quality spin.

Close of play: First day, Surrey 338-5 (Shahid 77*, Batty 2*); Second day, Somerset 111-6 (Burns 12*, Turner 3*).

Surrey

M. A. Butcher c Turner b Grove	82	A. J. Tudor lbw b Trego	27
I. J. Ward c Turner b Jones	0	I. D. K. Salisbury c Jones b Blackwell	23
G. P. Thorpe lbw b Jones	115	Saqlain Mushtaq c Holloway b Blackwell	11
N. Shahid b Jones	77		
A. D. Brown lbw b Jones	0	B 5, l-b 8, w 7, n-b 20	40
*A. J. Hollioake c Turner b Trescothick	39		
†J. N. Batty not out	100	1/1 2/191 3/242 4/242 5/321	548
M. P. Bicknell b Trego	34	6/343 7/403 8/457 9/516	

Bonus points – Surrey 5, Somerset 2 (Score at 130 overs: 466-8).

Bowling: Jones 37–11–103–4; Grove 24–3–113–1; Trego 22–4–79–2; Burns 20–3–70–0; Parsons 7–2–23–0; Blackwell 26.3–3–99–2; Cox 5–1–8–0; Trescothick 13–1–40–1.

Somerset

*J. Cox lbw b Saqlain Mushtaq	34	– (2) st Batty b Salisbury	36
M. E. Trescothick b Salisbury	45	– (1) c Hollioake b Tudor	13
P. C. L. Holloway c Batty b Salisbury	1	– lbw b Salisbury	24
P. D. Bowler c Shahid b Salisbury	0	– c Hollioake b Salisbury	37
K. A. Parsons b Saqlain Mushtaq	1	– c Hollioake b Saqlain Mushtaq	12
M. Burns lbw b Saqlain Mushtaq	17	– b Salisbury	3
P. D. Trego lbw b Saqlain Mushtaq	0	– (9) c Hollioake b Salisbury	4
†R. J. Turner c Tudor b Saqlain Mushtaq	3	– (7) lbw b Salisbury	1
I. D. Blackwell c and b Saqlain Mushtaq	16	– (8) not out	32
P. S. Jones lbw b Salisbury	0	– c Saqlain Mushtaq b Salisbury	9
J. O. Grove not out	12	– b Salisbury	1
B 7, l-b 3, w 2, n-b 4	16	B 4, l-b 2, w 2, n-b 10	18
1/73 2/95 3/95 4/96 5/98	145	1/13 2/66 3/83 4/111 5/118	190
6/98 7/112 8/122 9/123		6/120 7/155 8/161 9/189	

Bonus points – Surrey 3.

Bowling: *First Innings*—Bicknell 10–3–24–0; Tudor 6–3–25–0; Hollioake 5–2–8–0; Saqlain Mushtaq 25.2–11–47–6; Salisbury 17–6–31–4. *Second Innings*—Bicknell 7–2–21–0; Tudor 7–3–25–1; Salisbury 30.4–9–60–8; Saqlain Mushtaq 30–7–75–1; Brown 1–0–3–0.

Umpires: R. Julian and G. Sharp.

At The Oval, June 19. SURREY beat NEW ZEALAND A by 24 runs (See New Zealand A tour section).

At Southampton, June 29, 30, July 1, 2. SURREY beat HAMPSHIRE by 120 runs.

At Oakham School, July 7, 8, 9. SURREY beat LEICESTERSHIRE by an innings and 178 runs.

SURREY v YORKSHIRE

At The Oval, July 12, 13, 14, 15. Surrey won by 203 runs. Surrey 16 pts, Yorkshire 4 pts. Toss: Surrey.

Despite the exploits of Yorkshire's young seamers Sidebottom and Hoggard on the first day – when left-armer Sidebottom returned his fourth five-wicket haul in four matches – spin decided this top-of-the-table encounter. Needing to bat 90 overs to save the game – 330 was an unlikely target on a dry, turning surface – Yorkshire had no answer to Saqlain Mushtaq, who followed his first-innings six for 63 with another five, wrapping up proceedings before tea with four for nine in 14 balls. Defeat undermined Yorkshire's Championship challenge and underlined the imbalance of their team, whose main spinner, the inexperienced Middlebrook, ploughed a solitary furrow. Contrasting half-centuries, steady from Vaughan and speedy from Lehmann – whose dismissal gave Bicknell his 800th first-class wicket – put Yorkshire marginally ahead on first innings. However, Brown followed up his 295 not out in the previous match with another unbeaten hundred, reaching three figures in 106 balls, the season's fastest to date. With Shahid, his partner in a stand of 144, contributing an elegant 80, Surrey asserted their authority like true champions.

Close of play: First day, Yorkshire 33-1 (Vaughan 21*); Second day, Surrey 1-1 (Ward 0*, Salisbury 1*); Third day, Surrey 320-7 (Brown 130*, Bicknell 25*).

Surrey

M. A. Butcher c Blakey b Hoggard	5	–	lbw b Silverwood	0
I. J. Ward lbw b Hoggard	28	–	c Blakey b Middlebrook	39
N. Shahid b Sidebottom	36	– (4)	lbw b Middlebrook	80
*A. J. Hollioake c Blakey b Sidebottom	48	– (5)	c Blakey b Fellows	1
A. D. Brown c Byas b Silverwood	7	– (6)	not out	140
B. C. Hollioake c Fellows b Sidebottom	8	– (7)	lbw b Middlebrook	13
†J. N. Batty lbw b Hoggard	1	– (8)	c Fellows b Middlebrook	1
M. P. Bicknell lbw b Sidebottom	45	– (9)	c and b Silverwood	40
I. D. K. Salisbury not out	29	– (3)	lbw b Sidebottom	12
Saqlain Mushtaq b Sidebottom	1			
C. G. Greenidge b Hoggard	3			
B 5, l-b 8, n-b 2	15		B 2, l-b 5, w 10, n-b 2	19

1/5 2/66 3/82 4/105 5/127   226   1/0 2/28 3/84   (8 wkts dec.) 345
6/144 7/148 8/221 9/223   4/85 5/229 6/257
                                    7/265 8/345

Bonus points – Surrey 1, Yorkshire 3.

Bowling: *First Innings*—Silverwood 16–5–64–1; Hoggard 21.5–3–70–4; Sidebottom 20–8–40–5; Fellows 12–2–16–0; Middlebrook 8–1–19–0; Lehmann 2–2–0–0; Vaughan 2–1–4–0. *Second Innings*—Silverwood 15.5–4–51–2; Hoggard 11–3–35–0; Sidebottom 18–7–38–1; Middlebrook 33–5–119–4; Lehmann 10–1–34–0; Fellows 13–2–61–1.

Yorkshire

*D. Byas c A. J. Hollioake b Salisbury	9	– c Brown b Bicknell	7
M. P. Vaughan lbw b Saqlain Mushtaq	80	– b Bicknell	10
†R. J. Blakey c Shahid b Saqlain Mushtaq	10	– (6) lbw b Salisbury	0
D. S. Lehmann c Salisbury b Bicknell	55	– c Brown b Salisbury	17
A. McGrath c B. C. Hollioake		– (3) c A. J. Hollioake	
b Saqlain Mushtaq	26	b Saqlain Mushtaq	22
M. J. Wood c A. J. Hollioake b Salisbury	4	– (5) c A. J. Hollioake b Salisbury	5
G. M. Fellows not out	24	– c Shahid b Saqlain Mushtaq	18
J. D. Middlebrook b Saqlain Mushtaq	14	– c Salisbury b Saqlain Mushtaq	11
C. E. W. Silverwood lbw b Saqlain Mushtaq	1	– lbw b Saqlain Mushtaq	18
R. J. Sidebottom lbw b Saqlain Mushtaq	0	– not out	6
M. J. Hoggard lbw b Salisbury	0	– lbw b Saqlain Mushtaq	2
B 4, l-b 11, n-b 4	19	B 4, l-b 6	10

1/33 2/64 3/158 4/189 5/194   242   1/21 2/24 3/55 4/65 5/67   126
6/198 7/235 8/237 9/241   6/68 7/100 8/101 9/124

Bonus points – Yorkshire 1, Surrey 3.

Bowling: *First Innings*—Bicknell 24.1–8–40–1; Greenidge 6–3–18–0; B. C. Hollioake 2–1–1–0; Saqlain Mushtaq 30–8–63–6; Salisbury 24.3–2–105–3. *Second Innings*—Bicknell 8–4–17–2; Greenidge 6–2–18–0; Saqlain Mushtaq 17.4–5–41–5; B. C. Hollioake 2–0–4–0; Salisbury 15–4–36–3.

Umpires: N. G. Cowley and P. Willey.

SURREY v LEICESTERSHIRE

At Guildford, July 19, 20, 21. Surrey won by ten wickets. Surrey 17 pts, Leicestershire 6 pts. Toss: Leicestershire.

Bicknell, on his home ground, turned the game on its head with the best match return in England since 1956 – and the best by a fast bowler since 1952. But the bare figures, 16 for 119, scarcely capture the drama of his superb seam and swing bowling on a near-perfect pitch. With hundreds from Smith and Ward – both demonstrating what could be achieved with discipline and concentration – matched by seven first-innings wickets for Bicknell and six for Ormond, Leicestershire held a slim 30-run advantage when they batted again in the last hour of the second day. By the close, the game was as good as settled. Bicknell had captured five for 24 in seven

---

MOST WICKETS IN A MATCH IN ENGLAND SINCE 1945

19-90	J. C. Laker	England v Australia at Manchester	1956
16-83	B. Dooland	Nottinghamshire v Essex at Nottingham	1954
16-83	G. A. R. Lock	Surrey v Kent at Blackheath	1956
16-84	C. Gladwin	Derbyshire v Worcestershire at Stourbridge	1952
16-112	J. H. Wardle	Yorkshire v Sussex at Hull	1954
16-119	**M. P. Bicknell**	**Surrey v Leicestershire at Guildford**	**2000**
16-137	R. A. L. Massie	Australia v England at Lord's	1972
16-215	T. P. B. Smith	Essex v Middlesex at Colchester	1947
16-220	M. Muralitharan	Sri Lanka v England at The Oval	1998
16-225	J. E. Walsh	Leicestershire v Oxford University at Oxford	1953

---

overs, the first two, Maddy and Sutcliffe, with deliveries that would have bowled the best. Next morning, Wells and DeFreitas threw the bat at everything until, in his fourth over, Bicknell began a spell of four for four in 16 balls that brought him Championship-best figures of nine for 47 and made him the first to 50 first-class wickets in the season. Leicestershire's first-innings 318 was the highest total Surrey had conceded to date; in the second, 87 was the lowest. Ward followed the third hundred of his career with an unbeaten 61 as Surrey wrapped up victory by mid-afternoon.

Close of play: First day, Leicestershire 313-9 (Kumble 0*, Ormond 1*); Second day, Leicestershire 33-6 (Wells 0*).

Leicestershire

D. L. Maddy c Batty b Bicknell	3	– b Bicknell	0
I. J. Sutcliffe c Brown b Bicknell	37	– b Bicknell	7
D. I. Stevens c and b Bicknell	6	– (4) c Butcher b Bicknell	14
B. F. Smith c Butcher b Bicknell	102	– (3) lbw b Greenidge	8
A. Habib c Shahid b Saqlain Mushtaq	20	– (6) c Butcher b Bicknell	2
*V. J. Wells lbw b Bicknell	15	– (7) c Brown b Bicknell	17
P. A. J. DeFreitas c A. J. Hollioake			
b Saqlain Mushtaq	27	– (8) c Butcher b Bicknell	24
†N. D. Burns c Batty b Bicknell	4	– (5) lbw b Bicknell	0
D. Williamson c Batty b A. J. Hollioake	47	– not out	1
A. Kumble c Batty b Bicknell	2	– c B. C. Hollioake b Bicknell	5
J. Ormond not out	2	– b Bicknell	0
B 4, l-b 23, n-b 26	53	L-b 3, w 2, n-b 4	9

1/16 2/26 3/95 4/146 5/199   318
6/214 7/226 8/312 9/312

1/0 2/7 3/31 4/31 5/33   87
6/33 7/80 8/81 9/87

Bonus points – Leicestershire 3, Surrey 3.

Bowling: *First Innings*—Bicknell 28.1–5–72–7; Greenidge 12–2–35–0; B. C. Hollioake 19–5–74–0; Saqlain Mushtaq 39–9–93–2; A. J. Hollioake 4–2–8–1; Salisbury 6–1–9–0. *Second Innings*—Bicknell 12.5–3–47–9; Greenidge 11–6–35–1; Saqlain Mushtaq 1–0–2–0.

Surrey

M. A. Butcher c Burns b Ormond	0	– not out	47
I. J. Ward c Habib b DeFreitas	107	– not out	61
N. Shahid b Kumble	47		
*A. J. Hollioake c DeFreitas b Ormond	18		
A. D. Brown c Burns b Ormond	34		
B. C. Hollioake c Sutcliffe b Ormond	21		
†J. N. Batty c Habib b Kumble	3		
M. P. Bicknell lbw b Ormond	0		
I. D. K. Salisbury not out	10		
Saqlain Mushtaq c Habib b Ormond	1		
C. G. Greenidge lbw b Kumble	6		
B 12, l-b 8, w 4, n-b 22	41	B 3, l-b 6, n-b 2	11

1/2 2/93 3/123 4/198 5/209   288
6/266 7/270 8/272 9/273

(no wkt) 119

Bonus points – Surrey 2, Leicestershire 3.

In the first innings Brown, when 5, retired hurt at 138 and resumed at 209.

Bowling: *First Innings*—Ormond 29–6–87–6; DeFreitas 25–7–76–1; Wells 4–0–25–0; Williamson 6–0–17–0; Kumble 17–1–68–3. *Second Innings*—Ormond 3–1–14–0; DeFreitas 15–2–30–0; Williamson 7–2–17–0; Kumble 3–1–5–0; Wells 4–1–13–0; Maddy 3–0–11–0; Stevens 3–0–8–0; Sutcliffe 1.3–0–12–0.

Umpires: V. A. Holder and N. A. Mallender.

SURREY v LANCASHIRE

At The Oval, August 2, 3, 4, 5. Surrey won by 272 runs. Surrey 18 pts, Lancashire 3 pts. Toss: Surrey.

Lancashire arrived four points behind Championship leaders Surrey, but the gulf between them proved greater than that margin suggested. Had the weather not accounted for almost three sessions, Surrey's superiority would have been even more apparent. Neither team shone particularly with the bat – with Atherton at Old Trafford playing his 100th Test, Lancashire promoted Chapple to open – but Surrey's attack again demonstrated it could bowl sides out on most surfaces. A hard pitch with even bounce was exploited first time round by Tudor, who returned a career-best seven for 48 with exemplary fast bowling; then, on the final day, Salisbury and Saqlain Mushtaq spun Lancashire to their first Championship defeat. Fine seam bowling by Smethurst had Surrey 12 for three on the opening day, but depth down the order produced a useful total that became competitive once Lancashire failed to meet the follow-on target. When Adam Hollioake did not enforce it, Butcher and Shahid batted the game beyond their reach. Surrey had won the psychological battle long before the visitors were asked to confront a deficit of 417 with a day remaining. During Fairbrother's second innings, he became the tenth-highest scorer in Lancashire's history, overtaking Alan Wharton's 17,921.

Close of play: First day, Surrey 191-6 (Batty 3*, Bicknell 3*); Second day, Surrey 310; Third day, Lancashire 19-0 (Chapple 7*, Crawley 10*).

Surrey

M. A. Butcher c Fairbrother b Smethurst	4	– c and b Schofield 95
I. J. Ward c Flintoff b Smethurst	6	– c Hegg b Schofield 20
N. Shahid lbw b Smethurst	1	– c sub b Keedy 62
*A. J. Hollioake c Hegg b Scuderi	80	– st Hegg b Keedy 18
A. D. Brown c Flintoff b Smethurst	54	– not out 19
B. C. Hollioake lbw b Scuderi	24	– not out 2
†J. N. Batty b Chapple	12	
M. P. Bicknell c Flintoff b Smethurst	28	
I. D. K. Salisbury lbw b Smethurst	35	
A. J. Tudor b Flintoff	35	
Saqlain Mushtaq not out	4	
B 1, l-b 16, w 8, n-b 2	27	L-b 9, n-b 2 11

1/10 2/11 3/12 4/108 5/164   310   1/74 2/183   (4 wkts dec.) 227
6/185 7/217 8/237 9/294   3/191 4/219

Bonus points – Surrey 3, Lancashire 3.

Bowling: *First Innings*—Chapple 32–8–78–1; Smethurst 29–12–63–6; Scuderi 21–5–65–2; Keedy 13–3–38–0; Flintoff 4.5–1–14–1; Schofield 11–2–35–0. *Second Innings*—Chapple 4–0–13–0; Smethurst 7–2–39–0; Keedy 22–2–79–2; Schofield 12.5–1–65–2; Scuderi 6–0–22–0.

Lancashire

G. Chapple c Butcher b Tudor	4	– c B. C. Hollioake b Tudor 7
*J. P. Crawley lbw b Bicknell	1	– c A. J. Hollioake b Saqlain Mushtaq 21
A. Flintoff c Shahid b Saqlain Mushtaq	36	– c B. C. Hollioake b Tudor 10
S. C. Ganguly hit wkt b Tudor	0	– b Salisbury 27
N. H. Fairbrother c Butcher b Tudor	15	– c Brown b Salisbury 47
G. D. Lloyd c Batty b Tudor	0	– c A. J. Hollioake b Saqlain Mushtaq 1
J. C. Scuderi c Batty b Saqlain Mushtaq	25	– c Batty b Salisbury 21
†W. K. Hegg b Tudor	12	– c Butcher b Salisbury 4
C. P. Schofield c Saqlain Mushtaq b Tudor	4	– c Butcher b Saqlain Mushtaq 1
G. Keedy c B. C. Hollioake b Tudor	2	– not out 0
M. P. Smethurst not out	0	– c Bicknell b Salisbury 0
B 3, l-b 4, w 4, n-b 10	21	W 2, n-b 4 6

1/5 2/7 3/7 4/33 5/33   120   1/23 2/37 3/45 4/89 5/94   145
6/85 7/96 8/103 9/119   6/132 7/136 8/137 9/145

Bonus points – Surrey 3.

Bowling: *First Innings*—Bicknell 10–3–20–1; Tudor 15.1–6–48–7; Saqlain Mushtaq 10–4–28–2; B. C. Hollioake 4–0–17–0. *Second Innings*—Bicknell 11–4–12–0; Tudor 11–2–42–2; Saqlain Mushtaq 20–8–45–3; Salisbury 14–4–46–5.

Umpires: R. Palmer and J. F. Steele.

SURREY v DERBYSHIRE

At The Oval, August 16, 17. Surrey won by an innings and 45 runs. Surrey 17 pts, Derbyshire 3 pts. Toss: Derbyshire.

This was Surrey's seventh consecutive Championship victory since their last defeat – by Derbyshire. Completed by tea on the second day, it was determined 24 hours earlier when Gary Butcher's swing bowling claimed four wickets in four balls, starting with the last delivery of the 52nd over. The first three went to slip catches. Butcher, making his first appearance of the season after Ben Hollioake was dropped, was the first to achieve the feat in the Championship since Surrey's Pat Pocock in 1972. Five for 18 was his best return since joining Surrey from Glamorgan in 1999, and only his second five-wicket haul ever. Then it was brother Mark's turn, putting on 137 with Ward. Despite losing eight for 99 next morning, as Dean took six for 14 in 9.3 overs, Surrey led by 142. Stubbings and Sutton had almost halved that before Salisbury, in his first over, had Stubbings and Di Venuto caught at forward short leg off consecutive balls. That stung Saqlain Mushtaq into action: with seven wickets for just five runs, on a pitch providing pace and bounce, it took him less than an hour to wrap up another abysmal Derbyshire batting effort.

Close of play: First day, Surrey 161-2 (Shahid 13*, Salisbury 4*).

Derbyshire

S. D. Stubbings lbw b Bicknell	11	– c Shahid b Salisbury	41
S. J. Lacey not out	7	– (7) c Shahid b Saqlain Mushtaq	0
M. J. Di Venuto b Tudor	10	– c Shahid b Salisbury	0
R. J. Bailey lbw b G. P. Butcher	9	– c Brown b Saqlain Mushtaq	0
M. P. Dowman c Shahid b Bicknell	36	– c Batty b Saqlain Mushtaq	9
†L. D. Sutton c M. A. Butcher b Bicknell	26	– (2) c Hollioake b Saqlain Mushtaq	23
M. E. Cassar lbw b Saqlain Mushtaq	1	– (6) b Saqlain Mushtaq	0
P. Aldred c M. A. Butcher b G. P. Butcher	6	– st Batty b Salisbury	4
*T. A. Munton c Bicknell b G. P. Butcher	0	– c and b Saqlain Mushtaq	13
K. J. Dean c Bicknell b G. P. Butcher	0	– lbw b Saqlain Mushtaq	0
L. J. Wharton lbw b G. P. Butcher	0	– not out	0
B 4, l-b 4, w 2, n-b 2	12	B 1, l-b 4, w 2	7

1/24 2/30 3/59 4/85 5/106   118   1/68 2/68 3/69 4/70 5/70   97
6/106 7/116 8/118 9/118   6/70 7/75 8/90 9/94

Bonus points – Surrey 3.

In the first innings Lacey, when 5, retired hurt at 15 and resumed at 106-6.

Bowling: *First Innings*—Bicknell 19–7–36–3; Tudor 15–4–34–1; Hollioake 5–2–10–0; G. P. Butcher 7.3–3–18–5; Saqlain Mushtaq 7–2–12–1. *Second Innings*—Bicknell 7–2–16–0; Tudor 5–1–27–0; G. P. Butcher 4–0–13–0; Saqlain Mushtaq 9.3–5–11–7; Salisbury 8–1–25–3.

Surrey

M. A. Butcher c Stubbings b Aldred	78	M. P. Bicknell lbw b Munton	3
I. J. Ward lbw b Cassar	57	A. J. Tudor not out	0
N. Shahid lbw b Munton	17	Saqlain Mushtaq lbw b Dean	0
I. D. K. Salisbury b Dean	24		
*A. J. Hollioake c Di Venuto b Dean	42	B 4, l-b 11, w 2	17
A. D. Brown c Stubbings b Dean	15		
G. P. Butcher c Aldred b Dean	7	1/137 2/152 3/165 4/219 5/238	260
†J. N. Batty b Dean	0	6/255 7/256 8/257 9/259	

Bonus points – Surrey 2, Derbyshire 3.

Bowling: Munton 20–3–69–2; Dean 19.3–5–51–6; Aldred 21–8–68–1; Wharton 8–1–13–0; Cassar 11–2–44–1.

Umpires: R. Julian and B. Leadbeater.

At Scarborough, August 30, 31, September 1, 2. SURREY drew with YORKSHIRE.

SURREY v DURHAM

At The Oval, September 6, 7, 8, 9. Surrey won by an innings and 68 runs. Surrey 20 pts, Durham 2 pts. Toss: Surrey.

Surrey's ninth victory left them needing one point to retain their Championship title. They took heavy revenge on Durham, who had started their own Championship campaign by crushing them in May, but ended it here with relegation. First, left-handers Mark Butcher and Ward wore Durham down by compiling 359, Surrey's fourth-highest opening partnership; then Salisbury bowled them to an innings defeat with his second ten-wicket return of the summer – his sixth in all. Butcher's 191 (one six, 23 fours) was only his second hundred of the season, but his third against Durham in five years, each of them over 150, while Ward's 144 went some way to ensuring

---

HIGHEST OPENING PARTNERSHIPS FOR SURREY

428	J. B. Hobbs (261) and A. Sandham (183) v Oxford University at The Oval	1926
379	R. Abel (173) and W. Brockwell (225) v Hampshire at The Oval.	1897
364	R. Abel (193) and D. L. A. Jephson (213) v Derbyshire at The Oval	1900
359	**M. A. Butcher (191) and I. J. Ward (144) v Durham at The Oval**	**2000**
352	T. W. Hayward (204*) and J. B. Hobbs (159) v Warwickshire at The Oval	1909
321	D. J. Bicknell (169) and G. S. Clinton (146) v Northamptonshire at The Oval . . .	1990
313	T. W. Hayward (146) and J. B. Hobbs (184) v Worcestershire at Worcester	1913

---

another England A place. Katich, Durham's left-handed Australian, played Salisbury and Saqlain particularly well for his first-innings 77 but, other than Pratt, another left-hander, and Phillips, the visitors looked bankrupt. Hollioake had eschewed the follow-on three times out of five; now, with the weather closing in, he went for the kill. Durham, 212 behind, were batting again before the shortened third day was over.

Close of play: First day, Surrey 243-0 (M. A. Butcher 100*, Ward 103*); Second day, Durham 165-6 (Pratt 15*, Phillips 0*); Third day, Durham 10-0 (Lewis 4*, Gough 5*).

Surrey

M. A. Butcher b Harmison	191	G. P. Butcher not out	10
I. J. Ward lbw b Brown	144	B 11, l-b 19, w 20.	50
N. Shahid c Collingwood b Phillips	33		
*A. J. Hollioake c Brown b Harmison . .	20	1/359 2/413 (4 wkts dec.) 453	
A. D. Brown not out.	5	3/421 4/437	

†J. N. Batty, M. P. Bicknell, A. J. Tudor, I. D. K. Salisbury and Saqlain Mushtaq did not bat.

Bonus points – Surrey 5, Durham 1.

Bowling: Brown 26–7–77–1; Harmison 26–6–105–2; Killeen 19–4–60–0; Collingwood 14–2–53–0; Phillips 39.5–7–110–1; Gough 2–0–9–0; Katich 2–0–9–0.

Durham

*J. J. B. Lewis b Bicknell	1	– lbw b Tudor	8
M. A. Gough lbw b Saqlain Mushtaq	28	– c Salisbury b Tudor	20
S. M. Katich st Batty b Salisbury	77	– b Batty b Tudor	0
P. D. Collingwood c Tudor b Salisbury	4	– run out	4
J. A. Daley c Ward b Salisbury	14	– b Salisbury	2
M. P. Speight c Hollioake b Salisbury	12	– c Hollioake b Salisbury	48
†A. Pratt st Batty b Salisbury	36	– c Shahid b Bicknell	31
N. C. Phillips c Shahid b Saqlain Mushtaq	29	– c Batty b Saqlain Mushtaq	14
N. Killeen lbw b Salisbury	8	– c Batty b Salisbury	14
S. J. Harmison lbw b Salisbury	9	– b Salisbury	0
S. J. E. Brown not out	0	– not out	0
B 6, l-b 5, n-b 12	23	B 3, l-b 5, n-b 8	16

1/22 2/66 3/89 4/113 5/137   241   1/16 2/16 3/30 4/43 5/43   144
6/162 7/205 8/225 9/237   6/120 7/129 8/133 9/133

Bonus points – Durham 1, Surrey 3.

Bowling: *First Innings*—Bicknell 7–3–20–1; Tudor 6–1–14–0; Saqlain Mushtaq 35–8–91–2; Salisbury 34.3–8–105–7. *Second Innings*—Saqlain Mushtaq 12–3–23–1; Salisbury 20.3–8–49–4; Tudor 11–2–41–3; Bicknell 11–5–23–1.

Umpires: J. W. Lloyds and N. A. Mallender.

At Manchester, September 13, 14, 15, 16. SURREY drew with LANCASHIRE.

DATES OF WINNING COUNTY CHAMPIONSHIP

The dates on which the County Championship has been settled since 1979 are as follows:

			Final margin
1979	Essex	August 21	77 pts
1980	Middlesex	September 2	13 pts
1981	Nottinghamshire	September 14	2 pts
1982	Middlesex	September 11	39 pts
1983	Essex	September 13	16 pts
1984	Essex	September 11	14 pts
1985	Middlesex	September 17	18 pts
1986	Essex	September 10	28 pts
1987	Nottinghamshire	September 14	4 pts
1988	Worcestershire	September 16	1 pt
1989	Worcestershire	August 31	6 pts
1990	Middlesex	September 20	31 pts
1991	Essex	September 19	13 pts
1992	Essex	September 3	41 pts
1993	Middlesex	August 30	36 pts
1994	Warwickshire	September 2	42 pts
1995	Warwickshire	September 16	32 pts
1996	Leicestershire	September 21	27 pts
1997	Glamorgan	September 20	4 pts
1998	Leicestershire	September 19	15 pts
1999	Surrey	September 2	56 pts
2000	Surrey	September 13	20 pts

Note: The earliest date on which the Championship has been won since it was expanded in 1895 was August 12, 1910, by Kent.

SUSSEX

James Kirtley

President: The Duke of Richmond and Gordon

Chairman: D. G. Trangmar

Chief Executive: D. R. Gilbert

Captain: C. J. Adams

Cricket Manager and Senior Coach: P. Moores

Head Groundsman: D. J. Traill

Scorer: L. V. Chandler

A season that promised so much at the halfway mark tailed off alarmingly, leaving Sussex with the wooden spoon in the Championship and relegation in the National League, after just one season in the top flight. It led to some serious soul-searching, with captain Chris Adams confirming he would step down if there was no big improvement in 2001. For coach Peter Moores and the 11 players out of contract at the end of it, the new season would be equally important.

It was a difficult third year in charge for Adams, although he brought some of the pressures upon himself. After a winter in which he had struggled to justify his England selection, he found himself embroiled in controversy early in the season. He was fined by the ECB for pushing Essex's Danny Law during the Benson and Hedges Cup tie at Chelmsford. Three weeks later, he initiated a heated exchange with David Constant in the umpires' room at Hove, after an lbw verdict had gone against him in the innings defeat by Warwickshire. Sussex stood by their captain, while warning him there could be no repeat. Adams knuckled down, but by the end of the season his patience was understandably wearing thin with his underperforming team.

In terms of results, Sussex fared as badly as in 1997. Bearing in mind the money invested in strengthening the team since then, 2000 was far more disappointing. The batting, so dependent on Michael Bevan and Adams, remained brittle, and Sussex seemed no nearer to solving this major weakness. Bevan had an excellent season, scoring 2,183 runs in all competitions, and his four Championship hundreds in five innings in July helped Sussex head Division Two. They were also improving in the League after a poor start. But Bevan was needed for a one-day tournament in Australia, and with him went Sussex's prospects. He missed four of their last five Championship games and Sussex lost all four.

For the second year running, no one apart from the overseas player scored 1,000 first-class runs, and several batsmen performed below expectations. Tony Cottey and Richard Montgomerie each hit two Championship centuries, but 740 and 769 runs respectively were modest returns, bearing in mind the considerable sums invested in bringing them to Hove. Will House, a winter signing from Kent, proved a reliable one-day performer but struggled to make an impact in the Championship.

The county were still looking for a dependable opening partnership, and Toby Peirce, deemed not to be the answer, was released at the end of the season, along with Wasim Khan, Justin Bates and Irishman Andy Patterson. The search also rumbled on for a wicket-keeper whose batting would boost the lower middle order. Shaun Humphries had plenty of sympathisers when he left halfway through the season; Patterson was promoted after scoring heavily in the Second Eleven, but at times he batted like a man in a fog, and was not in Humphries's class as a wicket-keeper; by the end of the season, Nick Wilton had the gloves and was showing some consistent form with the bat. The challenge to him in 2001 comes from Australian-born Tim Ambrose and Matthew Prior, the only player from the club's youth academy taken on the staff.

Much was expected of Robin Martin-Jenkins after he had found himself on the fringe of England A selection. A career-best 86 at Arundel and 77 amid the carnage at Colwyn Bay offered evidence of his undoubted ability, but the perception remained that he was a decent first-change seamer who could bat a bit.

It wasn't all doom and gloom. James Kirtley again led the attack with gusto, taking 95 wickets in all cricket, and was offered an improved contract as Sussex sought to hold on to a prized asset. Jason Lewry supported him well, but it was something of a mystery that this talented left-armer did not play any League matches. Umer Rashid took a modest 23 Championship wickets with his left-arm spin, but his batting was a revelation. He made a maiden century at Colwyn Bay, and the improvements in his fielding and overall attitude were manifest. It will be interesting to see if his bowling develops along similar lines in 2001 when Mark Davis, a South African off-spinner with a considerable reputation and a British parent, comes to Hove.

In the League, Sussex made a habit of losing games they should have won. Despite Bevan's half-centuries in his last four innings as he increased his League aggregate to 706 runs at 117.66, four defeats in the last five games condemned them to bottom place. For once, Sussex progressed from the group stage of the Benson and Hedges Cup, but they were well beaten in the quarter-finals by Gloucestershire and similarly outplayed by Surrey in the NatWest Trophy.

At the end of the season, Bevan asked to be excused from the second year of his three-year contract so he could rest, and Sussex moved quickly to sign Murray Goodwin, the former Zimbabwean Test batsman. Chairman Don Trangmar and chief executive Dave Gilbert proved more than capable administrators in their first season together. Prudent housekeeping turned a big loss in 1998 into a modest profit and Sussex decided that, in the absence of suitable alternative sites, they would undertake a redevelopment of the County Ground rather than seek a new home.

One familiar face missing in 2000 was groundsman Peter Eaton, who died suddenly in February after more than 30 years of unstinting service to the county. The new net area at Hove was dedicated to his memory. By the end of the season his successor, Derek Traill, was digging up the moribund Hove square for the first time in living memory. – ANDY ARLIDGE.

SUSSEX 2000

[*Bill Smith*]

Back row: S. Osborne (*physiotherapist*), D. A. Clapp, M. H. Yardy, J. J. Bates, W. J. House, J. R. Carpenter, B. V. Taylor, P. M. Havell, T. Wright (*physiotherapist*).
Middle row: L. J. Lenham (*education coach*), R. A. Harley (*fitness coach*), N. J. Wilton, M. T. E. Peirce, S. Humphries, R. S. C. Martin-Jenkins, U. B. A. Rashid, W. G. Khan, B. Zuiderent. *Front row*: R. R. Montgomerie, P. A. Cottey, J. D. Lewry, P. Moores (*cricket manager/senior coach*), C. J. Adams (*captain*), K. Greenfield (*Second Eleven coach*), M. A. Robinson, R. J. Kirtley. *Inset*: M. G. Bevan.

SUSSEX RESULTS

All first-class matches – Played 17: Won 3, Lost 7, Drawn 7.

County Championship matches – Played 16: Won 3, Lost 6, Drawn 7.

PPP Healthcare County Championship, 9th in Division 2; NatWest Trophy, 4th round;
Benson and Hedges Cup, q-f; Norwich Union National League, 9th in Division 1.

COUNTY CHAMPIONSHIP AVERAGES

BATTING

Cap		M	I	NO	R	HS	100s	50s	Avge	Ct
1998	M. G. Bevan§	12	18	3	1,124	174	5	1	74.93	2
1998	C. J. Adams	16	26	3	913	156	1	7	39.69	15
	U. B. A. Rashid	14	20	3	560	110	1	4	32.94	6
1999	P. A. Cottey	16	23	0	740	154	2	2	32.17	8
1999	R. R. Montgomerie . . .	16	28	2	769	133	2	3	29.57	17
2000	R. S. C. Martin-Jenkins	14	21	1	465	86	0	2	23.25	3
	W. G. Khan	2	4	0	85	74	0	1	21.25	0
	M. T. E. Peirce	13	22	1	401	86	0	2	19.09	3
	N. J. Wilton	8	11	2	150	46	0	0	16.66	19
	W. J. House	5	8	1	90	35	0	0	12.85	3
1996	J. D. Lewry†	16	22	4	149	39	0	0	8.27	5
	J. J. Bates	3	4	0	33	17	0	0	8.25	1
1998	R. J. Kirtley†	16	22	4	146	26*	0	0	8.11	5
	M. H. Yardy	3	6	1	39	14	0	0	7.80	0
1997	M. A. Robinson	9	11	8	19	8*	0	0	6.33	3
	B. V. Taylor	5	6	4	9	6	0	0	4.50	0
	A. D. Patterson	7	9	0	37	8	0	0	4.11	15

Also batted: S. Humphries† (1 match) 4, 18 (3 ct, 1 st).

* Signifies not out.   † Born in Sussex.   § Overseas player.

BOWLING

	O	M	R	W	BB	5W/i	Avge
R. J. Kirtley	521.4	138	1,559	63	6-41	4	24.74
J. D. Lewry	494.4	122	1,507	51	6-66	3	29.54
M. A. Robinson	228	77	537	16	3-88	0	33.56
R. S. C. Martin-Jenkins	335.1	71	1,135	32	5-94	1	35.46
U. B. A. Rashid	297.5	73	892	23	5-103	1	38.78

Also bowled: C. J. Adams 27–3–110–2; J. J. Bates 79–14–254–3; M. G. Bevan
103.4–11–400–5; P. A. Cottey 1–1–0–0; W. J. House 17–2–62–1; W. G. Khan 7–0–22–0;
M. T. E. Peirce 11–3–37–1; B. V. Taylor 118–28–405–6; M. H. Yardy 5–0–17–0.

COUNTY RECORDS

Highest score for:	333	K. S. Duleepsinhji v Northamptonshire at Hove . .	1930
Highest score against:	322	E. Paynter (Lancashire) at Hove	1937
Best bowling for:	10-48	C. H. G. Bland v Kent at Tonbridge	1899
Best bowling against:	9-11	A. P. Freeman (Kent) at Hove	1922
Highest total for:	705-8 dec.	v Surrey at Hastings	1902
Highest total against:	726	by Nottinghamshire at Nottingham	1895
Lowest total for:	{ 19	v Surrey at Godalming	1830
	{ 19	v Nottinghamshire at Hove	1873
Lowest total against:	18	by Kent at Gravesend	1867

At Bristol, April 26, 27, 28, 29. SUSSEX drew with GLOUCESTERSHIRE.

At Hastings, May 7. SUSSEX lost to ZIMBABWEANS by eight wickets (See Zimbabwean tour section).

SUSSEX v WARWICKSHIRE

At Hove, May 11, 12, 13, 14. Warwickshire won by an innings and 47 runs. Warwickshire 20 pts, Sussex 3 pts. Toss: Sussex.

This was not a happy game for Sussex. Not only were they soundly beaten after two limp batting displays but their captain, Adams, found himself in hot water for marching into the umpires' room to confront David Constant, who had given him out lbw to Giles. Adams, who said he only wanted to know where the ball pitched in case he needed to sort out his technique, later apologised and, although a clearly shaken Constant mentioned the incident in his report, Lord's took no further action. The fracas overshadowed a thumping triumph for Warwickshire. On a slow, flat pitch, Sussex's first-innings 224 was clearly insufficient. Warwickshire also began shakily, but the later batsmen piled into some wayward bowling. Brown capitalised most with a maiden double-hundred, full of flowing drives and meaty cuts, hitting 30 fours from 335 balls in 407 minutes; with Giles, whose unbeaten 128 was also a career-best, he put on 289, a Warwickshire seventh-wicket record, in five hours. Facing a deficit of 324 on a pitch offering increasing help to the spinners, Sussex never looked likely to save the game. Only the obdurate Montgomerie offered prolonged resistance.

Close of play: First day, Warwickshire 70-2 (Knight 21*, Hemp 9*); Second day, Warwickshire 439-6 (Brown 157*, Giles 70*); Third day, Sussex 220-6 (House 35*, Lewry 31*).

Sussex

R. R. Montgomerie b Richardson	6	– b Giles		51
M. T. E. Peirce c Piper b Giddins	10	– c Piper b Richardson		8
M. G. Bevan c Knight b Giddins	30	– lbw b Smith		36
*C. J. Adams lbw b Richardson	70	– lbw b Giles		23
P. A. Cottey lbw b Richardson	42	– b Giddins		26
W. J. House b Richardson	9	– c Brown b Smith		35
R. S. C. Martin-Jenkins c Piper b Brown	31	– lbw b Giddins		0
J. D. Lewry c Piper b Giles	2	– c Ostler b Smith		39
†S. Humphries hit wkt b Brown	4	– b Giles		18
R. J. Kirtley c Knight b Brown	2	– b Giddins		14
M. A. Robinson not out	0	– not out		7
L-b 15, w 3	18	B 6, l-b 5, w 5, n-b 4		20

1/7 2/45 3/54 4/149 5/159   224   1/12 2/81 3/116 4/131 5/169   277
6/197 7/206 8/215 9/217   6/169 7/220 8/233 9/257

Bonus points – Sussex 1, Warwickshire 3.

Bowling: *First Innings*—Giddins 18–12–37–2; Richardson 20–3–69–4; Giles 16–4–48–1; Brown 14.2–0–55–3. *Second Innings*—Giddins 23.3–9–50–3; Richardson 17–3–53–1; Brown 7–2–22–0; Giles 33–13–61–3; Smith 26–5–80–3.

Warwickshire

M. J. Powell c Adams b Robinson	19	D. R. Brown st Humphries b Peirce	203
N. V. Knight c House b Kirtley	38	A. F. Giles not out	128
D. P. Ostler b Martin-Jenkins	13	B 3, l-b 23, n-b 24	50
D. L. Hemp c Humphries b Kirtley	90		
T. L. Penney c Humphries b Robinson	7	1/35 2/50 3/133 (7 wkts dec.)	548
*N. M. K. Smith c Humphries b Robinson	0	4/158 5/158	
		6/259 7/548	

†K. J. Piper, A. Richardson and E. S. H. Giddins did not bat.

Bonus points – Warwickshire 5, Sussex 2 (Score at 130 overs: 443-6).

Bowling: Lewry 38–9–123–0; Kirtley 30–9–101–2; Robinson 35–14–88–3; Martin-Jenkins 36–5–133–1; Adams 4–1–16–0; Bevan 3–0–17–0; Peirce 11–3–37–1; House 3–1–7–0.

Umpires: D. J. Constant and G. Sharp.

SUSSEX v WORCESTERSHIRE

At Hove, May 18, 19, 20, 21. Worcestershire won by seven wickets. Worcestershire 18 pts, Sussex 4 pts. Toss: Sussex. Championship debut: A. D. Patterson.

More inept batting by Sussex on a perfectly good pitch condemned them to a second successive home defeat, though they were almost reprieved by rain. Worcestershire eventually reached their target of 96 – in what had been reduced to 26 overs – with 11 balls to spare. The weather also curtailed the first day, allowing only an hour's play. When Sussex resumed next morning, they had no answer to the sustained hostility of McGrath, who claimed five in an innings for the first time for Worcestershire. Lampitt gave good support and removed Bevan as he was threatening to cut loose. Despite numerous stoppages, which extended the second day's play beyond 8 p.m., Worcestershire steadily built a lead, thanks to Solanki's attractive strokeplay. If anything, Sussex's second-innings batting was more flaccid than the first; McGrath took his match haul to nine, with six for the persevering Lampitt.

Close of play: First day, Sussex 51-1 (Montgomerie 20*, Bevan 0*); Second day, Worcestershire 89-2 (Solanki 8*, Spiring 20*); Third day, Sussex 114-7 (Rashid 10*, Lewry 1*).

Sussex

R. R. Montgomerie lbw b McGrath	25	– lbw b Lampitt	24
M. T. E. Peirce lbw b McGrath	21	– lbw b McGrath	2
M. G. Bevan lbw b Lampitt	41	– b McGrath	26
*C. J. Adams c Illingworth b Lampitt	36	– c Leatherdale b Sheriyar	8
P. A. Cottey lbw b Lampitt	0	– b McGrath	21
†A. D. Patterson c Rhodes b Ali	5	– c Illingworth b Sheriyar	0
U. B. A. Rashid lbw b McGrath	37	– c Solanki b McGrath	14
R. S. C. Martin-Jenkins c Solanki b McGrath	29	– c Lampitt b Solanki	6
J. D. Lewry c Rhodes b Sheriyar	0	– c Rhodes b Lampitt	18
R. J. Kirtley c Rhodes b McGrath	12	– lbw b McGrath	0
M. A. Robinson not out	0	– not out	1
L-b 12, w 7, n-b 33	52	B 4, l-b 2, n-b 22	28

1/43 2/86 3/114 4/114 5/127	258	1/13 2/53 3/70 4/70 5/81	148
6/173 7/206 8/209 9/237		6/99 7/113 8/144 9/144	

Bonus points – Sussex 2, Worcestershire 3.

Bowling: *First Innings*—McGrath 23.5–5–54–5; Sheriyar 18–1–101–1; Lampitt 12–1–50–3; Ali 8–1–36–1; Illingworth 2–0–5–0. *Second Innings*—McGrath 14–5–30–4; Sheriyar 17–2–69–2; Lampitt 10.2–3–35–3; Illingworth 3–2–1–0; Solanki 2–0–7–1.

Worcestershire

E. J. Wilson lbw b Lewry	22	– lbw b Robinson	47
R. C. Driver lbw b Robinson	32	– c Patterson b Martin-Jenkins	4
V. S. Solanki c and b Rashid	98	– b Robinson	33
K. R. Spiring c Rashid b Robinson	38	– not out	4
D. A. Leatherdale lbw b Rashid	35	– not out	0
*†S. J. Rhodes not out	34		
S. R. Lampitt c Martin-Jenkins b Kirtley	7		
R. K. Illingworth lbw b Kirtley	1		
G. D. McGrath c and b Kirtley	15		
B 5, l-b 8, w 6, n-b 10	29	L-b 6, n-b 2	8

1/55 2/55 3/147 4/227   (8 wkts dec.) 311   1/11 2/91 3/92   (3 wkts) 96
5/250 6/271 7/283 8/311

Kabir Ali and A. Sheriyar did not bat.

Bonus points – Worcestershire 3, Sussex 2.

Bowling: *First Innings*—Lewry 23–5–77–1; Kirtley 19.5–4–79–3; Robinson 19–4–52–2; Rashid 21–6–56–2; Martin-Jenkins 11–0–34–0. *Second Innings*—Lewry 6–0–27–0; Kirtley 5.1–1–19–0; Martin-Jenkins 7–1–26–1; Robinson 6–1–18–2.

Umpires: K. E. Palmer and R. A. White.

At Chelmsford, May 23, 24, 25, 26. SUSSEX drew with ESSEX.

SUSSEX v GLAMORGAN

At Hove, May 31, June 1, 2, 3. Sussex won by ten wickets. Sussex 20 pts, Glamorgan 2 pts. Toss: Glamorgan.

From the moment Lewry removed the cream of Glamorgan's batting in his opening spell, until they cruised to victory on the final morning, Sussex were in command. It was their first win of the season and lifted them four places from the bottom of the table. Only the determined Dale made anything of the ideal batting conditions in Glamorgan's first innings, and while the visitors' bowlers subsequently stuck to their task, Sussex were in no mood to surrender the initiative. Montgomerie and Peirce shared their first century opening stand of the season, after which Bevan and Adams pressed home the advantage. Bevan made Sussex's first Championship hundred at Hove for almost a year, while Adams was at his belligerent best, hitting nine fours and three sixes, one of which shattered the calm of the committee-room. Sussex, 278 ahead, steadily chipped away at the opposition batting, with Martin-Jenkins claiming the second five-wicket haul of his career – both against Glamorgan at Hove. Maynard, handicapped by a knee injury, batted at No. 7 with a runner, who duly ran him out, and Glamorgan needed Croft's intransigence to take the match to a fourth day.

Close of play: First day, Sussex 62-0 (Montgomerie 33*, Peirce 23*); Second day, Sussex 433-8 (Rashid 32*, Kirtley 0*); Third day, Glamorgan 242-6 (Shaw 34*, Croft 23*).

Glamorgan

M. T. G. Elliott c Adams b Lewry	14	– (2) c Montgomerie b Martin-Jenkins	42
S. P. James lbw b Lewry	8	– (1) lbw b Robinson	32
M. J. Powell c Adams b Kirtley	46	– lbw b Rashid	26
*M. P. Maynard b Lewry	5	– (7) run out	3
A. Dale lbw b Martin-Jenkins	75	– c Patterson b Martin-Jenkins	41
W. L. Law c Patterson b Lewry	1	– (4) lbw b Rashid	23
†A. D. Shaw c Adams b Martin-Jenkins	6	– (6) c Montgomerie b Martin-Jenkins	45
R. D. B. Croft c and b Kirtley	10	– c Adams b Martin-Jenkins	31
S. D. Thomas b Martin-Jenkins	0	– c and b Martin-Jenkins	0
S. L. Watkin not out	0	– not out	7
S. P. Jones b Kirtley	0	– c Robinson b Kirtley	13
B 1, l-b 13, w 2, n-b 4	20	B 9, l-b 6, w 2, n-b 4	21
	185		**284**

1/20 2/25 3/41 4/121 5/139   185   1/80 2/88 3/135 4/136 5/197   284
6/172 7/177 8/185 9/185   6/204 7/255 8/257 9/263

Bonus points – Sussex 3.

Bowling: *First Innings*—Lewry 14–3–40–4; Kirtley 17–4–48–3; Robinson 13–7–7–0; Martin-Jenkins 14–6–28–3; Rashid 17–5–36–0; Bevan 3–0–12–0. *Second Innings*—Lewry 13–1–46–0; Kirtley 21.2–8–52–1; Martin-Jenkins 31–7–94–5; Rashid 16–7–28–2; Bevan 3–1–5–0; Robinson 23–9–44–1; Cottey 1–1–0–0.

Sussex

R. R. Montgomerie c Shaw b Thomas	71	– not out	1
M. T. E. Peirce c Law b Croft	60	– not out	6
M. G. Bevan c Elliott b Watkin	107		
*C. J. Adams b Thomas	90		
P. A. Cottey c Shaw b Watkin	7		
R. S. C. Martin-Jenkins c Powell b Dale	25		
†A. D. Patterson c Shaw b Watkin	8		
U. B. A. Rashid not out	51		
J. D. Lewry c Elliott b Dale	7		
R. J. Kirtley c Shaw b Watkin	2		
M. A. Robinson not out	8		
B 5, l-b 8, w 8, n-b 6	27		
	(9 wkts dec.) 463		**(no wkt) 7**

1/106 2/186 3/317 4/359 5/359   (9 wkts dec.) 463   (no wkt) 7
6/370 7/417 8/429 9/451

Bonus points – Sussex 5, Glamorgan 2 (Score at 130 overs: 441-8).

Bowling: *First Innings*—Watkin 36–8–102–4; Thomas 27–5–103–2; Dale 21–4–63–2; Jones 29.3–4–97–0; Croft 27–6–85–1. *Second Innings*—Thomas 1–0–4–0; Jones 0.2–0–3–0.

Umpires: T. E. Jesty and A. A. Jones.

SUSSEX v MIDDLESEX

At Horsham, June 7, 8, 9, 10. Drawn. Sussex 10 pts, Middlesex 11 pts. Toss: Middlesex.

A third-day washout, together with the captains' inability to agree on a run-chase, condemned Horsham's annual Championship fixture to dreary deadlock. By the last afternoon, those spectators who had not headed down the road to watch Brian Lara making hay at Arundel were slow hand-clapping Roseberry – though his fifty was greeted by a resounding silence. The first two days had been keenly fought and full of good cricket. Martin-Jenkins, who was capped on his home ground, reduced Middlesex to 220 for six, but Nash grittily helped the tail add another 150. Most Sussex batsmen then made starts, and Bevan hit 15 boundaries in a thrilling 72, but Johnson, among the wickets again after long-term injury problems, put Middlesex in a strong position. Despite the rain and the drab conclusion, the host club were happy. They had paid Sussex £7,500 to stage the festival, which had lost money for years, but good crowds – as well as insurance against the weather – delivered a healthy profit.

Close of play: First day, Middlesex 340-8 (Nash 54*, Batt 18*); Second day, Sussex 284-9 (Rashid 44*, Kirtley 9*); Third day, No play.

Middlesex

A. J. Strauss b Martin-Jenkins	26	– (2) c Montgomerie b Martin-Jenkins	33
M. R. Ramprakash lbw b Lewry	0	– (1) c Patterson b Lewry	20
*J. L. Langer lbw b Martin-Jenkins	64	– c and b Bates	45
O. A. Shah c Bates b Rashid	60	– lbw b Rashid	55
P. N. Weekes lbw b Martin-Jenkins	23	– c and b Bates	23
M. A. Roseberry lbw b Martin-Jenkins	35	– c Montgomerie b Lewry	87
†D. C. Nash not out	75	– not out	47
R. L. Johnson c Rashid b Bevan	10	– not out	7
A. R. C. Fraser run out	26		
C. J. Batt b Lewry	21		
P. C. R. Tufnell c Adams b Lewry	4		
B 7, l-b 12, w 5, n-b 2	26	B 9, l-b 3, w 6, n-b 2	20

1/5 2/93 3/98 4/134 5/216   370   1/36 2/86 3/155   (6 wkts dec.) 337
6/220 7/239 8/298 9/364   4/185 5/198 6/321

Bonus points – Middlesex 4, Sussex 3.

Bowling: *First Innings*—Lewry 29.4–7–84–3; Kirtley 30–8–75–0; Martin-Jenkins 24–6–66–4; Bates 17–3–51–0; Rashid 6–2–19–1; Bevan 15–2–54–1; Adams 1–0–2–0. *Second Innings*—Lewry 15–4–43–2; Kirtley 4–1–21–0; Martin-Jenkins 7–1–25–1; Rashid 31–5–132–1; Bates 27–4–85–2; Bevan 8–1–19–0.

Sussex

R. R. Montgomerie c Fraser b Johnson	12	J. J. Bates b Johnson	1
M. T. E. Peirce lbw b Fraser	2	J. D. Lewry b Johnson	0
M. G. Bevan b Johnson	72	R. J. Kirtley not out	17
*C. J. Adams lbw b Batt	35	B 6, l-b 11, w 6, n-b 8	31
P. A. Cottey lbw b Johnson	36		
R. S. C. Martin-Jenkins lbw b Shah	35	1/3 2/52 3/103 (9 wkts dec.) 300	
U. B. A. Rashid not out	51	4/131 5/194 6/217	
†A. D. Patterson b Johnson	8	7/247 8/255 9/257	

Bonus points – Sussex 3, Middlesex 3.

Bowling: Fraser 22–4–69–1; Batt 12–3–44–1; Tufnell 23–6–69–0; Johnson 27–10–71–6; Shah 5–0–23–1; Weekes 1–0–7–0.

Umpires: R. Julian and R. Palmer.

At Worcester, June 15, 16. SUSSEX beat WORCESTERSHIRE by eight wickets.

At Hove, June 28, 29, 30, July 1. SUSSEX lost to NEW ZEALAND A by an innings and 57 runs (See New Zealand A tour section).

At Birmingham, July 7, 8, 9, 10. SUSSEX drew with WARWICKSHIRE.

SUSSEX v ESSEX

At Arundel, July 12, 13, 14, 15. Drawn. Sussex 9 pts, Essex 9 pts. Toss: Sussex.

Essex, set 310 in 73 overs, called off the chase when Stuart Law, batting down the order because of back spasms, was caught in the 53rd over with the score 189. Prichard and Robinson had provided an ideal platform with 126 for the second wicket. Sussex's declaration arose out of Bevan's undefeated 151, his 44th first-class hundred and his highest for them yet in the Championship. Batting almost six hours, he hit ten fours and four sixes. On the first day, Sussex had slipped to 45 for four through a mixture of movement and misjudgment, then recovered through a stand of 150 between Cottey and Martin-Jenkins, who scored a career-best 86. Light rain took 30 overs out of the second day, but solid middle-order batting gave Essex the prospect of a useful lead until Kirtley's three quick wickets next morning – giving him six for the innings – left the teams level-pegging.

Close of play: First day, Essex 30-2 (Robinson 7*, S. G. Law 10*); Second day, Essex 234-6 (Peters 46*, D. R. Law 8*); Third day, Sussex 243-5 (Bevan 105*).

Sussex

R. R. Montgomerie lbw b Irani	14	– lbw b Such	18
M. T. E. Peirce c Hyam b Ilott	0	– c and b Ilott	13
M. G. Bevan b Ilott	0	– not out	151
*C. J. Adams b Cowan	11	– c S. G. Law b Irani	53
P. A. Cottey c Hyam b D. R. Law	83	– lbw b Irani	0
R. S. C. Martin-Jenkins c S. G. Law b D. R. Law	86	– c Hyam b Such	37
U. B. A. Rashid c Hyam b Cowan	35	– b Grayson	16
†A. D. Patterson lbw b D. R. Law	3	– b Grayson	8
J. D. Lewry c Hyam b Cowan	12	– c Hyam b Grayson	5
R. J. Kirtley c Hyam b Cowan	0	– not out	1
M. A. Robinson not out	1		
L-b 10, w 6, n-b 4	20	B 2, l-b 11, w 2, n-b 4	19

1/13 2/13 3/23 4/45 5/195   265   1/17 2/51 3/154   (8 wkts dec.) 321
6/210 7/222 8/256 9/258   4/154 5/243 6/270
                               7/308 8/314

Bonus points – Sussex 2, Essex 3.

Bowling: *First Innings*—Ilott 20–5–50–2; Irani 14–4–29–1; Cowan 14.4–2–61–4; D. R. Law 15–2–74–3; Such 23–4–41–0. *Second Innings*—Ilott 13–3–30–1; Cowan 14–4–37–0; Irani 16–6–35–2; Such 41–7–113–2; D. R. Law 7–1–38–0; Grayson 15–5–55–3.

Essex

P. J. Prichard c Patterson b Kirtley	4	– c Patterson b Martin-Jenkins	66
A. P. Grayson lbw b Lewry	5	– c Montgomerie b Kirtley	1
D. D. J. Robinson c and b Kirtley	61	– b Martin-Jenkins	65
S. G. Law c Patterson b Martin-Jenkins	40	– (6) c Robinson b Martin-Jenkins	12
*R. C. Irani c Patterson b Kirtley	21	– c Cottey b Bevan	4
S. D. Peters c Adams b Kirtley	46	– (7) not out	22
†B. J. Hyam c Montgomerie b Martin-Jenkins	9	– (8) c Rashid b Bevan	10
D. R. Law not out	32	– (4) c Lewry b Bevan	49
A. P. Cowan lbw b Kirtley	4	– not out	5
M. C. Ilott b Kirtley	1		
P. M. Such c Patterson b Martin-Jenkins	2		
B 10, l-b 28, w 2, n-b 12	52	L-b 8, w 10, n-b 2	20

1/5 2/9 3/88 4/137 5/177   277   1/8 2/134 3/147 4/162   (7 wkts) 254
6/210 7/234 8/244 9/250   5/189 6/231 7/249

Bonus points – Essex 2, Sussex 3.

Bowling: *First Innings*—Lewry 22–11–35–1; Kirtley 29–7–85–6; Robinson 25–9–37–0; Martin-Jenkins 21–4–56–3; Rashid 8–1–19–0; Bevan 2–0–7–0. *Second Innings*—Lewry 8–3–18–0; Kirtley 14.4–3–38–1; Martin-Jenkins 17–4–75–3; Robinson 10–6–13–0; Rashid 6–0–28–0; Bevan 17–2–74–3.

Umpires: N. A. Mallender and A. G. T. Whitehead.

SUSSEX v NOTTINGHAMSHIRE

At Hove, July 19, 20, 21, 22. Drawn. Sussex 12 pts, Nottinghamshire 10 pts. Toss: Nottinghamshire.
Bevan followed 151 not out in his previous Championship innings with 166 and 174, to become the 14th player to make two hundreds in a match for Sussex, and the seventh to reach three in succession. Yet his achievement was nearly trumped by Nottinghamshire's bid to score 407 in 103 overs. Gallian and Morris shared a superb third-wicket stand of 222, with Morris hitting his 50th first-class century and first for Nottinghamshire; Gallian, without a Championship fifty all season, equalled his best for them. Only when Afzaal was out at 374 did Nottinghamshire abandon the pursuit, leaving Reiffel and Harris to survive the final 34 balls. Gallian, having put Sussex in, had to watch Montgomerie and Bevan add 292 for their second wicket, the basis of a first-innings lead of 128; both reached county-best scores. But for a ninth-wicket stand of 59 by Read and Harris, Nottinghamshire might have followed on. As it was, another double-century stand between Montgomerie and Bevan, 265 in 54 overs, set up the fascinating final day. Bevan raised his Championship-best for the second time in the match, his 174 in 178 balls containing 22 fours, two sixes and an exquisite range of strokes. Montgomerie was five runs from emulating him and thus providing the fourth instance of players on the same side each hitting two hundreds in a match. The only Championship occurrence was by Worcestershire's R. E. and W. L. Foster against Hampshire in 1899.
Close of play: First day, Sussex 404-5 (Adams 35*, House 0*); Second day, Nottinghamshire 240-3 (Morris 75*, Afzaal 35*); Third day, Nottinghamshire 19-0 (Bicknell 7*, Welton 6*).

Sussex

R. R. Montgomerie c Gallian b Stemp	133	– c Read b Afzaal	95
M. T. E. Peirce b Harris	18	– lbw b Millns	0
M. G. Bevan b Millns	166	– c Gallian b Afzaal	174
*C. J. Adams c Gallian b Reiffel	55	– not out	1
P. A. Cottey b Reiffel	17		
R. J. Kirtley lbw b Reiffel	0		
W. J. House c Harris b Gallian	24		
U. B. A. Rashid lbw b Reiffel	0		
†N. J. Wilton c Afzaal b Gallian	6		
J. D. Lewry b Harris	7		
B. V. Taylor not out	1		
B 4, l-b 7, w 14, n-b 20	45	L-b 2, n-b 6	8

1/45 2/337 3/341 4/404 5/404   472   1/0 2/265 3/278   (3 wkts dec.) 278
6/455 7/455 8/464 9/466

Bonus points – Sussex 5, Nottinghamshire 3.

Bowling: *First Innings*—Millns 24–3–120–1; Reiffel 32–10–85–4; Harris 25–4–111–2; Gallian 13–0–42–2; Stemp 25–4–85–1; Afzaal 3–0–18–0. *Second Innings*—Reiffel 11–1–31–0; Millns 10–0–56–1; Stemp 13–3–62–0; Harris 11–0–52–0; Gallian 9–1–55–0; Afzaal 3.2–0–20–2.

Nottinghamshire

D. J. Bicknell c Cottey b Bevan	45	– c Montgomerie b Rashid	23
G. E. Welton c Cottey b Kirtley	9	– lbw b Kirtley	6
*J. E. R. Gallian run out	44	– b Rashid	120
J. E. Morris c Wilton b Kirtley	76	– c Adams b Kirtley	115
U. Afzaal lbw b Kirtley	43	– b Lewry	54
P. Johnson c House b Lewry	1	– c Cottey b Rashid	9
†C. M. W. Read not out	38	– (8) c Rashid b Lewry	9
D. J. Millns lbw b Kirtley	1	– (7) b Rashid	0
P. R. Reiffel c Wilton b Lewry	7	– not out	9
A. J. Harris c House b Kirtley	31	– not out	2
R. D. Stemp b Kirtley	4		
B 11, l-b 13, w 2, n-b 19	45	L-b 20, n-b 12	32

1/12 2/77 3/163 4/241 5/246   344   1/20 2/59 3/281   (8 wkts) 379
6/250 7/252 8/265 9/324   4/297 5/317 6/317
                                     7/342 8/374

Bonus points – Nottinghamshire 3, Sussex 3.

Bowling: *First Innings*—Lewry 28–7–57–2; Kirtley 29–10–90–6; Taylor 16–5–42–0; Rashid 17–5–45–0; Bevan 24–3–65–1; House 4–1–21–0; Adams 1–1–0–0. *Second Innings*—Lewry 26.5–7–64–2; Kirtley 29–5–89–2; Taylor 14–2–69–0; Rashid 23–3–93–4; Bevan 10–1–44–0.

Umpires: B. Dudleston and J. W. Lloyds.

At Southgate, July 28, 29, 30, 31. SUSSEX beat MIDDLESEX by seven wickets.

At Northampton, August 9, 10, 11, 12. SUSSEX lost to NORTHAMPTONSHIRE by an innings and 17 runs.

SUSSEX v NORTHAMPTONSHIRE

At Eastbourne, August 16, 17, 18. Northamptonshire won by 162 runs. Northamptonshire 15 pts, Sussex 3 pts. Toss: Northamptonshire.

Northamptonshire strengthened their position as division leaders with a fourth successive victory, and their second back-to-back over Sussex, who were beginning to look increasingly adrift without Bevan. Nineteen wickets fell on the first day, more because of excessive swing and atrocious batting than the greenest pitch at the Saffrons for years. After Kirtley, on his home ground, had claimed a season's best return that took him past 50 first-class wickets, Adams, outclassing everyone in his judicious shot selection, put Sussex 43 ahead. Northamptonshire erased that soon enough, but were only 69 on when their fifth wicket fell. Cook, driving and cutting ferociously, turned the tide with his second Championship hundred, and Sussex needed 228 to win. An hour's woeful batting on the second evening, against quality swing bowling from Cousins and Taylor, saw them reduced to 45 for seven, albeit a recovery from 13 for six; only Adams's determination took the match into the third day. The corporate guests had not started their soup by the time Taylor swept aside the tail to complete his own season's best figures and dent Sussex's promotion chances.

Close of play: First day, Sussex 151-9 (Adams 82*); Second day, Sussex 45-7 (Adams 16*, Wilton 14*).

Northamptonshire

A. S. Rollins c Kirtley b Lewry	2	– (2) c Cottey b Kirtley	15
*M. L. Hayden lbw b Kirtley	6	– (1) c Peirce b Martin-Jenkins	21
J. W. Cook b Lewry	4	– b Rashid	116
D. J. Sales lbw b Kirtley	9	– lbw b Robinson	5
R. J. Warren b Kirtley	29	– lbw b Robinson	0
A. L. Penberthy c Wilton b Robinson	8	– lbw b Lewry	10
G. P. Swann c Robinson b Kirtley	20	– c Peirce b Kirtley	24
†D. Ripley b Lewry	5	– not out	39
J. P. Taylor b Kirtley	0	– c Adams b Lewry	8
D. M. Cousins not out	17	– c Adams b Lewry	2
J. F. Brown b Kirtley	0	– c Wilton b Lewry	0
B 1, l-b 1, n-b 8	10	B 14, l-b 10, n-b 6	30

1/4 2/12 3/20 4/28 5/50   110   1/22 2/46 3/65 4/65 5/112   270
6/80 7/89 8/89 9/101   6/169 7/236 8/264 9/270

Bonus points – Sussex 3.

Bowling: *First Innings*—Lewry 15–6–38–3; Kirtley 15.2–4–41–6; Martin-Jenkins 8–5–17–0; Robinson 7–3–12–1. *Second Innings*—Lewry 19.4–4–57–4; Kirtley 17–8–52–2; Robinson 20–7–58–2; Martin-Jenkins 20–3–55–1; Rashid 9–2–24–1.

Sussex

R. R. Montgomerie b Taylor	7	– lbw b Cousins	1
M. T. E. Peirce c Hayden b Taylor	6	– c Swann b Cousins	0
W. G. Khan lbw b Cousins	1	– lbw b Cousins	0
*C. J. Adams lbw b Cousins	84	– not out	24
P. A. Cottey lbw b Cousins	17	– b Cousins	1
R. S. C. Martin-Jenkins c Hayden b Penberthy	5	– c Ripley b Taylor	5
U. B. A. Rashid c Ripley b Penberthy	1	– (8) c Ripley b Taylor	4
†N. J. Wilton lbw b Taylor	14	– (9) c Hayden b Taylor	19
R. J. Kirtley lbw b Swann	0	– (7) lbw b Taylor	0
J. D. Lewry b Taylor	4	– c Hayden b Taylor	0
M. A. Robinson not out	0	– lbw b Taylor	0
L-b 6, w 8	14	B 1, l-b 8, w 2	11

1/16 2/17 3/29 4/72 5/77   153   1/1 2/1 3/2 4/6 5/13   65
6/83 7/115 8/138 9/151   6/13 7/25 8/61 9/61

Bonus points – Northamptonshire 3.

Bowling: *First Innings*—Cousins 14.3–2–39–3; Taylor 18–4–42–4; Penberthy 10–3–26–2; Brown 9 1 33 0; Swann 5–1–7–1. *Second Innings*—Cousins 13–6–25–4; Taylor 15.3–7–27–6; Brown 4–3–3–0; Swann 1–0–1–0.

Umpires: T. E. Jesty and A. A. Jones.

At Colwyn Bay, August 22, 23, 24, 25. SUSSEX lost to GLAMORGAN by an innings and 60 runs.

At Nottingham, August 30, 31, September 1, 2. SUSSEX drew with NOTTINGHAMSHIRE.

SUSSEX v GLOUCESTERSHIRE

At Hove, September 7, 8. Gloucestershire won by an innings and 18 runs. Gloucestershire 16 pts, Sussex 3 pts. Toss: Sussex.

Less than six weeks after Sussex headed the division, defeat in two days effectively condemned them to bottom place. There was no excuse; the batting was awful. They had now lost all four of their games without Bevan, three by an innings. After their openers put on 35 in untroubled fashion, Harvey cut a swathe through the Sussex order, taking four for seven in 11 overs before lunch and finishing with a Championship-best six for 19. He then put Gloucestershire ahead in a third-wicket stand of 105 with Windows. However, Martin-Jenkins dismissed them both, and Kirtley's hostile spell after lunch on the second day restricted their lead to 89. Once again, the home openers prospered, but 40 without loss was just an illusion. Sussex lost all ten wickets for 31 in 16 overs, with 26 of their final total of 71 coming in extras. The whole innings lasted less than two hours. Harvey had match figures of ten for 32, but even he must have been surprised by the Sussex batsmen's abject lack of application.

Close of play: First day, Gloucestershire 74-2 (Windows 19*, Harvey 12*).

Sussex

M. H. Yardy c Ball b Harvey	14	– lbw b Alleyne	12
R. R. Montgomerie c Windows b Gannon	30	– c Russell b Harvey	10
W. J. House c Russell b Harvey	9	– c Gannon b Alleyne	0
*C. J. Adams lbw b Harvey	1	– c Harvey b Alleyne	1
P. A. Cottey c Russell b Harvey	11	– c Russell b Lewis	9
R. S. C. Martin-Jenkins lbw b Gannon	5	– lbw b Harvey	6
U. B. A. Rashid b Lewis	17	– c Russell b Harvey	0
†N. J. Wilton lbw b Lewis	12	– c Alleyne b Harvey	0
R. J. Kirtley c Hancock b Harvey	19	– b Lewis	0
J. D. Lewry c Lewis b Harvey	8	– not out	1
B. V. Taylor not out	0	– b Lewis	6
B 1, l-b 3, w 8	12	B 6, l-b 6, w 14	26

1/35 2/53 3/55 4/71 5/79   138   1/40 2/40 3/40 4/42 5/49   71
6/79 7/100 8/115 9/130   6/51 7/51 8/60 9/65

Bonus points – Gloucestershire 3.

Bowling: First Innings—Lewis 19–3–62–2; Gannon 9–2–33–2; Harvey 15–6–19–6; Alleyne 9–2–20–0. *Second Innings*—Lewis 6–1–20–3; Gannon 2–0–16–0; Harvey 10–2–13–4; Alleyne 7–3–10–3.

Gloucestershire

T. H. C. Hancock b Kirtley	3	M. C. J. Ball not out	21
D. R. Hewson c Wilton b Martin-Jenkins	35	B. W. Gannon lbw b Kirtley	4
M. G. N. Windows b Martin-Jenkins	49	J. Lewis c Lewry b Kirtley	4
I. J. Harvey lbw b Martin-Jenkins	60		
*M. W. Alleyne lbw b Lewry	4	L-b 10, w 8, n-b 14	32
J. N. Snape lbw b Lewry	0		
C. G. Taylor c Wilton b Kirtley	15	1/9 2/54 3/159 4/164 5/171	227
†R. C. Russell c Wilton b Lewry	0	6/174 7/174 8/215 9/223	

Bonus points – Gloucestershire 1, Sussex 3.

Bowling: Lewry 16–4–51–3; Kirtley 19.3–8–53–4; Martin-Jenkins 19–8–51–3; Taylor 18–3–62–0.

Umpires: M. J. Harris and R. Julian.

WARWICKSHIRE

Michael Powell

President: The Rt Hon. The Lord Guernsey
Chairman: M. J. K. Smith
Chief Executive: D. L. Amiss
Chairman, Cricket Committee: T. A. Lloyd
Captain: 2000 – N. M. K. Smith
         2001 – M. J. Powell
Director of Coaching: R. A. Woolmer
Head Groundsman: S. J. Rouse
Scorer: D. Wainwright

National League promotion and a Lord's final, even one lost unsatisfactorily under Duckworth/Lewis rules, would have satisfied any number of counties. Not Warwickshire. Within 24 hours of the season's end, Neil Smith was sacked as captain and replaced by 25-year-old Michael Powell, the youngest club captain since Smith's father, current chairman M.J.K., took over in 1957. Capped only in 1999, he would also be Warwickshire's fifth captain in six seasons, and his appointment was an admission that a new start was essential at Edgbaston, following a decline in results and occasional, clumsy maladministration off the field.

Captaincy changes generally come later in the year, but coach Bob Woolmer's input brought an earlier decision because of his pending return to South Africa. He also had a major influence in the decision not to offer Ed Giddins another contract once the fast bowler had not committed himself to a long-term future at the club. Smith's quiet approach seemed to count against him, as well as the fact that, with Ashley Giles's star in the ascendant, he needed to bat and bowl well to justify playing two spinners. The management believed that the balance of the side suffered sometimes when both played. Smith averaged 25 with the bat, hitting four Championship fifties, and his 28 wickets were bettered only by Giles's 52. He was not helped by the relatively poor returns of Donald and Giddins – 38 wickets between them at a cost of 30 – or the weather.

More than 1,600 overs were lost in the Championship – the equivalent of four games – and yet Warwickshire would have finished second instead of sixth had they beaten Essex in the rain-affected final game. As it was, they won only twice and failed to win at home for the first time since 1982. An analysis of their bonus points – they won more batting and fewer bowling than the other 17 counties – highlights a bowling weakness that will not be remedied easily. Giddins's release, after 39 Championship games and 151 wickets at 24.21 apiece in three years, and Allan Donald's departure followed hard on Gladstone Small's retirement in 1999 and Tim Munton's move to Derbyshire. Signing Melvyn Betts from Durham and Neil Carter, who bowls left-arm seam for Boland and has British citizenship, helps fill the gap. International commitments ruled out Shaun Pollock's return as Donald's replacement, so the club turned to the much-travelled Vasbert Drakes.

Powell's first full season in the side – he has still played only 44 first-class matches – produced 1,046 runs at an average of 43.58, including two hundreds and eight half-centuries in 26 innings. England calls and injury limited Nick Knight to five Championship games, in which a career-best 233 helped him average 67.42, while Dominic Ostler, benefiting from Woolmer's return as coach, regained top form after several moderate seasons. Superb slip fielding and 19 catches accompanied his first 1,000 runs since 1994. Mark Wagh progressed in the second half of the season and was awarded his cap in the final game, but Anurag Singh, whose career ran parallel with that of Wagh through school and Oxbridge, was allowed to join Worcestershire. Wagh's method and approach were considered more solid. David Hemp and Trevor Penney disappointed, with only one hundred and six fifties from 40 combined Championship innings; all-rounder Graeme Welch moved to Derbyshire in the winter.

Giles had his best all-round season, averaging 40.36 with the bat and heading the county's Championship averages with 52 wickets at 23.07. Called to the England squad for the final Test at The Oval, he subsequently emerged as England's leading wicket-taker in Pakistan. His success there raised the question of why he had played in only five one-day internationals prior to the tour, despite being in more than 30 one-day squads. Keith Piper had a splendid return to first-team cricket, with wicket-keeping of such a high standard that recently capped Tony Frost never played a Championship game. Dougie Brown had a much better season with the bat than the ball, hitting a maiden double-hundred at Hove as he and Giles set a club record for the seventh wicket. Alan Richardson bowled tirelessly, but is essentially a support bowler, and Charlie Dagnall showed promise late in the season.

Knight was outstanding in the League, scoring 378 runs in nine innings, while Brown and Giles took the bowling honours with 25 and 22 wickets respectively, as well as making runs. A poor performance at Bristol precluded progress to the knockout stage of the Benson and Hedges Cup, but successive home NatWest Trophy wins, helped along by a hundred from Giles and consecutive ones from Knight, took Warwickshire to Lord's. Rain late on the reserve day exposed a weakness in the rule that prevented any play after 6.30 p.m., leaving frustrated and disappointed Warwickshire supporters to wend their way home in sunshine.

Donald took a wicket with his last ball at Edgbaston, thus bringing to an end a magnificent career in which he took 536 first-class wickets in 11 seasons since 1987. International calls and injuries, however, limited him to only 80 wickets in 21 games after 1995. No more popular cricketer has graced Edgbaston, and he will be sorely missed. – JACK BANNISTER.

WARWICKSHIRE 2000

[*Bill Smith*]

Back row: I. R. Bell, G. D. Franklin, C. E. Dagnall, A. Richardson, R. E. Sierra, N. A. Warren, D. A. Altree, B. W. O'Connell. *Middle row:* D. L. Amiss (*chief executive*), S. Hollyhead (*sports science manager*), M. A. Wagh, M. J. Powell, D. L. Hemp, E. S. H. Giddins, T. Frost, A. Singh, M. A. Sheikh, R. N. Abberley (*head coach, indoor cricket centre*), S. Nottingham (*physiotherapist*). *Front row:* S. P. Perryman (*Second Eleven coach*), T. L. Penney, D. R. Brown, A. F. Giles, N. V. Knight, M. J. K. Smith (*chairman*), N. M. K. Smith (*captain*), R. A. Woolmer (*director of coaching*), A. A. Donald, D. P. Ostler, K. J. Piper, G. Welch.

WARWICKSHIRE RESULTS

All first-class matches – Played 17: Won 2, Lost 3, Drawn 12.

County Championship matches – Played 16: Won 2, Lost 3, Drawn 11.

PPP Healthcare County Championship, 6th in Division 2; NatWest Trophy, finalists;
Benson and Hedges Cup, 3rd in Midlands/Wales/West Group;
Norwich Union National League, 3rd in Division 2.

COUNTY CHAMPIONSHIP AVERAGES

BATTING

Cap		M	I	NO	R	HS	100s	50s	Avge	Ct/St
1995	N. V. Knight	5	7	0	472	233	1	1	67.42	4
1991	D. P. Ostler†	15	23	2	1,021	145	2	6	48.61	19
2000	M. A. Wagh†	9	16	3	592	137	2	3	45.53	4
1999	M. J. Powell	16	25	2	1,006	145	2	8	43.73	9
1996	A. F. Giles	12	14	3	444	128*	1	1	40.36	4
1995	D. R. Brown	15	21	5	618	203	1	2	38.62	11
1997	D. L. Hemp	16	23	2	738	129	1	4	35.14	9
1994	T. L. Penney	12	17	3	469	85	0	2	33.50	8
1993	N. M. K. Smith† . . .	16	19	2	436	87	0	4	25.64	8
	A. Singh	5	7	0	156	79	0	1	22.28	1
	A. Richardson	13	9	7	43	17*	0	0	21.50	3
1992	K. J. Piper	16	18	3	260	69	0	1	17.33	28/3
1997	G. Welch	7	8	1	116	55	0	1	16.57	1
1989	A. A. Donald§	7	9	2	69	18	0	0	9.85	3
1998	E. S. H. Giddins . . .	8	6	1	15	14	0	0	3.00	1

Also batted: D. A. Altree† (1 match) 4; C. E. Dagnall (2 matches) 5*, 6*; M. A. Sheikh† (1 match) 58*.

* Signifies not out.   *† Born in Warwickshire.*   *§ Overseas player.*

BOWLING

	O	M	R	W	BB	5W/i	Avge
A. F. Giles	526.4	163	1,200	52	8-90	5	23.07
A. A. Donald	201.3	56	530	18	4-59	0	29.44
N. M. K. Smith	310.4	70	875	28	5-66	1	31.25
E. S. H. Giddins	234.5	78	642	20	4-70	0	32.10
D. R. Brown	268.2	49	917	24	5-87	1	38.20
A. Richardson	368.2	96	1,040	27	4-69	0	38.51

Also bowled: D. A. Altree 20.1–1–77–0; C. E. Dagnall 54.4–16–181–5; D. L. Hemp 20–3–80–2; D. P. Ostler 5–0–46–1; M. J. Powell 24–6–80–2; M. A. Sheikh 23–7–68–1; A. Singh 6.5–0–66–0; M. A. Wagh 25–9–55–0; G. Welch 156–32–564–3.

COUNTY RECORDS

Highest score for:	501*	B. C. Lara v Durham at Birmingham	1994
Highest score against:	322	I. V. A. Richards (Somerset) at Taunton.	1985
Best bowling for:	10-41	J. D. Bannister v Combined Services at Birmingham . .	1959
Best bowling against:	10-36	H. Verity (Yorkshire) at Leeds	1931
Highest total for:	810-4 dec.	v Durham at Birmingham	1994
Highest total against:	887	by Yorkshire at Birmingham	1896
Lowest total for:	16	v Kent at Tonbridge	1913
Lowest total against:	15	by Hampshire at Birmingham	1922

At Oxford, April 26, 27, 28. WARWICKSHIRE drew with OXFORD UNIVERSITIES.

WARWICKSHIRE v GLAMORGAN

At Birmingham, May 3, 4, 5, 6. Drawn. Warwickshire 12 pts, Glamorgan 10 pts. Toss: Warwickshire.

Knight dominated the first two days with his maiden double-hundred, batting six minutes short of nine hours and facing 402 balls. Drizzle and bad light curtailed the opening day, but pitch conditions were ideal as he and Powell put on 172, the first century opening partnership at Edgbaston in the Championship since September 1998. Knight, who hit 27 fours, also added 170 with Penney, before Warwickshire declared, giving themselves some 220 overs to take 20 wickets. But Glamorgan responded with an even higher opening stand, 203 by Elliott and James. The fluent Elliott hit 19 fours and two sixes in his first Championship innings, while James batted nearly eight hours, Thursday through to Saturday, for his 40th first-class century. James was on the brink of saving the follow-on, but on the final morning Glamorgan's last three wickets fell in four overs, leaving them two short. Batting again, he was out third ball to begin a slide to 95 for five. It was as close as Warwickshire got. Giles furthered his earlier efforts with another marathon stint of left-arm spin, but dogged half-centuries from Maynard and Shaw, and the placid pitch, saved Glamorgan.

Close of play: First day, Warwickshire 252-2 (Knight 127*, Hemp 7*); Second day, Glamorgan 64-0 (Elliott 37*, James 15*); Third day, Glamorgan 387-7 (James 165*, Thomas 7*).

Warwickshire

M. J. Powell c Shaw b Watkin	73	G. Welch not out		35
N. V. Knight b Watkin	233	A. F. Giles not out		4
D. P. Ostler c Shaw b Jones	24	B 3, l-b 21, w 2, n-b 8		34
D. L. Hemp c James b Thomas	32			
T. L. Penney b Watkin	85	1/172 2/242 3/290	(6 wkts dec.)	551
*N. M. K. Smith c Watkin b Croft	31	4/460 5/489 6/517		

†K. J. Piper, A. Richardson and E. S. H. Giddins did not bat.

Bonus points – Warwickshire 5, Glamorgan 1 (Score at 130 overs: 452-3).

Bowling: Watkin 35–7–97–3; Thomas 30–4–119–1; Jones 28–1–106–1; Dale 13–1–56–0; Croft 41–11–136–1; Elliott 3–0–13–0.

Glamorgan

M. T. G. Elliott c and b Powell	117	lbw b Giddins	37
S. P. James c Piper b Giles	166	c and b Richardson	0
A. Dale c Knight b Giles	24	c Ostler b Giles	13
*M. P. Maynard b Giles	1	c Knight b Smith	52
M. J. Powell c Piper b Richardson	10	c Hemp b Richardson	18
W. L. Law c Welch b Giles	4	c Ostler b Giles	1
†A. D. Shaw lbw b Giddins	10	not out	56
R. D. B. Croft c Ostler b Welch	16	not out	2
S. D. Thomas c and b Giddins	15		
S. P. Jones c Ostler b Giles	0		
S. L. Watkin not out	4		
B 3, l-b 8, w 2, n-b 20	33	L-b 9, n-b 6	15

1/203 2/245 3/247 4/268 5/277	400	1/0 2/50 3/62 (6 wkts) 194
6/346 7/370 8/392 9/396		4/94 5/95 6/176

Bonus points – Glamorgan 5, Warwickshire 3.

Bowling: *First Innings*—Giddins 24–4–92–2; Richardson 25–7–57–1; Giles 42–17–89–5; Welch 22–3–97–1; Smith 14–3–36–0; Powell 3–0–18–1. *Second Innings*—Giddins 17–7–30–1; Richardson 16–5–28–2; Giles 39–14–72–2; Welch 5–1–22–0; Smith 15–6–32–1; Powell 2–1–1–0.

Umpires: V. A. Holder and K. E. Palmer.

At Hove, May 11, 12, 13, 14. WARWICKSHIRE beat SUSSEX by an innings and 47 runs.

WARWICKSHIRE v ESSEX

At Birmingham, May 17, 18, 19, 20. Drawn. Warwickshire 10 pts, Essex 8 pts. Toss: Warwickshire.

Rain washed out the second day, disrupted the other three and reduced the match to a contest for bonus points. Warwickshire's batsmen took the honours, securing their third maximum "five" after totalling 400 in three consecutive innings for the first time. Ostler's 144, his first Championship hundred for five years and only his second at Edgbaston, provided the core, while Brown's bravura hitting in a stand of 90 with Smith highlighted the waywardness of the Essex seam bowling. Danny Law was rather flattered by his five wickets; Stuart Law not at all by his 83 in 101 balls on the last day. Irani was nine runs short of a century and Essex two from their third batting point when the rain had its final say.

Close of play: First day, Warwickshire 160-2 (Ostler 93*, Hemp 14*); Second day, No play; Third day, Essex 8-0 (Prichard 3*, Grayson 5*).

Warwickshire

M. J. Powell c Hyam b Cowan	30	G. Welch b D. R. Law	0
M. A. Wagh c Mason b Irani	7	†K. J. Piper not out	12
D. P. Ostler c Hyam b D. R. Law	144		
D. L. Hemp b Anderson	16	B 4, l-b 3, n-b 28	35
T. L. Penney b D. R. Law	39		
*N. M. K. Smith not out	68	1/12 2/100 3/182 (8 wkts dec.) 400	
D. R. Brown c Mason b D. R. Law	42	4/265 5/268 6/358	
A. F. Giles c Hyam b D. R. Law	7	7/366 8/366	

A. Richardson did not bat.

Bonus points – Warwickshire 5, Essex 2.

Bowling: Cowan 25–7–60–1; Irani 24.3–7–63–1; Anderson 25–3–105–1; D. R. Law 21–5–78–5; Mason 31–7–82–0; Grayson 2–0–5–0.

Essex

P. J. Prichard b Brown	36	S. D. Peters not out	34
A. P. Grayson lbw b Richardson	15		
D. D. J. Robinson c Piper b Richardson	32	L-b 5, n-b 2	7
S. G. Law c Piper b Brown	83		
*R. C. Irani not out	91	1/25 2/74 3/115 4/196 (4 wkts) 298	

D. R. Law, T. J. Mason, †B. J. Hyam, A. P. Cowan and R. S. G. Anderson did not bat.

Bonus points – Essex 2, Warwickshire 1.

Bowling: Richardson 23–4–74–2; Welch 18–6–41–0; Brown 18–3–85–2; Giles 21–3–58–0; Powell 2–0–10–0; Smith 7–2–25–0.

Umpires: J. W. Lloyds and D. R. Shepherd.

At Cardiff, May 23, 24, 25, 26. WARWICKSHIRE drew with GLAMORGAN.

WARWICKSHIRE v NOTTINGHAMSHIRE

At Birmingham, June 2, 3, 4, 5. Drawn. Warwickshire 4 pts, Nottinghamshire 12 pts. Toss: Warwickshire.

A record-breaking opening partnership of 406 between Welton and Bicknell set Nottinghamshire up to become only the second county to win a first-class game without losing a wicket, following Lancashire against Leicestershire in 1956. But rain on the final afternoon, coupled with half-centuries from Ostler and Brown, narrowly saved Warwickshire from defeat and the indignity of finishing without a point. Instead, four from the draw took them back to the top of the table; without rain on all four days, it must have been a different story. They batted poorly on the opening day against the moving ball, losing nine wickets in 41 overs. Just how poorly was underlined when Nottinghamshire's openers remained unbeaten for eight hours 22 minutes. Their stand was the highest for any Nottinghamshire wicket, beating 398 by Arthur Shrewsbury and William Gunn against Sussex at Trent Bridge in 1890, and the fourth-highest, and highest unbroken, for the first wicket in the Championship. Welton advanced from a maiden first-class hundred to become Nottinghamshire's youngest double-century-maker at 22 years 31 days. He faced 385 balls, Bicknell 397, and each hit 23 fours against an attack deprived of Donald (injured), Giddins (on Test duty) and Brown, whose shoulder injury kept him from bowling.

Close of play: First day, Warwickshire 104-9 (Richardson 7*, Altree 0*); Second day, Nottinghamshire 194-0 (Bicknell 90*, Welton 89*); Third day, Warwickshire 82-2 (Ostler 18*, Hemp 29*).

Warwickshire

M. J. Powell c Read b Millns	0	– c Stemp b Millns	7
G. Welch c Millns b Franks	0	– c Welton b Franks	16
D. P. Ostler c Stemp b Millns	28	– b Millns	93
D. L. Hemp b Millns	4	– b Lucas	38
T. L. Penney c Read b Stemp	37	– c Welton b Stemp	43
*N. M. K. Smith c Read b Franks	1	– (7) c Franks b Millns	0
D. R. Brown c Gallian b Stemp	11	– (6) not out	51
A. F. Giles run out	10	– c Read b Stemp	5
†K. J. Piper c Gallian b Lucas	0	– b Stemp	8
A. Richardson not out	9	– not out	0
D. A. Altree b Franks	4		
L-b 4, w 2	6	B 1, l-b 9, w 2, n-b 32	44

1/1 2/5 3/9 4/60 5/69	110	1/33 2/33 3/103 (8 wkts) 305
6/84 7/97 8/97 9/97		4/232 5/232 6/232
		7/253 8/305

Bonus points – Nottinghamshire 3.

Bowling: *First Innings*—Franks 15.5–4–27–5; Millns 11–0–44–3; Lucas 11–4–22–1; Stemp 7–3–13–2. *Second Innings*—Franks 15–0–72–1; Millns 16–4–67–3; Stemp 38–19–46–3; Afzaal 17–7–43–0; Lucas 13–0–62–1; Gallian 2–1–5–0.

Nottinghamshire

D. J. Bicknell not out	180
G. E. Welton not out	200
B 13, l-b 11, n-b 2	26

(no wkt dec.) 406

U. Afzaal, J. E. Morris, *J. E. R. Gallian, C. M. Tolley, †C. M. W. Read, P. J. Franks, D. J. Millns, D. S. Lucas and R. D. Stemp did not bat.

Bonus points – Nottinghamshire 5 (Score at 130 overs: 405-0).

Bowling: Richardson 24–7–68–0; Altree 20.1–1–77–0; Welch 29–8–94–0; Giles 39–10–89–0; Powell 5–3–9–0; Smith 13–1–45–0.

Umpires: G. I. Burgess and G. Sharp.

At Northampton, June 14, 15, 16, 17. WARWICKSHIRE beat NORTHAMPTONSHIRE by an innings and 53 runs.

WARWICKSHIRE v GLOUCESTERSHIRE

At Birmingham, June 28, 29, 30, July 1. Drawn. Warwickshire 8 pts, Gloucestershire 11 pts. Toss: Gloucestershire.

Although rain limited the last day's play to 33 overs, making Warwickshire's target of 350 quite irrelevant, the points from their fourth successive home draw helped them leapfrog back over Worcestershire to head Division Two. Donald's return from injury brought his first Championship wickets at Edgbaston since Gloucestershire's visit in September 1997, but there was no brushing Barnett aside. His first Championship hundred of the season, and 57th first-class all told, frustrated Warwickshire for four and a quarter hours – and for half that time Russell doubled the aggravation as they added 104. Next day, Powell occupied five hours, including 50 minutes on 96 before he edged Gannon to slip. But his discipline and Neil Smith's less restrained fifty were all that stood between Gloucestershire's nagging all-seam attack and the follow-on. Donald sustained a thigh strain on the third day, when fifties from Hewson and Windows increased Gloucestershire's lead and, in theory, gave their bowlers a full day to dismiss Warwickshire again.

Close of play: First day, Gloucestershire 316-6 (Russell 67*, Snape 14*); Second day, Warwickshire 218-9 (Smith 44*, Richardson 0*); Third day, Gloucestershire 232-7 (Snape 20*, Russell 16*).

Gloucestershire

R. J. Cunliffe lbw b Brown	36	–	(2) lbw b Richardson	7
D. R. Hewson c Ostler b Donald	0	–	(1) b Giles	58
M. G. N. Windows c Piper b Donald	36	–	c Ostler b Hemp	56
K. J. Barnett c Powell b Smith	106	–	c Hemp b Giles	37
I. J. Harvey lbw b Brown	31	–	c Smith b Hemp	0
C. G. Taylor c Wagh b Giles	0	–	c Smith b Giles	25
*†R. C. Russell lbw b Richardson	70	–	(9) not out	16
J. N. Snape c Hemp b Donald	21	–	(7) not out	20
B. W. Gannon c Smith b Donald	6			
J. Lewis c Giles b Richardson	7	–	(8) b Richardson	8
A. M. Smith not out	2			
B 9, l-b 20, n-b 6	35		L-b 5	5

1/1 2/71 3/116 4/180 5/189   350   1/12 2/114 3/130   (7 wkts dec.) 232
6/293 7/325 8/337 9/344   4/132 5/185
                                  6/189 7/208

Bonus points – Gloucestershire 4, Warwickshire 3.

Bowling: *First Innings*—Donald 22–4–59–4; Richardson 26.5–8–72–2; Welch 8–0–41–0; Brown 16–4–46–2; Giles 34–9–65–1; Smith 9–0–34–1; Powell 1–0–4–0. *Second Innings*—Donald 7–1–16–0; Richardson 17–5–39–2; Brown 7–0–28–0; Welch 14–5–47–0; Giles 20–4–68–3; Hemp 8–1–29–2.

Warwickshire

M. J. Powell c Cunliffe b Gannon	96	– c Cunliffe b Lewis	6
M. A. Wagh c Russell b Smith	1	– not out	52
D. P. Ostler c Snape b Smith	10	– c Harvey b Lewis	11
D. L. Hemp c Cunliffe b Gannon	18	– not out	36
D. R. Brown b Lewis	11		
G. Welch c Hewson b Gannon	10		
A. F. Giles c Smith b Harvey	19		
*N. M. K. Smith not out	58		
†K. J. Piper c Lewis b Gannon	4		
A. A. Donald c Russell b Gannon	0		
A. Richardson c Russell b Harvey	0		
L-b 6	6	L-b 1, n-b 2	3

1/4 2/26 3/48 4/65 5/82   233   1/27 2/41   (2 wkts) 108
6/132 7/209 8/217 9/217

Bonus points – Warwickshire 1, Gloucestershire 3.

Bowling: *First Innings*—Lewis 24–9–66–1; Smith 19–3–59–2; Harvey 19.3–7–44–2; Gannon 21–6–58–5. *Second Innings*—Smith 8–3–17–0; Lewis 10–2–36–2; Gannon 5–1–33–0; Harvey 3–1–13–0; Snape 4–3–4–0; Taylor 3–2–4–0.

Umpires: J. H. Harris and T. E. Jesty.

WARWICKSHIRE v SUSSEX

At Birmingham, July 7, 8, 9, 10. Drawn. Warwickshire 9 pts, Sussex 7 pts. Toss: Warwickshire.
    Giles, with a hundred off Sussex in May and 107 against Derbyshire two days before in the NatWest Trophy, was just the man for the crisis Warwickshire found themselves in at 33 for five, soon 39 for six. Lewry and Kirtley did the damage with sharp movement off a green-tinged pitch; Giles and Smith repaired it with a partnership of 178 in 51 overs that ended with Giles two short of another century. Neither he nor Smith was through with Sussex. Whereas ten wickets fell to seam and swing on the opening day, eight went to spin on a murky, rain-cut second. Giles finished with six and Smith three as Sussex lost their last six batsmen for 23 in 18 overs. But Warwickshire's chances of a first home win were ruined by the weather, which allowed only 33 overs – around five interruptions – on Sunday and none on Monday. Ostler raised his first-class aggregate to 648, the highest of the season by an England-qualified player, when he and Powell added 131 in 28 overs.
    Close of play: First day, Sussex 55-2 (Peirce 28*, Kirtley 2*); Second day, Warwickshire 25-1 (Powell 14*, Piper 5*); Third day, Warwickshire 165-2 (Powell 70*, Ostler 66*).

Warwickshire

M. J. Powell b Lewry	4	– not out	70
M. A. Wagh b Kirtley	1	– lbw b Lewry	2
D. P. Ostler c Montgomerie b Lewry	13	– (4) not out	66
D. L. Hemp lbw b Kirtley	5		
T. L. Penney lbw b Lewry	4		
D. R. Brown c Rashid b Kirtley	1		
A. F. Giles c Bevan b Rashid	98		
*N. M. K. Smith b Lewry	87		
†K. J. Piper not out	13	– (3) run out	13
A. A. Donald lbw b Lewry	9		
E. S. H. Giddins b Lewry	0		
L-b 9, w 2, n-b 6	17	L-b 8, n-b 6	14

1/6 2/18 3/28 4/28 5/33   252   1/19 2/34   (2 wkts) 165
6/39 7/217 8/236 9/252

Bonus points – Warwickshire 2, Sussex 3.

Bowling: *First Innings*—Lewry 24–9–66–6; Kirtley 21–5–57–3; Taylor 12–3–37–0; Martin-Jenkins 11–2–40–0; Rashid 13–3–35–1; Adams 2–0–8–0; Bevan 1–1–0–0. *Second Innings*—Lewry 16–3–64–1; Kirtley 12–4–31–0; Martin-Jenkins 11.1–1–46–0; Rashid 4–1–16–0.

Sussex

R. R. Montgomerie c Powell b Donald . .	7	†A. D. Patterson lbw b Giles	1
M. T. E. Peirce c Brown b Giles	41	J. D. Lewry c Donald b Smith	7
M. G. Bevan c Ostler b Giles	13	B. V. Taylor not out	0
R. J. Kirtley b Giles	2		
*C. J. Adams c and b Smith.	38	L-b 2, w 4.	6
P. A. Cottey st Piper b Giles	36		
R. S. C. Martin-Jenkins c Piper b Giles .	4	1/16 2/44 3/55 4/82 5/135	158
U. B. A. Rashid c Brown b Smith	3	6/145 7/149 8/150 9/150	

Bonus points – Warwickshire 3.

Bowling: Donald 14–8–26–1; Giddins 13–4–38–0; Brown 4–0–13–0; Giles 27–10–58–6; Smith 13.5–7–21–3.

Umpires: B. Leadbeater and J. F. Steele.

At Cheltenham, July 19, 20, 21, 22. WARWICKSHIRE drew with GLOUCESTERSHIRE.

WARWICKSHIRE v NORTHAMPTONSHIRE

At Birmingham, July 28, 29, 30. Northamptonshire won by 54 runs. Northamptonshire 18 pts, Warwickshire 4 pts. Toss: Northamptonshire.

Displaced England seamer Giddins was rested, fuelling speculation about his future at Edgbaston, and the wicket attracted the attention of pitch liaison officer Tony Brown. He took no action, although generous turn from the first day ultimately resulted in match figures of 11 for 196 for Warwickshire's Giles (who had taken 12 at Northampton in June), and 11 for 178 for Northamptonshire's Jason Brown. Only five wickets fell to the seam bowlers. Hayden, who had scored twin hundreds, one a double, against Warwickshire for Hampshire in 1997, provided a positive start with 122, hitting four sixes off Giles and 14 fours. Ostler continued his good season with 88, but from 168 for three Warwickshire added only 68. Though Northamptonshire's own last six managed only 46 second time round, thanks to Hayden's 72 they led by 258. This time, Warwickshire's tail did better, after they were 99 for seven. Smith added 67 runs to his earlier five for 66 – his best return for five years – but it was not enough to prevent Warwickshire's first Championship defeat of the season.

Close of play: First day, Northamptonshire 296-7 (Bailey 21*, Taylor 0*); Second day, Northamptonshire 44-2 (Hayden 35*).

Northamptonshire

A. S. Rollins c Ostler b Giles.	19	– lbw b Giles	8
*M. L. Hayden c Richardson b Smith	122	– b Smith	72
M. B. Loye c Ostler b Giles.	2	– (4) c Ostler b Smith	25
D. J. Sales c Ostler b Giles	18	– (5) b Smith	17
J. W. Cook c Ostler b Giles	27	– (6) c Brown b Giles	3
A. L. Penberthy run out	22	– (7) not out.	18
G. P. Swann c and b Donald	58	– (8) c Brown b Smith.	8
†T. M. B. Bailey c Penney b Donald	21	– (9) b Giles	6
J. P. Taylor b Piper b Giles.	11	– (3) c Hemp b Smith	0
D. M. Cousins c Powell b Giles	10	– c Penney b Giles	7
J. F. Brown not out.	0	– lbw b Giles	0
B 2, l-b 2, n-b 4	8	B 4, l-b 8	12
1/40 2/42 3/86 4/144 5/200	318	1/43 2/44 3/90 4/130 5/131	176
6/240 7/291 8/296 9/317		6/137 7/148 8/159 9/169	

Bonus points – Northamptonshire 3, Warwickshire 3.

Bowling: *First Innings*—Donald 16–1–50–2; Richardson 19–7–39–0; Brown 13–0–50–0; Giles 32.3–6–118–6; Smith 19–3–57–1. *Second Innings*—Donald 2–0–6–0; Richardson 2–0–14–0; Smith 26–3–66–5; Giles 25.4–3–78–5.

Warwickshire

M. J. Powell c Penberthy b Brown	9	– c and b Taylor	0
N. V. Knight c Rollins b Taylor	12	– lbw b Brown	43
D. P. Ostler c Rollins b Brown	88	– lbw b Cousins	13
D. L. Hemp c Swann b Brown	26	– c and b Brown	3
T. L. Penney st Bailey b Swann	32	– c Bailey b Brown	2
D. R. Brown b Swann	5	– b Brown	8
A. F. Giles c Rollins b Swann	17	– b Brown	2
*N. M. K. Smith c and b Brown	28	– lbw b Brown	67
†K. J. Piper c Bailey b Swann	1	– c Sales b Swann	24
A. A. Donald c Taylor b Brown	5	– c Taylor b Swann	18
A. Richardson not out	0	– not out	12
B 8, l-b 5	13	B 2, l-b 4, w 6	12

1/16 2/51 3/109 4/168 5/174   236   1/5 2/24 3/30 4/32 5/42   204
6/188 7/214 8/228 9/236   6/48 7/99 8/134 9/180

Bonus points – Warwickshire 1, Northamptonshire 3.

Bowling: *First Innings*—Cousins 6–0–20–0; Taylor 12–2–41–1; Brown 34.1–9–88–5; Swann 29–9–74–4. *Second Innings*—Cousins 6–2–14–1; Taylor 12–2–29–1; Brown 27–4–90–6; Swann 20.2–2–65–2.

Umpires: A. Clarkson and P. Willey.

At Nottingham, August 3, 4, 5, 6. WARWICKSHIRE drew with NOTTINGHAMSHIRE.

WARWICKSHIRE v MIDDLESEX

At Birmingham, August 17, 18, 19, 20. Drawn. Warwickshire 7 pts, Middlesex 9 pts. Toss: Middlesex.

The loss of more than a day to rain resulted in recourse to a once-familiar formula – declaration bowling and a negotiated target. With promotion an issue, however, and points available for a draw, Warwickshire opted in the end for safety, rather than risking defeat by trying to score 296 in 80 overs. Victory would have lifted Middlesex from eighth to third; defeat would have demoted Warwickshire to the bottom three. With Donald and Giddins injured, Langer and Ramprakash prospered, both passing 1,000 runs for the season: Ramprakash was the first Englishman to do so. Langer, having raced to 50 off 46 balls, hit 109 in 158, while Ramprakash's unbeaten 120 was his fourth hundred in nine innings since England omitted him. The final morning produced Ostler's maiden first-class wicket, when Strauss hoisted him to deep square leg, but the three Warwickshire wickets that Cook and Tufnell took in eight overs either side of tea had a greater influence on the endgame.

Close of play: First day, Middlesex 292-6 (Ramprakash 77*, Hutton 0*); Second day, No play; Third day, Warwickshire 211-4 (Hemp 78*, Brown 36*).

Middlesex

A. J. Strauss lbw b Richardson	19	– c Wagh b Ostler	10
M. A. Roseberry c Piper b Smith	62	– not out	47
*J. L. Langer c Piper b Richardson	109	– not out	69
M. R. Ramprakash not out	120		
E. C. Joyce c Piper b Richardson	0		
†D. C. Nash c Richardson b Giles	13		
T. F. Bloomfield lbw b Richardson	0		
B. L. Hutton c sub b Brown	5		
S. J. Cook c Ostler b Welch	23		
R. L. Johnson not out	9		
L-b 10, w 2, n-b 8	20		

1/30 2/164 3/255 4/257   (8 wkts dec.) 380   1/16   (1 wkt dec.) 126
5/292 6/292 7/305 8/361

P. C. R. Tufnell did not bat.

Bonus points – Middlesex 4, Warwickshire 2.

Bowling: *First Innings*—Richardson 30–9–99–4; Brown 21–5–65–1; Welch 16–2–56–1; Giles 29–4–87–1; Smith 15–0–63–1. *Second Innings*—Ostler 5–0–46–1; Singh 6.5–0–66–0; Powell 2–0–14–0.

Warwickshire

M. J. Powell b Bloomfield	8	– c Roseberry b Cook	55
M. A. Wagh lbw b Hutton	40	– c Tufnell b Bloomfield	20
D. P. Ostler run out	29	– c and b Johnson	5
D. L. Hemp not out	78	– b Tufnell	44
A. Singh c Nash b Johnson	13	– c Johnson b Tufnell	11
D. R. Brown not out	36	– not out	15
A. F. Giles (did not bat)		– not out	30
L-b 5, n-b 2	7	L-b 9, w 2	11

1/17 2/74   (4 wkts dec.) 211   1/32 2/48 3/131   (5 wkts) 191
3/90 4/125   4/137 5/146

G. Welch, *N. M. K. Smith, †K. J. Piper and A. Richardson did not bat.

Bonus points – Warwickshire 1, Middlesex 1.

Bowling: *First Innings*—Johnson 12–2–43–1; Bloomfield 13–5–31–1; Cook 13–5–41–0; Hutton 7–2–30–1; Tufnell 16–3–45–0; Ramprakash 8–2–16–0. *Second Innings*—Johnson 17–8–27–1; Bloomfield 15–2–47–1; Tufnell 30–11–69–2; Cook 11–2–28–1; Ramprakash 7–3–11–0.

Umpires: N. A. Mallender and J. F. Steele.

At Worcester, August 21, 22, 23. WARWICKSHIRE lost to WORCESTERSHIRE by nine wickets.

WARWICKSHIRE v WORCESTERSHIRE

At Birmingham, August 30, 31, September 1, 2. Drawn. Warwickshire 12 pts, Worcestershire 8 pts. Toss: Worcestershire.

Rain and bad light claimed 101 overs on the second and third days, but bonus points and the draw kept both sides in contention for promotion. A slow pitch meant that Donald had to toil for his last four Championship wickets at Edgbaston, as did McGrath, who took six when Warwickshire replied. Solanki's sparkling first-innings 71 for Worcestershire took him past 1,000 runs for the season, while Ostler, in a more conservative manner, reached the same mark for the first time since 1994. Warwickshire's innings spread over all four days, and, on the second, openers Wagh and Powell set them in line for a full hand of bonus points, putting on 166 in 55 overs. Wagh reached a Championship-best 130, after being dropped in the slips off McGrath before scoring; Powell was missed at the wicket when 28. The draw left Warwickshire without a home Championship win for the first time since 1982.

Close of play: First day, Warwickshire 28-0 (Powell 17*, Wagh 9*); Second day, Warwickshire 224-1 (Wagh 118*, Ostler 26*); Third day, Warwickshire 367-5 (Singh 42*, Smith 0*).

Worcestershire

W. P. C. Weston lbw b Brown	23	– not out	58
E. J. Wilson c Brown b Donald	34	– c Donald b Smith	51
V. S. Solanki c Piper b Donald	71	– not out	57
D. A. Leatherdale b Richardson	42		
R. C. Driver b Smith	2		
D. J. Pipe c Hemp b Smith	30		
*†S. J. Rhodes not out	39		
S. R. Lampitt lbw b Smith	2		
M. J. Rawnsley b Donald	4		
C. G. Liptrot b Donald	0		
G. D. McGrath lbw b Richardson	7		
L-b 5, n-b 4	9	B 7, l-b 8	15

1/51 2/61 3/151 4/168 5/182   263   1/96   (1 wkt) 181
6/226 7/237 8/246 9/250

Bonus points – Worcestershire 2, Warwickshire 3.

Bowling: *First Innings*—Donald 23–9–69–4; Giddins 11–2–46–0; Richardson 15–3–47–2; Brown 16–4–45–1; Smith 23–6–51–3; Wagh 1–1–0–0. *Second Innings*—Donald 7–1–18–0; Richardson 11–5–12–0; Brown 10–3–24–0; Smith 17–6–41–1; Wagh 14–6–30–0; Powell 8–1–24–0; Hemp 5–1–17–0.

Warwickshire

M. J. Powell c and b McGrath	69	†K. J. Piper not out	11
M. A. Wagh lbw b McGrath	130	A. A. Donald c Rhodes b McGrath	16
D. P. Ostler run out	88	B 5, l-b 7, n-b 16	28
D. L. Hemp c Solanki b McGrath	10		
A. Singh c Lampitt b McGrath	46	1/166 2/239 3/263 (8 wkts dec.) 407
D. R. Brown lbw b Lampitt	4	4/360 5/366 6/374
*N. M. K. Smith c Solanki b McGrath	5	7/381 8/407

A. Richardson and E. S. H. Giddins did not bat.

Bonus points – Warwickshire 5, Worcestershire 2.

Bowling: McGrath 42.4–11–90–6; Liptrot 22–5–94–0; Lampitt 34–5–117–1; Rawnsley 19–5–48–0; Leatherdale 7–0–27–0; Solanki 5–0–19–0.

Umpires: J. W. Lloyds and R. Palmer.

At Lord's, September 5, 6, 7, 8. WARWICKSHIRE drew with MIDDLESEX.

At Chelmsford, September 13, 14, 15, 16. WARWICKSHIRE lost to ESSEX by six wickets.

WORCESTERSHIRE

Vikram Solanki

President: 2000 – R. Booth
               2001 – M. G. Jones
Chairman: J. W. Elliott
Secretary: The Rev. M. D. Vockins
Chairman, Cricket Committee: M. J. Horton
Captain: 2000 – G. A. Hick
Coach: 2000 – C. W. J. Athey
Director of Cricket: 2001 – T. M. Moody
Head Groundsman: R. McLaren
Scorer: S. S. Hale

No one connected with Worcestershire was surprised when the Severn burst its banks and flooded the County Ground in October: 2000 had been one of those years. Their season, full of promise early on, had fallen away so catastrophically that it was difficult to know what caused greatest disappointment. After leading the Championship second division several times, and being in the top three for much of the summer, they still failed to secure promotion. In the National League, they led Division One by six points at the halfway stage, and looked capable of going one better than their runners-up position in 1999. Instead, they failed to win any of their remaining matches and were relegated.

It did not help that it was Gloucestershire who ended their unbeaten League run of seven games and went on to take the title. There had been acrimony between the neighbours ever since Gloucestershire overturned the result of their NatWest Trophy third-round tie. Worcestershire had unwittingly fielded a cup-tied player, 19-year-old Kabir Ali, in their three-wicket win over the holders and, when this was drawn to their notice, the ECB ruled that the match be replayed. Given a second chance, Gloucestershire won by five runs.

Coach Bill Athey insisted that the players' reaction to losing the replay had dissolved within 48 hours and could not be used as an excuse for their slump in fortunes. By the end of the season, however, he had seen enough and resigned. In an attempt to recapture the glory years of the late 1980s and early 1990s, the club appointed their former captain and overseas player, Tom Moody, as director of cricket.

Worcestershire certainly have promising youngsters in Kabir Ali, his cousin Kadeer Ali, Elliott Wilson, who made two Championship hundreds, and wicket-keeper/batsman Jamie Pipe. Ryan Driver moved to Lancashire, but they managed to talk Alamgir Sheriyar out of his request to be released from his contract. The arrival of Anurag Singh from Warwickshire strengthened the batting, but recruitment remained a prime concern.

Batting cover is needed for Graeme Hick and Vikram Solanki should their England commitments continue in 2001. A question mark remains over the future of Reuben Spiring after his seventh knee operation, and such key performers as Steve Rhodes and Stuart Lampitt are in the twilight of their career, despite having excellent seasons. Injury forced Gavin Haynes's retirement, and the defeat by Kent that sealed Worcestershire's fate in the National League was a sad backdrop against which to bid farewell to him and left-arm spinner Richard Illingworth, who was released after 19 years at New Road.

Only Solanki, who passed 1,000 runs for the second successive season, and David Leatherdale batted consistently in the four-day game, although Paul Pollard was more dependable when he switched from opener to the middle order. Hick was absent for half the Championship campaign and his runs and experience were sorely missed. The county were forced to blood too many youngsters in the top six at the same time, with the result that the bowlers were often left with too much ground to make up.

No more could have been asked of Glenn McGrath, in his first year of a split two-season contract which should see him return in 2002. He bowled with hostility and enthusiasm to finish as the country's leading wicket-taker with 80 in 14 first-class games, and 114 in all cricket; his economy in the League was the meanest on record. There was never any question that he would be Worcestershire's Player of the Year.

The problem was that his only worthwhile support came from Lampitt, who picked up 56 first-class wickets and bowled with great heart in his benefit season. Sheriyar, who himself had been the country's leading wicket-taker 12 months earlier with 92 victims, was expected to be the perfect foil for McGrath. But he tinkered with his run-up, almost halving it, and lost the knack of bowling wicket-taking deliveries. Ultimately he lost his place in the side. Kabir Ali's call-up by England Under-19 and a subsequent back problem limited his appearances in the second half of the season, and it is important that he uses 2001 to build on the promise he showed after breaking into the first team. Queenslander Andy Bichel was Worcestershire's choice to replace McGrath, though his selection for Australia in their home series against West Indies cast some doubt on his availability.

Rhodes's 55 first-class dismissals put him joint-top of the wicket-keeping list, and he also chipped in with late-order runs to repair the failings of the front-line batsmen. He deputised as captain for long spells when Hick was absent, and his unfailing enthusiasm was never more needed than in the testing last three months of the season. It was far from ideal that Hick should be in charge of team affairs when he was away so much with England. In fairness, he had been willing to stand down once awarded a central contract, but was asked to carry on by the county, and this is one of several issues on which Moody is sure to have a strong influence.

Worcestershire will be looking to make 2001 a fitting summer to mark the retirement of their secretary, Mike Vockins, who leaves in June after 30 years with the club. In that time he has seen them win three Championships, two Lord's finals and three Sunday League titles; off the field, his stewardship helped Worcestershire secure the freehold of the County Ground. By making his decision early, Vockins gave the club time to find a suitable replacement, but forward planning was always one of his strengths. – JOHN CURTIS.

WORCESTERSHIRE 2000

[Mike Pollard]

Back row: Kabir Ali, C. G. Liptrot, D. B. Patel, D. N. Catterall, D. J. Pipe, Kadeer Ali. *Middle row:* M. M. Mirza, E. J. Wilson, M. J. Rawnsley, K. R. Spiring, D. A. Leatherdale, A. Sheriyar, V. S. Solanki, P. R. Pollard, R. C. Driver, J. Rees (*physiotherapist*). *Front row:* D. B. D'Oliveira (*assistant coach*), S. R. Lampitt, R. K. Illingworth, G. A. Hick (*captain*), R. Murray (*chief executive, Midlands Electricity*), S. J. Rhodes, G. R. Haynes, C. W. J. Athey (*first-team coach*). *Insets:* G. D. McGrath, W. P. C. Weston.

WORCESTERSHIRE RESULTS

All first-class matches – Played 18: Won 5, Lost 5, Drawn 8.

County Championship matches – Played 16: Won 5, Lost 5, Drawn 6.

PPP Healthcare County Championship, 5th in Division 2; NatWest Trophy, 3rd round;
Benson and Hedges Cup, 5th in Midlands/Wales/West Group;
Norwich Union National League, 7th in Division 1.

COUNTY CHAMPIONSHIP AVERAGES

BATTING

Cap		M	I	NO	R	HS	100s	50s	Avge	Ct/St
1998	V. S. Solanki	14	25	2	1,062	161*	2	7	46.17	17
1986	G. A. Hick‡	8	14	2	521	122	2	2	43.41	8
1994	D. A. Leatherdale . .	16	28	4	953	132*	2	7	39.70	9
1997	K. R. Spiring	3	4	1	96	38	0	0	32.00	0
1986	S. J. Rhodes	16	26	6	583	103	1	1	29.15	49/1
	P. R. Pollard	12	21	1	560	123*	1	4	28.00	3
	E. J. Wilson	15	28	1	647	104*	2	2	23.96	9
	D. J. Pipe	3	5	0	107	54	0	1	21.40	0
	R. C. Driver	9	17	2	283	64	0	1	18.86	2
	Kabir Ali	9	14	3	201	50*	0	1	18.27	5
1995	W. P. C. Weston . . .	9	18	2	264	58*	0	2	16.50	1
1989	S. R. Lampitt	16	25	7	290	56*	0	1	16.11	10
1986	R. K. Illingworth . . .	8	11	2	140	44*	0	0	15.55	3
2000	G. D. McGrath§ . . .	13	15	3	112	55	0	1	9.33	3
1997	A. Sheriyar	10	11	3	69	17	0	0	8.62	0
	M. J. Rawnsley	9	13	0	102	18	0	0	7.84	5
	Kadeer Ali	3	6	0	10	8	0	0	1.66	1

Also batted: C. G. Liptrot (3 matches) 1, 0 (2 ct).

* *Signifies not out.*   ‡ *ECB contract.*   § *Overseas player.*

BOWLING

	O	M	R	W	BB	5W/i	Avge
G. D. McGrath	404.4	125	1,047	76	8-41	6	13.77
S. R. Lampitt	361.5	91	1,050	50	7-45	2	21.00
D. A. Leatherdale	137	28	473	16	3-17	0	29.56
A. Sheriyar	254	50	1,010	27	4-51	0	37.40
Kabir Ali	180	34	661	17	4-114	0	38.88

Also bowled: R. C. Driver 11.2–2–44–2; G. A. Hick 45–6–135–1; R. K. Illingworth 157.5–45–382–9; C. G. Liptrot 67–10–281–7; P. R. Pollard 0.1–0–4–0; M. J. Rawnsley 204–55–573–9; V. S. Solanki 62.3–7–202–6.

COUNTY RECORDS

Highest score for:	405*	G. A. Hick v Somerset at Taunton	1988
Highest score against:	331*	J. D. Robertson (Middlesex) at Worcester	1949
Best bowling for:	9-23	C. F. Root v Lancashire at Worcester	1931
Best bowling against:	10-51	J. Mercer (Glamorgan) at Worcester	1936
Highest total for:	670-7 dec.	v Somerset at Worcester	1995
Highest total against:	701-4 dec.	by Leicestershire at Worcester	1906
Lowest total for:	24	v Yorkshire at Huddersfield	1903
Lowest total against:	30	by Hampshire at Worcester	1903

WORCESTERSHIRE v GLAMORGAN

At Worcester, April 26, 27, 28, 29. Drawn. Worcestershire 5 pts, Glamorgan 6 pts. Toss: Glamorgan. Championship debuts: G. D. McGrath; M. T. G. Elliott.

Worcestershire lost the opening two days of their first-class season for the first time since 1968 and, with the heavens opening again to wash out the final day, the only play was on the third. That was dominated by their new captain, Hick, the only batsman to master the damp, seamer-friendly pitch, and Watkin, the one bowler to use it properly. The others all bowled too short, and Hick pulled and cut to good effect, hitting 13 fours in his 76 from 80 balls. Even so, it was Glamorgan's day on bonus points. McGrath did not take the field on his home debut for Worcestershire, and his compatriot Elliott did not bat for Glamorgan.

Close of play: First day, No play; Second day, No play; Third day, Worcestershire 206-7 (Rhodes 30*, Illingworth 3*).

Worcestershire

E. J. Wilson b Jones	16	S. R. Lampitt c Elliott b Watkin	5
P. R. Pollard lbw b Thomas	0	R. K. Illingworth not out	3
*G. A. Hick c Shaw b Thomas	76		
V. S. Solanki b Jones	1	L-b 5, w 2	7
K. R. Spiring c Shaw b Dale	26		
D. A. Leatherdale c Elliott b Watkin	42	1/0 2/49 3/51 4/119 (7 wkts) 206	
†S. J. Rhodes not out	30	5/123 6/178 7/184	

A. Sheriyar and G. D. McGrath did not bat.

Bonus points – Worcestershire 1, Glamorgan 2.

Bowling: Watkin 19–10–33–2; Thomas 13–2–55–2; Jones 9.1–0–66–2; Dale 12–1–47–1.

Glamorgan

M. T. G. Elliott, S. P. James, A. Dale, *M. P. Maynard, M. J. Powell, W. L. Law, †A. D. Shaw, R. D. B. Croft, S. D. Thomas, S. L. Watkin and S. P. Jones.

Umpires: J. H. Harris and T. E. Jesty.

At Cambridge, May 2, 3, 4. WORCESTERSHIRE drew with CAMBRIDGE UNIVERSITY.

WORCESTERSHIRE v MIDDLESEX

At Worcester, May 11, 12, 13. Worcestershire won by seven wickets. Worcestershire 15 pts, Middlesex 3 pts. Toss: Middlesex.

Hick's 115 off 106 balls saw Worcestershire to victory before lunch on the third day, after 31 wickets had fallen on the first two. The normally aggressive Solanki, who contributed 19 to a stand of 97, could only stand and admire. Hick hit two sixes and 15 of his 19 fours as he scored 90 of Worcestershire's last 111 in 79 minutes. It was so different from what had gone before. A pitch saturated a fortnight earlier gave the seam bowlers all manner of assistance, although some of the batsmen showed little technique. Opposing openers illustrated the difference of approach: Middlesex's Strauss scored 47 off 59 balls in their dismal 161; Worcestershire's Wilson, who made his maiden hundred when these teams met here in the final match of 1999, carried his bat for 104 out of 182, lasting four and a quarter hours. He hit 18 fours and almost single-handedly ensured the last five wickets added 78. As Langer consolidated on a still tricky pitch (cleared by ECB pitch liaison officer David Hughes), Middlesex looked capable of setting a substantial target. Once Illingworth snared him, however, their familiar failings resurfaced.

Close of play: First day, Worcestershire 147-8 (Wilson 75*, McGrath 0*); Second day, Worcestershire 50-1 (Wilson 19*, Hick 25*).

Middlesex

A. J. Strauss c Rhodes b Lampitt	47	– c Solanki b McGrath	37
M. R. Ramprakash b McGrath	6	– lbw b Lampitt	14
*J. L. Langer b Sheriyar	1	– c Solanki b Illingworth	73
O. A. Shah b McGrath	6	– c Rhodes b McGrath	0
R. M. S. Weston c Leatherdale b Lampitt	16	– c Rhodes b Hick	15
P. N. Weekes c Wilson b Lampitt	21	– c Ali b Illingworth	5
†D. C. Nash c Rhodes b Lampitt	12	– c Hick b Illingworth	3
R. L. Johnson c Lampitt b Sheriyar	21	– c Rhodes b Sheriyar	14
A. R. C. Fraser not out	9	– b Sheriyar	4
T. F. Bloomfield b Sheriyar	4	– c Leatherdale b McGrath	0
P. C. R. Tufnell c Rhodes b Sheriyar	0	– not out	0
L-b 6, n-b 12	18	B 5, l-b 3, n-b 8	16

1/29 2/36 3/59 4/78 5/95   161   1/33 2/66 3/70 4/141 5/155   181
6/122 7/135 8/157 9/161   6/158 7/166 8/178 9/181

Bonus points – Worcestershire 3.

Bowling: *First Innings*—McGrath 15–6–30–2; Sheriyar 10–1–55–4; Ali 8–1–26–0; Lampitt 13–3–44–4. *Second Innings*—McGrath 17–6–36–3; Sheriyar 16.2–2–45–2; Lampitt 10–4–27–1; Ali 7–2–18–0; Illingworth 16–5–34–3; Hick 6–0–13–1.

Worcestershire

P. R. Pollard c Nash b Fraser	0	– lbw b Johnson	3
E. J. Wilson not out	104	– c Langer b Johnson	19
*G. A. Hick c Langer b Johnson	4	– not out	115
V. S. Solanki c Nash b Bloomfield	30	– c Langer b Fraser	19
D. A. Leatherdale c Nash b Johnson	2	– not out	0
†S. J. Rhodes c Strauss b Bloomfield	9		
S. R. Lampitt lbw b Bloomfield	0		
R. K. Illingworth c Johnson b Bloomfield	4		
Kabir Ali b Fraser	8		
G. D. McGrath c Ramprakash b Fraser	1		
A. Sheriyar c Nash b Fraser	0		
B 5, l-b 7, n-b 8	20	L-b 3, n-b 2	5

1/0 2/9 3/71 4/76 5/104   182   1/17 2/50 3/147   (3 wkts) 161
6/104 7/110 8/144 9/180

Bonus points – Middlesex 3.

Bowling: *First Innings*—Fraser 20–9–29–4; Johnson 21–5–63–2; Bloomfield 13–1–57–4; Tufnell 11–6–21–0. *Second Innings*—Fraser 10–2–30–1; Johnson 14–4–49–2; Bloomfield 6–1–29–0; Tufnell 6–1–35–0; Weekes 1.4–0–15–0.

Umpires: N. G. Cowley and B. Leadbeater.

At Hove, May 18, 19, 20, 21. WORCESTERSHIRE beat SUSSEX by seven wickets.

At Bristol, May 23, 24, 25, 26. WORCESTERSHIRE drew with GLOUCESTERSHIRE.

At Worcester, June 2, 3, 4. WORCESTERSHIRE drew with WEST INDIANS (See West Indian tour section).

At Nottingham, June 7, 8, 9, 10. WORCESTERSHIRE beat NOTTINGHAMSHIRE by 106 runs.

WORCESTERSHIRE v SUSSEX

At Worcester, June 15, 16. Sussex won by eight wickets. Sussex 17 pts, Worcestershire 4 pts.
Toss: Sussex.

Another poor pitch, described by McGrath as one of the slowest he had bowled on, produced a harvest of 32 wickets in two days, and cost Division Two leaders Worcestershire their first Championship defeat. Overcast conditions on the opening day encouraged Sussex's swing bowlers, and a combined tally of 23 fours in half-centuries by Leatherdale and Driver, whose 64 was a career-best, suggested they thought their salvation lay in strokeplay. Although Kabir Ali struck back, removing Montgomerie and Bevan with successive balls to halt a virtual run-a-minute start by Sussex, Peirce's three-hour stay, Adams's 71-ball fifty and Cottey's equally fluent 76 underwrote a first-innings lead of 47. Worcestershire lost three wickets making up the arrears. With Lewry bowling in a finely fashioned groove for his five wickets, and Taylor thriving on his second Championship outing, they sorely needed someone to stay with Wilson. No one did, and Sussex required only 64 to earn two days off.

Close of play: First day, Sussex 144-3 (Peirce 33*, Kirtley 0*).

Worcestershire

P. R. Pollard lbw b Lewry	8	– (8) c Patterson b Taylor	3
E. J. Wilson c Patterson b Taylor	14	– (1) c Adams b Lewry	36
V. S. Solanki lbw b Lewry	0	– c Peirce b Kirtley	8
D. A. Leatherdale b Taylor	56	– c Patterson b Robinson	2
R. C. Driver c Adams b Robinson	64	– (2) b Lewry	0
*†S. J. Rhodes c Patterson b Kirtley	4	– (5) c Adams b Lewry	14
S. R. Lampitt lbw b Lewry	20	– (6) c Patterson b Taylor	2
R. K. Illingworth lbw b Robinson	10	– (7) b Taylor	1
Kabir Ali lbw b Lewry	24	– not out	15
G. D. McGrath b Kirtley	0	– lbw b Lewry	0
A. Sheriyar not out	11	– b Lewry	14
B 1, l-b 10, n-b 8	19	B 5, l-b 6, n-b 4	15

1/12 2/16 3/63 4/94 5/107   230   1/1 2/23 3/30 4/62 5/67   110
6/160 7/184 8/192 9/192   6/69 7/71 8/75 9/80

Bonus points – Worcestershire 1, Sussex 3.

Bowling: *First Innings*—Lewry 11.4–3–71–3; Kirtley 18–1–60–3; Taylor 18–5–44–2; Robinson 17–6–36–2; Rashid 1–0–8–0. *Second Innings*—Lewry 15.4–7–29–5; Kirtley 6–1–21–1; Robinson 6–1–22–1, Taylor 14–5–27–3.

Sussex

R. R. Montgomerie c and b Ali	37	– b Sheriyar	5
M. T. E. Peirce c Rhodes b Sheriyar	42	– c Solanki b Sheriyar	2
M. G. Bevan c Rhodes b Ali	0	– not out	23
*C. J. Adams c Rhodes b McGrath	55	– not out	32
R. J. Kirtley c Rhodes b Ali	7		
P. A. Cottey b McGrath	76		
U. B. A. Rashid c Rhodes b Lampitt	15		
†A. D. Patterson run out	4		
J. D. Lewry b McGrath	9		
B. V. Taylor run out	2		
M. A. Robinson not out	0		
L-b 6, w 4, n-b 20	30	N-b 2	2

1/61 2/61 3/144 4/154 5/191   277   1/7 2/18   (2 wkts) 64
6/222 7/228 8/247 9/258

Bonus points – Sussex 2, Worcestershire 3.

Bowling: *First Innings*—McGrath 21.2–11–39–3; Sheriyar 14–2–65–1; Lampitt 13–3–43–1; Ali 16–2–66–3; Illingworth 13–4–46–0; Leatherdale 1–0–12–0. *Second Innings*—McGrath 6.2–1–20–0; Sheriyar 5–1–29–2; Ali 1–0–15–0.

Umpires: G. I. Burgess and M. J. Kitchen.

At Worcester, June 26. WORCESTERSHIRE lost to NEW ZEALAND A by four wickets (See New Zealand A tour section).

At Swansea, June 28, 29, 30, July 1. WORCESTERSHIRE lost to GLAMORGAN by 81 runs.

At Southgate, July 7, 8, 9, 10. WORCESTERSHIRE drew with MIDDLESEX.

WORCESTERSHIRE v NOTTINGHAMSHIRE

At Worcester, July 12, 13, 14, 15. Drawn. Worcestershire 9 pts, Nottinghamshire 11 pts. Toss: Worcestershire.

Rhodes's first hundred for two years earned the draw that put Worcestershire back on top of Division Two. It seemed unlikely at the start of the day, when they were only 79 ahead with five wickets remaining. But Stemp, who took four wickets the previous evening through spin and misjudged shots, could not press home the advantage, though he finished with five for the first time since joining Nottinghamshire. Rhodes's relish for a fight, plus Pollard's highest score since leaving Nottinghamshire in 1998, made the game safe; the last-wicket stand of 103 between Kabir Ali and McGrath, both hitting maiden fifties, amplified the visitors' frustration. Having watched Wilson grind out 102 over six and a half hours in the first innings – he and Weston shared Worcestershire's first century start in the Championship for a year – Nottinghamshire had taken fresh heart when they claimed nine for 68 on a sluggish pitch. They themselves were 145 for five before Afzaal nearly repeated his hundred against Worcestershire in June. He and Read took the initiative, adding 106, and Millns and Reiffel built on their good work.

Close of play: First day, Worcestershire 248-5 (Leatherdale 5*, Kadeer Ali 0*); Second day, Nottinghamshire 235-5 (Afzaal 65*, Read 43*); Third day, Worcestershire 153-5 (Pollard 45*, Rhodes 14*).

Worcestershire

W. P. C. Weston c Read b Reiffel	52	– (2) c Morris b Stemp	15
E. J. Wilson c Gallian b Harris	102	– (1) lbw b Stemp	34
P. R. Pollard b Gallian	53	– c Read b Stemp	74
D. A. Leatherdale b Millns	18	– c Morris b Stemp	4
M. J. Rawnsley lbw b Reiffel	8	– (9) lbw b Harris	7
R. C. Driver lbw b Harris	0	– c Welton b Stemp	30
Kadeer Ali c Read b Reiffel	2	– (6) lbw b Harris	0
*†S. J. Rhodes c and b Millns	0	– (7) c Morris b Afzaal	103
S. R. Lampitt b Millns	5	– (8) run out	20
Kabir Ali not out	8	– not out	50
G. D. McGrath b Harris	4	– c Johnson b Morris	55
L-b 12, w 6, n-b 14	32	B 5, l-b 10, w 6, n-b 18	39
	284		**431**

1/123 2/216 3/228 4/241 5/246   284   1/42 2/74 3/78 4/130 5/131   431
6/265 7/266 8/272 9/279   6/216 7/273 8/291 9/328

Bonus points – Worcestershire 2, Nottinghamshire 3.

Bowling: *First Innings*—Reiffel 25–4–59–3; Millns 21-3–58–3; Stemp 26–12–45–0; Harris 25.4–5–84–3; Gallian 15–6–17–1; Afzaal 10–4–9–0. *Second Innings*—Millns 15-2–54–0; Reiffel 25–6–53–0; Harris 32–9–101–2; Stemp 51–17–123–5; Afzaal 13–3–45–1; Gallian 4–2–14–0; Morris 2.4–0–26–1.

Nottinghamshire

D. J. Bicknell lbw b McGrath	16	– not out		11
G. E. Welton c Rhodes b Kabir Ali	32	– not out		9
*J. E. R. Gallian b McGrath	45			
J. E. Morris c Lampitt b Kabir Ali	8			
U. Afzaal run out	86			
P. Johnson lbw b Driver	0			
†C. M. W. Read b Kabir Ali	50			
D. J. Millns b Leatherdale	35			
P. R. Reiffel not out	45			
A. J. Harris b Leatherdale	0			
R. D. Stemp c Leatherdale b McGrath	3			
B 4, l-b 6, w 2, n-b 26	38	L-b 2, n-b 2		4
	358	(no wkt)		24

1/32 2/64 3/74 4/134 5/145
6/251 7/285 8/353 9/353

Bonus points – Nottinghamshire 4, Worcestershire 3.

Bowling: *First Innings*—McGrath 23.2–5–70–3; Kabir Ali 23–3–81–3; Rawnsley 20–7–57–0; Lampitt 17–4–63–0; Leatherdale 13–4–46–2; Driver 8–2–31–1. *Second Innings*—Kabir Ali 4–0–19–0; Rawnsley 3–1–3–0.

Umpires: G. I. Burgess and K. E. Palmer.

At Chelmsford, July 19, 20, 21. WORCESTERSHIRE lost to ESSEX by four wickets.

WORCESTERSHIRE v GLOUCESTERSHIRE

At Worcester, July 28, 29, 30. Worcestershire won by 52 runs. Worcestershire 15 pts, Gloucestershire 3 pts. Toss: Worcestershire.

After five games without a win, Worcestershire revived their promotion prospects in a rain-hit match of barely two days' playing time. Another pitch of unreliable bounce, lacking in pace yet bringing McGrath his second ten-wicket Championship return, held the key. Despite Hick's first Championship appearance in seven weeks, Worcestershire were routed for 98 by Smith, Gannon (with three wickets in his first five overs) and Harvey. But McGrath, like Harvey about to fly home for one-day commitments, earned an 11-run lead with seven for 29 in 16 hostile overs that took him past 50 Championship wickets. Though Worcestershire were in further difficulty at 98 for five, with Harvey on his way to county-best figures, fifties by Leatherdale and Rhodes left a target of 237. McGrath and Sheriyar ruled that out, reducing the visitors to 69 for six. Lampitt's three in 13 balls effectively wrapped up the win after Russell and Snape had held out for 16 overs. Rhodes, with nine catches, again equalled Worcestershire's record of dismissals in a match.

Close of play: First day, Gloucestershire 57-5 (Windows 2*, Harvey 10*); Second day, Worcestershire 218-9 (Rhodes 50*, Sheriyar 2*).

Worcestershire

W. P. C. Weston c Russell b Gannon	5	– (2) c Russell b Smith	0
E. J. Wilson b Gannon	1	– (1) lbw b Harvey	11
*G. A. Hick c Russell b Harvey	17	– lbw b Harvey	10
V. S. Solanki lbw b Gannon	0	– c Ball b Harvey	41
P. R. Pollard lbw b Harvey	23	– c Hewson b Gannon	20
D. A. Leatherdale c Ball b Harvey	5	– c Russell b Harvey	56
†S. J. Rhodes c Mohammed b Smith	15	– not out	52
S. R. Lampitt not out	20	– lbw b Harvey	7
M. J. Rawnsley lbw b Smith	3	– lbw b Gannon	3
G. D. McGrath c Russell b Smith	6	– b Gannon	7
A. Sheriyar c Ball b Smith	0	– c Russell b Harvey	7
L-b 1, w 2	3	B 4, l-b 7	11

1/4 2/13 3/13 4/36 5/50   98   1/3 2/20 3/37 4/66 5/98   225
6/59 7/78 8/84 9/98   6/161 7/175 8/180 9/204

Bonus points – Gloucestershire 3.

Bowling: *First Innings*—Smith 17.2–8–16–4; Gannon 10–4–35–3; Harvey 18–7–37–3; Alleyne 5–2–9–0. *Second Innings*—Smith 23–8–39–1; Gannon 14–4–53–3; Harvey 30.3–8–100–6; Alleyne 7–3–22–0.

Gloucestershire

T. H. C. Hancock lbw b McGrath	10	– (2) c Rawnsley b Sheriyar	6
D. R. Hewson c Rhodes b McGrath	4	– (1) c Pollard b McGrath	4
†R. C. Russell c Solanki b Sheriyar	0	– (7) c Pollard b Lampitt	18
I. Mohammed c Wilson b McGrath	14	– (3) c Rhodes b McGrath	15
M. G. N. Windows c Rhodes b McGrath	10	– (4) lbw b McGrath	0
*M. W. Alleyne c Rhodes b McGrath	4	– (5) c Rhodes b Sheriyar	10
I. J. Harvey c Rhodes b McGrath	27	– (6) lbw b Leatherdale	25
J. N. Snape lbw b Lampitt	4	– c Rhodes b Lampitt	43
M. C. J. Ball c Rawnsley b McGrath	4	– not out	30
B. W. Gannon not out	0	– c Rhodes b Lampitt	8
A. M. Smith b Lampitt	0	– c Rhodes b Sheriyar	12
L-b 2, n-b 12	14	B 2, l-b 1, n-b 10	13

1/15 2/20 3/40 4/40 5/44   87   1/10 2/10 3/10 4/33 5/65   184
6/80 7/83 8/87 9/87   6/69 7/132 8/135 9/149

Bonus points – Worcestershire 3.

Bowling: *First Innings*—McGrath 16–9–29–7; Sheriyar 13–3–51–1; Lampitt 2.5–0–5–2. *Second Innings*—McGrath 15–3–40–3; Sheriyar 14–3–69–3; Lampitt 15–6–27–3; Leatherdale 8–0–39–1; Rawnsley 4–2–6–0.

Umpires: G. Sharp and D. R. Shepherd.

At Northampton, August 4, 5, 6, 7. WORCESTERSHIRE lost to NORTHAMPTONSHIRE by an innings and 72 runs.

WORCESTERSHIRE v ESSEX

At Kidderminster, August 9, 10, 11, 12. Essex won by ten wickets. Essex 20 pts, Worcestershire 6 pts. Toss: Essex.

Essex won with two sessions to spare, inflicting Worcestershire's fourth successive Championship defeat at Chester Road. But for Pollard, they might have won in three days. Benefiting from a bland pitch, a fast outfield and his switch from opener to the middle order, he made his first

Championship hundred for five years, sharing stands of 92 with Solanki and 124 with Leatherdale. His unbeaten 123 included 18 fours, and he hit one six on to the railway embankment, but Stuart Law's glorious 189, containing 30 fours, outshone it. Law added 166 at five an over with Prichard, then 185 with Peters, an Essex fifth-wicket record against Worcestershire. When the home side resumed, there were further century partnerships, between Hick, hitting his first fifty in 11 first-class innings, and Solanki, followed by a stubborn effort from Pollard and Leatherdale, but the last six wickets fell for 36. Cowan and Irani turned in their best figures of the season, with five apiece. Prichard hit his second half-century of the game as he and Grayson made light of Essex's 123-run target.

Close of play: First day, Essex 35-1 (Prichard 10*, Hussain 9*); Second day, Essex 461-9 (Hyam 24*, McGarry 0*); Third day, Essex 6-0 (Prichard 3*, Grayson 1*).

Worcestershire

W. P. C. Weston lbw b Irani	11	– (2) lbw b Irani	5
E. J. Wilson c Hyam b Cowan	5	– (1) b Cowan	1
*G. A. Hick b Irani	1	– b Irani	75
V. S. Solanki c Hyam b Cowan	55	– c S. G. Law b Cowan	56
P. R. Pollard not out	123	– c Prichard b Cowan	69
D. A. Leatherdale lbw b Cowan	52	– c Hyam b Irani	36
†S. J. Rhodes c S. G. Law b Cowan	8	– c Grayson b Cowan	0
S. R. Lampitt b D. R. Law	6	– c Hyam b Cowan	0
Kabir Ali c Hyam b D. R. Law	0	– lbw b Irani	1
M. J. Rawnsley run out	0	– c Hyam b Irani	10
A. Sheriyar st Hyam b Grayson	1	– not out	0
B 1, l-b 9, w 12, n-b 18	40	L-b 3, w 16, n-b 10	29
	302		**282**

1/7 2/12 3/17 4/109 5/233   302   1/8 2/10 3/146 4/146 5/246   282
6/247 7/287 8/289 9/294   6/247 7/251 8/256 9/278

Bonus points – Worcestershire 3, Essex 3.

Bowling: *First Innings*—Cowan 20–8–69–4; Irani 19–11–24–2; D. R. Law 22–1–85–2; McGarry 8–1–44–0; Such 6–0–36–0; Grayson 17–6–34–1. *Second Innings*—Cowan 24–8–54–5; Irani 25.5–5–79–5; McGarry 8–0–44–0; Such 12–3–36–0; D. R. Law 7–3–23–0; Grayson 16–2–43–0.

Essex

P. J. Prichard c Leatherdale b Ali	74	– not out	62
A. P. Grayson b Ali	4	– not out	50
N. Hussain c Rhodes b Ali	10		
S. G. Law c Solanki b Sheriyar	189		
*R. C. Irani b Lampitt	14		
S. D. Peters b Sheriyar	67		
†B. J. Hyam c Rhodes b Sheriyar	25		
D. R. Law b Rawnsley	1		
A. P. Cowan lbw b Sheriyar	0		
P. M. Such c Rawnsley b Ali	2		
A. C. McGarry not out	0		
B 5, l-b 11, w 8, n-b 52	76	L-b 5, w 2, n-b 6	13
	462	(no wkt)	**125**

1/6 2/38 3/204 4/233 5/418   462   (no wkt) 125
6/421 7/426 8/433 9/457

Bonus points – Essex 5, Worcestershire 3.

Bowling: *First Innings*—Sheriyar 28.2–3–110–4; Ali 20–2–114–4; Lampitt 23–7–60–1; Rawnsley 28–8–91–1; Leatherdale 10–1–40–0; Hick 7–0–31–0. *Second Innings*—Lampitt 10–3–34–0; Ali 15–4–36–0; Sheriyar 2–0–22–0; Rawnsley 8–2–24–0; Pollard 0.1–0–4–0.

Umpires: J. W. Holder and J. F. Steele.

WORCESTERSHIRE v WARWICKSHIRE

At Worcester, August 21, 22, 23. Worcestershire won by nine wickets. Worcestershire 18 pts, Warwickshire 3 pts. Toss: Worcestershire. Championship debut: D. J. Pipe.

This Midlands derby was brought forward 24 hours to give Warwickshire a free day before the NatWest final; early defeat gave them two free days. The changed schedule deprived Worcestershire of McGrath, still returning from Australia, but with Liptrot and Lampitt both achieving career-bests, he was hardly missed. Solanki had set up their winning position, reaching his first Championship fifty at New Road in 2000, and going on to 160, with 25 fours, to help Worcestershire to their highest first-innings total at home for the season. Jamie Pipe, their reserve wicket-keeper playing as a specialist batsman, contributed 54 in 64 balls on Championship debut. In reply, Warwickshire were bowled over by Liptrot, making his first Championship appearance of the season, although Powell survived for 51 overs. When they followed on, 196 behind, they came up against Lampitt, whose spell of four for 16 in 28 balls completed a three-day win that took Worcestershire back to second place. While this was Lampitt's 19th five-wicket return, he had never before gone on to six, let alone seven. Only Singh, with 15 fours and a six in his 79, and Penney's fifty delayed the outcome.

Close of play: First day, Worcestershire 231-5 (Solanki 113*, Rhodes 20*); Second day, Warwickshire 140-8 (Welch 0*).

Worcestershire

W. P. C. Weston lbw b Giddins	0	– not out		11
P. R. Pollard c Piper b Giddins	5			
*G. A. Hick c Piper b Richardson	0	– not out		0
V. S. Solanki c sub b Brown	160			
D. A. Leatherdale lbw b Welch	18			
D. J. Pipe c Smith b Richardson	54	– (2) lbw b Powell		17
†S. J. Rhodes c Powell b Giddins	46			
S. R. Lampitt not out	25			
M. J. Rawnsley b Richardson	3			
C. G. Liptrot run out	1			
A. Sheriyar b Giddins	0			
B 1, l-b 11, w 2, n-b 12	26	B 4, n-b 4		8
	338		(1 wkt)	**36**

1/3 2/8 3/8 4/75 5/175   1/29
6/287 7/313 8/334 9/338

Bonus points – Worcestershire 3, Warwickshire 3.

Bowling: *First Innings*—Richardson 32–8–81–3; Giddins 30.2–10–75–4; Brown 23–5–78–1; Welch 24–5–87–1; Smith 3–2–5–0; Wagh 1–1–0–0. *Second Innings*—Giddins 2–0–13–0; Richardson 2.3–0–19–0; Powell 1–1–0–1.

Warwickshire

M. J. Powell c Rhodes b Liptrot	75	– c Leatherdale b Sheriyar		0
M. A. Wagh lbw b Liptrot	4	– lbw b Lampitt		25
A. Singh c Hick b Liptrot	0	– b Liptrot		79
D. L. Hemp c Solanki b Liptrot	4	– c Liptrot b Lampitt		9
T. L. Penney lbw b Sheriyar	3	– c Weston b Leatherdale		51
D. R. Brown c Pollard b Lampitt	13	– (7) c Hick b Lampitt		27
*N. M. K. Smith lbw b Leatherdale	10	– (6) c Rhodes b Lampitt		11
†K. J. Piper b Liptrot	18	– lbw b Lampitt		10
G. Welch c Hick b Liptrot	0	– lbw b Lampitt		0
A. Richardson not out	2	– not out		3
E. S. H. Giddins b Sheriyar	0	– c Liptrot b Lampitt		0
L-b 7, n-b 6	13	B 1, l-b 5, w 4, n-b 6		16
	142			**231**

1/8 2/10 3/24 4/47 5/76   1/2 2/70 3/92 4/136 5/170
6/89 7/135 8/140 9/141   6/206 7/216 8/216 9/231

Bonus points – Worcestershire 3.

Bowling: *First Innings*—Sheriyar 18.2–6–52–2; Liptrot 15–2–44–6; Lampitt 12–6–23–1; Leatherdale 9–3–16–1. *Second Innings*—Sheriyar 21–6–60–1; Liptrot 16–3–68–1; Lampitt 18.4–3–45–7; Leatherdale 16–6–36–1; Rawnsley 4–1–16–0.

Umpires: M. R. Benson and B. Leadbeater.

At Birmingham, August 30, 31, September 1, 2. WORCESTERSHIRE drew with WARWICKSHIRE.

WORCESTERSHIRE v NORTHAMPTONSHIRE

At Worcester, September 13, 14, 15, 16. Drawn. Worcestershire 7 pts, Northamptonshire 8 pts. Toss: Worcestershire. First-class debut: M. J. Powell.

The loss of the second and third days dashed Worcestershire's hopes of the win that might have secured promotion along with Northamptonshire, already confirmed as Division Two champions. Put in, the visitors were 96 for seven at lunch, but Bailey's unbeaten 96 from 127 balls resuscitated them. He looked set for a maiden hundred until last man Cousins, who helped add 59, had the misfortune to play on. Cousins's response was to plunge Worcestershire's fragile batting into deep trouble. But the follow-on, a real possibility at 50 for five as the first day ended, was averted once the rain relented. Rhodes declared soon afterwards, whereupon McGrath, with his season's best eight for 41 – giving him career-best match figures of 12 for 116 – bowled Northamptonshire out for 125 to offer his side an unexpected chance of victory. Needing 262 from 43 overs, they lost wickets at regular intervals before Driver and Rhodes shepherded them to safety.

Close of play: First day, Worcestershire 50-5 (Leatherdale 20*, Rhodes 3*); Second day, No play; Third day, No play.

Northamptonshire

A. S. Rollins c Rawnsley b McGrath	0	– b McGrath	0
A. J. Swann lbw b Lampitt	19	– b McGrath	13
J. W. Cook b McGrath	9	– b McGrath	21
R. J. Warren lbw b Leatherdale	11	– b Lampitt	15
M. J. Powell lbw b Lampitt	1	– b McGrath	1
*A. L. Penberthy c Solanki b Lampitt	48	– c Wilson b McGrath	0
G. P. Swann lbw b Leatherdale	2	– lbw b Lampitt	11
K. J. Innes c Driver b McGrath	5	– c Rhodes b McGrath	25
†T. M. B. Bailey not out	96	– lbw b McGrath	22
J. P. Taylor b McGrath	14	– c Rhodes b McGrath	0
D. M. Cousins b Driver	24	– not out	5
B 5, l-b 4, w 14, n-b 8	31	L-b 4, n-b 8	12

1/0 2/44 3/46 4/58 5/67   260   1/0 2/32 3/45 4/59 5/59   125
6/69 7/96 8/149 9/201   6/61 7/85 8/110 9/110

Bonus points – Northamptonshire 2, Worcestershire 3.

Bowling: *First Innings*—McGrath 25–10–75–4; Liptrot 7–0–49–0; Lampitt 22–3–58–3; Leatherdale 14–3–44–2; Driver 3.2–0–13–1; Rawnsley 2–1–12–0. *Second Innings*—McGrath 13.5–2–41–8; Liptrot 7–0–26–0; Lampitt 11–1–36–2; Leatherdale 5–1–18–0.

Worcestershire

P. R. Pollard c Bailey b Taylor	10	– c Bailey b Cousins	0
E. J. Wilson b Cousins	10	– c Bailey b Taylor	0
V. S. Solanki c Cook b Taylor	0	– b Taylor	30
D. A. Leatherdale b Taylor	46	– b Taylor	3
R. C. Driver c Penberthy b Cousins	0	– not out	47
D. J. Pipe b Cousins	5	– b Taylor	1
*†S. J. Rhodes c Rollins b Innes	42	– lbw b Cousins	24
S. R. Lampitt not out	5	– not out	1
L-b 4, n-b 2	6	L-b 7, w 6	13

1/21 2/21 3/29 4/30	(7 wkts dec.) 124	1/6 2/12 3/20
5/35 6/108 7/124		4/47 5/59 6/114

(6 wkts) 119

M. J. Rawnsley, C. G. Liptrot and G. D. McGrath did not bat.

Bonus points – Northamptonshire 2.

Bowling: *First Innings*—Cousins 18–4–61–3; Taylor 18–4–51–3; Innes 1.3–0–8–1. *Second Innings*—Cousins 10.3–2–54–2; Taylor 12–4–27–4; Penberthy 5–1–11–0; Innes 3–0–20–0.

Umpires: V. A. Holder and J. F. Steele.

CRICKET SOCIETY AWARDS, 2000

Kabir Ali of Worcestershire won the Cricket Society's Most Promising Young Cricketer Award. The A. A. Thomson Fielding Prize, for the best schoolboy fielder, went to Tim Rees of Canon Slade Church of England School, Bolton. The Sir John Hobbs Memorial Prize, for the outstanding Under-16 schoolboy, was won by Tom New of Quarrydale Comprehensive, Sutton-in-Ashfield. Wetherall awards went to Martin Bicknell of Surrey as the outstanding all-rounder in the first-class game, with the schools award going to Richard Wilkinson of RGS Worcester.

YORKSHIRE

Matthew Hoggard

President: R. A. Smith
Chairman: K. H. Moss
Chief Executive: C. D. Hassell
Chairman, Cricket Committee: R. K. Platt
Captain: D. Byas
Director of Coaching: 2000 – M. D. Moxon
First-Team Coach: 2001 – W. M. Clark
Cricket Development Manager: S. Oldham
Head Groundsman: A. W. Fogarty
Scorer: J. T. Potter

With Darren Gough, Craig White and Michael Vaughan regularly missing on Test calls, and Matthew Hoggard making his England debut, Yorkshire did well to finish third in the Championship – a position not bettered in 25 years – and second in the National League. Such high placings were even more commendable considering the number of injuries they sustained. Resources were so stretched at times that they blooded nine players during the summer, six of them in the Championship.

Though overall a satisfactory season, it again revealed Yorkshire's long-standing weakness of failing to grasp the moment, which cost them crucial matches. Having finished top of their group in the Benson and Hedges Cup, they lost to Surrey in the quarter-finals by a margin far wider than seven runs would suggest. Their performance against Northamptonshire in the fourth round of the NatWest Trophy was simply dire – and inexcusable. All the Test players were available; in fact, they were so "strong" that Hoggard could not get into the side. And they went down by 69 runs.

It was a similar story in the National League. First they lost ground with an inexplicably poor display against Gloucestershire at Bristol, David Byas using eight bowlers in a forlorn attempt to get a grip on the game. Yorkshire later pulled themselves together with five consecutive victories to head the table, but when it mattered, in their final fixture under the Canterbury floodlights, they went to pieces. The Championship was the same: they lost only twice, but significantly these defeats were against the top two teams, Surrey and Lancashire. They began and ended their Championship season with two consecutive wins, and only briefly fell outside the top three.

More than once, Yorkshire had pitch liaison officers breathing down their necks at Headingley, and were lucky to get away without losing points against Kent when A. C. Smith felt he had not seen enough of the match to make a judgment. They were not so fortunate in the final home game of the season against Surrey at Scarborough. Mike Denness convened the pitches panel, despite Surrey reaching 330 for eight on the first day on an unarguably green top, and docked eight points. Yorkshire decided an appeal but were furious at the harsh way in which they felt they were treated. Salt was rubbed into their wounds when the deduction ultimately cost them the runners-up spot and £50,000. There was no prize money for finishing third.

Along with their disappointments, Yorkshire had many outstanding moments, and Darren Lehmann and Hoggard mainly laid down the foundations on which their successes were built. The Australian was as flamboyant as ever in his third season with Yorkshire, and by the time it drew to a close he had been appointed vice-captain, with his contract extended to the end of 2003. His reliability was such that he rarely knew the meaning of failure; in 23 Championship innings he piled up 1,477 runs at an average of 67.13 to become the heaviest scorer in the country. His century against Kent at Canterbury was the fastest of the season, coming off 89 balls, and it was also his sixth consecutive Championship score of 50 or more.

Hoggard stayed firmly on his feet all summer while fast-bowling colleagues fell around him. As well as being the club's only bowler to boast 50 first-class wickets for the club, he also claimed the country's top haul in the National League, his 37 beating Yorkshire's previous record in League cricket of 29 set by Howard Cooper in 1975. Distinctly unfriendly on but not off the field, Hoggard achieved accuracy and movement without sacrificing his natural pace. Once his ferocity had been noted on television during the Benson and Hedges game with Surrey, he found himself on the threshold of an England place. It came against West Indies at Lord's – and, as with Brian Close over half a century earlier, before he had received his Yorkshire cap. That was handed over during the match against Somerset at Scarborough in mid-July, when Ryan Sidebottom was also capped. By then, though, the left-arm swing bowler had been stretchered off with a serious hip injury which ended his season. It also halted a remarkable run of form during which Sidebottom had grabbed 22 wickets in the four previous matches, starting with career-best figures of 11 for 43 against Kent at Headingley.

Vaughan, who hit 155 at the start of the season against Derbyshire before retiring hurt with a broken hand, later returned to add consistency to his elegance and style. But Byas, in his benefit season, struggled to find any sort of form. Matthew Wood also began with a hundred against Derbyshire but faded away for the second summer in succession, while it was well into the season before Anthony McGrath was able to show his pedigree after being absent with knee problems. Gavin Hamilton did well enough with bat and ball to make up for his winter disappointments with England in South Africa, but the days of Richard Blakey, Yorkshire's longest-serving player, looked numbered. Even though he had claimed 40 Championship dismissals behind the stumps, he was axed at the start of August because of insufficient runs, and his livewire replacement, Simon Guy, gave little indication that he would willingly give up the gloves.

At the end of the season, work began on the £10 million redevelopment of Headingley, which included demolition of the notorious Western Terrace. Yorkshire had to fund £4 million themselves, and borrowing put their finances under considerable strain. This led indirectly to Martyn Moxon's shock resignation in January 2001 as director of coaching and his move to Durham. A hugely popular figure within his native county, Moxon had become disenchanted with the increasing pressure to make financial cuts and decided to take up a "new challenge". His replacement as first-team coach, Wayne Clark, has no experience of English conditions; but in his six years with Western Australia, they have won both the Sheffield Shield and Mercantile Mutual Cup. Yorkshire will be hoping his methods travel well. – DAVID WARNER.

YORKSHIRE 2000

[Bill Smith]

Back row: S. M. Guy, C. J. Ellison, R. K. J. Dawson, J. W. Inglis, S. Widdup, M. Thewlis, V. J. Craven, R. A. Stead, M. J. Lumb. *Middle row:* C. A. Becker (*physiotherapist*), S. Oldham (*cricket development manager*), M. J. Wood, I. D. Fisher, R. J. Sidebottom, M. J. Hoggard, J. D. Middlebrook, G. M. Fellows, A. Sidebottom (*Second E'even coach*), R. Jones (*Second E'even physiotherapist*). *Front row:* C. E. W. Silverwood, C. White, R. J. Harden, D. S. Lehmann, D. Gough, M. P. Vaughan, D. Byas (*captain*), G. M. Hamilton, P. M. Hutchison, R. J. Blakey, A. McGrath, M. D. Moxon (*director of coaching*).

YORKSHIRE RESULTS

All first-class matches – Played 18: Won 7, Lost 4, Drawn 7.

County Championship matches – Played 16: Won 7, Lost 2, Drawn 7.

PPP Healthcare County Championship, 3rd in Division 1; NatWest Trophy, 4th round; Benson and Hedges Cup, q-f; Norwich Union National League, 2nd in Division 1.

COUNTY CHAMPIONSHIP AVERAGES
BATTING

Cap		M	I	NO	R	HS	100s	50s	Avge	Ct/St
1997	D. S. Lehmann§ . . .	16	23	1	1,477	136	4	9	67.13	8
1995	M. P. Vaughan‡	9	15	1	697	155*	2	3	49.78	2
1998	G. M. Hamilton. . . .	12	14	2	375	125	1	2	31.25	6
1999	A. McGrath†	10	14	1	375	133	1	1	28.84	8
	I. D. Fisher†	5	8	2	167	68*	0	1	27.83	1
	V. J. Craven†	6	7	1	164	58	0	1	27.33	6
1991	D. Byas†	15	22	1	523	84	0	2	24.90	22
	G. M. Fellows†	13	18	4	305	46	0	0	21.78	7
	M. J. Wood†	10	15	3	224	100*	1	0	18.66	5
	S. Widdup†	8	12	1	195	44	0	0	17.72	6
1987	R. J. Blakey†	11	16	1	262	56	0	1	17.46	38/2
1996	C. E. W. Silverwood†	9	11	1	173	48	0	0	17.30	1
	J. D. Middlebrook† .	9	11	0	184	45	0	0	16.72	3
	S. M. Guy†	5	7	1	97	42	0	0	16.16	17/2
2000	M. J. Hoggard†	14	15	3	80	20*	0	0	6.66	2
2000	R. J. Sidebottom† . .	6	7	2	15	6*	0	0	3.00	2
1998	P. M. Hutchison† . .	5	5	2	3	3*	0	0	1.00	2

Also batted: C. J. Elstub† (3 matches) 4*, 2* (1 ct); D. Gough†‡ (cap 1993) (3 matches) 23, 5 (1 ct); R. J. Harden (1 match) 0; G. A. Lambert (2 matches) 1, 3*, 2* (1 ct); G. Ramsden† (1 match) 0*; C. White†‡ (cap 1993) (3 matches) 17, 11, 10.

* Signifies not out.   † Born in Yorkshire.   ‡ ECB contract.   § Overseas player.

BOWLING

	O	M	R	W	BB	5W/i	Avge
R. J. Sidebottom.	134.2	46	300	24	6-16	4	12.50
D. Gough	100.5	22	245	16	6-63	1	15.31
C. White	76	18	194	12	3-12	0	16.16
J. D. Middlebrook. . . .	237.5	58	650	27	6 82	1	24.07
G. M. Hamilton	286	68	820	33	4-34	0	24.84
P. M. Hutchison	100.4	22	350	14	3-62	0	25.00
M. J. Hoggard	456.4	121	1,216	46	5-50	2	26.43
C. E. W. Silverwood . .	292.3	80	762	26	4-60	0	29.30
I. D. Fisher	187.1	43	541	15	3-40	0	36.06

Also bowled: D. Byas 0.1–0–0–0; V. J. Craven 8–1–15–0; C. J. Elstub 50–10–138–5; G. M. Fellows 121–28–361–7; S. M. Guy 4–1–8–0; G. A. Lambert 46–7–133–4; D. S. Lehmann 112–18–310–8; G. Ramsden 12–1–68–1; M. P. Vaughan 51.5–12–127–6; S. Widdup 2.3–0–22–1.

COUNTY RECORDS

Highest score for:	341	G. H. Hirst v Leicestershire at Leicester	1905
Highest score against:	318*	W. G. Grace (Gloucestershire) at Cheltenham. . . .	1876
Best bowling for:	10-10	H. Verity v Nottinghamshire at Leeds	1932
Best bowling against:	10-37	C. V. Grimmett (Australians) at Sheffield	1930
Highest total for:	887	v Warwickshire at Birmingham	1896
Highest total against:	681-7 dec.	by Leicestershire at Bradford	1996
Lowest total for:	23	v Hampshire at Middlesbrough	1965
Lowest total against:	13	by Nottinghamshire at Nottingham	1901

YORKSHIRE v DERBYSHIRE

At Leeds, May 3, 4, 5. Yorkshire won by an innings and 79 runs. Yorkshire 20 pts, Derbyshire 2 pts. Toss: Yorkshire.

The only blot on an otherwise unblemished start to Yorkshire's Championship campaign was the loss of Vaughan, who was struck by a bouncer from Cassar, which broke a knuckle on his left hand. Vaughan had compiled an elegant 155, with nine fours and two sixes, the first of which took him to his maiden century at Headingley. He gave just one chance in seven and three-quarter hours. The untimely blow robbed Vaughan of his Test place against Zimbabwe. Yorkshire took charge from the moment Hoggard destroyed Derbyshire's early batting with a burst of three for ten in eight balls. Only Di Venuto showed form, in an attacking 88-ball 70, striking eight fours and two sixes. He added 33 more runs in the second innings, when Gough wiped out the middle order with three for two in 16 balls. In between, Vaughan set up the innings victory by putting Yorkshire on their way to 508 for five; there was a flamboyant 95 from Lehmann, while Wood rediscovered his touch in his first century since September 1998.

Close of play: First day, Yorkshire 74-0 (Byas 28*, Vaughan 41*); Second day, Yorkshire 407-4 (Wood 38*, Fellows 20*).

Derbyshire

M. P. Dowman c Blakey b Hoggard	7	– (2) c Hamilton b Hoggard	4
S. D. Stubbings b Hoggard	0	– (1) c Byas b White	4
M. J. Di Venuto c Byas b Sidebottom	70	– c Wood b White	33
S. P. Titchard lbw b Hoggard	4	– c Byas b Hamilton	11
R. J. Bailey b Sidebottom	14	– not out	54
M. E. Cassar b Hamilton	9	– c Blakey b Gough	24
*†K. M. Krikken c Byas b Hamilton	38	– lbw b Gough	0
P. Aldred c Byas b Vaughan	38	– c Byas b Gough	0
T. A. Munton not out	16	– retired hurt	4
T. M. Smith c Blakey b White	15	– b Hamilton	21
K. J. Dean c Blakey b White	0	– b White	15
B 6, l-b 2, w 2, n-b 18	28	L-b 2, n-b 18	20
	239		190

1/6 2/13 3/17 4/66 5/79   1/8 2/28 3/53 4/67 5/112
6/130 7/192 8/202 9/239   6/114 7/114 8/169 9/190

Bonus points – Derbyshire 1, Yorkshire 3.

In the second innings Munton retired hurt at 127.

Bowling: *First Innings*—Gough 14–1–68–0; Hoggard 16–4–36–3; Sidebottom 9–0–44–2; Hamilton 13–2–42–2; White 15–5–20–2; Fellows 4–0–11–0; Vaughan 4–1–10–1. *Second Innings*—Gough 17–4–34–3; Hoggard 15.5–7–25–1; White 11–2–47–3; Hamilton 12.1–1–41–2; Sidebottom 6–0–22–0; Lehmann 5–0–19–0.

Yorkshire

*D. Byas lbw b Aldred	49	G. M. Fellows lbw b Smith	37
M. P. Vaughan retired hurt	155	G. M. Hamilton not out	10
†R. J. Blakey lbw b Aldred	13	B 13, l-b 11, w 4, n-b 4	32
D. S. Lehmann c Krikken b Aldred	95		
C. White b Aldred	17	1/119 2/141 3/293 (5 wkts dec.) 508
M. J. Wood not out	100	4/319 5/459	

D. Gough, R. J. Sidebottom and M. J. Hoggard did not bat.

Bonus points – Yorkshire 5, Derbyshire 1 (Score at 130 overs: 409-4).

Vaughan retired hurt at 365.

Bowling: Smith 26.3–4–102–1; Munton 43–6–117–0; Dean 19–2–74–0; Aldred 33–7–97–4; Cassar 24–8–72–0; Bailey 3–0–11–0; Dowman 2–1–7–0; Titchard 2–0–4–0.

Umpires: A. A. Jones and A. G. T. Whitehead.

YORKSHIRE v HAMPSHIRE

At Leeds, May 12, 13, 14. Yorkshire won by an innings and 100 runs. Yorkshire 19 pts, Hampshire 3 pts. Toss: Hampshire. First-class debut: V. J. Craven.

One of the few things Hampshire got right was the toss, but it was perhaps unwise to bat first on an awkward pitch of variable bounce (though pitch liaison officer Mike Denness pronounced himself satisfied). No one came to terms with Gough or White, who did most of the damage between them. In reply, Vic Craven, a 19-year-old left-hander introduced in place of Vaughan, played some crisp shots, and Lehmann batted with his usual fluency, but it was Hamilton who led Yorkshire's recovery from 160 for six. He rushed from 90 to a maiden century in consecutive balls – upper-cutting Hartley for six and cover-driving a half-volley for four. Hamilton struck 15 fours altogether in 206 balls, and was last out seeking one run for maximum batting points. Hampshire's batsmen continued to show little stomach for a fight, though Kendall defended solidly for an unbeaten 78. It was another depressing game for Warne, who took only two wickets and bagged a pair for the second match running as Yorkshire completed victory on the third morning.

Close of play: First day, Yorkshire 144-4 (Lehmann 37*, Wood 8*); Second day, Hampshire 84-4 (Kendall 26*, Morris 4*).

Hampshire

G. W. White st Blakey b Middlebrook	13	– lbw b Hoggard	1
J. S. Laney b Gough	13	– c Blakey b Gough	19
W. S. Kendall lbw b Gough	3	– not out	78
*R. A. Smith c Blakey b White	15	– lbw b White	22
†D. A. Kenway b Gough	14	– c Craven b Middlebrook	7
J. P. Stephenson lbw b White	6	– (7) c Craven b Gough	6
A. D. Mascarenhas b White	3	– (8) c Blakey b Hamilton	25
S. K. Warne lbw b Middlebrook	0	– (9) c Wood b Hamilton	0
S. D. Udal c Blakey b Hamilton	6	– (10) c Craven b Middlebrook	0
A. C. Morris lbw b Gough	0	– (6) b White	4
P. J. Hartley not out	5	– c Byas b Hamilton	22
B 1, l-b 6, n-b 16	23	B 10, l-b 2, n-b 2	14
	101		**198**

1/27 2/31 3/61 4/61 5/70   101   1/17 2/23 3/54 4/78 5/84   198
6/74 7/77 8/87 9/90   6/105 7/152 8/152 9/153

Bonus points – Yorkshire 3.

Bowling: *First Innings*—Gough 14.3–6–23–4; Hoggard 8–3–22–0; Hamilton 12–5–20–1; Middlebrook 9–3–17–2; White 9–3–12–3. *Second Innings*—Gough 15–4–29–2; Hoggard 13–2–47–1; White 14–3–30–2; Hamilton 10.5–1–43–3; Middlebrook 8–1–37–2; Lehmann 1–1–0–0.

Yorkshire

*D. Byas c Stephenson b Morris	8	J. D. Middlebrook c Stephenson b Warne	1
V. J. Craven lbw b Hartley	29	D. Gough c Stephenson b Morris	23
†R. J. Blakey c White b Hartley	19	M. J. Hoggard not out	20
D. S. Lehmann c Laney b Mascarenhas	85		
C. White c Kenway b Stephenson	11	B 15, l-b 16, w 12, n-b 25	68
M. J. Wood c Kenway b Hartley	9		
G. M. Fellows lbw b Mascarenhas	1	1/15 2/65 3/68 4/90 5/155	**399**
G. M. Hamilton b Warne	125	6/160 7/271 8/272 9/355	

Bonus points – Yorkshire 4, Hampshire 3.

Bowling: Hartley 26–5–91–3; Morris 21–3–72–2; Warne 26.3–3–81–2; Udal 10–4–20–0; Stephenson 17–3–53–1; Mascarenhas 20–3–51–2.

Umpires: A. Clarkson and N. A. Mallender.

At Derby, May 17, 18, 19, 20. YORKSHIRE drew with DERBYSHIRE.

At Leeds, May 24, 25, 26, 27. YORKSHIRE lost to ZIMBABWEANS by 32 runs (See Zimbabwean tour section).

YORKSHIRE v LEICESTERSHIRE

At Leeds, May 31, June 1, 2, 3. Drawn. Yorkshire 7 pts, Leicestershire 7 pts. Toss: Leicestershire. First-class debut: C. J. Elstub.

This clash between the Championship's two top sides was ruined by bad weather, which interrupted the second day and washed out all play after midday on the third. Leicestershire failed to capitalise on their best start of the season to date, 84 in 21 overs from Ward and Maddy. It was DeFreitas who made sure of their two batting points by adding 100 for the last two wickets, assisted by Ormond and Boswell. While never missing a scoring opportunity, DeFreitas showed commendable restraint until Hutchison bowled him for 70, attempting to drive a ninth four which would have raised 300 and a third point. The same tail-end trio then combined to keep Yorkshire on a tight rein. Only Lehmann batted freely; he seemed in complete control until an on-drive by Byas was deflected off Ormond's hand into the stumps to run him out.

Close of play: First day, Yorkshire 1-0 (Byas 0*, Craven 1*); Second day, Yorkshire 107-4 (Wood 2*, Fellows 0*); Third day, Yorkshire 146-4 (Wood 17*, Fellows 19*).

Leicestershire

T. R. Ward c Byas b Hamilton	24		P. A. J. DeFreitas b Hutchison		70
D. L. Maddy c Byas b Middlebrook	63		J. Ormond b Middlebrook		20
*V. J. Wells b Hutchison	19		S. A. J. Boswell not out		12
B. F. Smith lbw b Middlebrook	30				
A. Habib c Lehmann b Hutchison	6		B 3, l-b 6, n-b 14		23
D. I. Stevens c Craven b Elstub	9				—
I. J. Sutcliffe lbw b Hoggard	14		1/84 2/106 3/133 4/149 5/160		296
†N. D. Burns b Hamilton	6		6/164 7/171 8/196 9/257		

Bonus points – Leicestershire 2, Yorkshire 3.

Bowling: Hoggard 21–6–55–1; Hutchison 15.5–3–62–3; Hamilton 21–6–80–2; Elstub 13–3–36–1; Middlebrook 22–9–39–3; Lehmann 9–2–15–0.

Yorkshire

*D. Byas c Burns b Boswell	44		G. M. Fellows not out		19
V. J. Craven lbw b Ormond	1				
†R. J. Blakey lbw b Wells	9		B 4, l-b 5, n-b 8		17
D. S. Lehmann run out	39				
M. J. Wood not out	17		1/3 2/18 3/94 4/106	(4 wkts)	146

C. J. Elstub, G. M. Hamilton, J. D. Middlebrook, P. M. Hutchison and M. J. Hoggard did not bat.

Bonus point – Leicestershire 1.

Bowling: Ormond 24–11–50–1; Boswell 9.4–3–18–1; DeFreitas 23–6–40–0; Wells 6–1–25–1; Maddy 2–1–4–0.

Umpires: D. R. Shepherd and R. A. White.

At Chester-le-Street, June 7, 8, 9. YORKSHIRE beat DURHAM by six wickets.

YORKSHIRE v KENT

At Leeds, June 14, 15, 16. Yorkshire won by six wickets. Yorkshire 15 pts, Kent 3 pts. Toss: Yorkshire.

Yorkshire were highly relieved when ECB pitch liaison officer A. C. Smith did not dock them eight points. He said he had not seen enough play to judge the pitch – hardly surprising, as 23 wickets had already toppled before he arrived. The match lasted barely 214 overs. Low bounce was the main problem; the wicket was never dangerous. Sidebottom, a last-minute selection ahead of Hutchison, routed Kent as he twice improved his career-best figures and finished with 11 for 43. On the first day, he seized four for two in 11 balls, reducing them to 26 for five; on the third, three for nought in nine balls as they succumbed for 82. Despite lacking anyone with his penetration, Kent restricted their first-innings deficit to 20. Vaughan, withdrawn on the first evening to join England at Edgbaston as cover for Ramprakash, was allowed to bat when sent home, the ECB waiving their usual regulation and Kent raising no objection. He went in at No. 6 after Middlebrook stood in as opener and Lehmann topped 3,000 runs for his adopted county in 50 innings. Victory on the third afternoon extended Yorkshire's Championship lead to 16 points, cut to 13 next day when the round was completed.

Close of play: First day, Kent 127-7 (Dravid 45*, Patel 0*); Second day, Kent 36-3 (Key 10*, Walker 6*).

Kent

D. P. Fulton lbw b Hoggard	3	– c Lehmann b Hoggard	1
R. W. T. Key c Middlebrook b Sidebottom	3	– c Lehmann b Hoggard	12
R. Dravid b Sidebottom	46	– c Blakey b Silverwood	6
A. P. Wells c Blakey b Sidebottom	2	– lbw b Sidebottom	7
M. J. Walker lbw b Sidebottom	0	– lbw b Hamilton	14
M. A. Ealham c Blakey b Sidebottom	0	– c Byas b Sidebottom	8
†P. A. Nixon lbw b Hoggard	27	– b Sidebottom	7
*M. V. Fleming c Blakey b Silverwood	29	– lbw b Sidebottom	0
M. M. Patel c Blakey b Hamilton	1	– b Sidebottom	0
D. D. Masters c Blakey b Hamilton	0	– c Wood b Sidebottom	12
M. J. Saggers not out	0	– not out	6
B 7, l-b 9, n-b 2	18	B 4, l-b 1, n-b 4	9

1/5 2/18 3/26 4/26 5/26   129   1/1 2/12 3/25 4/46 5/52   82
6/78 7/121 8/129 9/129   6/58 7/58 8/58 9/67

Bonus points – Yorkshire 3.

Bowling: *First Innings*—Silverwood 17–7–31–1; Hoggard 17–10–16–2; Hamilton 18–9–27–2; Sidebottom 18.2–8–27–5; Middlebrook 5–1–12–0. *Second Innings*—Silverwood 15–9–12–1; Hoggard 13–6–22–2; Sidebottom 12.5–7–16–6; Hamilton 12–3–27–1; Middlebrook 1–1–0–0.

Yorkshire

*D. Byas c Nixon b Masters	14	– c Saggers b Masters	10
J. D. Middlebrook lbw b Ealham	18		
†R. J. Blakey run out	22	– lbw b Ealham	4
D. S. Lehmann c Nixon b Masters	28	– not out	29
M. J. Wood c Dravid b Ealham	0	– c Nixon b Saggers	4
M. P. Vaughan c Nixon b Masters	9	– (2) b Saggers	0
G. M. Fellows c Patel b Saggers	13	– (6) not out	11
G. M. Hamilton lbw b Saggers	18		
C. E. W. Silverwood not out	23		
R. J. Sidebottom lbw b Fleming	1		
M. J. Hoggard c Fulton b Fleming	0		
L-b 3	3	B 1, l-b 2, w 2	5

1/21 2/54 3/84 4/84 5/88   149   1/1 2/11 3/40 4/47   (4 wkts) 63
6/99 7/117 8/128 9/149

Bonus points – Kent 3.

Bowling: *First Innings*—Ealham 19–6–41–2; Saggers 17–4–35–2; Masters 13–5–33–2; Fleming 16–6–37–3; Patel 3–3–0–0. *Second Innings*—Saggers 9–3–26–2; Masters 5–0–20–1; Ealham 3.1–0–14–1.

Umpires: J. H. Hampshire and P. Willey.

At Manchester, June 29, 30, July 1. YORKSHIRE lost to LANCASHIRE by nine wickets.

YORKSHIRE v DURHAM

At Leeds, July 7, 8, 9, 10. Drawn. Yorkshire 7 pts, Durham 10 pts. Toss: Yorkshire.

After winning eight out of nine Championship encounters with Durham, Yorkshire looked to be heading for their first defeat when they followed on 185 behind. But centuries from Vaughan and Lehmann, the first conceded by Durham's bowlers in 2000, put them 201 in front as the game meandered to a close in bitter cold. Byas even suggested that, if the weather had spared the third morning, he might have set a target. It was Lehmann's ninth hundred for Yorkshire, but first at Headingley; he scored 136 in 146 balls, with 18 fours, using a runner from 49 because of a back strain. Vaughan's flawless 118 contained ten fours and took 306 deliveries. Solid half-centuries from Lewis, Katich and Speak had given Durham a respectable total, while there were another five wickets for Sidebottom; Hamilton pulled up with a side strain. Yorkshire batted lamentably in reply, against a sharp pace attack spearheaded by Brown. Michael Gough's first Championship outing of the year ended abruptly when he was admitted to an isolation ward for tests on a chest infection, which it was thought might date from England A's tour of Bangladesh.

Close of play: First day, Durham 253-8 (Speak 37*, Harmison 7*); Second day, Yorkshire 9-0 (Byas 5*, Vaughan 3*); Third day, Yorkshire 149-1 (Vaughan 94*, Blakey 12*).

Durham

J. J. B. Lewis c Middlebrook b Vaughan .	66	M. M. Betts c Blakey b Silverwood	5
M. A. Gough b Sidebottom	24	N. Killeen lbw b Silverwood	2
S. M. Katich c Middlebrook		S. J. Harmison b Sidebottom	10
b Silverwood .	55	S. J. E. Brown c Sidebottom b Vaughan .	19
P. D. Collingwood c Byas b Sidebottom .	23	B 3, l-b 15, w 6, n-b 19	43
*N. J. Speak not out	61		
S. M. Ali lbw b Sidebottom	0	1/60 2/167 3/179 4/214 5/214	314
†M. P. Speight c Blakey b Sidebottom . .	6	6/226 7/237 8/241 9/284	

Bonus points – Durham 3, Yorkshire 3.

Bowling: Silverwood 33–6–97–3; Hoggard 31–12–68–0; Hamilton 4.5–0–14–0; Sidebottom 33–12–66–5; Byas 0.1–0–0–0; Middlebrook 8–3–13–0; Vaughan 12.5–5–33–2; Lehmann 3–0–5–0.

Yorkshire

*D. Byas c Collingwood b Harmison	6	– c and b Betts	18
M. P. Vaughan lbw b Collingwood	34	– b Killeen	118
†R. J. Blakey c Katich b Harmison	3	– c Speight b Betts	15
D. S. Lehmann c sub b Betts	28	– c Ali b Killeen	136
A. McGrath not out	29		
M. J. Wood c Katich b Brown	1	– (5) not out	48
G. M. Hamilton c Collingwood b Brown	0	– (6) not out	17
J. D. Middlebrook c Collingwood b Killeen	9		
C. E. W. Silverwood c Speak b Betts	6		
R. J. Sidebottom c Katich b Brown	4		
M. J. Hoggard b Brown	0		
L-b 2, w 3, n-b 4	9	B 13, l-b 13, w 4, n-b 4 . . .	34
1/13 2/17 3/63 4/84 5/85	129	1/67 2/157 (4 wkts dec.)	386
6/85 7/111 8/118 9/127		3/259 4/341	

Bonus points – Durham 3.

Bowling: *First Innings*—Brown 15.4–5–33–4; Harmison 14–4–21–2; Killeen 14–5–36–1; Betts 12–2–32–2; Collingwood 5–3–5–1. *Second Innings*—Brown 27–6–80–0; Harmison 23–5–50–0; Killeen 37–14–70–2; Betts 25–3–71–2; Collingwood 25–11–58–0; Katich 8–0–22–0; Ali 3–0–9–0.

Umpires: M. J. Kitchen and R. Palmer.

At The Oval, July 12, 13, 14, 15. YORKSHIRE lost to SURREY by 203 runs.

YORKSHIRE v SOMERSET

At Scarborough, July 19, 20, 21. Yorkshire won by an innings and six runs. Yorkshire 20 pts, Somerset 3 pts. Toss: Yorkshire.

Yorkshire capped Hoggard on the first day, and he responded with career-best match figures of eight for 97. Sidebottom, who should have shared in the ceremony, was less lucky; he tore a hip muscle and had to be stretchered off. Even without him, Somerset were dismissed in 61 overs on a green but true pitch. Their own weakened pace attack could not prevent Yorkshire collecting maximum batting points with one ball to spare. Silverwood thrashed three sixes and five fours as the last two wickets added 52 in seven overs – Sidebottom batted with a runner. Hoggard then removed Cox cheaply for the second time, and later sent back Bowler and Burns within four balls. A large holiday crowd, which had basked in the sunshine for three days, enjoyed a brief fling from last man Jones, who blasted a Championship-best 56 from 50 balls. They still had plenty of time to make it back to their digs for high tea when Widdup claimed his maiden first-class wicket to complete Yorkshire's fifth win.

Close of play: First day, Yorkshire 144-3 (Lehmann 21*, Byas 10*); Second day, Somerset 12-2 (Holloway 1*).

Somerset

M. N. Lathwell b Silverwood	1	– (2) lbw b Lehmann	4
*J. Cox c Blakey b Hoggard	10	– (1) lbw b Hoggard	7
P. C. L. Holloway lbw b Fellows	27	– b Hoggard	1
P. D. Bowler c Blakey b Hutchison	15	– c Fellows b Hoggard	15
K. A. Parsons c Fellows b Silverwood	20	– lbw b Hutchison	38
M. Burns c Blakey b Hoggard	14	– c Widdup b Hoggard	0
†R. J. Turner b Lehmann	38	– c McGrath b Hoggard	20
I. D. Blackwell c Blakey b Hoggard	16	– c McGrath b Silverwood	24
G. D. Rose c Fellows b Hutchison	2	– lbw b Widdup	20
P. D. Trego not out	27	– b Hutchison	0
P. S. Jones b Lehmann	0	– not out	56
L-b 5, n-b 7	12	B 4, l-b 9, w 6, n-b 8	27
	182		**212**

1/14 2/14 3/57 4/57 5/89
6/99 7/116 8/138 9/182

1/8 2/12 3/12 4/68 5/68
6/74 7/121 8/138 9/139

Bonus points – Yorkshire 3.

Bowling: *First Innings*—Silverwood 14–5–30–2; Hoggard 18–7–47–3; Sidebottom 3.1–1–12–0; Hutchison 12.5–4–44–2; Fellows 9–2–35–1; Lehmann 4–1–9–2. *Second Innings*—Hoggard 21–7–50–5; Silverwood 20–9–65–1; Hutchison 16–4–42–2; Lehmann 9–3–17–1; Fellows 2–1–3–0; Widdup 2.3–0–22–1.

Yorkshire

S. Widdup c Blackwell b Trego	44	P. M. Hutchison lbw b Burns 0
M. P. Vaughan c Parsons b Rose	30	M. J. Hoggard b Trego 7
A. McGrath c Parsons b Trego	27	R. J. Sidebottom not out 4
D. S. Lehmann c Cox b Blackwell	77	
*D. Byas lbw b Jones	84	L-b 13, w 8, n-b 12 33
†R. J. Blakey b Burns	24	
G. M. Fellows lbw b Rose	22	1/49 2/99 3/114 4/244 5/296 400
C. E. W. Silverwood b Trego	48	6/321 7/342 8/348 9/371

Bonus points – Yorkshire 5, Somerset 3 (Score at 130 overs: 400-9).

Bowling: Rose 27–3–90–2; Jones 24–5–67–1; Burns 20–5–75–2; Trego 26.1–6–84–4; Parsons 18–5–42–0; Blackwell 15–7–29–1.

Umpires: M. R. Benson and T. E. Jesty.

At Leeds, July 24, 25. YORKSHIRE lost to WEST INDIANS by ten wickets (See West Indian tour section).

YORKSHIRE v LANCASHIRE

At Leeds, July 28, 29, 30, 31. Drawn. Yorkshire 11 pts, Lancashire 9 pts. Toss: Yorkshire.

Rain, which had already cut into the first two days, wiped out the last one when Yorkshire held a slight advantage: Lancashire were 18 runs on with eight second-innings wickets in hand. Two extra batting points meant that Yorkshire supplanted them in second place in the table; a win for either side would have put them above Surrey. A dark pitch appeared damp at the start, but ECB officer A. C. Smith was satisfied with the way it played. Lancashire faltered after a bright opening and had to be rescued from 128 for six by Hegg's fine assault, including nine fours. Yorkshire took a lead of 109 through eighties from the fluent Lehmann and the more restrained Byas. Their century stand was interrupted when a torrential downpour flooded the ground on the second afternoon, but next day Fellows, with a Championship-best 46, and Silverwood helped to gain Yorkshire four batting points. Lancashire quickly set about clearing the arrears with some positive strokeplay, though 19-year-old Elstub added another notable scalp, Atherton, to his first-innings victims, Fairbrother and Flintoff.

Close of play: First day, Yorkshire 4-0 (Widdup 4*, Vaughan 0*); Second day, Yorkshire 203-4 (Lehmann 83*, Byas 31*); Third day, Lancashire 127-2 (Crawley 46*, Fairbrother 26*).

Lancashire

M. A. Atherton c Blakey b Hoggard	21	– c Blakey b Elstub	17
*J. P. Crawley c Byas b White	23	– not out	46
A. Flintoff lbw b Elstub	28	– c Byas b Silverwood	25
S. C. Ganguly c Blakey b Hoggard	28		
N. H. Fairbrother b Elstub	5	– (4) not out	26
G. D. Lloyd c McGrath b Silverwood	12		
†W. K. Hegg c Blakey b Hoggard	75		
G. Chapple c Byas b Vaughan	19		
R. J. Green not out	29		
G. Keedy b Hoggard	7		
M. P. Smethurst b White	0		
L-b 8, n-b 12	20	B 5, l-b 2, n-b 6	13

1/46 2/78 3/84 4/89 5/122   267   1/31 2/74   (2 wkts) 127
6/128 7/216 8/248 9/266

Bonus points – Lancashire 2, Yorkshire 3.

Bowling: *First Innings*—Silverwood 22–3–49–1; Hoggard 23–4–70–4; White 20–4–59–2; Elstub 13–2–40–2; Fellows 6–1–24–0; Vaughan 8–2–17–1. *Second Innings*—Silverwood 12–2–34–1; Hoggard 13–3–32–0; Elstub 7–2–18–1; White 7–1–26–0; Vaughan 3–1–10–0.

Yorkshire

S. Widdup c Hegg b Chapple	16	C. E. W. Silverwood c Fairbrother	
M. P. Vaughan c and b Smethurst	31	b Keedy	34
A. McGrath c Flintoff b Smethurst	17	M. J. Hoggard c Keedy b Flintoff	14
D. S. Lehmann lbw b Smethurst	83	C. J. Elstub not out	4
C. White lbw b Green	10	B 1, l-b 10, w 10, n-b 19	40
*D. Byas c Hegg b Fairbrother	81		
†R. J. Blakey lbw b Chapple	0	1/20 2/75 3/94 4/108 5/208	376
G. M. Fellows c Atherton b Chapple	46	6/209 7/291 8/337 9/367	

Bonus points – Yorkshire 4, Lancashire 3.

Bowling: Chapple 30–6–80–3; Smethurst 31–5–101–3; Ganguly 12.4–2–33–0; Green 18–4–68–1; Keedy 27–4–73–1; Fairbrother 2.2–0–5–1; Flintoff 3.5–2–5–1.

Umpires: A. A. Jones and N. A. Mallender.

At Taunton, August 2, 3, 4, 5. YORKSHIRE drew with SOMERSET.

At Leicester, August 16, 17, 18, 19. YORKSHIRE drew with LEICESTERSHIRE.

YORKSHIRE v SURREY

At Scarborough, August 30, 31, September 1, 2. Drawn. Yorkshire 7 pts, Surrey 11 pts. Toss: Yorkshire. First-class debut: G. A. Lambert.

Rivalry between these old opponents bubbled over into acrimony when the pitches panel docked Yorkshire eight points for a wicket considered too grassy, causing undue movement and uneven bounce. Rightly or wrongly, the home side felt Surrey knew in advance that pitch liaison officer Mike Denness would attend and were only too gleeful at the forfeiture. With leaders Surrey starting 18 points ahead, and two rounds after this, it was a severe blow to Yorkshire's challenge. There was no doubting the pitch was green; the panel concluded that it was dry, but that excessive grass had attracted moisture. Yet in spite of being classed "poor", it yielded 356 runs after Surrey were put in, thanks to the tail who, marshalled by Salisbury, exploited some poorly directed bowling. Yorkshire lost Widdup and McGrath to the first two balls of their innings, from Tudor, and next over Ben Hollioake yorked Craven. Lehmann edged a no-ball to Batty, then thrashed 66 off 74 balls, but no one else survived long. Yorkshire might have thought the pitch penalty harsh, but they were thoroughly outplayed; Surrey could have won had they enforced the follow-on. In the event, bad light halted the second day, only 11 overs were possible on the third, and the final day began at 4 p.m. The delays were prolonged by unsatisfactory covering of the bowler's run-up at the Pavilion End, which created a muddy patch, frustrating a large crowd – over 10,000 watched during the first two days – and Surrey. They had only 32 overs to dismiss Yorkshire, and Widdup and Craven held out comfortably. The players made some attempt to repair bridges by shaking hands at the end.

Close of play: First day, Surrey 330-8 (Salisbury 47*, Tudor 23*); Second day, Surrey 53-2 (M. A. Butcher 30*, A. J. Hollioake 5*); Third day, Surrey 89-3 (M. A. Butcher 49*, Brown 4*).

Surrey

M. A. Butcher c Guy b Hamilton	8	– not out	49
I. J. Ward c Widdup b Hoggard	59	– c Guy b Silverwood	0
N. Shahid lbw b Fellows	29	– b Hamilton	13
*A. J. Hollioake c Guy b Hoggard	37	– c Craven b Silverwood	13
A. D. Brown c Guy b Lambert	2	– not out	4
G. P. Butcher c Lehmann b Hamilton	27		
B. C. Hollioake c Guy b Fellows	4		
†J. N. Batty c Hamilton b Lehmann	47		
I. D. K. Salisbury not out	57		
A. J. Tudor lbw b Hoggard	24		
Saqlain Mushtaq c Guy b Silverwood	12		
B 15, l-b 15, w 6, n-b 14	50	B 6, l-b 2, w 2	10

1/29 2/93 3/147 4/158 5/168   356   1/5 2/32 3/67   (3 wkts dec.) 89
6/185 7/197 8/275 9/333

Bonus points – Surrey 4, Yorkshire 3.

Bowling: *First Innings*—Silverwood 23.3–6–76–1; Hoggard 30–1–100–3; Hamilton 20–6–53–2; Lambert 14–2–36–1; Fellows 14–5–27–2; Lehmann 9–0–34–1. *Second Innings*—Silverwood 13–2–24–2; Hoggard 15–2–36–0; Hamilton 5–1–11–1; Lambert 4–0–10–0.

Yorkshire

S. Widdup lbw b Tudor	0	– not out	38
V. J. Craven b B. C. Hollioake	2	– not out	17
A. McGrath c Batty b Tudor	0		
D. S. Lehmann run out	66		
*D. Byas c Shahid b B. C. Hollioake	19		
G. M. Fellows c Batty b Tudor	16		
G. M. Hamilton b Saqlain Mushtaq	23		
†S. M. Guy lbw b Tudor	0		
C. E. W. Silverwood c and b B. C. Hollioake	3		
M. J. Hoggard not out	10		
G. A. Lambert c A. J. Hollioake b Saqlain Mushtaq	1		
L-b 3, w 2, n-b 13	18	L-b 7, n-b 6	13

1/0 2/0 3/4 4/73 5/112   158   (no wkt) 68
6/123 7/125 8/130 9/156

Bonus points – Surrey 3.

Bowling: *First Innings*—Tudor 17–1–75–4; B. C. Hollioake 19–1–67–3; G. P. Butcher 4–1–13–0; Saqlain Mushtaq 1.1–1–0–2. *Second Innings*—Tudor 6–1–13–0; B. C. Hollioake 4–0–15–0; Saqlain Mushtaq 8–1–18–0; Salisbury 6–2–13–0; Brown 1–0–2–0.

Umpires: B. Dudleston and J. H. Harris.

At Canterbury, September 7, 8, 9, 10. YORKSHIRE beat KENT by 32 runs.

At Southampton, September 13, 14, 15, 16. YORKSHIRE beat HAMPSHIRE by 72 runs.

NATWEST TROPHY, 2000

Ian Harvey

For 20 years the NatWest Trophy final, like the Last Night of the Proms, had signalled the dying fall of summer. Not any more. National Westminster Bank's decision to concentrate its corporate beneficence on English cricket's new midsummer one-day international tournament left the county game's oldest limited-overs competition in need of a new sponsor. And now that the final is played on August Bank Holiday weekend, rather than the first dewy Saturday of September, it is not quite the same harbinger of autumn.

By a cruel twist of fate, NatWest's farewell final, between holders Gloucestershire and Warwickshire, was more like the middle of winter. Saturday's play was washed out and Sunday's brought to a sodden, sudden end by heavy downpours, to the accompaniment of lightning. Not that the rain, any more than losing to neighbours Worcestershire in the third round, could prevent Gloucestershire from retaining the trophy by winning their fourth consecutive Lord's final – an unprecedented back-to-back Benson and Hedges Cup–NatWest Trophy double.

Ten days later, Gloucestershire's supremacy in the county one-day game was affirmed when they won the Norwich Union National League, becoming the first to win all three one-day titles in a season. It was a fairy-tale Indian summer for Gloucestershire's Kim Barnett, who, as well as having the distinction of being on winning sides in the first and last NatWest finals, had now received four successive winners' medals at Lord's since changing counties in 1999. The year before, he was with Derbyshire when they lost the NatWest final to Lancashire.

Gloucestershire's third-round defeat had been overturned on a technicality: Worcestershire's Kabir Ali was ineligible to play in the match because he had previously played for their Board XI after making first-team appearances earlier in the season. Under the regulations, this cup-tied him. Worcestershire had been sufficiently perplexed by the regulation's wording to ask the ECB for clarification before playing Ali; either they asked the wrong question or they received the wrong answer. But while the board decided Worcestershire had not deliberately infringed the rules, they did insist that the tie be replayed. This time Gloucestershire won, and next day they came from behind to pip Leicestershire in the fourth round. Doubly reprieved, there was no stopping Mark Alleyne's men after that; even the Duckworth/Lewis numbers came up in their favour when the rain stopped Warwickshire's rampant Allan Donald in his tracks at Lord's.

Unlike the previous year, when the Dutch knocked out Durham, there were no other upsets in the early rounds; indeed, Holland, who went on to win the European Championships, failed to get past Lincolnshire in the second round this time. In instances when a Minor County or Board XI did threaten a reverse, by restricting a first-class county to a low total, the full-time bowlers proved too accurate and experienced for the recreational cricketers.

Prize money

£53,000 for winners: GLOUCESTERSHIRE.
£27,000 for runners-up: WARWICKSHIRE.
£16,500 for each losing semi-finalist: HAMPSHIRE, LANCASHIRE.
£11,500 for each losing quarter-finalist: GLAMORGAN, MIDDLESEX, NORTHAMPTONSHIRE, SURREY.

Man of the Match award winners received £1,750 in the final, £550 in the semi-finals, £500 in the quarter-finals, £450 in the fourth round, £350 in the third round, £325 in the second round and £300 in the first round. The prize money was increased from £174,750 in the 1999 tournament to £182,150.

In the following scores, * by the name of a team indicates that they won the toss.

FIRST ROUND

At Boughton Hall, Chester, May 2. Lincolnshire won by virtue of losing fewer wickets. Cheshire* 204 (50 overs) (G. I. Foley 38, I. Cockbain 65, Extras 43; R. J. Chapman three for 34); Lincolnshire 204 for nine (50 overs) (S. G. Plumb 48; C. C. Finegan three for 31).
Man of the Match: R. J. Chapman.

At Truro, May 2. Norfolk won by four wickets. Cornwall 170 for six (50 overs) (S. M. Williams 32, S. C. Pope 56; S. C. Goldsmith three for 34); Norfolk* 171 for six (47.5 overs) (C. J. Rogers 83 not out; J. P. Kent three for 21).
Man of the Match: C. J. Rogers.

At Gateshead Fell, May 2. Durham Board XI won by three wickets. Leicestershire Board XI 192 for nine (50 overs) (A. S. Wright 112, Extras 30; S. Chapman three for 39); Durham Board XI* 195 for seven (49.5 overs) (S. Chapman 64, I. Pattison 48 not out, Extras 40; N. J. Pullen three for 25).
Man of the Match: A. S. Wright.

At Cheltenham, May 2. Gloucestershire Board XI won by eight wickets. Nottinghamshire Board XI 125 for nine (50 overs) (S. M. Brogan 33; A. N. Bressington three for 21); Gloucestershire Board XI* 126 for two (28.5 overs) (I. Mohammed 53, Extras 47).
Man of the Match: I. Mohammed.

At Cove, May 2. Huntingdonshire Board XI won by 28 runs. Huntingdonshire Board XI 148 for eight (50 overs) (Extras 43; C. J. Yates three for 17); Hampshire Board XI* 120 (46 overs) (R. L. A. Hunter 33; B. Young three for 22).
Man of the Match: B. Young.

At Colwall, May 2. Sussex Board XI won by six runs. Sussex Board XI 215 for seven (50 overs) (K. Ibrahim 63, H. F. G. Southwell 36, Extras 42); Herefordshire* 209 for nine (50 overs) (I. Dawood 39, C. W. Boroughs 34, Extras 38; D. A. Clapp three for 46).
Man of the Match: K. Ibrahim.

At Welwyn Garden City, May 2. Cambridgeshire won by four wickets. Hertfordshire 114 (47.1 overs) (K. Jahangir 30; D. G. Wilson three for 30, A. G. Tapp three for 17); Cambridgeshire* 115 for six (46 overs) (S. A. Kellett 42; J. M. Engelke three for eight).
Man of the Match: M. J. G. Mason.
In a match that included 36 maidens, Mason had figures of 10–8–5–1 while his Cambridgeshire new-ball partner, Ajaz Akhtar, conceded just one run in his 43 balls; for Hertfordshire, Engelke's complete figures were 10–8–8–3.

At Castle Avenue, Dublin, May 2. Shropshire won by five wickets. Ireland 140 (44.3 overs) (A. R. Dunlop 56; A. B. Byram three for 30, A. B. Byram four for 24); Shropshire* 141 for five (49 overs) (T. Parton 51 not out, Extras 31).
Man of the Match: A. B. Byram.

At Northampton, May 2. Northumberland won by six wickets. Northamptonshire Board XI* 173 for eight (50 overs) (R. E. Falkner 46, A. J. Swann 40; S. J. Foster three for 23, L. J. Crozier three for 30); Northumberland 175 for four (48.2 overs) (A. T. Heather 79, B. Parker 50).
Man of the Match: A. T. Heather.

At Walsall, May 2. Staffordshire won by seven wickets. Somerset Board XI 124 (45.4 overs) (D. Follett three for ten, I. D. Carr three for 34); Staffordshire* 127 for three (29 overs) (L. Potter 37, G. F. Archer 32 not out).
Man of the Match: L. Potter.
Potter had figures of 10–5–9–1.

At Mildenhall, May 2. Lancashire Board XI won by four wickets. Suffolk 145 (49.4 overs) (C. P. Seal 34, Extras 31; S. E. Dearden four for 31); Lancashire Board XI* 146 for six (38.2 overs) (Extras 32; I. D. Graham three for 25).
Man of the Match: S. E. Dearden.

At Pontarddulais, May 2. Wales won by 11 runs. Wales 212 for six (50 overs) (M. J. Newbold 35, P. V. Simmons 82, Extras 33; K. L. T. Arthurton three for 46); Buckinghamshire* 201 for nine (50 overs) (K. L. T. Arthurton 48, K. J. Locke 41).
Man of the Match: P. V. Simmons.

At South Wiltshire CC, May 2. Wiltshire won by seven wickets. Scotland 93 (29.5 overs) (K. J. Nash three for ten, R. J. Bates three for 16); Wiltshire* 94 for three (31.1 overs) (D. A. Winter 37 not out, J. L. Taylor 36 not out).
Man of the Match: J. L. Taylor.

At Kidderminster, May 2. Kent Board XI won by 50 runs. Kent Board XI 239 for nine (50 overs) (J. D. P. Bowden 98, Extras 30); Worcestershire Board XI* 189 (44.2 overs) (D. J. Pipe 56, G. R. Hill 40, C. W. Henderson 32; E. J. Stanford three for 38).
Man of the Match: J. D. P. Bowden.

SECOND ROUND

At March Town, May 16. Cumberland won by nine wickets. Cambridgeshire 123 (45.1 overs) (N. T. Gadsby 42; D. B. Pennett four for 20, M. A. Sharp three for eight); Cumberland* 126 for one (32.2 overs) (S. T. Knox 40 not out, A. A. Metcalfe 51 not out).
Man of the Match: M. A. Sharp.
Cambridgeshire were one for three, then nine for four. Sharp also held three catches.

At Heanor Town, May 16. Derbyshire Board XI won by 50 runs. Derbyshire Board XI 222 for eight (50 overs) (A. J. Marsh 53, I. J. Darlington 32; A. N. Edwards three for 38); Gloucestershire Board XI* 172 (43.3 overs) (C. R. J. Budd 52, A. N. Bressington 44; I. J. Darlington three for 19).
Man of the Match: A. J. Marsh.

At Torquay, May 16. Devon won by 192 runs. Devon 238 (49.5 overs) (R. I. Dawson 61, A. J. Pugh 41, Extras 38; L. Potter four for nine); Staffordshire* 46 (20.5 overs) (M. C. Theedom five for 18).
Man of the Match: M. C. Theedom.
Staffordshire slumped to 13 for six. At one stage, Theedom had taken five for two from 21 balls. Potter's full figures were 10–5–9–4.

At Bournemouth, May 16. Dorset won by 110 runs. Dorset* 181 for eight (50 overs) (A. J. Sexton 34, G. D. Reynolds 32); Norfolk 71 (33.2 overs) (V. J. Pike five for ten).
Man of the Match: V. J. Pike.
Seven of Pike's ten overs were maidens. Norfolk collapsed from 61 for four.

At Hartlepool, May 16. Durham Board XI won by five wickets. Denmark 218 (50 overs) (A. Ahmed 94, Extras 47; S. Ball three for 45); Durham Board XI* 223 for five (38.3 overs) (S. D. Birbeck 32, S. Chapman 60, M. J. North 69 not out, Extras 39).

Man of the Match: M. J. North.

North, a professional from Western Australia playing for Gateshead Fell in the North-East Premier League, faced 51 balls.

At Chelmsford, May 16. Essex Board XI won by 15 runs. Essex Board XI* 266 (50 overs) (A. J. E. Hibbert 59, G. W. Ecclestone 35, G. R. Napier 79, Extras 33; S. E. Dearden three for 50); Lancashire Board XI 251 for nine (50 overs) (N. D. R. Bannister 62, S. E. Dearden 44, G. A. Knowles 33, S. C. Catterall 37 not out).

Man of the Match: G. R. Napier.

At Godmanchester, May 16. Yorkshire Board XI won by five wickets. Huntingdonshire Board XI* 204 for eight (50 overs) (V. P. Winn 50, N. Pishon 38); Yorkshire Board XI 207 for five (45 overs) (A. E. McKenna 43, M. J. Doidge 54 not out, A. J. Walker 30 not out).

Man of the Match: M. J. Doidge.

At Grantham, May 16. Lincolnshire won by 95 runs. Lincolnshire* 210 for eight (50 overs) (S. N. Warman 33, P. C. Trend 52, Extras 35; R. P. Lefebvre four for 37); Holland 115 (37.2 overs) (K. J. J. van Noortwijk 33; S. G. Plumb four for 16).

Man of the Match: P. C. Trend.

At Southgate, May 16. Middlesex Board XI won by three runs. Middlesex Board XI* 203 for eight (50 overs) (R. K. Rao 49, S. K. Ranasinghe 34, A. G. J. Fraser 38; R. J. Sillence three for 47, J. P. Searle three for 40); Wiltshire 200 for nine (50 overs) (R. J. Rowe 47, J. L. Taylor 49; R. O. Jones three for 24).

Man of the Match: A. G. J. Fraser.

Alastair Fraser, brother of England seam bowler Angus, also took two for 36.

At Jesmond, May 16. Northumberland won by seven wickets. Bedfordshire* 164 (48 overs) (J. R. Page 61, Extras 33; S. J. Foster three for 21); Northumberland 167 for three (33.2 overs) (W. Falla 64, A. T. Heather 36, S. J. Foster 38 not out).

Man of the Match: S. J. Foster.

At Shifnal, May 16. Shropshire won by six wickets. Surrey Board XI 233 for nine (50 overs) (T. P. Hodgson 33, Z. de Bruyn 43, M. R. Bainbridge 38; K. P. Evans three for 37); Shropshire* 239 for four (49.2 overs) (J. B. R. Jones 76, J. V. Anders 51, Asif Din 32 not out, Extras 41).

Man of the Match: J. B. R. Jones.

At Hastings, May 16. Berkshire won by five wickets. Sussex Board XI 206 (49.4 overs) (G. R. A. Campbell 59, K. Ibrahim 57); Berkshire* 207 for five (47.2 overs) (L. H. Nurse 81, H. M. Hall 32, S. S. Patel 53 not out).

Man of the Match: L. H. Nurse.

At the age of 47, John Emburey, the former Middlesex and England off-spinner, came out of retirement and took two for 45 for Berkshire. Nurse is great-nephew of West Indies Test batsman Seymour Nurse.

At Cardiff, May 16. Wales won by eight wickets. Oxfordshire* 120 (49.1 overs); Wales 122 for two (35.3 overs) (A. J. Jones 43 not out, M. J. Newbold 34).

Man of the Match: A. J. Jones.

For Wales, Steve Barwick had figures of 9.1–5–7–2.

At Stratford-upon-Avon, May 16. Kent Board XI won by 45 runs. Kent Board XI* 208 for eight (50 overs) (H. Iqbal 31, S. L. Williams 32, Extras 40; J. O. Troughton three for 34); Warwickshire Board XI 163 (47.3 overs) (D. A. T. Dalton 30; A. P. Walton three for 31, E. J. Stanford three for 29).

Man of the Match: S. L. Williams.

Warwickshire Board XI conceded 30 wides and four no-balls.

THIRD ROUND

BERKSHIRE v DURHAM

At Finchampstead, June 21. Durham won by 43 runs. Toss: Berkshire.

Emburey's four wickets for 13 tell their own story. Durham's batsmen had no answer to the 47-year-old former England off-spinner, now Berkshire's coach, and few answers in general on a slow pitch. They hit only six fours, with five coming from the Australian, Katich. Ali batted almost an hour and a quarter for five; Speak spent 30 overs making 33 not out. But with an upset on the cards, Berkshire found Durham's bowlers just as troublesome and folded inside 29 overs.

Man of the Match: J. E. Emburey.

Durham

P. D. Collingwood c Lane b Barrow	3		J. Wood b Fusedale	4	
S. M. Ali c and b Fusedale	5		N. C. Phillips b Emburey	5	
S. M. Katich b Emburey	40		N. Killeen b Emburey	2	
*N. J. Speak not out	33		B 4, l-b 5, w 23, n-b 2	34	
J. J. B. Lewis c Loveday b Emburey	10				
†M. P. Speight c Lane b Myles	1		1/6 2/60 3/70	(49.4 overs) 140	
M. M. Betts c Willoughby b Myles	2		4/84 5/88 6/95		
I. D. Hunter run out	1		7/102 8/125 9/136		

Bowling: Willoughby 10–2–27–0; Barrow 6–1–19–1; Fusedale 10–2–19–2; Myles 10–1–43–2; Emburey 9.4–3–13–4; Patel 4–0–10–0.

Berkshire

*G. E. Loveday lbw b Killeen	1		N. A. Fusedale lbw b Collingwood	1	
L. H. Nurse b Wood	26		J. K. Barrow b Killeen	16	
S. D. Myles lbw b Betts	5		C. M. Willoughby c Speak b Phillips	0	
J. R. Wood lbw b Betts	1		L-b 2, w 6, n-b 12	20	
H. M. Hall lbw b Betts	1				
S. S. Patel b Betts	0		1/1 2/19 3/31	(28.5 overs) 97	
†M. G. Lane not out	24		4/35 5/38 6/55		
J. E. Emburey b Collingwood	2		7/70 8/73 9/94		

Bowling: Betts 8–0–34–4; Killeen 8–1–15–2; Hunter 4–0–18–0; Wood 5–2–15–1; Collingwood 2–0–7–2; Phillips 1.5–0–6–1.

Umpires: A. R. Bundy and K. E. Palmer.

CUMBERLAND v KENT

At Carlisle, June 21. Kent won by six wickets. Toss: Kent.

Batting first was never easy after a rain-delayed start. Adams, left-arm fast and in his first season with Kent, made it look impossible as he skimmed the top off Cumberland's batting, taking a wicket with his first ball. John Lewis's eight fours in his 65 gave the local crowd something to cheer, until Adams docked the tail to finish with six for 24. Kent's greatest concern was the threat of rain and, driven by Dravid's half-century, they narrowly beat it.

Man of the Match: K. Adams.

Cumberland

S. T. Knox lbw b Adams	1	D. B. Pennett c Wells b Adams	2
D. J. Pearson c Marsh b Ealham	8	M. A. Sharp not out	4
A. A. Metcalfe b Adams	6	D. M. Wheatman b Adams	1
J. D. Glendenen b Adams	0	L-b 2, w 11, n-b 2	15
S. J. O'Shaughnessy st Nixon b Patel	14		
*†S. M. Dutton lbw b Adams	1	1/1 2/16 3/16	(48.1 overs) 140
J. M. Lewis run out	65	4/16 5/22 6/75	
J. M. Fielding st Nixon b Patel	23	7/127 8/129 9/132	

Bowling: Ealham 10–2–16–1; Adams 9.1–0–24–6; Fleming 9–2–26–0; Masters 10–0–36–0; Patel 10–1–36–2.

Kent

D. P. Fulton lbw b Sharp	9	M. A. Ealham not out	8
S. A. Marsh lbw b Sharp	23	B 5, w 6, n-b 14	25
R. Dravid b Fielding	54		
A. P. Wells b Fielding	7	1/24 2/111	(4 wkts, 39 overs) 141
M. J. Walker not out	15	3/111 4/125	

†P. A. Nixon, *M. V. Fleming, M. M. Patel, D. D. Masters and K. Adams did not bat.

Bowling: Pennett 10–3–38–0; Sharp 10–2–23–2; Lewis 2–0–20–0; Wheatman 8–2–29–0; Fielding 9–3–26–2.

Umpires: J. W. Holder and N. A. Mallender.

DERBYSHIRE BOARD XI v DERBYSHIRE

At Derby, June 21. Derbyshire won by 223 runs. Toss: Derbyshire.

This local derby was not so much a mismatch as a rout. Di Venuto's unbeaten 173, off 152 balls with 21 fours, was a personal and county one-day best; Cork's highest one-day score, 93 off 77 balls, featured two sixes and eight fours as he and Di Venuto added 177 in 25 overs. The Board XI were 20 for four in the tenth over, but Ian Darlington, a county Second Eleven player, marshalled the lower order so well that Derbyshire had to field the full 50 overs.

Man of the Match: M. J. Di Venuto.

Derbyshire

L. D. Sutton c Smit b Gofton	45	
M. J. Di Venuto not out	173	
*D. G. Cork c Marples b Gofton	93	
R. J. Bailey not out	20	
B 2, l-b 2, w 13, n-b 8	25	

1/105 2/282   (2 wkts, 50 overs) 356

M. P. Dowman, S. D. Stubbings, †K. M. Krikken, S. J. Lacey, T. M. Smith, T. A. Munton and K. J. Dean did not bat.

Bowling: Darlington 10–0–76–0; Dodds 10–2–76–0; Gofton 10–0–76–2; Hall 10–0–66–0; Parkin 10–0–58–0.

Derbyshire Board XI

A. J. Marsh b Dean	5	I. C. Parkin c Cork b Smith	8
J. R. Benstead lbw b Dean	0	†K. J. Hollis not out	7
D. Smit lbw b Munton	4	D. H. Dodds not out	0
P. G. T. Davies lbw b Munton	0	L-b 15, w 8, n-b 2	25
A. F. Gofton run out	17		
I. J. Darlington c Dowman b Dean	58	1/5 2/10 3/12 (9 wkts, 50 overs) 133	
*C. Marples run out	2	4/20 5/58 6/69	
M. Hall b Cork	7	7/91 8/125 9/126	

Bowling: Munton 5–3–4–2; Dean 10–3–14–3; Smith 10–1–25–1; Dowman 10–0–22–0; Lacey 10–3–25–0; Cork 5–0–28–1.

Umpires: G. I. Burgess and R. Palmer.

DEVON v SURREY

At Exmouth, June 21. Surrey won by eight wickets. Toss: Surrey.

Bicknell's accuracy and late swing never allowed Devon to settle. Bowling his ten overs off the reel, he removed the first three batsmen and conceded only 19 runs. Matt Wood and David Lye added 100 in more or less even time, with Lye going to a 59-ball half-century which included a six over mid-wicket off Saqlain Mushtaq. Stewart anchored Surrey's reply; Brown, before the break for rain at 30 overs, and afterwards Thorpe outscored him in untroubled partnerships.

Man of the Match: D. F. Lye.

Devon

G. T. J. Townsend c Stewart b Bicknell	17	A. J. Procter not out	21
R. I. Dawson b Bicknell	0	†A. K. Hele not out	10
*N. A. Folland c Brown b Bicknell	18	B 1, l-b 8, w 8	17
M. J. Wood b Saqlain Mushtaq	43		
D. F. Lye c Bicknell b Saqlain Mushtaq	56	1/3 2/37 3/44 (6 wkts, 50 overs) 194	
I. Gompertz c Brown b Hollioake	12	4/144 5/150 6/174	

M. C. Theedom, R. Horrell and P. M. Warren did not bat.

Bowling: Bicknell 10–3–19–3; Greenidge 10–0–54–0; Ratcliffe 8–1–31–0; Saqlain Mushtaq 10–0–36–2; Salisbury 10–0–30–0; Hollioake 2–0–15–1.

Surrey

M. A. Butcher c Hele b Warren	5		
A. D. Brown b Horrell	59		
†A. J. Stewart not out	70		
G. P. Thorpe not out	46		
B 4, l-b 3, w 5, n-b 6	18		

1/13 2/103   (2 wkts, 44 overs) 198

*A. J. Hollioake, I. J. Ward, J. D. Ratcliffe, M. P. Bicknell, I. D. K. Salisbury, Saqlain Mushtaq and C. G. Greenidge did not bat.

Bowling: Theedom 10–0–56–0; Warren 8–1–39–1; Gompertz 7–0–34–0; Procter 10–2–29–0; Horrell 9–2–33–1.

Umpires: D. L. Burden and M. J. Kitchen.

DORSET v GLAMORGAN

At Bournemouth, June 21. Glamorgan won by 139 runs. Toss: Dorset.

Newell and Elliott put Glamorgan on course to their fourth-highest one-day total with 246, a county first-wicket record in one-day competitions: the previous best was 192 unbroken by Steve James and Hugh Morris against the same opponents in 1995. Newell, out in the 40th over, faced 123 balls for his 129, hitting three sixes and 15 fours. His first six crashed through the press-box roof; his third smashed the rear window of team-mate Croft's car. Elliott's run-a-ball 156 contained four sixes and 17 fours. Glamorgan's pace men quickly scythed away Dorset's top-order batting, leaving Vyv Pike, better known in Minor County circles as a record-breaking leg-spinner, to amuse the crowd with two successive leg-side sixes off the hapless Croft. Maynard handed the captaincy to Watkin for the day.

Man of the Match: M. T. G. Elliott.

Glamorgan

K. Newell st Miller b Pike	129		A. Dale not out		4
M. T. G. Elliott c Reynolds b Forshaw	156		B 2, l-b 3, w 8		13
A. G. Wharf lbw b Pike	6				—
S. D. Thomas c Pike b Sharpe	11		1/246 2/270	(4 wkts, 50 overs)	333
S. P. James not out	14		3/301 4/318		

M. P. Maynard, †A. D. Shaw, R. D. B. Croft, *S. L. Watkin and O. T. Parkin did not bat.

Bowling: Forshaw 10–0–59–1; Sharpe 10–0–56–1; Hicks 10–0–61–0; Pike 10–0–82–2; Treagus 10–0–70–0.

Dorset

M. Swarbrick c Shaw b Thomas	5		V. J. Pike b Parkin		45
G. R. Treagus lbw b Thomas	8		T. J. Sharpe b Parkin		0
A. J. Sexton lbw b Parkin	1		S. M. Forshaw not out		7
P. J. Deakin c James b Watkin	9		B 5, l-b 8, w 10, n-b 2		25
*S. W. D. Rintoul lbw b Thomas	9				—
G. D. Reynolds b Thomas	4		1/5 2/14 3/14	(48.5 overs)	194
†M. G. Miller c Shaw b Watkin	81		4/26 5/33 6/68		
T. C. Hicks b Wharf	0		7/69 8/151 9/159		

Bowling: Parkin 10·2–37–3; Thomas 8–1–27–4; Watkin 7.5–2–16–2; Wharf 10–2–17–1; Dale 4–0–16–0; Croft 6–1–52–0; Newell 3–0–16–0.

Umpires: P. Adams and T. E. Jesty.

DURHAM BOARD XI v NORTHAMPTONSHIRE

At Chester-le-Street, June 21. Northamptonshire won by eight wickets. Toss: Northamptonshire.

Two hours' batting was enough for Northamptonshire and their captain, Hayden, to reach their target, although Sales gave the impression they would have got there sooner had he come to the wicket earlier. It was never so straightforward for the Board XI. Quentin Hughes, the 1999 Cambridge captain, played with some fluency, making 37 from 57 balls, but Stephen Ball, taking an hour and a half for 13, plainly emphasised the gulf in standards.

Man of the Match: M. L. Hayden.

Durham Board XI

S. D. Birbeck c Ripley b Cousins	8		B. C. Usher c Swann b Brown		5
S. Ball c Hayden b Swann	13		G. Smith not out		9
S. Chapman c Ripley b Brown	5		A. M. Davies b Cousins		0
M. J. North c Penberthy b Malcolm	37		B 1, l-b 11, w 8, n-b 2		22
I. Pattison run out	8				—
Q. J. Hughes lbw b Cousins	37		1/13 2/27 3/60	(49.5 overs)	167
*G. K. Brown c Innes b Swann	15		4/82 5/90 6/113		
†P. Mustard b Brown	8		7/137 8/151 9/167		

Bowling: Malcolm 10–1–25–1; Cousins 9.5–1–39–3; Brown 10–1–35–3; Penberthy 10–1–31–0; Swann 10–1–25–2.

Northamptonshire

*M. L. Hayden not out	77
M. B. Loye lbw b Smith	14
J. W. Cook b Usher	37
D. J. Sales not out	19
L-b 6, w 8, n-b 8	22

1/35 2/142   (2 wkts, 32.2 overs) 169

A. L. Penberthy, G. P. Swann, †D. Ripley, K. J. Innes, D. M. Cousins, J. F. Brown and D. E. Malcolm did not bat.

Bowling: Smith 8–3–30–1; Davies 7–1–25–0; North 8–0–42–0; Ball 2–0–22–0; Hughes 4–0–22–0; Usher 2.2–0–14–1; Chapman 1–0–8–0.

Umpires: B. Leadbeater and R. A. White.

ESSEX BOARD XI v WARWICKSHIRE

At Billericay, June 21. Warwickshire won by 11 runs. Toss: Essex Board XI.

Warwickshire never found the going simple against steady early bowling and might have been embarrassed had Penney, 45 not out off 52 balls, not engineered 112 from the later order. After a good start, the Board XI openers found themselves up against Donald, playing his first game since breaking his ribs at Southampton seven weeks earlier. So, when 34 were required from the last two overs, did Andrew MacKinlay (who had hit Welch for six) and Simon Fitzgerald. Ten off Donald and 12 off Brown was good going but not enough, leaving MacKinlay 33 not out from 27 balls.

Man of the Match: T. L. Penney.

Warwickshire

N. V. Knight c Saeed b Moore	1	M. J. Powell c Ecclestone b MacKinlay .	10
G. Welch c Ecclestone b Churchill	41	D. R. Brown c Ecclestone b Moore	7
*N. M. K. Smith c Richards b Saeed . . .	5	L-b 8, w 24	32
D. P. Ostler c Saeed b Jones.	16		
D. L. Hemp c Fitzgerald b Churchill . . .	35	1/11 2/17 3/62 (8 wkts, 50 overs) 214
T. L. Penney not out.	45	4/102 5/132 6/172	
A. F. Giles run out	22	7/199 8/214	

†K. J. Piper and A. A. Donald did not bat.

Bowling: MacKinlay 9–3–31–1; Moore 10–3–25–2; Saeed 10–1–37–1; Jones 10–0–52–1; Ecclestone 3–0–29–0; Churchill 8–0–32–2.

Essex Board XI

A. J. E. Hibbert c Penney b Donald. . . .	29	†S. D. Fitzgerald c Hemp b Brown	10
N. Carlier run out.	56	S. Moore not out	9
*G. W. Ecclestone c Powell b Smith . . .	9		
A. C. Richards run out	16	B 1, l-b 8, w 1, n-b 6	16
A. J. Churchill st Piper b Giles.	10		
R. A. Smith b Giles	6	1/50 2/78 3/123 (8 wkts, 50 overs) 203
A. I. MacKinlay not out	33	4/127 5/140 6/145	
T. D. Jones b Donald	9	7/172 8/191	

A. Saeed did not bat.

Bowling: Brown 10–1–40–1; Welch 10–0–50–0; Donald 10–1–37–2; Giles 10–0–34–2; Smith 10–0–33–1.

Umpires: C. S. Kelly and J. W. Lloyds.

KENT BOARD XI v HAMPSHIRE

At Canterbury, June 21. Hampshire won by eight wickets. Toss: Hampshire.

The Sevenoaks Vine pair, John Bowden and Shami Iqbal, son of former Kent and Pakistan captain Asif Iqbal, batted soundly for an hour and a half, putting on 76 for the first wicket. But the return of Mascarenhas, with a three-wicket burst, exposed the remaining batsmen to the contrasting spin of Udal and Warne. Only Simon Williams survived, 45 not out from 54 balls. Mascarenhas was soon back in action, seeing Hampshire to an easy win with his run-a-ball 67.

Man of the Match: A. D. Mascarenhas.

Kent Board XI

J. D. P. Bowden c Stephenson			D. J. Trigger c Stephenson b Warne	0
b Mascarenhas	30		A. Tutt st Aymes b Warne	4
H. Iqbal c Smith b Mascarenhas	33		K. D. Masters st Aymes b Warne	0
M. R. Featherstone lbw b Mascarenhas	0			
M. S. Alexander c Stephenson b Udal	2		L-b 7, w 15	22
J. C. Tredwell run out	0			
†S. L. Williams not out	45		1/76 2/76 3/82	(50 overs) 149
A. P. Walton lbw b Warne	0		4/82 5/91 6/94	
*E. J. Stanford b Udal	13		7/129 8/143 9/149	

Bowling: Francis 6–1–10–0; Mascarenhas 10–2–25–3; Mullally 10–2–37–0; Stephenson 4–1–12–0; Udal 10–2–24–2; Warne 10–0–34–4.

Hampshire

G. W. White c Williams b Masters	15
J. P. Stephenson b Stanford	40
A. D. Mascarenhas not out	67
*R. A. Smith not out	20
L-b 2, w 4, n-b 2	8

1/20 2/111   (2 wkts, 36.5 overs) 150

W. S. Kendall, J. S. Laney, S. K. Warne, S. D. Udal, †A. N. Aymes, A. D. Mullally and S. R. G. Francis did not bat.

Bowling: Masters 8–1–28–1; Tutt 6–3–6–0; Trigger 10–3–27–0; Walton 1.5–0–23–0; Tredwell 4–0–27–0; Stanford 7–0–37–1.

Umpires: C. T. Puckett and G. Sharp.

LINCOLNSHIRE v LANCASHIRE

At Cleethorpes, June 21. Lancashire won by ten wickets. Toss: Lancashire.

While some Lancashire bowlers looked to be going through the motions, Ganguly was exempt from criticism – with bat or ball. He wrapped up Lincolnshire's batting, then took their bowling apart with his first county hundred. It, and Lancashire's victory, came in an over of medium-pace from David Pipes costing 28 (444664) which left the Indian captain 120 not out from 100 balls; he hit 18 fours as well as those two sixes. Atherton, who assisted him in Lancashire's highest opening stand and first ten-wicket win in this competition, was doubtless relieved to have reached his fifty before Ganguly cut loose. Richard Howitt, who a month earlier had hit his maiden first-class hundred for Cambridge University against Middlesex, sustained the Lincolnshire innings with a half-century that lost little in comparison to Atherton's.

Man of the Match: S. C. Ganguly.

Lincolnshire

J. C. Harrison c Hegg b Chapple	6	D. A. Christmas c Hegg b Ganguly	26
S. G. Plumb c Lloyd b Austin	10	S. Oakes c Austin b Ganguly	0
R. W. J. Howitt st Hegg b Schofield	52	D. J. Pipes not out	0
S. N. Warman lbw b Smethurst	17	L-b 18, w 9	27
*M. A. Fell c Chapple b Ganguly	22		
J. Clarke c Schofield b Chapple	8	1/22 2/26 3/67 (9 wkts, 50 overs) 190	
†P. C. Trend run out	5	4/115 5/124 6/134	
R. J. Chapman not out	17	7/139 8/184 9/184	

Bowling: Chapple 9–1–39–2; Austin 10–3–23–1; Flintoff 3–1–12–0; Smethurst 8–0–33–1; Schofield 10–0–39–1; Ganguly 10–2–26–3.

Lancashire

M. A. Atherton not out	52
S. C. Ganguly not out	120
L-b 3, w 10, n-b 8	21

(no wkt, 30 overs) 193

*J. P. Crawley, N. H. Fairbrother, A. Flintoff, G. D. Lloyd, †W. K. Hegg, I. D. Austin, G. Chapple, M. P. Smethurst and C. P. Schofield did not bat.

Bowling: Chapman 6–0–35–0; Christmas 8–2–30–0; Oakes 6–0–55–0; Pipes 7–0–60–0; Plumb 3–0–10–0.

Umpires: J. H. Evans and A. G. T. Whitehead.

MIDDLESEX v NOTTINGHAMSHIRE

At Lord's, June 21. Middlesex won by 128 runs. Toss: Middlesex. County debut: P. R. Reiffel.

Nottinghamshire had beaten Middlesex emphatically in the Championship several days earlier. Now it was Middlesex's turn, prompted by another century from Langer. Dropped when 15 by Read, he added 115 with Strauss in 25 overs and 103 in 17 with Shah. Dutch's 29 from 18 balls closed the door on the visitors; Fraser locked it with two of the four wickets that fell inside 13 overs. It was a sobering start for Reiffel, just two days after flying in from Australia to replace Shoaib Akhtar as Nottinghamshire's overseas player.

Man of the Match: J. L. Langer.

Middlesex

A. J. Strauss c Reiffel b Stemp	56	S. J. Cook not out	2
M. R. Ramprakash b Franks	5		
*J. L. Langer run out	100	L-b 13, w 13	26
O. A. Shah st Read b Tolley	49		
P. N. Weekes b Franks	7	1/17 2/132 3/235 (5 wkts, 50 overs) 274	
K. P. Dutch not out	29	4/236 5/256	

†D. C. Nash, R. L. Johnson, A. R. C. Fraser and A. W. Laraman did not bat.

Bowling: Franks 10–0–47–2; Harris 10–0–77–0; Tolley 10–0–38–1; Reiffel 10–0–52–0; Stemp 10–0–47–1.

Nottinghamshire

D. J. Bicknell lbw b Fraser	1	P. R. Reiffel b Laraman	19
G. E. Welton c Ramprakash b Cook	16	A. J. Harris not out	3
*J. E. R. Gallian c Langer b Johnson	8	R. D. Stemp lbw b Laraman	0
J. E. Morris c Johnson b Fraser	18	L-b 4, w 6	10
U. Afzaal run out	31		
C. M. Tolley c Ramprakash b Laraman	20	1/7 2/20 3/47	(37 overs) 146
†C. M. W. Read run out	13	4/48 5/82 6/113	
P. J. Franks c Dutch b Laraman	7	7/117 8/141 9/146	

Bowling: Johnson 5–0–34–1; Fraser 7–2–19–2; Cook 10–2–29–1; Laraman 9–1–39–4; Dutch 6–0–21–0.

Umpires: A. Clarkson and N. G. Cowley.

MIDDLESEX BOARD XI v SUSSEX

At Southgate, June 21. Sussex won by nine wickets. Toss: Sussex.

Lively, accurate bowling by the Sussex seamers, headed by Taylor, illustrated the difference between club and county cricket; their opening batsmen rammed the message home. While there was no shortage of players with first-class experience in the Board side, no one imposed himself on bowlers encouraged by the early conditions. Most could survive; scoring runs was the problem.

Man of the Match: B. V. Taylor.

Middlesex Board XI

D. M. Bowen lbw b Robinson	29	K. Marc b Kirtley	7
T. W. Harrison c Patterson b Taylor	12	R. A. Fay b Kirtley	16
R. K. Rao c House b Taylor	2	R. D. Nelson not out	5
R. O. Jones lbw b Taylor	1	B 1, l-b 3, w 6	10
S. K. Ranasinghe c House b Rashid	15		
*A. G. J. Fraser c Taylor b Rashid	32	1/15 2/23 3/24	(50 overs) 153
C. C. Remy c House b Rashid	18	4/59 5/69 6/114	
†N. F. Sargeant c Kirtley b Taylor	6	7/116 8/132 9/134	

Bowling: Lewry 10–2–20–0; Taylor 10–2–26–4; Robinson 10–0–26–1; Kirtley 10–1–45–2; Rashid 10–2–32–3.

Sussex

*C. J. Adams c Remy b Jones	64
R. R. Montgomerie not out	68
P. A. Cottey not out	13
L-b 1, w 2, n-b 6	9

1/132	(1 wkt, 27.1 overs) 154

M. G. Bevan, W. J. House, U. B. A. Rashid, †A. D. Patterson, J. D. Lewry, R. J. Kirtley, B. V. Taylor and M. A. Robinson did not bat.

Bowling: Fay 7–1–32–0; Marc 4–0–32–0; Fraser 3–0–22–0; Ranasinghe 5–1–15–0; Nelson 5–0–29–0; Jones 2–0–14–1; Rao 1.1–0–9–0.

Umpires: K. Coburn and J. H. Harris.

NORTHUMBERLAND v LEICESTERSHIRE

At Jesmond, June 21. Leicestershire won by 226 runs. Toss: Northumberland.

Wells began as if intent on beating his Leicestershire record of 201 for the competition, hitting 11 fours and a six before he was second out for 60 from 42 balls. Smith's wicket soon afterwards lifted North Country hearts; Stevens broke them with 133 from 111 balls, including 16 fours and two sixes. He was finally bowled by Steve Foster, the ECB XI captain in 2000, who finished with six for 52. Northumberland in reply had nothing to offer against an attack that had recently made Derbyshire follow on. Kumble was a mystery to them.

Man of the Match: D. I. Stevens.

Leicestershire

*V. J. Wells c Angus b Foster	60	†N. D. Burns c and b Foster	7
D. L. Maddy c Parker b Foster	18	A. Kumble not out	1
A. Habib st Nicholson b Crozier	27	J. Ormond not out	1
B. F. Smith c Parker b Foster	9	L-b 17, w 18	35
D. I. Stevens b Foster	133		
C. C. Lewis c Stewart	32	1/69 2/93 3/104 (9 wkts, 50 overs) 328	
J. M. Dakin c Hallam b Foster	5	4/158 5/284 6/311	
D. Williamson run out	0	7/312 8/325 9/326	

Bowling: Angus 10–1–72–0; Rutherford 10–0–68–0; Stewart 10–0–58–1; Crozier 10–0–61–1; Foster 10–0–52–6.

Northumberland

W. Falla c Burns b Ormond	23	L. J. Crozier not out	3
A. T. Heather c Lewis b Kumble	12	G. Angus b Williamson	0
S. J. Foster c Burns b Wells	3	B. Stewart lbw b Kumble	2
B. Parker b Dakin	7	B 1, l-b 13, w 15, n-b 6	35
G. Hallam lbw b Kumble	0		
J. B. Windows lbw b Kumble	5	1/40 2/61 3/61 (33.3 overs) 102	
*†P. J. Nicholson c Habib b Kumble	6	4/61 5/81 6/89	
D. J. Rutherford c Burns b Williamson	6	7/94 8/96 9/96	

Bowling: Ormond 7–1–22–1; Lewis 7–1–22–0; Wells 4–1–11–1; Kumble 9.3–2–27–5; Dakin 4–1–5–1; Williamson 2–1–1–2.

Umpires: J. H. Hampshire and M. J. Harris.

SHROPSHIRE v SOMERSET

At Telford, June 21. Somerset won by 27 runs. Toss: Somerset.

Although Shropshire's 24-year-old batsman James Ralph took the match award, the decisive contributions came from Somerset's Trescothick. He dominated early stands with Cox and Holloway; his 87 from 97 balls, helped along by three sixes and nine fours, provided the platform for a final assault. Later, he effectively ended the contest with two wickets, including the threatening Jon Anders. Ralph's three sixes and 11 fours were good entertainment, but his 102 from 81 balls was always in a losing cause.

Man of the Match: J. T. Ralph.

Somerset

M. E. Trescothick c Ralph b Simmons .	87	K. A. Parsons not out	37
*J. Cox lbw b G. J. Byram	27	†R. J. Turner not out	16
P. C. L. Holloway c Tilt b A. B. Byram .	22	B 5, l-b 4, w 11, n-b 2	22
P. D. Bowler c Ralph b G. J. Byram . . .	8		
M. Burns b Shimmons	11	1/71 2/118 3/157 (6 wkts, 50 overs) 262
I. D. Blackwell c A. B. Byram b Evans .	32	4/157 5/169 6/213

A. R. Caddick, P. D. Trego and P. S. Jones did not bat.

Bowling: Evans 10–1–44–1; Shimmons 10–1–56–2; Asif Din 10–0–53–0; G. J. Byram 9–0–40–2; A. B. Byram 10–0–49–1; Jones 1–0–11–0.

Shropshire

T. Parton run out	1	K. P. Evans c Bowler b Trego	9
*J. B. R. Jones b Parsons	29	A. M. Shimmons b Trego	0
J. V. Anders c Turner b Trescothick	43	†M. A. Tilt not out	0
A. N. Johnson b Trescothick	0	B 4, l-b 7, w 7, n-b 8	26
J. T. Ralph not out	102		
Asif Din c Turner b Parsons	9	1/4 2/72 3/76 (9 wkts, 50 overs) 235
G. J. Byram lbw b Blackwell	0	4/88 5/117 6/118
A. B. Byram c Holloway b Burns	16	7/177 8/215 9/216

Bowling: Caddick 10–1–27–0; Jones 8–0–48–0; Trego 6–0–30–2; Parsons 10–0–33–2; Trescothick 7–0–23–2; Blackwell 5–0–20–1; Burns 4–0–43–1.

Umpires: D. J. Constant and W. E. Smith.

WALES v ESSEX

At Swansea, June 21. Essex won by 103 runs. Toss: Essex.

David Towse, who was on the MCC groundstaff in 1987 and had a game for Yorkshire against Cambridge University a year later, rocked Essex with three early wickets. He removed Prichard with the first ball of the match, caught behind by former Glamorgan wicket-keeper Colin Metson, and Essex were 15 for four after 11 overs. Irani and Peters pulled them round with a stand of 84. There was still too much movement for the bowlers when Wales batted, and Essex had an experienced quartet to exploit it. Only Towse managed as long as half an hour at the crease.

Man of the Match: S. D. Peters.

Essex

P. J. Prichard c Metson b Towse	0	†B. J. Hyam run out	4
S. G. Law c and b George	4	T. J. Mason lbw b Barwick	6
N. Hussain lbw b Towse	8	M. C. Ilott not out	6
A. P. Cowan lbw b Towse	0	L-b 2, w 4, n-b 6	12
*R. C. Irani c Simmons b L. O. Jones . .	45		
S. D. Peters b Barwick	58	1/0 2/10 3/14 (48.1 overs) 154
A. P. Grayson run out	3	4/15 5/99 6/107
D. R. Law b L. O. Jones	8	7/120 8/131 9/147

Bowling: Towse 10–5–19–3; George 8–3–13–1; Barwick 9.1–0–18–2; Simmons 9–0–37–0; Davies 4–0–31–0; L. O. Jones 8–0–34–2.

Wales

A. J. Jones c Peters b Irani	5		*†C. P. Metson run out	4
M. J. Newbold c Hyam b Ilott	16		P. S. George c Peters b D. R. Law	1
J. H. Langworth lbw b Irani	0		S. R. Barwick not out	1
P. V. Simmons lbw b Irani	2		B 1, w 1, n-b 4	6
R. W. Sylvester lbw b Ilott	4			
L. O. Jones c S. G. Law b Ilott	3		1/22 2/22 3/23 (21 overs) 51	
M. Davies c Hyam b Cowan	0		4/24 5/28 6/31	
A. D. Towse c Ilott b D. R. Law	9		7/35 8/43 9/46	

Bowling: Ilott 8–2–20–3; Irani 6–2–15–3; Cowan 4–1–7–1; D. R. Law 3–0–8–2.

Umpires: V. A. Holder and M. P. Moran.

WORCESTERSHIRE v GLOUCESTERSHIRE

At Worcester, June 21. Worcestershire won by three wickets. The result was subsequently declared void because Worcestershire fielded an ineligible player. Toss: Gloucestershire.

Gloucestershire's defence of the trophy looked to have ended at the first hurdle. But they challenged Worcestershire's inclusion of 19-year-old Kabir Ali, pointing out that he had become ineligible by appearing in the first round for the county's Board XI having already played first-team cricket for Worcestershire in 2000 – three games in the Benson and Hedges Cup. While concluding that the mistake had been inadvertent, the ECB ruled that the match be replayed. This would not have been necessary had Gloucestershire made the total that looked likely when Russell and Cunliffe were adding 109 in 28 overs. But from 146 for one, they lost their way. Worcestershire struggled early on. However, Driver, expertly pacing his innings, put on 89 with Leatherdale and, after the loss of three wickets for one run, Illingworth helped him score the 54 needed from the last ten overs.

Man of the Match: R. C. Driver.

Gloucestershire

R. J. Cunliffe c Illingworth b Ali	69		M. C. J. Ball c Hick b Illingworth	10
K. J. Barnett c Hick b Ali	16		J. M. M. Averis not out	2
†R. C. Russell c Pollard b Illingworth	84			
M. G. N. Windows run out	1		L-b 3, w 7, n-b 4	14
*M. W. Alleyne c Rhodes b Lampitt	0			
I. J. Harvey st Rhodes b Leatherdale	5		1/37 2/146 3/148 (8 wkts, 50 overs) 211	
J. N. Snape c Ali b Illingworth	6		4/149 5/177 6/195	
C. G. Taylor not out	4		7/195 8/208	

A. M. Smith did not bat.

Bowling: McGrath 10–1–23–0; Ali 10–0–45–2; Lampitt 10–1–30–1; Leatherdale 5–0–40–1; Illingworth 10–0–43–3; Hick 5–0–27–0.

Worcestershire

P. R. Pollard c and b Harvey	12		S. R. Lampitt c Russell b Ball	0
E. J. Wilson st Russell b Ball	21		R. K. Illingworth not out	25
*G. A. Hick c Snape b Smith	13		B 1, l-b 5, w 10, n-b 4	20
V. S. Solanki lbw b Smith	7			
D. A. Leatherdale c and b Harvey	53		1/14 2/32 3/51 (7 wkts, 48.5 overs) 212	
R. C. Driver not out	61		4/68 5/157	
†S. J. Rhodes run out	0		6/158 7/158	

Kabir Ali and G. D. McGrath did not bat.

Bowling: Smith 10–3–39–2; Harvey 9–1–45–2; Averis 8.5–0–41–0; Ball 9–1–31–2; Alleyne 8–0–31–0; Snape 4–0–19–0.

Umpires: J. F. Steele and P. Willey.

YORKSHIRE BOARD XI v YORKSHIRE

At Harrogate, June 21. Yorkshire won by 130 runs. Toss: Yorkshire Board XI.

Taking first use of a seaming pitch was always the Board XI's best chance of an upset, but an hour passed before a wicket fell. Vaughan continued his comeback from injury with a sensible 70 off 113 balls, which Lehmann consolidated by hitting 48 off 35 balls as Yorkshire's last ten overs brought 74 runs. It was more than the Board could afford. Rain interrupted their innings; Gough, who took two early wickets, finished it with three in seven balls.

Man of the Match: M. P. Vaughan.

Yorkshire

G. M. Fellows c Brook b Kettleborough	18	G. M. Hamilton not out	1
M. P. Vaughan b McCarthy	70		
†R. J. Blakey c Gill b McKenna	41	L-b 14, w 15, n-b 2	31
D. S. Lehmann not out	48		—
*D. Byas lbw b Carruthers	15	1/49 2/143 3/156 (5 wkts, 50 overs)	240
C. White b Gill	16	4/197 5/234	

J. D. Middlebrook, C. E. W. Silverwood, R. J. Sidebottom and D. Gough did not bat.

Bowling: Carruthers 10–2–38–1; McCarthy 10–2–44–1; Kettleborough 10–1–37–1; Gill 10–1–47–1; Walker 6–0–35–0; McKenna 4–0–25–1.

Yorkshire Board XI

J. Proud lbw b Gough	1	R. McCarthy c Middlebrook b Gough	1
*A. J. Bethel lbw b Gough	4	†G. Brook lbw b Gough	3
M. Gilliver lbw b Hamilton	13	J. R. Carruthers lbw b Gough	0
R. A. Kettleborough c Middlebrook b Sidebottom	31	L-b 1, w 10, n-b 14	25
A. E. McKenna lbw b Hamilton	0		
M. J. Doidge c Lehmann b White	14	1/3 2/15 3/49 (38.5 overs)	110
A. J. Walker b Vaughan	10	4/49 5/71 6/80	
N. S. Gill not out	8	7/93 8/105 9/109	

Bowling: Gough 8.5–1–30–5; Silverwood 7–1–15–0; Hamilton 7–2–24–2; White 4–0–12–1; Middlebrook 6–1–15–0; Sidebottom 4–2–9–1; Vaughan 2–0–4–1.

Umpires: A. A. Jones and K. Shuttleworth.

WORCESTERSHIRE v GLOUCESTERSHIRE

At Worcester, July 4. Gloucestershire won by five runs. Toss: Gloucestershire.

It was close-run at the end but Gloucestershire, availing themselves of the ECB's reprieve, lived to defend the NatWest Trophy. A slow, uncertain pitch made most batsmen wary and, even when Worcestershire's last pair needed just six in two overs, the bowlers dictated terms. Harvey bowled a maiden to McGrath; Rhodes played on to Ball, who had earlier taken two outstanding catches – Hick at slip, Catterall at backward point. Worcestershire's day was summed up by the sixth-ball duck that befell Driver, man of the original match.

Man of the Match: M. C. J. Ball.

Gloucestershire

R. J. Cunliffe lbw b McGrath	0	M. J. Cawdron b McGrath		17
K. J. Barnett c Hick b Leatherdale	26	J. M. M. Averis c McGrath b Catterall		12
*†R. C. Russell b Lampitt	8	A. M. Smith not out		2
M. G. N. Windows c Pollard b Lampitt	20	L-b 7, w 5, n-b 2		14
I. J. Harvey c Rhodes b McGrath	32			
C. G. Taylor c Pollard b McGrath	1	1/0 2/41 3/43	(49.3 overs)	163
J. N. Snape run out	12	4/85 5/87 6/102		
M. C. J. Ball lbw b Leatherdale	19	7/121 8/142 9/161		

Bowling: McGrath 10–3–23–4; Catterall 9.3–1–40–1; Lampitt 10–1–25–2; Leatherdale 10–1–42–2; Rawnsley 10–0–26–0.

Worcestershire

P. R. Pollard run out	55	D. N. Catterall c Ball b Barnett		1
E. J. Wilson b Harvey	0	M. J. Rawnsley lbw b Averis		5
*G. A. Hick c Ball b Averis	23	G. D. McGrath not out		1
V. S. Solanki c Barnett b Averis	0	L-b 6, w 16		22
D. A. Leatherdale c Russell b Averis	5			
R. C. Driver c Russell b Cawdron	0	1/3 2/33 3/39	(49.3 overs)	158
†S. J. Rhodes b Ball	43	4/57 5/61 6/122		
S. R. Lampitt lbw b Smith	3	7/131 8/134 9/141		

Bowling: Harvey 10–5–15–1; Smith 10–0–29–1; Averis 10–1–36–4; Cawdron 10–1–27–1; Barnett 5–0–27–1; Ball 4.3–0–18–1.

Umpires: R. Julian and G. Sharp.

FOURTH ROUND

DURHAM v HAMPSHIRE

At Chester-le-Street, July 5. Hampshire won by five wickets. Toss: Durham.

Winning only his fifth toss in 23 competitive matches, Speak chose to bat first on a damp pitch that proved a seamer's paradise. It was a flawed decision and Durham could manage only 91, with Speak's 15 not out in 80 balls their best off the bat. Katich was 37 balls over his four runs. Hampshire might have struggled in turn had Harmison not conceded 34 from three overs in the middle of their reply. He bowled five wides and was cut for three boundaries by Smith in one over. Extras top-scored for both sides, but the match award went to Stephenson, who followed his two for 31 with 20 runs and dominated the opening stand of 40 with White.

Man of the Match: J. P. Stephenson.

Durham

M. A. Gough c Aymes b Mascarenhas	10	J. Wood lbw b Warne		7
S. M. Ali lbw b Mascarenhas	11	N. Killeen run out		1
S. M. Katich c Aymes b Mullally	4	S. J. Harmison lbw b Hartley		0
*N. J. Speak not out	15	B 1, l-b 7, w 13, n-b 8		29
J. J. B. Lewis b Mullally	1			
P. D. Collingwood b Stephenson	3	1/25 2/31 3/41	(42.4 overs)	91
†M. P. Speight c Aymes b Warne	10	4/49 5/52 6/63		
M. M. Betts b Stephenson	0	7/66 8/88 9/89		

Bowling: Mascarenhas 10–2–13–2; Hartley 7.4–2–19–1; Mullally 8–3–8–2; Stephenson 10–3–31–2; Warne 7–1–12–2.

Hampshire

G. W. White b Killeen	6	S. K. Warne not out		0
J. P. Stephenson c Speight b Harmison	20			
J. S. Laney c and b Betts	5	L-b 10, w 10, n-b 15		35
*R. A. Smith not out	23			
W. S. Kendall c Katich b Wood	1	1/40 2/48 3/75	(5 wkts, 24.3 overs)	92
A. D. Mascarenhas lbw b Betts	2	4/76 5/85		

S. D. Udal, †A. N. Aymes, P. J. Hartley and A. D. Mullally did not bat.

Bowling: Betts 10–1–26–2; Killeen 6–1–10–1; Harmison 3–0–34–1; Wood 5.3–1–12–1.

Umpires: B. Dudleston and R. Palmer.

KENT v GLAMORGAN

At Canterbury, July 5, 6. Glamorgan won by five wickets. Toss: Glamorgan.

Play started at 3.15 p.m. on the first day, and when the umpires called a halt at 8 p.m. Glamorgan, needing only 57 more to win, would apparently have been happy to continue. Kent's batting had failed to develop any momentum in the bowler-friendly conditions that Wharf used skilfully. He was also responsible for running out Fleming. Whereas Kent managed only four boundaries, Newell and Elliott doubled that in their opening stand, and Newell remained unbeaten next day as Ealham's four for three in 22 balls delayed, but could not stop, Glamorgan's passage into the quarter-finals.

Man of the Match: K. Newell.

Close of play: Glamorgan 65-1 (13 overs) (Newell 30*, James 8*).

Kent

R. Dravid lbw b Wharf	22	M. M. Patel c Parkin b Croft		7
D. P. Fulton c Shaw b Parkin	14	D. D. Masters c Shaw b Croft		1
J. B. Hockley c James b Dale	8	K. Adams c Powell b Parkin		2
A. P. Wells b Wharf	0	L-b 6, w 9		15
M. A. Ealham lbw b Dale	0			
M. J. Walker b Wharf	6	1/32 2/47 3/52	(48.4 overs)	121
†P. A. Nixon not out	38	4/56 5/56 6/66		
*M. V. Fleming run out	8	7/86 8/100 9/111		

Bowling: Watkin 10–1–23–0; Parkin 9.4–0–24–2; Wharf 10–1–18–3; Dale 10–4–23–2; Croft 8–0–17–2; Newell 1–0–10–0.

Glamorgan

K. Newell not out	62	†A. D. Shaw not out		7
M. T. G. Elliott lbw b Masters	21			
S. P. James c Fulton b Ealham	15	L-b 5, w 8		13
*M. P. Maynard c Nixon b Ealham	0			
A. Dale c Nixon b Ealham	3	1/46 2/72 3/80	(5 wkts, 37.1 overs)	122
M. J. Powell c Nixon b Ealham	1	4/84 5/86		

R. D. B. Croft, A. G. Wharf, O. T. Parkin and S. L. Watkin did not bat.

Bowling: Ealham 10–1–36–4; Adams 10–1–35–0; Masters 8.1–0–23–1; Fleming 7–2–20–0; Walker 2–1–3–0.

Umpires: R. Julian and D. R. Shepherd.

LANCASHIRE v ESSEX

At Manchester, July 5. Lancashire won by 68 runs. Toss: Lancashire.

Atherton and Ganguly picked up where they left off in the third round, with another century stand. By the time Ganguly was caught at long-on, aiming for his fifth six and his hundred, Flintoff was charging into the Essex bowlers. Ganguly's 97 came in 119 balls; Flintoff's 43 in 29, with four fours and a six. It was all too much for Essex. Prichard and Stuart Law gave them a bright start, and Danny Law blazed 45 in 44 balls, but their last five wickets went for 19. Spinners Yates and Schofield, matching his county one-day best with four for 34, more than compensated for the absence of seamers Martin, Austin and Chapple through injury or illness.

Man of the Match: S. C. Ganguly.

Lancashire

M. A. Atherton b Ilott	70	G. D. Lloyd not out		2
S. C. Ganguly c S. G. Law b Grayson	97	L-b 6, w 11		17
A. Flintoff run out	43			
*J. P. Crawley c Irani b D. R. Law	15	1/163 2/195 3/212	(5 wkts, 50 overs)	251
N. H. Fairbrother c D. R. Law b Irani	7	4/228 5/251		

†W. K. Hegg, C. P. Schofield, J. C. Scuderi, G. Yates and M. P. Smethurst did not bat.

Bowling: Ilott 10–0–45–1; Irani 10–1–41–1; Cowan 10–0–52–0; Mason 7–0–27–0; Grayson 7–0–34–1; D. R. Law 6–0–46–1.

Essex

P. J. Prichard lbw b Flintoff	26	T. J. Mason c Yates b Schofield		3
S. G. Law c and b Smethurst	27	A. P. Cowan not out		1
*R. C. Irani c Ganguly b Yates	10	M. C. Ilott c Yates b Smethurst		0
S. D. Peters c Scuderi b Yates	6	B 10, l-b 13, w 6		29
A. P. Grayson c Yates b Schofield	18			
D. R. Law c Fairbrother b Schofield	45	1/62 2/76 3/86	(42.3 overs)	183
G. R. Napier lbw b Flintoff	17	4/93 5/121 6/164		
†B. J. Hyam c Yates b Schofield	1	7/174 8/181 9/181		

Bowling: Smethurst 8.3–0–30–2; Ganguly 8–1–32–0; Flintoff 8–1–21–2; Scuderi 3–1–8–0; Yates 8–0–35–2; Schofield 7–0–34–4.

Umpires: D. J. Constant and T. E. Jesty.

LEICESTERSHIRE v GLOUCESTERSHIRE

At Leicester, July 5. Gloucestershire won by ten runs. Toss: Gloucestershire.

Lingering doubts that the one-day force was still with Gloucestershire should have been dispelled by this match. Leicestershire, needing 20 off the last five overs with five wickets remaining, were virtually through to the quarter-finals. Instead, all five fell for nine runs in 18 balls and Gloucestershire, even with captain Alleyne and deputy Hancock still absent, survived once more; 24 hours earlier they had beaten Worcestershire in their replayed third-round tie. Excellent catches by Barnett at mid-wicket – ending Maddy's splendid 72 in 83 balls on a sluggish pitch – and Ball at point symbolised the difference. Leicestershire had twice dropped Barnett when he was in single figures, and he went on to anchor Gloucestershire to their match-winning total.

Man of the Match: K. J. Barnett.

Gloucestershire

D. R. Hewson c Lewis b Ormond	11	M. J. Cawdron run out		5
K. J. Barnett c Smith b Ormond	86	M. C. J. Ball not out		2
I. J. Harvey c Burns b Lewis	5	L-b 6, w 5		11
M. G. N. Windows c Habib b DeFreitas	23			
*†R. C. Russell c Burns b Dakin	13	1/23 2/34 3/99	(8 wkts, 50 overs)	210
C. G. Taylor b Kumble	41	4/122 5/164 6/201		
J. N. Snape run out	13	7/203 8/210		

J. M. M. Averis and A. M. Smith did not bat.

Bowling: Ormond 10–1–52–2; Lewis 10–2–35–1; Dakin 7–1–35–1; DeFreitas 10–0–29–1; Kumble 10–0–33–1; Wells 3–0–20–0.

Leicestershire

*V. J. Wells lbw b Smith	5	†N. D. Burns lbw b Averis		0
D. I. Stevens c Taylor b Ball	55	A. Kumble c Taylor b Harvey		1
A. Habib c and b Harvey	1	J. Ormond not out		0
B. F. Smith c Russell b Cawdron	6	L-b 7, w 10		17
D. L. Maddy c Barnett b Harvey	72			
P. A. J. DeFreitas b Ball	15	1/6 2/20 3/46	(48.1 overs)	200
C. C. Lewis c Ball b Averis	28	4/101 5/138 6/191		
J. M. Dakin lbw b Harvey	0	7/191 8/193 9/200		

Bowling: Harvey 9–1–40–4; Smith 10–2–28–1; Averis 9.1–1–41–2; Cawdron 7–1–29–1; Ball 10–0–38–2; Snape 3–0–17–0.

Umpires: B. Leadbeater and N. A. Mallender.

MIDDLESEX v SOMERSET

At Southgate, July 5, 6. Middlesex won by 165 runs. Toss: Somerset.

Somerset were dismissed for their lowest total in the competition, one less than their 59 against the same opposition at Lord's in 1977, and equalled their lowest in all one-day games – 58 against Essex at Chelmsford in the Sunday League, also in 1977. Bloomfield's three wickets in seven balls had them nine for four in the sixth over and, after he came back to end Parsons's hour and a quarter of resistance, Laraman nipped in with three wickets in 17 balls to complete Somerset's humiliation. That Middlesex got through their innings on the first day was due to the excellent work of the local club's groundstaff after heavy rain had delayed the start until mid-afternoon. Ramprakash's 42 off 68 balls, with only one four, indicated how difficult it was to score runs. But nothing suggested how straightforward wicket-taking would be the next day.

Man of the Match: T. F. Bloomfield.

Close of play: Middlesex 223-4 (50 overs).

Middlesex

A. J. Strauss b Jarvis	30	†D. Alleyne c Turner b Jones		7
M. A. Roseberry retired hurt	21	K. P. Dutch not out		12
*J. L. Langer b Jarvis	18	L-b 3, w 15, n-b 4		22
M. R. Ramprakash c Caddick				
b Blackwell	42	1/76 2/83	(4 wkts, 50 overs)	223
P. N. Weekes not out	71	3/166 4/189		

A. W. Laraman, A. R. C. Fraser, R. L. Johnson and T. F. Bloomfield did not bat.

Roseberry retired hurt at 43.

Bowling: Caddick 10–0–31–0; Jones 10–0–59–1; Parsons 10–2–30–0; Jarvis 9–1–43–2; Trescothick 2–0–13–0; Blackwell 6–0–27–1; Burns 3–0–17–0.

Somerset

M. E. Trescothick c Weekes b Bloomfield	1	A. R. Caddick c and b Laraman	0
*J. Cox lbw b Fraser	2	P. W. Jarvis not out	2
P. C. L. Holloway c Ramprakash b Fraser	11	P. S. Jones c Ramprakash b Laraman	1
P. D. Bowler c Weekes b Bloomfield	0	W 6, n-b 8	14
M. Burns b Alleyne b Bloomfield	0		
K. A. Parsons lbw b Bloomfield	24	1/7 2/9 3/9 (28.3 overs)	58
†R. J. Turner c Ramprakash b Laraman	2	4/9 5/42 6/52	
I. D. Blackwell run out	1	7/53 8/54 9/54	

Bowling: Fraser 10–2–19–2; Bloomfield 8–1–17–4; Johnson 6–2–16–0; Laraman 4.3–1–6–3.

Umpires: M. J. Kitchen and K. E. Palmer.

NORTHAMPTONSHIRE v YORKSHIRE

At Northampton, July 5. Northamptonshire won by 69 runs. Toss: Northamptonshire.

Strong, who moved to Northamptonshire from Sussex in the winter, stunned Yorkshire with an opening spell that removed Fellows, Blakey and Lehmann in the space of 20 balls. Byas and McGrath did their best to repair the damage, adding 73 in 18 overs, but Yorkshire were always behind the clock and duly recorded their fourth defeat in as many ties between these sides in this competition. Hayden, 63 in 69 balls, and Sales had earlier laid the foundation for a solid Northamptonshire total, putting on 118 for the third wicket; Gough brushed the tail aside with four wickets in eight balls, bowling the last three with trademark yorkers.

Man of the Match: M. R. Strong.

Northamptonshire

A. S. Rollins lbw b Hamilton	20	M. R. Strong b Gough	1
M. B. Loye lbw b Hamilton	24	J. F. Brown not out	1
*M. L. Hayden c Byas b Hamilton	63	D. E. Malcolm b Gough	0
D. J. Sales lbw b Lehmann	65	B 4, l-b 12, w 5, n-b 4	25
G. P. Swann c Byas b Lehmann	18		
J. W. Cook c Byas b Gough	20	1/48 2/51 3/169 (50 overs)	252
A. L. Penberthy c Middlebrook b Lehmann	11	4/207 5/208 6/244	
†D. Ripley b Gough	4	7/247 8/249 9/252	

Bowling: Gough 10–1–36–4; Silverwood 10–0–50–0; White 8–0–39–0; Hamilton 10–1–39–3; Middlebrook 2–0–23–0; McGrath 4–0–23–0; Lehmann 6–0–26–3.

Yorkshire

G. M. Fellows b Strong	2	C. E. W. Silverwood c Sales b Swann	2
M. P. Vaughan c Hayden b Malcolm	16	J. D. Middlebrook not out	6
†R. J. Blakey c Ripley b Strong	0	D. Gough run out	3
D. S. Lehmann c Swann b Strong	7	B 1, l-b 11, w 9, n-b 2	23
*D. Byas c Hayden b Penberthy	33		
A. McGrath c Swann b Penberthy	64	1/13 2/13 3/28 (43.5 overs)	183
C. White b Penberthy	26	4/36 5/109 6/160	
G. M. Hamilton c Hayden b Swann	1	7/170 8/171 9/178	

Bowling: Malcolm 9–1–31–1; Strong 7–3–10–3; Brown 10–1–41–0; Swann 9.5–0–45–2; Penberthy 8–0–44–3.

Umpires: M. R. Benson and A. Clarkson.

SURREY v SUSSEX

At The Oval, July 5, 6. Surrey won by seven wickets. Toss: Surrey.

Stewart and Butcher set up Surrey's pursuit of a Sussex total that always looked inadequate on a good batting pitch. After they put on 85, Butcher then added 90 with Ward in even time. Sussex had never found a way to accelerate against admirably tight bowling from Bicknell and spinners Salisbury and Saqlain Mushtaq. Bevan put on 104 for the third wicket with Montgomerie but was unable to deliver the necessary fireworks. Adam Holtioake's three-wicket burst left the target well below par.

Man of the Match: M. A. Butcher.

Close of play: Sussex 5-0 (2 overs) (Adams 5*, Montgomerie 0*).

Sussex

*C. J. Adams c Butcher b Tudor	8	†A. D. Patterson lbw b A. J. Holioake. .	1
R. R. Montgomerie c Saqlain Mushtaq		R. J. Kirtley not out	7
b A. J. Hollioake .	53	B. V. Taylor c Tudor b Bicknell	1
P. A. Cottey c Brown b Ratcliffe	17	M. A. Robinson not out.	8
M. G. Bevan c Stewart b Salisbury	60	L-b 3, w 6, n-b 2	11
W. J. House lbw b A. J. Hollioake.	5		
U. B. A. Rashid c Butcher		1/13 2/39 3/143 (9 wkts, 50 overs) 192	
b Saqlain Mushtaq .	5	4/150 5/154 6/162	
R. S. C. Martin-Jenkins run out	16	7/165 8/179 9/184	

Bowling: Bicknell 10–1–26–1; Tudor 8–0–36–1; Ratcliffe 2–0–17–1; Saqlain Mushtaq 10–0–30–1; Salisbury 10–1–30–1; B. C. Hollioake 4–0–27–0; A. J. Hollioake 6–0–23–3.

Surrey

M. A. Butcher not out.	87	*A. J. Hollioake not out	13
A. D. Brown c Patterson			
b Martin-Jenkins .	1	L-b 13, w 20, n-b 2	35
†A. J. Stewart b Martin-Jenkins	31		
I. J. Ward b Taylor	29	1/7 2/92 3/182 (3 wkts, 47.4 overs) 196	

B. C. Hollioake, M. P. Bicknell, J. D. Ratcliffe, A. J. Tudor, I. D. K. Salisbury and Saqlain Mushtaq did not bat.

Bowling: Martin-Jenkins 10–1–28–2; Kirtley 10–0–29–0; Taylor 5 0 23 1; Robinson 10–0–33–0; Rashid 5–0–25–0; Bevan 7.4–1–45–0.

Umpires: G. I. Burgess and M. J. Harris.

WARWICKSHIRE v DERBYSHIRE

At Birmingham, July 5. Warwickshire won by 40 runs. Toss: Warwickshire.

Giles's maiden one-day hundred gave Warwickshire a grip on the match that they never relaxed. Promoted to No. 3, he reached 50 off 49 balls, 100 off 45 more, and his 107 from 97 contained 12 fours and two sixes. A target of 258 was quite beyond Derbyshire, despite Di Venuto's brisk 84. Krikken, playing solely as a batsman because of back trouble, helped him add 87 at a run a ball, but Derbyshire's game was over once Donald dismissed Di Venuto. Giles completed a memorable all-round match with a stunning boundary catch and two wickets with successive deliveries.

Man of the Match: A. F. Giles.

Warwickshire

M. J. Powell c Sutton b Shah	25		*N. M. K. Smith run out	17
G. Welch c Krikken b Cork	11		†K. J. Piper not out	6
A. F. Giles c Cork b Dowman	107		B 8, l-b 10, w 1, n-b 2	21
D. P. Ostler lbw b Dowman	32			
D. L. Hemp lbw b Shah	3		1/21 2/73 3/133 (8 wkts, 50 overs)	257
T. L. Penney b Cork	34		4/137 5/222 6/229	
D. R. Brown b Lacey	1		7/229 8/257	

A. A. Donald and E. S. H. Giddins did not bat.

Bowling: Cork 10–1–40–2; Munton 10–3–18–0; Lungley 4–0–24–0; Shah 8–0–46–2; Lacey 9–0–62–1; Dowman 9–0–49–2.

Derbyshire

S. P. Titchard c Piper b Giddins	13		T. A. Munton b Donald	2
M. J. Di Venuto c Penney b Donald	84		T. Lungley c Smith b Donald	3
*D. G. Cork b Giles b Brown	6		K. Z. Shah not out	1
M. P. Dowman b Giles	18		B 1, l-b 10, w 7	18
K. M. Krikken c Giddins b Brown	35			
S. D. Stubbings run out	16		1/21 2/44 3/164 (46.5 overs)	217
†L. D. Sutton c Powell b Donald	21		4/169 5/201 6/202	
S. J. Lacey b Giles	0		7/202 8/206 9/215	

Dowman, when 18, retired hurt at 77 and resumed at 202-6.

Bowling: Welch 10–0–50–0; Giddins 10–1–34–1; Brown 9–1–35–2; Donald 8.5–0–42–4; Giles 9–0–45–2.

Umpires: N. G. Cowley and J. W. Holder.

QUARTER-FINALS

MIDDLESEX v HAMPSHIRE

At Lord's, July 25. Hampshire won by seven wickets. Toss: Hampshire.

Batting was never easy on a worn pitch previously used for two one-day internationals, but neither that nor Mascarenhas's penetrating opening spell could excuse another pusillanimous Middlesex display. Once again, Langer came in too late. They were 42 for four before he faced a ball, and in worse trouble when, having scored only eight, he chopped the second-last ball from Mascarenhas on to his stumps. Skilful variations of pace and swing lay behind Mascarenhas's best one-day figures of four for 25. With Smith letting him bowl his ten overs off the reel, it was the 24th over before Warne joined the attack, and by then Middlesex were out of the running. Dutch and Johnson saw the total into three figures but Hampshire could afford to jog through to the semi-finals.

Man of the Match: A. D. Mascarenhas.

Middlesex

A. J. Strauss c and b Mullally	24		S. J. Cook c Stephenson b Warne	7
M. A. Roseberry b Mascarenhas	3		R. L. Johnson b Udal	21
†D. Alleyne c Stephenson b Mascarenhas	1		A. R. C. Fraser not out	8
M. R. Ramprakash lbw b Mascarenhas	8		L-b 4, w 9	13
*J. L. Langer b Mascarenhas	8			
P. N. Weekes lbw b Hartley	6		1/9 2/17 3/41 (44 overs)	127
K. P. Dutch c Aymes b Hartley	26		4/42 5/57 6/57	
A. W. Laraman lbw b Warne	2		7/61 8/73 9/107	

Bowling: Mascarenhas 10–3–25–4; Hartley 9–2–20–2; Stephenson 1–0–3–0; Mullally 10–2–27–1; Warne 10–1–38–2; Udal 4–0–10–1.

Hampshire

G. W. White c Alleyne b Laraman	18	W. S. Kendall not out	25
J. P. Stephenson c Ramprakash b Dutch	35	B 2, l-b 1	3
S. K. Warne c Langer b Dutch	20		
J. S. Laney not out	27	1/50 2/71 3/82 (3 wkts, 34.5 overs)	128

*R. A. Smith, †A. N. Aymes, A. D. Mascarenhas, S. D. Udal, P. J. Hartley and A. D. Mullally did not bat.

Bowling: Johnson 5–1–21–0; Fraser 7–1–23–0; Laraman 10–1–21–1; Dutch 8–1–37–2; Cook 2–0–10–0; Weekes 2.5–0–13–0.

Umpires: V. A. Holder and R. A. White.

WARWICKSHIRE v GLAMORGAN

At Birmingham, July 25. Warwickshire won by 81 runs. Toss: Glamorgan.

Warwickshire took control through a magnificent 118 from Knight, who – dropped when nine – held the innings together after the loss of two early wickets. Just back from injury and unable to regain his England place, he added 123 in 25 overs with Ostler and 71 in 11 with Penney, hitting 11 fours in all in 143 balls. Glamorgan needed at least one major innings, but Elliott, Maynard and James aggregated only 67 against a rejuvenated Warwickshire attack. Captain Smith played a decisive role when he prised out three of Glamorgan's top five, and Donald was always on hand to see off the tail.

Man of the Match: N. V. Knight.

Warwickshire

M. J. Powell c Shaw b Wharf	11	*N. M. K. Smith not out	11
N. V. Knight c Maynard b Parkin	118	†K. J. Piper not out	2
A. F. Giles c James b Wharf	0	B 8, l-b 3, w 2, n-b 4	17
D. P. Ostler c Maynard b Croft	63		
D. L. Hemp c and b Croft	0	1/21 2/25 3/148 (7 wkts, 50 overs)	273
T. L. Penney c Powell b Newell	42	4/148 5/219	
D. R. Brown b Thomas	9	6/249 7/260	

A. A. Donald and E. S. H. Giddins did not bat.

Bowling: Wharf 10–2–44–2; Parkin 10–0–54–1; Thomas 9–0–46–1; Dale 6–0–39–0; Croft 10–0–48–2; Newell 5–0–31–1.

Glamorgan

K. Newell b Smith	35	S. D. Thomas c Giles b Donald	3
M. T. G. Elliott c Powell b Brown	4	A. G. Wharf b Giles	0
S. P. James run out	27	O. T. Parkin b Donald	0
*M. P. Maynard b Smith	36	L-b 4, w 8, n-b 6	18
A. Dale st Piper b Smith	4		
M. J. Powell lbw b Giles	3	1/9 2/77 3/77 (44.4 overs)	192
†A. D. Shaw c Smith b Donald	32	4/99 5/104 6/130	
R. D. B. Croft not out	30	7/175 8/187 9/189	

Bowling: Giddins 9–0–55–0; Brown 8–0–32–1; Donald 8.4–1–29–3; Giles 9–0–35–2; Smith 10–0–37–3.

Umpires: M. J. Kitchen and J. F. Steele.

GLOUCESTERSHIRE v NORTHAMPTONSHIRE

At Bristol, July 26. Gloucestershire won by 62 runs. Toss: Gloucestershire.

The drinks tray troubled Gloucestershire more than their opponents' indifferent bowling on a slow pitch. Three deliveries after the first break, Hewson was caught behind; two balls after the second, Barnett lost his off stump, having added 121 in 22 overs with Hancock. These, however, were minor setbacks. Hancock set the pace with a bravura maiden one-day hundred – getting there with six off Swann over long-on – until he was smartly stumped off a widish delivery from Penberthy for 110 in 131 balls. A target of 281 asked a lot of Northamptonshire, and Smith, bowling through his ten overs for 24 runs, gave Gloucestershire a vital edge. Cook hit 48 off 50 balls before tipping up a catch to cover, while Penberthy made a valiant 54 in 71 balls. Northamptonshire were well behind the clock by the time he became Harvey's fourth victim.

Man of the Match: T. H. C. Hancock.

Gloucestershire

T. H. C. Hancock st Ripley b Penberthy	110		C. G. Taylor not out	6
D. R. Hewson c Ripley b Strong	38		M. C. J. Ball run out	1
K. J. Barnett b Cousins	51		L-b 3, w 7, n-b 6	16
I. J. Harvey c Sales b Brown	20			
*M. W. Alleyne c Cousins b Strong	17		1/69 2/190 3/234 (8 wkts, 50 overs) 280	
J. N. Snape b Cousins	7		4/238 5/251 6/273	
†R. C. Russell c Swann b Cousins	14		7/274 8/280	

J. M. M. Averis and A. M. Smith did not bat.

Bowling: Cousins 10–2–42–3; Strong 10–0–62–2; Penberthy 10–1–44–1; Brown 10–0–61–1; Swann 8–0–55–0; Sales 2–0–13–0.

Northamptonshire

*M. L. Hayden c Taylor b Harvey	11		M. R. Strong b Snape	21
M. B. Loye c Averis b Ball	24		D. M. Cousins not out	10
J. W. Cook c Snape b Alleyne	48		J. F. Brown not out	0
D. J. Sales c Taylor b Ball	17		L-b 7, w 6	13
R. J. Warren c Russell b Ball	1			
A. L. Penberthy c Hancock b Harvey	54		1/20 2/86 3/98 (9 wkts, 50 overs) 218	
G. P. Swann b Harvey	17		4/101 5/116 6/149	
†D. Ripley c Barnett b Harvey	2		7/155 8/192 9/218	

Bowling: Smith 10–0–24–0; Harvey 10–1–37–4; Averis 7–0–45–0; Alleyne 6–0–31–1; Ball 10–0–39–3; Snape 7–0–35–1.

Umpires: A. A. Jones and P. Willey.

SURREY v LANCASHIRE

At The Oval, July 26. Lancashire won by eight wickets. Toss: Surrey.

"We have just watched one of the most awesome innings we are ever going to see on a cricket field," said David Gower, the former England captain, after Flintoff's match-winning 135 not out. In preceding weeks, Flintoff had been stung by accusations in the press that he was overweight, and Surrey's bowlers felt the full force of his poundage as he pummelled them for four sixes and 19 fours until Lancashire were in the semi-finals. His first delivery, a leg-side half-volley, was clipped to the square-leg boundary, cleanly struck off-drives followed, and if he appeared to be lbw on 67, deceived on the back foot by Salisbury's googly, umpire Sharp deemed otherwise. He reached 100 in 88 balls; his whole innings took just 111, and he put on 190 with Ganguly, a Lancashire second-wicket record in this competition. Surrey were without Bicknell, who had a back injury, but they possessed enough front-line bowlers to keep most batsmen in check. As it was, Saqlain Mushtaq and Salisbury's thunder was stolen by the Lancashire spinners, and only Thorpe and Stewart managed any kind of score. The rest of Surrey's batting fell woefully short of what was needed, even before Flintoff went ballistic.

Man of the Match: A. Flintoff.

Surrey

I. J. Ward st Hegg b Yates	28	I. D. K. Salisbury not out	21
†A. J. Stewart b Keedy	49	A. J. Tudor not out	10
G. P. Thorpe c Ganguly b Schofield	55	L-b 7, w 5, n-b 2	14
A. D. Brown c Crawley b Yates	3		
*A. J. Hollioake b Schofield	17	1/80 2/99 3/109 (7 wkts, 50 overs)	210
B. C. Hollioake st Hegg b Schofield	0	4/139 5/139	
J. D. Ratcliffe c Lloyd b Schofield	13	6/165 7/182	

C. G. Greenidge and Saqlain Mushtaq did not bat.

Bowling: Chapple 9–3–23–0; Ganguly 8–1–45–0; Flintoff 3–0–14–0; Keedy 10–0–40–1; Schofield 10–1–41–4; Yates 10–0–40–2.

Lancashire

M. A. Atherton b Tudor	0		
S. C. Ganguly c Thorpe b Tudor	51		
A. Flintoff not out	135		
*J. P. Crawley not out	12		
B 2, l-b 6, w 6, n-b 2	16		

1/0 2/190   (2 wkts, 36 overs) 214

N. H. Fairbrother, G. D. Lloyd, †W. K. Hegg, C. P. Schofield, G. Yates, G. Chapple and G. Keedy did not bat.

Bowling: Tudor 10–1–48–2; Greenidge 4–0–33–0; Ratcliffe 2–0–13–0; Saqlain Mushtaq 7–1–30–0; Salisbury 6–0–31–0; A. J. Hollioake 3–0–17–0; B. C. Hollioake 3–0–25–0; Brown 1–0–9–0.

Umpires: G. Sharp and D. R. Shepherd.

SEMI-FINALS

WARWICKSHIRE v HAMPSHIRE

At Birmingham, August 12. Warwickshire won by 19 runs. Toss: Hampshire.

Given first use of a good batting pitch, Knight and Singh put on 185 in 39 overs, a record for Warwickshire's first wicket in one-day games. Singh scored 85 in 114 balls, with a wristy six off Mullally and ten fours, while Knight went on to his second successive NatWest hundred before he was out in the 43rd over, having hit 11 fours. Without Warne, back in Melbourne for Australia's one-day series against South Africa, the Hampshire attack contained little beyond line and length. Warwickshire, on the other hand, discovered turn for their spinners as the pitch began to wear. Hampshire's Robin Smith set about their quicker bowling as if chasing five an over was a stroll, punching 61 off 67 balls and taking his side to 102 before he was bowled by his namesake and opposing captain Neil. Without him, Hampshire lacked the blazing bats that would stay in touch with the run-rate; as it escalated, so their dreams of a fourth Lord's final vanished.

Man of the Match: N. V. Knight.

Warwickshire

N. V. Knight c Kendall b Morris	100	D. R. Brown not out	6
A. Singh c Laney b Mullally	85	B 4, l-b 8, w 4, n-b 2	18
D. P. Ostler lbw b Mascarenhas	20		
T. L. Penney not out	29	1/185 2/212 (4 wkts, 50 overs)	262
M. J. Powell b Mullally	4	3/228 4/243	

A. F. Giles, *N. M. K. Smith, †K. J. Piper, A. A. Donald and G. Welch did not bat.

Bowling: Hartley 10–1–54–0; Mascarenhas 10–2–29–1; Mullally 10–0–55–2; Morris 8–0–45–1; Udal 10–0–48–0; Stephenson 2–0–19–0.

Hampshire

J. P. Stephenson c Powell b Brown	15	S. D. Udal c Brown b Giles	8
*R. A. Smith b Smith	61	A. C. Morris not out	3
G. W. White c Knight b Smith	28	B 2, l-b 4, w 4, n-b 2	12
J. S. Laney c Powell b Donald	43		
W. S. Kendall run out	27	1/66 2/102 3/121 (7 wkts, 50 overs) 243	
A. D. Mascarenhas c Ostler b Brown	13	4/174 5/184	
†A. N. Aymes not out	33	6/204 7/225	

P. J. Hartley and A. D. Mullally did not bat.

Bowling: Welch 10–0–60–0; Brown 10–2–37–2; Donald 10–1–48–1; Giles 10–0–45–1; Smith 10–0–47–2.

Umpires: B. Dudleston and J. W. Lloyds.

GLOUCESTERSHIRE v LANCASHIRE

At Bristol, August 13, 14. Gloucestershire won by 98 runs. Toss: Lancashire.

Gloucestershire's veterans, Barnett (40) and Russell (on the eve of his 37th birthday), pointed them towards a record fourth consecutive limited-overs final at Lord's. In a reprise of the teams' Benson and Hedges Cup semi-final here at the end of May, the match was put back 24 hours because of rain. This time, the pitch was bowler-friendly, but Lancashire squandered the advantage of winning the toss: no one managed a consistently tight line, and 19 wides were profligate. Barnett's imperturbability – Lancashire were convinced he was caught behind in the first over, when umpire Whitehead called wide – and Russell's terrier-like eagerness realised 125 for the second wicket, and Alleyne's 36 off 27 balls at the end charged Lancashire with chasing 249. After losing Atherton, Ganguly and Flintoff in the first 14 overs for 43, they were overwhelmed by Gloucestershire's typically combative bowling and fielding. Harvey's absence in Australia was scarcely noticed.

Man of the Match: M. W. Alleyne.

Gloucestershire

T. H. C. Hancock c Atherton b Martin	26	M. C. J. Ball b Austin	1
K. J. Barnett c Ganguly b Martin	80	J. Lewis not out	4
†R. C. Russell c and b Schofield	55	B 5, l-b 6, w 19	30
J. N. Snape c Hegg b Martin	8		
*M. W. Alleyne not out	36	1/55 2/180 3/186 (7 wkts, 50 overs) 248	
M. G. N. Windows run out	3	4/196 5/209	
C. G. Taylor b Schofield	5	6/230 7/241	

J. M. M. Averis and A. M. Smith did not bat.

Bowling: Chapple 9–1–53–0; Austin 9–0–29–1; Martin 10–0–44–3; Flintoff 4–0–16–0; Scuderi 4–0–23–0; Ganguly 4–0–20–0; Schofield 10–0–52–2.

Lancashire

M. A. Atherton c Alleyne b Lewis	2	G. Chapple c and b Smith	6
S. C. Ganguly c Lewis b Smith	4	I. D. Austin not out	18
A. Flintoff c Hancock b Averis	22	P. J. Martin st Russell b Averis	18
*J. P. Crawley run out	41	B 1, l-b 6, w 4, n-b 2	13
N. H. Fairbrother c Lewis b Alleyne	15		
J. C. Scuderi lbw b Ball	7	1/3 2/21 3/43 (45.2 overs) 150	
†W. K. Hegg run out	3	4/88 5/90 6/98	
C. P. Schofield b Ball	1	7/99 8/110 9/114	

Bowling: Lewis 9–1–30–1; Smith 10–4–18–2; Averis 7.2–1–34–2; Alleyne 10–1–20–1; Ball 9–1–41–2.

Umpires: T. E. Jesty and A. G. T. Whitehead.

FINAL

GLOUCESTERSHIRE v WARWICKSHIRE

At Lord's, August 26, 27. Gloucestershire won by 22 runs (D/L method). Toss: Gloucestershire.

Rain washed out the scheduled day, truncated the reserve one, and brought Duckworth/Lewis into play for the first time in a Lord's final. It may have made history – doubly so with Gloucestershire winning their fourth successive final – but it was an unsatisfactory and anticlimactic way for the curtain to fall on the NatWest Trophy after 20 years.

A patient crowd waited until 5.15 p.m. on Saturday before play was called off – the regulations allowed for play to continue until 8 p.m. on the first day in the event of time lost and a possible finish – and a much thinner gathering reconvened under gloomy skies next morning. Gloucestershire wasted no time in asserting their authority. Although Harvey, recently returned from Australia, looked out of sorts, Mike Smith dismissed Knight in the second over, forcing him to follow a ball which moved away, and bowled Singh in the tenth.

Giles, his inclusion in England's squad for the Fifth Test made public while he batted, looked purposeful as he added 49 in 11 overs with Ostler, but with Averis bowling as tightly as Smith – and Russell standing up to Averis – Warwickshire struggled. Alleyne offered some respite by bowling himself, only to tighten the screw when he brought on Hancock. Hancock should have had Giles caught at mid-on when 58, and soon had him caught at mid-wicket for 60 in 104 balls. Warwickshire's scoring remained well below par until their captain, Neil Smith, struck a lusty 28 in 29 balls, with Piper helping him take 35 off the last four overs and get their side past 200.

If only psychologically, Warwickshire needed an inspirational opening burst from Donald. Instead, Brown conceded three boundaries to Hancock in a wayward first over and, though Giddins was tighter and had Hancock dropped at slip, the Gloucestershire openers were not rattled until Donald's arrival in the ninth over. Bursting with energy on his last big occasion for Warwickshire, roared in by an appreciative following, he unnerved Hancock in a ferocious first over before defeating him with a slower sixth delivery. His first spell of 4–1–4–1 earned rapturous applause but, while he rested, Harvey and Barnett, playing in a fifth consecutive Lord's final, helped themselves to 39 risk-free runs in eight overs against the spinners. They had registered the only fifty partnership of the match by the time Donald returned for two overs and, with his second ball, bowled Barnett middle stump. Russell and Harvey then added 29 untroubled runs under darkening skies before the Australian, scenting his half-century and conscious of the perplexities of the Duckworth/Lewis tables, took to Brown and was caught by Powell just inside the mid-wicket rope. As he walked off, a sudden downpour sent the other players hurrying after him.

Torrential rain and lightning made further play unlikely – the scheduled close was 6.30 p.m. – and at 5.45 p.m. the match was called off, with Gloucestershire safely ahead on the Duckworth/Lewis reckonings. The announcement sparked an incongruous outburst of rain-sodden joy as Gloucestershire supporters slid across the outfield, apparent despair from Donald, whose efforts earned him the match award, and a touch of the absurd as Channel 4 staff belatedly rushed the NatWest Trophy from their television studio to the Pavilion so the winning captain could hold it aloft for the final time. – MATTHEW HANCOCK.

Man of the Match: A. A. Donald. *Attendance:* 20,442; *receipts* £520,263.

Warwickshire

N. V. Knight c Russell b Smith	1	†K. J. Piper not out		8
A. Singh b Smith	10			
A. F. Giles c Barnett b Hancock	60	L-b 12, w 22		34
D. P. Ostler c Harvey b Averis	19			
T. L. Penney c Alleyne b Smith	20	1/9 (1) 2/32 (2)	(7 wkts, 50 overs)	205
M. J. Powell b Harvey	21	3/81 (4) 4/129 (3)		
D. R. Brown c Barnett b Hancock	4	5/134 (5) 6/147 (7)		
*N. M. K. Smith not out	28	7/170 (6)	Score at 15 overs: 46-2	

A. A. Donald and E. S. H. Giddins did not bat.

Bowling: Harvey 10–0–47–1; Smith 10–3–18–3; Averis 10–1–50–1; Alleyne 6–0–28–0; Hancock 10–1–34–2; Ball 4–0–16–0.

Gloucestershire

T. H. C. Hancock b Donald	18
K. J. Barnett b Donald	45
I. J. Harvey c Powell b Brown	47
†R. C. Russell not out	6
L-b 5, w 1	6

1/40 (1) 2/93 (2)   (3 wkts, 29.4 overs) 122
3/122 (3)   Score at 15 overs: 54-1

M. G. N. Windows, *M. W. Alleyne, C. G. Taylor, J. N. Snape, M. C. J. Ball, J. M. M. Averis and A. M. Smith did not bat.

Bowling: Brown 5.4–0–38–1; Giddins 7–0–20–0; Donald 6–2–7–2; Smith 4–0–23–0; Giles 7–0–29–0.

Umpires: J. H. Hampshire and R. Julian.

NATWEST TROPHY RECORDS

(Including Gillette Cup, 1963-80)

65-over games in 1963; 60-over games 1964-98; 50-over games 1999 onwards.

Batting

Highest individual scores: 206, A. I. Kallicharran, Warwickshire v Oxfordshire, Birmingham, 1984; 201, V. J. Wells, Leicestershire v Berkshire, Leicester, 1996; 180*, T. M. Moody, Worcestershire v Surrey, The Oval, 1994; 177, C. G Greenidge, Hampshire v Glamorgan, Southampton, 1975; 177, A. J. Wright, Gloucestershire v Scotland, Bristol, 1997; 173*, M. J. Di Venuto, Derbyshire v Derbyshire Board XI, Derby, 2000; 172*, G. A. Hick, Worcestershire v Devon, Worcester, 1987; 165*, V. P. Terry, Hampshire v Berkshire, Southampton, 1985; 162*, C. J. Tavaré, Somerset v Devon, Torquay, 1990; 162*, I. V. A. Richards, Glamorgan v Oxfordshire, Swansea, 1993. *In the final:* 146, G. Boycott, Yorkshire v Surrey, 1965. (343 hundreds have been scored in the competition. The most hundreds in one season was 26 in 1996.)

Most runs: 2,547, G. A. Gooch; 2,309, R. A. Smith; 2,148, M. W. Gatting; 1,998, A. J. Lamb; 1,992, K. J. Barnett; 1,950, D. L. Amiss.

Fastest hundred: G. D. Rose off 36 balls, Somerset v Devon, Torquay, 1990.

Most hundreds: 8, R. A. Smith; 7, C. L. Smith; 6, G. A. Gooch; 5, D. I. Gower, I. V. A. Richards and G. M. Turner.

Highest totals: 413 for four, Somerset v Devon, Torquay, 1990; 406 for five, Leicestershire v Berkshire, Leicester, 1996; 404 for three, Worcestershire v Devon, Worcester, 1987; 392 for five, Warwickshire v Oxfordshire, Birmingham, 1984; 386 for five, Essex v Wiltshire, Chelmsford, 1988; 384 for six, Kent v Berkshire, Finchampstead, 1994; 384 for nine, Sussex v Ireland, Belfast, 1996; 381 for three, Lancashire v Hertfordshire, Radlett, 1999; 373 for seven, Glamorgan v Bedfordshire, Cardiff, 1998; 372 for five, Lancashire v Gloucestershire, Manchester, 1990; 371 for four, Hampshire v Glamorgan, Southampton, 1975. *In the final:* 322 for five, Warwickshire v Sussex, Lord's, 1993.

Highest total by a minor county: 323 for seven, Hertfordshire v Leicestershire Board XI, Radlett, 1999.

Highest total by a side batting first and losing: 327 for eight (60 overs), Derbyshire v Sussex, Derby, 1997. *In the final:* 321 for six (60 overs), Sussex v Warwickshire, 1993.

Highest totals by a side batting second: 350 (59.5 overs), Surrey lost to Worcestershire, The Oval, 1994; 339 for nine (60 overs), Somerset lost to Warwickshire, Birmingham, 1995; 329 for five (59.2 overs), Sussex beat Derbyshire, Derby, 1997; 326 for nine (60 overs), Hampshire lost to Leicestershire, Leicester, 1987; 322 for five (60 overs), Warwickshire beat Sussex, Lord's, 1993 (*in the final*); 319 for nine (59.5 overs), Essex beat Lancashire, Chelmsford, 1992.

Lowest completed totals: 39 (26.4 overs), Ireland v Sussex, Hove, 1985; 41 (20 overs), Cambridgeshire v Buckinghamshire, Cambridge, 1972; 41 (19.4 overs), Middlesex v Essex, Westcliff, 1972; 41 (36.1 overs), Shropshire v Essex, Wellington, 1974. *In the final:* 57 (27.2 overs), Essex v Lancashire, 1996.

Lowest total by a side batting first and winning: 98 (56.2 overs), Worcestershire v Durham, Chester-le-Street, 1968.

Shortest innings: 10.1 overs (60 for one), Worcestershire v Lancashire, Worcester, 1963.

Matches rearranged on a reduced number of overs are excluded from the above.

Record partnerships for each wicket

311	for 1st	A. J. Wright and N. J. Trainor, Gloucestershire v Scotland at Bristol ..	1997
286	for 2nd	I. S. Anderson and A. Hill, Derbyshire v Cornwall at Derby	1986
309*	for 3rd	T. S. Curtis and T. M. Moody, Worcestershire v Surrey at The Oval ..	1994
234*	for 4th	D. Lloyd and C. H. Lloyd, Lancashire v Gloucestershire at Manchester .	1978
166	for 5th	M. A. Lynch and G. R. J. Roope, Surrey v Durham at The Oval	1982
226	for 6th	N. J. Llong and M. V. Fleming, Kent v Cheshire at Bowdon	1999
160*	for 7th	C. J. Richards and I. R. Payne, Surrey v Lincolnshire at Sleaford	1983
112	for 8th	A. L. Penberthy and J. E. Emburey, Northamptonshire v Lancashire at Manchester	1996
87	for 9th	M. A. Nash and A. E. Cordle, Glamorgan v Lincolnshire at Swansea ..	1974
81	for 10th	S. Turner and R. E. East, Essex v Yorkshire at Leeds	1982

Bowling

Most wickets: 81, G. G. Arnold; 80, C. A. Connor; 79, J. Simmons.

Best bowling (12 overs unless stated): eight for 21 (10.1 overs), M. A. Holding, Derbyshire v Sussex, Hove, 1988; eight for 31 (11.1 overs), D. L. Underwood, Kent v Scotland, Edinburgh, 1987; seven for 15, A. L. Dixon, Kent v Surrey, The Oval, 1967; seven for 15 (9.3 overs), R. P. Lefebvre, Somerset v Devon, Torquay, 1990; seven for 19, N. V. Radford, Worcestershire v Bedfordshire, Bedford, 1991; seven for 27 (9.5 overs), D. Gough, Yorkshire v Ireland, Leeds, 1997; seven for 30, P. J. Sainsbury, Hampshire v Norfolk, Southampton, 1965; seven for 32, S. P. Davis, Durham v Lancashire, Chester-le-Street, 1983; seven for 33, R. D. Jackman, Surrey v Yorkshire, Harrogate, 1970; seven for 35 (10.1 overs), D. E. Malcolm, Derbyshire v Northamptonshire, Derby, 1997; seven for 37, N. A. Mallender, Northamptonshire v Worcestershire, Northampton, 1984. *In the final:* six for 18 (6.2 overs), G. Chapple, Lancashire v Essex, 1996.

Most economical analysis: 12–9–3–1, J. Simmons, Lancashire v Suffolk, Bury St Edmunds, 1985.

Most expensive analysis: 12–0–107–2, C. C. Lovell, Cornwall v Warwickshire, St Austell, 1996.

Hat-tricks (11): J. D. F. Larter, Northamptonshire v Sussex, Northampton, 1963; D. A. D. Sydenham, Surrey v Cheshire, Hoylake, 1964; R. N. S. Hobbs, Essex v Middlesex, Lord's, 1968; N. M. McVicker, Warwickshire v Lincolnshire, Birmingham, 1971; G. S. le Roux, Sussex v Ireland, Hove, 1985; M. Jean-Jacques, Derbyshire v Nottinghamshire, Derby, 1987; J. F. M. O'Brien, Cheshire v Derbyshire, Chester, 1988; R. A. Pick, Nottinghamshire v Scotland, Nottingham, 1995; J. E. Emburey, Northamptonshire v Cheshire, Northampton, 1996; A. R. Caddick, Somerset v Gloucestershire, Taunton, 1996; D. Gough, Yorkshire v Ireland, Leeds, 1997.

Four wickets in five balls: D. A. D. Sydenham, Surrey v Cheshire, Hoylake, 1964.

Wicket-keeping and Fielding

Most dismissals: 82 (69 ct, 13 st), R. C. Russell; 66 (58 ct, 8 st), R. W. Taylor; 65 (59 ct, 6 st), A. P. E. Knott.

Most dismissals in an innings: 7 (all ct), A. J. Stewart, Surrey v Glamorgan, Swansea, 1994.

Most catches by a fielder: 27, J. Simmons; 26, M. W. Gatting and G. A. Gooch; 25, G. Cook; 24, P. J. Sharpe.

Most catches by a fielder in an innings: 4 – A. S. Brown, Gloucestershire v Middlesex, Bristol, 1963; G. Cook, Northamptonshire v Glamorgan, Northampton, 1972; C. G. Greenidge, Hampshire v Cheshire, Southampton, 1981; D. C. Jackson, Durham v Northamptonshire, Darlington, 1984; T. S. Smith, Hertfordshire v Somerset, St Albans, 1984; H. Morris, Glamorgan v Scotland, Edinburgh, 1988; C. C. Lewis, Nottinghamshire v Worcestershire, Nottingham, 1992; G. Yates, Lancashire v Essex, Manchester, 2000.

Results

Largest victories in runs: Somerset by 346 runs v Devon, Torquay, 1990; Sussex by 304 runs v Ireland, Belfast, 1996; Worcestershire by 299 runs v Devon, Worcester, 1987; Essex by 291 runs v Wiltshire, Chelmsford, 1988; Sussex by 244 runs v Ireland, Hove, 1985; Lancashire by 241 runs v Gloucestershire, Manchester, 1990.

Victories by ten wickets (19): By Essex, Glamorgan, Hampshire (twice), Holland, Lancashire, Middlesex, Northamptonshire, Nottinghamshire, Somerset, Surrey, Sussex (twice), Warwickshire (twice), Yorkshire (four times).

Earliest finishes: both at 2.20 p.m. Worcestershire beat Lancashire by nine wickets at Worcester, 1963; Essex beat Middlesex by eight wickets at Westcliff, 1972.

Scores level (11): Nottinghamshire 215, Somerset 215 for nine at Taunton, 1964; Surrey 196, Sussex 196 for eight at The Oval, 1970; Somerset 287 for six, Essex 287 at Taunton, 1978; Surrey 195 for seven, Essex 195 at Chelmsford, 1980; Essex 149, Derbyshire 149 for eight at Derby, 1981; Northamptonshire 235 for nine, Derbyshire 235 for six at Lord's, 1981 (*in the final*); Middlesex 222 for nine, Somerset 222 for eight at Lord's, 1983; Hampshire 224 for eight, Essex 224 for seven at Southampton, 1985; Essex 307 for six, Hampshire 307 for five at Chelmsford, 1990; Hampshire 204 for nine, Leicestershire 204 for nine at Leicester, 1995; Cheshire 204, Lincolnshire 204 for nine at Chester, 2000.
Note: Under the rules the side which lost fewer wickets won; at Leicester in 1995, Leicestershire won by virtue of their higher total after 30 overs.

Match Awards

Most awards: 9, G. A. Gooch and R. A. Smith; 8, C. H. Lloyd and C. L. Smith.

WINNERS 1963-2000

Gillette Cup

		Man of the Match
1963	SUSSEX* beat Worcestershire by 14 runs.	N. Gifford†
1964	SUSSEX beat Warwickshire* by eight wickets.	N. I. Thomson
1965	YORKSHIRE beat Surrey* by 175 runs.	G. Boycott
1966	WARWICKSHIRE* beat Worcestershire by five wickets.	R. W. Barber
1967	KENT* beat Somerset by 32 runs.	M. H. Denness
1968	WARWICKSHIRE beat Sussex* by four wickets.	A. C. Smith
1969	YORKSHIRE beat Derbyshire* by 69 runs.	B. Leadbeater
1970	LANCASHIRE* beat Sussex by six wickets.	H. Pilling
1971	LANCASHIRE* beat Kent by 24 runs.	Asif Iqbal†
1972	LANCASHIRE* beat Warwickshire by four wickets.	C. H. Lloyd

		Man of the Match
1973	GLOUCESTERSHIRE* beat Sussex by 40 runs.	A. S. Brown
1974	KENT* beat Lancashire by four wickets.	A. P. E. Knott
1975	LANCASHIRE* beat Middlesex by seven wickets.	C. H. Lloyd
1976	NORTHAMPTONSHIRE* beat Lancashire by four wickets.	P. Willey
1977	MIDDLESEX* beat Glamorgan by five wickets.	C. T. Radley
1978	SUSSEX* beat Somerset by five wickets.	P. W. G. Parker
1979	SOMERSET beat Northamptonshire* by 45 runs.	I. V. A. Richards
1980	MIDDLESEX* beat Surrey by seven wickets.	J. M. Brearley

NatWest Trophy

1981	DERBYSHIRE* beat Northamptonshire by losing fewer wickets with the scores level.	G. Cook†
1982	SURREY* beat Warwickshire by nine wickets.	D. J. Thomas
1983	SOMERSET beat Kent* by 24 runs.	V. J. Marks
1984	MIDDLESEX beat Kent* by four wickets.	C. T. Radley
1985	ESSEX beat Nottinghamshire* by one run.	B. R. Hardie
1986	SUSSEX* beat Lancashire by seven wickets.	D. A. Reeve
1987	NOTTINGHAMSHIRE* beat Northamptonshire by three wickets.	R. J. Hadlee
1988	MIDDLESEX* beat Worcestershire by three wickets.	M. R. Ramprakash
1989	WARWICKSHIRE beat Middlesex* by four wickets.	D. A. Reeve
1990	LANCASHIRE* beat Northamptonshire by seven wickets.	P. A. J. DeFreitas
1991	HAMPSHIRE* beat Surrey by four wickets.	R. A. Smith
1992	NORTHAMPTONSHIRE* beat Leicestershire by eight wickets.	A. Fordham
1993	WARWICKSHIRE* beat Sussex by five wickets.	Asif Din
1994	WORCESTERSHIRE* beat Warwickshire by eight wickets.	T. M. Moody
1995	WARWICKSHIRE beat Northamptonshire* by four wickets.	D. A. Reeve
1996	LANCASHIRE beat Essex* by 129 runs.	G. Chapple
1997	ESSEX* beat Warwickshire by nine wickets.	S. G. Law
1998	LANCASHIRE* beat Derbyshire by nine wickets.	I. D. Austin
1999	GLOUCESTERSHIRE beat Somerset* by 50 runs.	R. C. Russell
2000	GLOUCESTERSHIRE* beat Warwickshire by 22 runs (D/L method).	A. A. Donald†

* *Won toss.*   † *On losing side.*

TEAM RECORDS 1963-2000

	Rounds reached				Matches		
	W	F	SF	QF	P	W	L
Derbyshire........	1	3	4	13	79*	42	37
Durham	0	0	0	1	44	14	30
Essex	2	3	6	15	84	48	36
Glamorgan	0	1	4	16	82	44	38
Gloucestershire.	3	3	7	16	85	49	36
Hampshire........	1	1	10	22	98	61	37
Kent.............	2	5	7	15	87	51	36
Lancashire.......	7	10	16	22	110	79	31
Leicestershire......	0	1	4	15	79	41	38
Middlesex	4	6	13	21	102	68	34
Northamptonshire . . .	2	7	10	21	97	61	36
Nottinghamshire	1	2	3	13	79	42	37
Somerset.........	2	5	10	18	93	57	36
Surrey	1	4	11	23	98*	61	37
Sussex	4	8	13	19	97	63	34
Warwickshire	5	11	17	22	111	78	33
Worcestershire	1	4	10	14	85	48	37
Yorkshire........	2	2	7	11	83	47	36

* Derbyshire and Surrey totals each include a bowling contest after their first-round matches were abandoned in 1991; Derbyshire lost to Hertfordshire and Surrey beat Oxfordshire.

MINOR COUNTY RECORDS

From 1964 to 1979 the previous season's top five Minor Counties were invited to take part in the competition. In 1980 these were joined by Ireland, and in 1983 the competition was expanded to embrace 13 Minor Counties, Ireland and Scotland. The number of Minor Counties dropped to 12 in 1992 when Durham attained first-class status, and 11 in 1995 when Holland were admitted to the competition.

Between 1964 and 1991 Durham qualified 21 times, including 15 years in succession from 1977-91. They reached the second round a record six times.

Up to the 1998 tournament, Staffordshire qualified most among the remaining Minor Counties, 20 times, followed by Devon, 19. Only Hertfordshire have ever reached the quarter-finals, in 1976.

From 1999, the competition was reformed and two preliminary rounds introduced, in which 42 teams compete for the right to join the first-class counties in the third round. They are all 20 Minor Counties (including Wales), plus Huntingdonshire Board XI, the first-class county Board XIs (excluding Glamorgan, who are covered by Wales) and the national teams of Denmark, Holland, Ireland and Scotland.

Wins by a minor team over a first-class county (10): Durham v Yorkshire (by five wickets), Harrogate, 1973; Lincolnshire v Glamorgan (by six wickets), Swansea, 1974; Hertfordshire v Essex (by 33 runs), 2nd round, Hitchin, 1976; Shropshire v Yorkshire (by 37 runs), Telford, 1984; Durham v Derbyshire (by seven wickets), Derby, 1985; Buckinghamshire v Somerset (by seven runs), High Wycombe, 1987; Cheshire v Northamptonshire (by one wicket), Chester, 1988; Hertfordshire v Derbyshire (2–1 in a bowling contest after the match was abandoned), Bishop's Stortford, 1991; Scotland v Worcestershire (by four runs), Edinburgh, 1998; Holland v Durham (by five wickets), Amstelveen, 1999.

WOMBWELL CRICKET LOVERS' SOCIETY AWARDS, 2000

Courtney Walsh of West Indies was voted George Spofforth Cricketer of the Year by members of the Wombwell Cricket Lovers' Society. Other award winners were: C. B. Fry Young Cricketer of the Year – Marcus Trescothick; Brian Sellers Captain of the Year – Mark Alleyne; Arthur Wood Wicket-keeper of the Year – Jack Russell; Les Bailey Best Yorkshire Newcomer – Matthew Hoggard; Learie Constantine Best Fielder in NatWest Final – Jeremy Snape; Denis Compton Memorial Award for Flair – Darren Lehmann; J. M. Kilburn Cricket Writer of the Year – Stephen Chalke; Jack Fingleton Cricket Commentator of the Year – Ralph Dellor; Ted Umbers Services to Yorkshire Cricket – Jack Lee.

BENSON AND HEDGES CUP, 2000

Matthew Maynard

Gloucestershire, returning to Lord's for their third consecutive final, uniquely made it three separate knockout trophies in a row when they beat Glamorgan by seven wickets. When Somerset and Lancashire had won successive Benson and Hedges finals, in 1982 and 1996 respectively, they were presented with the same cup they won the previous year. Not so Gloucestershire, who would now have something old and something new in their trophy cabinet. Alongside the one-off Benson and Hedges Super Cup, which they won in 1999, went the original Benson and Hedges Cup, which was taken out of mothballs when the ECB returned the competition to its initial format of qualifying and knockout rounds.

For Glamorgan, in their first Lord's final since losing to Middlesex in the 1977 Gillette Cup, there was only the consolation of Matthew Maynard's century, which graced the occasion and brought him the Gold Award. It was, coincidentally, the second successive century by a county captain in the final. Gloucestershire's Mark Alleyne had made 112 against Yorkshire the previous year.

The first Lord's final of the new century was also its earliest, and it was attended, if not by a full house, by good weather at least. Until then, the competition that had refused to lie down, brought back to life in 2000 by demand of the counties, had fallen foul of the third-wettest April on record. Only one third of the group games was not abbreviated or abandoned: Middlesex did not take the field until their fifth and final fixture. (The northern group had easily the best record of completed matches, suggesting rather that the north of England's reputation for rain has been mischievously exaggerated.) With 15 games abandoned before the players could take the field, it came as no surprise when counties began to call for a later start to the competition. Such a move, of course, would be sure to guarantee April sunshine. Not that the inclement weather seemed to bother Benson and Hedges, who announced they would continue to sponsor the competition in its present format for two more years, which was good news for county coffers.

Prize money

£52,000 for winners: GLOUCESTERSHIRE.
£26,000 for runners-up: GLAMORGAN.
£15,500 for each losing semi-finalist: LANCASHIRE, SURREY.
£10,500 for each losing quarter-finalist: DURHAM, HAMPSHIRE, SUSSEX, YORKSHIRE.

Gold Award winners received £1,750 in the final, £550 in the semi-finals, £500 in the quarter-finals and £300 in the group matches. Because of the restoration of the group rounds, the total prize money awarded increased from £149,300 in the 1999 Benson and Hedges Super Cup to £163,650; the total sponsorship rose from £800,000 to £850,000.

FINAL GROUP TABLES

	Played	Won	Lost	No result	Points	Net run-rate
Midlands/Wales/West Group						
GLAMORGAN.	5	2	1	2	6	−0.43
GLOUCESTERSHIRE	5	2	1	2	6	1.03
Warwickshire	5	1	1	3	5	−1.79
Northamptonshire	5	1	1	3	5	−0.35
Worcestershire	5	1	1	3	5	2.03
Somerset	5	0	2	3	3	−0.23
North Group						
YORKSHIRE	5	3	1	1	7	0.31
LANCASHIRE	5	3	2	0	6	0.06
DURHAM*	5	3	2	0	6	0.64
Derbyshire	5	2	1	2	6	0.11
Leicestershire	5	1	2	2	4	−0.04
Nottinghamshire	5	0	4	1	1	−1.47
South Group						
SUSSEX	5	2	1	2	6	0.28
HAMPSHIRE.	5	2	1	2	6	0.06
SURREY*	5	1	1	3	5	1.10
Kent	5	1	1	3	5	0.84
Essex	5	1	2	2	4	−0.52
Middlesex	5	0	1	4	4	−1.54

* Durham and Surrey qualified as the most successful third-placed teams.

Where two or more counties finished with an equal number of points, the positions were decided by (a) most wins (b) most points in head-to-head matches (c) net run-rate (runs scored per 100 balls minus runs conceded per 100 balls, revising figures in matches where the Duckworth/Lewis method was used and discounting those not played to a result).

MIDLANDS/WALES/WEST GROUP

GLAMORGAN v GLOUCESTERSHIRE

At Cardiff, April 15. Glamorgan won by three wickets. Toss: Glamorgan. County debut: M. T. G. Elliott. First-team debut: C. G. Taylor.

With two balls to spare, Thomas hit Smith to the square-leg boundary and ensured Glamorgan had the better of a cold, wet day than holders Gloucestershire, unbeaten in both knockout competitions in 1999. The game, reduced to 25 overs a side after a rain-delayed start, seemed to be heading Gloucestershire's way when Glamorgan collapsed from 59 without loss to 71 for four. But James and then Newell kept the asking-rate within bounds: 34 from four overs became eight from the last. Gloucestershire had earlier sped from the blocks when Jones conceded 17 in his first over, and it needed the experience of Watkin, who took three for seven from his five overs, to rein them in.

Gold Award: S. L. Watkin.

Gloucestershire

J. N. Snape b Watkin	26	J. Lewis not out	15
K. J. Barnett c Elliott b Watkin.	0		
M. G. N. Windows b Watkin	0	L-b 12, w 8	20
T. H. C. Hancock c Elliott b Thomas. . .	24		
*M. W. Alleyne run out	50	1/17 2/26 3/57 (6 wkts, 25 overs) 148
D. R. Hewson run out	13	4/67 5/114 6/148

†R. C. Russell, C. G. Taylor, J. M. M. Averis and A. M. Smith did not bat.

Bowling: Jones 5–0–47–0; Watkin 5–2–7–3; Thomas 5–0–21–1; Newell 3–0–14–0; Dale 4–0–20–0; Croft 3–0–27–0.

Glamorgan

M. T. G. Elliott c Smith b Alleyne	29	S. D. Thomas not out	6
R. D. B. Croft b Barnett	25	†A. D. Shaw not out	1
M. J. Powell lbw b Alleyne	0	L-b 5, w 2	7
*M. P. Maynard c Snape b Averis	21		
A. Dale st Russell b Barnett	6	1/59 2/59 3/60 (7 wkts, 24.4 overs) 150	
S. P. James run out	34	4/71 5/95	
K. Newell run out	21	6/138 7/145	

S. P. Jones and S. L. Watkin did not bat.

Bowling: Smith 4.4–0–25–0; Lewis 5–0–28–0; Averis 5–0–36–1; Alleyne 5–0–28–2; Barnett 5–0–28–2.

Umpires: V. A. Holder and A. G. T. Whitehead.

NORTHAMPTONSHIRE v WORCESTERSHIRE

At Northampton, April 15. No result (abandoned).

WARWICKSHIRE v SOMERSET

At Birmingham, April 15. No result. Toss: Warwickshire.
The weather limited play to just under an hour, enough time for Trescothick to reach 29 from 45 balls.

Somerset

M. E. Trescothick not out	29
*J. Cox c Piper b Giddins	6
P. C. L. Holloway b Sheikh	2
M. Burns not out	4
B 1, l-b 2, w 4	7

1/25 2/29   (2 wkts, 14 overs) 48

†R. J. Turner, I. D. Blackwell, K. A. Parsons, G. D. Rose, A. R. Caddick, P. W. Jarvis and P. S. Jones did not bat.

Bowling: Giddins 7–0–19–1; Brown 3–1–17–0; Sheikh 4–1–9–1.

Warwickshire

N. V. Knight, *N. M. K. Smith, D. L. Hemp, D. P. Ostler, T. L. Penney, D. R. Brown, M. A. Sheikh, †K. J. Piper, A. F. Giles, A. A. Donald and E. S. H. Giddins.

Umpires: M. J. Harris and J. F. Steele.

GLOUCESTERSHIRE v WARWICKSHIRE

At Bristol, April 16. Gloucestershire won by five wickets. Toss: Gloucestershire.

Generous lateral movement on a sluggish pitch made batting awkward, especially early on, and Gloucestershire's bowlers capitalised on winning the toss. They had Warwickshire eight for two, then 66 for six. Penney and Giles shored up the innings for a while, but once they were caught by Russell – his five catches were a county record in the competition – the end came swiftly. Averis finished with four for eight, including two in two balls, his best one-day figures; Warwickshire finished with their lowest Benson and Hedges total. Their bowlers then failed to match their opponents' accuracy, with Donald's nine wides a factor in extras being more than a third of the Gloucestershire total. Only Hewson's determined 30 came close to matching them.

Gold Award: J. M. M. Averis.

Warwickshire

N. V. Knight lbw b Alleyne	17	†K. J. Piper c Russell b Averis			0
*N. M. K. Smith c Russell b Smith	4	A. A. Donald b Averis			2
D. L. Hemp b Averis	1	E. S. H. Giddins not out			0
D. P. Ostler c Russell b Cawdron	11	L-b 1, w 3			4
T. L. Penney c Russell b Alleyne	25				
D. R. Brown c Averis b Cawdron	8	1/5 2/8 3/36		(35.4 overs)	94
M. A. Sheikh b Cawdron	7	4/36 5/45 6/66			
A. F. Giles c Russell b Averis	15	7/92 8/92 9/92			

Bowling: Smith 7–0–25–1; Averis 7.4–2–8–4; Alleyne 8–2–18–2; Cawdron 10–2–30–3; Barnett 3–0–12–0.

Gloucestershire

T. H. C. Hancock c Penney b Giddins	5	†R. C. Russell not out		1
K. J. Barnett b Giddins	5			
M. G. N. Windows b Sheikh	7	B 2, l-b 12, w 15, n-b 4		33
*M. W. Alleyne b Sheikh	6			
D. R. Hewson not out	30	1/18 2/24 3/37	(5 wkts, 28.1 overs)	96
C. G. Taylor c Piper b Giddins	9	4/49 5/84		

M. J. Cawdron, J. N. Snape, J. M. M. Averis and A. M. Smith did not bat.

Bowling: Donald 7–0–25–0; Giddins 9–2–22–3; Sheikh 7.1–2–20–2; Brown 4–0–14–0; Giles 1–0–1–0.

Umpires: J. H. Harris and A. G. T. Whitehead.

SOMERSET v NORTHAMPTONSHIRE

At Taunton, April 16. Northamptonshire won by seven wickets (D/L method). Toss: Northamptonshire. County debuts: D. M. Cousins, A. S. Rollins.

Until rain interrupted play nearly an hour before the scheduled close, the game looked set for an intriguing climax. Play resumed 45 minutes later, but by then Northamptonshire's target had been revised from 76 in 10.3 overs to just six from nine balls. They made no mistake: Sales, who had twice lofted Blackwell for straight sixes, guided Northamptonshire home and finished undefeated on 64 off 72 balls. Somerset had set a competitive target, helped by fifties from Cox and Holloway, who added 120 for the second wicket.

Gold Award: D. J. Sales.

Somerset

M. E. Trescothick c Loye b Malcolm	7	G. D. Rose not out		15
*J. Cox c Malcolm b Penberthy	59	A. R. Caddick not out		3
P. C. L. Holloway c Ripley b Swann	78	L-b 8, w 7, n-b 2		17
M. Burns c Warren b Cousins	40			
I. D. Blackwell c Warren b Swann	3	1/13 2/133 3/180	(7 wkts, 50 overs)	257
†R. J. Turner run out	29	4/186 5/205		
K. A. Parsons lbw b Cousins	6	6/213 7/247		

P. S. Jones and P. W. Jarvis did not bat.

Bowling: Malcolm 10–0–45–1; Cousins 8–0–37–2; Penberthy 10–0–24–1; Logan 7–0–49–0; Innes 10–0–63–0; Swann 5–0–31–2.

Northamptonshire

A. S. Rollins c Holloway b Rose	1	A. L. Penberthy not out		28
M. B. Loye c Blackwell b Jarvis	57	L-b 7, w 8, n-b 2		17
R. J. Warren c Blackwell b Jarvis	23			
D. J. Sales not out	64	1/1 2/55 3/126	(3 wkts, 40.1 overs)	190

G. P. Swann, K. J. Innes, *†D. Ripley, R. J. Logan, D. M. Cousins and D. E. Malcolm did not bat.

Bowling: Caddick 10–1–32–0; Rose 6–2–18–1; Jones 7.1–0–40–0; Jarvis 5–0–21–1; Parsons 8–0–43–0; Blackwell 4–0–29–0.

Umpires: R. Palmer and D. R. Shepherd.

WORCESTERSHIRE v GLAMORGAN

At Worcester, April 16. Worcestershire won by nine wickets. Toss: Worcestershire. County debut: A. G. Wharf.

Worcestershire, in the youthful guise of Kabir Ali, a 19-year-old seam bowler, and the experienced form of Hick, proved far too strong for Glamorgan. Ali, in his first one-day game at county level, removed Elliott with his third ball and Croft two overs later, then came back to finish the innings with consecutive balls. Maynard threatened a recovery, but it was left to Dale to offer prolonged resistance. When Worcestershire batted, all hostility seemed to vanish from the pitch, and Hick brought matters to an explosive conclusion with 20 overs to spare: he struck the last four balls, bowled by Wharf, for successive leg-side boundaries, one of them clearing the ropes. Ice had to be removed from the covers before play could start.

Gold Award: Kabir Ali.

Glamorgan

M. T. G. Elliott lbw b Ali	1	†A. D. Shaw c Hick b Sheriyar		8
R. D. B. Croft c Hick b Ali	12	A. G. Wharf c Leatherdale b Ali		15
M. J. Powell b Sheriyar	0	S. L. Watkin lbw b Ali		0
*M. P. Maynard c Sheriyar b Lampitt	31	L-b 5, w 6		11
A. Dale not out	49			
S. P. James b Leatherdale	1	1/6 2/12 3/16	(46.4 overs)	147
K. Newell b Leatherdale	12	4/57 5/63 6/88		
S. D. Thomas c and b Lampitt	7	7/100 8/122 9/147		

Bowling: Sheriyar 10–0–44–2; Ali 8.4–2–29–4; Lampitt 10–0–16–2; Leatherdale 10–1–23–2; Illingworth 8–0–30–0.

Worcestershire

P. R. Pollard not out	54
K. R. Spring c Shaw b Watkin	10
*G. A. Hick not out	55
L-b 11, w 18	29

1/24   (1 wkt, 29.4 overs) 148

V. S. Solanki, E. J. Wilson, D. A. Leatherdale, †S. J. Rhodes, S. R. Lampitt, R. K. Illingworth, Kabir Ali and A. Sheriyar did not bat.

Bowling: Watkin 10–1–22–1; Wharf 6.4–2–40–0; Dale 5–0–21–0; Thomas 5–0–29–0; Newell 3–0–25–0.

Umpires: A. Clarkson and M. J. Harris.

WARWICKSHIRE v NORTHAMPTONSHIRE

At Birmingham, April 18. No result (abandoned).

WORCESTERSHIRE v GLOUCESTERSHIRE

At Worcester, April 18. No result. Toss: Worcestershire.

Just ten overs had been bowled when the game was called off. Ali, the hero of Worcestershire's victory against Glamorgan, struggled to recapture that form and his first four overs cost 34. Despite the rain, there was good news for Worcestershire: their overseas signing, Australian Test bowler Glenn McGrath, arrived after the one-day series in South Africa.

Gloucestershire

T. H. C. Hancock c Solanki b Sheriyar . .	22
K. J. Barnett not out	18
M. G. N. Windows not out	7
L-b 2, w 6, n-b 2	10

1/31   (1 wkt, 10 overs) 57

†R. C. Russell, *M. W. Alleyne, D. R. Hewson, C. G. Taylor, M. J. Cawdron, J. N. Snape, J. M. M. Averis and A. M. Smith did not bat.

Bowling: Sheriyar 4–0–16–1; Ali 5–1–34–0; Lampitt 1–0–5–0.

Worcestershire

P. R. Pollard, K. R. Spring, *G. A. Hick, V. S. Solanki, E. J. Wilson, D. A. Leatherdale, †S. J. Rhodes, S. R. Lampitt, R. K. Illingworth, Kabir Ali and A. Sheriyar.

Umpires: A. Clarkson and B. Dudleston.

SOMERSET v GLAMORGAN

At Taunton, April 19. No result (abandoned). Toss: Glamorgan.

A break in the weather fleetingly hinted that there would be time for a ten-over thrash, but the teams never took the field.

Somerset

*J. Cox, M. E. Trescothick, P. C. L. Holloway, M. Burns, †R. J. Turner, K. A. Parsons, I. D. Blackwell, P. W. Jarvis, A. R. Caddick, P. S. Jones and M. P. L. Bulbeck.

Glamorgan

M. T. G. Elliott, R. D. B. Croft, M. J. Powell, *M. P. Maynard, A. Dale, S. P. James, K. Newell, S. D. Thomas, †A. D. Shaw, A. G. Wharf and S. L. Watkin.

NORTHAMPTONSHIRE v GLOUCESTERSHIRE

At Northampton, April 20. No result (abandoned).

SOMERSET v WORCESTERSHIRE

At Taunton, April 21. No result (abandoned).

GLAMORGAN v WARWICKSHIRE

At Cardiff, April 22. No result (abandoned).

GLOUCESTERSHIRE v SOMERSET

At Bristol, April 24. Gloucestershire won by ten runs (D/L method). Toss: Gloucestershire.

Harvey's blistering 35 in 29 balls, building on sensible batting by Windows, was enough to nose Gloucestershire in front on the Duckworth/Lewis reckoning before rain forced a premature finish. Conditions never favoured batting, and Somerset, despite reaching 45 without loss, had struggled to 139 for five before the left-handed pair of Holloway and Blackwell added 73 in ten overs. Averis took four wickets for the second innings in succession; captain Alleyne held four catches. If 226 looked formidable, Gloucestershire's revised target after a shower – 206 from 42 overs – was more so. However, the interruption galvanised Harvey and, when more rain came, Gloucestershire were ten runs to the good and through to the quarter-finals.

Gold Award: I. J. Harvey.

Somerset

*J. Cox c Alleyne b Smith	13	P. W. Jarvis run out	1
M. E. Trescothick c Alleyne b Averis	19	P. S. Jones b Averis	0
P. C. L. Holloway c Alleyne b Averis	72	M. P. L. Bulbeck not out	1
M. Burns c Hancock b Alleyne	14	B 8, l-b 9, w 17, n-b 2	36
†R. J. Turner c Hancock b Lewis	12		
K. A. Parsons c and b Barnett	15	1/45 2/45 3/68 (49.5 overs) 225
I. D. Blackwell c Hewson b Harvey	41	4/105 5/139 6/212
A. R. Caddick c Alleyne b Averis	1	7/218 8/218 9/222

Bowling: Smith 10–4–22–1; Harvey 9.5–1–33–1; Averis 10–0–48–4; Alleyne 8–0–45–1; Lewis 9–0–43–1; Barnett 3–0–17–1.

Gloucestershire

T. H. C. Hancock c Turner b Jarvis	29	†R. C. Russell not out	5
K. J. Barnett c Turner b Caddick	8		
M. G. N. Windows not out	42	L-b 3, w 16	19
*M. W. Alleyne b Jones	8		
D. R. Hewson b Parsons	8	1/24 2/51 3/67 (5 wkts, 32 overs) 154
I. J. Harvey c Parsons b Burns	35	4/86 5/147

J. Lewis, J. N. Snape, A. M. Smith and J. M. M. Averis did not bat.

Bowling: Caddick 9–2–30–1; Bulbeck 7–1–27–0; Jarvis 3–0–21–1; Jones 6–1–20–1; Parsons 4–0–32–1; Burns 2–0–14–1; Trescothick 1–0–7–0.

Umpires: D. J. Constant and J. F. Steele.

NORTHAMPTONSHIRE v GLAMORGAN

At Northampton, April 24. Glamorgan won by 39 runs. Toss: Northamptonshire.

A convincing victory over Northamptonshire ensured Glamorgan finished top of their group and gained a home tie in the next round. On a pitch helpful to seam bowling, no batsman ever felt entirely comfortable, but James and Dale showed how to master the conditions by placement and good running, rather than boundary hitting. Their 73 in ten overs for the fifth wicket contained only six fours. In reply, Northamptonshire set off at a lick, and appeared the likelier winners at 74 for one in the 17th over. Two quick wickets, and then Croft's dismissal of Hayden, 67 in 72 balls, changed the complexion. This was Hayden's first game of the season for Northamptonshire after playing for Australia in South Africa and, at his request, Ripley continued to lead the county. Penberthy typified their lack of subsequent endeavour with 18 from 56 balls.

Gold Award: R. D. B. Croft.

Glamorgan

M. T. G. Elliott c Ripley b Cousins	14	†A. D. Shaw run out	2
R. D. B. Croft c Ripley b Logan	35	O. T. Parkin not out	1
M. J. Powell c Warren b Cousins	42		
*M. P. Maynard c Warren b Cousins	48	L-b 4, w 12, n-b 4	20
A. Dale b Logan	34		
S. P. James not out	33	1/33 2/72 3/146 (8 wkts, 50 overs) 238	
K. Newell b Innes	4	4/149 5/222 6/227	
S. D. Thomas c Ripley b Logan	5	7/234 8/236	

S. L. Watkin did not bat.

Bowling: Malcolm 10–2–33–0; Cousins 10–1–36–3; Logan 10–0–52–3; Penberthy 10–0–46–0; Innes 4–0–38–1; Swann 6–0–29–0.

Northamptonshire

M. B. Loye c Shaw b Watkin	19	R. J. Logan st Shaw b Dale	1
M. L. Hayden b Croft	67	D. M. Cousins c Shaw b Thomas	10
R. J. Warren run out	10	D. E. Malcolm c and b Watkin	6
D. J. Sales lbw b Dale	0	L-b 3, w 9	12
A. L. Penberthy c Elliott b Thomas	18		
G. P. Swann c Shaw b Parkin	28	1/40 2/74 3/75 (46 overs) 199	
K. J. Innes b Thomas	19	4/105 5/136 6/163	
*†D. Ripley not out	9	7/170 8/175 9/192	

Bowling: Parkin 8–0–39–1; Watkin 10–3–35–2; Thomas 10–0–49–3; Dale 8–1–37–2; Croft 10–1–36–1.

Umpires: J. H. Harris and M. J. Kitchen.

WARWICKSHIRE v WORCESTERSHIRE

At Birmingham, April 24. Warwickshire won by seven wickets. Toss: Warwickshire. County debut: G. D. McGrath.

After six hours' hanging around and a ten-over slog, the net result was that neither county qualified for the quarter-finals. Worcestershire would have, had the game been abandoned, but Warwickshire, needing a win to have any chance of progressing, were desperate to play. It gave McGrath a bizarre introduction to county cricket, particularly as results elsewhere meant the thrash counted for nought in the end.

Gold Award: G. Welch.

Worcestershire

P. R. Pollard c Ostler b Welch	30	D. A. Leatherdale not out		17
*G. A. Hick c Penney b Giddins	0	W 2		2
V. S. Solanki b Welch	1			
K. R. Spiring c Penney b Smith	17	1/2 2/23	(4 wkts, 10 overs)	91
E. J. Wilson not out	24	3/34 4/63		

†S. J. Rhodes, S. R. Lampitt, R. K. Illingworth, Kabir Ali and G. D. McGrath did not bat.

Bowling: Giddins 2–0–10–1; Brown 1–0–13–0; Welch 2–0–9–2; Giles 2–0–24–0; Donald 2–0–25–0; Smith 1–0–10–1.

Warwickshire

N. V. Knight c Hick b Lampitt	30	*N. M. K. Smith not out		3
G. Welch c sub b Illingworth	29	W 3, n-b 2		5
D. L. Hemp run out	9			
D. P. Ostler not out	16	1/53 2/69 3/89	(3 wkts, 9.5 overs)	92

T. L. Penney, D. R. Brown, †K. J. Piper, A. F. Giles, A. A. Donald and E. S. H. Giddins did not bat.

Bowling: McGrath 2–0–21–0; Ali 2–0–31–0; Leatherdale 2–0–20–0; Lampitt 2–0–11–1; Illingworth 1.5–0–9–1.

Umpires: A. A. Jones and R. Palmer.

NORTH GROUP

DERBYSHIRE v LEICESTERSHIRE

At Derby, April 15. No result. Toss: Derbyshire. County debuts: R. J. Bailey, M. J. Di Venuto, M. P. Dowman, T. A. Munton; N. D. Burns, A. Kumble, T. R. Ward.

Rain set in two overs too soon to implement Duckworth/Lewis, but hardly soon enough for players and spectators alike on a cold, gloomy day. Only Ward managed double figures for Leicestershire as the ball darted about, and he needed 92 balls for his 34. Lewis, who injured a hand while batting, claimed two early wickets when Derbyshire's batsmen struggled in turn.

Leicestershire

*V. J. Wells b Cork	2	J. M. Dakin b Smith		5
D. L. Maddy lbw b Cork	8	A. Kumble c Cork b Aldred		1
T. R. Ward b Smith	34	J. Ormond c Krikken b Cork		1
B. F. Smith b Munton	3	L-b 12, w 4		16
A. Habib lbw b Munton	0			
C. C. Lewis not out	5	1/7 2/12 3/18	(37 overs)	86
†N. D. Burns lbw b Smith	9	4/18 5/54 6/71		
P. A. J. DeFreitas c Bailey b Aldred	2	7/71 8/82 9/84		

Lewis, when 3, retired hurt at 26 and resumed at 84.

Bowling: Cork 9–0–27–3; Munton 10–3–15–2; Aldred 10–3–18–2; Smith 8–2–14–3.

Derbyshire

M. E. Cassar c Habib b Lewis	4	S. D. Stubbings not out		0
M. J. Di Venuto c DeFreitas b Lewis	4	W 3		3
M. P. Dowman c and b Ormond	1			
R. J. Bailey not out	10	1/4 2/6 3/15	(3 wkts, 8 overs)	22

*D. G. Cork, S. P. Titchard, †K. M. Krikken, P. Aldred, T. A. Munton and T. M. Smith did not bat.

Bowling: Ormond 4–1–16–1; Lewis 4–2–6–2.

Umpires: N. A. Mallender and R. A. White.

DURHAM v YORKSHIRE

At Chester-le-Street, April 15. Durham won by ten runs. Toss: Yorkshire. County debut: S. M. Katich. First-team debut: N. Peng.

Speak underwrote the propitious start to his Durham captaincy in a match reduced to 40 overs a side, putting on 102 in 19 overs with Lewis. His 72, coming off 98 balls, was brisk batting on a slow pitch. Yorkshire, well on course at 122 for two, collapsed badly against Killeen and Collingwood and lost seven wickets for 46. Collingwood's return of four for 31 was his best in limited-overs cricket.

Gold Award: N. J. Speak.

Durham

J. A. Daley lbw b Hamilton	15	J. J. B. Lewis not out		55
†M. P. Speight c Sidebottom		P. D. Collingwood not out		18
b Silverwood	1	B 2, l-b 5, w 3, n-b 6		16
S. M. Katich lbw b Silverwood	1			—
*N. J. Speak b Gough	72	1/4 2/7 3/41 4/143	(4 wkts, 40 overs)	178

N. Peng, J. Wood, N. Killeen, S. J. Harmison and S. J. E. Brown did not bat.

Bowling: Gough 8–2–23–1; Silverwood 8–0–42–2; White 8–1–38–0; Sidebottom 8–2–35–0; Hamilton 8–2–33–1.

Yorkshire

*D. Byas lbw b Brown	17	D. Gough not out		0
C. White b Killeen	45	C. E. W. Silverwood c Katich		
†R. J. Blakey c Speight b Harmison	8	b Collingwood		4
D. S. Lehmann c Katich b Killeen	40	L-b 9, w 20, n-b 2		31
M. P. Vaughan b Collingwood	11			—
G. M. Fellows c Speight b Collingwood	1	1/25 2/53 3/122	(9 wkts, 40 overs)	168
G. M. Hamilton c Killeen b Collingwood	0	4/146 5/152 6/152		
M. J. Wood c Brown b Harmison	11	7/164 8/164 9/168		

R. J. Sidebottom did not bat.

Bowling: Brown 8–1–34–1; Wood 8–1–23–0; Harmison 8–0–42–2; Killeen 8–1–29–2; Collingwood 8–0–31–4.

Umpires: B. Dudleston and J. W. Holder.

LANCASHIRE v NOTTINGHAMSHIRE

At Manchester, April 15. Lancashire won by eight wickets. Toss: Nottinghamshire. County debuts: S. C. Ganguly; D. J. Bicknell, A. J. Harris, J. E. Morris.

Given the degree of sideways movement that the Lancashire bowlers obtained, it was surprising Nottinghamshire chose to bat first. Ufzaal stayed two and a quarter hours, but no one batted in the assured way in which Atherton and Crawley took charge of Lancashire's reply. They put on 115 in as many minutes after Ganguly, caught at slip, had lasted just six balls.

Gold Award: M. A. Atherton.

Nottinghamshire

D. J. Bicknell lbw b Martin	2	P. J. Franks not out		10
U. Afzaal c Hegg b Austin	45	D. J. Millns not out		6
*J. E. R. Gallian c Hegg b Chapple	14	B 4, l-b 12, w 11, n-b 2		29
P. Johnson c and b Martin	33			—
J. E. Morris c Crawley b Austin	2	1/2 2/42 3/94	(7 wkts, 50 overs)	164
†C. M. W. Read lbw b Austin	15	4/98 5/115		
C. M. Tolley c Flintoff b Chapple	8	6/135 7/152		

A. J. Harris and R. D. Stemp did not bat.

Bowling: Martin 8–2–15–2; Austin 10–2–26–3; Chapple 9–0–34–2; Flintoff 10–1–23–0; Ganguly 10–0–38–0; Yates 3–0–12–0.

Lancashire

M. A. Atherton not out	81
S. C. Ganguly c Gallian b Harris	0
*J. P. Crawley c Afzaal b Stemp	61
N. H. Fairbrother not out	15
L-b 1, w 7	8

1/0 2/115   (2 wkts, 46.5 overs) 165

A. Flintoff, G. D. Lloyd, †W. K. Hegg, I. D. Austin, P. J. Martin, G. Chapple and G. Yates did not bat.

Bowling: Franks 8–3–11–0; Harris 8–2–23–1; Millns 7.5–1–45–0; Tolley 9–0–36–0; Stemp 10–1–28–1; Gallian 2–0–17–0; Afzaal 2–1–4–0.

Umpires: M. R. Benson and J. H. Hampshire.

LEICESTERSHIRE v DURHAM

At Leicester, April 16. Leicestershire won by 20 runs. Toss: Durham.

Bowlers held sway, and not always with the ball. Chris Lewis, ostensibly playing as a bowler following his previous day's hand injury, boosted Leicestershire's total in a last-wicket 47 with Ormond after six wickets had gone for 36. Ormond then had Durham's top three back in the pavilion with 12 on the board. Despite 84 between Speak and Collingwood, the asking-rate, climbing above seven an over, was rarely in the visitors' favour.

Gold Award: J. Ormond.

Leicestershire

*V. J. Wells c Speak b Brown	40	A. Kumble b Harmison	1
D. L. Maddy b Killeen	1	J. Ormond not out	14
T. R. Ward c Speight b Wood	9	C. C. Lewis b Wood	29
B. F. Smith b Wood	16	L-b 10, w 19, n-b 2	31
A. Habib c Speight b Harmison	19		
†N. D. Burns c Lewis b Collingwood . . .	3	1/4 2/36 3/66 (49.3 overs) 187
P. A. J. DeFreitas c Speight b Wood . . .	20	4/104 5/104 6/125
J. M. Dakin b Killeen	4	7/135 8/140 9/140

Bowling: Brown 10–1–38–1; Killeen 10–2–30–2; Wood 9.3–2–28–4; Collingwood 10–0–47–1; Harmison 10–2–34–2.

Durham

J. A. Daley lbw b Ormond	3	N. Killeen b DeFreitas	3
†M. P. Speight c Wells b Ormond	8	S. J. Harmison c Habib b Ormond	8
S. M. Katich c Burns b Ormond	1	S. J. E. Brown not out	3
*N. J. Speak b Kumble	49	L-b 6, w 6	12
J. J. B. Lewis lbw b Kumble	10		
P. D. Collingwood c Burns b Kumble . .	35	1/10 2/11 3/12 (9 wkts, 50 overs) 167
N. Peng b DeFreitas	7	4/31 5/115 6/124
J. Wood not out	28	7/128 8/142 9/161

Bowling: Ormond 10–1–27–4; Lewis 10–1–36–0; DeFreitas 10–0–32–2; Kumble 10–2–26–3; Wells 5–0–24–0; Dakin 5–0–16–0.

Umpires: A. A. Jones and R. A. White.

NOTTINGHAMSHIRE v DERBYSHIRE

At Nottingham, April 16. Derbyshire won by nine wickets. Toss: Derbyshire.

Cork reinforced the value of winning the toss by taking three wickets in his first two overs. Bicknell went first ball, Gallian two later. Aldred's three wickets at the other end of the innings had Nottinghamshire losing their last five for 14. Batting was a different story for Di Venuto. Hitting 12 fours, including five off Franks in one over, he rattled to 61 in 42 balls, and Derbyshire won inside 12 overs against some poor bowling. Harris, up against his former county, broke a finger trying to stop one of Di Venuto's return drives.

Gold Award: D. G. Cork.

Nottinghamshire

D. J. Bicknell lbw b Cork	0	D. J. Millns c Titchard b Aldred	0
U. Afzaal lbw b Cork	5	A. J. Harris c Krikken b Aldred	1
*J. E. R. Gallian lbw b Cork	2	R. D. Stemp c Krikken b Aldred	2
P. Johnson c Aldred b Munton	13	L-b 8, w 13, n-b 2	23
J. E. Morris b Cassar	39		
†C. M. W. Read run out	5	1/0 2/2 3/12	(33.3 overs) 94
C. M. Tolley lbw b Cassar	2	4/44 5/78 6/80	
P. J. Franks not out	2	7/84 8/85 9/86	

Bowling: Cork 7–2–17–3; Munton 10–0–21–1; Smith 6–0–28–0; Aldred 6.3–0–12–3; Cassar 4–0–8–2.

Derbyshire

M. E. Cassar b Stemp	22
M. J. Di Venuto not out	61
M. P. Dowman not out	10
W 5	5

1/84　　　　　　　　(1 wkt, 11.4 overs) 98

R. J. Bailey, S. D. Stubbings, *D. G. Cork, S. P. Titchard, †K. M. Krikken, P. Aldred, T. A. Munton and T. M. Smith did not bat.

Bowling: Franks 3–0–30–0; Harris 2.3–0–16–0; Stemp 3.1–0–23–1; Millns 2–0–25–0; Tolley 1–0–4–0.

Umpires: J. H. Hampshire and J. F. Steele.

YORKSHIRE v LANCASHIRE

At Leeds, April 16. Yorkshire won by four wickets. Toss: Yorkshire.

White's all-round effort – he even kept wicket while Blakey had a dislocated finger put back in place – illustrated why England had called him up for their winter's limited-overs programme. His one-day best of five for 21 against Zimbabwe in February just shaded his return here. Hamilton, too, underlined the thinking behind his selection for the South African tour, taking three wickets and, when victory might have slipped away, helping Blakey add the 64 Yorkshire needed to win. Batting was never straightforward on a slow pitch of uneven bounce, and Extras was Yorkshire's highest score. All told, both sides' bowlers gave away 46 runs in wides.

Gold Award: C. White.

Lancashire

M. A. Atherton b Hamilton	3	G. Chapple not out	3
*J. P. Crawley c Blakey b White	45	G. Yates c Vaughan b White	1
N. H. Fairbrother c Blakey b White	11		
S. C. Ganguly c Vaughan b White	5	L-b 7, w 17, n-b 2	26
A. Flintoff c Vaughan b Hamilton	35		
G. D. Lloyd c Wood b Hamilton	24	1/38 2/72 3/80 (9 wkts, 50 overs) 166	
†W. K. Hegg c Blakey b Gough	4	4/86 5/148 6/148	
I. D. Austin c Blakey b White	9	7/159 8/164 9/166	

P. J. Martin did not bat.

Bowling: Gough 10–1–23–1; Hoggard 10–3–33–0; Hamilton 8–2–24–3; Sidebottom 6–0–37–0; White 10–4–25–5; Vaughan 6–0–17–0.

Yorkshire

*D. Byas b Martin	10	†R. J. Blakey not out	33
C. White lbw b Ganguly	21	G. M. Hamilton not out	28
M. P. Vaughan lbw b Ganguly	6	B 1, l-b 6, w 29, n-b 4	40
D. S. Lehmann c Crawley b Ganguly	0		
M. J. Wood lbw b Flintoff	11	1/30 2/47 3/47 (6 wkts, 45.3 overs) 167	
G. M. Fellows c Fairbrother b Austin	18	4/62 5/74 6/103	

D. Gough, R. J. Sidebottom and M. J. Hoggard did not bat.

Bowling: Martin 8–0–39–1; Austin 7.3–1–39–1; Chapple 10–0–33–0; Ganguly 10–2–31–3; Flintoff 10–3–18–1.

Umpires: M. R. Benson and B. Dudleston.

DURHAM v LANCASHIRE

At Chester-le-Street, April 18. Lancashire won by nine wickets. Toss: Lancashire.

When play was eventually possible, there was time for only ten overs apiece, but that was time enough for Ganguly to make his mark. He took wickets with his second and third balls; later, he won the match, with three overs to spare, by hitting Killeen for six then four. Durham, in contrast, had managed only two boundaries in their entire innings.

Gold Award: S. C. Ganguly.

Durham

†M. P. Speight c Hegg b Martin	6	M. M. Betts not out	0
S. M. Katich c Flintoff b Martin	1	S. J. Harmison not out	1
*N. J. Speak c Crawley b Ganguly	7		
P. D. Collingwood c Lloyd b Ganguly	1	L-b 3, w 3	6
J. J. B. Lewis b Ganguly	10		
J. A. Daley run out	9	1/6 2/8 3/19 (8 wkts, 10 overs) 53	
N. Peng b Flintoff	3	4/19 5/35 6/42	
J. Wood lbw b Chapple	9	7/46 8/52	

N. Killeen did not bat.

Bowling: Austin 2–0–9–0; Martin 2–0–6–2; Ganguly 2–0–7–3; Chapple 2–0–15–1; Flintoff 2–0–13–1.

Lancashire

*J. P. Crawley b Wood		20
A. Flintoff not out		12
S. C. Ganguly not out		22
	W 1	1

1/25   (1 wkt, 6.5 overs) 55

M. A. Atherton, N. H. Fairbrother, G. D. Lloyd, J. C. Scuderi, †W. K. Hegg, I. D. Austin, P. J. Martin and G. Chapple did not bat.

Bowling: Wood 2–0–12–1; Harmison 2–0–19–0; Killeen 1.5–0–20–0; Betts 1–0–4–0.

Umpires: J. W. Holder and N. A. Mallender.

YORKSHIRE v LEICESTERSHIRE

At Leeds, April 19. Yorkshire won by five wickets. Toss: Leicestershire. County debut: W. F. Stelling.

Interviewed the previous day by the ECB about his match-fixing claims, Lewis was omitted here "because it was better for him and the team if he didn't play," according to Leicestershire coach Birkenshaw. But it didn't help Leicestershire that Wells was also out with a hamstring injury, or that DeFreitas bowled only three overs before being sent home, suffering from flu. With all three playing, they might have defended their 191, which owed much to an unbroken stand of 122 between Habib and Billy Stelling – formerly of Western Province and Boland – after miserly spells by Gough. Instead, once Byas had added 69 in 18 overs with Blakey, a stand of 53 in 13 between Lehmann and Fellows took Yorkshire to within five runs of a comfortable victory.

Gold Award: D. Byas.

Leicestershire

D. L. Maddy c Lehmann b Gough	0		W. F. Stelling not out	50
D. I. Stevens lbw b Gough	2			
T. R. Ward c Lehmann b White	22		B 1, l-b 9, w 13, n-b 4	27
*B. F. Smith c and b Sidebottom	19			
A. Habib not out	70		1/0 2/3 3/36 (5 wkts, 50 overs) 191	
†N. D. Burns lbw b Vaughan	1		4/66 5/69	

P. A. J. DeFreitas, J. M. Dakin, A. Kumble and J. Ormond did not bat.

Bowling: Gough 10–4–19–2; Hoggard 9–1–34–0; Sidebottom 10–0–54–1; Hamilton 5–0–12–0; White 10–2–44–1; Vaughan 6–1–18–1.

Yorkshire

*D. Byas b Dakin	71		M. J. Wood not out	1
C. White c Smith b Dakin	23			
†R. J. Blakey run out	19		L-b 5, w 14, n-b 2	21
D. S. Lehmann st Burns b Kumble	26			
M. P. Vaughan c Burns b Kumble	5		1/43 2/112 3/129 (5 wkts, 45.5 overs) 192	
G. M. Fellows not out	26		4/134 5/187	

G. M. Hamilton, D. Gough, R. J. Sidebottom and M. J. Hoggard did not bat.

Bowling: Ormond 10–2–20–0; DeFreitas 3–1–17–0; Dakin 10–1–28–2; Kumble 10–1–42–2; Maddy 6.5–0–34–0; Stelling 6–0–46–0.

Umpires: J. H. Hampshire and V. A. Holder.

DERBYSHIRE v LANCASHIRE

At Derby, April 20. Derbyshire won by six wickets. Toss: Derbyshire.

Flintoff, dropped by bowler Aldred when four, made nonsense of a slow, seaming pitch by thumping eight fours and a six in 70 from 75 balls. Even so, when he and Fairbrother both fell to Dowman at 129, having put on 96 in 20 overs, Lancashire would have struggled without Lloyd and Scuderi's 84-run partnership. Dowman and Cassar more than matched them with 100 for Derbyshire's second wicket, and Bailey saw his new county home with an unbeaten 50. Lancashire dropped three catches as Derbyshire, needing 65 from the last ten overs, got them with one to spare.

Gold Award: M. P. Dowman.

Lancashire

*J. P. Crawley c Krikken b Munton	12		J. C. Scuderi c Cork b Aldred	42
M. A. Atherton lbw b Munton	7		†W. K. Hegg not out	0
S. C. Ganguly c Cork b Aldred	10		B 4, l-b 5, w 10	19
A. Flintoff c Krikken b Dowman	70			
N. H. Fairbrother c Bailey b Dowman	23		1/14 2/27 3/33	(6 wkts, 50 overs) 218
G. D. Lloyd not out	35		4/129 5/129 6/213	

I. D. Austin, P. J. Martin and M. P. Smethurst did not bat.

Bowling: Cork 10–1–35–0; Munton 10–3–20–2; Aldred 10–1–59–2; Smith 4–0–21–0; Cassar 9–0–46–0; Dowman 7–0–28–2.

Derbyshire

M. E. Cassar c Hegg b Smethurst	43		*D. G. Cork not out	26
M. J. Di Venuto b Austin	9		L-b 7, w 3, n-b 2	12
M. P. Dowman c Lloyd b Ganguly	65			
R. J. Bailey not out	50		1/18 2/118	(4 wkts, 49 overs) 219
S. D. Stubbings c Hegg b Flintoff	14		3/134 4/168	

S. P. Titchard, †K. M. Krikken, P. Aldred, T. A. Munton and T. M. Smith did not bat.

Bowling: Martin 9–0–53–0; Austin 10–4–21–1; Ganguly 8–0–42–1; Smethurst 10–0–43–1; Flintoff 9–1–40–1; Scuderi 3–0–13–0.

Umpires: G. I. Burgess and J. W. Holder.

NOTTINGHAMSHIRE v DURHAM

At Nottingham, April 20. Durham won by two runs. Toss: Nottinghamshire. County debut: G. R. Haywood.

A game of 28 overs a side allows for few errors, yet Durham got away with dropping Gallian twice, off Harmison, and Bicknell on 15 as this pair added 98 for Nottinghamshire's third wicket. Crucially, however, Killeen gave little away when Nottinghamshire needed nine off the final over. Earlier, Katich had come good for Durham, hitting 50 in 54 balls, and Speak and Collingwood consolidated his effort by adding 55 in 33 balls together.

Gold Award: D. J. Bicknell.

Durham

†M. P. Speight c and b Millns	3		J. Wood b Franks	1
N. Peng b Lucas	14		M. M. Betts b Franks	0
S. M. Katich c Haywood b Stemp	50		L-b 4, w 7, n-b 6	17
R. Robinson run out	19			
*N. J. Speak c Bicknell b Millns	34		1/6 2/46 3/81	(8 wkts, 28 overs) 174
P. D. Collingwood c Haywood b Millns	31		4/113 5/168 6/168	
J. J. B. Lewis not out	5		7/174 8/174	

N. Killeen and S. J. Harmison did not bat.

Bowling: Millns 6–1–35–3; Franks 6–2–32–2; Haywood 2–0–9–0; Lucas 5–0–33–1; Stemp 6–0–39–1; Gallian 3–0–22–0.

Nottinghamshire

J. E. Morris c Speak b Wood	5	P. J. Franks b Killeen		6
U. Afzaal lbw b Betts	0			
D. J. Bicknell not out	71	L-b 4, w 6, n-b 6		16
*J. E. R. Gallian b Harmison	47			
P. Johnson run out	11	1/5 2/6 3/104	(7 wkts, 28 overs)	172
†C. M. W. Read c Killeen b Harmison	15	4/130 5/160		
G. R. Haywood run out	1	6/162 7/172		

D. J. Millns, D. S. Lucas and R. D. Stemp did not bat.

Bowling: Betts 5–0–44–1; Wood 6–0–16–1; Collingwood 5–0–29–0; Killeen 6–0–41–1; Harmison 6–0–38–2.

Umpires: J. F. Steele and A. G. T. Whitehead.

DERBYSHIRE v YORKSHIRE

At Derby, April 22. No result. Toss: Derbyshire.

Play began at one o'clock, but gave way to oncoming rain within an hour and a half. Derbyshire's point kept them top of the table and, unbeaten to date, seemingly in line to qualify for the quarter-finals.

Yorkshire

*D. Byas c Cork b Munton	2
C. White not out	40
†R. J. Blakey b Aldred	35
D. S. Lehmann not out	1
L-b 2, w 2	4

1/3 2/76   (2 wkts, 21.2 overs) 82

M. P. Vaughan, G. M. Fellows, M. J. Wood, G. M. Hamilton, D. Gough, R. J. Sidebottom and M. J. Hoggard did not bat.

Bowling: Cork 5.2–1–21–0; Munton 6–0–21–1; Aldred 7–0–21–1; Smith 3–0–17–0.

Derbyshire

M. E. Cassar, M. J. Di Venuto, M. P. Dowman, R. J. Bailey, S. D. Stubbings, *D. G. Cork, S. P. Titchard, †K. M. Krikken, P. Aldred, T. A. Munton and T. M. Smith.

Umpires: G. I. Burgess and D. R. Shepherd.

LEICESTERSHIRE v NOTTINGHAMSHIRE

At Leicester, April 22. No result (abandoned).

DURHAM v DERBYSHIRE

At Chester-le-Street, April 24. Durham won by 138 runs. Toss: Derbyshire. County debut: L. D. Sutton.

Durham's victory had a sting in its tail for Derbyshire. While both finished the group matches with six points, the win let Durham into the quarter-finals as one of the two leading third-placed teams and dropped Derbyshire back to fourth. Robinson, yet to make his first-class debut, spurred the home side with 68 in 38 balls, hitting four sixes, all off Munton, and six fours before Bailey restored order with his best-ever figures. Though Derbyshire were missing captain Cork, who had flu, his absence could not excuse some indisciplined seam bowling – there were 25 wides – or the batsmen's subsequent surrender.

Gold Award: R. Robinson.

Durham

J. A. Daley lbw b Munton	0	N. C. Phillips lbw b Bailey	16
†M. P. Speight c Smith b Munton	41	S. J. Harmison lbw b Bailey	0
S. M. Katich st Krikken b Aldred	1	N. Killeen not out	11
*N. J. Speak c Di Venuto b Dowman	14	B 1, l-b 11, w 25	37
R. Robinson lbw b Bailey	68		
J. J. B. Lewis not out	35	1/0 2/2 3/76 (9 wkts, 50 overs)	245
P. D. Collingwood c Cassar b Bailey	22	4/142 5/162 6/202	
J. Wood b Bailey	4	7/203 8/227 9/227	

Bowling: Munton 10–1–52–2; Aldred 8–0–47–1; Smith 10–0–38–0; Cassar 8–1–28–0; Dowman 4–0–23–1; Bailey 10–0–45–5.

Derbyshire

M. E. Cassar c Speight b Killeen	0	P. Aldred c Speight b Phillips	7
M. J. Di Venuto run out	46	T. A. Munton not out	8
M. P. Dowman c Katich b Killeen	2	T. M. Smith c and b Phillips	0
R. J. Bailey c Collingwood b Wood	3		
S. D. Stubbings c Katich b Collingwood	0	B 4, l-b 4, w 11, n-b 2	21
L. D. Sutton c Speight b Wood	0		
S. P. Titchard c and b Phillips	7	1/0 2/3 3/39 (40.4 overs)	107
*†K. M. Krikken c Collingwood		4/40 5/41 6/68	
b Harmison	13	7/79 8/98 9/98	

Bowling: Killeen 9–3–13–2; Wood 8–2–25–2; Collingwood 6–1–8–1; Harmison 8–0–28–1; Phillips 8.4–2–17–3; Katich 1–0–8–0.

Umpires: B. Leadbeater and D. R. Shepherd.

LANCASHIRE v LEICESTERSHIRE

At Manchester, April 24. Lancashire won by one wicket. Toss: Lancashire.

Austin and last man Smethurst batted through the final nine overs, picking off the 25 runs Lancashire needed to be sure of a quarter-final place. Initially, with Atherton at the helm, they looked to be cruising to victory, but Kumble's four wickets dispersed the middle order and swung the tie Leicestershire's way. Schofield's leg-spin had done something similar to Leicestershire's middle order, while Lewis, booed by some spectators on his return after making match-fixing allegations, was run out without facing a ball. But for Smith's 64 in 91 balls, Austin might not have had to play his familiar role of Lancashire's best man in a crisis.

Gold Award: I. D. Austin.

Leicestershire

*V. J. Wells b Smethurst	33	A. Kumble c Fairbrother b Smethurst	9
D. L. Maddy lbw b Austin	2	J. M. Dakin c Hegg b Martin	10
T. R. Ward b Flintoff	18	J. Ormond b Austin	0
B. F. Smith not out	64	L-b 8, w 10, n-b 8	26
A. Habib c Martin b Schofield	7		
C. C. Lewis run out	0	1/7 2/50 3/56　(47.3 overs)	172
†N. D. Burns b Schofield	1	4/91 5/92 6/96	
P. A. J. DeFreitas c Hegg b Schofield	2	7/108 8/141 9/169	

Bowling: Martin 10–2–36–1; Austin 9.3–2–22–2; Smethurst 6–0–34–2; Flintoff 9–1–28–1; Schofield 10–1–33–3; Ganguly 3–1–11–0.

Lancashire

M. A. Atherton b Ormond	40	I. D. Austin not out	24
*J. P. Crawley lbw b Lewis	16	P. J. Martin b Dakin	0
S. C. Ganguly c Smith b DeFreitas	16	M. P. Smethurst not out	10
A. Flintoff st Burns b Kumble	16	L-b 8, w 9, n-b 4	21
N. H. Fairbrother c Maddy b Kumble	17		
G. D. Lloyd b Kumble	0	1/22 2/69 3/97　(9 wkts, 46.3 overs)	176
†W. K. Hegg lbw b Kumble	0	4/97 5/104 6/104	
C. P. Schofield lbw b Lewis	16	7/128 8/143 9/148	

Bowling: Ormond 10–3–37–1; Lewis 10–2–37–2; DeFreitas 7–0–29–1; Dakin 9–0–33–1; Kumble 10–2–28–4; Wells 0.3–0–4–0.

Umpires: K. E. Palmer and P. Willey.

NOTTINGHAMSHIRE v YORKSHIRE

At Nottingham, April 24. Yorkshire won by six wickets (D/L method). Toss: Yorkshire.

Gough and Hoggard were near-unplayable at the start in swinging, seaming conditions. Gough took four wickets at a cost of eight runs in his first 27 balls, the basis of competition-best figures, and Nottinghamshire had no way back from 21 for five. Rain in the 18th over not only made a recovery less likely, by limiting the innings to 35 overs, but the subsequent Duckworth/Lewis formula made Yorkshire's 35-over target ten runs less than Nottinghamshire's total. Yorkshire's win put them at the head of the group.

Gold Award: D. Gough.

Nottinghamshire

D. J. Bicknell c Blakey b Gough	2	G. R. Haywood lbw b White	5
U. Afzaal b Hoggard	0	P. J. Franks run out	14
*J. E. R. Gallian run out	22	L-b 7, w 15, n-b 8	30
P. Johnson b Gough	3		
J. E. Morris c Blakey b Gough	0	1/2 2/2 3/13　(8 wkts, 35 overs)	129
†C. M. W. Read b Gough	4	4/13 5/21 6/52	
C. M. Tolley not out	49	7/64 8/129	

D. S. Lucas and R. D. Stemp did not bat.

Bowling: Gough 7–1–17–4; Hoggard 7–2–18–1; Hamilton 7–0–21–0; White 7–0–33–1; Sidebottom 4–1–21–0; Fellows 3–0–12–0.

Yorkshire

*D. Byas b Gallian	6	G. M. Fellows not out	9
C. White c Read b Franks	9	L-b 4, w 23, n-b 2	29
†R. J. Blakey b Gallian	30		
D. S. Lehmann c Read b Franks	21	1/12 2/48	(4 wkts, 28.2 overs) 119
M. P. Vaughan not out	15	3/78 4/103	

M. J. Wood, G. M. Hamilton, D. Gough, R. J. Sidebottom and M. J. Hoggard did not bat.

Bowling: Franks 7–0–14–2; Lucas 4–0–28–0; Tolley 7–1–18–0; Gallian 5–0–34–2; Stemp 3.2–1–15–0; Haywood 2–0–6–0.

Umpires: R. Julian and K. J. Lyons.

SOUTH GROUP

ESSEX v SURREY

At Chelmsford, April 15. No result (abandoned).

HAMPSHIRE v MIDDLESEX

At Southampton, April 15. No result (abandoned).

KENT v SUSSEX

At Canterbury, April 15. No result (abandoned).

MIDDLESEX v ESSEX

At Lord's, April 16. No result (abandoned).

SURREY v KENT

At The Oval, April 16. No result (abandoned).

KENT v ESSEX

At Canterbury, April 18. Essex won by two runs. Toss: Kent. County debuts: R. Dravid, P. A. Nixon. First-team debut: D. D. Masters.

Kent went into the final over needing 16 to win. Ealham's six off the penultimate ball reduced the target to three, but Ilott bowled straight and full and Ealham missed. He had been a thorn in Essex's side throughout, taking four wickets in two tidy spells and picking up the pace after Wells had shaped Kent's reply. Danny Law's 34 off 24 balls, including two straight sixes, sealed Essex's recovery from 36 for four at 16 overs. Morning rain had delayed the start and reduced the match to 39 overs a side.

Gold Award: M. A. Ealham.

Essex

*N. Hussain b Ealham	12	A. P. Cowan not out		15
P. J. Prichard c Golding b Phillips	0	M. C. Ilott not out		0
S. G. Law c Nixon b Ealham	1			
R. C. Irani c Nixon b Phillips	37	B 3, l-b 2, w 12		17
A. P. Grayson b Masters	7			
S. D. Peters c Fleming b Ealham	42		(8 wkts, 39 overs)	175
D. R. Law c Golding b Ealham	34	1/1 2/10 3/18		
†B. J. Hyam c Fleming b Golding	10	4/36 5/83 6/138		
		7/156 8/166		

R. S. G. Anderson did not bat.

Bowling: Ealham 8–4–17–4; Phillips 8–1–28–2; Golding 8–3–49–1; Masters 7–1–19–1; Patel 2–0–13–0; Fleming 6–0–44–0.

Kent

E. T. Smith b Cowan	18	†P. A. Nixon not out		19
M. J. Walker lbw b Irani	0	L-b 6, w 10		16
R. Dravid lbw b Anderson	23			
A. P. Wells b Irani	36	1/1 2/50 3/50	(5 wkts, 39 overs)	173
M. A. Ealham b Ilott	61	4/137 5/173		

*M. V. Fleming, J. M. Golding, B. J. Phillips, M. M. Patel and D. D. Masters did not bat.

Bowling: Ilott 8–0–39–1; Irani 8–1–23–2; Anderson 8–0–33–1; Cowan 8–0–38–1; D. R. Law 7–0–34–0.

Umpires: N. G. Cowley and J. W. Lloyds.

SUSSEX v SURREY

At Hove, April 18. Surrey won by 35 runs (D/L method). Toss: Surrey. County debut: W. J. House.
From 30 without loss after ten overs, Sussex lost seven wickets in another ten and could not even rely on the miserable weather to help them. Surrey were comfortably ahead of the Duckworth/Lewis rate when heavy rain drove the players off – a sad conclusion to a match dedicated to the memory of Peter Eaton, the Sussex groundsman for 30 years until his death in February, aged 57.

Gold Award: I. E. Bishop.

Sussex

R. R. Montgomerie lbw b Tudor	28	†N. J. Wilton b Ratcliffe		3
W. J. House b Bicknell	8	R. J. Kirtley not out		10
*C. J. Adams c Hollioake b Bishop	0	M. A. Robinson run out		5
B. Zuiderent b Bishop	2			
P. A. Cottey lbw b Tudor	0	B 3, l-b 1, w 12, n-b 2		25
R. S. C. Martin-Jenkins c Butcher				
b Ratcliffe	2	1/30 2/37 3/49	(44 overs)	97
U. B. A. Rashid c Brown b Ratcliffe	6	4/50 5/51 6/52		
J. D. Lewry c Stewart b Bicknell	8	7/62 8/72 9/72		

Bowling: Bicknell 10–4–15–2; Tudor 10–2–28–2; Bishop 10–3–22–2; Ratcliffe 9–3–15–3; Salisbury 4–0–4–0; Hollioake 1–0–2–0.

Surrey

M. A. Butcher not out............	23		
A. D. Brown b Lewry............	15		
†A. J. Stewart not out...........	9		
L-b 9, w 5.............	14		

1/28   (1 wkt, 20 overs) 61

I. J. Ward, G. P. Thorpe, *A. J. Hollioake, J. D. Ratcliffe, M. P. Bicknell, I. D. K. Salisbury, A. J. Tudor and I. E. Bishop did not bat.

Bowling: Lewry 5–1–16–1; Kirtley 5–0–18–0; Robinson 5–0–9–0; Martin-Jenkins 5–1–9–0.

Umpires: D. J. Constant and J. H. Harris.

ESSEX v HAMPSHIRE

At Chelmsford, April 19. Hampshire won by five wickets. Toss: Hampshire. County debut: S. K. Warne.

Warne's introduction to county cricket, a day after flying in from South Africa, included being clobbered into the backyard of neighbouring flats, much to the delight of some 3,000 spectators. The striker was Irani, whose half-century, along with another 40-something from Peters, put Essex on track. In reply, Smith and Aymes made light of Ilott's early two-wicket strike – Kenway was caught and bowled via his own boot – and Mascarenhas hurried up the win by taking 16 off Ilott's last over.

Gold Award: A. N. Aymes.

Essex

*N. Hussain b Mascarenhas.........	20	A. P. Cowan c and b Mullally........	2
P. J. Prichard c Hartley b Udal.......	28	M. C. Ilott not out...............	0
S. G. Law c Stephenson b Hartley.....	5		
R. C. Irani c Kenway b Hartley......	50	B 2, l-b 5, w 19, n-b 2......	28
D. R. Law c and b Udal...........	0		
A. P. Grayson lbw b Mascarenhas.....	17	1/32 2/44 3/71 (9 wkts, 50 overs) 201	
S. D. Peters c White b Hartley.......	43	4/72 5/110 6/177	
†B. J. Hyam run out..............	8	7/193 8/195 9/201	

R. S. G. Anderson did not bat.

Bowling: Mullally 10–4–44–1; Hartley 10–1–38–3; Mascarenhas 10–0–41–2; Warne 10–0–44–0; Udal 10–0–27–2.

Hampshire

J. S. Laney lbw b Ilott...........	2	A. D. Mascarenhas not out.........	21
D. A. Kenway c and b Ilott.........	2		
†A. N. Aymes b Cowan............	63	L-b 14, w 11............	25
*R. A. Smith b Grayson...........	56		
G. W. White c Hyam b Anderson.....	27	1/10 2/11 3/131 (5 wkts, 47.3 overs) 202	
J. P. Stephenson not out...........	6	4/170 5/180	

S. K. Warne, S. D. Udal, P. J. Hartley and A. D. Mullally did not bat.

Bowling: Irani 6–2–7–0; Ilott 10–0–53–2; Cowan 8.3–0–24–1; Anderson 10–1–48–1; Grayson 10–0–39–1; S. G. Law 3–0–17–0.

Umpires: B. Leadbeater and R. A. White.

HAMPSHIRE v KENT

At Southampton, April 20. No result (abandoned).

MIDDLESEX v SUSSEX

At Lord's, April 20. No result (abandoned).

MIDDLESEX v SURREY

At Southgate, April 21. No result (abandoned).

With Lord's, the scheduled venue, still waterlogged, the match was switched to Southgate in the hope that Middlesex might play their first game. It was all to no avail. Conditions there proved just as unplayable and the match was called off at lunchtime.

SUSSEX v HAMPSHIRE

At Hove, April 23. Sussex won by two wickets. Toss: Sussex.

Bevan, in his first match of the season, won both the game and the game within a game between Australians. Warne's consolation was his first wicket for his county. Bevan and Martin-Jenkins put on 97 in 28 overs to rescue Sussex from an unpromising 29 for five, and 16 needed from the last two overs became an easy three when Mascarenhas went for 13. Hampshire had been early strugglers also, but 50 for the ninth wicket between Hartley and Udal, followed by 40-year-old Hartley's best one-day figures of five for 20, meant Sussex were thankful for Bevan's supremacy. Kenway kept wicket for Hampshire after Aymes twisted his knee while walking back to his position.

Gold Award: M. G. Bevan.

Hampshire

J. S. Laney b Lewry	0	S. D. Udal b Kirtley		19
D. A. Kenway c Rashid b Martin-Jenkins	36	P. J. Hartley not out		32
†A. N. Aymes lbw b Lewry	2	A. D. Mullally not out		2
*R. A. Smith c Wilton b Martin-Jenkins	5	L-b 8, w 21, n-b 6		35
G. W. White run out	6			
J. P. Stephenson c Adams b Rashid	17	1/4 2/12 3/36	(9 wkts, 50 overs)	166
A. D. Mascarenhas b Rashid	11	4/48 5/64 6/101		
S. K. Warne b Kirtley	1	7/102 8/102 9/152		

Bowling: Lewry 10–0–32–2; Kirtley 10–2–24–2; Martin-Jenkins 10–1–30–2; Rashid 10–3–25–2; Adams 8–0–31–0; Bevan 2–0–16–0.

Sussex

R. R. Montgomerie lbw b Hartley	11	U. B. A. Rashid lbw b Warne		0
W. J. House b Hartley	7	J. D. Lewry run out		10
*C. J. Adams lbw b Mullally	4	†N. J. Wilton not out		7
M. G. Bevan not out	65	B 2, l-b 6, w 13		21
P. A. Cottey c Kenway b Hartley	0			
J. R. Carpenter c Kenway b Hartley	0	1/20 2/25 3/25	(8 wkts, 49.2 overs)	170
R. S. C. Martin-Jenkins c Kenway b Hartley	45	4/27 5/29 6/126		
		7/130 8/149		

R. J. Kirtley did not bat.

Bowling: Hartley 10–2–20–5; Mullally 9.2–1–28–1; Mascarenhas 10–0–45–0; Warne 10–1–22–1; Udal 7–0–30–0; Stephenson 3–0–17–0.

Umpires: N. G. Cowley and J. W. Lloyds.

ESSEX v SUSSEX

At Chelmsford, April 24. Sussex won by 62 runs. Toss: Essex.

This game had ramifications beyond the victory that put Sussex rather than Essex into the quarter-finals. Following complaints by Essex to the ECB, the Sussex captain, Adams, was charged with pushing Danny Law, a former Sussex player, and using abusive language. Law had been caught off a full toss and was awaiting the umpires' ruling on the legitimacy of the delivery. On May 30, Adams was fined £500 on the first charge and cleared on the second. Back in April, the talking-point was not his behaviour but his batting as he and Bevan added 271 in 41 overs, a third-wicket record for the competition; Bevan's 157 not out, off 136 balls with a six and 18 fours, was a Benson and Hedges best for Sussex. Adams hit four sixes and ten fours. Essex began their reply confidently but never overcame losing Stuart Law and Hussain in the same over.

Gold Award: M. G. Bevan.

Sussex

R. R. Montgomerie b Ilott	7	P. A. Cottey not out		2
W. J. House b Irani	0	B 1, l-b 9, w 16, n-b 2		28
*C. J. Adams b Cowan	122			
M. G. Bevan not out	157	1/1 2/28 3/299	(3 wkts, 50 overs)	316

J. R. Carpenter, R. S. C. Martin-Jenkins, U. B. A. Rashid, J. D. Lewry, †N. J. Wilton and R. J. Kirtley did not bat.

Bowling: Irani 10–1–59–1; Ilott 10–2–68–1; Cowan 10–0–54–1; Anderson 5–0–28–0; Grayson 9–0–56–0; D. R. Law 4–0–27–0; S. G. Law 2–0–14–0.

Essex

*N. Hussain b Martin-Jenkins	40	A. P. Cowan not out		34
P. J. Prichard c Wilton b Lewry	34	M. C. Ilott not out		26
S. G. Law c Adams b Martin-Jenkins	9			
R. C. Irani c Martin-Jenkins b House	6	B 1, l-b 8, w 15, n-b 4		28
A. P. Grayson c Adams b House	4			
S. D. Peters c Montgomerie b House	21	1/66 2/98 3/99	(8 wkts, 50 overs)	254
D. R. Law c Martin-Jenkins b Kirtley	28	4/107 5/111 6/152		
†B. J. Hyam c Cottey b House	24	7/173 8/193		

R. S. G. Anderson did not bat.

Bowling: Lewry 8–0–44–1; Kirtley 10–3–42–1; Martin-Jenkins 10–2–38–2; Rashid 10–1–55–0; House 8–0–41–4; Bevan 4–0–25–0.

Umpires: A. Clarkson and V. A. Holder.

KENT v MIDDLESEX

At Canterbury, April 24. Kent won by 77 runs. Toss: Middlesex. County debut: R. M. S. Weston.

It took Middlesex five games to get to the middle, and they'd have finished two places higher in their group if this game had been another washout. Kent dismissed them with almost 14 of their overs unused. Langer's unbeaten 66 from 85 balls put the conditions, not ideal but all right, into a better perspective, as did Kent's total.

Gold Award: P. A. Nixon.

Kent

M. J. Walker c Roseberry b Fraser	17	B. J. Phillips run out	0
*M. V. Fleming c Weekes b Hewitt	4	M. M. Patel not out	8
R. Dravid b Tufnell	27	D. D. Masters not out	12
A. P. Wells c Langer b Shah	34	L-b 7, w 12, n-b 8	27
†P. A. Nixon c Nash b Weekes	37		
M. A. Ealham c Fraser b Shah	17	1/6 2/38 3/77 (9 wkts, 50 overs)	204
J. B. Hockley st Nash b Weekes	14	4/106 5/138 6/170	
J. M. Golding c Nash b Tufnell	7	7/178 8/178 9/181	

Bowling: Fraser 10–3–30–1; Hewitt 8–3–40–1; Johnson 10–1–29–0; Tufnell 10–1–38–2; Shah 7–0–35–2; Weekes 5–0–25–2.

Middlesex

O. A. Shah lbw b Ealham	0	J. P. Hewitt c Nixon b Ealham	8
M. R. Ramprakash c Nixon b Ealham	6	A. R. C. Fraser c Masters b Phillips	3
†D. C. Nash b Phillips	1	P. C. R. Tufnell b Ealham	6
*J. L. Langer not out	66	L-b 5, w 5	10
R. M. S. Weston c Dravid b Fleming	18		
M. A. Roseberry b Golding	3	1/1 2/8 3/8 (36.2 overs)	127
P. N. Weekes c Nixon b Golding	4	4/65 5/76 6/82	
R. L. Johnson c Nixon b Golding	2	7/84 8/110 9/118	

Bowling: Ealham 9.2–2–32–4; Phillips 7–0–25–2; Fleming 8–0–19–1; Patel 3–0–14–0; Golding 6–1–20–3; Masters 3–1–12–0.

Umpires: B. Dudleston and N. A. Mallender.

SURREY v HAMPSHIRE

At The Oval, April 24. Hampshire won by two runs. Toss: Surrey.

It was only a ten-over slog, played in shifting light after a five o'clock start, but it put both counties into the quarter-finals. Surrey went through on net run-rate as one of the two best third-placed teams. Kenway's 29-ball 47, with four sixes and two fours, bankrolled Hampshire's opening bid, helped along by Laney as 50 came from four overs. Surrey looked on course at 60 for three after six overs, but Warne changed that. In two frugal overs, he accounted for Surrey's danger men, as well as seeing Butcher dropped by the wicket-keeper. Ten runs from Mullally's final over proved beyond Surrey.

Gold Award: S. K. Warne.

Hampshire

†D. A. Kenway b Ratcliffe	47	S. D. Udal c B. C. Hollioake b Ratcliffe	0
*R. A. Smith b Tudor	1	G. W. White not out	0
A. D. Mascarenhas run out	2	W. S. Kendall not out	2
J. P. Stephenson c Brown b B. C. Hollioake	4	B 1, l-b 2, w 4	7
J. S. Laney c Bishop b Tudor	17	1/7 2/9 3/14 4/64 (7 wkts, 10 overs)	87
S. K. Warne run out	7	5/82 6/82 7/85	

P. J. Hartley and A. D. Mullally did not bat.

Bowling: Bicknell 2–0–10–0; Tudor 2–0–12–2; B. C. Hollioake 2–0–10–1; Bishop 1–0–22–0; A. J. Hollioake 2–0–25–0; Ratcliffe 1–0–5–2.

Surrey

A. D. Brown c Stephenson b Hartley	17	J. D. Ratcliffe not out		6
†A. J. Stewart b Mascarenhas	8			
B. C. Hollioake c Udal b Hartley	1	L-b 8, w 5		13
G. P. Thorpe c Udal b Warne	16			—
*A. J. Hollioake b Warne	16	1/25 2/27 3/37	(5 wkts, 10 overs)	85
M. A. Butcher not out	8	4/62 5/78		

I. J. Ward, M. P. Bicknell, A. J. Tudor and I. E. Bishop did not bat.

Bowling: Mullally 2–0–16–0; Mascarenhas 2–0–22–1; Hartley 2–0–22–2; Udal 2–0–11–0; Warne 2–0–6–2.

Umpires: R. A. White and A. G. T. Whitehead.

QUARTER-FINALS

GLAMORGAN v HAMPSHIRE

At Cardiff, May 9. Glamorgan won by 113 runs. Toss: Hampshire.

After Hampshire were dismissed in 34.2 overs, Smith, their captain, described the Sophia Gardens pitch as "atrocious" and "not a ground where I would want to play my cricket". The entire square had been covered by tarpaulin under a large tent for commercial activities during the previous autumn's rugby union World Cup and this had caused the grass to die. Re-seeding had not taken as quickly as hoped. Even so, Hampshire's batsmen contributed to their own downfall with an abysmal batting performance that left them 16 for five inside 12 overs. Their top order were so preoccupied with playing across the line that it was no surprise when five of the first six were lbw. Glamorgan had been in trouble themselves at 83 for five, but reached a useful total through a partnership of 99 in 18 overs between Dale and Newell.

Gold Award: A. Dale.

Glamorgan

R. D. B. Croft c Kenway b Hartley	11	S. P. James c Stephenson b Warne		9
M. T. G. Elliott lbw b Hartley	1	K. Newell run out		49
M. J. Powell st Kenway b Warne	29	B 2, l-b 9, w 3		14
*M. P. Maynard c Kendall				—
b Mascarenhas	6	1/7 2/16 3/31	(6 wkts, 50 overs)	182
A. Dale not out	63	4/67 5/83 6/182		

†A. D. Shaw, A. G. Wharf, O. T. Parkin and S. L. Watkin did not bat.

Bowling: Hartley 10–4–22–2; Mascarenhas 10–4–16–1; Mullally 10–2–45–0; Warne 10–0–40–2; Udal 8–0–43–0; Stephenson 2–0–5–0.

Hampshire

J. S. Laney lbw b Parkin	5	S. D. Udal c and b Newell		15
†D. A. Kenway lbw b Parkin	1	A. D. Mullally c Powell b Newell		13
W. S. Kendall lbw b Parkin	0	P. J. Hartley not out		1
*R. A. Smith c Elliott b Watkin	9	L-b 7, w 1		8
G. W. White lbw b Dale	12			—
J. P. Stephenson lbw b Watkin	0	1/5 2/5 3/16	(34.2 overs)	69
A. D. Mascarenhas c Shaw b Dale	0	4/16 5/16 6/33		
S. K. Warne b Wharf	5	7/34 8/38 9/63		

Bowling: Parkin 8–4–16–3; Watkin 7–5–3–2; Wharf 8–0–22–1; Dale 8–4–11–2; Croft 2–0–4–0; Newell 1.2–0–6–2.

Umpires: G. I. Burgess and N. A. Mallender.

LANCASHIRE v DURHAM

At Manchester, May 9. Lancashire won by three wickets. Toss: Lancashire.

Schofield, the Lancashire leg-spinner, who was in line for his Test debut the following week, left his mark on a lack-lustre quarter-final. Durham, with only one win over Lancashire in any competition, back in 1992, were threatening a formidable total until he ripped the heart out of their innings by removing Robinson, Katich and Speak. The last seven wickets fell for 25 inside ten overs, and Schofield, adding Peng to his list, finished with his best county one-day figures. Even so, Lancashire had to rely on all the experience of Fairbrother to steer them through after a series of shocks. Wood bowled beautifully, probably one of the best spells of his career, and at 35 for five Lancashire faced an embarrassing exit. Fairbrother rescued them with an unbeaten 57 in 117 balls, supported by Hegg and Austin, to reinforce his supporters' claims that he was still one of the country's best one-day batsmen.

Gold Award: N. H. Fairbrother.

Durham

J. J. B. Lewis c Hegg b Martin	0	M. M. Betts b Martin	4
†M. P. Speight b Flintoff	36	N. Killeen b Flintoff	0
S. M. Katich c Flintoff b Schofield	62	S. J. Harmison not out	8
R. Robinson c Ganguly b Schofield	10	B 1, l-b 4, w 3, n-b 4	12
*N. J. Speak c Ganguly b Schofield	14		
P. D. Collingwood b Austin	2	1/0 2/87 3/104 (46.5 overs) 154	
N. Peng c Hegg b Schofield	6	4/129 5/133 6/134	
J. Wood b Austin	0	7/140 8/140 9/142	

Bowling: Martin 7.5–2–25–2; Austin 10–3–16–2; Chapple 6–1–24–0; Flintoff 10–1–30–2; Schofield 10–1–34–4; Ganguly 3–0–20–0.

Lancashire

M. A. Atherton b Betts	2	C. P. Schofield c Katich b Wood	3
*J. P. Crawley c Collingwood b Wood	1	I. D. Austin not out	16
A. Flintoff b Wood	10	L-b 2, w 13, n-b 8	23
S. C. Ganguly b Wood	9		
N. H. Fairbrother not out	57	1/4 2/6 3/21 (7 wkts, 45 overs) 158	
G. D. Lloyd b Killeen	1	4/32 5/35	
†W. K. Hegg b Harmison	36	6/108 7/126	

P. J. Martin and G. Chapple did not bat.

Bowling: Wood 10–0–26–4; Betts 9–1–47–1; Killeen 10–2–27–1; Collingwood 8–0–22–0; Harmison 8–0–34–1.

Umpires: J. H. Hampshire and T. E. Jesty.

SUSSEX v GLOUCESTERSHIRE

At Hove, May 9. Gloucestershire won by 29 runs. Toss: Gloucestershire.

As if it were needed, Harvey provided compelling evidence of his limited-overs skills, beginning with a supremely entertaining 88 in 68 balls that lifted Gloucestershire from the insecurity of 54 for four in the 21st over. Martin-Jenkins was responsible for their uncertain start, running out Hancock with a direct hit and removing Snape and Windows in his first two overs. But Harvey, hitting two sixes and 11 fours, added 132 in 20 overs with Alleyne, whose straight drive, deflected by bowler Adams, inadvertently ran Harvey out. Alleyne, in contrast, was 78 balls over his 42. Sussex, 30 for two in the 12th over, looked to their own Australian, Bevan, to break down Gloucestershire's trademark control in the field. For all his brilliant strokeplay and fast running between the wickets, however, the run-rate was up to eight an over from the last 11 when he was fifth out, sweeping Ball to mid-wicket.

Gold Award: I. J. Harvey.

Gloucestershire

T. H. C. Hancock run out	7	C. G. Taylor not out	23
J. N. Snape c Carpenter b Martin-Jenkins	6	M. C. J. Ball not out	10
M. G. N. Windows c Rashid			
b Martin-Jenkins	18	L-b 4, w 9, n-b 4	17
K. J. Barnett run out	14		
*M. W. Alleyne b House	42	1/8 2/33 3/42	(7 wkts, 50 overs) 237
I. J. Harvey run out	88	4/54 5/186	
†R. C. Russell c Carpenter b Kirtley	12	6/191 7/220	

J. M. M. Averis and A. M. Smith did not bat.

Bowling: Lewry 10–2–33–0; Kirtley 10–0–46–1; Martin-Jenkins 10–5–24–2; Rashid 7–1–41–0; House 8–0–53–1; Bevan 3–0–21–0; Adams 2–0–15–0.

Sussex

R. R. Montgomerie run out	36	J. D. Lewry st Russell b Harvey	10
*C. J. Adams c Ball b Harvey	1	†S. Humphries c Alleyne b Harvey	0
P. A. Cottey c Russell b Averis	4	R. J. Kirtley not out	4
M. G. Bevan c Alleyne b Ball	71	L-b 6, w 7	13
U. B. A. Rashid b Ball	6		
J. R. Carpenter not out	53	1/8 2/30 3/84	(9 wkts, 50 overs) 208
W. J. House run out	5	4/91 5/152 6/160	
R. S. C. Martin-Jenkins c Smith b Averis	5	7/182 8/199 9/199	

Bowling: Smith 8–2–20–0; Harvey 10–1–28–3; Averis 10–0–55–2; Alleyne 10–1–35–0; Ball 8–0–39–2; Snape 4–0–25–0.

Umpires: N. G. Cowley and M. J. Harris.

YORKSHIRE v SURREY

At Leeds, May 9. Surrey won by seven runs. Toss: Yorkshire.

Surrey were indebted to Stewart for his unbeaten 97 off 142 balls, which rebuilt the innings after Hoggard had emphasised his England potential with a menacing new-ball spell that reduced them to 39 for four. The young fast bowler was unfortunate not to claim more. Ben Hollioake, having survived a concerted appeal for caught behind when two – Surrey were then 75 for five – added 96 in 21 overs with Stewart. He played an equally significant part in Yorkshire's downfall: first holding two superb catches at backward point, later ending Wood's threatening innings at 59, and finally running out Hamilton, the third consecutive run-out as panic set in. Wood's 109-run stand with Lehmann, unlucky to be adjudged caught down the leg side when the ball clipped a pad buckle, had pulled Yorkshire back into contention after three early wickets.

Gold Award: A. J. Stewart.

Surrey

M. A. Butcher b Hoggard	3	B. C. Hollioake c Craven b White	44
A. D. Brown b Hoggard	2	J. D. Ratcliffe not out	15
†A. J. Stewart not out	97	L-b 8, w 8, n-b 2	18
G. P. Thorpe lbw b Hoggard	0		
*A. J. Hollioake c Byas b Hoggard	10	1/5 2/19 3/20	(6 wkts, 50 overs) 198
I. J. Ward c Byas b Hamilton	9	4/39 5/71 6/167	

C. G. Greenidge, A. J. Tudor and M. P. Bicknell did not bat.

Bowling: Gough 10–1–50–0; Hoggard 10–1–39–4; Sidebottom 10–4–24–0; Hamilton 8–1–17–1; White 9–0–50–1; Lehmann 3–0–10–0.

Yorkshire

*D. Byas lbw b Bicknell	0		D. Gough run out	4	
C. White c B. C. Hollioake b Tudor	4		R. J. Sidebottom b Ratcliffe	8	
†R. J. Blakey c B. C. Hollioake b Tudor	5		M. J. Hoggard not out	2	
D. S. Lehmann c Stewart					
b A. J. Hollioake	50		L-b 2, w 12, n-b 8	22	
M. J. Wood c Stewart b B. C. Hollioake	59				
V. J. Craven c Ward b A. J. Hollioake	1		1/5 2/6 3/15	(49.5 overs) 191	
G. M. Fellows run out	28		4/124 5/130 6/166		
G. M. Hamilton run out	8		7/170 8/177 9/183		

Bowling: Bicknell 10–2–22–1; Tudor 10–1–39–2; Greenidge 4–0–22–0; B. C. Hollioake 10–0–43–1; Ratcliffe 5.5–0–33–1; A. J. Hollioake 10–1–30–2.

Umpires: A. Clarkson and J. H. Harris.

SEMI-FINALS

GLAMORGAN v SURREY

At Cardiff, May 27, 28. Glamorgan won by 32 runs (D/L method). Toss: Glamorgan.

Glamorgan qualified for their first appearance in a Lord's final since 1977, when they lost to Middlesex in the Gillette Cup. Maynard set up the victory with a chanceless century, having gone to the crease with his side 27 for two. He and Powell put on 133 in 27 overs, but his dismissal for 109 in 115 balls began a collapse, with the next six wickets adding only 25 runs. Rain had prevented play until late afternoon on Saturday and, with more stoppages on the reserve day, Surrey's target was set at 245 from 46 overs. They were quickly in trouble when Parkin was on a hat-trick in his second over. Butcher put on 54 with Stewart but was stumped off Croft's third ball, and three wickets in successive overs from Wharf effectively ended Surrey's hopes. Stewart, supported by Ratcliffe and Bicknell, struck out boldly until Parkin, amid joyous scenes, had him caught with three overs left.

Gold Award: M. P. Maynard.

Close of play: Glamorgan 99-2 (24.1 overs) (Powell 48*, Maynard 34*).

Glamorgan

R. D. B. Croft c and b Tudor	1		†A. D. Shaw b A. J. Hollioake	0	
M. T. G. Elliott b Bicknell	6		S. L. Watkin run out	1	
M. J. Powell b Tudor	67		O. T. Parkin not out	0	
*M. P. Maynard c Salisbury					
b A. J. Hollioake	109		L-b 14, w 10, n-b 2	26	
A. Dale run out	25				
S. P. James run out	10		1/3 2/27 3/160	(49.1 overs) 251	
K. Newell b A. J. Hollioake	6		4/226 5/231 6/241		
A. G. Wharf run out	0		7/250 8/250 9/251		

Bowling: Bicknell 10–0–40–1; Tudor 10–2–46–2; B. C. Hollioake 7.1–0–49–0; Ratcliffe 7–0–26–0; Salisbury 8–0–40–0; A. J. Hollioake 7–0–36–3.

Surrey

M. A. Butcher st Shaw b Croft	32		J. D. Ratcliffe c Dale b Croft	24	
A. D. Brown c Elliott b Parkin	0		M. P. Bicknell b James b Parkin	25	
A. J. Tudor lbw b Parkin	0		I. D. K. Salisbury not out	0	
†A. J. Stewart c James b Parkin	85		L-b 13, w 5	18	
G. P. Thorpe b Wharf	21				
*A. J. Hollioake lbw b Wharf	1		1/11 2/11 3/65	(43 overs) 212	
B. C. Hollioake c Newell b Wharf	4		4/101 5/105 6/121		
I. J. Ward b Croft	2		7/125 8/170 9/201		

Bowling: Parkin 8–0–60–4; Watkin 9–0–30–0; Wharf 9–1–37–3; Dale 7–0–30–0; Croft 10–0–42–3.

Umpires: D. J. Constant and J. W. Holder.

GLOUCESTERSHIRE v LANCASHIRE

At Bristol, May 28, 29. Gloucestershire won by 15 runs. Toss: Gloucestershire.

Cunliffe went to Nevil Road on the reserve day as a spectator – the first day was washed out – and left with the match award, having been given 25 minutes' notice to replace Harvey, who failed a hamstring test. Without the Australian, such a major factor in their one-day success, Gloucestershire were the underdogs against a side with a formidable history in limited-overs cricket. Cunliffe might have gone twice in single figures, but survived to share three stands worth 167 while scoring 71 off 114 balls. The slow pitch favoured his method – he hit only four fours – while robbing Lancashire's attack, Austin apart, of any real venom. Austin had only 17 runs taken off him, and four of those came from a boundary. If Lancashire felt that 221 was a passport to their 17th Lord's final, they were jolted by the loss of three wickets for 19 in the first ten overs. As ever, Fairbrother did his best to prompt them, whipping 74 runs off 102 balls despite the inconvenience of a pulled calf muscle and needing a runner. But it was not enough to prevent him from finishing on the losing side for the first time in 11 semi-finals. For holders Gloucestershire, however, victory meant a third successive Lord's final.

Gold Award: R. J. Cunliffe.

Gloucestershire

T. H. C. Hancock c Hegg b Chapple	39	†R. C. Russell not out	1
K. J. Barnett c Hegg b Martin	14		
R. J. Cunliffe c Martin b Flintoff	71	L-b 10, w 7	17
M. G. N. Windows c Martin b Watkinson	43		
*M. W. Alleyne run out	32	1/38 2/78 3/149 (6 wkts, 50 overs)	220
J. N. Snape c Flintoff b Martin	3	4/205 5/216 6/220	

C. G. Taylor, J. Lewis, J. M. M. Averis and A. M. Smith did not bat.

Bowling: Martin 9–0–49–2; Austin 10–2–17–0; Chapple 9–1–41–1; Schofield 7–0–37–0; Flintoff 10–0–40–1; Watkinson 5–0–26–1.

Lancashire

M. Watkinson b Lewis	8	I. D. Austin not out	11
M. A. Atherton c Windows b Snape	27	G. Chapple b Smith	2
*J. P. Crawley b Smith	0		
A. Flintoff b Smith	0	B 1, l-b 16, w 6, n-b 2	25
N. H. Fairbrother c Windows b Lewis	74		
G. D. Lloyd lbw b Snape	5	1/12 2/13 3/19 (9 wkts, 50 overs)	205
†W. K. Hegg b Averis	30	4/71 5/87 6/159	
C. P. Schofield b Smith	23	7/163 8/201 9/205	

P. J. Martin did not bat.

Bowling: Lewis 10–1–32–2; Smith 10–1–27–4; Averis 9–1–37–1; Snape 10–0–48–2; Alleyne 7–0–28–0; Barnett 4–0–16–0.

Umpires: B. Leadbeater and R. Palmer.

FINAL

GLAMORGAN v GLOUCESTERSHIRE

At Lord's, June 10. Gloucestershire won by seven wickets. Toss: Glamorgan.

Gloucestershire, who won both knockout trophies in 1999, became the first county to win three in a row with a convincing victory in the earliest ever Lord's final. But Maynard, Glamorgan's captain, stole most of the acclaim and the Gold Award with a century of rare quality. He alone ensured that Glamorgan's long-awaited return to a Lord's showpiece was not a complete anticlimax.

Despite bright sunshine and clear skies, the ground was only three-quarters full; many had been deterred by ticket prices of up to £45. Maynard won the toss and soon found himself in the middle after the departure of both openers by the time Glamorgan reached 24. He dominated the remainder of the innings: with calculating drives and pulls he garnered ones and twos, and calmly struck ten fours when the invitation was there. These were met with strains of *Hymns and Arias* from the travelling Welsh support, and Maynard and Powell added 137 in 31 overs. But after Powell had fallen to a return catch at the end of the 40th over, there was little to sing about. Glamorgan subsided, losing their last eight wickets for 64 inside ten overs.

That Gloucestershire fought back so strongly was down to Harvey, who gave a fine demonstration in the art of varying pace. Having already dismissed both openers, he induced a lob into the covers from Newell with a slower ball, trapped Wharf on the crease with a quicker one, and yorked Watkin to become only the third man in the 29 Benson and Hedges finals to finish with five wickets. Maynard, denied the strike, could only stand and watch. The ball after Watkin's dismissal he attempted a dicey single, only to be run out by Barnett coming in from cover, whereupon both sets of partisan supporters rose to salute him. His 104 from 118 balls made him the fifth century-maker in the final of this competition.

Glamorgan's woes were compounded in the first 15 overs of Gloucestershire's reply, as Hancock and Barnett punished some wayward bowling from Parkin and Watkin to reach 79 without loss. Barnett, enjoying his fourth successive Lord's final (he played for Derbyshire in the 1998 NatWest), overtook Mike Gatting as the second-highest scorer in Benson and Hedges cricket when 21. After Hancock went to a stunning full-length return catch by Parkin, Alleyne and Windows steered Gloucestershire home with ease, Windows reaching his 59-ball half-century in the nick of time before his captain hit the winning run with three overs to spare. – MATTHEW HANCOCK.

Gold Award: M. P. Maynard. *Attendance:* 20,189; *receipts* £581,990.

Glamorgan

R. D. B. Croft c Lewis b Harvey	11	S. L. Watkin b Harvey	10
M. T. G. Elliott b Harvey	9	O. T. Parkin not out	0
M. J. Powell c and b Snape	48	L-b 5, w 8, n-b 8	21
*M. P. Maynard run out	104		
A. Dale run out	5	1/18 (1) 2/24 (2) 3/161 (3) (49.3 overs) 225	
S. P. James b Averis	7	4/178 (5) 5/192 (6)	
K. Newell c Cunliffe b Harvey	1	6/195 (7) 7/202 (8)	
†A. D. Shaw c Barnett b Averis	1	8/213 (9) 9/225 (10)	
A. G. Wharf lbw b Harvey	8	10/225 (4) Score at 15 overs: 43-2	

Bowling: Harvey 9.3–1–34–5; Smith 10–1–44–0; Lewis 5–0–23–0; Averis 10–0–49–2; Alleyne 7–0–33–0; Snape 8–0–37–1.

Gloucestershire

T. H. C. Hancock c and b Parkin	60
K. J. Barnett b Croft	39
R. J. Cunliffe c Shaw b Watkin	24
M. G. N. Windows not out	53
*M. W. Alleyne not out	40
B 1, l-b 4, w 3, n-b 2	10

1/80 (2) 2/118 (3) (3 wkts, 46.5 overs) 226
3/131 (1) Score at 15 overs: 79-0

I. J. Harvey, †R. C. Russell, J. N. Snape, J. Lewis, J. M. M. Averis and A. M. Smith did not bat.

Bowling: Parkin 8–1–46–1; Watkin 10–1–42–1; Wharf 10–0–48–0; Croft 10–0–39–1; Dale 8.5–0–46–0.

Umpires: K. E. Palmer and G. Sharp.

BENSON AND HEDGES CUP RECORDS

55 overs available in all games 1972-95, 50 overs in 1996-2000.
Only eight teams took part in 1999.

Batting

Highest individual scores: 198*, G. A. Gooch, Essex v Sussex, Hove, 1982; 177, S. J. Cook, Somerset v Sussex, Hove, 1990; 173*, C. G. Greenidge, Hampshire v Minor Counties (South), Amersham, 1973; 167*, A. J. Stewart, Surrey v Somerset, The Oval, 1994; 160, A. J. Stewart, Surrey v Hampshire, The Oval, 1996; 158*, B. F. Davison, Leicestershire v Warwickshire, Coventry, 1972; 158, W. J. Cronje, Leicestershire v Lancashire, Manchester, 1995; 157*, M. G. Bevan, Sussex v Essex, Chelmsford, 2000; 155*, M. D. Crowe, Somerset v Hampshire, Southampton, 1987; 155*, R. A. Smith, Hampshire v Glamorgan, Southampton, 1989; 154*, M. J. Procter, Gloucestershire v Somerset, Taunton, 1972; 154*, C. L. Smith, Hampshire v Combined Universities, Southampton, 1990; 151*, M. P. Maynard, Glamorgan v Middlesex, Lord's, 1996; 151, D. L. Maddy, Leicestershire v Minor Counties, Leicester, 1998. *In the final:* 132*, I. V. A. Richards, Somerset v Surrey, 1981. (320 hundreds have been scored in the competition. The most hundreds in one season was 26 in 1996.)

Most runs: 5,176, G. A. Gooch; 2,940, K. J. Barnett; 2,921, M. W. Gatting; 2,814, A. J. Stewart; 2,795, N. H. Fairbrother; 2,772, G. A. Hick; 2,761, C. J. Tavaré; 2,718, W. Larkins; 2,689, R. J. Bailey; 2,663, D. W. Randall; 2,636, A. J. Lamb; 2,567, R. T. Robinson; 2,551, C. W. J. Athey.

Fastest hundred: M. A. Nash in 62 minutes, Glamorgan v Hampshire at Swansea, 1976.

Most hundreds: 15, G. A. Gooch; 7, G. A. Hick and W. Larkins; 6, M. P. Maynard and N. R. Taylor; 5, C. G. Greenidge, A. J. Lamb and R. A. Smith.

Highest totals: 388 for seven, Essex v Scotland, Chelmsford, 1992; 382 for six, Leicestershire v Minor Counties, Leicester, 1998; 371 for six, Leicestershire v Scotland, Leicester, 1997; 369 for eight, Warwickshire v Minor Counties, Jesmond, 1996; 366 for four, Derbyshire v Combined Universities, Oxford, 1991; 359 for seven, Essex v Ireland, Chelmsford, 1998; 353 for seven, Lancashire v Nottinghamshire, Manchester, 1995; 350 for three, Essex v Oxford & Cambridge Univs, Chelmsford, 1979; 349 for seven, Somerset v Ireland, Taunton, 1997; 338 for six, Kent v Somerset, Maidstone, 1996; 333 for four, Essex v Oxford & Cambridge Univs, Chelmsford, 1985; 333 for six, Surrey v Hampshire, The Oval, 1996; 331 for five, Surrey v Hampshire, The Oval, 1990; 331 for five, Essex v British Univs, Chelmsford, 1996; 330 for four, Lancashire v Sussex, Manchester, 1991. *In the final:* 291 for nine, Gloucestershire v Yorkshire, 1999.

Highest total by a side batting second and winning: 318 for five (54.3 overs), Lancashire v Leicestershire (312 for five), Manchester, 1995. *In the final:* 244 for six (55 overs), Yorkshire v Northamptonshire (244 for seven), 1987; 244 for seven (55 overs), Nottinghamshire v Essex (243 for seven), 1989.

Highest total by a side batting second and losing: 303 for seven (55 overs), Derbyshire v Somerset (310 for three), Taunton, 1990. *In the final:* 255 (51.4 overs), Surrey v Essex (290 for six), 1979.

Highest match aggregates: 631 for 15 wickets, Kent (338 for six) v Somerset (293 for nine), Maidstone, 1996; 630 for ten wickets, Leicestershire (312 for five) v Lancashire (318 for five), Manchester, 1995; 629 for 14 wickets, Lancashire (353 for seven) v Nottinghamshire (276 for seven), Manchester, 1995; 628 for 15 wickets, Warwickshire (312 for six) v Lancashire (316 for nine), Manchester, 1996; 626 for ten wickets, British Univs (312 for eight) v Glamorgan (314 for two), Cambridge, 1996; 615 for 11 wickets, Gloucestershire (307 for four) v Surrey (308 for seven), The Oval, 1996; 613 for ten wickets, Somerset (310 for three) v Derbyshire (303 for seven), Taunton, 1990; 610 for eight wickets, Sussex (303 for six) v Kent (307 for two), Hove, 1995; 610 for 14 wickets, Warwickshire (304 for eight) v Kent (306 for six), Canterbury, 1997.

Lowest totals: 50 in 27.2 overs, Hampshire v Yorkshire, Leeds, 1991; 52 in 26.5 overs, Minor Counties v Lancashire, Lakenham, 1998; 56 in 26.2 overs, Leicestershire v Minor Counties, Wellington, 1982; 59 in 34 overs, Oxford & Cambridge Univs v Glamorgan, Cambridge, 1983; 60 in 26 overs, Sussex v Middlesex, Hove, 1978; 61 in 25.3 overs, Essex v Lancashire, Chelmsford, 1992; 62 in 26.5 overs, Gloucestershire v Hampshire, Bristol, 1975. *In the final:* 76 in 27.4 overs, Leicestershire v Essex, 1998.

Shortest completed innings: 21.4 overs (156), Surrey v Sussex, Hove, 1988.

Record partnership for each wicket

252	for 1st	V. P. Terry and C. L. Smith, Hampshire v Combined Universities at Southampton	1990
285*	for 2nd	C. G. Greenidge and D. R. Turner, Hampshire v Minor Counties (South) at Amersham	1973
271	for 3rd	C. J. Adams and M. G. Bevan, Sussex v Essex at Chelmsford	2000
207	for 4th	R. C. Russell and A. J. Wright, Gloucestershire v British Universities at Bristol	1998
160	for 5th	A. J. Lamb and D. J. Capel, Northamptonshire v Leicestershire at Northampton	1986
167*	for 6th	M. G. Bevan and R. J. Blakey, Yorkshire v Lancashire at Manchester. . .	1996
149*	for 7th	J. D. Love and C. M. Old, Yorkshire v Scotland at Bradford.	1981
109	for 8th	R. E. East and N. Smith, Essex v Northamptonshire at Chelmsford	1977
83	for 9th	P. G. Newman and M. A. Holding, Derbyshire v Nottinghamshire at Nottingham	1985
80*	for 10th	D. L. Bairstow and M. Johnson, Yorkshire v Derbyshire at Derby	1981

Bowling

Most wickets: 149, J. K. Lever; 132, I. T. Botham.

Best bowling: seven for 12, W. W. Daniel, Middlesex v Minor Counties (East), Ipswich, 1978; seven for 22, J. R. Thomson, Middlesex v Hampshire, Lord's, 1981; seven for 24, Mushtaq Ahmed, Somerset v Ireland, Taunton, 1997; seven for 32, R. G. D. Willis, Warwickshire v Yorkshire, Birmingham, 1981. *In the final:* five for 13, S. T. Jefferies, Hampshire v Derbyshire, 1988.

Hat-tricks (12): G. D. McKenzie, Leicestershire v Worcestershire, Worcester, 1972; K. Higgs, Leicestershire v Surrey in the final, Lord's, 1974; A. A. Jones, Middlesex v Essex, Lord's, 1977; M. J. Procter, Gloucestershire v Hampshire, Southampton, 1977; W. Larkins, Northamptonshire v Oxford & Cambridge Univs, Northampton, 1980; E. A. Moseley, Glamorgan v Kent, Cardiff, 1981; G. C. Small, Warwickshire v Leicestershire, Leicester, 1984; N. A. Mallender, Somerset v Combined Universities, Taunton, 1987; W. K. M. Benjamin, Leicestershire v Nottinghamshire, Leicester, 1987; A. R. C. Fraser, Middlesex v Sussex, Lord's, 1988; S. M. Pollock (four in four balls), Warwickshire v Leicestershire, Birmingham, 1996; Saqlain Mushtaq, Surrey v Lancashire, The Oval, 1998.

Wicket-keeping and Fielding

Most dismissals: 122 (117 ct, 5 st), D. L. Bairstow; 100 (90 ct, 10 st), S. J. Rhodes.

Most dismissals in an innings: 8 (all ct), D. J. S. Taylor, Somerset v Oxford & Cambridge Univs, Taunton, 1982.

Most catches by a fielder: 68, G. A. Gooch; 55, C. J. Tavaré; 53, I. T. Botham.

Most catches by a fielder in an innings: 5, V. J. Marks, Oxford & Cambridge Univs v Kent, Oxford, 1976.

Results

Largest victories in runs: Essex by 272 runs v Scotland, Chelmsford, 1992; Leicestershire by 256 runs v Minor Counties, Leicester, 1998; Somerset by 233 runs v Ireland, Eglinton, 1995; Somerset by 221 runs v Ireland, Taunton, 1997; Glamorgan by 217 runs v Combined Universities, Cardiff, 1995; Essex by 214 runs v Oxford & Cambridge Univs, Chelmsford, 1979; Derbyshire by 206 runs v Combined Universities, Oxford, 1991; Warwickshire by 195 runs v Minor Counties, Jesmond, 1996.

Victories by ten wickets (19): By Derbyshire, Essex (twice), Glamorgan, Hampshire, Kent (twice), Lancashire, Leicestershire (twice), Middlesex, Northamptonshire, Somerset, Warwickshire, Worcestershire (twice), Yorkshire (three times).

Gold Awards

Most awards: 22, G. A. Gooch; 11, K. J. Barnett, M. W. Gatting, G. A. Hick, T. E. Jesty and B. Wood.

WINNERS 1972-2000

		Gold Award
1972	LEICESTERSHIRE* beat Yorkshire by five wickets.	J. C. Balderstone
1973	KENT* beat Worcestershire by 39 runs.	Asif Iqbal
1974	SURREY* beat Leicestershire by 27 runs.	J. H. Edrich
1975	LEICESTERSHIRE beat Middlesex* by five wickets.	N. M. McVicker
1976	KENT* beat Worcestershire by 43 runs.	G. W. Johnson
1977	GLOUCESTERSHIRE* beat Kent by 64 runs.	A. W. Stovold
1978	KENT beat Derbyshire* by six wickets.	R. A. Woolmer
1979	ESSEX beat Surrey* by 35 runs.	G. A. Gooch
1980	NORTHAMPTONSHIRE* beat Essex by six runs.	A. J. Lamb
1981	SOMERSET* beat Surrey by seven wickets.	I. V. A. Richards
1982	SOMERSET* beat Nottinghamshire by nine wickets.	V. J. Marks
1983	MIDDLESEX beat Essex* by four runs.	C. T. Radley
1984	LANCASHIRE* beat Warwickshire by six wickets.	J. Abrahams
1985	LEICESTERSHIRE* beat Essex by five wickets.	P. Willey
1986	MIDDLESEX beat Kent* by two runs.	J. E. Emburey
1987	YORKSHIRE* beat Northamptonshire, having taken more wickets with the scores tied.	J. D. Love
1988	HAMPSHIRE* beat Derbyshire by seven wickets.	S. T. Jefferies
1989	NOTTINGHAMSHIRE beat Essex* by three wickets.	R. T. Robinson
1990	LANCASHIRE beat Worcestershire* by 69 runs.	M. Watkinson
1991	WORCESTERSHIRE beat Lancashire* by 65 runs.	G. A. Hick
1992	HAMPSHIRE beat Kent* by 41 runs.	R. A. Smith
1993	DERBYSHIRE beat Lancashire* by six runs.	D. G. Cork
1994	WARWICKSHIRE* beat Worcestershire by six wickets.	P. A. Smith
1995	LANCASHIRE beat Kent* by 35 runs.	P. A. de Silva†
1996	LANCASHIRE* beat Northamptonshire by 31 runs.	I. D. Austin
1997	SURREY beat Kent* by eight wickets.	B. C. Hollioake
1998	ESSEX beat Leicestershire* by 192 runs.	P. J. Prichard
1999‡	GLOUCESTERSHIRE* beat Yorkshire by 124 runs.	M. W. Alleyne
2000	GLOUCESTERSHIRE beat Glamorgan* by seven wickets.	M. P. Maynard†

* Won toss.   † On losing side.   ‡ Super Cup.

WINS BY NON-CHAMPIONSHIP TEAMS

1973	OXFORD beat Northamptonshire at Northampton by two wickets.
1975	{ OXFORD & CAMBRIDGE beat Worcestershire at Cambridge by 66 runs. { OXFORD & CAMBRIDGE beat Northamptonshire at Oxford by three wickets.
1976	OXFORD & CAMBRIDGE beat Yorkshire at Barnsley by seven wickets.
1980	MINOR COUNTIES beat Gloucestershire at Chippenham by three runs.
1981	MINOR COUNTIES beat Hampshire at Southampton by three runs.
1982	MINOR COUNTIES beat Leicestershire at Wellington by 131 runs.
1984	OXFORD & CAMBRIDGE beat Gloucestershire at Bristol by 27 runs.
1986	SCOTLAND beat Lancashire at Perth by three runs.
1987	MINOR COUNTIES beat Glamorgan at Oxford (Christ Church) by seven wickets.
1989	{ COMBINED UNIVERSITIES beat Surrey at Cambridge by nine runs. { COMBINED UNIVERSITIES beat Worcestershire at Worcester by five wickets.
1990	{ COMBINED UNIVERSITIES beat Yorkshire at Leeds by two wickets. { SCOTLAND beat Northamptonshire at Northampton by two runs.
1992	MINOR COUNTIES beat Sussex at Marlow by 19 runs.
1995	MINOR COUNTIES beat Leicestershire at Leicester by 26 runs.
1997	{ IRELAND beat Middlesex at Dublin (Castle Avenue) by 46 runs. { BRITISH UNIVERSITIES beat Sussex at Cambridge by 19 runs.
1998	BRITISH UNIVERSITIES beat Gloucestershire at Bristol by seven runs.

TEAM RECORDS 1972-2000

	Rounds reached					Matches			
	W	F	SF	QF	P	W	L	NR	
Derbyshire	1	3	4	9	126	65	51	10	
Durham	0	0	0	2	32	14	16	2	
Essex	2	6	9	16	141	85	50	6	
Glamorgan	0	1	2	9	122	54	61	7	
Gloucestershire	3	3	4	9	127	64	57	6	
Hampshire	2	2	5	14	132	64	61	7	
Kent	3	8	13	19	150	94	49	7	
Lancashire	4	6	11	19	148	94	47	7	
Leicestershire	3	5	8	12	137	74	54	9	
Middlesex	2	3	5	15	134	67	55	12	
Northamptonshire	1	3	6	11	128	59	58	11	
Nottinghamshire	1	2	5	13	130	71	51	8	
Somerset	2	2	8	13	132	69	57	6	
Surrey	2	4	10	15	140	79	54	7	
Sussex	0	0	2	11	123	58	61	4	
Warwickshire	1	2	8	15	136	74	52	10	
Worcestershire	1	5	8	15	136	69	60	7	
Yorkshire	1	3	8	14	133	73	52	8	
Cambridge University	0	0	0	0	8	0	8	0	
Oxford University	0	0	0	0	4	1	3	0	
Oxford & Cambridge Universities	0	0	0	0	48	4	42	2	
Combined/British Universities . . .	0	0	0	1	47	5	41	1	
Minor Counties	0	0	0	0	75	6	65	4	
Minor Counties (North)	0	0	0	0	20	0	20	0	
Minor Counties (South)	0	0	0	0	20	0	19	1	
Minor Counties (East)	0	0	0	0	12	0	12	0	
Minor Counties (West)	0	0	0	0	12	0	12	0	
Scotland	0	0	0	0	70	2	64	4	
Ireland	0	0	0	0	17	1	14	2	

Middlesex beat Gloucestershire on the toss of a coin in their quarter-final in 1983. Derbyshire, Kent, Somerset and Warwickshire totals each include a bowling contest; Derbyshire beat Somerset and Warwickshire beat Kent when their quarter-finals, in 1993 and 1994 respectively, were abandoned. In 1999, only eight counties took part; from 2000, the competition was restricted to the 18 first-class counties.

NORWICH UNION NATIONAL LEAGUE, 2000

Glenn McGrath

So many ingredients were there. Ebb and flow, a faltering and ultimately failing pace-maker, a climax that produced an unprecedented one-day treble when Gloucestershire, straight from winning their fourth Lord's final in a row, stormed to the front to add the League title to their knockout trophies double. Yet throughout the season the unfolding drama was often impossible to follow. With only nine counties in each division, matches played at irregular intervals, and the weekly tables usually revealing teams with games in hand, the true state of play was not always obvious. There was one entire weekend of League cricket in late June, beginning with three floodlit games on Friday night and continuing until the Tuesday evening. But there were other weekends when there were no, or next to no, games.

When Gloucestershire's NatWest semi-final win over Lancashire took them to their second Lord's final of the summer, they were third in the table behind Worcestershire and Somerset, and had just entered a period of two and a half weeks without a League game. By the time they won the NatWest final, they were down to fifth, with a game postponed from May in hand. Next day, they embarked on a run of three wins in nine days to go top, as previous leaders Yorkshire ended their campaign with defeat away to Kent. Once Somerset, the only other challenger, were beaten by Lancashire, Gloucestershire could afford to lose their last game – and did.

Rival neighbours Worcestershire, meanwhile, were still coming to terms with the hand fate had dealt them. After losing their opening fixture, they had gone seven games without defeat to head Division One by six points at the halfway stage. They then failed to win one of their last eight and were relegated, even though their Australian fast bowler, Glenn McGrath, had conceded fewer runs per over (2.16) and per wicket (8.13) than any other bowler, and had bettered the previous lowest marks: Derek Shackleton's economy-rate of 2.23 for Hampshire in 1969 and James Ormond's average of 8.68 for Leicestershire in 1998.

Worcestershire could point to the absence of Graeme Hick, their captain and outstanding batsman, for more than half their matches, owing to England calls. Lancashire, champions the previous two years, and Sussex, both of whom spent almost all season in the relegation zone, dropped into Division Two with them. Sussex had the League's leading run-scorer in Michael Bevan, who hit 706 runs, but like McGrath he returned to Australia to fulfil international commitments at a crucial time.

Division Two was more or less a two-horse race once Warwickshire, winners in their first four outings, went three weeks without a game. That let Nottinghamshire take up the running, until their four-week break let unbeaten Surrey gallop into the lead. Surrey were 14 points clear with three to play and, when Nottinghamshire lost to Middlesex, it did not matter that they lost all of them.

NORWICH UNION NATIONAL LEAGUE

Division One

	M	W	L	T	NR	Pts	Net run-rate
1 – Gloucestershire Gladiators (4) . . .	16	9	6	0	1	38	1.25
2 – Yorkshire Phoenix (5).	16	9	7	0	0	36	5.97
3 – Northamptonshire Steelbacks (3) .	16	9	7	0	0	36	–3.98
4 – Leicestershire Foxes (6)	16	7	6	2	1	34	–0.45
5 – Kent Spitfires (1)	16	7	7	0	2	32	6.17
6 – Somerset Sabres (2).	16	7	8	0	1	30	0.59
7 – Worcestershire Royals (2).	16	6	8	0	2	28	–4.23
8 – Lancashire Lightning (1)	16	6	8	1	1	28	–5.82
9 – Sussex Sharks (1)	16	5	8	1	2	26	0.34

Division Two

	M	W	L	T	NR	Pts	Net run-rate
1 – Surrey Lions (6)	16	11	3	0	2	48	11.93
2 – Nottinghamshire Outlaws (5). . . .	16	11	4	0	1	46	–2.17
3 – Warwickshire Bears (7)	16	10	5	1	0	42	7.09
4 – Middlesex Crusaders (7).	16	8	5	1	2	38	–0.26
5 – Essex Eagles (9).	16	7	7	0	2	32	0.35
6 – Glamorgan Dragons (4)	16	7	7	2	0	32	–2.18
7 – Durham Dynamos (9)	16	5	11	0	0	20	0.32
8 – Hampshire Hawks (8)	16	5	11	0	0	20	–5.78
9 – Derbyshire Scorpions (8)	16	2	13	0	1	10	–8.99

1999 positions are shown in brackets: Division One in bold, Division Two in italic.

The bottom three teams in Division One are relegated for 2001, the top three teams in Division Two are promoted.

When two or more counties finished with an equal number of points, positions were decided by a) most wins, b) higher net run-rate (runs scored per 100 balls minus runs conceded per 100 balls).

Prize money

Division One
£54,000 for winners: GLOUCESTERSHIRE.
£27,000 for runners-up: YORKSHIRE.

Division Two
£20,000 for winners: SURREY.
£11,000 for runners-up: NOTTINGHAMSHIRE.

Winners of each match (both divisions): £600.

Leading run-scorers: M. G. Bevan 706, *P. D. Collingwood* 607, *S. M. Katich* 598, S. C. Ganguly 569, D. S. Lehmann 564, D. J. Sales 547, *D. J. Bicknell* 537, B. F. Smith 508, *M. P. Maynard* 501.

Leading wicket-takers: M. J. Hoggard 37, I. J. Harvey 34, G. D. McGrath 30, J. M. M. Averis and *N. Killeen* 29, P. S. Jones 28, R. J. Kirtley 26, *D. R. Brown, P. J. Franks* and *S. K. Warne* 25.

Most economical bowlers (runs per over, minimum 100 overs): G. D. McGrath 2.16, A. M. Smith 2.78, I. J. Harvey 3.31, *R. C. Irani* 3.33, *T. A. Munton* 3.35, S. R. Lampitt 3.73, P. A. J. DeFreitas 3.74.

Leading wicket-keepers: N. D. Burns 30 (28 ct, 2 st), *C. M. W. Read* 27 (25 ct, 2 st), R. J. Blakey 26 (21 ct, 5 st) and P. A. Nixon 26 (22 ct, 4 st), R. C. Russell 25 (17 ct, 8 st).

Leading fielders: C. J. Adams, *P. D. Collingwood* and *J. L. Langer* 11, M. G. Bevan, D. Byas and J. Cox 10.

Players who appeared in Division Two are shown in italics.

DIVISION ONE

GLOUCESTERSHIRE

GLOUCESTERSHIRE v SUSSEX

At Bristol, April 30. Gloucestershire won by ten runs. Toss: Sussex.

Adams's bowlers justified his decision to put Gloucestershire in. Despite Barnett's stands of 60 with Alleyne and 43 with Russell, they mustered only 145. Sussex, with six wickets in hand, were 21 runs off the points, but seamers Averis and Harvey undid them on an old pitch that ought to have favoured spin. While Bevan stood stranded off the strike, those last six wickets tumbled for ten runs in 43 balls.

Gloucestershire

T. H. C. Hancock c Montgomerie		M. C. J. Ball c Robinson b House	3
b Kirtley	11	J. M. M. Averis b Kirtley	0
J. N. Snape c Adams b Martin-Jenkins	3	A. M. Smith not out	2
M. G. N. Windows lbw b Martin-Jenkins	2		
K. J. Barnett c Carpenter b House	55	L-b 4, w 3, n-b 2	9
*M. W. Alleyne st Wilton b Rashid	30		
I. J. Harvey c Adams b Robinson	1	1/4 2/16 3/16 (43.5 overs) 145	
†R. C. Russell c Adams b House	23	4/76 5/79 6/122	
D. R. Hewson b Kirtley	6	7/134 8/139 9/141	

Bowling: Kirtley 8–1–18–3; Martin-Jenkins 9–1–34–2; Robinson 9–1–28–1; Rashid 9–2–20–1; House 6.5–0–34–3; Bevan 2–0–7–0.

Sussex

R. R. Montgomerie lbw b Harvey	7	†N. J. Wilton c Barnett b Averis	1
W. J. House b Smith	26	R. J. Kirtley c Harvey b Averis	0
*C. J. Adams run out	12	M. A. Robinson lbw b Averis	0
M. G. Bevan not out	52	L-b 1, w 5	6
P. A. Cottey c Alleyne b Snape	2		
J. R. Carpenter b Harvey	29	1/29 2/35 3/83 (43.4 overs) 135	
R. S. C. Martin-Jenkins b Averis	0	4/88 5/125 6/126	
U. B. A. Rashid run out	0	7/130 8/133 9/135	

Bowling: Smith 9–3–34–1; Harvey 9–2–15–2; Averis 8.4–2–21–4; Alleyne 6–1–24–0; Ball 5–0–20–0; Snape 6–1–20–1.

Umpires: J. H. Hampshire and N. A. Mallender.

At Taunton, May 1. GLOUCESTERSHIRE lost to SOMERSET by eight runs.

At Northampton, May 7. GLOUCESTERSHIRE beat NORTHAMPTONSHIRE by 49 runs (D/L method).

At Leeds, May 21. GLOUCESTERSHIRE lost to YORKSHIRE by 35 runs (D/L method).

At Tunbridge Wells, June 4. GLOUCESTERSHIRE beat KENT by six runs.

At Worcester, June 14 (day/night). GLOUCESTERSHIRE lost to WORCESTERSHIRE by 21 runs.

GLOUCESTERSHIRE v YORKSHIRE

At Bristol, June 24. Gloucestershire won by 51 runs. Toss: Gloucestershire.

Alleyne, nursing a strained back, missed his first competitive game for Gloucestershire in ten seasons, but stand-in captain Russell made sure they moved into third place in Division One. He and Harvey added 77 in 14 overs, with Harvey's 52 coming from 45 balls, before a remarkable sequence saw Vaughan take four for 27 in 5.5 overs. If Yorkshire hadn't sensed it was not their day when Hoggard's first two overs cost 22 runs, including seven wides and a no-ball, they should have guessed it when Fellows was leg-before to the first ball of their reply. Byas resisted for 62 balls then fell to Harvey, who promptly bowled Middlebrook.

Gloucestershire

R. J. Cunliffe c Blakey b Hamilton	34	M. J. Cawdron b White		0
K. J. Barnett b White	18	J. M. M. Averis b Vaughan		6
*†R. C. Russell c Blakey b Hoggard	37	A. M. Smith not out		3
M. G. N. Windows c Byas b Hamilton	10	L-b 6, w 15, n-b 2		23
I. J. Harvey st Blakey b Vaughan	52			
C. G. Taylor c Fellows b Vaughan	15	1/47 2/73 3/90	(44.5 overs)	211
J. N. Snape c Byas b Vaughan	11	4/167 5/169 6/197		
R. C. J. Williams c Vaughan b White	2	7/200 8/201 9/208		

Bowling: Silverwood 4–0–13–0; Hoggard 4–0–38–1; Sidebottom 5–0–17–0; White 7–0–30–3; Hamilton 7–0–29–2; Middlebrook 9–0–29–0; Lehmann 3–0–22–0; Vaughan 5.5–1–27–4.

Yorkshire

G. M. Fellows lbw b Smith	0	C. E. W. Silverwood c Harvey b Averis		4
M. P. Vaughan st Russell b Smith	6	R. J. Sidebottom st Russell b Averis		3
†R. J. Blakey c Russell b Smith	27	M. J. Hoggard not out		1
D. S. Lehmann c Cunliffe b Cawdron	22	B 1, l-b 5, w 11		17
*D. Byas b Harvey	38			
C. White c Taylor b Cawdron	11	1/0 2/38 3/41	(42 overs)	160
G. M. Hamilton b Averis	31	4/76 5/106 6/135		
J. D. Middlebrook b Harvey	0	7/135 8/148 9/159		

Bowling: Smith 9–2–20–3; Harvey 7–1–24–2; Averis 8–0–26–3; Cawdron 9–1–37–2; Snape 9–0–47–0.

Umpires: N. A. Mallender and G. Sharp.

At Leicester, June 25. GLOUCESTERSHIRE lost to LEICESTERSHIRE by 38 runs.

GLOUCESTERSHIRE v WORCESTERSHIRE

At Cheltenham, July 16. Gloucestershire won by three wickets. Toss: Worcestershire.

McGrath took three wickets in seven balls but, after Gloucestershire plummeted from 76 for three to 76 for seven, he was taken off. This allowed Taylor and Ball to engineer a most unlikely escape, putting on 73 in 13 overs, with Ball hitting the winning cover boundary off the penultimate delivery. Worcestershire's batting had never got going: there were four run-outs, and Gloucestershire's sharpness in the field reached its height in the final five overs, when Harvey and Averis conceded only 11 runs.

Worcestershire

P. R. Pollard b Smith	8	Kabir Ali run out	1
E. J. Wilson c Ball b Harvey	4	M. J. Rawnsley not out	4
V. S. Solanki c Averis b Alleyne	45	G. D. McGrath not out	0
D. A. Leatherdale c Williams b Alleyne	6	L-b 2, w 7	9
R. C. Driver run out	29		
*†S. J. Rhodes c Alleyne b Harvey	27	1/15 2/17 3/33 (9 wkts, 45 overs)	145
S. R. Lampitt run out	7	4/90 5/107 6/131	
R. K. Illingworth run out	5	7/137 8/140 9/142	

Bowling: Smith 9–5–9–1; Harvey 9–0–25–2; Averis 9–1–23–0; Alleyne 9–0–38–2; Ball 9–1–48–0.

Gloucestershire

†R. C. Russell c and b Lampitt	7	R. C. J. Williams c Rhodes b McGrath	0
D. R. Hewson run out	34	M. C. J. Ball not out	30
I. J. Harvey b Illingworth	11	B 3, l-b 4, w 2, n-b 2	11
*M. W. Alleyne b Rawnsley	12		
M. G. N. Windows lbw b McGrath	7	1/40 2/56 3/56 (7 wkts, 44.5 overs)	149
C. G. Taylor not out	37	4/76 5/76	
J. N. Snape lbw b McGrath	0	6/76 7/76	

J. M. M. Averis and A. M. Smith did not bat.

Bowling: McGrath 9–4–15–3; Ali 9–1–25–0; Lampitt 9–1–31–1; Leatherdale 1–0–5–0; Illingworth 8.5–1–33–1; Rawnsley 8–2–33–1.

Umpires: D. J. Constant and M. J. Harris.

GLOUCESTERSHIRE v KENT

At Cheltenham, July 23. Gloucestershire won by five wickets. Toss: Kent.

Russell and Alleyne led Gloucestershire to their sixth League win and a double over Kent. On a good surface, their target of 200 should have been higher, and Hewson and Harvey made quick inroads, taking 72 off 13 overs. Kent were still in with a chance as Gloucestershire fell away to 109 for five by the 26th over, but Russell came along to hit 55 at a run a ball. Ealham's unbeaten 49 for Kent had included quick-scoring stands of 38, 23 and 33, the last with Fleming coming off four overs.

Kent

R. Dravid c Russell b Averis	16	†P. A. Nixon c Hewson b Averis	12
E. T. Smith lbw b Smith	14	*M. V. Fleming not out	15
J. B. Hockley c Snape b Ball	29	B 2, l-b 5, w 3	10
A. P. Wells c Hancock b Ball	38		
M. A. Ealham not out	49	1/34 2/36 3/103 (6 wkts, 45 overs)	199
M. J. Walker c Windows b Alleyne	16	4/105 5/143 6/166	

M. M. Patel, D. D. Masters and M. J. McCague did not bat.

Bowling: Harvey 9–0–47–0; Smith 9–1–28–1; Averis 9–1–43–2; Ball 9–0–45–2; Alleyne 9–0–29–1.

Gloucestershire

T. H. C. Hancock c Nixon b McCague	4	*M. W. Alleyne not out	35
D. R. Hewson c Ealham b Patel	45		
I. J. Harvey b Fleming	41	L-b 2, w 7	9
J. N. Snape lbw b Patel	4		
M. G. N. Windows lbw b Ealham	7	1/4 2/76 3/81 (5 wkts, 40.1 overs)	200
†R. C. Russell not out	55	4/100 5/109	

C. G. Taylor, J. M. M. Averis, M. C. J. Ball and A. M. Smith did not bat.

Bowling: McCague 5–0–40–1; Ealham 7–0–23–1; Masters 8–0–41–0; Fleming 8.1–0–44–1; Patel 9–1–33–2; Walker 2–0–13–0; Dravid 1–0–4–0.

Umpires: R. Julian and R. A. White.

GLOUCESTERSHIRE v SOMERSET

At Bristol, August 9 (day/night). No result. Toss: Somerset.

It was a huge disappointment for a 6,500 crowd when heavy drizzle saw the match called off at the end of Somerset's innings. The two points were enough to move them to the top of the division because of a superior run-rate to Worcestershire and Gloucestershire, all tied on 26 points. Powerful driving by Trescothick – he hit eight fours – carried him to 50 off 59 balls. His opening partnership with Lathwell, worth 80 in 16 overs, put Somerset in a strong position.

Somerset

M. E. Trescothick run out	53	G. D. Rose c Ball b Cawdron		3
M. N. Lathwell lbw b Alleyne	37	A. R. Caddick run out		1
I. D. Blackwell c Russell b Alleyne	0	P. S. Jones not out		3
*J. Cox run out	26	B 1, l-b 4, w 7, n-b 4		16
P. D. Bowler c Russell b Alleyne	23			
K. A. Parsons c Hancock b Smith	47	1/80 2/80 3/101	(45 overs)	223
†R. J. Turner lbw b Ball	2	4/134 5/151 6/154		
M. Burns c Alleyne b Averis	12	7/183 8/199 9/202		

Bowling: Smith 8–2–46–1; Cawdron 9–0–55–1; Averis 8–0–38–1; Alleyne 9–0–36–3; Ball 7–0–30–1; Hancock 4–0–13–0.

Gloucestershire

T. H. C. Hancock, D. R. Hewson, M. G. N. Windows, *M. W. Alleyne, C. G. Taylor, †R. C. Russell, J. N. Snape, M. C. J. Ball, M. J. Cawdron, J. M. M. Averis and A. M. Smith.

Umpires: B. Dudleston and T. E. Jesty.

At Manchester, August 11. GLOUCESTERSHIRE lost to LANCASHIRE by ten wickets.

GLOUCESTERSHIRE v LEICESTERSHIRE

At Bristol, August 28 (day/night). Gloucestershire won by 47 runs. Toss: Gloucestershire.

The day after retaining the NatWest Trophy, Gloucestershire amassed 269 for nine, their highest League score of the season. Harvey, playing despite a badly bruised thigh, hit a dozen fours in his 66 off 35 balls (and later took four wickets), after which Snape and Windows put on 130 in 23 overs. Leicestershire's Smith and Maddy bettered this with 138 off 22, but they were already well behind the run-rate. Gloucestershire's seventh win took them back to third place.

Gloucestershire

T. H. C. Hancock c Dakin b Kumble	28	M. C. J. Ball b Maddy		4
K. J. Barnett b Ormond	5	J. M. M. Averis not out		1
I. J. Harvey c Habib b Kumble	66	A. M. Smith not out		1
J. N. Snape c Kumble b Wells	71	B 1, l-b 5, w 4, n-b 4		14
M. G. N. Windows c and b Kumble	61			
*M. W. Alleyne b DeFreitas	12	1/9 2/92 3/109	(9 wkts, 45 overs)	269
C. G. Taylor lbw b DeFreitas	3	4/239 5/249 6/260		
†R. C. Russell c Kumble b Maddy	3	7/263 8/267 9/267		

Bowling: Ormond 7–0–43–1; Dakin 5–0–46–0; Kumble 9–1–42–3; Wells 9–0–42–1; DeFreitas 8–0–46–2; Maddy 7–0–44–2.

Leicestershire

T. R. Ward c Russell b Averis	17	†N. D. Burns b Averis	5
*V. J. Wells run out	1	A. Kumble c Snape b Harvey	7
A. Habib b Harvey	1	J. Ormond not out	0
B. F. Smith c Ball b Snape	77	B 1, l-b 3, w 8	12
D. L. Maddy b Harvey	86		
D. I. Stevens b Alleyne	1	1/10 2/15 3/28 (45 overs) 222
P. A. J. DeFreitas c Smith b Alleyne	7	4/166 5/170 6/194
J. M. Dakin b Harvey	8	7/203 8/210 9/220

Bowling: Harvey 9–1–26–4; Smith 9–1–28–0; Averis 9–0–54–2; Ball 7–0–38–0; Alleyne 7–0–47–2; Snape 4–0–25–1.

Umpires: D. J. Constant and A. A. Jones.

GLOUCESTERSHIRE v LANCASHIRE

At Bristol, September 4. Gloucestershire won by five wickets. Toss: Lancashire.

Lancashire's batting was lacklustre on a slow pitch after Smith had stifled their start by bowling through his nine overs for a return of two for 13. Fairbrother and Lloyd put on a sensible 56, but 157 was never going to trouble a bubbling Gloucestershire side scenting a third one-day trophy. Hancock and Barnett got the reply off to a strong start, and Harvey capitalised on it with six boundaries in his quickfire 34. The fixture was originally scheduled for May 28, but the two counties were drawn to play each other in a Benson and Hedges Cup semi-final that day.

Lancashire

M. J. Chilton b Smith	1	G. Chapple b Alleyne	3
S. C. Ganguly c Harvey b Smith	15	I. D. Austin c Taylor b Harvey	9
A. Flintoff lbw b Averis	13	G. Keedy not out	0
*J. P. Crawley c Russell b Averis	4	L-b 1, w 4	5
N. H. Fairbrother b Ball	31		
G. D. Lloyd c Russell b Alleyne	46	1/2 2/28 3/34 (45 overs) 157
†W. K. Hegg c and b Ball	0	4/45 5/101 6/105
C. P. Schofield b Harvey	30	7/123 8/129 9/157

Bowling: Harvey 9–0–35–2; Smith 9–1–13–2; Averis 8–1–28–2; Ball 9–0–41–2; Alleyne 7–0–30–2; Snape 3–0–9–0.

Gloucestershire

T. H. C. Hancock c Fairbrother b Keedy	44	†R. C. Russell not out	5
K. J. Barnett run out	22		
I. J. Harvey b Keedy	34	L-b 2, w 1	3
J. N. Snape lbw b Ganguly	20		
M. G. N. Windows b Chapple	18	1/64 2/73 3/107 (5 wkts, 38.3 overs) 160
*M. W. Alleyne not out	14	4/125 5/143

C. G. Taylor, M. C. J. Ball, J. M. M. Averis and A. M. Smith did not bat.

Bowling: Austin 9–4–15–0; Chapple 8–1–43–1; Flintoff 2–0–7–0; Schofield 8–0–37–0; Keedy 7.3–0–41–2; Ganguly 4–0–15–1.

Umpires: N. G. Cowley and R. Julian.

At Hove, September 5 (day/night). GLOUCESTERSHIRE beat SUSSEX by six wickets (D/L method).

GLOUCESTERSHIRE v NORTHAMPTONSHIRE

At Bristol, September 17. Northamptonshire won by 27 runs (D/L method). Toss: Northamptonshire.
A crowd of 3,500 defied the weather to salute Gloucestershire's all-conquering season in the limited-overs game. Russell's two victims took his season's dismissals to 25 (17 caught and eight stumped), a Gloucestershire record in the League, and on a poor, uneven pitch two bowlers returned their best League figures. Harvey took five for 19 to finish the season with a county-best 34 wickets, while Penberthy, having scored 30 of Northamptonshire's modest 129, oversaw a home collapse from 65 for four to finish with five for 29. Victory gave Northamptonshire third place.

Northamptonshire

J. W. Cook b Harvey	0		J. P. Taylor lbw b Harvey	3
G. P. Swann c Alleyne b Smith	16		D. M. Cousins not out	5
*M. L. Hayden c Russell b Harvey	9		J. F. Brown b Harvey	4
D. J. Sales c Alleyne b Smith	0		B 1, l-b 6, w 3, n-b 2	12
R. J. Warren c Snape b Averis	1			
A. L. Penberthy st Russell b Harvey	30		1/0 2/28 3/29	(42.5 overs) 129
†D. Ripley b Ball	17		4/32 5/32 6/68	
K. J. Innes b Alleyne	32		7/110 8/116 9/124	

Bowling: Harvey 8.5–1–19–5; Smith 9–1–22–2; Averis 8–1–15–1; Ball 9–0–38–1; Alleyne 8–1–28–1.

Gloucestershire

T. H. C. Hancock b Cousins	7		M. C. J. Ball c Warren b Penberthy	1
K. J. Barnett lbw b Cousins	10		J. M. M. Averis c and b Brown	1
I. J. Harvey b Penberthy	43		A. M. Smith c Hayden b Innes	2
J. N. Snape run out	4		L-b 1, w 2	3
M. G. N. Windows c Sales b Penberthy	2			
*M. W. Alleyne c Ripley b Penberthy	3		1/12 2/41 3/50	(33.4 overs) 101
†R. C. Russell not out	17		4/65 5/68 6/69	
C. G. Taylor c Ripley b Penberthy	8		7/87 8/91 9/93	

Bowling: Cousins 9–0–25–2; Taylor 5–0–31–0; Penberthy 9–3–29–5; Brown 9–2–12–1; Swann 1–0–2–0; Innes 0.4–0–1–1.

Umpires: M. R. Benson and K. E. Palmer.

KENT

KENT v LANCASHIRE

At Canterbury, April 30. No result (abandoned).

KENT v NORTHAMPTONSHIRE

At Canterbury, May 1. Kent won by seven wickets. Toss: Kent.
Northamptonshire never recovered from an indifferent start that saw them 18 for four. Phillips, sidelined by a broken collarbone throughout 1999, enjoyed his best one-day return in what proved to be his last game of 2000 because of a back injury. Ealham conceded just five runs in his first seven overs, and run-scoring was never easy. Northamptonshire's 76 contained only four boundaries. Kent took 19 overs to reach their target, thanks to 54 in 12 between the enterprising Hockley and Dravid, after losing Walker to the first ball and Key inside four overs.

Northamptonshire

*M. L. Hayden c Masters b Phillips. . . .	0	R. J. Logan b Golding.	0
M. B. Loye lbw b Masters	16	D. M. Cousins b Fleming.	4
R. J. Warren c Nixon b Ealham	1	D. E. Malcolm run out	3
D. J. Sales b Phillips.	1	L-b 2, w 9.	11
G. P. Swann lbw b Phillips.	4		
A. L. Penberthy c Dravid b Masters. . . .	8	1/5 2/9 3/13	(40.4 overs) 76
K. J. Innes c Fleming b Phillips	16	4/18 5/35 6/42	
†D. Ripley not out	12	7/55 8/57 9/68	

Bowling: Ealham 8.4–4–10–1; Phillips 7–0–25–4; Masters 9–3–10–2; Golding 9–2–18–1; Fleming 7–1–11–1.

Kent

M. J. Walker lbw b Malcolm	0	A. P. Wells not out	2
R. W. T. Key lbw b Cousins.	3	L-b 3, w 10, n-b 2.	15
J. B. Hockley c Sales b Innes	26		
R. Dravid not out	31	1/0 2/9 3/63	(3 wkts, 18.5 overs) 77

*M. V. Fleming, M. A. Ealham, †P. A. Nixon, J. M. Golding, B. J. Phillips and D. D. Masters did not bat.

Bowling: Malcolm 4–0–12–1; Cousins 6–0–19–1; Logan 5.5–0–35–0; Innes 3–0–8–1.

Umpires: M. J. Harris and B. Leadbeater.

At Leicester, May 21. KENT lost to LEICESTERSHIRE by three wickets.

KENT v SUSSEX

At Tunbridge Wells, May 28. No result (abandoned).

KENT v GLOUCESTERSHIRE

At Tunbridge Wells, June 4. Gloucestershire won by six runs. Toss: Gloucestershire.

Fulton, with his first one-day half-century, and Wells looked to have put Kent in command, adding 71 in 17 overs. Instead, seven wickets fell for 51, and the last pair were unable to squeeze 11 runs from the final over. Harvey was the pick of Gloucestershire's bowlers on a slow pitch, and earlier had given their innings added momentum with his 43-ball 58. He and Russell put on 55 in seven overs after Barnett's more restrained half-century.

Gloucestershire

T. H. C. Hancock b Patel.	33	†R. C. Russell not out.	18
J. N. Snape c Fulton b Adams	4		
K. J. Barnett lbw b Fleming.	62	L-b 4, w 6.	10
M. G. N. Windows c Nixon b Patel. . . .	4		
*M. W. Alleyne st Nixon b Masters. . . .	3	1/6 2/86 3/90	(5 wkts, 45 overs) 192
I. J. Harvey not out	58	4/95 5/137	

R. J. Cunliffe, C. G. Taylor, J. M. M. Averis and A. M. Smith did not bat.

Bowling: Ealham 9–0–24–0; Adams 9–1–36–1; Fleming 9–1–37–1; Masters 9–0–54–1; Patel 9–1–37–2.

Kent

M. J. Walker c Russell b Harvey	4
R. W. T. Key c Russell b Averis	12
D. P. Fulton c Hancock b Barnett	69
A. P. Wells st Russell b Smith	41
M. A. Ealham lbw b Snape	5
†P. A. Nixon b Harvey	13
*M. V. Fleming b Averis	7
J. B. Hockley not out	15
M. M. Patel b Harvey	1
D. D. Masters run out	2
K. Adams run out	1
B 1, l-b 4, w 11	16
	—
1/5 2/59 3/130 (44.4 overs)	186
4/141 5/143 6/161	
7/173 8/175 9/181	

Bowling: Smith 9–1–34–1; Harvey 8.4–1–19–3; Averis 9–0–42–2; Alleyne 7–0–32–0; Snape 5–0–30–1; Barnett 6–0–24–1.

Umpires: D. J. Constant and R. Julian.

At Taunton, June 11. KENT lost to SOMERSET by nine wickets.

At Leeds, June 18. KENT lost to YORKSHIRE by 24 runs.

At Hove, June 23 (day/night). KENT beat SUSSEX by three runs.

KENT v SOMERSET

At Maidstone, July 2. Somerset won by 54 runs. Toss: Kent.

Though Kent's spirited run-chase came to nothing, the 3,000 crowd at The Mote were given superb value for money throughout. Trescothick and Cox had Somerset's 100 on the board in 15 overs, with Trescothick, dropped on five, roaring to 71 in 50 balls, his fourth half-century in six League innings. Nor did the pace slacken after that. In reply, Wells hit his second successive fifty, and Kent were on course as Walker and Fleming added 69 for the sixth wicket. Both fell to Blackwell in the same over, and that was it for Kent.

Somerset

M. E. Trescothick run out	71
*J. Cox c Nixon b Fleming	51
P. C. L. Holloway c Walker b Patel	14
P. D. Bowler c Marsh b Patel	9
I. D. Blackwell run out	39
M. Burns c Patel b Walker	18
K. A. Parsons not out	49
†R. J. Turner run out	7
G. D. Rose not out	17
B 5, l-b 6, w 7, n-b 2	20
	—
1/114 2/145 3/148 (7 wkts, 45 overs)	295
4/158 5/200	
6/240 7/251	

P. W. Jarvis and P. S. Jones did not bat.

Bowling: Ealham 9–0–58–0; Adams 6–0–51–0; Patel 9–0–56–2; Masters 5–0–40–0; Fleming 9–0–36–1; Walker 7–0–43–1.

Kent

D. P. Fulton lbw b Rose	13
R. Dravid lbw b Jones	10
M. A. Ealham b Rose	28
A. P. Wells c Turner b Trescothick	59
M. J. Walker c and b Blackwell	63
†P. A. Nixon b Trescothick	7
*M. V. Fleming c Burns b Blackwell	28
S. A. Marsh b Blackwell	4
M. M. Patel c Blackwell b Trescothick	1
D. D. Masters c Turner b Jarvis	4
K. Adams not out	0
L-b 14, w 6, n-b 4	24
	—
1/22 2/32 3/77 (40.2 overs)	241
4/148 5/162 6/231	
7/233 8/234 9/237	

Bowling: Rose 9–0–51–2; Jones 6–0–43–1; Jarvis 6.2–0–37–1; Parsons 2–0–21–0; Trescothick 9–0–45–3; Blackwell 8–0–30–3.

Umpires: B. Dudleston and J. F. Steele.

At Cheltenham, July 23. KENT lost to GLOUCESTERSHIRE by five wickets.

KENT v LEICESTERSHIRE

At Canterbury, August 6. Kent won by 75 runs. Toss: Leicestershire.

Coach John Wright and captain Matthew Fleming set Kent the target of winning five of their last six League games in an attempt to remain in Division One. This victory was inspired by McCague's 25-ball 56, a tremendous innings with eight fours and three sixes. Even with Ealham unable to bowl – he fractured his right index finger while batting – Leicestershire showed little inclination to threaten Kent's comeback.

Kent

M. J. Walker c Williamson b Lewis	13	M. J. McCague c Burns b Williamson . .	56
R. Dravid c Burns b Ormond	6	D. D. Masters not out	8
M. A. Ealham run out	25	M. J. Saggers lbw b Williamson	0
A. P. Wells run out	0	B 1, l-b 3, w 15, n-b 2	21
†P. A. Nixon run out	20		
J. B. Hockley c Williamson b Wells	44	1/21 2/24 3/30 (44.2 overs) 214
*M. V. Fleming lbw b Kumble	7	4/82 5/105 6/134
S. A. Marsh c Burns b Williamson	14	7/185 8/207 9/208

Ealham, when 24, retired hurt at 62 and resumed at 208.

Bowling: Ormond 8–0–32–1; Lewis 7–1–35–1; Kumble 9–1–28–1; Dakin 8–0–37–0; Wells 8–0–46–1; Williamson 4.2–0–32–3.

Leicestershire

T. R. Ward lbw b Saggers	6	†N. D. Burns c Marsh b Masters	6
*V. J. Wells c Masters b McCague	6	A. Kumble b Saggers	1
A. Habib c Nixon b Fleming	24	J. Ormond not out	5
B. F. Smith lbw b Fleming	38	L-b 5, w 10	15
D. L. Maddy c sub b McCague	22		
C. C. Lewis lbw b Fleming	4	1/14 2/17 3/80 (38.4 overs) 139
J. M. Dakin b Walker	0	4/89 5/105 6/108
D. Williamson b Saggers	12	7/114 8/130 9/132

Bowling: Saggers 8.4–0–26–3; McCague 9–1–40–2; Masters 5–0–24–1; Fleming 7–2–7–3; Walker 9–1–37–1.

Umpires: B. Dudleston and J. W. Holder.

At Manchester, August 15 (day/night). KENT beat LANCASHIRE by seven wickets.

KENT v WORCESTERSHIRE

At Canterbury, August 27. Kent won by 44 runs. Toss: Kent.

Worcestershire's dramatic collapse from 81 without loss off 11 overs to 110 for seven inside the next 13 helped Kent to their third successive League victory. Rhodes tried to get them back on course, but they were well off the pace when he holed out with four overs remaining. Kent's innings had revolved around Dravid's first one-day hundred for them. His 104, off 98 balls, featured 12 fours and two sixes, and included partnerships of 99 in 26 overs with Hockley and 85 in 11 with Nixon.

Kent

S. A. Marsh c Hick b McGrath	7	D. D. Masters c Leatherdale b McGrath	7
M. J. Walker c Weston b Liptrot	0	M. J. Saggers not out	3
J. B. Hockley b Illingworth	64		
R. Dravid c Leatherdale b Liptrot	104	L-b 4, w 8, n-b 2	14
A. P. Wells c Hick b McGrath	0		
†P. A. Nixon c McGrath b Liptrot	23	1/3 2/23 3/122 (8 wkts, 45 overs)	228
M. J. McCague run out	0	4/123 5/208 6/212	
*M. V. Fleming not out	6	7/212 8/221	

D. A. Scott did not bat.

Bowling: McGrath 9–3–17–3; Liptrot 6–0–44–3; Lampitt 9–1–25–0; Leatherdale 7–0–53–0; Illingworth 9–0–37–1; Hick 5–0–48–0.

Worcestershire

W. P. C. Weston c Nixon b Saggers	47	R. K. Illingworth c McCague b Scott	21
D. J. Pipe c Dravid b McCague	45	C. G. Liptrot not out	15
*G. A. Hick lbw b Fleming	0	G. D. McGrath c and b Scott	0
V. S. Solanki c Nixon b McCague	0	B 2, l-b 4, w 4	10
D. A. Leatherdale c Nixon b Fleming	6		
E. J. Wilson lbw b Fleming	0	1/81 2/81 3/84 (41 overs)	184
†S. J. Rhodes c Hockley b Scott	40	4/95 5/96 6/110	
S. R. Lampitt lbw b Saggers	0	7/110 8/155 9/183	

Bowling: Saggers 7–1–44–2; Masters 9–0–43–0; McCague 9–1–29–3; Fleming 7–1–22–2; Walker 4–0–19–0; Scott 5–0–21–3.

Umpires: V. A. Holder and T. E. Jesty.

At Northampton, September 3. KENT lost to NORTHAMPTONSHIRE by five runs.

KENT v YORKSHIRE

At Canterbury, September 5 (day/night). Kent won by 64 runs. Toss: Kent.

The St Lawrence Ground's first floodlit game attracted a crowd of 7,000, who saw Kent register their fourth win in five starts and move out of the relegation zone. Yorkshire's defeat, their first in six matches, ended their hopes of lifting the trophy. Fleming's 79 from 85 balls gave Kent a solid base; Nixon raised their 200 with successive sixes off Hoggard, who responded with three wickets to lift this season's tally to a Yorkshire-record 37. Marsh, playing his last innings at Canterbury after announcing his retirement earlier in the day, was given a standing ovation. Hamilton kept Yorkshire in the game with 44 off 70 balls, but Fleming's economy and three wickets prevented the much-needed middle-order acceleration.

Kent

*M. V. Fleming run out	79	J. M. Golding lbw b Hoggard	0
S. A. Marsh c McGrath b Hamilton	14	M. J. Saggers not out	10
J. B. Hockley lbw b Vaughan	18	D. D. Masters b Silverwood	2
R. Dravid c Byas b Fellows	36	L-b 6, w 2	8
M. J. McCague c Byas b Hamilton	4		
†P. A. Nixon b Hoggard	30	1/76 2/105 3/136 (44.4 overs)	217
M. A. Ealham run out	3	4/141 5/162 6/170	
M. J. Walker b Hoggard	13	7/201 8/201 9/208	

Bowling: Silverwood 7.4–0–48–1; Hoggard 9–2–46–3; Hamilton 7–0–36–2; Fisher 9–0–29–0; Vaughan 7–0–36–1; Fellows 5–1–16–1.

Yorkshire

*D. Byas lbw b Masters	4		C. E. W. Silverwood c and b Saggers	8
M. P. Vaughan c and b Ealham	39		I. D. Fisher lbw b Saggers	0
D. S. Lehmann c Nixon b Saggers	1		M. J. Hoggard not out	0
G. M. Hamilton c Dravid b Ealham	44		L-b 3, w 1	4
A. McGrath c Dravid b Fleming	11			
†R. J. Blakey c Nixon b Fleming	30		1/16 2/17 3/88	(40.2 overs) 153
G. M. Fellows st Nixon b Fleming	9		4/91 5/112 6/138	
S. Widdup c Walker b McCague	3		7/143 8/153 9/153	

Bowling: Saggers 8–1–22–3; Masters 6–0–29–1; McCague 7.2–1–33–1; Ealham 9–1–34–2; Fleming 9–0–19–3; Walker 1–0–13–0.

Umpires: A. Clarkson and D. J. Constant.

At Worcester, September 17. KENT beat WORCESTERSHIRE by eight wickets.

LANCASHIRE

At Canterbury, April 30. KENT v LANCASHIRE. No result (abandoned).

LANCASHIRE v LEICESTERSHIRE

At Manchester, May 7. Tied. Toss: Leicestershire.

Dakin, having just hit Martin for six, needed two off the last ball, missed it, but snatched a bye with Kumble for Leicestershire's second successive tie. Hegg's underarm throw just missed the stumps. Smith, captaining Leicestershire, made their late surge possible with 90 in 118 balls, only to be run out in the 42nd over. A first-ball duck for DeFreitas and another run-out swung the match Lancashire's way but, with 11 required, Dakin produced his final-over flourish. Chapple's two sixes in Lancashire's last over had lifted a total owing much to Atherton's technique on a sluggish pitch and to Ganguly's first half-century for them.

Lancashire

M. A. Atherton c Smith b DeFreitas	46		I. D. Austin c Burns b Ormond	3
*J. P. Crawley c Burns b Ormond	1		G. Chapple not out	14
A. Flintoff c Kumble b Dakin	7		B 2, l-b 6, w 2, n-b 2	12
S. C. Ganguly b Lewis	61			
N. H. Fairbrother b Lewis	1		1/7 2/17 3/112	(7 wkts, 45 overs) 177
G. D. Lloyd c Burns b Lewis	10		4/119 5/124	
†W. K. Hegg not out	22		6/143 7/154	

G. Yates and P. J. Martin did not bat.

Bowling: Ormond 9–0–31–2; Dakin 7–1–33–1; DeFreitas 9–1–32–1; Maddy 2–0–13–0; Kumble 9–1–31–0; Lewis 9–0–29–3.

Leicestershire

T. R. Ward lbw b Austin	1		P. A. J. DeFreitas b Martin	0
D. I. Stevens lbw b Chapple	16		J. Ormond run out	1
C. C. Lewis c Hegg b Austin	4		A. Kumble not out	2
*B. F. Smith run out	90		B 1, l-b 3, w 1, n-b 2	7
D. L. Maddy c Yates b Flintoff	16			
A. Habib b Chapple	6		1/1 2/7 3/28	(9 wkts, 45 overs) 177
†N. D. Burns run out	16		4/79 5/104 6/152	
J. M. Dakin not out	18		7/160 8/160 9/163	

Bowling: Martin 9–0–43–1; Austin 9–3–20–2; Chapple 9–2–32–2; Flintoff 9–1–26–1; Yates 5–0–29–0; Ganguly 4–0–23–0.

Umpires: A. Clarkson and R. Julian.

At Northampton, June 4. LANCASHIRE lost to NORTHAMPTONSHIRE by seven wickets.

LANCASHIRE v WORCESTERSHIRE

At Manchester, June 11. Worcestershire won by 12 runs. Toss: Worcestershire.

The Red Rose flew at half-mast in memory of Brian Statham, who had died the day before. Glenn McGrath, another metronomic fast bowler, paid his own tribute, wrecking Lancashire's reply with three for 11 in nine high-class overs. The only side with a League victory at Old Trafford the previous season, Worcestershire became the first to win here in 2000, building consistently on an opening stand of 81 between Pollard and Wilson. Pollard was dropped at slip on two. In reply, Flintoff hit 64 (50 in boundaries) in 47 balls, and Fairbrother reached his fourth successive one-day fifty with a six.

Worcestershire

P. R. Pollard b Flintoff	40	D. N. Catterall b Chapple		2
E. J. Wilson b Ganguly	38	R. K. Illingworth not out		1
*G. A. Hick c Hegg b Schofield	21	B 2, l-b 12, w 9		23
V. S. Solanki not out	59			—
D. A. Leatherdale b Flintoff	26	1/81 2/104 3/122	(7 wkts, 45 overs)	216
†S. J. Rhodes b Flintoff	3	4/179 5/189		
S. R. Lampitt b Austin	3	6/211 7/214		

Kabir Ali and G. D. McGrath did not bat.

Bowling: Chapple 9–1–26–1; Austin 8–0–33–1; Smethurst 6–0–37–0; Flintoff 9–0–41–3; Schofield 9–0–51–1; Ganguly 4–0–14–1.

Lancashire

M. A. Atherton b Ali	1	I. D. Austin not out		1
*J. P. Crawley c Ali b Lampitt	8	G. Chapple b McGrath		2
A. Flintoff c Hick b Leatherdale	64	M. P. Smethurst run out		0
N. H. Fairbrother b Ali	75	L-b 6, w 7		13
S. C. Ganguly c Catterall b Illingworth	2			—
G. D. Lloyd lbw b McGrath	2	1/1 2/38 3/106	(43.4 overs)	204
†W. K. Hegg c Leatherdale b Ali	33	4/114 5/138 6/182		
C. P. Schofield b McGrath	3	7/197 8/198 9/204		

Bowling: McGrath 8.4–0–11–3; Ali 6–0–44–3; Lampitt 9–2–40–1; Catterall 4–0–31–0; Illingworth 7–1–34–1; Leatherdale 9–0–38–1.

Umpires: A. Clarkson and D. J. Constant.

LANCASHIRE v NORTHAMPTONSHIRE

At Manchester, June 23 (day/night). Lancashire won by 24 runs (D/L method). Toss: Lancashire.

Lancashire ended one of their worst starts to a League campaign, but they suffered a blow when Austin limped off with a calf strain which would keep him out for almost a month. Despite unpleasant weather, some 5,000 turned out for Old Trafford's first day/night game of the year, though strong winds prevented the floodlights being used until Northamptonshire were well into their innings. Atherton and Ganguly made sure Lancashire, chasing a revised target of 182 in 42 overs, were ahead of the Duckworth/Lewis rate before the rain set in.

Northamptonshire

G. P. Swann c Atherton b Austin	1	D. M. Cousins b Flintoff		1
M. B. Loye run out	26	J. F. Brown st Hegg b Ganguly		1
*M. L. Hayden c and b Watkinson	48	D. E. Malcolm c and b Ganguly		1
D. J. Sales b Flintoff	32	B 1, l-b 7, w 9, n-b 2		19
J. W. Cook lbw b Schofield	23			
A. L. Penberthy b Watkinson	1	1/2 2/70 3/86	(41 overs)	178
†D. Ripley b Ganguly	5	4/136 5/141 6/146		
K. J. Innes not out	20	7/171 8/175 9/176		

Bowling: Chapple 7–0–29–0; Austin 3–0–14–1; Flintoff 8–0–30–2; Ganguly 8–1–22–3; Watkinson 9–1–46–2; Schofield 6–0–29–1.

Lancashire

M. A. Atherton c Ripley b Innes	43	N. H. Fairbrother not out		13
S. C. Ganguly not out	47	L-b 1, w 6		7
A. Flintoff b Swann	7			
*J. P. Crawley lbw b Innes	1	1/73 2/85 3/86	(3 wkts, 25.5 overs)	118

G. D. Lloyd, M. Watkinson, †W. K. Hegg, C. P. Schofield, I. D. Austin and G. Chapple did not bat.

Bowling: Malcolm 5–0–27–0; Brown 5–0–23–0; Innes 6–2–14–2; Penberthy 2–0–18–0; Swann 5.5–0–22–1; Cousins 2–0–13–0.

Umpires: B. Leadbeater and D. R. Shepherd.

LANCASHIRE v YORKSHIRE

At Manchester, June 27 (day/night). Yorkshire won by 69 runs (D/L method). Toss: Yorkshire.

It was a good night for conspiracy theorists. As happened in this fixture the previous year, a generator failed and blacked out a bank of floodlights, causing an 18-minute stoppage just when Lancashire were in trouble at 96 for four, still needing 130 over 19 overs. When play resumed, they then required 112 off 14 and, against the probing Yorkshire attack, they were never in the hunt. Early stands of 66 in 15 overs and 85 in 18 had launched Yorkshire to their handy total.

Yorkshire

G. M. Fellows c Crawley b Scuderi	57	G. M. Hamilton not out		7
M. J. Wood b Schofield	31			
D. S. Lehmann b Chapple	62	L-b 7, w 19, n-b 2		28
†R. J. Blakey run out	5			
A. McGrath not out	32	1/66 2/151 3/158	(5 wkts, 45 overs)	225
*D. Byas b Chapple	3	4/193 5/201		

J. D. Middlebrook, C. E. W. Silverwood, R. J. Sidebottom and P. M. Hutchison did not bat.

Bowling: Chapple 9–1–40–2; Smethurst 4–0–23–0; Scuderi 7–0–38–1; Ganguly 7–0–33–0; Schofield 9–1–37–1; Watkinson 9–0–47–0.

Lancashire

M. J. Chilton b Silverwood	0	C. P. Schofield st Blakey b Lehmann		6
S. C. Ganguly c Wood b Silverwood	5	G. Chapple lbw b Middlebrook		3
*J. P. Crawley not out	71	M. P. Smethurst st Blakey b Lehmann		3
N. H. Fairbrother b Hutchison	5	B 1, l-b 3, w 5		9
G. D. Lloyd lbw b Hamilton	22			
J. C. Scuderi run out	3	1/0 2/10 3/22	(34.4 overs)	138
M. Watkinson st Blakey b Middlebrook	9	4/87 5/96 6/115		
†W. K. Hegg run out	2	7/119 8/130 9/133		

Bowling: Silverwood 5–0–25–2; Hutchison 6–1–16–1; Hamilton 9–1–25–1; Sidebottom 5–0–24–0; Middlebrook 6–0–31–2; Lehmann 3.4–0–13–2.

Umpires: N. G. Cowley and V. A. Holder.

At Taunton, July 16. LANCASHIRE beat SOMERSET by seven wickets.

At Leicester, July 23. LANCASHIRE lost to LEICESTERSHIRE by seven wickets.

At Hove, August 7 (day/night). LANCASHIRE lost to SUSSEX by 27 runs (D/L method).

At Leeds, August 9 (day/night). LANCASHIRE lost to YORKSHIRE by nine wickets.

LANCASHIRE v GLOUCESTERSHIRE

At Manchester, August 11. Lancashire won by ten wickets. Toss: Gloucestershire.

These sides were to meet in the NatWest semi-finals two days later, and Lancashire could not have wished for a more impressive return to form after recent League losses. In seaming conditions, Gloucestershire made a dreadful start against Chapple and Austin, while Martin came back well from his long injury lay-off. Hegg claimed his 200th League catch to dismiss Alleyne. With time no object, Ganguly began patiently then accelerated to reach a century off 108 balls. It was Lancashire's best League win of the season, but someone should have remembered the adage about dress rehearsals.

Gloucestershire

T. H. C. Hancock lbw b Chapple	0	M. C. J. Ball c Lloyd b Schofield	20
K. J. Barnett lbw b Austin	11	J. M. M. Averis not out	23
D. R. Hewson lbw b Chapple	0	A. M. Smith not out	2
M. G. N. Windows b Austin	7	L-b 3, w 5, n-b 2	10
†R. C. Russell run out	40		
*M. W. Alleyne c Hegg b Austin	2	1/3 2/6 3/17 (9 wkts, 45 overs) 137	
C. G. Taylor c Hegg b Austin	1	4/22 5/26 6/28	
J. N. Snape run out	21	7/52 8/91 9/134	

Bowling: Chapple 9–1–17–2; Austin 9–2–14–4; Martin 9–3–27–0; Scuderi 7–2–25–0; Ganguly 5–0–23–0; Schofield 6–1–28–1.

Lancashire

*J. P. Crawley not out	32
S. C. Ganguly not out	101
B 1, l-b 1, w 3	5

(no wkt, 32.1 overs) 138

N. H. Fairbrother, G. D. Lloyd, J. C. Scuderi, †W. K. Hegg, I. D. Austin, G. Chapple, P. J. Martin, C. P. Schofield and G. Keedy did not bat.

Bowling: Smith 5–0–10–0; Averis 6–0–29–0; Alleyne 7–1–21–0; Ball 6–0–32–0; Snape 6–0–28–0; Hancock 2.1–0–16–0.

Umpires: B. Leadbeater and G. Sharp.

LANCASHIRE v KENT

At Manchester, August 15 (day/night). Kent won by seven wickets. Toss: Kent.

Dravid won the battle of the Indian stars, his unbeaten 60 off 43 balls containing some fine shots and enabling Kent to reach their target comfortably in a game reduced to 21 overs each. Ganguly had gone past 50 for the fifth time, at a run a ball, but he was involved in the run-outs of Flintoff and Fairbrother, and no one appeared on the Lancashire dressing-room balcony to applaud his effort.

Lancashire

A. Flintoff run out	15	I. D. Austin b Walker		0
S. C. Ganguly c Wells b Patel	52	M. J. Chilton not out		0
*J. P. Crawley c Hockley b Masters	32	B 1, l-b 6, w 4		11
N. H. Fairbrother run out	8			
J. C. Scuderi not out	13	1/23 2/81 3/101	(7 wkts, 21 overs)	136
†W. K. Hegg c Hockley b Patel	0	4/126 5/129		
C. P. Schofield b Walker	5	6/135 7/135		

G. Chapple and P. J. Martin did not bat.

Bowling: McCague 3–0–24–0; Saggers 5–0–29–0; Masters 4–0–22–1; Fleming 2–0–14–0; Walker 4–0–27–2; Patel 3–0–13–2.

Kent

M. J. Walker lbw b Martin	7	M. J. McCague not out		31
*M. V. Fleming c Scuderi b Chapple	17	L-b 4, w 2, n-b 2		8
R. Dravid not out	60			
A. P. Wells c Fairbrother b Scuderi	18	1/9 2/50 3/94	(3 wkts, 18.5 overs)	141

M. M. Patel, †P. A. Nixon, J. B. Hockley, S. A. Marsh, D. D. Masters and M. J. Saggers did not bat.

Bowling: Martin 3–0–19–1; Austin 3–0–19–0; Chapple 2–0–19–1; Flintoff 5–0–20–0; Scuderi 4–0–37–1; Ganguly 1–0–7–0; Schofield 0.5–0–16–0.

Umpires: J. H. Hampshire and K. E. Palmer.

At Worcester, September 3. LANCASHIRE beat WORCESTERSHIRE by two wickets.

At Bristol, September 4. LANCASHIRE lost to GLOUCESTERSHIRE by five wickets.

LANCASHIRE v SOMERSET

At Manchester, September 6 (day/night). Lancashire won by ten runs. Toss: Lancashire.

Defending title-holders Lancashire handed Gloucestershire the National League, and an unprecedented one-day treble, by eliminating their only possible challenger. Again Ganguly dominated Lancashire's innings, hitting his second League hundred from 134 balls, supported by a quickfire display from Fairbrother. Somerset's Cox threatened to keep Gloucestershire waiting, but his run-out by Chapple's direct hit, for 110 in 104 balls, left his side 20 short with two overs remaining. This proved beyond them.

Lancashire

M. J. Chilton c Turner b Rose	35	C. P. Schofield not out		0
S. C. Ganguly c Cox b Jarvis	102	L-b 10, w 11, n-b 2		23
J. J. Haynes c and b Kerr.	12			
N. H. Fairbrother b Jarvis	62	1/82 2/107	(4 wkts, 45 overs)	236
G. D. Lloyd not out	2	3/232 4/235		

*†W. K. Hegg, G. Chapple, G. Keedy, I. D. Austin and M. P. Smethurst did not bat.

Bowling: Jones 9–2–48–0; Rose 9–2–35–1; Jarvis 9–0–48–2; Blackwell 9–0–40–0; Kerr 6–0–30–1; Cox 3–0–25–0.

Somerset

P. D. Bowler c Hegg b Chapple	14	G. D. Rose c Smethurst b Austin		4
M. N. Lathwell b Keedy	53	J. I. D. Kerr not out		0
*J. Cox run out	110	L-b 4, w 4		8
M. Burns c and b Schofield	3			
I. D. Blackwell c Haynes b Schofield	18	1/32 2/107 3/112	(8 wkts, 45 overs)	226
K. A. Parsons run out	2	4/170 5/184 6/217		
†R. J. Turner c Keedy b Austin	14	7/226 8/226		

P. W. Jarvis and P. S. Jones did not bat.

Bowling: Chapple 9–1–50–1; Austin 9–0–34–2; Smethurst 6–0–32–0; Ganguly 4–0–18–0; Keedy 8–0–41–1; Schofield 9–0–47–2.

Umpires: R. A. White and P. Willey.

LANCASHIRE v SUSSEX

At Manchester, September 17. Lancashire won by six wickets (D/L method). Toss: Sussex.

Defeat in funereal gloom dragged Sussex into Division Two along with Lancashire, National League champions for the previous two years. Keedy's five for 30, his one-day best, including two wickets in an over twice, undid Montgomerie and Bevan's early good work for Sussex. By hitting his sixth successive half-century, Bevan equalled the League-best sequence held by three other overseas players: Hampshire's Barry Richards in 1976, Durham's Dean Jones in 1992 and Kent's Carl Hooper in 1994. Atherton ended his one-day season as he began it, with a half-century, and, after their target was adjusted by rain, Lancashire won with three overs in hand.

Sussex

U. B. A. Rashid c Fairbrother b Martin	9	R. J. Kirtley c Haynes b Keedy		2
R. R. Montgomerie b Smethurst	44	B. V. Taylor run out		5
*M. G. Bevan b Schofield	52	M. A. Robinson not out		15
B. Zuiderent b Keedy	1			
W. J. House b Keedy	0	B 2, l-b 6, w 13		21
P. A. Cottey not out	45			
R. S. C. Martin-Jenkins st Haynes b Keedy	1	1/22 2/93 3/97	(9 wkts, 45 overs)	195
		4/98 5/135 6/140		
†N. J. Wilton c Austin b Keedy	0	7/140 8/149 9/163		

Bowling: Martin 9–1–24–1; Austin 9–1–44–0; Smethurst 9–0–35–1; Schofield 9–0–54–1; Keedy 9–0–30–5.

Lancashire

M. A. Atherton run out	51	C. P. Schofield not out	24
S. C. Ganguly c Bevan b Martin-Jenkins	22		
M. J. Chilton st Wilton b Rashid	19	L-b 3, w 7, n-b 4	14
*N. H. Fairbrother c Martin-Jenkins b Robinson	6	1/30 2/85 (4 wkts, 30 overs) 154	
G. D. Lloyd not out	18	3/98 4/103	

†J. J. Haynes, I. D. Austin, P. J. Martin, G. Keedy and M. P. Smethurst did not bat.

Bowling: Kirtley 5–0–31–0; Martin-Jenkins 7–0–32–1; Taylor 5–0–36–0; Robinson 7–0–28–1; Rashid 6–0–24–1.

Umpires: R. Julian and G. Sharp.

LEICESTERSHIRE

LEICESTERSHIRE v SUSSEX

At Leicester, May 1. Tied. Toss: Sussex.

Ten were needed off the last over for a Sussex win and, after Lewis conceded eight but also took two wickets, the last pair, Robinson and non-striker Kirtley, scampered through for a bye off the last ball to level the scores. With 52 runs required off ten overs, and eight wickets remaining, Sussex should have won, despite the difficulties of a slow "stopping" pitch. Bevan's 66 in 19 overs with Montgomerie was easily the highest partnership on both sides, though Habib and Burns, adding 38 for Leicestershire's ninth wicket, had given their bowlers something to defend. Robinson's four for 23 equalled his best limited-overs figures.

Leicestershire

*V. J. Wells c Wilton b Martin-Jenkins	5	P. A. J. DeFreitas c Wilton b House	1
D. I. Stevens c Montgomerie b Robinson	32	†N. D. Burns not out	16
T. R. Ward c Rashid b Martin-Jenkins	4		
B. F. Smith c Carpenter b Robinson	19	L-b 3, w 6	9
D. L. Maddy c Kirtley b Robinson	24		
J. M. Dakin c Rashid b Robinson	2	1/5 2/15 3/56 (8 wkts, 45 overs) 164	
A. Habib not out	39	4/75 5/89 6/89	
C. C. Lewis lbw b House	13	7/124 8/126	

A. Kumble did not bat.

Bowling: Kirtley 9–0–31–0; Martin-Jenkins 7–0–31–2; Robinson 9–1–23–4; Rashid 9–0–34–0; House 9–1–27–2; Adams 2–0–15–0.

Sussex

R. R. Montgomerie c Burns b Lewis	42	†N. J. Wilton b Lewis	0
W. J. House c Burns b Lewis	4	R. J. Kirtley not out	1
*C. J. Adams c DeFreitas b Wells	18	M. A. Robinson not out	0
M. G. Bevan b Dakin	59	B 5, l-b 1, w 3, n-b 2	11
P. A. Cottey run out	7		
J. R. Carpenter c Wells b Dakin	3	1/9 2/47 3/113 (9 wkts, 45 overs) 164	
R. S. C. Martin-Jenkins run out	9	4/133 5/138 6/149	
U. B. A. Rashid b Lewis	10	7/150 8/158 9/163	

Bowling: Lewis 9–0–34–4; DeFreitas 9–2–36–0; Kumble 9–1–18–0; Dakin 8–1–36–2; Wells 9–1–28–1; Maddy 1–0–6–0.

Umpires: M. R. Benson and D. R. Shepherd.

At Manchester, May 7. LEICESTERSHIRE tied with LANCASHIRE.

LEICESTERSHIRE v KENT

At Leicester, May 21. Leicestershire won by three wickets. Toss: Leicestershire. First-team debut: K. Adams.

After two successive ties, Leicestershire eased to their first win, with Ward in sparkling form against his old county. Although debutant left-arm seamer Kristian Adams reduced Leicestershire to 23 for four in a lively five-over spell, taking three wickets with his first 11 balls, Ward was already on his way to 53 in 57 balls; he hit seven fours and a six. Tight bowling by Vince Wells and Kumble had kept Kent in check and, once they lost six for 21 in six overs, Leicestershire's target was always going to be modest.

Kent

M. J. Walker c Burns b Wells	48	M. M. Patel not out	14
R. W. T. Key lbw b DeFreitas	10	D. D. Masters c Ward b Wells	0
R. Dravid c Burns b Dakin	10	K. Adams not out	6
A. P. Wells run out	6	B 1, l-b 12, w 9	22
M. A. Ealham b Kumble	24		
†P. A. Nixon c Burns b Kumble	1	1/35 2/58 3/65	(9 wkts, 45 overs) 141
*M. V. Fleming lbw b Kumble	0	4/105 5/111 6/111	
J. M. Golding lbw b Wells	0	7/115 8/120 9/126	

Bowling: DeFreitas 9–2–22–1; Lewis 9–1–26–0; Wells 9–1–32–3; Dakin 9–2–22–1; Kumble 9–0–26–3.

Leicestershire

T. R. Ward run out	53	C. C. Lewis not out	26
D. I. Stevens c Nixon b Adams	0	J. M. Dakin not out	17
*V. J. Wells lbw b Adams	0	L-b 3, w 4, n-b 2	9
B. F. Smith c Nixon b Adams	0		
D. L. Maddy c Nixon b Adams	2	1/3 2/9 3/9	(7 wkts, 39 overs) 142
A. Habib st Nixon b Patel	28	4/23 5/76	
†N. D. Burns c Fleming b Patel	7	6/87 7/100	

P. A. J. DeFreitas and A. Kumble did not bat.

Bowling: Ealham 9–1–16–0; Adams 5–0–19–4; Masters 4–0–23–0; Golding 4–0–20–0; Fleming 7–0–28–0; Patel 9–2–26–2; Dravid 1–0–7–0.

Umpires: D. J. Constant and G. Sharp.

At Leeds, June 4. LEICESTERSHIRE beat YORKSHIRE by three wickets.

At Horsham, June 11. LEICESTERSHIRE lost to SUSSEX by 11 runs.

LEICESTERSHIRE v GLOUCESTERSHIRE

At Leicester, June 25. Leicestershire won by 38 runs. Toss: Gloucestershire.

One-day specialists Gloucestershire, with captain Alleyne resting a sore back, were comfortably beaten after deciding to chase runs rather than set a target. Maddy led the way for Leicestershire with 87 not out off 76 balls, going past 50 with a six on to the players' balcony and completing 2,000 runs in the League during his innings. Wells, dropped on seven, laid the foundations with a more conservative half-century. Barnett and Russell batted solidly in reply, but with little support. Even though DeFreitas limped off with a groin strain after one over, Leicestershire were never under pressure.

Leicestershire

T. R. Ward b Harvey	0	C. C. Lewis not out		5
*V. J. Wells lbw b Snape	59			
D. I. Stevens c Snape b Harvey	6	L-b 7, w 2		9
B. F. Smith run out	22			
D. L. Maddy not out	87	1/2 2/12 3/75	(5 wkts, 45 overs)	218
P. A. J. DeFreitas lbw b Averis	30	4/120 5/195		

J. Ormond, J. M. Dakin, †N. D. Burns and A. Kumble did not bat.

Bowling: Smith 9–2–24–0; Harvey 9–1–33–2; Lewis 7–1–39–0; Averis 9–0–56–1; Cawdron 6–0–28–0; Snape 5–0–31–1.

Gloucestershire

R. J. Cunliffe c Lewis b Ormond	9	J. M. M. Averis st Burns b Kumble		3
K. J. Barnett b Kumble	45	J. Lewis b Ormond		16
M. G. N. Windows b Ormond	4	A. M. Smith run out		0
*†R. C. Russell b Maddy	49	L-b 8, w 5		13
I. J. Harvey c sub b Wells	5			
C. G. Taylor c Burns b Dakin	2	1/16 2/34 3/100	(43.3 overs)	180
J. N. Snape not out	30	4/113 5/120 6/126		
M. J. Cawdron c Ormond b Kumble	4	7/133 8/142 9/180		

Bowling: Ormond 8.3–1–43–3; Lewis 7–3–14–0; DeFreitas 1–0–3–0; Kumble 9–1–28–3; Wells 9–0–30–1; Dakin 8–0–43–1; Maddy 1–0–11–1.

Umpires: B. Dudleston and T. E. Jesty.

At Worcester, July 2. WORCESTERSHIRE v LEICESTERSHIRE. No result (D/L method).

LEICESTERSHIRE v NORTHAMPTONSHIRE

At Leicester, July 16. Northamptonshire won by four wickets. Toss: Leicestershire.

A late-order collapse, then dropped catches, cost Leicestershire dearly. Hayden, let off on 15 and 61, steered Northamptonshire to victory with an unbeaten 96 off 110 balls, hitting eight fours and three sixes. He shared stands of 70 in 16 overs with Sales and 50 in nine with Penberthy, whose earlier dismissal of Habib had sparked the slump in which six Leicestershire wickets fell for 26 in seven overs.

Leicestershire

*V. J. Wells c Penberthy b Cousins	6	†N. D. Burns run out		4
D. I. Stevens c Strong b Cousins	15	A. Kumble c Swann b Strong		13
A. Habib c Rollins b Penberthy	70	J. Ormond not out		3
B. F. Smith c Rollins b Penberthy	14	L-b 5, w 6		11
D. L. Maddy c Cook b Penberthy	8			
P. A. J. DeFreitas run out	40	1/8 2/42 3/68	(44.4 overs)	187
C. C. Lewis c Brown b Swann	3	4/88 5/161 6/165		
D. Williamson b Cousins	0	7/166 8/166 9/182		

Bowling: Strong 7.4–0–36–1; Cousins 9–0–27–3; Penberthy 9–1–37–3; Brown 9–1–32–0; Sales 4–0–17–0; Swann 6–0–33–1.

Northamptonshire

A. S. Rollins c Maddy b Ormond	. . . .	0	G. P. Swann b Kumble	 6
M. B. Loye c Wells b Ormond	. . . .	19	†D. Ripley not out	 4
*M. L. Hayden not out	. . . .	96	L-b 5, w 3	 8
D. J. Sales b Williamson	. . . .	40		—
J. W. Cook c DeFreitas b Williamson	. . .	2	1/0 2/39 3/109	(6 wkts, 43.3 overs) 192
A. L. Penberthy c Ormond b DeFreitas. .		17	4/117 5/167 6/180	

M. R. Strong, J. F. Brown and D. M. Cousins did not bat.

Bowling: Ormond 8–2–26–2; Lewis 7–2–20–0; DeFreitas 9–0–36–1; Kumble 9–0–52–1; Williamson 4–0–23–2; Wells 5–0–22–0; Maddy 1.3–0–8–0.

Umpires: J. H. Harris and D. R. Shepherd.

LEICESTERSHIRE v LANCASHIRE

At Leicester, July 23. Leicestershire won by seven wickets. Toss: Leicestershire.

Habib and Smith, putting on 133 in 27 overs, guided Leicestershire to the easiest of wins against the 1999 League champions. Lancashire, with Martin and Austin injured, had matched some disappointing batting with a below-par performance in the field. Having lost seven for 58 – as many runs as Ganguly made off his own bat – in 14 overs, they did not need their bowlers, particularly England men Flintoff and Schofield, to give away 23 wides in Leicestershire's reply.

Lancashire

M. A. Atherton c Burns b Ormond	. . . .	12	G. Chapple c Burns b Williamson	 14
S. C. Ganguly c Sutcliffe b Kumble.	. . .	58	R. J. Green not out	 3
A. Flintoff c Burns b Ormond	. . . .	10		
*J. P. Crawley c and b Lewis	. . . .	19	B 1, l-b 3, w 8, n-b 2	 14
N. H. Fairbrother c Lewis b Kumble	. . .	0		—
G. D. Lloyd run out	. . . .	0	1/25 2/51 3/104	(9 wkts, 45 overs) 162
†W. K. Hegg c Sutcliffe b Williamson . .		24	4/105 5/106 6/113	
C. P. Schofield c and b Kumble	. . . . . .	8	7/132 8/150 9/162	

M. P. Smethurst did not bat.

Bowling: Ormond 9–1–25–2; Lewis 8–1–19–1; DeFreitas 7–0–29–0; Wells 5–1–22–0; Kumble 9–1–29–3; Williamson 7–0–34–2.

Leicestershire

C. C. Lewis c Hegg b Chapple	. . . .	0	D. L. Maddy not out.	 16
*V. J. Wells b Ganguly	. . . .	6	L-b 3, w 23	 26
A. Habib c Smethurst b Schofield	. . . . .	63		—
B. F. Smith not out	. . . .	54	1/0 2/9 3/142	(3 wkts, 36.5 overs) 165

I. J. Sutcliffe, D. Williamson, P. A. J. DeFreitas, †N. D. Burns, A. Kumble and J. Ormond did not bat.

Bowling: Chapple 7–1–22–1; Ganguly 7–1–28–1; Green 4.5–1–24–0; Smethurst 6–0–27–0; Schofield 9–0–43–1; Flintoff 3–0–18–0.

Umpires: G. I. Burgess and J. F. Steele.

At Canterbury, August 6. LEICESTERSHIRE lost to KENT by 75 runs.

At Northampton, August 13. LEICESTERSHIRE lost to NORTHAMPTONSHIRE by eight wickets (D/L method).

LEICESTERSHIRE v YORKSHIRE

At Leicester, August 20. Yorkshire won by eight wickets. Toss: Leicestershire.

Not even a pitch of low bounce could excuse Leicestershire's lamentable batting performance. "We shouldn't be bowled out for 53 on any pitch in the world," said cricket manager Jack Birkenshaw after not one Leicestershire player had reached double figures. Extras, with wides to the fore, top-scored with 15. Hoggard's five for 28 was his one-day best; Silverwood's four for 11 a competition-best. Yorkshire knocked off the runs inside 15 overs to move up to second in the division, completing the game in two hours 32 minutes – a minute less than they had taken to beat Lancashire 11 days earlier.

Leicestershire

T. R. Ward c McGrath b Hoggard	8	†N. D. Burns c Blakey b Hoggard		0
*V. J. Wells b Hoggard	6	A. Kumble c Craven b Silverwood		7
A. Habib c Craven b Hoggard	3	J. Ormond b Silverwood		0
B. F. Smith lbw b Silverwood	1	L-b 2, w 11, n-b 2		15
D. L. Maddy not out	8			
D. I. Stevens run out	1	1/16 2/21 3/25	(20.3 overs)	53
P. A. J. DeFreitas b Silverwood	0	4/29 5/34 6/36		
D. Williamson b Hoggard	4	7/46 8/46 9/53		

Bowling: Gough 6–1–12–0; Hoggard 9–1–28–5; Silverwood 5.3–1–11–4.

Yorkshire

V. J. Craven c Burns b Kumble	14
M. P. Vaughan lbw b DeFreitas	12
*D. S. Lehmann not out	18
A. McGrath not out	9
W 1	1

1/27 2/29   (2 wkts, 14.5 overs) 54

†R. J. Blakey, C. White, G. M. Fellows, G. M. Hamilton, D. Gough, C. E. W. Silverwood and M. J. Hoggard did not bat.

Bowling: Ormond 4–0–12–0; DeFreitas 7–2–15–1; Kumble 3.5–0–27–1.

Umpires: M. R. Benson and M. J. Harris.

At Bristol, August 28 (day/night). LEICESTERSHIRE lost to GLOUCESTERSHIRE by 47 runs.

At Taunton, August 30 (day/night). LEICESTERSHIRE beat SOMERSET by 62 runs.

LEICESTERSHIRE v WORCESTERSHIRE

At Leicester, September 8 (day/night). Leicestershire won by seven runs. Toss: Leicestershire.

Worcestershire, without a win since late June, lost a low-scoring but thrilling game after their bowlers had restricted Leicestershire to a seemingly inadequate total. Having matched the home side's start, they lost three wickets in six balls, recovered, then lost the next four for two runs in five overs. A final-over demand of 13 proved out of the question. Kumble, in his last match for Leicestershire, went wicketless but was no less influential, conceding a miserly 14 runs from his nine overs.

Leicestershire

T. R. Ward c Rhodes b Leatherdale	....	16
I. J. Sutcliffe st Rhodes b Leatherdale	..	18
*V. J. Wells c Lampitt b Rawnsley	.....	21
A. Habib st Rhodes b Rawnsley	......	20
B. F. Smith c Driver b Rawnsley	......	5
D. L. Maddy c Rhodes b McGrath	.....	20
P. A. J. DeFreitas b Illingworth	......	0
†N. D. Burns c Weston b Leatherdale	..	18

A. Kumble b Lampitt	....	1
J. Ormond b McGrath	....	5
S. A. J. Boswell not out	....	5
L-b 13, w 4, n-b 6	......	23

1/41 2/52 3/73   (44.2 overs) 152
4/89 5/106 6/107
7/127 8/129 9/137

Bowling: McGrath 9–2–18–2; Lampitt 9–0–36–1; Leatherdale 8.2–0–30–3; Rawnsley 9–0–31–3; Illingworth 9–0–24–1.

Worcestershire

W. P. C. Weston c Kumble b DeFreitas	..	19
D. J. Pipe run out	....	22
P. R. Pollard b Maddy	....	11
V. S. Solanki b DeFreitas	....	0
D. A. Leatherdale c Burns b Ormond	...	39
R. C. Driver c Burns b Wells	....	1
*†S. J. Rhodes c Ward b Maddy	......	16
S. R. Lampitt run out	....	0

R. K. Illingworth st Burns b Wells	....	13
M. J. Rawnsley not out	....	5
G. D. McGrath run out	....	1
L-b 10, w 8	....	18

1/41 2/42 3/42   (45 overs) 145
4/102 5/103 6/103
7/104 8/139 9/143

Bowling: Ormond 9–2–38–1; DeFreitas 7–0–24–2; Kumble 9–3–14–0; Boswell 4–0–14–0; Wells 8–2–26–2; Maddy 8–1–19–2.

Umpires: J. H. Harris and G. Sharp.

LEICESTERSHIRE v SOMERSET

At Leicester, September 17. Leicestershire won by 77 runs. Toss: Leicestershire.

So tight was Division One that Leicestershire could have been relegated had they lost, while victory might have placed them third. In the event, they won comfortably and finished fourth. Sutcliffe's half-century, in his second one-day innings of the season, laid the foundations for Leicestershire's competitive total; their seam bowlers then kept Somerset's batsmen on the back foot. Four more catches capped Burns's comeback season with 30 League dismissals (28 catches and two stumpings), a county record.

Leicestershire

T. R. Ward c Cox b Jones	....	4
I. J. Sutcliffe run out	....	53
*V. J. Wells b Jarvis	....	31
A. Habib c and b Pierson	....	29
B. F. Smith c Turner b Blackwell	.....	16
D. L. Maddy run out	....	28
†N. D. Burns c Lathwell b Jones	......	29
P. A. J. DeFreitas lbw b Jones	....	2

W. F. Stelling not out	....	10
J. Ormond not out	....	2
L-b 4, w 12	....	16

1/19 2/75 3/111   (8 wkts, 45 overs) 220
4/147 5/151 6/202
7/208 8/209

S. A. J. Boswell did not bat.

Bowling: Jones 9–1–45–3; Rose 7–0–30–0; Jarvis 8–0–42–1; Burns 3–0–21–0; Pierson 9–0–34–1; Blackwell 9–0–44–1.

Somerset

P. D. Bowler c Maddy b Ormond	2		A. R. K. Pierson c Burns b Maddy	8	
M. N. Lathwell c Burns b Ormond	3		P. W. Jarvis b Wells	7	
*J. Cox c Burns b Boswell	24		P. S. Jones not out	1	
M. Burns run out	5		L-b 13, w 7, n-b 4	24	
K. A. Parsons b Stelling	38				
I. D. Blackwell c Ward b Boswell	9		1/2 2/12 3/32	(39.1 overs) 143	
†R. J. Turner c Burns b Stelling	2		4/44 5/79 6/84		
G. D. Rose b Stelling	20		7/106 8/132 9/137		

Bowling: Ormond 9–2–31–2; DeFreitas 9–1–20–0; Boswell 9–0–37–2; Stelling 9–2–35–3; Maddy 2–0–7–1; Wells 1.1–1–0–1.

Umpires: R. Palmer and A. G. T. Whitehead.

NORTHAMPTONSHIRE

At Canterbury, May 1. NORTHAMPTONSHIRE lost to KENT by seven wickets.

NORTHAMPTONSHIRE v GLOUCESTERSHIRE

At Northampton, May 7. Gloucestershire won by 49 runs (D/L method). Toss: Gloucestershire. First-team debut: J. W. Cook.

Rain interrupted Gloucestershire's innings at 75 for two in the 19th over, after which the match was reduced to 35 overs per side. This resulted in Northamptonshire being set a target of 162, once Snape, Barnett and Russell had played major hands in getting Gloucestershire to 150, and they never really challenged it. Averis, continuing his impressive early-season form, finished the match with three wickets in five balls, but Ball's fine return catch to dismiss Cook had effectively settled the issue.

Gloucestershire

T. H. C. Hancock lbw b Cousins	4		M. C. J. Ball c Penberthy b Swann	7	
J. N. Snape c Ripley b Penberthy	39		J. M. M. Averis c Warren b Penberthy	11	
M. G. N. Windows c Ripley b Malcolm	0		A. M. Smith not out	0	
K. J. Barnett run out	30		B 2, l-b 11, w 8	21	
†R. C. Russell not out	28				
*M. W. Alleyne c Malcolm b Davies	3		1/7 2/8 3/89	(9 wkts, 35 overs) 150	
I. J. Harvey c Warren b Innes	1		4/93 5/106 6/109		
C. G. Taylor c Innes b Davies	6		7/121 8/133 9/148		

Bowling: Malcolm 7–2–31–1; Cousins 7–1–23–1; Penberthy 6–0–20–2; Innes 6–0–28–1; Davies 7–0–29–2; Swann 2–0–6–1.

Northamptonshire

A. S. Rollins b Smith	6		D. E. Malcolm c Snape b Averis	3	
G. P. Swann b Smith	2		M. K. Davies not out	0	
*M. L. Penberthy c Barnett b Alleyne	22		D. M. Cousins b Averis	0	
R. J. Warren c Russell b Averis	4		L-b 1, w 13	14	
A. L. Penberthy b Averis	11				
J. W. Cook c and b Ball	33		1/9 2/12 3/25	(29.5 overs) 112	
†D. Ripley b Alleyne	10		4/44 5/65 6/88		
K. J. Innes b Averis	7		7/98 8/107 9/107		

Bowling: Smith 7–1–25–2; Harvey 4–0–12–0; Averis 4.5–0–20–5; Ball 7–1–27–1; Alleyne 7–0–27–2.

Umpires: J. W. Holder and P. Willey.

At Taunton, May 21. NORTHAMPTONSHIRE lost to SOMERSET by four wickets.

At Worcester, May 28. NORTHAMPTONSHIRE lost to WORCESTERSHIRE by 47 runs (D/L method).

NORTHAMPTONSHIRE v LANCASHIRE

At Northampton, June 4. Northamptonshire won by seven wickets. Toss: Lancashire.

Northamptonshire gained their first League victory of the season at the fifth attempt, easing home thanks to a robust unbeaten 51 off 53 balls from Sales. Solid contributions from Loye and Cook had already exposed the inadequacy of Lancashire's total. The visitors had struggled to make any headway against tight bowling until Fairbrother and Watkinson provided some impetus with a stand of 58 in 13 overs.

Lancashire

P. C. McKeown lbw b Cousins	1	†W. K. Hegg c Penberthy b Innes	20
*J. P. Crawley b Brown	19	I. D. Austin not out	0
J. C. Scuderi lbw b Malcolm	14	L-b 13, w 14	27
N. H. Fairbrother not out	66		
G. D. Lloyd c Innes b Brown	7	1/7 2/34 3/66 (6 wkts, 45 overs)	187
M. Watkinson c Sales b Swann	33	4/81 5/139 6/186	

G. Chapple, M. P. Smethurst and G. Yates did not bat.

Bowling: Malcolm 8–0–25–1; Cousins 6–0–22–1; Penberthy 9–1–27–0; Brown 8–0–32–2; Swann 7–1–28–1; Innes 7–0–40–1.

Northamptonshire

*M. L. Hayden lbw b Austin	19	A. L. Penberthy not out	5
M. B. Loye c Yates b Watkinson	61	B 3, l-b 2, w 5	10
J. W. Cook c sub b Scuderi	45		
D. J. Sales not out	51	1/30 2/128 3/136 (3 wkts, 43.2 overs)	191

G. P. Swann, †D. Ripley, K. J. Innes, D. M. Cousins, J. F. Brown and D. E. Malcolm did not bat.

Bowling: Chapple 9–1–39–0; Austin 9–0–31–1; Smethurst 9–0–33–0; Scuderi 6–0–30–1; Yates 4–0–20–0; Watkinson 6–0–29–1; McKeown 0.2–0–4–0.

Umpires: B. Dudleston and M. J. Harris.

NORTHAMPTONSHIRE v SOMERSET

At Northampton, June 18. Northamptonshire won by 22 runs. Toss: Northamptonshire.

Sales played another dynamic and decisive National League innings, scoring his 72 from 55 balls and sharing a third-wicket stand of 107 in 16 overs with the more restrained Loye. Somerset began briskly in defence of their unbeaten record but, despite Bowler's half-century in the anchor role, lost too many wickets to sustain the chase. Northamptonshire were already safe by the time Pierson and Jones, the last pair, added their 40.

Northamptonshire

*M. L. Hayden b Jarvis............	39
M. B. Loye c Burns b Trescothick.....	54
J. W. Cook b Pierson	0
D. J. Sales c Blackwell b Pierson	72
A. L. Penberthy c Blackwell	
b Trescothick .	25
G. P. Swann b Trescothick	12
K. J. Innes b Trescothick	8

†D. Ripley not out	9
M. R. Strong run out	1
D. M. Cousins not out.............	1
B 1, l-b 6, w 23	30
	—
1/63 2/65 3/172 (8 wkts, 45 overs)	251
4/187 5/230 6/233	
7/243 8/246	

J. F. Brown did not bat.

Bowling: Jones 9–1–43–0; Jarvis 9–0–48–1; Pierson 9–0–50–2; Blackwell 6–0–31–0; Parsons 3–0–22–0; Trescothick 9–0–50–4.

Somerset

M. E. Trescothick lbw b Penberthy	34
*J. Cox st Ripley b Brown..........	2
P. C. L. Holloway c Cousins b Strong ..	14
P. D. Bowler st Ripley b Swann	69
M. N. Lathwell b Brown	19
K. A. Parsons lbw b Innes	0
†M. Burns b Swann	12
I. D. Blackwell b Strong	8

P. W. Jarvis run out	0
A. R. K. Pierson not out	31
P. S. Jones b Innes	27
L-b 10, w 3	13
	—
1/11 2/48 3/64 (44.1 overs)	229
4/104 5/105 6/128	
7/153 8/153 9/189	

Bowling: Brown 9–0–46–2; Cousins 5–0–32–0; Penberthy 9–2–36–1; Strong 8–1–38–2; Innes 5.1–0–32–2; Swann 8–0–35–2.

Umpires: J. W. Holder and A. G. T. Whitehead.

At Manchester, June 23 (day/night). NORTHAMPTONSHIRE lost to LANCASHIRE by 24 runs (D/L method).

At Leeds, June 25. NORTHAMPTONSHIRE beat YORKSHIRE by 60 runs.

NORTHAMPTONSHIRE v SUSSEX

At Northampton, July 2. Sussex won by 43 runs. Toss: Sussex.
    Sussex meted out severe punishment to Northamptonshire's bowlers in a match reduced by rain to 33 overs a side. Adams hit three sixes and 11 fours in his 95-ball century, adding 98 with Cottey, but the fireworks came when Bevan and House piled on 58 in the last four overs. Northamptonshire began promisingly, but no one made the substantial contribution needed to put the Sussex bowlers – and a run-rate of eight an over – under pressure.

Sussex

*C. J. Adams c Rollins b Penberthy....	100
R. R. Montgomerie c Penberthy b Brown	16
P. A. Cottey st Ripley b Penberthy.....	47
M. G. Bevan not out..............	54

W. J. House not out	26
L-b 6, w 11	17
	—
1/65 2/163 3/202 (3 wkts, 33 overs)	260

U. B. A. Rashid, R. S. C. Martin-Jenkins, †A. D. Patterson, R. J. Kirtley, B. V. Taylor and M. A. Robinson did not bat.

Bowling: Malcolm 5–0–43–0; Strong 6–0–41–0; Penberthy 7–0–49–2; Brown 7–0–38–1; Swann 7–0–63–0; Hayden 1–0–20–0.

Northamptonshire

*M. L. Hayden c Bevan b Martin-Jenkins	45		M. R. Strong b Rashid	0
M. B. Loye c Bevan b Taylor	13		J. F. Brown not out	3
G. P. Swann c House b Kirtley	30		D. E. Malcolm b Rashid	6
D. J. Sales c Rashid b Robinson	35			
J. W. Cook c Adams b Robinson	3		B 5, l-b 9, w 7, n-b 6	27
A. L. Penberthy c Adams				
b Martin-Jenkins	10		1/21 2/68 3/132	(30.5 overs) 217
A. S. Rollins b Kirtley	28		4/137 5/138 6/156	
†D. Ripley c Bevan b Rashid	17		7/207 8/208 9/209	

Bowling: Martin-Jenkins 7–0–48–2; Taylor 5–0–36–1; Kirtley 6–0–39–2; Robinson 7–0–42–2; Rashid 5.5–0–38–3.

Umpires: D. J. Constant and B. Leadbeater.

At Leicester, July 16. NORTHAMPTONSHIRE beat LEICESTERSHIRE by four wickets.

NORTHAMPTONSHIRE v WORCESTERSHIRE

At Northampton, August 2 (day/night). Northamptonshire won by seven wickets. Toss: Worcestershire.

Wantage Road's first experience of floodlit cricket proved a conspicuous success, both on and off the field. A crowd of 5,000 enjoyed the spectacle of Northamptonshire coasting home against League-leaders Worcestershire with more than eight overs to spare. Loye and Sales shared a decisive partnership of 105 in 17 overs, with each boundary greeted by a pyrotechnic display on top of the main scoreboard. The match had begun poorly for Northamptonshire, as Cousins conceded seven runs in wides before bowling a legal delivery, but Worcestershire's batsmen failed to develop sufficient momentum.

Worcestershire

P. R. Pollard run out	3		R. K. Illingworth run out	6
W. P. C. Weston c Bailey b Taylor	15		Kabir Ali not out	2
V. S. Solanki lbw b Cousins	3		G. D. McGrath not out	0
D. A. Leatherdale c and b Swann	40		B 3, l-b 8, w 10	21
E. J. Wilson c Bailey b Penberthy	5			
R. C. Driver c Taylor b Penberthy	2		1/14 2/26 3/30	(9 wkts, 45 overs) 179
*†S. J. Rhodes c Loye b Swann	43		4/50 5/56 6/83	
S. R. Lampitt c Bailey b Cousins	39		7/156 8/176 9/178	

Bowling: Cousins 9–1–29–2; Taylor 9–1–27–1; Penberthy 9–0–37–2; Brown 9–1–32–0; Swann 9–0–43–2.

Northamptonshire

A. S. Rollins lbw b Leatherdale	13		R. J. Warren not out	7
M. B. Loye c Ali b McGrath	75		B 2, l-b 1, w 12, n-b 6	21
J. W. Cook c Rhodes b Lampitt	9			
D. J. Sales not out	58		1/39 2/59 3/164	(3 wkts, 36.4 overs) 183

G. P. Swann, *A. L. Penberthy, †T. M. B. Bailey, J. P. Taylor, D. M. Cousins and J. F. Brown did not bat.

Bowling: McGrath 9–0–35–1; Ali 5.4–0–45–0; Lampitt 9–0–43–1; Leatherdale 5–0–19–1; Illingworth 5–0–24–0; Solanki 3–0–14–0.

Umpires: D. J. Constant and J. W. Lloyds.

NORTHAMPTONSHIRE v LEICESTERSHIRE

At Northampton, August 13. Northamptonshire won by eight wickets (D/L method). Toss: Leicestershire.

Hayden and Sales made light work of a revised target after rain had intervened with Northamptonshire 103 for two from 25 overs against Leicestershire's makeshift attack. When play resumed 65 minutes later, they needed 19 from three overs and accomplished that with five balls remaining. Leicestershire were indebted to Ward and Habib's 82 in 15 overs, and to Stevens, who was chiefly responsible for 47 coming from their last six overs. Ward's 61 included his 5,000th run in the League.

Leicestershire

T. R. Ward st Ripley b Brown	61	†N. D. Burns b Swann	2
*V. J. Wells b Taylor	22	C. D. Crowe not out	5
A. Habib c Cook b Brown	28	L-b 6, w 3	9
B. F. Smith c Cook b Innes	34		
D. L. Maddy c Cook b Innes	18	1/30 2/112 3/118 (7 wkts, 45 overs) 220
D. I. Stevens not out	30	4/163 5/173
D. Williamson lbw b Cousins	11	6/201 7/210

S. A. J. Boswell and A. A. Khan did not bat.

Bowling: Cousins 8–0–53–1; Taylor 6–1–24–1; Innes 9–0–39–2; Penberthy 9–0–28–0; Brown 9–0–47–2; Swann 4–0–23–1.

Northamptonshire

J. W. Cook lbw b Boswell	2
M. B. Loye run out	2
*M. L. Hayden not out	69
D. J. Sales not out	43
W 7	7

1/5 2/21   (2 wkts, 27.1 overs) 123

A. L. Penberthy, G. P. Swann, K. J. Innes, †D. Ripley, J. P. Taylor, D. M. Cousins and J. F. Brown did not bat.

Bowling: Boswell 7–1–20–1; Wells 7–1–31–0; Maddy 6–0–25–0; Williamson 5 0–23–0; Crowe 1–0–10–0; Khan 1.1–0–14–0.

Umpires: N. G. Cowley and R. Palmer.

At Eastbourne, August 20. NORTHAMPTONSHIRE beat SUSSEX by six wickets.

NORTHAMPTONSHIRE v YORKSHIRE

At Northampton, August 28. Yorkshire won by six wickets. Toss: Northamptonshire.

Yorkshire's pace attack decided this vital match for both sides, with Hoggard and Gough celebrating their selection earlier in the day for England's winter tours. Swinging the ball at a lively pace, they had Northamptonshire 22 for five in the tenth over. Hoggard took five League wickets for the second time in nine days. Innes and Cousins added 40 to carry the total into three figures, but Lehmann and McGrath put Yorkshire on course for the top of Division One. Defeat ended Northamptonshire's run of seven wins in the Championship and League.

Northamptonshire

J. W. Cook c Blakey b Gough	10	J. P. Taylor c McGrath b Gough	0
M. B. Loye b Hoggard	3	D. M. Cousins b Fisher	18
*M. L. Hayden lbw b Gough	0	J. F. Brown c Blakey b White	1
D. J. Sales b Hoggard	4	L-b 2, w 7, n-b 2	11
G. P. Swann b Hoggard	25		
A. L. Penberthy c Blakey b Hoggard	1	1/6 2/7 3/14	(37.3 overs) 109
†D. Ripley c McGrath b Hoggard	9	4/21 5/22 6/40	
K. J. Innes not out	27	7/62 8/62 9/102	

Bowling: Gough 9–1–19–3; Hoggard 9–1–30–5; Silverwood 6–1–22–0; White 6.3–3–11–1; Hamilton 4–0–19–0; Fisher 3–1–6–1.

Yorkshire

V. J. Craven c Penberthy b Taylor	8	C. White not out	6
M. P. Vaughan b Cousins	10	L-b 3, w 8, n-b 2	13
*D. S. Lehmann b Brown	37		
A. McGrath not out	36	1/25 2/27	(4 wkts, 30.3 overs) 111
G. M. Hamilton lbw b Penberthy	1	3/81 4/82	

†R. J. Blakey, I. D. Fisher, D. Gough, C. E. W. Silverwood and M. J. Hoggard did not bat.

Bowling: Cousins 7–1–17–1; Taylor 6–0–20–1; Penberthy 9–0–29–1; Innes 4–0–24–0; Brown 4.3–0–18–1.

Umpires: N. G. Cowley and R. Julian.

NORTHAMPTONSHIRE v KENT

At Northampton, September 3. Northamptonshire won by five runs. Toss: Northamptonshire.

The result kept Kent in the relegation zone, and secured Northamptonshire's place in Division One for another season. Dravid had boosted Kent's prospects by adding 44 in eight overs with McCague and 47 with Scott, so that they reached the final over, bowled by Cousins, needing eight with two wickets standing. Only two came from the first four balls; then Dravid fell to a brilliant catch at long-on, and Scott holed out at extra cover. Batting first, Northamptonshire subsided from 111 for two but rallied thanks to Penberthy's 39 not out in 48 balls.

Northamptonshire

M. B. Loye run out	19	J. P. Taylor b Ealham	11
*M. L. Hayden lbw b McCague	47	D. M. Cousins c Nixon b Walker	1
R. J. Warren b Scott	10	J. F. Brown not out	1
D. J. Sales c Nixon b McCague	24	B 1, l-b 12, w 6	19
G. P. Swann c Nixon b Scott	11		
A. L. Penberthy not out	39	1/41 2/75 3/111	(9 wkts, 45 overs) 195
†D. Ripley c Marsh b Saggers	12	4/122 5/127 6/156	
K. J. Innes lbw b Saggers	1	7/158 8/182 9/185	

Bowling: Saggers 9–0–41–2; Masters 9–0–27–0; Ealham 9–1–44–1; Scott 9–0–40–2; McCague 7–0–25–2; Walker 2–0–5–1.

Kent

M. J. Walker lbw b Cousins	0	D. D. Masters b Brown	0
*M. V. Fleming b Innes	29	D. A. Scott c Hayden b Cousins	27
J. B. Hockley c Sales b Taylor	4	M. J. Saggers not out	0
R. Dravid c Brown b Cousins	68	L-b 1, w 8	9
M. A. Ealham c Warren b Innes	5		
†P. A. Nixon b Innes	19	1/1 2/7 3/54	(45 overs) 190
S. A. Marsh lbw b Innes	0	4/71 5/99 6/99	
M. J. McCague c Warren b Brown	29	7/143 8/143 9/190	

Bowling: Cousins 9–3–32–3; Taylor 8–0–30–1; Penberthy 9–0–41–0; Innes 9–3–36–4; Brown 9–0–42–2; Swann 1–0–8–0.

Umpires: G. I. Burgess and P. Willey.

At Bristol, September 17. NORTHAMPTONSHIRE beat GLOUCESTERSHIRE by 27 runs (D/L method).

SOMERSET

SOMERSET v GLOUCESTERSHIRE

At Taunton, May 1. Somerset won by eight runs. Toss: Somerset.

Revenge was overdue for Somerset after too many recent defeats by their regional rivals, most painfully in the 1999 NatWest final. Gloucestershire had every chance to sustain the sequence after a useful reply by their top-order batsmen, but Jones ran through the tail and, with 11 needed off the final over, last man Smith was run out by Holloway's direct hit. Somerset had earlier been steadied by Parsons's highest score in one-day cricket until, caught on the mid-wicket boundary, he contributed to Harvey's best return in the League to date.

Somerset

M. E. Trescothick b Harvey	7	A. R. Caddick st Russell b Averis		16
*J. Cox c Russell b Smith	6	P. S. Jones not out		12
P. C. L. Holloway c Russell b Harvey	2	M. P. L. Bulbeck st Russell b Averis		1
M. Burns b Smith	0	B 4, l-b 6, w 7, n-b 4		21
K. A. Parsons c Taylor b Harvey	66			
†R. J. Turner c Hancock b Lewis	22	1/9 2/19 3/19	(43.5 overs)	181
I. D. Blackwell c Windows b Harvey	28	4/20 5/71 6/139		
G. D. Rose b Harvey	0	7/140 8/159 9/178		

Bowling: Smith 9–2–11–2; Harvey 8–1–33–5; Averis 8.5–0–42–2; Lewis 9–0–39–1; Snape 5–0–19–0; Alleyne 4–0–27–0.

Gloucestershire

T. H. C. Hancock lbw b Jones	33	J. Lewis b Jones		0
J. N. Snape b Bulbeck	22	J. M. M. Averis c Blackwell b Jones		1
M. G. N. Windows run out	38	A. M. Smith run out		3
K. J. Barnett c Rose b Parsons	15	L-b 5, w 2		7
I. J. Harvey lbw b Parsons	1			
*M. W. Alleyne not out	44	1/48 2/58 3/98	(44.2 overs)	173
†R. C. Russell c Bulbeck b Blackwell	6	4/100 5/135 6/151		
C. G. Taylor b Jones	3	7/159 8/159 9/165		

Bowling: Caddick 8.2–1–32–0; Rose 5–0–23–0; Bulbeck 6–1–23–1; Jones 9–0–32–4; Blackwell 9–1–33–1; Parsons 7–0–25–2.

Umpires: J. W. Holder and V. A. Holder.

SOMERSET v NORTHAMPTONSHIRE

At Taunton, May 21. Somerset won by four wickets. Toss: Northamptonshire.

Somerset's immediate response to Northamptonshire's weighty total was a confident and beefy 68 from Trescothick. On a bitter day, Hayden, Sales, Swann, with 57 in 40 balls, and Ripley had put Northamptonshire in a strong position, while Jones had again taken four wickets to underline his value in limited-overs cricket. Trescothick soon put the rapid departure of his captain behind him, one over from Malcolm bringing him 14 runs, including a six over the stand. After he went, amid some irresolute Somerset batting, Parsons and Blackwell steadied the innings and, in some style, won the game with 85 from 11 overs.

Northamptonshire

M. B. Loye lbw b Jones	8	M. K. Davies b Jones		4
*M. L. Hayden c Cox b Jarvis	47	D. E. Malcolm run out		3
A. L. Penberthy c Turner b Jones	4	D. M. Cousins not out		3
D. J. Sales c Lathwell b Rose	30	B 1, l-b 12, w 11, n-b 4		28
J. W. Cook c Turner b Jarvis	11			—
G. P. Swann b Trescothick	57	1/20 2/27 3/86	(44.4 overs)	240
†D. Ripley c and b Blackwell	30	4/108 5/115 6/203		
K. J. Innes c Cox b Jones	15	7/205 8/226 9/237		

Bowling: Rose 9–0–46–1; Jones 8.4–1–36–4; Jarvis 7–0–35–2; Parsons 7–0–40–0; Blackwell 8–0–41–1; Trescothick 5–0–29–1.

Somerset

M. E. Trescothick c Hayden b Davies	68	†R. J. Turner lbw b Cousins		8
*J. Cox lbw b Cousins	0	I. D. Blackwell not out		45
P. C. L. Holloway run out	15	L-b 8, w 18, n-b 2		28
M. Burns c Cousins b Penberthy	19			—
M. N. Lathwell lbw b Innes	6	1/9 2/37 3/98	(6 wkts, 42.1 overs)	243
K. A. Parsons not out	54	4/110 5/119 6/158		

G. D. Rose, P. W. Jarvis and P. S. Jones did not bat.

Bowling: Malcolm 8–0–53–0; Cousins 8–0–45–2; Penberthy 9–0–36–1; Innes 7.1–0–38–1; Davies 5–0–28–1; Swann 4–0–29–0; Hayden 1–0–6–0.

Umpires: G. I. Burgess and B. Dudleston.

SOMERSET v SUSSEX

At Bath, June 4. Somerset won by 16 runs. Toss: Sussex.

Somerset opened the Bath Festival by maintaining their 100 per cent record in the National League, although Sussex had been well placed while Adams and Bevan were going steadily. But when Adams was bowled, aiming ambitiously for a boundary, there was still too much for Bevan to do. Somerset had relied on Trescothick's confidence to overcome a slow pitch, and he hit four sixes in his 72 off 84 balls before being run out when Burns's drive was deflected on to the stumps by bowler Robinson. Trescothick had been similarly dismissed by Robinson at Taunton the previous season in the Championship.

Somerset

M. E. Trescothick run out	72	†R. J. Turner not out		19
*J. Cox run out	12	G. D. Rose c Cottey b Kirtley		7
P. C. L. Holloway c Patterson b Martin-Jenkins	4	P. D. Trego c Cottey b Kirtley		0
P. D. Bowler c Carpenter b Taylor	35	P. S. Jones c Cottey b Bevan		0
M. Burns c Patterson b Bevan	28	L-b 4, w 3		7
I. D. Blackwell c Martin-Jenkins b Robinson	1	1/20 2/24 3/103	(44.1 overs)	197
K. A. Parsons lbw b Bevan	12	4/142 5/155 6/164		
		7/181 8/196 9/196		

Bowling: Kirtley 9–2–28–2; Martin-Jenkins 9–1–32–1; Taylor 7–0–25–1; Rashid 6–0–52–0; Robinson 9–1–31–1; Adams 1–0–8–0; Bevan 3.1–0–17–3.

Sussex

R. R. Montgomerie c Holloway b Rose .	4	R. J. Kirtley not out	4
U. B. A. Rashid c Blackwell b Rose . . .	16	B. V. Taylor not out	1
*C. J. Adams b Parsons	33		
M. G. Bevan c Rose b Trescothick	69	L-b 12, w 7	19
P. A. Cottey c Holloway b Parsons	2		
J. R. Carpenter c Parsons b Burns	1	1/29 2/30 3/118 (8 wkts, 45 overs) 181
R. S. C. Martin-Jenkins b Jones	20	4/123 5/141 6/143
†A. D. Patterson c Bowler b Burns	12	7/169 8/179

M. A. Robinson did not bat.

Bowling: Rose 9–4–18–2; Jones 9–1–25–1; Trego 6–0–32–0; Parsons 9–1–32–2; Trescothick 9–0–38–1; Burns 3–0–24–2.

Umpires: V. A. Holder and P. Willey.

SOMERSET v KENT

At Taunton, June 11. Somerset won by nine wickets. Toss: Somerset.

The opening stand of 145 by Trescothick and Cox guaranteed Somerset's fourth win in their first four League games. Indeed, Trescothick, increasingly becoming an England target, was seldom out of the action. He started by taking two wickets, though 21 off a later over rather ruined his figures, and "ran out" Wells with a throw from second slip. The batsman was recalled after it was ruled that the ball was already dead. Fleming's bold strokeplay, including two sixes, gave late substance to a Kent innings in which Turner brought off two fine leg-side stumpings, standing up to the medium-pacers.

Kent

M. J. Walker c Trego b Jones	5	M. M. Patel run out	2
R. W. T. Key b Caddick	16	D. D. Masters not out	10
D. P. Fulton c Burns b Jones	9	K. Adams not out	1
R. Dravid c Turner b Caddick	1	L-b 3, w 6, n-b 2	11
A. P. Wells st Turner b Parsons	25		
M. A. Ealham st Turner b Trescothick . .	27	1/5 2/23 3/24 (9 wkts, 45 overs) 179
†P. A. Nixon c and b Trescothick	9	4/43 5/61 6/84
*M. V. Fleming b Jones	63	7/98 8/112 9/178

Bowling: Caddick 9–2–15–2; Jones 9–0–39–3; Trego 6–0–24–0; Parsons 4–0–21–1; Trescothick 8–1–42–2; Blackwell 9–1–35–0.

Somerset

M. E. Trescothick not out	92
*J. Cox c Walker b Adams	62
P. C. L. Holloway not out	8
L-b 1, w 17	18

1/145 (1 wkt, 35.1 overs) 180

P. D. Bowler, M. Burns, †R. J. Turner, K. A. Parsons, I. D. Blackwell, P. D. Trego, A. R. Caddick and P. S. Jones did not bat.

Bowling: Ealham 4–1–16–0; Adams 8–0–41–1; Masters 4.1–0–24–0; Patel 9–3–41–0; Fleming 3–1–11–0; Dravid 4–0–26–0; Walker 3–0–20–0.

Umpires: A. A. Jones and J. W. Lloyds.

At Northampton, June 18. SOMERSET lost to NORTHAMPTONSHIRE by 22 runs.

SOMERSET v WORCESTERSHIRE

At Taunton, June 24. Worcestershire won by four runs. Toss: Somerset.

Worcestershire's narrow win, maintaining their lead of Division One, owed much to Hick, who hit the first League hundred of 2000 – the latest date in the competition's history for the season's first. He came to the wicket when Solanki was out to the first ball of the day and faced 108 deliveries, hitting ten fours. Kabir Ali rocked Somerset by bowling Trescothick and Holloway with successive balls, but while Bowler and Burns were together they still had a chance. This was Worcestershire's sixth consecutive League victory, but it proved to be their last.

Worcestershire

V. S. Solanki c Trescothick b Caddick . .	0	S. R. Lampitt run out	16
E. J. Wilson c Turner b Jones	6	R. K. Illingworth b Jones	0
*G. A. Hick b Jarvis.	101	L-b 2, w 6	8
D. A. Leatherdale c Turner b Parsons . . .	35		
R. C. Driver lbw b Parsons	0	1/0 2/31 3/89 (8 wkts, 45 overs) 222	
Kadeer Ali b Blackwell	20	4/89 5/137 6/191	
†S. J. Rhodes not out	36	7/222 8/222	

Kabir Ali and G. D. McGrath did not bat.

Bowling: Caddick 9–4–18–1; Jones 9–2–42–2; Jarvis 9–0–63–1; Parsons 9–0–50–2; Trescothick 5–0–31–0; Blackwell 4–0–16–1.

Somerset

M. E. Trescothick b Kabir Ali	14	A. R. Caddick run out.	2
*J. Cox lbw b Leatherdale	20	P. W. Jarvis not out.	0
P. C. L. Holloway b Kabir Ali	0		
P. D. Bowler st Rhodes b Lampitt	67	L-b 3, w 3, n-b 4	10
M. Burns c and b Illingworth	56		
K. A. Parsons c Hick b Kabir Ali	12	1/23 2/23 3/64 (8 wkts, 45 overs) 218	
†R. J. Turner not out.	18	4/150 5/178 6/178	
I. D. Blackwell c Rhodes b McGrath . . .	19	7/209 8/217	

P. S. Jones did not bat.

Bowling: McGrath 9–0–37–1; Kabir Ali 9–1–44–3; Lampitt 9–1–23–1; Leatherdale 9–1–49–1; Illingworth 9–0–62–1.

Umpires: J. H. Hampshire and J. W. Lloyds.

At Maidstone, July 2. SOMERSET beat KENT by 54 runs.

SOMERSET v LANCASHIRE

At Taunton, July 16. Lancashire won by seven wickets. Toss: Somerset.

Somerset's decision to omit Lathwell, and play a bowler instead, resulted in a modest total which, on a pitch shimmering with runs, Atherton and Ganguly ridiculed with a record start for Lancashire in the League. Atherton's second hundred at Taunton in five days contained 14 fours, Ganguly hit a six and ten fours, and their effortless 192 in 34 overs was only five short of the county's all-wicket record for the competition. If Somerset lacked sparkle, at least Bowler had sunshine, a big crowd and full buckets in his benefit match.

Somerset

*J. Cox lbw b Yates	45	J. I. D. Kerr b Chapple		13
†R. J. Turner c Lloyd b Chapple	20	P. W. Jarvis c Ganguly b Scuderi		18
P. C. L. Holloway lbw b Ganguly	0	P. S. Jones not out		5
P. D. Bowler c Hegg b Yates	27	L-b 4, w 10, n-b 2		16
M. Burns c Ganguly b Schofield	6			
K. A. Parsons b Chapple	25	1/46 2/58 3/103	(44 overs)	198
I. D. Blackwell c Ganguly b Schofield	12	4/108 5/118 6/136		
G. D. Rose c Hegg b Smethurst	11	7/156 8/162 9/183		

Bowling: Chapple 9–2–23–3; Smethurst 6–1–36–1; Ganguly 5–0–27–1; Scuderi 6–0–35–1; Schofield 9–0–37–2; Yates 9–0–36–2.

Lancashire

M. A. Atherton c Jones b Jarvis	105	N. H. Fairbrother not out		4
S. C. Ganguly b Jones	82	L-b 1, w 4		5
G. D. Lloyd not out	4			
*J. P. Crawley b Jones	2	1/192 2/192 3/198	(3 wkts, 38 overs)	202

J. C. Scuderi, †W. K. Hegg, C. P. Schofield, G. Chapple, G. Yates and M. P. Smethurst did not bat.

Bowling: Jones 8–1–47–2; Rose 7–2–24–0; Jarvis 8–1–45–1; Cox 6–0–29–0; Blackwell 6–0–31–0; Kerr 2–0–14–0; Parsons 1–0–11–0.

Umpires: A. Clarkson and B. Leadbeater.

At Scarborough, July 23. SOMERSET beat YORKSHIRE by two wickets.

SOMERSET v YORKSHIRE

At Taunton, August 6. Yorkshire won by 32 runs. Toss: Yorkshire.

Title-contenders Somerset were badly served by their fielding, while their bowlers conceded 54 runs in the last five overs to McGrath and Hamilton, who finished with 124 in 18 overs together. Jarvis suffered particularly, going for 19 in his final over and finishing with one for 67 against his native county. McGrath continued his comeback from injury with a delightful 85 in 77 balls. Somerset began well but, to the dismay of an almost packed ground, never overcame the loss of Cox and Turner in the 21st over. Lehmann captained Yorkshire in the absence of the injured Byas.

Yorkshire

S. Widdup b Jarvis	38	G. M. Hamilton not out		43
V. J. Craven c Turner b Jones	24	L-b 6, w 13, n-b 2		21
*D. S. Lehmann c Turner b Blackwell	38			
A. McGrath not out	85	1/46 2/90 3/125	(3 wkts, 45 overs)	249

†R. J. Blakey, G. M. Fellows, C. J. Elstub, J. D. Middlebrook, I. D. Fisher and M. J. Hoggard did not bat.

Bowling: Rose 9–0–47–0; Jones 9–1–51–1; Jarvis 9–0–67–1; Trego 8–0–39–0; Blackwell 9–0–37–1; Burns 1–0–2–0.

Somerset

M. N. Lathwell b Hoggard	27	P. D. Trego b Hamilton		14
†R. J. Turner c Fellows b Fisher	44	P. W. Jarvis b Hoggard		2
*J. Cox c Blakey b Fisher	18	P. S. Jones not out		0
P. D. Bowler c and b Fellows	40	B 1, l-b 4, w 1		6
I. D. Blackwell c Widdup b Middlebrook	23			—
K. A. Parsons c Craven b Fisher	12	1/47 2/91 3/94	(43.3 overs)	217
M. Burns c Craven b Hamilton	22	4/125 5/152 6/190		
G. D. Rose b Hoggard	9	7/190 8/213 9/216		

Bowling: Hoggard 8.3–1–32–3; Elstub 7–0–36–0; Hamilton 6–0–35–2; Middlebrook 9–0–37–1; Fisher 9–0–53–3; Fellows 4–0–19–1.

Umpires: G. I. Burgess and N. G. Cowley.

At Bristol, August 9 (day/night). GLOUCESTERSHIRE v SOMERSET. No result.

At Worcester, August 20. SOMERSET beat WORCESTERSHIRE by 53 runs.

At Hove, August 28 (day/night). SOMERSET lost to SUSSEX by six wickets.

SOMERSET v LEICESTERSHIRE

At Taunton, August 30 (day/night). Leicestershire won by 62 runs. Toss: Leicestershire.

A win would have put Somerset on top of the League table and, while Michael Burns was going so well, it looked within reach. He and Parsons added 134 in 24 overs after Somerset were four down inside eight; when he was brilliantly caught, three short of a century, by his namesake Neil, the former Somerset wicket-keeper, the challenge fell away. Dakin's competition-best 68 in 49 balls, with three sixes and three fours, had earlier capped a solid batting display by Leicestershire.

Leicestershire

T. R. Ward c Cox b Rose	7	D. L. Maddy c Burns b Blackwell		29
A. Kumble c Cox b Jones	0	D. I. Stevens not out		18
*V. J. Wells c Turner b Jarvis	40	L-b 4, w 6, n-b 2		12
A. Habib c Rose b Kerr	45			—
B. F. Smith c Cox b Kerr	48	1/1 2/25 3/67	(6 wkts, 45 overs)	267
J. M. Dakin not out	68	4/137 5/158 6/222		

P. A. J. DeFreitas, †N. D. Burns and S. A. J. Boswell did not bat.

Bowling: Jones 9–0–65–1; Rose 9–0–39–1; Jarvis 9–1–47–1; Kerr 9–0–53–2; Blackwell 6–0–40–1; Parsons 3–0–19–0.

Somerset

P. D. Bowler c Smith b DeFreitas	1	J. I. D. Kerr not out		1
M. N. Lathwell c Wells b Boswell	5	P. W. Jarvis b Maddy		0
*J. Cox c Burns b Boswell	0	P. S. Jones b Dakin		2
M. Burns c Burns b Dakin	97	L-b 6, w 2		8
I. D. Blackwell c Burns b Boswell	14			—
K. A. Parsons c Stevens b Maddy	69	1/6 2/6 3/10	(38.3 overs)	205
†R. J. Turner c Stevens b Maddy	7	4/41 5/175 6/194		
G. D. Rose b Maddy	1	7/200 8/202 9/202		

Bowling: DeFreitas 7–0–28–1; Boswell 7–0–38–3; Wells 7–0–41–0; Dakin 6.3–0–46–2; Kumble 7–0–30–0; Maddy 4–0–16–4.

Umpires: V. A. Holder and K. Shuttleworth.

At Manchester, September 6 (day/night). SOMERSET lost to LANCASHIRE by ten runs.

At Leicester, September 17. SOMERSET lost to LEICESTERSHIRE by 77 runs.

SUSSEX

At Bristol, April 30. SUSSEX lost to GLOUCESTERSHIRE by ten runs.

At Leicester, May 1. SUSSEX tied with LEICESTERSHIRE.

SUSSEX v WORCESTERSHIRE

At Hove, May 17 (day/night). Worcestershire won by four runs (D/L method). Toss: Worcestershire. County debut: A. D. Patterson.

The Sussex reply was held up for 15 minutes after 11 overs when two of the floodlights, which had not been serviced over the winter, went out. This interruption, following an earlier stoppage for rain, left Sussex chasing 184 from 36 overs, but more rain 13 overs later ended play. Sussex had done well to restrict Worcestershire to 206 on a good pitch after Pollard and Spiring fluently put on 99 for the first wicket. But they found McGrath in inspired form. In the final reckoning, his three for 19 proved more decisive than the 66-run partnership in 13 overs between Montgomerie and Bevan. With the crowd less than 1,500, on a cold, drizzly evening, Sussex quickly announced that, in future, floodlit matches would be staged later in the season.

Worcestershire

P. R. Pollard c Patterson b Robinson	49	R. K. Illingworth lbw b Kirtley	2
K. R. Spiring c Adams b Kirtley	71	Kabir Ali not out	2
V. S. Solanki st Patterson b Rashid	8		
E. J. Wilson b House	7	B 4, l-b 5, w 7, n-b 2	18
D. A. Leatherdale c Bevan b Kirtley	28		
*†S. J. Rhodes c Martin-Jenkins b Kirtley	11	1/99 2/110 3/129 (7 wkts, 45 overs) 206
S. R. Lampitt not out	10	4/163 5/178
		6/186 7/197

G. D. McGrath and A. Sheriyar did not bat.

Bowling: Kirtley 9–0–41–4; Martin-Jenkins 9–1–40–0; Robinson 9–0–37–1; House 8–1–33–1; Rashid 9–0–39–1; Adams 1–0–7–0.

Sussex

R. R. Montgomerie c Wilson b Ali	30	J. R. Carpenter not out	16
W. J. House b McGrath	1	N-b 6	6
*C. J. Adams c Spiring b McGrath	0		
M. G. Bevan not out	49	1/1 2/7 (4 wkts, 23.1 overs) 103
P. A. Cottey c Rhodes b McGrath	1	3/73 4/76

R. S. C. Martin-Jenkins, U. B. A. Rashid, †A. D. Patterson, R. J. Kirtley and M. A. Robinson did not bat.

Bowling: McGrath 8–3–19–3; Sheriyar 5–0–23–0; Ali 6–0–34–1; Lampitt 3.1–0–23–0; Illingworth 1–0–4–0.

Umpires: K. E. Palmer and R. A. White.

At Tunbridge Wells, May 28. KENT v SUSSEX. No result (abandoned).

At Bath, June 4. SUSSEX lost to SOMERSET by 16 runs.

SUSSEX v LEICESTERSHIRE

At Horsham, June 11. Sussex won by 11 runs. Toss: Leicestershire.

Sussex recorded their first win of the season, defending what looked an under-par total with accurate seam bowling appreciated by a crowd of more than 3,000. Adams, promoting himself to open, got Sussex away well, and House and Patterson provided much-needed impetus after Wells and Maddy had checked the mid-innings acceleration. When Ward and Wells were belting 69 off the first ten overs, the visitors' unbeaten record seemed safe. But three wickets fell in eight overs, and Lewis and Dakin were brilliantly run out by Martin-Jenkins and House respectively as Sussex strangled the reply with energetic out-cricket.

Sussex

*C. J. Adams c Lewis b Maddy	52	R. J. Kirtley not out	13
R. R. Montgomerie lbw b DeFreitas	35	B. V. Taylor run out	0
U. B. A. Rashid c Burns b DeFreitas	34	M. A. Robinson run out	1
P. A. Cottey run out	10	B 1, l-b 5, w 5, n-b 2	13
M. G. Bevan c Ormond b Wells	7		
W. J. House b Maddy	33	1/64 2/109 3/129 (45 overs)	219
R. S. C. Martin-Jenkins b Wells	1	4/140 5/154 6/158	
†A. D. Patterson lbw b Dakin	20	7/204 8/204 9/207	

Bowling: Ormond 7–0–45–0; Lewis 4–0–24–0; DeFreitas 9–1–40–2; Dakin 7–2–41–1; Wells 9–0–29–2; Maddy 9–1–34–2.

Leicestershire

T. R. Ward b Robinson	33	A. Habib lbw b Taylor	13
*V. J. Wells b Kirtley	81	†N. D. Burns c Kirtley b Rashid	2
D. I. Stevens c Bevan b Taylor	2	J. Ormond not out	3
B. F. Smith c Bevan b Robinson	2	B 2, l-b 8, w 7	17
D. L. Maddy c Rashid b Martin-Jenkins	21		
P. A. J. DeFreitas b Martin-Jenkins	7	1/76 2/81 3/84 (44.4 overs)	208
C. C. Lewis run out	15	4/140 5/152 6/165	
J. M. Dakin run out	12	7/189 8/192 9/196	

Bowling: Kirtley 7–0–45–1; Martin-Jenkins 9–1–38–2; Taylor 8.4–0–30–2; Robinson 9–3–35–2; House 4–0–21–0; Rashid 7–0–29–1.

Umpires: R. Julian and R. Palmer.

SUSSEX v KENT

At Hove, June 23 (day/night). Kent won by three runs. Toss: Kent.

Sussex had victory in their grasp when, with Bevan in full flow and wickets in hand, they needed five off the last over. Yet Walker, an occasional bowler at best, bowled it so well that Bevan needed to hit the final ball for four and, instead, holed out to deep mid-wicket. It was Kent's first League win for six games. Earlier, Wells had been warmly applauded by the 3,500-strong crowd for an entertaining 90 against his old county, hitting nine fours and two sixes, but Sussex were well in control as Adams and Montgomerie rattled along at five an over to set up what should have been a winning position.

Kent

D. P. Fulton b Kirtley	0	†P. A. Nixon not out	6
S. A. Marsh c Patterson b Kirtley	1		
R. Dravid b Rashid	37	B 1, l-b 9, w 2, n-b 2	14
A. P. Wells b Bevan	90		—
M. J. Walker c and b Taylor	37	1/0 2/7 3/85 (7 wkts, 45 overs) 215
*M. V. Fleming b Kirtley	22	4/161 5/197
M. A. Ealham c Adams b Kirtley	8	6/201 7/215

M. M. Patel, D. D. Masters and K. Adams did not bat.

Bowling: Kirtley 9–1–32–4; Taylor 9–2–37–1; Robinson 9–0–38–0; Yardy 3–0–15–0; Rashid 8–0–37–1; House 4–0–19–0; Bevan 3–0–27–1.

Sussex

*C. J. Adams b Fleming	82
R. R. Montgomerie c Dravid b Masters	65
P. A. Cottey b Fleming	1
M. G. Bevan c Fulton b Walker	41
W. J. House not out	4
L-b 7, w 10, n-b 2	19

1/126 2/127 (4 wkts, 45 overs) 212
3/206 4/212

U. B. A. Rashid, M. H. Yardy, †A. D. Patterson, R. J. Kirtley, B. V. Taylor and M. A. Robinson did not bat.

Bowling: Ealham 9–1–35–0; Adams 9–0–31–0; Fleming 9–0–44–2; Patel 8–0–51–0; Masters 9–1–43–1; Walker 1–0–1–1.

Umpires: A. Clarkson and N. G. Cowley.

At Northampton, July 2. SUSSEX beat NORTHAMPTONSHIRE by 43 runs.

SUSSEX v YORKSHIRE

At Arundel, July 16. Sussex won by 70 runs. Toss: Sussex.

Under-strength Yorkshire slumped to their third mid-term defeat in four games after Bevan's sparkling 89 in 81 balls had underpinned a formidable Sussex total. Montgomerie and Adams laid the foundations; Bevan, in his first match against his former employers, helped Sussex plunder 93 from the last ten overs against an attack missing four England caps. Yorkshire made a decent start but no one stayed with Lehmann long enough. Taking their cue from Robinson, another Yorkshire outcast, the Sussex bowlers maintained admirable discipline on a pitch that allowed no margin for error. Yorkshire's preparations were not helped by a 3.30 a.m. false fire alarm at their hotel.

Sussex

*C. J. Adams b Sidebottom	54	R. S. C. Martin-Jenkins run out	5
R. R. Montgomerie c Byas b Hoggard	44	†N. J. Wilton not out	3
U. B. A. Rashid lbw b Fisher	12	L-b 12, w 11	23
M. G. Bevan not out	89		
P. A. Cottey c Blakey b Middlebrook	11	1/76 2/106 3/154 (6 wkts, 45 overs) 272
W. J. House b Lehmann	31	4/174 5/232 6/254

R. J. Kirtley, B. V. Taylor and M. A. Robinson did not bat.

Bowling: Hoggard 9–1–59–1; Hutchison 8–0–49–0; Sidebottom 9–0–36–1; Fisher 9–0–38–1; Middlebrook 7–0–53–1; Lehmann 3–0–25–1.

Yorkshire

*D. Byas run out	29	R. J. Sidebottom c Montgomerie	
M. J. Wood lbw b Robinson	21	b Rashid	21
A. McGrath lbw b Taylor	1	M. J. Hoggard st Wilton b Rashid	1
D. S. Lehmann b Kirtley	89	P. M. Hutchison not out	0
†R. J. Blakey lbw b House	1	L-b 18, w 4, n-b 2	24
G. M. Fellows c Rashid b Robinson	6		
J. D. Middlebrook b House	5	1/49 2/54 3/80 4/83 5/100 (42 overs) 202	
I. D. Fisher lbw b Rashid	4	6/116 7/130 8/198 9/202	

Bowling: Kirtley 6–0–31–1; Martin-Jenkins 4–0–17–0; Taylor 6–1–18–1; Robinson 9–0–20–2; House 9–0–49–2; Rashid 8–0–49–3.

Umpires: N. A. Mallender and A. G. T. Whitehead.

SUSSEX v LANCASHIRE

At Hove, August 7 (day/night). Sussex won by 27 runs (D/L method). Toss: Sussex.

Lancashire were outplayed by a home side for whom House and Zuiderent more than covered Bevan's absence. They lifted Sussex from 64 for four with 141 in 24 overs, Dutchman Zuiderent impressing the crowd of 4,500 – the largest yet for floodlit cricket at Hove – with his imperious straight driving. Both made their highest scores for the county. A shower had Lancashire's target adjusted to 220 in 41 overs, but they lost their way after Flintoff and Fairbrother, who added 75 in 13 overs, were parted. Some batsmen found the bungee jumping, situated behind the sightscreen, a distraction.

Sussex

*C. J. Adams c Flintoff b Austin	0	R. S. C. Martin-Jenkins run out	5
R. R. Montgomerie c Hegg b Flintoff	19		
U. B. A. Rashid c Fairbrother b Chapple	13	L-b 3, w 14, n-b 4	21
P. A. Cottey run out	7		
B. Zuiderent b Chapple	68	1/0 2/26 3/35 (6 wkts, 41 overs) 213	
W. J. House not out	80	4/64 5/205 6/213	

†N. J. Wilton, R. J. Kirtley, B. V. Taylor and M. A. Robinson did not bat.

Bowling: Austin 9–1–32–1; Chapple 8–0–62–2; Flintoff 8–1–37–1; Chilton 1–0–12–0; Yates 4–0–18–0; Schofield 6–0–29–0; Keedy 5–0–20–0.

Lancashire

M. J. Chilton lbw b Kirtley	3	G. Chapple not out	11
*J. P. Crawley c Montgomerie b Kirtley	5	G. Yates b Kirtley	3
A. Flintoff c and b Rashid	41	G. Keedy b Taylor	1
N. H. Fairbrother b Robinson	41	B 3, l-b 10, w 6, n-b 2	21
G. D. Lloyd c Cottey b Martin-Jenkins	28		
†W. K. Hegg b Martin-Jenkins	20	1/12 2/17 3/92 (39.2 overs) 192	
C. P. Schofield c Adams b Taylor	15	4/100 5/142 6/166	
I. D. Austin b Kirtley	3	7/177 8/179 9/189	

Bowling: Martin-Jenkins 8–1–37–2; Kirtley 7–1–45–4; Robinson 9–0–33–1; Taylor 7.2–1–30–2; Rashid 8–0–34–1.

Umpires: B. Dudleston and J. H. Hampshire.

At Worcester, August 13. WORCESTERSHIRE v SUSSEX. No result.

SUSSEX v NORTHAMPTONSHIRE

At Eastbourne, August 20. Northamptonshire won by six wickets. Toss: Sussex.

Sales, at the time the League's leading run-scorer, made light of a testing target on a well-grassed pitch, condemning Sussex to their third defeat by their visitors in nine days: Northamptonshire had won home and away in the Championship. Batting with increasing assurance, Sales added 102 with Loye and struck 13 fours in his run-a-ball 84 – as many boundaries as Sussex managed in all. Adams was run out soon after hitting his 5,000th League run, but Montgomerie stayed from first over till last for 89. To complete a miserable festival week for Sussex, the Saffrons crowd was less than 1,500; not surprising as the fixture list put the game up against a popular local air show.

Sussex

R. R. Montgomerie c Brown b Penberthy	89	R. J. Kirtley b Taylor		3
*C. J. Adams run out	15	B. V. Taylor not out		3
U. B. A. Rashid c Taylor b Penberthy	10	M. A. Robinson b Penberthy		0
P. A. Cottey c Hayden b Penberthy	1	B 1, l-b 8, w 14		23
B. Zuiderent run out	22			
W. J. House c Penberthy b Taylor	28	1/47 2/75 3/80	(45 overs)	196
R. S. C. Martin-Jenkins run out	1	4/117 5/169 6/173		
†N. J. Wilton b Cousins	1	7/180 8/192 9/196		

Bowling: Taylor 9–0–32–2; Cousins 9–0–40–1; Penberthy 8–1–32–4; Innes 9–0–36–0; Brown 7–0–28–0; Swann 3–0–19–0.

Northamptonshire

J. W. Cook c Kirtley b Taylor	15	A. L. Penberthy not out		19
M. B. Loye c Martin-Jenkins b House	54	L-b 1, w 5		6
*M. L. Hayden b Taylor	8			
D. J. Sales not out	84	1/21 2/38	(4 wkts, 39 overs)	199
G. P. Swann c Montgomerie b Robinson	13	3/140 4/174		

K. J. Innes, †D. Ripley, J. P. Taylor, D. M. Cousins and J. F. Brown did not bat.

Bowling: Martin-Jenkins 9–0–41–0; Taylor 9–0–51–2; Kirtley 7–0–27–0; Rashid 4–0–25–0; Robinson 6–0–36–1; House 4–0–18–1.

Umpires: T. E. Jesty and A. A. Jones.

SUSSEX v SOMERSET

At Hove, August 28 (day/night). Sussex won by six wickets. Toss: Somerset.

Bevan, in his first county game for four weeks, lifted Sussex out of the relegation zone with his match-winning single off the last ball. Jones's over had begun with seven needed. Although Somerset's total looked inadequate – it took enterprising strokeplay from Parsons and Turner to get it to 200 – a slow pitch and accurate bowling yielded runs grudgingly. The situation was tailor-made for Bevan, whose unbeaten 85 in 82 balls contained only five fours. Despite falling foul of the weather in May, Sussex, who had decided to play all their League games at Hove under lights, were again supported by a crowd in excess of 3,500.

Somerset

M. E. Trescothick c Zuiderent b Martin-Jenkins	16	†R. J. Turner not out		34
M. N. Lathwell c Zuiderent b Kirtley	15	G. D. Rose run out		4
*J. Cox c Adams b House	49			
P. D. Bowler c Bevan b Rashid	22	L-b 9, w 1, n-b 2		12
M. Burns b Rashid	32	1/26 2/43 3/84	(8 wkts, 45 overs)	212
K. A. Parsons c Bevan b Taylor	27	4/130 5/157 6/158		
I. D. Blackwell c Bevan b Kirtley	1	7/199 8/212		

A. R. Caddick and P. S. Jones did not bat.

Bowling: Martin-Jenkins 9–0–35–1; Kirtley 9–0–56–2; Taylor 7–0–35–1; Robinson 9–0–33–0; Rashid 9–0–35–2; House 2–0–9–1.

Sussex

R. R. Montgomerie c Lathwell b Caddick	11	W. J. House not out		3
*C. J. Adams c Blackwell b Trescothick .	68	L-b 1, w 4, n-b 2		7
U. B. A. Rashid lbw b Jones	32			
M. G. Bevan not out	85	1/21 2/70	(4 wkts, 45 overs)	213
B. Zuiderent run out	7	3/180 4/203		

M. A. Robinson, R. S. C. Martin-Jenkins, †N. J. Wilton, R. J. Kirtley and B. V. Taylor did not bat.

Bowling: Caddick 9–1–33–1; Rose 9–1–40–0; Jones 9–0–39–1; Trescothick 9–0–44–1; Blackwell 8–0–48–0; Parsons 1–0–8–0.

Umpires: R. Palmer and A. G. T. Whitehead.

At Scarborough, September 3. SUSSEX lost to YORKSHIRE by 49 runs.

SUSSEX v GLOUCESTERSHIRE

At Hove, September 5 (day/night). Gloucestershire won by six wickets (D/L method). Toss: Sussex.

Victory here, Yorkshire's defeat at Canterbury, and Somerset's the next night at Old Trafford, guaranteed Gloucestershire the League title and a clean sweep of one-day honours. Bevan's eighth League fifty of the season, 82 in 87 balls, went largely unsupported; a recalculated target of 171 from 31 overs was always within Gloucestershire's range once Hancock and Barnett had opened with 69 in 15 overs. Harvey's 43 from 29 balls got them closer, and dropped Sussex back into the relegation zone.

Sussex

R. R. Montgomerie c Hancock b Harvey	4	†N. J. Wilton lbw b Harvey		0
*C. J. Adams c Russell b Harvey	0	R. J. Kirtley not out		1
U. B. A. Rashid lbw b Averis	11			
M. G. Bevan not out	82	L-b 1		1
B. Zuiderent b Hancock	29			
W. J. House c Taylor b Ball	19	1/3 2/12 3/43	(8 wkts, 31 overs)	148
P. A. Cottey c Alleyne b Ball	0	4/98 5/123 6/124		
R. S. C. Martin-Jenkins run out	1	7/141 8/141		

M. A. Robinson did not bat.

Bowling: Harvey 6–0–25–3; Smith 7–1–25–0; Averis 6–0–32–1; Alleyne 6–0–27–0; Ball 5–0–28–2; Hancock 1–0–10–1.

Gloucestershire

T. H. C. Hancock c Zuiderent b Martin-Jenkins .	51	M. G. N. Windows not out		9
K. J. Barnett c Martin-Jenkins b Rashid .	29	L-b 6, w 9, n-b 4		19
I. J. Harvey run out	43			
J. N. Snape b Kirtley	9	1/69 2/135	(4 wkts, 29.1 overs)	174
†R. C. Russell not out	14	3/141 4/159		

*M. W. Alleyne, C. G. Taylor, M. C. J. Ball, J. M. M. Averis and A. M. Smith did not bat.

Bowling: Martin-Jenkins 6–1–23–1; Kirtley 6–0–36–1; Robinson 6–0–46–0; House 4–0–21–0; Rashid 4.1–0–25–1; Adams 3–0–17–0.

Umpires: M. J. Harris and R. Julian.

At Manchester, September 17. SUSSEX lost to LANCASHIRE by six wickets (D/L method).

WORCESTERSHIRE

WORCESTERSHIRE v YORKSHIRE

At Worcester, April 30. Yorkshire won by 19 runs. Toss: Worcestershire.

McGrath reeled off six maidens in his first spell at New Road and conceded only five scoring strokes in a return of 9–6–9–4, but Yorkshire's greater depth of bowling prevailed on a seaming pitch providing pace and bounce. Gough almost matched McGrath's economy with an opening spell of 5–4–2–1, and Yorkshire were favourites from the moment Hick's mistimed pull found Hoggard. Rhodes's eighth-wicket 43 with Illingworth turned Worcestershire round from 85 for seven, but their last three wickets fell for four runs. Blakey and Lehmann, carrying Yorkshire to 90 for two, had made the biggest impact when they batted.

Yorkshire

*D. Byas c Rhodes b Sheriyar	4	D. Gough not out	15
C. White b McGrath	1	R. J. Sidebottom not out	2
†R. J. Blakey c Hick b Lampitt	27		
D. S. Lehmann b Illingworth	46	B 1, l-b 8, w 15	24
M. P. Vaughan c Wilson b McGrath	11		
G. M. Fellows lbw b Leatherdale	3	1/3 2/11 3/90	(8 wkts, 45 overs) 151
M. J. Wood c Rhodes b McGrath	13	4/103 5/106 6/123	
G. M. Hamilton b McGrath	5	7/127 8/140	

M. J. Hoggard did not bat.

Bowling: McGrath 9–6–9–4; Sheriyar 9–1–37–1; Lampitt 9–2–14–1; Leatherdale 6–0–38–1; Hick 3–0–18–0; Illingworth 9–0–26–1.

Worcestershire

P. R. Pollard c Blakey b Hamilton	24	R. K. Illingworth c Blakey b Hoggard	16
V. S. Solanki c Blakey b Gough	1	G. D. McGrath lbw b White	0
*G. A. Hick c Hoggard b Sidebottom	7	A. Sheriyar not out	1
K. R. Spiring b White	0	B 1, l-b 5, w 11, n-b 4	21
E. J. Wilson c Wood b Hamilton	17		
D. A. Leatherdale c Blakey b Hamilton	0	1/10 2/24 3/25	(43.2 overs) 132
†S. J. Rhodes b White	42	4/56 5/57 6/72	
S. R. Lampitt c Gough b Hoggard	3	7/85 8/128 9/129	

Bowling: Gough 8–4–12–1; Hoggard 8–0–29–2; Sidebottom 8–2–23–1; White 8.2–0–26–3; Hamilton 9–1–29–3; Vaughan 2–0–7–0.

Umpires: J. H. Harris and T. E. Jesty.

At Leeds, May 7. WORCESTERSHIRE beat YORKSHIRE by nine runs.

At Hove, May 17 (day/night). WORCESTERSHIRE beat SUSSEX by four runs (D/L method).

WORCESTERSHIRE v NORTHAMPTONSHIRE

At Worcester, May 28. Worcestershire won by 47 runs (D/L method). Toss: Northamptonshire.

Pollard's 89 from 90 balls, his highest score since joining Worcestershire in 1999, made light of any irritation at Hick being ordered to rest by the England management when other ECB-contracted players were available for the weekend's Benson and Hedges semi-finals. Stands of 62 with Solanki and 69 with Wilson, rattling along at six and seven an over, set a target that was challenging from 45 overs, never mind the 34 allocated after the delayed start. Rain at tea meant another reduction, requiring Northamptonshire to chase 181 from 27 overs. Their fourth consecutive League defeat was guaranteed once McGrath removed both openers with successive balls and Ali reduced them to 17 for four soon afterwards. The win took Worcestershire to the top of Division One.

Worcestershire

P. R. Pollard lbw b Cousins	89		*†S. J. Rhodes not out	1
K. R. Spiring c Hayden b Innes	15		B 4, l-b 8, w 11	23
V. S. Solanki c and b Swann	30			—
E. J. Wilson not out	32		1/46 2/108	(4 wkts, 34 overs) 207
D. A. Leatherdale run out	17		3/177 4/204	

S. R. Lampitt, R. K. Illingworth, Kabir Ali, D. N. Catterall and G. D. McGrath did not bat.

Bowling: Malcolm 5–0–28–0; Cousins 6–0–38–1; Innes 7–0–31–1; Logan 4–0–47–0; Swann 7–0–20–1; Hayden 7–0–31–0.

Northamptonshire

M. B. Loye c Wilson b McGrath	5		R. J. Logan c Ali b Illingworth	17
*M. L. Hayden c Rhodes b McGrath	6		D. M. Cousins not out	7
J. W. Cook b Ali	0		D. E. Malcolm not out	0
D. J. Sales b Ali	2		L-b 4, w 3, n-b 2	9
A. S. Rollins st Rhodes b Illingworth	23			—
G. P. Swann c Rhodes b Ali	8		1/12 2/12 3/12	(9 wkts, 27 overs) 133
†D. Ripley b Lampitt	1		4/17 5/31 6/32	
K. J. Innes c Leatherdale b Illingworth	55		7/80 8/118 9/128	

Bowling: McGrath 6–2–15–2; Ali 6–1–19–3; Lampitt 5–1–39–1; Catterall 5–0–30–0; Illingworth 5–0–26–3.

Umpires: J. H. Harris and P. Willey.

At Manchester, June 11. WORCESTERSHIRE beat LANCASHIRE by 12 runs.

WORCESTERSHIRE v GLOUCESTERSHIRE

At Worcester, June 14 (day/night). Worcestershire won by 21 runs. Toss: Worcestershire.

New Road's inaugural day/night game 11 months earlier had realised nearly 500 runs; for the second, conditions were difficult for batting and Worcestershire were initially grateful for Pollard's patient 41 in 34 overs. However, 142 proved well beyond Gloucestershire. McGrath, taking three wickets in one over, and Ali quickly reduced them to 27 for five and, with Lampitt accounting for the lower middle order, Worcestershire's fifth successive League win – their best run since 1995 – was as good as settled.

Worcestershire

P. R. Pollard lbw b Averis	41		Kabir Ali run out	0
E. J. Wilson c Russell b Smith	10		G. D. McGrath st Russell b Harvey	0
V. S. Solanki c Russell b Smith	6		A. Sheriyar not out	1
D. A. Leatherdale c Russell b Snape	18		B 2, l-b 10, w 17	29
R. C. Driver b Harvey	19			—
*†S. J. Rhodes c and b Harvey	12		1/39 2/46 3/87	(44.4 overs) 141
S. R. Lampitt c Alleyne b Harvey	5		4/101 5/129 6/135	
R. K. Illingworth c Alleyne b Averis	0		7/136 8/139 9/140	

Bowling: Harvey 8.4–3–23–4; Smith 9–0–22–2; Averis 9–0–26–2; Alleyne 9–0–26–0; Cawdron 4–0–13–0; Snape 5–1–19–1.

Gloucestershire

T. H. C. Hancock lbw b McGrath	5	M. J. Cawdron c Rhodes b McGrath	26
K. J. Barnett c Leatherdale b Ali	11	J. M. M. Averis c Rhodes b Ali	13
R. J. Cunliffe b Ali	6	A. M. Smith not out	2
M. G. N. Windows c Solanki b McGrath	0	L-b 4, w 7, n-b 6	17
*M. W. Alleyne c Rhodes b McGrath	0		
I. J. Harvey c Illingworth b Lampitt	12	1/14 2/19 3/19	(29.5 overs) 120
†R. C. Russell c Wilson b Lampitt	5	4/19 5/27 6/35	
J. N. Snape c Rhodes b Lampitt	23	7/58 8/78 9/106	

Bowling: McGrath 9–3–12–4; Ali 5.5–1–34–3; Lampitt 9–3–32–3; Sheriyar 6–1–38–0.

Umpires: G. I. Burgess and M. J. Kitchen.

At Taunton, June 24. WORCESTERSHIRE beat SOMERSET by four runs.

WORCESTERSHIRE v LEICESTERSHIRE

At Worcester, July 2. No result (D/L method). Toss: Worcestershire.

Even with McGrath to exploit the conditions, top-of-the-table Worcestershire were relieved when a thunderstorm prevented Leicestershire from tackling a Duckworth/Lewis target of 118. But their relief was tempered by the thigh injury that ruled Illingworth out of their controversial NatWest third-round replay against Gloucestershire two days later. It happened as he helped rescue Worcestershire from the embarrassment of 41 for six.

Worcestershire

P. R. Pollard run out	6	D. N. Catterall not out	9
E. J. Wilson c Ward b Lewis	2	Kabir Ali not out	2
V. S. Solanki c Burns b Lewis	7		
D. A. Leatherdale c Stevens b Ormond	0	L-b 7, w 13	20
R. C. Driver c Ormond b Wells	10		
*†S. J. Rhodes c sub b Kumble	2	1/12 2/26 3/27	(8 wkts, 38 overs) 108
S. R. Lampitt c and b Maddy	20	4/27 5/41 6/41	
R. K. Illingworth c Stevens b Wells	30	7/89 8/103	

G. D. McGrath did not bat.

Bowling: Ormond 9–2–17–1; Lewis 7–2–18–2; Wells 8–1–32–2; Kumble 8–2–21–1; Williamson 4–0–9–0; Maddy 2–0–4–1.

Leicestershire

T. R. Ward, *V. J. Wells, D. I. Stevens, B. F. Smith, D. L. Maddy, A. Habib, C. C. Lewis, D. Williamson, †N. D. Burns, A. Kumble and J. Ormond.

Umpires: A. Clarkson and R. Palmer.

At Cheltenham, July 16. WORCESTERSHIRE lost to GLOUCESTERSHIRE by three wickets.

At Northampton, August 2 (day/night). WORCESTERSHIRE lost to NORTHAMPTONSHIRE by seven wickets.

WORCESTERSHIRE v SUSSEX

At Worcester, August 13. No result. Toss: Worcestershire.
The two points took Worcestershire back to the top of Division One.

Sussex

*C. J. Adams c Hick b Liptrot	2
R. R. Montgomerie not out	9
U. B. A. Rashid not out.	0
W 4	4

1/15   (1 wkt, 3.1 overs) 15

P. A. Cottey, B. Zuiderent, W. J. House, R. S. C. Martin-Jenkins, †N. J. Wilton, R. J. Kirtley,
B. V. Taylor and M. A. Robinson did not bat.

Bowling: Ali 2–0–9–0; Liptrot 1.1–0–6–1.

Worcestershire

W. P. C. Weston, P. R. Pollard, *G. A. Hick, V. S. Solanki, D. A. Leatherdale, D. J. Pipe, †S. J.
Rhodes, S. R. Lampitt, R. K. Illingworth, Kabir Ali and C. G. Liptrot.

Umpires: J. W. Holder and J. F. Steele.

WORCESTERSHIRE v SOMERSET

At Worcester, August 20. Somerset won by 53 runs. Toss: Somerset.
Worcestershire surrendered to Somerset the League leadership they had enjoyed for much of
the campaign. Their bowlers struggled to contain Somerset's strokemakers after young openers
Kabir Ali and Liptrot conceded 36 runs in four wayward overs; their batsmen were never really
in the hunt once Hick went after eight balls. Having to accelerate on a slow pitch, they lost a
cluster of wickets to Blackwell's spin.

Somerset

M. E. Trescothick c Hick b Lampitt. . . .	25	G. D. Rose c Lampitt b Hick	0
M. N. Lathwell run out	29	P. W. Jarvis run out	6
*J. Cox c Lampitt b Leatherdale	57	P. S. Jones not out	4
P. D. Bowler run out.	8	L-b 10, w 17	27
M. Burns b Leatherdale.	51		
K. A. Parsons b Illingworth	12	1/68 2/73 3/108 (9 wkts, 45 overs) 227
I. D. Blackwell run out	0	4/182 5/205 6/205
†R. J. Turner not out.	8	7/212 8/213 9/222

Bowling: Ali 5–0–32–0; Liptrot 4–0–30–0; Lampitt 9–1–36–1; Leatherdale 9–1–34–2; Hick
9–0–50–1; Illingworth 9–0–35–1.

Worcestershire

P. R. Pollard run out.	26	R. K. Illingworth b Blackwell.	0
W. P. C. Weston c Cox b Rose	14	Kabir Ali c Cox b Trescothick	7
*G. A. Hick c Cox b Jones	3	C. G. Liptrot not out.	1
V. S. Solanki c Turner b Trescothick . . .	32	L-b 8, w 11, n-b 2.	21
D. A. Leatherdale c Turner b Blackwell . .	43		
D. J. Pipe b Blackwell.	5	1/23 2/26 3/63 (40.3 overs) 174
†S. J. Rhodes c Jarvis b Blackwell	16	4/115 5/126 6/145
S. R. Lampitt run out	6	7/155 8/157 9/166

Bowling: Jones 7–0–32–1; Rose 9–1–23–1; Jarvis 6–0–20–0; Burns 3–0–21–0; Trescothick
8–0–34–2; Blackwell 7.3–0–36–4.

Umpires: N. G. Cowley and D. R. Shepherd.

At Canterbury, August 27. WORCESTERSHIRE lost to KENT by 44 runs.

WORCESTERSHIRE v LANCASHIRE

At Worcester, September 3. Lancashire won by two wickets. Toss: Worcestershire.

Needing two off the last ball, Austin straight-drove Illingworth for four to leave Worcestershire likelier to join Lancashire in the relegation zone than challenge for the title. In 1999, these counties were the League's top two. Worcestershire owed much to Driver's first League fifty and Rhodes's 35-ball 48 not out. Lancashire lost wickets at regular intervals but, with 37 required from five overs, Schofield and Chapple scrambled 32 in four and set up the finale for Austin.

Worcestershire

W. P. C. Weston b Austin	4	R. K. Illingworth b Flintoff	3
D. J. Pipe c Chapple b Flintoff	23	C. G. Liptrot not out	2
V. S. Solanki lbw b Austin	0		
D. A. Leatherdale st Hegg b Schofield	24	B 3, l-b 13, w 5	21
R. C. Driver b Keedy	52		
E. J. Wilson c Hegg b Flintoff	8	1/12 2/20 3/35	(8 wkts, 45 overs) 188
*†S. J. Rhodes not out	48	4/95 5/117 6/143	
S. R. Lampitt b Chapple	3	7/155 8/186	

G. D. McGrath did not bat.

Bowling: Chapple 8–0–35–1; Austin 9–3–18–2; Flintoff 9–3–39–3; Schofield 9–0–31–1; Ganguly 6–0–32–0; Keedy 4–0–17–1.

Lancashire

M. J. Chilton c and b Illingworth	37	G. Chapple not out	15
S. C. Ganguly c Rhodes b McGrath	11	I. D. Austin not out	5
A. Flintoff c Rhodes b Lampitt	6		
*J. P. Crawley c Lampitt b Liptrot	11	L-b 1, w 9, n-b 2	12
N. H. Fairbrother run out	35		
G. D. Lloyd b Leatherdale	17	1/19 2/26 3/44	(8 wkts, 45 overs) 191
†W. K. Hegg c Leatherdale b Driver	8	4/93 5/124 6/125	
C. P. Schofield b McGrath	34	7/152 8/184	

G. Keedy did not bat.

Bowling: McGrath 9–2–21–2; Lampitt 9–1–34–1; Leatherdale 9–0–37–1; Liptrot 6–0–37–1; Illingworth 9–0–44–1; Driver 3–0–17–1.

Umpires: R. Julian and N. A. Mallender.

At Leicester, September 8 (day/night). WORCESTERSHIRE lost to LEICESTERSHIRE by seven runs.

WORCESTERSHIRE v KENT

At Worcester, September 17. Kent won by eight wickets. Toss: Worcestershire.

Defeat meant Worcestershire's relegation while Kent stayed up at their expense, thanks to their fifth win in six games. Since heading the table by eight points in late June, Worcestershire had now gone nine games without a win, and 98 was their lowest League total of the season. McGrath, who operated with six slips and a gully, failed to pick up a wicket but ended with the best-ever economy rate and average for a League season: 2.16 runs an over, with 30 wickets at 8.13. Former Kent captain Marsh enjoyed a winning send-off into retirement, while Nixon, his successor behind the stumps, finished with a county League-record 26 dismissals (22 catches and four stumpings). But it was a sad farewell for Illingworth after 19 summers at New Road.

Worcestershire

W. P. C. Weston c Nixon b Saggers	1	R. K. Illingworth c Nixon b Saggers	4
D. J. Pipe lbw b Masters	11	M. J. Rawnsley b Saggers	4
P. R. Pollard c Ealham b Masters	1	G. D. McGrath not out	0
V. S. Solanki c Nixon b McCague	28	L-b 2, w 5	7
D. A. Leatherdale c Saggers b Ealham	11		
R. C. Driver c Fulton b Ealham	15	1/10 2/16 3/17	(36.3 overs) 98
*†S. J. Rhodes c Walker b McCague	0	4/45 5/69 6/70	
S. R. Lampitt lbw b Fleming	16	7/77 8/92 9/98	

Bowling: Masters 9–2–34–2; Saggers 9–1–25–3; Ealham 9–1–15–2; McCague 6–1–15–2; Fleming 3.3–1–7–1.

Kent

D. P. Fulton c Rawnsley b Lampitt	13	
S. A. Marsh b Rawnsley	38	
J. B. Hockley not out	36	
R. Dravid not out	9	
L-b 1, w 4	5	
1/23 2/73	(2 wkts, 26.5 overs) 101	

M. J. Walker, M. A. Ealham, †P. A. Nixon, M. J. McCague, M. J. Saggers, *M. V. Fleming and D. D. Masters did not bat.

Bowling: McGrath 9–3–13–0; Lampitt 7–2–24–1; Driver 3–0–25–0; Rawnsley 4.5–0–26–1; Leatherdale 1–0–3–0; Illingworth 2–0–9–0.

Umpires: B. Leadbeater and J. F. Steele.

YORKSHIRE

At Worcester, April 30. YORKSHIRE beat WORCESTERSHIRE by 19 runs.

YORKSHIRE v WORCESTERSHIRE

At Leeds, May 7. Worcestershire won by nine runs. Toss: Worcestershire. First-team debut: V. J. Craven.

A competition-best three for 20 by Hoggard helped keep Worcestershire in check, but Pollard's rugged half-century, combined with some less inhibited batting by Spiring, had already ensured a useful total. It proved too much for Yorkshire, who were undone by three Bradford-born exiles: Illingworth and Leatherdale each captured three wickets and Rhodes made two catches and a stumping. Newcomer Vic Craven almost turned the tables with a spirited 28 off 33 balls, but 24 from the last three overs was asking a lot when McGrath would bowl two of them.

Worcestershire

P. R. Pollard c Blakey b Hoggard	55	R. K. Illingworth run out	1
V. S. Solanki c Blakey b Hoggard	7	Kabir Ali not out	0
*G. A. Hick lbw b Hamilton	16		
K. R. Spiring run out	49	L-b 4, w 9, n-b 6	19
E. J. Wilson c Blakey b Hoggard	2		
D. A. Leatherdale run out	21	1/26 2/73 3/134	(8 wkts, 45 overs) 173
†S. J. Rhodes not out	3	4/138 5/156 6/172	
S. R. Lampitt c Lehmann b Gough	0	7/172 8/173	

G. D. McGrath did not bat.

Bowling: Gough 9–0–40–1; Hoggard 9–3–20–3; Sidebottom 3–0–37–0; Hamilton 7–0–35–1; White 9–1–18–0; Lehmann 8–1–19–0.

Yorkshire

*D. Byas c Rhodes b McGrath	7	D. Gough not out		15
C. White run out	14	R. J. Sidebottom st Rhodes b Illingworth		0
†R. J. Blakey c Spring b Illingworth	31	M. J. Hoggard not out		0
D. S. Lehmann c Rhodes b Illingworth	39	B 1, l-b 4, w 4, n-b 4		13
M. J. Wood lbw b Leatherdale	8			
V. J. Craven c Spring b Leatherdale	28	1/20 2/27 3/98	(9 wkts, 45 overs)	164
G. M. Fellows lbw b Leatherdale	1	4/98 5/111 6/121		
G. M. Hamilton c Ali b McGrath	8	7/147 8/151 9/155		

Bowling: McGrath 9–2–22–2; Ali 9–0–32–0; Lampitt 9–2–26–0; Leatherdale 7–0–39–3; Illingworth 9–1–30–3; Hick 2–0–10–0.

Umpires: A. A. Jones and A. G. T. Whitehead.

YORKSHIRE v GLOUCESTERSHIRE

At Leeds, May 21. Yorkshire won by 35 runs (D/L method). Toss: Gloucestershire.

Yorkshire avenged their two 1999 knockout defeats by Gloucestershire through two young bowlers with only one previous county League game between them. After 17-year-old seamer Ramsden had picked up two important wickets in Hancock and Barnett, Middlebrook unstitched the middle order with his well-directed off-spin. Light rain early on had reduced the game to 33 overs a side and, with Duckworth/Lewis now operating, Lehmann and Blakey lost little time building on Yorkshire's solid opening of 77 in 18 overs.

Yorkshire

*D. Byas st Russell b Cawdron	48	R. J. Harden not out		2
G. M. Fellows lbw b Alleyne	30	B 1, l-b 6, w 6		13
†R. J. Blakey not out	43			
D. S. Lehmann c Cawdron b Averis	24	1/77 2/108 3/149	(3 wkts, 33 overs)	160

G. Ramsden, M. J. Wood, G. M. Hamilton, J. D. Middlebrook, P. M. Hutchison and M. J. Hoggard did not bat.

Bowling: Smith 7–1–19–0; Harvey 7–0–36–0; Cawdron 6–0–33–1; Averis 6–0–42–1; Alleyne 7–0–23–1.

Gloucestershire

T. H. C. Hancock lbw b Ramsden	19	M. J. Cawdron c Byas b Hoggard		8
R. J. Cunliffe b Hoggard	0	J. M. M. Averis not out		6
M. G. N. Windows c Blakey b Hamilton	26	A. M. Smith c Byas b Hamilton		0
K. J. Barnett b Ramsden	3	B 1, l-b 5, w 9, n-b 4		19
*M. W. Alleyne c Byas b Middlebrook	10			
I. J. Harvey lbw b Middlebrook	31	1/1 2/44 3/58	(30.2 overs)	129
J. N. Snape lbw b Middlebrook	4	4/60 5/96 6/108		
†R. C. Russell run out	3	7/113 8/118 9/128		

Bowling: Hoggard 5–0–14–2; Hutchison 5–1–21–0; Hamilton 5.2–1–12–2; Ramsden 4–0–26–2; Lehmann 5–0–24–0; Middlebrook 5–0–16–3; Fellows 1–0–10–0.

Umpires: M. J. Harris and J. W. Holder.

YORKSHIRE v LEICESTERSHIRE

At Leeds, June 4. Leicestershire won by three wickets. Toss: Leicestershire.

Smith's no-frills 88 not out off 106 balls maintained Leicestershire's unbeaten League record after Hutchison's pace had them 41 for three. In poor light, Wells launched their innings with 19 off 16 balls, including four boundaries, to make sure they were ahead after ten overs. But while the conditions never improved, there was no call upon Duckworth/Lewis. The game would have tilted Yorkshire's way had Middlebrook held a return catch from Smith on 55; that would have left Leicestershire 141 for seven in the 34th over. Bringing back novice seamer Elstub with 22 wanted from four overs also favoured the visitors, for he conceded 11 runs to seal Yorkshire's fate. Fellows had earlier struck a career-best 65 for Yorkshire, his progress being slowed by the wet outfield.

Yorkshire

*D. Byas c Burns b Lewis	10	M. P. Vaughan not out		2
G. M. Fellows c DeFreitas b Dakin	65	B 1, l-b 10, w 3, n-b 6		20
†R. J. Blakey c Maddy b Lewis	62			—
D. S. Lehmann not out	30	1/24 2/137 3/185	(3 wkts, 45 overs)	189

C. J. Elstub, M. J. Wood, G. M. Hamilton, J. D. Middlebrook, P. M. Hutchison and M. J. Hoggard did not bat.

Bowling: Ormond 9–1–41–0; Lewis 9–3–19–2; Dakin 9–1–44–1; DeFreitas 9–1–43–0; Wells 5–0–15–0; Maddy 4–0–16–0.

Leicestershire

T. R. Ward c Wood b Hutchison	9	D. L. Maddy c Lehmann b Hoggard		8
*V. J. Wells b Hutchison	19	A. Habib not out		15
D. I. Stevens b Hutchison	0	B 4, l-b 1, w 7, n-b 2		14
B. F. Smith not out	88			
P. A. J. DeFreitas c Vaughan b Lehmann	28	1/28 2/33 3/41	(7 wkts, 43.2 overs)	193
J. M. Dakin b Middlebrook	5	4/111 5/118		
C. C. Lewis b Lehmann	7	6/134 7/157		

†N. D. Burns and J. Ormond did not bat.

Bowling: Hoggard 9–0–38–1; Hutchison 6–1–27–3; Hamilton 5–0–30–0; Elstub 5.2–0–31–0; Lehmann 9–0–33–2; Middlebrook 9–0–29–1.

Umpires: D. R. Shepherd and R. A. White.

YORKSHIRE v KENT

At Leeds, June 18. Yorkshire won by 24 runs. Toss: Yorkshire.

White's hat-trick, in his first game for five weeks after recovering from injuries and illness, snatched from Kent the victory that looked increasingly likely as Nixon and Fleming took them to 138 for six by the 42nd over. Yorkshire's earlier recovery from 44 for five was due to a gritty half-century from Byas, and Dravid played a similar role for Kent after Silverwood bowled openers Fulton and Key without scoring.

Yorkshire

G. M. Fellows b Ealham	11	C. E. W. Silverwood c Patel b Fleming		12
M. P. Vaughan c Dravid b Adams	9	R. J. Sidebottom not out		7
†R. J. Blakey c Nixon b Ealham	10	M. J. Hoggard not out		2
D. S. Lehmann c Nixon b Adams	2	B 4, l-b 15, w 3, n-b 2		24
*D. Byas c Walker b Ealham	52			
C. White run out	4	1/17 2/32 3/38	(9 wkts, 45 overs)	163
G. M. Hamilton c Nixon b Patel	21	4/38 5/44 6/95		
J. D. Middlebrook st Nixon b Patel	9	7/125 8/143 9/160		

Bowling: Ealham 9–1–38–3; Adams 7–1–17–2; Masters 9–2–19–0; Fleming 6–0–26–1; Patel 9–1–25–2; Dravid 5–0–19–0.

Kent

D. P. Fulton b Silverwood	0	M. M. Patel lbw b White	0
R. W. T. Key b Silverwood	0	D. D. Masters lbw b White	0
R. Dravid lbw b Hoggard	49	K. Adams b Silverwood	0
M. J. Walker lbw b Middlebrook	18	L-b 6, w 1	7
A. P. Wells b Middlebrook	5		
M. A. Ealham b Middlebrook	1	1/0 2/10 3/57 (42.4 overs)	139
†P. A. Nixon not out	30	4/63 5/73 6/97	
*M. V. Fleming c Vaughan b White	29	7/138 8/138 9/138	

Bowling: Silverwood 7.4–2–16–3; Hoggard 9–2–31–1; Sidebottom 6–1–19–0; White 8–0–27–3; Middlebrook 9–0–24–3; Lehmann 3–0–16–0.

Umpires: J. H. Hampshire and P. Willey.

At Bristol, June 24. YORKSHIRE lost to GLOUCESTERSHIRE by 51 runs.

YORKSHIRE v NORTHAMPTONSHIRE

At Leeds, June 25. Northamptonshire won by 60 runs. Toss: Northamptonshire.

Yorkshire raised a few eyebrows by "resting" White and Silverwood, a move believed to be a disciplinary measure, and Northamptonshire were never in much trouble after recovering from early wickets by Hoggard, who had just heard he was in England's Test squad for the first time. Sales mastered a sluggish pitch with an unbeaten 71 off 96 balls, four times driving Middlebrook for six, and Northamptonshire remained in charge as Brown and Swann dominated the Yorkshire batting with their off-spin.

Northamptonshire

A. S. Rollins c Byas b Hoggard	1	†D. Ripley b Gough	0
M. B. Loye c Fellows b Hamilton	16	M. R. Strong not out	1
*M. L. Hayden c McGrath b Hoggard	7	L-b 5, w 12	17
D. J. Sales not out	71		
J. W. Cook c Hamilton b Lehmann	33	1/1 2/23 3/34 (7 wkts, 45 overs)	189
A. L. Penberthy b Gough	27	4/104 5/164	
G. P. Swann c Fellows b Hoggard	16	6/183 7/188	

J. F. Brown and D. E. Malcolm did not bat.

Bowling: Gough 9–0–29–2; Hoggard 9–1–43–3; Hamilton 7–0–23–1; Sidebottom 7–1–27–0; Middlebrook 8–0–48–0; Lehmann 5–0–14–1.

Yorkshire

G. M. Fellows c Sales b Brown	20	D. Gough not out	6
M. P. Vaughan c Ripley b Malcolm	8	R. J. Sidebottom b Swann	3
*D. Byas lbw b Brown	21	M. J. Hoggard b Swann	0
D. S. Lehmann b Strong	4	L-b 6, w 7	13
A. McGrath c Cook b Swann	32		
G. M. Hamilton c Hayden b Penberthy	5	1/14 2/50 3/55 (39 overs)	129
†R. J. Blakey b Swann	16	4/69 5/80 6/115	
J. D. Middlebrook c Swann b Hayden	1	7/118 8/120 9/129	

Bowling: Strong 6–0–23–1; Malcolm 9–2–24–1; Brown 9–1–28–2; Penberthy 6–0–18–1; Swann 5–0–14–4; Hayden 4–0–16–1.

Umpires: J. F. Steele and R. A. White.

At Manchester, June 27 (day/night). YORKSHIRE beat LANCASHIRE by 69 runs (D/L method).

At Arundel, July 16. YORKSHIRE lost to SUSSEX by 70 runs.

YORKSHIRE v SOMERSET

At Scarborough, July 23. Somerset won by two wickets. Toss: Yorkshire.

Blackwell drove Hutchison out of the ground to reach 50 off 41 balls and bring Somerset a win that appeared unlikely at 74 for seven. Byas, who earlier had reached 5,000 League runs, paid the penalty for placing too much faith in the slow bowling of Middlebrook and Lehmann; pace might have knocked over the tail. Jones, who dismissed both Yorkshire openers and later claimed the last two wickets, had pegged the home side back to 141. He was well supported by Jarvis, with three for 23 against his former county, while Trescothick made his dawn dash from the England team hotel in London worthwhile by capturing two wickets in one over. He managed only 12 with the bat, however.

Yorkshire

S. Widdup lbw b Jones	8	C. E. W. Silverwood b Jarvis		1
*D. Byas b Jones	14	M. J. Hoggard b Jones		0
A. McGrath c Holloway b Jarvis	17	P. M. Hutchison not out		1
D. S. Lehmann b Rose	18	L-b 10, w 4		14
†R. J. Blakey b Jarvis	33			
G. M. Fellows c and b Trescothick	15	1/25 2/26 3/55	(43 overs)	141
J. D. Middlebrook lbw b Trescothick	0	4/63 5/97 6/97		
I. D. Fisher st Turner b Jones	20	7/127 8/135 9/136		

Bowling: Rose 9–3–21–1; Jones 8–1–33–4; Jarvis 8–0–23–3; Burns 5–1–22–0; Trescothick 6–1–16–2; Blackwell 7–0–16–0.

Somerset

M. E. Trescothick c Blakey b Hoggard	12	I. D. Blackwell not out		50
*J. Cox c Byas b Hoggard	3	G. D. Rose not out		13
P. C. L. Holloway lbw b Silverwood	1			
P. D. Bowler lbw b Silverwood	4	B 4, l-b 4, w 13		21
M. Burns c Hutchison b Fisher	26			
K. A. Parsons c Blakey b Hutchison	11	1/18 2/25 3/35	(8 wkts, 40.3 overs)	146
†R. J. Turner lbw b Fisher	5	4/37 5/59 6/74		
P. S. Jones lbw b Fisher	0	7/74 8/107		

P. W. Jarvis did not bat.

Bowling: Silverwood 9–1–33–2; Hoggard 8–1–19–2; Hutchison 6.3–1–28 1; Fisher 9 0 20–3; Middlebrook 6–0–26–0; Lehmann 2–0–12–0.

Umpires: M. R. Benson and T. E. Jesty.

At Taunton, August 6. YORKSHIRE beat SOMERSET by 32 runs.

YORKSHIRE v LANCASHIRE

At Leeds, August 9 (day/night). Yorkshire won by nine wickets. Toss: Lancashire.

So much for the floodlights: the sun was still shining when Yorkshire dashed to victory by nine wickets. The game had lasted only two hours 33 minutes – and that after Lancashire chose to bat in reasonable conditions. Their 68 eclipsed their previous lowest League score of 71 against Essex at Chelmsford in 1987. Lehmann, leading Yorkshire in Byas's absence through injury, showed the way home with his unbeaten 54 off 43 balls, including eight fours.

Lancashire

*J. P. Crawley b Hoggard	3	G. Chapple run out	0
S. C. Ganguly c Craven b Hoggard	11	G. Yates c Vaughan b Hamilton	4
A. Flintoff b White	28	M. P. Smethurst not out	3
N. H. Fairbrother run out	7	B 3, n-b 2	5
G. D. Lloyd b Blakey b White	1		
J. C. Scuderi b White	0	1/7 2/14 3/21	(23.3 overs) 68
†W. K. Hegg c Lehmann b White	4	4/32 5/32 6/40	
I. D. Austin b Hoggard	2	7/43 8/47 9/62	

Bowling: Gough 6–2–24–0; Hoggard 9–4–15–3; White 6–0–14–4; Hamilton 2.3–0–12–1.

Yorkshire

V. J. Craven c Fairbrother b Austin	3
M. P. Vaughan not out	11
*D. S. Lehmann not out	54
L-b 1, w 3	4

1/4   (1 wkt, 13.5 overs) 72

A. McGrath, G. M. Fellows, †R. J. Blakey, G. M. Hamilton, C. White, I. D. Fisher, M. J. Hoggard and D. Gough did not bat.

Bowling: Chapple 5–0–17–0; Austin 6.5–1–39–1; Smethurst 2–0–15–0.

Umpires: J. W. Lloyds and A. G. T. Whitehead.

At Leicester, August 20. YORKSHIRE beat LEICESTERSHIRE by eight wickets.

At Northampton, August 28. YORKSHIRE beat NORTHAMPTONSHIRE by six wickets.

YORKSHIRE v SUSSEX

At Scarborough, September 3. Yorkshire won by 49 runs. Toss: Yorkshire.

A fifth consecutive win, keeping Yorkshire on top of the table, was engineered mainly by Hamilton, who followed his brisk unbeaten fifty with five for 34 as Sussex slumped so dramatically that they lost their last eight wickets for 28. While Bevan and Adams were adding 113 in 26 overs, Sussex looked to be cruising. But after Hamilton bowled Bevan, they fell apart. Six batsmen failed to score, matching the dismal record of Gloucestershire in 1981 and Nottinghamshire in 1982 – both against Somerset at Bath. Earlier, Lehmann, who had succeeded Bevan at Yorkshire, overcame the loss of early wickets with 80 in 99 balls, and when he was out Hamilton maintained the momentum.

Yorkshire

*D. Byas lbw b Kirtley	0	C. E. W. Silverwood b Taylor	1
S. Widdup c Adams b Martin-Jenkins	0	J. D. Middlebrook not out	15
D. S. Lehmann c House b Robinson	80		
A. McGrath c Adams b Robinson	1	L-b 8, w 5	13
†R. J. Blakey c Wilton b Taylor	5		
G. M. Fellows c Wilton b Martin-Jenkins	15	1/0 2/3 3/37	(8 wkts, 45 overs) 192
G. M. Hamilton not out	57	4/56 5/92 6/129	
I. D. Fisher b Kirtley	5	7/156 8/163	

M. J. Hoggard did not bat.

Bowling: Kirtley 9–1–39–2; Martin-Jenkins 9–1–30–2; Robinson 9–1–30–2; Taylor 9–0–42–2; House 6–0–28–0; Adams 3–0–15–0.

Sussex

R. R. Montgomerie c Blakey b Hoggard	0	R. J. Kirtley c Widdup b Fisher	11
*C. J. Adams run out	47	B. V. Taylor c Fellows b Hamilton	0
U. B. A. Rashid c Fellows b Hoggard	0	M. A. Robinson not out	0
M. G. Bevan b Hamilton	67		
B. Zuiderent lbw b Hamilton	0	B 1, l-b 5, w 3, n-b 2	11
W. J. House c Blakey b Hamilton	4		
R. S. C. Martin-Jenkins c McGrath b Hamilton	0	1/1 2/2 3/115 (35.3 overs) 143
†N. J. Wilton st Blakey b Fisher	3	4/115 5/125 6/125
		7/132 8/132 9/133

Bowling: Hoggard 7–1–16–2; Silverwood 7–2–26–0; Hamilton 8–1–34–5; Middlebrook 5–0–27–0; Fellows 3–0–9–0; Fisher 5.3–1–25–2.

Umpires: B. Dudleston and J. H. Harris.

At Canterbury, September 5 (day/night). YORKSHIRE lost to KENT by 64 runs.

DIVISION TWO

DERBYSHIRE

DERBYSHIRE v MIDDLESEX

At Derby, May 1. Middlesex won by 71 runs. Toss: Middlesex.

Middlesex made far better use of the conditions to win with more than eight overs to spare. In contrast to the previous day's performance at Chelmsford, their innings was a series of useful contributions, helped by 19 wides. Dean made his first senior appearance for Derbyshire since July 1999, following a back operation in the winter. Derbyshire's response was feeble, and off-spinner Weekes returned his best one-day figures.

Middlesex

M. A. Roseberry b Cork	10	A. W. Laraman not out	11
M. R. Ramprakash c Krikken b Aldred	38		
*J. L. Langer lbw b Aldred	12	B 4, l-b 8, w 19	31
O. A. Shah c Krikken b Cork	37		
R. M. S. Weston c Krikken b Dowman	28	1/16 2/62 3/75 (6 wkts, 45 overs) 185
P. N. Weekes b Aldred	18	4/151 5/153 6/185

†D. C. Nash, R. L. Johnson, A. R. C. Fraser and J. P. Hewitt did not bat.

Bowling: Cork 9–0–34–2; Munton 9–0–23–0; Dean 9–0–38–0; Aldred 8–0–31–3; Cassar 9–0–45–0; Dowman 1–0–2–1.

Derbyshire

M. E. Cassar c Roseberry b Johnson	20	P. Aldred c Fraser b Weekes	4
M. J. Di Venuto b Fraser	4	T. A. Munton c Hewitt b Weekes	16
M. P. Dowman c Weston b Fraser	0	K. J. Dean run out	4
R. J. Bailey c Nash b Hewitt	11	L-b 1, w 2	3
S. D. Stubbings lbw b Laraman	14		
†K. M. Krikken not out	34	1/21 2/25 3/25 (36.5 overs) 114
B. L. Spendlove c Langer b Weekes	4	4/46 5/51 6/59
*D. G. Cork c and b Weekes	0	7/61 8/69 9/107

Bowling: Fraser 5–3–7–2; Johnson 6–1–18–1; Laraman 9–1–38–1; Hewitt 9–1–24–1; Weekes 7.5–1–26–4.

Umpires: A. Clarkson and A. G. T. Whitehead.

At Nottingham, May 21. DERBYSHIRE lost to NOTTINGHAMSHIRE by four wickets.

At Cardiff, May 29. DERBYSHIRE lost to GLAMORGAN by six wickets.

DERBYSHIRE v SURREY

At Derby, June 11. Surrey won by three wickets. Toss: Surrey.

Another poor performance by Derbyshire led to their fourth consecutive defeat. They began well through Cassar and Di Venuto, but the promise of 135 for two in 28 overs evaporated as the last five wickets managed only 31. Thorpe, gradually and grittily regaining his touch, steered Surrey to victory after his deflected drive had resulted in Ward's run-out for 53 in 69 balls. Cork took his 100th wicket in the competition when he dismissed Hollioake and so became the second, after Geoff Miller, to score 1,000 runs and take 100 wickets for Derbyshire.

Derbyshire

M. E. Cassar c Hollioake b Brown	56	P. Aldred not out	8
M. J. Di Venuto b Bishop	31	T. A. Munton c Greenidge b Tudor	7
M. P. Dowman b Hollioake	10	K. J. Dean not out	1
S. P. Titchard lbw b Ratcliffe	15		
R. J. Bailey c and b Saqlain Mushtaq	23	L-b 7, w 15, n-b 6	28
S. D. Stubbings c Brown b Saqlain Mushtaq	7		
*D. G. Cork b Hollioake	11	1/52 2/93 3/135 (9 wkts, 45 overs) 197
†K. M. Krikken b Saqlain Mushtaq	0	4/141 5/166 6/177
		7/181 8/185 9/192

Bowling: Tudor 4–0–36–1; Bishop 9–1–22–1; Greenidge 2–0–11–0; Saqlain Mushtaq 9–0–36–3; Ratcliffe 9–1–25–1; Hollioake 8–0–42–2; Brown 4–0–18–1.

Surrey

M. A. Butcher lbw b Munton	14	A. J. Tudor b Cassar	7
I. J. Ward run out	53	Saqlain Mushtaq not out	2
†A. J. Stewart lbw b Dean	19	B 4, l-b 7, w 11	22
G. P. Thorpe not out	45		
A. D. Brown lbw b Cork	34	1/49 2/87 3/102 (7 wkts, 42 overs) 198
*A. J. Hollioake st Krikken b Cork	2	4/158 5/178
J. D. Ratcliffe lbw b Cork	0	6/178 7/194

I. E. Bishop and C. G. Greenidge did not bat.

Bowling: Cork 8–1–31–3; Munton 9–0–53–1; Aldred 6–0–24–0; Dean 7–1–26–1; Cassar 9–0–35–1; Bailey 3–0–18–0.

Umpires: B. Dudleston and V. A. Holder.

At Lord's, June 18. DERBYSHIRE beat MIDDLESEX by 15 runs.

DERBYSHIRE v NOTTINGHAMSHIRE

At Derby, June 26 (day/night). Nottinghamshire won by 30 runs. Toss: Nottinghamshire.

The first match under lights at the County Ground was a successful occasion except that, from a home perspective, local rivals Nottinghamshire maintained their surge at the top of Division Two with a comfortable victory, and Bailey, injuring a calf muscle when he set off for a routine single, was expected to be out for a month. Cork took the spotlight with four wickets and a half-century, adding 92 in 19 overs with Di Venuto and threatening to eclipse Bicknell's earlier 90 for Nottinghamshire. Stemp removed them both and Lucas bowled a decisive last spell, four for four in three overs, as batsmen struggled to line up the ball early enough. Lucas's return was his second one-day best in three days.

Nottinghamshire

D. J. Bicknell c Cork b Dean	90	P. J. Franks not out		2
G. E. Welton c and b Cork	12	D. S. Lucas b Cork		0
*J. E. R. Gallian c Di Venuto b Dean	16	L-b 4, w 6		10
J. E. Morris c Bailey b Lacey	33			
U. Afzaal c Cork b Dean	30	1/22 2/64 3/119	(8 wkts, 45 overs)	212
C. M. Tolley b Cork	13	4/180 5/203 6/207		
†C. M. W. Read lbw b Cork	6	7/212 8/212		

A. J. Harris and R. D. Stemp did not bat.

Bowling: Cork 9–0–40–4; Munton 9–1–28–0; Dean 9–1–37–3; Smith 5–0–33–0; Lacey 8–0–48–1; Dowman 5–0–22–0.

Derbyshire

M. E. Cassar c Welton b Harris	2	T. M. Smith b Lucas		3
M. J. Di Venuto c Read b Stemp	46	T. A. Munton b Franks		1
*D. G. Cork b Stemp	51	K. J. Dean not out		4
M. P. Dowman run out	6	B 4, l-b 7, w 5, n-b 2		18
R. J. Bailey run out	30			
S. D. Stubbings b Lucas	16	1/10 2/102 3/117	(42.3 overs)	182
†K. M. Krikken b Lucas	4	4/121 5/162 6/171		
S. J. Lacey b Lucas	1	7/174 8/177 9/178		

Bowling: Harris 9–2–40–1; Lucas 8–0–27–4; Franks 7.3–0–35–1; Tolley 9–0–35–0; Stemp 9–0–34–2.

Umpires: J. H. Harris and R. Julian.

At Darlington, July 2. DERBYSHIRE lost to DURHAM by 95 runs.

DERBYSHIRE v WARWICKSHIRE

At Derby, July 16. Warwickshire won by 45 runs. Toss: Warwickshire.

Dean marked his return from injury with three wickets in his first three overs, but a stand of 48 between Ostler and Brown pointed Warwickshire towards a useful total on a desperately slow pitch. Just how slow was evident when Krikken and Lungley took 15 overs to score 36 after Brown's three for one in nine balls had derailed Derbyshire's reply. Giles put them out of their misery; fellow-spinner Smith consigned Derbyshire to their seventh defeat in eight games with four overs to spare.

Warwickshire

N. V. Knight c Krikken b Dean	6	†K. J. Piper not out	12

N. V. Knight c Krikken b Dean 6
G. Welch b Dean 2
D. P. Ostler b Lungley 27
T. L. Penney b Dean 0
D. R. Brown c Dean b Cork 24
M. J. Powell c Krikken b Lungley 20
A. F. Giles c Cork b Dean 18
*N. M. K. Smith st Krikken b Shah . . . 16
E. S. H. Giddins did not bat.

†K. J. Piper not out 12
A. A. Donald not out 3

L-b 9, w 11, n-b 2 22

1/9 2/17 3/17   (8 wkts, 45 overs) 150
4/65 5/78 6/105
7/119 8/143

Bowling: Munton 9–2–18–0; Dean 9–1–30–4; Cork 9–1–31–1; Shah 9–0–36–1; Lungley 9–0–26–2.

Derbyshire

L. D. Sutton b Giddins 1
M. J. Di Venuto c Ostler b Brown 15
*D. G. Cork b Giddins 11
S. D. Stubbings b Brown 21
J. P. Pyemont lbw b Brown 0
†K. M. Krikken b Giles 19
T. Lungley st Piper b Giles 15
T. A. Munton c Giddins b Smith 2

K. Z. Shah c Giddins b Smith 3
K. J. Dean c and b Smith 2
L. J. Wharton not out 0
B 3, l-b 3, w 10 16

1/3 2/16 3/53   (40.5 overs) 105
4/53 5/57 6/93
7/95 8/101 9/105

Bowling: Giddins 7–1–15–2; Welch 4–1–18–0; Donald 7–1–20–0; Brown 7–2–13–3; Giles 9–2–23–2; Smith 6.5–0–10–3.

Umpires: M. J. Kitchen and J. W. Lloyds.

At Chelmsford, July 23. DERBYSHIRE lost to ESSEX by six runs.

DERBYSHIRE v HAMPSHIRE

At Derby, August 6. Hampshire won by 36 runs. Toss: Derbyshire.

Kendall and Smith put on 111 in the last 12 overs as Kendall hit 73 off 42 balls, including three sixes and eight fours. Derbyshire responded brightly but, once Di Venuto was third out, they lost ground. Their last six wickets fell in eight overs. Kenway made three stumpings in five dismissals to add to his earlier fifty.

Hampshire

†D. A. Kenway run out 53
J. P. Stephenson b Aldred 27
*R. A. Smith not out 61
J. S. Laney c Pyemont b Cassar 8

W. S. Kendall not out 73
B 1, l-b 4, w 6 11

1/47 2/103 3/122   (3 wkts, 45 overs) 233

G. W. White, S. D. Udal, A. D. Mascarenhas, S. J. Renshaw, A. C. Morris and C. M. Tremlett did not bat.

Bowling: Dean 9–1–33–0; Munton 9–1–34–0; Aldred 8–1–41–1; Shah 6–0–45–0; Lacey 9–0–57–0; Cassar 4–0–18–1.

Derbyshire

M. E. Cassar c Kenway b Morris	44	S. J. Lacey lbw b Stephenson	2
M. J. Di Venuto b Tremlett	47	*T. A. Munton st Kenway b Stephenson	0
M. P. Dowman c Kenway b Morris	0	K. J. Dean not out	3
J. P. Pyemont b Stephenson	27		
S. D. Stubbings st Kenway		L-b 6, w 10, n-b 4	20
b Mascarenhas	20		
†L. D. Sutton b Stephenson	26	1/87 2/87 3/111 (42.4 overs) 197	
K. Z. Shah st Kenway b Mascarenhas	7	4/149 5/157 6/174	
P. Aldred run out	1	7/177 8/188 9/190	

Bowling: Mascarenhas 9–1–37–2; Renshaw 5–0–30–0; Stephenson 8.4–0–40–4; Morris 6–2–16–2; Udal 9–0–48–0; Tremlett 5–0–20–1.

Umpires: N. A. Mallender and D. R. Shepherd.

DERBYSHIRE v ESSEX

At Derby, August 13. No result (D/L method). Toss: Essex. County debut: J. S. Foster.

Napier demonstrated his recovery from back trouble with an entertaining 78, including three sixes, on a sluggish pitch. He added 111 with Irani. Despite interruption by rain, Essex completed their 45 overs, but more rain during the interval meant a revised target of 193 in 40 overs for Derbyshire. Only four overs were possible, the abandonment giving Derbyshire their first League points since beating Middlesex on June 18.

Essex

P. J. Prichard c Di Venuto b Munton	24	T. J. Mason b Cork	1
S. G. Law c Lacey b Dean	21	J. E. Bishop not out	1
G. R. Napier b Aldred	78		
*R. C. Irani b Cork	35	B 1, l-b 5, w 3	9
S. D. Peters st Sutton b Aldred	14		
D. R. Law c Wharton b Aldred	2	1/42 2/48 3/159 (8 wkts, 45 overs) 204	
A. P. Grayson c Cassar b Dean	6	4/177 5/180 6/183	
†J. S. Foster not out	13	7/197 8/203	

A. C. McGarry did not bat.

Bowling: Munton 9–3–13–1; Dean 7–0–45–2; Aldred 9–1–34–3; Cork 9–0–43–2; Wharton 7–0–40–0; Lacey 4–0–23–0.

Derbyshire

M. E. Cassar not out	3
M. J. Di Venuto lbw b D. R. Law	0
M. P. Dowman not out	6
L-b 2, w 3	5

1/1 (1 wkt, 4 overs) 14

*D. G. Cork, S. D. Stubbings, †L. D. Sutton, S. J. Lacey, P. Aldred, T. A. Munton, K. J. Dean and L. J. Wharton did not bat.

Bowling: D. R. Law 2–0–6–1; McGarry 2–0–6–0.

Umpires: D. J. Constant and P. Willey.

At The Oval, August 20. DERBYSHIRE lost to SURREY by six wickets.

DERBYSHIRE v GLAMORGAN

At Derby, August 27. Glamorgan won by one wicket. Toss: Derbyshire.

Derbyshire's flying start, 31 from the first three overs, could not be maintained against spinners Cosker and Croft. Even Bailey was unable to break free, hitting only three fours in 109 balls. James and Powell survived chances to give Glamorgan's reply substance, but, from the comfort of 197 for six, they needed their last pair, Cosker and Parkin, to get ten from 14 balls. There was one to spare when Parkin hit Cassar wide of mid-on.

Derbyshire

M. E. Cassar c Croft b Parkin	44	*T. A. Munton not out		3
M. J. Di Venuto c Evans b Parkin	16	K. J. Dean not out		0
R. J. Bailey b Dale	64			
M. P. Dowman c Maynard b Croft	33	B 5, l-b 2, w 7		14
S. D. Stubbings c James b Cosker	11			
†L. D. Sutton c Croft b Newell	11	1/44 2/80 3/130	(8 wkts, 45 overs)	211
J. P. Pyemont run out	15	4/157 5/186 6/200		
S. J. Lacey run out	0	7/200 8/209		

L. J. Wharton did not bat.

Bowling: Parkin 9–1–38–2; Harrison 6–0–52–0; Dale 7–0–34–1; Newell 5–1–19–1; Cosker 9–0–30–1; Croft 9–0–31–1.

Glamorgan

K. Newell c Wharton b Dean	13	D. S. Harrison b Cassar		4
I. J. Thomas c Sutton b Dean	23	D. A. Cosker not out		5
S. P. James c Munton b Dowman	56	O. T. Parkin not out		5
*†M. P. Maynard b Wharton	25	L-b 1, w 5		6
A. Dale c Sutton b Cassar	8			
M. J. Powell run out	53	1/29 2/41 3/77	(9 wkts, 44.5 overs)	212
A. W. Evans lbw b Cassar	6	4/88 5/168 6/180		
R. D. B. Croft c Bailey b Dowman	8	7/197 8/202 9/202		

Bowling: Munton 9–0–27–0; Dean 8–0–53–2; Cassar 8.5–0–42–3; Wharton 9–0–43–1; Lacey 3–1–18–0; Bailey 2–0–12–0; Dowman 5–0–16–2.

Umpires: A. Clarkson and G. Sharp.

At Birmingham, September 3. DERBYSHIRE lost to WARWICKSHIRE by 44 runs.

At Southampton, September 10. DERBYSHIRE beat HAMPSHIRE by four runs.

DERBYSHIRE v DURHAM

At Derby, September 17. Durham won by one run. Toss: Durham.

Cassar's excellent 126 in 136 balls (three sixes, 12 fours) put Derbyshire in reach of what would have been only their third League win. They needed 27 from five overs with six wickets standing, then six from the last. But Killeen bowled it expertly, taking three wickets to complete his best one-day figures, six for 31, and equal Anderson Cummins's 1993 county-best 29 wickets in a League season. Durham's total had been built around fifties from Daley and Collingwood, his seventh of the League season. Derbyshire marked umpire John Harris's retirement with a pre-match presentation.

Durham

J. A. Daley c Munton b Cassar	54	M. M. Betts b Dowman	16
M. P. Speight c Bailey b Dean	11	N. Killeen not out	20
S. M. Katich lbw b Munton	16	L-b 3, w 16	19
P. D. Collingwood b Wharton	52		
*J. J. B. Lewis lbw b Wharton	2	1/18 2/66 3/131 (7 wkts, 45 overs) 229	
†A. Pratt c Dowman b Wharton	10	4/134 5/154	
N. C. Phillips not out	29	6/157 7/203	

I. D. Hunter and S. J. E. Brown did not bat.

Bowling: Munton 9–0–43–1; Dean 3–1–19–1; Cassar 7–0–48–1; Dowman 5–0–38–1; Wharton 9–2–29–3; Lacey 9–0–32–0; Bailey 3–0–17–0.

Derbyshire

M. E. Cassar b Killeen	126	S. J. Lacey c Katich b Killeen	0
M. J. Di Venuto c Katich b Betts	13	*T. A. Munton not out	1
R. J. Bailey b Killeen	9	B 2, l-b 9, w 9	20
M. P. Dowman c Speight b Killeen	4		
S. D. Stubbings b Hunter	32	1/19 2/51 3/61 (8 wkts, 45 overs) 228	
†L. D. Sutton b Killeen	20	4/148 5/221 6/227	
J. P. Pyemont b Killeen	3	7/227 8/228	

K. J. Dean and L. J. Wharton did not bat.

Bowling: Betts 7–1–22–1; Brown 7–0–22–0; Killeen 7–0–31–6; Hunter 9–0–65–1; Collingwood 6–0–34–0; Phillips 9–0–43–0.

Umpires: J. H. Harris and N. A. Mallender.

DURHAM

At Nottingham, April 30. DURHAM lost to NOTTINGHAMSHIRE by four wickets.

DURHAM v SURREY

At Chester-le-Street, May 6. Surrey won by 66 runs. Toss: Durham.

The entertainment matched the drab weather; Durham's introduction of a party zone, complete with hot tub, fell as flat as their abject performance. There were 51 extras, 26 of them from wides, in Surrey's total, and 55 runs came in the last five overs, mainly off Harmison. Adam Hollioake picked up five easy wickets for career-best one-day figures as Durham hit out in desperation.

Surrey

M. A. Butcher b Phillips	27	J. D. Ratcliffe not out	25
A. D. Brown c Katich b Killeen	19	A. J. Tudor not out	5
†A. J. Stewart c Lewis b Harmison	41	B 5, l-b 14, w 26, n-b 6	51
G. P. Thorpe b Phillips	0		
*A. J. Hollioake b Killeen	17	1/36 2/71 3/85 (7 wkts, 45 overs) 230	
B. C. Hollioake st Speight b Collingwood	42	4/120 5/149	
I. J. Ward lbw b Killeen	3	6/157 7/219	

M. P. Bicknell and C. G. Greenidge did not bat.

Bowling: Betts 9–0–31–0; Killeen 9–2–37–3; Harmison 9–0–66–1; Phillips 9–0–31–2; Collingwood 9–0–46–1.

Durham

S. M. Katich lbw b Bicknell.	6	M. M. Betts c B. C. Hollioake	
†M. P. Speight c Bicknell b Tudor.	21	b A. J. Hollioake .	4
J. A. Daley lbw b Tudor	5	N. Killeen c Stewart b A. J. Hollioake . .	4
P. D. Collingwood run out	28	S. J. Harmison not out	1
*N. J. Speak b A. J. Hollioake	24	L-b 11, w 16, n-b 4	31
R. Robinson b Ratcliffe.	7		
J. J. B. Lewis b A. J. Hollioake.	16	1/30 2/38 3/42 4/99 5/114 (41.3 overs) 164
N. C. Phillips b A. J. Hollioake.	17	6/129 7/140 8/156 9/159

Bowling: Bicknell 7–2–15–1; Tudor 7–0–26–2; Greenidge 8–1–29–0; B. C. Hollioake 6–0–27–0; A. J. Hollioake 7.3–0–29–5; Ratcliffe 6–0–27–1.

Umpires: G. I. Burgess and T. E. Jesty.

DURHAM v GLAMORGAN

At Chester-le-Street, May 21. Glamorgan won by 15 runs (D/L method). Toss: Glamorgan.
Durham were four for two when the first shower brought a reduction to 38 overs a side. That came down by ten more following another interruption at 57 for two after 19 overs. Durham failed to push on in the remaining nine overs, whereas Glamorgan, chasing a target of 105, made sure they were ahead of requirements before further rain ended play. Glamorgan's first League win left Durham still to open their account.

Durham

S. M. Katich not out.	47	J. J. B. Lewis not out	14
N. Peng c Shaw b Thomas.	0	L-b 2, w 4.	6
P. D. Collingwood c Elliott b Parkin . . .	0		
*N. J. Speak lbw b Newell	24	1/2 2/4 3/64 (3 wkts, 28 overs) 91

†M. P. Speight, N. C. Phillips, J. Wood, M. M. Betts, I. D. Hunter and S. J. Harmison did not bat.

Bowling: Thomas 6–0–19–1; Parkin 6–0–17–1; Dale 6–0–23–0; Wharf 3–1–7–0; Croft 5–0–14–0; Newell 2–0–9–1.

Glamorgan

R. D. B. Croft b Betts.	13
M. T. G. Elliott not out	26
M. J. Powell b Harmison	5
*M. P. Maynard not out.	16
B 4, w 6	10

1/19 2/28 (2 wkts, 18 overs) 70

A. Dale, S. P. James, K. Newell, S. D. Thomas, †A. D. Shaw, O. T. Parkin and A. G. Wharf did not bat.

Bowling: Wood 5–0–21–0; Betts 5–1–14–1; Harmison 6–1–23–1; Phillips 1–0–7–0; Hunter 1–0–1–0.

Umpires: J. H. Hampshire and B. Leadbeater.

DURHAM v NOTTINGHAMSHIRE

At Chester-le-Street, May 28. Nottinghamshire won by three runs (D/L method). Toss: Durham.
Returning to the ground where he spent six seasons before released at the end of 1999, Morris made 73 in 82 deliveries, took two catches and offered an offensive gesture to a section of the crowd. A stoppage saw Durham's target revised to 194 off 43 overs, and they were always just ahead of the rate until Katich fell at 128, pulling a long-hop fiercely to Morris at mid-wicket. With 17 required from the last two overs, Franks claimed three more wickets to finish

with six for 27, his best figures in limited-overs cricket, and consign Durham to their fourth successive defeat.

Nottinghamshire

D. J. Bicknell c Katich b Harmison	5	P. J. Franks not out	6
G. E. Welton b Collingwood	32	D. J. Millns not out	8
*J. E. R. Gallian b Hunter	19	B 1, l-b 9, w 14, n-b 4	28
J. E. Morris c Hunter b Phillips	73		
C. M. Tolley run out	24	1/18 2/55 3/87 (6 wkts, 45 overs) 199	
†C. M. W. Read c Daley b Collingwood	4	4/164 5/182 6/183	

D. S. Lucas, A. J. Harris and R. D. Stemp did not bat.

Bowling: Wood 9–1–28–0; Harmison 9–0–38–1; Hunter 9–0–29–1; Collingwood 9–0–46–2; Phillips 9–0–48–1.

Durham

J. A. Daley c Gallian b Franks	18	N. C. Phillips b Franks	0
N. Peng c Morris b Stemp	36	I. D. Hunter not out	3
S. M. Katich c Morris b Franks	45		
*N. J. Speak b Stemp	10	L-b 11, w 8, n-b 2	21
J. J. B. Lewis c Harris b Franks	17		
P. D. Collingwood b Franks	28	1/32 2/93 3/122 (8 wkts, 43 overs) 190	
†M. P. Speight c Millns b Franks	3	4/128 5/167 6/178	
J. Wood not out	9	7/179 8/180	

S. J. Harmison did not bat.

Bowling: Millns 8–0–35–0; Lucas 8–1–38–0; Harris 9–0–44–0; Franks 9–0–27–6; Stemp 9–0–35–2.

Umpires: M. R. Benson and N. A. Mallender.

At Ilford, June 4. DURHAM beat ESSEX by seven runs.

At Basingstoke, June 18. DURHAM lost to HAMPSHIRE by 18 runs.

DURHAM v MIDDLESEX

At Chester-le-Street, June 25. Middlesex won by 53 runs. Toss: Middlesex.

Harmison made a surprise return from a ten-day lay-off with a suspected stress fracture of the shin to record his best one-day figures. But his opening five overs cost 33 runs and set Strauss and Ramprakash on their way to a century opening stand, an ultimate match-winner given that Middlesex lost nine wickets for 53 in their last ten overs. There was an even more spectacular spell by Laraman in Durham's reply, reduced to 43 overs by their own slow over-rate. Taken off with none for 20 after two overs, he returned to take the last six Durham wickets with his gentle swing bowling and record career-best figures.

Middlesex

A. J. Strauss c Speak b Phillips	90	A. W. Laraman c Speight b Harmison	0
M. R. Ramprakash c Speight b Killeen	46	J. P. Hewitt lbw b Phillips	2
O. A. Shah c Speight b Hunter	29	A. R. C. Fraser not out	6
S. J. Cook b Harmison	17	L-b 6, w 9, n-b 4	19
P. N. Weekes b Killeen	5		
*J. L. Langer run out	1	1/112 2/180 3/186 (44.2 overs) 233	
K. P. Dutch c Ali b Wood	17	4/200 5/202 6/209	
†D. Alleyne c Collingwood b Harmison	1	7/210 8/210 9/226	

Bowling: Harmison 9–1–45–3; Wood 9–2–44–1; Killeen 9–0–28–2; Hunter 6–0–42–1; Phillips 8.2–0–52–2; Collingwood 3–0–16–0.

Durham

P. D. Collingwood st Alleyne b Dutch . .	47	I. D. Hunter b Laraman	0
S. M. Ali c Langer b Fraser	13	N. Killeen lbw b Laraman	2
S. M. Katich c Alleyne b Weekes	7	S. J. Harmison c Alleyne b Laraman . . .	2
*N. J. Speak not out	53	L-b 7, w 4, n-b 6	17
J. J. B. Lewis run out	9		
†M. P. Speight c Cook b Laraman	17	1/26 2/75 3/75 (40.1 overs) 180
N. C. Phillips c Weekes b Laraman	6	4/87 5/128 6/148
J. Wood b Laraman	7	7/158 8/159 9/163

Bowling: Fraser 6–2–7–1; Hewitt 6–0–33–0; Cook 6–0–20–0; Laraman 8.1–0–51–6; Dutch 6–0–24–1; Weekes 8–0–38–1.

Umpires: D. J. Constant and V. A. Holder.

DURHAM v DERBYSHIRE

At Darlington, July 2. Durham won by 95 runs. Toss: Derbyshire.

Woeful batting resulted in Derbyshire's dismissal for 87, the lowest total against Durham in the League. Making his second appearance in the competition almost two years after his first, 19-year-old Davies took three for 15 despite bowling seven wides. Extras, in fact, were Derbyshire's top score. A third-wicket stand of 70 between Speight and Katich had helped Durham to a useful total in a match reduced to 37 overs a side by an hour's delay, and Speight went on to add three catches and two stumpings to his fifty.

Durham

P. D. Collingwood b Munton	0	M. J. Symington b Smith	16
S. M. Ali b Smith	24		
†M. P. Speight c Shah b Lungley	55	L-b 3, w 7, n-b 2	12
S. M. Katich not out	67		
*N. J. Speak b Dowman	3	1/0 2/47 3/117 (6 wkts, 37 overs) 182
J. J. B. Lewis lbw b Lungley	5	4/128 5/134 6/182

N. C. Phillips, I. D. Hunter, N. Killeen and A. M. Davies did not bat.

Bowling: Munton 7–0–41–1; Shah 8–1–21–0; Smith 7–1–41–2; Lungley 8–0–31–2; Lacey 3–0–24–0; Dowman 4–0–21–1.

Derbyshire

S. D. Stubbings c Speight b Davies	1	T. M. Smith b Phillips	4
M. J. Di Venuto run out	12	T. A. Munton not out	1
S. P. Titchard lbw b Hunter	8	K. Z. Shah st Speight b Phillips	2
M. P. Dowman b Davies	14	B 1, l-b 4, w 15	20
L. D. Sutton c Speight b Davies	1		
*†K. M. Krikken c Speight b Killeen . . .	2	1/9 2/18 3/38 (24 overs) 87
S. J. Lacey st Speight b Phillips	7	4/41 5/52 6/52
T. Lungley c Phillips b Symington	15	7/67 8/81 9/85

Bowling: Killeen 7–0–33–1; Davies 6–0–15–3; Hunter 6–1–15–1; Phillips 3–1–4–3; Symington 2–0–15–1.

Umpires: G. Sharp and P. Willey.

At Southgate, July 16. DURHAM lost to MIDDLESEX by one run.

At Birmingham, July 23. DURHAM beat WARWICKSHIRE by 50 runs.

At Cardiff, August 6. DURHAM lost to GLAMORGAN by three wickets.

DURHAM v WARWICKSHIRE

At Chester-le-Street, August 14. Warwickshire won by seven wickets. Toss: Warwickshire.

Two days after his century in the NatWest semi-final, Knight hit 75 in 100 balls to leave Warwickshire needing 32 from seven overs with seven wickets remaining. Put in, Durham had batted with the constant threat of rain, and were indebted to their visitors' profligate extras and Collingwood's skilful working of the gaps; he hit only three fours in his 73 not out. Warwickshire in reply took 19 off the first two overs and were never in trouble in much improved conditions.

Durham

M. A. Gough run out	9	J. Wood st Piper b Giles	9
*N. J. Speak b Richardson	6	N. C. Phillips not out	6
S. M. Katich c Knight b Sheikh	32	L-b 14, w 14, n-b 12	40
P. D. Collingwood not out	73		
J. J. B. Lewis b Richardson	18	1/14 2/25 3/97 (7 wkts, 45 overs) 202	
J. A. Daley b Giles	8	4/144 5/181	
†A. Pratt st Piper b Giles	1	6/183 7/195	

N. Killeen and I. D. Hunter did not bat.

Bowling: Welch 7–2–26–0; Richardson 9–0–43–2; Brown 9–1–36–0; Sheikh 9–1–32–1; Giles 9–0–40–3; Smith 2–0–11–0.

Warwickshire

N. V. Knight lbw b Phillips	75	T. L. Penney not out	11
A. Singh b Wood	14	B 1, l-b 5, w 10, n-b 4	20
A. F. Giles c Katich b Killeen	45		
D. P. Ostler not out	38	1/29 2/108 3/171 (3 wkts, 42.3 overs) 203	

G. Welch, D. R. Brown, *N. M. K. Smith, †K. J. Piper, M. A. Sheikh and A. Richardson did not bat.

Bowling: Wood 8–0–38–1; Killeen 9–0–43–1; Hunter 6–0–30–0; Collingwood 8.3–0–30–0; Phillips 8–0–39–1; Gough 3–0–17–0.

Umpires: V. A. Holder and D. R. Shepherd.

DURHAM v ESSEX

At Chester-le-Street, August 27. Essex won by one wicket (D/L method). Toss: Durham. County debut: W. I. Jefferson.

Durham announced that their captain, Speak, had been rested; next day, he was relieved of the captaincy. Katich and Collingwood were again their mainstays, but a total of 188 from 43 overs seemed inadequate, even when Essex's target was calculated as 167 in 33 because of two rain breaks. They were cruising at 92 for two in the 21st, thanks to newcomer Will Jefferson's 65-ball 50, but, with 31 needed off the last five overs, Killeen took three wickets. As he came on to bowl the final over, Essex still needed 12 with one wicket left. One legitimate ball later, they had won. Danny Law smashed a high full toss over square leg for eight (six, plus two for the no-ball) and another full toss, not as high, for four to the same boundary.

Durham

M. A. Gough lbw b Irani	18	M. J. Symington run out	1
N. Peng c Irani b Cowan	7	I. D. Hunter not out	2
S. M. Katich b Anderson	63		
P. D. Collingwood b Cowan	50	L-b 3, w 8, n-b 6	17
*J. J. B. Lewis not out	21		
R. Robinson b Grayson	3	1/21 2/69 3/140 (8 wkts, 43 overs) 188	
†A. Pratt run out	2	4/155 5/164 6/172	
N. C. Phillips b Cowan	4	7/178 8/180	

N. Killeen did not bat.

Bowling: Cowan 8–0–51–3; D. R. Law 7–0–31–0; Irani 8–2–16–1; McGarry 3–0–18–0; Anderson 8–0–31–1; Grayson 9–0–38–1.

Essex

S. G. Law c Collingwood b Killeen	1	A. P. Cowan b Killeen	0
W. I. Jefferson b Phillips	50	R. S. G. Anderson lbw b Hunter	1
G. R. Napier c Symington b Robinson	25	A. C. McGarry not out	0
*R. C. Irani c Killeen b Phillips	23	L-b 3, w 4, n-b 2	9
D. R. Law not out	27		
S. D. Peters c Robinson b Phillips	2	1/5 2/48 3/92 (9 wkts, 32.1 overs) 167	
A. P. Grayson b Killeen	19	4/106 5/110 6/140	
†J. S. Foster st Pratt b Killeen	10	7/152 8/152 9/153	

Bowling: Killeen 6.1–1–32–4; Symington 5–0–28–0; Hunter 5–0–23–1; Robinson 4–0–17–1; Phillips 7–0–34–3; Collingwood 5–0–30–0.

Umpires: B. Dudleston and R. A. White.

DURHAM v HAMPSHIRE

At Chester-le-Street, August 29 (day/night). Hampshire won by seven wickets. Toss: Durham.

Durham's dismal failure to set a competitive target was ruthlessly exploited by Hampshire, a place above them in the lower reaches of Division Two. Gough batted half the innings for his best one-day score, 36, after which acting-captain Lewis tried to gather some momentum with 40 not out off 55 balls, without hitting a boundary. A breezy 29 from Warne entertained the crowd of just over 4,000, and Smith's measured 88 saw Hampshire to victory with five overs to spare.

Durham

J. A. Daley b Mullally	18	M. J. Symington b Morris	0
M. A. Gough lbw b Warne	36	I. D. Hunter not out	14
S. M. Katich c and b Mascarenhas	7		
P. D. Collingwood st Aymes b Udal	11	B 1, l-b 5, w 9	15
*J. J. B. Lewis not out	40		
R. Robinson lbw b Udal	0	1/30 2/44 3/81 (8 wkts, 45 overs) 161	
†A. Pratt c Smith b Warne	3	4/89 5/94 6/105	
N. C. Phillips b Mascarenhas	17	7/138 8/142	

N. Killeen did not bat.

Bowling: Mascarenhas 9–1–31–2; Morris 9–0–52–1; Mullally 9–1–26–1; Warne 9–2–19–2; Udal 9–0–27–2.

Hampshire

*R. A. Smith not out	88	W. S. Kendall not out	20
G. W. White c Symington b Phillips	11	B 1, l-b 3, w 13	17
S. K. Warne c Phillips b Collingwood	29		
J. S. Laney lbw b Hunter	0	1/42 2/107 3/109 (3 wkts, 39.1 overs) 165	

L. R. Prittipaul, A. D. Mascarenhas, S. D. Udal, †A. N. Aymes, A. C. Morris and A. D. Mullally did not bat.

Bowling: Killeen 8–2–26–0; Symington 6–0–25–0; Phillips 9–0–40–1; Hunter 7–0–25–1; Collingwood 7–1–32–1; Robinson 2.1–0–13–0.

Umpires: J. F. Steele and R. A. White.

At The Oval, September 10. DURHAM beat SURREY by 59 runs.

At Derby, September 17. DURHAM beat DERBYSHIRE by one run.

ESSEX

At Chelmsford, April 30. ESSEX beat MIDDLESEX by 60 runs.

ESSEX v NOTTINGHAMSHIRE

At Chelmsford, May 7. Nottinghamshire won by three runs. Toss: Essex.

Essex looked to be coasting to victory at 121 for two. But Hussain was caught behind, cutting, in the 29th over and the innings disintegrated to a combination of poor shots and suicidal run-outs. Tolley's 38 from 33 deliveries, building on good work by Johnson and Morris, had proved decisive when Nottinghamshire batted, but a side strain prevented him bowling his full allocation of overs.

Nottinghamshire

D. J. Bicknell c Peters b D. R. Law	15	P. J. Franks not out		23
U. Afzaal run out	15	†C. M. W. Read not out		6
*J. E. R. Gallian c Hussain b D. R. Law	4	L-b 3, w 14		17
P. Johnson c Cowan b Grayson	37			—
J. E. Morris st Hyam b Grayson	27	1/33 2/43 3/44	(7 wkts, 42 overs)	190
C. M. Tolley c D. R. Law b Irani	38	4/111 5/116		
G. R. Haywood lbw b Grayson	8	6/142 7/174		

D. S. Lucas and R. D. Stemp did not bat.

Bowling: Irani 9-0-34-1; Ilott 5-0-26-0; D. R. Law 6-0-21-2; Cowan 9-1-39-0; Mason 7-0-44-0; Grayson 6-1-23-3.

Essex

N. Hussain c Read b Haywood	55	†B. J. Hyam c sub b Afzaal		5
P. J. Prichard c Read b Franks	9	A. P. Cowan run out		3
S. G. Law c Morris b Haywood	39	M. C. Ilott not out		2
*R. C. Irani not out	42	B 1, l-b 5, w 5, n-b 2		13
A. P. Grayson c Read b Afzaal	2			—
S. D. Peters run out	15	1/23 2/94 3/121	(9 wkts, 42 overs)	187
D. R. Law c Franks b Stemp	1	4/126 5/154 6/160		
T. J. Mason c Read b Franks	1	7/166 8/171 9/182		

Bowling: Franks 9-0-40-2; Lucas 8-0-34-0; Tolley 3.1-1-8-0; Stemp 8-0-35-1; Haywood 8.5-0-34-2; Afzaal 5-0-30-2.

Umpires: M. R. Benson and B. Leadbeater.

At The Oval, May 29. SURREY v ESSEX. No result (abandoned).

ESSEX v DURHAM

At Ilford, June 4. Durham won by seven runs. Toss: Essex.

Durham broke their duck at the fifth attempt, though Essex had looked the likelier winners when they reached three figures in the 24th over with eight wickets remaining. But once Stuart Law's luck ran out – he was dropped three times before Collingwood took a sharp return catch – Durham clawed their way back with a career-best performance from 20-year-old Hunter. Earlier, Katich and Lewis had revived the visitors with a century stand in 25 overs that included just five boundaries.

Durham

J. A. Daley c Hyam b Irani	0	J. Wood c Napier b Cowan	0
†M. P. Speight c Prichard b Cowan	16	M. M. Betts not out	2
S. M. Katich c Robinson b Grayson	61	L-b 3, w 7	10
*N. J. Speak b D. R. Law	0		
J. J. B. Lewis c S. G. Law b Napier	60	1/0 2/24 3/25	(7 wkts, 45 overs) 182
P. D. Collingwood not out	26	4/133 5/154	
I. D. Hunter c Irani b Cowan	7	6/172 7/172	

N. C. Phillips and S. J. Harmison did not bat.

Bowling: Irani 9–1–37–1; Cowan 9–2–24–3; D. R. Law 6–0–15–1; Grayson 9–0–34–1; Napier 6–0–32–1; Mason 6–0–37–0.

Essex

P. J. Prichard c Speight b Hunter	14	†B. J. Hyam c Betts b Collingwood	0
S. G. Law c and b Collingwood	63	A. P. Cowan run out	1
S. D. Peters c Collingwood b Harmison	19	T. J. Mason not out	1
*R. C. Irani c Katich b Hunter	23	L-b 5, w 2	7
A. P. Grayson lbw b Hunter	32		
D. D. J. Robinson b Hunter	4	1/53 2/86 3/108	(44.5 overs) 175
D. R. Law run out	2	4/128 5/137 6/141	
G. R. Napier c Hunter b Collingwood	9	7/158 8/159 9/161	

Bowling: Wood 4–0–12–0; Harmison 9–0–32–1; Hunter 8.5–1–29–4; Betts 9–0–40–0; Collingwood 9–0–29–3; Phillips 5–0–28–0.

Umpires: N. G. Cowley and J. F. Steele.

At Cardiff, June 13 (day/night). ESSEX lost to GLAMORGAN by 20 runs.

At Nottingham, June 24. ESSEX lost to NOTTINGHAMSHIRE by four wickets.

At Birmingham, June 25. ESSEX beat WARWICKSHIRE by 24 runs.

ESSEX v MIDDLESEX

At Chelmsford, July 2. Essex won by seven wickets. Toss: Middlesex.

Stuart Law's unbeaten 104 from 96 balls, containing a straight six off Fraser and ten fours, his sixth century in the League, earned Essex their first home win in the competition since August 1998. It was, for all that, their second win of the season at Chelmsford against Middlesex, whose *home* fixture was played here in April. Without a major input from Langer, the Middlesex innings had revolved around Roseberry's 72 in two and a half hours. The inadequacy of their total was starkly apparent as Law and Grayson hit 73 in nine overs to ring up victory with eight unused.

Middlesex

A. J. Strauss c Mason b Ilott	1	A. W. Laraman not out	8
M. A. Roseberry b D. R. Law	72	J. P. Hewitt run out	3
*J. L. Langer b Irani	7	A. R. C. Fraser not out	5
P. N. Weekes st Hyam b Grayson	28	L-b 14, w 15, n-b 2	31
O. A. Shah c and b Grayson	10		
†D. Alleyne run out	33	1/17 2/35 3/95	(9 wkts, 45 overs) 213
K. P. Dutch b Grayson	1	4/117 5/167 6/171	
S. J. Cook run out	14	7/186 8/198 9/203	

Bowling: Irani 8–1–32–1; Ilott 8–0–36–1; Cowan 9–0–44–0; D. R. Law 7–0–24–1; Grayson 9–0–31–3; Mason 4–0–32–0.

Essex

P. J. Prichard c Alleyne b Fraser	18	A. P. Grayson not out	36
S. G. Law not out	104	B 1, l-b 3, w 4, n-b 2	10
*R. C. Irani st Alleyne b Dutch	21		
S. D. Peters lbw b Shah	25	1/44 2/93 3/141 (3 wkts, 37 overs)	214

G. R. Napier, D. R. Law, †B. J. Hyam, A. P. Cowan, T. J. Mason and M. C. Ilott did not bat.

Bowling: Fraser 7–2–19–1; Hewitt 5–0–27–0; Cook 4–0–36–0; Dutch 8–1–51–1; Laraman 5–0–36–0; Weekes 4–0–20–0; Shah 4–0–21–1.

Umpires: J. W. Holder and D. R. Shepherd.

ESSEX v DERBYSHIRE

At Chelmsford, July 23. Essex won by six runs. Toss: Essex.

Derbyshire's gallant effort narrowly failed when Mason held two fine boundary catches, just as Munton and Shah looked like winning it for them. Shah had blitzed 20 from his previous eight deliveries. Hussain, with 47 in 87 balls, provided the cornerstone of the Essex innings, adding 80 in 19 overs with Peters, and the tail helped Grayson get the rate up by taking 68 from the last ten. Derbyshire's defeat was their eighth in nine games.

Essex

P. J. Prichard c Krikken b Munton	4	G. R. Napier b Cork	8
S. G. Law b Munton	24	A. P. Cowan c Pyemont b Shah	7
N. Hussain c Sutton b Lungley	47	L-b 15, w 5, n-b 2	22
*R. C. Irani c Cork b Munton	1		
S. D. Peters c Munton b Dean	38	1/9 2/30 3/34 (8 wkts, 45 overs)	203
A. P. Grayson not out	37	4/114 5/141 6/178	
D. R. Law b Cork	15	7/192 8/203	

†B. J. Hyam and T. J. Mason did not bat.

Bowling: Dean 9–0–41–1; Munton 9–2–24–3; Cork 9–0–33–2; Lungley 9–1–47–1; Shah 9–0–43–1.

Derbyshire

L. D. Sutton lbw b D. R. Law	17	T. A. Munton c Mason b Grayson	18
M. J. Di Venuto run out	18	K. Z. Shah c Mason b Grayson	20
S. D. Stubbings run out	24	K. J. Dean not out	6
J. P. Pyemont run out	34	B 1, l-b 8, w 8, n-b 2	14
*D. G. Cork b Cowan	24		
†K. M. Krikken c and b D. R. Law	1	1/29 2/47 3/89 (44.5 overs)	197
S. J. Lacey c Hussain b D. R. Law	6	4/122 5/123 6/126	
T. Lungley run out	15	7/136 8/165 9/188	

Bowling: Cowan 8.5–2–35–1; Irani 9–4–20–0; D. R. Law 9–0–41–3; Mason 3–0–18–0; Grayson 9–0–53–2; Napier 6–0–26–0.

Umpires: A. Clarkson and A. A. Jones.

At Southampton, July 30. ESSEX lost to HAMPSHIRE by six wickets.

At Derby, August 13. DERBYSHIRE v ESSEX. No result (D/L method).

ESSEX v HAMPSHIRE

At Colchester, August 20. Hampshire won by six wickets. Toss: Essex.

Mullally, returning his best one-day figures of the season, cut Essex down as their middle-order batsmen struggled to make an impact after early setbacks. Danny Law and Bishop smashed 34 in four lively overs at the end, but Kenway and Smith countered with an opening stand of 120 in 24. Laney chipped in with 30 in 27 balls and Hampshire powered to victory with eight overs to spare.

Essex

P. J. Prichard c Kenway b Mascarenhas .	5	T. J. Mason c White b Mullally	7
S. G. Law b Mascarenhas	8	J. E. Bishop not out	16
G. R. Napier c Mascarenhas b Mullally .	11		
*R. C. Irani b Tremlett	24	B 1, l-b 4, w 4	9
S. D. Peters c and b Udal	21		
A. P. Grayson c Udal b Mullally	37	1/13 2/23 3/28 (8 wkts, 45 overs) 184
†J. S. Foster c Kenway b Mullally	12	4/70 5/82 6/124
D. R. Law not out	34	7/124 8/150

A. C. McGarry did not bat.

Bowling: Morris 9–0–33–0; Mascarenhas 9–1–35–2; Mullally 9–1–30–4; Tremlett 9–0–29–1; Udal 9–1–52–1.

Hampshire

†D. A. Kenway c Foster b Mason	56	L. R. Prittipaul not out	1
*R. A. Smith c Foster b Grayson	62	L-b 4, w 9	13
G. W. White lbw b Bishop	18		
J. S. Laney c Mason b Irani	30	1/120 2/136 (4 wkts, 36.3 overs) 188
W. S. Kendall not out	8	3/164 4/181

A. D. Mascarenhas, A. C. Morris, S. D. Udal, C. M. Tremlett and A. D. Mullally did not bat.

Bowling: Irani 8.3–0–34–1; D. R. Law 8–1–36–0; McGarry 4–0–19–0; Mason 8–0–42–1; Bishop 4–0–29–1; Grayson 4–0–24–1.

Umpires: G. I. Burgess and B. Dudleston.

ESSEX v SURREY

At Colchester, August 23 (day/night). Essex won by 23 runs. Toss: Essex.

A capacity crowd, approaching 6,000 for the first competitive floodlit match in Essex, watched the home side inflict the season's first defeat on Surrey. A win for them would have clinched the Division Two title. Hussain and Stuart Law put on 161 in 32 overs, Law setting the pace with 92 in 94 balls (one six, 11 fours). Hussain, 57 in 102, continued his good League form, but the next eight batsmen managed only 41 between them. Surrey's reply never consolidated and, needing 63 from ten overs, they lost their last six batsmen for 39 inside nine.

Essex

N. Hussain c Stewart b Hollioake	57	A. P. Cowan c Shahid b Hollioake	3
S. G. Law c Hollioake b Salisbury	92	T. J. Mason not out	8
G. R. Napier c Bicknell b Salisbury	2		
*R. C. Irani c Bicknell b Hollioake	8	B 5, l-b 4, w 3, n-b 4	16
S. D. Peters c Brown b Salisbury	7		
A. P. Grayson c Stewart b Salisbury . . .	0	1/161 2/164 3/168 (8 wkts, 45 overs) 206
†J. S. Foster not out	11	4/180 5/180 6/180
D. R. Law c Thorpe b Hollioake	2	7/187 8/197

A. C. McGarry did not bat.

Bowling: Bicknell 7–0–27–0; Tudor 6–0–44–0; Saqlain Mushtaq 9–1–34–0; Ratcliffe 5–0–22–0; Salisbury 9–2–32–4; Hollioake 9–0–38–4.

Surrey

A. D. Brown b McGarry	27	M. P. Bicknell not out 15
†A. J. Stewart c D. R. Law b Cowan	13	I. D. K. Salisbury run out 0
N. Shahid c Foster b Irani	14	Saqlain Mushtaq c D. R. Law b Cowan . 4
G. P. Thorpe c Mason b Grayson	19	L-b 9, w 7, n-b 2 18
I. J. Ward b D. R. Law	25	
*A. J. Hollioake c Napier b D. R. Law..	36	1/28 2/58 3/58 (43.3 overs) 183
J. D. Ratcliffe c Cowan b McGarry	9	4/95 5/149 6/154
A. J. Tudor c Irani b D. R. Law	3	7/161 8/164 9/164

Bowling: Cowan 8.3–0–38–2; D. R. Law 8–1–45–3; Irani 8–1–23–1; McGarry 8–2–20–2; Mason 6–0–29–0; Grayson 5–0–19–1.

Umpires: J. H. Hampshire and D. R. Shepherd.

At Chester-le-Street, August 27. ESSEX beat DURHAM by one wicket (D/L method).

ESSEX v GLAMORGAN

At Southend, September 3. Essex won by four runs. Toss: Essex.

Four wickets in the final over denied Glamorgan the six runs they needed and brought Essex a thrilling victory. After Darren Thomas was run out from the first delivery, trying to keep James on strike, Cowan bowled Cosker, Wallace and Parkin with his third, fifth and sixth balls. Mason's magnificent diving catch on the mid-wicket boundary, getting rid of Maynard, had set off a chain reaction that cost Glamorgan their last eight wickets for 31 inside five overs, and left James stranded on 88 from 101 balls. He hit just one four. Essex's Jefferson, in contrast, hit 11 in his 65 and set the tone for the subsequent run-feast as he and another 20-year-old, Napier, put on 95.

Essex

S. G. Law b S. D. Thomas	8	†J. S. Foster not out 22
W. I. Jefferson b Dale	65	
G. R. Napier c Maynard b Cosker	52	B 1, l-b 13, w 9, n-b 2 25
*R. C. Irani c James b Croft	33	
S. D. Peters not out	73	1/14 2/109 3/147 (5 wkts, 45 overs) 289
A. P. Grayson b Cosker	11	4/189 5/215

D. R. Law, A. P. Cowan, T. J. Mason and R. S. G. Anderson did not bat.

Bowling: S. D. Thomas 9–0–56–1; Parkin 7–0–67–0; Dale 6–0–31–1; Newell 5–0–28–0; Croft 9–0–50–1; Cosker 9–0–43–2.

Glamorgan

K. Newell c Grayson b Irani	78	D. A. Cosker b Cowan 0
I. J. Thomas c Foster b Cowan	21	†M. A. Wallace b Cowan............ 0
S. P. James not out	88	O. T. Parkin b Cowan 0
*M. P. Maynard c Mason b Grayson	61	L-b 8, w 10, n-b 2........... 20
A. Dale run out	1	
M. J. Powell st Foster b Grayson	4	1/48 2/130 3/254 (45 overs) 285
R. D. B. Croft b Irani	8	4/266 5/271 6/280
S. D. Thomas run out	0	7/285 8/285 9/285

Bowling: Cowan 9–0–44–4; D. R. Law 8–0–53–0; Anderson 7–0–51–0; Irani 9–0–48–2; Grayson 9–0–58–2; Mason 3–0–23–0.

Umpires: M. J. Harris and K. E. Palmer.

ESSEX v WARWICKSHIRE

At Chelmsford, September 17. Warwickshire won by six wickets. Toss: Essex.

Warwickshire won with nearly ten overs in hand to confirm third place in Division Two and so gain promotion. The day before, Essex had beaten them to win promotion in the Championship. Smith sealed the win with a six off Mason to finish with 75 from 106 balls; earlier, he took three wickets as Essex partially recovered from losing half their side for 33. Grayson and Danny Law set the visitors something of a challenge, even if it never really tested them.

Essex

D. D. J. Robinson lbw b Brown	5	A. P. Cowan c Piper b Smith	0
W. I. Jefferson b Powell	2	T. J. Mason not out	5
G. R. Napier c Piper b Dagnall	12	R. S. G. Anderson b Richardson	1
*R. C. Irani c Penney b Dagnall	0	L-b 3, w 10	13
S. D. Peters c Ostler b Brown	3		
A. P. Grayson b Richardson	64	1/4 2/22 3/22 (41.2 overs) 152	
†J. S. Foster c Piper b Smith	13	4/22 5/33 6/53	
D. R. Law c Singh b Smith	34	7/131 8/132 9/150	

Bowling: Powell 8–0–34–1; Dagnall 9–2–32–2; Brown 8–2–22–2; Richardson 7.2–0–34–2; Smith 9–0–27–3.

Warwickshire

M. A. Wagh c Foster b Cowan	3	T. L. Penney not out	26
A. Singh c Jefferson b Cowan	17	L-b 2, w 8, n-b 2	12
*N. M. K. Smith not out	75		
D. P. Ostler c Foster b Irani	12	1/20 2/32 (4 wkts, 35.1 overs) 153	
D. L. Hemp c Cowan b Irani	8	3/64 4/88	

M. J. Powell, D. R. Brown, †K. J. Piper, C. E. Dagnall and A. Richardson did not bat.

Bowling: Cowan 7–1–18–2; Law 5–0–36–0; Anderson 8–2–27–0; Irani 7–0–19–2; Grayson 4–0–23–0; Mason 4.1–0–28–0.

Umpires: B. Dudleston and J. H. Hampshire.

GLAMORGAN

GLAMORGAN v SURREY

At Cardiff, April 30. Surrey won by ten runs. Toss: Surrey.

Elliott withdrew from the Glamorgan team ten minutes before the start after his two-year-old son was taken to hospital, and Wharf, a bowler, had to open their innings as they were without a reserve batsman. Butcher and Thorpe put on 91 for Surrey's second wicket, but the next seven added only 69. Glamorgan's reply faded when Maynard was caught off a Salisbury long-hop. Needing 22 from the last three overs, with three wickets in hand, they conceded to Adam Hollioake.

Surrey

M. A. Butcher b Wharf	47	I. D. K. Salisbury b Thomas	2
A. D. Brown c and b Parkin	16	A. J. Tudor not out	0
G. P. Thorpe b Parkin	61		
†J. N. Batty c Powell b Croft	8	B 1, l-b 5, w 6	12
*A. J. Hollioake c and b Watkin	16		
B. C. Hollioake b Croft	1	1/25 2/116 3/135 (9 wkts, 45 overs) 185	
I. J. Ward c Maynard b Parkin	10	4/144 5/147 6/167	
M. P. Bicknell run out	12	7/177 8/185 9/185	

I. E. Bishop did not bat.

Bowling: Watkin 9–0–38–1; Parkin 9–0–39–3; Thomas 9–0–38–1; Wharf 9–0–36–1; Croft 9–0–28–2.

Glamorgan

R. D. B. Croft c Salisbury b Bicknell...	3	†A. D. Shaw lbw b A. J. Hollioake	3	
A. G. Wharf b Bicknell............	4	O. T. Parkin b A. J. Hollioake........	1	
M. J. Powell c Butcher b A. J. Hollioake	30	S. L. Watkin not out.............	0	
*M. P. Maynard c Batty b Salisbury ...	46	B 1, l-b 5, w 12, n-b 3......	21	
A. Dale c A. J. Hollioake b Salisbury ..	19			
S. P. James b A. J. Hollioake	22	1/8 2/13 3/72	(44.1 overs) 175	
K. Newell c Thorpe b Bicknell	6	4/103 5/130 6/145		
S. D. Thomas b Tudor.............	20	7/149 8/167 9/175		

Bowling: Bicknell 9–2–28–3; Tudor 6–1–0–25–1; Bishop 3–0–26–0; B. C. Hollioake 9–0–19–0; A. J. Hollioake 8.1–0–39–4; Salisbury 9–0–32–2.

Umpires: A. A. Jones and R. Julian.

At Birmingham, May 7. GLAMORGAN lost to WARWICKSHIRE by nine wickets.

At Chester-le-Street, May 21. GLAMORGAN beat DURHAM by 15 runs (D/L method).

GLAMORGAN v DERBYSHIRE

At Cardiff, May 29. Glamorgan won by six wickets. Toss: Glamorgan.

The previous night's celebrations, following their Benson and Hedges semi-final win over Surrey, did not inhibit Glamorgan as they overcame Derbyshire's challenge with two overs remaining. Their reply was built around Elliott, who shared a partnership of 92 in 22 overs with Maynard but ran himself out eight short of victory. For Derbyshire, put in on a slow pitch, nearly all their batsmen made decent starts but failed to consolidate.

Derbyshire

M. E. Cassar b Wharf.............	29	†K. M. Krikken run out	1	
M. J. Di Venuto b Parkin...........	25			
M. P. Dowman st Shaw b Croft.......	25	B 8, l-b 6, w 12..........	26	
S. P. Titchard c James b Dale........	33			
R. J. Bailey c Thomas b Dale........	39	1/48 2/75 3/107	(7 wkts, 45 overs) 185	
*D. G. Cork c Maynard b Parkin......	2	4/170 5/178		
S. D. Stubbings not out...........	5	6/183 7/185		

S. J. Lacey, P. Aldred and T. A. Munton did not bat.

Bowling: Thomas 9–0–38–0; Parkin 9–1–40–2; Wharf 9–1–39–1; Dale 9–1–24–2; Croft 9–0–30–1.

Glamorgan

R. D. B. Croft c Dowman b Aldred	19	S. P. James not out...............	5	
M. T. G. Elliott run out............	88	L-b 3, w 7..............	10	
M. J. Powell c Krikken b Aldred	1			
*M. P. Maynard c Aldred b Munton....	40	1/35 2/38	(4 wkts, 43 overs) 186	
A. Dale not out.................	23	3/130 4/178		

K. Newell, †A. D. Shaw, S. D. Thomas, A. G. Wharf and O. T. Parkin did not bat.

Bowling: Cork 9–0–38–0; Munton 9–2–28–1; Aldred 9–1–36–2; Cassar 4–0–22–0; Lacey 7–0–37–0; Bailey 4–0–18–0; Dowman 1–0–4–0.

Umpires: N. G. Cowley and B. Dudleston.

At Lord's, June 4. GLAMORGAN tied with MIDDLESEX.

GLAMORGAN v ESSEX

At Cardiff, June 13 (day/night). Glamorgan won by 20 runs. Toss: Glamorgan.

The sizeable crowd who turned out for Glamorgan's first home game under lights were rewarded by their third win of the season. Newell, replacing Croft at the top of the batting, struck seven fours while putting on 59 in 11 overs with Elliott, who then added 98 with Maynard. The last five wickets going for 17 did not prevent Glamorgan setting a useful challenge. Essex looked in contention at 113 for two, but they never overcame losing the next six wickets for 48.

Glamorgan

K. Newell c Peters b Ilott	38
M. T. G. Elliott c Grayson b Cowan . . .	94
M. J. Powell c Mason b Ilott	2
*M. P. Maynard c Napier b Mason	50
A. Dale c and b Mason.	0
S. P. James c Ilott b Law.	7
S. D. Thomas c and b Cowan	11
†A. D. Shaw b Cowan.	3
A. G. Wharf c Grayson b Cowan	2
D. A. Cosker not out.	4
O. T. Parkin lbw b Grayson	0
L-b 5, w 4.	9

1/59 2/69 3/167   (44.2 overs) 220
4/168 5/185 6/203
7/213 8/213 9/220

Bowling: Ilott 7–1–31–2; Irani 4–1–23–0; Cowan 9–1–39–4; Law 7–0–42–1; Mason 9–0–43–2; Grayson 8.2–0–37–1.

Essex

P. J. Prichard b Thomas	21
G. R. Napier lbw b Parkin	11
D. D. J. Robinson c Elliott b Newell . . .	51
*R. C. Irani lbw b Cosker	40
A. P. Grayson c Elliott b Newell	8
S. D. Peters b Cosker	23
D. R. Law lbw b Cosker	0
†B. J. Hyam c Napier b Newell	0
A. P. Cowan b Thomas	24
T. J. Mason not out.	5
M. C. Ilott c Maynard b Thomas.	10
L-b 5, w 2.	7

1/35 2/35 3/113   (42.4 overs) 200
4/127 5/147 6/147
7/150 8/161 9/188

Bowling: Thomas 8.4–2–30–3; Parkin 8–0–47–1; Wharf 4–0–21–0; Dale 4–0–24–0; Cosker 9–0–36–3; Newell 9–1–37–3.

Umpires: M. J. Harris and N. A. Mallender.

GLAMORGAN v HAMPSHIRE

At Cardiff, June 24. Glamorgan won by 51 runs. Toss: Glamorgan.

Hampshire fared better than in their Benson and Hedges quarter-final here the previous month, but never threatened to win after slipping to 91 for seven chasing 237. Thomas, having started with four wides in his first over, set up the slide when he dismissed Stephenson and Mascarenhas in three balls. Maynard and Powell had provided the high points in Glamorgan's innings, with each striking Warne for successive sixes. One of Maynard's straight blows disrupted a hockey tournament outside the ground. Glamorgan's fifth successive League game without defeat – the tie against Middlesex interrupted a winning sequence – lifted them into third place in Division Two.

Glamorgan

K. Newell c White b Udal	43	†A. D. Shaw run out 5
M. T. G. Elliott c and b Mascarenhas	0	R. D. B. Croft not out 1
S. P. James c Aymes b Mullally	32	B 1, l-b 3, w 3 7
*M. P. Maynard c Warne b Mascarenhas	67	
A. Dale c White b Udal	17	1/6 2/63 3/107 (7 wkts, 45 overs) 236
M. J. Powell not out	43	4/155 5/169
S. D. Thomas c Udal b Warne	21	6/208 7/215

A. G. Wharf and O. T. Parkin did not bat.

Bowling: Mascarenhas 8–0–43–2; Francis 5–1–15–0; Mullally 9–1–39–1; Stephenson 6–0–29–0; Warne 8–0–58–1; Udal 9–0–48–2.

Hampshire

G. W. White b Dale	24	†A. N. Aymes c Elliott b Newell 17
J. P. Stephenson c Shaw b Thomas	5	A. D. Mullally b Parkin 6
A. D. Mascarenhas c Shaw b Thomas	0	S. R. G. Francis not out 8
*R. A. Smith c Croft b Parkin	9	L-b 11, w 11, n-b 4 26
W. S. Kendall b Croft	28	
J. S. Laney b Wharf	7	1/20 2/20 3/38 (9 wkts, 45 overs) 185
S. K. Warne c Dale b Croft	4	4/71 5/83 6/88
S. D. Udal not out	51	7/91 8/142 9/164

Bowling: Thomas 9–1–47–2; Parkin 9–2–32–2; Wharf 9–1–29–1; Dale 5–1–19–1; Croft 9–1–22–2; Newell 4–0–25–1.

Umpires: J. H. Harris and K. E. Palmer.

GLAMORGAN v WARWICKSHIRE

At Swansea, July 2. Tied (D/L method). Toss: Glamorgan.

Glamorgan's second tie of the season rested on Dale preventing Smith taking a single off the last ball. In the event, he bowled him. Nine from Parkin's last over had cut the visitors' requirement to seven, but Dale's accuracy prevailed. After Newell's dismissal, providing Piper with his 100th League catch and Giddins with his 100th wicket, Elliott and James set Glamorgan up with a century stand; rain prevented the later batsmen from capitalising on it. Warwickshire's target was set at 202 from 38 overs. At 134 for six, this looked out of reach, but Powell and Smith took the game to the wire.

Glamorgan

K. Newell c Piper b Giddins	0	M. J. Powell not out 11
M. T. G. Elliott not out	84	L-b 1, w 4, n-b 2 7
S. P. James c Piper b Welch	53	
*M. P. Maynard c Sheikh b Giles	11	1/3 2/104 (4 wkts, 38 overs) 167
A. Dale c Smith b Welch	1	3/129 4/133

†A. D. Shaw, S. D. Thomas, A. G. Wharf, R. D. B. Croft and O. T. Parkin did not bat.

Bowling: Giddins 7–1–26–1; Welch 9–0–35–2; Sheikh 7–1–31–0; Brown 5–0–24–0; Giles 9–0–43–1; Smith 1–0–7–0.

Warwickshire

G. Welch c Dale b Parkin	16	*N. M. K. Smith b Dale 27
A. Singh c Shaw b Thomas	3	
A. F. Giles c Maynard b Dale	40	B 1, l-b 5, w 7, n-b 2 15
D. P. Ostler c Wharf b Thomas	14	
D. L. Hemp c Parkin b Wharf	12	1/13 2/30 3/54 (7 wkts, 38 overs) 201
D. R. Brown c and b Newell	35	4/85 5/117
M. J. Powell not out	39	6/134 7/201

M. A. Sheikh, †K. J. Piper and E. S. H. Giddins did not bat.

Bowling: Parkin 8–0–41–1; Thomas 8–0–48–2; Wharf 8–0–38–1; Croft 5–0–28–0; Dale 6–0–20–2; Newell 3–0–20–1.

Umpires: M. R. Benson and R. A. White.

At The Oval, July 16. GLAMORGAN lost to SURREY by 67 runs.

GLAMORGAN v DURHAM

At Cardiff, August 6. Glamorgan won by three wickets. Toss: Durham.

With Glamorgan needing two to win, Harrison edged the penultimate ball to the third-man boundary. At the start of the chase, Elliott had retired hurt with a back spasm after three balls, James was lbw first ball, and later Maynard had to bat with a runner. No one took on Phillips's off-spin (13 from nine overs) but Dale and Powell set up the victory with a partnership of 91. Dale's straight six off Wood, with two overs left, eased Welsh nerves. Durham's innings was built on similar foundations, with Katich and Collingwood adding 92 in 17 overs.

Durham

N. Peng c Parkin b Wharf	3	†A. Pratt not out		0
*N. J. Speak st Maynard b Cosker	30			
S. M. Katich c Maynard b Thomas	70	B 3, l-b 3, w 1, n-b 6		13
P. D. Collingwood lbw b Dale	66			
J. J. B. Lewis run out	16	1/8 2/66 3/158	(5 wkts, 45 overs)	202
M. A. Gough not out	4	4/193 5/201		

N. C. Phillips, N. Killeen, J. Wood and I. D. Hunter did not bat.

Bowling: Wharf 7–0–27–1; Parkin 9–1–26–0; Thomas 9–0–48–1; Harrison 5–1–20–0; Cosker 9–1–42–1; Dale 6–0–33–1.

Glamorgan

M. T. G. Elliott c Pratt b Hunter	14	A. G. Wharf run out		5
K. Newell c Wood b Phillips	15	D. S. Harrison not out		5
S. P. James lbw b Killeen	0	L-b 3, w 1, n-b 2		6
*†M. P. Maynard c Phillips b Killeen	37			
A. Dale not out	73	1/4 2/37 3/72	(7 wkts, 44.5 overs)	205
M. J. Powell c Gough b Katich	48	4/163 5/180		
S. D. Thomas c Collingwood b Wood	2	6/183 7/198		

D. A. Cosker and O. T. Parkin did not bat.

Elliott, when 4, retired hurt at 4-0 and resumed at 163.

Bowling: Killeen 9–1–34–2; Wood 9–1–42–1; Phillips 9–2–13–1; Hunter 9–0–47–1; Gough 2–0–13–0; Collingwood 4.5–0–28–0; Katich 2–0–25–1.

Umpires: J. H. Harris and R. A. White.

At Southampton, August 14. GLAMORGAN beat HAMPSHIRE by five runs.

GLAMORGAN v NOTTINGHAMSHIRE

At Colwyn Bay, August 20. Nottinghamshire won by eight wickets (D/L method). Toss: Glamorgan.
Reiffel removed Glamorgan's first three batsmen in nine balls, but Maynard and Dale added 54 before two breaks for rain reduced the match to 26 overs. When Dale and Powell smashed 30 from the three overs remaining after the resumption, Nottinghamshire were set a target of 131. Although Watkin, playing his first League game since May, took two wickets in successive overs, Nottinghamshire had started well enough; Bicknell and Johnson's unbroken 95 put paid to Glamorgan's promotion prospects.

Glamorgan

K. Newell c Afzaal b Reiffel	9	M. J. Powell not out		20
M. T. G. Elliott c Tolley b Reiffel	4	L-b 1, w 6		7
S. P. James c Read b Reiffel	0			
*†M. P. Maynard c Read b Franks	36	1/15 2/16	(4 wkts, 26 overs)	104
A. Dale not out	28	3/19 4/73		

R. D. B. Croft, S. D. Thomas, A. G. Wharf, S. L. Watkin and O. T. Parkin did not bat.

Bowling: Reiffel 7–3–8–3; Harris 5–0–29–0; Franks 7–1–20–1; Tolley 5–0–29–0; Stemp 2–0–17–0.

Nottinghamshire

D. J. Bicknell not out	59
*J. E. R. Gallian c Maynard b Watkin	17
J. E. Morris b Watkin	0
P. Johnson not out	49
L-b 4, w 2	6

1/32 2/36   (2 wkts, 21.3 overs) 131

U. Afzaal, †C. M. W. Read, C. M. Tolley, P. J. Franks, P. R. Reiffel, A. J. Harris and R. D. Stemp did not bat.

Bowling: Wharf 3–0–19–0; Parkin 1–0–15–0; Watkin 5–0–28–2; Thomas 3–0–21–0; Dale 5–0–18–0; Croft 4.3–0–26–0.

Umpires: J. W. Holder and J. W. Lloyds.

At Derby, August 27. GLAMORGAN beat DERBYSHIRE by one wicket.

At Southend, September 3. GLAMORGAN lost to ESSEX by four runs.

At Nottingham, September 10. GLAMORGAN lost to NOTTINGHAMSHIRE by three runs.

GLAMORGAN v MIDDLESEX

At Cardiff, September 17. Middlesex won by six wickets. Toss: Glamorgan. First-team debut: J. W. M. Dalrymple.
Joyce's outside edge to the third-man boundary off the last ball meant Glamorgan's third successive defeat and, looking ahead, a tie against Derbyshire, instead of a non-first-class county, in the third round of the 2001 successor to the NatWest Trophy. Powell continued his recent good form to rescue Glamorgan from 42 for four, but Laraman returned to account for him and finished with a career-best six for 42. Langer carried on from where he left off in the Championship game. Middlesex needed ten from the last over and, although Langer lost strike, having to score three off the last ball did not discompose Joyce.

Glamorgan

I. J. Thomas b Cook	20	D. A. Cosker c Strauss b Laraman	0
K. Newell c Joyce b Laraman	14	S. L. Watkin b Laraman	2
S. P. James lbw b Laraman	0	O. T. Parkin not out	5
*M. P. Maynard c Langer b Fraser	0	L-b 4, w 2, n-b 2	8
A. Dale st Nash b Dalrymple	32		
M. J. Powell c Langer b Laraman	86	1/27 2/27 3/28 (9 wkts, 42 overs) 191	
R. D. B. Croft c Cook b Laraman	16	4/42 5/129 6/176	
†M. A. Wallace not out	8	7/176 8/178 9/185	

Bowling: Fraser 7–0–18–1; Laraman 9–1–42–6; Cook 5–0–24–1; Hutton 6–0–36–0; Dalrymple 7–1–37–1; Ramprakash 8–0–30–0.

Middlesex

O. A. Shah c Wallace b Watkin	21	E. C. Joyce not out	13
A. J. Strauss lbw b Cosker	40	L-b 6, w 2	8
*J. L. Langer not out	76		
M. R. Ramprakash c Croft b Dale	34	1/35 2/109 (4 wkts, 42 overs) 193	
A. W. Laraman b Parkin	1	3/169 4/171	

†D. C. Nash, B. L. Hutton, J. W. M. Dalrymple, A. R. C. Fraser and S. J. Cook did not bat.

Bowling: Parkin 9–1–35–1; Watkin 9–1–29–1; Newell 3–0–13–0; Dale 8–0–40–1; Cosker 5–0–31–1; Croft 8–0–39–0.

Umpires: G. I. Burgess and D. J. Constant.

HAMPSHIRE

HAMPSHIRE v WARWICKSHIRE

At Southampton, May 1. Warwickshire won by 97 runs. Toss: Hampshire.

A serious injury to Donald overshadowed Warne's home debut before a crowd of some 3,000. The car park was full an hour and a half before the start. Donald, having effectively won the match earlier with a hostile spell of three in eight balls, broke two ribs when he stepped back into advertising boards in an attempt to catch Warne off Smith at long-on. He was taken from the field by stretcher and then by ambulance to hospital. Warne did eventually perish to a catch at long-on.

Warwickshire

N. V. Knight c and b Udal	46	M. A. Sheikh st Kenway b Warne	36
G. Welch run out	39	†K. J. Piper not out	1
*N. M. K. Smith c Kendall b Mascarenhas	1	B 4, l-b 9	13
D. P. Ostler c Kenway b Mullally	9		
D. L. Hemp c Mullally b Udal	13	1/70 2/74 3/98 (8 wkts, 45 overs) 215	
T. L. Penney c Kenway b Warne	51	4/98 5/129 6/153	
M. J. Powell b Mascarenhas	6	7/213 8/215	

A. A. Donald and E. S. H. Giddins did not bat.

Bowling: Stephenson 9–0–46–0; Mullally 9–1–38–1; Mascarenhas 9–1–40–2; Warne 9–1–31–2; Udal 9–0–47–2.

Hampshire

J. S. Laney c Penney b Giddins	13	S. K. Warne c Welch b Powell	7
†D. A. Kenway run out	12	S. D. Udal not out	5
*R. A. Smith b Donald	12	A. D. Mullally lbw b Powell	1
G. W. White c Piper b Donald	9	L-b 6, w 8	14
W. S. Kendall b Sheikh	0		
J. P. Stephenson c Piper b Donald	0	1/26 2/32 3/52　(35.5 overs)	118
A. D. Mascarenhas c and b Smith	20	4/57 5/58 6/58	
L. Savident b Smith	25	7/94 8/107 9/114	

Bowling: Giddins 6–1–26–1; Welch 7–1–18–0; Donald 6–2–9–3; Sheikh 7–1–27–1; Smith 6–0–19–2; Powell 3.5–0–13–2.

Umpires: D. J. Constant and B. Dudleston.

At Lord's, May 7. HAMPSHIRE lost to MIDDLESEX by four wickets.

At Birmingham, May 21. HAMPSHIRE lost to WARWICKSHIRE by five wickets.

At The Oval, May 30 (day/night). HAMPSHIRE lost to SURREY by seven wickets.

At Nottingham, June 11. HAMPSHIRE lost to NOTTINGHAMSHIRE by eight wickets.

HAMPSHIRE v DURHAM

At Basingstoke, June 18. Hampshire won by 18 runs. Toss: Hampshire.

More than 2,500 spectators crammed into May's Bounty on a brilliant summer's day for the final county match scheduled there. They saw Stephenson go past 4,000 League runs and – for a record fifth time in the competition – bat through a completed innings without being dismissed. Durham were well placed at 95 without loss in the 21st over, but were unable to capitalise on Collingwood and Ali's brisk start, slumping to 126 for seven. Lewis's 55 not out in 53 balls could not prevent Hampshire's first League win of the season.

Hampshire

G. W. White c Katich b Wood	0	J. S. Laney b Wood	27
J. P. Stephenson not out	83	S. K. Warne not out	18
A. D. Mascarenhas lbw b Killeen	11	B 4, l-b 6, w 3, n-b 4	17
*R. A. Smith c Collingwood b Phillips	43		
W. S. Kendall c Symington		1/2 2/20 3/99　(5 wkts, 45 overs)	222
b Collingwood	23	4/153 5/188	

S. D. Udal, †A. N. Aymes, S. R. G. Francis and A. D. Mullally did not bat.

Bowling: Killeen 9–1–36–1; Wood 9–0–42–2; Collingwood 9–0–34–1; Hunter 8–0–47–0; Phillips 7–1–30–1; Katich 3–0–23–0.

Durham

P. D. Collingwood run out	51	J. Wood b Mullally	8
S. M. Ali st Aymes b Warne	36	N. C. Phillips run out	3
S. M. Katich c Aymes b Mullally	8	N. Killeen b Mascarenhas	21
†M. P. Speight lbw b Udal	0	L-b 3, w 12	15
*N. J. Speak lbw b Warne	0		
J. J. B. Lewis not out	55	1/95 2/100 3/100	(44 overs) 204
M. J. Symington c Warne b Mullally	5	4/101 5/116 6/122	
I. D. Hunter c Aymes b Mullally	2	7/126 8/158 9/172	

Bowling: Mullally 9–1–40–4; Mascarenhas 8–0–54–1; Francis 9–2–41–0; Warne 9–1–40–2; Udal 9–1–26–1.

Umpires: A. Clarkson and T. E. Jesty.

At Cardiff, June 24. HAMPSHIRE lost to GLAMORGAN by 51 runs.

HAMPSHIRE v SURREY

At Southampton, June 27. Surrey won by 43 runs. Toss: Surrey.

Good bowling and poor batting from both sides contributed to a low-scoring match on a pitch marked above average by the umpires. Surrey could hardly have expected to defend such a small total, which owed everything to Ben Hollioake's top score of 37 and the late-order partnerships he nurtured. But they had reckoned without Hampshire's self-destructive tendency and, from the moment Bicknell removed White and Mascarenhas in his first over, there was no serious challenge.

Surrey

M. A. Butcher c Smith b Mascarenhas	21	A. J. Tudor lbw b Warne	0
A. D. Brown lbw b Mascarenhas	0	I. D. K. Salisbury b Udal	13
I. J. Ward c Warne b Mullally	14	Saqlain Mushtaq not out	7
*A. J. Hollioake c Aymes b Mullally	3	L-b 2, w 4	6
B. C. Hollioake st Aymes b Mascarenhas	37		
J. D. Ratcliffe run out	9	1/3 2/40 3/40	(38 overs) 116
†J. N. Batty c Aymes b Warne	6	4/44 5/63 6/73	
M. P. Bicknell c Aymes b Udal	0	7/74 8/75 9/97	

Bowling: Francis 4–0–23–0; Mascarenhas 8–1–21–3; Mullally 9–1–20–2; Warne 9–2–32–2; Udal 8–1–18–2.

Hampshire

G. W. White b Bicknell	0	S. D. Udal c B. C. Hollioake	
J. P. Stephenson b Salisbury	23	b Saqlain Mushtaq	1
A. D. Mascarenhas c Tudor b Bicknell	4	A. D. Mullally lbw b Saqlain Mushtaq	0
*R. A. Smith b Tudor	5	S. R. G. Francis not out	1
D. A. Kenway lbw b Bicknell	2		
J. S. Laney c Saqlain Mushtaq		L-b 2, w 5	7
b Salisbury	29		
S. K. Warne lbw b Saqlain Mushtaq	1	1/0 2/5 3/15 4/18 5/57	(32.4 overs) 73
†A. N. Aymes run out	0	6/60 7/60 8/67 9/67	

Bowling: Bicknell 9–4–14–3; Tudor 7–2–7–1; Saqlain Mushtaq 9–4–12–3; Salisbury 7.4–0–38–2.

Umpires: M. J. Harris and B. Leadbeater.

HAMPSHIRE v MIDDLESEX

At Portsmouth, July 23. Middlesex won by four wickets. Toss: Middlesex.

A crowd of 2,500 witnessed the United Services Ground's last rites, but there was little for home supporters to cheer. Middlesex won more easily than a last-over victory would suggest. Smith pulled a hamstring just as he was showing glimpses of his best form, and was immediately run out when his runner, White, attempted a risky third. Hampshire's total never looked enough once Roseberry and Ramprakash put on 82 for Middlesex's fourth wicket.

Hampshire

G. W. White c Langer b Dutch	27	†A. N. Aymes not out	13
J. P. Stephenson c Alleyne b Laraman	32	S. J. Renshaw run out	0
*R. A. Smith run out	42	P. J. Hartley not out	1
J. S. Laney c and b Weekes	28	L-b 3, w 3	6
A. D. Mascarenhas c Langer b Johnson	30		
W. S. Kendall c Cook b Weekes	2	1/58 2/68 3/121 (9 wkts, 45 overs) 190	
S. K. Warne c Laraman b Johnson	7	4/134 5/139 6/158	
S. D. Udal c Ramprakash b Fraser	2	7/168 8/183 9/184	

Bowling: Fraser 9–1–39–1; Johnson 9–0–42–2; Laraman 9–0–26–1; Cook 5–0–26–0; Dutch 9–0–36–1; Weekes 4–0–18–2.

Middlesex

A. J. Strauss c sub b Hartley	9	P. N. Weekes not out	7
†D. Alleyne c Aymes b Hartley	33	K. P. Dutch not out	2
M. A. Roseberry c Stephenson b Udal	54	L-b 3, w 11, n-b 6	20
R. L. Johnson c sub b Renshaw	0		
M. R. Ramprakash c Warne b Hartley	46	1/36 2/51 3/52 (6 wkts, 44.2 overs) 192	
*J. L. Langer c sub b Warne	21	4/134 5/183 6/185	

A. W. Laraman, S. J. Cook and A. R. C. Fraser did not bat.

Bowling: Renshaw 6–0–26–1; Hartley 9–1–41–3; Mascarenhas 7–0–35–0; Stephenson 5–0–22–0; Udal 9–0–35–1; Warne 8.2–0–30–1.

Umpires: J. H. Hampshire and J. H. Harris.

HAMPSHIRE v ESSEX

At Southampton, July 30. Hampshire won by six wickets. Toss: Hampshire.

Having set Essex back with a superb one-handed slip catch to dismiss Stuart Law, Warne put Hampshire on track for their first win of the season at Northlands Road – in any competition – with bowling of high quality. Only Peters blocked his path, finally stumped off the last delivery. Though Warne was subsequently out first ball, it did not matter: Hampshire always had wickets and overs to spare.

Essex

P. J. Prichard lbw b Mullally	10	T. J. Mason c Laney b Mullally	1
S. G. Law c Warne b Hartley	9	†B. J. Hyam not out	16
N. Hussain lbw b Warne	34		
*R. C. Irani b Stephenson	7	L-b 3, w 5	8
S. D. Peters st Aymes b Warne	51		
A. P. Grayson c Aymes b Warne	8	1/12 2/34 3/53 (9 wkts, 45 overs) 158	
D. R. Law b Warne	8	4/78 5/92 6/102	
A. P. Cowan lbw b Udal	6	7/115 8/131 9/158	

M. C. Ilott did not bat.

Bowling: Hartley 7–3–20–1; Mascarenhas 7–2–18–0; Stephenson 5–0–15–1; Mullally 9–1–34–2; Warne 9–1–32–4; Udal 8–0–36–1.

Hampshire

D. A. Kenway c Irani b Ilott	26	A. D. Mascarenhas not out	26
J. P. Stephenson b D. R. Law	19	L-b 13, w 7	20
S. K. Warne b D. R. Law	0		
J. S. Laney b Grayson	25	1/46 2/46	(4 wkts, 42.2 overs) 162
W. S. Kendall not out	46	3/54 4/89	

L. R. Prittipaul, *S. D. Udal, †A. N. Aymes, P. J. Hartley and A. D. Mullally did not bat.

Bowling: Cowan 7.2–1–34–0; Irani 7–2–13–0; D. R. Law 8–2–24–2; Ilott 5–2–19–1; Grayson 9–1–33–1; Mason 6–0–26–0.

Umpires: R. Julian and J. F. Steele.

At Derby, August 6. HAMPSHIRE beat DERBYSHIRE by 36 runs.

HAMPSHIRE v GLAMORGAN

At Southampton, August 14. Glamorgan won by five runs. Toss: Glamorgan.

Hampshire's last pair put on 53 in three overs in a brave but fruitless charge for victory. Tremlett smashed three sixes in his 15-ball 30 and Kendall (eight fours, two sixes) matched him for ferocity, ending with 85 in 77 balls. Newell, dropped before scoring, and Elliott had set Glamorgan up with 126 for the first wicket, James punched a run-a-ball fifty, and 264 looked beyond Hampshire until the final derring-do. For a moment, their NatWest semi-final defeat two days earlier was forgotten.

Glamorgan

K. Newell c Laney b Udal	64	R. D. B. Croft not out	16
M. T. G. Elliott c White b Tremlett	68		
*M. P. Maynard run out	24	L-b 5, w 6, n-b 2	13
S. P. James not out	50		
A. Dale c Kendall b Morris	21	1/126 2/153 3/169	(5 wkts, 45 overs) 263
M. J. Powell lbw b Mascarenhas	7	4/215 5/230	

S. D. Thomas, A. G. Wharf, †M. A. Wallace and O. T. Parkin did not bat.

Bowling: Morris 9–0–63–1; Mascarenhas 9–1–49–1; Tremlett 9–0–45–1; Mullally 9–0–56–0; Udal 9–0–45–1.

Hampshire

D. A. Kenway c Wallace b Thomas	47	A. C. Morris c Wallace b Thomas	0
*R. A. Smith c Maynard b Parkin	20	A. D. Mullally c and b Parkin	7
G. W. White run out	1	C. M. Tremlett not out	30
J. S. Laney c and b Thomas	17	L-b 3, w 5	8
W. S. Kendall not out	85		
A. D. Mascarenhas b Croft	33	1/45 2/50 3/87	(9 wkts, 45 overs) 258
†A. N. Aymes st Wallace b Croft	3	4/92 5/173 6/179	
S. D. Udal b Thomas	7	7/196 8/196 9/205	

Bowling: Wharf 9–0–53–0; Parkin 9–0–59–2; Thomas 9–0–42–4; Dale 9–0–65–0; Croft 9–0–36–2.

Umpires: M. J. Kitchen and R. A. White.

At Colchester, August 20. HAMPSHIRE beat ESSEX by six wickets.

At Chester-le-Street, August 29 (day/night). HAMPSHIRE beat DURHAM by seven wickets.

HAMPSHIRE v DERBYSHIRE

At Southampton, September 10. Derbyshire won by four runs. Toss: Derbyshire.

Hampshire, six down, needed nine runs off the last over. But Cassar bowled Aymes with the third ball, then top-scorer Kenway and Tremlett with the last two, to gain Derbyshire only their second League win of the season. Earlier, Warne had also taken three wickets in four balls, after Sutton and Pyemont had rescued Derbyshire with a stand of 99.

Derbyshire

M. E. Cassar c Aymes b Mascarenhas	13	P. Aldred b Warne		0
M. J. Di Venuto lbw b Hartley	10	*T. A. Munton st Aymes b Hartley		0
R. J. Bailey c Tremlett b Mascarenhas	0	K. J. Dean not out		6
M. P. Dowman b Mascarenhas	4	B 1, l-b 12, w 13		26
S. D. Stubbings c Aymes b Warne	33			
†L. D. Sutton not out	53	1/17 2/18 3/24	(9 wkts, 45 overs)	195
J. P. Pyemont b Warne	50	4/37 5/85 6/184		
S. J. Lacey lbw b Warne	0	7/184 8/184 9/185		

Bowling: Hartley 9–1–36–2; Mascarenhas 9–2–40–3; Tremlett 9–0–45–0; Warne 9–2–23–4; Udal 9–0–38–0.

Hampshire

S. K. Warne lbw b Munton	0	S. D. Udal not out		1
*R. A. Smith c Sutton b Dean	14	C. T. Tremlett b Cassar		0
D. A. Kenway b Cassar	90			
J. S. Laney c Pyemont b Cassar	22	L-b 7, w 4		11
W. S. Kendall run out	1			
L. R. Prittipaul b Dowman	19	1/0 2/30 3/79	(9 wkts, 45 overs)	191
A. D. Mascarenhas c Di Venuto b Aldred	26	4/87 5/129 6/178		
†A. N. Aymes b Cassar	7	7/190 8/191 9/191		

P. J. Hartley did not bat.

Bowling: Munton 9–0–27–1; Dean 8–0–45–1; Cassar 8–0–29–4; Aldred 9–1–32–1; Lacey 6–0–24–0; Dowman 5–0–27–1.

Umpires: V. A. Holder and A. A. Jones.

HAMPSHIRE v NOTTINGHAMSHIRE

At Southampton, September 17. Nottinghamshire won by three runs. Toss: Hampshire.

A Royal Marines bugler played "Sunset" on the players' balcony as chairman Brian Ford ceremoniously lowered the Hampshire flag at the end of 115 years at Northlands Road. Warne threw his kit to eager hands below, and there were tears among a 2,500 crowd. For Hampshire to celebrate the occasion with a win, Udal had needed to hit the final ball, from Tolley, for four; typical of their season, he missed it.

Nottinghamshire

D. J. Bicknell b Morris	8	C. M. Tolley c Prittipaul b Warne		24
M. N. Bowen b Morris	31	P. J. Franks run out		0
*J. E. R. Gallian b Morris	0	L-b 1, w 16		17
U. Afzaal not out	95			
P. Johnson c Morris b Udal	43	1/25 2/25 3/50	(8 wkts, 45 overs)	234
G. E. Welton run out	7	4/144 5/156 6/170		
†C. M. W. Read c Aymes b Tremlett	9	7/225 8/234		

A. J. Harris and R. D. Stemp did not bat.

Bowling: Mascarenhas 9–2–52–0; Morris 9–0–59–3; Tremlett 9–0–46–1; Warne 9–0–49–1; Udal 9–0–27–1.

Hampshire

D. A. Kenway c Afzaal b Harris	17	S. D. Udal not out	7
*R. A. Smith b Bowen	0	A. C. Morris not out	16
S. K. Warne c Afzaal b Bowen	29		
J. S. Laney c Tolley b Franks	9	B 1, l-b 7, w 8, n-b 2	18
W. S. Kendall run out	63		
L. R. Prittipaul c Welton b Stemp	61	1/1 2/38 3/57	(8 wkts, 45 overs) 231
A. D. Mascarenhas b Tolley	7	4/69 5/196 6/197	
†A. N. Aymes c Bicknell b Tolley	4	7/208 8/208	

C. T. Tremlett did not bat.

Bowling: Harris 7–2–29–1; Bowen 9–0–49–2; Franks 9–0–40–1; Tolley 9–0–45–2; Stemp 9–0–44–1; Afzaal 2–0–16–0.

Umpires: J. W. Holder and T. E. Jesty.

MIDDLESEX

MIDDLESEX v ESSEX

At Chelmsford, April 30. Essex won by 60 runs. Toss: Middlesex.

Middlesex's *home* tie against Essex had been scheduled for Chelmsford because it was known that no pitch would be available at Lord's. While it might be open to debate whether or not Essex's victory constituted their first home win in the League since August 1998, there was no disputing their superiority in a match reduced to 23 overs each. Hussain's 60 from 52 deliveries, containing three sixes and five fours, provided the backbone to the Essex innings on a pitch that favoured seam. Fraser dismissed him in a spell of three for three in eight balls. Middlesex collapsed alarmingly in reply, losing seven wickets for only 16 inside eight overs.

Essex

P. J. Prichard c Langer b Fraser	8	A. P. Cowan c Weekes b Fraser	1
S. G. Law c Langer b Laraman	10	†B. J. Hyam c Roseberry b Johnson	6
N. Hussain c Laraman b Fraser	60	M. C. Ilott not out	0
*R. C. Irani run out	6	W 4	4
D. R. Law c Ramprakash b Weekes	37		
S. D. Peters c Weston b Fraser	0	1/11 2/28 3/59	(22.4 overs) 143
A. P. Grayson c Hewitt b Weekes	1	4/124 5/125 6/125	
T. J. Mason c Weekes b Johnson	10	7/128 8/134 9/141	

Bowling: Fraser 5–0–18–4; Johnson 4.4–0–31–2; Laraman 5–1–16–1; Hewitt 4–0–31–0; Weekes 3–0–28–2; Shah 1–0–19–0.

Middlesex

O. A. Shah c Hyam b Ilott	3	J. P. Hewitt st Hyam b Mason	12
M. R. Ramprakash c Hussain b Irani	10	R. L. Johnson c Peters b Mason	2
A. W. Laraman c Hyam b Ilott	0	A. R. C. Fraser not out	6
*J. L. Langer lbw b Irani	0	L-b 10, w 12, n-b 2	24
R. M. S. Weston lbw b Ilott	0		
M. A. Roseberry b Cowan	1	1/9 2/9 3/12	(9 wkts, 23 overs) 83
P. N. Weekes c Hyam b Irani	0	4/14 5/14 6/14	
†D. C. Nash not out	25	7/16 8/69 9/75	

Bowling: Irani 5–2–10–3; Ilott 5–1–13–3; Cowan 3–1–5–1; D. R. Law 4–0–21–0; S. G. Law 3–0–10–0; Mason 3–0–14–2.

Umpires: M. J. Harris and R. Palmer.

At Derby, May 1. MIDDLESEX beat DERBYSHIRE by 71 runs.

MIDDLESEX v HAMPSHIRE

At Lord's, May 7. Middlesex won by four wickets. Toss: Hampshire.

Only Smith batted with any conviction in the face of accurate, aggressive Middlesex bowling that had Hampshire 17 for three in four overs. Not that the home side's batting was much more convincing. Had Hampshire been sharper in the field, the result could just as easily have gone the other way.

Hampshire

J. S. Laney c Nash b Johnson	0	S. D. Udal st Nash b Weekes	14
L. Savident b Johnson	2	P. J. Hartley b Fraser	14
†D. A. Kenway lbw b Fraser	13	A. D. Mullally not out	1
*R. A. Smith b Johnson	71	L-b 1, w 5, n-b 2	8
G. W. White c sub b Cook	7		
J. P. Stephenson b Cook	3	1/1 2/13 3/17 (44.5 overs)	147
A. D. Mascarenhas c and b Weekes	4	4/45 5/60 6/80	
S. K. Warne b Laraman	10	7/103 8/125 9/141	

Bowling: Johnson 9–1–37–3; Fraser 8.5–2–24–2; Cook 9–2–22–2; Laraman 9–0–32–1; Weekes 9–0–31–2.

Middlesex

M. A. Roseberry lbw b Mascarenhas	15	S. J. Cook lbw b Warne	0
M. R. Ramprakash c Udal b Mascarenhas	8	A. W. Laraman not out	7
*J. L. Langer c Kenway b Mullally	20	L-b 4, w 10, n-b 2	16
O. A. Shah c Stephenson b Warne	39		
R. M. S. Weston c Mascarenhas b Warne	16	1/27 2/27 3/55 (6 wkts, 43.2 overs)	148
P. N. Weekes not out	27	4/99 5/125 6/125	

†D. C. Nash, R. L. Johnson and A. R. C. Fraser did not bat.

Bowling: Hartley 8–0–40–0; Mascarenhas 8–1–32–2; Mullally 9–0–16–1; Udal 6.2–0–16–0; Warne 9–2–33–3; Stephenson 3–1–7–0.

Umpires: M. J. Kitchen and R. A. White.

At The Oval, May 21. SURREY v MIDDLESEX. No result (abandoned).

MIDDLESEX v GLAMORGAN

At Lord's, June 4. Tied. Toss: Middlesex.

Having twice squandered a strong position, Middlesex were delighted to salvage the tie when Weekes ran out Wharf as he dived to make the winning single off the last ball. At 124 for one in the 32nd over, the home side looked on course for a big total, only to lose eight wickets while 58 came off 81 balls. Crucially, however, Glamorgan were docked an over from their innings. They were 77 for six after 22 overs, but Middlesex let them escape. Acting-captain James and Shaw added 62 off 88 balls to set up the League season's third tie to date.

Middlesex

M. A. Roseberry run out	41	R. L. Johnson b Dale	1
*J. L. Langer c Elliott b Thomas	16	C. J. Batt not out	3
P. N. Weekes c Parkin b Dale	43	A. R. C. Fraser not out	2
O. A. Shah lbw b Wharf	13	L-b 13, w 16, n-b 4	33
A. J. Strauss c Shaw b Thomas	19		
R. M. S. Weston b Parkin	8	1/36 2/124 3/126 (9 wkts, 45 overs) 185
†D. Alleyne b Parkin	6	4/152 5/160 6/174
S. J. Cook run out	0	7/177 8/180 9/182

Bowling: Thomas 9–1–24–2; Parkin 9–0–40–2; Wharf 9–1–44–1; Dale 9–0–27–2; Croft 9–0–37–0.

Glamorgan

R. D. B. Croft b Batt	18	S. D. Thomas c Batt b Johnson	13
M. T. G. Elliott lbw b Batt	22	A. G. Wharf run out	5
M. J. Powell lbw b Fraser	16		
K. Newell c Alleyne b Johnson	3	B 4, l-b 7, w 10, n-b 2	23
A. Dale c Weekes b Cook	7		
*S. P. James not out	54	1/28 2/45 3/49 (9 wkts, 44 overs) 185
W. L. Law lbw b Fraser	0	4/69 5/77 6/77
†A. D. Shaw run out	24	7/139 8/162 9/185

O. T. Parkin did not bat.

Bowling: Fraser 9–0–55–2; Batt 9–0–23–2; Johnson 9–0–23–2; Cook 9–1–25–1; Shah 3–0–14–0; Weekes 5–0–34–0.

Umpires: B. Leadbeater and A. G. T. Whitehead.

MIDDLESEX v DERBYSHIRE

At Lord's, June 18. Derbyshire won by 15 runs. Toss: Derbyshire.

Winning the toss for the first time in the current League programme, Cork elected to bat, came in at the fall of the first wicket, and hit a responsible 64 off 111 balls, with eight fours. It was the basis of both a respectable total and Derbyshire's first win in five attempts. Middlesex were 53 for four in the 20th over before Langer faced a ball, and at 77 for six his decision to bat at No. 5 was decidedly questionable. When he was ninth out, bowled by Cork for 56, they still needed 18 from 14 balls – a task too far for Fraser with Batt.

Derbyshire

M. E. Cassar c Cook b Johnson	19	P. Aldred not out	8
M. J. Di Venuto c Alleyne b Batt	8	L. J. Wharton not out	0
*D. G. Cork lbw b Johnson	64		
M. P. Dowman c Alleyne b Fraser	12	B 5, l-b 2, w 4	11
R. J. Bailey st Alleyne b Dutch	18		
†K. M. Krikken lbw b Cook	5	1/14 2/28 3/69 (8 wkts, 45 overs) 186
S. P. Titchard run out	1	4/105 5/114 6/115
S. J. Lacey c Fraser b Weekes	40	7/170 8/186

T. A. Munton did not bat.

Bowling: Batt 4–0–27–1; Fraser 7–0–35–1; Johnson 9–2–39–2; Dutch 9–2–23–1; Cook 9–0–20–1; Weekes 7–0–35–1.

Middlesex

O. A. Shah c Aldred b Cassar	9	R. L. Johnson c Cork b Lacey	14
A. J. Strauss b Munton	27	A. R. C. Fraser c Lacey b Cassar	7
K. P. Dutch st Krikken b Aldred	1	C. J. Batt not out	1
P. N. Weekes lbw b Aldred	10	B 4, l-b 5, w 11	20
*J. L. Langer b Cork	56		
R. M. S. Weston st Krikken b Aldred	4	1/38 2/39 3/53 (43.5 overs) 171	
†D. Alleyne c and b Cassar	0	4/53 5/75 6/77	
S. J. Cook c Cork b Lacey	22	7/127 8/149 9/169	

Bowling: Cork 9–2–26–1; Munton 9–2–18–1; Aldred 8–1–34–3; Cassar 6.5–0–33–3; Lacey 7–0–32–2; Wharton 4–0–19–0.

Umpires: J. W. Lloyds and R. A. White.

At Chester-le-Street, June 25. MIDDLESEX beat DURHAM by 53 runs.

At Chelmsford, July 2. MIDDLESEX lost to ESSEX by seven wickets.

MIDDLESEX v DURHAM

At Southgate, July 16. Middlesex won by one run. Toss: Middlesex.

As so often in the League, a dull game was saved by a close finish. Strauss top-scored for Middlesex with 43 in 58 balls, but Killeen's three for two in eight balls meant they failed to bat out their overs. Katich, whose unbeaten 70 was his one-day best in England, added 61 in 15 overs with Collingwood and 37 for the last wicket with Killeen, for whom three off Cook's final delivery proved too much.

Middlesex

O. A. Shah c Katich b Killeen	13	S. J. Cook b Killeen	1
A. J. Strauss b Phillips	43	R. L. Johnson not out	3
*J. L. Langer c Speight b Hunter	16	A. R. C. Fraser c Collingwood b Killeen	1
M. R. Ramprakash c Wood b Collingwood	20	B 3, l-b 14, w 1	18
P. N. Weekes lbw b Phillips	31		
K. P. Dutch c Collingwood b Phillips	8	1/32 2/80 3/80 (43.4 overs) 173	
†D. Alleyne c Wood b Katich	5	4/132 5/148 6/149	
B. L. Hutton c Ali b Killeen	14	7/157 8/169 9/170	

Bowling: Wood 8–0–30–0; Hunter 7–0–33–1; Killeen 7.4–0–18–4; Phillips 9–1–29–3; Katich 9–1–31–1; Collingwood 3–0–15–1.

Durham

J. Wood c Langer b Johnson	9	N. C. Phillips run out	0
S. M. Ali b Johnson	14	I. D. Hunter c Ramprakash b Dutch	2
S. M. Katich not out	70	N. Killeen not out	13
M. J. Symington c Alleyne b Fraser	1	L-b 11, w 4	15
P. D. Collingwood b Weekes	36		
*N. J. Speak b Cook	11	1/25 2/30 3/32 (9 wkts, 45 overs) 172	
J. J. B. Lewis b Cook	1	4/93 5/121 6/126	
†M. P. Speight lbw b Cook	0	7/126 8/126 9/135	

Bowling: Johnson 7–0–26–2; Fraser 7–2–24–1; Cook 9–1–31–3; Dutch 6–1–18–1; Weekes 7–1–36–1; Ramprakash 9–2–26–0.

Umpires: B. Dudleston and R. Julian.

At Portsmouth, July 23. MIDDLESEX beat HAMPSHIRE by four wickets.

MIDDLESEX v SURREY

At Lord's, August 6. Surrey won by five wickets. Toss: Middlesex.

Except for Ramprakash, this was another mediocre batting display by Middlesex, with Bicknell starting the rot when he took his 200th League wicket. All Surrey had to do was concentrate on the basic disciplines. Anchored by Shahid's 50 and propelled by Adam Hollioake's 43-ball 47, they made light of recording their seventh successive League win.

Middlesex

A. J. Strauss lbw b Bicknell	0	S. J. Cook not out	28
*J. L. Langer c Brown b Tudor	8	R. L. Johnson b B. C. Hollioake	4
M. R. Ramprakash b B. C. Hollioake . . .	53	A. W. Laraman not out	3
P. N. Weekes b Saqlain Mushtaq	16	L-b 7, w 17	24
R. M. S. Weston st Batty			
b Saqlain Mushtaq .	0	1/1 2/35 3/65 (8 wkts, 45 overs) 167
†D. Alleyne lbw b Ratcliffe	2	4/67 5/83 6/118
B. L. Hutton c Brown b A. J. Hollioake .	29	7/156 8/163

A. R. C. Fraser did not bat.

Bowling: Bicknell 9–0–24–1; Tudor 7–2–24–1; Saqlain Mushtaq 9–1–45–2; Ratcliffe 9–1–21–1; B. C. Hollioake 7–0–32–2; A. J. Hollioake 4–0–14–1.

Surrey

M. A. Butcher run out	17	J. D. Ratcliffe not out	4
I. J. Ward b Laraman	10		
N. Shahid not out	50	L-b 8, w 9	17
A. D. Brown c Langer b Cook	23		
*A. J. Hollioake st Alleyne b Weekes . . .	47	1/32 2/32 3/77 (5 wkts, 39.1 overs) 170
B. C. Hollioake c Strauss b Weekes	2	4/152 5/158

†J. N. Batty, M. P. Bicknell, A. J. Tudor and Saqlain Mushtaq did not bat.

Bowling: Fraser 9–1–27–0; Laraman 9–1–34–1; Cook 7–0–31–1; Johnson 6.1–1–23–0; Weekes 6–1–25–2; Hutton 2–0–22–0.

Umpires: J. H. Hampshire and G. Sharp.

At Nottingham, August 13. NOTTINGHAMSHIRE v MIDDLESEX. No result (D/L method).

At Birmingham, August 16 (day/night). MIDDLESEX beat WARWICKSHIRE by 15 runs.

MIDDLESEX v NOTTINGHAMSHIRE

At Richmond, August 28. Middlesex won by 23 runs. Toss: Nottinghamshire.

Heavy showers delayed the start of Middlesex's first game at Old Deer Park until there was time for only 21 overs each. There was some fierce hitting by Ramprakash, with four fours and two sixes towards 53 in 31 balls, and Joyce (two sixes). Ramprakash hit Franks for six twos in the final over. From 18 for two in the fifth, Nottinghamshire were always struggling. Although defeat did not affect their second place in the table, it guaranteed Surrey the Division Two title (with two games to play) and let Middlesex move up briefly to third in the promotion challenge.

Middlesex

A. J. Strauss c Read b Reiffel	16	E. C. Joyce not out	23
†D. Alleyne c Afzaal b Bowen	32	L-b 12, w 2	14
*J. L. Langer run out	10		
M. R. Ramprakash not out	53	1/34 2/70 3/73 (3 wkts, 21 overs)	148

K. P. Dutch, B. L. Hutton, S. J. Cook, R. L. Johnson, A. R. C. Fraser and T. F. Bloomfield did not bat.

Bowling: Reiffel 5–1–12–1; Harris 4–0–42–0; Bowen 4–0–33–1; Franks 4–0–28–0; Tolley 4–0–21–0.

Nottinghamshire

D. J. Bicknell c Alleyne b Fraser	8	C. M. Tolley not out	1
*J. E. R. Gallian c Strauss b Cook	43	P. R. Reiffel not out	5
J. E. Morris c Johnson b Bloomfield	1		
P. Johnson b Johnson	8	B 4, l-b 2, w 3	9
U. Afzaal b Fraser	30		
M. N. Bowen c Hutton b Johnson	13	1/15 2/18 3/42 (7 wkts, 21 overs)	125
†C. M. W. Read c Ramprakash b Johnson	7	4/92 5/110 6/119 7/119	

P. J. Franks and A. J. Harris did not bat.

Bowling: Bloomfield 4–0–20–1; Fraser 4–0–18–2; Johnson 5–0–26–3; Cook 4–0–28–1; Dutch 3–0–19–0; Hutton 1–0–8–0.

Umpires: J. H. Harris and M. J. Harris.

MIDDLESEX v WARWICKSHIRE

At Lord's, September 9. Warwickshire won by 37 runs. Toss: Middlesex.

Given that five of Middlesex's seven wins had come when batting first, including a 15-run win at Edgbaston, it was hard to understand why Langer chose to field. True, his bowlers did well to restrict Warwickshire to 172, which owed much to Singh's 125-ball 74. But, to climax a season of dismal batting displays, Middlesex crashed to 24 for five in 11 overs. Only some late hitting by Hutton avoided complete ignominy. The result ruled Middlesex out of the promotion race and assured Warwickshire of Division One League cricket in 2001.

Warwickshire

M. A. Wagh lbw b Cook	24	†K. J. Piper not out	4
A. Singh b Johnson	74	A. A. Donald b Cook	1
*N. M. K. Smith run out	1	C. E. Dagnall b Cook	1
D. P. Ostler b Johnson	6	B 4, l-b 16, w 10	30
D. L. Hemp c Alleyne b Hutton	11		
T. L. Penney b Bloomfield	13	1/72 2/77 3/94 (42.5 overs)	172
D. R. Brown run out	2	4/111 5/140 6/152	
M. J. Powell b Johnson	5	7/160 8/161 9/168	

Bowling: Fraser 9–1–31–0; Bloomfield 7–1–20–1; Cook 8.5–1–22–3; Weekes 3–0–17–0; Johnson 8–1–26–3; Hutton 7–0–36–1.

Middlesex

A. J. Strauss lbw b Dagnall	5	R. L. Johnson run out	16
†D. Alleyne c Smith b Brown	4	A. R. C. Fraser c Ostler b Smith	1
*J. L. Langer run out	9	T. F. Bloomfield not out	1
M. R. Ramprakash lbw b Dagnall	2	L-b 6, w 8, n-b 4	18
E. C. Joyce c Smith b Donald	0		
P. N. Weekes run out	15	1/5 2/9 3/23	(41 overs) 135
B. L. Hutton lbw b Dagnall	49	4/24 5/24 6/70	
S. J. Cook c Ostler b Brown	15	7/103 8/132 9/134	

Bowling: Brown 8–2–26–2; Dagnall 9–2–33–3; Donald 7–2–8–1; Smith 8–2–28–1; Powell 5–0–19–0; Wagh 4–0–15–0.

Umpires: J. W. Holder and K. E. Palmer.

At Cardiff, September 17. MIDDLESEX beat GLAMORGAN by six wickets.

NOTTINGHAMSHIRE

NOTTINGHAMSHIRE v DURHAM

At Nottingham, April 30. Nottinghamshire won by four wickets. Toss: Nottinghamshire.

Ten days after needing to get two off the last ball to beat Durham at Trent Bridge in the Benson and Hedges Cup, Franks found himself in an identical situation. Having failed on that occasion, this time he hurtled through for the bye that would tie the game. But umpire Shepherd was already signalling Harmison's delivery a wide, so the bye proved the winning run. Earlier, Daley and Katich hit 55 from the first ten overs for Durham before Franks, Tolley and Lucas slowed the flow with accurate spells. In reply, Morris passed 5,000 League runs on the way to his 47-ball 50, and Gallian anchored the innings until the penultimate ball, bringing in Franks to end Nottinghamshire's run of four one-day defeats since the season's start.

Durham

J. A. Daley b Lucas	53	J. Wood not out	28
†M. P. Speight c Read b Millns	0	N. C. Phillips not out	8
S. M. Katich c Stemp b Franks	33	B 3, l-b 15, w 10, n-b 2	30
R. Robinson c Read b Franks	0		
*N. J. Speak b Franks	49	1/1 2/85 3/85	(6 wkts, 45 overs) 208
J. J. B. Lewis c Read b Lucas	7	4/136 5/152 6/174	

M. M. Betts, N. Killeen and S. J. Harmison did not bat.

Bowling: Millns 9–1–52–1; Lucas 9–0–34–2; Tolley 9–1–24–0; Franks 9–0–33–3; Stemp 5–1–26–0; Gallian 4–0–21–0.

Nottinghamshire

D. J. Bicknell c Speight b Betts	19	C. M. Tolley not out	13
U. Afzaal run out	26	P. J. Franks not out	0
*J. E. R. Gallian run out	74	L-b 7, w 7, n-b 10	24
P. Johnson b Harmison	1		
J. E. Morris c Betts b Wood	50	1/25 2/71 3/83	(6 wkts, 44.5 overs) 209
†C. M. W. Read c Speight b Killeen	2	4/162 5/179 6/207	

D. J. Millns, D. S. Lucas and R. D. Stemp did not bat.

Bowling: Wood 9–0–28–1; Betts 9–1–32–1; Killeen 9–0–30–1; Phillips 9–0–58–0; Harmison 8.5–0–54–1.

Umpires: A. Clarkson and D. R. Shepherd.

At Chelmsford, May 7. NOTTINGHAMSHIRE beat ESSEX by three runs.

NOTTINGHAMSHIRE v DERBYSHIRE

At Nottingham, May 21. Nottinghamshire won by four wickets. Toss: Nottinghamshire.

Nottinghamshire cruised to their third successive League win as all five of their domestic winter signings took the field together for the first time. Derbyshire set off at a fearsome pace, plundering 34 runs from the first 15 balls, but Harris and Franks had them 88 for five and the impetus was gone. Nottinghamshire's target of 187 presented few problems as Bicknell put on 76 with Gallian and 48 with Morris.

Derbyshire

M. E. Cassar b Harris	35	P. Aldred c Read b Lucas		11
M. J. Di Venuto b Lucas	13	T. M. Smith c Harris b Lucas		12
M. P. Dowman c Franks b Harris	20	K. J. Dean not out		6
R. J. Bailey c Read b Franks	0	L-b 6, w 4		10
S. D. Stubbings run out	59			
†K. M. Krikken c Gallian b Franks	10	1/34 2/70 3/70	(44.3 overs)	186
*D. G. Cork c Read b Millns	6	4/70 5/88 6/112		
S. J. Lacey lbw b Stemp	4	7/123 8/142 9/172		

Bowling: Millns 9–1–52–1; Lucas 8.3–0–55–3; Harris 9–0–38–2; Franks 9–2–16–2; Stemp 9–1–19–1.

Nottinghamshire

D. J. Bicknell c Cork b Smith	51	D. J. Millns not out		4
G. E. Welton lbw b Smith	0	G. R. Haywood not out		16
*J. E. R. Gallian st Krikken b Aldred	37	L-b 2, w 7, n-b 4		13
J. E. Morris c Di Venuto b Cassar	54			
†C. M. W. Read c Lacey b Smith	5	1/3 2/79 3/127	(6 wkts, 41.2 overs)	189
P. J. Franks run out	9	4/139 5/164 6/170		

D. S. Lucas, A. J. Harris and R. D. Stemp did not bat.

Bowling: Cork 9–0–39–0; Smith 9–1–45–3; Dean 4.2–1–22–0; Aldred 9–0–41–1; Cassar 6–0–26–1; Lacey 4–1–14–0.

Umpires: A. A. Jones and M. J. Kitchen.

At Chester-le-Street, May 28. NOTTINGHAMSHIRE beat DURHAM by three runs (D/L method).

At Birmingham, May 31 (day/night). NOTTINGHAMSHIRE lost to WARWICKSHIRE by 38 runs.

NOTTINGHAMSHIRE v HAMPSHIRE

At Nottingham, June 11. Nottinghamshire won by eight wickets. Toss: Nottinghamshire.

Hampshire crashed to a fifth consecutive League defeat. With Lucas and Millns injured, Harris took the new ball and reaped full benefit by returning one-day best figures as Hampshire's fragile batting folded on a featherbed pitch. In reply, Bicknell hit eight boundaries – more than Hampshire managed between them – to guide Nottinghamshire to their fifth win in the competition with eight overs to spare.

Hampshire

G. W. White c Harris b Stemp	27		S. D. Udal c Bicknell b Harris		5
D. A. Kenway c Read b Harris	7		A. D. Mullally not out		6
†A. N. Aymes c Read b Harris	7		S. R. G. Francis b Harris		0
*R. A. Smith b Franks	9		L-b 7, w 3		10
L. R. Prittipaul b Franks	6				
W. S. Kendall lbw b Harris	39		1/9 2/25 3/46	(44 overs)	135
S. K. Warne c Welton b Tolley	12		4/58 5/67 6/93		
L. Savident b Stemp	7		7/110 8/126 9/134		

Bowling: Harris 9–0–35–5; Bowen 9–0–23–0; Tolley 9–1–21–1; Franks 8–0–22–2; Stemp 9–0–27–2.

Nottinghamshire

D. J. Bicknell not out	58
G. E. Welton c and b Francis	11
J. E. Morris b Warne	38
U. Afzaal not out	12
L-b 6, w 9, n-b 2	17

1/42 2/113   (2 wkts, 36.4 overs) 136

*P. Johnson, C. M. Tolley, †C. M. W. Read, P. J. Franks, M. N. Bowen, A. J. Harris and R. D. Stemp did not bat.

Bowling: Mullally 7–2–19–0; Francis 6–1–22–1; Savident 7–1–20–0; Prittipaul 1–0–14–0; Warne 9–2–32–1; Udal 5–0–14–0; White 1.4–0–9–0.

Umpires: M. J. Harris and P. Willey.

NOTTINGHAMSHIRE v ESSEX

At Nottingham, June 24. Nottinghamshire won by four wickets. Toss: Essex.

Lucas's one-day best set up the victory that took Nottinghamshire back to the top of Division Two. But it was a less satisfactory day for the out-of-form England captain, Hussain. Caught at point early on, he later broke his thumb fielding and withdrew from England's team for the Lord's Test against West Indies. Only a restrained half-century from their normally ebullient captain, Irani, ensured Essex reached a respectable total. Welton anchored Nottinghamshire's response, allowing Gallian to hit an aggressive 41, and, after some mid-innings jitters, Read and Franks added the last 51 in ten easy overs.

Essex

D. D. J. Robinson c Read b Lucas	10		†B. J. Hyam b Lucas		0
S. G. Law b Lucas	20		T. J. Mason c Afzaal b Lucas		12
N. Hussain c Tolley b Franks	3				
*R. C. Irani c Harris b Franks	52		L-b 5, w 7		12
S. D. Peters st Read b Tolley	10				
A. P. Grayson lbw b Tolley	7		1/31 2/34 3/46	(9 wkts, 45 overs)	177
D. R. Law c Read b Reiffel	22		4/76 5/86 6/129		
A. P. Cowan not out	29		7/149 8/153 9/177		

M. C. Ilott did not bat.

Bowling: Reiffel 9–3–32–1; Lucas 9–1–38–4; Franks 9–1–32–2; Harris 9–1–36–0; Tolley 9–0–34–2.

Nottinghamshire

D. J. Bicknell c Mason b Ilott	9	†C. M. W. Read not out		29
G. E. Welton lbw b D. R. Law	40	P. J. Franks not out		23
*J. E. R. Gallian c Robinson b Irani	41	L-b 8, w 8, n-b 2		18
J. E. Morris c Hyam b Ilott	15			
U. Afzaal run out	2	1/12 2/78 3/103	(6 wkts, 42.3 overs)	179
C. M. Tolley c Hyam b D. R. Law	2	4/111 5/115 6/128		

P. R. Reiffel, D. S. Lucas and A. J. Harris did not bat.

Bowling: Irani 7.3–3–26–1; Ilott 9–1–37–2; D. R. Law 8–0–43–2; Cowan 9–0–38–0; Mason 9–0–27–0.

Umpires: T. E. Jesty and J. F. Steele.

At Derby, June 26 (day/night). NOTTINGHAMSHIRE beat DERBYSHIRE by 30 runs.

At Guildford, July 23. NOTTINGHAMSHIRE lost to SURREY by 127 runs.

NOTTINGHAMSHIRE v WARWICKSHIRE

At Nottingham, August 1 (day/night). Warwickshire won by 95 runs. Toss: Warwickshire.

Nottinghamshire saved their worst batting of the season for their biggest crowd. After Warwickshire had predictably elected to bat in sunshine, rather than electric light, openers Knight and Singh gave them a racing start with 91 at a run a ball, which Ostler augmented with 79 from 93 deliveries. The home team's reply fell behind the rate as they stalled in the twilight zone; only Bicknell's half-century and a fine cameo from Franks prevented a three-figure defeat.

Warwickshire

N. V. Knight c Lucas b Stemp	50	M. J. Powell b Stemp		1
A. Singh c Gallian b Stemp	43	*N. M. K. Smith not out		6
D. P. Ostler not out	79	L-b 5, w 8, n-b 6		19
T. L. Penney b Afzaal	30			
A. F. Giles st Read b Afzaal	10	1/91 2/118 3/185	(6 wkts, 45 overs)	244
D. R. Brown lbw b Stemp	6	4/205 5/225 6/227		

†K. J. Piper, A. A. Donald and E. S. H. Giddins did not bat.

Bowling: Reiffel 8–1–40–0; Lucas 8–1–43–0; Harris 8–0–49–0; Franks 7–0–40–0; Stemp 9–0–36–4; Afzaal 5–0–31–2.

Nottinghamshire

D. J. Bicknell c Powell b Brown	61	D. S. Lucas lbw b Brown		5
G. E. Welton b Brown	10	A. J. Harris run out		9
P. Johnson b Donald	7	R. D. Stemp c and b Powell		5
*J. E. R. Gallian c Penney b Giles	1	L-b 5, w 8		13
U. Afzaal b Smith	6			
†C. M. W. Read c Brown b Smith	0	1/32 2/49 3/50	(43.5 overs)	149
P. R. Reiffel c Penney b Smith	1	4/71 5/71 6/73		
P. J. Franks not out	31	7/99 8/110 9/139		

Bowling: Giddins 7–1–24–0; Brown 9–1–28–3; Donald 6–0–17–1; Giles 9–2–23–1; Smith 9–1–38–3; Powell 3.5–0–14–1.

Umpires: T. E. Jesty and B. Leadbeater.

NOTTINGHAMSHIRE v MIDDLESEX

At Nottingham, August 13. No result (D/L method). Toss: Middlesex.

Persistent drizzle robbed Middlesex of an almost certain win after dashing strokeplay had rattled their innings along at more than a run a ball. Showers reduced their allocation to 41 then 37 overs, and spurred Ramprakash and Joyce to blast 68 in the six overs following the second stoppage. The Duckworth/Lewis calculation set Nottinghamshire 257 at seven an over, an unlikely target had the weather relented.

Middlesex

A. J. Strauss c Read b Reiffel	13	E. C. Joyce not out		40
†D. Alleyne c Afzaal b Tolley	58	B 2, l-b 20, w 1, n-b 2		40
*J. L. Langer b Tolley	29			
M. R. Ramprakash not out	61	1/41 2/118 3/155	(3 wkts, 37 overs)	241

P. N. Weekes, B. L. Hutton, S. J. Cook, R. L. Johnson, J. P. Hewitt and T. F. Bloomfield did not bat.

Bowling: Reiffel 8–1–31–1; Lucas 7–0–50–0; Franks 7–0–55–0; Tolley 9–0–27–2; Stemp 3–0–30–0; Gallian 3–0–26–0.

Nottinghamshire

D. J. Bicknell, *J. E. R. Gallian, P. Johnson, J. E. Morris, U. Afzaal, †C. M. W. Read, P. J. Franks, P. R. Reiffel, D. S. Lucas, C. M. Tolley and R. D. Stemp.

Umpires: M. J. Harris and A. A. Jones.

At Colwyn Bay, August 20. NOTTINGHAMSHIRE beat GLAMORGAN by eight wickets (D/L method).

At Richmond, August 28. NOTTINGHAMSHIRE lost to MIDDLESEX by 23 runs.

NOTTINGHAMSHIRE v SURREY

At Nottingham, September 3. Nottinghamshire won by 63 runs. Toss: Nottinghamshire. County debut: T. J. Murtagh. First-team debut: P. J. Sampson.

With the division won, and the County Championship still to clinch, Surrey fielded a weakened side. Bicknell and Gallian revelled against second-string bowling to register Nottinghamshire's highest opening stand in the League, 196 at a run a ball, and Bicknell went on to a century against his former county. Read hit 22 off the last over. Shahid excluded – his 109 came from 108 balls – the Surrey batsmen bizarrely ignored their formidable target and looked content to settle for defeat.

Nottinghamshire

D. J. Bicknell run out	115	†C. M. W. Read not out		26
*J. E. R. Gallian c and b Brown	84	B 3, l-b 4, w 15, n-b 2		24
J. E. Morris c Greenidge b Brown	9			
P. Johnson c Ratcliffe b Brown	8	1/196 2/208	(4 wkts, 45 overs)	288
U. Afzaal not out	22	3/222 4/247		

P. J. Franks, P. R. Reiffel, D. S. Lucas, A. J. Harris and R. D. Stemp did not bat.

Bowling: Greenidge 3–0–25–0; Murtagh 8–1–52–0; Sampson 5–0–43–0; Ratcliffe 9–0–46–0; Butcher 4–0–28–0; G. J. Batty 9–0–48–0; Brown 7–0–39–3.

Surrey

I. J. Ward c Read b Franks	46	G. J. Batty not out		26
A. D. Brown c Read b Reiffel	5	B 4, l-b 6, w 11, n-b 4		25
N. Shahid not out	109			
G. P. Butcher run out	14	1/14 2/99 3/138	(3 wkts, 45 overs)	225

*A. J. Hollioake, J. D. Ratcliffe, †J. N. Batty, T. J. Murtagh, P. J. Sampson and C. G. Greenidge did not bat.

Bowling: Reiffel 7–1–16–1; Harris 9–0–42–0; Lucas 9–0–60–0; Franks 9–0–42–1; Stemp 9–0–45–0; Afzaal 1–0–4–0; Bicknell 1–0–6–0.

Umpires: D. J. Constant and R. A. White.

NOTTINGHAMSHIRE v GLAMORGAN

At Nottingham, September 10. Nottinghamshire won by three runs. Toss: Nottinghamshire.

Nervy Nottinghamshire secured the win they required to guarantee promotion, but were taken to the last ball by batting of the highest class from Maynard. Having threatened a huge total as Afzaal and Johnson's century stand took the score to 163 from 30 overs, they lost ground when the remaining 15 overs produced only 66 more runs. In reply, Glamorgan were well on course until Stemp and Tolley pegged them back. Maynard was too long off the strike in the later stages and, in appalling light, failed to hit Harris for either six to win or four to tie. Read's three catches brought him a Nottinghamshire-record 27 dismissals (25 catches, two stumpings) in a League season.

Nottinghamshire

D. J. Bicknell c and b Parkin	14	P. J. Franks lbw b Watkin		6
M. N. Bowen c Newell b Parkin	4	A. J. Harris not out		4
*J. E. R. Gallian c and b Watkin	31	R. D. Stemp not out		4
U. Afzaal c Thomas b Croft	51	L-b 6, w 6, n-b 2		14
P. Johnson c Thomas b Croft	62			
†C. M. W. Read c Harrison b Newell	17	1/4 2/41 3/57	(9 wkts, 45 overs)	229
C. M. Tolley c James b Newell	5	4/164 5/174 6/190		
P. R. Reiffel b Newell	17	7/195 8/212 9/222		

Bowling: Watkin 9–1–40–2; Parkin 9–1–51–2; Harrison 3–0–24–0; Dale 7–0–33–0; Croft 9–0–43–2; Newell 8–0–32–3.

Glamorgan

K. Newell c Stemp b Reiffel	0	D. S. Harrison b Harris		2
I. J. Thomas c and b Franks	36	S. L. Watkin run out		1
S. P. James c Read b Tolley	29	O. T. Parkin not out		0
*M. P. Maynard not out	88	L-b 2, w 10		12
A. Dale c Read b Stemp	20			
M. J. Powell b Franks	28	1/0 2/63 3/87	(9 wkts, 45 overs)	226
R. D. B. Croft c Read b Franks	3	4/137 5/192 6/201		
†M. A. Wallace run out	7	7/214 8/220 9/225		

Bowling: Reiffel 9–1–43–1; Harris 6–0–51–1; Franks 9–0–41–3; Tolley 9–0–43–1; Stemp 9–0–32–1; Bowen 3–0–14–0.

Umpires: B. Dudleston and A. G. T. Whitehead.

At Southampton, September 17. NOTTINGHAMSHIRE beat HAMPSHIRE by three runs.

SURREY

At Cardiff, April 30. SURREY beat GLAMORGAN by ten runs.

At Chester-le-Street, May 6. SURREY beat DURHAM by 66 runs.

SURREY v MIDDLESEX

At The Oval, May 21. No result (abandoned).

SURREY v ESSEX

At The Oval, May 29. No result (abandoned).

SURREY v HAMPSHIRE

At The Oval, May 30 (day/night). Surrey won by seven wickets. Toss: Hampshire.

Supporters were denied the drama of floodlit cricket, for the match was over long before the sun set. Tudor, earning one-day best figures, and Bicknell proved unplayable on a lively, seaming pitch; Hampshire's batting, by and large, proved incapable. Warne, signed for his bowling, was forced to earn his corn with the bat, not that it did his team any good. Brown and Ward, who faced 51 balls for 44, reduced the chase to simplicity itself.

Hampshire

J. S. Laney c Batty b Tudor	2	S. K. Warne c Salisbury b B. C. Hollioake	34
D. A. Kenway b Bicknell	0	S. D. Udal c Thorpe b Ratcliffe	1
†A. N. Aymes c Thorpe b Tudor	0	A. D. Mullally lbw b Tudor	0
*R. A. Smith lbw b Ratcliffe	20	S. R. G. Francis not out	8
G. W. White c Thorpe b Bicknell	2	L-b 11, w 8, n-b 4	23
J. P. Stephenson c Batty b Bicknell	3		
A. D. Mascarenhas c B. C. Hollioake		1/2 2/5 3/6 4/15 5/38 (30.2 overs) 94	
b Tudor	1	6/42 7/74 8/80 9/81	

Bowling: Bicknell 9–2–18–3; Tudor 9–2–26–4; Ratcliffe 8–1–19–2; B. C. Hollioake 4.2–0–20–1.

Surrey

M. A. Butcher c Udal b Mullally	0	*A. J. Hollioake not out	6
A. D. Brown c Francis b Mascarenhas	23	L-b 1, w 5, n-b 2	8
I. J. Ward b Warne	44		
G. P. Thorpe not out	14	1/0 2/63 3/81 (3 wkts, 21.1 overs) 95	

B. C. Hollioake, J. D. Ratcliffe, †J. N. Batty, A. J. Tudor, M. P. Bicknell and I. D. K. Salisbury did not bat.

Bowling: Mullally 5–2–23–1; Francis 3–0–17–0; Warne 7.1–1–26–1; Mascarenhas 6–1–28–1.

Umpires: J. W. Holder and R. Palmer.

At Derby, June 11. SURREY beat DERBYSHIRE by three wickets.

At Birmingham, June 23 (day/night). SURREY beat WARWICKSHIRE by seven wickets.

At Southampton, June 27. SURREY beat HAMPSHIRE by 43 runs.

SURREY v GLAMORGAN

At The Oval, July 16. Surrey won by 67 runs. Toss: Surrey.

The Hollioakes took unbeaten Surrey to the top of Division Two, Adam hitting his maiden one-day hundred (more than doubling his season's one-day aggregate) and Ben picking up four wickets. Adam, adding 181 in 30 overs with Ward, faced only 96 balls for his 111; the second of his two sixes landed in the seventh row of the pavilion middle balcony. He then took a wicket and two catches as third-placed Glamorgan tumbled to their first defeat in seven games.

Surrey

M. A. Butcher b Wharf	2	J. D. Ratcliffe not out		4
I. J. Ward not out	90			
N. Shahid b Wharf	5	L-b 13, w 6		19
A. D. Brown c James b Dale	26			
*A. J. Hollioake b Dale	111	1/2 2/9 3/72	(5 wkts, 45 overs)	268
B. C. Hollioake c Wharf b Parkin	11	4/253 5/264		

†J. N. Batty, M. P. Bicknell, C. G. Greenidge and Saqlain Mushtaq did not bat.

Bowling: Wharf 9–1–37–2; Parkin 9–0–70–1; Dale 9–0–43–2; Croft 9–0–41–0; Cosker 7–0–47–0; Newell 2–0–17–0.

Glamorgan

K. Newell c A. J. Hollioake b Ratcliffe	32	R. D. B. Croft c Ratcliffe		
M. T. G. Elliott c Batty b Greenidge	9	b B. C. Hollioake	24	
*S. P. James lbw b B. C. Hollioake	36	A. G. Wharf lbw b Saqlain Mushtaq	4	
M. J. Powell c A. J. Hollioake		D. A. Cosker b Greenidge	17	
b B. C. Hollioake	31	O. T. Parkin not out	5	
A. Dale c Butcher b A. J. Hollioake	9	L-b 13, w 4, n-b 6	23	
A. W. Evans run out	5			
†A. D. Shaw c Ratcliffe		1/21 2/65 3/113 4/114	(41.2 overs)	201
b B. C. Hollioake	6	5/130 6/130 7/147 8/178 9/180		

Bowling: Bicknell 7–0–16–0; Greenidge 7.2–0–43–2; Saqlain Mushtaq 7–0–31–1; Ratcliffe 5–0–29–1; B. C. Hollioake 9–0–42–4; A. J. Hollioake 6–0–27–1.

Umpires: N. G. Cowley and P. Willey.

SURREY v NOTTINGHAMSHIRE

At Guildford, July 23. Surrey won by 127 runs. Toss: Surrey.

Surrey showed second-placed Nottinghamshire how tough it was at the top, winning handsomely to stretch their lead. Thorpe hit a 127-ball 126 (14 fours) and added 139 in 27 overs with the consistent Ward. A target of 274 asked far too much of the visitors on a hard, bouncy pitch. Franks's fruitless double-strike in Surrey's last over – Adam Hollioake off a no-ball, Thorpe from the subsequent "free hit" delivery – should have warned Nottinghamshire it was not their day; Darren Bicknell's run-out on his homecoming, followed by Saqlain Mushtaq's three top-order wickets in 11 balls, made it obvious.

Surrey

M. A. Butcher c Reiffel b Lucas	6	*A. J. Hollioake not out		21
I. J. Ward run out	51	L-b 11, w 8, n-b 13		32
G. P. Thorpe not out	126			
A. D. Brown b Lucas	37	1/10 2/149 3/223	(3 wkts, 45 overs)	273

B. C. Hollioake, J. D. Ratcliffe, †J. N. Batty, M. P. Bicknell, Saqlain Mushtaq and C. G. Greenidge did not bat.

Bowling: Lucas 9–0–68–2; Franks 9–0–50–0; Harris 9–2–33–0; Reiffel 6–0–41–0; Tolley 9–0–44–0; Gallian 3–0–26–0.

Nottinghamshire

D. J. Bicknell run out	14	
*J. E. R. Gallian c Ward b Ratcliffe	42	
J. E. Morris c Ratcliffe		
b Saqlain Mushtaq	7	
P. Johnson b Saqlain Mushtaq	9	
U. Afzaal c A. J. Hollioake		
b Saqlain Mushtaq	3	
†C. M. W. Read b Ratcliffe	8	
C. M. Tolley lbw b Ratcliffe	7	

P. R. Reiffel c Greenidge
    b B. C. Hollioake . 18
P. J. Franks not out 14
D. S. Lucas lbw b A. J. Hollioake 4
A. J. Harris lbw b B. C. Hollioake 1
    L-b 7, w 10, n-b 2 19

1/57 2/66 3/70 4/76 5/87   (35.2 overs) 146
6/91 7/111 8/141 9/145

Bowling: Bicknell 7–0–26–0; Greenidge 5–0–28–0; Ratcliffe 9–0–39–3; Saqlain Mushtaq 9–1–25–3; B. C. Hollioake 3.2–0–13–2; A. J. Hollioake 2–0–8–1.

Umpires: V. A. Holder and N. A. Mallender.

At Lord's, August 6. SURREY beat MIDDLESEX by five wickets.

SURREY v WARWICKSHIRE

At Whitgift School, August 9. Surrey won by 103 runs. Toss: Surrey.

A crowd of more than 3,000 in a picturesque setting saw Surrey go 16 points clear in Division Two's promotion race. Third-placed Warwickshire, 24 for four inside ten overs, subsided meekly to accurate, penetrative seam and spin bowling. They were unlucky earlier when Giddins broke down with back spasms in his third over, for the slow pitch and uncertain bounce favoured his strengths. But Thorpe's 62 in 57 balls was masterly, befitting Whitgift's first county game: part of their 400th anniversary celebrations.

Surrey

I. J. Ward st Piper b Powell	8	
†A. J. Stewart c Ostler b Giles	19	
N. Shahid run out	32	
G. P. Thorpe c Giles b Smith	62	
A. D. Brown c Singh b Powell	16	
*A. J. Hollioake c Singh b Smith	21	
J. D. Ratcliffe c Smith b Donald	2	
A. J. Tudor c Brown b Donald	7	

M. P. Bicknell c Smith b Donald 10
I. D. K. Salisbury not out 8
Saqlain Mushtaq not out 2
    B 4, l-b 4, w 16 24

1/13 2/56 3/82   (9 wkts, 45 overs) 211
4/127 5/170 6/180
7/182 8/193 9/206

Bowling: Brown 9–3–23–0; Giddins 2.4–0–5–0; Powell 6.2–0–44–2; Donald 9–1–40–3; Giles 9–0–41–1; Smith 9–0–50–2.

Warwickshire

N. V. Knight c Thorpe b Bicknell	1	
A. Singh c Salisbury b Tudor	5	
D. P. Ostler run out	5	
T. L. Penney c Salisbury		
b Saqlain Mushtaq	35	
D. R. Brown c Hollioake b Tudor	3	
M. J. Powell c Shahid b Saqlain Mushtaq	7	
A. F. Giles c Shahid b Hollioake	28	
*N. M. K. Smith c Shahid b Ratcliffe	0	

†K. J. Piper b Hollioake 10
A. A. Donald not out 0
E. S. H. Giddins absent hurt

    L-b 4, w 8, n-b 2 14

1/2 2/13 3/20   (30 overs) 108
4/24 5/56 6/68
7/73 8/108 9/108

Bowling: Bicknell 7–0–23–1; Tudor 7–1–23–2; Ratcliffe 6–0–25–1; Saqlain Mushtaq 7–1–19–2; Salisbury 2–0–7–0; Hollioake 1–0–7–2.

Umpires: M. R. Benson and G. I. Burgess.

SURREY v DERBYSHIRE

At The Oval, August 20. Surrey won by six wickets. Toss: Derbyshire.

Unbeaten Surrey's 11th League win, their ninth on the trot, guaranteed promotion to Division One. It owed as much to bottom-side Derbyshire's ineptness as to Hollioake and Ratcliffe's matter-of-fact, unbroken stand of 93. Ward and Shahid had earlier put on 55 for the second wicket. Batting was never straightforward, and without Bailey's gritty 43 in 76 balls, Derbyshire would have struggled to set a reasonable target. The Surrey spinners ensured it never moved out of reach.

Derbyshire

M. E. Cassar c Salisbury b Tudor	9	*T. A. Munton c and b Salisbury	1
M. J. Di Venuto c Batty b Bicknell	30	K. J. Dean not out	8
R. J. Bailey b Hollioake	43	L. J. Wharton not out	7
M. P. Dowman c Brown b Saqlain Mushtaq	24	L-b 5, w 10	15
S. D. Stubbings run out	0		
†L. D. Sutton b Saqlain Mushtaq	3	1/16 2/51 3/89 (9 wkts, 45 overs) 175	
J. P. Pyemont c Shahid b Salisbury	10	4/91 5/105 6/118	
P. Aldred c Ward b Salisbury	25	7/143 8/154 9/155	

Bowling: Bicknell 7–0–21–1; Saqlain Mushtaq 9–1–34–2; Tudor 6–1–29–1; Ratcliffe 7–0–34–0; Salisbury 9–0–32–3; Hollioake 7–1–20–1.

Surrey

M. A. Butcher run out	2	J. D. Ratcliffe not out	42
I. J. Ward c Sutton b Aldred	34	B 3, l-b 2, w 14	19
N. Shahid st Sutton b Wharton	23		
A. D. Brown b Aldred	8	1/11 2/66 (4 wkts, 44 overs) 176	
*A. J. Hollioake not out	48	3/79 4/83	

†J. N. Batty, M. P. Bicknell, A. J. Tudor, I. D. K. Salisbury and Saqlain Mushtaq did not bat.

Bowling: Munton 9–1–29–0; Dean 8–1–31–0; Aldred 9–0–26–2; Wharton 9–0–36–1; Cassar 3–0–20–0; Bailey 6–0–29–0.

Umpires: R. Julian and B. Leadbeater.

At Colchester, August 23 (day/night). SURREY lost to ESSEX by 23 runs.

At Nottingham, September 3. SURREY lost to NOTTINGHAMSHIRE by 63 runs.

SURREY v DURHAM

At The Oval, September 10. Durham won by 59 runs. Toss: Durham.

Surrey's third successive defeat since sealing promotion on August 20 was an unsatisfactory preliminary to their official recognition as Division Two winners. Again, however, they fielded a below-strength side, and Durham made all the running. Daley, batting from first ball to last, hit his maiden one-day hundred after putting on 177 in 33 overs with Collingwood, whose 86 was his fifth half-century in six League games. Brown and Ward replied with 87 in 12 overs, but Hunter and then off-spinner Phillips, with his season's best, stymied Surrey's chase.

Durham

J. A. Daley c Butcher b Hollioake	105	J. Wood not out		0
M. P. Speight c G. J. Batty b Greenidge	15	B 1, l-b 11, w 2, n-b 4		18
S. M. Katich c G. J. Batty b Greenidge	2			
P. D. Collingwood b Murtagh	86	1/23 2/31 3/208	(5 wkts, 45 overs)	251
*J. J. B. Lewis c Shahid b Hollioake	25	4/245 5/251		

†A. Pratt, N. C. Phillips, M. M. Betts, I. D. Hunter and N. Killeen did not bat.

Bowling: Greenidge 9–0–49–2; Murtagh 9–0–50–1; Ratcliffe 7–0–33–0; Sampson 7–0–24–0; Butcher 4–0–28–0; G. J. Batty 2–0–16–0; Hollioake 7–0–39–2.

Surrey

I. J. Ward c Speight b Hunter	41	T. J. Murtagh c and b Phillips		0
A. D. Brown c Killeen b Hunter	51	P. J. Sampson c Lewis b Collingwood		4
N. Shahid c Pratt b Hunter	6	C. G. Greenidge not out		3
G. P. Butcher b Killeen	37	L-b 9		9
G. J. Batty b Phillips	20			
*A. J. Hollioake b Phillips	5	1/87 2/94 3/99	(40.3 overs)	192
J. D. Ratcliffe c Phillips b Collingwood	12	4/137 5/153 6/171		
†J. N. Batty c Lewis b Phillips	4	7/180 8/181 9/184		

Bowling: Killeen 7–0–43–1; Betts 4–0–26–0; Wood 8–1–31–0; Hunter 5–0–23–3; Phillips 9–0–30–4; Collingwood 7.3–1–30–2.

Umpires: J. W. Lloyds and N. A. Mallender.

WARWICKSHIRE

At Southampton, May 1. WARWICKSHIRE beat HAMPSHIRE by 97 runs.

WARWICKSHIRE v GLAMORGAN

At Birmingham, May 7. Warwickshire won by nine wickets. Toss: Glamorgan.

Penney's fielding was too much for Glamorgan: he caught Elliott brilliantly at backward point, one-handed to his right, then ran out Maynard and Shaw with direct hits. Without Dale's 47 off 80 balls, they would not have made 125, and it was witless cricket to be bowled out with more than five overs unused. Knight and Welch put on 91 in 18 overs, with Knight's unbeaten 68 giving him an aggregate of 301 for once out in five days against Glamorgan.

Glamorgan

R. D. B. Croft c Giles b Welch	10	†A. D. Shaw run out		14
M. T. G. Elliott c Penney b Brown	20	O. T. Parkin b Brown		4
M. J. Powell c Piper b Brown	11	S. L. Watkin not out		0
*M. P. Maynard run out	0	L-b 2, w 7		9
A. Dale c Hemp b Sheikh	47			
S. P. James c Welch b Sheikh	7	1/25 2/44 3/45	(39.2 overs)	125
K. Newell c and b Giles	2	4/48 5/73 6/81		
S. D. Thomas c Piper b Giles	1	7/85 8/120 9/125		

Bowling: Giddins 7–0–25–0; Welch 9–0–27–1; Brown 8–1–23–3; Sheikh 8.2–0–26–2; Giles 7–0–22–2.

Warwickshire

N. V. Knight not out	. . . .	68
G. Welch c Maynard b Thomas	. . . . . .	38
D. P. Ostler not out	. . . .	19
L-b 1, w 1	. . . .	2

1/91　　　　　　(1 wkt, 26.5 overs) 127

D. L. Hemp, T. L. Penney, D. R. Brown, *N. M. K. Smith, M. A. Sheikh, A. F. Giles, †K. J. Piper and E. S. H. Giddins did not bat.

Bowling: Parkin 6–3–19–0; Watkin 5–0–27–0; Thomas 5–0–27–1; Croft 3–0–21–0; Newell 4.5–1–22–0; Elliott 3–1–10–0.

Umpires: V. A. Holder and K. E. Palmer.

WARWICKSHIRE v HAMPSHIRE

At Birmingham, May 21. Warwickshire won by five wickets. Toss: Hampshire.

Warwickshire's third successive League win left Hampshire still searching for their first. It had looked vaguely possible when Warwickshire lost half their side for 71, but Brown and Penney put on 87 in 20 overs to run up victory with 5.3 overs to spare. Hampshire did not help themselves by conceding 17 wides. Opting to bat first, they had surrendered the initiative by slumping from 100 for three to 154 all out against an accurate attack in which spinners Giles and Smith shared four wickets.

Hampshire

J. S. Laney c Welch b Smith	. . . .	69	S. D. Udal c Smith b Brown	. . . .	3
†D. A. Kenway b Dagnall	. . . .	7	S. J. Renshaw c Brown b Smith	. . . . . .	1
S. K. Warne c Piper b Dagnall	. . . . . .	0	P. J. Hartley run out	. . . .	3
*R. A. Smith b Giles	. . . .	8	L-b 1, w 4	. . . .	5
G. W. White run out	. . . .	21		
W. S. Kendall c Piper b Giles	. . . .	0	1/18 2/18 3/57	(44.4 overs) 154
J. P. Stephenson not out	. . . .	33	4/100 5/102 6/111	
A. D. Mascarenhas b Sheikh	. . . .	4	7/132 8/142 9/143	

Bowling: Welch 9–2–22–0; Dagnall 6–0–21–2; Brown 7–0–30–1; Giles 9–2–21–2; Sheikh 9–0–34–1; Smith 4.4–0–25–2.

Warwickshire

M. J. Powell lbw b Hartley	. . . .	21	D. R. Brown not out	. . . .	45
G. Welch b Renshaw	. . . .	7		
*N. M. K. Smith c Kendall b Hartley	. .	0	L-b 8, w 17	. . . .	25
D. P. Ostler b Warne	. . . .	8		
D. L. Hemp lbw b Stephenson	. . . . . .	16	1/33 2/37 3/37	(5 wkts, 39.3 overs) 158
T. L. Penney not out	. . . .	36	4/63 5/71	

M. A. Sheikh, A. F. Giles, †K. J. Piper and C. E. Dagnall did not bat.

Bowling: Hartley 9–3–24–2; Renshaw 6–1–19–1; Mascarenhas 5–0–25–0; Stephenson 6–0–26–1; Warne 8.3–1–33–1; Udal 5–0–23–0.

Umpires: J. W. Lloyds and D. R. Shepherd.

WARWICKSHIRE v NOTTINGHAMSHIRE

At Birmingham, May 31 (day/night). Warwickshire won by 38 runs. Toss: Warwickshire.

Warwickshire had the advantage of batting in daylight – Edgbaston's temporary floodlights were barely adequate – and made the most of it in this top-of-the-table meeting between unbeaten sides. A total of 200 or more had become something of a rarity here and proved too much for

Nottinghamshire. They never came to grips with the home attack in which Giles was again outstanding. Although they passed 100 with only two wickets down, the required run-rate eventually rose to double figures.

Warwickshire

M. J. Powell run out	26	A. F. Giles b Franks 0
G. Welch c Welton b Tolley	55	M. A. Sheikh not out 0
D. P. Ostler c Franks b Millns	55	L-b 10, w 7, n-b 2 19
D. L. Hemp c Read b Harris	45	
*N. M. K. Smith c Bicknell b Millns	6	1/80 2/110 3/176 (7 wkts, 45 overs) 222
T. L. Penney not out	14	4/192 5/219
D. R. Brown run out	2	6/221 7/222

†K. J. Piper and C. E. Dagnall did not bat.

Bowling: Millns 7–0–46–2; Lucas 7–0–28–0; Franks 9–0–41–1; Harris 9–1–52–1; Stemp 9–1–24–0; Tolley 4–0–21–1.

Nottinghamshire

D. J. Bicknell c Piper b Dagnall	11	D. S. Lucas run out 0
G. E. Welton lbw b Giles	42	A. J. Harris not out 7
J. E. Morris c Dagnall b Brown	16	
*J. E. R. Gallian c Piper b Giles	30	B 8, l-b 4, w 7, n-b 2 21
C. M. Tolley b Welch	7	
†C. M. W. Read st Piper b Giles	5	1/26 2/58 3/102 (8 wkts, 45 overs) 184
P. J. Franks not out	32	4/107 5/117 6/123
D. J. Millns c Giles b Brown	13	7/157 8/165

R. D. Stemp did not bat.

Bowling: Dagnall 9–1–22–1; Welch 9–0–32–1; Sheikh 9–0–43–0; Brown 9–1–43–2; Giles 9–1–32–3.

Umpires: G. I. Burgess and G. Sharp.

WARWICKSHIRE v SURREY

At Birmingham, June 23 (day/night). Surrey won by seven wickets. Toss: Warwickshire.

Despite the advantage of batting first under lights, Warwickshire always struggled on a slow pitch. Only Knight, with 82 in 42 overs, came to terms with the conditions, although he was dropped twice, and the fact that only 29 runs were scored between the 20th and 30th overs speaks volumes for the Surrey bowlers' control. Brown and Stewart settled the match with a second-wicket partnership of 75 in 18 overs after Warwickshire's experiment of opening with Giles's spin had flattered to deceive. Surrey's win, stretching their unbeaten run to seven and ending Warwickshire's, took them to the top of Division Two.

Warwickshire

N. V. Knight c Thorpe b Bicknell	82	A. F. Giles c Ratcliffe b B. C. Hollioake	1
G. Welch c Ward b Bicknell	13	M. A. Sheikh not out 2
D. P. Ostler st Stewart		
b Saqlain Mushtaq	25	L-b 6, w 3 9
D. L. Hemp lbw b Saqlain Mushtaq	0	
T. L. Penney lbw b Tudor	5	1/25 2/93 3/93 (7 wkts, 45 overs) 162
*N. M. K. Smith b B. C. Hollioake	4	4/115 5/128
D. R. Brown not out	21	6/146 7/150

†K. J. Piper and E. S. H. Giddins did not bat.

Bowling: Bicknell 9–1–29–2; Tudor 9–2–41–1; Ratcliffe 9–0–34–0; Saqlain Mushtaq 9–1–24–2; B. C. Hollioake 9–0–28–2.

Surrey

M. A. Butcher lbw b Giles	2	*A. J. Hollioake not out	13
A. D. Brown lbw b Giles	45	B 3, l-b 2, w 8, n-b 4	17
†A. J. Stewart not out	72		
G. P. Thorpe run out	17	1/19 2/94 3/129 (3 wkts, 41.1 overs)	166

I. J. Ward, J. D. Ratcliffe, A. J. Tudor, Saqlain Mushtaq, B. C. Hollioake and M. P. Bicknell did not bat.

Bowling: Giles 9–1–43–2; Welch 9–2–24–0; Brown 7–0–30–0; Giddins 3–0–20–0; Sheikh 7.1–0–25–0; Smith 6–0–19–0.

Umpires: J. W. Holder and A. A. Jones.

WARWICKSHIRE v ESSEX

At Birmingham, June 25. Essex won by 24 runs. Toss: Essex.

Warwickshire's second League defeat, coming just two days after their first, rested again on their batsmen's failure to adjust to a slow pitch. Essex had found strokeplay equally difficult, with their best partnership 53 in ten overs between Grayson and Peters, but 163 proved more than enough. Once Knight went for 42 out of 66, Warwickshire's middle order were squeezed out by Grayson's nagging spin. With the target down to 64 in 20 overs, he dismissed Sheikh, Hemp and Brown in four overs to reach 100 League wickets (for Yorkshire and Essex). Earlier in the day he had scored his 1,000th League run for Essex.

Essex

S. G. Law c Knight b Sheikh	14	A. P. Cowan lbw b Brown	2
D. D. J. Robinson b Giles	31		
*R. C. Irani b Sheikh	14	B 2, l-b 5, w 2	9
S. D. Peters c Penney b Smith	39		
A. P. Grayson not out	41	1/41 2/61 3/77 (7 wkts, 45 overs)	163
D. R. Law c Giddins b Brown	9	4/130 5/146	
G. R. Napier c Ostler b Welch	4	6/153 7/163	

†B. J. Hyam, T. J. Mason and M. C. Ilott did not bat.

Bowling: Giddins 9–1–21–0; Welch 9–1–39–1; Sheikh 9–1–24–2; Giles 9–1–22–1; Smith 4–0–23–1; Brown 5–0–27–2.

Warwickshire

N. V. Knight c Napier b Mason	42	*N. M. K. Smith b D. R. Law	4
G. Welch c and b Ilott	0	†K. I. Piper not out	0
D. P. Ostler c Grayson b Ilott	18	E. S. H. Giddins lbw b Cowan	0
M. A. Sheikh lbw b Grayson	18	L-b 9, w 1	10
T. L. Penney b Cowan	28		
D. L. Hemp b Grayson	1	1/8 2/61 3/66 (40.2 overs)	139
D. R. Brown lbw b Grayson	8	4/100 5/102 6/110	
A. F. Giles b D. R. Law	10	7/133 8/139 9/139	

Bowling: Irani 7–1–19–0; Ilott 7–0–35–2; Cowan 6.2–0–24–2; Mason 9–0–27–1; Grayson 9–0–21–3; D. R. Law 2–0–4–2.

Umpires: B. Leadbeater and P. Willey.

At Swansea, July 2. WARWICKSHIRE tied with GLAMORGAN (D/L method).

At Derby, July 16. WARWICKSHIRE beat DERBYSHIRE by 45 runs.

WARWICKSHIRE v DURHAM

At Birmingham, July 23. Durham won by 50 runs. Toss: Durham.

Warwickshire's third successive home defeat dropped them to fourth in Division Two. Yet again, they batted ineptly on a substandard one-day pitch, and too many runs were given away by poor spin bowling and shoddy fielding. Katich hit an attractive 64 off 85 balls and, in a partnership marked by good running, added 118 in 25 overs with Collingwood. A rare failure by Knight exposed his colleagues' shortcomings, with only Brown getting beyond 20. Brown was earlier involved in an incident which led to umpire Whitehead being fined £250 for "a breach of the ECB directive relating to fair and proper conduct on the field of play".

Durham

J. J. B. Lewis b Brown	16	J. Wood not out		5
M. A. Gough b Giddins	25	†A. Pratt not out		1
S. M. Katich c Welch b Donald	64	L-b 9, w 15, n-b 2		26
P. D. Collingwood c Smith b Brown	53			
*N. J. Speak b Giles b Donald	2	1/42 2/54 3/172	(6 wkts, 45 overs)	198
M. P. Speight b Brown	6	4/182 5/188 6/197		

N. C. Phillips, I. D. Hunter and N. Killeen did not bat.

Bowling: Giddins 9–2–20–1; Welch 6–0–31–0; Brown 9–0–45–3; Donald 9–1–28–2; Giles 9–0–43–0; Smith 3–0–22–0.

Warwickshire

N. V. Knight lbw b Killeen	8	†T. Frost lbw b Collingwood		18
G. Welch b Killeen	10	A. A. Donald b Killeen		11
A. F. Giles c Collingwood b Hunter	17	E. S. H. Giddins not out		0
D. P. Ostler b Hunter	10	L-b 3, w 7		10
T. L. Penney st Pratt b Wood	12			
D. R. Brown c Collingwood b Wood	30	1/17 2/20 3/45	(40.1 overs)	148
M. J. Powell c Collingwood b Phillips	2	4/46 5/84 6/93		
*N. M. K. Smith c Killeen b Phillips	20	7/94 8/134 9/148		

Bowling: Wood 9–1–29–2; Killeen 8–1–24–3; Hunter 7–1–21–2; Collingwood 5–0–25–1; Phillips 8.1–1–31–2; Katich 3–0–15–0.

Umpires: M. J. Kitchen and A. G. T. Whitehead.

At Nottingham, August 1 (day/night). WARWICKSHIRE beat NOTTINGHAMSHIRE by 95 runs.

At Whitgift School, August 9. WARWICKSHIRE lost to SURREY by 103 runs.

At Chester-le-Street, August 14. WARWICKSHIRE beat DURHAM by seven wickets.

WARWICKSHIRE v MIDDLESEX

At Birmingham, August 16 (day/night). Middlesex won by 15 runs. Toss: Middlesex.

A slow pitch with little bounce, and Edgbaston's inadequate floodlights, made the toss too important. Middlesex lost Strauss first ball, but Langer built a useful platform in stands with Ramprakash, who went past 5,000 League runs, and Joyce. Although six wickets fell, 37 runs in Middlesex's last seven overs put the game out of Warwickshire's reach. Batting second was too big a handicap and they were rarely up with the required run-rate.

Middlesex

A. J. Strauss lbw b Welch	0	P. N. Weekes run out	4
†D. Alleyne c Penney b Welch	5	B. L. Hutton not out	5
*J. L. Langer run out	93	T. F. Bloomfield not out	3
M. R. Ramprakash st Piper b Giles	37	L-b 1, w 6	7
E. C. Joyce c Penney b Brown	34		
K. P. Dutch c Powell b Sheikh	3	1/0 2/23 3/91	(9 wkts, 45 overs) 201
S. J. Cook b Brown	10	4/164 5/167 6/179	
R. L. Johnson b Brown	0	7/179 8/191 9/195	

Bowling: Welch 9–1–32–2; Richardson 7–1–32–0; Sheikh 5–0–38–1; Brown 9–1–35–3; Giles 9–0–37–1; Smith 6–0–26–0.

Warwickshire

G. Welch b Johnson	21	†K. J. Piper not out	5
A. Singh c Ramprakash b Cook	28	M. A. Sheikh run out	16
A. F. Giles st Alleyne b Hutton	16	A. Richardson run out	0
D. P. Ostler lbw b Hutton	24	B 1, l-b 11, w 5	17
T. L. Penney lbw b Hutton	24		
M. J. Powell b Hutton	13	1/41 2/58 3/86	(44 overs) 186
D. R. Brown c Langer b Dutch	14	4/109 5/133 6/140	
*N. M. K. Smith b Bloomfield	8	7/162 8/162 9/186	

Bowling: Johnson 9–1–47–1; Bloomfield 9–0–25–1; Cook 8–2–30–1; Dutch 9–0–40–1; Hutton 9–2–32–4.

Umpires: N. A. Mallender and J. F. Steele.

WARWICKSHIRE v DERBYSHIRE

At Birmingham, September 3. Warwickshire won by 44 runs. Toss: Warwickshire.

Donald, in his farewell match at Edgbaston, received an emotional ovation after wrapping up the victory that kept Warwickshire in the promotion frame. Batting first, they looked shaky at 136 for five, but Powell and Brown's partnership of 78 eased them towards a more secure total of 233. Di Venuto's 84 in 88 balls was threatening until he became Dagnall's fourth wicket in a career best return.

Warwickshire

M. A. Wagh c Pyemont b Munton	31	†K. J. Piper not out	12
A. Singh c Sutton b Aldred	11	A. A. Donald not out	4
A. F. Giles c Sutton b Cassar	36		
D. P. Ostler b Wharton	36	L-b 6, w 11	17
T. L. Penney c Sutton b Cassar	6		
M. J. Powell c Di Venuto b Aldred	41	1/47 2/49 3/119	(8 wkts, 45 overs) 233
D. R. Brown lbw b Munton	36	4/129 5/136 6/214	
*N. M. K. Smith c Pyemont b Aldred	3	7/216 8/220	

C. E. Dagnall did not bat.

Bowling: Munton 9–2–40–2; Dean 7–0–41–0; Aldred 9–0–49–3; Cassar 9–1–29–2; Wharton 8–0–49–1; Dowman 3–0–19–0.

Derbyshire

M. E. Cassar c Ostler b Dagnall	5	*T. A. Munton c Piper b Brown	4
M. J. Di Venuto c Giles b Dagnall	84	K. J. Dean c Giles b Donald	8
R. J. Bailey c Brown b Dagnall	6	L. J. Wharton not out	1
M. P. Dowman c Piper b Dagnall	6	L-b 2, w 7	9
S. D. Stubbings st Piper b Giles	41		
†L. D. Sutton lbw b Smith	1	1/10 2/28 3/40	(43 overs) 189
J. P. Pyemont b Giles	24	4/146 5/149 6/155	
P. Aldred b Giles	0	7/156 8/180 9/183	

Bowling: Brown 8–0–42–1; Dagnall 9–2–34–4; Donald 8–1–26–1; Giles 9–0–45–3; Smith 9–0–40–1.

Umpires: J. W. Lloyds and R. Palmer.

At Lord's, September 9. WARWICKSHIRE beat MIDDLESEX by 37 runs.

At Chelmsford, September 17. WARWICKSHIRE beat ESSEX by six wickets.

NATIONAL LEAGUE RECORDS

40 overs available in all games up to 1998, except for 1993, when teams played 50 overs;
45 overs since 1999.

Batting

Highest individual scores: 203, A. D. Brown, Surrey v Hampshire, Guildford, 1997; 176, G. A. Gooch, Essex v Glamorgan, Southend, 1983; 175*, I. T. Botham, Somerset v Northamptonshire, Wellingborough School, 1986.

Most runs: 8,573, G. A. Gooch; 8,447, K. J. Barnett; 7,526, C. W. J. Athey; 7,499, W. Larkins; 7,183, G. A. Hick; 7,062, D. W. Randall; 7,040, D. L. Amiss; 6,695, R. T. Robinson; 6,690, P. Johnson; 6,673, M. W. Gatting; 6,650, C. T. Radley. **In a season:** 917, T. M. Moody, Worcestershire, 1991.

Most hundreds: 14, W. Larkins; 12, G. A. Gooch; 11, C. G. Greenidge and G. A. Hick; 10, T. M. Moody and R. A. Smith; 9, K. S. McEwan and B. A. Richards. 630 hundreds have been scored in the League. The most in one season is 40 in 1990.

Most sixes in an innings: 13, I. T. Botham, Somerset v Northamptonshire, Wellingborough School, 1986. **By a team in an innings:** 18, Derbyshire v Worcestershire, Knypersley, 1985, and Surrey v Yorkshire, Scarborough, 1994. **In a season:** 26, I. V. A. Richards, Somerset, 1977.

Highest total: 375 for four, Surrey v Yorkshire, Scarborough, 1994. **By a side batting second:** 317 for six, Surrey v Nottinghamshire, The Oval, 1993 (50-overs match).

Highest match aggregate: 631 for 13 wickets, Nottinghamshire (314 for seven) v Surrey (317 for six), The Oval, 1993 (50-overs match).

Lowest total: 23 (19.4 overs), Middlesex v Yorkshire, Leeds, 1974.

Shortest completed innings: 16 overs (59), Northamptonshire v Middlesex, Tring, 1974.

Record partnerships for each wicket

239	for 1st	G. A. Gooch and B. R. Hardie, Essex v Nottinghamshire at Nottingham .	1985
273	for 2nd	G. A. Gooch and K. S. McEwan, Essex v Nottinghamshire at Nottingham	1983
223	for 3rd	S. J. Cook and G. D. Rose, Somerset v Glamorgan at Neath	1990
219	for 4th	C. G. Greenidge and C. L. Smith, Hampshire v Surrey at Southampton .	1987
220*	for 5th	C. C. Lewis and P. A. Nixon, Leicestershire v Kent, Canterbury	1999
137	for 6th	M. P. Speight and I. D. K. Salisbury, Sussex v Surrey at Guildford	1996
132	for 7th	K. R. Brown and N. F. Williams, Middlesex v Somerset at Lord's	1988
110*	for 8th	C. L. Cairns and B. N. French, Nottinghamshire v Surrey at The Oval . .	1993
105	for 9th	D. G. Moir and R. W. Taylor, Derbyshire v Kent at Derby	1984
82	for 10th	G. Chapple and P. J. Martin, Lancashire v Worcestershire at Manchester .	1996

Bowling

Most wickets: 386, J. K. Lever; 368, J. E. Emburey; 346, D. L. Underwood; 307, J. Simmons; 303, S. Turner; 284, N. Gifford; 281, E. E. Hemmings; 267, J. N. Shepherd; 264, R. K. Illingworth; 261, G. C. Small; 260, A. C. S. Pigott; 256, I. T. Botham. **In a season:** 39, A. J. Hollioake, Surrey, 1996.

Best bowling: eight for 26, K. D. Boyce, Essex v Lancashire, Manchester, 1971; seven for 15, R. A. Hutton, Yorkshire v Worcestershire, Leeds, 1969; seven for 16, S. D. Thomas, Glamorgan v Surrey, Swansea, 1998; seven for 30, M. P. Bicknell, Surrey v Glamorgan, The Oval, 1999; seven for 39, A. Hodgson, Northamptonshire v Somerset, Northampton, 1976; seven for 41, A. N. Jones, Sussex v Nottinghamshire, Nottingham, 1986; six for six, R. W. Hooker, Middlesex v Surrey, Lord's, 1969; six for seven, M. Hendrick, Derbyshire v Nottinghamshire, Nottingham, 1972; six for nine, N. G. Cowans, Middlesex v Lancashire, Lord's, 1991.

Most economical analysis: 8–8–0–0, B. A. Langford, Somerset v Essex, Yeovil, 1969.

Most expensive analyses: 8–0–96–1, D. G. Cork, Derbyshire v Nottinghamshire, Nottingham, 1993; 8–0–94–2, P. N. Weekes, Middlesex v Leicestershire, Leicester, 1994; 7.5–0–89–3, G. Miller, Derbyshire v Gloucestershire, Gloucester, 1984; 8–0–88–1, E. E. Hemmings, Nottinghamshire v Somerset, Nottingham, 1983.

Hat-tricks: There have been 31 hat-tricks, four of them for Glamorgan.

Four wickets in four balls: A. Ward, Derbyshire v Sussex, Derby, 1970; V. C. Drakes, Nottinghamshire v Derbyshire, Nottingham, 1999.

Wicket-keeping and Fielding

Most dismissals: 336 (259 ct, 77 st), S. J. Rhodes; 257 (234 ct, 23 st), D. L. Bairstow; 244 (199 ct, 45 st), R. C. Russell; 236 (187 ct, 49 st), R. W. Taylor; 235 (203 ct, 32 st), W. K. Hegg; 223 (184 ct, 39 st), E. W. Jones; 220 (197 ct, 23 st), S. A. Marsh. **In a season:** 32 (26 ct, 6 st), R. J. Blakey, Yorkshire, 1999. **In an innings:** 7 (6 ct, 1 st), R. W. Taylor, Derbyshire v Lancashire, Manchester, 1975.

Most catches in an innings: 6, K. Goodwin, Lancashire v Worcestershire, Worcester, 1969; R. W. Taylor, Derbyshire v Lancashire, Manchester, 1975; K. M. Krikken, Derbyshire v Hampshire, Southampton, 1994; and P. A. Nixon, Leicestershire v Essex, Leicester, 1994.

Most stumpings in an innings: 4, S. J. Rhodes, Worcestershire v Warwickshire, Birmingham, 1986 and N. D. Burns, Somerset v Kent, Taunton, 1991.

Most catches by a fielder: 103, V. P. Terry; 101, J. F. Steele; 100, K. J. Barnett and G. A. Gooch; 97, D. P. Hughes; 95, C. W. J. Athey†; 94, G. Cook and P. W. G. Parker. **In a season:** 16, J. M. Rice, Hampshire, 1978. **In an innings:** 5, J. M. Rice, Hampshire v Warwickshire, Southampton, 1978.

† C. W. J. Athey also took two catches as a wicket-keeper.

Results

Largest victory in runs: Somerset by 220 runs v Glamorgan, Neath, 1990.

Victories by ten wickets (33): By Derbyshire, Durham, Essex (four times), Glamorgan (twice), Hampshire (twice), Kent, Lancashire, Leicestershire (twice), Middlesex (twice), Northamptonshire, Nottinghamshire, Somerset (twice), Surrey (three times), Warwickshire, Worcestershire (six times) and Yorkshire (three times). This does not include those matches in which the side batting second was set a reduced target but does include matches where both sides faced a reduced number of overs.

Ties: There have been 55 tied matches. Worcestershire have tied 11 times.

Shortest match: 1 hr 53 min (26.3 overs), Surrey v Leicestershire, The Oval, 1996.

CHAMPIONS 1969-2000

John Player's County League
1969   Lancashire

John Player League
1970   Lancashire
1971   Worcestershire
1972   Kent
1973   Kent
1974   Leicestershire
1975   Hampshire
1976   Kent
1977   Leicestershire
1978   Hampshire
1979   Somerset
1980   Warwickshire
1981   Essex
1982   Sussex
1983   Yorkshire

John Player Special League
1984   Essex
1985   Essex
1986   Hampshire

Refuge Assurance League
1987   Worcestershire
1988   Worcestershire
1989   Lancashire
1990   Derbyshire
1991   Nottinghamshire

Sunday League
1992   Middlesex

AXA Equity & Law League
1993   Glamorgan
1994   Warwickshire
1995   Kent
1996   Surrey

AXA Life League
1997   Warwickshire

AXA League
1998   Lancashire

CGU National League
1999   Lancashire

Norwich Union National League
2000   Gloucestershire

MATCH RESULTS 1969-2000

	P	W	L	T	NR	1st	2nd	3rd
			Matches				*League positions*	
Derbyshire	519	210	250	5	54	1	0	1
Durham	151	41	90	3	17	0	0	0
Essex	519	262	204	9	44	3	5*	4
Glamorgan	519	188	270	7	54	1	0	0
Gloucestershire	519	185	268	4	62	1	1	1
Hampshire	519	241	228	7	43	3	1	3
Kent	519	279	184	6	50	4	4	5
Lancashire	519	268	183	10	58	5	2	3
Leicestershire	519	224	226	5	64	2	2*	2
Middlesex	519	230	226	9	54	1	1	3
Northamptonshire	519	208	251	6	54	0	0	2
Nottinghamshire	519	223	245	4	47	1	3	1
Somerset	519	248	218	3	50	1	6*	0
Surrey	519	231	227	5	56	1	0	1
Sussex	519	222	236	6	55	1	2*	1
Warwickshire	519	227	231	7	54	3	2	1
Worcestershire	519	253	206	11	49	3	4	2
Yorkshire	519	235	232	3	49	1	2	1

* *Includes one shared 2nd place in 1976.*

UMPIRES FOR 2001

FIRST-CLASS UMPIRES

M. R. Benson, G. I. Burgess, A. Clarkson, D. J. Constant, N. G. Cowley, B. Dudleston, J. H. Evans, J. H. Hampshire, M. J. Harris, J. W. Holder, V. A. Holder, T. E. Jesty, A. A. Jones, R. Julian, M. J. Kitchen, B. Leadbeater, J. W. Lloyds, N. A. Mallender, K. E. Palmer, R. Palmer, G. Sharp, D. R. Shepherd, J. F. Steele, R. A. White, A. G. T. Whitehead and P. Willey. *Reserves:* P. Adams, N. L. Bainton, M. Dixon, I. J. Gould, C. S. Kelly, N. J. Llong, K. J. Lyons, K. Shuttleworth.

MINOR COUNTIES UMPIRES

P. Adams, N. L. Bainton, S. F. Bishopp, P. Brown, A. R. Bundy, D. L. Burden, P. D. Clubb, K. Coburn, M. Dixon, A. J. Hardy, J. Ilott, J. H. James, M. A. Johnson, C. S. Kelly, P. W. Kingston-Davey, S. W. Kuhlmann, G. I. McLean, C. Megennis, M. P. Moran, W. Morgan, C. T. Puckett, G. P. Randall-Johnson, J. G. Reed, T. R. Riley, G. Ripley, K. S. Shenton, W. E. Smith, R. M. Sutton, J. M. Tythcott, T. G. Wilson and R. Wood. *Reserves:* J. T. Brady, A. C. Briggs, R. G. Eagleton, H. Evans, J. S. Johnson, P. W. Joy, C. L. McNamee, S. Marszal, C. G. Pocock, A. P. Price, D. G. Tate, G. Watkins, M. C. White, J. Wilkinson.

CAREER FIGURES

Players not expected to appear in county cricket in 2001.

BATTING

	M	I	NO	R	HS	100s	Avge	1,000r/ season
S. M. Ali	4	5	0	25	18	0	5.00	0
D. A. Altree	6	8	3	6	4	0	1.20	0
J. J. Bates	21	32	2	411	57	0	13.70	0
C. J. Batt	12	17	2	177	43	0	11.80	0
M. N. Bowen	67	92	26	817	32	0	12.37	0
M. T. Brimson	66	66	27	459	54*	0	11.76	0
M. K. Davies	26	38	9	261	32*	0	9.00	0
R. L. Eagleson	2	3	2	91	50*	0	91.00	0
I. N. Flanagan	18	32	1	580	61	0	18.70	0
G. A. Gooch	581	990	75	44,846	333	128	49.01	21‡
D. J. Goodchild	9	18	1	354	105	1	20.82	0
R. J. Harden	253	417	63	13,336	187	28	37.67	7
P. J. Hartley	232	283	66	4,321	127*	2	19.91	0
M. E. Harvey	7	11	1	155	39	0	15.50	0
G. R. Haynes	100	155	16	4,173	158	3	30.02	1
G. R. Haywood	1	2	0	15	14	0	7.50	0
S. Humphries	31	47	5	555	66	0	13.21	0
J. W. Inglis	1	2	0	4	2	0	2.00	0
P. W. Jarvis	215	268	67	3,373	80	0	16.78	0
G. J. Kennis	12	23	1	436	175	1	19.81	0
A. A. Khan	24	29	5	337	52	0	14.04	0
W. G. Khan	57	101	8	2,834	181	5	30.47	0
S. J. Lacey	26	36	10	553	55*	0	21.26	0
W. L. Law	23	35	4	883	131	1	28.48	0
C. C. Lewis	189	275	34	7,406	247	9	30.73	0
P. C. McKeown	19	27	1	679	75	0	26.11	0
S. A. Marsh	291	429	69	10,098	142	9	28.05	0
M. M. Mirza	6	7	4	17	10*	0	5.66	0
A. R. Oram	19	28	13	53	13	0	3.53	0
A. D. Patterson	9	13	0	125	31	0	9.61	0
M. T. E. Peirce	69	122	2	2,928	123	2	24.40	0
S. J. Renshaw	39	48	20	459	56	0	16.39	0
P. M. Ridgway	5	7	3	48	35	0	12.00	0
D. J. Roberts	17	30	1	751	117	1	25.89	0
P. E. Robinson	159	261	35	7,617	189	7	33.70	0
A. Sachdeva	1	2	1	0	0*	0	0.00	0
L. Savident	4	6	2	32	10*	0	8.00	0
†M. Saxelby	61	106	7	2,916	181	2	29.45	1
D. A. Scott	8	10	8	46	17*	0	23.00	0
K. Z. Shah	4	6	2	102	38*	0	25.50	0
R. V. Sutcliffe	2	2	1	9	9*	0	9.00	0
D. J. Thompson	11	13	0	109	22	0	8.38	0
J. B. D. Thompson	36	48	19	546	65*	0	18.82	0
D. Williamson	9	13	4	273	47	0	30.33	0
N. T. Wood	30	45	5	1,179	155	1	29.47	0

* *Signifies not out.*
† *Died October 12, 2000.*
‡ *Includes 1,363 runs scored overseas in India, Sri Lanka and South Africa in 1981-82.*

BOWLING AND FIELDING

	R	W	BB	Avge	5W/i	10W/m	Ct/St
S. M. Ali	9	0	–	–	–	–	1
D. A. Altree	497	8	3-41	62.12	–	–	1
J. J. Bates	1,528	49	5-67	31.18	4	0	17
C. J. Batt	1,092	37	6-101	29.51	2	0	3
M. N. Bowen	5,925	183	7-73	32.37	7	1	17
M. T. Brimson	4,069	124	5-12	32.81	3	0	11
M. K. Davies	2,062	79	6-49	26.10	–	–	7
R. L. Eagleson	183	4	2-50	45.75	–	–	3
I. N. Flanagan	51	1	1-50	51.00	–	–	19
G. A. Gooch	8,457	246	7-14	34.37	3	0	555
D. J. Goodchild	88	0	–	–	–	–	1
R. J. Harden	1,023	20	2-7	51.15	–	–	3
P. J. Hartley	20,635	683	9-41	30.21	23	3	68
M. E. Harvey	48	0	–	–	–	–	3
G. R. Haynes	3,541	96	6-50	36.88	2	0	39
G. R. Haywood	66	0	–	–	–	–	0
P. W. Jarvis	18,914	654	7-55	28.92	22	3	67
G. J. Kennis	4	0	–	–	–	–	13
A. A. Khan	2,009	48	5-137	41.85	1	0	9
W. G. Khan	62	0	–	–	–	–	36
S. J. Lacey	1,429	30	4-84	47.63	–	–	8/1
W. L. Law	89	3	2-29	29.66	–	–	11
C. C. Lewis	16,225	543	6-22	29.88	20	3	154
S. A. Marsh	240	2	2-20	120.00	–	–	688/61
M. M. Mirza	620	19	4-51	32.63	–	–	1
A. R. Oram	1,653	57	4-37	29.00	–	–	6
M. T. E. Peirce	272	3	1-16	90.66	–	–	30
S. J. Renshaw	3,580	93	5-110	38.49	1	0	14
P. M. Ridgway	301	6	3-51	50.16	–	–	0
P. E. Robinson	329	3	1-10	109.66	–	–	130
A. Sachdeva	54	1	1-32	54.00	–	–	0
L. Savident	286	4	2-86	71.50	–	–	2
M. Saxelby	903	11	3-41	82.09	–	–	18
D. A. Scott	613	13	4-151	47.15	–	–	3
K. Z. Shah	260	4	2-24	65.00	–	–	0
R. V. Sutcliffe	164	4	2-88	41.00	–	–	0
D. J. Thompson	914	29	4-46	31.51	–	–	1
J. B. D. Thompson	3,103	122	7-81	25.43	5	0	5
D. Williamson	529	14	3-19	37.78	–	–	5
N. T. Wood	154	0	–	–	–	–	5

Note: The following players did not bowl but made fielding or wicket-keeping dismissals:
S. Humphries 56 ct, 3 st; P. C. McKeown 14 ct; A. D. Patterson 16 ct; D. J. Roberts 8 ct.

THE UNIVERSITIES IN 2000

OXFORD

President: A. C. Smith (Brasenose)
Hon. Treasurer: Dr S. R. Porter (St Cross College)

Captain: T. C. Hicks (Lord Wandsworth College and St Catherine's)
Secretary: R. G. Smalley (RGS, Newcastle and Keble)

Captain for 2001: N. Millar (Fettes and Christ Church)
Secretary: C. P. Stearn (Bedford and Worcester)

It was in 1827 that Oxford and Cambridge first met at Lord's, but the 2000 fixture, washed out on its final day, marked the close of an era. As the England and Wales Cricket Board's reform of university cricket saw Oxford become one of six University Centres of Excellence in 2001, it was decided that the first-class Varsity Match should alternate between Fenner's and The Parks. The one-day fixture, introduced in the 1990s, would be played at Lord's instead, the day after the Centre of Excellence final.

Oxford were already preparing for their new status in 2000 when, for the first time, they played under the title Oxford Universities; cricketers from Oxford Brookes University, formerly Oxford Polytechnic, were eligible to wear the Dark Blue cap alongside students from the traditional institution, though not in the Varsity Match itself (nor, in 2000, in the BUSA league, in which Oxford reached the semi-finals). Eventually, it was hoped, extending the franchise would lift playing standards to accommodate first-class status more comfortably. By the end of the season, there were reports that more than a team's worth of contracted county players had applied to Oxford Brookes, where the academic entry requirements were less daunting to those who have spent summers developing their cricketing as well as scholastic skills.

The full effect was not yet felt in 2000. Of the four Brookes players who appeared in first-class matches, only Joe Porter was in the side that achieved the season's most notable success. That was a three-wicket victory over Northamptonshire – Oxford's first win against county opposition since they won at Canterbury in 1998, and their first first-class win in The Parks since they beat Glamorgan in 1997.

Apart from that memorable event, it was business as usual. At the start of the term, when counties were keen to put out virtually full sides and the students were still settling in to the requirements of first-class cricket, it was a struggle to avoid embarrassment, and there were heavy defeats by Somerset and Glamorgan. Later, more acceptable scorecards were evident, and it was significant that the victory over Northamptonshire came in the last home fixture of the season. The visitors were not seriously depleted, and were prepared to make a genuine contest with two declarations, albeit with seven and eight wickets down.

Even so, there were some laudable individual performances in other games. New Zealander Scott Weenink marked his first-class debut with a polished 72 at Taunton, where Richard Smalley, a more than competent wicket-keeper, showed the first signs of being a productive batsman as well. He was easily the season's leading run-scorer, with 272, and maintained an average above 30, a fine effort. Promoted to open, he started with a duck, but in his next innings scored 83 at Bristol. Porter, like Smalley a left-hander, showed he had adapted to his new surroundings in that match, with the first of three first-class fifties; he was the only other player to reach 200 runs. Soccer blue James Redmayne was not always available, for academic reasons, but he also managed a fifty. Byron Byrne batted usefully on his two appearances, as did Alan Gofton, most notably in a last-wicket century partnership against Northamptonshire with the expansive Salman Khan.

OXFORD UNIVERSITY 2000

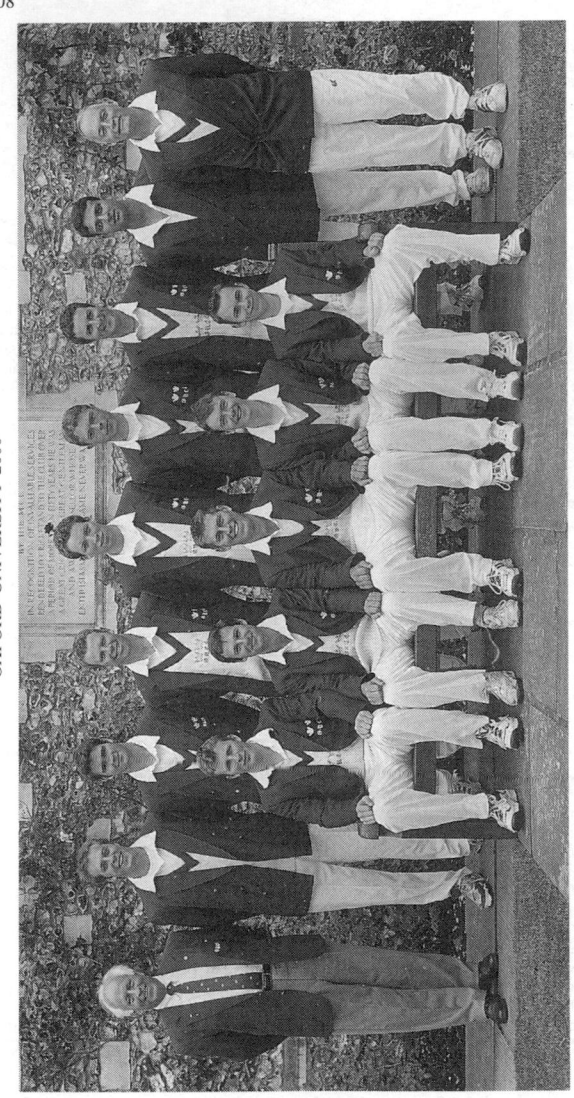

[*Bill Smith*]

Back row: N. T. Harris (*scorer*), C. C. M. Warren, N. Millar, S. W. Weenink, J. R. S. Redmayne, A. F. Gofton, R. Garland, Salman Khan, J. Potter (*coach*).
Front row: A. Claughton, B. W. Byrne, T. C. Hicks (*captain*), D. P. Mather, R. G. Smalley.

The captain, Tom Hicks, disappointed with the bat after his promise of the previous season, but his off-breaks came into their own when he took nine wickets against Northamptonshire. Otherwise, the attack lacked penetration, especially as medical studies and injury restricted the appearances of left-arm seamer David Mather, who made his debut back in 1995. He played in the first match of the season, at Taunton, but did not reappear in a first-class fixture until Lord's, where the bowlers struggled to contain the Cambridge batsmen. Cambridge won the one-day game in June. – RALPH DELLOR.

OXFORD UNIVERSITIES RESULTS

First-class matches – Played 6: Won 1, Lost 2, Drawn 3. Abandoned 1.

FIRST-CLASS AVERAGES

BATTING AND FIELDING

	M	I	NO	R	HS	100s	50s	Avge	Ct/St
Salman Khan	5	5	1	143	87	0	1	35.75	2
R. G. Smalley	6	10	1	272	83	0	1	30.22	6/4
J. R. S. Redmayne	4	6	1	139	68	0	1	27.80	0
J. J. Porter	5	9	0	204	67	0	3	22.66	0
A. F. Gofton	6	7	1	117	47*	0	0	19.50	0
S. W. Weenink	6	9	2	124	72*	0	1	17.71	4
J. A. Claughton	3	5	1	45	19*	0	0	11.25	0
C. C. M. Warren	3	5	1	41	21	0	0	10.25	1
R. Garland	4	6	1	27	15	0	0	5.40	1
A. M. T. Janmohamed	3	4	1	16	6	0	0	5.33	0
T. C. Hicks	6	6	1	20	10	0	0	4.00	5
A. S. Bones	4	7	0	24	7	0	0	3.42	0

Also batted: B. W. Byrne (2 matches) 30, 34 (1 ct); R. W. S. Carroll (1 match) 0*; D. P. Mather (2 matches) 13, 5; N. Millar (2 matches) 0 (1 ct); Ali Sawal (1 match) 2*, 0; B. M. Vonwiller (2 matches) 0, 1* (2 ct). J. A. D. Brooker (1 match) (1 ct) did not bat.

* *Signifies not out.*

BOWLING

	O	M	R	W	BB	5W/i	Avge
T. C. Hicks	147	29	570	14	5-54	1	40.71
B. M. Vonwiller	30	4	137	3	2-59	0	45.66
R. Garland	68.3	8	325	7	2-73	0	46.42
D. P. Mather	54.2	11	202	3	2-73	0	67.33
Salman Khan	135	25	417	6	2-34	0	69.50
S. W. Weenink	127	13	480	6	3-121	0	80.00

Also bowled: Ali Sawal 28–9–96–2; J. A. D. Brooker 6–0–38–0; R. W. S. Carroll 7–0–52–0; A. F. Gofton 88.2–7–386–1; A. M. T. Janmohamed 6–0–29–0; N. Millar 3–0–17–0; J. J. Porter 4–0–43–0.

Salman Khan was known as S. H. Khan in Wisden 2000.

Note: Matches in this section which were not first-class are signified by a dagger.

At Taunton, April 7, 8, 9. OXFORD UNIVERSITIES lost to SOMERSET by 404 runs.

OXFORD UNIVERSITIES v HAMPSHIRE

At Oxford, April 11, 12, 13. Abandoned. Toss: Oxford Universities.

Heavy rain ten minutes before the start prevented Hampshire from starting their innings on the first day; the entire match was abandoned at nine o'clock on the second morning, when the players arrived at the ground to find a covering of snow.

†At Oxford, April 17. No result. Toss: Oxford Universities. Hertfordshire 73 for three (24.4 overs) v Oxford Universities.

†At Oxford, April 21. No result. Toss: Wiltshire. Wiltshire 207 for six (45 overs) (B. L. Crosdale 82, J. L. Taylor 52); Oxford Universities 96 for three (25 overs) (A. S. Bones 43 not out).

†At Bournemouth, April 24. No result. Toss: Oxford Universities. Oxford Universities 178 (49.5 overs) (R. G. Smalley 55; V. J. Pike three for 29, G. R. Treagus four for 42); Dorset 55 for one (19 overs).

OXFORD UNIVERSITIES v WARWICKSHIRE

At Oxford, April 26, 27, 28. Drawn. Toss: Oxford Universities. First-class debut: J. A. D. Brooker.

After four full days had been lost to the weather, The Parks finally saw some first-class cricket on the second day here. Warwickshire's top order made full use of a benign pitch and attack, running up 356 at four an over after Knight made an early exit, bowled by Salman Khan's in-swinger. Penney scored his first county century in nearly four years, and Hemp fell only four short of another. In the seven overs possible after Smith declared, Oxford's first three batsmen were all dismissed for nought; then it was back to the rain.

Close of play: First day, No play; Second day, Oxford Universities 10-3 (Weenink 9*, Warren 1*).

Warwickshire

M. J. Powell c Salman Khan b Vonwiller	40		D. R. Brown not out	4
N. V. Knight b Salman Khan	2			
D. P. Ostler c Brooker b Vonwiller	75		L-b 1, w 6, n-b 4	11
D. L. Hemp c and b Weenink	96			
T. L. Penney not out	100		1/13 2/58	(5 wkts dec.) 356
*N. M. K. Smith c Salman Khan b Weenink	28		3/155 4/287	
			5/343	

A. F. Giles, †T. Frost, A. A. Donald and E. S. H. Giddins did not bat.

Bowling: Salman Khan 17–4–52–1; Vonwiller 14–2–59–2; Gofton 15–2–81–0; Hicks 13–1–54–0; Brooker 6–0–38–0; Weenink 22.4–4–71–2.

Oxford Universities

A. S. Bones c Powell b Donald	0
†R. G. Smalley lbw b Giddins	0
J. J. Porter b Donald	0
S. W. Weenink not out	9
C. C. M. Warren not out	1

1/0 2/0 3/4   (3 wkts) 10

A. F. Gofton, A. M. T. Janmohamed, *T. C. Hicks, Salman Khan, J. A. D. Brooker and B. M. Vonwiller did not bat.

Bowling: Donald 4–4–0–2; Giddins 3–0–10–1.

Umpires: G. J. Burgess and J. H. Evans.

†At Oxford, April 29. Oxford Universities won by 14 runs. Toss: Oxford Universities. Oxford Universities 246 for six (45 overs) (J. A. Claughton 71, B. W. Byrne 58, J. R. S. Redmayne 48 not out, Extras 35; C. A. Haupt three for 49); Oxfordshire 232 for eight (45 overs) (C. A. Haupt 61, R. J. Williams 38, A. P. Cook 48 not out; Salman Khan three for 18, B. W. Byrne four for 56).

†At Oxford, May 1. Buckinghamshire won by ten wickets. Toss: Oxford Universities. Oxford Universities 218 for four (50 overs) (R. Garland 45, A. F. Gofton 93, J. J. Porter 32 not out); Buckinghamshire 219 for no wkt (30.1 overs) (P. D. Atkins 102 not out, R. P. Lane 89 not out).

At Bristol, May 3, 4, 5. OXFORD UNIVERSITIES drew with GLOUCESTERSHIRE.

†At Arundel, May 11. Drawn. Toss: Oxford Universities. Earl of Arundel's XI 176 (J. J. B. van Bunge 62; C. P. Stearn four for 34); Oxford Universities 158 for seven (T. C. Hicks 49).

†At Wormsley, May 14. Drawn. Toss: Sir Paul Getty's XI. Oxford University 199 for nine dec. (C. C. M. Warren 32, J. R. S. Redmayne 100 not out, N. Millar 37; B. L. Hutton five for 40); Sir Paul Getty's XI 137 for nine (S. W. Weenink four for 41).

OXFORD UNIVERSITIES v GLAMORGAN

At Oxford, May 16, 17, 18. Glamorgan won by an innings and 203 runs. Toss: Oxford Universities. First-class debut: Ali Sawal.

Alarming collapses at either end of the match saw Oxford go down to an innings defeat. On the opening day, they slid to 74 for six, and only a partnership of 53 in 50 minutes between Redmayne and Warren provided a degree of respectability. In their second innings, a reshuffled order fared even worse, three men falling first ball as Parkin and Thomas reduced them to 18 for four. Porter, aided by Gofton and two lengthy rain-breaks, made Glamorgan wait for their victory. On the second day, the county had piled on the runs; their innings was stuffed with fifties, while Wharf recorded a maiden century.

Close of play: First day, Glamorgan 99-0 (Evans 52*, Law 40*); Second day, Oxford Universities 0-1 (Warren 0*).

Oxford Universities

R. Garland lbw b Parkin	2	– (9) lbw b Parkin	0
†R. G. Smalley b Parkin	9	– (3) c and b Cosker	31
A. F. Gofton b Newell	14	– (7) c Shaw b Jones	11
J. J. Porter c Law b Newell	15	– (6) c Shaw b Thomas	50
A. S. Bones lbw b Jones	4	– (4) lbw b Thomas	0
S. W. Weenink lbw b Parkin	7	– (5) lbw b Thomas	0
J. R. S. Redmayne c Cosker b Jones	68	– (8) lbw b Parkin	8
C. C. M. Warren lbw b Thomas	21	– (1) c Shaw b Parkin	7
*T. C. Hicks lbw b Cosker	5	– (10) not out	0
Salman Khan b Cosker	0	– (11) c Cosker b Thomas	4
Ali Sawal not out	2	– (2) lbw b Parkin	0
B 1, l-b 10, n-b 2	13	B 1	1

1/10 2/15 3/41 4/44 5/54   160   1/0 2/17 3/18 4/18 5/55   112
6/74 7/127 8/154 9/158   6/82 7/104 8/108 9/108

Bowling: *First Innings*—Thomas 11–3–19–1; Parkin 10–2–34–3; Wharf 12–1–34–0; Jones 11–1–32–2; Newell 11–6–18–2; Cosker 6.5–2–12–2. *Second Innings*—Thomas 8.2–2–14–4; Parkin 10–4–14–4; Jones 12–5–23–1; Wharf 7–1–25–0; Cosker 15–6–35–1.

Glamorgan

A. W. Evans lbw b Ali Sawal	58	A. G. Wharf not out	100
W. L. Law c Warren b Garland	85	S. D. Thomas not out	18
M. J. Powell c Weenink b Hicks	46	L-b 9, w 2, n-b 8	19
*M. P. Maynard c Smalley b Ali Sawal	71		
K. Newell b Garland	64	1/111 2/172 3/274 (6 wkts dec.) 475	
†A. D. Shaw b Hicks	14	4/274 5/322 6/415	

D. A. Cosker, S. P. Jones and O. T. Parkin did not bat.

Bowling: Salman Khan 27–2–102–0; Ali Sawal 28–9–96–2; Garland 17–1–73–2; Weenink 14–0–70–0; Hicks 21–4–80–2; Gofton 9–0–45–0.

Umpires: B. Leadbeater and K. J. Lyons.

†At Oxford, May 24, 25, 26. Drawn. Toss: Oxford Universities. Oxford Universities 232 (A. S. Bones 36, N. Millar 59, R. G. Smalley 48; R. Clarke three for 49, A. Gidman six for 53); MCC Young Cricketers 244 for one (T. D. Fray 134 not out, A. Duncan 85).

†At Oxford, May 29. Harlequins won by four wickets. Toss: Oxford University. Oxford University 178 (A. F. Gofton 71; I. J. Curtis four for 60); Harlequins 180 for six (J. A. M. Molins 44, J. H. Louw 50, B. W. Byrne 35, L. G. Buchanan 37 not out; D. P. Mather three for 54).

OXFORD UNIVERSITIES v NORTHAMPTONSHIRE

At Oxford, June 6, 7, 8. Oxford Universities won by three wickets. Toss: Oxford Universities. First-class debuts: N. Millar; R. A. White. County debut: M. R. Strong.

Improved bowling paved the way, but two dynamic innings from tailender Salman Khan were the key to Oxford's first victory over Northamptonshire since 1974, when Imran Khan starred. On the opening day, the student bowlers did good work, despite a hundred from Alec Swann. Their batsmen seemed to throw it all away, though, and 87 for nine told a familiar story. However, Khan and Gofton set about the county attack to add a remarkable 134 in 34 overs: Khan cracked 87 from 102 balls. Off-spinner Hicks then claimed a career-best five wickets, taking his match haul to nine, and Northamptonshire's last pair were together when the declaration set Oxford 243 in 68 overs. It looked possible while Porter, with his third fifty in successive matches, and Byrne were batting, but when Strong removed both the chance seemed wasted – until Khan joined Redmayne. Needing 61 from 15 overs, they did it with three to spare.

Close of play: First day, Oxford Universities 16-1 (Smalley 7*, Claughton 1*); Second day, Northamptonshire 114-4 (Bailey 38*, White 0*).

Northamptonshire

R. A. White c Smalley b Garland	11	– (6) c and b Hicks	20
A. J. Swann st Smalley b Hicks	108	– (7) c and b Hicks	0
J. W. Cook c Hicks b Salman Khan	32	– (2) c Smalley b Salman Khan	5
R. J. Warren c Smalley b Salman Khan	27	– (1) lbw b Garland	6
G. P. Swann b Hicks	16	– (3) c Byrne b Hicks	57
K. J. Innes not out	32	– (5) c Weenink b Hicks	4
*†T. M. B. Bailey st Smalley b Hicks	13	– (4) retired hurt	38
M. K. Davies c and b Hicks	6	– lbw b Salman Khan	8
M. R. Strong not out	10	– b Hicks	14
J. A. R. Blain (did not bat)		– not out	31
J. F. Brown (did not bat)		– not out	1
L-b 2, w 2, n-b 16	20	B 2, n-b 2	4

1/21 2/119 3/176 4/198 (7 wkts dec.) 275	1/11 2/11 3/102 (8 wkts dec.) 188
5/208 6/239 7/259	4/112 5/114 6/133
	7/149 8/160

In the second innings Bailey retired hurt at 114-4.

Bowling: *First Innings*—Salman Khan 23–3–80–2; Garland 12–4–51–1; Gofton 8–1–23–0; Weenink 18.4–3–56–0; Hicks 17–5–63–4. *Second Innings*—Salman Khan 13–4–34–2; Garland 5–0–34–1; Hicks 22–5–54–5; Gofton 5–0–29–0; Weenink 9–1–35–0.

Oxford Universities

R. Garland b Blain	3	– lbw b Strong	1
†R. G. Smalley lbw b Strong	18	– b Innes	29
J. A. Claughton lbw b Strong	4	– c White b Brown	18
J. J. Porter lbw b Innes	1	– b Strong	54
B. W. Byrne c White b Brown	30	– c Warren b Strong	34
S. W. Weenink b Innes	0	– (8) b Innes	13
J. R. S. Redmayne lbw b Davies	7	– not out	43
A. F. Gofton not out	47	– (6) c Warren b Strong	1
N. Millar c G. P. Swann b Brown	0		
*T. C. Hicks c Blain b Brown	10		
Salman Khan b Innes	87	– (9) not out	39
L-b 6, n-b 8	14	L-b 5, n-b 6	11

1/8 2/25 3/32 4/44 5/44	221	1/6 2/42 3/69 4/143	(7 wkts) 243
6/65 7/71 8/71 9/87		5/145 6/148 7/182	

Bowling: *First Innings*—Blain 13–1–37–1; Brown 23–3–60–3; Strong 12–5–31–2; Innes 7.4–1–23–3; Davies 19–7–40–1; G. P. Swann 6–1–24–0. *Second Innings*—Strong 15–3–46–4; Blain 9–2–37–0; Innes 10–3–31–2; Brown 9.5–1–49–1; Davies 5–1–26–0; G. P. Swann 16–2–49–0.

Umpires: N. L. Bainton and K. E. Palmer.

†At Oxford, June 9. Oxford Universities won by ten wickets. Toss: De Flamingo's. De Flamingo's 154 for eight (45 overs) (M. van Nierop 50; C. P. Stearn three for 33); Oxford Universities 155 for no wkt (27.5 overs) (A. S. Bones 92 not out, G. R. Butcher 52 not out).

†At Oxford, June 13, 14, 15. Drawn. Toss: Combined Services. Oxford University 248 (J. A. Claughton 30, J. R. S. Redmayne 67, M. K. Floyd 55; CPOMEA D. Garbutt three for 41, Lt C. R. Phillips five for 39) and 238 for five dec. (T. A. Swerling 31, J. R. S. Redmayne 109; Lt C. R. Phillips three for 71); Combined Services 284 for eight dec. (Lt P. Andrew 110, Cpl I. Redfern 76; A. F. Gofton four for 99) and 177 for seven (JT M. Bray 65; B. M. Vonwiller three for 58, T. C. Hicks four for 64).

†At Oxford, June 18. Cambridge University won by two wickets. Toss: Oxford University. Oxford University 233 for nine (50 overs) (J. A. Claughton 39, N. Millar 42, J. R. S. Redmayne 50, S. W. Weenink 43, Extras 31; S. M. Sheikh three for 37); Cambridge University 234 for eight (50 overs) (J. P. Pyemont 36, B. J. Collins 41, C. A. Sayers 33, Extras 33).

Cambridge lead 4–2 in the Johnson Fry limited-overs Varsity series.

†At Oxford, June 26, 27, 28. MCC won by 65 runs. Toss: MCC. MCC 306 for five dec. (Asif Mujtaba 117, D. J. Callaghan 63, B. W. Byrne 35 not out, C. Patel 35 not out) and 143 for four dec. (H. Pedrola 43, D. J. Callaghan 46 not out); Oxford University 174 (C. C. M. Warren 58, M. K. Floyd 33; Asif Mujtaba four for 28) and 210 (S. W. Weenink 37, D. C. Cohen 72; Asif Mujtaba four for 61).

†At Oxford, July 6, 7. Oxford University won by four wickets. Toss: Oxford University. Oxfordshire A 141 (D. P. Mather three for 32, A. F. Gofton three for 25) and 199 (J. France 52, S. Bates 36, A. P. Cook 45; T. C. Hicks three for 19, S. W. Weenink four for 30); Oxford University 211 for six dec. (J. A. Claughton 77, B. W. Byrne 50, Extras 32; S. J. Ali four for 42) and 132 for six (R. Garland 50 not out).

At Lord's, July 11, 12, 13. OXFORD UNIVERSITY drew with CAMBRIDGE UNIVERSITY.

CAMBRIDGE

President: Professor A. D. Buckingham (Pembroke)

Captain: J. P. Pyemont (Tonbridge and Trinity Hall)
Secretary: B. J. Collins (St Albans School and Girton)

Captain for 2001: B. J. Collins (St Albans School and Girton)
Vice-captain: J. P. Pyemont (Tonbridge and Trinity Hall)
Secretary: C. A. Sayers (Millfield and Trinity Hall)

Oxbridge cricket as it has been known for more than a century came to a damp and dismal end when the last first-class Varsity Match to be played at Lord's was drawn with no play possible on the final day. Wet surrounds had already prevented play for much of the opening day, offering a good deal of opportunity for members and dignitaries in the hospitality boxes to discuss the future of university cricket.

Views were sharply divided between those who saw the changes brought about by the England and Wales Cricket Board as a great opportunity and those who considered the plans no more than wanton vandalism. The truth probably lay somewhere between the two. In recent years, it has been increasingly difficult to defend the first-class status enjoyed by Oxford and Cambridge while denying the claims of other universities. The proposed six Centres of Excellence offer a bold vision, but are born of muddled thinking, certainly where Cambridge are concerned.

The advent of a cricket school to which students must offer commitment is hardly likely to encourage Cambridge admission tutors to welcome a new breed of cricketing undergraduate. They have already found it difficult to offer places to cricketers, however gifted academically; it was not insignificant that there were no freshmen in the first Light Blue side of the new millennium, while at least two applicants with all the necessary academic entry requirements were rejected, only to be quickly offered places at other universities.

It is sad, too, that the three-day Varsity Match is to be relegated to Fenner's and The Parks, with only a one-day game at Lord's. Even if it were to lose first-class status, the three-day game at Lord's seemed like one tradition worth preserving.

The current uncertainty over the future role of cricket at Fenner's prompted the Blues, at their annual captaincy elections during the Varsity Match, to name, in effect, two captains for 2001. Ben Collins was elected captain of Cambridge University Cricket Club and James Pyemont moved sideways to the new post of vice-captain, with the intention that he should lead the newly formed Cambridge Centre of Excellence team, for which players from Anglia Polytechnic University will also be eligible.

Despite the problems off the field and appalling early-season weather that interfered with the majority of their matches, Cambridge generally gave a good account of themselves. Altogether there were four centuries – by Andrew Danson and Richard Howitt against the counties and by Pyemont and Quentin Hughes, captains present and past, against Oxford. For Pyemont, a Derbyshire-contracted player, to score his maiden century at Lord's was a particular delight for both team and supporters. Generally, Cambridge had the edge over Oxford; their narrow victory in the one-day Varsity Match, played in The Parks, was testimony to the team ethic that Pyemont and coach Derek Randall had instilled in the side.

It was true that the whole proved greater than the sum of the parts. The highlights of the Fenner's term came right in the middle, with student centuries in successive innings. Danson, who had played in all the Derbyshire age-group sides before arriving at Cambridge, scored an unbeaten 117 against his county. He was followed by Richard Howitt, a batsman with some experience in Nottinghamshire's Second Eleven, who scored 118 not out when the University elected to bat against Middlesex.

CAMBRIDGE UNIVERSITY 2000

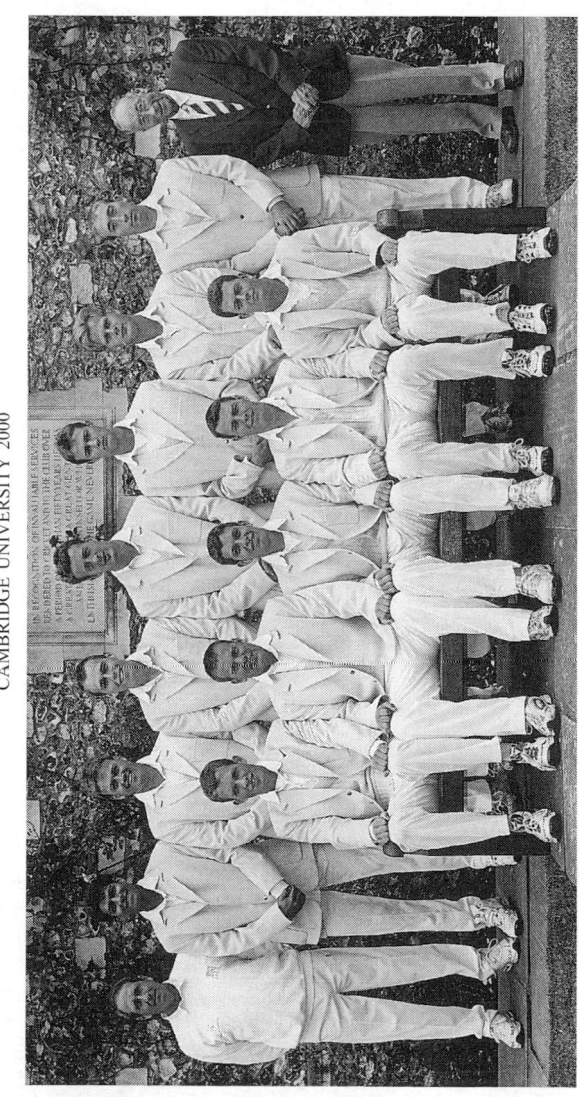

Back row: D. W. Randall (*coach*), S. M. Sheikh, R. W. J. Howit, S. J. W. Lewis, C. R. Pimlott, C. A. Sayers, T. R. Hughes, A. R. Danson, A. R. May (*scorer*).
Front row: M. J. Birks, B. J Collins, J. P. Pyemont (*captain*), J. P. Lowe, Q. J. Hughes.

[*Bill Smith*]

The bowling relied heavily on seam, with no specialist spinner available. The pick of the pace bowlers was Charlie Pimlott who, when fit, bowled a line and length that demanded respect and earned him a place in the British Universities side. As ever, Malcolm Birks kept wicket cheerfully and batted doggedly, setting an example in application to many of his colleagues. His durability meant he was often night-watchman. Never did he fill the role better than when batting for two and a half hours for 25 against a Worcestershire attack headed by Glenn McGrath. – DAVID HALLETT.

CAMBRIDGE UNIVERSITY RESULTS

First-class matches – Played 6: Lost 1, Drawn 5. Abandoned 1.

FIRST-CLASS AVERAGES
BATTING AND FIELDING

	M	I	NO	R	HS	100s	50s	Avge	Ct/St
R. W. J. Howitt.	6	10	2	274	118*	1	1	34.25	0
Q. J. Hughes	6	10	3	237	119	1	1	33.85	0
A. R. Danson.	6	9	2	211	117*	1	0	30.14	4
J. P. Pyemont	6	9	1	230	124	1	0	28.75	4
C. R. Pimlott	4	3	1	31	31*	0	0	15.50	2
M. J. Birks	6	7	0	107	32	0	0	15.28	8/2
T. R. Hughes	6	3	2	14	13*	0	0	14.00	1
C. A. Sayers	6	8	2	71	46	0	0	11.83	4
S. J. W. Lewis	6	10	1	98	26	0	0	10.88	2
S. A. A. Block	2	4	0	31	23	0	0	7.75	0
J. P. Lowe	3	3	1	7	6*	0	0	3.50	0
B. J. Collins.	4	4	0	11	6	0	0	2.75	0

Also batted: J. W. S. Piper (1 match) 19; J. S. Ross (2 matches) 0, 2; S. M. Sheikh (2 matches) 17, 0*.

* *Signifies not out.*

BOWLING

	O	M	R	W	BB	5W/i	Avge
C. R. Pimlott	78	26	265	11	3-42	0	24.09
A. R. Danson.	76	21	218	5	3-20	0	43.60
T. R. Hughes	121	30	408	9	3-55	0	45.33
R. W. J. Howitt.	60	8	254	4	2-54	0	63.50

Also bowled: Q. J. Hughes 20–2–97–1; J. P. Lowe 79–30–181–1; J. W. S. Piper 7–1–30–2; J. P. Pyemont 46.1–18–106–1; J. S. Ross 39–11–108–1; S. M. Sheikh 22–3–99–0.

Note: Matches in this section which were not first-class are signified by a dagger.

†At Cambridge, April 4. Cambridge University v Northamptonshire Second Eleven. Abandoned.

CAMBRIDGE UNIVERSITY v LANCASHIRE

At Cambridge, April 7, 8, 9. Lancashire won by 170 runs. Toss: Cambridge University. First-class debuts: R. W. J. Howitt, T. R. Hughes. County debut: J. C. Scuderi.

The earliest start to an English cricket season got under way in surprisingly warm weather, and Crawley, a former Cambridge captain, made the most of it with his first century at Fenner's. He shared hundred partnerships with Joe Scuderi, formerly of South Australia but with an Italian passport, and Fairbrother. Then Flintoff smashed the student attack to pieces, hitting four sixes, ten fours and 80 runs in all from just 35 balls. The Cambridge top order struggled in reply, but Lancashire waived the follow-on, taking further batting practice before leg-spinner Schofield, recently awarded an England contract, wrapped up the game with five for 48, his best figures yet in county cricket.

Close of play: First day, Cambridge University 24-1 (Lewis 9*, Danson 10*); Second day, Lancashire 56-2 (Atherton 15*, Schofield 13*).

Lancashire

*J. P. Crawley st Birks b Q. J. Hughes	126		
M. A. Atherton c Birks b Pimlott	8	– b T. R. Hughes	19
J. C. Scuderi c Birks b T. R. Hughes	51		
N. H. Fairbrother not out	69		
A. Flintoff not out	80		
G. D. Lloyd (did not bat)		– (1) c Birks b T. R. Hughes	13
†W. K. Hegg (did not bat)		– (3) lbw b Pimlott	8
C. P. Schofield (did not bat)		– (4) lbw b Pimlott	36
G. Chapple (did not bat)		– (5) c Pyemont b T. R. Hughes	0
P. J. Martin (did not bat)		– (6) not out	14
M. P. Smethurst (did not bat)		– (7) not out	3
B 1, l-b 7, w 14, n-b 8	30	L-b 1, w 12	13

1/21 2/134 3/252   (3 wkts dec.) 364   1/17 2/28 3/60   (5 wkts dec.) 106
                                                     4/64 5/96

Bowling: *First Innings*—Pimlott 20–1–113–1; Howitt 4–0–32–0; Lowe 17–6–44–0; T. R. Hughes 16–2–73–1; Q. J. Hughes 19–2–90–1; Pyemont 1–0–4–0. *Second Innings*—Pimlott 14–8–34–2; T. R. Hughes 15–4–55–3; Lowe 4–3–5–0; Danson 4–1–11–0; Pyemont 1–1–0–0.

Cambridge University

S. J. W. Lewis c Fairbrother b Smethurst	26	– c Fairbrother b Chapple	10
R. W. J. Howitt c Hegg b Chapple	0	– c Hegg b Schofield	34
A. R. Danson c Flintoff b Smethurst	11	– (6) c Fairbrother b Chapple	1
Q. J. Hughes b Smethurst	0	– (3) c sub b Smethurst	14
*J. P. Pyemont c Hegg b Scuderi	1	– (4) not out	38
B. J. Collins b Schofield	5	– (5) c Crawley b Schofield	6
C. A. Sayers lbw b Chapple	46	– st Hegg b Schofield	3
†M. J. Birks c Atherton b Smethurst	31	– c Fairbrother b Martin	2
C. R. Pimlott lbw b Scuderi	0	– c Crawley b Martin	0
J. P. Lowe lbw b Chapple	1	– lbw b Schofield	0
T. R. Hughes not out	13	– c sub b Schofield	0
L-b 17, w 7, n-b 10	34	B 4, l-b 8, w 2, n-b 10	24

1/6 2/37 3/41 4/44 5/56   168   1/17 2/58 3/70 4/90 5/93   132
6/64 7/133 8/134 9/139   6/114 7/127 8/131 9/132

Bowling: *First Innings*—Martin 20–9–31–0; Chapple 20–11–22–3; Smethurst 20.1–9–34–4; Flintoff 7–4–8–0; Scuderi 12–2–42–2; Schofield 9–3–14–1. *Second Innings*—Martin 13–9–16–2; Chapple 13–1–27–2; Smethurst 12–3–23–1; Schofield 22.5–5–48–5; Scuderi 3–0–6–0.

Umpires: N. J. Llong and A. G. T. Whitehead.

At Nottingham, April 11, 12, 13. NOTTINGHAMSHIRE v CAMBRIDGE UNIVERSITY. Abandoned.

†At Cambridge, April 18. Cambridge University v Cambridgeshire. Abandoned.

†At Cambridge, April 19. Cambridge University won by 11 runs. Toss: Loughborough Students. Cambridge University 213 for five (50 overs) (R. W. J. Howitt 34, Q. J. Hughes 41, J. P. Pyemont 64, Extras 31); Loughborough Students 202 (49.1 overs) (R. Moyser 30, L. Hilton 43, Extras 55; A. R. Danson three for 28).

†At Cambridge, April 20. No result. Toss: Cambridge University. Loughborough Students 27 for two (17 overs) v Cambridge University.

†At Hoddesdon, April 25. Hertfordshire v Cambridge University. Abandoned.

CAMBRIDGE UNIVERSITY v ESSEX

At Cambridge, April 26, 27, 28. Drawn. Toss: Essex. County debut: T. J. Mason.

The first day was washed out, and damp conditions dictated the rest of the match. Pimlott and Toby Hughes made the most of them to pin back Essex on the second day, when only Law made much headway for the visitors. Essex eventually declared, but the outfield was so soggy on the final morning that they were reluctant to risk their fielders. To keep the match going, Cambridge declared at their overnight total, and reduced the county to 99 for seven by lunch, with Danson picking up three wickets for the first time. Then rain ended proceedings.

Close of play: First day, No play; Second day, Cambridge University 50-1 (Lewis 15*, Q. J. Hughes 10*).

Essex

*A. P. Grayson c Lewis b Pimlott	11	– c Danson b Pimlott	9
I. N. Flanagan c Birks b T. R. Hughes	23	– (8) c and b Danson	5
D. D. J. Robinson c Pyemont b T. R. Hughes	37	– (7) not out	5
S. D. Peters c Sayers b Pimlott	1	– c T. R. Hughes b Lowe	25
T. J. Mason c Birks b Pimlott	10	– (2) lbw b Pimlott	0
D. R. Law not out	55	– c Sayers b Danson	8
†B. J. Hyam c Pimlott b Howitt	9	– (3) run out	21
A. P. Cowan not out	5	– (5) st Birks b Danson	4
P. M. Such (did not bat)		– not out	3
B 2, l-b 4, w 4, n-b 12	22	L-b 5, w 2, n-b 12	19

1/19 2/73 3/82   (6 wkts dec.) 173   1/9 2/20 3/54   (7 wkts dec.) 99
4/86 5/115 6/139   4/62 5/72 6/73 7/84

R. S. G. Anderson and D. J. Thompson did not bat.

Bowling: *First Innings*—T. R. Hughes 14–2–29–2; Lowe 18–8–35–0; Pimlott 15–5–42–3; Howitt 11–1–43–1; Danson 3–1–7–0; Pyemont 3–1–11–0. *Second Innings*—Pimlott 6–1–24–2; T. R. Hughes 6–2–12–0; Lowe 8–3–21–1; Danson 6–0–20–3; Howitt 3–0–17–0.

Cambridge University

S. J. W. Lewis not out		15
R. W. J. Howitt c Hyam b Law		21
Q. J. Hughes not out		10
B 1, l-b 3		4

1/35	(1 wkt dec.) 50

*J. P. Pyemont, B. J. Collins, A. R. Danson, C. A. Sayers, †M. J. Birks, C. R. Pimlott, J. P. Lowe and T. R. Hughes did not bat.

Bowling: Cowan 6–2–11–0; Thompson 6–3–10–0; Law 5–2–8–1; Anderson 5–2–6–0; Mason 4–2–4–0; Such 6–3–5–0; Grayson 2–1–2–0.

Umpires: P. Adams and R. Palmer.

CAMBRIDGE UNIVERSITY v WORCESTERSHIRE

At Cambridge, May 2, 3, 4. Drawn. Toss: Cambridge University. First-class debut: Kadeer Ali.

After rain prevented him from bowling in Worcestershire's opening Championship match, Australian Test star McGrath asked for a game here. He claimed four wickets, three of them ducks, and conceded ten runs in his 11 overs – of which only four came off the bat. Night-watchman Birks batted bravely for two and a half hours, but the students were much relieved when it was announced that McGrath was returning to Worcester after lunch on the second day, for treatment on his hamstring. Having saved the follow-on, Cambridge declared overnight, and Rhodes set them 276 on the final afternoon. Despite McGrath's absence, there was no chase and Quentin Hughes used the time profitably to make an unbeaten fifty. On the first day, Pollard and Wilson opened with 167 before Pimlott had both caught behind, but further success for the University bowlers was merely the prelude to the advent of McGrath.

Close of play: First day, Cambridge University 15-2 (Howitt 11*, Birks 2*); Second day, Cambridge University 109-8 (Pimlott 31*, Lowe 6*).

Worcestershire

P. R. Pollard c Birks b Pimlott	72	– c Sayers b Howitt	20
E. J. Wilson c Birks b Pimlott	77	– retired hurt	50
V. S. Solanki c Pimlott b Danson	0	– c Sayers b T. R. Hughes	25
D. A. Leatherdale c Lewis b Pimlott	11	– not out	11
R. C. Driver not out	34	– not out	8
Kadeer Ali c Birks b T. R. Hughes	3		
*†S. J. Rhodes lbw b T. R. Hughes	4		
S. R. Lampitt not out	15		
B 2, l-b 12, w 20, n-b 4	38	B 1, l-b 5, n-b 10	16

1/167 2/168 3/193	(6 wkts dec.) 254	1/56 2/113	(2 wkts dec.) 130
4/196 5/203 6/209			

R. K. Illingworth, G. D. McGrath and A. Sheriyar did not bat.

In the second innings Wilson retired hurt at 101.

Bowling: *First Innings*—Pimlott 19–9–42–3; T. R. Hughes 19–7–62–2; Lowe 24–8–60–0; Howitt 3–0–25–0; Danson 15–4–46–1; Pyemont 4–3–5–0. *Second Innings*—T. R. Hughes 9–3–28–1; Lowe 8–2–16–0; Howitt 11–3–33–1; Danson 7–1–31–0; Pyemont 3.1–0–16–0.

Cambridge University

S. J. W. Lewis b McGrath	0	– c Illingworth b Lampitt	1
R. W. J. Howitt hit wkt b McGrath	14	– c Solanki b Lampitt	9
Q. J. Hughes c Rhodes b McGrath	0	– not out	50
†M. J. Birks lbw b Solanki	25		
*J. P. Pyemont b McGrath	0	– (4) c Solanki b Leatherdale	19
B. J. Collins lbw b Sheriyar	0	– (5) c Solanki b Leatherdale	0
A. R. Danson c Lampitt b Solanki	15	– (6) not out	7
C. A. Sayers c Solanki b Leatherdale	1		
C. R. Pimlott not out	31		
J. P. Lowe not out	6		
L-b 5, n-b 12	17	B 2, l-b 7, n-b 10	19

1/4 2/6 3/23 4/23   (8 wkts dec.) 109   1/9 2/24 3/87 4/91   (4 wkts) 105
5/33 6/66 7/69 8/79

T. R. Hughes did not bat.

Bowling: First Innings—McGrath 11–7–10–4; Sheriyar 14.2–5–22–1; Lampitt 11–4–21–0; Leatherdale 9–2–18–1; Illingworth 3–0–11–0; Solanki 7–1–22–2. *Second Innings*—Sheriyar 10–4–16–0; Lampitt 11–3–39–2; Illingworth 12–7–11–0; Leatherdale 8–4–17–2; Solanki 6–1–13–0.

Umpires: N. A. Mallender and P. Willey.

†At Shenley Park, May 8, 9, 10. MCC won by 332 runs. Toss: MCC. MCC 318 (Z. de Bruyn 38, I. A. Wrigglesworth 116, O. A. Dawkins 30, C. E. Sketchley 34; J. S. Ross four for 51, C. A. Sayers four for 81) and 242 for four dec. (C. E. Sketchley 63, P. D. Atkins 100 not out); Cambridge University 157 (J. P. Pyemont 45, Extras 30; C. E. Sketchley seven for 38) and 71 (C. E. Sketchley four for 31).

CAMBRIDGE UNIVERSITY v DERBYSHIRE

At Cambridge, May 12, 13, 14. Drawn. Toss: Cambridge University. First-class debuts: S. A. A. Block; Z. M. Khan, T. Lungley, L. J. Wharton.

Pyemont's decision to bat backfired when his team were bowled out inside 50 overs for 84 – which Derbyshire's openers needed only 15 overs to overtake. Dean claimed five wickets, and Stubbings and Dowman cashed in to put on 215, though both fell to Howitt a little short of their hundreds. An unbeaten 77 from Cassar extended the county's lead to 253, and defeat looked certain when Cambridge slumped again to 21 for four on the second evening. However, Derbyshire-bred Danson, promoted to open after top-scoring in the first innings, stood firm and on the final day advanced to a maiden hundred, with ten fours. Finding support at last from debutant Stuart Block and the reliable Birks, he steered the University to safety.

Close of play: First day, Derbyshire 139-0 (Stubbings 71*, Dowman 52*); Second day, Cambridge University 25-4 (Danson 11*, Block 0*).

Cambridge University

S. J. W. Lewis c Sutton b Dean	0	– lbw b Dean		0
R. W. J. Howitt b Dean	0	– (5) c Dowman b Lacey		8
Q. J. Hughes lbw b Lungley	4	– lbw b Lungley		0
*J. P. Pyemont lbw b Cassar	5	– b Lungley		2
A. R. Danson c Sutton b Lungley	25	– (2) not out		117
C. A. Sayers lbw b Lungley	1	– (7) c Spendlove b Cassar		1
S. A. A. Block c Spendlove b Dean	7	– (6) c Lacey b Lungley		23
†M. J. Birks lbw b Dowman	10	– c Sutton b Khan		32
S. M. Sheikh c Wharton b Dean	17	– not out		0
J. S. Ross lbw b Dean	0			
T. R. Hughes not out	1			
B 6, l-b 4, w 2, n-b 2	14	B 8, l-b 5, w 2, n-b 10		25

1/3 2/8 3/8 4/18 5/25   84   1/0 2/1 3/3 4/21   (7 wkts) 208
6/42 7/57 8/80 9/80   5/85 6/94 7/206

Bowling: *First Innings*—Dean 13–5–18–5; Cassar 10–4–11–1; Lungley 9.2–6–10–3; Khan 6–1–13–0; Dowman 11–3–22–1. *Second Innings*—Dean 10–7–13–1; Lungley 14–5–31–3; Lacey 29–14–42–1; Wharton 25–10–37–0; Khan 14–4–32–1; Cassar 7–2–16–1; Dowman 13–6–23–0; Titchard 3–2–1–0.

Derbyshire

S. D. Stubbings c Pyemont b Howitt	92	S. J. Lacey not out	2
M. P. Dowman b Howitt	94		
*S. P. Titchard b Ross	8	L-b 10, w 16, n-b 20	46
M. E. Cassar not out	77		
B. L. Spendlove c and b Danson	0	1/215 2/220 3/254 (5 wkts dec.) 337
†L. D. Sutton b Pyemont	18	4/276 5/321

K. J. Dean, Z. M. Khan, L. J. Wharton and T. Lungley did not bat.

Bowling: Sheikh 17–3–80–0; T. R. Hughes 13–2–64–0; Howitt 16–4–54–2; Ross 19–5–46–1; Danson 24–8–57–1; Pyemont 19–9–26–1.

Umpires: M. R. Benson and M. J. Kitchen.

CAMBRIDGE UNIVERSITY v MIDDLESEX

At Cambridge, May 16, 17, 18. Drawn. Toss: Cambridge University. First-class debut: J. W. S. Piper.

Cambridge had beaten Middlesex 11 months earlier, but looked unlikely to repeat the feat when Bloomfield and Laraman reduced them to 34 for four. Pyemont and Howitt rallied, however, and Howitt, looking more comfortable at No. 6 than as an opener, eventually reached his maiden hundred with a six off Dutch, the second of two sixes as well as ten fours in his unbeaten 118. He added 75 with Pyemont and 94 for the eighth wicket with debutant James Piper, whose contribution was 19. Roseberry responded with his first century in a year, hitting 17 fours and a six in five hours against an attack weakened by the loss of Pimlott to injury. Weekes declared shortly after Roseberry retired with a hamstring strain, and had three Cambridge wickets down by the close. In the 34 overs spared by rain on the final day, Quentin Hughes cleared the deficit and ensured the draw.

Close of play: First day, Middlesex 18-0 (Hutton 6*, Roseberry 0*); Second day, Cambridge University 10-3 (Lewis 8*, Q. J. Hughes 0*).

Cambridge University

S. J. W. Lewis c Dutch b Laraman	8	– b Weekes	26
A. R. Danson c Dutch b Bloomfield	4	– lbw b Bloomfield	0
†M. J. Birks c Weekes b Bloomfield	6	– b Bloomfield	1
Q. J. Hughes c Dutch b Laraman	4	– (5) not out	36
*J. P. Pyemont c Dutch b Bloomfield	38	– (6) c Laraman b Dutch	3
R. W. J. Howitt not out	118	– (7) b Cook	20
C. A. Sayers lbw b Laraman	1	– (8) not out	0
S. A. A. Block lbw b Laraman	0	– (4) c Weston b Dutch	1
J. W. S. Piper c Dutch b Weekes	19		
J. S. Ross b Weekes	2		
L-b 9, n-b 9	18	W 6, n-b 2	8

1/9 2/20 3/24 4/34 5/109   (9 wkts dec.) 218   1/1 2/9 3/10   (6 wkts) 95
6/110 7/114 8/208 9/218   4/32 5/39 6/88

T. R. Hughes did not bat.

Bowling: *First Innings*—Bloomfield 21–3–58–3; Cook 16–5–29–0; Laraman 15–4–33–4; Hutton 10–3–17–0; Weekes 13.4–0–45–2; Dutch 9–1–27–0. *Second Innings*—Bloomfield 9–1–25–2; Cook 6–0–25–1; Dutch 13–6–16–2; Weekes 8–4–7–1; Laraman 6–0–22–0.

Middlesex

B. L. Hutton c Pyemont b Piper	31	*P. N. Weekes not out	5
M. A. Roseberry retired hurt	139	B 4, l-b 4, w 16, n-b 22	46
O. A. Shah c Danson b Piper	43		
R. M. S. Weston not out	32	1/114 2/192 (2 wkts dec.) 296

A. J. Strauss, †D. C. Nash, A. W. Laraman, K. P. Dutch, T. F. Bloomfield and S. J. Cook did not bat.

Roseberry retired hurt at 288.

Bowling: T. R. Hughes 26–8–70–0; Howitt 9–0–40–0; Ross 20–6–62–0; Danson 14–5–42–0; Piper 7–1–30–2; Pyemont 15–4–44–0.

Umpires: N. L. Bainton and N. G. Cowley.

†At Cambridge, May 28. Cambridge University v Free Foresters. Abandoned.

†At Cambridge, June 7. Cambridge University won by 73 runs. Toss: Cambridge University. Cambridge University 231 for eight (50 overs) (J. P. Pyemont 72, Extras 44; V. Grandia four for 34, F. Zaaman three for 43); De Flamingo's 158 (43.4 overs) (Extras 32; T. R. Hughes four for 30).

†At Cambridge, June 16. Cambridge University won by seven wickets. Toss: MCC Young Cricketers. MCC Young Cricketers 227 for six (50 overs) (M. Curry 45, R. K. Lynch 35, P. Sawyer 76 not out); Cambridge University 228 for three (48.4 overs) (S. J. W. Lewis 93 not out, J. P. Pyemont 31, C. A. Sayers 62 not out).

At Oxford, June 18. CAMBRIDGE UNIVERSITY beat OXFORD UNIVERSITY by two wickets.

†At Arundel, June 27. Drawn. Toss: Cambridge University. Cambridge University 236 for three dec. (A. R. Danson 88 not out, J. P. Pyemont 50, B. J. Collins 30); Earl of Arundel's XI 222 for nine (M. Winson 32, J. P. Arscott 33, D. R. H. Churton 75, R. O. Jones 33).

†At Cambridge, July 3, 4, 5. Drawn. Toss: Combined Services. Cambridge University 269 for six dec. (A. R. Danson 37, Q. J. Hughes 31, J. P. Pyemont 31, R. W. J. Howitt 80 not out, Extras 35) and 65 for no wkt (A. R. Danson 34 not out); Combined Services 263 for six dec. (Wtr C. Potter 76, Capt. A. G. Grinonneau 72, Sgt N. Palmer 51).

†At Cambridge, July 9. Tied. Toss: Cambridge University. Cambridge University 216 for nine (50 overs) (Q. J. Hughes 72, J. P. Pyemont 33; I. Mohammed four for 53); Quidnuncs 216 for nine (50 overs) (G. W. Jones 79, R. G. Halsall 61; J. P. Pyemont three for 39).

THE UNIVERSITY MATCH, 2000

OXFORD UNIVERSITY v CAMBRIDGE UNIVERSITY

At Lord's, July 11, 12, 13. Drawn. Toss: Cambridge University.

First-class university cricket at Lord's quietly petered out, with no play surviving the weather on the final day. In 2001, these two teams were scheduled to meet at Lord's only for a one-day game, with the three-day match held at Fenner's. Cambridge had the better of what play there was – damp and drizzle had also threatened the opening day, which finally got under way at 4.10 p.m. Pyemont chose to bat and, coming to the crease on the second morning, scored a maiden first-class hundred, having fallen just short the previous year. As in 1999, he shared a century partnership with Hughes, who hit his second successive hundred in this fixture. Together, they added 187 for Cambridge's third wicket; Hughes hit 13 fours, Pyemont 12 and two sixes, and each faced 213 balls. There was time for a brisk fifty from Howitt before the declaration. Oxford's openers were undaunted, however; Smalley led the way as they put on 71 in 19 overs before bad light ended play. Speculation that the captains would contrive a run-chase on the final day was ended by the weather.

Close of Play: First day, Cambridge University 90-2 (Q. J. Hughes 39*); Second day, Oxford University 71-0 (Claughton 19*, Smalley 42*).

Cambridge University

S. J. W. Lewis (*Ermysted's GS and Jesus*) lbw b Garland		12
A. R. Danson (*Birkdale, Sheffield and Pembroke*) c Millar b Hicks		31
Q. J. Hughes (*Durham Johnston and St Edmund's*) b Hicks		119
*J. P. Pyemont (*Tonbridge and Trinity Hall*) c and b Weenink		124
R. W. J. Howitt (*Denstone, Swansea U., and Homerton*) not out		50
C. A. Sayers (*Millfield and Trinity Hall*) not out		18
L-b 12, w 8, n-b 8		28

1/26 2/90 3/277 4/325   (4 wkts dec.) 382

B. J. Collins (*St Albans and Girton*), †M. J. Birks (*South Craven CS and Jesus*) S. M. Sheikh (*KCS, Wimbledon, and St John's*), C. R. Pimlott (*Stockport GS and Downing*) and T. R. Hughes (*Oldbury Wells S. and Homerton*) did not bat.

Bowling: Mather 25.2–5–86–0; Salman Khan 22–4–50–0; Garland 17–2–64–1; Gofton 11–1–40–0; Hicks 23–6–69–2; Weenink 13–0–44–1; Millar 3–0–17–0.

Oxford University

J. A. Claughton (*King Edward VI, Southampton, and Keble*) not out		19
†R. G. Smalley (*RGS, Newcastle, and Keble*) not out		42
B 4, l-b 2, w 2, n-b 2		10

(no wkt) 71

S. W. Weenink (*Rongotai Boys' C, Wellington, and Wolfson*), B. W. Byrne (*Esperance HS, W. Australia U. and Magdalen*), J. R. S. Redmayne (*Eton and Trinity*), A. F. Gofton (*Tapton S. and Wadham*), R. Garland (*Durban HS, Natal U. and Brasenose*), Salman Khan (*Islamabad GS, UCL and Wadham*), N. Millar (*Fettes and Christ Church*), *T. C. Hicks (*Lord Wandsworth and St Catherine's*) and D. P. Mather (*Wirral GS and Green*) did not bat.

Bowling: Pimlott 4–2–10–0; Sheikh 5–0–19–0; T. R. Hughes 3–0–15–0; Howitt 3–0–10–0; Danson 3–1–4–0; Q. J. Hughes 1–0–7–0.

Umpires: J. H. Hampshire and A. A. Jones.

OXFORD v CAMBRIDGE, NOTES

The University Match dates back to 1827. Altogether there have been 155 official matches, Cambridge winning 56 and Oxford 48, with 51 drawn. Since the war Cambridge have won ten times (1949, 1953, 1957, 1958, 1972, 1979, 1982, 1986, 1992 and 1998) and Oxford nine (1946, 1948, 1951, 1959, 1966, 1976, 1984, 1993 and 1995). All other matches have been drawn; the 1988 fixture was abandoned without a ball being bowled.

One hundred and seven three-figure innings have been played in the University matches, 50 for Oxford and 57 for Cambridge. For the fullest lists see the 1940 and 1993 *Wisdens*. There have been three double-centuries for Cambridge (211 by G. Goonesena in 1957, 201 by A. Ratcliffe in 1931 and 200 by Majid Khan in 1970) and two for Oxford (238* by Nawab of Pataudi, sen. in 1931 and 201* by M. J. K. Smith in 1954). Ratcliffe's score was a record for the match for only one day, before being beaten by Pataudi's. M. J. K. Smith and R. J. Boyd-Moss (Cambridge) are the only players to score three hundreds.

The highest totals in the fixture are 513 for six in 1996, 503 in 1900, 457 in 1947, 453 for eight in 1931 and 453 for nine in 1994, all by Oxford. Cambridge's highest is 432 for nine in 1936. The lowest totals are 32 by Oxford in 1878 and 39 by Cambridge in 1858.

F. C. Cobden, in the Oxford v Cambridge match in 1870, performed the hat-trick by taking the last three wickets and won an extraordinary game for Cambridge by two runs. Other hat-tricks, all for Cambridge, have been achieved by A. G. Steel (1879), P. H. Morton (1880), J. F. Ireland (1911) and R. G. H. Lowe (1926). S. E. Butler, in the 1871 match, took all ten wickets in the Cambridge first innings.

D. W. Jarrett (Oxford 1975, Cambridge 1976), S. M. Wookey (Cambridge 1975-76, Oxford 1978) and G. Pathmanathan (Oxford 1975-78, Cambridge 1983) gained Blues for both Universities.

A full list of Blues from 1837 may be found in Wisdens *published between 1923 and 1939. The lists thereafter were curtailed, covering more recent years only, and dropped after 1992.*

THE HALIFAX BUSA CHAMPIONSHIP, 2000

By GRENVILLE HOLLAND

In the last final staged by the British Universities Sports Association before the advent of the Centres of Excellence, Durham University came within one ball of a remarkable treble. They took the junior and ladies championships, the juniors winning their final against Exeter, and the women defeating UWIC (University of Wales Institute, Cardiff). But in the senior championship, Durham were foiled at the death by arch-rivals Loughborough, who won by a single wicket. The final in Cambridge was the closest and most exciting in the 73-year history of BUSA and its predecessor, the Universities Athletic Union.

The 2001 season sees the start of the new venture. The ECB have invested £1 million over three years in university cricket in an attempt to lift the sport to new levels, with the establishment of six University Centres of Cricketing Excellence. BUSA finalists Durham and Loughborough take their places in this select group, as do Oxford (in partnership with their neighbours, Oxford Brookes University) and Cambridge (in association with Anglia). In Yorkshire, Leeds University, Bradford and Leeds Metropolitan combine to form a fifth Centre, with Cardiff, UWIC and Glamorgan providing a sixth in Wales. Each of the Centres was to play three three-day matches against the counties, and two-day games against each other, but only those between a county and Oxford, Cambridge or Durham would be given first-class status. The six Centres would also take part in the BUSA Premier League, now streamlined to 12 teams (Liverpool, Nottingham, Bristol, Exeter, Reading and St Mary's University College, Twickenham, plus the six Centres) divided into two groups.

There were few surprises in the 2000 BUSA Premier League. Durham, though not in vintage form, were still impressive; Loughborough were as competitive as ever; Oxford at last recognised that only their Blues team was good enough for BUSA and almost went the distance; and Exeter had something to prove, after failing to be chosen as a Centre of Excellence.

Exeter were unbeaten in the South, with four straight wins and the walkover conceded by London. But the previous year's finalists, UWIC, declined in disappointing fashion; they won only once on the field, against Reading, finished fourth thanks to a walkover against Southampton, and failed to reach the quarter-finals. Oxford and Loughborough headed the Midlands table. Oxford were undefeated, dropping points only in a washout. Victory away to Loughborough proved they were, at last, a force to be reckoned with; Byron Byrne and Alan Gofton led them to 178 for six, then Tom Hicks bowled some deadly off-spin, claiming five wickets as Loughborough crumbled for 81. That was Loughborough's only reverse of the campaign. Meanwhile, Durham romped home in the North with four convincing victories; Leeds just pipped Liverpool for second place on net run-rate.

The quarter-finals all ran to form. Durham totalled 308 against Reading before demolishing them for 142. Oxford's Scott Weenink seized five Leeds wickets and David Mather four, and an unbeaten 55 from Ross Garland helped them saunter home. Exeter's Chris Ellison routed Nottingham with six for 26, and Loughborough overwhelmed Bristol by seven wickets.

The semi-finals were almost as clear cut. At Dean Park, Bournemouth, Exeter stumbled at last. They never came to terms with the bowling of Loughborough's Mark Tournier and Michael Dobson, who picked up three cheap wickets apiece, and succumbed for a modest 122. The talented Richard Dawson and Stephen Moore restricted Loughborough to 67 for four by the halfway stage, but an undefeated 40 from Dan Furnivall saw them home without further loss. The semi-final between Durham and Oxford, both unbeaten to date, was rescheduled at The Parks after torrential rain at Stockton. Batting first, Durham were sustained by a century from Matt Banes and useful contributions from Michael Brown and Jamie Rowe as they reached 262. Oxford's reply was fitful and uncertain; although Byrne briefly threatened, a brilliant catch in the deep by Alex Stead removed him. Despite a belated frolic by Garland and Neil Millar, Oxford were bowled out well short of their target and Durham joined Loughborough in the final.

BUSA PREMIER GROUP

South	P	W	L	NR	Pts
EXETER	5	5	0	0	15
BRISTOL.	5	3	2	0	9
READING	5	3	2	0	9
UWIC	5	2	2	1	7
Southampton.	5	1	4	0	0*
London	5	0	4	1	−2*
Midlands					
OXFORD.	5	4	0	1	13
LOUGHBOROUGH	5	4	1	0	12
NOTTINGHAM.	5	3	2	0	9
Cambridge	5	1	3	1	4
Birmingham	5	1	3	1	4
Nottingham Trent.	5	0	4	1	1

North	P	W	L	NR	Pts
DURHAM	5	4	0	1	13
LEEDS	5	2	2	1	7
Liverpool	5	2	2	1	7
Manchester	5	2	3	0	6
Northumbria	5	2	2	1	4*
Sheffield	5	1	4	0	3

Where two or more teams finished level on points, the positions were decided by net run-rate.

* *Southampton, London and Northumbria were each docked three points for forfeiting a match, and eliminated from the competition in 2001 for failing to complete the fixture list.*

QUARTER-FINALS

Durham beat Reading by 166 runs; **Oxford** beat Leeds by eight wickets; **Exeter** beat Nottingham by nine wickets; **Loughborough** beat Bristol by seven wickets.

SEMI-FINALS

At Bournemouth, June 5. Loughborough won by six wickets. Toss: Loughborough. Exeter 122 (49.2 overs) (M. A. Tournier three for 13, A. M. Dobson three for 26); Loughborough 125 for four (43.5 overs) (D. W. Furnivall 40 not out).

At Oxford, June 10. Durham won by 90 runs. Toss: Durham. Durham 262 for seven (50 overs) (M. J. Brown 43, M. J. Banes 102, J. R. Rowe 41); Oxford 172 (41.1 overs) (R. Garland 33).

FINAL

DURHAM v LOUGHBOROUGH

At Cambridge, June 12. Loughborough won by one wicket. Toss: Loughborough.

Invited to bat on a good pitch, Durham made steady progress, thanks to half-centuries from Will Jefferson and Matt Banes, but the middle order for once failed to put the match beyond recall. Worcestershire's Ryan Driver was bowled by Scottish off-spinner Gregor Maiden for only 13. However, an unbroken partnership of 67 between wicket-keeper Jamie Foster, later selected for England A's tour of the West Indies, and captain Gavin Franklin enabled them to leave a target of 247. Loughborough's reply was well calculated. Matthew Byrne and Mark Powell contributed fifties and, at 217 for four, victory seemed assured. But four quick wickets tipped the balance, and Loughborough entered the final over needing ten runs to win, with two wickets left. Dan Furnivall, having guided Loughborough so close, fell to its third ball when Yorkshire seamer Alex Stead had him caught at mid-wicket, and by the last delivery the requirement was two. Chris Coleman edged it and, with Foster standing up, that was enough to secure the title.

Durham

W. I. Jefferson c Selwood b Parkin	51	†J. S. Foster not out	42
J. R. Rowe c Powell b Watts	12	*G. D. Franklin not out	34
M. J. Banes c Tournier b Dobson	67	B 1, l-b 5, w 5, n-b 4	15
R. C. Driver b Maiden	13		
H. J. H. Loudon c Selwood b Parkin . . .	1	1/54 2/87 3/125 (6 wkts, 50 overs) 246
R. A. Stead c Coleman b Bourke	11	4/128 5/145 6/179

I. J. W. McCarter, C. G. van der Gucht and J. T. Bruce did not bat.

Bowling: Tournier 10–2–31–0; Dobson 6–0–48–1; Watts 9–1–51–1; Maiden 10–1–28–1; Parkin 10–0–45–2; Bourke 5–0–37–1.

Loughborough

S. A. Selwood lbw b Driver	29	M. A. Tournier st Foster b Bruce	0
M. T. Byrne b Driver	53	†C. P. Coleman not out	14
*N. A. Bourke lbw b van der Gucht	12	A. M. Dobson not out	0
M. J. Powell c Jefferson b Driver	50	B 2, l-b 8, w 6, n-b 4	20
D. W. Furnivall c Driver b Stead	44		
D. F. Watts c Jefferson b Franklin	21	1/51 2/77 3/158 (9 wkts, 50 overs) 249	
G. I. Maiden run out	5	4/171 5/217 6/225	
I. C. Parkin c van der Gucht b Stead	1	7/227 8/233 9/241	

Bowling: Bruce 10–1–31–1; Stead 7–0–32–2; Driver 10–0–49–3; van der Gucht 10–1–50–1; Franklin 6–0–37–1; McCarter 5–0–23–0; Banes 2–0–17–0.

Umpires: K. Hopley and S. W. Poole.

WINNERS 1927–2000

The UAU Championship was replaced by the BUSA Championship after 1994.

1927 Manchester	1957 Loughborough Colls.	1979 Manchester
1928 Manchester	1958 Null and void	1980 Exeter
1929 Nottingham	1959 Liverpool	1981 Durham
1930 Sheffield	1960 Loughborough Colls.	1982 Exeter
1931 Liverpool	1961 Loughborough Colls.	1983 Exeter
1932 Manchester	1962 Manchester	1984 Bristol
1933 Manchester	1963 Loughborough Colls.	1985 Birmingham
1934 Leeds	1964 Loughborough Colls.	1986 Durham
1935 Sheffield	1965 Hull	1987 Durham
1936 Sheffield	1966 { Newcastle / Southampton	1988 Swansea
1937 Nottingham		1989 Loughborough
1938 Durham	1967 Manchester	1990 Durham
1939 Durham	1968 Southampton	1991 Durham
1946 Not completed	1969 Southampton	1992 Durham
1947 Sheffield	1970 Southampton	1993 Durham
1948 Leeds	1971 Loughborough Colls.	1994 Swansea
1949 Leeds	1972 Durham	1995 Durham
1950 Manchester	1973 { Leicester / Loughborough Colls.	1996 Loughborough
1951 Manchester		1997 Durham
1952 Loughborough Colls.	1974 Durham	1998 { Durham / Loughborough
1953 Durham	1975 Loughborough Colls.	
1954 Manchester	1976 Loughborough	1999 Durham
1955 Birmingham	1977 Durham	2000 Loughborough
1956 Null and void	1978 Manchester	

OTHER FIRST-CLASS MATCH, 2000

SCOTLAND v IRELAND

At Ayr, August 19, 20, 21. Scotland won by six wickets. Toss: Ireland. First-class debuts: M. A. Gillespie, R. S. Haire, A. Joyce, G. J. Neely.

Scotland beat Ireland for the first time in their annual three-day encounter since 1988, tying the series at 20 wins apiece. But the match was dominated by Angus Dunlop, who scored 150 on the opening day. He batted for 283 minutes, faced 230 balls and hit 20 fours and a six; it was Ireland's highest score in this fixture, and their fourth-highest in all. Dunlop added 73 with Joyce and 104 with Mark Gillespie, making his debut for Ireland. Next day, Scotland matched their total of 259 exactly, thanks to an unbeaten 43 from No. 8 Brinkley, who followed up with two early strikes when the visitors batted again. Asim Butt soon added Dunlop and, on the final day, Ireland were dismissed for a disappointing 121. Scotland had 75 minutes plus the mandatory 16 overs for the run-chase, but lost half an hour to a thunderstorm. Patterson and Williamson launched them on their way with 67, however, and the winning runs arrived with ten balls to spare.

Close of play: First day, Scotland 24-1 (Patterson 11*, Smith 10*); Second day, Ireland 54-3 (Shields 30*, Gillespie 12*).

Ireland

I. P. Shields c Lockhart b Asim Butt	7	– b Asim Butt.	31
A. Joyce lbw b Asim Butt	29	– c Patterson b Brinkley	2
R. S. Haire c Smith b Asim Butt	0	– b Brinkley	0
A. R. Dunlop c Brinkley b Tennant	150	– c Smith b Asim Butt	10
M. A. Gillespie c Brinkley b Maiden	34	– lbw b Brinkley	22
*W. K. McCallan lbw b Maiden	0	– b Maiden	17
†A. D. Patterson not out	20	– c Brinkley b Tennant	10
P. J. K. Mooney run out	2	– c Lockhart b Tennant	9
M. D. Dwyer b Brinkley	2	– not out	4
G. J. Neely (did not bat)		– lbw b Tennant	0
A. G. A. M. McCoubrey (did not bat)		– b Asim Butt	0
B 1, l-b 9, w 1, n-b 4	15	B 3, l-b 8, n-b 5	16

1/17 2/17 3/90 4/194   (8 wkts dec.) 259   1/2 2/4 3/33 4/61 5/73   121
5/202 6/247 7/249 8/259   6/96 7/110 8/115 9/115

Bowling: *First Innings*—Brinkley 19.5–7–40–1; Asim Butt 22–6–63–3; Wright 9–2–25–0; Williamson 9–1–26–0; Tennant 13–5–45–1; Maiden 15–1–50–2. *Second Innings*—Brinkley 14–6–31–3; Asim Butt 20.2–8–25–3; Wright 3–0–6–0; Tennant 21–12–20–3; Maiden 11–3–28–1.

Scotland

D. M. W. Patterson c Patterson b Mooney	31	– b Gillespie	24
D. R. Lockhart c Patterson b McCoubrey	0		
†C. J. O. Smith lbw b Dwyer	24	– (4) c Joyce b Dwyer	7
R. A. Parsons b Gillespie	20	– (5) not out	27
*G. Salmond c Joyce b Dwyer	36	– (3) lbw b Dwyer	0
J. G. Williamson lbw b Gillespie	7	– (2) b Gillespie	41
C. M. Wright b McCallan	40	– (6) not out	15
J. E. Brinkley not out	43		
G. I. Maiden b Dwyer	7		
Asim Butt b Neely	10		
A. M. Tennant b Neely	5		
B 12, l-b 15, n-b 9	36	L-b 10	10

1/8 2/56 3/62 4/102 5/116   259   1/67 2/70 3/97 4/101   (4 wkts) 124
6/153 7/191 8/216 9/243

Bowling: *First Innings*—Mooney 6–0–26–1; McCoubrey 16–2–43–1; McCallan 25–6–54–1; Neely 8.2–1–29–2; Dwyer 24–7–39–3; Gillespie 17–4–41–2. *Second Innings*—McCoubrey 2–0–16–0; McCallan 9–0–39–0; Dwyer 6–0–25–2; Gillespie 7.2–1–34–2.

Umpires: J. Thallon and D. Walker.

MCC MATCHES IN 2000

By STEVEN LYNCH

MCC arranged more than 400 matches against schools, clubs and representative bodies for the second year running. Of 411 matches, 164 were won, 126 drawn (21 with significant weather interference), one tied, 72 lost and 48 abandoned without a ball bowled.

The tie came in a match to mark the Queen Mother's 100th birthday in August. MCC took on Royal Ascot, who play within the confines of the famous racecourse. Nick Gifford, son of former champion jockey Josh, scored 55 for Royal Ascot, who also included Michael Scudamore, son of another champion, Peter.

MCC's only first-class match, against New Zealand A, was marked by the return of former England captain Graham Gooch, three years retired and just short of his 47th birthday. He signed up because he had never played in The Parks for Essex, and was slightly surprised to discover that it was a four-day game, and first-class to boot. Gooch warmed up with a century against MCC at Wormsley, but found the young New Zealanders more of a handful. Bravely opening the batting, he fell second ball in the first innings, and eighth in the second. His side, though, won an exciting match by three runs.

Gooch's old Essex team-mate, Brian Hardie, now in charge of cricket at Brentwood School, lived up to his nickname of "Lager" by providing mid-innings drinks when MCC visited. Unfortunately, that was in the middle of one of 2000's many cold and wet spells. It was observed that Hardie took the drinks out of the fridge to cool them down even more.

In all, 74 centuries were scored for MCC during the season, the highest being 161 by Sussex left-hander Toby Peirce against the Isle of Wight. Guy Bucknell, Neil Davis, Neil Millar, Toby Sawrey-Cookson, Zahid Sadiq and Tim Shaw made two hundreds each. Robert Hillman and Damien Cummins shared an unbroken opening partnership of 245 against St Benedict's School. The best bowling figures were Major Jez Bennett's nine for 15 against Latymer Upper School. Off-spinner Chris Sketchley fell three runs short of the match double, combining 97 runs with 11 wickets in the crushing defeat of Cambridge. MCC were surprised to be confronted by a girl at Yorkshire's South Craven School – Laura Spragg, an 18-year-old left-arm seamer who played for England during the summer. She took three for 26. MCC's own women's team played ten matches, winning three, drawing five and losing two. Jan Godman, the former England player, hit 103 not out against Surrey Under-21s.

Overseas, a strong MCC team visited Bangladesh in January: Anthony McGrath of Yorkshire and Leicestershire's Ben Smith scored two hundreds apiece, while, in the drawn representative match at Dhaka, Shahriar Hossain became the first Bangladeshi to make twin first-class centuries. MCC also toured South Africa (beating Western Province in a one-day match at Newlands), Denmark, Belgium and Luxembourg, and Gibraltar and Spain. On two forays to North America, they won all eight matches in Canada, and all six in Philadelphia. This made up for MCC's surprise home defeat by the USA in Castleford. Finally, two MCC teams travelled to the Chiang Mai Sixes tournament in Thailand – defeating all comers to contest the final.

MCC's Young Cricketers enjoyed a respectable season, winning 16 of their 37 matches, including victories over Surrey and Sussex in the AON Trophy, the county Second Eleven limited-overs cup. Four young players signed up for counties in 2001: Andrew Sexton and Irfan Shah with Hampshire, and Ricky Clarke and Ben Scott with Surrey.

Note: Matches in this section were not first-class except for the game v New Zealand A.

At Lord's, April 28. MCC v MCC Young Cricketers. Abandoned.

At Bovey Tracey, May 1. MCC won by 27 runs. Toss: Devon. MCC 219 for eight (55 overs) (Z. A. Sadiq 81; R. I. Horrell three for 32); Devon 192 for seven (55 overs) (A. M. Small 48, D. F. Lye 32, I. Gompertz 53; P. M. Roebuck three for 28).

At Shenley Park, May 8, 9, 10. MCC beat CAMBRIDGE UNIVERSITY by 332 runs (See The Universities section).

At Derry, May 23, 24, 25. MCC won on scoring-rate. Toss: MCC. MCC 171 (46.3 overs) (Sadiq Mohammad 59; P. J. K. Mooney three for 22); Ireland 73 for four (23.3 overs) (R. S. Haire 31 not out).
A one-innings match was played on May 25, after only 22 overs were possible on the first two days, during which MCC scored 96 for five.

At Castleford, May 28. MCC lost to ZIMBABWEANS by 22 runs (See Zimbabwean tour section).

At Finchampstead, May 31. Club Cricket Conference won by two wickets. Toss: MCC. MCC 183 for five dec. (S. J. Dean 69, D. A. Banks 85 not out); Club Cricket Conference 184 for eight (G. Martin 45, A. Richards 38, K. M. Wijesuriya 34; A. I. Carrington four for 48).
For the Conference, S. F. Stanway returned an analysis of 20–10–18–1.

At Beaconsfield, June 15. England Board XI won by five runs. Toss: England Board XI. England Board XI 173 for six (50 overs) (R. G. Halsall 45, R. G. Hignett 30); MCC 168 (46.5 overs) (J. R. Carruthers four for 38, I. Parkin four for 28).

At Durham University, June 21, 22, 23. MCC won by 11 runs. Toss: MCC. MCC 304 for seven dec. (J. D. Bean 69, D. F. Watts 101, M. P. W. Jeh 57 not out) and 43 for two dec.; Durham University 26 for no wkt dec. and 310 (A. P. Hollingsworth 59, C. P. R. Hodgson 131, H. J. H. Loudon 44; H. Pedrola seven for 137).

At Arundel, June 25. Earl of Arundel's XI won by six wickets. Toss: Earl of Arundel's XI. MCC 212 (J. R. Wileman 42, D. C. Sandiford 44 not out; M. Pasupati four for 44, C. Mansell five for 69); Earl of Arundel's XI 213 for four (M. Tickle 46, M. J. Prior 32, J. Golding 58 not out, G. Morgan 48 not out).

At Oxford, June 26, 27, 28. MCC beat OXFORD UNIVERSITY by 65 runs (See The Universities section).

At Aldershot, July 11. MCC won by 107 runs. Toss: Combined Services. MCC 191 for eight dec. (T. P. Newman 38, I. A. Wrigglesworth 34, C. M. Pitcher 47 not out; Sgt S. D. P. Cornhill four for 25); Combined Services 84 (C. M. Pitcher four for 20, M. G. Boocock three for 26).

At Finchampstead, July 12. Midlands Club Cricket Conference won by six wickets. Toss: MCC. MCC 131 (G. Morgan 52; G. Wagg three for 42, A. Stevenson five for 20); Midlands Club Cricket Conference 132 for four (N. Davies 59).

At Swansea, July 12, 13, 14. Drawn. Toss: Wales. MCC 250 for five dec. (J. E. M. Nicolson 63, Z. A. Sadiq 109, C. F. B. P. Rudd 33 not out) and 197 for nine dec. (C. F. B. P. Rudd 62 not out; P. S. George four for 49); Wales 232 for six dec. (J. P. J. Sylvester 126) and 168 for eight (M. J. Haswell 49, P. S. George 40 not out; M. J. G. Davis four for 37).

At Castleford, July 13. United States of America Cricket Association won by four wickets. Toss: MCC. MCC 209 for seven (50 overs) (S. T. Crawley 79, O. A. Dawkins 38, A. Schwass 33 not out); United States of America CA 211 for six (49.3 overs) (M. Johnson 37, N. Hafiz 33, S. Massiah 71 not out).

At Wormsley, July 16. Sir Paul Getty's XI won by three wickets. Toss: Sir Paul Getty's XI. MCC 201 for eight dec. (S. J. Dean 69, W. S. Kendall 60, K. C. Williams 32); Sir Paul Getty's XI 202 for seven (G. A. Gooch 101, B. W. Byrne 46; R. Clarke three for 29).

At Oxford, July 18, 19, 20, 21. MCC beat NEW ZEALAND A by three runs (See New Zealand A tour section).

At Exmouth, August 8. Minor Counties won by six wickets. Toss: MCC. MCC 196 (47 overs) (H. Pedrola 65, R. J. Falconer 34; A. J. Procter three for 54); Minor Counties 197 for four (47.2 overs) (N. A. Folland 55 not out, I. Dawood 36 not out).

At Lord's, August 15, 16. Drawn. Toss: MCC. MCC 184 (B. W. Byrne 53, Z. de Bruyn 78; J. E. Brinkley three for 40, Asim Butt six for 42) and 260 for four dec. (G. W. White 118, Z. de Bruyn 100 not out); Scotland 177 for four dec. (D. R. Lockhart 58, D. F. Watts 33, R. A. Parsons 52) and 119 for eight (D. J. Pryke four for 21).

At Lord's, August 17. No result. Toss: MCC. MCC 282 for six (50 overs) (D. M. Ward 113, S. P. Moffat 45, L. Potter 47, W. S. Kendall 40; D. J. P. Boden three for 79); Minor Counties 80 for two (18 overs) (G. M. Thomas 43 not out).

PRESIDENTS OF MCC SINCE 1946

1946	General Sir Ronald Adam, Bart	1971-72	F. R. Brown
1947	Captain Lord Cornwallis	1972-73	A. M. Crawley
1948	Brig.-Gen. The Earl of Gowrie	1973-74	Lord Caccia
1949	HRH The Duke of Edinburgh	1974-75	HRH The Duke of Edinburgh
1950	Sir Pelham Warner	1975-76	C. G. A. Paris
1951-52	W. Findlay	1976-77	W. H. Webster
1952-53	The Duke of Beaufort	1977-78	D. G. Clark
1953-54	The Earl of Rosebery	1978-79	C. H. Palmer
1954-55	Viscount Cobham	1979-80	S. C. Griffith
1955-56	Field Marshal Earl Alexander of Tunis	1980-81	P. B. H. May
		1981-82	G. H. G. Doggart
1956-57	Viscount Monckton of Brenchley	1982-83	Sir Anthony Tuke
1957-58	The Duke of Norfolk	1983-84	A. H. A. Dibbs
1958-59	Marshal of the RAF Viscount Portal of Hungerford	1984-85	F. G. Mann
		1985-86	J. G. W. Davies
1959-60	H. S. Altham	1986-87	M. C. Cowdrey
1960-61	Sir Hubert Ashton	1987-88	J. J. Warr
1961-62	Col. Sir William Worsley, Bart	1988-89	Field Marshal The Lord Bramall
1962-63	Lt-Col. Lord Nugent	1989-90	The Hon. Sir Denys Roberts
1963-64	G. O. B. Allen	1990-91	The Rt Hon. The Lord Griffiths
1964-65	R. H. Twining	1991-92	M. E. L. Melluish
1965-66	Lt-Gen. Sir Oliver Leese, Bart	1992-94	D. R. W. Silk
1966-67	Sir Alec Douglas-Home	1994-96	The Hon. Sir Oliver Popplewell
1967-68	A. E. R. Gilligan	1996-98	A. C. D. Ingleby-Mackenzie
1968-69	R. Aird	1998-2000	A. R. Lewis
1969-70	M. J. C. Allom	2000-01	Lord Alexander of Weedon
1970-71	Sir Cyril Hawker		

Since 1951, Presidents of MCC have taken office on October 1. Previously they took office immediately after the annual general meeting at the start of the season. From 1992 to 2000, Presidents were eligible for two consecutive years of office; since then the period has reverted to one year.

OTHER MATCHES, 2000

Note: Matches in this section were not first-class.

TRIPLE CROWN TOURNAMENT

At Northop Hall, July 4. Scotland won on scoring-rate. Toss: England Board XI. Scotland 157 for nine (45 overs) (C. J. O. Smith 65; J. R. Carruthers three for 40); England Board XI 114 for nine (36.1 overs) (D. J. Cox five for 23).

At Brymbo, July 4. No result. Wales and Ireland tied 4–4 in a bowling contest.

At Brymbo, July 5. No result. Scotland beat Ireland 4–3 in a bowling contest.

At Northop Hall, July 5. No result. Wales and England Board XI tied 4–4 in a bowling contest.

At Northop Hall, July 6. No result. Ireland beat England Board XI 4–1 in a bowling contest.
  Ireland completed the tournament without playing a single match.

At Colwyn Bay, July 6. Scotland won by 157 runs. Toss: Wales. Scotland 266 for seven (50 overs) (B. M. W. Patterson 109, G. Salmond 59, Extras 33); Wales 109 (34 overs) (Extras 30; Asim Butt four for 34).
  Scotland completed their third straight win (including one in a bowling contest) and retained the Triple Crown.

Final table

	Played	Won	Lost	Tied	Points
Scotland	3	3	0	0	6
Ireland	3	1	1	1	3
Wales	3	0	1	2	2
England Board XI	3	0	2	1	1

EUROPEAN CHAMPIONSHIP

At Ayr, July 21. England Board XI won by eight wickets. Toss: Denmark. Denmark 133 (48.5 overs) (M. D. Nielsen 31; S. J. Foster four for 21); England Board XI 135 for two (34.2 overs) (S. J. Foster 46 not out, Extras 30).

At Hamilton Crescent, Glasgow, July 21. Holland won by seven wickets. Toss: Holland. Ireland 164 (49.3 overs) (A. R. Dunlop 43; Asim Khan three for 19, T. B. M. de Leede three for 22); Holland 165 for three (44.1 overs) (Ahmed Zulfiqar 85 not out, R. A. F. Bradley 43).

At Uddingston, July 21. Scotland won by nine wickets. Toss: Italy. Italy 139 (47.5 overs) (A. Bonora 30, A. G. Corbellari 32; G. I. Maiden three for 11); Scotland 145 for one (27.4 overs) (B. M. W. Patterson 37, B. G. Lockie 45 not out, C. J. O. Smith 45 not out).

At Linlithgow, July 22. Italy won by nine runs. Italy 242 for seven (50 overs) (P. Di Venuto 90, B. Giordano 76; A. Khan four for 45); Denmark 233 for nine (50 overs) (S. Hansen 68, T. M. Hansen 35 not out; A. G. Corbellari three for 57).

At Titwood, Glasgow, July 22. England Board XI won by 34 runs. Toss: England Board XI. England Board XI 213 for eight (50 overs) (C. Amos 50, P. R. J. Bryson 70; A. R. White four for 37); Ireland 179 (50 overs) (W. K. McCallan 30, P. G. Gillespie 54, B. J. Archer 30; S. J. Foster three for 22).

At Ayr, July 22. Holland won by two wickets. Toss: Holland. Scotland 201 for eight (50 overs) (B. G. Lockie 38, R. A. Parsons 47); Holland 202 for eight (50 overs) (R. F. van Oosterom 110). *Holland needed 16 off the last over; Roland Scholte hit two sixes to help see them home.*

At Uddingston, July 24. Ireland won by 73 runs. Toss: Ireland. Ireland 234 for nine (50 overs) (A. R. White 111; A. Khan four for 49, B. Chawla three for 35); Denmark 161 (40.5 overs) (A. Ahmed 30, A. Khan 34, T. M. Hansen 49 not out).

At Titwood, Glasgow, July 24. Holland won by seven wickets. Toss: Holland. Italy 114 (41.5 overs) (H. Jayasena 34; Asim Khan three for 26, L. van Troost three for 24); Holland 118 for three (34.5 overs) (R. R. A. F. Bradley 39 not out, L. van Troost 30 not out).

At Hamilton Crescent, Glasgow, July 24. England Board XI won by 105 runs. Toss: Scotland. England Board XI 209 for four (50 overs) (P. R. J. Bryson 70, S. J. Foster 71 not out); Scotland 104 (35.3 overs) (G. Salmond 31; S. J. Foster five for 19).

At Linlithgow, July 25. Holland won by six wickets. Toss: England Board XI. England Board XI 138 for nine (50 overs) (R. P. Lefebvre four for 24); Holland 141 for four (47.5 overs) (R. R. A. F. Bradley 37 not out, T. B. M. de Leede 47 not out).

At Ayr, July 25. Ireland won by six wickets. Toss: Italy. Italy 74 (36.5 overs) (M. D. Dwyer three for ten, W. K. McCallan five for 23); Ireland 78 for four (19.3 overs) (H. Jayasena three for 18).

At Uddingston, July 26. Scotland won by nine wickets. Toss: Denmark. Denmark 85 (29.3 overs) (C. M. Wright four for 27); Scotland 86 for one (19.3 overs) (D. R. Lockhart 45 not out).
Originally scheduled for Titwood the previous day; the umpires ended that match after 2.1 overs, with Scotland 13-0, because of a dangerous pitch.

At Hamilton Crescent, Glasgow, July 27. Holland won by eight wickets. Denmark 186 for seven (50 overs) (A. Ahmed 31, M. Siddiq 51, T. M. Hansen 33 not out; R. P. Lefebvre three for 36); Holland 188 for two (42.2 overs) (R. F. van Oosterom 58, Ahmed Zulfiqar 85).
Victory clinched the title for Holland.

At Uddingston, July 27. England Board XI won by three wickets. Toss: England Board XI. Italy 139 for nine (50 overs) (A. Qureshi 31; M. A. Sharp three for 24, S. J. Foster three for 20); England Board XI 143 for seven (36 overs) (C. M. Mole 51, S. A. Stoneman 37; A. G. Corbellari three for 38).

At Linlithgow, July 27. Scotland won by five wickets, their target having been revised to 176 in 48 overs. Toss: Scotland. Ireland 183 for nine (50 overs) (W. K. McCallan 39, D. Joyce 37); Scotland 176 for five (39.1 overs) (R. A. Parsons 70, J. G. Williamson 58 not out; P. J. K. Mooney three for 28).

Division One

	Played	Won	Lost	Points	Run-rate
Holland	5	5	0	10	2.23
England Board XI	5	4	1	8	1.72
Scotland	5	3	2	6	1.42
Ireland.	5	2	3	4	0.91
Italy	5	1	4	2	0.51
Denmark	5	0	5	0	0.41

Division Two

	Played	Won	Lost	Points	Run-rate
Gibraltar	5	5	0	10	1.69
Germany	5	4	1	8	1.39
Portugal.	5	2	3	4	1.08
France.	5	2	3	4	1.03
Israel	5	2	3	4	0.83
Greece.	5	0	5	0	0.46

Run-rate is calculated by dividing each team's scoring-rate (runs scored divided by wickets lost) by that of their opponents.

At Honourable Artillery Company Ground, London, July 27. Malcolm Marshall XVII won by five wickets. Toss: Malcolm Marshall XVII. International PCA Bunbury XVIII 238 for five (35 overs) (G. P. Thorpe 36, M. C. J. Nicholas 32, A. J. Lamb 70, M. A. Butcher 55 not out); Malcolm Marshall XVII 239 for five (32.5 overs) (C. G. Greenidge 63, D. L. Haynes 53, Sir Vivian Richards 35, A. I. Kallicharran 39 not out).

This match was held to raise funds for the late Malcolm Marshall's son, Mali. In all, 35 players participated; of these, 11 from each side bowled at least two overs. For the Bunbury team, comedian Rory Bremner scored ten not out and bowled Brian Lara.

At The Oval, July 29. Rest of the World XI won by 15 runs. Toss: Rest of the World XI. Rest of the World XI 219 for eight (50 overs) (N. Hussain 45, N. J. Astle 51; Saqlain Mushtaq four for 45); Asia XI 204 (48.5 overs) (P. A. de Silva 35, M. Azharuddin 33, N. Chopra 30; A. D. Mullally three for 41, C. L. Cairns three for 29).

This match was held to raise funds for development of The Oval. Sachin Tendulkar was forced to withdraw by chicken-pox.

I ZINGARI RESULTS, 2000

Matches 23: Won 7, Lost 4, Drawn 12. Abandoned 4.

April 27	Eton College	Abandoned
April 30	Charterhouse School	Lost by four wickets
May 7	Hampshire Hogs	Abandoned
May 13	Eton Ramblers	Won by 54 runs
May 14	Stragglers of Asia	Won by one run
May 27	Royal Armoured Corps	Abandoned
June 3	Harrow School	Drawn
June 4	Bradfield Waifs	Won by two wickets
June 4	Earl of Carnarvon's XI	Drawn
June 13	Winchester College	Drawn
June 24	Guards CC	Won by six wickets
June 25	Sir Paul Getty's XI	Drawn
July 2	Hagley CC	Drawn
July 8	Green Jackets Club	Won by eight wickets
July 9	Old Wykehamists	Drawn
July 15	Lord Stafford's XI	Abandoned
July 16	Sir John Starkey's XI	Won by seven wickets
July 22	Hurlingham CC	Lost by five wickets
July 29	Willow Warblers	Drawn
July 30	Earl of Arundel's XI	Drawn
August 6	Band of Brothers	Drawn
August 7	South Wales Hunts	Won by four wickets
August 8	Gentlemen of Cheshire	Lost by 55 runs
August 9	Free Foresters	Drawn
August 10	Stanley	Lost by 45 runs
August 15	Lord Vestey's XI	Drawn
September 5	J. H. Pawle's XI	Drawn

THE MINOR COUNTIES IN 2000

By MIKE BERRY

It was third time lucky for Dorset, whose first Minor Counties Championship title came in their third consecutive play-off and after 99 years of trying. Stuart Rintoul's side had amassed a record 140 points in completing their hat-trick of Western Division triumphs, doing so with what was predominantly a young, locally nurtured squad of players. The average age in the final was just 24, compared to Cumberland's 31.

After the success of the three-day final, introduced in 1999, a proposal to revamp the Championship to a three-day format was put before the October meeting of the MCCA, where the counties voted 15–3 in favour, with two abstentions. Consequently, in 2001 each team plays six three-day matches, rather than the traditional nine two-day games. As the two divisions remain the same, there will be a three-year cycle before each county has played all nine other teams in their section on a home and away basis. In the ECB 38-County Cup, won by Herefordshire, a newcomer in 2001 will be the Channel Islands.

MINOR COUNTIES CHAMPIONSHIP, 2000

Eastern Division	P	W	L	D	NR	Bonus Points Batting	Bowling	Total Points
Cumberland	9	5	0	2	2	8	14	112
Lincolnshire	9	3	0	4	2	10	22	90
Suffolk.	9	2	3†	4	0	15	21	73
Northumberland	9	2	2	3	2	3	18	63
Bedfordshire	9	1	2	5	1	23	19	63
Buckinghamshire	9	2	3	4	0	11	19	62
Cambridgeshire	9	1	1	6	1	12	24	57
Norfolk	9	1	3	3	2	7	21	54
Staffordshire	9	0	0	7	2	10	22	42
Hertfordshire	9	0	3	4	2	12	16	36*

Western Division	P	W	L	D	NR	Bonus Points Batting	Bowling	Total Points
Dorset	9	6	0	2	1	22	19	140*
Oxfordshire	9	5	2	2	0	19	25	124
Shropshire	9	4	2†	3	0	17	20	106
Herefordshire	9	3	3	2	1	18	24	95
Devon	9	2	3	2	2	21	25	88
Wiltshire	9	3	3	2	1	8	19	80
Berkshire	9	2	1	4	2	19	16	77
Cornwall	9	2	4	2	1	9	28	74
Cheshire.	9	0	5†	3	1	10	21	41
Wales	9	0	4†	4	1	4	13	27

Final: Dorset beat Cumberland by five wickets.

Win = 16 points. No result = 5 points.
* 2 points deducted for slow over-rate.
† Includes 5 points gained for losing match reduced to one day.

Eastern Division

Richard Dalton ended his two-year reign as captain of **Bedfordshire** by topping the national bowling averages with 22 wickets at just 10.63 each, which won him the Frank Edwards Trophy for the second time in five years. Andy Roberts, who takes over from Dalton in 2001, scored 557 runs and took 21 wickets, while his brother Tim made 365 runs in only four appearances in his debut season. Bedfordshire gained more batting bonus points than any other county but recorded only one win, over Buckinghamshire.

Having lost the services of wicket-keeper/batsman Neil Burns (to Leicestershire), leg-spinner Andy Clarke (to Norfolk) and slow left-armer Tim Scriven (retired), **Buckinghamshire** looked to their seamers more in 2000. Three hit the 20-wicket mark: Simon Stanway 25, Jamie Bovill 24 and Steve Naylor, a newcomer from Huntingdonshire, 20, including a match return of ten for 38 in the innings victory over Hertfordshire. Naylor, who took a hat-trick in the ECB 38-County Cup game against the Surrey Board, also made 309 Championship runs, a figure bettered only by captain Paul Atkins (521) and Graeme Paskins (314). Buckinghamshire led the table for a time but picked up only six points from their final three games and fell away.

Opening batsmen Simon Kellett and Nigel Gadsby dominated **Cambridgeshire's** campaign. Both topped 500 runs and shared in three unbroken partnerships of over 200, including two in the same fixture when they put on 241 and 265 against Suffolk. Kellett finished with 572 runs at 63.55 to top the national batting averages and win the Wilfred Rhodes Trophy. Gadsby, who was close behind with 561 at 56.10, became the county's leading Championship run-scorer during his partnership of 215 with Kellett against Buckinghamshire; he overhauled Maurice Crouch's aggregate of 8,474 between 1936 and 1963 and finished the season on 8,612. Ajaz Akhtar, the captain, took 37 wickets, including the 250th of his Championship career.

Cumberland's achievement in winning the Eastern Division for the second successive season was partly overshadowed by the unorthodox manner of their last-match victory over Northumberland. Teatime discussions on the first day, instigated by what Simon Dutton, their captain, called a "brainstorm", resulted in Northumberland declaring at ten for two from 13 overs in reply to 293 for two from 67, whereupon Cumberland forfeited their second innings to leave Northumberland a target of 284 in more than 150 overs. The move virtually eliminated the possibility of a draw, and Cumberland completed a 155-run win soon after lunch. Dutton, accused of subterfuge by Lincolnshire, who were also in contention, stood down at the end of the season after nine years in charge, but insisted his actions were more creative than duplicitous. Ashley Metcalfe, one of five Cumberland batsmen to score centuries, made 418 runs while David Pennett, with 32 wickets, and Marcus Sharp, with 29, maintained their reputation as the best new-ball pairing in the Championship.

In another productive summer with **Hertfordshire**, David Ward was the Championship's leading run-scorer with 835. His 202 not out (ten sixes, 16 fours, 167 balls) against Norfolk at Lakenham was the highest innings of the season, and he also scored centuries against Suffolk, Staffordshire (for the third year in four) and Lincolnshire. Of the other batsmen, Stephen Lowe made 420 runs in his first full season. However, the bowling lacked bite, with no fewer than 22 different players called upon, and Hertfordshire, with a new captain in Martin James, finished with the regional wooden spoon, reversing their recovery to third the previous season.

Despite being severely affected by the inclement weather that dogged much of the season, and cost them four of their first six days on home territory, **Lincolnshire** still managed to put together a title challenge. The key to a late-season flourish of three wins in four matches was the form of their seam bowlers: David Pipes and Simon Oakes both finished with 24 wickets, while 22 fell to Elliot Wilson, who moved on to Warwickshire for 2001. Richard Howitt, the Cambridge University left-hander, scored 240 runs in three appearances, including 143 not out against Hertfordshire.

Norfolk's season began with the controversial announcement that 2000 was to be their last at Lakenham, their Norwich-based home for more than 100 years, and that they would relocate to Manor Park, home of Horsford CC, for 2001. The move was influenced by the prohibitive cost of staging matches at Lakenham, a site formerly owned by Colman's and recognised as one of the leading Minor Counties venues. Leg-spinner Andy Clarke, who had joined the side from

Buckinghamshire, was the leading wicket-taker with 27, while Paul Newman took 23 – including a hat-trick against Hertfordshire – and Steve Goldsmith 22. The batting was a disappointment, with no one passing 300 runs.

Northumberland, fourth in the Eastern Division, finished in the top half of the table for only the second time in 14 years. Their run-scoring rewards were meagre, with just three batting bonus points, although Steve Foster, captain of the England Board XI, showed what might have been with 218 runs in only four appearances as one of their professionals; he also took ten wickets. Seam bowler Graeme Angus was leading wicket-taker with 23.

Though unbeaten in the Championship, **Staffordshire** failed to record a win for the first time since 1973, and ninth was their lowest Eastern Division placing. Laurie Potter again earned his money with 546 runs and 14 wickets, while Graeme Archer, back with his native county after leaving Nottinghamshire, contributed 476 runs; slow left-armer Guy Bulpitt claimed 25 wickets.

Derek Randall brought the curtain down on his **Suffolk** career by extending his runs for them to 3,927 in 50 appearances at an average of 45.66. The former England batsman, now 50, signed initially for just two seasons but surprised everyone by staying for seven. The three Catley brothers, none of whom was born when Randall made his first-class debut for Nottinghamshire in 1972, scored over 1,000 runs between them – Russell hit 458, Matthew 403 and Tim 213. Pace man Richard Pineo, who had taken only 27 wickets in 17 previous appearances, came good with 31, and Gary Kirk took 24, as well as performing a hat-trick in the ECB 38-County Cup win over Hertfordshire.

Western Division

Berkshire engaged John Emburey, the former Middlesex and England spinner, as their player-coach, and his impact was substantial: in all competitions he claimed 57 wickets, 36 in the Championship. Neil Fusedale, a slow left-armer back from South Africa, matched Emburey's tally of two-day victims, while Julian Wood dominated the Berkshire run-scoring with 620. Gary Loveday, who made 536, announced he was to give up the captaincy after five years.

Two relative newcomers were the stars of an indifferent season for **Cheshire**. Mark Currie made 352 runs in five games, including 171 against Wiltshire and 109 not out against Wales. Chris Brown, an off-spinner formerly with Lancashire, made a spectacular entrance with a match return of ten for 141 against Dorset and a hat-trick against Wales among his 26 wickets. Cheshire lost five of their nine matches and finished without a Championship win for the first time in 20 years, though they came close to beating Dorset in a tense finish. They did, however, reach the final of the ECB 38-County Cup.

Cornwall's new professional, Neil Williams, the former Middlesex, Essex and England bowler, was overshadowed by James Hands, a slow left-armer who bagged 32 wickets and hit 331 runs. Williams managed only 13 wickets in seven games, but chipped in with some useful runs in making 300. Gary Thomas, the captain, scored 345 runs, while seamers Charlie Shreck (19 wickets), Nick George (18) and Justin Stephens (17) all had their moments.

For **Devon**, 2000 was a transitional year following Peter Roebuck's decision to step down as captain. His successor, Nick Folland, led by example with 607 runs, and Bobby Dawson, back from Gloucestershire, contributed 550. Andy Procter, an off-spinner, emerged as a major influence with 34 wickets. Devon's inconsistent season was best illustrated by their making 372 for five against Cheshire, then 12 days later folding from 43 for one to 59 all out – the lowest Championship total of the summer – as they lost by an innings to Herefordshire.

Vyvian Pike, **Dorset's** prolific leg-spinner, was once more the jewel in their crown. His 57 wickets took his aggregate to 125 in two years and included five or more in an innings on six occasions. He had match figures of 13 for 78 against Cornwall, ten for 131 against Cheshire and then 13 for 178 in the final regional fixture against Wiltshire, in which Dorset knocked off a target of 304 in 57.2 overs to achieve a fourth successive win and leapfrog Oxfordshire at the head of the table. Their batting benefited from the explosive talent of left-hander Darren Cowley, who made 615 runs, while Matthew Swarbrick (740) and new boy Glyn Treagus (550) also scored freely. Of the bowlers, two young seamers, Toby Sharpe (aged 19) and David Kidner (18), both distinguished themselves.

Ismail Dawood, the former Worcestershire and Glamorgan wicket-keeper, established a new **Herefordshire** record of 30 victims in his debut season and also scored 497 runs. The only player with more was Paul Lazenbury, a left-hander who had joined the side from Gloucestershire and whose tally of 723 was boosted by a purple patch of three hundreds in four days, including two in the same game against Cornwall. Dawood (142 not out) and Lazenbury (134) rewrote the county record book with a second-wicket partnership of 287 against Shropshire, the highest for any Herefordshire wicket since they became a Minor County. A third newcomer, John Shaw, finished as leading wicket-taker with 28, including a hat-trick in the victory over Dorset and a spell of 3–2–4–4 in the defeat of Devon. Herefordshire were challenging for the title until well beaten by Oxfordshire, but there was consolation for them at Lord's when they beat Cheshire to win the ECB 38-County Cup for the first time.

Oxfordshire were agonisingly close to topping the Western Division for the first time in nine years. They went into the final round of fixtures three points clear, but only drew with Berkshire while Dorset defeated Wiltshire. Keith Arnold, in his 21st season, was a major factor in their record of five victories; his career-best 62 wickets took him beyond 500 in all and contained the season's best innings analysis of nine for 19 in the ten-wicket win over Herefordshire. Arnold ended the match with figures of 15 for 76. Craig Haupt, a South African-born batsman who had qualified by residence, overcame the disappointment of a king pair against Shropshire on his debut to make 484 runs, while Stewart Laudat hit 468 and took 20 wickets.

A final position of third equalled **Shropshire's** best Western Division performance, and their total of 106 points was their highest ever. Kevin Evans, formerly with Nottinghamshire, was good value as their new professional, taking 34 wickets, while Adam Simmons backed him up with 29, including match figures of 11 for 103 in the win over Oxfordshire. The batting was a disappointment overall, but Ben Platt's exploits in the draw with Herefordshire at Whitchurch will live long in the memory. His unbeaten 104 off only 76 balls was part of a record last-wicket stand of 107 with Matthew Tilt, who contributed just two not out.

Wales were an unsettled side under their fifth captain in five years and, led in 2000 by Colin Metson, finished bottom of the Western Division for the second successive season. They gave debuts to no fewer than 19 players, and used 40 in all. A meagre return of four batting bonus points told its own story, although Jamie Sylvester, their 1999 captain, hit 296 in four games after deciding against a possible return to Herefordshire.

Wiltshire made a flying start by winning their opening two Championship matches, and also beat Scotland in the first round of the NatWest Trophy, but went on to lose three of their seven subsequent Championship matches. Their leading performers were all-rounders Richard Sillence, with 500 runs and 22 wickets, and Richard Bates, with 358 runs and 29 wickets, including a hat-trick against Wales.

LEADING AVERAGES, 2000

BATTING

(Qualification: 8 completed innings, average 30.00)

	M	I	NO	R	HS	100s	Avge
S. A. Kellett (*Cambridgeshire*)	6	12	3	572	127*	3	63.55
N. A. Folland (*Devon*)	9	15	5	607	110	2	60.70
A. A. Metcalfe (*Cumberland*)	7	11	4	418	105*	1	59.71
N. T. Gadsby (*Cambridgeshire*)	7	13	3	561	133*	2	56.10
D. J. Cowley (*Dorset*)	9	15	4	615	103*	1	55.90
D. M. Ward (*Hertfordshire*)	9	16	1	835	202*	4	55.66
J. R. Wood (*Berkshire*)	9	15	3	620	100	1	51.66
T. C. Z. Lamb (*Dorset*)	8	12	3	465	116	1	51.66
P. S. Lazenbury (*Herefordshire*)	9	16	2	723	134	4	51.64
P. D. Atkins (*Buckinghamshire*)	9	15	4	521	102*	1	47.36
M. Swarbrick (*Dorset*)	10	17	1	740	114	2	46.25

	M	I	NO	R	HS	100s	Avge
T. W. Roberts (*Bedfordshire*)	4	8	0	365	139	1	45.62
L. Potter (*Staffordshire*)	8	13	1	546	146*	1	45.50
A. R. Roberts (*Bedfordshire*)	8	15	2	557	140	1	42.84
J. M. Lewis (*Cumberland*)	8	12	4	342	128*	1	42.75
P. J. Caley (*Suffolk*)	9	15	7	341	50*	0	42.62
R. J. Sillence (*Wiltshire*)	7	13	1	500	150	2	41.66
S. T. Knox (*Cumberland*)	8	12	2	397	158*	1	39.70
R. J. Williams (*Oxfordshire*)	8	14	5	340	61*	0	37.77
K. Pearson (*Herefordshire*)	9	13	4	336	76	0	37.33
R. I. Dawson (*Devon*)	9	15	0	550	151	1	36.66
H. V. Patel (*Herefordshire*)	8	13	3	363	91*	0	36.30
L. H. Nurse (*Berkshire*)	6	11	1	361	108	1	36.10
R. J. Bates (*Wiltshire*)	8	13	3	358	67	0	35.80
J. C. Harrison (*Lincolnshire*)	8	11	2	322	74	0	35.77
G. E. Loveday (*Berkshire*)	9	16	1	536	98	0	35.73
B. W. W. Platt (*Shropshire*)	6	11	2	321	104*	1	35.66
I. Dawood (*Herefordshire*)	9	16	2	497	142*	1	35.50
O. J. Clayson (*Bedfordshire*)	8	16	3	455	74*	0	35.00
C. A. Haupt (*Oxfordshire*)	9	17	3	484	121*	1	34.57
G. R. Treagus (*Dorset*)	9	16	0	550	85	0	34.37
C. Amos (*Norfolk*)	6	11	3	275	102*	1	34.37
C. S. Knightley (*Oxfordshire*)	8	14	5	302	94*	0	33.55
D. J. M. Mercer (*Bedfordshire*)	7	14	3	368	98*	0	33.45
S. V. Laudat (*Oxfordshire*)	8	15	1	468	118	1	33.42
N. F. Williams (*Cornwall*)	7	12	3	300	67	0	33.33
S. A. Seymour (*Berkshire*)	7	12	2	331	79	0	33.10
N. W. Round (*Herefordshire*)	9	15	5	324	98*	0	32.40
R. J. Rollins (*Cambridgeshire*)	6	9	1	257	56	0	32.12
G. F. Archer (*Staffordshire*)	9	15	0	476	113	1	31.73
G. T. J. Townsend (*Devon*)	7	11	1	317	81	0	31.70
A. J. Trott (*Bedfordshire*)	6	11	3	253	63	0	31.62
M. D. Catley (*Suffolk*)	7	13	0	403	110	1	31.00
S. P. Naylor (*Buckinghamshire*)	9	13	3	309	74*	0	30.90
R. J. Rowe (*Wiltshire*)	8	14	1	392	65*	0	30.15

* *Signifies not out.*

BOWLING

(Qualification: 10 wickets, average 22.00)

	O	M	R	W	BB	5W/i	Avge
R. N. Dalton (*Bedfordshire*)	88.5	22	234	22	6-28	1	10.63
S. Oakes (*Lincolnshire*)	127	37	279	24	6-27	3	11.62
K. A. Arnold (*Oxfordshire*)	348.1	98	838	62	9-19	6	13.51
D. J. Pipes (*Lincolnshire*)	142.3	48	348	24	5-41	2	14.50
M. A. Sharp (*Cumberland*)	194.5	67	422	29	5-49	1	14.55
K. P. Evans (*Shropshire*)	235.4	68	530	34	4-7	0	15.58
S. P. Naylor (*Buckinghamshire*)	88.4	14	328	20	7-22	1	16.40
A. M. Simmmons (*Shropshire*)	159.5	34	487	29	6-42	2	16.79
E. J. Wilson (*Lincolnshire*)	138.5	34	372	22	7-61	1	16.90
D. B. Pennett (*Cumberland*)	180.2	46	543	32	7-33	2	16.96
C. Brown (*Cheshire*)	125.5	19	448	26	5-41	3	17.23
J. M. Hands (*Cornwall*)	157.5	27	553	32	6-39	2	17.28
R. W. Pineo (*Suffolk*)	173	43	544	31	5-29	1	17.54
S. C. Goldsmith (*Norfolk*)	158.3	46	387	22	5-28	1	17.59
V. J. Pike (*Dorset*)	334.1	87	1,045	57	7-27	6	18.33
G. M. Kirk (*Suffolk*)	149.4	41	451	24	5-30	2	18.79
P. G. Newman (*Norfolk*)	163.5	50	443	23	6-31	1	19.26

	O	M	R	W	BB	5W/i	Avge
J. W. Shaw (*Herefordshire*)	159	31	555	28	6-44	1	19.82
T. J. Sharpe (*Dorset*)	147.5	33	476	24	6-60	1	19.83
A. Akhtar (*Cambridgeshire*).	288.3	91	735	37	8-44	3	19.86
A. J. Procter (*Devon*)	205	43	676	34	6-77	3	19.88
J. E. Emburey (*Berkshire*)	277.5	58	759	36	7-74	1	21.08
C. R. Gibbens (*Wiltshire*)	120.2	22	427	20	6-21	1	21.35
R. J. Bates (*Wiltshire*).	174.1	35	632	29	7-38	2	21.79
J. N. B. Bovill (*Buckinghamshire*) .	174.2	37	526	24	6-38	1	21.91
G. Angus (*Northumberland*).	165	31	505	23	5-87	1	21.95

Eastern Division

At Barrow, May 21, 22. Cumberland won by four wickets. Hertfordshire 212 for seven dec. and 212; Cumberland 228 for six dec. and 197 for six (S. M. Dutton 106*). *Cumberland 23 pts, Hertfordshire 5 pts.*

At Bourne, May 21, 22. Drawn (no result). Staffordshire 157 for seven. *Lincolnshire 5 pts, Staffordshire 5 pts.*

At Jesmond, May 23, 24. Drawn (no result). Northumberland 268 for five dec.; Hertfordshire 168 for seven. *Northumberland 5 pts, Hertfordshire 5 pts.*

At Sleaford, May 28, 29. Abandoned (no result). *Lincolnshire 5 pts, Bedfordshire 5 pts.*

At Sleaford, May 31, June 1. Drawn. Northumberland 176 for six dec.; Lincolnshire 178 for four dec. *Lincolnshire 4 pts, Northumberland 1 pt.*

At Flitwick, June 4, 5. Drawn. Northumberland 161 for three dec. and 240 for eight dec.; Bedfordshire 175 for seven dec. and 174 for six. *Bedfordshire 3 pts, Northumberland 4 pts.*

At Netherfield, June 5, 6. Drawn (no result). Cumberland 135 (P. G. Newman six for 31); Norfolk 106 for seven. *Cumberland 5 pts, Norfolk 5 pts.*

At Wisbech, June 6, 7. Drawn. Cambridgeshire 160 for seven dec. and 170 for six dec.; Northumberland 119 (A. Akhtar five for 37) and 114 for five. *Cambridgeshire 4pts, Northumberland 3 pts.*

At Stone, June 7, 8. Drawn. Staffordshire 158 for five dec. and 222 for seven dec.; Norfolk 150 for eight dec. and 214 for nine. *Staffordshire 4 pts, Norfolk 2 pts.*

At Bedford Town, June 11, 12. Cumberland won by 86 runs. Cumberland 278 for five dec. and 252 for three dec. (J. M. Lewis 128*, A. A. Metcalfe 105*); Bedfordshire 227 for three dec. and 217 (M. A. Sharp five for 49). *Cumberland 19 pts, Bedfordshire 6 pts.*

At Cannock, June 13, 14. Drawn. Buckinghamshire 206 for six dec. and 12 for no wkt; Staffordshire 181 for four dec. *Staffordshire 4 pts, Buckinghamshire 2 pts.*

At Saffron Walden, June 14, 15. Drawn. Cambridgeshire 241 for no wkt dec. (S. A. Kellett 127*) and 265 for no wkt dec. (N. T. Gadsby 133*, S. A. Kellett 115*); Suffolk 200 for four dec. and 291 for nine (M. D. Catley 110). *Cambridgeshire 4 pts, Suffolk 3 pts.*

At March, June 28, 29. Drawn. Cambridgeshire 186 for eight dec. and 204 for three dec.; Staffordshire 164 for eight dec. and 93 for three. *Cambridgeshire 4 pts, Staffordshire 4 pts.*

At Beaconsfield, July 2, 3. Buckinghamshire won by 85 runs. Buckinghamshire 195 and 189 for six dec.; Norfolk 137 for six dec. and 162. *Buckinghamshire 18 pts, Norfolk 4 pts.*

At Long Marston, July 2, 3. Drawn. Hertfordshire 171 and 251 for eight dec. (D. M. Ward 100); Suffolk 169 for eight dec. and 117 for seven. *Hertfordshire 4 pts, Suffolk 5 pts.*

At Lincoln Lindum, July 2, 3. Drawn. Lincolnshire 172 (D. M. Wheatman six for 34) and 108 for no wkt dec.; Cumberland 59 for six dec. *Lincolnshire 3 pts, Cumberland 4 pts.*

At Saffron Walden, July 4, 5. Drawn (no result). Cambridgeshire 168; Cumberland 136 for nine (A. Akhtar five for 19). *Cambridgeshire 5 pts, Cumberland 5 pts.*

At South Northumberland, July 9, 10. Drawn (no result). Staffordshire 153 for eight dec.; Northumberland 77 for five. *Northumberland 5 pts, Staffordshire 5 pts.*

At Askam, July 11, 12. Drawn. Cumberland 153 (G. Bulpitt six for 71) and 149 (L. Potter six for 32); Staffordshire 140 for six dec. and 134 for eight (D. B. Pennett seven for 33). *Cumberland 2 pts, Staffordshire 4 pts.*

At Fenner's, Cambridge, July 12, 13. Drawn. Buckinghamshire 209 for seven dec. and 261; Cambridgeshire 215 for no wkt dec. (S. A. Kellett 103*, N. T. Gadsby 100*) and 179 for six. *Cambridgeshire 6 pts, Buckinghamshire 2 pts.*

At Bishop's Stortford, July 16, 17. Buckinghamshire won by an innings and 66 runs. Buckinghamshire 278 for four dec.; Hertfordshire 122 (S. P. Naylor seven for 22) and 90. *Buckinghamshire 24 pts, Hertfordshire 1 pt.*

At Grantham, July 16, 17. Lincolnshire won by an innings and 12 runs. Lincolnshire 253 for five dec.; Cambridgeshire 142 (E. J. Wilson seven for 61) and 99. *Lincolnshire 21 pts, Cambridgeshire 2 pts.*

At Ipswich School, July 16, 17. Suffolk won by four wickets. Bedfordshire 226 and 175; Suffolk 227 for seven dec. and 175 for six. *Suffolk 24 pts, Bedfordshire 7 pts.*

At Marlow, July 23, 24. Bedfordshire won by 47 runs. Bedfordshire 178 (J. N. B. Bovill six for 38) and 235; Buckinghamshire 174 (R. N. Dalton six for 28) and 192. *Bedfordshire 22 pts, Buckinghamshire 5 pts.*

At Lakenham, July 23, 24. Drawn. Norfolk 204 for five dec. and 188; Lincolnshire 187 for eight dec. and 106 for five. *Norfolk 5 pts, Lincolnshire 3 pts.*

At Ransomes, Ipswich, July 23, 24. Northumberland won by 16 runs. Northumberland 218 for eight dec. and 108 (G. M. Kirk five for 30); Suffolk 156 (G. Angus five for 87) and 154. *Northumberland 22 pts, Suffolk 4 pts.*

At Brewood, July 24, 25. Drawn. Staffordshire 242 for eight dec. (G. F. Archer 113; S. P. White five for 48) and 262 for eight dec. (L. Potter 146*); Hertfordshire 300 (D. M. Ward 160) and 41 for three. *Staffordshire 6 pts, Hertfordshire 7 pts.*

At Lakenham, July 25, 26. Norfolk won by 95 runs. Norfolk 230 for seven dec. and 158 for six dec.; Northumberland 151 and 142 (S. C. Goldsmith five for 28). *Norfolk 24 pts, Northumberland 3 pts.*

At Ransomes, Ipswich, July 25, 26. Lincolnshire won by nine wickets. Lincolnshire 208 for eight dec. (G. M. Kirk five for 61) and 41 for one; Suffolk 89 (S. Oakes five for 38) and 159 (D. J. Pipes five for 41). *Lincolnshire 20 pts, Suffolk 3 pts.*

At Dunstable, July 30, 31. Drawn. Hertfordshire 207 for seven dec. and 320 for eight dec.; Bedfordshire 225 for three dec. and 246 for eight. *Bedfordshire 7 pts, Hertfordshire 4 pts.*

At Millom, July 31, August 1. Cumberland won by three wickets (one innings). Suffolk 174 (D. B. Pennett five for 79); Cumberland 176 for seven. *Cumberland 16 pts, Suffolk 5 pts.*

At Lakenham, July 31, August 1. Cambridgeshire won by three wickets. Norfolk 123 (A. Akhtar eight for 44) and 210 for seven dec.; Cambridgeshire 156 (A. R. Clarke five for 48) and 180 for seven. *Cambridgeshire 21 pts, Norfolk 4 pts.*

At Lakenham, August 2, 3. Drawn (no result). Hertfordshire 295 for four dec. (D. M. Ward 202*); Norfolk 19 for no wkt. *Norfolk 5 pts, Hertfordshire 5 pts.*

At Leek, August 2, 3. Drawn. Suffolk 205 for eight dec. and 199 for five dec.; Staffordshire 177 for seven dec. and 129 for eight (R. W. Pineo five for 29). *Staffordshire 5 pts, Suffolk 4 pts.*

At Luton, August 6, 7. Drawn. Norfolk 198 for seven dec. (S. R. Rashid five for 49) and 328 for three dec. (C. Amos 102*); Bedfordshire 226 for four dec. and 271 for eight (T. W. Roberts 139). *Bedfordshire 7 pts, Norfolk 2 pts.*

At Milton Keynes, August 6, 7. Drawn. Buckinghamshire 191 and 285 for five dec. (B. S. Percy 106, P. D. Atkins 102*); Suffolk 207 for eight dec. and 198 for six. *Buckinghamshire 5 pts, Suffolk 7 pts.*

At Radlett, August 6, 7. Lincolnshire won by nine wickets. Hertfordshire 114 and 205 (D. M. Ward 101; S. Oakes six for 27); Lincolnshire 275 for seven dec. (R. W. J. Howitt 143*) and 45 for one. *Lincolnshire 21 pts, Hertfordshire 3 pts.*

At Southill Park, August 13, 14. Drawn. Bedfordshire 167 for eight dec. and 207 for seven dec.; Cambridgeshire 162 for five dec. and 188 for nine (A. J. Trott five for 66). *Bedfordshire 2 pts, Cambridgeshire 3 pts.*

At Jesmond, August 13, 14. Northumberland won by one wicket. Buckinghamshire 186 and 107 for one dec.; Northumberland 39 for three dec. and 255 for nine. *Northumberland 20 pts, Buckinghamshire 2 pts.*

At Carlisle, August 15, 16. Cumberland won by five wickets. Buckinghamshire 137 and 159 for one dec.; Cumberland 122 for seven dec. (S. F. Stanway six for 47) and 175 for five. *Cumberland 20 pts, Buckinghamshire 3 pts.*

At High Wycombe, August 20, 21. Drawn. Lincolnshire 225 for four dec. (J. Clarke 100*) and 195 for three dec.; Buckinghamshire 139 (S. Oakes six for 45) and 179 for three. *Buckinghamshire 1 pt, Lincolnshire 8 pts.*

At Stevenage, August 20, 21. Drawn. Hertfordshire 197 and 293 for six dec.; Cambridgeshire 262 for eight dec. and 198 for nine. *Hertfordshire 4 pts, Cambridgeshire 8 pts.*

At Jesmond, August 20, 21. Cumberland won by 155 runs. Cumberland 293 for two dec. (S. T. Knox 158*) and forfeited second innings; Northumberland ten for two dec. and 128. *Cumberland 18 pts.*

At Walsall, August 20, 21. Drawn. Bedfordshire 246 for seven dec. and 264 for eight dec. (A. R. Roberts 140), Staffordshire 225 for four dec. and 269 for eight. *Staffordshire 5 pts, Bedfordshire 4 pts.*

At Bury St Edmunds, August 20, 21. Suffolk won by 225 runs. Suffolk 252 for seven dec. and 57 for one dec.; Norfolk nine for no wkt dec. and 75 (A. Poole six for 19). *Suffolk 18 pts, Norfolk 3 pts.*

Western Division

At Hungerford, May 21, 22. Drawn. Berkshire 204 for five dec. and 236 for five dec.; Wales 175 for two dec. and 215 for eight. *Berkshire 3 pts, Wales 4 pts.*

At Colwall, May 21, 22. Dorset won by eight wickets. Herefordshire 225 for two dec. and 178 for five dec.; Dorset 181 (J. W. Shaw six for 44) and 225 for two (M. Swarbrick 114). *Dorset 18 pts, Herefordshire 8 pts.*

At Shrewsbury, May 21, 22. Shropshire won by seven wickets. Oxfordshire 94 (A. M. Shimmons five for 61) and 99 (A. M. Shimmons six for 42); Shropshire 93 (K. A. Arnold six for 32) and 101 for three. *Shropshire 20 pts, Oxfordshire 4 pts.*

At Alderley Edge, May 23, 24. Oxfordshire won by two runs (one innings). Oxfordshire 123; Cheshire 121 (K. A. Arnold five for 46). *Oxfordshire 16 pts, Cheshire 5 pts.*

At Finchampstead, May 28, 29. Drawn (no result). Herefordshire 223 (N. A. Fusedale five for 55); Berkshire 52 for no wkt. *Berkshire 5 pts, Herefordshire 5 pts.*

At Torquay, May 28, 29. Drawn (no result). Devon 183 for seven dec. (N. A. Folland 101*); Dorset 106 for one. *Devon 5 pts, Dorset 5 pts.*

At Westbury, May 28, 29. Wiltshire won by 30 runs (one innings). Wiltshire 183; Wales 153 (R. J. Bates seven for 38). *Wiltshire 16 pts, Wales 5 pts.*

At Wellington, June 4, 5. Wiltshire won by 24 runs (one innings). Wiltshire 150 for six dec.; Shropshire 126 (R. J. Sillence seven for 38). *Wiltshire 16 pts, Shropshire 5 pts.*

At Weymouth, June 11, 12. Drawn. Dorset 176 for seven dec. and 262 for nine dec.; Shropshire 237 for seven dec. *Dorset 3 pts, Shropshire 7 pts.*

At Banbury CC, June 11, 12. Oxfordshire won by 31 runs. Oxfordshire 229 for five dec. and 214 for five dec.; Wales 153 (G. S. Peddy five for 36) and 259. *Oxfordshire 24 pts, Wales 3 pts.*

At Warminster, June 11, 12. Drawn. Berkshire 170 (J. P. Searle five for 47) and 247 for eight dec. (L. H. Nurse 108); Wiltshire 166 for nine dec. (J. E. Emburey seven for 74) and 88 for nine. *Wiltshire 4 pts, Berkshire 5 pts.*

At Truro, June 12, 13. Drawn. Cheshire 199 for five dec. and 182 for two dec.; Cornwall 155 and 28 for one. *Cornwall 3 pts, Cheshire 6 pts.*

At Bovey Tracey, June 14, 15. Devon won by nine wickets. Devon 372 for five dec. (R. I. Dawson 151, N. A. Folland 110) and 97 for one; Cheshire 106 and 359 (J. Cornford 145). *Devon 24 pts, Cheshire 2 pts.*

At Kington, June 25, 26. Herefordshire won by an innings and 90 runs. Devon 224 for seven dec. (P. J. Humphries six for 75) and 59; Herefordshire 373 for five dec. *Herefordshire 23 pts, Devon 4 pts.*

At Hurst, July 2, 3. Berkshire won by two wickets. Berkshire 261 (N. T. P. George five for 43) and 119 for eight; Cornwall 96 and 283. *Berkshire 22 pts, Cornwall 4 pts.*

At Colwyn Bay, July 2, 3. Drawn. Wales 31 for three dec. and 62 for one; Shropshire forfeited first innings. *Shropshire 1 pt.*

At The Parks, Oxford, July 4, 5. Oxfordshire won by six wickets. Cornwall 185 and 75 (S. V. Laudat seven for 38); Oxfordshire 182 for eight dec. and 80 for four. *Oxfordshire 22 pts, Cornwall 3 pts.*

At Penzance, July 16, 17. Dorset won by 121 runs. Dorset 216 (T. C. Z. Lamb 116) and 241 for nine dec.; Cornwall 210 (V. J. Pike six for 51) and 126 (V. J. Pike seven for 27). *Dorset 22 pts, Cornwall 4 pts.*

At Cheadle Hulme, July 16, 17. Herefordshire won by 168 runs. Herefordshire 200 for eight dec. (C. C. Finegan five for 60) and 287 for six dec.; Cheshire 184 for eight dec. and 135. *Herefordshire 22 pts, Cheshire 5 pts.*

At Marlborough CC, July 16, 17. Oxfordshire won by eight wickets. Wiltshire 91 (K. A. Arnold seven for 36) and 227 (I. J. Curtis five for 66); Oxfordshire 220 for eight dec. and 101 for two. *Oxfordshire 22 pts, Wiltshire 3 pts.*

At Dean Park, Bournemouth, July 23, 24. Drawn. Berkshire 294 for three dec. and 258 for eight dec.; Dorset 285 for four dec. (M. Swarbrick 102). *Dorset 3 pts, Berkshire 3 pts.*

At Christ Church, Oxford, July 23, 24. Drawn. Devon 227 for four dec. and 271 for eight dec.; Oxfordshire 224 (A. J. Procter five for 76) and 240 for eight. *Oxfordshire 2 pts, Devon 8 pts.*

At Whitchurch, July 23, 24. Drawn. Herefordshire 313 for two dec. (I. Dawood 142*, P. S. Lazenbury 134) and 195; Shropshire 235 for nine dec. (B. W. W. Platt 104*) and 227 for eight. *Shropshire 4 pts, Herefordshire 8 pts.*

At Neath, July 23, 24. Cornwall won by five wickets. Wales 168 for seven dec. (J. C. J. Stephens five for 47) and 245 for six dec. (J. P. J. Sylvester 120); Cornwall 181 for eight dec. and 235 for five. *Cornwall 21 pts, Wales 3 pts.*

At South Wilts CC, Salisbury, July 23, 24. Drawn. Wiltshire 229 for six dec. and 165 for eight; Cheshire 96 (C. R. Gibbens six for 21) and 344 for six dec. (M. R. Currie 171; R. J. Bates five for 87). *Wiltshire 6 pts, Cheshire 2 pts.*

At Falkland CC, Newbury, July 25, 26. Berkshire won by 75 runs. Berkshire 227 for seven dec. and 257 for seven dec.; Devon 198 for seven dec. and 211 (N. A. Fusedale five for 83). *Berkshire 23 pts, Devon 5 pts.*

At Dean Park, Bournemouth, July 25, 26. Dorset won by one wicket. Cheshire 206 for six dec. (V. J. Pike five for 57) and 187 (V. J. Pike five for 74); Dorset 229 for seven dec. (C. Brown five for 79) and 165 for nine (C. Brown five for 62). *Dorset 22 pts, Cheshire 6 pts.*

At Dales CC, Leominster, July 25, 26. Herefordshire won by 132 runs. Herefordshire 222 (P. S. Lazenbury 121) and 268 for five dec. (P. S. Lazenbury 118); Cornwall 227 for eight dec. and 131. *Herefordshire 20 pts, Cornwall 8 pts.*

At Oxton, July 30, 31. Drawn. Cheshire 223 for two dec. (M. R. Currie 109*) and 28 for two; Wales 156 (C. Brown five for 41). *Cheshire 7 pts, Wales 1 pt.*

At Budleigh Salterton, July 30, 31. Shropshire won by 101 runs. Shropshire 224 for nine dec. (A. J. Procter five for 75) and 230 (A. J. Procter six for 77); Devon 228 for five dec. and 125. *Shropshire 20 pts, Devon 8 pts.*

At Dean Park, Bournemouth, July 30, 31. Dorset won by seven wickets. Oxfordshire 232 for three dec. (C. A. Haupt 121*) and 190; Dorset 247 for five dec. (D. J. Cowley 103*) and 176 for three. *Dorset 21 pts, Oxfordshire 5 pts.*

At Luctonians, Kingsland, July 30, 31. Wiltshire won by seven wickets. Herefordshire 294 for seven dec. and 165 for eight dec.; Wiltshire 260 for six dec. and 200 for three (R. J. Sillence 106*). *Wiltshire 21 pts, Herefordshire 4 pts.*

At Camborne, August 1, 2. Cornwall won by 146 runs. Cornwall 188 and 249 for five dec. (G. M. Thomas 101); Shropshire 196 for nine dec. and 95 (C. E. Shreck seven for 41). *Cornwall 20 pts, Shropshire 6 pts.*

At Exmouth, August 6, 7. Devon won by 168 runs. Devon 243 for three dec. and 235 for eight dec. (S. C. B. Tomlinson 119*); Wiltshire 167 and 143. *Devon 24 pts, Wiltshire 2 pts.*

At Thame, August 6, 7. Oxfordshire won by ten wickets. Herefordshire 164 (K. A. Arnold six for 57) and 83 (K. A. Arnold nine for 19); Oxfordshire 226 for four dec. and 27 for no wkt. *Oxfordshire 24 pts, Herefordshire 1 pt.*

At Ynysygerwn, August 6, 7. Dorset won by an innings and 14 runs. Wales 105 (D. A. Kidner five for 18) and 169 (T. J. Sharpe six for 60); Dorset 288 for five dec. *Dorset 24 pts, Wales 2 pts.*

At Neston, August 13, 14. Drawn (no result). Berkshire 83 for five v Cheshire. *Cheshire 5 pts, Berkshire 5 pts.*

At Falmouth, August 13, 14. Abandoned (no result). *Cornwall 5 pts, Wiltshire 5 pts.*

At Pontarddulais, August 13, 14. Drawn (no result). Wales 60 for two v Devon. *Wales 5 pts, Devon 5 pts.*

At Bridgnorth, August 15, 16. Shropshire won by 22 runs. Shropshire 226 for seven dec. and 257 for seven dec.; Berkshire 215 for six dec. and 246 (B. W. W. Platt six for 92). *Shropshire 20 pts, Berkshire 6 pts.*

At Reading, August 20, 21. Drawn. Berkshire 225 for six dec. and 241 for nine dec. (J. R. Wood 100; K. A. Arnold five for 86); Oxfordshire 216 for three dec. (S. V. Laudat 118) and 115 for six. *Berkshire 5 pts, Oxfordshire 5 pts.*

At Bowdon, August 20, 21. Shropshire won by eight runs. Shropshire 225 for eight dec. and 179 for nine dec.; Cheshire 144 and 252 (Asif Din five for 64). *Shropshire 23 pts, Cheshire 3 pts.*

At St Austell, August 20, 21. Drawn. Devon 183 (J. M. Hands six for 39) and 123 for four; Cornwall 191 for nine dec. *Cornwall 6 pts, Devon 5 pts.*

At Brockhampton, August 20, 21. Drawn. Herefordshire 98 and 259 for six dec. (P. S. Lazenbury 103); Wales 107 and 193 for eight. *Herefordshire 4 pts, Wales 4 pts.*

At Corsham, August 20, 21. Dorset won by two wickets. Wiltshire 222 (V. J. Pike seven for 61) and 333 for six dec. (R. J. Sillence 150; V. J. Pike six for 117); Dorset 252 for nine dec. and 307 for eight. *Dorset 24 pts, Wiltshire 7 pts.*

CHAMPIONSHIP FINAL

DORSET v CUMBERLAND

At Bournemouth SC, September 10, 11, 12. Dorset won by five wickets. Toss: Dorset.

Dorset's victory brought them a first Championship title and avenged their defeat by the same opponents in the 1999 final. Cumberland began strongly with a first-innings lead that owed much to an unbeaten 108 from left-handed opener David Pearson, playing in his last game for the county. In the second innings, though, teenage seamers Kidner and Sharpe provided some quality back-up for Pike's leg-breaks to bowl Cumberland out cheaply and leave Dorset a target of 193. This was reached comfortably through a robust 63 off 55 balls from Cowley, who had also dominated their first innings.

Cumberland

S. T. Knox c Lamb b Pike	59	– c Rintoul b Kidner		2
D. J. Pearson not out	108	– b Sharpe		7
A. A. Metcalfe c Forshaw b Pike	30	– c Swarbrick b Treagus		47
J. M. Lewis c sub b Treagus	60	– (7) c Lamb b Kidner		18
S. J. O'Shaughnessy st Lamb b Treagus	4	– (5) c Deakin b Pike		8
*†S. M. Dutton b Pike	5	– (6) b Pike		23
J. M. Fielding not out	3	– (9) b Pike		0
D. E. Barnes (did not bat)		– (4) b Sharpe		2
S. A. J. Kippax (did not bat)		– (8) lbw b Sharpe		13
D. B. Pennett (did not bat)		– c Lamb b Sharpe		9
M. A. Sharp (did not bat)		– not out		7
B 2, l-b 7, w 2, n-b 2	13	B 4, l-b 8, n-b 4		16

1/113 2/167 3/268 (5 wkts, 70 overs) 282 1/7 2/39 3/43 4/66 5/78 152
4/274 5/279 6/102 7/118 8/118 9/130

Bowling: *First Innings*—Forshaw 6–1–20–0; Sharpe 8–2–22–0; Pike 32–8–115–3; Kidner 14–3–53–0; Cowley 5–1–26–0; Treagus 5–0–37–2. *Second Innings*—Forshaw 6–2–22–0; Kidner 15–3–32–2; Sharpe 10.3–4–19–4; Pike 21–6–55–3; Treagus 7–3–12–1.

Dorset

G. R. Treagus b Pennett	2	– (2) lbw b Pennett	27
M. Swarbrick c and b Fielding	52	– (1) c Dutton b Pennett	4
N. J. Thurgood c Lewis b O'Shaughnessy	13	– b Fielding	62
D. J. Cowley st Dutton b Fielding	75	– b Pennett	63
P. J. Deakin c Sharp b Kippax	20	– c Pearson b Kippax	5
†T. C. Z. Lamb c Kippax b Fielding	17	– not out	24
*S. W. D. Rintoul not out	34	– not out	8
D. A. Kidner run out	1		
T. J. Sharpe c and b Kippax	2		
V. J. Pike lbw b Kippax	5		
S. Forshaw not out	1		
B 2, l-b 6, n-b 12	20	L-b 3	3

1/24 2/39 3/131   (9 wkts, 70 overs) 242   1/4 2/71 3/151   (5 wkts) 196
4/164 5/184 6/201   4/159 5/177
7/206 8/211 9/233

Bowling: *First Innings*—Pennett 18–4–73–1; Sharp 14–4–45–0; Fielding 14–4–56–3; O'Shaughnessy 6–1–18–1; Kippax 18–4–42–3. *Second Innings*—Pennett 12–3–19–3; Sharp 14–4–38–0; Fielding 18–4–56–1; Kippax 15.3–2–65–1; O'Shaughnessy 3–1–5–0; Lewis 6–3–10–0.

Umpires: D. L. Burden and J. H. Evans.

THE MINOR COUNTIES CHAMPIONS

1895 {	Norfolk	1928	Berkshire	1967	Cheshire
	Durham	1929	Oxfordshire	1968	Yorkshire II
	Worcestershire	1930	Durham	1969	Buckinghamshire
1896	Worcestershire	1931	Leicestershire II	1970	Bedfordshire
1897	Worcestershire	1932	Buckinghamshire	1971	Yorkshire II
1898	Worcestershire	1933	Undecided	1972	Bedfordshire
1899 {	Northamptonshire	1934	Lancashire II	1973	Shropshire
	Buckinghamshire	1935	Middlesex II	1974	Oxfordshire
	Glamorgan	1936	Hertfordshire	1975	Hertfordshire
1900 {	Durham	1937	Lancashire II	1976	Durham
	Northamptonshire	1938	Buckinghamshire	1977	Suffolk
1901	Durham	1939	Surrey II	1978	Devon
1902	Wiltshire	1946	Suffolk	1979	Suffolk
1903	Northamptonshire	1947	Yorkshire II	1980	Durham
1904	Northamptonshire	1948	Lancashire II	1981	Durham
1905	Norfolk	1949	Lancashire II	1982	Oxfordshire
1906	Staffordshire	1950	Surrey II	1983	Hertfordshire
1907	Lancashire II	1951	Kent II	1984	Durham
1908	Staffordshire	1952	Buckinghamshire	1985	Cheshire
1909	Wiltshire	1953	Berkshire	1986	Cumberland
1910	Norfolk	1954	Surrey II	1987	Buckinghamshire
1911	Staffordshire	1955	Surrey II	1988	Cheshire
1912	In abeyance	1956	Kent II	1989	Oxfordshire
1913	Norfolk	1957	Yorkshire II	1990	Hertfordshire
1914	Staffordshire†	1958	Yorkshire II	1991	Staffordshire
1920	Staffordshire	1959	Warwickshire II	1992	Staffordshire
1921	Staffordshire	1960	Lancashire II	1993	Staffordshire
1922	Buckinghamshire	1961	Somerset II	1994	Devon
1923	Buckinghamshire	1962	Warwickshire II	1995	Devon
1924	Berkshire	1963	Cambridgeshire	1996	Devon
1925	Buckinghamshire	1964	Lancashire II	1997	Devon
1926	Durham	1965	Somerset II	1998	Staffordshire
1927	Staffordshire	1966	Lincolnshire	1999	Cumberland
				2000	Dorset

† *Disputed. Most sources claim the Championship was never decided.*

ECB 38-COUNTY CUP FINAL

CHESHIRE v HEREFORDSHIRE

At Lord's, August 30. Herefordshire won by 42 runs. Toss: Herefordshire.

Herefordshire celebrated their first major trophy only nine years after becoming a Minor County. Harshad Patel, their captain and the sole survivor of the side beaten by Cambridgeshire in the 1995 MCC Trophy final, saw his decision to bat vindicated as Lazenbury and Chris Boroughs shared a third-wicket stand of 203 in 33 overs. Taking advantage of a short Tavern boundary, they blazed 11 sixes and Herefordshire piled up a significant total. In reply, Cheshire reached 92 for one off 23 overs before Kevin Cooper had Ian Cockbain caught behind with his first ball and caught James Cornford off his own bowling. On changing ends, he bowled Paul Bryson with the first ball of his second spell and then had Stuart Stoneman caught behind without scoring. Some lusty blows from Richard Hignett, a fifth victim for Cooper, and Brown came too late for Cheshire to claim a record fourth victory in one-day finals.

Herefordshire

*H. V. Patel c Bramhall b Finegan	20	N. W. Round run out	1
R. D. Hughes c Bryson b Lamb	8	A. Farooque not out	13
P. S. Lazenbury c Finegan b Stoneman	118	L-b 6, w 18	24
C. W. Boroughs b Lamb	94		
†I. Dawood not out	5	1/10 2/47 3/250 (6 wkts, 50 overs) 291	
J. E. Brinkley run out	8	4/262 5/273 6/274	

K. Pearson, K. E. Cooper and P. J. Humphries did not bat.

Bowling: Stoneman 10–0–45–1; Lamb 10–1–54–2; Finegan 9–0–64–1; Cross 7–0–39–0; Brown 9–1–42–0; Hall 5–0–41–0.

Cheshire

P. R. J. Bryson b Cooper	73	C. Brown not out	39
N. D. Cross c Pearson b Brinkley	7	C. Lamb b Round	15
*I. Cockbain c Dawood b Cooper	14	C. C. Finegan not out	6
J. Cornford c and b Cooper	12	L-b 11, w 10, n-b 4	25
R. G. Hignett c Humphries b Cooper	38		
S. A. Stoneman c Dawood b Cooper	0	1/40 2/92 3/110 (9 wkts, 50 overs) 249	
C. J. Hall c Pearson b Humphries	14	4/142 5/142 6/169	
†S. Bramhall c Round b Humphries	6	7/175 8/191 9/226	

Bowling: Brinkley 10–2–27–1; Humphries 10–0–58–2; Boroughs 3–0–18–0; Farooque 10–0–53–0; Pearson 5–0–35–0; Cooper 10–3–29–5; Round 2–0–18–1.

Umpires: S. W. Kuhlmann and W. E. Smith.

WINNERS 1983-2000

1983	Cheshire	1989	Cumberland	1995	Cambridgeshire
1984	Hertfordshire	1990	Buckinghamshire	1996	Cheshire
1985	Durham	1991	Staffordshire	1997	Norfolk
1986	Norfolk	1992	Devon	1998	Devon
1987	Cheshire	1993	Staffordshire	1999	Bedfordshire
1988	Dorset	1994	Devon	2000	Herefordshire

SECOND ELEVEN CHAMPIONSHIP, 2000

Middlesex became only the third team to retain the Second Eleven Championship, after Worcestershire in 1963 and Kent in 1970. Victory at Hastings in the last match of the season ensured they won the trophy for the fourth time in 12 seasons, averaging over a point more than second-placed Kent.

The strength of Middlesex's batting proved crucial. They totalled 43 batting points, by far the most, even though only two counties played fewer matches. Against Derbyshire at Uxbridge, they scored 632 for nine declared, the fourth-highest total in the competition. Their leading run-scorer, Robin Weston, scored 558 runs at 55.80, and was named Second Eleven Player of the Year.

Unlike the previous three seasons, no batsman hit a triple-century in 2000. The best came from Hampshire's John Stephenson, who made an undefeated 208 against Derbyshire at Bournemouth. There were two other double-centuries: Warwickshire's Anurag Singh scored 205 not out against Worcestershire at Stratford-upon-Avon and Graham Lloyd of Lancashire thrashed 202 off 205 balls against Warwickshire at Manchester. A 20-year-old left-hander from Yorkshire, Michael Lumb, was the most prolific batsman of the summer, with 885 runs at 44.25. The son of Yorkshire stalwart Richard, he finished well ahead of Glamorgan's Ian Thomas, who had almost reached 800 before being promoted to the first team.

The outstanding bowling performance of the season came at Harrow, where Middlesex seamer Jamie Hewitt took eight for 55 to secure victory over Worcestershire. Bowlers generally had the better of the summer – 719 bonus points for bowling compared to 522 for batting – and four took 50 or more wickets in the season, a feat last achieved in 1997. Richard Green, the Lancashire medium-pacer, led the way with 54 wickets at 20.01.

From 2001, each side must play a minimum of ten Championship games (two fewer than in 2000), at least four of which must be four-day fixtures. This reflects the ECB's eagerness to accommodate counties with smaller playing staffs, especially those with young cricketers who might miss the early part of the summer through academic commitments.

SECOND ELEVEN CHAMPIONSHIP, 2000

	P	W	L	D	Bonus points Batting	Bonus points Bowling	Points	Avge
1 – Middlesex (1).	13	6	1	6	43	39	178	13.69
2 – Kent (5)	14	7	3	4	33	44	177	12.64
3 – Warwickshire (10). . .	14	6	2	6	36	42	174	12.42
4 – Nottinghamshire (11) .	16	7	3	6	36	50	194	12.12
5 – Yorkshire (14)	15	5	2	8	37	42	173*	11.53
6 – Sussex (3).	12	5	4	3	22	37	131	10.91
7 – Lancashire (4)	15	5	4	6	30	43	157	10.46
8 – Surrey (9)	14	4	3	7	33	37	146	10.42
9 – Gloucestershire (15). .	14	4	1	9	21	33	138	9.85
10 – Essex (12).	14	4	5	5	28	40	136	9.71
11 – Hampshire (7)	14	4	7	3	25	44	129	9.21
12 – Durham (8)	13	3	4	6	18	40	118	9.07
13 – Glamorgan (17)	14	3	5	6	29	36	125	8.92
14 – Northamptonshire (13)	16	3	4	9	21	48	141	8.81
15 – Leicestershire (16). . .	12	2	6	4	29	33	102	8.50
16 – Somerset (18).	13	2	6	5	30	35	109	8.38
17 – Worcestershire (6). . .	14	2	7	5	30	37	111	7.92
18 – Derbyshire (2)	15	3	8	4	21	39	112	7.46

1999 positions are shown in brackets.

Win = 12 pts; draw = 4 pts.

* Includes 2 pts for draw in which scores were level.

After the departure of a number of senior players, a young **Derbyshire** side fell 16 places and finished last. There were some individual successes: all-rounder Nathan Dumelow scored 403 runs, took 25 wickets with off-spin and was given another season on a match-by-match contract, and Lian Wharton, in his first year on the staff, bowled well enough to gain promotion to the first team. Rawait Khan, aged 18, scored 106 not out on debut against Sussex at Hove and ended with the most runs in the summer, though Scotland international Doug Lockhart led the averages. The most pleasing performance, however, came at Chesterfield, when James Pyemont's first-innings five for 21 inspired a five-wicket victory over a strong Nottinghamshire side.

Durham fielded 12 academy players and, by the end of a difficult summer, had fallen to 12th place. Their three wicket-keepers topped the batting: Martin Speight averaged 51.85 from four matches, Andrew Pratt, who kept wicket most impressively, was the highest run-scorer with 557 from 13 innings, while next came Philip Mustard. Pratt's good form earned him elevation to the first team for the last third of the season. Marc Symington and Ian Hunter each took 33 wickets, Hunter also contributing 281 runs at more than 25.

Essex continued their progress of recent seasons and finished tenth, their best position since 1993, though they were squeezed out of a tight group in the AON Trophy. Wicket-keeper/batsman Jamie Foster and Will Jefferson, both Durham University students, showed promising form and stepped up to the first team towards the end of the season. Meanwhile, Graham Napier, who took 25 wickets and scored 386 runs, was given an extended run in the senior one-day side. Also encouraging was the form of Tim Phillips, a left-arm spinner from Felsted School.

An uneventful season nevertheless saw **Glamorgan** rise four places to 13th. They were not helped by the weather, which prevented any play at home to Gloucestershire or away to Kent, or by the depletion of the squad by first-team calls. Ian Thomas, who totalled 792 runs in 17 innings, was deservedly elevated when he looked set to reach 1,000 for the season. David Harrison, the most successful bowler with 31 wickets, was selected to attend the Dennis Lillee academy in Chennai.

Gloucestershire were frustrated by the wet summer – nine of their 14 matches were affected, including one abandoned without a ball bowled – but still finished in the top half. After they lost their first match to Somerset by one wicket, they remained unbeaten for the rest of the season. They won four games, but it could easily have been more: in three of their eight draws the opposition clung on with nine wickets down. Michael Sutliff, on trial from Leicestershire, carried his bat for 90 against Hampshire, and was later awarded a contract for 2001. Reg Williams kept wicket tidily and held the batting together on several occasions, while the bowlers, though rarely spectacular, performed well as a unit.

A young **Hampshire** team, well coached by Tony Middleton, reached the final of the AON Trophy for the second year running. They went unbeaten in the zonal matches but, after narrowly beating Durham in the semi-final, threw away a commanding position in the final against Leicestershire at Southampton, collapsing from 112 for two to 180 all out to lose by 25 runs. A win over Yorkshire in the last Championship match of the season lifted them to 11th place. On largely seamer-friendly pitches the chief run-makers were Andrew Sexton, Lawrence Prittipaul and, in the latter part of the season, John Stephenson. Off-spinner Irfan Shah was the leading wicket-taker, closely followed by Zac Morris, who resourcefully switched between left-arm spin and swing.

Kent enjoyed an encouraging summer, finishing as Championship runners-up and reaching the semi-final of the AON Trophy. At one stage, they strung together a run of 11 wins, five in the Championship and six in the one-day competition. In the Championship victory over Leicestershire, David Fulton, 197, and Matthew Walker, 162, put on a county-record 299 for the third wicket. Wicket-keeper and leading run-scorer Geraint Jones, as well as Paul Lazenbury, the next-highest scorer, earned contracts for 2001, but captain Steve Marsh's long involvement with the county ended. He scored a magnificent 196 not out in the AON Trophy against Essex, and his buoyant, aggressive attitude was instrumental in moulding the team into a competitive unit.

Lancashire began the summer fielding several players with first-team experience, and results reflected this. Later a number of trialists were introduced, but with less success. Seventh place showed how a few poor sessions can turn a win into a draw – or a draw into defeat. Seamer Richard Green was the mainstay of the bowling attack, claiming 54 Championship wickets, while the talented spin trio of Gary Yates, Gary Keedy and Chris Schofield all had their moments. The batting tended more to the satisfactory than to the spectacular: both wicket-keeper Jamie Haynes and Graham Lloyd scored over 500 Championship runs – the latter from only four games – while Paddy McKeown again showed an ability to destroy attacks at this level.

Leicestershire won the AON Trophy with an excellent victory over Hampshire at Southampton. Opener Steve Adshead, whose form had earned him a first-class debut against the West Indians, scored 58, the cornerstone of a modest – but ultimately sufficient – total of 205. Their Championship performances, however, were disappointing. The policy of blooding younger players impeded short-term success, though Leicestershire did finish 15th, one up on 1999. Ashley Wright rounded off an excellent season with 148 against Glamorgan, while two other batsmen had memorable debuts: Nick Ferraby hit an impressive 73 against Northamptonshire, and Tom Huggins 55 against a strong Surrey side. The bowlers worked hard all summer long, with five taking five wickets in an innings.

Middlesex retained the Championship thanks to some destructive batting. Five batsmen averaged more than 50 and, against Derbyshire at Uxbridge, the team made a county-record 632 for nine declared, including an opening partnership of 235 between Robin Weston and Mike Roseberry, both of whom hit centuries. In the last game, at Hastings, Middlesex recovered from 56 for five, Aaron Laraman (158) and Keerthi Ranasinghe (78) adding 122 for the ninth wicket; they went on to win the match. Jamie Hewitt shone with the ball, taking a career-best eight for 55 in the second innings against Worcestershire at Harrow. He dominated the seam attack with 31 wickets at 22.12.

Inclement weather frustrated the first half of **Northamptonshire's** season. In the second, they fielded a number of trialists and, in all, 38 players turned out in the Championship. The leading run-scorers were Mark Powell (711 runs at 39.50) and Alec Swann (746 at 39.26), but the batting was largely disappointing. The bowlers achieved more, with six taking a five-wicket haul at least once. Monty Panesar, a left-arm spinner, was rewarded for his progress with an England Under-19 place. Toby Bailey, outstanding behind the stumps, captained the side with skill and maturity – and was selected for the first team as a specialist batsman.

An incisive attack guided **Nottinghamshire** to seven victories, and they rose seven places to fourth in the table. In all, their bowlers ensured 50 bonus points, more than any other county. Matthew Whiley took 52 wickets, and several young batsmen impressed, including Gareth Clough, whose 37 at 19.05 earned him a full-time contract. The batsmen contributed effectively too: captain Mike Newell averaged 50 and Chris Hewison, an ever-present, scored 709 runs. A home-grown talent, Samit Patel, who played for England in the Under-15 World Challenge, was awarded a contract for 2001.

Somerset endured another disappointing season, though they did lift themselves two places off the foot of the Championship. And by including at least five Under-19s in each game, they ensured youth was given a chance. One to make the most of the opportunity was all-rounder Peter Trego, who soon advanced to the first team. Former England opener Mark Lathwell led the batting before he too stepped up to the first-class game. The form of Joe Tucker was particularly heartening: after suffering from a back injury in 1999 and from glandular fever, jaundice and hepatitis in 2000, he returned to finish fourth in the bowling averages. He took five for 24 as Hampshire were bowled out for 81 in the fourth innings at Clevedon, and made a notable first-class debut against the West Indians.

A combination of poor weather and inconsistent performances restricted **Surrey** to a mid-table position in the Championship and little progress in the AON Trophy. Gary Butcher led from the front to finish at the top of both averages – enough to warrant a late-season promotion to the first team, whereupon he took four Derbyshire wickets in four balls. Gareth Batty produced useful all-round performances while Joe Porter prospered with the bat. Carl Greenidge, who bowled with hostility, took 37 wickets, including a match-winning seven for 57 against Lancashire.

Though they never reached the heights of previous seasons, a young and relatively inexperienced **Sussex** side secured sixth place. They gave a modest showing in the AON Trophy, but won four of their last six Championship matches. Coach Keith Greenfield ably oversaw the campaign and contributed a fine century against Hampshire. Will House, newly arrived from Kent, headed the averages and hit one hundred and three fifties. The leading bowler, Billy Taylor, claimed 35 Championship wickets and was rewarded with first-team cricket. Other notable bowling feats included Wasim Khan's hat-trick in the AON Trophy match against Surrey, and a five-wicket haul on debut by leg-spinner Patrick Spencer.

Strength in depth served **Warwickshire** well, and they finished third. All told, 17 players passed 50, and the season included seven centuries. Three came from Mark Wagh, whose exceptional form – 533 runs at 66.62 – brought first-team selection and his county cap. All-rounder Ryan Sierra, born in South Africa of British parents, scored over 600 runs but a side injury prevented him from bowling in the Championship. Charlie Dagnall, a seamer, also earned elevation to the first team, as did left-armer Darren Altree, who topped the bowling averages with 51 wickets at 17.49, was not retained.

It was a tricky season for **Worcestershire**, who won just two matches and fell 11 places to 17th. Injuries to first-team players ensured a steady flow of first-class calls and an unsettled side, for which 37 players turned out at least once. Right-armer Chris Liptrot came through a mid-season loss of form and confidence to end the summer in breathtaking style: he finished with 53 wickets at 25.11. Trialist Nick Boulton, the one ever-present in the Championship side, scored 778 runs, and earned a contract for 2001.

Yorkshire's policy of giving match experience to younger players paid off: fifth place was nine higher than in 1999. The leading run-scorer was Michael Lumb, the 20-year-old son of former Yorkshire batsman Richard. Though born in South Africa, he is England-qualified for the 2001 season. He scored 885 runs at 44.25, with a highest innings of 191 against Nottinghamshire at Middlesbrough; Matthew Wood hit the same score against Derbyshire at Rotherham. Ian Fisher and James Middlebrook were the most successful bowlers, Middlebrook's 28 wickets coming from just five matches.

DERBYSHIRE SECOND ELEVEN

Matches 15: Won – Glamorgan, Leicestershire, Nottinghamshire. Lost – Durham, Essex, Gloucestershire, Hampshire, Lancashire, Middlesex, Nottinghamshire, Yorkshire. Drawn – Northamptonshire, Somerset, Sussex, Warwickshire.

Batting Averages

	M	I	NO	R	HS	100s	Avge
†D. R. Lockhart	6	12	0	383	112	2	31.91
J. E. K. Schofield	4	8	1	214	65	0	30.57
*†L. D. Sutton	7	12	0	363	51	0	30.25
J. P. Pyemont	3	6	0	155	51	0	25.83
*A. M. Brown	12	19	6	305	67	0	23.46
A. J. Marsh	3	5	0	97	35	0	19.40
S. B. Ellis	3	5	0	95	31	0	19.00
S. A. Selwood.	7	14	0	258	49	0	18.42
A. Bowman	6	12	0	218	59	0	18.16
R. M. Khan	15	28	1	473	106*	1	17.51
S. J. Lacey.	3	4	0	70	58	0	17.50
K. J. Dean	3	4	0	69	42	0	17.25
B. L. Spendlove	8	14	1	224	48*	0	17.23
K. Z. Shah.	10	18	4	228	41*	0	16.28
W. A. Kirby	3	6	0	97	28	0	16.16
N. R. C. Dumelow	14	27	2	403	97	0	16.12
T. M. Smith	3	4	0	63	22	0	15.75
T. Lungley	7	13	0	203	71	0	15.61
S. J. Hassan	2	4	0	56	28	0	14.00
J. E. Brinkley	3	6	2	52	25*	0	13.00
L. J. Wharton	7	11	7	49	18*	0	12.25
D. C. Ward	8	12	1	92	38	0	8.36
Z. M. Khan	11	18	7	61	20	0	5.54
I. J. Darlington	3	6	0	32	23	0	5.33

Played in two matches: A. M. Reynolds 2, 0, 3. Played in one match: C. M. Brittain 35, 15; *M. E. Cassar 112, 4; †C. P. Coleman 0, 0; A. R. Danson 2, 2; M. P. Dowman 56, 14; J. D. J. Frith 23, 4; C. J. Hall 1, 5; †K. J. Hollis 6, 7*; *†K. M. Krikken 14, 10; A. J. Maiden 2, 1; G. Moulds 0*, 0*; B. Nash 20, 55; P. J. Swanepoel 1, 23.

Note: In the match v Leicestershire at Hinckley, T. M. Smith, called up for a first-team match, was replaced by D. C. Ward.

Bowling Averages

	O	M	R	W	BB	Avge
J. E. Brinkley............	101	29	255	15	4-60	17.00
P. J. Swanepoel..........	24.4	4	98	5	5-98	19.60
S. B. Ellis...............	74.1	12	267	12	4-45	22.25
J. P. Pyemont............	78	18	217	9	5-21	24.11
L. J. Wharton...........	199.1	56	616	24	6-71	25.66
K. J. Dean..............	62	16	210	8	2-9	26.25
I. J. Darlington..........	57	10	190	7	4-52	27.14
T. Lungley..............	164	36	522	19	4-68	27.47
K. Z. Shah	195	37	635	23	4-27	27.60
S. J. Lacey	67	18	170	5	4-93	34.00
Z. M. Khan	130.1	22	508	14	3-32	36.28
D. C. Ward	105	19	305	8	2-17	38.12
J. E. K. Schofield	69.2	8	255	6	3-23	42.50
N. R. C. Dumelow	355.2	92	1,125	25	6-78	45.00

Also bowled: C. M. Brittain 10–0–40–2; M. E. Cassar 3–0–10–0; J. D. J. Frith 21–3–82–0; C. J. Hall 29.1–3–69–2; G. Moulds 10–1–53–0; A. M. Reynolds 32–10–105–2; S. A. Selwood 3–0–21–0; T. M. Smith 67–14–257–3.

DURHAM SECOND ELEVEN

Matches 13: Won – Derbyshire, Glamorgan, Lancashire. Lost – Essex, Northamptonshire, Nottinghamshire, Sussex. Drawn – Gloucestershire, Kent, Surrey, Worcestershire, Yorkshire. Abandoned – Yorkshire.

Batting Averages

	M	I	NO	R	HS	100s	Avge
*†M. P. Speight	4	8	1	363	131	1	51.85
†A. Pratt	7	13	0	557	107	1	42.84
†P. Mustard	5	10	1	273	51	0	30.33
N. Peng..............	2	4	0	120	86	0	30.00
*N. C. Phillips	5	9	1	238	80	0	29.75
*J. A. Daley..........	5	10	2	224	62	0	28.00
J. Graham	2	4	0	112	51	0	28.00
J. Harmison	2	4	2	56	55*	0	28.00
I. D. Hunter	9	16	5	281	69*	0	25.54
S. M. Ali.............	11	22	2	510	100*	1	25.50
I. Pattison	4	8	0	200	55	0	25.00
*R. Robinson	6	12	0	242	43	0	20.16
G. J. Pratt	6	11	0	218	47	0	19.81
P. Chivers	2	4	1	50	28	0	16.66
G. D. Bridge	12	23	1	365	55	0	16.59
*A. Walker.	6	9	4	78	16*	0	15.60
M. J. Symington	9	17	1	191	42	0	11.93
C. Mann	3	5	0	51	16	0	10.20
G. J. Muchall	3	6	0	61	23	0	10.16
K. D. Gresham	4	8	0	51	23	0	6.37

	M	I	NO	R	HS	100s	Avge
Q. J. Hughes	2	4	0	25	14	0	6.25
N. Killeen	2	4	0	24	15	0	6.00
H. Marambe	3	6	0	29	27	0	4.83
A. M. Davies	3	5	0	19	13	0	3.80
N. G. Hatch	4	6	1	18	14*	0	3.60
G. Taylor	2	4	1	9	7	0	3.00

Played in two matches: G. M. Scott 39*, 14, 40. Played in one match: M. M. Betts 20; M. I. Cannon 7*, 0; M. A. Gough 34, 32; S. J. Harmison 4*, 1; †T. C. Londesborough 17*, 4; G. Shaw 3*; O. W. Stacey 41, 21*.

Bowling Averages

	O	M	R	W	BB	Avge
N. Killeen	55	19	136	14	4-33	9.71
A. M. Davies	82	27	148	10	3-29	14.80
R. Robinson	131.3	41	342	21	6-38	16.28
M. J. Symington	205.2	46	605	33	5-11	18.33
J. A. Daley	44	9	149	8	2-27	18.62
N. C. Phillips	104.1	43	217	10	6-30	21.70
I. D. Hunter	248.2	46	758	33	7-75	22.96
G. D. Bridge	307.4	95	809	31	6-94	26.09
I. Pattison	66.4	19	180	6	4-5	30.00
P. Chivers	40	9	134	4	4-73	33.50
N. G. Hatch	53	15	139	4	1-12	34.75

Also bowled: S. M. Ali 23–1–66–0; M. M. Betts 12–1–42–0; M. A. Gough 6–1–15–1; K. D. Gresham 10.1–2–44–2; J. Harmison 42.4–8–200–2; S. J. Harmison 15–4–32–0; C. Mann 13–4–35–0; G. J. Muchall 29–8–103–2; G. M. Scott 7–1–24–1; G. Shaw 17–4–57–0; O. W. Stacey 3–0–23–0; G. Taylor 34.1–9–98–1.

ESSEX SECOND ELEVEN

Matches 14: Won – Derbyshire, Durham, Middlesex, Somerset. Lost – Hampshire, Kent, Lancashire, Surrey, Warwickshire. Drawn – Gloucestershire, Leicestershire, Northamptonshire, Worcestershire, Yorkshire.

Batting Averages

	M	I	NO	R	HS	100s	Avge
†C. J. Warn	3	5	3	124	79*	0	62.00
*†B. J. Hyam	4	6	2	207	73*	0	51.75
A. J. Clarke	4	5	2	149	59	0	49.66
†J. S. Foster	6	11	3	372	116	1	46.50
W. I. Jefferson	6	10	1	334	102	1	37.11
R. J. Mansfield	6	11	1	341	98*	0	34.10
*D. D. J. Robinson	2	4	0	124	97	0	31.00
J. E. Bishop	6	9	2	204	85	0	29.14
*I. N. Flanagan	12	20	1	531	95	0	27.94
M. W. Page	2	4	0	103	70	0	25.75
Z. K. Sharif	2	4	0	102	38	0	25.50
*T. J. Mason	5	9	1	192	52	0	24.00
G. R. Napier	11	17	0	386	98	0	22.70
T. J. Phillips	10	17	1	362	82	0	22.62
D. G. Brandy	4	8	0	178	67	0	22.25
D. J. Thompson	9	14	3	227	62	0	20.63

	M	I	NO	R	HS	100s	Avge
N. L. Williams	3	4	0	54	48	0	13.50
J. C. Powell	8	12	0	142	44	0	11.83
M. C. Ilott.	4	7	2	57	26*	0	11.40
D. J. Roberts	3	6	0	56	29	0	9.33
*P. M. Such	6	9	2	60	30	0	8.57
A. C. McGarry.	7	10	0	5	2	0	0.50

Played in two matches: A. Akram 4, 5, 1; R. S. G. Anderson 25, 22, 0; D. R. Ellison 0, 0, 4*; P. B. C. James 0, 6*; P. S. Lazenbury 17, 4, 46; M. L. Pettini 14*, 50*, 36; J. G. C. Rowe 46, 8, 6; C. A. Swallow 0, 4, 2; J. C. Went 3*, 18*. Played in one match: C. W. G. Bassano 0, 10; N. E. Batson 6, 0; A. N. Cook 1, 26*; A. P. Cowan 8; D. R. Drepaul 1, 22*; S. B. Ellis 0*, 0; †I. D. Letch 0, 50; M. Patel 4; S. D. Peters 0, 15; †S. Salejee 0; K. D. E. Stewart 13*, 9; S. A. Twigg 8, 0; M. A. Wolstenholme 17. A. P. Palladino did not bat.

Note: In the match v Kent at Chelmsford, I. N. Flanagan, called up for a first-team match, was replaced by A. J. Clarke.

Bowling Averages

	O	M	R	W	BB	Avge
J. C. Went	29.5	4	84	8	3-28	10.50
D. G. Brandy	18.2	7	83	7	3-39	11.85
M. C. Ilott.	84.5	35	156	11	4-36	14.18
T. J. Mason	174.2	65	396	21	6-32	18.85
A. C. McGarry.	112.5	21	417	21	4-54	19.85
Z. K. Sharif	25.2	4	91	4	2-58	22.75
P. M. Such	186	56	364	14	4-16	26.00
T. J. Phillips	249.4	83	615	21	3-8	29.28
G. R. Napier	210.5	46	733	25	4-36	29.32
J. E. Bishop.	126.4	27	413	14	3-65	29.50
A. J. Clarke	73.1	19	243	8	2-38	30.37
R. S. G. Anderson	44	6	203	6	3-88	33.83
N. L. Williams	49.5	15	140	4	3-8	35.00
D. J. Thompson	198	44	646	17	5-51	38.00

Also bowled: A. Akram 1–0–1–0; A. P. Cowan 20–9–34–2; S. B. Ellis 24–3–86–2; D. R. Ellison 30–5–143–2; I. N. Flanagan 2–0–16–0; P. B. C. James 37–11–84–2; R. J. Mansfield 12–1–27–3; A. P. Palladino 12–0–88–0; J. C. Powell 15.3–4–62–3; K. D. E. Stewart 14–1–62–2; C. A. Swallow 8–4–8–1; M. A. Wolstenholme 6–1–21–1.

GLAMORGAN SECOND ELEVEN

Matches 14: Won – Surrey, Warwickshire, Worcestershire. Lost – Derbyshire, Durham, Hampshire, Lancashire, Yorkshire. Drawn – Leicestershire, Middlesex, Somerset, Surrey. Abandoned – Gloucestershire, Kent.

Batting Averages

	M	I	NO	R	HS	100s	Avge
I. J. Thomas	9	17	1	792	143	2	49.50
*J. Derrick	9	15	9	276	47*	0	46.00
*†A. W. Evans	10	19	1	714	158	3	39.66
D. D. Cherry	10	18	1	463	103	1	27.23
†M. A. Wallace.	6	10	0	260	83	0	26.00
J. Hughes.	11	19	2	425	101	1	25.00
W. L. Law	9	18	1	409	99	0	24.05
A. P. Davies	7	12	2	223	63*	0	22.30
†N. D. Buttigieg	3	5	1	73	37	0	18.25

	M	I	NO	R	HS	100s	Avge
S. M. A. Bukhari	4	6	1	83	23	0	16.60
I. M. Bird	9	17	3	228	37*	0	16.28
D. S. Harrison	9	16	0	251	43	0	15.68
A. J. Davies	3	4	0	56	34	0	14.00
C. M. Roberts	7	11	5	84	28	0	14.00
S. P. Jones	2	4	0	25	13	0	6.25
G. H. Bowers	3	4	0	10	9	0	2.50

Played in two matches: D. A. Cosker 19*, 40; A. N. French 2, 10, 12; P. S. George 0, 0, 0; K. Newell 28, 17, 19; O. T. Parkin 12, 8, 30; A. G. Wharf 28, 1*, 0; *J. R. A. Williams 11, 30, 73*. Played in one match: N. A. Gage 13*; †J. D. Larner 5; †R. M. Lewis 0; M. J. Powell 87, 9; D. Sutton 4, 25; A. J. Syddall 11, 5*; T. A. Wright 4.

Bowling Averages

	O	M	R	W	BB	Avge
A. J. Syddall	22	5	53	4	3-37	13.25
A. G. Wharf	51	16	127	9	5-34	14.11
D. A. Cosker	71.2	26	165	7	4-103	23.57
S. P. Jones	56.2	8	214	9	3-37	23.77
G. H. Bowers	54.1	10	181	7	4-35	25.85
J. Derrick	118.3	15	367	14	3-66	26.21
A. W. Evans	32.4	7	112	4	3-30	28.00
A. P. Davies	205.1	42	706	25	6-89	28.24
D. S. Harrison	226.4	30	907	31	5-85	29.25
I. J. Thomas	35	4	120	4	3-70	30.00
O. T. Parkin	69.3	13	215	7	5-59	30.71
S. M. A. Bukhari	143	19	531	15	5-44	35.40
A. N. French	62.4	15	169	4	2-4	42.25
J. Hughes	110.3	12	487	11	5-101	44.27
C. M. Roberts	167.5	20	734	15	4-86	48.93
A. J. Davies	78	8	284	5	3-53	56.80

Also bowled: N. A. Gage 23–6–72–0; P. S. George 26–6–94–1; W. L. Law 48–4–161–1; K. Newell 3–1–6–1; M. J. Powell 4–0–25–0; T. A. Wright 21–2–100–1.

GLOUCESTERSHIRE SECOND ELEVEN

Matches 14: Won – Derbyshire, Hampshire, Leicestershire, Worcestershire. Lost – Somerset. Drawn – Durham, Essex, Lancashire, Middlesex, Northamptonshire, Nottinghamshire, Sussex, Warwickshire. Abandoned – Glamorgan.

Batting Averages

	M	I	NO	R	HS	100s	Avge
*†R. C. J. Williams	10	13	6	497	115*	1	71.00
M. D. R. Sutliff	4	7	2	353	90*	0	70.60
*M. C. J. Ball	5	5	2	188	109*	1	62.66
N. C. Willis-Stovold	5	7	2	249	65*	0	49.80
I. Mohammed	12	19	1	739	122	1	41.05
B. R. F. Staunton	2	4	1	120	94*	0	40.00
D. R. Hewson	6	10	1	340	126*	2	37.77
C. W. G. Bassano	6	10	1	302	100*	1	33.55
*M. J. Cawdron	8	9	1	215	100	1	26.87
J. M. M. Averis	3	4	2	52	24*	0	26.00
M. A. Hardinges	11	16	3	297	54*	0	22.84

	M	I	NO	R	HS	100s	Avge
C. R. J. Budd	6	8	2	125	45	0	20.83
*R. J. Cunliffe	6	7	0	144	63	0	20.57
*A. J. Wright	7	7	1	119	54	0	19.83
R. J. Sillence	3	4	0	73	62	0	18.25
B. W. Gannon	5	4	1	30	13	0	10.00
D. J. Forder	7	5	1	28	13	0	7.00
A. N. Bressington	8	9	0	55	15	0	6.11
T. P. Cotterell	7	7	3	11	4	0	2.75

Played in three matches: J. Woosey 2. Played in two matches: N. S. Bressington 0, 0; A. N. Edwards 0, 16; C. M. Gomm 1, 1; C. G. Taylor 65, 63. Played in one match: †O. E. Burford 4; †J. F. Cotterell 0, 3; S. T. J. Cowley 11*, 3; J. Pearson 12, 2; D. J. Peiris 0, 4; †S. P. Pope 25; S. Sergeant 1; A. M. Smith 3; J. N. Snape 103*, 12; J. W. White 0; N. A. Willis-Stovold 10*; M. A. Wolstenholme 10; D. R. Womble 0, 21.

Note: Owing to first-team calls, T. P. Cotterell and R. J. Cunliffe were replaced by M. J. Cawdron and C. G. Taylor in the match v Somerset at Bristol.

Bowling Averages

	O	M	R	W	BB	Avge
C. G. Taylor	27	14	57	5	5-57	11.40
R. J. Sillence	42.1	14	92	7	3-20	13.14
D. R. Womble	19.4	1	55	4	4-32	13.75
I. Mohammed	57.3	11	188	10	6-74	18.80
M. C. J. Ball	114.4	33	221	11	4-83	20.09
T. P. Cotterell	178.1	78	325	15	6-64	21.66
M. J. Cawdron	207.3	39	559	24	5-49	23.29
M. A. Hardinges	226.4	46	674	27	3-10	24.96
A. N. Bressington	159	30	529	21	5-35	25.19
D. J. Forder	113.5	22	362	13	4-71	27.84
J. Woosey	65.5	16	197	7	4-26	28.14
J. M. M. Averis	79.2	14	275	8	3-64	34.37
B. W. Gannon	111.2	21	365	6	3-17	60.83

Also bowled: N. S. Bressington 17.4–3–67–2; R. J. Cunliffe 1–0–15–0; A. N. Edwards 4–0–9–0; C. M. Gomm 18–2–76–2; D. R. Hewson 16.3–6–36–1; S. Sergeant 25–9–59–2; A. M. Smith 16–2–38–0; J. N. Snape 42–10–96–3; J. W. White 9–0–62–2; N. C. Willis-Stovold 1.1–0–7–2; M. A. Wolstenholme 6–0–32–1.

HAMPSHIRE SECOND ELEVEN

Matches 14: Won – Derbyshire, Essex, Glamorgan, Yorkshire. Lost – Gloucestershire, Kent, Lancashire, Northamptonshire, Somerset, Sussex, Warwickshire. Drawn – Nottinghamshire, Surrey, Worcestershire.

Batting Averages

	M	I	NO	R	HS	100s	Avge
*J. P. Stephenson	5	9	2	500	208*	1	71.42
A. J. Sexton	12	22	3	575	111	1	30.26
L. R. Prittipaul	11	19	1	526	132	1	29.22
Z. C. Morris	11	19	2	466	64*	0	27.41
†I. Brunnschweiler	14	22	6	432	116*	1	27.00
*S. J. Renshaw	10	17	1	366	79	0	22.87
J. H. K. Adams	12	23	2	468	87	0	22.28
*A. C. Morris	4	7	0	145	58	0	20.71

	M	I	NO	R	HS	100s	Avge
J. D. Francis..........	6	11	0	218	104	1	19.81
D. A. Kenway.........	3	5	0	95	43	0	19.00
J. R. C. Hamblin.......	6	8	0	143	36	0	17.87
I. H. Shah	14	23	5	294	70	0	16.33
A. H. D. Perry	6	10	0	142	52	0	14.20
D. Jackson...........	8	12	0	169	40	0	14.08
C. G. van der Gucht	7	9	6	38	13*	0	12.66
*L. Savident.........	5	8	0	69	22	0	8.62
K. D. E. Stewart.......	2	4	0	31	23	0	7.75

Played in two matches: D. C. Shirazi 15, 0, 28; C. T. Tremlett 9, 0*, 6; C. J. Yates 0, 12. Played in one match: C. C. Benham 53; J. Cornford 8, 5*; S. R. G. Francis 13*, 5; J. S. Laney 68, 20; J. Moss 0*; M. A. Richards 0, 0; D. J. Roberts 33, 30; T. J. Sharpe 3, 0; A. J. Syddall 0, 1*; N. J. Thurgood 5, 0; B. J. Trott 6, 5; *S. D. Udal 12.

Bowling Averages

	O	M	R	W	BB	Avge
J. Moss..............	54.5	21	117	9	5-54	13.00
C. J. Yates...........	27	9	87	5	3-34	17.40
J. P. Stephenson	147.2	31	428	24	7-81	17.83
T. J. Sharpe	17	1	73	4	2-28	18.25
L. Savident	130	33	372	17	5-93	21.88
Z. C. Morris	217.5	48	702	32	6-43	21.93
J. R. C. Hamblin	138.3	22	522	22	5-27	23.72
S. J. Renshaw	235.3	65	644	26	5-85	24.76
I. H. Shah	307	78	930	34	5-26	27.35
A. C. Morris	70	14	253	9	2-15	28.11
C. G. van der Gucht	178.1	53	457	15	4-76	30.46
L. R. Prittipaul.......	70	26	182	5	1-5	36.40
S. R. G. Francis	33	0	147	4	3-28	36.75

Also bowled: D. A. Kenway 1–0–4–0; K. D. E. Stewart 33–5–97–3; A. J. Syddall 14–3–58–1; C. T. Tremlett 34–11–69–2; B. J. Trott 25–2–100–0; S. D. Udal 1–0–3–0.

KENT SECOND ELEVEN

Matches 14: Won – Essex, Hampshire, Leicestershire, Northamptonshire, Nottinghamshire, Somerset, Worcestershire. Lost – Middlesex, Sussex, Warwickshire. Drawn – Durham, Lancashire, Yorkshire. Abandoned – Glamorgan.

Batting Averages

	M	I	NO	R	HS	100s	Avge
M. J. Walker..........	2	4	1	245	162	1	81.66
D. P. Fulton	3	4	0	315	197	1	78.75
P. S. Lazenbury........	7	12	0	479	114	1	39.91
†G. O. Jones	14	19	3	638	127	1	39.87
*M. J. McCague	6	9	1	305	63	0	38.12
E. T. Smith	5	7	0	236	151	1	33.71
*J. M. Golding	8	12	2	303	89	0	30.30
R. S. Ferley	6	10	2	240	63	0	30.00
*S. A. Marsh	11	16	2	403	89	0	28.78
A. G. R. Loudon.......	9	12	1	296	92	0	26.90
M. J. Banes	6	9	0	241	86	0	26.77
J. B. Hockley	5	8	0	187	92	0	23.37
B. J. Phillips..........	4	5	1	85	35	0	21.25

	M	I	NO	R	HS	100s	Avge
D. A. Scott.	9	7	2	90	23	0	18.00
J. C. Tredwell	4	6	0	97	40	0	16.16
J. D. Watson	6	5	0	75	22	0	15.00
B. J. Trott	6	7	2	68	35	0	13.60
J. E. P. Walford.	5	7	0	81	23	0	11.57
K. Adams	4	4	2	23	19	0	11.50
*R. S. Clinton	5	8	0	77	32	0	9.62
A. R. Bray	3	5	0	35	18	0	7.00
R. H. Joseph	5	8	3	25	9	0	5.00
A. Khan	4	6	1	11	5	0	2.20

Played in two matches: P. J. Bradshaw 8, 10; M. J. G. Davis 89; A. P. Wells 26, 0, 21. M. J. Saggers did not bat. Played in one match: C. W. G. Bassano 7, 8; R. W. J. Howitt 42; L. J. P. Jenkins 87*; R. W. T. Key 8, 53; T. J. Sharpe 24; D. J. Trigger 4, 13*; G. A. White 6; J. W. White 0, 9; D. R. Womble 11, 0. K. J. Locke did not bat.

Note: In the match v Somerset at Taunton, D. A. Scott, called up for a first-team match, was replaced by A. R. Bray.

Bowling Averages

	O	M	R	W	BB	Avge
D. R. Womble	25	10	27	4	2-7	6.75
J. E. P. Walford	32	15	55	7	4-27	7.85
B. J. Phillips	61.2	23	118	11	6-50	10.72
M. J. G. Davis	120	53	145	11	6-19	13.18
D. J. Trigger	38.3	6	100	6	3-46	16.66
M. J. Walker	39.4	15	68	4	2-9	17.00
B. J. Trott	151.2	34	449	26	6-39	17.26
K. Adams	101	25	311	15	7-73	20.73
M. J. McCague.	198	65	455	21	6-27	21.66
R. H. Joseph	137.5	29	455	19	5-72	23.94
A. R. Bray	56	8	217	9	3-38	24.11
P. J. Bradshaw	48	9	134	5	2-26	26.80
R. S. Ferley	204	43	683	24	4-59	28.45
A. Khan	90.4	19	259	9	5-22	28.77
D. A. Scott	220.1	63	536	16	4-64	33.50
J. C. Tredwell.	151	45	411	12	4-71	34.25
J. D. Watson	78.1	14	349	8	3-65	43.62

Also bowled: M. J. Banes 1–0–12–0; R. S. Clinton 19–1–82–3; J. M. Golding 17.4–6–41–2; J. B. Hockley 15–4–61–1; A. G. R. Loudon 30–12–49–0; M. J. Saggers 18–6–33–1; T. J. Sharpe 14–3–58 1; J. W. White 34–3–127–2.

LANCASHIRE SECOND ELEVEN

Matches 15: Won – Derbyshire, Essex, Glamorgan, Hampshire, Yorkshire. Lost – Durham, Leicestershire, Surrey, Warwickshire. Drawn – Gloucestershire, Kent, Middlesex, Northamptonshire, Somerset, Worcestershire.

Batting Averages

	M	I	NO	R	HS	100s	Avge
*G. D. Lloyd	4	7	0	522	202	2	74.57
M. J. Chilton	6	9	0	423	169	1	47.00
*M. Watkinson	12	14	2	475	139	1	39.58
J. R. M. Lee	4	6	1	173	72	0	34.60
†J. J. Haynes	14	19	4	501	66*	0	33.40

	M	I	NO	R	HS	100s	Avge
P. C. McKeown........	11	17	2	463	85	0	30.86
N. T. Wood..........	8	12	2	266	78	0	26.60
G. Keedy...........	5	4	2	47	25*	0	23.50
T. Roberts..........	7	12	1	255	60	0	23.18
S. J. Marshall........	3	4	2	42	23*	0	21.00
R. J. Green.........	15	17	1	308	49*	0	19.25
M. E. Harvey........	15	23	3	384	54	0	19.20
P. M. Ridgway.......	8	7	1	112	58	0	18.66
*G. Yates...........	8	9	1	128	56	0	16.00
K. Hogg...........	6	6	1	74	39	0	14.80
C. M. Barrow........	6	5	3	26	14	0	13.00
J. M. Anderson.......	4	4	3	13	12*	0	13.00
M. Taylor..........	3	6	0	20	11	0	3.33
C. M. Ferguson.......	3	4	0	5	3	0	1.25

Played in three matches: C. P. Schofield 31, 5, 27. Played in two matches: P. Green 0, 49; J. C. Scuderi 16, 20, 0; M. P. Smethurst 10, 32. Played in one match: S. J. Airey 4, 0; I. D. Austin 57, 35; L. Crilly 7, 4; M. R. Currie 5; L. Daggett 11, 4*; U. Janjua 0; S. I. Mahmood 11; H. J. H. Marshall 48; P. J. Martin 2*; B. Nash 0; S. C. Oddie 4*, 0; K. S. Pickering 32, 19; A. J. Scholefield 46; A. J. Syddall 8*, 0*; C. J. Warren 7, 4*; †R. Whalley 3; J. W. White 9.

Note: Owing to first-team calls R. J. Green was replaced by C. P. Schofield in the match v Somerset at Middleton, P. J. Martin was replaced by J. R. M. Lee in the match v Glamorgan at Southport and N. T. Wood was replaced by M. P. Smethurst in the match v Derbyshire at Dunstall.

Bowling Averages

	O	M	R	W	BB	Avge
C. P. Schofield.........	62	24	135	12	6-51	11.25
P. J. Martin...........	37	11	74	6	4-42	12.33
M. Watkinson.........	97.2	27	240	16	4-38	15.00
S. I. Mahmood........	32.1	6	117	7	4-44	16.71
S. C. Oddie...........	30	10	90	5	4-31	18.00
L. Crilly.............	35.3	7	128	7	4-67	18.28
G. Yates............	177.5	50	448	23	7-47	19.47
R. J. Green..........	383.1	84	1,081	54	5-42	20.01
K. Hogg............	55	14	165	8	3-18	20.62
G. Keedy............	122	33	338	16	5-79	21.12
P. M. Ridgway,.	160	51	356	15	3-31	23.73
M. Taylor...........	50	18	102	4	3-53	25.50
J. M. Anderson........	76	15	291	4	1-23	72.75

Also bowled: S. J. Airey 29-6-102-2; I. D. Austin 34-10-61-1; C. M. Barrow 47-17-117-3; M. J. Chilton 39-14-95-3; L. Daggett 21-4-81-0; P. Green 1-1-0-0; U. Janjua 18-7-48-3; P. C. McKeown 6-0-24-0; H. J. H. Marshall 5-2-12-0; S. J. Marshall 49-8-172-3; B. Nash 1-0-2-0; K. S. Pickering 28-4-100-4; T. Roberts 5.2-2-15-2; A. J. Scholefield 13-2-34-1; J. C. Scuderi 53.3-19-109-3; M. P. Smethurst 34-9-106-3; A. J. Syddall 22.5-3-130-0; C. J. Warren 19-2-75-2; J. W. White 17.5-4-48-1.

LEICESTERSHIRE SECOND ELEVEN

Matches 12: Won – Lancashire, Worcestershire. Lost – Derbyshire, Gloucestershire, Kent, Nottinghamshire, Surrey, Sussex. Drawn – Essex, Glamorgan, Northamptonshire, Yorkshire.

Batting Averages

	M	I	NO	R	HS	100s	Avge
*T. R. Ward..........	3	5	0	316	125	1	63.20
S. A. J. Boswell	8	10	6	240	77	0	60.00
*P. E. Robinson	5	6	2	182	111	1	45.50

	M	I	NO	R	HS	100s	Avge
D. I. Stevens	2	4	0	150	70	0	37.50
*I. J. Sutcliffe	6	10	0	374	142	1	37.40
D. Williamson	6	10	0	372	127	1	37.20
O. Banks	5	9	2	257	62*	0	36.71
M. D. R. Sutliff	4	8	2	213	59*	0	35.50
†S. J. Adshead	12	23	1	769	94	0	34.95
S. Vesty	2	4	1	98	51*	0	32.66
A. S. Wright	12	23	1	704	148	1	32.00
W. F. Stelling	6	10	1	243	95	0	27.00
C. D. Crowe	5	9	1	214	92*	0	26.75
P. Kumar	3	5	0	133	57	0	26.60
P. Griffiths	8	12	7	125	40	0	25.00
L. Reeves	4	7	0	161	76	0	23.00
T. B. Huggins	2	4	0	87	55	0	21.75
C. P. Crowe	10	17	2	236	57	0	15.73
A. A. Khan	10	14	2	169	57*	0	14.08
M. T. Brimson	5	6	0	75	40	0	12.50
A. Sachdeva	3	5	0	32	28	0	6.40

Played in two matches: D. S. Brignull 2, 0, 0; S. B. Ellis 60, 10, 15. Played in one match: D. E. Barnes 1, 15; N. J. Ferraby 73, 5; R. Harris 5, 5; S. Kirby 0, 0*; *D. L. Maddy 36, 14; R. C. Towler 1; S. Twist 0. T. M. Hansen did not bat.

Note: In the match v Yorkshire at Harrogate, I. J. Sutcliffe, called up for a first-team match, was replaced by P. E. Robinson.

Bowling Averages

	O	M	R	W	BB	Avge
S. Kirby	13	2	53	5	5-33	10.60
D. S. Brignull	35.4	8	119	5	2-38	23.80
R. Harris	21.4	2	105	4	4-84	26.25
M. T. Brimson	89.4	16	239	9	5-43	26.55
C. P. Crowe	153	32	591	22	5-73	26.86
D. Williamson	63	17	193	7	3-69	27.57
W. F. Stelling	67	20	175	6	3-20	29.16
A. A. Khan	217.4	49	652	21	5-42	31.04
S. B. Ellis	49	12	165	5	2-47	33.00
P. Griffiths	176.4	52	467	14	2-47	33.35
A. Sachdeva	109.4	26	318	9	3-17	35.33
S. A. J. Boswell	225.3	39	741	18	5-95	41.16
C. D. Crowe	111.5	20	359	6	3-90	59.83

Also bowled: O. Banks 42–7–127–3; T. M. Hansen 10–2–26–2; P. Kumar 37–8–147–3; D. L. Maddy 16–4–57–3; P. E. Robinson 10–4–28–0; I. J. Sutcliffe 5–0–33–1; M. D. R. Sutliff 3–0–58–0; R. C. Towler 18–2–100–2; S. Twist 17–5–57–2; A. S. Wright 8.3–0–63–3.

MIDDLESEX SECOND ELEVEN

Matches 13: Won – Derbyshire, Kent, Northamptonshire, Surrey, Sussex, Worcestershire. Lost – Essex. Drawn – Glamorgan, Gloucestershire, Lancashire, Nottinghamshire, Warwickshire, Yorkshire.

Batting Averages

	M	I	NO	R	HS	100s	Avge
E. C. Joyce	3	4	1	273	128*	1	91.00
*O. A. Shah	6	9	1	545	141	2	68.12
R. M. S. Weston	7	10	0	558	176	2	55.80
*P. N. Weekes	8	11	2	501	154	1	55.66

	M	I	NO	R	HS	100s	Avge
S. J. Cook	6	5	2	157	70	0	52.33
A. W. Laraman	9	9	0	334	158	1	37.11
*K. P. Dutch	5	8	0	271	142	1	33.87
J. K. Maunders	10	17	3	451	106	1	32.21
†D. Alleyne	10	15	1	333	93	0	23.78
B. L. Hutton.	4	6	0	135	74	0	22.50
M. J. Brown	6	10	2	171	41	0	21.37
J. W. M. Dalrymple	7	9	1	165	37	0	20.62
D. J. Goodchild.	5	8	1	135	59*	0	19.28
C. J. Batt.	9	10	2	94	37	0	11.75
J. P. Hewitt.	11	12	4	74	24*	0	9.25
A. D. Edwards	5	6	1	37	10	0	7.40

Played in four matches: T. F. Bloomfield 4, 0, 0; †D. C. Nash 51*, 142, 173. Played in three matches: *M. A. Roseberry 76*, 56, 142. Played in two matches: R. B. Bryan 3*, 1*; M. L. Creese 0; *I. J. Gould 9*, 4, 0*; T. A. Hunt 0*, 0*; S. K. Ranasinghe 2, 78; †B. J. M. Scott 10, 12. Played in one match: T. J. Aldiss 10; A. J. Coleman 10*; O. A. Dawkins 0; M. R. Gillespie 1; D. R. Holt 20; S. Katariwala 0; S. P. Naylor 0; *M. R. Ramprakash 23, 0; J. A. Rayment 7; T. J. Sharpe 4; A. J. Strauss 14, 1.

Note: Owing to first-team calls, D. C. Nash and A. W. Laraman were replaced by D. Alleyne and C. J. Batt in the match v Essex at Harrow.

Bowling Averages

	O	M	R	W	BB	Avge
T. F. Bloomfield	113.3	23	315	20	4-43	15.75
K. P. Dutch	146.2	49	315	18	7-75	17.50
A. W. Laraman	104.5	29	250	14	3-4	17.85
B. L. Hutton	39.2	10	108	6	4-41	18.00
S. P. Naylor	20.5	5	76	4	3-47	19.00
S. J. Cook.	111.2	32	288	14	4-53	20.57
P. N. Weekes	176.1	71	294	14	4-38	21.00
S. K. Ranasinghe	46.1	12	107	5	3-54	21.40
C. J. Batt	146.5	41	408	19	6-68	21.47
J. P. Hewitt	208.4	51	686	31	8-55	22.12
J. W. M. Dalrymple.	164	52	397	16	5-93	24.81
A. D. Edwards	72	15	200	7	4-49	28.57

Also bowled: R. B. Bryan 15–2–46–0; A. J. Coleman 5–3–7–1; M. L. Creese 32–8–85–0; O. A. Dawkins 11–2–39–1; M. R. Gillespie 7.4–1–23–0; I. J. Gould 1–0–10–0; T. A. Hunt 24–3–89–2; E. C. Joyce 15–3–51–1; S. Katariwala 9–3–22–2; J. K. Maunders 13.5–3–35–2; D. C. Nash 1–0–5–0; J. A. Rayment 5–2–15–0; O. A. Shah 19–6–50–2; T. J. Sharpe 11–3–12–1; R. M. S. Weston 3–0–27–0.

NORTHAMPTONSHIRE SECOND ELEVEN

Matches 16: Won – Durham, Hampshire, Somerset. Lost – Kent, Middlesex, Nottinghamshire, Worcestershire. Drawn – Derbyshire, Essex, Gloucestershire, Lancashire, Leicestershire, Nottinghamshire, Surrey, Warwickshire, Yorkshire.

Batting Averages

	M	I	NO	R	HS	100s	Avge
D. J. Roberts	3	4	2	82	41*	0	41.00
M. J. Powell.	10	19	1	711	131*	1	39.50
A. J. Swann	11	20	1	746	123	1	39.26
T. J. Roberts.	2	4	0	150	81	0	37.50

	M	I	NO	R	HS	100s	Avge
K. J. Innes	7	10	0	368	104	1	36.80
R. J. Warren	6	11	2	313	120*	1	34.77
*†T. M. B. Bailey	14	22	4	536	52	0	29.77
M. C. Dobson	10	16	3	311	85	0	23.92
R. A. White	11	20	1	402	106	1	21.15
M. K. Davies	10	15	4	216	67*	0	19.63
J. F. Brown	6	7	3	72	39*	0	18.00
J. W. Cook	3	6	0	100	30	0	16.66
D. E. Malcolm	5	7	1	95	42	0	15.83
J. A. R. Blain	9	12	4	123	30	0	15.37
S. Whitwam	5	9	0	131	69	0	14.55
J. P. Taylor	3	5	1	58	21	0	14.50
J. Wade	8	12	2	135	61	0	13.50
M. S. Panesar	5	8	5	35	25	0	11.66
M. R. Strong	10	11	2	93	19	0	10.33
R. J. Logan	8	12	2	69	23	0	6.90
A. A. Duncan	2	4	0	26	19	0	6.50
R. McLean	6	5	3	7	3*	0	3.50

Played in three matches: *N. G. B. Cook 1*, 2; W. E. Sneath 5, 7*, 0, 1. Played in two matches: T. Dann 7, 2; O. A. Dawkins 6, 5; D. M. Yeomans 15, 0, 0. Played in one match: N. J. Clewley 0, 8; S. M. Eustace 0, 10; K. J. Locke 0, 8; M. B. Loye 0, 149; R. McNeilly 11*, 3; R. Robinson 0, 2; A. S. Rollins 0; G. P. Swann 5, 10. T. M. Hansen, B. Ingery and S. P. Naylor did not bat.

Note: In the match v Middlesex at Northampton, T. M. B. Bailey, called up for a first-team match, was replaced by T. Dann.

Bowling Averages

	O	M	R	W	BB	Avge
D. M. Yeomans	11	3	22	4	4-22	5.50
A. J. Swann	78.4	33	162	12	4-25	13.50
R. J. Logan	182.5	51	527	26	6-53	20.26
D. E. Malcolm	202.1	41	609	28	7-91	21.75
K. J. Innes	154	24	514	23	5-45	22.34
J. P. Taylor	118.5	33	316	14	7-89	22.57
J. F. Brown	209	91	388	16	5-75	24.25
M. S. Panesar	111	41	257	10	3-19	25.70
M. R. Strong	176.2	29	635	24	5-21	26.45
R. McLean	82	20	234	8	2-35	29.25
G. P. Swann	33.2	7	120	4	3-32	30.00
J. A. R. Blain	151.1	16	692	15	3-55	46.13
M. C. Dobson	83.3	25	289	6	3-103	48.16
M. K. Davies	245.3	80	674	10	3-45	67.40

Also bowled: N. J. Clewley 8–6–3–0; J. W. Cook 49–16–113–2; O. A. Dawkins 14–2–55–2; A. A. Duncan 8–2–21–0; T. M. Hansen 18–1–113–1; R. McNeilly 10–1–34–1; S. P. Naylor 11.1–1–54–1; M. J. Powell 5–0–49–0; R. Robinson 23–4–43–1; W. E. Sneath 44–12–118–1; R. J. Warren 1–0–15–1; R. A. White 31–5–131–2; S. Whitwam 30.5–7–104–1.

NOTTINGHAMSHIRE SECOND ELEVEN

Matches 16: Won – Derbyshire, Durham, Leicestershire, Northamptonshire, Somerset, Warwickshire, Worcestershire. Lost – Derbyshire, Kent, Yorkshire. Drawn – Gloucestershire, Hampshire, Middlesex, Northamptonshire, Surrey (twice).

Batting Averages

	M	I	NO	R	HS	100s	Avge
C. M. Tolley	5	9	2	384	130*	1	54.85
*†M. Newell	9	8	4	200	80	0	50.00
G. S. Kandola	6	7	0	287	75	0	41.00
M. N. Bowen	8	12	2	403	67	0	40.30
*†W. M. Noon	13	18	2	633	144	1	39.56
C. J. Hewison	16	24	4	709	98*	0	35.45
M. W. Page	5	5	0	157	61	0	31.40
G. E. Welton	4	4	1	94	57	0	31.33
G. R. Haywood	14	20	2	489	102*	1	27.16
G. D. Clough	12	17	2	400	68	0	26.66
D. S. Lucas	5	6	1	111	39*	0	22.20
V. Atri	8	10	1	181	70	0	20.11
W. R. Smith	6	8	0	157	61	0	19.62
R. Wyld	5	5	2	56	34*	0	18.66
S. J. Randall	14	15	0	213	56	0	14.20
B. M. Shafayat	4	4	1	39	29	0	13.00
N. Malik	5	5	0	11	4	0	2.20
M. J. A. Whiley	16	16	4	23	5	0	1.91

Played in five matches: S. B. Ellis 13, 17, 9. Played in two matches: Z. Iqbal 26*, 7*. Played in one match: U. Afzaal 1; P. J. Franks 66; A. J. Harris 4; P. Johnson 20; W. A. Kirby 2, 27; P. S. Lazenbury 14; D. J. Millns 23*, 18; †C. M. Mole 7; S. Patel 4, 5*; D. J. Saker 0; T. E. Savill 0; K. D. E. Stewart 2, 12*; M. A. Wolstenholme 1, 6. J. Clarke and P. Scott did not bat.

Note: In the match v Northamptonshire at Boots Ground, Nottingham, C. J. Hewison, called up for a first-team match, was replaced by P. Scott.

Bowling Averages

	O	M	R	W	BB	Avge
G. D. Clough	256.2	66	705	37	5-40	19.05
N. Malik	83.2	19	291	15	3-34	19.40
R. Wyld	76.3	32	141	7	2-12	20.14
M. N. Bowen	270.5	70	715	35	4-54	20.42
A. J. Harris	39.2	13	82	4	4-41	20.50
G. R. Haywood	54	13	162	7	3-4	23.14
M. J. A. Whiley	404.3	103	1,281	52	6-107	24.63
D. S. Lucas	116.3	30	321	13	4-19	24.69
S. B. Ellis	97	26	275	11	5-61	25.00
S. J. Randall	422.5	123	1,001	39	5-67	25.66
C. M. Tolley	70.1	22	199	4	2-29	49.75

Also bowled: U. Afzaal 11–4–30–1; P. J. Franks 30–8–90–2; C. J. Hewison 3–0–11–0; Z. Iqbal 33–5–155–2; P. S. Lazenbury 1–0–3–0; D. J. Millns 6–1–20–2; D. J. Saker 21–4–73–1; T. E. Savill 4–1–9–0; P. Scott 1–0–5–1; W. R. Smith 5–0–17–1; K. D. E. Stewart 7–4–17–2; M. A. Wolstenholme 8–1–24–2.

SOMERSET SECOND ELEVEN

Matches 13: Won – Gloucestershire, Hampshire. Lost – Essex, Kent, Northamptonshire, Nottinghamshire, Surrey, Yorkshire. Drawn – Derbyshire, Glamorgan, Lancashire, Sussex, Worcestershire.

Batting Averages

	M	I	NO	R	HS	100s	Avge
*M. N. Lathwell	6	12	1	618	185	1	56.18
†J. A. Knott	5	9	1	420	98	0	52.50
C. A. Hunkin	10	18	7	394	76*	0	35.81
M. J. Wood	8	15	0	471	95	0	31.40
J. C. Williams	4	7	1	171	77	0	28.50
W. J. Durston	9	18	0	505	117	1	28.05
J. P. Tucker	6	11	3	215	54	0	26.87
J. I. D. Kerr	10	17	1	429	96	0	26.81
P. D. Trego	8	15	2	336	77*	0	25.84
M. Burns	2	4	1	75	37	0	25.00
†C. M. Gazzard	7	13	0	295	72	0	22.69
J. E. K. Schofield	4	7	0	137	64	0	19.57
*G. J. Kennis	13	26	1	450	76	0	18.00
*A. R. K. Pierson	8	11	2	145	54*	0	16.11
M. Coles	6	10	2	114	34*	0	14.25
*P. C. L. Holloway	3	6	0	82	30	0	13.66
I. Gompertz	3	6	0	68	32	0	11.33
A. V. Suppiah	4	8	0	90	35	0	11.25
J. O. Grove	4	7	1	64	25	0	10.66
M. T. Gitsham	3	5	1	30	18	0	7.50
R. Jones	4	7	2	35	16	0	7.00

Played in two matches: D. P. Britton 14*, 8*, 0; C. Brown 5, 57, 32; D. G. Court 21, 2, 7*; K. Farooq 4*; R. W. Selway 22, 3, 18*. Played in one match: C. W. G. Bassano 77, 7*; E. D. Craik 15, 23; C. Guerrea 6*, 2; J. Hudson 0, 30; P. W. Jarvis 32, 20; K. A. Parsons 12, 8; †J. Payne 2; T. Webley 0, 5. †J. P. Harrison did not bat.

Note: Owing to first-team calls, A. R. K. Pierson was replaced by R. W. Selway v Gloucestershire at Bristol and J. I. D. Kerr was replaced by M. T. Gitsham v Surrey at North Perrott. C. M. Gazzard was called up for the England Under-19 squad and was replaced by J. P. Harrison.

Bowling Averages

	O	M	R	W	BB	Avge
K. A. Parsons	33	2	115	7	4-44	16.42
C. Guerrea , , , , , , , , , ,	26	0	92	5	3-34	18.40
P. W. Jarvis	42	12	120	5	3-48	24.00
J. P. Tucker	118.5	23	425	17	5-24	25.00
C. A. Hunkin	141.3	27	471	18	4-3	26.16
K. Farooq	40	8	165	6	5-86	27.50
J. O. Grove	96.3	10	360	13	5-67	27.69
P. D. Trego	205.5	26	814	29	6-89	28.06
J. E. K. Schofield	76.2	12	307	8	3-90	38.37
J. I. D. Kerr	75.4	22	242	5	2-30	48.40
E. D. Craik	53	9	211	4	2-81	52.75
W. J. Durston	108	18	334	6	2-44	55.66
R. Jones	67.4	14	242	4	2-20	60.50
A. V. Suppiah	72.1	15	245	4	1-15	61.25
A. R. K. Pierson	146.5	28	447	7	4-55	63.85

Also bowled: D. P. Britton 30–5–144–3; C. Brown 47–12–99–3; M. Burns 28–9–60–1; M. Coles 32–11–96–0; D. G. Court 27–6–85–1; M. T. Gitsham 18–0–93–2; I. Gompertz 9–0–41–1; J. Hudson 4–0–15–0; G. J. Kennis 25–5–81–0; J. A. Knott 3–0–30–0; M. N. Lathwell 5–0–23–0; R. W. Selway 17–6–55–1; T. Webley 3.3–0–6–0.

SURREY SECOND ELEVEN

Matches 14: Won – Essex, Lancashire, Leicestershire, Somerset. Lost – Glamorgan, Middlesex, Sussex. Drawn – Durham, Glamorgan, Hampshire, Northamptonshire, Nottinghamshire (twice), Warwickshire.

Batting Averages

	M	I	NO	R	HS	100s	Avge
*G. P. Butcher	10	16	2	627	153	2	44.78
*N. Shahid	4	6	0	248	129	1	41.33
J. J. Porter	9	14	2	490	111*	1	40.83
†J. N. Batty	6	8	0	320	135	1	40.00
*G. J. Batty	14	23	1	761	146	2	34.59
J. G. E. Benning	2	4	0	118	45	0	29.50
M. A. Carberry	12	20	0	538	136	1	26.90
T. J. Murtagh	6	9	1	214	53	0	26.75
B. C. Hollioake	3	5	0	128	44	0	25.60
S. A. Newman	10	18	1	417	47	0	24.52
R. Clarke	3	4	0	94	38	0	23.50
J. D. Ratcliffe	6	12	1	210	77	0	19.09
†E. P. Cruz	2	4	1	57	29	0	19.00
K. A. O. Barrett	6	10	0	172	43	0	17.20
P. J. Sampson	11	17	2	237	62	0	15.80
C. G. Greenidge	8	12	2	136	35	0	13.60
I. E. Bishop	8	11	5	66	16	0	11.00
†M. R. Duce	2	4	0	21	11	0	5.25
R. M. Amin	13	18	7	53	10*	0	4.81
†M. A. Tilt	3	4	1	7	3*	0	2.33

Played in two matches: S. J. Andrews 55, 23*, 49; B. Hooper 8, 4*, 3; M. A. Lewis 5*, 8, 5; A. K. Moon 1, 13, 2; P. Pemberton 12*, 14, 20; †B. J. M. Scott 5, 16, 70*. Played in one match: *A. R. Butcher 32; †S. M. Eustace 0; T. Howes 3; T. J. Sharpe 0, 0.

Bowling Averages

	O	M	R	W	BB	Avge
G. P. Butcher	150.4	31	503	29	5-53	17.34
J. D. Ratcliffe	40	15	95	5	3-43	19.00
C. G. Greenidge	217	26	707	37	7-57	19.10
I. E. Bishop	135	42	372	19	4-42	19.57
B. C. Hollioake	45.5	4	158	7	4-69	22.57
T. J. Murtagh	149.5	32	518	21	4-28	24.66
G. J. Batty	208.4	51	619	22	4-59	28.13
R. M. Amin	352.4	115	873	28	4-90	31.17
P. J. Sampson	190	37	700	14	3-44	50.00

Also bowled: K. A. O. Barrett 14-1-66-0; J. G. E. Benning 5-2-12-0; M. A. Carberry 2-0-10-0; R. Clarke 24-1-100-0; B. Hooper 16-4-44-2; M. A. Lewis 33-7-142-3; A. K. Moon 17-6-47-3; T. J. Sharpe 11-3-44-1.

SUSSEX SECOND ELEVEN

Matches 12: Won – Durham, Hampshire, Kent, Leicestershire, Surrey. Lost – Middlesex, Warwickshire, Worcestershire, Yorkshire. Drawn – Derbyshire, Gloucestershire, Somerset.

Batting Averages

	M	I	NO	R	HS	100s	Avge
W. J. House	7	9	0	404	100	1	44.88
N. J. K. Creed	5	6	2	152	51*	0	38.00
*J. J. Bates.	9	12	2	356	119*	1	35.60
M. H. Yardy	6	10	2	272	94	0	34.00
W. G. Khan	9	15	3	394	72	0	32.83
*J. R. Carpenter	11	18	2	502	132	1	31.37
S. B. Ellis	3	6	3	93	54	0	31.00
C. D. Nash.	2	4	1	76	42	0	25.33
†M. J. Prior	4	6	0	140	50	0	23.33
B. Zuiderent.	10	17	0	364	87	0	21.41
D. A. Clapp	9	15	0	275	64	0	18.33
B. V. Taylor	7	7	2	71	40*	0	14.20
†S. Humphries	3	4	0	51	27	0	12.75
P. M. Havell	11	13	7	43	24	0	7.16
M. A. Robinson	4	7	3	11	5	0	2.75

Played in four matches: †N. J. Wilton 2, 1, 1. Played in three matches: *K. Greenfield 113, 7, 32. Played in two matches: S. R. Ades 30, 3; T. A. Ambrose 0, 20, 41; R. N. Jackson 6, 19, 34; †A. D. Patterson 15, 43, 132; M. T. E. Peirce 26, 12, 16*; G. G. Read 3; P. J. S. Spencer 13, 4, 28; B. J. Trott 8, 12, 2. Played in one match: †A. D. Bairstow 31, 23; J. Chadburn 1; M. J. G. Davis 39, 29; J. D. Lewry 23, 4; *R. R. Montgomerie 30, 25; A. Perry 2, 8; A. J. Sartor 55; †C. J. O. Smith 0, 84; T. van Noort 27, 5.

Bowling Averages

	O	M	R	W	BB	Avge
M. J. G. Davis	52.3	19	78	8	5-46	9.75
M. A. Robinson	94.5	23	219	18	6-68	12.16
P. J. S. Spencer	37.1	7	99	6	5-42	16.50
B. V. Taylor	244.5	81	612	35	7-34	17.48
N. J. K. Creed	61.2	13	222	10	4-35	22.20
G. G. Read	44	11	131	5	3-23	26.20
S. B. Ellis	71.4	18	201	6	4-69	33.50
J. J. Bates	303.3	82	744	22	4-97	33.81
M. H. Yardy	142.1	46	378	11	3-35	34.36
B. J. Trott	40	5	147	4	2-73	36.75
W. J. House.	94.2	26	310	8	2-14	38.75
P. M. Havell	223.2	51	823	19	3-38	43.31

Also bowled: S. R. Ades 20–3–73–0; J. R. Carpenter 27–4–76–2; D. A. Clapp 2–0–23–0; K. Greenfield 2–1–10–0; R. N. Jackson 15–1–49–2; W. G. Khan 4.5–0–9–1; C. D. Nash 37–4–150–3; A. J. Sartor 14–3–41–1; T. van Noort 11–4–23–1.

WARWICKSHIRE SECOND ELEVEN

Matches 14: Won – Essex, Hampshire, Kent, Lancashire, Sussex, Worcestershire. Lost – Glamorgan, Nottinghamshire. Drawn – Derbyshire, Gloucestershire, Middlesex, Northamptonshire, Surrey, Yorkshire.

Batting Averages

	M	I	NO	R	HS	100s	Avge
M. A. Wagh	7	10	2	533	142	3	66.62
D. A. T. Dalton	2	4	0	218	72	0	54.50
*A. Singh	8	13	2	474	205*	2	43.09
M. A. Sheikh	10	16	1	621	78	0	41.40

	M	I	NO	R	HS	100s	Avge
I. R. Bell............	7	12	1	436	94	0	39.63
*G. Welch............	7	10	0	375	81	0	37.50
J. Troughton.........	6	8	2	210	104	1	35.00
R. E. Sierra.........	13	20	1	632	90	0	33.26
G. D. Franklin.......	8	11	2	262	52	0	29.11
E. J. Wilson.........	6	6	5	29	12*	0	29.00
†T. Frost............	14	21	2	507	89	0	26.68
H. R. Jones.........	5	6	1	129	54	0	25.80
B. W. O'Connell......	13	16	2	321	100*	1	22.92
C. E. Dagnall........	12	14	1	220	63*	0	16.92
A. Richardson.......	4	5	3	31	22	0	15.50
D. A. Altree........	13	13	7	64	19*	0	10.66
J. A. Spires........	8	10	1	48	21	0	5.33
N. A. Warren........	2	4	1	4	3*	0	1.33

Played in two matches: S. P. Byng 9, 7; D. L. Hemp 8, 2, 56. Played in one match: D. J. Barr 13, 6; D. R. Brown 5, 74; R. A. Harris 24; T. L. Penney 60; K. P. Pietersen 92. T. Mees did not bat.

Note: In the match v Surrey at Leamington Spa, M. A. Wagh, called up for a first-team match, was replaced by H. R. Jones.

Bowling Averages

	O	M	R	W	BB	Avge
D. A. Altree...........	300.3	71	892	51	6-37	17.49
M. A. Wagh...........	88.3	28	181	10	6-71	18.10
C. E. Dagnall..........	252.3	73	693	36	5-22	19.25
M. A. Sheikh..........	182.5	70	419	19	4-41	22.05
B. W. O'Connell........	286.5	101	751	32	6-56	23.46
N. A. Warren..........	30	11	125	5	2-15	25.00
A. Richardson	137.3	43	329	12	4-60	27.41
G. Welch.............	182.1	35	566	18	5-79	31.44
E. J. Wilson..........	82	19	253	7	2-6	36.14
J. A. Spires..........	222.5	55	655	14	3-67	46.78

Also bowled: I. R. Bell 25-5-77-2; D. R. Brown 30-14-32-3; D. A. T. Dalton 5-0-32-0; G. D. Franklin 51-8-212-1; R. A. Harris 11-1-50-1; D. L. Hemp 8-1-25-1; H. R. Jones 2-0-23-0; T. Mees 0.5-0-0-1; K. P. Pietersen 20-3-71-2; A. Singh 2-0-10-0; J. Troughton 11-1-35-2.

WORCESTERSHIRE SECOND ELEVEN

Matches 14: Won – Northamptonshire, Sussex. Lost – Glamorgan, Gloucestershire, Kent, Leicestershire, Middlesex, Nottinghamshire, Warwickshire. Drawn – Durham, Essex, Hampshire, Lancashire, Somerset.

Batting Averages

	M	I	NO	R	HS	100s	Avge
D. N. Catterall	7	7	2	294	102	1	58.80
Kadeer Ali...........	11	18	3	753	126*	2	50.20
D. E. Paynter........	6	12	0	520	98	0	43.33
Kabir Ali............	4	4	2	78	34	0	39.00
*N. R. Boulton.......	14	24	4	778	146	2	38.90
G. S. Kandola........	5	10	1	284	85	0	31.55
G. R. Treagus........	6	12	1	312	62	0	28.36
D. J. Roberts	2	4	0	87	60	0	21.75
*†D. J. Pipe	12	21	1	423	109*	1	21.15

	M	I	NO	R	HS	100s	Avge
C. R. Howell	8	14	2	223	69	0	18.58
*M. J. Rawnsley	7	9	0	154	34	0	17.11
G. Prince	3	4	1	49	19*	0	16.33
J. Burgoyne	8	12	2	142	42*	0	14.20
R. Wilkinson	4	5	1	40	18	0	10.00
C. G. Liptrot	12	17	5	102	23	0	8.50
R. C. Driver	3	4	0	31	15	0	7.75
M. M. Mirza	5	4	1	12	12*	0	4.00
J. P. Searle	7	10	2	30	13	0	3.75
D. B. Patel	7	10	1	22	5	0	2.44

Played in three matches: *A. Sheriyar 13, 25. Played in two matches: S. J. Ali 10, 8, 13; R. J. Sillence 23, 1, 16*; W. P. C. Weston 65, 32*, 19. Played in one match: J. Cornford 50, 38*; O. A. Dawkins 41, 5*; N. Din 19*, 10; †S. M. Eustace 2*; *G. R. Haynes 3; T. P. Hodgson 7; *R. K. Illingworth 12; †C. M. Mole 2, 38; K. J. Nash 1, 4; P. R. Pollard 20, 52; A. J. Syddall 1, 15; J. M. Tandy 23, 18; R. M. Wilkinson 3; E. J. Wilson 4.

Bowling Averages

	O	M	R	W	BB	Avge
K. J. Nash	23.2	5	88	5	3-47	17.60
C. G. Liptrot	352	65	1,331	53	7-27	25.11
M. J. Rawnsley	211.5	75	486	19	4-28	25.57
D. B. Patel	133.5	31	480	17	5-70	28.23
R. J. Sillence	41	12	116	4	3-57	29.00
G. Prince	97.1	20	414	14	5-62	29.57
J. Burgoyne	172.3	25	628	17	4-64	36.94
A. Sheriyar	106.4	17	374	10	5-61	37.40
J. P. Searle	263.1	72	785	17	3-53	46.17
D. N. Catterall	121.3	21	382	8	2-30	47.75
M. M. Mirza	99.1	19	441	9	2-65	49.00
Kabir Ali	79.5	15	287	5	2-80	57.40

Also bowled: Kadeer Ali 44–4–169–3; S. J. Ali 3–0–24–0; N. R. Boulton 5–0–24–1; J. Cornford 3–0–12–0; O. A. Dawkins 21–2–73–1; N. Din 12–2–54–3; R. C. Driver 2–0–8–0; C. R. Howell 4–0–29–0; R. K. Illingworth 33–12–62–0; D. E. Paynter 25–4–84–3; A. J. Syddall 29–8–110–2; G. R. Treagus 2–0–6–0; R. Wilkinson 16.5–2–60–2.

YORKSHIRE SECOND ELEVEN

Matches 15: Won – Derbyshire, Glamorgan, Nottinghamshire, Somerset, Sussex. Lost – Hampshire, Lancashire. Drawn – Durham, Essex, Kent, Leicestershire, Middlesex, Northamptonshire, Warwickshire. Abandoned – Durham.

Batting Averages

	M	I	NO	R	HS	100s	Avge
*†R. J. Blakey	2	4	1	198	86	0	66.00
*R. J. Harden	3	5	1	234	148	1	58.50
*M. J. Wood	7	14	1	590	191	1	45.38
M. J. Lumb	13	22	2	885	191	1	44.25
S. A. Richardson	11	18	4	615	104	2	43.92
C. R. Taylor	5	6	1	219	104*	1	43.80
J. D. Middlebrook	5	7	3	154	75*	0	38.50
V. J. Craven	6	12	0	415	136	1	34.58
T. M. Baker	5	5	2	99	31*	0	33.00
I. D. Fisher	8	12	1	316	69	0	28.72
R. A. Stead	7	11	2	240	73	0	26.66

	M	I	NO	R	HS	100s	Avge
*S. Widdup	8	13	0	290	81	0	22.30
C. J. Elstub	7	5	4	19	9*	0	19.00
J. W. Inglis.	10	19	2	295	66	0	17.35
†S. M. Guy	9	11	1	166	87*	0	16.60
A. McGrath	4	7	1	77	25	0	12.83
R. K. J. Dawson	6	7	0	52	22	0	7.42
P. M. Hutchison	3	5	1	20	17	0	5.00
G. Ramsden	3	4	2	4	4	0	2.00

Played in five matches: G. A. Lambert 0, 40, 0. Played in three matches: C. J. Ellison 7*, 2, 24*; J. L. Sadler 5, 5, 26; D. H. Wigley 12*, 9. Played in two matches: C. T. Brice 2, 7*; D. L. Broadbent 11, 0; J. J. Sayers 44, 2*; T. J. Sharpe 9, 0; †M. Thewlis 6, 57. Played in one match: †M. D. Beckett 9; †M. R. Duce 9*, 2; G. M. Hamilton 0, 15*; N. J. Harris 0; S. Mason 16, 6*; G. J. Newton 0; A. Roberts 1; C. E. W. Silverwood 33; L. C. Weekes 12.

Note: In the match v Essex at Chelmsford, S. M. Guy, called up for a first-team match, was replaced by M. Thewlis.

Bowling Averages

	O	M	R	W	BB	Avge
P. M. Hutchison	98	32	219	11	5-53	19.90
J. D. Middlebrook	256.5	92	573	28	7-51	20.46
T. M. Baker	136.2	36	438	21	6-19	20.85
G. Ramsden.	65	16	210	9	4-49	23.33
I. D. Fisher	302.2	100	741	29	5-105	25.55
C. T. Brice	61.2	18	162	5	2-46	32.40
R. A. Stead	142	41	390	12	3-39	32.50
D. H. Wigley	49	15	131	4	2-43	32.75
V. J. Craven	50.3	17	135	4	1-0	33.75
G. A. Lambert	149.5	34	490	14	3-42	35.00
C. J. Elstub	131.1	26	429	12	3-66	35.75
R. K. J. Dawson	273.1	72	837	22	6-92	38.04
D. L. Broadbent	58	18	158	4	1-30	39.50
M. J. Lumb	65.1	9	310	5	3-43	62.00

Also bowled: C. J. Ellison 54–11–186–3; R. J. Harden 18–0–110–0; S. A. Richardson 3–0–20–0; A. Roberts 20–2–111–3; J. L. Sadler 3–0–14–0; T. J. Sharpe 13.2–4–44–3; C. E. W. Silverwood 16–7–38–3; C. R. Taylor 3–0–10–0; L. C. Weekes 6–1–12–0; S. Widdup 49.5–5–189–3; M. J. Wood 33–6–88–1.

SECOND ELEVEN CHAMPIONS

1959	Gloucestershire	1974	Middlesex	1988	Surrey
1960	Northamptonshire	1975	Surrey	1989	Middlesex
1961	Kent	1976	Kent	1990	Sussex
1962	Worcestershire	1977	Yorkshire	1991	Yorkshire
1963	Worcestershire	1978	Sussex	1992	Surrey
1964	Lancashire	1979	Warwickshire	1993	Middlesex
1965	Glamorgan	1980	Glamorgan	1994	Somerset
1966	Surrey	1981	Hampshire	1995	Hampshire
1967	Hampshire	1982	Worcestershire	1996	Warwickshire
1968	Surrey	1983	Leicestershire	1997	Lancashire
1969	Kent	1984	Yorkshire	1998	Northamptonshire
1970	Kent	1985	Nottinghamshire	1999	Middlesex
1971	Hampshire	1986	Lancashire	2000	Middlesex
1972	Nottinghamshire	1987	{ Kent / Yorkshire }		
1973	Essex				

AON TROPHY, 2000

A Zone	Played	Won	Lost	No result	Points	Net run-rate
Leicestershire	8	6	0	2	14	40.32
Gloucestershire	8	5	1	2	12	4.48
Glamorgan.	8	2	4	2	6	0.00
Nottinghamshire	8	0	4	4	4	−29.41
Minor Counties	8	0	4	4	4	−30.31

B Zone	Played	Won	Lost	No result	Points	Net run-rate
Durham	8	4	1	3	11	22.08
Lancashire	8	5	2	1	11	11.19
Warwickshire	8	4	3	1	9	−0.84
Worcestershire	8	3	4	1	7	−10.74
Yorkshire.	8	0	6	2	2	−18.11

C Zone	Played	Won	Lost	No result	Points	Net run-rate
Hampshire.	8	6	0	2	14	14.85
Surrey	8	3	3	2	8	6.29
Somerset	8	3	4	1	7	2.34
Sussex	8	2	4	2	6	−8.17
MCC Young Cricketers . . .	8	2	5	1	5	−12.89

D Zone	Played	Won	Lost	No result	Points	Net run-rate
Kent	8	7	0	1	15	30.60
Middlesex	8	2	3	3	7	−1.60
Northamptonshire	8	3	4	1	7	−6.72
Essex	8	3	4	1	7	−10.27
Derbyshire.	8	2	6	0	4	−7.03

Semi-finals

At West End, Southampton, August 7. Hampshire won by three wickets. Toss: Durham. Durham 198 for eight (50 overs) (J. A. Daley 33, A. Pratt 30, I. D. Hunter 40 not out; Z. C. Morris four for 36); Hampshire 199 for seven (49.4 overs) (J. H. K. Adams 51, A. J. Sexton 72; G. D. Bridge three for 22).

At Canterbury, August 7. Leicestershire won by 150 runs. Toss: Leicestershire. Leicestershire 239 (50 overs) (W. F. Stelling 35, D. Williamson 72, C. D. Crowe 39); Kent 89 (21.5 overs) (J. B. Hockley 23; P. Griffiths three for 32, A. A. Khan four for seven).

Final

At Northlands Road, Southampton, September 4. Leicestershire won by 25 runs. Toss: Hampshire. Leicestershire 205 (49.4 overs) (S. J. Adshead 58, P. E. Robinson 35); Hampshire 180 (47.3 overs) (A. J. Sexton 58, L. R. Prittipaul 39; P. Griffiths three for 27, C. D. Crowe three for 41).

WINNERS 1986-2000

1986	Northamptonshire	1991	Nottinghamshire	1996	Leicestershire
1987	Derbyshire	1992	Surrey	1997	Surrey
1988	Yorkshire	1993	Leicestershire	1998	Northamptonshire
1989	Middlesex	1994	Yorkshire	1999	Kent
1990	Lancashire	1995	Leicestershire	2000	Leicestershire

LEAGUE CRICKET IN ENGLAND AND WALES IN 2000

By GEOFFREY DEAN

In the first year of the new century, the ECB could finally claim that a national network of premier leagues was in place. After ten leagues had met the criteria for premier status in 1999, the number doubled to 20 in 2000, with hopes that as many as 25 might be up and running for 2001.

Having originally insisted that premier leagues must play 120 overs per day, the ECB agreed in the winter of 1999-2000 that 110 would be acceptable, but only on condition that the side batting first could bat beyond 55 overs; the board did not want a 50:50 split of overs. At the end of the 2000 season, however, it decided to drop its opposition to such a split if individual leagues favoured one. "We prefer time games," said Frank Kemp, the ECB's operations manager for recreational cricket. "But the consensus was that it can be very difficult to play a time game within 110 overs. That doesn't mean a return to compulsory result cricket though – draws must still be possible."

The board's flexibility on this issue encouraged further leagues to join the premier family in 2001. The North Staffordshire & South Cheshire League was given accreditation as a premier league. So was Cornwall, where a new Premier Division, created by invitation, was set up. In Wales, the North Wales League was accredited and, after unsuccessful attempts to persuade the East Wales League and the South Wales Cricket Association to unite in one Premier League, East Wales gained Premier League status, with a structure allowing South Wales clubs, or the Association itself, to join in the future. Discussions continued with Leicestershire, but opposition to any change remained resolute in both the Lancashire and Central Lancashire Leagues.

Undoubtedly, the team of the season were Sheffield Collegiate who, in the same September weekend, won first the Yorkshire League and then the National Club Championship final. Collegiate pipped Harrogate, runners-up for the second successive year, by a single point to the League title. By contrast, Bowdon won the Cheshire County League by a massive 81 points from 1999 champions Macclesfield, and Wanstead won the Essex League by 73 points, winning 14 of their 18 matches. Indian Test player Devang Gandhi scored 800 runs and took 46 wickets to help Hadleigh & Thundersley into third place. Wimbledon, in their first season after being promoted, were equally convincing winners of the Surrey Championship, after a poor start when they failed to win a game before June. They were unbeaten thereafter and secured the title by August 19. Spencer were certain of relegation even earlier than that, after being docked 41 points for fielding an ineligible overseas player. Weybridge, champions the year before, were much less potent a force once Martin Love, their Queensland opener, flew home early. He broke an ankle after making three hundreds in six innings.

The oldest league in the world, the Birmingham and District, was won by a club enjoying only their second season at this level. Runners-up at their first attempt in 1999, Cannock were crowned champions this time; their captain, Laurie Potter, once of Kent and Leicestershire, combined 740 runs with 32 wickets. A similarly solid all-round performance from Anthony Woolley (637 runs and 37 wickets) helped Alvaston & Boulton to the Derbyshire Premier League title. Phil Simmons, the former West Indies all-rounder, made 1,065 runs at 62 for runners-up Dunstall, although Heanor Town's Mark Saxelby was the league's leading run-scorer with 1,193, simply emphasising the tragic circumstances of his death in October (see Obituary). Across the M1, New Zealander Andrew Adams played a key part in Kimberley's Nottinghamshire Cricket Board title triumph with a double of over 500 runs and 50 wickets. Further south in the Midlands, Wellingborough seamer Richard Dalton returned the best figures in a Northamptonshire Championship match, nine for 20, to dismiss Peterborough for 36.

Two new regional premier leagues enjoyed successful inaugural seasons. Sunderland, without a title since 1971, were the first champions of the North East League, helped along by St Vincent professional Cameron Cuffy's 54 wickets. The Home Counties League, whose clubs were drawn from as many as six shires, became a two-horse race between Banbury and High Wycombe, who regularly exchanged the leadership. Craig Haupt's consistency – he scored 813 runs, including a match-winning century on the crucial final day of the season – and former Worcestershire seamer Neal Radford's 66 wickets were the key to Banbury's title. Finchampstead beat Banbury home and away, however; their Australian all-rounder, Jon Moss, managed the remarkable feat of a hundred plus a hat-trick in *each* game against the eventual champions. Moss finished with 878 runs and 53 victims.

In the East Anglian League, the 1999 winners, Vauxhall Mallards, and runners-up, Norwich, changed places, Norwich clinching the title on the final day of the season. The Devon League was also decided in the final round, when Exeter beat off Exmouth's bid for a third successive championship. Bath easily maintained their dominance in the West of England Premier League, averaging ten points more per game than runners-up Cheltenham. Brighton & Hove picked up both the Sussex League and Cup titles, bolstered by Dutch batsman Bas Zuiderent. Richard Howitt of Cambridge University helped Bourne to claim the Lincolnshire League, scoring 657 runs. Netherfield won the Northern League for the third time in four seasons, while Wallasey took the Liverpool and District Competition premiership, finishing 68 points ahead of previous winners Bootle.

In the Kent League, where games were again played over two days as in Australian grade cricket, the longer duration allowed Simon Willis (234) and Ian Baldock (138) to put on 379 for the first wicket for St Lawrence against reigning champions The Mote. While St Lawrence's title was their third in seven seasons, Havant won the Southern League for a record seventh time. In the Middlesex League, Brondesbury, champions for the first time in 1999, retained their crown, despite a rancorous August meeting with Finchley, then leaders. Finchley batted all day to make 200 for eight from 108 overs, thereby ensuring they would stay top as each side received one point. A cap on the length of the first innings in the Middlesex League was expected as a result.

Away from the Premier Leagues, Greenfield secured their first Saddleworth League title since 1953. Saddleworth professional Peter Skuse amassed more than 1,800 runs, 228 of them in one innings against Micklehurst. Across the Pennines, Townville won the Central Yorkshire League in controversial circumstances, when the league management decided to cancel the final round because of the fuel crisis. Several clubs expressed outrage, as no great distances were involved for away teams. The Merseyside Competition did the sensible thing and postponed games for a week.

With bad on-field behaviour by some players still a recurring problem, it was heartening that one premier league, Essex, took drastic action in a notable case. Khalid Ishmail of Hainault & Clayhall was banned for five years for punching a member of the Fives & Heronians side. The Middlesex League also suspended five Enfield players following incidents in a second-division match at Shepherd's Bush. In a Middlesex Championship match between Southall and Osterley, a brawl resulted in one player needing hospital treatment after being hit with a bat.

ECB PREMIER LEAGUE TABLES, 2000

Birmingham and District Premier Cricket League

	P	W	L	Pts
Cannock	22	10	2	237
Stratford	22	9	4	229
Walsall	22	8	2	227
Halesowen	22	7	2	226
Old Hill	22	6	2	194
Coventry & N. Warwicks	22	6	4	184
Barnt Green	22	5	5	169
Kidderminster	22	4	8	162
West Brom. Dartmouth	22	3	5	146
Wolverhampton	22	3	8	146
Harborne	22	1	5	145
Smethwick	22	0	15	49

Devon Cricket League

	P	W	L	Pts
Exeter	18	13	0	289
Exmouth	18	11	2	279
Bovey Tracey	18	10	5	251
Paignton	18	6	6	208
Torquay	18	5	6	191
Plympton	18	4	4	189
Sidmouth	18	4	7	179
Cornwood	18	2	7	150
North Devon	18	2	9	132
Seaton	18	1	12	112

Cheshire County Cricket League

	P	W	L	Pts
Bowdon	22	16	0	418
Macclesfield	22	9	5	337
Toft	22	8	5	284
Oxton	22	7	5	281
Chester Boughton Hall	22	7	6	276
Nantwich	22	8	5	268
Hyde	22	4	8	251
Didsbury	22	6	5	249
Neston	22	8	8	247
Cheadle Hulme	22	6	7	247
Alsager	22	2	14	183
Birkenhead Park	22	1	14	122

East Anglian Premier Cricket League

	P	W	L	Pts	Avge
Norwich	18	11	1	274	17.13
Vauxhall Mallards	18	9	1	228	16.29
Swardeston	18	8	5	207	14.79
Cambridge Granta	18	7	5	201	12.56
Clacton	18	5	5	167	10.44
Mildenhall	18	4	6	145	10.36
Bury St Edmunds	18	4	7	161	9.47
Halstead	18	3	8	129	8.60
Godmanchester	18	1	7	92	6.57
Cambridge St Giles	18	2	9	104	6.50

Derbyshire Premier League

	P	W	L	Pts
Alvaston & Boulton	22	8	1	342
Dunstall	22	7	2	323
Ockbrook & Borrowash	22	7	2	321
Sandiacre Town	22	7	3	315
Stainsby Hall	22	8	7	285
Chesterfield	22	5	4	264
Quarndon	22	4	4	259
Heanor Town	22	5	5	243
Ilkeston Rutland	22	3	4	234
Denby	22	1	6	228
Langley Mill United	22	2	7	167
Shipley Hall	22	1	13	126

Essex League

	P	W	L	Pts
Wanstead	18	14	3	296
Saffron Walden	18	8	5	223
Hadleigh & Thundersley	18	8	4	216
Loughton	18	5	5	178
Hainault & Clayhall	18	5	4	172
Shenfield	18	5	7	170
Fives & Heronians	18	5	7	162
Gidea Park & Romford	18	3	4	155
Chelmsford	18	4	9	144
Billericay	18	2	11	108

Home Counties Premier Cricket League

	P	W	L	Pts
Banbury	18	13	3	344
High Wycombe	18	12	3	333
Reading	18	8	3	258
Beaconsfield	18	8	6	248
Finchampstead	18	6	7	221
Basingstoke & N. Hants	18	6	7	200
Bicester & N. Oxford	18	5	8	175
Radlett	18	4	6	172
Luton Town	18	3	9	148
Bletchley Town	18	1	14	60

Liverpool and District Cricket Competition

	P	W	L	Pts
Wallasey	22	15	2	361
Bootle	22	11	3	293
Ormskirk	22	11	2	287
Northern	22	9	4	255
Lytham	22	10	6	252*
Leigh	22	6	10	211
Northop Hall	22	7	10	197
Colwyn Bay	22	6	11	188
Wigan	22	5	10	174
New Brighton	22	5	8	169
Formby	22	5	14	162
Southport & Birkdale	22	3	13	128

* Match pts plus extra 10 pts deducted for fielding an unregistered player.

Kent Cricket League

	P	W	L	Pts
St Lawrence	9	6	2	278
Bromley	9	7	1	275
Bexley	9	5	2	223
Folkestone	9	4	3	212
Beckenham	9	6	3	206
Sevenoaks Vine	9	2	4	166
The Mote	9	2	3	165
Ashford	9	1	4	135
Bickley Park	9	1	7	119
Orpington	9	1	6	102

Middlesex County Cricket League

	P	W	L	T	Pts
Brondesbury	18	9	3	1	109
Finchley	18	7	1	0	92
Teddington	18	8	5	1	89
Winchmore Hill	18	7	6	0	81
Eastcote	18	6	5	0	76
Brentham	18	4	5	0	58
Uxbridge	18	4	5	0	45*
Wembley	18	3	8	0	43
Hornsey	18	2	8	0	37
Stanmore	18	2	6	0	35*

* 10 pts deducted for fielding an unregistered player.

Lincolnshire Cricket Board Premier League

	P	W	L	Pts	%
Bourne	14	12	2	219	78.2
Sleaford	17	13	4	244	71.8
Grimsby	15	11	4	212	70.7
Messingham	16	10	6	205	64.1
Market Rasen	16	9	7	188	58.8
Market Deeping	15	8	7	170	56.7
Lindum	13	6	7	128	49.2
Caistor	14	3	11	93	33.2
Long Sutton	15	2	13	70	23.3
Grantham	15	1	14	53	17.7

Northamptonshire Cricket Championship

	P	W	L	Pts
Finedon Dolben	20	12	1	142
County Colts	20	8	2	118
Peterborough Town	20	9	5	116
Brixworth	20	7	7	91
Wellingborough Town	20	6	5	75
Bedford Town	20	4	3	70
Horton House	20	4	5	62
Old Northamptonians	20	4	9	58
Northampton Saints	20	3	7	45
Irthlingborough Town	20	3	9	42
Old Wellingburians	20	1	8	28

North East Premier League

	P	W	L	Pts
Sunderland	20	8	1	261
Durham Cricket Academy	20	6	3	223
Blaydon	20	6	4	209
South Northumberland	20	5	3	209
Norton	20	3	3	208
Chester-le-Street	20	3	2	202
Benwell Hill	20	3	2	195
Gateshead Fell	20	4	4	183
Stockton	20	3	6	176
Tynemouth	20	1	5	151
Newcastle	20	0	9	106

Southern Premier Cricket League

	P	W	L	Pts	Avge
Havant	18	11	2	250	17.86
Calmore Sports	18	8	5	206	13.73
BAT Sports	18	9	6	213	13.31
Andover	18	6	6	180	12.00
Bournemouth	18	7	6	195	11.47
South Wiltshire	18	7	8	180	11.25
Bashley (Rydal) I.	18	6	7	176	11.00
Hungerford	18	5	7	172	10.75
Burridge	18	2	8	110	7.33
Cove	18	2	8	107	7.13

Northern Premier League

	P	W	L	Pts
Netherfield	22	13	1	220
Darwen	22	12	2	188
Chorley	22	9	5	169
Morecambe	22	8	4	151
Blackpool	22	7	3	147
St Annes	22	5	2	143
Fleetwood	22	8	7	141
Kendal	22	4	9	110
Lancaster	22	4	6	110
Leyland	22	4	10	93
Leyland DAF	22	2	12	66
Preston	22	1	16	39

Surrey Championship

	P	W	L	Pts
Wimbledon	18	10	1	149
Sunbury	18	8	4	115
Banstead	18	8	5	115
Sutton	18	7	2	111
Guildford	18	8	6	110
Weybridge	18	5	5	85
Esher	18	3	5	63
Reigate Priory	18	4	11	55
Cheam	18	3	9	44
Spencer	18	3	11	5*

* 41 pts deducted for fielding an unregistered player.

Nottinghamshire Cricket Board

	P	W	L	Pts
Kimberley	22	13	2	328
Welbeck	22	9	3	263
West Indian Cavaliers	22	8	3	261
Bracebridge	22	5	5	226
Craythorpe	22	4	7	218
Radcliffe	22	5	6	205
Bridon	22	5	5	193
Wollaton	22	4	5	188
Clifton	22	2	7	184
Notts Unity Casuals	22	6	7	179
Arnold	22	4	10	171
Southwell	22	2	7	160

Sussex Cricket League

	P	W	L	Pts
Brighton & Hove	16	10	4	332
Hastings	16	9	4	325
Three Bridges	16	7	4	268
Crowborough	16	7	5	267
Horsham	16	6	6	242
Haywards Heath	16	6	7	233
Eastbourne	16	5	4	227
Chichester	16	4	10	187
Bexhill	16	1	11	107

West of England Premier League

	P	W	L	Pts	Avge
Bath	13	11	0	385	29.61
Cheltenham	14	8	4	279	19.93
Chippenham	14	7	4	262	18.71
Thornbury	17	8	5	309	18.18
Taunton St Andrews . .	15	8	6	272	18.13
Downend	14	7	4	244	17.43
Clifton Flax Bourton. .	12	3	5	164	13.67
Keynsham.	15	4	5	199	13.27
Weston-super-Mare . . .	15	2	7	158	10.53
Optimists	14	1	8	104	7.43
Stroud	14	0	9	85	6.07

Wins and losses columns do not balance because a mix-up over rules led to Chippenham and Downend each being awarded a win in matches for which their opponents were awarded a draw.

Yorkshire ECB County Premier League

	P	W	L	Pts
Sheffield Collegiate	26	15	4	137
Harrogate.	26	16	4	136
Sheffield United	26	16	7	129
Doncaster.	26	13	7	114
York	26	12	8	104
Hull	26	11	8	104
Yorkshire Academy	26	11	9	99
Scarborough	26	11	10	92
Castleford	26	8	9	89
Cleethorpes	26	7	10	83
Appleby Frodingham	26	8	12	63
Rotherham	26	5	17	55
Driffield.	26	5	17	50
Barnsley	26	2	18	39

OTHER LEAGUE WINNERS, 2000

Airedale & Wharfedale	Guiseley
Bassetlaw	Blidworth
Bolton	Kearsley
Bradford	Pudsey Congs
Central Yorkshire	Townville
Cherwell	Banbury XX
Cornwall	St Buryan
Durham County	Leadgate
Durham Senior	Horden
East Wales	Newport
East Yorkshire	Wrigglesworth Fruit Trades
Hertfordshire	Hoddesdon
Huddersfield	Scholes
Lancashire County	Irlam
Leeds	Leeds Police
Leicestershire County	Kibworth
Merseyside Competition	Wavertree
Norfolk Alliance	Cromer
North Lancs & Cumbria	Barrow
North Staffs & South Cheshire	Audley
Northumberland & Tyneside Senior	Tynedale
North Wales	Bangor
North Yorks & South Durham	Saltburn
Pembrokeshire	Lamphey
Ribblesdale	Ribblesdale Wanderers
Saddleworth	Greenfield
Shropshire	Shrewsbury
Somerset	Wellington
South Wales	Ynysygerwn
Thames Valley	Burnham
Two Counties	Maldon
West Wales	Swansea

THE LANCASHIRE LEAGUES, 2000

By CHRIS ASPIN

The 2000 season was the most closely contested in the Lancashire League in recent years, while the Central Lancashire League will remember it for the record-breaking performance of Brandon Nash, the Oldham professional. He scored more runs in a season than any other batsman in the competition's 108-year history.

At the end of July, with ten games to play, only 14 points separated the Lancashire League's top eight sides. By the final weekend three teams were still in contention and, on the last afternoon, Bacup clinched the title after a gap of 40 years. Their success owed much to the seam bowling of Australian Adam Dale and amateur David Ormerod, who bowled unchanged for most of the season, the pair claiming 194 out of 219 wickets. Dale took 109 at 10.00 apiece, Ormerod 85 at 12.29. Ramsbottom, despite winning the most games and losing the fewest, had to be content with second place, thanks to rules that reward losing sides generously with bonus points; East Lancashire were third. In the Worsley Cup final, Todmorden trounced Haslingden by 124 runs.

Three Australian professionals – Matthew Mott of Rawtenstall, Ramsbottom's Brad Hodge and Ben Johnson of Colne – topped 1,000 runs, but amateur batsmen had a poor year: Liam Jackson's 597 for Enfield was the highest aggregate. Mott hit 155 not out against Todmorden, for whom Richard Baigent, in another game, made an unbeaten 147 to break the club record for an amateur; it helped his side, chasing 214, to a last-ball win against Accrington. Dale was the only Lancashire League bowler to reach 100 wickets, though Rawtenstall spinner Keith Roscoe went close with 91 at 10.58, beating a club record dating back to 1921. It was also the best return by any amateur in the League since 1945.

After scoring 1,810 runs to set a Huddersfield League record in 1999, Yorkshire-based South African Brandon Nash did even better in the Central Lancashire League as Oldham's professional. His 2,197 runs overtook Carl Hooper's 2,144 for Werneth in 1989 and, with an unbeaten 245 against Ashton, he also smashed the record for the highest individual score, beating Brad Osborne's 223 not out for Middleton against Hyde in 1991. That innings lifted Oldham to 360 for three, whereupon Nash seized four for five as Ashton were dismissed for 110. He hit another eight centuries, two of them against Milnrow: 156 in a league game and an unbeaten 154 off 125 balls, with three sixes and 21 fours, in the first round of the Wood Cup. Nash looked to be steering Oldham to victory in the Cup final when they were 137 for one in pursuit of Rochdale's 179, but he was out for 78 and the last eight wickets scraped together only 29 more.

The Championship was won by Middleton, their first since 1988. Captain and left-arm spinner Lee Wolstenholme took 100 wickets for the second successive season, finishing with 107 at 12.02, while pace bowler Dave Norris's 82 at 13.21 included seven for 17 – and a hat-trick – to rout Stand for 24. Professional Ruwin Peiris hit 142 out of 306 for three against Werneth on a weekend (May 13–14) that saw five centuries in the CLL. Asif Mujtaba completed the double for Norden, combining 1,255 runs with 124 wickets. Only he and Wolstenholme took 100 wickets, the next best return being 90 by Steve Dearden. Formerly an amateur with Ramsbottom and Haslingden, Dearden joined Radcliffe as a professional after they took the wooden spoon in 1997; in 2000, they were fourth. The leading amateur run-makers were Simon North of Norden, with 961, and Bruce Cruse of Radcliffe, with 901. Chris Dearden of Littleborough, who has played in the Central Lancashire League since 1975, took his aggregate to 15,000 runs.

Rochdale won the Inter-League Cup, defeating Norden by 33 runs. Most of the Lancashire League sides lost in the first round on bowl-outs.

TRANSCO LANCASHIRE LEAGUE

	P	W	L	NR	Bonus Pts	Pts	Professional	Runs	Avge	Wkts	Avge
Bacup......	26	16	9	0	51	218*	A. C. Dale......	552	25.09	109	10.00
Ramsbottom..	26	17	5	3	27	212*†	B. J. Hodge.....	1,183	59.15	14	26.21
E. Lancs....	26	16	7	2	36	209*	C. W. Henderson..	515	32.18	88	13.26
Colne.....	26	15	9	2	30	186	B. A. Johnson....	1,067	53.35	51	19.01
Nelson.....	26	14	10	2	29	175	K. L. T. Arthurton.	758	50.53	40	14.67
Church.....	26	13	12	1	31	163†	‡M. Watkinson...	544	32.00	45	18.00
Todmorden...	26	12	10	3	21	157*	D. J. Marsh......	782	37.23	64	17.95
Lowerhouse..	26	13	11	2	20	155†	M. van Jaarsveld..	879	43.95	33	20.48
Accrington...	26	11	14	1	31	144	‡N. J. Astle......	812	47.76	60	12.96
Haslingden...	26	7	15	4	63	144†	‡P. A. Strang......	391	26.06	31	20.64
Rawtenstall..	26	10	15	1	40	143	M. P. Mott......	1,317	59.86	38	22.94
Rishton.....	26	8	15	3	46	134†	‡J. N. Gillespie...	169	16.90	45	11.91
Enfield.....	26	7	16	3	31	110	D. J. Saker......	424	22.31	66	16.63
Burnley.....	26	7	18	1	37	109†	‡G. I. Foley......	931	46.55	37	24.40

Notes: Ten points awarded for a win; seven for a tie; two points for dismissing opposition and three for an uncompleted game. A maximum of five bonus points available to losing sides for batting and bowling.

  * Includes seven points for a tie.

  † One point deducted for slow over-rates.

  ‡ Did not play the whole season.

CENTRAL LANCASHIRE LEAGUE

	P	OW	LW	L	D	Pts	Professional	Runs	Avge	Wkts	Avge
Middleton ...	28	17	5	3	3	111	G. R. P. Peiris....	1,163	50.56	37	17.51
Norden.....	28	14	6	6	2	100	Asif Mujtaba.....	1,255	62.75	124	9.08
Littleborough .	28	13	7	5	3	99	C. T. Perren....	970	46.19	68	15.48
Radcliffe....	28	14	3	6	5	94	S. E. Dearden....	467	23.35	90	14.56
Rochdale....	28	11	7	6	4	93	D. J. J. de Vos...	1,196	74.75	31	13.80
Werneth.....	28	9	5	10	4	75	B. Nash......	1,029	46.77	56	20.80
Oldham.....	28	9	3	13	3	64	B. A. Nash......	2,197	95.52	47	20.00
Unsworth....	28	8	3	14	3	60	W. M. P. N. Wanasinghe....	1,026	42.75	81	14.30
Heywood....	28	6	5	13	4	60	B. D. Hara.....	746	29.84	52	18.92
Royton.....	28	5	3	14	6	52	G. A. Roe......	582	21.55	71	18.67
Milnrow....	28	4	5	15	4	51	M. A. Conyers....	818	35.56	53	20.79
Walsden	28	6	2	16	4	50	G. J. Kruis......	894	37.25	65	16.40
Stand	28	4	3	19	2	41	B. Flegg........	1,026	41.04	38	32.73
Ashton	28	0	3	21	4	24	S. A. Deitz.....	844	42.20	22	29.77
Crompton ...	28	1	2	22	3	20	Zafar Iqbal.....	878	33.76	67	22.50

Notes: Five points awarded for an outright win; four points for a limited win. A team achieves an outright win by bowling out the opposition. CLL averages include cup games.

NATIONAL CLUB CHAMPIONSHIP, 2000

The day after winning the Yorkshire Premier League, Sheffield Collegiate became national club champions when they defeated Sussex club Eastbourne at the second attempt. The final originally began on September 1 at Lord's, its traditional venue, but was rained off after Sheffield had made a strong start; it was rescheduled 16 days later at Southgate, where they won a low-scoring match convincingly.

The victorious team included spinner John Hespe, a management consultant who had flown back (business class) from Philadelphia, where he was working on a deal, every weekend for two months to make sure Sheffield Collegiate reached the final for the first time. They had a little good fortune – Townville conceded their third-round fixture – but won their six remaining games, including a 20-run victory over Ormskirk of Lancashire in the semi-final.

Eastbourne, who won the title in 1997 against another Yorkshire side, Harrogate, had their closest squeak in the third round, needing their last-wicket pair to overtake Finchley's 168 for seven. In the semi-final, they came up against Teddington, four-time finalists, who ran up 181 for nine; rain shortened the game, and Eastbourne won on scoring-rate.

After two years without a sponsor for the Club Championship it was announced that Play-cricket.com, a website for recreational cricketers, supported by the England and Wales Cricket Board, would fill the role from 2001 to 2003.

FINAL

EASTBOURNE v SHEFFIELD COLLEGIATE

At Lord's, September 1. No result. Toss: Sheffield Collegiate. Sheffield Collegiate 123 for two (30.3 overs) (N. R. Gaywood 32, N. Priestley 36) v Eastbourne.

At Southgate, September 17. Sheffield Collegiate won by 60 runs. Toss: Sheffield Collegiate.
Sheffield Collegiate again chose to bat, and in damp conditions found it tough going. Paul Hacker bowled nine overs for 11 runs, Devon opener Nick Gaywood took 84 balls to score 30, and three wickets fell for two runs in mid-innings. Only 31 in 38 balls from Jim Tasker lifted the total to 135, and Eastbourne's target was just three an over. But Richard Kettleborough, the former Middlesex and Yorkshire player, and Andrew Wylie reduced them to 13 for four. Eastbourne were all out with more than ten overs to spare when Wylie returned to take a third wicket, last man Hacker, whom he also trumped by conceding a mere nine runs in 8.3 overs.
Man of the Match: A. J. Wylie.

Sheffield Collegiate

N. R. Gaywood b R. S. Myall	30		J. P. Hespe c Lord b R. S. Myall	1
†N. Priestley st P. J. Stevens b Lord	23		M. B. Ivill c and b Lord	0
R. A. Kettleborough c Meacher b Smith	9		A. J. Wylie not out	1
*A. E. McKenna lbw b Halsall	11			
C. E. Wall c Hacker b Halsall	0		B 1, l-b 10	11
M. E. Root lbw b Smith	0			
J. A. R. Tasker b R. S. Myall	31		1/35 2/47 3/72 4/74 5/74 (45 overs)	135
M. G. Boocock run out	18		6/96 7/130 8/131 9/132	

Bowling: R. S. Myall 9–3–25–3; Hacker 9–4–11–0; Lord 9–1–29–2; Halsall 9–1–28–2; Smith 9–2–31–2.

Eastbourne

**†P. J. Stevens c Tasker b Kettleborough.	2	R. S. Myall not out	7
R. G. Halsall lbw b Wylie	0	R. J. Smith run out.	3
D. P. Stevens c Wall b Wylie	6	P. S. Hacker lbw b Wylie.	2
D. Kirtley c Hespe b Boocock	18		
D. Cumming c Priestley b Kettleborough	1	L-b 2, w 1, n-b 1	4
D. Meacher c Priestley b Hespe	11		
S. Myall b Hespe.	9	1/2 2/11 3/11 4/13 5/41 (34.3 overs) 75
J. Lord run out	12	6/43 7/58 8/65 9/72	

Bowling: Kettleborough 6–2–10–2; Wylie 8.3–3–9–3; Hespe 9–3–19–2; Ivill 2–0–10–0; Boocock 9–1–25–1.

Umpires: A. Bayley and S. Poole.

WINNERS 1969–2000

1969	Hampstead	1980	Moseley	1991	Teddington
1970	Cheltenham	1981	Scarborough	1992	Optimists
1971	Blackheath	1982	Scarborough	1993	Old Hill
1972	Scarborough	1983	Shrewsbury	1994	Chorley
1973	Wolverhampton	1984	Old Hill	1995	Chorley
1974	Sunbury	1985	Old Hill	1996	Walsall
1975	York	1986	Stourbridge	1997	Eastbourne
1976	Scarborough	1987	Old Hill	1998	Doncaster Town
1977	Southgate	1988	Enfield	1999	Wolverhampton
1978	Cheltenham	1989	Teddington	2000	Sheffield Collegiate
1979	Scarborough	1990	Blackpool		

NATIONAL VILLAGE CHAMPIONSHIP, 2000

Four of the side who won the championship for Derbyshire village Elvaston in 1994 returned to Lord's to claim a second title. But the star of their victory over Eversholt of Bedfordshire was 20-year-old Lee Archer, who followed 81 runs with two catches and a stumping.

Eversholt reached the final during a thunderstorm, seizing Timsbury's last seven wickets for 24 to scrape home by eight runs in the southern semi-final. Elvaston had an easier win over the North Yorkshire side, Folkton and Flixton: seamer Sean Murray, who took a hat-trick in their quarter-final against Plumtree, claimed another three wickets as Folkton crumbled for 108. Archer had flown back from a holiday in Spain for the match.

The 2000 tournament, sponsored by Wadworth, hit the national headlines when Welsh team Usk took the organisers to court after being expelled. They had reached the quarter-finals for the first time, beating Werrington by a single run, before the visitors noticed the road sign "Historic Town of Usk" on their way home to Cornwall. The judge agreed that Usk should be excluded as a town, despite a population of only 2,187, within the competition requirements, and Werrington were reinstated, only to lose by nine wickets to Timsbury. There had been controversy, too, over the eligibility of Jerry Frith of Sparsholt, who had appeared for Hampshire Board XI in the NatWest Trophy. A committee decided that, while two matches for the Board XI would have disqualified him, he was in the clear, having been thirteenth man the second time. Frith later helped to knock out 1999 champions Linton Park, and contributed three wickets and 85 runs in the quarter-final, but Sparsholt still succumbed to Eversholt.

A competition record was set in Cornwall when the match between Gorran and Clyst Hydon, of Devon, produced 608 runs for eight wickets. Clyst Hydon made 373 for three, with Richard Baggs hitting 169 from 83 balls (34 in one over), and Gorran replied with 235 for five.

FINAL

ELVASTON v EVERSHOLT

At Lord's, September 3. Elvaston won by 16 runs. Toss: Elvaston.

Richard Johnson gave his team an excellent start, winning the toss and falling only one short of a century stand with his opening partner, Lee Archer, who went on to 81 in 114 balls, with seven fours. But no one else passed 20 as seamer Simon Davis claimed five wickets; trainee chef Peter Moult, weighing in at 23 stone with a 56-inch chest, went first ball. Eversholt were soon in trouble. Captain Alan Garratt was struck by a ball from Andrew Barrett, who then had him caught behind; the top three batsmen totalled 24. Davis fought back until smartly stumped by Archer, and Warren Davies scored a run-a-ball 37, but the ninth wicket fell with 33 still required. That was 22 by the final over; Sean Murray conceded five.

Elvaston

*R. D. Johnson st A. C. Garratt		J. R. Bodill b Turner	1
b D. C. Garratt .	40	P. I. Moult b Turner	0
†L. D. Archer c A. C. Litchfield b Davis	81	D. J. Randle not out	7
P. E. Birch c A. C. Garratt b Davis	5	L-b 11, w 4, n-b 5	20
A. Brear c P. A. Litchfield b Turner	12		
M. White c Munro-Hall b Davis	8	1/99 2/111 3/150 (9 wkts, 40 overs) 191
R. A. Torry b Davis	1	4/153 5/162 6/164
S. R. Murray c S. M. Litchfield b Davis	16	7/165 8/165 9/191

A. R. Barrett did not bat.

Bowling: P. A. Litchfield 4–0–21–0; Davies 5–0–17–0; Turner 9–1–41–3; D. C. Garratt 9–1–32–1; Morgan 7–0–31–0; Davis 6–0–38–5.

Eversholt

*†A. C. Garratt c Archer b Barrett	9	P. A. Litchfield c Johnson b Murray	13
S. M. Litchfield c White b Birch	8	P. J. Morgan not out	6
R. J. Munro-Hall b White	7	D. C. Turner not out	7
S. D. L. Davis st Archer b Barrett	32	L-b 10, w 12, n-b 1	23
P. A. Garratt c Johnson b Bodill	19		
W. B. Davies c White b Barrett	37	1/14 2/26 3/48 (9 wkts, 40 overs) 175
A. C. Litchfield c Archer b Murray	9	4/80 5/100 6/130
D. C. Garratt run out	5	7/143 8/148 9/159

Bowling: Murray 9–2–40–2; Barrett 9–0–36–2; White 9–1–33–1; Birch 9–1–33–2; Brear 2–0–11–0; Bodill 2–0–12–1.

Umpires: J. Dimery and R. McLeod.

WINNERS 1972–2000

1972	Troon (Cornwall)	1987	Longparish (Hampshire)
1973	Troon (Cornwall)	1988	Goatacre (Wiltshire)
1974	Bomarsund (Northumberland)	1989	Toft (Cheshire)
1975	Gowerton (Glamorgan)	1990	Goatacre (Wiltshire)
1976	Troon (Cornwall)	1991	St Fagans (Glamorgan)
1977	Cookley (Worcestershire)	1992	Hursley Park (Hampshire)
1978	Linton Park (Kent)	1993	Kington (Herefordshire)
1979	East Bierley (Yorkshire)	1994	Elvaston (Derbyshire)
1980	Marchwiel (Clwyd)	1995	Woodhouse Grange (Yorkshire)
1981	St Fagans (Glamorgan)	1996	Caldy (Cheshire)
1982	St Fagans (Glamorgan)	1997	Caldy (Cheshire)
1983	Quarndon (Derbyshire)	1998	Methley (Yorkshire)
1984	Marchwiel (Clwyd)	1999	Linton Park (Kent)
1985	Freuchie (Fife)	2000	Elvaston (Derbyshire)
1986	Forge Valley (Yorkshire)		

IRISH CRICKET IN 2000

By DEREK SCOTT

The Irish season was dominated by thoughts of the ICC Trophy in Toronto in July 2001. Five stalwarts from the 1997 Trophy – Angus Dunlop, Alan Lewis, Neil Doak, Justin Benson and Garfield Harrison – were no longer available, and only two new players of their calibre have emerged, in Ed Joyce and Matt Dwyer. In Ireland's favour, however, is the timing of the tournament, during their normal season, and, most importantly, its being played on grass pitches. An improvement on fourth place last time would see Ireland into the 2003 World Cup.

The squad's selection on players' form in 2000 lent extra significance to Ireland's games between April, when they attended the Emerging Nations Tournament in Harare, and August, when they played their traditional first-class match with Scotland. With a full-strength party in Harare, Ireland finished third behind Kenya and Holland. But from then on, they were unable to pick their first-choice team. Only two players appeared in all their remaining fixtures, with 25 used in total.

They lost badly to Shropshire in the NatWest first round in May, and MCC's visit was ruined by rain. In June, Zimbabwe won two limited-overs matches in Dublin, despite the presence in the Irish side of Australian Mark Waugh, on an ICC coaching and public relations mission, and Paul Mooney's four wickets in five overs in the second game.

The Triple Crown, held in North Wales in July, was so wet that all Ireland's fixtures were decided by bowl-outs. Bizarrely, if they had hit the stumps three more times, out of 30 attempts, they could have claimed the trophy without setting foot on the field; instead, they were runners-up to Scotland. Ireland also finished behind hosts Scotland in the European Championship; they beat Denmark and Italy, but three defeats and fourth place were disappointing.

The season closed in Ayr with the three-day match, which Scotland won even though Dunlop became only the fourth player to hit 150 for Ireland. Two months later, he retired. In 114 matches since 1990, he had scored 3,164 runs at 29.29; 428 of those came in 2000, when only two others, Kyle McCallan and Peter Gillespie, totalled more than 200. Joyce, often absent with Middlesex, scored 169 at 33.80. Dwyer was the leading wicket-taker, with 21 at 21.04, while Mooney headed the averages with 17 at 16.29. The season's finds were 19-year-old Andrew White, who made 111 against Denmark, and Mark Gillespie, Peter's older brother, a fine left-hand batsman and leg-spinner.

Donemana won the Royal Liver Irish Senior Cup, depriving North-West rivals Limavady of a treble, but lost the final of the new Ulster Cup to Lisburn. Limavady won their seventh successive North-West League title, and third League–Cup double in four years. In Dublin, Clontarf completed their third double in nine seasons; leading League challengers Merrion lost points for unruly behaviour. For the third year running, the Northern Union League was won by a newly promoted team, this time Waringstown, who pipped Cliftonville with nine wins in their last ten matches. North Down took the Cup, though Woodvale reached their third successive final. Cork County retained the Munster League but lost the Cup final to University College Cork.

Ireland's women played their maiden Test at Dublin in July, defeating Pakistan in two days by an innings and 54 runs. Isobel Joyce, Ed's sister, took six for 21 in the second innings, including debutante Sajjida Shah who, at 12 years 35 days, was the youngest full international cricketer. She made two and nought.

Winners of Irish Leagues and Cups
Royal Liver Irish Senior Cup: Donemana. **Dublin Senior League:** Clontarf. **Dublin Senior Cup:** Clontarf. **Ulster Cup:** Lisburn. **Munster League:** Cork County. **Munster Cup:** University College Cork. **Northern Union League:** Waringstown. **Northern Union Cup:** North Down. **North-West League:** Limavady. **North-West Cup:** Limavady.

SCOTTISH CRICKET IN 2000

By J. WATSON BLAIR

After the excitement of their World Cup appearance in 1999, it was business as usual for Scotland, though they hoped to win entry to the World Cup for a second time through the 2001 ICC Trophy in Toronto. They met several of their rivals for that prize in the Emerging Nations Tournament, held in Harare in April 2000. But Scottish results were disappointing, with only one win, over Denmark. They lost to Ireland, Kenya, Zimbabwe A and Holland, and finished bottom of the table.

Back at home, bad weather left the national side short of practice. They were knocked out of the NatWest Trophy's first round by Wiltshire in May. But they retained the Triple Crown, staged in North Wales, in July. Scotland beat the England Board XI in a rain-affected game, defeated Ireland in a bowl-out, and routed Wales in the one match played to a finish. Later that month, they hosted the third European Championship, contested by 12 nations in ideal conditions. The undisputed champions of Division One were Holland, who won all their five matches, with Robert van Oosterom scoring 110 against Scotland at Ayr. Scotland finished third, behind the England Board XI, with wins over Italy, Denmark and Ireland.

August saw the West Indians – minus Brian Lara – in action against Scotland at Uddingston, where they won a low-scoring game by 21 runs. The international programme ended with two two-day fixtures, a draw against MCC at Lord's and a victory over Ireland at Ayr, their first in this series in 12 years.

On the domestic front, the second year of the Scottish National Cricket League saw some tight tussles. Edinburgh club Grange became Premier League champions, but were only half a percentage point ahead of Heriot's FP, who beat them next day in the Scottish Cup final. Greenock were relegated to the first division after a 75-point penalty was imposed following allegations of making improper approaches to players at other clubs. They responded with a writ against the SNCL and Scottish Cricket Union but eventually dropped the action. Promotion and relegation between the second division and the feeder leagues was now in full swing, though Strathmore Union winners Inverurie relinquished their chance of promotion because of their geographical remoteness. Runners-up Dundee HSFP replaced them in the play-offs and lost, only to go up – along with Western Union champions Glasgow Academicals – when their opponents were ruled to have fielded an ineligible player.

In October, the Famous Grouse awards were held for the 13th and, apparently, last year. Grange and Heriot's shared the team award. Asim Butt of Heriot's was best bowler and Bruce Patterson of Ayr best batsman, West of Scotland's Douglas Wright best all-rounder (for the third time), and Colin Smith of Aberdeenshire best wicket-keeper. Ricky Bawa of Uddingston was named best Under-23 player, and a special award went to Bob McFarlane for his many years of service to Rossie Priory.

Encouragement for the future came when Timmergreens Primary School of Arbroath emerged from the 5,000 schools who entered the Wrigley UK Schools Kwik Cricket tournament to win the final in Nottingham in July.

After some ten years as general manager of the SCU, Alan Ritchie retired. His extensive knowledge of the game, as player and administrator, served Scotland well during a period of extensive expansion.

Winners of Scottish Leagues and Cups
Scottish National Cricket League: *Premier Division* – Grange; *First Division* – Watsonians; *Second Division* – Stirling County. **Scottish Cup:** Heriot's FP. **SCU Trophy:** Poloc. **Small Clubs' Cup:** Renfrew. **Border League:** Berwick. **East of Scotland League:** Pakistan Association. **Strathmore Union:** Inverurie. **Western Union:** Glasgow Academicals. **Regional Championship:** Strathmore Union. **North of Scotland League:** Buckie. **Perthshire League:** Rossie Priory. **West League Cup:** West of Scotland. **Rowan Cup:** Ayr.

SRI LANKA UNDER-19 IN ENGLAND, 2000

By GERALD HOWAT

Sri Lanka sent an Under-19 side to England after an interval of eight years. Like their predecessors, they came to the deciding Test with honours even. But unlike 1992, when England were the victors, these Sri Lankans won a close match to take the series 2–1. Of the players from that earlier visit, Russel Arnold, Naveed Nawaz, Jayantha Silva and Chaminda Vaas had gone on to play senior international cricket, and manager Anuruddha Polonowita expected a similar future for some of his side. He was impressed, but not surprised, by how far the team advanced.

Losing all three one-day internationals in the first seven days was a blow. But the first two defeats were by narrow margins, and any of the games could have gone the other way. What they exposed early on were weaknesses including running between the wickets, pushing for singles and judging the pace of the game. In the three-day matches before the Tests, the Sri Lankans showed themselves capable of large scores, making 379 against a Development of Excellence XI and 443 for five against ECB North Under-19.

Defeat by an innings in the First Test was a setback from which immediate lessons were learned; the tourists went on to win the Second Test handsomely. Coming back from such a heavy loss, and eventually winning the series, was no mean achievement for a side of schoolboys who, on paper, lacked the experience of their English counterparts, all of whom were under contract to counties. But schools cricket in Sri Lanka enjoys a higher profile than in England. There are two-day matches before large crowds with good press coverage. What was new to the Sri Lankans was the longer game, of three and four days. By mid-tour they had adapted, learning both to be patient and to concentrate.

Seven of the team could make runs, while the attack's strength lay in five spinners. Jehan Mubarak, a tall, elegant, left-handed strokeplayer, was their leading batsman, with 570 runs at 47.50; Muthumudalige Pushpakumara, the main all-rounder and another left-hander, provided 456 runs at 45.60, including a vital century in the Second Test, plus 20 wickets at 24.20 with his off-spin. The openers – wicket-keeper Nimesh Perera and the dashing Ian Daniel (534 at 33.37) – never really established a partnership, but hit hundreds in the minor matches. Thilina Kandambi supplemented three half-centuries with some useful leg-spin. The leading bowler was leg-spinner Kausbal Lokuarachchi, with 23 wickets at 9.78, and, when the seamers came into their own in the final Test, Akalanka Ganegama's ten wickets took his tour aggregate to 18 at 27.00 apiece. Kaushalya Weeraratne led his side well, almost secured victory in the second one-day international, and played two crucial innings in the Third Test.

England, despite their one-day triumphs, were understandably disappointed at losing the Test series. No one dominated as Marcus Trescothick and Andrew Flintoff had in earlier years, but there was obvious talent in Nicky Peng of Durham, who had already caught the eye with 98 against Surrey on first-class debut, and in Warwickshire's Ian Bell, an unbeaten caretaker-captain before he returned the reins to wicket-keeper Mark Wallace of Glamorgan. Wallace had broken a finger on the eve of the one-day series; he returned for the Second Test, but Bell was restored, less successfully, to the captaincy for the Third. Somerset's jaunty all-rounder, Peter Trego, made a particular impression until a side strain ruled him out after the First Test, and two other seamers, Justin Bishop of Essex and Tim Murtagh of Surrey, both performed consistently. Bishop's seven for 42 in the Third Test was the third-best return for England at this level.

SRI LANKA UNDER-19 TOURING PARTY

K. Weeraratne (*captain*), A. Bandaranayake, G. I. Daniel, D. G. R. Dhammika, K. M. Gajanayake, W. C. A. Ganeghama, S. H. T. Kandambi, K. S. Lokuarachchi, J. Mubarak, R. A. P. Nissanka, R. T. Peiris, M. Perera, N. Perera, M. Pushpakumara, T. Thushara.

Manager: A. Polonowita.   *Coach:* O. Mattau.

SRI LANKA UNDER-19 TOUR RESULTS

Matches – Played 13: Won 7, Lost 4, Drawn 2.

Note: Matches in this section were not first-class.

At Abergavenny, July 25. Sri Lanka Under-19 won by eight wickets. Toss: ECB Schools. ECB Schools 107 (42.1 overs) (J. Tredwell 40; K. S. Lokuarachchi three for 27); Sri Lanka Under-19 109 for two (23 overs) (K. M. Gajanayake 53 not out, S. H. T. Kandambi 39 not out).

At Abergavenny, July 26. Sri Lanka Under-19 won by 92 runs. Toss: ECB Schools. Sri Lanka Under-19 272 for five (50 overs) (K. S. Lokuarachchi 35, G. I. Daniel 83, M. Pushpakumara 67 not out, Extras 35); ECB Schools 180 for six (50 overs) (D. Fairbanks 33, J. G. E. Benning 38, J. Tredwell 38 not out).

At Cardiff, July 28. First one-day international: England Under-19 won by 15 runs. Toss: England Under-19. England Under-19 238 for six (42 overs) (N. Peng 89, I. R. Bell 62); Sri Lanka Under-19 223 (41 overs) (G. I. Daniel 43, S. H. T. Kandambi 50).

At Cardiff, July 29. Second one-day international: England Under-19 won by two runs. Toss: England Under-19. England Under-19 211 for seven (50 overs) (N. Peng 50, P. D. Trego 53 not out; M. Pushpakumara three for 34); Sri Lanka Under-19 209 (47.2 overs) (S. H. T. Kandambi 38, K. Weeraratne 58, Extras 30; P. D. Trego three for 41).

At Hove, July 31 (day/night). Third one-day international: England Under-19 won by three wickets. Toss: Sri Lanka Under-19. Sri Lanka Under-19 177 (43.5 overs) (M. Pushpakumara 48, K. Weeraratne 31; A. M. Davies three for 32, J. W. M. Dalrymple three for 32); England Under-19 178 for seven (48.5 overs) (N. Peng 43, I. R. Bell 52; K. S. Lokuarachchi four for 26).
England won the one-day series 3–0.

At Arundel, August 2, 3, 4. Drawn. Toss: ECB South Under-19. ECB South Under-19 344 (J. H. K. Adams 49, I. Pattison 54, T. J. Phillips 42, M. H. Yardy 59, Extras 33); Sri Lanka Under-19 234 for six (G. I. Daniel 31, J. Mubarak 104 not out, M. Pushpakumara 45; T. J. Phillips four for 75).

At Brighton College, August 5, 6, 7. Sri Lanka Under-19 won by an innings and 60 runs. Toss: Development of Excellence XI. Development of Excellence XI 140 (M. J. Powell 46) and 179 (M. J. Prior 44, D. Holt 31; M. Pushpakumara three for 49, K. Weeraratne three for 20); Sri Lanka Under-19 379 (N. Perera 100, M. Perera 59, J. Mubarak 75, K. M. Gajanayake 70; N. Weekes four for 64).

At Sleaford, August 9, 10, 11. Drawn. Toss: ECB North Under-19. ECB North Under-19 255 for eight dec. (B. M. Shafayat 32, J. Sayers 31, G. J. Muchall 66, G. Scott 38 not out; K. S. Lokuarachchi four for 42) and 239 for four (K. J. Locke 30, B. M. Shafayat 34, J. Sayers 45, G. J. Muchall 52 not out, A. Roberts 44 not out); Sri Lanka Under-19 443 for five dec. (G. I. Daniel 149, M. Perera 36, J. Mubarak 128 not out, M. Pushpakumara 31, K. M. Gajanayake 34 not out, Extras 38).
Daniel scored his 149 from 144 balls, with 22 fours and one five; Mubarak also struck 22 fours, in 161 balls.

At Oakham School, August 13. Sri Lanka Under-19 won by seven wickets (D/L method). Toss: England Board XI. England Board XI 217 for eight (50 overs) (C. Amos 39, P. R. J. Bryson 30, S. Chapman 50 not out); Sri Lanka Under-19 154 for three (30.2 overs) (G. I. Daniel 77 not out, K. Weeraratne 31 not out).

Sri Lanka's target was revised to 152 from 35 overs.

ENGLAND v SRI LANKA

First Under-19 Test

At Nottingham, August 15, 16, 17. England won by an innings and 22 runs. Toss: Sri Lanka Under-19.

Sri Lanka, on a wicket offering bounce and pace, batted attractively though scarcely prudently for a four-day match. Mubarak's half-century, which included 22 in five balls off Trego, summed up their general approach. Murtagh was the most consistent home bowler. Confident England then batted through five sessions to establish a winning platform. Pratt and Bell laid the foundations in a second-wicket partnership of 164; Kadeer Ali and Trego hammered home the advantage with 126 for the sixth wicket, Trego hitting a swashbuckling 90 in 112 balls. All were severe on wasteful Sri Lankan seam bowling, though leg-spinner Kandambi struck back with three for four in 17 deliveries. Despite being 206 behind, Sri Lanka batted in much the same way second time round and were all out on the third afternoon. Mubarak, with 44 in 45 balls, including ten fours, again set an example that was both good and bad. The Sri Lankan manager ordered an immediate net practice, only for it to be curtailed by a cloudburst.

Close of play: First day, England Under-19 5-1 (Pratt 0*); Second day, England Under-19 325-5 (Kadeer Ali 55*, Trego 56*).

Sri Lanka Under-19

†N. Perera c Gazzard b Murtagh	16	– c Peng b Kabir Ali	31
G. I. Daniel c Kadeer Ali b Panesar	43	– b Kabir Ali	4
M. Perera c Kabir Ali b Murtagh	18	– c Gazzard b Murtagh	16
S. H. T. Kandambi b Trego	11	– c Peng b Pattison	11
J. Mubarak lbw b Dalrymple	54	– c Bell b Panesar	44
K. M. Gajanayake c Pratt b Murtagh	40	– c Gazzard b Kabir Ali	14
M. Pushpakumara c Kadeer Ali b Pattison	11	– c Gazzard b Panesar	14
*K. Weeraratne c Peng b Pattison	11	– c Bell b Panesar	8
K. S. Lokuarachchi c Kadeer Ali b Panesar	1	– lbw b Kabir Ali	9
D. G. R. Dhammika not out	3	– lbw b Murtagh	9
R. A. P. Nissanka lbw b Murtagh	0	– not out	7
B 1, l-b 3, n-b 10	14	B 4, l-b 7, n-b 6	17

1/53 2/69 3/72 4/95 5/147   211   1/25 2/42 3/62 4/97 5/117   184
6/172 7/184 8/195 9/211   6/141 7/141 8/156 9/164

Bowling: First Innings—Kabir Ali 13–3–43–0; Trego 7–1–48–1; Murtagh 15–7–29–4; Pattison 9–1–32–2; Panesar 20–9–30–2; Dalrymple 10–3–25–1. *Second Innings*—Kabir Ali 14–4–49–4; Murtagh 9–2–46–2; Panesar 13–3–53–3; Dalrymple 4–1–8–0; Pattison 7–2–17–1.

England Under-19

G. J. Pratt c Daniel b Kandambi	75	†C. M. Gazzard b Dhammika	1
N. Peng c M. Perera b Weeraratne	0	T. J. Murtagh c Gajanayake	
*I. R. Bell c N. Perera b Kandambi	72	b Pushpakumara	16
Kadeer Ali c Daniel b Nissanka	59	M. S. Panesar not out	1
I. Pattison c N. Perera b Kandambi	3	B 4, l-b 23, w 7, n-b 8	42
J. W. M. Dalrymple c and b Kandambi	30		
P. D. Trego b Dhammika	90	1/5 2/169 3/170 4/174 5/230 417
Kabir Ali st N. Perera b Pushpakumara	28	6/356 7/391 8/397 9/414

Bowling: Nissanka 20–0–75–1; Weeraratne 17–2–76–1; Dhammika 29–8–61–2; Mubarak 4–0–7–0; Pushpakumara 18.2–5–39–2; Lokuarachchi 18–4–57–0; Kandambi 26–2–75–4.

Umpires: A. Clarkson and J. W. Lloyds.

ENGLAND v SRI LANKA

Second Under-19 Test

At Northampton, August 21, 22, 23, 24. Sri Lanka Under-19 won by 151 runs. Toss: England Under-19.

The match was well-balanced until the middle of the third day, when Pushpakumara cut loose with a century that allowed Sri Lanka's spin attack free rein. Wallace, back as England's captain, had put Sri Lanka in on a pitch expected to turn later. Although 30 overs were lost on the opening day, they achieved a useful 223 for five after a quick-scoring start from Perera and Daniel, and a stylish fourth-wicket 98 between Kandambi and Mubarak. England's reply produced a fine century by Peng, who hit two sixes and 18 fours, but Dhammika and his fellow-spinners made the greater impression. England gained a brief mastery by reducing Sri Lanka to 51 for five, a lead of 74, but Pushpakumara's onslaught snatched the game from them. When last out, he had scored 135 from 251 balls and left an unlikely target of 309. Four spinners on a turning pitch were too much for England. Though Wallace rallied them from 51 for six, the last wicket fell with 15 minutes remaining.

Close of play: First day, Sri Lanka Under-19 223-5 (Weeraratne 14*, Pushpakumara 23*); Second day, England Under-19 222-6 (Pattison 21*, Harrison 0*); Third day, Sri Lanka Under-19 268-8 (Pushpakumara 125*, Ganegama 6*).

Sri Lanka Under-19

†N. Perera c Bell b Murtagh	27	– c Bell b Pattison 33
G. I. Daniel c Bishop b Harrison	38	– c Panesar b Murtagh 0
K. M. Gajanayake c Peng b Bishop	1	– lbw b Harrison 4
S. H. T. Kandambi lbw b Bishop	58	– b Murtagh 1
J. Mubarak b Panesar	46	– lbw b Murtagh 0
*K. Weeraratne c Bell b Bishop	28	– b Bishop 10
M. Pushpakumara not out	42	– c Dalrymple b Harrison 135
K. S. Lokuarachchi lbw b Bishop	0	– b Panesar 63
D. G. R. Dhammika b Murtagh	8	– c Wallace b Panesar 0
W. C. A. Ganegama lbw b Murtagh	6	– b Harrison 13
R. A. P. Nissanka c Wallace b Harrison	9	– not out 0
B 6, l-b 9, w 4, n-b 4	23	B 17, l-b 8, n-b 1 26

1/51 2/52 3/79 4/177 5/177   **286**   1/10 2/19 3/26 4/26 5/51   **285**
6/240 7/240 8/260 9/272   6/74 7/203 8/229 9/282

Bowling: *First Innings*—Harrison 15–4–51–2; Murtagh 23–5–66–3; Bishop 24–9–71–4; Panesar 13–6–33–1; Dalrymple 12–7–25–0; Pattison 12–6–25–0. *Second Innings*—Harrison 20.3–5–55–3; Murtagh 16–5–36–3; Pattison 9–2–22–1; Bishop 9–0–39–1; Dalrymple 11–1–37–0; Panesar 23–6–71–2.

England Under-19

G. J. Pratt c Daniel b Ganegama	25	– c Mubarak b Dhammika 17
N. Peng c Gajanayake b Dhammika	123	– c Perera b Nissanka 4
I. R. Bell c Pushpakumara b Kandambi	31	– c Dhammika b Nissanka 0
Kadeer Ali c Perera b Kandambi	3	– c Perera b Lokuarachchi 12
I. Pattison c Mubarak b Pushpakumara	39	– c Pushpakumara b Kandambi 7
J. W. M. Dalrymple c Daniel b Dhammika . . .	1	– c Weeraratne b Kandambi 3
**†M. A. Wallace c Mubarak b Dhammika	1	– (8) c Mubarak b Pushpakumara . . . 47
D. S. Harrison c Perera b Dhammika	12	– (7) run out 28
J. E. Bishop b Pushpakumara	0	– (10) c Dhammika b Lokuarachchi . . 5
T. J. Murtagh c and b Dhammika	6	– (9) c Mubarak b Pushpakumara . . . 9
M. S. Panesar not out	0	– not out 0
B 7, l-b 1, n-b 10	18	B 14, l-b 1, w 1, n-b 9 . . . 25

1/64 2/140 3/164 4/199 5/220   **263**   1/7 2/7 3/28 4/37 5/42   **157**
6/222 7/239 8/246 9/263   6/51 7/134 8/142 9/157

Bowling: *First Innings*—Nissanka 5–0–41–0; Ganegama 6–0–29–1; Dhammika 37–14–59–5; Weeraratne 5–2–16–0; Lokuarachchi 14–5–34–0; Pushpakumara 12–2–36–2; Kandambi 18–6–40–2. *Second Innings*—Nissanka 8–4–15–2; Ganegama 6–1–12–0; Dhammika 24–12–29–1; Kandambi 19–7–37–2; Lokuarachchi 14–12–6–2; Pushpakumara 20–12–31–2; Weeraratne 3–0–12–0.

Umpires: J. H. Evans and R. A. White.

At Milton Keynes, August 26, 27. Sri Lanka Under-19 won by three wickets. Toss: England Under-18. England Under-18 154 for nine dec. (B. M. Shafayat 39; R. A. P. Nissanka three for 33, K. S. Lokuarachchi three for 31); Sri Lanka Under-19 155 for seven (S. H. T. Kandambi 68; K. Hogg three for 34).

The first day was completely lost to rain.

ENGLAND v SRI LANKA

Third Under-19 Test

At Worcester, August 29, 30, 31. Sri Lanka Under-19 won by two wickets. Toss: England Under-19.

Seam bowlers dictated a low-scoring match by exploiting the awkward bounce. England's batsmen set the pattern by collapsing to 25 for six before lunch on the first day, and needed Tremlett, on his debut, to get them past their lowest total, 71. Bishop, having ably assisted him, then reduced Sri Lanka to six for four when he bowled Perera, and came back to claim the tail and return England's third-best figures in Under-19 Tests. In between, however, the elegant Mubarak had put his side on course for a vital lead of 46. On the second afternoon, England were again dismissed cheaply, with Ganegama achieving match figures of ten for 87. Sri Lanka's target was only 109, but they collapsed to 26 for five; closing on 57 without further loss left the game tantalisingly poised. The excitement continued on the third morning as Bishop took the seventh and eighth wickets with five runs needed, but a boundary by Gajanayake in the same over saw Sri Lanka scramble home. A match that had started at 12.15 p.m. finished 48 hours later.

Close of play: First day, Sri Lanka Under-19 124-7 (Weeraratne 24*, Dhammika 0*); Second day, Sri Lanka Under-19 57-5 (Daniel 24*, Gajanayake 15*).

England Under-19

G. J. Pratt c Weeraratne b Nissanka	0	–	c Mubarak b Ganegama	21
N. Peng b Ganegama	8	–	(4) c Perera b Weeraratne	14
*I. R. Bell run out	7	–	c Perera b Ganegama	18
J. H. K. Adams c Perera b Ganegama	7	–	(2) c Mubarak b Ganegama	13
Kadeer Ali c Kandambi b Weeraratne	0	–	c Mubarak b Ganegama	1
†M. A. Wallace c Perera b Ganegama	0	–	c Perera b Lokuarachchi	12
D. S. Harrison c Gajanayake b Ganegama	16	–	lbw b Lokuarachchi	11
C. T. Tremlett not out	39	–	c Kandambi b Pushpakumara	10
T. J. Murtagh b Ganegama	0	–	c Perera b Weeraratne	32
J. E. Bishop c Perera b Ganegama	24	–	b Weeraratne	4
M. S. Panesar b Lokuarachchi	6	–	not out	0
L-b 3, w 1, n-b 1	5		B 2, l-b 5, w 4, n-b 7	18

1/9 2/9 3/19 4/20 5/25	112	1/29 2/40 3/73 4/75 5/75
6/25 7/46 8/46 9/89		6/103 7/104 8/142 9/151

154

Bowling: *First Innings*—Nissanka 10–5–15–1; Ganegama 18–4–43–6; Weeraratne 7–1–25–1; Pushpakumara 4–1–7–0; Lokuarachchi 8–2–15–2; Dhammika 2–0–13–0. *Second Innings*—Nissanka 8–3–22–0; Ganegama 20–6–44–4; Weeraratne 17.1–3–51–3; Mubarak 3–1–6–0; Daniels 4–4–0–0; Lokuarachchi 8–2–15–2; Pushpakumara 5–2–9–1.

Sri Lanka Under-19

	First Innings			Second Innings	
†N. Perera b Bishop	0	– c Harrison b Murtagh	0
G. I. Daniel lbw b Bishop	4	– b Murtagh	29
K. S. Lokuarachchi c Adams b Bishop	0	– run out	1
S. H. T. Kandambi lbw b Murtagh	1	– c Bell b Tremlett	4
J. Mubarak c Pratt b Tremlett	49	– lbw b Murtagh	4
M. Pushpakumara c Wallace b Harrison	22	– c Wallace b Tremlett	0
K. M. Gajanayake lbw b Bishop	6	– not out	36
*K. Weeraratne b Bishop	24	– c Wallace b Bishop	19
D. G. R. Dhammika c Harrison b Bishop	13	– c Peng b Bishop	0
W. C. A. Ganegama b Bishop	15	– not out	1
R. A. P. Nissanka not out	0		
B 6, l-b 7, w 7, n-b 4	24	B 4, l-b 6, w 5	15
	158	(8 wkts)	**109**

1/5 2/5 3/6 4/6 5/57 6/83 7/110 8/124 9/150   158

1/0 2/7 3/20 4/25 5/26 6/67 7/104 8/104   (8 wkts) 109

Bowling: *First Innings*—Murtagh 14–3–52–1; Bishop 15.3–4–42–7; Harrison 11–4–22–1; Tremlett 7–1–22–1; Panesar 2–0–7–0. *Second Innings*—Murtagh 13–4–32–3; Bishop 8.5–2–26–2; Tremlett 11–3–26–2; Harrison 6–3–9–0; Panesar 2–0–6–0.

Umpires: N. G. Cowley and J. W. Holder.

YOUNG CRICKETER OF THE YEAR

(Elected by the Cricket Writers' Club)

1950	R. Tattersall	1976	G. Miller
1951	P. B. H. May	1977	I. T. Botham
1952	F. S. Trueman	1978	D. I. Gower
1953	M. C. Cowdrey	1979	P. W. G. Parker
1954	P. J. Loader	1980	G. R. Dilley
1955	K. F. Barrington	1981	M. W. Gatting
1956	B. Taylor	1982	N. G. Cowans
1957	M. J. Stewart	1983	N. A. Foster
1958	A. C. D. Ingleby-Mackenzie	1984	R. J. Bailey
1959	G. Pullar	1985	D. V. Lawrence
1960	D. A. Allen	1986	{ A. A. Metcalfe / J. J. Whitaker }
1961	P. H. Parfitt		
1962	P. J. Sharpe	1987	R. J. Blakey
1963	G. Boycott	1988	M. P. Maynard
1964	J. M. Brearley	1989	N. Hussain
1965	A. P. E. Knott	1990	M. A. Atherton
1966	D. L. Underwood	1991	M. R. Ramprakash
1967	A. W. Greig	1992	I. D. K. Salisbury
1968	R. M. H. Cottam	1993	M. N. Lathwell
1969	A. Ward	1994	J. P. Crawley
1970	C. M. Old	1995	A. Symonds
1971	J. Whitehouse	1996	C. E. W. Silverwood
1972	D. R. Owen-Thomas	1997	B. C. Hollioake
1973	M. Hendrick	1998	A. Flintoff
1974	P. H. Edmonds	1999	A. J. Tudor
1975	A. Kennedy	2000	P. J. Franks

An additional award, in memory of Norman Preston, Editor of *Wisden* from 1951 to 1980, was made to C. W. J. Athey in 1980.

UNDER-15 WORLD CHALLENGE, 2000

By GERALD HOWAT

The second Under-15 World Challenge, sponsored by supermarket company Costcutter, saw West Indies and Pakistan contest the final at Lord's, though in less dramatic circumstances than surrounded Pakistan's final against India in 1996. There were no pitch invasions – the authorities were prepared for any eventuality, none the less – and a much smaller crowd. While Pakistan's supporters again turned out *en masse*, there were few to cheer West Indies to their eventual victory.

Eight countries took part, with Canada and Australia not reappearing from the ten participants of four years earlier. The Australians, who had won only one match then, felt that their structure did not lend itself to national representation at this level. (The qualifying date meant players could be within three weeks of their 16th birthday.) This is something on which even the host country has divided opinions. While the substantial efforts of the English Schools' Cricket Association are widely recognised, and England Under-15 cricketers emerge from competitions such as the annual Bunbury Festival, not everyone supports international cricket for the age group. There are great disparities in height, weight and maturity, and, although this can sometimes be balanced by displays of considerable skill, the ability to make judgments, whether in captaincy, batting or bowling, is often less certain.

The Challenge was launched at Lord's on July 29 with lunch, music and a dance display. The cricket began in earnest next day, with league rounds at Eton and Wellington Colleges. Holland, without a win in 1996, chose to bat at Agar's Plough, Eton's Second XI ground, and slumped to seven for five against West Indies, who went on to win by nine wickets. The match was over well before lunch. England set out their stall at Upper Club, the First XI pitch, with an 81-run victory over defending champions India, coached by the former Test all-rounder, Roger Binny, and a day later beat the future champions, West Indies, by six wickets. Off-spinners Dan Broadbent and James Beaumont took command in both games and English hopes were high as they advanced to win Group A. West Indies joined them in the semi-finals by virtue of a superior run-rate to India, with whom they tied after chasing a Duckworth/Lewis target following rain. At Wellington, meanwhile, South Africa, a side of multiracial composition, claimed Group B with victories over Pakistan and Zimbabwe. Pakistan progressed as a result of beating Sri Lanka.

The semi-finals pitted group winners against the runners-up, and England travelled to the county ground at Chelmsford as favourites to beat Pakistan. When it came to the big occasion, however, they played well below form. Broadbent conceded only 17 runs in his ten overs, Beaumont claimed two wickets, and Nic Swetman closed Pakistan's innings with three wickets in four balls. But 19 wides, several dropped catches, two missed stumpings and wasted run-out chances told another story. So did the three run-outs as England stuttered to 132 and defeat. Only Samit Patel, with 48 to accompany his earlier dismissal of the attacking Zulqarnain Haider, took the game to the opposition.

Rain delayed the start of the second semi-final, at Hove, and after three hours of play in sweltering heat the match was interrupted by a thunderstorm of monsoon proportions, with South Africa 191 for five from 42.5 overs. This owed much to a fourth-wicket partnership of 105 between the left-handed Divan van Wyk and Vaughan van Jaarsveld against a West Indian attack in which opening bowler Ravi Rampaul impressed. Next day, as West Indies chased a stiff target of 226, 14-year-old Aaron Ragoonath hit a splendid 93 not out in 130 balls to lead his side to Lord's. With the scores level, the South African captain, Mandilakhe Dipha, dislocated his shoulder in bowling the last delivery and was no-balled for over-stepping as he collapsed to the ground. Ragoonath struck the ball to the boundary for good measure, and Dipha remained immobilised beside the pitch until an ambulance came to the edge of the square to collect him.

The final was all the promoters could have wished for. The sun shone, a military band played, and Sky TV provided live coverage. Pakistan's total, after being put in, was built around a fifth-wicket partnership of 63 between Shahid Yousuf and Zulqarnain, but wickets then fell with frequency before a last-wicket stand of 26 took Pakistan to 175. It assumed even more significance when West Indies were 133 for five and the pitch was encouraging the Pakistani spinners, among them opening batsman Mohammad Naeem, who bowled slow left-arm to right-handers and right-arm off-spin to left-handers. When Guyana's Assad Fudadin was sixth out at 145 for a solid 55, West Indies still had some way to go, but runs were scampered and there were overs in hand when their ninth-wicket pair secured victory and the trophy.

The West Indian coach, former Test batsman Gus Logie, praised his players' rapid improvement during their two weeks in England. "They exceeded all my expectations way and above their experience. I would have been satisfied if they had won or lost." He believed that tournaments like this, taking place every two years instead of four, "would give the impetus to develop cricket at grassroots level" in the West Indies.

David English, who along with ESCA's Ken Lake was the driving force behind the whole enterprise, spoke of Philadelphia as a possible venue for the next tournament. More realistically, South Africa was mooted, with the competition centred on Cape Town, while sponsors Costcutter promised to underwrite it again if it were held in England. Whatever the venue, however, all associated with the Under-15 Challenge were united in their opinion that it had come to stay.

GROUP TABLES

Group A	Played	Won	Lost	No result	Points	Net run-rate
England........	3	3	0	0	6	0.87
West Indies.....	3	1	1	1	3	1.08
India..........	3	1	1	1	3	0.40
Holland........	3	0	3	0	0	−2.41

West Indies qualified for the semi-finals on net run-rate, having shared the points in their head-to-head match with India. Net run-rate is calculated by subtracting runs conceded per over from runs scored per over.

Group B	Played	Won	Lost	No result	Points	Net run-rate
South Africa.....	3	2	0	1	5	1.16
Pakistan........	3	1	1	1	3	−0.05
Sri Lanka.......	3	1	1	1	3	1.55
Zimbabwe	3	0	2	1	1	−2.80

Pakistan qualified for the semi-finals, having beaten Sri Lanka in their head-to-head match.

SEMI-FINALS

At Chelmsford, August 5. Pakistan won by 58 runs. Toss: Pakistan. Pakistan 190 (49.4 overs) (Shahid Yousuf 42, Zulqarnain Haider 41, Extras 36; N. T. Swetman four for 39); England 132 (44.4 overs) (S. Patel 48).

At Hove, August 8, 9. West Indies won by two wickets. Toss: South Africa. South Africa 225 for seven (50 overs) (D. van Wyk 85, V. van Jaarsveld 55; T. Maraj three for 21); West Indies 230 for eight (49.5 overs) (A. Ragoonath 93 not out).

FINAL

PAKISTAN v WEST INDIES

At Lord's, August 10. West Indies won by two wickets. Toss: West Indies.
Man of the Match: A. Fudadin.

Pakistan

Mohammad Naeem b Santokie	7	Talal Zia c Fudadin b Rampaul	19
Masood Asim b Liburd	6	Umair Rao lbw b Maraj	0
Subtain Raza c Maraj b Santokie	13	Shahryar Khan not out	8
Shahid Yousuf b Punoo	46		
*†Kashif Mahmood b Punoo	5	L-b 6, w 15, n-b 1	22
Zulqarnain Haider b Maraj	48		
Adnan Raza st Ramdin b Marshall	0	1/15 2/39 3/51 4/69 5/132 (49.3 overs) 175
Azhar Ali c and b Marshall	1	6/133 7/141 8/149 9/149

Bowling: Rampaul 9.3–0–41–1; Santokie 8–0–34–2; Liburd 7–0–20–1; Punoo 10–0–32–2; Marshall 9–1–27–2; Maraj 6–1–15–2.

West Indies

R. Rampaul b Shahryar Khan	24	†D. Ramdin c Subtain Raza	
X. Marshall lbw b Umair Rao	0	b Shahid Yousuf	12
L. Simmons c Zulqarnain Haider		K. Santokie not out	13
b Subtain Raza	24	S. Liburd not out	2
A. Fudadin c Kashif Mahmood			
b Shahid Yousuf	55	B 5, l-b 7, w 12, n-b 1	25
A. Ragoonath c Subtain Raza			
b Azhar Ali	10	1/3 2/37 3/100 (8 wkts, 46.1 overs) 176
H. Powell b Shahid Yousuf	1	4/121 5/133 6/145
*T. Maraj run out	10	7/155 8/170

H. Punoo did not bat.

Bowling: Shahryar Khan 7–2–24–1; Umair Rao 5–0–26–1; Mohammad Naeem 7–0–34–0; Talal Zia 2–1–8–0; Subtain Raza 10–3–24–1; Azhar Ali 9.1–1–32–1; Shahid Yousuf 6–1–16–3.

Umpires: N. A. Mallender and K. E. Palmer.

ENGLAND SQUAD

T. I. New (Quarrydale School/Nottinghamshire) (*captain*), J. Beaumont (Ian Ramsey CES/ Cleveland), T. T. Bresnan (Hemsworth HS/Yorkshire), D. L. Broadbent (Ryedale School/ Yorkshire), J. A. Chervak (Ashville College/Yorkshire), A. N. Cook (Bedford School/Essex), C. M. Goode (Huxlow School/Northamptonshire), A. J. Harrison (West Monmouth School/Glamorgan), J. C. Hildreth (Millfield/Somerset), A. W. Parkin-Coates (Worksop College/Yorkshire), S. Patel (Worksop College/Nottinghamshire), T. M. Rees (Canon Slade CES/Lancashire), D. A. Stiff (Batley GS/ Yorkshire), N. T. Swetman (Westbourne College/Glamorgan).
Coach: P. Farbrace.

TEST MATCH SPECIAL UNDER-15 YOUNG CRICKETER OF THE YEAR

Samit Patel of Worksop College, Nottinghamshire, won the inaugural BBC *Test Match Special* Under-15 Young Cricketer of the Year Award. He scored 159 runs and took seven wickets with his left-arm spin in four games for England in the Under-15 World Challenge in August. The award was given to him by a panel of judges consisting of Paul Farbrace (England Under-15 coach), John Weitzel (England Under-15 manager), Hugh Morris (ECB technical director) and Ken Lake (general secretary of the England Schools Cricket Association).

SCHOOLS CRICKET IN 2000

For most schools, this was a trying season. Coaching staff could partly blame the atrocious weather, though they also faced mounting difficulties motivating players wrestling with the rigours of the academic timetable. Rain cancelled or curtailed play the length and breadth of the land: Malvern abandoned eight of their 23 fixtures, one more than in 1999. The theoretically drier south-east appeared particularly hard hit, with three Kentish schools having an appalling time of it: like Malvern, The Harvey GS called off eight games, Simon Langton GS described their season as "totally disrupted", while Sir Roger Manwood's played just two matches in dry conditions. Similar reports came from Haberdashers' Aske's and Christ's, Finchley. Amid all this Home Counties dampness, however, Merchiston Castle in Edinburgh reported perhaps the driest May and June for 15 years. Schools from the north-west also seemed largely unconcerned by the weather.

The pressure of examinations stripped many teams of their most experienced players, limited opportunities for travel to midweek games and disrupted practice, claimed Elizabeth College. Even when senior students were available, coaches reported periods of play when "minds were not sufficiently focused on the game" (Bancroft's) or that "lapses in concentration were a problem throughout" (QEGS, Wakefield). And there were misgivings about a new exam for lower-sixth students in 2001, which, it was felt, would do little to help. These difficulties, however, did allow many young players an opportunity to make their mark, and King Edward VII and Queen Mary, Lytham, and Tiffin both noted the progress of talented 13-year-olds.

The damp conditions were not ideal for strokeplay, and only two batsmen passed 1,000 runs, six fewer than in 1999. One was Gordon Muchall of Durham, who did so for the second year in succession, managing 1,003 runs from 11 innings at 167.16, the country's highest average. The most prolific, though, was Christopher Warde of Dauntsey's, who gathered 1,352 at 75.11, having batted 21 times. These two were well clear of the field, which was headed by Brendan McKerchar of Merchiston Castle with 871 – his 41 wickets at 13.95 made him the leading all-rounder. Then came Ben Graham of Bradford GS, with 820, and Brighton's Matthew Prior, with 801.

Muchall, who made five centuries, hit the summer's only double-hundred, 204 not out against St Peter's, York. Among batsmen who passed 500 runs, four others recorded three-figure averages: Jean-Paul Duminy of Wrekin with 150.50, Robert Ferley of Sutton Valence (126.50), Clifton's Nick Willis-Stovold (114.66) and Matthew Bennett of Cranbrook (100.66). South Craven's Chris Meehan hit three unbeaten hundreds from seven innings.

Plenty to smile about: Christopher Warde of Dauntsey's (*left*) was the season's leading batsman with 1,352 runs, Brendan McKerchar of Merchiston Castle the most successful all-rounder with 871 runs and 41 wickets.

Pranay Sanklecha of Brighton College bowled 256 overs, more than anyone else, and, with 45, was the joint-leading wicket-taker with Owen Burwell of Stamford, whose average was a mere 7.33. Others to reach 40 wickets were Neil Bezodis of Reigate GS (42 at 12.35), Tim Denyer of Royal GS, Worcester, John Reynolds of Wellington School, and McKerchar (41 each), and Nick Murrills of Manchester GS (40). No one took nine wickets in an innings, the best return coming from Norwich's George Walker, who captured eight for eight against Colford. William Bates of Queen's, Taunton, dismissed 37 batsmen at 8.75 each, including seven for four against Wycliffe College. Four bowlers did the hat-trick, including Westminster's Pierre Bell, who went one better and claimed four in four.

Leading all-rounders – McKerchar aside – were Sanklecha, who complemented his 45 wickets with 631 runs, the Oundle pair of Martin Dobson (677 runs and 32 wickets) and Jonathan Outar (583 and 30), and Trevor Smith of St Peter's, York (570 and 33).

Of the six unbeaten schools, Royal GS, Worcester, had by far the best record, winning 18 of their 22 fixtures, the sixth-best season reported in *Wisden* since 1980. The others were Bedford Modern, Durham, Plymouth, St Paul's and, for a fourth consecutive year, Radley College. King's, Taunton, won 12 of their 13 matches, losing only to Millfield. The absence of draws hints at the move in schools cricket towards limited-overs games; almost all of Taunton's home games are 50-over matches.

The fact that 33 schools could not find a single bowler with 15 wickets (the threshold for qualification) – and a further 30 could offer just one – was not entirely the fault of the weather. Several thought 15 wickets too high, given that the ECB limits quicker bowlers to eight-over spells; others blamed the trend towards starting games after lunch.

The five British schools who took part in the 14th Sir Garfield Sobers Schools Cricket Festival, held in Barbados in July, were Alleyn's, Dauntsey's, Pangbourne, St George's, Weybridge, and Wallington HS. As in 1999, Grenada Schools won the competition.

Details of records broken, other outstanding performances and interesting features of the season may be found in the returns of the schools that follow.

ECB SCHOOLS EAST v ECB SCHOOLS WEST

At RAF Vine Lane, Uxbridge, July 11, 12. ECB Schools East won by 32 runs. Toss: ECB Schools East.

Sterling work by groundsman Doug New allowed a prompt start to the second day after torrential rain had washed out the first. With half the match lost, it was agreed to adopt a 55-overs-a-side format. The East chose to bat on a good pitch, but soon lost both openers to Morris. Unfazed, Prior and Clarke rebuilt the innings, taking the score from 24 to 74. Then Benning, who made an unbeaten 75, shared fifty partnerships with Andrews and Wyld, and guided the East to 229. In reply, the West never quite hit their stride: they preserved their wickets, yet could not break free from some tight spin bowling. Watson hit 46 from 73 balls, but neither Thompson nor Evans could increase the tempo when they were falling behind the asking-rate. Benning added to his impressive batting display with an economical spell of six overs, including three successive maidens. The West eventually lost by 32 runs – the margin of their 1999 victory.

ECB Schools East

P. S. Coverdale (*Wellingborough School*) c Mumford b Morris .	8	
M. R. Calnan (*St Olave's Grammar School, Orpington*) b Morris .	12	
*M. J. Prior (*Brighton College*) c Watson b Ades .	30	
B. T. Clarke (*Ratcliffe College*) c Nair b Murrills .	29	
J. G. E. Benning (*Caterham School*) not out .	75	

S. J. Andrews (*Radley College*) c Smart b Evans .	15
R. M. Wyld (*Colonel Frank Seely School, Calverton*) c Fairbanks b Ades .	35
†D. Rock (*Orwell High School*) not out	3
B 4, l-b 4, w 10, n-b 4	22
1/14 2/24 3/74 (6 wkts, 55 overs) 229	
4/93 5/146 6/223	

K. Dudhareja (*Soar Valley Community College*), G. G. Read (*Midhurst Grammar School*) and N. Weekes (*Collyer's*) did not bat.

Bowling: Morris 8–2–45–2; Smart 9–2–28–0; Ades 14–1–57–2; Evans 9–1–19–1; Murrills 6–1–40–1; Nair 9–0–32–0.

ECB Schools West

*K. Watson (King Edward's School, Bath)
  c Coverdale b Dudharejia . 46
D. Fairbanks (Clough Hall Technology
  College) c Andrews b Read . 16
P. Thompson (Oldbury Wells School)
  not out . 66
S. Nair (Millfield School) st Rock
  b Coverdale . 16

P. J. Evans (Lord Williams's School)
  run out . 26
†G. J. Mumford (Bridgnorth Endowed
  School) not out . 0
  B 5, l-b 2, w 19, n-b 1 27

1/44 2/93   (4 wkts, 55 overs) 197
3/148 4/197

S. R. Ades (Brighton and Hove Sixth Form College), N. P. Murrills (Manchester Grammar School),
S. L. Smart (Stowe School), G. E. Morris (Millfield School) and N. C. Willis-Stovold (Clifton
College) did not bat.

Bowling: Weekes 9–1–36–0; Read 11–0–38–1; Wyld 7–2–15–0; Dudharejia 15–0–68–1;
Benning 6–3–6–0; Coverdale 7–0–27–1.

Umpires: G. J. Bullock and K. Coburn.

ETON v HARROW

At Lord's, May 25. Harrow won by 19 runs. Toss: Eton.

Harrow won the traditional fixture for the first time since 1975, when it was still played over
two days. This was its first year as a simple limited-overs match, to circumvent over-cautious
declarations; the change had been thwarted by a washout the previous season. Another wet morning
delayed the start until 2 p.m. and reduced each innings from 55 to 40 overs. Nick Compton, whose
grandfather Denis had made the first of his many appearances at Lord's 70 years earlier, was soon
at the crease. He added 68 in 18 overs with Dunbar, who hit six fours and a six, before both fell
to Aubrey-Fletcher's spin. Eton seemed well on course for victory when their captain, Ferreira,
steered them to 98 for two. But Compton and Willetts snatched three wickets for no runs in seven
balls, triggering a fatal collapse of eight for 26 in six overs.

Harrow

T. G. Dunbar c Ferreira
  b Aubrey-Fletcher . 46
K. Motaung c Ferreira b Williams 0
N. R. D. Compton b Aubrey-Fletcher . . 20
M. J. S. Willetts c and b McCall 0
*†L. F. de Rougemont b Aubrey-Fletcher 16
W. M. F. Scott lbw b Dalrymple 6

S. R. L. Maydon b Dalrymple 8
C. J. M. Cooke-Hurle not out 4
S. W. MacDonald not out 9
  B 1, l-b 19, w 12, n-b 2 34

1/2 2/70 3/76 4/87   (7 wkts, 40 overs) 143
5/110 6/122 7/124

J. M. Kostoris and J. G. B. Dick-Cleland did not bat.

Bowling: Collins 8–1–17–0; Williams 6–1–30–1; McCall 8–1–25–1; Dalrymple 7–0–23–2;
Aubrey-Fletcher 8–2–19–3; Lowe 3–0–9–0.

Eton

T. H. McL. Hawk run out 21
A. M. Goldberg st de Rougemont
  b Kostoris . 13
*†D. C. Ferreira lbw b Willetts 38
T. P. McCall c de Rougemont
  b Compton . 1
M. Lowe not out 17
E. C. J. Fielding b Willetts 0
A. P. Kindersley c Kostoris b Compton . 4
A. N. Dalrymple run out 1

E. D. Williams run out 4
H. B. Aubrey-Fletcher c Maydon
  b Cooke-Hurle . 0
S. W. F. Collins c de Rougemont
  b Cooke-Hurle . 0
  B 4, l-b 8, w 8, n-b 5 25

1/40 2/74 3/98   (36.4 overs) 124
4/98 5/98 6/106
7/107 8/119 9/124

Bowling: Cooke-Hurle 6.4–0–22–2; Dick-Cleland 6–1–32–0; Willetts 8–1–18–2; Kostoris
8–2–10–1; Compton 8–2–30–2.

Umpires: I. Dunbar Sutherland and N. M. Freeman.

Schools Cricket in 2000

Of the 163 matches played between the two schools since 1805, Eton have won 52, Harrow 45 and 66 have been drawn. Matches during the two world wars are excluded from the reckoning. The fixture was reduced from a two-day, two-innings-a-side match to one day in 1982, and became a limited-overs fixture from 1999. Forty-nine centuries have been scored, the highest being 183 by D. C. Boles of Eton in 1904; M. C. Bird of Harrow is the only batsman to have made two hundreds in a match, in 1907. The highest score since the First World War is 161 not out by M. K. Fosh of Harrow in 1975, Harrow's last victory before 2000. Since then Eton have won in 1977, 1985, 1990 and 1991, Harrow in 2000, the 1997 and 1999 matches were abandoned and all other games have been drawn. A full list of centuries since 1918 and results from 1950 can be found in Wisdens prior to 1994.

REPORTS AND AVERAGES

(Qualification: Batting 150 runs; Bowling 15 wickets)

* *On name indicates captain.*   * *On figures indicates not out.*

Note: The line for batting reads Innings–Not Outs–Runs–Highest Score–100s–Average; that for bowling reads Overs–Maidens–Runs–Wickets–Best Bowling–Average.

ABINGDON SCHOOL   *Played 15: W 3, L 8, D 4. A 2*

Master i/c: J. R. W. Beasley

Batting—*S. C. T. Dexter 12–2–283–62–0–28.30; T. W. S. Bracher 12–1–265–79–0–24.09; E. J. M. Webber 11–1–233–69–0–23.30; M. T. Armitage 12–0–159–59–0–13.25.

Bowling—S. C. T. Dexter 121–21–400–22–5/21–18.18; B. J. L. Garner 120.2–35–359–17–3/21–21.11; A. W. Hunter 158.1–25–586–16–4/69–36.62.

ALDENHAM SCHOOL   *Played 10: W 4, L 5, D 1. A 2*

Master i/c: A. P. Stephenson

Batting—M. S. Tennant 8–1–184–66–0–26.28.

Bowling—R. L. Brant 78.3–15–201–15–5/16–13.40.

ALLEYN'S SCHOOL   *Played 17: W 9, L 3, D 5. A 1*

Master i/c: R. Ody   Professional: P. H. Edwards

Batting—D. Ellis 16–2–630–103–1–45.00; N. Dasandi 17–3–546–96–0–39.00; T. Arul-Pragasam 8–2–204–56–0–34.00; E. Postma 13–2–194–45–0–17.63.

Bowling—T. Hunt 126–25–362–22–5/29–16.45; N. Dasandi 138–36–386–22–4/9–17.54; E. Postma 102–23–381–21–3/25–18.14; P. Baker 80–10–308–15–4/10–20.53.

AMPLEFORTH COLLEGE   *Played 12: W 2, L 2, D 8. A 4*

Master i/c: G. D. Thurman   Professional: D. Wilson

Batting—P. Gretton 12–1–395–85–0–35.90; B. Fitzherbert 12–2–274–78–0–27.40; S. Phillips 12–2–274–73–0–27.40; J. Tussaud 10–0–246–67–0–24.60; *D. Ansell 12–2–243–63–0–24.30.

Bowling—J. Tussaud 162–30–546–22–5/63–24.81.

ARDINGLY COLLEGE *Played 12: W 7, L 5, D 0. A 2*

Master i/c: G. W. Hart   Professional: D. Frame

Nick Patterson, grandson of former West Indies captain Denis Atkinson, bowled at a fearsome pace and hit a hundred against MCC.

Batting—A. J. Virgo 12–2–367–90–0–36.70; N. W. B. Patterson 12–0–370–132–1–30.83; S. J. Kingcome 10–1–244–101*–1–27.11; D. E. Brooker 13–1–287–66–0–23.91; A. J. Beer 13–0–248–87–0–19.07.

Bowling—N. W. B. Patterson 137.4–29–283–29–5/12–9.75; S. J. Kingcome 67–13–169–15–3/15–11.26; A. J. Beer 123.5–30–355–25–5/28–14.20.

ARNOLD SCHOOL *Played 8: W 1, L 6, D 1. A 6*

Master i/c: A. Crowther

Batting—No batsman scored 150 runs. The leading batsman was J. Webb 6–0–142–88–0–23.66.

Bowling—No bowler took 15 wickets. The leading bowler was D. Atkinson 23.3–5–67–10–3/10–6.70.

BABLAKE SCHOOL *Played 8: W 2, L 4, D 2. A 4*

Master i/c: R. E. Jones   Professional: M. Bell

Batting—*P. Jones 7–4–151–37–0–50.33; I. Cure 8–2–152–46–0–25.33.

Bowling—P. Jones 67.2–11–229–15–4/12–15.26.

BANCROFT'S SCHOOL *Played 17: W 2, L 5, D 10. A 2*

Master i/c: J. K. Lever

An ostensibly strong side had a disappointing season, with the bowlers' lack of penetration and consistency undermining several sound batting displays. The captain, Duncan O'Leary, led by example, but could not inspire all his team-mates. Joseph Johnson proved a strong wicket-keeper/batsman and Michael Levis a useful all-rounder. Off-spinner Mark Mariathas was the pick of the attack.

Batting—*D. C. O'Leary 15–0–415–72–0–27.66; C. F. Leech 13–0–251–85–0–19.30; J. Johnson 15–2–250–42–0–19.23; J. Rolfe 15–4–206–43–0–18.72; M. Levis 14–0–247–71–0–17.64; S. Gevertz 15–0–256–52–0–17.06.

Bowling—M. N. Mariathas 94.5–7–423–26–5/47–16.26; M. Levis 79–8–303–15–3/28–20.20; J. Pittal 110–15–456–21–6/36–21.71.

BANGOR GRAMMAR SCHOOL *Played 25: W 11, L 8, D 6. A 2*

Master i/c: D. J. Napier   Professional: C. C. J. Harte

After a shaky start, an experienced but young side had improved enough by late August to defeat Foyle in the final of the McCullough Cup. Two all-rounders, captain Ryan Bell and Paul McKenzie, represented Ireland Under-17.

Batting—*R. M. Bell 15–4–300–48–0–27.27; P. D. McKenzie 20–5–398–79*–0–26.53; C. J. R. Kane 19–2–350–74*–0–20.58; J. E. McClaughlin 20–0–339–102–1–16.95; M. D. Montgomery 22–3–279–80*–0–14.68; A. J. Ritchie 16–1–177–44–0–11.80.

Bowling—T. E. Macauley 98.2–12–310–29–4/13–10.68; R. M. Bell 147–28–419–32–6/11–13.09; A. W. Gowdy 175.3–41–520–35–4/5–14.85; A. G. Andrews 98.3–12–374–24–5/14–15.58; C. S. Scott 79–11–245–15–3/14–16.33; P. D. McKenzie 143–26–405–24–3/8–16.87.

BARNARD CASTLE SCHOOL   *Played 9: W 2, L 6, D 1. A 1*

Master i/c: B. C. Usher

Batting—T. Foster 3–0–162–75–0–54.00; R. Wood 7–1–197–62*–0–32.83; P. Clarke 8–0–185–60–0–23.12; J. Wren 9–0–205–74–0–22.77.

Bowling—D. Warnock-Smith 78–17–194–17–5/19–11.41; E. Williamson 102–19–329–15–3/39–21.93; S. McLennan 98–13–363–16–4/37–22.68.

BEDFORD SCHOOL   *Played 17: W 9, L 5, D 3. A 2*

Master i/c: J. J. Farrell   Professional: R. T. Bates

Adrian Shankar led the team to good wins over Rugby, Haileybury and the XL Club, before playing for Middlesex Second Eleven and Bedfordshire. Other representative honours came to Alastair Cook, selected for the England Under-15 World Cup campaign, and to William Smith, who appeared for England Under-17 and Nottinghamshire Second Eleven.

Batting—J. Stedman 18–3–696–95–0–46.40; W. Smith 16–2–620–156–1–44.28; A. N. Cook 12–3–311–89–0–34.55; E. O'Callaghan 15–6–243–63–0–27.00; R. Wycherly 14–6–214–42–0–26.75; *A. Shankar 12–2–286–61–0–19.06.

Bowling—A. Shankar 79.2–14–248–20–5/30–12.40; J. Stedman 184–45–474–28–6/21–16.92; P. Heady 130.1–25–366–17–3/2–21.52; R. Ward 104–14–362–15–3/35–24.13; W. Smith 185–35–567–23–3/40–24.65.

BEDFORD MODERN SCHOOL   *Played 12: W 7, L 0, D 5. A 6*

Master i/c: N. J. Chinneck

The only games lost by Bedford Modern were to the weather – in all, a third of their fixtures fell victim. Nitin Parsooth headed the batting averages and took most wickets, including eight for 60 against Berkhamsted, while left-arm spinner Monty Panesar went on to play for Northamptonshire Second Eleven and England Under-19.

Batting—N. Parsooth 10–4–217–58*–0–36.16; O. Chinneck 11–2–277–53–0–30.77; D. Myers 9–1–210–56–0–26.25; J. Clulow 11–2–182–46*–0–20.22; R. King 12–0–206–41–0–17.16; A. Griffin 11–0–165–43–0–15.00.

Bowling—M. S. Panesar 89–21–215–20–7/50–10.75; N. Parsooth 173–34–484–37–8/60–13.08; N. Lockwood 130–25–362–24–6/37–15.08.

BERKHAMSTED COLLEGIATE SCHOOL   *Played 14: W 5, L 4, D 5. A 3*

Master i/c: J. G. Tolchard   Professional: M. R. Herring

A tour of Barbados in April provided good preparation for the season, and five victories were scored by mid-term. However, injuries to key players – most notably captain Damian Horton – sapped confidence, and the side, which took part in the Castle Festival at Kimbolton, failed to win again.

Batting—I. A. Bartholomew 12–1–298–73–0–27.09; T. W. Warren 11–2–196–56–0–21.77; M. R. Herring 11–0–223–55–0–20.27; A. P. Williamson 9–1–155–49–0–19.37; J. A. Hallan 10–0–166–62–0–16.60.

Bowling—M. R. Herring 100.3–23–286–17–4/11–16.82.

BIRKENHEAD SCHOOL   *Played 19: W 8, L 4, D 6, T 1*

Master i/c: M. H. Bowyer   Professional: H. L. Alleyne

Anthony Birley struck 124 in 90 minutes against Ellesmere, including 11 fours and eight sixes. He shared a stand of 170 with Simon Marshall, while Elliot Berstock and David Milligan went seven better in an undefeated partnership against UCS, London. Berstock's regular opening partner was his brother, James.

Batting—D. Milligan 5–1–194–70*–0–48.50; A. Birley 10–1–351–124–1–39.00; E. Berstock 13–5–298–72*–0–37.25; J. Berstock 17–4–340–109–1–26.15; *S. Marshall 10–1–209–70–0–23.22; T. Cottrell 15–4–151–28–0–13.72.

Bowling—S. Marshall 146–51–259–27–5/5–9.59; C. Kirk 114.5–23–318–25–6/11–12.72.

BLOXHAM SCHOOL   *Played 11: W 1, L 6, D 4. A 3*

Master i/c: N. C. W. Furley

Batting—C. de Weymarn 11–1–326–116*–2–32.60; R. Crofts 11–1–187–41*–0–17.00.

Bowling—J. P. Burrough 91–23–220–17–6/15–12.94; R. Foxon 83–10–312–15–3/38–20.80.

BLUNDELL'S SCHOOL   *Played 19: W 12, L 6, D 1. A 2*

Master i/c: N. A. Folland

The outstanding player in a good season was Tom Wright, a member of the England Under-17 squad. The school's most successful bowler for the fourth season running, he also hit 568 runs in aggressive style and played for Devon alongside coach Nick Folland. Captain and wicket-keeper Philip Arnold also had trials for Devon.

Batting—T. A. Wright 15–2–568–96*–0–43.69; *P. W. T. Arnold 15–3–384–69–0–32.00; J. C. Dark 13–1–303–80–0–25.25; E. N. Buckland 11–4–166–62*–0–23.71; J. H. K. White 12–1–255–65–0–23.18; C. I. Hill 12–2–180–38–0–18.00.

Bowling—T. A. Wright 110–15–305–23–4/22–13.26; A. M. O. Berry 88–7–225–15–3/8–15.00; E. N. Buckland 99–7–342–18–5/31–19.00; C. I. Hill 101–11–297–15–3/13–19.80.

BRADFIELD COLLEGE   *Played 12: W 3, L 4, D 5. A 1*

Master i/c: C. C. Ellison   Professional: J. F. Harvey

Batting—C. P. Hose 11–2–307–86–0–34.11; *A. J. J. Jeffries 11–2–283–92*–0–31.44; A. S. G. Tod 12–1–322–103*–1–29.27; M. D. Clark 8–0–178–46–0–22.25; W. M. H. Edes 9–1–162–38–0–20.25; D. R. W. Irens 12–1–203–54*–0–18.45.

Bowling—E. G. Dillon 172.4–50–408–24–6/36–17.00.

BRADFORD GRAMMAR SCHOOL   *Played 18: W 5, L 4, D 9. A 1*

Master i/c: A. G. Smith

Ben Graham hit three centuries in his 820 runs, but was let down by poor bowling. The exception was slow left-armer Nick Cockcroft, who took 34 wickets and raised his career total to 153, second on the school's all-time list.

Batting—*B. R. Graham 16–2–820–146–3–58.57; J. A. S. Benzafar 13–2–331–58–0–30.09; N. R. Cockcroft 16–3–258–50*–0–19.84; T. D. Ambepitiya 17–1–289–51–0–18.06; J. R. Topham 13–1–189–50–0–15.75; M. J. Dillingham 15–0–212–37–0–14.13.

Bowling—R. M. Harland 159.4–30–516–28–6/60–18.42; N. R. Cockcroft 242.4–51–765–34–5/89–22.50.

BRENTWOOD SCHOOL   *Played 16: W 6, L 4, D 6*

Master i/c: B. R. Hardie

Batting—P. R. Gray 14–2–428–93–0–35.66; E. J. Bowler 16–2–465–101*–1–33.21; D. P. Selby 11–3–254–77*–0–31.75; *A. M. Szczuka 14–2–330–68*–0–27.50; J. G. Redwood 8–0–160–74–0–20.00; D. E. Johnson 13–1–221–41–0–18.41.

Bowling—E. J. Gooday 156.2–36–406–28–4/43–14.50; D. P. Selby 104.3–29–351–18–3/3–19.50; N. C. S. Hobbs 171–32–501–25–4/28–20.04; E. J. Bowler 171.4–33–580–22–6/64–26.36.

BRIGHTON COLLEGE   *Played 21: W 16, L 2, D 3*

Master i/c: J. Spencer   Professional: R. Halsall

Ten straight wins represented the college's best-ever start to a season, and their total of 16 was second only to 1999. Major contributions came from all-rounders Pranay Sanklecha and Carl Hopkinson, while Matthew Prior scored most runs by some distance and went on England's Under-19 tour to India.

Batting—M. J. Prior 21–2–801–145–2–42.15; P. Sanklecha 20–4–631–100–1–39.43; C. D. Hopkinson 20–1–630–111–1–33.15; M. J. Brackpool 17–4–316–48–0–24.30; B. R. Stubbs 13–3–201–41–0–20.10; T. R. Burton 13–1–218–55–0–18.16; N. C. F. Woodbridge 18–4–254–64–0–18.14.

Bowling—N. A. Epstein 124–22–398–33–4/12–12.06; S. Murphy 118–28–353–27–4/10–13.07; C. D. Hopkinson 153–51–320–24–4/8–13.33; P. Sanklecha 256–78–625–45–5/38–13.88; O. W. Phillips 108–16–411–22–5/18–18.68.

BRISTOL GRAMMAR SCHOOL   *Played 14: W 5, L 6, D 3. A 1*

Master i/c: G. Clark   Professional: S. McDermott

Batting—*D. W. Hayward 11–2–314–102*–1–34.88; S. Douglas 11–0–298–63–0–27.09; P. W. Morris 12–1–272–79–0–24.72; A. J. Staniforth 9–1–160–31*–0–20.00.

Bowling—No bowler took 15 wickets. The leading bowler was D. W. Hayward 57.1–10–174–14–6/21–12.42.

BRYANSTON SCHOOL   *Played 9: W 6, L 3, D 0. A 5*

Master i/c: T. J. Hill

In the opening match, against Prior Park, Will Heath (123 not out) and Ben Edgell (85) set a school first-wicket record of 216. However, strike bowler Bevan Hornby damaged a shoulder and failed to appear again. The final game, in which identical twins James and William Morris made their debuts, saw the school rattle up 285 in 35 overs, eventually beating Exeter by 133 runs.

Batting—*D. A. W. Heath 7–2–329–123*–2–65.80; B. C. Edgell 7–0–232–85–0–33.14; N. J. P. Brunner 9–0–260–68–0–28.88.

Bowling—No bowler took 15 wickets. The leading bowler was A. M. Whiteley 42–11–129–12–4/18–10.75.

CAMPBELL COLLEGE   *Played 12: W 7, L 4, D 1. A 1*

Master i/c: G. Fry   Professional: D. Anderson

Batting—*C. Fuller 10–2–422–110–1–52.75; A. Heasley 9–2–160–39*–0–22.85; R. Turtle 9–1–154–32–0–19.25.

Bowling—No bowler took 15 wickets. The leading bowler was C. Fuller 47–5–199–14–4/20–14.21.

CANFORD SCHOOL   *Played 13: W 6, L 4, D 3*

Master i/c: A. Copp   Professionals: L. Ferreira, J. J. E. Hardy and J. H. Shackleton

Batting—*A. Bell 12–0–438–71–0–36.50; J. Martin 10–1–315–70*–0–35.00; M. Spitteler 13–0–363–50–0–27.92; H. Stead 13–0–232–55–0–17.84.

Bowling—E. Howat 83.3–18–293–17–5/12–17.23.

CHARTERHOUSE SCHOOL   *Played 16: W 9, L 5, D 2*

Master i/c: P. J. Deakin   Professional: R. V. Lewis

With several tight limited-overs games going against them, the school were unable to maintain the excellent start, which saw six wins in seven games. The highlights were dominant victories against Bradfield and Winchester, and impressive first seasons by Simon Hollingsworth and Andrew Gloak. Hollingsworth hit a classy hundred against Wellington College and took a hat-trick against I Zingari, and Gloak headed the bowling averages. Captain and wicket-keeper James Toller gave the batting much-needed stability.

Batting—J. W. L. Toller 12–3–316–57*–0–35.11; S. C. Hollingsworth 12–1–382–108–1–34.72; H. B. Bourne 12–1–303–78*–0–27.54; J. A. Gilbert 10–3–190–77*–0–27.14; P. L. Hunt 10–1–234–83–0–26.00; W. J. S. Clark 15–2–288–74–0–22.15; J. C. Hare 12–2–187–77*–0–18.70.

Bowling—A. J. Gloak 93.3–16–339–19–3/17–17.84; O. W. J. Gray 123–27–368–18–4/35–20.44; S. C. Hollingsworth 120–8–407–17–4/27–23.94; I. T. MacAuslan 131–28–409–16–3/4–25.56; A. G. Gordon-Martin 128–12–559–19–5/60–29.42.

CHELTENHAM COLLEGE   *Played 12: W 3, L 3, D 6. A 4*

Master i/c: M. W. Stovold   Professional: M. P. Briers

Batting—*R. T. J. Howell 12–1–613–129*–2–55.72; J. A. Hayes 9–4–277–50*–0–55.40; E. B. H. Shaw 10–0–316–61–0–31.60; G. P. Tyndall 10–3–214–82*–0–30.57.

Bowling—R. T. J. Howell 119–28–299–21–5/30–14.23.

CHIGWELL SCHOOL   *Played 12: W 4, L 2, D 6. A 4*

Master i/c: D. N. Morrison   Professional: F. W. Griffiths

Batting—O. M. Compton 11–1–349–100*–1–34.90; R. W. Gull 12–1–316–66–0–28.72; *A. S. N. Kurukulaswooriya 10–0–220–59–0–22.00; C. S. Benn 11–0–236–56–0–21.45; R. Radia 9–0–187–52–0–20.77.

Bowling—O. M. Hashmi 67–5–278–15–4/65–18.53; A. S. N. Kurukulaswooriya 116.2–14–467–24–5/53–19.45; M. C. Woda 106–11–413–16–3/16–25.81.

CHRIST COLLEGE, BRECON   *Played 12: W 3, L 6, D 3. A 2*

Masters i/c: N. C. Blackburn and T. J. P. Davenport   Professional: A. P. Davies

Batting—*J. R. P. Davenport 11–3–345–125*–1–43.12; W. J. Hitch 7–3–168–61*–0–42.00; R. J. Price 10–0–318–93–0–31.80; G. H. Bowers 10–1–165–50–0–18.33.

Bowling—G. H. Bowers 117–26–335–22–6/22–15.22.

CHRIST'S COLLEGE, FINCHLEY   *Played 9: W 5, L 3, D 1. A 7*

Master i/c: S. S. Goldsmith

In a campaign ruined by the weather, the most memorable game was a battling draw with Delhi Blues, fresh from a match against Yorkshire Second Eleven. On several occasions, leading bowler Divyesh Depala played beside his two younger brothers, Darshan and Chetan.

Batting—A. J. Hunter 7–3–174–64*–0–43.50; S. Hingorani 6–0–204–104–1–34.00.

Bowling—D. Depala 58.4–15–157–16–6/12–9.81.

CHRIST'S HOSPITAL, HORSHAM   *Played 18: W 7, L 10, D 1*

Master i/c: H. P. Holdsworth   Professional: L. J. Lenham

Batting—M. A. Jackson 17–3–430–73–0–30.71; N. J. Green 17–1–425–92–0–26.56; S. Curtin 17–1–276–55–0–17.25.

Bowling—B. J. Walker 134.1–16–384–35–5/22–10.97; J. S. E. Busby 121.4–15–475–27–4/23–17.59; A. E. Woodbridge 90–14–307–17–4/42–18.05; M. Y. Annoh 91–13–356–17–3/16–20.94; M. A. Jackson 99–13–356–15–4/21–23.73; J. W. S. Sheppard-Burgess 102.4–10–379–15–3/19–25.26.

CLAYESMORE SCHOOL   *Played 13: W 4, L 4, D 5*

Master i/c: D. I. Rimmer

Batting—T. J. C. Lack 13–0–465–112–2–35.76; R. Roe 13–2–323–67–0–29.36; T. Bryson 13–1–246–115*–1–20.50; C. Haniff 13–1–238–43*–0–19.83.

Bowling—T. J. C. Lack 82–18–323–20–3/9–16.15; T. Bryson 124.2–34–353–19–3/14–18.57; C. Haniff 115.2–25–360–15–4/33–24.00.

CLIFTON COLLEGE   *Played 13: W 8, L 3, D 2. A 5*

Master i/c: D. C. Henderson   Professional: P. W. Romaines

The outstanding player was Nick Willis-Stovold, who struck 688 runs in ten innings at 114.66. Ian Simmonds, who got the best from a useful bowling attack, captained with flair.

Batting—N. C. Willis-Stovold 10–4–688–134*–4–114.66; D. B. Romain 9–3–227–48*–0–37.83; *I. D. Simmonds 11–1–225–78*–0–22.50; M. Houcke 12–1–231–52–0–21.00.

Bowling—R. A. Yates 76–19–207–22–4/13–9.40; W. D. Rudge 94–16–226–19–4/28–11.89.

COLFE'S SCHOOL   *Played 15: W 5, L 5, D 5. A 3*

Master i/c: G. S. Clinton

Batting—B. Khan 7–3–284–93–0–71.00; M. Brown 9–2–196–104*–1–28.00; *V. German 12–1–246–61–0–22.36; G. Fitzgerald 8–0–159–47–0–19.87; P. S. Clinton 11–0–159–62–0–14.45.

Bowling—P. S. Clinton 53–8–183–16–4/6–11.43; B. Khan 94–20–319–15–3/9–21.26.

CRANBROOK SCHOOL   *Played 14: W 10, L 1, D 3*

Master i/c: A. J. Presnell

Matthew Bennett hit four undefeated 90s, but never reached three figures. By way of compensation, he became the first student to average over a hundred.

Batting—*M. Bennett 12–6–604–96*–0–100.66; J. Spencer 11–3–288–53–0–36.00; C. Sorensen 12–1–261–119*–1–23.72; T. Page 13–0–190–46–0–14.61.

Bowling—R. Pickerill 131–25–387–26–6/19–14.88; A. Barrett 85–12–293–15–4/52–19.53; J. Spencer 132–24–412–16–3/32–25.75.

CRANLEIGH SCHOOL   *Played 17: W 8, L 3, D 6. A 1*

Master i/c: D. C. Williams

Three players dominated the averages and saw the school to a successful summer. Robert Campbell, Alex Craven and Richard Hume each scored over 300 runs and took 24 or more wickets. Hume ended his school career the most accomplished all-rounder of recent years.

Batting—R. L. Campbell 16–3–445–117–1–34.23; A. D. Craven 14–4–333–85–0–33.30; R. T. Hume 16–0–445–126–1–27.81; S. R. Langmead 13–4–249–48–0–27.66; S. C. Worthy 15–0–403–103–1–26.86; *D. J. Groenveld 16–1–306–69–0–20.40; A. R. Houston 10–1–153–45–0–17.00; G. J. Starling 17–0–283–76–0–16.64.

Bowling—A. D. Craven 129–21–411–24–4/17–17.12; R. T. Hume 177–35–496–28–7/52–17.71; R. L. Campbell 182–29–584–24–4/32–24.33.

CULFORD SCHOOL   *Played 12: W 4, L 4, D 4. A 2*

Master i/c: R. P. Shepperson   Professional: D. Gibson

Batting—H. C. Jones 11–1–357–103–1–35.70; *N. J. Harrington 11–1–277–70–0–27.70; S. M. Hamshere 10–2–221–102*–1–27.62; M. K. S. Ampomah 11–0–195–102–1–17.72.

Bowling—N. J. Harrington 110–27–364–25–5/35–14.56; I. Beeby 104–23–293–16–3/35–18.31.

DARTFORD GRAMMAR SCHOOL   *Played 10: W 7, L 2, D 1*

Master i/c: A. Futter

A talented side, regularly fielding four Under-15s, concluded a fine season with a nine-wicket win against MCC.

Batting—S. Richards 6–1–289–89*–0–57.80; R. Hallam 4–1–152–127–1–50.66; M. Jobling 8–0–202–42–0–25.25.

Bowling—No bowler took 15 wickets. The leading bowler was C. Round 35.4–8–117–11–4/11–10.63.

DAUNTSEY'S SCHOOL   *Played 23: W 9, L 9, D 5. A 2*

Master i/c: A. J. Palmer   Professional: R. Chaudhuri

Against Prior Park, two players, Christopher Warde and Oliver Smith, hit maiden centuries in the same game – the first time this had happened. Warde finished the season with 1,352 runs, another record. In July, the side took part in the 14th Sir Garfield Sobers Festival in Barbados and finished the best-placed British team.

Batting—*C. J. Warde 21–3–1,352–103–2–75.11; O. L. Smith 22–2–574–105*–1–28.70; D. J. A. Neale 21–2–290–78*–0–15.26; T. G. A. Sterling 17–0–201–41–0–11.82.

Bowling—T. J. Sebright 164–17–597–32–6/37–18.65; N. J. Warde 149.4–18–548–28–3/14–19.57; C. J. Warde 159–23–610–28–4/39–21.78; D. J. A. Neale 144–16–551–25–4/18–22.04.

DEAN CLOSE SCHOOL   *Played 13: W 6, L 3, D 4. A 3*

Master i/c: C. J. Townsend   Professional: P. Fourie

A strong batting line-up preferred chasing to setting targets, and all six wins came bowling first. Alex Fateh and Matthew Shayle added exactly 200 for the third wicket against King's, Gloucester, a school record. Nine different bowlers were given the new ball, none with particular success.

Batting—T. Judge 8–5–177–100*–1–59.00; A. Fateh 12–5–316–124*–1–45.14; M. Shayle 10–1–349–89–0–38.77; G. Curry 11–4–224–60*–0–32.00; M. Whitney 12–1–343–59–0–31.18.

Bowling—N. Anderson 61–8–223–15–3/20–14.86.

DENSTONE COLLEGE   *Played 15: W 6, L 5, D 4. A 3*

Master i/c: A. N. James

Iain MacKinnon epitomised the team's improved late-season form with a spectacular 120 before lunch against Wirral GS. Good cricket continued on an end-of-term tour of Barbados, where three strong teams were beaten in six games.

Batting—I. C. MacKinnon 12–0–522–120–1–43.50; M. Johnson 12–6–189–53–0–31.50; A. A. Siddique 14–3–291–110–1–26.45; A. A. Easter 14–1–342–71*–0–26.30; *P. K. Riley 15–2–324–83–0–24.92; B. J. Young 10–1–185–48–0–20.55.

Bowling—M. Johnson 96–15–298–20–3/17–14.90; P. K. Riley 107–15–504–19–3/34–26.52.

DOLLAR ACADEMY   *Played 10: W 7, L 2, D 1. A 6*

Master i/c: J. G. A. Frost   Professional: L. Spendlove

A successful season comprised seven wins from ten matches. Barbadian all-rounder Marvin Forde played the major part, taking 23 wickets at 9.17 and averaging 71.00 with the bat. Kari Anderson became the first girl to represent the school at this level, and she went on to play for Scotland.

Batting—M. Forde 6–2–284–104*–1–71.00; *C. Butcher 7–2–212–110*–1–42.40; J. Miller 7–0–179–56–0–25.57.

Bowling—E. Wilson 74–17–182–20–5/13–9.10; M. Forde 89–26–211–23–5/13–9.17.

DOVER COLLEGE   *Played 10: W 1, L 7, D 2. A 1*

Master i/c: D. C. Butler

Alexei Korobkin, a 16-year-old from St Petersburg, took six for 24 against the XL Club in just his second season of cricket.

Batting—No batsman scored 150 runs. The leading batsman was J. Fung 8–2–106–30*–0–17.66.

Bowling—No bowler took 15 wickets. The leading bowler was A. Korobkin 59–8–180–13–6/24–13.84.

DOWNSIDE SCHOOL   *Played 16: W 7, L 6, D 3*

Master i/c: A. P. Smerdon

Batting—D. Smit 16–1–568–91–0–37.86; A. Van der Merwe 16–3–435–105*–1–33.46; R. Minnie 16–1–499–126–1–33.26; *J. Cook 13–3–163–39–0–16.30.

Bowling—A. Van der Merwe 153–19–485–34–4/22–14.26; R. Minnie 132–27–388–24–4/27–16.16; H. C. Monro 134–20–462–21–4/15–22.00.

DUKE OF YORK'S ROYAL MILITARY SCHOOL   *Played 10: W 3, L 3, D 4. A 4*

Master i/c: S. Salisbury   Professional: N. J. Llong

Batting—P. J. Jefferson 10–2–209–36–0–26.12.

Bowling—No bowler took 15 wickets. The leading bowler was S. Rennalls 134–23–310–13–4/30–23.84.

DULWICH COLLEGE   *Played 16: W 8, L 2, D 6. A 4*

Master i/c: D. J. Cooper   Professionals: D. Berry and A. Ranson

The summer ended as it began: under umbrellas. In between, Adam Moon took his side to eight victories and his first-team career to 62 matches, finishing with 146 wickets at 17.82.

Batting—M. J. Easter 16–2–552–99*–0–39.42; P. R. J. Hazell 13–1–330–57–0–27.50; I. Nasser 12–1–295–71–0–26.81; B. M. Patel 16–2–371–77*–0–26.50; *A. K. Moon 13–2–247–64*–0–22.45.

Bowling—A. K. Moon 213.1–56–545–32–6/26–17.03; P. R. J. Hazell 136–26–362–21–4/15–17.23.

DURHAM SCHOOL   *Played 13: W 5, L 0, D 7, T 1. A 2*

Master i/c: M. E. Hirsch

After setting records for runs and centuries in 1999, Gordon Muchall turned his attention to his average in 2000. He achieved 167.16, another record, and hit five hundreds, one of which was a double – 204 not out against St Peter's, York. Having led the side through an unbeaten season, Muchall was chosen for the England Under-19 tour of India. Nick Hooper and Robert Flunder made solid all-round contributions, while left-arm spinner David Burgess bowled with good control.

Batting—*G. J. Muchall 11–5–1,003–204*–5–167.16; J. McCreedy 8–6–167–44*–0–83.50; N. Hooper 7–3–307–102–1–76.75; R. Flunder 13–6–209–47–0–29.85; P. Curry 10–0–217–47–0–21.70.

Bowling—D. Burgess 165–17–559–30–6/56–18.63; N. Hooper 90–13–317–15–4/52–21.13; R. Flunder 152–35–455–19–5/27–23.94; G. J. Muchall 122–14–446–15–4/32–29.73.

EASTBOURNE COLLEGE   *Played 17: W 7, L 4, D 6. A 1*

Master i/c: N. L. Wheeler   Professional: D. Kotze

A visit to Barbados in April whetted appetites for the season – the high point of which was Henry Stafford's 118 before lunch against Sevenoaks. Two players had connections with Sussex: leading wicket-taker Eliot Pigott is the son of Tony, the former opening bowler and chief executive, and Timothy Langridge is the grandson of Test umpire and *Wisden* Cricketer of the Year, John.

Batting—O. L. Gale 11–5–242–75*–0–40.33; T. A. Eyre 13–0–449–78–0–34.53; H. E. Stafford 14–1–380–118–1–29.23; T. J. Langridge 13–0–328–72–0–25.23; P. A. Fleming 11–2–226–71*–0–25.11; *M. D. Firth 10–3–154–48–0–22.00; L. J. A. Burgess 12–2–152–40–0–15.20.

Bowling—A. P. Rowe 45–9–165–17–5/32–9.70; E. S. Pigott 141.5–29–438–24–4/62–18.25; M. D. Firth 145–34–414–18–4/19–23.00.

THE EDINBURGH ACADEMY   *Played 15: W 7, L 3, D 4, T 1*

Master i/c: G. R. Bowe

High points of an enjoyable campaign were a nine-wicket victory over a strong MCC side and a tie in the festival match against King's, Macclesfield.

Batting—C. M. Hillyard 15–3–474–89*–0–39.50; C. P. Muldoon 16–2–387–80*–0–27.64; *D. F. Paterson 11–2–193–47–0–21.44; A. G. H. Moffat 14–2–241–68–0–20.08; D. W. Blair 13–2–213–32–0–19.36; E. C. Mitchell 12–2–186–52*–0–18.60.

Bowling—D. F. Paterson 104–35–273–21–5/18–13.00; R. B. Callicott 111–19–337– 24–4/28–14.04; A. G. H. Moffat 88–19–294–16–5/25–18.37.

ELIZABETH COLLEGE, GUERNSEY   *Played 14: W 7, L 6, D 1*

Master i/c: M. E. Kinder

The season finally came alive with a six-wicket win over Victoria College, Jersey, after academic demands had restricted both practice and midweek games. Further successes – including festival victories against Loretto, Rossall and Merchant Taylors', Northwood – were based on sound batting from Alex Hunter, the seam bowling of Chris Van Vliett and the all-round skills of Mark Betts.

Batting—*A. R. Hunter 13–2–409–92–0–37.18; M. J. S. Betts 9–3–161–102*–1–26.83; M. C. Greenfield 13–2–277–84*–0–25.18; A. Harbour 12–0–150–40–0–12.50.

Bowling—C. Van Vliett 127.2–28–387–30–6/23–12.90; C. J. Blackburn 117–23–343– 23–4/15–14.91; M. J. S. Betts 132.1–36–383–24–6/27–15.95.

ELLESMERE COLLEGE   *Played 11: W 3, L 4, D 4. A 1*

Master i/c: P. J. Hayes

The high point of the summer came when a young side put in an outstanding team effort to score 279 for eight and overhaul the XL Club.

Batting—P. Kukreja 6–1–214–109*–1–42.80; *R. M. Furniss 10–2–252–93–0–31.50; S. J. Watson-Jones 9–2–217–66–0–31.00; R. M. Molvihill 10–1–269–56–0–29.88; E. J. Rowe 9–1–150–75–0–18.75.

Bowling—P. Singh 96.5–15–360–15–5/33–24.00.

ELTHAM COLLEGE   *Played 12: W 5, L 3, D 4. A 2*

Masters i/c: P. C. McCartney and B. M. Withecombe   Professional: R. W. Hills

Expectations were high after a successful South African tour in February, but rain, injuries and unavailability marred the season. However, 14-year-old Johan Malcolm-Hansen made good progress, hitting a century against Sutton Valence and bowling some tidy off-spin, while Will Goodyear bowled with pace and scored runs freely.

Batting—R. J. Malcolm-Hansen 9–1–372–129–1–46.50; P. J. Selvey-Clinton 8–3–196– 63*–0–39.20; W. S. Goodyear 8–1–232–66–0–33.14; J. R. Sheikh 7–1–154–70*–0–25.66.

Bowling—W. S. Goodyear 128.1–24–355–22–5/57–16.13; A. J. Ring 102.5–23–281– 17–3/13–16.52.

ENFIELD GRAMMAR SCHOOL   *Played 19: W 7, L 8, D 4. A 1*

Master i/c: S. Pickering

Batting—A. Herron 7–1–221–80–0–36.83; E. Barber 17–0–518–95–0–30.47; M. Feeney 7–0–180–73–0–25.71; D. Keerthichandra 17–0–253–68–0–14.88; S. Morrison 12–1–154– 29–0–14.00; *V. Jethwa 15–0–193–54–0–12.86.

Bowling—T. Miller 63.3–7–212–17–4/16–12.47; S. Morrison 98–10–311–15–3/39–20.73; E. Barber 124–18–458–21–5/71–21.80.

EPSOM COLLEGE   *Played 13: W 3, L 8, D 2*

Master i/c: P. J. Williams   Professional: S. Cloete

The captain, Henry Kingham, ended his school career with a record 122 wickets. He had strong support from Jonathan Gale, who scored a century against Dulwich and topped both averages. That said, the side could achieve only three wins.

Batting—J. P. A. Gale 12–0–363–101–1–30.25; A. L. Riggs 13–1–285–66*–0–23.75; A. A. J. Robinson 13–1–218–39–0–18.16; *H. P. E. Kingham 12–0–202–36–0–16.83; T. J. Sinnett 13–0–214–41–0–16.46.

Bowling—J. P. A. Gale 118.1–19–389–25–3/20–15.56; H. P. E. Kingham 127.5–13–457–25–5/39–18.28; N. Tanna 112–18–409–17–3/19–24.05.

ETON COLLEGE   *Played 16: W 7, L 6, D 2, T 1. A 3*

Master i/c: R. D. Oliphant-Callum   Professional: J. M. Rice

An acceptable summer would have been better had inexperience not played a part in several close games. Even so, the only side to outplay them was Maritzburg College, from South Africa. Schools defeated included Bradfield, Charterhouse and Oundle, while a game with Tonbridge was tied for the second year running.

Batting—D. C. Ferreira 16–3–568–97*–0–43.69; T. H. McL. Hawk 17–2–511–102*–2–34.06; B. R. Thompson 10–1–258–60*–0–28.66; T. P. McCall 15–4–193–55–0–17.54; E. C. J. Fielding 14–2–207–47*–0–17.25; A. M. Goldberg 15–0–197–40–0–13.13.

Bowling—S. W. F. Collins 163.5–31–483–29–6/28–16.65; E. D. Williams 106.5–21–362–17–2/4–21.29; T. P. McCall 180.5–32–532–21–3/21–25.33; A. M. Goldberg 113–18–397–15–4/24–26.46.

EXETER SCHOOL   *Played 13: W 6, L 7, D 0. A 2*

Master i/c: W. Hughes

Batting—*R. Martin 14–2–358–60*–0–29.83; D. Saunders 14–0–315–48–0–22.50; A. Ash 12–0–224–86–0–18.66; A. Milton 10–0–154–63–0–15.40.

Bowling—T. Giles 70.5–12–262–19–5/31–13.78; A. Ash 108.1–14–405–24–5/10–16.87.

FELSTED SCHOOL   *Played 15: W 6, L 4, D 5*

Master i/c: M. E. Allbrook   Professional: N. J. Lockhart

Batting—*T. Ballentyne 14–0–445–71–0–31.78; N. J. Phillips 13–1–329–65*–0–27.41; P. E. Wilkinson 13–1–282–63–0–23.50; T. Peacock 13–1–276–58–0–23.00; E. T. Thorogood 12–1–237–83–0–21.54.

Bowling—T. Ballentyne 97–17–337–21–4/40–16.04; N. E. J. Porter 128–25–391–21–4/24–18.61.

FETTES COLLEGE   *Played 11: W 5, L 3, D 3. A 1*

Master i/c: C. S. Thomson   Professional: B. Russell

Batting—N. Abernethy 9–4–185–43*–0–37.00; *A. Millar 11–3–176–46–0–22.00; E. A. M. Murray 12–0–261–64–0–21.75; D. G. B. Trodd 13–1–246–59–0–20.50; A. R. Edington 14–1–235–78–0–18.07; J. F. Jackson 12–2–180–58*–0–18.00; A. W. Rathie 11–0–151–58–0–13.72.

Bowling—R. F. Jackson 125.2–41–290–25–6/44–11.60; A. Millar 121–44–249–17–3/1–14.64.

FOREST SCHOOL   *Played 15: W 9, L 3, D 3. A 3*

Master i/c: S. Turner

Batting—D. Stevens 13–2–505–115–1–45.90; J. Lawes 11–1–325–119–1–32.50; *M. Patel 10–1–241–88–0–26.77; M. Westwood 9–2–183–63*–0–26.14; K. Paul 10–2–202–66*–0–25.25; K. Bhachu 12–0–244–64–0–20.33.

Bowling—J. Lawes 52.4–10–152–17–5/24–8.94; J. Kay 146–30–380–30–6/28–12.66; T. Watkins 100–18–281–16–4/24–17.56.

FOYLE AND LONDONDERRY COLLEGE   *Played 19: W 10, L 5, D 4*

Master i/c: G. R. McCarter

Batting—*I. R. Donaghey 18–3–491–92–0–32.73; D. J. Fleming 17–2–337–63*–0–22.46; P. H. J. McCartney 17–1–300–76–0–18.75; D. T. Robb 18–2–288–52–0–18.00.

Bowling—M. D. Nesbitt 59–9–159–17–5/13–9.35; R. J. Doherty 54.4–7–191–17–4/24–11.23; S. Qureshi 113.5–25–331–16–3/50–20.68; D. T. Robb 115–12–490–23–3/9–21.30.

FRAMLINGHAM COLLEGE   *Played 10: W 3, L 5, D 2. A 2*

Master i/c: R. Curtis

Batting—A. J. Blemings 10–0–278–73–0–27.80; W. T. Gallagher 10–0–204–52–0–20.40.

Bowling—No bowler took 15 wickets. The leading bowler was G. W. Lucking 90–18–283–14–5/33–20.21.

GIGGLESWICK SCHOOL   *Played 12: W 6, L 2, D 4. A 3*

Master i/c: N. A. Gemmell   Professional: A. G. Lawson

Nick Harrison scored two centuries to set up comfortable wins against Ermysted GS and Rossall. Captain and slow left-armer Stephen Langstaff took over 100 wickets in his five-year career.

Batting—N. J. Harrison 11–1–455–158–2–45.50; J. W. Hird 12–2–322–68*–0–32.20; T. M. Canaway 11–0–177–39–0–16.09.

Bowling—*S. J. Langstaff 137–32–389–26–5/47–14.96; A. Nawaz 99–15–310–20–5/77–15.50.

GLASGOW ACADEMY   *Played 9: W 2, L 7, D 0*

Master i/c: A. Lyall   Professional. V. Hariharan

Searching for consistency, particularly in batting, proved a real problem as a young side wrestled with the demands of first-team cricket. There was clear potential amongst the bowlers: Peter Gettinby took 11 wickets from just 28 overs.

Batting—No batsman scored 150 runs. The leading batsman was R. Andrew 9–0–109–38–0–12.11.

Bowling—No bowler took 15 wickets. The leading bowler was R. Andrew 63.1–10–229–13–3/28–17.61.

GLENALMOND COLLEGE   *Played 11: W 3, L 5, D 3. A 2*

Master i/c: A. Norton

Freddie Weld Forester and Christopher Murray dominated the scoring (putting on an unbeaten 219 for the second wicket against Gordonstoun), but the middle order proved liable to collapse. The pick of a more consistent bowling line-up was Andrew Peters.

Batting—F. Weld Forester 9–1–330–104*–1–41.25; C. Murray 10–0–271–98–0–27.10.

Bowling—A. Peters 111.5–29–307–22–5/43–13.95.

GORDONSTOUN SCHOOL   *Played 9: W 3, L 5, D 1. A 1*

Master i/c: A. T. Greaves

Batting—A. D. D. Morbey 10–1–297–103–1–33.00; A. T. C. Cannon 6–1–158–51*–0–31.60; B. Schwartz 7–1–171–63–0–28.50.

Bowling—R. S. R. Pyper 99–15–314–19–4/9–16.52; A. D. D. Morbey 91–10–383–16–5/53–23.93; O. Valliani 90–12–378–15–3/68–25.20.

GRESHAM'S SCHOOL   *Played 12: W 8, L 3, D 1. A 1*

Master i/c: A. M. Ponder

Batting—*T. Hedley 11–1–375–116–1–37.50; M. Hedley 10–2–250–44–0–31.25; M. Pickett 11–0–291–73–0–26.45; J. Pearse 12–1–281–59–0–25.54; R. Lintott 11–4–165–31–0–23.57; R. Fulford 7–0–150–33–0–21.42.

Bowling—P. Dudman 193.2–63–511–33–7/24–15.48; C. Morrison 117.1–27–401–19–4/66–21.10; A. Welham 112–13–377–17–4/12–22.17; R. Lintott 118.1–27–389–17–4/12–22.88.

HABERDASHERS' ASKE'S SCHOOL   *Played 18: W 8, L 3, D 7. A 5*

Master i/c: S. D. Charlwood

A good team spirit, combined with some useful performances, helped to compensate for a disappointingly wet summer. Highlights were the first win against MCC since the mid-1980s, victory over Trinity GS, Sydney, and Ian Pryor's undefeated century against Sidmouth CC.

Batting—K. Manzoor 13–6–241–67*–0–34.42; P. B. Duffy 11–5–200–50*–0–33.33; I. J. Pryor 15–2–400–106*–1–30.76; K. Sethi 17–2–305–63*–0–20.33; A. D. Cohen 10–0–197–54–0–19.70; J. Hills 15–1–243–41–0–17.35; B. L. Ruben 15–2–190–51–0–14.61.

Bowling—N. McGarry 91.3–21–295–21–4/35–14.04; A. M. Theivendra 136–36–362–25–4/33–14.48; *A. R. Jayaweera 140–29–450–28–6/50–16.07; P. B. Duffy 188–49–546–32–4/44–17.06.

HAILEYBURY COLLEGE   *Played 12: W 4, L 6, D 2. A 1*

Master i/c: T. Newman   Professional: J. Williams

A young side, well led by Philip Reid, grew in confidence as the season progressed. Victories included Bishop's Stortford and Felsted.

Batting—D. Gerard 13–1–391–98–0–32.58; N. Walker 12–2–288–66–0–28.80; *P. Reid 13–1–268–72–0–22.33; Y. Qureshi 11–1–194–38–0–19.40; J. Kachel 13–0–178–65–0–13.69.

Bowling—N. Walker 136–24–524–24–4/28–21.83; P. Lundi 164–34–543–19–4/76–28.57; D. Gerard 139–29–483–16–4/42–30.18.

HAMPTON SCHOOL   *Played 14: W 9, L 4, D 1. A 3*

Master i/c: E. M. Wesson

Batting—N. Khanna 12–2–387–79*–0–38.70; *A. G. Pittard 14–1–390–73*–0–30.00; J. D. Irons 11–2–248–52–0–27.55; J. M. Chapple 13–1–261–89–0–21.75; O. J. Wootton 11–2–163–43*–0–18.11.

Bowling—N. E. Baker 50.3–10–174–16–8/34–10.87; M. E. Jones 127.5–27–407–24–4/20–16.95; J. D. Irons 162.5–49–468–21–3/17–22.28.

HARROW SCHOOL   *Played 15: W 6, L 2, D 7. A 1*

Master i/c: S. J. Halliday   Professional: R. K. Sethi

The team defeated Eton at Lord's for the first time in 25 years (see page 995). Nick Compton, who headed both averages, is the grandson of Denis Compton.

Batting—N. R. D. Compton 13–3–416–100*–1–41.60; T. G. Dunbar 15–2–478–81–0–36.76; L. F. de Rougemont 13–2–282–117*–1–25.63; S. W. MacDonald 11–1–229–104–1–22.90.

Bowling—N. R. D. Compton 148.4–37–400–24–4/6–16.66; M. J. S. Willetts 117.2–21–386–23–4/16–16.78; C. J. M. Cooke-Hurle 122–22–350–19–4/7–18.42; J. M. Kostoris 147–31–360–18–3/22–20.00.

THE HARVEY GRAMMAR SCHOOL   *Played 17: W 5, L 7, D 5. A 8*

Master i/c: P. J. Harding

Batting—*S. J. Hagger 13–2–378–129–2–34.36; M. S. Gamlyn 11–4–164–46–0–23.42; R. A. Hall 14–1–276–107*–1–21.23.

Bowling—O. G. Mitchell 88–15–277–15–4/20–18.46.

HEREFORD CATHEDRAL SCHOOL   *Played 15: W 1, L 11, D 3. A 2*

Master i/c: A. H. Connop

Batting—T. DeSouza 14–1–369–84–0–28.38; A. J. Hewlett 15–2–253–69–0–19.46; E. Tomlinson 12–1–195–68*–0–17.72; H. W. E. Warren 13–1–183–37–0–15.25.

Bowling—T. DeSouza 110–17–398–17–5/10–23.41; H. Hopkins 113.5–14–427–15–4/54–28.46.

HIGHGATE SCHOOL   *Played 14: W 1, L 11, D 2. A 1*

Master i/c: R. J. Davis   Professional: R. E. Jones

Batting—J. Book 14–0–217–46–0–15.50; T. Atchinson 13–0–171–47–0–13.15; B. Dewhirst 14–0–180–42–0–12.85.

Bowling—S. Whiteside-McFadden 110.1–30–400–25–5/13–16.00.

HURSTPIERPOINT COLLEGE   *Played 14: W 4, L 7, D 3. A 1*

Master i/c: C. W. Gray   Professional: D. J. Semmence

Batting—*K. Singh 15–1–660–135–1–47.14; M. Khan 13–4–241–64*–0–26.77; J. Harrison 11–0–263–63–0–23.90; D. Jones 11–3–164–50*–0–20.50; J. Marsh 14–3–212–55–0–19.27.

Bowling—J. Marsh 113–16–363–19–4/16–19.10; K. Singh 128–21–468–18–4/10–26.00.

IPSWICH SCHOOL   *Played 13: W 8, L 4, D 1. A 3*

Master i/c: A. K. Golding   Professional: R. E. East

Batting—J. Southgate 5–4–173–61*–0–173.00; M. Elliot 15–6–440–116*–1–48.88; R. Mann 15–2–512–73*–0–39.38; *C. Swallow 11–2–321–79*–0–35.66; E. Flather 14–1–275–57*–0–21.15; N. Parry 11–3–151–42–0–18.87.

Bowling—C. Swallow 156.5–27–455–30–6/51–15.16; G. Ingham 112–23–310–20–4/40–15.50; N. Parry 99.2–12–295–15–5/62–19.66; O. Didham 105–14–315–15–3/38–21.00.

THE JOHN LYON SCHOOL   *Played 11: W 2, L 4, D 5. A 4*

Master i/c: I. R. Parker

Batting—N. Packianathan 10–3–187–59–0–26.71; N. Tanna 11–0–227–48–0–20.63; S. Singh 11–1–163–29–0–16.30.

Bowling—N. Smart 102.1–17–370–18–4/27–20.55; N. Tanna 115–21–392–19–4/27–20.63.

KELLY COLLEGE   *Played 7: W 1, L 4, D 2. A 4*

Master i/c: T. Ryder

Only a handful of players with first-team experience were available and the rebuilt team found success elusive. The sole victory came against the Old Boys; Tom Ingram bowled outstandingly to take six for 16.

Batting—O. Pitts 7–1–174–50–0–29.00.

Bowling—No bowler took 15 wickets. The leading bowler was T. Ingram 31.5–7–149–11–6/16–13.54.

KIMBOLTON SCHOOL   *Played 14: W 7, L 3, D 4. A 3*

Master i/c: A. G. Tapp

Thomas Huggins was the dominant figure in a successful season. He averaged 47 with the bat, took useful wickets and went on to play for Leicestershire Second Eleven. Term concluded with the school hosting – and winning – the Castle Festival.

Batting—T. B. Huggins 14–5–423–74*–0–47.00; E. Longmate 13–4–318–86*–0–35.33; A. Lacey 9–4–167–73–0–33.40.

Bowling—C. McCarthy 121.5–17–391–26–4/14–15.03; T. B. Huggins 148.4–41–389–20–4/33–19.45; A. Lacey 121.5–26–390–20–5/27–19.50.

KING EDWARD VI COLLEGE, STOURBRIDGE   *Played 9: W 4, L 3, D 2. A 3*

Masters i/c: M. L. Ryan and R. A. Williams

Opening batsman Alastair Maiden remained undefeated in all but two of his seven innings and averaged 183.50. He played for Staffordshire and ESCA Midlands Under-18. Fellow-opener Mark Fisher represented Worcestershire's County Board and Under-17 sides. The achievement of the season was a ten-wicket win over Bishop Vesey's GS.

Batting—A. J. Maiden 7–5–367–119*–1–183.50; M. S. Fisher 8–1–178–65*–0–25.42.

Bowling—No bowler took 15 wickets. The leading bowler was I. Gill 54.3–9–173–10–4/12–17.30.

KING EDWARD VI SCHOOL, SOUTHAMPTON   *Played 19: W 11, L 5, D 3. A 2*

Master i/c: R. J. Putt

A young side, without (as yet) any outstanding players, pulled together to transform a season of rebuilding into one of achievement.

Batting—I. A. Strother 15–2–426–84*–0–32.76; T. C. Moore 12–5–203–78*–0–29.00; J. P. Dixon 15–0–368–62–0–24.53; *A. M. Paul 13–4–214–70*–0–23.77; W. G. Dineen 12–0–231–60–0–19.25; C. E. Boyd 14–2–205–36–0–17.08.

Bowling—N. S. Greaves 107.1–14–287–26–5/25–11.03; R. M. Noble 100.1–14–367–22–5/27–16.68.

Youth policy: Jack Kelliher of King Edward VII and Queen Mary, Lytham (*left*) and Arun Harinath of Tiffin School both made significant impacts at the age of 13.

KING EDWARD VII AND QUEEN MARY SCHOOL, LYTHAM

Played 25: W 13, L 6, D 6. A 1

Master i/c: A. M. Weston   Professionals: D. J. Callaghan and C. Rogers

Plenty of fine weather brought the best from the side: 13 wins equalled the school record, set in 1999. Thirteen-year-old Jack Kelliher, after playing the early part of the season with his own age group, broke into the senior team and topped the batting averages.

Batting—J. Kelliher 12–3–396–75*–0–44.00; C. Roberts 15–3–359–47*–0–29.91; B. J. James 24–3–540–84–0–25.71; *J. M. Hill 23–2–520–77–0–24.76; B. Garthwaite 10–2–151–41–0–18.87; T. J. Thompson 14–2–208–51–0–17.33; T. Eastham 25–4–322–51*–0–15.33; B. M. Ourin 19–4–210–51*–0–14.00; C. L. Blackett 24–4–195–44*–0–9.75.

Bowling—C. L. Blackett 176.3–29–532–37–6/13–14.37; J. M. Hill 169.1–20–554–34–4/22–16.29; S. Holliday 137.3–24–386–23–4/9–16.78; C. D. Pickles 167.4–18–645–35–5/12–18.42; J. Kelliher 101–11–317–16–4/17–19.81.

KING EDWARD'S SCHOOL, BIRMINGHAM   *Played 19: W 2, L 8, D 9. A 4*

Master i/c: M. D. Stead   Professionals: D. Collins and R. J. Newman

A very young side – only three regulars were sixth formers – had a difficult summer, with several talented players failing to develop as expected.

Batting—D. J. F. Shilvock 19–3–420–72–0–26.25; A. Singh 18–0–433–92–0–24.05; B. N. Patel 12–2–225–32*–0–22.50; N. C. Brandrick 15–3–251–74–0–20.91; G. J. E. Brandrick 17–5–242–57*–0–20.16.

Bowling—V. Banerjee 115–18–347–18–4/47–19.27.

KING EDWARD'S SCHOOL, WITLEY   *Played 15: W 1, L 9, D 5. A 3*

Master i/c: D. H. Messenger   Professional: C. Mahachi

Injuries to two senior batsmen, Mark Josling and James Hamilton, hampered run-scoring but gave opportunities to younger players. Robert Ledger took his chance, played well above his 15 years and was dismissed only three times in ten innings. Charlie Crowne, who turned to off-spin during the winter nets, was the most successful bowler.

Batting—R. C. Ledger 10–7–194–39*–0–64.66; J. R. Hamilton 9–1–211–57*–0–26.37; W. C. Acquaye 9–1–184–56–0–23.00.

Bowling—M. T. Owoade 103–15–266–15–5/40–17.73; C. A. Crowne 73.4–7–357–17–4/32–21.00; M. R. K. Amberton 112.4–43–445–15–3/45–29.66.

KING HENRY VIII SCHOOL, COVENTRY   *Played 11: W 5, L 4, D 2. A 3*

Master i/c: A. M. Parker

Batting—J. M. Whittingham 10–4–391–94–0–65.16; M. P. Windridge 6–3–160–62*–0–53.33; S. E. Bowers 11–1–198–61*–0–19.80.

Bowling—R. Mistry 70–15–223–21–6/26–10.61; H. S. Kalirai 94–13–361–15–3/13–24.06.

KING WILLIAM'S COLLEGE   *Played 8: W 3, L 2, D 3*

Master i/c: A. Maree   Professional: D. Mark

Batting—M. Green 5–0–216–90–0–43.20; *P. Richards 5–1–166–50*–0–41.50; G. Barrett 7–0–197–48–0–28.14.

Bowling—No bowler took 15 wickets. The leading bowler was A. Corrin 67–6–187–12–7/27–15.58.

KING'S COLLEGE, TAUNTON   *Played 13: W 12, L 1, D 0. A 2*

Master i/c: H. R. J. Trump   Professional: D. J. Breakwell

Batting—T. Webley 12–2–604–128–2–60.40; J. Payn 12–1–492–100–1–44.72; *C. Stafford 11–4–271–52–0–38.71; J. Hudson 12–1–354–124–1–32.18.

Bowling—P. Lewis 118–19–318–23–5/21–13.82; T. Webley 92–29–260–15–3/30–17.33; C. Stafford 92–15–343–18–3/34–19.05.

KING'S COLLEGE SCHOOL, WIMBLEDON   *Played 12: W 4, L 5, D 3. A 3*

Master i/c: G. C. McGinn   Professional: M. Church

Zaheen Mir framed his season with unbeaten hundreds; he scored 115 in the first game of the summer, against St John's, Leatherhead, and 161 in the last, versus Victoria College. Also catching the eye was wicket-keeper/batsman Oliver Fernie.

Batting—*Z. Mir 12–2–533–161*–2–53.30; O. M. Fernie 11–2–265–62*–0–29.44; H. F. Jones 8–0–164–82–0–20.50; D. E. Hitchman 9–0–156–55–0–17.33.

Bowling—P. M. Smith 90–20–257–16–3/29–16.06; M. E. C. Jones 89–18–276–15–3/18–18.40; B. H. Woodbridge 93–13–336–15–4/32–22.40; L. T. D. Finch 88–16–342–15–3/37–22.80.

KING'S SCHOOL, BRUTON   *Played 16: W 2, L 12, D 2. A 2*

Master i/c: J. D. Roebuck   Professional: A. P. Davis

Several respectable bowling performances – leading to gettable targets – came to nothing as the batting fell apart under pressure. The problem was highlighted when Sherborne, dismissed for 137 (Tristan Lark five for 14), still won by 78. Even so, Chris Davis marshalled his side well, and slow left-armer Ali Lund was backed up by improved fielding.

Batting—M. Green 8–2–150–66–0–25.00; R. Tulloch 15–1–287–78–0–20.50; A. Grazette 14–1–198–30–0–15.23; C. Pratt 14–2–169–41–0–14.08; C. Davis 14–1–160–55–0–12.30.

Bowling—A. Lund 150–30–481–25–4/11–19.24; C. Pratt 88–12–339–15–3/12–22.60; T. Lark 119–15–504–16–5/14–31.50.

KING'S SCHOOL, CANTERBURY   *Played 12: W 4, L 2, D 6. A 1*

Master i/c: M. Afzal   Professional: A. G. E. Ealham

One of the better seasons in recent years owed much to the shrewd captaincy of Matthew Chataway.
His bowlers supported him well, often dismissing opponents on good batting pitches. However,
the batting was less assured: only Tom Bruce and Sam Traill contributed consistently.

Batting—T. O. Bruce 12–1–339–61–0–30.81; S. G. Traill 11–1–293–81–0–29.30; H. J. M.
Wacher 12–0–213–70–0–17.75; J. D. E. Stubbs 10–0–153–66–0–15.30; *C. M. C. Chataway
11–0–155–49–0–14.09.

Bowling—T. W. Morey 94–32–195–20–5/12–9.75; E. C. Eccles 78–21–214–17–5/24–12.58;
S. A. F. Darroch 124–25–405–21–4/59–19.28; T. O. Bruce 103–25–300–15–3/19–20.00.

THE KING'S SCHOOL, CHESTER   *Played 11: W 7, L 3, D 1. A 3*

Master i/c: S. Neal

Despite poor weather, the side performed well, though three close games were hard on the nerves:
MCC were vanquished with eight wickets down and one ball remaining; the last pair for Merchant
Taylors', Crosby, gained the nine they needed for victory; and, chasing 131 against King's,
Macclesfield, the side slid from 124 for four to 129 all out.

Batting—T. D. Bonser 9–2–270–82–0–38.57; J. P. McKay 7–1–188–53–0–31.33; R. D. G.
Brown 9–2–195–66–0–27.85; *E. W. D. Francis 10–0–177–46–0–17.70.

Bowling—E. W. Mason 91.2–26–244–23–4/13–10.60.

KING'S SCHOOL, ELY   *Played 10: W 0, L 9, D 1*

Masters i/c: T. Firth and W. J. Marshall

Batting—T. M. F. Sale 10–1–242–65–0–26.88.

Bowling—No bowler took 15 wickets. The leading bowler was T. W. Wilkins
68.2–13–242–8–3/6–30.25.

KING'S SCHOOL, MACCLESFIELD   *Played 17: W 7, L 5, D 5. A 2*

Master i/c: J. D. Nuttall   Professional: S. Moores

The school achieved a dramatic one-run victory against King's, Chester when their last six wickets
– including a hat-trick for Ashley Sharp – tumbled for five runs.

Batting—J. P. Keep 11–6–296–78–0–59.20; A. M. Day 14–1–394–69*–0–30.30; *J. A. O. Duffy
16–1–443–112–1–29.53; T. M. Isherwood 15–3–272–63–0–22.66; O. D. Kenyon 16–2–295–
46*–0–21.07; O. C. W. Rushton 14–1–260–60*–0–20.00.

Bowling—T. A. Davenport 92.5–12–300–16–3/31–18.75; J. M. Arnfield 103.3–22–310–
15–4/28–20.66.

KING'S SCHOOL, ROCHESTER   *Played 13: W 1, L 10, D 2. A 1*

Master i/c: G. R. Williams

Batting—*R. W. Hughes 14–2–396–63–0–33.00; S. J. Baker 13–0–177–74–0–13.61.

Bowling—R. H. Barrett 89–15–352–18–6/31–19.55; R. W. Hughes 146.5–27–486–
24–5/82–20.25.

THE KING'S SCHOOL, TYNEMOUTH   *Played 10: W 3, L 3, D 4. A 5*

Masters i/c: W. Ryan and P. J. Nicholson

After a slow start, the mature captaincy of Marcus Turner galvanised a workmanlike side into one capable of excellent performances. He also dominated the batting, contributing almost three times more than the next-highest scorer.

Batting—M. J. Turner 10–0–564–148–2–56.40; R. J. Gardham 10–1–190–47–0–21.11.

Bowling—J. P. Taylor 69.3–15–256–15–5/20–17.06.

KING'S SCHOOL, WORCESTER   *Played 17: W 9, L 2, D 6. A 1*

Master i/c: D. P. Iddon   Professional: A. A. D. Gillgrass

A batting order that had strength in depth secured nine wins; the only school side to defeat the XI was Maritzburg College, on tour from South Africa.

Batting—S. A. Ott 14–1–388–111–1–29.84; R. J. Hallett 10–4–150–51–0–25.00; J. W. Robinson 15–1–343–62–0–24.50; N. O. S. Major 14–1–302–65–0–23.23; P. A. Burdon 13–1–241–77–0–20.08; *N. J. D. Dale-Lace 15–3–214–67–0–17.83; R. W. Fardon 14–1–213–62–0–16.38; J. R. Gwynne 14–3–151–34–0–13.72.

Bowling—J. R. Hill 128–29–325–21–6/36–15.47; R. W. Seeley 171.2–47–444–27–4/12–16.44; *N. J. D. Dale-Lace 213.4–48–669–34–5/25–19.67.

KINGSTON GRAMMAR SCHOOL   *Played 10: W 2, L 5, D 3. A 2*

Master i/c: D. Wethey

Batting—*O. M. Smith 8–0–293–70–0–36.62; R. Trivedi 10–1–164–34–0–18.22.

Bowling—No bowler took 15 wickets. The leading bowler was J. Webber 47.3–16–95–11–6/14–8.63.

KINGSWOOD SCHOOL   *Played 11: W 7, L 2, D 2*

Master i/c: G. Opie

A young side, well led by Tim Ward, fought hard to win seven of their 11 matches – the best tally for 39 years. For the second year running, James Thorne hit most runs, backed up by Sam Kelly's all-round skills.

Batting—J. E. G. Thorne 9–1–312–81–0–39.00; S. R. Kelly 9–2–182–69*–0–26.00; *T. Ward 8–0–183–45–0–22.87; J. A. Seddon 11–2–182–44*–0–20.22.

Bowling—H. F. Seddon 66–10–194–16–3/13–12.12; S. R. Kelly 82.4–13–249–18–3/14–13.83; M. N. Raisbeck 66.1–9–234–16–5/13–14.62.

LANCING COLLEGE   *Played 15: W 10, L 3, D 2*

Master i/c: M. P. Bentley   Professional: R. J. Davies

Batting—R. Wakeford 15–1–459–117–2–32.78; I. Higgins 12–1–302–64–0–27.45; N. Wood 14–1–327–106–1–25.15; Y. Salameh 11–2–216–60–0–24.00; J. Wood 12–0–235–61–0–19.58.

Bowling—J. Lepar 115.1–30–270–19–5/27–14.21; J. Vokins 93–23–284–15–5/33–18.93.

Alex Blakeborough (*left*) slotted easily into Leeds Grammar School's batting line-up, while George Walker was a mainstay of Norwich School's attack.

LANGLEY PARK SCHOOL   *Played 9: W 3, L 4, D 1, T 1*

Master i/c: J. Cockcroft

Batting—No batsman scored 150 runs. The leading batsman was S. B. Painter 7–0–136–42–0–19.42.

Bowling—No bowler took 15 wickets. The leading bowler was S. B. Painter 35–5–140–14–4/22–10.00.

LEEDS GRAMMAR SCHOOL   *Played 13: W 4, L 5, D 4. A 2*

Master i/c: R. Hill

The high points of the season were the 631 runs scored by Alex Blakeborough in his first year in the side, and a one-wicket victory over Manchester GS.

Batting—A. J. Blakeborough 13–2–631–116–2–57.36; A. Von Hirschberg 13–6–214–31*–0–30.57; G. O. E. James 13–0–270–67–0–20.76; C. J. Smith 12–2–171–57*–0–17.10; *C. J. Leadbeater 12–0–185–46–0–15.41.

Bowling—B. R. Maude 131.2–27–423–21–4/19–20.14; E. J. Manning 105.4–18–357–15–2/14–23.80.

THE LEYS SCHOOL   *Played 12: W 6, L 4, D 2. A 1*

Master i/c: A. R. C. Batterham   Professional: R. Lawson

Batting—S. O'Shea 10–3–219–61–0–31.28; D. Jordan 12–1–300–68–0–27.27; K. Coetzee 12–0–236–97–0–19.66; C. Walker-Smith 11–0–195–47–0–17.72; J. Houlder 13–1–184–41–0–15.33.

Bowling—G. Houghton 63–15–196–28–5/18–7.00; C. Walker-Smith 74–21–206–18–4/32–11.44; C. Dyson 66–17–225–15–2/31–15.00.

LIVERPOOL COLLEGE   *Played 11: W 1, L 10, D 0. A 4*

Master i/c: A. Fox   Professional: B. Mukherjee

Batting—No batsman scored 150 runs. The leading batsman was J. Howarth 12–2–98–28–0–9.80.

Bowling—No bowler took 15 wickets. The leading bowler was B. Ridgway 156–21–426–11–2/41–38.72.

LLANDOVERY COLLEGE   *Played 6: W 2, L 3, D 1. A 4*

Master i/c: T. G. Marks

For the third year running, the term was spoilt by the weather. Even so, the school triumphed over the Old Llandoverians for the first time in six years and battled to a worthy draw against a strong MCC. In the win over M. Smith's Eleven, Barry Esterhuizen captured four for one, including a hat-trick.

Batting—R. J. Coles 6–1–212–64–0–42.40.

Bowling—No bowler took 15 wickets. The leading bowler was B. Esterhuizen 40–3–127–8–4/1–15.87.

LORD WANDSWORTH COLLEGE   *Played 12: W 5, L 5, D 2. A 5*

Master i/c: M. C. Russell   Professional: D. M. Thomas

George Bayer and Simon Kent began the season in cracking form – prepared to chase any target – and four of the first five matches were won. However, the middle order seldom gave the expected support. Adam Askew and Toby Martin performed reliably with the ball but, like the batting, the bowling lacked depth. The side contained four qualified coaches.

Batting—S. A. Kent 12–1–357–89–0–32.45; *G. W. Bayer 11–2–279–73*–0–31.00; J. J. Ablett 10–1–232–49–0–25.77.

Bowling—A. F. Askew 104.2–24–393–21–5/50–18.71; T. Martin 134.4–39–316–16–4/39–19.75.

LORD WILLIAMS'S SCHOOL   *Played 12: W 3, L 4, D 5*

Master i/c: J. E. Fulkes

Batting—*A. Krol 12–2–330–82–0–33.00; P. J. Evans 9–2–196–50*–0–28.00; I. J. Evans 10–1–247–69*–0–27.44; T. Morgan 10–2–204–58*–0–25.50.

Bowling—A. Krol 86.4–16–297–16–3/21–18.56; I. J. Evans 89.1–11–319–17–4/35–18.76.

LOUGHBOROUGH GRAMMAR SCHOOL   *Played 16: W 4, L 7, D 5. A 4*

Master i/c: J. S. Weitzel   Professional: H. T. Tunnicliffe

Batting—*A. Bull 14–1–346–121–1–26.61; M. Alderson 14–0–228–54–0–16.28; P. Broster 13–1–154–57*–0–12.83; R. Martin 15–1–161–31–0–11.50.

Bowling—No bowler took 15 wickets. The leading bowler was E. Barnet 98–13–334–13–2/15–25.69.

MAGDALEN COLLEGE SCHOOL   *Played 13: W 2, L 3, D 8. A 2*

Master i/c: P. Askew

Batting—A. L. Capek 15–0–418–90–0–27.86; J. K. Neilson 15–3–266–54–0–22.16; N. D. Cook 14–0–283–74–0–20.21; R. S. Craig 14–0–282–84–0–20.14; *K-L. H. E. Noll 13–1–179–52–0–14.91.

Bowling—J. K. Neilson 198–47–612–39–6/41–15.69; K-L. H. E. Noll 137.3–26–546–23–5/72–23.73; A. I. Robinson 143–28–455–19–4/30–23.94.

MALVERN COLLEGE   *Played 15: W 7, L 6, D 2. A 8*

Master i/c: A. J. Murtagh   Professional: R. W. Tolchard

Batting—*J. D. Kontarines 14–2–460–101*–1–38.33; W. A. Murtagh 8–3–159–46–0–31.80; W. M. Gifford 10–4–188–55*–0–31.33; C. Wood 8–0–221–62–0–27.62; J. J. C. Lewis 11–3–176–67*–0–22.00; J. E. P. Cartwright 12–0–151–55–0–12.58.

Bowling—J. D. Kontarines 122.4–23–299–24–4/22–12.45; J. J. C. Lewis 102.3–17–346–19–4/26–18.21; J. M. Murtagh 138.1–27–472–20–4/24–23.60.

MANCHESTER GRAMMAR SCHOOL   *Played 15: W 5, L 1, D 9. A 1*

Master i/c: D. Moss

Several drawn matches were nearly won – including three with the opposition nine wickets down – and more was achieved than the results might indicate. Sandip Kotecha showed a mature grasp of tactics, cleverly switching his resources to get the best from leg-spinner Nick Murrills and opening pair Rana Malook and John Whitaker. The batting was dependable, with five players totalling 200 or more.

Batting—N. P. Murrills 9–3–237–66–0–39.50; *S. J. Kotecha 13–0–364–76–0–28.00; M. B. Filson 12–4–215–48*–0–26.87; M. R. A. Tufft 14–1–309–49–0–23.76; R. A. Buchan 12–2–209–57–0–20.90; V. Y. Ahuja 12–0–154–40–0–12.83.

Bowling—R. J. Malook 162.4–47–358–36–4/18–9.94; J. K. H. Whitaker 119.5–30–232–22–5/11–10.54; N. P. Murrills 237.1–62–584–40–5/15–14.60.

MARLBOROUGH COLLEGE   *Played 10: W 4, L 2, D 4. A 4*

Master i/c: N. E. Briers   Professional: R. M. Ratcliffe

In the first innings of a two-day match against Rugby, captain and wicket keeper Matthew Pocock made four stumpings and took three catches.

Batting—H. G. Ingham 8–3–207–58*–0–41.40; A. J. E. Coventry 6–1–162–43–0–32.40; M. G. Jacob 10–2–178–53*–0–22.25; H. R. D. Twort 9–2–152–57–0–21.71.

Bowling—E. J. Carpenter 185.1–66–393–28–7/27–14.03; A. C. R. Bush 96.1–20–282–18–5/21–15.66; A. R. G. Armstrong 118.2–25–336–18–5/24–18.66.

MERCHANT TAYLORS' SCHOOL, CROSBY   *Played 13: W 9, L 2, D 2. A 4*

Master i/c: Rev. D. A. Smith

Batting—*M. S. Cowdy 10–3–211–56*–0–30.14; G. A. Barry 10–2–218–51–0–27.25; J. F. Wildman 11–1–150–82*–0–15.00.

Bowling—P. K. Battersby 107–26–312–27–5/15–11.55; J. F. Wildman 91–22–267–21–6/42–12.71; G. A. Barry 110–36–278–21–4/22–13.23.

MERCHANT TAYLORS' SCHOOL, NORTHWOOD   *Played 17: W 10, L 1, D 6*

Master i/c: C. R. Evans-Evans   Professional: H. C. Latchman

The batting was again strong, and results were better than 1999 thanks to a more incisive attack. Andrew Nicholson led by example: his undefeated 126 against the touring Trinity GS, Sydney, was a highlight. Other key players were the fast-improving all-rounder Stuart Simons, and Simon Noach – who took hundreds off St Benedict's and St Paul's.

Batting—S. M. Simons 7–4–234–71–0–78.00; *A. P. Nicholson 13–4–447–126*–1–49.66; S. Noach 15–2–542–104–2–41.69; S. G. James 11–4–264–75–0–37.71; R. J. C. Wise 13–1–377–75–0–31.41; S. Woolf 9–2–175–41–0–25.00; R. J. M. Booth 13–5–169–54*–0–21.12.

Bowling—S. M. Simons 161–40–379–28–6/9–13.53; R. J. M. Booth 124.2–22–357–19–3/13–18.78; S. G. James 156.3–22–460–24–4/45–19.16.

MERCHISTON CASTLE SCHOOL   *Played 16: W 11, L 1, D 4. A 1*

Master i/c: C. W. Swan

The team flourished in the driest May and June for perhaps 15 years, winning nine and losing only one in 13 matches against other schools. Brendan McKerchar had a fine all-round season with 871 runs – including hundreds against Lothian Schools and Hereford Cathedral – and 41 wickets. He captained the Scotland Under-17 side and was selected for Scotland Under-19. Off-spinner Peter Swan is the son of former Scotland captain Richard.

Batting—B. T. McKerchar 17–2–871–145–2–58.06; A. W. Sharpe 11–4–296–55*–0–42.28; *A. R. Donaldson 12–1–272–97–0–24.72; J. M. R. Robertson 17–3–297–54*–0–21.21; O. D. Abram 12–3–187–46–0–20.77.

Bowling—L. W. Murray 193–50–409–36–5/7–11.36; B. T. McKerchar 197–39–572–41–4/9–13.95; P. A. Swan 167–57–405–22–5/32–18.40.

MILLFIELD SCHOOL   *Played 19: W 10, L 4, D 4, T 1. A 3*

Master i/c: R. M. Ellison   Professional: M. R. Davis

Batting—A.V. Suppiah 18–4–519–147–1–37.07; *J. G. S. Haggie 16–4–365–59–0–30.41; J. C. Hildreth 14–1–395–75*–0–30.38; R. L. S. Stokes 18–1–457–87–0–26.88; J. A. Elliot-Square 7–0–170–104–1–24.28; S. Nair 15–3–257–61–0–21.41; O. T. Harker-Smith 13–3–185–41–0 18.50; N. S. Goodman 19–2–279–72–0–16.41.

Bowling—S. Nair 133–23–375–24–4/33–15.62; A. V. Suppiah 199.2–55–433–24–3/21–18.04; J. G. S. Haggie 170.5–24–613–31–5/21–19.77; G. E. Morris 116.1–27–408–20–5/36–20.40.

MILL HILL SCHOOL   *Played 15: W 8, L 3, D 4. A 2*

Master i/c: P. H. Edwards   Professional: I. J. F. Hutchinson

Batting—J. Le Fort 11–3–387–109*–1–48.37; M. Hirsch 13–3–302–100*–1–30.20; L. Blair 11–3–213–65–0–26.62; V. Bhimjiyani 12–3–238–62*–0–26.44; T. Clarke 13–2–218–57–0–19.81; S. Da Re 13–1–185–42–0–15.41.

Bowling—V. Bhimjiyani 176–62–357–35–6/19–10.20; J. Le Fort 93–13–257–19–4/11–13.52; S. Da Re 89–20–300–17–4/53–17.64.

MONKTON COMBE SCHOOL   *Played 13: W 4, L 7, D 2*

Master i/c: P. R. Wickens   Professional: N. D. Botton

An experienced team generally performed well in the field and, despite inconsistent batting, the playing record was an improvement on the past two seasons.

Batting—*T. Hamilton 13–1–270–54*–0–22.50; M. A. Lynch 12–0–221–71–0–18.41; N. Wheeler 12–0–189–32–0–15.75; T. St John 12–2–156–36–0–15.60; O. Anderson 13–1–182–52–0–15.16; D. Thompson 11–0–156–30–0–14.18.

Bowling—T. Hamilton 126–27–335–20–5/36–16.75; N. Wheeler 94–14–343–20–4/24–17.15; M. E. Lynch 112–30–317–18–6/32–17.61.

MONMOUTH SCHOOL   *Played 14: W 4, L 6, D 4. A 2*

Master i/c: A. J. Jones   Professional: G. I. Burgess

Kunnal Khanna scored 109 and took five for 28 against Colston's.

Batting—K. Khanna 10–1–320–109–1–35.55; J. Wyatt 11–1–291–68–0–29.10; I. Clayton 7–0–158–42–0–22.57; A. D. Smith 9–0–180–73–0–20.00.

Bowling—J. Harrisson 95–10–342–15–5/58–22.80.

NEWCASTLE-UNDER-LYME SCHOOL   *Played 9: W 1, L 6, D 2. A 3*

Master i/c: S. A. Robson   Professional: O. D. Gibson

The school endured its worst-ever season; even when the bowling and fielding were competitive, the batting remained brittle and immature. John James, the captain, was alone in achieving the required standard, and went on to lead the Staffordshire Under-17 side.

Batting—*J. W. James 9–0–308–88–0–34.22.

Bowling—J. W. James 97–25–268–18–5/32–14.88.

NORWICH SCHOOL   *Played 12: W 5, L 3, D 4. A 2*

Master i/c: T. J. W. Day   Professionals: R. A. Bunting and S. C. Goldsmith

Left-arm spinner George Walker had figures of 9.1–5–8–8 as Norwich bundled out Culford for 68, and eventually won by nine wickets.

Batting—E. D. Hopkins 10–1–304–71*–0–33.77; W. J. V. Prewer 8–1–184–73–0–26.28; E. J. Foster 9–1–202–47–0–25.25; N. G. Pinder 8–1–161–47–0–23.00; C. W. Jones 11–0–198–47–0–18.00; *J. C. L. Marczewski 10–0–166–55–0–16.60.

Bowling—G. W. Walker 135.1–54–291–30–8/8–9.70; W. J. V. Prewer 103–24–243–16–3/44–15.18; A. J. Robinson 90.2–13–330–16–4/58–20.62.

NOTTINGHAM HIGH SCHOOL   *Played 12: W 7, L 1, D 4. A 2*

Master i/c: J. Lamb   Professional: K. E. Cooper

Batting—R. L. Pilgrim 10–2–402–157*–1–50.25; R. J. M. Wild 11–3–272–67*–0–34.00; *M. L. M. T. Marenah 9–1–194–67–0–24.25; G. J. Middleton 10–1–186–43–0–20.66.

Bowling—R. J. M. Wild 129.1–25–339–31–6/13–10.93; R. L. Pilgrim 82.5–20–240–15–3/5–16.00.

OAKHAM SCHOOL   *Played 17: W 8, L 4, D 5*

Master i/c: F. C. Hayes   Professional: D. S. Steele

Richard Mockford equalled the school record for wicket-keeping dismissals when he claimed six victims against St Edward's, Oxford, while George Firmin's average of 69.40 was the best since 1934.

Batting—G. R. Firmin 15–5–694–112*–2–69.40; *D. N. Jackson 16–6–459–84*–0–45.90; R. O. Mockford 9–5–178–50*–0–44.50; N. J. Ferraby 15–3–414–64*–0–34.50; J. E. B. A. Hamilton-Kennaway 11–2–234–55*–0–26.00; M. A. G. Boyce 9–0–162–46–0–18.00.

Bowling—N. J. Ferraby 182–36–573–28–5/36–20.46; J. E. B. A. Hamilton-Kennaway 184.2–23–645–30–5/22–21.50; M. S. Pilling 169.4–40–533–24–3/28–22.20.

Spin twins: between them, Oundle's identical twins Jonathan (*left*) and David Outar took 55 wickets with their left-arm spin. Jonathan also contributed 583 runs.

THE ORATORY SCHOOL   *Played 13: W 6, L 3, D 4*

Master i/c: P. L. Tomlinson   Professional: J. B. K. Howell

Batting—N. R. H. Lo 13–1–406–75–0–33.83; *D. E. Pike 12–1–361–55–0–32.81; A. J. Wight 11–4–224–54*–0–32.00; M. W. Housego 9–1–207–68–0–25.87; A. D. S. Critien 9–2–155–52–0–22.14; D. Campbell 13–1–200–50–0–16.66.

Bowling—D. E. Pike 148–28–229–22–5/5–10.40; M. J. Farmar 137.5–24–435–24–5/20–18.12; A. J. Wight 117.4–21–319–15–3/13–21.26.

OSWESTRY SCHOOL   *Played 9: W 1, L 7, D 1. A 2*

Master i/c: P. S. Jones

Batting—No batsman scored 150 runs. The leading batsman was A. Blaney 8–0–95–34–0–11.87.

Bowling—M. J. Nicholson 112–22–329–18–4/58–18.27.

OUNDLE SCHOOL   *Played 16: W 7, L 3, D 6. A 2*

Master i/c: J. R. Wake   Professional: T. Howorth

Martyn Dobson captained an inexperienced side to seven wins, shouldering all-rounder duties with Jonathan Outar. As well as contributing two centuries each, they – together with Jonathan's twin, David – bore the brunt of the bowling.

Batting—J. Outar 14–1–583–110*–2–44.84; *M. C. Dobson 16–0–677–137–2–42.31; R. P. de Pree 12–0–382–102–1–31.83; D. Outar 11–5–186–54–0–31.00; J. A. R. Wilson 13–4–170–54*–0–18.88; B. Redmond 15–2–239–51*–0–18.38; C. J. Wake 13–4–151–40–0–16.77.

Bowling—D. Outar 110–16–429–25–6/34–17.16; J. Outar 162.3–35–516–30–5/47–17.20; M. C. Dobson 218–70–569–32–5/40–17.78.

PANGBOURNE COLLEGE   *Played 8: W 3, L 3, D 2. A 1*

Master i/c: R. H. A. Brodhurst

Batting—C. J. Sutton 7–1–319–137–1–53.16; *J. Allsop 7–0–195–53–0–27.85.

Bowling—No bowler took 15 wickets. The leading bowler was J. P. Lewis 59–17–239–13–4/9–18.38.

THE PERSE SCHOOL   *Played 14: W 3, L 8, D 3. A 2*

Master i/c: M. A. Judson   Professional: D. C. Collard

A youthful side reached the final of the Cambridgeshire Under-19 Cup, but otherwise results were disappointing.

Batting—O. Gregory 14–0–308–54–0–22.00; J. Hayden-Smith 11–1–201–63–0–20.10; S. Smith 12–2–200–69–0–20.00.

Bowling—S. Duke 98–26–288–19–4/8–15.15; J. Unwin 85.2–14–261–17–4/26–15.35; *J. Ing 143.5–27–410–23–5/25–17.82; D. Hawkins 86.1–9–327–18–3/8–18.16.

PLYMOUTH COLLEGE   *Played 11: W 8, L 0, D 3*

Masters i/c: G. Lane and G. C. Roderick

An undefeated season culminated in victory at the end-of-term festival, contested by Bryanston, Lord Wandsworth College and hosts Clayesmore. At the Past v Present match in early July, former cricket master John Stevens accepted a presentation to mark 31 years' service.

Batting—*D. Pope 9–2–251–71–0–35.85; A. Egford 7–1–194–73*–0–32.33; I. Wheaton 9–3–194–69*–0–32.33; J. Green 7–1–171–69*–0–28.50; J. Toms 10–0–183–61–0–18.30.

Bowling—A. Lampe 70–15–272–21–7/42–12.95; R. Williams 103–23–301–21–4/36–14.33; T. Lane 118–24–361–24–5/25–15.04.

POCKLINGTON SCHOOL   *Played 14: W 5, L 4, D 5. A 4*

Master i/c: R. Smith

Batting—*A. N. Mitchell 12–3–338–97*–0–37.55; H. J. Mitchell 13–2–299–70–0–27.18; R. G. Booth 12–0–261–100–1–21.75; P. G. Priestley 13–0–248–42–0–19.07; D. P. C. Izzard 10–0–173–47–0–17.30.

Bowling—R. G. Booth 174.5–41–383–30–5/13–12.76; A. N. Mitchell 150.1–43–405–25–4/19–16.20; R. J. G. Owen 111.3–26–310–17–3/12–18.23.

PORTSMOUTH GRAMMAR SCHOOL   *Played 12: W 2, L 8, D 2. A 5*

Master i/c: G. D. Payne   Professional: R. J. Parks

Batting—*A. C. Saunders 12–0–321–61–0–26.75; O. Jones 10–0–258–52–0–25.80; I. R. Butler 11–2–189–34–0–21.00.

Bowling—I. R. Butler 148.5–25–379–21–3/26–18.04; B. Morgan 102.1–12–452–17–4/36–26.58.

PRIOR PARK COLLEGE   *Played 14: W 4, L 8, D 2*

Master i/c: D. R. Holland   Professional: M. D. Browning

Batting—R. Maunder 9–2–245–93–0–35.00; H. Blathwayt 10–0–294–68–0–29.40; H. J. Kidd 14–1–279–68–0–21.46.

Bowling—B. Beardmore 93–17–335–15–5/17–22.33.

QUEEN ELIZABETH GS, WAKEFIELD   *Played 13: W 3, L 4, D 6. A 1*

Master i/c: T. Barker   Professional: C. Jackson

The high point of the season was Simon Kelly's century against Bradford GS. Generally, the team played positively, though lapses in concentration were a persistent problem.

Batting—*S. Kelly 9–0–306–113–1–34.00; J. Anderson 12–1–327–69*–0–29.72; T. Bradley 9–1–229–79*–0–28.62; G. Fearns 12–1–284–62–0–25.81.

Bowling—No bowler took 15 wickets. The leading bowler was R. Wainwright 119–28–365–11–3/40–33.18.

QUEEN ELIZABETH'S HOSPITAL, BRISTOL   *Played 10: W 1, L 5, D 4. A 2*

Master i/c: P. Joslin

Batting—M. Beale 10–1–241–76–0–26.77.

Bowling—No bowler took 15 wickets. The leading bowler was L. Brown 56.3–8–244–14–6/17–17.42.

QUEEN'S COLLEGE, TAUNTON   *Played 16: W 11, L 2, D 3. A 3*

Master i/c: A. S. Free

An excellent season saw two new school records: Oliver Bailey took his career total to 2,220 runs (including seven centuries), while Matthew Gitsham became the leading all-rounder with 1,698 runs and 98 wickets over the same four-year period. William Bates added a final flourish to his career with seven for four against Wycliffe College.

Batting—O. J. Bailey 14–3–717–124*–3–65.18; *M. T. Gitsham 14–2–548–79–0–45.66; J. E. Trundley 14–4–393–92–0–39.30; S. A. Butt 14–0–234–85–0–16.71.

Bowling—W. R. Bates 145.3–36–324–37–7/4–8.75;   M. T. Gitsham 131.3–28–377–30–4/9–12.56.

RADLEY COLLEGE   *Played 13: W 4, L 0, D 9*

Master i/c: W. J. Wesson   Professionals: A. G. Robinson and A. R. Wagner

Radley went undefeated, though the weather had the last laugh in many games. The captain, Sam Andrews, scored runs consistently, bowled outstandingly without luck, and later played for Surrey Second Eleven. Simon Dalrymple is the brother of 1999 captain Jamie, who appeared for England against Sri Lanka in the Under-19 Test series.

Batting—*S. J. Andrews 13–2–564–125*–2–51.27; T. P. Hodgson 8–4–181–50–0–45.25; J. Waddell 13–0–414–87–0–31.84; S. H. Dalrymple 10–4–150–53*–0–25.00; L. D. McLaren 12–0–237–60–0–19.75; R. D. M. Kirkness 12–1–155–34–0–14.09.

Bowling—J. Waddell 114–18–324–19–5/20–17.05; C. R. Langton 134–18–405–23–3/38–17.60; M. C. Cooper 166–38–423–22–5/43–19.22.

RATCLIFFE COLLEGE   *Played 12: W 4, L 6, D 2. A 2*

Master i/c: R. Hughes   Professional: D. Collard

Batting—L. J. Wright 9–2–483–130–3–69.00; *B. T. Clarke 8–0–382–66–0–47.75.

Bowling—A. Ekanayake 69–5–250–22–7/50–11.36.

Left-arm spinners Daniel Mendis (*left*) and Neil Bezodis proved a potent combination for Reigate Grammar School.

READING SCHOOL   *Played 11: W 7, L 1, D 3. A 2*

Masters i/c: J. E. Bonneywell and R. F. Perkins

Batting—H. H. Griffiths 7–2–260–123–1–52.00; M. Bushell 9–1–383–78*–0–47.87; *M. J. Leary 9–1–376–112*–1–47.00; T. G. Burrows 6–2–160–81–0–40.00; M. J. Orford 7–1–156–59–0–26.00.

Bowling—M. G. R. Ball 78.2–12–228–20–4/20–11.40; M. R. Jubb 60–6–196–16–5/43–12.25; H. H. Griffiths 80.1–12–293–16–3/23–18.31.

REIGATE GRAMMAR SCHOOL   *Played 17: W 8, L 2, D 7. A 3*

Master i/c: D. C. R. Jones   Professional: B. J. Oldroyd

Chief architects of the side's success were slow left-armers Neil Bezodis and captain Daniel Mendis, who between them took nearly 80 wickets. However, the batting was fragile and the school did not pass 200 all term. Cricket master David Jones completed 25 years and 500 matches with the team.

Batting—*D. C. Mendis 17–5–381–59–0–31.75; A. C. H. Diggles 14–1–299–77*–0–23.00; N. R. Bezodis 16–2–259–66–0–18.50.

Bowling—N. R. Bezodis 228–73–519–42–4/1–12.35; D. C. Mendis 144.4–26–497–36–7/21–13.80; J. A. R. Brickley 178.5–45–466–24–3/13–19.41.

RENDCOMB COLLEGE   *Played 11: W 4, L 5, D 2. A 1*

Master i/c: B. L. North

Batting—W. Witchell 12–3–282–68–0–31.33; N. Hall 9–1–192–60–0–24.00.

Bowling—B. Stanfield 65–14–176–16–5/2–11.00; N. Hall 56.1–7–185–16–5/24–11.56; C. Henson 61–7–197–15–5/58–13.13.

REPTON SCHOOL   *Played 13: W 5, L 5, D 3. A 5*

Master i/c: F. P. Watson   Professional: M. K. Kettle

Batting—J. W. Stevenson 13–2–442–85–0–40.18; R. T. Alsop 13–0–405–83–0–31.15; D. A. Exley 12–2–186–48–0–18.60; *M. Hall 12–1–173–45–0–15.72.

Bowling—B. D. E. Dewhirst 87–20–279–17–4/14–16.41; J. W. Stevenson 108.4–20–400–19–5/20–21.05.

ROSSALL SCHOOL   *Played 15: W 1, L 10, D 4*

Master i/c: A. D. Todd   Professional: Abbus Ali

Batting—J. E. Bruck 15–1–181–43–0–12.92; *J. M. Ferguson 14–1–167–66*–0–12.84; M. Webster 15–0–174–41–0–11.60.

Bowling—R. Dingle 149–15–495–23–3/10–21.52.

ROYAL GRAMMAR SCHOOL, COLCHESTER   *Played 22: W 2, L 12, D 8. A 4*

Master i/c: R. L. Bayes

The school had a disappointing season in both timed and limited-overs cricket. Only Chris Dingley, with 781, scored the expected runs, but the bowling was a little stronger: three students, all of whom return for the 2001 season, averaged under 20.

Batting—C. H. Dingley 22–0–781–123–1–35.50; *M. R. Cranley 22–2–496–61–0–24.80; T. W. R. George 19–0–448–79–0–23.57; T. W. Bradshaw 21–0–435–81–0–20.71; M. Tyler 20–2–208–32–0–11.55; A. E. Cook 16–2–152–39–0–10.85; S. R. Plant 20–1–166–40*–0–8.73.

Bowling—P. C. Smith 109–18–330–21–4/22–15.71; M. Tyler 202–49–566–31–5/39–18.25; K. Patel 102–24–274–15–4/27–18.26; C. H. Dingley 173–26–677–25–4/33–27.08; S. R. Plant 195.3–30–646–22–6/45–29.36; A. E. Cook 172.5–33–549–17–4/62–32.29.

ROYAL GRAMMAR SCHOOL, GUILDFORD   *Played 18: W 9, L 4, D 5. A 1*

Master i/c: S. B. R. Shore   Professional: M. A. Lynch

The team won a gratifying nine of their 18 fixtures, including a first-ever victory over MCC. There was a tense draw at Charterhouse, which ended with the scores level.

Batting—T. G. Markham 6–3–225–83*–0–75.00; P. J. Hosier 7–2–272–55*–0–54.40; A. Tucker 13–3–300–50*–0–30.00; S. P. Barnsley 9–1–221–67*–0–27.62; T. H. Dickson 11–4–180–36–0–25.71; *G. E. Hughes 12–0–252–65–0–21.00; S. P. Peel 12–0–215–87–0–17.91; S. K. T. Elliott 15–1–209–65*–0–14.92.

Bowling—S. K. T. Elliott 101.4–14–378–23–6/55–16.43; A. Tucker 156–24–447–24–5/43–18.62; D. J. Jones 110.2–17–380–19–4/25–20.00.

ROYAL GRAMMAR SCHOOL, HIGH WYCOMBE   *Played 15: W 9, L 2, D 4. A 1*

Master i/c: P. R. Miles

Batting—C. Allfrey 14–3–489–80*–0–44.45; H. Matcham 10–3–252–76–0–36.00; R. Bentall 12–3–290–67–0–32.22; M. Honeyben 13–3–297–67–0–29.70.

Bowling—C. Langley 110.5–29–289–26–4/13–11.11; J. Nicholas 140.1–41–367–31–7/11–11.83; J. Mahood 139–41–359–28–4/2–12.82.

ROYAL GRAMMAR SCHOOL, LANCASTER   *Played 15: W 7, L 3, D 5. A 1*

Master i/c: I. D. Whitehouse   Professional: D. H. Cameron

Batting—D. J. Hagen 14–0–555–104–1–39.64; G. J. Hiron 11–1–248–44*–0–24.80; D. M. Kidd 12–1–206–64*–0–18.72; B. S. Simm 14–1–188–42–0–14.46.

Bowling—R. N. Kidd 112–33–311–19–5/18–16.36; C. R. Glover 161–22–434–24–4/43–18.08; B. S. Simm 202–51–581–30–5/51–19.36; D. M. Kidd 142–26–415–16–3/20–25.93.

ROYAL GRAMMAR SCHOOL, NEWCASTLE   *Played 17: W 5, L 8, D 4. A 2*

Master i/c: O. L. Edwards

Batting—A. J. Nairn 16–1–435–92–0–29.00; C. W. Robson 13–1–302–67–0–25.16; A. S. Ladhar 13–2–268–89*–0–24.36; R. J. McSherry 11–1–171–38–0–17.10; *D. F. Carr 12–2–157–53–0–15.70.

Bowling—M. C. D. Lewis 132–26–376–20–3/25–18.80; C. W. Robson 145.3–21–427–21–4/40–20.33.

ROYAL GRAMMAR SCHOOL, WORCESTER   *Played 22: W 18, L 0, D 4*

Master i/c: B. M. Rees   Professional: P. J. Newport

An impressive battery of five seamers – led by Tim Denyer and David Taylor – carried all before them, resulting in an unbeaten season and a record 18 wins. Together they grabbed 157 wickets at 11.26. Richard Wilkinson, the captain, and wicket-keeper Chris Edwards were the mainstays of the batting, each contributing over 500. Wilkinson became a founder member of the Worcestershire Academy.

Batting—*R. M. Wilkinson 16–6–555–84*–0–55.50; J. R. Watkins 11–4–294–48–0–42.00; C. J. Edwards 20–5–522–69–0–34.80; S. D. Emson 14–3–265–71*–0–24.09; A. D. Millington 10–1–210–63–0–23.33; J. S. Smith 13–0–236–87–0–18.15.

Bowling—T. S. Denyer 161.2–46–417–41–6/27–10.17; J. A. Hayden 134.4–29–310–29–4/31–10.68; D. C. Taylor 154.3–24–444–39–5/18–11.38; R. M. Wilkinson 154–30–389–32–3/19–12.15; S. D. Emson 65.5–5–208–16–3/9–13.00.

RUGBY SCHOOL   *Played 12: W 5, L 3, D 4. A 2*

Master i/c: P. J. Rosser   Professional: L. Tennant

Batting—R. Menon 8–2–319–70–0–53.16; J. Jarvis 12–2–293–68*–0–29.30; T. Clark 9–1–185–48–0–23.12.

Bowling—P. Sinclair 99–32–224–15–4/24–14.93; J. Noble 157–39–413–23–4/54–17.95

RYDAL PENRHOS   *Played 8: W 4, L 3, D 1*

Master i/c: M. T. Leach

Gareth Van Heerden scored an undefeated 125 against Liverpool College, and leg-spinning all-rounder David Watkins was selected for Wales Under-16.

Batting—*G. Van Heerden 8–1–322–125*–1–46.00; P. J. H. Leach 6–0–237–86–0–39.50; D. Watkins 7–2–185–74*–0–37.00.

Bowling—P. J. H. Leach 60–15–199–17–6/13–11.70.

RYDE SCHOOL   *Played 6: W 2, L 3, D 1*

Master i/c: M. Mairis

Alex Baker, with 96, and younger brother Danny (67) did most to secure an honourable draw with MCC, the highlight of a short season. Victories over Winchester and Churchers gave a small pool of players a much-needed boost.

Batting—A. Baker 5–0–203–96–0–40.60; D. Baker 6–0–189–83–0–31.50.

Bowling—No bowler took 15 wickets. The leading bowler was A. Baker 29–6–132–8–4/36–16.50.

ST ALBANS SCHOOL   *Played 16: W 5, L 5, D 6*

Masters i/c: C. C. Hudson and R. Wright   Professional: P. Knight

The season got under way with a bang when captain Siran Seevaratnam ran his car into a wall. His unavailability deprived the team of an opening bowler and forcing batsman. Poor weather discouraged run-scoring, though Andrew Brazier managed almost 400 in conditions favouring bowlers. Left-arm pace man Jonathan Bateman exploited them to take 27 wickets.

Batting—A. Brazier 13–0–392–92–0–30.15; *M. Jacobs 15–1–278–94–0–19.85; E. Charlesworth 15–6–177–27*–0–19.66; A. Sheridan 14–2–218–68–0–18.16; M. Searle 9–0–152–40–0–16.88.

Bowling—J. Bateman 139.4–46–319–27–4/28–11.81; T. Perry 110.1–22–311–22–4/30–14.13; K. Coulson 100.4–14–330–16–3/30–20.62; M. Pettit 113.2–17–404–19–4/38–21.26.

ST DUNSTAN'S COLLEGE   *Played 12: W 2, L 8, D 2*

Master i/c: N. R. Taylor

Batting—*B. Postma 10–3–236–82*–0–33.71; S. Giddins 11–1–206–31–0–20.60.

Bowling—No bowler took 15 wickets. The leading bowler was B. Postma 75.2–15–328–13–4/41–25.23.

ST EDMUND'S COLLEGE   *Played 6: W 0, L 5, D 1. A 2*

Master i/c: J. Faithfull

Batting—No batsman scored 150 runs. The leading batsman was M. Emmanuel 5–0–72–38–0–14.40.

Bowling—No bowler took 15 wickets. The leading bowler was A. Taylor 42–13–91–8–3/29–11.37.

ST EDMUND'S SCHOOL, CANTERBURY   *Played 9: W 3, L 5, D 1. A 1*

Master i/c: M. C. Dobson   Professional: M. Jenkinson

A talented group of batsmen, led by Dominic Chambers, regularly manoeuvred the side into a strong position only for it to be squandered by inconsistent bowling and careless fielding. However, in the best match of the summer, against Cheadle Hulme, bowlers and fielders held their nerve, and victory came by 15 runs.

Batting—D. J. Chambers 10–5–450–89*–0–90.00; *G. S. Haji 6–1–265–126–1–53.00; A. W. Gerrard 7–2–243–97–0–48.60; S. S. Bokhari 9–1–310–96–0–38.75.

Bowling—J. P. Tinto 90–15–323–16–3/7–20.18; A. W. Gerrard 87–10–357–15–4/23–23.80.

ST EDWARD'S, OXFORD   *Played 10: W 3, L 5, D 2. A 3*

Master i/c: J. Mills

In an end-of-season flourish, David Leadbitter amassed over 250 runs in his last four innings.

Batting—D. Leadbitter 10–2–342–89*–0–42.75; T. Newell 8–2–178–53*–0–29.66; *F. Cross 9–1–196–46–0–24.50; P. Swainson 10–1–217–42–0–24.11.

Bowling—T. Conibear 73–13–195–15–4/21–13.00.

ST GEORGE'S COLLEGE, WEYBRIDGE   *Played 23: W 4, L 13, D 6. A 2*

Master i/c: R. Ambrose

Despite mixed fortunes, contesting the Sir Garfield Sobers Schools Festival in Barbados was the pinnacle of the summer. James Tindall and Tim Frost were selected for a representative side to challenge a team made up of Caribbean players.

Batting—J. R. Tindall 20–0–637–65–0–31.85; A. J. Fraser 20–3–402–78–0–23.64; T. J. S. Frost 21–2–402–53–0–21.15; *A. J. T. O'Sullivan 20–3–331–55–0–19.47; A. D. R. Stanier 18–3–202–59*–0–13.46; C. J. J. Caswell 16–2–165–39–0–11.78.

Bowling—A. D. R. Stanier 79.5–10–320–20–7/42–16.00; T. J. S. Frost 163.5–40–552–34–6/10–16.23; A. A. S. Holman 157.1–23–582–21–2/14–27.71; A. J. Fraser 172.1–33–742–26–3/28–28.53.

ST JOHN'S SCHOOL, LEATHERHEAD   *Played 14: W 9, L 3, D 2. A 2*

Master i/c: A. B. Gale

Batting—D. M. Eaton 11–3–289–77*–0–36.12; D. S. Blows 14–2–358–80*–0–29.83; D. J. Balcombe 8–1–179–55–0–25.57; S. R. S. Bennett 14–2–217–69–0–18.08.

Bowling—W. S. A. Palmer 103.3–16–325–25–3/20–13.00; J. T. E. Balcombe 93.4–13–279–17–5/36–16.41; L. E. Hudson 110.5–19–330–18–4/22–18.33; *T. J. H. Clegg 110.1–15–394–21–3/13–18.76.

ST JOSEPH'S COLLEGE, IPSWICH   *Played 10: W 2, L 5, D 3. A 1*

Master i/c: M. Davey   Professional: K. Brooks

Batting—T. Hembry 10–2–387–97–0–48.37; K. Mildenhall 9–0–168–55–0–18.66; *N. Barratt 10–1–156–59*–0–17.33.

Bowling—K. Mildenhall 81–16–202–23–7/20–8.78; M. Dias 100–13–328–16–5/60–20.50.

ST PAUL'S SCHOOL   *Played 13: W 6, L 0, D 7. A 3*

Master i/c: G. Hughes   Professional: M. Heath

The season sparked into life with two confidence-boosting ten-wicket victories – against Royal GS, Guildford, and St Dunstan's – and the team remained unbeaten. Ben Duncan batted particularly well on rain-affected wickets, while Lachlan Nieboer spearheaded the attack, bowling 19 of his 26 victims.

Batting—B. J. Duncan 13–5–616–131*–1–77.00; *T. R. Pugh 12–3–229–75*–0–25.44; J. J. Segall 11–2–189–58–0–21.00; R. V. Kapadia 10–2–161–49–0–20.12.

Bowling—L. B. S. Nieboer 112.3–25–288–26–6/36–11.07; L. A. Wilson 120.1–30–346–24–4/10–14.41.

ST PETER'S SCHOOL, YORK   *Played 18: W 7, L 2, D 9. A 3*

Master i/c: D. Kirby   Professional: K. F. Mohan

Trevor Smith made major contributions with both bat and ball as the school – which hosted the Six Schools' Festival – enjoyed a successful season.

Batting—T. C. Smith 18–4–570–86*–0–40.71; T. Main 12–4–320–71*–0–40.00; *A. T. Main 19–4–477–78*–0–31.80; P. A. Bainbridge 18–2–498–124*–1–31.12; G. Mackfall 14–7–173–35*–0–24.71; J. E. Taylor 15–1–286–51–0–20.42; R. N. R. Gibbon 15–4–206–36–0–18.72; M. W. Spilman 16–0–211–47–0–13.18.

Bowling—T. C. Smith 201.3–59–660–33–4/30–20.00; G. Mackfall 169.1–45–488–24–3/12–20.33; T. T. Bainbridge 159.4–42–534–25–4/27–21.36.

SEDBERGH SCHOOL   *Played 16: W 6, L 4, D 6. A 1*

Master i/c: J. C. Bobby   Professional: R. E. Veenstra

Christian Howard took eight for 81 against Barnard Castle.

Batting—R. M. Bean 16–1–452–65–0–30.13; R. W. G. Ross 16–1–432–84*–0–28.80; A. C. Robertson 12–5–150–36*–0–21.42; A. H. Clappison 16–0–279–52–0–17.43; M. W. E. Lofthouse 15–0–237–67–0–15.80; A. H. Robson 14–0–220–51–0–15.71; *J. C. Goulding 16–2–193–35–0–13.78.

Bowling—P. Howell 155–39–385–22–5/29–17.50; J. C. Goulding 194.2–46–465–24–4/29–19.37; R. M. Talbot 174.3–45–456–21–4/27–21.71.

SEVENOAKS SCHOOL   *Played 13: W 2, L 7, D 4. A 2*

Master i/c: C. J. Tavaré

Batting—*B. E. Sergeant 12–2–250–81*–0–25.00; D. A. Showell 11–2–225–51–0–25.00; A. M. Gill 10–1–169–59–0–18.77; B. P. Spokes 11–1–185–79–0–18.50; O. T. R. Jones 12–0–214–50–0–17.83.

Bowling—S. J. G. Wilkin 94–26–259–15–4/6–17.26.

SHEBBEAR COLLEGE   *Played 8: W 4, L 4, D 0. A 2*

Master i/c: A. Bryan

Batting—E. Neill-Hall 7–1–210–63–0–35.00.

Bowling—No bowler took 15 wickets. The leading bowler was J. Sanders 32–6–94–11–6/20–8.54.

SHERBORNE SCHOOL   *Played 13: W 5, L 6, D 2. A 2*

Master i/c: M. D. Nurton   Professional: A. Willows

Against King's, Bruton, Peter Langly-Smith became the first student to carry his bat, while all-rounder Ben Adams took an undefeated century off Taunton.

Batting—B. W. Adams 15–2–485–100*–1–37.30; T. R. Dowdall 15–1–433–97–0–30.92; W. P. Fegen 13–2–223–42–0–20.27; P. F. C. Langly-Smith 15–1–209–72*–0–14.92.

Bowling—T. R. Dowdall 148–40–277–28–6/10–9.89; W. P. Fegen 76–8–223–16–3/28–13.93; B. W. Adams 119–21–327–20–4/2–16.35; C. J. P. Hopkins 134–22–413–17–4/42–24.29.

SHREWSBURY SCHOOL   *Played 19: W 5, L 6, D 8. A 2*

Master i/c: M. J. Lascelles   Professional: A. P. Pridgeon

Batting—L. Briggs 16–3–371–56–0–28.53; T. G. F. Wainright-Lee 11–4–195–32–0–27.85; *B. J. N. Chapman 20–1–504–93–0–26.52; A. C. McLaren 16–4–314–72–0–26.16; C. R. H. Stockbridge 18–2–409–82–0–25.56; C. J. G. Owen 16–0–255–49–0–15.93; C. H. C. Marlow 14–2–169–43–0–14.08.

Bowling—R. F. N. Champion 183–41–513–27–3/26–19.00; T. G. F. Wainright-Lee 140–20–378–18–3/21–21.00; N. J. Bevan 240–40–763–36–5/29–21.19; T. W. Graham 141–22–437–17–4/23–25.70; A. C. McLaren 111–20–414–16–3/32–25.87.

SIMON LANGTON GRAMMAR SCHOOL   *Played 6: W 4, L 1, D 1. A 2*

Master i/c: R. H. Green

Batting—K. Marsh 3–0–192–93–0–64.00; M. Paine 5–0–190–61–0–38.00.

Chris Meehan *(left)* regularly saw South Craven off to a good start. Queen's College, Taunton, will miss Matthew Gitsham's all-round abilities.

Bowling—No bowler took 15 wickets. The leading bowler was O. Janaway 48–9–105–12–4/15–8.75.

SIR ROGER MANWOOD'S SCHOOL   *Played 4: W 0, L 2, D 2*

Master i/c: J. F. Willmott

The sole bright spot in a season ruined by rain was the performance of Lewis Jenkins, who later turned out for Kent Second Eleven.

Batting—No batsman scored 150 runs. The leading batsman was L. J. P. Jenkins 3–0–129–88–0–43.00.

Bowling—No bowler took 15 wickets. The leading bowler was L. J. P. Jenkins 43–9–120–9–4/58–13.33.

SOLIHULL SCHOOL   *Played 12: W 7, L 3, D 2. A 1*

Master i/c: S. A. Morgan   Professional: Aamir Farooque

Batting—J. Robinson 10–1–333–77*–0–37.00; J. Hemming 13–3–274–66–0–27.40; *T. Moore 11–0–249–54–0–22.63; N. Hemming 10–1–200–53–0–22.22; D. Birch 11–0–203–62–0–18.45.

Bowling—N. Hemming 60–12–212–21–5/24–10.09.

SOUTH CRAVEN SCHOOL   *Played 7: W 2, L 5, D 0. A 3*

Master i/c: D. M. Birks

Opening batsman Chris Meehan set two school records – for hundreds and for runs in a season. His three centuries were all unbeaten, two coming on successive days against Queen Elizabeth GS, Wakefield, and Grange GS, Bradford.

Batting—C. M. Meehan 7–3–377–120*–3–94.25.

Bowling—No bowler took 15 wickets. The leading bowler was T. E. Hodgson 32–5–143–7–3/11–20.42.

STAMFORD SCHOOL   *Played 15: W 11, L 3, D 1. A 3*

Master i/c: A. N. Pike   Professional: J. E. Hindson

A record 11 wins included victories over local rivals Oakham and over Lincolnshire Gentlemen, the first in 51 years of the fixture. The captain, Oliver Burwell, bowled fast and straight – he collected seven for 19 against Gresham's – and finished with 45 wickets at 7.33. Runs came consistently, with six batsmen totalling 200 or more.

Batting—M. P. Williams 15–3–598–105*–2–49.83; J. D. Barker 12–4–229–65*–0–28.62; T. E. Lloyd 15–2–328–110*–1–25.23; J. R. Feetham 14–2–277–52*–0–23.08; M. J. L. Albinson 13–3–200–33*–0–20.00; D. B. South 12–0–237–76–0–19.75.

Bowling—*O. D. Burwell 138–42–330–45–7/19–7.33; M. N. Taylor 89–14–310–15–4/7–20.66; M. P. Williams 119–30–375–18–4/48–20.83.

STOCKPORT GRAMMAR SCHOOL   *Played 10: W 4, L 3, D 3*

Master i/c: A. Brett   Professional: D. J. Makinson

Batting—E. Daber 10–1–450–101–1–50.00.

Bowling—*C. Longden 132–27–347–27–6/43–12.85; P. Cowling 110–28–318–15–3/39–21.20.

STOWE SCHOOL   *Played 10: W 3, L 3, D 4. A 4*

Master i/c: R. C. Sutton   Professional: H. Rhodes

Batting—N. A. Oldridge 8–2–217–51–0–36.16; R. D. Large 9–1–267–71–0–33.37; A. G. Pearson 10–1–230–103*–1–25.55; O. R. Cullingworth 10–0–238–83–0–23.80.

Bowling—R. C. Worrall 117.1–22–390–22–5/74–17.72; *S. L. Smart 132–32–373–18–5/36–20.72.

STRATHALLAN SCHOOL   *Played 11: W 6, L 1, D 4. A 1*

Master i/c: R. H. Fitzsimmons

Outstanding fielding and teamwork, exemplified by wicket-keeper/batsman Tom Booth, delivered the most successful season for several years. The captain, Andrew Moodie, and Booth headed the batting, while Hamish Forbes and Colin Thwaites maintained pressure on opponents, each taking five or more wickets on four occasions. There were good wins against the XL Club and MCC, while Merchiston Castle inflicted the sole defeat.

Batting—*A. R. Moodie 10–1–305–78*–0–33.88; T. M. Booth 10–1–289–89*–0–32.11; L. V. Court 8–1–151–40–0–21.57; W. Bowry 11–1–198–35*–0–19.80.

Bowling—N. J. McIlwraith 73–26–152–18–5/38–8.44; C. A. Thwaites 124–29–298–29–7/36–10.27; H. D. Forbes 167.2–48–412–32–6/34–12.87.

SUTTON VALENCE SCHOOL   *Played 11: W 4, L 1, D 6. A 2*

Masters i/c: J. H. Kittermaster and W. D. Buck   Professional: A. P. Igglesden

Robert Ferley and Robert Joseph were selected for Kent Second Eleven, with Joseph making his first-class debut for the Counties Select XI against New Zealand A. Ferley later went on the England Under-19 tour of India. Their unavailability gave younger players a chance but, despite victories over the XL Club and the touring Australians from Scotch College, results were generally disappointing.

Batting—*R. S. Ferley 6–2–506–151*–2–126.50; R. H. Joseph 5–0–151–75–0–30.20; D. Julian 8–1–210–72*–0–30.00; R. Bradstock 11–2–262–74–0–29.11.

Bowling—R. S. Ferley 90.2–22–244–20–6/9–12.20.

TAUNTON SCHOOL   *Played 14: W 3, L 9, D 2. A 2*

Master i/c: S. T. Hogg   Professional: A. Kennedy

The Collins family were involved on and off the pitch: 16-year-old Martin was by some distance the leading batsman, while his sister, Danielle, proved a capable scorer. Joey Rose, the captain, is the youngest son of the former Somerset captain, Brian.

Batting—M. Collins 12–0–476–78–0–39.66; P. Dunn 11–0–278–88–0–25.27; P. Read 11–0–239–70–0–21.72; C. Bradbury 11–1–201–120*–1–20.10; L. Fishlock 12–2–186–40–0–18.60; *J. Rose 10–1–160–41–0–17.77.

Bowling—W. Penny 96.4–15–309–23–4/6–13.43; J. Kennedy 74–8–292–15–5/37–19.46.

TIFFIN SCHOOL   *Played 18: W 6, L 3, D 9. A 3*

Master i/c: M. J. Williams

Thirteen-year-old Arun Harinath became the youngest student to reach the First Eleven – even old boy Alec Stewart was 15 before getting his chance! Harinath was averaging over 150 for the Under-13s before making an immediate impact in the senior side.

Batting—S. Subesinghe 7–4–151–46*–0–50.33; C. N. Weerasinghe 16–1–424–84–0–28.26; A. E. Sacher 9–1–210–67*–0–26.25; R. M. O'Brien 14–4–238–64–0–23.80; A. Harinath 8–1–154–64–0–22.00; *S. R. Toama 14–1–286–65–0–22.00; D. W. Bates 15–4–163–23–0–14.81.

Bowling—A. Harinath 61–17–189–17–4/19–11.11; G. J. Nutt 83.4–8–299–17–3/13–17.58; S. Subesinghe 125.4–25–427–23–4/45–18.56; D. W. Bates 125.2–27–461–23–5/4–20.04; R. M. Cunningham 145.2–33–459–16–5/33–28.68.

TONBRIDGE SCHOOL   *Played 14: W 6, L 4, D 3, T 1. A 1*

Master i/c: N. A. Leamon   Professional: D. Chadwick

Batting—*J. Atkinson 17–1–666–93–0–41.62; N. Bluett 16–0–421–69–0–26.31; J. Aylward 17–2–393–82–0–26.20; R. Evans 10–1–216–61–0–24.00; W. Montgomery 13–0–302–65–0–23.23; S. Ulpy 10–3–151–29–0–21.57; N. Taylor 15–2–269–52*–0–20.69; G. Adams 16–1–304–76–0–20.26.

Bowling—J. Moses 125–16–468–29–4/17–16.13; J. Aylward 152–25–510–31–6/24–16.45; W. Murday 98–16–346–16–4/15–21.62; N. Bluett 163–22–585–15–3/53–39.00.

TRENT COLLEGE   *Played 13: W 9, L 3, D 1. A 3*

Master i/c: J. T. Jordison   Professional: J. A. Afford

Batting—J. Siddall 8–3–226–60–0–45.20; P. Scott 8–1–301–139–1–43.00; J. Tunnicliffe 11–3–223–72–0–27.87; C. Newman 13–2–257–69–0–23.36; W. Rolt 14–2–261–58–0–21.75; A. Allcock 12–0–202–34–0–16.83.

Bowling—C. Wood 81.2–10–294–16–3/14–18.37; W. Rolt 153.1–33–377–17–3/31–22.17.

TRINITY SCHOOL, CROYDON   *Played 14: W 3, L 6, D 5. A 1*

Master i/c: C. R. Burke

Richard Piggin, in his first year as captain, thrived on the new responsibility, and his cricket matured significantly. He headed both batting and bowling averages.

Batting—*R. Piggin 11–1–282–90*–0–28.20; M. Handley 12–4–203–40–0–25.37; A. Fifield 11–3–200–64–0–25.00; M. Amin 12–1–203–46–0–18.45; D. Rapley 12–1–200–74–0–18.18; G. Barker 13–0–185–52–0–14.23.

Bowling—R. Piggin 110–20–217–20–5/21–10.85; J. Broadfoot 135–38–339–19–7/12–17.84; M. Amin 122–15–364–16–4/44–22.75.

TRURO SCHOOL   *Played 10: W 3, L 3, D 4. A 3*

Master i/c: D. M. Phillips

Off-spinner Laura Harper made her international debut for England against South Africa, taking one for 39 from her ten overs.

Batting—*P. M. Ellis 9–2–397–121–1–56.71; D. J. Pollard 8–0–232–99–1–29.00; O. J. Turnbull 6–0–162–49–0–27.00; D. W. Miller 8–2–158–67–0–26.33.

Bowling—No bowler took 15 wickets. The leading bowler was D. J. Pollard 40–7–184–9–4/18–20.44.

UNIVERSITY COLLEGE SCHOOL   *Played 11: W 2, L 9, D 0. A 2*

Masters i/c: S. M. Bloomfield and C. P. Mahon   Professional: W. G. Jones

Batting—N. R. C. Jones 9–1–292–106*–1–36.50; J. S. Nissan 8–0–266–73–0–33.25; T. J. Banks 8–0–180–61–0–22.50; *J. D. Ricketts 10–0–210–49–0–21.00.

Bowling—P. J. Harrington 65.5–5–219–15–3/18–14.60.

UPPINGHAM SCHOOL   *Played 21: W 7, L 6, D 8. A 2*

Master i/c: C. C. Stevens   Professional: B. T. P. Donelan

In the two-innings match against Shrewsbury, opening bat and wicket-keeper Josh Branson spent all but ten overs of the game on the field. He scored 80 and 60 not out as well as making five dismissals. The game ended with Shrewsbury two runs and Uppingham one wicket from victory.

Batting—S. T. P. Pearson 9–4–216–45*–0–43.20; T. H. Gibbs 16–3–397–64–0–30.53; *O. C. W. Williams 22–3–500–73*–0–26.31; W. G. Hodson 17–2–362–58*–0–24.13; J. T. Branson 18–2–336–80–0–21.00; B. J. Branson 12–1–221–70–0–20.09; C. G. B. Bond 16–2–189–32–0–13.50.

Bowling—T. H. Gibbs 165.1–48–467–36–4/17–12.97; W. E. Crowder 175.2–40–518–35–4/18–14.80; W. G. Hodson 180.5–39–619–32–5/19–19.34; O. C. W. Williams 80–13–320–15–2/4–21.33.

VICTORIA COLLEGE, JERSEY   *Played 16: W 6, L 6, D 4*

Master i/c: D. A. R. Ferguson   Professional: C. Minty

Batting—B. J. Vautier 7–1–227–69*–0–37.83; A. S. J. Dewhurst 14–1–341–100*–1–26.23; P. W. Gough 14–1–324–53*–0–24.92; *G. O. Hughes 12–1–273–119*–1–24.81; T. J. Perchard 12–0–297–70–0–24.75; J. M. Gough 14–3–257–42–0–23.36.

Bowling—J. M. Gough 137–34–342–30–5/33–11.40; G. O. Hughes 142–38–337–27–4/5–12.48; A. S. J. Dewhurst 87–13–266–17–4/46–15.64.

WARWICK SCHOOL   *Played 12: W 5, L 4, D 3. A 5*

Master i/c: G. A. Tedstone

Batting—T. A. Qadri 10–3–266–81*–0–38.00; J. P. Montanaro 11–2–322–50–0–35.77; *J. M. G. Meredith 11–1–238–56*–0–23.80; S. H. Pangli 9–0–201–37–0–22.33; O. C. Higgens 8–0–163–44–0–20.37.

Bowling—No bowler took 15 wickets. The leading bowler was T. A. Qadri 84.4–10–316–14–3/26–22.57.

WATFORD GRAMMAR SCHOOL　　*Played 14: W 1, L 5, D 8*

Master i/c: R. Panter

Batting—*A. Hodgkinson 14–3–465–85–0–42.27; R. Shafe 11–1–192–38–0–19.20; S. Long 12–1–154–34–0–14.00.

Bowling—J. Kamruddin 98–18–262–15–3/20–17.46; C. Cobb 83.2–18–293–16–7/14–18.31.

WELLINGBOROUGH SCHOOL　　*Played 10: W 4, L 5, D 1. A 4*

Master i/c: M. H. Askham　　　　　　　　　　　　　　Professional: J. C. J. Dye

Batting—P. S. Coverdale 7–1–222–114*–1–37.00; T. C. Gee 10–2–285–105*–1–35.62; W. J. Tooley 8–1–223–59*–0–31.85; M. G. Carter 9–3–186–51–0–31.00; A. D. Daniels 9–1–220–78*–0–27.50.

Bowling—A. E. M. Tailor 60.5–10–208–17–5/28–12.23; C. E. Johnson 92.5–21–276–17–4/28–16.23.

WELLINGTON COLLEGE　　*Played 14: W 7, L 4, D 3. A 3*

Masters i/c: C. M. Oliphant-Callum and R. I. H. B. Dyer　　　Professional: P. J. Lewington

Tight bowling, good fielding and astute captaincy by Kai Horstmann ensured a competitive side played some impressive cricket, including a three-wicket victory over Eton, the first in 25 years. This result was of particular interest to the two schools' cricket masters.

Batting—A. T. Jarvis 15–1–454–60*–0–32.42; M. E. T. Briers 9–1–212–101–1–26.50; E. A. Bostock 14–2–297–70*–0–24.75; J. A. F. Robertson 12–1–229–62*–0–20.81; A. J. Bell 12–3–165–31*–0–18.33; G. M. Phillips 14–1–237–50–0–18.23; *K. G. Horstmann 12–0–205–79–0–17.08; W. H. Evered 10–1–152–71–0–16.88.

Bowling—W. H. Evered 126–21–315–23–3/11–13.69; B. T. Russell 108.2–12–317–19–4/20–16.68.

WELLINGTON SCHOOL　　*Played 18: W 6, L 7, D 5. A 3*

Master i/c: P. M. Pearce

Batting—R. C. Edwards 10–4–253–50*–0–42.16; B. J. Rogers 17–2–492–97–0–32.80; J. W. Reynolds 18–2–390–79–0–24.37; W. G. Sheppard 12–4–177–53*–0–22.12; S. W. Turner 11–1–180–47–0–18.00; J. T. House 10–1–161–43–0–17.88.

Bowling—S. W. Turner 245.1–32–522–33–4/8–15.81; J. W. Reynolds 172.2–25–663–41–4/20–16.17; J. T. House 110.5–16–408–23–5/31–17.73.

WELLS CATHEDRAL SCHOOL　　*Played 14: W 5, L 4, D 5*

Master i/c: M. Stringer

Batting—J. Hill 12–2–349–67–0–34.90; *M. Truman 14–1–387–85–0–29.76.

Bowling—A. Mufti 139.4–29–459–28–5/44–16.39; J. Hill 87–16–300–15–3/36–20.00; A. Cowley 92–16–361–18–4/24–20.05; H. Freeman 126–16–560–22–4/19–25.45.

WEST BUCKLAND SCHOOL　　*Played 13: W 2, L 5, D 5, T 1. A 3*

Master i/c: L. Whittal-Williams

Batting—C. M. Welch 12–1–324–58*–0–29.45; *I. T. Gear 9–1–210–65*–0–26.25; M. J. Brayley 11–2–157–29–0–17.44.

Bowling—G. E. T. Cornish 93–20–246–17–3/21–14.47; I. T. Gear 90–15–325–17–6/45–19.11.

WESTMINSTER SCHOOL *Played 13: W 3, L 6, D 4. A 4*

Master i/c: M. H. Feltham Professional: R. O. Butcher

The side was more competitive than in 1999 and enjoyed a successful visit to Barbados. Against Deighton Griffith School, Pierre Bell wrapped up the match with four wickets in four balls.

Batting—D. M. H. Stranger-Jones 12–3–394–111*–1–43.77; I. A. Coomaraswamy 10–0–237–80–0–23.70.

Bowling—No bowler took 15 wickets. The leading bowler was P. O. A. Bell 33–5–103–13–6/10–7.92.

WHITGIFT SCHOOL *Played 11: W 5, L 2, D 4. A 4*

Master i/c: P. C. Fladgate Professional: D. M. Ward

A season characterised by poor weather failed to dampen the spirits of a capable batting side who gained good wins against Trinity, Colfe's and Kingston GS. The consistent Daniel Watson, strongly supported by James Pearce and Sam Woodward, led the batting. Six bowlers took more than ten but fewer than 15 wickets.

Batting—D. Watson 9–3–341–112–1–56.83; J. R. Pearce 11–1–402–138*–1–40.20; S. J. Woodward 8–1–273–94*–0–39.00; K. K. A. Lakhani 9–1–197–54–0–24.62.

Bowling—No bowler took 15 wickets. The leading bowler was J. R. Pearce 102.1–23–316–14–3/23–22.57.

WILSON'S SCHOOL *Played 10: W 3, L 1, D 6. A 2*

Master i/c: J. Molyneux

Batting—G. Lambe 8–2–305–119*–1–50.83; J. Parkinson 11–1–305–68–0–30.50; A. Parkinson 10–0–194–45–0–19.40.

Bowling—N. Ansari 124–23–364–26–5/13–14.00.

WINCHESTER COLLEGE *Played 13: W 5, L 4, D 4. A 4*

Master i/c: C. J. Good Professional: J. R. Ayling

For the first time in 25 years, the college defeated Eton, while for the first time ever three brothers – Alex, James and Chris Walters – appeared in the same Winchester team.

Batting—R. H. W. Readhead 10–3–403–100*–1–57.57; *P. M. Nevin 12–1–400–97–0–36.36; J. H. Walters 10–4–190–56*–0–31.66; A. K. Walters 13–2–294–84–0–26.72; J. E. R. Williams 13–0–202–46–0–15.53.

Bowling—T. A. M. Sutton 148–32–389–29–5/16–13.41; T. E. White 115–22–353–21–4/36–16.80; E. A. J. Marsh 126–27–358–15–3/39–23.86.

WOLVERHAMPTON GRAMMAR SCHOOL *Played 11: W 4, L 7, D 0. A 4*

Master i/c: N. H. Crust Professional: T. King

Batting—*S. Drury 7–0–204–69–0–29.14; N. Gray 10–0–185–41–0–18.50; D. Bowyer 11–1–162–76–0–16.20.

Bowling—No bowler took 15 wickets. The leading bowler was A. Fleet 65–14–213–14–5/23–15.21.

WOODBRIDGE SCHOOL   *Played 12: W 6, L 5, D 1*

Master i/c: C. Seal

Batting—O. King 8–4–201–69*–0–50.25; P. Steen 10–1–253–81–0–28.11; M. Lincoln 10–2–211–55–0–26.37; G. Booth 11–0–194–51–0–17.63.

Bowling—P. Nicholls 105.5–28–324–26–5/15–12.46; P. Steen 132.5–24–399–17–4/36–23.47.

WOODHOUSE GROVE SCHOOL   *Played 18: W 9, L 2, D 7*

Master i/c: R. I. Frost   Professional: G. R. J. Roope

Nine wins made this the most successful season for seven years; the only disappointment was the defeat at Hymer's College, which ended a two-year unbeaten run against schools. Rhodri Jones, Martyn Bray and Sam Anderson all played for Yorkshire Schools' Under-19.

Batting—T. E. Bould 16–1–523–132–1–34.86; R. W. Jones 16–1–507–83–0–33.80; *J. I. Henry 16–5–263–73*–0–23.90; R. W. Verity 13–1–284–76–0–23.66; S. King 15–2–269–63–0–20.69; M. A. Bray 16–4–248–56*–0–20.66; K. Cholmondeley 17–3–258–59–0–18.42.

Bowling—M. A. Bray 159–42–341–34–5/16–10.02; R. W. Jones 117.3–22–375–24–5/1–15.62; M. Greenwood 113–15–336–20–4/20–16.80; M. S. Bottomley 119.3–23–396–18–5/31–22.00.

WORKSOP COLLEGE   *Played 16: W 8, L 2, D 6. A 2*

Master i/c: C. G. Paton   Professional: A. Kettleborough

Batting—T. M. Gray 13–7–321–96–0–53.50; S. Clark 16–2–576–88–0–41.14; A. W. Parkin-Coates 11–4–230–43–0–32.85; H. E. Straw 9–0–248–78–0–27.55; D. H. Coote 15–0–325–63–0–21.66.

Bowling—S. Clark 159–38–401–30–6/18–13.36; S. Patel 174–54–376–27–6/17–13.92; G. A. H. Wilkinson 166–43–400–17–5/10–23.52.

WREKIN COLLEGE   *Played 11: W 6, L 2, D 3. A 2*

Master i/c: M. de Weymarn   Professional: P. Dawson

South African exchange student Jean-Paul Duminy made an immediate impact when he dropped a skier off the first ball of the season. After that, however, he never looked back, hitting 602 runs at an average of 150.50, thought to be a school record. Stuart Blount had a happier season than in 1999; now recovered from injury and with a remodelled action, he gave the attack a much-needed cutting-edge.

Batting—J-P. Duminy 10–6–602–121*–2–150.50; C. Catling 8–1–256–106*–1–36.57; S. Blount 8–2–195–51–0–32.50.

Bowling—S. Blount 106.5–21–243–21–5/31–11.57; J-P. Duminy 111.4–23–343–19–6/35–18.05; *N. Lamont 95–14–286–15–4/39–19.06.

YOUTH CRICKET, 2000

UNDER-19 CRICKET

Sussex won the ECB Under-19 County Championship, beating Warwickshire by 145 runs in the two-day final at Hinckley, Leicestershire. Sussex ran up 345 for six in their 100 overs, thanks to 106 not out from James Chadburn, who shared a sixth-wicket partnership of 148 with Andrew Hodd; opener Matthew Prior hit 55. In reply, Warwickshire were dismissed for 200; only Guriq Randawa, with 71, put up much resistance. Glen Read (three for 43) and Chris Baker (three for 32) did the damage.

UNDER-17 CRICKET

Yorkshire beat Essex by virtue of a faster scoring-rate in the final of the ECB Under-17 County Championship, also held over two days at Hinckley. Yorkshire's total of 316 for five was based around an opening stand of 156 between Joe Sayers, who hit 114, and Andrew Gale, who made 86; Adnam Akram took four for 55. Essex then struggled, reaching 73 for five before the rain came. In the semi-finals, Yorkshire had beaten Staffordshire by six wickets, while Essex had overcome Somerset by 67 runs.

UNDER-16 CRICKET

The Britvic Inner Cities Cup, run in association with the Lord's Taverners and now in its fifth year, again took place over three days at Arundel. Eight teams qualified for the final stages: Birmingham, Bristol, Glasgow, Leeds, Leicester, London North, Manchester and Swansea. In a hard-fought final, Manchester made 175 for nine, before restricting Bristol to 166 for seven to win by nine runs. Players were eligible only if they lived within a ten-mile radius of their city centre and had not previously played at county or national level.

The Lord's Taverners Under-16 County Championship finals were contested over two days at Haileybury College. In the final, Devon won by 38 runs, making 220 for eight off 50 overs before restricting Warwickshire to 182 for nine.

UNDER-15 CRICKET

At the 14th annual Bunbury/ESCA Festival at Ampleforth College, the North won all three matches in the round-robin regional competition. They went on to become the first winners of the Hubert Doggart Cup, beating the South by 67 runs in the final; Tim Bresnan took four for 33, and captain Tim Rees scored 115. In the group games, the North dismissed the West for just 62, while David Wainwright, also of the North, took five for 38 against the South. James Hildreth, of the West, smashed 151 against the Midlands, from a total of 207 for eight; the next-highest score was 16. Bresnan won the Dunlop Slazenger equipment contract awarded to the outstanding player of the tournament: he took 11 wickets and hit 71 not out against the South. All matches were 50 overs a side.

Lancashire beat Surrey by five wickets to win the ESCA Under-15 County Championship finals at Oundle School. Replying to Surrey's 189 for six in 55 overs, Lancashire reached 190 for five with 13 balls to spare; Tim Rees hit 66. Staffordshire, for whom Robert Jones took four for eight, beat Cornwall by four wickets to win the third-place play-off. In the semi-finals, Lancashire's Bilal Mustafa returned figures of 17–6–23–9 as Cornwall were dismissed for just 83. Mustafa took the first nine wickets to fall, and was denied all ten when No. 10 Mike Munday was lbw to Rees.

Banstead became the first Surrey side to win the Sun Life of Canada Under-15 Championship, when they beat Diss, from Norfolk, by four runs in the final at Basingstoke. Coached by former Surrey players David Ward and Neil Kendrick, Banstead made 115 for six in their 20 overs, with Sam Woodward hitting 45 not out from just 39 balls; he and younger brother Nick smashed 31 off the final two overs. Diss began well, reaching 52 for no wicket, but then lost six for 20, and reached the final over still needing 11; they managed just six. Among the spectators were Nasser Hussain, fresh from England's triumph at Headingley, and Brian Lara.

Malvern College lifted the Lord's Taverners/*Cricketer* Colts Trophy, after winning a tense final against Whitgift at Trent Bridge by two wickets. Whitgift scraped together 149 for seven in their 40 overs, a total boosted by a hard-hitting undefeated 50 from Adam Clarke; Malvern captain Will Gifford took three for 28 with his medium-pace. At 83 for two in reply, Malvern were coasting, but opener Chris Wood fell for 49, and the middle order folded to the leg-spin of Shahnawaz Malik, who claimed three for 26. By the start of the final over, Malvern needed three runs with two wickets in hand. Thanks to an overthrow, they got there with three balls to spare.

UNDER-14 CRICKET

All six matches at the Lord's Taverners Under-14 Festival at Coventry were drawn, but there were still some tight finishes. The North closed just 12 runs short of the South's 157 for five, which relied on 102 from Johan Malcolm. And the West hung on, nine down, after their final pair had batted out the last 15 overs against the South, for whom David Hammond scored 83. Hammond was the tournament's top-scorer with 180 runs, followed by Will Gifford of the Midlands, whose aggregate of 168 included an unbeaten 103 against the North. Mark Mitchell claimed five for 53 for the West against the South. All the games took place at the Peugeot Cricket Club and Kenilworth Wardens grounds over four days, and although rain affected two of the matches, the decision to move the festival from May to August proved a success.

UNDER-13 CRICKET

Shrewsbury won the Subaru Under-13 National Club Championship – the Ken Barrington Cup – held over four days at Oakham School in Rutland. They became the second side from Shropshire to win the competition, after Wem in 1981. From an original entry of about 1,600 sides, eight reached the round-robin finals. Shrewsbury won all seven of their games, inflicting the only defeat on Horsley and Send, who came second. The finalists, in finishing order, were: Shrewsbury, Horsley and Send, Waresley, Worcester Nomads – who also reached the final stages in 1999 – Letchworth, South Wilts, Sheffield United and Tynemouth.

Millfield Preparatory School beat Nottingham High by 54 runs to win the Under-12/13 Calypso Cup at Headingley, after 37 teams had made it through to the regional finals. Millfield, beaten finalists in 1999, reached 167 for four in their 35 overs, with opener Liam Lewis hitting 81. Nottingham were skittled for 113 in reply as Robin Lett picked up four for 20.

The ECB/ESCA Under-13 Festival at Taunton was ruined by the weather, with three of the six games abandoned. In the three played to a finish, the South beat the North by two wickets and drew with the West, who beat the Midlands by nine wickets.

WOMEN'S CRICKET, 2000

By CAROL SALMON

SOUTH AFRICA WOMEN IN ENGLAND, 2000

Success in the five-match series against South Africa was essential if England were to recover from their humiliation in Australia and New Zealand during the winter, and build up confidence for December's World Cup. A 3–2 win was not as clear-cut as hoped, but South Africa were much improved since their last visit three years earlier. Nine of that party returned for a tour which, as in 1997, was dogged by rain; only two of the five internationals were not shortened by the weather.

Clare Connor was confirmed as England captain, having taken over in New Zealand after Karen Smithies resigned, and another three teenagers were introduced. This was in addition to Nicki Shaw and Dawn Holden, who were blooded in Australasia. Arran Thompson, the 18-year-old captain of England Under-19s, came in for the first match at Chelmsford and held her place in the top order, though missing one game because of A-levels. Her superb fielding considerably lifted that department. After the series was secured at Taunton, 16-year-old off-spinner Laura Harper and Leanne Davis, at 15 years and 66 days England's youngest international, played in the final game at Worcester. Davis, called up after Laura Newton damaged her knee, opened the bowling and took an early wicket, while Harper completed her ten overs, competently mastering an increasingly damp ball. Claire Taylor kept wicket in that game to end Jane Cassar's unbroken run in the side since 1993.

South Africa had discovered a powerful teenager of their own in 16-year-old Sunnette Viljoen, who made a considerable all-round impression. But later in July came news of the youngest international cricketer yet, when Pakistan unveiled 12-year-old Sajjida Shah in their one-off Test defeat by Ireland.

As well as the influx of talented youngsters – England's best bat, Charlotte Edwards, was still only 20 – another major plus was Barbara Daniels's return to form. So bad were her batting returns down under that Daniels, then the ECB's manager for women's cricket, was a controversial selection. Critics soon felt the middle of her bat, however: she was the leading run-scorer, with 231 runs at 57.75. At Taunton, she and Edwards, who aggregated 194 at 48.50, put on 182 to win the match and series. Daniels attributed her recovery to the fact that she had already decided to resign from her stressful and demanding post with the ECB. Though she did not make her debut until the 1993 World Cup, when she was 28, Daniels became England's second-heaviest one-day scorer during this series, overtaking Carole Hodges. In 44 games she had made 1,123 at an average of 29.55, with only Janette Brittin, now retired, ahead on 2,121 at 42.42. Edwards became the fourth Englishwoman to reach four figures during her 96 not out at Taunton.

Despite the success of Edwards and Daniels, now club-mates at Kent Invicta, England's batting, particularly the top order, remained their Achilles heel. Nor did anyone new emerge at the County Championship which followed to demand selection. The seam attack performed competently, although the leading wicket-taker on either side was Yorkshire leg-spinner Kathryn Leng, with seven. For South Africa, Helen Davies and Cindy Eksteen both passed 100 runs, while Davies also took five wickets.

SOUTH AFRICAN TOURING PARTY

K. Price (Western Province) (*captain*), C. E. Eksteen (Free State) (*vice-captain*), A. A. Burger (Northerns), H. A. Davies (Western Province), A. Hodgkinson (Northerns), A. Kuylaars (Western Province), K. A. Laing (Gauteng), L. P. Lewis (Western Province), N. Ndzundzu (Border), L. Olivier (Gauteng), D. J. Reid (Western Province), R. Scheepers (Northerns), M. Terblanche (Gauteng), Y. van der Merwe (Northerns), S. S. Viljoen (North West).

Manager: S. Cade.   *Coach:* R. Willemburg.   *Physiotherapist:* M. van der Merwe.

SOUTH AFRICAN TOUR RESULTS

Matches – Played 7: Won 3, Lost 3, Tied 1.

Note: Matches in this section were not first-class.

At Shenley Park, June 14. South Africa won by three wickets. Toss: South Africa. England A 164 for eight (50 overs) (M. Godliman 34); South Africa 165 for seven (48 overs) (H. A. Davies 47, C. E. Eksteen 43).

At Shenley Park, June 16. Tied. Toss: South Africa. England A 169 for eight (50 overs) (K. Lowe 45, K. Wilkins 47); South Africa 169 for eight (50 overs).

At Chelmsford, June 20. First one-day international: England won by 20 runs. Toss: England. England 159 (43.4 overs) (B. A. Daniels 49, M. A. Reynard 46 not out); South Africa 139 for nine (44 overs) (L. Olivier 52, S. S. Viljoen 31).
    A rain-affected match was reduced to 44 overs.

At Nottingham, June 22. Second one-day international: England won by nine wickets. Toss: England. South Africa 151 for nine (35 overs) (H. A. Davies 43, C. E. Eksteen 41; L. C. Pearson three for 14); England 91 for one (18 overs) (C. M. Edwards 36, S. C. Taylor 47 not out).
    England's target was revised to 91 from 21 overs.

At Canterbury, June 25. Third one-day international: South Africa won by one wicket. Toss: England. England 203 for six (50 overs) (B. A. Daniels 74, A. Thompson 33, M. A. Reynard 33 not out, Extras 31); South Africa 204 for nine (49.4 overs) (A. Hodgkinson 32, H. A. Davies 47, S. S. Viljoen 30 not out; K. M. Leng four for 47).
    Daniels passed 1,000 runs in her 42nd one-day international.

At Taunton, June 28. Fourth one-day international: England won by eight wickets. Toss: England. South Africa 222 for seven (50 overs) (C. E. Eksteen 62, A. Kuylaars 57 not out); England 225 for two (46.2 overs) (C. M. Edwards 96 not out, B. A. Daniels 95).
    Edwards passed 1,000 runs in her 30th one-day international, adding 182 with Daniels for England's second wicket.

At Worcester, July 1. Fifth one-day international: South Africa won by five runs. Toss: England. South Africa 156 for six (39 overs) (K. A. Laing 47, H. A. Davies 34); England 123 for eight (32 overs) (C. M. Edwards 57; H. A. Davies three for 34).
    Leanne Davis became England's youngest player at 15 years and 66 days. England failed to reach a revised target of 129 in 32 overs, but took the series 3–2.

ENGLISH WOMEN'S CRICKET, 2000

Yorkshire claimed their eighth County Championship in nine years, winning all five games. In their decisive match against Nottinghamshire, who as East Midlands had interrupted Yorkshire's reign in 1999, new captain (and England vice-captain) Melissa Reynard led from the front with 70 out of 273 for four. England wicket-keeper Jane Cassar replied with 96, but Nottinghamshire closed on 198 for nine. These two sides have monopolised the Championship since 1986, when Middlesex and Kent shared the title. Kent were third this time, thanks to Charlotte Edwards, recently recruited from East Anglia, who scored 374 runs at 93.50.

    The Championship's format continues to be revised: from 2001, all Second Elevens have been removed from the competition and East Anglia divide into Hertfordshire and Cambridgeshire. Counties may also include one overseas player without the usual eight-month qualifying procedure.

    As the standard of county cricket has improved, so have the representative age-group sides. England Under-19 and Under-17 won one-day series against Ireland and Holland respectively at Peterborough during preparations for the senior World Cup in New Zealand. Four players from England's own World Cup squad, Laura Harper, Sarah Collyer, Nicki Shaw and Arran Thompson, helped the Under-19s beat Ireland 2–1; Harper and another full England international, Leanne Davis, also appeared for the Under-17s, who defeated Holland by the same margin.

Kent Invicta retained the National League title in a one-sided match against Wakefield, while Middlesex club Gunnersbury won the National Club Knockout for the first time since 1982, beating Redoubtables on a rain-affected pitch at Horsley and Send CC in Wisley, Surrey. The Knockout and Plate finals had been scheduled for Sheffield, but the national petrol crisis forced a change of venue. The Plate final, in which Hambledon were to meet Brighton and Hove, did not take place. The crisis also caused the Under-19 county final, between Sussex and Staffordshire, to be postponed to 2001. However, the other age-group finals were played: Sussex Under-17s beat Derbyshire, and Kent Under-15s beat Nottinghamshire.

Club cricket has so far not matched the improvement at county and representative level. The ECB responded by appointing four club development officers, responsible for revitalising the game in the North, the East Midlands, the Home Counties, and Devon, Cornwall, Somerset and Dorset. Another initiative during 2000 was the first floodlit women's match in England: at Hove on August 30, Surrey defeated Sussex in the final over.

Barbara Daniels, who became the national manager for women's cricket at the ECB after negotiating the Women's Cricket Association's merger with the board, resigned during the summer to concentrate on her playing career. Gill McConway took over in October. New Zealand-born but UK-resident since 1973, McConway played 14 Tests for England between 1984 and 1987, taking 40 wickets with a best return of seven for 34 against India in 1986. England coach Paul Farbrace also announced that he would stand down at the end of the World Cup in December to concentrate on his position coaching England Under-15 boys. Jane Horwood, chair of the first Women's Advisory Group at the ECB, completed her two-year term and was re-elected for a further year.

Note: Matches in this section were not first-class.

COUNTY CHAMPIONSHIP, 2000

Division One

	Played	Won	Lost	Points
Yorkshire	5	5	0	102
Nottinghamshire	5	4	1	84
Kent	5	2	3	54.5
Berkshire	5	2	3	53
Surrey	5	1	4	43.5
Sussex	5	1	4	42

Division Two

	Played	Won	Lost	Points
Staffordshire	5	5	0	99
Lancashire	5	3	2	74
Somerset	5	3	2	73.5
Yorkshire Second XI	5	1	4	53.5
Cheshire	5	2	3	43
East Anglia	5	1	4	34

Division Three

	Played	Won	Lost	Points
Derbyshire	5	5	0	100
Middlesex	5	3	2	76
Surrey Second XI	5	3	2	73
Hampshire	5	3	2	69
Sussex Second XI	5	1	4	42.5
Northumberland	5	0	5	20.5

NATIONAL LEAGUE FINAL, 2000

At Milton Keynes, September 10. Kent Invicta won by 114 runs. Toss: Kent Invicta. Kent Invicta 201 for two (50 overs) (B. A. Daniels 99 not out, P. Arnold 45 not out); Wakefield 87 (43.5 overs) (P. Weeks four for 18, M. Davies three for 20).

NATIONAL CLUB KNOCKOUT FINAL, 2000

At Wisley, September 16. Gunnersbury won by eight wickets. Toss: Gunnersbury. Redoubtables 99 for six (40 overs) (B. Morgan three for 27); Gunnersbury 100 for two (34.4 overs) (S. Donaldson 32).

FIFTY YEARS AGO

From WISDEN CRICKETERS' ALMANACK 1951

WEST INDIES IN ENGLAND, 1950, by N. Preston – "Worrell, Weekes and Walcott stood out in a class on their own. For beauty of stroke no one in the history of the game can have excelled Worrell. A fairly tall, lean figure, there was something like a dreamy casualness about the way he flicked the ball with nonchalant ease: but how it sped to the boundary! Worrell's masterpiece was his 261 in the Third Test at Trent Bridge, where he and Weekes surpassed anything previously accomplished for West Indies in Test cricket by adding 283 for the third wicket. Weekes, shorter and stockier than Worrell, imparted more force into his strokes. Quick on his feet, he would go back on his right foot and cut mercilessly… Walcott, too, specialised with the square cut and drive, and of the three he looked the best on wet wickets, for his defence was so sound."

FIVE CRICKETERS OF THE YEAR, E. D. WEEKES, by F. L. Belson – "Perhaps no batsman since Bradman has made such an impression on his first English tour as a ruthless compiler of big scores as did Everton de Courcy Weekes of the West Indies in the 1950 season. There were many sceptical of his ability to reproduce on English county grounds the form by which he made so many high scores at home and broke records in India and in Lancashire League cricket. Weekes, in a predominantly wet summer, soon proved them wrong by revealing a propensity for reaching his hundred and settling down for another hundred by methods heartbreakingly safe from the bowlers' point of view yet aggressive enough to carry his score along deceptively fast and afford the richest entertainment to the spectators. By mid-July he reached three figures five times, and not once did he stop short of a double century."

NOTES BY THE EDITOR, Hubert Preston – "Frank Chester standing in the Test Match at Trent Bridge… called 'out' to an appeal for leg-before against D. J. Insole and insisted that his ruling should go on the score sheet although the ball went off the batsman's pads on to the stumps; surely this meant bowled. How Chester contrived to signal 'out' before the ball reached the stumps is difficult to realise, but, however that may be, his refusal to withdraw his verdict in favour of the more definite and satisfactory form of dismissal cannot be understood. Both for bowler and batsman 'bowled' looks far better than 'l.b.w.' in the score, and the obstinacy of such an expert as Frank Chester, regarded as the most sagacious, quickest and reliable umpire for many years, in declining to alter his attitude is more than surprising. Can it be that having given his decision he regarded the ball as 'dead' before it reached the stumps?"

PART FIVE: OVERSEAS CRICKET IN 1999-2000

FEATURES OF 1999-2000

Double-Hundreds (39)

353	V. V. S. Laxman	Hyderabad v Karnataka at Bangalore.
305*‡	P. Dharmani	Punjab v Jammu and Kashmir at Ludhiana.
288†	S. Sriram	Tamil Nadu v Uttar Pradesh at Kanpur.
275	G. Kirsten	South Africa v England (Third Test) at Durban.
274	V. Shewag	North Zone v South Zone at Agartala.
271	R. Nayyar	Himachal Pradesh v Jammu and Kashmir at Chamba.
265	Jai P. Yadav	Madhya Pradesh v Railways at Indore.
248*‡	A. V. Kale	Maharashtra v Baroda at Pune.
245	J. Cox	Tasmania v New South Wales at Hobart.
240	Asif Mujtaba	PIA v Lahore Division at Sheikhupura.
238*	M. van Jaarsveld	Northerns v Griqualand West at Kimberley.
237*	C. C. Williams	Baroda v Saurashtra at Rajkot.
233‡	S. R. Tendulkar	Mumbai v Tamil Nadu at Mumbai.
228	M. L. Love	Queensland v New South Wales at Brisbane.
223	J. L. Langer	Australia v India (Third Test) at Sydney.
220	D. J. Watson	KwaZulu-Natal v North West at Potchefstroom.
219‡	A. V. Kale	Maharashtra v Gujarat at Ahmedabad.
217‡	S. R. Tendulkar	India v New Zealand (Third Test) at Ahmedabad.
216*‡	M. S. Atapattu	Sri Lanka v Zimbabwe (First Test) at Bulawayo.
216*	S. Chanderpaul	West Indians v New Zealand A at Taupo.
214	J. L. Arnberger	Victoria v Tasmania at Richmond.
214	M. S. Sinclair	New Zealand v West Indies (Second Test) at Wellington.
213	S. K. L. de Silva	Colombo v Sinhalese at Colombo.
213	Rafatullah Mohmand	Redco v Faisalabad at Faisalabad.
212*†	R. S. Gavaskar	Bengal v Tripura at Agartala.
210*	I. Mohammed	Pakistan Customs v Gujranwala at Sialkot.
207*‡	M. S. Atapattu	Sri Lanka v Pakistan (Third Test) at Kandy.
205†	S. Sharath	Tamil Nadu v Uttar Pradesh at Kanpur.
204*	Imran Abbas	ADBP v Karachi Blues at Karachi.
203*	H. P. Tillekeratne	Nondescripts v Singha at Colombo.
203	R. J. Campbell	Western Australia v Queensland at Perth.
202*‡	P. Dharmani	Punjab v Services at Mohali.
202*	N. D. Modi	Gujarat v Baroda at Baroda.
202*‡	Younis Khan	Habib Bank v Islamabad at Rawalpindi.
200*	M. Azharuddin	Hyderabad v Goa at Panaji.
200*	H. H. Dippenaar	Free State v Boland at Bloemfontein.
200*†	S. J. Kalyani	Bengal v Tripura at Agartala.
200*	Rizwan-uz-Zaman	PIA v Hyderabad at Hyderabad.
200*‡	Younis Khan	Habib Bank v Redco at Islamabad.

† *Gavaskar and Kalyani scored their double-hundreds in one innings, as did Sharath and Sriram.*
‡ *Atapattu, Kale, Dharmani, Tendulkar and Younis Khan each scored two double-hundreds, Dharmani in consecutive innings.*

Hundred on First-Class Debut

158	K. D. Aphale	Maharashtra v Saurashtra at Pune.
118*	A. S. Naidu	Vidarbha v Uttar Pradesh at Kanpur (2nd innings).
106	B. M. Rowland	Karnataka v Kerala at Bangalore.
187	G. C. Smith	UCB Invitation XI v Griqualand West at Kimberley.

Three or More Hundreds in Successive Innings

S. L. Campbell (West Indians)	112 and 109* v Auckland at Auckland
	170 v New Zealand (First Test) at Hamilton.
P. Dharmani (Punjab)	202* v Services at Mohali
	305* v Jammu and Kashmir at Ludhiana
	101 v Delhi at Ludhiana.
V. V. S. Laxman (Hyderabad)	131 v Goa at Panaji
	104 v Andhra at Secunderabad
	113 Indians v Queensland at Brisbane.
V. V. S. Laxman (Hyderabad)	128 and 177* v Uttar Pradesh at Kanpur
	353 v Karnataka at Bangalore.
J. D. Wells (Wellington)	143 v Canterbury at Wellington
	107 and 132* v Central Districts at New Plymouth.
Younis Khan (Habib Bank)	101 v Faisalabad at Faisalabad
	132 and 142* v Peshawar at Peshawar
	202* v Islamabad at Rawalpindi.

Hundred in Each Innings of a Match

J. D. C. Bryant	131	129	Eastern Province v Western Province at Cape Town.
S. L. Campbell	112	109*	West Indians v Auckland at Auckland.
V. V. S. Laxman	128	177*	Hyderabad v Uttar Pradesh at Kanpur.
D. S. Lehmann	101*	113	South Australia v Tasmania at Hobart.
P. M. Mullick	108	111*	Orissa v Bengal at Cuttack.
Rizwan Malik	109	169*	Gujranwala v National Bank at Sialkot.
R. R. Sarwan	100	111	President's XI v Zimbabweans at Pointe-à-Pierre.
Shahriar Hossain . . .	133	121*	Bangladesh v MCC at Dhaka.
J. D. Wells	107	132*	Wellington v Central Districts at New Plymouth.
Younis Khan	132	142*	Habib Bank v Peshawar at Peshawar.

Most Consecutive Scoreless Innings

Seven	L. J. Hamilton (Central Districts)	*Five ducks, two not out.*
Five	A. B. Agarkar (India)	*Four first-ball ducks, one second-ball duck.*

Carrying Bat Through Completed Innings

R. P. Arnold	104*	Sri Lanka (231) v Zimbabwe (Third Test) at Harare.
M. S. Atapattu	216*	Sri Lanka (428) v Zimbabwe (First Test) at Bulawayo.
Faisal Naved	114*	Gujranwala (209) v Lahore City at Lahore.
Faisal Naved	109*	Gujranwala (210) v Bahawalpur at Bahawalpur.
Faisal Naved	151*	Gujranwala (270) v PNSC at Sialkot.
		(in three consecutive matches).
D. A. Fitzgerald	111*	South Australia (250) v Pakistanis at Adelaide.
A. Haniff	84*	Guyana (172) v Windward Islands at St Vincent.
M. E. Hussey	172*	Western Australia (392) v South Australia at Perth.
K. Y. P. Sanjeewa	38*	Matara (76) v Kurunegala Youth at Kurunegala.
Shoaib Mohammad . . .	147*	PIA (334) v WAPDA at Karachi.
H. S. G. Silva	28*	Police (115) v Galle at Colombo.
W. T. Siziba	40*	Matabeleland (150) v Manicaland at Harare
		(on first-class debut).
Wasim Jaffer	173*	West Zone (367) v North Zone at Calcutta.
C. C. Williams.	237*	Baroda (487) v Saurashtra at Rajkot.

Long Innings

Mins
1,015	R. Nayyar (271)	Himachal Pradesh v Jammu and Kashmir at Chamba.
878	G. Kirsten (275)	South Africa v England (Third Test) at Durban.
759	V. V. S. Laxman (353) . .	Hyderabad v Karnataka at Bangalore.

An Hour Without Adding to the Score

N. Hussain (146*)	73 mins on 15	England v South Africa at Durban.
G. J. Denton (8*)	93 mins on 0	Tasmania v Queensland at Hobart.

First-Wicket Partnerships of 100 in Each Innings

102	112.	C. M. Spearman/D. P. Kelly, Central Districts v Wellington at New Plymouth.
126	155.	G. J. Rennie/T. R. Gripper, Mashonaland v Manicaland at Harare.
130	130.	D. F. Hills/J. Cox, Tasmania v Western Australia at Hobart.

Other Notable Partnerships

First Wicket
403	Rizwan-uz-Zaman/Shoaib Mohammad, PIA v Hyderabad at Hyderabad.
353	M. T. G. Elliott/J. L. Arnberger, Victoria v Tasmania at Richmond.
340	M. L. Bruyns/D. J. Watson, KwaZulu-Natal v North West at Potchefstroom.
335	M. S. Atapattu/S. T. Jayasuriya, Sri Lanka v Pakistan (Third Test) at Kandy.
304	Rizwan-uz-Zaman/Shoaib Mohammad, PIA v Lahore City at Lahore.
276	A. F. G. Griffith/S. L. Campbell, West Indies v New Zealand (First Test) at Hamilton.

Second Wicket
294	J. Cox/M. J. di Venuto, Tasmania v New South Wales at Hobart.
257	Mohammad Ramzan/Faisal Athar, PNSC v Hyderabad at Hyderabad.
254	A. Jain/R. J. Kanwat, Rajasthan v Bengal at Calcutta.

Third Wicket
406*	R. S. Gavaskar/S. J. Kalyani, Bengal v Tripura at Agartala.
367	Shoaib Mohammad/Asif Mujtaba, PIA v Lahore Division at Sheikhupura.
288	V. V. S. Laxman/M. Azharuddin, Hyderabad v Karnataka at Bangalore.
288	Tariq Aziz/Hasan Adnan, WAPDA v Bahawalpur at Bahawalpur.
286	A. V. Kale/S. S. Sugwekar, Maharashtra v Gujarat at Ahmedabad.
254	S. R. Waugh/M. E. Waugh, Australians v ZCU President's XI at Bulawayo.
253	D. Makalima/J. M. Kemp, Eastern Province/Border XI v Sri Lanka A at Port Elizabeth.

Fourth Wicket
330†	D. P. Viljoen/C. N. Evans, Mashonaland v Matabeleland at Bulawayo.
306	Afsar Nawaz/Saad Wasim, Karachi Blues v ADBP at Karachi.
285	H. P. Tillekeratne/C. P. Mapatuna, Nondescripts v Singha at Colombo.
281	S. R. Tendulkar/S. C. Ganguly, India v New Zealand (Third Test) at Ahmedabad.
269*	Mohammad Masroor/Asim Kamal, Karachi Whites v Hyderabad at Karachi.

Fifth Wicket
381	R. Nayyar/V. Shewag, North Zone v South Zone at Agartala.
327	J. L. Langer/R. T. Ponting, Australia v Pakistan (Third Test) at Perth.
254	H. K. Badani/R. R. Singh, Tamil Nadu v Mumbai at Mumbai.
239	S. R. Waugh/R. T. Ponting, Australia v India (First Test) at Adelaide.
237	J. D. C. Bryant/J. M. Kemp, Eastern Province v Easterns at Port Elizabeth.

Sixth Wicket
256   Sajid Ali/Fahadullah Khan, National Bank v Karachi Whites at Karachi.
255   Y. Gowda/S. V. Wankhede, Railways v Baroda at Delhi.
238   J. L. Langer/A. C. Gilchrist, Australia v Pakistan (Second Test) at Hobart.

Seventh Wicket
231* P. Dharmani/H. S. Jugnu, Punjab v Jammu and Kashmir at Ludhiana.
159* E. L. R. Stewart/E. A. E. Baptiste, KwaZulu-Natal v Western Province at Cape Town.
153   V. Shewag/H. Chowdhury, Delhi v Punjab at Ludhiana.
151   D. D. Wickremasinghe/C. P. H. Ramanayake, Galle v Colts at Colombo.

Eighth Wicket
198   A. V. Kale/S. V. Aradhye, Maharashtra v Baroda at Pune.
194* A. P. Katti/D. J. Johnson, Karnataka v Goa at Bangalore.
181   Yasir Hameed/Nauman Habib, Peshawar v KRL at Peshawar.

Ninth Wicket
188   N. R. Parlane/D. R. Tuffey, Northern Districts v Wellington at Wellington.

Tenth Wicket
137   R. Bhatia/J. Gokulkrishnan, Tamil Nadu v Orissa at Cuttack.
122* Kamran Akmal/Salman Fazal, National Bank v WAPDA at Karachi.
112   Naumanullah/Imran Tahir, Redco v Pakistan Reserves at Lahore.
103   G. Dros/G. J-P. Kruger, South Africa A v Windward Islands at St Vincent.

   † *National record.*

Eight or More Wickets in an Innings (9)

9-45	A. W. Zaidi.	Uttar Pradesh v Vidarbha at Kanpur.
8-23	G. Dutta.	Assam v Tripura at Mangoldoi.
8-52	Shahid Iqbal	Karachi Whites v Gujranwala at Karachi.
8-72	Iqbal Siddiqui	Maharashtra v Saurashtra at Pune.
8-76	Imran Tahir.	Redco v Karachi Blues at Lahore.
8-79	Aamir Nazir	Allied Bank v Faisalabad at Faisalabad.
8-83	W. C. Labrooy.	Burgher v Matara at Colombo.
8-88	P. V. Gandhe	Vidarbha v Railways at Nagpur.
8-110	Arshad Khan.	Allied Bank v Redco at Islamabad.

Twelve or More Wickets in a Match (15)

15-192	A. W. Zaidi.	Uttar Pradesh v Vidarbha at Kanpur.
13-66	H. D. P. K. Dharmasena	Bloomfield v Antonians at Colombo.
13-171	M. Muralitharan.	Sri Lanka v South Africa (First Test) at Galle.
12-55	B. P. Martin	Northern Districts v Auckland at Taupo.
12-77	Nadeem Iqbal	Pakistan Customs v Hyderabad at Hyderabad.
12-93	M. Kartik	Railways v Vidarbha at Nagpur.
12-94	M. Hayward	Eastern Province v Easterns at Port Elizabeth.
12-121	M. Diwakar	Bihar v Railways at Ranchi.
12-122	S. Weerakoon	Burgher v Tamil Union at Colombo.
12-128	T. C. B. Fernando	Panadura v Bloomfield at Colombo.
12-138	Danish Kaneria	Pakistan Reserves v KRL at Rawalpindi.
12-148	P. J. Wiseman	South Island v North Island at Christchurch.
12-149	Arshad Khan.	Allied Bank v Sargodha at Sargodha.
12-149	D. L. Vettori	New Zealand v Australia (First Test) at Auckland.
12-169	N. R. Odedra	Saurashtra v Orissa at Rajkot.

Hat-Tricks (8)

Abdur Razzaq	Pakistan v Sri Lanka (Second Test) at Galle.
T. K. Canning	Auckland v Central Districts at Auckland.
M. H. W. Inness	Victoria v New South Wales at Richmond.
M. Ntini	Border v Free State at Bloemfontein.
F. A. Rose	Jamaica v Barbados at Kingston.
N. S. Rupasinghe	Colombo v Singha at Colombo.
B. S. M. Warnapura	Burgher v Singha at Colombo.
D. N. T. Zoysa	Sri Lanka v Zimbabwe (Second Test) at Harare *(his first three balls of the match).*

Wicket with First Ball in First-Class Cricket

Khawar Ali	Rawalpindi v Sargodha at Rawalpindi.
D. J. Wates	Western Australia v Queensland at Brisbane *(first legitimate ball, after a no-ball).*

Most Overs Bowled in an Innings

77–18–172–4	Avinash Kumar	Bihar v Bengal at Jamshedpur.
77–32–117–4	Sanjay Sharma	Jammu and Kashmir v Himachal Pradesh at Chamba.

Most Runs Conceded in an Innings

63–24–235–3	N. S. Kalekar	Goa v Karnataka at Bangalore.
53–6–205–1	S. B. Joshi	Karnataka v Hyderabad at Bangalore.
57–5–200–4	D. L. Vettori	New Zealand v India (Third Test) at Ahmedabad.

Outstanding Innings Analyses

9.1–6–5–5	R. A. D. C. Perera	Sebastianites v Kurunegala Youth at Kurunegala.
7.1–5–4–4	W. Majumder	Bengal v Tripura at Agartala.

Six or More Wicket-Keeping Dismissals in an Innings

7 ct.	Aamer Iqbal	Pakistan Customs v Karachi Whites at Karachi.
7 ct.	H. A. P. W. Jayawardene	Sebastianites v Sinhalese at Colombo.
6 ct.	Atiq-uz-Zaman	Pakistan Reserves v KRL at Rawalpindi.
4 ct, 2 st . .	R. B. Jhalani	Rajasthan v Mumbai at Mumbai.
4 ct, 2 st . . .	Mohammad Shahbaz	Islamabad v Sargodha at Islamabad.
5 ct, 1 st . . .	Moin Khan	Pakistanis v South Australia at Adelaide.
6 ct.	S. Soysa	Singha v Antonians at Kadana.
6 ct.	Tariq Sabzwari	Karachi Blues v Sargodha at Karachi *(on first-class debut).*

Nine or More Wicket-Keeping Dismissals in a Match

11 ct.	Aamer Iqbal	Pakistan Customs v Karachi Whites at Karachi.
10 ct.	A. C. Gilchrist	Australia v New Zealand (Third Test) at Hamilton.
10 ct.	H. A. P. W. Jayawardene	Sebastianites v Sinhalese at Colombo.
9 ct.	D. S. Berry	Victoria v Queensland at Brisbane.
9 ct.	R. J. Campbell	Western Australia v South Australia at Perth.
8 ct, 1 st . . .	Khalid Mahmood	Gujranwala v Lahore Division at Gujranwala.
6 ct, 3 st . . .	Moin Khan	Pakistanis v South Australia at Adelaide.
9 ct.	R. Paul	Tamil Nadu v Punjab at Chennai.

Five Catches in an Innings in the Field

Babar Naeem. . . . . . .   Rawalpindi v Allied Bank at Rawalpindi.
J. Gokulkrishnan . . . .   Tamil Nadu v Andhra at Vishakhapatnam.

Seven Catches in a Match in the Field

S. C. Oasis . . . .   Kerala v Andhra at Kozhikode.

No Byes Conceded in Total of 500 or More

Faisal Qazi . . . .   Hyderabad v Lahore Division (505-8 dec.) at Hyderabad.
Khalid Mahmood . . . .   Gujranwala v PNSC (505) at Sialkot.
E. G. Poole . . . .   North West v KwaZulu-Natal (504-3 dec.) at Potchefstroom.
Sarabjit Singh . . . . . .   Services v Punjab (533-6 dec.) at Mohali.

Unusual Dismissal

Hit the Ball Twice
Maqsood Raza.   115   Lahore Division v PNSC at Sheikhupura.

Highest Innings Totals

711-8 dec. . . . .   Hyderabad v Karnataka at Bangalore.
696-5 dec. . . . .   Tamil Nadu v Uttar Pradesh at Kanpur.
640-5 dec. . . . .   Gauteng v Griqualand West at Kimberley.
620-6 dec. . . . .   Punjab v Jammu and Kashmir at Ludhiana.
604-8 dec. . . . .   National Bank v Pakistan Customs at Karachi.
600-8 dec. . . . .   West Zone v East Zone at Calcutta.
600-8 dec. . . . .   Pakistan v Sri Lanka (Second Test) at Galle.

Lowest Innings Totals

31† . . . .   Midlands v Mashonaland at Harare (1st innings).
41 . . . .   Kurunegala Youth v Sebastianites at Kurunegala.
44 . . . .   Zimbabwe Academy v Sri Lankans at KweKwe.
50 . . . .   Sebastianites v Colombo at Colombo (1st innings).
52 . . . .   Panadura v Tamil Union at Panadura.
56 . . . .   Midlands v Mashonaland at Harare (2nd innings).
57 . . . .   Tripura v Assam at Mangoldoi.
58 . . . .   Hyderabad v Pakistan Customs at Hyderabad.
60 . . . .   Sebastianites v Colombo at Colombo (2nd innings).
63 . . . .   Zimbabwe v West Indies (First Test) at Port-of-Spain.
67 . . . .   Police v Nondescripts at Colombo.
68 . . . .   Colts v Sinhalese at Colombo.
68 . . . .   Panadura v Nondescripts at Panadura.
69 . . . .   Matara v Antonians at Matara.

† *National record.*

Highest Fourth-Innings Total

443-4 . . . .   Free State v KwaZulu-Natal at Durban (set 443).

Victory Losing Only One Wicket

PIA (412-1 dec.) beat Hyderabad (226 and 102) at Hyderabad.

Match Aggregate of 1,500 Runs

1,504 for 24 . . . . . . Hyderabad (711-8 dec. and 236-6 dec.) v Karnataka (557) at Bangalore.

Fewest Runs in a Full Day's Play

83 in 104 overs . . . . Railways (3-0 to 86-5) v Madhya Pradesh at Indore.

Most Extras in an Innings

	b	l-b	w	n-b	
70	28	23	3	16	Pakistan Customs (439-6 dec.) v Bahawalpur at Rahimyar Khan.
65	28	1	2	34	President's XI (417) v Zimbabweans at Pointe-à-Pierre.
64	32	15	3	14	Galle (401-7 dec.) v Singha at Galle.
61	14	16	6	25	West Zone (600-8 dec.) v East Zone at Calcutta.
60	11	16	8	25	Pakistan Reserves (476-9 dec.) v Sargodha at Lahore.

Career Aggregate Milestones

10,000 runs	G. S. Blewett, J. Cox, Ajay Sharma.
500 wickets	M. S. Kasprowicz, A. D. Mullally, Nadeem Khan, S. L. V. Raju.

INTERNATIONAL UMPIRES' PANEL

On December 21, 1993, the International Cricket Council announced the formation of an international umpires' panel. Each full member of ICC was to nominate two officials – apart from England, who named four, because of their large number of professional umpires and the fact that most Tests take place during the English winter. A third-country member of the panel has stood with a "home" umpire, not necessarily from the panel, in every Test staged from February 1994. The ICC plans to have two panels from April 2002: an elite group of up to eight full-time umpires, contracted to the ICC, and an emerging panel of 25 to 30.

The following umpires were on the panel from September 2000: S. A. Bucknor (West Indies), B. C. Cooray (Sri Lanka), D. B. Cowie (New Zealand), R. S. Dunne (New Zealand), D. B. Hair (Australia), J. H. Hampshire (England), D. J. Harper (Australia), A. V. Jayaprakash (India), R. E. Koertzen (South Africa), P. Manuel (Sri Lanka), Mian Aslam (Pakistan), E. A. Nicholls (West Indies), D. L. Orchard (South Africa), Riazuddin (Pakistan), I. D. Robinson (Zimbabwe), G. Sharp (England), D. R. Shepherd (England), R. B. Tiffin (Zimbabwe), S. Venkataraghavan (India), P. Willey (England).

Note: Compared with the 1999-2000 list, Mian Aslam has replaced Athar Zaidi of Pakistan.

ENGLAND IN SOUTH AFRICA AND ZIMBABWE, 1999-2000

Review by COLIN BATEMAN

A unique and totally unexpected victory in the Fifth and final Test against South Africa – albeit subsequently devalued – could not mask another disappointing overseas trip by England. The South Africans were much too strong and confident, and the revenge they sought for their series defeat in England in 1998, when they believed fate conspired against them, was obtained more comfortably than the 2–1 margin might suggest. England's status as one of the weakest teams in the world did not improve, despite the new stewardship of Nasser Hussain and Duncan Fletcher.

The tour took place against a background of political unrest in South African cricket, which was promoting a policy of "affirmative action". Provincial unions were expected to field teams of mixed colour, making allowances for the degree of ability. It was a thorny issue, and a few consciences were pricked when an all-white Northerns/Gauteng combined eleven was named to play England before the First Test. Displeasure turned to outrage when it was discovered that Geoffrey Toyana, a black batsman from Soweto, had been replaced in the original squad by Sven Koenig, a move prompted by the United Cricket Board president, Ray White. Although injury to David Townsend subsequently allowed the Board to bring in Walter Masimula, a black fast bowler who played at the expense of Townsend's original replacement, Rudi Bryson, this eleventh-hour decision smacked of tokenism and the row rumbled on. It ended with White's resignation during the one-day triangular tournament that followed the Test series.

The political brouhaha did not improve the demeanour of South Africa's captain, Hansie Cronje, often a brooding figure, unhappy with his masters and his own form. Already disgruntled at starting the series with a short-term appointment for two Tests only, subsequently extended to cover the remaining Tests and the one-day games against England and Zimbabwe, he reportedly offered to drop himself before the Third at Durban because he strongly opposed the selectors' decision to leave out Jonty Rhodes. Throughout, Cronje was widely criticised for being too cautious tactically, yet at the end he was again a national champion, hailed both for the series victory and for his initiative on the last day at Centurion Park.

Within months, however, his career, possibly his life, was in ruins. His captaincy of South Africa had become a source of national shame rather than pride. In April, following allegations of match-fixing by the Indian police – South Africa toured there after England's visit – Cronje confessed to accepting a bookmaker's money in return for "detailed information and forecasting" on the one-day series between India and South Africa. He was immediately stripped of the captaincy, and South Africa set up an inquiry into match-fixing, the King Commission, which heard in June that Cronje's involvement with bookmakers went back to 1995.

Not even the history-making Fifth Test escaped untarnished. After rain for three and a half days, this match at Centurion had appeared destined for a watery grave, the fate it suffered when England played in the inaugural Test there in November 1995. With South Africa still in the first innings of the match on the last morning, Cronje approached Hussain about a contrived finish, suggesting they each forfeit an innings to make a contest of it. Permitted in domestic competitions in similar circumstances, the forfeiting of one innings, let alone two, had never been seen in Test cricket before. At the time the Laws, subject to local playing conditions, allowed the forfeit only of a second innings. After some bartering, a deal was struck and England chased 249 to win in 76 overs, a target they reached with two wickets and five balls to spare.

Defeat ended South Africa's unbeaten sequence of 14 Tests since Headingley 1998, and some traditionalists held up their hands in horror at the "cheapening" of the five-day game. But most agreed, including match referee Barry Jarman and the travelling England supporters who had endured three miserable days without play, that Cronje's enterprise was to be applauded. What subsequently emerged at the King Commission hearing was that Cronje's initiative had been motivated by a Johannesburg bookmaker, Marlon Aronstam, who rewarded the South African captain with 53,000 rand (around £5,000) and a woman's leather jacket. As the odds favoured a draw, a win by either side was the most satisfactory result for bookmakers.

At the time, it seemed Cronje had little to lose, having taken the series. England, in contrast, had arrived in South Africa ranked bottom of the Test nations after their home defeat by New Zealand. They came with a new management team and an experimental squad of 17 players, eight of whom had nine caps between them. Four of those – Michael Vaughan, Chris Adams, Gavin Hamilton and Graeme Swann – had still to make their Test debut. Left at home for a variety of reasons were experienced players such as Graham Thorpe, Mark Ramprakash and Graeme Hick.

By the end of what was England's longest tour for nine years – 122 days including four one-day internationals in Zimbabwe – they had called up 26 players and made little progress, despite the optimistic reports from Hussain and Fletcher. Two players were the victims of injury and both were costly losses. Fast bowler Dean Headley suffered a stress fracture of the back before the Test series started, and Andrew Flintoff, having set aside early concerns about his back, broke a toe during the Fourth Test, just as he was beginning to look a genuinely exciting all-rounder. Chris Silverwood was drafted in from the A tour of New Zealand as cover for Headley and Flintoff, then stayed on when Headley returned home. Craig White left his winter employment, also in New Zealand, with Central Districts, to replace Flintoff for the one-day tournament. Ramprakash was denied Christmas at home when he was called up as temporary cover for Vaughan, who had bruised a finger, but was not needed and returned for his cold turkey without having faced a ball. The rest of those wearing England shirts were the one-day specialists, flown out for the triangular tournament in South Africa and the series in Zimbabwe at the end. If somewhat spurious in the context of a major tour, the visit to Zimbabwe did give England the opportunity, by winning 3–0, to correct the embarrassing imbalance that existed between the sides in one-day international results.

The most encouraging aspect of the tour was Hussain's impact as captain. Appointed the previous summer after the World Cup, he stamped his authority impressively on a team containing his two predecessors, Mike Atherton and Alec Stewart. His batting flourished with the extra responsibility, and he was by some distance his team's best player. Often regarded as a confrontational character, intense about his personal success, Hussain handled his players with thoughtful attention to detail. Tactically, he outplayed Cronje and, off the field, he proved more adept at public relations than any England captain since Tony Greig.

Coach Fletcher, another summer appointment, made a contrasting figure. Quiet, undemonstrative and camera-shy, he none the less won the respect of the players with his knowledge and organisational skills. Zimbabwe-born and bred, well-versed in the methods of Southern African sport, he was a stickler for punctuality and self-discipline; as a few players discovered, he was not to be crossed. Phil Tufnell and Swann both ran into trouble for missing early-morning buses, while Flintoff was left in no doubt about the fitness levels expected of him.

Fletcher and Hussain, the two tour selectors, soon made up their minds about the Test team, whereupon the rest of the squad became peripheral figures. Swann, only 20, played just two first-class games, in which he took one wicket and had one innings; he did make his England debut against South Africa in England's first match of the triangular tournament, but that was his last appearance. Little more was seen of the reserve wicket-keeper, Chris Read, before the one-dayers, while Alex Tudor, Darren Maddy and Hamilton failed to make the impact hoped of them. Consequently, and worryingly for the long term, it was left to the old hands to make England competitive, something they achieved in the Second and Third Tests before South Africa finally asserted themselves at Cape Town.

England's batting was held together by Hussain, Atherton and wicket-keeper Stewart, with Stewart finishing 1999 as the world's leading run-maker of the decade, having scored 6,407 in his 93 Tests. Other than them, no one managed a Test half-century until Vaughan's 69 on the last day at Centurion, and this was England's biggest failing. South Africa could always rely on someone – Lance Klusener's 174 in the Second Test, batting at No. 7, being a spectacular example. If England's main three did not produce, the innings crumbled. Mark Butcher had another torrid time as Atherton's opening partner and Adams was not up to the challenge of Test cricket, averaging only 13 despite being given the chance to play in all five. Of the newcomers, only Vaughan returned home with his reputation enhanced.

South Africa outbowled England in every department. Andrew Caddick was England's best by some distance, but he and Darren Gough's were never as effective as Allan Donald and Shaun Pollock as a new-ball pair. South Africa's newcomer, Mornantau "Nantie" Hayward, was quicker and more successful than England's novice, Silverwood, and even in spin, which played a pitifully small part in the series, Paul Adams's left-arm wrist-spin posed more threat than Tufnell's conventional finger-spin.

The First Test was won by Donald and Pollock, who took 19 wickets between them on a substandard Wanderers pitch. England, having prepared well for a month, felt they had been ambushed, and few could blame them. For Donald, however, out of form and injured before the series, the match was a triumph: his 11 for 127 brought him closer to becoming the first South African to take 300 Test wickets. He started the series on 268, but any prospect of reaching his target against England disappeared when he withdrew on the morning of the last Test with gout, and 290 wickets to his credit.

That England regrouped and fought back so keenly in the Second and Third Tests owed much to Hussain's leadership and his batting. In Port Elizabeth he inspired the fightback, then ensured safety; in the Christmas Test at Durban, where England shocked a nation by making South Africa follow on for the first time in 73 Tests, since January 1967 against Australia at Cape Town, Hussain was the architect with 146 not out over ten hours 35 minutes. It seemed a marathon until Gary Kirsten batted more than two days to save the match.

Several days later at Cape Town, for what was called the Millennium Test, the toll of that Third Test on the England players became apparent. A good start was squandered, Daryll Cullinan and Jacques Kallis exploited the weariness of the bowlers, and England, the ship holed and down to ten men, ran up the white flag. It meant that, for the first time since the West Indies in 1993-94, they went into the final Test of a tour with the rubber decided. While there was cheer in the final hour at Centurion, there was little consolation or convincing evidence that any corner had been turned.

ENGLAND TOURING PARTY

N. Hussain (Essex) (*captain*), C. J. Adams (Sussex), M. A. Atherton (Lancashire), M. A. Butcher (Surrey), A. R. Caddick (Somerset), A. Flintoff (Lancashire), D. Gough (Yorkshire), G. M. Hamilton (Yorkshire), D. W. Headley (Kent), D. L. Maddy (Leicestershire), A. D. Mullally (Leicestershire), C. M. W. Read (Nottinghamshire), A. J. Stewart (Surrey), G. P. Swann (Northamptonshire), A. J. Tudor (Surrey), P. C. R. Tufnell (Middlesex), M. P. Vaughan (Yorkshire).

C. E. W. Silverwood (Yorkshire) later joined the tour as cover for Flintoff and Headley, and remained when Headley returned home. M. R. Ramprakash (Middlesex) flew out briefly as cover for Vaughan.

After the Test series, Atherton, Butcher, Stewart, Swann, Tudor, Tufnell and Vaughan flew home. The squad for the one-day series was reinforced by M. W. Alleyne (Gloucestershire), M. A. Ealham (Kent), A. F. Giles (Warwickshire), G. A. Hick (Worcestershire), N. V. Knight (Warwickshire), V. S. Solanki (Worcestershire) and C. White (Yorkshire), who was added to the squad after Flintoff was injured in the Fourth Test.

Tour manager: P. A. Neale. *Coach:* D. A. G. Fletcher. *Assistant coach:* R. M. H. Cottam. *Scorer:* M. N. Ashton. *Physiotherapist:* D. O. Conway. *Fitness consultant:* N. P. Stockill. *Media Relations Managers:* A. J. Walpole and D. A. Clarke.

ENGLAND TOUR RESULTS

Test matches – Played 5: Won 1, Lost 2, Drawn 2.
First-class matches – Played 11: Won 3, Lost 2, Drawn 6.
Wins – South Africa, Combined Free State/Griqualand West XI, Combined Northerns/Gauteng XI.
Losses – South Africa (2).
Draws – South Africa (2), Combined Western Province/Boland XI, KwaZulu-Natal, Combined Border/Eastern Province XI, South African Invitation XI.
One-day internationals – Played 11: Won 5, Lost 4, No result 2. *Wins* – South Africa, Zimbabwe (4). *Losses* – South Africa (3), Zimbabwe. *No result* – Zimbabwe (2).
Other non-first-class matches – Played 5: Won 4, Lost 1. *Wins* – Easterns, Gauteng Invitation XI, Combined Border/Eastern Province Invitation XI, North West. *Loss* – N. F. Oppenheimer's XI.

TEST MATCH AVERAGES

SOUTH AFRICA – BATTING

	T	I	NO	R	HS	100s	50s	Avge	Ct
L. Klusener	5	6	1	370	174	1	2	74.00	4
G. Kirsten	5	7	0	396	275	1	1	56.57	4
D. J. Cullinan	5	7	0	386	120	2	1	55.14	3
J. N. Rhodes	3	4	1	149	57*	0	2	49.66	3
J. H. Kallis	5	7	1	297	105	1	2	49.50	2
M. V. Boucher	5	6	1	212	108	1	0	42.40	19
H. H. Gibbs	5	7	0	203	85	0	1	29.00	2
S. M. Pollock	5	6	1	114	64	0	1	22.80	3
P. R. Adams	4	4	3	16	9	0	0	16.00	0
W. J. Cronje	5	7	0	102	44	0	0	14.57	0
A. A. Donald	4	4	0	16	9	0	0	4.00	1

Played in three Tests: M. Hayward 10*, 0*. Played in one Test: P. C. Strydom 30.

* *Signifies not out.*

BOWLING

	O	M	R	W	BB	5W/i	Avge
A. A. Donald	145.2	41	422	22	6-53	3	19.18
S. M. Pollock	184.2	69	396	19	4-16	0	20.84
M. Hayward	85.2	21	265	10	4-75	0	26.50
P. R. Adams	95.3	32	190	7	3-42	0	27.14
J. H. Kallis	72.2	18	184	5	2-22	0	36.80
L. Klusener	118	40	276	5	2-8	0	55.20

Also bowled: W. J. Cronje 48–24–84–3; P. C. Strydom 6–0–27–0.

ENGLAND – BATTING

	T	I	NO	R	HS	100s	50s	Avge	Ct/St
N. Hussain	5	8	2	370	146*	1	2	61.66	2
A. J. Stewart	5	8	0	342	95	0	3	42.75	13/1
M. P. Vaughan	4	7	0	204	69	0	1	29.14	6
M. A. Atherton	5	8	0	225	108	1	1	28.12	3
A. Flintoff	4	6	0	155	42	0	0	25.83	2
M. A. Butcher	5	8	0	166	48	0	0	20.75	0
D. Gough	5	7	3	64	16*	0	0	16.00	0
A. R. Caddick	5	8	1	105	48	0	0	15.00	1
C. J. Adams	5	8	0	104	31	0	0	13.00	6
C. E. W. Silverwood	4	5	3	19	7*	0	0	9.50	1
P. C. R. Tufnell	3	4	2	9	7*	0	0	4.50	0

Played in two Tests: D. L. Maddy 24, 3 (3 ct); A. D. Mullally 10, 0 (1 ct). Played in one Test: G. M. Hamilton 0, 0.

* *Signifies not out.*

BOWLING

	O	M	R	W	BB	5W/i	Avge
A. D. Mullally	58	17	122	5	3-80	0	24.40
A. R. Caddick	185	51	468	16	7-46	1	29.25
D. Gough	171	34	527	14	5-70	1	37.64
A. Flintoff.	66.5	16	190	5	2-31	0	38.00
C. E. W. Silverwood	109	19	344	7	5-91	1	49.14
P. C. R. Tufnell	171.4	35	433	6	4-124	0	72.16

Also bowled: C. J. Adams 20–5–59–1; M. A. Butcher 11.2–0–41–2; G. M. Hamilton 15–1–63–0; N. Hussain 5–1–15–0; D. L. Maddy 14–1–40–0; M. P. Vaughan 18–1–73–0.

ENGLAND TOUR AVERAGES – FIRST-CLASS AVERAGES

BATTING

	M	I	NO	R	HS	100s	50s	Avge	Ct/St
N. Hussain	9	14	3	559	146*	2	2	50.81	5
A. Flintoff.	7	11	2	396	89*	0	2	44.00	6
M. A. Atherton.	9	15	0	603	108	1	4	40.20	7
M. P. Vaughan	10	15	2	435	85	0	2	33.46	11
A. J. Stewart	9	13	1	399	95	0	3	33.25	21/1
C. J. Adams.	10	14	1	376	89	0	3	28.92	11
A. J. Tudor	5	5	2	76	45	0	0	25.33	0
M. A. Butcher	10	16	1	348	87*	0	1	23.20	5
G. M. Hamilton	6	7	2	93	64*	0	1	18.60	3
A. R. Caddick	8	12	2	137	48	0	0	13.70	3
D. L. Maddy	6	6	0	81	38	0	0	13.50	7
D. Gough	8	9	3	68	16*	0	0	11.33	0
C. E. W. Silverwood	5	5	3	19	7*	0	0	9.50	1
A. D. Mullally	5	5	0	30	20	0	0	6.00	1
P. C. R. Tufnell	5	6	3	16	7*	0	0	5.33	0

Played in three matches: C. M. W. Read 14, 15* (7 ct). Played in two matches: G. P. Swann 13. Played in one match: M. A. Ealham 26; G. A. Hick 57 (1 ct); N. V. Knight 111; V. S. Solanki 40 (1 ct).

* *Signifies not out.*

BOWLING

	O	M	R	W	BB	5W/i	Avge
A. Flintoff.	98.3	23	285	12	3-6	0	23.75
A. R. Caddick	298.2	88	690	29	7-46	2	23.79
A. D. Mullally	182	64	390	15	3-31	0	26.00
A. J. Tudor	128	24	444	15	3-61	0	29.60
D. Gough	264.1	56	849	27	5-70	1	31.44
G. M. Hamilton	130	30	394	11	3-28	0	35.81
M. P. Vaughan	95.1	12	302	8	2-22	0	37.75
C. E. W. Silverwood	138	29	409	8	5-91	1	51.12
P. C. R. Tufnell	258.4	62	619	11	4-124	0	56.27

Also bowled: C. J. Adams 26–6–79–1; M. A. Butcher 25.2–2–92–3; M. A. Ealham 22–8–55–3; G. A. Hick 1–0–5–0; N. Hussain 5–1–15–0; D. L. Maddy 29–1–83–0; G. P. Swann 52.4–8–210–1.

Note: Matches in this section which were not first-class were signified by a dagger.

†At Randjesfontein, November 1. N. F. Oppenheimer's XI won by six wickets. Toss: England XI. England XI 203 for seven dec. (M. A. Atherton 72, M. P. Vaughan 59 not out; J. M. Kemp four for 33); N. F. Oppenheimer's XI 207 for four (M. van Jaarsveld 40, D. M. Benkenstein 41, J. M. Kemp 81 not out, N. Pothas 39 not out).

This was the first victory over a touring side by an Oppenheimer XI. Dean Headley withdrew because of a back spasm after bowling ten balls for England; substitute Gavin Hamilton was allowed to bowl and took two for 51.

†At Benoni, November 2. England XI won by 19 runs. Toss: Easterns. England XI 234 for nine (50 overs) (N. Hussain 64, A. Flintoff 54; A. Nel four for 33); Easterns 215 for seven (50 overs) (D. J. Smith 75).

COMBINED WESTERN PROVINCE/BOLAND XI v ENGLAND XI

At Cape Town, November 5, 6, 7, 8. Drawn. Toss: Combined Western Province/Boland XI.

England's plans had been upset even before their first-class programme began. Fast bowlers Gough and Headley came out of the Oppenheimer XI game with back problems, and Flintoff had also suffered some back discomfort in training. Tudor, still feeling his way to full fitness after his knee operation in the autumn, was required to bowl here. At least Atherton's troublesome back stood the strain of six and a half hours at the crease in the first innings, and Caddick continued his good form of the English summer. On a slow pitch, however, the support bowling revealed England's slim reserves: even without Test players Gibbs, Kallis and Kirsten, the Combined team got out of trouble in both innings. Atherton apart, only two England batsmen reached double figures first time round – Vaughan impressed with his composure; Adams's 89 was as chancy as it was unique – and the collapse of the last six wickets for 15 in ten overs had the hallmark of all-too-familiar failings. A target of 250 in 47 overs held no attraction when the tourists batted a second time.

Close of play: First day, Combined Western Province/Boland XI 247-5 (Jackson 69*, C. W. Henderson 2*); Second day, England XI 78-2 (Atherton 26*, Vaughan 33*); Third day, Combined Western Province/Boland XI 51-4 (Prince 1*).

Combined Western Province/Boland XI

R. Magiet b Caddick		3	– b Caddick	12
J. M. Henderson c Butcher b Caddick		6	– c Butcher b Mullally	3
*L. J. Koen c Maddy b Caddick		96	– lbw b Mullally	25
H. D. Ackerman b Butcher		35	– c Hamilton b Tudor	10
A. G. Prince c Vaughan b Tudor		21	– c Caddick b Vaughan	31
K. C. Jackson b Mullally		80	– c Maddy b Mullally	2
C. W. Henderson c Atherton b Caddick		7		
†S. J. Palframan lbw b Caddick		72	– (7) not out	43
D. M. Koch c Adams b Tudor		0	– (8) not out	10
R. Telemachus not out		13		
L-b 11, w 3, n-b 11		25	L-b 2, n-b 2	4

1/4 2/11 3/70 4/117 5/243   (9 wkts dec.) 358   1/6 2/36 3/47   (6 wkts dec.) 140
6/263 7/274 8/302 9/358   4/51 5/54 6/109

C. M. Willoughby did not bat.

Bowling: First Innings—Caddick 33.2–11–53–5; Mullally 36–16–54–1; Hamilton 20–3–65–0; Tudor 23–3–76–2; Butcher 8–1–34–1; Vaughan 16–1–65–0. *Second Innings*—Caddick 14–7–24–1; Mullally 14–5–31–3; Tudor 11–4–18–1; Vaughan 12–2–31–1; Hamilton 5–1–19–0; Butcher 3–1–3–0; Maddy 4–0–12–0.

England XI

M. A. Butcher b Willoughby	0	– run out	3
M. A. Atherton b C. W. Henderson	83	– c Magiet b Koch	24
*N. Hussain c Willoughby b Telemachus	9	– not out	33
M. P. Vaughan lbw b Willoughby	36	– not out	16
†A. J. Stewart b Telemachus	1		
C. J. Adams c C. W. Henderson b Koch	89		
D. L. Maddy c Palframan b Koch	2		
G. M. Hamilton not out	4		
A. J. Tudor c Telemachus b Koch	0		
A. R. Caddick c Palframan b Telemachus	8		
A. D. Mullally c Palframan b Telemachus	0		
B 1, l-b 4, w 2, n-b 10	17	B 2, l-b 1, n-b 3	6

1/2 2/14 3/86 4/87 5/234	249	1/11 2/30	(2 wkts) 82
6/236 7/236 8/236 9/247			

Bowling: *First Innings*—Willoughby 26–6–62–2; Telemachus 23.3–5–64–4; Koch 25–4–73–3; C. W. Henderson 25–17–22–1; J. M. Henderson 7–1–22–0. *Second Innings*—Telemachus 7–1–20–0; Willoughby 7–3–8–0; C. W. Henderson 14–5–24–0; Koch 6–2–12–1; J. M. Henderson 7–2–15–0.

Umpires: R. Brooks and I. L. Howell.

COMBINED FREE STATE/GRIQUALAND WEST XI v ENGLAND XI

At Bloemfontein, November 12, 13, 14, 15. England XI won by 153 runs. Toss: Combined Free State/Griqualand West XI.

Against another Combined side without current internationals, England's Test team began to take shape, with Flintoff joining fellow all-rounder Hamilton to bolster the batting. Along with a more disciplined 84 by Adams, both hit half-centuries to revive England's first innings and set up a morale-boosting win. The tourists' mood was also lifted by Gough's return: he took four wickets as the home side's reply fell away against England's purposeful, well-drilled cricket. Mullally initiated the collapse when he ended Liebenberg's dogged four-and-three-quarter-hour stay and dismissed Bosman in three balls. There was further encouragement from Butcher's 87 not out in the second innings. His stand of 141 with Atherton, plus some lusty hitting by Flintoff, allowed Hussain to declare late on the third evening, and next day his bowlers won the game with ten overs to spare.

Close of play: First day, England XI 271-7 (Hamilton 8*); Second day, Combined Free State/Griqualand West XI 156-3 (Liebenberg 80*, van Wyk 20*); Third day, Combined Free State/Griqualand West XI 15-0 (Liebenberg 3*, Gidley 10*).

England XI

M. A. Butcher c Liebenberg b Bakkes	3	– not out	87
M. A. Atherton b Vorster	26	– c Bossenger b Vorster	81
*N. Hussain c Bossenger b Bakkes	41		
M. P. Vaughan c Gidley b van der Wath	14		
†A. J. Stewart b Roe	19		
C. J. Adams c Brooker b van der Wath	84		
A. Flintoff lbw b Bakkes	65	– (3) not out	37
G. M. Hamilton not out	64		
D. Gough c Gidley b Roe	0		
A. D. Mullally c van der Wath b Vorster	20		
P. C. R. Tufnell not out	7		
B 5, l-b 4, w 1, n-b 5	15	B 1, l-b 4, w 1	6

1/25 2/33 3/86 4/94 5/127	(9 wkts dec.) 358	1/141	(1 wkt dec.) 211
6/259 7/271 8/290 9/344			

Bowling: *First Innings*—van der Wath 25–1–84–2; Bakkes 25–8–53–3; Vorster 17–4–88–2; Roe 28–7–80–2; Gidley 23–5–44–0. *Second Innings*—Gidley 12–3–43–0; Bakkes 4–1–16–0; van der Wath 8–2–29–0; Vorster 12–1–67–1; Bosman 8–0–27–0; Roe 6–0–24–0.

Combined Free State/Griqualand West XI

*G. F. J. Liebenberg c Hussain b Mullally	92	– c sub (D. L. Maddy) b Hamilton . . 12
M. I. Gidley b Gough	37	– b Gough 11
F. C. Brooker c Butcher b Vaughan	0	– b Vaughan 56
P. H. Barnard c Atherton b Hamilton	3	– b Hamilton 16
M. N. van Wyk lbw b Gough	31	– c Adams b Tufnell 21
L. L. Bosman c Stewart b Mullally	0	– lbw b Mullally 40
J. J. van der Wath run out	0	– c Hamilton b Tufnell 11
†W. Bossenger c Stewart b Gough	3	– b Gough 9
H. C. Bakkes c Adams b Gough	8	– c Stewart b Tufnell 2
G. A. Roe c Hussain b Tufnell	1	– not out 14
C. J. Vorster not out	2	– b Vaughan 18
L-b 12, w 1, n-b 4	17	L-b 7, n-b 5 12

1/81 2/90 3/101 4/170 5/170   194   1/20 2/33 3/53   222
6/170 7/180 8/183 9/192   4/83 5/162 6/166
                                                  7/186 8/188 9/189

Bowling: *First Innings*—Gough 21–6–60–4; Mullally 19–11–24–2; Hamilton 10–1–40–1; Tufnell 24–11–31–1; Vaughan 13–2–26–1; Butcher 1–0–1–0. *Second Innings*—Gough 19–5–52–2; Hamilton 14–2–39–2; Tufnell 17–6–27–3; Vaughan 7.1–0–37–2; Mullally 20–7–60–1.

Umpires: D. F. Becker and R. E. Koertzen.

COMBINED NORTHERNS/GAUTENG XI v ENGLAND XI

At Centurion, November 18, 19, 20, 21. England XI won by 102 runs. Toss: Combined Northerns/Gauteng XI.

During this game, England's last before the First Test, a scan revealed that Headley had what was suspected to be a stress fracture in his lower back. As a result, Silverwood, who had arrived as cover during the previous match, became a permanent member of the tour party. A more positive note was struck by Flintoff, bowling again a week ahead of schedule and returning match figures of five for 23 from his first overs of the tour. Apart from Tudor, who replaced the resting Mullally, this was England's intended Test side, and they took heart from the way they outplayed opposition containing five Test cricketers and a potential one in McKenzie. A former Under-19 captain, McKenzie cut and pulled powerfully in his two half-centuries, giving England's bowlers a timely reminder of the cost of pitching short. The batting of Atherton and Vaughan was reassuring in the first innings. Less reassuring was the second-innings collapse in which England's top five went in the space of nine runs.

Close of play: First day, England XI 238-6 (Adams 11*, Flintoff 2*); Second day, Combined Northerns/Gauteng XI 85-3 (McKenzie 56*, van Jaarsveld 5*); Third day, England XI 136-7 (Adams 8*, Tudor 1*).

England XI

M. A. Butcher lbw b Smith	15	– c van Jaarsveld b Eksteen	39
M. A. Atherton b Smith	81	– c Cullinan b Eksteen	39
*N. Hussain b Terbrugge	1	– c Cullinan b Eksteen	2
M. P. Vaughan lbw b Elworthy	85	– c Pothas b Masimula	2
†A. J. Stewart c Pothas b Terbrugge	20	– c van Jaarsveld b Masimula	1
C. J. Adams c van Jaarsveld b Smith	19	– (8) c Bacher b Eksteen	21
A. R. Caddick lbw b Terbrugge	0	– (10) not out	24
A. Flintoff b Elworthy	26	– (6) c van Jaarsveld b Elworthy	24
G. M. Hamilton c van Jaarsveld b Terbrugge	16	– (7) c Cullinan b Elworthy	7
A. J. Tudor not out	4	– (9) not out	19
D. Gough c Eksteen b Elworthy	4		
B 8, l-b 9, n-b 15	32	B 8, l-b 3, n-b 6	17

1/43 2/44 3/176 4/218 5/234   303   1/88 2/91 3/93   (8 wkts dec.) 195
6/235 7/252 8/295 9/295   4/96 5/97 6/127
    7/130 8/156

Bowling: *First Innings*—Elworthy 26.4–5–73–3; Smith 24–4–77–3; Terbrugge 30–6–67–4; Masimula 11–0–33–0; Eksteen 20–7–36–0; McKenzie 1–1–0–0. *Second Innings*—Elworthy 16–3–46–2; Smith 4–0–34–0; Eksteen 26–8–72–4; Terbrugge 4–1–15–0; Bacher 1–0–5–0; Masimula 10–5–12–2.

Combined Northerns/Gauteng XI

S. G. Koenig lbw b Gough	0	– (2) c Vaughan b Gough	6
A. M. Bacher c Stewart b Caddick	4	– (1) c Hussain b Vaughan	18
N. D. McKenzie lbw b Gough	62	– b Gough	87
D. J. Cullinan lbw b Hamilton	11	– c Vaughan b Gough	32
M. van Jaarsveld c Atherton b Hamilton	13	– lbw b Caddick	5
†N. Pothas c Stewart b Hamilton	29	– c sub (D. L. Maddy) b Hamilton	3
S. Elworthy c Stewart b Flintoff	43	– c and b Flintoff	6
*C. E. Eksteen c Stewart b Caddick	7	– c Vaughan b Flintoff	0
D. J. Terbrugge c Vaughan b Flintoff	7	– lbw b Hamilton	4
G. J. Smith c Stewart b Flintoff	4	– b Vaughan	18
W. B. Masimula not out	2	– not out	2
B 1, l-b 5, w 1, n-b 12	19	L-b 10, w 1, n-b 3	14

1/0 2/37 3/73 4/94 5/130   201   1/9 2/46 3/107 4/119 5/125   195
6/139 7/158 8/191 9/195   6/138 7/138 8/145 9/193

Bowling: *First Innings*—Gough 16–3–69–2; Caddick 25–7–57–2; Tudor 8–2–35–0; Hamilton 14–6–28–3; Flintoff 4.1–0–6–3. *Second Innings*—Gough 13.1–1–69–3; Caddick 12–5–24–1; Tudor 2–0–13–0; Vaughan 8–1–27–2; Hamilton 8–1–35–2; Flintoff 5–2–17–2.

Umpires: W. A. Diedricks and D. L. Orchard.

SOUTH AFRICA v ENGLAND

First Test Match

At Johannesburg, November 25, 26, 27, 28. South Africa won by an innings and 21 runs. Toss: South Africa. Test debuts: C. J. Adams, G. M. Hamilton, M. P. Vaughan.

South Africa overpowered a new-look England side who went to the Wanderers full of optimism and left realising the scale of the task ahead. It was South Africa's tenth consecutive home Test win, equalling India's winning sequence from December 1988 to November 1994, and only their second victory by an innings against England. The first had been in 1905-06 at Cape Town, by an innings and 16 runs. This later one was completed before lunch on the fourth morning but, with rain and bad light causing interruptions, there were less than three days of playing time.

[*Patrick Eagar*

The worst possible start to a series: Donald bowls Atherton (1), Pollock bounces out Hussain (2), then with consecutive balls Donald has Butcher caught behind (3) and Stewart lbw (4). England are two for four in the third over.

The match was dominated by South Africa's peerless new-ball pairing of Donald and Pollock, who exploited perfect conditions for fast bowling to claim 19 wickets between them. Poor England. They turned up on the first morning to find a damp, spongy pitch underfoot and heavy, low clouds overhead. Then Cronje won the toss. It took just 17 deliveries to put all England's plans and preparation through a shredder as they lost four wickets for two runs, their worst start to a Test match.

Donald did the principal damage, bowling Atherton second ball with a late in-swinger. Four years earlier, Atherton had batted here for ten hours 43 minutes, scoring an unbeaten 185 to save the Second Test. Donald's devastating first two overs also accounted for Butcher and Stewart, out first ball, so that Chris Adams, coming in at No. 6, found himself batting to prevent a hat-trick within 15 minutes of his debut. With Hussain out third ball to an almost unplayable lifter from Pollock in between, any contest was as good as over. That England achieved 122 owed much to Vaughan, who impressed on his first outing, and some controlled hitting by Flintoff, back in Test cricket after 15 months' absence. But with the ball swinging through the air and seaming off the pitch, batting was a lottery.

WORST STARTS TO A TEST INNINGS

7 for 6	Australia v England at Manchester	1888
6 for 5	India v England at The Oval	1952
0 for 4	India v England at Leeds	1952
*2 for 4	**England v South Africa at Johannesburg**	**1999-2000**
5 for 4	England v Australia at Melbourne	1903-04
7 for 4	Australia v England at The Oval	1896
7 for 4	Australia v England at Brisbane	1936-37
8 for 4	England v India at Bangalore	1976-77
9 for 4	Australia v Sri Lanka at Moratuwa	1992-93
9 for 4	West Indies v Australia at Brisbane	1992-93

* England's 2 for 4 is the only instance in this list to occur in the first innings of a Test.

Research: Gordon Vince

Or it appeared that way until England had the ball in their hands. Gough, Caddick and Mullally lacked the potency of South Africa's fast men and, when Hussain turned to his support bowlers, the home team plundered runs at will on the second day as the sun shone and the pitch dried out. Without a specialist spinner to call on, he was unable to assert the necessary control over events. Gibbs and Cullinan were allowed to leave alone far too often against some wasteful bowling as they ensured that South Africa would build a commanding lead – the 15th time in consecutive Tests that England had conceded a first-innings deficit. Gibbs, recalled after missing the two preceding Tests against Zimbabwe through injury, fell 15 short of his first Test century at home, but Cullinan was in no mood to miss out on his fourth Test hundred of 1999. His 108 in four and a quarter hours, including 17 fours, put him alongside Dudley Nourse and Kirsten on a record nine hundreds for South Africa.

Three quick wickets on the third morning gave Gough a flattering five-wicket return. But, after removing Pollock and Donald with successive balls, he was denied the chance of a hat-trick – he had achieved one in his previous Test, back in January at Sydney – by the weather. Before Paul Adams could take guard, the umpires offered the light and the players went off. During the hour-long delay, Cronje declared.

Needing 281 to avoid an innings defeat, England were instantly in trouble. Pollock unleashed a wickedly fast, rising delivery that Atherton could only glove behind to be out first ball, his second pair and 19th duck in Tests. Only Derek Underwood, an *habitué* of the other end of the innings, had made as many for England. Stubborn resistance from Butcher, who spent 220 minutes grafting for 32, and Stewart meant England's innings was not always one-way traffic. Stewart, struck in the ribs by Pollock, put attack before occupation and hit a bold 86, with a six and 14 fours, before becoming Donald's tenth victim of the match. His 11th, Hamilton, was also his 75th against England, equalling in 14 Tests Hugh Tayfield's record from 15 games. More bad light meant the match went into the fourth day, when the lower-order antics of Flintoff and Caddick, who made a Test-best 48, persuaded Cronje to turn to Adams. Spin did the trick, extracting a return catch out of Flintoff, but it also prevented Pollock and Donald from becoming only the seventh pair to claim all 20 wickets in a Test. – COLIN BATEMAN.

Man of the Match: A. A. Donald.   *Attendance:* 35,943.

Close of play: First day, South Africa 64-1 (Gibbs 28*, Kallis 6*); Second day, South Africa 386-6 (Klusener 61*, Pollock 0*); Third day, England 188-7 (Flintoff 26*, Caddick 4*).

England

M. A. Butcher c Boucher b Donald	1	– lbw b Donald	32
M. A. Atherton b Donald	0	– c Boucher b Pollock	0
*N. Hussain c Klusener b Pollock	0	– b Pollock	16
M. P. Vaughan c Boucher b Pollock	33	– lbw b Donald	5
†A. J. Stewart lbw b Donald	0	– c Rhodes b Donald	86
C. J. Adams c Boucher b Donald	16	– c Boucher b Donald	1
A. Flintoff c Boucher b Pollock	38	– c and b Adams	36
G. M. Hamilton c Pollock b Donald	0	– c Pollock b Donald	0
A. R. Caddick c Boucher b Donald	4	– b Pollock	48
D. Gough not out	15	– not out	16
A. D. Mullally lbw b Pollock	10	– c Kallis b Pollock	0
L-b 3, w 2	5	B 4, l-b 10, w 6	20
	122		**260**

1/1 (2) 2/2 (3) 3/2 (1) 4/2 (5)   1/0 (2) 2/31 (3) 3/41 (4)
5/34 (6) 6/90 (4) 7/91 (8)   4/145 (5) 5/147 (6) 6/166 (5)
8/91 (7) 9/103 (9) 10/122 (11)   7/166 (8) 8/218 (7)
    9/260 (9) 10/260 (11)

Bowling: *First Innings*—Donald 15-3-53-6; Pollock 14.4-6-16-4; Cronje 5-2-15-0; Klusener 6-1-30-0; Adams 1-0-5-0. *Second Innings*—Donald 23-7-74-5; Pollock 24.4-11-64-4; Klusener 19-3-55-0; Adams 11-1-31-1; Cronje 6-3-22-0.

South Africa

G. Kirsten lbw b Mullally	13	A. A. Donald b Gough	0
H. H. Gibbs b Mullally	85	P. R. Adams not out	0
J. H. Kallis c Stewart b Gough	12	B 7, l-b 18, w 2, n-b 10	37
D. J. Cullinan b Caddick	108		
*W. J. Cronje b Gough	44	1/37 (1) 2/79 (3)	(9 wkts dec.) 403
J. N. Rhodes lbw b Mullally	26	3/175 (2) 4/284 (4)	
L. Klusener b Gough	72	5/299 (5) 6/378 (6)	
S. M. Pollock c Stewart b Gough	2	7/398 (7) 8/403 (8)	
†M. V. Boucher not out	4	9/403 (10)	

Bowling: Gough 30-8-70-5; Caddick 34-12-81-1; Mullally 34-7-80-3; Flintoff 14-5-45-0; Hamilton 15-1-63-0; Vaughan 11-1-39-0.

Umpires: S. Venkataraghavan (India) and D. L. Orchard.
Referee: B. N. Jarman (Australia).

†At Lenasia, December 1. England XI won by 38 runs. Toss: Gauteng Invitation XI. England XI 274 for five (50 overs) (M. A. Butcher 47, D. L. Maddy 79 not out, C. J. Adams 37; A. J. Hall three for 35); Gauteng Invitation XI 236 for nine (50 overs) (A. J. Hall 48, Z. de Bruyn 82, S. Ndima 52; D. Gough three for 48, C. E. W. Silverwood three for 45).

KWAZULU-NATAL v ENGLAND XI

At Durban, December 3, 4, 5, 6. Drawn. Toss: KwaZulu-Natal. First-class debut: H. Amla.

Kingsmead provided a tranquil pitch for batsmen needing to regroup after their traumatic experiences at Johannesburg. KwaZulu-Natal also made life easier by putting out a young team, giving a first-class debut to 16-year-old Hashim Amla, captain of Durban High School and brother of Ahmed, aged 20. England were without Mullally, who had strained his side in the Test match, and Silverwood, who had damaged an ankle at Lenasia. However, Tudor failed to impress in their absence – not that he was alone in this – as the home team ran up 310, at times with panache. Kent, another 20-year-old, batted well for his second first-class hundred, despite interruptions for poor weather, while Pietersen and Gilder collared Tufnell in a jolly last-wicket stand of 69 in ten overs. England's measured response was to grind their way into the fourth day, building a lead of 111. Hussain spent five and a half hours making sure he posted the first century for England in a first-class match in 1999. Flintoff was poised to become the second but was 11 short of his first hundred for England when Tudor, with whom he added 105, and Tufnell succumbed to successive deliveries.

Close of play: First day, KwaZulu-Natal 136-5 (Kent 50*, Veenstra 14*); Second day, England XI 163-2 (Hussain 54*, Vaughan 27*); Third day, England XI 401-8 (Flintoff 74*, Tudor 40*).

KwaZulu-Natal

M. L. Bruyns c Butcher b Caddick	1	– b Tudor	12
D. J. Watson lbw b Caddick	12	– not out	52
A. M. Amla c Atherton b Tudor	4	– c Flintoff b Tufnell	53
*D. M. Benkenstein lbw b Tudor	45	– not out	20
J. C. Kent b Maddy b Flintoff	103		
H. Amla c Flintoff b Caddick	1		
R. E. Veenstra run out	20		
†D. L. Brown c and b Caddick	7		
K. P. Pietersen not out	61		
G. H. Bodi c Flintoff b Tudor	5		
G. M. Gilder c Read b Flintoff	28		
B 2, l-b 7, w 2, n-b 12	23	B 4, n-b 11	15

1/7 2/19 3/23 4/97 5/110   310   1/32 2/126   (2 wkts) 152
6/152 7/203 8/226 9/241

Bowling: *First Innings*—Caddick 29–7–64–4; Tudor 25–1–91–3; Flintoff 11.3–0–47–2; Tufnell 26–5–86–0; Butcher 2–0–13–0. *Second Innings*—Tudor 16–3–48–1; Flintoff 11–5–25–0; Tufnell 20–5–42–1; Adams 4–1–12–0; Vaughan 10–1–21–0.

England XI

M. A. Butcher c A. M. Amla b Gilder	35	A. R. Caddick c and b A. M. Amla	0
M. A. Atherton st Brown b Pietersen	44	A. J. Tudor c Brown b Veenstra	45
*N. Hussain b Pietersen	103	P. C. R. Tufnell c Watson b Veenstra	0
M. P. Vaughan c Brown b Pietersen	46		
C. J. Adams b Pietersen	0	B 2, l-b 3, n-b 2	7
D. L. Maddy c A. M. Amla b Veenstra	38		
A. Flintoff not out	89	1/76 2/86 3/201 4/201 5/262	421
†C. M. W. Read c Watson b A. M. Amla	14	6/282 7/313 8/316 9/421	

Bowling: Veenstra 29.2–9–47–3; Gilder 22–4–56–1; Pietersen 55.5–14–141–4; Kent 19–5–51–0; Bodi 17.1–4–46–0; A. M. Amla 17–1–53–2; Benkenstein 4–0–22–0.

Umpires: W. A. Diedricks and D. L. Orchard.

SOUTH AFRICA v ENGLAND

Second Test Match

At Port Elizabeth, December 9, 10, 11, 12, 13. Drawn. Toss: England. Test debut: M. Hayward.

A much improved performance by England denied South Africa their 11th successive home victory. Indeed, had the tourists seized the initiative when South Africa were 146 for five in their first innings, they might have gained an unexpected success. But not for the first time, South Africa's middle and late order, led by the dashing Klusener, enabled their side to reach a substantial total. Klusener was named Man of the Match, but there was not a lot in it between him and Hussain. The England captain, as resolute and single-minded as Atherton had been at Johannesburg when captain on the previous tour, defied South Africa's five-man pace attack for five hours two minutes as England battled for the draw they deserved.

They were not helped by some debatable decisions from umpire Rudi Koertzen, who after the match offered a public apology for his mistakes. Unlike Bob Woolmer, who as South Africa's coach had openly criticised the umpires in the Second Test of

---

HIGHEST TEST SCORES BY No. 7 BATSMEN

270	D. G. Bradman.	Australia v England at Melbourne	1936-37
219	D. St E. Atkinson	West Indies v Australia at Bridgetown	1954-55
201*	J. Ryder	Australia v England at Adelaide	1924-25
182	D. T. Lindsay	South Africa v Australia at Johannesburg	1966-67
175	K. S. Ranjitsinhji	England v Australia at Sydney	1897-98
174	**L. Klusener**	**South Africa v England at Port Elizabeth**	**1999-2000**
169*	J. Hardstaff, jun.	England v Australia at The Oval	1938
164	D. W. Randall	England v New Zealand at Wellington	1983-84
163	Kapil Dev	India v Sri Lanka at Kanpur.	1986-87
161*	I. A. Healy	Australia v West Indies at Brisbane	1996-97

Research: Gordon Vince

---

the 1995-96 series, England coach Fletcher refused to comment on five questionable decisions made by Koertzen: Boucher and Kirsten not out in the first and second innings respectively; Butcher, Vaughan and Adams out in the second. Koertzen was also involved when Dave Orchard, the third official, using television replays from South African Broadcasting's coverage, gave the green light to Kallis who, on 12 in the second innings, appeared to have been caught inches from the ground by Adams at silly point off Tufnell. Orchard had been unable to find conclusive evidence that the ball carried; had he consulted Sky Television's pictures, which revealed a fair catch, Kallis would have been out. The incident emphasised that the TV umpire should have access to all available evidence, regardless of the host broadcaster.

After South Africa had left out their spinner, Adams, to bring in fast bowler Nantie Hayward, England surprisingly included Tufnell, who rewarded his captain by containing more effectively than the seamers. Hamilton was dropped, while Silverwood replaced the injured Mullally. Gough bowled poorly, conceding five runs an over throughout South Africa's first innings, but when Tufnell had Cullinan stumped, England might have sensed a breakthrough. Instead Klusener counter-attacked with relish, reaching 50 in 72 minutes and raising the 100 partnership with Rhodes by driving Tufnell for six. Flintoff broke the stand by dismissing Rhodes, but the following

United they stand; divided, England could fall: Nasser Hussain and Mike Atherton carried the fight to South Africa at Port Elizabeth with a second-wicket partnership of 155.

morning Klusener reached three figures off just 127 balls. He went on to achieve the highest individual Test score at St George's Park, also a personal best, and share with Boucher a record eighth-wicket stand of 119 against England – surpassing the unbroken 109 between Bruce Mitchell and Lindsay Tuckett at The Oval in 1947. Klusener's 174 contained two sixes and 25 fours and was the sixth-highest score by a Test batsman coming in at No. 7. England had not bowled intelligently to him by feeding his strength outside off stump.

Butcher was bowled in the second over, but Hussain soon made his intentions clear, hitting Pollock for 4, 6, 6 off the second, fourth and fifth balls he received. Atherton, no match for Donald in the First Test, struck his adversary for four fours in one over as they raced to 139 for one, on a day when 336 runs were scored. The partnership ended when Hussain gloved Donald to the wicket-keeper, but Atherton continued to his 13th Test hundred; England's first in a Test since Stewart's 107 at Melbourne almost 12 months earlier. He was eventually one of four wickets for Hayward, making his debut on his home ground, who bowled faster than anyone else and appeared to be Donald's natural successor. Flintoff set pulses racing when he hit Pollock for four fours in five balls, but such derring-do inevitably exposed the suspect tail.

England were 77 runs adrift on first innings but Gough, with a better performance, and Caddick pegged South Africa back to 50 for three when they batted a second time. The bowlers' accuracy was reflected in South Africa's slow progress, and any ideas Cronje might have had of declaring on the fourth evening were dispelled as Kallis and Rhodes crawled along at barely two an over. He had to wait another half-hour on the final morning before setting England 302 in 79 overs.

They were five for two in the seventh over, with Atherton and Butcher out in the space of six balls. But Vaughan, again playing in his correct and measured fashion, added 75 with his captain, and there was further resistance from Stewart. However, 20 overs remained when Stewart was lbw to Pollock, to be followed by Adams – though replays showed that the ball ricocheted to cover from the batsman's pad. Hussain continued to look secure; it was the other end that was vulnerable. With four overs to go, Flintoff became Boucher's 100th Test victim (and 98th catch), the wicket-keeper getting to that milestone in fewer Tests, 23, than his predecessor for South Africa, Dave Richardson, and Australia's Wally Grout, who had shared the record with 24. Caddick was sufficiently resolute for Cronje to accept the draw with two overs remaining. – EDWARD BEVAN.

Man of the Match: L. Klusener.　　　*Attendance:* 30,524.

Close of play: First day, South Africa 253-6 (Klusener 63*, Pollock 1*); Second day, England 139-1 (Atherton 58*, Hussain 70*); Third day, England 364-9 (Caddick 33*); Fourth day, South Africa 189-4 (Kallis 74*, Rhodes 35*).

South Africa

G. Kirsten c Hussain b Caddick	15	– c Vaughan b Gough	2
H. H. Gibbs run out	48	– c Flintoff b Caddick	10
J. H. Kallis c Caddick b Silverwood	1	– not out	85
D. J. Cullinan st Stewart b Tufnell	58	– b Caddick	18
*W. J. Cronje c Flintoff b Tufnell	2	– c Vaughan b Flintoff	27
J. N. Rhodes c Atherton b Flintoff	50	– not out	57
L. Klusener c Adams b Gough	174		
S. M. Pollock c Vaughan b Flintoff	7		
†M. V. Boucher c Stewart b Tufnell	42		
A. A. Donald c Hussain b Tufnell	9		
M. Hayward not out	10		
B 10, l-b 5, w 1, n-b 18	34	B 4, l-b 11, w 1, n-b 9	25

1/28 (1) 2/57 (3) 3/87 (2) 4/91 (5)　　　　450　　1/5 (1) 2/17 (2)　　　(4 wkts dec.) 224
5/146 (4) 6/252 (6) 7/268 (8)　　　　　　　　　 3/50 (4) 4/98 (5)
8/387 (9) 9/401 (10) 10/450 (7)

Bowling: *First Innings*—Gough 21.1–1–107–1; Caddick 31–5–100–1; Silverwood 24–4–57–1; Tufnell 42–9–124–4; Vaughan 3–0–16–0; Flintoff 7–0–31–2. *Second Innings*—Gough 19–6–52–1; Caddick 18–4–29–2; Silverwood 10–1–24–0; Tufnell 35–9–71–0; Vaughan 2–0–9–0; Flintoff 8.5–2–24–1.

England

M. A. Butcher b Pollock	4	– lbw b Hayward	1
M. A. Atherton b Hayward	108	– b Pollock	3
*N. Hussain c Boucher b Donald	82	– not out	70
M. P. Vaughan b Hayward	21	– c Boucher b Kallis	29
†A. J. Stewart b Donald	15	– lbw b Pollock	28
C. J. Adams c Kallis b Pollock	25	– c Rhodes b Cronje	1
A. Flintoff b Pollock	42	– c Boucher b Kallis	12
A. R. Caddick b Hayward	35	– not out	4
D. Gough b Donald	6		
C. E. W. Silverwood c Klusener b Hayward	6		
P. C. R. Tufnell not out	7		
B 1, l-b 8, n-b 13	22	L-b 2, n-b 3	5

1/5 (1) 2/160 (3) 3/228 (4) 4/229 (2)　　　373　　1/5 (2) 2/5 (1)　　　(6 wkts) 153
5/264 (5) 6/281 (6) 7/336 (7)　　　　　　　　　 3/80 (4) 4/125 (5)
8/349 (9) 9/364 (10) 10/373 (8)　　　　　　　　 5/137 (6) 6/149 (7)

Bowling: *First Innings*—Donald 34–9–109–3; Pollock 34–7–112–3; Hayward 28.1–7–75–4; Klusener 25–9–48–0; Cronje 16–5–20–0. *Second Innings*—Donald 13–4–37–0; Pollock 17–8–18–2; Hayward 20–8–55–1; Kallis 7–1–22–2; Klusener 14–9–17–0; Cronje 6–4–2–1.

Umpires: S. A. Bucknor (West Indies) and R. E. Koertzen.
Referee: B. N. Jarman (Australia).

†At Alice, December 16. England XI won by 153 runs. Toss: England XI. England XI 309 for eight (50 overs) (M. A. Atherton 51, D. L. Maddy 133, Extras 30; R. J. Peterson four for 43); Combined Border/Eastern Province Invitation XI 156 (36.4 overs) (M. R. Benfield 58; G. P. Swann three for 38, P. C. R. Tufnell three for 34).

Maddy scored his 133 from 117 balls, with 11 fours and three sixes.

COMBINED BORDER/EASTERN PROVINCE XI v ENGLAND XI

At East London, December 18, 19, 20, 21. Drawn. Toss: Combined Border/Eastern Province XI.

England's preparations for the back-to-back Third and Fourth Tests fell foul of the weather, with rain preventing further play after tea on the second day. They had hoped for signs of good form from Butcher, Maddy and Adams; instead they lost Vaughan for the Durban Test, his right index finger severely bruised by Kruger. On one of the best batting surfaces England had encountered, their bowlers did well to dismiss the home side for 384, Strydom, the captain, imposing himself until he was bowled by Silverwood 14 short of his century. England started poorly in response. Butcher was out in the first over and Maddy, a century-maker three days earlier, went in the 13th. Adams's breezy half-century, containing 11 boundaries, brought some cheer before the clouds rolled in over Buffalo Park.

Close of play: First day, Combined Border/Eastern Province XI 331-5 (Strydom 66*, Peterson 41*); Second day, England XI 113-2 (Adams 59*, Stewart 16*); Third day, No play.

Combined Border/Eastern Province XI

B. M. White lbw b Swann	48	†L. Masikazana c Adams b Hamilton		6
C. C. Bradfield c Butcher b Gough	11	G. J-P. Kruger not out		6
J. D. C. Bryant c Read b Hamilton	72	M. Ntini c Read b Tudor		4
W. Wiblin c Read b Tudor	63	B 4, l-b 13, w 4, n-b 17		38
*P. C. Strydom b Silverwood	86			
L. L. Gamiet b Tudor	0	1/29 2/123 3/161		384
R. J. Peterson c Adams b Gough	42	4/241 5/253 6/333		
T. Henderson c Read b Hamilton	8	7/351 8/372 9/372		

Bowling: Gough 24–7–72–2; Silverwood 29–10–65–1; Tudor 15.1–1–72–3; Hamilton 21–7–61–3; Swann 17–3–79–1; Adams 2–0–8–0; Maddy 3–0–10–0.

England XI

M. A. Butcher c Bradfield b Ntini	0	*A. J. Stewart not out		16
D. L. Maddy c Henderson b Kruger	14	B 11, l-b 1, n-b 5		17
C. J. Adams not out	59			
M. P. Vaughan retired hurt	7	1/2 2/43	(2 wkts)	113

G. M. Hamilton, G. P. Swann, †C. M. W. Read, A. J. Tudor, D. Gough and C. E. W. Silverwood did not bat.

Vaughan retired hurt at 64.

Bowling: Ntini 9–1–36–1; Henderson 7–1–19–0; Kruger 6–1–35–1; White 4–3–1–0; Peterson 2–0–10–0.

Umpires: I. L. Howell and C. M. Schoof.

SOUTH AFRICA v ENGLAND

Third Test Match

At Durban, December 26, 27, 28, 29, 30. Drawn. Toss: England.

Played in high humidity and at times searing heat, this was a tedious Test match, the sort for which the word attritional might have been coined. Occasionally, as when Stewart or Pollock was batting, or when Caddick was bowling in dramatic fashion and to devastating effect in South Africa's first innings, the torpor was lifted. But for the most part, marathons rather than sprints were the norm. Hussain must have come close to going into reverse at one time during his eighth Test century, and Kirsten spent the last 878 minutes of the match rooted defiantly to the crease. His 275 was a record tenth hundred for South Africa and equalled their highest in a Test, by Cullinan in New Zealand ten months earlier. Only Hanif Mohammad, who at Bridge-town in January 1958 made 337 in 970 minutes, had batted longer in a Test.

In dismissing South Africa for 156, having made 366 for nine themselves, England not only gained a first-innings lead for the first time in 17 Tests since the two teams met at Edgbaston 18 months earlier, but were able to enforce the follow-on, something they had not managed in 59 matches since they played New Zealand at Old Trafford in 1994. For South Africa, it was the first time in eight matches that their wonderfully deep batting had not reached 400 in the first innings, and they had not been asked to follow on for 73 Tests.

LONGEST TEST INNINGS

Mins

970	Hanif Mohammad (337)	Pakistan v West Indies at Bridgetown	1957-58
878	**G. Kirsten (275)**	**South Africa v England at Durban**	**1999-2000**
799	S. T. Jayasuriya (340)	Sri Lanka v India at Colombo (RPS)	1997-98
797	L. Hutton (364)	England v Australia at The Oval	1938
777	D. S. B. P. Kuruppu (201*)	Sri Lanka v New Zealand at Colombo (CCC) .	1986-87
766	B. C. Lara (375)	West Indies v England at St John's.	1993-94
762	R. B. Simpson (311)	Australia v England at Manchester.	1964
753	R. S. Mahanama (225)	Sri Lanka v India at Colombo (RPS)	1997-98

The initial shock for South Africans, however, was the omission on his home ground of the talismanic Rhodes, who had made half-centuries in each innings at Port Elizabeth. The effect this had in undermining the team could not be underestimated, and it was rumoured that Cronje, on a poor run of form, had offered to stand down himself. Paul Adams returned, while Maddy replaced the injured Vaughan in England's line-up.

Hussain's strategy after winning the toss was to keep South Africa in the field and build a total at any price. On the opening day, hampered by a slow pitch and the haste with which Cronje went on the defensive when deprived of Donald's bowling – he had a stomach ailment – England mustered only 135 for two from 85 overs. Hussain made just 51 in all but 35 minutes of the day's ration, but the foundation he wanted had been laid. Next morning, Stewart, playing wonderfully well, belied the conditions and struck 95 of a stand of 156 in 50 overs. Despite a typical England collapse lower down the order – five wickets fell for 26 runs – Hussain was able to declare overnight, unbeaten with 146 after 635 minutes. He had reached three figures in 467 minutes,

[*Laurence Griffiths, Allsport*

Too good on the day: Andrew Caddick turned in his finest Test performance yet to make South Africa follow on at Kingsmead. Mark Boucher, bowled second ball, was the middleman when Caddick took three wickets in five balls.

the third-slowest hundred by an England batsman after Peter Richardson (488 minutes) and Clive Radley (487), and, including his second innings of the previous Test, Hussain had now batted 63 minutes short of an unprecedented 1,000 minutes without being dismissed.

The pitch had gained some pace and Caddick, striding downwind from the Umgeni End, responded with his finest bowling for England. Steep bounce, lateral movement and at last a modicum of luck brought him seven wickets for 46 – six for 18 at one point – not only his best figures but the best by a visiting bowler in a Test on this ground. His first three wickets, which included his 100th, came in 11 balls; the next three, in five balls of his 11th over, left South Africa tottering on 84 for eight. Pollock's forthright 64 helped them to 156.

The final two days belonged to South Africa and Kirsten. Caddick removed Gibbs early on the fourth day to raise England hopes of pushing home their advantage, but the pitch, far from deteriorating, had become increasingly moribund. England were destined to labour long and hard. Kirsten and Kallis added 152 for the second wicket before Kallis was caught behind, nibbling at the second new ball, and only a massive effort from Flintoff in the last 30 minutes of a ridiculously long day brought further reward. The playing-time had been increased to seven and a half hours in an effort to make up time lost earlier to bad weather.

What was to prove a key moment had come hours earlier, however. Kirsten, then 33 and batting with all the co-ordination of Bambi on ice, played back to Tufnell and must have been lbw had not the bowler, unforgivably for a spinner, overstepped the crease. For the remainder of the fourth day, and all of the fifth, until Butcher spun the last ball of the match behind his legs to clip the leg stump, Kirsten gave no further hint of a chance. He reached his second double-hundred for South Africa in 741 minutes; only Brendon Kuruppu, who took 777 minutes for Sri Lanka against New Zealand at Colombo in 1986-87, had been slower. In all, Kirsten faced 642 balls and hit 26 fours.

England could not be faulted for effort, either with the ball or in the field, but the game was taken out of their hands by the fifth-wicket partnership of 192, a South African record against all countries, between Kirsten and Boucher. Missed off a return catch to Maddy when 66 – the score was 369 for four – Boucher moved on to his third Test hundred, his second as night-watchman, before presenting Chris Adams with his first Test wicket. England's agony was then compounded by a 92-minute stand of 101 between Kirsten and Klusener. In effecting their great escape, South Africa compiled their highest total against England. More significantly, the immense effort of more than two days in the field would cost England dear in the Fourth Test that followed in three days' time. – MIKE SELVEY.

Men of the Match: A. R. Caddick and G. Kirsten.   *Attendance:* 45,559.

Close of play: First day, England 135-2 (Hussain 51*, Maddy 24*); Second day, England 366-9 (Hussain 146*, Tufnell 0*); Third day, South Africa 27-0 (Kirsten 3*, Gibbs 24*); Fourth day, South Africa 251-4 (Kirsten 126*, Boucher 1*).

England

M. A. Butcher c Klusener b Adams	48	C. E. W. Silverwood c Boucher b Pollock	0
M. A. Atherton b Hayward	1	P. C. R. Tufnell not out	0
*N. Hussain not out	146	B 1, l-b 14, w 3, n-b 1	19
D. L. Maddy c Adams b Donald	24		
†J. Stewart lbw b Hayward	95	1/7 (2) 2/82 (1)	(9 wkts dec.) 366
C. J. Adams b Adams	19	3/138 (4) 4/294 (5)	
A. Flintoff lbw b Cronje	5	5/336 (6) 6/345 (7)	
A. R. Caddick lbw b Donald	0	7/345 (8) 8/362 (9)	
D. Gough c Klusener b Donald	9	9/362 (10)	

Bowling: Donald 23.4–3–67–2; Pollock 33–14–55–1; Hayward 20–3–74–2; Kallis 23–9–38–0; Klusener 17–5–38–0; Adams 43–17–74–2; Cronje 7–5–5–2.

South Africa

G. Kirsten c Stewart b Caddick	11	– b Butcher	275
H. H. Gibbs c Stewart b Caddick	2	– c Maddy b Caddick	26
J. H. Kallis c Stewart b Caddick	0	– c Stewart b Gough	69
D. J. Cullinan b Gough	20	– c Stewart b Flintoff	16
*W. J. Cronje c Stewart b Caddick	28	– c Stewart b Flintoff	1
L. Klusener c Maddy b Tufnell	15	– (7) b Butcher	45
S. M. Pollock b Caddick	64	– (8) not out	7
†M. V. Boucher b Caddick	0	– (6) c Stewart b Adams	108
A. A. Donald c Atherton b Caddick	0		
P. R. Adams c Silverwood b Gough	9		
M. Hayward not out	0		
B 4, l-b 1, w 1, n-b 1	7	B 5, l-b 13, w 2, n-b 5	25

1/11 (2) 2/11 (3) 3/24 (1) 4/57 (4)   156
5/74 (6) 6/84 (5) 7/84 (8)
8/84 (9) 9/154 (7) 10/156 (10)

1/41 (2) 2/193 (3)   (7 wkts) 572
3/242 (4) 4/244 (5)
5/436 (6) 6/537 (7) 7/572 (1)

Bowling: *First Innings*—Gough 15.5–6–36–2; Caddick 16–5–46–7; Silverwood 6–1–38–0; Tufnell 10–1–24–1; Flintoff 3–0–7–0. *Second Innings*—Caddick 36–12–70–1; Silverwood 30–6–89–0; Gough 28–5–82–1; Flintoff 30–9–67–2; Tufnell 45–6–117–0; Adams 13–3–42–1; Maddy 14–1–40–0; Butcher 8.2–0–32–2; Hussain 5–1–15–0.

Umpires: D. B. Cowie (New Zealand) and D. L. Orchard.
Referee: B. N. Jarman (Australia).

SOUTH AFRICA v ENGLAND

Fourth Test Match

At Cape Town, January 2, 3, 4, 5. South Africa won by an innings and 37 runs. Toss: England.

For England's second South African tour in succession, the balance of power turned against them at Newlands. They were beaten before tea on the fourth day, leaving the large contingent of English supporters extra time to go to the beaches and moan. Yet it was not a match England had lost from the start. They controlled much of the first day, and on the third produced an exceptionally game performance in most unpromising circumstances. What decided the issue, and handed the series to South Africa, were two horrific batting collapses. It may have been a new millennium. It was an old, familiar failing by England.

As expected, Vaughan was preferred to Maddy, but Silverwood held on to his place at the last minute because Mullally had flu. This turned out to be a bit of luck. South Africa had an embarrassment of riches. The omission of Rhodes at Durban was accepted as a mistake, but it was hard deciding who should make way for him. There were even arguments that it should be Cronje, about to captain South Africa for the 50th time, though in the event Hayward was the one to go. When Atherton and Butcher took England past 100, this looked like a bad call, not helped by Rhodes ("of all people," said everyone) dropping a simple chance offered by Atherton on 15. However, Donald and Adams pegged England back after lunch, and eventually frustration became impatience. Even Atherton, caught hooking for 71, was culpable, and after he departed England managed only 26 runs in as many overs. Finally disaster struck: 213 for three late on the first day became 258 all out before lunch on the second.

South Africa now seized command with awesome strokeplay against bowling that was demoralised even before Flintoff broke a toe during his fourth over and vanished from the tour. They began the third day, a hot one, just 58 behind with nine wickets standing and the pitch playing beautifully. One half-expected England to surrender. Instead, they played some of their best cricket of the series.

Chris Silverwood was England's hero at Newlands, with five wickets, but had to concede his place in the sun as the irrepressible Daryll Cullinan hit his second hundred of the series.

Their spearhead, Caddick, was clearly paying the price of his exertions in Durban. But Silverwood led the way with a courageous bowling performance, generating surprising pace from an unyielding surface to capture five wickets in a Test for the first time. He was backed by outstanding ground fielding. Kirsten, 80 overnight, edged a catch off the first ball he faced, and when they had South Africa 307 for seven there was a chance that England could get back in the contest. The depth of South Africa's batting saw them through. Cullinan followed Kallis to a hundred, but perhaps the decisive innings was Boucher's 36, a typical contribution that stretched the lead to 163. There was no route back for England, and they made no effort to find it. Their second-innings was pathetic, and the total only just passed their first-innings opening stand.

As happened in England 17 months earlier, the crucial game was marked by poor third-party umpiring. The Sri Lankan B. C. Cooray, perhaps reasoning that it is an itchy trigger-finger that gets umpires into trouble, spent most of the game immovable and inscrutable behind his dark glasses, refusing even the most promising appeals. On day four, however, he gave an lbw decision against Hussain when he had not merely hit the ball but hit it for four without it ever touching the pad. This was some compensation for South Africa after an earlier wrong decision by Cyril Mitchley had seen off Boucher. Not that the result was affected.

The game ended amid mild confusion with nine England wickets down. Spectators were unsure whether it was tea, whether the injured Flintoff might suddenly appear, or whether it was indeed all over. Though there were almost 20,000 in the ground every day, the atmosphere was restrained throughout, in contrast to the highly charged mood on the field, where all kinds of bitter, semi-private sub-plots were acted out. Silverwood aside, no Englishman could really leave Cape Town with any personal satisfaction to ease the collective misery. Not so the victors. Cullinan's century was his third in a row in Newlands Tests, and his tenth for South Africa, equalling Kirsten's record set several days earlier at Durban. Donald finished the match with 86 wickets against England, putting him three ahead of Sydney Barnes, the previous record-holder for games between these countries. And – the telling statistic – it was South Africa's biggest win over England, their third by an innings, increasing the margin of victory obtained in the First Test. – MATTHEW ENGEL.

Man of the Match: D. J. Cullinan. *Attendance:* 65,289.

Close of play: First day, England 215-5 (Vaughan 40*, Adams 0*); Second day, South Africa 200-1 (Kirsten 80*, Kallis 80*); Third day, England 4-0 (Butcher 4*, Atherton 0*).

England

M. A. Butcher c Kirsten b Donald	40	– c Boucher b Pollock	4
M. A. Atherton c Kirsten b Donald	71	– c Cullinan b Pollock	35
*N. Hussain c Boucher b Adams	15	– lbw b Klusener	16
M. P. Vaughan c Kirsten b Donald	42	– c Boucher b Klusener	5
†A. J. Stewart c Kirsten b Donald	40	– b Adams	5
A. R. Caddick c Cullinan b Donald	0	– (7) c Gibbs b Donald	14
C. J. Adams c Pollock b Kallis	10	– (6) b Adams	31
A. Flintoff c Rhodes b Klusener	22	– absent hurt	
D. Gough c Boucher b Klusener	4	– (8) c Donald b Kallis	8
C. E. W. Silverwood not out	1	– (9) not out	5
P. C. R. Tufnell b Kallis	2	– (10) c Cullinan b Adams	0
L-b 6, w 2, n-b 3	11	L-b 3	3
1/115 (2) 2/125 (1) 3/141 (3) 4/213 (5) 5/213 (6) 6/218 (4) 7/231 (7) 8/253 (8) 9/255 (9) 10/258 (11)	258	1/4 (1) 2/40 (3) 3/59 (4) 4/62 (2) 5/66 (5) 6/105 (7) 7/113 (6) 8/125 (8) 9/126 (10)	126

Bowling: *First Innings*—Donald 26–13–47–5; Pollock 27–8–59–0; Kallis 20–4–61–2; Klusener 16–5–42–2; Cronje 3–2–5–0; Adams 21–9–38–1. *Second Innings*—Adams 19.3–5–42–3; Donald 10.4–2–35–1; Pollock 14–8–19–2; Kallis 9.2–2–19–1; Klusener 7–4–8–2.

South Africa

G. Kirsten c Stewart b Silverwood	80
H. H. Gibbs c Vaughan b Silverwood	29
J. H. Kallis c Atherton b Gough	105
D. J. Cullinan c Vaughan b Tufnell	120
*W. J. Cronje c Vaughan b Caddick	0
J. N. Rhodes c Adams b Silverwood	16
L. Klusener b Gough	3
S. M. Pollock c Adams b Caddick	4
†M. V. Boucher lbw b Silverwood	36
A. A. Donald c Adams b Silverwood	7
P. R. Adams not out	3
B 1, l-b 7, n-b 10	18
1/43 (2) 2/201 (1) 3/246 (3) 4/247 (5) 5/279 (6) 6/290 (7) 7/307 (8) 8/397 (9) 9/405 (10) 10/421 (4)	421

Bowling: Gough 37–6–88–2; Caddick 31–6–95–2; Silverwood 32–6–91–5; Flintoff 4–0–16–0; Tufnell 39.4–10–97–1; Butcher 3–0–9–0; Adams 7–2–17–0.

Umpires: B. C. Cooray (Sri Lanka) and C. J. Mitchley
Referee: B. N. Jarman (Australia).

SOUTH AFRICAN INVITATION XI v ENGLAND XI

At Port Elizabeth, January 9, 10, 11. Drawn. Toss: South African Invitation XI.

After the exertions and disappointments of the Christmas and New Year Tests, the tour management decided to rest the ten who played in both games and drafted in four of the six one-day specialists who had joined the party. One of them, Hick, was made captain. He was joined by Ealham, Solanki and Knight in a side that never seemed sure about the point of the exercise. While some, like Mullally, were pushing for a Test place, others took it as a useful workout for the one-day series ahead. Knight, whose last Test had been against South Africa in 1998, made a pleasant 111 from 166 balls, with 14 fours, and Hick hit a characteristic 57. But it seemed pointless for England to bat into the third and last day for a lead of 78. Having declared his own first innings at a challenging 253 for seven on the opening day, the Invitation XI's captain, McKenzie, could justifiably accuse England of "killing the game". He now instructed his side to bat it out.

Close of play: First day, England XI 16-0 (Knight 14*, Maddy 0*); Second day, England XI 312-7 (Swann 9*, Read 8*).

South African Invitation XI

P. J. R. Steyn c Hamilton b Ealham	93	– (2) c Hick b Tudor	0
C. C. Bradfield b Mullally	0	– (1) c Solanki b Mullally	6
J. D. C. Bryant b Mullally	69	– retired hurt	4
*N. D. McKenzie b Tudor	7	– b Vaughan	80
A. G. Prince c Read b Ealham	32	– b Tudor	0
J. L. Ontong lbw b Tudor	33	– c Read b Ealham	34
†W. Bossenger b Tudor	13	– c Maddy b Vaughan	3
R. Telemachus not out	2	– not out	50
G. J. Smith (did not bat)	–	not out	35
N-b 4	4	B 1, l-b 7, w 1, n-b 2	11

1/8 2/126 3/145 4/181	(7 wkts dec.) 253	1/9 2/13 3/17 (6 wkts) 223
5/221 6/242 7/253		4/131 5/131 6/141

G. J-P. Kruger and C. K. Langeveldt did not bat.

In the second innings Bryant retired hurt at 13-2.

Bowling: *First Innings*—Tudor 15.5–6–61–3; Mullally 20–3–61–2; Hamilton 14–4–32–0; Swann 19–3–61–0; Ealham 15–6–35–2; Maddy 3–0–3–0. *Second Innings*—Tudor 12–4–30–2; Mullally 15–5–38–1; Hamilton 9–4–12–0; Ealham 7–2–20–1; Swann 16.4–2–70–0; Hick 1–0–5–0; Vaughan 11–4–22–2; Maddy 5–0–18–0.

England XI

N. V. Knight c Telemachus b Kruger	111	†C. M. W. Read not out	15
D. L. Maddy c Bryant b Telemachus	0	A. J. Tudor b Smith	8
M. P. Vaughan c Bossenger b Telemachus	25	A. D. Mullally c Bossenger b Smith	0
*G. A. Hick b Kruger	57		
V. S. Solanki c Ontong b Langeveldt	40	B 4, l-b 8, n-b 22	34
G. M. Hamilton c Bossenger b Kruger	2		
M. A. Ealham c Kruger b Ontong	26	1/44 2/115 3/214 4/225 5/242	331
G. P. Swann b Smith	13	6/294 7/300 8/317 9/327	

Bowling: Telemachus 20–2–109–2; Smith 17.2–4–51–3; Langeveldt 16–7–28–1; Kruger 19–1–60–3; Ontong 16–3–67–1; McKenzie 2–0–4–0.

Umpires: B. G. Jerling and R. E. Koertzen.

SOUTH AFRICA v ENGLAND

Fifth Test Match

At Centurion, January 14, 15, 16, 17, 18. England won by two wickets. Toss: England. Test debut: P. C. Strydom.

History was made on the final day when a match apparently reduced to the deadliest of finishes, following three consecutive playless days, was brought back to life by the captains. For the first time in Test cricket, innings were forfeited and this produced a memorable, entertaining climax. When play resumed, with South Africa still in the first innings, the many hundreds of travelling English supporters and a few hundred hardy locals had every reason to expect the worst. What they were treated to was a gripping finale that saw England win with five balls and two wickets remaining.

Five months after the match, however, came the bitterness of deceit when Cronje, South Africa's captain, admitted receiving 53,000 rand (around £5,000) and a leather jacket from a bookmaker, who had urged him to initiate a positive result, rather than let the match peter out as a draw. At the King Commission inquiry into match-fixing, which opened in Cape Town in June, he insisted that his motives were "for the good of cricket", but the fact that financial reward formed a part of his motivation tainted the match for ever. History would also record that it was the first Test in which "fixing" was proven.

South Africa, who had been inserted on a fresh pitch under overcast skies, were a precarious 155 for six when play was halted after 45 overs on the first day. In truth, England should have done even better, but Gough, Caddick, Mullally and Silverwood, encouraged by the bounce, all bowled too many short, and so wasted, deliveries. The unseasonal rain made the next three days deeply depressing for the local Cricket Union, Northerns. They were not insured – the cost had been prohibitive, president Richard Harrison announced – and the estimated loss was more than two million rand.

Some 30 minutes into play on the final day, the first rumour of what was about to happen reached the media. Cronje had approached his opposite number, Hussain, half an hour before the start and offered to "make a game of it". His offer was a target of 255 runs in 73 overs, based on the premise that South Africa could score another 100 runs in 30 overs on the extended final morning, followed by a double forfeiture of innings – England's first and South Africa's second. Hussain declined. "The wicket might have been sweating under those covers for three days. It might have been unplayable. I couldn't take that chance," he said later. Ten overs into the session, however, having seen how well the pitch was playing under sunny skies, he left the field and sought out Cronje. "Is the offer still open?" he enquired. The answer was "Yes."

There was never any suggestion that scoring runs would be made easy. Indeed, Hussain's magnificent direct hit from mid-on to run out Pollock for 30 might have derailed the initiative. Klusener, though, batted smoothly to reach an unbeaten 61 from 95 balls. Yet when the declaration came, Cronje's original offer had become even more generous, particularly as Donald, the series' leading wicket-taker, had dropped out before the game with gout. To win, and so limit their series defeat to 2–1, England had to score 249 in 76 overs.

When Paul Adams broke a finger on his bowling hand early on, crashing into an advertising hoarding, Cronje's only spin option was the slow left-arm of debutant Pieter Strydom, a 30-year-old all-rounder called up because Rhodes had a hamstring injury. Donald's replacement, Hayward, had had to fly from Port Elizabeth on the first morning, arriving in time for the delayed start after lunch. For England, Maddy had come in for the injured Flintoff, and Mullally returned instead of Tufnell.

Between innings, the chairman of the England Management Advisory Committee, Brian Bolus, pointed out that no provision existed in the Laws for the forfeiture of a first innings, although domestic playing conditions had sanctioned it in first-class cricket for some years. As it happened, a new code of the Laws, already in draft form and to take effect later in the year, would allow first-innings forfeitures, so Cronje and Hussain were simply months ahead of time. Like almost everyone at the ground, however, Bolus was effusive in his praise for the captains' ingenuity and insisted that "sanity had prevailed". The scorers were officially instructed to record England's first innings as nought for no wicket declared, even though they never took the field.

By the 38th over, with England 102 for four, Hussain could have been forgiven if he was regretting the whole business. Atherton had edged Pollock to the keeper, Butcher was lbw to Klusener's slower ball, the captain himself had chipped another slower ball, from Pollock, to cover, and Chris Adams had just fended a Hayward bouncer rather lamely to Boucher. Vaughan, criticised earlier in the tour for batting too slowly and now demoted two places, walked out to salvage the draw. Or so it was thought. During an innings rich in cover drives, he added 126 with Stewart. When Stewart was caught behind, England were 21 runs from victory with five wickets still in hand.

Nerves now played a part. Maddy was run out from the cover boundary attempting a second run, Caddick was caught behind two balls later, and then Vaughan, backing away to hit Hayward through the covers, was bowled for 69 from 108 balls with nine fine boundaries. England needed nine runs from the final 13 balls. Silverwood took a single, chipped the first ball of the penultimate over agonisingly close to extra cover but scrambled two, then failed to score from the next four. The sixth delivery, however, he drove towards the cover boundary where Strydom, staring straight into the setting sun, failed to see the ball until the last moment. What should have been two became four. Gough then pulled the first ball of Hayward's final over triumphantly for the winning boundary.

Inevitably, some wondered whether Test cricket had been compromised, even belittled, by the contrived result. Cronje was adamant that, should the game's administrators at the ICC be among those showing disapproval, he "wouldn't want to be a part of cricket any more. What is wrong with trying to make a game of it?" he said afterwards. But his previous dealings with bookmakers, as revealed at the King Commission, had forced him into that position. It was the first, albeit oblique, evidence of what had become a sadly corrupted outlook on the game and his responsibilities. "Test cricket needs to do everything it can to advertise itself and be competitive in a buoy sporting market," he went on. "It hurts to lose – we lost a 14-match unbeaten run because of this – but it was a fabulous game in the end and people deserve to be entertained."

Hussain, understandably delighted, paid special tribute to Cronje at the time. "It was a very special thing that Hansie did and I hope he gets the credit he deserves. It certainly was a great finish to be a part of." But later, when it emerged that corruption had played its regrettable part in the shaping of the final day, he would write in his newspaper column that England's win had been ruined. "We can't get away from that," he said. "It will always be remembered as a Test that was fixed."

Yet the cricket was played as hard as both teams were able, and that is some consolation. Cronje's goal was to achieve a positive result and, while a captain without thought of personal gain might have opted for defence and the safety of a draw when the match was slipping away, South Africa did almost pull off a remarkable win. – NEIL MANTHORP.

Man of the Match: M. P. Vaughan.

Man of the Series: D. J. Cullinan.

Close of play: First day, South Africa 155-6 (Klusener 22*, Pollock 9*); Second day, No play; Third day, No play; Fourth day, No play.

South Africa

G. Kirsten c Adams b Gough	0	†M. V. Boucher b Mullally	22
H. H. Gibbs c Adams b Caddick	3	P. R. Adams not out	4
J. H. Kallis b Caddick	25	B 2, l-b 11, w 3, n-b 11	27
D. J. Cullinan c and b Mullally	46		
*W. J. Cronje c Maddy b Gough	0	1/1 (1) 2/15 (2)	(8 wkts dec.) 248
P. C. Strydom c Stewart b Silverwood	30	3/50 (3) 4/55 (5)	
L. Klusener not out	61	5/102 (6) 6/136 (4)	
S. M. Pollock run out	30	7/196 (8) 8/243 (9)	

M. Hayward did not bat.

Bowling: Gough 20–2–92–2; Caddick 19–7–47–2; Mullally 24–10–42–2; Silverwood 7–1–45–1; Vaughan 2–0–9–0.

South Africa forfeited their second innings.

England

M. A. Butcher (did not bat)		– lbw b Klusener	36
M. A. Atherton (did not bat)		– c Boucher b Pollock	7
*N. Hussain (did not bat)		– c Gibbs b Pollock	25
†A. J. Stewart (did not bat)		– c Boucher b Hayward	73
C. J. Adams (did not bat)		– c Boucher b Hayward	1
M. P. Vaughan (did not bat)		– b Hayward	69
D. L. Maddy (did not bat)		– run out	3
A. R. Caddick (did not bat)		– c Boucher b Pollock	0
D. Gough (did not bat)		– not out	6
C. E. W. Silverwood (did not bat)		– not out	7
		B 4, l-b 9, w 4, n-b 7	24

(no wkt dec.) 0   1/28 (2) 2/67 (1)   (8 wkts) 251
3/90 (3) 4/102 (5)
5/228 (4) 6/236 (7)
7/236 (8) 8/240 (6)

A. D. Mullally did not bat.

Bowling: Pollock 20–7–53–3; Hayward 17.1–3–61–3; Klusener 14–4–38–1; Kallis 13–2–44–0; Cronje 5–3–15–0; Strydom 6–0–27–0.

Umpires: D. B. Hair (Australia) and R. E. Koertzen.
Referee: B. N. Jarman (Australia).

†At Potchefstroom, January 20. England XI won by 41 runs. Toss: England XI. England XI 264 for nine (50 overs) (G. A. Hick 77, C. J. Adams 47, V. S. Solanki 38, C. White 50; D. J. Pryke five for 34, D. Roussouw three for 70); North West 223 for eight (50 overs) (G. Outram 34, H. M. de Vos 30, A. Jacobs 36).

England's matches v South Africa and Zimbabwe in the Standard Bank International Series (January 23–February 13) may be found in that section.

[*Patrick Eagar*

At Bulawayo, as the weather threatened an early finish to the first one-day international, Graeme Hick made regular checks on England's progress against Duckworth/Lewis tables. Umpire Evans looks on.

†ZIMBABWE v ENGLAND

First One-Day International

At Bulawayo, February 16. England won by five wickets (D/L method). Toss: Zimbabwe.

This was an important match both for Hick and his adopted country. In six innings against his former compatriots, he had managed just 78 runs; England on their one previous visit to Zimbabwe had lost all three one-day internationals and drawn both Tests. But now Hick, playing his first one-day international there, more than doubled his personal aggregate and brought a morale-boosting win when he drove Olonga for six. Batting first, Zimbabwe initially made light of a slow pitch and sodden outfield, with 50 coming up in the 11th over. Against tighter bowling, though, the second 50 did not arrive until the 31st, so Grant Flower's unbeaten half-century was welcome. Chasing 199 – a first-innings shower docked two overs; Duckworth/Lewis increased the target by four – England reached 116 for five as storm clouds gathered. With 14 overs left, Hick consulted the tables he had prudently taken with him and discovered England were behind on the Duckworth/Lewis reckoning. He and Ealham promptly clubbed 15 from Viljoen's next over and soon ensured that, whenever the game finished, England would have their noses in front. Their only mistake after that was returning to the wrong ends after a drinks break.

Man of the Match: G. A. Hick.

Zimbabwe

N. C. Johnson b Mullally	21	D. P. Viljoen not out	0
A. D. R. Campbell run out	29		
S. V. Carlisle c Hussain b White	30	L-b 8, w 5, n-b 3	16
M. W. Goodwin lbw b White	2		
*†A. Flower c Knight b Mullally	19	1/43 (1) 2/83 (3) (7 wkts, 48 overs) 194	
G. W. Flower not out	55	3/87 (4) 4/93 (2)	
C. B. Wishart c Read b Mullally	6	5/124 (5) 6/160 (7)	
H. H. Streak c Hussain b White	16	7/192 (8) Score at 15 overs: 57-1	

G. B. Brent and H. K. Olonga did not bat.

Bowling: Caddick 10–0–36–0; Gough 10–2–47–0; Mullally 10–1–37–3; Ealham 9–0–37–0; White 9–1–29–3.

England

*N. Hussain b Olonga	3	M. A. Ealham not out	36
N. V. Knight b Streak	20	B 1, l-b 6, w 11	18
G. A. Hick not out	87		
D. L. Maddy c Streak b G. W. Flower	24	1/13 (1) 2/37 (2) (5 wkts, 46.3 overs) 199	
V. S. Solanki b G. W. Flower	11	3/90 (4) 4/107 (5)	
C. White c Olonga b G. W. Flower	0	5/109 (6) Score at 14 overs: 45-2	

†C. M. W. Read, A. R. Caddick, D. Gough and A. D. Mullally did not bat.

Bowling: Olonga 8.3–1–47–1; Johnson 6–0–24–0; Streak 9–2–39–1; Brent 8–0–31–0; G. W. Flower 10–1–27–3; Viljoen 5–0–24–0.

Umpires: G. R. Evans and I. D. Robinson.

†ZIMBABWE v ENGLAND

Second One-Day International

At Bulawayo, February 18. England won by one wicket. Toss: England.

Needing just 12 for victory with half their wickets in hand, England conspired to lose four for five runs, and left themselves reliant upon the dubious batting talent of Mullally, a practising No. 11, to see them home. In a match reduced to 48 overs a side before the start, Zimbabwe had again begun confidently, only to lose their way: 60 for one became 102 for eight against the brisk medium-pace of White, who orchestrated the collapse with a second spell of four for nine in seven overs. He had previously dismissed Johnson. England lost both openers to Streak for six, but the middle order seemed to have settled matters until the late clatter of wickets. Gough's fine-leg four and Mullally's winning boundary through third man ensured that England could no longer lose the four-match series.

Man of the Match: C. White.

BEST BOWLING FOR ENGLAND IN ONE-DAY INTERNATIONALS

5-15	**M. A. Ealham v Zimbabwe at Kimberley**	**1999-2000**
5-20	V. J. Marks v New Zealand at Wellington	1983-84
5-21	**C. White v Zimbabwe at Bulawayo**	**1999-2000**
5-31	M. Hendrick v Australia at The Oval	1980
5-32	M. A. Ealham v Sri Lanka at Perth	1998-99
5-33	**G. A. Hick v Zimbabwe at Harare**	**1999-2000**
5-35	P. W. Jarvis v India at Bangalore	1992-93
5-39	V. J. Marks v Sri Lanka at Taunton	1983
5-44	D. Gough v Zimbabwe at Sydney	1994-95
5-44	D. Gough v Australia at Lord's	1997

Zimbabwe

N. C. Johnson c Hussain b White	30	G. B. Brent b Ealham	10	
A. D. R. Campbell c Hick b Caddick	6	H. K. Olonga b Ealham	0	
S. V. Carlisle c Read b White	31	W 1, n-b 6	7	
M. W. Goodwin c Hick b Mullally	21			
*†A. Flower c Read b White	3	1/16 (2) 2/60 (1) 3/76 (3)	(47.3 overs) 131	
G. W. Flower b White	2	4/80 (5) 5/84 (6)		
D. P. Viljoen c Read b White	2	6/98 (7) 7/98 (4)		
H. H. Streak c Hick b Caddick	1	8/102 (8) 9/131 (10)		
J. A. Rennie not out	18	10/131 (11)	Score at 14 overs: 58-1	

Bowling: Caddick 10–4–24–2; Gough 9–1–31–0; Mullally 10–0–28–1; White 10–1–21–5; Ealham 8.3–0–27–2.

England

*N. Hussain lbw b Streak	2	D. Gough not out	4	
N. V. Knight c A. Flower b Streak	0	A. D. Mullally not out	5	
G. A. Hick c A. Flower b Streak	13			
D. L. Maddy c Olonga b Brent	13	L-b 5, w 8, n-b 2	15	
V. S. Solanki c Streak b G. W. Flower	24			
C. White c Goodwin b Olonga	26	1/2 (2) 2/6 (1)	(9 wkts, 44.2 overs) 134	
M. A. Ealham lbw b Brent	32	3/30 (3) 4/58 (4)		
†C. M. W. Read c sub (C. B. Wishart)		5/73 (5) 6/120 (6)		
b Brent	0	7/124 (8) 8/125 (7)		
A. R. Caddick c sub b Viljoen	0	9/125 (9)	Score at 14 overs: 39-3	

Bowling: Streak 10–1–26–3; Rennie 5–0–17–0; Olonga 10–1–29–1; Brent 5.2–0–29–3; G. W. Flower 10–2–18–1; Viljoen 4–1–10–1.

Umpires: J. F. Fenwick and R. B. Tiffin.

†ZIMBABWE v ENGLAND

Third One-Day International

At Harare, February 20. England won by 85 runs. Toss: Zimbabwe.

This was Hick's match: booed as he walked to the crease – some in his native land still harboured resentment that he preferred to play for England – he produced the perfect riposte. His commanding innings, which included ten fours, quickly compensated for the early loss of Hussain, and he looked set for a sixth one-day century when he was narrowly run out for 80. Maddy, with a maiden one-day international fifty, provided useful support, but when Viljoen took three wickets in five balls England needed some hefty blows from White and Caddick to hoist a challenging total. Hick, though, had not yet finished. After tight, penetrative spells from the new-ball bowlers – Caddick conceded only seven runs in eight overs – he capitalised on Zimbabwe's need for brisk runs. Two smart stumpings, two sharp catches by Mullally and one by Ealham brought him five for 33, and there were no jeers as he collected the match award. England, moreover, had won a one-day competition for the first time in eight attempts.

Man of the Match: G. A. Hick.

England

*N. Hussain c Campbell b Strang	1	A. R. Caddick not out	21	
N. V. Knight c Strang b Olonga	26			
G. A. Hick run out	80	L-b 4, w 17, n-b 3	24	
D. L. Maddy c Brent b Viljoen	53			
V. S. Solanki c Carlisle b Brent	14	1/4 (1) 2/85 (2)	(7 wkts, 50 overs) 248	
C. White not out	27	3/149 (3) 4/171 (5)		
M. A. Ealham c Viljoen	0	5/198 (4) 6/198 (7)		
†C. M. W. Read c and b Viljoen	2	7/207 (8)	Score at 15 overs: 84-1	

D. Gough and A. D. Mullally did not bat.

Bowling: Streak 8–0–44–0; Strang 10–0–34–1; Johnson 2–0–16–0; Olonga 6–0–44–1; G. W. Flower 10–0–37–0; Brent 7–0–42–1; Viljoen 6–0–20–3; Campbell 1–0–7–0.

Zimbabwe

N. C. Johnson b Gough	7	G. B. Brent not out	13
A. D. R. Campbell c White b Gough	2	H. K. Olonga c Knight b White	11
S. V. Carlisle run out	41	L-b 7, w 3, n-b 1	11
M. W. Goodwin c Mullally b Hick	28		
*†A. Flower st Read b Hick	21	1/5 (2) 2/16 (1) 3/83 (4) (46.5 overs) 163	
G. W. Flower st Read b Hick	5	4/91 (3) 5/104 (6)	
D. P. Viljoen c Ealham b Hick	4	6/112 (7) 7/124 (5)	
H. H. Streak c Hussain b Mullally	7	8/126 (8) 9/146 (9)	
B. C. Strang c Mullally b Hick	13	10/163 (11) Score at 15 overs: 34-2	

Bowling: Caddick 8–4–7–0; Gough 6–2–10–2; Mullally 10–1–43–1; White 5.5–0–35–1; Ealham 7–0–28–0; Hick 10–2–33–5.

Umpires: G. R. Evans and I. D. Robinson.
Series referee: Naushad Ali (Pakistan).

†ZIMBABWE v ENGLAND

Fourth One-Day International

At Harare, February 23. No result (abandoned).

The final match of the tour was washed out without a ball bowled, leaving England 3–0 victors and bringing revenge for their whitewash in the equivalent series three years earlier.

CORNHILL INSURANCE ENGLAND PLAYER OF THE YEAR

The Cornhill Insurance England Player of the Year Award was won in April 2000 by Andrew Caddick of Somerset. He received £10,000. Nasser Hussain, the England captain, received a special award for improving the image of the national side with the public.

ENGLAND A IN BANGLADESH AND NEW ZEALAND, 1999-2000

By RALPH DELLOR

Though the purpose of an A tour must be to prepare promising players for full Test level, the players and management of this England party could nevertheless also be proud of their record in Bangladesh and New Zealand. With three wins and four draws, they extended the A team's unbeaten first-class record to 36 matches since Hugh Morris's team was beaten by Natal in 1993-94, and they won both the Test and the one-day series against New Zealand A.

The two legs of the tour provided considerable evidence of improvement, both in individuals and in team performance. Their progress had to be welcomed with caution, however; it has been shown that players who shine at this level, and in the special atmosphere that envelops successful touring parties, do not necessarily make a satisfactory transition to full international exposure.

It is difficult to imagine a greater contrast between the two countries visited. Bangladesh, with huge crowds whose enthusiasm knew no bounds, seemed to encapsulate the whole Asian cricketing experience, while New Zealand – the one Test-playing country England A had not previously visited – lacked the intensity of life but offered cricket of a higher standard.

In both countries, Vikram Solanki stood out as the batsman who appeared ready to step up. Not only did he score 597 first-class runs – no one else reached 400 – at an average of 59.70, but there was an unmistakable touch of class about the way he made them. Just because he shaped to drive through mid-off, it did not mean that the ball would end up travelling in that direction. By using his wrists to open or close the face of the bat, he could place it anywhere between third man and fine leg, a rare talent among England batsmen and one that should be given free rein. Solanki could eliminate some impetuosity, and a slightly tighter technique would not come amiss, provided it was not at the expense of his other priceless gifts. David Sales proved himself another batsman who could destroy attacks, or be destroyed of his own doing. It seemed he would be unlucky not to play Test cricket, for he had ability in abundance, and was learning quickly how to make the most of it. Aftab Habib had already tasted Test cricket in 1999 and suggested that he would again. He scored a fine century to help save the First Test against New Zealand A, following a fifty in Bangladesh, and averaged 51.

Of the other batsmen, it had been hoped that Ian Ward, a compact, organised left-hander, might develop into a genuine Test candidate. Despite diligent practice, however, he rather lost his way as the tour progressed. Michael Gough, his regular opening partner, turned 20 on the last weekend of the trip, so still had plenty of time to expand his game; there is nothing wrong with concentrating on a sound technique at this stage of his career if he can add a touch of aggression later.

Marcus Trescothick's top score of 45 in eight first-class innings in no way reflected his potential, but did not advance his claims either. His close-catching was world-class, however, and he occasionally bowled useful spells of medium-pace. Of the genuine all-rounders, Ronnie Irani had a disappointing time, though this was not his fault: batting down the order gave him little opportunity, while the Bangladeshi pitches hardly added venom to his bowling. When he got to New Zealand, which should have suited him better, he was laid low with chicken-pox, and it was not until the final one-day matches that he came into his own.

With Chris Silverwood called up to join the senior touring party in South Africa, Paul Franks emerged as the most promising of the quicker bowlers. At his best, he was the typical fast-medium bowler on whom so much of England's success has traditionally been founded. Alamgir Sheriyar had a wretched time in Bangladesh, where he bowled only 12 overs and was involved in an unseemly incident with an umpire, but he took the eye for more salutary reasons in New Zealand, where conditions were more akin to those in which he had taken 92 wickets the previous English summer. James Kirtley arrived as a replacement for the injured Steve Harmison, and did enough to suggest he might have been an original selection. The other pace bowler was Darren Thomas, who took Silverwood's place and, with very limited opportunities, managed to top the first-class bowling averages.

Of the spinners, left-armer Michael Davies made a very favourable impression on his first A tour, while Chris Schofield suggested he could be the answer to England's search for a quality leg-spinner. He was the leading wicket-taker in first-class matches, with 23, and in all matches he claimed 35; he started taking them on turning pitches in Bangladesh and continued on seamers' pitches in New Zealand. A live-wire in the field and an unorthodox batsman good enough to record three first-class fifties – the first of his career – he did more than enough to warrant his subsequent inclusion among the 12 players awarded ECB central contracts, and could develop into a formidable cricketer.

Rob Turner had an impeccable tour as wicket-keeper, but after his successful season in 1999, scoring 1,000 runs in the Championship, he endured a miserable time with the bat in New Zealand. He missed only one match, back in Chittagong, where Mark Alleyne, the captain, kept wicket. Alleyne's tour was more notable for his telling contributions with bat or ball, however: he was the second leading scorer in the first-class programme, with 359, and he earned the label of genuine all-rounder. He also performed well as a captain of the undemonstrative school who commanded the unwavering respect of his side.

Alleyne formed just one part of a well-balanced management team. Mike Gatting has had a troubled history in the subcontinent, but in New Zealand his stature in the game gave him an imposing authority. Martyn Moxon, on his first tour as coach, impressed everyone with his methodical approach. Practice sessions were always well thought out and interesting, and the players responded readily to his quiet, reasoned methods. Physiotherapist Ann Brentnall worked tirelessly to get them on to the field, while Richard Smith, the tourists' physiologist, ensured they were well prepared when they got there.

The party triumphantly achieved their playing objectives, and on and off the field were splendid ambassadors for English cricket, the glitch with the umpires in Chittagong apart. It remained to be seen whether the lessons learned would help to produce a significant number of players to enhance the full England Test team.

ENGLAND A TOURING PARTY

M. W. Alleyne (Gloucestershire) (*captain*), R. J. Turner (Somerset) (*vice-captain*), M. K. Davies (Northamptonshire), P. J. Franks (Nottinghamshire), M. A. Gough (Durham), A. Habib (Leicestershire), R. C. Irani (Essex), R. J. Kirtley (Sussex), D. J. Sales (Northamptonshire), C. P. Schofield (Lancashire), A. Sheriyar (Worcestershire), C. E. W. Silverwood (Yorkshire), V. S. Solanki (Worcestershire), M. E. Trescothick (Somerset), I. J. Ward (Surrey).

Kirtley replaced S. J. Harmison (Durham), who withdrew injured before the start of the tour. S. D. Thomas (Glamorgan) replaced Silverwood when he was promoted to the senior England tour.

Tour manager: M. W. Gatting. *Coach:* M. D. Moxon. *Physiotherapist:* A. E. Brentnall. *Physiologist:* R. Smith.

ENGLAND A TOUR RESULTS

First-class matches – Played 7: Won 3, Drawn 4.
Wins – South Island, Central Districts, New Zealand A.
Draws – Bangladesh (2), North Island, New Zealand A.
Non-first-class matches – Played 8: Won 7, No result 1. *Wins* – Bangladesh Youth XI, Bangladesh Cricket Board XI, Bangladesh, New Zealand Academy (2), New Zealand A (2). *No result* – New Zealand A.

ENGLAND A AVERAGES – FIRST-CLASS MATCHES

BATTING

	M	I	NO	R	HS	100s	50s	Avge	Ct/St
V. S. Solanki	7	11	1	597	185	1	6	59.70	10
A. Habib	4	6	1	255	101*	1	1	51.00	1
D. J. Sales	6	9	1	354	115	2	1	44.25	6
M. W. Alleyne	7	10	1	359	152*	1	1	39.88	2
M. A. Gough	4	7	1	194	78	0	1	32.33	3
C. P. Schofield	6	8	0	236	74	0	3	29.50	2
M. E. Trescothick	5	8	1	199	45	0	0	28.42	8
M. K. Davies	5	6	4	55	20*	0	0	27.50	1
I. J. Ward	7	12	1	287	72	0	3	26.09	8
P. J. Franks	6	9	3	101	19	0	0	16.83	4
R. J. Turner	6	9	0	105	40	0	0	11.66	25/1
R. J. Kirtley	5	5	0	37	32	0	0	7.40	1
A. Sheriyar	5	5	2	22	12*	0	0	7.33	0

Played in two matches: R. C. Irani 22, 8 (3 ct); S. D. Thomas 18, 31, 0.

* *Signifies not out.*

BOWLING

	O	M	R	W	BB	5W/i	Avge
S. D. Thomas	49	7	138	8	4-56	0	17.25
P. J. Franks	168.2	49	395	21	5-26	1	18.80
R. J. Kirtley	145	47	368	19	5-54	1	19.36
A. Sheriyar	162.4	33	457	22	6-70	2	20.77
M. K. Davies	165.3	55	363	14	4-71	0	25.92
C. P. Schofield	208.1	52	608	23	6-120	2	26.43
M. W. Alleyne	100	32	244	6	2-70	0	40.66

Also bowled: M. A. Gough 1–0–2–0; R. C. Irani 39–14–100–0; V. S. Solanki 51–8–167–3; M. E. Trescothick 10–3–33–0.

Note: Matches in this section which were not first-class are signified by a dagger.

†At Savar, October 22. England A won by 69 runs (D/L method). Toss: England A. England A 208 for eight (40 overs) (V. S. Solanki 73, D. J. Sales 60); Bikash Das three for 33, Mushfiqur Rehman three for 37); Bangladesh Youth XI 150 for nine (40 overs) (Mazharul Haq 46, Extras 30).

> *Mushfiqur Rehman took a hat-trick when he dismissed Turner, Schofield and Franks with the last three balls of the innings. Rain halfway through England A's innings reduced the match to 40 overs a side; Bangladesh Youth XI's target was revised to 220.*

†At Dhaka, October 23 (day/night). England A won by six wickets. Toss: Bangladesh Cricket Board XI. Bangladesh Cricket Board XI 244 for nine (50 overs) (Harunur Rashid 55, Habibul Bashar 83; C. E. W. Silverwood three for 40, C. P. Schofield five for 40); England A 245 for four (49 overs) (D. J. Sales 33, A. Habib 41, M. W. Alleyne 66 not out, R. J. Turner 46 not out).

BANGLADESH v ENGLAND A

At Chittagong, October 25, 26, 27. Drawn. Toss: Bangladesh.

International cricket returned to Chittagong, which staged two Asia Cup games in 1988-89, and the townspeople turned out in vast numbers. On the final day it was estimated that there were some 30,000 inside the M. A. Aziz Stadium, with another 5,000 outside trying to get in. Habibul Bashar gave the crowd a polished, unbeaten hundred to celebrate on the first day, batting four and a half hours, while Schofield recorded a career-best six for 120. But Bashar was later eclipsed by Solanki, who hit 20 fours and seven sixes in five and three-quarter hours, an innings of the highest quality. Bangladesh lost only two wickets in wiping out first-innings arrears of 73, and soon secured the draw, but their innings was not without incident. Sheriyar had to be ushered away forcibly from umpire Chowdhury by his team-mates after querying the rejection of an lbw appeal by Franks. The ICC subsequently confirmed the match's first-class status.

Close of play: First day, England A 15-0 (Gough 12*, Ward 3*); Second day, England A 269-7 (Solanki 106*, Kirtley 7*).

Bangladesh

Shahriar Hossain c Trescothick b Franks	9	– b Schofield	27
Javed Omar c Trescothick b Schofield	53	– c Ward b Schofield	19
Habibul Bashar not out	143	– c Habib b Davies	35
*Aminul Islam c Gough b Schofield	47	– b Franks	44
Akram Khan c Solanki b Schofield	0		
Khaled Mahmud c Ward b Solanki	0	– (5) c Alleyne b Schofield	15
†Khaled Masud b Schofield	1	– (6) not out	2
Enamul Haque c Solanki b Schofield	11	– (7) not out	14
Shabbir Khan c Franks b Schofield	20		
Shafiuddin Ahmed not out	3		
B 10, l-b 2, w 6, n-b 10	28	N-b 2	2

1/34 (1) 2/105 (2) 3/219 (4)   (8 wkts dec.) 315   1/44 (1) 2/55 (2)   (5 wkts) 158
4/219 (5) 5/220 (6) 6/225 (7)   3/104 (3) 4/142 (4)
7/239 (8) 8/285 (9)   5/142 (5)

Manjurul Islam did not bat.

Bowling: *First Innings*—Sheriyar 6–0–30–0; Kirtley 10–4–17–0; Franks 8–0–34–1; Schofield 30–4–120–6; Davies 14–3–47–0; Solanki 10–0–36–1; Trescothick 3–0–19–0. *Second Innings*—Kirtley 3–0–11–0; Sheriyar 3–0–18–0; Davies 14–5–35–2; Schofield 13–0–56–2; Solanki 8–1–33–0; Franks 5–3–3–1; Gough 1–0–2–0

England A

M. A. Gough lbw b Shabbir Khan	29	R. J. Kirtley c sub (Al-Shahriar Rokon)	
I. J. Ward c Akram Khan		b Habibul Bashar	32
b Shabbir Khan	53	M. K. Davies not out	12
M. E. Trescothick st Khaled Masud		A. Sheriyar st Khaled Masud	
b Enamul Haque	29	b Enamul Haque	1
V. S. Solanki b Habibul Bashar	185		
A. Habib run out	33	B 5, l-b 2, n-b 1	8
*†M. W. Alleyne b Enamul Haque	0		
C. P. Schofield c sub (Al-Shahriar Rokon)		1/82 (2) 2/93 (1) 3/160 (3)	388
b Enamul Haque	1	4/218 (5) 5/234 (6) 6/236 (7)	
P. J. Franks c Khaled Masud		7/258 (8) 8/373 (4)	
b Shabbir Khan	5	9/382 (9) 10/388 (11)	

Bowling: Manjurul Islam 17–5–53–0; Shafiuddin Ahmed 18–3–58–0; Enamul Haque 49.2–16–107–4; Shabbir Khan 31–9–87–3; Aminul Islam 3–0–17–0; Khaled Mahmud 5–1–29–0; Habibul Bashar 7–2–28–2; Javed Omar 1–0–2–0.

Umpires: S. B. Chowdhury and Manjur Rahman.

†At Dhaka, October 29 (day/night). England A won by five wickets. Toss: Bangladesh. Bangladesh 226 (49.5 overs) (Shahriar Hossain 34, Javed Omar 48, Khaled Mahmud 32, Aminul Islam 30; P. J. Franks three for 35, C. P. Schofield four for 49); England A 229 for five (49.1 overs) (I. J. Ward 31, M. E. Trescothick 44, M. W. Alleyne 66 not out).

BANGLADESH v ENGLAND A

At Dhaka, November 1, 2, 3, 4. Drawn. Toss: England A.

Although runs came throughout the order for England A, with three fifties in the top four and a maiden one for Schofield later on, they could not score quickly enough to establish a winning position. Repeated interruptions for rain did not help their progress. Bangladesh's response was equally slow as they concentrated on trying to avoid the follow-on, which they failed to achieve by 21 runs on the final morning. By the 15th over of the second innings, England A's bowlers had reduced the home side to 28 for three, but the pitch was bland enough to draw the fire from the attack after that initial burst. Khaled Masud's unbeaten century frustrated England A's hopes of a win, and left them complaining that they found the local umpiring "inconsistent".

Close of play: First day, England A 192-3 (Habib 18*, Alleyne 26*); Second day, England A 279-6 (Turner 10*, Schofield 12*); Third day, Bangladesh 186-9 (Hasibul Hussain 3*, Bikash Das 2*).

England A

I. J. Ward c Khaled Masud b Hasibul Hussain .	19	C. P. Schofield b Bikash Das 54
D. J. Sales c sub (Nasirul Alam) b Habibul Bashar .	63	P. J. Franks not out 18
V. S. Solanki c Khaled Masud b Habibul Bashar .	55	R. J. Kirtley b Hasibul Hussain. 0
A. Habib run out	51	M. K. Davies lbw b Hasibul Hussain. . . 0
*M. W. Alleyne lbw b Hasibul Hussain .	32	B 10, l-b 3, w 1, n-b 4 18
R. C. Irani c Khaled Masud b Hasibul Hussain .	22	
†R. J. Turner c Aminul Islam b Enamul Haque .	24	356

1/47 (1) 2/139 (2) 3/150 (3) 4/208 (5) 5/244 (4) 6/261 (6) 7/309 (7) 8/355 (8) 9/356 (10) 10/356 (11)

Bowling: Hasibul Hussain 30.3–5–85–5; Bikash Das 18–5–48–1; Mushfiqur Rehman 4–0–18–0; Enamul Haque 41–17–77–1; Shabbir Khan 16–3–70–0; Habibul Bashar 18–3–38–2; Al-Shahriar Rokon 1–0–7–0.

Bangladesh

Shahriar Hossain c Kirtley b Schofield.	20	– b Franks	8
Javed Omar b Kirtley	11	– c Turner b Franks	1
Habibul Bashar c Solanki b Franks	2	– c Turner b Schofield	3
*Aminul Islam c Turner b Kirtley	6	– (6) not out.	37
Al-Shahriar Rokon c Franks b Kirtley	73	– b Davies.	56
†Khaled Masud c Solanki b Schofield	30	– (4) not out.	105
Mushfiqur Rehman c Turner b Davies	9	
Enamul Haque c Ward b Davies	7	
Shabbir Khan lbw b Kirtley	8	
Hasibul Hussain not out	3	
Bikash Das b Davies	2	
L-b 8, w 1, n-b 6	15	B 10, l-b 6, n-b 6	22

1/26 (2) 2/30 (3) 3/39 (4) 4/54 (1)   186   1/12 (1) 2/17 (2)   (4 wkts) 232
5/124 (6) 6/160 (7) 7/168 (8)   3/28 (3) 4/164 (5)
8/180 (5) 9/181 (9) 10/186 (11)

Bowling: *First Innings*—Kirtley 16–6–36–4; Franks 9–0–23–1; Irani 5–1–10–0; Schofield 20–4–66–2; Davies 21.2–10–43–3. *Second Innings*—Kirtley 11–6–15–0; Franks 11–3–33–2; Schofield 28–8–76–1; Davies 28–10–60–1; Solanki 6–1–31–0; Irani 1–0–1–0; Alleyne 1–1–0–0.

Umpires: Akhteruddin Shaheen and Syed Mahbubullah.

†At BIL Oval, Lincoln, November 10. England A won by six wickets. Toss: England A. NZ Academy 183 for nine (50 overs) (N. R. Parlane 40, T. K. Canning 43, Extras 51; M. W. Alleyne three for 43); England A 184 for four (39 overs) (A. Habib 46 not out, M. W. Alleyne 53, Extras 31; T. K. Canning three for 19).

†At BIL Oval, Lincoln, November 11. England A won by two wickets. Toss: England A. NZ Academy 200 (49.5 overs) (H. J. H. Marshall 86); England A 203 for eight (49 overs) (M. A. Gough 41, I. J. Ward 32, C. E. W. Silverwood 38 not out; H. J. Shaw four for 34, T. K. Canning three for 46).

NORTH ISLAND v ENGLAND A

At BIL Oval, Lincoln, November 15, 16, 17, 18. Drawn. Toss: England A.
    This match, and the one that followed, formed part of the triangular Conference series, in which England A competed with North and South Islands. In the strong, blustery winds that characterised England A's stay in the Christchurch area, Gough and Ward shared a century opening partnership, but the loss of six wickets for 34 demanded a certain amount of rebuilding from Sales and Schofield, who put on 109 for the seventh wicket. Sales batted just over four and a quarter hours for his first century of the tour, only for Sinclair and North Island's middle order to negate his effort. Sinclair batted nearly seven and a half hours for 182, adding 102 with Vincent and 154 with Marshall. The pitch of Waikari soil proved much too resilient to cause batsmen any concern in the second innings. England A ran up the third total of 300-plus in the match, enough to prevent any other result than a draw, and certainly North Island showed no interest in pursuing a token target of 267 from 43 overs in the bitterly cold conditions.
    Close of play: First day, England A 275-7 (Sales 65*, Franks 4*); Second day, North Island 228-3 (Sinclair 112*, Marshall 52*), Third day, England A 106-1 (Gough 44*, Solanki 21*).

England A

M. A. Gough c Walmsley b Penn	48	– c Vincent b Tuffey	78
I. J. Ward b Tuffey	72	– c Marshall b Walker	38
V. S. Solanki c Bell b Penn	4	– lbw b Penn	78
A. Habib lbw b Tuffey	4	– lbw b Walker	47
*M. W. Alleyne b Jefferson	10	– run out	4
D. J. Sales b Walker	115	– (7) not out	19
†R. J. Turner lbw b Jefferson	2	– (8) c Bell b Tuffey	2
C. P. Schofield c Vincent b Walmsley	52	– (6) b Tuffey	3
P. J. Franks c Bell b Walker	9	– not out	8
R. J. Kirtley c Pocock b Walker	2		
M. K. Davies not out	4		
L-b 4, n-b 10	14	B 6, l-b 8, w 3, n-b 7	24

1/125 2/125 3/131 4/138 5/151	336	1/80 2/171 3/250	(7 wkts dec.) 301
6/159 7/268 8/303 9/317		4/264 5/266	
		6/272 7/280	

Bowling: *First Innings*—Penn 32–8–92–2; Walmsley 26–4–85–1; Tuffey 21–5–55–2; Jefferson 27–5–62–2; Pocock 4–1–6–0; Walker 9.3–4–32–3. *Second Innings*—Penn 19–2–60–1; Walmsley 5.4–1–11–0; Tuffey 26–3–82–3; Walker 28–6–65–2; Jefferson 15–5–47–0; Pocock 6.2–1–22–0.

North Island

M. D. Bell b Franks	0	– (2) not out	32
*B. A. Pocock lbw b Kirtley	2	– (1) lbw b Davies	11
M. S. Sinclair c Sales b Schofield	182	– c Turner b Davies	44
L. Vincent c Solanki b Schofield	45	– not out	6
J. A. H. Marshall c Ward b Kirtley	61		
†C. J. Nevin c Sales b Schofield	23		
B. G. K. Walker c Ward b Schofield	0		
M. R. Jefferson c Ward b Schofield	19		
A. J. Penn lbw b Kirtley	11		
D. R. Tuffey c Turner b Kirtley	1		
K. P. Walmsley not out	3		
L-b 6, w 1, n-b 17	24	L-b 3, n-b 1	4

1/1 2/13 3/115 4/269 5/329   371   1/13 2/88   (2 wkts) 97
6/337 7/338 8/361 9/364

Bowling: *First Innings*—Franks 27–7–76–1; Kirtley 25.5–5–80–4; Alleyne 21–8–45–0; Davies 29–10–52–0; Schofield 45–13–107–5; Solanki 1–0–5–0. *Second Innings*—Kirtley 5–3–16–0; Franks 4–1–12–0; Davies 11–1–23–2; Schofield 5–0–29–0; Solanki 3–1–14–0.

Umpires: D. M. Quested and G. J. Stewart.

SOUTH ISLAND v ENGLAND A

At Hagley Park, Christchurch, November 21, 22, 23, 24. England A won by eight wickets. Toss: England A.

The match was originally scheduled for the Test ground in Christchurch, to be played on a pitch produced in an aluminium tray and dropped in by crane. But when the experimental pitch was damaged by a stray firework while still in storage, the venue was moved to one of the city's public parks. To date, the English batsmen had displayed a disturbing tendency to become established, then give their wickets away, and Alleyne showed them here how to reverse that trend, batting 11 minutes short of six hours before declaring. His innings was the heart of an excellent team performance in miserably cold and windy conditions. Thomas bowled admirably, just a few days after arriving to replace Silverwood, and his four wickets helped ensure that South Island would get nowhere near the follow-on target of 306. The home batsmen fought harder in their second innings but were bowled out again only 99 ahead. England A had 38 overs in which to reach their first first-class win of the tour, and with Solanki and Trescothick mounting a blistering assault, they did it inside 15.

Close of play: First day, England A 294-5 (Alleyne 53*, Turner 29*); Second day, South Island 135-5 (Redmond 25*, Hopkins 10*); Third day, South Island 139-3 (Richardson 35*, Englefield 32*).

England A

M. A. Gough c Wiseman b Martin	17	– c Gaffaney b Wisneski	7
I. J. Ward c Hopkins b Wisneski	60	– lbw b Wisneski	5
V. S. Solanki b Wisneski	59	– not out	52
M. E. Trescothick run out	45	– not out	30
*M. W. Alleyne not out	152		
D. J. Sales c Lawson b Wisneski	22		
†R. J. Turner c Wiseman b Wisneski	40		
R. C. Irani c Englefield b Wiseman	8		
S. D. Thomas b Wisneski	18		
M. K. Davies b Wiseman	17		
B 4, l-b 7, n-b 6	17	L-b 1, w 1, n-b 4	6

1/59 2/114 3/170 4/199 5/237   (9 wkts dec.) 455   1/11 2/31   (2 wkts) 100
6/317 7/355 8/401 9/455

A. Sheriyar did not bat.

Bowling: *First Innings*—Bulfin 25–3–111–0; Wisneski 37–16–98–5; Martin 27–11–64–1; Wiseman 45.4–10–120–2; Redmond 13–1–41–0; Richardson 1–0–6–0; Cumming 1–0–4–0. *Second Innings*—Bulfin 6–0–41–0; Wisneski 6–1–34–2; Martin 1.3–0–16–0; Redmond 1–0–8–0.

South Island

*R. A. Lawson lbw b Alleyne	46	– c Gough b Thomas	20
C. D. Cumming c Ward b Sheriyar	18	– lbw b Davies	11
C. B. Gaffaney c Irani b Sheriyar	2	– c Irani b Davies	29
M. H. Richardson c Turner b Thomas	27	– b Solanki	45
J. I. Englefield c Irani b Thomas	3	– b Alleyne	37
A. J. Redmond b Davies	51	– c Solanki b Sheriyar	23
†G. J. Hopkins c Turner b Thomas	35	– c Turner b Alleyne	32
W. A. Wisneski b Thomas	0	– c Gough b Davies	60
P. J. Wiseman not out	23	– lbw b Davies	39
C. E. Bulfin lbw b Davies	4	– c Turner b Sheriyar	12
C. S. Martin b Sheriyar	1	– not out	0
N-b 7	7	B 5, l-b 15, w 4, n-b 5	29

1/28 2/30 3/73 4/79 5/111   217   1/34 2/60 3/76 4/144 5/173   337
6/176 7/176 8/195 9/203   6/195 7/249 8/311 9/337

Bowling: *First Innings*—Sheriyar 24.1–6–60–3; Thomas 21–2–56–4; Irani 17–7–50–0; Alleyne 11–2–26–1; Davies 10–4–25–2. *Second Innings*—Sheriyar 28–7–66–2; Irani 16–6–39–0; Trescothick 7–3–14–0; Davies 36.1–14–71–4; Thomas 7–1–29–1; Solanki 12–4–28–1; Alleyne 20–5–70–2.

Umpires: G. A. Baxter and R. S. Dunne.

NEW ZEALAND A v ENGLAND A

First A-team Test

At BIL Oval, Lincoln, November 28, 29, 30, December 1, 2. Drawn. Toss: England A.

With temperatures on the second day lower than those in wintry London, additional hand-warmers were needed by the fielders and had to be borrowed from the International Antarctic Centre in Christchurch. The groundsman used a blowtorch to dry a damp patch mid-pitch where rain had leaked under the covers. Sinclair and Richardson gave New Zealand A's first innings respectability – a commodity lacking in the tourists' reply. After a first-day washout, the follow-on margin was reduced from 200 (for a five-day match) to 150, under Law 13.2, even though extra time was played on the remaining four days. That meant England A needed 112, and though they recovered from 41 for five, they were still three runs short of the follow-on when the last pair came together to complete the job. New Zealand A over-extended their second innings, when the English bowlers, especially Sheriyar, made progress difficult, but they still gave themselves more than a day to bowl England A out a second time. Ward fell first ball, but by late on the final day it seemed the players were on the field principally to allow Alleyne his hundred. When Styris dismissed him and Turner in four balls, however, the New Zealanders continued, trying to force the win, until Habib reached three figures.

Close of play: First day, No play; Second day, New Zealand A 235-7 (Hopkins 20*, Penn 14*); Third day, New Zealand A 102-2 (Bell 45*, Vincent 37*); Fourth day, England A 6-1 (Trescothick 2*, Solanki 2*).

New Zealand A

*G. R. Stead c Trescothick b Franks	3	– c Trescothick b Sheriyar.	12
M. D. Bell c Turner b Kirtley	7	– c Franks b Alleyne	58
M. S. Sinclair c Trescothick b Kirtley	62	– c Solanki b Kirtley	3
L. Vincent c Turner b Alleyne	13	– c Turner b Sheriyar	64
M. H. Richardson lbw b Kirtley	74	– not out	67
S. B. Styris lbw b Schofield	0	– c Sales b Sheriyar.	14
†G. J. Hopkins b Franks	20	– c Trescothick b Sheriyar.	7
W. A. Wisneski c Turner b Schofield	23	– c Turner b Sheriyar	9
A. J. Penn lbw b Kirtley	27	– c Turner b Sheriyar	0
P. J. Wiseman c Turner b Kirtley	9	– c Trescothick b Franks.	22
C. J. Drum not out	4	– not out	4
B 5, l-b 7, n-b 7	19	B 5, l-b 8, w 3, n-b 2	18

1/11 (1) 2/25 (2) 3/56 (4) 4/149 (3)   261   1/21 (1) 2/32 (3)   (9 wkts dec.) 278
5/158 (6) 6/184 (5) 7/213 (8)   3/123 (2) 4/153 (4)
8/235 (7) 9/256 (9) 10/261 (10)   5/182 (6) 6/198 (7)
                                                      7/222 (8) 8/222 (9)
                                                      9/261 (10)

Bowling: *First Innings*—Franks 21–7–44–2; Sheriyar 24–3–74–0; Kirtley 18.5–4–54–5; Alleyne 11–5–22–1; Schofield 24–9–55–2. *Second Innings*—Franks 23–5–56–1; Sheriyar 26–5–70–6; Kirtley 28–11–65–1; Schofield 12–1–42–0; Alleyne 16–5–32–1.

England A

I. J. Ward b Drum	8	– b Drum.	0
M. E. Trescothick c Penn b Drum	8	– c Hopkins b Wisneski	6
V. S. Solanki c Hopkins b Drum	2	– b Wisneski	97
D. J. Sales b Penn	8	– c Drum b Penn	22
*M. W. Alleyne c Styris b Penn	8	– c Sinclair b Styris	96
A. Habib c Stead b Penn	19	– not out	101
†R. J. Turner c Sinclair b Wisneski	12	– c and b Styris	0
C. P. Schofield c Styris b Wisneski	23		
P. J. Franks c Vincent b Wiseman	17	– (8) not out.	1
R. J. Kirtley c Vincent b Penn	3		
A. Sheriyar not out	5		
L-b 7, n-b 3	10	B 1, l-b 5, n-b 2	8

1/8 (1) 2/12 (3) 3/26 (2) 4/33 (4)   123   1/0 (1) 2/19 (2)   (6 wkts) 331
5/41 (5) 6/73 (7) 7/73 (6)   3/70 (4) 4/164 (3)
8/98 (9) 9/109 (10) 10/123 (8)   5/317 (5) 6/317 (7)

Bowling: *First Innings*—Drum 11–4–34–3; Wisneski 16.5–5–32–2; Penn 14–5–21–4; Styris 6–1–17–0; Wiseman 4–0–12–1. *Second Innings*—Drum 18–6–59–1; Wisneski 23–3–82–2; Wiseman 32.4–9–75–0; Styris 15–5–40–2; Penn 17–3–63–1; Richardson 2–0–6–0.

Umpires: R. D. Anderson and B. F. Bowden.

CENTRAL DISTRICTS v ENGLAND A

At Palmerston North, December 5, 6, 7. England A won by 95 runs. Toss: Central Districts.

Alleyne lost the toss for the only time in New Zealand and was invited to bat first on a damp, green pitch that was invaded by a duck on the opening day, a companion for those made by Sales and Turner as England A struggled to 76 for seven. A fifty partnership between Franks and Thomas avoided total embarrassment. The England bowlers also illustrated how awkward batting could be made on such a surface, Sheriyar claiming five wickets as Central Districts, the reigning national champions, were dismissed for 111. England A were batting again by the first evening, but next morning their mood bordered on reckless and they were again in trouble at 83 for six. Once more the lower order came to the rescue, notably Schofield with a series of unorthodox but effective strokes. He and Davies put on 70 for the ninth wicket to take the game out of Central Districts' reach; 208 was too high a target in such a low-scoring game.

Close of play: First day, England A 35-0 (Ward 7*, Trescothick 24*); Second day, Central Districts 60-4 (Douglas 11*, Oram 4*).

England A

I. J. Ward lbw b Mason	12	– c Furlong b Hamilton			9
M. E. Trescothick c Sigley b Hamilton	13	– c Spearman b Mason			25
V. S. Solanki c Spearman b Hamilton	11	– b Mason b Hamilton			0
D. J. Sales b Hamilton	0	– c Spearman b Mason			0
†R. J. Turner lbw b Hamilton	0	– c Furlong b Mason			24
*M. W. Alleyne c Sulzberger b Oram	14	– b Hamilton			5
C. P. Schofield c Sigley b Mason	13	– c Sigley b Craik			74
P. J. Franks b Craik	19	– c Sigley b Craik			9
S. D. Thomas c Sigley b Furlong	31	– b Craik			0
M. K. Davies not out	2	– not out			20
A. Sheriyar b Furlong	4	– c Douglas b Craik			0
B 1, l-b 2, n-b 10	13	L-b 14, n-b 6			20

1/28 2/38 3/39 4/39 5/47	132	1/37 2/37 3/37 4/40 5/51
6/76 7/76 8/126 9/126		6/83 7/116 8/116 9/186

186

Bowling: *First Innings*—Mason 13–2–43–2; Hamilton 14–3–38–4; Craik 14–5–26–1; Oram 4–1–11–1; Furlong 2.2–1–11–2. *Second Innings*—Hamilton 17–3–41–3; Mason 14–5–49–3; Craik 11–4–25–4; Oram 8–4–18–0; Furlong 13–2–39–0.

Central Districts

D. P. Kelly b Alleyne	27	– (2) b Franks			6
G. S. Milnes lbw b Sheriyar	0	– (1) lbw b Sheriyar			2
*C. M. Spearman lbw b Sheriyar	8	– b Franks			23
G. P. Sulzberger c Sales b Thomas	26	– c Turner b Franks			7
M. W. Douglas run out	2	– c Solanki b Sheriyar			11
J. D. P. Oram c Turner b Franks	19	– c Schofield b Franks			6
†M. A. Sigley b Franks	21	– c Alleyne b Thomas			11
C. J. M. Furlong b Sheriyar	2	– lbw b Schofield			14
M. J. Mason c Turner b Sheriyar	0	– c Davies b Thomas			6
L. J. Hamilton c Sales b Sheriyar	0	– not out			0
E. Craik not out	2	– c Solanki b Franks			18
N-b 4	4	L-b 6, n-b 2			8

1/0 2/10 3/62 4/64 5/70	111	1/7 2/20 3/33 4/48 5/62
6/103 7/109 8/109 9/109		6/62 7/83 8/94 9/94

112

Bowling: *First Innings*—Franks 12–6–18–2; Sheriyar 10.3–2–35–5; Thomas 11–3–26–1; Davies 2–0–7–0; Alleyne 10–3–25–1. *Second Innings*—Franks 19.2–9–26–5; Sheriyar 15–5–39–2; Thomas 10–1–27–2; Alleyne 3–1–11–0; Schofield 4–3–3–1.

Umpires: R. D. Anderson and M. George.

NEW ZEALAND A v ENGLAND A

Second A-team Test

At Basin Reserve, Wellington, December 10, 11, 12. England A won by ten wickets. Toss: England A.

England A took the series 1–0 by winning with more than two days to spare – despite rain shortening the second day. Although a green, moist pitch did nothing to discourage them, the English bowlers deserved full credit for their efficient demolition of the opposition. The tourists' reply centred on a century from Sales. Ignoring a chest infection, he made his positive intentions obvious from the outset and was able to shepherd the lower order to a total that almost doubled New Zealand A's effort. Sales reached his hundred on the third morning, from 147 balls, and after he was last out the England bowlers claimed three wickets in the ten overs before lunch, followed by another shortly afterwards. Richardson and Styris fought back to add 57, but once their partnership was broken, wickets fell at regular intervals. England A needed only six runs for victory – a target achieved in ten balls on the third evening.

Close of play: First day, England A 51-2 (Solanki 28*); Second day, England A 235-7 (Sales 60*, Franks 0*).

New Zealand A

G. R. Stead c Turner b Sheriyar	5	– b Sheriyar 3
M. D. Bell c Trescothick b Sheriyar	5	– c Sales b Kirtley 5
M. S. Sinclair lbw b Franks	44	– lbw b Franks 3
L. Vincent lbw b Kirtley	0	– c Turner b Franks 0
*M. H. Richardson c Turner b Kirtley	30	– c Schofield b Kirtley 43
S. B. Styris c Turner b Franks	12	– c sub (M. K. Davies) b Franks . 29
†G. J. Hopkins lbw b Kirtley	29	– c Solanki b Schofield 33
W. A. Wisneski st Turner b Schofield	0	– c Turner b Sheriyar 15
P. J. Wiseman lbw b Schofield	4	– c Franks b Solanki 2
C. J. Drum c Ward b Schofield	0	– (11) run out 0
M. J. Mason not out	10	– (10) not out 20
L-b 13, w 1, n-b 2	16	B 2, l-b 3, w 1 6

1/8 (1) 2/24 (2) 3/25 (4) 4/81 (5)   155   1/3 (1) 2/7 (3) 3/7 (4)   159
5/106 (3) 6/109 (6) 7/117 (8)   4/20 (2) 5/77 (6) 6/102 (5)
8/127 (9) 9/127 (10) 10/155 (7)   7/125 (7) 8/130 (9)
     9/142 (8) 10/159 (11)

Bowling: *First Innings*—Franks 17–5–38–2; Sheriyar 14–2–32–2; Kirtley 15.2–4–43–3; Schofield 12–5–16–3; Alleyne 7–2–13–0. *Second Innings*—Franks 12–3–32–3; Sheriyar 12–3–33–2; Kirtley 12–4–31–2; Schofield 15.1–5–38–1; Solanki 11–1–20–1.

England A

M. A. Gough c Vincent b Mason	10	– not out 5
I. J. Ward c Stead b Wisneski	10	– not out 1
V. S. Solanki c Sinclair b Styris	54	
M. E. Trescothick c Drum b Mason	43	
*M. W. Alleyne c Hopkins b Drum	38	
D. J. Sales c Wiseman b Mason	105	
†R. J. Turner c Vincent b Wiseman	1	
C. P. Schofield c Hopkins b Wiseman	16	
P. J. Franks c Styris b Wisneski	15	
R. J. Kirtley c Hopkins b Drum	0	
A. Sheriyar not out	12	
L-b 1, n-b 4	5	

1/15 (2) 2/51 (1) 3/101 (3) 4/133 (4)   309   (no wkt) 6
5/194 (5) 6/203 (7) 7/235 (8)
8/269 (6) 9/270 (10) 10/309 (9)

Bowling: *First Innings*—Drum 27.5–8–63–2; Mason 19–3–60–3; Wisneski 29–8–98–2; Wiseman 11–3–29–2; Styris 11–3–58–1. *Second Innings*—Mason 1–0–4–0; Wisneski 0.4–0–2–0.

Umpires: D. M. Quested and E. A. Watkin.

†At Nelson Park, Napier, December 16. First A-team one-day international: England A won by nine runs. Toss: England A. England A 213 for seven (50 overs) (M. E. Trescothick 69, R. C. Irani 62; M. J. Mason three for 51); New Zealand A 204 (48.5 overs) (C. J. Nevin 68, J. D. P. Oram 41; P. J. Franks three for 28, R. C. Irani three for 25).

New Zealand A, having been 131 for one, lost their last six wickets for 27.

†At Eden Park Outer Oval, Auckland, December 18. Second A-team one-day international: England A won by three wickets. Toss: England A. New Zealand A 216 (49.4 overs) (J. D. P. Oram 44, S. B. Styris 56; R. C. Irani three for 47); England A 219 for seven (49 overs) (M. A. Gough 31, V. S. Solanki 34, M. W. Alleyne 38 not out, Extras 45).

†At Eden Park Outer Oval, Auckland, December 19. Third A-team one-day international: No result. Toss: England A. England A 187 for seven (45.4 overs) (I. J. Ward 31, M. W. Alleyne 54) v New Zealand A.

Rain ended play, leaving England A 2–0 winners of the one-day series.

PWC TEST RATINGS

Introduced in 1987, the PricewaterhouseCoopers (PwC) Ratings (originally the Deloitte Ratings, and later the Coopers & Lybrand Ratings) rank Test cricketers on a scale up to 1,000 according to their performances in Test matches. The ratings take into account playing conditions, the quality of the opposition and the result of the matches. In August 1998, a similar set of ratings for one-day internationals was added (see page 1120).

The leading 20 batsmen and bowlers in the Test ratings after the 2000 Test series between England and West Indies which ended on September 4 were:

	Batsmen	Rating		Bowlers	Rating
1.	S. R. Tendulkar (*Ind.*)	863	1.	S. M. Pollock (*SA*)	900
2.	S. R. Waugh (*Aus.*)	841	2.	G. D. McGrath (*Aus.*)	896
3.	Saeed Anwar (*Pak.*)	808	3.	A. A. Donald (*SA*)	851
4.	R. T. Ponting (*Aus.*)	804	4.	C. A. Walsh (*WI*)	836
5.	Inzamam-ul-Haq (*Pak.*)	786	5.	C. E. L. Ambrose (*WI*)	830
6.	J. L. Langer (*Aus.*)	767	6.	M. Muralitharan (*SL*)	822
7.	B. C. Lara (*WI*)	766	7.	B. Lee (*Aus.*)	735
8.	A. Flower (*Zim.*)	732	8.	Wasim Akram (*Pak.*)	725
9.	J. H. Kallis (*SA*)	727	9.	A. Kumble (*Ind.*)	722
10.	A. J. Stewart (*Eng.*)	723	10.	A. R. Caddick (*Eng.*)	718
11.	M. A. Atherton (*Eng.*)	709	11.	D. Gough (*Eng.*)	706
	D. P. M. D. Jayawardene	709			
13.	D. J. Cullinan (*SA*)	696	12.	H. H. Streak (*Zim.*)	701
14.	C. D. McMillan (*NZ*)	686	13.	D. W. Fleming (*Aus.*)	699
15.	P. A. de Silva (*SL*)	680	14.	Waqar Younis (*Pak.*)	692
16.	M. J. Slater (*Aus.*)	675	15.	C. L. Cairns (*NZ*)	683
17.	C. L. Cairns (*NZ*)	670	16.	D. J. Nash (*NZ*)	674
18.	A. C. Gilchrist (*Aus.*)	664	17.	S. K. Warne (*Aus.*)	652
19.	L. Klusener (*SA*)	661	18.	J. Srinath (*Ind.*)	640
20.	R. Dravid (*Ind.*)	660	19.	D. L. Vettori (*NZ*)	604
	M. E. Waugh (*Aus.*)	660	20.	D. G. Cork (*Eng.*)	602
22.	G. Kirsten (*SA*)	649	21.	Saqlain Mushtaq (*Pak.*)	590
23.	S. T. Jayasuriya (*SL*)	641	22.	S. B. Doull (*NZ*)	577
24.	S. Chanderpaul (*WI*)	637	23.	W. P. U. J. C. Vaas (*SL*)	533
25.	M. S. Atapattu (*SL*)	635	24.	J. H. Kallis (*SA*)	529
26.	N. J. Astle (*NZ*)	630	25.	J. N. Gillespie (*Aus.*)	527
27.	S. P. Fleming (*NZ*)	625	26.	C. R. Miller (*Aus.*)	520
28.	S. C. Ganguly (*Ind.*)	622	27.	Arshad Khan (*Pak.*)	517
	N. Hussain (*Eng.*)	622	28.	D. W. Headley (*Eng.*)	507
30.	Yousuf Youhana (*Pak.*)	620	29.	Mushtaq Ahmed (*Pak.*)	495
			30.	R. D. King (*WI*)	479

THE AUSTRALIANS IN SRI LANKA AND ZIMBABWE, 1999-2000

By MALCOLM CONN

Not in anyone's wildest dreams could the painful revamping of Sri Lankan cricket have been so emphatically endorsed. The unwieldy and factionalised Board of Control had been tossed out and replaced by an interim committee of respected businessmen, the canny but difficult Arjuna Ranatunga was deposed as captain, and Dav Whatmore returned as coach. Building for the future, after three years basking in past glory, had become essential after a dreadful World Cup. Sanath Jayasuriya was appointed captain, while Ranatunga and Aravinda de Silva were left out of the one-day side.

Bold moves indeed, because the Australians were coming. What would the World Cup champions and Test leaders do against such an unsettled side? Answer: receive the shock of their lives. An upset win over Australia in the final of the Aiwa Cup one-day competition was just the fillip Whatmore and Jayasuriya needed in their drive for youth and fitness. But it was surely an aberration. Australia, after all, had dominated the triangular tournament until then.

Nine days later, Australia tumbled to 60 for seven before lunch on the opening day of the First Test in Kandy. In a flash, the series was decided. Despite some heroics, Australia never recovered; the next two rain-marred games would be drawn. It was their first Test failure against Sri Lanka in 11 matches going back to their inaugural meeting, on the same ground, 16 years earlier.

There were two major factors in Sri Lanka's unexpected success: excellent and exhaustive preparation by Whatmore, assisted by physiotherapist Alex Kountouri, both Australian nationals, and the bowling of Muttiah Muralitharan. Whatever questions remained about his action, particularly the top-spinner, Muralitharan baffled most of the Australian batsmen. His wonderful control and use of flight on slow, turning pitches once again exposed their vulnerabilities on the subcontinent. "He turns it more than any other spinner going around at the moment and I guess we're facing something like the opposition has faced with Shane Warne over the years," said Australian captain Steve Waugh. The left-handed Justin Langer was the one most traumatised by Muralitharan, as the ball constantly turned across him.

Murali was easily the leading wicket-taker in the series, with 15, and might have doubled that if rain had not washed out much of the last two Tests. He was well supported by Chaminda Vaas, who claimed ten wickets. Sri Lanka's batting, however, revolved almost solely around de Silva, recalled alongside Ranatunga for the Tests. He was dismissed only twice in four innings and averaged 96.

But the Man of the Series was Ricky Ponting, with 253 runs at 84.33, including the only century on either side. The one Australian middle-order batsman to pass 50 in the series, doing so three times in four innings that stretched across almost ten hours, he was described by Steve Waugh as the future of Australian cricket. By contrast, Mark Waugh had another nightmare tour of Sri Lanka. In 1992-93, he averaged ten, finishing with four successive ducks. In 1999-2000, he averaged seven.

Warne reclaimed his place after being dropped for the last Test of the previous series, in the West Indies: he and off-spinner Colin Miller were Australia's most successful bowlers, with eight wickets each. Glenn McGrath, however, was out of sorts from the start and seized up completely late in the First Test; his under-used muscles became so tight that he could not bend and consequently missed a vital catch off Ranatunga. But Australia's misery at Kandy was epitomised by the loss of Jason Gillespie, who broke his right leg and injured his wrist in a dreadful on-field collision with Steve Waugh as they both went for a catch behind square leg. The fast bowler had been Australia's leading wicket-taker in the one-day tournament. A disastrous tour for injuries and illness continued when Gillespie's replacement, Scott Muller, split the webbing in his right hand four days after arriving and left again; meanwhile, Simon Katich, an uncapped left-handed batsman from Western Australia, was sent back to Colombo and put in isolation after being diagnosed with chicken-pox. Another departure was Geoff Marsh, who, having coached the side since 1996, resigned unexpectedly to spend more time with his family and returned to Australia after the Sri Lankan Tests. Former captain Allan Border was released from his television commitments so he could cover as coach for the Zimbabwean leg of the tour.

This was a tough time for Waugh as captain. Australia had underperformed in the West Indies, drawing 2–2 against weakened opponents. Had he been able to bat again in the Kandy Test, Australia might have scrambled a victory. Instead, he had a badly broken nose and was being flown by helicopter to a Colombo hospital with Gillespie; he could not even see his men go down fighting. However, Waugh insisted on returning for the Second Test. His presence was not enough to prevent another poor performance, but by the Third his side were playing the better cricket. The weather denied them in Colombo, having rescued them at Galle. As four of Australia's last six Tests on the island had now been ruined by rain, there was a good argument for them visiting Sri Lanka during April in future, rather than the monsoon months of August and September.

By the time they moved on to Zimbabwe for the overdue inaugural Test between the two countries, the Australians' cricket was back on song. Greeted by the dry warmth and big blue skies so typical of Australia, the players felt at home and performed accordingly, winning the only Test by ten wickets and crushing Zimbabwe 3–0 in the one-day series. Both Steve and Mark Waugh recaptured their form, with centuries in the Test and limited-overs games respectively, while McGrath picked up six Test wickets. Zimbabwe fought well, but were clearly outmatched and made basic mistakes at crucial moments. For the Australians, however, after their trials in Sri Lanka, the Test match marked the start of a record-breaking run of success.

AUSTRALIAN TOURING PARTY

S. R. Waugh (New South Wales) (*captain*), S. K. Warne (Victoria) (*vice-captain*), G. S. Blewett (South Australia), D. W. Fleming (Victoria), J. N. Gillespie (South Australia), M. L. Hayden (Queensland), I. A. Healy (Queensland), S. M. Katich (Western Australia), J. L. Langer (Western Australia), S. C. G. MacGill (New South Wales), G. D. McGrath (New South Wales), C. R. Miller (Tasmania), R. T. Ponting (Tasmania), M. J. Slater (New South Wales), M. E. Waugh (New South Wales).

S. A. Muller (Queensland) replaced the injured Gillespie and when also injured was replaced by M. J. Nicholson (Western Australia). Katich went home after contracting chicken-pox.

M. G. Bevan (New South Wales), A. C. Dale (Queensland), A. C. Gilchrist (Western Australia), D. S. Lehmann (South Australia), D. R. Martyn (Western Australia), T. M. Moody (Western Australia) and A. Symonds (Queensland) were in Australia's one-day squads in Sri Lanka and Zimbabwe; Blewett, Hayden, Healy, Katich, Langer, MacGill, Miller and Slater were not included for the one-day games.

A. R. Border took over from Marsh as coach for the Zimbabwean leg of the tour.

Team manager: S. R. Bernard. *Coach:* G. R. Marsh. *Scorer:* M. K. Walsh. *Physiotherapist:* E. Alcott. *Fitness advisor:* D. Misson.

AUSTRALIAN TOUR RESULTS

Test matches – Played 4: Won 1, Lost 1, Drawn 2.
First-class matches – Played 7: Won 4, Lost 1, Drawn 2.
Wins – Zimbabwe, Sri Lankan Board XI (2), ZCU President's XI.
Loss – Sri Lanka.
Draws – Sri Lanka (2).
One-day internationals – Played 8: Won 7, Lost 1. *Wins* – Sri Lanka (2), India (2), Zimbabwe (3). *Loss* – Sri Lanka.
Other non-first-class match – Won v Sri Lankan Board President's XI.

TEST MATCH AVERAGES – SRI LANKA v AUSTRALIA

SRI LANKA – BATTING

	T	I	NO	R	HS	100s	50s	Avge	Ct/St
P. A. de Silva	3	4	2	192	78	0	2	96.00	2
D. P. M. D. Jayawardene . .	3	4	0	122	46	0	0	30.50	2
R. P. Arnold.	3	3	0	69	50	0	1	23.00	1
M. S. Atapattu	3	5	1	84	29	0	0	21.00	7
A. Ranatunga.	3	4	2	34	19*	0	0	17.00	4
S. T. Jayasuriya	3	5	1	57	21*	0	0	14.25	1
R. S. Kaluwitharana	3	3	0	39	25	0	0	13.00	2/3

Played in three Tests: M. Muralitharan 0, 7* (1 ct); W. P. U. J. C. Vaas 2*, 41 (1 ct); D. N. T. Zoysa 7, 1. Played in two Tests: R. Herath 3. Played in one Test: U. D. U. Chandana 12.

* Signifies not out.

BOWLING

	O	M	R	W	BB	5W/i	Avge
W. P. U. J. C. Vaas	63.4	17	143	10	4-54	0	14.30
M. Muralitharan	141.1	24	349	15	5-71	1	23.26
R. Herath	69.3	16	195	6	4-97	0	32.50
D. N. T. Zoysa	39	10	98	3	3-38	0	32.66

Also bowled: R. P. Arnold 7–4–3–1; U. D. U. Chandana 10.2–1–48–1; P. A. de Silva 3–0–5–0; S. T. Jayasuriya 27–4–41–0.

AUSTRALIA – BATTING

	T	I	NO	R	HS	100s	50s	Avge	Ct
R. T. Ponting	3	4	1	253	105*	1	2	84.33	3
M. J. Slater	3	4	0	182	96	0	2	45.50	1
G. S. Blewett.	3	4	0	146	70	0	2	36.50	2
S. R. Waugh	3	3	0	52	19	0	0	17.33	1
G. D. McGrath.	3	4	3	14	10*	0	0	14.00	1
J. L. Langer.	3	4	0	51	32	0	0	12.75	1
M. E. Waugh	3	4	0	29	13	0	0	7.25	2
I. A. Healy	3	4	0	25	11	0	0	6.25	4
C. R. Miller.	3	4	0	14	8	0	0	3.50	2
S. K. Warne.	3	4	0	6	6	0	0	1.50	2

Played in two Tests: D. W. Fleming 16, 32. Played in one Test: J. N. Gillespie 41.

* Signifies not out.

BOWLING

	O	M	R	W	BB	5W/i	Avge
S. K. Warne.	56.1	20	115	8	5-52	1	14.37
D. W. Fleming	32.5	6	103	5	3-14	0	20.60
C. R. Miller.	60.3	10	193	8	4-62	0	24.12
G. D. McGrath.	68.5	19	214	6	3-81	0	35.66

Also bowled: G. S. Blewett 3–0–12–0; J. N. Gillespie 12–2–43–0; R. T. Ponting 4–1–7–0; M. E. Waugh 2–1–9–0.

Note: Matches in this section which were not first-class are signified by a dagger.

†At Sinhalese Sports Club, Colombo, August 19. Australians won by five wickets. Toss: Sri Lankan Board President's XI. Sri Lankan Board President's XI 208 for five (50 overs) (S. I. Fernando 67, L. P. C. Silva 45); Australians 212 for five (45.1 overs) (A. C. Gilchrist 45, R. T. Ponting 60 retired, D. S. Lehmann 37).
   The Australian team contained 13 players.

Australia's matches v Sri Lanka and India in the Aiwa Cup (August 22–31) may be found in that section.

At P. Saravanamuttu Stadium, Colombo, September 3, 4, 5, 6. Australians won by four wickets. Toss: Sri Lankan Board XI. Sri Lankan Board XI 228 (R. P. Arnold 63, S. I. de Saram 67; G. D. McGrath four for 52) and 271 (R. P. Arnold 79, L. P. C. Silva 70; C. R. Miller six for 57, S. K. Warne three for 74); Australians 179 (S. R. Waugh 43, R. T. Ponting 35; R. Herath four for 57, M. M. D. N. R. G. Perera three for 50) and 321 for six (G. S. Blewett 148, M. J. Slater 51, J. L. Langer 52).

SRI LANKA v AUSTRALIA

First Test Match

At Kandy, September 9, 10, 11. Sri Lanka won by six wickets. Toss: Australia.
   The drama of Test cricket rose to new heights as the sound of a helicopter filled Asgiriya Stadium. Reminiscent of a scene from *Apocalypse Now*, the machine had appeared, dark green and menacing, over the adjoining hill, out of tropical vegetation, and play stopped as it swept low over the back of the ground, touched down briefly, then headed towards Colombo. With it went any possible chance Australia might have had of turning round a Test Sri Lanka always deserved to win.
   On board were Steve Waugh, with a badly broken nose, and Gillespie, with a broken leg that would keep him out of the national side throughout the Australian season. They had crashed, horrifically, as Waugh ran back from square leg and Gillespie came in from the boundary, both trying to catch the Sri Lankan vice-captain, Jayawardene. The ball always seemed destined to fall between them.
   This freak accident represented Australia's lowest point on a rare lowly tour. When it happened on the second morning, Sri Lanka were already 139 for three in reply to Australia's 188, and threatening to bat them out of the match. Jayawardene and de Silva ran two but abandoned a third when they saw the Australians had forgotten the ball and were huddled around their fallen colleagues. Play was held up for six minutes while they received treatment before Gillespie was carried from the field.
   Little had gone right for Steve Waugh since winning the toss had given Australia a record 13 in succession. Minutes before lunch on the opening day, Australia had crumbled to a staggering 60 for seven, first against the left-arm seam attack of Vaas and Zoysa, then the off-spin of Muralitharan. A face-saving century partnership between Ponting and Gillespie was the only high point of a dreadful day's batting. Gillespie stuck for more than two hours, scoring 41, while Ponting remained until the end. On 96, with only McGrath for support, he was in two minds about how best to snatch a hundred and pushed a catch back to Murali.
   Sri Lanka were coasting at 177 for three in reply, but fell victim to Warne and inexperience: they were all out for 234, a lead of just 46. Back in the Test side after being dropped in the West Indies, and now acting-captain in Waugh's absence, Warne bowled beautifully for five wickets. Only de Silva, with a patient and polished 78, lasting three hours and containing 13 fours, and Jayawardene, with a more fortunate 46, offered significant contributions. But Australia's batting soon failed again. Without their captain and down to nine men, they mustered only 140, Murali and Vaas grabbing three wickets each. This time Ponting stood alone, with another fifty.
   Sri Lanka needed just 95 for a historic first Test victory over Australia, but it was no simple affair. They had stumbled to 39 for three when the new batsman, Jayawardene, spooned the ball towards cover and bowler Miller gathered it left-handed at ground level after a desperate lunge. Australian celebrations were cut short, however. Umpire Manuel, apparently fooled by a puff of dust from Jayawardene's bat, believed it had been a bump ball, despite its slow, looping trajectory, and did not choose to consult either his colleague at square leg or the third umpire. Miller did remove Jayawardene a few overs later, leaving Sri Lanka an uneasy 60 for four, but the old firm

of Ranatunga and de Silva ensured glory would not drown in a sea of panic. Riding his luck with the cheeky approach that so annoys the Australians, Ranatunga survived a desperately close lbw appeal and a dropped catch before scoring, then broke the game open with a four and six off successive balls from Warne.

Excitement mounted with every delivery, amid rhythmic clapping and wild cheering. The small and picturesque ground was suddenly so full that the crowd spilled out in front of the sightscreen at one end and could not be moved by police. In the end, Sri Lanka scrambled to a six-wicket victory after three days of drama, tension and controversy. It was 14 years to the day since they won their first Test – against India at the P. Sara Stadium in Colombo. Well as Australia fought, the better team won.

Men of the Match: P. A. de Silva and R. T. Ponting.

Close of play: First day, Sri Lanka 69-2 (Atapattu 25*); Second day, Australia 89-6 (Ponting 22*, Miller 0*).

Australia

M. J. Slater lbw b Vaas	0	– (2) lbw b Muralitharan	27
G. S. Blewett lbw b Zoysa	0	– (1) c Atapattu b Muralitharan	14
J. L. Langer c de Silva b Vaas	7	– lbw b Vaas	5
M. E. Waugh c and b Vaas	6	– b Vaas	0
*S. R. Waugh c de Silva b Zoysa	19	– absent hurt	
R. T. Ponting c and b Muralitharan	96	– (5) c Jayasuriya b Chandana	51
†I. A. Healy st Kaluwitharana b Muralitharan	11	– (6) b Muralitharan	3
S. K. Warne c Atapattu b Zoysa	0	– (7) run out	6
J. N. Gillespie lbw b Muralitharan	41	– absent hurt	
C. R. Miller c Atapattu b Muralitharan	0	– (8) b Vaas	8
G. D. McGrath not out	4	– (9) not out	10
N-b 4	4	B 6, l-b 5, w 1, n-b 4	16

1/0 (1) 2/4 (2) 3/9 (3) 4/16 (4)   188   1/37 (2) 2/49 (3) 3/49 (4)   140
5/40 (5) 6/59 (7) 7/60 (8)   4/49 (1) 5/58 (6) 6/75 (7)
8/167 (9) 9/171 (10) 10/188 (6)   7/99 (8) 8/140 (5)

Bowling: *First Innings*—Vaas 16–2–43–3; Zoysa 13–2–38–3; Muralitharan 25.1–4–63–4; Jayasuriya 5–0–5–0; Chandana 8–1–39–0. *Second Innings*—Vaas 15–7–15–3; Zoysa 10–3–28–0; de Silva 3–0–5–0; Muralitharan 26–5–65–3; Jayasuriya 4–1–7–0; Chandana 2.2–0–9–1.

Sri Lanka

*S. T. Jayasuriya lbw b McGrath	18	– c sub (M. L. Hayden) b Miller	18
M. S. Atapattu c Langer b Miller	25	– c Blewett b McGrath	0
R. P. Arnold lbw b Miller	19		
P. A. de Silva c Ponting b Warne	78	– not out	31
D. P. M. D. Jayawardene c Ponting b Warne	46	– c Slater b Miller	9
A. Ranatunga c Healy b Warne	4	– not out	19
†R. S. Kaluwitharana b Miller	9	– (3) b Miller	5
U. D. U. Chandana c sub (M. L. Hayden) b Warne	12		
W. P. U. J. C. Vaas not out	2		
D. N. T. Zoysa c Miller b Warne	7		
M. Muralitharan c McGrath b Miller	0		
B 4, l-b 7, n-b 3	14	B 8, l-b 2, n-b 3	13

1/22 (1) 2/69 (3) 3/70 (2) 4/177 (5)   234   1/12 (2) 2/24 (1)   (4 wkts) 95
5/181 (6) 6/197 (7) 7/223 (8)   3/39 (3) 4/60 (5)
8/226 (4) 9/234 (10) 10/234 (11)

Bowling: *First Innings*—McGrath 18–5–66–1; Gillespie 12–2–43–0; Miller 20.3–6–62–4; Warne 16–4–52–5. *Second Innings*—McGrath 7–2–19–1; Miller 13–2–48–3; Warne 6.5–3–18–0.

Umpires: S. Venkataraghavan (India) and P. T. Manuel.
Referee: C. W. Smith (West Indies).

At Maitland Crescent, Colombo, September 17, 18, 19. Australians won by 247 runs. Toss: Sri Lankan Board XI. Australians 226 (J. L. Langer 47, S. M. Katich 40, I. A. Healy 32; K. R. Pushpakumara five for 37) and 296 for five dec. (M. J. Slater 119, M. E. Waugh 43, S. M. Katich 36 not out); Sri Lankan Board XI 185 (L. P. C. Silva 66, A. S. A. Perera 46; D. W. Fleming four for 40, S. A. Muller five for 64) and 90 (H. A. P. W. Jayawardene 40; D. W. Fleming three for 25).

Muller, who had flown out to replace Gillespie, took a wicket with his first ball.

SRI LANKA v AUSTRALIA

Second Test Match

At Galle, September 22, 23, 24, 25, 26. Drawn. Toss: Sri Lanka. Test debut: R. Herath.

With Muralitharan's deceptive spinners still causing profound embarrassment, Australia received a "get out of jail free" card when rain limited play on the last three days to little more than two hours. One full day should have been enough for a dominant Sri Lanka to apply more pressure on the Australians' brittle batting and clinch the series.

Steve Waugh defied medical advice and four broken bones in his nose to lead Australia. Having decided against fielding in a helmet, he also took up his normal position in the gully instead of the safer option of mid-on. There was instant jubilation for the Australians when McGrath had Jayasuriya caught at second slip by Mark Waugh with the first ball of the match. But overall it was a mixed day for them, despite more vintage bowling from Warne. Sri Lanka were 254 for six by stumps; again, de Silva, batting three and a half hours for 64, was their mainstay.

Next morning, Vaas advanced to a breezy 41 which ended when he tried to slog his third boundary in four balls. As the ball flew up in the air and Ponting took the catch, Fleming continued directly down the pitch and firmly brushed Vaas with his right shoulder before turning to celebrate with his team-mates. Referee Cammie Smith conducted a hearing but refused to disclose what action he had taken; the ICC confirmed that Fleming was fined half his match fee.

Replying to Sri Lanka's eventual total of 296, Slater and Blewett appeared to put Australia in a sound position with an opening stand of 138 – only the third, and the highest, century partnership for Australia's first wicket in 40 Tests. Blewett, Slater's opening partner since the Caribbean Tests, hit only his second half-century in his last 20 innings, but their good work was undone after tea when Muralitharan exploited a pitch aiding turn with a wicket-to-wicket spell of five for 22 in 13.1 overs. Slater missed his 13th Test century by four, his sixth score in the nineties.

Not even the weather could disguise the ineptitude of Australia's batting. On the third day, which was restricted to a late final session after heavy overnight rain, they lost their remaining five wickets inside an hour to be all out for 228, 68 behind on first innings. This time it was Sri Lanka's debutant left-arm finger-spinner, Rangana Herath, who did the damage. Having begun the day with nought for 78, he now claimed four for 19 from 6.3 overs and demonstrated a wonderful delivery, bowled out of the front of his hand, which turned back into right-handers.

In the event, it was all to little avail. The fourth day was washed out completely and only 18 minutes' play was possible on the fifth before another tropical storm flooded the ground. Sri Lanka, 55 without loss and leading by 123, could reflect on what they might have achieved; Australia had fewer reasons to be cheerful, other than the fact that the series remained open.

Man of the Match: M. J. Slater.

Close of play: First day, Sri Lanka 254-6 (Kaluwitharana 24*, Vaas 14*); Second day, Australia 188-5 (S. R. Waugh 2*, Ponting 0*); Third day, Sri Lanka 44-0 (Jayasuriya 19*, Atapattu 21*); Fourth day, No play.

Sri Lanka

*S. T. Jayasuriya c M. E. Waugh b McGrath	0	– not out	21
M. S. Atapattu c Healy b Warne	29	– not out	28
R. P. Arnold c Warne b Miller	50		
P. A. de Silva c S. R. Waugh b Fleming	64		
D. P. M. D. Jayawardene c Blewett b Warne	46		
A. Ranatunga c Miller b Warne	10		
†R. S. Kaluwitharana b McGrath	25		
W. P. U. J. C. Vaas c Ponting b Fleming	41		
R. Herath run out	3		
D. N. T. Zoysa c M. E. Waugh b McGrath	1		
M. Muralitharan not out	7		
B 4, l-b 8, n-b 8	20	L-b 3, n-b 3	6

1/0 (1) 2/80 (2) 3/100 (3) 4/193 (5)   296   (no wkt) 55
5/206 (6) 6/226 (4) 7/262 (7)
8/288 (8) 9/288 (9) 10/296 (10)

Bowling: *First Innings*—McGrath 26.5–7–81–3; Fleming 23–6–74–2; Miller 23–1–72–1; Warne 25–11–29–3; Ponting 4–1–7–0; M. E. Waugh 2–1–9–0; Blewett 3–0–12–0. *Second Innings*—McGrath 7–2–23–0; Fleming 4–0–15–0; Miller 3–1–9–0; Warne 3.2–1–5–0.

Australia

M. J. Slater st Kaluwitharana b Muralitharan		S. K. Warne c Atapattu b Herath	0
G. S. Blewett b Muralitharan	96	D. W. Fleming b Herath	16
J. L. Langer c Ranatunga b Muralitharan	62	C. R. Miller run out	6
M. E. Waugh c Ranatunga	7	G. D. McGrath not out	0
b Muralitharan	10	B 1, l-b 4, n-b 2	7
*S. R. Waugh c Kaluwitharana b Herath	19		
†I. A. Healy c Jayawardene		1/138 (2) 2/160 (3) 3/179 (1)	228
b Muralitharan	4	4/182 (4) 5/188 (6) 6/189 (7)	
R. T. Ponting c Ranatunga b Herath	1	7/189 (8) 8/215 (9)	
		9/228 (10) 10/228 (5)	

Bowling: Vaas 9–3–31–0; Zoysa 6–1–9–0; Herath 34.3–6–97–4; Muralitharan 38–10–71–5; Jayasuriya 9–1–15–0.

Umpires: D. B. Cowie (New Zealand) and B. C. Cooray.
Referee: C. W. Smith (West Indies).

SRI LANKA v AUSTRALIA

Third Test Match

At Sinhalese Sports Club, Colombo, September 30, October 1, 2, 3, 4. Drawn. Toss: Australia.

Rain dominated the final Test to such an extent that commentator David Hookes, the former Test batsman, wanted to present the match award to the overworked Super Sopper. That the game began at all was a miracle, and there was never a realistic chance of a result. Nevertheless, it was Australia's best Test and they dominated Sri Lanka from the time Steve Waugh won the toss.

Slater and Blewett again opened with a hundred partnership, putting on 126 on a pitch that was underprepared because of the bad weather. The ball began to jump and turn sharply from the first day. Australia had not managed a century opening stand in consecutive Tests since November 1995, against Pakistan, and not in consecutive innings since January that same year, against England, 50 Tests before this one. Slater was involved in each instance, though his partner then was Mark Taylor.

Slater was first out, once more a victim of his own impetuosity, advancing to push the modest off-spin of Arnold into the covers and being stumped for 59. It was a replica of his dismissal by Muralitharan in the previous Test. By the close, Australia were well set at 203 for four but, because of the rain, it would take Ponting three days to compile the only hundred of the series. Unbeaten on 105 when Australia were bowled out for 342, he struck 11 fours in three and three-quarter hours.

Jayasuriya created a small piece of history on the fourth day, which saw just 91 minutes of play. He was out to the first ball of the innings, again to McGrath, for the second time in successive Tests: a sad end to a bitter-sweet series for him. He became the first Sri Lankan captain to win a Test series against Australia, yet scored just 57 runs in three Tests at 14.25. Sri Lanka collapsed to ten for three, thanks to a brilliant opening spell from Fleming, and were 61 for four when the final day was completely washed out.

Man of the Match: R. T. Ponting.   *Man of the Series:* R. T. Ponting.

Close of play: First day, Australia 203-4 (S. R. Waugh 10*, Ponting 11*); Second day, Australia 318-7 (Ponting 90*, Fleming 23*); Third day, Australia 342; Fourth day, Sri Lanka 61-4 (de Silva 19*, Ranatunga 1*).

Australia

G. S. Blewett c Atapattu b Herath	70	C. R. Miller lbw b Vaas		0
M. J. Slater st Kaluwitharana b Arnold	59	G. D. McGrath c Atapattu b Vaas		0
J. L. Langer c Ranatunga b Muralitharan	32			
M. E. Waugh c Arnold b Muralitharan	13	N-b 10		10
*S. R. Waugh c Kaluwitharana b Herath	14			
R. T. Ponting not out	105			342
†I. A. Healy c Jayawardene b Vaas	7	1/126 (2) 2/147 (1) 3/182 (4)		
S. K. Warne lbw b Vaas	0	4/183 (3) 5/221 (5) 6/253 (7)		
D. W. Fleming c Atapattu b Muralitharan	32	7/255 (8) 8/335 (9)		
		9/342 (10) 10/342 (11)		

Bowling: Vaas 23.4–5–54–4; Zoysa 10–4–23–0; Herath 35–10–98–2; Muralitharan 52–5–150–3; Jayasuriya 9–2–14–0; Arnold 7–4–3–1.

Sri Lanka

*S. T. Jayasuriya c Warne b McGrath	0	A. Ranatunga not out		1
M. S. Atapattu c Healy b Fleming	2			
R. P. Arnold lbw b Fleming	0	B 8, l-b 1, w 5, n-b 4		18
P. A. de Silva not out	19			
D. P. M. D. Jayawardene c Healy b Fleming	21	1/0 (1) 2/7 (2)	(4 wkts)	61
		3/10 (3) 4/60 (5)		

†R. S. Kaluwitharana, W. P. U. J. C. Vaas, R. Herath, D. N. T. Zoysa and M. Muralitharan did not bat.

Bowling: McGrath 10–3–25–1; Fleming 5.5–0–14–3; Warne 5–1–11–0; Miller 1–0–2–0.

Umpires: P. Willey (England) and K. T. Francis.
Referee: C. W. Smith (West Indies).

At Queens Sports Club, Bulawayo, October 9, 10, 11. Australians won by 244 runs. Toss: ZCU President's XI. Australians 335 for seven dec. (J. L. Langer 148, M. E. Waugh 63; J. A. Rennie three for 72) and 304 for five dec. (S. R. Waugh 161, M. E. Waugh 116); ZCU President's XI 219 (T. R. Gripper 59, T. N. Madondo 59, E. A. Brandes 30, Extras 41; G. D. McGrath five for 36, D. W. Fleming three for 41) and 176 (G. A. Lamb 47, J. A. Rennie 50; D. W. Fleming three for 16, S. K. Warne three for 50).

In their second innings, the Australians lost both openers for one run before the Waugh twins added 254 for the third wicket.

ZIMBABWE v AUSTRALIA

Inaugural Test Match

At Harare, October 14, 15, 16, 17. Australia won by ten wickets. Toss: Zimbabwe. Test debut: T. R. Gripper.

Seven years had passed since Zimbabwe's elevation to Test status but their long overdue first Test against Australia never looked like becoming a David and Goliath story. In the end, Australia required only five runs for a remarkably easy victory, and they managed those within an over with more than a day to spare.

After their disappointing tour of Sri Lanka, the Australians ruthlessly set about restoring cricket's pecking order, beginning with an unsettling display of fast bowling. Zimbabwe's captain, Campbell, was left to rue his decision to bat first on a pitch that Steve Waugh said he would have been bowled on had he won the toss. Zimbabwe had tumbled to 37 for four in the 19th over before Johnson and the dour Andy Flower, who occupied more than two and a half hours scoring 28, added 70 for the fifth wicket. Johnson, top scorer with a spirited 75, clubbed a four and a six off successive balls from Warne to rekindle memories of his World Cup century against Australia, when he hit Warne for four fours in an over. But these were fleeting high points: Zimbabwe were dismissed for 194 on the first evening.

In circumstances that might have been designed for him, Mark Waugh took the opportunity to revive his flagging career as Australia took control next day. Arriving in the second over of the morning, with his side an embarrassing seven for two, he ran up his best score in 14 Test innings – 90 in three and a half hours, with 13 fours. When he passed 78, Waugh overtook Neil Harvey's 6,149 Test runs to become Australia's seventh highest run-scorer.

But it was his brother who ensured that only one team could win. By the time Steve Waugh had finished with Zimbabwe's bowlers on the third day, Australia had amassed a devastatingly unspectacular 422, a first-innings lead of 228, and Waugh, unbeaten on 151, had joined the exclusive 20-Test-century club as the 17th member, three days after the 16th, Sachin Tendulkar. He batted for seven hours and 14 minutes, and faced 352 balls for 18 fours. Olonga dropped Waugh on the second day, when he was only 39, and the usually reliable Grant Flower spilled a straightforward chance at point a day later, when he was 94. On both occasions the unlucky bowler was Streak, who in spite of these misfortunes snared five for 93.

Fleming also had two lives as he helped his captain add 114 in 134 minutes for the eighth wicket. A tailender with a good eye, using much the same technique for cricket and golf, he reached his second fifty in 13 Tests in just 55 balls, with ten boundaries, before deciding to play like a batsman. He then used up another 39 balls scoring 15, without another four.

Zimbabwe seemed capable of better things at their second attempt, when they ground their way to 200 for two. But they could not sustain the fight, and lost their last eight in a spectacular collapse for 32 runs in 25 overs. McGrath and Miller bowled economically for three wickets each, while Warne cleaned up the tail and finally claimed Goodwin, caught at cover off a wide long-hop, in a spell of three for nought in 13 balls. Goodwin fell nine short of his century after five and a half hours. The match would prove to be the last of Healy's 119 Tests for Australia.

Man of the Match: S. R. Waugh.

Close of play: First day, Australia 6-0 (Slater 4*, Blewett 1*); Second day, Australia 275-5 (S. R. Waugh 90*, Healy 5*); Third day, Zimbabwe 80-1 (Gripper 25*, Goodwin 11*).

Zimbabwe

G. J. Rennie c Ponting b McGrath	18	–	(4) c McGrath b Miller		23
G. W. Flower c Ponting b Fleming	1	–	lbw b McGrath		32
M. W. Goodwin run out	0	–	c S. R. Waugh b Warne		91
*A. D. R. Campbell c Slater b Fleming	5	–	(5) run out		1
†A. Flower c M. E. Waugh b McGrath	28	–	(6) c Healy b McGrath		0
N. C. Johnson c M. E. Waugh b McGrath	75	–	(7) c M. E. Waugh b McGrath		5
T. R. Gripper lbw b Warne	4	–	(1) lbw b Miller		60
H. H. Streak c M. E. Waugh b Warne	3	–	(9) lbw b Warne		0
G. J. Whittall c Healy b Warne	27	–	(8) c M. E. Waugh b Warne		2
B. C. Strang run out	17	–	c Langer b Miller		0
H. K. Olonga not out	0	–	not out		0
B 2, l-b 4, n-b 10	16		B 9, l-b 2, w 1, n-b 6		18

1/6 (2) 2/6 (3) 3/22 (4) 4/37 (1)   194   1/56 (2) 2/154 (1) 3/200 (4)   232
5/107 (5) 6/119 (6) 7/125 (8)   4/208 (5) 5/211 (6) 6/220 (7)
8/165 (9) 9/190 (6) 10/194 (10)   7/227 (8) 8/227 (9)
9/232 (10) 10/232 (3)

Bowling: *First Innings*—McGrath 23–7–44–3; Fleming 15–6–22–2; Miller 19–6–36–0; Warne 23–2–69–3; Ponting 1–1–0–0; S. R. Waugh 4–1–17–0. *Second Innings*—McGrath 31–12–46–3; Fleming 21–6–31–0; Miller 34–10–66–3; Ponting 1–1–0–0; Warne 30.1–11–68–3; Blewett 5–1–10–0.

Australia

M. J. Slater c A. Flower b Strang	4	– (2) not out	0
G. S. Blewett c Campbell b Streak	1	– (1) not out	4
J. L. Langer run out	44		
M. E. Waugh c and b G. W. Flower	90		
*S. R. Waugh not out	151		
R. T. Ponting c Johnson b Streak	31		
†I. A. Healy c A. Flower b Strang	5		
S. K. Warne c A. Flower b Streak	6		
D. W. Fleming lbw b Streak	65		
C. R. Miller c Johnson b Streak	2		
G. D. McGrath c Johnson b Whittall	13		
L-b 5, w 4, n-b 1	10	W 1	1
	422	(no wkt)	**5**

1/6 (2) 2/7 (1) 3/96 (3) 4/174 (4)
5/253 (6) 6/275 (7) 7/282 (8)
8/396 (9) 9/398 (10) 10/422 (11)

Bowling: *First Innings*—Olonga 17–1–83–0; Streak 34–8–93–5; Strang 44–14–96–2; Johnson 2–0–14–0; Whittall 21.4–3–74–1; G. W. Flower 18–3–38–1; Gripper 3–0–19–0. *Second Innings*—Strang 0.4–0–5–0.

Umpires: G. Sharp (England) and I. D. Robinson.
Referee: G. R. Viswanath (India).

†ZIMBABWE v AUSTRALIA

First One-Day International

At Bulawayo, October 21. Australia won by 83 runs. Toss: Zimbabwe.

The last one-day encounter between these sides was their World Cup game at Lord's four months earlier, and there were several striking instances of *déjà vu*. Once more, Australia were asked to bat and, led by another century from Mark Waugh, responded with the same total, 303. Again, Johnson, Zimbabwe's free-flowing left-hander, replied with his own hundred in a losing cause, hitting 12 fours and two sixes. But whereas other Australians had joined Waugh in the run-feast, Johnson played a lone hand. Zimbabwe's next highest score was 27. Waugh's 106, his 13th one-day century, came from 97 balls, with 11 fours and two sixes, while Martyn completed the Australian innings with 57 in 38 balls.

Man of the Match: M. E. Waugh.

Australia

M. E. Waugh run out	106	A. Symonds c G. W. Flower b Blignaut	1
†A. C. Gilchrist c G. W. Flower b Mutendera	14	T. M. Moody not out	3
R. T. Ponting st A. Flower b Brent	67	L-b 5, w 10, n-b 1	16
M. G. Bevan st A. Flower b Brent	25		
*S. R. Waugh c Johnson b A. R. Whittall	14	1/39 2/198 3/201 (6 wkts, 50 overs)	303
D. R. Martyn not out	57	4/223 5/280 6/292	

S. K. Warne, D. W. Fleming and G. D. McGrath did not bat.

Bowling: Mutendera 8–0–42–1; Brent 10–0–63–2; Blignaut 10–0–60–1; A. R. Whittall 10–0–57–1; G. J. Whittall 5–0–31–0; G. W. Flower 7–0–45–0.

Zimbabwe

N. C. Johnson c Ponting b Fleming	110	G. B. Brent c M. E. Waugh		
G. W. Flower c Gilchrist b Fleming	0		b McGrath	5
M. W. Goodwin c Martyn b Symonds	19	A. R. Whittall c M. E. Waugh b Warne		2
*A. D. R. Campbell c Ponting		D. T. Mutendera not out		0
b Symonds	6			
†A. Flower st Gilchrist b Warne	11	B 4, l-b 4, w 4, n-b 4		16
G. J. Rennie run out	22			
G. J. Whittall lbw b Fleming	2	1/7 2/69 3/77	(43.4 overs)	220
A. M. Blignaut c M. E. Waugh		4/106 5/162 6/180		
b Symonds	27	7/201 8/212 9/220		

Bowling: McGrath 6.4–0–21–1; Fleming 8–1–33–3; Moody 5–0–30–0; Symonds 8–0–52–3; M. E. Waugh 3–0–14–0; Warne 9–1–40–2; Bevan 4–0–22–0.

Umpires: G. R. Evans and R. B. Tiffin.

†ZIMBABWE v AUSTRALIA

Second One-Day International

At Harare, October 23. Australia won by nine wickets. Toss: Australia.

Zimbabwe's batting was embarrassed to such an extent that Steve Waugh briefly lined up all nine fieldsmen in an arc from slips to point, probably a first in one-day cricket. The home side had crashed to 98 for nine in Fleming's final over, the 33rd of the innings, and No. 11 Mutendera had just come in when Waugh gradually called his players into the cordon. Fleming finished with three for 14, which included three wides and a no-ball, from his ten overs. Needing a mere 117, Australia lost only Gilchrist as they won with more than 21 overs to spare. Mark Waugh led the way again, with an unbeaten fifty.

Man of the Match: D. W. Fleming.

Zimbabwe

*A. D. R. Campbell c M. E. Waugh		J. A. Rennie c Gilchrist b Fleming	5
b Dale	5	A. R. Whittall c Ponting b Fleming	0
N. C. Johnson c Ponting b Fleming	2	D. T. Mutendera b Symonds	10
T. N. Madondo c Warne b Moody	29		
†A. Flower b Dale	0	L-b 9, w 5, n-b 2	16
G. W. Flower c Gilchrist b Martyn	17		
M. W. Goodwin c Gilchrist b Martyn	11	1/9 2/10 3/10	(37.3 overs) 116
G. J. Rennie c Gilchrist b Moody	0	4/63 5/71 6/75	
A. M. Blignaut not out	21	7/75 8/87 9/98	

Bowling: Fleming 10–4–14–3; Dale 9–3–24–2; Moody 7–1–25–2; Symonds 3.3–0–23–1; Martyn 8–1–21–2.

Australia

†A. C. Gilchrist c Johnson b Blignaut	18
M. E. Waugh not out	54
R. T. Ponting not out	31
L-b 5, w 5, n-b 4	14

1/31	(1 wkt, 28.3 overs) 117

M. G. Bevan, *S. R. Waugh, D. R. Martyn, A. Symonds, T. M. Moody, S. K. Warne, D. W. Fleming and A. C. Dale did not bat.

Bowling: J. A. Rennie 8.3–2–31–0; Mutendera 10–2–40–0; Blignaut 6–0–24–1; Whittall 4–0–17–0.

Umpires: K. C. Barbour and I. D. Robinson.

†ZIMBABWE v AUSTRALIA

Third One-Day International

At Harare, October 24. Australia won by nine wickets. Toss: Australia.

A spirited 99 not out from Andy Flower could not prevent Australia from cruising to another nine-wicket victory and a clean sweep in the three-match series. Mark Waugh was rested, but Ponting stepped up to finish his great tour of Sri Lanka and Zimbabwe with an unbeaten 87, adding 157 with Bevan. Flower's brave innings was all the more impressive given his lack of support. In 109 balls, he hit seven fours and concluded with two sixes off Symonds in the final over. Steve Waugh had left himself an over short when he bowled out McGrath and Dale, and Symonds's last over cost 20: Flower scored 15 of them. It made little difference as Australia coasted home with 11 overs in hand.

Man of the Match: A. Flower.

Zimbabwe

*A. D. R. Campbell b McGrath	18	G. B. Brent lbw b Moody	0
N. C. Johnson c Warne b McGrath	5	A. R. Whittall run out	1
T. N. Madondo c Gilchrist b Moody	6	D. T. Mutendera not out	8
†A. Flower not out	99	L-b 7, w 6, n-b 4	17
G. W. Flower c Martyn b Symonds	21		
M. W. Goodwin c Symonds b Warne	14	1/24 2/29 3/38	(9 wkts, 50 overs) 200
A. M. Blignaut c Bevan b Warne	1	4/81 5/120 6/125	
J. A. Rennie run out	10	7/154 8/156 9/167	

Bowling: McGrath 10–4–18–2; Dale 10–0–35–0; Moody 10–2–34–2; Symonds 8–0–52–1; Warne 10–0–42–2; Martyn 2–0–12–0.

Australia

R. T. Ponting not out	87
†A. C. Gilchrist c A. Flower b Mutendera	28
M. G. Bevan not out	77
L-b 3, w 6	9
1/44 (1 wkt, 39 overs)	201

D. S. Lehmann, *S. R. Waugh, D. R. Martyn, A. Symonds, T. M. Moody, S. K. Warne, A. C. Dale and G. D. McGrath did not bat.

Bowling: Rennie 6–1–46–0; Mutendera 6–0–42–1; Blignaut 6–1–25–0; Whittall 8–0–30–0; Brent 10–1–44–0; G. W. Flower 3–0–11–0.

Umpires: I. D. Robinson and R. B. Tiffin.
Series referee: G. R. Viswanath (India).

THE NEW ZEALANDERS IN INDIA, 1999-2000

By DICKY RUTNAGUR

With the pitches slow, the cricket in this series was largely attritional and did little to restore the falling popularity of Test cricket in a country where, before India's World Cup success in 1983, Test match tickets sold at a premium. A deplorable pitch at Kanpur provided the springboard from which India leapt to victory in the Second Test, but while they also had the better of the Mohali and Ahmedabad Tests, both were drawn. So were two of the New Zealanders' other first-class games. They lost the third, to the Ranji Trophy champions, Karnataka.

Where India had the edge was in the sheer weight of runs accumulated by their top order, the bulk of them, 435 at 108.75, coming from Sachin Tendulkar, who eschewed flamboyance and daredevilry to fulfil his responsibility as captain. The new opening partnership of Devang Gandhi, making his Test debut, and Sadagoppan Ramesh was consistent, Sourav Ganguly was productive and entertaining, and Rahul Dravid played an exquisite innings of 144 in the second innings of the First Test at Mohali. Put in on a pitch containing some moisture, India had been routed for a paltry 83. They responded to the shock of this débâcle by piling up a big score in the second innings, and they batted in the following Tests as if chastened by the initial experience.

New Zealand's batting never came to terms with the slow pitches and each time, except in their final innings of the series, it suffered from the openers' failure to lay a foundation. No one recorded a century on their behalf (the Indians compiled five) and only Stephen Fleming, the captain, finished with an average higher than 40 (52.20). That said, however, their batsmen were full of fight, and the middle order usually kept the Indian bowlers at bay long enough to prevent them from forcing home their advantage.

Neither side's attack was razor sharp. India were heavily dependent on Javagal Srinath and Anil Kumble, who took 13 and 20 wickets respectively, while the other seven bowlers managed only 16 between them. Even so, Kumble gathered half his aggregate at Kanpur, where the bounce of the pitch was horrendously erratic, and Srinath captured six wickets in the first innings of the opening Test. Thereafter, his effectiveness was dulled by the lack of pace in the pitches and, no less, from being overworked.

Not surprisingly, considering the nature of the pitches, slow left-armer Daniel Vettori was New Zealand's main wicket-taker. He took six for 127 in India's first innings at Kanpur, but 12 wickets were an inadequate return from 191.3 overs in the series. He was the best finger-spinner on either side, impressing with his variations of pace and flight and his subtle use of the crease, so it was a pity that often, and sometimes for long periods, he bowled negatively from over the wicket into the rough outside leg stump. Still only 20, Vettori left India's shores with sore fingers and an aching body, but a better bowler for the experience of jousting with some of the best players of spin.

The pitches reduced New Zealand's strike bowlers, Chris Cairns and Dion Nash, to workhorses. Nash started off with a bag of six wickets, but could scrape up only two more in the series, while Cairns had to be content with five. However, they bowled with immense discipline in a containing role, as did Nathan Astle, who delivered his 79 overs with commendable economy. The quality of fielding on both sides was variable, more unexpectedly on New Zealand's part considering the standard achieved in England a few months earlier. Missed chances cost them dearly in every Test.

India also won the series of five one-day internationals, though it stayed open until the final encounter. The high point was provided by Tendulkar and Dravid, whose second-wicket partnership of 331 at Hyderabad set a world record for any wicket in one-day internationals.

NEW ZEALAND TOURING PARTY

S. P. Fleming (Canterbury) (*captain*), N. J. Astle (Canterbury), M. D. Bell (Wellington), C. L. Cairns (Canterbury), C. J. Drum (Auckland), C. Z. Harris (Canterbury), M. J. Horne (Otago), C. D. McMillan (Canterbury), D. J. Nash (Auckland), S. B. O'Connor (Otago), A. C. Parore (Auckland), A. J. Penn (Central Districts), C. M. Spearman (Central Districts), D. L. Vettori (Northern Districts), P. J. Wiseman (Otago).

G. R. Stead (Canterbury) replaced McMillan, who returned home injured. R. G. Twose (Wellington) and S. B. Styris (Northern Districts) replaced Bell, Penn and Wiseman for the one-day series; A. R. Tait (Northern Districts) replaced Nash, who returned home injured.

Manager: J. J. Crowe.　　　*Coach:* D. G. Trist.

NEW ZEALAND TOUR RESULTS

Test matches – Played 3: Lost 1, Drawn 2.
First-class matches – Played 6: Lost 2, Drawn 4.
Losses – India, Karnataka.
Draws – India (2), India A, Board President's XI.
One-day internationals – Played 5: Won 2, Lost 3.

TEST MATCH AVERAGES

INDIA – BATTING

	T	I	NO	R	HS	100s	50s	Avge	Ct
S. R. Tendulkar	3	6	2	435	217	2	0	108.75	2
S. C. Ganguly	3	5	1	244	125	1	2	61.00	6
D. J. Gandhi	3	5	1	200	88	0	2	50.00	2
S. Ramesh.	3	6	0	287	110	1	0	47.83	5
R. Dravid	3	6	0	239	144	1	0	39.83	3
J. Srinath.	3	4	2	72	33*	0	0	36.00	0
A. Kumble	3	3	1	39	27*	0	0	19.50	2
M. S. K. Prasad	3	4	1	54	19	0	0	18.00	5

Played in two Tests: R. V. Bharadwaj 0, 22 (3 ct); Harbhajan Singh 1*; S. B. Joshi 0, 19; B. K. V. Prasad 0. Played in one Test: A. Jadeja 13, 12*.

* *Signifies not out.*

BOWLING

	O	M	R	W	BB	5W/i	Avge
A. Kumble	197.4	76	364	20	6-67	2	18.20
J. Srinath.	134	46	313	13	6-45	1	24.07
S. B. Joshi.	85	33	150	5	2-38	0	30.00
Harbhajan Singh.	88.4	25	196	6	3-33	0	32.66
B. K. V. Prasad.	74	24	168	3	2-52	0	56.00

Also bowled: R. V. Bharadwaj 29.1–7–72–1; R. Dravid 1–1–0–0; S. C. Ganguly 12–1–40–1; S. R. Tendulkar 11–4–30–0.

NEW ZEALAND – BATTING

	T	I	NO	R	HS	100s	50s	Avge	Ct/St
S. P. Fleming	3	6	1	261	73	0	2	52.20	3
N. J. Astle	3	5	0	192	74	0	1	38.40	4
C. M. Spearman	3	6	1	170	54*	0	2	34.00	4
C. L. Cairns	3	5	1	134	72	0	2	33.50	0
A. C. Parore	3	5	1	114	48	0	0	28.50	8/1
D. J. Nash	3	4	2	57	41*	0	0	28.50	2
C. D. McMillan	2	4	0	105	34	0	0	26.25	0
M. J. Horne	3	6	0	90	41	0	0	15.00	0
M. D. Bell.	2	4	0	29	15	0	0	7.25	1
D. L. Vettori	3	4	1	11	8*	0	0	3.66	2
P. J. Wiseman.	2	3	0	3	3	0	0	1.00	0

Played in one Test: C. Z. Harris 12; S. B. O'Connor 2; G. R. Stead 17, 78.

* *Signifies not out.*

BOWLING

	O	M	R	W	BB	5W/i	Avge
D. J. Nash	110	36	279	8	6-27	1	34.87
N. J. Astle.	79	22	177	5	2-27	0	35.40
D. L. Vettori	191.3	42	543	12	6-127	1	45.25
C. L. Cairns	82	22	254	5	2-23	0	50.80

Also bowled: C. Z. Harris 28–3–108–2; C. D. McMillan 2–0–8–0; S. B. O'Connor 25–4–93–2; P. J. Wiseman 58–12–205–2.

Note: Matches in this section which were not first-class are signified by a dagger.

At Pune, September 30, October 1, 2. Drawn. Toss: New Zealanders. New Zealanders 135 for six v India A.
   Rain washed out play on the first and third days, and all but 44 overs of the second.

At Jodhpur, October 5, 6, 7. Drawn. Toss: Board President's XI. Board President's XI 298 (G. K. Khoda 32, P. M. Mullick 67, H. H. Kanitkar 99, S. S. Dighe 32; S. B. O'Connor three for 62, D. J. Nash three for 54) and 79 for four (G. K. Khoda 49); New Zealanders 444 for five dec. (M. J. Horne 85, C. M. Spearman 56, S. P. Fleming 32, C. D. McMillan 168 not out, A. C. Parore 72 not out; Harbhajan Singh four for 91).
   McMillan and Parore shared an unbroken sixth-wicket stand of 212.

INDIA v NEW ZEALAND

First Test Match

At Mohali, October 10, 11, 12, 13, 14. Drawn. Toss: New Zealand. Test debuts: R. V. Bharadwaj, D. J. Gandhi, M. S. K. Prasad.
   Even though 20 wickets fell in less than a day and a half, the match remained unfinished, the principal reason being the steady decline in the pace of the pitch. At the start it contained sufficient

moisture, partly from sweating under the covers, to make batting a trial, and New Zealand reaped a rich dividend from putting India in. A proliferation of damp patches delayed the start by 45 minutes, but the conditions could hardly be blamed for the speed with which India capitulated. Four wickets down for ten runs in six overs, they were all out for 83 in 27, equalling their second-lowest total at home. New Zealand's three seamers had the discipline to exploit a succession of inept shots by the Indians, who were palpably unprepared for a Test match. They had played no first-class cricket earlier in the season, having instead spent the preceding weeks participating in inconsequential one-day tournaments in various parts of the world. Nash bowled outstandingly to capture six for 27, his best figures in Test cricket.

New Zealand also lost their openers quickly, recovered, then faltered again – and that despite a marked improvement in batting conditions on the second day. With Srinath probing away, a model of accuracy in line and length, the last six wickets added just 59 runs.

India's openers wiped off a deficit of 132, although Ramesh, sometimes tentative against balls outside the off stump, could have been caught three times while making 73. His first chance was offered at 17 in a total of 28. Gandhi, in a more sedate innings of 75, survived him for another 25 overs in partnership with Dravid, who batted on and on for a faultless 144 spread over seven hours, during which time he received 327 balls and hit 18 fours. Even before the second-wicket partnership was broken in the 88th over, when India were still less than 50 ahead, Vettori was bowling from over the wicket.

Off the first ball Tendulkar received, bowled by Astle, he survived the first of several appeals for lbw. Out of the game for a month because of back trouble, he played within the limitations imposed by uncertain form, batting steadfastly for more than six and a half hours and completing his 20th Test hundred. When the time came for the offensive, he let first Dravid and then Ganguly head the charge. Dravid made bold to sweep Vettori out of the rough and inevitably paid the penalty. But Vettori's tactic was unavailing against the left-handed Ganguly, who put him to the sword and scored 64 of the last 95 runs off 75 balls.

India became the first Test side to follow being dismissed for under 100 with a second innings of more than 500. They led by 373 and had 135 overs in which to dismiss New Zealand. But while the ball turned, it turned slowly. Thanks mainly to Fleming, who batted almost five and a half hours, and was out to the last ball of the match, New Zealand survived. It might have been different had he been caught 27 minutes before lunch, and McMillan soon after tea, but both were difficult chances close to the wicket. The match entered the final hour with five wickets standing.

Man of the Match: J. Srinath.

Close of play: First day, New Zealand 119-3 (Fleming 38*, Astle 12*); Second day, India 115-0 (Gandhi 52*, Ramesh 58*); Third day, India 303-2 (Dravid 87*, Tendulkar 54*); Fourth day, New Zealand 80-1 (Horne 26*, Spearman 30*).

India

D. J. Gandhi c Parore b Nash	0	– lbw b Astle	75
S. Ramesh b Nash	0	– c and b Vettori	73
R. Dravid c Astle b Cairns	1	– b Vettori	144
*S. R. Tendulkar b O'Connor	18	– not out	126
S. C. Ganguly b Nash	2	– not out	64
R. V. Bharadwaj c Parore b Cairns	0		
†M. S. K. Prasad not out	16		
S. B. Joshi c Spearman b O'Connor	0		
A. Kumble c Spearman b Nash	7		
J. Srinath c Astle b Nash	20		
B. K. V. Prasad c Fleming b Nash	0		
B 8, l-b 5, n-b 6	19	B 9, l-b 7, n-b 7	23

1/2 (2) 2/3 (3) 3/7 (1) 4/10 (5)   83   1/137 (2) 2/181 (1)   (3 wkts dec.) 505
5/22 (6) 6/38 (4) 7/38 (8)   3/410 (3)
8/53 (9) 9/83 (10) 10/83 (11)

Bowling: *First Innings*—Cairns 9–4–23–2; Nash 11–3–27–6; O'Connor 7–1–20–2. *Second Innings*—Cairns 24–3–76–0; Nash 37–16–79–0; Vettori 71–24–171–2; O'Connor 18–3–73–0; Astle 31–8–82–1; McMillan 2–0–8–0.

New Zealand

M. J. Horne c Ganguly b Srinath	6	– c Ganguly b Joshi	33
M. D. Bell b Srinath	0	– lbw b Srinath	7
C. M. Spearman c and b Kumble	51	– c Ganguly b Joshi	35
*S. P. Fleming lbw b Srinath	43	– c Ganguly b Kumble	73
N. J. Astle c Kumble b Srinath	45	– c M. S. K. Prasad b Srinath	34
C. D. McMillan lbw b Joshi	22	– c Ramesh b Kumble	18
†A. C. Parore not out	13	– c Gandhi b Kumble	7
C. L. Cairns b B. K. V. Prasad	7	– not out	0
D. J. Nash c M. S. K. Prasad b Srinath	2		
D. L. Vettori b Srinath	0		
S. B. O'Connor c Gandhi b Bharadwaj	2		
B 5, l-b 11, n-b 8	24	B 24, l-b 15, n-b 5	44

1/7 (2) 2/8 (1) 3/99 (3) 4/156 (4)   215
5/179 (5) 6/181 (6) 7/199 (8)
8/207 (9) 9/212 (10) 10/215 (11)

1/24 (2) 2/95 (1)   (7 wkts) 251
3/108 (3) 4/186 (5)
5/227 (6) 6/246 (7) 7/251 (4)

Bowling: *First Innings*—Srinath 22–9–45–6; B. K. V. Prasad 19–6–56–1; Ganguly 1–0–1–0; Kumble 18–3–49–1; Bharadwaj 14.1–4–26–1; Joshi 17–8–22–1. *Second Innings*—Srinath 31–9–63–2; B. K. V. Prasad 16–7–24–0; Kumble 41–19–42–3; Joshi 28–12–38–2; Bharadwaj 13–3–34–0; Tendulkar 6–2–11–0.

Umpires: P. T. Manuel (Sri Lanka) and S. Venkataraghavan.
Referee: R. S. Madugalle (Sri Lanka).

At Bangalore, October 17, 18, 19. Karnataka (Ranji Trophy Champions) won by seven wickets. Toss: Karnataka. New Zealanders 249 for six dec. (S. P. Fleming 115 not out, N. J. Astle 58; M. A. Khan three for 56) and 105 (N. J. Astle 33; D. Ganesh three for 41, S. B. Joshi four for 17); Karnataka 269 for nine dec. (J. Arun Kumar 31, R. V. Bharadwaj 96, V. S. T. Naidu 52, Extras 36; C. J. Drum four for 19, P. J. Wiseman three for 99) and 86 for three (R. V. Bharadwaj 33 not out).

INDIA v NEW ZEALAND

Second Test Match

At Kanpur, October 22, 23, 24, 25. India won by eight wickets. Toss: New Zealand.
As if the pitch's appearance was not tell-tale enough, India's inclusion of an extra spinner, Harbhajan Singh, in place of a seam bowler, Venkatesh Prasad, confirmed the belief that it would break up sooner rather than later. New Zealand also excluded a seamer, O'Connor, to make room for a second spinner in Wiseman.
If the groundsman, by shaving the pitch and leaving it underprepared, had bestowed on India an advantage that the uncommitted spectator might consider unfair, providence attempted to redress the balance by favouring New Zealand with the toss. They squandered their good fortune, conceding four wickets before lunch through poor batting, and only the determination of the lower middle order saw the innings into the second day. Kumble took the bowling honours with four for 67, but Srinath's performance in taking three top-order wickets for 62 was more distinguished.
New Zealand's recovery was wasted by indifferent bowling and two significant missed catches. Gandhi and Ramesh were allowed to add 103 between lunch and tea on a pitch that had already become uneven in pace and bounce. Gandhi, who batted four hours for 88, with 14 fours and a six, was dropped at silly point when only four; Ramesh was missed at slip, off Vettori, when 48.
On the third morning, however, Vettori bowled with flair, accuracy and craft, while the seamers kept the batsmen on a tight rein. Run-getting was reduced to a crawl, but the contest was always absorbing. He removed Tendulkar and Ganguly with successive balls, though an over apart, and soon afterwards ended a tidy three and a quarter hours by Dravid. A frustrated Tendulkar, who scored 15 off 54 balls, holed out; a ball that "stopped" did for Ganguly; Dravid was defeated by

one that turned to take the edge. India were still behind at this stage, albeit by a single run, but eventually led by 74.

The match seemed nicely poised, but not for long. In the 14 overs left on the third day, Kumble captured three New Zealand wickets, including his 250th in Tests. Night-watchman Nash lasted just one ball. Next morning two more wickets fell in the first five overs while the total reached 33, and even honour in defeat looked to be beyond New Zealand.

However, Fleming fought for 21 overs till he met one from Harbhajan Singh that fizzed and took his bat on the way to silly mid-off. Parore and McMillan, who came in at No. 8 with a broken finger, then batted with composure for the seventh wicket until a dubious lbw decision against McMillan ended the struggle. Parore batted on without taking risks until Cairns was out. Kumble, revelling on the fractious pitch, took six for 67 to gain match figures of ten for 134. A target of 82 was too small for India to be undermined by the loss of two wickets in the first four overs. Tendulkar, rushing to 44 in 39 balls, and Gandhi swiftly bridged the gap to put them one up in the series with a day to spare.

Man of the Match: A. Kumble.

Close of play: First day, New Zealand 217-7 (Cairns 42*, Nash 19*); Second day, India 212-1 (Ramesh 81*, Dravid 29*); Third day, New Zealand 17-3 (Spearman 1*, Fleming 0*).

New Zealand

M. J. Horne c Prasad b Ganguly	5	– lbw b Kumble	3
M. D. Bell lbw b Srinath	15	– lbw b Kumble	7
C. M. Spearman c Ramesh b Kumble	12	– (4) c Tendulkar b Harbhajan Singh	1
*S. P. Fleming b Srinath	2	– (5) c Dravid b Harbhajan Singh	31
N. J. Astle lbw b Srinath	39	– (6) c Bharadwaj b Kumble	0
C. D. McMillan c Ramesh b Joshi	34	– (8) lbw b Kumble	31
†A. C. Parore c Dravid b Kumble	35	– b Harbhajan Singh	48
C. L. Cairns c Tendulkar b Kumble	53	– (9) b Joshi	2
D. J. Nash not out	41	– (3) b Kumble	0
D. L. Vettori c Bharadwaj b Harbhajan Singh	0	– not out	8
P. J. Wiseman c Bharadwaj b Kumble	0	– lbw b Kumble	0
B 7, n-b 13	20	B 5, l-b 9, n-b 10	24

1/7 (1) 2/33 (3) 3/40 (4) 4/50 (2)   256   1/16 (2) 2/16 (3) 3/17 (1)   155
5/112 (6) 6/130 (5) 7/172 (7)   4/28 (4) 5/33 (6) 6/71 (5)
8/255 (8) 9/255 (10) 10/256 (11)   7/128 (8) 8/138 (9)
                                     9/150 (7) 10/155 (11)

Bowling: *First Innings*—Srinath 22–9–62–3; Ganguly 4–0–15–1; Kumble 32.5–12–67–4; Harbhajan Singh 17–6–30–1; Joshi 25–7–63–1; Bharadwaj 2–0–12–0. *Second Innings*—Srinath 9–5–12–0; Ganguly 1–0–2–0; Kumble 26.5–5–67–6; Joshi 15–6–27–1; Harbhajan Singh 15–3–33–3.

India

D. J. Gandhi c Fleming b Astle	88	– not out	31
S. Ramesh c Parore b Astle	83	– b Cairns	5
R. Dravid c Parore b Vettori	48	– lbw b Nash	1
*S. R. Tendulkar c Astle b Vettori	15	– not out	44
S. C. Ganguly c and b Vettori	0		
R. V. Bharadwaj c Spearman b Wiseman	22		
†M. S. K. Prasad c Fleming b Vettori	19		
S. B. Joshi c Bell b Vettori	19		
A. Kumble st Parore b Vettori	5		
J. Srinath c Astle b Wiseman	0		
Harbhajan Singh not out	1		
B 14, l-b 6, n-b 10	30	L-b 1, n-b 1	2

1/162 (1) 2/214 (2) 3/243 (4) 4/246 (5)   330   1/5 (2) 2/7 (3)   (2 wkts) 83
5/255 (3) 6/293 (6) 7/311 (7)
8/321 (8) 9/326 (10) 10/330 (9)

Bowling: *First Innings*—Cairns 16–8–34–0; Nash 22–10–41–0; Vettori 55.1–11–127–6; Wiseman 29–10–81–2; Astle 26–12–27–2. *Second Innings*—Cairns 3–1–10–1; Nash 4–1–11–1; Vettori 6.2–2–22–0; Wiseman 5–0–39–0.

Umpires: D. J. Harper (Australia) and A. V. Jayaprakash.
Referee: R. S. Madugalle (Sri Lanka).

INDIA v NEW ZEALAND

Third Test Match

At Ahmedabad, October 29, 30, 31, November 1, 2. Drawn. Toss: India.

Three of the four previous Tests played on the Motera ground had finished decisively, and more than once its pitches had been rated as "poor". This time the pitch was so firm that it produced one of the most boring draws in recent memory. It became slower and slower by the day.

With the dry atmosphere denying the bowlers any assistance from swing, it took New Zealand the best part of two sessions to exploit Ramesh's vulnerability around the off stump, in which time he compiled his second Test hundred. His wicket, captured by Harris with a subtle variation of angle, was their last success until halfway between lunch and tea on the second day when Ganguly, who made 125 (20 fours), failed to get sufficient carry on a lofted on-drive off Astle. By then, he and Tendulkar had added 281 – breaking the Indian fourth-wicket Test record that they themselves had set at 256 against Sri Lanka two years earlier – and Tendulkar was well on his way to his first Test double-century and highest first-class score. Acquiring steadily over eight and a quarter hours, he may have been slow by his own standards, but few loose balls among 343 escaped punishment. He hit 29 fours.

Yet twice the Indian captain might have been out in the 90s late on the first day. Till then he had refrained from going for bouncers but he was unable to resist the short one that Cairns slipped him in his first over with the second new ball. Astle, running back from second slip, narrowly failed to complete what would have been a stunning catch off a top edge. A run later, there was not much daylight between the ball and Tendulkar's outside edge as he played a forcing shot at Nash. The dramatic effect was heightened by Parore dropping the ball. Tendulkar was eventually out shortly after tea on the second day, magnificently held just off the ground at straightish mid-wicket by Nash from a full-blooded pull at Vettori. The left-arm spinner took four wickets, but in 57 overs conceded 200, and India declared at 583, their highest total against New Zealand.

The tourists lost Horne in negotiating the remains of the day, and three more wickets fell on the third morning. A hardy stand of 70 between Fleming and Astle halted the collapse, and it was a gem of a reverse-swinging ball by Srinath that took Fleming's edge. Astle, batting with immense concentration yet missing no scoring opportunity, stayed until the close, but next morning he met a deadly out-swinger from Venkatesh Prasad before he had his eye in against the new ball. He was seventh out, but the recovery was sustained, Cairns remaining at the heart of it with 72 in four hours. New Zealand's innings lasted 55 minutes beyond lunch, which was long enough to persuade Tendulkar to rest his bowlers before mounting another assault.

India, 275 ahead, increased their lead to 423 with a rush of merry batting that brought up 100 in 93 minutes. Tendulkar declared with time for 13 overs that evening, but Horne and Stead, who had come from New Zealand to replace the injured McMillan, put on 131 in 55 overs before falling in the space of seven balls. These reverses proved to be a minor tremor: Spearman and Fleming shut the door in India's face with an unbroken stand of 121.

Man of the Match: S. R. Tendulkar.   *Man of the Series:* A. Kumble.

Close of play: First day, India 311-3 (Tendulkar 104*, Ganguly 51*); Second day, New Zealand 18-1 (Stead 11*, Vettori 0*); Third day, New Zealand 211-6 (Astle 68*, Cairns 18*); Fourth day, New Zealand 21-0 (Horne 10*, Stead 10*).

India

D. J. Gandhi c Parore b Cairns	6				
S. Ramesh c Spearman b Harris	110	– (1) c Parore b Nash	16
R. Dravid c Parore b Vettori	33	– run out	12
*S. R. Tendulkar c Nash b Vettori	217	– (2) c Cairns	15
S. C. Ganguly c Nash b Astle	125	– (4) b Harris	53
A. Jadeja b Vettori	13	– (7) not out	12
†M. S. K. Prasad b Vettori	2	– c Parore b Astle	17
A. Kumble not out	27		
J. Srinath not out	33	– (6) not out	19
B 4, l-b 7, n-b 6	17	L-b 4	4

1/20 (1) 2/102 (3) 3/182 (2)   (7 wkts dec.) 583   1/21 (2) 2/35 (1)   (5 wkts dec.) 148
4/463 (5) 5/502 (6)   3/68 (3) 4/114 (5)
6/518 (7) 7/521 (4)   5/122 (4)

B. K. V. Prasad and Harbhajan Singh did not bat.

Bowling: *First Innings*—Cairns 24–5–82–1; Nash 28–6–86–0; Vettori 57–5–200–4; Astle 17–2–55–1; Harris 17–3–64–1; Wiseman 24–2–85–0. *Second Innings*—Cairns 6–1–29–1; Nash 8–0–35–1; Vettori 2–0–23–0; Harris 11–0–44–1; Astle 5–0–13–1.

New Zealand

G. R. Stead c Ganguly b Kumble	17	– (2) c M. S. K. Prasad	
		b Harbhajan Singh	78
M. J. Horne c Dravid b Kumble	2	– (1) c sub (R. V. Bharadwaj)	
		b Kumble	41
D. L. Vettori c sub (R. V. Bharadwaj) b Kumble	3		
C. M. Spearman c Ramesh b B. K. V. Prasad	17	– (3) not out	54
*S. P. Fleming c M. S. K. Prasad b Srinath	48	– (4) not out	64
N. J. Astle c Ganguly b B. K. V. Prasad	74		
†A. C. Parore lbw b Kumble	11		
C. L. Cairns b Kumble	72		
C. Z. Harris c Ramesh b Srinath	12		
D. J. Nash not out	14		
P. J. Wiseman lbw b Harbhajan Singh	3		
B 8, l b 14, n-b 13	35	B 1, l-b 5, n-b 9	15

1/13 (2) 2/29 (3) 3/33 (1) 4/65 (4)   308   1/131 (1) 2/131 (2)   (2 wkts) 252
5/135 (5) 6/166 (7) 7/231 (6)
8/284 (9) 9/294 (8) 10/308 (11)

Bowling: *First Innings*—Srinath 35–11–72–2; B. K. V. Prasad 26–9–52–2; Kumble 48–21–82–5; Harbhajan Singh 30.4–8–78–1; Ganguly 2–1–2–0. *Second Innings*—Srinath 15–3–59–0; B. K. V. Prasad 13–2–36–0; Kumble 31–16–57–1; Harbhajan Singh 26–8–55–1; Tendulkar 5–2–19–0; Ganguly 4–0–25–0; Dravid 1–1–0–0.

Umpires: R. E. Koertzen (South Africa) and V. K. Ramaswamy.
Referee: R. S. Madugalle (Sri Lanka).

†INDIA v NEW ZEALAND

First One-Day International

At Rajkot, November 5. New Zealand won by 43 runs. Toss: New Zealand. International debut: S. B. Styris.

New Zealand obtained their first win of the tour by amassing their biggest limited-overs total, which was also – for three days – the highest one-day international score on Indian soil. The previous record was New Zealand's 348 for eight at Nagpur, in 1995-96, which was overshadowed by the deaths of nine spectators when a wall collapsed. This time, the tourists could celebrate, especially Astle, who had scored a hundred at Nagpur and now hit 120 from 136 balls, including 12 fours and two sixes. He shared century stands with Spearman, who smashed 68 in 44 balls, and Twose. An even bigger total seemed likely when they were 187 for one at the halfway mark, but India still needed seven an over to win. Tendulkar and Ganguly matched that rate, racing to 87 in 12 overs, and Jadeja scored 95 in 97 balls. They were all out, however, with three overs to spare, having raised the match aggregate to 655, nine short of another record.

Man of the Match: N. J. Astle.

New Zealand

C. M. Spearman c Bharadwaj		D. J. Nash not out	6
b B. K. V. Prasad .	68	S. B. Styris st M. S. K. Prasad b Kumble	1
N. J. Astle c Dravid b B. K. V. Prasad . .	120	D. L. Vettori c Jadeja b Kumble	0
R. G. Twose b Srinath	56	S. B. O'Connor not out	0
*S. P. Fleming c Dravid		L-b 5, w 13, n-b 5	23
b B. K. V. Prasad .	10		
C. L. Cairns run out	24	1/115 2/224 3/244 (9 wkts, 50 overs)	349
C. Z. Harris c Tendulkar b Bharadwaj . .	23	4/277 5/310 6/336	
†A. C. Parore c Chopra b Bharadwaj . . .	18	7/343 8/345 9/345	

Bowling: Srinath 10–2–51–1; B. K. V. Prasad 10–0–75–3; Kumble 10–0–64–2; Chopra 10–0–72–0; Tendulkar 3–0–18–0; Bharadwaj 5–0–44–2; Singh 2–0–20–0.

India

S. C. Ganguly c Harris b O'Connor	41	J. Srinath c sub (M. J. Horne) b Styris . .	19
*S. R. Tendulkar c Cairns b Styris	32	A. Kumble not out	15
R. Dravid lbw b Astle	39	B. K. V. Prasad c Astle b Styris	9
A. Jadeja c sub (M. J. Horne) b Astle . .	95	B 1, l-b 7, w 19, n-b 3	30
R. R. Singh c Spearman b Harris	23		
R. V. Bharadwaj c Twose b Vettori	1	1/87 2/90 3/171 (47 overs)	306
N. Chopra st Parore b Vettori	0	4/240 5/247 6/248	
†M. S. K. Prasad b Astle	2	7/251 8/268 9/288	

Bowling: Nash 1–0–2–0; O'Connor 3–0–42–1; Cairns 8–0–47–0; Styris 10–0–63–3; Harris 10–0–56–1; Vettori 8–0–48–2; Astle 7–0–40–3.

Umpires: K. Hariharan and I. Shivaram.

†INDIA v NEW ZEALAND

Second One-Day International

At Hyderabad, November 8. India won by 174 runs. Toss: India.

India hit back with a vengeance and a clutch of records. Their total of 376 for two was second at this level only to Sri Lanka's 398 for five against Kenya in the 1996 World Cup. Tendulkar and Dravid added 331 for the second wicket in 46 overs, an all-wicket record for any side in one-day internationals, beating Dravid's 318 with Ganguly in a World Cup game against Sri Lanka six months earlier. In that match Ganguly had made 183, the highest limited-overs score for India, but now Tendulkar surpassed him, batting throughout the innings for an unbeaten 186, then the fourth-highest score in any one-day international. It was his 24th century in such games, coming nine days after his 21st Test hundred, and he hit 20 fours and three sixes in 150 balls. Dravid partnered him with a run-a-ball 153, striking 15 fours and two sixes. New Zealand lost both openers in the first five overs and lasted only two-thirds of their batting allocation. But for Styris, last out for 43 in only his second international, they would not have reached 200.

Man of the Match: S. R. Tendulkar.

India

S. C. Ganguly run out	4
*S. R. Tendulkar not out	186
R. Dravid c Fleming b Cairns	153
A. Jadeja not out	2
B 5, l-b 8, w 3, n-b 15	31

1/10 2/341   (2 wkts, 50 overs) 376

R. R. Singh, R. V. Bharadwaj, N. Chopra, †M. S. K. Prasad, J. Srinath, A. Kumble and B. K. V. Prasad did not bat.

Bowling: Cairns 10–0–73–1; O'Connor 7–0–61–0; Drum 9–0–85–0; Styris 10–0–58–0; Harris 3–0–27–0; Astle 3–0–20–0; Vettori 8–0–39–0.

New Zealand

C. M. Spearman c Tendulkar b B. K. V. Prasad	15	S. B. Styris c M. S. K. Prasad b B. K. V. Prasad	43
N. J. Astle c Jadeja b Srinath	9	D. L. Vettori run out	5
†A. C. Parore st M. S. K. Prasad b Bharadwaj	39	S. B. O'Connor run out	1
R. G. Twose lbw b Chopra	28	C. J. Drum not out	7
*S. P. Fleming c Srinath b Kumble	12	L-b 8, w 12, n-b 8	28
C. L. Cairns run out	13	1/23 2/27 3/67 4/101 5/120 (33.1 overs) 202
C. Z. Harris c Chopra b Kumble	2	6/127 7/140 8/152 9/156

Bowling: Srinath 6–0–37–1; B. K. V. Prasad 5.1–0–38–2; Chopra 7–0–38–1; Kumble 10–0–39–2; Bharadwaj 4–0–27–1; Ganguly 1–0–15–0.

Umpires: Jasbir Singh and S. K. Tarapore.

†INDIA v NEW ZEALAND

Third One-Day International

At Gwalior, November 11. India won by 14 runs. Toss: India.

Another day, another Indian century. This time it was Ganguly's turn to bat through 50 overs, scoring 153 in 150 balls, with 18 fours and three sixes. But he had little support, his colleagues faltering on a damp pitch, until Robin Singh joined him at 142 for five in the 39th over. They added 119 in 69 balls, Singh smiting three sixes to reach 45 in 34 deliveries, with the final three overs yielding 55 runs. A fluent Astle led New Zealand's reply, but his dismissal, three short of a second hundred in the series, swiftly followed by Fleming's, was a severe setback. At least they reduced the margin of defeat from 174 runs at Hyderabad to 14.

Man of the Match: S. C. Ganguly.

India

S. C. Ganguly not out	153	R. R. Singh not out	45
*S. R. Tendulkar c Fleming b Drum	1		
R. Dravid sub (M. J. Horne) b Tait	14	B 1, l-b 5, w 7, n-b 3	16
N. Chopra b Astle	15		
A. Jadeja c and b Astle	15	1/23 2/63 3/97 (5 wkts, 50 overs) 261
R. V. Bharadwaj run out	2	4/138 5/142

†M. S. K. Prasad, A. B. Agarkar, A. Kumble and D. S. Mohanty did not bat.

Bowling: Cairns 10–1–56–0; Drum 10–2–58–1; Styris 6–0–37–0; Tait 7–0–23–1; Harris 7–0–34–0; Astle 10–0–47–2.

New Zealand

C. M. Spearman c Dravid b Chopra. . . .	32	A. R. Tait b Chopra	1
N. J. Astle b Kumble	97	D. L. Vettori not out	2
†A. C. Parore b Ganguly	3		
*S. P. Fleming lbw b Chopra	27	B 1, l-b 11, w 7, n-b 2.	21
R. G. Twose run out	9		
C. L. Cairns c Mohanty b Agarkar	8	1/99 2/113 3/170 (8 wkts, 50 overs) 247
C. Z. Harris not out	22	4/172 5/190 6/198
S. B. Styris b Kumble.	25	7/237 8/240

C. J. Drum did not bat.

Bowling: Agarkar 10–0–42–1; Mohanty 5–0–38–0; Kumble 8–0–38–2; Chopra 9–1–32–3; Ganguly 8–1–33–1; Bharadwaj 8–0–41–0; Singh 2–0–11–0.

Umpires: S. C. Gupta and K. Parthasarathy.

†INDIA v NEW ZEALAND

Fourth One-Day International

At Gauhati, November 14. New Zealand won by 48 runs. Toss: India. International debut: T. Kumaran.

New Zealand squared the series, despite losing their top three cheaply after being asked to bat. Twose and Cairns fought back against an inexperienced attack, India having rested three key bowlers ahead of the Australian tour, and Cairns hit three sixes as he steered New Zealand past 200. India also made a poor start: within seven overs they had lost the three century-makers in the earlier games. Joshi, coming in at 88 for six, was the only home batsman to reach 30 and was unbeaten on 61 when Styris wrapped up the innings in the 46th over.

Man of the Match: C. L. Cairns.

New Zealand

C. M. Spearman run out	25	A. R. Tait not out.	13
N. J. Astle lbw b Kumaran.	1	D. L. Vettori c and b Chopra	11
*S. P. Fleming c Ganguly b Agarkar . . .	4	C. J. Drum not out.	2
R. G. Twose c Singh b Chopra	46	B 1, l-b 7, w 9, n-b 2	19
C. L. Cairns run out	80	
†A. C. Parore run out.	3	1/17 2/30 3/32 (9 wkts, 50 overs) 236
C. Z. Harris c Kumaran b Bharadwaj. . .	29	4/128 5/143 6/202
S. B. Styris b Bharadwaj	3	7/206 8/210 9/233

Bowling: Agarkar 10–1–68–1; Kumaran 8–1–29–1; Ganguly 3–1–18–0; Singh 6–0–20–0; Joshi 4–0–19–0; Bharadwaj 10–0–41–2; Chopra 9–0–33–2.

India

S. C. Ganguly lbw b Drum	17	N. Chopra run out	13
*S. R. Tendulkar c Spearman b Drum . .	2	A. B. Agarkar lbw b Styris	4
R. Dravid c Parore b Cairns	5	T. Kumaran c Astle b Styris.	8
A. Jadeja c Parore b Vettori	27	L-b 1, w 5	6
R. V. Bharadwaj b Harris.	27	
R. R. Singh run out	2	1/22 2/27 3/27 (45.3 overs) 188
†M. S. K. Prasad c Twose b Vettori	16	4/83 5/85 6/88
S. B. Joshi not out	61	7/126 8/172 9/178

Bowling: Drum 6–1–31–2; Cairns 5–1–14–1; Styris 9.3–0–39–2; Tait 2–0–9–0; Vettori 10–1–37–2; Harris 6–0–25–1; Astle 7–0–32–0.

Umpires: S. K. Bansal and S. Chowdhury.

†INDIA v NEW ZEALAND

Fifth One-Day International

At Delhi, November 17. India won by seven wickets. Toss: New Zealand.

India sealed the series 3–2, winning with six overs in hand, but it was a low-key finale. Both New Zealand openers were out in controversial circumstances, Astle lbw to a ball that seemed to be going down the leg side, Spearman caught when Kumaran was overstepping. Again, Twose and Cairns shored up the innings, but it totalled a disappointing 179. Gandhi, in his first one-day international, and Ganguly opened with 117 in reply. Ganguly went on to take his aggregate for the series to 301. He outshone all other batsmen in the match in scoring 86, with 12 fours and a six. Though Vettori dismissed him and Tendulkar in four balls, Dravid saw India to a comfortable victory. Both umpires were the sons of Test umpires, M. Y. Gupte and H. P. Sharma.

Man of the Match: S. C. Ganguly.   *Man of the Series:* S. C. Ganguly.

New Zealand

C. M. Spearman c Dravid b Kumaran	3	A. R. Tait c Singh b Kumaran		4
N. J. Astle lbw b Srinath	7	D. L. Vettori run out		2
*S. P. Fleming lbw b Ganguly	22			
R. G. Twose c Bharadwaj b Joshi	47	L-b 13, w 9, n-b 4		26
C. L. Cairns lbw b Singh	41			
†A. C. Parore b Kumaran	13	1/11 2/23 3/58	(9 wkts, 50 overs)	179
C. Z. Harris not out	12	4/124 5/152 6/161		
S. B. Styris run out	2	7/165 8/172 9/179		

C. J. Drum did not bat.

Bowling: Srinath 10–1–31–1; Kumaran 9–3–24–3; Chopra 5–1–16–0; Ganguly 6–1–29–1; Singh 10–0–28–1; Joshi 10–0–38–1.

India

D. J. Gandhi lbw b Drum	30	R. V. Bharadwaj not out		17
S. C. Ganguly st Parore b Vettori	86	L-b 2, w 12, n-b 5		19
R. Dravid not out	29			
*S. R. Tendulkar c and b Vettori	0	1/117 2/156 3/156	(3 wkts, 44 overs)	181

R. R. Singh, †M. S. K. Prasad, S. B. Joshi, N. Chopra, J. Srinath and T. Kumaran did not bat.

Bowling: Cairns 7–4–10–0; Drum 5–0–41–1; Styris 10–2–23–0; Astle 4–0–19–0; Harris 6–0–30–0; Vettori 10–2–46–2; Tait 2–0–10–0.

Umpires: V. M. Gupte and S. K. Sharma.
Series referee: R. S. Madugalle (Sri Lanka).

CEAT CRICKETER OF THE YEAR

The fifth CEAT International Cricketer of the Year was Sourav Ganguly of India. The CEAT formula awarded him 98 points for his performances in Tests and limited-overs internationals to April 30, 2000; Ganguly's team-mate Sachin Tendulkar and New Zealand's Chris Cairns were runners-up with 95 each. Previous winners were Brian Lara of West Indies, Venkatesh Prasad of India, Sanath Jayasuriya of Sri Lanka and Jacques Kallis of South Africa. Australia won the team award with 154 points to South Africa's 101.

THE WEST INDIANS IN BANGLADESH, 1999-2000

As part of the mission to broaden Bangladesh's international experience while they campaigned for Test status, the West Indians visited Dhaka briefly in October before going on to the Coca-Cola Champions' Trophy in Sharjah. Bangladesh had already hosted one-day tournaments and A-team tours, as well as playing first-class cricket against regional sides in New Zealand. This visit was a further step in their development, because they played a first-class match against a Test nation and performed encouragingly. They restricted the West Indians to a 20-run lead on first innings, but rain prevented the match reaching a conclusion. The short limited-overs series for the Biman Millennium Cup was much more one-sided, with West Indies taking full advantage of the toss to cruise home in both matches; captain Brian Lara scored the second-fastest hundred in one-day internationals in the second game.

Large crowds proved once again that Bangladesh compared favourably with any Test country when it came to an enthusiastic fan base. The Bangabandhu Stadium was overflowing for the one-day games, which attracted more than 40,000 each, though only a tenth of that number turned out for the first-class match.

WEST INDIAN TOURING PARTY

B. C. Lara (Trinidad & Tobago) (*captain*), J. C. Adams (Jamaica), C. E. L. Ambrose (Leeward Islands), S. L. Campbell (Barbados), S. Chanderpaul (Guyana), P. T. Collins (Barbados), M. Dillon (Trinidad & Tobago), C. H. Gayle (Jamaica), A. F. G. Griffith (Barbados), W. W. Hinds (Jamaica), R. D. Jacobs (Leeward Islands), R. D. King (Guyana), N. A. M. McLean (Windward Islands), N. O. Perry (Jamaica), R. L. Powell (Jamaica).

Manager: C. H. Lloyd.

WEST INDIAN TOUR RESULTS

First-class match – Drew v Bangladeshis.
One-day internationals – Played 2: Won 2.

Note: Matches in this section which were not first-class are signified by a dagger.

At Dhaka, October 4, 5, 6. Drawn. Toss: Bangladesh. Bangladeshis 229 (Javed Omar 53, Khaled Mahmud 40, Khaled Masud 59 not out, Enamul Haque 32; N. O. Perry five for 84) and 59 for three; West Indians 249 (W. W. Hinds 70, B. C. Lara 87; Manjurul Islam three for 64, Enamul Haque five for 57).
The third day was washed out.

†BANGLADESH v WEST INDIES

At Dhaka, October 8 (day/night). West Indies won by 73 runs. Toss: West Indies.
Lara opted to bat and returned to the top of the order, but he and fellow-opener Campbell were out by the fifth over. There were no further failures, however, as half-centuries from Adams and Chanderpaul steadied the batting before Powell and McLean lashed out to lift the scoring-rate to nearly six an over. Rain prolonged the break between innings; no overs were lost, but batting conditions were more difficult when Bangladesh replied. Shahriar Hossain managed 45 before Adams claimed three wickets in his first three overs. With Bangladesh out of the running at 96 for five, Lara chose not to turn the screw. Instead, having experimented with Perry's off-spin as an opening gambit, he now gave everyone a bowl except for wicket-keeper Jacobs and himself. This allowed Al-Shahriar Rokon and wicket-keeper Khaled Masud to save national honour in an unbroken stand of 123.
Man of the Match: J. C. Adams.

West Indies

*B. C. Lara c Khaled Mahmud		R. L. Powell c Khaled Masud	
b Manjurul Islam .	2	b Hasibul Hussain .	34
S. L. Campbell c Enamul Haque		N. A. M. McLean c Aminul Islam	
b Hasibul Hussain .	13	b Manjurul Islam .	39
J. C. Adams c Khaled Mahmud		N. O. Perry not out.	1
b Aminul Islam .	56	L-b 3, w 9, n-b 3	15
W. W. Hinds c Habibul Bashar			
b Khaled Mahmud .	40	1/13 2/29 3/83 (6 wkts, 50 overs) 292	
S. Chanderpaul not out	92	4/175 5/224 6/290	

†R. D. Jacobs, C. E. L. Ambrose and M. Dillon did not bat.

Bowling: Hasibul Hussain 9–1–66–2; Manjurul Islam 10–0–63–2; Naimur Rahman 7–1–33–0; Khaled Mahmud 10–0–44–1; Enamul Haque 9–0–49–0; Aminul Islam 5–0–34–1.

Bangladesh

Shahriar Hossain lbw b Adams	45	†Khaled Masud not out	53
Javed Omar c Jacobs b Dillon	4		
Habibul Bashar st Jacobs b Adams	25	L-b 9, w 14, n-b 5	28
*Aminul Islam c Campbell b Adams . . .	0		
Al-Shahriar Rokon not out	62	1/22 2/73 3/73 (5 wkts, 50 overs) 219	
Khaled Mahmud c Jacobs b McLean . . .	2	4/88 5/96	

Naimur Rahman, Enamul Haque, Hasibul Hussain and Manjurul Islam did not bat.

Bowling: Perry 10–0–45–0; Dillon 5–1–19–1; Ambrose 5–0–9–0; Adams 7–1–24–3; Chanderpaul 7–0–25–0; McLean 5–0–17–1; Hinds 6–0–35–0; Powell 3–0–20–0; Campbell 2–0–16–0.

Umpires: B. C. Cooray and Riazuddin.

†BANGLADESH v WEST INDIES

At Dhaka, October 9 (day/night). West Indies won by 109 runs. Toss: West Indies. International debut: Ahmed Kamal.

Lara hit the second-fastest century in limited-overs internationals. He carved his way to 50 in 26 balls, passing 6,000 one-day international runs in the process, and needed just 45 balls in all to complete his first hundred at this level since April 1998. Only Shahid Afridi of Pakistan had been quicker than Lara, taking 37 balls against Sri Lanka at Nairobi in 1996-97. Lara's eventual 117 in 62 balls contained 18 fours and four sixes. West Indies were 158 for one before the fielding restrictions were lifted at the end of the 15th over. The home spinners later slowed the scoring slightly, and Chanderpaul's 77 from 87 balls, his second unbeaten half-century in successive days, was comparatively stately as the total rose to 314. Campbell then emerged as the unexpected destroyer of the Bangladeshi batting by seizing four wickets, while Jacobs equalled the then world record of five dismissals in a one-day international for the third time.

Man of the Match: B. C. Lara.

West Indies

S. L. Campbell c Khaled Masud		J. C. Adams b Enamul Haque	15
b Ahmed Kamal .	28	N. O. Perry not out	19
*B. C. Lara b Habibul Bashar	117		
R. L. Powell c Enamul Haque			
b Khaled Mahmud .	21	L-b 1, w 10, n-b 1	12
W. W. Hinds b Enamul Haque	14		
S. Chanderpaul not out	77	1/98 2/161 (6 wkts, 50 overs) 314	
†R. D. Jacobs c Khaled Masud		3/185 4/187	
b Aminul Islam .	11	5/218 6/257	

N. A. M. McLean, C. E. L. Ambrose and M. Dillon did not bat.

Bowling: Manjurul Islam 4–0–38–0; Shafiuddin Ahmed 3–0–32–0; Ahmed Kamal 5–0–39–1; Enamul Haque 10–0–45–2; Khaled Mahmud 8–0–78–1; Habibul Bashar 10–0–31–1; Aminul Islam 10–0–50–1.

Bangladesh

Shahriar Hossain st Jacobs b Campbell	47	Ahmed Kamal c Chanderpaul b Perry	11
Javed Omar c Hinds b McLean	18	Shafiuddin Ahmed c Ambrose b Lara	0
Habibul Bashar c Jacobs b Dillon	0	Manjurul Islam not out	5
*Aminul Islam st Jacobs b Lara	66	L-b 3, w 19, n-b 4	26
Al-Shahriar Rokon c Jacobs b Campbell	12		
Khaled Mahmud b Campbell	2	1/65 2/66 3/79	(49.1 overs) 205
†Khaled Masud st Jacobs b Campbell	5	4/106 5/108 6/135	
Enamul Haque c Adams b Perry	13	7/162 8/184 9/190	

Bowling: McLean 8–0–44–1; Ambrose 7–1–21–0; Dillon 7–0–29–1; Campbell 10–0–30–4; Powell 8–0–47–0; Perry 7–0–19–2; Lara 2.1–0–12–2.

Umpires: B. C. Cooray and Riazuddin.
Series referee: P. L. van der Merwe (South Africa).

PWC ONE-DAY INTERNATIONAL RATINGS

The PricewaterhouseCoopers (PwC) One-Day International Ratings, introduced in August 1998, follow similar principles to the Test Ratings (see page 1093).

The leading 20 batsmen and bowlers in the One-Day International Ratings after the indoor series between Australia and South Africa in Melbourne which ended on August 20 were:

	Batsmen	Rating		Bowlers	Rating
1.	M. G. Bevan (*Aus.*)	799	1.	G. D. McGrath (*Aus.*)	862
2.	3. C. Ganguly (*Ind.*)	764	2.	A. D. Mullally (*Eng.*)	810
3.	N. J. Astle (*NZ*)	740	3.	M. Muralitharan (*SL*)	805
4.	J. H. Kallis (*SA*)	708	4.	D. Gough (*Eng.*)	785
5.	Inzamam-ul-Haq (*Pak.*)	697	5.	S. M. Pollock (*SA*)	767
	S. R. Tendulkar (*Ind.*)	697	6.	R. D. King (*WI*)	752
7.	L. Klusener (*SA*)	696	7.	S. K. Warne (*Aus.*)	750
8.	R. T. Ponting (*Aus.*)	694	8.	M. A. Ealham (*Eng.*)	728
9.	A. C. Gilchrist (*Aus.*)	693	9.	A. R. Caddick (*Eng.*)	707
10.	R. G. Twose (*NZ*)	670	10.	Wasim Akram (*Pak.*)	702
11.	B. C. Lara (*WI*)	661	11.	Abdur Razzaq (*Pak.*)	701
12.	M. S. Atapattu (*SL*)	656	12.	D. W. Fleming (*Aus.*)	666
13.	G. Kirsten (*SA*)	652	13.	A. Kumble (*Ind.*)	665
14.	S. R. Waugh (*Aus.*)	650	14.	A. A. Donald (*SA*)	659
15.	G. A. Hick (*Eng.*)	646		L. Klusener (*SA*)	659
16.	A. J. Stewart (*Eng.*)	640	16.	C. L. Cairns (*NZ*)	652
17.	R. Dravid (*Ind.*)	638		H. H. Streak (*Zim.*)	652
18.	G. P. Thorpe (*Eng.*)	637	18.	Saqlain Mushtaq (*Pak.*)	651
19.	M. E. Waugh (*Aus.*)	630	19.	D. L. Vettori (*NZ*)	650
20.	S. T. Jayasuriya (*SL*)	618	20.	C. Z. Harris (*NZ*)	649
	Saeed Anwar (*Pak.*)	618			

THE ZIMBABWEANS IN SOUTH AFRICA, 1999-2000

In advance of South Africa's 1999-2000 series against England, the Zimbabweans crossed the Limpopo River for their first Test in South Africa, the first to be staged at Bloemfontein's Springbok Park. South Africa won both that match and the one in Harare a fortnight later. The games were not regarded as constituting a series. The results emphasised the disparity between the two countries, although neither was at full strength. The gap was less apparent at one-day level when Zimbabwe returned to South Africa, later in the season, to join England and the hosts in a triangular tournament.

ZIMBABWEAN TOURING PARTY

A. D. R. Campbell (Mashonaland) (*captain*), A. Flower (Mashonaland), G. W. Flower (Mashonaland), M. W. Goodwin (Mashonaland), T. R. Gripper (Mashonaland), N. C. Johnson (Matabeleland), M. Mbangwa (Matabeleland), D. T. Mutendera (Midlands), H. K. Olonga (Matabeleland), G. J. Rennie (Mashonaland), B. C. Strang (Mashonaland), A. R. Whittall (Manicaland), G. J. Whittall (Manicaland).

A. M. Blignaut (Mashonaland) and H. H. Streak (Matabeleland) withdrew from the squad through injury.

Coach: D. L. Houghton.

SOUTH AFRICA v ZIMBABWE

Test Match

At Bloemfontein, October 29, 30, 31, November 1. South Africa won by an innings and 13 runs. Toss: South Africa. Test debut: H. H. Dippenaar.

Bloemfontein's Springbok Park became the world's 80th Test venue and South Africa's sixth current Test ground. And with the country's most-capped players, Cronje and Donald, making no secret of their emotions at the prospect of playing a Test in front of their home Free State crowd, Zimbabwe had every reason to feel apprehensive when Cronje opted to field first. The pitch might have enjoyed a reputation for producing large scores in domestic cricket, but it was obvious that Donald was raring to bowl. As it happened, he bowled poorly; his partner Pollock, on the other hand, was outstanding. Perhaps he enjoyed some fortune with the lbw decision that removed Grant Flower in his first over, but his other four victims were outclassed.

At 79 for six, the visitors were in danger of humiliation. Campbell, under increasing pressure for his batting place, let alone the captaincy, had battled gamely for his 27 from 83 deliveries, and the ball with which Pollock dismissed him, climbing steeply and flying off the edge to gully, was simply unplayable. Whittall, however, more than doubled the score off his own bat with a rousing 85 from 114 balls, three of his 14 fours coming in one over as he gave himself room and cracked Donald through the covers.

Even so, Zimbabwe's 192 looked woefully inadequate for a side deprived of two key bowlers in Streak and Paul Strang, and with all-rounder Johnson unfit to bowl more than two tentative overs. Their seamers consigned themselves to bowling wide of the off stump and hoping for mistakes. In the meantime, with eight batsmen and Extras contributing between 20 and 70, South Africa compiled a total of 417 and an intimidating lead of 225. Debutant Boeta Dippenaar and Bacher, opening in place of Gibbs and Kirsten (injured after 53 consecutive Tests – a South African record) gave them a steady start, which Kallis developed with a patient 64. Cronje helped him add 90, in the course of which Cronje leapfrogged over Bruce Mitchell and Kirsten to become South Africa's leading run-maker in Tests, and Rhodes batted pleasantly in top-scoring with 70 until he played around a straight delivery from Olonga.

Zimbabwe's second innings began no better than their first. Kallis, bowling as fast as Donald in Cronje's estimation, did the initial damage with swing and pace, claiming his 50th Test wicket when he had Gripper leg-before, and Pollock again ended a determined Campbell innings with an angry delivery that flew to fourth slip. Kallis beat Andy Flower with speed, and, when Pollock nipped one back to trap Johnson in front, the match seemed all over at 123 for six. However, a change of pace by way of Adams's spin offered the later batsmen something to hit before getting the ball that was too good for them. This gave Whittall the opportunity to record his second half-century of the match, from 91 deliveries with nine boundaries, but nothing could prevent South Africa from winning with a day in hand.

"To win by an innings is always an achievement, even though Zimbabwe had problems with injuries and were under strength," Cronje said afterwards, while Campbell admitted they had been "outplayed and outclassed. It's going to be hard to regroup after this, but that's what we have to do. We must try to learn from defeats like this." – NEIL MANTHORP.

Man of the Match: J. H. Kallis.   *Attendance:* 17,353.

Close of play: First day, South Africa 29-0 (Dippenaar 17*, Bacher 9*); Second day, South Africa 253-4 (Cronje 60*, Rhodes 24*); Third day, Zimbabwe 123-5 (Johnson 23*, Rennie 4*).

Zimbabwe

G. W. Flower lbw b Pollock	0	– b Kallis	8
T. R. Gripper run out	16	– lbw b Kallis	11
M. W. Goodwin c Boucher b Pollock	7	– c Boucher b Kallis	0
*A. D. R. Campbell c Klusener b Pollock	27	– c Cronje b Pollock	33
†A. Flower lbw b Pollock	13	– lbw b Kallis	39
N. C. Johnson c Boucher b Donald	6	– lbw b Pollock	23
G. J. Rennie c Cullinan b Kallis	14	– c Boucher b Adams	10
G. J. Whittall c Boucher b Kallis	85	– b Adams	51
B. C. Strang c Cronje b Pollock	9	– lbw b Adams	0
H. K. Olonga b Kallis	1	– c Rhodes b Adams	24
M. Mbangwa not out	0	– not out	0
L-b 6, w 3, n-b 5	14	L-b 4, w 5, n-b 4	13

1/1 (1) 2/14 (3) 3/41 (2) 4/63 (5)   192   1/11 (1) 2/19 (3) 3/24 (2)   212
5/78 (6) 6/79 (4) 7/117 (7)   4/77 (4) 5/115 (5) 6/123 (6)
8/140 (9) 9/183 (10) 10/192 (8)   7/166 (7) 8/166 (9)
                                   9/202 (8) 10/212 (10)

Bowling: *First Innings*—Donald 18–5–58–1; Pollock 21–6–39–5; Klusener 16–5–40–0; Kallis 17–4–44–3; Adams 3–1–5–0. *Second Innings*—Donald 15–6–25–0; Pollock 19–5–62–2; Kallis 21–3–68–4; Adams 12.1–5–31–4; Klusener 4–0–22–0.

South Africa

H. H. Dippenaar lbw b Olonga	20	A. A. Donald b Olonga	2
A. M. Bacher c Goodwin b Mbangwa	42	P. R. Adams c Gripper b Olonga	20
J. H. Kallis lbw b Whittall	64		
D. J. Cullinan c G. W. Flower b Whittall	27	L-b 3, w 1, n-b 22	26
*W. J. Cronje c A. Flower b Mbangwa	64		
J. N. Rhodes lbw b Olonga	70	1/43 (1) 2/72 (2) 3/128 (4)	417
S. M. Pollock c Campbell b Strang	8	4/218 (3) 5/266 (5) 6/278 (7)	
L. Klusener lbw b G. W. Flower	19	7/310 (8) 8/342 (6)	
†M. V. Boucher not out	55	9/363 (10) 10/417 (11)	

Bowling: Olonga 33.1–7–93–4; Strang 27–6–99–1; Johnson 2–0–8–0; G. W. Flower 23–5–44–1; Mbangwa 35–9–75–2; Whittall 30–9–95–2.

Umpires: R. S. Dunne (New Zealand) and D. L. Orchard.
Referee: J. L. Hendriks (West Indies).

THE PAKISTANIS IN AUSTRALIA, 1999-2000

By PETER DEELEY

Pakistan's cricketers left for Australia following a string of upheavals that seem part and parcel of life in their country. A military coup days before their departure not only overthrew the elected, if almost universally unpopular, government; it also detained the newly appointed chairman of the Pakistan Cricket Board, Mujeeb-ur-Rehman, and replaced the board members with yet another *ad hoc* committee. The new chairman, Zafar Altaf, had been manager of Pakistan's World Cup team in England.

This was shortly preceded by the reinstatement as captain of Wasim Akram, who had been suspended after the World Cup following allegations of match-fixing. Also reinstated, albeit for a short term, was Richard Pybus, Pakistan's technical coach at the World Cup, who was appointed coach after Wasim Raja had resigned. Pybus lasted a month and a half before being replaced in turn by the former captain and manager, Intikhab Alam, but at least he got to Australia. Shabbir Ahmed, a 23-year-old fast bowler, was withdrawn from the original tour party after the ICC questioned his bowling action. He had been reported by Peter van der Merwe, the tournament referee at Toronto, where he made his one-day international debut in September. Shabbir's place was filled by the experienced Waqar Younis.

There was a particular piquancy in this meeting between two of the world's leading sides. Four and a half months earlier, Steve Waugh's Australians had trounced Pakistan in the embarrassingly one-sided final of the World Cup at Lord's. And beyond that lay the tension provoked by it being a previous Australian team, under Mark Taylor, which made the match-fixing allegations that led to the judicial inquiry into Pakistan cricket.

Waugh could hardly have dared hope for a clean sweep against a side boasting an all-round attack probably without parallel in the contemporary game. Yet, for a variety of reasons, Pakistan's bowlers failed to live up to their promise. There was never room for both spinners, Mushtaq Ahmed and Saqlain Mushtaq, and Shoaib Akhtar was often too carried away by his reputation as the world's fastest bowler to reproduce his form of earlier in the year. Waqar Younis played in only one Test and appeared to be nearing the end of a wonderful international career. We learned that he felt slighted by the way Wasim had overlooked him. He could respect his captain as a cricketer, he said, but not as a leader.

Despite these problems, Pakistan had their moments. They were in with a chance of victory in a rousing First Test until the fourth afternoon, and they should have won the Second. Indeed, they would have but for an epic partnership between the left-handed Western Australian team-mates, Justin Langer and Adam Gilchrist, and an umpiring decision that swayed the game Australia's way.

Australia played the series without Jason Gillespie, still recovering from the injury sustained in Sri Lanka in September when he collided with Steve Waugh. In his place they gave two Tests to Queensland's Scott Muller, but he was clearly not up to standard. Certainly not in the opinion of a Channel 9 cameraman, whose "Can't bowl, can't throw" jibe in Hobart, caught on a sound-effects microphone, caused a furore when it was made public during the Perth Test and mistakenly attributed to Shane Warne. By this time, Muller was back in Brisbane, playing against the Indian tourists and twice taking the wicket of Sachin Tendulkar, his Test place claimed by fellow-Queenslander Michael Kasprowicz, back after a year's absence.

Perth proved to be a dreadful anticlimax. One almost has to think the unthinkable and ask whether the WACA ground is a fitting stage for Test cricket. For the third time in four Tests there, the match finished inside three days, and for much of the time there was an unevenness about the contest between bat and ball that did not make for satisfying cricketing entertainment. Yet by the same criteria Hobart, which had also had its critics, offered five gripping days of Test cricket.

Shoaib had special reasons for not thinking kindly of Perth. In a one-day warm-up game there, his bowling action was secretly filmed by a posse of Western Australian umpires and the tape was sent to the Australian Cricket Board. As the game was not under the jurisdiction of the ICC, however, the ACB chose to take no further action and the doubts over the legitimacy of Shoaib's action were widely rubbished as a tasteless whispering campaign. What few people knew at the time was that the series' match referee, John Reid, was sufficiently concerned to have Shoaib filmed in all three Test matches, with the support of the umpires. After the Perth Test, the evidence, suggesting that the fast bowler might sometimes throw his bouncer, was sent to the ICC. By the end of the year he had been banned from playing international cricket – though not for long, it transpired. In a dramatic about-turn, Shoaib was reprieved on the eve of the Carlton & United one-day series.

Australia were faced at the outset with filling the void left by the retirement of Ian Healy, their wicket-keeper in 119 Tests since 1988-89. Healy was accorded a hero's farewell at the First Test in his home city, Brisbane, as he drove around the boundary in an open-top car, and Gilchrist, his successor, came in for some unfavourable comparison from the Queensland locals until they saw the quality of the man with gloves and bat. Langer was under scrutiny for different reasons and was in danger of losing the No. 3 place after a run of poor form up to the Hobart Test. That he responded with back-to-back hundreds said much for his character, and by the end of the series he was something of a celebrity.

Steve Waugh, though averaging only 14.50 with the bat, showed a sure touch throughout his first home series as captain. He created a stir by inserting Pakistan in the first two Tests, and both decisions could have backfired. Instead, it all came up roses. "We believe we can win from any situation, and that is the great asset this team has," he said. Given the quality of players he could call on, he thought Australia were near-invincible at home, and nothing happened all summer to prove him wrong.

PAKISTANI TOURING PARTY

Wasim Akram (PIA) (*captain*), Moin Khan (PIA) (*vice-captain*), Abdur Razzaq (PIA), Azhar Mahmood (PIA), Ghulam Ali (PIA), Ijaz Ahmed, sen. (Habib Bank), Inzamam-ul-Haq, Mohammad Akram (Allied Bank), Mohammad Wasim (KRL), Mushtaq Ahmed (National Bank), Saeed Anwar (ADBP), Saqlain Mushtaq (PIA), Shoaib Akhtar (KRL), Wajahatullah Wasti (Allied Bank), Waqar Younis (Redco), Yousuf Youhana (PIA).

Shahid Afridi (Habib Bank) and Shoaib Malik (Pakistan Reserves) replaced Ghulam Ali, Mohammad Akram and Mushtaq Ahmed; Brigadier Mohammad Nasir Ahmed replaced Yawar Saeed as manager, and Intikhab Alam replaced Pybus as coach for the Carlton & United one-day series.

Manager: Yawar Saeed.   *Coach:* R. A. Pybus.

PAKISTANI TOUR RESULTS

Test matches – Played 3: Lost 3.
First-class matches – Played 5: Won 1, Lost 4.
Win – South Australia.
Losses – Australia (3), Queensland.
One-day internationals – Played 10: Won 4, Lost 6. *Wins* – Australia (1), India (3). *Losses* – Australia (5), India (1).
Other non-first-class matches – Played 6: Won 1, Lost 5. *Win* – Australian Country XI. *Losses* – ACB Chairman's XII, Western Australia, Australia A (2), Queensland.

TEST MATCH AVERAGES

AUSTRALIA – BATTING

	T	I	NO	R	HS	100s	50s	Avge	Ct/St
A. C. Gilchrist	3	4	1	264	149*	1	1	88.00	12/1
J. L. Langer	3	4	0	331	144	2	1	82.75	0
M. J. Slater	3	5	1	325	169	1	1	81.25	3
G. S. Blewett	3	5	1	204	89	0	1	51.00	2
R. T. Ponting	3	4	0	197	197	1	0	49.25	5
S. K. Warne	3	4	1	99	86	0	1	33.00	4
M. E. Waugh	3	4	0	105	100	1	0	26.25	7
S. R. Waugh	3	4	0	58	28	0	0	14.50	3
G. D. McGrath	3	3	0	8	7	0	0	2.66	3
D. W. Fleming	3	3	0	0	0	0	0	0.00	2

Played in two Tests: S. A. Muller 6*, 0* (2 ct). Played in one Test: M. S. Kasprowicz 9*.

* *Signifies not out.*

BOWLING

	O	M	R	W	BB	5W/i	Avge
M. S. Kasprowicz	28	5	132	7	4-53	0	18.85
D. W. Fleming	137.4	29	401	18	5-59	1	22.27
G. D. McGrath	134	37	393	14	4-49	0	28.07
S. K. Warne	130	37	370	12	5-110	1	30.83
S. A. Muller	58	8	258	7	3-68	0	36.85

Also bowled: G. S. Blewett 9–2–32–0; R. T. Ponting 11–2–31–0; M. E. Waugh 2–0–6–0; S. R. Waugh 5–1–20–0.

PAKISTAN – BATTING

	T	I	NO	R	HS	100s	50s	Avge	Ct/St
Saeed Anwar	3	6	0	282	119	1	2	47.00	0
Inzamam-ul-Haq	3	6	0	260	118	1	1	43.33	2
Ijaz Ahmed, sen.	3	6	0	209	115	1	1	34.83	3
Yousuf Youhana	3	6	0	207	95	0	2	34.50	3
Mohammad Wasim	2	4	0	129	91	0	1	32.25	1
Wasim Akram	3	6	1	154	52	0	1	30.80	1
Moin Khan	3	6	0	139	61	0	1	23.16	5/2
Azhar Mahmood	3	6	0	124	39	0	0	20.66	2
Saqlain Mushtaq	2	4	0	30	12	0	0	7.50	1
Shoaib Akhtar	3	6	2	23	8	0	0	5.75	0

Played in one Test: Abdur Razzaq 11, 2 (1 ct); Mohammad Akram 0, 10*; Mushtaq Ahmed 0, 1* (1 ct); Wajahatullah Wasti 5, 7; Waqar Younis 12*, 0.

* *Signifies not out.*

BOWLING

	O	M	R	W	BB	5W/i	Avge
Saqlain Mushtaq	94.5	24	251	10	6-46	1	25.10
Mohammad Akram	27.5	1	138	5	5-138	1	27.60
Azhar Mahmood	69.2	8	229	5	2-43	0	45.80
Wasim Akram	90.1	13	275	5	2-87	0	55.00
Shoaib Akhtar	93	11	406	6	4-153	0	67.66
Mushtaq Ahmed	40	3	214	3	3-194	0	71.33

Also bowled: Abdur Razzaq 17–3–66–0; Ijaz Ahmed, sen. 2–0–8–0; Wajahatullah Wasti 1–1–0–0; Waqar Younis 23–3–80–2.

Note: Matches in this section which were not first-class are signified by a dagger.

†At Lilac Hill, Perth, October 26. ACB Chairman's XII won by seven wickets. Toss: Pakistanis. Pakistanis 168 (44 overs) (Azhar Mahmood 43, Moin Khan 60 not out; D. K. Lillee three for eight, A. Lillee three for 29); ACB Chairman's XII 171 for three (23.3 overs) (M. L. Hayden 32, R. J. Campbell 103).

Dennis Lillee, now 50, opened the bowling with his son Adam and had figures of 8–4–8–3 in what he said would be his last appearance in a major match.

†At Perth, October 27 (day/night). Western Australia won by three runs. Toss: Western Australia. Western Australia 253 for seven (50 overs) (A. C. Gilchrist 37, B. P. Julian 64, J. L. Langer 62 not out, Extras 33; Abdur Razzaq four for 46); Pakistanis 250 for nine (47 overs) (Saeed Anwar 31, Mohammad Wasim 100, Ijaz Ahmed, sen. 35; M. P. Atkinson three for 49, K. M. Harvey four for 40).

The Pakistanis faced only 47 overs because of their slow over-rate.

At Allan Border Field, Brisbane, October 30, 31, November 1, 2. Queensland won by 112 runs. Toss: Queensland. Queensland 274 (J. P. Maher 70, A. Symonds 78, W. A. Seccombe 33; Mushtaq Ahmed four for 103) and 318 for five dec. (M. L. Hayden 128, S. G. Law 100); Pakistanis 276 (Abdur Razzaq 30, Inzamam-ul-Haq 37, Azhar Mahmood 83, Moin Khan 70; A. C. Dale five for 58) and 204 (Saeed Anwar 54, Inzamam-ul-Haq 57; G. I. Foley five for 25).

The inaugural first-class match at Allan Border Field.

AUSTRALIA v PAKISTAN

First Test Match

At Brisbane, November 5, 6, 7, 8, 9. Australia won by ten wickets. Toss: Australia. Test debuts: A. C. Gilchrist, S. A. Muller; Abdur Razzaq.

Steve Waugh's decision to put Pakistan in, influenced by a green-tinged pitch and his opponents' reputation as notoriously slow starters on overseas tours, was open to debate for much of the first day. The Gabba pitch proved to be an excellent batting surface – it ultimately provided 1,297 runs for the loss of 30 wickets – and the Australian captain owed much to Fleming, who outshone McGrath in the attack. Fleming took two wickets in four balls in mid-morning and finished the day by having Yousuf Youhana and Mushtaq Ahmed, the night-watchman, caught behind in his last two overs. In between, Pakistan had threatened a shut-out total as Youhana (16 fours) and Inzamam-ul-Haq (15 fours) consolidated a good morning's work by Saeed Anwar. They added 152 in 51 overs before McGrath trapped Inzamam with the new ball. When Moin Khan hit 61 from 68 balls next morning, including a six over long-on off Muller, Pakistan's final 367 left Waugh still at the mercy of his critics.

Slater and Blewett swung the game Australia's way with their third century opening partnership in their last four Test innings. By the close they were unbeaten with 233, already past Slater's first-wicket record against Pakistan with Taylor in 1994-95, and they increased it on the third day to 269, Australia's third-highest opening stand. Slater against Shoaib Akhtar added spice to the occasion, with the crowd wanting to see if Shoaib could outpace their own Jeff Thomson, once measured at 99.7mph. There were two rival speed guns on the ground, but they varied considerably in their measurements, which in any case were calibrated in kph.

HIGHEST OPENING PARTNERSHIPS FOR AUSTRALIA

382	W. M. Lawry (210) and R. B. Simpson (201) v West Indies at Bridgetown ..	1964-65
329	G. R. Marsh (138) and M. A. Taylor (219) v England at Nottingham	1989
269	**M. J. Slater (169) and G. S. Blewett (89) v Pakistan at Brisbane**	**1999-2000**
260	M. A. Taylor (111) and M. J. Slater (152) v England at Lord's	1993
244	R. B. Simpson (225) and W. M. Lawry (119) v England at Adelaide	1965-66
233	W. A. Brown (121) and J. H. W. Fingleton (112) v South Africa at Cape Town.	1935-36
228	M. J. Slater (219) and M. A. Taylor (96) v Sri Lanka at Perth...........	1995-96

Research: Gordon Vince

Shoaib once put Slater on his back, was unofficially rebuked by the match referee for making faces at the batsman, and had him dropped at second slip on 99. Slater had already been dropped when 78 off Wasim Akram at mid-off. It was obviously his day. He passed 4,000 runs in Tests and went on to his third-highest score for Australia, hitting a six and 25 fours in a stay of almost six hours (271 balls). Shoaib had a moment of triumph when he sent back Steve Waugh and Ponting in quick succession, but there was no respite for the Pakistanis. Mark Waugh scored a typically high-class hundred (148 balls, 17 fours), though he should have been stumped in the 90s; Gilchrist helped him add 123 in 113 minutes and looked on course for a debut hundred until Shoaib yorked him for 81, and followed up with Fleming's wicket three deliveries later. A hailstorm brought the third day to an early close, but next morning Warne raced from 34 not out to a career-best 86 off 90 balls in a last-wicket stand of 86 with Muller. Warne's four sixes all came off fellow-leg-spinner Mushtaq, three in one over, and he also hit nine fours.

Five missed chances and sloppy ground fielding contributed to Pakistan's 208-run deficit. However, an uncharacteristic Australian fumble, by Mark Waugh at slip, let them claw their way back after early setbacks. Anwar, only four when he was dropped, fought on to 119 (174 balls, 20 fours). He and Youhana added a record 177 runs for Pakistan's fourth wicket against Australia and, when rain stopped play at tea on the fourth day, he was still there, with Pakistan 15 runs ahead and six wickets in hand. The first of those went to Warne off the first ball of the final morning, McGrath quickly ended Anwar's resistance, and Fleming claimed the tail to finish with five wickets, and nine for the match – an excellent return in a game so dominated by batsmen. It left Australia requiring 74 runs to win, and Slater and Blewett knocked them off in 56 minutes to let Steve Waugh take an early flight to Sydney to await the birth of his second child: his first son, as it happened.

Man of the Match: M. J. Slater.   *Attendance:* 41,636.

Close of play: First day, Pakistan 280-6 (Azhar Mahmood 7*, Abdur Razzaq 0*); Second day, Australia 233-0 (Slater 134*, Blewett 77*); Third day, Australia 515-9 (Warne 34*, Muller 1*); Fourth day, Pakistan 223-4 (Saeed Anwar 118*, Abdur Razzaq 2*).

Pakistan

Saeed Anwar c M. E. Waugh b Warne	61	– c Gilchrist b McGrath	119
Mohammad Wasim c Gilchrist b Fleming	18	– lbw b Fleming	0
Ijaz Ahmed, sen. c Warne b Fleming	0	– c Gilchrist b McGrath	5
Inzamam-ul-Haq lbw b McGrath	88	– c Ponting b Fleming	12
Yousuf Youhana c Gilchrist b Fleming	95	– c M. E. Waugh b Muller	75
Azhar Mahmood c Slater b McGrath	13	– (8) st Gilchrist b Warne	0
Mushtaq Ahmed c Gilchrist b Fleming	0	– (10) not out	1
Abdur Razzaq c M. E. Waugh b Muller	11	– (6) c Ponting b Warne	2
†Moin Khan run out	61	– (7) c Muller b Fleming	17
*Wasim Akram c and b Muller	9	– (9) b Fleming	28
Shoaib Akhtar not out	0	– b Fleming	5
B 4, l-b 2, n-b 5	11	B 6, l-b 6, n-b 5	17

1/42 (2) 2/42 (3) 3/113 (1) 4/265 (4)　　367　　1/3 (2) 2/8 (3) 3/37 (4)　　281
5/280 (5) 6/280 (7) 7/288 (6)　　　　　　　4/214 (5) 5/223 (6) 6/225 (1)
8/334 (8) 9/356 (10) 10/367 (9)　　　　　7/227 (8) 8/273 (9)
　　　　　　　　　　　　　　　　　　　　9/276 (7) 10/281 (11)

Bowling: *First Innings*—McGrath 28–4–116–2; Fleming 31–5–65–4; Muller 19–4–72–2; Warne 28.1–11–73–1; Blewett 5–1–22–0; Ponting 5–1–12–0; S. R. Waugh 1–0–1–0. *Second Innings*—McGrath 21–9–63–2; Fleming 14.1–2–59–5; Muller 10–1–55–1; Warne 25–8–80–2; Ponting 4–0–12–0.

Australia

M. J. Slater c Yousuf Youhana b Azhar Mahmood	169	– (2) not out	32
G. S. Blewett lbw b Mushtaq Ahmed	89	– (1) not out	40
J. L. Langer c Abdur Razzaq b Mushtaq Ahmed	1		
M. E. Waugh c Wasim Akram b Mushtaq Ahmed	100		
*S. R. Waugh c Moin Khan b Shoaib Akhtar	1		
R. T. Ponting lbw b Shoaib Akhtar	0		
†A. C. Gilchrist b Shoaib Akhtar	81		
S. K. Warne c Mushtaq Ahmed b Wasim Akram	86		
D. W. Fleming lbw b Shoaib Akhtar	0		
G. D. McGrath c Yousuf Youhana b Wasim Akram	1		
S. A. Muller not out	6		
B 3, l-b 12, n-b 26	41	L-b 2	2

1/269 (2) 2/272 (3) 3/311 (1) 4/328 (5)　　575　　　　　　　　　　　(no wkt) 74
5/342 (6) 6/465 (4) 7/485 (7)
8/486 (9) 9/489 (10) 10/575 (8)

Bowling: *First Innings*—Wasim Akram 31.1–6–87–2; Shoaib Akhtar 32–2–153–4; Abdur Razzaq 17–3–66–0; Azhar Mahmood 19–2–52–1; Mushtaq Ahmed 38–3–194–3; Ijaz Ahmed 2–0–8–0. *Second Innings*—Wasim Akram 4–0–14–0; Shoaib Akhtar 5–0–25–0; Azhar Mahmood 3.2–0–13–0; Mushtaq Ahmed 2–0–20–0.

Umpires: E. A. Nicholls (West Indies) and D. J. Harper.
Referee: J. R. Reid (New Zealand).

At Adelaide, November 12, 13, 14, 15. Pakistanis won by an innings and 26 runs. Toss: Pakistanis. South Australia 250 (D. S. Lehmann 136 not out, J. M. Vaughan 40, C. J. Davies 31; Waqar Younis three for 64, Mohammad Akram three for 64, Mushtaq Ahmed three for 46) and 250 (D. A. Fitzgerald 111 not out, C. J. Davies 38, B. A. Johnson 32; Waqar Younis four for 61, Mushtaq Ahmed four for 74); Pakistanis 526 (Ghulam Ali 31, Wajahatullah Wasti 74, Mohammad Wasim 50, Ijaz Ahmed, sen. 141, Yousuf Youhana 90, Moin Khan 66, Saeed Anwar 37; P. Wilson six for 106).

Fitzgerald carried his bat through South Australia's second innings.

[*Jack Atley, Allsport*

Beauty! Pumped-up Adam Gilchrist responds to dressing-room applause for his maiden Test hundred as Justin Langer – fellow Western Australian in a match-winning partnership – adds his own congratulations.

AUSTRALIA v PAKISTAN

Second Test Match

At Hobart, November 18, 19, 20, 21, 22. Australia won by four wickets. Toss: Australia.

Australia achieved an extraordinary victory to secure the series, registering the third-highest fourth-innings total to win a Test match. They had been on the ropes at 126 for five, but Langer and Gilchrist put on 238 in 59 overs, a sixth-wicket record by any country against Pakistan, to take their side to within five runs of their goal.

The win was not without controversy. Umpire Parker's refusal to judge Langer caught at the wicket in the first hour of the final morning left Wasim Akram, Pakistan's captain and also the unlucky bowler, almost incandescent with rage. A breakthrough then would have made Pakistan strong favourites. Unfortunately, it was already public knowledge that Parker had apologised to Langer the previous day for giving him out wrongly in the first innings, and in Pakistani minds it all added up to a suspicion that they were not getting a fair rub of the green. Certainly, neither the situation nor the umpire was helped by the fact that, as in Brisbane, the "snickometer" reading was played over and over on the ground television screen and appeared to indicate some contact. Replays of debatable decisions were shown much too frequently. After this latest incident, series referee Reid concluded that they were undermining the umpires and took action to limit their use. Before the final Test the ACB drew the line at one slow-motion replay and one at normal speed.

Waugh again put Pakistan in, declaring that the days when captains won the toss and almost always batted were over. He looked to have got it right when Pakistan were all out for 222, an hour after tea on the first day. McGrath, always hostile and accurate, claimed his 250th Test wicket to leave Pakistan 18 for two, and only Mohammad Wasim, severe on Warne early on, successfully carried the fight to the Australian bowlers, hitting 12 fours.

Slater and Blewett again set up Australia, having survived a torrid late-afternoon start against Wasim and Shoaib Akhtar. But it was guile rather than brute pace that effected a remarkable transition on the second day. Australia had reached 191 for one with Slater, dropped three times, three runs away from centuries in successive Tests when he pulled Saqlain Mushtaq high to mid-wicket. It was Slater's seventh dismissal in the 90s in Tests and opened the way to a remarkable spell of spin bowling. With his 'wrong 'un' causing mayhem, Saqlain – fit again and preferred to Mushtaq Ahmed – took six for 17 in eight overs. Fleming narrowly averted a hat-trick in a three-wicket over, and Australia lost nine for 55, their lead restricted to 24. Saqlain's six for 46 were his best Test figures, while Gilchrist provided him with his 100th wicket in his 23rd Test. Waqar Younis contributed two wickets and brought memories flooding back when Ponting shouldered arms to a trademark in-swinger timed at 90mph.

Warne produced something special himself on the third day, pitching in the rough outside the left-handed Saeed Anwar's off stump and hitting leg. By then, though, Anwar had given Pakistan a good start, and Ijaz Ahmed and Inzamam-ul-Haq improved on it with 134 runs in 34 overs. Inzamam's century belied his reputation for plodding between the wickets: more than a stone lighter thanks to a new training regime, he ran and ran and ran. His unbeaten 116 at the close contained nine threes as well as 12 fours, but next morning he added only two runs before Mark Waugh took an astounding catch at slip, holding on to a fierce top edge as the ball passed him.

It took Australia almost until lunch to capture the last two wickets, leaving them just over five sessions in which to score 369. Shoaib had Slater caught at slip early in the afternoon off a ball measured at 95mph, the fastest legitimate delivery of the series. The full toss that jammed Langer's index finger against his bat handle was quicker but a no-ball. Azhar Mahmood's double strike just before tea put him on a hat-trick, and by the close Australia still needed 181 with their last recognised batsmen at the wicket. The bookmakers were offering 9–1 against them winning. Ponting, on his home ground, had been dismissed for his third nought in a row.

HIGHEST TEST PARTNERSHIPS BETWEEN LEFT-HANDERS

322	for 5th†	B. C. Lara (213) and J. C. Adams (94)	WI v A	Kingston	1998-99
279	for 2nd	M. A. Taylor (334*) and J. L. Langer (116)	A v P	Peshawar	1998-99
259	for 2nd	W. B. Phillips (159) and G. N. Yallop (141)	A v P	Perth	1983-84
240*	for 4th	A. P. Gurusinha (116*) and A. Ranatunga (135*)	SL v P	Colombo (PSS)	1985-86
238	**for 6th**	**J. L. Langer (127) and A. C. Gilchrist (149*)** .	**A v P**	**Hobart**	**1999-2000**
237	for 4th	H. A. Gomes (123) and C. H. Lloyd (143)	WI v I	Port-of-Spain	1982-83
230	for 4th	A. P. Gurusinha (137) and A. Ranatunga (127) . .	SL v A	Colombo (SSC)	1992-93
224	for 2nd	W. Bardsley (132) and C. Hill (191)	A v SA	Sydney	1910-11
221	for 3rd	B. C. Lara (147) and J. C. Adams (151)	WI v NZ	Wellington	1994-95

† *The fifth wicket added 344, right-hander P. T. Collins retiring hurt after 22 had been added.*

Wasim's curiously negative approach to the first hour's play on the final day allowed Langer and Gilchrist to gain the ascendancy. Saqlain could not repeat his feats of the first innings, and Waqar appeared handicapped by ankle trouble. Gilchrist's attitude to batting was so relaxed that his captain said of him, "He could be playing in his own back yard." His unbeaten 149 came off only 163 balls in four and a half hours, with a six and 13 fours. Langer, on the other hand, took more than seven hours (295 balls, 12 fours) for his 127. When it was all over, Waugh described the Test as one of the "great wins" of his career. Wasim was so distraught that he could not face the press and sent a messenger to say he was feeling unwell.

Man of the Match: J. L. Langer.   *Attendance:* 20,754.

Close of play: First day, Australia 29-0 (Slater 16*, Blewett 9*); Second day, Pakistan 61-1 (Saeed Anwar 36*, Saqlain Mushtaq 0*); Third day, Pakistan 351-7 (Inzamam-ul-Haq 116*, Wasim Akram 1*); Fourth day, Australia 188-5 (Langer 52*, Gilchrist 45*).

Pakistan

Saeed Anwar c Warne b McGrath	0	– b Warne	78
Mohammad Wasim c Gilchrist b Muller	91	– c McGrath b Muller	20
Ijaz Ahmed, sen. c Slater b McGrath	6	– (4) c S. R. Waugh b McGrath	82
Inzamam-ul-Haq b Muller	12	– (5) c M. E. Waugh b Warne	118
Yousuf Youhana c M. E. Waugh b Fleming	17	– (6) c Ponting b Fleming	2
Azhar Mahmood b Warne	27	– (7) lbw b Warne	28
†Moin Khan c McGrath b Muller	1	– (8) c Gilchrist b Fleming	6
*Wasim Akram c Gilchrist b Warne	29	– (9) c Blewett b Warne	31
Saqlain Mushtaq lbw b Warne	3	– (3) lbw b Warne	8
Waqar Younis not out	12	– run out	0
Shoaib Akhtar c Gilchrist b Fleming	5	– not out	5
B 10, l-b 6, w 3	19	L-b 6, w 1, n-b 7	14

1/4 (1) 2/18 (3) 3/71 (4) 4/120 (5)   222
5/148 (2) 6/153 (7) 7/188 (6)
8/198 (9) 9/217 (8) 10/222 (11)

1/50 (2) 2/100 (3) 3/122 (1)   392
4/256 (4) 5/263 (6) 6/320 (7)
7/345 (8) 8/357 (5)
9/358 (10) 10/392 (9)

Bowling: *First Innings*—McGrath 18–8–34–2; Fleming 24.5–7–54–2; Muller 12–0–68–3; Warne 16–6–45–3; Blewett 2–1–5–0. *Second Innings*—McGrath 27–8–87–1; Fleming 29–5–89–2; Warne 45.5–11–110–5; Muller 17–3–63–1; S. R. Waugh 4–1–19–0; M. E. Waugh 2–0–6–0; Ponting 2–1–7–0; Blewett 2–0–5–0.

Australia

M. J. Slater c Ijaz Ahmed b Saqlain Mushtaq	97	– (2) c Azhar Mahmood b Shoaib Akhtar	27
G. S. Blewett c Moin Khan b Azhar Mahmood	35	– (1) c Moin Khan b Azhar Mahmood	29
J. L. Langer c Mohammad Wasim b Saqlain Mushtaq	59	– c Inzamam-ul-Haq b Saqlain Mushtaq	127
M. E. Waugh lbw b Waqar Younis	5	– lbw b Azhar Mahmood	0
*S. R. Waugh c Ijaz Ahmed b Wasim Akram	24	– c and b Saqlain Mushtaq	28
R. T. Ponting b Waqar Younis	0	– lbw b Wasim Akram	0
†A. C. Gilchrist st Moin Khan b Saqlain Mushtaq	6	– not out	149
S. K. Warne b Saqlain Mushtaq	0	– not out	0
D. W. Fleming lbw b Saqlain Mushtaq	0		
G. D. McGrath st Moin Khan b Saqlain Mushtaq	7		
S. A. Muller not out	0		
B 2, l-b 6, n-b 5	13	B 1, l-b 4, n-b 4.	9

1/76 (2) 2/191 (1) 3/206 (4) 4/206 (3)   246
5/213 (6) 6/236 (7) 7/236 (8)
8/236 (9) 9/246 (5) 10/246 (10)

1/39 (2) 2/81 (1)   (6 wkts) 369
3/81 (4) 4/125 (5)
5/126 (6) 6/364 (3)

Bowling: *First Innings*—Wasim Akram 20–4–51–1; Shoaib Akhtar 17–2–69–0; Waqar Younis 12–1–42–2; Saqlain Mushtaq 24–8–46–6; Azhar Mahmood 7–1–30–1. *Second Innings*—Wasim Akram 18–1–68–1; Waqar Younis 11–2–38–0; Shoaib Akhtar 23–5–85–1; Saqlain Mushtaq 44.5–9–130–2; Azhar Mahmood 17–3–43–2.

Umpires: P. Willey (England) and P. D. Parker.
Referee: J. R. Reid (New Zealand).

AUSTRALIA v PAKISTAN

Third Test Match

At Perth, November 26, 27, 28. Australia won by an innings and 20 runs. Toss: Pakistan.

Completed by tea on the third day, this match was a sorry anticlimax after the fluctuations of the first two absorbing Tests. It certainly didn't help that 14 wickets fell on the opening day. Pakistan, still in a state of some demoralisation after the Hobart game, lost five wickets before lunch after choosing to bat on a typically bouncy Perth pitch and were all out in three and three-quarter hours. Australia's fast bowlers held an off-side line, just short of a length, and left it to the batsmen to feed the close catchers. Gilchrist's leg-side catch to dismiss Yousuf Youhana was in a class of its own. Four Australian wickets then fell for 54 inside 12 overs, but Langer, the local hero, and Ponting made a nonsense of all that had gone before. Together for almost six and a half hours, they shut Pakistan out of the game by adding 327, a record for any Australian wicket against these opponents and the highest fifth-wicket partnership against them by any country.

Langer batted seven and a quarter hours for his 144, his second successive century; only weeks before, the critics were calling for his head. Even more significant for Australia was 24-year-old Ponting's return to form after three consecutive noughts. He admitted he had been the butt of some teasing in the dressing-room, but his Test-highest 197 (288 balls, 22 fours), compiled in seven hours, silenced the mockers. Handsomely executed drives from both men repeatedly beat the fielders across the fast outfield, with Ponting always looking to dominate the bowling.

Left with 15 overs to bat on the second evening, after Australia's last five wickets went for 27 runs, Pakistan lost two wickets. Next morning, Saqlain Mushtaq was unable to resume his night-watchman's duties because of food poisoning. He returned when his fellow overnight batsman, Ijaz Ahmed, mishooked Kasprowicz to deep square leg to end a brave, brilliantly counter-attacking innings of 115. It was his 12th hundred in Tests and his sixth against Australia. For a time, Wasim Akram ignored his disappointments, as well as the groin injury suffered the previous day, and bludgeoned 52 from 40 balls. It was great fun but all in a lost cause. The Pakistanis could not even make Australia bat again for their victory.

Man of the Match: R. T. Ponting.　　　　*Attendance:* 40,449.

Man of the Series: J. L. Langer.

Close of play: First day, Australia 171-4 (Langer 63*, Ponting 62*); Second day, Pakistan 40-2 (Ijaz Ahmed 19*, Saqlain Mushtaq 4*).

Pakistan

Saeed Anwar c Ponting b McGrath	18	– c Gilchrist b Fleming	6
Wajahatullah Wasti c Ponting b McGrath	5	– c Fleming b McGrath	7
Ijaz Ahmed, sen. b Fleming	1	– c Slater b Kasprowicz	115
Inzamam-ul-Haq c S. R. Waugh b Kasprowicz	22	– (5) c M. E. Waugh b McGrath	8
Yousuf Youhana c Gilchrist b McGrath	18	– (6) c S. R. Waugh b McGrath	0
Azhar Mahmood b Warne b Fleming	39	– (7) b Warne	17
†Moin Khan c and b Fleming	28	– (8) c Gilchrist b McGrath	26
*Wasim Akram not out	5	– (9) c McGrath b Kasprowicz	52
Saqlain Mushtaq c Blewett b Kasprowicz	7	– (4) lbw b Kasprowicz	12
Shoaib Akhtar b Kasprowicz	0	– c Warne b Fleming	8
Mohammad Akram c M. E. Waugh b Kasprowicz	0	– not out	10
L-b 4, n-b 8	12	L-b 6, n-b 9	15

1/18 (2) 2/26 (3) 3/26 (1) 4/51 (5)　　　　　155　　1/15 (1) 2/25 (2) 3/53 (5) 4/56 (6)　　　276
5/83 (4) 6/135 (6) 7/142 (7)　　　　　　　　　　　5/114 (7) 6/168 (8) 7/230 (3)
8/155 (9) 9/155 (10) 10/155 (11)　　　　　　　　　8/256 (4) 9/261 (9) 10/276 (10)

In the second innings Saqlain Mushtaq, when 4, retired ill at 40, and resumed at 230.

Bowling: *First Innings*—McGrath 19-3-44-3; Fleming 19-7-48-3; Kasprowicz 12-2-53-4; Warne 2-0-6-0. *Second Innings*—McGrath 21-5-49-4; Fleming 19.4-3-86-2; Kasprowicz 16-3-79-3; Warne 13-1-56-1.

Australia

M. J. Slater lbw b Wasim Akram	0
G. S. Blewett c Inzamam-ul-Haq b Mohammad Akram	11
J. L. Langer c Moin Khan b Shoaib Akhtar	144
M. E. Waugh c sub (Ghulam Ali) b Mohammad Akram	0
*S. R. Waugh c Yousuf Youhana b Mohammad Akram	5
R. T. Ponting c Ijaz Ahmed b Azhar Mahmood	197
†A. C. Gilchrist b Mohammad Akram	28
S. K. Warne c Moin Khan b Saqlain Mushtaq	13
M. S. Kasprowicz not out	9
D. W. Fleming lbw b Saqlain Mushtaq	0
G. D. McGrath c Azhar Mahmood b Mohammad Akram	0
B 9, l-b 9, n-b 26	44

1/0 (1) 2/28 (2) 3/48 (4) 4/54 (5)　　　　　451
5/381 (3) 6/424 (7) 7/424 (6)
8/448 (8) 9/450 (10) 10/451 (11)

Bowling: Wasim Akram 17–2–55–1; Mohammad Akram 27.5–1–138–5; Shoaib Akhtar 16–2–74–1; Azhar Mahmood 23–2–91–1; Saqlain Mushtaq 26–7–75–2; Wajahatullah Wasti 1–1–0–0.

Umpires: P. Willey (England) and D. B. Hair.
Referee: J. R. Reid (New Zealand).

†At Perth, January 2 (day/night). Australia A won by 52 runs. Toss: Pakistanis. Australia A 281 for nine (50 overs) (M. L. Hayden 128, D. A. Fitzgerald 85; Saqlain Mushtaq five for 40); Pakistanis 229 (41.5 overs) (Azhar Mahmood 100 not out, Abdur Razzaq 35; S. Lee four for 32, P. Wilson three for 34).

†At Adelaide, January 4 (day/night). Australia A won by six wickets. Toss: Pakistanis. Pakistanis 167 (47.5 overs) (Wajahatullah Wasti 31, Yousuf Youhana 63; P. Wilson three for 14, S. C. G. MacGill three for 26); Australia A 168 for four (33.4 overs) (B. J. Hodge 46, S. Lee 60 not out).

†At Brisbane, January 6 (day/night). Queensland won by four wickets. Toss: Pakistanis. Pakistanis 169 (40.4 overs) (Moin Khan 77 not out; M. S. Kasprowicz three for 40); Queensland 173 for six (44.5 overs) (G. I. Foley 64, W. A. Seccombe 64 not out; Waqar Younis three for 40).

Pakistan's matches v Australia and India in the Carlton & United Series (January 9–February 4) may be found in that section.

†At Canberra, January 12. Pakistanis won by 37 runs (D/L method). Toss: Pakistanis. Pakistanis 283 for six (48 overs) (Wajahatullah Wasti 54, Yousuf Youhana 152, Mohammad Wasim 33); Australian Country XI 245 for six (48 overs) (A. A. Shields 65, B. K. D. May 83, G. Smith 38). *The Australian Country XI's target was revised to 283 from 48 overs.*

TEST RESULTS, 1999-2000

	P	W	L	D	% W
Australia	13	10	1	2	76.92
South Africa	12	7	2	3	58.33
England	12	5	3	4	41.66
Sri Lanka	15	5	4	6	33.33
West Indies	12	4	5	3	33.33
Pakistan	12	3	6	3	25.00
New Zealand	8	2	4	2	25.00
India	8	1	5	2	12.50
Zimbabwe	10	0	7	3	00.00

THE SOUTH AFRICANS IN ZIMBABWE, 1999-2000

SOUTH AFRICAN TOURING PARTY

W. J. Cronje (Free State) (*captain*), P. R. Adams (Western Province), A. M. Bacher (Gauteng), N. Boje (Free State), M. V. Boucher (Border), D. J. Cullinan (Gauteng), H. H. Dippenaar (Free State), A. A. Donald (Free State), J. H. Kallis (Western Province), L. Klusener (KwaZulu-Natal), S. M. Pollock (KwaZulu-Natal), J. N. Rhodes (KwaZulu-Natal).

Manager: Goolam Rajah.   *Coach:* G. X. Ford.

ZIMBABWE v SOUTH AFRICA

Test Match

At Harare, November 11, 12, 13, 14. South Africa won by an innings and 219 runs. Toss: South Africa.

Zimbabwe suffered their heaviest defeat in seven years of Test cricket, giving South Africa their biggest-ever victory. The previous records for both countries had involved Sri Lanka, beaten by South Africa by an innings and 208 runs at Colombo in 1993-94 but winners over Zimbabwe by an innings and 77 runs, also at Colombo, in 1996-97.

The omens for Zimbabwe had not been good in the lead-up to the match. Campbell unexpectedly resigned as captain 48 hours before the start, to be replaced by Andy Flower, his predecessor; the attack was still severely weakened by the absence through injury of Streak and Paul Strang, as well as by Johnson being unfit to bowl; confidence was low after the two crushing losses, to Australia and South Africa, of the past month; and an unresolved pay dispute with their Board had badly affected morale, according to one senior player. It was a burden Zimbabwe could not carry.

Had Zimbabwe been able to bowl first, in conditions overwhelmingly favouring the bowlers, the game might have been more evenly contested. On a truncated first day, when only 23 overs were possible because of rain, South Africa, notably Donald, bowled erratically yet claimed three wickets, thanks partly to poor batting. On the second morning, the result was effectively decided. More injudicious strokes against persistent bowling on a helpful pitch saw Zimbabwe bowled out before lunch for 102, then their lowest Test total. Only Johnson, the victim of a poor decision, offered protracted resistance, surviving 99 minutes for 20. Pollock, swinging the ball out on a good line, was the pick of the bowlers, while Cronje returned Test-best figures of three for 14. Klusener claimed his 50th Test wicket when he dismissed Whittall, who fell to the best of five good slip catches. South Africa dropped nothing.

Although the well-grassed pitch still offered assistance in the first few hours of the South African innings, the Zimbabwean seamers' inability to hit as hard, or bowl with the same discipline, as South Africa's bowlers proved all-important. Kallis's defence was watertight, his attacking strokes well selected and executed as he compiled a masterly 115 in five hours 39 minutes, with 13 fours and three sixes, his fifth Test hundred. A less fluent Cronje helped him add 100 in 38 overs. By the third morning the pitch had flattened out, an important factor in Boucher and Pollock's South African eighth-wicket record of 148 in 37 overs. Boucher went on to record not only his second Test hundred of the year but also the highest Test score by a night-watchman, 125 in 322 minutes with 18 fours, most of which came from cuts and drives. It was a chanceless innings, a personal best, and he could not hide his disappointment when he mis-hit to mid-on to give part-time off-spinner Gripper his first Test wicket.

With two days in which to save the match, following Cronje's declaration at South Africa's overnight score, Zimbabwe succumbed in less than three and a half hours. An improved Donald removed Grant Flower with the second ball of the innings, a near unplayable delivery, and returned to bowl brother Andy with another rapid off-cutter. Pollock was again impressive, but the dispirited and inept Zimbabwean batting showed no backbone whatever. – GEOFFREY DEAN.

Men of the Match: M. V. Boucher and S. M. Pollock.

Close of play: First day, Zimbabwe 48-3 (Johnson 18*, A. Flower 2*); Second day, South Africa 207-4 (Kallis 101*, Boucher 1*); Third day, South Africa 462-9 (Donald 17*, Adams 3*).

Zimbabwe

G. W. Flower c Kallis b Klusener	5	– b Donald	0
T. R. Gripper b Pollock	1	– c Kallis b Cronje	18
M. W. Goodwin c Cronje b Pollock	17	– lbw b Pollock	7
N. C. Johnson c Boucher b Pollock	20	– c Boucher b Klusener	9
*†A. Flower c Boucher b Pollock	8	– b Donald	14
A. D. R. Campbell c Pollock b Cronje	15	– c Rhodes b Adams	25
G. J. Rennie c Cullinan b Klusener	11	– c Donald b Adams	34
G. J. Whittall c Pollock b Klusener	3	– c Dippenaar b Pollock	17
B. C. Strang lbw b Cronje	11	– lbw b Pollock	0
H. K. Olonga c Boucher b Cronje	0	– not out	4
M. Mbangwa not out	1	– lbw b Adams	3
L-b 7, n-b 3	10	L-b 4, w 2, n-b 4	10

1/6 (1) 2/6 (2) 3/35 (3) 4/59 (5)   102
5/64 (4) 6/79 (6) 7/86 (8)
8/101 (7) 9/101 (9) 10/102 (10)

1/0 (1) 2/17 (3) 3/33 (2)   141
4/37 (4) 5/73 (5) 6/83 (6)
7/128 (8) 8/128 (9)
9/132 (7) 10/141 (11)

Bowling: First Innings—Donald 10–5–10–0; Pollock 17–7–32–4; Klusener 12–3–39–3; Cronje 7.5–2–14–3. *Second Innings*—Donald 9–2–25–2; Pollock 16–9–23–3; Klusener 9–1–29–1; Cronje 6–1–20–1; Adams 10.5–0–40–3.

South Africa

A. M. Bacher c A. Flower b Strang	8	S. M. Pollock c Campbell b Olonga	61
H. H. Dippenaar c Johnson b Olonga	33	A. A. Donald not out	17
J. H. Kallis lbw b Strang	115	P. R. Adams not out	3
D. J. Cullinan c A. Flower b Strang	0	L-b 3, n-b 10	13
*W. J. Cronje c Rennie b Olonga	58		
†M. V. Boucher c Goodwin b Gripper	125	1/20 (1) 2/96 (2) (9 wkts dec.) 462	
J. N. Rhodes c G. W. Flower		3/105 (4) 4/205 (5)	
b Mbangwa	4	5/230 (3) 6/237 (7)	
L. Klusener c Olonga b Mbangwa	25	7/281 (8) 8/429 (9) 9/451 (6)	

Bowling: Olonga 33–7–107–3; Strang 38–10–92–3; Mbangwa 28–6–91–2; Whittall 27–8–78–0; G. W. Flower 18–3–52–0; Goodwin 2–0–11–0; Gripper 8–1–28–1.

Umpires: D. B. Hair (Australia) and R. B. Tiffin.
Referee: J. L. Hendriks (West Indies).

ICC REFEREES' PANEL

On July 10, 1991, the International Cricket Council agreed to form a panel of referees to enforce the new Code of Conduct for Tests and one-day internationals, to impose penalties for slow over-rates, breaches of the Code and other ICC regulations, and to support the umpires in upholding the conduct of the game. ICC referees began to supervise Tests and one-day internationals under a pilot scheme in the 1991-92 season.

The following referees were on the panel from September 2000: P. J. Burge (Australia), M. H. Denness (England), G. T. Dowling (New Zealand), A. Ebrahim (Zimbabwe), H. Gardiner (Zimbabwe), Hanumant Singh (India), B. F. Hastings (New Zealand), J. L. Hendriks (West Indies), B. N. Jarman (Australia), D. T. Lindsay (South Africa), R. S. Madugalle (Sri Lanka), Naushad Ali (Pakistan), J. R. Reid (New Zealand), A. C. Smith (England), C. W. Smith (West Indies), R. Subba Row (England), Talat Ali (Pakistan), G. R. Viswanath (India), B. Warnapura (Sri Lanka), M. R. Wilson (South Africa).

Note: Compared with the 1999-2000 list, D. T. Lindsay and M. R. Wilson have replaced E. Isaacs and P. L. van der Merwe of South Africa; Talat Ali and B. Warnapura have joined from Pakistan and Sri Lanka respectively.

THE SRI LANKANS IN ZIMBABWE, 1999-2000

By JOHN WARD

When Sri Lanka visited Zimbabwe five years earlier for the initial Test series between the two countries, negative cricket by the tourists and Zimbabwe's inexperience in forcing victory resulted in three somewhat dreary draws. Since then, Zimbabwe had won their first Test matches and Sri Lanka, with spectacular success, had won the World Cup in 1995-96. But less happy recent events, rather than past triumphs, provided the background to this latest tour. Sri Lanka had endured a disastrous World Cup in 1999, though they were picking themselves up under a new captain, Sanath Jayasuriya, while Zimbabwe were still reeling from heavy defeats by Australia and South Africa in the last month.

Victory in the Second Test gave Sri Lanka the series 1–0. The only match of the three not seriously affected by the weather, it will be remembered for Nuwan Zoysa's first-over hat-trick in his only international match of the tour. Having missed the First Test through illness, he returned home after this one because of a groin strain. Less deserving of memory was the controversial run-out of Zimbabwe's Murray Goodwin later in the same match. Assuming the ball was dead, he left his crease and Tillekeratne Dilshan, playing in only his second Test, broke his wicket. This incident led to a serious deterioration in the relationship between the teams. Three Zimbabweans, Goodwin, Alistair Campbell and Neil Johnson, were fined and given suspended sentences for persistent sledging during the Third Test, the one match of the series in which the sides were evenly balanced almost throughout. Had the rain held off, it might have had a fascinating finish.

During the Tests, Zimbabwe still seemed to attract the ill-fortune that dogged them earlier in the season. They lost all three tosses, making it seven lost out of the last nine, and suffered more than their share of dubious umpiring decisions. By the one-day series, Lady Luck had relented a little. Zimbabwe won the toss in the first four matches although, ironically, their only victory came on the one occasion they lost it. Sri Lanka took the series 3–1, the opening match falling victim to rain.

Without Arjuna Ranatunga, not selected, and Aravinda de Silva, who withdrew from the tour for personal reasons, Sri Lanka's batting was young and inexperienced. The poor form of Jayasuriya was both a disappointment and a handicap. Yet, until the final one-day international, someone always rose to the occasion, and young players such as Russel Arnold and Dilshan showed great promise. Marvan Atapattu and Arnold carried their bats in the First and Third Tests respectively, the first time two players from the same country had done so in a series. The home side were over-reliant on their captain and wicket-keeper, Andy Flower, who hit a hundred and three fifties in the Tests and whose handling of Muttiah Muralitharan was particularly impressive. Grant Flower, struggling for form, had a different opening partner in each of the Tests but, going in together in the one-day series, he and Campbell only once failed to put on 50.

Both series were decided, in the main, by Sri Lanka's disciplined bowlers. Their seamers were invariably persistent, with Chaminda Vaas the pick, while Muralitharan's off-spin, though rarely returning outstanding figures, always presented the batsmen with problems. Zimbabwe's bowling was much more fragile. Heath Streak and Paul Strang missed the entire tour through injury, Neil Johnson was still unable to bowl, and Adam Huckle, who might have deputised for Strang as the leg-spinner, had unexpectedly retired. Henry Olonga and the left-arm seamer, Bryan Strang, recalled as a stock bowler, did a fine job with little incisive support, while the surprise return of Eddo Brandes, for his first Test since the England tour of 1996-97, boosted Zimbabwe's morale in the final match.

Andy Flower, having resumed the captaincy for the return match against South Africa, handled his team and his own game well, and Jayasuriya won acclaim for his astute leadership. Even if spectators rarely saw his true form with the bat, he several times played a crucial role with the ball and in the field. And the standard of fielding, from both sides, was excellent.

Given that there was much fascinating cricket, public support was disappointing. No doubt this could be attributed to the poor showing of the home team and the perception that Sri Lanka were not such attractive opponents as Zimbabwe's recent visitors, Australia and South Africa. But it cannot have helped that Zimbabwe played host to such a glut of international cricket in a two-month period.

SRI LANKAN TOURING PARTY

S. T. Jayasuriya (Bloomfield) (*captain*), D. P. M. D. Jayawardene (Sinhalese) (*vice-captain*), R. P. Arnold (Nondescripts), M. S. Atapattu (Sinhalese), S. I. de Saram (Tamil Union), T. M. Dilshan (Sebastianites), I. S. Gallage (Colombo), R. Herath (Moors), H. P. W. Jayawardene (Sebastianites), R. S. Kaluwitharana (Colts), M. Muralitharan (Tamil Union), A. S. A. Perera (Sinhalese), L. P. C. Silva (Panadura), W. P. U. J. C. Vaas (Colts), G. P. Wickremasinghe (Sinhalese), D. N. T. Zoysa (Sinhalese).

Dilshan replaced P. A. de Silva (Nondescripts), who withdrew for personal reasons. K. R. Pushpakumara (Nondescripts) joined the party as cover for Perera and Zoysa, who were unfit; they flew home while U. D. U. Chandana (Tamil Union) and K. S. C. de Silva (Burgher) reinforced the party for the one-day internationals.

Manager: S. Jayasinghe.   *Coach:* D. F. Whatmore.

Jayasinghe replaced the original manager, C. T. A. Schaffter.

SRI LANKAN TOUR RESULTS

Test matches – Played 3: Won 1, Drawn 2.
First-class matches – Played 5: Won 2, Drawn 3.
Wins – Zimbabwe, CFX Academy.
Draws – Zimbabwe (2), ZCU President's XI.
One day internationals – Played 5: Won 3, Lost 1, No result 1.

TEST MATCH AVERAGES

ZIMBABWE – BATTING

	T	I	NO	R	HS	100s	50s	Avge	Ct
A. Flower	3	6	2	388	129	1	3	97.00	13
N. C. Johnson	3	6	1	162	70	0	2	32.40	1
G. J. Whittall	3	5	1	111	53*	0	1	27.75	0
M. W. Goodwin	3	6	0	160	61	0	1	26.66	2
G. W. Flower	3	6	0	123	48	0	0	20.50	4
B. C. Strang	3	4	0	76	41	0	0	19.00	0
A. D. R. Campbell	3	5	0	77	36	0	0	15.40	3
H. K. Olonga	3	4	3	14	10*	0	0	14.00	0
G. B. Brent	2	3	0	3	3	0	0	1.00	0

Played in one Test: E. A. Brandes 9, 1*; T. R. Gripper 0, 4 (3 ct); E. Z. Matambanadzo 6, 0; R. W. Price 2, 4; G. J. Rennie 16, 2; A. R. Whittall 8; C. B. Wishart 1, 9.

* *Signifies not out.*

BOWLING

	O	M	R	W	BB	5W/i	Avge
E. A. Brandes	21	5	65	4	3-45	0	16.25
G. B. Brent	61.2	19	144	5	3-21	0	28.80
H. K. Olonga	93.4	15	270	9	4-103	0	30.00
B. C. Strang	95	31	239	7	3-91	0	34.14
G. J. Whittall	50	14	145	3	2-37	0	48.33

Also bowled: G. W. Flower 13.3–4–37–1; T. R. Gripper 1–0–6–0; E. Z. Matambanadzo 31–6–95–2; R. W. Price 8–3–22–0; A. R. Whittall 35–6–105–1.

SRI LANKA – BATTING

	T	I	NO	R	HS	100s	50s	Avge	Ct
T. M. Dilshan	3	4	1	209	163*	1	0	69.66	6
M. S. Atapattu	3	5	1	265	216*	1	0	66.25	3
R. P. Arnold	3	5	2	175	104*	1	0	58.33	7
D. P. M. D. Jayawardene	3	4	1	116	91	0	1	38.66	5
S. I. de Saram	3	3	0	94	39	0	0	31.33	0
R. S. Kaluwitharana	3	4	1	70	30	0	0	23.33	6
S. T. Jayasuriya	3	5	1	82	49	0	0	20.50	0
G. P. Wickremasinghe	3	3	0	38	18	0	0	12.66	0
M. Muralitharan	3	3	0	16	6	0	0	5.33	1
W. P. U. J. C. Vaas	3	3	0	14	9	0	0	4.66	0

Played in one Test: I. S. Gallage 3; K. R. Pushpakumara 7; D. N. T. Zoysa 5.

* *Signifies not out.*

BOWLING

	O	M	R	W	BB	5W/i	Avge
D. N. T. Zoysa	24	6	46	4	3-22	0	11.50
K. R. Pushpakumara	46	10	95	5	5-56	1	19.00
S. T. Jayasuriya	35.4	10	77	4	4-40	0	19.25
W. P. U. J. C. Vaas	154.4	37	347	14	4-56	0	24.78
G. P. Wickremasinghe	112.2	36	233	9	6-60	1	25.88
M. Muralitharan	165.5	50	329	9	3-44	0	36.55

Also bowled: R. P. Arnold 14–5–30–0; I. S. Gallage 25–5–77–0; D. P. M. D. Jayawardene 6–2–19–0.

Note: Matches in this section which were not first-class are signified by a dagger.

At Bulawayo, November 7, 8, 9. Drawn. Toss: ZCU President's XI. ZCU President's XI 325 (G. J. Rennie 127, G. B. Brent 55, J. A. Rennie 48 not out, A. J. Mackay 33; I. S. Gallage six for 60); Sri Lankans 438 (M. S. Atapattu 48, T. M. Dilshan 35, R. P. Arnold 75, D. P. M. D. Jayawardene 38, L. P. C. Silva 32, S. I. de Saram 49, A. S. A. Perera 46, I. S. Gallage 36; A. R. Whittall six for 151).

  Gavin Rennie earned himself a last-minute reprieve from being dropped from the Test team with his highest career score to date.

At Kwekwe, November 12, 13. Sri Lankans won by an innings and 132 runs. Toss: Sri Lankans. Sri Lankans 302 (M. S. Atapattu 40, S. T. Jayasuriya 39, D. P. M. D. Jayawardene 50, A. S. A. Perera 38; G. B. Brent five for 84); CFX Academy 126 (W. P. U. J. C. Vaas four for 43, M. Muralitharan four for 24) and 44 (G. P. Wickremasinghe four for five, R. P. Arnold three for ten).

The Academy's 44 in their second innings was then the lowest total in a first-class match in Zimbabwe. Wickremasinghe's analysis was 8–6–5–4.

ZIMBABWE v SRI LANKA

First Test Match

At Bulawayo, November 18, 19, 20, 21, 22. Drawn. Toss: Sri Lanka. Test debuts: G. B. Brent; S. I. de Saram, T. M. Dilshan, I. S. Gallage.

Zimbabwe were glad to play at Bulawayo after their recent experiences against Australia and South Africa on bowler-friendly pitches in Harare. The Queens Sports Club pitch favoured batsmen, though giving a little help to bowlers prepared to work hard, and Sri Lanka appeared to have misinterpreted its grass covering when they put Zimbabwe in. Their innings was built around a determined stand of 99 between Goodwin and Andy Flower, after the earlier batsmen had made a start but failed to build on it. Flower, eager to monopolise the strike because of his team's long tail, threw away the chance of a century, but a lusty innings from Strang, in his usual block-and-bang style, took the total close to 300 before he was last out to Wickremasinghe, who returned career-best figures of six for 60.

Sri Lanka's reply revolved around Atapattu, who became only the second Sri Lankan to carry his bat in Test cricket, after Sidath Wettimuny against New Zealand in 1982-83. Jayasuriya looked in deceptively good form in their opening stand of 85, but thereafter only Kaluwitharana and the patient de Saram lent significant support as the persistent Zimbabwe bowlers worked their way down the order. Atapattu played a percentage game throughout, content to wait for the bad ball and accumulate steadily. The Zimbabweans were convinced they should have won an lbw decision against him just after he reached his fifty, but he gave no actual chances while batting for ten hours 27 minutes, during which he faced 437 balls and hit 24 fours. His unbeaten 216 was his second double-century against Zimbabwe.

Only half a day's play was possible on the third day before a torrential downpour enveloped the ground, and play began an hour late on the fourth, when Sri Lanka's main aim seemed to be continued accumulation rather than quick runs. Rain clouds were building up again by the time Zimbabwe began their second innings, shortly after lunch, but the first interruption was not caused by the weather. In the first over, Grant Flower glanced the new ball to the fine-leg boundary, where it rolled into a hole filled with water on the building site of the new media centre and had to be replaced.

Flower, putting behind him the loss of two partners early on, looked set for his first Test fifty of the season before being given out, somewhat unluckily, caught at short leg. Then came an intriguing battle between Muralitharan and the left-handers, Johnson and Andy Flower. Johnson, in particular, struggled, spending 72 minutes on nine. Ultimately, Muralitharan changed his tactics and tossed the ball up more, which the batsman appreciated to the tune of three fours in one over and, later, a six over long-on. He had just reached a fine fifty in the final session when the light deteriorated and the players came off. Another downpour that evening and prolonged rain the following morning left areas of the ground waterlogged, making play impossible on the final day.

Man of the Match: M. S. Atapattu.

Close of play: First day, Zimbabwe 256-8 (Strang 21*, A. R. Whittall 0*); Second day, Sri Lanka 232-4 (Atapattu 109*, Kaluwitharana 27*); Third day, Sri Lanka 358-6 (Atapattu 178*, Vaas 6*); Fourth day, Zimbabwe 136-3 (Johnson 52*, A. Flower 15*).

Zimbabwe

G. W. Flower c Arnold b Wickremasinghe	....	17	– c Dilshan b Muralitharan 48
G. J. Rennie lbw b Wickremasinghe	....	16	– c Kaluwitharana b Vaas 2
M. W. Goodwin c Arnold b Wickremasinghe	...	61	– c Dilshan b Vaas 2
N. C. Johnson c Arnold b Vaas	....	17	– not out 52
*†A. Flower c Muralitharan b Wickremasinghe	.	86	– not out 15
A. D. R. Campbell run out	....	0	
G. J. Whittall run out	....	11	
G. B. Brent c Jayawardene b Muralitharan	..	0	
B. C. Strang c Kaluwitharana b Wickremasinghe		41	
A. R. Whittall c Kaluwitharana b Wickremasinghe		8	
H. K. Olonga not out	....	1	
L-b 5, n-b 23	....	28	B 1, l-b 4, n-b 12 17

1/37 (1) 2/38 (2) 3/68 (4) 4/167 (3)   286   1/8 (2) 2/27 (3) 3/72 (1)   (3 wkts) 136
5/167 (6) 6/212 (7) 7/214 (8)
8/250 (5) 9/275 (10) 10/286 (9)

Bowling: *First Innings*—Vaas 28–3–88–1; Gallage 14–1–53–0; Wickremasinghe 21.2–6–60–6; Muralitharan 20–3–61–1; Arnold 6–3–8–0; Jayasuriya 7–1–11–0. *Second Innings*—Vaas 13–4–27–2; Gallage 11–4–24–0; Wickremasinghe 8–1–20–0; Muralitharan 14–3–50–1; Arnold 2–0–9–0; Jayasuriya 1–0–1–0.

Sri Lanka

M. S. Atapattu not out	 216	G. P. Wickremasinghe c A. Flower	
*S. T. Jayasuriya lbw b A. R. Whittall	.. 49	b Strang .	13
R. P. Arnold c A. Flower b Olonga	 7	M. Muralitharan c G. W. Flower	
D. P. M. D. Jayawardene lbw b Brent	... 17	b Olonga .	6
T. M. Dilshan lbw b Olonga	 9	B 12, l-b 11, w 1, n-b 6	30
†R. S. Kaluwitharana c A. Flower			
b Olonga . 30	1/85 (2) 2/98 (3) 3/141 (4)	428
S. I. de Saram c A. Flower b Brent	 39	4/159 (5) 5/238 (6) 6/345 (7)	
W. P. U. J. C. Vaas c Campbell b Strang .		7/372 (8) 8/390 (9)	
I. S. Gallage c G. W. Flower b Strang	.. 3	9/417 (10) 10/428 (11)	

Bowling: Olonga 32–6–103–4; Strang 30–9–91–3; Brent 32–12–55–2; A. R. Whittall 35–6–105–1; G. J. Whittall 14–3–48–0; G. W. Flower 4–2–3–0.

Umpires: E. A. Nicholls (West Indies) and K. C. Barbour.
Referee: J. L. Hendriks (West Indies).

ZIMBADWE v SRI LANKA

Second Test Match

At Harare, November 26, 27, 28, 29, 30. Sri Lanka won by six wickets. Toss: Sri Lanka.

Seldom has a Test match had as sensational a start as this one. No bowler had previously taken a hat-trick with his first three deliveries in a Test, or as early as its second over, which is when Zoysa accomplished Sri Lanka's first hat-trick in their 95th Test. Gripper, opening in place of Rennie, padded up to a ball that nipped back, Goodwin got a faint touch to one that lifted and moved away, and finally Johnson, moving forward and across, was also given lbw by umpire Bucknor. Unfortunately, only the first two parts of the hat-trick were recorded for posterity because a power failure interrupted television coverage.

Only India had lost more wickets without a run on the board at the start of a Test innings – four against England at Headingley in 1952 – and Australia were the only other side to have lost their first three wickets for nought, against England at Brisbane in 1950-51. But both these instances had been in the third innings of the match, in difficult conditions. While the Harare pitch had been expected to help bowlers early on, Zimbabwe had not been unduly concerned when put in. There was less grass on it than there had been against South Africa, or in the one-day matches against Australia, and Sri Lanka's bowling was not considered as lethal as either of those attacks. In the event, there was just enough movement for the ball to beat the bat, and this proved crucial.

Zimbabwe could not have had two better men than the Flower brothers to stand in the breach, and they survived until lunch. Andy, in fact, stayed almost to the close, when he received a harsh lbw decision, but he had little support after Campbell, who had batted well, paid the price for playing across the line. Ironically, Zoysa posed little threat after his initial breakthrough. Vaas was generally more dangerous and took his 100th wicket in 33 Tests when Strang was brilliantly caught by Dilshan in the gully off a thick edge.

Jayawardene and Dilshan took Sri Lanka well ahead with a fourth-wicket stand of 178, with the latter going on to a fine century in his second Test. He showed admirable restraint as Zimbabwe curtailed his favourite pull and cover drive and, although he played and missed frequently, he batted for a minute under eight hours, facing 343 balls and hitting 18 fours. However, the Zimbabweans did at last discover how to dismiss Atapattu; they ran him out twice in the match. In the first innings he was undone by Johnson's throw from the fine-leg boundary as he attempted a third run.

Zimbabwe, 258 behind with more than two days remaining and the weather good, appeared to have nothing to play for, especially when they lost three wickets before the close. But, on the fourth day, Goodwin and Andy Flower showed tremendous fighting spirit and, as they survived well into the afternoon session, the Sri Lankans grew increasingly frustrated. So hysterical did their appeals become that the match referee, Jackie Hendriks, spoke to them during the tea interval, after which their behaviour was impeccable.

By then, however, Zimbabwe's defences had been breached in a way that caused great offence. Goodwin and Flower had not long reached their century partnership when Goodwin played the last delivery of Vaas's over, the fifth before tea, back to the bowler. Vaas, rather than pick the ball up, kicked it back towards the slips, Goodwin himself aiming a light-hearted kick as it passed him before he wandered down the pitch to do some "gardening". But the umpire had not called "over", and Dilshan, picking up the ball, threw down his wicket.

Flower then found a staunch partner in Whittall, and they took the match into the final day, adding 125 before the Zimbabwean captain was caught at backward point off Jayasuriya, who wrapped up the tail in his next 14 balls with the help of two dubious lbw decisions. Flower had batted seven hours for his sixth Test hundred, a Zimbabwean record, faced 304 balls and hit just eight boundaries. Sri Lanka needed only 35, and failed to take their target seriously at first; the fired-up Zimbabwean bowlers and fielders embarrassed them by claiming four wickets, three of them for Brent, before Kaluwitharana hit the winning boundary.

Man of the Match: T. M. Dilshan.

Close of play: First day, Zimbabwe 163-9 (Olonga 4*, Matambanadzo 2*); Second day, Sri Lanka 236-3 (Jayawardene 71*, Dilshan 57*); Third day, Zimbabwe 34-3 (Goodwin 6*, Johnson 5*); Fourth day, Zimbabwe 235-6 (A. Flower 107*, Whittall 27*).

Zimbabwe

G. W. Flower b Muralitharan	19	– c Kaluwitharana b Muralitharan	13
T. R. Gripper lbw b Zoysa	0	– c Arnold b Vaas	4
M. W. Goodwin c Kaluwitharana b Zoysa	0	– run out	48
N. C. Johnson lbw b Zoysa	0	– (5) c Atapattu b Zoysa	14
*†A. Flower lbw b Vaas	74	– (6) c Atapattu b Jayasuriya	129
A. D. R. Campbell lbw b Wickremasinghe	36	– (7) lbw b Muralitharan	5
G. J. Whittall b Muralitharan	1	– (8) not out	53
G. B. Brent c Kaluwitharana b Vaas	3	– (9) lbw b Jayasuriya	0
B. C. Strang c Dilshan b Vaas	4	– (10) c Jayawardene b Jayasuriya	3
H. K. Olonga not out	10	– (11) lbw b Jayasuriya	0
E. Z. Matambanadzo c Jayawardene b Muralitharan	6	– (4) run out	0
B 2, l-b 8, n-b 11	21	B 3, l-b 15, n-b 5	23
	174		**292**

1/0 (2) 2/0 (3) 3/0 (4) 4/53 (1) 5/133 (6) 6/134 (7) 7/152 (8) 8/153 (5) 9/161 (9) 10/174 (11)

1/5 (2) 2/28 (1) 3/28 (4) 4/51 (5) 5/152 (3) 6/159 (7) 7/284 (6) 8/284 (9) 9/292 (10) 10/292 (11)

Bowling: *First Innings*—Vaas 27–8–50–3; Zoysa 13–4–22–3; Wickremasinghe 18–7–31–1; Muralitharan 29.5–11–44–3; Jayasuriya 3–1–7–0; Arnold 5–2–10–0. *Second Innings*—Vaas 35–7–78–1; Zoysa 11–2–24–1; Wickremasinghe 28–10–51–0; Muralitharan 43–15–71–2; Jayasuriya 12.4–3–40–4; Arnold 1–0–3–0; Jayawardene 4–2–7–0.

Sri Lanka

M. S. Atapattu run out	37	– run out	6
*S. T. Jayasuriya c A. Flower b Olonga	6	– c Gripper b Brent	7
R. P. Arnold c Campbell b Strang	49	– c A. Flower b Brent	1
D. P. M. D. Jayawardene c A. Flower b Strang.	91	– not out	6
T. M. Dilshan not out	163	– lbw b Brent	0
†R. S. Kaluwitharana run out	19	– not out	14
S. I. de Saram c Goodwin b Matambanadzo	17		
W. P. U. J. C. Vaas c Gripper b Matambanadzo	5		
G. P. Wickremasinghe c A. Flower b Whittall	7		
M. Muralitharan c G. W. Flower b Olonga	5		
D. N. T. Zoysa c Gripper b G. W. Flower	5		
B 1, l-b 10, w 7, n-b 10	28	L-b 1, w 2, n-b 1	4

1/17 (2) 2/97 (1) 3/105 (3) 4/283 (4)   432
5/323 (6) 6/371 (7) 7/381 (8) 8/403 (9)
9/408 (10) 10/432 (11)

1/10 (1) 2/15 (2)   (4 wkts) 38
3/19 (3) 4/20 (5)

Bowling: *First Innings*—Olonga 30–5–88–2; Brent 22–4–68–0; Matambanadzo 31–6–95–2; Strang 37–13–70–2; Gripper 1–0–6–0; Whittall 19–2–60–1; G. W. Flower 9.3–2–34–1. *Second Innings*—Olonga 5–1–14–0; Brent 7.2–3–21–3; Strang 3–1–2–0.

Umpires: S. A. Bucknor (West Indies) and R. B. Tiffin.
Referee: J. L. Hendriks (West Indies).

ZIMBABWE v SRI LANKA

Third Test Match

At Harare, December 4, 5, 6, 7, 8. Drawn. Toss: Sri Lanka. Test debut: R. W. Price.

For the first time in the season, Zimbabwe got themselves on level terms in a Test match. They conceded a lead of only 13 to Sri Lanka on first innings and, batting a second time on a pitch still assisting the seam bowlers, were 35 runs ahead with eight wickets standing when rain washed out the fourth day. This left Sri Lanka the only team with enough time for a possible victory, and all Zimbabwe could do was ensure a draw.

Zimbabwe selected their side entirely with a view to winning. The most interesting change was the unexpected recall of the 36-year-old Brandes, for his first Test since the England tour of 1996-97, and the move was an undoubted success, with his seam bowling inspiring the home side after another disappointing batting performance. Of the other changes, Craig Wishart failed to fulfil his role of aggressive opener, though he did have to bat when the pitch was at its trickiest, while Raymond Price, nephew of international golfer Nick Price, had little opportunity to display his left-arm spin bowling in his first Test. Sri Lanka replaced the injured Zoysa with Pushpakumara, who had taken seven for 116 in the Third Test here on the previous tour and now, along with Vaas, exploited the helpful conditions superbly; they took all but one of Zimbabwe's first-innings wickets. Only Johnson and Whittall survived for long against the moving ball, adding 61 for the sixth wicket, and it took some unorthodox hitting by Strang on the second morning to lift the total beyond 200.

Olonga and Brandes soon had the tourists in similar trouble, with Atapattu adjudged caught at second slip off a lifting delivery in the first over, and Jayawardene brilliantly taken at short leg. Jayasuriya, having moved himself down two places after a poor Second Test, was still required early at the crease and failed again, becoming Andy Flower's 100th dismissal in 39 Tests. Earlier, Flower had been the first to score 2,500 Test runs for Zimbabwe. Dilshan, driving superbly but riskily for 37 in 42 balls, and de Saram played useful innings, but the pillar was undoubtedly Arnold, who emulated Atapattu in the First Test by carrying his bat through a Test innings. Restrained but determined, he reached his century, and also put Sri Lanka ahead, with his last partner, Muralitharan, at the crease. All told, he faced 243 balls and hit 14 fours in six and a quarter hours.

Zimbabwe batted again in humid conditions and lost both openers before bad light stopped play midway through the third afternoon. The match was in an interesting position, considering Sri Lanka would have to bat last. But once the fourth day was lost, it was unrealistic to expect Zimbabwe to set Sri Lanka a target. On a pitch damp in patches, and with the bounce and movement unreliable, Andy Flower played another innings of fine judgment and determination to make sure his team avoided any possibility of another defeat in Harare's fourth Test match in two months.

Man of the Match: R. P. Arnold.   *Man of the Series:* A. Flower.

Close of play: First day, Zimbabwe 178-8 (Brandes 1*, Strang 3*); Second day, Sri Lanka 159-7 (Arnold 65*, Pushpakumara 0*); Third day, Zimbabwe 48-2 (Goodwin 15*, Johnson 9*); Fourth day, No play.

Zimbabwe

G. W. Flower c Dilshan b Pushpakumara	13	– c Dilshan b Vaas	13
C. B. Wishart lbw b Vaas	1	– b Vaas	9
M. W. Goodwin b Pushpakumara	11	– c Jayawardene b Muralitharan	38
N. C. Johnson lbw b Wickremasinghe	70	– c Dilshan b Wickremasinghe	9
*†A. Flower c Arnold b Vaas	14	– not out	70
A. D. R. Campbell lbw b Pushpakumara	9	– c Jayawardene b Vaas	27
G. J. Whittall c Arnold b Pushpakumara	37	– c Arnold b Muralitharan	9
R. W. Price lbw b Pushpakumara	2	– run out	4
E. A. Brandes b Vaas	9	– not out	1
B. C. Strang c Atapattu b Vaas	28		
H. K. Olonga not out	3		
L-b 4, w 2, n-b 15	21	B 3, l-b 5, n-b 9	17

1/5 (2) 2/24 (3) 3/33 (1) 4/67 (5) 218 1/14 (1) 2/28 (2) (7 wkts dec.) 197
5/82 (6) 6/143 (4) 7/174 (7) 3/51 (4) 4/93 (3)
8/175 (8) 9/196 (9) 10/218 (10) 5/151 (6) 6/174 (7) 7/184 (8)

Bowling: *First Innings*—Vaas 29.4–10–56–4; Pushpakumara 25–5–56–5; Wickremasinghe 16–6–41–1; Muralitharan 24–6–51–0; Jayasuriya 4–1–10–0. *Second Innings*—Vaas 22–5–48–3; Pushpakumara 21–5–39–0; Wickremasinghe 21–6–30–1; Jayawardene 2–0–12–0; Muralitharan 35–12–52–2; Jayasuriya 8–4–8–0.

Sri Lanka

M. S. Atapattu c Johnson b Olonga	0	– c A. Flower b Brandes	6
R. P. Arnold not out	104	– (3) not out	14
D. P. M. D. Jayawardene c Goodwin b Brandes	2		
*S. T. Jayasuriya c A. Flower b Brandes	4	– (2) not out	16
T. M. Dilshan c A. Flower b Strang	37		
†R. S. Kaluwitharana c A. Flower b Whittall	7		
S. I. de Saram c G. W. Flower b Whittall	38		
W. P. U. J. C. Vaas c Campbell b Brandes	0		
K. R. Pushpakumara lbw b Strang	7		
G. P. Wickremasinghe c A. Flower b Olonga	18		
M. Muralitharan b Olonga	5		
L-b 2, w 2, n-b 5	9		

1/1 (1) 2/4 (3) 3/29 (4) 4/82 (5) 231 1/7 (1) (1 wkt) 36
5/90 (6) 6/158 (7) 7/159 (8)
8/178 (9) 9/208 (10) 10/231 (11)

Bowling: *First Innings*—Olonga 22.4–2–54–3; Brandes 17–5–45–3; Strang 24–8–71–2; Whittall 17–9–37–2; Price 8–3–22–0. *Second Innings*—Olonga 4–1–11–0; Brandes 4–0–20–1; Strang 1–0–5–0.

Umpires: S. Venkataraghavan (India) and I. D. Robinson.
Referee: J. L. Hendriks (West Indies).

†ZIMBABWE v SRI LANKA

First One-Day International

At Bulawayo, December 11. No result. Toss: Zimbabwe.

Zimbabwe went into the one-day series without all-rounder Johnson, who was having treatment on the groin injury that had prevented him bowling in the Tests. They won the toss, for a change, but inaccurate bowling allowed Jayasuriya, finding his best form of the tour, to race to 54 in 44 balls, including three sixes over point. After his dismissal, the bowlers regained a measure of control. A target of 285 looked unlikely, but Grant Flower and Campbell made a good start, reaching 51 in 11 overs, before rain ended their pursuit.

Sri Lanka

*S. T. Jayasuriya c G. J. Whittall b Brent	54	W. P. U. J. C. Vaas b Brent 12
†R. S. Kaluwitharana run out	54	M. Muralitharan b Olonga 6
M. S. Atapattu c Goodwin		G. P. Wickremasinghe not out 2
b G. J. Whittall .	33	K. S. C. de Silva not out 1
D. P. M. D. Jayawardene		
lbw b G. J. Whittall .	3	L-b 5, w 8, n-b 2 15
R. P. Arnold c A. Flower b G. J. Whittall	56	
T. M. Dilshan st A. Flower b Brent	35	1/96 2/143 3/150 (9 wkts, 50 overs) 284
U. D. U. Chandana c A. R. Whittall		4/157 5/228 6/251
b Brent .	13	7/267 8/276 9/283

Bowling: Olonga 8–0–42–1; Mbangwa 6–0–59–0; A. R. Whittall 9–0–44–0; Brent 10–0–53–4; G. W. Flower 10–0–45–0; G. J. Whittall 7–0–36–3.

Zimbabwe

A. D. R. Campbell not out	22
G. W. Flower b de Silva	30
T. N. Madondo not out	2
L-b 3, w 3, n-b 5	11

1/51   (1 wkt, 14.5 overs) 65

*†A. Flower, M. W. Goodwin, G. J. Whittall, G. J. Rennie, G. B. Brent, A. R. Whittall, H. K. Olonga and M. Mbangwa did not bat.

Bowling: Vaas 7–0–34–0; de Silva 7–0–28–1; Wickremasinghe 0.5–0–0–0.

Umpires: G. R. Evans and R. B. Tiffin.

†ZIMBABWE v SRI LANKA

Second One-Day International

At Bulawayo, December 12. Sri Lanka won by 13 runs. Toss: Zimbabwe.

On a superb batting pitch, outstanding Zimbabwean bowling reduced Sri Lanka to 103 for seven before Arnold, after a cautious start, galvanised his last three partners sufficiently to double the score and, with a straight six – his third – reach an invaluable century off the penultimate ball of the innings. De Silva contributed just two runs in their Sri Lankan tenth-wicket record of 51. Zimbabwe looked likely winners following an opening stand of 91 but, as Campbell and Madondo became bogged down, the run-rate increased. Even so, with five wickets in hand, the later batsmen should have been able to handle 19 off the final three overs. Instead, they all fell for just five runs to frenetic batting as first Muralitharan and then Jayasuriya turned up the pressure.

Man of the Match: R. P. Arnold.

Sri Lanka

*S. T. Jayasuriya lbw b J. A. Rennie	9	G. P. Wickremasinghe c Goodwin		
†R. S. Kaluwitharana hit wkt b Olonga	0		b G. J. Whittall	19
M. S. Atapattu c A. R. Whittall b Brent	15	M. Muralitharan c A. Flower		
D. P. M. D. Jayawardene b Olonga	16		b G. J. Whittall	2
R. P. Arnold lbw b J. A. Rennie	103	K. S. C. de Silva not out		2
T. M. Dilshan b G. J. Whittall	6	L-b 9, w 20		29
U. D. U. Chandana c A. Flower				
	b G. J. Whittall	10	1/10 2/14 3/49 4/52 5/66 (50 overs)	213
W. P. U. J. C. Vaas lbw b Brent	2	6/100 7/103 8/160 9/162		

Bowling: Olonga 10–0–51–2; J. A. Rennie 10–0–40–2; Brent 10–0–37–2; G. J. Whittall 10–0–35–4; A. R. Whittall 5–0–18–0; G. W. Flower 5–0–23–0.

Zimbabwe

A. D. R. Campbell c Chandana		G. J. Rennie lbw b Jayasuriya		8
	b Jayasuriya	56	J. A. Rennie run out	0
G. W. Flower c Wickremasinghe		G. B. Brent c Jayasuriya b de Silva		3
	b Chandana	48	A. R. Whittall b Jayasuriya	1
*†A. Flower c Chandana b Jayasuriya	24	H. K. Olonga not out		0
T. N. Madondo st Kaluwitharana		L-b 7, w 3, n-b 2		12
	b Chandana	4			
M. W. Goodwin c Chandana		1/91 2/127 3/142 (49.1 overs)	200
	b Muralitharan	14	4/144 5/184 6/196	
G. J. Whittall c Vaas b Muralitharan	30	7/196 8/197 9/200	

Bowling: Vaas 6–0–20–0; de Silva 7.1–0–24–1; Wickremasinghe 8–0–27–0; Muralitharan 10–0–48–2; Chandana 7–1–28–2; Arnold 1–0–5–0; Jayasuriya 10–0–41–4.

Umpires: I. D. Robinson and R. B. Tiffin.

†ZIMBABWE v SRI LANKA

Third One-Day International

At Harare, December 15. Sri Lanka won by 98 runs. Toss: Zimbabwe.

The Zimbabwean bowlers, with Olonga the most impressive, kept Sri Lanka's batsmen in check until their final flurry brought 47 in the last four overs. Zimbabwe were well on target, reaching 100 with one wicket down, but Grant Flower's dismissal was the signal for one batsman after another to hurl himself over the cliff. Whittall was an honourable exception to this self-destruction, but Chandana removed his last three partners in ten balls to end the game with 13 overs to spare.

Man of the Match: U. D. U. Chandana.

Sri Lanka

*S. T. Jayasuriya c Campbell b Olonga	1	U. D. U. Chandana c Brent b Olonga		26
†R. S. Kaluwitharana c G. J. Rennie		W. P. U. J. C. Vaas not out		19
	b J. A. Rennie	12	G. P. Wickremasinghe not out		11
M. S. Atapattu c A. Flower b Olonga	69	B 4, l-b 7, w 17		28
D. P. M. D. Jayawardene c A. Flower				
	b Brent	18	1/12 2/25 3/59 (7 wkts, 50 overs)	248
R. P. Arnold c Olonga b Brent	37	4/154 5/160	
T. M. Dilshan b Olonga	27	6/208 7/222	

M. Muralitharan and K. S. C. de Silva did not bat.

Bowling: J. A. Rennie 10–0–32–1; Olonga 10–0–51–4; Brent 10–0–63–2; G. J. Whittall 10–1–41–0; A. R. Whittall 7–0–34–0; Goodwin 3–0–16–0.

Zimbabwe

A. D. R. Campbell run out.	38	G. J. Rennie run out	2
G. W. Flower c Jayasuriya		G. B. Brent b Muralitharan	2
b Muralitharan .	47	J. A. Rennie c Atapattu b Chandana.	5
M. W. Goodwin c Wickremasinghe		A. R. Whittall b Chandana.	2
b Muralitharan .	25	H. K. Olonga lbw b Chandana	0
*†A. Flower c Wickremasinghe		L-b 5, w 1	6
b Jayawardene .	0		
S. V. Carlisle c Kaluwitharana		1/81 2/100 3/101 (37 overs) 150	
b Muralitharan .	0	4/102 5/123 6/129	
G. J. Whittall not out	23	7/132 8/140 9/150	

Bowling: Vaas 7–0–25–0; de Silva 2–0–20–0; Wickremasinghe 4–0–26–0; Arnold 3–0–15–0; Jayawardene 5–0–14–1; Muralitharan 7–0–16–4; Chandana 7–1–21–3; Jayasuriya 2–0–8–0.

Umpires: G. R. Evans and I. D. Robinson.

†ZIMBABWE v SRI LANKA

Fourth One-Day International

At Harare, December 18. Sri Lanka won by six wickets. Toss: Zimbabwe.

Carlisle, for so long a fringe player batting at No. 7 or No. 8, where he had little chance of building an innings, seized the opportunity to bat first wicket down by hitting a maiden international hundred, off 138 balls with eight fours and four sixes. With Andy Flower adding a blistering 53 off 30 balls in a 131-run stand that took only 13 overs, Sri Lanka faced a difficult task. Despite taking two early wickets, though, the Zimbabwean bowlers were unable to deliver victory. Kaluwitharana and Jayawardene hit back against some undisciplined bowling, raising 100 in the 16th over as they put on 144 together. Kaluwitharana's powerful 99 came in 86 balls.

Man of the Match: S. V. Carlisle.

Zimbabwe

A. D. R. Campbell c sub (L. P. C. Silva)		*†A. Flower c Muralitharan	
b Chandana .	43	b Wickremasinghe .	53
G. W. Flower c Arnold b Vaas	7	L-b 8, w 2	10
S. V. Carlisle not out.	121		
M. W. Goodwin b Jayasuriya	26	1/17 2/79 3/129 4/260 (4 wkts, 50 overs) 260	

G. J. Whittall, G. J. Rennie, G. B. Brent, J. A. Rennie, E. A. Brandes and H. K. Olonga did not bat.

Bowling: Vaas 10–0–44–1; Pushpakumara 8–1–37–0; Wickremasinghe 8–0–30–1; Muralitharan 10–1–52–0; Chandana 5–0–25–1; Jayasuriya 7–0–46–1; Arnold 2–0–18–0.

Sri Lanka

*S. T. Jayasuriya c G. J. Rennie		R. P. Arnold not out	42
b J. A. Rennie .	8	T. M. Dilshan not out	20
†R. S. Kaluwitharana b Olonga.	99		
M. S. Atapattu c A. Flower		L-b 2, w 15, n-b 7.	24
b J. A. Rennie .	6		
D. P. M. D. Jayawardene c A. Flower		1/25 2/44 (4 wkts, 44.4 overs) 262	
b Brandes .	63	3/188 4/213	

U. D. U. Chandana, W. P. U. J. C. Vaas, G. P. Wickremasinghe, M. Muralitharan and K. R. Pushpakumara did not bat.

Bowling: Brandes 10–0–52–1; J. A. Rennie 8–0–36–2; Brent 5.4–0–48–0; Whittall 3–0–34–0; Olonga 10–0–54–1; G. W. Flower 6–0–27–0; Campbell 2–0–9–0.

Umpires: M. A. Esat and R. B. Tiffin.

†ZIMBABWE v SRI LANKA

Fifth One-Day International

At Harare, December 19. Zimbabwe won by six wickets. Toss: Sri Lanka.

Sri Lanka rested three key bowlers, only for their batting to let them down against a Zimbabwean attack determined to rectify their aberrations of the previous day. Once again, Campbell and Grant Flower put Zimbabwe on course with a confident opening stand of 94 in 18 overs, but four soft dismissals in quick succession gave rise to all the usual spectres. The turning-point came when Jayasuriya, who had played a crucial role so often in the series, dropped a return catch off Whittall when he was two. After that, Whittall, who earlier on had taken three mid-order wickets, and Goodwin coolly took their team through to a consolation victory.

Man of the Match: G. J. Whittall.

Sri Lanka

*S. T. Jayasuriya c A. Flower		
b J. A. Rennie .	6	
†R. S. Kaluwitharana c Goodwin		
b Olonga .	7	
M. S. Atapattu b G. J. Whittall	25	
D. P. M. D. Jayawardene c Strang		
b J. A. Rennie .	17	
R. P. Arnold c A. Flower b G. J. Whittall	39	
T. M. Dilshan c Carlisle b Strang	53	
S. I. de Saram c G. W. Flower		
b G. J. Whittall .	7	

U. D. U. Chandana c A. R. Whittall	
b Olonga .	17
I. S. Gallage run out	14
K. R. Pushpakumara c A. Flower	
b Strang .	0
K. S. C. de Silva not out	0
B 1, l-b 3, w 11, n-b 2.	17
1/14 2/14 3/36 (48.2 overs) 202	
4/96 5/110 6/118	
7/161 8/202 9/202	

Bowling: Olonga 8–0–42–2; J. A. Rennie 9.2–2–21–2; Strang 10–1–36–2; G. J. Whittall 8–0–37–3; A. R. Whittall 10–0–45–0; G. W. Flower 3–0–17–0.

Zimbabwe

A. D. R. Campbell c Kaluwitharana		
b Jayawardene .	36	
G. W. Flower run out	52	
S. V. Carlisle c Dilshan b Chandana. . . .	10	
M. W. Goodwin not out.	47	
*†A. Flower run out	9	

G. J. Whittall not out	37
B 1, l-b 1, w 8, n-b 5	15
1/94 2/110 (4 wkts, 46.2 overs) 206	
3/111 4/128	

G. J. Rennie, B. C. Strang, J. A. Rennie, A. R. Whittall and H. K. Olonga did not bat.

Bowling: Pushpakumara 9–1–35–0; Gallage 8–2–36–0; de Silva 3.2–0–23–0; Arnold 5–0–16–0; Jayawardene 3–0–24–1; Chandana 10–0–33–1; Jayasuriya 8–0–37–0.

Umpires: K. C. Barbour and I. D. Robinson.
Series referee: J. L. Hendriks (West Indies).

PWC AWARDS

The Federation of International Cricketers' Associations/PricewaterhouseCoopers Test Player of the Year Trophy was won in July 2000 by Glenn McGrath of Australia. Fellow Australian Brett Lee was named International Young Player of the Year.

THE INDIANS IN AUSTRALIA, 1999-2000

By DICKY RUTNAGUR

The Indians failed to live up to having top billing in a season of twin tours. Never before in almost 68 years as a Test nation had an Indian national team been so completely overwhelmed. It wasn't just that they were outclassed in all three Tests. They lost to Queensland on the fourth morning, were soundly beaten by 164 runs in a one-day fixture against the Prime Minister's XI, a team of young aspirants, and lost seven of their eight games in the Carlton & United series. Their only win, other than beating Pakistan once in the one-day series, was against New South Wales, who fielded a depleted side.

Apart from Sachin Tendulkar and Sourav Ganguly, India's batsmen could not come to terms with the pace and bounce of Australia's pitches. Tendulkar, despite being the victim of dubious umpiring decisions in both innings of the First Test, averaged 46.33, scoring a splendid 116 in the Second and two half-centuries. However, V. V. S. Laxman, with some substantial innings early on the tour and a gloriously elegant 167 in the final innings of the rubber, showed that he could have made a bigger impact batting lower down the order. Not yet an established Test player, he was pitchforked by circumstances into opening the innings in the Second and Third Tests. The big disappointment was Rahul Dravid who, to date, had an impressive overseas record. He made a hundred on a lifeless pitch in the drawn game against Tasmania but gathered just 93 runs in six Test innings.

Javagal Srinath was India's best bowler, and his new-ball partner, Ajit Agarkar, toiled hard and bowled at a rapid pace for one who is small of build and whose career had been blighted by frequent injury. Between them they claimed 21 of the 38 Australian wickets in the series, whereas Anil Kumble, who was expected to be a big force on resilient Australian pitches, obtained no more than five. India took early wickets in every innings of the Test matches – Australia's highest opening stand was nine – but never managed to restrict the home side's first innings to under 400, which was a clear reflection of their meagre bowling resources.

So pronounced was the disparity between the two sides that Australia's selectors never contemplated replacing two batsmen who were palpably out of form, Greg Blewett and Mark Waugh. Whenever Australia were hard pressed for runs or momentum, they were unfailingly invigorated by Ricky Ponting, the top run-scorer on either side with 375, and Adam Gilchrist (221), whose wicket-keeping, too, was consistently excellent.

A pace attack headed by Glenn McGrath, at the height of his form, and Damien Fleming was enough of a handful in the opening Test before the Australians further sharpened its edge by introducing 23-year-old Brett Lee, who had hitherto played only 16 first-class matches. The younger brother of Shane Lee, Australia's one-day international all-rounder, he showed remarkable maturity as he combined genuine pace with admirable control, subtlety and an ability to reverse-swing the old ball. Lee had match figures of seven for 78 at Melbourne, including five wickets in the first innings, and he followed up with six wickets in the final Test. Fleming, the principal wicket-taker in the First Test, also bowled well in the Third, but with little luck.

Eight wickets at 41.87 apiece do no justice to Shane Warne's part in a series in which the fast bowlers were the main destroyers. On an easy pitch in Adelaide, however, he took six wickets and in the first innings skimmed off the cream of India's batting: Dravid, Tendulkar and Ganguly. He again bowled superbly in the Second Test and, although his reward was merely two wickets, struck the mortal blow by dismissing Tendulkar in the second innings.

INDIAN TOURING PARTY

S. R. Tendulkar (Mumbai) (*captain*), S. C. Ganguly (Bengal) (*vice-captain*), A. B. Agarkar (Mumbai), R. V. Bharadwaj (Karnataka), R. Dravid (Karnataka), D. J. Gandhi (Bengal), Harbhajan Singh (Punjab), H. H. Kanitkar (Maharashtra), T. Kumaran (Tamil Nadu), A. Kumble (Karnataka), V. V. S. Laxman (Hyderabad), D. S. Mohanty (Orissa), B. K. V. Prasad (Karnataka), M. S. K. Prasad (Andhra), S. Ramesh (Tamil Nadu), J. Srinath (Karnataka).

Kanitkar replaced A. Jadeja (Haryana), who withdrew injured; N. R. Mongia (Baroda) reinforced the party before the First Test and returned home after playing against Tasmania. N. Chopra (Delhi), S. S. Dighe (Mumbai), S. B. Joshi (Karnataka), J. J. Martin (Baroda) and R. R. Singh (Tamil Nadu) replaced Harbhajan Singh, Kumaran, M. S. K. Prasad and Ramesh for the Carlton & United one-day series.

Manager: Dr M. K. Bhargawa. *Coach:* Kapil Dev.

INDIAN TOUR RESULTS

Test matches – Played 3: Lost 3.
First-class matches – Played 6: Won 1, Lost 4, Drawn 1.
Win – New South Wales.
Losses – Australia (3), Queensland.
Draw – Tasmania.
One-day internationals – Played 8: Won 1, Lost 7. *Win* – Pakistan. *Losses* – Pakistan (3), Australia (4).
Other non-first-class match – Lost v Prime Minister's XI.

TEST MATCH AVERAGES

AUSTRALIA – BATTING

	T	I	NO	R	HS	100s	50s	Avge	Ct/St
R. T. Ponting	3	5	2	375	141*	2	1	125.00	3
J. L. Langer.	3	5	0	289	223	1	0	57.80	6
A. C. Gilchrist	3	5	1	221	78	0	2	55.25	9/1
S. R. Waugh	3	5	0	276	150	1	1	55.20	4
M. E. Waugh	3	5	1	137	51*	0	1	34.25	8
S. K. Warne.	3	3	0	88	86	0	1	29.33	3
G. S. Blewett	3	5	0	144	88	0	1	28.80	1
M. J. Slater	3	5	0	123	91	0	1	24.60	3

Played in three Tests: D. W. Fleming 12*, 31*; G. D. McGrath 4, 1 (1 ct). Played in two Tests: B. Lee 27. Played in one Test: M. S. Kasprowicz 4, 21* (1 ct).

* *Signifies not out.*

BOWLING

	O	M	R	W	BB	5W/i	Avge
G. D. McGrath	113	34	248	18	5-48	2	13.77
B. Lee	69	19	184	13	5-47	1	14.15
D. W. Fleming	96.2	25	279	12	5-30	1	23.25
S. K. Warne.	127	35	335	8	4-92	0	41.87

Also bowled: G. S. Blewett 14–4–49–2; M. S. Kasprowicz 17–2–85–0; R. T. Ponting 1–0–8–0; M. J. Slater 1–0–2–0; M. E. Waugh 5–1–17–2.

INDIA – BATTING

	T	I	NO	R	HS	100s	50s	Avge	Ct
S. R. Tendulkar	3	6	0	278	116	1	2	46.33	0
V. V. S. Laxman	3	6	0	221	167	1	0	36.83	2
S. C. Ganguly	3	6	0	177	60	0	1	29.50	3
A. Kumble	3	6	2	102	28*	0	0	25.50	0
S. Ramesh	2	4	1	60	28	0	0	20.00	1
H. H. Kanitkar	2	4	0	74	45	0	0	18.50	0
R. Dravid	3	6	0	93	35	0	0	15.50	1
M. S. K. Prasad	3	6	0	52	14	0	0	8.66	10
J. Srinath	3	6	1	42	15*	0	0	8.40	3
B. K. V. Prasad	3	6	3	22	10	0	0	7.33	1
A. B. Agarkar	3	6	0	19	19	0	0	3.16	1

Played in one Test: R. V. Bharadwaj 6; D. J. Gandhi 4, 0 (1 ct).

* *Signifies not out.*

BOWLING

	O	M	R	W	BB	5W/i	Avge
A. B. Agarkar	108	24	351	11	3-43	0	31.90
J. Srinath	126	18	461	10	4-130	0	46.10
B. K. V. Prasad	106.3	25	356	7	3-83	0	50.85
A. Kumble	146.2	22	450	5	2-72	0	90.00

Also bowled: R. V. Bharadwaj 12–1–35–0; S. C. Ganguly 21–2–90–2; H. H. Kanitkar 1–0–2–0; V. V. S. Laxman 3–1–2–0; S. R. Tendulkar 9–0–46–1.

Note: Matches in this section which were not first-class are signified by a dagger.

At Brisbane, November 26, 27, 28, 29. Queensland won by ten wickets. Toss: Queensland. Indians 277 (S. Ramesh 43, V. V. S. Laxman 113, S. R. Tendulkar 83; S. A. Muller three for 27) and 204 (V. V. S. Laxman 73, R. Dravid 42; S. A. Muller three for 37, M. A. Anderson four for 50); Queensland 401 (M. L. Hayden 44, M. L. Love 120, A. Symonds 161; T. Kumaran five for 68) and 82 for no wkt (S. G. Law 60 not out).
Love and Symonds added 204 for Queensland's fourth wicket.

At Sydney, December 2, 3, 4, 5. Indians won by 93 runs. Toss: Indians. Indians 185 (V. V. S. Laxman 37, S. C. Ganguly 38; B. Lee three for 56) and 331 (S. Ramesh 74, S. C. Ganguly 81, A. B. Agarkar 65 not out, Extras 31; B. Lee four for 77, S. C. G. MacGill four for 84); New South Wales 231 (G. J. Mail 31, C. J. Richards 51, S. Lee 39, B. J. Haddin 60; A. Kumble four for 50) and 192 (G. J. Hayne 89; A. Kumble four for 38).

†At Canberra, December 7. Prime Minister's XI won by 164 runs. Toss: Indians. Prime Minister's XI 334 for five (50 overs) (D. A. Fitzgerald 115, A. Symonds 101, S. Lee 55 not out; T. Kumaran three for 63); Indians 170 (44.4 overs) (R. V. Bharadwaj 45, S. C. Ganguly 46; B. Lee four for 25).

AUSTRALIA v INDIA

First Test Match

At Adelaide, December 10, 11, 12, 13, 14. Australia won by 285 runs. Toss: Australia.

Losing their top four for 52 on the opening morning proved only a pinprick for Australia. Their batting had enough depth to overcome periodic slumps and, with Warne's powers restored, their bowling was not stretched in subduing opposition whose own batting strength was concentrated on three high-class performers.

With Tendulkar employing Ganguly after lunch, rather than one of his front-line bowlers, and keeping him on too long, Steve Waugh and Ponting were under little pressure as they prepared the ground for Australia's largest fifth-wicket partnership against India, 239. Audacious and versatile in his range of strokes, Ponting contributed 125, hitting 15 fours and looking impregnable until he was run out through a dreadful misunderstanding five minutes before the close. If more watchful, Waugh left nothing loose unpunished and had 17 fours in his 150, scored off 323 balls. His innings gave him not only hundreds against the other eight Test-playing countries – the first to achieve this – but also 150 against all of them except New Zealand, and took him past 8,000 Test runs. He batted on beyond lunch on the second day – Gilchrist was victim to its first ball – and Warne, let off at backward point when 12, equalled his recent career-best with a swashbuckling 86.

India, beginning their reply 40 minutes before tea, lost both openers for just nine. Ramesh was beaten by Blewett's direct hit from long-off as he tried to complete a fourth. But Laxman batted with freedom, unlike his more experienced partner Dravid, as they put on 81 before he paid the penalty for square-cutting McGrath without getting on top of a high-bouncing ball. McGrath in that spell bowled eight overs for one run, and he and Warne, subtle and accurate, allowed Dravid and Tendulkar little licence. Dravid did not survive until stumps, caught at short leg off Warne; Tendulkar, weighed down by the crisis, managed only 12 off 69 balls.

He cast off his shackles the following morning. With Ganguly also at ease and free with his strokes, particularly the square cut, India added 92 in 22 overs before Tendulkar, having scored his last 49 off 64 balls, was adjudged caught at short leg off Warne. The videotape proved him unlucky. However, Warne's dismissal of Ganguly, 14 runs later, was a masterpiece. He drew the left-hander out to scotch the menace of a ball pitched into the rough outside his off stump, beat him with a googly and had him stumped. The lower order struggled manfully, but India were left with a deficit of 156.

As the pitch became uneven in bounce, India made Australia fight for runs by bowling with zest and discipline, and Waugh felt unable to declare until 25 minutes after tea on the fourth afternoon. Blewett, with a sturdy 88 off 262 balls, held the innings together; Gilchrist gave it late momentum at almost a run a ball.

In the 26 overs remaining to the close, McGrath, Fleming and Warne virtually settled the issue by reducing India to 76 for five, still 319 behind. Any hope of a significant revival had been extinguished when Tendulkar ducked to evade a short delivery from McGrath. The ball did not get up, he was struck on the shoulder, and umpire Harper deemed contact had been made in line with the stumps and within his height. Next morning, Fleming claimed four of the remaining wickets; those of Ganguly, acrobatically caught by Gilchrist, and Agarkar with successive balls. A second Test hat-trick was denied him when Warne, at first slip, failed to take a face-high chance offered by Srinath.

Man of the Match: S. R. Waugh.   *Attendance:* 65,610.

[*Hamish Blair, Allsport*

Down and out: umpire Harper was sufficiently sure Sachin Tendulkar was in line with the stumps when Glenn McGrath's no-rise short delivery struck him on the shoulder.

Close of play: First day, Australia 298-5 (S. R. Waugh 117*, Gilchrist 0*); Second day, India 123-4 (Tendulkar 12*, Ganguly 12*); Third day, Australia 71-2 (Blewett 26*, M. E. Waugh 0*); Fourth day, India 76-5 (Ganguly 31*, M. S. K. Prasad 6*).

Australia

G. S. Blewett c M. S. K. Prasad b Srinath	4	– (2) b Agarkar	88
M. J. Slater c Ramesh b Ganguly	28	– (1) c Ganguly b Srinath	0
J. L. Langer lbw b B. K. V. Prasad	11	– c Gandhi b Kumble	38
M. E. Waugh c M. S. K. Prasad b B. K. V. Prasad	5	– c Laxman b Agarkar	8
*S. R. Waugh c M. S. K. Prasad b Agarkar	150	– c M. S. K. Prasad b Agarkar	5
R. T. Ponting run out	125	– c M. S. K. Prasad b B. K. V. Prasad	21
†A. C. Gilchrist c and b Agarkar	0	– c Laxman b Srinath	43
S. K. Warne lbw b Kumble	86	– c Dravid b Srinath	0
M. S. Kasprowicz b Kumble	4	– not out	21
D. W. Fleming not out	12		
G. D. McGrath c M. S. K. Prasad b B. K. V. Prasad	4		
B 1, l-b 5, n-b 6	12	B 3, l-b 8, w 2, n-b 2	15

1/8 (1) 2/29 (3) 3/45 (2) 4/52 (4)   441   1/1 (1) 2/65 (3)   (8 wkts dec.) 239
5/291 (6) 6/298 (7) 7/406 (5)   3/95 (4) 4/113 (5)
8/417 (9) 9/424 (8) 10/441 (11)   5/153 (6) 6/204 (2)
                                                     7/205 (8) 8/239 (7)

Bowling: *First Innings*—Srinath 29-3-117-1; Agarkar 26-5-86-2; B. K. V. Prasad 24.3-4-83-3; Ganguly 7-1-34-1; Kumble 34-1-101-2; Tendulkar 2-0-12-0; Laxman 3-1-2-0. *Second Innings*—Srinath 21.5-4-64-3; Agarkar 18-6-43-3; B. K. V. Prasad 18-5-48-1; Kumble 32-9-73-1.

India

D. J. Gandhi c Kasprowicz b McGrath	4	– c Gilchrist b McGrath	0
S. Ramesh run out	2	– lbw b Warne	28
V. V. S. Laxman c S. R. Waugh b McGrath	41	– b Fleming	0
R. Dravid c Langer b Warne	35	– c Gilchrist b Warne	6
*S. R. Tendulkar c Langer b Warne	61	– lbw b McGrath	0
S. C. Ganguly st Gilchrist b Warne	60	– c Gilchrist b Fleming	43
†M. S. K. Prasad b Warne	14	– c Langer b Fleming	11
A. B. Agarkar b Fleming	19	– c S. R. Waugh b Fleming	0
J. Srinath c S. R. Waugh b Fleming	11	– c Slater b McGrath	11
A. Kumble not out	17	– b Fleming	3
B. K. V. Prasad lbw b Fleming	0	– not out	2
L-b 1, w 1, n-b 19	21	L-b 1, n-b 5	6

1/7 (2) 2/9 (1) 3/90 (3) 4/107 (4) 285 1/0 (1) 2/3 (3) 3/24 (4) 110
5/215 (5) 6/229 (6) 7/240 (7) 4/27 (5) 5/48 (2) 6/93 (6)
8/266 (9) 9/275 (8) 10/285 (11) 7/93 (8) 8/102 (7)
9/108 (9) 10/110 (10)

Bowling: First Innings—McGrath 30–13–49–2; Fleming 24.4–7–70–3; Kasprowicz 11–2–62–0; Warne 42–12–92–4; Blewett 6–1–11–0. *Second Innings*—McGrath 12–2–35–3; Fleming 9.1–2–30–5; Warne 10–6–21–2; Kasprowicz 6–0–23–0; M. E. Waugh 1–1–0–0.

Umpires: R. S. Dunne (New Zealand) and D. J. Harper.
Referee: R. S. Madugalle (Sri Lanka).

At Hobart, December 17, 18, 19, 20. Drawn. Toss: Indians. Indians 316 for nine dec. (S. Ramesh 34, R. Dravid 107, H. H. Kanitkar 58; A. G. Downton five for 90) and 130 for three (V. V. S. Laxman 58); Tasmania 548 for five dec. (D. F. Hills 84, J. Cox 139, J. A. Dykes 61, D. J. Marsh 157, S. Young 62 not out, Extras 32; R. V. Bharadwaj three for 105).
Hills and Cox put on 205 in their opening stand. All 11 Tasmania players bowled in the Indians' second innings.

AUSTRALIA v INDIA

Second Test Match

At Melbourne, December 26, 27, 28, 29, 30. Australia won by 180 runs. Toss: India. Test debuts: B. Lee; H. H. Kanitkar.

Australia's elation at winning this Test, and with it the series, was all the greater for the contribution of their new recruit, Brett Lee, who took seven wickets in the match, including five for 47 in the first innings. Lee for Kasprowicz was the only change from the eleven that won the First Test, while India left out Gandhi, clearly shell-shocked, promoted Laxman to open in his place, and took aboard the left-handed Hrishikesh Kanitkar to bat in the middle order.

India's fast bowlers were not disciplined enough to capitalise on first use of a bouncy pitch which, having sweated under the covers, also provided movement off the seam. Slater was in splendid touch and, with Mark Waugh patient in the absence of form, Australia rallied from a poor start to share the honours of a rain-shortened first day. Play had not got under way until the afternoon. Srinath and Agarkar were accurate and hostile in later spells, but by then Slater and Waugh were well entrenched.

There were further interruptions for rain on the second day. India's bowlers, not allowing for the fact that the ball was in middle age and less resilient, pitched too short and again paid a high price for the two wickets captured. Slater hooked a wide ball high and straight to long leg – his eighth Test dismissal in the 90s – while misjudgment of width in square-cutting toppled Steve Waugh. Bad light, immediately followed by a thunderstorm, ended play early, but the Delegates Room at the MCG was lit till late as the referee, Ranjan Madugalle, conducted a lengthy hearing on Venkatesh Prasad's conduct after dismissing Slater. He had pumped the air with upturned fists in the batsman's face as he departed, and it earned him a heavy fine plus a suspension held in abeyance.

When Australia resumed at 332 for five on the third day, India's hopes of a win were already distant. By the close, the spectre of defeat was staring at them. The satisfaction of removing Ponting, the rapacious Gilchrist – this pair had put on 144 for the sixth wicket, mostly the previous day – and Warne in the space of four runs all came to nothing once the tail wagged furiously. Lee, the debutant, spent 77 productive minutes in the middle with Fleming, adding 59.

This cameo helped ensure that Lee was free of stage fright when Waugh brought him on to bowl the sixth over of the Indian innings. He struck with only his fourth ball, bowling Ramesh off the inside edge, and later in the day was in line for a hat-trick, reverse-swinging a ball almost 59 overs old to dismiss Mannava Prasad and Agarkar. By then, the innings was a shambles, for all that Tendulkar remained unscathed, gathering runs with deft placements and assaults on the rare loose ball. He and the equally defiant Kumble saved the follow-on but, with only five overs left to the close, Tendulkar pulled a long-hop straight to square leg. He had made 116 out of a total of 212, with a straight six off Warne but only nine fours.

Gilchrist's previous mastery over Kumble saw him come in at No. 4 to provide Australia with quick runs after the early loss of two second-innings wickets. He obliged with 55 off 73 balls, and Waugh declared with a lead of 375 and a minimum of 126 overs remaining.

Laxman again fell cheaply, and Ramesh batted for only one over on the final morning before retiring hurt, his left thumb broken the previous evening when he fended a bouncer from Lee on to his helmet. Lee produced another very fast delivery to get rid of Dravid. However, it was an inspired move by Waugh, giving Blewett a short spell just before lunch, that breached the remaining partnership that could have frustrated Australia. With his penultimate ball before the interval, Blewett bowled Ganguly with one that skidded through low. Soon after the resumption, Warne's only wicket of the innings sealed India's doom, for it was Tendulkar. Absolutely composed hitherto in making 52, Tendulkar misread his old adversary's intentions, shouldered arms and was lbw. Kanitkar and Mannava Prasad held the Australians up, but Waugh again proved the adage that fortune favours a winning captain. Turning to his brother Mark's off-spin, he was rewarded with consecutive wickets. Kumble was able to prevent a hat-trick but not the defeat.

Man of the Match: S. R. Tendulkar.   *Attendance:* 134,554.

Close of play: First day, Australia 138-3 (Slater 64*, S. R. Waugh 5*); Second day, Australia 332-5 (Ponting 59*, Gilchrist 77*); Third day, India 235-9 (Kumble 26*, B. K. V. Prasad 10*); Fourth day, India 40-1 (Ramesh 26*, Dravid 10*).

Australia

G. S. Blewett b Srinath	2	– (2) c Ganguly b Kumble	31
M. J. Slater c Srinath b B. K. V. Prasad	91	– (1) lbw b Agarkar	3
J. L. Langer lbw b Srinath	8	– c M. S. K. Prasad b Agarkar	9
M. E. Waugh lbw b Agarkar	41	– (5) not out	51
*S. R. Waugh c M. S. K. Prasad b B. K. V. Prasad	32	– (6) lbw b Agarkar	32
R. T. Ponting lbw b Srinath	67	– (7) not out	21
†A. C. Gilchrist c Ganguly b Agarkar	78	– (4) c Srinath b Kumble	55
S. K. Warne c M. S. K. Prasad b Agarkar	2		
D. W. Fleming not out	31		
B. Lee c and b Srinath	27		
G. D. McGrath run out	1		
B 1, l-b 9, w 1, n-b 14	25	L-b 2, w 1, n-b 3	6
	405	(5 wkts dec.)	**208**

1/4 (1) 2/28 (3) 3/123 (4) 4/192 (2)   405
5/197 (5) 6/341 (7) 7/343 (6)
8/345 (8) 9/404 (10) 10/405 (11)

1/5 (1) 2/32 (3)   (5 wkts dec.) 208
3/91 (2) 4/109 (4)
5/167 (6)

Bowling: *First Innings*—Srinath 33.1–7–130–4; Agarkar 28–7–76–3; B. K. V. Prasad 26–6–101–2; Ganguly 2–0–10–0; Kumble 29–3–78–0. *Second Innings*—Srinath 14–0–45–0; Agarkar 17–3–51–3; B. K. V. Prasad 10–0–38–0; Kumble 18–3–72–2.

India

V. V. S. Laxman c M. E. Waugh b McGrath ...	5	– c McGrath b Fleming	1
S. Ramesh b Lee	4	– retired hurt	26
R. Dravid c Gilchrist b Lee	9	– c Gilchrist b Lee	14
*S. R. Tendulkar c Langer b Fleming.	116	– lbw b Warne	52
S. C. Ganguly c M. E. Waugh b McGrath	31	– b Blewett	17
H. H. Kanitkar lbw b Warne	11	– lbw b Fleming	45
†M. S. K. Prasad b Lee	6	– c Warne b M. E. Waugh	13
A. B. Agarkar lbw b Lee...............	0	– c Blewett b M. E. Waugh.......	0
J. Srinath c M. E. Waugh b Lee	1	– (10) c Warne b Lee...........	1
A. Kumble not out....................	28	– (9) run out	13
B. K. V. Prasad c M. E. Waugh b McGrath ..	10	– not out	6
L-b 8, n-b 9	17	L-b 4, n-b 3	7

1/11 (2) 2/11 (1) 3/31 (4) 4/108 (5)   238   1/5 (1) 2/72 (3) 3/110 (5)   195
5/138 (6) 6/167 (7) 7/167 (8)   4/133 (4) 5/162 (7) 6/162 (8)
8/169 (9) 9/212 (4) 10/238 (11)   7/184 (6) 8/185 (10) 9/195 (9)

In the second innings Ramesh retired hurt at 40.

Bowling: *First Innings*—McGrath 18.1–3–39–3; Fleming 15–0–62–1; Lee 18–2–47–5; Warne 24–5–77–1; M. E. Waugh 1–0–5–0. *Second Innings*—McGrath 17–8–22–0; Fleming 21.3–7–46–2; Warne 26–7–63–1; Lee 19–6–31–2; Blewett 3–1–17–1; M. E. Waugh 3–0–12–2.

Umpires: D. R. Shepherd (England) and S. J. Davis.
Referee: R. S. Madugalle (Sri Lanka).

AUSTRALIA v INDIA

Third Test Match

At Sydney, January 2, 3, 4. Australia won by an innings and 141 runs. Toss: India.

At the instigation of Steve Waugh, the Australians marked their first Test of the new century with a one-off appearance in caps of the style and shade of green worn in 1900. Having made this concession to history, they got down to business as remorselessly as ever, winning in three days to complete their second clean sweep of the summer and extend their run of Test victories to seven. India, their morale in tatters, were ready victims.

Australia remained unchanged. They had called up Colin Miller to provide spin options but, with the pitch firm and grassy, did not include him. As for India, Ramesh's Melbourne injury ruled him out and, in another makeshift arrangement, they promoted wicket-keeper Mannava Prasad to open the batting with Laxman. The vacant place went to Bharadwaj, who had made his debut against New Zealand three months earlier.

Although rain before the start produced conditions choice for pace bowlers, Tendulkar opted to bat first – and duly came to grief. McGrath and Lee went through India in 68 overs, all except Tendulkar looking hopelessly out of their depth. For the fourth time in succession, Agarkar was dismissed first ball – unprecedented in Tests, and another unwelcome record was in store for him. Tendulkar batted with greater abandon than at Adelaide and Melbourne, hitting eight fours in 45 from 53 balls. His dismissal was the climax of a rousing duel with McGrath, who, having been hooked, pulled and driven earlier in the over, sent Tendulkar on his way with an ill-tempered verbal assault. Yet it brought him no more than a mild censure from referee Madugalle, a distinct contrast to the punishment imposed on Venkatesh Prasad in the previous Test.

The pitch rolled out true on the sunny second day, but India had Australia 49 for two, and a further setback looked imminent as Langer struggled. He hung on, though, found his fluency after reaching 50 and prospered to compile the highest score by an Australian against India. His 223 was spread over eight hours 43 minutes, in which he faced 355 balls and hit 30 fours. The Waugh twins – Mark was playing his 100th Test – helped Langer put on 218 and then Ponting, in irresistible form, joined him to add another 190. When Langer finally lifted Tendulkar's off-spin to mid-on, Ponting and Gilchrist savaged the limp attack for another 18 overs until the declaration. Ponting's unbeaten 141 included 17 fours and a six.

MOST DUCKS IN A TEST SERIES

	Tests	Inns	Series	
Six				
*A. G. Hurst	6	12	Australia v England	1978-79
Five				
Pankaj Roy	4	7	India v England	1952
N. A. T. Adcock	5	8	South Africa v Australia	1957-58
R. C. Motz	5	9	New Zealand v South Africa	1961-62
W. M. Clark	4	7	Australia v West Indies	1977-78
M. Amarnath	3	6	India v West Indies	1983-84
G. D. McGrath	5	7	Australia v England	1998-99
A. D. Mullally	4	7	England v Australia	1998-99
A. B. Agarkar	**3**	**6**	**India v Australia**	**1999-2000**
G. P. Wickremasinghe	**3**	**6**	**Sri Lanka v Pakistan**	**1999-2000**

* A. G. Hurst also had one innings of 0 not out in this series.

Any significant Indian reply was snuffed out when Tendulkar, off the fourth ball he faced, ladled a catch to cover. McGrath methodically unpicked the innings, taking five wickets for the second time in the match. His last was that of poor Agarkar, this time out second ball without scoring to equal the unenviable record of five successive ducks in Test innings. Australia's Bob Holland made two against England in 1985 and three against New Zealand in 1985-86, including consecutive pairs. India's honour was saved by a quite remarkable 167 off 198 balls by Laxman, who at the start of his innings had taken a staggering blow on the visor of his helmet. Tall and elegant, he drove with classic grace to all points between cover and mid-wicket and was just as assertive against anything short, cutting and pulling with power. Ganguly kept him company for 17 overs, but his only other ally was Kumble, who doggedly defended against 45 deliveries while Laxman went from 88 to 158 in 19 overs.

Man of the Match: G. D. McGrath.   *Attendance:* 106,637.

Man of the Series: S. R. Tendulkar.

Close of play: First day, India 121-8 (Kumble 1*, Srinath 2*); Second day, Australia 331-4 (Langer 167*, Ponting 34*).

India

†M. S. K. Prasad c M. E. Waugh b McGrath . .	5	– (2) c M. E. Waugh b McGrath . . .	3
V. V. S. Laxman c Slater b Lee	7	– (1) c Gilchrist b Lee	167
R. Dravid c Ponting b McGrath	29	– c Warne b McGrath	0
*S. R. Tendulkar lbw b McGrath	45	– c Langer b Fleming	4
S. C. Ganguly c S. R. Waugh b Blewett	1	– c M. E. Waugh b McGrath	25
H. H. Kanitkar c Gilchrist b Lee	10	– c Slater b Lee	8
R. V. Bharadwaj c Gilchrist b Lee	6	– absent hurt	
A. Kumble c Langer b McGrath	26	– (7) c Ponting b McGrath	15
A. B. Agarkar c M. E. Waugh b Lee	0	– (8) c Gilchrist b McGrath	0
J. Srinath c Ponting b McGrath	3	– (9) not out	15
B. K. V. Prasad not out	1	– (10) run out	3
L-b 12, w 1, n-b 4	17	B 4, l-b 2, w 1, n-b 14 . . .	21

1/10 (1) 2/27 (2) 3/68 (3) 4/69 (5)   150   1/22 (2) 2/26 (3) 3/33 (4)   261
5/95 (4) 6/118 (6) 7/119 (7)   4/101 (5) 5/145 (6) 6/234 (7)
8/119 (9) 9/126 (10) 10/150 (8)   7/234 (8) 8/258 (1) 9/261 (10)

Bowling: *First Innings*—McGrath 18.5–7–48–5; Fleming 13–7–24–0; Lee 21–9–39–4; Warne 12–4–22–0; Blewett 3–2–5–1. *Second Innings*—McGrath 17–1–55–5; Fleming 13–2–47–1; Lee 11–2–67–2; Blewett 2–0–16–0; Warne 13–1–60–0; Ponting 10–8–0; Slater 1–0–2–0.

Australia

G. S. Blewett b B. K. V. Prasad	19	R. T. Ponting not out	141
M. J. Slater c M. S. K. Prasad b Srinath	1	†A. C. Gilchrist not out	45
J. L. Langer c B. K. V. Prasad		B 2, l-b 21, n-b 11	34
b Tendulkar	223		
M. E. Waugh b Ganguly	32	1/9 (2) 2/49 (1) 3/146 (4) (5 wkts dec.) 552	
*S. R. Waugh lbw b Srinath	57	4/267 (5) 5/457 (3)	

S. K. Warne, D. W. Fleming, B. Lee and G. D. McGrath did not bat.

Bowling: Srinath 28–4–105–2; Agarkar 19–3–95–0; B. K. V. Prasad 28–10–86–1; Kumble 33.2–6–126–0; Ganguly 12–1–46–1; Bharadwaj 12–1–35–0; Tendulkar 7–0–34–1; Kanitkar 1–0–2–0.

Umpires: I. D. Robinson (Zimbabwe) and D. B. Hair.
Referee: R. S. Madugalle (Sri Lanka).

India's matches v Pakistan and Australia in the Carlton & United Series (January 10–30) may be found in that section.

ONE HUNDRED YEARS AGO

From JOHN WISDEN'S CRICKETERS' ALMANACK FOR 1901

FIELDING IN 1900, by D. L. A. Jephson – "Taken as a whole the fielding has been bad, thoroughly bad. Men stand in the field to day like... waxen figures in a third-rate tailor's shop. The energy, the life, the ever-watchfulness of ten years ago is gone, and in their place are lethargy, laziness, and a wonderful yearning for rest. To day a ball is driven through two so-called fieldsmen, and instead of a simultaneous rush to gather it, to hurl it to one end or the other, the two... stand facing each other with a lingering hope in their eyes that they will not be compelled to fetch it... There is another feature that strikes the interested spectator, namely, the growing inclination on the part of certain fieldsmen to remove themselves as far as possible from the *dangerous* ball that travels at *too great a speed*."

THE WEST INDIANS IN ENGLAND, 1900, by P. F. Warner – "On Monday, June 11th, the first West Indian eleven made its appearance in England, on the Crystal Palace ground, against an eleven collected by W. G. Grace... The tour was a success [given]... that the team had never played together before, [and] that they were quite unaccustomed to the strain of three day cricket... Of the seventeen matches played, five were won, four drawn, and eight lost, and bearing in mind all the circumstances and the opponents they had to meet this was a very creditable performance."

SOUTH AUSTRALIA v. NEW SOUTH WALES, 1899-1900 – "In this match New South Wales made a record score in first-class cricket in the Colonies, their total of 807 beating the 803 obtained by the Non-Smokers against the Smokers at Melbourne in 1887, and the previous record in Inter-colonial matches, 775 by New South Wales against Victoria, at Sydney, in 1882. Under the circumstances it is not at all surprising that New South Wales won the match by an innings and 392 runs – one of the most decisive victories ever known."

THE LEADING COUNTIES IN 1900 – "The Championship in 1900 was from first to last simply a race between Yorkshire and Lancashire, no other county being in the running for first place. For a long time the two elevens remained on even terms. Their matches with each other could not be played out, and at the beginning of the last week in July both were unbeaten. Then, however, Lancashire sustained an unexpected defeat at the hands of Gloucestershire, and as it turned out this one reverse would have been sufficient to put them out of court, Yorkshire to the end of the season enjoying a career of uninterrupted success in county matches."

THE WEST INDIANS IN NEW ZEALAND, 1999-2000

By GEOFFREY DEAN

Less than 12 months after their disastrous tour of South Africa, West Indies' away form showed no signs of improving. Beaten by New Zealand in a Test match for the first time since 1986-87, they went on to suffer only their second series defeat at their hands. Brian Lara's side were then whitewashed 5–0 in the one-day series by a country that had won just four of their previous 25 limited-overs meetings. Lara admitted afterwards: "Everyone is hurt, but there is no one to blame but us. It's a greater hurt than in South Africa because it's a year later and you expect it to make a difference."

A complete management clearout followed the tour, with Lara resigning from the captaincy, Clive Lloyd stepping down as manager and Sir Viv Richards, who was appointed as coach in a caretaker capacity after Malcolm Marshall had fallen ill, being overlooked when the position was advertised on the party's return home. Even Dennis Waight, West Indies' Australian-born physiotherapist, left his job after more than 20 years. Lloyd declared that his frustration in being unable to take part in selection had been a major factor in his decision to resign. "I dislike my contract and my fulfilment of it," he said, having been in the post three years. "These are traumatic times for West Indies cricket. There are a lot of things wrong at the moment."

Personal problems, coupled with a disillusionment with the game, caused Lara not only to give up the leadership of the side but also to take a four-month sabbatical from all cricket. Mentally stale, he made himself unavailable for both home series, against Zimbabwe and Pakistan, that followed the tour. In New Zealand, he appeared weighed down by responsibilities and, while he was not exactly out of form, two fatally irresponsible strokes in the First Test played a large part in what was a catastrophic defeat. Another, West Indies' tenth in succession on foreign soil, followed in the Second Test at the Basin Reserve.

Adrian Griffith had an excellent Test series, his four innings spanning a combined total of more than 18 hours, but the rest of the batting was inconsistent. Of the bowlers, only Reon King did himself justice. Courtney Walsh was ineffective in both Tests; Curtly Ambrose, rested with his own agreement in the hope of extending his Test career, was badly missed.

For New Zealand, their twin series victories further enhanced their growing reputation as an international force although, a couple of months later, Australia again suggested that the gulf between the sides was as wide as the Tasman Sea. Chris Cairns confirmed his status as a world class all-rounder with telling performances with the ball in both Tests as well as a crucial innings in the First. He finished with 17 wickets at the remarkable average of 9.94 apiece. His contributions in the one-day series were also important, as was the form of Nathan Astle, who totalled 320 runs at an average of 80. Daniel Vettori continued to suggest that he was the best left-arm spinner in world cricket in both forms of the game.

WEST INDIAN TOURING PARTY

B. C. Lara (Trinidad & Tobago) (*captain*), J. C. Adams (Jamaica), S. L. Campbell (Barbados), S. Chanderpaul (Guyana), P. T. Collins (Barbados), M. Dillon (Trinidad & Tobago), D. Ganga (Trinidad & Tobago), A. F. G. Griffith (Barbados), W. W. Hinds (Jamaica), R. D. Jacobs (Leeward Islands), R. D. King (Guyana), N. O. Perry (Jamaica), R. L. Powell (Jamaica), D. Ramnarine (Trinidad & Tobago), F. A. Rose (Jamaica), C. A. Walsh (Jamaica).
Manager: C. H. Lloyd.　　*Coach:* Sir Vivian Richards.

WEST INDIAN TOUR RESULTS

Test matches – Played 2: Lost 2.
First-class matches – Played 4: Drawn 2, Lost 2.
Losses – New Zealand (2).
Draws – New Zealand A, Auckland.
One-day internationals – Played 5: Lost 5.
Other non-first-class match – Lost v New Zealand Max Blacks.

Note: Matches in this section which were not first-class are signified by a dagger.

†At Christchurch, December 3. New Zealand Max Blacks won by eight wickets. Toss: West Indians. West Indians 99 for five (10 overs) (R. L. Powell 42) and 92 for five (7 overs) (B. C. Lara 40; C. E. Bulfin three for four); New Zealand Max Blacks 145 for five (10 overs) (C. L. Cairns 44, R. G. Twose 43 not out) and 47 for two (5.1 overs).
West Indians should have faced eight overs in the second innings of this game of Super Max cricket, but were docked one for a slow over-rate.

At Taupo, December 5, 6, 7. Drawn. Toss: West Indians. West Indians 450 for five dec. (S. Chanderpaul 216 not out, R. L. Powell 86, J. C. Adams 46; P. J. Wiseman three for 107) and 64 for four dec. (A. J. Penn three for 24); New Zealand A 140 (M. S. Sinclair 38; C. A. Walsh three for 49, M. Dillon four for 48) and 58 for two.
Chanderpaul's 216 not out lasted 560 minutes and 397 balls and included 34 fours and one six.

At Eden Park Outer Oval, Auckland, December 10, 11, 12, 13. Drawn. Toss: West Indians. West Indians 380 (S. L. Campbell 112, J. C. Adams 65, R. D. Jacobs 86 not out; K. D. Mills three for 104, R. G. Morgan five for 75) and 228 for no wkt (S. L. Campbell 109 retired hurt, D. Ganga 100 not out); Auckland 369 (T. G. McIntosh 30, J. M. Aiken 84, A. C. Barnes 52, K. D. Mills 45 not out, Extras 51; P. T. Collins three for 77).
Campbell hit a hundred in each innings for the first time, though in the second innings, when 13, he was bowled by a no-ball from Mills. He completed his second century from 99 balls.

NEW ZEALAND v WEST INDIES

First Test Match

At Hamilton, December 16, 17, 18, 19, 20. New Zealand won by nine wickets. Toss: West Indies. Test debut: R. L. Powell.
That West Indies lost this match after being 276 without loss shortly before the close of the first day will long haunt them. From that seemingly impregnable position, they batted so poorly on a docile pitch that they managed only 186 more runs in the match for the loss of 20 wickets. The transformation in New Zealand's bowling, which had been so disappointing on the first day, was equally marked. Their batsmen all made useful contributions against indifferent West Indian bowling, but it was a magnificent all-round effort from Cairns that was primarily responsible for this extraordinary victory. Coming to the wicket at 258 for six, he played some superb attacking shots in a belligerent 72 that gave his side an unexpected first-innings lead of 28. Then he demolished West Indies' second innings, ending with seven for 27, his best figures in Test cricket. In all, he claimed ten for 100, meaning that he and Lance Cairns became the first father and son each to take ten wickets in a Test.

Campbell, hitting his third hundred in successive first-class innings, and Griffith, who made a maiden Test century off 261 balls, had dominated the first day with a West Indian all-wicket record against New Zealand. Sixteen of Campbell's 23 fours were struck behind square on the off side, mostly from cuts, an indication of the width he was given. He also pulled two sixes off McMillan before he was out for 170 from 262 balls, trying to hook the second new ball.

On the second day, Cairns, by going round the wicket to the left-handers, was much more effective, taking three for 14 from 15 overs – compared to none for 59 from 16 on the first. But Vettori played the key role, dismissing Lara and Griffith with successive balls; his second-day figures were four for 27 in 13.1 overs. Lara, caught at mid-off from a leading edge, was one of several batsmen to gift his wicket.

New Zealand owed much to Fleming for holding their innings together with a responsible 66 in three and three-quarter hours. They were fortunate, too, that Cairns, apparently run out off his first ball by a direct hit from Chanderpaul at cover, was given the benefit of the doubt – when none seemed to exist – by the third umpire, Dave Quested. Cairns went on to bludgeon nine fours and two sixes, one an enormous blow over wide long-on off Rose, and passed 2,000 Test runs.

West Indies, batting again, lost their first three wickets for one run, including Lara when he drove recklessly at a half-volley without moving his feet. Ricardo Powell, who collected a duck in his debut innings, tried to hit his way out of trouble and found the boundary with his first six scoring shots in Test cricket before a wild heave cost him his wicket. Almost all the last two sessions of the fourth day were washed out, and, next morning, resuming 38 ahead, West Indies surrendered their last six wickets in 100 minutes. Cairns ended Griffith's two-and-a-half-hour stay when he went round the wicket and, after Jacobs was needlessly run out, his change of pace confounded the tail. Vettori kept the other end tight by bowling into the bowlers' footmarks. Adams was last out, top-edging a hook to give Cairns the third-best Test figures for New Zealand after Sir Richard Hadlee's nine for 52 against Australia at Brisbane in 1985-86 and seven for 23 against India at Wellington in 1975-76. New Zealand needed only 15 overs to reach their target, though Horne had a finger broken by Rose in that time.

Lara confessed afterwards that his side had been complacent after the first day. "We came out on the second day and took things for granted. We sat back on our laurels and just waited for the Test to take its course. I take full responsibility for what happened out there and was very disappointed in myself." Coach Richards admitted that the New Zealand bowlers used the pitch conditions much better than the West Indians.

Man of the Match: C. L. Cairns.

Close of play: First day, West Indies 282-1 (Griffith 103*, Ramnarine 5*); Second day, New Zealand 113-3 (Fleming 18*, Vettori 5*); Third day, West Indies 0-0 (Griffith 0*, Campbell 0*); Fourth day, West Indies 66-4 (Griffith 14*, Adams 14*).

West Indies

A. F. G. Griffith c Parore b Vettori	114	– c Parore b Cairns	18
E. L. Campbell c Parore b Nash	170	– b Cairns	0
D. Ramnarine c Parore b Cairns	8	– (9) c and b Cairns	0
S. Chanderpaul c Fleming b Astle	14	– (3) c Parore b Cairns	0
*B. C. Lara c Nash b Vettori	24	– (4) c Parore b Nash	1
R. L. Powell c Wiseman b Cairns	0	– (5) c Spearman b Vettori	30
J. C. Adams not out	17	– (6) c sub (S. B. O'Connor) b Cairns	25
†R. D. Jacobs c Spearman b Vettori	5	– (7) run out	2
F. A. Rose c Wiseman b Cairns	4	– (8) lbw b Cairns	3
R. D. King b Nash	1	– lbw b Cairns	0
C. A. Walsh b Vettori	0	– not out	5
L-b 6, n-b 2	8	B 7, l-b 3, n-b 3	13

1/276 (2) 2/289 (3) 3/311 (4) 4/336 (5)   365   1/0 (2) 2/0 (3) 3/1 (4)   97
5/336 (1) 6/336 (6) 7/345 (8)   4/36 (5) 5/78 (1) 6/85 (7)
8/352 (9) 9/362 (10) 10/365 (11)   7/90 (8) 8/90 (9)
                                                                              9/90 (10) 10/97 (6)

Bowling: *First Innings*—Cairns 31–11–73–3; Nash 28–12–63–2; Vettori 34.1–9–83–4; Astle 16–2–67–1; Wiseman 22–10–51–0; McMillan 4–1–22–0. *Second Innings*—Vettori 22–12–20–1; Cairns 22.5–10–27–7; Nash 7–1–37–1; Wiseman 2–0–3–0.

New Zealand

G. R. Stead b Walsh	22	– b Walsh	16
M. J. Horne c Rose b King	32	– retired hurt	5
C. M. Spearman b Ramnarine	27	– not out	30
*S. P. Fleming c Jacobs b Ramnarine	66		
D. L. Vettori c Adams b King	29		
N. J. Astle c Ramnarine b Walsh	48	– (4) not out	7
C. D. McMillan c Jacobs b King	51		
C. L. Cairns c Campbell b Ramnarine	72		
†A. C. Parore run out	8		
D. J. Nash c Powell b King	6		
P. J. Wiseman not out	0		
B 4, l-b 9, w 3, n-b 16	32	B 4, l-b 1, n-b 7	12

1/61 (2) 2/67 (1) 3/107 (3) 4/162 (5)   **393**   1/59 (1)   (1 wkt) **70**
5/215 (4) 6/258 (6) 7/374 (8)
8/379 (7) 9/388 (9) 10/393 (10)

In the second innings Horne retired hurt at 16.

Bowling: *First Innings*—Walsh 29–4–81–2; Rose 27–4–103–0; Ramnarine 36–10–82–3; King 26.2–2–81–4; Powell 5–2–13–0; Adams 7–1–20–0. *Second Innings*—Walsh 8–1–33–1; Rose 6–0–28–0; Ramnarine 1–0–4–0.

Umpires: D. R. Shepherd (England) and D. B. Cowie.
Referee: R. Subba Row (England).

NEW ZEALAND v WEST INDIES

Second Test Match

At Basin Reserve, Wellington, December 26, 27, 28, 29. New Zealand won by an innings and 105 runs. Toss: West Indies. Test debut: M. S. Sinclair.

Having put New Zealand in, West Indies were dismayed to find that the green, evenly grassed pitch offered neither bounce nor movement. They bowled without discipline, giving too much width to Mathew Sinclair, 24, who made easily the highest score by a New Zealander on debut, a chanceless 214 in 534 minutes. With the series effectively lost by the end of the second day,

DOUBLE-HUNDREDS ON TEST DEBUT

287, 19	R. E. Foster	England v Australia at Sydney	1903-04
214, 100*	L. G. Rowe	West Indies v New Zealand at Kingston	1971-72
214	**M. S. Sinclair**	**New Zealand v West Indies at Wellington**	**1999-2000**
201*	D. S. B. P. Kuruppu	Sri Lanka v New Zealand at Colombo (CCC)	1986-87

West Indies batted with neither sufficient skill nor stomach, though they were handicapped by the absence of Ganga in both innings after he fractured a finger in the field. New Zealand impressed with thoughtful, at times aggressive, bowling and tenacious fielding. Nash received a warning from the match referee, Raman Subba Row, for verbal abuse.

Only R. E. "Tip" Foster, with 287 for England at Sydney in 1903-04, made more as a debutant than Sinclair, who had replaced the injured Horne. After getting off the mark with an inside edge

[*Phil Walter/Fotopress*

At Wellington, Mathew Sinclair became the fifth New Zealander to hit a century on Test debut.
But none of the others – all left-handers – had managed to make it a double.

for four off Walsh, Sinclair barely put a foot wrong, playing positively at first to reach 50 off 65
balls. Having made his hundred off 164, he then dug in, facing 451 in all. He hit all but four of
his 22 boundaries – most off the back foot – in an arc between third man and extra cover, an
area that was heavily patrolled, and only two on his much weaker leg side, both behind square.
Only once did West Indies persuade him to hook or pull; their fault lay in failing to bowl straight
enough at him.

Fleming, with whom Sinclair added 164 in 57 overs for the third wicket, made a disciplined
67 in three and a half hours. Astle's stay of just over four – in which they added 189, a New
Zealand fourth-wicket record against West Indies – featured rasping drives and cuts, and ended
when Rose ran him out, going for the second run that would have brought up Sinclair's double-
hundred. By the time Rose cut through the tail as the third new ball, unlike the first two, swung
generously, New Zealand were already comfortably past their previous highest total against West
Indies on home soil.

New Zealand then dismissed their opponents cheaply, thanks to Cairns's aggression and Vettori's
attrition. Cairns claimed his ninth five-wicket haul in Tests, while Vettori, bowling into Wellington's

notoriously strong wind, simply wore the many left-handers down by pitching into the rough outside their off stump. Only Lara played him with conviction until, trying for the umpteenth time to kick him away, he was bowled by a ball that rebounded on to his stumps via pad flap and glove. It was a cruel end to the sort of responsible innings that had been so badly needed in the First Test. Once his partnership of 112 with Griffith was broken, West Indies quickly subsided and were asked to follow on. Griffith, a model of concentration, resisted 345 minutes for his 67.

West Indies began their second innings, 339 adrift, just before the end of the third day. They looked to have an outside chance of survival at 148 for two a few overs before tea on the fourth day, particularly as Cairns was restricted by a sore back. Lara and Chanderpaul had added 65 in 22 overs without any real difficulty, but then a familiar collapse ensued. Nash, bowling well on a pitch that had become low and slow, had Chanderpaul and Adams caught behind with two good deliveries from round the wicket, the first straightening, the second lifting off a length, and he and Parore combined again to end another responsible innings from Lara, who was palpably unlucky with the decision. Nash's influence extended to his fielding, for he ran out the adhesive Griffith with an athletic dive and pinpoint throw on the turn. New Zealand completed their first innings victory over West Indies, and a 2–0 series win, when Cairns trapped Rose, his 150th Test victim.

Man of the Match: M. S. Sinclair.

Close of play: First day, New Zealand 263-3 (Sinclair 123*, Astle 8*); Second day, West Indies 5-1 (Griffith 2*, Perry 3*); Third day, West Indies 2-0 (Griffith 0*, Campbell 2*).

New Zealand

C. M. Spearman c Walsh b King	24	D. L. Vettori c Campbell b Rose	2
G. R. Stead c Campbell b King	17	S. B. O'Connor not out	0
M. S. Sinclair b King	214	B 5, l-b 12, w 1, n-b 14	32
*S. P. Fleming c Adams b Chanderpaul	67		
N. J. Astle run out	93	1/33 (2) 2/76 (1)	(9 wkts dec.) 518
C. D. McMillan c Jacobs b King	31	3/240 (4) 4/429 (5)	
C. L. Cairns c Adams b Rose	31	5/456 (3) 6/507 (7)	
†A. C. Parore b Rose	5	7/507 (6) 8/514 (8)	
D. J. Nash not out	2	9/518 (10)	

Bowling: Walsh 41–5–112–0; King 36–11–96–4; Rose 32.3–5–113–3; Perry 32–5–120–0; Adams 26–9–45–0; Chanderpaul 6–1–15–1.

West Indies

A. F. G. Griffith c Fleming b Nash	67	– run out	45
S. L. Campbell lbw b Cairns	0	– lbw b Cairns	3
N. O. Perry c Parore b Cairns	3	– (7) lbw b Astle	0
S. Chanderpaul c Parore b Cairns	5	– (3) c Parore b Nash	70
*B. C. Lara b Vettori	67	– (4) c Parore b Nash	75
J. C. Adams c Stead b Vettori	8	– (5) c Parore b Nash	4
†R. D. Jacobs not out	19	– (6) c Stead b Vettori	20
F. A. Rose c Parore b Cairns	0	– lbw b Cairns	10
R. D. King run out	0	– (10) not out	4
C. A. Walsh b Cairns	0	– (9) lbw b Nash	0
D. Ganga absent hurt		– absent hurt	
B 2, l-b 4, w 2, n-b 2	10	B 1, l-b 1, w 1	3

1/1 (2) 2/5 (3) 3/17 (4) 4/129 (5)	179	1/8 (2) 2/83 (1) 3/148 (3)	234
5/141 (6) 6/174 (1) 7/175 (8)		4/154 (5) 5/189 (6) 6/204 (7)	
8/176 (9) 9/179 (10)		7/225 (4) 8/225 (9) 9/234 (8)	

Bowling: *First Innings*—Cairns 19–5–44–5; Nash 18–8–23–1; Vettori 31–10–69–2; O'Connor 19–8–25–0; Astle 4–1–12–0. *Second Innings*—O'Connor 16–3–50–0; Vettori 32–8–86–1; Nash 16–4–38–4; Cairns 12.1–4–25–2; Astle 7–0–33–1.

Umpires: R. B. Tiffin (Zimbabwe) and E. A. Watkin.
Referee: R. Subba Row (England).

†NEW ZEALAND v WEST INDIES

First One-Day International

At Auckland, January 2. New Zealand won by three wickets (D/L method). Toss: West Indies.

Set a revised target of 250 in 46 overs after an interruption, New Zealand won with five deliveries to spare. They were helped by the fact that West Indies had to bowl with a wet ball after fielding through further rain. Astle and Cairns, joining forces at 62 for three, put on a match-winning stand of 136 in 25 overs. Cairns hit six sixes in his 88-ball 75, while Astle reached his fifty from only 57 deliveries. For West Indies, Jacobs and Campbell had raised 100 in the 16th over, and the impetus was maintained by Lara and Powell, who both scored at around a run a ball.

Man of the Match: N. J. Astle.

West Indies

S. L. Campbell st Parore b Vettori	51	J. C. Adams c Fleming b Astle	0
†R. D. Jacobs lbw b Harris	65	M. Dillon not out	13
*B. C. Lara c Nash b O'Connor	76	B 4, l-b 6, w 3	13
S. Chanderpaul run out	11		
R. L. Powell c Twose b Nash	35	1/111 2/131 3/158 (7 wkts, 50 overs) 268
F. A. Rose c McMillan b O'Connor	2	4/249 5/253
N. O. Perry not out	2	6/253 7/255

R. D. King and C. A. Walsh did not bat.

Bowling: Nash 8–0–62–1; Cairns 5–0–29–0; O'Connor 8–0–62–2; Harris 10–0–40–1; Vettori 10–1–28–1; Astle 9–0–37–1.

New Zealand

C. M. Spearman c Jacobs b Walsh	25	†A. C. Parore c Dillon b King	4
N. J. Astle b Rose	77	D. J. Nash not out	12
*S. P. Fleming c Jacobs b King	1	L-b 14, w 6, n-b 7	27
C. D. McMillan c Rose b King	1		
C. L. Cairns c Powell b Rose	75	1/44 2/48 3/62 (7 wkts, 45.1 overs) 250
C. Z. Harris not out	22	4/198 5/198
R. G. Twose c Jacobs b Rose	6	6/211 7/226

D. L. Vettori and S. B. O'Connor did not bat.

Bowling: Walsh 10–0–48–1; Rose 9–0–71–3; King 8.1–3–24–3; Dillon 9–1–41–0; Perry 9–0–52–0.

Umpires: B. F. Bowden and D. M. Quested.

†NEW ZEALAND v WEST INDIES

Second One-Day International

At Taupo, January 4 (day/night). New Zealand won by seven wickets. Toss: New Zealand.

Vettori's best return in one-day internationals, four for 24, was a key factor in restricting West Indies to 192 after rain reduced the match to a 43-over affair. Cairns also played a leading part with two early wickets in a fine opening spell – he removed Campbell with the first ball of the game – and a hard-hitting unbeaten 27 later on. Astle, with 32 off 25 balls, gave New Zealand a flier as 56 came off the first eight overs. Fleming ensured the good start was not wasted with 59 not out.

Man of the Match: D. L. Vettori.

West Indies

S. L. Campbell c Fleming b Cairns	0	M. Dillon c Astle b Vettori	10
†R. D. Jacobs c Cairns b O'Connor	13	R. D. King lbw b Astle	0
J. C. Adams b Vettori	69	C. A. Walsh c Twose b Nash	0
*B. C. Lara c Vettori b Cairns	2	B 5, l-b 4, w 5, n-b 2	16
S. Chanderpaul c Vettori b Harris	26		
R. L. Powell c Cairns b Vettori	35	1/0 2/29 3/31 (41.3 overs) 192
N. O. Perry b Vettori.	0	4/88 5/150 6/151
F. A. Rose not out	21	7/171 8/183 9/187

Bowling: Cairns 9–1–25–2; O'Connor 5–0–39–1; Nash 6.3–0–27–1; Harris 9–1–42–1; Vettori 8–1–24–4; Astle 4–0–26–1.

New Zealand

C. M. Spearman c Jacobs b Dillon	42	C. L. Cairns not out	27
N. J. Astle c Dillon b Adams	32	L-b 4, w 5, n-b 12.	21
*S. P. Fleming not out.	59		
C. D. McMillan c Jacobs b Rose.	13	1/56 2/98 3/137 (3 wkts, 35.4 overs) 194

R. G. Twose, C. Z. Harris, †A. C. Parore, D. J. Nash, D. L. Vettori and S. B. O'Connor did not bat.

Bowling: Walsh 6–0–32–0; King 5–0–27–0; Adams 3.4–0–29–1; Perry 5–0–24–0; Dillon 9–0–37–1; Campbell 1–0–4–0; Rose 6–0–37–1.

Umpires: R. S. Dunne and D. M. Quested.

†NEW ZEALAND v WEST INDIES

Third One-Day International

At Napier, January 6 (day/night). New Zealand won by four wickets. Toss: West Indies.

Another poor performance with the bat saw West Indies fall some 50 runs short of par. Once more Cairns bowled a superb new-ball spell, again dismissing Campbell with the first legitimate ball of the match, and Harris tied up the middle order. When Harris caught and bowled Lara, sixth out at 70, any hope of a competitive total was lost, though Perry batted sensibly for a maiden international fifty. Astle and Fleming launched the reply with 105 in 21 overs before Fleming guided his side home with more than 12 overs to spare.

Man of the Match: S. P. Fleming.

West Indies

S. L. Campbell c Parore b Cairns	0	M. Dillon c Parore b Astle.	15
†R. D. Jacobs lbw b Cairns	4	D. Ramnarine b Styris.	2
J. C. Adams c Parore b Nash	2	R. D. King lbw b Nash	5
S. Chanderpaul b Cairns	10	L-b 1, w 9	10
*B. C. Lara c and b Harris	30		
R. L. Powell c Astle b Harris	11	1/1 2/6 3/15 (49.5 overs) 159
W. W. Hinds c and b Harris	18	4/33 5/62 6/70
N. O. Perry not out.	52	7/97 8/145 9/147

Bowling: Cairns 8–0–25–3; Nash 4.5–0–11–2; Styris 10–1–31–1; Vettori 10–1–40–0; Harris 10–1–28–3; Astle 7–0–23–1.

New Zealand

C. M. Spearman c Jacobs b Dillon	0	C. Z. Harris c Adams b King	10
N. J. Astle c Chanderpaul b Perry	50	†A. C. Parore not out	9
*S. P. Fleming not out	66	B 4, l-b 2, w 2, n-b 3	11
R. G. Twose c Adams b King	0		—
C. L. Cairns c Campbell b King	8	1/1 2/106 3/106 (6 wkts, 37.2 overs) 160	
C. D. McMillan c and b Hinds	6	4/114 5/126 6/142	

D. J. Nash, S. B. Styris and D. L. Vettori did not bat.

Bowling: Dillon 8–0–45–1; King 10–1–35–3; Ramnarine 6.2–2–23–0; Perry 10–0–37–1; Hinds 3–0–14–1.

Umpires: D. B. Cowie and E. A. Watkin.

†NEW ZEALAND v WEST INDIES

Fourth One-Day International

At WestpacTrust Stadium, Wellington, January 8, 9. New Zealand won by eight wickets. Toss: New Zealand.

The first international at Wellington's new stadium was blighted by bad weather and, after rain allowed less than 11 overs on the Saturday, the match was concluded on the reserve day. West Indies never came to terms with a sporting pitch against good bowling, of which Harris was the pick, and later they dropped vital catches, reprieving both Astle, in his 100th one-day international, and Twose before they were established. Their unbroken partnership of 149 was a New Zealand all-wicket record against West Indies – until they broke it two days later.

Man of the Match: C. Z. Harris.

Close of play: West Indies 43-1 (10.5 overs) (Jacobs 10*).

West Indies

†R. D. Jacobs c Parore b Styris	24	M. Dillon c sub (S. B. O'Connor) b Vettori	0
S. Chanderpaul c Twose b Cairns	27	P. T. Collins not out	10
J. C. Adams c Parore b Harris	24	R. D. King not out	7
*B. C. Lara lbw b Styris	5	L-b 11, w 7, n-b 1	19
S. L. Campbell c Parore b Styris	30		—
W. W. Hinds c McMillan b Vettori	7	1/43 2/73 3/79 (9 wkts, 50 overs) 171	
R. L. Powell run out	9	4/105 5/116 6/131	
N. O. Perry st Parore b Astle	9	7/146 8/147 9/153	

Bowling: Cairns 10–2–27–1; Nash 8–0–35–0; Styris 10–0–37–3; Harris 10–3–15–1; Vettori 10–0–33–2; Astle 2–0–13–1.

New Zealand

C. M. Spearman c Jacobs b Dillon	0
N. J. Astle not out	76
*S. P. Fleming c Adams b King	10
R. G. Twose not out	68
L-b 7, w 6, n-b 5	18

1/0 2/23   (2 wkts, 36.3 overs) 172

C. L. Cairns, C. D. McMillan, C. Z. Harris, †A. C. Parore, D. J. Nash, S. B. Styris and D. L. Vettori did not bat.

Bowling: Dillon 9–0–52–1; King 6–1–20–1; Collins 5.3–0–37–0; Perry 6–0–22–0; Adams 10–1–34–0.

Umpires: R. S. Dunne and E. A. Watkin.

†NEW ZEALAND v WEST INDIES

Fifth One-Day International

At Christchurch, January 11 (day/night). New Zealand won by 20 runs. Toss: New Zealand.

New Zealand achieved a 5–0 whitewash thanks to some superb batting against inconsistent bowling on a good pitch. It was the first time they had scored 300 against West Indies in a one-day international. This time, the chief aggressor in another record-breaking stand, 170 at more than a run a ball, was Twose rather than Astle, who hit his fourth fifty of the series. Twose faced only 90 balls for his 97, a personal best in international cricket. West Indies raced to 100 for two in 15 overs, but when Lara holed out to long-on at 111, their chances were all but scuppered. Campbell struck a brisk 71 to entertain a crowd of 12,200.

Man of the Match: R. G. Twose.

New Zealand

C. M. Spearman run out	5		C. D. McMillan c Lara b Walsh	23
N. J. Astle c Lara b Campbell	85		†A. C. Parore not out	2
*S. P. Fleming c Adams b Perry	8		B 1, l-b 5, w 10, n-b 5	21
R. G. Twose b King	97			
C. Z. Harris not out	37		1/8 2/35 3/205	(6 wkts, 50 overs) 302
C. L. Cairns b Campbell	24		4/217 5/255 6/297	

A. J. Penn, S. B. Styris and D. L. Vettori did not bat.

Bowling: Dillon 10–1–42–0; Walsh 10–0–70–1; Perry 10–0–63–1; Adams 3–0–21–0; King 10–0–54–1; Campbell 7–0–46–2.

West Indies

†R. D. Jacobs c Twose b Cairns	4		M. Dillon c Penn b Styris	8
S. Chanderpaul c Parore b Vettori	30		R. D. King not out	7
A. F. G. Griffith c Spearman b Styris	35		C. A. Walsh b Styris	18
*B. C. Lara c Twose b Harris	37		B 1, l-b 6, w 7, n-b 2	16
J. C. Adams c Styris b Harris	26			
S. L. Campbell c Astle b Styris	71		1/4 2/58 3/102	(49.5 overs) 282
R. L. Powell run out	2		4/111 5/164 6/167	
N. O. Perry c Harris b Vettori	28		7/221 8/242 9/261	

Bowling: Cairns 4–0–31–1; Penn 6–0–49–0; Styris 9.5–0–57–4; Vettori 10–0–40–2; Harris 10–1–44–2; Astle 10–0–54–0.

Umpires: A. L. Hill and E. A. Watkin.
Series referee: R. Subba Row (England).

THE SRI LANKANS IN PAKISTAN, 1999-2000

By SAMIUL HASAN

Muttiah Muralitharan was the obvious and outstanding difference between competitive, focused Sri Lanka and injury-plagued Pakistan in an entertaining three-Test series that the Sri Lankans won 2–1. Thanks to him, they became the first team to win successive Test series in Pakistan (excluding the drawn game in the Asian Test Championship the previous year). He had been their leading wicket-taker with 15 when Sri Lanka toured Pakistan in 1995-96; now he bagged eight wickets at Rawalpindi, ten at Peshawar and eight at Karachi to finish the series with 26 – the best return by any Test bowler visiting Pakistan. The Pakistani strokemakers, once considered to be among the best players of spin, were repeatedly shown up by the menace of his prodigious and varied turn.

While the series confirmed the revival of Sri Lankan cricket after their disastrous World Cup nine months earlier, finalists Pakistan continued to plunge deeper into crisis. Prior to the series, Wasim Akram had paid the price for his side's débâcle in the World Cup final and for their defeat in all three Tests, and six out of ten one-day internationals, in Australia. His successor – not for the first time – was Saeed Anwar, reappointed after wicket-keeper Moin Khan had rejected the offer to lead his country. But it turned out to be a short-term succession. Anwar not only failed to inspire his team; he turned out to be a man of limited ideas when he opted to bat last in all three one-day internationals, despite having an inexperienced middle order. This series, a drab affair for which the selectors omitted Ijaz Ahmed, Inzamam-ul-Haq and Shahid Afridi, preceded the Test matches and was won 3–0 by Sri Lanka.

Anwar suffered also from the loss of key players. The recently married Waqar Younis was excused the one-day series, and Shoaib Akhtar was unavailable for the first international because the Pakistan Cricket Board had suspended him for a match, following an unauthorised night out in Australia. He then missed the third one-day game and the opening Test because of a groin injury incurred in the second, while a side strain in the third international ruled Azhar Mahmood out of the Test series. But the most cruel blow came when Wasim Akram limped off after bowling just 13 deliveries in the First Test. In that same match, Saqlain Mushtaq was taken to hospital suffering from dehydration and showed a lot of courage to bowl 33 overs virtually unchanged on the fifth day. Neither took any further part in the series, by the end of which Pakistan had called up 19 players.

Anwar was himself injured when he collided with an umpire in the Second Test and, in his absence, Moin Khan led the team in the Third. On the second day of that match, however, Anwar announced that he was stepping down permanently, to concentrate on his batting, and Moin was appointed to replace him for a four-month programme that would take Pakistan to Sharjah, the West Indies and Sri Lanka. Only a week earlier, the Board had confirmed Anwar's appointment until July.

As if Pakistan did not have enough to contend with, battling to overcome injuries and poor performances in the field, the Board triggered an avoidable controversy by confirming, on the opening day's play in the Second Test, that Javed Miandad would replace Intikhab Alam as coach for the forthcoming tours. Next morning, an angry and offended Intikhab announced that he had packed his bags and was quitting the team. Although he subsequently agreed to a request that he see out the match, the PCB penalised him for his outburst by cancelling his nomination for the ICC panel of match referees. Miandad took over as coach for the Third Test, earlier than planned and for the second time in less than a year.

Controversy dogged the final Test at Karachi as well, which Pakistan won to preserve their unbeaten record at the National Stadium. After the third day's play, Inzamam alleged that the Sri Lankan close-in fielders had been trying to break his concentration with abusive sledging, a comment which earned him the displeasure of the match referee, Brian Hastings of New Zealand, and a suspended fine of 25 per cent of his match fee. Along with his team-mates, he lost an actual 25 per cent when Pakistan were fined for their slow over-rate. Also on the third day, local umpire Riazuddin had an exchange with Jayasuriya after Tillekeratne Dilshan had appeared to throw the ball at him on several occasions – an unsportsmanlike protest against decisions by Riaz which, the tourists obviously felt, deprived them of vital wickets. While no formal complaints were lodged with the referee, the Sri Lankans did make a verbal protest about Riazuddin's umpiring and Hastings was later reported to have given him zero marks.

SRI LANKAN TOURING PARTY

S. T. Jayasuriya (Bloomfield) (*captain*), D. P. M. D. Jayawardene (Sinhalese) (*vice-captain*), R. P. Arnold (Nondescripts), M. S. Atapattu (Sinhalese), U. D. U. Chandana (Tamil Union), S. I. de Saram (Tamil Union), P. A. de Silva (Nondescripts), T. M. Dilshan (Sebastianites), I. S. Gallage (Colombo), R. Herath (Moors), R. S. Kaluwitharana (Colts), M. Muralitharan (Tamil Union), K. R. Pushpakumara (Nondescripts), M. Pushpakumara, A. Ranatunga (Sinhalese), L. P. C. Silva (Panadura), W. P. U. J. C. Vaas (Colts), G. P. Wickremasinghe (Sinhalese), D. N. T. Zoysa (Sinhalese).

De Saram, M. Pushpakumara and Silva went home after the one-day leg of the tour, when de Silva, Herath and Ranatunga joined the party for the first-class programme; de Saram later returned after Ranatunga flew home injured.

Manager: T. B. Kehelgamuwa.   *Coach:* D. F. Whatmore.

SRI LANKAN TOUR RESULTS

Test matches – Played 3: Won 2, Lost 1.
First-class matches – Played 4: Won 2, Lost 1, Drawn 1.
Wins – Pakistan (2).
Loss – Pakistan.
Draw – Pakistan Cricket Board XI.
One-day internationals – Played 3: Won 3.
Other non-first-class matches – Won v Pakistan Cricket Board XI (2).

TEST MATCH AVERAGES

PAKISTAN – BATTING

	T	I	NO	R	HS	100s	50s	Avge	Ct/St
Inzamam-ul-Haq	3	6	1	355	138	1	2	71.00	0
Saeed Anwar	2	4	0	217	84	0	2	54.25	0
Shahid Afridi	2	4	0	143	74	0	1	35.75	1
Younis Khan	3	6	0	201	107	1	1	33.50	2
Yousuf Youhana	3	6	0	164	88	0	1	27.33	4
Moin Khan	2	4	0	107	70	0	1	26.75	8/1
Shoaib Akhtar	2	4	1	35	26	0	0	11.66	1
Aamir Sohail	2	4	0	46	24	0	0	11.50	2
Waqar Younis	3	6	0	66	39	0	0	11.00	2
Abdur Razzaq	2	4	0	17	9	0	0	4.25	0

Played in one Test: Arshad Khan 0, 5; Atiq-uz-Zaman 1, 25 (5 ct); Ijaz Ahmed, sen. 7, 3 (1 ct); Irfan Fazil 1*, 3 (2 ct); Mohammad Akram 0, 1*; Naved Ashraf 5, 27; Saqlain Mushtaq 3*, 2* (2 ct); Wajahatullah Wasti 17, 1 (2 ct); Wasim Akram 0, 79.

* Signifies not out.

BOWLING

	O	M	R	W	BB	5W/i	Avge
Aamir Sohail	42.2	9	99	5	2-20	0	19.80
Shoaib Akhtar	67.5	9	238	11	5-75	1	21.63
Waqar Younis	96.5	18	310	13	4-103	0	23.84
Shahid Afridi	27	4	121	5	3-50	0	24.20
Abdur Razzaq	92.5	28	221	8	4-56	0	27.62
Arshad Khan	65	21	151	4	3-81	0	37.75
Saqlain Mushtaq	67	16	152	3	2-78	0	50.66

Also bowled: Irfan Fazil 8–0–65–2; Mohammad Akram 24.1–3–93–2; Wajahatullah Wasti 1–1–0–0; Wasim Akram 2.1–0–8–0.

SRI LANKA – BATTING

	T	I	NO	R	HS	100s	50s	Avge	Ct/St
P. A. de Silva	2	4	0	197	112	1	0	49.25	2
W. P. U. J. C. Vaas	3	6	3	128	53*	0	1	42.66	1
R. P. Arnold	3	6	0	189	99	0	1	31.50	7
D. P. M. D. Jayawardene . .	3	6	0	153	42	0	0	25.50	9
M. S. Atapattu	3	6	0	148	75	0	1	24.66	2
S. T. Jayasuriya	3	6	0	143	56	0	1	23.83	1
R. S. Kaluwitharana	3	6	1	115	42	0	0	23.00	7/2
M. Muralitharan	3	5	2	50	22	0	0	16.66	1
K. R. Pushpakumara	2	4	0	66	44	0	0	16.50	1
T. M. Dilshan	2	4	0	56	31	0	0	14.00	4
G. P. Wickremasinghe	3	6	0	5	5	0	0	0.83	6

Played in one Test: S. I. de Saram 5, 18 (1 ct); A. Ranatunga 49, 29* (1 ct); D. N. T. Zoysa 26, 13.

* *Signifies not out.*

BOWLING

	O	M	R	W	BB	5W/i	Avge
M. Muralitharan	213.1	50	516	26	6-71	1	19.84
S. T. Jayasuriya	26.5	5	92	3	1-9	0	30.66
W. P. U. J. C. Vaas	146	29	408	13	3-69	0	31.38
D. N. T. Zoysa	39	10	101	3	3-64	0	33.66
K. R. Pushpakumara	57.5	10	170	5	4-66	0	34.00
G. P. Wickremasinghe	105.5	27	306	8	4-37	0	38.25

Also bowled: R. P. Arnold 5–1–15–0; P. A. de Silva 6–2–10–0; D. P. M. D. Jayawardene 5–3–7–1.

Note: Matches in this section which were not first-class are signified by a dagger.

†At National Stadium, Karachi, February 8. Sri Lankans won by eight wickets. Toss: Sri Lankans. Pakistan Cricket Board XI 250 for six (50 overs) (Aamir Sohail 63, Imran Abbas 79, Faisal Iqbal 31); Sri Lankans 251 for two (40.3 overs) (S. T. Jayasuriya 37, M. S. Atapattu 122 not out, D. P. M. D. Jayawardene 62 not out).

†At UBL Sports Complex, Karachi, February 10. Sri Lankans won by nine wickets. Toss: Sri Lankans. Pakistan Cricket Board XI 48 (33 overs) (M. Muralitharan three for 12, U. D. U. Chandana four for 12); Sri Lankans 49 for one (6.5 overs) (S. T. Jayasuriya 35 not out).

Only Hasan Raza, with 18, reached double figures for the Board XI. Chandana's full analysis was 9–3–12–4 and Muralitharan's 10–4–12–3. As the game ended before lunch, a 25-over exhibition match was staged, which the Board XI won by seven wickets.

†PAKISTAN v SRI LANKA

First One-Day International

At Karachi, February 13. Sri Lanka won by 29 runs. Toss: Pakistan. International debuts: Imran Abbas, Yasir Arafat, Younis Khan.

Atapattu's third century in 90 one-day internationals, after he had added 111 for the second wicket with Jayasuriya, propelled Sri Lanka to an imposing total after being sent in. His elegant, unbeaten 119 in 135 balls contained seven boundaries. Pakistan made a positive start, Saeed Anwar and Aamir Sohail putting on 71 in the first 15 overs, but Muralitharan's control backed by alert fielding had them struggling at 166 for six by the 37th. A flurry from debutant Younis Khan and Abdur Razzaq, putting on 61 in eight overs, saved some blushes but never threatened to snatch victory. This match was former Test batsman Sadiq Mohammad's debut as an international umpire.

Man of the Match: M. S. Atapattu.

Sri Lanka

*S. T. Jayasuriya c Wasim Akram b Yasir Arafat .	54	U. D. U. Chandana c Younis Khan b Saqlain Mushtaq .	3
†R. S. Kaluwitharana lbw b Shahid Nazir	1	W. P. U. J. C. Vaas run out	2
M. S. Atapattu not out	119		
D. P. M. D. Jayawardene c Imran Abbas b Shahid Nazir .	27	L-b 15, w 5, n-b 7	27
R. P. Arnold b Shahid Nazir	2	1/10 2/121 3/177 (8 wkts, 50 overs)	274
T. M. Dilshan b Wasim Akram	34	4/185 5/250 6/259	
S. I. de Saram lbw b Saqlain Mushtaq . .	5	7/269 8/274	

G. P. Wickremasinghe and M. Muralitharan did not bat.

Bowling: Wasim Akram 10–0–48–1; Shahid Nazir 10–0–58–3; Abdur Razzaq 9–1–31–0; Saqlain Mushtaq 10–0–60–2; Aamir Sohail 6–0–34–0; Yasir Arafat 5–0–28–1.

Pakistan

*Saeed Anwar lbw b Arnold	36	Abdur Razzaq c Atapattu b Muralitharan	24
Aamir Sohail run out	47	Yasir Arafat b Vaas	6
Imran Abbas c and b Muralitharan	28	Saqlain Mushtaq c de Saram b Vaas . . .	3
Yousuf Youhana run out	6	Shahid Nazir not out	0
Wasim Akram c Chandana b Muralitharan	23	L-b 4, w 4, n-b 5	13
†Moin Khan c Kaluwitharana b Chandana .	13	1/71 2/101 3/112 (48 overs)	245
Younis Khan run out	46	4/147 5/149 6/166	
		7/227 8/242 9/243	

Bowling: Vaas 9–0–32–2; Wickremasinghe 10–0–65–0; Arnold 9–0–37–1; Muralitharan 10–0–31–3; Chandana 5–0–38–1; Jayasuriya 5–0–38–0.

Umpires: Sadiq Mohammad and Salim Badar.

†PAKISTAN v SRI LANKA

Second One-Day International

At Gujranwala, February 16. Sri Lanka won by 34 runs. Toss: Pakistan.

Jayasuriya produced an inspirational performance in his 200th one-day international to give Sri Lanka the three-match series with a game to play. He hit a polished 65 off 78 balls, with nine fours, and capped it with two wickets as the game was won with 23 balls to spare. The Pakistanis had been docked an over for their slow bowling-rate. Their misfortunes began when Shoaib Akhtar limped off with a groin injury after bowling five overs, and neither a sedate 68 by Yousuf Youhana nor Wasim Akram's four sixes in his 29-ball 34 provided much consolation.

Man of the Match: S. T. Jayasuriya.

Sri Lanka

*S. T. Jayasuriya c Moin Khan b Saqlain Mushtaq .	65	W. P. U. J. C. Vaas c and b Wasim Akram 34
†R. S. Kaluwitharana c Moin Khan b Abdur Razzaq .	32	R. P. Arnold not out 36
M. S. Atapattu c Yousuf Youhana b Saqlain Mushtaq .	57	S. I. de Saram run out 12
D. P. M. D. Jayawardene st Moin Khan b Aamir Sohail .	9	T. M. Dilshan not out 0
		L-b 6, w 9, n-b 3 18

1/84 2/121 3/147   (6 wkts, 50 overs) 263
4/199 5/236 6/262

U. D. U. Chandana, G. P. Wickremasinghe and M. Muralitharan did not bat.

Bowling: Wasim Akram 10–1–45–1; Shoaib Akhtar 5–1–34–0; Abdur Razzaq 10–0–42–1; Azhar Mahmood 10–0–51–0; Saqlain Mushtaq 10–0–48–2; Aamir Sohail 5–0–37–1.

Pakistan

*Saeed Anwar c Chandana b Vaas	17	Azhar Mahmood c Dilshan b Chandana . 2
Aamir Sohail c Dilshan b Wickremasinghe .	23	Wasim Akram b Muralitharan 34
Imran Abbas run out	1	Saqlain Mushtaq b Jayasuriya 3
Yousuf Youhana c Chandana b Wickremasinghe .	68	Shoaib Akhtar not out 1
Younis Khan b Muralitharan	28	B 4, l-b 7, w 10, n-b 2 23
†Moin Khan b Jayasuriya	15	
Abdur Razzaq c Kaluwitharana b Vaas . .	14	

1/23 2/32 3/50   (45.1 overs) 229
4/118 5/143 6/176
7/181 8/198 9/209

Bowling: Wickremasinghe 9–0–43–2; Vaas 9–0–38–2; Arnold 6–0–34–0; Chandana 5–0–28–1, Muralitharan 9.1–0–45–2; Jayasuriya 7 0 30 2.

Umpires: Aleem Dar and Asad Rauf.

†PAKISTAN v SRI LANKA

Third One-Day International

At Lahore, February 19. Sri Lanka won by 104 runs. Toss: Pakistan. International debut: Faisal Iqbal.

The Sri Lankans wrapped up the series 3–0 with a cakewalk win, even though Pakistan's bowlers, with Abdur Razzaq and Wasim Akram to the fore, kept the tourists' strong batting line-up under 250 for the first time. However, Pakistan's own batting never threatened Sri Lanka's total, losing five for 60 by the 22nd over. Saeed Anwar, whose 200th one-day international this was, came under fire for inserting Sri Lanka in all three games, while Pakistan's policy of blooding youngsters, albeit forward-thinking, met with only limited success. Atapattu passed 50 for the third time in the series to aggregate 253 runs at 126.50.

Man of the Match: M. S. Atapattu.   *Man of the Series:* M. S. Atapattu.

Sri Lanka

*S. T. Jayasuriya c Azhar Mahmood b Wasim Akram .	10
†R. S. Kaluwitharana lbw b Abdur Razzaq .	35
M. S. Atapattu c Saeed Anwar b Wasim Akram .	77
D. P. M. D. Jayawardene c and b Saqlain Mushtaq .	43
R. P. Arnold run out .	4
T. M. Dilshan c Moin Khan b Abdur Razzaq .	17

W. P. U. J. C. Vaas c sub (Zahid Saeed) b Abdur Razzaq .	6
U. D. U. Chandana b Wasim Akram .	16
M. Muralitharan b Abdur Razzaq .	0
G. P. Wickremasinghe not out .	10
D. N. T. Zoysa not out .	3
L-b 11, w 8, n-b 1 .	20
	—
1/19 2/64 3/148 (9 wkts, 50 overs)	241
4/161 5/196 6/205	
7/224 8/224 9/228	

Bowling: Wasim Akram 10–3–38–3; Shahid Nazir 10–0–48–0; Abdur Razzaq 10–0–36–4; Azhar Mahmood 1–0–6–0; Saqlain Mushtaq 10–1–43–1; Aamir Sohail 7–0–43–0; Faisal Iqbal 2–0–16–0.

Pakistan

*Saeed Anwar c Arnold b Wickremasinghe .	30
Aamir Sohail c Kaluwitharana b Zoysa .	6
Younis Khan lbw b Zoysa .	11
Yousuf Youhana run out .	7
Faisal Iqbal run out .	4
†Moin Khan b Jayasuriya .	14
Abdur Razzaq b Muralitharan .	22
Wasim Akram b Jayasuriya .	29

Saqlain Mushtaq lbw b Vaas .	2
Shahid Nazir not out .	0
Azhar Mahmood absent hurt	
L-b 7, w 5 .	12
	—
1/26 2/48 3/48 (39.3 overs)	137
4/57 5/60 6/96	
7/112 8/125 9/137	

Bowling: Zoysa 8–2–30–2; Vaas 7–0–12–1; Wickremasinghe 7–0–19–1; Muralitharan 8–2–29–1; Chandana 2–0–13–0; Jayasuriya 7.3–0–27–2.

Umpires: Mian Aslam and Nadeem Ghauri.
Series referee: B. F. Hastings (New Zealand).

At KRL Cricket Ground, Rawalpindi, February 21, 22, 23. Drawn. Toss: Sri Lankans. Sri Lankans 278 (S. T. Jayasuriya 60, D. P. M. D. Jayawardene 39, A. Ranatunga 47, R. S. Kaluwitharana 36, U. D. U. Chandana 31 not out, Extras 35; Mohammad Akram four for 91, Irfan Fazil five for 120) and 253 for four (R. P. Arnold 39, P. A. de Silva 74 not out, A. Ranatunga 86 not out); Pakistan Cricket Board XI 290 (Naved Ashraf 62, Wajahatullah Wasti 85, Rashid Latif 56; D. N. T. Zoysa three for 53, K. R. Pushpakumara four for 83).

PAKISTAN v SRI LANKA

First Test Match

At Rawalpindi, February 26, 27, 28, 29, March 1. Sri Lanka won by two wickets. Toss: Sri Lanka. Test debut: Younis Khan.

When Sri Lanka, chasing 220 for victory, slumped to 177 for eight in the final session, Pakistan looked as if they could pull off a sensational win. But Ranatunga, batting with a broken thumb, joined Kaluwitharana in a fighting stand of 43 that saw their team to victory with 9.1 overs remaining. Ranatunga had retired hurt earlier after being struck on the hand by Waqar Younis, and might have been run out soon after his return. That escape, along with a missed catch at 172 for six when Kaluwitharana hit Abdur Razzaq to Waqar at mid-on, swung the gripping climax Sri Lanka's way.

The Pakistanis had looked dead and buried after the first day. Muralitharan and Wickremasinghe caused their batting to collapse from 135 for four to 182 all out, Pakistan's lowest against Sri Lanka at home. And Wasim Akram had limped off with a groin strain after bowling just 13 deliveries, leaving them with three front-line bowlers. (Saqlain Mushtaq, despite suffering from dehydration during the match, bowled 33 overs unchanged, except to switch ends, on the fifth day.) On the second day, de Silva, who played in the Tests after being overlooked for the one-day series, put Sri Lanka in a position of strength with a delightful 112, his 18th century in 80 Tests and his eighth in 17 against Pakistan. Together with Ranatunga, dropped third ball by Moin Khan before scoring, he put on 129 for the fifth wicket in 59 overs. When he was seventh out, having batted for more than six hours, faced 276 balls and stroked 12 forceful fours, Vaas took on the responsibility of extending Sri Lanka's lead to 171. Hitting an unbeaten 53, he added 51 for the ninth wicket with Zoysa and 22 more with Muralitharan.

Pakistan pulled back much of the deficit before a lapse of concentration and fading light ended Saeed Anwar's gritty 219-ball 84 two overs before stumps. At 148 for four, the advantage was back with Sri Lanka but, on the fourth day, debutant Younis Khan and Wasim gave Pakistan a glimmer of hope with a series-record ninth-wicket stand of 145. Pakistan were just 65 ahead when Wasim joined 22-year-old Younis Khan, who became the seventh Pakistani, and 66th overall, to make a century on Test debut. Surviving two dropped chances, he batted more than five hours for his 107, during which he hit 11 boundaries in 250 balls; Wasim, using a runner, was three and a quarter hours over his 79, which included ten fours. Muralitharan picked up another four wickets to finish with match figures of eight for 172.

Waqar removed Atapattu and Arnold in his first six overs, but Jayasuriya's sensibly paced half-century, his first as captain, looked to have booked a straightforward passage for Sri Lanka. If it did not turn out to be quite so simple, Jayasuriya never doubted which way the finish would go. "As long as Ranatunga was there, we were convinced we could win," he said. "He played a gem of an innings, like an injured tiger."

Man of the Match: P. A. de Silva.

Close of play: First day, Sri Lanka 58-2 (Arnold 23*, de Silva 10*); Second day, Sri Lanka 290-8 (Vaas 21*, Zoysa 6*); Third day, Pakistan 154-4 (Yousuf Youhana 6*, Waqar Younis 0*); Fourth day, Sri Lanka 11-0 (Atapattu 6*, Jayasuriya 5*).

Pakistan

*Saeed Anwar c Arnold b Vaas	23	– b Vaas	84
Wajahatullah Wasti c Arnold b Wickremasinghe	17	– c Wickremasinghe b Zoysa	1
Aamir Sohail c Kaluwitharana b Vaas	0	– c Jayawardene b Muralitharan	24
Inzamam-ul-Haq c Arnold b Wickremasinghe	44	– c sub (U. D. U. Chandana) b Zoysa	20
Yousuf Youhana c Arnold b Muralitharan	32	– c Jayawardene b Muralitharan	18
Younis Khan lbw b Wickremasinghe	12	– (7) c de Silva b Muralitharan	107
†Moin Khan c Kaluwitharana b Wickremasinghe	21	– (8) lbw b Vaas	10
Abdur Razzaq st Kaluwitharana b Muralitharan	9	– (9) c Kaluwitharana b Zoysa	3
Wasim Akram c Wickremasinghe b Muralitharan	0	– (10) c Jayawardene b Muralitharan	79
Saqlain Mushtaq not out	3	– (11) not out	2
Waqar Younis c Ranatunga b Muralitharan	0	– (6) c and b Vaas	8
L-b 9, n-b 12	21	B 4, l-b 12, n-b 18	34

1/44 (1) 2/46 (3) 3/59 (2) 4/125 (5)   **182**   1/9 (2) 2/72 (3) 3/136 (4)   **390**
5/135 (4) 6/166 (6) 7/167 (7)   4/148 (1) 5/169 (6) 6/189 (5)
8/168 (9) 9/179 (8) 10/182 (11)   7/224 (8) 8/236 (9)
                                       9/381 (10) 10/390 (7)

Bowling: First Innings—Vaas 20-4-54-2; Zoysa 13-2-37-0; Wickremasinghe 20-5-37-4; Muralitharan 20.5-7-45-4. *Second Innings*—Vaas 38-7-85-3; Zoysa 26-8-64-3; Wickremasinghe 24-4-76-0; Muralitharan 54.1-14-127-4; Arnold 1-1-0-0; de Silva 6-2-10-0; Jayasuriya 3-0-12-0.

Sri Lanka

M. S. Atapattu c Wajahatullah Wasti b Waqar Younis .	8	– c Saqlain Mushtaq b Waqar Younis	10
*S. T. Jayasuriya c Moin Khan b Waqar Younis .	17	– c Aamir Sohail b Abdur Razzaq . .	56
R. P. Arnold c Moin Khan b Waqar Younis	26	– c Saqlain Mushtaq b Waqar Younis	6
P. A. de Silva lbw b Saqlain Mushtaq	112	– c Moin Khan b Abdur Razzaq. . . .	21
D. P. M. D. Jayawardene run out.	42	– c Yousuf Youhana b Saqlain Mushtaq .	35
A. Ranatunga b Abdur Razzaq	49	– not out	29
†R. S. Kaluwitharana lbw b Abdur Razzaq	0	– not out	36
W. P. U. J. C. Vaas not out.	53	– run out	0
G. P. Wickremasinghe c sub (Shahid Afridi) b Saqlain Mushtaq .	0	– (10) b Abdur Razzaq.	0
D. N. T. Zoysa c Yousuf Youhana b Waqar Younis .	26	– (9) c Wajahatullah Wasti b Abdur Razzaq .	13
M. Muralitharan st Moin Khan b Aamir Sohail .	7		
B 2, l-b 8, n-b 3	13	B 1, l-b 11, n-b 2	14

1/9 (1) 2/38 (2) 3/69 (3) 4/117 (5)   353   1/16 (1) 2/34 (3)   (8 wkts) 220
5/246 (6) 6/246 (7) 7/280 (4)   3/73 (4) 4/116 (2)
8/280 (9) 9/331 (10) 10/353 (11)   5/144 (5) 6/152 (8)
    7/177 (9) 8/177 (10)

In the second innings Ranatunga, when 8, retired hurt at 146 and resumed at 177-8.

Bowling: *First Innings*—Wasim Akram 2.1–0–8–0; Waqar Younis 30–3–103–4; Abdur Razzaq 32.5–7–99–2; Saqlain Mushtaq 34–9–78–2; Aamir Sohail 23.2–5–55–1; Wajahatullah Wasti 1–1–0–0. *Second Innings*—Waqar Younis 24.5–6–78–2; Abdur Razzaq 26–6–56–4; Saqlain Mushtaq 33–7–74–1.

Umpires: D. L. Orchard (South Africa) and Athar Zaidi.
Referee: B. F. Hastings (New Zealand).

PAKISTAN v SRI LANKA

Second Test Match

At Peshawar, March 5, 6, 7, 8, 9. Sri Lanka won by 57 runs. Toss: Pakistan. Test debut: Atiq-uz-Zaman.

Victory gave Jayasuriya his third successive Test series win since taking over the team the previous July. Four and a half years earlier, he had been carrying the towels when Sri Lanka lost by an innings here, before coming back to win that series 2–1 under Ranatunga. Now he was proving himself to be Ranatunga's legitimate heir as Sri Lanka's captain.

His triumph could not have been in greater contrast to Saeed Anwar's latest term in charge of Pakistan; he had lost all three limited-overs internationals and now two Tests. This latest Test defeat was Pakistan's fifth on the trot, and their third successive series defeat at home after losing to Australia and Zimbabwe in 1998-99. To compound Anwar's misery, he was left nursing a bruised nose and sprained neck after running into umpire Mohammad Nazir in his second innings.

With Wasim Akram, Saqlain Mushtaq and Moin Khan unavailable through injury or illness, Pakistan's plight had worsened since their narrow defeat at Rawalpindi. In their place came Shoaib Akhtar, off-spinner Arshad Khan and debutant wicket-keeper Atiq-uz-Zaman, while Shahid Afridi replaced Wajahatullah Wasti. Sri Lanka brought in Dilshan and Pushpakumara for the injured Ranatunga and Zoysa.

The match was one of fluctuating fortunes, with 27 wickets, 17 of them Pakistan's, falling on the third and fourth days. When the dust settled, Pakistan were 222 for eight, still 72 from victory, and on the final morning Sri Lanka needed just nine balls, three of which were hit for boundaries, to beat the country once reckoned to be nigh invincible at home.

Their hero was spin wizard Muralitharan, who captured ten for 148 runs, taking his tally to 18 in the series. In the first innings, Pakistan had been shaping well at 154 for three in reply to Sri Lanka's 268 but, falling prey to Muralitharan's guile, they lost seven wickets for 45 in 19 overs. Anwar looked to have laid the foundation for a big score with his second successive half-century, only to give his wicket away attempting a second six in four balls. Other than Inzamam-ul-Haq's patient, unbeaten 58, before he ran out of partners, there was little else on offer.

Sri Lanka's first innings, beginning after the first two sessions of the opening day were lost to rain, had revolved around a measured 75 in 254 balls by opener Atapattu. Shoaib claimed five for 75 on his return to Test cricket after being cleared by the ICC following his brief ban for having a suspect bowling action. Second time round, building on a cushion of 69 runs, Sri Lanka accumulated 224 through an enterprising 99 by Arnold, who hit 13 fours and a six in his 192-ball innings spanning five hours. The 53rd player to miss a century by one run – there have been 60 instances in all, but no previous Sri Lankan - Arnold added 79 with de Silva, who batted with a runner after pulling a hamstring earlier in the match. When the stand was broken, Sri Lanka lost their remaining four wickets for 36 runs in 12 overs to give Pakistan a slight chance of squaring the series.

Once more their openers sent them off with a half-century stand. But Inzamam and Aamir Sohail fell victim to controversial decisions, and soon afterwards Anwar had to retire after his collision with umpire Nazir, whose 54th birthday this fourth day was. Pakistan never recovered from these setbacks, despite a dogged 88 from Yousuf Youhana, who completed 1,000 runs in his 17th Test when 45. He hit eight fours and three sixes, and added 63 with Atiq-uz-Zaman before Anwar returned to the fray. As if there had not been enough drama already, Muralitharan brought the day to a grandstand finale by removing Youhana and Waqar Younis with successive balls. He had to wait until the final morning to attempt his hat-trick; it eluded him, but not the tenth wicket that sealed Pakistan's fate.

Man of the Match: M. Muralitharan.

Close of play: First day, Sri Lanka 88-2 (Atapattu 29*, de Silva 18*); Second day, Pakistan 67-1 (Saeed Anwar 37*, Yousuf Youhana 3*); Third day, Sri Lanka 129-5 (Arnold 63*, de Silva 7*); Fourth day, Pakistan 222-8 (Saeed Anwar 32*).

Sri Lanka

M. S. Atapattu b Shoaib Akhtar	75	– c Aamir Sohail b Arshad Khan	29
*S. T. Jayasuriya b Shoaib Akhtar	30	– lbw b Waqar Younis	6
R. P. Arnold c Atiq-uz-Zaman b Abdur Razzaq	2	– c Yousuf Youhana b Arshad Khan	99
P. A. de Silva lbw b Aamir Sohail	33	– (7) c Waqar Younis b Aamir Sohail	31
D. P. M. D. Jayawardene c Shahid Afridi b Aamir Sohail	36	– (4) lbw b Waqar Younis	10
T. M. Dilshan b Arshad Khan	13	– (5) c Atiq-uz-Zaman b Aamir Sohail	7
†R. S. Kaluwitharana c Atiq-uz-Zaman b Shoaib Akhtar	4	– (6) lbw b Shoaib Akhtar	0
W. P. U. J. C. Vaas not out	17	– (8) c Yousuf Youhana b Arshad Khan	5
G. P. Wickremasinghe b Shoaib Akhtar	0	– (10) c Younis Khan b Shoaib Akhtar	5
K. R. Pushpakumara c Atiq-uz-Zaman b Abdur Razzaq	7	– (9) c Atiq-uz-Zaman b Waqar Younis	14
M. Muralitharan b Shoaib Akhtar	22	– not out	2
B 1, l-b 8, n-b 20	29	B 4, l-b 7, n-b 5	16
	268		**224**

1/58 (2) 2/67 (3) 3/121 (4) 4/186 (5) 5/207 (6) 6/209 (1) 7/221 (7) 8/223 (9) 9/241 (10) 10/268 (11)

1/7 (2) 2/69 (1) 3/90 (4) 4/108 (5) 5/109 (6) 6/188 (7) 7/201 (3) 8/206 (8) 9/222 (9) 10/224 (10)

Bowling: *First Innings*—Waqar Younis 5–0–20–0; Shoaib Akhtar 24.3–3–75–5; Arshad Khan 45–18–70–1; Abdur Razzaq 17–6–39–2; Shahid Afridi 7–0–31–0; Aamir Sohail 11–1–24–2. *Second Innings*—Waqar Younis 16–3–38–3; Shoaib Akhtar 12.2–1–47–2; Arshad Khan 20–3–81–3; Abdur Razzaq 17–9–27–0; Aamir Sohail 8–3–20–2.

Pakistan

*Saeed Anwar c Muralitharan b Jayasuriya	74	– c Wickremasinghe b Vaas	36
Aamir Sohail c de Silva b Jayawardene	22	– (4) c Dilshan b Jayasuriya	0
Yousuf Youhana c Kaluwitharana b Vaas	8	– (5) lbw b Muralitharan	88
Inzamam-ul-Haq not out	58	– (3) c Jayawardene b Muralitharan	9
Younis Khan c Jayawardene b Muralitharan	8	– (6) c Arnold b Vaas	6
Shahid Afridi c Arnold b Vaas	4	– (2) st Kaluwitharana b Muralitharan	31
Abdur Razzaq c Jayawardene b Muralitharan	0	– lbw b Muralitharan	5
†Atiq-uz-Zaman c Kaluwitharana b Wickremasinghe	1	– b Vaas	25
Waqar Younis c Jayawardene b Muralitharan	3	– c Jayawardene b Muralitharan	0
Arshad Khan lbw b Muralitharan	0	– c Jayawardene b Muralitharan	5
Shoaib Akhtar c Atapattu b Wickremasinghe	5	– not out	4
L-b 1, w 1, n-b 14	16	B 9, l-b 6, n-b 12	27

1/54 (2) 2/82 (3) 3/137 (1) 4/154 (5) 199
5/165 (6) 6/166 (7) 7/174 (8)
8/177 (9) 9/177 (10) 10/199 (11)

1/59 (2) 2/77 (3) 3/82 (4) 236
4/103 (6) 5/145 (7) 6/208 (8)
7/222 (5) 8/222 (9)
9/226 (1) 10/236 (10)

In the second innings Saeed Anwar, when 30, retired hurt at 85 and resumed at 208.

Bowling: *First Innings*—Vaas 20–3–44–2; Pushpakumara 11–2–36–0; Muralitharan 39–10–77–4; Jayawardene 5–3–7–1; Jayasuriya 3–1–9–1; Wickremasinghe 10.5–4–25–2. *Second Innings*—Vaas 16–3–69–3; Pushpakumara 10–1–31–0; Wickremasinghe 12–5–22–0; Muralitharan 27.1–4–71–6; Jayasuriya 5–1–28–1.

Umpires: J. H. Hampshire (England) and Mohammad Nazir.
Referee: B. F. Hastings (New Zealand).

PAKISTAN v SRI LANKA

Third Test Match

At Karachi, March 12, 13, 14, 15. Pakistan won by 222 runs. Toss: Sri Lanka. Test debut: Irfan Fazil.

Pakistan salvaged some pride with a consolation win inside four days to extend their unbeaten record at Karachi's National Stadium to 34 Tests and set aside fears of a first-ever whitewash on home soil. It was certainly a felicitous result for captain Moin Khan, who had returned to the side and was initially deputising for the injured Saeed Anwar; he found himself doing the job on a more permanent basis when Anwar relinquished it. Inzamam-ul-Haq celebrated his promotion to vice-captain with two match-winning innings.

Other changes saw Naved Ashraf come in to open the innings with Shahid Afridi, so providing Pakistan's fourth opening partnership in three Tests – Afridi was promoted from the middle order at Peshawar – while Ijaz Ahmed returned in place of Aamir Sohail. Out went off-spinner Arshad Khan as Pakistan turned to a four-man pace attack, supplemented by Afridi's leg-spin: Mohammad Akram was recalled and the Lahore 18-year-old, Irfan Fazil, introduced. Sri Lanka's only change was de Saram for the injured de Silva.

Muralitharan, with match figures of eight for 196, was again outstanding for the visitors and, in his 51st Test, became the first Sri Lankan to claim 250 wickets when he had Naved lbw in the second innings. This time, however, Sri Lanka's batting gave ground to the home team, and in particular Inzamam. On the opening day, he soon lost Afridi – whose 74 in 92 balls, after Pakistan were put in, contained 12 fours and a six – and Pakistan were seven wickets down before Shoaib Akhtar helped him add 50. Shoaib then had a hand in Inzamam's run-out for a watchful 86 in four hours. Sri Lanka were batting by the close, but next day, without a major contribution, they conceded a first-innings lead for the first time in the series.

Inzamam lit up the third day with his ninth Test hundred, a magnificent 138 in five and a half hours replete with 17 signature fours and a six (off Muralitharan). He was dropped on 56, ten runs before becoming the fifth Pakistani to score 4,000 Test runs. Not even the Sri Lankans' sledging could interrupt his progress, although Inzamam, son of an Islamic saint, was drawn to complain to umpire Tiffin about the language used. "They [the close fielders] were sometimes sledging and continuously tried to disturb my concentration," he was quoted as saying.

Sparkling half-centuries by Younis Khan, who put on 124 for the sixth wicket with Inzamam, and by Moin meant that Sri Lanka faced a daunting target of 451 as they began their second innings nine overs before lunch on the fourth day. When half the side were out within 22 overs, Pakistan's victory was assured. Pushpakumara's hard-hit 44 from 45 balls down the order gave the total some respectability, but a second pair by Wickremasinghe put him among a small group with five ducks in a series (see table, page 1156).

Man of the Match: Inzamam-ul-Haq.

Men of the Series: M. Muralitharan and Waqar Younis.

Close of play: First day, Sri Lanka 10-0 (Atapattu 1*, Jayasuriya 5*); Second day, Pakistan 88-3 (Inzamam-ul-Haq 12*, Shoaib Akhtar 0*); Third day, Pakistan 375-7 (Moin Khan 51*, Waqar Younis 18*).

Pakistan

Naved Ashraf b Pushpakumara	5	– lbw b Muralitharan 27
Shahid Afridi c Wickremasinghe b Muralitharan.	74	– b Pushpakumara 34
Ijaz Ahmed, sen. lbw b Vaas	7	– c Dilshan b Muralitharan 3
Inzamam-ul-Haq run out	86	– c Wickremasinghe b Muralitharan . 138
Yousuf Youhana c Wickremasinghe		– (6) c Kaluwitharana
b Muralitharan.	7	b Pushpakumara . 11
Younis Khan lbw b Vaas	7	– (7) c Kaluwitharana
		b Wickremasinghe . 61
*†Moin Khan c de Saram b Wickremasinghe . .	6	– (8) c Arnold b Pushpakumara 70
Waqar Younis c Dilshan b Muralitharan	16	– (9) c Dilshan b Muralitharan. 39
Shoaib Akhtar c Pushpakumara b Muralitharan .	26	– (5) lbw b Vaas 0
Irfan Fazil not out	1	– c Jayasuriya b Pushpakumara 3
Mohammad Akram c Atapattu b Jayasuriya	0	– not out 1
L-b 2, n-b 19	21	L-b 16, n-b 18 34

1/40 (1) 2/82 (3) 3/111 (2) 4/135 (5)	256	1/70 (2) 2/70 (1) 3/84 (3) 421
5/152 (6) 6/164 (7) 7/197 (8)		4/106 (5) 5/159 (6) 6/283 (7)
8/247 (4) 9/255 (9) 10/256 (11)		7/320 (4) 8/408 (8)
		9/419 (9) 10/421 (10)

Bowling: *First Innings*—Vaas 18–4–49–2; Pushpakumara 16–4–37–1; Wickremasinghe 13–4–64–1; Muralitharan 32–10–89–4; Jayasuriya 6.5–2–15–1. *Second Innings*—Vaas 34–8–107–1; Pushpakumara 20.5–3–66–4; Wickremasinghe 26–7–82–1; Muralitharan 40–5–107–4; Jayasuriya 9–1–28–0; Arnold 4–0–15–0.

Sri Lanka

M. S. Atapattu lbw b Waqar Younis	3	c Moin Khan b Mohammad Akram 23
*S. T. Jayasuriya c Ijaz Ahmed b Shoaib Akhtar	24	– lbw b Waqar Younis 10
R. P. Arnold c Younis Khan b Irfan Fazil	48	– c Moin Khan b Waqar Younis 8
D. P. M. D. Jayawardene c Moin Khan		
b Waqar Younis .	1	– b Irfan Fazil 29
T. M. Dilshan c Moin Khan b Shahid Afridi . . .	31	– run out 5
†R. S. Kaluwitharana run out.	42	– b Shoaib Akhtar 33
S. I. de Saram c Waqar Younis b Shahid Afridi .	5	– lbw b Shahid Afridi 18
W. P. U. J. C. Vaas not out.	25	– c Shoaib Akhtar b Shahid Afridi . . 28
K. R. Pushpakumara c Moin Khan		
b Shoaib Akhtar .	1	– c Irfan Fazil b Shahid Afridi. 44
G. P. Wickremasinghe b Shoaib Akhtar	0	– run out 0
M. Muralitharan c Irfan Fazil		
b Mohammad Akram .	14	– not out 5
B 10, l-b 2, n-b 21	33	B 1, l-b 7, n-b 17. 25

1/17 (1) 2/41 (2) 3/46 (4) 4/100 (3)	227	1/27 (2) 2/41 (1) 3/41 (3) 228
5/154 (6) 6/164 (7) 7/188 (5)		4/59 (5) 5/86 (4) 6/121 (6)
8/206 (9) 9/206 (10) 10/227 (11)		7/145 (7) 8/191 (8)
		9/199 (10) 10/228 (9)

Bowling: *First Innings*—Waqar Younis 10–2–39–2; Shoaib Akhtar 18–4–52–3; Mohammad Akram 14.1–2–49–1; Irfan Fazil 4–0–35–1; Shahid Afridi 12–3–40–2. *Second Innings*—Waqar Younis 11–4–32–2; Shoaib Akhtar 13–1–64–1; Mohammad Akram 10–1–44–1; Irfan Fazil 4–0–30–1; Shahid Afridi 8–1–50–3.

Umpires: R. B. Tiffin (Zimbabwe) and Riazuddin.
Referee: B. F. Hastings (New Zealand).

ERRATA

WISDEN, 1988

Page 939   In the third one-day International between India and Australia at Hyderabad on September 24, Azharuddin scored 8*, not 9; there were three leg-byes and one wide, and Davis conceded 17.

WISDEN, 1999

Page 166   S. K. L. de Silva appeared for Colombo, not Kurunegala Youth, in 1997-98.
Pages 1018   A. Jaffer took a wicket with his first ball in first-class cricket for Uttar Pradesh v
and 1335   Tamil Nadu at Chennai.
Page 1019   N. Boje scored 104* and 9* and took 5-84 and 6-34 for Free State v Northerns at Bloemfontein.

WISDEN, 2000

Page 12   The traditional starter at the annual Master's Club dinner in memory of Sir Jack Hobbs is game pâté, not tomato soup.
Page 16   Electors of the Cricketers of the Century who themselves played Test cricket before World War II also included Bill Brown and Walter Hadlee.
Page 41   Dera Ismail Khan's defeat by an innings and 851 runs was not their only first-class game; they reappeared for ten matches between 1983-84 and 1985-86.
Page 410   Krikken and DeFreitas added 152 for Derbyshire's eighth wicket, not the ninth.
Page 495   England failed to score a Test century at home in 1963 or 1972 as well as in 1999.
Page 504   The list of two completed Test innings on the same day should include Australia 147, England 119 at Manchester (1st day) in 1909; the Test was drawn.
Page 538   In the table of County Championship statistics, some of the totals for wickets conceded/taken by individual counties are incorrect, owing to the misplacing of wickets falling to run-outs. Derbyshire took 262 wickets, and averaged 26.66 runs scored per wicket lost; Lancashire 221 (31.56); Somerset 226 (37.12); Sussex 278 (27.16); Warwickshire 255 (24.64). Essex took 261 wickets, and averaged 29.80 runs conceded per wicket taken; Kent 259 (29.45); Lancashire 249 (27.34); Northamptonshire 249 (29.87); Nottinghamshire 250 (30.57); Worcestershire 242 (30.40).
Page 739   Michael Pearce of the Surrey Statistical Group provided the list of Consecutive Wins.
Page 802   K. J. Parsons, not his twin K. A., scored 65 for the Somerset Board XI against Bedfordshire on May 17.
Page 978   A. Y. Karim scored 35 not out for the Kenyans against Somerset on May 7.
Page 1202   G. Fowler scored 201 not 210 at Madras in 1984-85.
Page 1224   India v Sri Lanka at Chandigarh, 1990-91, was also a three-innings Test.
Page 1236   In the seventh one-day international between West Indies and Australia, S. L. Campbell was Man of the Match. He was also Man of the Series.
Page 1313   The picture is of Mark Boucher not Boeta Dippenaar. *Wisden* apologises for the error.
Page 1359   In the match between Mumbai and Gujarat, A. S. Kotecha's six consecutive fours came in the first over of Gujarat's second innings; he also hit his seventh delivery for four.
Page 1413   Mr Wally Glynn informs us that, while he did play for Malta when aged 65, it was not against Switzerland, but against Greece in Switzerland, and the match was in August 1997. His father was British, his mother Maltese.

THE AUSTRALIANS IN NEW ZEALAND, 1999-2000

By DON CAMERON

The Australians arrived in New Zealand in mid-February with drums banging and cymbals clanging, the most successful act in world cricket and confident they would add more headlines to their superb summer of achievements. Having overwhelmed Zimbabwe in Harare, and accounted for Pakistan and India in Australia, they needed one more win to equal the Australian record of eight consecutive Test victories, set by Warwick Armstrong's side in 1920-21 and 1921 against England. They had also won nine successive one-day internationals against Pakistan and India, and were keen to extend that winning sequence in six more games. In addition, Shane Warne was on the threshold of Dennis Lillee's record of 355 Test wickets for Australia. New Zealand seemed destined to linger among the side-shows while their visitors dominated the big top.

After wet weather delayed, interrupted and finally curtailed the first one-day international, Australia won the next four to create a record unbeaten run of 14 (13 victories) before losing the last game to New Zealand. Warne got his Australian record in the First Test, at Eden Park, and Australia's wins there and in the next two Tests gave them ten in a row – one away from the record established by Clive Lloyd's West Indians between April and December 1984. Australia had ended that run; to equal it, fate had already decreed, they would have to beat West Indies at Brisbane in November 2000.

Yet there were times when the Australians almost got themselves in a tangle, and they were gracious enough to suggest that New Zealand gave them much stiffer opposition in the Tests than Pakistan and India had. Steve Waugh, masterly as captain, batsman, and provider of straight-from-the-shoulder comments at press conferences, several times mentioned the way the New Zealanders kept fighting back, whether it was through their middle-order batsmen or with bowlers of modest fire-power. At Eden Park, on a surprisingly frisky pitch, New Zealand needed 281 to win, the highest score of the match, and, despite the habitual top-order batting failure, seemed possible winners at one stage. Overall, though, Waugh was closer to the truth when he maintained that his was one of the very best Australian sides. New Zealand, however gritty and competitive, were not strong enough to spoil their parade.

While the Australian batting also drew only modest opening stands, they had strong and consistent success after that from Damien Martyn, Justin Langer, whose aggregate of 288 took him past 1,000 Test runs for the summer, Steve and Mark Waugh, and the ballistic Adam Gilchrist. Michael Slater's century at Wellington more than offset his low scores otherwise. Brett Lee arrived in New Zealand as a novice Test fast bowler, took 18 Test wickets at 17.44, and returned home having displayed the skill and artistry of a future champion. Warne never seemed at peak form, but still claimed 15 wickets, while Glenn McGrath, the man of classical style, and Colin Miller each had 12. The Australian fielding was as aggressive as their batting and as accurate as their bowling.

The New Zealanders invariably suffered from weak starts by Matt Horne and Craig Spearman, and Mathew Sinclair's debut 214 against West Indies at the end of December was sadly reduced to a faint memory. The fact that New Zealand remained competitive was greatly to the credit of Stephen Fleming, a restored Craig McMillan and a belligerent Chris Cairns, the series' leading run-scorer with 341. There were useful contributions, too, from Adam Parore and Nathan Astle. When left-arm spinner Daniel Vettori took 12 wickets at Eden Park, including career-best figures and his 100th Test wicket, New Zealand could claim to have a subtle complement to Cairns's increasingly successful fast bowling. Unfortunately, Vettori damaged his back in the Second Test and could not play in the Third. For all that Shayne O'Connor and Paul Wiseman showed improvement as Test cricketers, Vettori's absence was confirmation, were it needed, that New Zealand still lacked another strike bowler of the highest class.

AUSTRALIAN TOURING PARTY

S. R. Waugh (New South Wales) (*captain*), S. K. Warne (Victoria) (*vice-captain*), M. G. Bevan (New South Wales), G. S. Blewett (South Australia), D. W. Fleming (Victoria), A. C. Gilchrist (Western Australia), I. J. Harvey (Victoria), M. L. Hayden (Queensland), M. S. Kasprowicz (Queensland), J. L. Langer (Western Australia), B. Lee (New South Wales), S. Lee (New South Wales), G. D. McGrath (New South Wales), D. R. Martyn (Western Australia), C. R. Miller (Tasmania), M. J. Slater (New South Wales), A. Symonds (Queensland), M. E. Waugh (New South Wales).

Bevan, Harvey, S. Lee and Symonds went home after the one-day leg of the tour, when Blewett, Kasprowicz, Langer, Miller and Slater joined the party for the first-class programme. R. T. Ponting (Tasmania) was originally selected for both legs, but withdrew because of injury; he was replaced by Hayden for the one-day games and Martyn in the Test squad.

Manager: S. R. Bernard.　　*Coach:* J. M. Buchanan.

AUSTRALIAN TOUR RESULTS

Test matches – Played 3: Won 3.
First-class matches – Played 5: Won 4, Drawn 1.
Wins – New Zealand (3), Northern Districts.
Draw – Central Districts.
One-day internationals – Played 6: Won 4, Lost 1, No result 1.

TEST MATCH AVERAGES

NEW ZEALAND – BATTING

	T	I	NO	R	HS	100s	50s	Avge	Ct/St
C. L. Cairns	3	6	0	341	109	1	2	56.83	1
C. D. McMillan	3	6	0	194	79	0	2	32.33	2
A. C. Parore	3	6	1	144	46	0	0	28.80	7/3
N. J. Astle	3	6	0	167	61	0	1	27.83	4
S. B. Doull	2	4	1	69	40	0	0	23.00	0
S. P. Fleming	3	6	0	137	60	0	1	22.83	4
C. M. Spearman	3	6	0	105	38	0	0	17.50	5
D. L. Vettori	2	4	1	50	27	0	0	16.66	0
M. S. Sinclair	3	6	0	61	24	0	0	10.16	3
M. J. Horne	3	6	0	44	14	0	0	7.33	2
P. J. Wiseman	2	4	0	27	16	0	0	6.75	2
S. B. O'Connor	2	4	2	6	4*	0	0	3.00	0

Played in one Test: D. R. Tuffey 3, 1* (1 ct).

* *Signifies not out.*

BOWLING

	O	M	R	W	BB	5W/i	Avge
D. L. Vettori	83	21	218	14	7-87	2	15.57
S. B. O'Connor	63.5	11	224	11	5-51	1	20.36
C. D. McMillan	25.3	10	74	3	3-57	0	24.66
P. J. Wiseman	67.5	12	232	9	3-49	0	25.77
C. L. Cairns	93.3	13	379	10	3-80	0	37.90

Also bowled: N. J. Astle 25.1–9–69–0; S. B. Doull 48–12–142–1; D. R. Tuffey 20–1–127–0.

AUSTRALIA – BATTING

	T	I	NO	R	HS	100s	50s	Avge	Ct/St
D. R. Martyn	3	6	2	241	89*	0	2	60.25	2
J. L. Langer	3	6	1	288	122*	1	1	57.60	3
S. R. Waugh	3	6	2	214	151*	1	0	53.50	4
M. E. Waugh	3	6	2	190	72*	0	1	47.50	4
A. C. Gilchrist	3	5	1	144	75	0	2	36.00	17/1
M. J. Slater	3	6	0	177	143	1	0	29.50	1
G. S. Blewett	2	4	0	50	25	0	0	12.50	3
S. K. Warne	3	4	0	36	12	0	0	9.00	4
G. D. McGrath	3	4	0	30	14	0	0	7.50	0
B. Lee	3	4	1	20	8	0	0	6.66	1
C. R. Miller	3	4	0	14	8	0	0	3.50	1

Played in one Test: M. L. Hayden 2, 37.

* *Signifies not out.*

BOWLING

	O	M	R	W	BB	5W/i	Avge
B. Lee	100.4	26	314	18	5-77	1	17.44
G. D. McGrath	115.2	40	269	12	4-33	0	22.41
C. R. Miller	112	29	311	12	5-55	1	25.91
S. K. Warne	129.2	33	414	15	4-68	0	27.60

Also bowled: G. S. Blewett 11–1–39–1; D. R. Martyn 7–4–12–0; S. R. Waugh 7–0–20–0.

Note: Matches in this section which were not first-class are signified by a dagger.

†NEW ZEALAND v AUSTRALIA

First One-Day International

At WestpacTrust Stadium, Wellington, February 16, 17 (day/night). No result. Toss: New Zealand. International debut: W. A. Wisneski.

The second international at Wellington's new stadium was even more severely affected by rain than the first, against West Indies in January. Play was not possible on the first day because the bowlers' run-ups were wet and, to the disappointment of the large crowd, the reserve day fared little better. With players and umpires in position for a 2 p.m. start, more rain meant a delay until 3.30 and a match reduced to 43 overs each. Gilchrist was caught at slip off the third legitimate ball, but Mark Waugh and Hayden punished some wayward New Zealand bowling. Hayden raced to 64 from 68 balls before the rain set in again. The Australians had been more inconvenienced off the field when it was revealed that their game plan, aggressive in content, had been pushed by mistake under the doors of fellow hotel guests.

Australia

†A. C. Gilchrist c Fleming b Cairns	...	0
M. E. Waugh not out	....	45
M. L. Hayden not out	....	64
B 2, l-b 2, w 4, n-b 2	......	10

1/1	(1 wkt, 23 overs) 119

M. G. Bevan, *S. R. Waugh, A. Symonds, D. R. Martyn, S. Lee, S. K. Warne, B. Lee and G. D. McGrath did not bat.

Bowling: Cairns 5–0–21–1; Wisneski 6–0–30–0; Styris 2–0–12–0; Vettori 5–0–19–0; Harris 3–0–16–0; Astle 2–0–17–0.

New Zealand

C. M. Spearman, N. J. Astle, *S. P. Fleming, R. G. Twose, C. L. Cairns, C. D. McMillan, C. Z. Harris, †A. C. Parore, S. B. Styris, D. L. Vettori and W. A. Wisneski.

Umpires: R. S. Dunne and E. A. Watkin.

†NEW ZEALAND v AUSTRALIA

Second One-Day International

At Auckland, February 19 (day/night). Australia won by five wickets. Toss: New Zealand.

In what was to become a pattern for most of the series, New Zealand's batting started badly. Spearman and Astle were out in the first seven balls without a run to the total; Fleming, Cairns and Twose had gone for 52 by the 14th over against a hostile, efficient attack taking its lead from McGrath and Brett Lee. The Australian reply was a light-hearted affair. After early setbacks, Hayden saw them home with 50 from 49 balls, all but two of his runs coming from boundaries (two sixes, nine fours).

Man of the Match: B. Lee.

New Zealand

C. M. Spearman c Gilchrist b McGrath	.	0	S. B. Styris c M. E. Waugh b Warne	... 1
N. J. Astle c M. E. Waugh b B. Lee	...	0	D. L. Vettori c Symonds b McGrath	 22
*S. P. Fleming c S. Lee b B. Lee	.....	14	P. J. Wiseman not out	 1
R. G. Twose b Warne	....	25	L-b 6, w 6, n-b 2	 14
C. L. Cairns c B. Lee b McGrath	...	1		
C. D. McMillan c Gilchrist b B. Lee	...	35	1/0 2/0 3/30	(30.1 overs) 122
C. Z. Harris c Gilchrist b S. Lee	......	9	4/31 5/52 6/81	
†A. C. Parore b S. Lee	....	0	7/81 8/84 9/119	

Bowling: McGrath 8.1–2–33–3; B. Lee 7–1–21–3; Warne 10–0–35–2; S. Lee 5–1–27–2.

Australia

M. E. Waugh c Parore b Cairns	......	2	D. R. Martyn not out	 8
†A. C. Gilchrist c Twose b Vettori	.....	10		
A. Symonds c Styris b Vettori	....	33	L-b 1, w 3, n-b 4	 8
M. L. Hayden c Vettori b Wiseman	....	50		
M. G. Bevan c Cairns b Wiseman	.....	8	1/13 2/17 3/62	(5 wkts, 24.4 overs) 123
*S. R. Waugh not out	....	4	4/98 5/112	

S. Lee, S. K. Warne, B. Lee and G. D. McGrath did not bat.

Bowling: Cairns 5–0–39–1; Vettori 10–1–37–2; Styris 4–0–21–0; Wiseman 5–0–21–2; McMillan 0.4–0–4–0.

Umpires: B. F. Bowden and D. B. Cowie.

†NEW ZEALAND v AUSTRALIA

Third One-Day International

At Dunedin, February 23 (day/night). Australia won by 50 runs. Toss: New Zealand.

If New Zealand hoped for quick success by sending Australia in, they were rudely disillusioned. In ideal batting conditions, Gilchrist and Mark Waugh had 114 up before being parted after 20 overs, Gilchrist providing great entertainment with his 77 from 65 balls. Symonds, who came in after Steve Waugh twisted his ankle, was equally destructive, taking Australia beyond 300 with 34 off 13 balls. Astle hit 81 from 84 balls to lead New Zealand's counter-offensive, adding 121 with Twose; once he was fourth out in the 29th over, the asking-rate rose. Parore's dismissal – when his helmet fell on his wicket after being struck by Brett Lee's bouncer – was a signal for the crowd to vent its disappointment; play was held up for ten minutes as objects were thrown on the field. Excluding the recent no-result in Wellington, this victory extended Australia's winning sequence to 11 and put them level with West Indies (June 1984–February 1985) and England (May 1991–March 1992, also interrupted by a no-result).

Man of the Match: A. C. Gilchrist.

Australia

†A. C. Gilchrist c Cairns b Vettori	 77	D. R. Martyn not out	....	1
M. E. Waugh b Cairns	 75			
M. L. Hayden c Cairns b Harris	 20	L-b 2, w 1, n-b 5	....	8
M. G. Bevan c Harris b Cairns	 52			
*S. R. Waugh retired hurt	 43	1/114 2/166	(4 wkts, 50 overs)	310
A. Symonds not out	 34	3/185 4/291		

S. K. Warne, D. W. Fleming, B. Lee and G. D. McGrath did not bat.

S. R. Waugh retired hurt at 270.

Bowling: Cairns 10–0–61–2; Wisneski 8–0–58–0; Styris 6–0–56–0; Vettori 10–0–48–1; Harris 10–0–37–1; Astle 6–0–48–0.

New Zealand

C. M. Spearman lbw b Fleming	 2	S. B. Styris c Symonds b Lee	....	19
N. J. Astle b Warne	 81	D. L. Vettori c Symonds b McGrath	....	0
*S. P. Fleming c Hayden b Fleming	 24	W. A. Wisneski c M. E. Waugh		
R. G. Twose lbw b Martyn	 62		b McGrath .	6
C. L. Cairns c Gilchrist b Martyn	 13	B 4, l-b 5, w 2, n-b 8	......	19
C. D. McMillan c sub (I. J. Harvey)				
	b Warne . 1	1/13 2/48 3/169	(45 overs)	260
C. Z. Harris not out	 25	4/187 5/197 6/199		
†A. C. Parore hit wkt b Lee	 8	7/223 8/246 9/247		

Bowling: McGrath 9–1–35–2; Fleming 6–0–42–2; Lee 9–0–51–2; Symonds 3–0–39–0; Warne 10–1–50–2; Martyn 8–0–34–2.

Umpires: D. B. Cowie and R. S. Dunne.

†NEW ZEALAND v AUSTRALIA

Fourth One-Day International

At Christchurch, February 26 (day/night). Australia won by 48 runs. Toss: New Zealand.

Fleming again tempted fate by giving away first use of an excellent batting strip and was punished as the Australians raced past their previous international best: 337 for seven against Pakistan three weeks earlier in the second Carlton & United final. Gilchrist was at his most irrepressible, delighting the crowd with seven sixes and nine fours before he was first out after 28 overs. His 128, out of 189, came from only 98 balls and made Mark Waugh's 70 from 88 look pedestrian. Steve Waugh, recovered after twisting his ankle at Dunedin, hit five sixes and two fours in his 54. New Zealand's reply began badly, opener Sinclair out first ball in his first one-day international, but brave batting – Astle and Fleming added 127 in 19 overs – won them respect as they reached 301. The match aggregate of 650 was the fifth-highest in limited-overs internationals.

Man of the Match: A. C. Gilchrist.

Australia

M. E. Waugh b Vettori	70	D. R. Martyn not out		29
†A. C. Gilchrist c and b Harris	128	S. Lee not out		4
A. Symonds run out	0	B 2, l-b 2, w 2, n-b 2		8
*S. R. Waugh b Harris	54			
I. J. Harvey lbw b Styris	19	1/189 2/190 3/233	(6 wkts, 50 overs)	349
M. G. Bevan c Wisneski b Vettori	37	4/267 5/285 6/343		

S. K. Warne, D. W. Fleming and B. Lee did not bat.

Bowling: Cairns 10–0–76–0; Wisneski 5–0–35–0; Styris 9–0–60–1; Vettori 10–0–71–2; Astle 4–0–28–0; Harris 10–0–58–2; McMillan 2–0–17–0.

New Zealand

M. S. Sinclair c Gilchrist b Fleming	0	S. B. Styris b S. Lee		9
N. J. Astle lbw b Warne	45	D. L. Vettori b Warne		3
*S. P. Fleming c S. R. Waugh b Warne	82	W. A. Wisneski not out		4
R. G. Twose c Gilchrist b Fleming	35	L-b 13, w 9, n-b 2		24
C. L. Cairns c S. Lee b Fleming	25			
C. D. McMillan run out	4	1/0 2/127 3/159	(9 wkts, 50 overs)	301
C. Z. Harris not out	59	4/201 5/202 6/209		
†A. C. Parore c Warne b S. Lee	11	7/252 8/276 9/292		

Bowling: Fleming 10–0–58–3; B. Lee 9–0–59–0; S. Lee 9–0–51–2; Harvey 10–0–52–0; Warne 9–0–50–3; Symonds 3–0–18–0.

Umpires: B. F. Bowden and D. M. Quested.

†NEW ZEALAND v AUSTRALIA

Fifth One-Day International

At Napier, March 1 (day/night). Australia won by five wickets. Toss: Australia. International debut: C. J. Nevin.

Winning the toss for the first time, Australia chose to play the chasing game and, had New Zealand found a steady partner for Astle, they might just have had a hard night. Astle batted superbly for 104 from 128 balls, but only Twose and Cairns, whose boundary ratio was confined to two sixes and no fours, gave him a modicum of support. Cairns struck two early blows with the ball – Mark Waugh went in the first over – but Hayden stuck fast and Bevan confirmed his genius for one-day batting. His 107 steered Australia to the brink of victory with overs to spare. The win took Australia's record sequence of wins (interrupted by the Wellington no-result) to 13.

Man of the Match: M. G. Bevan.

New Zealand

N. J. Astle c Gilchrist b Fleming	104	D. L. Vettori c Hayden b Fleming	17
M. S. Sinclair lbw b Fleming	0	S. B. Doull not out	0
*S. P. Fleming c S. R. Waugh b Fleming	10		
R. G. Twose b M. E. Waugh	32	L-b 7, w 12, n-b 4	23
C. L. Cairns c Warne b McGrath	31		
C. Z. Harris c Hayden b Harvey	15	1/2 2/26 3/115 (9 wkts, 50 overs) 243	
S. B. Styris b McGrath	0	4/177 5/207 6/208	
†C. J. Nevin c Martyn b Warne	11	7/223 8/232 9/243	

P. J. Wiseman did not bat.

Bowling: McGrath 10–0–61–2; Fleming 8–0–41–4; Harvey 10–0–35–1; Lee 5–0–23–0; Warne 10–2–34–1; M. E. Waugh 7–0–42–1.

Australia

†A. C. Gilchrist c Styris b Cairns	14	D. R. Martyn not out	4
M. E. Waugh c Astle b Cairns	0		
M. L. Hayden st Nevin b Wiseman	57	B 3, l-b 3, w 2	8
M. G. Bevan c Styris b Doull	107		
S. K. Warne c Nevin b Vettori	12	1/1 2/34 3/130 (5 wkts, 45.4 overs) 245	
*S. R. Waugh not out	43	4/155 5/237	

I. J. Harvey, S. Lee, D. W. Fleming and G. D. McGrath did not bat.

Bowling: Cairns 8–0–31–2; Doull 7–0–36–1; Styris 6.4–0–46–0; Wiseman 10–0–52–1; Vettori 10–0–47–1; Harris 2–0–17–0; Astle 2–0–10–0.

Umpires: D. B. Cowie and E. A. Watkin.

†NEW ZEALAND v AUSTRALIA

Sixth One-Day International

At Auckland, March 3 (day/night). New Zealand won by seven wickets. Toss: Australia.

With the series won 4–0, the Australians were more relaxed. Only Martyn, batting throughout the innings for 116, with 13 fours and a six, his first hundred for Australia, seemed intent on extending their unbeaten streak. The rest of the batting was untidy, and Nevin, New Zealand's sprightly wicket-keeper, upstaged everyone with a sparkling 74 from 94 balls after being promoted to open in his second international. His century partnership with Fleming left the captain with the reasonably easy target of another 26 to get New Zealand home, which he achieved with nine overs to spare.

Man of the Match: C. J. Nevin.

Australia

M. L. Hayden c Twose b Cairns	0	S. K. Warne c Nevin b Cairns	7
D. R. Martyn not out	116	B. Lee c Fleming b Wiseman	3
*S. R. Waugh c Fleming b Cairns	1	G. D. McGrath c Nevin b Styris	11
M. G. Bevan c Fleming b Doull	2	L-b 3, w 6	9
M. E. Waugh run out	14		
†A. C. Gilchrist c Cairns b Harris	22	1/2 2/8 3/22 (46.2 overs) 191	
A. Symonds run out	6	4/86 5/125 6/141	
S. Lee lbw b Vettori	0	7/143 8/155 9/160	

Bowling: Cairns 9–1–33–3; Doull 5–1–26–1; Vettori 10–0–39–1; Styris 3.2–0–10–1; Harris 7–0–31–1; Astle 2–0–15–0; Wiseman 10–0–34–1.

New Zealand

†C. J. Nevin lbw b Symonds	74	R. G. Twose not out		13
N. J. Astle b McGrath	12	B 5, l-b 3, w 5, n-b 3		16
M. S. Sinclair c S. Lee b Warne	19			
*S. P. Fleming not out	60	1/28 2/66 3/166 (3 wkts, 41 overs)		194

C. L. Cairns, C. Z. Harris, S. B. Styris, D. L. Vettori, S. B. Doull and P. J. Wiseman did not bat.

Bowling: McGrath 6–1–29–1; B. Lee 8–0–39–0; Warne 10–1–25–1; M. E. Waugh 5–0–24–0; Bevan 6–0–37–0; S. Lee 3–1–8–0; Symonds 2–0–6–1; Hayden 1–0–18–0.

Umpires: D. B. Cowie and R. S. Dunne.
Series referee: M. H. Denness (England).

At Hamilton, March 5, 6, 7, 8. Australians won by five wickets. Toss: Northern Districts. Northern Districts 300 (J. A. H. Marshall 64, M. D. Bailey 32, N. R. Parlane 47, H. J. H. Marshall 45, J. A. F. Yovich 35, Extras 47; G. D. McGrath three for 40) and 280 (J. A. H. Marshall 40, M. D. Bailey 32, H. J. H. Marshall 50, S. B. Styris 31, G. E. Bradburn 63; G. D. McGrath three for 37, C. R. Miller three for 68); Australians 383 for four dec. (G. S. Blewett 34, J. L. Langer 155, D. R. Martyn 109, M. L. Hayden 67 not out) and 198 for five (G. S. Blewett 83 not out, B. Lee 39).

NEW ZEALAND v AUSTRALIA

First Test Match

At Auckland, March 11, 12, 13, 14, 15. Australia won by 62 runs. Toss: Australia.

There was no keeping Warne out of the limelight. Fellow-spinners Vettori and Miller may have outbowled him; Steve Waugh, his captain, might have kept him sidelined as Miller and Lee worked through New Zealand's lower-order batting on the final day. But, with the last pair at the wicket, Warne returned. Wiseman hit him for two fours then swung again, missed and could do nothing as the ball looped from glove, arm and shoulder to wicket-keeper Gilchrist. Warne, having gone into the match needing five for the record, had captured his 356th Test wicket to overtake Dennis Lillee as Australia's leading wicket-taker and complete Australia's eighth consecutive Test victory.

It was a little ironic that Warne, the most prolific spinner in cricket history, had to wait to the last, given that spin accounted for 28 of the 40 wickets. It was certainly a contrast to the Test at Eden Park a year earlier, when New Zealand and South Africa ran up 1,217 runs for 18 wickets, only five to slow bowlers. This time the pitch was grassy enough to favour seamers, but it also offered the spinners turn and a tricky, tennis-ball bounce. Vettori was in action from the tenth over on the first morning, Langer immediately greeting him with a four and a six, as if aware that batting was already a matter of trusting to luck. Langer rushed to 46 from 47 balls before he was stumped off Wiseman's off-spin, Blewett went to the same bowler two overs later and, after that, only Mark Waugh, unbeaten for three and a quarter hours, had a satisfactory answer to the questions set by Vettori and Wiseman. Vettori bowled his left-arm spin unchanged from lunch until the end of the innings.

McGrath and Lee presided over the almost ritual removal of the New Zealand openers, with the drama heightened by the first use of floodlights in a New Zealand Test, owing to the poor light. Warne chipped away at the middle order the following morning and, soon after lunch, McGrath finished his previous evening's work with three for 21 from his last 25 balls. Australia had a lead of 51, which was just as well. After Cairns had again closed the Blewett–Slater opening partnership, Vettori took the ninth over and embarked on one of the great New Zealand spin-bowling passages. Langer corrected the faulty start with a brisk 47; Vettori fought back and got him in the 27th over. When both Waughs had gone at 107 for five, a winning door was opening for New Zealand.

Stout batting by Martyn and Gilchrist amid the third-morning showers helped Australia out of the danger zone, but Vettori and Wiseman took the last five wickets in 11 overs either side of an early lunch prolonged by more rain. When Vettori bowled Martyn, he had his 100th wicket in 29

[*Phil Walter, Fotopress*

The one they were waiting for: Shane Warne goes one better than Dennis Lillee as Australia's
leading wicket-taker, thanks to keeper Adam Gilchrist catching Paul Wiseman.

Tests and, at the age of 21 years 46 days, he supplanted Saqlain Mushtaq as the youngest spinner
to this landmark by a year and 279 days. Only Kapil Dev, a fast bowler, had reached his century
at a younger age. Vettori's seven for 87 in Australia's second innings were his best figures yet,
while his match return of 12 for 149, his first ten-wicket take, was the second best for New
Zealand behind Sir Richard Hadlee's 15 for 123, also against Australia, at Brisbane in 1985-86.

   Showers, bad light and overnight thunderstorms all conspired against New Zealand's attempt
on a winning score of 281. There was also the depressingly familiar scenario of second-innings
wickets falling early, with four gone for 43 by the 18th over. Astle and McMillan applied a
tourniquet, adding 78 in 17 overs before Warne bowled Astle around his legs to equal Lillee's
record. With McMillan, whose fifty came off 50 balls, and Cairns still together at stumps, and
New Zealand 130 from their target, victory was not completely out of the question with two days
to play. But rain washed out the fourth day and delayed the start of the fifth, when New Zealand
immediately lost Cairns. Parore stayed for an hour, but when Lee struck twice, removing him and
McMillan in successive overs, that was it. All that remained was for Miller to complete his first
five-wicket return in Tests, and for Warne to pursue the victim who would take him past Lillee.
   Man of the Match: D. L. Vettori.

Close of play: First day, New Zealand 26-4 (Fleming 0*); Second day, Australia 114-5 (Martyn 10*, Gilchrist 4*); Third day, New Zealand 151-5 (McMillan 57*, Cairns 20*); Fourth day, No play.

Australia

M. J. Slater b Cairns	5	– (2) c Horne b Cairns	6
G. S. Blewett c Astle b Wiseman	17	– (1) c Spearman b Vettori	8
J. L. Langer st Parore b Wiseman	46	– c Astle b Vettori	47
M. E. Waugh not out	72	– c Parore b Vettori	25
*S. R. Waugh c Spearman b Vettori	17	– c and b Wiseman	10
D. R. Martyn c Astle b Vettori	17	– b Vettori	36
†A. C. Gilchrist lbw b Wiseman	7	– c Fleming b Vettori	59
S. K. Warne c Fleming b Vettori	7	– c Wiseman b Vettori	12
B. Lee c Parore b Vettori	6	– not out	6
C. R. Miller b Cairns	0	– st Parore b Vettori	8
G. D. McGrath c Spearman b Vettori	8	– lbw b Wiseman	1
B 7, l-b 4, n-b 1	12	B 7, l-b 4	11

1/10 (1) 2/77 (3) 3/78 (2) 4/114 (5)   214   1/7 (2) 2/46 (1) 3/67 (3)   229
5/138 (6) 6/161 (7) 7/184 (8)   4/81 (5) 5/107 (4) 6/174 (6)
8/192 (9) 9/193 (10) 10/214 (11)   7/202 (8) 8/214 (7)
    9/226 (10) 10/229 (11)

Bowling: *First Innings*—Cairns 18–0–71–2; Doull 14–6–21–0; Vettori 25–8–62–5; Wiseman 14–2–49–3. *Second Innings*—Cairns 4–1–13–1; Wiseman 33.5–6–110–2; Vettori 35–11–87–7; Doull 5–1–8–0.

New Zealand

M. J. Horne c Blewett b McGrath	3	– c Langer b Miller	11
C. M. Spearman c Martyn b Lee	12	– lbw b McGrath	4
M. S. Sinclair lbw b Warne	8	– lbw b Miller	6
P. J. Wiseman b Lee	1	– (11) c Gilchrist b Warne	9
*S. P. Fleming st Gilchrist b Miller	21	– (4) c Gilchrist b Miller	8
N. J. Astle c M. E. Waugh b Warne	31	– (5) b Warne	35
C. D. McMillan lbw b Warne	6	– (6) c Warne b Lee	78
C. L. Cairns c Gilchrist b McGrath	35	– (7) c S. R. Waugh b Miller	20
†A. C. Parore c Gilchrist b McGrath	11	– (8) c S. R. Waugh b Lee	26
D. L. Vettori not out	15	– (9) c Warne b Miller	0
S. B. Doull c Lee b McGrath	12	– (10) not out	5
B 4, l-b 1, n-b 3	8	B 7, l-b 7, n-b 2	16

1/4 (1) 2/25 (3) 3/25 (2) 4/26 (4)   163   1/15 (1) 2/25 (3) 3/25 (2)   218
5/80 (6) 6/80 (5) 7/102 (7)   4/43 (4) 5/121 (5) 6/151 (7)
8/134 (8) 9/143 (9) 10/163 (11)   7/195 (8) 8/204 (6)
    9/204 (9) 10/218 (11)

Bowling: *First Innings*—McGrath 11.1–2–33–4; Miller 22–8–38–1; Warne 22–4–68–3; Lee 7–4–19–2. *Second Innings*—McGrath 23–8–33–1; Lee 12–4–36–2; Miller 18–5–55–5; Warne 20.3–5–80–2.

Umpires: S. Venkataraghavan (India) and B. F. Bowden.
Referee: M. H. Denness (England).

At Napier, March 18, 19, 20. Drawn. Toss: Australians. Central Districts 160 (M. W. Douglas 30; D. W. Fleming five for 21) and 320 for nine dec. (D. P. Kelly 67, M. S. Sinclair 75, J. D. P. Oram 78, M. J. Mason 30 not out; D. W. Fleming three for 55, M. S. Kasprowicz three for 73); Australians 207 (M. E. Waugh 93 not out; L. J. Hamilton four for 76, A. J. Penn three for 59) and 186 for four (J. L. Langer 79, D. R. Martyn 61 not out; L. J. Hamilton three for 67).

NEW ZEALAND v AUSTRALIA

Second Test Match

At Basin Reserve, Wellington, March 24, 25, 26, 27. Australia won by six wickets. Toss: New Zealand.

New Zealand stiffened their pace attack by bringing in the left-arm seamer, O'Connor, ahead of off-spinner Wiseman. The obvious plan, or so it appeared, was to attack on what looked a lively pitch. Yet, on winning the toss, Fleming decided to put his own brittle batting line-up under pressure first. It was quickly exposed. Lee, using his speed rather than extravagant movement, had brushed aside Spearman and Horne by his second over, Miller trapped Sinclair lbw with a straight medium-pacer in the tenth, and Fleming and McMillan were also out by the time New Zealand struggled to lunch at 69 for five.

[*Ross Land, Fotopress*

New Zealand was the only Test country missing from Steve Waugh's innings of 150 or more, but he settled that score at the Basin Reserve.

The afternoon, however, produced New Zealand's best hours of Test cricket since they outplayed West Indies either side of Christmas. While Astle bustled away, Cairns flexed his batting muscles and in half an hour they added 46. Cairns should have been caught when 38, but their fightback had added 72 off 88 balls when Mark Waugh helped Warne remove Astle with one of his artistic first-slip catches. Undeterred, Cairns charged past fifty from 54 balls, steadied a little and was 82 at tea, 135 runs having come in the 32 overs since lunch. He lost Parore after the interval, their partnership worth 109 in 113 minutes, but there was no stopping his third Test hundred. From 138 balls, his 109 contained 14 fours and two sixes, its end just as dramatic as its compilation. Cairns hit Miller high and straight, and Blewett at long-on wobbled about under the ball until he dragged in the catch as he was falling to the ground.

New Zealand built on their recovery by whisking out Blewett and night-watchman Warne for 29 in the last seven overs, and enjoyed further success next morning with Langer and Mark Waugh out within eight more overs. However, Slater and Steve Waugh drew from their deep well of experience and slowly worked Australia clear. When the bowling lost its sharp edge as Vettori began to feel the effects of a back strain, the two New South Welshmen were away. Slater took 97 balls for his first fifty, only 54 for his second, and while Waugh's 22nd Test century was more circumspect – 94 balls for the first fifty, 113 for the second – their stand was worth 199 by the time Slater was caught behind for 143, having hit a six and 23 fours. Waugh and Martyn added 68, mostly off the new ball, before bad light stopped play, and the runs continued to flow on the third morning as they extended their partnership to 114. Even after McMillan and O'Connor broke through, New Zealand had to endure a run-a-minute last-wicket stand of 33 between Waugh and McGrath that saw Australia's captain to 151 not out, so completing scores of 150 against the other eight Test countries. He had batted seven minutes short of seven hours and hit 23 fours, establishing a lead of 121.

Horne and Spearman put on 46 for the first wicket, New Zealand's best start of the series. But when Horne and Sinclair left in four balls, Spearman at 69 and Astle and McMillan at 88, putting Warne on a hat-trick, New Zealand were still 33 behind. Once again, Cairns came to the rescue – and with a full cavalry charge. He belted Warne for four, six, six, then flicked a ball from Lee over the long-leg fence and away down Kent Terrace. Next came the shot of the Test, perhaps the season. Cairns rocked slightly back and hit Lee high and straight over the sightscreen. The Australian batsmen in the slip cordon almost clapped. He hit two more sixes and another four as he reached his fifty in 54 balls for the second time in the match, and he was unbeaten on 61 when bad light left New Zealand 189 for five. Fleming had seemed almost anonymous during their century stand. Both went in the first hour on the fourth morning, though, and it needed another tidy innings by Parore and a roistering 40 from Doull to set Australia as many as 174. By now the pitch had flattened out and, with most of the afternoon ahead of them, the Australians were able to bat well within themselves and still win with a day to spare.

Man of the Match: M. J. Slater.

Close of play: First day, Australia 29-2 (Slater 22*); Second day, Australia 318-5 (S. R. Waugh 109*, Martyn 41*); Third day, New Zealand 189-5 (Fleming 53*, Cairns 61*).

New Zealand

M. J. Horne c Warne b Lee	4	– b Lee	14
C. M. Spearman c Gilchrist b Lee	4	– c Langer b Miller	38
M. S. Sinclair lbw b Miller	4	– b Lee	0
*S. P. Fleming c Miller b Warne	16	– c Blewett b Miller	60
N. J. Astle c M. E. Waugh b Warne	61	– b Warne	14
C. D. McMillan c Gilchrist b Lee	1	– c M. E. Waugh b Warne	0
C. L. Cairns c Blewett b Miller	109	– lbw b McGrath	69
†A. C. Parore c Gilchrist b Blewett	46	– run out	33
D. L. Vettori c Langer b Warne	27	– c S. R. Waugh b Lee	8
S. B. Doull c Slater b Warne	12	– c S. R. Waugh b Warne	40
S. B. O'Connor not out	2	– not out	4
B 1, l-b 8, n-b 3	12	B 3, l-b 8, n-b 3	14

1/4 (2) 2/9 (1) 3/18 (3) 4/53 (4)   298   1/46 (1) 2/46 (3) 3/69 (2)   294
5/66 (6) 6/138 (5) 7/247 (8)   4/88 (5) 5/88 (6) 6/198 (7)
8/282 (7) 9/287 (9) 10/298 (10)   7/205 (4) 8/222 (9)
                                                    9/276 (10) 10/294 (8)

Bowling: *First Innings*—McGrath 17–4–60–0; Lee 17–2–49–3; Miller 20–2–78–2; Warne 14.5–1–68–4; Blewett 8–1–24–1; S. R. Waugh 4–0–10–0. *Second Innings*—McGrath 22.2–11–35–1; Lee 23–6–87–3; Miller 21–5–54–2; Warne 27–7–92–3; Blewett 3–0–15–0.

Australia

M. J. Slater c Parore b McMillan	143	– (2) st Parore b Vettori		12
G. S. Blewett c Astle b Doull	0	– (1) b Cairns		25
S. K. Warne lbw b Vettori	7			
J. L. Langer c Parore b Cairns	12	– (3) c Spearman b O'Connor		57
M. E. Waugh c Sinclair b Cairns	3	– (4) not out		44
*S. R. Waugh not out	151	– (5) c Fleming b O'Connor		15
D. R. Martyn c Parore b McMillan	78	– (6) not out		17
†A. C. Gilchrist c Parore b O'Connor	3			
B. Lee lbw b O'Connor	0			
C. R. Miller c and b McMillan	4			
G. D. McGrath c and b Cairns	14			
L-b 1, n-b 3	4	B 2, l-b 2, w 3		7

1/8 (2) 2/29 (3) 3/47 (4) 4/51 (5)   419   1/22 (2) 2/83 (1)   (4 wkts) 177
5/250 (1) 6/364 (7) 7/375 (8)   3/110 (3) 4/144 (5)
8/375 (9) 9/386 (10) 10/419 (11)

Bowling: *First Innings*—Cairns 26.3–2–110–3; Doull 19–3–78–1; Vettori 15–1–50–1; O'Connor 26–2–78–2; Astle 11–2–45–0; McMillan 23–10–57–3. *Second Innings*—Cairns 13–2–45–1; O'Connor 11–3–42–2; Vettori 8–1–19–1; Doull 10–2–35–0; McMillan 2–0–13–0; Astle 10.1–4–19–0.

Umpires: Riazuddin (Pakistan) and D. M. Quested.
Referee: M. H. Denness (England).

NEW ZEALAND v AUSTRALIA

Third Test Match

At Hamilton, March 31, April 1, 2, 3. Australia won by six wickets. Toss: Australia. Test debut: D. R. Tuffey.

The Australians brought in the left-handed Hayden to open with Slater in place of the out-of-touch Blewett, while New Zealand recalled Wiseman for the injured Vettori and, omitting Doull, gave a first Test to the burly Maori, Daryl Tuffey. Steve Waugh, hoping for early help from the grassy pitch, bowled first and, though the pitch had no mischief in it, the New Zealand batting contained its usual ration of ups and downs. Lee, using his speed well, took five consecutive wickets in the middle of the innings, including Astle second ball. Had McMillan not stayed almost three and a quarter hours for his 79, adding 77 with Cairns, New Zealand would have been on the back foot throughout. As it was, they had Australia in that position 13 overs into their reply. O'Connor removed Hayden just before stumps, and on the second morning, gaining sharp natural in-swing to the right-handers, he had Slater and Warne lbw. When Cairns bowled Langer and had Steve Waugh caught at slip, Australia were 29 for five.

Afterwards, Steve Waugh said he had such confidence in his team that he was not worried when the first innings was on the brink of ruin. Someone would come to the rescue. He could hardly have expected that the "someone" would be his opposite number, the New Zealand captain. But with O'Connor seemingly poised for the killing blow, Fleming removed him from the attack after five overs of his morning spell and introduced the new boy, Tuffey. Immediately the match turned towards Australia, with Mark Waugh and Martyn finding progress easy against Tuffey and the tiring Cairns before lunch. The second session belonged to Gilchrist, who launched a spectacular counter-attack in which he cracked 16 fours in 75 from only 80 balls. He and Martyn put on 119 for the seventh wicket in an hour and a half and Australia were off the hook. O'Connor came back to take the last two wickets and finish with his first five-wicket return in his 12 Tests.

Yet again, New Zealand started badly, with Miller running out Horne in the third over. Spearman batted two hours until the close but was soon out on the third morning, one of ten catches for

Gilchrist, an Australian record. Once more Cairns mounted the main challenge and his 71, including two typical sixes and ten fours, lifted his aggregate for the series to 341 at 56.83. When he was ninth out, just before tea, Australia were in line for their third successive clean-sweep in a three-Test series and their tenth consecutive Test victory, half of them won with a day or more to spare. Requiring 210 for victory, they strolled to 137 for three in the third session; all they needed on the fourth morning were 14 overs as Langer put the finishing touches to his golden summer. He reached 50 from 42 deliveries and his 122 not out came at a run a ball, with 19 fours. Australia had bolted home.

Man of the Match: A. C. Gilchrist.

Close of play: First day, Australia 4-1 (Slater 2*, Warne 0*); Second day, New Zealand 58-3 (Spearman 29*, Astle 2*); Third day, Australia 137-3 (Langer 72*, S. R. Waugh 1*).

New Zealand

M. J. Horne c Gilchrist b McGrath	12	– run out	0
C. M. Spearman c Gilchrist b McGrath	12	– c Gilchrist b Lee	35
M. S. Sinclair c Warne b Lee	19	– lbw b Miller	24
*S. P. Fleming lbw b Lee	30	– c Gilchrist b Miller	2
N. J. Astle lbw b Lee	0	– c Gilchrist b Warne	26
C. D. McMillan c Gilchrist b Lee	79	– c M. E. Waugh b Warne	30
C. L. Cairns c Martyn b Lee	37	– b McGrath	71
†A. C. Parore not out	12	– c Gilchrist b McGrath	16
P. J. Wiseman b Warne	1	– c Gilchrist b Lee	16
D. R. Tuffey c Gilchrist b McGrath	3	– not out	1
S. B. O'Connor c Gilchrist b McGrath	0	– lbw b Lee	0
B 5, l-b 7, w 2, n-b 13	27	L-b 4, n-b 4	8

1/22 (2) 2/42 (1) 3/53 (3) 4/53 (5)   232   1/3 (1) 2/49 (3) 3/53 (4)   229
5/131 (4) 6/208 (6) 7/212 (7)   4/71 (2) 5/111 (5) 6/130 (6)
8/224 (9) 9/227 (10) 10/232 (11)   7/165 (8) 8/220 (9)
                                              9/228 (7) 10/229 (11)

Bowling: *First Innings*—McGrath 21.5–8–58–4; Lee 23–8–77–5; Warne 20–5–45–1; Miller 11–4–28–0; Martyn 7–4–12–0. *Second Innings*—McGrath 20–7–50–2; Lee 18.4–2–46–3; Miller 20–5–58–2; Warne 25–11–61–2; S. R. Waugh 3–0–10–0.

Australia

M. L. Hayden c Parore b O'Connor	2	– (2) c Spearman b Wiseman	37
M. J. Slater lbw b O'Connor	2	– (1) lbw b O'Connor	9
S. K. Warne lbw b O'Connor	10		
J. L. Langer b Cairns	4	– (3) not out	122
M. E. Waugh c Sinclair b Wiseman	28	– (4) c Sinclair b Wiseman	18
*S. R. Waugh c Fleming b Cairns	3	– (5) retired hurt	18
D. R. Martyn not out	89	– (6) lbw b O'Connor	4
†A. C. Gilchrist c Horne b Wiseman	75	– (7) not out	0
B. Lee c McMillan b Cairns	8		
G. D. McGrath b O'Connor	7		
C. R. Miller c Tuffey b O'Connor	2		
B 4, l-b 6, n-b 12	22	L-b 1, n-b 3	4

1/3 (1) 2/16 (2) 3/17 (3) 4/25 (4)   252   1/13 (1) 2/96 (2)   (4 wkts) 212
5/29 (6) 6/104 (5) 7/223 (8)   3/124 (4) 4/190 (6)
8/233 (9) 9/248 (10) 10/252 (11)

In the second innings S. R. Waugh retired hurt at 175.

Bowling: *First Innings*—Cairns 22–7–80–3; O'Connor 15.5–5–51–5; Tuffey 9–0–75–0; Astle 4–3–5–0; Wiseman 11–3–31–2. *Second Innings*—Cairns 10–1–60–0; O'Connor 11–1–53–2; Wiseman 9–1–42–2; Tuffey 11–1–52–0; McMillan 0.3–0–4–0.

Umpires: A. V. Jayaprakash (India) and R. S. Dunne.
Referee: M. H. Denness (England).

THE SOUTH AFRICANS IN INDIA, 1999-2000

By DICKY RUTNAGUR

By beating India 2–0 in a two-match rubber, South Africa ended India's sequence of 14 unbeaten home series since Pakistan won there in March 1987. Consequently, victory also gave them the distinction of becoming the only country in that 13-year period to win series in all three countries of the subcontinent. Sadly, South Africa's achievement would be first undermined by accusations of match-fixing against their captain, Hansie Cronje, and four team-mates, then overshadowed by Cronje's admission to the King Commission in June that he had accepted money from bookmakers since South Africa's tour of India in 1996. Cronje continued to deny all allegations of match-fixing, but the integrity of his captaincy, along with his team's record, had been seriously besmirched.

For India, the losses, coming on top of the 0–3 whitewash in Australia, extended their run of consecutive defeats to five. And as if their morale was not already low after the calamitous time in Australia, it suffered further when Sachin Tendulkar announced four days before the start of the Test series that he would relinquish the captaincy immediately it ended. The timing of his resignation roused speculation that it was linked to the reinstatement of Mohammad Azharuddin and Nayan Mongia – out of the side since Tendulkar's return as captain and the coinciding appointment of Kapil Dev as coach. In the unpleasant atmosphere that prevailed, India were vulnerable.

South Africa, despite the subsequent revelations by and about Cronje, nevertheless deserve credit for their triumph. They were given just one first-class match, of three days, to accustom themselves to India's slow, turning pitches. Moreover, Daryll Cullinan, their leading batsman, was injured during that match and could not play in the First Test. He just made the Second. Cronje's poor luck with the toss must also rank prominently among South Africa's handicaps, for both Test pitches were prepared to nullify South Africa's fast bowlers and give India's spinners an extra edge. For the Second Test, India included three front-line spinners, with Anil Kumble opening the bowling.

South Africa's superiority was testimony to thorough tactical planning, disciplined bowling on and around off stump, and batting that was resolute, if seldom spectacular. Outstanding fast bowlers prevail on all surfaces, and Allan Donald, Shaun Pollock and Nantie Hayward certainly left bold marks on the series. Cronje and Jacques Kallis took important wickets by dint of swing and, with a match haul of seven wickets at Bangalore in only his second Test, left-arm spinner Nicky Boje hoist India with their own petard. He also made 85 there as night-watchman.

Kallis, the Man of the Series, batted in subdued style but played crucial innings in both Tests. His temperament was undoubtedly the decisive factor in the low-scoring, closely fought First Test. South Africa had lost four middle-order wickets for 21 in the second innings, leaving them to get 35 more with four wickets in hand while Kumble and Murali Kartik were bowling venomously on a pitch that had become vicious. Kallis, who had made a tormented, undignified start, held his ground for three hours 11 minutes, if for only 36 not out. In the Second Test, he made 95 and his partnership of 164 with Lance Klusener virtually secured the series for South Africa.

It is ironic that an Indian, Azharuddin, made the only hundred in the Tests, for their batting was deplorably poor. Tendulkar may have been a reluctant captain, but as a batsman he was not wanting for courage and grit. He made 97 in his first innings of the series, but as India's fortunes declined he seemed hard put to sustain his concentration. India's bowling, apart from Kumble and Javagal Srinath, was pedestrian.

For the Pepsi Cup one-day tournament that followed, India's captaincy passed to Sourav Ganguly, who immediately led them to victory in the first two games and went on to win the series 3–2. But the sweet smell of success did not last long. Within three weeks, Delhi police investigations into match-fixing, following intercepted phone calls between Indian bookmakers and between Cronje and a bookmaker, cast doubt on the games at Kochi, Faridabad and Nagpur. And even without this breaking scandal, there were good reasons for not viewing the one-day series as a consolation prize. The dismay and disappointment occasioned by the succession of Test defeats put into perspective the decline of Indian cricket brought about by the cynical downgrading of their domestic competitions, and demanded that the issue be addressed.

SOUTH AFRICAN TOURING PARTY

W. J. Cronje (Free State) (*captain*), S. M. Pollock (KwaZulu-Natal) (*vice-captain*), N. Boje (Free State), M. V. Boucher (Border), D. J. Cullinan (Gauteng), H. H. Dippenaar (Free State), A. A. Donald (Free State), C. E. Eksteen (Gauteng), H. H. Gibbs (Western Province), M. Hayward (Eastern Province), J. H. Kallis (Western Province), G. Kirsten (Western Province), L. Klusener (KwaZulu-Natal), P. C. Strydom (Border).

Cullinan, Dippenaar, Donald and Eksteen were replaced by D. M. Benkenstein (KwaZulu-Natal), D. N. Crookes (Gauteng), S. Elworthy (Northerns), N. D. McKenzie (Northerns) and H. S. Williams (Boland) for the one-day international series.

Manager: Goolam Rajah.   *Coach:* G. X. Ford.

SOUTH AFRICAN TOUR RESULTS

Test matches – Played 2: Won 2.
First-class matches – Played 3: Won 2, Drawn 1.
Wins – India (2).
Draw – Board President's XI.
One-day internationals – Played 5: Won 2, Lost 3.

Note: Matches in this section which were not first-class are signified by a dagger.

At Brabourne Stadium, Mumbai, February 19, 20, 21. Drawn. Toss: South Africans. South Africans 293 for six dec. (G. Kirsten 56, H. H. Gibbs 53, J. H. Kallis 50, D. J. Cullinan 43, W. J. Cronje 33, M. V. Boucher 33 not out) and 207 for five dec. (W. J. Cronje 55, P. C. Strydom 63 not out); Board President's XI 172 (Harbhajan Singh 38, A. Bhandari 30 not out; M. Hayward four for 68, C. E. Eksteen three for 51) and 181 for eight (Wasim Jaffer 47, M. Kaif 33, Harbhajan Singh 39; C. E. Eksteen five for 79).

Mohammad Azharuddin's thumb injury, forcing him to retire hurt, and the groin strain sustained by Cullinan kept them out of the First Test.

INDIA v SOUTH AFRICA

First Test Match

At Mumbai, February 24, 25, 26. South Africa won by four wickets. Toss: India. Test debuts: M. Kartik, Wasim Jaffer; N. Boje.

A pitch made to order could not mask India's shortcomings, but highlighting their weaknesses would not do justice to South Africa's achievement, particularly that of their fast bowlers, in winning with two days to spare. From its appearance – the surface was not just shorn by the mower but also scraped with a wire brush – it was clear that the ball would turn wickedly, and South Africa were persuaded to include both left-arm spinners, Eksteen and Boje, at the expense of the speed of Hayward. Instead it was Donald, Pollock and Kallis, backed up by Cronje, who determined the course of the match with skill and swing more than sheer pace.

Donald struck quickly to spoil Wasim Jaffer's debut, and vitally when he went through Dravid's "gate". Pollock's slower ball, inviting Ganguly to his doom, had India 96 for four, of which an unbeaten 44 came from Tendulkar. The captain kept the innings breathing until, three runs short of his century, he half-heartedly glanced at Kallis and was taken low down by Boucher. Batting responsibly, yet without being inhibited, he hit 12 fours, as well as two sixes off Eksteen; if his bat was passed on occasions, all credit to the bowlers, who harnessed the breeze that got up with the afternoon tide. A gallant last-wicket stand of 52 between Agarkar and newcomer Kartik helped the total to minor respectability, with Agarkar making 41 not out off 42 balls in his first Test outing since his five successive ducks in Australia.

South Africa failed to build on the splendid start of 90 given them by Kirsten and Gibbs. Tendulkar, bowling a medley of off and leg-spin, made the initial breakthrough and took two more wickets in a later brief stint. Between these strikes, Kumble also made inroads and, although Klusener batted defiantly, all ten South African wickets fell for 86 more runs. India's lead of 49 was substantial, considering the rate at which the pitch was deteriorating, but generally woeful batting against Donald, Pollock and Cronje stretched it only to 162.

Kirsten, batting staunchly, and Gibbs, using his feet to attack the spinners, took South Africa almost a third of the way there. Kumble removed them both and, in having Kirsten caught behind, became India's second-highest wicket-taker ahead of Bishan Bedi (266). But it was the run-out of Cronje at 107, an agile piece of fielding by Jaffer at short leg, that triggered a collapse. Three more wickets went in the space of 21 runs, leaving South Africa 128 for six and turning the finish into a fierce test of nerves. Kartik, playing his first Test, could not rise to the challenge. His brief, as the slow left-armer, was to bowl into the rough from over the wicket, but when Boucher, the new batsman, took his courage in his hands and swept him for four, Kartik lost control. Under assault, he was swept and pulled by Boucher for three more fours to narrow the gap, and the final runs came easily. Kallis, unbeaten for 129 balls, could reflect on a job well done, having kept one end stable when the innings was at its most turbulent.

Man of the Match: S. R. Tendulkar.

Close of play: First day, South Africa 27-0 (Kirsten 8*, Gibbs 15*); Second day, India 75-5 (Dravid 27*, Kumble 0*).

India

Wasim Jaffer b Donald	4	– c Klusener b Pollock	6
V. V. S. Laxman c Eksteen b Kallis	16	– c Boucher b Donald	0
R. Dravid b Donald	22	– b Pollock	37
*S. R. Tendulkar c Boucher b Kallis	97	– lbw b Cronje	8
S. C. Ganguly c Strydom b Pollock	2	– c Klusener b Pollock	31
A. Jadeja c Pollock b Cronje	12	– c Boucher b Donald	1
†N. R. Mongia c Boucher b Cronje	0	– (11) not out	19
A. Kumble run out	4	– (7) c Boucher b Cronje	4
A. B. Agarkar not out	41	– (8) c Boucher b Cronje	3
J. Srinath b Kallis	0	– run out	0
M. Kartik b Pollock	14	– (9) c Boucher b Pollock	2
L-b 7, w 1, n-b 5	13	L-b 1, n-b 1	2
	225		**113**

1/8 (1) 2/39 (2) 3/69 (3) 4/96 (5)
5/147 (6) 6/151 (7) 7/167 (8)
8/173 (4) 9/173 (10) 10/225 (11)

1/5 (2) 2/13 (1) 3/24 (4) 4/73 (5)
5/75 (6) 6/80 (7) 7/92 (8) 8/92 (3)
9/92 (10) 10/113 (9)

Bowling: *First Innings*—Donald 16–6–23–2; Pollock 19.2–6–43–2; Klusener 10–0–53–0; Kallis 16–8–30–3; Eksteen 6–0–26–0; Boje 5–0–17–0; Cronje 7–1–26–2. *Second Innings*—Donald 14–6–23–2; Pollock 12.2–6–24–4; Kallis 5–1–21–0; Cronje 12–5–23–3; Eksteen 7–3–21–0.

South Africa

G. Kirsten b Tendulkar	50	– c Mongia b Kumble	20
H. H. Gibbs c Ganguly b Tendulkar	47	– b Dravid b Kumble	46
J. H. Kallis c Laxman b Kumble	5	– not out	36
*W. J. Cronje c Laxman b Kumble	0	– run out	13
P. C. Strydom c Agarkar b Kartik	2	– c Ganguly b Kartik	3
L. Klusener c Laxman b Srinath	33	– c Srinath b Kumble	1
S. M. Pollock c Jadeja b Tendulkar	0	– lbw b Kumble	5
†M. V. Boucher c Mongia b Kartik	3	– not out	27
N. Boje b Srinath	14		
C. E. Eksteen b Srinath	4		
A. A. Donald not out	1		
B 8, l-b 8, n-b 1	17	B 4, l-b 9	13

1/90 (2) 2/102 (3) 3/102 (4) 4/105 (5)	176
5/131 (1) 6/131 (7) 7/144 (8)	
8/169 (6) 9/173 (10) 10/176 (9)	

1/51 (1) 2/76 (2)	(6 wkts) 164
3/107 (4) 4/110 (5)	
5/115 (6) 6/128 (7)	

Bowling: *First Innings*—Srinath 12–1–45–3; Agarkar 7–1–15–0; Kumble 22–1–62–2; Kartik 18–6–28–2; Tendulkar 5–1–10–3. *Second Innings*—Srinath 11–3–26–0; Agarkar 4–1–15–0; Kumble 28–12–56–4; Kartik 19–5–50–1; Tendulkar 1–0–4–0.

Umpires: D. R. Shepherd (England) and S. Venkataraghavan.
Referee: R. Subba Row (England).

INDIA v SOUTH AFRICA

Second Test Match

At Bangalore, March 2, 3, 4, 5, 6. South Africa won by an innings and 71 runs. Toss: India. Test debuts: N. Chopra, M. Kaif.

Once again the loss of the toss did not inconvenience the South Africans. Their bowlers turned in another superlative effort to dismiss India on the first day, when the pitch was at its best for batting. Then, as it began to help the spinners, as anticipated, their batsmen played with determination and discipline to put the game and the series out of India's reach.

India had brought in the uncapped off-spinner, Nikhil Chopra, at the expense of Agarkar, but even on the slow, turning pitch he proved innocuous, failing to take a wicket. There were also changes in their batting. Laxman was dropped, Dravid was promoted to open, and Azharuddin – forced out of the First Test by injury – returned to make his 99th Test appearance. Mohammad Kaif came in for Jadeja to make his first. South Africa ignored the obvious qualities of the pitch and reinforced their pace attack with Hayward, who had bowled with awesome speed against the Board President's XI on the drowsy Brabourne Stadium pitch. Cullinan's return from injury strengthened their batting.

Little went right for the Indians on the opening day, other than winning the toss at the start and dismissing Gibbs cheaply in the closing stages. Of their four leading batsmen, Ganguly and Azharuddin, whom Donald removed with a deadly off-stump bouncer, made minute contributions. Dravid and Tendulkar faced 75 and 76 balls, but could score no more than 17 and 21 respectively, with Tendulkar in his 76th Test reaching 6,000 runs. But for the unbeaten Kumble, who batted with courage and good sense for 95 balls to make India's top score, their day would have been even more disastrous. All the South African bowlers drew blood, emphasising their efficiency and the extent of their resources.

South Africa were in the lead before they lost their second wicket, that of night-watchman Boje shortly before tea on the second day. Apart from a low caught-and-bowled chance to Kumble, at 37, he had always looked secure and, with well-chosen shots square of the wicket and the occasional sumptuous drive, he outscored Kirsten. When 58, Kirsten became the first South African to 4,000 Test runs. Both fell to the admirable Kumble in the space of eight overs – Boje playing down the wrong line, Kirsten beaten by bounce and caught at short leg – but India had to wait until the next morning for further success.

Kallis was again the stumbling-block. Though frequently discomforted by Srinath's leg-cutters, he stayed more than seven hours and faced 359 balls for his 95, adding 85 with the ebullient Cullinan and 164 in just over four hours with an uncharacteristically workmanlike Klusener, who was moved up the order because India's bowlers were less happy against left-handers. Klusener had faced 169 balls when, with a century in his grasp, he lost patience; Kallis fell soon after to a vicious ball from Kumble. He and Kartik were both turning the ball at will now and, with the bounce also awkward, the last four wickets added only 38. Kumble's marathon effort earned him six wickets and he remained a strong contender for the match award even after Boje, linking accuracy and available turn, had picked up five wickets in India's second innings. Kumble was also a dedicated ally in a partnership of 96 that saw Azharuddin reach the only century of the series for either side. It contained two sixes and 13 fours, and no sooner was it completed than Azharuddin holed out with a wanton shot.

Man of the Match: N. Boje.						*Man of the Series:* J. H. Kallis.

Close of play: First day, South Africa 11-1 (Kirsten 5*, Boje 0*); Second day, South Africa 254-3 (Kallis 21*, Cullinan 46*); Third day, South Africa 472-8 (Boucher 14*, Donald 1*); Fourth day, India 196-5 (Azharuddin 73*, Kumble 14*).

India

Wasim Jaffer c Boucher b Hayward	13	– (2) c Kallis b Boje		23
R. Dravid c Boucher b Cronje	17	– (1) c Pollock b Boje		18
S. C. Ganguly lbw b Pollock	1	– lbw b Boje		13
*S. R. Tendulkar c Cronje b Hayward	21	– c Gibbs b Donald		20
M. Azharuddin c Klusener b Donald	9	– c Kirsten b Pollock		102
M. Kaif lbw b Kallis	12	– lbw b Kallis		23
†N. R. Mongia lbw b Boje	20	– absent hurt		
A. Kumble not out	36	– (7) lbw b Boje		28
N. Chopra c Pollock b Boje	4	– (8) c Boucher b Donald		3
M. Kartik run out	0	– (9) c Gibbs b Boje		2
J. Srinath c Gibbs b Pollock	4	– (10) not out		1
B 8, l-b 8, n-b 5	21	B 8, l-b 5, n-b 4		17

1/29 (1) 2/30 (3) 3/58 (2) 4/69 (5)					158				1/47 (1) 2/48 (2) 3/71 (3)					250
5/77 (4) 6/104 (6) 7/114 (7)								4/95 (4) 5/144 (6) 6/240 (5)
8/138 (9) 9/139 (10) 10/158 (11)								7/244 (7) 8/246 (9) 9/250 (8)

Bowling: *First Innings*—Donald 14-2-31-1; Pollock 17.3-5-26-2; Hayward 15-2-40-2; Cronje 12-6-17-1; Kallis 9-5-18-1; Boje 15-7-10-2. *Second Innings*—Donald 14-5-56-2; Pollock 24-14-40-1; Hayward 16-4-31-0; Boje 38-11-83-5; Cronje 3-0-17-0; Kallis 6-3-10-1.

South Africa

G. Kirsten c Wasim Jaffer b Kumble	79	A. A. Donald lbw b Kumble		7
H. H. Gibbs lbw b Kumble	4	M. Hayward not out		0
N. Boje b Kumble	85			
J. H. Kallis c Wasim Jaffer b Kumble	95	B 24, l-b 3, n-b 4		31
D. J. Cullinan c Wasim Jaffer b Kumble	53			
L. Klusener c Tendulkar b Kartik	97	1/10 (2) 2/171 (3) 3/186 (1)		479
*W. J. Cronje b Srinath	12	4/271 (5) 5/435 (6) 6/441 (4)		
S. M. Pollock c Tendulkar b Kartik	1	7/449 (8) 8/468 (7)		
†M. V. Boucher b Kartik	15	9/477 (9) 10/479 (10)		

Bowling: Srinath 30-6-53-1; Kumble 68.4-15-143-6; Chopra 24-3-78-0; Kartik 50-11-123-3; Tendulkar 10-2-33-0; Ganguly 6-1-18-0; Kaif 3-0-4-0.

Umpires: R. B. Tiffin (Zimbabwe) and A. V. Jayaprakash.
Referee: R. Subba Row (England).

†INDIA v SOUTH AFRICA

First One-Day International

At Kochi, March 9. India won by three wickets. Toss: South Africa.

Farce at the finish made a nonsense of the batting feast that preceded it. The last over began with eight needed. Pollock's second delivery was called no-ball – television indicated no overstepping – and the target soon became four from four balls. Kumble's steer to third man brought three, but in stopping the ball Kallis crossed the boundary and umpire Singh signalled four. Stumps were drawn and the players left the field. The TV umpire then pointed out that Kallis was not touching the ball when he went over the line and, after some delay, the players were ordered back for Robin Singh to face one more delivery. Kirsten and Gibbs had set up the game with a 235-run opening stand in 40 overs, Gibbs taking flight with two sixes over cover in the third over. Ganguly, India's new captain, responded in kind, hitting three fours in Pollock's first over and three more in Kallis's second. Still, it needed Jadeja, with three sixes and eight fours, to get India within striking distance of such a challenging target.

Man of the Match: A. Jadeja.

South Africa

G. Kirsten c Jadeja b Dravid	115	*W. J. Cronje not out	19
H. H. Gibbs c Agarkar b Joshi	111	L-b 6, w 9, n-b 4	19
J. H. Kallis not out	37		
L. Klusener c and b Dravid	0	1/235 2/249 3/249 (3 wkts, 50 overs)	301

N. Boje, S. M. Pollock, †M. V. Boucher, D. N. Crookes, H. S. Williams and M. Hayward did not bat.

Bowling: Agarkar 7–0–55–0; Kumaran 5–0–41–0; Kumble 8–0–48–0; Joshi 10–0–52–1; Tendulkar 10–0–44–0; Dravid 9–1–43–2; Singh 1–0–12–0.

India

*S. C. Ganguly c Boucher b Pollock	31	†S. S. Dighe c Cronje b Pollock	5
S. R. Tendulkar c Williams b Hayward	26	A. Kumble not out	7
R. Dravid c Williams b Cronje	17	B 1, l-b 6, w 13, n-b 7	27
S. B. Joshi run out	13		
M. Azharuddin c Pollock b Kallis	42	1/45 2/70 3/82 (7 wkts, 49.4 overs)	302
A. Jadeja c Crookes b Cronje	92	4/101 5/180	
R. R. Singh not out	42	6/272 7/287	

A. B. Agarkar and T. Kumaran did not bat.

Bowling: Pollock 9.4–0–59–2; Kallis 6–0–42–1; Cronje 8–0–48–2; Hayward 6–0–35–1; Williams 9–1–40–0; Boje 6–0–34–0; Crookes 5–0–37–0.

Umpires: M. R. Singh and C. R. Vijayaraghavan.

†INDIA v SOUTH AFRICA

Second One-Day International

At Jamshedpur, March 12. India won by six wickets. Toss: South Africa.

Keenan Stadium's reputation for being a high-scoring ground did not daunt the Indian bowlers, backed by run-saving ground fielding and improved close catching. South Africa could not even bat through their full quota of overs and only Cronje, staying for 27 overs, managed a substantial contribution. India's reply was completely dominated by Ganguly's 12th one-day international hundred. Severe on the spinners, he hit four sixes and ten fours in a delightful exhibition that put his team 2–0 ahead in the series and gave India their first win in their six one-day internationals at this venue.

Man of the Match: S. C. Ganguly.

South Africa

G. Kirsten b Agarkar	0		D. N. Crookes c Ganguly b Joshi	0	
H. H. Gibbs c Dighe b Joshi	27		P. C. Strydom lbw b Kumble	1	
J. H. Kallis c Dighe b Agarkar	18		S. Elworthy c and b Agarkar	3	
L. Klusener c Dighe b Tendulkar	19		L-b 6, w 4, n-b 1	11	
*W. J. Cronje c Singh b Joshi	71				
N. Boje c Dighe b Kumaran	28		1/0 2/41 3/59	(47.2 overs) 199	
S. M. Pollock b Joshi	7		4/88 5/158 6/178		
†M. V. Boucher not out	14		7/182 8/182 9/185		

Bowling: Agarkar 9.2–1–34–3; Kumaran 8–0–37–1; Joshi 10–1–38–4; Kumble 10–0–36–1; Tendulkar 9–0–39–1; Dravid 1–0–9–0.

India

*S. C. Ganguly not out	105		A. Jadeja not out	2	
S. R. Tendulkar c Cronje b Pollock	21		L-b 3, w 5, n-b 2	10	
S. B. Joshi lbw b Crookes	0				
R. Dravid c Gibbs b Boje	36		1/33 2/33	(4 wkts, 47.1 overs) 203	
M. Azharuddin b Cronje	29		3/121 4/194		

R. R. Singh, †S. S. Dighe, A. Kumble, A. B. Agarkar and T. Kumaran did not bat.

Bowling: Pollock 8–0–25–1; Elworthy 3–1–17–0; Boje 10–2–34–1; Crookes 10–2–44–1; Strydom 10–0–57–0; Kallis 5–0–19–0; Cronje 1.1–1–4–1.

Umpires: Jasbir Singh and C. R. Mohite.

†INDIA v SOUTH AFRICA

Third One-Day International

At Faridabad, March 15. South Africa won by two wickets. Toss: South Africa.

South Africa came back into the series, winning with an over to spare despite being penalised one over for their slow rate in India's innings. The chase was anything but straightforward, however, from the time Tendulkar ended a century partnership between Kirsten and Cronje in the 38th over until Boucher joined Pollock in the 44th and steadied dressing-room nerves. Earlier, Ganguly had again made the running for India. His 56 from 54 balls put 80 on the board inside 16 overs but, with Dravid and Jadeja unable to match his fluency during their fourth-wicket partnership of 62, the flying start was eventually grounded.

Man of the Match: W. J. Cronje.

India

*S. C. Ganguly c Boucher b Elworthy	56		†S. S. Dighe not out	17	
S. R. Tendulkar lbw b Pollock	12		A. B. Agarkar b Kallis	8	
R. Dravid run out	73		B 1, l-b 4, w 9, n-b 3	17	
M. Azharuddin c Boucher b Kallis	2				
A. Jadeja c Kallis b Cronje	31		1/61 2/80 3/85	(8 wkts, 50 overs) 248	
S. B. Joshi run out	23		4/147 5/182 6/209		
R. R. Singh run out	9		7/238 8/248		

A. Kumble and T. Kumaran did not bat.

Bowling: Pollock 10–1–36–1; Elworthy 10–1–44–1; Cronje 10–0–69–1; Kallis 10–0–37–2; Klusener 2–0–11–0; Boje 4–0–22–0; Benkenstein 1–0–9–0; Strydom 3–0–15–0.

South Africa

G. Kirsten b Tendulkar	93	†M. V. Boucher not out	17
H. H. Gibbs c Tendulkar b Kumble	19	P. C. Strydom not out	1
N. Boje c Agarkar b Tendulkar	14		
J. H. Kallis b Joshi	10	B 1, w 8, n-b 2	11
*W. J. Cronje lbw b Tendulkar	66		
D. M. Benkenstein b Kumble	0	1/42 2/63 3/91 (8 wkts, 48 overs) 251	
L. Klusener c Ganguly b Tendulkar	6	4/204 5/205 6/217	
S. M. Pollock b Dravid	14	7/219 8/244	

S. Elworthy did not bat.

Bowling: Agarkar 8–0–36–0; Kumaran 5–0–31–0; Joshi 10–0–56–1; Kumble 10–0–39–2; Tendulkar 10–0–56–4; Ganguly 3–0–16–0; Dravid 2–0–16–1.

Umpires: V. Chopra and T. R. Kashyappan.

†INDIA v SOUTH AFRICA

Fourth One-Day International

At Baroda, March 17. India won by four wickets. Toss: South Africa.

India secured the one-day series in a finish far more tense than looked likely during their opening stand of 153 in 25 overs. Ganguly made a riotous 87 with 12 fours and two sixes, and Tendulkar, almost back to his best, cut loose on Ganguly's departure to bring India's target down to 27 from 29 balls when he was third out for 122, his 25th one-day international hundred. Pollock's two wickets in the penultimate over upped the ante but South African nerve failed first, Klusener dropping Robin Singh at mid-on with four runs needed and three balls remaining. Cronje's decision to bat first on an easy pitch had gone against him. Kirsten and Gibbs again got South Africa going, taking 43 from Srinath's first five overs, and Kallis atoned for Kirsten's run-out by remaining unbeaten for 81. His quickfire stands with Benkenstein and Klusener propelled his side to a formidable total. India's captains present and past wasted no time putting it into perspective.

Man of the Match: S. R. Tendulkar.

South Africa

G. Kirsten run out	72	L. Klusener not out	14
H. H. Gibbs lbw b Joshi	37		
J. H. Kallis not out	81	L-b 5, w 7, n-b 4	16
*W. J. Cronje c Agarkar b Joshi	26		
N. Boje c Joshi b Kumble	9	1/99 2/136 3/181 (5 wkts, 50 overs) 282	
D. M. Benkenstein b Srinath	27	4/199 5/256	

S. M. Pollock, †M. V. Boucher, P. C. Strydom and S. Elworthy did not bat.

Bowling: Srinath 9–0–60–1; Agarkar 10–0–61–0; Kumble 9–0–32–1; Joshi 10–0–69–2; Singh 3–0–12–0; Tendulkar 9–1–43–0.

India

*S. C. Ganguly c Pollock b Strydom	87	S. B. Joshi b Pollock	4
S. R. Tendulkar c Elworthy b Kallis	122	†S. S. Karim not out	2
R. Dravid c Cronje b Boje	3	L-b 3, w 5, n-b 3	11
M. Azharuddin c and b Kallis	39		
A. Jadeja b Pollock	5	1/153 2/176 3/256 (6 wkts, 49.5 overs) 283	
R. R. Singh not out	10	4/267 5/273 6/277	

A. B. Agarkar, A. Kumble and J. Srinath did not bat.

Bowling: Pollock 9–0–54–2; Elworthy 7–0–52–0; Kallis 8.5–0–50–2; Cronje 6–0–33–0; Boje 10–0–43–1; Strydom 9–0–48–1.

Umpires: K. Hariharan and I. Shivaram.

†INDIA v SOUTH AFRICA

Fifth One-Day International

At Nagpur, March 19. South Africa won by ten runs. Toss: India. International debut: S. Sriram.

Klusener bludgeoned 75 of the 115 runs that came from South Africa's final 17.3 overs to set India a target no country had achieved to win a one-day international. He hit three sixes and eight fours in 58 balls, having gone half of those before hitting his first boundary. Later, when India were threatening victory, he shut them out by removing Karim and Robin Singh in four balls. With Gibbs hitting 13 fours and a six, South Africa had raced to 160 for four off 20 overs, but the Indian spinners pegged them back to 72 off the next 20. Klusener's return to form was vital. That India came so near to winning owed everything to a rollicking partnership of 180 in 24 overs between Tendulkar and Dravid, feeding off Cronje's decision to put off-spinner Crookes first-up in the firing line. South Africa's other opener, Williams, failed to complete his second over after aggravating a shoulder injury suffered before the second one-day international. Delhi police accused Cronje of informing a bookmaker that these two would open the bowling. Williams and Gibbs subsequently testified to the King Commission that Cronje offered them \$US15,000 (£10,000) each to play poorly in this game: Gibbs was to score less than 20, Williams to concede more than 50. During his 93, which included four sixes and seven fours, Tendulkar became the second batsman after Azharuddin to reach 9,000 runs in one-day internationals.

Man of the Match: L. Klusener.   *Man of the Series:* S. R. Tendulkar.

South Africa

G. Kirsten run out	1	L. Klusener not out	75
H. H. Gibbs run out	74	P. C. Strydom not out	0
N. D. McKenzie c Karim b Kumble	13	L-b 1, w 2, n-b 10	13
D. N. Crookes b Kumble	14		—
*W. J. Cronje c Dravid b Chopra	38	1/9 2/42 3/66 (7 wkts, 50 overs)	320
†M. V. Boucher c Kumble b Prasad	68	4/126 5/161	
D. M. Benkenstein b Tendulkar	24	6/205 7/319	

S. Elworthy and H. S. Williams did not bat.

Bowling: Srinath 6–0–65–0; Prasad 6–1–46–1; Kumble 10–0–61–2; Chopra 10–0–57–1; Sriram 6–0–36–0; Singh 1–0–6–0; Tendulkar 10–0–31–1; Ganguly 1–0–17–0.

India

*S. C. Ganguly c Elworthy b Williams	6	N. Chopra run out	3
S. R. Tendulkar c Elworthy b Crookes	93	A. Kumble run out	5
R. Dravid run out	79	B. K. V. Prasad not out	0
A. Jadeja b Elworthy	10	D 4, l b 8, w 14, n-b 5	31
S. Sriram c Boucher b Elworthy	12		—
J. Srinath c Strydom b Klusener	20	1/13 2/193 3/193 (48.5 overs)	310
R. R. Singh c Cronje b Klusener	29	4/214 5/221 6/259	
†S. S. Karim c and b Klusener	22	7/290 8/304 9/310	

Bowling: Williams 1.5–0–11–1; Crookes 10–1–69–1; McKenzie 0.1–0–0–0; Elworthy 8–0–50–2; Cronje 9.5–0–62–0; Klusener 9–0–59–3; Strydom 10–0–47–0.

Umpires: S. K. Bansal and F. Gomes.
Series referee: R. Subba Row (England).

FICA/WCM INTERNATIONAL MOMENT IN TIME AWARD

The Federation of International Cricketers' Associations/*Wisden Cricket Monthly* International Moment in Time 2000 award went to Courtney Walsh for overtaking Kapil Dev's record of 434 Test wickets in West Indies' Test against Zimbabwe at Kingston in March 2000.

THE ZIMBABWEANS IN THE WEST INDIES, 1999-2000

By CRAIG COZIER

West Indies began their first home international season of the new millennium, combining Test series against Zimbabwe and Pakistan with the first triangular one-day tournament in the Caribbean, in a state of uncertainty. Smarting from yet another overseas catastrophe – losing both Tests and all five one-day internationals in New Zealand – Brian Lara not only resigned as captain but, reportedly contemplating retirement, took a break from the game, leaving West Indies without their star batsman. Meanwhile, controversy surrounded the appointment of Roger Harper as coach, replacing Sir Viv Richards after just one assignment, the New Zealand tour. When the decision to sack Richards was announced in February, the outcry was most vehement in his native island of Antigua, which is also the headquarters of the West Indies Cricket Board. A large crowd marched through the streets with placards; a window was smashed and a gate vandalised at the Board's offices.

A month later, new captain Jimmy Adams joined his players and thousands of fans in a lap around Kingston's Sabina Park to acclaim hard-fought victories in both Tests of the inaugural series against Zimbabwe. The success was made sweeter by the fact that, a day earlier and in front of his Jamaican countrymen, 37-year-old Courtney Walsh had passed India's Kapil Dev as Test cricket's leading wicket-taker. But the ensuing euphoria could not mask the fact that West Indies had been outplayed by Zimbabwe for long periods.

In the First Test at Port-of-Spain, they were let off the hook when Zimbabwe's inexperience and lack of confidence, combined with their own disciplined fast bowling and fielding, saw them home: Zimbabwe collapsed for 63 in pursuit of a mere 99. "We simply did not seem to have that belief in our ability to win," said coach David Houghton. "We led for four days and about one session."

Once more, the bowlers had had to pull West Indies from a perilous position. Walsh and Curtly Ambrose, team-mates since 1988 and creators of several West Indian escapes to victory over the past decade, were again to the forefront. But their back-up also proved up to the task, with Reon King and Franklyn Rose enhancing their reputations. King had already served notice as the stand-out bowler in New Zealand. The renaissance of Rose, named Man of the Series, was more heartening, however. His steady decline through injury and poor attitude had been halted, and he reaped nine wickets with consistent line, length and swing, none more crucial than his four for 19 as Zimbabwe slid to defeat at Port-of-Spain. Just as encouraging was Rose's batting. Its continuing development and maturity were manifested in his maiden half-century during the stand with Adams that proved to be the turning-point of the Second Test.

Adams clearly thrived in his unsolicited role as leader, scoring his first Test century for four years. The management team he formed with Ricky Skerritt, a St Kitts businessman who had succeeded Clive Lloyd as manager, Harper, assistant coach Jeffrey Dujon, physio/trainer Ronald Rogers and performance consultant Dr Rudi Webster united his side, as witnessed by their commitment on the field and comfortable interaction with fans off it.

Zimbabwe, their focus distracted by violence and political unrest back home, had a disappointing first visit to the Caribbean. They played much good cricket, yet did not manage a single win. Their captain, Andy Flower, was the series' leading run-scorer, with 194 at 64.66, and his determined hundred in the low-scoring First Test – when no one else reached 50 – should have put him on the winning team. At Kingston, in the Second Test, he added 176 with Murray Goodwin, who showed his class with a century of his own, and pushed his team to a satisfying first-innings total of 308. But Zimbabwe, like West Indies, lacked batting consistency; none of their other batsmen contributed a Test fifty. One of the biggest disappointments was former captain Alistair

Campbell, whose tour started with two unbeaten centuries in the opening first-class matches. Test failures saw his form and confidence dip to such an extent that he was dropped during the triangular series, in which Zimbabwe lost all four games.

ZIMBABWEAN TOURING PARTY

A. Flower (Mashonaland) (*captain*), H. H. Streak (Matabeleland) (*vice-captain*), A. M. Blignaut (Mashonaland), A. D. R. Campbell (Mashonaland), S. V. Carlisle (Mashonaland), G. W. Flower (Mashonaland), M. W. Goodwin (Mashonaland), T. R. Gripper (Mashonaland), N. C. Johnson (Matabeleland), M. Mbangwa (Matabeleland), B. A. Murphy (Mashonaland), M. L. Nkala (Matabeleland), H. K. Olonga (Matabeleland), B. C. Strang (Mashonaland), C. B. Wishart (Mashonaland).

T. Taibu joined the tour as cover for A. Flower. G. B. Brent (Manicaland), D. P. Viljoen (Mashonaland) and G. J. Whittall (Manicaland) replaced Gripper, Strang and Mbangwa for the Cable & Wireless one-day series, during which Murphy flew back to Cape Town to resume his university studies.

Manager: A. H. Shah.   *Coach:* D. L. Houghton.

ZIMBABWEAN TOUR RESULTS

Test matches – Played 2: Lost 2.
First-class matches – Played 5: Lost 2, Drawn 3.
Losses – West Indies (2).
Draws – West Indies Board XI, West Indies President's XI, West Indies Select XI.
One-day internationals – Played 4: Lost 4. *Losses* – West Indies (2), Pakistan (2).

At St George's, March 4, 5, 6. Drawn. Toss: Zimbabweans. Zimbabweans 428 (G. W. Flower 69, T. R. Gripper 61, A. D. R. Campbell 116 not out, S. V. Carlisle 69; K. C. B. Jeremy six for 81) and 24 for no wkt; West Indies Board XI 198 (D. Ganga 57, R. O. Hinds 31, C. O. Browne 34; G. W. Flower three for 15).

At Pointe-à-Pierre, March 10, 11, 12, 13. Drawn. Toss: Zimbabweans. West Indies President's XI 349 (P. A. Wallace 34, S. C. Joseph 100, R. R. Sarwan 100, Extras 52; H. K. Olonga three for 103, B. C. Strang four for 36) and 417 (D. Ganga 41, D. Rampersad 34, S. C. Joseph 51, R. R. Sarwan 111, R. N. Lewis 62, C. E. Cuffy 37, Extras 65; H. K. Olonga three for 98, B. A. Murphy four for 71); Zimbabweans 394 (T. R. Gripper 30, M. W. Goodwin 30, A. D. R. Campbell 158 not out, S. V. Carlisle 86; C. E. Cuffy three for 69, M. I. Black four for 87).

Sarwan scored two hundreds in the match. The Zimbabweans conceded a total of 117 extras, including 64 in no-balls.

WEST INDIES v ZIMBABWE

Inaugural Test Match

At Port-of-Spain, March 16, 17, 18, 19, 20. West Indies won by 35 runs. Toss: Zimbabwe. Test debuts: C. H. Gayle, W. W. Hinds; B. A. Murphy.

A stirring display of fast bowling on the final day saved West Indies from adding another embarrassing chapter to their recent book of woes. Zimbabwe's bowlers, inspired by Streak, had routed them twice to present their own batsmen with a target of 99 on a worn but still firm pitch. But against Walsh and Ambrose, and with Rose and King rising to the occasion, the Zimbabweans could not grasp the gilt-edged chance, slumping to 63 all out, their first Test total under 100. Ambrose returned figures of 11–6–8–3; there was only one, edged, boundary in 47 overs, and Zimbabwean coach Houghton said that "there was hardly a ball to be hit anywhere off the square". West Indies' escape, one of a number throughout the Walsh–Ambrose era, provided only the second instance of a Test side successfully defending a target below 100 (Australia dismissed England for 77 chasing 85 at The Oval in 1882).

Zimbabwe owed their ascendancy to Andy Flower's seventh Test century, sandwiched between two disciplined bowling performances. Streak, on his 26th birthday, removed Griffith third ball after Flower sent West Indies in on the rain-spoilt first day, and added three more next day. Leg-spinner Brian Murphy, a law student from Cape Town University, picked up three on debut to ensure a modest total. Fellow-debutants Chris Gayle and Wavell Hinds, two Jamaican left-handers, were the most enterprising West Indians. Tall and powerful, Gayle stroked six fours before Murphy's athleticism ran him out, while Hinds, unbeaten for almost three hours, held the lower order together while the score was more than doubled.

Zimbabwe's reply stuttered for a time after Ambrose trapped Johnson first ball, but Gripper and Andy Flower fashioned a determined stand of 117, spanning four and a half hours. Flower benefited before scoring from umpire Bucknor's not-out decision on a gloved, leg-side deflection to the wicket-keeper off Walsh, and later from four missed chances as he moved towards an unbeaten hundred containing 12 fours. He remained entrenched for 431 minutes and 290 balls. Streak helped him add 68 before three swift wickets for Gayle's off-spin kept the lead to 49.

West Indies' batting let them down again as Streak struck twice in his first over. Although Chanderpaul and Adams dragged the score up from 37 for three to 115, the remaining batsmen managed just 32 runs. At the start of the final day, when Streak took his match haul to a Test-best nine for 72, Zimbabwe were on the verge of a historic victory.

Instead, the traditional West Indian four-pronged pace attack wrote history in their own favour. After Johnson was despatched in Walsh's second over, Grant Flower and Gripper dug deep for an hour until King broke through. Rose flattened the middle order, all to catches by wicket-keeper Jacobs, while at the other end Walsh bowled Grant Flower with one that kept low. In frustration, Flower demolished the stumps to earn a suspended ban and fine; apart from him, no one reached double figures. Ambrose returned before tea to remove the last three in 13 balls and draw alongside Malcolm Marshall on 376 wickets, with only Walsh among West Indians ahead of him.

Victory complete, Adams gathered his elated troops in a huddle of prayer on the outfield before setting off on a joyous lap of honour in front of the sparse crowd.

Man of the Match: C. E. L. Ambrose.

Close of play: First day, West Indies 79-3 (Campbell 20*, Ambrose 5*); Second day, Zimbabwe 109-3 (Gripper 31*, A. Flower 52*); Third day, Zimbabwe 236; Fourth day, West Indies 147-9 (King 1*, Walsh 0*).

West Indies

A. F. G. Griffith lbw b Streak	0	– lbw b Streak	0
S. L. Campbell lbw b Streak	24	– run out	23
C. H. Gayle run out	33	– b Streak	0
S. Chanderpaul c A. Flower b Olonga	12	– lbw b Streak	49
C. E. L. Ambrose c A. Flower b Streak	7	– (8) c Johnson b Murphy	1
*J. C. Adams lbw b Murphy	17	– (5) c Murphy b Olonga	27
W. W. Hinds not out	46	– (6) run out	9
†R. D. Jacobs c and b Murphy	10	– (7) lbw b Olonga	0
F. A. Rose b Johnson	1	– c A. Flower b Streak	9
R. D. King lbw b Streak	2	– c A. Flower b Streak	1
C. A. Walsh lbw b Murphy	11	– not out	0
B 7, l-b 6, n-b 11	24	B 11, l-b 6, w 3, n-b 8	28
	187		**147**

1/5 (1) 2/49 (3) 3/72 (4) 4/81 (5) 5/87 (2) 6/121 (6) 7/136 (8) 8/149 (9) 9/161 (10) 10/187 (11)

1/0 (1) 2/0 (3) 3/37 (2) 4/115 (5) 5/115 (4) 6/118 (7) 7/119 (8) 8/142 (9) 9/146 (6) 10/147 (10)

Bowling: *First Innings*—Streak 24–9–45–4; Olonga 18–7–44–1; Mbangwa 10–3–21–0; Johnson 13–4–26–1; Murphy 13.4–7–32–3; G. W. Flower 2–0–6–0. *Second Innings*—Streak 17–8–27–5; Olonga 13–3–28–2; Mbangwa 15–10–15–0; Murphy 15–3–23–1; Johnson 4–0–18–0; Gripper 2–0–6–0; G. W. Flower 9–4–13–0.

Zimbabwe

N. C. Johnson lbw b Ambrose	0	– (2) c Adams b Walsh	3
G. W. Flower c Campbell b Walsh	0	– (1) b Walsh	26
T. R. Gripper c Gayle b Ambrose	41	– lbw b King	3
M. W. Goodwin c Gayle b Walsh	20	– c Jacobs b Rose	8
*†A. Flower not out	113	– c Jacobs b Rose	5
A. D. R. Campbell c Jacobs b Ambrose	0	– b Ambrose	6
S. V. Carlisle b Ambrose	17	– c Jacobs b Rose	3
H. H. Streak c Campbell b Gayle	20	– lbw b Rose	0
B. A. Murphy lbw b Rose	1	– not out	0
H. K. Olonga b Gayle	2	– c Chanderpaul b Ambrose	0
M. Mbangwa b Gayle	0	– b Ambrose	0
B 2, l-b 6, w 1, n-b 13	22	L-b 7, n-b 2	9
	236		**63**

1/0 (1) 2/0 (2) 3/27 (4) 4/144 (3)   236
5/144 (6) 6/164 (7) 7/232 (8)
8/233 (9) 9/236 (10) 10/236 (11)

1/4 (2) 2/20 (3) 3/37 (4)   63
4/47 (5) 5/51 (1) 6/57 (7)
7/57 (8) 8/62 (6)
9/63 (10) 10/63 (11)

Bowling: *First Innings*—Ambrose 25–13–42–4; Walsh 28–9–49–2; Rose 19–6–41–1; King 20–2–71–0; Gayle 15–2–25–3. *Second Innings*—Ambrose 11–6–8–3; Walsh 14–8–18–2; King 9–2–11–1; Rose 13–4–19–4.

Umpires: G. Sharp (England) and S. A. Bucknor.
Referee: R. S. Madugalle (Sri Lanka).

WEST INDIES v ZIMBABWE

Second Test Match

At Kingston, March 24, 25, 26, 27, 28. West Indies won by ten wickets. Toss: Zimbabwe.

Jamaica's favourite cricketer became Test cricket's leading wicket-taker in front of several thousand ecstatic countrymen. In his 16th international season and 114th Test, Courtney Walsh reached the magical mark of 435 at 5.12 p.m. on the fourth day when Zimbabwe's last man, Olonga, pushed a lifting ball to short leg, where Hinds pouched it left-handed. The catch took Walsh past India's Kapil Dev, who took 434 wickets in 131 Tests.

Two other Jamaicans – there were five in the eleven – Adams and Rose, had already transformed the match with an eighth-wicket stand of 147, a West Indian Test record, to establish an unexpected first-innings lead. Up until then, Zimbabwe had matched West Indies for two and a half days, despite their top order again being found wanting. Walsh had broken through swiftly, taking Grant Flower's edge to go level with Sir Richard Hadlee on 431 wickets, and King struck twice before lunch. However, Andy Flower and Goodwin launched a spirited revival, adding 176 in the last two sessions with enterprising strokeplay until they perished off successive deliveries: Goodwin was run out by Hinds's swoop and accurate return; Flower played no shot at Rose's next delivery and lost his off stump. Goodwin's 113, his second Test century, lasted 324 minutes and 239 balls; though he favoured the off side, his ten fours were hit to all parts of the ground.

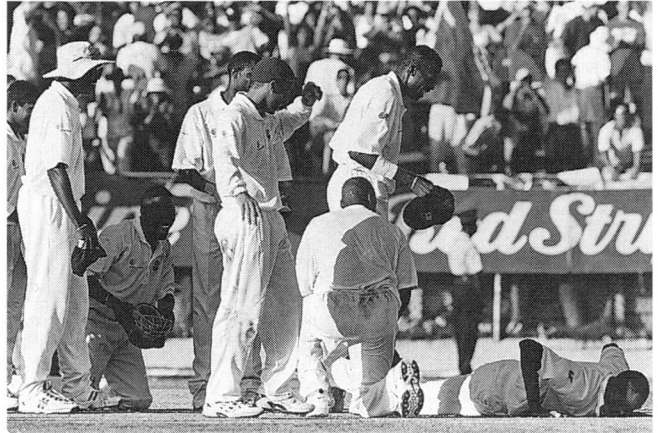

[*Laurence Griffiths, Allsport*

Courtney Walsh kisses the Sabina Park pitch after becoming Test cricket's leading wicket-taker.
Henry Olonga, caught at short leg, was victim 435.

Next day, King completed his first five-wicket haul in his fifth Test, but Carlisle and Olonga added 54, a Zimbabwe tenth-wicket record, and had stretched the total to 308 when Carlisle became Walsh's 432nd victim. Already, though, Zimbabwe had suffered a severe handicap, with Streak forced to miss the rest of the match because of muscle spasms and strained ligaments in his back. His team-mates did not let him down, however, bowling with discipline and accuracy. Only Sherwin Campbell, with 48 in two hours, broke their stranglehold on the second day.

West Indies deteriorated to 171 for seven after lunch on the third day before Adams and Rose turned things around, advancing the score to 318 on the fourth morning. Rose lashed 12 boundaries in his career-best 69 before he was caught behind, leaving Adams on 89. He lost Walsh three balls later but, with last man King safely negotiating 19 balls, eventually reached his sixth Test hundred – the first since his 208 not out against New Zealand in 1995-96 and, at 496 minutes (71 more than Larry Gomes took against Australia at Perth in 1984-85), the slowest Test century for West Indies. In 366 deliveries, Adams hit only six fours.

The scene was now set for Walsh. With the Blue Mountains at his back, he despatched Gripper and Grant Flower in his seventh over, both to outside edges, to draw level with Kapil. The crowd sensed history, but they, and Walsh, were kept waiting until the end as Zimbabwe's middle order was swept away by Walsh's colleagues. When he returned for his third spell, at 98 for seven with Streak unable to bat, the tension grew – and became electric when Rose accounted for Strang. But the fifth ball of Walsh's 16th over was short of a length, jagging back into Olonga's rib cage, and produced the desired result. It was the signal for wild celebrations. Walsh started with high fives, then kissed the pitch where he had taken 42 wickets in ten Tests. There were hugs and kisses from his mother, Joan Wollaston, and 13-year-old son Courtney Junior, a lap of honour after the day's play, and special tributes from Kapil (live from Sharjah, where he was coaching India) and Jamaica's prime minister. The next night, Walsh was honoured by the government and presented with a plot of land. Long before that, of course, West Indies had raced to their ten-wicket win, spurred on by Griffith's frenetic 54 in 41 balls with its 11 fours.

Man of the Match: J. C. Adams.   *Man of the Series:* F. A. Rose.

Close of play: First day, Zimbabwe 220-5 (Murphy 0*, Campbell 0*); Second day, West Indies 106-4 (Adams 9*, Hinds 12*); Third day, West Indies 295-7 (Adams 87*, Rose 53*); Fourth day, West Indies 8-0 (Campbell 3*, Griffith 4*).

Zimbabwe

G. W. Flower c Jacobs b Walsh	2	– c Campbell b Walsh	11
T. R. Gripper c Walsh b King	11	– c Jacobs b Walsh	0
M. W. Goodwin run out	113	– b King	9
N. C. Johnson c Gayle b King	0	– (6) b Rose	29
*†A. Flower b Rose	66	– b King	10
B. A. Murphy b Rose	0	– (8) not out	0
A. D. R. Campbell lbw b King	1	– (4) lbw b Ambrose	22
S. V. Carlisle c Jacobs b Walsh	44	– (7) lbw b Gayle	7
H. H. Streak b King	2	– absent hurt	
B. C. Strang c Jacobs b King	13	– (9) c Ambrose b Rose	3
H. K. Olonga not out	22	– (10) c Hinds b Walsh	2
B 4, l-b 12, w 2, n-b 16	34	L-b 4, n-b 5	9
	308		**102**

1/5 (1) 2/40 (2) 3/40 (4) 4/216 (3)   1/12 (2) 2/14 (1) 3/37 (3)
5/216 (5) 6/223 (7) 7/229 (6)   4/48 (5) 5/72 (4) 6/90 (7)
8/234 (9) 9/254 (10) 10/308 (8)   7/96 (6) 8/100 (9) 9/102 (10)

Bowling: *First Innings*—Ambrose 25–8–36–0; Walsh 22.4–6–46–2; King 23–8–51–5; Rose 24–8–69–2; Gayle 10–0–46–0; Adams 9–2–32–0; Chanderpaul 2–0–12–0. *Second Innings*—Ambrose 16–9–14–1; Walsh 15.5–6–21–3; Rose 12–5–24–2; King 10–1–30–2; Gayle 6–3–9–1.

West Indies

A. F. G. Griffith b Johnson	6	– (2) not out	54
S. L. Campbell c Campbell b Murphy	48	– (1) not out	16
C. H. Gayle c A. Flower b Olonga	13		
S. Chanderpaul c A. Flower b Strang	12		
*J. C. Adams not out	101		
W. W. Hinds c Campbell b Murphy	14		
†R. D. Jacobs c A. Flower b Olonga	27		
C. E. L. Ambrose c Carlisle b Johnson	7		
F. A. Rose c A. Flower b Johnson	69		
C. A. Walsh c G. W. Flower b Johnson	0		
R. D. King b Olonga	4		
B 8, l-b 18, n-b 12	38	N-b 5	5
	339	(no wkt)	**75**

1/37 (1) 2/69 (3) 3/85 (2) 4/85 (4)   (no wkt) 75
5/122 (6) 6/161 (7) 7/171 (8)
8/318 (9) 9/318 (10) 10/339 (11)

Bowling: *First Innings*—Olonga 31.1–8–65–3; Strang 36–17–43–1; Johnson 37–14–77–4; Murphy 36–17–99–2; G. W. Flower 18–9–14–0; Gripper 6–2–15–0. *Second Innings*—Strang 3–0–21–0; Johnson 5–1–27–0; Olonga 3–0–20–0; G. W. Flower 1–1–0–0; Gripper 0.4–0–7–0.

Umpires: Athar Zaidi (Pakistan) and E. A. Nicholls.
Referee: R. S. Madugalle (Sri Lanka).

At St George's, April 8, 9, 10. Drawn. Toss: Zimbabweans. West Indies Select XI 257 (M. N. Samuels 59, K. F. Semple 58, N. Deonarine 36; A. M. Blignaut four for 46, M. L. Nkala three for 35); Zimbabweans 170 for four (C. B. Wishart 94).

Zimbabwe's matches v West Indies and Pakistan in the Cable & Wireless Trophy (April 1–15) may be found in that section.

THE PAKISTANIS IN THE WEST INDIES, 1999-2000

By FAZEER MOHAMMED

Building on the successes of the previous series against Zimbabwe, and benefiting from generous slices of outrageous good fortune at crucial moments, West Indies narrowly turned back the threat of Pakistan to triumph 1–0 in the three-Test series. The one-wicket victory, earned amid heart-stopping drama and sensational controversy in Antigua on the final day of the tour, was a much-needed fillip for a team going through a period of rehabilitation in the wake of humiliating defeats away from home. Pakistan's expectations had been high when they won the Cable & Wireless triangular one-day tournament that preceded the Tests; instead, they became the latest touring team to leave the Caribbean agonising over lost opportunities.

For the new West Indies captain, Jimmy Adams, and their reconstituted team management, the rediscovery of a sense of determination and team spirit in the continued absence of Brian Lara was as important as the result. More than once, they wriggled out of tight spots as some of their talented young batsmen made vital contributions alongside the dour defiance of their captain. Wavell Hinds's aggregate of 340 runs – the highest by any batsman on either side – was an outstanding mark for the 23-year-old Jamaican. Less than eight months earlier, in one-day tournaments in Toronto and Sharjah, he had struggled to come to terms with the bowlers he now bludgeoned at Bridgetown on the way to his maiden Test hundred: the only century by a West Indian in the series. He made two half-centuries as well, including the top score of 63 in the final run-chase at St John's, and few questioned his nomination as Man of the Series.

Ramnaresh Sarwan, an elegant 19-year-old from the Essequibo region of Guyana, marked his Test debut with an unbeaten 84, while also providing a different challenge to bowlers accustomed to the array of left-handers in West Indies' batting order. Adams, the very antithesis of elegance, gave solidity to a vulnerable middle order and averaged more than 50 for the second consecutive series.

Pakistan, in the middle of a rebuilding programme themselves and haunted by the spectre of bribery and match-fixing, were buoyed by Yousuf Youhana's fluent centuries in the Second and Third Tests. Inzamam-ul-Haq furthered his already considerable reputation for reliability, making a hundred in the rain-ruined opener at Georgetown and two other scores over 50, and 18-year-old Imran Nazir displayed abundant gifts in his stroke-filled 131 at Bridgetown. Like so many of the batsmen on both sides, however, the young opener lacked the discipline to be consistently successful.

Domination of four of the game's greatest fast bowlers was always unlikely. In what was assumed to be their last home appearance together for West Indies, the veteran partnership of Courtney Walsh and Curtly Ambrose accounted for 25 Pakistani wickets. And if Waqar Younis could only occasionally produce the pace and hostility of old, Wasim Akram was a constant threat, although he left it until the final Test to stamp his mark on the rubber. Then he captured 11 wickets in a valiant effort to achieve Pakistan's first series win in five West Indian tours. Shoaib Akhtar's continuing problems with injury were a blow to Pakistan, as well as depriving the series of a great attraction. Spinners Mushtaq Ahmed and Saqlain Mushtaq offered variety, but at a price: their 14 wickets cost 43 each, in contrast to Mushtaq Ahmed's more economical 20 apiece in the one-day series.

With both Adams and Moin Khan ultra-cautious in their approach, much of the cricket lacked the intensity normally associated with these two teams. But the combination of umpiring errors, Pakistani panic and the West Indian captain's resolution on the final day put a memorable seal on an otherwise ordinary contest. It also allowed the West Indians to set off on their tour of England in better heart than seemed credible when they returned from New Zealand earlier in the year.

PAKISTANI TOURING PARTY

Moin Khan (PIA) (*captain*), Inzamam-ul-Haq (*vice-captain*), Abdur Razzaq (PIA), Arshad Khan (Allied Bank), Atiq-uz-Zaman (Pakistan Reserves), Imran Nazir (Pakistan Reserves), Irfan Fazil (Habib Bank), Mohammad Akram (Allied Bank), Mohammad Wasim (KRL), Mushtaq Ahmed (National Bank), Naved Ashraf (Redco), Saqlain Mushtaq (PIA), Shabbir Ahmed (Pakistan Reserves), Shahid Afridi (Habib Bank), Shoaib Akhtar (KRL), Shoaib Malik (Pakistan Reserves), Wajahatullah Wasti (Allied Bank), Waqar Younis (Redco), Wasim Akram (PIA), Younis Khan (Habib Bank), Yousuf Youhana (PIA).

Saeed Anwar (ADBP) withdrew because of injury. Saqlain Mushtaq arrived during the triangular series, after which Atiq-uz-Zaman, Irfan Fazil, Naved Ashraf and Shoaib Malik flew home. Shabbir Ahmed was added to the squad as cover for Shoaib Akhtar.

Manager: Brigadier Mohammad Nasir Ahmed.   *Coach:* Javed Miandad.

PAKISTANI TOUR RESULTS

Test matches – Played 3: Lost 1, Drawn 2.
First-class matches – Played 5: Won 1, Lost 2, Drawn 2.
Win – West Indies Under-23.
Losses – West Indies, West Indies A.
Draws – West Indies (2).
One-day internationals – Played 7: Won 4, Lost 3. *Wins* – West Indies (2), Zimbabwe (2).
   Losses – West Indies (3).
Other non-first-class matches – Played 2: Won 1, Lost 1. *Win* – West Indies Select XI.
   Loss – West Indies Select XI.

TEST MATCH AVERAGES

WEST INDIES – BATTING

	T	I	NO	R	HS	100s	50s	Avge	Ct
W. W. Hinds	3	5	0	340	165	1	2	68.00	3
J. C. Adams	3	5	2	170	60	0	1	56.66	7
R. R. Sarwan	2	4	2	111	84*	0	1	55.50	2
S. Chanderpaul	3	5	1	191	89	0	1	47.75	2
C. A. Walsh	3	3	2	28	22	0	0	28.00	1
S. L. Campbell	3	5	0	104	58	0	1	20.80	6
A. F. G. Griffith	3	5	0	88	34	0	0	17.60	2
C. E. L. Ambrose	3	4	1	32	22	0	0	10.66	0
R. D. Jacobs	3	4	0	21	10	0	0	5.25	8
R. D. King	3	3	0	5	3	0	0	1.66	0

Played in two Tests: N. A. M. McLean 46, 1. Played in one Test: C. H. Gayle 13 (2 ct); F. A. Rose 15, 4 (2 ct).

* *Signifies not out.*

BOWLING

	O	M	R	W	BB	5W/i	Avge
C. E. L. Ambrose	118.3	42	219	11	4-43	0	19.90
C. A. Walsh.	123	26	292	14	5-22	2	20.85
R. D. King	111	26	291	12	4-48	0	24.25
F. A. Rose	39	6	117	3	2-48	0	39.00
N. A. M. McLean	65.4	12	268	5	2-93	0	53.60
J. C. Adams	72	13	186	3	2-52	0	62.00

Also bowled: S. Chanderpaul 4–0–16–0; C. H. Gayle 9–4–16–0; R. R. Sarwan 2–0–16–0.

PAKISTAN – BATTING

	T	I	NO	R	HS	100s	50s	Avge	Ct/St
Yousuf Youhana	3	5	1	279	115	2	0	69.75	4
Inzamam-ul-Haq	3	5	0	295	135	1	2	59.00	2
Imran Nazir	2	4	0	143	131	1	0	35.75	0
Abdur Razzaq	3	5	0	162	87	0	2	32.40	1
Mohammad Wasim	3	5	0	124	82	0	1	24.80	1
Wasim Akram	3	5	0	108	42	0	0	21.60	3
Moin Khan	3	5	0	92	38	0	0	18.40	4/1
Saqlain Mushtaq	3	5	1	72	33	0	0	18.00	0
Waqar Younis	3	5	1	48	16	0	0	12.00	1
Younis Khan	3	5	0	31	23	0	0	6.20	4
Mushtaq Ahmed	3	4	2	9	4	0	0	4.50	1

Played in one Test: Wajahatullah Wasti 8.

BOWLING

	O	M	R	W	BB	5W/i	Avge
Wasim Akram	116.2	35	264	15	6-61	2	17.60
Abdur Razzaq	49	9	121	3	1-13	0	40.33
Waqar Younis	68	13	212	5	2-72	0	42.40
Saqlain Mushtaq	127	35	259	6	5-121	1	43.16
Mushtaq Ahmed	115	18	349	8	3-91	0	43.62

Note: Matches in this section which were not first-class are signified by a dagger.

Pakistan's matches v Zimbabwe and West Indies in the Cable & Wireless Trophy (April 5–23) may be found in that section.

†At St John's, April 8. West Indies Select XI won by nine runs. Toss: West Indies Select XI. West Indies Select XI 168 for nine (35 overs) (R. S. Morton 34, M. V. Nagamootoo 32 not out; Mohammad Akram three for 24, Shoaib Malik three for 48); Pakistanis 159 (34.3 overs) (Naved Ashraf 31, Younis Khan 52; N. A. M. McLean five for 26).

†At St John's, April 9. Pakistanis won by 14 runs. Toss: Pakistanis. Pakistanis 183 for nine (50 overs) (Mohammad Wasim 50); West Indies Select XI 169 (40.3 overs) (R. R. Sarwan 47, Extras 38; Mohammad Akram four for 28).

At Uitvlugt, Guyana, April 27, 28, 29, 30. Pakistanis won by 107 runs. Toss: Pakistanis. Pakistanis 299 (Mohammad Wasim 59, Yousuf Youhana 81, Mushtaq Ahmed 39; K. C. B. Jeremy three for 46) and 172 for four dec. (Younis Khan 103 not out); West Indies Under-23 143 (A. Haniff 46, S. C. Joseph 45; Mohammad Akram five for 16) and 221 (A. Haniff 75, M. N. Samuels 61, Extras 44; Saqlain Mushtaq three for 37).

The match was moved from Everest CC in Georgetown, which was waterlogged.

WEST INDIES v PAKISTAN

First Test Match

At Georgetown, May 5, 6, 7, 8, 9. Drawn. Toss: West Indies.

A finely balanced contest was reduced to a saturated anticlimax when torrential rain forced the abandonment of the final two days. Yet again, the authorities were left to ponder the wisdom of scheduling Test matches in Georgetown, given the almost perennial threat of rain in this equatorial region.

Inzamam-ul-Haq's tenth Test century, and his 206-run sixth-wicket partnership with Abdur Razzaq, lifted Pakistan from 39 for five after the West Indian fast bowlers had wreaked havoc under grey skies on the first morning. Ambrose led the assault with three wickets, while Walsh and King provided potent support. King dismissed Moin Khan with his first ball in a Test on his home ground and had Inzamam missed at second slip by the diving Campbell before lunch. It proved a costly chance as Inzamam, finding a resolute partner in the unflappable Razzaq, wrested the initiative with a mixture of watchful defence and effortless strokeplay. Fifteen boundaries – he was to hit 20 in all, most of them caressed with typical nonchalance – took him to a hundred, while their partnership broke Pakistan's sixth-wicket record against West Indies, set by Wazir Mohammad and Abdul Kardar in 1957-58. King, in a reprise of his opening-day feat, made the breakthrough when he had Inzamam lbw with his first delivery of the second day, and Pakistan lost their last five wickets for 43. Razzaq failed to capitalise on two dropped catches, falling 13 short of a maiden Test hundred.

West Indies made heavy weather of their reply after the early loss of Campbell, caught at slip. Griffith took four boundaries off Waqar Younis before falling lbw to Razzaq, whereupon Mushtaq Ahmed claimed the next three wickets and the home side were 139 for six by mid-afternoon on a rain-shortened third day. Only Chanderpaul, returning after he missed the one-day series because of exhaustion, showed the confidence to use his feet to Mushtaq's leg-spin. With McLean crashing his way to a Test-best 46 in their stand of 74, a record for West Indies' seventh wicket against Pakistan, the balance was redressed somewhat before Waqar and the second new ball saw off McLean. Shortly afterwards, ominous clouds approaching off the Atlantic confirmed the considerable risk of planning for five consecutive dry days on the northern fringe of one of the rainiest places on earth.

Man of the Match: Inzamam-ul-Haq.

Close of play: First day, Pakistan 221-5 (Inzamam-ul-Haq 117*, Abdur Razzaq 80*); Second day, West Indies 101-3 (Adams 16*, Chanderpaul 9*); Third day, West Indies 222-7 (Chanderpaul 46*, Ambrose 2*); Fourth day, No play.

Pakistan

Mohammad Wasim b Ambrose	4	Saqlain Mushtaq not out	8
Wajahatullah Wasti b Walsh	8	Mushtaq Ahmed c Gayle b Ambrose	4
Younis Khan lbw b Ambrose	2		
Inzamam-ul-Haq lbw b King	135	L-b 2, n-b 3	5
Yousuf Youhana c Jacobs b Ambrose	0		
*†Moin Khan c Adams b King	6		288
Abdur Razzaq c Gayle b McLean	87		
Wasim Akram c Jacobs b Walsh	16		
Waqar Younis b McLean	13		

1/12 (2) 2/12 (1) 3/21 (3) 4/21 (5) 5/39 (6) 6/245 (4) 7/262 (8) 8/266 (7) 9/277 (9) 10/288 (11)

Bowling: Ambrose 25.3–10–43–4; Walsh 28–10–46–2; McLean 26–5–93–2; King 26–7–57–2; Gayle 9–4–16–0; Adams 9–0–31–0.

West Indies

S. L. Campbell c Younis Khan b Wasim Akram	1	†R. D. Jacobs run out	6
A. F. G. Griffith lbw b Abdur Razzaq	34	N. A. M. McLean c Inzamam-ul-Haq b Waqar Younis	46
W. W. Hinds st Moin Khan b Mushtaq Ahmed	34	C. E. L. Ambrose not out	2
*J. C. Adams c Younis Khan b Mushtaq Ahmed	20	L-b 2, n-b 18	20
S. Chanderpaul not out	46		
C. H. Gayle c Wasim Akram b Mushtaq Ahmed	13	(7 wkts) 222	

1/2 (1) 2/69 (2) 3/79 (3) 4/106 (4) 5/130 (6) 6/139 (7) 7/213 (8)

R. D. King and C. A. Walsh did not bat.

Bowling: Wasim Akram 20–6–46–1; Waqar Younis 15–3–46–1; Mushtaq Ahmed 32–5–91–3; Abdur Razzaq 10–2–13–1; Saqlain Mushtaq 10–1–24–0.

Umpires: R. E. Koertzen (South Africa) and S. A. Bucknor.
Referee: P. J. Burge (Australia).

At Bridgetown, May 12, 13, 14, 15. West Indies A won by 65 runs. Toss: West Indies A. West Indies A 160 (D. Ganga 54, R. R. Sarwan 32, M. N. Samuels 31; Saqlain Mushtaq six for 48) and 396 (R. L. Powell 43, R. R. Sarwan 75, C. O. Browne 46, D. Ganga 63 not out, M. V. Nagamootoo 59, Extras 51; Shabbir Ahmed three for 71); Pakistanis 346 (Mohammad Wasim 111, Yousuf Youhana 58, Shahid Afridi 38, Saqlain Mushtaq 31; M. Dillon three for 52, P. T. Collins three for 84) and 145 (Imran Nazir 39, Mohammad Wasim 47; M. Dillon six for 40).

WEST INDIES v PAKISTAN

Second Test Match

At Bridgetown, May 18, 19, 20, 21, 22. Drawn. Toss: Pakistan. Test debut: R. R. Sarwan.

Fearful of offering the opposition the faintest whiff of victory, Moin Khan chose the safety-first option on a docile pitch to condemn the match to a draw. It was the first stalemate over an uninterrupted five days at Kensington Oval since February 1977, when the same opponents scored 1,398 runs for 38 wickets and produced a tension-filled finale in which West Indies' last-wicket pair, Andy Roberts and Colin Croft, staved off defeat.

Similar drama seemed possible when the home team were 41 for three before tea on the final day, having been set an improbable target of 275 in 57 overs. But Hinds's aggressive 52 and a watchful unbeaten 34 from Adams dispelled West Indian fears of an ignominious collapse to

Pakistan's varied armoury. Indeed, this was Hinds's Test, with that match-saving half-century following the maiden Test hundred which built the platform for West Indies' first-innings lead of 145. His 165, spanning almost six hours, was spiced with 24 rasping boundaries; coming in only his fourth Test, along with debutant Ramnaresh Sarwan's elegant, unbeaten 84, it raised hopes for the coming of a new era of West Indian batting champions.

On a more responsive surface, Pakistan's deficit would have been daunting; here, it merely spurred their openers on. They had cleared the arrears by stumps on the third day and proceeded to a partnership of 219, an all-wicket record for Pakistan in the Caribbean. Imran Nazir's felicitous 131 underlined the teenager's rich promise in only his second Test, while Mohammad Wasim's studious 82 proved the ideal foil. But, although they had a lead of 200 and three wickets in hand, Pakistan started the final day with any sense of enterprise stifled by an overwhelming desire to avoid defeat: they scored only 18 runs in the first 18 overs. Their declaration ten balls after lunch, following a laborious 72 by Abdur Razzaq, batting with a runner, meant they could be the only winner. Despite the swift removal of the openers and then Chanderpaul, that possibility had evaporated long before the captains agreed not to extend the match through the full final 15 overs.

YOUNGEST PLAYERS TO SCORE A TEST HUNDRED

Years	Days				
17	82	Mushtaq Mohammad .	101	Pakistan v India at Delhi	1960-61
17	112	S. R. Tendulkar.	119*	India v England at Manchester . . .	1990
18	**157**	**Imran Nazir**	**131**	**Pakistan v West Indies at**	
				Bridgetown	**1999-2000**
18	328	Salim Malik	100*	Pakistan v Sri Lanka at Karachi . .	1981-82
19	26	Mohammad Ilyas. . . .	126	Pakistan v New Zealand at Karachi	1964-65

The sedate conclusion contrasted sharply with another sensational opening day as the West Indian fast bowlers repeated their feat of the First Test, skittling half the Pakistan side for less than 40 runs, after they chose to bat. This time, Yousuf Youhana led the rescue act with a classy 115 in six hours, with 14 fours. His dismissal shortly before stumps brought the innings to an end and gave the persevering Walsh his 18th five-wicket innings return in Tests. However, the tourists' first-innings total of 253 was put into proper perspective by a West Indian reply that fell just short of 400, and it was obvious that Pakistan would have to be reckless in the extreme not to stage a worthy fightback on a pitch that drained the enthusiasm of even the most tireless triers.

Man of the Match: W. W. Hinds.

Close of play: First day, West Indies 2-0 (Campbell 2*, Griffith 0*); Second day, West Indies 283-5 (Sarwan 28*, Ambrose 0*); Third day, Pakistan 152-0 (Mohammad Wasim 53*, Imran Nazir 94*); Fourth day, Pakistan 345-7 (Abdur Razzaq 32*, Saqlain Mushtaq 2*).

Pakistan

Mohammad Wasim c Adams b Walsh	4	– lbw b King	82
Imran Nazir c Campbell b Ambrose.	2	– c Adams b King.	131
Younis Khan c Chanderpaul b Walsh	0	– c Jacobs b King	23
Inzamam-ul-Haq c Adams b King	8	– c and b Walsh	29
Yousuf Youhana c Campbell b Walsh	115	– c Adams b McLean.	19
Abdur Razzaq c Hinds b McLean	1	– c sub (C. H. Gayle) b King	72
*†Moin Khan c Chanderpaul b Walsh	38	– b Adams	14
Wasim Akram b Ambrose	42	– c Hinds b Adams	0
Saqlain Mushtaq c Campbell b Adams	12	– b McLean	33
Waqar Younis c Griffith b Walsh	14	– not out	1
Mushtaq Ahmed not out	2		
B 2, l-b 9, n-b 4	15	L-b 4, w 1, n-b 10	15

1/7 (1) 2/7 (2) 3/7 (3) 4/34 (4)   253   1/219 (1) 2/232 (2)   (9 wkts dec.) 419
5/37 (6) 6/110 (7) 7/179 (8)   3/248 (3) 4/294 (4)
8/220 (9) 9/248 (10) 10/253 (5)   5/294 (5) 6/341 (7)
                                                             7/341 (8) 8/411 (6) 9/419 (9)

Bowling: *First Innings*—Ambrose 21–7–53–2; Walsh 13–4–22–5; King 17–1–56–1; McLean 16–3–63–1; Adams 17–1–45–1; Chanderpaul 2–0–3–0. *Second Innings*—Ambrose 37–16–54–0; Walsh 36–6–102–1; King 29–9–82–4; McLean 23.4–4–112–2; Adams 26–9–52–2; Chanderpaul 2–0–13–0.

West Indies

S. L. Campbell b Saqlain Mushtaq	58	– c sub (Shahid Afridi) b Wasim Akram .	8
A. F. G. Griffith c Moin Khan b Waqar Younis .	4	– lbw b Waqar Younis	5
W. W. Hinds c Inzamam-ul-Haq b Waqar Younis.	165	– c Moin Khan b Mushtaq Ahmed . .	52
S. Chanderpaul c Moin Khan b Abdur Razzaq.	9	– c Mohammad Wasim b Mushtaq Ahmed .	16
*J. C. Adams c Younis Khan b Saqlain Mushtaq	8	– not out	34
R. R. Sarwan not out	84	– not out	11
C. E. L. Ambrose c Younis Khan b Wasim Akram .	22		
†R. D. Jacobs b Saqlain Mushtaq	10		
N. A. M. McLean c Yousuf Youhana b Wasim Akram .	1		
R. D. King c Mushtaq Ahmed b Saqlain Mushtaq .	2		
C. A. Walsh c Moin Khan b Saqlain Mushtaq . .	22		
L-b 6, n-b 7	13	B 1, l-b 1, n-b 4	6
	398	(4 wkts)	**132**

1/11 (2) 2/144 (1) 3/176 (4) 4/213 (5) 5/282 (3) 6/321 (7) 7/338 (8) 8/339 (9) 9/362 (10) 10/398 (11)

1/15 (2) 2/15 (1) 3/41 (4) 4/113 (3)

Bowling: *First Innings*—Wasim Akram 33–9–84–2; Waqar Younis 17–2–72–2; Mushtaq Ahmed 22–2–65–0; Abdur Razzaq 16–3–50–1; Saqlain Mushtaq 51–10–121–5. *Second Innings*—Wasim Akram 7–1–24–1; Waqar Younis 4–0–14–1; Saqlain Mushtaq 21–12–28–0; Mushtaq Ahmed 20–5–64–2.

Umpires: R. E. Koertzen (South Africa) and E. A. Nicholls.
Referee: P. J. Burge (Australia).

WEST INDIES v PAKISTAN

Third Test Match

At St John's, May 25, 26, 27, 28, 29. West Indies won by one wicket. Toss: West Indies.

Amid scenes reminiscent of Brian Lara's heroics against Australia in Barbados a year earlier, Adams piloted his team to a nerve-jangling one-wicket victory and West Indies' fourth triumph in five unbeaten home series against Pakistan. Yet a reasoned appraisal of the events of that last afternoon left no doubt that West Indies were extremely fortunate to reach their target of 216. They benefited from two glaring umpiring errors and Saqlain Mushtaq's raw panic when the match was literally in his hands.

Wasim Akram, in an inspired spell of fast bowling as devastating as his first-innings six for 61, had a confident appeal for a catch by Moin Khan off Adams turned down by umpire Doctrove, while an equally vehement claim for a bat-pad dismissal of last man Walsh, off Saqlain, was denied by umpire Cowie. Television replays confirmed that both should have been out. Yet Pakistani fury at the officiating was tempered by Saqlain's bungling of two run-out chances, the second opportunity producing one of the more amazing scenes in the history of Test cricket: both Adams and Walsh seemed hopelessly stranded at the striker's end, only for Saqlain to fail to gather the return cleanly. As the ball ran away from him, Walsh hared through for the leg-bye Adams intended.

After such incredible escapes, it was almost inevitable that the last pair would make the 19 runs they required, and Adams was engulfed by joyous team-mates after scampering the winning run. For Antiguans in particular, it was cause for a double celebration, following the investiture of the former West Indies captain and master batsman, Sir Vivian Richards, at the lunch interval.

Even though Adams's painstaking 48 was the match-winner – he did not hit a single four in five and a half hours – his effort could not take the lustre off Wasim's Test-best return of 11 for 110, which left him two wickets from becoming only the fourth bowler to claim 400 wickets in Tests. Publication on the eve of the match of Justice Qayyum's long-awaited report on bribery and match-fixing in Pakistan seemed to spur Wasim on; his rout of West Indies' first innings on the third day – six wickets for four runs in 28 balls – limited their advantage to a negligible four runs. The way Chanderpaul and Adams were batting the previous afternoon, when they added 130 for the fourth wicket, the lead promised to be considerably greater.

Pakistan's first innings of 269 had featured another polished century by Yousuf Youhana, and one more five-wicket feast for the irresistible Walsh. Inzamam-ul-Haq's first-innings fifty was a vital contribution, and his contentious dismissal for a top score of 68 in the second was another grievance for the tourists. (Inzamam was fined for lingering after Doctrove gave him out caught behind.) Wasim put it in the background for the time being by taking three of the four wickets that fell on the fourth afternoon. They included that of Hinds, whose 63 was tilting the balance in the home team's favour, whereupon rain ended play for the day, leaving West Indies in need of 72 more runs. They would take 41 nail-biting overs. When, with the last ball before lunch, Saqlain removed Ambrose, making his farewell Test appearance on his home island, and King was bowled offering no shot to Wasim, the game was as good as Pakistan's. At 197 for nine, West Indies needed a miracle or considerable good fortune. As it turned out, they got both in adequate supply.

Man of the Match: Wasim Akram. *Man of the Series:* W. W. Hinds.

Close of play: First day, Pakistan 267-8 (Yousuf Youhana 102*, Waqar Younis 4*); Second day, West Indies 214-3 (Chanderpaul 68*, Adams 60*); Third day, Pakistan 157-5 (Yousuf Youhana 41*, Saqlain Mushtaq 2*); Fourth day, West Indies 144-4 (Adams 15*).

Pakistan

Mohammad Wasim c and b Rose	13	– b King 21
Imran Nazir c Rose b Ambrose	10	– c Sarwan b Walsh 0
Younis Khan c Jacobs b Ambrose	4	– lbw b Ambrose 2
Inzamam-ul-Haq c Griffith b Walsh	55	– c Jacobs b Rose 68
Yousuf Youhana not out	103	– lbw b King 42
Abdur Razzaq c Jacobs b Walsh	2	– (8) run out 0
*†Moin Khan c Jacobs b Rose	24	– (6) c Hinds b King 10
Wasim Akram c Campbell b King	26	– (9) c Adams b King 24
Saqlain Mushtaq c Campbell b Walsh	4	– (7) c Campbell b Ambrose 15
Waqar Younis c Sarwan b Walsh	4	– c Adams b Ambrose 16
Mushtaq Ahmed c Jacobs b Walsh	0	– not out 3
L-b 4, n-b 20	24	B 2, l-b 4, n-b 12 18

1/21 (2) 2/27 (3) 3/33 (1) 4/130 (4)   269   1/0 (2) 2/3 (3) 3/49 (1)   219
5/132 (6) 6/173 (7) 7/209 (8)   4/129 (4) 5/150 (6) 6/162 (5)
8/247 (9) 9/268 (10) 10/269 (11)   7/163 (8) 8/186 (7)
                                                    9/213 (10) 10/219 (9)

Bowling: *First Innings*—Ambrose 14–4–30–2; Walsh 26–2–83–5; Rose 19–4–48–2; King 16–3–48–1; Adams 14–2–40–0; Sarwan 2–0–16–0. *Second Innings*—Ambrose 21–5–39–3; Walsh 20–4–39–1; Rose 20–2–69–1; King 23–6–48–4; Adams 6–1–18–0.

West Indies

S. L. Campbell c Yousuf Youhana			
b Mushtaq Ahmed .	31	– c Yousuf Youhana b Wasim Akram .	6
A. F. G. Griffith b Mushtaq Ahmed	22	– c Waqar Younis b Wasim Akram . .	23
W. W. Hinds run out	26	– b Wasim Akram	63
S. Chanderpaul b Wasim Akram	89	– lbw b Abdur Razzaq	31
*J. C. Adams lbw b Waqar Younis.	60	– not out	48
R. R. Sarwan lbw b Wasim Akram	10	– lbw b Wasim Akram	6
†R. D. Jacobs lbw b Wasim Akram	0	– run out	5
F. A. Rose c Abdur Razzaq b Wasim Akram . . .	15	– c Wasim Akram b Mushtaq Ahmed	4
C. E. L. Ambrose c Yousuf Youhana			
b Wasim Akram .	0	– lbw b Saqlain Mushtaq	8
R. D. King c and b Wasim Akram	3	– b Wasim Akram	0
C. A. Walsh not out	2	– not out	4
B 1, l-b 10, n-b 4	15	B 8, l-b 7, n-b 3.	18

1/40 (1) 2/73 (2) 3/84 (3) 4/218 (5)   273   1/16 (1) 2/31 (2)   (9 wkts) 216
5/235 (6) 6/243 (7) 7/254 (4)   3/84 (4) 4/144 (3)
8/258 (9) 9/269 (8) 10/273 (10)   5/161 (6) 6/169 (7)
  7/177 (8) 8/194 (9) 9/197 (10)

Bowling: *First Innings*—Wasim Akram 26.2–7–61–6; Waqar Younis 21–8–41–1; Mushtaq Ahmed 24–3–68–2; Saqlain Mushtaq 23–5–48–0; Abdur Razzaq 12–1–44–0. *Second Innings*—Wasim Akram 30–12–49–5; Waqar Younis 11–0–39–0; Mushtaq Ahmed 17–3–61–1; Abdur Razzaq 11–3–14–1; Saqlain Mushtaq 22–7–38–1.

Umpires: D. B. Cowie (New Zealand) and B. R. Doctrove.
Referee: P. J. Burge (Australia).

ONE-DAY INTERNATIONAL COMPETITIONS, 1999-2000

Competition	Winners	Runners-up	Others
Aiwa Cup.	**Sri Lanka**	Australia	India
Coca-Cola Singapore Challenge . . .	**West Indies**	India	Zimbabwe
LG Cup	**South Africa**	India	Zimbabwe, Kenya
Coca-Cola Champions Trophy	**Pakistan**	Sri Lanka	West Indies
Carlton & United Series	**Australia**	Pakistan	India
Standard Bank International Series .	**South Africa**	England	Zimbabwe
Coca-Cola Cup	**Pakistan**	South Africa	India
Cable & Wireless Trophy.	**Pakistan**	West Indies	Zimbabwe
Pepsi Asia Cup	**Pakistan**	Sri Lanka	India, Bangladesh
Singer Triangular Series	**Sri Lanka**	South Africa	Pakistan
NatWest Series	**England**	Zimbabwe	West Indies

Note: Only competitions held during 1999-2000 and 2000 seasons involving three or more teams are included.

THE PAKISTANIS IN SRI LANKA, 2000

By SA'ADI THAWFEEQ

Sri Lanka's joy at winning their Test series in Pakistan in March evaporated three months later when Pakistan extracted revenge with a remorseless 2–0 victory in the three-Test series played in Sri Lanka. It was not that the Sri Lankans underperformed; they simply came up against a Pakistan team playing at their peak.

The result was not one many would have forecast. For a start, Pakistan had been playing almost non-stop cricket for five months and had every reason to be exhausted. The Coca-Cola Cup in Sharjah, a gruelling and ultimately heartbreaking tour of the Caribbean, and then the Asia Cup in Bangladesh had preceded this tour. Sanath Jayasuriya's team, on the other hand, were playing on familiar terrain and appeared confident of repeating their series win in Pakistan. They also had the incentive of the opening Test in Colombo being their country's 100th. But logic went by the board as Pakistan dominated the first two Tests.

The touring team were led admirably by wicket-keeper/batsman Moin Khan. He and Javed Miandad, reinstated as coach during the series between these sides in Pakistan, looked to have formed a vital partnership for their country. They could point to a number of fine individual performances in the first two Tests, but none to compare with those of former captain Wasim Akram, whose all-round skills gave his side a distinct edge. He might have been under considerable pressure after the publication of the Qayyum Report into match-fixing but, as in the West Indies, he put aside the allegations to produce cricket of the highest quality. The irony was that Wasim would have missed the series but for Qayyum; he would have been in England working for Channel 4 TV. He withdrew from their commentary team when the report was severely critical of him. At Colombo, his 96th Test, he became the fourth bowler to reach 400 wickets in Tests, after Sir Richard Hadlee, Kapil Dev and Courtney Walsh, and the first to take 400 in both Tests and one-day internationals. By way of celebration, he helped himself to a rapid hundred at Galle, the last of four in Pakistan's match-winning 600 for eight declared, and was their leading run-scorer in the series, heading the averages with 99.

Although the pace men grabbed the headlines – at Galle, all-rounder Abdur Razzaq became the youngest to take a hat-trick in Tests – Pakistan owed much to the off-spin bowling of Arshad Khan for their series success. So often in the shadow of Saqlain Mushtaq, who was in England playing for Surrey, Arshad now matched the great Muttiah Muralitharan with 12 wickets at almost the same cost. Waqar Younis, with 11, again demonstrated that reports of his demise were an exaggeration.

For the Sri Lankans, the series provided little pleasure once the celebrations to mark their 100th Test passed and the cricket began in earnest. Even their enormous opening partnership of 335 between Marvan Atapattu and Jayasuriya at Kandy, the fifth-highest in all Tests, was ultimately robbed of relevance by the rain. They had to wait for the Singer Triangular Series that followed the Tests to settle the score, and did so to great effect. For Pakistan, however, the one-day tournament was disappointing. After winning their last three one-day tournaments, they now failed to win any of their four games against South Africa or the hosts.

PAKISTANI TOURING PARTY

Moin Khan (PIA) (*captain*), Inzamam-ul-Haq (*vice-captain*), Abdur Razzaq (PIA), Arshad Khan (Allied Bank), Azhar Mahmood (PIA), Imran Nazir (Pakistan Reserves), Mohammad Akram (Allied Bank), Mohammad Wasim (KRL), Mushtaq Ahmed (National Bank), Qaiser Abbas (Pakistan Reserves), Saeed Anwar (ADBP), Shabbir Ahmed (Pakistan Reserves), Shoaib Malik (Pakistan

Reserves), Waqar Younis (Redco), Wasim Akram (PIA), Younis Khan (Habib Bank), Yousuf Youhana (PIA).

Wasim Akram flew home after the Tests, while Mohammad Wasim and Qaiser Abbas returned to join Pakistan A's tour of Kenya. Shahid Afridi (Habib Bank) reinforced the party for the Singer Triangular Series.

Manager: Brigadier Mohammad Nasir Ahmed.   *Coach:* Javed Miandad.

PAKISTANI TOUR RESULTS

Test matches – Played 3: Won 2, Drawn 1.
One-day internationals – Played 4: Lost 4. *Losses* – Sri Lanka (2), South Africa (2).
Other non-first-class match – Abandoned v Sri Lankan Board XI.

TEST MATCH AVERAGES

SRI LANKA – BATTING

	T	*I*	*NO*	*R*	*HS*	*100s*	*50s*	*Avge*	*Ct/St*
M. S. Atapattu	3	5	1	380	207*	1	2	95.00	1
S. T. Jayasuriya	3	5	0	275	188	1	0	55.00	0
D. P. M. D. Jayawardene . .	3	5	0	161	77	0	2	32.20	2
A. Ranatunga.	3	5	0	135	65	0	2	27.00	2
M. Muralitharan	3	4	2	43	22	0	0	21.50	0
P. A. de Silva	3	5	0	66	30	0	0	13.20	0
W. P. U. J. C. Vaas	3	4	0	48	20	0	0	12.00	0
R. P. Arnold.	3	5	0	60	26	0	0	12.00	3
R. S. Kaluwitharana	2	4	0	23	9	0	0	5.75	2/1

Played in two Tests: D. N. T. Zoysa 17, 13 (1 ct). Played in one Test: H. D. P. K. Dharmasena 12*; C. R. D. Fernando 5*, 0 (3 ct); R. Herath 0, 0; K. R. Pushpakumara 0, 0* (1 ct); H. A. P. W. Jayawardene did not bat.

* *Signifies not out.*

BOWLING

	O	*M*	*R*	*W*	*BB*	*5W/i*	*Avge*
D. N. T. Zoysa	32	5	68	4	2-30	0	17.00
M. Muralitharan	114	28	306	12	5-115	1	25.50

Also bowled: R. P. Arnold 21–4–73–1; P. A. de Silva 3–1–4–0; C. R. D. Fernando 18.5–1–67–2; R. Herath 36–7–115–0; S. T. Jayasuriya 6–3–28–0; D. P. M. D. Jayawardene 5.2–1–34–2; K. R. Pushpakumara 29–6–116–1; A. Ranatunga 2–1–13–0; W. P. U. J. C. Vaas 71–17–154–0.

PAKISTAN – BATTING

	T	*I*	*NO*	*R*	*HS*	*100s*	*50s*	*Avge*	*Ct/St*
Wasim Akram	3	3	1	198	100	1	1	99.00	3
Younis Khan	3	3	1	171	116	1	0	85.50	5
Saeed Anwar	3	3	0	185	123	1	1	61.66	2
Inzamam-ul-Haq.	3	3	0	137	112	1	0	45.66	3
Moin Khan	3	3	1	61	47	0	0	30.50	6/1
Mohammad Wasim	2	3	0	67	30	0	0	22.33	6
Yousuf Youhana	3	3	0	54	41	0	0	18.00	1

Played in three Tests: Abdur Razzaq 0, 48; Arshad Khan 9*; Waqar Younis 4. Played in two Tests: Mushtaq Ahmed 2 (1 ct). Played in one Test: Azhar Mahmood 0; Imran Nazir did not bat.

* *Signifies not out.*

BOWLING

	O	M	R	W	BB	5W/i	Avge
Azhar Mahmood	26.3	7	84	4	2-36	0	21.00
Waqar Younis	75.1	12	244	11	4-40	0	22.18
Wasim Akram	95.3	23	234	9	5-45	1	26.00
Arshad Khan.	139	32	317	12	4-62	0	26.41
Abdur Razzaq	92	21	225	6	3-35	0	37.50

Also bowled: Mushtaq Ahmed 41–3–153–1.

Note: Matches in this section which were not first-class are signified by a dagger.

†At Police Park, Colombo, June 10, 11. Sri Lankan Board XI v Pakistanis. Abandoned.
The match was moved from Moratuwa after a bomb exploded in the area, but was washed out at the new venue.

SRI LANKA v PAKISTAN

First Test Match

At Sinhalese Sports Club, Colombo, June 14, 15, 16, 17. Pakistan won by five wickets. Toss: Sri Lanka. Test debut: C. R. D. Fernando.

Wasim Akram upstaged Sri Lanka's 100th-Test celebrations with a virtuoso performance. On the third day, he kept Pakistan in contention with a fighting innings of 78, adding 90 for the last wicket with Arshad Khan to restrict Sri Lanka's first-innings lead to seven. Next, he demolished the home side's second innings with his 25th five-wicket return in Tests, including his 400th Test wicket, and set Pakistan up for victory inside four days.

With the start being delayed until three o'clock because of the wet outfield, and bad light bringing an early close, the first day contained only 42 overs. Atapattu, promoted to vice-captain, took three hours to reach fifty, but responsible batting was essential after Waqar Younis removed Jayasuriya and Arnold in successive overs. Jayawardene, the former deputy, was also steadfast, batting three and three-quarter hours, but Waqar and Arshad worked away at the innings. When Wasim caught Muralitharan at mid-on to end the innings, Waqar in his 65th Test became the third Pakistan bowler to take 300 wickets, after Wasim himself and Imran Khan.

Pakistan were batting just before tea on the second day, and after losing five for 17 next morning to Muralitharan and Zoysa they were down to their last pair before lunch. Murali already had his 19th five-wicket haul and Sri Lanka were looking forward to extending their lead through the afternoon. Instead, Wasim and Arshad were still there at tea, having added 87; their eventual 90 together, of which Arshad's share was nine, set a tenth-wicket record for Tests between these countries. By his usual batting standards, Wasim's 78 off 204 balls was a circumspect affair, and the way he shielded his partner for three hours showed his commitment to the team effort. Nor was he finished with the Sri Lankans.

He began their second innings with a piece of history of his own: Arnold, caught at second slip, was his 400th Test wicket. He wrapped it up with a clatter of wickets, removing Vaas and Zoysa with successive balls and firing out debutant seamer Dilhara Fernando in his next over. It was Wasim at his wicked best, swinging the ball fast and late and hitting the seam. His other wicket was Ranatunga, himself making history as the first player to appear in his country's first and 100th Test matches. But that was Ranatunga's only mark. In the first innings, he was run out for six by Mushtaq Ahmed's direct hit; second time round, he made just seven. Bundled out for a shocking 123, the Sri Lankans left Pakistan more than four and a half sessions to make 131.

They looked to be cruising as Mohammad Wasim and Yousuf Youhana reached 50 on the stroke of tea. Immediately after the break, though, Muralitharan removed them both in three balls, and soon accounted for Inzamam-ul-Haq. Murali was turning the ball prodigiously and, with more runs to play with, would have proved a handful. However, Wasim, batting higher up the order than usual, was already settling in, and his presence calmed Pakistan's nerves as he guided them to victory.

Man of the Match: Wasim Akram.

Close of play: First day, Sri Lanka 115-3 (Atapattu 50*, Jayawardene 2*); Second day, Pakistan 130-3 (Saeed Anwar 56*, Moin Khan 31*); Third day, Sri Lanka 53-2 (Atapattu 33*, de Silva 10*).

Sri Lanka

M. S. Atapattu c Mohammad Wasim b Arshad Khan .	73	– c Saeed Anwar b Arshad Khan ... 40
*S. T. Jayasuriya c Younis Khan b Waqar Younis	26	– lbw b Waqar Younis 8
R. P. Arnold b Waqar Younis	4	– c Mohammad Wasim b Wasim Akram . 1
P. A. de Silva c Wasim Akram b Arshad Khan..	30	– c Inzamam-ul-Haq b Abdur Razzaq 21
D. P. M. D. Jayawardene c Moin Khan b Wasim Akram .	77	– c Mohammad Wasim b Arshad Khan . 1
A. Ranatunga run out	6	– c Saeed Anwar b Wasim Akram .. 7
†R. S. Kaluwitharana c Mohammad Wasim b Arshad Khan .	4	– c Younis Khan b Arshad Khan.... 6
W. P. U. J. C. Vaas b Mushtaq Ahmed	3	– c and b Wasim Akram......... 20
D. N. T. Zoysa st Moin Khan b Arshad Khan ..	17	– c Inzamam-ul-Haq b Wasim Akram 13
M. Muralitharan c Wasim Akram b Waqar Younis .	18	– (11) not out................. 3
C. R. D. Fernando not out	5	– (10) b Wasim Akram......... 0
B 5, l-b 1, n-b 4	10	L-b 1, w 1, n-b 1 3

1/52 (2) 2/56 (3) 3/109 (4) 4/176 (1)   273
5/187 (6) 6/193 (7) 7/206 (8)
8/245 (9) 9/257 (5) 10/273 (10)

1/14 (2) 2/25 (3) 3/67 (1)   123
4/71 (5) 5/73 (4) 6/82 (7)
7/88 (6) 8/120 (8)
9/120 (9) 10/123 (10)

Bowling: *First Innings*—Wasim Akram 20–6–55–1; Waqar Younis 14.2–0–50–3; Abdur Razzaq 18–1–58–0; Mushtaq Ahmed 14–1–42–1; Arshad Khan 31–8–62–4. *Second Innings*—Waqar Younis 9–3–21–1; Wasim Akram 15.3–1–45–5; Abdur Razzaq 14–6–23–1; Arshad Khan 22–8–30–3; Mushtaq Ahmed 1–0–3–0.

Pakistan

Saeed Anwar c Ranatunga b Muralitharan.....	56	– c Fernando b Zoysa.......... 6
Mohammad Wasim c Arnold b Fernando	8	– lbw b Muralitharan 30
Younis Khan c Fernando b Muralitharan.....	23	– (7) not out................. 32
Yousuf Youhana c Jayawardene b Muralitharan..	2	– (3) b Muralitharan 11
*†Moin Khan c Fernando b Zoysa..........	47	– (6) lbw b Zoysa 11
Inzamam-ul-Haq c Jayawardene b Zoysa......	12	– (4) c Arnold b Muralitharan 13
Abdur Razzaq run out................	0	
Wasim Akram b Fernando	78	– (5) not out............. 20
Waqar Younis c Zoysa b Muralitharan	4	
Mushtaq Ahmed c Arnold b Muralitharan.....	2	
Arshad Khan not out	9	
L-b 4, w 3, n-b 18	25	B 4, n-b 4............. 8

1/16 (2) 2/67 (3) 3/75 (4) 4/130 (1)   266
5/159 (6) 6/160 (7) 7/165 (5)
8/173 (9) 9/176 (10) 10/266 (8)

1/19 (1) 2/51 (3)   (5 wkts) 131
3/52 (2) 4/66 (4) 5/89 (6)

Bowling: *First Innings*—Vaas 29–7–52–0; Zoysa 19–4–30–2; de Silva 3–1–4–0; Fernando 15.5–1–53–2; Muralitharan 47–12–115–5; Jayawardene 2–1–2–0; Jayasuriya 4–3–6–0; Ranatunga 1–1–0–0. *Second Innings*—Vaas 8–3–20–0; Zoysa 13–1–38–2; Muralitharan 17–3–53–3; Fernando 3–0–14–0; Arnold 1–0–2–0.

Umpires: S. A. Bucknor (West Indies) and B. C. Cooray.
Referee: J. R. Reid (New Zealand).

SRI LANKA v PAKISTAN

Second Test Match

At Galle, June 21, 22, 23, 24. Pakistan won by an innings and 163 runs. Toss: Sri Lanka.

Still shaken after the First Test, the Sri Lankans were not ready for a rampant Pakistan display in the Second. Their first innings was a disaster, picked open by vintage fast bowling from Waqar Younis and parcelled up by a hat-trick from young all-rounder Abdur Razzaq. Four Pakistani batsmen then made hundreds and the tourists were on course for an unbeatable 2–0 series lead. Again, they won with a day to spare.

The battle was lost on the first day when Sri Lanka, after winning the toss, were shot out for 181. There was a distinct lack of application on the part of the batsmen, with too many going for their strokes early on. Apart from Jayawardene and Ranatunga, no one seemed to have the will to make a fight of it. These two forged a useful 116-run partnership for the fifth wicket after Waqar, with help from Wasim Akram, had reduced Sri Lanka to a groggy 47 for four. But just when Sri Lanka were on the recovery track at 163 for four, Ranatunga was run out for 51 in the

---

MOST HUNDREDS IN A TEST INNINGS

5	Australia (758-8 dec.) v West Indies at Kingston	1954-55
4	England (658-8 dec.) v Australia at Nottingham	1938
4	West Indies (631) v India at Delhi.............................	1948-49
4	Pakistan (652) v India at Faisalabad	1982-83
4	West Indies (550) v India at St John's	1982-83
4	**Pakistan (600-8 dec.) v Sri Lanka at Galle**...................	**2000 (SL)**

---

fourth over after tea, looking for a second on an overthrow. This opened the floodgates; the next five wickets went for 18. Razzaq, at 20 years 202 days, became the youngest bowler to claim a Test hat-trick – the first in Sri Lanka – when he sent back Kaluwitharana, Herath and Pushpakumara off the last three balls of his 11th over. He was only the second Pakistani to achieve a hat-trick; Wasim Akram had taken two, also against Sri Lanka, in consecutive Tests in the 1998-99 Asia Championship. Jayawardene once again battled with great flair in scoring 72 off 127 balls, but the scorecard made sorry reading. Only three batsmen reached double figures.

In stark contrast, four Pakistanis reached three figures. Saeed Anwar set the ball rolling with a quality innings of 123, his tenth Test century, which took 237 balls and included two sixes and 12 fours. But that was a quiet effort. Inzamam dismantled the Sri Lankan bowling with a ruthless attack that produced 18 fours in 112 from 163 balls. The four successive boundaries off Jayasuriya to raise his 11th Test hundred were breathtaking batsmanship. He and Anwar put on 105 for the fourth wicket.

Next in line was Younis Khan, who had made a hundred on debut against Sri Lanka three and a half months earlier at Rawalpindi. Following a poor series in the Caribbean against West Indies' pace attack, Younis found the Sri Lankan medium-fast bowlers more to his liking. He added 106 for the sixth wicket with Razzaq, and 120 for the seventh – a Pakistani record against Sri Lanka – with Wasim before he was out for 116 from 281 balls. Wasim was severe on the tiring bowlers, smashing six sixes and eight fours to reach his third Test century off just 86 balls. It was only the sixth instance of four or more batsmen making hundreds in the same Test innings, and Pakistan's 600 for eight was their highest total against Sri Lanka.

Trailing by 419, the Sri Lankan batsmen found the pressure and Pakistan's pace attack too much to cope with. Jayasuriya and de Silva again failed to provide a major innings, and it was left to Atapattu and Ranatunga to delay the inevitable. Atapattu batted four hours for 59, while Ranatunga's two-hour response was typically aggressive. He hit 13 fours and had faced 80 balls for his 65 when he was lbw to Wasim's in-swinging yorker. Waqar picked up four wickets with a mixture of out-swingers and in-dippers for match figures of seven for 79. Pakistan's only setback came when referee John Reid fined Arshad Khan 30 per cent of his match fee for persistent appealing. Asoka de Silva, the first Sri Lankan Test cricketer to umpire in a Test match, must have wished his debut had been less traumatic for his countrymen.

Man of the Match: Wasim Akram.

Close of play: First day, Pakistan 74-2 (Saeed Anwar 42*, Yousuf Youhana 0*); Second day, Pakistan 341-5 (Younis Khan 24*, Abdur Razzaq 0*); Third day, Sri Lanka 45-1 (Atapattu 17*, Arnold 4*).

Sri Lanka

M. S. Atapattu c Moin Khan b Waqar Younis ..	1	– c Moin Khan b Arshad Khan	59
*S. T. Jayasuriya b Wasim Akram	32	– c Inzamam-ul-Haq b Waqar Younis.	21
R. P. Arnold c Yousuf Youhana b Waqar Younis .	5	– lbw b Waqar Younis	26
P. A. de Silva c Moin Khan b Waqar Younis ..	4	– c Mohammad Wasim b Arshad Khan .	11
D. P. M. D. Jayawardene c Mohammad Wasim b Azhar Mahmood .	72	– lbw b Wasim Akram	9
A. Ranatunga run out	51	– lbw b Wasim Akram	65
†R. S. Kaluwitharana c Moin Khan b Abdur Razzaq .	4	– lbw b Waqar Younis	9
W. P. U. J. C. Vaas c Younis Khan b Azhar Mahmood .	5	– c sub (Imran Nazir) b Azhar Mahmood .	20
R. Herath lbw b Abdur Razzaq.............	0	– lbw b Azhar Mahmood	0
K. R. Pushpakumara lbw b Abdur Razzaq	0	– not out	0
M. Muralitharan not out	0	– b Waqar Younis	22
B 1, l-b 1, w 2, n-b 3	7	L-b 12, w 1, n-b 1	14
	181		**256**

1/13 (1) 2/23 (3) 3/43 (2) 4/47 (4)
5/163 (6) 6/173 (5) 7/177 (7)
8/177 (9) 9/177 (10) 10/181 (8)

1/33 (2) 2/91 (3) 3/123 (1)
4/130 (4) 5/156 (5) 6/187 (7)
7/230 (6) 8/234 (8)
9/234 (9) 10/256 (11)

Bowling: *First Innings*—Wasim Akram 13–3–40–1; Waqar Younis 13–2–39–3; Abdur Razzaq 12–2–35–3; Azhar Mahmood 16.3–5–36–2; Arshad Khan 10–0–29–0. *Second Innings*—Waqar Younis 19.1–7–40–4; Wasim Akram 22–7–53–2; Abdur Razzaq 15–2–44–0; Arshad Khan 24–9–59–2; Azhar Mahmood 10–2–48–2.

Pakistan

Saeed Anwar c Kaluwitharana b Arnold .	123	Abdur Razzaq b Muralitharan........	48
Mohammad Wasim c Ranatunga b Muralitharan .	29	Wasim Akram c Atapattu b Jayawardene .	100
Azhar Mahmood b Muralitharan	0	*†Moin Khan not out	3
Yousuf Youhana st Kaluwitharana b Muralitharan .	41	B 5, l-b 6, n-b 17	28
Inzamam-ul-Haq c Kaluwitharana b Pushpakumara .	112		
Younis Khan c Pushpakumara b Jayawardene .	116		(8 wkts dec.) **600**

1/71 (2) 2/72 (3)
3/161 (4) 4/266 (1)
5/340 (5) 6/446 (7)
7/566 (6) 8/600 (8)

Waqar Younis and Arshad Khan did not bat.

Bowling: Vaas 34–7–82–0; Pushpakumara 29–6–116–1; Herath 36–7–115–0; Muralitharan 50–13–138–4; Arnold 20–4–71–1; Jayasuriya 2–0–22–0; Jayawardene 3.2–0–32–2; Ranatunga 1–0–13–0.

Umpires: R. B. Tiffin (Zimbabwe) and E. A. R. de Silva.
Referee: J. R. Reid (New Zealand).

SRI LANKA v PAKISTAN

Third Test Match

At Kandy, June 28, 29, 30, July 1, 2. Drawn. Toss: Sri Lanka. Test debut: H. A. P. W. Jayawardene.

Just when Sri Lanka looked to have the measure of the Pakistan bowling, running up their highest total at home against them, foul weather allowed only restricted play on the first three days and washed out the last two. In the 11 hours and four minutes of play that were possible, nearly eight were occupied by the opening pair, Atapattu and Jayasuriya, who put together Sri Lanka's highest first-wicket partnership in Test cricket, 335, the fifth-best start in Test cricket and the first over 300 since Australia's Mark Taylor and Geoff Marsh put on 329 against England at Nottingham in 1989. It was also Sri Lanka's highest for any wicket against Pakistan.

For 114 overs, Sri Lanka's captain and vice-captain blunted and then mastered the bowling with an approach that had been lacking previously in the series. Jayasuriya certainly rode his luck; he was missed four times between 50 and 140 as he marked his 50th Test with his first hundred as captain. His eventual 188, containing two sixes and 17 fours, was the highest innings by a Sri Lankan captain and took him past 3,000 runs.

Atapattu batted in copybook fashion for his third Test double-hundred, and his second at Kandy. He came in on the second evening unbeaten on 199, and in the 15 minutes of play that was possible late on the third day he moved on to 207, made from 457 balls with a six and 19 fours. While Atapattu stood rocklike at one end, Pakistan had their little moments of success at the other, when Abdur Razzaq and off-spinner Arshad Khan picked up four middle-order wickets for 33.

Man of the Series: Wasim Akram.

Close of play: First day, Sri Lanka 140-0 (Atapattu 50*, Jayasuriya 82*); Second day, Sri Lanka 449-5 (Atapattu 199*, Dharmasena 4*); Third day, Sri Lanka 467-5 (Atapattu 207*, Dharmasena 12*); Fourth day, No play.

Sri Lanka

M. S. Atapattu not out 207	A. Ranatunga c Mushtaq Ahmed		
*S. T. Jayasuriya c Younis Khan		b Arshad Khan .	6
b Abdur Razzaq . 188	H. D. P. K. Dharmasena not out		12
R. P. Arnold c Moin Khan			
b Abdur Razzaq . 24	B 14, l-b 8, w 1, n-b 5.		28
P. A. de Silva c Younis Khan			
b Arshad Khan . 0	1/335 (2) 2/401 (3) 3/402 (4) (5 wkts) 467		
D. P. M. D. Jayawardene b Arshad Khan . 2	4/412 (5) 5/434 (6)		

†H. A. P. W. Jayawardene, W. P. U. J. C. Vaas, D. N. T. Zoysa and M. Muralitharan did not bat.

Bowling: Wasim Akram 25–6–41–0; Waqar Younis 19.4–0–94–0; Arshad Khan 52–7–137–3; Abdur Razzaq 33–10–65–2; Mushtaq Ahmed 26–2–108–0.

Pakistan

Saeed Anwar, Imran Nazir, Yousuf Youhana, Inzamam-ul-Haq, Younis Khan, Abdur Razzaq, Wasim Akram, *†Moin Khan, Waqar Younis, Mushtaq Ahmed and Arshad Khan.

Umpires: S. A. Bucknor (West Indies) and P. T. Manuel.
Referee: J. R. Reid (New Zealand).

Pakistan's matches v Sri Lanka and South Africa in the Singer Triangular Series (July 5–12) may be found in that section.

THE SOUTH AFRICANS IN SRI LANKA, 2000

By NEIL MANTHORP

Hansie Cronje and South Africa's King Commission into match-fixing did not hang heavily on the minds of the country's cricketers when they departed for Sri Lanka on June 30, even though five of the nine players who testified at the inquiry were on the plane to Colombo. As soon as they arrived, however, many began to realise just how much emotion they had suppressed. Their former captain was everywhere and nowhere, his ghost haunting the senior players and confusing the new faces in the squad.

Shaun Pollock was diplomacy personified, accepting his responsibility as captain to speak honestly and answer questions whenever they were asked. At a packed news conference on the second day, he admitted there were many disillusioned cricket followers in South Africa whose trust and respect had to be regained. He promised that his new-look squad would never contemplate communication, let alone dealings, with bookmakers and that they would give "110 per cent effort" in every game they played.

It took three weeks at least for the players to settle, and to come to terms with the realisation that – for the first time in their careers – Cronje was not on tour. And would not be again. Jonty Rhodes admitted to looking for him at every practice during the first ten days, and while many were still smarting over his betrayal of them as a friend, they none the less missed him as both player and disciplinarian. The team stayed close to their hotel when they were not playing, and they were understandably reserved, waiting to see how they were regarded.

The tour – which after the Sri Lankan leg was to incorporate the world's first indoor one-day internationals, in Melbourne's new Colonial Stadium, followed by a triangular tournament with New Zealand and Pakistan in Singapore – was seen as a time for rebuilding the social structures of the squad, as well as the team on the field. Without Allan Donald, honouring his last contract with Warwickshire, there were few of the old guard alongside Pollock and vice-captain Mark Boucher. Herschelle Gibbs's last-minute removal from the tour party, as a result of his admissions to the King Commission, resulted in a place for Boeta Dippenaar, and there were opportunities for Andrew Hall, Neil McKenzie, David Terbrugge and Roger Telemachus to establish their credentials.

Without their best player of spin, Cronje, to counter the expected troop of spinners led by Muttiah Muralitharan, many expected Pollock's team to struggle in Sri Lanka. The squad duly assembled a week before departure in Durban to practise on deliberately under-prepared pitches. The topic of Cronje's demise was raised in team meetings, and a determination to put it behind them prevailed. When the time came, however, the team looked disorientated, and initially could not get to grips with a Sri Lankan side brimming with confidence. Pollock began his reign as Test captain with an innings defeat, Sri Lanka's first victory in six Tests between the two nations. That he and his team fought back to square the series spoke volumes for their character.

Sri Lanka won all three of their encounters in the one-day Singer Triangular Series that preceded the Tests, and South Africa's two wins over Pakistan, who had just beaten Sri Lanka 2–0 in a three-Test series, were a minor comfort. Muralitharan took five South African wickets in the one-day final; he claimed 13 more in the First Test at Galle, and finished the series with 26, equalling his own Sri Lankan record set in Pakistan five months earlier. Captain Sanath Jayasuriya and Mahela Jayawardene shared the glory of the innings win at Galle, with centuries that underpinned Sri Lanka's highest total against South Africa, and were the leading run-scorers in the series. But Lance Klusener was close behind. His daring unbeaten hundred in the Second Test at Kandy saved South Africa from a disastrous start and eventually enabled them to claim a tense seven-run win. In the final game at Colombo, he scored another 95 not out, but rain and determined play from both sides meant that honours finished even. Pollock flung himself into the task of leading the attack and was rewarded with 11 wickets in the series, while slow left-armer Nicky Boje concluded the trip with a career-best five for 62. The series ended with celebrations of Arjuna Ranatunga's 18-year Test career; he completed his 93rd and final game with 5,105 runs at 35.69.

SOUTH AFRICAN TOURING PARTY

S. M. Pollock (KwaZulu-Natal) (*captain*), M. V. Boucher (Border) (*vice-captain*), P. R. Adams (Western Province), N. Boje (Free State), D. J. Cullinan (Gauteng), H. H. Dippenaar (Free State), A. J. Hall (Gauteng), M. Hayward (Eastern Province), J. H. Kallis (Western Province), G. Kirsten (Western Province), L. Klusener (KwaZulu-Natal), N. D. McKenzie (Northerns), M. Ntini (Border), J. N. Rhodes (KwaZulu-Natal), R. Telemachus (Western Province), D. J. Terbrugge (Gauteng).

Manager: Goolam Rajah. *Coach:* G. X. Ford.

Dippenaar replaced H. H. Gibbs (Western Province), who was originally named but withdrawn from the party. R. J. Peterson (Eastern Province) joined the party as cover for Adams. D. Russell managed the tour until Goolam Rajah arrived after an operation.

SOUTH AFRICAN TOUR RESULTS

Test matches – Played 3: Won 1, Lost 1, Drawn 1.
One-day internationals – Played 5: Won 2, Lost 3. *Wins* – Pakistan (2). *Losses* – Sri Lanka (3).
Other non-first-class matches – Played 3: Won 1, Drawn 2. *Win* – Sri Lankan Board XI.
Draws – Sri Lankan Board XI, Sri Lankan Board President's XI.

TEST MATCH AVERAGES

SRI LANKA – BATTING

	T	I	NO	R	HS	100s	50s	Avge	Ct
D. P. M. D. Jayawardene . .	3	5	1	321	167	2	0	80.25	4
S. T. Jayasuriya	3	5	0	278	148	1	1	55.60	1
A. Ranatunga	3	5	1	197	88	0	2	49.25	3
M. S. Atapattu	3	5	0	184	120	1	1	36.80	4
R. P. Arnold.	3	4	0	101	40	0	0	25.25	5
U. D. U. Chandana	3	4	1	57	32	0	0	19.00	2
W. P. U. J. C. Vaas	3	4	0	68	54	0	1	17.00	0
K. Sangakkara	3	5	0	83	25	0	0	16.60	9
D. N. T. Zoysa	2	3	1	15	10	0	0	7.50	0
H. D. P. K. Dharmasena. . .	2	3	0	8	4	0	0	2.66	1
M. Muralitharan	3	4	2	2	2*	0	0	1.00	1

Played in one Test: P. A. de Silva 2, 41 (1 ct); P. D. R. L. Perera 10.

* *Signifies not out.*

BOWLING

	O	M	R	W	BB	5W/i	Avge
M. Muralitharan	227.4	52	480	26	7-84	3	18.46
S. T. Jayasuriya	48	5	135	5	2-45	0	27.00
W. P. U. J. C. Vaas	87	30	169	6	4-85	0	28.16
U. D. U. Chandana	82.1	11	262	9	2-21	0	29.11
H. D. P. K. Dharmasena. . .	71	11	212	5	3-58	0	42.40

Also bowled: R. P. Arnold 6.1–1–11–0; P. A. de Silva 29.5–9–65–1; P. D. R. L. Perera 20–3–73–2; D. N. T. Zoysa 20–5–56–2.

SOUTH AFRICA – BATTING

	T	I	NO	R	HS	100s	50s	Avge	Ct/St
L. Klusener	3	6	2	275	118*	1	1	68.75	2
J. N. Rhodes	3	6	1	195	63*	0	2	39.00	4
D. J. Cullinan	3	6	1	175	114*	1	0	35.00	3
J. H. Kallis	3	6	0	191	87	0	1	31.83	1
N. Boje	3	6	1	124	35	0	0	24.80	2
G. Kirsten	3	6	0	131	55	0	1	21.83	3
M. V. Boucher	3	6	0	111	60	0	1	18.50	6/1
S. M. Pollock	3	6	0	87	33	0	0	14.50	1
N. D. McKenzie	3	6	0	54	25	0	0	9.00	2
P. R. Adams	3	6	1	44	15	0	0	8.80	0
M. Hayward	2	4	1	16	13	0	0	5.33	1

Played in one Test: M. Ntini 8, 0.

* *Signifies not out.*

BOWLING

	O	M	R	W	BB	5W/i	Avge
S. M. Pollock	94	30	247	11	3-40	0	22.45
M. Hayward	56	10	171	7	2-15	0	24.42
N. Boje	101.1	20	273	10	5-62	1	27.30
J. H. Kallis	53.4	17	136	4	2-18	0	34.00
L. Klusener	60.1	15	149	3	2-34	0	49.66
P. R. Adams	78	11	326	4	3-184	0	81.50

Also bowled: D. J. Cullinan 4–0–17–1; M. Ntini 19–1–73–1.

Note: Matches in this section which were not first-class are signified by a dagger.

†At Moratuwa, July 4. South Africans won by six runs. Toss: Sri Lankan Board XI. South Africans 234 for seven (50 overs) (J. H. Kallis 56, J. N. Rhodes 46, M. V. Boucher 30); Sri Lankan Board XI 228 for nine (50 overs) (D. A. Gunawardene 53, K. E. A. Upashantha 63 not out, Extras 30).
   Upashantha's 48-ball innings contained five sixes and two fours.

South Africa's matches v Sri Lanka and Pakistan in the Singer Triangular Series (July 6–14) may be found in that section.

†At P. Saravanamuttu Stadium, Colombo, July 16, 17. Drawn. Toss: Sri Lankan Board XI. South Africans 441 for seven dec. (M. V. Boucher 75, N. D. McKenzie 181, L. Klusener 36, S. M. Pollock 65, Extras 30; D. Hettiarachchi three for 88) and 82 for three dec.; Sri Lankan Board XI 109 (K. Weeraratne 38) and 74 for no wkt (D. A. Gunawardene 40 not out).

SRI LANKA v SOUTH AFRICA

First Test Match

At Galle, July 20, 21, 22, 23. Sri Lanka won by an innings and 15 runs. Toss: Sri Lanka. Test debuts: K. Sangakkara; N. D. McKenzie.
   Sri Lanka's victory in four days was a triumph of planning and execution, with the match following a course prescribed and predicted from three days before it began. For match-winner Muralitharan, his second-best Test analysis of 13 for 171 provided further evidence that he was the complete off-spinner, the ultimate attacking bowler. For South Africa, it was like being trapped

in a nightmare. Everything pointed towards a contest between Muralitharan and the touring batsmen after his domination of them in the preceding Singer Triangular Series. Not one South African had felt comfortable against him; none even pretended to. Consequently, no one was surprised that the match started on a dry, cracked pitch that might have been ready for play two days earlier.

In such conditions, a captain's most important job can be to win the toss and bat. But Jayasuriya accomplished much more. He seized control on the first morning with an innings of such brutality and speed that Pollock, in his first Test as captain, had neither time nor inclination to consider a contingency plan. Before the match was even warm, the left-handed Jayasuriya upper-cut him high over gully for a one-bounce four that crashed into a van selling chicken snacks. Pollock looked more bewildered than offended. Jayasuriya slashed again, with the same result, and so began a game of chicken that Pollock was to lose emphatically.

The more Jayasuriya went over the top, the more Pollock kept his field up, intent on not being the first to give way. Kallis and Ntini suffered just as much, if not worse, forcing Pollock to bring on spinner Adams after 80 minutes of play. Jayasuriya stroked, clipped and thumped his first three balls to the boundary, and a sense of desperation settled on the fielding side.

At lunch, Sri Lanka were 145 without loss; Jayasuriya had missed, by four runs, becoming the fifth player to score a century before lunch on the first day of a Test. By the time he heaved Adams to deep mid-wicket, he had hit 24 fours and a six in 148 from 156 balls; the scoreboard was changing to 211 for two. He and Atapattu had put on 193 in 44 overs for the first wicket, Sri Lanka's highest partnership against South Africa. Nor was the visitors' ordeal over. Jayasuriya's replacement, Jayawardene, displayed marvellous technical skills, confirming his reputation as the future of Sri Lankan batting with 167 in five and a half hours. He never had to wait longer than six balls for a bad one, and finished with 22 fours and two sixes. He and Vaas put on 117 for the eighth wicket, a Sri Lankan record against all-comers, helping them towards the first 500-run total in Tests between these sides.

Then it was Murali's turn. Maintaining complete control over the degree of spin of his stock off-break, revelling in both his "mystery ball", which turned the other way, and a top-spinner that darted towards the knees of the batsman, he reduced batting to a lottery. Cullinan played with immense skill to remain unbeaten with 114 after four and a half hours, yet admitted: "I could have been out three or four times. He's unique." On occasions, Muralitharan almost toyed with the batsmen as he gleefully tossed high, looping deliveries wide and short of off stump, teasing them into stepping back to cut. Rhodes and Boucher were both bowled, and embarrassed, when the ball spun back prodigiously.

BOWLERS DISMISSING ALL 11 BATSMEN IN A TEST

J. C. Laker	19-90	E v A	Manchester	1956
S. Venkataraghavan	12-152	I v NZ	Delhi	1964-65
G. Dymock	12-166	A v I	Kanpur	1979-80
Abdul Qadir	13-101	P v E	Lahore	1987-88
Waqar Younis	12-130	P v NZ	Faisalabad	1990-91
M. Muralitharan	**13-171**	**SL v SA**	**Galle**	**2000 (SL)**

Research: M. L. Fernando

When South Africa followed on, 284 behind, leg-spinner Chandana had the temerity to take two of the first three wickets to fall. But Murali claimed the last seven to become only the sixth bowler in Tests to dismiss all 11 opposing batsmen. When he achieved his career-best 16 for 220 against England at The Oval in 1998, Alec Stewart's wicket had evaded him.

Pollock said afterwards that, with hindsight, he should have defended against Jayasuriya's onslaught much earlier, but always believed the edge was coming. The Sri Lankan captain admitted it was impossible to plan an innings such as his. And, in a delightful moment of understatement, he summarised his side's success: "Murali bowled very well and everything else just fell into place."

Man of the Match: M. Muralitharan.

Close of play: First day, Sri Lanka 341-5 (Jayawardene 78*, Dharmasena 4*); Second day, South Africa 81-2 (Kallis 27*, Cullinan 27*); Third day, South Africa 112-2 (Kallis 25*).

Sri Lanka

M. S. Atapattu c Boje b Ntini	54	W. P. U. J. C. Vaas b Pollock	54
*S. T. Jayasuriya c McKenzie b Adams	148	D. N. T. Zoysa c and b Cullinan	10
R. P. Arnold c Boucher b Adams	5	M. Muralitharan not out	2
D. P. M. D. Jayawardene c Boucher b Pollock	167	B 15, l-b 16, n-b 3	34
†K. Sangakkara lbw b Boje	23		
A. Ranatunga c Pollock b Adams	13	1/193 (1) 2/211 (2) 3/216 (3)	522
H. D. P. K. Dharmasena c Klusener b Pollock	4	4/297 (5) 5/318 (6) 6/341 (7) 7/365 (8) 8/482 (4)	
U. D. U. Chandana c Cullinan b Kallis	8	9/500 (10) 10/522 (9)	

Bowling: Pollock 30.4–8–73–3; Kallis 17–7–41–1; Ntini 19–1–73–1; Adams 45–6–184–3; Klusener 15–4–38–0; Boje 22–2–72–1; Cullinan 2–0–10–1.

South Africa

G. Kirsten c Sangakkara b Muralitharan	12	– run out	55
N. D. McKenzie b Muralitharan	11	– c Ranatunga b Chandana	25
J. H. Kallis c Arnold b Muralitharan	29	– c Muralitharan b Chandana	40
D. J. Cullinan not out	114	– c Arnold b Muralitharan	12
J. N. Rhodes b Muralitharan	12	– not out	63
L. Klusener c Chandana b Dharmasena	19	– c Sangakkara b Muralitharan	4
†M. V. Boucher b Muralitharan	0	– lbw b Muralitharan	7
*S. M. Pollock c Dharmasena b Muralitharan	4	– c Arnold b Muralitharan	12
N. Boje c Atapattu b Jayasuriya	12	– lbw b Muralitharan	35
P. R. Adams c Atapattu b Chandana	4	– b Muralitharan	2
M. Ntini c Ranatunga b Chandana	8	– b Muralitharan	0
B 2, l-b 1, n-b 10	13	B 3, l-b 5, n-b 6	14

1/25 (2) 2/30 (1) 3/86 (4) 4/119 (5)   238   1/58 (2) 2/112 (1) 3/139 (3)   269
5/162 (6) 6/168 (7) 7/198 (8)   4/141 (4) 5/153 (6) 6/163 (7)
8/213 (9) 9/223 (10) 10/238 (11)   7/193 (8) 8/263 (9)
     9/269 (10) 10/269 (11)

Bowling: *First Innings*—Vaas 12–6–16–0; Zoysa 4–1–12–0; Dharmasena 25–5–70–1; Muralitharan 41–8–87–6; Chandana 14–3–46–2; Jayasuriya 3–0–4–1. *Second Innings*—Vaas 7–2–18–0; Zoysa 5–2–11–0; Dharmasena 10–1–37–0; Muralitharan 35–5–84–7; Chandana 29–6–88–2; Jayasuriya 5–0–21–0; Arnold 1–0–2–0.

Umpires: D. J. Harper (Australia) and P. T. Manuel.
Referee: B. F. Hastings (New Zealand).

†At Moratuwa, July 26, 27. Drawn. Toss: Sri Lankan Board President's XI. Sri Lankan Board President's XI 135 (T. M. Dilshan 37; M. Hayward five for 32) and 141 for six (R. S. Kaluwitharana 32, T. M. Dilshan 53 not out); South Africans 302 for five dec. (G. Kirsten 53, N. D. McKenzie 75, H. H. Dippenaar 60, D. J. Cullinan 66; D. Hettiarachchi three for 73).

SRI LANKA v SOUTH AFRICA

Second Test Match

At Kandy, July 30, 31, August 1, 2. South Africa won by seven runs. Toss: Sri Lanka.

South Africa avenged their innings defeat at Galle with a narrow victory in a match that was compulsive viewing from first ball to last, attracting larger crowds each day as it neared its climax. They came to see Sri Lanka clinch the series; instead South Africa delivered a knockout blow on the fourth day to square the series.

Winning the toss meant a gamble, for the pitch was a strange hybrid. Prepared as a dry turner, it had then sweated profusely under two days under heavy, tarpaulin covers while it rained incessantly. Jayasuriya unsurprisingly let his bowlers loose on it and South Africa crashed to 34 for five in 19 overs. The recovery was effected by Klusener and Boucher, who opted for a thrilling counter-attack rather than attritional repair work. Hitting the spinners over the top, and thrashing anything vaguely short, they put on 124, a sixth-wicket record for South Africa against Sri Lanka, before Klusener misjudged Muralitharan's agility off his own bowling and Boucher was run out. However, Klusener used his anger at himself constructively, and forged on towards his third Test hundred, squeezing 80 runs from the last two wickets and encouraging rare discipline from Adams and Hayward, who had replaced Ntini. The total slipped past 250 before Klusener was left unbeaten on 118, containing 13 fours and two sixes in 220 balls, an innings he described as his best yet.

In reply, Atapattu produced an exhibition of such impeccable, straight-bat technique that it resembled illustrations from a coaching manual. Together with the pugnacious Ranatunga, in his penultimate Test, he took the score to 286 for four, a lead of 33: Atapattu had a century, Ranatunga a half-century. But a desperate Pollock, bowling with skill and passion, instigated a collapse worth six for 22 in seven overs. Ranatunga had more than one reason to look watery-eyed at umpire Harper when lbw to a rising delivery that struck him on the box.

South Africa lost three wickets working off the arrears, but for almost four hours Kallis survived on a pitch that, by the third day, was offering exotic and quirky bounce. His 87 contained long periods of defence, mainly on the back foot reading the spinners off the pitch, but there were also moments of aggression when he used his feet and charged the bowling. Even so, South Africa's lead was only 137 with two wickets left when they resumed on the fourth morning. Boje, a No. 9 with four first-class hundreds, coaxed another partnership out of Adams, but ultimately Sri Lanka had more than five sessions to make 177.

The start was sensational: Atapattu and Jayasuriya were both lbw first ball, and at lunch Sri Lanka were 41 for four, with Ranatunga already on his way to a 36-ball 50 that made him the second Sri Lankan to pass 5,000 Test runs. No matter what Pollock tried, no matter how defensive his field-settings or the bowling, Ranatunga found the middle of the bat and the gaps in the field. Arnold dropped anchor and admired his former captain during a stand of 109 that seemed to be winning the match. Then he lost concentration and was lbw to Boje for 40. Ranatunga's innings, with 15 fours, ended just before tea when Rhodes snapped up a reflex catch at short leg off the full face of the bat. Suddenly South Africa sniffed victory, although Sri Lanka then needed only 16 with three wickets still in hand.

Klusener, bowling slow, awkward cutters and "grippers" off just five paces, yorked Chandana first ball after the break, and five overs later Vaas, jittery and nervous, was run out by the injured Zoysa's runner, Jayasuriya, who had gone out himself to avoid exactly this possibility. Muralitharan was then unkindly given out caught behind off his first ball, which summed up an unhappy match for umpires Harper and Gamini Silva, standing in his first Test.

Men of the Match: L. Klusener and A. Ranatunga.

Close of play: First day, Sri Lanka 15-0 (Atapattu 1*, Jayasuriya 10*); Second day, Sri Lanka 260-4 (Atapattu 107*, Ranatunga 34*); Third day, South Africa 192-8 (Boje 0*, Adams 6*).

South Africa

G. Kirsten lbw b Vaas.................	0	– b Dharmasena 13
N. D. McKenzie c Jayawardene b Zoysa......	0	– b Zoysa 1
I H. Kallis lbw b Muralitharan.............	16	– b Muralitharan 87
D. J. Cullinan b Dharmasena	2	– b Muralitharan 6
J. N. Rhodes b Dharmasena	12	– c Sangakkara b Jayasuriya 33
L. Klusener not out	118	– c Sangakkara b Jayasuriya 4
†M. V. Boucher run out.................	60	– c Atapattu b Muralitharan....... 15
*S. M. Pollock c Jayawardene b Chandana	5	– c Sangakkara b Vaas 20
N. Boje lbw b Chandana	0	– c sub (T. M. Dilshan) b Chandana 27
P. R. Adams c Jayawardene b Dharmasena	6	– not out 14
M. Hayward b Muralitharan	13	– lbw b Chandana 0
B 9, l-b 6, n-b 6	21	B 7, l-b 1, n-b 3........ 11

253   231

1/0 (1) 2/4 (2) 3/16 (4) 4/34 (5)   1/10 (2) 2/37 (1) 3/50 (4)
5/34 (3) 6/158 (7) 7/173 (8)   4/121 (5) 5/128 (6) 6/153 (7)
8/173 (9) 9/210 (10) 10/253 (11)   7/186 (8) 8/186 (3)
                                 9/231 (9) 10/231 (11)

Bowling: First Innings—Vaas 8–5–11–1; Zoysa 6–2–16–1; Dharmasena 20–3–58–3; Muralitharan 30.5–3–95–2; Chandana 20–2–58–2. *Second Innings*—Vaas 14–6–17–1; Zoysa 5–0–17–1; Dharmasena 16–2–47–1; Muralitharan 36–8–76–3; Chandana 9.5–0–21–2; Jayasuriya 13–1–45–2.

Sri Lanka

M. S. Atapattu lbw b Pollock	120	– lbw b Pollock	0
*S. T. Jayasuriya c Kallis b Hayward	28	– lbw b Hayward	0
R. P. Arnold run out	28	– lbw b Boje	40
D. P. M. D. Jayawardene c Cullinan b Boje	18	– c Boucher b Hayward	1
†K. Sangakkara run out	24	– c Hayward b Kallis	5
A. Ranatunga lbw b Hayward	54	– c Rhodes b Boje	88
H. D. P. K. Dharmasena c Boucher b Pollock	3	– c Rhodes b Klusener	1
W. P. U. J. C. Vaas c Rhodes b Pollock	4	– (9) run out	5
U. D. U. Chandana not out	1	– (8) b Klusener	16
D. N. T. Zoysa b Kallis	3	– not out	2
M. Muralitharan b Kallis	0	– c Boucher b Boje	0
B 6, l-b 12, n-b 7	25	B 1, l-b 6, w 2, n-b 2	11

1/53 (2) 2/109 (3) 3/142 (4) 4/182 (5)	308	1/0 (1) 2/5 (2) 3/9 (4)	169
5/286 (1) 6/296 (6) 7/300 (7)		4/21 (5) 5/130 (3) 6/133 (7)	
8/303 (8) 9/308 (10) 10/308 (11)		7/161 (6) 8/161 (8)	
		9/169 (9) 10/169 (11)	

Bowling: *First Innings*—Pollock 24–5–83–3; Hayward 22–6–67–2; Kallis 11.4–4–18–2; Boje 15–2–50–1; Klusener 11–2–21–0; Adams 14–1–44–0; Cullinan 2–0–7–0. *Second Innings*—Pollock 11–4–38–1; Hayward 5–1–15–2; Kallis 8–1–25–1; Adams 3–1–26–0; Klusener 13–3–34–2; Boje 10.1–4–24–3.

Umpires: D. J. Harper (Australia) and G. Silva.
Referee: B. F. Hastings (New Zealand).

SRI LANKA v SOUTH AFRICA

Third Test Match

At Sinhalese Sports Club, Colombo, August 6, 7, 8, 9, 10. Drawn. Toss: Sri Lanka.

Ranatunga's farewell to international cricket after 93 Tests loomed over the deciding match, despite both teams entertaining genuine hopes of a series win. Sri Lanka's former captain, an 18-year-old schoolboy when he played in their inaugural Test, against England in February 1982, had announced his pending retirement during the First Test, and emotions had been building up ever since. The selectors even recalled de Silva, many believing it inconceivable that the two great men of Sri Lankan cricket could be separated for Ranatunga's last game. The only other change was Zoysa's replacement by another left-arm seamer, Perera, returning to Test cricket after more than a year out with back problems.

Many of SSC's most loyal servants, Ranatunga's friends and colleagues, formed a guard of honour as he trotted on to the field after Jayasuriya chose to bowl under grey skies at a venue well known for assisting seamers. Perera struck with his first ball, helped by McKenzie's slash at a wide half-volley, and the dismissal set off a top-order quake. South Africa crumbled to 117 for six before Klusener again came to the rescue with an unbeaten 95 that was two-sided in character but packed with power and craft. He blasted 50 from 64 balls before a sensational rainstorm ended play at 194 for seven. Next morning saw him push and prod for another 111 deliveries, getting South Africa up to 279 before he ran out of partners when Hayward spooned a full toss to square leg.

Sri Lanka's reply was dominated by left-arm spinner Boje, who displayed every facet of his attacking armoury in his second five-wicket haul in six months – only the third by a South African slow bowler since their return to Test cricket in 1992. Meanwhile, Adams, the only other spinner to achieve one, was not trusted with a single over after his hammering in the first two Tests. Chandana's selective hitting reduced South Africa's lead to just 21, with the result that their second innings was governed by caution. Kirsten's 40 occupied three and a quarter hours, while Rhodes took 151 balls over 54; Muralitharan made South Africa battle for every run. Klusener, Boucher and Boje frustrated Sri Lanka every time they sensed a breakthrough, and finally Pollock set a target of 263 in two sessions, totalling 68 overs.

Adams, given a bowl at last, dismissed Jayasuriya in his first over to cut the run-chase to 37 for three, but his wild celebrations were sadly premature, for Jayawardene, de Silva and Ranatunga all went after him. De Silva displayed brief touches of silk until departing an hour before the final curtain, whereupon Ranatunga entered to huge applause from a crowd given free entrance for this moment. After defending a couple of deliveries, he launched several more down the ground in defiance of Father Time, chuckled with the bowlers and walked his singles as if he owned the turf. In fact, he looked just as he had for the past decade and more.

Jayawardene kept the players on the field virtually until the final over to complete his fourth Test century, but by then all attention had turned to the marching band, the stage and the fanfare being prepared to bid farewell to the hero. Jayasuriya was not alone in wiping away tears as he applauded the man from whom he inherited the leadership of Sri Lankan cricket.

Man of the Match: M. Muralitharan.   *Man of the Series:* L. Klusener.

Close of play: First day, South Africa 194-7 (Klusener 50*, Boje 2*); Second day, Sri Lanka 138-4 (Jayawardene 4*, Vaas 1*); Third day, South Africa 27-0 (Kirsten 18*, McKenzie 6*); Fourth day, South Africa 157-5 (Klusener 27*, Boucher 2*).

South Africa

G. Kirsten c Ranatunga b Perera	11	– lbw b Muralitharan	40
N. D. McKenzie c Arnold b Perera	0	– run out	17
J. H. Kallis c Sangakkara b Vaas	19	– b de Silva	0
D. J. Cullinan c Atapattu b Vaas	38	– c Arnold b Muralitharan	3
J. N. Rhodes b Muralitharan	21	– c Jayawardene b Muralitharan	54
L. Klusener not out	95	– c Sangakkara b Muralitharan	35
†M. V. Boucher c Chandana b Vaas	4	– b Muralitharan	25
*S. M. Pollock b Muralitharan	33	– c Sangakkara b Jayasuriya	13
N. Boje c Sangakkara b Vaas	21	– not out	29
P. R. Adams lbw b Muralitharan	15	– c b Jayasuriya	3
M. Hayward c de Silva b Chandana	0	– not out	3
B 2, l-b 8, n-b 12	22	L-b 4, n-b 15	19

1/0 (2) 2/23 (3) 3/57 (1) 4/89 (5)   279   1/50 (2) 2/50 (3)   (9 wkts dec.) 241
5/103 (4) 6/117 (7) 7/186 (8)   3/59 (4) 4/107 (1)
8/240 (9) 9/278 (10) 10/279 (11)   5/152 (5) 6/169 (6)
                                                       7/197 (7) 8/220 (8) 9/236 (10)

Bowling: *First Innings*—Vaas 36–9–85–4; Perera 18–3–60–2; de Silva 5–2–16–0; Muralitharan 39–14–70–3; Chandana 4.2–0–16–1; Jayasuriya 3–0–9–0; Arnold 3–1–3–0. *Second Innings*—Vaas 10–2–22–0; Perera 2–0–13–0; Arnold 2.1–0–6–0; de Silva 24.5–7–49–1; Muralitharan 45.5–14–68–5; Jayasuriya 24–4–56–2; Chandana 5–0–23–0.

Sri Lanka

M. S. Atapattu b Hayward	10	– c Kirsten b Pollock	0
*S. T. Jayasuriya c Kirsten b Boje	85	– b Adams	17
R. P. Arnold c Klusener b Boje	28		
P. A. de Silva st Boucher b Boje	2	– (5) lbw b Klusener	41
D. P. M. D. Jayawardene c Kirsten b Boje	34	– (4) not out	101
W. P. U. J. C. Vaas lbw b Pollock	5		
A. Ranatunga b Boje	14	– (6) not out	28
†K. Sangakkara c Boucher b Hayward	25	– (3) c Rhodes b Hayward	6
U. D. U. Chandana c McKenzie b Pollock	32		
P. D. R. L. Perera c Boje b Pollock	10		
M. Muralitharan not out	0		
B 3, l-b 1, w 1, n-b 8	13	N-b 2	2

1/19 (1) 2/122 (3) 3/130 (4) 4/135 (2)   258   1/6 (1) 2/20 (3)   (4 wkts) 195
5/170 (6) 6/180 (5) 7/201 (7)   3/37 (2) 4/119 (5)
8/223 (8) 9/257 (10) 10/258 (9)

Bowling: *First Innings*—Pollock 22.2–10–40–3; Hayward 20–2–68–2; Kallis 13–3–48–0; Klusener 9–2–36–0; Boje 34–8–62–5. *Second Innings*—Pollock 6–3–13–1; Hayward 9–1–21–1; Kallis 4–2–4–0; Klusener 12.1–4–20–1; Adams 16–3–72–1; Boje 20–4–65–0.

Umpires: E. A. Nicholls (West Indies) and B. C. Cooray.
Referee: B. F. Hastings (New Zealand).

AIWA CUP, 1999-2000

This tournament in Sri Lanka in August 1999 saw the first one-day international cricket since the end of the World Cup in England, two months earlier. At first, the Aiwa Cup looked as if it would have the same winner: Steve Waugh's Australians, who won all four qualifying matches. Instead, Sri Lanka completed a hat-trick in one-day finals against Australia, which had begun with their greatest triumph, the World Cup of 1996, and continued in the Singer World Series later that year. Those victories had come under the leadership of Arjuna Ranatunga, but he had been sacked and banished from the team, along with vice-captain Aravinda de Silva, after the wretched 1999 World Cup campaign. The tournament provided the first success for the new captain, Sanath Jayasuriya – he was their leading player, too, with 169 runs and eight wickets – and an encouraging return as coach for Dav Whatmore.

The third participants were India, who had also sacked and dropped their captain since the World Cup: Sachin Tendulkar now replaced Mohammad Azharuddin for his second spell in charge. He had a less happy tournament, however, despite scoring its only century. A back injury forced him to sit out India's second match against Australia, when his team went down to their third successive defeat, and while they managed to beat Sri Lanka in their final game, India could not raise their net run-rate sufficiently to reach the final.

There were no such doubts about Australia, until the final. Their unbeaten progress was led by wicket-keeper and opening batsman Adam Gilchrist, the leading scorer of the tournament with 231 runs, and Jason Gillespie, the leading bowler with ten wickets. Their final slip was a pointer to the Test series with Sri Lanka that immediately followed; their earlier success a harbinger of their dominance over the rest of the summer of 1999-2000.

Note: Matches in this section were not first-class.

SRI LANKA v AUSTRALIA

At Galle, August 22. Australia won by 50 runs (D/L method). Toss: Sri Lanka. International debut: S. I. de Saram.

Bad weather continued to dog Galle, whose first three scheduled one-day internationals in June 1998 were all washed out. This time, the consequences were less severe. Arriving midway through Australia's innings, rain reduced the match to 43 overs a side, and eventually caused Sri Lanka's target to be set at 211. Australian openers Gilchrist and Mark Waugh had raised 60 by the 11th over but, after Gilchrist was controversially given run out by third umpire Pathirana, Jayasuriya seized three key wickets. He finished with five for 28. Bevan regained the initiative, hitting 42 in 44 balls, then Gillespie made three early strikes as Sri Lanka struggled to 41 for four. The middle order could not regain momentum as Warne overtook Craig McDermott's Australian record of 203 wickets in one-day internationals.

Man of the Match: J. N. Gillespie.

Australia

†A. C. Gilchrist run out	27	S. K. Warne c Chandana b Jayasuriya	3
M. E. Waugh c Chandana b Perera	28	J. N. Gillespie st Kaluwitharana	
R. T. Ponting st Kaluwitharana		b Jayasuriya	0
b Jayasuriya	38	D. W. Fleming not out	4
D. S. Lehmann run out	26		
T. M. Moody st Kaluwitharana		L-b 4, w 8, n-b 5	17
b Jayasuriya	6		
*S. R. Waugh b Jayasuriya	6	1/60 2/62 3/110 (9 wkts, 43 overs) 205	
M. G. Bevan not out	42	4/119 5/127 6/160	
A. Symonds run out	8	7/171 8/182 9/183	

Bowling: Vaas 9–0–61–0; Zoysa 8–2–39–0; Perera 7–0–25–1; Muralitharan 9–0–38–0; Jayasuriya 9–0–28–5; Chandana 1–0–10–0.

Sri Lanka

*S. T. Jayasuriya c Moody b Fleming . . .	1	A. S. A. Perera c Bevan b Warne	26
D. A. Gunawardene c Gilchrist		W. P. U. J. C. Vaas not out	5
b Gillespie .	8	D. N. T. Zoysa c Lehmann b Warne. . . .	4
M. S. Atapattu b Gillespie	5	M. Muralitharan c Ponting b Lehmann . .	2
D. P. M. D. Jayawardene c S. R. Waugh			
b Gillespie .	7	B 4, l-b 6, w 5	15
S. I. de Saram b Moody	24		
†R. S. Kaluwitharana c Gilchrist		(37.4 overs)	160
b Fleming .	33	1/7 2/17 3/25	
U. D. U. Chandana run out	30	4/41 5/78 6/98	
		7/145 8/149 9/154	

Bowling: Gillespie 6–1–26–3; Fleming 9–0–40–2; Warne 9–1–39–2; Moody 7–1–21–1; Lehmann 6.4–0–24–1.

Umpires: E. A. R. de Silva and P. T. Manuel.

AUSTRALIA v INDIA

At Galle, August 23. Australia won by eight wickets (D/L method). Toss: India.

Duckworth/Lewis came into play for the second day running; India were interrupted at 65 for three, the match was cut to 38 overs a side and Australia were asked to make 159 to win. They did that with almost nine overs to spare after Gilchrist and Symonds had added 132 for the second wicket. Each contributed 68, with seven fours; Symonds, promoted to No. 3, outpaced his partner by scoring at a run a ball, and also hit a six. India's performance was disappointing. Their pace bowlers pitched too short, and earlier Tendulkar, suffering from a bad back, occupied 51 minutes in making 14. Only Jadeja and Robin Singh made much headway with the bat, and not enough to set a challenging target.

Man of the Match: A. Symonds.

India

S. C. Ganguly lbw b Gillespie	10	N. Chopra not out	18
*S. R. Tendulkar c Lehmann b Moody . .	14	A. Kumble not out	3
R. Dravid c Gilchrist b Symonds.	5		
A. Jadeja c Fleming b Warne	30	L-b 4, w 6, n-b 2	12
A. R. Khurasiya c and b Moody	17		
R. R. Singh lbw b Gillespie	38	1/25 2/32 3/38 4/66 (7 wkts, 38 overs)	151
†M. S. K. Prasad b Warne	4	5/92 6/103 7/139	

J. Srinath and B. K. V. Prasad did not bat.

Bowling: Gillespie 8–0–30–2; Fleming 8–0–31–0; Moody 8–0–25–2; Symonds 7–0–25–1; Warne 7–0–36–2.

Australia

M. E. Waugh c M. S. K. Prasad		R. T. Ponting not out	1
b B. K. V. Prasad .	12	L-b 6, w 1, n-b 3	10
†A. C. Gilchrist c Dravid b Ganguly . . .	68		
A. Symonds not out	68	1/23 2/155 (2 wkts, 29.1 overs)	159

D. S. Lehmann, *S. R. Waugh, M. G. Bevan, T. M. Moody, S. K. Warne, J. N. Gillespie and D. W. Fleming did not bat.

Bowling: Srinath 5–0–26–0; B. K. V. Prasad 5.1–0–37–1; Kumble 6–0–35–0; Chopra 8–0–33–0; Singh 4–0–18–0; Ganguly 1–0–4–1.

Umpires: L. V. Jayasundera and P. T. Manuel.

SRI LANKA v INDIA

At R. Premadasa Stadium, Colombo, August 25 (day/night). Sri Lanka won by seven wickets. Toss: India.

Sri Lanka gained revenge for their mauling by India at Taunton in the World Cup three months earlier. Then, Ganguly and Dravid scored 328 between them; this time, they totalled 31. Tendulkar was one of four men run out, having survived one run-out attempt earlier and also being dropped on his way to 37. Only Jadeja came close to 50 as India declined sharply from 155 for three. In reply, Jayasuriya hurried to 61 in 62 balls, with eight fours, out of a first-wicket stand of 83. His new opening partner, Atapattu, anchored the innings and was still there when Sri Lanka achieved their target in the 47th over.

Man of the Match: M. S. Atapattu.

India

S. C. Ganguly run out	9	A. Kumble run out	3
*S. R. Tendulkar run out	37	J. Srinath not out	12
R. Dravid c Kaluwitharana b Vaas	22		
A. Jadeja c Jayawardene b Chandana	49	B 4, l-b 3, w 13, n-b 8	28
A. R. Khurasiya c de Saram b Chandana	29		
R. R. Singh c Vaas b Muralitharan	4	1/49 2/83 3/93 (8 wkts, 50 overs) 205
†M. S. K. Prasad run out	0	4/155 5/169 6/170
N. Chopra not out	12	7/173 8/182

B. K. V. Prasad did not bat.

Bowling: Vaas 8–0–46–1; Zoysa 8–0–25–0; Perera 5–0–32–0; Muralitharan 10–1–31–1; Jayasuriya 9–0–29–0; Chandana 10–0–35–2.

Sri Lanka

*S. T. Jayasuriya st M. S. K. Prasad b Chopra	61	D. P. M. D. Jayawardene b Singh	27
M. S. Atapattu not out	71	S. I. de Saram not out	24
D. A. Gunawardene c M. S. K. Prasad b Chopra	7	L-b 7, w 5, n-b 4	16
		1/83 2/100 3/148 (3 wkts, 46.4 overs) 206

†R. S. Kaluwitharana, U. D. U. Chandana, A. S. A. Perera, W. P. U. J. C. Vaas, M. Muralitharan and D. N. T. Zoysa did not bat.

Bowling: Srinath 10–0–28–0; B. K. V. Prasad 10–0–35–0; Kumble 8–0–50–0; Chopra 9–2–37–2; Ganguly 6.4–0–31–0; Singh 3–0–18–1.

Umpires: E. A. R. de Silva and D. N. Pathirana.

SRI LANKA v AUSTRALIA

At R. Premadasa Stadium, Colombo, August 26 (day/night). Australia won by 27 runs. Toss: Australia. International debut: L. P. C. Silva.

Mark Waugh was back in form, running up 83 in 15 overs with Gilchrist and continuing to 84 from 94 balls, though he struck only five fours. The Sri Lankan spinners managed to slow down the later innings as Muralitharan and Chandana picked up three wickets apiece. Their batsmen were less impressive, slumping to 87 for five, with McGrath claiming two victims in his first appearance of the tournament. However, Chamara Silva marked his international debut with a fifty, and Vaas and Chandana stepped up the pace. Chandana, smashing 35 in 31 balls, gave Australia a few anxious moments before he was last out with three overs to go. Australia's third victory ensured their entry to the final.

Man of the Match: M. E. Waugh.

Australia

†A. C. Gilchrist c Muralitharan	
b Jayawardene .	38
M. E. Waugh c de Saram b Chandana . .	84
R. T. Ponting c de Saram b Muralitharan	14
D. S. Lehmann b Chandana	5
*S. R. Waugh c Kaluwitharana	
b Chandana .	12
M. G. Bevan b Muralitharan.	23
D. R. Martyn b Muralitharan	17

A. Symonds c Muralitharan b Arnold . . .	14
S. K. Warne run out	15
A. C. Dale not out	4
G. D. McGrath not out	2
B 2, l-b 3, w 4, n-b 4	13

1/83 2/122 3/131   (9 wkts, 50 overs) 241
4/160 5/167 6/200
7/211 8/231 9/235

Bowling: Vaas 6–0–32–0; Perera 4–0–31–0; Arnold 8–0–34–1; Jayawardene 4–0–16–1; Chandana 10–0–35–3; Muralitharan 10–0–50–3; Jayasuriya 8–0–38–0.

Sri Lanka

*S. T. Jayasuriya c Ponting b McGrath . .	10
M. S. Atapattu run out	14
R. P. Arnold run out	41
D. P. M. D. Jayawardene c Gilchrist	
b McGrath .	0
S. I. de Saram b Dale	1
L. P. C. Silva st Gilchrist b Warne	55
†R. S. Kaluwitharana run out	10
W. P. U. J. C. Vaas b Martyn	23

U. D. U. Chandana c Symonds	
b S. R. Waugh .	35
A. S. A. Perera st Gilchrist b Warne . . .	6
M. Muralitharan not out	0
L-b 5, w 11, n-b 3	19

1/15 2/45 3/45   (47.1 overs) 214
4/48 5/87 6/114
7/157 8/197 9/214

Bowling: McGrath 10–0–52–2; Dale 10–2–27–1; Symonds 5–0–22–0; Martyn 10–0–30–1; Warne 9–0–52–2; S. R. Waugh 3.1–0–26–1.

Umpires: K. T. Francis and L. V. Jayasundera.

AUSTRALIA v INDIA

At Sinhalese Sports Club, Colombo, August 28. Australia won by 41 runs. Toss: India.

India went down to their third successive defeat. With the injured Tendulkar forced to drop out, their regular wicket-keeper, Mannava Prasad, handed the gloves to Dravid so that they could bolster the batting by introducing Ramesh and Kambli. Ramesh, who needed a runner in the later stages, added 123 in 28 overs with Robin Singh – but only after McGrath and Gillespie had reduced India to 44 for five. Gilchrist had responded eagerly to India's invitation to bat, hitting 77 from 84 balls, including nine fours, and Australia's total was built on his second-wicket partnership of 110 in 20 overs with Symonds. India had only 49 overs to chase 253, after being penalised one for their own slow over-rate.

Man of the Match: A. C. Gilchrist.

Australia

M. E. Waugh c Dravid b Srinath	18
†A. C. Gilchrist c Srinath b Chopra	77
A. Symonds c Dravid b Srinath	45
R. T. Ponting c sub (L. R. Shukla)	
b Prasad .	32
D. S. Lehmann run out	28
*S. R. Waugh c and b Singh	6
M. G. Bevan b Prasad.	7
T. M. Moody not out	14

S. K. Warne c sub (L. R. Shukla)	
b Kumble .	4
J. N. Gillespie not out	2
B 1, l-b 10, w 5, n-b 3	19

1/40 2/150 3/152   (8 wkts, 50 overs) 252
4/200 5/213 6/227
7/234 8/244

G. D. McGrath did not bat.

Bowling: Srinath 10–1–43–2; Prasad 10–0–29–2; Chopra 10–0–62–1; Kumble 9–0–48–1; Singh 8–0–41–1; Ganguly 3–0–18–0.

India

S. C. Ganguly c Warne b McGrath	8	J. Srinath c Gilchrist b Gillespie	15
S. Ramesh c M. E. Waugh b Symonds	71	A. Kumble b Lehmann	4
A. R. Khurasiya b Gillespie	12	B. K. V. Prasad not out	0
†R. Dravid c Gilchrist b Gillespie	0	L-b 4, w 10, n-b 4	18
*A. Jadeja lbw b McGrath	0		
V. G. Kambli c Gilchrist b Gillespie	3	1/8 2/31 3/31 (48.3 overs) 211	
R. R. Singh c Symonds b Lehmann	75	4/32 5/44 6/167	
N. Chopra run out	5	7/173 8/198 9/211	

Bowling: McGrath 10–0–55–2; Gillespie 9–1–26–4; Moody 10–4–28–0; Symonds 7–0–32–1; Bevan 5–0–21–0; Warne 7–0–41–0; Lehmann 0.3–0–4–2.

Umpires: B. C. Cooray and T. H. Wijewardene.

SRI LANKA v INDIA

At Sinhalese Sports Club, Colombo, August 29. India won by 23 runs (D/L method). Toss: Sri Lanka.

India won at last to draw level with Sri Lanka on points, but remained bottom on net run-rate. After rain sent them off five overs into their pursuit of 297, Sri Lanka were set a revised target of 271 in 42 overs to win, or 232 to beat India's net run-rate. (Under new ICC regulations that came into force three days later, all matches settled by Duckworth/Lewis would have been excluded from the calculations, and India would have been doomed the moment Sri Lanka's innings was interrupted.) Jayasuriya, who took only 53 balls for his 71, and Atapattu opened with 105 in just 17 overs, while Jayawardene scored the third fifty of the innings. That proved enough to achieve their preliminary target, though with victory now meaningless, the tail fell away rapidly. Earlier, Tendulkar returned from injury to score his 23rd hundred in one-day internationals, 120 in 141 balls, with 11 fours and two sixes. His principal ally was Ganguly, who helped him add 127 in 22 overs as India advanced towards an imposing 296, easily the highest total of the tournament. Unexpectedly, Robin Singh earned the match award for his tight bowling and two key wickets.

Man of the Match: R. R. Singh.

India

*S. R. Tendulkar c Muralitharan b Zoysa	120	R. R. Singh not out	4
S. Ramesh c Kaluwitharana b Perera	32	B 4, l-b 4, w 9, n-b 6	23
†R. Dravid c Kaluwitharana b Chandana	13		
S. C. Ganguly c Arnold b Jayasuriya	85	1/75 2/112 (4 wkts, 50 overs) 296	
A. Jadeja not out	19	3/239 4/279	

A. R. Khurasiya, J. Srinath, A. Kumble, B. K. V. Prasad and N. Chopra did not bat.

Bowling: Vaas 7–0–59–0; Zoysa 10–1–50–1; Perera 6–1–41–1; Muralitharan 10–0–42–0; Chandana 10–0–49–1; Jayasuriya 6–0–33–1; Arnold 1–0–14–0.

Sri Lanka

*S. T. Jayasuriya c Dravid b Singh	71	W. P. U. J. C. Vaas run out	0
M. S. Atapattu c Ganguly b Kumble	55	M. Muralitharan not out	5
†R. S. Kaluwitharana b Singh	7	D. N. T. Zoysa not out	0
D. P. M. D. Jayawardene c Chopra b Prasad	62	B 1, l-b 11, w 5, n-b 2	19
L. P. C. Silva c Prasad b Chopra	5		
U. D. U. Chandana c Chopra b Kumble	0	1/105 2/119 3/193 (9 wkts, 42 overs) 247	
R. P. Arnold c Singh b Prasad	19	4/205 5/205 6/238	
A. S. A. Perera run out	4	7/238 8/238 9/243	

Bowling: Srinath 8–0–40–0; Prasad 9–0–59–2; Chopra 7–0–40–1; Kumble 9–0–57–2; Singh 7–0–27–2; Ganguly 2–0–12–0.

Umpires: G. Silva and E. K. G. Wijewardene.

QUALIFYING TABLE

	Played	Won	Lost	Points	Net run-rate
Australia	4	4	0	8	0.89
Sri Lanka.	4	1	3	2	−0.36
India	4	1	3	2	−0.53

Sri Lanka finished ahead of India on net run-rate, having shared the points in their head-to-head matches. Net run-rate is calculated by subtracting runs conceded per over from runs scored per over.

FINAL

SRI LANKA v AUSTRALIA

At R. Premadasa Stadium, Colombo, August 31 (day/night). Sri Lanka won by eight wickets. Toss: Australia.

After 11 one-day internationals without defeat, Australia finally stumbled against Sri Lanka, to the home crowd's delight. They chose to bat, on a slow pitch, but were restricted by the spinners – Sri Lanka boldly omitted Vaas – to 202. Only Steve Waugh, who equalled Allan Border's record of 273 one-day internationals for Australia, and his twin Mark reached 30; both were bowled by Muralitharan. For their reply, Sri Lanka restored Kaluwitharana to open the innings with Atapattu, while Jayasuriya held himself back in case of a crisis. Kaluwitharana rose to the occasion with an unbeaten 95, off 117 balls, with 11 fours. He was denied his hundred only by the speed with which Jayasuriya hastened to victory. Coming in with 29 runs required, Sri Lanka's captain hit 26 off 23 balls, lifting the winning six with ten overs in hand.

Man of the Match: R. S. Kaluwitharana. *Man of the Series:* A. C. Gilchrist.

Australia

†A. C. Gilchrist c Jayawardene b Wickremasinghe	.	21
M. E. Waugh b Muralitharan	. . . .	32
R. T. Ponting run out	. . . .	18
D. S. Lehmann c and b Chandana	. . . . .	21
*S. R. Waugh b Muralitharan	. . . .	43
M. G. Bevan b Chandana	. . . .	0
A. Symonds not out	. . . .	22
S. K. Warne c Silva b Arnold	. . . .	21
J. N. Gillespie b Arnold	. . . .	14

D. W. Fleming st Kaluwitharana b Jayasuriya	.	0
G. D. McGrath st Kaluwitharana b Jayasuriya	.	1
L-b 2, w 3, n-b 3	. . . .	9

1/37 2/74 3/75 (50 overs) 202
4/126 5/126 6/144
7/178 8/197 9/198

Bowling: Zoysa 7–0–31–0; Arnold 8–0–42–2; Wickremasinghe 8–0–24–1; Muralitharan 10–1–36–2; Chandana 10–0–33–2; Jayasuriya 7–0–33–2.

Sri Lanka

M. S. Atapattu c Gilchrist b Fleming	. . .	24
†R. S. Kaluwitharana not out	. . . .	95
R. P. Arnold b Gillespie.	. . . .	47
*S. T. Jayasuriya not out	. . . .	26
L-b 5, w 5, n-b 6	. . . .	16

1/64 2/174 (2 wkts, 39.3 overs) 208

D. P. M. D. Jayawardene, S. I. de Saram, L. P. C. Silva, U. D. U. Chandana, G. P. Wickremasinghe, M. Muralitharan and D. N. T. Zoysa did not bat.

Bowling: McGrath 7–0–47–0; Gillespie 9–0–37–1; Fleming 7–1–28–1; Warne 8–0–46–0; Symonds 3–0–14–0; S. R. Waugh 3–0–16–0; Lehmann 1.3–0–13–0; Ponting 1–0–2–0.

Umpires: B. C. Cooray and K. T. Francis.
Series referee: C. W. Smith (West Indies).

COCA-COLA SINGAPORE CHALLENGE, 1999-2000

Just as at Singapore's first senior one-day international tournament three and a half years earlier, so batsmen dominated the second. The venue had changed, but the short boundaries had not. At the Padang in April 1996, Sanath Jayasuriya hit what was then the fastest hundred in this form of cricket (48 balls). No one could quite match that now, but the Kallang ground was just as inviting for the big hitters. In the first game, 16 sixes sailed over the ropes. In the three completed matches that followed there were another 35. As in 1996, rain interfered, shortening two of the three preliminary matches, and the final had to be played on the reserve day after a false start. West Indies enjoyed a rare tournament success, with Ricardo Powell's breathtaking 124 propelling them to victory over India.

Powell's one previous game for West Indies before arriving in Singapore was in their unhappy World Cup campaign. In his three innings here, he smashed 221 runs from just 175 balls, including 13 sixes. He exhibited such fluency and natural aggression that pundits (inevitably) compared him with Viv Richards. It wasn't just Powell: the whole team oozed confidence, and Brian Lara hit his 126 runs from 98 balls. It may not have been a bowlers' tournament, but West Indies had two stars. Reon King took nine wickets – the same as Debasis Mohanty, for India, and five more than anyone else – while Courtney Walsh was alone in costing less than four an over: his 27 averaged 2.62 apiece.

Rahul Dravid, who kept wicket in three of India's four matches, played with control rather than flamboyance, but was the leading run-scorer after Powell, with 183. Andy Flower and Alistair Campbell both hit form for Zimbabwe with the bat, but had scant support from their colleagues. Their bowlers were out of sorts from the start, and Heath Streak, with an injured knee, was badly missed.

Three days after the final, West Indies took on India again, in the DMC Festival in Toronto. They left Singapore victorious and in high spirits, but in the morass of one-day cricket that lay ahead (after India they played Pakistan, also in Canada, then toured Bangladesh, Sharjah and New Zealand before entertaining Zimbabwe and Pakistan), there would be few similar moments to savour.

Note: Matches in this section were not first-class.

WEST INDIES v ZIMBABWE

At Kallang Ground, Singapore, September 2. West Indies won by six wickets. Toss: Zimbabwe. International debut: A. M. Blignaut.

Effervescent West Indian batting, particularly from Powell, made light of an apparently stiff target. After Zimbabwe had lost their third wicket at 38, Alistair Campbell and Andy Flower added 114 at more than six an over. Both hit brisk eighties, but they had next to no support. West Indies' pace quartet took all nine wickets cheaply, their two slow bowlers none, rather more expensively. Chasing 245, West Indies rushed to 100 without loss in the 15th over. This time it was Jacobs and the other Campbell, Sherwin, who shared a partnership of 114 at more than a run a ball. Three wickets fell for six, but there was no let-up for Zimbabwe. Lara, with 48 from 44 balls, and then Powell, who rocketed to a 38-ball fifty, each struck four sixes to achieve victory with more than six overs to spare. In all, there were 16 sixes, an indication of the compact size of the ground.

Man of the Match: R. D. Jacobs.

Zimbabwe

N. C. Johnson c Jacobs b Dillon	3	P. A. Strang b Walsh	3
G. W. Flower c Lara b Bryan	12	A. R. Whittall not out	0
*A. D. R. Campbell c Jacobs b King	80	H. K. Olonga not out	2
M. W. Goodwin c Powell b King	2	B 2, l-b 5, w 10, n-b 8	25
†A. Flower b Dillon	89		
A. M. Blignaut c Jacobs b King	1	1/3 2/31 3/38　(9 wkts, 50 overs) 244	
S. V. Carlisle c Jacobs b Bryan	27	4/152 5/159 6/230	
C. N. Evans b Bryan	0	7/230 8/240 9/240	

Bowling: Walsh 10–4–31–1; Dillon 9–1–34–2; King 8–0–37–3; Bryan 10–1–36–3; Perry 7–0–53–0; Adams 6–0–46–0.

West Indies

S. L. Campbell b G. W. Flower	63	R. L. Powell not out	51
†R. D. Jacobs run out	47	W 7, n-b 1	8
J. C. Adams b G. W. Flower	1		
*B. C. Lara c Campbell b Strang	48	1/114 2/115　(4 wkts, 43.4 overs) 247	
S. Chanderpaul not out	29	3/120 4/176	

N. O. Perry, H. R. Bryan, M. Dillon, R. D. King and C. A. Walsh did not bat.

Bowling: Johnson 4–0–29–0; Whittall 8–1–34–0; Strang 6–0–42–1; Olonga 6–1–49–0; Evans 6–0–28–0; G. W. Flower 10–0–39–2; Blignaut 3.4–0–26–0.

Umpires: D. B. Hair and Riazuddin.

INDIA v ZIMBABWE

At Kallang Ground, Singapore, September 4. India won by 115 runs. Toss: Zimbabwe.

Overnight rain reduced this match to 30 overs a side, but India set a target Zimbabwe would have found awkward in 50. Tendulkar reached his half-century off 50 balls, yet was outpaced by Jadeja, who took 39. Together they piled on 143 for the third wicket in 17 overs. A calf-muscle injury eventually forced Jadeja to retire after facing just 61 balls for his 88. All Zimbabwe's bowlers came in for punishment, notably Grant Flower, whose single over went for 20, including three sixes. A slow over-rate – perhaps understandable given the ball-chasing – cost Zimbabwe an over from their reply, but from 19 for four that was academic.

Man of the Match: S. R. Tendulkar.

India

S. C. Ganguly c and b Johnson	6	S. B. Joshi not out	16
*S. R. Tendulkar c Carlisle b Whittall	85	A. Kumble not out	0
†R. Dravid c Johnson b Blignaut	12		
A. Jadeja retired hurt	88	L-b 5, w 14, n-b 2	21
A. R. Khurasiya c A. Flower b Blignaut	5		
R. R. Singh c Whittall b Evans	8	1/38 2/60 3/203　(6 wkts, 30 overs) 245	
N. Chopra c Blignaut b Johnson	4	4/216 5/222 6/233	

B. K. V. Prasad and D. S. Mohanty did not bat.

Jadeja retired hurt at 212.

Bowling: Johnson 6–0–39–2; Mbangwa 6–0–54–0; Blignaut 6–0–35–2; Whittall 6–0–42–1; Evans 5–0–50–1; G. W. Flower 1–0–20–0.

Zimbabwe

N. C. Johnson c Ganguly b Prasad	....	8	C. N. Evans c Dravid b Joshi	2
G. W. Flower c Dravid b Mohanty	.....	5	A. M. Blignaut b Kumble	0
C. B. Wishart b Mohanty	......	0	A. R. Whittall not out	11
*A. D. R. Campbell c sub (L. R. Shukla)			B 1, l-b 3, w 2, n-b 1	7
b Kumble .	27			
M. W. Goodwin c Joshi b Mohanty	....	3	1/15 2/15 3/15	(8 wkts, 29 overs) 130
†A. Flower not out	....	63	4/19 5/66 6/87	
S. V. Carlisle c Chopra b Joshi	....	4	7/92 8/93	

M. Mbangwa did not bat.

Bowling: Prasad 5–2–17–1; Mohanty 6–1–28–3; Chopra 6–0–27–0; Kumble 6–0–30–2; Joshi 5–1–16–2; Singh 1–0–8–0.

Umpires: D. B. Hair and R. E. Koertzen.

INDIA v WEST INDIES

At Kallang Ground, Singapore, September 5. West Indies won by 42 runs. Toss: West Indies. International debut: W. W. Hinds.

With both teams having qualified for the final, several key players were rested: Tendulkar for India, Walsh and Campbell for West Indies. For the second day running, rain reduced the game to a 30-over contest. India began in style when Jacobs lofted the first ball straight to mid-on, but it did not prevent a steady flow of runs, which became a torrent while Powell and Lara were batting. Powell scored 46 in 44 balls, Lara 60 in just 43. When India replied, Ganguly and Dravid put on 73 for the second wicket before Ganguly was stumped. Apparently more concerned with an appeal for lbw or caught behind, he was too casual in regaining his ground – and the opportunistic Jacobs, standing back to McLean, threw down the stumps. Soon afterwards, India lost three more wickets for five runs and gave up a largely pointless run-chase.

Man of the Match: B. C. Lara.

West Indies

†R. D. Jacobs c Chopra b Mohanty	....	0	N. O. Perry not out	14
S. Chanderpaul c Chopra b Mohanty	...	23	H. R. Bryan not out	9
J. C. Adams c Singh b Shukla	....	8	L-b 4, w 3, n-b 5	12
N. A. M. McLean c Mohanty b Ramesh	.	23		
W. W. Hinds c Prasad b Chopra	......	1	1/0 2/32 3/45	(7 wkts, 30 overs) 196
R. L. Powell st Prasad b Chopra	......	46	4/49 5/85	
*B. C. Lara c Khurasiya b Mohanty	...	60	6/146 7/176	

M. Dillon and R. D. King did not bat.

Bowling: Mohanty 6–0–52–3; Shukla 5–0–25–1; Chopra 6–0–23–2; Joshi 6–0–29–0; Ramesh 3–0–23–1; Singh 3–0–28–0; Ganguly 1–0–12–0.

India

S. Ramesh c Perry b King	....	0	†M. S. K. Prasad c Perry b Hinds	5
*S. C. Ganguly st Jacobs b McLean	...	32	S. B. Joshi not out	4
R. Dravid c Bryan b McLean	....	39		
V. G. Kambli run out	....	11	L-b 1, w 13, n-b 2	16
A. R. Khurasiya c and b Perry	....	3		
R. R. Singh not out	....	23	1/5 2/78 3/96	(8 wkts, 30 overs) 154
L. R. Shukla b Dillon	....	13	4/96 5/101 6/115	
N. Chopra c Jacobs b King	....	8	7/135 8/148	

D. S. Mohanty did not bat.

Bowling: Dillon 6–0–27–1; King 5–0–25–2; Bryan 6–0–33–0; Perry 6–1–30–1; McLean 6–0–32–2; Hinds 1–0–6–1.

Umpires: R. E. Koertzen and Riazuddin.

QUALIFYING TABLE

	Played	Won	Lost	Points	Net run-rate
West Indies	2	2	0	4	1.04
India.	2	1	1	2	1.12
Zimbabwe	2	0	2	0	−1.94

Net run-rate is calculated by subtracting runs conceded per over from runs scored per over.

FINAL

INDIA v WEST INDIES

At Kallang Ground, Singapore, September 7. No result. Toss: India.

The weather, which had shortened the two previous games, ended play with India a precarious 149 for six. When the downpour started, Ganguly had just been run out for an unconvincing 23, leaving Robin Singh, eight not out, the last recognised batsman. King was the pick of the West Indian bowlers, generating good pace and relentlessly finding a line just outside off.

India

*S. R. Tendulkar c Jacobs b Walsh	40	R. R. Singh not out	8
S. Ramesh c Perry b King	15		
†R. Dravid c Campbell b King	29	L-b 7, w 11, n-b 6.	24
S. C. Ganguly run out.	23		
V. G. Kambli c Jacobs b King	1	1/42 2/102 3/105 (6 wkts, 38.2 overs) 149
N. Chopra c and b Dillon	9	4/111 5/137 6/149

S. B. Joshi, A. Kumble, B. K. V. Prasad and D. S. Mohanty did not bat.

Bowling: Walsh 7–1–21–1; Dillon 9–0–38–1; King 8–1–25–3; Adams 5–0–27–0; Bryan 5–0–12–0; Perry 4.2–0–19–0.

West Indies

S. L. Campbell, †R. D. Jacobs, J. C. Adams, *B. C. Lara, S. Chanderpaul, R. L. Powell, N. O. Perry, H. R. Bryan, M. Dillon, R. D. King and C. A. Walsh.

Umpires: D. B. Hair and R. E. Koertzen.

INDIA v WEST INDIES

At Kallang Ground, Singapore, September 8. West Indies won by four wickets. Toss: West Indies.

The previous day's rain granted India only a brief stay of execution. After a shaky start, West Indies ran out deserved winners, 20-year-old Powell concluding a successful tournament with a whirlwind 124, his first one-day international hundred in his fourth innings. It was an astonishing performance, the more remarkable because West Indies, chasing 255, were struggling at 67 for four in the 17th over when he reached the crease. By the time he was out, top-edging a pull, he had hit nine fours and eight sixes in his 93 balls – and West Indies were only nine short of victory. He added 61 with Chanderpaul and 118 with Perry, who gave vital, intelligent support. Earlier, India had lost Tendulkar to the last ball of the first over, but were held together by Dravid, who batted with mounting confidence to finish unbeaten on 103. Chopra filled the support role with an accomplished maiden half-century in limited-overs internationals. He also accounted for two important batsmen to tilt matters India's way – until Powell took over.

Man of the Match: R. L. Powell.   *Man of the Series:* R. L. Powell.

India

*S. R. Tendulkar c Bryan b Walsh.	0	S. B. Joshi not out	13	
S. Ramesh c Lara b King	13			
†R. Dravid not out	103			
S. C. Ganguly c Dillon b Perry.	46	L-b 5, w 7, n-b 3	15	
V. G. Kambli st Jacobs b Perry.	1	—		
N. Chopra c Jacobs b Perry	61	1/0 2/27	(6 wkts, 50 overs) 254	
R. R. Singh c sub (A. F. G. Griffith)		3/105 4/108		
b Adams .	2	5/210 6/224		

A. Kumble, B. K. V. Prasad and D. S. Mohanty did not bat.

Bowling: Walsh 10–2–19–1; Dillon 9–0–46–0; King 8–1–44–1; Bryan 6–0–30–0; Perry 10–0–65–3; Adams 7–0–45–1.

West Indies

S. L. Campbell lbw b Mohanty.	1	N. O. Perry not out.	38	
†R. D. Jacobs b Mohanty.	20	H. R. Bryan not out	6	
J. C. Adams c Ganguly b Chopra	21	L-b 2, w 3, n-b 2	7	
*B. C. Lara b Chopra	18	—		
S. Chanderpaul c Chopra b Kumble. . . .	20	1/2 2/31 3/60	(6 wkts, 47.4 overs) 255	
R. L. Powell c Dravid b Mohanty	124	4/67 5/128 6/246		

M. Dillon, R. D. King and C. A. Walsh did not bat.

Bowling: Prasad 10–0–50–0; Mohanty 8.4–1–33–3; Chopra 8–0–43–2; Kumble 10–1–51–1; Joshi 10–1–63–0; Ganguly 1–0–13–0.

Umpires: D. B. Hair and R. E. Koertzen.
Series referee: R. S. Madugalle (Sri Lanka).

DMC FESTIVAL, 1999-2000

Political tensions between India and Pakistan threatened their return to Toronto, where they had met in bilateral one-day series for the previous three years. Barely a fortnight before the start of the tournament, a compromise was reached: West Indies were invited to Canada to play three matches against India followed by three against Pakistan, thus keeping the Asian neighbours apart. As it happened, India and West Indies played in the final of another one-day competition, in Singapore, only three days before they met again in Toronto. In between, they had a 30-hour journey, changing planes in London. India's captain, Sachin Tendulkar, and vice-captain, Ajay Jadeja, did not travel with them as both were resting injuries; Sourav Ganguly stepped up to take charge. But West Indies looked the worse for the ordeal, and their captain, Brian Lara, complained about the pressure of non-stop cricket when they went down by eight wickets in the first game. Though they fought back in the next match, it was their only victory: they lost 2–1 to India and were whitewashed by Pakistan.

Pakistan, by contrast, had not played since the disappointment of their World Cup final defeat by Australia in June. Since then, captain Wasim Akram and two other players had been suspended while allegations of match-fixing were investigated. Wicket-keeper Moin Khan was named to lead the team in Canada. But a few days before their arrival, the Pakistan board announced that nothing had yet been disclosed to justify Wasim's suspension and he was reinstated as captain. They, too, had to cope without a star player, as Shoaib Akhtar was being treated for a shoulder strain, though they scarcely missed him. In a generally low-scoring tournament, Yousuf Youhana reinforced his reputation for reliability in the middle order, making the only century of the week, while young all-rounder Abdur Razzaq struck two fifties. For India, Ganguly and his vice-captain, Rahul Dravid, were the leading batsmen, and off-spinner Nikhil Chopra took eight wickets at eight runs apiece. Understandably, as they played twice as many matches, West Indies had the leading run-scorer, Sherwin Campbell, who numbered three fifties among his 230 runs, and the leading wicket-taker, Mervyn Dillon, who took 11 in five games at wildly varying cost. But the overall results served to boost the subcontinent, while the late-invited West Indians suffered a further blow to their already shaky morale.

Note: Matches in this section were not first-class.

DMC CUP

INDIA v WEST INDIES

First One-Day International

At Toronto, September 11. India won by eight wickets. Toss: India. International debuts: J. J. Martin; C. H. Gayle.

India's captain Ganguly guided them to victory and claimed his sixth match award at Toronto – he was actually named "Royal Stag of the Match" after a sponsor's product. The Indians had lost to West Indies in Singapore three days earlier, but looked to have recovered far better from jetlag as they now reduced them to 57 for four on a damp pitch. Campbell anchored the innings with 62, but only Powell, with 37 from 34 balls, lent him momentum in a stand of 64 in nine overs. Chasing only 164, India experimented by opening with Ramesh and wicket-keeper Mannava Prasad, who ran up 54 by the 13th over. Prasad and Dravid went in quick succession, but Ganguly hit seven fours and a six in 69 balls in an unbroken century partnership with Ramesh, and the win came with 12 overs to spare.

Man of the Match: S. C. Ganguly.

West Indies

S. L. Campbell st M. S. K. Prasad b Joshi .	62	H. R. Bryan lbw b Joshi	1
A. F. G. Griffith b Mohanty	1	C. D. Collymore not out	13
S. Chanderpaul st M. S. K. Prasad b Chopra .	16	R. D. King c Martin b Mohanty	0
C. H. Gayle b Singh	1	C. A. Walsh c Martin b B. K. V. Prasad .	1
*B. C. Lara c Kanitkar b Singh	2	B 2, l-b 2, w 4, n-b 2	10
R. L. Powell c Martin b Singh	37		
†R. D. Jacobs lbw b Chopra	19		

1/8 2/43 3/48   (46.2 overs) 163
4/57 5/121 6/135
7/141 8/155 9/160

Bowling: B. K. V. Prasad 8.2–0–38–1; Mohanty 10–2–31–2; Singh 10–1–43–3; Chopra 10–3–17–2; Joshi 8–0–30–2.

India

†M. S. K. Prasad c Griffith b Collymore	24
S. Ramesh not out	55
R. Dravid c Jacobs b Walsh	5
*S. C. Ganguly not out	54
L-b 11, w 14, n-b 2	27

1/54 2/59   (2 wkts, 37.3 overs) 165

H. H. Kanitkar, R. R. Singh, J. J. Martin, N. Chopra, S. B. Joshi, B. K. V. Prasad and D. S. Mohanty did not bat.

Bowling: Collymore 8–1–29–1; Bryan 8–0–22–0; Walsh 7–2–20–1; King 8–0–39–0; Gayle 6–0–37–0; Powell 0.3–0–7–0.

Umpires: D. J. Harper and D. L. Orchard.

INDIA v WEST INDIES

Second One-Day International

At Toronto, September 12. West Indies won by 70 runs. Toss: West Indies.

Campbell's second fifty in two days was rewarded this time as West Indies levelled the series. Lara, Ganguly's third victim thanks to a diving catch by the wicket-keeper, was the only other batsman to reach 30 in the match, and he was correct when he said that 190 should be enough on this pitch. India's new openers both fell in the second over of their reply, and incisive bowling meant their side were a wretched 43 just after the halfway mark. They were saved from undercutting India's lowest one-day total, 63 against Australia in 1980-81, by Chopra and Joshi, who carried them to 100. But the last three wickets fell in as many overs. Dillon, who conceded only one run an over, and Walsh bowled with particular thrift.

Man of the Match: S. L. Campbell.

West Indies

S. L. Campbell lbw b Joshi	59	J. C. Adams not out	22
†R. D. Jacobs b Chopra	11	M. Dillon not out	21
S. Chanderpaul c M. S. K. Prasad b Ganguly	7	L-b 7, w 8	15
C. H. Gayle lbw b Ganguly	15		
*B. C. Lara c M. S. K. Prasad b Ganguly	34	1/43 2/64 (6 wkts, 50 overs)	190
R. L. Powell c M. S. K. Prasad b Mohanty	6	3/89 4/119	
		5/126 6/154	

C. D. Collymore, R. D. King and C. A. Walsh did not bat.

Bowling: B. K. V. Prasad 9–0–36–0; Mohanty 10–0–36–1; Chopra 10–2–26–1; Joshi 9–0–35–1; Ganguly 9–1–37–3; Kanitkar 1–0–3–0; Singh 2–0–10–0.

India

†M. S. K. Prasad run out	0	S. B. Joshi c Powell b Adams	25
S. Ramesh c Powell b King	0	B. K. V. Prasad c Walsh b Gayle	18
R. Dravid lbw b Dillon	16	D. S. Mohanty not out	0
*S. C. Ganguly c Chanderpaul b Collymore	1	L-b 5, w 19, n-b 2	26
H. H. Kanitkar c Jacobs b Dillon	2		
R. R. Singh run out	4	1/0 2/2 3/12 (41.5 overs)	120
J. J. Martin b King	7	4/26 5/27 6/42	
N. Chopra b Gayle	21	7/43 8/100 9/115	

Bowling: Walsh 7–2–13–0; King 10–2–33–2; Collymore 10–0–27–1; Dillon 8–2–8–2; Gayle 4.5–0–18–2; Adams 2–0–16–1.

Umpires: R. S. Dunne and D. J. Harper.

INDIA v WEST INDIES

Third One-Day International

At Toronto, September 14. India won by 88 runs. Toss: West Indies.

India took the series 2–1 and would have won their final game far more quickly but for Powell, whose 76 in 73 balls echoed his dazzling century in Singapore a week earlier. He hit seven sixes and three fours, but West Indies' next highest score was 26, and they were beaten with 15 overs to spare. Chopra collected five for 21; earlier, Dillon had taken five Indian wickets, though at greater cost. Ganguly resumed opening, but it was Dravid who dominated their innings with 77 in 87 balls, hitting six fours plus two sixes over long-on off successive balls from Adams. He later took four catches to line up the match award. Mohanty removed the in-form Campbell with the first ball of West Indies' reply, and they were 52 for seven by the 18th over. However, Powell's pyrotechnics added 84, a West Indian eighth-wicket record to which Collymore contributed two.

Man of the Match: R. Dravid.   *Man of the Series:* S. C. Ganguly.

India

†M. S. K. Prasad c Jacobs b Walsh	2	N. Chopra not out		4
*S. C. Ganguly b Dillon	34			
S. Ramesh c Campbell b Dillon	2	L-b 6, w 16, n-b 14		36
J. J. Martin c Jacobs b Walsh	33			
R. Dravid b Dillon	77	1/10 2/24 3/61	(7 wkts, 50 overs)	225
V. G. Kambli c Jacobs b Dillon	26	4/120 5/197		
R. R. Singh c Lara b Dillon	11	6/203 7/225		

S. B. Joshi, B. K. V. Prasad and D. S. Mohanty did not bat.

Bowling: Walsh 10–1–30–2; King 10–0–37–0; Dillon 10–1–51–5; Adams 8–0–47–0; Collymore 10–0–36–0; Powell 2–0–18–0.

West Indies

S. L. Campbell b Mohanty	0	C. D. Collymore lbw b Chopra		3
†R. D. Jacobs c Dravid b B. K. V. Prasad	0	R. D. King c Kambli b Singh		0
S. Chanderpaul c Dravid		C. A. Walsh not out		0
b B. K. V. Prasad .	12			
C. H. Gayle c Ganguly b Mohanty	7	L-b 2, w 4, n-b 4		10
*B. C. Lara c Dravid b Chopra	26			
J. C. Adams c Dravid b Chopra	3	1/0 2/6 3/20	(34.2 overs)	137
R. L. Powell c Singh b Chopra	76	4/20 5/49 6/52		
M. Dillon b Chopra	0	7/52 8/136 9/137		

Bowling: Mohanty 9–2–35–2; B. K. V. Prasad 8–1–30–2; Ganguly 1–0–16–0; Chopra 6.2–2–21–5; Joshi 7–1–21–0; Singh 3–0–12–1.

Umpires: R. S. Dunne and D. L. Orchard.
Series referee: P. L. van der Merwe (South Africa).

DMC TROPHY

PAKISTAN v WEST INDIES

First One-Day International

At Toronto, September 16. Pakistan won by 15 runs. Toss: Pakistan.

This was the 1,500th one-day international: Walsh had played in 200 of them and Wasim Akram in 276. Seizing the advantage after they were both given lives, Saeed Anwar and Wajahatullah Wasti opened with 131 in 29 overs, a Pakistani first-wicket record against West Indies. The middle order flagged, but Azhar Mahmood lashed out at the end with 25 from 13 balls. Dillon, so miserly four days earlier, conceded 19 – including a six and three fours – in his final over, and 65 in all. Even so, West Indies might have won had they not given away 33 in wides and no-balls. Campbell, missed on one, hit his third half-century in four innings, but Powell's promotion to No. 3 was not a success. Although managing a six and a four, he was only 12 when he lost his middle stump. Adams batted valiantly for 35 in 33 balls, but the last over, from Saqlain Mushtaq, yielded just one run while Moin Khan made his 50th one-day stumping.

Man of the Match: Saeed Anwar.

Pakistan

Saeed Anwar b Dillon	63
Wajahatullah Wasti c Chanderpaul b Adams	40
Aamir Sohail c and b Adams	8
Inzamam-ul-Haq c Hinds b Dillon	24
Yousuf Youhana c Jacobs b Walsh	25
†Moin Khan run out	1
Azhar Mahmood not out	25
Abdur Razzaq not out	1
L-b 10, w 23, n-b 10	43
1/131 2/141 3/147 (6 wkts, 50 overs)	230
4/187 5/190 6/209	

*Wasim Akram, Saqlain Mushtaq and Waqar Younis did not bat.

Bowling: Walsh 10–0–44–1; King 10–2–38–0; Bryan 10–1–32–0; Dillon 10–0–65–2; Hinds 3–0–22–0; Adams 7–1–19–2.

West Indies

S. L. Campbell run out	69
†R. D. Jacobs lbw b Waqar Younis	4
R. L. Powell b Abdur Razzaq	12
W. W. Hinds run out	16
*B. C. Lara c sub (Hasan Raza) b Wasim Akram	20
S. Chanderpaul c Waqar Younis b Aamir Sohail	29
J. C. Adams not out	35
H. R. Bryan run out	4
M. Dillon b Azhar Mahmood	7
R. D. King st Moin Khan b Saqlain Mushtaq	1
C. A. Walsh not out	0
L-b 5, w 12, n-b 1	18
1/7 2/31 3/99 (9 wkts, 50 overs)	215
4/133 5/137 6/177	
7/189 8/211 9/215	

Bowling: Waqar Younis 8–0–44–1; Wasim Akram 10–1–41–1; Abdur Razzaq 10–2–26–1; Azhar Mahmood 10–1–55–1; Saqlain Mushtaq 10–2–30–1; Aamir Sohail 2–0–14–1.

Umpires: D. J. Harper and D. L. Orchard.

PAKISTAN v WEST INDIES

Second One-Day International

At Toronto, September 18. Pakistan won by 42 runs. Toss: Pakistan.

Pakistan made sure of the series despite a doubtful start. Choosing to bat, they faced an unlikely opening bowler in off-spinner Gayle, who removed Saeed Anwar in the fifth over, and after 22 overs they were 68 for four. Yousuf Youhana and Abdur Razzaq regrouped and they put on 149 together. Razzaq was run out in the final over, trying to help his colleague to his century, which Youhana reached just afterwards; he finished with 104 from 114 balls, having hit 13 fours. His second fifty took only 25 balls as the last ten overs cost 100 runs. In reply, Campbell and his latest opening partner, Chanderpaul, fell cheaply. Though Lara hit 26 in 21 balls, only Hinds stood firm for long. When Wasim Akram bowled him in the 45th over, it was soon over.

Man of the Match: Yousuf Youhana.

Pakistan

Saeed Anwar b Gayle	6
Wajahatullah Wasti b Bryan	14
Inzamam-ul-Haq c Jacobs b Dillon	14
Aamir Sohail c Adams b Dillon	21
Yousuf Youhana not out	104
Abdur Razzaq run out	55
†Moin Khan not out	0
L-b 1, w 6, n-b 1	8
1/13 2/36 3/46 (5 wkts, 50 overs)	222
4/68 5/217	

*Wasim Akram, Arshad Khan, Saqlain Mushtaq and Waqar Younis did not bat.

Bowling: Gayle 10–1–41–1; Walsh 10–4–40–0; Dillon 10–0–42–2; Bryan 10–0–58–1; Adams 10–0–40–0.

West Indies

S. L. Campbell c Yousuf Youhana			
b Wasim Akram .	8	†R. D. Jacobs b Saqlain Mushtaq	1
		H. R. Bryan b Saqlain Mushtaq	11
S. Chanderpaul c Moin Khan		M. Dillon not out.	2
b Waqar Younis .	9	C. A. Walsh b Abdur Razzaq	1
W. W. Hinds b Wasim Akram	65		
*B. C. Lara lbw b Saqlain Mushtaq. . . .	26	B 6, l-b 6, w 9, n-b 1	22
R. L. Powell lbw b Abdur Razzaq	1		
J. C. Adams c Wasim Akram		1/21 2/23 3/59 (46.2 overs) 180	
b Arshad Khan .	28	4/60 5/128	
C. H. Gayle c Abdur Razzaq		6/148 7/149	
b Arshad Khan .	6	8/174 9/179	

Bowling: Wasim Akram 10–2–44–2; Waqar Younis 8–2–32–1; Abdur Razzaq 7.2–1–31–2; Saqlain Mushtaq 8–2–18–3; Arshad Khan 10–0–27–2; Aamir Sohail 3–1–16–0.

Umpires: R. S. Dunne and R. J. Harper.

PAKISTAN v WEST INDIES

Third One-Day International

At Toronto, September 19. Pakistan won by seven wickets. Toss: West Indies. International debut: Shabbir Ahmed.

Pakistan completed a clean sweep as Shabbir Ahmed made a dramatic debut. A tall, 23-year-old fast bowler with an unconventional action, he took the new ball in the absence of Wasim Akram and Waqar Younis, who were rested. His first over saw three leg-side wides run to the boundary, but also the wicket of Griffith, clean bowled; in a later spell, he bowled Powell and Gayle with consecutive deliveries to round off a West Indian collapse of five for six in 47 balls. Though their team was supposedly packed with batsmen, West Indies were only 161 when Mushtaq Ahmed, in his first one-day international for 17 months, finished them off with his third wicket. Walsh checked Pakistan momentarily, bowling Wajahatullah Wasti first ball, but he later left the field with a side strain. Abdur Razzaq and Inzamam-ul-Haq both hit fifties, with eight fours apiece, and Pakistan won comfortably with ten overs in hand.

Man of the Match: Abdur Razzaq.

West Indies

S. L. Campbell lbw b Saqlain Mushtaq .	32	†R. D. Jacobs c Moin Khan	
A. F. G. Griffith b Shabbir Ahmed.	3	b Abdur Razzaq .	10
W. W. Hinds c Wajahatullah Wasti		M. Dillon c Yousuf Youhana	
b Saqlain Mushtaq .	27	b Mushtaq Ahmed .	9
S. Chanderpaul st Moin Khan		C. A. Walsh not out	0
b Arshad Khan .	3		
*B. C. Lara c Shabbir Ahmed		L-b 8, w 27, n-b 2	37
b Mushtaq Ahmed .	12		
R. L. Powell b Shabbir Ahmed	1	1/11 2/86 3/91 (44.4 overs) 161	
C. H. Gayle b Shabbir Ahmed	0	4/91 5/92	
J. C. Adams c Inzamam-ul-Haq		6/92 7/113	
b Mushtaq Ahmed .	27	8/133 9/156	

Bowling: Abdur Razzaq 8–2–31–1; Shabbir Ahmed 10–1–52–3; Arshad Khan 10–1–21–1; Saqlain Mushtaq 8–2–18–2; Mushtaq Ahmed 8.4–0–31–3.

Pakistan

Wajahatullah Wasti b Walsh	0
Abdur Razzaq c Powell b Chanderpaul . .	57
Hasan Raza c Hinds b Adams	11
Inzamam-ul-Haq not out	55

Yousuf Youhana not out	8
L-b 2, w 19, n-b 10	31
1/0 2/50 3/136   (3 wkts, 39.4 overs) 162

Saeed Anwar, *†Moin Khan, Arshad Khan, Mushtaq Ahmed, Saqlain Mushtaq and Shabbir Ahmed did not bat.

Bowling: Walsh 7–1–24–1; Dillon 9–2–31–0; Adams 7–0–36–1; Gayle 9–0–31–0; Chanderpaul 6–0–33–1; Campbell 1.4–0–5–0.

Umpires: R. S. Dunne and D. L. Orchard.
Series referee: P. L. van der Merwe (South Africa).

LG CUP, 1999-2000

South Africa's new coach, Graham Ford, guided his side to the LG Cup, the third senior one-day international tournament held in Kenya. The other participants were India, playing their fourth limited-overs competition in six weeks – and on three different continents – Zimbabwe, and the hosts, Kenya. It was rated a reasonable success, and attendances were noticeably up on two years earlier, when Zimbabwe had won the President's Cup in front of near-empty houses. The Kenyan Cricket Association had failed to secure the participation of India on that occasion, and their presence this time made all the difference.

When India were involved, the ground was full to capacity, and many would-be spectators climbed trees outside the Gymkhana Club to glimpse their heroes. Kenya may have been the home nation, but it was India who enjoyed the most partisan support, since almost all the spectators came from the Asian population. Some lessons had been learned from the President's Cup, though, and schoolchildren – predominantly African – were granted free admission to less popular matches.

Not that they would have found the cricket especially exciting. The one tense game was the first, between Kenya and Zimbabwe, and even that warmed up only for the last ten overs. Kenya lost their three games, but were never humiliated. They batted with distinction – Ravindu Shah and Steve Tikolo both hit half-centuries – and, more encouragingly, they bowled well. They took seven wickets in each game; and on both occasions the Kenyans put their opponents in to bat, they restricted them to 220. Even so, no home player took more than four wickets in the competition. They gave debuts to two young seam bowlers, Josephat Ababu and Peter Ochieng, and both turned in tidy performances.

After a promising World Cup, Zimbabwe fell significantly short of expectations, and lost heavily to the Test-playing nations. The top order made runs, but never dominated the bowling the way opponents dominated theirs. Both the tournament's centuries, by Lance Klusener and Sourav Ganguly, were scored against their attack, weakened by the continued absence of Heath Streak.

India were also without a leading light: Sachin Tendulkar was in Australia consulting a specialist on his problematic lower back. Even so, they coasted through the preliminary rounds with three polished performances. Their spin bowlers proved too much for South Africa – Sunil Joshi claimed five for six, though he could not take another wicket in the tournament – while their batsmen, Ganguly in particular, savaged Zimbabwe. Vijay Bharadwaj, an all-rounder making his international debut, was the find of the tournament. Dismissed only once in four innings, he totalled 89 at precisely a run a ball, and his off-spin brought ten wickets at 12.20.

An under-strength South African side – Allan Donald, Gary Kirsten and Daryll Cullinan were all unavailable – looked rusty in their first match, but peaked when it mattered. Klusener continued his phenomenal World Cup batting form in the early part of the tournament: after the second game, against Zimbabwe, he had hit 575 runs in his past 14 one-day international innings, at an average of 287.50. And when Klusener failed in the final, Herschelle Gibbs stepped up. The bowling was carried by Shaun Pollock, quietly assisted by off-spinner Derek Crookes.

Note: Matches in this section were not first-class.

KENYA v ZIMBABWE

At Gymkhana, Nairobi, September 25. Zimbabwe won by three wickets. Toss: Zimbabwe. International debuts: J. Ababu; D. T. Mutendera.

Zimbabwe did their best to squander a seemingly indomitable position, though the momentum gained from Goodwin's undefeated 76 was just enough to carry them home with four balls to spare. Kenya had started well, reaching 121 for one in the 33rd over thanks to a partnership of 100 between Shah and Tikolo. But wickets then fell with regularity, and Kenya could set a target of only 200 on a good pitch. With their reply stuck on 31, Zimbabwe lost both openers – Johnson to the first ball of 19-year-old Josephat Ababu's international career. Goodwin and Andy Flower added 109 for the fourth wicket and took Zimbabwe to within 19 of victory with almost ten overs left. Those 19 eventually came, but for the loss of four wickets and a fair bit of face.

Man of the Match: M. W. Goodwin.

Kenya

†K. O. Otieno c Goodwin b Johnson	7	J. K. Kamande not out		2
R. D. Shah c and b G. J. Whittall	71	M. A. Suji not out		0
S. O. Tikolo run out	33			
*M. O. Odumbe lbw b Campbell	12	B 4, l-b 10, w 4, n-b 1		19
H. S. Modi c Mutendera b A. R. Whittall	31			
T. M. Odoyo c Johnson b Campbell	8	1/21 2/121 (8 wkts, 50 overs)		199
A. O. Suji c Strang b G. J. Whittall	8	3/133 4/156		
Mohammad Sheikh c Carlisle		5/170 6/184		
b G. J. Whittall	8	7/193 8/198		

J. Ababu did not bat.

Bowling: Johnson 7–0–24–1; Mutendera 5–0–20–0; A. R. Whittall 9–0–31–1; Blignaut 1–0–5–0; Strang 5–0–21–0; G. J. Whittall 10–1–29–3; G. W. Flower 10–0–35–0; Campbell 3–0–20–2.

Zimbabwe

N. C. Johnson b Ababu	8	A. M. Blignaut c Modi b Tikolo		0
G. W. Flower lbw b Odoyo	18	P. A. Strang not out		0
*A. D. R. Campbell st Otieno b Odumbe	27			
M. W. Goodwin not out	76	B 2, l-b 4, w 5		11
†A. Flower c Ababu b Tikolo	55			
G. J. Whittall c Tikolo		1/31 2/31 3/72 (7 wkts, 49.2 overs)		200
b Mohammad Sheikh	5	4/181 5/192		
S. V. Carlisle c Otieno b Tikolo	0	6/197 7/197		

A. R. Whittall and D. T. Mutendera did not bat.

Bowling: M. A. Suji 5–0–21–0; Odoyo 8.2–1–32–1; Ababu 6–1–26–1; Mohammad Sheikh 10–0–57–1; Odumbe 10–2–31–1; Tikolo 9–3–22–3; Shah 1–0–5–0.

Umpires: Athar Zaidi and E. A. Nicholls.

INDIA v SOUTH AFRICA

At Gymkhana, Nairobi, September 26. India won by eight wickets. Toss: South Africa. International debuts: R. V. Bharadwaj; H. H. Dippenaar.

On a wicket perfect for spin, South Africa foundered to their second-lowest total in limited-overs internationals. India's two off-break bowlers, Chopra and Vijay Bharadwaj, playing his first international, took four for 42 from their combined 20 overs. Slow left-armer Joshi did even better, finishing with five for six from his ten, the best figures by any bowler against South Africa and, at the time, the third most economical analysis by anyone completing his full quota of overs (see page 1257). Of the South African batsmen, Kallis alone coped with the turning ball, though he too eventually succumbed to spin. India lost two wickets to Crookes – South Africa's one slow bowler after they had misread the pitch and omitted Adams – but were never in trouble, sailing home with more than half their overs unused.

Man of the Match: S. B. Joshi.

South Africa

H. H. Dippenaar b Joshi	17	D. N. Crookes c M. S. K. Prasad	
H. H. Gibbs c Dravid b Joshi	18	b Chopra .	8
†M. V. Boucher run out	0	S. Elworthy c Jadeja b Chopra	0
J. H. Kallis c Mohanty b Bharadwaj	38		
*W. J. Cronje c Ramesh b Joshi	2	B 4, l-b 4	8
D. M. Benkenstein c and b Chopra	18		
J. N. Rhodes c Chopra b Joshi	1	1/32 2/32 3/39 (48 overs) 117	
S. M. Pollock c Dravid b Joshi	0	4/45 5/83 6/85	
L. Klusener not out	7	7/85 8/104 9/117	

Bowling: B. K. V. Prasad 9–1–23–0; Mohanty 6–1–21–0; Joshi 10–6–6–5; Chopra 10–0–26–3; Bharadwaj 10–3–16–1; Ramesh 2–0–7–0; Dravid 1–0–10–0.

India

S. Ramesh c Pollock b Crookes	36
S. C. Ganguly c Pollock b Crookes	38
R. V. Bharadwaj not out	18
R. Dravid not out	9
B 4, l-b 7, w 6, n-b 2	19

1/72 2/104 (2 wkts, 22.4 overs) 120

*A. Jadeja, R. R. Singh, N. Chopra, S. B. Joshi, †M. S. K. Prasad, B. K. V. Prasad and D. S. Mohanty did not bat.

Bowling: Pollock 3–0–17–0; Kallis 1–0–12–0; Klusener 3–0–19–0; Crookes 8.4–0–47–2; Elworthy 7–2–14–0.

Umpires: E. A. Nicholls and G. Sharp.

SOUTH AFRICA v ZIMBABWE

At Gymkhana, Nairobi, September 28. South Africa won by nine wickets. Toss: South Africa.

South Africa returned to form after their drubbing by India, and avenged their defeat by Zimbabwe in the World Cup four months earlier. At 170 for two in the 39th over, Zimbabwe were cruising towards a challenging total. Then they lost Grant Flower for a pugnacious 91 and began to haemorrhage wickets. When South Africa batted, Gibbs and Klusener shot out of the blocks, zooming to 101 by the end of the 15th over. Kallis replaced Gibbs, forced to retire with an injured foot, and continued the momentum; Cronje did likewise when a wicket at last fell, at 174. Klusener reached his second one-day international hundred, off 104 balls, just before victory arrived. Each opening partnership was a limited-overs record against the opposition.

Man of the Match: L. Klusener.

Zimbabwe

N. C. Johnson b Crookes	35	P. A. Strang c Boucher b Adams	0
G. W. Flower c and b Kallis	91	A. R. Whittall b Pollock	1
*A. D. R. Campbell c Gibbs b Klusener	7	D. T. Mutendera lbw b Adams	2
M. W. Goodwin c Boucher b Dawson	27	L-b 5, w 11, n-b 1	17
†A. Flower b Dawson	6		
G. J. Rennie not out	20	1/99 2/124 3/170 (47.4 overs) 216	
S. V. Carlisle c Pollock b Dawson	0	4/172 5/186 6/186	
G. J. Whittall c and b Adams	10	7/198 8/207 9/213	

Bowling: Pollock 9–2–30–1; Dawson 9–1–36–3; Kallis 9–1–35–1; Klusener 7–0–30–1; Crookes 5–0–37–1; Adams 8.4–0–43–3.

South Africa

H. H. Gibbs retired hurt	48
L. Klusener not out	101
J. H. Kallis b G. J. Whittall	25
*W. J. Cronje not out	31
L-b 4, w 5, n-b 3	12

1/174 (1 wkt, 35 overs) 217

J. N. Rhodes, D. M. Benkenstein, S. M. Pollock, †M. V. Boucher, D. N. Crookes, A. C. Dawson and P. R. Adams did not bat.

Gibbs retired hurt at 125.

Bowling: Johnson 4–0–26–0; Mutendera 4–0–26–0; A. R. Whittall 10–0–46–0; G. W. Flower 5–1–35–0; G. J. Whittall 10–0–46–1; Strang 2–0–34–0.

Umpires: Athar Zaidi and G. Sharp.

KENYA v INDIA

At Gymkhana, Nairobi, September 29. India won by 58 runs. Toss: Kenya.

A slow pitch made run-scoring difficult for both sides. After 22 overs, India had trudged to just 56, also held back by inspired Kenyan fielding. Importantly, however, they had lost only one wicket, allowing more expansive batting later on. Although the opener, Ramesh, needed 116 balls for his half-century, Jadeja hit 31 at a run a ball – and Bharadwaj savaged an unbeaten 41 from just 30. When the Kenyans batted, they showed no such patience – and paid the price. Otieno, having already dropped Chopra and missed a stumping chance against Jadeja, edged the first ball of the innings from the hand of one Prasad into the gloves of the other. Tikolo followed next over and, by the end of the tenth, Kenya were a desperate 42 for four. There was no way back. Mannava Prasad made five dismissals to share what was then the record in one-day internationals.

Man of the Match: R. V. Bharadwaj.

India

S. Ramesh st Otieno b Odumbe	50	S. B. Joshi c and b Odumbe	6
S. C. Ganguly c Odoyo b M. A. Suji	21	†M. S. K. Prasad not out	4
R. Dravid c Vadher b Odumbe	30	B 3, l-b 1, w 17	21
*A. Jadeja run out	31		
N. Chopra c and b Tikolo	13	1/35 2/111 3/116 (7 wkts, 50 overs) 220	
R. V. Bharadwaj not out	41	4/134 5/189	
R. R. Singh b Odoyo	3	6/198 7/211	

B. K. V. Prasad and D. S. Mohanty did not bat.

Bowling: M. A. Suji 8–1–25–1; Odoyo 10–0–35–1; A. O. Suji 7–1–24–0; Ababu 4–1–15–0; Tikolo 10–0–49–1; Mohammad Sheikh 3–0–17–0; Odumbe 8–1–51–3.

Kenya

†K. O. Otieno c M. S. K. Prasad		A. O. Suji c M. S. K. Prasad	
b B. K. V. Prasad .	0	b Bharadwaj .	27
R. D. Shah c Joshi b Mohanty	26	Mohammad Sheikh c M. S. K. Prasad	
S. O. Tikolo c Chopra b Mohanty	8	b B. K. V. Prasad .	1
*M. O. Odumbe c M. S. K. Prasad		M. A. Suji not out	11
b B. K. V. Prasad .	5	J. Ababu b Chopra	11
A. V. Vadher c and b Bharadwaj	18	L-b 7, w 5	12
H. S. Modi st M. S. K. Prasad b Chopra	10		
T. M. Odoyo c B. K. V. Prasad		1/0 2/11 3/21 4/42 5/65 (50 overs) 162	
b Bharadwaj .	33	6/76 7/133 8/138 9/140	

Bowling: B. K. V. Prasad 9–2–26–3; Mohanty 8–2–25–2; Joshi 10–3–24–0; Chopra 10–2–18–2; Bharadwaj 7–0–38–3; Singh 6–1–24–0.

Umpires: Athar Zaidi and E. A. Nicholls.

KENYA v SOUTH AFRICA

At Gymkhana, Nairobi, September 30. South Africa won by 24 runs. Toss: Kenya. International debut: P. Ochieng.

A spirited Kenyan all-round performance fleetingly threatened an upset, but in the end South Africa's bowlers – in particular Pollock, who took three for ten – snuffed out the challenge. Earlier, Cronje had unexpectedly decided to open the batting, a gamble that did not pay off. Rhodes, who could have been caught at backward point before scoring, hit 45 from 46 balls, and in general the South African batsmen played themselves in, only to get out when going well. Kenya were never up with the asking-rate but, until Tikolo and Odoyo were parted at 156, there was a glimmer of hope. In a beautiful innings, Tikolo cut and pulled the quicker bowlers and punished anything short from Adams.

Man of the Match: S. O. Tikolo.

South Africa

H. H. Dippenaar c Shah b Ochieng	26	†M. V. Boucher not out	28
*W. J. Cronje c Otieno b M. A. Suji . . .	2	S. Elworthy not out	2
L. Klusener c Odoyo b A. O. Suji	22		
J. H. Kallis c Odumbe b A. O. Suji	39	B 4, l-b 2, w 4, n-b 4	14
D. M. Benkenstein c Odoyo			
b Mohammad Sheikh .	12	1/23 2/55 3/56 (7 wkts, 50 overs) 220	
J. N. Rhodes c Ochieng b M. A. Suji . . .	45	4/83 5/156	
S. M. Pollock b Odoyo	30	6/157 7/207	

P. V. Mpitsang and P. R. Adams did not bat.

Bowling: M. A. Suji 9–1–37–2; Odoyo 10–1–37–1; A. O. Suji 7–1–24–2; Ochieng 4–0–10–1; Mohammad Sheikh 6–0–31–1; Odumbe 10–0–45–0; Tikolo 4–0–30–0.

Kenya

†K. O. Otieno lbw b Kallis	7	Mohammad Sheikh c Klusener b Pollock	9
R. D. Shah c Boucher b Pollock	9	M. A. Suji b Kallis	0
A. V. Vadher c Boucher b Klusener	17	P. Ochieng not out	0
S. O. Tikolo lbw b Cronje	67	L-b 17, w 15, n-b 1	33
*M. O. Odumbe b Klusener	3		
H. S. Modi c Cronje b Adams	10	1/20 2/28 3/60 (48.1 overs) 196	
T. M. Odoyo c Boucher b Pollock	41	4/74 5/96 6/156	
A. O. Suji c Rhodes b Adams	0	7/167 8/195 9/196	

Bowling: Pollock 8.1–3–10–3; Kallis 9–1–27–2; Elworthy 7–1–21–0; Klusener 8–0–29–2; Adams 10–0–57–2; Mpitsang 3–1–14–0; Cronje 3–0–21–1.

Umpires: E. A. Nicholls and G. Sharp.

INDIA v ZIMBABWE

At Gymkhana, Nairobi, October 1. India won by 107 runs. Toss: Zimbabwe.

Ganguly's eighth hundred in 120 limited-overs internationals took the game far beyond Zimbabwe's reach and saw India, unbeaten in the preliminary games, to the final. Cloud cover encouraged Campbell to field, but the pitch proved perfect for batting. Ganguly started at a restrained pace, putting on 70 for the first wicket in 16 overs with Ramesh, then accelerated. Though he was dropped by Mbangwa when 67, it was otherwise one-way traffic. In a coruscating innings, he hit 11 fours and five sixes, finishing on 139 from 147 balls in the 47th over. As others joined in the attack, India pillaged 94 off the last ten overs. For Zimbabwe, victory was not enough: to reach the final on net run-rate they needed 278 in 42.1 overs, an asking-rate of 6.59. They had made 52 without loss after ten overs but, once the openers went, no one else stayed for long.

Man of the Match: S. C. Ganguly.

India

S. Ramesh b G. J. Whittall	31	S. B. Joshi b G. J. Whittall	25
S. C. Ganguly c Campbell b Olonga . . .	139	N. Chopra not out	2
R. R. Singh c sub (A. M. Blignaut)			
b G. J. Whittall .	41	L-b 5, w 8	13
R. Dravid lbw b Goodwin	12		
*A. Jadeja c Johnson b Olonga	8	1/70 2/177 3/213 (6 wkts, 50 overs)	277
R. V. Bharadwaj not out	6	4/224 5/245 6/274	

†M. S. K. Prasad, B. K. V. Prasad and D. S. Mohanty did not bat.

Bowling: Johnson 4–0–14–0; Mbangwa 10–1–54–0; Olonga 10–0–48–2; A. R. Whittall 10–0–68–0; G. J. Whittall 10–0–55–3; G. W. Flower 4–0–21–0; Goodwin 2–0–12–1.

Zimbabwe

N. C. Johnson c Joshi b Chopra	52	A. R. Whittall c Jadeja b Bharadwaj . . .	6
G. W. Flower c Dravid b B. K. V. Prasad .	38	H. K. Olonga c Ramesh b Chopra	4
*A. D. R. Campbell run out	2	M. Mbangwa not out	0
S. V. Carlisle c Dravid b Mohanty	21		
M. W. Goodwin c Jadeja b Chopra	11	L-b 1, w 2, n-b 2	5
†A. Flower lbw b Chopra	0		
G. J. Rennie c Singh b Bharadwaj	20	1/52 2/65 3/92 (38.3 overs)	170
G. J. Whittall c B. K. V. Prasad		4/120 5/120 6/131	
b Bharadwaj .	11	7/158 8/160 9/170	

Bowling: B. K. V. Prasad 8–1–23–1; Mohanty 8–0–45–1; Chopra 8.3–0–33–4; Joshi 7–0–26–0; Bharadwaj 6–0–34–3; Ramesh 1–0–8–0.

Umpires: E. A. Nicholls and G. Sharp.

QUALIFYING TABLE

	Played	Won	Lost	Points	Net run-rate
India	3	3	0	6	2.04
South Africa	3	2	1	4	−0.23
Zimbabwe	3	1	2	2	−1.21
Kenya	3	0	3	0	−0.57

Net run-rate is calculated by subtracting runs conceded per over from runs scored per over.

FINAL

INDIA v SOUTH AFRICA

At Gymkhana, Nairobi, October 3. South Africa won by 26 runs. Toss: India.

South Africa won an entertaining game despite struggling to 18 for three in 11 overs. The Indian seam bowlers dominated until Cronje joined Gibbs; together they rallied the innings, adding 78 at almost a run a ball. Crookes helped maintain the recovery after Cronje misread a flighted delivery from Chopra, and South Africa reached 187 before Gibbs was sixth out for a resolute 84. India wrested the initiative back with another wicket three balls later, but a quick-fire 23 from Pollock finished the innings with a flourish. Needing 236, India also faltered early on, losing both openers for 25, before rebuilding. Mannava Prasad, promoted to No. 4, battled both accurate bowling and cramp to keep India in the hunt. And although he was forced to retire at 134 for three, the runs continued to come: with 46 required from seven overs, and five wickets remaining, the game was wide open. Prasad returned, but the close finish never materialised.

Man of the Match: H. H. Gibbs.   *Man of the Series:* R. V. Bharadwaj.

South Africa

H. H. Gibbs b Bharadwaj	84	S. M. Pollock not out		23
L. Klusener b Mohanty	0	†M. V. Boucher c Jadeja b Bharadwaj		10
J. H. Kallis c Dravid b B. K. V. Prasad	9	A. C. Dawson run out		6
J. N. Rhodes c Ganguly		S. Elworthy not out		9
b B. K. V. Prasad	0	B 2, l-b 5, w 2, n-b 3		12
*W. J. Cronje b Chopra	39			
D. N. Crookes c M. S. K. Prasad		1/2 2/12 3/18	(9 wkts, 50 overs)	235
b Mohanty	25	4/96 5/149 6/187		
D. M. Benkenstein b Bharadwaj	18	7/188 8/212 9/219		

Bowling: B. K. V. Prasad 10–5–21–2; Mohanty 10–2–36–2; Joshi 10–0–55–0; Chopra 9–0–48–1; Singh 2–0–18–0; Ganguly 1–0–16–0; Bharadwaj 8–0–34–3.

India

S. Ramesh c Crookes b Dawson	8	N. Chopra c Crookes b Klusener		5
S. C. Ganguly c Boucher b Pollock	10	B. K. V. Prasad not out		3
R. Dravid c Rhodes b Crookes	30	D. S. Mohanty lbw b Kallis		0
†M. S. K. Prasad run out	63			
*A. Jadeja c sub (H. H. Dippenaar)		L-b 4, w 5, n-b 3		12
b Pollock	30			
R. V. Bharadwaj c Pollock b Klusener	24	1/18 2/25 3/90	(47.3 overs)	209
R. R. Singh b Crookes	6	4/141 5/163 6/190		
S. B. Joshi st Boucher b Crookes	18	7/196 8/201 9/208		

M. S. K. Prasad, when 56, retired hurt at 134 and resumed at 196.

Bowling: Pollock 9–0–28–2; Dawson 10–1–43–1; Kallis 8.3–0–33–1; Klusener 7–0–33–2; Crookes 9–0–47–3; Elworthy 4–0–21–0.

Umpires: E. A. Nicholls and G. Sharp.
Referee: M. H. Denness (England).

COCA-COLA CHAMPIONS' TROPHY, 1999-2000

Against a background of rumours that Justice Qayyum's report into match-fixing would recommend bans or fines for their key players, Pakistan turned on a display of cricket of the highest quality to take their 11th Sharjah tournament. Even in the last preliminary game, when they had guaranteed a place in the final, they did not let their standards drop. Four wins and a tie took their unbeaten sequence to eight – including five wins against West Indies – since their abject performance in the World Cup final.

True, their opponents, Sri Lanka and West Indies, were not the forces in the one-day game they once were, but Pakistan – apart from the tied match with Sri Lanka – barely needed to break into a sweat. Their margins of victory tell the story: 130, 118, 138 and 88 runs. They also show how lucky they were with the toss, winning five out of five and electing to bat each time. As all games were day/night fixtures, this allowed the Pakistan bowlers to exploit evening dew and generate considerable reverse swing. Azhar Mahmood proved especially adept, picking up 13 wickets at 9.69, including 11 in the last two games, while Abdur Razzaq took five in the first match against Sri Lanka.

Pakistan may have been without the injured Shoaib Akhtar (shoulder) and Saqlain Mushtaq (knee), but they had much the strongest attack, bowling out their opponents in each game. They also had the tournament's best batsmen. In conditions that never favoured strokeplay, Inzamam-ul-Haq was the epitome of consistency with scores of 71, 42, 33, 61 and 54. Yousuf Youhana prospered, too, hitting 175 at 43.75.

Sri Lanka and West Indies had a less happy time. Sri Lanka lost a tight game when the two first met, choked spectacularly but clung on for a tie against Pakistan, then crushed West Indies in the return match. It proved enough to take them to the final.

After an initial success, West Indies lurched from disaster to catastrophe. In a tournament characterised by collapse, they got it down to a fine art. Their last three games saw them lose five wickets for 16 runs, seven for 19 and seven for 25. Before the last qualifying match, team sponsors Cable & Wireless promised $US50,000 if West Indies won the competition. They could safely have offered the world. West Indies were unlucky to lose Jimmy Adams during the second game, but the dire state of their batting was illustrated by the fact that just one player, Wavell Hinds, averaged above 18. As part of their policy of alternating Courtney Walsh and Curtly Ambrose between one-day tournaments, to conserve their energy, Walsh was rested, but Ambrose, though economical, was less penetrative than usual.

Note: Matches in this section were not first-class.

SRI LANKA v WEST INDIES

At Sharjah, October 13 (day/night). West Indies won by three wickets. Toss: Sri Lanka.

On a lifeless pitch, West Indies made a meal of overhauling a modest target, eventually winning with four balls to spare thanks to a gritty unbeaten 74 from Adams. It was their sole success in the tournament. Though Adams claimed the match award, West Indies' victory owed as much to Ambrose, who bowled his ten overs in a single spell at a cost of just five runs. Only his erstwhile colleague, Phil Simmons, had bowled a full quota of overs for fewer runs, against Pakistan at Sydney in 1992-93. Useful, if more expensive, support came from the occasional off-spin of Campbell, who removed de Silva as he looked to increase the tempo.

Man of the Match: J. C. Adams.

MOST ECONOMICAL BOWLING IN LIMITED-OVERS INTERNATIONALS

(Minimum 10 overs)

10–8–3–4	P. V. Simmons	West Indies v Pakistan at Sydney	1992-93
10–5–5–1	**C. E. L. Ambrose**	**West Indies v Sri Lanka at Sharjah . . . . . .**	**1999-2000**
12–8–6–1	B. S. Bedi	India v East Africa at Leeds	1975
10–6–6–5	**S. B. Joshi**	**India v South Africa at Nairobi . . . .**	**1999-2000**
10–5–8–4	C. M. Old	England v Canada at Manchester	1979
10–4–8–1	E. J. Chatfield	New Zealand v Sri Lanka at Dunedin	1982-83
10–4–8–2	C. E. L. Ambrose	West Indies v Scotland at Leicester	1999
10–4–8–4	**G. D. McGrath**	**Australia v India at Sydney . . . .**	**1999-2000**
10–5–9–2	M. F. Malone	Australia v West Indies at Melbourne	1981-82
10–4–9–4	Abdul Qadir	Pakistan v New Zealand at Sharjah	1985-86

Research: Gordon Vince

Sri Lanka

M. S. Atapattu c Powell b Dillon	10	G. P. Wickremasinghe not out	4
*S. T. Jayasuriya c Jacobs b Ambrose . .	28	D. N. T. Zoysa run out	6
P. A. de Silva c Jacobs b Campbell	31	M. Muralitharan b McLean	0
R. P. Arnold b Campbell	20	L-b 6, w 15, n-b 1	22
D. P. M. D. Jayawardene run out	6		
L. P. C. Silva c Jacobs b Adams	4	1/39 2/55 3/90 (49.3 overs) 178
†R. S. Kaluwitharana b McLean	36	4/104 5/110 6/118
W. P. U. J. C. Vaas c Powell b Perry . . .	11	7/162 8/169 9/178

Bowling: McLean 8.3–1–40–2; Ambrose 10–5–5–1; Dillon 7–0–23–1; Perry 6–0–29–1; Adams 10–1–23–1; Campbell 8–0–52–2.

West Indies

S. L. Campbell hit wkt b Vaas	1	N. O. Perry c Jayasuriya b Arnold	21
*B. C. Lara c Kaluwitharana b Vaas . . .	0	N. A. M. McLean not out	3
J. C. Adams not out	74	B 1, l-b 4, w 4, n-b 1	10
W. W. Hinds c de Silva b Muralitharan. .	35		
S. Chanderpaul c Atapattu b de Silva . . .	22	1/1 2/4 3/52 (7 wkts, 49.2 overs) 181
R. L. Powell b Muralitharan	15	4/89 5/114
†R. D. Jacobs run out	0	6/115 7/164

M. Dillon and C. E. L. Ambrose did not bat.

Bowling: Vaas 9–2–22–2; Zoysa 6.2–1–24–0; Wickremasinghe 6–0–26–0; Muralitharan 10–1–24–2; Arnold 10–1–36–1; de Silva 6–0–28–1; Jayasuriya 1–0–9–0; Jayawardene 1–0–7–0.

Umpires: R. S. Dunne and D. R. Shepherd.

PAKISTAN v WEST INDIES

At Sharjah, October 14 (day/night). Pakistan won by 130 runs. Toss: Pakistan. International debut: Shoaib Malik.

A disastrous match for the West Indians saw them not only plummet to what was briefly their heaviest defeat in terms of runs – nine worse than when Australia beat them by 121 at Adelaide in 1995-96 – but also lose their only in-form batsman to injury. Adams had just been hit for two sixes in three balls by Saeed Anwar when he damaged his knee ligaments and was unable to continue. Anwar fell soon afterwards for a crisp 72, but Inzamam-ul-Haq, with an equally aggressive

71, and then Moin Khan, crashing 27 from 16 balls, built on Pakistan's sound base. Even the metronomic Ambrose went for 33 in his last five overs. For West Indies, there were thirties from Campbell and – at a run a ball – Powell, but the result was never in doubt. Seventeen-year-old off-spinner Shoaib Malik, on debut, removed them both.

Man of the Match: Saeed Anwar.

Pakistan

Saeed Anwar c Lara b McLean	72	Azhar Mahmood not out	2
Aamir Sohail b Perry	18		
Inzamam-ul-Haq run out	71	L-b 4, w 8, n-b 1	13
Yousuf Youhana run out	48		
†Moin Khan not out	27	1/49 2/121 3/218 (5 wkts, 50 overs) 260	
*Wasim Akram c Powell b Perry	9	4/223 5/237	

Hasan Raza, Abdur Razzaq, Shoaib Malik and Arshad Khan did not bat.

Bowling: McLean 10–0–55–1; Ambrose 10–0–41–0; Dillon 9–1–31–0; Perry 9–0–53–2; Adams 1.4–0–16–0; Chanderpaul 8.2–0–50–0; Campbell 2–0–10–0.

West Indies

S. L. Campbell lbw b Shoaib Malik	34	N. A. M. McLean lbw b Abdur Razzaq	0
*B. C. Lara c Moin Khan		C. E. L. Ambrose c Shoaib Malik	
b Wasim Akram	8	b Arshad Khan	3
W. W. Hinds c Aamir Sohail		M. Dillon st Moin Khan b Aamir Sohail	0
b Azhar Mahmood	13	J. C. Adams absent hurt	
S. Chanderpaul run out	5		
R. L. Powell st Moin Khan		L-b 4, w 7, n-b 1	12
b Shoaib Malik	36		
†R. D. Jacobs not out	16	1/23 2/45 3/58 (34.4 overs) 130	
N. O. Perry c Wasim Akram		4/79 5/114 6/120	
b Abdur Razzaq	3	7/120 8/127 9/130	

Bowling: Wasim Akram 6–1–15–1; Abdur Razzaq 8–1–26–2; Azhar Mahmood 5–0–24–1; Shoaib Malik 8–1–34–2; Arshad Khan 6–0–24–1; Aamir Sohail 1.4–0–3–1.

Umpires: D. B. Cowie and R. S. Dunne.

PAKISTAN v SRI LANKA

At Sharjah, October 15 (day/night). Tied. Toss: Pakistan.

In an astonishing nine-ball spell, Abdur Razzaq took four for nought to snatch a tie from what seemed a certain Sri Lankan victory. At one stage, they needed just 24 from ten overs with eight wickets remaining. But when Razzaq returned to bowl three of the last five overs, the Sri Lankan collapse had already started. Even so, with 14 required from 30 balls and five wickets left, they still looked safe. Razzaq, whose previous seven overs had gone for 28, conceded three runs (two were overthrows) to tilt matters further Sri Lanka's way. Then he sliced through the lower order with unplayable reverse swing, hitting the stumps three times to complete a career-best five for 31. Earlier, the Pakistan batsmen never fully coped with a turning ball, though at 131 for two they would have hoped for a larger total. For Sri Lanka, Kaluwitharana and Arnold put on 115 for the second wicket to manoeuvre them into an ostensibly impregnable position. It was the 16th tie in 1,514 one-day internationals.

Man of the Match: Abdur Razzaq.

Pakistan

Saeed Anwar c and b Vaas	30	Abdur Razzaq not out	7
Aamir Sohail b Vaas	6	Shoaib Malik c and b Jayasuriya	0
Inzamam-ul-Haq c Jayasuriya b Arnold	42	Arshad Khan b Arnold	2
Yousuf Youhana run out	48	B 4, l-b 8, w 8, n-b 2	22
Hasan Raza c Jayasuriya b Muralitharan	14		
†Moin Khan b Muralitharan	6	1/37 2/38 3/131 (49.4 overs) 196	
*Wasim Akram run out	2	4/157 5/163 6/168	
Azhar Mahmood run out	17	7/185 8/188 9/189	

Bowling: Vaas 8–2–29–2; Zoysa 8–0–24–0; Perera 5–0–28–0; Muralitharan 10–1–22–2; Jayasuriya 9–0–43–1; Arnold 9.4–0–38–2.

Sri Lanka

M. S. Atapattu c Moin Khan b Wasim Akram	11	L. P. C. Silva b Abdur Razzaq	13
†R. S. Kaluwitharana c Moin Khan b Abdur Razzaq	75	A. S. A. Perera b Abdur Razzaq	0
		W. P. U. J. C. Vaas b Abdur Razzaq	0
R. P. Arnold b Shoaib Malik	61	M. Muralitharan run out	1
P. A. de Silva b Wasim Akram	9	D. N. T. Zoysa not out	0
*S. T. Jayasuriya c Moin Khan b Wasim Akram	1	B 2, l-b 9, w 11, n-b 2	24
D. P. M. D. Jayawardene c Moin Khan b Abdur Razzaq	1	1/42 2/157 3/173 (49.1 overs) 196	
		4/174 5/177 6/186	
		7/186 8/194 9/196	

Bowling: Wasim Akram 10–1–38–3; Abdur Razzaq 9.1–2–31–5; Azhar Mahmood 9–2–33–0; Shoaib Malik 10–0–42–1; Arshad Khan 8–0–33–0; Aamir Sohail 3–1–8–0.

Umpires: D. B. Cowie and D. R. Shepherd.

SRI LANKA v WEST INDIES

At Sharjah, October 17 (day/night). Sri Lanka won by nine wickets. Toss: West Indies.

After losing their previous match by more runs than ever before, West Indies ensured an unwelcome symmetry by losing this one by a record number of wickets. The openers departed quickly, but Hinds, first with Lara (run out at the non-striker's end by a direct hit from Muralitharan at short third man) and then Chanderpaul, effected a slow recovery. At 126 for three in the 41st over, they needed to accelerate. But the search for runs brought only wickets, the last seven falling for 19. Three went to Muralitharan, who bamboozled the lower order. Jayasuriya then came out with all guns blazing, hitting Dillon for two sixes and a four in four balls. He faced only 80 deliveries for his 88, which took him past 5,000 runs in one-day internationals.

Man of the Match: S. T. Jayasuriya.

West Indies

S. L. Campbell c Chandana b Zoysa	6	C. E. L. Ambrose st Kaluwitharana b Muralitharan	4
†R. D. Jacobs c Chandana b Vaas	1	M. Dillon c de Silva b Muralitharan	0
W. W. Hinds c and b de Silva	58	R. D. King not out	0
*B. C. Lara run out	29	L-b 6, w 2, n-b 1	9
S. Chanderpaul c Kaluwitharana b Arnold	31		
R. L. Powell run out	0	1/3 2/21 3/62 (49.3 overs) 145	
C. H. Gayle c Jayawardene b Muralitharan	7	4/126 5/127 6/134	
N. O. Perry b Arnold	0	7/134 8/142 9/145	

Bowling: Vaas 7–3–15–1; Zoysa 7–2–14–1; Arnold 10–1–32–2; Muralitharan 9.3–0–22–3; Chandana 6–0–28–0; de Silva 10–3–28–1.

Sri Lanka

*S. T. Jayasuriya b Perry	88
†R. S. Kaluwitharana not out	44
R. P. Arnold not out	8
L-b 2, w 3, n-b 1	6

1/128   (1 wkt, 28 overs) 146

M. S. Atapattu, P. A. de Silva, D. P. M. D. Jayawardene, L. P. C. Silva, U. D. U. Chandana, W. P. U. J. C. Vaas, D. N. T. Zoysa and M. Muralitharan did not bat.

Bowling: Dillon 6–1–40–0; Ambrose 4–0–21–0; King 7–0–33–0; Perry 8–0–45–1; Gayle 3–0–5–0.

Umpires: R. S. Dunne and D. R. Shepherd.

PAKISTAN v SRI LANKA

At Sharjah, October 18 (day/night). Pakistan won by 118 runs. Toss: Pakistan.

This was a notable victory for Pakistan's youth policy, with three teenagers playing prominent roles in their handsome win. Their innings was built around whirlwind fifties from two 19-year-old all-rounders: Shahid Afridi clobbered five sixes from his 50 balls, Abdur Razzaq four from 51. More sedate support came from most of the middle order. After Shabbir Ahmed, playing his second one-day international, had decapitated Sri Lanka's reply, removing both openers in his first three overs, they regrouped through de Silva and Atapattu. But the latter's departure was the signal for a rush of Sri Lankan wickets: seven went for 37, two to Afridi's leg-spin and two to 17-year-old Shoaib Malik, who also ran out Silva. Pakistan's success saw them safely to the final.

Man of the Match: Shahid Afridi.

Pakistan

Saeed Anwar c Jayasuriya b Zoysa	0	*Wasim Akram st Kaluwitharana
Shahid Afridi c Jayawardene b Vaas	58	b Jayasuriya . 3
Wajahatullah Wasti st Kaluwitharana		Azhar Mahmood b Vaas . 16
b Chandana .	21	Shoaib Malik not out . 3
Inzamam-ul-Haq st Kaluwitharana		L-b 6, w 5, n-b 3 . 14
b Jayasuriya .	33	
Yousuf Youhana c and b Muralitharan	3	1/1 2/70 3/96 (8 wkts, 50 overs) 239
†Moin Khan b Jayasuriya	29	4/105 5/137 6/184
Abdur Razzaq not out	59	7/196 8/231

Shabbir Ahmed did not bat.

Bowling: Vaas 9 1 38 2; Zoysa 8 0 32 1; Muralitharan 10–1–57–1; Chandana 10–0–38–1; Jayasuriya 10–0–41–3; Arnold 3–0–27–0.

Sri Lanka

*S. T. Jayasuriya c Saeed Anwar		U. D. U. Chandana b Shahid Afridi . 5
b Shabbir Ahmed .	5	W. P. U. J. C. Vaas c Azhar Mahmood
†R. S. Kaluwitharana b Moin Khan		b Shahid Afridi . 7
b Shabbir Ahmed .	2	D. N. T. Zoysa c and b Shoaib Malik . 1
R. P. Arnold c and b Wasim Akram	4	M. Muralitharan not out . 2
P. A. de Silva run out	35	
M. S. Atapattu c Inzamam-ul-Haq		L-b 6, w 4, n-b 11. 21
b Azhar Mahmood .	29	
D. P. M. D. Jayawardene		1/9 2/15 3/15 (33.4 overs) 121
c Shabbir Ahmed b Shoaib Malik .	2	4/84 5/91 6/103
L. P. C. Silva run out	8	7/110 8/111 9/118

Bowling: Wasim Akram 6–1–16–1; Shabbir Ahmed 6–2–11–2; Azhar Mahmood 5–0–23–1; Abdur Razzaq 5–0–23–0; Shoaib Malik 8.4–0–36–2; Shahid Afridi 3–1–6–2.

Umpires: D. B. Cowie and D. R. Shepherd.

PAKISTAN v WEST INDIES

At Sharjah, October 19 (day/night). Pakistan won by 138 runs. Toss: Pakistan.

Another day, another West Indian collapse. For the third successive match their last five wickets crumpled for less than 20. This defeat was, again, their heaviest by runs, beating their loss by 130 against Pakistan five days earlier. To reach the final, West Indies had to win, but that never seemed likely; Pakistan had won their last five meetings, and had hit impressive form. To make matters worse, Ambrose had a hand injury and did not play. For Pakistan, yet another precocious talent, 17-year-old Hasan Raza, compiled a measured 77, and Yousuf Youhana cut loose at the end: his unbeaten 71, with four sixes and three fours, spanned 46 balls as Pakistan plundered 99 from the last ten overs. At 92 for three in the 20th over, West Indies were just about on course. Then Azhar Mahmood clicked into gear. Swinging the ball both ways, he ended with a career-best six for 18, then the seventh-best return in limited-overs internationals.

Man of the Match: Azhar Mahmood.

Pakistan

Shahid Afridi lbw b King	4	Abdur Razzaq not out		8
Wajahatullah Wasti c King b Chanderpaul	19			
Hasan Raza b King	77			
Inzamam-ul-Haq c Powell b Perry	61	L-b 4, w 8, n-b 3		15
Yousuf Youhana not out	71	1/5 2/47 3/145	(5 wkts, 50 overs)	255
*†Moin Khan run out	0	4/226 5/226		

Azhar Mahmood, Shabbir Ahmed, Mohammad Akram and Shoaib Malik did not bat.

Bowling: King 10–2–52–2; Dillon 10–0–26–0; Collins 10–0–58–0; Chanderpaul 5–0–23–1; Gayle 9–0–55–0; Perry 6–0–37–1.

West Indies

†R. D. Jacobs b Azhar Mahmood	28	W. W. Hinds c Moin Khan		
S. L. Campbell c Moin Khan		b Azhar Mahmood	8	
b Mohammad Akram	4	N. O. Perry lbw b Azhar Mahmood	1	
C. H. Gayle c Inzamam-ul-Haq		M. Dillon run out	0	
b Azhar Mahmood	22	R. D. King lbw b Azhar Mahmood	0	
*B. C. Lara c Wajahatullah Wasti		P. T. Collins not out	0	
b Shoaib Malik	30			
S. Chanderpaul c Inzamam-ul-Haq		B 2, l-b 3, w 2, n-b 3	10	
b Shoaib Malik	14			
R. L. Powell c Moin Khan		1/8 2/55 3/64 4/92 5/93	(31.3 overs)	117
b Azhar Mahmood	0	6/109 7/111 8/111 9/111		

Bowling: Mohammad Akram 6–1–18–1; Shabbir Ahmed 4–0–27–0; Abdur Razzaq 5–0–28–0; Azhar Mahmood 10–2–18–6; Shoaib Malik 6.3–1–21–2.

Umpires: D. B. Cowie and R. S. Dunne.

QUALIFYING TABLE

	Played	Won	Lost	Tied	Points	Net run-rate
Pakistan	4	3	0	1	7	1.93
Sri Lanka	4	1	2	1	3	−0.22
West Indies	4	1	3	0	2	−1.84

Net run-rate is calculated by subtracting runs conceded per over from runs scored per over.

FINAL

PAKISTAN v SRI LANKA

At Sharjah, October 22 (day/night). Pakistan won by 88 runs. Toss: Pakistan.

Another spell of accomplished swing bowling from Azhar Mahmood – as well as two unfortunate umpiring decisions – ensured a convincing Pakistan victory. Fifties from Saeed Anwar and Inzamam-ul-Haq, playing his 200th limited-overs international, were the mainstay of the innings, which, despite their efforts, never quite took off. Wasim Akram did his best late on, hitting 30 from 26 balls, though leg-spinner Chandana, with three for 40, helped restrict the target to a gettable 212. However, Sri Lanka lost their captain fourth ball, before Kaluwitharana and de Silva put on 49. Then de Silva edged to first slip, where Inzamam claimed a catch with the ball lodged between his knees. Third umpire Steve Dunne scrutinised countless replays, which suggested the ball had bounced on the ground – and then gave him out. One run later, Kaluwitharana was ruled lbw by umpire Shepherd after deflecting the ball on to his pads. After that, Mahmood ran through the batting and ended with five for 28 from his ten-over spell.

Man of the Match: Azhar Mahmood.   *Man of the Series:* Inzamam-ul-Haq.

Pakistan

Saeed Anwar c Kaluwitharana b Chandana .	53	†Moin Khan run out . . . .
Shahid Afridi c Jayawardene b Vaas	2	Azhar Mahmood not out . . . .
Abdur Razzaq c Atapattu b Zoysa	6	Shoaib Malik st Kaluwitharana b Jayasuriya .
Inzamam-ul-Haq c Zoysa b Jayasuriya . .	54	B 1, l-b 4, w 5, n-b 1 . . . .
Yousuf Youhana b Chandana	5	
Hasan Raza st Kaluwitharana b Chandana .	18	1/12 2/25 3/96 (9 wkts, 50 overs) 211
*Wasim Akram c Jayasuriya b Zoysa . . .	30	4/106 5/145 6/148
		7/179 8/194 9/211

Saeed Anwar c Kaluwitharana b Chandana . 53
Shahid Afridi c Jayawardene b Vaas 2
Abdur Razzaq c Atapattu b Zoysa 6
Inzamam-ul-Haq c Zoysa b Jayasuriya . . 54
Yousuf Youhana b Chandana 5
Hasan Raza st Kaluwitharana b Chandana . 18
*Wasim Akram c Jayasuriya b Zoysa . . . 30

†Moin Khan run out 7
Azhar Mahmood not out 13
Shoaib Malik st Kaluwitharana b Jayasuriya . 12
B 1, l-b 4, w 5, n-b 1 11

1/12 2/25 3/96   (9 wkts, 50 overs) 211
4/106 5/145 6/148
7/179 8/194 9/211

Mohammad Akram did not bat.

Bowling: Vaas 8–0–20–1; Zoysa 10–0–34–2; Wickremasinghe 4–0–31–0; Muralitharan 10–0–39–0; Chandana 10–0–40–3; Jayasuriya 8–0–42–2.

Sri Lanka

*S. T. Jayasuriya c Shahid Afridi b Wasim Akram . 0
†R. S. Kaluwitharana lbw b Wasim Akram . 10
P. A. de Silva c Inzamam-ul-Haq b Abdur Razzaq . 25
D. P. M. D. Jayawardene c Moin Khan b Azhar Mahmood . 8
M. S. Atapattu c Moin Khan b Azhar Mahmood . 3
R. P. Arnold not out 27

U. D. U. Chandana c Moin Khan b Azhar Mahmood . 0
W. P. U. J. C. Vaas c Inzamam-ul-Haq b Azhar Mahmood . 9
G. P. Wickremasinghe b Azhar Mahmood 1
D. N. T. Zoysa c and b Shoaib Malik . . . 22
M. Muralitharan b Shoaib Malik 0
L-b 5, w 9, n-b 4 18

1/0 2/49 3/50 4/57 5/66   (36 overs) 123
6/70 7/85 8/89 9/117

Bowling: Wasim Akram 8–2–21–2; Mohammad Akram 7–1–26–0; Abdur Razzaq 5–0–13–1; Azhar Mahmood 10–2–28–5; Shoaib Malik 6–1–30–2.

Umpires: D. B. Cowie and D. R. Shepherd.
Series referee: P. L. van der Merwe (South Africa).

CARLTON & UNITED SERIES, 1999-2000

Having beaten Pakistan and India 3–0 each in Test series earlier in the summer, Australia confirmed their ranking as No. 1 in both forms of the game by dominating the one-day Carlton & United Series. They lost only once, to Pakistan right at the start, and completely overwhelmed them in the finals.

Steve Waugh's Australians had the tournament's outstanding bowler in Glenn McGrath, who took 19 wickets at 15.31, and there was excellent back-up from the Lee brothers, Shane and Brett (16 each). Shane Warne's absence through injury for most of the qualifying games went unnoticed. As for the batsmen, someone was always in control, whether it was Ricky Ponting, who top-scored with 404 runs in spite of three successive mid-term ducks, Michael Bevan, Mark Waugh or Adam Gilchrist. India's Sourav Ganguly, with 356 runs from seven games, rivalled them as a main attraction, and the young Pakistani, Abdur Razzaq, shone as an all-rounder, scoring 225 runs and taking 14 wickets – sufficient to win him the Man of the Series award.

The one-sided nature of the tournament soon became apparent. India in particular were a disappointing side, out of sorts much of the time, and managed only one win in eight games. After their opening match, and a flight from Brisbane to Melbourne, Sachin Tendulkar, their captain, criticised the non-stop schedule. "It's unfair," he said. "If you want to see quality cricket, you need to give the players recovery time." Tendulkar's own sketchy form, 198 runs at 24.75, undoubtedly contributed to his team's malaise.

Although the series began with a degree of controversy, nothing matched the inflammatory circumstances of the previous season, when Muttiah Muralitharan was called for throwing. A fuse was laid, waiting for a torch, when the ICC lifted its suspension of the Pakistani fast bowler, Shoaib Akhtar, but it was never lit.

The ban was imposed after a nine-man ICC panel, acting on doubts raised by the umpires and referee during the Test series against Australia, ruled that Shoaib's action was sometimes illegal. Suspicion centred on his bouncer, which it was said he threw. Pakistan, however, appealed to the ICC, in particular to the president, Jagmohan Dalmiya, and cricket chairman Sir Clyde Walcott, and included Shoaib in their squad. The suspension, claimed the Pakistan Cricket Board's secretary, Shafqat Rana, was racially motivated. While his team-mates prepared for the series by losing to Australia A and Queensland, Shoaib remained in Perth to work on his action.

The likeliest outcome was that Shoaib would return to Pakistan without playing. Instead, the ICC relented on the eve of the tournament. By some strange logic, it was decided that an illegal action need not be considered so if the resulting delivery is a no-ball. "Since bouncers are not used in one-day cricket," Dalmiya reasoned, "as these are called no-balls, it would be best to permit Shoaib to play for Pakistan in the triangular series. Remedial coaching will be continued by the Pakistan board."

Meanwhile, Darrell Hair, one of the umpires who drew attention to Shoaib's action (and who called Muralitharan seven times at Melbourne in December 1995) rebutted claims that he and his colleagues on Australia's five-man international panel were biased and racist. In a statement read by Hair at a pre-series meeting of team officials in Brisbane, convened by the tournament referee, Cammie Smith, the umpires expressed their discontent with the criticism. The most apparent consequence of the statement was that Hair was not selected to stand in the final matches.

Note: Matches in this section were not first-class.

AUSTRALIA v PAKISTAN

At Brisbane, January 9 (day/night). Pakistan won by 45 runs. Toss: Pakistan.

Shoaib Akhtar, his ban suspended at the last minute, made a trans-continental dash from Perth and played a crucial role in his side's victory, dismissing Ponting and Steve Waugh with successive balls. Abdur Razzaq quickly trumped him with three wickets in six balls and Australia, having lost five for seven runs, were on course for their second defeat in 16 one-day internationals. Shoaib guaranteed it when he broke the eighth-wicket stand of 33 between a defiant Bevan and Dale. He had arrived at the Gabba 12 minutes after play began to find Pakistan batting and a wicket down from Dale's first over. They looked out of contention at 60 for six, but first Moin Khan and Wasim Akram (a victim of Ponting's arm from extra cover), then Saqlain Mushtaq and Waqar Younis built a total they could defend. The final over, bowled by McGrath, yielded 18 runs.

Man of the Match: Abdur Razzaq. *Attendance:* 35,738.

Pakistan

Saeed Anwar c Gilchrist b McGrath. . . .	12	Saqlain Mushtaq not out	37
Mohammad Wasim lbw b Dale.	0	Waqar Younis not out	23
Abdur Razzaq c Gilchrist b Symonds. . . .	9		
Ijaz Ahmed, sen. c Gilchrist b Symonds .	8	L-b 5, w 8, n-b 2	15
Inzamam-ul-Haq lbw b Warne	12		
Yousuf Youhana c Gilchrist b Symonds. .	0	1/2 2/20 3/24 (8 wkts, 50 overs)	184
†Moin Khan c M. E. Waugh b Warne . .	33	4/32 5/34 6/60	
*Wasim Akram run out	35	7/103 8/127	

Shoaib Akhtar did not bat.

Bowling: McGrath 10–1–35–1; Dale 10–2–19–1; Symonds 10–1–34–3; Lee 10–1–39–0; Warne 10–0–52–2.

Australia

†A. C. Gilchrist c Moin Khan		B. Lee b Abdur Razzaq.	2
b Abdur Razzaq .	27	A. C. Dale c Saeed Anwar	
M. E. Waugh lbw b Waqar Younis.	1	b Shoaib Akhtar .	15
R. T. Ponting c Mohammad Wasim		S. K. Warne c Ijaz Ahmed	
b Shoaib Akhtar .	32	b Waqar Younis .	9
M. G. Bevan not out	31	G. D. McGrath run out	0
*S. R. Waugh lbw b Shoaib Akhtar	0	B 2, l-b 7, w 3, n-b 6	18
D. R. Martyn c Ijaz Ahmed			
b Abdur Razzaq .	4	1/7 2/60 3/72 (39 overs)	139
A. Symonds c Mohammad Wasim		4/72 5/77 6/77	
b Abdur Razzaq .	0	7/79 8/112 9/132	

Bowling: Wasim Akram 8–0–39–0; Waqar Younis 8–2–25–2; Shoaib Akhtar 7–1–31–3; Abdur Razzaq 8–1–23–4; Saqlain Mushtaq 8–2–12–0.

Umpires: D. J. Harper and P. D. Parker.

INDIA v PAKISTAN

At Brisbane, January 10 (day/night). Pakistan won by two wickets. Toss: India. International debut: S. S. Dighe.

For the second night in a row, Saqlain Mushtaq and Waqar Younis starred as batsmen, this time with an entertaining if chancy stand of 43 from 37 balls that ran India ragged. Even so, it took a scampered bye off the last delivery to bring victory. Pakistan, docked one over for their slow over-rate, had been 71 for six before Yousuf Youhana's exhilarating 63 made light of conditions offering bowlers generous movement. Batting first, India had managed only eight from their first six overs and, when Abdur Razzaq ripped out Tendulkar's middle stump, the portents were ominous. Only solid fifties from Ganguly and Robin Singh saved them. Shoaib Akhtar continued to make headlines, both for initiating another collapse and, dramatically, for pulling a young fan from the path of a speeding taxi after the game. The boy had run across the road to where Shoaib was signing autographs. "He saved the kid's life," said a police sergeant.

Man of the Match: Yousuf Youhana.   *Attendance:* 15,583.

India

V. V. S. Laxman c Shahid Afridi		A. Kumble run out	16
b Waqar Younis .	9	A. B. Agarkar run out	2
S. C. Ganguly b Shoaib Akhtar.	61	J. Srinath b Wasim Akram	0
R. Dravid c Moin Khan b Shoaib Akhtar	8	B. K. V. Prasad not out	0
*S. R. Tendulkar b Abdur Razzaq	13		
H. H. Kanitkar c Moin Khan		B 1, l-b 8, w 14, n-b 7	30
b Saqlain Mushtaq .	0		
R. R. Singh c Waqar Younis		1/15 2/50 3/76 (48.5 overs)	195
b Saqlain Mushtaq .	50	4/77 5/143 6/150	
†S. S. Dighe lbw b Shoaib Akhtar.	6	7/186 8/194 9/195	

Bowling: Wasim Akram 9.5–1–45–1; Waqar Younis 8–0–30–1; Abdur Razzaq 8–1–31–1; Shoaib Akhtar 8–1–19–3; Saqlain Mushtaq 9–0–35–2; Shahid Afridi 6–0–26–0.

Pakistan

Saeed Anwar c Singh b Srinath	24	Saqlain Mushtaq not out	27
Shahid Afridi c Laxman b Srinath	0	Waqar Younis not out	13
Ijaz Ahmed, sen. lbw b Agarkar	13		
Inzamam-ul-Haq lbw b Agarkar	4	B 1, l-b 9, w 6, n-b 3	19
Yousuf Youhana c Dighe b Srinath	63		
Abdur Razzaq lbw b Kumble	6	1/7 2/36 3/42 (8 wkts, 49 overs)	196
†Moin Khan c Dravid b Srinath	3	4/55 5/64 6/71	
*Wasim Akram b Ganguly	24	7/120 8/153	

Shoaib Akhtar did not bat.

Bowling: Srinath 10–0–49–4; Agarkar 10–0–39–2; Prasad 10–2–27–0; Kumble 10–0–35–1; Ganguly 6–1–26–1; Singh 3–0–10–0.

Umpires: S. J. Davis and S. J. A. Taufel.
(D. J. Harper deputised for Davis in Pakistan's innings.)

AUSTRALIA v INDIA

At Melbourne, January 12 (day/night). Australia won by 28 runs. Toss: Australia.

Spectators in the lower Southern Stand, angered when Ganguly was run out in the 40th over, held up play for 17 minutes by hurling plastic bottles on to the outfield. Ganguly had scored his tenth one-day hundred, off 127 balls, and added 109 with Dravid, when he failed to ground his bat as Symonds's throw from cover broke the wicket. Those watching replays mistakenly believed Ganguly was safely in. Not that India looked like preventing the first win in Australia's record run of 14 one-day internationals without defeat. They were always off the pace after a slow start, not helped by two other run-outs. Australia had lost their openers inside four overs but then their batting caught fire, sparked by Ponting's sixth one-day century. His 115 off 121 balls iced the cake after his appointment as vice-captain in place of Warne, who tore a side muscle at Brisbane. The inclusion of Shane Lee for Warne provided the first instance of two sets of brothers playing for Australia.

Man of the Match: R. T. Ponting.   *Attendance:* 73,219.

Australia

M. E. Waugh c Laxman b Agarkar	7	S. Lee not out	22
†A. C. Gilchrist c Laxman b Srinath	3	D. W. Fleming not out	14
R. T. Ponting c Tendulkar b Srinath	115	B 1, l-b 2, w 8	11
M. G. Bevan c Agarkar b Singh	41		
*S. R. Waugh run out	23	1/10 2/19 3/118 (7 wkts, 50 overs)	269
D. R. Martyn c Tendulkar b Kumble	30	4/156 5/227	
A. Symonds run out	3	6/232 7/234	

B. Lee and G. D. McGrath did not bat.

Bowling: Srinath 10–0–52–2; Agarkar 9–0–47–1; Prasad 10–0–52–0; Tendulkar 3–0–23–0; Kumble 10–0–57–1; Singh 3–0–19–1; Ganguly 5–0–16–0.

India

V. V. S. Laxman c Gilchrist b McGrath	2	J. J. Martin run out	0
S. C. Ganguly run out	100	A. B. Agarkar not out	6
†S. S. Dighe c M. E. Waugh b Fleming	3	L-b 8, w 10, n-b 7	25
*S. R. Tendulkar run out	12		
R. Dravid c Martyn b S. Lee	60	1/7 2/31 3/68 (6 wkts, 50 overs)	241
R. R. Singh not out	33	4/177 5/212 6/212	

A. Kumble, J. Srinath and B. K. V. Prasad did not bat.

Bowling: McGrath 10–1–32–1; Fleming 10–1–39–1; B. Lee 10–0–49–0; S. Lee 10–0–57–1; Symonds 5–0–28–0; Martyn 5–0–28–0.

Umpires: D. J. Harper and S. J. A. Taufel.

AUSTRALIA v INDIA

At Sydney, January 14 (day/night). Australia won by five wickets. Toss: India.

The crowd may have missed out on a full evening's entertainment, but they went home happy with Australia's ruthless demolition of the Indian batting. Tendulkar elected to bat first and also chose to promote himself to open with Ganguly. That was all the spur McGrath needed: the Indian captain became his first victim in an unforgiving ten-over master-class that produced four wickets for eight runs. India's demoralisation was completed by the medium-pace of Symonds, who twice took two wickets in two balls in his three and a half overs. Without substantial help from Extras, the total would not have reached 100. Srinath then reduced the Australians to 59 for five, highlighting Mark Waugh's continuing poor form, but the target meant there was little other cause for concern.

Man of the Match: A. Symonds.   *Attendance:* 38,831.

India

S. C. Ganguly c Gilchrist b McGrath . . .	5	N. Chopra lbw b Symonds	14
*S. R. Tendulkar c Gilchrist b McGrath .	1	J. Srinath not out	5
V. V. S. Laxman b McGrath	2	B. K. V. Prasad b Symonds	0
R. Dravid lbw b Symonds	22	L-b 14, w 15, n-b 3	32
D. J. Gandhi c Bevan b B. Lee	6		
R. R. Singh c Martyn b S. Lee	11	1/6 2/9 3/18 (36.3 overs) 100	
†S. S. Dighe b Martyn b McGrath	2	4/29 5/71 6/74	
A. Kumble c Gilchrist b Symonds	0	7/74 8/82 9/100	

Bowling: McGrath 10–4–8–4; Fleming 6–0–18–0; B. Lee 10–0–29–1; S. Lee 7–0–20–1; Symonds 3.3–0–11–4.

Australia

†A. C. Gilchrist c Dravid b Srinath	37	A. Symonds not out	28
M. E. Waugh lbw b Srinath	3		
R. T. Ponting c Laxman b Prasad	0	L-b 7, w 2, n-b 5	14
M. G. Bevan c Kumble b Srinath	2		
*S. R. Waugh lbw b Srinath	4	1/28 2/29 3/55 (5 wkts, 26.5 overs) 101	
D. R. Martyn not out	13	4/56 5/59	

S. Lee, D. W. Fleming, B. Lee and G. D. McGrath did not bat.

Bowling: Srinath 10–2–30–4; Prasad 10–0–29–1; Ganguly 3.5–0–22–0; Singh 2–1–1–0; Kumble 1–0–12–0.

Umpires: P. D. Parker and S. J. A. Taufel.

AUSTRALIA v PAKISTAN

At Melbourne, January 16. Australia won by six wickets. Toss: Australia.

Pakistan made heavy weather of batting in humid, overcast conditions. Morning drizzle had delayed the start by two and a half hours, reducing the match to 41 overs a side, and the ball kicked off a length and swung prodigiously. Only two of their first seven reached double figures, and when three wickets fell in nine balls, Pakistan and the game were thankful for Abdur Razzaq's 54-ball half-century. Australia set off in a hurry, Mark Waugh and Gilchrist reaching 32 in four overs before Shoaib Akhtar reined them back with two wickets from his first four balls. Youhana ran out Mark Waugh in the seventh over, but brother Steve steadied the innings from 38 for three and was still there, 81 not out from 92 balls, when Australia eased home.

Man of the Match: S. R. Waugh.   *Attendance:* 37,325.

Pakistan

Saeed Anwar c Bevan b Symonds	49	Saqlain Mushtaq c S. R. Waugh b B. Lee	11
Wajahatullah Wasti c Gilchrist b McGrath	8	Waqar Younis c Gilchrist b McGrath	8
Ijaz Ahmed, sen. lbw b Fleming	0		
Inzamam-ul-Haq c Symonds b S. Lee	8	L-b 7, w 7, n-b 2	16
Yousuf Youhana c M. E. Waugh b S. Lee	20		
†Moin Khan c Martyn b Symonds	5	1/15 2/22 3/42 (9 wkts, 41 overs)	176
*Wasim Akram c Gilchrist b S. Lee	0	4/87 5/92 6/92	
Abdur Razzaq not out	51	7/106 8/144 9/176	

Shoaib Akhtar did not bat.

Bowling: McGrath 9–1–48–2; Fleming 8–0–33–1; B. Lee 8–0–37–1; S. Lee 8–1–24–3; Symonds 8–0–27–2.

Australia

M. E. Waugh run out	12	D. R. Martyn not out	39
†A. C. Gilchrist lbw b Shoaib Akhtar	21		
R. T. Ponting c Wajahatullah Wasti b Shoaib Akhtar	0	L-b 3, w 6	9
M. G. Bevan run out	15	1/32 2/32 (4 wkts, 38.5 overs)	177
*S. R. Waugh not out	81	3/38 4/92	

A. Symonds, S. Lee, D. W. Fleming, B. Lee and G. D. McGrath did not bat.

Bowling: Wasim Akram 7–0–29–0; Waqar Younis 6.5–0–48–0; Shoaib Akhtar 8–2–32–2; Abdur Razzaq 8–0–35–0; Saqlain Mushtaq 9–0–30–0.

Umpires: P. D. Parker and S. J. A. Taufel.

AUSTRALIA v PAKISTAN

At Sydney, January 19 (day/night). Australia won by 81 runs. Toss: Australia.

On dismissing Martyn, Wasim Akram became the first bowler to take 400 one-day international wickets: no one else had yet taken 300, but then only Mohammad Azharuddin had played more games than Wasim's 285. Later, however, the spotlight fell on a bowler playing his first one-day international. Leg-spinner MacGill's return of four for 19 was the second-best by an Australian on one-day debut after Tony Dodemaide's five for 21 against Sri Lanka in 1987-88. With 29 coming from McGrath's first two overs, and Abdur Razzaq cracking five consecutive fours from his fifth, the Pakistanis had raced to 100 inside 13 overs. MacGill put a stop to the mayhem with his sixth ball; the next 50 took almost 20 overs and cost six wickets. Batting first on a hot, sticky afternoon, Australia had called all the shots after Wasim's double strike in the ninth over. Mark Waugh became the first Australian to reach 7,000 one-day international runs, and with Bevan added 90 in 16 overs. Symonds, hitting 47 in 26 balls, and Shane Lee (26 in 13) supplied the fireworks as the final ten overs realised 101.

Man of the Match: S. C. G. MacGill.   *Attendance:* 38,006.

Australia

†A. C. Gilchrist c Moin Khan b Wasim Akram	13	S. Lee c Shoaib Akhtar b Saqlain Mushtaq	26
M. E. Waugh b Shoaib Akhtar	43	D. W. Fleming b Abdur Razzaq	0
R. T. Ponting lbw b Wasim Akram	0	S. C. G. MacGill run out	1
M. G. Bevan c Shoaib Akhtar b Azhar Mahmood	77	G. D. McGrath not out	0
*S. R. Waugh b Shoaib Akhtar	6	B 1, l-b 6, w 12, n-b 4	23
D. R. Martyn c Ijaz Ahmed b Wasim Akram	50	1/23 2/23 3/113 (49.4 overs)	286
A. Symonds c Azhar Mahmood b Abdur Razzaq	47	4/132 5/177 6/245 7/265 8/266 9/286	

Bowling: Wasim Akram 9–1–40–3; Waqar Younis 7–0–32–0; Abdur Razzaq 10–0–56–2; Shoaib Akhtar 7–0–50–2; Azhar Mahmood 8–0–37–1; Saqlain Mushtaq 8.4–0–64–1.

Pakistan

Saeed Anwar run out	23	Saqlain Mushtaq lbw b MacGill	2
Ijaz Ahmed, sen. c S. R. Waugh		Waqar Younis lbw b Symonds	37
b Fleming	23	Shoaib Akhtar not out	3
Abdur Razzaq c McGrath b MacGill	40		
Inzamam-ul-Haq lbw b Lee	12	B 1, l-b 4, w 8, n-b 5	18
Yousuf Youhana c Gilchrist b MacGill	10		
†Moin Khan c Symonds b McGrath	13	1/34 2/62 3/100	(45.2 overs) 205
Azhar Mahmood c Lee b MacGill	1	4/116 5/122 6/124	
*Wasim Akram c MacGill b Lee	23	7/138 8/143 9/186	

Bowling: McGrath 8–0–67–1; Fleming 10–0–48–1; Martyn 1–0–11–0; Lee 9–0–25–2; MacGill 10–2–19–4; M. E. Waugh 2–0–8–0; Bevan 3–0–17–0; Symonds 2.2–0–5–1.

Umpires: S. J. Davis and D. J. Harper.

INDIA v PAKISTAN

At Hobart, January 21. Pakistan won by 32 runs. Toss: India.

A tremendous all-round performance by 20-year-old Abdur Razzaq left India marooned without a point at the bottom of the table and half their games played. First, capitalising on a gem-like 67 from Ijaz Ahmed, he took Pakistan to 262 for seven with an unbeaten 70 off 52 balls, including two sixes and four fours. Next, he claimed five for 48 as India tried to beat this challenging total in only 48 overs. As if misjudging the pitch and inserting Pakistan were not bad enough, they were fined for their slow over-rate. Tendulkar and Ganguly made a good start, but Razzaq had Ganguly caught at cover, soon accounted for Laxman and had the distinction of bowling Tendulkar – who hit ten fours – for the second match in succession.

Man of the Match: Abdur Razzaq.   *Attendance:* 6,128.

Pakistan

Saeed Anwar c Dighe b Ganguly	43	*Wasim Akram c Dighe b Mohanty	2
Shahid Afridi c Tendulkar b Mohanty	12	Waqar Younis not out	3
Ijaz Ahmed, sen. b Prasad	67	L-b 6, w 5, n-b 3	14
Inzamam-ul-Haq c Dighe b Ganguly	6		
Yousuf Youhana c Mohanty b Kumble	45	1/22 2/82 3/96	(7 wkts, 50 overs) 262
†Moin Khan c Dighe b Prasad	0	4/156 5/156	
Abdur Razzaq not out	70	6/223 7/243	

Saqlain Mushtaq and Shoaib Akhtar did not bat.

Bowling: Srinath 10–0–55–0; Mohanty 10–0–76–2; Prasad 10–0–41–2; Kumble 10–2–25–1; Ganguly 8–0–43–2; Singh 1–0–10–0; Tendulkar 1–0–6–0.

India

*S. R. Tendulkar b Abdur Razzaq	93	A. Kumble b Abdur Razzaq	14
S. C. Ganguly c Shahid Afridi		J. Srinath b Abdur Razzaq	2
b Abdur Razzaq	43	B. K. V. Prasad lbw b Wasim Akram	5
V. V. S. Laxman c Moin Khan		D. S. Mohanty b Wasim Akram	0
b Abdur Razzaq	7	L-b 5, w 13, n-b 4	22
R. Dravid lbw b Wasim Akram	15		
J. J. Martin run out	16	1/99 2/111 3/156	(46.5 overs) 230
R. R. Singh c and b Shoaib Akhtar	2	4/177 5/193 6/194	
†S. S. Dighe not out	11	7/219 8/221 9/230	

Bowling: Wasim Akram 9.5–1–34–3; Shoaib Akhtar 10–0–49–1; Saqlain Mushtaq 8–0–42–0; Abdur Razzaq 10–0–48–5; Waqar Younis 2–0–19–0; Shahid Afridi 7–0–33–0.

Umpires: D. J. Harper and P. D. Parker.

AUSTRALIA v PAKISTAN

At Melbourne, January 23 (day/night). Australia won by 15 runs. Toss: Australia.

Australia reached the finals with another convincing display, but Pakistan contributed just as much to a thrilling game. Once again they set off at a cracking pace and were 88 for one when Shahid Afridi was run out in a mix-up with Ijaz Ahmed over Symonds's reactions at point. That start meant Pakistan were ahead on the Duckworth/Lewis method when rain stopped play in the 40th over, but only 20 minutes were lost and the Australians, Shane Lee to the fore, came back to snatch the last six wickets for 48. Australia's innings had again revolved around Bevan, while Ponting made amends for three successive ducks with a quick 53 and Symonds scored 35 from 36 balls. Two wickets from Shoaib Akhtar might have then curtailed Australia, but they always had sufficient in reserve. Moin Khan made five dismissals for the second time in limited-overs internationals.

Man of the Match: M. G. Bevan.   *Attendance:* 56,815.

Australia

M. E. Waugh c Moin Khan		S. Lee run out	17
b Abdur Razzaq	20	D. R. Martyn not out	12
†A. C. Gilchrist c Yousuf Youhana		D. W. Fleming st Moin Khan	
b Wasim Akram	13	b Saqlain Mushtaq	10
R. T. Ponting lbw b Shahid Afridi	53	B. Lee st Moin Khan b Saqlain Mushtaq	1
M. G. Bevan c Moin Khan		S. C. G. MacGill not out	0
b Shahid Afridi	83	L-b 3, w 2, n-b 5	10
A. Symonds c Moin Khan			
b Shoaib Akhtar	35	1/29 2/56 3/122 (9 wkts, 50 overs)	260
*S. R. Waugh c Wasim Akram		4/188 5/203 6/234	
b Shoaib Akhtar	6	7/235 8/253 9/255	

Bowling: Wasim Akram 10–1–42–1; Shoaib Akhtar 9–1–49–2; Abdur Razzaq 8–0–42–1; Azhar Mahmood 6–0–34–0; Saqlain Mushtaq 8–0–45–2; Shahid Afridi 9–0–45–2.

Pakistan

Saeed Anwar c Martyn b B. Lee	11	*Wasim Akram c M. E. Waugh b S. Lee	14
Shahid Afridi run out	45	Saqlain Mushtaq b S. Lee	2
Ijaz Ahmed, sen. b S. Lee	85	Shoaib Akhtar not out	0
Inzamam-ul-Haq c and b S. Lee	5	B 6, l-b 8, w 6, n-b 1	21
Yousuf Youhana c S. Lee b M. E. Waugh	12		
†Moin Khan lbw b B. Lee	33	1/27 2/88 3/108 (48.5 overs)	245
Abdur Razzaq run out	12	4/140 5/201 6/215	
Azhar Mahmood b MacGill	5	7/226 8/238 9/245	

Bowling: Fleming 9–0–44–0; B. Lee 10–1–48–2; MacGill 10–1–48–1; S. Lee 8.5–0–37–4; Symonds 5–0–26–0; M. E. Waugh 6–0–28–1.

Umpires: D. B. Hair and P. D. Parker.

INDIA v PAKISTAN

At Adelaide, January 25 (day/night). India won by 48 runs. Toss: India.

India opened their account in the series on the back of scintillating batting by their left-handed opener, Ganguly. On a true pitch, he rolled out his full repertoire of strokes, scoring 141 from 145 balls. Ganguly put on 88 in 15 overs with Tendulkar for the first wicket, 87 in 20 with Dravid for the second, and made sure the good work was not squandered by remaining until the 49th over. Pakistan's reply had little to offer. Ijaz Ahmed stayed 77 balls for his third successive fifty and it was not until Azhar Mahmood arrived that they looked competitive. Azhar struck 67 from 50 balls but when he was last out the Indians finally had a victory to celebrate. A charge of ball-tampering against Tendulkar was dismissed as "frivolous and without foundation" by tournament referee Smith.

Man of the Match: S. C. Ganguly.   *Attendance:* 11,263.

India

*S. R. Tendulkar c Moin Khan		J. J. Martin not out	10
b Abdur Razzaq .	41	J. Srinath st Moin Khan	
S. C. Ganguly lbw b Wasim Akram	141	b Saqlain Mushtaq .	4
R. Dravid c Inzamam-ul-Haq		†S. S. Dighe not out	0
b Shahid Afridi .	32	L-b 6, w 1, n-b 5	12
H. H. Kanitkar c Inzamam-ul-Haq			
b Shoaib Akhtar .	6	1/88 2/175 3/186 (6 wkts, 50 overs) 267	
R. R. Singh c and b Saqlain Mushtaq . .	21	4/234 5/257 6/262	

A. Kumble, B. K. V. Prasad and D. S. Mohanty did not bat.

Bowling: Wasim Akram 10–0–55–1; Shoaib Akhtar 8–0–39–1; Abdur Razzaq 7–0–37–1; Azhar Mahmood 9–1–42–0; Saqlain Mushtaq 10–0–56–2; Shahid Afridi 6–0–32–1.

Pakistan

Saeed Anwar c Martin b Mohanty	8	*Wasim Akram c Srinath b Mohanty . . .	4
Shahid Afridi c Dighe b Srinath	9	Saqlain Mushtaq c Tendulkar b Srinath . .	1
Ijaz Ahmed, sen. c Dravid b Kumble	54	Shoaib Akhtar not out	1
Inzamam-ul-Haq c Kanitkar b Prasad . . .	15	L-b 4, w 2, n-b 7	13
Yousuf Youhana c Martin b Kumble	19		
†Moin Khan lbw b Kumble	15	1/20 2/21 3/62 (44.4 overs) 219	
Abdur Razzaq c Kumble b Prasad	13	4/109 5/124 6/128	
Azhar Mahmood c Kanitkar b Kumble . .	67	7/200 8/207 9/210	

Bowling: Srinath 8–0–47–2; Mohanty 10–0–42–2; Prasad 8–0–41–2; Singh 9–0–45–0; Kumble 9.4–0–40–4.

Umpires: S. J. Davis and D. B. Hair.

AUSTRALIA v INDIA

At Adelaide, January 26 (day/night). Australia won by 152 runs. Toss: Australia.

India's batting of the previous day was eclipsed by an awesome Australia Day performance from the home side that produced 329 runs, then their highest total in one-day internationals in Australia, beating 323 for two against Sri Lanka, also at Adelaide, in 1984-85. Mark Waugh and Gilchrist got away to a blazing start, putting on 163 in 30 overs, to which Waugh and Ponting added 100 more in little over 13. Symonds and Shane Lee, who faced 15 balls each, delivered the *coup de grâce*. Waugh, his form indifferent of late, took 131 balls for his 116; after hitting the first for four, he managed only five more boundaries. Australia's fast bowlers allowed the Indian openers no leeway, with Brett Lee's pace in particular rubbing in his side's fire-power. Dravid hit ten fours in his top-scoring 63.

Man of the Match: M. E. Waugh.   *Attendance:* 29,506.

Australia

†A. C. Gilchrist c Dravid b Kumble	92	M. G. Bevan not out	11
M. E. Waugh st Dighe b Tendulkar	116		
R. T. Ponting c Dravid b Kumble	43	L-b 8, w 2, n-b 4	14
A. Symonds c Dravid b Srinath	26		
S. Lee not out	27	1/163 2/263 3/279 (5 wkts, 50 overs) 329	
I. J. Harvey run out	0	4/305 5/306	

*S. R. Waugh, B. Lee, S. C. G. MacGill and G. D. McGrath did not bat.

Bowling: Srinath 10–0–55–1; Mohanty 6–0–39–0; Kumble 10–0–71–2; Prasad 9–0–50–0; Ganguly 2–0–19–0; Kanitkar 5–0–29–0; Tendulkar 7–0–48–1; Singh 1–0–10–0.

India

*S. R. Tendulkar c MacGill b B. Lee	18	J. Srinath c Gilchrist b B. Lee	0
S. C. Ganguly c S. Lee b McGrath	5	B. K. V. Prasad not out	5
R. Dravid c Gilchrist b S. Lee	63	D. S. Mohanty b B. Lee	1
H. H. Kanitkar lbw b B. Lee	0	B 1, l-b 1, w 7, n-b 7	16
J. J. Martin lbw b Symonds	17		
R. R. Singh b S. Lee	1	1/12 2/39 3/39	(46.5 overs) 177
†S. S. Dighe c McGrath b MacGill	25	4/107 5/111 6/111	
A. Kumble b B. Lee	26	7/163 8/166 9/174	

Bowling: McGrath 5–1–13–1; Harvey 8–0–39–0; S. Lee 7–0–35–2; B. Lee 8.5–1–27–5; MacGill 10–1–38–1; Symonds 6–0–18–1; S. R. Waugh 2–0–5–0.

Umpires: D. J. Harper and S. J. A. Taufel.

INDIA v PAKISTAN

At Perth, January 28 (day/night). Pakistan won by 104 runs. Toss: Pakistan.

Waqar and Wasim's destructive pace had India reeling at 33 for five and consigned to their sixth defeat in seven games. Poor India: they even had the embarrassment of a batsman ordered back by the umpires without facing a ball. Martin had come in at No. 4 to replace Tendulkar, out to a controversial caught-behind decision after hitting four fours in 14 balls. But as he had been off the field injured for two hours in Pakistan's innings, Martin was told he must wait until the fall of the fifth wicket. At least he then had the consolation of adding 86 with Robin Singh. Batting first, the Pakistanis had profited from consistency down the order after the openers put on 77 by the 14th over. Victory guaranteed them a place in the finals.

Man of the Match: Wasim Akram. *Attendance:* 10,531.

Pakistan

Saeed Anwar b Srinath	44	Shoaib Malik c Srinath b Kumble	5
Shahid Afridi c Prasad b Ganguly	41	Waqar Younis not out	3
Ijaz Ahmed, sen. run out	13		
Inzamam-ul-Haq c Ganguly b Singh	35	B 4, l-b 2, w 13, n-b 5	24
Yousuf Youhana c Dravid b Ganguly	18		
†Moin Khan c Tendulkar b Ganguly	23	1/77 2/96 3/133	(8 wkts, 50 overs) 261
Azhar Mahmood c Tendulkar b Prasad	24	4/165 5/180 6/202	
*Wasim Akram not out	31	7/236 8/254	

Shoaib Akhtar did not bat.

Bowling: Srinath 9–0–42–1; Agarkar 8–0–60–0; Prasad 10–0–51–1; Kumble 8–1–36–1; Ganguly 10–1–34–3; Singh 5–0–32–1.

India

*S. R. Tendulkar c Moin Khan b Waqar Younis	17	A. B. Agarkar c Wasim Akram b Shahid Afridi	0
S. C. Ganguly c Moin Khan b Waqar Younis	1	A. Kumble c Azhar Mahmood b Shahid Afridi	7
R. Dravid c Moin Khan b Wasim Akram	3	J. Srinath not out	8
V. V. S. Laxman lbw b Wasim Akram	1	B. K. V. Prasad run out	14
R. R. Singh c and b Shahid Afridi	51	L-b 4, w 6, n-b 4	14
†S. S. Dighe c Moin Khan b Wasim Akram	2	1/7 2/20 3/23 4/24 5/33	(46 overs) 157
J. J. Martin run out	39	6/119 7/119 8/133 9/133	

Bowling: Wasim Akram 7–4–10–3; Waqar Younis 8–0–33–2; Shoaib Akhtar 5–1–16–0; Azhar Mahmood 6–1–11–0; Shoaib Malik 10–0–41–0; Shahid Afridi 10–0–42–3.

Umpires: D. B. Hair and S. J. A. Taufel.

AUSTRALIA v INDIA

At Perth, January 30. Australia won by four wickets. Toss: India.

Having already lost Ganguly and Kumble to injury, India were further handicapped by yet another poor start. Both openers went in the first nine overs. This time, though, the later batsmen were helped by the Australians' uncharacteristic fielding errors and generous bowling from the two Shanes, Warne and Lee. This was Warne's first game since his injury at Brisbane. Dravid and Kanitkar put on 81 in 15 overs but Ponting broke the stand with a brilliant catch, running and then diving full-length at cover. A stand of 73 from ten overs between Robin Singh and Dighe kept the momentum going. Even so, 226 never looked enough, not with the Indian bowlers feeding the Australian strokemakers a steady diet of short-pitched deliveries. Bevan, in particular, relished them.

Man of the Match: M. G. Bevan.   *Attendance:* 26,116.

India

V. V. S. Laxman c Warne b B. Lee	3	†S. S. Dighe not out..............	36
*S. R. Tendulkar b Fleming	3	S. B. Joshi not out	2
R. Dravid c M. E. Waugh b S. Lee	65	L-b 14, w 7, n-b 8.........	29
H. H. Kanitkar c Ponting b Martyn ...	30		
D. J. Gandhi c Martyn b Warne	13	1/11 2/11 3/92 (6 wkts, 50 overs)	226
R. R. Singh c M. E. Waugh b McGrath .	45	4/113 5/145 6/218	

A. B. Agarkar, J. Srinath and B. K. V. Prasad did not bat.

Bowling: McGrath 9–3–22–1; Fleming 8–2–37–1; B. Lee 7–0–22–1; S. Lee 8–0–38–1; Martyn 5–0–19–1; Warne 9–0–57–1; S. R. Waugh 4–0–17–0.

Australia

M. E. Waugh c Dighe b Joshi........	40	S. Lee run out..................	2
†A. C. Gilchrist c Singh b Agarkar	6	S. K. Warne not out	16
R. T. Ponting c Agarkar b Joshi	33	L-b 7, w 9, n-b 8	24
M. G. Bevan c Tendulkar b Singh	71		
*S. R. Waugh b Singh.............	19	1/39 2/78 3/136 (6 wkts, 49.3 overs)	230
D. R. Martyn not out	19	4/190 5/201 6/205	

D. W. Fleming, B. Lee and G. D. McGrath did not bat.

Bowling: Srinath 10–0–55–0; Agarkar 10–1–39–1; Prasad 9.3–0–59–0; Joshi 10–1–33–2; Singh 10–1–37–2.

Umpires: S. J. Davis and D. B. Hair.

QUALIFYING TABLE

	Played	Won	Lost	Points	Net run-rate
Australia........	8	7	1	14	0.92
Pakistan	8	4	4	8	0.07
India	8	1	7	2	–0.97

Net run-rate is calculated by subtracting runs conceded per over from runs scored per over.

AUSTRALIA v PAKISTAN

First Final Match

At Melbourne, February 2 (day/night). Australia won by six wickets. Toss: Pakistan.

Pakistan's nightmare start to the 1999 World Cup final came back to haunt them, only this time it was worse. Two days after receiving the inaugural Allan Border Medal, McGrath demonstrated why fellow-players, umpires and media had proclaimed him Australia's outstanding player of the year. He was fast, relentlessly accurate, as hostile as Melbourne's heat-wave, and inside two overs he had Pakistan in ruins, with four runs on the board and three wickets down. When the Lee brothers chipped in with another three wickets, they were as good as out of the game at 78 for seven. Moin Khan's rally spared Pakistan from complete humiliation, yet even he rather gave his wicket away. "Glenn was awesome," Steve Waugh said afterwards. "A real match-winner." Steady half-centuries from Ponting, in his 100th one-day international, and Bevan stifled whatever hopes Pakistan might have entertained when Shoaib Akhtar removed Australia's openers early on.

Man of the Match: G. D. McGrath.   *Attendance:* 39,041.

Pakistan

Saeed Anwar c Warne b B. Lee	7	*Wasim Akram b Symonds	15
Shahid Afridi c Gilchrist b McGrath	0	Saqlain Mushtaq b B. Lee	16
Ijaz Ahmed, sen. c Warne b McGrath	0	Shoaib Akhtar not out	3
Inzamam-ul-Haq lbw b McGrath	0	L-b 2, w 9, n-b 1	12
Yousuf Youhana lbw b S. Lee	14		
Abdur Razzaq c S. R. Waugh b B. Lee	24	1/1 2/4 3/4	(47.2 overs) 154
Azhar Mahmood c S. R. Waugh b Bevan	4	4/12 5/28 6/59	
†Moin Khan c Martyn b Warne	47	7/78 8/108 9/147	

Bowling: McGrath 9–1–17–3; B. Lee 8.2–2–18–3; Warne 10–2–33–1; S. Lee 10–1–37–1; Symonds 7–1–24–1; Bevan 2–0–16–1; M. E. Waugh 1–0–7–0.

Australia

†A. C. Gilchrist c Azhar Mahmood b Shoaib Akhtar	9	*S. R. Waugh not out	19
M. E. Waugh lbw b Shoaib Akhtar	10	D. R. Martyn not out	4
R. T. Ponting c Abdur Razzaq b Shahid Afridi	50	L-b 4, n-b 5	9
M. G. Bevan c Abdur Razzaq b Saqlain Mushtaq	54	1/11 2/27	(4 wkts, 42.4 overs) 155
		3/104 4/147	

A. Symonds, S. Lee, S. K. Warne, B. Lee and G. D. McGrath did not bat.

Bowling: Wasim Akram 6–0–26–0; Shoaib Akhtar 7–1–26–2; Abdur Razzaq 3.5–0–19–0; Azhar Mahmood 7–1–22–0; Ijaz Ahmed 0.5–0–2–0; Saqlain Mushtaq 10–0–27–1; Shahid Afridi 8–0–29–1.

Umpires: D. J. Harper and S. J. A. Taufel.

AUSTRALIA v PAKISTAN

Second Final Match

At Sydney, February 4 (day/night). Australia won by 152 runs. Toss: Australia.

A capacity crowd was treated to another devastating display of one-day cricket by Australia. Just as they did at Adelaide against India, Mark Waugh and Gilchrist (dropped at square leg when seven) laid the foundation for a record score – this time 337, Australia's one-day best, surpassing 332 for three against Sri Lanka at Sharjah in 1989-90. They put on 74 before Gilchrist's explosive fifty (42 balls, one five, eight fours – four in one Wasim Akram over) ended in the 11th over. Ponting also survived an early chance, then hit a merciless 78 from 80 balls; Symonds, Steve Waugh and Martyn drove the hapless Pakistanis to distraction as the total mounted at a breathless rate. Nor did McGrath and Brett Lee offer any consolation prizes when Pakistan replied. Their first four went down blazing for 43 runs in the first six overs. There was a semblance of a recovery from the middle order but, when McGrath returned to claim another three wickets, the match and the series were wrapped up with more than 13 overs remaining. It was Australia's ninth consecutive victory. "They are definitely worthy world champions," Wasim Akram said of Australia. Nothing in the two finals, little throughout the series, suggested otherwise.

Man of the Match: R. T. Ponting.   *Attendance:* 38,123.

Man of the Series: Abdur Razzaq.

Australia

M. E. Waugh run out	53	S. Lee c Yousuf Youhana		
†A. C. Gilchrist c Moin Khan			b Saqlain Mushtaq	12
b Azhar Mahmood	51	D. R. Martyn not out		23
R. T. Ponting c Moin Khan		S. K. Warne not out		4
b Shahid Afridi	78	L-b 14, w 12, n-b 5		31
A. Symonds st Moin Khan				
b Saqlain Mushtaq	45	1/74 2/170 3/220	(7 wkts, 50 overs)	337
M. G. Bevan b Wasim Akram	3	4/224 5/290		
*S. R. Waugh run out	37	6/297 7/308		

B. Lee and G. D. McGrath did not bat.

Bowling: Wasim Akram 10–1–65–1; Shoaib Akhtar 9–0–61–0; Waqar Younis 4–0–38–0; Azhar Mahmood 7–0–51–1; Saqlain Mushtaq 10–0–54–2; Shahid Afridi 10–0–54–1.

Pakistan

Saeed Anwar c Gilchrist b McGrath	16	Saqlain Mushtaq c Gilchrist b McGrath		0
Shahid Afridi c Bevan b B. Lee	18	Waqar Younis run out		15
Ijaz Ahmed, sen. c Gilchrist b McGrath	0	Shoaib Akhtar not out		1
Yousuf Youhana c Warne b S. Lee	41			
Mohammad Wasim lbw b B. Lee	0	L-b 7, w 3, n-b 6		16
Azhar Mahmood c S. Lee b B. Lee	27			
†Moin Khan b McGrath	33	1/20 2/21 3/42	(36.3 overs)	185
*Wasim Akram c S. R. Waugh		4/43 5/80 6/131		
b McGrath	18	7/149 8/153 9/177		

Bowling: McGrath 9.3–2–49–5; B. Lee 9–0–51–3; Warne 7–2–28–0; S. Lee 6–0–20–1; Symonds 5–0–30–0.

Umpires: S. J. Davis and P. D. Parker.
Series referee: C. W. Smith (West Indies).

STANDARD BANK INTERNATIONAL SERIES, 1999-2000

Few observers believed that either England or Zimbabwe would pose any real threat to host country South Africa in the one-day tournament that followed the Test series against England, and so it proved. Hansie Cronje's team, whose one-day form was second only to Australia's, duly overcame the visitors, but it was drab fare. Most games were played on lifeless pitches that largely ruled out attacking strokeplay. There were no centuries, and the highest total in 18 innings was 233. Some close finishes provided entertainment, but for the most part this was a tournament best forgotten.

South Africa may have emerged victorious, but their progress was not always straightforward. After six qualifying matches, each team had won and lost two games: on net run-rate Zimbabwe were top and South Africa bottom. The South Africans picked up speed from there on in, though never quite fired on all cylinders.

Their most serious shortcoming was their top-order batting. With Daryll Cullinan having announced his retirement from one-day cricket before the tournament, with Gary Kirsten and Jonty Rhodes hopelessly out of touch and Cronje – hindsight might suggest – often seeming distracted and introverted, they were over-reliant on Jacques Kallis. He did all that was required of him, hitting 290 runs at an average of 48.33, and there was good support from Lance Klusener, even if his 225 runs were delivered at, by his standards, a restrained strike-rate of 70 per 100 balls. Shaun Pollock, taking 14 wickets at 15.64, carried the bowling almost single-handed after his long-term opening partner, Allan Donald, had been omitted, following his decision to cut back on his international commitments later in the year. South Africa's selection policy was apparently to build a squad for the 2003 World Cup.

England began in swashbuckling style when they brushed the hosts aside by nine wickets. Unused to such giddy heights, they returned to earth with a bump, losing their next two games, the first by a whisker, the second by a mile when Henry Olonga's six for 19 destroyed them. Revenge came two days later in the unassuming guise of Mark Ealham, who had half the Zimbabwean team trapped in front of their stumps. Nick Knight was England's most successful batsman with 258 runs at 64.50, casting doubt on his exclusion from the previous summer's World Cup, while Darren Gough was the tournament's leading wicket-taker with Pollock, averaging an even better 14.43 from his 14 wickets.

The last qualifying match, between England and Zimbabwe, effectively became a semi-final – or would have, had rain allowed play. England probably deserved to go through on run-rate, for Zimbabwe, who had struggled in subsequent tournaments to match their World Cup results, ultimately proved too erratic. Olonga's six-wicket haul apart, they did not have the ability to bowl opponents out. Neil Johnson prospered with the bat, but could offer little with the ball. Heath Streak, back after a knee injury, was at best tidy.

The tournament won, Cronje and his South African team set off for India and further success in the Test series there. What no one could have imagined was that the Standard Bank final against England would be Cronje's last home appearance for his country. In April, already under suspicion as a result of Indian police investigations into match-fixing, he admitted receiving between $US10,000 and $US15,000 from a bookmaker during the triangular tournament – ostensibly for forecasts on games in India – and was sacked. However, it emerged at the King Commission in June that Cronje had received the money, during the Centurion Test against England, to fix a qualifying match in this tournament if South Africa were sure of a place in the final.

Match reports by Edward Bevan and Colin Bryden.

Note: Matches in this section were not first-class.

SOUTH AFRICA v ZIMBABWE

At Johannesburg, January 21 (day/night). South Africa won by six wickets. Toss: Zimbabwe.

After a poor Test series against England, Cronje was in match-winning form with an unbeaten 83 from 112 balls, during which he became the first South African to score 5,000 runs in limited-overs internationals. His stand of 104 with Gibbs enabled South Africa to recover from a stuttering start in pursuit of a modest target. Cronje hit eight fours and would have had a six had a steward not stepped over the boundary rope and tried, unsuccessfully, to catch the ball. Earlier, Goodwin, with 73 off 71 balls, had helped Zimbabwe overcome a mid-innings wobble that saw them lose three wickets for 11 in 34 balls.

Man of the Match: W. J. Cronje.   *Attendance*: 25,080.

Zimbabwe

N. C. Johnson run out	33	G. B. Brent not out		1
G. W. Flower b Klusener	19	J. A. Rennie lbw b Pollock		0
A. D. R. Campbell c Hayward b Kallis	29	A. R. Whittall run out		1
M. W. Goodwin b Pollock	73	L-b 11, w 7, n-b 3		21
*†A. Flower c Boucher b Kallis	2			
S. V. Carlisle b Klusener	38	1/38 2/94 3/95	(49.5 overs)	226
G. J. Whittall c Kirsten b Cronje	3	4/105 5/184 6/187		
H. H. Streak b Pollock	6	7/212 8/225 9/225		

Bowling: Pollock 9.5–0–31–3; Kallis 10–1–34–2; Hayward 10–0–55–0; Klusener 9–0–47–2; Boje 10–1–40–0; Cronje 1–0–8–1.

South Africa

G. Kirsten lbw b Rennie	8	L. Klusener not out		26
H. H. Gibbs c Streak b Johnson	65	B 2, l-b 11, w 25, n-b 3		41
J. H. Kallis c A. R. Whittall b Streak	4			
D. M. Benkenstein b Johnson	2	1/27 2/38	(4 wkts, 48.1 overs)	229
*W. J. Cronje not out	83	3/55 4/159		

†M. V. Boucher, P. C. Strydom, S. M. Pollock, N. Boje and M. Hayward did not bat.

Bowling: Streak 10–2–31–1; Rennie 8.1–0–34–1; Johnson 10–0–61–2; Brent 6–0–28–0; G. J. Whittall 4–1–18–0; A. R. Whittall 10–0–44–0.

Umpires: S. B. Lambson and C. J. Mitchley.

SOUTH AFRICA v ENGLAND

At Bloemfontein, January 23. England won by nine wickets. Toss: South Africa. International debuts: V. S. Solanki, G. P. Swann.

The highest opening partnership against South Africa in one-day internationals gained England a comprehensive victory with more than ten overs remaining. After choosing to bat, South Africa were soon in trouble against the new ball, plummeting to 23 for four by the seventh over as Gough put a disappointing Test series behind him. Kallis played a watchful innings, adding 69 in 17 overs with Strydom, but accurate, economical bowling from Caddick and Ealham, along with excellent fielding, restricted South Africa to a modest total on a reasonable pitch. Hussain and Knight had reached 165, just 20 short of the target, when Hussain was caught at cover. It was only the fourth time in 302 limited-overs games that England had won by nine wickets.

Man of the Match: D. Gough.   *Attendance*: 11,912.

South Africa

G. Kirsten c Read b Gough	1	S. M. Pollock not out		19
H. H. Gibbs lbw b Caddick	9	N. Boje c Adams b White		2
J. H. Kallis b Gough	57	D. J. Terbrugge b White		5
D. M. Benkenstein b Gough	2	B 4, l-b 5, w 4, n-b 2		15
*W. J. Cronje c Read b Gough	2			
†M. V. Boucher c Gough b White	11	1/3 2/18 3/21	(49.5 overs)	184
P. C. Strydom c Caddick b Ealham	34	4/23 5/53 6/122		
L. Klusener c Caddick b Hick	27	7/137 8/172 9/176		

Bowling: Gough 10–1–29–4; Caddick 10–1–23–1; White 8.5–0–45–3; Swann 5–0–24–0; Ealham 10–1–22–1; Hick 6–0–32–1.

England

*N. Hussain c Gibbs b Boje	85		
N. V. Knight not out	71		
G. A. Hick not out	12		
L-b 10, w 6, n-b 1	17		

1/165	(1 wkt, 39.3 overs)	185

V. S. Solanki, C. J. Adams, C. White, M. A. Ealham, G. P. Swann, †C. M. W. Read, A. R. Caddick and D. Gough did not bat.

Bowling: Pollock 8–2–22–0; Terbrugge 6–1–23–0; Kallis 4–0–34–0; Boje 10–1–47–1; Strydom 2–0–7–0; Klusener 5–0–25–0; Cronje 4.3–0–17–0.

Umpires: D. F. Becker and D. L. Orchard.

SOUTH AFRICA v ENGLAND

At Cape Town, January 26 (day/night). South Africa won by one run. Toss: South Africa.

England began the final over nine runs from victory, but Kallis bowled Caddick with the second ball and maintained a full length that gave little away. Gough, needing four from the last ball, could manage only two. England had been well placed at 72 for one in the 18th over, but Hick and Knight fell in successive overs and the momentum was lost. By the time Adams was out for 42 in the 43rd over, the asking-rate had risen above seven. Read and Ealham raised hopes as they put on 39, taking 16 off the parsimonious Pollock in the penultimate over, but the final task proved too great. Kallis had already played a vital hand when South Africa batted, top-scoring with 43; Cronje shared important partnerships with him and Klusener. Gough continued to thrive and his three wickets took his total in one-day internationals to 115, level with Phillip DeFreitas. Only Ian Botham, with 145, had more for England.

Man of the Match: J. H. Kallis.   *Attendance:* 20,008.

South Africa

G. Kirsten lbw b Gough	13	†M. V. Boucher c Ealham b Alleyne	15
H. H. Gibbs c and b Gough	13	S. M. Pollock not out	13
J. H. Kallis run out	43	L-b 3, w 7	10
J. N. Rhodes c Caddick b White	14		
*W. J. Cronje c Read b Gough	39	1/26 2/32 3/71 (7 wkts, 50 overs) 204	
L. Klusener not out	42	4/109 5/147	
P. C. Strydom b Caddick	2	6/153 7/182	

H. S. Williams and M. Hayward did not bat.

Bowling: Gough 10–0–36–3; Caddick 10–0–29–1; White 10–0–36–1; Ealham 6–0–33–0; Alleyne 10–0–42–1; Hick 4–0–25–0.

England

*N. Hussain c Boucher b Hayward	1	†C. M. W. Read not out	26
N. V. Knight c Boucher b Williams	36	A. R. Caddick b Kallis	0
G. A. Hick c Boucher b Kallis	25	D. Gough not out	3
V. S. Solanki c Kallis b Klusener	7	L-b 5, w 9, n-b 6	20
C. J. Adams c Pollock b Klusener	42		
M. W. Alleyne c Boucher b Hayward	12	1/4 2/72 3/72 (9 wkts, 50 overs) 203	
C. White c Rhodes b Williams	6	4/86 5/121 6/138	
M. A. Ealham c Rhodes b Pollock	25	7/152 8/191 9/197	

Bowling: Pollock 10–0–48–1; Hayward 10–0–39–2; Williams 10–0–36–2; Kallis 10–0–41–2; Klusener 10–0–34–2.

Umpires: W. A. Diedricks and R. E. Koertzen.

ENGLAND v ZIMBABWE

At Cape Town, January 28 (day/night). Zimbabwe won by 104 runs. Toss: Zimbabwe.

Olonga's six for 19, the best figures by a Zimbabwean in limited-overs internationals and the best by any bowler on African soil, guaranteed that England would be beaten for the sixth time in their eight one-day meetings with Zimbabwe. He claimed their top five for 18 in his first eight-over spell. It took England's last-wicket pair, Read and Caddick, to guide them past their lowest one-day total: 93 against Australia at Leeds in their 1975 World Cup semi-final. Several batsmen brought about their own downfall in rash strokes. Zimbabwe's innings was dominated by Johnson, who stayed until the 46th over. From the start, he took the fight to the English attack, especially Gough, and missed his hundred by three when Hick held a steepling catch on the mid-wicket boundary.

Man of the Match: H. K. Olonga.   *Attendance:* 8,612.

Zimbabwe

N. C. Johnson c Hick b Ealham	97	H. H. Streak b White	18
G. W. Flower c Hick b Alleyne	23	J. A. Rennie not out	1
A. D. R. Campbell run out	0	L-b 4, w 3, n-b 1	8
M. W. Goodwin c Read b Hick	21		
*†A. Flower c Solanki b Caddick	20	1/56 2/56 3/111 (7 wkts, 50 overs) 211	
S. V. Carlisle c Alleyne b Gough	2	4/151 5/163	
G. J. Whittall not out	21	6/181 7/210	

H. K. Olonga and A. R. Whittall did not bat.

Bowling: Gough 10–1–42–1; Caddick 10–1–30–1; Ealham 9–0–35–1; Alleyne 7–0–30–1; Hick 4–0–25–1; White 10–0–45–1.

England

*N. Hussain b Olonga	15	†C. M. W. Read c G. J. Whittall	
N. V. Knight lbw b Olonga	5	b Olonga	23
G. A. Hick c A. Flower b Olonga	0	D. Gough c Carlisle b A. R. Whittall	3
V. S. Solanki c Goodwin b Olonga	14	A. R. Caddick not out	4
C. J. Adams b Johnson b Olonga	1	B 4, l-b 1, w 13	18
M. W. Alleyne c A. Flower b Rennie	4		
C. White c Campbell b Johnson	18	1/11 2/11 3/37 4/42 5/47 (34.2 overs) 107	
M. A. Ealham run out	2	6/47 7/63 8/73 9/91	

Bowling: Olonga 8.2–3–19–6; Rennie 8–1–22–1; Streak 6–0–24–0; Johnson 4–0–12–1; G. J. Whittall 5–0–17–0; A. R. Whittall 3–0–8–1.

Umpires: I. L. Howell and C. J. Mitchley.

ENGLAND v ZIMBABWE

At Kimberley, January 30. England won by eight wickets. Toss: Zimbabwe.

Ealham turned in the best figures by an England bowler in limited-overs internationals and helped his team to a victory as emphatic as their defeat at the hands of Olonga two days earlier had been humiliating. His five for 15 surpassed Vic Marks's five for 20 against New Zealand at Wellington in 1983-84, and made him only the ninth to 50 one-day wickets for England. All five were lbw, unparalleled in this form of the game, and all five were sent on their way by umpire Orchard. Zimbabwe collapsed from 71 for one to 98 for seven as Ealham seized five for eight in 24 balls before Streak and Rennie put on 62 in 21 overs. With Olonga seldom the force he was in Cape Town, Knight and Hussain shared their second century partnership of the tournament until Hussain was caught at long-off, aiming for a third six in his haste to improve England's net run-rate. Hick's dismissal for two took his tally against Zimbabwe in his last three innings to six runs.

Man of the Match: M. A. Ealham.   *Attendance:* 7,188.

Zimbabwe

N. C. Johnson c Hussain b Caddick	11	J. A. Rennie c Hussain b Gough	23
G. W. Flower lbw b Ealham	28	H. K. Olonga b Gough	0
A. D. R. Campbell c Solanki b Alleyne	28		
M. W. Goodwin lbw b Ealham	15	L-b 4, w 6, n-b 1	11
*†A. Flower lbw b Ealham	8		
S. V. Carlisle lbw b Ealham	2	1/15 2/71 3/73 (9 wkts, 50 overs) 161	
G. J. Whittall lbw b Ealham	0	4/92 5/96 6/97	
H. H. Streak not out	35	7/98 8/160 9/161	

A. R. Whittall did not bat.

Bowling: Gough 10–2–31–2; Caddick 10–2–21–1; White 10–1–44–0; Alleyne 10–0–46–1; Ealham 10–3–15–5.

England

*N. Hussain c Rennie b Olonga	64
N. V. Knight not out	72
G. A. Hick b Streak	2
V. S. Solanki not out	16
B 4, l-b 1, w 2, n-b 1	8

1/128 2/140   (2 wkts, 32.1 overs) 162

D. L. Maddy, M. W. Alleyne, C. White, M. A. Ealham, †C. M. W. Read, A. R. Caddick and D. Gough did not bat.

Bowling: Olonga 9–0–52–1; Rennie 7–0–27–0; Streak 7.1–0–26–1; A. R. Whittall 4–1–25–0; G. J. Whittall 5–0–27–0.

Umpires: S. B. Lambson and D. L. Orchard.

SOUTH AFRICA v ZIMBABWE

At Durban, February 2 (day/night). Zimbabwe won by two wickets. Toss: South Africa. International debut: N. D. McKenzie.

Zimbabwe's win off the last ball put all three teams level on points with three qualifying matches left. Both sides suffered top-order collapses before being revived by big seventh-wicket stands. Kallis and Klusener put on 82 for South Africa but their effort was bettered by Andy Flower and Whittall, with 91; both were national records for that wicket. When Flower slashed a catch to Rhodes at backward point, his side still needed 25 off 24 balls with three wickets in hand, and Whittall's run-out by a backhand flick from mid-on by Gibbs left ten to win from nine. By the last over the requirement was four. With the scores level, Streak squeezed the final ball from Kallis to leg; Boucher collected, threw at the stumps and missed by inches as Brent scrambled home.

Man of the Match: A. Flower.   *Attendance:* 18,114.

South Africa

H. H. Gibbs c A. Flower b Olonga	20	L. Klusener not out	65
L. J. Koen c Goodwin b Olonga	19	S. M. Pollock not out	14
J. H. Kallis c Wishart b Brent	52		
N. D. McKenzie c Carlisle b Streak	7	B 1, l-b 1, w 11, n-b 1	14
*W. J. Cronje c A. Flower b Johnson	10		
J. N. Rhodes c Brent b Johnson	13	1/40 2/41 3/49 4/69 (7 wkts, 50 overs) 222
†M. V. Boucher c Johnson b Brent	8	5/92 6/112 7/194	

H. S. Williams and M. Hayward did not bat.

Bowling: Olonga 8–0–34–2; Johnson 10–0–53–2; Streak 10–0–53–1; Brent 10–0–32–2; G. W. Flower 10–0–37–0; Whittall 2–0–11–0.

Zimbabwe

N. C. Johnson c McKenzie b Kallis	35	H. H. Streak not out	20
G. W. Flower lbw b Hayward	0	G. B. Brent not out	1
C. B. Wishart c Kallis b Williams	18		
A. D. R. Campbell c Boucher b Williams	11	L-b 2, w 5, n-b 11	18
M. W. Goodwin lbw b Klusener	16		
*†A. Flower c Rhodes b Williams	59	1/13 2/57 3/65 (8 wkts, 50 overs) 223
S. V. Carlisle lbw b Hayward	6	4/85 5/90 6/107	
G. J. Whittall run out	39	7/198 8/213	

H. K. Olonga did not bat.

Bowling: Pollock 10–0–55–0; Hayward 10–0–42–2; Williams 10–0–38–3; Kallis 10–0–41–1; Klusener 10–0–45–1.

Umpires: W. A. Diedricks and D. L. Orchard.

SOUTH AFRICA v ENGLAND

At East London, February 4 (day/night). South Africa won by two wickets. Toss: South Africa.

With South Africa needing seven from four balls, Pollock hit successive full tosses from Ealham to the boundary. Initially they had been tied down by an England attack that included Mullally for the first time in the tournament, and at 126 for five in the 32nd over, with 106 still needed, the game was intriguingly poised. First Rhodes and then Klusener, taking ten off his first three balls, from Caddick, provided the acceleration. Alleyne was instrumental in removing both – bowling Klusener and holding a blinding catch off Rhodes – just as earlier he had ensured a respectable England total by putting on 74 with Ealham. Knight struck his third fifty of the competition but Hick's poor form continued. His five innings had contributed 50 runs.

Man of the Match: M. W. Alleyne.   *Attendance:* 16,070.

England

*N. Hussain c Boucher b Pollock	10	M. A. Ealham not out		29
N. V. Knight c and b Strydom	64	†C. M. W. Read not out		10
G. A. Hick c Koen b Hayward	11	L-b 4, w 13, n-b 5		22
V. S. Solanki c Pollock b Kallis	10			
D. L. Maddy c Strydom b Cronje	22	1/22 2/35 3/61	(6 wkts, 50 overs)	231
M. W. Alleyne c Kallis b Pollock	53	4/105 5/144 6/218		

A. R. Caddick, D. Gough and A. D. Mullally did not bat.

Bowling: Pollock 10–0–36–2; Hayward 8–0–46–1; Cronje 10–0–25–1; Kallis 8–0–51–1; Klusener 9–0–51–0; Strydom 5–0–18–1.

South Africa

H. H. Gibbs c Read b Mullally	14	P. C. Strydom not out		7
L. J. Koen c Read b Ealham	28	S. M. Pollock not out		9
†M. V. Boucher c Knight b Caddick	5			
J. H. Kallis c Read b Alleyne	36	L-b 5, w 7, n-b 7		19
N. D. McKenzie run out	37			
*W. J. Cronje c Ealham b Alleyne	10	1/36 2/46 3/79	(8 wkts, 49.4 overs)	233
J. N. Rhodes c Alleyne b Gough	42	4/110 5/126 6/163		
L. Klusener b Alleyne	26	7/201 8/221		

M. Hayward did not bat.

Bowling: Gough 10–0–46–1; Caddick 10–0–50–1; Mullally 10–1–24–1; Ealham 9.4–0–53–1; Alleyne 10–0–55–3.

Umpires: I. L. Howell and R. E. Koertzen.

SOUTH AFRICA v ZIMBABWE

At Port Elizabeth, February 6. South Africa won by 53 runs. Toss: South Africa.

The skill and patience of Kallis's batting, combined with a devastating opening spell from Pollock, saw South Africa safely into the final. Accurate bowling and excellent fielding by Zimbabwe left Kallis two short of a century at the end, having faced 132 balls, and even Klusener was kept in check: the two put on a sedate 58 in 18 overs for the sixth wicket. On another slow pitch, however, South Africa's eventual total was sufficiently competitive; more so when Pollock had Grant Flower caught in the slips off the second ball of the innings, quickly following up by dismissing Wishart and Campbell. Pollock's final figures were 8–4–7–3. Johnson batted aggressively before he was caught at mid-off, and Zimbabwe's last hopes died when Andy Flower was run out by a direct hit from Gibbs at mid-wicket.

Man of the Match: J. H. Kallis.   *Attendance:* 10,073.

South Africa

H. H. Gibbs run out	11	S. M. Pollock b Streak	8
L. J. Koen b Olonga	13	†M. V. Boucher not out	6
J. H. Kallis not out	98		
N. D. McKenzie c Goodwin b Brent	6	B 1, l-b 3, w 10, n-b 3	17
*W. J. Cronje c Carlisle b Brent	13		
J. N. Rhodes c Brent b Whittall	3	1/23 2/37 3/66 4/97 (7 wkts, 50 overs) 204	
L. Klusener run out	29	5/106 6/164 7/188	

H. S. Williams and N. Boje did not bat.

Bowling: Olonga 7–0–43–1; Johnson 8–0–33–0; Brent 10–0–48–2; Streak 8–0–21–1; Whittall 9–0–34–1; G. W. Flower 8–0–21–0.

Zimbabwe

N. C. Johnson c Cronje b Klusener	56	H. H. Streak c Klusener b Cronje	4
G. W. Flower c Koen b Pollock	0	G. B. Brent not out	2
C. B. Wishart b Pollock	0	H. K. Olonga b Williams	0
A. D. R. Campbell c Boucher b Pollock	4	B 1, l-b 3, w 7, n-b 1	12
M. W. Goodwin lbw b Cronje	7		
*†A. Flower run out	37	1/1 2/9 3/25 (46 overs) 151	
S. V. Carlisle b Williams	17	4/52 5/97 6/120	
G. J. Whittall c Koen b Klusener	12	7/135 8/148 9/151	

Bowling: Pollock 8–4–7–3; Kallis 8–2–26–0; Williams 10–1–30–2; Cronje 7–0–28–2; Boje 3–0–19–0; Klusener 10–0–37–2.

Umpires: D. F. Becker and R. E. Koertzen.

ENGLAND v ZIMBABWE

At Centurion, February 9. Abandoned.

As a victory would have taken either side into the final against South Africa, it was England, with a superior run-rate, who benefited from the rain.

QUALIFYING TABLE

	Played	Won	Lost	No result	Points	Net run-rate
South Africa	6	4	2	0	8	0.07
England	6	2	3	1	5	0.03
Zimbabwe	6	2	3	1	5	−0.12

England finished ahead of Zimbabwe on net run-rate, having shared the points in their head-to-head matches. Net run-rate is calculated by subtracting runs conceded per over from runs scored per over.

FINAL

SOUTH AFRICA v ENGLAND

At Johannesburg, February 12, 13 (day/night). South Africa won by 38 runs. Toss: England.

After a week of torrential rain, said to be the worst at the Wanderers in 40 years, there were fears the final would be abandoned and the trophy shared. However, play eventually began at 4.30 p.m. on the reserve day, with the match reduced to 45 overs each. When the pitch, which had spent almost a week under covers, at last saw the light of day, it turned out to be a seam bowler's dream. Hussain won his first toss of the tournament and, after nine overs, South Africa were reeling at 21 for five. But shortly afterwards Gough and then Caddick were taken off. This allowed Cronje and Boucher to consolidate – they added 74 for the sixth wicket – and the opportunity to dismiss South Africa for a small total was lost. When England batted, Cronje did not repeat Hussain's mistake. Pollock, getting such extravagant movement as to make him often unplayable, bowled his nine overs in a single spell and returned his best one-day figures against England. All five of his wickets came from catches to the wicket-keeper and slips.

Man of the Match: S. M. Pollock.
Man of the Series: S. M. Pollock.   *Attendance:* 24,691.

South Africa

H. H. Gibbs c Knight b Gough	8		P. C. Strydom c Maddy b Caddick	3
N. D. McKenzie b Caddick	4		S. Elworthy not out	8
J. H. Kallis b Gough	0		H. S. Williams run out	7
*W. J. Cronje c Knight b Mullally	56		L-b 5, w 6, n-b 1	12
J. N. Rhodes c Hick b Caddick	5			
S. M. Pollock c White b Caddick	0		1/14 2/14 3/14 (45 overs)	149
†M. V. Boucher c Hick b Alleyne	36		4/21 5/21 6/95	
L. Klusener c Hussain b Pollock	10		7/129 8/132 9/134	

Bowling: Caddick 9–1–19–4; Gough 9–2–18–3; Mullally 9–3–22–1; White 7–0–38–0; Ealham 5–0–24–0; Alleyne 6–0–23–1.

England

*N. Hussain c Boucher b Pollock	8		A. R. Caddick c Boucher b Kallis	7
N. V. Knight c Boucher b Pollock	10		D. Gough c Boucher b Kallis	1
G. A. Hick c Kallis b Pollock	12		A. D. Mullally not out	14
D. L. Maddy c Kallis b Pollock	0		L-b 1, w 21, n-b 2	24
M. W. Alleyne c Cronje b Pollock	6			
C. White b Klusener	16		1/16 2/22 3/23 (38 overs)	111
M. A. Ealham c Boucher b Klusener	4		4/41 5/45 6/64	
†C. M. W. Read lbw b Williams	9		7/72 8/83 9/87	

Bowling: Pollock 9–1–20–5; Kallis 8–0–25–2; Elworthy 6–0–19–0; Williams 6–0–18–1; Klusener 9–1–28–2.

Umpires: R. E. Koertzen and D. L. Orchard.
Series referee: Hanumant Singh (India).

COCA-COLA CUP, 1999-2000

Pakistan won their third title at Sharjah in 11 months, having overcome Sri Lanka and West Indies in October, and India and England the previous April. This time, their opponents were India and South Africa, who had just met in Test and one-day series in the subcontinent.

Pakistan arrived in disarray after their unsuccessful tour of Australia and subsequent home defeats by Sri Lanka, which had precipitated the resignations of first Wasim Akram and then Saeed Anwar as captain. Moin Khan resumed the position and turned initial reverses into ultimate triumph. Their player of the series was Waqar Younis, who had recently been sidelined, but hit back with 13 wickets at 13.46. In the process he became only the second bowler to take 300 one-day international wickets, following Wasim Akram. Just as important was Inzamam-ul-Haq, who scored 239 runs at 59.75. The only other batsman to approach 200 was the 18-year-old opener, Imran Nazir, who made a very favourable impression.

India had a disappointing tournament, with a single win over Pakistan their only reward, whereas South Africa started in stunning form, winning their first three matches. They had won all five on their only previous visit to Sharjah, in 1995-96, and seemed to be heading for a repeat performance until, already sure of going through, they relaxed in the last qualifying game and were routed by Shoaib Akhtar's pace. Their subsequent defeat by Pakistan in the final proved to be Hansie Cronje's last bow; a week later, Indian police accused him of match-fixing. Since South Africa's readmission to world cricket in 1991-92, he had played in all but two of their Tests and all but six of their one-day internationals, but the revelations that followed brought a once-distinguished career to an end.

Note: Matches in this section were not first-class.

INDIA v SOUTH AFRICA

At Sharjah, March 22 (day/night). South Africa won by ten wickets. Toss: India.

Kirsten and Gibbs swept South Africa to their first ten-wicket victory in one-day internationals with 20 overs to spare. Each hit nine fours, though Gibbs topped them off with three sixes. India had subsided to 89 for eight by the 21st over, with Ntini grabbing three wickets on his first international appearance since his conviction for rape was overturned. Elworthy, whose ten overs cost only 17 runs, also collected three, and India were heading for their lowest total in Sharjah until Jadeja shared easily the biggest stand of the innings with last man Srinath. Their 62 were an Indian tenth-wicket record.

Man of the Match: S. Elworthy.

India

*S. C. Ganguly c Boje b Kallis	27	A. B. Agarkar b Ntini	1
S. R. Tendulkar b Pollock	5	A. Kumble c and b Elworthy	8
R. Dravid b Kallis	8	J. Srinath c Gibbs b Boje	30
S. B. Joshi b Ntini	24	L-b 3, w 7	10
M. Azharuddin c Boucher b Ntini	7		
A. Jadeja not out	43	1/9 2/42 3/50 (45.2 overs) 164	
R. R. Singh lbw b Elworthy	1	4/72 5/81 6/82	
†S. S. Karim b Elworthy	0	7/82 8/89 9/102	

Bowling: Pollock 8–0–35–1; Kallis 10–1–43–2; Ntini 10–2–36–3; Elworthy 10–3–17–3; Klusener 4–0–21–0; Boje 3.2–0–9–1.

South Africa

G. Kirsten not out	71
H. H. Gibbs not out	87
L-b 3, w 5, n-b 2	10

(no wkt, 29.2 overs) 168

J. H. Kallis, N. D. McKenzie, *W. J. Cronje, †M. V. Boucher, L. Klusener, S. M. Pollock, N. Boje, S. Elworthy and M. Ntini did not bat.

Bowling: Srinath 4–0–25–0; Agarkar 5–0–29–0; Kumble 7–0–37–0; Joshi 5–0–32–0; Tendulkar 6–0–32–0; Singh 2–1–6–0; Jadeja 0.2–0–4–0.

Umpires: J. H. Hampshire and D. J. Harper.

INDIA v PAKISTAN

At Sharjah, March 23 (day/night). India won by five wickets. Toss: Pakistan.

Choosing to bat backfired on Pakistan, who were two down by the third over. But, after Imran Nazir scored a brisk 43, Inzamam-ul-Haq steered them to 108 for three, only to be involved, once again, in a run-out. Wicket-keeper Karim threw down the stumps at the bowler's end as striker Yousuf Youhana went for a single. Inzamam, rather than go on, tried to regain his ground, and it took the third umpire to decide that it was Youhana who should leave. Next ball, Inzamam was caught behind and Pakistan's last seven wickets fell for 38 runs. India needed only 147, but their chase dragged into the 44th over. Azharuddin made sure of victory with the match's only fifty, striking seven fours.

Man of the Match: M. Azharuddin.

Pakistan

Imran Nazir b Joshi	43	Waqar Younis run out		0
Shahid Afridi c Azharuddin b Prasad	0	Arshad Khan b Kumble		1
Abdur Razzaq c Jadeja b Agarkar	2	Shoaib Akhtar not out		9
Inzamam-ul-Haq c Karim b Singh	41	L-b 4, w 4, n-b 1		9
Yousuf Youhana run out	17			
Younis Khan b Kumble	0	1/1 2/5 3/62	(45.3 overs)	146
*†Moin Khan lbw b Joshi	14	4/108 5/108 6/110		
Wasim Akram b Prasad	10	7/128 8/128 9/131		

Bowling: Agarkar 8–1–31–1; Prasad 10–0–29–2; Kumble 10–4–26–2; Joshi 9.3–1–29–2; Tendulkar 4–0–21–0; Singh 4–0–6–1.

India

*S. C. Ganguly c Moin Khan		A. Jadeja not out		11
b Wasim Akram	25	R. R. Singh run out		7
S. R. Tendulkar lbw b Shoaib Akhtar	11	†S. S. Karim not out		0
R. Dravid c sub (Shoaib Malik)		L-b 4, w 7, n-b 4		15
b Abdur Razzaq	26			
M. Azharuddin c Younis Khan		1/39 2/41 3/111	(5 wkts, 43.3 overs)	149
b Arshad Khan	54	4/132 5/145		

S. B. Joshi, A. B. Agarkar, A. Kumble and B. K. V. Prasad did not bat.

Bowling: Wasim Akram 8–1–33–1; Waqar Younis 7–2–15–0; Shoaib Akhtar 8–3–19–1; Abdur Razzaq 8–1–42–1; Arshad Khan 7.3–3–21–1; Shahid Afridi 5–1–15–0.

Umpires: J. H. Hampshire and P. T. Manuel.

PAKISTAN v SOUTH AFRICA

At Sharjah, March 24 (day/night). South Africa won by three wickets. Toss: Pakistan.

Pakistan suffered their seventh consecutive defeat in one-day internationals – and their 14th in succession against South Africa, going back to January 1995. Both sides were below full strength, with Wasim Akram, Shoaib Akhtar and Pollock all unfit. But Pakistan put up a fight this time. Imran Nazir and Younis Khan added 115 for the second wicket, though a little too slowly, before Klusener struck four times in 11 balls, finishing with five wickets in a single ten-over spell. South Africa had to chase 197, but their reply looked shaky after some early strikes from Waqar Younis. Boje, coming in at 136 for six, won back the initiative with 35 from 42 balls.

Man of the Match: L. Klusener.

Pakistan

Imran Nazir b Klusener	71	Shoaib Malik not out	3
Shahid Afridi c McKenzie b Elworthy	6	Arshad Khan not out	1
Younis Khan c Elworthy b Klusener	48		
*†Moin Khan lbw b Klusener	0	L-b 7, w 6, n-b 1	14
Inzamam-ul-Haq c Boucher b Klusener	7		
Yousuf Youhana b Klusener	15	1/14 2/129 3/129 (8 wkts, 50 overs)	196
Abdur Razzaq c Gibbs b Elworthy	23	4/142 5/145 6/165	
Waqar Younis c Boje b Ntini	8	7/192 8/193	

Mohammad Akram did not bat.

Bowling: Hayward 10–1–21–0; Kallis 3–1–3–0; Elworthy 10–1–43–2; Ntini 9–1–38–1; Cronje 4–0–24–0; Klusener 10–0–47–5; Boje 4–0–13–0.

South Africa

G. Kirsten c Inzamam-ul-Haq b Waqar Younis	20	L. Klusener c Moin Khan b Shoaib Malik	5
H. H. Gibbs c Inzamam-ul-Haq b Waqar Younis	0	N. Boje not out	35
J. H. Kallis c Moin Khan b Abdur Razzaq	35	S. Elworthy not out	4
N. D. McKenzie lbw b Arshad Khan	31	B 10, w 8, n-b 10	28
*W. J. Cronje c Shoaib Malik b Arshad Khan	14	1/1 2/45 3/69 (7 wkts, 44.3 overs)	199
†M. V. Boucher c and b Shahid Afridi	27	4/98 5/124	
		6/136 7/163	

M. Hayward and M. Ntini did not bat.

Bowling: Waqar Younis 7–0–28–2; Mohammad Akram 7.3–0–44–0; Abdur Razzaq 10–1–47–1; Arshad Khan 10–2–34–2; Shoaib Malik 7–0–33–1; Shahid Afridi 3–0–3–1.

Umpires: D. J. Harper and P. T. Manuel.

INDIA v PAKISTAN

At Sharjah, March 26 (day/night). Pakistan won by 98 runs. Toss: Pakistan.

Returning after a day off, Pakistan ended their losing streak in style. For the third time running, they chose to bat, but this time it paid off. No team had yet reached 200 in this tournament, but Inzamam-ul-Haq and Yousuf Youhana coasted past in an unbroken partnership of 151 in 22 overs – the last two yielded 93. Inzamam struck nine fours and five sixes in his 121 from 113 balls. Waqar Younis then took over. His first spell removed Ganguly and Joshi, promoted to No. 4 as a pinch-hitter, his second saw off Azharuddin and Jadeja and left India 99 for six in the 29th over. Waqar collected five wickets for the tenth time in one-day internationals, and shared the match award with Inzamam.

Men of the Match: Inzamam-ul-Haq and Waqar Younis.

Pakistan

Imran Nazir c Kumble b Agarkar	11	Yousuf Youhana not out	56
Shahid Afridi st Karim b Kumble	28	L-b 2, w 8, n-b 2	12
Younis Khan c Azharuddin b Joshi	44		
Inzamam-ul-Haq not out	121	1/20 2/55 3/121 (3 wkts, 50 overs)	272

*†Moin Khan, Abdur Razzaq, Wasim Akram, Waqar Younis, Arshad Khan and Shoaib Akhtar did not bat.

Bowling: Agarkar 10–0–50–1; Prasad 10–0–63–0; Kumble 9–0–66–1; Singh 10–1–34–0; Joshi 9–2–42–1; Ganguly 1–0–4–0; Tendulkar 1–0–11–0.

India

*S. C. Ganguly c and b Waqar Younis	7	A. B. Agarkar b Waqar Younis	20
S. R. Tendulkar b Wasim Akram	10	A. Kumble not out	14
R. Dravid c Moin Khan b Shoaib Akhtar	29	B. K. V. Prasad not out	0
S. B. Joshi c Moin Khan b Waqar Younis	3		
M. Azharuddin c Moin Khan		L-b 2, w 11, n-b 3	16
b Waqar Younis	20		
A. Jadeja b Waqar Younis	20	1/12 2/20 3/25 (9 wkts, 50 overs) 174	
R. R. Singh c Moin Khan b Arshad Khan	22	4/63 5/90	
†S. S. Karim c Younis Khan		6/99 7/131	
b Arshad Khan	13	8/137 9/172	

Bowling: Wasim Akram 7–2–16–1; Waqar Younis 10–1–31–5; Abdur Razzaq 5–1–29–0; Shoaib Akhtar 5–0–24–1; Arshad Khan 10–0–32–2; Shahid Afridi 8–0–21–0; Younis Khan 4–0–17–0; Imran Nazir 1–0–2–0.

Umpires: D. J. Harper and P. T. Manuel.

INDIA v SOUTH AFRICA

At Sharjah, March 27 (day/night). South Africa won by six wickets. Toss: India.

Cronje struck Robin Singh for six over long-on to complete South Africa's eighth straight win at Sharjah and seal their place in the final. They had faltered when Prasad extracted Gibbs and Klusener with successive balls; had Jadeja held a catch offered by Kallis in the 27th over, they would have been five. Instead, Kallis and Cronje made certain there were no further alarms. India's innings had started quite smoothly, reaching 80 for one before McKenzie's direct hit dismissed Azharuddin. Tendulkar was also run out in the subsequent flurry of wickets, and Hayward, opening the bowling because Pollock was injured, picked up a career-best four for 31. As in their previous encounter, South Africa bowled India out for 164.

Man of the Match: M. Hayward.

India

S. R. Tendulkar run out	39	N. Chopra not out	1
*S. C. Ganguly c Boucher b Hayward	6	A. B. Agarkar lbw b Hayward	4
M. Azharuddin run out	36	B. K. V. Prasad c Boucher b Ntini	1
A. Jadeja lbw b Elworthy	0	L-b 5, w 4	9
R. Dravid c McKenzie b Klusener	26		
R. R. Singh c Boucher b Hayward	28	1/10 2/80 3/80 (48.5 overs) 164	
†S. S. Karim c McKenzie b Hayward	12	4/93 5/124 6/154	
A. Kumble b Klusener	2	7/157 8/159 9/163	

Bowling: Hayward 10–2–31–4; Kallis 10–2–30–0; Ntini 8.5–1–25–1; Elworthy 8–1–28–1; Klusener 10–1–35–2; Boje 2–0–10–0.

South Africa

G. Kirsten c Ganguly b Kumble	31	*W. J. Cronje not out	42
H. H. Gibbs c Ganguly b Prasad	8	B 5, l-b 2, w 4, n-b 3	14
L. Klusener lbw b Prasad	0		
J. H. Kallis not out	53	1/30 2/30 (4 wkts, 42.4 overs) 167	
N. D. McKenzie c Jadeja b Chopra	19	3/50 4/96	

†M. V. Boucher, N. Boje, S. Elworthy, M. Hayward and M. Ntini did not bat.

Bowling: Agarkar 10–1–44–0; Prasad 10–1–30–2; Kumble 10–1–26–1; Chopra 8–0–36–1; Tendulkar 1–0–3–0; Singh 3.4–1–21–0.

Umpires: J. H. Hampshire and D. J. Harper.

PAKISTAN v SOUTH AFRICA

At Sharjah, March 28 (day/night). Pakistan won by 67 runs. Toss: Pakistan. International debut: C. M. Willoughby.

South Africa's 100 per cent record at Sharjah was blown away as Pakistan booked a place in the final. Several players were resting, including Cronje after an unbroken run of 162 limited-overs internationals since September 1993. Pollock returned to captain his country for the first time in a full international (he had led them to victory in the Commonwealth Games 18 months earlier). He started well when Pakistan were dismissed for 168; only Yousuf Youhana, last out for 65, made much headway. But after Kirsten had retired with back spasms, South Africa's batting folded, with their last eight wickets going for 27 while Gibbs carried his bat for 59. Waqar Younis struck first, getting McKenzie lbw for his 300th one-day international wicket, but Shoaib Akhtar did the damage with three wickets in his fourth over. The strain – his pace had been recorded at 97 mph – was too much, however: a groin injury forced him off midway through his next over. He returned to bowl two more balls before breaking down again, and was forced to miss the final.

Man of the Match: Shoaib Akhtar.

Pakistan

Imran Nazir b Pollock	0	Waqar Younis b Crookes	2
Shahid Afridi b Klusener	26	Shoaib Akhtar c Boucher b Hayward	7
Younis Khan c Boucher b Willoughby	5	Arshad Khan not out	2
Inzamam-ul-Haq lbw b Klusener	17	B 1, l-b 2, w 7, n-b 1	11
Yousuf Youhana run out	65		
*†Moin Khan c and b Hayward	0	1/0 2/12 3/43 (49.2 overs) 168
Abdur Razzaq run out	14	4/60 5/61 6/96
Wasim Akram c Crookes b Willoughby	19	7/124 8/139 9/161

Bowling: Pollock 9.2–2–28–1; Willoughby 10–2–39–2; Hayward 10–1–35–2; Klusener 10–0–27–2; Crookes 7–0–22–1; Strydom 3–0–14–0.

South Africa

G. Kirsten retired hurt	8	P. C. Strydom lbw b Abdur Razzaq	0
H. H. Gibbs not out	59	D. N. Crookes run out	5
N. D. McKenzie lbw b Waqar Younis	1	M. Hayward b Waqar Younis	1
†M. V. Boucher c Moin Khan b Shoaib Akhtar	14	C. M. Willoughby b Abdur Razzaq	0
D. M. Benkenstein b Shoaib Akhtar	0	B 7, w 4, n-b 2	13
L. Klusener b Shoaib Akhtar	0		
*S. M. Pollock c Inzamam-ul-Haq b Wasim Akram	0	1/27 2/74 3/74 (26.5 overs) 101
		4/75 5/75 6/80
		7/89 8/94 9/101

Kirsten retired hurt at 22.

Bowling: Wasim Akram 8–0–26–1; Waqar Younis 8–0–39–2; Shoaib Akhtar 4.5–2–9–3; Shahid Afridi 2–0–10–0; Abdur Razzaq 4–1–10–2.

Umpires: J. H. Hampshire and P. T. Manuel.

QUALIFYING TABLE

	Played	Won	Lost	Points	Net run-rate
South Africa	4	3	1	6	0.35
Pakistan	4	2	2	4	0.60
India	4	1	3	2	−1.01

Net run-rate is calculated by subtracting runs conceded per over from runs scored per over.

FINAL

PAKISTAN v SOUTH AFRICA

At Sharjah, March 31 (day/night). Pakistan won by 16 runs. Toss: Pakistan.

Pakistan claimed the cup and completed their reversal of fortune after Waqar Younis had taken four wickets in as many overs to end South Africa's challenge. Moin Khan won the toss for the fifth time, whereupon Imran Nazir, surviving a run-out chance in the first over, and Shahid Afridi gave their side the perfect platform with 123 in 21 overs. Afridi struck a belligerent 48-ball 52 before a brilliant running, diving catch by Kallis sent him back. His team-mates could not quite sustain that rate, but Inzamam-ul-Haq added another fifty and Pakistan beat their previous best against these opponents. South Africa in reply lost two wickets by the eighth over, which brought in Cronje for what was to be his final international innings. Hitting 79 in 73 balls, with six fours and three sixes, he put on 105 with McKenzie, who went on to add 61 with Boucher. Off-spinner Arshad Khan broke both these stands, and Waqar eventually saw off the threat from Boucher, 57 in 49 balls, to conclude his own irresistible breakthrough.

Man of the Match: Waqar Younis.   *Man of the Series:* Waqar Younis.

Pakistan

Imran Nazir st Boucher b Crookes....	69	Abdur Razzaq not out.............	28
Shahid Afridi c Kallis b Klusener	52	Wasim Akram not out.............	5
Younis Khan lbw b Klusener	4	L-b 10, w 10, n-b 4...........	24
Inzamam-ul-Haq b Pollock..........	53		
Yousuf Youhana c Cronje b Kallis	26	1/123 2/135 3/139 (6 wkts, 50 overs)	263
*†Moin Khan lbw b Kallis..........	2	4/204 5/209 6/256	

Waqar Younis, Arshad Khan and Mohammad Akram did not bat.

Bowling: Pollock 10–1–54–1; Hayward 9–0–52–0; Kallis 10–0–57–2; Elworthy 3–0–21–0; Klusener 10–1–27–2; Crookes 5–0–20–1; Cronje 3–0–22–0.

South Africa

H. H. Gibbs c Inzamam-ul-Haq b Wasim Akram .	5	N. Boje c Moin Khan b Waqar Younis ..	0
N. D. McKenzie c Mohammad Akram b Arshad Khan .	58	L. Klusener b Waqar Younis.........	0
		S. M. Pollock b Waqar Younis	14
J. H. Kallis c Moin Khan b Mohammad Akram .	11	S. Elworthy not out...............	5
*W. J. Cronje c Younis Khan b Arshad Khan .	79	M. Hayward b Abdur Razzaq........	4
		L-b 6, w 4, n-b 3	13
D. N. Crookes b Arshad Khan .....,	1	1/12 2/30 3/135 (49 overs)	247
†M. V. Boucher b Waqar Younis	57	4/137 5/198 6/199	
		7/199 8/224 9/239	

Bowling: Wasim Akram 9–2–23–1; Waqar Younis 10–0–62–4; Mohammad Akram 9–0–42–1; Abdur Razzaq 9–0–33–1; Shahid Afridi 4–0–30–0; Arshad Khan 8–0–51–3.

Umpires: D. J. Harper and P. T. Manuel.
Series referee: R. Subba Row (England).

CABLE & WIRELESS SERIES, 1999-2000

By CRAIG COZIER

Pakistan won the Caribbean's first triangular tournament, defeating the home team 2–1 in the finals after West Indies had cruised through the qualifiers with a 100 per cent record. The third side, Zimbabwe, their confidence undermined after losing the Test series, were beaten in all four group matches, a disappointing end to a tour that had promised much.

Inzamam-ul-Haq was one of the main architects of Pakistan's performance. He was named Man of the Series for his 295 runs at 59.00, in a competition where the bowlers dominated and there was only one total over 250. Mushtaq Ahmed, recalled and seemingly refreshed after missing Pakistan's home series against Sri Lanka and a recent tournament in Sharjah, confused all batsmen with his leg-breaks and googlies, conceded just over three runs an over and produced a telling four-wicket haul in the decisive final.

West Indies carried into the tournament the self-assurance born of their Test series victory over Zimbabwe, and started off with four comprehensive wins. Sherwin Campbell, who scored 316 in all, and Wavell Hinds notched maiden centuries in the one-day game. The bowlers, even without Courtney Walsh, resting after the euphoria of his record 435th Test wicket in preparation for the series against Pakistan, were consistently impressive: Reon King claimed 17 wickets at 11.52. Captain Jimmy Adams and 20-year-old Chris Gayle advertised their all-round worth.

But their batting faltered when it really mattered, in the face of Pakistan's versatile, high-quality attack. West Indies failed to reach 198 on a good Kensington Oval pitch in the opening final and, with the trophy on the line, collapsed for 114 in the decider. It was only the second time West Indies had lost a series of home one-day internationals. Allan Border's Australians won 4–1 in 1990-91, though Sri Lanka also won a one-off match five years later.

Note: Matches in this section were not first-class.

WEST INDIES v ZIMBABWE

At Kingston, April 1. West Indies won by 87 runs. Toss: Zimbabwe.

West Indies' vice-captain and captain made the difference between the teams. Campbell hit eight fours in a chanceless 103 off 130 balls, his maiden century in 71 one-day internationals, adding 141 with Adams, who struck just one four in 86 balls. Both were among four run-outs as West Indies went from 181 for two to 237 for nine in the last ten overs. Zimbabwe, docked two overs because of their slow over-rate, lost both openers cheaply, then Carlisle and Goodwin rebuilt the innings in an 86-run stand. When King bowled Carlisle off an inside edge, and Goodwin (52 off 57 balls) fell to Adams at the same score, the visitors collapsed, losing their last eight wickets for 34. Adams's economical left-arm spin earned three wickets.

Man of the Match: S. L. Campbell.

West Indies

P. A. Wallace b Olonga	6	M. Dillon run out	1
S. L. Campbell run out	103	C. E. L. Ambrose not out	0
C. H. Gayle c A. Flower b Brent	4	R. D. King not out	0
*J. C. Adams run out	60	L-b 4, w 12, n-b 4	20
R. L. Powell c Wishart b Nkala	0		
†R. D. Jacobs c Olonga b Brent	32	1/31 2/41 3/182 (9 wkts, 50 overs) 237
W. W. Hinds run out	10	4/188 5/190 6/228
F. A. Rose b Streak	1	7/234 8/237 9/237

Bowling: Streak 10–0–44–1; Olonga 8–0–36–1; Brent 10–0–49–2; Nkala 7–0–36–1; G. W. Flower 10–0–44–0; Johnson 3–0–15–0; Goodwin 2–0–9–0.

Zimbabwe

N. C. Johnson c Gayle b King	6	M. L. Nkala b Dillon		1
G. W. Flower c Rose b Ambrose	9	G. B. Brent lbw b Powell		2
S. V. Carlisle b King	37	H. K. Olonga not out		5
M. W. Goodwin c Wallace b Adams	52	L-b 7, w 3, n-b 5		15
*†A. Flower c Powell b Dillon	7			—
A. D. R. Campbell st Jacobs b Adams	1	1/7 2/30 3/116	(41.4 overs)	150
C. B. Wishart st Jacobs b Powell	15	4/116 5/118 6/128		
H. H. Streak c Jacobs b Adams	0	7/129 8/136 9/141		

Bowling: Ambrose 7-1-18-1; King 8-0-30-2; Dillon 9-0-34-2; Rose 6-1-21-0; Gayle 3-0-16-0; Adams 7-0-19-3; Powell 1.4-0-5-2.

Umpires: S. A. Bucknor and B. E. W. Morgan.

WEST INDIES v ZIMBABWE

At Kingston, April 2. West Indies won by 41 runs. Toss: West Indies.

A batting feast, led by Hinds's aggressive maiden century and augmented by his fellow Jamaican left-handers Adams and Gayle, swept West Indies to their third victory over Zimbabwe on this ground in six days. Adams helped Hinds add 95, but the acceleration really started after he was again run out: Hinds and Gayle then amassed 125 in 15 overs, including 100 in the last ten, to reach a formidable 280 for three. Gayle's career-best 58 took 45 deliveries and included five fours and a six; Hinds, dropped at 82 by Grant Flower, stroked 12 fours and a six in his 116 off 125 balls. Carlisle and Andy Flower batted enterprisingly for fifties, but wickets fell too regularly for Zimbabwe to mount a realistic challenge.

Man of the Match: W. W. Hinds.

West Indies

P. A. Wallace b Brent	18	C. H. Gayle not out		58
S. L. Campbell b Brent	21	B 4, l-b 7, w 10, n-b 5		26
W. W. Hinds not out	116			—
*J. C. Adams run out	41	1/53 2/60 3/155	(3 wkts, 50 overs)	280

R. L. Powell, †R. D. Jacobs, F. A. Rose, M. Dillon, C. E. L. Ambrose and R. D. King did not bat.

Bowling: Streak 8-0-51-0; Olonga 7-0-40-0; Nkala 10-1-38-0; Brent 8-0-34 2; Whittall 6-0-53-0; Viljoen 5-1-31-0; G. W. Flower 6-0-22-0.

Zimbabwe

G. W. Flower b Ambrose	15	M. L. Nkala st Jacobs b Powell		17
C. B. Wishart c Jacobs b King	7	G. B. Brent not out		3
S. V. Carlisle c Hinds b King	57			
M. W. Goodwin b Rose	20	B 4, l-b 6, w 9, n-b 9		28
*†A. Flower c Ambrose b Adams	52			—
D. P. Viljoen c Powell b King	4	1/23 2/25 3/72	(8 wkts, 50 overs)	239
G. J. Whittall not out	29	4/141 5/146 6/189		
H. H. Streak run out	7	7/208 8/231		

H. K. Olonga did not bat.

Bowling: Ambrose 10-1-19-1; King 8-3-27-3; Dillon 10-0-58-0; Rose 9-0-52-1; Powell 7-0-42-1; Campbell 1-0-7-0; Adams 5-0-24-1.

Umpires: S. A. Bucknor and B. E. W. Morgan.

PAKISTAN v ZIMBABWE

At St John's, April 5. Pakistan won by five wickets. Toss: Zimbabwe.

Pakistan's first match of the tour ended in a comfortable victory. But Zimbabwe's third defeat gave West Indies a final berth and almost certainly meant their own elimination. Spin stifled the Zimbabweans after their openers had laid solid foundations. Arshad Khan and Mushtaq Ahmed had combined figures of two for 56 off 20 overs, while Shahid Afridi removed the dangerous Goodwin and Andy Flower. A total of 199 never looked enough, though Zimbabwe still had a chance when Pakistan were 153 for five. Afridi had blazed a forthright, run-a-ball 69, laced with five fours and three sixes, adding 68 with Inzamam-ul-Haq. But when both fell to Viljoen's left-arm spin and Yousuf Youhana was run out, Moin Khan and Abdur Razzaq steadied the nerves with an unfussy stand of 47.

Man of the Match: Shahid Afridi.

Zimbabwe

N. C. Johnson c Imran Nazir			H. H. Streak c Moin Khan	
b Arshad Khan .	20		b Mohammad Akram .	15
G. W. Flower c Younis Khan			M. L. Nkala c Yousuf Youhana	
b Abdur Razzaq .	36		b Waqar Younis .	1
S. V. Carlisle c Yousuf Youhana			B. A. Murphy not out	1
b Mushtaq Ahmed .	30		G. B. Brent not out	4
M. W. Goodwin c Imran Nazir				
b Shahid Afridi .	17		B 9, l-b 2, w 9, n-b 3	23
*†A. Flower c Imran Nazir				
b Shahid Afridi .	16		1/59 2/61 3/100 (9 wkts, 50 overs) 199	
D. P. Viljoen run out	5		4/108 5/118 6/151	
G. J. Whittall b Mohammad Akram	31		7/188 8/191 9/195	

Bowling: Waqar Younis 7–0–26–1; Mohammad Akram 8–0–31–2; Abdur Razzaq 9–0–40–1; Arshad Khan 10–3–26–1; Mushtaq Ahmed 10–1–30–1; Shahid Afridi 6–0–35–2.

Pakistan

Imran Nazir c Carlisle b Johnson	6		Abdur Razzaq not out	28
Shahid Afridi c Johnson b Viljoen	69			
Younis Khan lbw b Streak	6		L-b 1, w 10, n-b 2	13
Inzamam-ul-Haq c Nkala b Viljoen	32			
Yousuf Youhana run out	21		1/12 2/41 3/109 (5 wkts, 47.1 overs) 200	
*†Moin Khan not out	25		4/136 5/153	

Waqar Younis, Mushtaq Ahmed, Arshad Khan and Mohammad Akram did not bat.

Bowling: Streak 8–0–33–1; Johnson 3–0–23–1; Brent 7–0–29–0; Nkala 3–0–24–0; Murphy 10–0–30–0; Viljoen 10–1–30–2; G. W. Flower 6.1–0–30–0.

Umpires: B. R. Doctrove and E. A. Nicholls.

WEST INDIES v PAKISTAN

At St Vincent, April 12. West Indies won by 96 runs. Toss: West Indies.

West Indies continued their dominant form when the tournament resumed after the ICC's Cricket Week, which had taken several players to Bangladesh. Pakistan took five overs to score their first run, and then crumbled to the lowest score in ten one-day internationals on St Vincent as Rose's career-best, five-wicket strike gunned down their middle order. Inzamam-ul-Haq's unbeaten half-century offered the sole resistance. Vincentian Nixon McLean, in his first international since October, claimed two late wickets, delighting a capacity crowd of 11,000 that included Rolling Stone Mick Jagger, who had flown over from neighbouring Mustique. Wallace and Campbell had earlier given West Indies a steady start, and then Adams, with an even fifty, shared a vital 84-run stand with Hinds. When the lower order knocked 76 off the last ten overs, lifting the total to 213 for seven, West Indies were well placed to gain their first win over Pakistan for seven internationals.

Man of the Match: F. A. Rose.

West Indies

P. A. Wallace b Mushtaq Ahmed		21
S. L. Campbell c Inzamam-ul-Haq		
b Abdur Razzaq		22
W. W. Hinds b Mushtaq Ahmed		39
*J. C. Adams c Yousuf Youhana		
b Arshad Khan		50
C. H. Gayle c Imran Nazir		
b Arshad Khan		15
†R. D. Jacobs not out		14

R. L. Powell c Younis Khan
     b Wasim Akram . 12
F. A. Rose b Abdur Razzaq 6
N. A. M. McLean not out 1
L-b 13, w 15, n-b 5 33

1/49 2/54 3/138   (7 wkts, 50 overs) 213
4/170 5/171
6/198 7/209

C. E. L. Ambrose and R. D. King did not bat.

Bowling: Wasim Akram 10-2-44-1; Waqar Younis 10-0-50-0; Mushtaq Ahmed 10-0-34-2; Abdur Razzaq 9-3-30-2; Arshad Khan 10-2-38-2; Shahid Afridi 1-0-4-0.

Pakistan

Imran Nazir c Jacobs b Ambrose		0
Shahid Afridi c Wallace b King		5
Younis Khan c King b Rose		15
Inzamam-ul-Haq not out		51
Yousuf Youhana c Hinds b Rose		0
Abdur Razzaq b Rose		2
*†Moin Khan c Jacobs b Rose		20
Wasim Akram c Adams b Rose		3

Waqar Younis lbw b McLean 8
Mushtaq Ahmed b McLean 0
Arshad Khan b Gayle 0
L-b 4, w 3, n-b 6 13

1/0 2/12 3/32   (41.3 overs) 117
4/32 5/41 6/88
7/92 8/115 9/116

Bowling: Ambrose 8-2-12-1; King 8-3-17-1; Rose 10-1-23-5; McLean 7-1-27-2; Adams 4-0-15-0; Gayle 4.3-0-19-1.

Umpires: S. A. Bucknor and B. E. W. Morgan.

PAKISTAN v ZIMBABWE

At St George's, April 15. Pakistan won by six wickets. Toss: Zimbabwe.

Teenager Imran Nazir's thrilling maiden international hundred powered Pakistan to a comprehensive win and ended Zimbabwe's tour without a victory. Nazir easily outscored the usually dynamic Shahid Afridi, who made only 19 of their 49 off 48 balls together; in all, his 105 took 135 balls, with ten fours and two huge sixes. He also shared key stands with Inzamam-ul-Haq and Moin Khan, who hit a six and five fours. Zimbabwe had begun positively as Johnson and Wishart compiled 84 in 23 overs, but Pakistan's varied attack began to cull batsmen and never allowed an increase in tempo. Mushtaq Ahmed's miserly leg-spin was always impressive, and a target of 205 was below par on a perfect pitch and fast outfield. Wasim Akram became the second player after India's Mohammad Azharuddin to appear in 300 one-day internationals.

Man of the Match: Imran Nazir.

Zimbabwe

N. C. Johnson c Arshad Khan		
b Mushtaq Ahmed		43
C. B. Wishart c Younis Khan		
b Abdur Razzaq		45
S. V. Carlisle b Arshad Khan		5
M. W. Goodwin c sub (Shoaib Malik)		
b Arshad Khan		35
*†A. Flower c and b Arshad Khan		31
A. M. Blignaut b Abdur Razzaq		3

G. W. Flower not out 9
G. J. Whittall c sub (Shoaib Malik)
     b Wasim Akram . 7
D. P. Viljoen not out 0
L-b 14, w 9, n-b 3 26

1/84 2/98 3/118   (7 wkts, 50 overs) 204
4/177 5/182
6/186 7/200

H. H. Streak and M. L. Nkala did not bat.

Bowling: Wasim Akram 8-1-27-1; Waqar Younis 10-0-44-0; Abdur Razzaq 10-2-32-2; Mushtaq Ahmed 10-1-29-1; Arshad Khan 10-0-45-3; Shahid Afridi 2-0-13-0.

Pakistan

Imran Nazir not out	105	*†Moin Khan not out	35
Shahid Afridi c Viljoen b Blignaut	19	L-b 6, w 4, n-b 1	11
Younis Khan c and b Viljoen	1		
Yousuf Youhana b Streak	0	1/49 2/77 (4 wkts, 43.1 overs) 205	
Inzamam-ul-Haq c A. Flower b Whittall	34	3/78 4/141	

Abdur Razzaq, Wasim Akram, Waqar Younis, Mushtaq Ahmed and Arshad Khan did not bat.

Bowling: Johnson 4–0–26–0; Blignaut 7–0–37–1; Streak 9–0–33–1; Nkala 4–0–23–0; Viljoen 10–1–34–1; G. W. Flower 4.1–0–24–0; Whittall 5–0–22–1.

Umpires: S. A. Bucknor and B. E. W. Morgan.

WEST INDIES v PAKISTAN

At St George's, April 16. West Indies won by 17 runs. Toss: West Indies.

With both sides already qualified, fast bowlers Ambrose and Wasim Akram were rested before the three-match final. Contrasting fifties from Campbell and Powell boosted West Indies to a satisfying 248 for six. Campbell's 89-ball 56 laid the platform from which Powell launched his power-hitting, with two sixes and a four in 36 balls. Abdur Razzaq and Arshad Khan both went for 16 in an over. After King quickly despatched the Pakistani openers, with a run-out in between, Inzamam-ul-Haq and Yousuf Youhana sensibly plotted a path to revival. Their stand was worth 123 when Inzamam was run out, for the 32nd time in 218 one-day internationals. Youhana fell two overs later, King bowled Razzaq, and the lower order could not threaten West Indies' 100 per cent record.

Man of the Match: R. D. King.

West Indies

P. A. Wallace lbw b Abdur Razzaq	17	R. L. Powell not out	50
S. L. Campbell c Yousuf Youhana b Arshad Khan	56	†R. D. Jacobs run out	25
		F. A. Rose not out	2
W. W. Hinds c Mohammad Wasim b Mushtaq Ahmed	24		
C. H. Gayle c Wajahatullah Wasti b Waqar Younis	42	B 1, l-b 5, w 12, n-b 3	21
*J. C. Adams run out	11	1/35 2/88 3/127 (6 wkts, 50 overs) 248	
		4/147 5/170 6/232	

N. O. Perry, N. A. M. McLean and R. D. King did not bat.

Bowling: Waqar Younis 10–1–43–1; Irfan Fazil 6–0–46–0; Abdur Razzaq 10–2–45–1; Mushtaq Ahmed 10–0–33–1; Arshad Khan 10–0–46–1; Wajahatullah Wasti 4–0–29–0.

Pakistan

Imran Nazir c Jacobs b King	9	Irfan Fazil c Adams b McLean	15
Wajahatullah Wasti b King	10	Mushtaq Ahmed st Jacobs b Adams	4
Mohammad Wasim run out	0	Arshad Khan not out	2
Inzamam-ul-Haq run out	69	L-b 5, w 7, n-b 8	20
Yousuf Youhana c Adams b Rose	56		
*†Moin Khan c Rose b Perry	16	1/19 2/19 3/24 (48.1 overs) 231	
Abdur Razzaq b King	24	4/147 5/162 6/200	
Waqar Younis c Hinds b Perry	6	7/206 8/214 9/229	

Bowling: King 10–0–38–3; Rose 10–3–36–1; McLean 9.1–0–47–1; Perry 10–0–54–2; Adams 5–0–28–1; Gayle 4–0–23–0.

Umpires: S. A. Bucknor and B. E. W. Morgan.

QUALIFYING TABLE

	Played	Won	Lost	Points	Net run-rate
West Indies	4	4	0	8	1.14
Pakistan	4	2	2	4	−0.34
Zimbabwe	4	0	4	0	−0.84

Net run-rate is calculated by subtracting runs conceded per over from runs scored per over.

WEST INDIES v PAKISTAN

First Final Match

At Bridgetown, April 19. Pakistan won by 17 runs. Toss: Pakistan. International debut: S. C. Joseph.

A tense, low-scoring game was clinched by Pakistan, who won their first toss of the tournament and held their nerve when it mattered. Only Inzamam-ul-Haq, with seven fours in an accomplished 86-ball 66, broke free against the disciplined home attack; he became the tenth batsman to score 7,000 one-day international runs and also passed 1,000 against West Indies. However, his 49-run stand with Younis Khan took up 18 overs, and wickets fell when Pakistan tried to accelerate. West Indies were in control at 144 for eight before Wasim Akram, coolly supported by Mushtaq Ahmed, smashed 42 off 36 balls: the last two overs cost 28. Wasim and Waqar Younis then stalled West Indies' reply, which laboured to 21 for one in 12 overs. A second-wicket stand of 86 had lasted almost 25 overs when Wallace fell to Mushtaq's final ball; Hinds soon followed as five wickets tumbled for 24. Only Sylvester Joseph, playing because Powell injured his ankle, raised hopes with a busy 28 off 32 balls, but Shahid Afridi completed victory with his career-best three for 16.

Man of the Match: Wasim Akram.

Pakistan

Imran Nazir c Wallace b King	12	
Shahid Afridi c Jacobs b Ambrose.	17	
Younis Khan run out.	23	
Inzamam-ul-Haq c and b McLean	66	
Yousuf Youhana lbw b King	8	
*†Moin Khan b Adams	0	
Abdur Razzaq run out.	7	
Wasim Akram not out	42	

Waqar Younis c Jacobs b Gayle.	0
Mushtaq Ahmed not out	11
L-b 2, w 6, n-b 3	11
1/24 2/32 3/81 (8 wkts, 50 overs)	197

Arshad Khan did not bat.

1/24 2/32 3/81 (8 wkts, 50 overs) 197
4/100 5/101 6/137
7/140 8/144

Bowling: Ambrose 10–0–35–1; King 10–1–37–2; McLean 10–1–36–1; Rose 10–1–41–0; Gayle 6–0–26–1; Adams 4–1–20–1.

West Indies

P. A. Wallace c Yousuf Youhana		
b Mushtaq Ahmed .	47	
S. L. Campbell c Moin Khan		
b Waqar Younis .	11	
W. W. Hinds c Moin Khan		
b Waqar Younis .	35	
C. H. Gayle run out	8	
*J. C. Adams b Abdur Razzaq	7	
†R. D. Jacobs c Younis Khan		
b Arshad Khan .	0	
S. C. Joseph b Shahid Afridi	28	

F. A. Rose b Shahid Afridi.	11
N. A. M. McLean run out	1
C. E. L. Ambrose c sub (Shoaib Malik)	
b Shahid Afridi .	11
R. D. King not out	2
B 1, l-b 4, w 12, n-b 2.	19
1/13 2/99 3/105 (49.3 overs)	180

1/13 2/99 3/105 (49.3 overs) 180
4/121 5/122 6/123
7/145 8/146 9/175

Bowling: Wasim Akram 10–3–30–0; Waqar Younis 9–0–34–2; Abdur Razzaq 10–1–38–1; Mushtaq Ahmed 10–2–23–1; Arshad Khan 7–0–34–1; Shahid Afridi 3.3–0–16–3.

Umpires: B. R. Doctrove and E. A. Nicholls.

WEST INDIES v PAKISTAN

Second Final Match

At Port-of-Spain, April 22. West Indies won by 60 runs. Toss: West Indies.

A professional West Indian performance levelled the series to ensure the third match, also at Queen's Park Oval, would draw a bumper Sunday crowd (it was to be played even if one team led 2–0). Campbell's 77 took him past 2,000 one-day runs, and his stands with left-handers Hinds and Gayle paced the innings: he added 58 with Hinds and 50 in 12 overs with Gayle, who hit four fours in 35 balls. Pakistan reached a promising 72 for one in the 16th over before three wickets fell for seven runs in 16 balls. McLean trapped Imran Nazir, while King removed Inzamam-ul-Haq, who had scored three half-centuries against West Indies in this series, and Yousuf Youhana with successive deliveries. The contrasting spin of Adams and Gayle further undermined Pakistan: together they shared five wickets for 49 off 20 overs.

Man of the Match: S. L. Campbell.

West Indies

P. A. Wallace lbw b Wasim Akram	....	8	F. A. Rose c Abdur Razzaq	
S. L. Campbell c Waqar Younis			b Wasim Akram .	5
	b Wasim Akram .	77	N. A. M. McLean not out	1
W. W. Hinds c Shahid Afridi			C. E. L. Ambrose not out	4
	b Abdur Razzaq .	24		
*J. C. Adams run out		5	B 2, l-b 4, w 8	14
C. H. Gayle run out		33		
R. L. Powell c Arshad Khan			1/11 2/69 3/84 (8 wkts, 50 overs) 208	
	b Shahid Afridi .	21	4/134 5/171 6/189	
†R. D. Jacobs b Abdur Razzaq		16	7/202 8/203	

R. D. King did not bat.

Bowling: Wasim Akram 10–2–34–3; Waqar Younis 8–1–26–0; Mushtaq Ahmed 10–0–34–0; Abdur Razzaq 10–0–42–2; Arshad Khan 7–0–31–0; Shahid Afridi 5–0–35–1.

Pakistan

Imran Nazir lbw b McLean	22	Waqar Younis run out	23	
Shahid Afridi c Jacobs b McLean	21	Mushtaq Ahmed b Adams	3	
Younis Khan lbw b Gayle	31	Arshad Khan not out.............	5	
Inzamam-ul-Haq lbw b King	4	B 1, l-b 4, w 8, n-b 6	18	
Yousuf Youhana lbw b King.........	0			
Abdur Razzaq b Adams............	6	1/34 2/72 3/79 (45 overs) 148		
*†Moin Khan c Hinds b Adams	11	4/79 5/98 6/98		
Wasim Akram st Jacobs b Gayle	4	7/108 8/124 9/138		

Bowling: Ambrose 7–0–23–0; King 6–1–22–2; McLean 6–0–33–2; Rose 6–1–17–0; Adams 10–0–21–3; Gayle 10–0–28–2.

Umpires: B. R. Doctrove and E. A. Nicholls.

WEST INDIES v PAKISTAN

Third Final Match

At Port-of-Spain, April 23. Pakistan won by four wickets. Toss: West Indies.

Mushtaq Ahmed, who had bowled with immaculate control throughout the tournament, effectively decided its outcome with four cheap wickets. West Indies were all out inside 34 overs for 114, equalling England's total at Bridgetown in 1985-86 as the lowest in 92 one-day internationals in the Caribbean. Their humbling could hardly have been predicted when Campbell and Wallace were opening with 61 in 17 overs. But once they fell, at the same score, the innings disintegrated. Mushtaq Ahmed bamboozled Hinds, Gayle and Powell, the young Jamaicans, within five balls, while Shoaib Akhtar and Saqlain Mushtaq, making their first appearance in this series, grabbed two wickets apiece. Despite the meagre target, the home bowlers made Pakistan struggle; King, hostile and accurate, had them 19 for three in the tenth over. But Inzamam-ul-Haq steadied the innings, adding 42 with Younis Khan, and despite needing a runner after King's yorker cannoned into his heel, his calm assurance never wavered. Though he took 98 balls for his 39, he always had overs in hand.

Man of the Match: Mushtaq Ahmed.   *Man of the Series:* Inzamam-ul-Haq.

West Indies

P. A. Wallace st Moin Khan		†R. D. Jacobs c Imran Nazir		
b Mushtaq Ahmed .	30	b Saqlain Mushtaq .	7
S. L. Campbell c Inzamam-ul-Haq		F. A. Rose not out	9
b Abdur Razzaq .	26	C. E. L. Ambrose b Shoaib Akhtar	0
W. W. Hinds b Mushtaq Ahmed	7	N. A. M. McLean c and b Saqlain Mushtaq	15
*J. C. Adams b Shoaib Akhtar	9	R. D. King run out.	0
C. H. Gayle c Shahid Afridi		L-b 2, w 6, n-b 3	11
b Mushtaq Ahmed .	0		
R. L. Powell c Shahid Afridi		1/61 2/61 3/71 4/71 5/71 (33.2 overs) 114	
b Mushtaq Ahmed .	0	6/83 7/97 8/97 9/114	

Bowling: Wasim Akram 7–0–22–0; Shoaib Akhtar 7–0–31–2; Abdur Razzaq 6–1–17–1; Mushtaq Ahmed 8–1–22–4; Saqlain Mushtaq 5.2–0–20–2.

Pakistan

Imran Nazir c Jacobs b King	4	*†Moin Khan c Jacobs b King	10
Shahid Afridi c Rose b King	13	Wasim Akram not out	10
Younis Khan c and b Adams	17	L-b 7, w 7, n-b 5	19
Abdur Razzaq c Jacobs b King	0		
Inzamam-ul Haq not out , ...	39	1/13 2/18 3/19 (6 wkts, 45.1 overs) 116	
Yousuf Youhana c Campbell b Adams . .	4	4/61 5/73 6/93	

Saqlain Mushtaq, Mushtaq Ahmed and Shoaib Akhtar did not bat.

Bowling: Ambrose 10–4–15–0; King 10–1–25–4; Rose 10–0–30–0; McLean 8.1–2–20–0; Adams 5–0–17–2; Gayle 2–1–2–0.

Umpires: B. R. Doctrove and E. A. Nicholls.
Series referee: R. S. Madugalle (Sri Lanka).

STANDARD BANK CHALLENGE SERIES, 1999-2000

By COLIN BRYDEN

This short series was completely overtaken by events, the cricket lost in the frenzied coverage of Hansie Cronje's fall from grace. He did not appear at any of the three matches, but his presence was ubiquitous: his name was on the lips of every spectator and writ large on every banner; it dominated every press interview.

The idea behind the games, forgotten in the media mêlée, was simple: this was the first leg of a money-spinning home-and-away series between the two strongest teams in one-day cricket. The second leg was scheduled to be played in an indoor stadium in Melbourne in August. It was a mouth-watering prospect. For South Africa, it was a chance for revenge after two titanic battles in the World Cup had seen Australia come off best. But then the roof caved in on South African cricket. The morning before the first match in Durban, their captain, Cronje, admitted he had "not been entirely honest" when, two days earlier, he denied involvement with Indian bookmakers. He was peremptorily sacked. The games went ahead, against a backdrop of one of the biggest scandals in cricket's history.

In the circumstances, South Africa's 2–1 victory was remarkable, given that the form of the teams had appeared to be travelling in opposite directions. Since the World Cup, Australia had won 20 of their 24 matches, including an unprecedented sequence of 13 interrupted by only one no-result, while South Africa's record was 13 from 21. Maybe Shaun Pollock, appointed South African captain at the age of 26, took heart from the 1998 Commonwealth Games, where he had led a young team to the gold medal by defeating a full-strength Australian side in the final. South Africa, though, had never won an official one-day series including Australia, despite each country having beaten the other 19 times, and Steve Waugh claimed that his current side was, if anything, more talented than the one that won the World Cup ten months earlier.

Even before the Cronje crisis, South Africa had been struggling to get into their stride in the absence of several experienced players. Paul Adams was injured, Daryll Cullinan had announced his retirement from the one-day game (a decision he later revoked) and Allan Donald had been dropped in advance of taking a sabbatical from international cricket to fulfil his commitment to Warwickshire. Yet when it mattered, the South Africans rose to the challenge. Showing the resilience of youth, they put the Cronje controversy from their minds and easily beat the jetlagged world champions at Kingsmead. They were outplayed at Newlands as the Australians reasserted their discipline, but bounced back impressively to take the series at the Wanderers. All three games were won by the side winning the toss and fielding, but only the last lived up to expectations.

Waugh was gracious in defeat. South Africa's recovery from the events that cost Cronje the captaincy had not surprised him, he said. It emphasised again that in cricket no individual was indispensable.

Note: Matches in this section were not first-class.

SOUTH AFRICA v AUSTRALIA

First One-Day International

At Durban, April 12 (day/night). South Africa won by six wickets. Toss: South Africa.

Pollock marked his ascent to the captaincy with a superb opening spell, trapping Mark Waugh with his seventh delivery and not conceding a run until his 22nd. Despite a belligerent 51 off 40 balls by Gilchrist, Australia were in dire straits at 120 for seven. Martyn then played superbly, doubling that score with lower-order support. Boucher, who had already equalled the wicket-keeping record in limited-overs internationals by holding five catches, dropped what looked like a straightforward sixth when the ball looped off the top edge of Lee's bat. Only 15 days earlier, Kirsten had been carried off the field at Sharjah with a spine injury. Now, showing immense character, he and Kallis pulled South Africa's innings around after a shaky start. Evening dew made conditions awkward for Warne, and McGrath alone bowled consistently. Rhodes concluded matters with a lively 46 from 40 balls.

Man of the Match: G. Kirsten.   *Attendance:* 21,638.

Australia

M. E. Waugh lbw b Pollock	0	D. W. Fleming c Ntini b Kallis	29
†A. C. Gilchrist c Boucher b Hayward	51	B. Lee not out	24
M. L. Hayden run out	0		
M. G. Bevan c Boucher b Ntini	31	L-b 3, w 5, n-b 1	9
*S. R. Waugh c Boucher b Ntini	2		
D. R. Martyn run out	74	1/10 2/13 3/72 (9 wkts, 50 overs)	240
A. Symonds c Boucher b Ntini	20	4/81 5/92 6/120	
S. K. Warne c Boucher b Ntini	0	7/120 8/185 9/240	

G. D. McGrath did not bat.

Bowling: Pollock 10–3–43–1; Kallis 10–0–53–1; Hayward 10–0–58–1; Ntini 10–0–56–4; Klusener 10–2–27–0.

South Africa

G. Kirsten b Lee	97	L. Klusener not out	4
H. H. Gibbs c S. R. Waugh b McGrath	0	B 1, l-b 2, w 9, n-b 7	19
N. D. McKenzie c Symonds b Lee	14		
J. H. Kallis c Gilchrist b McGrath	61	1/12 2/32 (4 wkts, 48 overs)	241
J. N. Rhodes not out	46	3/161 4/228	

D. J. Callaghan, †M. V. Boucher, *S. M. Pollock, M. Hayward and M. Ntini did not bat.

Bowling: McGrath 9–2–21–2; Fleming 10–0–60–0; Lee 10–0–57–2; Warne 8–0–47–0; Symonds 5–0–21–0; S. R. Waugh 3–0–18–0; M. E. Waugh 3–0–14–0.

Umpires: C. J. Mitchley and D. L. Orchard.

SOUTH AFRICA v AUSTRALIA

Second One-Day International

At Cape Town, April 14 (day/night). Australia won by five wickets. Toss: Australia.

Australia levelled the series with a one-sided win, using less than half their allocation of overs. Although batting first in floodlit matches at Newlands has historically paid off, Steve Waugh's decision to bowl was justified by what he described as his team's best bowling and fielding performance since the World Cup. At 54 for one, South Africa had built a reasonable foundation, but McGrath, the Lee brothers and Warne – who bowled scarcely a loose ball between them – wore down the batsmen. In the process, Gilchrist became the first wicket-keeper to make six dismissals in limited-overs internationals; his counterpart, Boucher, was one of 18 sharing the previous record of five. Kallis took three wickets in ten deliveries to give South Africa a flicker of hope, but aggressive batting by Martyn – who played some glorious strokes in a 32-ball half-century that included ten fours – and by Bevan carried Australia to within sight of victory.

Man of the Match: D. R. Martyn.   *Attendance:* 21,110.

South Africa

G. Kirsten c Warne b S. Lee	34	*S. M. Pollock c Gilchrist b McGrath	4
H. H. Gibbs c Gilchrist b McGrath	5	M. Hayward c Martyn b Symonds	4
N. D. McKenzie c Gilchrist b B. Lee	22	M. Ntini not out	3
J. H. Kallis c Warne b S. Lee	5	W 9, n-b 1	10
J. N. Rhodes c Gilchrist b B. Lee	8		
D. J. Callaghan c Gilchrist b Warne	15	1/15 2/54 3/65 (9 wkts, 50 overs)	144
†M. V. Boucher c Gilchrist b B. Lee	0	4/75 5/88 6/88	
L. Klusener not out	34	7/101 8/117 9/124	

Bowling: McGrath 10–1–13–2; B. Lee 10–2–32–3; S. Lee 7–1–19–2; Harvey 9–0–44–0; Warne 10–1–21–1; Symonds 4–0–15–1.

Australia

†A. C. Gilchrist b Kallis	8	I. J. Harvey not out	11
M. E. Waugh c Boucher b Kallis.	2		
S. Lee c Kirsten b Kallis	8	L-b 5, w 2, n-b 1	8
D. R. Martyn b Ntini	50		
M. G. Bevan c Boucher b Hayward	39	1/10 2/14 3/21 (5 wkts, 24.3 overs)	145
A. Symonds not out	19	4/104 5/116	

*S. R. Waugh, S. K. Warne, B. Lee and G. D. McGrath did not bat.

Bowling: Pollock 6–1–31–0; Kallis 6–1–40–3; Hayward 6.3–1–42–1; Ntini 6–0–27–1.

Umpires: R. E. Koertzen and D. L. Orchard.

SOUTH AFRICA v AUSTRALIA

Third One-Day International

At Johannesburg, April 16. South Africa won by four wickets. Toss: South Africa.

In front of an enthusiastic capacity crowd, South Africa gained an exciting win in a day game that had to be completed under floodlights. Pollock bowled another outstanding opening spell to seize the initiative, Bevan and Steve Waugh survived dropped catches to stage a recovery, and the fighting eighth-wicket partnership of 52 between Harvey and Warne guaranteed a competitive target. South Africa lost two batsmen to an onslaught from McGrath and Brett Lee. But Hall and Kallis seemed to swing the match South Africa's way when they took 37 off four overs from Shanes Warne and Lee – including 20 off Warne's first two overs. Then came a dramatic change of fortune. Hall drove Warne to cover, whereupon Waugh brought back Brett Lee, who dismissed Kallis and Boje without further addition. From his last eight overs, Warne took two for ten: his second wicket, Rhodes, made just four from 29 deliveries. Boucher took time to start, but Klusener was soon on song for the 50-ball 52 that dominated their match-winning stand of 87.

Man of the Match: L. Klusener.

Man of the Series: L. Klusener.   *Attendance:* 30,888.

Australia

M. E. Waugh c Boucher b Hayward	9	S. K. Warne c Boje b Pollock	32
†A. C. Gilchrist c Kirsten b Pollock	10	B. Lee b Pollock	1
D. R. Martyn c Boucher b Pollock	6	G. D. McGrath not out	0
M. G. Bevan b Klusener	33	L-b 6, w 8, n-b 3	17
*S. R. Waugh b Hayward.	51		
A. Symonds c Hall b Klusener	6	1/22 2/28 3/37 (49.5 overs)	205
S. Lee b Kallis	2	4/82 5/107 6/114	
I. J. Harvey b Kallis	38	7/149 8/201 9/205	

Bowling: Pollock 9.5–1–37–4; Hayward 10–0–37–2; Kallis 7–1–38–2; Ntini 10–2–30–0; Klusener 10–1–45–2; Hall 3–0–12–0.

South Africa

G. Kirsten b B. Lee	1	†M. V. Boucher not out	55
A. J. Hall c Symonds b Warne	46	L. Klusener not out	52
H. H. Gibbs lbw b McGrath.	4		
J. H. Kallis c M. E. Waugh b B. Lee	30	B 1, l-b 2, w 10, n-b 4	17
J. N. Rhodes c sub (M. L. Hayden) b Warne	4	1/9 2/19 3/91 (6 wkts, 47.5 overs)	209
N. Boje lbw b B. Lee	0	4/91 5/91 6/122	

*S. M. Pollock, M. Hayward and M. Ntini did not bat.

Bowling: McGrath 9–1–37–1; B. Lee 10–2–32–3; Harvey 5.5–1–32–0; S. Lee 7–0–47–0; Warne 10–2–30–2; M. E. Waugh 1–0–6–0; Bevan 3–0–11–0; Symonds 2–0–11–0.

Umpires: R. E. Koertzen and C. J. Mitchley.

Series referee: A. C. Smith (England).

PEPSI ASIA CUP, 1999-2000

Pakistan won the Asia Cup for the first time since the competition began in 1983-84. It was their third consecutive one-day triumph under Moin Khan's captaincy after successes in Sharjah and the Caribbean. They arrived in Bangladesh on June 1 – straight from a punishing tour of the West Indies, with the tournament already under way – and won four games in six days to become undisputed one-day champions of the subcontinent.

No side could contain Pakistan's wonderfully destructive batsmen, who scored 1,085 runs for the loss of 17 wickets in all, an average of 63.82 per wicket. In Yousuf Youhana, they possessed a batsman in blistering form – he hit 80, 100 not out, 90 not out and 25 to average 147.50 – while their 233-run win against Bangladesh was, until Sri Lanka beat India by 245 runs in October, the largest victory in limited-overs internationals.

Sri Lanka, the defending champions, lost twice to Pakistan but convincingly beat Bangladesh and India. Marvan Atapattu was their dominant batsman with an aggregate of 245 runs, including a brave 100 in the final. But Sri Lanka's lower order fell away in both matches against Pakistan: the last five wickets caved in for 25 runs in the group match and 42 in the final. India, who had won four of the six previous Asia Cups, found their bowling too inexperienced – they conceded 249 to Bangladesh – and they were well beaten by both Pakistan and Sri Lanka. Meanwhile, hosts Bangladesh, who were looking to advance their case for Test status, were comprehensively defeated in all three games.

The tournament, originally planned for early 1999, but deferred because the three Test countries were contesting the Pepsi Cup in India, came under threat from two different sources. Torrential rain in Dhaka leading up to the tournament ceased just in time, though the opening match had to be put back by 24 hours. Before that, Indian coach Kapil Dev, who in the aftermath of the Cronje affair had been accused of match-fixing, wanted his side to pull out. "It is my personal opinion not to play because of the prevalent atmosphere," he said. The Indian authorities refused to sanction their withdrawal. However, in the tense mood that pervaded international cricket, Saber Hussain Chowdhury, president of the Bangladesh Cricket Board, did ask the grounds committee not to divulge information about the weather or the pitch to anyone.

Note: Matches in this section were not first-class.

BANGLADESH v SRI LANKA

At Dhaka, May 28, 29 (day/night). Sri Lanka won by nine wickets. Toss: Sri Lanka. International debut: K. Weeraratne.

After heavy rain had delayed the match by 24 hours, Bangladesh struggled for runs in overcast conditions. Vaas's tight opening burst undermined them, and they were 27 for three in the 12th over when captain Aminul Islam was removed by medium-pacer Kaushalya Weeraratne's fifth ball in international cricket. Javed Omar and Akram Khan then added 75 for the fourth wicket. Javed, whose fighting 85 was his maiden international half-century, became the first Bangladesh batsman to bat through a completed innings. Needing just 176, Sri Lanka pushed de Silva to the top of the order, where he destroyed Bangladesh with a dazzling 96 in 93 balls, hitting three sixes and 13 fours.

Man of the Match: P. A. de Silva.

Bangladesh

Shahriar Hossain c de Silva b Vaas	....	2	†Khaled Masud c Jayawardene	
Javed Omar not out	....	85	b Muralitharan .	18
Habibul Bashar c Chandana b Vaas	....	1	Mohammad Rafiq not out	 11
*Aminul Islam c Chandana			B 2, l-b 4, w 3, n-b 3	 12
b Weeraratne .		5		
Akram Khan c Vaas b de Silva	....	41	1/6 2/11 3/27 (6 wkts, 50 overs)	175
Naimur Rahman run out	....	0	4/102 5/102 6/159	

Manjurul Islam, Hasibul Hussain and Khaled Mahmud did not bat.

Bowling: Vaas 10–0–28–2; Zoysa 7–0–30–0; Weeraratne 7–1–18–1; Muralitharan 10–0–35–1; Chandana 4–0–17–0; Jayasuriya 8–0–23–0; de Silva 4–1–18–1.

Sri Lanka

*S. T. Jayasuriya st Khaled Masud		
b Mohammad Rafiq .		28
P. A. de Silva not out	....	96
M. S. Atapattu not out	....	41
L-b 2, w 6, n-b 5	....	13
1/66	(1 wkt, 30.4 overs)	178

R. P. Arnold, D. P. M. D. Jayawardene, †R. S. Kaluwitharana, U. D. U. Chandana, W. P. U. J. C. Vaas, M. Muralitharan, D. N. T. Zoysa and K. Weeraratne did not bat.

Bowling: Hasibul Hussain 5–0–38–0; Manjurul Islam 7–0–33–0; Khaled Mahmud 4.4–0–40–0; Mohammad Rafiq 10–0–42–1; Naimur Rahman 4–0–23–0.

Umpires: Salim Badar and S. Venkataraghavan.

BANGLADESH v INDIA

At Dhaka, May 30, 31 (day/night). India won by eight wickets. Toss: Bangladesh. International debuts: Mushfiqur Rehman; H. K. Badani.

Despite a much-improved performance, Bangladesh were crushed again as India's batsmen replied in determined mood. When rain ended play on the first day, the hosts were handily placed at 98 for two. Next day, Habibul Bashar and Aminul Islam extended their partnership to 94 before both fell to Tendulkar, India's eighth bowler, and Akram Khan hit a whirlwind 64 as 97 came from the final ten overs. Ganguly, fearful of more rain, hit back with a breathtaking 135 from 124 balls, including seven sixes and six fours. He and Tendulkar, who took 22 off one over from Manjurul Islam, opened with 85 runs from 11 overs, and Hemang Badani scored a competent 35 on debut before Azharuddin and Ganguly saw India home, adding 100 in 15 overs. Earlier, Karim, India's wicket-keeper, was ruled out of the tournament after being hit near the eye by a rising delivery from Kumble; Dravid replaced him behind the stumps.

Man of the Match: S. C. Ganguly.

Close of play: Bangladesh 98-2 (25.2 overs) (Habibul Bashar 45*, Aminul Islam 32*).

Bangladesh

Shahriar Hossain c Joshi b Kumaran	...	11	Mohammad Rafiq b Kumaran	 8
Javed Omar b Kumaran	....	1	Enamul Haque not out	 5
Habibul Bashar c Azharuddin b Tendulkar		57	L-b 8, w 3, n-b 6	 17
*Aminul Islam c Kumble b Tendulkar	..	47		
Akram Khan c Badani b Agarkar	.....	64	1/2 2/30 3/124 (6 wkts, 50 overs)	249
Naimur Rahman not out	....	39	4/131 5/234 6/243	

†Khaled Masud, Mushfiqur Rehman and Manjurul Islam did not bat.

Bowling: Agarkar 10–2–37–1; Kumaran 9–0–54–3; Ganguly 4–0–35–0; Kumble 9–0–43–0; Joshi 7–0–31–0; Badani 1–0–6–0; Singh 4–0–11–0; Tendulkar 6–0–24–2.

India

*S. C. Ganguly not out	135	M. Azharuddin not out	35
S. R. Tendulkar c Habibul Bashar			
b Mushfiqur Rehman	36	L-b 4, w 5, n-b 2	11
H. K. Badani c Aminul Islam			
b Enamul Haque	35	1/85 2/152 (2 wkts, 40.1 overs)	252

R. Dravid, R. R. Singh, A. B. Agarkar, †S. S. Karim, A. Kumble, T. Kumaran and S. B. Joshi did not bat.

Bowling: Manjurul Islam 7–0–54–0; Mohammad Rafiq 7–0–48–0; Mushfiqur Rehman 9.1–0–59–1; Naimur Rahman 10–0–45–0; Enamul Haque 5–0–28–1; Habibul Bashar 2–0–14–0.

Umpires: B. C. Cooray and Mohammad Nazir.

INDIA v SRI LANKA

At Dhaka, June 1 (day/night). Sri Lanka won by 71 runs. Toss: Sri Lanka.

Jayasuriya's eighth century in one-day internationals was a commanding innings that contained 11 fours in 116 balls. With Atapattu, he put on a risk-free 104 for the second wicket. A mid-innings wobble saw Sri Lanka lose four batsmen – including Jayasuriya, run out after a mix-up with Kaluwitharana – for 26 in 36 balls. Kaluwitharana then made amends in a 55-run seventh-wicket stand with Vaas, who hit two sixes in one Agarkar over. A brisk 93 from Tendulkar made headway against a stiff target, but no one other than Dravid offered much support. The match effectively ended with Tendulkar's dismissal, caught on the boundary behind square leg, the first of three wickets which went down at 174 in eight balls.

Man of the Match: S. T. Jayasuriya.

Sri Lanka

*S. T. Jayasuriya run out	105	W. P. U. J. C. Vaas not out	34
P. A. de Silva c and b Kumaran	23	K. Weeraratne run out	2
M. S. Atapattu c Dravid b Tendulkar	42	M. Muralitharan not out	1
D. P. M. D. Jayawardene lbw b Agarkar	7	B 2, l-b 11, w 9, n-b 1	23
R. P. Arnold c Dravid b Tendulkar	5		
†R. S. Kaluwitharana c Ganguly		1/58 2/162 3/183 (8 wkts, 50 overs)	276
b Agarkar	33	4/191 5/202 6/209	
T. M. Dilshan c Ganguly b Chopra	1	7/264 8/273	

D. N. T. Zoysa did not bat.

Bowling: Agarkar 10–1–55–2; Kumaran 9–0–46–1; Chopra 10–0–49–1; Kumble 8–0–36–0; Singh 3–0–22–0; Joshi 2–0–11–0; Tendulkar 8–0–44–2.

India

*S. C. Ganguly c Kaluwitharana b Zoysa	13	A. B. Agarkar c de Silva b Zoysa	0
S. R. Tendulkar c Jayawardene		A. Kumble not out	18
b Weeraratne	93	N. Chopra run out	5
S. B. Joshi c Kaluwitharana b Vaas	11	T. Kumaran c Vaas b Jayasuriya	7
†R. Dravid c and b Muralitharan	24	L-b 3, w 11, n-b 3	17
M. Azharuddin run out	3		
A. Jadeja c Kaluwitharana b Weeraratne	8	1/38 2/56 3/123 (45 overs)	205
R. R. Singh c Kaluwitharana		4/139 5/156 6/174	
b Weeraratne	6	7/174 8/174 9/194	

Bowling: Vaas 6–1–24–1; Zoysa 10–0–47–2; Weeraratne 9–2–46–3; Muralitharan 9–1–38–1; Jayasuriya 9–0–39–1; de Silva 2–1–8–0.

Umpires: Mohammad Nazir and Salim Badar.

BANGLADESH v PAKISTAN

At Dhaka, June 2 (day/night). Pakistan won by 233 runs. Toss: Pakistan.

Pakistan entered the tournament in style by recording what was then the widest margin of victory in a limited-overs international, surpassing Australia's 232-run defeat of Sri Lanka at Adelaide in 1984-85. They also ran up the highest total in the Asia Cup, and dismissed their hosts for the lowest, which was also Bangladesh's lowest score in any one-day international. Saeed Anwar and Imran Nazir raced away at eight an over against indifferent bowling and the onslaught continued with Nazir and Yousuf Youhana both reaching 80. Inzamam-ul-Haq reinforced Pakistan's dominance with a dazzling 61-ball 75. In reply, only two Bangladeshis reached double figures. After Habibul Bashar steered them to 47 for one in the 14th over, they lost six wickets for nine runs in 30 balls. It was a third thrashing in three games for Bangladesh – and emphatic revenge for Pakistan after their embarrassing defeat in the 1999 World Cup.

Man of the Match: Imran Nazir.

Pakistan

Saeed Anwar b Naimur Rahman	31	Shahid Afridi not out 45
Imran Nazir run out	80	
Yousuf Youhana st Khaled Masud		
b Enamul Haque .	80	W 7, n-b 2 9
Inzamam-ul-Haq not out 75		1/83 2/158 3/236 (3 wkts, 50 overs) 320

Abdur Razzaq, *†Moin Khan, Wasim Akram, Azhar Mahmood, Mohammad Akram and Arshad Khan did not bat.

Bowling: Mushfiqur Rehman 8–0–61–0; Shafiuddin Ahmed 9–0–65–0; Khaled Mahmud 10–0–81–0; Naimur Rahman 10–0–41–1; Enamul Haque 10–0–50–1; Aminul Islam 3–0–22–0.

Bangladesh

Javed Omar c Azhar Mahmood		Mushfiqur Rehman lbw
b Wasim Akram .	7	b Mohammad Akram . 11
Habibul Bashar c Inzamam-ul-Haq		Enamul Haque c Shahid Afridi
b Abdur Razzaq .	23	b Arshad Khan . 7
Naimur Rahman lbw b Abdur Razzaq . .	7	Shafiuddin Ahmed not out 3
*Aminul Islam run out	0	Shahriar Hossain absent hurt
Akram Khan lbw b Abdur Razzaq	2	L-b 8, w 8, n-b 6 22
†Khaled Masud lbw b Azhar Mahmood .	1	
Khaled Mahmud c Saeed Anwar		1/25 2/47 3/48 4/50 5/51 (34.2 overs) 87
b Azhar Mahmood .	4	6/55 7/56 8/74 9/87

Bowling: Wasim Akram 5–0–13–1; Mohammad Akram 7.2–1–23–1; Azhar Mahmood 6–0–22–2; Abdur Razzaq 4–1–5–3; Arshad Khan 8–4–5–1; Shahid Afridi 4–2–11–0.

Umpires: E. A. R. de Silva and A. V. Jayaprakash.

INDIA v PAKISTAN

At Dhaka, June 3 (day/night). Pakistan won by 44 runs. Toss: Pakistan. International debut: A. Bhandari.

Pakistan made another flying start; Saeed Anwar and Imran Nazir hit 14 fours between them as they put on 74 in 12.2 overs. But both fell within four balls to Kumble's leg-spin and, when Agarkar bowled Inzamam-ul-Haq next over, Pakistan were on the back foot. Yousuf Youhana led the recovery with a canny 100, his first fifty occupying 90 balls, his second just 23, with the last ball of the innings, from Kumaran, despatched over long-on for six. India's batsmen were unable to settle: Abdur Razzaq again proved the pick of the bowlers, with four for 29, after Wasim Akram's dismissal of Ganguly set Pakistan on their way. Jadeja scored a brave 93 in what quickly became a lost cause – made all the more difficult because two overs were docked for a slow over-rate. Defeat eliminated India from the competition.

Man of the Match: Yousuf Youhana.

Pakistan

Saeed Anwar c Kumaran b Kumble	....	43	Wasim Akram c Dravid b Bhandari	 9
Imran Nazir c Agarkar b Kumble	.....	29	Azhar Mahmood not out	 9
Yousuf Youhana not out	....	100	L-b 3, w 8, n-b 5	 16
Inzamam-ul-Haq b Agarkar	....	1		
Shahid Afridi c Tendulkar b Kumble	...	21	1/74 2/74 3/75	(7 wkts, 50 overs) 295
*†Moin Khan c Mongia b Agarkar	....	46	4/103 5/195	
Abdur Razzaq c Agarkar b Bhandari	...	21	6/246 7/277	

Mohammad Akram and Arshad Khan did not bat.

Bowling: Agarkar 10–1–47–2; Kumaran 10–0–86–0; Bhandari 10–0–75–2; Kumble 10–1–43–3; Tendulkar 10–0–41–0.

India

*S. C. Ganguly c Mohammad Akram b Wasim Akram .	8	A. Kumble st Moin Khan b Arshad Khan	10
S. R. Tendulkar lbw b Abdur Razzaq ...	25	A. B. Agarkar b Abdur Razzaq	21
R. Dravid lbw b Abdur Razzaq	26	T. Kumaran run out	4
M. Azharuddin c Imran Nazir b Abdur Razzaq .	1	A. Bhandari not out	0
A. Jadeja st Moin Khan b Imran Nazir..	93	L-b 16, w 16, n-b 6........	38
R. R. Singh run out	21		
†N. R. Mongia c Shahid Afridi b Arshad Khan .	4	1/26 2/68 3/74	(47.4 overs) 251
		4/75 5/124 6/142	
		7/183 8/235 9/249	

Bowling: Wasim Akram 7–0–30–1; Mohammad Akram 7–0–39–0; Abdur Razzaq 8–0–29–4; Azhar Mahmood 6–0–20–0; Arshad Khan 10–0–59–2; Shahid Afridi 9–0–55–0; Imran Nazir 0.4–0–3–1.

Umpires: B. C. Cooray and E. A. R. de Silva.

PAKISTAN v SRI LANKA

At Dhaka, June 5 (day/night). Pakistan won by seven wickets. Toss: Sri Lanka.

Pakistan rested three key players for this meaningless match – both sides, hitherto unbeaten, had already qualified for the final – and still won convincingly. Jayasuriya chose to bat in humid conditions, but was one of just three Sri Lankan batsmen to pass 20 as they conceded five run-outs in a sloppy display. Azhar Mahmood, making his comeback in this tournament after being laid up since February, claimed three top-order wickets for 24, including the prize scalp of Atapattu, who fell to a stunning but controversial catch by Imran Nazir at point. The third umpire decided it had carried. Yousuf Youhana extended his good run, steering Pakistan to victory with an unbeaten 90.

Man of the Match: Yousuf Youhana.

Sri Lanka

*S. T. Jayasuriya c Arshad Khan b Azhar Mahmood .	28	W. P. U. J. C. Vaas c Shoaib Malik b Shahid Afridi .	7
P. A. de Silva run out	2	K. Weeraratne run out.............	11
M. S. Atapattu c Imran Nazir b Azhar Mahmood .	62	M. Muralitharan run out	0
D. P. M. D. Jayawardene c Moin Khan b Azhar Mahmood .	2	K. S. C. de Silva not out...........	1
R. P. Arnold run out	17	L-b 1, w 4, n-b 7	12
†R. S. Kaluwitharana run out	4	1/16 2/41 3/47	(49 overs) 192
U. D. U. Chandana c Shoaib Malik b Shabbir Ahmed .	46	4/97 5/105 6/167	
		7/178 8/181 9/182	

Bowling: Shabbir Ahmed 9–0–40–1; Mohammad Akram 10–1–41–0; Azhar Mahmood 8–2–24–3; Arshad Khan 10–1–34–0; Shoaib Malik 9–0–46–0; Shahid Afridi 3–0–6–1.

Pakistan

Imran Nazir lbw b K. S. C. de Silva	15	Shahid Afridi not out	2	
Mohammad Wasim c Chandana				
b Jayasuriya	44	B 5, l-b 1, w 5, n-b 4	15	
Yousuf Youhana not out	90			
Inzamam-ul-Haq c Arnold		1/24 2/131	(3 wkts, 48.2 overs) 193	
b K. S. C. de Silva	27	3/188		

Shoaib Malik, *†Moin Khan, Shabbir Ahmed, Azhar Mahmood, Mohammad Akram and Arshad Khan did not bat.

Bowling: Vaas 7.2–0–25–0; K. S. C. de Silva 6–0–34–2; Weeraratne 4–2–11–0; P. A. de Silva 7–0–35–0; Muralitharan 10–2–18–0; Chandana 7–0–30–0; Jayasuriya 7–0–34–1.

Umpires: A. V. Jayaprakash and S. Venkataraghavan.

QUALIFYING TABLE

	Played	Won	Lost	Points	Net run-rate
Pakistan	3	3	0	6	1.86
Sri Lanka	3	2	1	4	1.08
India	3	1	2	2	−0.34
Bangladesh	3	0	3	0	−2.80

Net run-rate is calculated by subtracting runs conceded per over from runs scored per over.

FINAL

PAKISTAN v SRI LANKA

At Dhaka, June 7 (day/night). Pakistan won by 39 runs. Toss: Pakistan.

Yet again Pakistan's batsmen revelled in the Bangabandhu pitch, producing three individual fifties. The last was the most devastating: captain Moin Khan came in at the end of the 40th over and destroyed Sri Lanka's bowling with an unbeaten 56 that included four sixes and took just 31 balls. Together with Inzamam-ul-Haq, he added 104 in the last ten overs. Inzamam, who hit 72 from 66 balls, batted in part with a runner, a request initially refused because he had begun the match with a leg injury. But Jayasuriya later relented: "He was really suffering, so we gave it to him." Saeed Anwar had earlier laid solid foundations with 82. The Sri Lankans were left to rue their shoddy fielding: they dropped seven catches in all, including Moin on 17. When they batted, Atapattu fought back with a round century from 124 balls but, after he and Arnold had put on 79, Sri Lanka lost their momentum. The last four wickets realised just 42 before the injured Weeraratne walked under – but it was just to congratulate Pakistan on their first Asia Cup.

Man of the Match: Moin Khan.   *Man of the Series:* Yousuf Youhana.

Pakistan

Saeed Anwar c Muralitharan b Jayasuriya	82	*†Moin Khan not out	56	
Imran Nazir c and b Zoysa	3	B 3, l-b 7, w 2, n-b 5	17	
Shahid Afridi c Arnold b Zoysa	22			
Yousuf Youhana c and b Chandana	25	1/17 2/56	(4 wkts, 50 overs) 277	
Inzamam-ul-Haq not out	72	3/124 4/173		

Abdur Razzaq, Wasim Akram, Azhar Mahmood, Arshad Khan and Mohammad Akram did not bat.

Bowling: Vaas 8–0–52–0; Zoysa 8–1–44–2; Weeraratne 6–0–23–0; Muralitharan 10–0–42–0; Chandana 10–0–43–1; Jayasuriya 8–0–63–1.

Sri Lanka

*S. T. Jayasuriya			
c and b Mohammad Akram .	22	U. D. U. Chandana b Wasim Akram....	24
†R. S. Kaluwitharana run out........	0	D. N. T. Zoysa not out	6
W. P. U. J. C. Vaas b Mohammad Akram.	10	M. Muralitharan c sub (Shoaib Malik)	
M. S. Atapattu c Moin Khan		b Abdur Razzaq .	0
b Wasim Akram .	100	K. Weeraratne absent hurt	
P. A. de Silva c Yousuf Youhana			
b Arshad Khan .	20	L-b 8, w 5, n-b 2	15
R. P. Arnold c Shahid Afridi			
b Arshad Khan .	41	1/6 2/21 3/46 (45.2 overs)	238
D. P. M. D. Jayawardene run out......	0	4/117 5/196 6/202	
		7/220 8/237 9/238	

Bowling: Wasim Akram 8–0–38–2; Mohammad Akram 8–0–50–2; Abdur Razzaq 7.2–0–40–1; Azhar Mahmood 10–0–40–0; Arshad Khan 10–0–42–2; Shahid Afridi 2–0–20–0.

Umpires: S. K. Bansal and A. V. Jayaprakash.
Series referee: J. R. Reid (New Zealand).

SINGER TRIANGULAR SERIES, 2000

By SA'ADI THAWFEEQ

Signs that Sri Lanka were coming out of a slump were evident in the final Test against Pakistan at Kandy, where they ran up an impressive 467 for five before the rain settled in with a vengeance. But there could be no escaping the hard truth that Sri Lanka had lost that series emphatically. When they bagged the Singer Triangular Series, therefore, with a hundred per cent record against two of the finest one-day sides, South Africa and Pakistan, it was truly a moment to savour.

Sri Lanka's bold policy of sticking to youngsters for their one-day games paid off handsomely. Avishka Gunawardene and Kumar Sangakkara, along with Mahela Jayawardene and Russel Arnold, not only gave the batting stability but also raised the standard of fielding to a plane similar to that when Sri Lanka won the World Cup in 1996. Newcomer Sangakkara, a 22-year-old left-handed wicket-keeper/batsman, emerged as the star of the tournament, scoring 199 runs at 66.33. Filling the batting spot vacated by another left-hander, Arjuna Ranatunga, he played some superlative innings, mostly under pressure, to justify his selection ahead of the experienced Romesh Kaluwitharana.

Opener Gunawardene, with 230 runs at 46, was the tournament's second-highest scorer after South African opener Gary Kirsten (236 at 47.20). Gunawardene's 87 against South Africa was the tournament's highest score. Muttiah Muralitharan returned the best bowling figures, five for 44 against South Africa in the final, to become the leading wicket-taker with nine at 19.11.

By virtue of beating Pakistan twice in the qualifying games, South Africa met Sri Lanka in the final. Jacques Kallis was their key player, hitting 211 runs at 52.75 including back-to-back innings of 83 against Pakistan and Sri Lanka. He went on to win the series award, which many thought should have gone to Sangakkara. Pakistan, at the end of a long and weary programme of international cricket, looked jaded. They were nowhere near the form that won them successive one-day tournaments in Sharjah, the West Indies and Bangladesh, followed by the recent Test victories over Sri Lanka, and failed to win a game. The absence of their influential all-rounder, Wasim Akram, who had returned home, was another factor weighing against them.

When Sanath Jayasuriya held the Singer Trophy aloft, Sri Lanka celebrated their second one-day tournament success under his leadership. The first was the Aiwa Cup the previous August, also at home.

Note: Matches in this section were not first-class.

SRI LANKA v PAKISTAN

At Galle, July 5. Sri Lanka won by five wickets. Toss: Sri Lanka. International debut: K. Sangakkara.

Pakistan, put in to bat after the match was reduced to 45 overs a side because of early rain, floundered to 53 for six. They recovered through a classy 83 off 118 balls from Inzamam-ul-Haq, who resumed after being hit in the groin and held the innings together. Zoysa, Sri Lanka's left-arm fast bowler, recorded career-best international figures. A target of 165 never troubled the Sri Lankans, even after losing two early wickets to Waqar Younis – who then succumbed to cramp. Atapattu adopted the anchor role, making 62 in 92 balls, and the match was won with seven overs in hand. Two left-armers, Vaas and Zoysa, opened the bowling for Sri Lanka and two left-handers, Jayasuriya and Gunawardene, opened the batting.

Man of the Match: D. N. T. Zoysa.

Pakistan

Saeed Anwar c and b Zoysa	20	Azhar Mahmood c Arnold b Muralitharan	14	
Imran Nazir run out	0	Waqar Younis b Zoysa	22	
Shahid Afridi c Dharmasena b Vaas	5	Mohammad Akram not out	1	
Yousuf Youhana c Sangakkara b Zoysa	0	L-b 5, w 5, n-b 3	13	
Inzamam-ul-Haq not out	83			
Abdur Razzaq lbw b Zoysa	0	1/0 2/20 3/22 (8 wkts, 45 overs)	164	
*†Moin Khan c Jayawardene		4/38 5/43 6/53		
b Upashantha	6	7/84 8/153		

Arshad Khan did not bat.

Inzamam-ul-Haq, when 13, retired hurt at 38-3 and resumed at 43.

Bowling: Vaas 9–0–38–1; Zoysa 9–2–34–4; Upashantha 9–0–29–1; Muralitharan 9–1–27–1; Dharmasena 4–0–12–0; Jayasuriya 5–1–19–0.

Sri Lanka

*S. T. Jayasuriya c Moin Khan		R. P. Arnold not out	22	
b Waqar Younis	11	H. D. P. K. Dharmasena not out	5	
D. A. Gunawardene lbw b Waqar Younis	0			
M. S. Atapattu lbw b Abdur Razzaq	62	L-b 4, w 12, n-b 1	17	
D. P. M. D. Jayawardene				
c Yousuf Youhana b Abdur Razzaq	14	1/1 2/19 3/65 (5 wkts, 37.3 overs)	166	
†K. Sangakkara run out	35	4/131 5/146		

W. P. U. J. C. Vaas, M. Muralitharan, D. N. T. Zoysa and K. E. A. Upashantha did not bat.

Bowling: Waqar Younis 5–2–11–2; Mohammad Akram 8–0–42–0; Abdur Razzaq 9–0–45–2; Azhar Mahmood 6.3–0–30–0; Arshad Khan 6–0–23–0; Shahid Afridi 3–0–11–0.

Umpires: P. T. Manuel and G. Silva.

SRI LANKA v SOUTH AFRICA

At Galle, July 6. Sri Lanka won by 37 runs. Toss: South Africa.

Sangakkara showed maturity beyond his years when he rescued his side from a shaky start with a stroke-filled 85 from 115 balls (11 fours). He and another left-hander, Arnold, with 59 off 70 balls, added 120 for the fifth wicket. Even so, a final total of 249 looked insufficient when South Africa's opening partnership of Kirsten and Hall put on 150. Then Muralitharan bowled Kirsten and, as magnificent Sri Lankan fielding helped put the brakes on the remaining batting, South Africa lost their next nine wickets for 62. Hall's fine 81 off 114 balls included three sixes and six fours.

Man of the Match: K. Sangakkara.

Sri Lanka

*S. T. Jayasuriya run out	0	H. D. P. K. Dharmasena c Pollock		
D. A. Gunawardene c Boucher b Ntini	47		b Kallis	4
M. S. Atapattu c Boucher b Hayward	3	W. P. U. J. C. Vaas not out		5
D. P. M. D. Jayawardene c Boucher			L-b 5, w 24, n-b 7	36
b Kallis	8			
†K. Sangakkara run out	85	1/0 2/14 3/35	(7 wkts, 50 overs)	249
R. P. Arnold not out	59	4/101 5/221		
U. D. U. Chandana b Kallis	2	6/226 7/242		

M. Muralitharan and D. N. T. Zoysa did not bat.

Bowling: Pollock 10−1−34−0; Hayward 5−0−47−1; Kallis 10−0−42−3; Klusener 10−0−45−0; Ntini 8−0−42−1; Boje 7−0−34−0.

South Africa

G. Kirsten b Muralitharan	59	N. Boje b Muralitharan		1
A. J. Hall c and b Chandana	81	M. Hayward not out		3
J. H. Kallis c Chandana b Dharmasena	11	M. Ntini run out		0
D. J. Cullinan c sub (T. M. Dilshan)				
b Chandana	14		B 4, l-b 4, w 8	16
J. N. Rhodes c Sangakkara b Chandana	0			
L. Klusener run out	20	1/150 2/157 3/176	(48.2 overs)	212
†M. V. Boucher run out	2	4/176 5/192		
*S. M. Pollock c Jayawardene		6/194 7/206		
b Chandana	5	8/208 9/211		

Bowling: Vaas 6−0−27−0; Zoysa 7−1−27−0; Dharmasena 10−0−41−1; Muralitharan 10−0−34−2; Chandana 10−0−44−4; Jayasuriya 2.2−0−15−0; Arnold 3−0−16−0.

Umpires: L. V. Jayasundera and G. Silva.

PAKISTAN v SOUTH AFRICA

At R. Premadasa Stadium, Colombo, July 8 (day/night). South Africa won by 18 runs. Toss: South Africa.

Choosing to bat first, South Africa rode on Kallis's splendid 83 off 111 balls to total 241 for six. Pakistan began their reply boldly, with an opening stand of 101 in 20 overs between Saeed Anwar and Imran Nazir, whose 80 off 86 balls contained ten fours. But Klusener's first spell, which brought him three wickets in consecutive overs, put paid to Pakistan's hopes, and helped Boucher to 100 dismissals in only 65 internationals. Left-arm spinner Boje then destroyed their later batting with career-best one-day international figures of four for 25. Waqar Younis received a one-match suspension and a 50 per cent match-fee fine, and Azhar Mahmood a 30 per cent fine, from referee John Reid for tampering with the ball; their captain, Moin Khan, was reprimanded.

Man of the Match: J. H. Kallis.

South Africa

G. Kirsten c Abdur Razzaq		L. Klusener c Imran Nazir		
b Mushtaq Ahmed	52		b Azhar Mahmood	14
A. J. Hall lbw b Abdur Razzaq	27	†M. V. Boucher not out		2
J. H. Kallis c sub (Shoaib Malik)			B 2, l-b 2, w 6, n-b 2	12
b Abdur Razzaq	83			
D. J. Cullinan run out	38	1/64 2/114 3/175	(6 wkts, 50 overs)	241
J. N. Rhodes b Abdur Razzaq	13	4/220 5/232 6/241		

*S. M. Pollock, N. Boje, M. Hayward and M. Ntini did not bat.

Bowling: Waqar Younis 10−0−51−0; Azhar Mahmood 10−0−47−1; Abdur Razzaq 10−2−36−3; Arshad Khan 10−0−44−0; Mushtaq Ahmed 10−0−59−1.

Pakistan

Saeed Anwar lbw b Ntini	39	Waqar Younis c Klusener b Boje	3	
Imran Nazir b Klusener	80	Mushtaq Ahmed c Rhodes b Boje	2	
Azhar Mahmood c Boucher b Klusener	19	Arshad Khan not out	11	
Inzamam-ul-Haq c Boucher b Klusener	6	L-b 4, w 5, n-b 3	12	
Yousuf Youhana b Boje	2			
Younis Khan not out	38	1/101 2/144 3/149 (9 wkts, 50 overs)	223	
*†Moin Khan lbw b Pollock	7	4/154 5/154 6/170		
Abdur Razzaq lbw b Boje	4	7/179 8/183 9/192		

Bowling: Pollock 9–1–35–1; Kallis 8–0–47–0; Hayward 7–0–45–0; Ntini 6–0–30–1; Klusener 10–0–37–3; Boje 10–1–25–4.

Umpires: E. A. R. de Silva and P. T. Manuel.

SRI LANKA v PAKISTAN

At R. Premadasa Stadium, Colombo, July 9 (day/night). Sri Lanka won by six wickets. Toss: Pakistan.

Pakistan made their highest total of the tournament, but it was not enough. For long periods, their innings had not promised as many runs, but Azhar Mahmood slammed an unbeaten 43 off 25 balls at the end, hitting a six and four fours while adding 58 off 39 balls with Abdur Razzaq. Sri Lanka launched their reply with an opening stand of 96 in 17 overs between Jayasuriya and Gunawardene, and were able to measure the run-chase comfortably after that. They won with four balls to spare.

Man of the Match: S. T. Jayasuriya.

Pakistan

Saeed Anwar b Vaas	13	Abdur Razzaq not out	17	
Imran Nazir run out	2	Azhar Mahmood not out	43	
Younis Khan b Jayasuriya	59			
Inzamam-ul-Haq c Atapattu b Jayasuriya	47	L-b 2, w 4, n-b 4	10	
Yousuf Youhana c Jayawardene b Dharmasena	39	1/16 2/19 3/101 (6 wkts, 50 overs)	240	
*†Moin Khan c Atapattu b Muralitharan	10	4/146 5/175 6/182		

Shoaib Malik, Shabbir Ahmed and Arshad Khan did not bat.

Bowling: Vaas 8–0–44–1; Zoysa 9–1–47–0; Dharmasena 7–0–38–1; Muralitharan 10–0–35–1; Chandana 10–0–41–0; Jayasuriya 6–0–33–2.

Sri Lanka

*S. T. Jayasuriya c Moin Khan b Shoaib Malik	54	†K. Sangakkara not out	36	
D. A. Gunawardene b Abdur Razzaq	47	R. P. Arnold not out	13	
M. S. Atapattu c Moin Khan b Shabbir Ahmed	25	B 1, l-b 10, w 5, n-b 4	20	
D. P. M. D. Jayawardene b Abdur Razzaq	49	1/96 2/126 (4 wkts, 49.2 overs)	244	
		3/167 4/219		

H. D. P. K. Dharmasena, U. D. U. Chandana, W. P. U. J. C. Vaas, M. Muralitharan and D. N. T. Zoysa did not bat.

Bowling: Shabbir Ahmed 10–0–52–1; Azhar Mahmood 9.2–0–48–0; Abdur Razzaq 10–0–50–2; Arshad Khan 10–0–43–0; Shoaib Malik 10–0–40–1.

Umpires: B. C. Cooray and T. H. Wijewardene.

SRI LANKA v SOUTH AFRICA

At Sinhalese Sports Club, Colombo, July 11. Sri Lanka won by eight wickets. Toss: Sri Lanka.

South Africa, again on the receiving end of brilliant Sri Lankan fielding in support of penetrative bowling, were totally outplayed. Kallis's unbeaten 83 off 148 balls, with three sixes and four fours, stood out like a beacon in their disappointing 167. After the early loss of Jayasuriya, Sri Lanka were powered to victory by fellow-opener Gunawardene, whose 87 off 77 balls sparkled with 14 fours. He and Atapattu added 129 in 19 overs for the second wicket, and Sri Lanka romped home with 22 overs unused.

Man of the Match: D. A. Gunawardene.

South Africa

G. Kirsten b Zoysa	3	N. Boje st Sangakkara b Dharmasena	19
L. Klusener c Atapattu b Wickremasinghe	0	M. Hayward run out	0
A. J. Hall c Jayawardene b Dharmasena	32	M. Ntini b Jayasuriya	1
J. H. Kallis not out	83		
D. J. Cullinan run out	8	L-b 1, w 3, n-b 4	8
J. N. Rhodes run out	5		
†M. V. Boucher c Jayawardene b Chandana	8	(49.2 overs)	167
*S. M. Pollock lbw b Chandana	0		

1/0 2/4 3/64
4/84 5/94 6/110
7/110 8/148 9/158

Bowling: Zoysa 7–2–23–1; Wickremasinghe 6–0–41–1; Dharmasena 10–0–37–2; Muralitharan 10–0–32–0; Chandana 10–1–20–2; Jayasuriya 6.2–2–13–1.

Sri Lanka

*S. T. Jayasuriya c Ntini b Pollock	1
D. A. Gunawardene lbw b Boje	87
M. S. Atapattu not out	44
D. P. M. D. Jayawardene not out	14
B 4, l-b 9, w 8, n-b 1	22

1/11 2/140   (2 wkts, 27.3 overs) 168

†K. Sangakkara, R. P. Arnold, U. D. U. Chandana, H. D. P. K. Dharmasena, G. P. Wickremasinghe, M. Muralitharan and D. N. T. Zoysa did not bat.

Bowling: Pollock 6–0–22–1; Hayward 2–0–26–0; Ntini 5–0–35–0; Hall 3–0–11–0; Boje 6.3–0–39–1; Klusener 4–0–18–0; Cullinan 1–0–4–0.

Umpires: B. C. Cooray and E. A. R. de Silva.

PAKISTAN v SOUTH AFRICA

At Sinhalese Sports Club, Colombo, July 12. South Africa won by seven wickets. Toss: Pakistan.

Pakistan still had a chance of reaching the final, but crashed in ignominy. Terbrugge, in only his second international, after a six-month gap, bowled impressively to claim four for 20 as he and his captain, Pollock, ran through Pakistan's top order with the new ball. They were 19 for six before Azhar Mahmood organised some resistance. Shoaib Malik and Mushtaq Ahmed added 55 at the end to lift the total to 153, but South Africa cruised past that in the 38th over and left Pakistan without a win.

Man of the Match: D. J. Terbrugge.

Pakistan

Saeed Anwar b Pollock	6	Shoaib Malik c Cullinan b Adams	28
Imran Nazir c Boucher b Pollock	0	Arshad Khan c and b Adams	1
Younis Khan c Boucher b Terbrugge	3	Mushtaq Ahmed not out	34
Inzamam-ul-Haq c Boucher b Terbrugge	0	L-b 6, w 11, n-b 6	23
Yousuf Youhana c Boucher b Terbrugge	2		
Azhar Mahmood run out	36	1/2 2/5 3/6	(44.1 overs) 153
Abdur Razzaq lbw b Terbrugge	1	4/13 5/18 6/19	
*†Moin Khan c Boucher b Kallis	19	7/49 8/90 9/98	

Bowling: Pollock 8–0–23–2; Terbrugge 8–1–20–4; Kallis 7–2–18–1; Klusener 5–1–26–0; Boje 7–1–24–0; Hall 2–0–12–0; Adams 7.1–2–24–2.

South Africa

G. Kirsten c Azhar Mahmood		D. J. Cullinan not out	35
b Mushtaq Ahmed	46	J. N. Rhodes not out	12
A. J. Hall c Inzamam-ul-Haq			
b Azhar Mahmood	15	L-b 4, w 14, n-b 3	21
J. H. Kallis c Azhar Mahmood			
b Shoaib Malik	27	1/26 2/82 3/122	(3 wkts, 37.3 overs) 156

L. Klusener, †M. V. Boucher, *S. M. Pollock, N. Boje, P. R. Adams and D. J. Terbrugge did not bat.

Bowling: Azhar Mahmood 5–1–26–1; Abdur Razzaq 3–1–15–0; Mushtaq Ahmed 10–2–31–1; Arshad Khan 7–2–24–0; Shoaib Malik 8–0–30–1; Younis Khan 2–0–12–0; Imran Nazir 2.3–0–14–0.

Umpires: E. A. R. de Silva and G. Silva.

QUALIFYING TABLE

	Played	Won	Lost	Points	Net run-rate
Sri Lanka	4	4	0	8	1.01
South Africa	4	2	2	4	−0.32
Pakistan	4	0	4	0	−0.62

Net run-rate is calculated by subtracting runs conceded per over from runs scored per over.

FINAL

SRI LANKA v SOUTH AFRICA

At R. Premadasa Stadium, Colombo, July 14 (day/night). Sri Lanka won by 30 runs. Toss: Sri Lanka.

Sri Lanka set South Africa an imposing 295 runs to chase after Jayasuriya and Gunawardene had provided a blazing start with 84 off 12 overs. The tempo was maintained by Sangakkara and Arnold, and only spinner Adams escaped punishment. Jayasuriya made 68 off 86 balls, Gunawardene 49 off 47, Sangakkara 43 off 49, and Arnold 51 off 53. South Africa began promisingly as Kirsten and Hall put on 91 in 18 overs, but Muralitharan dismissed them both. From 175 for six in the 36th over, South Africa were put on track again by Rhodes and Klusener, who added 54. Pollock also threatened, until Muralitharan was brought back to end their challenge and collect his third five-wicket haul in one-day internationals.

Man of the Match: M. Muralitharan.   *Man of the Series:* J. H. Kallis.

Sri Lanka

*S. T. Jayasuriya run out	68	W. P. U. J. C. Vaas not out	17
D. A. Gunawardene b Adams	49	U. D. U. Chandana c Boucher b Pollock	1
M. S. Atapattu c Kirsten b Kallis	11	L-b 10, w 10, n-b 7	27
D. P. M. D. Jayawardene c McKenzie			
b Boje	27	1/84 2/110 3/167 (7 wkts, 50 overs) 294	
†K. Sangakkara c Rhodes b Klusener	43	4/174 5/254	
R. P. Arnold c Klusener b Pollock	51	6/291 7/294	

H. D. P. K. Dharmasena, M. Muralitharan and D. N. T. Zoysa did not bat.

Bowling: Pollock 9–0–54–2; Terbrugge 4–0–38–0; Adams 10–1–29–1; Kallis 10–1–64–1; Boje 10–0–56–1; Klusener 7–0–43–1.

South Africa

G. Kirsten st Sangakkara b Muralitharan.	76	*S. M. Pollock c Sangakkara	
A. J. Hall b Muralitharan	35	b Muralitharan	22
J. H. Kallis run out.	7	P. R. Adams not out	2
N. D. McKenzie lbw b Chandana	10	D. J. Terbrugge not out	0
N. Boje st Sangakkara b Muralitharan	11	B 4, l-b 8, w 3, n-b 3	18
J. N. Rhodes lbw b Dharmasena	43		
†M. V. Boucher lbw b Chandana	1	1/91 2/102 3/127 (9 wkts, 50 overs) 264	
L. Klusener st Sangakkara		4/142 5/170 6/175	
b Muralitharan .	39	7/229 8/251 9/264	

Bowling: Vaas 7–0–29–0; Zoysa 6–0–40–0; Arnold 2–0–11–0; Dharmasena 10–1–39–1; Muralitharan 10–0–44–5; Jayasuriya 6–0–35–0; Chandana 9–0–54–2.

Umpires: B. C. Cooray and P. T. Manuel.
Series referee: J. R. Reid (New Zealand).

SUPER CHALLENGE, 2000

By NEIL MANTHORP

Steve Waugh wondered if August 16, 2000 might be remembered as the day when cricket changed for ever – and just in case it was, he hit a hundred to be remembered by. Four days later, when South Africa squared the first official one-day international series played indoors, Australia's captain might have been quite content for cricket's latest innovation to be little more than a footnote in the game's history.

Played beneath the roof of Melbourne's Colonial Stadium, and accompanied by the kind of razzamatazz that appears compulsory on such occasions, the Super Challenge formed the second leg of a six-match home-and-away programme. Each series, however, had its own sponsor and trophy. In April, the South Africans had won 2–1. In Melbourne, after losing the first game, they fought back characteristically to tie the second and win the third. It was their usual team effort: whereas Steve Waugh and Michael Bevan hit hundreds for the Australians, only two South Africans reached 50 throughout. What kept them in the series was the way they put the Australian batting under pressure, and the home side's failure to meet the challenge.

The Australians saw the indoor experiment as a novel way of bringing cricket to the people in winter – and people to cricket. The overall attendance was 94,278, which was in line with expectations if some way short of the stadium's potential: the capacity for a cricket game was 48,000. The South Africans looked to the series to serve a higher purpose than mere revenue generation. Interest in cricket was at an all-time low in the Republic in the wake of Hansie Cronje's disgrace. It was hoped that success in Melbourne, following on from the Test team's dramatic comeback in Sri Lanka, would give the game's image a much-needed boost.

[Hamish Blair, Allsport

A sign of things to come: the pitch arrives at the Colonial Stadium.

That batsmen did not ultimately dominate the series was no reflection on the high-quality drop-in pitches prepared by Les Burdett. The outfield, having hosted Australian Football League and rugby union games, was a little damp and soft, but the short square boundaries swung the balance back towards the batsmen – as well as bringing out the best in two athletic fielding sides. The umpires had been told to declare the ball "dead" if it hit the roof, but there was never a likelihood of that.

Note: Matches in this section were not first-class.

AUSTRALIA v SOUTH AFRICA

First One-Day International

At Colonial Stadium, Melbourne, August 16 (day/night). Australia won by 94 runs. Toss: South Africa.

Put in, Australia were at a crossroads when 37 for three in the 12th over. Bevan (106 balls) and Steve Waugh (103 balls) steered them on the road to victory with centuries and a stand worth 222 in 212 balls, an Australian fourth-wicket record in one-day internationals. When Shane Lee took 17 off Pollock, including two successive sixes over cover, South Africa needed something special. Instead, they batted as tepidly as they had bowled: wickets fell regularly and the asking-rate stretched beyond their reach. Fiercely determined to live up to the occasion, they had played with uncharacteristic inertia.

Man of the Match: S. R. Waugh.　　　*Attendance:* 25,785.

Australia

†A. C. Gilchrist run out	1		I. J. Harvey not out	1
M. E. Waugh c Hayward b Telemachus	17			
R. T. Ponting c Rhodes b Telemachus	16		B 2, l-b 2, w 3, n-b 5	12
M. G. Bevan c Kallis b Pollock	106			
*S. R. Waugh not out	114		1/1 2/32 3/37	(5 wkts, 50 overs) 295
S. Lee c Cullinan b Kallis	28		4/259 5/289	

D. R. Martyn, S. K. Warne, B. Lee and G. D. McGrath did not bat.

Bowling: Pollock 10–0–46–1; Telemachus 10–1–54–2; Kallis 10–0–74–1; Hayward 6–0–45–0; Klusener 8–0–43–0; Hall 6–0–29–0.

South Africa

G. Kirsten st Gilchrist b Warne	43		†M. V. Boucher c Bevan b S. Lee	6
A. J. Hall c Gilchrist b Harvey	11		*S. M. Pollock not out	4
J. H. Kallis lbw b Harvey	42		L-b 2, w 1	3
D. J. Cullinan b Harvey	29			
J. N. Rhodes c Martyn b Warne	16		1/37 2/70 3/124	(7 wkts, 50 overs) 201
L. Klusener not out	25		4/137 5/148	
N. D. McKenzie b S. Lee	22		6/179 7/189	

M. Hayward and R. Telemachus did not bat.

Bowling: McGrath 10–2–28–0; B. Lee 10–0–51–0; Harvey 10–0–41–3; S. Lee 10–0–41–2; Warne 10–0–38–2.

Umpires: D. B. Hair and S. J. A. Taufel.

AUSTRALIA v SOUTH AFRICA

Second One-Day International

At Colonial Stadium, Melbourne, August 18 (day/night). Tied. Toss: South Africa.

The tie emulated the famous 1999 World Cup semi-final result that inspired this home-and-away series. Yet South Africa were not in contention until the final three overs. Batting first this time, they limped to 95 for four before half-centuries from Rhodes and Boucher allowed them to reach a sub-par 226. Australia set off at a sparkling rate but Boje, who missed the first game with a hand injury, put a brake on the runs. As South Africa found a way into the game, the Australians missed Bevan's limited-overs nous in the middle order: he had broken a knuckle on his right hand, trying to catch Boucher, and came in at No. 8. When Hall, an unexpected hero, bowled the 47th and 49th overs for three runs and two wickets, Australia required 13 from the last over. Pollock's first three balls conceded nine, but then he ran out Gillespie, playing his first game for Australia since breaking his leg in Sri Lanka. Warne needed two off the last ball but could only cannon a yorker to mid-on via the non-striker's stumps for a single.

Man of the Match: A. J. Hall.   *Attendance:* 35,724.

South Africa

A. J. Hall c M. E. Waugh b Symonds	37		N. Boje not out	8
G. Kirsten lbw b Harvey	22		R. Telemachus not out	6
J. H. Kallis b Gillespie	22			
D. J. Cullinan c Warne b Symonds	0		B 4, l-b 3, w 1, n-b 2	10
J. N. Rhodes c sub (S. Lee) b McGrath	54			
†M. V. Boucher c Warne b Harvey	51		1/43 2/70 3/78	(8 wkts, 50 overs) 226
L. Klusener c M. E. Waugh b Gillespie	12		4/95 5/182 6/201	
*S. M. Pollock c sub (S. Lee) b Gillespie	4		7/210 8/210	

D. J. Terbrugge did not bat.

Bowling: McGrath 10–0–47–1; Gillespie 10–0–40–3; Harvey 10–1–43–2; Warne 10–0–33–0; Symonds 10–0–56–2.

Australia

M. E. Waugh c Hall b Boje	48		S. K. Warne not out		9
†A. C. Gilchrist c Pollock b Kallis	37		J. N. Gillespie run out		0
R. T. Ponting b Telemachus	39		G. D. McGrath not out		0
D. R. Martyn b Boje	18		L-b 11, w 4, n-b 3		18
A. Symonds b Klusener	17				
*S. R. Waugh b Hall	30		1/78 2/105 3/146	(9 wkts, 50 overs)	226
I. J. Harvey c Hall b Klusener	7		4/164 5/177 6/193		
M. G. Bevan c Boucher b Hall	3		7/213 8/214 9/223		

Bowling: Pollock 10–0–51–0; Telemachus 10–1–37–1; Terbrugge 3–0–24–0; Kallis 4–1–21–1; Klusener 10–0–41–2; Boje 10–1–33–2; Hall 3–0–8–2.

Umpires: D. J. Harper and P. D. Parker.

AUSTRALIA v SOUTH AFRICA

Third One-Day International

At Colonial Stadium, Melbourne, August 20. South Africa won by eight runs. Toss: South Africa.
Dismal batting under pressure again cost Australia a match they should have won, even allowing for the two-over deduction for their slow over-rate. Gilchrist hit 63 of their first 75, but the middle order choked in the face of fine bowling from Boje, Telemachus and Pollock, backed by customary brilliance in the field. Pollock and Boje had earlier saved their side with the bat, adding 56 in 45 balls at the end after McGrath and Brett Lee had South Africa 19 for four, then 119 for six. McKenzie and Klusener effected the first recovery with 98 in 156 balls. Without time to fly in a replacement for Boucher, who had sliced his fingers cutting dried meat, Hall took the gloves for South Africa. Kirsten kept in the 47th over when Hall came on to bowl; he was at long-on next over when he caught Gillespie.

Man of the Match: N. Boje.   *Attendance:* 32,769.
Man of the Series: N. Boje.

South Africa

†A. J. Hall c M. E. Waugh b McGrath	1		*S. M. Pollock not out		34
G. Kirsten c M. E. Waugh b McGrath	9		N. Boje not out		28
J. H. Kallis c Gilchrist b B. Lee	3		B 4, l-b 6, w 1, n-b 5		16
D. J. Cullinan b B. Lee	0				
N. D. McKenzie b McGrath	45		1/16 2/19 3/19	(7 wkts, 50 overs)	206
L. Klusener c Gilchrist b B. Lee	49		4/19 5/117		
H. H. Dippenaar run out	21		6/119 7/150		

R. Telemachus and M. Ntini did not bat.

Bowling: McGrath 10–4–26–3; B. Lee 10–1–56–3; Warne 10–2–30–0; Gillespie 10–1–39–0; S. Lee 5–0–23–0; Bevan 5–0–22–0.

Australia

†A. C. Gilchrist c McKenzie b Ntini	63		J. N. Gillespie c Kirsten b Kallis		10
M. E. Waugh b Pollock	1		B. Lee not out		6
R. T. Ponting c Ntini b Pollock	5		G. D. McGrath not out		0
M. G. Bevan run out	33		L-b 9, w 1, n-b 3		13
*S. R. Waugh c Pollock b Klusener	17				
D. R. Martyn b Telemachus	31		1/21 2/31 3/75	(9 wkts, 48 overs)	198
S. K. Warne c Kirsten b Boje	7		4/114 5/130 6/143		
S. Lee c McKenzie b Boje	12		7/171 8/176 9/195		

Bowling: Pollock 8–0–36–2; Telemachus 10–2–36–1; Kallis 8–0–37–1; Ntini 6–0–19–1; Klusener 5–0–27–1; Boje 10–0–29–2; Hall 1–0–5–0.

Umpires: D. B. Hair and D. J. Harper.
Series referee: B. F. Hastings (New Zealand).

OTHER A-TEAM TOURS

SRI LANKA A IN SOUTH AFRICA, 1999-2000

Sri Lanka A toured South Africa in October and November 1999, playing five first-class matches and three one-day games. They won two and lost two of their first-class matches, with one draw, losing the two-match series against South Africa A 1–0, and lost their one-day international series 2–1.

The squad of 16 named for the tour was: M. N. Nawaz (Nondescripts) (*captain*), D. A. Gunawardene (Sinhalese) (*vice-captain*), M. K. D. I. Amerasinghe (Colts), M. R. C. N. Bandaratilleke (Tamil Union), S. I. de Saram (Tamil Union), K. S. C. de Silva (Burgher), T. M. Dilshan (Sebastianites), S. I. Fernando (Colts), R. P. Hewage (Nondescripts), S. Kalawithigoda (Sinhalese), R. A. P. Nissanka (Matara), W. M. B. Perera (Colombo), M. M. D. N. R. G. Perera (Sebastianites), K. R. Pushpakumara (Nondescripts), T. T. Samaraweera (Sinhalese), K. Sangakkara (Nondescripts). *Manager:* S. Jayasinghe. *Coach:* H. H. Devapriya. S. Jayasinghe subsequently took over the management of the Test side's tour of Zimbabwe, and was replaced on the A-team tour by D. S. B. P. Kuruppu. S. K. L. de Silva (Colombo), U. A. Fernando (Sinhalese) and D. P. Samaraweera (Colts) replaced de Saram and Dilshan, who also joined the Zimbabwean tour; later, Pushpakumara and de Silva were also promoted.

At Potchefstroom, October 24, 25, 26. North West/Free State/Griqualand West XI won by six wickets. Toss: North West/Free State/Griqualand West XI. Sri Lanka A 99 (T. M. Dilshan 37; J. N. Dreyer three for 32, H. C. Bakkes six for 33) and 264 (T. M. Dilshan 96, S. I. Fernando 55, M. M. D. N. R. G. Perera 44; J. N. Dreyer five for 81); North West/Free State/Griqualand West XI 270 for eight dec. (G. F. J. Liebenberg 126, F. C. Brooker 39) and 97 for four (N. Boje 39 not out).

At Johannesburg, October 29, 30, 31. Sri Lanka A won by five wickets. Toss: Gauteng/Northerns XI. Gauteng/Northerns XI 255 (Q. R. Still 84, N. Pothas 32; K. S. C. de Silva three for 51, W. M. B. Perera three for 43) and 134 (M. van Jaarsveld 45; K. R. Pushpakumara five for 51); Sri Lanka A 207 (D. A. Gunawardene 41, S. I. Fernando 30, W. M. B. Perera 51 not out, K. R. Pushpakumara 31; S. Jacobs four for 37, I. R. Kuiler three for 33) and 186 for five (R. P. Hewage 71, K. Sangakkara 35, S. I. Fernando 50).

At Port Elizabeth, November 5, 6, 7. Sri Lanka A won by two wickets. Toss: Sri Lanka A. Eastern Province/Border XI 330 for six dec. (D. Makalima 78, J. M. Kemp 166, L. L. Gamiet 35; S. I. Fernando four for 30) and 159 for five dec. (D. Makalima 42; S. I. Fernando three for 33); Sri Lanka A 277 for nine dec. (R. P. Hewage 45, K. Sangakkara 55, T. T. Samaraweera 69, M. M. D. N. R. G. Perera 48; J. M. Kemp four for 38) and 214 for eight (R. P. Hewage 35, S. Kalawithigoda 45, K. Sangakkara 36).

In Eastern Province/Border's first innings, Makalima and Kemp added 253 for the third wicket.

At Centurion, November 11, 12, 13. First A-team Test: South Africa A won by an innings and 116 runs. Toss: Sri Lanka A. South Africa A 460 for five dec. (M. L. Bruyns 144, D. J. Watson 31, N. D. McKenzie 102, A. G. Prince 68, P. C. Strydom 61 not out, Extras 39); Sri Lanka A 161 (S. I. Fernando 38; M. Hayward five for 40) and 183 (S. I. Fernando 36, T. T. Samaraweera 59; D. J. Terbrugge four for 69, P. V. Mpitsang three for 42).

Wicket-keeper Nic Pothas took eight catches for South Africa A in the match.

At Pietermaritzburg, November 18, 19, 20, 21. Second A-team Test: Drawn. Toss: South Africa A. South Africa A 296 (D. M. Benkenstein 84, A. G. Prince 45, J. M. Kemp 39; R. A. P. Nissanka five for 59) and 91 for one (M. L. Bruyns 58 not out); Sri Lanka A 242 (U. A. Fernando 65, S. K. L. de Silva 44, M. R. C. N. Bandaratilleke 44; M. Hayward three for 78, S. Abrahams three for 63).

INDIA A IN THE WEST INDIES, 1999-2000

India A toured the West Indies in November and December 1999, playing four first-class matches and four one-day games. They drew the whole of their first-class programme, including the two-match series against West Indies A, and lost their one-day international series 1–0, with the second match abandoned and the third ending in no result because of rain. They also lost another one-day game against Guyana.

The squad of 15 originally named for the tour was: H. H. Kanitkar (Maharashtra) (*captain*), G. K. Khoda (Rajasthan) (*vice-captain*), J. Arun Kumar (Karnataka), A. Bhandari (Delhi), D. S. Bundela (Madhya Pradesh), S. S. Dighe (Mumbai), D. Ganesh (Karnataka), M. Kaif (Uttar Pradesh), M. Kartik (Railways), J. J. Martin (Baroda), P. Mullick (Orissa), R. L. Sanghvi (Delhi), L. R. Shukla (Bengal), H. S. Sodhi (Madhya Pradesh), S. Sriram (Tamil Nadu). *Manager:* S. C. Khanna. *Coach:* R. M. H. Binny. S. H. Kotak (Saurashtra) replaced Kanitkar, who was called up to reinforce the Test side in Australia after the First A-team Test.

At Peñal (Trinidad), November 12, 13, 14, 15. Drawn. Toss: India A. India A 227 (J. Arun Kumar 37, J. J. Martin 82, H. H. Kanitkar 57; M. Persad three for 63, D. Ramnarine five for 66) and 163 (S. S. Dighe 49, H. S. Sodhi 31; M. Persad five for 46, D. Ramnarine three for 53); Trinidad & Tobago 124 (L. A. Roberts 30, R. A. M. Smith 35; R. L. Sanghvi four for 23) and 14 for no wkt.

At Port-of-Spain, November 19, 20, 21, 22. First A-team Test: Drawn. Toss: India A. India A 226 (G. K. Khoda 50, M. Kaif 40, S. S. Dighe 32; D. H. Mais three for 40) and 283 for six (J. J. Martin 75, J. Arun Kumar 48, H. H. Kanitkar 30, M. Kaif 54 not out); West Indies A 289 (S. C. Joseph 58, J. C. Adams 35, R. O. Hinds 62, R. N. Lewis 64; D. Ganesh three for 41, M. Kartik six for 75).

At Uitvlugt, Guyana, November 25, 26, 27. Drawn. Toss: Guyana. Guyana 222 (A. Haniff 60, N. Deonarine 52 not out; R. L. Sanghvi three for 65, S. Sriram four for 26) and 193 for one (A. Haniff 102 not out, R. R. Sarwan 56 not out); India A 324 for nine dec. (J. Arun Kumar 110, P. Mullick 62, D. S. Bundela 42, S. S. Dighe 48 not out; C. E. L. Stuart three for 63, M. V. Nagamootoo three for 91).

At Georgetown, November 30, December 1, 2, 3. Second A-team Test: Drawn. Toss: West Indies A. West Indies A 238 (R. R. Sarwan 89, R. O. Hinds 68; H. S. Sodhi three for 42, M. Kartik three for 64) and 206 (L. A. Roberts 74, R. N. Lewis 48; M. Kartik five for 73); India A 251 (J. Arun Kumar 74, M. Kaif 69 not out; N. A. M. McLean four for 45, D. H. Mais three for 63) and 147 for six (S. Sriram 39; R. N. Lewis three for 45).

ZIMBABWE A IN SRI LANKA, 1999-2000

Zimbabwe A toured Sri Lanka in April and May 2000, playing five first-class matches and four one-day games. They lost their three-match series with Sri Lanka A 2–0, suffering innings defeats in the last two after drawing the opening three first-class games of the programme. They also lost their one-day international series 2–0, after the first match was ended in the third over by rain, and lost another one-day game against a Sri Lankan Board XI.

The squad of 15 named for the tour was: A. J. Mackay (Mashonaland) (*captain*), E. Z. Matambanadzo (Mashonaland) (*vice-captain*), A. M. Blignaut (Mashonaland), D. J. R. Campbell (Mashonaland), D. D. Ebrahim (Matabeleland), N. R. Ferreira (Manicaland), G. A. Lamb (CFX Academy), A. Maregwede (CFX Academy), D. A. Marillier (Midlands), D. T. Mutendera (Midlands), D. J. Peacock (Mashonaland), R. W. Price (Midlands), G. J. Rennie (Mashonaland), M. A. Vermeulen (Matabeleland), C. B. Wishart (Mashonaland). *Manager:* K. Gokal. *Coach:* K. M. Curran. B. T. Watambwa (Mashonaland) joined the party for the one-day internationals. A. R. Whittall was originally named captain, but withdrew through injury; T. N. Madondo (Mashonaland) was dropped for disciplinary reasons.

At P. Saravanamuttu Stadium, Colombo, April 19, 20, 21. Drawn. Toss: Zimbabwe A. Zimbabwe A 344 (N. R. Ferreira 52, M. A. Vermeulen 152, G. A. Lamb 31; K. Weeraratne four for 67, M. R. C. N. Bandaratilleke three for 67) and 105 for four (G. J. Rennie 48 not out); Sri Lanka A 283 for seven dec. (D. A. Gunawardene 72, L. P. C. Silva 100 not out).

At Kurunegala, April 24, 25, 26, 27. First A-team Test: Drawn. Toss: Zimbabwe A. Zimbabwe A 306 (N. R. Ferreira 35, D. J. Peacock 62, A. M. Blignaut 93, A. J. Mackay 35 not out; I. S. Gallage three for 42, K. Weeraratne four for 108) and 174 for eight (G. J. Rennie 90; T. T. Samaraweera three for 39); Sri Lanka A 474 (D. A. Gunawardene 129, R. P. Hewage 135, T. M. Dilshan 37, L. P. C. Silva 38, K. Weeraratne 33, Extras 30; D. J. Peacock three for 121, R. W. Price five for 171).

Gunawardene and Hewage put on 228 for Sri Lanka A's first wicket.

At Moratuwa, April 30, May 1, 2. Drawn. Toss: Sri Lankan Board XI. Sri Lankan Board XI 212 (K. Sangakkara 90, U. A. Fernando 46; D. T. Mutendera three for 28, D. J. Peacock three for 64, R. W. Price three for 73) and 229 for six dec. (S. Kalawithigoda 73, G. I. Daniel 52, K. Sangakkara 48 not out, A. S. A. Perera 38; G. J. Rennie four for 42); Zimbabwe A 173 (D. A. Marillier 81; A. S. A. Perera three for 27, D. Hettiarachchi three for 25) and 81 for four.

At Galle, May 5, 6, 7, 8. Second A-team Test: Sri Lanka A won by an innings and 134 runs. Toss: Zimbabwe A. Sri Lanka A 431 for eight dec. (D. A. Gunawardene 140, S. I. de Saram 61, L. P. C. Silva 34, T. T. Samaraweera 106 not out; A. J. Mackay three for 100, D. J. Peacock three for 70); Zimbabwe A 221 (C. B. Wishart 103, A. M. Blignaut 34; K. A. D. M. Fernando three for 47, K. Weeraratne three for 66) and 76 (K. A. D. M. Fernando three for nine, C. R. D. Fernando four for 35).

At Matara, May 11, 12, 13, 14. Third A-team Test: Sri Lanka A won by an innings and 21 runs. Toss: Sri Lanka A. Zimbabwe A 126 (T. T. Samaraweera four for 39) and 97 (R. Herath three for 23, T. T. Samaraweera four for 25); Sri Lanka A 244 (S. I. de Saram 143; A. J. Mackay three for 46, R. W. Price four for 67).

In Zimbabwe A's second innings, Herath's full figures were 35–19–23–3 and Samaraweera's 29.5–14–25–5.

PAKISTAN A IN KENYA, 2000

Pakistan A toured Kenya in July 2000, playing one first-class match and six one-day games. They drew their first-class match against the Kenyans but, after winning their first limited-overs game, against Kenya A, lost their one-day series against the full Kenyan side 4–1.

The squad of 14 for the tour was: Salim Elahi (Habib Bank) (*captain*), Bazid Khan (Pakistan Reserves) (*vice-captain*), Ali Naqvi (Pakistan Customs), Atiq-uz-Zaman (Pakistan Reserves), Danish Kaneria (Pakistan Reserves), Faisal Iqbal (Pakistan Reserves), Hasan Raza (Habib Bank), Imran Farhat (Pakistan Reserves), Kashif Raza (Pakistan Reserves), Qaiser Abbas (Pakistan Reserves), Sajid Shah (Habib Bank), Yasir Arafat (Pakistan Reserves), Yasir Hameed (Peshawar), Zahid Saeed (Pakistan Reserves). *Manager:* Syed Asif Shah. *Coach:* Mohsin Kamal. Mohammad Wasim (KRL) was originally named captain, but withdrew through injury. His place was taken by Hasan Raza.

At Aga Khan Sports Club, Nairobi, July 18, 19, 20, 21. Drawn. Toss: Pakistan A. Pakistan A 352 (Yasir Hameed 42, Faisal Iqbal 39, Imran Farhat 43, Atiq-uz-Zaman 94, Extras 31; A. O. Suji four for 62) and 305 for four dec. (Salim Elahi 30, Hasan Raza 106 not out, Faisal Iqbal 99); Kenyans 219 (Mohsin Ali 47, T. M. Odoyo 59; Sajid Shah five for 72) and 274 for eight (K. O. Otieno 86, T. M. Odoyo 82, Extras 57; Zahid Saeed four for 71).

Danish Kaneria had figures of 23–13–22–1 in the Kenyans' first innings. In Pakistan A's second innings, Hasan Raza and Faisal Iqbal added 201 for the fourth wicket.

SOUTH AFRICA A IN THE WEST INDIES, 2000

South Africa A toured the West Indies in August and September 2000, playing five first-class matches and four one-day games. They drew the whole of their first-class programme, including the two-match series against West Indies A, and won the one-day international series 2–0, with the third match abandoned. They also won one-day games against Barbados and a Jamaica Select XI.

The squad of 16 for the tour was: D. M. Benkenstein (KwaZulu-Natal) (*captain*), M. L. Bruyns (KwaZulu-Natal), J. D. C. Bryant (Eastern Province), G. Dros (Northerns), J. M. Kemp (Eastern Province), G. J-P. Kruger (Eastern Province), C. K. Langeveldt (Boland), P. V. Mpitsang (Free State), M. Ngam (Eastern Province), J. L. Ontong (Boland), R. J. Peterson (Eastern Province), N. Pothas (Gauteng), A. G. Prince (Western Province), G. C. Smith (Western Province), D. J. Watson (KwaZulu-Natal), C. M. Willoughby (Boland). *Manager:* H. Paulse. *Coaches:* H. D. Ackerman and S. Conrad. Kruger replaced the injured D. Pretorius (Free State) and Watson replaced H. H. Dippenaar (Free State), who had been promoted to the Test side touring Sri Lanka.

At St Philip, Barbados, August 22, 23, 24, 25. Drawn. Toss: Barbados. South Africa A 282 for nine dec. (D. J. Watson 30, J. L. Ontong 57, D. M. Benkenstein 57, A. G. Prince 69; I. D. R. Bradshaw four for 61, H. R. O. Graham three for 74) and 228 for eight dec. (M. L. Bruyns 85, G. C. Smith 30, D. M. Benkenstein 57; C. F. Lopez five for 61, R. O. Hinds three for 73); Barbados 287 (D. M. Richards 53, R. O. Hinds 54, I. D. R. Bradshaw 62 not out, Extras 48; M. Ngam three for 56) and 140 for six (K. J. Wilkinson 48 not out, C. A. Glasgow 31).

At St Vincent, September 1, 2, 3. Drawn. Toss: South Africa A. South Africa A 195 (G. Dros 67 not out, G. J-P. Kruger 58; D. Butler four for 51, K. Peters three for 25) and 70 for no wkt (D. J. Watson 35 not out, G. C. Smith 32 not out); Windward Islands 276 (D. S. Smith 31, J. Eugene 130 not out, U. Pope 31, Extras 39; R. J. Peterson five for 68).
    In South Africa A's first innings, Dros and Kruger added 103 for the last wicket.

At St Vincent, September 6, 7, 8, 9. First A-team Test: Drawn. Toss: South Africa A. South Africa A 144 (G. C. Smith 34; M. Dillon three for 32, C. E. L. Stuart four for 42) and 194 (G. C. Smith 47, N. Pothas 42 not out; C. E. L. Stuart four for 50); West Indies A 202 (D. Ramnarine 38, M. Dillon 52, Extras 50; C. M. Willoughby three for 38, G. J-P. Kruger four for 39) and 128 for two (A. Haniff 50, R. S. Morton 36 not out).

At Uitvlugt, Guyana, September 12, 13, 14. Drawn. Toss: Guyana. Guyana 189 (T. M. Dowlin 46, V. Nagamootoo 32) and 81 for four; South Africa A 215 (D. J. Watson 69, J. L. Ontong 35; R. Griffith three for 41, E. Katchay three for 46).

At Georgetown, September 16, 17, 18, 19. Second A-team Test: Drawn. Toss: South Africa A. West Indies A 95 (C. M. Willoughby three for 35, M. Ngam three for 21, C. K. Langeveldt three for 15) and 125 for three (R. S. Morton 60 not out); South Africa A 285 (M. L. Bruyns 126, D. J. Watson 33; C. E. L. Stuart four for 60, D. Ramnarine three for 66).

ONE-DAY INTERNATIONAL RESULTS, 1999-2000

	P	W	L	T	NR	% W (excl. NR)
Australia	30	22	6	1	1	75.86
Sri Lanka	27	16	9	1	1	61.53
England	18	9	6	0	3	60.00
South Africa	32	18	13	1	0	56.25
Pakistan	41	22	18	1	0	53.65
New Zealand	16	8	7	0	1	53.33
India	40	16	23	0	1	41.02
West Indies	34	13	19	0	2	40.62
Zimbabwe	34	8	23	0	3	25.80
Bangladesh	5	0	5	0	0	0.00
Kenya.	3	0	3	0	0	0.00

UNDER-19 WORLD CUP, 1999-2000

By JOHN STERN

To the disappointment of a large, excitable crowd at the Sinhalese Sports Club in Colombo, Sri Lanka fell at the final hurdle in the third Under-19 World Cup. Granted free admission, local schoolchildren forsook books for national flags to support their heroes in the biggest match of their burgeoning careers. But they were conquered in a relatively one-sided final by India, who fielded three players from the Under-15 team that won the Lombard World Challenge in England in 1996.

The format of the competition, now a biennial event, was similar to that of its 1998 predecessor in South Africa. The nine Test-playing nations were joined by seven other teams: Bangladesh, Kenya, Ireland and Namibia returned, while the Americas (drawn from Argentina, Bermuda, Canada and the United States), Holland and Nepal made their debuts at this level. They all played initially in four groups of four, followed by a Super League stage for the top two from each group, semi-finals (the only change from South Africa) and a final. As before, there was a Plate competition for the remaining eight teams.

India were deserving champions, the only unbeaten side in the tournament, their highlights being two victories over Sri Lanka and a crushing 170-run semi-final win over Australia. To no one's surprise, Pakistan, with several players from the previous Under-19 World Cup still eligible, also reached the semis, where they lost by ten runs to Sri Lanka in front of a 5,000-strong partisan crowd at Galle.

So the subcontinental venue ultimately yielded three Asian semi-finalists. But they owed their success to more than familiarity with local conditions. In the case of Pakistan, their vast experience – both their captain, Hasan Raza, and vice-captain Imran Nazir had already played Test cricket – counted for much. Pakistan boasted the tournament's leading wicket-taker in Zahid Saeed, a left-arm pace bowler who claimed 15 victims at only 7.60 apiece. And India and Sri Lanka each had a glorious lack of inhibition with the bat, accurate and awkward spinners and a credible opening bowler.

India were indebted to their prolific opening batsmen, Ravneet Ricky and Manish Sharma, who shared three century stands and one fifty partnership in eight innings. Although Ricky was the tournament's second-highest scorer, with 340 runs at 42.50 including a century in the semi-final against Australia, it was Sharma, with 257 at 42.83, who looked the more complete batsman. India unearthed a powerhouse in the middle order. Yuvraj Singh, a left-hander from Punjab who had scored 358 in an Indian Under-19 domestic final in December, proved a batsman of rare vigour, scoring an aggregate of 203 from 196 balls. His most explosive innings came against Australia: 58 off only 25 balls, smashing five sixes and five fours. Consequently, the modest harvest of runs from their highly rated captain, Mohammad Kaif, was never a setback. Reetinder Sodhi, who had captained India to the Under-15 title in 1996, excelled against Sri Lanka, hitting a vital 74 in their Super League game and then winning the match award in the final with an all-round performance of great maturity.

Sri Lanka, unbeaten except by India, suffered a heavy blow in that final with the early loss of their leading batsman, Ian Daniel, who was averaging 99.66 from 299 runs before he was out in the first over for a duck. Their only man in form on the day was left-hander Jehan Mubarak, who made a forceful fifty. The most successful home bowlers were seamer Kaushalya Weeraratne, with 12 wickets, and leg-spinner Ranil Dhammika, with 13.

Australia lost their captain, Michael Clarke, the day before the semi-final with India, because he was required by New South Wales in the Pura Milk Cup. Whether this was the reason or not, they looked dispirited as India ran up 284 for six, and they folded for 114. Having made a statement of intent by scoring 321 for two against Namibia, the Australian batsmen rarely delivered on that early promise, but their bowlers saw them through to the semi-finals with a remarkable victory over 1998 finalists New Zealand. Australia were bowled out for 122 on a desperately slow, low pitch at Moratuwa, but then dismissed New Zealand for 53. There were 11 lbw decisions in the match, four of them for their opening bowler, Tim Welsford, who finished with five for 22.

Defending champions England were extremely disappointing, even allowing for the alien conditions and the loss of John Sadler, an opening batsman, to a knee injury on the eve of the tournament. Their only victory over a Test-playing nation came off the last ball of their final group match against Zimbabwe. Either side of that win were heavy defeats by West Indies, Sri Lanka and India, all of whom were more confident and better drilled.

West Indies, under the enthusiastic tutelage of Gus Logie, hinted at the roots of a cricketing recovery in the Caribbean. In addition to a trio of erratic but promising quick bowlers, off-spinner Rodney Sooklal made life awkward for batsmen with his bounce, and his 35 overs averaged just 1.6 runs each. Their unorthodox captain, Ryan Hinds, a feisty left-handed batsman, and deputy Marlon Samuels both scored more than 200 runs.

South Africa arrived as one of the favourites and left thoroughly frustrated and disillusioned, winners only of the Plate competition, in which they completed a straightforward win over Bangladesh in the final. The weather allowed them cricket in only one of their three group matches, against Nepal, and even then not enough (only the final of the main competition had a reserve day) to complete the expected victory. This misfortune meant that they finished the group with three points from three no-results, while Nepal, with four points, thanks to two no-results and a victory over Kenya, qualified ahead of them, together with Pakistan, for the Super League. By way of consolation for South Africa, their left-handed batsman, Graeme Smith, was the tournament's leading run-scorer with 348 at 87.00.

There were more sad tales, on and off the field. A bomb near the Prime Minister's residence in Colombo, which killed 13 people five days before the start of the tournament, cast a shadow, although most participants shrugged this off once they started playing. There was also the death of an umpire, Annesley Jayasundera, who suffered a fatal stroke on his way to officiate in Namibia's match against Ireland. One of his colleagues, Test umpire B. C. Cooray, was hospitalised after being hit on the head by a wayward throw during Zimbabwe's game against Bangladesh.

Note: Matches in this section were not first-class.

Group A

At Braybrooke Place, Colombo, January 11. **England won by eight wickets.** Toss: Americas. Americas 105 (33.1 overs) (T. J. Murtagh four for 33); England 109 for two (19.1 overs) (I. R. Bell 41, M. A. Carberry 42 not out).

At Nondescripts Cricket Club, Colombo, January 11. **West Indies won by 124 runs (D/L method).** Toss: West Indies. West Indies 234 for six (50 overs) (K. J. Wilkinson 31, R. O. Hinds 58, M. N. Samuels 83); Zimbabwe 92 for nine (31 overs) (T. J. Friend 39; C. F. Lopez three for 16, J. J. C. Lawson four for six).

Lawson's full figures were 4–2–6–4, including a hat-trick. When rain ended Zimbabwe's innings at 31 overs, the Duckworth/Lewis par score was 216.

At Kadirana Ground, Gampaha, January 13. **Zimbabwe won by eight wickets.** Toss: Zimbabwe. Americas 95 (42.1 overs); Zimbabwe 96 for two (23.2 overs) (G. M. Croxford 34 not out).

At Sinhalese Sports Club, Colombo, January 13. **West Indies won by 98 runs.** Toss: West Indies. West Indies 196 (48.3 overs) (N. Deonarine 44, R. O. Hinds 69; T. J. Murtagh four for 26, A. G. R. Loudon three for 41); England 98 (36 overs).

At Kadirana Ground, Gampaha, January 15. West Indies won by 142 runs. Toss: Americas. West Indies 216 for six (50 overs) (Z. R. Ali 31, C. F. Lopez 42 not out, C. C. Alexander 33 not out); Americas 74 (40.1 overs) (M. N. Samuels three for 20).

At Maitland Crescent, Colombo, January 15. England won by three runs. Toss: Zimbabwe. England 187 for eight (50 overs) (J. H. K. Adams 31, G. J. Pratt 68 not out, Extras 32); Zimbabwe 184 for six (50 overs) (G. M. Croxford 63 not out, M. L. Nkala 53; T. J. Phillips three for 38).

West Indies 6 pts, England 4 pts, Zimbabwe 2 pts, Americas 0 pts. West Indies and England qualified for the Super League.

Group B

At Moratuwa, January 12. India won by 122 runs. Toss: Bangladesh. India 235 for five (50 overs) (R. S. Ricky 61, Manish Sharma 55, M. Kaif 30, N. K. Patel 31 not out; Rajin Saleh three for 44); Bangladesh 113 (34.5 overs) (A. M. Dave four for 15).

At Matara, January 12. New Zealand won by 151 runs. Toss: Holland. New Zealand 206 for six (32 overs) (J. M. How 43, J. E. C. Franklin 38 not out, Extras 30); Holland 55 for nine (32 overs) (G. Hayne three for nine).

At Galle, January 14. Bangladesh v New Zealand. No result (abandoned).

At Matara, January 14. No result. Toss: Holland. Holland 58 (29.2 overs) (A. M. Dave three for seven); India 15 for three (4 overs) (V. Tewarie three for eight).

At Moratuwa, January 16. Bangladesh won by 41 runs (D/L method). Toss: Holland. Holland 137 (46.5 overs) (Extras 42; Bikash Das four for seven); Bangladesh 119 for five (25.3 overs) (Hannan Sarker 30; K. Kout three for 39).
   When rain halted Bangladesh's innings, they were 41 ahead of the par score of 78.

At Galle, January 16. India won by 28 runs. Toss: India. India 199 (49.1 overs) (Yuvraj Singh 68; T. P. Robin four for 26, G. D. Irwin three for 13); New Zealand 171 (49.3 overs) (J. P. McNamee 56; Yuvraj Singh four for 36).

India 5 pts, New Zealand 3 pts, Bangladesh 3 pts, Holland 1 pt. India and New Zealand (on net run-rate) qualified for the Super League.

Group C

At Radella, January 12. Pakistan won by eight wickets. Toss: Pakistan. Kenya 66 (25 overs) (Extras 32; Zahid Saeed three for 15); Pakistan 67 for two (15.5 overs).

At Katunayake, January 12. No result. Toss: South Africa. South Africa 295 for five (50 overs) (G. C. Smith 74, J. A. Rudolph 156 not out, J. Trott 39; B. K. Das three for 54); Nepal 24 for four (12 overs).
   Smith and Rudolph added 160 in 30 overs for South Africa's second wicket. Rudolph's 156 not out was the highest individual score of the tournament.

At Kurunegala, January 14. Kenya v South Africa. No result (abandoned).

At Kandy, January 14. Nepal v Pakistan. No result (abandoned).

At Kandy, January 16. Nepal won by 14 runs. Toss: Kenya. Nepal 107 (44.3 overs) (Extras 48); Kenya 93 (24.5 overs) (M. Sheikh 46; B. K. Das three for 25, M. Alam three for 36).

At Kurunegala, January 16. Pakistan v South Africa. No result (abandoned).

Pakistan 4 pts, Nepal 4 pts, South Africa 3 pts, Kenya 1 pt. Pakistan and Nepal qualified for the Super League.

Group D

At P. Saravanamuttu Stadium, Colombo, January 11. Australia won by 266 runs. Toss: Australia. Australia 321 for two (50 overs) (E. J. M. Cowan 69, S. E. Marsh 61, S. R. Watson 100 not out, A. B. McDonald 63 not out); Namibia 55 (30.4 overs).
Cowan and Marsh put on 129 in 21 overs for Australia's first wicket; Watson and McDonald shared an unbroken partnership of 143 in 17 overs for the third.

At Sinhalese Sports Club, Colombo, January 11. Sri Lanka won by eight wickets. Toss: Ireland. Ireland 134 (47.1 overs) (R. S. Haire 39, J. Mooney 34; W. C. A. Ganegama three for 11, K. Weeraratne three for 26); Sri Lanka 135 for two (23.2 overs) (G. I. Daniel 72 not out).

At Maitland Crescent, Colombo, January 13. Australia won by 63 runs. Toss: Ireland. Australia 240 (49.4 overs) (L. G. Buchanan 58, S. E. Marsh 58; J. Gardiner three for 46, C. Armstrong three for 23); Ireland 177 for nine (50 overs) (K. Spelman 34; M. J. Clarke three for 17).

At P. Saravanamuttu Stadium, Colombo, January 13. Sri Lanka won by seven wickets. Toss: Namibia. Namibia 93 (44.2 overs) (K. S. Lokuarachchi three for 24); Sri Lanka 96 for three (20.4 overs) (K. M. Gajanayake 43 not out).

At Braybrooke Place, Colombo, January 15. Tied (D/L method). Toss: Ireland. Namibia 186 for seven (48 overs) (S. Swanepoel 39, M. van der Merwe 70, S. Ludick 34 not out; A. White three for 31); Ireland 127 for five (36 overs) (D. Joyce 43).
Ireland's target was revised to 128 from 36 overs.

At R. Premadasa Stadium, Colombo, January 15. Sri Lanka won by eight wickets. Toss: Australia. Australia 90 (37.1 overs); Sri Lanka 91 for two (27 overs) (G. I. Daniel 40 not out).

Sri Lanka 6 pts, Australia 4 pts, Ireland 1 pt, Namibia 1 pt. Sri Lanka and Australia qualified for the Super League.

Super League Group One

At Sinhalese Sports Club, Colombo, January 18. Australia won by four wickets. Toss: Australia. West Indies 199 for six (50 overs) (M. N. Samuels 54, R. O. Hinds 33); Australia 202 for six (48.5 overs) (S. R. Watson 72, N. M. Hauritz 34).

At R. Premadasa Stadium, Colombo, January 18. Pakistan won by six wickets. Toss: Pakistan. New Zealand 90 (42.3 overs) (Zahid Saeed five for 14); Pakistan 94 for four (31.4 overs) (Taufiq Umar 31 not out).

At R. Premadasa Stadium, Colombo, January 20. Pakistan won by four wickets. Toss: Pakistan. Australia 112 (47.5 overs) (Zahid Saeed three for 13, Danish Kaneria five for 17); Pakistan 113 for six (39.1 overs) (Humayun Farhat 38 not out).

At Nondescripts Cricket Club, Colombo, January 20. West Indies won by 57 runs. Toss: West Indies. West Indies 218 for eight (50 overs) (B. A. Parchment 57, M. N. Samuels 36); New Zealand 161 (43.1 overs) (C. C. Alexander three for 49).

At Moratuwa, January 22. Australia won by 69 runs. Toss: Australia. Australia 122 (42.2 overs) (T. H. Welsford 30; J. E. C. Franklin four for 18); New Zealand 53 (27 overs) (T. H. Welsford five for 22).

At Maitland Crescent, Colombo, January 22. Pakistan won by three wickets. Toss: Pakistan. West Indies 182 (49.4 overs) (R. O. Hinds 32, S. Chattergoon 44, Extras 31; Zahid Saeed four for 27); Pakistan 185 for seven (43.1 overs) (Taufiq Umar 65, Faisal Iqbal 67 not out; R. O. Hinds four for 19).

Pakistan 6 pts, Australia 4 pts, West Indies 2 pts, New Zealand 0 pts. Pakistan and Australia qualified for the semi-finals.

Super League Group Two

At Police Park, Colombo, January 18. India won by eight wickets. Toss: India. Nepal 101 for nine (44 overs) (Yuvraj Singh four for 15); India 105 for two (25.2 overs) (R. S. Ricky 35, M. Kaif 57 not out).

The match was moved from Katunayake because of a waterlogged pitch.

At P. Saravanamuttu Stadium, Colombo, January 18. Sri Lanka won by seven wickets. Toss: Sri Lanka. England 123 (47.3 overs) (D. G. R. Dhammika four for 13); Sri Lanka 124 for three (24.5 overs) (G. I. Daniel 46, J. Mubarak 36).

At Maitland Crescent, Colombo, January 20. India won by nine wickets. Toss: India. England 182 for nine (50 overs) (J. K. Maunders 32, M. A. Carberry 36, G. J. Pratt 56); India 183 for one (42.3 overs) (R. S. Ricky 68, Manish Sharma 86 not out).

At Matara, January 20. Sri Lanka won by nine wickets. Toss: Nepal. Nepal 89 (34.2 overs) (K. Weeraratne three for 15); Sri Lanka 92 for one (18.3 overs) (G. I. Daniel 44 not out, J. Mubarak 31 not out).

At Braybrooke Place, Colombo, January 22. England won by 64 runs. Toss: Nepal. England 260 for seven (50 overs) (I. Pattison 97, G. J. Pratt 51; A. Akhtar three for 57); Nepal 196 (46.3 overs) (V. V. Shah 32, P. Lunia 37 not out, Extras 50; J. E. Bishop three for 39, G. D. Bridge three for 28).

At R. Premadasa Stadium, Colombo, January 22. India won by 41 runs. Toss: India. India 242 for seven (50 overs) (R. S. Ricky 32, Yuvraj Singh 36, R. S. Sodhi 74, N. K. Patel 43; D. G. R. Dhammika four for 43); Sri Lanka 201 (45.4 overs) (J. Mubarak 30, R. T. Peiris 66; M. Kaif three for 29).

India 6 pts, Sri Lanka 4 pts, England 2 pts, Nepal 0 pts. India and Sri Lanka qualified for the semi-finals.

Plate League Group One

At Matara, January 19. Bangladesh won by seven wickets. Toss: Bangladesh. Namibia 57 (28.3 overs) (Hannan Sarker five for 15); Bangladesh 58 for three (11.1 overs).

At Galle, January 19. Zimbabwe won by six wickets. Toss: Zimbabwe. Kenya 162 (44.2 overs) (A. G. Gore 34, J. S. Ababu 40, Extras 30; H. Henderson three for 35); Zimbabwe 165 for four (31.4 overs) (C. Brewer 34, T. Taibu 40, G. A. Lamb 41 not out).

At Matara, January 21. Bangladesh won by 125 runs. Toss: Bangladesh. Bangladesh 198 (50 overs) (Extras 37; M. Sheikh four for 37); Kenya 73 (37.3 overs) (Anwar Hossain three for 21).

At Galle, January 21. Zimbabwe won by three wickets. Toss: Namibia. Namibia 231 for five (50 overs) (M. van der Merwe 44, S. Swanepoel 38, J. B. Burger 69, P. Burger 36 not out); Zimbabwe 233 for seven (48.2 overs) (T. Taibu 59, G. M. Croxford 41 not out, T. J. Friend 37; B. van Rooi three for 53).

At Nondescripts Cricket Club, Colombo, January 23. Bangladesh won by 75 runs. Toss: Bangladesh. Bangladesh 270 for seven (50 overs) (Nahidul Haque 54, Mohammad Salim 54, Mahfuz Kabir 41 not out, Tariqul Hasan 35, Extras 36; G. Ewing three for 31); Zimbabwe 195 for nine (50 overs) (M. G. Munson 41; Anwar Hossain three for 39).

At Katunayake, January 23. Kenya won by 54 runs. Toss: Kenya. Kenya 220 (48 overs) (A. K. P. Bhudia 30, C. O. Obuya 42, M. A. Ouma 44, Extras 38; B. van Rooi three for 47); Namibia 166 (44.2 overs) (P. Burger 69).

Bangladesh 6 pts, Zimbabwe 4 pts, Kenya 2 pts, Namibia 0 pts. Bangladesh and Zimbabwe qualified for the semi-finals.

Plate League Group Two

At Kurunegala, January 19. South Africa won by 151 runs. Toss: South Africa. South Africa 264 for three (50 overs) (G. C. Smith 59, A. G. Puttick 75, J. A. Rudolph 38, J. Trott 60 not out); Americas 113 (40 overs) (A. Bagai 53 not out; J. A. Morkel five for 25).

At Radella, January 19. Ireland won by 19 runs. Toss: Ireland. Ireland 149 for eight (40 overs) (D. Joyce 59; V. Tewarie three for 24); Holland 130 (38.3 overs) (A. Raja 43; C. Armstrong three for 13).

At Radella, January 21. Ireland won by 85 runs. Toss: Ireland. Ireland 183 (48.5 overs) (A. White 76); Americas 98 (36.3 overs) (R. D. McGerrigle three for 24, J. Mooney three for 25).

At Kandy, January 21. South Africa won by 154 runs. Toss: Holland. South Africa 278 for six (50 overs) (A. G. Puttick 33, G. C. Smith 44, J. G. Myburgh 53, U. Abrahams 40; R. de Graaf four for 53); Holland 124 for eight (49 overs) (R. van Ierschot 31, Extras 30).

At Radella, January 23. Holland won by seven runs. Toss: Americas. Holland 226 for seven (50 overs) (K. Shafiq 49, E. Nawaz 58 not out, F. Nijman 30 not out, Extras 43; K. Sanders three for 33); Americas 219 for eight (50 overs) (C. Foggo 91, A. Bagai 36, O. Pitcher 35).

At Kurunegala, January 23. South Africa won by ten wickets. Toss: Ireland. Ireland 78 (30 overs) (D. Senekal five for 28); South Africa 82 for no wkt (13.4 overs) (G. C. Smith 38 not out, J. A. Rudolph 40 not out).

South Africa 6 pts, Ireland 4 pts, Holland 2 pts, Americas 0 pts. South Africa and Ireland qualified for the semi-finals.

Plate Semi-finals

At Kurunegala, January 25. Bangladesh won by 67 runs. Toss: Bangladesh. Bangladesh 196 (48.5 overs) (Nahidul Haque 32, Mohammad Kalim 58; R. D. McGerrigle four for 54, C. Armstrong three for 44); Ireland 129 (43.3 overs) (N. O'Brien 36; Bikash Das four for 19).

At Kandy, January 25. South Africa won by eight wickets. Toss: Zimbabwe. Zimbabwe 179 for seven (50 overs) (S. M. Ervine 61, G. A. Lamb 63); South Africa 180 for two (35.2 overs) (G. C. Smith 82 not out, A. G. Puttick 37, J. G. Myburgh 31 not out).

Plate Final

At Kandy, January 27. South Africa won by 80 runs. Toss: South Africa. South Africa 213 (49.4 overs) (G. C. Smith 51, J. Trott 41; Bikash Das three for 43); Bangladesh 133 (47.5 overs) (Hannan Sarker 51; D. Senekal three for 20).

Super League Semi-finals

At Galle, January 24. Sri Lanka won by ten runs. Toss: Sri Lanka. Sri Lanka 219 (49.1 overs) (G. I. Daniel 58, M. Pushpakumara 47); Pakistan 209 (50 overs) (Hasan Raza 44, Faisal Iqbal 53).
Five Sri Lankans were run out.

At P. Saravanamuttu Stadium, Colombo, January 25. India won by 170 runs. Toss: India. India 284 for six (50 overs) (R. S. Ricky 108, Manish Sharma 65, Yuvraj Singh 58); Australia 114 (34.5 overs) (S. R. Watson 38; A. M. Dave three for 25).
Australia's captain, Michael Clarke, left the day before the game because he was required by New South Wales; Nathan Hauritz deputised.

FINAL

INDIA v SRI LANKA

At Sinhalese Sports Club, Colombo, January 28. India won by six wickets. Toss: Sri Lanka.

India controlled the final on a slow turner from the moment that Sriwastava, their left-arm swing bowler, brought the fourth ball of the match back into the right-handed Daniel and had him leg-before. Only Mubarak, an aggressive left-hander, whipped up any momentum for Sri Lanka. His innings of 58 came from 108 balls, with five fours, before he drove the off-spin of Kaif, the Indian captain, straight back to him. Sriwastava returned to take two more wickets in his second spell, and Sodhi's medium-pace was miserly. He also took a fine diving catch at mid-wicket to dismiss Dhammika and ran out Ganegama – one of four Sri Lankan run-outs. When India batted, it was Sodhi who provided a steady hand on the rudder, reaching 39 not out from 43 balls to make sure of the match award. He won the trophy for India with nearly ten overs in hand when he cut Weeraratne through third man for four.

Man of the Match: R. S. Sodhi.   *Man of the Series:* Yuvraj Singh.

Sri Lanka

†R. T. Peiris c Dave b Tripathi	17	W. C. A. Ganegama run out	2
G. I. Daniel lbw b Sriwastava	0	R. A. P. Nissanka not out	2
J. Mubarak c and b Kaif	58		
S. H. T. Kandambi run out	10	B 2, l-b 10, w 9, n-b 2	23
*K. M. Gajanayake c Ratra b Dave	6		
M. Pushpakumara run out	17	1/1 (2) 2/43 (1)	(48.1 overs) 178
K. S. Lokuarachchi b Sriwastava	14	3/84 (4) 4/100 (5)	
K. Weeraratne run out	23	5/118 (3) 6/125 (6)	
D. G. R. Dhammika c Sodhi		7/158 (7) 8/171 (8)	
b Sriwastava	6	9/174 (9) 10/178 (10)	

Bowling: Sriwastava 9–2–33–3; Tripathi 9.1–1–38–1; Sodhi 10–0–26–0; Kaif 10–1–31–1; Dave 9–1–33–1; Yuvraj Singh 1–0–5–0.

India

Manish Sharma lbw b Dhammika	27	N. K. Patel not out	34
R. S. Ricky b Lokuarachchi	18	B 4, l-b 4, w 5, n-b 4	17
*M. Kaif b Ganegama	18		
Yuvraj Singh lbw b Pushpakumara	27	1/53 (2) 2/63 (1)	(4 wkts, 40.4 overs) 180
R. S. Sodhi not out	39	3/94 (3) 4/116 (4)	

†A. Ratra, Y. Venugopala Rao, A. M. Dave, M. Tripathi and S. Sriwastava did not bat.

Bowling: Nissanka 5–0–25–0; Ganegama 6–1–28–1; Dhammika 9.2–28–1; Lokuarachchi 6–0–20–1; Pushpakumara 10–2–34–1; Kandambi 3–0–24–0; Weeraratne 1.4–0–13–0.

Umpires: E. A. R. de Silva and P. Manuel.

UNDER-19 WORLD CUP WINNERS

ICC CRICKET WEEK, 1999-2000

By RALPH DELLOR

The International Cricket Council's concept of a worldwide cricket awareness week in April 2000 was admirable. The intention was to enhance the game's profile in territories where it was already established, and to push back the boundaries into regions where it was yet to be developed. In reality, it was perceived by most of the world as an Asian exercise, with little relevance elsewhere. Furthermore, the scandal surrounding Hansie Cronje, which broke on the very eve of the showcase match in Dhaka, did more to promote global awareness of cricket than any of the scheduled activities.

That point aside, given that the ICC was, perhaps unfairly, renowned for lacking enterprise, the events planned did have a cohesion and purpose. Twenty-four cricket ambassadors were appointed from among the great and the good to attend functions around the world and promote the game. Events ranged from Allan Border opening a refurbished cricket pavilion in Shanghai to Michael Holding attending a coaching clinic in New York.

Competitions, festivals and special matches were held, from the Playground League in Hong Kong to the Emerging Nations Tournament in Zimbabwe for the designated fast-track developing countries, intended to advance their progress towards competing on reasonably equal terms with Full Members in one-day internationals. Denmark, Holland, Ireland, Kenya and Scotland joined Zimbabwe A in Harare; an unbeaten Kenyan side were clear winners, with Holland runners-up. In addition, a series of television programmes was made to capture the flavour of the game: these included profiles of all-time cricketing greats, a quiz, a look at cricket in some far-flung locations, classic matches and a feature called "The Spirit of Cricket".

The United Nations backed the concept, recognising cricket's potential in promoting peace and harmony. Secretary-General Kofi Annan recorded a special message, revealing that he had played and enjoyed cricket as a boy in Ghana, and remembered some of its finer qualities. "The very essence of cricket is that both sides agree on the rules and they respect each other, which is precisely what the peoples of the world need to do if this new century is to be more peaceful and civilised than the last one. All of us know what is not cricket. Racism, prejudice, intolerance and hostile behaviour. We know that what unites us – the love of the game – is far more important than what separates us. So let us resolve to live our lives as good cricketers both on the field and off it." Cricket could adopt his words as a mission statement.

The culmination of Cricket Week was a one-day game between teams representing Asia and the Rest of the World. This was held in Dhaka, allowing Bangladesh, soon to become the tenth Test nation, to demonstrate its insatiable fascination with the game. The fact that the Asia XI was largely as selected was testimony to the power of the political wheels set in motion; several players flew over from the Caribbean, where Pakistan were touring, helping to provide a memorable match to round off the week.

Note: The following match did not have official one-day international status.

ASIA XI v REST OF THE WORLD XI

At Dhaka, April 8 (day/night). Asia XI won by one run. Toss: Asia XI.

A crowd of 50,000 witnessed a feast of runs. Tendulkar and Ganguly set the tone, adding 114 runs from 17 overs. Both were dropped by Tufnell off his own left-arm spin, but he finally had Tendulkar caught at long-on, then accounted for Ganguly in identical fashion. Tendulkar hit 11 fours in 77 balls, Ganguly six fours and three sixes in 66. Further attractive contributions from Asia set a target of 321, which looked beyond the Rest of the World when they limped to 196 for seven. But Bevan, supported by Caddick, then put on 119 in 13 overs. Widely regarded as the world's best one-day batsman, Bevan produced some devastating strokeplay, while Caddick played admirably until carelessly failing to ground his bat with one ball to go. Needing six, Bevan managed four, and Asia won by a single run. He remained unbeaten on 185 from 132 balls, with five sixes and 19 fours. Television later suggested that one of those, a straight drive, should have been signalled as six.

Man of the Match: M. G. Bevan.

Asia XI

S. T. Jayasuriya c Bevan b Hayward	12	A. Kumble not out	14
S. R. Tendulkar c Rose b Tufnell	80	W. P. U. J. C. Vaas run out	0
S. C. Ganguly c Rose b Tufnell	67	M. Muralitharan not out	0
P. A. de Silva c Gilchrist b Bevan	39	L-b 9, w 16, n-b 3	28
A. Jadeja c Johnson b Waugh	28		
Abdur Razzaq b Waugh	3	1/49 2/163 3/183 (9 wkts, 50 overs) 320	
†Moin Khan c and b Hayward	34	4/242 5/248 6/248	
*Wasim Akram b Hayward	15	7/291 8/314 9/319	

P. C. R. Tufnell did not bat.

Bowling: Caddick 4–0–27–0; Hayward 7–0–39–3; Rose 6–0–44–0; Cairns 4–0–22–0; Tufnell 9–0–68–2; Klusener 4–0–22–0; Bevan 10–0–61–1; Waugh 6–0–28–2.

Rest of the World XI

N. C. Johnson c Jadeja b Wasim Akram	2	A. R. Caddick run out	23
*M. E. Waugh c and b Vaas	28	M. Hayward not out	0
J. H. Kallis lbw b Kumble	27		
M. G. Bevan not out	185	B 5, l-b 13, w 2, n-b 2	22
C. L. Cairns c and b Muralitharan	8		
L. Klusener c Jayasuriya b Muralitharan	16	1/28 2/46 3/97 (8 wkts, 50 overs) 319	
†A. C. Gilchrist b Abdur Razzaq	1	4/134 5/180 6/186	
F. A. Rose lbw b Abdur Razzaq	7	7/196 8/315	

P. C. R. Tufnell did not bat.

Bowling: Wasim Akram 5–1–27–1; Vaas 10–1–57–1; Abdur Razzaq 10–0–68–2; Kumble 9–0–59–1; Muralitharan 9–1–45–2; Tendulkar 7–0–45–0.

Umpires: D. L. Orchard and S. Venkataraghavan.
Referee: P. L. van der Merwe.

HONOURS' LIST, 2000-01

In 2000-01, the following were decorated for their services to cricket:

Queen's Birthday Honours, 2000: B. G. K. Downing (former chairman of ECB Marketing Advisory Committee; services to England and Wales Cricket Board) OBE, N. Kirk (services to community, especially Goole Town Cricket Club) MBE, C. E. Taylor (England Women; services to cricket, Association Football and hockey) MBE.

Queen's Birthday Honours (Australia), 1999: Dr C. Battersby (Australian Cricket Board director; services to medicine) AM, W. A. Brown (Australia) OAM.

New Year's Honours, 2001: C. O. L. Deane (Barbados scorer; services to cricket) MBE, E. R. Dexter (England; services to cricket) CBE, C. Young (services to Southborough Cricket Club, Kent) MBE.

Australia Day Honours, 2001: C. L. Batt (services to Tasmanian community and cricket clubs) OAM, M. Lilienthal (services to NSW County Cricket Association) OAM, Dr J. C. Lill (South Australia; services to Melbourne Cricket Club and Lord's Taverners Australia) OAM.

ENGLAND WOMEN IN AUSTRALIA AND NEW ZEALAND, 1999-2000

By CAROL SALMON

Karen Smithies resigned the captaincy halfway through a tour that saw England plunge to a new low: they were whitewashed 9–0 in limited-overs internationals either side of the Tasman Sea. Nearly seven years after her greatest triumph, leading England to the 1993 World Cup, she stood down after losing the fourth and last one-day international with Australia by 220 runs. She said she felt unable to continue, and some of the team appeared unwilling to play under her leadership.

Tour vice-captain and Sussex skipper Clare Connor took over for the New Zealand leg. Smithies kept her place for the first two internationals against the Kiwis but was then dropped, and failed to regain her place for the ensuing home series against South Africa. She had played 69 one-day games and 15 Tests since her England debut in 1986, and remained one of a handful of players combining 500 runs with 50 wickets in limited-overs internationals.

England's problems began even before they left home, when they were forced into two late changes. Katharine Winks replaced Sarah Collyer, who was unable to get leave of absence from her university, and 18-year-old Nicki Shaw came in for Suzanne Redfern, who failed the pre-tour medical. It was always going to be a demanding trip. Apart from the 1997 World Cup in India, England had not toured overseas since 1995-96; they were some three months out of season, and had lost all their ten one-day games against Australia and New Zealand, the strongest women's teams, since beating them in the 1993 World Cup. Only two warm-up matches were arranged for the Australian leg, and losing both of them set the tone for the tour.

The batting was abysmal. Charlotte Edwards's aggregate of 214 runs in nine international innings was almost 100 ahead of the next-best, Kathryn Leng's 125. By way of contrast, Australian captain Belinda Clark scored 283 for two dismissals in four games against England, and Lisa Keightley made 185 for once out. However, Australia's player of the series was opening bowler Charmaine Mason, who took 15 wickets at 6.60 each, including two five-wicket hauls. England's bowlers, on the other hand, all suffered at the hands of the rampant Australians. Debutante Dawn Holden, a 19-year-old spinner, looked to have potential, but a side that bats as poorly as England cannot afford to concede an average of ten wides per international.

New Zealand also visited Australia and lost 3–0 before returning home to take on the tourists. They, too, were under a new captain, Emily Drumm having taken over from the experienced Debbie Hockley for the Australian series, but if England hoped to find New Zealand vulnerable, they were soon disillusioned. Drumm led her side to a 5–0 win and was the highest scorer with 171. At least England gave Claire Taylor an overdue opportunity; she responded with two fifties, including 83 in a warm-up against Wellington, the solitary success of the trip. Edwards also hit two half-centuries but there were no others. Barbara Daniels, on her return to the team after a year concentrating on ECB duties, averaged 6.33 over the tour.

ENGLAND WOMEN TOURING PARTY

K. Smithies (East Midlands) *(captain)*, C. J. Connor (Sussex) *(vice-captain)*, J. Cassar (East Midlands), B. A. Daniels (West Midlands), C. M. Edwards (East Anglia), D. Holden (East Midlands), K. M. Leng (Yorkshire), L. K. Newton (Cheshire), L. C. Pearson (East Anglia), M. A. Reynard (Yorkshire), N. Shaw (East Midlands), C. E. Taylor (Yorkshire), S. C. Taylor (Thames Valley), K. Winks (Western Counties).

S. V. Collyer (Cheshire) and S. Redfern (Derbyshire) were originally selected, but Collyer withdrew and Redfern failed a fitness test. They were replaced by Shaw and Winks.

Manager/coach: P. Farbrace.   *Assistant coach:* G. R. Dilley.
Physiotherapist: K. Giles.   *Sports scientist:* J. Brooks.

Note: Matches in this section were not first-class.

At Parramatta, January 26. New South Wales XII won by five wickets. Toss: New South Wales XII. England 104 (49.5 overs); New South Wales XII 105 for five (34.3 overs) (L. M. Keightley 39, M. A. J. Goszko 34; D. Holden four for 31).

At Bankstown, January 27. New South Wales Second XII won by eight runs. Toss: England. New South Wales Second XII 165 for eight (45 overs) (A. Owens 47, T. Roach 30); England 157 for six (45 overs) (C. M. Edwards 55, L. K. Newton 31).

At Sydney, January 29. First one-day international: Australia won by 86 runs. Toss: Australia. Australia 241 for seven (50 overs) (L. M. Keightley 127 not out, B. J. Clark 47); England 155 for seven (50 overs) (C. M. Edwards 55).
Keightley, who made 113 not out in her previous one-day international against England at Lord's in 1998, scored 127 in 152 balls; she and Clark opened with 123 in 21 overs. England wicket-keeper Jane Cassar reached 50 one-day international dismissals.

At Sydney, January 30. Second one-day international: Australia won by 87 runs. Toss: Australia. Australia 249 for six (50 overs) (C. Bambury 66, K. L. Rolton 40, M. A. Winch 54); England 162 (49.4 overs) (C. L. Mason five for 30).

At Bowral, February 1. Third one-day international: Australia won by ten wickets. Toss: Australia. England 106 (45.5 overs) (C. L. Mason four for 27, C. Smith three for 17); Australia 108 for no wkt (24.5 overs) (L. M. Keightley 38 not out, B. J. Clark 66 not out).

At Newcastle, February 3. Fourth one-day international: Australia won by 220 runs. Toss: Australia. Australia 299 for two (50 overs) (B. J. Clark 146 not out, J. Broadbent 85, C. Bambury 53); England 79 (40 overs) (C. L. Mason five for nine).
Clark, making a record 59th one-day appearance for Australia, shared her third century opening partnership in four games, this time 179 in 32 overs with Broadbent. Her 151-ball 146 and the total of 299 were Australian one-day records against England and Mason's 6–3–9–5 were the best figures by any Australian woman in a one-day international. England succumbed to their heaviest defeat by Australia, who took the series 4–0.

At Basin Reserve, Wellington, February 8. England won by 11 runs. Toss: England. England 196 for eight (50 overs) (S. C. Taylor 83, Extras 31; F. A. Stickney three for 38); Wellington XII 185 for eight (50 overs) (L. R. V. S. Harford 56, F. A. Stickney 40, A. Cooper 50 not out).

At Palmerston North, February 12. First one-day international: New Zealand won by seven wickets. Toss: New Zealand. England 157 for nine (50 overs) (C. M. Edwards 37; K. M. Keenan three for 34); New Zealand 161 for three (45.1 overs) (D. A. Hockley 40, E. C. Drumm 45, H. M. Tiffen 42 not out).

At WestpacTrust Stadium, Wellington, February 15. Second one-day international: New Zealand won by eight wickets. Toss: New Zealand. England 141 (47 overs) (S. C. Taylor 56, C. M. Edwards 38; K. M. Keenan three for 15); New Zealand 142 for two (40.2 overs) (D. A. Hockley 64 not out, E. C. Drumm 39).

At Eden Park Outer Oval, Auckland, February 17. Third one-day international: New Zealand won by four wickets. Toss: England. England 146 for eight (50 overs); New Zealand 147 for six (46.2 overs) (E. C. Drumm 59).
Aged 15 years 359 days, Munokoa Tunupopo became New Zealand's youngest player.

At Hamilton, February 20. Fourth one-day international: New Zealand won by five wickets. Toss: England. England 117 (48.5 overs) (J. Cassar 32 not out; R. J. Pullar three for 15); New Zealand 118 for five (33.3 overs) (H. M. Tiffen 32 not out).

At Napier, February 22 (day/night). Fifth one-day international: New Zealand won by six wickets, their target having been revised to 63 in 29 overs. Toss: New Zealand. England 86 (37.2 overs) (R. J. Pullar four for 11); New Zealand 63 for four (25.4 overs).
New Zealand completed a 5–0 series win. The match went ahead as a day/night fixture despite one of the five banks of floodlights being stolen beforehand.

CRICKET IN AUSTRALIA, 1999-2000

By JOHN MacKINNON

Darren Lehmann

The season was already a month old when the venerated Sheffield Shield, awarded to the Australian champions since 1892-93, became just a memory and the Pura Milk Cup emerged as the new symbol of interstate supremacy. The four-year sponsorship by National Foods Limited, valued at $A22 million per year, should pay a lot of bills at the Australian Cricket Board, which explained that the deal would enable it to "concentrate on strengthening the interstate competition as the best domestic cricket in the world". Given the increasingly rare state appearances by the country's cricketing élite, the status claimed for the tournament could be questioned. Meanwhile, the old Shield rests in peace in the board's offices, out of sight but never quite out of mind.

The new cup's inaugural winners were Queensland, who had won the Shield twice in its last five seasons. They took the title after drawing the final with Victoria, whose opening batsman, Matthew Elliott, described them as "the strongest side I've ever played against in a domestic competition". Queensland's dominance of the earlier rounds was without precedent. They won eight of their ten games, including five out of five at home, plus two against the Pakistani and Indian tourists. It was a great start for their new coach, Bennett King, who was promoted after five years assisting John Buchanan. Buchanan himself was coaching Australia to nine straight Test wins – and a 14-match unbeaten run in one-day internationals. King's man-management skills were warmly embraced by Stuart Law, confirmed in his *de facto* role of captain after Ian Healy announced his retirement. Law relished being left to run things on the field, one area where he and Buchanan had not always hit it off.

Queensland's pace attack has long been the key to their success. After recovering from an early-season twinge, Michael Kasprowicz claimed 40 wickets in five matches when not required by Australia. Andy Bichel was the leading national wicket-taker, with 60; he also bowled more overs than anyone. Still under 30 at the end of the season, he should continue to star for his state, if not his country, for a few years yet. Adam Dale's brand of swing, cut and frugal accuracy earned handsome rewards, and Scott Muller recovered well from a traumatic Test debut and a brief relegation from the state side.

Seven century-makers suggested Queensland's strength in batting, in name if not always in deed. Andrew Symonds led the way with a scoring-rate of 85 per 100 balls. He was as dynamic in the field, could bowl some medium-pace, and soon became a fixture in Australia's limited-overs squad. Martin Love teed off with a career-best 228, while Law saved his best for the final, when his two innings occupied 13 hours and shut Victoria out of the match. Wade Seccombe, behind the stumps, was rarely out of the action: he claimed 67 first-class victims, equalling Rodney Marsh's 24-year-old record, and his 151 at the MCG confirmed a burgeoning batting talent. Queensland were runners-up in the one-day Mercantile Mutual Cup, thanks to Matthew Hayden, who compiled three hundreds and two fifties in six qualifying matches. Had he and Symonds not missed the final, because of the tour of New Zealand, they might have claimed the double.

Four consecutive wins before Christmas gave Victoria and their new captain, Paul Reiffel, the impetus for a successful campaign. Two heavy defeats by Queensland were then offset by two effortless wins over New South Wales, and they cruised into the final. Reiffel appeared to revel in the captaincy; he bowled his heart out, finishing with 59 wickets – one behind Bichel. He inspired some of his younger charges, notably left-armer Mathew Inness, whose high point was an unforgettable 11 wickets, including a hat-trick, against New South Wales. Even though Damien Fleming and Shane Warne were unavailable, the bowling resources were more than adequate, except possibly for spin: John Davison returned a meagre eight wickets. Once again, Elliott's batting carried all before him and, with his sheer volume of runs plus almost limitless ability, he looked ready for a recall to Test duties. His burly fellow-opener, Jason Arnberger, helped provide some memorable starts, including successive partnerships of 242 and 353 against South Australia and Tasmania. Down the order, Matthew Mott was a workmanlike No. 3, and Ian Harvey's batting, previously seen as a one-day asset, became increasingly valuable in the four-day game.

A dispute between the MCG and the ACB over advertising, during which the ground was threatened with the removal of its matches, was resolved before the season began. Two games were actually sent away to Richmond so that the MCG could stage a soccer international and a rugby league match. There was a time when the cricket club's trustees would have been apoplectic at the thought. Now, with virtually all sport governed by television revenue, interstate cricket's commercial appeal could not match that of football. More of the same can be expected.

Defending champions Western Australia finished with four wins, which took them into third place. Their innings defeat of Queensland in Perth came a week after Ryan Campbell had ransacked Queensland's star attack to set up Western Australia's victory in the Mercantile Mutual Cup final. Whether by strategy or just the WACA pitch, they always scored quickly, none more so than the rejuvenated Campbell. With Adam Gilchrist absent for all but one game, he also kept wicket until his knees gave way; Mark Walsh then took over, freeing Campbell to concentrate on his opening partnership with the talented Mike Hussey, which produced three century stands. Damien Martyn, who was recalled by Australia, and Justin Langer, whose batting took on a new dimension as he cemented his Test place, made the most of limited state opportunities. Simon Katich, such a prospect the previous year, was hindered by persistent illness but looked well on the way to recovery by season's end. With Tom Moody out all year, and Brendon Julian for most of it, there was a gap in the bowling. It was amply filled by the Victorian expat, Brad Williams, whose speed and aggression were well suited to the WACA. Jo Angel had his arm broken by a Brett Lee missile but was soon back in the fray, and with Sean Cary, always posed a challenge. Another seamer, Matthew Nicholson, just couldn't land a ball for a while, but he regained form after time off.

South Australia's fortunes rested largely on the broad shoulders of their captain, Darren Lehmann. Seven first-class hundreds, the highest national run-aggregate, and the umpires' vote as state player of the season at least earned him an ACB contract: that was as close as he came to playing for his country. Greg Blewett lost form, and Jamie Siddons generally struggled before acceding to the protests of his body and retiring, aged 35. Siddons had played seven seasons with Victoria and nine with South Australia. He scored 10,643 runs in interstate cricket – no one else had reached five figures – and made 146 appearances, 13 behind John Inverarity, with whom he shares the catching record of 189. His only game for Australia was a limited-overs international at Lahore in October 1988. Without him, much must depend on opener David Fitzgerald, who scored five first-class centuries and seemed to have established himself at last, and on middle-order batsman Ben Johnson. Paul Wilson and Brett Swain were the pick of the faster bowlers: Jason Gillespie missed all but the last two games, recovering from his freakish collision with Steve Waugh in Sri Lanka. Wilson's workload was exceeded only by Bichel and by his slow left-arm team-mate, Brad Young. Young and Peter McIntyre were match-winners against Western Australia and New South Wales, showing that spinners can prosper on the Adelaide Oval.

Tasmania beat New South Wales twice, but no one else. They lacked the bowling to expect much more; their spearhead was 39-year-old Mark Ridgway, who bowled his seam off a few paces in his final season. Colin Miller, a fit 36 and still an effective Test bowler, was a reluctant starter as he tried to move back to his native Victoria, which he managed for the 2000-01 season. Gerard Denton fell out with stress fractures early on, which hastened the state debut of Andrew Downton, left-arm, enthusiastic and very promising. Having honed his captaincy skills with Somerset, Jamie Cox led a formidable but inconsistent batting line-up. His four first-class hundreds included a career-best 245, against New South Wales. Five other Tasmanians scored hundreds. Daniel Marsh, with three, continued to improve, and Dene Hills came back well after a finger injury. While Ponting's batting for Australia won many plaudits, he made only one inconsequential appearance for his state.

New South Welshmen had blinked in disbelief at their unprecedented sixth place the previous season, but that was nothing compared to the débâcle of 1999-2000. Eight losses, not to mention a ninth to an insipid Indian team, left little to savour in Sydney. It was not an auspicious time for a new captain: Michael Bevan's many qualities have never included communication or leadership skills. To his credit, Bevan gave 100 per cent for his state, turning out whenever he could and scoring 600 runs in six matches. Not all his colleagues showed the same commitment. The captaincy issue was always contentious, and a newspaper column by Michael Slater ensured it remained so. He highlighted a lack of direction, poor spirit and wrong appointments, specifically when Shawn Bradstreet, in his second first-class match, was given the captaincy ahead of him at Adelaide. Slater withdrew from that match, but his own record of 194 runs at 24.25 suggested that his state credentials were not overwhelming.

New South Wales's only success came, of all places, in Perth, where recently they had lost in two or three days. They put out a near full-strength side (McGrath had not played for his state for two years). Pace bowler Brett Lee seized his chance, grabbed eight wickets and showed the world he was ready for the ultimate promotion. That was the last New South Wales saw of him as his international career took off. Meanwhile, Stuart MacGill's international career came to a halt; he worked hard enough, but his brand of wrist-spin did not suit a stock bowler's role. Don Nash, in his first season, enjoyed two seven-wicket returns and could be a real asset if he works on his basic fitness. New South Wales looked to a former player, Steve Rixon, to restore their fortunes. After a successful three years looking after New Zealand, he signed a two-year contract to coach his old team, replacing Steve Small.

FIRST-CLASS AVERAGES, 1999-2000

BATTING

(Qualification: 500 runs)

	M	I	NO	R	HS	100s	Avge
R. T. Ponting (*Tas*)	7	11	3	582	197	3	72.75
M. T. G. Elliott (*Vic*)	10	19	4	1,028	183*	4	68.53
J. L. Langer (*WA*)	10	17	0	1,108	223	5	65.17
D. S. Lehmann (*SA*)	10	20	2	1,142	149	7	63.44

	M	I	NO	R	HS	100s	Avge
A. C. Gilchrist (*WA*)	7	11	2	537	149*	1	59.66
D. R. Martyn (*WA*)	5	10	1	534	169	1	59.33
A. Symonds (*Qld*)	9	14	2	710	161	3	59.16
M. G. Bevan (*NSW*)	7	14	3	613	132	2	55.72
J. Cox (*Tas*)	11	19	1	967	245	4	53.72
M. E. Hussey (*WA*)	10	18	1	874	172*	3	51.41
M. L. Love (*Qld*)	12	18	2	792	228	3	49.50
I. J. Harvey (*Vic*)	9	15	4	543	107	1	49.36
R. J. Campbell (*WA*)	10	18	0	885	203	2	49.16
M. P. Mott (*Vic*)	11	20	2	841	148	2	46.72
D. A. Fitzgerald (*SA*)	11	22	1	935	159	5	44.52
M. J. Di Venuto (*Tas*)	11	18	0	793	136	1	44.05
J. L. Arnberger (*Vic*)	11	22	2	869	214	2	43.45
B. A. Johnson (*SA*)	11	22	7	637	104	2	42.46
D. J. Marsh (*Tas*)	11	18	1	698	157	3	41.05
S. G. Law (*Qld*)	13	20	2	713	129	2	39.61
M. L. Hayden (*Qld*)	10	18	3	573	128	2	38.20
M. J. Slater (*NSW*)	10	18	1	642	169	1	37.76
D. F. Hills (*Tas*)	10	18	1	628	139	1	36.94
J. A. Dykes (*Tas*)	10	16	0	589	153	2	36.81
G. S. Blewett (*SA*)	12	22	1	723	89	0	34.42
B. J. Haddin (*NSW*)	11	21	1	643	86	0	32.15
J. P. Maher (*Qld*)	13	25	7	508	102*	1	28.22

* *Signifies not out.*

BOWLING

(Qualification: 20 wickets)

	O	M	R	W	BB	5W/i	Avge
M. S. Kasprowicz (*Qld*)	247.3	69	706	49	5-32	4	14.40
P. R. Reiffel (*Vic*)	425.2	118	982	59	5-65	1	16.64
G. D. McGrath (*Australia*)	247	71	641	32	5-48	2	20.03
A. J. Bichel (*Qld*)	479.4	143	1,207	60	6-45	2	20.11
B. Lee (*NSW*)	313.3	78	892	44	5-47	1	20.27
A. C. Dale (*Qld*)	399.2	128	927	44	5-54	3	21.06
I. J. Harvey (*Vic*)	325.2	95	824	37	5-53	1	22.27
D. W. Fleming (*Australia*)	234	54	680	30	5-30	2	22.66
B. A. Williams (*WA*)	365.4	94	1,151	50	6-74	5	23.02
P. Wilson (*SA*)	428.4	123	1,063	44	6-106	2	24.15
B. A. Swain (*SA*)	231.1	70	610	25	4-37	0	24.40
S. A. Muller (*Qld*)	330	83	945	37	4-68	0	25.54
M. W. H. Inness (*Vic*)	294	77	829	31	6-70	2	26.74
J. Angel (*WA*)	243.3	65	697	26	6-64	1	26.80
D. A. Nash (*NSW*)	254	63	743	27	7-54	2	27.51
S. R. Cary (*WA*)	292.1	98	734	25	4-70	0	29.36
M. A. Anderson (*Qld*)	221.4	60	658	21	4-50	0	31.33
D. J. Saker (*Vic*)	276.4	76	787	25	4-37	0	31.48
A. G. Downton (*Tas*)	250.3	65	786	24	6-56	2	32.75
M. W. Ridgway (*Tas*)	331	85	1,012	30	6-38	1	33.73
P. E. McIntyre (*SA*)	249.2	54	811	24	5-55	1	33.79
S. K. Warne (*Australia*)	257	72	705	20	5-110	1	35.25
S. C. G. MacGill (*NSW*)	366.1	60	1,351	36	4-42	0	37.52
B. E. Young (*SA*)	463.4	114	1,433	31	6-85	2	46.22

PURA MILK CUP, 1999-2000

	Played	Won	Lost	Drawn	1st-inns Points	Points	Quotient
Queensland	10	8	1	1	0	48	1.386
Victoria	10	6	2	2	0	36	1.290
Western Australia . . .	10	4	4	2	6	30	1.125
South Australia.	10	3	5	2	6	24	0.948
Tasmania	10	2	4	4	6	18	0.968
New South Wales . . .	10	1	8	1	0	5.6*	0.657

* 0.4 points deducted for slow over-rate.
Outright win = 6 pts; lead on first innings in a drawn or lost game = 2 pts.
Quotient = runs per wicket scored divided by runs per wicket conceded.

Final: Queensland drew with Victoria, but took the Pura Milk Cup by virtue of heading the table.

Under Australian Cricket Board playing conditions, one extra is scored for every no-ball or wide bowled whether scored off or not. Any runs scored off the bat are credited to the batsman, while byes and leg-byes are counted as no-balls, in accordance with Law 24.9, in addition to the initial penalty.

Full scores, match reports and statistics of the 1999-2000 Australian season can be found in *Wisden Cricketers' Almanack Australia 2000-01.*

In the following scores, * by the name of a team indicates that they won the toss.

At Perth, October 14, 15, 16, 17. Drawn. Victoria 295 (M. T. G. Elliott 80, M. P. Mott 101, Extras 30; B. A. Williams six for 74) and 303 for four dec. (J. L. Arnberger 57, M. T. G. Elliott 37, M. P. Mott 89, B. J. Hodge 69 not out, I. J. Harvey 31); Western Australia* 299 for nine dec. (M. E. Hussey 80, R. M. Baker 33, M. G. Dighton 77, G. B. Hogg 35; P. R. Reiffel four for 65) and 196 for five (R. J. Campbell 57, R. M. Baker 77 not out; I. J. Harvey three for 29). *Western Australia 2 pts.*
Western Australian captain Brendon Julian took his 400th first-class wicket on the opening day. Williams returned career-best figures on debut for WA against his old team, Victoria, but was later fined $A300 for verbal abuse of a batsman.

At Brisbane, October 19, 20, 21, 22. Queensland won by nine wickets. Queensland 473 for eight dec. (J. P. Maher 31, M. L. Love 228, S. G. Law 39, G. I. Foley 90; B. Lee three for 95, S. Lee four for 87) and 81 for one (J. P. Maher 31 not out); New South Wales* 242 (G. J. Hayne 40, S. Lee 32, G. J. Mail 62, B. J. Haddin 33, B. Lee 34; S. A. Muller three for 34) and 311 (G. J. Hayne 41, C. J. Richards 54, S. Lee 98, B. J. Haddin 54; A. J. Bichel three for 76, S. A. Muller four for 68). *Queensland 6 pts.*
After Matthew Hayden was out to the first ball of the match – c S. Lee b B. Lee – Love scored 228 in 591 minutes and 444 balls, including 21 fours.

At Adelaide, October 21, 22, 23, 24. Victoria won by nine wickets. South Australia* 353 for seven dec. (D. A. Fitzgerald 159, C. J. Davies 40, B. A. Johnson 102 not out) and 220 for five dec. (D. A. Fitzgerald 84, J. M. Vaughan 70); Victoria 287 (M. T. G. Elliott 50, J. L. Arnberger 57, B. J. Hodge 30, D. S. Berry 44; M. A. Harrity three for 68, P. E. McIntyre three for 72) and 287 for one (J. L. Arnberger 123 not out, M. T. G. Elliott 137). *Victoria 6 pts, South Australia 2 pts.*
Set 287 in 79 overs, Victoria won inside 65. Arnberger and Elliott opened with 242 in 210 minutes.

At Perth, October 22, 23, 24, 25. Drawn. Tasmania* 467 for seven dec. (J. Cox 78, M. J. Di Venuto 74, J. A. Dykes 123, S. P. Kremerskothen 82 not out, Extras 58); Western Australia 220 (M. G. Dighton 41, S. M. Katich 55, B. P. Julian 40; M. W. Ridgway three for 49, D. J. Marsh four for six) and 313 for six (M. E. Hussey 112, R. J. Campbell 32, J. L. Langer 36, S. M. Katich 41, B. P. Julian 36 not out, M. J. Nicholson 38 not out; M. W. Ridgway four for 71). *Tasmania 2 pts.*

Debutant Scott Kremerskothen batted more than four hours, adding 157 with Dykes, a Tasmanian sixth-wicket record v Western Australia. Colin Miller withdrew from Tasmania's squad as he tried to secure a transfer to Victoria.

At Sydney, October 27, 28, 29, 30. Drawn. South Australia* 339 (D. S. Lehmann 121, B. A. Johnson 41, B. E. Young 114 not out; S. C. G. MacGill three for 78) and 194 (D. A. Fitzgerald 52, J. D. Siddons 40; B. Lee three for 59, S. Lee four for 35); New South Wales 268 (M. J. Slater 59, M. G. Bevan 77, B. J. Haddin 86; P. Wilson four for 38, P. E. McIntyre three for 38) and 143 for four (G. J. Hayne 33, M. G. Bevan 39 not out). *South Australia 2 pts.*

Both captains, Bevan and Lehmann, arrived back from Harare on the first morning. McIntyre ended New South Wales's first innings with three wickets in five balls.

At Hobart, November 5, 6, 7, 8. Drawn. Tasmania 153 (M. J. Di Venuto 44, D. J. Marsh 35; A. J. Bichel four for 47, A. C. Dale three for 54) and 183 (S. Young 103; A. J. Bichel six for 45, A. C. Dale three for 48); Queensland* 133 (D. G. Wright three for 45, M. W. Ridgway three for 40) and seven for no wkt. *Tasmania 2 pts.*

In Tasmania's second innings, No. 10 Gerard Denton took 93 minutes to get off the mark; Bichel returned career-best figures.

At Adelaide, November 18, 19, 20, 21. South Australia won by two runs. South Australia* 309 (D. S. Lehmann 120, J. D. Siddons 40; J. Angel three for 61, B. J. Oldroyd three for 71) and 195 (D. J. Harris 31, D. A. Fitzgerald 44, J. D. Siddons 39; B. A. Williams five for 49); Western Australia 314 for nine dec. (M. E. Hussey 67, R. J. Campbell 37, D. R. Martyn 59, G. B. Hogg 61 not out; B. E. Young four for 75) and 188 (S. M. Katich 31, D. R. Martyn 40; P. E. McIntyre five for 55). *South Australia 6 pts, Western Australia 2 pts.*

Lehmann hit his 40th first-class hundred. Chasing 191 to win, Western Australia collapsed from 129 for two, losing their last eight wickets for 59.

At Richmond, November 18, 19, 20, 21. Victoria won by six wickets. Victoria* 427 for two dec. (M. T. G. Elliott 183 not out, J. L. Arnberger 214) and 155 for four (M. P. Mott 36, L. D. Harper 70); Tasmania 244 (M. J. Di Venuto 54, J. A. Dykes 36, M. N. Atkinson 49 not out, D. G. Wright 35; P. R. Reiffel four for 43) and 334 (M. J. Di Venuto 45, D. J. Marsh 134; P. R. Reiffel four for 57). *Victoria 6 pts.*

Transferred to Punt Road Oval, Richmond, because Australia had played Brazil at soccer at the MCG the previous day. Arnberger's 214 lasted 391 minutes and 315 balls and included 31 fours and one six; he and Elliott, who passed 8,000 first-class runs, opened with 353, the fourth-highest opening partnership in Sheffield Shield/Pura Milk Cup cricket; they reached 320 on the first day.

At Sydney, November 19, 20, 21. Queensland won by ten wickets. Queensland* 291 (M. L. Hayden 101, J. P. Maher 44, W. A. Seccombe 47, M. S. Kasprowicz 37; B. Lee three for 77, G. R. Robertson three for 70, S. C. G. MacGill three for 70) and 17 for no wkt; New South Wales 131 (A. J. Bichel three for 49, M. S. Kasprowicz four for 31) and 176 (G. J. Mail 39, G. R. Robertson 30; M. S. Kasprowicz five for 68). *Queensland 6 pts.*

Hayden's 40th first-class hundred set up victory in just over two days.

At Melbourne, December 1, 2, 3, 4. Victoria won by 11 runs. Victoria* 292 (I. J. Harvey 107, D. S. Berry 83; B. A. Williams five for 79, S. R. Cary three for 60) and 169 (G. R. Vimpani 34, M. P. Mott 62 not out, I. J. Harvey 31; B. A. Williams four for 35, J. Angel four for 37); Western Australia 286 (M. E. Hussey 53, R. J. Campbell 59, D. R. Martyn 72, R. M. Baker 37, G. B. Hogg 32 not out; P. R. Reiffel three for 39, J. M. Davison three for 84) and 164 (R. J. Campbell 37, M. G. Dighton 36, D. R. Martyn 34; D. J. Saker four for 37, I. J. Harvey four for 44). *Victoria 6 pts.*

As in their previous game, Western Australia were 129 for two in the run-chase; this time, needing 176, they lost their last eight wickets for 35.

At Hobart, December 2, 3, 4, 5. Drawn. Tasmania 315 (J. Cox 154, C. R. Miller 32, Extras 30; P. Wilson four for 74, B. A. Swain three for 73) and 328 for eight dec. (D. F. Hills 93, M. J. Di Venuto 56, D. J. Marsh 45, M. N. Atkinson 37 not out); South Australia* 320 for four dec. (G. S. Blewett 82, D. A. Fitzgerald 114, D. S. Lehmann 101 not out) and 198 for six (D. S. Lehmann 113; D. G. Wright three for 75, C. R. Miller three for 33). *South Australia 2 pts.*

Jamie Siddons took his 200th first-class catch. Lehmann made a century in each innings, his fourth and fifth in four matches.

At Sydney, December 9, 10, 11, 12. Tasmania won by 101 runs. Tasmania* 226 (M. J. Di Venuto 76, S. P. Kremerskothen 42, D. G. Wright 45; D. A. Nash seven for 54) and 259 (J. A. Dykes 41, D. J. Marsh 104, M. N. Atkinson 39 not out; B. Lee three for 20, M. G. Bevan three for 40); New South Wales 138 (B. J. Haddin 57; M. W. Ridgway four for 28, D. J. Marsh three for 12) and 246 (G. J. Mail 40, M. J. Clarke 65, G. R. Robertson 67 not out; A. G. Downton six for 56). *Tasmania 6 pts.*

Tasmania were 13 for five on the first day; Nash took seven for 54 in his fifth match. New South Wales were 40 for six in their first innings; in the second, Downton took six for 56 on competition debut.

At Brisbane, December 9, 10, 11, 12. Queensland won by ten wickets. Western Australia 171 (D. R. Martyn 92; A. C. Dale five for 54) and 244 (D. R. Martyn 41, D. J. Wates 62; A. C. Dale five for 81, S. A. Muller three for 41); Queensland* 412 (M. L. Hayden 59, A. Symonds 158, G. I. Foley 39, W. A. Seccombe 31, Extras 56; B. A. Williams five for 86, S. R. Cary three for 81) and four for no wkt. *Queensland 6 pts.*

Wates's first ball in first-class cricket was a no-ball; he dismissed Martin Love with his next, and rounded off his debut with a half-century.

At Melbourne, December 9, 10, 11, 12. Victoria won by 203 runs. Victoria 169 (J. L. Arnberger 60, D. S. Berry 33; B. A. Swain four for 37, B. E. Young five for 24) and 304 for eight dec. (J. L. Arnberger 65, M. T. G. Elliott 56, M. P. Mott 44, L. D. Harper 47; M. A. Harrity three for 68); South Australia* 127 (D. S. Lehmann 46; P. R. Reiffel three for 41) and 143 (G. A. Manou 36, D. S. Lehmann 47; D. J. Saker three for 27, I. J. Harvey four for 38). *Victoria 6 pts.*

Lehmann passed 9,000 Sheffield Shield/Pura Milk Cup runs. Victoria completed their fourth successive win, their best run for 20 years.

At Brisbane, December 17, 18, 19. Queensland won by 121 runs. Queensland 189 (M. L. Hayden 38, S. G. Law 30, A. Symonds 59; P. R. Reiffel four for 42, I. J. Harvey five for 53) and 147 (W. A. Seccombe 31; P. R. Reiffel four for 38, M. L. Lewis three for 36); Victoria* 112 (D. S. Berry 30 not out; A. C. Dale four for 44, M. S. Kasprowicz three for 27) and 103 (I. J. Harvey 34 not out; A. J. Bichel four for 36, M. S. Kasprowicz three for 21). *Queensland 6 pts.*

Queensland wicket-keeper Seccombe made his 250th dismissal. The match effectively took two days, as the second day was washed out.

At Perth, December 17, 18, 19, 20. New South Wales won by 115 runs. New South Wales* 182 (M. J. Slater 38, M. G. Bevan 75; J. Angel three for 44, M. J. Nicholson four for 42) and 409 (S. R. Waugh 128, M. G. Bevan 119 not out, S. Lee 45; J. Angel four for 133, S. R. Cary four for 85); Western Australia 312 (R. J. Campbell 66, J. L. Langer 78, B. P. Julian 30, G. B. Hogg 39; B. Lee four for 84, S. Lee three for 37) and 164 (R. J. Campbell 58, A. C. Gilchrist 45; B. Lee four for 55, S. C. G. MacGill four for 42). *New South Wales 6 pts, Western Australia 2 pts.*

New South Wales's only win of the season. Set 280 in 82 overs, Western Australia were all out inside 41; Angel retired hurt after a ball from Brett Lee broke his forearm.

At Adelaide, January 6, 7, 8, 9. South Australia won by 78 runs. South Australia* 253 (D. A. Fitzgerald 47, C. J. Davies 69, G. A. Manou 78; D. A. Nash seven for 72) and 274 (D. A. Fitzgerald 102, J. D. Siddons 58, B. A. Johnson 44; D. A. Nash four for 61, G. R. Robertson four for 77); New South Wales 248 (G. J. Mail 58, M. J. Phelps 71; P. Wilson four for 61, B. A. Swain three for 29) and 201 (M. J. Phelps 54, S. D. Bradstreet 42, B. J. Haddin 43; B. E. Young six for 85). *South Australia 6 pts.*

Slater withdrew after Bradstreet was named New South Wales captain.

At Albion, January 14, 15, 16. Queensland won by an innings and 80 runs. Tasmania 130 (M. J. Di Venuto 38; M. S. Kasprowicz five for 56, S. A. Muller three for 31) and 155 (J. Cox 47, M. J. Di Venuto 50; A. J. Bichel three for 46, M. S. Kasprowicz five for 32); Queensland* 365 (S. G. Law 53, C. T. Perren 153, G. I. Foley 75; C. R. Miller three for 86, A. G. Downton three for 72). *Queensland 6 pts.*

Cox passed 10,000 first-class runs.

At Perth, January 14, 15, 16, 17. Western Australia won by three wickets. South Australia 330 (G. S. Blewett 42, J. D. Siddons 31, C. J. Davies 53, B. E. Young 55, P. Wilson 32 not out, Extras 47; B. A. Williams three for 84, S. R. Cary four for 70) and 317 (G. S. Blewett 76, D. S. Lehmann 43, B. A. Johnson 104, M. J. Smith 45; M. J. Nicholson three for 59, G. G. Swan five for 54); Western Australia* 392 (M. E. Hussey 172 not out, R. J. Campbell 32, J. L. Langer 120; P. Wilson five for 71) and 256 for seven (J. L. Langer 77, M. J. North 60, M. J. Nicholson 30 not out). _Western Australia 6 pts._

Hussey carried his bat through Western Australia's first innings. This was Siddons's final first-class match. He finished with 11,587 runs at 44.91 in 160 matches, with 206 catches.

At Hobart, January 27, 28, 29, 30. Tasmania won by ten wickets. New South Wales 84 (S. D. Bradstreet 30; M. W. Ridgway six for 38, C. R. Miller four for 24) and 496 (G. J. Mail 30, M. J. Slater 44, C. J. Richards 111, M. J. Phelps 192, M. J. Clarke 73; A. G. Downton four for 123); Tasmania* 510 for five dec. (J. Cox 245, M. J. Di Venuto 136, J. A. Dykes 35, Extras 35) and 74 for no wkt (D. F. Hills 47 not out). _Tasmania 6 pts._

Cox's 245, his third and highest double-hundred, lasted 496 minutes and 391 balls and included 28 fours and one six; he and Di Venuto added 294 in 290 minutes, a Tasmanian second-wicket record. Stuart MacGill was fined $A500 for dissent and crude language.

At Melbourne, January 27, 28, 29, 30. Queensland won by nine wickets. Victoria 222 (J. L. Arnberger 81; M. S. Kasprowicz four for 49, A. A. Noffke four for 46) and 266 (M. T. G. Elliott 88, L. D. Harper 58, M. P. Mott 34; M. S. Kasprowicz four for 65); Queensland* 455 (M. L. Hayden 83, M. L. Love 52, G. I. Foley 56, W. A. Seccombe 151, M. S. Kasprowicz 50; M. W. H. Inness three for 102, M. L. Lewis four for 101) and 37 for one. _Queensland 6 pts._

Victorian wicket-keeper Darren Berry reached 450 first-class dismissals.

At Hobart, February 8, 9, 10, 11. Western Australia won by 125 runs. Western Australia* 457 for nine dec. (M. E. Hussey 43, J. L. Langer 37, D. R. Martyn 169, S. M. Katich 73, M. J. Nicholson 39; C. R. Miller four for 109) and 280 for four dec. (R. J. Campbell 111, J. L. Langer 129); Tasmania 351 for four dec. (D. F. Hills 139, J. Cox 66, M. J. Di Venuto 91, D. J. Marsh 30 not out) and 261 (D. F. Hills 52, J. Cox 101, D. J. Marsh 34, S. Young 32; G. B. Hogg four for 56). _Western Australia 6 pts._

Langer reached 1,000 runs for the season, in his tenth match.

At Adelaide, February 9, 10, 11. Queensland won by eight wickets. Queensland* 345 (J. P. Maher 55, M. L. Love 56, S. G. Law 54, A. Symonds 49, A. J. Bichel 34 not out, A. C. Dale 48; G. S. Blewett three for 47) and 99 for two; South Australia 146 (B. A. Johnson 47 not out; A. J. Bichel three for 32, M. S. Kasprowicz five for 42) and 297 (G. S. Blewett 86, D. S. Lehmann 58, Extras 38; M. S. Kasprowicz three for 70, A. J. Bichel three for 41). _Queensland 6 pts._

Queensland won their sixth successive victory in the competition, their seventh in first-class cricket. Seccombe made his 50th dismissal of the season in his tenth match.

At Sydney, February 10, 11, 12, 13. Victoria won by 148 runs. Victoria* 435 for six dec. (M. T. G. Elliott 48, J. L. Arnberger 46, M. P. Mott 148, B. J. Hodge 61, I. J. Harvey 57 not out; S. C. G. MacGill four for 156) and 178 (M. T. G. Elliott 32, M. P. Mott 77, M. Klinger 35; J. M. Heath three for 37, S. C. G. MacGill three for 34); New South Wales 349 (M. G. Bevan 132, M. J. Clarke 75, B. J. Haddin 58, Extras 32; P. R. Reiffel four for 74, I. J. Harvey four for 103) and 116 (M. G. Bevan 44 not out; P. R. Reiffel three for 23). _Victoria 6 pts._

Only nine wickets fell over the first two days, but 16 on the last.

At Adelaide, March 2, 3, 4, 5. South Australia won by 99 runs. South Australia* 502 for five dec. (D. A. Fitzgerald 128, S. A. Deitz 85, D. S. Lehmann 149, B. A. Johnson 65 not out) and 178 for six dec. (D. A. Fitzgerald 50, C. J. Davies 50); Tasmania 337 (D. F. Hills 63, J. Cox 38, M. J. Di Venuto 30, D. J. Marsh 72, M. N. Atkinson 30 not out, M. W. Ridgway 30; P. Wilson four for 43) and 244 (D. F. Hills 50, M. J. Di Venuto 61, M. N. Atkinson 36; B. E. Young three for 36). _South Australia 6 pts._

Lehmann reached 1,000 runs for the season, in nine matches, during his sixth hundred. Jason Gillespie of South Australia bowled for the first time since breaking his leg in Sri Lanka, and took two wickets in each innings.

At Richmond, March 2, 3, 4. Victoria won by ten wickets. New South Wales* 148 (G. J. Mail 35; P. R. Reiffel four for 33, M. W. H. Inness five for 38) and 290 (G. J. Mail 97, C. J. Richards 76, M. J. Clarke 45; P. R. Reiffel three for 67, M. W. H. Inness six for 70); Victoria 410 for eight dec. (M. T. G. Elliott 101 not out, M. P. Mott 65, L. D. Harper 92, D. S. Berry 106; M. A. Higgs three for 59) and 30 for no wkt. *Victoria 6 pts.*

Transferred from the MCG because of a rugby league game. Inness took a hat-trick in New South Wales's second innings.

At Perth, March 2, 3, 4. Western Australia won by an innings and 257 runs. Western Australia 558 for nine dec. (M. E. Hussey 33, R. J. Campbell 203, M. G. Dighton 182 not out, M. J. Walsh 50, M. J. Nicholson 39; A. C. Dale four for 120); Queensland* 173 (M. L. Love 44, G. I. Foley 38; J. Angel three for 56, B. A. Williams five for 38) and 128 (S. G. Law 68; S. R. Cary three for 14, B. A. Williams three for 34, M. J. Nicholson three for 37). *Western Australia 6 pts.*

Queensland's only first-class defeat of the season. Campbell's 203 lasted 302 minutes and 222 balls and included 27 fours and two sixes.

At Sydney, March 9, 10, 11, 12. Western Australia won by an innings and 34 runs. New South Wales* 255 (G. J. Mail 37, M. J. Clarke 58, B. J. Haddin 67; J. Angel six for 64) and 149 (M. G. Bevan 49; G. B. Hogg five for 53, M. J. North three for 23); Western Australia 438 for seven dec. (M. E. Hussey 172, R. J. Campbell 93, S. M. Katich 76, M. J. Nicholson 32 not out). *Western Australia 6 pts.*

Angel returned career-best figures before leaving to attend his wife in childbirth. Brad Williams reached 50 wickets for the season, in his tenth match.

At Albion, March 9, 10, 11, 12. Queensland won by 56 runs. Queensland* 290 for nine dec. (T. J. Dixon 30, A. Symonds 140 not out, A. C. Dale 35) and 158 for five dec. (J. P. Maher 102 not out, W. A. Seccombe 30 not out); South Australia 175 for six dec. (S. A. Deitz 45, D. S. Lehmann 104; A. J. Bichel four for 44) and 217 (S. A. Deitz 85, J. M. Vaughan 56; M. A. Anderson three for 79). *Queensland 6 pts.*

Lehmann scored his seventh hundred of the season; Bichel reached 50 wickets, in his 12th match.

At Hobart, March 9, 10, 11, 12. Drawn. Victoria 279 for nine dec. (M. P. Mott 61, I. J. Harvey 92, P. R. Reiffel 46 not out; D. G. Wright three for 53, D. J. Marsh three for 24) and 477 for five (J. L. Arnberger 45, M. T. G. Elliott 100, M. P. Mott 86, B. J. Hodge 96, L. D. Harper 92, I. J. Harvey 78 not out); Tasmania* 421 (J. A. Dykes 153, S. Young 106, M. N. Atkinson 62, Extras 34; P. R. Reiffel four for 79, D. J. Saker three for 98). *Tasmania 2 pts.*

Reiffel reached 50 wickets for the season, in his tenth match.

FINAL

QUEENSLAND v VICTORIA

At Albion, March 17, 18, 19, 20, 21. Drawn. Toss: Queensland.

A forgettable final produced the draw that leaders Queensland needed to win the cup. With the Gabba being spruced up for the Olympic soccer tournament, the teams played on a slow pitch and heavy outfield at Allan Border Field. Nearly 16,000 spectators attended, but rarely saw the scoring-rate rise above two an over before bad light ended play midway through the final day.

Victorians had little to cheer after the first afternoon, when Queensland were struggling at 111 for five. Then Law, aided by Seccombe, began to turn things round. He survived a passionate appeal for a catch at the wicket just before the close, and eventually batted for nearly seven and a half hours of stern attrition before he was last out. Queensland's pace bowlers made short work of Victoria; Bichel especially revelled in the conditions and gave the keeper, Seccombe, a feast of chances. Trailing by 103, Victoria were frustrated when a number of close decisions went against them in Queensland's second innings. For Saker, it was all too much when umpire Hair turned down an lbw appeal; he was fined $A1,950 for dissent plus "crude and abusive language". Law and Love, meanwhile, batted relentlessly for more than five hours to add 174 for the third wicket. Victorian captain Reiffel took nine wickets in all, but his opposite number, Law, deservedly claimed the match award.

Man of the Match: S. G. Law.

Close of play: First day, Queensland 198-5 (Law 77*, Seccombe 44*); Second day, Victoria 94-6 (Harvey 20*, Reiffel 0*); Third day, Queensland 105-2 (Love 46*, Law 35*); Fourth day, Queensland 274-7 (Bichel 8*, Dale 9*).

Queensland

J. P. Maher c Elliott b Reiffel	2	– lbw b Reiffel	2
T. J. Dixon c Berry b Inness	14	– lbw b Harvey	21
M. L. Love c Elliott b Reiffel	32	– c Berry b Saker	100
*S. G. Law c and b Reiffel	129	– b Mott	84
A. Symonds c Elliott b Reiffel	0	– c Harper b Mott	18
G. I. Foley c and b Inness	9	– c Elliott b Reiffel	16
†W. A. Seccombe c Hodge b Inness	49	– c Berry b Reiffel	3
A. J. Bichel c Arnberger b Reiffel	1	– b Saker	8
A. C. Dale c Mott b Saker	18	– hit wkt b Reiffel	42
S. A. Muller c Arnbergher b Inness	6	– lbw b Mott	20
M. A. Anderson not out	0	– not out	7
B 4, l-b 6, n-b 15	25	L-b 7, w 2, n-b 13	22

1/4 2/32 3/82 4/82 5/111   285
6/215 7/216 8/242 9/280

1/6 2/39 3/213 4/222 5/239   343
6/252 7/257 8/285 9/326

Bowling: *First Innings*—Reiffel 29.4–8–65–5; Inness 33–7–73–4; Saker 26–6–67–1; Harvey 26–8–53–0; Davison 10–4–17–0. *Second Innings*—Reiffel 40–11–65–4; Inness 28–11–64–0; Saker 38–14–84–2; Davison 26–12–43–0; Mott 19.5–5–35–3; Harvey 9–0–29–1; Elliott 3–3–0–0; Hodge 12–4–16–0.

Victoria

M. I. O. Elliott c Seccombe b Bichel	29	– (2) not out	14
J. L. Arnberger c Love b Bichel	8	– (1) c Seccombe b Dale	9
M. P. Mott c Seccombe b Bichel	3	– not out	6
B. J. Hodge lbw b Dale	0		
L. D. Harper c Seccombe b Muller	17		
I. J. Harvey c Seccombe b Muller	50		
†D. S. Berry lbw b Bichel	9		
*P. R. Reiffel c Seccombe b Bichel	3		
D. J. Saker not out	25		
J. M. Davison lbw b Dale	19		
M. W. H. Inness c Dixon b Bichel	3		
L-b 6, n-b 10	16	W 1, n-b 1	2

1/17 2/21 3/26 4/51 5/71   182   1/12   (1 wkt) 31
6/89 7/108 8/135 9/163

Bowling: *First Innings*—Bichel 27.5–9–47–6; Dale 34–13–53–2; Muller 22–7–53–2; Anderson 2–1–1–0; Symonds 3–0–22–0. *Second Innings*—Bichel 6–4–6–0; Dale 8.1–2–20–1; Muller 3–0–5–0.

Umpires: S. J. Davis and D. B. Hair.

CHAMPIONS

Sheffield Shield

1892-93	Victoria
1893-94	South Australia
1894-95	Victoria
1895-96	New South Wales
1896-97	New South Wales
1897-98	Victoria
1898-99	Victoria
1899-1900	New South Wales
1900-01	Victoria
1901-02	New South Wales
1902-03	New South Wales
1903-04	New South Wales
1904-05	New South Wales
1905-06	New South Wales
1906-07	New South Wales
1907-08	Victoria
1908-09	New South Wales
1909-10	South Australia
1910-11	New South Wales
1911-12	New South Wales
1912-13	South Australia
1913-14	New South Wales
1914-15	Victoria
1915-19	No competition
1919-20	New South Wales
1920-21	New South Wales
1921-22	Victoria
1922-23	New South Wales
1923-24	Victoria
1924-25	Victoria
1925-26	New South Wales
1926-27	South Australia
1927-28	Victoria
1928-29	New South Wales
1929-30	Victoria
1930-31	Victoria
1931-32	New South Wales
1932-33	New South Wales
1933-34	Victoria
1934-35	Victoria
1935-36	South Australia
1936-37	Victoria
1937-38	New South Wales
1938-39	South Australia
1939-40	New South Wales
1940-46	No competition
1946-47	Victoria
1947-48	Western Australia
1948-49	New South Wales
1949-50	New South Wales
1950-51	Victoria

1951-52	New South Wales
1952-53	South Australia
1953-54	New South Wales
1954-55	New South Wales
1955-56	New South Wales
1956-57	New South Wales
1957-58	New South Wales
1958-59	New South Wales
1959-60	New South Wales
1960-61	New South Wales
1961-62	New South Wales
1962-63	Victoria
1963-64	South Australia
1964-65	New South Wales
1965-66	New South Wales
1966-67	Victoria
1967-68	Western Australia
1968-69	South Australia
1969-70	Victoria
1970-71	South Australia
1971-72	Western Australia
1972-73	Western Australia
1973-74	Victoria
1974-75	Western Australia
1975-76	South Australia
1976-77	Western Australia
1977-78	Western Australia
1978-79	Victoria
1979-80	Victoria
1980-81	Western Australia
1981-82	South Australia
1982-83	New South Wales
1983-84	Western Australia
1984-85	New South Wales
1985-86	New South Wales
1986-87	Western Australia
1987-88	Western Australia
1988-89	Western Australia
1989-90	New South Wales
1990-91	Victoria
1991-92	Western Australia
1992-93	New South Wales
1993-94	New South Wales
1994-95	Queensland
1995-96	South Australia
1996-97	Queensland
1997-98	Western Australia
1998-99	Western Australia

Pura Milk Cup

1999-2000	Queensland

New South Wales have won the title 42 times, Victoria 25, Western Australia 15, South Australia 13, Queensland 3, Tasmania 0.

MERCANTILE MUTUAL CUP, 1999-2000

One-day 50-over tournament between the six first-class states and Australian Capital Territory. The top four in the league qualified for the semi-finals. Teams included 12 players, one of whom was not allowed to bat; only 11 players were allowed to field at any time. The ACT team was dropped from the competition in 2000-01.

Note: Matches in this section were not first-class.

At North Sydney, October 10. Victoria won by seven wickets. New South Wales* 240 for six (50 overs) (C. J. Richards 75, M. G. Bevan 41, G. C. Rummans 45, Extras 30); Victoria 241 for three (47.5 overs) (M. T. G. Elliott 103, G. R. Vimpani 92).

At Adelaide, October 17. Tasmania won by six wickets. South Australia 235 for seven (50 overs) (J. D. Siddons 102, B. A. Johnson 65 not out; D. G. Wright three for 29); Tasmania* 238 for four (46.5 overs) (J. Cox 48, S. Young 64, D. J. Marsh 78 not out).

At Brisbane, October 24. New South Wales won by four wickets. Queensland* 247 for nine (50 overs) (J. P. Maher 87, M. L. Hayden 104; S. Lee three for 45, S. C. G. MacGill three for 45); New South Wales 250 for six (46 overs) (G. C. Rummans 67, S. Lee 112).

At Sydney, October 31. New South Wales v South Australia. Abandoned.

At Brisbane, November 12 (day/night). Western Australia won by four wickets. Queensland* 260 for eight (50 overs) (M. L. Hayden 98, J. P. Maher 62); Western Australia 264 for six (41.3 overs) (A. C. Gilchrist 115, S. M. Katich 42, B. P. Julian 38, R. M. Baker 31 not out).

At Richmond, November 13. Victoria won by 18 runs. Victoria 259 for eight (50 overs) (B. J. Hodge 110, I. J. Harvey 47; A. M. Stuart three for 51); Australian Capital Territory* 241 (48.4 overs) (A. D. McQuire 58, G. T. Cunningham 72, C. M. Smart 44; I. J. Harvey five for 34).

At North Sydney, November 14. New South Wales won by 21 runs. New South Wales 277 for nine (50 overs) (M. J. Slater 45, C. J. Richards 70, M. G. Bevan 46, S. Lee 46, G. C. Rummans 37; G. J. Denton three for 53); Tasmania* 256 for eight (50 overs) (J. Cox 54, S. Young 33, D. J. Marsh 30, D. F. Hills 49 not out).

At Adelaide, November 26 (day/night). South Australia won by 93 runs. South Australia* 287 for three (50 overs) (D. S. Lehmann 36, D. A. Fitzgerald 114, C. J. Davies 57, J. D. Siddons 57 not out); Victoria 194 (41.1 overs) (G. R. Vimpani 38, B. J. Hodge 38, L. D. Harper 61; B. E. Young four for 24).

At Canberra, December 4. Queensland won by 26 runs. Queensland 280 for three (50 overs) (M. L. Hayden 113, J. P. Maher 128); Australian Capital Territory* 254 (47.3 overs) (P. J. Solway 51, R. J. Tucker 85, A. M. Stuart 38).
   Hayden and Maher opened with 250, a Queensland first-wicket record in this competition.

At Melbourne, December 5. Western Australia won by 29 runs. Western Australia* 239 for five (50 overs) (R. J. Campbell 31, M. E. Hussey 100 not out, G. B. Hogg 53 not out, Extras 36; M. L. Lewis three for 51); Victoria 210 (48.3 overs) (G. R. Vimpani 87, L. D. Harper 36; S. Nikitaras three for 32, M. E. Hussey three for 52).
   Hussey and Hogg shared an unbroken stand of 173, a sixth-wicket record in this competition.

At Brisbane, December 22 (day/night). Queensland won by eight wickets. Victoria* 193 (48.2 overs) (B. J. Hodge 42, M. P. Mott 32; M. S. Kasprowicz three for 29); Queensland 194 for two (31.3 overs) (M. L. Hayden 78 not out, S. G. Law 60, A. Symonds 45 not out).

At Perth, January 7 (day/night). Western Australia won by six wickets. Australian Capital Territory* 226 for nine (50 overs) (P. J. Solway 71, R. J. Tucker 31, G. T. Cunningham 39, D. J. MacDonald

31 not out; S. Nikitaras three for 30, R. M. Baker three for 25); Western Australia 230 for four (46.3 overs) (J. L. Langer 84 not out, S. M. Katich 62).

Baker took a hat-trick for Western Australia.

At Hobart, January 9. Queensland won by 122 runs. Queensland 224 for nine (50 overs) (M. L. Love 63, W. A. Seccombe 41); Tasmania* 102 (38.4 overs) (A. J. Bichel three for 22, M. S. Kasprowicz three for 18).

At Perth, January 12 (day/night). South Australia won by 33 runs. South Australia* 302 for seven (50 overs) (D. A. Fitzgerald 52, G. S. Blewett 66, C. J. Davies 90, D. S. Lehmann 42; D. J. Wates three for 54); Western Australia 269 (46.5 overs) (J. L. Langer 146, G. B. Hogg 30).

At Canberra, January 16. New South Wales won by 118 runs (D/L method). New South Wales* 252 for nine (47 overs) (B. J. Haddin 70, M. A. Higgs 77; A. M. Stuart three for 32); Australian Capital Territory 136 (35.1 overs) (R. J. Tucker 43; D. A. Nash three for 31).

Australian Capital Territory's target was revised to 255 from 47 overs.

At Perth, January 21 (day/night). Western Australia won by six wickets (D/L method). New South Wales 249 (48 overs) (B. J. Haddin 70, M. A. Higgs 40; M. P. Atkinson four for 38, D. J. Wates three for 45); Western Australia* 246 for four (45.2 overs) (J. L. Langer 53, M. E. Hussey 81 not out, R. M. Baker 42 not out).

Western Australia's target was revised to 243 from 47 overs.

At Hobart, January 23. Tasmania won by 51 runs (D/L method). Tasmania* 241 for five (45 overs) (J. Cox 47, S. Young 89, D. J. Marsh 38); Australian Capital Territory 196 (41.5 overs) (R. J. Tucker 42; D. J. Marsh three for 47).

Australian Capital Territory's target was revised to 248 from 45 overs.

At Canberra, January 30. South Australia won by 40 runs. South Australia* 226 for seven (50 overs) (D. A. Fitzgerald 32, D. S. Lehmann 83 not out, B. A. Swain 35 not out; K. P. French three for 38); Australian Capital Territory 186 (47 overs) (A. D. McQuire 68; P. Wilson four for 23, P. E. McIntyre four for 39).

At Melbourne, February 5. Victoria won by six wickets. Tasmania* 215 (50 overs) (S. Young 54, M. J. Di Venuto 30; S. H. Cook four for 42); Victoria 217 for four (49.1 overs) (B. J. Hodge 55, M. Klinger 80 not out, M. P. Mott 55 not out).

At Hobart, February 12. Tasmania won by 46 runs (D/L method). Tasmania 233 for seven (50 overs) (D. J. Marsh 67 not out, D. F. Hills 64); Western Australia* 182 (42.4 overs) (D. R. Martyn 36, M. E. Hussey 53, G. B. Hogg 34; S. Young three for 24).

Western Australia's target was revised to 229 from 48 overs.

At Adelaide, February 13. Queensland won by nine wickets. South Australia 193 (46.4 overs) (G. S. Blewett 101 not out, B. E. Young 31; S. A. Prestwidge three for 25); Queensland* 197 for one (35.5 overs) (M. L. Hayden 120 not out, J. P. Maher 49).

Blewett carried his bat through South Australia's innings.

Western Australia 8 pts, Queensland 8 pts, New South Wales 7 pts, South Australia 7 pts, Victoria 6 pts, Tasmania 6 pts, Australian Capital Territory 0 pts.

Semi-finals

At Perth, February 19. Western Australia won by 29 runs. Western Australia 246 for seven (50 overs) (S. M. Katich 116, G. B. Hogg 36 not out); South Australia* 217 (46.4 overs) (D. S. Lehmann 85, J. M. Vaughan 31; G. B. Hogg three for 37).

At Albion, February 20. Queensland won by three wickets. New South Wales* 210 for six (50 overs) (C. J. Richards 30, G. C. Rummans 37, M. A. Higgs 74 not out); Queensland 214 for seven (46.2 overs) (S. G. Law 33, C. T. Perren 86 not out).

Final

At Perth, February 27. Western Australia won by 45 runs. Western Australia* 301 for six (50 overs) (R. J. Campbell 108, J. L. Langer 42, S. M. Katich 43, G. B. Hogg 40 not out); Queensland 256 (45.2 overs) (M. L. Love 73, J. P. Maher 102; J. Angel three for 49).

Campbell scored his 108 from 85 balls, with 14 fours and two sixes. Love and Maher opened with 186 at seven an over, then all ten Queensland wickets fell for 70 in 19 overs.

PURA MILK CUP PLAYER OF THE YEAR

The Pura Milk Cup Player of the Year award for 1999-2000 was won by Darren Lehmann of South Australia. The award, instituted in 1975-76, is adjudicated by the umpires over the course of the season. Each of the two umpires standing in each of the 30 Pura Milk Cup matches (excluding the final) allocated marks of 3, 2 and 1 to the three players who most impressed them during the game. Lehmann won $A8,000. The Mercantile Mutual Player of the Year was Matthew Hayden of Queensland, who won $A5,000.

SHEFFIELD SHIELD/PURA MILK CUP FINALS

1982-83	NEW SOUTH WALES* beat Western Australia by 54 runs.
1983-84	WESTERN AUSTRALIA beat Queensland by four wickets.
1984-85	NEW SOUTH WALES beat Queensland by one wicket.
1985-86	NEW SOUTH WALES drew with Queensland.
1986-87	WESTERN AUSTRALIA drew with Victoria.
1987-88	WESTERN AUSTRALIA beat Queensland by five wickets.
1988-89	WESTERN AUSTRALIA drew with South Australia.
1989-90	NEW SOUTH WALES beat Queensland by 345 runs.
1990-91	VICTORIA beat New South Wales by eight wickets.
1991-92	WESTERN AUSTRALIA beat New South Wales by 44 runs.
1992-93	NEW SOUTH WALES beat Queensland by eight wickets.
1993-94	NEW SOUTH WALES beat Tasmania by an innings and 61 runs.
1994-95	QUEENSLAND beat South Australia by an innings and 101 runs.
1995-96	SOUTH AUSTRALIA drew with Western Australia.
1996-97	QUEENSLAND* beat Western Australia by 160 runs.
1997-98	WESTERN AUSTRALIA beat Tasmania by seven wickets.
1998-99	WESTERN AUSTRALIA* beat Queensland by an innings and 31 runs.
1999-2000	QUEENSLAND drew with Victoria.

Note: The team that finishes top of the table has home advantage against the runners-up. A draw means the home team wins the title.

 * *Denotes victory for the away team.*

CRICKET IN SOUTH AFRICA, 1999-2000

By COLIN BRYDEN and ANDREW SAMSON

Vasbert Drakes

A successful season for South African cricket on the field was overshadowed by two events off it: the resignation of its president and the dismissal of its captain. While the first was a strictly domestic matter, the circumstances surrounding the second reverberated around the world.

Ray White resigned as president of the United Cricket Board of South Africa in January, after his ability to lead the UCB through the process of racial transformation was questioned. White later claimed the game in South Africa had become "a cesspool of self-interest and politics". Despite this upheaval in the boardroom, though, the national team led by Hansie Cronje carried on winning. Since the start of the season, they had already won a quadrangular one-day tournament in Kenya, home and away Tests against Zimbabwe, and the Test series against England. Following White's departure, they went on to claim the honours in the limited-overs series with England and Zimbabwe before achieving one of their greatest triumphs, travelling to India, unbeaten in a home Test series for 13 years, to win 2–0.

It was that Indian tour, though, that led to the discovery of South African cricket's greatest betrayal. During the one-day series which replaced what was originally scheduled to be a third Test, Cronje was taped by Indian police in telephone discussions on match-fixing with a bookmaker. The storm broke shortly after South Africa returned home, via yet another one-day tournament in Sharjah. Having initially denied any involvement with bookmakers, Cronje admitted he had been "less than honest" and that he had accepted cash from an Indian bookmaker in Johannesburg on the eve of the one-day series with England and Zimbabwe, before touring India. He was sacked just before a three-match limited-overs series against Australia, the World Cup champions; Shaun Pollock led the side to what was, in the circumstances, a surprising 2–1 win. But the crisis was only just beginning, as the King Commission set up to investigate the match-fixing allegations elicited further damaging revelations from Cronje and other witnesses. Three of these – Herschelle Gibbs, Pieter Strydom and Henry Williams, all current internationals – were suspended as a result of their testimony and ruled out of selection for South Africa's tour of Sri Lanka, Australia and Singapore in July and August.

The resignation of White could be linked directly to South African cricket's struggle to transform itself into a sport reflecting the nation's many colours and cultures. Administrators had had to juggle cricketing and political considerations, which were not always in total harmony. White was criticised by an independent transformation monitoring committee, appointed by the board, after he made personal comments about political interference when he unveiled the UCB's Transformation Charter in January 1999. He came under further fire when he backed the selection of an all-white combined Northerns/Gauteng team to play the England tourists in November, a move which seemed against the spirit of a UCB policy that provincial and representative teams should include players of colour.

Matters came to a head when Gerald Majola, a black UCB member and national selector, wrote to White expressing "dismay" at the way he had managed transformation. One issue Majola raised was the role of Dr Ali Bacher, the board's managing director. It had been decided that Bacher should step down during 2000 to concentrate on organising the 2003 World Cup. But, according to Majola, White had been behind a move to keep Bacher in charge of both the World Cup planning and the day-to-day affairs of the UCB. Majola said it was time to appoint a black chief executive to succeed Bacher.

His letter was discussed at a board meeting on January 22, after which White resigned. "It has become clear to me that my continued presence as UCB president has become divisive in terms of the administration of the game in this country," he announced. "In the interest of cricket in South Africa, which I love passionately, I have decided to step down." Within months, the UCB advertised for a managing director, making it clear they were looking for a "previously disadvantaged" person, although Bacher insisted that, initially at least, the appointee would work under his supervision. In October, it was announced that Majola would take up the appointment in January 2001.

The transformation process may also have influenced the Cronje affair. The captain had stormed out of a meeting with Bacher after the Test series against West Indies in January 1999. Bacher had said it was necessary to include more black players in the one-day squad; Cronje was adamant that caps should be won on merit alone. In September, the national selectors, under new convenor Rushdie Magiet, a former player from the "non-racial" SA Cricket Board of Control (SACBOC), named Cronje as captain for only the first half of 1999-2000. Cronje's reaction was to accept, without consulting the UCB, an invitation to coach Glamorgan in 2000, which would have prevented his joining the Test tour of Sri Lanka in July and August. With his contract expiring in April, he felt the board had offered him no job security. Bacher had to engage in frantic diplomacy to persuade Cronje to commit himself to South Africa and to extricate him from the Glamorgan deal.

In retrospect, it might have been better if the UCB had accepted what was effectively the resignation of a man who was beginning to show the strain of being South Africa's longest-serving captain. The bribery scandal brought to an abrupt and ignominious end a career in which Cronje captained South Africa in 53 Tests, winning 27, with 15 drawn and 11 lost. In one-day internationals, Cronje had 99 wins in 138 matches, with 35 defeats, one tie and three no-results.

Race was an issue in provincial cricket, too, although here the results were largely pleasing. It was the first season in which provinces were compelled to include at least one player of colour in all teams, and the transition was relatively smooth. Several provinces, notably Western Province, Boland and Eastern Province, had no difficulty in meeting the requirement. Elsewhere, black players fitted into provincial sides with varying degrees of competence. By season's end, the selectors named four players of colour in the senior team touring Sri Lanka and five to visit the West Indies with South Africa A. Age-group teams routinely included a significant number of black players, most of whom had attended traditional cricket schools in an education system recently integrated. A further sign of black cricket's progress was that black clubs won the league titles in Border and Griqualand West.

For the first time, all 11 provinces competed in a single SuperSport Series competition, with eight advancing to a Super Eight stage, similar to the Super Six in the 1999 World Cup, and the bottom three playing in a Shield competition.

Four provinces started the season with new captains, and another three finished with a change at the helm. One of the new captains was Clive Eksteen, who led Gauteng to their first first-class title since 1987-88, when the province then known as Transvaal won what was then the Currie Cup. Gauteng, consistently among the front-runners, finished top of the Super Eight league and won a hard-fought final against Border at the Wanderers. They seemed on course for a double when they headed the league stage of the 45-overs Standard Bank Cup and won the first leg of the best-of-three semi-final away to Eastern Province, only to lose the next two at home.

Ken Rutherford, the former New Zealand captain, had a splendid swansong for Gauteng, leading the competition run-scorers with 818 at 51.12, while West Indian import Kenny Benjamin added firepower to their bowling, taking 38 wickets at 15.63. Gauteng had more strength in depth than most of their rivals; batsmen Adam Bacher and Daryll Cullinan, when not required for South Africa, and all-rounder Andrew Hall had good seasons.

Border reached the SuperSport final for the second year running, and owed much to West Indian Vasbert Drakes, who set a new competition record of 60 wickets at 16.31. Captain Pieter Strydom batted well enough to earn a Test call-up at the age of 30, while Mark Boucher shone when he was not on national duty, hitting a century in the final.

Boland seemed in disarray when their coach, Hylton Ackerman, was fired early in the season after a dispute with the executive, causing a protest by the players. But they went on to have their best year yet, finishing third in the Super Eight and winning the one-day Standard Bank Cup, the first major title in their history. Well led by Louis Koen, returning to his native province after a lengthy stint with Eastern Province, Boland also benefited from the input of Andre Bruyns, their chief executive and a former Western Province captain. Seamer Henry Williams headed the national averages, and with left-armer Charl Willoughby formed an effective new-ball pair. It was to Boland's credit that they won the Cup final despite both being absent, Willoughby having been called up to join the national side in Sharjah as the replacement for Williams, who had been injured in India. The batting relied greatly on Koen and the promising Justin Ontong. The perennial problem faced by small provinces like Boland was illustrated at the end of the season when Willoughby was tempted away by neighbours Western Province. Charl Langeveldt, another talented bowler, was on the verge of signing for Northerns before deciding to stay in the winelands.

KwaZulu-Natal headed Pool B in the SuperSport first round, and carried 40 points through to the Super Eight, just one behind Border. But they did not win again, and finished fourth. The Natalians batted well, with Doug Watson and Mark Bruyns proving a prolific opening pair, backed by Andrew Hudson and Errol Stewart, who headed the national averages with 553 runs at 92.16. Their bowling lacked penetration.

Free State were unsettled. Gerhardus Liebenberg gave up the captaincy early on to concentrate on his batting; Cronje took over for a while, and Nicky Boje finished up holding the reins. One highlight came when they scored 443 to beat KwaZulu-Natal in Durban, a record fourth-innings run-chase by a provincial team, thanks to centuries from Andrew Gait and Cronje. One of the finds of the season was the fast-medium bowler, Dewald Pretorius, who made rapid strides.

Eastern Province produced some of the country's most exciting new talent. James Bryant batted superbly – 928 runs made him the season's leading scorer in all first-class cricket – as did left-handed opener Carl Bradfield on occasion. Pace bowlers Garnett Kruger and Mfuneko Ngam showed rich promise and Robin Peterson emerged as a capable left-arm spinner. The 35-year-old Dave Callaghan was the leading run-maker of the Standard Bank Cup, sweeping them into the final.

Northerns were disappointing, although they were hard hit by exceptionally heavy rain in the later season; the union's finances suffered when three days of the Fifth Test against England, plus a one-day international between England and Zimbabwe, were washed out. Neil McKenzie took over as captain and showed promise in the new role, while continuing to make substantial contributions with the bat and going on to win promotion to the national team. Peter Kirsten, the coach, resigned after the campaign, returning to Cape Town.

Western Province, the defending champions, barely scraped into the Super Eight – they had to beat fellow-stragglers North West in their final Pool B match – and finished eighth, with no other wins. They were also tenth, out of 11, in the Standard Bank Cup, and the poor performances prompted an inquiry. Vincent Barnes, the first former SACBOC player to be awarded a major provincial coaching job, had been unable to get the best out of his players and captain Craig Matthews retired. Hylton "H.D." Ackerman succeeded Matthews for 2000-01, following in the footsteps of his father, Hylton, who captained the province in the late 1970s. Meanwhile, Eric Simons, who coached Western Province B to the three-day Bowl title, was to share coaching duties with Barnes, with Peter Kirsten helping the senior batsmen in addition to coaching the B team.

Easterns, in their first SuperSport season, failed to advance to the Super Eight, but played respectable cricket with a young side, directed by their new coach, Ray Jennings, and captain Deon Jordaan, who proved a reliable batsman. Easterns came into their own in the Standard Bank Cup, reaching the semi-finals before losing to Boland.

North West batted reasonably well on the shirt-front pitches at the impressive new North West Stadium in Potchefstroom, with Glen Hewitt adapting successfully to the demands of the top league, but their bowling was innocuous. They did win the inaugural Shield competition, for those not qualifying for the Super Eight, when a daring declaration by Easterns in the deciding match backfired.

After winning the Standard Bank Cup the previous year, Griqualand West sank ignominiously. Kepler Wessels, recently appointed to the national selection panel, decided to stand down as captain after just one match, having battled in vain to overcome an old knee injury. Another international veteran, Pat Symcox, took over, but without success; he, too, retired before the season ended, handing the job to Martyn Gidley, the side's most successful batsman. The retirement of Wessels ended a 27-year career in which he scored nearly 25,000 runs at an average above 50. He played 40 Tests: 24 for Australia, while South Africa were outlawed from international cricket because of the apartheid regime, and then 16 as captain of his native country after their return in 1992. He was succeeded in 1994 by Cronje. – C.B.

FIRST-CLASS AVERAGES, 1999-2000

BATTING

(Qualification: 8 innings, average 40.00)

	M	I	NO	R	HS	100s	Avge
E. L. R. Stewart (*KwaZulu-Natal*)	8	11	5	553	151*	2	92.16
D. Jordaan (*Easterns*)	7	13	3	648	106	1	64.80
P. C. Strydom (*Border*)	10	14	2	759	125	2	63.25
L. Klusener (*KwaZulu-Natal*)	9	11	2	545	174	1	60.55
D. J. Cullinan (*Gauteng*)	12	17	1	916	135	5	57.25
B. M. McMillan (*W. Province*)	5	8	2	334	104*	1	55.66
J. D. C. Bryant (*E. Province*)	11	19	2	928	149	4	54.58
K. R. Rutherford (*Gauteng*)	10	18	2	818	195*	3	51.12
M. L. Bruyns (*KwaZulu-Natal*)	10	16	2	708	144	3	50.57
M. V. Boucher (*Border*)	10	14	2	598	112	2	49.83
G. Kirsten (*W. Province*)	9	13	1	590	275	1	49.16
N. D. McKenzie (*Northerns*)	12	19	1	861	175	2	47.83
G. M. Hewitt (*North West*)	7	13	3	476	151	1	47.60
D. J. Watson (*KwaZulu-Natal*)	10	16	2	659	220	4	47.07
J. N. Rhodes (*KwaZulu-Natal*)	6	9	1	375	124	1	46.87
J. M. Arthur (*Griqualand W.*)	7	14	1	606	128	3	46.61
J. H. Kallis (*W. Province*)	8	12	1	508	105	1	46.18
N. Pothas (*Gauteng*)	8	13	4	415	109*	1	46.11

	M	I	NO	R	HS	100s	Avge
D. M. Benkenstein (*KwaZulu-Natal*)...	10	14	3	499	84	0	45.36
L. J. Koen (*Boland*)	9	16	2	634	113	1	45.28
M. van Jaarsveld (*Northerns*)	11	18	5	568	238*	1	43.69
C. Light (*North West*)	6	9	1	347	108*	1	43.37
H. H. Dippenaar (*Free State*)	9	17	1	653	200*	2	40.81
P. J. R. Steyn (*Northerns*).	10	17	1	650	145	1	40.62
A. M. Bacher (*Gauteng*)	11	19	0	768	195	2	40.42

* *Signifies not out.*

BOWLING

(Qualification: 20 wickets, average 30.00)

	O	M	R	W	BB	5W/i	Avge
H. S. Williams (*Boland*)	264.5	73	551	42	6-27	3	13.11
K. C. G. Benjamin (*Gauteng*).	250	78	594	38	6-48	3	15.63
H. C. Bakkes (*Free State*)	251.4	74	617	39	6-33	3	15.82
V. C. Drakes (*Border*).	319.2	52	979	60	5-26	3	16.31
C. M. Willoughby (*Boland*)	404.4	134	878	50	5-87	1	17.56
M. Hayward (*E. Province*)	330.1	100	854	46	6-31	4	18.56
D. J. Terbrugge (*Gauteng*)	396	122	870	44	5-45	1	19.77
S. Elworthy (*Northerns*).	292.1	74	735	37	7-105	1	19.86
P. J. Botha (*Border*)	203.2	60	453	21	4-27	0	21.57
A. A. Donald (*Free State*)	272.3	83	693	32	6-53	4	21.65
A. J. Hall (*Gauteng*).	333.4	99	890	40	5-20	2	22.25
J. H. Kallis (*W. Province*).	176.2	47	447	20	6-60	1	22.35
S. M. Pollock (*KwaZulu-Natal*) . . .	356.3	119	757	32	5-39	1	23.65
R. E. Veenstra (*KwaZulu-Natal*) . . .	333.3	91	832	35	5-95	1	23.77
P. R. Adams (*W. Province*)	344.5	81	836	32	6-78	3	26.12
M. Ntini (*Border*).	186.4	32	582	22	4-55	0	26.45
G. J-P. Kruger (*E. Province*).	312.5	52	955	36	7-64	1	26.52
T. Henderson (*Border*).	261.1	66	649	24	3-14	0	27.04
O. D. Gibson (*Griqualand W.*).	172.5	23	604	22	7-141	1	27.45
M. J. Lavine (*North West*)	186	43	578	21	5-44	1	27.52
P. V. Mpitsang (*Free State*).	252	72	664	24	4-42	0	27.66
G. M. Gilder (*KwaZulu-Natal*)	241.5	60	654	23	6-61	1	28.43
R. J. Peterson (*E. Province*)	322	83	967	34	6-67	2	28.44

SUPERSPORT SERIES, 1999-2000

First Round

Pool A

	Played	Won	Lost	Drawn	Batting	Bowling	Points
					Bonus Points		
Border	5	3	0	2	16	20	66
Gauteng	5	3	1	1	19	13	62
Eastern Province	5	2	2	1	13	18	51
Northerns	5	2	1	2	14	15	49
Griqualand West	5	0	3	2	14	7	21
Easterns	5	0	3	2	9	12	15*

* *6 points deducted for fielding an ineligible player.*

Pool B

	Played	Won	Lost	Drawn	Bonus Points Batting	Bonus Points Bowling	Points
KwaZulu-Natal	4	2	1	1	17	11	48
Free State.	4	2	0	2	9	11	40
Boland.	4	1	1	2	7	15	32
Western Province	4	1	1	2	8	8	26
North West	4	0	3	1	6	12	18

The top four teams from each pool advanced to the Super Eight; the remaining three contested the Shield Series.

Super Eight

	Played	Won	Lost	Drawn	Bonus Points Batting	Bonus Points Bowling	Points
Gauteng	7	4	1	2	24	25	89
Border.	7	4	1	2	17	28	85
Boland.	7	3	2	2	10	27	67
KwaZulu-Natal	7	2	2	3	19	16	55
Free State.	7	2	2	3	10	20	50
Eastern Province	7	1	4	2	13	20	43
Northerns	7	1	2	4	8	17	35
Western Province	7	0	3	4	14	8	22

Super Eight teams carried forward results and points gained against fellow-qualifiers in the first round, but not those gained against the teams eliminated.

Final

Gauteng beat Border by three wickets.

Shield Series

	Played	Won	Lost	Drawn	Bonus Points Batting	Bonus Points Bowling	Points*
North West	2	1	0	1	3	4	21.5
Easterns . . . . , . . .	2	0	1	1	3	8	14
Griqualand West	2	0	0	2	4	5	13.2

* Teams carried forward their average points gained per match in the first round.

Outright win = 10 pts.
Bonus points were awarded for the first 100 overs of each team's first innings. One batting point was awarded for the first 150 runs and for every subsequent 50. One bowling point was awarded for the third wicket taken and for every subsequent two.

In the following scores, * by the name of a team indicates that they won the toss.

Pool A

At Benoni, October 7, 8, 9. Northerns won by 222 runs. Northerns* 352 for eight dec. (Q. R. Still 52, N. D. McKenzie 79, G. Dros 67, J. G. Myburgh 55, Extras 47) and 191 for four dec. (P. J. R. Steyn 49, M. van Jaarsveld 51 not out); Easterns 140 (A. M. van den Berg 41; M. J. G. Davis three for 51) and 181 (D. Jordaan 75, R. T. Coetzee 39; G. J. Smith three for 47). *Northerns 17 pts, Easterns 1 pt.*

In Easterns' first SuperSport match, their openers, Philip Hearle and Hussain Manack, both made pairs. It was Hearle's debut for Easterns; he had also made a pair on debut for Boland. Team-mate Jordaan was appearing for his fifth province, after Free State, Griqualand West, Western Province and Northerns.

At Kimberley, October 7, 8, 9, 10. Gauteng won by an innings and 93 runs. Griqualand West* 400 for four dec. (J. M. Arthur 128, M. I. Gidley 100, P. H. Barnard 73 not out, K. C. Wessels 30, F. C. Brooker 35 not out) and 147 (W. Bossenger 38; D. J. Terbrugge three for 33, C. E. Eksteen five for 54); Gauteng 640 for five dec. (S. G. Koenig 99, A. M. Bacher 195, K. R. Rutherford 34, D. J. Cullinan 119, D. N. Crookes 126, N. Pothas 49 not out). *Gauteng 14 pts, Griqualand West 3 pts.*

Gauteng's 640 for five was their highest total, the fifth-highest in South African first-class cricket, and the second-highest in the Currie/Castle/SuperSport tournament after Natal's 664 for six v Western Province at Durban in 1936-37. This was Wessels's final first-class match; he ended his career with 24,738 runs at 50.58.

At East London, October 14, 15, 16, 17. Drawn. Border* 453 for eight dec. (P. J. Botha 31, W. Wiblin 80, M. V. Boucher 48, P. C. Strydom 125, L. L. Gamiet 43, Extras 49; P. V. Simmons three for 37); Easterns 238 (P. de Bruyn 34, G. A. Pollock 40, D. J. Smith 48; V. C. Drakes four for 85, T. Henderson three for 47) and 69 for three (D. Jordaan 31 not out). *Border 7 pts, Easterns 4 pts.*

At Port Elizabeth, October 14, 15, 16, 17. Drawn. Griqualand West* 351 (J. M. Arthur 32, P. H. Barnard 76, L. L. Bosman 57, W. Bossenger 32, O. D. Gibson 62, Extras 36; M. Hayward six for 90) and 186 (M. I. Gidley 55; M. Hayward four for 53); Eastern Province 359 (M. R. Benfield 60, C. C. Bradfield 65, J. D. C. Bryant 48, S. Abrahams 63 not out, D. W. Murray 40, Extras 37; O. D. Gibson four for 80) and eight for no wkt. *Eastern Province 6 pts, Griqualand West 5 pts.*

At Centurion, October 14, 15, 16, 17. Drawn. Northerns* 396 (N. D. McKenzie 175, G. Dros 94, J. G. Myburgh 32; D. J. Terbrugge five for 45) and 237 for five dec. (Q. R. Still 45, P. J. R. Steyn 89, M. van Jaarsveld 49 not out); Gauteng 337 (S. G. Koenig 46, A. M. Bacher 33, N. Pothas 109 not out, A. J. Hall 36; G. J. Smith three for 108, D. H. Townsend four for 102) and 175 for five (A. M. Bacher 65, A. J. Seymore 39; G. J. Smith three for 37). *Northerns 7 pts, Gauteng 5 pts.*

At Johannesburg, October 21, 22, 23. Gauteng won by an innings and 22 runs. Eastern Province* 99 (A. J. Hall five for 20, W. B. Masimula four for 35) and 279 (C. C. Bradfield 44, M. R. Benfield 31, G. V. Grace 34, D. W. Murray 36, M. W. Pringle 83; D. J. Terbrugge four for 66, D. N. Crookes three for 20); Gauteng 400 for nine dec. (A. M. Bacher 34, K. R. Rutherford 100, D. J. Cullinan 135, N. Pothas 89; M. W. Pringle four for 103, M. Hayward three for 121). *Gauteng 20 pts, Eastern Province 4 pts.*

At Centurion, October 21, 22, 23, 24. Drawn. Border 318 (P. J. Botha 52, B. M. White 76, S. C. Pope 32, M. V. Boucher 54, P. C. Strydom 60; S. Elworthy seven for 105) and 80 for five (S. Elworthy three for 11); Northerns* 249 (P. J. R. Steyn 48, N. D. McKenzie 46, S. Elworthy 43, M. L. G. Pedi 39, G. J. Smith 30; V. C. Drakes four for 50, G. T. Love three for 99). *Northerns 5 pts, Border 8 pts.*

White took 296 minutes and 183 balls to reach 50, the slowest half-century in South African interprovincial first-class cricket.

At East London, October 28, 29, 30, 31. Border won by eight wickets. Border 426 (P. J. Botha 47, S. C. Pope 77, W. Wiblin 56, P. C. Strydom 100, I. Mitchell 32, V. C. Drakes 33, T. Henderson 37 not out, Extras 33; O. D. Gibson seven for 141) and 162 for two (P. J. Botha 64, S. C. Pope 52 not out); Griqualand West* 238 (W. M. Dry 64, O. D. Gibson 42, P. L. Symcox 35; V. C. Drakes four for 77, T. Henderson three for 27) and 349 (M. I. Gidley 71, P. H. Barnard 64, F. C. Brooker 59, P. L. Symcox four for 124). *Border 18 pts, Griqualand West 4 pts.*

Wendell Bossenger became the first wicket-keeper to complete 100 first-class dismissals for Griqualand West.

At Port Elizabeth, October 28, 29, 30, 31. Eastern Province won by nine wickets. Easterns 284 (D. Jordaan 57, P. V. Simmons 122; M. Hayward six for 63) and 185 (P. K. Hearle 31, D. Jordaan 91; M. Hayward six for 31); Eastern Province* 375 (J. D. C. Bryant 125, J. M. Kemp 120, Extras 56; A. Nel five for 61, F. Erasmus three for 79) and 95 for one (M. R. Benfield 50 not out, J. D. C. Bryant 31 not out). *Eastern Province 18 pts, Easterns 7 pts.*

At Johannesburg, November 4, 5, 6, 7. Gauteng won by 200 runs. Gauteng* 311 (G. Toyana 32, K. R. Rutherford 52, D. N. Crookes 74, N. Pothas 50; M. J. Mostert three for 80, D. Jordaan three for nine) and 122 (A. J. Hall 62 not out; F. Erasmus three for 35, A. Nel four for 25); Easterns 150 (D. Jordaan 73 not out; K. C. G. Benjamin five for 22, C. E. Eksteen three for 25) and 83 (D. J. Terbrugge three for 17, K. C. G. Benjamin three for 27). *Gauteng 17 pts, Easterns 3 pts.*

At Kimberley, November 4, 5, 6, 7. Northerns won by ten wickets. Northerns* 562 for seven dec. (P. J. R. Steyn 145, N. D. McKenzie 41, M. van Jaarsveld 238 not out, S. Elworthy 38, Extras 31) and four for no wkt; Griqualand West 228 (M. I. Gidley 38, O. D. Gibson 33, G. A. Roe 38 not out, G. J. Kruis 47; S. Elworthy four for 51) and 337 (M. I. Gidley 136, W. M. Dry 32, Extras 33; S. Elworthy four for 77). *Northerns 19 pts, Griqualand West 3 pts.*

Northerns' 562 for seven was their highest total, and van Jaarsveld's unbeaten 238 was their highest individual score. His innings lasted 466 minutes and 345 balls and included 27 fours and one six.

At Port Elizabeth, November 11, 12, 13. Eastern Province won by an innings and 179 runs. Northerns* 146 (J. G. Myburgh 38; R. J. Peterson four for 55) and 201 (P. J. R. Steyn 83; R. J. Peterson five for 56); Eastern Province 526 (M. R. Benfield 90, C. C. Bradfield 67, J. D. C. Bryant 149, M. W. Rushmere 41, J. M. Kemp 82, Extras 37; M. J. G. Davis three for 92, G. Dros three for 21). *Eastern Province 18 pts, Northerns 1 pt.*

At Johannesburg, November 11, 12, 13, 14. Border won by seven wickets. Gauteng* 224 (A. J. Seymore 42, K. R. Rutherford 38, C. E. Eksteen 35, D. Jennings 30; V. C. Drakes five for 73) and 277 (S. G. Koenig 43, D. N. Crookes 46, A. J. Hall 52, D. Jennings 36 not out; V. C. Drakes three for 44, G. T. Love four for 84); Border 253 (P. J. Botha 71, L. L. Gamiet 32, I. Mitchell 34, G. T. Love 30 not out; K. C. G. Benjamin four for 56) and 251 for three (P. J. Botha 57, S. C. Pope 81 not out, W. Wiblin 54, I. Mitchell 35 not out). *Border 17 pts, Gauteng 6 pts.*

This was Border's first win over Gauteng in Johannesburg.

At East London, November 18, 19, 20. Border won by 188 runs. Border* 210 (P. J. Botha 30, M. V. Boucher 91, I. Mitchell 35; G. J-P. Kruger seven for 64) and 208 (S. C. Pope 31, W. Wiblin 81; G. J-P. Kruger three for 73, R. J. Peterson six for 67); Eastern Province 152 (D. J. Callaghan 30; V. C. Drakes four for 55) and 78 (P. J. Botha four for 27, G. T. Love four for 12). *Border 16 pts, Eastern Province 5 pts.*

At Benoni, November 18, 19, 20, 21. Drawn. Griqualand West* 313 (J. M. Arthur 60, M. I. Gidley 46, L. L. Bosman 59, O. D. Gibson 55, Extras 36; A. Nel three for 45, A. G. Botha four for 89) and 276 for seven dec. (J. M. Arthur 113 not out, M. I. Gidley 43, P. H. Barnard 63; A. G. Botha four for 101); Easterns 334 (D. Jordaan 96, Shakeel Ahmed 59, P. V. Simmons 53, D. J. Smith 58; P. L. Symcox four for 111) and 116 for three (D. Jordaan 40 not out, Shakeel Ahmed 66 not out). *Easterns 6 pts, Griqualand West 6 pts.*

Easterns were fined six points for playing Gareth Flusk who was ineligible at the time, having played for Gauteng B earlier in the season.

Pool B

At Bloemfontein, October 7, 8, 9, 10. Drawn. Free State* 284 (H. H. Dippenaar 64, W. J. Cronje 43, J. F. Venter 34, N. Boje 55, J. J. van der Wath 57 not out) and 344 for seven (A. I. Gait 56, H. H. Dippenaar 200 not out, G. L. Brophy 31; H. S. Williams three for 59); Boland 413 (J. M. Henderson 60, L. J. Koen 74, K. C. Jackson 106, S. J. Palframan 43, B. T. Player 46; H. C. Bakkes three for 58, P. V. Mpitsang four for 114). *Free State 4 pts, Boland 6 pts.*

Dippenaar's 200 not out lasted 522 minutes and 426 balls and included 24 fours and one six.

At Potchefstroom, October 7, 8, 9, 10. Drawn. KwaZulu-Natal* 504 for three dec. (M. L. Bruyns 142, D. J. Watson 220, A. C. Hudson 31, D. M. Benkenstein 54 not out, E. L. R. Stewart 34 not out) and 254 for two dec. (M. L. Bruyns 65, D. J. Watson 32, A. C. Hudson 106 not out, D. M. Benkenstein 32 not out); North West 362 (A. Jacobs 44, G. M. Hewitt 151, M. J. Lavine 41, E. G. Poole 35; R. E. Veenstra five for 95) and 198 for three (H. M. de Vos 61 not out, A. Jacobs 66). *North West 4 pts, KwaZulu-Natal 8 pts.*

North West's first SuperSport match. Watson's 220 lasted 433 minutes and 352 balls and included 30 fours and one six; he and Bruyns opened for KwaZulu-Natal with 340.

At Bloemfontein, October 14, 15, 16, 17. Drawn. Western Province 284 (J. H. Kallis 40, H. D. Ackerman 64, J. B. Commins 60; A. A. Donald five for 47, P. V. Mpitsang four for 61) and 278 (J. H. Kallis 44, H. D. Ackerman 91, A. G. Prince 41; P. V. Mpitsang four for 42); Free State* 444 for nine dec. (A. I. Gait 59, H. H. Dippenaar 128, W. J. Cronje 124, N. Boje 37, G. L. Brophy 40, Extras 32; A. C. Dawson four for 77, P. R. Adams five for 143) and 117 for six (G. F. J. Liebenberg 34, W. J. Cronje 39; R. Telemachus three for 30). *Free State 5 pts, Western Province 3 pts.*

At Durban, October 14, 15, 16, 17. KwaZulu-Natal won by two wickets. Boland 306 (C. R. Wilson 60, J. M. Henderson 35, L. J. Koen 61, P. K. Amre 71 not out; R. E. Veenstra three for 56, L. Klusener three for 102) and 110 (L. J. Koen 30, J. L. Ontong 30; S. M. Pollock three for 31, R. E. Veenstra four for 33); KwaZulu-Natal* 323 for eight dec. (M. L. Bruyns 105, D. J. Watson 44, S. M. Pollock 49, L. Klusener 37 not out) and 97 for eight (H. S. Williams five for 51, C. M. Willoughby three for 41). *KwaZulu-Natal 16 pts, Boland 5 pts.*

Eldine Baptiste, who had recently moved from Eastern Province to KwaZulu-Natal, became the first overseas player to take 200 wickets in this tournament.

At Paarl, October 21, 22, 23, 24. Drawn. Boland 247 (L. J. Koen 113, J. L. Ontong 50; A. C. Dawson three for 54, J. H. Kallis six for 60) and 255 for nine dec. (J. M. Henderson 70, L. J. Koen 60, J. L. Ontong 40, S. J. Palframan 50; C. W. Henderson four for 101, P. R. Adams three for 88); Western Province* 137 (J. H. Kallis 58; H. S. Williams three for 24, C. M. Willoughby four for 29) and 178 for three (B. M. McMillan 104 not out, T. L. Tsolekile 33). *Boland 6 pts, Western Province 3 pts.*

At Cape Town, October 28, 29, 30, 31. KwaZulu-Natal won by ten wickets. Western Province* 222 (R. Magiet 46, A. G. Prince 73; R. B. MacQueen four for 65) and 260 (J. B. Commins 56, B. M. McMillan 95 not out, R. Telemachus 46; G. M. Gilder six for 61); KwaZulu-Natal 451 for six dec. (M. L. Bruyns 30, D. J. Watson 62, D. M. Benkenstein 71, E. L. R. Stewart 151 not out, E. A. E. Baptiste 75 not out, Extras 33; R. Telemachus three for 77) and 34 for no wkt. *KwaZulu-Natal 16 pts, Western Province 3 pts.*

At Potchefstroom, November 4, 5, 6, 7. Free State won by four wickets. North West 205 (C. Light 34, E. G. Poole 31; H. C. Bakkes three for 37) and 276 (H. M. de Vos 51, G. M. Hewitt 63, C. Light 36, M. J. Lavine 30; H. C. Bakkes three for 51); Free State* 244 (G. F. J. Liebenberg 46, N. Boje 35, G. L. Brophy 66; M. J. Lavine five for 44) and 238 for six (A. I. Gait 40, W. J. Cronje 44, J. F. Venter 33, N. Boje 76 not out; J. N. Dreyer three for 70). *Free State 16 pts, North West 6 pts.*

At Paarl, November 11, 12, 13. Boland won by seven wickets. North West 101 (H. S. Williams six for 27, C. M. Willoughby four for 37) and 153 (G. M. Hewitt 57; H. S. Williams three for 39, C. M. Willoughby three for 41, B. T. Player three for 26); Boland* 191 (J. M. Henderson 40, P. K. Amre 36; M. J. Lavine four for 31, D. Rossouw four for 52) and 66 for three. *Boland 15 pts, North West 4 pts.*

At Durban, November 18, 19, 20, 21. Free State won by six wickets. KwaZulu-Natal* 341 (C. B. Sugden 43, J. N. Rhodes 124, S. M. Pollock 50; H. C. Bakkes six for 46) and 299 for eight dec. (A. M. Amla 35, E. L. R. Stewart 64 not out, S. M. Pollock 54, L. Klusener 73, R. E. Veenstra 33); Free State 198 (J. F. Venter 85; R. E. Veenstra three for 25, L. Klusener three for 47) and 443 for four (G. F. J. Liebenberg 58, A. I. Gait 101, W. J. Cronje 151 not out, J. F. Venter 46, N. Boje 67 not out; G. M. Gilder three for 66). *Free State 15 pts, KwaZulu-Natal 8 pts.*

Free State's 443 for four was the highest fourth-innings total to win an interprovincial match in South Africa, and the second-highest to win in all South African first-class cricket.

At Cape Town, November 18, 19, 20. Western Province won by nine wickets. North West* 148 (G. M. Hewitt 40, M. J. Lavine 59; R. Telemachus three for 24, C. R. Matthews three for 21) and 200 (A. G. Lawson 30, C. Light 91, C. T. Enslin 36; R. Telemachus three for 41, P. R. Adams six for 78); Western Province 284 (G. Kirsten 59, L. D. Ferreira 50, J. B. Commins 95 not out; J. N. Dreyer five for 97) and 66 for one (G. Kirsten 48 not out). *Western Province 17 pts, North West 4 pts.*

Super Eight

At Bloemfontein, December 3, 4, 5, 6. Border won by 102 runs. Border 325 (P. J. Botha 51, P. C. Strydom 72, I. Mitchell 72, L. L. Gamiet 44, V. C. Drakes 30; D. Pretorius three for 86, H. C. Bakkes five for 61) and 151 (P. C. Strydom 55; M. J. Hoggard four for 34, H. C. Bakkes three for 42); Free State* 170 (G. F. J. Liebenberg 42; M. Ntini four for 55) and 204 (G. L. Brophy 73, N. Boje 38; V. C. Drakes three for 53, M. Ntini three for 40). *Border 17 pts, Free State 3 pts.*

   Ntini took a hat-trick in Free State's first innings. His victims were Brophy, Pretorius and Yorkshireman Matthew Hoggard.

At Centurion, December 3, 4, 5. Boland won by an innings and six runs. Northerns 98 (H. S. Williams six for 39, C. M. Willoughby three for 16) and 185 (N. D. McKenzie 38, G. Dros 35; H. S. Williams three for 52); Boland* 289 (J. L. Ontong 78, S. J. Palframan 96; S. Elworthy four for 74). *Boland 17 pts, Northerns 4 pts.*

At Cape Town, December 3, 4, 5, 6. Drawn. Eastern Province* 338 (M. R. Benfield 55, J. D. C. Bryant 131, M. W. Rushmere 60; R. Telemachus four for 56, P. R. Adams five for 110) and 270 for four (J. D. C. Bryant 129, D. J. Callaghan 48, M. W. Rushmere 38 not out); Western Province 473 for seven dec. (G. Kirsten 63, H. H. Gibbs 119, H. D. Ackerman 86, A. G. Prince 117, A. C. Dawson 33 not out, Extras 37). *Western Province 5 pts, Eastern Province 4 pts.*

   Bryant hit two centuries in the match.

At Paarl, December 10, 11, 12. Gauteng won by 175 runs. Gauteng 233 (G. Toyana 36, K. R. Rutherford 93, M. R. Street 31; C. M. Willoughby three for 44, N. M. Carter three for 48) and 143 (S. G. Koenig 43; C. M. Willoughby four for 53, H. S. Williams three for 41); Boland* 95 (L. J. Koen 38 not out; K. C. G. Benjamin four for 17, A. J. Hall three for 17) and 106 (D. J. Terbrugge four for 16, A. J. Hall three for 23, C. E. Eksteen three for 21). *Gauteng 16 pts, Boland 4 pts.*

At Durban, December 10, 11, 12, 13. Drawn. Eastern Province 266 (J. D. C. Bryant 62, M. W. Creed 61, S. Abrahams 40; R. E. Veenstra four for 52, J. C. Kent three for 58) and 342 for six (M. R. Benfield 43, C. C. Bradfield 154 not out, M. W. Rushmere 94); KwaZulu-Natal* 462 for five dec. (M. L. Bruyns 93, D. J. Watson 48, A. C. Hudson 102, E. L. R. Stewart 109 not out, J. C. Kent 34, Extras 45). *KwaZulu-Natal 7 pts, Eastern Province 4 pts.*

At Centurion, December 10, 11, 12, 13. Drawn. Western Province 287 for eight dec. (B. M. McMillan 47, A. G. Prince 77 not out, A. C. Dawson 48, Extras 38; G. J. Smith five for 81); Northerns* 132 for three (P. J. R. Steyn 58, M. van Jaarsveld 34 not out). *Northerns 2 pts, Western Province 4 pts.*

At Bloemfontein, December 17, 18, 19, 20. Northerns won by two wickets. Free State* 160 (H. H. Dippenaar 30, J. F. Venter 31; D. J. J. de Vos six for 32) and 151 (G. L. Brophy 50; D. J. J. de Vos five for 68); Northerns 215 (P. Joubert 30 not out, G. J. Smith 33; J. F. Venter six for 78) and 99 for eight (J. G. Myburgh 37 not out; N. Boje five for 38, J. F. Venter three for 54). *Northerns 16 pts, Free State 5 pts.*

At Johannesburg, December 17, 18, 19, 20. Gauteng won by nine wickets. KwaZulu-Natal* 264 (E. L. R. Stewart 63, A. M. Amla 49, J. C. Kent 32, E. A. E. Baptiste 36 not out; K. C. G. Benjamin five for 34) and 252 (D. J. Watson 84, D. M. Benkenstein 50, A. M. Amla 36 not out, Extras 34; K. C. G. Benjamin three for 63, A. J. Hall four for 41); Gauteng 373 (A. M. Bacher 32, S. G. Koenig 30, K. R. Rutherford 195 not out, D. J. Cullinan 32, A. J. Hall 56; G. M. Gilder three for 90) and 147 for one (A. M. Bacher 78, S. G. Koenig 43 not out). *Gauteng 17 pts, KwaZulu-Natal 4 pts.*

At East London, January 7, 8, 9, 10. Drawn. Border 361 (S. C. Pope 45, W. Wiblin 31, I. Mitchell 84, V. C. Drakes 71; K. P. Pietersen three for 69) and 190 (P. C. Strydom 50, V. C. Drakes 32 not out; R. E. Veenstra three for 31, E. A. E. Baptiste four for 18); KwaZulu-Natal* 225 (A. M. Amla 104; V. C. Drakes four for 65, P. C. Strydom three for eight) and 293 for nine (D. M. Benkenstein 55, E. L. R. Stewart 84 not out, J. C. Kent 59; V. C. Drakes four for 52). *Border 7 pts, KwaZulu-Natal 4 pts.*

At Johannesburg, January 7, 8, 9, 10. Drawn. Free State* 143 (N. Boje 32; D. J. Terbrugge four for 41, A. J. Hall four for 35) and 366 (A. I. Gait 80, H. H. Dippenaar 91, N. Boje 33, J. A. Beukes 97; C. E. Eksteen four for 83); Gauteng 306 (K. R. Rutherford 134, D. N. Crookes 39; H. C. Bakkes four for 71) and 36 for three (N. Boje three for three). *Gauteng 8 pts, Free State 4 pts.*

At Paarl, January 14, 15. Boland won by eight wickets. Border* 110 (V. C. Drakes 52; H. S. Williams four for 20, C. M. Willoughby three for 38) and 105 (C. M. Willoughby four for 44, B. T. Player four for 19); Boland 139 (C. R. Wilson 32; V. C. Drakes five for 26) and 79 for two. *Boland 14 pts, Border 4 pts.*

At Port Elizabeth, January 14, 15, 16, 17. Free State won by 185 runs. Free State* 296 (A. I. Gait 30, G. F. J. Liebenberg 67, J. F. Venter 42, H. C. Bakkes 62; G. J-P. Kruger four for 56, M. Ngam three for 52) and 226 for six dec. (H. H. Dippenaar 33, G. L. Brophy 34, N. Boje 58 not out; S. Abrahams four for 67); Eastern Province 227 for eight dec. (J. D. C. Bryant 37, D. J. Callaghan 100 not out, M. W. Pringle 43; D. Pretorius five for 58) and 110 (M. W. Rushmere 52 not out; D. Pretorius three for 30, J. F. Venter four for 47). *Free State 14 pts, Eastern Province 4 pts.*

Liebenberg took his 21st catch of the season, equalling the South African record.

At Durban, January 14, 15, 16, 17. Drawn. Northerns 139 for two (P. J. R. Steyn 39, N. D. McKenzie 34 not out, M. van Jaarsveld 38 not out) v KwaZulu-Natal*.

At Cape Town, January 14, 15, 16, 17. Gauteng won by 93 runs. Gauteng* 411 for six dec. (A. M. Bacher 128, S. G. Koenig 104, G. Toyana 46, Z. de Bruyn 50 not out, M. R. Street 33 not out; R. Telemachus three for 84) and 164 for six dec. (S. G. Koenig 43, G. Toyana 62; C. W. Henderson four for 72); Western Province 240 (H. D. Ackerman 119, A. C. Dawson 54; D. J. Terbrugge three for 52, A. J. Hall three for 71) and 242 (B. M. McMillan 54, A. G. Prince 50, A. C. Dawson 57 not out; C. E. Eksteen three for 70, W. B. Masimula three for 37). *Gauteng 17 pts, Western Province 2 pts.*

At East London, January 21, 22, 23. Border won by an innings and 74 runs. Western Province 111 (R. Magiet 35; V. C. Drakes five for 37, T. Henderson three for 14) and 155 (A. G. Prince 51, S. Ackermann 31; M. Ntini three for 42); Border* 340 (B. M. White 44, G. T. Love 52, S. C. Pope 39, L. L. Gamiet 44, Extras 41; A. C. Dawson six for 51, C. W. Henderson three for 97). *Border 16 pts, Western Province 2 pts.*

At Port Elizabeth, January 21, 22, 23, 24. Boland won by ten runs. Boland* 193 (L. J. Koen 42, P. K. Amre 30, C. K. Langeveldt 32 not out; R. J. Peterson three for 66) and 232 (L. J. Koen 37, K. C. Jackson 61, C. K. Langeveldt 56, N. M. Carter 37; J. M. Kemp four for 30, R. J. Peterson four for 52); Eastern Province 87 (C. M. Willoughby four for 42, B. T. Player three for 14) and 328 (D. J. Callaghan 118, M. W. Rushmere 48, J. M. Kemp 43, R. J. Peterson 31 not out; C. M. Willoughby five for 87). *Boland 15 pts, Eastern Province 4 pts.*

Koen equalled the South African record of 21 catches in a season.

FINAL

GAUTENG v BORDER

At Johannesburg, January 28, 29, 30, 31. Gauteng won by three wickets. Toss: Gauteng.

Gauteng won with a day to spare, but not nearly as easily as they expected after reducing Border to 113 for six on the opening day. From there, Strydom checked the rampages of Hall and Benjamin, holding firm for four and a half hours to add 170 with the lower order; then Henderson, who struck nine fours and three sixes in a career-best 81, put on another 63 with Ntini. When Gauteng replied, Rutherford scored his last half-century before retirement, after which Cullinan and Toyana advanced the score to 301 for three. But the remaining seven wickets fell for just 86. Trailing by 41, Border's batsmen faltered again; this time, Strydom was out first ball, and only a century from Boucher raised the target to 182. Benjamin completed match figures of ten for 150, before his fellow-West Indian, Drakes, gave Gauteng a scare. He and Botha knocked over their top six for 74; Drakes also claimed a tournament record of 60 wickets for the season, beating Mike Procter's 59 for Natal in 1976-77. But he could not secure Border's first title; Hall steered Gauteng home in an unbroken eighth-wicket stand with Eksteen.

Man of Match: A. J. Hall.

Close of play: First day, Border 260-8 (Strydom 78*, Henderson 43*); Second day, Gauteng 221-3 (Cullinan 55*, Toyana 27*); Third day, Border 130-5 (Boucher 70*, Mitchell 13*).

Border

B. M. White lbw b Hall	0	– (2) c Hall b Benjamin	6
P. J. Botha c Crookes b Hall	14	– (1) c Pothas b Benjamin	1
S. C. Pope c Bacher b Benjamin	16	– c Cullinan b Hall	28
W. Wiblin c Pothas b Benjamin	25	– c Toyana b Benjamin	4
†M. V. Boucher c Rutherford b Hall	18	– b Benjamin	112
*P. C. Strydom b Benjamin	88	– lbw b Benjamin	0
I. Mitchell c Rutherford b Eksteen	0	– c Pothas b Crookes	36
V. C. Drakes b Hall	45	– b Eksteen	2
G. T. Love c Crookes b Benjamin	3	– not out	9
T. Henderson c Crookes b Hall	81	– c Pothas b Benjamin	0
M. Ntini not out	34	– c Crookes b Hall	11
B 4, l-b 10, w 4, n-b 4	22	L-b 7, w 2, n-b 4	13

1/5 2/29 3/42 4/83 5/112   346   1/2 2/17 3/21 4/99 5/105   222
6/113 7/198 8/205 9/283   6/184 7/187 8/200 9/200

Bowling: *First Innings*—Benjamin 31–10–102–4; Hall 27.4–11–67–5; Masimula 15–3–27–0; Eksteen 34–9–101–1; Crookes 10–3–35–0. *Second Innings*—Benjamin 26–8–48–6; Hall 19.2–5–42–2; Eksteen 26–3–65–1; Masimula 7–0–13–0; Crookes 12–1–32–1; Bacher 4–0–15–0.

Gauteng

S. G. Koenig c Boucher b Henderson	33	– lbw b Drakes	4
A. M. Bacher lbw b Drakes	17	– b Drakes	20
K. R. Rutherford c Mitchell b Ntini	79	– c Botha b Drakes	23
D. J. Cullinan c Mitchell b Ntini	120	– c Mitchell b Botha	7
G. Toyana c Drakes b Ntini	63	– lbw b Botha	5
D. N. Crookes c Wiblin b Botha	1	– b Botha	0
†N. Pothas lbw b Drakes	12	– b Ntini	30
A. J. Hall c Boucher b Drakes	8	– not out	57
*C. E. Eksteen b Henderson	16	– not out	20
K. C. G. Benjamin not out	12		
W. B. Masimula run out	0		
B 1, l-b 8, w 7, n-b 10	26	B 4, l-b 5, w 1, n-b 6	16

1/29 2/101 3/166 4/301 5/312   387   1/4 2/54 3/55 4/65   (7 wkts) 182
6/330 7/349 8/364 9/376   5/65 6/74 7/112

Bowling: *First Innings*—Drakes 29–2–97–3; Botha 16–2–53–1; Henderson 23.5–6–66–2; Ntini 21–2–71–3; Love 22–2–73–0; Strydom 7–1–18–0. *Second Innings*—Drakes 16–1–81–3; Henderson 8–0–35–0; Botha 11.2–2–43–3; Ntini 8–2–14–1.

Umpires: D. F. Becker and R. E. Koertzen.

CHAMPIONS

Currie Cup	
1889-90	Transvaal
1890-91	Kimberley
1892-93	Western Province
1893-94	Western Province
1894-95	Transvaal
1896-97	Western Province
1897-98	Western Province
1902-03	Transvaal
1903-04	Transvaal
1904-05	Transvaal
1906-07	Transvaal
1908-09	Western Province
1910-11	Natal
1912-13	Natal
1920-21	Western Province
1921-22	Transvaal/Natal/W. Prov. (Tied)
1923-24	Transvaal
1925-26	Transvaal
1926-27	Transvaal
1929-30	Transvaal
1931-32	Western Province
1933-34	Natal
1934-35	Transvaal
1936-37	Natal
1937-38	Natal/Transvaal (Tied)
1946-47	Natal
1947-48	Natal
1950-51	Transvaal
1951-52	Natal
1952-53	Western Province
1954-55	Natal
1955-56	Western Province
1958-59	Transvaal
1959-60	Natal
1960-61	Natal
1962-63	Natal
1963-64	Natal
1965-66	Natal/Transvaal (Tied)

1966-67	Natal
1967-68	Natal
1968-69	Transvaal
1969-70	Transvaal/W. Province (Tied)
1970-71	Transvaal
1971-72	Transvaal
1972-73	Transvaal
1973-74	Natal
1974-75	Western Province
1975-76	Natal
1976-77	Natal
1977-78	Western Province
1978-79	Transvaal
1979-80	Transvaal
1980-81	Natal
1981-82	Western Province
1982-83	Transvaal
1983-84	Transvaal
1984-85	Transvaal
1985-86	Western Province
1986-87	Transvaal
1987-88	Transvaal
1988-89	Eastern Province
1989-90	E. Province/W. Province (Shared)
Castle Cup	
1990-91	Western Province
1991-92	Eastern Province
1992-93	Orange Free State
1993-94	Orange Free State
1994-95	Natal
1995-96	Western Province
SuperSport Series	
1996-97	Natal
1997-98	Free State
1998-99	Western Province
1999-2000	Gauteng

Transvaal/Gauteng have won the title outright 25 times, Natal 20, Western Province 16, Orange Free State/Free State 3, Eastern Province 2, Kimberley 1. The title has been shared five times as follows: Transvaal 4, Natal and Western Province 3, Eastern Province 1.

Shield Series

At Potchefstroom, December 3, 4, 5, 6. Drawn. Griqualand West 308 (J. M. Arthur 44, P. P. J. Koortzen 58, W. Bossenger 80 not out, Extras 35; M. J. Lavine three for 80, C. T. Enslin three for 58) and 267 for eight (J. M. Arthur 66, M. I. Gidley 32, O. D. Gibson 39, G. J. Kruis 57 not out; M. Strydom four for 65, C. Light four for 42); North West* 352 (M. Strydom 30, M. C. Venter 57, G. M. Hewitt 52, C. Light 108 not out; O. D. Gibson four for 65, G. J. Kruis four for 56). *North West 7 pts, Griqualand West 7 pts.*

At Kimberley, December 17, 18, 19, 20. Drawn. Easterns 421 for seven dec. (A. G. Botha 79, D. Brand 45, D. Jordaan 106, P. V. Simmons 60, D. J. Smith 54, Extras 31; Z. A. Abrahim three for 71); Griqualand West* 231 (D. K. Dobson 36, L. L. Bosman 42, P. P. J. Koortzen 60; J. A. Morkel six for 36) and 219 for eight (D. K. Dobson 37, P. P. J. Koortzen 32, G. D. Elliott 58, W. Bossenger 41). *Griqualand West 2 pts, Easterns 7 pts.*

At Benoni, January 7, 8, 9, 10. North West won by five wickets. Easterns 114 for two dec. (D. Jordaan 45) and 145 (M. A. Conyers 32; J. N. Dreyer three for 36, D. Rossouw three for 23); North West* 141 (A. G. Lawson 35; F. Erasmus three for 28) and 121 for five (A. Jacobs 50 not out; F. Erasmus three for 27). *North West 10 pts, Easterns 4 pts.*

Other First-Class Match

At Kimberley, February 5, 6, 7. UCB Invitation XI won by 141 runs. UCB Invitation XI* 342 for six dec. (G. C. Smith 187, G. Toyana 47, L. L. Gamiet 44) and 219 (M. R. Street 47, L. L. Gamiet 36; Z. A. Abrahim six for 53); Griqualand West 322 for seven dec. (J. M. Arthur 105, W. M. Dry 40, F. C. Brooker 44, G. J. Kruis 43 not out; J. A. Rudolph three for 74) and 98 (G. J-P. Kruger three for 24, R. J. Peterson three for 18).

Graeme Smith's 187 was the second-highest score on first-class debut by a South African, after 240 by W. F. E. Marx for Transvaal v Griqualand West at Johannesburg in 1920-21.

Sri Lanka A's first-class matches may be found in the Other A-Team Tours section.

STANDARD BANK CUP, 1999-2000

	Played	Won	Lost	No Result	Bonus Points	Points
Gauteng	10	8	2	0	3	35
Boland	10	7	3	0	3	31
Easterns	10	5	2	3	4	30
Eastern Province	10	6	4	0	3	27
KwaZulu-Natal	10	6	4	0	2	26
Northerns	10	4	4	2	5	25
Border	10	3	5	2	2	18
Griqualand West	10	4	6	0	2	18
Free State	10	3	6	1	3	17
Western Province	10	2	6	2	1	13
North West	10	1	7	2	0	8

Semi-finals
1st leg

At Benoni, March 8. Boland won by 25 runs. Boland* 190 for three (45 overs) (I. J. L. Trott 76, J. L. Ontong 32, P. K. Amre 42 not out); Easterns 165 (42.4 overs) (D. Brand 51; N. M. Carter four for 31).

2nd leg

At Paarl, March 10. Boland won by 30 runs. Boland* 240 for seven (45 overs) (J. M. Henderson 60, P. K. Amre 38, Extras 34); Easterns 210 (43.4 overs) (P. V. Simmons 39, D. Jordaan 35, J. A. Morkel 40, P. de Bruyn 32 not out; C. K. Langeveldt three for 46, B. T. Player three for 39).

1st leg

At Port Elizabeth, March 15. Gauteng won by six wickets (D/L method). Eastern Province* 179 for eight (38 overs) (K. D. Duckworth 43, D. J. Callaghan 47, J. M. Kemp 31; A. J. Hall three for 44, C. E. Eksteen three for 23); Gauteng 182 for four (35.5 overs) (A. J. Hall 32, K. R. Rutherford 59 not out, Z. de Bruyn 36).

2nd leg

At Johannesburg, March 17. Eastern Province won by 24 runs. Eastern Province 225 for eight (45 overs) (D. J. Callaghan 107 not out, M. W. Creed 47); Gauteng* 201 (44 overs) (A. J. Hall 37, Z. de Bruyn 58; M. W. Pringle three for 24, D. J. Callaghan three for 32).

3rd leg

At Johannesburg, March 19, 20. No result. Gauteng* 193 for six (32 overs) (A. M. Bacher 51, A. J. Hall 69, Z. de Bruyn 36 not out; M. Ngam three for 38, D. J. Callaghan three for 40); Eastern Province 31 for two (nine overs).

3rd leg replay

At Johannesburg, March 24. Eastern Province won by 62 runs. Eastern Province* 187 for eight (45 overs) (M. R. Benfield 33, D. J. Callaghan 65); Gauteng 125 (38.2 overs) (A. M. Bacher 59; D. J. Callaghan four for 31).

Final

At Paarl, March 29. Boland won by 36 runs. Boland* 209 for six (45 overs) (L. J. Koen 31, J. L. Ontong 67, S. J. Palframan 38); Eastern Province 173 for eight (45 overs) (D. J. Callaghan 42).

CRICKET IN THE WEST INDIES, 1999-2000

By TONY COZIER

Chris Gayle

West Indies cricket found itself in such decline that the relevant Caribbean Community governments and the University of the West Indies convened a conference in Barbados in June 2000 to analyse the crisis. The two-day forum followed three months of consultations with players, administrators, sponsors and fans, and its recommendations were presented to the annual Caricom summit in July. It was the first time politicians and academics had felt the need to become directly involved in a game that had always looked after itself. But the West Indies Cricket Board's credibility had been so badly damaged by fiascos off the field and defeat on it that there was no public outcry against the possibility of government intervention.

The optimism sparked by the drawn series when Australia toured in 1998-99 reverted to disillusionment, with early elimination from the World Cup, heavy one-day defeats in Toronto and Sharjah and, most humiliating of all, the loss of both Tests and all five one-day internationals in New Zealand. The upshot was the resignation of captain Brian Lara, whose remarkable batting had inspired the revival against Australia. "After two years, the moderate success and devastating failure that has engulfed West Indies cricket has brought me to the realisation that there is a need for me to withdraw from my present leadership position," Lara explained in February. A week later, he declared he was taking a break from the game "to seek the assistance of appropriate professionals".

Jimmy Adams succeeded him, West Indies' fourth captain in four years, backed by a new management team. Ricky Skerritt, a business executive from St Kitts, took over as manager from former Test captain Clive Lloyd, who chose to stand down. More controversially, Roger Harper replaced Sir Viv Richards as coach, with Jeffrey Dujon taking the new post of assistant coach. Richards, a commanding personality who had never lost a series as West Indies captain, had deputised for the ailing Malcolm Marshall during the World Cup, remained for the harrowing New Zealand tour, and hoped to continue. His rejection, reportedly for a lack of official certificates, sparked such anger in his home island, Antigua, that protesters stormed the WICB's headquarters there. To complete the changes, Dennis Waight, the Australian who had joined the West Indies of World Series Cricket as trainer and physiotherapist in 1977-78, and remained with the official Test side, was supplanted by Ronald Rogers, formerly of the Trinidad & Tobago army. Ill health obliged Steve Camacho to step down as the board's chief executive after 18 years.

Meanwhile, a fierce contest developed for the leadership of the WICB. For the first time since the board was established in 1927, the president was challenged at its AGM in May. Pat Rousseau, the Jamaican attorney who took office in 1996, and his vice-president, Antiguan businessman Clarvis Joseph, just fought off Alloy Lequay, the 73-year-old president of the Trinidad & Tobago Board, and his running-mate, former Test bowler Wes Hall. Lequay and Hall spoke of "deception" and "betrayal" after the vote; Rousseau said the prelude had been "tainted by unpleasant tactics". Rousseau had asked to be judged on his record, especially the WICB's improved finances, and played a late trump card. A fortnight earlier, he had signed a $US40 million contract with British broadcaster BSkyB for exclusive television rights to all cricket in the Caribbean from 2004 to 2008. It superseded the board's 1990 agreement with Trans World International.

Such upheavals were compounded by the premature deaths of Marshall, Sir Conrad Hunte and Sylvester Clarke, all eminent Test players, all Barbadian and all within a month in late 1999. Marshall, aged 41, had been West Indies' coach for three years until struck down by colon cancer during the World Cup; Hunte, 67, had been elected president of the Barbados Cricket Association only a month before succumbing to a heart attack. Both had much more to contribute to West Indies cricket.

Yet hopes were renewed by triumph in the home Tests against Zimbabwe and Pakistan. Spirits were lifted when, in his native Kingston, Courtney Walsh surpassed Kapil Dev's 434 Test wickets to become Test cricket's leading bowler. And when West Indies won the First Test of their subsequent series in England, ending a sequence of ten overseas Test defeats, and led by 133 on first innings in the Second, it seemed as if Adams and the new management had made a difference. The illusion was shattered in two breathtaking hours at Lord's, when West Indies were routed for 54. After that, their cricket reverted to its accustomed inconsistency, culminating in the surrender of the Wisden Trophy, theirs since 1973.

There were a host of reasons for such events, and the Barbados conference sought to source and correct them. They included a lack of proper planning and facilities, poor pitches and players' attitudes. The effect had been evident for some time in the domestic first-class tournament, known since 1998-99 as the Busta Cup, and chairman of selectors Mike Findlay lamented the "very poor" standards after the 1999-2000 competition. This was won by the best-balanced team, Jamaica, who had also triumphed in the one-day Red Stripe Bowl. But in the 18 Busta Cup matches, the highest total was 398 for eight declared, by the Leeward Islands; there were only five more totals above 300, against 12 under 150 and a further 12 between 150 and 200.

The only batsman to pass 600 runs in the tournament was Chris Gayle, Jamaica's 20-year-old left-handed opener, named the Cup's Most Valuable Player for his 623 at 56.63. The next highest aggregate was 379 by his team-mate Laurie Williams, whose medium-pace swing also brought him 20 wickets. Apart from Gayle, only Shivnarine Chanderpaul of Guyana and 34-year-old Windwards all-rounder Roy Marshall averaged above 40 in the competition. There were only 12 hundreds, with two each from Gayle and Barbados captain Philo Wallace. Given such statistics, it is little wonder that, between December and August, West Indies were bowled out for 97 (by New Zealand), 147 (Zimbabwe), and 54, 61 and 125 (England), or that bowlers continued to dominate the domestic game.

In his last home season, Curtly Ambrose was too good for most batsmen, despite the remnants of an arm injury that kept him in the Caribbean while West Indies were in New Zealand. Bowling 247 overs in seven matches for the Leeward Islands, he took 31 wickets at 12.03 each. Guyanese leg-spinner Mahendra Nagamootoo also claimed 31, at 20.83, and his consistency earned him selection for the England tour. Another leg-spinner, Dave Marshall, finally gained a regular place with Barbados when their prolific left-arm spinner, Winston Reid, retired. Marshall made the most of his opportunity, with 28 wickets at 16.17.

Jamaica's success, in both competitions, was based on all-round depth and a mix of experience and youth. Their batting was based around two established left-handers, Adams and former Test opener Robert Samuels, and three up-and-comers in left-handers Gayle and Hinds and the explosive, if disappointing, Ricardo Powell. The bowling was mainly in the hands of Walsh (who handed the captaincy to Adams after the Bowl), Franklyn Rose, Williams and Nehemiah Perry, all of whom had international experience.

In both Bowl and Cup, Jamaica overcame the Leeward Islands in the final. Barbados, the 1998-99 champions, led the Busta Cup table after the round-robin matches but were outplayed by Leewards in the semi-final, their last pair just avoiding outright defeat. Jamaica, too, went through to the final on first-innings lead, knocking out Guyana on the back of 168 from Gayle and six for 71 from Rose, despite a century from Chanderpaul. They were happy to settle for a first-innings win in the final as well, spurning the chance to enforce the follow-on after they scored 333, thanks to 127 from Hinds, and Leewards collapsed to 142. Administrators were left to ponder a more challenging method for the future.

The Windward Islands were again in the bottom half of the table but lost only once, to Barbados on a shocking pitch at Dominica's Botanical Gardens, hosting their first first-class match in more than 20 years. However, a concerted WICB coaching programme aimed at strengthening Windward Islands cricket began to bear fruit. In Guyana, in August 2000, they captured the Under-19 championship for the first time.

Trinidad & Tobago endured their worst season in living memory. Diminished by the retirement of three top players – Ian Bishop, Phil Simmons and David Williams – and with Lara distracted, they did not win a match at first-class or one-day level, finishing bottom in the Busta Cup and in their zone of the Bowl. Their board even threatened to withhold players' match fees after a two-day loss to Jamaica. This did not materialise, but there were six team changes for the next and final match – which they lost to Barbados, albeit by a single run.

The WICB sent teams to the Under-19 World Cup, in Sri Lanka in January, and the Under-15 World Challenge, in England later in the year. The Under-19s reached the Super League stage, numbering Zimbabwe, England and New Zealand among their victories – a considerable improvement on 1998, when they were knocked out in the preliminaries. The Under-15s, benefiting from a more strategic selection policy than in 1996, provided a significant fillip by winning their tournament, defeating Pakistan in the final at Lord's.

A-teams from India and South Africa toured the Caribbean. Because neither could be accommodated into the crowded itinerary of the dry months between January and May, however, both came when the weather was less predictable: India in late 1999 and South Africa in August and September 2000. Both visits were severely affected by rain; none of the four Tests – two against each touring side – produced a result. To counter the problem, the WICB came up with a novel idea for England A's visit in 2000-01, and for those of future A-teams. They would play in the Busta Cup, with a combined West Indies youth team bringing the participants to eight. The board believed it would be "a major motivational factor to heighten competitiveness and effort of national teams", arguing that whichever team won the Cup was "of limited importance compared to the priority of creating a stronger West Indies team".

Not everyone saw it that way. "The board should understand that there is more than cricket at stake... there is also national pride," wrote Tony Becca, sports editor of Jamaica's *Daily Gleaner*. "The regional four-day competition is for West Indian teams and should remain so." In an editorial, the *Jamaica Observer* charged that "for a lack of imagination, we are willing to subsume West Indian sovereignty and trade our nationalism". The fear, according to some cynics, was that England A would become West Indian champions.

In the end, the board resolved the dilemma by instituting a new tournament altogether – the Busta International Series. The six territories, West Indies B (an Under-23 side) and England A would play each other in a preliminary round leading to semi-finals and a final for the Busta Shield. The Busta Cup, meanwhile, would be won by the territory that gained most points in the preliminary matches.

FIRST-CLASS AVERAGES, 1999-2000

BATTING

(Qualification: 250 runs)

	M	I	NO	R	HS	100s	Avge
R. R. Sarwan (*Guyana*)	13	24	4	906	111	2	45.30
S. Chanderpaul (*Guyana*)	9	15	2	579	112	1	44.53
W. W. Hinds (*Jamaica*)	10	18	2	682	165	2	42.62
C. H. Gayle (*Jamaica*)	12	21	3	711	168	2	39.50
J. C. Adams (*Jamaica*)	11	18	3	552	101*	1	36.80
R. A. Marshall (*Windward I.*)	6	9	1	289	70	0	36.12
L. R. Williams (*Jamaica*)	7	12	1	379	135	1	34.45
R. S. Morton (*Leeward I.*)	10	17	3	475	110	1	33.92
A. Haniff (*Guyana*)	11	21	2	625	102*	1	32.89
R. I. C. Holder (*Barbados*)	6	10	1	271	66*	0	30.11
P. A. Wallace (*Barbados*)	9	16	1	443	117	2	29.53
D. Ganga (*T & T*)	9	15	2	379	63*	0	29.15
K. F. Semple (*Guyana*)	8	13	0	359	67	0	27.61
R. G. Samuels (*Jamaica*)	7	13	1	325	73*	0	27.08
K. L. T. Arthurton (*Leeward I.*)	7	11	0	296	88	0	26.90
T. M. Dowlin (*Guyana*)	8	13	1	319	102	1	26.58
R. N. Lewis (*Windward I.*)	8	13	2	292	64	0	26.54
D. Rampersad (*T & T*)	7	11	0	281	107	1	25.54
S. C. Joseph (*Leeward I.*)	14	25	2	583	100	1	25.34
C. O. Browne (*Barbados*)	11	17	2	380	109*	1	25.33
R. O. Hinds (*Barbados*)	9	14	0	337	68	0	24.07
D. S. Smith (*Windward I.*)	7	13	1	263	59	0	21.91
S. L. Campbell (*Barbados*)	9	17	2	322	58	0	21.46
M. V. Nagamootoo (*Guyana*)	8	13	1	254	59	0	21.16
A. F. G. Griffith (*Barbados*)	9	16	1	300	90	0	20.00

* *Signifies not out.*

BOWLING

(Qualification: 15 wickets)

	O	M	R	W	BB	5W/i	Avge
M. Dillon (*T & T*)	138	39	305	23	6-40	2	13.26
C. E. L. Ambrose (*Leeward I.*)	443	188	692	50	5-39	2	13.84
L. R. Williams (*Jamaica*)	142.1	45	315	20	6-45	1	15.75
D. K. Marshall (*Barbados*)	194.1	52	453	28	7-49	2	16.17
M. Persad (*T & T*)	216.2	60	488	29	5-46	2	16.82
F. A. Rose (*Jamaica*)	194.4	40	594	34	6-71	3	17.47
C. A. Walsh (*Jamaica*)	325.2	90	687	39	5-22	2	17.61
R. D. King (*Guyana*)	310	78	755	42	5-24	3	17.97
C. M. Tuckett (*Leeward I.*)	132.1	44	290	15	4-77	0	19.33
H. R. Bryan (*Barbados*)	217.1	69	496	25	5-38	1	19.84
D. Ramnarine (*T & T*)	268.2	80	532	26	5-31	2	20.46
K. C. B. Jeremy (*Leeward I.*)	253.4	72	656	32	6-81	2	20.50
D. R. Maynard (*Barbados*)	155.4	32	454	22	4-51	0	20.63
C. E. L. Stuart (*Guyana*)	238.4	58	626	30	4-42	0	20.86
M. V. Nagamootoo (*Guyana*)	346.3	81	821	37	4-45	0	22.18
N. A. M. McLean (*Windward I.*)	272.1	66	733	30	5-37	1	24.43
R. A. Marshall (*Windward I.*)	168.3	38	379	15	4-84	0	25.26
R. N. Lewis (*Windward I.*)	241.2	43	639	18	4-66	0	35.50

Note: Averages include South Africa A's tour in August and September 2000.

BUSTA CUP, 1999-2000

	Played	Won	Lost	Drawn	1st-inns Points	Points
Barbados.........	5	2	1	2	8	48
Jamaica	5	2	1	2	4	44
Guyana..........	5	1	0	4	8	40
Leeward Islands	5	1	1	3	9	37
Windward Islands ...	5	0	1	4	12	28
Trinidad & Tobago ..	5	0	2	3	5	17

Win = 16 pts; draw = 4 pts; 1st-innings lead in a drawn match = 4 pts; 1st-innings lead in a lost match = 5 pts.

Semi-finals: Leeward Islands drew with Barbados, but qualified for the final on first-innings lead; Jamaica drew with Guyana, but qualified for the final on first-innings lead.

Final: Jamaica drew with Leeward Islands, but took the Cup by virtue of their first-innings lead.

*In the following scores, * by the name of a team indicates that they won the toss.*

At Wilson Road Recreation Ground, Peñal (Trinidad), January 6, 7, 8, 9. Drawn. Trinidad & Tobago 114 (A. J. A. Lake three for 20); Leeward Islands* 263 for nine (S. C. Williams 84, C. D. Cannonier 30, K. L. T. Arthurton 32, C. M. Tuckett 51 not out; M. Persad five for 63). *Trinidad & Tobago 4 pts, Leeward Islands 8 pts.*
  The first two days were washed out.

At Kensington Oval, Bridgetown, January 7, 8, 9, 10. Drawn. Barbados* 272 (F. L. Reifer 37, R. O. Hurley 55, I. D. R. Bradshaw 39, H. R. Bryan 76 not out; C. E. L. Stuart three for 51, M. V. Nagamootoo three for 46) and 252 for six dec. (P. A. Wallace 117, R. I. C. Holder 39, C. O. Browne 30 not out; M. V. Nagamootoo three for 77); Guyana 198 (N. A. De Groot 31, R. R. Sarwan 65, M. V. Nagamootoo 32 not out; D. K. Marshall six for 51, R. O. Hurley three for 30) and 206 for eight (K. F. Semple 45, T. M. Dowlin 39, M. V. Nagamootoo 30; D. R. Maynard four for 51). *Barbados 8 pts, Guyana 4 pts.*
  In Guyana's second innings, Marshall had figures of 21–11–18–0.

At Arnos Vale, St Vincent, January 7, 8, 9, 10. Drawn. Jamaica 280 (C. D. Wright 70, L. R. Williams 135; C. E. Cuffy three for 60, R. N. Lewis four for 66) and 143 for five dec. (C. H. Gayle 86 not out); Windward Islands* 153 (J. R. Murray 55) and 106 for one (K. K. Sylvester 51 not out). *Windward Islands 4 pts, Jamaica 8 pts.*

At Kensington Oval, Bridgetown, January 14, 15, 16, 17. Drawn. Leeward Islands* 255 (S. C. Williams 62, R. S. Morton 54, C. M. Tuckett 31; H. R. Bryan five for 38) and 178 for eight (R. S. Morton 70 not out, C. M. Tuckett 36; D. R. Maynard three for 39); Barbados 266 (P. A. Wallace 32, C. O. Browne 109 not out, I. D. R. Bradshaw 30, H. R. Bryan 30; C. E. L. Ambrose four for 47, C. M. Tuckett four for 77). *Barbados 8 pts, Leeward Islands 4 pts.*

At Sabina Park, Kingston, January 14, 15, 16, 17. Drawn. Guyana 287 (N. A. De Groot 44, R. R. Sarwan 35, T. M. Dowlin 102, N. C. McGarrell 38; L. R. Williams six for 45) and 218 for eight dec. (A. Haniff 59, K. F. Semple 57, T. M. Dowlin 38 not out; C. H. Gayle three for 73); Jamaica* 206 (C. D. Wright 45, R. G. Samuels 71; C. E. L. Stuart four for 53, N. C. McGarrell four for 32) and 236 for six (C. H. Gayle 121 not out, T. O. Powell 57). *Jamaica 4 pts, Guyana 8 pts.*

At Mindoo Phillip Park, Castries (St Lucia), January 14, 15, 16, 17. Drawn. Windward Islands 238 (K. K. Sylvester 34, J. R. Murray 56, R. A. Marshall 36, M. J. Morgan 30 not out; A. I. Jan five for 67, M. Persad three for 63) and five for no wkt; Trinidad & Tobago* 122 (R. A. M. Smith 36; R. N. Lewis three for 35). *Windward Islands 8 pts, Trinidad & Tobago 4 pts.*
  Weather permitted only 17 balls on the final two days.

At Guaracara Park, Pointe-à-Pierre, January 20, 21, 22, 23. Drawn. Guyana 284 (K. F. Semple 67, R. R. Sarwan 79, S. Chanderpaul 36, M. V. Nagamootoo 38; M. Persad three for 80, A. Balliram three for eight) and 149 (K. F. Semple 65; D. Ramnarine five for 31, M. Persad three for 36); Trinidad & Tobago* 251 (I. H. Jan 43, D. Rampersad 107, Extras 31; R. D. King five for 71, C. E. L. Stuart three for 62) and 155 for nine (B. C. Lara 56, Extras 45; R. D. King five for 24). *Trinidad & Tobago 4 pts, Guyana 8 pts.*

At Sabina Park, Kingston, January 21, 22, 23, 24. Jamaica won by 114 runs. Jamaica* 195 (C. H. Gayle 39, L. R. Williams 48, F. A. Rose 32 not out; D. R. Maynard three for 29, H. R. Bryan three for 61, R. O. Hurley three for 31) and 318 (C. H. Gayle 69, W. W. Hinds 49, M. G. Sinclair 40, R. G. Samuels 55, Extras 31; D. R. Maynard four for 68, D. K. Marshall four for 96); Barbados 157 (R. I. C. Holder 43, R. O. Hurley 41; F. A. Rose six for 74) and 242 (A. F. G. Griffith 90, C. O. Browne 46; J. C. Adams four for 23). *Jamaica 16 pts.*
   Rose took a hat-trick in Barbados's first innings, composed of Test batsmen Sherwin Campbell, Griffith and Philo Wallace.

At Recreation Ground, St John's, January 21, 22, 23, 24. Drawn. Leeward Islands 85 (N. A. M. McLean five for 37, M. J. Morgan four for 27) and 398 for eight dec. (C. D. Cannonier 34, S. C. Joseph 43, K. L. T. Arthurton 79, R. D. Jacobs 117 not out, Extras 54; R. A. Marshall four for 107); Windward Islands* 230 (R. A. Marshall 70, D. Thomas 42; C. E. L. Ambrose three for 38) and 140 for five (R. A. Marshall 48; K. C. B. Jeremy three for 29). *Leeward Islands 4 pts, Windward Islands 8 pts.*
   The highest individual score in Leewards' first innings was Jacobs's 14.

At Botanical Gardens, Roseau (Dominica), January 27, 28, 29. Barbados won by ten wickets. Windward Islands* 120 (D. K. Marshall seven for 49) and 89 (D. K. Marshall four for 33, R. O. Hurley three for 15); Barbados 190 (P. A. Wallace 57, C. O. Browne 33; C. E. Cuffy three for 21, R. A. Marshall four for 84) and 25 for no wkt. *Barbados 16 pts.*

At Alpart Sports Club, St Elizabeth, January 28, 29. Jamaica won by nine wickets. Trinidad & Tobago* 72 (F. A. Rose five for 22, N. O. Perry four for ten) and 119 (L. A. Roberts 40; C. A. Walsh four for 18, L. R. Williams three for 34); Jamaica 181 (C. H. Gayle 69, F. A. Rose 30 not out; M. Persad four for 35, D. Ramnarine three for 78) and 11 for one. *Jamaica 16 pts.*

At Recreation Ground, St John's, January 28, 29, 30, 31. Guyana won by two wickets. Leeward Islands 221 (D. R. E. Joseph 60, W. D. Phillip 33; R. D. King four for 40, M. V. Nagamootoo four for 51) and 136 (F. A. Adams 34; R. D. King three for 43, M. V. Nagamootoo four for 45); Guyana* 204 (K. F. Semple 51, S. Chanderpaul 83; R. Christopher four for 47, K. C. B. Jeremy three for 35) and 157 for eight (N. C. McGarrell 54, S. Chanderpaul 31; C. E. L. Ambrose five for 39). *Guyana 16 pts, Leeward Islands 5 pts.*

At Queen's Park Oval, Port-of-Spain, February 3, 4, 5, 6. Barbados won by one run. Barbados 196 (R. I. C. Holder 40, R. O. Hinds 32; R. I. Sooklal three for 27) and 249 (P. A. Wallace 100; M. Dillon six for 54); Trinidad & Tobago* 283 (D. Ganga 39, R. A. M. Smith 65, K. Mason 82; D. R. Maynard four for 67) and 161 (D. Ganga 30, D. Rampersad 34, B. C. Lara 49, Extras 31; P. T. Collins three for 36, H. R. Bryan three for 38). *Barbados 16 pts, Trinidad & Tobago 5 pts.*

At Arnos Vale, St Vincent, February 3, 4, 5, 6. Drawn. Windward Islands 187 (D. S. Smith 59, J. R. Murray 32, R. N. Lewis 35; N. C. McGarrell four for 38, M. V. Nagamootoo four for 45) and 190 for seven dec. (J. R. Murray 56, R. A. Marshall 68; K. G. Darlington three for 37); Guyana* 172 (A. Haniff 84 not out; C. E. Cuffy four for 30) and 120 for three (A. Haniff 44, R. R. Sarwan 50 not out). *Windward Islands 8 pts, Guyana 4 pts.*
   Haniff carried his bat through Guyana's first innings, in which Cuffy's full figures were 30–11–30–4.

At Recreation Ground, St John's, February 4, 5, 6, 7. Leeward Islands won by an innings and 46 runs. Jamaica 153 (R. L. Powell 38, R. G. Samuels 45; C. E. L. Ambrose four for 15, C. M. Tuckett three for 32) and 139 (L. R. Williams 50; K. C. B. Jeremy five for 40); Leeward Islands* 338 (W. W. Cornwall 70, S. C. Joseph 32, R. S. Morton 110, C. E. L. Ambrose 34, Extras 41; C. A. Walsh three for 50, L. R. Williams three for 33). *Leeward Islands 16 pts.*
   Ambrose's match figures were 35–25–22–6.

Semi-finals

At Kensington Oval, Bridgetown, February 11, 12, 13, 14. Drawn. Leeward Islands qualified for the final by virtue of their first-innings lead. Leeward Islands 190 (R. S. Morton 60, W. D. Phillip 34; I. D. R. Bradshaw three for 50, R. O. Hurley three for 37) and 360 (D. R. E. Joseph 39, K. L. T. Arthurton 88, R. D. Jacobs 39, C. M. Tuckett 59 not out, W. D. Phillip 45; D. K. Marshall three for 61); Barbados* 148 (C. E. L. Ambrose five for 39) and 167 for nine (R. I. C. Holder 66 not out; W. W. Cornwall six for 53).

At Sabina Park, Kingston, February 18, 19, 20, 21. Drawn. Jamaica qualified for the final by virtue of their first-innings lead. Jamaica* 348 (C. H. Gayle 168, R. L. Powell 31, L. R. Williams 38 not out; N. C. McGarrell four for 82, M. V. Nagamootoo three for 89) and 192 for six (W. W. Hinds 39, R. G. Samuels 73 not out; R. D. King four for 30); Guyana 242 (S. Chanderpaul 112; F. A. Rose six for 71).

FINAL

JAMAICA v LEEWARD ISLANDS

At Sabina Park, Kingston, February 25, 26, 27, 28. Drawn. Toss: Leeward Islands.

Jamaica took the Cup by virtue of their first-innings lead; though they could have enforced the follow-on, they preferred to continue batting on the final day rather than seek an outright victory. Invited to bat by Leewards, Hinds obliged for eight hours, giving three chances, hitting 14 fours and sharing century partnerships with fellow left-handers Adams and Tony Powell. Jamaica failed to exploit their first-day 219 for two fully, but it hardly mattered; Leewards lost four wickets for five runs on the second evening, finishing on 78 for six. Their tail showed more spirit, but could only reduce the deficit to 191. When Jamaica chose to bat again, Hinds fell in Ambrose's first over, but Adams and Gayle set about making their position impregnable. Even the injured Powell and Walsh batted on the fourth day, aided by runners, and when Jamaica finally declared, Leewards' target was an impossible 353 in 50 overs. There was no attempt to chase it.

Man of the Match: W. W. Hinds. *Most Valuable Player of the Tournament:* C. H. Gayle.

Close of play: First day, Jamaica 219-2 (Hinds 116*, T. O. Powell 46*); Second day, Leeward Islands 78-6 (Arthurton 8*, Tuckett 5*); Third day, Jamaica 105-2 (Adams 44*, R. L. Powell 27*).

Jamaica

W. W. Hinds c Jacobs b Tuckett	127	– c Jacobs b Ambrose 0
C. H. Gayle c S. C. Joseph b Jeremy	8	– b Phillip 31
*J. C. Adams c Jacobs b Phillip	32	– c Jacobs b Ambrose 51
T. O. Powell c Jacobs b Cornwall	54	– (10) not out 4
R. L. Powell b Phillip	37	– (4) c S. C. Joseph b Ambrose 38
R. G. Samuels c Phillip b Cornwall	2	– (5) c and b Jeremy 7
L. R. Williams c Tuckett b Ambrose	15	– (6) c S. C. Joseph b Ambrose 0
N. O. Perry lbw b Ambrose	0	– (7) lbw b Jeremy 24
†M. G. Sinclair not out	9	– (8) b Jeremy 0
F. A. Rose c Jeremy b Phillip	10	– (9) c S. C. Joseph b Phillip 1
C. A. Walsh run out	10	– not out 1
B 4, l-b 10, n-b 15	29	N-b 4 4

1/20 2/121 3/247 4/248 5/255	333	1/0 2/49 3/123 (9 wkts dec.) 161
6/295 7/295 8/306 9/320		4/124 5/124 6/155
		7/155 8/156 9/156

Bowling: *First Innings*—Ambrose 34–16–62–2; Jeremy 23.5–8–71–1; Tuckett 24–13–32–1; Cornwall 28–8–65–2; Phillip 33–8–76–3; Arthurton 2–0–13–0. *Second Innings*—Ambrose 16–8–18–4; Jeremy 15–5–24–3; Cornwall 1–0–11–0; Tuckett 11–3–34–0; Phillip 37–11–46–2; Arthurton 10–2–19–0; S. C. Joseph 2–0–9–0.

Leeward Islands

*S. C. Williams lbw b Walsh	8	– c Sinclair b Williams	15
W. W. Cornwall lbw b Williams	29	– c Perry b Williams	43
S. C. Joseph c Sinclair b Walsh	1	– not out	36
D. R. E. Joseph c Sinclair b Williams	16	– not out	13
K. L. T. Arthurton lbw b Walsh	8		
R. S. Morton c T. O. Powell b Perry	1		
†R. D. Jacobs lbw b Perry	0		
C. M. Tuckett c Sinclair b Rose	28		
C. E. L. Ambrose c Samuels b Rose	2		
W. D. Phillip c Sinclair b Williams	24		
K. C. B. Jeremy not out	10		
B 3, l-b 1, n-b 11	15	B 2, l-b 1, n-b 4	7

1/16 2/27 3/61 4/62 5/66   142   1/42 2/67   (2 wkts) 114
6/66 7/93 8/102 9/109

Bowling: First Innings—Walsh 15–5–37–3; Rose 11–3–30–2; Williams 12.4–7–21–3; Perry 26–12–44–2; R. L. Powell 3–2–4–0; Adams 1–0–2–0. *Second Innings*—Rose 4–0–25–0; Williams 7–1–33–2; Hinds 3–1–12–0; Perry 9–2–17–0; R. L. Powell 12–5–16–0; Adams 6–2–4–0; Gayle 2–1–4–0.

Umpires: S. A. Bucknor and E. A. Nicholls.

REGIONAL CHAMPIONS

Shell Shield		1985-86	Barbados
1965-66	Barbados	1986-87	Guyana
1966-67	Barbados		
1967-68	No competition	*Red Stripe Cup*	
1968-69	Jamaica	1987-88	Jamaica
1969-70	Trinidad	1988-89	Jamaica
1970-71	Trinidad	1989-90	Leeward Islands
1971-72	Barbados	1990-91	Barbados
1972-73	Guyana	1991-92	Jamaica
1973-74	Barbados	1992-93	Guyana
1974-75	Guyana	1993-94	Leeward Islands
1975-76 { Trinidad		1994-95	Barbados
{ Barbados		1995-96	Leeward Islands
1976-77	Barbados	1996-97	Barbados
1977-78	Barbados		
1978-79	Barbados	*President's Cup*	
1979-80	Barbados	1997-98 { Leeward Islands	
1980-81	Combined Islands	{ Guyana	
1981-82	Barbados		
1982-83	Guyana	*Busta Cup*	
1983-84	Barbados	1998-99	Barbados
1984-85	Trinidad & Tobago	1999-2000	Jamaica

Barbados have won the title outright 15 times, Guyana and Jamaica 5, Leeward Islands and Trinidad/Trinidad & Tobago 3, Combined Islands 1. Barbados, Guyana, Leeward Islands and Trinidad have also shared the title.

The first-class matches played by India A and South Africa A may be found in the Other A-Team Tours section.

RED STRIPE BOWL, 1999-2000

Note: Matches in this section were not first-class.

Zone A (in Jamaica)

At Alpart Sports Club, St Elizabeth, October 27. Jamaica won by ten runs (D/L method). Jamaica 118 for six (41 overs) (P. Philpott three for 33); Bermuda* 95 for eight (25 overs) (C. H. Gayle four for 24).
   Bermuda's target was revised to 106 from 25 overs.

At Alpart Sports Club, St Elizabeth, October 28. Guyana won by three wickets. Windward Islands 76 (35 overs) (N. C. McGarrell five for 20); Guyana* 77 for seven (28.1 overs) (R. A. Marshall three for 22).

At Sabina Park, Kingston, October 30. Jamaica won by seven wickets. Windward Islands 101 (47.4 overs) (D. Thomas 30; F. A. Rose four for 16); Jamaica* 104 for three (29.3 overs).

At Sabina Park, Kingston, October 31. Jamaica won by seven wickets. Guyana 146 (49.5 overs) (S. Chanderpaul 46; C. A. Walsh three for 18, B. S. Murphy three for 29); Jamaica* 147 for three (42 overs) (C. H. Gayle 75 not out, R. G. Samuels 33).

At Kensington Park, Kingston, November 1. Guyana won by eight wickets. Bermuda 102 (42.1 overs) (C. M. Marshall 43; K. F. Semple three for 13); Guyana* 104 for two (18.1 overs) (N. A. De Groot 44, A. Gonsalves 46).

At Kensington Park, Kingston, November 2. Windward Islands won by 161 runs. Windward Islands 209 (49.4 overs) (J. R. Murray 40, R. N. Lewis 67; R. Basden five for 35, H. Durham three for 36); Bermuda* 48 (26.3 overs) (R. N. Lewis three for ten).

Jamaica 6 pts, Guyana 4 pts, Windward Islands 2 pts, Bermuda 0 pts.

Zone B (in Leeward Islands)

At Recreation Ground, St John's, October 29. Leeward Islands won by four wickets. Barbados* 120 (40 overs) (A. F. G. Griffith 31; W. W. Cornwall four for 23); Leeward Islands 121 for six (42.2 overs) (R. D. Jacobs 31).

At Recreation Ground, St John's, October 30. Barbados won by 114 runs (D/L method). Barbados 220 for eight (50 overs) (P. A. Wallace 45, S. L. Campbell 40, F. L. Reifer 48); Canada* 88 for seven (41 overs) (M. Croning 30 not out)
   Canada's target was revised to 203 from 41 overs.

At Ronald Webster Park, The Valley (Anguilla), October 30. Leeward Islands won by 47 runs. Leeward Islands* 260 for six (50 overs) (S. C. Joseph 83, K. L. T. Arthurton 93; D. Ramnarine three for 61); Trinidad & Tobago 213 (48 overs) (D. Rampersad 62, R. A. M. Smith 42, I. R. Bishop 34; G. T. Prince four for 46).

At Ronald Webster Park, The Valley (Anguilla), October 31. Barbados won by 101 runs. Barbados* 291 for seven (50 overs) (S. L. Campbell 102, R. I. C. Holder 31, H. R. Waldron 43, C. O. Browne 30); Trinidad & Tobago 190 (43.3 overs) (S. Ragoonath 37, D. Ganga 33; P. T. Collins four for 25).

At Ronald Webster Park, The Valley (Anguilla), November 1. Canada v Trinidad & Tobago. No result (abandoned).

At Ronald Webster Park, The Valley (Anguilla), November 2. Leeward Islands v Canada. No result (abandoned).

Leeward Islands 5 pts, Barbados 4 pts, Canada 2 pts, Trinidad & Tobago 1 pt.

Semi-finals (in Jamaica)

At Kaiser Sports Club, Discovery Bay, November 5. Leeward Islands won by five wickets (D/L method). Guyana 217 for six (50 overs) (N. A. De Groot 30, R. R. Sarwan 40, T. M. Dowlin 30; H. A. G. Anthony three for 28); Leeward Islands* 193 for five (45.1 overs) (S. C. Joseph 57, K. L. T. Arthurton 35, R. D. Jacobs 50, R. S. Morton 33 not out).
   Leewards' target was revised to 192 from 46 overs.

At Kaiser Sports Club, Discovery Bay, November 6. Jamaica v Barbados. No result (abandoned).
   Jamaica qualified for the final by virtue of scoring more points in the Zone games.

Final

At Kaiser Sports Club, Discovery Bay, November 7. Jamaica won by ten runs (D/L method). Leeward Islands 228 for seven (50 overs) (S. C. Williams 65, S. C. Joseph 100 not out); Jamaica* 177 for six (38 overs) (R. G. Samuels 77 not out).
   When bad light and rain ended Jamaica's innings, they were ten ahead of the par score of 167 from 38 overs. Joseph was named Most Valuable Player of the Final Four.

CRICKET IN NEW ZEALAND, 1999-2000

By DON CAMERON and FRANCIS PAYNE

Brooke Walker

After the giddy start offered by the wholesale defeat of an out-of-sorts West Indies, the new millennium left another frown-line on the forehead of New Zealand cricket. It was not solely because the New Zealanders were subsequently demolished by what the next visiting captain, Steve Waugh, believed to be one of the great Australian sides. Nor was it due to the difficulty, akin to that faced by England, of developing an intermediate grade at domestic level that would identify and promote promising players into international ranks.

The new worry was one of finding suitable playing and spectator facilities, and then providing matches to attract spectators. New Zealand has seven grounds worthy of international status – Eden Park in Auckland, WestpacTrust/Seddon Park in Hamilton, McLean Park in Napier, the Basin Reserve and the new WestpacTrust Stadium in Wellington, the Lancaster Park complex in Christchurch and Carisbrook in Dunedin. But at several of these, cricket has to compete for time and space with rugby.

In Christchurch, rugby and cricket combined happily in the use of Lancaster Park until a new administration took over. The main field, now known as Jade Stadium, may still serve for one-day internationals and Tests – provided they are over before rugby requires the park, from late February onward. The same applies to Carisbrook. Ironically, Jade Stadium/Lancaster Park and Carisbrook produce the finest batting pitches in New Zealand, which also encourage better bowlers. But the economical and geographical facts of cricket life mean they will be lucky to stage one major match each a year. Auckland could also be looking for another international cricket venue should rugby demand more time; Eden Park has a large new grandstand, lifting the reserved-seat capacity to 45,000, which makes it a rugby money-maker, but has lowered the standard of the Test facilities. Wellington's Basin Reserve is the only major cricket ground of the traditional type, and the capital city has virtually replaced Christchurch as the spiritual home of the game. However, Wellington also has a new purpose-built, multi-sport stadium, seating 35,000 and adequate for one-day internationals, the development of which was encouraged on the basis that it would also stage Tests.

Cricket does not draw big crowds in New Zealand; the national administration relies mostly on sponsorship, broadcasting rights and the astonishing money-raising ability of chief executive Christopher Doig. The Basin Reserve is the only ground likely to draw more than 10,000 to a Test on a favourable day; on bad days, it struggles to get past 1,000. One-day internationals occasionally attract above 20,000 to Eden Park, but the new Wellington stadium appears to be the only other 10,000-plus venue.

New Zealand Cricket has an annual problem trying to spread international fixtures as widely as possible, to present international-quality conditions, and to run games as close to break-even as possible. Uncertainty about the major venues does not make life easier for the selectors, coaches and administrators trying to develop a credible national team.

The provincial sides are further disadvantaged. Only Eden Park has a secondary oval worthy of first-class cricket. So the four-day and one-day Shell competitions, which frequently lose their best players to international duty, must also take place on secondary grounds, often without suitable facilities for spectators.

Northern Districts are more fortunate than most, with good playing facilities at Hamilton, Taupo, Mount Maunganui, Rotorua and Whangarei. In recent years, they have had another advantage: when the national selectors called, only bowlers Daniel Vettori and Simon Doull have been removed – joined in March 2000 by Daryl Tuffey, a burly young Maori seamer. Not surprisingly, Northern Districts dominated the four-day Shell Trophy. They won four of their five games outright, and claimed the title after crushing Auckland in the five-day final. Their find of the season was left-arm spinner Bruce Martin, who made his first-class debut, aged 19, in February and finished as the country's leading wicket-taker with 37 victims at 17.72 apiece, including two ten-wicket returns. The batting was led by Mark Bailey and another youngster, 21-year-old Jamie Marshall, who scored 569 runs in all first-class cricket.

An improving Auckland side reached three finals – the Shell Trophy, the one-day Shell Cup and the even shorter Super Max League – but lost them all. Like Northern Districts, they won four Trophy games. Tama Canning, Adelaide-born to New Zealand parents and a graduate of Australia's Cricket Academy, took 30 wickets, including Auckland's first hat-trick since 1912-13. Leg-spinner Brooke Walker began to look a promising all-rounder; only his captain, Blair Pocock, scored more than his 298 runs for Auckland in the Shell Trophy, in which Walker also took 21 wickets.

The only batsman to reach 1,000 runs in the home season was Mathew Sinclair, but his province, Central Districts, were not the primary beneficiaries. They once lost him to international duties in mid-match, just after he had scored a century against Otago, who went on to win by an innings. They still possessed the leading scorer in the Shell Trophy, Glen Sulzberger, who made 550 runs at 61.11 and gave an indication that he could develop as an off-spinner. But, by March, former Test player Mark Greatbatch had emerged from retirement to bolster a Central campaign which had gone downhill after two early victories – including the only reverse inflicted on Northern Districts.

Otago's innings win over Central Districts remained their only four-day victory. It was set up by centuries from Chris Gaffaney, who contributed 487 runs in all, and Test opener Matthew Horne, with seam bowlers Glenn Jonas and Shayne O'Connor, a lithe left-armer, accounting for the home team's batting. The same pair dismissed Northern Districts for 84 in March, only for Otago to crumble for 77 in reply. O'Connor later collected a five-wicket bag against Australia, and off-spinner Paul Wiseman showed progress at international level.

Wellington, too, had only one Shell Trophy victory. Jason Wells stood out, scoring 473 runs at 94.60, and became the first batsman to hit three hundreds in successive first-class innings for the province. They did pick up the Max title, beating league-leaders Auckland in the final, and signed Test captain Stephen Fleming and Jonas for 2000-01.

Canterbury, who won the one-day Shell Cup for the seventh time in nine years, typified the dilemma of the domestic game in New Zealand. They were at full strength as they retained their title, without serious challenge, over the first six weeks of 2000; inevitably, they beat Auckland in the final. But they lost five players to the national side as the Trophy began in mid-February, and could not win a single first-class match.

Canterbury's case was worrying proof that the gap between the thin layer of international players and the lower domestic stratum was growing. The Conference competition, originally devised as an intermediate grade, was reduced to three games in 1999-2000, and forgotten altogether the next year, when the Trophy expanded again to two full rounds – each team playing ten league matches instead of five. NZC had spent much money and effort on putting promising players through its Academy, and in arranging all manner of local and overseas competition in a bid to strengthen their resources. Yet during the season, the only players promoted to Test status were Sinclair, who started with 214 against West Indies but averaged only 10.16 against Australia, and Tuffey, who went wicketless in his one Test – though he won a pat on the back from Steve Waugh. Meanwhile, the previous year's debutants, Gary Stead, an ugly duckling who had missed the Academy but proved himself a doughty batsman for Canterbury, and Wellington's Matthew Bell, were soon discarded.

The need for reserve strength was clear. New Zealand's top three against Australia, Craig Spearman, Horne and Sinclair, totalled 210 runs at 11.66 between them. Fleming, one of New Zealand's most experienced batsmen, declined to move up from No. 4; Adam Parore, once commended for a sound batting technique, needed to concentrate on his shaky wicket-keeping. The selectors, Ross Dykes, Rick Pickard and coach David Trist, stolidly declared that no other top-order candidate had, as that wearying cliché goes, "put up his hand and said 'pick me' ". Apparently they never saw the up-raised hand of Wells, or the scoresheets for his three consecutive hundreds for Wellington. One fears that future selectors will be just as intractable. The situation recalls *Catch 22...* the players, especially batsmen, will not develop in the low-key competition of the Shell Trophy, but that low level will be reinforced by selectors unwilling to risk promoting someone who has not "put his hand up".

The bowling prospects looked slightly brighter, provided NZC could find a back-injury specialist. Geoff Allott, joint leading wicket-taker in the 1999 World Cup, missed the entire season with a bad back, and Dion Nash was laid low by the end of it. Doull's history of knee injuries caught up with him; he did eventually play against Australia, but possibly that owed more to his do-or-die character than to medical expertise. Then, the 21-year-old Vettori, who had just taken 12 wickets in the First Test against Australia, limped out of the series – with a stress fracture of the lower back.

One man transcended all New Zealand's trials. When the prizes for 1999-2000 were given out, Chris Cairns was named player of the international series, and best batsman and bowler of the season; he was rated overseas as the best all-rounder in world cricket, and was vice-captain when the Rest of the World played Asia at Dhaka. Cairns bowled superbly against West Indies, and batted like a tiger against Australia. At last, after ten years' effort of varying degree, he had made it to the top. New Zealand hoped that it would not be another ten years before the next match-winning crowd-puller came along. – D.C.

FIRST-CLASS AVERAGES, 1999-2000

BATTING

(Qualification: 5 completed innings, average 35.00)

	M	I	NO	R	HS	100s	Avge
J. D. Wells (*Wellington*)	4	6	1	473	143	3	94.60
C. B. Gaffaney (*Otago*)	7	13	2	624	140*	1	56.72
S. M. Lynch (*Auckland*)	4	7	2	280	81*	0	56.00
C. L. Cairns (*New Zealand*)	5	8	0	444	109	1	55.50
S. J. Blackmore (*Wellington*)	4	6	0	320	91	0	53.33
K. D. Mills (*Auckland*)	6	9	3	291	81*	0	48.50
G. P. Sulzberger (*C. Districts*)	7	13	0	628	159	2	48.30
S. R. Mather (*Otago*)	5	8	2	288	117*	1	48.00
M. H. W. Papps (*Canterbury*)	4	8	1	305	84	0	43.57
M. H. Richardson (*Otago*)	9	16	1	638	108	1	42.53
M. S. Sinclair (*C. Districts*)	14	26	2	1,004	214	3	41.83

	M	I	NO	R	HS	100s	Avge
M. D. Bailey (*N. Districts*)	7	12	0	497	100	1	41.41
J. D. P. Oram (*C. Districts*)	7	14	2	496	92*	0	41.33
N. J. Astle (*New Zealand*)	5	9	1	315	93	0	39.37
S. P. Fleming (*Canterbury*)	6	10	0	386	78	0	38.60
J. A. H. Marshall (*N. Districts*)	9	16	1	569	81	0	37.93
S. B. Doull (*N. Districts*)	4	7	2	182	63*	0	36.40
N. R. Parlane (*N. Districts*)	7	12	1	391	147	1	35.54
C. J. Nevin (*Wellington*)	6	9	1	284	72	0	35.50
T. A. Boyer (*Wellington*)	4	7	0	248	104	1	35.42

* Signifies not out.

BOWLING

(Qualification: 15 wickets)

	O	M	R	W	BB	5W/i	Avge
G. R. Jonas (*Otago*)	103.2	33	242	19	6-35	2	12.73
B. P. Martin (*N. Districts*)	237.3	51	656	37	7-33	5	17.72
T. K. Canning (*Auckland*)	281.3	105	577	30	5-47	2	19.23
L. J. Hamilton (*C. Districts*)	206.5	42	627	31	5-106	1	20.22
G. E. Bradburn (*N. Districts*)	176.1	55	405	20	4-37	0	20.25
C. L. Cairns (*New Zealand*)	178.3	43	548	27	7-27	2	20.29
S. B. O'Connor (*Otago*)	268.4	75	715	35	5-43	3	20.42
D. L. Vettori (*New Zealand*)	202.1	60	476	22	7-87	2	21.63
J. D. P. Oram (*C. Districts*)	158.4	47	407	18	5-30	1	22.61
A. R. Adams (*Auckland*)	115	30	399	15	5-64	1	26.60
S. B. Styris (*N. Districts*)	133.1	36	400	15	6-32	1	26.66
P. J. Wiseman (*Otago*)	388.4	102	980	34	7-113	2	28.82
J. A. F. Yovich (*N. Districts*)	176.1	27	581	20	4-19	0	29.05
C. S. Martin (*Canterbury*)	264.2	74	686	23	4-54	0	29.82
D. R. Tuffey (*N. Districts*)	265.5	62	763	25	4-31	0	30.52
K. D. Mills (*Auckland*)	215.2	59	622	20	3-16	0	31.10
W. A. Wisneski (*Canterbury*)	218.3	57	623	20	5-98	1	31.15
K. P. Walmsley (*Auckland*)	181.2	42	568	17	4-43	0	33.41
B. G. K. Walker (*Auckland*)	348.5	94	939	27	5-94	1	34.77
J. S. Patel (*Wellington*)	213	46	610	16	5-145	1	38.12

SHELL TROPHY, 1999-2000

	Played	Won	Lost	Drawn	1st-inns Points	Points
Northern Districts . . .	5	4	1	0	2	26
Auckland	5	4	1	0	0	24
Central Districts	5	2	2	1	2	14
Otago	5	1	3	1	2	8
Wellington	5	1	2	2	2	8
Canterbury	5	0	3	2	2	2

Final: Northern Districts beat Auckland by 267 runs.

Outright win = 6 pts; lead on first innings in a drawn or lost game = 2 pts.

Under New Zealand Cricket playing conditions, one extra was scored for every no-ball bowled whether scored off or not. Any runs scored off the bat were credited to the batsman, while byes and leg-byes were counted separately, in addition to the initial penalty.

In the following scores, * by the name of a team indicates that they won the toss.

At Eden Park Outer Oval, Auckland, February 12, 13, 14, 15. Auckland won by an innings and 35 runs. Wellington* 289 (M. D. Bell 68, J. D. Wells 67, R. G. Petrie 32, M. R. Jefferson 32; T. K. Canning five for 55) and 191 (G. T. Donaldson 60; K. D. Mills three for 16, B. G. K. Walker four for 85); Auckland 515 for seven dec. (T. G. McIntosh 52, B. A. Pocock 167, R. T. King 36, B. G. K. Walker 107 not out, K. D. Mills 81 not out, Extras 41; J. S. Patel five for 145). *Auckland 6 pts.*

Walker, scoring his maiden first-class hundred, and Mills, with his first fifty, added an unbroken 172 for Auckland's eighth wicket. Debutant Patel took five for 145 off 59 overs.

At Queen Elizabeth II Park, Christchurch, February 12, 13, 14, 15. Drawn. Otago* 349 (M. J. Horne 36, M. H. Richardson 70, S. R. Mather 117 not out, C. B. Gaffaney 56; C. S. Martin three for 99, H. J. Shaw five for 84) and 247 for four dec. (A. J. Hore 102, M. H. Richardson 30, S. R. Mather 74 not out); Canterbury 279 (M. H. W. Papps 84, A. J. Redmond 41, G. J. Hopkins 35, C. J. Anderson 50; S. B. O'Connor three for 82, P. J. Wiseman three for 57) and 240 for five (C. D. Cumming 35, B. J. K. Doody 54, J. I. Englefield 55, G. R. Stead 68 not out; W. C. McSkimming three for 58). *Otago 2 pts.*

At Seddon Park, Hamilton, February 12, 13, 14, 15. Central Districts won by three wickets. Northern Districts* 288 (J. A. H. Marshall 46, M. E. Parlane 60, H. J. H. Marshall 58, J. A. F. Yovich 44; J. D. P. Oram five for 30, T. R. Anderson four for 64) and 243 for five dec. (M. D. Bailey 85, N. R. Parlane 60); Central Districts 220 (D. P. Kelly 32, G. P. Sulzberger 76, J. D. P. Oram 38; G. E. Bradburn three for 41) and 313 for seven (G. P. Sulzberger 139, M. W. Douglas 34, C. J. M. Furlong 36 not out; D. R. Tuffey three for 66). *Central Districts 6 pts, Northern Districts 2 pts.*

This was Northern Districts' only defeat in the Shell Trophy; they won all their other matches outright.

At McLean Park, Napier, February 18, 19, 20, 21. Central Districts won by five wickets. Central Districts 358 (D. P. Kelly 43, G. P. Sulzberger 65, M. W. Douglas 46, J. D. P. Oram 90, C. J. M. Furlong 50 not out; H. J. Shaw three for 102) and 122 for five (D. P. Kelly 32, G. P. Sulzberger 33); Canterbury* 150 (B. J. K. Doody 40, C. J. Anderson 30 not out; K. Marc three for 32, C. J. M. Furlong four for 36) and 326 (C. D. Cumming 39, J. I. Englefield 65, M. H. W. Papps 81, A. J. Redmond 51, G. J. Hopkins 30; K. Marc three for 53, C. J. M. Furlong three for 105). *Central Districts 6 pts.*

With injuries depleting their pace attack, Central included 17-year-old Taraia Robin and former Middlesex player Kervin Marc.

At Carisbrook, Dunedin, February 18, 19, 20, 21. Auckland won by 70 runs. Auckland 285 (R. T. King 104, A. C. Barnes 47, Extras 30; D. G. Sewell three for 58, W. C. McSkimming four for 72) and 180 (A. C. Barnes 42, T. K. Canning 53; S. B. O'Connor five for 43, S. R. Mather three for 39); Otago* 185 (C. B. Gaffaney 82; T. K. Canning three for 50, K. P. Walmsley four for 43) and 210 (M. J. Horne 66, S. R. Mather 54; T. K. Canning five for 47, K. P. Walmsley three for 82). *Auckland 6 pts.*

The opening day's play started half an hour late when umpire Steve Dunne's flight was delayed. Paul Wiseman of Otago was called up for a one-day international after the match began, and replaced by Nathan Morland.

At Basin Reserve, Wellington, February 18, 19, 20, 21. Northern Districts won by ten wickets. Wellington 285 (M. D. Bell 77, T. A. Boyer 104, R. G. Petrie 32; A. R. Tait four for 59, G. E. Bradburn three for 37) and 177 (S. J. Blackmore 37, C. J. Nevin 31, T. A. Boyer 64; J. A. F. Yovich four for 68, G. E. Bradburn four for 37); Northern Districts* 436 (J. A. H. Marshall 52, M. D. Bailey 45, N. R. Parlane 147, D. R. Tuffey 89 not out, Extras 38) and 27 for no wkt. *Northern Districts 6 pts.*

Parlane, scoring his maiden first-class century, and Tuffey, whose previous best was 21 not out, added 188 for Northern Districts' ninth wicket.

At Fitzherbert Park, Palmerston North, February 24, 25, 26. Otago won by an innings and 125 runs. Central Districts* 165 (M. S. Sinclair 102; G. R. Jonas six for 39) and 215 (D. P. Kelly 30, C. M. Spearman 42, M. W. Douglas 64 not out, J. D. P. Oram 31; S. B. O'Connor five for 52);

Otago 505 (M. J. Horne 141, M. H. Richardson 61, R. A. Lawson 42, C. B. Gaffaney 140 not out, Extras 38; L. J. Hamilton three for 123, C. J. M. Furlong three for 128). *Otago 6 pts.*

After scoring 102, Sinclair left to join New Zealand's one-day side, replacing Spearman, who was given permission to bat in his place in Central Districts' second innings.

At Owen Delany Park, Taupo, February 24, 25, 26. Northern Districts won by an innings and 65 runs. Northern Districts* 345 (J. A. H. Marshall 54, M. E. Parlane 49, M. D. Bailey 100; T. K. Canning three for 76); Auckland 131 (B. G. K. Walker 47; S. B. Doull three for 22, B. P. Martin five for 22) and 149 (B. P. Martin seven for 33). *Northern Districts 6 pts.*

Martin, with five wickets in his two first-class matches to date, took 12 for 55.

At Basin Reserve, Wellington, February 24, 25, 26, 27. Drawn. Wellington* 390 (G. T. Donaldson 37, M. D. Bell 55, J. D. Wells 143, S. J. Blackmore 57, C. J. Nevin 43; C. S. Martin four for 67, A. J. Redmond three for 101); Canterbury 182 (A. J. Redmond 32; J. E. C. Franklin three for 58, J. S. Patel four for 42) and 384 for five (B. J. K. Doody 72, J. I. Englefield 76, G. R. Stead 125, M. H. W. Papps 49; R. G. Petrie three for 53). *Wellington 2 pts.*

At Eden Park Outer Oval, Auckland, March 5, 6, 7, 8. Auckland won by six wickets. Canterbury* 187 (S. P. Fleming 38, A. J. Redmond 72) and 258 (J. I. Englefield 50, S. P. Fleming 78, C. Z. Harris 60 not out; T. K. Canning three for 51, A. R. Adams four for 59); Auckland 285 (J. M. Aiken 40, B. A. Pocock 56, S. M. Lynch 42, L. G. Howell 34, B. G. K. Walker 37; A. J. Redmond four for 72, C. J. Anderson three for 41) and 161 for four (S. M. Lynch 46 not out, R. T. King 57; W. A. Wisneski three for 45). *Auckland 6 pts.*

At Pukekura Park, New Plymouth, March 5, 6, 7, 8. Drawn. Wellington* 438 (J. D. Wells 107, S. J. Blackmore 88, J. E. C. Franklin 41, R. G. Petrie 72, R. J. Kennedy 31; L. J. Hamilton five for 106) and 331 for four dec. (M. D. Bell 30, J. D. Wells 132 not out, T. A. Boyer 42, S. J. Blackmore 91); Central Districts 468 (C. M. Spearman 61, D. P. Kelly 62, G. P. Sulzberger 159, J. D. P. Oram 41, M. A. Sigley 35, C. J. M. Furlong 54 not out; R. J. Kennedy three for 70, J. S. Patel three for 145) and 202 for two (D. P. Kelly 104, C. M. Spearman 47, M. S. Sinclair 43 not out). *Central Districts 2 pts.*

A century in each innings made Wells the first player to score three successive first-class hundreds for Wellington. Spearman and Kelly opened with 102 in Central Districts' first innings and 112 in their second.

At Harry Barker Reserve, Gisborne, March 15, 16, 17. Northern Districts won by 65 runs. Northern Districts 84 (M. D. Bailey 47; S. B. O'Connor four for 29, G. R. Jonas six for 35) and 172 (M. E. Parlane 42; S. B. O'Connor three for 41, G. R. Jonas four for 54, W. C. McSkimming three for 41); Otago* 77 (C. B. Gaffaney 32; D. R. Tuffey four for 31, J. A. F. Yovich four for 19) and 114 (H. T. Anderson 36, C. B. Gaffaney 43; D. R. Tuffey three for 46, S. B. Styris six for 32). *Northern Districts 6 pts.*

A total of 24 wickets fell on the first day, rain washed out the second, and Northern Districts won on the third.

At Colin Maiden Park, Auckland, March 23, 24, 25, 26. Auckland won by eight runs. Auckland 291 (A. C. Barnes 65, K. D. Mills 76 not out; L. J. Hamilton four for 77) and 182 (B. A. Pocock 39, S. M. Lynch 48; L. J. Hamilton four for 46, J. D. P. Oram three for 18, T. R. Anderson three for 71); Central Districts* 194 (M. W. Douglas 38, J. D. P. Oram 54; K. D. Mills three for 44, A. R. Adams five for 64) and 271 (G. P. Sulzberger 42, M. W. Douglas 56, J. D. P. Oram 92 not out, M. J. Greatbatch 30; T. K. Canning three for 45, B. G. K. Walker five for 94). *Auckland 6 pts.*

Greatbatch came out of retirement. Hamilton scored 5 and 3, his first first-class runs of the season in his final match, after going scoreless in his previous seven innings. The game ended when Canning claimed the first first-class hat-trick for Auckland for 87 years.

At Queen Elizabeth II Park, Christchurch, March 23, 24, 25, 26. Northern Districts won by six wickets. Canterbury* 300 (C. D. Cumming 32, M. H. W. Papps 67, G. R. Stead 49, A. J. Redmond 45 not out; B. P. Martin five for 88) and 139 (A. J. Redmond 44; B. P. Martin six for 44); Northern Districts 191 (M. E. Parlane 57, G. E. Bradburn 35; C. S. Martin four for 54, C. Z. Harris four for 39) and 251 for four (M. E. Parlane 42, M. D. Bailey 44, J. A. H. Marshall 45, N. R. Parlane 61 not out; C. Z. Harris three for 87). *Northern Districts 6 pts, Canterbury 2 pts.*

Bruce Martin had his second ten-wicket haul in three games; he had not bowled in the middle match.

At Molyneux Park, Alexandra, March 23, 24, 25. Wellington won by nine wickets. Wellington 307 (M. D. Bell 54, S. J. Blackmore 47, C. J. Nevin 72, R. G. Petrie 36; N. L. McCullum four for 57) and 47 for one; Otago* 144 (W. C. McSkimming 31; J. E. C. Franklin four for 41) and 208 (M. H. Richardson 51, C. B. Gaffaney 68; M. R. Gillespie five for 58). *Wellington 6 pts.*

Nine years after his last game for Otago, 44-year-old Stu McCullum fielded as substitute alongside his sons Brendon and Nathan.

FINAL

NORTHERN DISTRICTS v AUCKLAND

At Owen Delany Park, Taupo, April 2, 3, 4, 5, 6. Northern Districts won by 267 runs. Toss: Northern Districts.

The final morning saw an unexpectedly dramatic finish. Needing a win to take the Trophy, Auckland launched a headlong assault on a target of 452, scored at six an over throughout, but were dismissed before lunch. Slow left-armer Martin ended the match with his eighth wicket – following 12 when the teams last met; Lynch was undefeated on 81 from 59 balls. Northern Districts' 267-run victory looked unlikely as they struggled through a gloomy opening day. Their eventual first-innings lead owed almost everything to Doull, who hit 63 in 59 balls and added 82 for the last wicket with Martin. Auckland's reply did not detain them long, but poor weather prolonged Northern Districts' second innings across three days. Leg-spinner Walker claimed four wickets for the second time in the game, but Yovich eluded him, batting six and a half hours before he was last out, one short of a maiden hundred. He compensated himself with the first three wickets in Auckland's helter-skelter run-chase.

Close of play: First day, Northern Districts 259-9 (Doull 43*, Martin 7*); Second day, Northern Districts 40-0 (J. A. H. Marshall 16*, M. E. Parlane 18*); Third day, Northern Districts 170-5 (Styris 26*, Yovich 3*); Fourth day, Northern Districts 367.

Northern Districts

J. A. H. Marshall lbw b Adams	81	– lbw b Adams	42
M. E. Parlane c Vincent b Canning	0	– c Vincent b Mills	18
M. D. Bailey lbw b Walker	13	– lbw b Walker	41
N. R. Parlane run out	2	– lbw b Walker	4
H. J. H. Marshall c Lynch b Walker	6	– lbw b Walker	24
S. B. Styris b Canning	81	– lbw b Adams	46
J. A. F. Yovich c Young b Walker	7	– c Young b Mills	99
G. E. Bradburn run out	0	– lbw b Canning	12
*†R. G. Hart c Aiken b Walker	2	– c Aiken b Mills	29
S. B. Doull not out	63	– b Walker	26
B. P. Martin c Young b Canning	2	– not out	0
B 2, l-b 4, w 5, n-b 6	17	B 4, l-b 17, w 1, n-b 4	26

1/8 2/49 3/51 4/67 5/156   292   1/41 2/93 3/106 4/130 5/155   367
6/205 7/205 8/205 9/210   6/214 7/264 8/323 9/362

Bowling: First Innings—Mills 18–2–77–0; Canning 22.1–7–53–3; Adams 18–1–95–1; Walker 27–7–61–4. *Second Innings*—Mills 30.2–10–98–3; Canning 40–19–78–1; Walker 50–17–95–4; Adams 21–8–54–2; Barnes 12–4–19–0; Vincent 3–1–2–0.

Auckland

J. M. Aiken c Hart b Yovich	6	– (9) c Hart b Bradburn	23
*B. A. Pocock lbw b Yovich	50	– (6) c Styris b Martin	6
S. M. Lynch lbw b Martin	29	– (4) not out	81
L. Vincent lbw b Doull	3	– (1) b Yovich	9
R. T. King c Hart b Yovich	8	– c Bradburn b Martin	0
A. C. Barnes not out	56	– (2) c J. A. H. Marshall b Yovich	17
B. G. K. Walker lbw b Styris	8	– (10) c Martin b Bradburn	9
K. D. Mills c J. A. H. Marshall b Bradburn	10	– (3) c H. J. H. Marshall b Yovich	22
T. K. Canning c Bailey b Martin	6	– (7) c Hart b Martin	6
†R. A. Young c Styris b Bradburn	1	– (11) b Martin	1
A. R. Adams b Martin	10	– (8) b Martin	8
L-b 14, w 1, n-b 6	21	L-b 1, w 1	2

1/13 2/74 3/80 4/110 5/113   208   1/15 2/45 3/62 4/67 5/81   184
6/148 7/165 8/176 9/181   6/101 7/115 8/144 9/170

Bowling: *First Innings*—Doull 12–3–34–1; Yovich 15–6–48–3; Styris 9–3–26–1; Martin 19.4–6–61–3; Bradburn 18–8–25–2. *Second Innings*—Doull 4–0–30–0; Yovich 9–0–47–3; Martin 11.5–0–75–5; Styris 2–0–16–0; Bradburn 4–0–15–2.

Umpires: D. M. Quested and E. A. Watkin.

CHAMPIONS

Plunket Shield					
1921-22	Auckland	1951-52	Canterbury	1976-77	Otago
1922-23	Canterbury	1952-53	Otago	1977-78	Auckland
1923-24	Wellington	1953-54	Central Districts	1978-79	Otago
1924-25	Otago	1954-55	Wellington	1979-80	Northern Districts
1925-26	Wellington	1955-56	Canterbury	1980-81	Auckland
1926-27	Auckland	1956-57	Wellington	1981-82	Wellington
1927-28	Wellington	1957-58	Otago	1982-83	Wellington
1928-29	Auckland	1958-59	Auckland	1983-84	Canterbury
1929-30	Wellington	1959-60	Canterbury	1984-85	Wellington
1930-31	Canterbury	1960-61	Wellington	1985-86	Otago
1931-32	Wellington	1961-62	Wellington	1986-87	Central Districts
1932-33	Otago	1962-63	Northern Districts	1987-88	Otago
1933-34	Auckland	1963-64	Auckland	1988-89	Auckland
1934-35	Canterbury	1964-65	Canterbury	1989-90	Wellington
1935-36	Wellington	1965-66	Wellington	1990-91	Auckland
1936-37	Auckland	1966-67	Central Districts	1991-92	{ Central Districts / Northern Districts
1937-38	Auckland	1967-68	Central Districts		
1938-39	Auckland	1968-69	Auckland	1992-93	Northern Districts
1939-40	Auckland	1969-70	Otago	1993-94	Canterbury
1940-45	No competition	1970-71	Central Districts	1994-95	Auckland
1945-46	Canterbury	1971-72	Otago	1995-96	Auckland
1946-47	Auckland	1972-73	Wellington	1996-97	Canterbury
1947-48	Otago	1973-74	Wellington	1997-98	Canterbury
1948-49	Canterbury	1974-75	Otago	1998-99	Central Districts
1949-50	Wellington			1999-2000	Northern Districts
1950-51	Otago	*Shell Trophy*			
		1975-76	Canterbury		

Auckland and Wellington have won the title outright 18 times, Canterbury 14, Otago 13, Central Districts 6, Northern Districts 4. Central Districts and Northern Districts also shared the title once.

SHELL CONFERENCE, 1999-2000

At Hagley Park, Christchurch, November 8, 9, 10, 11. North Island won by 32 runs. North Island*
174 (M. D. Bell 32, C. J. Nevin 36; W. A. Wisneski three for 42, P. J. Wiseman five for 35) and
355 for nine dec. (M. D. Bell 57, M. S. Sinclair 42, L. Vincent 46, B. G. K. Walker 34, M. R.
Jefferson 35; P. J. Wiseman seven for 113); South Island 162 (C. B. Gaffaney 91; A. C. Barnes
three for 21, M. R. Jefferson three for 36) and 335 (C. D. Cumming 30, M. H. Richardson 108,
J. I. Englefield 75, W. A. Wisneski 48; K. P. Walmsley three for 78, M. J. Mason three for 57).

*North Island v England A and South Island v England A may be found in the England A tour
section. No points were awarded in the 1999-2000 Conference, which was discontinued with the
expansion of the 2000-01 Shell Trophy.*

SHELL CUP, 1999-2000

Note: Matches in this section were not first-class.

Semi-final

At Eden Park, Auckland, January 28. Auckland won by one wicket. Northern Districts 150 (36.2
overs) (M. E. Parlane 40, M. D. Bailey 31; A. R. Adams five for seven); Auckland* 151 for nine
(50 overs) (J. M. Aiken 49, D. J. Nash 44 not out; D. L. Vettori three for 24).

Finals

At Eden Park, Auckland, February 4. Canterbury won by two runs. Canterbury* 185 for eight (50
overs) (G. R. Stead 35); Auckland 183 for nine (50 overs) (L. G. Howell 62, B. A. Pocock 32;
C. L. Cairns three for 39).

At Lancaster Park, Christchurch, February 6. Canterbury won by seven wickets. Auckland* 224
for six (50 overs) (A. C. Barnes 32, D. J. Nash 85 not out, T. K. Canning 58; W. A. Wisneski
three for 53); Canterbury 225 for three (41.5 overs) (B. J. K. Doody 44, N. J. Astle 76, S. P.
Fleming 57 not out).

  Canterbury won the best-of-three final 2–0.

CRICKET IN INDIA, 1999-2000

By R. MOHAN and MOHANDAS MENON

V. V. S. Laxman

So overwhelming was India's obsession with *l'affaire Hansie Cronje* that, while acres of newsprint and hours of television time were featuring the match-fixing scandal and its enormous fall-out, national cricket reached its climax in the 1999-2000 Ranji Trophy virtually unnoticed. The media were more interested in seeking denials of match-fixing rumours from the two captains, Mohammad Azharuddin, leading Hyderabad for the first time in a Ranji final, and Mumbai's Sachin Tendulkar. Not that denials satisfied the fascination as the story unfolded: few names, few reputations escaped scrutiny in the imbroglio of charges and counter-charges that surfaced in the coming months.

What began in March 2000 with intercepted phone conversations between South Africa's captain and an Indian bookmaker soon entangled India's leading cricketers. In September, national coach Kapil Dev resigned his position while he attempted, successfully, to clear his name. In December, Azharuddin, India's captain in 47 of his 99 Tests, was banned from cricket for life by the Board of Control, as was Ajay Sharma. A government-initiated inquiry by India's Central Bureau of Investigation "into match-fixing and related malpractices" had concluded that Azharuddin "took money from bookies/punters to fix cricket matches". Two other international players, Ajay Jadeja and Manoj Prabhakar, received five-year suspensions.

By then, Azharuddin's achievement in taking Hyderabad to the Ranji final back in April had become a distant, almost forgotten memory. Yet hindsight suggests he was already feeling the strain of the breaking stories and the constant media pressure. Setting off for an impossible single on a misfield, he ran out V. V. S. Laxman when they had been batting well together. It ruined Hyderabad's hopes, and they eventually lost by a massive 297 runs. Mumbai's 34th triumph in the 65-year history of the tournament was a vindication of the strategies of coach Ashok Mankad, whose first season in charge, 1998-99, had seen them fail to qualify for the knockout stage.

Laxman, a strokeplaying middle-order batsman who met with only partial success in international cricket after being asked to open in Tests, had had an extraordinary domestic season. He scored 1,415 runs in the Ranji Trophy, overhauling the record of 1,280 set by Karnataka's Vijay Bharadwaj in 1998-99, and eight hundreds, another tournament record. Laxman also became the first to hit two triple-centuries in Ranji cricket when he made 353 in Hyderabad's semi-final against Karnataka, to add to his 301 not out against Bihar in 1997-98. This propelled his team to a mammoth 711 for eight declared, well beyond the reach of defending champions Karnataka, who had put Hyderabad in to bat when acting-captain Venkatesh Prasad mistook some surface grass for the live variety. Mumbai captain Samir Dighe took the same decision in the other semi-final, against Tamil Nadu, only to see Hemang Badani and Robin Singh set up a total of 485. But that match turned out to be the highlight of the knockout stages, with Tendulkar, dropped early on the third morning in the slips when 42, swinging it Mumbai's way through his first Ranji double-century. Mumbai were still 37 short of a first-innings lead when the eighth wicket fell, but Tendulkar made all those as he squeezed out a five-run lead. Demoralised, Tamil Nadu went on to lose outright.

It did not go down well in Karnataka that, before the semi-final against Hyderabad, two of their leading players, Rahul Dravid and Anil Kumble, had already slipped away to England to keep county appointments. As the season was ending, the focus was on national cricket and how to improve it, particularly in the wake of India's drubbing on their tour of Australia, and it was generally agreed that the stars should play in domestic cricket to help raise its standards. Azharuddin's absence from the Indian team for much of the season meant that he played his fullest domestic programme for a long time, including eight Ranji matches. However, though named as captain, he did not join South Zone for their Duleep Trophy quarter-final against North Zone at Agartala in the remote north-east – to the disappointment of the many fans who assembled at the airport in the hope of welcoming him. But he did lead the Board President's XI to triumph in the limited-overs Wills Trophy. The debate over the availability of the Test stars continued into the Challenger series for the N. K. P. Salve Trophy. Most of the squad from the Australian tour turned out for the competition, although Tendulkar asked to rest, while many of the Under-19 side, whose victory in their World Cup in Sri Lanka was one of the highlights of the season, appeared in the tournament for India A and India B.

In the interzonal competitions, North Zone did the double, beating West Zone in the December final of the first-class Duleep Trophy, and then winning the limited-overs Deodhar Trophy league in January. West opener Wasim Jaffer carried his bat for 173 in the Duleep final, and North's careless second-innings batting gave West Zone a chance of an outright win until a 66-run last-wicket partnership staved off that possibility. With the Duleep Trophy now in its fourth season since reverting to a four-match knockout format, the Board again considered restoring the competition to its former primacy in the domestic season.

The Irani Cup match, the season's curtain-raiser in October, featured a ten-wicket return for Thirunavukkarasu Kumaran, a lanky fast bowler from Tamil Nadu who was making his first appearance for the Rest of India against the previous season's Ranji champions. His second-innings spell of 8.5–2–21–6 as he reverse-swung the old ball sent Karnataka tumbling to defeat by an innings and 60 runs with more than a day's play remaining. Shitanshu Kotak, a left-hander from Saurashtra, made 118 in more than six hours for the Rest. While Karnataka's batting was deprived of Dravid and Bharadwaj, with India in Kenya, Javagal Srinath, who was resting from India's one-day squad at his own request, found his form with six for 77 from 34.3 overs. The selectors promptly asked him to return for the Test series against New Zealand.

Laxman dominated the season's batting figures, with 1,432 in all first-class cricket at 89.50, though Sridharan Sriram, the only other batsman to reach four figures in Ranji cricket, with 1,075 for Tamil Nadu, averaged 97.72, and Tendulkar scored 1,008 at 100.80 including his performances for India. Pankaj Dharmani of Punjab, one of nine batsmen in all with 1,000 first-class runs, enjoyed an extraordinary run of form when he scored 608 in three innings between dismissals, including a triple-century. It was a fair comment on the dearth of bowling talent in the country that the leading wicket-taker should be the evergreen Hyderabad off-spinner, Kanwaljit Singh. In the Ranji final, a week after turning 42, he claimed his 62nd wicket of the season for them – two short of the Ranji record of 64, by Bishen Bedi for Delhi in 1974-75 – while team-mate Venkatapathy Raju finished with 52 from his left-arm spinners. Both benefited from the volume of runs gathered by Laxman and Azharuddin, who responded to his omission from the national side with 815 runs for his state. Another slow left-armer, Utpal Chatterjee of Bengal, also took 52 wickets, and there were 50 for Tamil Nadu off-spinner Aashish Kapoor. Ashish Winston Zaidi, a graduate of Dennis Lillee's pace school, returned the best figures of the season, nine for 45 in an innings and 15 for 192 in the match, for Uttar Pradesh against Vidarbha in December.

The season witnessed some classic marathons of slow batting: Rajiv Nayyar played the longest innings in first-class cricket, 271 in 1,015 minutes, for Himachal Pradesh against Jammu and Kashmir, while Railways managed only 83 runs in 104 overs, the fewest runs ever scored in a full day, to save their game against Madhya Pradesh. A livelier performance came from Rohan Gavaskar, a batsman with a famous name, who did his father Sunil proud when he and Shrikant Kalyani shared the season's best partnership, 406 unbroken, for Bengal against lowly Tripura. – R.M.

FIRST-CLASS AVERAGES, 1999-2000

BATTING

(Qualification: 600 runs)

	M	I	NO	R	HS	100s	Avge
S. R. Tendulkar (*Mumbai*)	7	14	4	1,008	233*	4	100.80
S. Sriram (*Tamil Nadu*)	9	12	1	1,075	288	5	97.72
V. V. S. Laxman (*Hyderabad*)	11	17	1	1,432	353	8	89.50
A. V. Kale (*Maharashtra*)	7	10	1	742	248*	3	82.44
P. Dharmani (*Punjab*)	13	18	3	1,194	305*	4	79.60
M. Azharuddin (*Hyderabad*)	10	15	3	935	200*	3	77.91
S. Sharath (*Tamil Nadu*)	11	17	4	1,012	205	3	77.84
R. Nayyar (*Himachal Pradesh*)	8	15	1	952	271	4	68.00
R. R. Parida (*Orissa*)	9	15	2	844	193	3	64.92
V. G. Kambli (*Mumbai*)	12	17	1	1,034	154	5	64.62
C. C. Williams (*Baroda*)	10	13	2	698	237*	3	63.45
V. Shewag (*Delhi*)	12	18	1	1,008	274	3	59.29
R. Puri (*Haryana*)	8	13	2	646	114*	3	58.72
D. Mongia (*Punjab*)	11	15	1	790	179	3	56.42
R. S. Gavaskar (*Bengal*)	9	13	1	637	212*	2	53.08
M. R. Beerala (*Karnataka*)	7	13	1	617	101*	1	51.41
A. A. Muzumdar (*Mumbai*)	13	20	4	814	131	1	50.87
J. V. Paranjpe (*Mumbai*)	9	15	2	652	185	3	50.15
V. Rathore (*Punjab*)	14	22	0	1,103	158	3	50.13
S. S. Das (*Orissa*)	9	17	1	799	110	2	49.93
A. Dani (*Delhi*)	12	19	1	892	140	2	49.55
Wasim Jaffer (*Mumbai*)	14	24	2	1,080	173*	2	49.09
H. K. Badani (*Tamil Nadu*)	11	16	0	775	162	2	48.43
S. S. Raul (*Orissa*)	8	14	1	608	120	2	46.76
R. S. Sodhi (*Punjab*)	12	19	1	803	114*	2	44.61
P. J. Bhatt (*Saurashtra*)	8	14	0	619	158	2	44.21
V. Pratap (*Hyderabad*)	12	19	3	672	100*	2	42.00
A. Nandakishore (*Hyderabad*)	13	23	2	867	135	2	41.28
V. S. T. Naidu (*Karnataka*)	13	22	4	628	93	0	34.88
J. R. Madanagopal (*Tamil Nadu*)	12	18	0	601	85	0	33.38

* *Signifies not out.*

BOWLING

(Qualification: 25 wickets)

	O	M	R	W	BB	5W/i	Avge
Sarandeep Singh (*Punjab*)	273.5	71	719	36	6-41	3	19.97
B. K. V. Prasad (*Karnataka*)	238.5	72	568	28	6-60	3	20.28
U. Chatterjee (*Bengal*)	573.1	186	1,172	57	7-45	6	20.56

	O	M	R	W	BB	5W/i	Avge
A. Kuruvilla (*Mumbai*)	229.2	39	660	32	5-32	2	20.62
R. V. Pawar (*Mumbai*)	379.4	111	916	44	7-103	4	20.81
M. Kartik (*Railways*)	227.4	65	547	26	6-31	2	21.03
J. Srinath (*Karnataka*)	245.3	73	578	26	6-45	2	22.23
P. K. Krishnakumar (*Rajasthan*) . . .	172.4	40	558	25	6-84	2	22.32
P. L. Mhambrey (*Mumbai*)	202.5	58	558	25	4-31	0	22.32
A. Kumble (*Karnataka*)	397.1	128	832	37	6-67	3	22.48
N. R. Odedra (*Saurashtra*)	290.4	75	841	37	6-52	3	22.72
R. S. Sodhi (*Punjab*)	256.2	75	679	29	5-30	2	23.41
A. Nehra (*Delhi*)	251.2	56	734	31	6-66	3	23.67
N. M. Kulkarni (*Mumbai*)	414	148	819	34	5-44	3	24.08
G. K. Pandey (*Uttar Pradesh*)	298	76	702	29	5-39	1	24.20
Navdeep Singh (*Punjab*)	357.1	114	768	31	5-28	1	24.77
Kanwaljit Singh (*Hyderabad*)	644.2	167	1,563	62	6-37	4	25.20
A. Bhandari (*Delhi*)	224.4	52	688	27	5-75	1	25.48
S. L. V. Raju (*Hyderabad*)	679	225	1,535	59	6-57	4	26.01
V. Jain (*Haryana*)	216.2	46	678	26	4-30	0	26.07
Harbhajan Singh (*Punjab*)	414	90	1,207	46	5-69	3	26.23
S. Mahesh (*Tamil Nadu*)	340.3	77	1,014	38	4-37	0	26.68
A. W. Zaidi (*Uttar Pradesh*)	424.4	78	1,316	49	9-45	3	26.85
R. Singh (*Delhi*)	279.5	62	803	29	7-80	3	27.68
S. K. Satpathy (*Orissa*)	357.2	86	1,053	38	6-86	3	27.71
Shakti Singh (*Himachal Pradesh*) . .	283.2	56	777	28	6-85	3	27.75
S. B. Joshi (*Karnataka*)	463.1	130	1,229	44	6-48	2	27.93
A. R. Kapoor (*Tamil Nadu*)	503.2	102	1,544	55	5-85	2	28.07
N. P. Singh (*Hyderabad*)	325.3	82	971	33	5-69	2	29.42
Iqbal Siddiqui (*Maharashtra*)	246.4	69	752	25	8-72	2	30.08
Zaheer Khan (*Baroda*)	394.5	77	1,321	42	5-43	3	31.45
J. Gokulkrishnan (*Tamil Nadu*)	289	70	859	25	5-42	1	34.36
D. Ganesh (*Karnataka*)	330.4	59	1,051	29	5-115	1	36.24

*In the following scores, * by the name of a team indicates that they won the toss.*

IRANI CUP, 1999-2000

Ranji Trophy Champions (Karnataka) v Rest of India

At M. Chinnaswamy Stadium, Bangalore, October 1, 2, 3, 4. Rest of India won by an innings and 60 runs. Karnataka 150 (J. Arun Kumar 30, S. Somasekhar 42; T. Kumaran four for 47, R. S. Sodhi four for 33) and 91 (H. S. Sodhi four for 41, T. Kumaran six for 39), Rest of India* 321 (N. L. Haldipur 40, S. H. Kotak 118, R. S. Sodhi 39, H. S. Sodhi 55; J. Srinath six for 77). *Rest of India beat the Ranji champions for the first time since 1993-94.*

DULEEP TROPHY, 1999-2000

Quarter-final

At Maharaja Bir Bikram College Stadium, Agartala, December 1, 2, 3, 4, 5. Drawn. North Zone were declared winners by virtue of their first-innings lead. North Zone* 589 (P. Dharmani 59, R. Nayyar 118, V. Shewag 274, Extras 36; S. B. Joshi four for 113) and 257 for eight dec. (V. Rathore 93, Shakti Singh 37; A. R. Kapoor three for 124, S. L. V. Raju five for 62); South Zone 424 (V. S. T. Naidu 55, J. R. Madanagopal 84, S. Sharath 149 not out, S. B. Joshi 75) and 100 for one (A. Nandakishore 51 not out, S. Mahesh 42).

Shewag's 274, his maiden double-hundred, lasted 416 minutes and 327 balls and included 36 fours and four sixes. With Nayyar, whose 118 occupied 603 minutes, he added 381 for North Zone's fifth wicket, an all-wicket Duleep record.

Semi-finals

At North-East Frontier Railway Stadium, Maligaon, Gauhati, December 9, 10, 11, 12, 13. Drawn. North Zone were declared winners by virtue of their first-innings lead. North Zone* 543 (A. Dani 53, V. Rathore 70, R. S. Sodhi 88, P. Dharmani 52, N. Chopra 132 not out, Shakti Singh 50, Extras 41; A. W. Zaidi three for 100, N. D. Hirwani three for 129) and 222 for four (P. Dharmani 121 not out, R. Nayyar 88); Central Zone 366 (Jyoti P. Yadav 70, S. Abbas Ali 31, Raja Ali 123, M. Saif 35; R. Singh five for 84).

At Eden Gardens, Calcutta, December 9, 10, 11, 12, 13. Drawn. West Zone were declared winners by virtue of their first-innings lead. West Zone* 600 for eight dec. (Wasim Jaffer 69, C. C. Williams 107, A. A. Muzumdar 90, V. G. Kambli 154, Iqbal Siddiqui 42, Extras 61; Javed Zaman three for 140, U. Chatterjee four for 138) and 260 for three dec. (Wasim Jaffer 94, C. C. Williams 41, A. V. Kale 105); East Zone 255 (S. S. Das 30, N. L. Haldipur 59, S. S. Karim 60, Sukhbinder Singh 51 not out) and 249 for three (S. S. Das 110, N. L. Haldipur 79).

Final

At Eden Gardens, Calcutta, December 17, 18, 19, 20, 21. Drawn. North Zone were declared winners by virtue of their first-innings lead. North Zone* 468 (A. Dani 43, V. Rathore 74, R. S. Sodhi 67, P. Dharmani 39, R. Nayyar 105 not out, Extras 48; N. M. Kulkarni five for 97) and 248 (V. Rathore 41, R. S. Sodhi 47, P. Dharmani 93; P. L. Mhambrey three for 48, Zaheer Khan four for 76, N. M. Kulkarni three for 42); West Zone 367 (Wasim Jaffer 173 not out, A. V. Kale 30, A. A. Muzumdar 52; R. Singh six for 63) and 64 for five (A. Bhandari three for 23).

Wasim Jaffer, who batted for 613 minutes, became the second player to carry his bat in the Duleep Trophy, following S. S. Bhave, also of West Zone, who scored 28 out of 103 against East Zone in 1993-94.

DULEEP TROPHY WINNERS

1961-62	West Zone	1976-77	West Zone	1990-91	North Zone
1962-63	West Zone	1977-78	West Zone	1991-92	North Zone
1963-64	West Zone	1978-79	North Zone	1992-93	North Zone
1964-65	West Zone	1979-80	North Zone	1993-94	North Zone
1965-66	South Zone	1980-81	West Zone	1994-95	North Zone
1966-67	South Zone	1981-82	West Zone	1995-96	South Zone
1967-68	South Zone	1982-83	North Zone	1996-97	Central Zone
1968-69	West Zone	1983-84	North Zone	1997-98	{ Central Zone { West Zone
1969-70	West Zone	1984-85	South Zone		
1970-71	South Zone	1985-86	West Zone	1998-99	Central Zone
1971-72	Central Zone	1986-87	South Zone	1999-2000	North Zone
1972-73	West Zone	1987-88	North Zone		
1973-74	North Zone	1988-89	{ North Zone { West Zone		
1974-75	South Zone				
1975-76	South Zone	1989-90	South Zone		

RANJI TROPHY, 1999-2000

Central Zone

At VCA Ground, Nagpur, October 23, 24, 25, 26. Drawn. Vidarbha* 263 (P. H. Sutane 66, M. S. Doshi 80, Extras 34; N. D. Hirwani four for 90, R. K. Chauhan three for 73) and 128 (M. S. Doshi 38 not out, Extras 32; M. S. Majithia three for 13); Madhya Pradesh 251 (D. S. Bundela 36, S. Abbas Ali 51, Raja Ali 40, Extras 39; P. V. Gandhe four for 84) and 50 for four. *Vidarbha 5 pts, Madhya Pradesh 3 pts.*

At Ravishankar Shukla Stadium, Durg, October 31, November 1, 2, 3. Drawn. Madhya Pradesh* 338 (A. R. Khurasiya 31, S. Abbas Ali 76, Raja Ali 104 not out, R. K. Chauhan 35; A. W. Zaidi three for 85, M. Raza three for 73) and 250 for nine (H. S. Sodhi 58, S. K. Sahu 99; S. Bajpai four for 76); Uttar Pradesh 383 (Jyoti P. Yadav 54, M. S. Mudgal 50, M. Kaif 46, Rizwan Shamshad 50, G. K. Pandey 33, S. A. Shukla 80, Extras 37; N. D. Hirwani three for 66). *Madhya Pradesh 3 pts, Uttar Pradesh 5 pts.*

At VCA Ground, Nagpur, October 31, November 1, 2, 3. Railways won by seven wickets. Vidarbha* 170 (U. V. Gandhe 85 not out; M. Kartik six for 62) and 172 (Extras 35; M. Kartik six for 31); Railways 270 (S. B. Bangar 84, Abhay Sharma 60, Devendra Singh 36 not out; P. V. Gandhe eight for 88) and 76 for three (S. B. Bangar 34). *Railways 8 pts.*

At Maharani Usharaje Trust Ground, Indore, November 11, 12, 13, 14. Drawn. Madhya Pradesh 538 for seven dec. (Jai P. Yadav 265, K. Rajagopalan 70, M. S. Majithia 34, S. Abbas Ali 67 not out, Extras 44); Railways* 216 (S. B. Bangar 34, Abhay Sharma 37, P. S. Rawat 58; R. K. Chauhan five for 99) and 86 for five (S. B. Bangar 39). *Madhya Pradesh 5 pts, Railways 3 pts.*

Yadav's 265, his maiden double-hundred, lasted 600 minutes and 429 balls and included 24 fours and six sixes. On the final day, Railways, following on, scored just 83 runs in 104 overs – the fewest runs in a full day of first-class cricket; left-arm spinner Majithia had figures of 20–20–0–1.

FEWEST RUNS IN A FULL DAY'S PLAY

Runs	Overs		
83	104	**Railways (3-0 to 86-5) v Madhya Pradesh at Indore (4th day)** .	**1999-2000**
95	67.5	Australia (80) v Pakistan (15-2) at Karachi (1st day)	1956-57
104	65	Pakistan (0-0 to 104-5) v Australia at Karachi (4th day)	1959-60
105	72*	Queensland (30-1 to 135-5) v MCC at Brisbane (3rd day).	1958-59
106	68.2*	England (92-2 to 198) v Australia at Brisbane (4th day)	1958-59
107	97	Pakistan XI (66-0 to 173-1) v MCC at Lahore (3rd day).	1955-56
110	59.6*	Combined XI (159-2 to 260) v MCC (9-1) at Perth (3rd day) . . .	1958-59
111	78	South Africa (48-2 to 130-6 dec.) v India (29-1) at Cape Town (5th day).	1992-93

* *Eight-ball overs; all other instances were six-ball overs.*

At K. L. Saini Stadium, Jaipur, November 11, 12, 13. Rajasthan won by an innings and 74 runs. Vidarbha 163 (P. H. Sutane 54; Sanjeev Sharma four for 56) and 205 (A. V. Deshpande 50, U. V. Gandhe 65; P. K. Krishnakumar five for 31); Rajasthan* 442 (A. Jain 78, Ajay Mehra 53, P. K. Krishnakumar 72, Sanjeev Sharma 117, D. P. Singh 56 not out; V. Boddlu three for 131). *Rajasthan 8 pts.*

Former Test medium-pacer Sanjeev Sharma played his first first-class match since the 1992-93 Duleep Trophy.

At Karnail Singh Stadium, Delhi, November 19, 20, 21, 22. Drawn. Uttar Pradesh* 439 (M. S. Mudgal 47, Jyoti P. Yadav 57, G. K. Pandey 107, S. A. Shukla 43, M. Saif 71, M. Raza 35) and eight for one; Railways 506 (S. B. Bangar 130, Abhay Sharma 99, Y. Gowda 84, P. S. Rawat 42, Zakir Hussain 89; G. K. Pandey four for 93). *Railways 5 pts, Uttar Pradesh 3 pts.*

At K. L. Saini Stadium, Jaipur, November 19, 20, 21, 22. Drawn. Madhya Pradesh 315 (Jai P. Yadav 50, S. Abbas Ali 159; P. K. Krishnakumar six for 84) and 203 for eight (Jai P. Yadav 48, Raja Ali 41; Mohammad Aslam three for 69); Rajasthan* 415 (A. Jain 50, N. Doru 87, S. Bhatia 90 not out, Sanjeev Sharma 54, Extras 55; Jai P. Yadav six for 74). *Rajasthan 5 pts, Madhya Pradesh 3 pts.*

At Sports Stadium, Meerut, November 26, 27, 28, 29. Drawn. Rajasthan 287 (A. Jain 90, P. K. Krishnakumar 56, Sanjeev Sharma 78 not out; M. Raza four for 81, P. Tewari four for 80) and 392 for six (A. Jain 31, Kuldeep Singh 92, Ajay Mehra 46, P. K. Krishnakumar 34, S. Bhatia 30, Sanjeev Sharma 100 not out); Uttar Pradesh* 224 (M. S. Mudgal 74, M. Saif 65, S. A. Shukla 30; Shamsher Singh three for 40, P. K. Krishnakumar four for 32). *Uttar Pradesh 3 pts, Rajasthan 5 pts.*

At Karnail Singh Stadium, Delhi, December 28, 29, 30, 31. Drawn. Railways* 132 (P. S. Rawat 51 not out; Sanjeev Sharma three for 39, Mohammad Aslam four for 35) and 294 for nine dec. (Abhay Sharma 65, Y. Gowda 59; Mohammad Aslam three for 54, R. J. Kanwat four for 65); Rajasthan 214 (N. Doru 35, P. K. Krishnakumar 39, R. B. Jhalani 40 not out; H. Singh four for 63, M. Kartik four for 53) and nought for no wkt. *Railways 3 pts, Rajasthan 5 pts.*

At Green Park, Kanpur, December 28, 29, 30, 31. Uttar Pradesh won by ten wickets. Vidarbha 98 (A. W. Zaidi nine for 45) and 331 (R. S. Paradkar 40, A. S. Naidu 118 not out, U. V. Gandhe 78, C. E. Atram 32; A. W. Zaidi six for 147, G. K. Pandey three for 69); Uttar Pradesh* 404 (Jyoti P. Yadav 46, M. Kaif 112, Rizwan Shamshad 95, M. Raza 42; A. Piprode three for 80) and 29 for no wkt. *Uttar Pradesh 8 pts.*

Naidu scored 118 not out on first-class debut. Zaidi claimed 15 for 192 in the match, improving on his own Uttar Pradesh record of 14 for 271 against Haryana at Faridabad in 1990-91.

Rajasthan 23 pts, Railways 19 pts, Uttar Pradesh 19 pts, Madhya Pradesh 14 pts, Vidarbha 5 pts. Rajasthan, Railways and Uttar Pradesh qualified for the Super League.

East Zone

At Eden Gardens, Calcutta, November 12, 13, 14, 15. Drawn. Assam* 347 (S. Saikia 124, S. R. Das 39, R. Bora 38, G. Dutta 34 not out; U. Chatterjee five for 54) and 228 for five (Tariq-ur-Rehman 103 not out, Sukhbinder Singh 37, V. R. Samant 30 not out); Bengal 351 (N. L. Haldipur 33, R. S. Gavaskar 63, S. J. Kalyani 59, W. Majumder 68 not out; Sukhbinder Singh five for 113). *Bengal 5 pts, Assam 3 pts.*

At Maharaja Bir Bikram College Stadium, Agartala, November 12, 13, 14, 15. Bihar won by 51 runs. Bihar* 174 (Avinash Kumar 43; S. Chowdhury three for two) and 231 (N. Ranjan 51, Vikash Kumar 42, Rajiv Kumar 45; S. Roy three for 38, A. Shukla three for 47); Tripura 172 (R. Chowdhury 31, A. A. Velaskar 34, V. Prajapati 37 not out, S. Chowdhury 34) and 182 (A. A. Velaskar 58; Avinash Kumar five for 47, K. V. P. Rao five for 65). *Bihar 8 pts.*

At Barabati Stadium, Cuttack, November 22, 23, 24, 25. Drawn. Orissa* 390 (S. S. Das 94, P. R. Mohapatra 38, R. R. Parida 115, S. K. Satpathy 54 not out; K. V. P. Rao three for 114) and 84 for no wkt (S. S. Das 44 not out, P. Jayachandra 39 not out); Bihar 386 (D. Chakraborty 57, V. Saxena 55, Avinash Kumar 96 not out; S. K. Satpathy four for 65). *Orissa 5 pts, Bihar 3 pts.*

At Maharaja Bir Bikram College Stadium, Agartala, November 22, 23, 24, 25. Bengal won by an innings and 252 runs. Bengal 533 for two dec. (N. L. Haldipur 47, D. Dasgupta 38, R. S. Gavaskar 212 not out, S. J. Kalyani 200 not out, Extras 36); Tripura* 163 (R. Ghosh 58; U. Chatterjee seven for 45) and 118 (R. Chowdhury 41; U. Chatterjee four for 16, W. Majumder four for four). *Bengal 8 pts.*

Gavaskar's 212 not out, his maiden double-hundred, lasted 506 minutes and 377 balls and included 18 fours and one six; Kalyani's 200 not out, his maiden hundred, lasted 460 minutes and 358 balls and included 17 fours; together, they shared an unbroken partnership of 406, a Ranji third-wicket record, in 460 minutes and 116 overs. Majumder's full second-innings analysis was 7.1-5-4-4. Bengal lost only two wickets in their innings win.

At DSA Stadium, Mangoldoi, December 25, 26. Assam won by an innings and 56 runs. Tripura* 57 (G. Dutta eight for 23) and 136 (G. Banik 40; Sukhbinder Singh three for 25); Assam 249 (S. Ghosh 52, G. Dutta 45, Sukhbinder Singh 73; R. Deb-Burman three for 67, G. Banik three for 49). *Assam 8 pts.*

On the opening day, Assam were 58 for six in reply to Tripura's 57; their last four wickets added 191 and they completed their innings victory on the second afternoon.

At Barabati Stadium, Cuttack, December 25, 26, 27, 28. Drawn. Orissa* 370 (S. S. Das 81, P. M. Mullick 108, S. S. Raul 53, P. Jayachandra 64 not out; L. R. Shukla six for 86) and 336 for five (S. S. Das 82, P. M. Mullick 111 not out, S. S. Raul 52; W. Majumder three for 110); Bengal 275 (R. S. Gavaskar 115, U. Chatterjee 34; A. Barik four for 83, J. Das three for 30). *Orissa 5 pts, Bengal 3 pts.*
  Mullick scored a century in each innings.

At Keenan Stadium, Jamshedpur, January 3, 4, 5, 6. Drawn. Bihar 341 (N. Ranjan 31, Rajiv Kumar 65, Sunil Kumar 35, S. Roy 46, Satish Singh 43, Avinash Kumar 32 not out; U. Chatterjee five for 90) and 51 for one; Bengal* 561 (N. Saha 60, R. S. Gavaskar 72, S. J. Kalyani 94, S. S. Karim 129, U. Chatterjee 30, W. Majumder 50, S. Panda 48; Avinash Kumar four for 172, Satish Singh four for 129). *Bihar 3 pts, Bengal 5 pts.*
  Avinash Kumar bowled 77 overs in Bengal's innings.

At Angul Stadium, Angul, January 3, 4, 5, 6. Drawn. Orissa* 425 (P. M. Mullick 40, S. S. Raul 120, P. Jayachandra 72, R. F. Morris 88, G. Gopal 30; G. Dutta three for 78, Sukhbinder Singh five for 129) and 202 for four dec. (S. S. Das 71, P. R. Mohapatra 62 not out); Assam 306 (Z. Zuffri 68, R. Bora 82, G. Dutta 55 not out; S. K. Satpathy six for 86) and 265 for seven (Z. Zuffri 144, S. Ghosh 47; S. S. Raul three for 49). *Orissa 5 pts, Assam 3 pts.*
  Bora and Dutta added 118 for the ninth wicket in Assam's first innings.

At Keenan Stadium, Jamshedpur, January 12, 13, 14, 15. Bihar won by 191 runs. Bihar* 258 (N. Ranjan 58, Sunil Kumar 68, M. S. Dhoni 40; Javed Zaman three for 45, O. Singh five for 81) and 343 (D. Chakraborty 32, A. Hashmi 53, Rajiv Kumar 84, Sunil Kumar 35, M. S. Dhoni 68 not out; O. Singh three for 88); Assam 247 (Z. Zuffri 37, R. Bora 39, V. R. Samant 43; Avinash Kumar four for 74, Vikash Kumar five for 98) and 163 (P. K. Das 30, Sukhbinder Singh 54; Avinash Kumar six for 43, Vikash Kumar three for 56). *Bihar 8 pts.*

At Samanta Chandrasekhar College Ground, Puri, January 12, 13, 14. Orissa won by an innings and 182 runs. Orissa* 545 for eight dec. (P. R. Mohapatra 54, P. K. Das 68, R. R. Parida 193, S. S. Raul 30, P. Jayachandra 53, R. R. Das 63, Y. Mohanty 31 not out, Extras 35; A. Shukla five for 182); Tripura 172 (R. Ghosh 31, C. Sachdev 45, S. Chowdhury 31; A. Barik three for 56, J. Das three for 29) and 191 (A. Pratap 58; J. Das five for 31). *Orissa 8 pts.*

Orissa 23 pts, Bihar 22 pts, Bengal 21 pts, Assam 14 pts, Tripura 0 pts. Orissa, Bihar and Bengal qualified for the Super League.

North Zone

At Nahar Singh Stadium, Faridabad, October 24, 25, 26, 27. Drawn. Haryana* 469 for eight dec. (Jitender Singh 36, Parender Sharma 79, R. Puri 109, A. S. Kaypee 95, S. Dalal 81, Extras 37; Vijay Sharma for 63, Sanjay Sharma three for 90); Jammu and Kashmir 242 (R. Bali 45, Kavaljit Singh 62; V. Jain four for 79, M. K. Shakalkar three for 58) and 155 for four (Amrit Pal Singh 35, Vijay Sharma 58 not out). *Haryana 5 pts, Jammu and Kashmir 3 pts.*

At PCA Stadium, Mohali, October 24, 25, 26, 27. Punjab won by 196 runs. Punjab* 354 (V. Rathore 44, R. S. Sodhi 79, P. Dharmani 70, Sarandeep Singh 57, Navdeep Singh 36 not out; Shakti Singh six for 107) and 176 for six dec. (D. Mongia 100, Amit Sharma 33); Himachal Pradesh 129 (Yashwinder Singh 32; Sandeep Sharma three for 46, R. S. Sodhi five for 30) and 205 (N. Gaur 37, R. Nayyar 85; R. S. Sodhi three for 40, Sarandeep Singh three for 48, Navdeep Singh three for 29). *Punjab 8 pts.*

At Harbax Singh Stadium, Delhi, October 24, 25, 26, 27. Delhi won by an innings and 45 runs. Services* 141 (S. Verma 37; A. Nehra five for 25) and 258 (Abu Samy 39, Sarabjit Singh 59, G. S. Thapa 40, Extras 31; A. Bhandari five for 75); Delhi 444 for eight dec. (A. Dani 76, A. Malhotra 42, Ajay Sharma 31, M. Manhas 125 not out, V. Shewag 70; M. V. Rao three for 104). *Delhi 8 pts.*

At Feroz Shah Kotla Ground, Delhi, October 31, November 1, 2, 3. Drawn. Haryana* 166 (Jasvir Singh 81 not out; A. Bhandari three for 39, A. Nehra three for 50) and 346 for five (Jasvir Singh 47, Parender Sharma 32, R. Puri 66, S. Dalal 107 not out, A. Ratra 61 not out); Delhi 470 for eight dec. (Devendra Sharma 56, A. Dani 89, Ajay Sharma 143, V. Shewag 47, A. Malhotra 45, Extras 31; F. Ghayas three for 90, S. Jhakar three for 159). *Delhi 5 pts, Haryana 3 pts.*

At Police Stadium, Chamba, October 31, November 1, 2, 3. Drawn. Jammu and Kashmir* 249 (R. Bali 80, Kavaljit Singh 38; Jaswant Rai three for 64) and 16 for one; Himachal Pradesh 567 (N. Gaur 69, R. Nayyar 271, Yashwinder Singh 55, Extras 45; Sanjay Sharma four for 117). *Himachal Pradesh 5 pts, Jammu and Kashmir 3 pts.*

Nayyar's 271, his maiden double-hundred, lasted 1,015 minutes and 728 balls and included 26 fours and one six. It was the longest innings in first-class cricket, outlasting Hanif Mohammad, who batted 970 minutes for Pakistan against West Indies at Bridgetown in 1957-58, scoring 337. Nayyar reached 200 in 810 minutes, 33 more than Brendon Kuruppu's record of 777 minutes for Sri Lanka against New Zealand at Colombo, 1986-87. Himachal Pradesh's innings lasted 255.2 overs; Sanjay Sharma bowled 77 of them.

At PCA Stadium, Mohali, October 31, November 1, 2, 3. Punjab won by an innings and 173 runs. Punjab* 533 for six dec. (V. Rathore 47, R. S. Sodhi 32, Amit Sharma 35, P. Dharmani 202 not out, D. Mongia 79, Sanjay Kumar 47, Sandeep Sharma 65); Services 171 (P. Maitreya 40; Sandeep Sharma three for 33, Sarandeep Singh six for 41) and 189 (S. Verma 67; Sarandeep Singh four for 50). *Punjab 8 pts.*

Dharmani's 202 not out, his third double-hundred, lasted 490 minutes and 384 balls and included 25 fours and one six.

At Nehru Stadium, Gurgaon, November 6, 7, 8. Haryana won by an innings and 94 runs. Haryana* 502 for four dec. (Jitender Singh 125, Jasvir Singh 116, Parender Sharma 53, A. S. Kaypee 108 not out, R. Puri 87); Services 100 (K. K. Dixit 36; V. Jain three for 32, F. Ghayas five for 39) and 308 (Narender Singh 41, C. D. Thomson 85 not out, P. Maitreya 52, S. Javed 47; F. Ghayas three for 82, P. Jain four for 50). *Haryana 8 pts.*

Javed scored 47 at No. 11 and added 68 for the last wicket with Thomson.

At Shaheed Krishan Chand Memorial Stadium, Mandi, November 6, 7, 8, 9. Delhi won by ten wickets. Delhi* 573 for seven dec. (A. Dani 126, V. Dahiya 63, Ajay Sharma 85, V. Shewag 165, M. Manhas 72, S. Joshi 35 not out) and ten for no wkt; Himachal Pradesh 244 (Yashwinder Singh 53, Jaswant Rai 70, Extras 41; S. Angurala four for 80) and 338 (N. Gaur 70, R. Nayyar 42, Yashwinder Singh 40, Sangram Singh 103, Jaswant Rai 30, Extras 34; R. Singh seven for 80). *Delhi 8 pts.*

At Punjab Agricultural University Ground, Ludhiana, November 6, 7, 8. Punjab won by an innings and 288 runs. Jammu and Kashmir* 171 (R. Bali 37, Kavaljit Singh 47, A. Gupta 40; Harbhajan Singh three for 63, Navdeep Singh five for 28) and 161 (Sanjay Sharma 46 not out, P. Bali 31; R. S. Sodhi five for 64, Navdeep Singh three for 47); Punjab 620 for six dec. (V. Rathore 114, P. Dharmani 305 not out, D. Mongia 31, Sanjay Kumar 36, H. S. Jugnu 106 not out; P. Bali four for 161). *Punjab 8 pts.*

Dharmani's 305 not out lasted 601 minutes and 482 balls and included 30 fours and two sixes; it followed an unbeaten 202 in his previous innings. He shared an unbroken seventh-wicket stand of 231 with Jugnu.

At Vishkarma High School Ground, Rohtak, November 13, 14, 15, 16. Haryana won by 248 runs. Haryana* 222 (A. S. Kaypee 35, V. Jain 30 not out; Shakti Singh six for 85, R. Panta three for 54) and 361 for nine dec. (Parender Sharma 36, R. Puri 56, S. Dalal 57, A. Ratra 75, Extras 48; Shakti Singh five for 84); Himachal Pradesh 152 (N. Gaur 50, R. Nayyar 31; V. Jain four for 30, F. Ghayas three for 49, P. Thakur three for 35) and 183 (R. Nayyar 33, S. Prakash 37, S. Modgil 30; P. Thakur three for 32, P. Jain four for 29). *Haryana 8 pts.*

At Punjab Agricultural University Ground, Ludhiana, November 13, 14, 15, 16. Drawn. Punjab* 530 for seven dec. (V. Rathore 75, R. S. Sodhi 104, P. Dharmani 101, D. Mongia 92, Sanjay Kumar 66, H. S. Jugnu 37 not out, Extras 30; H. Chowdhury three for 151) and 227 for three

(Yuvraj Singh 60, D. Mongia 101 not out); Delhi 527 (A. Dani 140, Ajay Sharma 36, V. Dahiya 42, V. Shewag 187, H. Chowdhury 32; Harbhajan Singh five for 156, Navdeep Singh three for 120). *Punjab 5 pts, Delhi 3 pts.*

Dharmani's third century in consecutive innings carried him to 608 runs before he was finally dismissed. Shewag's 187 included 20 fours and nine sixes.

At Harbax Singh Stadium, Delhi, November 13, 14, 15, 16. Jammu and Kashmir won by 30 runs. Jammu and Kashmir* 221 (R. Bali 31, Amrit Pal Singh 82, Kavaljit Singh 58; S. V. Ghag four for 24, S. K. Kulkarni three for 42) and 200 (R. Bali 31, Amrit Pal Singh 34, A. Gupta 33, Sanjay Sharma 31; S. Javed three for 24, S. K. Kulkarni four for 58); Services 263 (S. Verma 74, C. D. Thomson 74; Surendra Singh four for 67) and 128 (S. Verma 49; Surendra Singh three for 18, A. Gupta three for 29). *Jammu and Kashmir 8 pts.*

At Feroz Shah Kotla Ground, Delhi, November 20, 21, 22. Delhi won by an innings and three runs. Jammu and Kashmir 113 (R. Kaul 42; A. Nehra five for 52) and 320 (Amrit Pal Singh 123, D. M. Gupta 123; A. Nehra six for 66, N. Chopra three for 65); Delhi* 436 for nine dec. (Vishal Sharma 31, Devendra Sharma 91, M. Manhas 139, V. Dahiya 57, N. Chopra 54; Vijay Sharma three for 90). *Delhi 8 pts.*

At Nehru Stadium, Gurgaon, November 20, 21, 22, 23. Drawn. Haryana* 279 (Jitender Singh 102, Parender Sharma 36, P. Jain 38; Sarandeep Singh six for 98) and 251 for eight (A. S. Kaypee 46, R. Puri 100 not out, Extras 42; Sarandeep Singh three for 40); Punjab 379 (V. Rathore 80, Yuvraj Singh 149, D. Mongia 63; P. Thakur three for 126, P. Jain four for 97, S. Dalal three for 23). *Haryana 3 pts, Punjab 5 pts.*

At JNV Stadium, Una, November 20, 21, 22, 23. Drawn. Services* 355 (H. Bhaskar 51, Sarabjit Singh 32, S. Verma 68, S. V. Ghag 43; Shakti Singh four for 89) and 248 for eight dec. (H. Bhaskar 39, S. Dutta 30, S. K. Kulkarni 54, P. Maitreya 30; R. Panta six for 103); Himachal Pradesh 347 (R. Nayyar 112, S. Prakash 54, A. Verma 47, Extras 34; M. V. Rao three for 73, P. Maitreya four for 61) and 164 for five (R. Panta 100 not out). *Himachal Pradesh 3 pts, Services 5 pts.*

In Services' first innings Ghag, batting at No. 11, added 78 for the last wicket with S. K. Kulkarni.

Punjab 34 pts, Delhi 32 pts, Haryana 27 pts, Jammu and Kashmir 14 pts, Himachal Pradesh 8 pts, Services 5 pts. Punjab, Delhi and Haryana qualified for the Super League.

South Zone

At Indira Priyadarshini Stadium, Vishakhapatnam, November 7, 8, 9, 10. Drawn. Andhra* 305 (A. Pathak 72, Y. Venugopala Rao 33, H. Wadekar 41, Y. S. Ranganath 45, Extras 31; T. Kumaran three for 85, S. Vidyuth five for 61) and 307 for six (L. N. P. Reddy 101 not out, A. Pathak 85, Y. Venugopala Rao 55); Tamil Nadu 371 (J. R. Madanagopal 60, S. V. Saravanan 126, R. Paul 47, J. Gokulkrishnan 53; N. Madhukar six for 109). *Andhra 3 pts, Tamil Nadu 5 pts.*

Gokulkrishnan took five catches in the field in Andhra's first innings.

At Gymkhana Ground, Panaji, November 7, 8, 9. Hyderabad won by an innings and 352 runs. Hyderabad 592 for six dec. (D. Manohar 55, A. Nandakishore 88, V. V. S. Laxman 131, M. Azharuddin 200 not out, V. Pratap 54, Extras 33; S. Jakati three for 115); Goa* 140 (P. J. Rodrigues 30; Kanwaljit Singh six for 37, S. L. V. Raju four for 57) and 100 (S. L. V. Raju three for 39, Kanwaljit Singh four for 31). *Hyderabad 8 pts.*

Azharuddin's 200 not out, his fourth double-hundred, lasted 340 minutes and 256 balls and included 12 fours and six sixes.

At M. Chinnaswamy Stadium, Bangalore, November 7, 8, 9, 10. Karnataka won by an innings and 137 runs. Karnataka* 483 (B. M. Rowland 106, A. Vijay 122, V. S. T. Naidu 93, A. P. Katti 45, G. N. Umesh 32, Extras 30; B. Ramprakash three for 112); Kerala 172 (S. Shankar 36, A. S. Kudva 34; G. N. Umesh three for 46, A. R. Yalvigi three for 42) and 174 (S. C. Oasis 65; M. A. Khan six for 66, G. N. Umesh three for 47). *Karnataka 8 pts.*

Rowland scored 106 on first-class debut.

At Gymkhana Ground, Secunderabad, November 15, 16, 17, 18. Drawn. Andhra* 380 (L. N. P. Reddy 37, A. Pathak 56, Y. Venugopala Rao 95, R. V. C. Prasad 79, K. S. T. Sai 49; S. L. V. Raju five for 105, M. Azharuddin three for 36) and 141 for five (R. V. C. Prasad 45); Hyderabad 510 for six dec. (D. Manohar 72, V. V. S. Laxman 104, A. Nandakishore 65, M. Azharuddin 77, M. V. Sridhar 86, V. Pratap 64 not out; H. Ramkishen three for 181). *Hyderabad 5 pts, Andhra 3 pts.*

Ramkishen bowled 68.1 overs in Hyderabad's innings.

At M. Chinnaswamy Stadium, Bangalore, November 15, 16, 17. Karnataka won by an innings and 179 runs. Goa* 189 (V. V. Kolambkar 72; G. N. Umesh four for 42, A. P. Katti four for 29) and 136 (R. R. Naik 34; A. R. Yalvigi five for 43); Karnataka 504 for seven dec. (B. M. Rowland 48, V. S. T. Naidu 63, B. Akhil 80, A. R. Yalvigi 38, A. P. Katti 109 not out, D. J. Johnson 101 not out, Extras 38; N. S. Kalekar three for 235). *Karnataka 8 pts.*

Katti and Johnson shared an unbroken stand of 194 for Karnataka's eighth wicket. Kalekar conceded 235 runs in 63 overs.

At M. A. Chidambaram Stadium, Chennai, November 15, 16, 17, 18. Drawn. Tamil Nadu 305 (A. J. George 57, S. Sharath 91, R. Paul 36; R. Menon six for 70) and 250 for five (R. Paul 45, S. Sharath 106 not out, J. R. Madanagopal 41); Kerala* 290 (S. Shankar 52, K. N. A. Padmanabhan 70, S. R. Nair 39, B. Ramprakash 70 not out; J. Gokulkrishnan three for 61, A. R. Kapoor four for 73). *Tamil Nadu 5 pts, Kerala 3 pts.*

R. Menon claimed six wickets on debut.

At Trishna Stadium, Vishakhapatnam, November 24, 25, 26, 27. Andhra won by four wickets. Goa* 213 (P. J. Rodrigues 35, R. R. Naik 68; N. Madhukar three for 59, K. S. Shahabuddin five for 72) and 193 (P. J. Rodrigues 68, V. V. Kolambkar 34; N. Madhukar four for 44, Y. S. Ranganath four for 61); Andhra 250 (L. N. P. Reddy 51, V. Nagini Kumar 32, Y. Venugopala Rao 88; S. Jakati three for 54, N. S. Kalekar four for 79) and 157 for six (L. N. P. Reddy 52 not out, I. G. Srinivas 40; S. Jakati three for 41). *Andhra 8 pts.*

At M. Chinnaswamy Stadium, Bangalore, November 24, 25, 26, 27. Tamil Nadu won by 116 runs. Tamil Nadu 355 (A. R. Kapoor 64, S. Sharath 83, S. V. Saravanan 64; S. B. Joshi four for 83) and 246 for seven dec. (H. K. Badani 87, J. R. Madanagopal 66; S. B. Joshi four for 74); Karnataka* 221 (S. Somasunder 55, S. B. Joshi 30, B. Akhil 36; S. Mahesh three for 34) and 264 (A. Vijay 62, V. S. T. Naidu 53, S. Somasekhar 48, S. B. Joshi 60; A. R. Kapoor five for 98). *Tamil Nadu 8 pts.*

Ranji holders Karnataka suffered their first outright defeat since December 1996 when Kerala beat them by six wickets at Palghat.

At Regional Engineering College Ground, Kozhikode, November 24, 25, 26, 27. Hyderabad won by nine wickets. Kerala* 247 (S. Shankar 48, M. P. Sorab 35, S. C. Oasis 46, B. Ramprakash 34; Kanwaljit Singh six for 91, S. L. V. Raju three for 102) and 179 (M. Suresh Kumar 61; S. L. V. Raju four for 77, Kanwaljit Singh five for 63); Hyderabad 303 (M. Azharuddin 56, M. V. Sridhar 35, V. Pratap 56, N. P. Singh 59; S. R. Nair three for 56) and 127 for one (A. Nandakishore 44 not out, D. Vinay Kumar 60 not out). *Hyderabad 8 pts.*

At District Sports Stadium, Kakinada, December 25, 26, 27, 28. Karnataka won by 46 runs. Karnataka 248 (M. R. Beerala 83, V. S. T. Naidu 32, S. Somasekhar 43, A. R. Yalvigi 37 not out; Y. S. Ranganath five for 69) and 273 (J. Arun Kumar 53, M. R. Beerala 94, A. Vijay 47; H. Wadekar four for 47); Andhra* 331 (R. V. C. Prasad 78, I. G. Srinivas 85, Y. S. Ranganath 47, Extras 30; D. Ganesh five for 115) and 144 (K. S. Shahabuddin 45 not out; M. A. Khan six for 47). *Karnataka 8 pts.*

Beerala scored 83 and 94 on first-class debut.

At M. A. Chidambaram Stadium, Chennai, December 27, 28, 29, 30. Drawn. Tamil Nadu 404 (S. Sriram 121, H. K. Badani 52, J. R. Madanagopal 55, J. Gokulkrishnan 46, S. Mahesh 46, Extras 30; N. P. Singh five for 100); Hyderabad* 205 (D. Manohar 34, M. Azharuddin 34; S. Mahesh three for 53, A. R. Kapoor four for 30) and 338 for eight (A. Nandakishore 135, D. Vinay Kumar 36, M. Azharuddin 69, M. F. Ahmed 51; A. R. Kapoor four for 97). *Tamil Nadu 5 pts, Hyderabad 3 pts.*

At Dr Rajendra Prasad Stadium, Margao, December 28, 29. Kerala won by ten wickets. Goa* 105 (R. Menon five for 45, M. Suresh Kumar five for 21) and 134 (A. A. Ranade 32; B. Ramprakash three for 27, M. Suresh Kumar three for 21); Kerala 234 (S. C. Oasis 76, B. Ramprakash 53; A. I. Aware six for 97) and six for no wkt. *Kerala 8 pts.*
Aware claimed six wickets on first-class debut.

At Gymkhana Ground, Secunderabad, January 6, 7, 8, 9. Drawn. Hyderabad* 255 (D. Vinay Kumar 56, M. Azharuddin 43, J. S. Yadav 37; G. N. Umesh five for 61, A. P. Katti three for 53) and 312 for six dec. (G. Arvind Kumar 46, D. Vinay Kumar 93, P. Satwalkar 80, Extras 34; D. Ganesh three for 52); Karnataka 212 (J. Arun Kumar 37, B. M. Rowland 37, V. S. T. Naidu 45; Kanwaljit Singh three for 53, J. S. Yadav three for 63) and 239 for four (M. R. Beerala 46, B. M. Rowland 64, S. Somasunder 55 not out, V. S. T. Naidu 31 not out). *Hyderabad 5 pts, Karnataka 3 pts.*

At Regional Engineering College Ground, Kozhikode, January 6, 7, 8. Kerala won by three wickets. Andhra* 168 (L. N. P. Reddy 48, A. Pathak 31; K. N. A. Padmanabhan four for 42, B. Ramprakash six for 68) and 179 (L. N. P. Reddy 49, V. Nagini Kumar 47; B. Ramprakash four for 81, S. C. Oasis five for 27); Kerala 186 (S. Sasikanth 38, S. C. Oasis 33, B. Ramprakash 44, K. N. A. Padmanabhan 30; V. J. T. Ram Mohan four for 33, H. Wadekar three for 44) and 164 for seven (M. P. Sorab 52, S. Shankar 30). *Kerala 8 pts.*
Oasis took seven catches in the match in the field, four of them off the bowling of Ramprakash in Andhra's first innings.

At M. A. Chidambaram Stadium, Chennai, January 6, 7, 8. Tamil Nadu won by an innings and 197 runs. Tamil Nadu 446 for eight dec. (S. Sriram 147, S. Sharath 63, T. Jabbar 100 not out, S. Mahesh 77; A. I. Aware five for 125); Goa* 112 (Y. C. Barde 69; S. Mahesh four for 37, A. R. Kapoor three for 30) and 137 (A. C. Bhagwat 31, A. A. Ranade 44; S. Suresh three for 28, A. R. Kapoor four for 33). *Tamil Nadu 8 pts.*

Tamil Nadu 31 pts, Hyderabad 29 pts, Karnataka 27 pts, Kerala 19 pts, Andhra 14 pts, Goa 0 pts. Tamil Nadu, Hyderabad and Karnataka qualified for the Super League.

West Zone

At IPCL Ground, Baroda, November 15, 16, 17, 18. Drawn. Gujarat 295 (N. D. Modi 46, N. K. Patel 64, M. H. Parmar 32, T. N. Varsania 32, B. N. Patel 43; M. S. Kadri six for 46) and 414 for five (A. S. Kotecha 49, N. D. Modi 202 not out, T. N. Varsania 99); Baroda* 329 (H. R. Jadhav 148 not out; H. A. Majumdar four for 93, M. N. Sheth three for 61). *Baroda 5 pts, Gujarat 3 pts.*
Modi's 202 not out, his maiden double-hundred, lasted 535 minutes and 394 balls and included 29 fours.

At Wankhede Stadium, Mumbai, November 15, 16, 17. Mumbai won by an innings and 11 runs. Maharashtra* 142 (D. Jadhav 55; R. V. Pawar six for 19) and 148 (S. S. Bhave 49, D. Jadhav 33; N. M. Kulkarni four for 44, R. V. Pawar five for 49); Mumbai 301 (P. L. Mhambrey 117, S. Kannan 35; Iqbal Siddiqui seven for 69). *Mumbai 8 pts.*
Opener Jadhav, making his first-class debut, was the last man out in Maharashtra's first innings.

At IPCL Ground, Baroda, November 22, 23, 24, 25. Drawn. Mumbai 335 (Wasim Jaffer 93, A. A. Muzumdar 80, V. G. Kambli 32, R. J. Sutar 32, R. V. Pawar 36 not out; Zaheer Khan five for 125) and 228 for two (Wasim Jaffer 33, A. A. Rane 35, J. V. Paranjpe 116 not out, A. A. Muzumdar 35 not out); Baroda* 364 (C. C. Williams 56, S. S. Parab 122, M. P. Mewada 46; P. L. Mhambrey three for 53, N. M. Kulkarni five for 116). *Baroda 5 pts, Mumbai 3 pts.*

At Municipal Ground, Rajkot, November 22, 23, 24, 25. Drawn. Saurashtra* 503 for eight dec. (S. S. Tanna 53, R. C. Vasant Kumar 131, B. M. Jadeja 156 not out, H. J. Parsana 79, D. N. Chudasama 35 not out; B. N. Mehta five for 179); Gujarat 347 (N. D. Modi 59, N. K. Patel 58, K. S. Padia 37, K. A. Damani 39, P. H. Patel 55, H. A. Majumdar 35; H. J. Parsana three for 69, N. R. Odedra three for 76, D. N. Chudasama three for 112) and 156 for four (N. K. Patel 100 not out). *Saurashtra 5 pts, Gujarat 3 pts.*
Saurashtra captain S. H. Kotak pulled out after the second day to join India A in the West Indies.

At Lalabhai Contractor Stadium, Surat, December 27, 28, 29, 30. Mumbai won by ten wickets. Gujarat 305 (A. S. Kotecha 41, K. S. Padia 75, T. N. Varsania 53, P. H. Patel 39; P. L. Mhambrey four for 71) and 167 (N. D. Modi 54; P. L. Mhambrey four for 31); Mumbai* 419 (Wasim Jaffer 173, A. A. Pagnis 52, V. G. Kambli 116, Extras 39; B. H. Patel three for 87, H. A. Majumdar three for 70, L. A. Patel three for 75) and 55 for no wkt. *Mumbai 8 pts.*

At Deccan Gymkhana Ground, Pune, December 27, 28, 29, 30. Drawn. Saurashtra 217 (S. H. Kotak 36, P. J. Bhatt 46, H. J. Parsana 58 retired hurt; Iqbal Siddiqui eight for 72) and 374 for five (R. C. Vasant Kumar 46, S. H. Kotak 126, P. J. Bhatt 85, B. M. Jadeja 53 not out); Maharashtra* 431 (S. S. Bhave 30, A. V. Kale 84, K. D. Aphale 158, S. D. Lande 62; R. R. Garsondia five for 90). *Maharashtra 5 pts, Saurashtra 3 pts.*

Siddiqui became Maharashtra's leading wicket-taker, with 156 wickets in 38 matches. Aphale scored 158 on first-class debut.

At Deccan Gymkhana Ground, Pune, January 3, 4, 5, 6. Drawn. Baroda 393 (C. C. Williams 34, S. S. Parab 46, T. B. Arothe 60, A. C. Bedade 139, Zaheer Khan 48; M. S. Kulkarni three for 86, S. D. Lande three for 72) and 34 for no wkt; Maharashtra* 213 (S. S. Bhave 113; Zaheer Khan three for 65, R. A. Swarup three for 49) and 449 (A. V. Kale 248 not out, S. S. Sugwekar 34, K. D. Aphale 37, S. S. Shah 32, S. V. Aradhye 58; Zaheer Khan three for 100, R. A. Swarup four for 161). *Maharashtra 3 pts, Baroda 5 pts.*

Kale's 248 not out, his second double-hundred, lasted 548 minutes and 367 balls and included 32 fours and one six; he added 198 for Maharashtra's eighth wicket with Aradhye.

At Wankhede Stadium, Mumbai, January 3, 4, 5, 6. Drawn. Mumbai 297 (A. A. Pagnis 45, A. A. Rane 43, A. A. Muzumdar 51, P. L. Mhambrey 65 not out; D. N. Chudasama four for 67) and 372 for four dec. (A. A. Pagnis 50, A. A. Rane 30, A. A. Muzumdar 131, V. G. Kambli 125 not out; N. R. Odedra three for 130); Saurashtra* 183 (F. U. Bambhaniya 59, M. M. Parmar 32; P. L. Mhambrey three for 46, A. Kuruvilla five for 47) and 206 for eight (S. H. Kotak 52, M. M. Parmar 67; P. L. Mhambrey three for 35, A. Kuruvilla three for 49). *Mumbai 5 pts, Saurashtra 3 pts.*

At Sardar Patel Stadium, Ahmedabad, January 10, 11, 12, 13. Drawn. Maharashtra* 501 for seven dec. (A. V. Kale 219, S. S. Sugwekar 137, K. D. Aphale 43); Gujarat 309 (A. S. Kotecha 35, M. N. Sheth 48, K. A. Damani 58, K. Desai 36 not out, L. A. Patel 35; M. V. Sane seven for 83) and 194 for eight (A. S. Kotecha 48, K. A. Damani 33 not out; M. V. Sane four for 63). *Gujarat 3 pts, Maharashtra 5 pts.*

Kale scored his second double-hundred in successive innings. His 219 lasted 509 minutes and 406 balls and included 23 fours and one six; he added 286 for Maharashtra's third wicket with Sugwekar.

At Municipal Ground, Rajkot, January 10, 11, 12, 13. Drawn. Saurashtra* 437 (R. C. Vasant Kumar 84, S. H. Kotak 42, P. J. Bhatt 158; A. P. Bhohite three for 79) and 127 for four (R. C. Vasant Kumar 42, P. J. Bhatt 37, F. U. Bambhaniya 38 not out; V. N. Buch four for 55); Baroda 487 (C. C. Williams 237 not out, R. A. Swarup 88, Zaheer Khan 32; R. Dhruv three for 153, N. R. Odedra four for 151). *Saurashtra 3 pts, Baroda 5 pts.*

Williams carried his bat for 237 not out, his maiden double-hundred, which lasted 628 minutes and 480 balls and included 30 fours and one six.

Mumbai 24 pts, Baroda 20 pts, Saurashtra 14 pts, Maharashtra 13 pts, Gujarat 9 pts. Mumbai, Baroda and Saurashtra qualified for the Super League.

Super League Group A

At Feroz Shah Kotla Ground, Delhi, February 5, 6, 7, 8. Drawn. Delhi* 453 for nine dec. (A. Dani 82, G. Gambhir 33, Ajay Sharma 52, V. Shewag 64, M. Manhas 102 not out); Rajasthan 311 (A. Jain 64, G. K. Khoda 73, R. J. Kanwat 52, P. K. Krishnakumar 39; A. Bhandari four for 87). *Delhi 5 pts, Rajasthan 3 pts.*

At M. Chinnaswamy Stadium, Bangalore, February 5, 6, 7. Mumbai won by an innings and 74 runs. Karnataka* 209 (J. Arun Kumar 76, A. Vijay 41; S. Kannan four for 55, N. M. Kulkarni three for 41) and 108 (M. R. Beerala 34; A. Kuruvilla five for 32); Mumbai 391 (Wasim Jaffer 72, A. A. Pagnis 54, J. V. Paranjpe 107, R. V. Pawar 49, A. Kuruvilla 37 not out; D. Ganesh four for 113, S. B. Joshi five for 126). *Mumbai 8 pts.*

At Eden Gardens, Calcutta, February 16, 17, 18, 19. Drawn. Delhi* 236 (A. Chopra 95, A. Malhotra 34; L. R. Shukla four for 70, U. Chatterjee three for 47) and 261 (A. Chopra 42, V. Dahiya 32, M. Manhas 46, N. Chopra 39; S. C. Ganguly five for 91, U. Chatterjee four for 84); Bengal 374 for eight dec. (N. L. Haldipur 92, R. S. Gavaskar 53, S. J. Kalyani 90, S. S. Karim 46, W. Majumder 34; S. Gill three for 41) and 82 for four. *Bengal 5 pts, Delhi 3 pts.*

At Rajinder Singh Institute Ground, Bangalore, February 16, 17, 18, 19. Karnataka won by 139 runs. Karnataka 243 (M. R. Beerala 48, R. Dravid 71, V. S. T. Naidu 38, S. B. Joshi 34; D. P. Singh four for 44) and 326 for six dec. (M. R. Beerala 59, R. Dravid 149, V. S. T. Naidu 49); Rajasthan* 211 (N. Doru 66, Kuldeep Singh 33; S. B. Joshi six for 48) and 219 (A. Jain 32, D. P. Singh 85). *Karnataka 8 pts.*

At Eden Gardens, Calcutta, February 24, 25, 26, 27. Drawn. Rajasthan* 377 (A. Jain 115, R. J. Kanwat 143, N. Doru 45; U. Chatterjee five for 76) and 216 for eight dec. (S. Bhatia 48, Sanjeev Sharma 54; U. Chatterjee five for 84); Bengal 284 (D. J. Gandhi 89, S. J. Kalyani 83 not out, Extras 31; D. P. Singh four for 73) and 179 for five (D. J. Gandhi 67, S. J. Kalyani 56; D. P. Singh four for 56). *Bengal 3 pts, Rajasthan 5 pts.*

At Feroz Shah Kotla Ground, Delhi, February 24, 25, 26, 27. Mumbai won by 310 runs. Mumbai* 247 (A. A. Pagnis 31, A. A. Muzumdar 36, V. G. Kambli 88, S. V. Bahutule 33; A. Bhandari three for 69) and 453 for eight dec. (J. V. Paranjpe 185, A. A. Muzumdar 38, V. G. Kambli 114, Extras 38; V. Shewag four for 87); Delhi 200 (A. Dani 74, V. Shewag 50, Ajay Sharma 39 not out; R. V. Pawar four for 64) and 190 (Devendra Sharma 34, A. Dani 47, Extras 32; A. Kuruvilla three for 43, N. M. Kulkarni three for 37, S. V. Bahutule three for 18). *Mumbai 8 pts.*

Kambli reached 100 in 87 balls; his 114 came in 97 balls. In Delhi's second innings, No. 9 Ashish Nehra remained unbeaten on three after 162 minutes and 136 balls.

At Eden Gardens, Calcutta, March 4, 5, 6, 7. Drawn. Bengal* 316 (R. S. Gavaskar 44, S. S. Karim 129 not out, Charanjit Singh 36; B. K. V. Prasad four for 62, D. Ganesh three for 62) and 264 for nine dec. (N. L. Haldipur 43, D. J. Gandhi 88, S. S. Karim 55 not out, L. R. Shukla 37; S. B. Joshi three for 108, S. K. Vadiaraj four for 59); Karnataka 268 (M. R. Beerala 35, B. M. Rowland 53, A. Vijay 39, S. B. Joshi 34, D. Ganesh 31, B. K. V. Prasad 37; U. Chatterjee six for 102) and 52 for one (B. M. Rowland 36 not out). *Bengal 5 pts, Karnataka 3 pts.*

At Wankhede Stadium, Mumbai, March 4, 5, 6, 7. Mumbai won by 72 runs. Mumbai 336 (S. S. Dighe 32, A. A. Pagnis 47, A. A. Muzumdar 63, V. G. Kambli 59, S. E. Manjrekar 38, Extras 53; P. K. Krishnakumar four for 69, D. P. Singh three for 38) and 285 for five dec. (S. S. Dighe 64, J. V. Paranjpe 53, A. A. Muzumdar 63 not out, S. E. Manjrekar 61); Rajasthan* 229 (G. K. Khoda 83, Sanjeev Sharma 33, R. B. Jhalani 32, Extras 32; S. R. Saxena five for 56, A. Kuruvilla four for 77) and 320 (N. Doru 105, S. Bhatia 90, G. K. Khoda 70, Extras 37; R. V. Pawar four for 93, R. R. Powar three for 59). *Mumbai 8 pts.*

Rajasthan wicket-keeper Jhalani made four catches and two stumpings in Mumbai's first innings.

At Eden Gardens, Calcutta, March 13, 14, 15, 16. Mumbai won by 242 runs. Mumbai* 182 (A. A. Pagnis 43, A. A. Muzumdar 34; U. Chatterjee four for 48) and 315 (Wasim Jaffer 73, J. V. Paranjpe 34, R. R. Powar 92, R. V. Pawar 30; V. S. Yadav four for 70); Bengal 117 (A. Kuruvilla three for 12) and 138 (L. R. Shukla 33; R. V. Pawar five for 60, R. R. Powar five for 46). *Mumbai 8 pts.*

At M. Chinnaswamy Stadium, Bangalore, March 13, 14, 15, 16. Karnataka won by eight wickets. Delhi 342 (A. Chopra 101, G. Gambhir 73, V. Shewag 49, M. Manhas 54 not out; B. K. V. Prasad six for 60) and 191 (A. Chopra 36, A. Dani 52, G. Gambhir 30; B. K. V. Prasad five for 36, S. K. Vadiaraj four for 73); Karnataka* 359 (J. Arun Kumar 127, V. S. T. Naidu 36, B. Akhil 59, Extras 38; A. Nehra three for 89, R. Mehra three for 103) and 175 for two (J. Arun Kumar 32, M. R. Beerala 101 not out). *Karnataka 8 pts.*

Mumbai 32 pts, Karnataka 19 pts, Bengal 13 pts, Delhi 8 pts, Rajasthan 8 pts. Mumbai went straight to the semi-finals as qualifiers with most points, as did Karnataka as holders of the Ranji Trophy.

Super League Group B

At IPCL Ground, Baroda, February 5, 6, 7. Baroda won by an innings and 114 runs. Baroda 499 (R. A. Swarup 59, N. R. Mongia 65, T. B. Arothe 125, A. C. Bedade 49, H. R. Jadhav 98 not out, R. B. Patel 35, V. N. Buch 39; Dhiraj Kumar six for 167, M. Diwakar four for 125); Bihar* 119 (M. S. Dhoni 31, Dhiraj Kumar 34; Zaheer Khan five for 43, I. K. Pathan three for 31) and 266 (N. Ranjan 72, M. S. Dhoni 45, M. Diwakar 67; Zaheer Khan five for 67). *Baroda 8 pts.*

At PCA Stadium, Mohali, February 5, 6, 7, 8. Drawn. Hyderabad 117 (V. Pratap 31; Sandeep Sharma three for 36, Gagandeep Singh five for 49) and 244 for three (P. Satwalkar 53, A. Nandakishore 35, D. Vinay Kumar 67, M. Azharuddin 63 not out); Punjab* 363 for eight dec. (R. S. Ricky 134, P. Dharmani 46, H. S. Jugnu 32, Sandeep Sharma 68 not out; N. P. Singh five for 69). *Punjab 5 pts, Hyderabad 3 pts.*

At Gymkhana Ground, Secunderabad, February 16, 17, 18, 19. Drawn. Bihar* 381 (Rajiv Kumar 85, Sunil Kumar 80, Manish Kumar 48, M. Diwakar 86; N. P. Singh three for 78, P. Satwalkar three for 42) and 229 for nine (A. Hashmi 58, Rajiv Kumar 34, Sunil Kumar 71 not out; P. Satwalkar three for 43, Kanwaljit Singh four for 70); Hyderabad 440 for eight dec. (A. Nandakishore 82, V. V. S. Laxman 119, V. Pratap 100 not out, P. Satwalkar 73; S. Khan three for 82). *Hyderabad 5 pts, Bihar 3 pts.*

At Karnail Singh Stadium, Delhi, February 16, 17, 18, 19. Drawn. Railways* 506 (Vishal Sharma 43, Y. Gowda 182, Devendra Singh 47, S. V. Wankhede 139; Zaheer Khan three for 120, V. N. Buch four for 109); Baroda 516 for nine (C. C. Williams 123, H. R. Jadhav 109, M. P. Mewada 37, A. C. Bedade 51, T. B. Arothe 41, A. P. Bhohite 52, R. B. Patel 53 not out, Extras 31). *Railways 3 pts, Baroda 5 pts.*

Gowda batted for 681 minutes and faced 488 balls, hitting 15 fours, and added 255 for Railways' sixth wicket with Wankhede.

At Mecon Sail Stadium, Ranchi, February 24, 25, 26, 27. Railways won by 40 runs. Railways 130 (Dhiraj Kumar three for 64, M. Diwakar seven for 47) and 216 (Vishal Sharma 54, Y. Gowda 82 not out, Tejinder Singh 31; M. Diwakar five for 74); Bihar* 105 (Manish Kumar 31; Zakir Hussain five for 36, K. S. Parida four for 29) and 201 (N. Ranjan 51, Sunil Kumar 31; K. S. Parida four for 52). *Railways 8 pts.*

At Punjab CA Stadium, Mohali, February 24, 25, 26, 27. Drawn. Punjab* 245 (R. S. Ricky 83; R. B. Patel three for 66, V. N. Buch three for 23) and 274 for four (V. Rathore 46, R. S. Sodhi 114 not out, P. Dharmani 67, Yuvraj Singh 31 not out); Baroda 384 (C. C. Williams 31, H. R. Jadhav 54, J. J. Martin 118, T. B. Arothe 61, A. P. Bhohite 51 not out; Gagandeep Singh four for 65, Harbhajan Singh three for 101). *Punjab 3 pts, Baroda 5 pts.*

At Punjab CA Stadium, Mohali, March 4, 5, 6, 7. Punjab won by an innings and 20 runs. Bihar 244 (N. Ranjan 39, Javed Khan 60, Rajiv Kumar 55; Gagandeep Singh four for 44, Harbhajan Singh five for 69) and 239 (Sunil Kumar 51, Manish Kumar 51, S. Khan 30 not out; Gagandeep Singh three for 65, Harbhajan Singh four for 68); Punjab* 503 for nine dec. (V. Rathore 158, R. S. Ricky 50, D. Mongia 179, H. S. Jugnu 53, Sandeep Sharma 33; S. Gupta three for 125). *Punjab 8 pts.*

At Feroz Shah Kotla Ground, Delhi, March 4, 5, 6, 7. Drawn. Hyderabad* 347 (A. Nandakishore 119, V. V. S. Laxman 109; W. D. Balaji Rao five for 56, K. S. Parida three for 121) and 212 for seven dec. (V. V. S. Laxman 45, V. Pratap 38, P. Satwalkar 45, A. S. Yadav 43); Railways 229 (P. S. Rawat 35, Devendra Singh 87; N. P. Singh four for 58, V. V. S. Laxman three for 11) and 182 for seven (Abhay Sharma 59, P. S. Rawat 39 not out; Kanwaljit Singh four for 40). *Railways 3 pts, Hyderabad 5 pts.*

At Gymkhana Ground, Secunderabad, March 12, 13, 14, 15. Hyderabad won by 71 runs. Hyderabad* 204 (A. Nandakishore 31, V. Pratap 57; V. N. Buch three for 60) and 246

(A. Nandakishore 30, D. Vinay Kumar 33, V. V. S. Laxman 48, P. Satwalkar 56; V. N. Buch five for 79); Baroda 216 (H. R. Jadhav 84, A. P. Bhohite 42; N. P. Singh three for 54, S. L. V. Raju three for 56) and 163 (J. J. Martin 30, N. R. Mongia 34; P. Satwalkar four for 41, S. L. V. Raju three for 43, Kanwaljit Singh three for 49). *Hyderabad 8 pts.*

At Karnail Singh Stadium, Delhi, March 13, 14, 15. Punjab won by an innings and 64 runs. Punjab* 355 (R. S. Ricky 97, Yuvraj Singh 54, D. Mongia 34, H. S. Jugnu 30, Sarandeep Singh 44 not out, Navdeep Singh 42, Extras 34; K. S. Parida six for 84); Railways 195 (Y. Gowda 64, K. S. Parida 35 not out; Navdeep Singh four for 59, Harbhajan Singh three for 64) and 96 (Harbhajan Singh three for 57, Sarandeep Singh five for 22). *Punjab 8 pts.*

Punjab 24 pts, Hyderabad 21 pts, Baroda 18 pts, Railways 14 pts, Bihar 3 pts. Punjab and Hyderabad qualified for the quarter-finals.

Super League Group C

At Vishkarma High School Ground, Rohtak, February 5, 6, 7, 8. Drawn. Haryana 198 (Parender Sharma 30, Jasvir Singh 94, A. Ratra 37; S. Sriwastava six for 82, G. K. Pandey four for 24); Uttar Pradesh* 93 for five (F. Ghayas three for 32). *Haryana 3 pts, Uttar Pradesh 3 pts.*

At M. A. Chidambaram Stadium, Chennai, February 5, 6, 7. Tamil Nadu won by an innings and 26 runs. Tamil Nadu 471 (A. R. Kapoor 59, S. Sriram 98, H. K. Badani 86, S. Sharath 76, S. Mahesh 33 not out); Saurashtra* 217 (S. H. Kotak 35, P. J. Bhatt 61, H. J. Parsana 54 not out; J. Gokulkrishnan five for 42, S. Mahesh three for 57) and 228 (P. J. Bhatt 88, H. J. Parsana 36, N. P. Rana 37; S. Mahesh four for 61, A. R. Kapoor five for 85). *Tamil Nadu 8 pts.*

At Vishkarma High School Ground, Rohtak, February 16, 17, 18, 19. Saurashtra won by nine wickets. Saurashtra* 405 (S. H. Kotak 83, P. J. Bhatt 110, H. J. Parsana 43, M. M. Parmar 34, Extras 54; V. Jain four for 96) and 97 for one (A. A. Merchant 41 not out, R. C. Vasant Kumar 38); Haryana 224 (Jitender Singh 51, Parender Sharma 43, R. Puri 64; H. J. Parsana six for 68, S. H. Kotak three for 14) and 274 (R. Puri 114 not out, S. Olan 36; F. U. Bambhaniya five for 54). *Saurashtra 8 pts.*

At Green Park, Kanpur, February 16, 17, 18, 19. Uttar Pradesh won by ten wickets. Orissa* 241 (S. S. Raul 108 not out, P. Jayachandra 36; G. K. Pandey four for 42) and 257 (S. S. Raul 82, R. R. Parida 69, P. Jayachandra 65 not out; M. Raza five for 49); Uttar Pradesh 487 (M. S. Mudgal 62, Jyoti P. Yadav 32, Rizwan Shamshad 115, G. K. Pandey 163, S. A. Shukla 43; S. K. Satpathy six for 147) and 14 for no wkt. *Uttar Pradesh 8 pts.*

At Nehru Stadium, Gurgaon, February 24, 25, 26, 27. Tamil Nadu won by an innings and 40 runs. Haryana* 208 (Jitender Singh 40, P. Jain 57, P. Thakur 53; J. Gokulkrishnan three for 40, R. R. Singh three for 19) and 238 (Parender Sharma 33, Jitender Singh 100); Tamil Nadu 486 (A. R. Kapoor 55, S. Sriram 177, H. K. Badani 31, J. R. Madanagopal 74, S. Mahesh 32, J. Gokulkrishnan 31 not out; P. Jain five for 143). *Tamil Nadu 8 pts.*

At Municipal Ground, Rajkot, February 24, 25, 26. Orissa won by 209 runs. Orissa* 372 (S. S. Das 101, P. Das 69, R. R. Parida 76, Y. Mohanty 30; N. R. Odedra six for 117) and 181 (P. Das 49, S. K. Satpathy 43; N. R. Odedra six for 52); Saurashtra 238 (H. J. Parsana 76, M. M. Parmar 71 not out; D. S. Mohanty four for 47, S. K. Satpathy four for 76) and 106 (R. C. Vasant Kumar 33; D. S. Mohanty five for 28, S. K. Satpathy five for 65). *Orissa 8 pts.*

At Barabati Stadium, Cuttack, March 4, 5, 6, 7. Drawn. Tamil Nadu* 327 (S. Sharath 60, R. Bhatia 72, J. Gokulkrishnan 59 not out; D. S. Mohanty three for 95, A. Barik three for 89, Bipin Singh three for 59) and 309 for eight dec. (R. Bhatia 60, S. Sriram 31, J. R. Madanagopal 31, S. Sharath 42, R. Paul 44 not out; S. K. Satpathy three for 57); Orissa 195 (R. R. Parida 35, Y. Mohanty 59 not out, S. K. Satpathy 35; S. Mahesh three for 63, A. R. Kapoor three for 45) and 311 for three (S. S. Das 83, R. R. Parida 147 not out). *Orissa 3 pts, Tamil Nadu 5 pts.*

Nos 10 and 11 Bhatia and Gokulkrishnan added 137 for the last wicket in Tamil Nadu's first innings.

At Municipal Ground, Rajkot, March 4, 5, 6. Uttar Pradesh won by 235 runs. Uttar Pradesh* 206 (Parvinder Singh 59, M. Saif 31; N. R. Odedra four for 56, H. J. Parsana three for 36) and 300 (M. S. Mudgal 44, Rizwan Shamshad 81, M. Saif 83, Extras 31; N. R. Odedra six for 63); Saurashtra 118 (F. U. Bambhaniya 35 not out; G. K. Pandey five for 39) and 153 (S. H. Kotak 32, H. J. Parsana 41; A. W. Zaidi six for 42, G. K. Pandey three for 44). *Uttar Pradesh 8 pts.*

At Gopabandhu Stadium, Paradeep, March 13, 14, 15, 16. Drawn. Haryana* 206 (Padamjeet Singh 51, Parender Sharma 40; J. Das four for 62, S. S. Raul three for 37) and 298 for eight dec. (Jitender Singh 40, Jasvir Singh 82, I. Ganda 40, S. Dalal 62); Orissa 165 (R. R. Parida 39, S. S. Raul 51; Sonu Sharma seven for 32) and 210 for six (R. R. Parida 49, P. M. Mullick 38). *Orissa 3 pts, Haryana 5 pts.*

At Green Park, Kanpur, March 13, 14, 15, 16. Drawn. Tamil Nadu* 696 for five dec. (S. Sriram 288, H. K. Badani 62, J. R. Madanagopal 85, S. Sharath 205) and 264 (H. K. Badani 104, R. Paul 47, J. Gokulkrishnan 43; A. W. Zaidi four for 69, M. Raza three for 80); Uttar Pradesh 228 (S. A. Shukla 102) and 28 for no wkt. *Uttar Pradesh 3 pts, Tamil Nadu 5 pts.*

Sriram's 288, his second double-hundred, lasted 679 minutes and 469 balls and included 38 fours, while Sharath's 205 came in 400 minutes and 323 balls with 32 fours and one six. In the second innings, Sriram retired overnight on nought when he was called up by India for a one-day international against South Africa.

Tamil Nadu 26 pts, Uttar Pradesh 22 pts, Orissa 14 pts, Saurashtra 8 pts, Haryana 8 pts. Tamil Nadu and Uttar Pradesh qualified for the quarter-finals.

Quarter-finals

At M. A. Chidambaram Stadium, Chennai, March 30, 31, April 1, 2, 3. Tamil Nadu won by seven wickets. Punjab 258 (V. Rathore 57, Yuvraj Singh 44, D. Mongia 33, H. S. Jugnu 34; S. Mahesh three for 55) and 366 (V. Rathore 127, R. S. Sodhi 89, D. Mongia 35, Sandeep Sharma 51 not out; R. Bhatia three for 18); Tamil Nadu* 461 (S. Sriram 165, H. K. Badani 70, J. R. Madanagopal 35, S. Sharath 33, R. Paul 32, Extras 35; Harbhajan Singh five for 106) and 167 for three (S. Ramesh 77 not out, S. Sharath 53 not out).

Play was delayed for several minutes on the opening morning by a snake in the outfield, and for 20 minutes on the final morning by a swarm of bees, which stung spectators and caused the players to throw themselves to the ground, until the umpires decided to take an early lunch. Sriram passed 1,000 runs for the season in Tamil Nadu's first innings, and wicket-keeper Paul took nine catches in the match.

At Green Park, Kanpur, March 30, 31, April 1, 2, 3. Hyderabad won by 92 runs. Hyderabad* 291 (V. V. S. Laxman 128; A. W. Zaidi three for 70, R. Mishra four for 30) and 381 for five dec. (A. Nandakishore 93, V. V. S. Laxman 177 not out, D. Vinay Kumar 48); Uttar Pradesh 362 (Jyoti P. Yadav 61, M. Kaif 66, G. K. Pandey 47, A. W. Zaidi 52, Extras 30; Kanwaljit Singh six for 97) and 218 (M. Saif 57, M. Kaif 86; Kanwaljit Singh three for 78, S. L. V. Raju six for 57). *Laxman scored his fifth and sixth centuries of the season.*

Semi-finals

At M. Chinnaswamy Stadium, Bangalore, April 11, 12, 13, 14, 15. Drawn. Hyderabad were declared winners by virtue of their first-innings lead. Hyderabad 711 for eight dec. (D. Manohar 39, V. V. S. Laxman 353, M. Azharuddin 123, V. Pratap 45, P. Satwalkar 37, M. F. Ahmed 31, Extras 43; B. K. V. Prasad five for 121) and 236 for six dec. (V. Pratap 100, M. F. Ahmed 40 not out); Karnataka* 557 (J. Arun Kumar 71, M. R. Beerala 74, B. M. Rowland 65, R. V. Bharadwaj 90, B. Akhil 32, S. B. Joshi 72, D. Ganesh 76, Extras 56; M. F. Ahmed three for 114, S. L. V. Raju four for 144, Kanwaljit Singh three for 143).

Laxman's 353, his fourth score over 200, lasted 759 minutes and 559 balls and included 51 fours and two sixes. He became the first batsman in Ranji Trophy history to score two triple-hundreds, following his 301 not out against Bihar at Jamshedpur in 1997-98, and added 288 for Hyderabad's third wicket with Azharuddin. It was his third century in successive innings.

At Wankhede Stadium, Mumbai, April 11, 12, 13, 14, 15. Mumbai won by eight wickets. Tamil Nadu 485 (S. Ramesh 44, H. K. Badani 162, R. R. Singh 183 not out, Extras 38; A. B. Agarkar four for 83, S. R. Saxena three for 91) and 171 (H. K. Badani 63, R. Paul 46); Mumbai* 490 (S. S. Dighe 55, S. R. Tendulkar 233 not out, V. G. Kambli 75, A. A. Muzumdar 47; S. Mahesh three for 105, A. R. Kapoor three for 93) and 169 for two (S. S. Dighe 73, J. V. Paranjpe 55 not out).

Badani and Robin Singh added 254 for Tamil Nadu's fifth wicket. Tendulkar's career-best 233 not out, his third double-hundred but his first in Ranji cricket, lasted 565 minutes and 334 balls and included 21 fours and five sixes. He was dropped on 42, when Mumbai were 149 for four.

FINAL

MUMBAI v HYDERABAD

At Wankhede Stadium, Mumbai, April 19, 20, 21, 22, 23. Mumbai won by 297 runs. Toss: Hyderabad.

Mumbai secured the Ranji Trophy for the 34th time, defeating Hyderabad nine overs into the final morning. Azharuddin had put them in, counting on a grassy pitch, but Kambli hit a hundred – dedicated to his recently deceased mother – adding 104 in 15 overs with Tendulkar, and Mhambrey steered Mumbai towards 376. Hyderabad's response depended on Laxman and Azharuddin. When 23, Laxman became the highest run-scorer in a Ranji season, but Azharuddin ran him out for 46

1,000 RUNS IN A RANJI TROPHY SEASON

		M	I	NO	R	HS	100s	50s	Avge
1999-2000	**V. V. S. Laxman (*Hyderabad*)**	9	14	1	1,415	353	8	0	108.84
1998-99	R. V. Bharadwaj (*Karnataka*)	10	15	3	1,280	200*	4	7	106.66
1999-2000	**S. Sriram (*Tamil Nadu*)**	8	12	1	1,075	288	5	1	97.72
1998-99	J. J. Martin (*Baroda*)	8	13	3	1,037	242	5	2	103.70
1996-97	R. Lamba (*Delhi*)	10	14	0	1,034	250	3	4	73.85
1996-97	Ajay Sharma (*Delhi*)	8	10	1	1,033	220*	5	3	114.77
1988-89	W. V. Raman (*Tamil Nadu*)	7	9	2	1,018	313	3	1	145.42
1944-45	R. S. Modi (*Bombay*)	5	7	2	1,008	245*	5	1	201.60

---

and found no other allies. Cushioned by a lead of 181, Mumbai's top order came out blazing and compiled three century partnerships. Tendulkar dashed to 128 in 124 balls, this time adding 105 in 18 overs with Kambli. Although the Hyderabad spinners, Raju and Kanwaljit Singh, took nine wickets between them, Mumbai left a target of 591. Laxman scored his eighth hundred of the season – another Ranji record – and put on 188 with Manohar. But 20-year-old slow left-armer Rajesh Pawar, Mumbai's only front-line spinner, dismissed them both on his way to a career-best seven for 103 and ten wickets in the match. Kuruvilla, who had just announced his retirement, led his victorious team-mates off the field.

Close of play: First day, Mumbai 303-6 (Mhambrey 38*, Agarkar 14*); Second day, Hyderabad 195; Third day, Mumbai 409; Fourth day, Hyderabad 251-7 (Ahmed 11*, Raju 0*).

Mumbai

*†S. S. Dighe c Azharuddin b Ahmed	3	– lbw b Kanwaljit Singh	46
Wasim Jaffer c Raju b N. P. Singh	32	– c Raju b Kanwaljit Singh	55
J. V. Paranjpe lbw b Ahmed	10	– c Manohar b Raju	42
S. R. Tendulkar c Sheikh b Raju	53	– c and b N. P. Singh	128
V. G. Kambli c and b Ahmed	108	– c N. P. Singh b Kanwaljit Singh	56
A. A. Muzumdar c Satwalkar b Raju	13	– lbw b Raju	15
P. L. Mhambrey b Raju	75	– c Ahmed b Raju	31
A. B. Agarkar lbw b N. P. Singh	30	– c Kanwaljit Singh b Raju	1
R. V. Pawar c Sheikh b N. P. Singh	0	– lbw b Kanwaljit Singh	5
A. Kuruvilla not out	5	– c Manohar b Raju	13
S. R. Saxena c Sheikh b Raju	5	– not out	4
B 8, l-b 12, w 5, n-b 17	42	L-b 1, w 1, n-b 11	13

1/18 2/51 3/72 4/176 5/202　　　　　　376　1/103 2/106 3/215 4/320 5/344　　409
6/283 7/343 8/343 9/370　　　　　　　　　　6/376 7/378 8/389 9/397

Bowling: *First Innings*—N. P. Singh 21–6–74–3; Ahmed 22–2–73–3; Raju 37.2–11–110–4; Satwalkar 9–3–28–0; Pratap 2–1–8–0; Kanwaljit Singh 22–0–63–0. *Second Innings*—N. P. Singh 12–1–76–1; Ahmed 12–4–48–0; Manohar 5–0–25–0; Raju 28.3–7–123–5; Kanwaljit Singh 32–4–136–4.

Hyderabad

D. Manohar c Pawar b Agarkar	6	– (2) b Pawar 71
A. Nandakishore c Tendulkar b Kuruvilla	0	– (1) c Tendulkar b Agarkar 9
V. V. S. Laxman run out	46	– c sub b Pawar 111
*M. Azharuddin c Dighe b Saxena	76	– (7) c sub b Pawar 11
V. Pratap c Dighe b Pawar	8	– (4) lbw b Agarkar 2
P. Satwalkar c Saxena b Pawar	30	– (5) lbw b Pawar 22
†R. Sheikh c Tendulkar b Agarkar	11	– (6) b Agarkar 1
M. F. Ahmed b Saxena	0	– c sub b Pawar 21
S. L. V. Raju c Saxena b Pawar	6	– c Tendulkar b Pawar 16
N. P. Singh not out	1	– c Tendulkar b Pawar 14
Kanwaljit Singh b Agarkar	0	– not out 1
L-b 4, w 1, n-b 6	11	B 1, l-b 7, n-b 6. 14

1/7 2/7 3/96 4/110 5/166   195   1/10 2/198 3/202 4/202 5/212   293
6/178 7/184 8/192 9/194   6/239 7/240 8/263 9/286

Bowling: *First Innings*—Agarkar 14.4–3–26–3; Kuruvilla 8–0–37–1; Saxena 13–1–46–2; Mhambrey 8–1–38–0; Pawar 20–5–44–3; Tendulkar 1–1–0–0. *Second Innings*—Kuruvilla 9–1–24–0; Agarkar 21–4–46–3; Pawar 34.2–8–103–7; Saxena 8–2–26–0; Mhambrey 10–2–47–0; Tendulkar 15–2–38–0; Wasim Jaffer 1–0–1–0.

Umpires: Jasbir Singh and N. Menon.

RANJI TROPHY WINNERS

1934-35	Bombay	1956-57	Bombay	1978-79	Delhi
1935-36	Bombay	1957-58	Baroda	1979-80	Delhi
1936-37	Nawanagar	1958-59	Bombay	1980-81	Bombay
1937-38	Hyderabad	1959-60	Bombay	1981-82	Delhi
1938-39	Bengal	1960-61	Bombay	1982-83	Karnataka
1939-40	Maharashtra	1961-62	Bombay	1983-84	Bombay
1940-41	Maharashtra	1962-63	Bombay	1984-85	Bombay
1941-42	Bombay	1963-64	Bombay	1985-86	Delhi
1942-43	Baroda	1964-65	Bombay	1986-87	Hyderabad
1943-44	Western India	1965-66	Bombay	1987-88	Tamil Nadu
1944-45	Bombay	1966-67	Bombay	1988-89	Delhi
1945-46	Holkar	1967-68	Bombay	1989-90	Bengal
1946-47	Baroda	1968-69	Bombay	1990-91	Haryana
1947-48	Holkar	1969-70	Bombay	1991-92	Delhi
1948-49	Bombay	1970-71	Bombay	1992-93	Punjab
1949-50	Baroda	1971-72	Bombay	1993-94	Bombay
1950-51	Holkar	1972-73	Bombay	1994-95	Bombay
1951-52	Bombay	1973-74	Karnataka	1995-96	Karnataka
1952-53	Holkar	1974-75	Bombay	1996-97	Mumbai
1953-54	Bombay	1975-76	Bombay	1997-98	Karnataka
1954-55	Madras	1976-77	Bombay	1998-99	Karnataka
1955-56	Bombay	1977-78	Karnataka	1999-2000	Mumbai

Bombay/Mumbai have won the Ranji Trophy 34 times, Delhi and Karnataka 6, Baroda and Holkar 4, Bengal, Hyderabad, Madras/Tamil Nadu and Maharashtra 2, Haryana, Nawanagar, Punjab and Western India 1.

CRICKET IN PAKISTAN, 1999-2000

By ABID ALI KAZI

Younis Khan

In today's cricket world, where it has become almost impossible to decide where one season ends and the next begins, Pakistan's international schedule becomes ever more hectic. From September to July, they played 12 Test matches and 41 one-day internationals. Their overall performance was satisfactory but unpredictable, studded with occasional sparks of brilliance. After winning one-day tournaments in Toronto and Sharjah, they lost all three Tests in Australia, who also beat them in the final of the Carlton & United series. Saeed Anwar briefly inherited the captaincy when the Pakistan Cricket Board decided to remove Wasim Akram; he lost both one-day and Test series at home to Sri Lanka before suffering an injury which gave the selectors an excuse to turn to Moin Khan instead, while Intikhab Alam was unceremoniously removed as coach and replaced by Javed Miandad. The team's fortunes immediately improved: they won the final Test against Sri Lanka and proceeded to win three successive one-day trophies, in Sharjah, the Caribbean and Bangladesh, where they won the Asia Cup for the first time. Their success was interrupted only in the Test series against West Indies, which they lost by a single wicket, but they won the return Test series in Sri Lanka 2–0.

The match-fixing saga reached a new stage when the PCB published the report of Justice Malik Mohammad Qayyum's inquiry in May. It recommended life bans for Salim Malik and Ata-ur-Rehman, and fines for Wasim, Anwar, Waqar Younis, Inzamam ul-Haq, Mushtaq Ahmed and Akram Raza, all of whom Qayyum said had failed to co-operate.

National politics continued to overshadow the game. Lt-General Tauqir Zia took over as the PCB chief from Zafar Altaf, who had been appointed in October after the arrest of Mujeeb-ur-Rehman, a protégé of prime minister Nawaz Sharif, who was ousted by a military coup. But Mujeeb's short tenure had left its mark on the 1999-2000 domestic season. It was too late to change the format, which he had completely revised, bringing the commercial department teams into the Quaid-e-Azam Trophy, the premier first-class competition normally contested only by regional sides. This meant that 23 teams, including a Pakistan Reserves side, were scheduled to play a record 122 matches (two were abandoned). In 1998-99, the Quaid-e-Azam and the Patron's Trophy for the department sides totalled only 93. Mujeeb's own team, Redco (Reliable Efficient and Developing Company), who had earned promotion the previous season, initially withdrew after his downfall, but eventually made their first-class debut after all.

However, the new format rendered the regional sides extremely weak – Hyderabad played ten games without a single point – as most of the best players were employed by the department teams, and several more scooped up by Pakistan Reserves. The teams were divided into two pools. PIA led Pool A, with five wins; WAPDA and Lahore City, the one regional side to flourish, also won five each, but PIA were unbeaten and advanced to the final. There, they met another unbeaten team, Habib Bank, who had pulled clear of Pakistan Reserves in the closing stages of Pool B; both recorded seven victories. PIA won a low-scoring final by eight wickets inside two days of the allotted five. It was Salim Malik's last first-class appearance.

The Patron's Trophy was relegated to non-first-class status, which had previously happened from 1979-80 to 1982-83, when it was used as a qualifying competition for the Quaid-e-Azam. It was also contested by 23 teams, the weaker department and regional sides, divided into four groups. In the final, Lahore City Blues beat Karachi Colts by virtue of their first-innings lead. The trophy regained its first-class status in 2000-01, when both competitions reverted to their traditional format and the Quaid-e-Azam was once more left to the regional teams.

Two one-day tournaments were held. The Tissot Cup in October was won by PIA, who beat Redco in the final. In April, the board's new management staged another competition, the National Bank Cup, in whose final Habib Bank beat KRL. It was not clear which of the two tournaments should be regarded as the premier one-day competition and successor to the Wills Cup.

Younis Khan of Habib Bank was the country's leading run-scorer, in only his second season. He scored 1,102 runs at 110.20 in the Quaid-e-Azam Trophy, and 1,315 in all, with six hundreds, including four in successive innings and another on his Test debut against Sri Lanka. No one else managed 1,000 runs. The overall first-class averages were headed by Imran Abbas of ADBP, who averaged 89.36 from nine matches. PIA batsmen Shoaib Mohammad and Rizwan-uz-Zaman helped their team to the Quaid-e-Azam title with five hundreds each, while their captain, former Test all-rounder Asif Mujtaba, recorded the season's highest score, a career-best 240, and also topped the bowling averages with 50 wickets at 13.74 apiece; he took 11 in a match twice. Murtaza Hussain of KRL also took 50 wickets, but Athar Laeeq of National Bank was the leading wicket-taker with 51 at 16.47. Tahir Rashid of Habib Bank was the most successful wicket-keeper with 39 dismissals, closely followed by Mohammad Shahbaz of Islamabad, with 38. The fielders were headed by Zahid Fazal of PIA, who took 19 catches in 11 matches.

FIRST-CLASS AVERAGES, 1999-2000

BATTING

(Qualification: 600 runs, average 45.00)

	M	I	NO	R	HS	100s	Avge
Imran Abbas (*ADBP*)	9	14	3	983	204*	4	89.36
Shoaib Mohammad (*PIA*)	11	15	3	971	180	5	80.91
Younis Khan (*Habib Bank*)	14	21	4	1,315	202*	6	77.35
Naumanullah (*Redco*)	8	11	2	642	171*	3	71.33
Rashid Latif (*Allied Bank*)	9	12	2	674	131*	2	67.40
Hasan Adnan (*WAPDA*)	10	14	2	760	130	2	63.33
Rizwan-uz-Zaman (*PIA*)	11	15	2	768	200*	5	59.07
Faisal Naved (*Gujranwala*)	8	16	3	761	151*	4	58.53
Asif Mujtaba (*PIA*)	11	13	2	636	240	1	57.81
Asim Kamal (*Karachi Whites*)	10	17	4	728	122*	3	56.00

	M	I	NO	R	HS	100s	Avge
Yasir Hameed (*Peshawar*)	9	16	0	895	154	3	55.93
Saeed Anwar (*KRL*)	11	16	4	669	177	2	55.75
Afsar Nawaz (*Karachi Blues*)	10	17	2	819	178	1	54.60
Saleem Mughal (*Lahore Division*)	9	15	2	699	193	3	53.76
Maqsood Raza (*Lahore Division*)	9	14	2	640	115	1	53.33
Mujahid Jamshed (*Habib Bank*)	9	14	0	729	158	3	52.07
Mohammad Ramzan (*PNSC*)	10	15	0	774	150	3	51.60
Hasnain Qayyum (*Redco*)	10	13	1	614	161*	1	51.16
Shahid Anwar (*National Bank*)	10	15	0	762	160	3	50.80
Adil Nisar (*WAPDA*)	10	15	1	703	158	2	50.21
Suleman Huda (*Karachi Whites*)	10	17	1	792	166	2	49.50
Mansoor Rana (*ADBP*)	10	14	1	636	120	2	48.92
Shoaib Khan (*Peshawar*)	9	15	2	622	127	1	47.84
Ali Naqvi (*Pakistan Customs*)	10	14	0	669	111	2	47.78
Saad Wasim (*Karachi Blues*)	8	13	0	620	152	2	47.69
Aamir Sohail (*Allied Bank*)	10	16	0	759	164	3	47.43
Ijaz Ahmed, jun. (*Allied Bank*)	10	16	1	706	188	1	47.06

* *Signifies not out.*

BOWLING

(Qualification: 30 wickets)

	O	M	R	W	BB	5W/i	Avge
Asif Mujtaba (*PIA*)	335.2	100	687	50	6-17	6	13.74
Athar Laeeq (*National Bank*)	305.4	76	840	51	6-47	6	16.47
Akram Raza (*Habib Bank*)	290.1	67	759	45	6-45	4	16.86
Kabir Khan (*Habib Bank*)	229	42	815	48	6-37	4	16.97
Nadeem Iqbal (*Pakistan Customs*) . .	285	56	808	47	7-25	3	17.19
Sajid Shah (*Habib Bank*)	220.3	50	585	34	6-28	3	17.20
Arshad Khan (*Allied Bank*)	275.5	82	642	37	8-110	4	17.35
Zahid Saeed (*Pakistan Reserves*) . . .	195.5	30	614	34	6-86	3	18.05
Sarfraz Ahmed (*WAPDA*)	307.5	85	737	37	7-50	2	19.91
Naved ul-Hasan (*Lahore Division*) . .	300.1	64	912	45	7-60	5	20.26
Mohammad Aslam (*Peshawar*)	298.5	102	673	33	6-49	2	20.39
Ali Gauhar (*PIA*)	247.1	43	840	41	6-45	1	20.48
Imranullah (*Karachi Blues*)	205.2	45	658	31	5-53	2	20.58
Nadeem Khan (*PIA*)	400.1	131	845	41	5-78	1	20.60
Azhar Abbas (*ADBP*)	192.3	35	644	31	5-58	2	20.77
Mohammad Hussain (*Lahore City*) .	360.2	99	832	38	6-97	4	21.89
Imran Tahir (*Redco*)	333.4	71	955	43	8-76	4	22.20
Ata-ur-Rehman (*Allied Bank*)	245.5	45	797	33	5-83	2	24.15
Murtaza Hussain (*KRL*)	529.2	160	1,214	50	6-58	5	24.28
Farhan Rasheed (*WAPDA*)	398.3	103	1,010	40	6-103	3	25.25
Aamer Mahmood (*Peshawar*)	314.4	68	865	34	6-46	2	25.44
Yasir Ashfaq (*Rawalpindi*)	271.2	68	770	30	6-45	1	25.66
Waqas Ahmed (*Redco*)	249.2	51	784	30	6-26	1	26.13
Fazl-e-Akbar (*Pakistan Reserves*) . . .	311.1	62	965	36	4-60	0	26.80
Jaffer Qureshi (*Karachi Blues*)	374.3	103	1,006	35	6-51	1	28.74
Shafiq Ahmed (*WAPDA*)	333.1	80	935	32	6-48	2	29.21
Aamir Nazir (*Allied Bank*)	385	68	1,306	44	8-79	2	29.68
S. John (*Islamabad*)	411.3	84	1,252	41	5-53	2	30.53
Tahir Mughal (*ADBP*)	278.3	31	1,012	33	5-45	1	30.66
Imran Amin (*Gujranwala*)	350	66	1,176	32	4-76	0	36.75

QUAID-E-AZAM TROPHY, 1999-2000

Pool A

	Played	Won	Lost	Drawn	1st-inns Points	Points
PIA	10	5	0	5	27	72
WAPDA	10	5	2	3	21	66
Lahore City	10	5	2	3	18	63
National Bank	10	4	0	6	21	57
Pakistan Customs . .	10	4	1	5	21	57
Lahore Division . . .	10	2	3	5	15	33
PNSC.	10	2	2	6	12	30
Bahawalpur	10	2	5	3	12	30
Karachi Whites	10	1	3	6	9	18
Gujranwala	10	1	3	6	3	12
Hyderabad.	10	0	10	0	0	0

Pool B

	Played	Won	Lost	Drawn	1st-inns Points	Points
Habib Bank	11	7	0	4	30	93
Pakistan Reserves . .	11	7	2	2	18	81
Allied Bank	10	3	0	7	30	57
ADBP	11	3	2	6	18	45
Redco	10	3	1	6	15	42
KRL	11	3	2	6	15	42
Karachi Blues	11	3	5	3	6	33
Peshawar.	10	2	4	4	6	24
Faisalabad	11	2	7	2	6	24
Islamabad	10	1	1	8	9	18
Sargodha	11	0	5	6	9	9
Rawalpindi	11	0	5	6	6	6

Note: The matches between Islamabad and Redco, and Peshawar and Allied Bank, were abandoned.

Outright win = 9 pts; lead on first innings in a won or drawn game = 3 pts.

Final: PIA beat Habib Bank by eight wickets.

In the following scores, by the name of a team indicates that they won the toss.

Pool A

At Bahawal Stadium, Bahawalpur, October 16, 17, 18, 19. Drawn. WAPDA* 482 for six dec. (Tariq Aziz 194, Hasan Adnan 130, Extras 37; Farooq Hameed five for 127) and 178 for four dec. (Ijaz Mahmood 47, Hasan Adnan 52 not out, Zahid Umar 33); Bahawalpur 349 (Arshad Hayat 115, Hasan Adnan 52 not out, Zahid Umar 33); Bahawalpur 349 (Arshad Hayat 115, Aamir Sohail 90, Zia-ul-Hasan 43 not out, Inam-ul-Haq 50; Farhan Rasheed four for 108) and 85 for six (Zia-ul-Hasan 32; Ashraf Bashir three for 24). *WAPDA 3 pts.*
    In WAPDA's first innings, Tariq Aziz and Hasan Adnan added 288 for the third wicket.

At Gujranwala Cricket Academy Ground, Gujranwala, October 16, 17, 18. Gujranwala won by eight wickets. Hyderabad 214 (Iqbal Sheikh 45, Feroz Hussain 36, Imran Naseer 68, Sajid Iqbal 31; Zaman Haider three for 43) and 275 (Akhtar Bangash 112, Imran Naseer 49, Sohaib Hashmi 40 not out; Imran Amin four for 76); Gujranwala* 454 for six dec. (Faisal Naved 51, Ehtesham Younis 87, Majid Saeed 149, Shehzad Malik 42, Kamran Younis 64 not out, Khalid Mahmood 38; Iqbal Sheikh three for 73) and 38 for two. *Gujranwala 12 pts.*

At UBL Sports Complex, Karachi, October 16, 17, 18, 19. Drawn. Karachi Whites 311 (Suleman Huda 32, Zeeshan Siddiqi 70, Mohammad Masroor 72, Asim Kamal 31, Extras 53; Mohammad Zahid, jun. three for 72, Nadeem Khan three for 39) and 225 for six dec. (Zafar Jadoon 48, Zeeshan Siddiqi 56 not out, Arif Mahmood 46); PIA* 170 (Ghulam Ali 30; Lal Faraz four for 65, Sheraz Haider three for 36) and 145 for one (Shoaib Mohammad 60 not out, Ghulam Ali 30 not out). *Karachi Whites 3 pts.*

At LCCA Ground, Lahore, October 16, 17, 18, 19. Lahore City won by 148 runs. Lahore City 179 (Tariq Sheikh 31, Mohammad Hussain 69, Faisal Javed 32; Naved-ul-Hasan five for 30, Abdur Rauf four for 83) and 448 for nine dec. (Sher Ali 39, Shahid Nawaz 54, Babar Zaman 72, Mohammad Hussain 61, Tariq Sheikh 54 not out, Faisal Javed 34, Shahid Mahmood 31, Extras 53; Naved-ul-Hasan five for 156); Lahore Division* 341 (Majid Majeed 57, Maqsood Raza 32, Saleem Mughal 102, Zahid Javed 33, Extras 45; Mohammad Hussain six for 127) and 138 (Mohammad Sarwar 45; Mohammad Hussain five for 41, Shahid Mahmood three for 55). *Lahore City 9 pts.*

At Defence Cricket Stadium, Karachi, October 16, 17, 18, 19. Drawn. Pakistan Customs* 430 (Ali Naqvi 107, Javed Sami 112, Azam Khan 60, Rana Qayyum 44, Aamer Wasim 36; Riaz Sheikh three for 106); PNSC 164 (Mohammad Ramzan 62; Haaris Khan five for 48) and 243 for two (Mohammad Ramzan 85, Kashif Ahmed 38, Shahid Qambrani 52 not out, Iqbal Imam 50 not out). *Pakistan Customs 3 pts.*

At Bahawal Stadium, Bahawalpur, October 23, 24, 25. Bahawalpur won by an innings and 38 runs. Bahawalpur* 398 (Arshad Hayat 54, Zia-ul-Hasan 51, Aamir Sohail 69, Inam-ul-Haq 58, Sheharyar Afridi 70, Faisal Elahi 35; Haider Raza five for 100); Hyderabad 137 (Akhtar Bangash 34; Maqbool Hussain five for 38, Farooq Hameed three for 36) and 223 (Tariq Aziz 32, Ahmed Ali 45, Riaz Khan 61; Kamran Hussain four for 71, Farooq Hameed four for 54). *Bahawalpur 12 pts.*

At Gujranwala Cricket Academy Ground, Gujranwala, October 23, 24, 25, 26. Drawn. Lahore Division 313 (Mohammad Sarwar 100, Maqsood Raza 55, Abdur Rauf 31 not out; Imran Amin three for 56) and 244 for eight dec. (Usman Akram 57, Maqsood Raza 59 not out, Naved-ul-Hasan 42; Kamran Younis three for 23, Imran Amin three for 104); Gujranwala* 231 (Faisal Naved 108, Ehtesham Younis 36; Naved-ul-Hasan four for 65, Mumtaz Ali four for 75) and 144 for five (Shehzad Malik 61 not out). *Lahore Division 3 pts.*
  Gujranwala wicket-keeper Khalid Mahmood made eight catches and one stumping in the match.

At Defence Cricket Stadium, Karachi, October 23, 24, 25, 26. Drawn. Karachi Whites* 207 (Arif Mahmood 69 not out, Ali Hussain Rizvi 34; Sarfraz Ahmed three for 46, Farhan Rasheed five for 54) and 519 for seven (Zafar Jadoon 167, Suleman Huda 87, Asim Kamal 105 not out, Arif Mahmood 39, Shahid Iqbal 34; Anwar Ali three for 129); WAPDA 331 (Ijaz Mahmood 39, Hasan Adnan 70, Zahid Umar 55, Shafiq Ahmed 42, Sarfraz Ahmed 83, Shahid Iqbal five for 91). *WAPDA 3 pts.*
  In Karachi's second innings, Zafar Jadoon and Suleman Huda opened with 254 in 330 minutes.

At UBL Sports Complex, Karachi, October 23, 24, 25. National Bank won by 222 runs. National Bank 159 (Akhtar Sarfraz 50, Naeem Tayyab 32 not out; Umar Rasheed four for 45, Sajjad Ali five for 40) and 278 (Tariq Mohammad 43, Shahid Anwar 93, Athar Laeeq 36, Extras 48; Sajjad Ali four for 80, Kashif Ibrahim three for 66); PNSC* 80 (Athar Laeeq six for 18) and 135 (Extras 33; Athar Laeeq five for 39). *National Bank 12 pts.*

At National Stadium, Karachi, October 23, 24, 25, 26. Drawn. Pakistan Customs 268 (Ali Naqvi 48, Azam Khan 89, Aamer Bashir 42, Extras 38; Asfandyar Jafri five for 45, Nadeem Khan four for 83) and 279 for eight dec. (Ali Naqvi 56, Azam Khan 72, Naved Latif 32, Shakeel Ansar 41 not out; Nadeem Khan four for 94); PIA* 310 (Shoaib Mohammad 110, Kashif Siddiq 35, Asif Mujtaba 54, Sohail Jaffer 36, Extras 40; Aamer Wasim four for 84) and 71 for three (Kashif Siddiq 38). *PIA 3 pts.*

At Asghar Ali Shah Stadium, Karachi, October 30, 31, November 1. WAPDA won by an innings and 72 runs. Hyderabad* 73 (Shafiq Ahmed three for 15, Farhan Rasheed three for 19) and 168

(Ayaz Taifi 56, Akhtar Bangash 54; Shafiq Ahmed six for 48, Farhan Rasheed four for 56); WAPDA 313 (Adil Nisar 44, Kashif Rasheed 42, Tariq Aziz 44, Hasan Adnan 44, Shahid Mansoor 60; Haider Raza four for 96, Tariq Aziz four for 50). *WAPDA 12 pts.*

At Sheikhupura Stadium, Sheikhupura, October 30, 31, November 1, 2. Drawn. Karachi Whites* 141 (Arif Mahmood 36; Naved-ul-Hasan three for 28) and 541 for five (Suleman Huda 166, Mohammad Masroor 119, Arif Mahmood 53, Asim Kamal 101 not out, Iqbal Sikandar 53 not out, Extras 47); Lahore Division 406 for seven dec. (Majid Majeed 132, Maqsood Raza 47, Saleem Mughal 66, Usman Akram 68, Extras 42). *Lahore Division 3 pts.*
  In Karachi's second innings, Suleman Huda added 250 for the third wicket with Mohammad Masroor and 125 for the fourth with Arif Mahmood.

At Gaddafi Stadium, Lahore, October 30, 31, November 1. Lahore City won by eight wickets. Gujranwala 209 (Faisal Naved 114 not out, Sajjad-ul-Haq 33; Ashfaq Ahmed six for 63, Mohammad Hussain three for 57) and 135 (Fahad Masood four for 23); Lahore City* 283 (Shafqat Hussain 52, Sher Ali 32, Faisal Javed 39, Zia-ur-Rehman 32, Mohammad Hussain 57) and 62 for two. *Lahore City 12 pts.*
  Faisal Naved carried his bat through Gujranwala's first innings.

At UBL Sports Complex, Karachi, October 30, 31, November 1, 2. Drawn. National Bank 604 for eight dec. (Shahid Anwar 131, Tariq Mohammad 50, Saeed Azad 95, Akhtar Sarfraz 137 not out, Naeem Ashraf 33, Athar Laeeq 35 not out, Extras 55; Nadeem Iqbal four for 133); Pakistan Customs* 340 (Ali Naqvi 111, Azhar Shafiq 43, Azam Khan 36, Naved Latif 46, Extras 57; Naeem Ashraf three for 68, Athar Laeeq three for 93) and 104 for two (Javed Sami 30). *National Bank 3 pts.*

At National Stadium, Karachi, October 30, 31, November 1, 2. Drawn. PIA 402 for nine dec. (Rizwan-uz-Zaman 130, Sohail Jaffer 72, Ahmed Zeeshan 40, Nadeem Khan 50, Extras 45) and 25 for no wkt; PNSC* 335 (Mohammad Ramzan 42, Faisal Athar 36, Riaz Sheikh 37, Iqbal Imam 39, Sajjad Akbar 64 not out, Ali Raza 47; Nadeem Khan three for 70). *PIA 3 pts.*

At Bahawal Stadium, Bahawalpur, November 6, 7, 8, 9. Drawn. Bahawalpur* 451 (Mohammad Rashid 89, Rehan Rafiq 54, Aamir Sohail 61, Kamran Hussain 95, Inam-ul-Haq 46, Maqbool Hussain 42, Faisal Elahi 35; Imran Amin four for 97, Najam Sohail three for 151); Gujranwala 210 (Faisal Naved 109 not out, Basit Murtaza 30; Farooq Hameed four for 54) and 228 for six (Faisal Naved 30, Shehzad Malik 88; Maqbool Hussain three for 61). *Bahawalpur 3 pts.*
  Faisal Naved carried his bat through Gujranwala's first innings for the second time in successive matches.

At Niaz Stadium, Hyderabad, November 6, 7, 8, 9. National Bank won by 156 runs. National Bank 234 (Sajid Ali 42, Akhtar Sarfraz 35, Naeem Ashraf 34 not out; Tariq Aziz four for 68, Haider Raza three for 65) and 242 for four dec. (Shahid Anwar 40, Tariq Mohammad 102 not out, Akhtar Sarfraz 30, Sajid Ali 52); Hyderabad* 140 (Naeem Akhtar 47; Naeem Ashraf three for 32, Athar Laeeq six for 38) and 180 (Ayaz Taifi 36, Akhtar Bangash 48, Tariq Aziz 31 not out; Naeem Tayyab four for 41, Naeem Khan four for 43). *National Bank 12 pts.*

At National Stadium, Karachi, November 6, 7, 8, 9. Drawn. PNSC 420 (Mohammad Ramzan 78, Shahid Qambrani 33, Faisal Athar 97, Iqbal Imam 33, Riaz Sheikh 30, Sajjad Akbar 55, Extras 35; Shahid Iqbal three for 68) and 121 for five (Shahid Qambrani 31, Iqbal Imam 53 not out; Sheraz Haider four for 49); Karachi Whites* 321 (Suleman Huda 60, Asim Kamal 85, Mohammad Masroor 41, Shahid Iqbal 48, Extras 30; Riaz Sheikh four for 44). *PNSC 3 pts.*

At LCCA Ground, Lahore, November 6, 7, 8. Pakistan Customs won by eight wickets. Lahore City* 109 (Sher Ali 55; Nadeem Iqbal three for 19, Aamer Wasim five for 25) and 178 (Babar Zaman 53, Mohammad Hussain 67; Nadeem Iqbal four for 38, Aamer Wasim four for 52); Pakistan Customs 254 (Naved Latif 60, Nasim Khan 51, Azam Khan 37; Mohammad Hussain six for 97) and 34 for two. *Pakistan Customs 12 pts.*

At UBL Sports Complex, Karachi, November 6, 7, 8. PIA won by an innings and 63 runs. PIA* 334 (Shoaib Mohammad 147 not out, Zahid Fazal 75; Farhan Rasheed three for 111, Shafiq Ahmed six for 67); WAPDA 145 (Adil Nisar 38, Sarfraz Ahmed 34; Nadeem Khan three for 34, Ali Gauhar four for 40) and 126 (Adil Nisar 30; Nadeem Khan four for 44, Ali Gauhar three for 29). *PIA 12 pts.*

Shoaib Mohammad carried his bat through PIA's innings.

At Jinnah Stadium, Sialkot, November 13, 14, 15, 16. Drawn. PNSC 505 (Mohammad Ramzan 141, Iqbal Imam 77, Riaz Sheikh 83, Sajjad Akbar 67, Mutahir Shah 50, Mohtashim Rasheed 58 not out; Imran Amin three for 151); Gujranwala* 270 (Faisal Naved 151 not out, Khalid Mahmood 30, Najam Sohail 31; Sajjad Ali five for 89) and 350 for six (Rizwan Malik 40, Ataullah Butt 68, Basit Murtaza 67, Faisal Naved 52, Mohammad Shoaib 33, Khalid Mahmood 66 not out). *PNSC 3 pts.*

For the third match running, Faisal Naved carried his bat through Gujranwala's first innings; he scored his fourth hundred in successive matches.

At National Stadium, Karachi, November 13, 14, 15. Karachi Whites won by an innings and ten runs. Hyderabad 159 (Ayaz Taifi 57, Mansoor Ahmed 30; Haider Ali four for 35, Iqbal Sikandar three for two) and 208 (Ijaz Shah 69, Ayaz Taifi 42, Extras 39; Sheraz Haider five for 68); Karachi Whites* 377 for three dec. (Zafar Jadoon 79, Mohammad Masroor 150 not out, Asim Kamal 122 not out). *Karachi Whites 12 pts.*

Iqbal Sikandar's full first-innings analysis was 3.3–2–2–3. Mohammad Masroor and Asim Kamal added an unbroken 269 for Karachi's fourth wicket.

At LCCA Ground, Lahore, November 13, 14, 15, 16. Lahore City won by 192 runs. Lahore City* 291 (Ali Hussain 91, Tariq Mahmood 45, Babar Zaman 30; Kamran Hussain three for 85, Maqbool Hussain four for 61) and 238 for six dec. (Mustaqeem Ahmed 44, Sher Ali 62, Tariq Mahmood 73 not out, Babar Zaman 30; Kamran Hussain three for 78); Bahawalpur 147 (Extras 31; Sajid Ali four for 38, Mohammad Hussain three for 32) and 190 (Mohammad Rashid 37, Rehan Rafiq 34, Inam-ul-Haq 50; Mohammad Hussain five for 55, Shahid Mahmood three for 86). *Lahore City 12 pts.*

At Sheikhupura Stadium, Sheikhupura, November 14, 15, 16. Drawn. Lahore Division 367 (Usman Akram 73, Maqsood Raza 53, Saleem Mughal 59, Abdur Rauf 60 not out, Extras 57; Athar Laeeq six for 86) and 242 for four (Majid Majeed 83, Usman Akram 33, Saleem Mughal 67 not out, Shahid Tanvir 34; Tahir Shah three for 62); National Bank* 481 for five dec. (Shahid Anwar 118, Tariq Mohammad 165 retired hurt, Saeed Azad 77, Naeem Ashraf 55 not out, Wasim Arif 43 not out; Abdur Rauf five for 132). *National Bank 3 pts.*

At Iqbal Stadium, Faisalabad, November 13, 14, 15, 16. WAPDA won by 101 runs. WAPDA 305 (Adil Nisar 38, Tariq Aziz 43, Hasan Adnan 81, Shahid Mansoor 40, Extras 43; Nadeem Iqbal three for 45, Saad Janjua three for 70) and 227 for nine dec. (Adil Nisar 83, Ijaz Mahmood 33; Aamer Wasim four for 89), Pakistan Customs* 330 (Ameeruddin 71, Nasim Khan 127; Raees Amjad three for 84, Shafiq Ahmed four for 84) and 101 (Nasim Khan 52; Sarfraz Ahmed three for 22, Ijaz Mahmood three for 23). *WAPDA 9 pts.*

At Bahawal Stadium, Bahawalpur, November 20, 21, 22, 23. Bahawalpur won by 55 runs. Bahawalpur* 220 (Mohammad Rashid 30, Shahnawaz Adeel 30, Aamir Sohail 30, Zia-ul-Hasan 41, Amjad Jam 47; Arif Mahmood three for 52, Iqbal Sheikh three for 49, Rizwan Qureshi three for 36) and 303 (Rehan Rafiq 40, Aamir Sohail 41, Zia-ul-Hasan 79, Sheharyar Afridi 35; Iqbal Sheikh five for 79); Karachi Whites 183 (Mohammad Masroor 51, Iqbal Sheikh 65; Kamran Hussain five for 30, Maqbool Hussain three for 60) and 285 (Zafar Jadoon 74, Asim Kamal 41, Mohammad Masroor 38, Arif Mahmood 75; Kamran Hussain five for 68, Sheharyar Afridi three for 60). *Bahawalpur 12 pts.*

At Jinnah Stadium, Sialkot, November 20, 21, 22, 23. Drawn. Gujranwala 250 (Rizwan Malik 109, Ataullah Butt 36, Shehzad Malik 45; Athar Laeeq four for 52, Zafar Iqbal three for 49) and 288 for seven (Rizwan Malik 169 not out, Ataullah Butt 35); National Bank* 423 (Hanif-ur-Rehman 120, Saeed Azad 40, Sajid Ali 67, Kamran Akmal 75; Zaman Haider three for 98, Sajjad-ul-Haq five for 112). *National Bank 3 pts.*

Rizwan Malik scored a century in each innings, batting for 13 hours in all.

At Niaz Stadium, Hyderabad, November 20, 21, 22. PIA won by an innings and 84 runs. PIA 412 for one dec. (Rizwan-uz-Zaman 200 not out, Shoaib Mohammad 180); Hyderabad* 226 (Ayaz Taifi 98, Akhtar Bangash 30, Tariq Aziz 31; Asif Mujtaba five for 50, Ali Gauhar four for 51) and 102 (Akhtar Bangash 40; Asif Mujtaba six for 17). *PIA 12 pts.*

Rizwan-uz-Zaman's unbeaten 200 lasted 425 minutes and 333 balls; he and Shoaib Mohammad opened with 403 runs in 412 minutes.

At LCCA Ground, Lahore, November 20, 21, 22, 23. Lahore City won by ten wickets. Lahore City* 464 for six dec. (Ali Hussain 47, Fareed Butt 167 not out, Rizwan Aslam 36, Mohammad Hussain 50, Tariq Mahmood 101) and four for no wkt; WAPDA 251 (Maqsood Akbar 32, Tariq Aziz 65, Ijaz Mahmood 44, Jamshed Iqbal 38 not out; Mohammad Hussain three for 44, Kashif Shafi four for 83) and 214 (Maqsood Akbar 51, Hasan Adnan 74 not out; Mohammad Hussain four for 65, Kashif Shafi four for 71). *Lahore City 12 pts.*

At Sheikhupura Stadium, Sheikhupura, November 20, 21, 22, 23. Drawn. PNSC 277 (Faisal Athar 50, Iqbal Imam 50, Riaz Sheikh 62, Extras 30; Naved-ul-Hasan five for 79) and 381 for nine (Faisal Athar 75, Mohtashim Rasheed 76, Sajjad Akbar 99, Mutahir Shah 37); Lahore Division* 307 (Maqsood Raza 115, Babar Javed 59; Riaz Sheikh three for 81). *Lahore Division 3 pts.*

Maqsood Raza was out hit the ball twice.

At Bahawal Stadium, Bahawalpur, November 27, 28, 29, 30. Lahore Division won by eight wickets. Bahawalpur* 295 (Hammad Tariq 72, Shabbir Zafar 33, Rehan Rafiq 52, Inam-ul-Haq 40, Kamran Hussain 40; Kashif Mahmood four for 40) and 161 (Usman Tariq 35; Naved-ul-Hasan five for 53); Lahore Division 388 (Majid Majeed 42, Maqsood Raza 84, Zahid Javed 132, Mohammad Haroon 51; Tariq Hafeez three for 47, Usman Tariq four for 123) and 71 for two (Usman Akram 31 not out). *Lahore Division 12 pts.*

At Jinnah Stadium, Sialkot, November 27, 28, 29, 30. WAPDA won by an innings and 139 runs. Gujranwala 234 (Shehzad Malik 83 not out, Khalid Mahmood 40; Shahid Aslam three for 56, Farhan Rasheed three for 69) and 95 (Sarfraz Ahmed three for 42, Shahid Aslam three for 11); WAPDA* 468 for eight dec. (Tariq Aziz 75, Hasan Adnan 101, Bilal Moin 88, Shahid Aslam 68 not out, Jamshed Iqbal 54; Imran Amin three for 122). *WAPDA 12 pts.*

At Niaz Stadium, Hyderabad, November 27, 28. Pakistan Customs won by an innings and 84 runs. Hyderabad* 58 (Nadeem Iqbal seven for 25) and 136 (Ayaz Taifi 38, Kashif Alam 30, Faisal Qazi 35; Nadeem Iqbal five for 52); Pakistan Customs 278 for seven dec. (Ali Naqvi 69, I. Mohammed 65, Nasim Khan 51 not out). *Pakistan Customs 12 pts.*

Hyderabad fielded eight debutants.

At LCCA Ground, Lahore, November 27, 28, 29, 30. Drawn. PNSC* 318 (Mohtashim Rasheed 51, Faisal Athar 33, Iqbal Imam 79, Sajjad Akbar 68; Fahad Masood six for 81) and 11 for no wkt; Lahore City 530 (Ali Hussain 92, Fareed Butt 65, Tariq Sheikh 32, Babar Zaman 68, Tariq Mahmood 51, Shahid Nawaz 83, Imran Nazir 44, Mohammad Hussain 30, Extras 49; Yasir Shakeeb four for 93). *Lahore City 3 pts.*

At Sheikhupura Stadium, Sheikhupura, November 27, 28, 29, 30. Drawn. National Bank 254 (Tariq Mohammad 31, Hanif-ur-Rehman 101, Naeem Ashraf 36; Asif Mujtaba six for 52, Ali Gauhar four for 69) and 365 for seven dec. (Shahid Anwar 44, Tariq Mohammad 43, Sajid Ali 130, Zafar Iqbal 67, Kamran Akmal 30 not out; Ali Gauhar three for 104); PIA* 285 (Sohail Jaffer 71, Asif Mujtaba 87, Zahid Fazal 33, Sagheer Abbas 39; Athar Laeeq seven for 101) and 174 for three (Rizwan-uz-Zaman 101 not out, Sohail Jaffer 35). *PIA 3 pts.*

At Bahawal Stadium, Bahawalpur, December 4, 5, 6, 7. PNSC won by an innings and 122 runs. Bahawalpur* 163 (Rehan Rafiq 62; Iqbal Imam three for 43, Mohtashim Rasheed four for 43) and 104 (Mohammad Rashid 39 not out; Iqbal Imam five for 33); PNSC 389 for nine dec. (Mohammad Ramzan 34, Faisal Athar 99, Iqbal Imam 88, Sajjad Akbar 44, Kashif Ibrahim 30 not out; Usman Tariq five for 103). *PNSC 12 pts.*

At Jinnah Stadium, Gujranwala, December 4, 5, 6. PIA won by nine wickets. Gujranwala 146 (Ali Gauhar four for 40, Asif Mujtaba four for 55) and 286 (Rizwan Malik 58, Majid Saeed 30, Ataullah Butt 30, Asim Munir 42, Humayun Taj 59; Asif Mujtaba five for 67, Zahid Ahmed four for 66); PIA* 424 for seven dec. (Rizwan-uz-Zaman 127, Shoaib Mohammad 48, Ghulam Ali 40, Sohail Jaffer 58, Zahid Fazal 46, Extras 40) and nine for one. *PIA 12 pts.*

At Niaz Stadium, Hyderabad, December 4, 5, 6. Lahore Division won by an innings and 170 runs. Lahore Division 505 for eight dec. (Maqsood Raza 36, Saleem Mughal 193, Babar Javed 40, Mohammad Haroon 107, Naved-ul-Hasan 30 not out; Saleem Sheikh three for 60); Hyderabad* 162 (Ayaz Taifi 56, Irshad Ali 38; Kashif Mahmood three for 76, Yasir Bashir four for 28) and 173 (Ayaz Taifi 39, A. Waheed Rashid 53 not out; Naved-ul-Hasan seven for 60). *Lahore Division 12 pts.*

At National Stadium, Karachi, December 4, 5, 6. Pakistan Customs won by an innings and two runs. Karachi Whites 165 (Mohammad Masroor 35, Asim Kamal 60; Nadeem Iqbal five for 37) and 145 (Nadeem Iqbal three for 66, Saad Janjua five for 52); Pakistan Customs* 312 (Ameeruddin 30, Nasim Khan 117, Extras 46; Haider Ali three for 76, Iqbal Sheikh three for 47). *Pakistan Customs 12 pts.*
    Pakistan Customs wicket-keeper Aamer Iqbal took seven catches in Karachi Whites' second innings. In all he made 11 dismissals in the match.

At LCCA Ground, Lahore, December 4, 5, 6, 7. National Bank won by an innings and 84 runs. National Bank* 518 for eight dec. (Shahid Anwar 160, Saeed Azad 83, Akhtar Sarfraz 148, Tahir Shah 50, Extras 40; Sajid Ali three for 135, Shahid Ali Khan four for 112); Lahore City 218 (Shahid Nawaz 65; Salman Fazal three for 40, Naeem Khan three for 35) and 216 (Babar Zaman 40, Imran Nazir 43, Mohammad Hussain 61; Naeem Ashraf three for 66, Salman Fazal six for 85). *National Bank 12 pts.*

At National Stadium, Karachi, January 13, 14, 15, 16. Drawn. Gujranwala 214 (Ataullah Butt 36, Aamer Butt 55, Khalid Mahmood 37; Shahid Iqbal eight for 52) and 381 for six (Faisal Naved 51, Mudassar Mushtaq 66, Rizwan Malik 35, Ataullah Butt 150); Karachi Whites* 287 for eight dec. (Kamran Hussain 55, Sultan Ahmed 40, Asim Kamal 48, Iqbal Sheikh 59, Rizwan Qureshi 33 not out; Aamer Butt three for 52). *Karachi Whites 3 pts.*

At Bahawal Stadium, Bahawalpur, January 15, 16, 17. PIA won by ten wickets. Bahawalpur 146 (Hammad Tariq 38; Asif Mujtaba six for 32) and 116 (Asif Mujtaba five for 23, Nadeem Khan three for 32); PIA* 210 (Ghulam Ali 35, Asif Mujtaba 43, Zahid Fazal 32, Maisam Hasnain 32; Usman Tariq three for 39, Tariq Hafeez three for 33) and 54 for no wkt (Shoaib Mohammad 35 not out). *PIA 12 pts.*

At Niaz Stadium, Hyderabad, January 15, 16, 17. Lahore City won by an innings and 135 runs. Hyderabad* 99 (Kashif Alam 46 not out; Sajid Ali three for 50, Fahad Masood seven for 45) and 194 (Akhtar Bangash 52, Iqbal Sheikh 69; Sajid Ali three for 65, Kashif Shafi four for 24); Lahore City 428 for six dec. (Tahir Butt 90, Fareed Butt 64, Ghaffar Kazmi 118, Babar Zaman 108; Iqbal Sheikh three for 83). *Lahore City 12 pts.*

At Sheikhupura Stadium, Sheikhupura, January 15, 16, 17, 18. Drawn. Lahore Division 227 (Maqsood Raza 43, Sarfraz Kazmi 39; Saad Janjua three for 33, Haaris Khan four for 74, Tabish Nawab three for 64) and 371 (Shahid Naseer 46, Maqsood Raza 31, Saleem Mughal 120, Babar Javed 47, Mohammad Haroon 37, Extras 32; Tabish Nawab six for 122); Pakistan Customs* 323 (Ali Naqvi 63, I. Mohammed 54, Nasim Khan 66, Azam Khan 78 not out; Mohammad Haroon three for 68, Saleem Mughal three for 40) and 38 for one. *Pakistan Customs 3 pts.*
    Tabish Nawab took six for 122 on first-class debut.

At National Bank Sports Complex, Karachi, January 15, 16, 17, 18. Drawn. National Bank 210 (Hanif-ur-Rehman 60, Sajid Ali 71; Sarfraz Ahmed three for 52, Shahid Aslam four for 37) and 358 for nine (Saeed Azad 36, Sajid Ali 31, Zafar Iqbal 34, Kamran Akmal 123 not out, Extras 30; Sarfraz Ahmed five for 78); WAPDA* 371 (Adil Nisar 158, Tariq Aziz 50, Hasan Adnan 57, Extras 57; Athar Laeeq five for 97, Zafar Iqbal three for 85). *WAPDA 3 pts.*
    Kamran Akmal and Salman Fazal, who scored 13 not out, added an unbroken 122 for the tenth wicket in National Bank's second innings.

At National Bank Sports Complex, Karachi, January 22, 23, 24, 25. Drawn. National Bank 280 (Sajid Ali 40, Tahir Shah 33, Mohammad Javed 83, Kamran Akmal 34; Imran Adil three for 50,

Usman Tariq three for 50) and 164 for four (Shahid Anwar 35, Hanif-ur-Rehman 50); Bahawalpur* 438 (Hammad Tariq 107, Mohammad Tayyab 44, Usman Tariq 89, Rehan Rafiq 90 not out, Tariq Hafeez 46; Naeem Khan three for 95). *Bahawalpur 3 pts.*

At Jinnah Stadium, Sialkot, January 22, 23, 24, 25. Drawn. Pakistan Customs 498 for five dec. (Ali Naqvi 78, I. Mohammed 210 not out, Nasim Khan 73, Rana Qayyum 58, Aamer Iqbal 50 not out; Imran Amin four for 159); Gujranwala* 269 (Faisal Butt 44, Asim Munir 127; Saad Janjua four for 106, Tabish Nawab three for 78) and 141 for four (Rizwan Malik 50, Khalid Mahmood 38). *Pakistan Customs 3 pts.*
   Imraan Mohammed's 210 not out lasted 522 minutes and 382 balls.

At Defence Cricket Stadium, Karachi, January 22, 23, 24, 25. Drawn. Lahore City* 453 (Fareed Butt 77, Aamer Manzoor 73, Ghaffar Kazmi 125, Babar Zaman 86, Extras 34; Tahir Khan five for 131, Mohammad Masroor three for 14); Karachi Whites 257 (Zafar Jadoon 31, Suleman Huda 86, Iqbal Sheikh 51, Tahir Khan 48; Kashif Shafi five for 105, Amin Athar three for 26) and 278 for six (Suleman Huda 100 not out, Iqbal Sheikh 67; Kashif Shafi three for 89). *Lahore City 3 pts.*

At Sheikhupura Stadium, Sheikhupura, January 22, 23, 24. PIA won by an innings and 81 runs. PIA 550 for four dec. (Shoaib Mohammad 163, Asif Mujtaba 240, Sohail Jaffer 51 not out, Zahid Fazal 31 not out; Lahore Division* 238 (Maqsood Raza 65 not out, Mohammad Haroon 45, Sarfraz Kazmi 59; Ali Gauhar three for 49, Nadeem Khan five for 78) and 231 (Saleem Mughal 34, Mohammad Haroon 56 not out, Sarfraz Kazmi 47; Ali Gauhar four for 35). *PIA 12 pts.*
   Asif Mujtaba's 240 lasted 410 minutes and 335 balls; he added 367 for PIA's third wicket with Shoaib Mohammad.

At Asghar Ali Shah Stadium, WAPDA, January 22, 23, 24, 25. WAPDA won by ten wickets. WAPDA* 378 (Adil Nisar 82, Hasan Adnan 81, Bilal Moin 59, Shahid Mansoor 59; Iqbal Imam five for 76, Riaz Sheikh three for 108) and 15 for no wkt; PNSC 138 (Umar Rasheed 41 not out; Sarfraz Ahmed seven for 50) and 254 (Mohammad Ramzan 108, Sajjad Akbar 40; Sarfraz Ahmed three for 42, Farhan Rasheed five for 90). *WAPDA 12 pts.*

At Mahmood Stadium, Rahimyar Khan, January 29, 30, 31. Pakistan Customs won by an innings and 130 runs. Pakistan Customs 439 for six dec. (Ali Naqvi 42, Azhar Shafiq 42, Azam Khan 93, Aamer Bashir 130, Rana Qayyum 43 not out, Extras 70); Bahawalpur* 107 (Zia-ul-Hasan 37; Azhar Shafiq three for 11, Tabish Nawab three for 29) and 202 (Tariq Hafeez 40, Shehzad Arshad 40 not out; Saad Janjua three for 65, Nadeem Iqbal four for 55). *Pakistan Customs 12 pts.*

At Niaz Stadium, Hyderabad, January 29, 30, 31, February 1. PNSC won by an innings and 50 runs. PNSC 489 for eight dec. (Mohammad Ramzan 150, Faisal Athar 122, Iqbal Imam 35, Nasir Wasti 45, Kashif Ahmed 50, Mutahir Shah 41); Hyderabad* 299 (Akhtar Bangash 82, Iqbal Sheikh 140; Kashif Ibrahim three for 75, Riaz Sheikh four for 103) and 140 (Akhtar Bangash 39; Riaz Sheikh six for 58). *PNSC 12 pts.*

At National Bank Sports Complex, Karachi, January 29, 30, 31, February 1. National Bank won by ten wickets. Karachi Whites* 175 (Zafar Jadoon 33, Suleman Huda 75; Athar Laeeq three for 45, Mohammad Javed five for 66) and 221 (Suleman Huda 41, Asim Kamal 59 not out, Iqbal Sheikh 31; Athar Laeeq four for 77); National Bank 391 (Sajid Ali 149, Fahadullah Khan 106, Extras 30; Shahid Iqbal five for 97, Rizwan Qureshi three for 54) and ten for no wkt. *National Bank 12 pts.*
   Sajid Ali and Fahadullah Khan added 256 for the sixth wicket in National Bank's first innings.

At Gaddafi Stadium, Lahore, January 29, 30, 31, February 1. Drawn. PIA 504 for six dec. (Rizwan-uz-Zaman 137, Shoaib Mohammad 178, Asif Mujtaba 73, Sohail Jaffer 64 not out, Extras 31; Fahad Masood three for 135); Lahore City 187* (Rahat Abbas 48, Imran Nazir 30, Rizwan Arshad 31; Nadeem Afzal three for 32, Asif Mujtaba four for 18) and 260 for four (Rizwan Ahmed 64, Mustaqeem Ahmed 50 not out, Ghaffar Kazmi 102 not out; Nadeem Khan four for 102). *PIA 3 pts.*
   Rizwan-uz-Zaman and Shoaib Mohammad opened with 304 for PIA.

At Sheikhupura Stadium, Sheikhupura, January 29, 30, 31, February 1. WAPDA won by an innings and 133 runs. WAPDA* 564 for nine dec. (Adil Nisar 147, Tariq Aziz 77, Hasan Adnan 32, Bilal Moin 128, Jamshed Iqbal 69, Sarfraz Ahmed 42, Extras 55; Zakaullah Khan five for 137); Lahore Division 238 (Mohammad Haroon 130, Kashif Mahmood 31; Zaheer Khan three for 40, Farhan Rasheed three for 87) and 193 (Mohammad Haroon 73 not out; Sarfraz Ahmed three for 19, Farhan Rasheed six for 103). *WAPDA 12 pts.*

Pool B

At Arbab Niaz Stadium, Peshawar, October 16, 17, 18. Habib Bank won by 109 runs. Habib Bank 241 (Asadullah Butt 78, Tahir Rashid 58 not out; Mubashir Nazir four for 78, Faheem Fazal three for 35) and 192 (Moin-ul-Atiq 33, Asadullah Butt 49; Tahir Mughal three for 54, Javed Hayat three for 28); ADBP* 113 (Inam-ul-Haq 31, Extras 33; Shahid Nazir four for 41, Sajid Shah six for 28) and 211 (Mansoor Rana 47, Tahir Mughal 33, Extras 39; Shahid Nazir three for 55, Akram Raza four for 14). *Habib Bank 12 pts.*

At Chaudhry Rehmat Ali Cricket Ground, Islamabad, October 16, 17, 18, 19. Drawn. Faisalabad* 437 (Mohammad Saleem 123, Javed Iqbal 56, Farooq Iqbal 55 not out, Mohammad Wasim 48, Extras 32; S. John three for 106) and 222 for seven (Javed Iqbal 50, Farooq Iqbal 49 not out; S. John five for 78); Islamabad 329 (Bilal Asad 71, Zaheer Abbasi 64, Amjad Aziz 33, Rauf Akbar 65 not out; Aqeel Ahmed three for 131, Farooq Iqbal three for 62). *Faisalabad 3 pts.*
   Islamabad wicket-keeper Mohammad Shahbaz made seven catches and a stumping in the match.

At National Stadium, Karachi, October 16, 17, 18. Pakistan Reserves won by an innings and 28 runs. Karachi Blues 213 (Imran Khan 41, Yahya Tajveed 63, Mohammad Shakeel 30, Wasim Naeem 30; Yasir Arafat six for 53) and 205 (Mohammad Shakeel 36, Wasim Naeem 69; Yasir Arafat three for 50, Danish Kaneria four for 80); Pakistan Reserves* 446 for nine dec. (Imran Farhat 36, Taimur Khan 139, Bazid Khan 37, Faisal Iqbal 41, Atiq-uz-Zaman 81, Extras 44; Anwar Ali three for 161). *Pakistan Reserves 12 pts.*

At KRL Cricket Ground, Rawalpindi, October 16, 17, 18, 19. Drawn. Allied Bank* 349 (Mohammad Nawaz 105, Masroor Hussain 76, Ijaz Ahmed, jun. 49, Rashid Latif 48; Jaffer Nazir five for 87, Mohammad Sarfraz three for 62) and 284 for eight dec. (Mohammad Nawaz 64, Ijaz Ahmed, jun. 31, Aaley Haider 88, Rashid Latif 34, Extras 34; Naeem Akhtar three for 47, Mohammad Sarfraz three for 32); KRL 217 (Intikhab Alam 62, Naeem Akhtar 36, Extras 30; Aamir Nazir five for 97, Mohammad Zahid four for 41) and 108 for one (Arif Butt 61 not out, Saeed Anwar 39 not out). *Allied Bank 3 pts.*

At Pindi Cricket Stadium, Rawalpindi, October 16, 17, 18, 19. Drawn. Sargodha 249 (Misbah-ul-Haq 41, Mohammad Hasnain 32, Saboor Ahmed 30 not out, Mohammad Shafiq 39, Extras 37; Shakeel Nawaz three for 53, Yasir Ashfaq four for 73) and 174 (Misbah-ul-Haq 64, Saboor Ahmed 31; Shakeel Nawaz three for 46, Maqsood Aslam three for 26); Rawalpindi* 181 (Ahmed Said 45; Ahmed Hayat three for 59, Mohammad Shafiq three for 66, Saboor Ahmed three for 13) and 232 for nine (Ahmed Said 37, Maqsood Aslam 43, Salman Ahmed 47; Mohammad Hasnain four for 32). *Sargodha 3 pts.*
   Khawar Ali of Rawalpindi took a wicket with his first ball in first-class cricket.

At Arbab Niaz Stadium, Peshawar, October 23, 24, 25, 26. Drawn. Habib Bank 253 (Asadullah Butt 39, Younis Khan 36, Salim Malik 30, Tahir Rashid 37, Extras 30; Ata-ur-Rehman five for 83, Aamir Nazir three for 91) and 376 for seven (Moin-ul-Atiq 34, Salim Elahi 108, Younis Khan 85 not out, Salim Malik 44, Extras 32); Allied Bank* 298 (Masroor Hussain 61, Ijaz Ahmed, jun. 37, Aaley Haider 58, Rashid Latif 45, Extras 43; Shahid Nazir three for 62, Kabir Khan three for 66). *Allied Bank 3 pts.*

At Iqbal Stadium, Faisalabad, October 23, 24, 25, 26. Pakistan Reserves won by ten wickets. Pakistan Reserves 392 (Imran Nazir 53, Imran Farhat 75, Taimur Khan 62, Bazid Khan 59, Ahmer Saeed 41, Atiq-uz-Zaman 30; Saeed Ajmal five for 109) and 54 for no wkt (Imran Nazir 30 not out); Faisalabad* 229 (Javed Iqbal 36, Asif Hussain 40, Saadat Gul 58; Fazl-e-Akbar three for 85, Zahid Saeed four for 20) and 214 (Mohammad Saleem 34, Saadat Gul 51, Farooq Iqbal 55; Zahid Saeed six for 86). *Pakistan Reserves 12 pts.*

At Chaudhry Rehmat Ali Cricket Ground, Islamabad, October 23, 24, 25, 26. Drawn. Sargodha 452 (Javed Iqbal 81, Saboor Ahmed 76, Haroon Malik 67 not out, Mohammad Shafiq 101, Nasir Ali 43, Extras 31; Bilal Asad four for 58) and 105 for three (Tanvir Hussain 46, Misbah-ul-Haq 36); Islamabad* 313 (Ashar Zaidi 98, Ali Raza 62, Rauf Akbar 52 not out, Extras 41; Ahmed Hayat six for 74). *Sargodha 3 pts.*

Islamabad wicket-keeper Mohammad Shahbaz made four catches and two stumpings in Sargodha's first innings.

At KRL Cricket Ground, Rawalpindi, October 23, 24, 25, 26. Drawn. ADBP 318 (Inam-ul-Haq 35, Mohammad Nadeem 120 not out, Faheem Fazal 31, Extras 30; Mohammad Sarfraz four for 98) and 150 for five (Zahoor Elahi 52, Mansoor Rana 34 not out); KRL* 413 (Abdul Basit 114, Saeed Anwar 32, Naseer Ahmed 48, Nadeem Abbasi 36, Extras 43; Mubashir Nazir four for 82, Mohammad Asif four for 37). *KRL 3 pts.*

At Pindi Cricket Stadium, Rawalpindi, October 23, 24, 25, 26. Drawn. Peshawar 353 (Asmatullah Mohmand 53, Yasir Hameed 148, Shoaib Khan 41, Zulfiqar Jan 32 not out; Shakeel Nawaz five for 94) and 222 for four dec. (Yasir Hameed 81, Shoaib Khan 52 not out); Rawalpindi* 252 (Ahmed Said 32, Zia-ul-Haq Chaudhry 42, Yasir Ashfaq 42, Shakeel Nawaz 55 not out; Shakeel-ur-Rehman three for 49) and 151 for six (Ahmed Said 30, Salman Ahmed 37 not out; Mohammad Aslam five for 48). *Peshawar 3 pts.*

At Iqbal Stadium, Faisalabad, October 30, 31, November 1, 2. Allied Bank won by 129 runs. Allied Bank 258 (Ijaz Ahmed, jun. 39, Aamer Hanif 48, Aaley Haider 50, Ata-ur-Rehman 35 not out; Sarfraz Butt seven for 84) and 271 for four dec. (Aamir Sohail 79, Masroor Hussain 82, Ijaz Ahmed, jun. 58); Faisalabad* 159 (Saadat Gul 44 not out, Farooq Iqbal 36; Aamir Nazir eight for 79) and 241 (Asif Hussain 72, Fida Hussain 51, Sarfraz Butt 34; Aamir Nazir three for 80, Arshad Khan four for 83). *Allied Bank 12 pts.*

Sarfraz Butt took seven for 84 on first-class debut.

At Margalla Cricket Ground, Islamabad, October 30, 31, November 1, 2. Habib Bank won by an innings and 220 runs. Habib Bank* 565 for seven dec. (Salim Elahi 140, Hasan Raza 70, Younis Khan 200 not out, Salim Malik 37, Tahir Rashid 42); Redco 97 (Kabir Khan five for 50, Sajid Shah three for 27) and 248 (Zeeshan Pervez 86, Hasnain Qayyum 55; Kabir Khan five for 38). *Habib Bank 12 pts.*

Younis Khan's unbeaten 200 lasted 354 minutes and 269 balls.

At Arbab Niaz Stadium, Peshawar, October 30, 31, November 1, 2. Pakistan Reserves won by 12 runs. Pakistan Reserves 247 (Taimur Khan 39, Bazid Khan 60, Faisal Iqbal 35, Yasir Arafat 42; Ashar Zaidi three for 45) and 150 (Taimur Khan 37; Rauf Akbar four for 37, Amjad Aziz four for 17); Islamabad* 171 (Ashar Zaidi 46; Fazl-e-Akbar three for 50) and 214 (Ali Raza 32, Bilal Asad 91; Zahid Saeed three for 53, Shoaib Malik four for 65). *Pakistan Reserves 12 pts.*

Islamabad wicket-keeper Mohammad Shahbaz made five catches and three stumpings in the match, taking his aggregate in three consecutive games to 22 dismissals (16 catches and six stumpings).

At KRL Cricket Ground, Rawalpindi, October 30, 31, November 1, 2. Karachi Blues won by three wickets. KRL 289 (Naseer Ahmed 143, Intikhab Alam 47; Imranullah four for 59) and 303 for five dec. (Abdul Basit 110, Intikhab Alam 106, Nadeem Abbasi 35 not out; Jaffer Qureshi three for 69); Karachi Blues* 260 (Imran Khan 47, Afsar Nawaz 48, Wasim Naeem 33, Asad Ahmed 40; Murtaza Hussain six for 90) and 333 for seven (Imran Khan 119, Afsar Nawaz 90, Extras 47; Saeed Anwar three for 58). *Karachi Blues 9 pts.*

At Pindi Cricket Stadium, Rawalpindi, October 30, 31, November 1. ADBP won by an innings and 45 runs. Rawalpindi 227 (Arif Javed 42, Salman Ahmed 72, Yasir Ashfaq 39) and 172 (Tauseef Ali 33; Faheem Fazal three for 46); ADBP* 444 for eight dec. (Inam-ul-Haq 55, Imran Abbas 133, Mansoor Rana 76, Majid Jahangir 32, Mohammad Nadeem 32, Extras 49; Yasir Ashfaq three for 92, Shah Faisal three for 28). *ADBP 12 pts.*

At Sports Stadium, Sargodha, October 30, 31, November 1, 2. Drawn. Sargodha* 379 (Mohammad Hasnain 65, Haroon Malik 135, Azhar Hussain 36, Nasir Ali 30; Mohammad Aslam three for 72, Hadi Hasan four for 62) and 222 (Tanvir Hussain 56, Mohammad Shafiq 37; Aamer Mahmood three for 61, Mohammad Aslam six for 49); Peshawar 328 (Asmatullah Mohmand 56, Shoaib Khan 32, Yasir Hameed 94, Aamer Mahmood 31, Mohammad Bilal 52; Mohammad Shafiq three for 63, Azhar Hussain four for 29) and 25 for one. *Sargodha 3 pts.*

At Gaddafi Stadium, Lahore, November 6, 7, 8, 9. Drawn. ADBP 248 (Zahoor Elahi 102; Ata-ur-Rehman four for 61, Aamer Hanif three for 41) and 329 (Inam-ul-Haq 41, Imran Abbas 101, Mansoor Rana 38, Atif Rauf 59, Extras 36; Aamir Nazir three for 121, Arshad Khan five for 83); Allied Bank* 464 (Aamir Sohail 34, Masroor Hussain 34, Aaley Haider 92, Rashid Latif 104, Ata-ur-Rehman 80, Humayun Hussain 48; Tahir Mughal three for 137, Majid Jahangir three for 64) and 71 for eight (Faheem Fazal three for 27). *Allied Bank 3 pts.*

At Iqbal Stadium, Faisalabad, November 6, 7, 8, 9. Faisalabad won by an innings and 42 runs. Sargodha 163 (Mohammad Hafeez 34, Azhar Hussain 43; Aqeel Ahmed five for 50) and 226 (Misbah-ul-Haq 129; Saeed Ajmal four for 73, Aqeel Ahmed four for 70); Faisalabad* 431 (Asif Hussain 99, Mohammad Saleem 73, Wasim Haider 89, Saadat Gul 57; Saboor Ahmed three for 82, Tariq Munir three for 101). *Faisalabad 12 pts.*

At Chaudhry Rehmat Ali Cricket Ground, Islamabad, November 6, 7, 8, 9. Drawn. Karachi Blues 160 (Imran Khan 40, Yahya Tajveed 30; Iftikhar Anjum five for 46); Islamabad* 162 for eight (Atif Ashraf 61 not out; Imranullah five for 53). *Islamabad 3 pts.*
    The first two days were washed out.

At KRL Cricket Ground, Rawalpindi, November 6, 7, 8, 9. Drawn. KRL* 326 (Naseer Ahmed 34, Intikhab Alam 49, Saeed Bin Nasir 32, Tasawwur Hussain 45, Shakeel Ahmed 32 not out, Extras 37; Abdur Rehman four for 50) and 72 for two; Habib Bank 362 (Salim Elahi 43, Hasan Raza 60, Younis Khan 70, Salim Malik 77; Jaffer Nazir three for 83, Mohammad Sarfraz three for 80). *Habib Bank 3 pts.*

At Arbab Niaz Stadium, Peshawar, November 6, 7, 8, 9. Drawn. Peshawar* 376 (Sajjad Ahmed 38, Shoaib Khan 34, Yasir Hameed 134, Zulfiqar Jan 63; Danish Kaneria seven for 129); Pakistan Reserves 499 for five (Imran Nazir 164, Taufiq Umar 57, Bazid Khan 119, Ahmer Saeed 105 not out). *Pakistan Reserves 3 pts.*

At Margalla Cricket Ground, Islamabad, November 6, 7, 8, 9. Drawn. Redco 275 for four dec. (Naved Ashraf 81, Hasnain Qayyum 161 not out); Rawalpindi* 94 for four (Arif Javed 59).
    The first two days were washed out.

At KRL Cricket Ground, Rawalpindi, November 13, 14, 15, 16. Drawn. ADBP* 429 (Imran Abbas 50, Mansoor Rana 79, Atif Rauf 65, Javed Hayat 60, Mohammad Nadeem 78 not out, Fahad Khan 34, Extras 30; S. John four for 81, Iftikhar Anjum five for 129) and 323 for six (Zahoor Elahi 41, Imran Abbas 132 not out, Javed Hayat 31); Islamabad 331 (Bilal Asad 81, Fazal Abbas 39, Mohammad Shahbaz 69 not out, Extras 58; Fahad Khan four for 88, Inam-ul-Haq three for 36). *ADBP 3 pts.*

At Margalla Cricket Ground, Islamabad, November 13, 14, 15, 16. Drawn. Allied Bank* 471 for five dec. (Aamir Sohail 40, Masroor Hussain 54, Ijaz Ahmed, jun. 65, Aamer Hanif 129 not out, Rashid Latif 131 not out) and 273 for two (Mohammad Nawaz 88, Aamir Sohail 136); Redco 402 (Naved Ashraf 44, Shabbir Khan 33, Shadab Kabir 137 not out, Waqas Ahmed 30, Adnan Naeem 72; Arshad Khan eight for 110). *Allied Bank 3 pts.*
    In Allied Bank's first innings, Aamer Hanif and Rashid Latif shared an unbroken sixth-wicket stand of 218.

At Gaddafi Stadium, Lahore, November 13, 14, 15, 16. Habib Bank won by 67 runs. Habib Bank 308 (Asadullah Butt 80, Mujahid Jamshed 54, Hasan Raza 85; Shabbir Ahmed four for 106, Fazl-e-Akbar four for 60) and 168 (Younis Khan 48, Shahid Afridi 39; Shabbir Ahmed four for 61, Fazl-e-Akbar three for 73); Pakistan Reserves* 162 (Extras 37; Sajid Shah four for 46) and 247 (Qaiser Abbas 31, Asif Mahmood 65, Bazid Khan 68, Extras 35; Kabir Khan four for 70, Sajid Shah six for 55). *Habib Bank 12 pts.*

At Arbab Niaz Stadium, Peshawar, November 13, 14, 15, 16. Peshawar won by four wickets. Faisalabad 164 (Wasim Haider 31, Atif Baig 37, Mohammad Wasim 42; Aamer Mahmood five for 57) and 167 (Amjad Ali 33; Mohammad Aslam four for 36); Peshawar* 157 (Zulfiqar Jan 30; Nadeem Butt three for 48, Saeed Ajmal three for 18) and 175 for six (Sajjad Ahmed 45, Shoaib Khan 42, Mohammad Bilal 40 not out). *Peshawar 9 pts.*

At Army Sports Stadium, Rawalpindi, November 13, 14, 15, 16. Karachi Blues won by six wickets. Rawalpindi 179 (Salman Ahmed 43, Khawar Ali 42; Asad Ahmed four for 22, Imranullah three for 39) and 314 (Salman Ahmed 127 not out, Zia-ul-Haq Chaudhry 44, Yasir Ashfaq 37; Mansoor Ahmed five for 123); Karachi Blues* 384 for eight dec. (Saad Wasim 152, Afsar Nawaz 63, Asad Ahmed 45; Jawad Hameed five for 136, Khawar Ali three for 70) and 113 for four (Imran Khan 48, Afsar Nawaz 34 not out). *Karachi Blues 12 pts.*

At Sports Stadium, Sargodha, November 13, 14, 15. KRL won by an innings and 33 runs. KRL 389 (Saeed Anwar 177, Saeed Bin Nasir 36, Nadeem Abbasi 35, Murtaza Hussain 53 not out, Extras 30; Shahid Ali four for 138, Saboor Ahmed three for 51); Sargodha* 105 (Misbah-ul-Haq 46; Murtaza Hussain five for 43, Saeed Anwar three for 11) and 251 (Mohammad Hasnain 36, Misbah-ul-Haq 41, Azhar Hussain 50, Mohammad Shafiq 39; Shakeel Ahmed six for 98, Murtaza Hussain four for 101). *KRL 12 pts.*

At Gaddafi Stadium, Lahore, November 20, 21. Allied Bank won by an innings and 129 runs. Allied Bank 329 (Aamir Sohail 164, Rashid Latif 86, Extras 38; Fazl-e-Akbar four for 89, Yasir Arafat three for 67); Pakistan Reserves* 128 (Taimur Khan 44; Aqib Javed three for 44, Aamir Nazir three for 43, Ata-ur-Rehman three for 25) and 72 (Aqib Javed five for 15, Aamir Nazir three for 32). *Allied Bank 12 pts.*
 Aamir Sohail and Rashid Latif added 218 for Allied Bank's sixth wicket.

At Iqbal Stadium, Faisalabad, November 20, 21, 22. 23. Redco won by an innings and 48 runs. Redco 395 (Rafatullah Mohmand 213, Shadab Kabir 65, Extras 38; Sarfraz Butt three for 69, Saeed Ajmal four for 129); Faisalabad* 185 (Amjad Ali 33, Mohammad Zaman 59; Waqas Ahmed three for 67, Imran Tahir six for 32) and 162 (Wasim Haider 45, Mohammad Nawaz 47; Waqas Ahmed six for 26, Ahmed Kundi three for 42). *Redco 12 pts.*
 Rafatullah Mohmand's 213 lasted 524 minutes and 402 balls.

At KRL Cricket Ground, Rawalpindi, November 20, 21, 22, 23. Drawn. KRL* 445 for eight dec. (Abdul Basit 58, Naseer Ahmed 81, Intikhab Alam 40, Nadeem Abbasi 91, Naeem Akhtar 79; S. John four for 119); Islamabad 234 (Ashar Zaidi 97; Jaffer Nazir four for 75, Murtaza Hussain four for 49) and 206 for eight (Atif Ashraf 85, Fazal Abbas 30, Mahmood Alam 39 not out; Murtaza Hussain four for 69). *KRL 3 pts.*

At Arbab Niaz Stadium, Peshawar, November 20, 21, 22, 23. Peshawar won by four wickets. Peshawar 335 (Sajjad Ahmed 112 retired hurt, Shoaib Khan 92, Mohammad Bilal 31; Asad Ahmed three for 87, Imranullah three for 78) and 145 for six (Shoaib Khan 61 not out; Asad Ahmed three for 65); Karachi Blues* 175 (Afsar Nawaz 45, Extras 32; Aamer Mahmood six for 46, Mohammad Aslam three for 29) and 304 (Imran Khan 32, Afsar Nawaz 98, Saad Wasim 85, Extras 34; Aamer Mahmood four for 57). *Peshawar 12 pts.*

At Margalla Cricket Ground, Rawalpindi, November 20, 21, 22. Habib Bank won by an innings and 105 runs. Rawalpindi* 132 (Ahmed Said 34; Shahid Afridi four for 27, Akram Raza three for 16) and 184 (Pervez Iqbal 58; Shahid Nazir four for 73, Shahid Afridi four for 32); Habib Bank 421 for five dec. (Salim Elahi 76, Mujahid Jamshed 158, Hasan Raza 42, Kabir Khan 33 not out, Extras 43). *Habib Bank 12 pts.*

At Sports Stadium, Sargodha, November 20, 21, 22, 23. Drawn. Sargodha* 247 (Misbah-ul-Haq 41, Mohammad Shafiq 33, Saboor Ahmed 30) and 294 (Mohammad Hafeez 83, Misbah-ul-Haq 77; Tahir Mughal four for 74); ADBP 329 (Zahoor Elahi 133, Imran Abbas 63, Mansoor Rana 52; Tariq Munir four for 88, Saboor Ahmed four for 72, Azhar Hussain three for 82). *ADBP 3 pts.*

At Gaddafi Stadium, Lahore, November 27, 28, 29, 30. Pakistan Reserves won by three wickets. ADBP 318 (Zahoor Elahi 45, Imran Abbas 87, Majid Jahangir 57, Extras 35; Fazl-e-Akbar three for 105, Zahid Saeed five for 90) and 247 (Imran Abbas 77, Majid Jahangir 36, Atif Rauf 36; Fazl-e-Akbar four for 76, Shoaib Malik three for 53); Pakistan Reserves* 252 (Taufiq Umar 36,

Imran Farhat 48, Ahmer Saeed 42, Shoaib Malik 30; Tahir Mughal three for 85, Azhar Abbas five for 58) and 314 for seven (Taufiq Umar 92, Imran Farhat 100, Faisal Iqbal 33 not out; Mohammad Asif four for 96). *Pakistan Reserves 9 pts.*

At KRL Cricket Ground, Rawalpindi, November 27, 28, 29, 30. Drawn. Habib Bank* 449 (Asadullah Butt 68, Mujahid Jamshed 70, Hasan Raza 125, Farhan Adil 44, Shaukat Mirza 39, Tahir Rashid 30 not out, Extras 32; Jaffer Qureshi three for 145, Adnan Malik three for 112) and 205 for four (Mujahid Jamshed 104, Shahid Javed 44); Karachi Blues 375 (Imran Khan 80, Rizwan Umar 34, Mohammad Farrukh 68, Kamran Nafees 40, Wasim Naeem 76; Akram Raza six for 96). *Habib Bank 3 pts.*

At Iqbal Stadium, Faisalabad, November 27, 28, 29, 30. KRL won by an innings and 52 runs. KRL* 506 for six dec. (Saeed Anwar 112, Iftikhar Hussain 151, Saeed Bin Nasir 57, Intikhab Alam 49, Moazzam Shah 75); Faisalabad 182 (Mohammad Saleem 43, Amjad Ali 37; Naeem Akhtar three for 45, Murtaza Hussain six for 58) and 272 (Javed Iqbal 55, Mohammad Zaman 33, Saadat Gul 89; Murtaza Hussain five for 96, Saeed Anwar three for 24). *KRL 12 pts.*

At Arbab Niaz Stadium, Peshawar, November 27, 28, 29, 30. Drawn. Islamabad* 381 (Bilal Asad 63, Fazal Abbas 60, Mohammad Shahbaz 91, Iftikhar Anjum 35, Extras 38; Aamer Mahmood three for 94) and 270 for four (Ashar Zaidi 127, Mahmood Alam 101); Peshawar 320 (Shoaib Khan 127, Hameed Gul 39, Mohammad Asif 46, Extras 30; S. John three for 79). *Islamabad 3 pts.*

At Pindi Cricket Stadium, Rawalpindi, November 27, 28, 29, 30. Drawn. Rawalpindi 210 (Ahmed Said 38, Irfan Bhatti 60; Aamir Nazir three for 65, Mohammad Zahid three for 30) and 429 (Babar Naeem 86, Ahmed Said 59, Pervez Aziz 67, Irfan Bhatti 70, Pervez Iqbal 35, Extras 53; Ata-ur-Rehman three for 110, Mohammad Zahid five for 63); Allied Bank* 329 (Aamir Sohail 70, Mohammad Nawaz 73, Ijaz Ahmed, jun. 59, Aaley Haider 30, Extras 31; Yasir Ashfaq four for 83) and 76 for three (Ijaz Ahmed, jun. 49 not out). *Allied Bank 3 pts.*
   Babar Naeem took five catches in Allied Bank's first innings.

At Sports Stadium, Sargodha, November 27, 28, 29, 30. Drawn. Redco* 311 (Shadab Kabir 37, Hasnain Qayyum 43, Zeeshan Pervez 43, Wasim Yousufi 98, Waqas Ahmed 31; Ahmed Hayat four for 76, Saboor Ahmed three for 71) and 363 for seven (Naumanullah 146, Shadab Kabir 50, Hasnain Qayyum 71); Sargodha 309 (Mohammad Hafeez 32, Misbah-ul-Haq 77, Mohammad Hasnain 37, Azhar Hussain 35, Mohammad Shafiq 33, Shahid Mahmood 30 not out; Imran Tahir four for 114). *Redco 3 pts.*

At Gaddafi Stadium, Lahore, December 4, 5, 6, 7. Allied Bank won by seven wickets. Allied Bank 353 (Aamir Sohail 134, Ijaz Ahmed, jun. 43, Aamer Hanif 46, Extras 44; Mohammad Hasnain five for 133) and 138 for three (Ijaz Ahmed, jun. 83); Karachi Blues* 188 (Afsar Nawaz 61, Saad Wasim 41, Kamran Nafees 38; Aamir Nazir four for 78, Ata-ur-Rehman four for 54) and 300 (Rizwan Umar 39, Mohammad Farrukh 37, Afsar Nawaz 51, Saad Wasim 74, Kamran Nafees 44; Ata-ur-Rehman five for 95). *Allied Bank 12 pts.*

At Iqbal Stadium, Faisalabad, December 4, 5, 6. ADBP won by nine wickets. Faisalabad* 216 (Fida Hussain 97, Extras 32; Azhar Abbas three for 52) and 131 (Zeeshan Butt 36; Javed Hayat three for 28, Fahad Khan three for 15); ADBP 339 (Majid Jahangir 49, Mansoor Rana 120, Fahad Khan 80; Sarfraz Butt three for 80, Maqbool Ahmed four for 63) and nine for one. *ADBP 12 pts.*

At Arbab Niaz Stadium, Peshawar, December 4, 5, 6, 7. KRL won by seven wickets. KRL 373 (Saeed Anwar 58, Saeed Bin Nasir 75, Moazzam Shah 35, Nadeem Abbasi 41, Naeem Akhtar 39, Murtaza Hussain 46, Extras 30; Aamer Mahmood three for 46, Nauman Habib three for 99, Mohammad Aslam three for 63) and 41 for three (Saeed Anwar 33 not out); Peshawar* 192 (Yasir Hameed 38; Mohammad Sarfraz three for 46, Shakeel Ahmed three for 39) and 221 (Yasir Hameed 154, Nauman Habib 42; Naeem Akhtar five for 42, Mohammad Sarfraz four for 33). *KRL 12 pts.*
   In Peshawar's second innings, Yasir Hameed and Nauman Habib added 181 for the eighth wicket.

At Pindi Cricket Stadium, Rawalpindi, December 4, 5, 6, 7. Islamabad won by 11 runs. Islamabad 221 (Atif Ashraf 52, Mohammad Shahbaz 31; Irfan Bhatti three for 52, Shakeel Nawaz four for

63) and 184 (Ashar Zaidi 40, Ali Raza 34, Extras 35; Yasir Ashfaq six for 45); Rawalpindi* 157 (Nauman Ashraf 44; S. John five for 53, Rauf Akbar four for 36) and 237 (Babar Naeem 72, Munawar Abbasi 35, Pervez Aziz 50; S. John four for 96, Khalid Zafar four for 39). *Islamabad 12 pts.*

At Sports Stadium, Sargodha, December 5, 6, 7. Habib Bank won by an innings and 37 runs. Sargodha* 201 (Mohammad Hafeez 73, Zameer-ul-Hasan 44; Akram Raza six for 45) and 195 (Mohammad Hafeez 43, Haroon Malik 30, Mohammad Shafiq 58; Kabir Khan six for 37, Akram Raza four for 93); Habib Bank 433 for nine dec. (Asadullah Butt 141, Mujahid Jamshed 108, Hasan Raza 101 not out, Tahir Rashid 30; Mohammad Shafiq five for 80). *Habib Bank 12 pts.*
Asadullah Butt and Mujahid Jamshed opened for Habib Bank with 252 in 282 minutes.

At LCCA Ground, Lahore, December 9, 10, 11. Redco won by six wickets. Karachi Blues 144 (Bilal Murtaza 41; Waqas Ahmed four for 50) and 229 (Mohammad Farrukh 37, Mohammad Shakeel 36, Saad Wasim 43, Afsar Nawaz 45; Imran Tahir eight for 76); Redco* 159 (Shadab Kabir 40, Hasnain Qayyum 46; Jaffer Qureshi six for 51) and 216 for four (Shadab Kabir 100 not out, Naumanullah 52 not out). *Redco 12 pts.*

At Gaddafi Stadium, Lahore, December 10, 11, 12. Pakistan Reserves won by an innings and 121 runs. Sargodha 160 (Salman Shahid 47; Shabbir Ahmed six for 72, Kashif Raza three for 53) and 195 (Mohammad Hafeez 69, Tariq Munir 56; Kashif Raza three for 83, Shoaib Malik five for 30); Pakistan Reserves* 476 for nine dec. (Qaiser Abbas 168, Asif Mahmood 58, Humayun Farhat 33, Shoaib Malik 101 not out, Extras 60; Mohammad Shafiq three for 130, Umair Hasan four for 166). *Pakistan Reserves 12 pts.*

At KRL Cricket Ground, Rawalpindi, December 16, 17, 18, 19. Pakistan Reserves won by eight wickets. KRL* 315 (Saeed Anwar 31, Naseer Ahmed 103, Tasawwar Hussain 73, Extras 44; Danish Kaneria seven for 101) and 120 (Moazzam Shah 33; Fazl-e-Akbar three for 32, Danish Kaneria five for 37); Pakistan Reserves 293 (Qaiser Abbas 40, Imran Nazir 82, Asif Mahmood 36, Atiq-uz-Zaman 53, Extras 30; Naseem Hanif three for 54) and 143 for two (Qaiser Abbas 52 not out, Imran Nazir 68). *Pakistan Reserves 9 pts.*
Pakistan Reserves wicket-keeper Atiq-uz-Zaman took six catches in KRL's first innings.

At LCCA Ground, Lahore, December 16, 17, 18. Redco won by an innings and 36 runs. Peshawar* 91 (Yasir Hameed 39; Imran Tahir six for 26) and 143 (Zulfiqar Jan 62; Waqas Ahmed three for 42, Imran Tahir four for 53); Redco 270 (Hasnain Qayyum 33, Naumanullah 143, Shabbir Khan 34; Nauman Habib seven for 89). *Redco 12 pts.*

At Pindi Cricket Stadium, Rawalpindi, December 22, 23, 24. Pakistan Reserves won by an innings and two runs. Rawalpindi 200 (Salman Ahmed 31, Mohammad Saleem 71 not out; Kashif Raza four for 52, Zahid Saeed five for 44) and 175 (Mohammad Zubair 55, Mohammad Saleem 30; Zahid Saeed three for 23, Yasir Arafat three for 36); Pakistan Reserves* 377 (Taufiq Umar 176, Atiq-uz-Zaman 35, Yasir Arafat 50). *Pakistan Reserves 12 pts.*

At Gaddafi Stadium, Lahore, December 28, 29, 30, 31. Drawn. Pakistan Reserves 233 (Qaiser Abbas 53, Mohammad Ghazan 36, Ahmer Saeed 35; Adnan Naeem four for 34, Imran Tahir four for 98) and 297 for four (Qaiser Abbas 76, Ahmer Saeed 47, Taimur Khan 73 not out, Asif Mahmood 62 not out); Redco* 447 (Rafatullah Mohmand 46, Hasnain Qayyum 43, Naumanullah 171 not out, Shabbir Khan 36, Extras 43; Kashif Raza four for 97). *Redco 3 pts.*
Naumanullah and Imran Tahir, who scored 23, added 112 for Redco's tenth wicket.

At Iqbal Stadium, Faisalabad, January 15, 16, 17. Habib Bank won by ten wickets. Faisalabad 110 (Farooq Iqbal 37 not out; Kabir Khan five for 27, Akram Raza three for 47) and 170 (Mohammad Zaman 37, Saeed Ajmal 39; Shahid Nazir five for 60, Younis Khan three for 24); Habib Bank* 249 (Mujahid Jamshed 56, Younis Khan 101; Farooq Iqbal seven for 60) and 32 for no wkt. *Habib Bank 12 pts.*

At Margalla Cricket Ground, Islamabad, January 15, 16, 17, 18. Islamabad v Redco. Abandoned.

At Defence Cricket Stadium, Karachi, January 15, 16, 17, 18. Drawn. ADBP* 452 (Majid Jahangir 90, Mansoor Rana 107, Manzoor Elahi 134, Javed Hayat 52; Jaffer Qureshi three for 131, Tahir

Mahmood three for 104) and 419 for eight (Imran Abbas 204 not out, Manzoor Elahi 42, Javed Hayat 54, Fahad Khan 34; Jaffer Qureshi four for 156); Karachi Blues 424 (Afsar Nawaz 178, Saad Wasim 116, Imranullah 36 not out, Extras 34; Azhar Abbas three for 122, Javed Hayat four for 106). *ADBP 3 pts.*

Imran Abbas's 204 not out lasted 386 minutes and 282 balls. Afsar Nawaz and Saad Wasim added 306 for Karachi's fourth wicket.

At KRL Cricket Ground, Rawalpindi, January 15, 16, 17, 18. Drawn. KRL* 204 (Saeed Anwar 51 retired hurt, Naseer Ahmed 37, Rashid Iqbal 30; Mohammad Ghufran three for 48, Ghulam Shabbir three for 31); Rawalpindi 239 (Munawar Abbasi 40, Irfan Bhatti 61, Khawar Ali 57; Naeem Hanif four for 48). *Rawalpindi 3 pts.*

At Arbab Niaz Stadium, Peshawar, January 15, 16, 17, 18. Peshawar v Allied Bank. Abandoned.

At Margalla Cricket Ground, Islamabad, January 22, 23, 24, 25. Drawn. Redco 394 (Naved Ashraf 34, Rafatullah Mohmand 87, Shadab Kabir 61, Hasnain Qayyum 88, Naumanullah 54; Azhar Abbas five for 87); ADBP* 133 for one (Imran Abbas 41 not out, Majid Jahangir 47 not out).

At KRL Cricket Ground, Rawalpindi, January 22, 23, 24, 25. Drawn. Allied Bank 460 for six dec. (Aamir Sohail 30, Ijaz Ahmed, jun. 188, Manzoor Akhtar 36, Rashid Latif 98, Extras 36; S. John three for 113); Islamabad* 206 (Bilal Asad 55, Extras 40; Aqib Javed three for 29) and 70 for two (Atif Ashraf 30 not out). *Allied Bank 3 pts.*

Ijaz Ahmed and Rashid Latif added 218 for Allied Bank's fifth wicket; it was the third time Latif had shared a stand of 218 in consecutive matches.

At UBL Sports Complex, Karachi, January 22, 23, 24, 25. Karachi Blues won by eight wickets. Sargodha 138 (Ahmed Hayat 64; Imranullah five for 54) and 175 (Misbah-ul-Haq 53, Azhar Hussain 44, Ahmed Hayat 38; Tanvir Ahmed three for 54, Imranullah four for 60); Karachi Blues* 249 (Imran Khan 38, Saad Wasim 40, Tanvir Ahmed 55; Ahmed Hayat three for 71, Umair Hasan three for 55) and 65 for two (Nadeem Sheikh 31 not out). *Karachi Blues 12 pts.*

On first-class debut, Karachi Blues wicket-keeper Tariq Sabzwari took six catches in Sargodha's first innings – when Sargodha recovered from 72 for eight – and eight in the match.

At Arbab Niaz Stadium, Peshawar, January 22, 23, 24, 25. Habib Bank won by 125 runs. Habib Bank* 339 (Moin-ul-Atiq 91, Younis Khan 132; Nauman Habib four for 115, Fazal Akbar three for 56) and 268 for three dec. (Mujahid Jamshed 47, Younis Khan 142 not out, Farhan Adil 58 not out); Peshawar 276 (Arshad Khan, jun. 38, Yasir Hameed 42, Shoaib Khan 47, Abdul Hafeez 41, Zulfiqar Jan 41; Akram Raza six for 83) and 206 (Yasir Hameed 88, Zulfiqar Jan 36; Kabir Khan three for 19). *Habib Bank 12 pts.*

Younis Khan scored a century in each innings.

At Pindi Cricket Stadium, Rawalpindi, January 22, 23, 24, 25. Drawn. Faisalabad 275 (Mohammad Zaman 68, Fida Hussain 141; Khawar Ali three for 26) and 73 for three; Rawalpindi* 371 (Mohammad Zubair 71, Khawar Ali 36, Salman Ahmed 56, Pervez Aziz 101, Irfan Bhatti 31, Yasir Ashfaq 34, Extras 32; Moazzam Ali five for 96, Nadeem Butt three for 73). *Rawalpindi 3 pts.*

At Pindi Cricket Stadium, Rawalpindi, January 29, 30, 31, February 1. Drawn. Habib Bank 528 for seven dec. (Moin-ul-Atiq 71, Mujahid Jamshed 95, Younis Khan 202 not out, Farhan Adil 61; S. John three for 159); Islamabad* 252 (Aamer Munir 30, Bilal Asad 55, S. John 44; Akram Raza six for 91). *Habib Bank 3 pts.*

Younis Khan's 202 not out, his fourth century in consecutive innings and second double of the season, lasted 342 minutes and 265 balls.

At UBL Sports Complex, Karachi, January 29, 30, 31. Faisalabad won by five wickets. Karachi Blues 229 (Imran Khan 46, Afsar Nawaz 45, Saad Wasim 35, Aamer Ali 36; Yasir Mushtaq four for 56) and 119 (Aamer Ali 31; Yasir Mushtaq four for 48, Maqbool Ahmed three for 31); Faisalabad* 159 (Tanvir Ahmed three for 49, Mohammad Hasnain four for 46, Jaffer Qureshi three for 16) and 190 for five (Mohammad Salman 51, Fida Hussain 32, Mohammad Nawaz 37 not out; Imranullah three for 46). *Faisalabad 9 pts.*

At KRL Cricket Ground, Rawalpindi, January 29, 30, 31, February 1. Drawn. Redco* 351 (Shabbir Khan 111, Wasim Yousufi 36, Imran Tahir 48, Extras 34; Murtaza Hussain five for 125); KRL 285 for nine (Saeed Anwar 41, Saeed Bin Nasir 55, Naseer Ahmed 35, Jaffer Nazir 39 not out, Extras 32; Imran Tahir five for 109).

At Arbab Niaz Stadium, Peshawar, January 29, 30, 31, February 1. ADBP won by an innings and 65 runs. ADBP 384 (Imran Abbas 52, Majid Jahangir 40, Atif Rauf 113, Javed Hayat 37, Tahir Mughal 32, Extras 47; Nauman Habib four for 86); Peshawar* 204 (Mohammad Asad 34, Yasir Hameed 32, Munsif Khan 69 not out; Azhar Abbas four for 76, Tahir Mughal four for 55) and 115 (Azhar Abbas four for 65, Tahir Mughal five for 45). *ADBP 12 pts.*

At Sports Stadium, Sargodha, January 29, 30, 31, February 1. Drawn. Sargodha 234 (Misbah-ul-Haq 40, Haroon Malik 34; Arshad Khan seven for 86, Manzoor Akhtar three for 68) and 195 (Mohammad Hafeez 38, Misbah-ul-Haq 53; Mohammad Akram four for 41, Arshad Khan five for 63); Allied Bank* 257 (Masroor Hussain 66, Iqbal Saleem 44, Arshad Khan 39; Ahmed Hayat three for 46) and 73 for three (Mohammad Nawaz 30 not out). *Allied Bank 3 pts.*

FINAL

HABIB BANK v PIA

At Iqbal Stadium, Faisalabad, February 12, 13. PIA won by eight wickets. Toss: PIA.

Switched from Lahore because of preparations there for Sri Lanka's visit, and scheduled for five days, the final was over inside two. Conditions in Faisalabad were perfect for seam bowlers. The Sri Lankan tour also meant the call-up of the prolific Younis Khan, and without him Habib Bank crumbled. Nadeem Afzal removed their top four, three caught behind, and later took out the tail. PIA surrendered even more quickly. Though they scored at five an over, that did not amount to much in 22 overs. Only Nadeem Khan reached 20 as Kabir Khan and Sajid Shah cleaned up. By the close, Habib Bank led by 79 – but their openers had fallen for the second time that day. Though Mohammad Zahid had broken down after bowling four balls, Ali Gauhar ran riot next morning to finish with six for 45. PIA batted again needing 166 – from 11 sessions. At 25 for two, even this looked improbable. But Ghulam Ali and Asif Mujtaba played as if they were in a different match and added 141 in 29 overs to secure the title.

Close of play: First day, Habib Bank 20-2 (Sajid Shah 6*, Mujahid Jamshed 1*).

Habib Bank

Asadullah Butt c Ahmed Zeeshan			
b Nadeem Afzal .	31	– c Asif Mujtaba b Ali Gauhar.	3
Salim Elahi c Ahmed Zeeshan b Nadeem Afzal .	4	– c Shoaib Mohammad	
		b Nadeem Afzal .	8
Mujahid Jamshed c Ahmed Zeeshan			
b Nadeem Afzal .	5	– (4) c Ghulam Ali b Ali Gauhar . . .	1
Hasan Raza c Ghulam Ali b Nadeem Afzal. . . .	0	– (5) c Ghulam Ali b Ali Gauhar . . .	9
Sajid Shah b Ali Gauhar	10	– (3) c Zahid Fazal b Ali Gauhar . . .	12
Salim Malik b Ali Gauhar	16	– c sub (Kashif Siddiq) b Ali Gauhar	26
Shahid Afridi c Asif Mujtaba			
b Mohammad Zahid .	28	– b Sohail Jaffer	0
†Tahir Rashid c Zahid Fazal			
b Mohammad Zahid .	14	– b Ali Gauhar	21
Kabir Khan c Ahmed Zeeshan b Nadeem Afzal .	12	– (10) not out.	4
*Akram Raza not out	20	– (9) lbw b Nadeem Afzal	7
Irfan Fazil c Asif Mujtaba b Nadeem Afzal. . . .	12	– run out	7
L-b 5, n-b 14	19	L-b 3, w 1, n-b 4	8

1/10 2/23 3/23 4/49 5/70	171	1/13 2/13 3/21 4/28 5/63	106
6/74 7/110 8/125 9/151		6/64 7/67 8/90 9/96	

Bowling: *First Innings*—Mohammad Zahid 12–1–50–2; Nadeem Afzal 12.5–3–59–6; Ali Gauhar 12–0–57–2. *Second Innings*—Mohammad Zahid 0.4–0–0–0; Ali Gauhar 15.5–4–45–6; Nadeem Afzal 12–0–43–2; Sohail Jaffer 4–0–15–1.

PIA

Rizwan-uz-Zaman lbw b Kabir Khan	2	– c Tahir Rashid b Sajid Shah	0
Shoaib Mohammad c Hasan Raza b Sajid Shah	3	– c Sajid Shah b Kabir Khan	6
Ghulam Ali c Asadullah Butt b Kabir Khan	17	– not out	73
*Asif Mujtaba c Kabir Khan b Sajid Shah	5	– not out	54
Zahid Fazal c Tahir Rashid b Kabir Khan	11		
Sohail Jaffer c and b Irfan Fazil	16		
†Ahmed Zeeshan lbw b Sajid Shah	5		
Nadeem Khan not out	26		
Nadeem Afzal b Sajid Shah	0		
Mohammad Zahid, sen. c Sajid Shah b Kabir Khan	1		
Ali Gauhar c Kabir Khan b Sajid Shah	4		
B 3, w 1, n-b 18	22	B 4, l-b 9, w 1, n-b 19	33
	112	**(2 wkts)**	**166**

1/6 2/12 3/34 4/36 5/63 6/69 7/73 8/93 9/106   112   1/14 2/25   (2 wkts) 166

Bowling: *First Innings*—Kabir Khan 8–1–49–4; Sajid Shah 10.5–3–42–5; Irfan Fazil 3–1–18–1. *Second Innings*—Kabir Khan 11–2–54–1; Sajid Shah 12–3–32–1; Irfan Fazil 5–1–17–0; Asadullah Butt 4–0–22–0; Akram Raza 2–0–17–0; Shahid Afridi 1–0–11–0.

Umpires: Feroz Butt and Mohammad Nazir.

QUAID-E-AZAM TROPHY WINNERS

1953-54	Bahawalpur	1972-73	Railways	1986-87	National Bank
1954-55	Karachi	1973-74	Railways	1987-88	PIA
1956-57	Punjab	1974-75	Punjab A	1988-89	ADBP
1957-58	Bahawalpur	1975-76	National Bank	1989-90	PIA
1958-59	Karachi	1976-77	United Bank	1990-91	Karachi Whites
1959-60	Karachi	1977-78	Habib Bank	1991-92	Karachi Whites
1961-62	Karachi Blues	1978-79	National Bank	1992-93	Karachi Whites
1962-63	Karachi A	1979-80	PIA	1993-94	Lahore City
1963-64	Karachi Blues	1980-81	United Bank	1994-95	Karachi Blues
1964-65	Karachi Blues	1981-82	National Bank	1995-96	Karachi Blues
1966-67	Karachi	1982-83	United Bank	1996-97	Lahore City
1968-69	Lahore	1983-84	National Bank	1997-98	Karachi Blues
1969-70	PIA	1984-85	United Bank	1998-99	Peshawar
1970-71	Karachi Blues	1985-86	Karachi	1999-2000	PIA

Note: Matches in the following competitions were not first-class.

TISSOT CUP, 1999-2000

Semi-finals

At National Stadium, Karachi, October 7. PIA won by five wickets. Allied Bank 161 (47.4 overs) (Manzoor Akhtar 49; Asif Mujtaba three for 29); PIA* 162 for five (38.3 overs) (Ghulam Ali 69, Asif Mujtaba 36 not out; Manzoor Akhtar three for 34).

At Gaddafi Stadium, Lahore, October 8 (day/night). Redco won by eight wickets. National Bank 109 (36.1 overs) (Mushtaq Ahmed four for 22); Redco* 112 for two (32.3 overs) (Naved Ashraf 34 not out, Bazid Khan 43 not out).

Final

At Gaddafi Stadium, Lahore, October 10 (day/night). PIA won by 38 runs. PIA 310 for four (50 overs) (Rizwan-uz-Zaman 42, Ghulam Ali 70, Zahid Fazal 85, Moin Khan 35 not out, Wasim Akram 32 not out, Extras 33); Redco* 272 for nine (50 overs) (Bazid Khan 67, Naved Ashraf 70, Mushtaq Ahmed 33 not out; Shoaib Malik three for 56).

NATIONAL BANK CUP, 1999-2000

Semi-finals

At Gaddafi Stadium, Lahore, April 9. KRL won by eight wickets. WAPDA* 218 (50 overs) (Ijaz Mahmood 53, Adil Nisar 63; Jaffer Nazir three for 31, Saeed Anwar three for 41); KRL 222 for two (42.3 overs) (Iftikhar Hussain 76 not out, Saeed Anwar 90, Naseer Ahmed 31 not out).

At Gaddafi Stadium, Lahore, April 10. Habib Bank won by seven wickets. Pakistan Customs 189 (48.3 overs) (Nasim Khan 45, Fazl-e-Akbar 40; Sajid Shah three for 21); Habib Bank* 190 for three (33 overs) (Salim Elahi 74, Taufiq Umar 58 not out).

Final

At Gaddafi Stadium, Lahore, April 13. Habib Bank won by 19 runs. Habib Bank 182 (49.3 overs) (Hasan Raza 57; Jaffer Nazir three for 29, Yasir Arafat three for 31); KRL* 163 (47.5 overs) (Naseer Ahmed 41, Jaffer Nazir 40; Imran Farhat four for 37).

CRICKET IN SRI LANKA, 1999-2000

By SA'ADI THAWFEEQ and GERRY VAIDYASEKERA

Arjuna Ranatunga

Sri Lanka's international season lasted a full 12 months, from the arrival of Australia and India in August 1999 to the departure of South Africa in August 2000. New captain Sanath Jayasuriya began by beating world champions Australia in the final of a one-day tournament and in the Test series that followed; he also led Sri Lanka to Test wins in Zimbabwe and Pakistan, though they lost the return series against Pakistan in Sri Lanka. The season ended with another one-day trophy and a drawn series with South Africa, which also marked the international farewell of Jayasuriya's most famous predecessor as captain, Arjuna Ranatunga. The only surviving player from Sri Lanka's inaugural Test against England in 1981-82, and the man who led his country to the World Cup in 1996, Ranatunga played his last Test innings at his home ground, Sinhalese Sports Club. He scored an undefeated 28, just enough to make him the only batsman to reach 1,000 first-class runs in this extended season.

The domestic season was shorter: the first-class Premier Trophy ran from November to February. Sri Lankan cricket was still controlled by an interim committee appointed by the sports minister, after the fracas following the annual general meeting in 1999. Under its auspices, the tournament's format was remodelled on similar lines to the last World Cup: 16 teams were divided into two groups, the top four from each group advanced to a Super League, carrying through results against fellow-qualifiers, and the remaining eight competed for a Plate Championship. Tournament committee chairman Sriyan Samararatne said this should make the competition more meaningful, and reduce the chances of weaker clubs conceding to title-contenders without a fight, believed to be a frequent occurrence.

The group rounds were completed in early January, when the tournament paused for the Under-19 World Cup, in which hosts Sri Lanka reached the final. The Super League and Plate commenced at the end of the month. Matches did seem to be played on a more competitive note in these two leagues, which both produced unexpected finishes. The fancied teams in the Super League were Tamil Union, in their centenary year, and Sinhalese, a batting powerhouse – they had the season's four leading scorers in Ranatunga, his brother Sanjeeva, Avishka Gunawardene and Mahela Jayawardene. Going into the last weekend, less than two points separated these sides. But both drew their final games and, worse than that, conceded first-innings points. Even so, Tamil Union came agonisingly close to taking the title through an outright win, reducing Sebastianites to 156 for nine chasing 206, only for the last-wicket pair to deny them. Sinhalese, with several players on national duty in Pakistan, were outgunned by Colombo.

While attention was focused on these two games, however, a dark horse overtook the front-runners. Colts, led by former Test opener Dulip Samaraweera, dismissed Burgher for 248 and then piled up 406 to take maximum points for batting, as well as for the first-innings lead, and edge past the other two contenders. Colts, runners-up to Bloomfield in 1998-99, and always in the Super League's top four, had last been champions eight years earlier. Left-arm spinner Dinuka Hettiarachchi spearheaded their campaign and finished the season with 55 first-class wickets at 15.09, including ten in a match twice, against Police and Sebastianites.

Bloomfield were kept out of the Super League in bizarre circumstances. They were in the top half of Group A when they were penalised 18 points, the maximum possible, for walking out of a match against Kurunegala Youth at Welagedera Stadium. Matches in Colombo were officially halted on the same day, in mid-December, because of a curfew after the general election; they resumed in the new year. But the tournament committee refused Bloomfield's explanation that they had returned home to Colombo because of the curfew, as it was not in force in Kurunegala. They also suspended the captain, Pubudu Dassanayake, for two matches for bringing back the team without seeking permission. Bloomfield were effectively relegated to the Plate.

In this competition, Galle upset favourites Nondescripts in the final match to clinch the title. Again, it came down to first-innings points in a drawn game. Nondescripts started it with a six-point lead, but Galle, after scoring 239, bowled them out for 156. Nondescripts badly missed Aravinda de Silva, who was in Pakistan; he had won their previous three games with a century and match bags of seven and ten wickets.

Matara, meanwhile, were suspended from the Plate for violating tournament rules. They were found to have altered the condition of the pitch during their match against Antonians, hoping to retrieve a win and escape relegation, though they had little hope when they were all out for 69. Matara – who had already failed to produce a pitch for their game with Police – and Singha were expected to go down in 2000-01, with teams representing the Sri Lankan Air Force and Navy promoted, but both were spared when the number of clubs starting the Premier Trophy increased to 18.

Although deprived of what would have been their first first-class title, Tamil Union celebrated their centenary by beating Sinhalese in two finals, winning the limited-overs Premier Trophy and the Under-23 championship. They also won Division Two of the inter-club league.

The Premier Trophy season began and ended with double-centuries. Nondescripts captain Hashan Tillekeratne scored an unbeaten 203 against Singha during the opening round, which remained the highest score until the final weekend, when another former Test wicket-keeper/batsman, Lanka de Silva, eclipsed it with 213 for Colombo against Sinhalese. Sanjeeva Ranatunga headed the full season's batting averages with 63.63; he and Arjuna each scored three hundreds for Sinhalese. Bloomfield's A. P. R. Shaman hit the fastest century, off 77 balls against Antonians; his captain, Kumar Dharmasena, returned 13 of 66 in the same game. Burgher pace bowler Wendell Labrooy took eight for 83 in an innings against Matara. Test off-spinner Muttiah Muralitharan captured 62 wickets in the first-class season, though he managed only nine in two matches for his club, Tamil Union; Hettiarachchi was the only other bowler to reach 50. A 15-year-old schoolboy spinner from Dharmasoka College in Ambalangoda, Ishara Dilshan, in his second match for Singha, against Sebastianites, took five for 110; he improved on that with two returns of six wickets and one of seven.

At the other extreme, 63-year-old P. H. A. N. Dias, president of Dimbulla Club, who had recently recovered from a heart attack, played against Dickoya Maskeliya in Division Three. These teams' rivalry dates back to 1872; this time, Dimbulla won.

In schools cricket, Gamini Chandrakumara of Sri Palee, Horana, had an outstanding season, scoring 1,238 runs. He made 266, with 18 sixes and 21 fours, against Maliyadeva Model School, and twin hundreds against Kannangara. Suranga de Silva of St Sebastian's also reached 1,000, as did Nimesh Perera of President's College, who made 212 against St Aloysius College of Galle. The outstanding bowling performance came from Ishara Kadeer, who claimed all ten wickets for 76 for St Anne's, Kurunegala, against Zahira of Colombo. In Panadura, Sanjeeva Roshan of St John's took nine for 67 against Royal; Lakmal Fernando of St Thomas's collected eight for 16 against Wesley at Campbell Park.

FIRST-CLASS AVERAGES, 1999-2000

BATTING

(Qualification: 450 runs, average 30.00)

	M	I	NO	R	HS	100s	Avge
S. Ranatunga (*Sinhalese*)	10	15	4	700	145	3	63.63
S. K. L. de Silva (*Colombo*)	8	10	1	512	213	1	56.88
D. P. Samaraweera (*Colts*)	8	10	1	491	114	2	54.55
A. Ranatunga (*Sinhalese*)	16	23	4	1,005	141	3	52.89
M. S. Atapattu (*Sinhalese*)	10	17	2	696	207*	2	46.40
H. D. P. K. Dharmasena (*Bloomfield*)	12	14	3	500	104	1	45.45
H. P. Tillekeratne (*Nondescripts*)	11	15	1	615	203*	1	43.92
D. P. M. D. Jayawardene (*Sinhalese*)	11	18	1	742	167	2	43.64
S. T. Jayasuriya (*Sri Lanka*)	9	15	1	610	188	2	43.57
W. M. P. N. Wanasinghe (*Galle*)	10	15	2	544	102*	1	41.84
C. Mendis (*Colts*)	10	14	1	511	124	3	39.30
S. Jayantha (*Bloomfield*)	10	15	3	458	182	1	38.16
G. R. P. Peiris (*Tamil Union*)	11	18	2	608	132	1	38.00
D. A. Gunawardene (*Sinhalese*)	12	20	1	714	140	2	37.57
K. E. A. Upashantha (*Colts*)	10	13	0	470	82	0	36.15
C. U. Jayasinghe (*Burgher*)	10	15	2	464	142	1	35.69
B. S. M. Warnapura (*Colts*)	11	17	4	464	112	1	35.69
P. A. de Silva (*Nondescripts*)	10	16	2	471	110	1	33.64
R. P. Arnold (*Nondescripts*)	11	15	0	501	129	1	33.40
S. Jayawardene (*Panadura*)	9	15	0	488	74	0	32.53
R. P. Hewage (*Nondescripts*)	11	16	2	450	135	1	32.14
H. G. J. M. Kulatunga (*Colts*)	11	16	0	513	151	2	32.06
B. C. M. S. Mendis (*Burgher*)	11	16	1	465	81	0	31.00
A. S. Polonowita (*Colombo*)	11	15	0	464	123	1	30.93
C. P. Handunnettige (*Burgher*)	11	15	0	463	140	1	30.86
K. Sangakkara (*Nondescripts*)	13	20	2	540	97	0	30.00

* *Signifies not out.*

BOWLING

(Qualification: 30 wickets, average 25.00)

	O	M	R	W	BB	5W/i	Avge
N. S. Rupasinghe (*Colombo*)	312.1	99	676	47	7-19	3	14.38
R. A. D. C. Perera (*Sebastianites*)	165	36	495	33	7-95	3	15.00
J. W. H. D. Boteju (*Colombo*)	191.3	60	466	31	5-18	1	15.03
S. Weerakoon (*Burgher*)	308.2	82	707	47	7-74	3	15.04
D. Hettiarachchi (*Colts*)	309.3	83	830	55	5-20	5	15.09
P. P. Wickremasinghe (*Bloomfield*)	292.2	98	685	44	7-58	4	15.56
H. D. P. K. Dharmasena (*Bloomfield*)	327.5	92	732	47	7-30	3	15.57

	O	M	R	W	BB	5Wi	Avge
U. D. U. Chandana (*Tamil Union*)	276.2	75	656	41	7-82	2	16.00
M. R. C. N. Bandaratilleke (*Tamil Union*)	274	86	504	30	6-67	2	16.80
M. I. Abdeen (*Nondescripts*)	225.2	54	536	30	4-14	0	17.86
R. S. Kalpage (*Nondescripts*)	304.5	86	727	39	5-30	2	18.64
K. E. A. Upashantha (*Colts*)	243.2	57	757	40	5-67	1	18.92
C. R. B. Mudalige (*Colombo*)	289	77	692	36	6-62	2	19.22
T. T. Samaraweera (*Sinhalese*)	357	101	831	43	5-25	1	19.32
M. S. Villavarayen (*Tamil Union*)	304.3	66	788	39	6-50	2	20.20
K. A. D. M. Fernando (*Sebastianites*) . . .	262.2	46	845	41	5-58	2	20.60
T. C. B. Fernando (*Panadura*)	221.4	34	730	35	6-39	2	20.85
M. Muralitharan (*Tamil Union*)	556	141	1,309	62	7-84	6	21.11
A. W. Ekanayake (*Kurunegala Youth*)	282	64	727	34	5-39	3	21.38
T. A. V. H. K. Ranaweera (*Police*)	221.5	28	779	34	4-46	0	22.91
C. M. Bandara (*Nondescripts*)	253.1	49	722	31	6-41	1	23.29
C. R. D. Fernando (*Sinhalese*)	296.2	51	959	41	6-29	1	23.39
R. Herath (*Moors*)	462.1	142	1,027	42	5-40	2	24.45

Note: Averages include Pakistan and South Africa's tours in June to August 2000.

PREMIER TROPHY, 1999-2000

SUPER LEAGUE

	Played	Won	Lost	Drawn	1st-inns Lead	Points
Colts CC	7	2	0	5	3	70.065
Sinhalese SC	7	1	0	6	4	68.725
Tamil Union C and AC	7	3	1	3	1	68.555
Colombo CC	7	1	1	5	3	59.235
Burgher RC	7	2	0	5	1	56.510
Sebastianites C and AC	7	0	3	4	3	45.610
Moors SC	7	0	2	5	2	39.180
Kurunegala Youth CC	7	0	2	5	1	24.925

Super League teams carried forward results and points gained against fellow-qualifiers in the first round, but not those gained against the teams eliminated.

PLATE CHAMPIONSHIP

	Played	Won	Lost	Drawn	1st-inns Lead	Points
Galle CC	6	3	0	3	2	72.030
Nondescripts CC	5	4	0	1	0	65.110
Panadura SC	6	2	1	3	1	50.445
Police SC	6	1	3	2	1	37.315
Bloomfield C and AC	5	3	1	1	0	36.095
Antonians SC	6	0	4	2	1	24.585
Singha SC	6	0	4	2	1	21.340

Matara SC were suspended from the tournament for improper preparation of the pitch; all points from their fixtures were excluded from the table. The match between Bloomfield and Nondescripts was abandoned.

Teams carried forward results and points gained against fellow-group members in the first round, but not those gained against the teams who qualified for the Super League.

In the following scores, * by the name of a team indicates that they won the toss.

Group A

At Reid Avenue, Colombo, November 12, 13, 14. Bloomfield won by an innings and 111 runs. Matara* 154 (S. W. N. D. Chinthaka 57, S. M. Ramzan 55; P. P. Wickremasinghe five for 48) and 135 (J. Nandakumar 47 not out; H. S. H. Alles three for 31, P. P. Wickremasinghe three for 37); Bloomfield 400 for eight dec. (S. Jayantha 182, H. D. P. K. Dharmasena 35, A. P. R. Shaman 56; P. I. W. Jayasekera three for 79).

At Havelock Park, Colombo (BRC), November 12, 13, 14. Burgher won by 89 runs. Burgher* 300 (C. P. Handunettige 75, R. H. S. Silva 35, B. S. M. Warnapura 38, W. C. Labrooy 31, Extras 40; S. A. L. J. Fernando four for 47) and 171 (C. U. Jayasinghe 34; C. H. Liyanage four for 33); Sebastianites 196 (T. N. S. Warusamana 41, Extras 39; S. Weerakoon three for 49, W. C. Labrooy three for 61, B. S. M. Warnapura four for 54) and 186 (L. Fernando 66, Extras 48; S. Weerakoon three for 34, S. Madanayake three for 23).
Between them, the teams conceded 152 extras in the match.

At Maitland Place, Colombo (NCC), November 12, 13, 14. Nondescripts won by an innings and 160 runs. Singha* 110 (M. I. Abdeen three for 22, C. M. Bandara three for three) and 165 (S. Sanjeewa 36, H. Premasiri 34, H. W. M. Kumara 45; M. I. Abdeen three for 54); Nondescripts 435 for four dec. (K. Weeraratne 43, H. P. Tillekeratne 203 not out, C. P. Mapatuna 125, R. S. Kalpage 35 not out; T. Thushara three for 127).
Tillekeratne and Mapatuna added 285 for Nondescripts, a Sri Lankan fourth-wicket record.

At Maitland Crescent, Colombo (CCC), November 13, 14, 15. Drawn. Kurunegala Youth 227 (D. K. Ranaweera 71, D. K. Samarasinghe 38; J. W. H. D. Boteju three for 34) and 142 (D. K. Ranaweera 43; N. S. Rupasinghe three for 19, P. B. Ediriweera three for 30); Colombo* 218 (D. N. Hunukumbura 49, A. S. Polonowita 58, D. Arnolda 33; J. C. Gamage three for 25, A. W. Ekanayake three for 80) and 91 for eight (J. A. M. W. Kumara three for 31).

At Reid Avenue, Colombo, November 19, 20, 21. Drawn. Bloomfield 337 (M. T. Gunaratne 37, B. de Silva 33, P. B. Dassanayake 47, I. C. Soysa 102 not out, P. W. Gunaratne 34, Extras 49; W. C. Labrooy three for 84); Burgher* 179 for six (N. S. Bopage 54, B. C. M. S. Mendis 63).

At Maitland Crescent, Colombo (CCC), November 19, 20, 21. Colombo won by ten wickets. Matara* 157 (N. S. Rupasinghe four for 31, C. R. B. Mudalige three for 27) and 146 (S. W. Sameera 35; J. W. H. D. Boteju three for 47, P. B. Ediriweera three for 28, C. R. B. Mudalige three for 16); Colombo 276 (M. G. van Dort 46, D. N. Hunukumbura 46, D. Arnolda 58, J. W. H. D. Boteju 41, M. H. R. M. Fernando 39 not out; K. G. A. S. Kalum three for 59, N. R. C. K. Guruge three for 43) and 29 for no wkt.

At Maitland Place, Colombo (NCC), November 19, 20, 21. Drawn. Nondescripts 135 (R. S. Kalpage 37, D. Ramanayake 30; A. W. Ekanayake five for 39, R. P. Mapatuna three for 18) and 168 for seven dec. (M. D. J. Jayasuriya 41, S. Pradeep 32; D. N. Jayakody four for 50); Kurunegala Youth* 174 (D. N. Jayakody 31, D. K. Samarasinghe 72; S. Pradeep three for 17) and 57 for eight (M. I. Abdeen three for 14, R. S. Kalpage three for 13).

At St Sebastian's College Ground, Moratuwa, November 20, 21, 22. Drawn. Singha 184 (H. Premasiri 32, T. R. D. Mendis 32, Extras 33; R. A. D. C. Perera four for 31) and 298 (W. M. J. Kumudu 31, H. W. M. Kumara 45, H. Premasiri 41, H. E. Mendis 34 not out; R. A. D. C. Perera seven for 95); Sebastianites* 356 (H. M. P. Fernando 56, L. R. Fernando 71, T. S. M. Peiris 40, S. A. L. J. Fernando 75 not out, C. H. Liyanage 36; I. Dilshan five for 110).
L. R. Fernando reached his fifty in 24 balls; 15-year-old Dilshan took five wickets in his second first-class match.

At Havelock Park, Colombo (BRC), November 26, 27, 28. Burgher won by an innings and 85 runs. Singha 81 (H. Premasiri 36; W. C. Labrooy three for 33, M. J. H. Rushdie four for 33, S. Weerakoon three for five) and 106 (W. M. J. Kumudu 30; B. S. M. Warnapura six for 22); Burgher* 272 (N. S. Bopage 40, U. N. K. Fernando 30, W. C. Labrooy 101, S. Madanayake 48; T. Thushara three for 66, P. Milton three for 66).
Warnapura took a hat-trick in Singha's second innings.

At Maitland Crescent, Colombo (CCC), November 26, 27, 28. Drawn. Bloomfield* 169 (S. D. Abeynaike 41, P. B. Dassanayake 32; N. S. Rupasinghe five for 59) and 21 for one; Colombo 178 for nine dec. (M. G. van Dort 41, D. N. Hunukumbura 31, J. W. H. D. Boteju 31; P. P. Wickremasinghe seven for 58).

At Welagedera Stadium, Kurunegala, November 26, 27, 28. Drawn. Sebastianites* 137 (J. C. Gamage six for 23) and 127 for five dec.; Kurunegala Youth 41 (K. A. D. M. Fernando four for 18, R. A. D. C. Perera five for five) and 11 for no wkt.
In Kurunegala's first innings, which lasted 40.1 overs, the highest score was ten, by D. N. Jayakody; Perera's analysis was 9.1–6–5–5.

At Maitland Place, Colombo (NCC), November 26, 27, 28. Nondescripts won by ten wickets. Matara 144 (P. B. Buddika 55; R. S. Kalpage three for 23, P. K. Abeygunasekera four for 18) and 140 (N. H. V. Chinthaka 54; R. S. Kalpage three for 34, H. P. Tillekeratne three for 33); Nondescripts* 259 for seven dec. (D. M. Ramanayake 71, H. P. Tillekeratne 61, C. P. Mapatuna 42, R. S. Kalpage 34 not out; N. R. C. K. Guruge three for 63) and 29 for no wkt.

At Reid Avenue, Colombo, December 3, 4, 5. Bloomfield v Nondescripts. Abandoned.

At Havelock Park, Colombo (BRC), December 3, 4, 5. Drawn. Burgher 361 for six dec. (C. P. Handunettige 140, N. S. Bopage 34, B. C. M. S. Mendis 33, C. U. Jayasinghe 36, R. H. S. Silva 74); Kurunegala Youth* 187 for eight (Extras 40; C. U. Jayasinghe four for 31).

At Maitland Crescent, Colombo (CCC), December 3, 4, 5. Colombo won by ten wickets. Singha* 83 (N. S. Rupasinghe seven for 19) and 163 (S. Sanjeewa 33; J. W. H. D. Boteju three for 17, N. S. Rupasinghe three for 38, P. Seneviratne four for 55); Colombo 163 (M. G. van Dort 30, S. K. L. de Silva 81, A. S. Polonowita 30; I. Dilshan six for 24) and 88 for no wkt (M. G. van Dort 53 not out, D. N. Hunukumbura 32 not out).
Rupasinghe took a hat-trick in Singha's first innings.

At Havelock Park, Colombo (Colts), December 3, 4, 5. Sebastianites won by four wickets. Matara* 148 (N. H. V. Chinthaka 42, Extras 33; R. A. D. C. Perera three for 25) and 118 (M. M. D. N. R. G. Perera four for 46, S. A. L. J. Fernando three for 14); Sebastianites 127 (G. G. Ranga Yasalal 37, T. N. S. Warusamana 38; N. R. C. K. Guruge four for 41) and 145 for six (M. M. D. N. R. G. Perera 34 not out).

At Reid Avenue, Colombo, December 10, 11, 12. Drawn. Sebastianites 258 (S. K. Silva 34, T. S. M. Peiris 57, S. A. L. J. Fernando 42, K. A. D. M. Fernando 50 not out; A. P. R. Shaman three for 54) and 190 (T. N. S. Warusamana 49, K. A. D. M. Fernando 40; P. P. Wickremasinghe five for 73); Bloomfield* 269 (S. Jayantha 32, H. D. P. K. Dharmasena 104, W. D. D. S. Perera 45; K. A. D. M. Fernando four for 74, C. H. Liyanage three for 31) and 172 for six (H. D. P. K. Dharmasena 53 not out).
Needing 180 to win in 28 overs, Bloomfield scored 172.

At Havelock Park, Colombo (BRC), December 10, January 5, 6. Drawn. Matara 121 (N. H. V. Chinthaka 36, Extras 37; W. C. Labrooy eight for 83) and 193 for eight (K. Y. P. Sanjeewa 37, S. W. Sameera 68 not out, P. I. W. Jayasekera 32, Extras 30; S. Madanayake five for 41); Burgher* 380 (C. U. Jayasinghe 33, B. S. M. Warnapura 112, U. N. K. Fernando 87, C. P. Handunettige 45, S. Madanayake 31, Extras 34; P. I. W. Jayasekera four for 78, S. M. Ramzan three for 89).
Play was interrupted for nearly four weeks after Matara's kit was stolen. Umpires N. S. Anurasiri and T. H. Wijewardene replaced E. A. R. de Silva and D. N. Pathirana when the match resumed.

At Welagedera Stadium, Kurunegala, December 10, 11, 12. Drawn. Singha 155 (S. Sanjeewa 36; A. W. Ekanayake five for 44) and 215 for eight (W. M. J. Kumudu 60, H. W. M. Kumara 31, H. Premasiri 34; J. A. M. W. Kumara three for 50, D. K. Samarasinghe three for 75); Kurunegala Youth* 315 for nine dec. (N. Munasinghe 35, S. C. Gunasekera 121, R. R. Jaymon 39; P. Milton four for 80, I. Dilshan three for 102).

At Maitland Place, Colombo (NCC), December 10, 11, 12. Drawn. Nondescripts* 336 (K. Sangakkara 62, M. N. Nawaz 78, C. P. Mapatuna 37, R. S. Kalpage 45, K. Weeraratne 44; C. R. B. Mudalige five for 99) and 175 for five (R. P. Hewage 38, M. N. Nawaz 63); Colombo 339 for nine dec. (A. S. Polonowita 123, W. M. B. Perera 41; M. I. Abdeen four for 65, S. Pradeep three for 48).

At Maitland Crescent, Colombo (CCC), December 17, 18, January 2. Colombo won by an innings and 100 runs. Sebastianites* 50 (N. S. Rupasinghe five for 11, C. R. B. Mudalige three for nine) and 60 (J. W. H. D. Boteju five for 18, C. R. B. Mudalige three for 12); Colombo 210 (D. N. Hunukumbura 74, J. W. H. D. Boteju 33; K. A. D. M. Fernando five for 58).

This match and others on the same dates were interrupted for two weeks because of a curfew in Colombo during elections. Sebastianites totalled 110 over two innings; only two batsmen reached double figures.

At Welagedera Stadium, Kurunegala, December 17, 18, January 2. Drawn. Kurunegala Youth 336 (D. N. Jayakody 64, R. P. Mapatuna 45, J. A. M. W. Kumara 85 not out, J. C. Gamage 40, Extras 46; H. S. H. Alles seven for 90); Bloomfield* 16 for one.

Bloomfield were fined 18 points for returning to Colombo without authorisation; the curfew did not apply in Kurunegala. When the game resumed, Bloomfield could muster only nine players.

At Galle Esplanade, Galle, December 17, 18, 19. Drawn. Matara 240 (K. Y. P. Sanjeewa 71, N. R. C. K. Guruge 59, S. M. Ramzan 34; I. Dilshan six for 87); Singha* 234 (W. M. J. Kumudu 32, T. R. D. Mendis 45; P. I. W. Jayasekera three for 50, N. R. C. K. Guruge three for 58).

At Maitland Place, Colombo (NCC), December 17, 18, January 2. Drawn. Burgher 311 (B. C. M. S. Mendis 57, C. U. Jayasinghe 81, B. S. M. Warnapura 50, W. C. Labrooy 33; M. A. Samsudeen four for 58); Nondescripts* 309 (M. N. Nawaz 51, H. P. Tillekeratne 89, R. S. Kalpage 42; M. J. H. Rushdie three for 78, S. Weerakoon three for 23).

When the match resumed in January, umpire B. C. Cooray was in Cape Town, standing in the Fourth Test between South Africa and England; he was replaced here by T. H. Wijewardene.

At Reid Avenue, Colombo, December 26, 27, 28. Bloomfield won by an innings and 155 runs. Singha* 144 (S. W. C. Sanjeewa 48, V. B. de Silva 36 not out; P. P. Wickremasinghe three for 26, B. de Silva four for 31) and 96 (S. W. C. Sanjeewa 31; P. W. Gunaratne three for 18, P. P. Wickremasinghe three for 29, H. D. P. K. Dharmasena three for 25); Bloomfield 395 (S. D. Abeynaike 54, S. Jayantha 89, H. D. P. K. Dharmasena 65, W. D. D. S. Perera 34, P. B. Dassanayake 66 not out; I. Dilshan seven for 114).

At Havelock Park, Colombo (BRC), December 26, 27, 28. Drawn. Burgher 310 (B. C. M. S. Mendis 32, R. H. S. Silva 120, B. S. M. Warnapura 43; J. W. H. D. Boteju three for 29, N. S. Rupasinghe four for 68) and 133 (C. P. Handunettige 31, B. C. M. S. Mendis 40; N. S. Rupasinghe four for 30, C. R. B. Mudalige six for 62); Colombo* 238 (P. B. Ediriweera 32, S. K. L. de Silva 59, Extras 50; K. S. C. de Silva six for 57) and 143 for seven (C. U. Jayasinghe three for one, S. Madanayake three for 23).

At Welagedera Stadium, Kurunegala, December 26, 27, 28. Kurunegala Youth won by an innings and three runs. Matara 76 (K. Y. P. Sanjeewa 38 not out; A. S. Wewalwala four for 21) and 222 (N. H. V. Chinthaka 65, S. W. N. D. Chinthaka 36; A. W. Ekanayake four for 57, A. S. Wewalwala three for 30); Kurunegala Youth* 301 for eight dec. (R. R. Jaymon 51, A. S. Wewalwala 88, D. K. Samarasinghe 59; K. G. A. S. Kalum three for 92, P. I. W. Jayasekera three for 15).

Sanjeewa carried his bat through Matara's innings.

At Maitland Place, Colombo (NCC), December 26, 27, 28. Sebastianites won by 54 runs. Sebastianites 137 (S. K. Silva 37, H. A. P. W. Jayawardene 56; K. R. Pushpakumara three for 50, R. S. Kalpage four for 40) and 310 for nine dec. (S. K. Silva 66, T. M. Dilshan 89, M. M. D. N. R. G. Perera 38; R. S. Kalpage three for 93, C. M. Bandara three for 83); Nondescripts* 184 (D. Ramanayake 62 not out, K. R. Pushpakumara 30; T. M. Dilshan three for 40) and 209 (M. N. Nawaz 64, H. P. Tillekeratne 37; T. M. Dilshan three for 59).

Sebastianites reached 102 for one in their first innings before losing nine for 35.

Burgher, Colombo, Kurunegala and Sebastianites qualified for the Super League.

Group B

At Galle Esplanade, Galle, November 12, 13, 14. Drawn. Galle* 245 (D. D. Wickremasinghe 33, W. M. P. N. Wanasinghe 78, M. K. P. B. Kularatne 50 not out; U. D. U. Chandana seven for 82) and 70 for no wkt (T. K. D. Sudarshana 36 not out); Tamil Union 302 (N. Weeraman 39, U. D. U. Chandana 48, P. S. A. N. Shiroman 32, M. C. R. Fernando 33; A. Riddeegammanagedera five for 107).

At Braybrooke Place, Colombo (Moors), November 12, 13, 14. Drawn. Moors* 343 (A. A. W. Gunawardene 63, H. K. P. Rangana 40, U. C. Hathurusinghe 67, K. A. S. Jayasinghe 37, R. S. Priyadarshana 52 not out, Extras 39; I. Amithakeerthi four for 38) and 157 for six dec. (A. A. W. Gunawardene 72 not out, R. S. Priyadarshana 34; G. A. S. Perera four for 33); Panadura 195 (J. S. K. Peiris 30, K. R. R. K. Wimalasena 54, Extras 32; C. M. Hathurusinghe five for 62) and 136 for six (J. S. K. Peiris 35).

At Police Park, Colombo, November 12, 13, 14. Colts won by 107 runs. Colts 304 (M. T. Sampath 44, K. E. A. Upashantha 36, D. K. Liyanage 108 not out; R. C. R. P. Silva three for 54) and 188 for four dec. (C. Mendis 102 not out, G. V. S. Janaka 33, H. G. J. M. Kulatunga 40; T. A. V. H. K. Ranaweera three for 49); Police* 176 (H. P. A. Priyantha 72; M. J. Sigera three for 41, D. Hettiarachchi five for 36) and 209 (H. S. G. S. Silva 56, A. V. Senasinghe 54 not out; K. E. A. Upashantha four for 32, D. Hettiarachchi five for 79).

At Maitland Place, Colombo (SSC), November 12, 13, 14. Drawn. Sinhalese 362 (S. Ranatunga 107, A. Ranatunga 79, C. R. P. Galappathy 40, H. G. D. Nayanakantha 40; C. Samarasinghe four for 115) and 221 for five (A. Ranatunga 141, S. Ranatunga 37; C. Samarasinghe three for 64); Antonians* 318 (S. K. Perera 31, P. K. Siriwardene 47, Y. M. W. B. Ekanayake 84, U. Hettiarachchi 60, Extras 48; C. R. D. Fernando three for 78, I. R. Ratnaweera four for 70).

At Maitland Crescent, Colombo (CCC), November 19, 20, 21. Drawn. Colts* 289 (C. Mendis 124, K. E. A. Upashantha 60; S. N. Liyanage three for 48, M. M. P. Silva three for 47) and 306 for nine (H. G. J. M. Kulatunga 100, M. T. Sampath 58; T. C. B. Fernando four for 83); Panadura 193 (K. R. R. K. Wimalasena 39; K. E. A. Upashantha three for 55, D. Hettiarachchi three for 44).

At Braybrooke Place, Colombo (Moors), November 19, 20, 21. Drawn. Galle* 149 (W. M. P. N. Wanasinghe 36; U. C. Hathurusinghe three for 24) and 110 for one (T. K. D. Sudarshana 50 not out, A. Rideegammanagedera 50 not out); Moors CC 215 (N. de Silva 31, R. S. Priyadarshana 46, U. C. Hathurusinghe 41; K. G. Perera five for 65).

At Maitland Place, Colombo (SSC), November 19, 20, 21. Drawn. Sinhalese 310 (R. H. Sureshchandra 36, W. M. S. M. Perera 70, R. P. A. H. Wickremaratne 50, A. Ranatunga 42, C. R. P. Galappathy 41 not out; T. A. V. H. K. Ranaweera three for 57, I. D. Gunawardene four for 63); Police* 153 (C. R. D. Fernando three for 19, I. R. Ratnaweera three for 31) and 176 for nine (W. N. M. Soysa 65, I. D. Gunawardene 35 not out; H. G. D. Nayanakantha three for 50, I. R. Ratnaweera six for 62).

At P. Saravanamuttu Stadium, Colombo, November 19, 20, 21. Drawn. Tamil Union 385 for nine dec. (G. R. P. Peiris 90, U. D. U. Chandana 53, G. R. K. Wijekoon 69, M. C. R. Fernando 53; C. Samarasinghe four for 126); Antonians* 140 (M. S. Sampan 33, Extras 31; G. R. K. Wijekoon three for 30, U. D. U. Chandana five for 39) and 133 for eight (S. K. Perera 67; M. C. R. Fernando four for 19).

At Havelock Park, Colombo (Colts), November 26, 27, 28. Drawn. Colts* 68 (C. R. D. Fernando six for 29) and 183 for six (I. R. Ratnaweera three for 32); Sinhalese 372 for eight dec. (R. H. Sureshchandra 46, A. Ranatunga 134 not out, R. P. A. H. Wickremaratne 52, C. R. D. Fernando 42, Extras 30).

At Galle Esplanade, Galle, November 26, 27, 28. Drawn. Panadura 255 (S. Jayawardene 74, K. R. R. K. Wimalasena 38; S. Sanjeewa three for 57, W. M. P. N. Wanasinghe five for 41); Galle* 163 for three (W. M. P. N. Wanasinghe 67 not out, A. Rideegammanagedera 30 not out; G. A. S. Perera three for 29).

At Braybrooke Place, Colombo (Moors), November 26, 27, 28. Drawn. Moors 269 for nine dec. (N. de Silva 38, A. A. W. Gunawardene 56, U. C. Hathurusinghe 37, B. D. A. P. Ranaweera 64 not out; C. Samarasinghe four for 116, F. A. Joseph three for 70); Antonians* 74 for seven (R. S. Priyadarshana three for 23).

At P. Saravanamuttu Stadium, Colombo, November 26, 27, 28. Tamil Union won by eight wickets. Police 185 (P. R. T Fernando 42, K. Mahinda 30 not out, Extras 31; D. P. S. Jayaratne four for 42) and 96 (W. J. M. R. Dias four for 20, U. D. U. Chandana four for ten); Tamil Union* 208 for eight dec. (N. Weeraman 39, P. S. A. N. Shiroman 37, G. R. P. Peiris 35) and 75 for two (G. R. P. Peiris 37 not out).

At Galle Esplanade, Galle, December 3, 4, 5. Drawn. Galle 188 (T. K. D. Sudarshana 36, D. D. Wickremasinghe 52 not out; H. G. D. Nayanakantha three for 42, R. Dhammika four for 52); Sinhalese* 30 for four.

At Braybrooke Place, Colombo (Moors), December 3, 4, 5. Drawn. Police 166 (H. P. A. Priyantha 43; B. D. A. P. Ranaweera three for 39); Moors* 202 (C. I. Bandaratilleke 42, R. S. Priyadarshana 52; W. N. M. Soysa four for 74).

At Panadura Esplanade, Panadura, December 3, 4, 5. Drawn. Antonians 165 (M. S. Sampan 34, Extras 39; T. C. B. Fernando three for 52, S. N. Liyanage four for 29) and 225 (P. K. Siriwardene 31, W. M. J. Wannukuwatta 39, W. A. L. Chaturanga 43, K. A. D. C. Silva 37 not out; T. C. B. Fernando three for 39, J. S. K. Peiris three for 35); Panadura* 193 (S. N. Liyanage 71, G. A. S. Perera 31; S. C. U. K. Fernando four for 67, C. Samarasinghe four for 70).

At P. Saravanamuttu Stadium, Colombo, December 3, 4, 5. Drawn. Colts 170 (S. I. Fernando 71; W. J. M. R. Dias four for 40, G. R. K. Wijekoon four for 47) and 139 (G. V. S. Janaka 67; G. R. K. Wijekoon three for 25, B. C. Jeganathan three for 14); Tamil Union* 141 (M. J. Sigera four for 59, S. Alexander three for 34, D. K. Liyanage three for 31).

At Galle Esplanade, Galle, December 10, 11, 12. Galle won by five wickets. Galle 349 (T. K. D. Sudarshana 36, C. M. Withanage 32, W. M. P. N. Wanasinghe 75, A. Rideegammanagedera 31, C. K. Hewamanne 59; C. Samarasinghe six for 135, K. A. D. C. Silva four for 46) and 72 for five (T. K. D. Sudarshana 38; C. Samarasinghe four for 25); Antonians* 183 (S. K. Perera 43, Y. M. W. B. Ekanayake 31, S. C. U. K. Fernando 32; A. Rideegammanagedera three for 44, K. G. Perera four for 33) and 234 (Y. M. W. B. Ekanayake 71, W. M. J. Wannukuwatta 43, C. Samarasinghe 36; K. G. Perera five for 48).

At Braybrooke Place, Colombo (Moors), December 10, 11, 12. Drawn. Colts 291 (S. I. Fernando 39, G. V. S. Janaka 42, A. S. S. P. A. Attanayake 36, K. E. A. Upashantha 49, D. K. Liyanage 41; R. S. Priyadarshana three for 80, U. C. Hathurusinghe three for 67) and 214 for seven dec. (D. P. Samaraweera 110 not out, H. G. J. M. Kulatunga 38); Moors* 173 (H. A. H. U. Tillekeratne 61, R. S. Priyadarshana 61; K. E. A. Upashantha four for 38, D. Hettiarachchi three for 53) and 240 for nine (U. C. Hathurusinghe 77; D. Hettiarachchi five for 94).

At Panadura Esplanade, Panadura, December 10, 11, 12. Drawn. Panadura 138 (S. Jayawardene 38; W. N. M. Soysa four for 24) and 284 for nine (B. P. Perera 99, D. Prasanna 35, Extras 30; I. D. Gunawardene four for 58); Police* 346 for eight dec. (P. R. T. Fernando 40, A. V. Senasinghe 72, H. M. N. C. Silva 31, M. Y. Kudagodage 51 not out, I. D. Gunawardene 39, Extras 32; K. C. Silva three for 66).

At Maitland Place, Colombo (SSC), December 10, 11, 12. Sinhalese won by seven wickets. Tamil Union 149 (G. R. K. Wijekoon 37, E. M. I. Galagoda 35; R. Dhammika three for 38) and 154 (P. S. A. N. Shiroman 31, G. R. K. Wijekoon 38; H. G. D. Nayanakantha five for 53, R. Dhammika five for 45); Sinhalese* 185 (U. A. Fernando 53; M. S. Villavarayen three for 50) and 119 for three (S. Kalawithigoda 31, U. A. Fernando 38, S. Ranatunga 30 not out).

At Havelock Park, Colombo (Colts), December 17, 18. Colts won by an innings and 142 runs. Colts* 396 (H. G. J. M. Kulatunga 151, K. E. A. Upashantha 82, S. Alexander 35, D. Hettiarachchi 30, Extras 35; P. K. Siriwardene three for 37, K. A. D. C. Silva three for 57); Antonians 97 (S. C. U. K. Fernando 32; S. I. Fernando three for five, K. E. A. Upashantha three for 27) and 157 (P. K. Siriwardene 49, K. A. D. C. Silva 30; D. Hettiarachchi four for 29, K. E. A. Upashantha five for 67).

At Panadura Esplanade, Panadura, December 17, 18, 19. Tamil Union won by an innings and 60 runs. Panadura 52 (M. S. Villavarayen five for 23, W. J. M. R. Dias four for 15) and 134

(S. Jayawardene 52, M. M. P. Silva 33; G. R. K. Wijekoon four for 35, B. C. Jeganathan three for seven); Tamil Union* 246 (B. C. Jeganathan 42, G. R. P. Peiris 43, P. S. A. N. Shiroman 50; S. Perera four for 55).

At Maitland Place, Colombo (SSC), December 17, 18, January 4. Drawn. Sinhalese 318 (D. A. Gunawardene 75, S. Kalawithigoda 49, U. A. Fernando 33, R. P. A. H. Wickremaratne 61, C. R. P. Galappathy 30; U. C. Hathurusinghe five for 70, M. A. P. Salgado three for 29) and 91 for two dec. (S. Kalawithigoda 43, W. M. S. M. Perera 34 not out); Moors* 183 (Extras 31; T. T. Samaraweera three for 19) and 126 for six (H. A. H. U. Tillekeratne 31, H. K. P. Rangana 32; T. T. Samaraweera three for 34).

This match, like some of those in Group A, was interrupted by the curfew, and resumed 17 days later, to coincide with the final day of Police's match against Galle; both Moors and Police were contending for a place in the Super League.

At Havelock Park, Colombo (Colts), December 26, 27, 28. Drawn. Galle 136 (C. M. Withanage 32, S. Sanjeewa 47; D. K. Liyanage six for 20) and 300 for seven (T. K. D. Sudarshana 68, D. D. Wickremasinghe 82, C. P. H. Ramanayake 78 not out; D. K. Liyanage three for 50, D. Hettiarachchi three for 67); Colts* 400 for eight dec. (D. P. Samaraweera 56, C. Mendis 121, G. V. S. Janaka 57, H. G. J. M. Kulatunga 58; W. M. P. N. Wanasinghe four for 67).

In Galle's second innings, Wickremasinghe and Ramanayake added 151 for the seventh wicket.

At Panadura Esplanade, Panadura, December 26, 27, 28. Drawn. Sinhalese* 402 for six dec. (D. A. Gunawardene 42, S. Kalawithigoda 115, S. Ranatunga 33, R. P. A. H. Wickremaratne 32, W. M. S. M. Perera 50 not out, T. T. Samaraweera 58 not out, Extras 42; K. C. Silva three for 52) and 123 for five dec. (D. A. Gunawardene 66 not out); Panadura 263 (J. S. K. Peiris 52, M. M. P. Silva 65, Extras 31; H. G. D. Nayanakantha four for 53, I. R. Ratnaweera four for 76) and 152 for three (I. Amithakeerthi 52 not out, M. M. P. Silva 55 not out).

At Police Park, Colombo, December 26, 27, 28. Police won by 159 runs. Police* 245 (P. R. T. Fernando 102 not out, I. D. Gunawardene 30; S. C. U. K. Fernando three for 38, K. A. D. C. Silva three for 53) and 193 for seven dec. (H. S. G. S. Silva 36, P. R. T. Fernando 86 not out; P. K. Siriwardene three for 36); Antonians 158 (Y. M. W. B. Ekanayake 48, C. Samarasinghe 38; T. A. V. H. K. Ranaweera four for 52, H. M. N. C. Silva three for 35) and 121 (W. A. L. Chaturanga 53, P. K. Siriwardene 38; W. N. M. Soysa four for 24, H. M. N. C. Silva four for 21).

At P. Saravanamuttu Stadium, Colombo, December 26, 27, 28. Tamil Union won by 84 runs. Tamil Union* 298 (P. S. A. N. Shiroman 43, B. C. Jeganathan 36, M. R. C. N Bandaratilleke 47 not out, Extras 33; U. C. Hathurusinghe four for 69, R. Herath three for 68) and 94 (R. S. Priyadarshana five for 38, R. Herath three for 16); Moors 191 (A. A. W. Gunawardene 30, H. A. H. U. Tillekeratne 39; M. Muralitharan six for 51, U. D. U. Chandana three for 48) and 117 (M. S. Villavarayen six for 50, U. D. U. Chandana three for ten).

At Police Park, Colombo, January 2, 3, 4. Galle won by 115 runs. Galle* 200 (T. K. D. Sudarshana 33, W. M. P. N. Wanasinghe 82) and 109 (C. M. Withanage 37; T. A. V. H. K. Ranaweera three for 12); Police 115 (C. P. H. Ramanayake four for 42, M. M. D. P. V. Perera four for 16) and 79 (M. M. D. P. V. Perera four for 11).

This match was postponed from December 17–19 because the Police were required for election duties. H. S. G. S. Silva carried his bat for 28 not out in Police's first innings.

Colts, Moors, Sinhalese and Tamil Union qualified for the Super League.

Super League

At Havelock Park, Colombo (BRC), January 29, 30, 31. Burgher won by six wickets. Moors 200 (V. Wijegunawardene 40, D. W. A. N. D. Vitharana 40; K. S. C. de Silva four for 65, S. Madanayake three for 30) and 227 (A. A. W. Gunawardene 34, V. Wijegunawardene 33, C. Hewawitharana 65 not out; K. S. C. de Silva three for 50, S. Weerakoon six for 50); Burgher* 327 (C. P. Handunettige 30, B. C. M. S. Mendis 39, C. U. Jayasinghe 142, S. Mackay 33; R. Herath five for 105) and 102 for four (N. S. Bopage 37).

At Maitland Crescent, Colombo (CCC), January 29, 30, 31. Tamil Union won by 207 runs. Tamil Union* 201 (G. R. P. Peiris 70, S. I. de Saram 32; I. S. Gallage five for 58, H. K. P. Jayasuriya three for 32) and 294 for eight dec. (G. R. P. Peiris 92, P. S. A. N. Shiroman 84, S. I. de Saram 37); Colombo 191 (S. K. L. de Silva 33, A. S. Polonowita 78; U. D. U. Chandana three for 43) and 97 (U. D. U. Chandana three for 23).

At Havelock Park, Colombo (Colts), January 29, 30, 31. Colts won by an innings and 217 runs. Kurunegala Youth 113 (R. R. Jaymon 36; K. E. A. Upashantha four for 34, M. J. Sigera three for 42) and 101 (W. P. U. J. C. Vaas three for 32, D. Hettiarachchi three for 38); Colts* 431 for seven dec. (D. P. Samaraweera 50, S. I. Fernando 136, R. S. Kaluwitharana 68, K. E. A. Upashantha 34, W. P. U. J. C. Vaas 54 not out; A. W. Ekanayake five for 87).

At Maitland Place, Colombo (SSC), January 29, 30, 31. Drawn. Sinhalese 297 (M. S. Atapattu 41, D. P. M. D. Jayawardene 38, R. P. A. H. Wickremaratne 89, W. M. S. M. Perera 41; W. R. S. de Silva four for 109, T. S. M. Peiris four for 71) and 202 for nine dec. (D. P. M. D. Jayawardene 94; W. R. S. de Silva three for 81, T. S. M. Peiris six for 70); Sebastianites* 309 (G. G. Ranga Yasalal 140, N. S. Wijesinghe 43; G. P. Wickremasinghe three for 79, T. T. Samaraweera four for 117) and 156 for six (H. M. P. Fernando 56, G. G. Ranga Yasalal 34).
    Sebastianites wicket-keeper H. A. P. W. Jayawardene took seven catches in the Sinhalese first innings and ten in the match.

At Maitland Crescent, Colombo (CCC), February 4, 5, 6. Drawn. Colombo* 329 (S. K. L. de Silva 59, B. Perera 79, H. K. P. Jayasuriya 45; R. S. Priyadarshana three for 62) and 93 for one (M. G. van Dort 50 not out, P. B. Ediriweera 36 not out); Moors 228 (H. A. H. U. Tillekeratne 78, M. A. P. Salgado 48; J. W. H. D. Boteju four for 29).

At Havelock Park, Colombo (Colts), February 4, 5, 6. Colts won by an innings and eight runs. Sebastianites 84 (H. A. P. W. Jayawardene 31; K. E. A. Upashantha four for 33, D. Hettiarachchi five for 20) and 148 (G. G. Ranga Yasalal 30, T. N. S. Warusamana 58; S. Alexander three for 27, D. Hettiarachchi five for 46); Colts* 240 (D. P. Samaraweera 59, G. V. S. Janaka 63, K. E. A. Upashantha 54; W. R. S. de Silva three for 62, R. A. D. C. Perera five for 53).

At Maitland Place, Colombo (SSC), February 4, 5, 6. Drawn. Sinhalese 355 for three dec. (D. A. Gunawardene 62, U. A. Fernando 46, S. Ranatunga 117 not out, A. Ranatunga 121) and 125 for two dec. (D. A. Gunawardene 50, U. A. Fernando 42); Kurunegala Youth* 251 (D. K. Ranaweera 62, D. N. Jayakody 31, J. P. Weerabaddana 32 not out, Extras 36; C. R. D. Fernando four for 65) and 119 for seven (D. N. Jayakody 30, J. P. Weerabaddana 31; T. T. Samaraweera three for 41).
    In Sinhalese's first innings, the Ranatunga brothers added 227 for the third wicket.

At P. Saravanamuttu Stadium, Colombo, February 4, 5, 6. Drawn. Tamil Union 186 (K. S. D. Kumara 36, G. R. K. Wijekoon 44, E. M. I. Galagoda 33, M. R. C. N. Bandaratilleke 32; K. S. C. de Silva four for 73, S. Weerakoon five for 48) and 217 for eight dec. (B. C. Jeganathan 55, K. S. D. Kumara 59; S. Weerakoon seven for 74); Burgher* 176 (C. P. Handunettige 59, D. S M. Warnapura 30; M. S. Villavarayen three for 69, M. R. C. N. Bandaratilleke three for 31) and 73 for one.

At Havelock Park, Colombo (BRC), February 11, 12, 13. Drawn. Sinhalese* 328 (S. Ranatunga 145, A. Ranatunga 64, Extras 34; W. C. Labrooy four for 82) and 131 (A. Ranatunga 46, T. T. Samaraweera 47 not out; K. S. C. de Silva five for 34, S. Weerakoon four for 26); Burgher 205 (B. S. M. Warnapura 72, Extras 30; G. W. S. Arunakumara three for 27, R. Dhammika three for 81, T. T. Samaraweera three for 38) and 155 for five (C. U. Jayasinghe 32, I. P. P. Batuwitarachchi 46).

At Maitland Crescent, Colombo (CCC), February 11, 12, 13. Drawn. Colombo* 363 (P. B. Ediriweera 116, B. Perera 30, H. K. P. Jayasuriya 92 not out; K. E. A. Upashantha three for 81, C. Mendis three for 51) and 94 for four (D. N. Hunukumbura 30); Colts 248 (D. P. Samaraweera 34, S. I. Fernando 38, G. V. S. Janaka 30, K. E. A. Upashantha 66; J. W. H. D. Boteju four for 30, N. S. Rupasinghe three for 65).

At Welagedera Stadium, Kurunegala, February 11, 12, 13. Tamil Union won by eight wickets. Kurunegala Youth 200 (S. C. Gunasekera 33, D. K. Samarasinghe 31; M. C. R. Fernando five for 40, M. R. C. N. Bandaratilleke three for 31) and 139 (M. S. Villavarayen three for 39, M. R. C. N. Bandaratilleke five for 27); Tamil Union* 297 for nine dec. (G. R. P. Peiris 132, K. S. D. Kumara 47, R. G. D. Sanjeewa 30, E. M. I. Galagoda 38; J. A. M. W. Kumara three for 77, S. Jayawardene three for 24) and 44 for two.

At Braybrooke Place, Colombo (Moors), February 11, 12, 13. Drawn. Moors* 257 (M. A. P. Salgado 41, K. A. S. Jayasinghe 32, M. N. R. Cooray 44, D. W. A. N. D. Vitharana 31, Extras 33; T. S. M. Peiris five for 61) and 204 (H. A. H. U. Tillekeratne 41, V. Wijegunawardene 33, C. Hewawitharana 38; K. A. D. M. Fernando four for 61, W. R. S. de Silva four for 76); Sebastianites 130 (N. Silva 39; K. K. S. Jayasinghe five for 30, R. Herath five for 40) and 200 for four (N. S. Wijesinghe 54 not out, L. R. Fernando 95).

At Havelock Park, Colombo (BRC), February 18, 19, 20. Drawn. Burgher* 248 (B. C. M. S. Mendis 81, C. U. Jayasinghe 31, I. P. P. Batuwitarachchi 32, Extras 33; M. J. Sigera five for 59, S. Alexander four for 61) and 101 for three (B. C. M. S. Mendis 37 not out); Colts 406 for nine dec. (D. P. Samaraweera 114, C. Mendis 61, S. I. Fernando 37, N. Abeyratne 43, A. S. S. P. A. Attanayake 71 not out, Extras 30; C. U. Jayasinghe three for 67, S. Weerakoon three for 99).

At Braybrooke Place, Colombo (Moors), February 18, 19, 20. Drawn. Moors 200 (M. N. R. Cooray 90, K. K. S. Jayasinghe 34; J. A. M. W. Kumara four for 69) and 386 (B. D. A. P. Ranaweera 47, C. Hewawitharana 34, K. A. S. Jayasinghe 66, K. K. S. Jayasinghe 65 not out, D. W. A. N. D. Vitharana 44, Extras 34; J. A. M. W. Kumara three for 102); Kurunegala Youth* 132 (D. K. Ranaweera 33; M. A. P. Salgado four for 11) and 82 for seven.

At Maitland Place, Colombo (SSC), February 18, 19, 20. Drawn. Sinhalese 273 (S. Ranatunga 70, C. R. P. Galappathy 62, R. Dhammika 30; A. S. Polonowita three for 41) and 150 for two (W. M. S. M. Perera 83, S. Ranatunga 43); Colombo* 408 (D. N. Hunukumbura 55, S. K. L. de Silva 213, J. W. H. D. Boteju 52, Extras 43; G. W. S. Arunakumara three for 74, T. T. Samaraweera four for 90).

At P. Saravanamuttu Stadium, Colombo, February 18, 19, 20. Drawn. Tamil Union 177 (M. C. R. Fernando 38, Extras 40; K. A. D. M. Fernando five for 80, W. R. S. de Silva four for 52) and 219 (N. Weeraman 39, B. C. Jeganathan 40; W. R. S. de Silva four for 71, S. A. L. J. Fernando three for 37); Sebastianites* 191 (G. G. Ranga Yasalal 37, N. S. Wijesinghe 45 not out, T. S. M. Peiris 32; M. S. Villavarayen three for 70, M. R. C. N. Bandaratilleke six for 67) and 168 for nine (L. R. Fernando 77; M. S. Villavarayen three for 44).

Plate Championship

At Reid Avenue, Colombo, January 29, 30, 31. Panadura won by 26 runs. Panadura 216 (L. P. C. Silva 41, T. C. B. Fernando 51, S. Perera 36) and 218 (S. Jayawardene 72, V. Abeywardene 45, L. P. C. Silva 57; P. W. Gunaratne four for 56, H. D. P. K. Dharmasena five for 57); Bloomfield* 226 (S. D. Abeynaike 48, H. D. P. K. Dharmasena 90; T. C. B. Fernando six for 89, K. C. Silva three for 22) and 182 (B. Mendis 36, B. de Silva 61 not out; T. C. B. Fernando six for 39).

At Galle Esplanade, Galle, January 29, 30, 31. Galle won by an innings and 125 runs. Galle 401 for seven dec. (C. M. Withanage 33, H. S. S. Fonseka 49, A. Rideegammanagedera 60, D. D. Wickremasinghe 100 not out, C. P. H. Ramanayake 33, Extras 64); Singha* 151 (N. Sampath 47; C. P. H. Ramanayake four for 32) and 125 (P. Milton 44; W. M. P. N. Wanasinghe six for 36).

At Maitland Place, Colombo (NCC), January 29, 30, 31. Nondescripts won by 310 runs. Nondescripts 440 for six dec. (R. P. Arnold 129, K. Sangakkara 50, P. A. de Silva 110, H. P. Tillekeratne 30, C. P. Mapatuna 57 not out) and 194 for six dec. (K. Sangakkara 40, M. N. Nawaz 100 not out; C. Samarasinghe three for 36); Antonians* 190 (D. D. M. R. Alwis 34 not out; M. I. Abdeen three for 23, M. A. Samsudeen five for 54) and 134 (K. A. D. C. Silva 53, W. M. J. Wannakuwatta 31; P. A. de Silva three for 27, R. S. Kalpage four for 39).

At Panadura Esplanade, Panadura, February 4, 5, 6. Nondescripts won by ten wickets. Nondescripts 259 (K. Sangakkara 97, H. P. Tillekeratne 53, C. P. Mapatuna 30 not out; K. C. Silva three for 38) and six for no wkt; Panadura* 68 (M. I. Abdeen four for 14, M. A. Samsudeen four for 21) and 196 (M. M. P. Silva 60, S. N. Liyanage 34, K. C. Silva 36; P. A. de Silva five for 33).

In Panadura's first-innings 68, 20 came from extras.

At Reid Avenue, Colombo, February 4, 5, 6. Bloomfield won by an innings and 104 runs. Bloomfield 401 for six dec. (B. Mendis 85, S. D. Abeynaike 31, S. Jayantha 76, H. D. P. K. Dharmasena 64 not out, A. P. R. Shaman 105; D. D. M. R. Alwis four for 42); Antonians* 164 (P. K. Siriwardene 54; H. D. P. K. Dharmasena seven for 30) and 133 (H. D. P. K. Dharmasena six for 36).

Shaman reached his hundred in 77 balls, the fastest of the season; Dharmasena took 13 for 66 in the match, the season's best return.

At Police Park, Colombo, February 6, 7, 8. Drawn. Police* 174 (H. P. A. Priyantha 36, R. C. Liyanage 39; R. D. Kottachchi three for 43, S. Sanjeewa three for 33) and 149 (H. P. A. Priyantha 45, S. A. Wijeratne 41; R. D. Kottachchi six for 46); Singha 187 (S. Sanjeewa 36, R. D. Kottachchi 53) and 94 for seven (W. N. M. Soysa three for 13).

At Reid Avenue, Colombo, February 11, 12, 13. Drawn. Galle* 274 (C. M. Withanage 40, W. M. P. N. Wanasinghe 56, P. A. R. C. Karunasena 38, C. P. H. Ramanayake 56, Extras 32; P. W. Gunaratne four for 75, H. D. P. K. Dharmasena three for 68) and 177 (H. S. S. Fonseka 59, D. D. Wickremasinghe 32; A. P. R. Shaman three for 36, H. D. P. K. Dharmasena five for 38); Bloomfield 185 (P. B. Dassanayake 40; U. Irandika four for 48) and three for one.

At Uyanwatte Stadium, Matara, February 11, 12, 13. Drawn. Antonians 136 (C. Samarasinghe 45, W. M. J. Wannukuwatta 32; K. G. A. S. Kalum four for 49, S. M. Ramzan four for 15) and seven for two; Matara* 69 (P. K. Siriwardene six for 40).
The match was called off on the second day when Matara were ruled to have altered the condition of the pitch; they were suspended from the tournament.

At Panadura Esplanade, Panadura, February 11, 12, 13. Panadura won by 99 runs. Panadura* 261 (S. Jayawardene 64, I. Amithakeerthi 32, J. S. K. Peiris 46, S. Perera 31; T. Thushara three for 58, R. D. Kottachchi five for 68) and 240 for seven dec. (S. Jayawardene 41, B. P. Perera 93, J. S. K. Peiris 40; T. R. D. Mendis three for 39); Singha 185 (S. W. C. Sanjeewa 44; T. C. B. Fernando three for 37, I. Amithakeerthi four for 47) and 217 (S. Sanjeewa 36, S. Prasad 36, V. B. de Silva 33, Extras 42; T. C. B. Fernando three for 58).

At Police Park, Colombo, February 11, 12, 13. Nondescripts won by eight wickets. Police* 151 (R. R. Wimalasiri 45; P. A. de Silva six for 29) and 67 (P. A. de Silva four for 19, R. S. Kalpage four for 30); Nondescripts 166 (P. A. de Silva 36, R. P. Hewage 36, C. P. Mapatuna 46; T. A. V. H. K. Ranaweera four for 46, W. N. M. Soysa three for 38) and 53 for two.

At De Mazenod College, Kadana, February 18, 19, 20. Drawn. Antonians 155 (P. K. Siriwardene 55, W. M. J. Wannukuwatta 45; T. Thushara six for 83) and 60 for four; Singha* 135 (D. D. M. R. Alwis six for 48).
Singha wicket-keeper S. Soysa took six catches in Antonians' first innings.

At Maitland Place, Colombo (NCC), February 18, 19, 20. Drawn. Galle* 239 (C. M. Withanage 42, D. D. Wickremasinghe 56 not out; C. M. Bandara six for 41) and 223 for five (C. M. Withanage 30, W. M. P. N. Wanasinghe 102 not out; C. M. Bandara three for 89); Nondescripts 156 (H. P. Tillekeratne 45; W. M. P. N. Wanasinghe four for 29).

At Police Park, Colombo, February 18, 19, 20. Bloomfield won by ten wickets. Police* 111 (P. R. T. Fernando 45 not out; P. P. Wickremasinghe five for 42) and 113 (I. D. Gunawardene 39; A. P. R. Shaman three for 49, P. P. Wickremasinghe three for 28); Bloomfield 222 (S. Rodrigo 40, H. D. P. K. Dharmasena 53; T. A. V. H. K. Ranaweera three for 47, S. A. Wijeratne three for 37) and six for no wkt.

CHAMPIONS

Lakspray Trophy

1988-89	{ Nondescripts CC
	{ Sinhalese SC
1989-90	Sinhalese SC

P. Saravanamuttu Trophy

1990-91	Sinhalese SC
1991-92	Colts CC
1992-93	Sinhalese SC
1993-94	Nondescripts CC

1994-95	{ Bloomfield C and AC
	{ Sinhalese SC
1995-96	Colombo CC
1996-97	Bloomfield C and AC
1997-98	Sinhalese SC

Premier Trophy

1998-99	Bloomfield C and AC
1999-2000	Colts CC

The first-class matches played by Zimbabwe A may be found in the Other A-Team Tours section.

CRICKET IN ZIMBABWE, 1999-2000

By JOHN WARD

Tatenda Taibu

This was the season when Zimbabwe expected to build on the successes of 1998-99 and earn the respect of the other Test-playing nations. Instead, it became a season of unparalleled disappointment on the international field, despite unparalleled progress on the domestic front.

Zimbabwe performed poorly in one-day tournaments in Singapore and Kenya, then suffered crushing Test defeats by Australia and South Africa. Alistair Campbell, his leadership and batting form under fire, relinquished the captaincy, and though his successor, Andy Flower, who had himself resigned the job in 1996, had an exceptional season, leading wisely, keeping wicket immaculately, playing some remarkable innings, the failures of others denied him his due reward. The return match against South Africa saw Zimbabwe bowled out for 102, then their lowest Test score, and despite some improvement against Sri Lanka they lost the one completed Test. Zimbabwe also lost three home one-day internationals to England, and in March squandered a golden opportunity to win their first West Indian Test. Needing 99 to win, they crumbled for 63, a humiliating new low.

Numerous reasons were offered. They suffered an appalling spate of injuries, especially to the bowlers and in particular their spearhead, Heath Streak. Since the previous season, moreover, their fine spin attack had been reduced to nothing. A disgruntled Adam Huckle announced his retirement, aged 28, while an arm injury cast doubts over the future of his fellow leg-spinner, Paul Strang; off-spinner Andrew Whittall lost his penetration. In such circumstances, the consistency, fitness and occasional devastating success of Henry Olonga provided rare consolation. Yet it was the batting that failed most. Grant Flower lost form completely, Campbell never regained his, and six different players were tried as Grant's opening partner. Neil Johnson tailed off after some fine performances, while Murray Goodwin tended to fall in the twenties or thirties. One success was Stuart Carlisle, who had worked hard to overcome his back-foot weakness. Too often, though, he batted down the order behind established players who were failing.

In addition, the team often cracked under pressure and, just as tellingly, were unable to maintain it. Three Tests – against Australia and South Africa in Harare, and West Indies in Jamaica – were swung by a century stand from the opposition's eighth-wicket pair. Nor did it help that from September to July they switched countries nine times. This was easily Zimbabwe's busiest season. There was, too, some dissatisfaction over their contracts with the Zimbabwe Cricket Union, and the distraction of the unsettled political situation at home.

On the domestic scene, the ZCU reinvigorated the Logan Cup. In the past, only teams from Mashonaland and Matabeleland took part, and it was usually played when the international players were free. In 1999-2000, it was staged in March, with the national side in the West Indies, and teams from the CFX Cricket Academy and two minor provinces, Manicaland and Midlands, joined in. This gave valuable experience to cricketers who had rarely played over three days, and took first-class cricket to new areas, notably the cities of Mutare (Manicaland) and Kwekwe (Midlands). Cricket in these provinces had almost died but is now thriving, thanks largely to a few enthusiasts, notably Ken Connelly of Midlands, and Peter Gillies and Mark Burmester, the former Test player, in Manicaland. Both provinces, along with Matabeleland, were strengthened by 1999 Academy students. (Each Academy player is on a three-year contract, and spends the last two coaching and playing in the provinces.)

Manicaland actually headed the league, but in the final were outclassed by the far more experienced Mashonaland. Even so, Mashonaland failed at times to impress: their batting could be erratic, the bowlers had difficulty in dismissing stubborn opposition, and a few players were unnecessarily combative and ungracious on the field. Their captain, Gus Mackay, who later led Zimbabwe A's tour of Sri Lanka, was the tournament's top wicket-taker, with 18. Gavin Rennie, unluckily dropped by Zimbabwe, scored 435 and took ten wickets with his revitalised left-arm spin; Dirk Viljoen enjoyed similar all-round success.

Manicaland, led by Burmester, owed much to the grit of their wicket-keeper/opening batsman, Neil Ferreira, an Academy graduate, who accumulated three centuries in four league matches. Gary Brent was the leading bowler. The team received enthusiastic local support in Mutare, where Bill Flower, father of the Test brothers, had begun coaching. Manicaland fielded two family pairs: cousins Guy and Andrew Whittall, and Jon and Gary Brent, uncle and nephew. Jon played his first first-class match since Zimbabwe's England tour of 1990.

Midlands depended heavily on their former Academy students, batsman Doug Marillier and bowlers David Mutendera and Raymond Price. They defeated Matabeleland by 14 runs in an exciting chase, but a fortnight later had the lowest first-class total in Zimbabwean cricket, 31, when they were bowled out by Mashonaland on a pitch described by both captains as unsuitable for first-class cricket. It was the third new low in a year, after the Academy had totalled 49 against their Australian equivalents in 1998-99 and 44 against the Sri Lankans. Price and Mutendera featured on all three occasions.

Matabeleland, with only three of the team who won the previous Logan Cup, finished bottom, without a victory. However, their young side were nearly always competitive. Mark Vermeulen, a stylish former Under 19 and Academy player, scored 197 against Midlands, while opening batsman Wisdom Siziba, a development player from the Bulawayo western townships, carried his bat against Manicaland on his first-class debut.

The Academy were the best-balanced team, along with Mashonaland, who had lent them Paul Strang as captain. Greg Lamb and Alester Maregwede, both picked for the A tour of Sri Lanka, impressed with the bat, as did Lamb with his off-breaks, while Jason Young and Travis Friend showed the potential to be genuine all-rounders. One more victory would have seen them in the final.

The Zimbabwe Board XI again played in the non-first-class UCBSA Bowl in South Africa. Bad weather hindered them in the three-day competition, but they reached the one-day final, only to be narrowly defeated by Free State B. Meanwhile, the Under-19 team should have reached the Super League of their World Cup in Sri Lanka but, like their seniors, they froze when victory was there for the taking. In South African inter-provincial age-group cricket, Zimbabwe's Under-14s had an impressive record of four victories, a draw and a one-run defeat.

The subsequent selection of the Under-19s' wicket-keeper/batsman, 16-year-old Tatenda Taibu, for the senior team's tours of the West Indies and England, along with the emergence of Mutendera at Midlands, showed that the development programme in the townships was beginning to bear fruit. Both had attended cricket-playing high schools, Churchill and Prince Edward respectively, through the ZCU scholarship scheme. Under another ZCU initiative, Mutendera and Douglas Hondo attended the MRF Pace Foundation in Chennai.

At club level, Trevor Penney again led Old Hararians to the national league and knockout titles, although they were beaten by Alexandra Sports Club for the Vigne Cup. Winstonians, a predominantly black club but captained by Andy Flower when available, made good progress and hoped for promotion to the national first league in 2000-01. Off the field, ZCU chief executive Dave Ellman-Brown worked to bring facilities up to international standards. This was most evident at Zimbabwe's two Test venues, Harare Sports Club and Queens Club, Bulawayo, which saw considerable increases in ground capacity and improved facilities for the public, players and media.

FIRST-CLASS AVERAGES, 1999-2000

BATTING

(Qualification: 200 runs)

	M	I	NO	R	HS	100s	Avge
J. A. Young (*CFX Academy*)	4	6	2	228	89*	0	57.00
N. R. Ferreira (*Manicaland*)	6	10	1	511	133	3	56.77
A. Flower (*Zimbabwe*)	5	10	2	438	129	1	54.75
D. P. Viljoen (*Mashonaland*)	5	7	1	321	173*	1	53.50
G. J. Rennie (*Mashonaland*)	9	14	0	666	152	2	47.57
M. A. Vermeulen (*Matabeleland*)	6	12	1	473	197	2	43.00
A. Maregwede (*CFX Academy*)	4	7	1	246	59	0	41.00
D. A. Marillier (*Midlands*)	6	11	0	430	149	2	39.09
G. A. Lamb (*CFX Academy*)	7	11	2	299	100*	1	33.22
C. N. Evans (*Manicaland*)	5	8	0	262	153	1	32.75
T. R. Gripper (*Mashonaland*)	5	10	0	320	86	0	32.00
N. C. Johnson (*Zimbabwe*)	5	10	1	271	75	0	30.11
G. J. Whittall (*Manicaland*)	6	11	2	257	80	0	28.55
M. G. Burmester (*Manicaland*)	5	8	0	227	89	0	28.37
M. W. Goodwin (*Zimbabwe*)	5	10	0	275	91	0	27.50
R. W. Price (*Midlands*)	7	14	0	223	82	0	15.92

* *Signifies not out.*

BOWLING

(Qualification: 10 wickets)

	O	M	R	W	BB	5W/i	Avge
A. J. Mackay (*Mashonaland*)	93.5	34	213	18	6-16	2	11.83
G. J. Rennie (*Mashonaland*)	49.3	12	130	10	7-66	1	13.00
G. A. Lamb (*CFX Academy*)	69.4	16	227	16	7-73	1	14.18
D. P. Viljoen (*Mashonaland*)	127.4	28	283	17	6-73	1	16.64
G. B. Brent (*Manicaland*)	261.1	84	536	30	5-84	1	17.86
G. D. Ferreira (*Midlands*)	66.5	10	240	13	5-45	1	18.46
L. J. Soma (*Manicaland*)	95	22	251	13	4-43	0	19.30
T. J. Friend (*CFX Academy*)	84	28	215	11	3-33	0	19.54
M. G. Burmester (*Manicaland*)	109.2	39	288	12	3-45	0	24.00
J. A. Rennie (*Matabeleland*)	79.5	23	249	10	5-70	1	24.90
B. C. Strang (*Mashonaland*)	212.4	73	479	19	7-20	1	25.21
I. A. Engelbrecht (*Matabeleland*) . .	122	27	338	13	3-52	0	26.00
A. R. Whittall (*Manicaland*)	158	33	491	16	6-151	2	30.68

	O	M	R	W	BB	5W/i	Avge
D. J. Peacock (*Mashonaland*)	111.3	22	320	10	4-8	0	32.00
R. W. Price (*Midlands*)	213.2	55	596	18	3-14	0	33.11
H. K. Olonga (*Zimbabwe*)	143.4	23	460	12	4-103	0	38.33
E. Z. Matambanadzo (*Mashonaland*)	131	26	392	10	2-41	0	39.20
D. T. Mutendera (*Midlands*)	138.5	30	475	10	2-23	0	47.50
S. P. Lawson (*Manicaland*)	141.5	27	483	10	3-14	0	48.30

LOGAN CUP, 1999-2000

	Played	Won	Lost	Drawn	Bonus points Batting	Bonus points Bowling	Points
Manicaland	4	2	0	2	5	16	51
Mashonaland	4	2	0	2	6	14	50
CFX Academy	4	1	0	3	6	15	42
Midlands	4	1	3	0	1	12	25
Matabeleland	4	0	3	1	4	16	23

Final: Mashonaland beat Manicaland by 257 runs.

Outright win = 12 pts; drawn match = 3 pts.
Bonus points are awarded for the first 120 overs of each team's first innings. One batting point is awarded for the first 200 runs and for every subsequent 50, to a maximum of four points. One bowling point is awarded for the third wicket taken and for every subsequent two.

*In the following scores, * by the name of a team signifies that they won the toss.*

At Country Club, Harare, March 3, 4, 5. Drawn. CFX Academy* 245 (A. Maregwede 59, P. A. Strang 72, J. A. Young 47; D. P. Viljoen four for 42) and 221 for seven dec. (T. J. Friend 35, C. Delport 34, J. A. Young 34); Mashonaland 272 (G. J. Rennie 152; G. A. Lamb four for 12). *CFX Academy 8 pts, Mashonaland 9 pts.*

At Kwekwe Sports Club, Kwekwe, March 3, 4, 5. Manicaland won by an innings and four runs. Midlands* 95 (D. A. Marillier 30; G. B. Brent four for 12, T. G. Denyer three for 27) and 258 (R. W. Price 82, D. A. Marillier 65, Extras 34; L. J. Soma four for 43, G. B. Brent four for 65); Manicaland 357 for seven dec. (N. R. Ferreira 133, P. K. Gada 34, M. G. Burmester 89, Extras 30). *Manicaland 18 pts, Midlands 1 pt.*

At Harare Sports Club, Harare, March 10, 11, 12. Manicaland won by four wickets. Matabeleland* 175 (D. D. Ebrahim 76; G. B. Brent three for 67) and 150 (W. T. Siziba 40 not out; G. B. Brent four for 16, S. P. Lawson three for 14); Manicaland 116 (N. R. Ferreira 31, Extras 33) and 213 for six (M. G. Burmester 53, P. K. Gada 44; I. A. Engelbrecht three for 52). *Manicaland 16 pts, Matabeleland 4 pts.*
    This match was played at a neutral venue because of the distance and lack of air service between Bulawayo and Mutare. Siziba carried his bat through Matabeleland's second innings on first-class debut.

At Kwekwe Sports Club, Kwekwe, March 10, 11, 12. CFX Academy won by eight wickets. Midlands 183 (G. R. Savory 35, G. D. Ferreira 46, C. A. Grant 39; T. J. Friend three for 33) and 247 (D. A. Marillier 149; G. A. Lamb seven for 73); CFX Academy* 343 (A. Maregwede 52, R. J. King 38, T. J. Friend 38, J. A. Young 89 not out, C. Delport 33) and 90 for two (A. Maregwede 45 not out, C. Delport 36). *CFX Academy 18 pts, Midlands 3 pts.*
    Marillier hit 149 from 155 balls, with two sixes and 25 fours.

At Mutare Sports Club, Mutare, March 17, 18, 19. Drawn. Manicaland 287 (N. R. Ferreira 106, M. G. Burmester 39, G. J. Whittall 30; D. P. Viljoen six for 73) and 77 for two (N. R. Ferreira 32 not out); Mashonaland* 353 for nine dec. (G. J. Rennie 50, T. N. Madondo 32, D. P. Viljoen 66, D. J. Peacock 42, A. J. Mackay 51, A. P. Hoffman 37 not out; A. R. Whittall three for 126, S. P. Lawson three for 97). *Manicaland 9 pts, Mashonaland 9 pts.*
    The inaugural first-class match in Mutare.

At Kwekwe Sports Club, Kwekwe, March 17, 18, 19. Midlands won by 14 runs. Midlands 204 (D. A. Marillier 133, G. R. Savory 32; M. D. Abrams four for 46) and 282 (R. W. Price 76, D. A. Marillier 33, D. T. Mutendera 51, E. R. Marillier 46 not out; M. D. Abrams three for 34, I. A. Engelbrecht three for 70); Matabeleland* 292 (M. A. Vermeulen 197, M. W. Townshend 32 not out; R. W. Price three for 78, G. D. Ferreira four for 55) and 180 (W. T. Siziba 35, D. D. Ebrahim 43, W. Gilmour 33 not out; G. D. Ferreira five for 45). *Midlands 17 pts, Matabeleland 6 pts.*

Douglas Marillier scored 65 per cent of Midlands' first innings, and Vermeulen 67 per cent of Matabeleland's reply; Vermeulen batted 316 minutes and 268 balls for 197, his maiden first-class century, hitting eight sixes and 18 fours.

At Mutare Sports Club, Mutare, March 24, 25, 26. Drawn. CFX Academy* 191 (K. P. R. Went 37, G. A. Lamb 100 not out; A. R. Whittall five for 47) and 250 for five (M. J. Vaughan-Davies 61, T. J. Friend 39, P. A. Strang 74 not out); Manicaland 288 (N. R. Ferreira 121, A. R. Whittall 42, Extras 31; J. A. Young three for 30). *Manicaland 8 pts, CFX Academy 6 pts.*

Jon Brent, aged 44, returned to first-class cricket, alongside his nephew Gary, having last played on Zimbabwe's 1990 tour of England; he scored one run and took three wickets for Manicaland.

At Bulawayo Athletic Club, Bulawayo, March 24, 25, 26. Mashonaland won by 276 runs. Mashonaland 170 (G. J. Rennie 32, D. P. Viljoen 36, D. J. R. Campbell 32; J. A. Rennie five for 70) and 448 for four dec. (D. R. Matambanadzo 50, D. J. Peacock 41, D. P. Viljoen 173 not out, C. N. Evans 153); Matabeleland* 256 (M. A. Vermeulen 87, J. A. Rennie 63) and 86 (S. K. Nyakutse 41; A. J. Mackay four for 30, C. N. Evans four for five). *Mashonaland 16 pts, Matabeleland 6 pts.*

In the second innings, Viljoen and Evans added 330 in 51 overs (213 minutes) for Mashonaland's fourth wicket, an all-wicket Zimbabwean record. Evans's full analysis was 6–5–5–4.

At Country Club, Harare, March 31, April 1, 2. Drawn. Matabeleland 176 (C. K. Coventry 42, W. Gilmour 31) and 207 for two (W. T. Siziba 54, M. A. Vermeulen 103 not out); CFX Academy* 316 (A. Maregwede 45, G. A. Lamb 78, T. J. Friend 48, P. A. Strang 37, J. A. Young 32, G. H. Haakonsen 45; K. M. Dabengwa five for 76). *CFX Academy 10 pts, Matabeleland 7 pts.*

At Harare Sports Club, Harare, March 31, April 1, 2. Mashonaland won by 251 runs. Mashonaland 165 (K. J. Davies 45; R. W. Price three for 14) and 173 for eight dec. (G. J. Rennie 41, C. N. Evans 36, A. J. Mackay 41; C. J. Saunders three for 56); Midlands* 31 (A. J. Mackay six for 16, B. T. Watambwa four for 15) and 56 (A. J. Mackay five for 19, D. J. Peacock four for eight). *Mashonaland 16 pts, Midlands 4 pts.*

On a substandard pitch, Midlands scored 31 in 12.5 overs, the lowest total in Zimbabwean first-class cricket; their match aggregate of 87 was another low.

FINAL

MASHONALAND v MANICALAND

At Harare Sports Club, Harare, April 7, 8, 9. Mashonaland won by 257 runs. Mashonaland 19 pts, Manicaland 4 pts. Toss: Manicaland.

Though Manicaland headed the table, the final had been scheduled for Mashonaland's home ground; Manicaland were also missing several top players, and fielded four schoolboys. They fought gallantly, but were badly outclassed. Nerves resulted in vital dropped catches on the first day; Gripper had three lives and finished with 86. Next day, Manicaland struggled for runs. Hamilton Masakadza batted nearly four hours for a fifty on first-class debut, and Soma was the only other to reach double figures. Left-arm seamer Strang, like Gripper newly returned from the West Indies, picked up seven wickets while conceding less than a run an over. Mackay chose not to enforce the follow-on and, with Rennie and Gripper enjoying their second century opening stand, Mashonaland extended their lead to 497 by the close. On the third day, Rennie's left-arm spin brought him, too, seven wickets. He completed Mashonaland's victory shortly after tea, despite determined fifties from Ferreira and Stuart Matsikenyeri.

Close of play: First day, Manicaland 8-0 (Ferreira 4*, Masakadza 3*); Second day, Mashonaland 275-5 (Peacock 38*, E. Z. Matambanadzo 31*).

Mashonaland

G. J. Rennie c Gada b Burmester	52	– st Ferreira b Masakadza	87
T. R. Gripper c Ferreira b Soma	86	– c Gada b Burmester	78
D. R. Matambanadzo c Sparrow b Gada	22	– c Burmester b Lawson	19
D. J. Peacock b Lawson	0	– (5) not out	38
C. N. Evans lbw b Burmester	27	– (4) run out	10
B. I. Robinson b Soma	61		
†D. J. R. Campbell c Denyer b Masakadza	50		
*A. J. Mackay c Masakadza b Soma	13	– (6) st Ferreira b Matsikenyeri	5
B. C. Strang c James b Soma	14		
A. P. Hoffman c Ferreira b Burmester	0		
E. Z. Matambanadzo not out	4	– (7) not out	31
L-b 6, w 8, n-b 2	16	B 2, l-b 1, w 3, n-b 1	7

1/126 2/163 3/164 4/196 5/197   **345**   1/155 2/172 3/196   (5 wkts dec.) **275**
6/282 7/311 8/332 9/337   4/216 5/234

Bonus points – Mashonaland 3, Manicaland 4.

Bowling: *First Innings*—Soma 28–2–63–4; Sparrow 9–1–22–0; Burmester 15–3–45–3; Gada 19–2–70–1; Lawson 21–2–97–1; Denyer 3–0–20–0; Masakadza 7–1–22–1. *Second Innings*—Soma 5–0–21–0; Sparrow 3–0–31–0; Burmester 11.2–1–69–1; Gada 4–0–28–0; Lawson 16–0–78–1; Masakadza 3.4–1–9–1; Matsikenyeri 6–0–36–1.

Manicaland

†N. R. Ferreira b Strang	8	– c Mackay b Hoffman	55
H. Masakadza c Campbell b Strang	53	– (4) c and b Rennie	4
P. K. Gada b Strang	0	– lbw b Rennie	18
S. P. Lawson c Campbell b Hoffman	2	– (2) c E. Z. Matambanadzo b Mackay	7
*M. G. Burmester lbw b Rennie	9	– c Mackay b Rennie	20
S. Matsikenyeri c Campbell b Strang	9	– not out	73
D. Yatras b Strang	0	– c D. R. Matambanadzo b Rennie	32
T. G. Denyer b Strang	4	– lbw b Gripper	0
L. J. Soma st Campbell b Rennie	23	– c Evans b Rennie	7
J. W. Sparrow lbw b Strang	0	– (11) b Rennie	2
B. W. James not out	2	– (10) c and b Rennie	3
B 5, l-b 1, w 4, n-b 3	13	B 14, l-b 5	19

1/12 2/12 3/19 4/41 5/81   **123**   1/12 2/51 3/55 4/87 5/154   **240**
6/81 7/92 8/111 9/111   6/207 7/210 8/229 9/238

Bonus points – Mashonaland 4.

Bowling: *First Innings*—Mackay 11–3–28–0; Strang 21–12–20–7; Hoffman 7–4–6–1; E. Z. Matambanadzo 7–2–14–0; Peacock 6–1–15–0; Rennie 8.4–1–29–2; Gripper 1–0–5–0. *Second Innings*—Strang 14–6–27–0; Mackay 6–2–11–1; E. Z. Matambanadzo 5–1–11–0; Evans 2–1–2–0; Peacock 7–1–32–0; Rennie 23.5–4–66–7; Gripper 15–3–59–1; Hoffman 4–1–13–1.

Umpires: I. D. Robinson and R. B. Tiffin.

LOGAN CUP WINNERS

CRICKET IN BANGLADESH, 1999-2000

By UTPAL SHUVRO

For the second time in just over a year, Bangladesh turned its gaze towards England, and once again the news coming back to the subcontinent triggered an outpouring of national pride and joy. In 1999, the magical day was May 31, when Bangladesh beat Pakistan against the odds in the World Cup. But June 26, 2000 would become a much more significant date in the nation's cricket heart. It was then that the dream seed, planted as ICC associate membership in 1977, reached full bloom with the unanimous decision of the ICC Annual General Meeting at Lord's to welcome Bangladesh into the Test family as its tenth member.

The reality of Test cricket arrived on November 10, and for four historic days Bangladesh played host to India. It was an occasion for colourful, noisy celebration, which peaked when Aminul Islam marked his country's Test debut with a century. Aminul, who had lost the captaincy in between the granting of Test status and the inaugural match, became only the third batsman, after Australia's Charles Bannerman in 1877 and Zimbabwe's Dave Houghton in 1992, to achieve this feat. He went on to make 145, batting in all for almost nine hours. Bangladesh's first innings in the highest class produced 400 runs, but the Indians overtook this and then reminded the newcomers that cricket is a game with as many lows as highs. They bowled out Bangladesh for 91 and won by nine wickets.

Although the Bangladesh Cricket Board had been planning for Test cricket over some years, when the moment came they were left with little time to prepare a pitch for the maiden Test. Dhaka's Bangabandhu Stadium had been built primarily for cricket but, after Bangladesh's emergence as an independent nation, it had become a multi-purpose venue. While Bangladeshis looked forward to their own first Test there, the national stadium was being used for soccer. It was welcome news that the government was taking steps to have separate facilities for domestic cricket and soccer, so leaving the Bangabandhu for international events only.

The programme leading to Test-match status gave an international flavour to the 1999-2000 season. The ICC had specified that Bangladesh should satisfy certain standards in first-class matches against touring teams, and, to this end, there were visits from the West Indians in early October, England A later in October and November, and MCC in January. In April, Bangladesh had the pleasure of hosting the high point of ICC's cricket week, the one-day game between Asia and the Rest of the World. Some 50,000 watched in fascination as Michael Bevan's amazing 185 not out took his side to within one run of Asia's winning 320 for nine.

May and June brought the Asia Cup to Bangladesh. The monsoon threatened a washout, but the rains relented in time for the tournament to start a day late. Bangladesh lost all three games, and in the last were bowled out for their lowest one-day total, 87, as Pakistan won by 233 runs, at the time the widest margin of victory in a one-day international. The pessimists started questioning the possibility of Test status after this disaster.

Happily, the right impression had been registered in the earlier first-class matches. All four had been drawn, but this was an improvement on a first-class record that previously read played five, lost five. And whereas Bangladesh had recorded only one century in those five games, the first-class programme against their 1999-2000 visitors produced four centuries. Habibul Bashar made 143 not out in the three-day match against England A at Chittagong, while the four-day game at Dhaka saw wicket-keeper Khaled Masud save Bangladesh with his unbeaten 105 in the second innings. But the best was saved for MCC, a side full of county players. Opener Shahriar Hossain made 133 and 121 not out, the first Bangladeshi to hit a hundred in each innings, and captain Aminul hit 113 not out as Bangladesh compiled 303 for three on the first day.

Another ICC stipulation, however, provoked an unexpected reaction. Bangladesh had been urged to organise their domestic cricket to provide a first-class structure, and a National League was set up. It comprised six divisional teams – Dhaka, Chittagong, Khulna, Rajshahi, Barisal and Sylhet – who would play each other on a home and away basis. First, though, the new competition had to overcome opposition from the players. Generally speaking, cricketers had earned little for representing their nation; the clubs, being the target for sponsorship and funding, were their major source of earning. Consequently, the leading players felt that the authorities were adopting a stepmotherly attitude by transferring them out of their traditional harvesting ground to play in the National League divisions. They called a strike, with the result that the competition had to start with lesser-known names and unknown newcomers. When national team members boycotted the four-day match between Dhaka Metropolis XI and MCC, the BCB hurriedly filled the home side with budding stars. Finally the Board's president intervened in the dispute; within a week the stars were back on the field, representing Bangladesh against MCC at the National Stadium. Cricket was rolling nicely again.

With the leading players on board at last, the National League also enjoyed a happy conclusion. Chittagong dominated throughout to win the title, with Sylhet runners-up. Dhaka, with most of the national team at their disposal, fared poorly and were fifth. The 1999-2000 matches were not first-class, this status being held back until the 2000-01 competition.

The board sought to prevent future conflicts of interest between club and representative commitments by putting 18 select players under contract. There were three categories of contract, to be reviewed annually. In another move towards a more professional approach, the board appointed a chief executive, although he will be known as the general manager: the BCB prefer to be different in this regard.

While the 64-district National Championship gave way to the new National League, the attractive Dhaka Premier League continued to provide its usual charm. As always, the appearance of Test and first-class cricketers from India, Pakistan and Sri Lanka added interest to the club scene. Abahani clinched their sixth title in eight seasons, but it was a close-run thing. After losing their last three matches, they finished level on points with Kalabagan and needed their superior run-rate to win the day.

Abahani's coach, Sarwar Imran, was asked to look after the national team for the Asia Cup tournament after Eddie Barlow, the director of coaching, was partially paralysed by a stroke in April. Barlow, a former South African Test all-rounder, had been appointed in September with a brief to convince the ICC that Bangladesh were ready for Test cricket. After his stroke he was taken to Singapore for treatment, and then to a clinic in Cape Town to recuperate. His discharge could not have come at a more serendipitous time, just before the ICC met at Lord's in June. His subsequent return to Bangladesh, to take over his charges again, was welcomed warmly by the country's cricket-loving millions.

At Dhaka, January 25, 26, 27. Drawn. Toss: MCC. Bangladesh 303 for three dec. (Shahriar Hossain 133, Aminul Islam 113 not out) and 226 for two dec. (Shahriar Hossain 121 not out, Habibul Bashar 85); MCC 218 for three dec. (M. J. Wood 70, B. F. Smith 113 not out) and 234 for eight (W. J. House 50, B. F. Smith 56, A. McGrath 41, P. A. Nixon 36; Hasibul Hussain four for 46).
Shahriar Hossain was the first Bangladeshi to score twin first-class hundreds. Umpire Nadir Shah failed to arrive on time on the second day, and had to be replaced by reserve umpire Ashiqur Rahman.

Bangladesh's first-class matches v the West Indians and v England A may be found in the West Indians in Bangladesh and England A tour sections respectively.

CRICKET IN KENYA, 2000

By JASMER SINGH

A momentous year for Kenyan cricket reached its well-planned climax with the staging of the second ICC Knockout tournament at the Nairobi Gymkhana Club in October. The biggest sporting event to have taken place in Kenya, it was officially opened by President Daniel Arap Moi, making his first visit to a cricket match. The draw pitted the hosts against India in the opening game, and while Kenya were beaten they were not disgraced, making 208 for nine in their 50 overs after being put in.

The tournament had taken the Kenya Cricket Association one year to organise, with the ICC providing guidance and support to the 14 sub-committees set up to plan the event. Hundreds of workers were involved and could look back with justifiable pride on the success of a fortnight of wonderful cricket involving all 11 one-day international countries. In its editorial the day after New Zealand beat India in the final, the *East African Standard* wrote that "The tournament has come and gone, leaving Kenyans with fond memories of a world-class event at their doorstep. This was the start of a positing journey, that could see Kenya given much bigger events to host before finally taking her place among Test nations." Kenya's application to the ICC for Test status has been proposed by West Indies and seconded by Zimbabwe, and the country's cricket officials were pleased to welcome the governing body's administrators to Nairobi for various ICC board meetings during the Knockout tournament.

Alongside the administrative planning went the national team's own preparation on the playing field. It meant there was no break for the players when their domestic season ended in March, and April found them in Zimbabwe, where they won the Emerging Nations tournament that formed part of the ICC Cricket Week. The other teams were Zimbabwe A, Denmark, Holland, Ireland and Scotland; apart from their washed-out opening game, Kenya won all their matches by large margins. Star batsman Steve Tikolo was named Player of the Tournament for his 310 runs in five innings at an average of 103.33.

Two days after returning from Zimbabwe, the Kenyan team set off on a five-week tour of India. Overcoming the extreme May temperatures, they won three of their four one-day games and the two-day 90-over match against Maharashtra Cricket Association: Tikolo hit 173 off 199 balls and Ravindu Shah 103 as Kenya ran up 432 for eight on the first day. The three-day games against Mumbai CA President's XI, Baroda CA XI and Gujarat CA President's XI were drawn. To cope with Agra's oppressive heat, the hours of play against Baroda were 8 a.m. to 1.20 p.m. Shah hit another hundred in the Gujarat game, and Tikolo ended the tour with an average of 116.50 from his 466 runs.

Home again, the Kenyans hosted tours in quick succession from Pakistan A, Indian state side Karnataka, and the South Africa Academy. Pakistan boasts one of the stronger A teams in the game, and not even Tikolo's brilliant 131 not out could save Kenya from defeat in the opening one-day match in the coastal city of Mombasa. Undeterred by this setback, however, the home players rallied to win the series 4–1. Thomas Odoyo, Kenya's gifted young all-rounder, was Man of the Series after making successive scores of 59, 82, 62 not out, 65 and 76 not out and taking nine wickets. There were also good knocks of 95 not out, 86 and 66 from Kennedy Otieno. The four-day match against the tourists, Kenya's first over this distance, was drawn.

There were equally impressive results against Karnataka, Ranji Trophy champions three times in the previous five years and containing a number of Indian Test players. Kenya took the five-match one-day series 3–1, with one match abandoned, and had the upper hand in the drawn three-day fixture. Set 307 to win in 67 overs, they were 255 for two at the close, with Shah 114 not out and Tikolo 92 not out after adding 153. Kenya's 19-year-old slow left-armer, Mohammad Sheikh, outshone Test spinners Vijay Bharadwaj and Sunil Joshi in capturing 13 wickets during the tour games.

The day that Karnataka flew out, the Academy side flew in from South Africa. As Kenya lost one three-day match and drew the other, and shared the honours in the one-day games, it was beginning to look as if the demands of constant cricket were taking their toll. In the Africa Cup in Nairobi that followed, Kenya, who along with South Africa and Zimbabwe fielded a development side, won the tournament without losing a match.

There were also honours off the field for Kenyan cricket in 2000. As well as Jimmy Rayani, chairman of the Kenya Cricket Association, being on the ICC executive board, vice-chairman Harilal Shah was elected to the cricket committee. In October, the ICC appointed former Kenyan captain Tom Tikolo to be development officer for East Africa. Plans progressed to set up Kenya's first cricket academy, at the Simba Union club, and it was hoped this would be operational early in 2001. Another important development in nurturing cricket at grassroots and schools levels was the establishment of the Kenya Women's Cricket Association.

CRICKET IN DENMARK, 2000

By PETER S. HARGREAVES

Participation in the third European Championship, in Scotland in July, was the focal point of the year for the Danish *landshold*, or national team. As Denmark had finished third and second in the two previous tournaments, a fair result was expected. In the event, they lost all five matches and finished last in Division One, which created a crisis back home. In Denmark, the game's international activities are financed according to performance, so the worse the side does, the harder the way back is. It's a Catch-22 situation.

What went wrong? For a start, the tournament was played on grass pitches for the first time, which immediately made it a different and difficult proposition for the Danes. Denmark has only one natural square, in Copenhagen, on which the team could practise, so work elsewhere was imperative. The ICC Cricket Week in April provided the opportunity to travel to Harare for the Emerging Nations tournament. Results were moderate, but with two wins they finished ahead of hosts Zimbabwe A and Scotland. Before leaving for the European Championship, Denmark squared two matches against a good MCC side on the turf pitch in Copenhagen, and followed this with warm-up matches in England against Nottinghamshire and Derbyshire scratch sides.

It was at this point that injuries were revealed and the fitness of several key players came into doubt. By the final selection of the Championship squad, two of the faster bowlers were out of commission: Martin Jensen, Denmark's bowler of the year in 1999, and Lars Hedegaard. In addition, Lars's brother Morten, the captain and best all-rounder, was hampered by a bad leg, and eventually missed Denmark's final game, against Holland; Aftab Ahmed, the side's best batsman, played through the tournament with a finger injury. Two other batsmen also suffered injured fingers.

Out of this predicament it was not easy to select highlights in individual performances, but two who did stand out were the opening bowlers – Thomas Hansen, regarded as superfluous by Hampshire after they signed Alan Mullally, and Amjad Khan, who was due to join Kent in August. Once they finished their spells, however, the support offered little threat, in stark contrast to the position of previous years. With the exception of the Italy game, when Denmark made 233 for nine, chasing 243, the batting never gelled.

The next concern is how Denmark will fare in the 2001 ICC Trophy in Canada. The demands will be heavy, with much depending on the extent to which the younger players come on. The average age of the European Championship side was 23 – the youngest ever to represent Denmark. They have talent and are undaunted, at least.

Denmark's interest in the NatWest Trophy was limited to the second round, in which they were knocked out by the Durham Board XI at Hartlepool. It was there that the injuries to the bowlers first occurred. One Dane to emerge from this competition with credit, however, was the country's leading umpire, Johan Luther, who stood in the early rounds, and also umpired at the European Championship.

On the domestic scene, long-term champions Svanholm again successfully defended their title, though only after a play-off against Herning, who ran them close for the second year in succession, finishing equal on points in the eight-team elite division. The previous weekend, Herning had actually beaten Svanholm. At the foot of the division, KB and Chang had to give way to promoted Husum and Ishøj for 2001, when a reconstruction of the lower divisions takes effect. Herning won the knockout cup for the third time in four years, beating Glostrup in the final. In the women's competitions, a notable advance by Herning saw them finish as champions ahead of Glostrup, with Nykøbing Mors beating AB for third place. Herning show every sign of providing the basis for future national sides. Earlier in the season, for reasons not entirely of their own making, Glostrup had had to default to Nykøbing Mors in the knockout cup final.

CRICKET IN THE NETHERLANDS, 2000

By DAVID HARDY

The Dutch team's last full year of preparation for the 2001 ICC Trophy in Canada was a useful and generally successful one. The obvious highlights were the retention of the European Championship, contested in Scotland in July, and second place to Kenya in the ICC Emerging Nations tournament in Zimbabwe in April. Less convincing, however, was Holland's performance in the NatWest Trophy. In contrast to 1999, when they beat first-class Durham to reach the fourth round, the Dutch fell at the first hurdle to a minor county, Lincolnshire, losing by 95 runs at Grantham. A degree of complacency, the absence of their inspirational Barbadian coach, Emmerson Trotman (whose home in Enschede had been badly damaged a few days earlier when a nearby firework factory caught fire), and the bowlers' lack of penetration all contributed to their early exit.

Trotman's role in the continuing resurgence of the Dutch national team is an important one. The captain, Roland Lefebvre, has committed himself through to the World Cup in 2003, and a stable side has begun to emerge around a nucleus of players: opening batsmen Robert van Oosterom and Pakistani-born Ahmed Zulfiqar, middle-order batsmen Klaas Jan van Noortwijk, Tim de Leede and New Zealander Roger Bradley, heavy-hitting all-rounder Luuk van Troost, wicket-keeper/batsman Roland Scholte, and another Pakistani, Asim Khan, opening the bowling with Lefebvre. It is hoped that Andre van Troost, Luuk's brother, available for Holland since retiring from English county cricket, and Sussex professional Bas Zuiderent will also be available for major tournaments. Zuiderent is attempting to become the first Dutch cricketer to make his mark in county cricket purely as a batsman, his predecessors – Paul-Jan Bakker, Lefebvre and van Troost – all being bowlers. Feiko Kloppenburg, a useful all-rounder who starred in the 1999 NatWest run, ruled himself out in order to concentrate on his studies. What the side does need is a class spinner to give it balance, and hopes are high that the promising Pakistani teenager, Luqman Tariq, could fill this role.

European Championship success in Scotland was resounding, with all five matches – against Ireland, Italy, Denmark, England and hosts Scotland – won. The victory over Scotland was especially noteworthy. Holland began the last over, bowled by Greig Williamson, requiring 16 to win: Scholte hit the first ball for six, and another six off the penultimate ball was followed by two runs off the last to seal a sensational victory. Scholte was obviously a hero, but equally so was van Oosterom, who chose the right time to make his first century in more than 100 matches for Holland.

The Dutch Premier League (*Hoofdklasse*) was won by Excelsior '20 of Schiedam, whose 15 wins in 18 games put them two points (or one win) clear of HBS The Hague. A club with a village-cricket atmosphere and a small ground to match, Excelsior have been the success story of the past decade. Without a national championship title in 71 years before 1991, they have now made it six in ten seasons. Michael Dighton, their professional from Western Australia, was the Premier League's leading run-maker with 837 at 49.23. VRA Amstelveen's New Zealand professional, Craig Cumming, topped the batting averages with 789 runs at 56.35, and Luuk van Troost (45.30) had the best average of the Dutch players.

Former New Zealand Test bowler Chris Pringle, of HCC The Hague, finished best bowler for the third time in five seasons, with the most wickets (43) and the best average (11.90), while young bowlers Sebastiaan Gokke and Luqman Tariq also averaged under 15. Another New Zealander, Darron Reekers, professional at Quick CC The Hague, produced one of the home season's highlights when he made history by hitting six sixes in one over. The suffering bowler, of all people, was Dutch legend Steven Lubbers, playing for relegated Koninklijke UD of Deventer. It was the first time this feat had been achieved in a Premier League match.

A policy of adopting the playing conditions of international one-day cricket resulted in a number of changes in 2000. Most obvious was the introduction of coloured clothing, though only in pastel shades of blue, yellow and grey as a red ball was still being used. Matches were 50 overs a side, with a maximum of ten per bowler – and for the first time in living memory the lunch and tea intervals merged into a long lunch-cum-tea break between innings. Other regulations such as no-balls and wides counting double, and fielding restrictions, were also implemented.

Dutch teams participated in the year's two major international youth tournaments, the Under-19 World Cup in Sri Lanka in January and the Under-15 World Challenge (fielding an Under-16 team) in England during the summer. Neither met with conspicuous success but both gained invaluable experience. Cricket is not widely played by young people in The Netherlands, but the national age-group teams do enjoy excellent coaching facilities and the opportunity to compete at the highest level. Something like half, around 1,500, of the active cricketers in The Netherlands now come from non-Dutch backgrounds, and an interesting development has been the growing prominence of Pakistani-born cricketers in Dutch teams.

One-day international status remains Holland's ultimate goal. The hope is that further development of the facilities at the VRA club in Amstelveen, providing more and better grass pitches, will bring this ambition closer to reality. The appointment to the full ICC committee of the Royal Dutch Cricket Association (KNCB) chairman, Rene van Ierschot, himself an ex-international cricketer, will do the Dutch cause no harm.

CRICKET ROUND THE WORLD, 2000

ARGENTINA

The first-ever Americas' Cup, in Toronto, gave Argentina a chance to pit themselves against teams with far more cricketers to choose from. Despite a brave performance against the US, the Argentines, playing out of season, came last of five in a tournament won by hosts Canada. Even so, Grant Dugmore, the national coach, insisted Argentina were the keenest, best-disciplined and best-mannered of the sides. The local season was more successful. The idea of getting a professional to turn out with each of the four local first division sides was a good one and the overall standard of play benefited accordingly. St Alban's Scholars, with Dugmore on their side, ran away with the regular Premier League, suffering defeat only once, against Belgrano. Captain Chris Tuñón led from the front and had a solid batting and fielding side plus the crafty left-arm spinner, Hernán Pereyra. The 101st annual three-day North–South match resulted in a win for the South by 23 runs after a see-sawing match. Tommy Francis scored 104 for them. Against St Alban's Scholars, a Lomas batsman was given timed out for dawdling on his way to the wicket. Lomas were involved in another unusual scorecard entry when they reached 290 for six to beat Hurlingham with two balls to spare. They should have applauded their top scorer to the pavilion for making 105. However, his name was Extras: 78 of the runs were wides. – David Parsons.

BELGIUM

In 2000, Belgian cricket suffered downpours and floods until the end of July, and despite playing on magic carpets we had to abandon many games. Only in August did the sun finally shine. A wonderfully cheery and social MCC side then toured Belgium and Luxembourg, and even had the good grace to allow the XI raised by the Belgian Cricket Federation's president, Ken Farmiloe, to beat them at the idyllic Antwerp CC ground. Flemish cyclists stopped under the fruit trees on the boundary to watch as David Moyson, born and bred in Belgium, hit the winning runs. Belgium's ambitions have advanced since the 1996 MCC tour, when draws were the best that could be managed. In the domestic league (15 teams in two divisions), Pakistan (Greens) CC, led by all-rounder Wasiq Syed, yet again pipped Royal Brussels CC. With a steady stream of talented young newcomers from the subcontinent, the Greens are hard to beat. However, a new rival outfit, Khan CC, were promoted in their first season and should provide memorable clashes in 2001. Belgian cricket has now extended to the coast with the formation of Ostend CC, and touring sides, principally from the UK, with the strong pound in their pockets and the cheap beer flowing freely, provided social highlights to many weekends. For some reason, they usually scored more runs on the Saturday than the Sunday. – Colin Wolfe.

BRUNEI DARUSSALAM

Alas, a large window, broken by a well-struck straight six, resulted in cricket being banned from the Shell Recreation ground. Two years earlier, the siting of soccer goals 15 yards from the bat at short mid-wicket had added an interesting dimension to the game. Although not proving as inconvenient as one might imagine, it was a sign of things to come. Cricket in Brunei is now restricted to the Panaga ground, and is down to five teams including the now homeless Shell Recreation Club. An early-season match between Panaga and Manggis provided an astonishing result. Manggis won the toss and elected to bat, as their Pakistani players had been attending a function in honour of a visiting government minister and were due to arrive a little late. Unfortunately, they lost seven wickets for seven, and were thus all out before the missing players could arrive. Panaga won by eight wickets, and went on to win the league. Royal Brunei Yacht Club, as usual, won the Galfar Knockout Cup. Towards the end of the season, Brunei defeated Sabah and Sarawak to win the Borneo Cup, which Sabah had held for the previous two years. – Derek Thursby.

CANADA

Y2K bugs did not destroy our computers, but they did play havoc with Canada's plans, preparations and vision for the ICC Trophy 2001 in Toronto, and eventual one-day international status. The year was an emotional roller-coaster ride that threatened to derail us. The second successive cancellation of the Sahara Cup series between India and Pakistan was a serious blow. In 1999, West Indies had stepped in to lessen the financial punishment, but this time no replacement was available and the huge loss threatened our plans. Canada thank key ICC officials for their hard work. Faced with match-fixing and other nightmares, they stayed the course: optimism, patience and hard work were brought to bear to avoid cancellation of the largest international cricket tournament in the world, and plans are now back on course. Ten separate turf squares, prepared by Mike Corley, groundsman at Scarborough in England, will be ready to welcome the Associate Members striving for the last three places in the 2003 World Cup. As preparation, Canada hosted the inaugural Americas' Cup and had the added satisfaction of victory. They also won one game against a strong MCC contingent. Regrettably, the traditional fixture against the US – the world's oldest international fixture – was again cancelled, though the teams did meet in both the Americas' Cup and the Red Stripe Bowl in Jamaica. – Geoff Edwards.

CAYMAN ISLANDS

Cricket in Cayman received a major boost with admission as an Affiliate Member of ICC. This had a knock-on effect, as participation in the first ICC Americas' Cup and the West Indies Red Stripe Bowl followed. Cayman did well in the Americas' Cup: with more poise, they could have emerged victors. However, the Red Stripe revealed a gulf in standards and was very much a learning experience. Youth cricket has continued to develop under the guidance of national coach Theo Cuffy, with sponsorship from the government and from Cable & Wireless, who also ran their fourth "Cricket Crazy" weekend. This included a coaching clinic from Sir Vivian Richards and three current West Indian Test players. The domestic competitions were keenly contested: the first division title was shared by Byrle and Prison – Ivan Burges.

CHILE

In the last two years, cricket in Chile has undergone a revival. In 1999 it was reintroduced in several schools, with 50 or so boys and girls now enjoying the game. Though Chilean cricket has dwindled since its heyday in the 1920s, the game has been kept alive and is now thriving, thanks to the generosity of the Prince of Wales Country Club, which offers its splendid ground at the foot of the Andes to cricketers every summer. This offer is currently being taken up by some 50 enthusiasts, mainly British expats with a sprinkling of other cricketing nationalities, a few Chileans, plus the odd US baseball player. The club schedules about 20 games per season, mostly intra-club matches, with occasional visits from UK and Australian teams and a very welcome annual visit from the Argentine Cricket Association. Whenever the Antarctic Survey ship HMS *Endurance* docks in Valparaíso a game is arranged, thus taking us back to 1829 and the very origins of cricket in Chile – when teams from two Royal Navy ships met. Recent visitors included Rosslyn Cricket Club, Old Merchant Taylors', the Old Bedfordians, Stowe School and a Stockbrokers' XI. Until the Stockbrokers came, only the occasional Australian had been seen fielding with a glass (or more likely a bottle) of beer in his hand. However, some of the Stockbrokers astounded their opponents by going out to field with a gin and tonic in *each* hand! MCC are sending a team in 2001; they are not expected to match this. – Anthony Adams.

COSTA RICA

Cricket in Costa Rica, which had its heyday in the first half of the 20th century, is experiencing a modest revival, and a cricket association has been formed to seek affiliate membership of the ICC. The game took root in this part of Central America in the late 19th century after Jamaican workers were imported to help build the railway, replacing those of other nationalities who had succumbed to malaria. Many stayed to work in banana plantations or as cocoa planters and, between the two world wars, there were 45 teams in three leagues on the Caribbean coast. Eventually, the West Indian youth on the coast turned to football instead of cricket. However, in the 1970s Cavaliers CC was founded by English expats in the capital, San José, and in 1986 San José CC itself was revived. The rivalry between San José and Limón – the traditional coastal cricket centre – has continued sporadically. In recent years there have been testimonials for the 80th birthdays of two of Costa Rica's cricket luminaries: Stanford Barton, vice-captain of the Limón team that twice toured Jamaica in the 1930s, and Lance Binns, who scored 30 for a Jamaican Schoolboys XI in 1935-36 against a Yorkshire touring team including Len Hutton. Binns still plays for San José. In August 2000 San José, comprising young masters at the British School and not-so-young resident expats, beat Limón by an innings and 64. – T. R. Illingworth.

ESTONIA

Like most good ideas and institutions, the Estonian Cricket Club (*Esti Kriketi Klubi*) was born in a pub, in this case The Lost Continent in Tallinn. The first club e-mail from the chairman, Kristian Garancis, said "Practice will be on Sunday 1300hrs providing no snow". That was 1998, and from there we developed. The first pitch was an outdoor basketball court, with one old bat and a tennis ball. We progressed to a very bumpy soccer pitch in a lovely setting surrounded by forest (and topless lady sunbathers), but under threat from scheduled soccer matches. Later that same year the club moved to the Hippodroom, the trotting track, where the management have been excellent hosts – and most flexible, as we built an all-weather pitch in the middle of the racecourse. The European Cricket Council have been most helpful and provided two start-up cricket kits. EKK facilities are now excellent, with three bars and the best wicket in the region. There are 30 regular players from nine nations, including Estonia. We have played home fixtures against Helsinki, Riga and Stockholm, and have started a programme to develop cricket in Estonian schools. Touring sides are welcome: Tallinn is a wonderful old Hanseatic city, and an excellent place to visit. Contact (372) 6464258 or ilsinfo@online.ee. – Philip Marsdale.

FRANCE

France made history in August as the first non-UK side to compete in the prestigious Isle of Wight Youth Festival, which features county and minor county Under-16 sides. Although the French, playing on grass pitches for the first time, lost all their games, they nearly beat Oxfordshire and Shropshire. Former Test umpire Don Oslear accompanied the squad and, as well as standing in all of France's matches, offered daily advice to the youngsters. Children from all over France went to Picardy for the first-ever trials for a French *minimes* (Under-12) side. The effort was well worth it: they finished runners-up at the 24-team Kent Kwik Cricket Festival at Canterbury. Perhaps the brightest aspect of the senior side's season – apart from the sky-blue outfit worn at the European Championship in Scotland – were the performances of Sulanga Richmond, a 16-year-old Parisian with Sri Lankan parents. He took three for 40 against Greece, and shared a seventh-wicket partnership of 151 with captain Simon Hewitt – whose 162 was the highest score for France – as the French recovered from 20 for five to beat Luxembourg's 257 for nine with one ball left. Another highlight was the celebration of cricket's Olympic Centenary. On August 20, 100 years to the day after cricket's only Olympic appearance (at the Paris games of 1900), a commemorative game at the new Hastings ground saw France draw with Derek Underwood's Old England side. France remain Olympic silver-medal holders to this day. Back home, Paris Université won the national club championship after beating Dreux by two runs in a thrilling final. – Nicoline Palmier.

GERMANY

The main focus of the international programme in 2000 was participation in the European Championship in Scotland – for the first time since Germany became an ICC Associate Member. The team performed well, losing only one game to take second place in Group B. Gerrit Müller was the top German run-maker and hit a century, as he had in the 1998 tournament in The Netherlands. Zaheer Ahmed was the leading wicket-taker and picked up two match awards. The Under-15s also did well in their international competitions: the growing number of such tournaments is truly welcome, and schools in five centres offer cricket coaching. All the leagues expanded in 2000, and there are now 50 clubs in Germany. Rodgau CC, based round Frankfurt, won the German Club Championship, while the youngest league, North Rhine Westphalia, showed its growing strength by reaching the final of the five-region League Cup before losing to West League. In a qualifying game, Dulip Nair of the North German Federation took four wickets in four balls against North Rhine Westphalia. – Brian Fell.

GIBRALTAR

A visiting MCC team ended their tour in September by winning the first day/night game to be staged on the Rock. This salvaged some pride after they had been beaten in two earlier fixtures, against a Gibraltar Cricket Association XI and a Chairman's XI. The highlight from a playing point of view was Gibraltar's performance in the European Championship in Scotland, where they came top of Group B. At home, UK Civilians CC retained the Wiggins Shield, Calpe won the Senior League for the first time in their short history and Gibraltar CC won the Murto Cup. – T. J. Finlayson.

HONG KONG

Excellent news for Hong Kong was that the government has allocated a precious site for cricket. We are now pursuing funding to develop it as every existing ground is used to maximum capacity. Among the highlights of a busy year was the inaugural Playground League, which had 16 teams from 13 schools playing in basketball-sized courts, which suits the crowded conditions in Hong Kong; Quarry Bay School were champions. The adult Saturday League was won by Hong Kong Cricket Club Nomads, and HKCC Gap Ramblers won the Saturday Cup. JKN Little Sai Wan won the Sunday League, with the Sunday Cup going to Pakistan Association. – John Cribbin.

ICELAND

The most northerly and most remarkable of cricketing nations arrived on the scene in 2000, not, in the normal fashion, through the efforts of exiles, but owing to the extraordinary vision of a handful of Icelanders. The story of Icelandic cricket began at the University of Iceland a few years ago when some students caught a glimpse of the game on Sky News. "Everyone was dressed in white," said one of them, Ragnar Kristinsson, "with pressed trousers, and we wanted to do the same." But none of the TV channels available in Iceland showed more than snatches of this mysterious game. However, in 1999 Kristinsson was on holiday in Cyprus during the great World Cup semi-final between Australia and South Africa, and was entranced again. The following Sunday he and a friend were in London, and decided they had to be near Lord's for the final. Outside, they met some Pakistanis, leaving in disgust as their team hurtled to defeat, who readily handed over their tickets. Kristinsson was now firmly hooked. He wrote to the European Cricket Council, who sent a starter set of equipment, and a couple of teams emerged: Kylfan (Icelandic for "the bat") in Reykjavik and Ungmennafelagid Glaumur in Stykkisholmer (believed to be the world's most northerly club, as well as the most unpronounceable). The teams mostly comprised native Icelanders, with coaching from some better-informed expats. Iceland's entry into international cricket came in September 2000 when Manchester barrister and aspirant Liberal Democrat politician, Jonathan Rule, decided this was the perfect venue for his stag night. He assembled a group of friends in a beautiful valley outside Reykjavik to take on the locals. With the help of the *émigrés*, the Icelanders scored 107 on a bumpy football pitch. The visitors (said to be swaying slightly at the crease after the previous evening's entertainment) lurched to 94 in fading light, watched by rather more journalists and cameras than their cricket usually justifies. The headline "Iceland beats England at cricket" appeared in the following morning's paper.

ISRAEL

Another year of progress saw Israel's first all-weather practice facility inaugurated at the Hadar Yosef National Athletics Stadium in Tel Aviv by ICC chief executive David Richards. On his three-day visit, Richards also visited the new artificial turf pitch at Ashdod and presented the prizes at the Youth Cricket tournament, in which 200 boys and girls participated. There was extensive press and TV coverage of the visit. The local season ran well into November owing to the lateness of the Jewish religious holidays, which took up four Saturdays. The league was again won by Lod Lions, who contributed four players to the national team that took part in the European Championship in Scotland. Although the performance there was generally frustrating, wicket-keeper Paul Amit took seven catches against France and 15 overall, and the cricket of young players such as Steve Shein, Raymond Ashton and David Massil was very pleasing. – Stanley Perlman.

ITALY

Italy can report another excellent season. Victory over Denmark in the European Championship was the best moment, but the domestic season was full of interest. Capannelle captured the Eis Cup from Pianoro, whose four-year dominance of the National Championship ended in the semi-finals when they lost to Trentino. Capannelle beat Bologna and then took the final for the first time since 1991. Trentino were unquestionably the season's most improved team. They won the Italian Cup, played only by Italian players under the original Cricket Max rules, beating Lazio by five wickets with one over to spare. Lazio looked to be batting themselves into an impregnable position, but ice-cream man Aamir Shah saw it differently: he took six wickets as all ten fell for a paltry 16 runs, then hit an unbeaten 64 to win the match. – Simone Gambino.

MEXICO

What is said to be the oldest surviving sports photograph in Mexico, dating from 1865, shows a cricket team with Emperor Maximilian in their midst. And Mexico City CC, founded in 1894, has been playing on its present site for 40 years. The ground at the Reforma Club is picturesque – with a lush outfield set among giant eucalyptus trees – and the club is particularly vibrant and sociable. At 7,200 feet above sea level, it is believed to be the second-highest turf wicket in the world. At present, more than 150 cricketers play in competitions every year, between October and March. There is also now an Australian coach, Elliot Cartledge. In 2000, the club hosted touring teams from Belize, Memorial CC of Houston (for the 15th successive year) and the British and Dominion Club of Los Angeles. Although the game was introduced to Mexico by the English, the club has outgrown these roots and embraces players from all backgrounds and abilities. Information can be obtained through the British Embassy or via e-mail at procom@internet.com.mx. – Keith Foster.

MOROCCO

Moroccan cricket continued to flourish in 2000, with the lead being taken by the Sharjah-based sponsor, Abdul Rehman Bukhatir, whose $US30 million stadium at Tangier is progressing fast and will put Morocco on the cricket map. His HIST company has also made it possible to encourage youngsters by providing world-class coaches as well as facilities. Two important tournaments were held: one, sponsored by the Pakistan Embassy, was won by a Pakistan XI; the other, sponsored by HIST and lasting a week in October 2000, included seven Moroccan teams and was won by Casablanca. – Shujaat Ali Khan, Pakistani Ambassador.

NEPAL

The Jai Trophy tournament, held at the new venue of Rajbiraj, had 20 participating teams, four more than in 1999. Kathmandu won, beating Kapilbastu. This was the domestic highlight of a busy year in which Nepal took part in several regional competitions, with erstwhile Pakistani Test player Haroon Rashid as coach. In the Under-19 World Cup, Nepal beat Kenya and advanced to the Super League. Bob Simpson, the former Australian captain, visited Kathmandu for a four-day trip as Cricket Ambassador, and stayed an extra week to help coach the Under-19s to very good effect. – Jai Kumar Shah.

NORFOLK ISLAND

Cricket on Norfolk Island, an Australian outpost in the Western Pacific, looked like dying in the mid-1990s but has experienced a remarkable revival. The turning-point was the Bounty Day match in 1997, which rekindled interest after a four-year break. The fixture dates back at least to 1876: it commemorates (on June 8) the arrival of the Bounty mutineers on the island and is always played between the descendants of the mutineers, who were transferred here from Pitcairn in 1856, and all-comers. There is a re-enactment of the landing, followed by a community picnic within the walls of the ruined convict settlement, and then a friendly match, with many in period costume.

By the 1920s, as many as six teams were also playing routine matches, and there were scheduled fixtures against Lord Howe Island, but by 1993 it was impossible to find even 22 cricketers. Now there are three senior and two junior teams, and regular visiting sides from Australia. The ground, Kingston Oval, dates back to 1838; a 160th anniversary match in 1998 had to be postponed following 12 inches of overnight rain. There is very high humidity, and drinks breaks can be long and leisurely. Owing to a lack of qualified umpires, there are no lbw decisions, which creates interesting situations when newcomers appeal for a plumb leg-before. Further details are on our website: www.nlk.nf/cricket. – Haydn Evans and Bob Wellham.

NORWAY

There was a sensational development off the field when the board members who had worked to achieve ICC affiliate membership were sacked in November. Different groups in Norwegian cricket have conflicting ideas about the meaning of "progress and development" and how these should be achieved. The highlight of the year was being invited to send our first international team to the Austrian Cricket Festival in Vienna. Majid Butt bowled Austria's opening batsman with Norway's first ball in international cricket, and the team went through the tournament undefeated to lift the Festival trophy. On the domestic front, reasonable weather allowed the full programme of matches to be completed. The Oslo League winners were Sentrum CC, while Star CC won the Norwegian Championship and Nord won the Norway Cup. – Bob Gibb.

PANAMA

In 2000, Panama fielded a combined team – irrespective of religious ties – for what is believed to be the first time in 36 years. A national side played two fixtures against a touring Venezuelan XI, winning the first game and gaining the edge in the second before rain intervened. In the opening game, Asif Patel scored 34 of his 38 in one over. Unfortunately, we have no cricket grounds so the game has to be played in football or baseball stadiums. Cricket in Panama dates back to about 1900, when West Indians arrived to help build the Panama Canal. Cricket then faded away until the Asian community began to establish itself. Religious conflicts meant that separate tournaments for Muslims and Hindus evolved. Games continue to be controversial: last season, during their semi-final in the Muslim competition, Bhatan CC walked off the field in protest against time-wasting by Paraiso CC, who were due to win on run-rate if the game was not completed by six o'clock. – Saleh and Musaji Banah.

SOLOMON ISLANDS

In May 2000, an encouraging report could have been written about cricket in the Solomon Islands. A resurgence led by Australian and New Zealand expats was progressing well. However, all this went by the board following a political coup in June, after which many of them left. Cricket had already declined here after the departure of foreign teachers in the 1980s. Some Solomon Islanders have an aptitude for the game and were obviously coached in their youth: in the matches that were played, their fielding and throwing were of a good standard. There is matting and equipment to help any further revival, but only one pitch – a concrete wicket in the grounds of the country's main secondary school, King George VI: the outfield is not really suitable and is not maintained because the school cannot afford a groundsman. Maybe cricket will come again, but at the moment the sporting scene has to be left to soccer. – Alan Waters, British High Commissioner.

SPAIN

Stephen Tolputt, an Australian civil engineer, hit what may be the highest score ever seen on Continental Europe when he made 320 not out in a 40-over match for the Cricket World XI at Javea. The ground is a small one, famous for six-hitting, but Tolputt exceeded all expectations with 24 sixes and 32 fours, and raced to his triple century out of 468 for three. Javea themselves reached 331. More quietly, Spanish cricket made good progress generally in 2000. The European Indoor Tournament was held in various venues in Costa Blanca. Not merely was the organisation successful, but the Spanish team finished a creditable fifth. However, Spain's geography and the lack of financial support continued to hamper progress. It was impossible to organise a national league, but Sporting Alfas retained the Royal and Sun Alliance Cup by beating Javea in a rerun of the 1999 final. – Clive Woodbridge.

SWITZERLAND

In 2000, the number of participating teams in the Swiss League jumped from six to nine with three Zurich-based clubs, Nomads, Classic and Royal Lankans, joining the Eastern Group to joust against Basle and Winterthur. Berne transferred to the Western Group to do battle against Geneva, Cossonay and CERN. In the Eastern, Winterthur were surprise winners, thus qualifying for the semi-finals against Western runners-up Geneva while, in the Western, Berne steamrollered to six successive victories and a tie against Eastern runners-up Nomads. The final, played in Geneva on a sunny September day before a big crowd, saw Winterthur, in their first final, beat Berne by 93 runs. The Swiss senior side met with defeats in Luxembourg and Portugal, but shared honours with France in two contrasting games over a May weekend in Geneva. On Saturday, Switzerland's meagre 63 was easily seen off by France for the loss of one wicket. Next day, the French scored 356 but lost by one wicket, the winning runs coming in the last over with two Swiss-born players, Barone and von Tobel, at the crease. On European Cricket Day in August, cricket was demonstrated as part of the Hornüss Festival (*hornüss* being probably the only truly Swiss sport apart from yodelling) in Frauenfeld. For 2001 the outlook is bright, with two of the clubs, CERN and Cossonay, having already started work on new, permanent wickets at grounds to be used exclusively for cricket. – John McKillop.

UNITED STATES

A banner year on the field for the United States was matched by a continuation of the off-field shambles that has bedevilled American cricket for years. In October came what might have been the greatest day in the long but rarely glorious history of the game in the US – the national team beat Barbados (led by Courtney Browne and including four other internationals) in the Red Stripe tournament in Jamaica. Off-spinner Rudy Narine took four for 35 and Barbados were bowled out for 128: the US inched home by two wickets, raising eyebrows across the global cricketing community. The team never reached such heights in their other games in the tournament, nor in the Americas' Cup in Toronto – they lost to the Canadians in both. Earlier in the year, however, they had an equally eye-catching win when they beat MCC by four wickets at Castleford on their eight-match British tour. MCC made 209 for seven in their 50 overs, which the Americans passed with three balls to spare after an unbeaten 71 from Steve Massiah. The US also had victories over Yorkshire Second Eleven and Wales. Such triumphs were in stark contrast to events just a month after the Barbados win, when an extraordinary general meeting of the USA Cricket Association was held in a New York airport hotel. Uniformed security guards had to be hired to ensure that only legitimate members were allowed entry. "Paranoid though such measures might sound," wrote the US CricInfo co-ordinator, Deb K. Das, in advance, "it is clear that the organisers feel they are necessary to maintain order. That is a sad commentary on the current state of affairs in US cricket." But the atmosphere was entirely in keeping with recent history, riddled with allegations of incompetence and corruption. Earlier in the year, Ricky Craig, the president of the association, resigned, evidently in protest against the reinstatement of the secretary, Atul Rai. The New York meeting apparently went off peacefully, and new elections were to be held early in 2001. It seemed doubtful they would end the bickering.

VANUATU

Vanuatu cricket had a bumper year in 2000, witnessing the introduction of the first kids' cricket league with more than 300 boys and girls playing a seven-week season of Kanga Cricket. The winners were Vanda Juniors in the 11–13 age group and Freshwater School in the Under-11s. Their skills progressed rapidly from "chucking" to some smooth and smart actions. We have a lot of hope for the future. In the BDO Club Championship, North Efate Bushpigs led the table throughout, only to be toppled by the Mele Bulls in a very good Grand Final. It was the first Mele victory since Vanuatu gained independence in 1980. There was a new entrant from the French-speaking Lycée Louis Antoine de Bougainville. Half the team had not seen a cricket match before the season but they finished third in the competition. I also heard a story from Justice Robert Kent QC, the Acting Chief Justice of Vanuatu, who told me about a match being played on the island of Santo. An old chief happened to wander past and took an interest. He said: "*Mi wantem pleiplei smol tisfala gem*" ("I would like to play"). There was no objection. When his turn came, he swung a bat for the first time in his life and hit a six. We think that this could be a record. – Mark Stafford.

PART SIX:
ADMINISTRATION AND LAWS

INTERNATIONAL CRICKET COUNCIL

On June 15, 1909, representatives of cricket in England, Australia and South Africa met at Lord's and founded the Imperial Cricket Conference. Membership was confined to the governing bodies of cricket in countries within the British Commonwealth where Test cricket was played. India, New Zealand and West Indies were elected as members on May 31, 1926, Pakistan on July 28, 1952, Sri Lanka on July 21, 1981, Zimbabwe on July 8, 1992 and Bangladesh on June 26, 2000. South Africa ceased to be a member of ICC on leaving the British Commonwealth in May, 1961, but was elected as a Full Member on July 10, 1991.

On July 15, 1965, the Conference was renamed the International Cricket Conference and new rules were adopted to permit the election of countries from outside the British Commonwealth. This led to the growth of the Conference, with the admission of Associate Members, who were each entitled to one vote, while the Foundation and Full Members were each entitled to two votes, on ICC resolutions. On July 12, 13, 1989, the Conference was renamed the International Cricket Council and revised rules were adopted.

On July 7, 1993, ICC ceased to be administered by MCC and became an independent organisation with its own chief executive, the headquarters remaining at Lord's. The category of Foundation Member, with its special rights, was abolished. On October 1, 1993, Sir Clyde Walcott became the first non-British chairman of ICC.

On June 16, 1997, ICC became an incorporated body, with an executive board and a president instead of a chairman. Jagmohan Dalmiya became ICC's first president.

Officers

President: M. A. Gray (2000–02). *Chief Executive:* D. L. Richards.
Chairman of Committees: Cricket – Management: D. L. Richards; *Cricket – Playing:* S. M. Gavaskar; *Development:* D. L. Richards; *Finance and Marketing:* E. Mani.
Executive Board: The president and chief executive sit on the board and all committees *ex officio*. They are joined by Sir John Anderson (New Zealand), P. Chingoka (Zimbabwe), S. H. Chowdhury (Bangladesh), Lord MacLaurin (England), Dr A. C. Muthiah (India), J. Rayani (Kenya), D. W. Rogers (Australia), P. H. O. Rousseau (West Indies), P. H. F. Sonn (South Africa), T. Sumathipala (Sri Lanka), Tauqir Zia (Pakistan), HRH Tunku Imran (Malaysia), R. van Ierschot (Netherlands).
General Manager: R. M. G. Hill. *Cricket Operations Manager:* C. D. Hitchcock. *Development Manager:* A. Eade. *Financial/Project Manager:* D. C. Jamieson. *Communications Manager:* M. J. Harrison.

Constitution

President: Each Full Member has the right, by rotation, to appoint ICC's president. In 1997, India named J. Dalmiya to serve until June 2000, when M. A. Gray of Australia took over. Gray and subsequent presidents will serve for two years.

Chief Executive: Appointed by the Council. D. L. Richards was appointed in 1993; he has announced that he intends to step down in September 2001.

Membership

Full Members: Australia, Bangladesh, England, India, New Zealand, Pakistan, South Africa, Sri Lanka, West Indies and Zimbabwe.

Associate Members*: Argentina (1974), Bermuda (1966), Canada (1968), Denmark (1966), East and Central Africa (1966), Fiji (1965), France (1998), Germany (1999), Gibraltar (1969), Hong Kong (1969), Ireland (1993), Israel (1974), Italy (1995), Kenya (1981), Malaysia (1967), Namibia (1992), Nepal (1996), Netherlands (1966), Papua New Guinea (1973), Scotland (1994), Singapore (1974), Uganda (1998), United Arab Emirates (1990), USA (1965) and West Africa (1976).

Affiliate Members*: Austria (1992), Bahamas (1987), Belgium (1991), Belize (1997), Brunei (1992), Cayman Islands (1997), Cook Islands (2000), Czech Republic (2000), Cyprus (1999), Finland (2000), Greece (1995), Japan (1989), Kuwait (1998), Luxembourg (1998), Malta (1998), Morocco (1999), Norway (2000), Oman (2000), Philippines (2000), Portugal (1996), Qatar (1999), Samoa (2000), Spain (1992), Sweden (1997), Switzerland (1985), Thailand (1995), Tonga (2000) and Vanuatu (1995).

* *Year of election shown in parentheses.*

The following governing bodies for cricket shall be eligible for election.

Full Members: The governing body for cricket recognised by ICC of a country, or countries associated for cricket purposes, or a geographical area, from which representative teams are qualified to play official Test matches.

Associate Members: The governing body for cricket recognised by ICC of a country, or countries associated for cricket purposes, or a geographical area, which does not qualify as a Full Member but where cricket is firmly established and organised.

Affiliate Members: The governing body for cricket recognised by ICC of a country, or countries associated for cricket purposes, or a geographical area (which is not part of one of those already constituted as a Full or Associate Member) where ICC recognises that cricket is played in accordance with the Laws of Cricket. Affiliate Members have no right to vote or to propose or second resolutions at ICC meetings.

ENGLAND AND WALES CRICKET BOARD

The England and Wales Cricket Board (ECB) became responsible for the administration of all cricket – professional and recreational – in England and Wales on January 1, 1997. It took over the functions of the Cricket Council, the Test and County Cricket Board and the National Cricket Association which had run the game in England and Wales since 1968. The Management Board is answerable to the First-Class Forum on matters concerning the first-class game and to the Recreational Forum on matters concerning the non-professional game. The First-Class Forum elects five members to the Management Board and the Recreational Forum elects four.

Officers

Chairman: Lord MacLaurin of Knebworth. *Chief Executive:* T. M. Lamb.

Management Board: Lord MacLaurin (*chairman*), D. L. Acfield, P. W. Anderson, J. B. Bolus, D. G. Collier, S. P. Coverdale, B. G. Ford, P. W. Gooden, H. M. V. Gray, R. Jackson, R. D. V. Knight, F. D. Morgan, R. C. Moylan-Jones, J. B. Pickup, M. J. Soper.

Chairmen of Committees: First-Class Forum: F. D. Morgan; *Recreational Forum:* J. B. Pickup; *Cricket Advisory Committee:* D. L. Acfield; *England Management Advisory Committee:* J. B. Bolus; *Finance Advisory Committee:* B. G. Ford; *Marketing Advisory Committee:* H. M. V. Gray; *Discipline Standing Committee:* G. Elias QC; *Registration Standing Committee:* D. S. Kemp.

Finance Director: B. W. Havill; *Director of Cricket Operations:* J. D. Carr; *Commercial Director:* T. D. M. Blake; *Corporate Affairs Director:* J. C. Read; *Performance Director:* H. Morris; *National Development Director:* K. R. Pont; *National Manager of Women's Cricket:* G. E. McConway; *Cricket Operations Manager (First-Class):* A. Fordham; *Cricket Operations Manager (Recreational):* F. R. Kemp.

THE MARYLEBONE CRICKET CLUB

The Marylebone Cricket Club evolved out of the White Conduit Club in 1787, when Thomas Lord laid out his first ground in Dorset Square. Its members revised the Laws in 1788 and gradually took responsibility for cricket throughout the world. However, it relinquished control of the game in the UK in 1968 and the International Cricket Council finally established its own secretariat in 1993. MCC still owns Lord's and remains the guardian of the Laws. It calls itself "a private club with a public function" and aims to support cricket everywhere, especially at grassroots level and in countries where the game is least developed.

Patron: HER MAJESTY THE QUEEN

Officers

President: 2000–01 – Lord Alexander of Weedon.

Club Chairman: Sir Michael Jenkins.   *Chairman of Finance:* O. H. J. Stocken.

Trustees: A. C. D. Ingleby-Mackenzie, M. E. L. Melluish, D. R. W. Silk.

Hon. Life Vice-Presidents: Sir Alec Bedser, Sir Donald Bradman, Lord Bramall, D. G. Clark, G. H. G. Doggart, Lord Griffiths, D. J. Insole, F. G. Mann, C. H. Palmer, D. R. W. Silk, J. J. Warr.

Secretary and Chief Executive: R. D. V. Knight.   *Deputy Chief Executive:* D. N. Batts.

Head of Cricket: A. I. C. Dodemaide.   *Assistant Secretary (Membership):* C. Maynard.   *Personal Assistant to Secretary:* Miss S. A. Lawrence.   *Curator:* S. E. A. Green.

MCC Committee: J. A. Bailey, D. I. Gower, M. G. Griffith, W. R. Griffiths, R. G. Marlar, M. C. J. Nicholas, T. J. G. O'Gorman, D. A. Peck, N. M. Peters, Sir Timothy Rice, Lt-Col. J. R. Stephenson, M. O. C. Sturt.

Chairmen of main sub-committees: E. R. Dexter (Cricket); M. J. de Rohan (Estates); C. A. Fry (Membership); A. W. Wreford (Marketing); *Additional Member of the Cricket Committee:* G. J. Toogood.

PROFESSIONAL CRICKETERS' ASSOCIATION

The Professional Cricketers' Association was formed in 1967 (as the Cricketers' Association) to represent the first-class county playing staffs, and to promote and protect professional players' interests. During the 1970s, it succeeded in establishing pension schemes and a minimum wage. In 1995, David Graveney became the Association's general secretary and first full-time employee; in 1998, he became chief executive. In 1997, the organisation set up its own management company to raise regular revenue and fund improved benefits for members of the PCA during and after their playing careers.

President: M. W. Gatting.   *Chairman:* M. V. Fleming.   *Chief Executive:* D. A. Graveney. *Chairman, PCA Management:* P. M. Walker.   *Managing Director:* R. H. Bevan.   *Directors:* D. A. Graveney, T. J. G. O'Gorman.

EUROPEAN CRICKET COUNCIL

On June 16, 1997, the eight-year-old European Cricket Federation was superseded by the European Cricket Council, bringing together all European ICC members, plus Israel. In 2000, the Council consisted of England (Full Member); Denmark, France, Germany, Gibraltar, Ireland, Israel, Italy, Netherlands and Scotland (Associate Members); and Austria, Belgium, Cyprus, Czech Republic, Finland, Greece, Luxembourg, Malta, Norway, Portugal, Spain, Sweden and Switzerland (Affiliate Members).

Chairman: D. J. Insole.   *European Development Manager:* I. C. D. Stuart.

ADDRESSES

INTERNATIONAL CRICKET COUNCIL

D. L. Richards, The Clock Tower, Lord's Cricket Ground, London NW8 8QN (020 7266 1818; fax 020 7266 1777; website www.icc.cricket.org; e-mail icc@icc.cricket.org).

Full Members

AUSTRALIA: Australian Cricket Board, M. Speed, 90 Jolimont Street, Jolimont, Victoria 3002 (00 61 3 9653 9999; fax 00 61 3 9653 9911; website www.acb.com.au).

BANGLADESH: Bangladesh Cricket Board, Syed Ashraful Huq, Bangabandhu National Stadium, Dhaka 1000 (00 880 2 966 6805; fax 00 880 2 956 3844; e-mail bcb@bangla.net).

ENGLAND: England and Wales Cricket Board, T. M. Lamb, Lord's Ground, London NW8 8QZ (020 7432 1200; fax 020 7289 5619; website www.ecb.co.uk).

INDIA: Board of Control for Cricket in India, J. Y. Lele, Sanmitra, Anandpura, Baroda 390 001 (00 91 265 431233; fax 00 91 265 428833).

NEW ZEALAND: New Zealand Cricket Inc., C. Doig, PO Box 958, 109 Cambridge Terrace, Christchurch (00 64 3 366 2964; fax 00 64 3 365 7491; website www.nzcricket.org.nz).

PAKISTAN: Pakistan Cricket Board, Brig. Munawar Rana, Gaddafi Stadium, Ferozepur Road, Lahore 54600 (00 92 42 571 7231; fax 00 92 42 571 1860).

SOUTH AFRICA: United Cricket Board of South Africa, M. G. Majola, PO Box 55009, North Street, Illovo, Northlands 2116 (00 27 11 880 2810; fax 00 27 11 880 6578; website www.ucbsa.cricket.org; e-mail ucbsa@ucb.co.za).

SRI LANKA: Board of Control for Cricket in Sri Lanka, A. P. B. Tennekoon, 35 Maitland Place, Colombo 7 (00 94 1 691439/689551; fax 00 94 1 697405; e-mail cricket@sri.lanka.net).

WEST INDIES: West Indies Cricket Board, G. Shillingford, Factory Road, PO Box 616 W, Woods Centre, St John's, Antigua (00 1 268 481 2452; fax 00 1 268 481 2498; e-mail wicb@candw.ag).

ZIMBABWE: Zimbabwe Cricket Union, D. Ellman-Brown, PO Box 2739, Harare (00 263 4 704616; fax 00 263 4 729370; website www.zcu.cricket.org; e-mail zcu@samara.co.zw).

Associate and Affiliate Members

ARGENTINA: Argentine Cricket Association, D. Lord, ACA Scde Central, J. M. Gutierrez 3829, 1425 Buenos Aires (00 54 11 4802 6166; fax 00 54 11 4802 6692; website cricketargentina@mail.com).

AUSTRIA: Österreichischer Cricket Verband, A. Simpson-Parker, Apollogasse 3/42, A-1070 Vienna (00 43 1 524 9366; fax 00 43 1 524 9367; e-mail 10747.740@compuserve.com).

BAHAMAS: Bahamas Cricket Association, S. Deveaux, Government House, PO Box 1001, Nassau (00 1 242 322 1875; fax 00 1 242 322 4659).

BELGIUM: Belgian Cricket Federation, M. O'Connor, Koningin Astridlaan 98, B-2800 Mechelen (00 32 15 331 635; fax 00 32 15 331 639).

BELIZE: Belize National Cricket Association, Mrs V. Parks, Burnham Manse, 88 Albert Street, PO Box 619, Belize City (00 501 2 72201; fax 00 501 2 30936).

BERMUDA: Bermuda Cricket Board of Control, R. Horton, PO Box HM992, Hamilton HM DX (00 1 441 292 8958; fax 00 1 441 292 8959; website bcb@ibl.bm).

BRUNEI: Persatuan Keriket Negara Brunei Darussalam, S. Langton, PO Box 931, MPC-Old Airport, Berakas-BB 3577 (00 673 873 3737; fax 00 673 242 4088).

CANADA: Canadian Cricket Association, G. Edwards, 46 Port Street East, Mississauga, Ontario L5G 1C1 (00 1 905 278 5000; fax 00 1 905 278 5005).

CAYMAN ISLANDS: Cayman Islands Cricket Association, C. Myles, PO Box 1201 GT, George Town, Grand Cayman (00 1 345 945 5589; fax 00 1 345 945 5558).

COOK ISLANDS: Cook Islands Cricket Association, G. Hoskings, PO Box 139, Raratonga (00 682 29 312; fax 00 682 29 314).

CYPRUS: Cyprus Cricket Association, S. Carr, PO Box 3293, Limassol, Cyprus CY 3301 (00 357 5 354 371; fax 00 357 5 342 996).

CZECH REPUBLIC: Czech Republic Cricket Association, J. Locke, Na Berance 7, 160 00 Praha 6 (00 420 22 481 1672; fax 00 420 22 481 1608).

DENMARK: Dansk Cricket-Forbund, C. B. S. Hansen, Idraettens Hus, 2605 Brøndby (00 45 4326 2160; fax 00 45 4326 2163; e-mail dcf@cricket.dk).

EAST AND CENTRAL AFRICA: East and Central African Cricket Conference, T. B. McCarthy, PO Box 34321, Lusaka 1010, Zambia (00 260 1 226 228; fax 00 260 1 224 454).

FIJI: Fiji Cricket Association, P. I. Knight, PO Box 300, Suva (00 679 301 499/300 321; fax 00 679 301 618).

FINLAND: Finnish Cricket Association, A. Armitage, Coats Opti Oy, Ketjutie 3, Fin-04220, Kerava (00 358 927 487 327; fax 00 358 927 487 371).

FRANCE: Fédération Française de Cricket, D. Marchois, La Saunerie, 41 rue de Fecamp, 75012 Paris (00 33 5 5354 4095; fax 00 33 5 5354 2783).

GERMANY: Deutscher Cricket Bund, B. Fell, Luragogasse 5, D-94032 Passau (00 49 851 34307; fax 00 49 851 32815; e-mail fell02@fsuni.rzuni.passau.de).

GIBRALTAR: Gibraltar Cricket Association, T. J. Finlayson, 23 Merlot House, Vineyards Estate (00 350 79461; also fax).

GREECE: Greek Cricket Federation, C. Evangelos, Cat. Pappa 8, Corfu 49100 (00 30 661 47753; fax 00 30 661 47754).

HONG KONG: Hong Kong Cricket Association, J. A. Cribbin, Room 1019, Sports House, 1 Stadium Path, So Kon Po, Causeway Bay (00 852 250 48101; fax 00 852 257 78486; website www.hkabc.net; e-mail hcca@hkabc.net).

IRELAND: Irish Cricket Union, J. Wright, The Diamond, Malahide, Co Dublin 18 (00 353 1 845 0710; fax 00 353 1 845 5545; e-mail info@typetest.ie).

ISRAEL: Israel Cricket Association, S. Perlman, PO Box 65085, Tel-Aviv 61650 (00 972 3 642 5529; fax 00 972 3 641 7271).

ITALY: Federazione Cricket Italiana, S. Gambino, Via S. Ignazio 9, 00186 Roma (00 39 06 689 6989; fax 00 39 06 687 8684).

JAPAN: Japan Cricket Association, T. Bayley, Nankitsu Machi 15-5, Maebashi City 371-0043 (00 81 3 5772 3470; fax 00 81 3 5772 3471; website www.jca@cricket.ne.jp).

KENYA: Kenya Cricket Association, H. Shah, PO Box 45870, Nairobi (00 254 2 766447/764579; fax 00 254 2 765057; e-mail kcricket@iconnect.co.ke).

KUWAIT: Kuwait Cricket Association, Abdul Muttaleb Ahmad, PO Box 6706, Hawalli-32042 (00 965 572 6600; fax 00 965 573 4973).

LUXEMBOURG: Federation Luxembourgeoise de Cricket, T. Dunning, 87 rue de Gasperich, L-1617 Luxembourg-Ville (00 352 430 12964).

MALAYSIA: Malaysian Cricket Association, K. Selveratnam, 1st Floor, Wisma OCM, Jalan Hang Jebat, 50150 Kuala Lumpur (00 60 3 201 6761; fax 00 60 3 201 3878).

MALTA: Malta Cricket Association, P. Naudi, c/o Marsa Sports Club, Marsa HMR 15 (00 356 233 851; fax 00 356 231 809).

MOROCCO: Moroccan Cricket Association, C. Laroussi, 6 Rue Sefrou A8, Hassan-Rabat (00 212 7 766 453; fax 00 212 7 766 742).

NAMIBIA: Namibia Cricket Board, L. Pieters, PO Box 266, Windhoek 9000 (00 264 61 263128/263129; fax 00 264 61 215149).

NEPAL: Cricket Association of Nepal, B. R. Pandey, Heritage Plaza, 5th Floor, Kamaldi, PO Box 20291, Kathmandu (00 977 1 247485 ext. 252; fax 00 977 1 247946).

NETHERLANDS: Royal Netherlands Cricket Board, A. de la Mar, Nieuwe Kalfjeslaan 21-B, 1182 AA Amstelveen (00 31 20 645 1705; fax 00 31 20 645 1715; e-mail adelamar@kncb.nl).

NORWAY: Norway Cricket Association, R. Gibb, Geologsvingen 11, 0380 Oslo (fax 00 47 22 73 0653).

OMAN: Oman Cricket Association, A. M. Yousef, PO Box 3948, Ruwi 112, Muscat, Sultanate of Oman (00 968 79 6655; fax 00 968 70 6372).

PAPUA NEW GUINEA: Papua New Guinea Cricket Board of Control, W. Satchell, PO Box 83, Konedobu NCD (00 675 321 1070; fax 00 675 321 7974; e-mail imcsghai@loxinfo.co.th).

PHILIPPINES: Philippine Cricket Association, c/o Davies, Langdon & Search Philippines Inc., 4th Floor, 2129 Pasong Tamo, Makati City, Metro Manilla (00 63 2 524 1426; fax 00 63 2 525 2171; e-mail cjh@dls.com.ph).

PORTUGAL: Associação de Cricket de Portugal, J. Simonson, Largo de Academia Nacional de Belas Artes 16, Lisboa P-1200 (00 351 1 346 2277; fax 00 351 1 346 5079).

QATAR: Qatar Cricket Association, F. H. Alfardan, PO Box 339, Doha (00 974 433 461; fax 00 974 435 2978).

SAMOA: Samoa Cricket Association, S. Kohlhasse, Seb & Rene Sports, PO Box 9599 (00 685 22 480; also fax).

SCOTLAND: Scottish Cricket Union, R. W. Barclay, National Cricket Academy, MES Sports Centre, Ravelston, Edinburgh EH4 3NT (0131 313 7420; fax 0131 313 7430; website www.scu.org.uk; e-mail admin.scu@btinternet.com).

SINGAPORE: Singapore Cricket Association, A. Kalaver, 31 Stadium Crescent (South Entrance) Singapore 397639 (00 65 348 6566; fax 00 65 348 6506).

SPAIN: Asociacion Española de Cricket, M. de Careaga, Casa Desiderata, VA 153, 03737 Javea, Alicante (00 34 96 686 6965; also fax).

SWEDEN: Sweden Cricket Board, Mrs I. Persson, Hjulstabackar 19BV, SE16365 Spånga (00 46 8 6496167; fax 00 46 8 7188850).

SWITZERLAND: Swiss Cricket Association, A. MacKay, Wingertlistrasse 22, 8405 Winterthur (00 41 52 233 4601; fax 00 41 1 839 4999; e-mail alex_mackay@ibi.com).

THAILAND: Thailand Cricket League, R. Sharma, 25-27 Soi 32/1, Charoen Nakhorn Road, Klongsan, Bangkok 10600 (00 66 2 862 7101; fax 00 66 2 862 4407; e-mail imcsghai@loxinfo.co.th).

TONGA: Tonga Cricket Association, c/o PO Box 1278, Nuku' Alofa (00 676 23 066; fax 00 676 26 011).

UGANDA: Uganda Cricket Association, J. Ligya, c/o National Council of Sports, Lugogo Stadium, PO Box 8346, Kampala (00 256 41 349550; fax 00 256 41 231478).

UNITED ARAB EMIRATES: Emirates Cricket Board, M. Khan, Sharjah Cricket Stadium, PO Box 88, Sharjah (00 971 6 532 2991; fax 00 971 6 533 4741; e-mail cricket@emirates.net.ae).

USA: United States of America Cricket Association, K. Prasad, The Cricket Pavilion, Hoverford College, 387 West Lancaster Avenue, Hoverford, Pennsylvania 19041 (00 1 6101 896 3633; fax 00 1 6101 896 7122).

VANUATU: Vanuatu Cricket Association, M. Stafford, c/o BDO, PO Box 240, Port Vila, Vanuatu (00 678 22280; fax 00 678 22317; e-mail stafford@vanuatu.com.vu).

WEST AFRICA: West Africa Cricket Conference, Miss G. Ekwempu, Tafawa Balewa Square, Race Course, Lagos, PO Box 9309, Nigeria (00 234 1 545 4472; fax 00 234 1 585 0529).

UK ADDRESSES

ENGLAND AND WALES CRICKET BOARD: T. M. Lamb, Lord's Ground, London NW8 8QZ (020 7432 1200; fax 020 7289 5619; website www.ecb.co.uk).

MARYLEBONE CRICKET CLUB: R. D. V. Knight, Lord's Ground, London NW8 8QN (020 7289 1611; fax 020 7289 9100. Tickets 020 7432 1066; fax 020 7432 1061).

First-Class Counties

DERBYSHIRE: County Ground, Nottingham Road, Derby DE21 6DA (01332 383211; fax 01332 290251; e-mail post@dccc.org.uk).

DURHAM: County Ground, Riverside, Chester-le-Street, County Durham DH3 3QR (0191 387 1717; fax 0191 387 1616; e-mail marketing@durham-ccc.org.uk).

ESSEX: County Ground, New Writtle Street, Chelmsford CM2 0PG (01245 252420; fax 01245 254030; e-mail administration.essex@ecb.co.uk).

GLAMORGAN: Sophia Gardens, Cardiff CF11 9XR (029 2040 9380; fax 029 2040 9390; e-mail glam@ecb.co.uk).

GLOUCESTERSHIRE: Phoenix County Ground, Nevil Road, Bristol BS7 9EJ (0117 910 8000; fax 0117 924 1193; e-mail info@glosccc.co.uk).

HAMPSHIRE: The Hampshire Rose Bowl, Botley Road, West End, Southampton SO30 3XH (023 8047 2002; fax 023 8047 2122; e-mail enquiries.hants@ecb.co.uk).

KENT: St Lawrence Ground, Old Dover Road, Canterbury CT1 3NZ (01227 456886; fax 01227 762168; e-mail kent@ecb.co.uk).

LANCASHIRE: County Cricket Ground, Old Trafford, Manchester M16 0PX (0161 282 4000; fax 0161 282 4100; e-mail sales.lancs@ecb.co.uk).

LEICESTERSHIRE: County Ground, Grace Road, Leicester LE2 8AD (0116 283 2128; fax 0116 244 0363; e-mail kevin.hill.leics@ecb.co.uk).

MIDDLESEX: Lord's Cricket Ground, London NW8 8QN (020 7289 1300; fax 020 7289 5831; e-mail enquiries.middlesex@ecb.co.uk).

NORTHAMPTONSHIRE: County Ground, Wantage Road, Northampton NN1 4TJ (01604 514455; fax 01604 514488; e-mail post@nccc.co.uk).

NOTTINGHAMSHIRE: County Cricket Ground, Trent Bridge, Nottingham NG2 6AG (0115 982 3000; fax 0115 945 5730; e-mail administration.notts@ecb.co.uk).

SOMERSET: County Ground, St James's Street, Taunton TA1 1JT (01823 272946; fax 01823 332395; e-mail somerset@ecb.co.uk).

SURREY: The Oval, Kennington, London SE11 5SS (020 7582 6660; fax 020 7735 7769; e-mail tcodrington@surreyccc.co.uk).

SUSSEX: County Ground, Eaton Road, Hove BN3 3AN (01273 827100; fax 01273 771549; e-mail sccc@mistral.co.uk).

WARWICKSHIRE: County Ground, Edgbaston, Birmingham B5 7QU (0121 446 4422; fax 0121 446 4544; e-mail info@thebears.co.uk).

WORCESTERSHIRE: County Ground, New Road, Worcester WR2 4QQ (01905 748474; fax 01905 748005; e-mail joan.grundy@wccc.co.uk).

YORKSHIRE: Headingley Cricket Ground, Leeds LS6 3BU (0113 278 7394; fax 0113 278 4099; e-mail cricket@yorkshireccc.org.uk).

Minor Counties

MINOR COUNTIES CRICKET ASSOCIATION: D. J. M. Armstrong, Thorpe Cottage, Mill Common, Ridlington, North Walsham NR28 9TY (01692 650563).

BEDFORDSHIRE: P. G. M. August, 35 Amberley Gardens, Bedford MK40 3BT (01234 327935).

BERKSHIRE: R. New, 41 Holyrood Close, Caversham, Reading, Berkshire RG4 6PZ (0118 947 7959, 07831 746295 mobile).

BUCKINGHAMSHIRE: K. A. Beaumont, 49 Amersham Road, Little Chalfont, Amersham, Buckinghamshire HP6 6SW (01494 763516).

CAMBRIDGESHIRE: P. W. Gooden, The Redlands, Oakington Road, Cottenham, Cambridge CB4 8TW (01954 250429).

CHESHIRE: J. B. Pickup, 36 Landswood Park, Hartford, Northwich, Cheshire CW8 1NF (01606 74970 home; fax 01606 79357).

CORNWALL: Mrs A. M. George, The Logan Rock Inn, Treen, St Levan, Penzance, Cornwall TR19 6LG (01736 810495, 01736 810177 fax).

CUMBERLAND: K. Ion, 47 Beech Grove, Stanwix, Carlisle, Cumbria CA3 9BG (01228 528858, 07970 421589 mobile; e-mail kion47bg@aol.com).

DEVON: G. R. Evans, Blueberry Haven, 20 Boucher Road, Budleigh Salterton, Devon EX9 6JF (01395 445216 home, 01392 217733 business; fax 01392 411697; e-mail geoffrevans@hotmail.com).

DORSET: K. H. House, The Barn, Higher Farm, Bagber Common, Sturminster Newton, Dorset DT10 2HB (01258 473394, 07971 245889 mobile).

HEREFORDSHIRE: P. Sykes, 5 Dale Drive, Holmer Grange, Hereford HR4 9RF (01432 264703 home, 07809 026484 mobile).

HERTFORDSHIRE: D. S. Dredge, "Trevellis", 38 Santers Lane, Potters Bar, Hertfordshire EN6 2BX (01707 658377 home, 020 7359 3579 business).

LINCOLNSHIRE: C. A. North, Lincolnshire CCC, First Floor, 27 The Forum, North Hykeham, Lincoln LN6 9HW (01522 688073 office/fax, 01522 681636 home).

NORFOLK: S. J. Skinner, 27 Colkett Drive, Old Catton, Norwich NR6 7ND (01603 485940 home, 01603 624236 business, 07585 418993 mobile; e-mail s.skinner@barclays.net).

NORTHUMBERLAND: A. B. Stephenson, Northumberland CCC, Osborne Avenue, Jesmond, Newcastle-upon-Tyne NE2 1JS (0191 281 2738 office, 0191 213 1152 home).

OXFORDSHIRE: P. R. N. O'Neill, 4 Brookside, Thame, Oxfordshire OX9 3DE (01844 260439, also fax; 07411 943449 mobile).

SHROPSHIRE: N. H. Birch, Four Winds, 24 Ridgebourne Road, Shrewsbury, Shropshire SY3 9AB (01743 233650, 07974 000906 mobile).

STAFFORDSHIRE: W. S. Bourne, 10 The Pavement, Brewood, Staffordshire ST19 9BZ (01902 850325 home, 07979 498816 mobile).

SUFFOLK: T. J. Pound, 94 Henley Road, Ipswich IP1 4NJ (01473 213288 home, 01473 232121 business).

WALES MINOR COUNTIES: W. Edwards, 59a King Edward Road, Swansea SA1 4LN (01792 462233; fax 01792 643931).

WILTSHIRE: C. R. Sheppard, 18 Bath Road, Swindon SN1 4BA (07071 221293 business, 01793 530784 fax; e-mail chrisshep@droveinv.telme.com).

HUNTINGDONSHIRE (ECB 38-county) D. Swannell, 23 Popes Lane, Warboys, Huntingdon PE17 2RN (01487 823122).

Other Bodies

ASSOCIATION OF CRICKET STATISTICIANS AND HISTORIANS: P. Wynne-Thomas, 3 Radcliffe Road, West Bridgford, Nottingham NG2 5FF (0115 945 5407; website www.acs.cricket.org; e-mail acsoffice@cricket.org).

ASSOCIATION OF CRICKET UMPIRES AND SCORERS: G. J. Bullock, PO Box 399, Camberley, Surrey GU16 5ZJ (01276 27962).

BRITISH UNIVERSITIES SPORTS ASSOCIATION: J. Ellis, 8 Union Street, London SE1 1SZ (020 7357 8555; e-mail jim@busa.org.uk).

CLUB CRICKET CONFERENCE: D. Franklin, 361 West Barnes Lane, New Malden, Surrey KT3 6JF (020 8336 0586; fax 020 8336 0537).

ENGLISH SCHOOLS' CRICKET ASSOCIATION: K. S. Lake, 38 Mill House, Woods Lane, Cottingham, Hull HU16 4HQ.

EUROPEAN CRICKET COUNCIL: I. C. D. Stuart, Europe Office, Lord's Ground, London NW8 8QN (020 7432 1019; fax 020 7432 1018; website www.ecc.cricket.org).

LEAGUE CRICKET CONFERENCE: N. Edwards, 1 Longfield, Freshfield, Formby, Merseyside L37 3LD (01704 877103).

MIDLAND CLUB CRICKET CONFERENCE: D. Thomas, 4 Silverdale Gardens, Wordsley, Stowbridge, West Midlands DY8 5NY (01384 278107 home; 01902 864685 business).

PROFESSIONAL CRICKETERS' ASSOCIATION: D. A. Graveney, Suite 210, 68 Lombard Street, London EC3V 9LJ (020 7868 1610; fax 020 7868 1830). PCA MANAGEMENT: R. H. Bevan, Hawkstone Park, Weston-under-Redcastle, Shrewsbury, Shropshire SY4 5UY (01939 200202; fax 01939 200699; e-mail pcam@enta.net).

RUTLAND COUNTY CRICKET ASSOCIATION: I. H. S. Balfour, Nanjazel, 7 Nightingale Way, Oakham, Rutland LE15 6ES.

Cricket Associations and Societies

AUSTRALIAN CRICKET SOCIETY: Queensland – Mrs D. Durrand, 128 Somerset Road, Kedron, Qld 4031. Victoria – D. Manning, Ravenstone, 240-246 Oban Road, North Ringwood, Vic 3134.

CHELTENHAM CRICKET SOCIETY: P. Murphy, 1 Colesbourne Road, Benhall, Cheltenham, Gloucestershire GL51 6DJ.

CHESTERFIELD CRICKET SOCIETY: J. S. Cook, 44 Morris Avenue, Newbold, Chesterfield, Derbyshire S41 7BA.

COUNCIL OF CRICKET SOCIETIES, THE: B. Rickson, 31 Grange Avenue, Cheadle Hulme, Cheshire SK8 5EN.

COUNTY CRICKET SUPPORTERS ASSOCIATION: Miss F. J. Walker, 12 Grasmere Drive, Linton Croft, Wetherby, West Yorkshire LS22 6GP.

CRICKET FAN CLUB: 1407 Qasimjan Street, Ballimaran, Delhi 110006, India.

CRICKET MEMORABILIA SOCIETY: A. Sheldon, 29 Highclere Road, Manchester M8 4WH.

CRICKET SOCIETY, THE: E. R. Budd, 16 Storey Court, 39 St John's Wood Road, London NW8 8QX.

CRICKET STATISTICIANS AND SCORERS OF INDIA, ASSOCIATION OF: PO Box 7145, Wadala Post Office, Mumbai 400-041.

DERBYSHIRE CRICKET SOCIETY: G. N. Swift, 6 Devonshire Ave, Beeston, Notts NG9 1BS.

DUNELM CRICKET SOCIETY: Mrs M. Coombs, White Lodge, Halliford Road, Shepperton, Middlesex TW17 8RU.

DURHAM AND NORTH-EAST CRICKET SOCIETY: Prof. R. Storer, 164 Eastern Way, Darras Hall, Ponteland, Newcastle-upon-Tyne NE20 9RH.

EAST RIDING CRICKET SOCIETY: Mrs S. Forward, 121 Fairfax Avenue, Hull HU5 4QU.

ESSEX CRICKET SOCIETY: G. J. Webster, 3 Woodham Drive, Hatfield Peverel, Chelmsford, Essex CM3 2RR.

GLOUCESTERSHIRE CRICKET LOVERS' SOCIETY: M. Simpson, 318 Canford Lane, Westbury-on-Trym, Bristol BS9 3PL.

HAMPSHIRE CRICKET SOCIETY: J. Moore, 85 Kingsway, Chandlers Ford, Hants SO53 1FD.

HEREFORDSHIRE CRICKET SOCIETY: T. Lowe, Hereford Cathedral Junior School, 28 Castle Street, Hereford HR1 2NW.

HERTFORDSHIRE CRICKET SOCIETY: W. A. Powell, 17 Swan Mead, The Willows, Hemel Hempstead, Hertfordshire HP3 9DQ.

HIGH PEAK CRICKET SOCIETY: R. H. Wood, 3 Orchard Avenue, Whaley Bridge, Derbyshire SK43 7AH.

LANCASHIRE AND CHESHIRE CRICKET SOCIETY: J. L. Petch, 63 Linksway, Gatley, Cheshire SK8 4LA.

LINCOLNSHIRE CRICKET LOVERS' SOCIETY: C. Kennedy, 26 Eastwood Avenue, Great Grimsby, South Humberside DN34 5BE.

MERSEYSIDE CRICKET SOCIETY: W. T. Robins, 31 Elmswood Court, Palmerston Road, Liverpool L18 8DJ.

MIDLAND CRICKET SOCIETY: Miss H. Allen, 14 Merrions Close, Birmingham B43 7AT.

NATIONAL CRICKET MEMBERSHIP SCHEME: 22 Grazebrook Road, London N16 0HS.

NEEDWOOD CRICKET LOVERS' SOCIETY: A. D. Campion, 45 Fallowfield Drive, Barton-under-Needwood, Staffordshire DE13 8DH.

NEW ZEALAND, CRICKET SOCIETY OF: C. Rosie, Eden Park, PO Box 2860, Auckland 1.

NORFOLK CRICKET SOCIETY: A. V. Burgess, 41 Ashby Street, Norwich, Norfolk NR1 3PT.

NORTHERN CRICKET SOCIETY: H. Jackson, 20 Foxholes Lane, Calverley, Leeds LS8 5NS.

NOTTINGHAM CRICKET LOVERS' SOCIETY: G. Blagdurn, 2 Inham Circus, Chilwell, Nottingham NG9 4FN.

PAKISTAN ASSOCIATION OF CRICKET STATISTICIANS: Abid Ali Kazi and Nauman Bader, 256-N, Model Town Ext, Lahore 54700 (e-mail naumanb@brain.net.pk).

ROTHERHAM CRICKET SOCIETY: J. A. R. Atkin, 15 Gallow Tree Road, Rotherham S65 3FE.

SCOTLAND, CRICKET SOCIETY OF: A. J. Robertson, 5 Riverside Road, Eaglesham, Glasgow G76 0DQ.

SOUTH AFRICA, CRICKET SOCIETY OF: Mrs J. Gleason, PO Box 78040, Sandton, Gauteng 2146.

STOURBRIDGE AND DISTRICT CRICKET SOCIETY: M. Taylor, 26 Wrekin Walk, Stourport, Worcestershire DY13 0LR.

SUSSEX CRICKET SOCIETY: Mrs P. Brabyn, 4 Wolstonbury Walk, Shoreham-by-Sea, West Sussex BN43 5GU.

WEST LANCASHIRE CRICKET SOCIETY: G. D. Anderson, 32 Dunster Rd, Southport PR8 2EN.

WOMBWELL CRICKET LOVERS' SOCIETY: M. Pope, 32 Louden Road, Scholes, Rotherham, South Yorkshire S61 2SU.

WORCESTER CRICKET SOCIETY: M. Niccols, 70 Park Avenue, Worcester WR3 7AQ.

YORKSHIRE CCC SOUTHERN GROUP: D. M. Wood, 15 Rothschild Road, Linslade, Leighton Buzzard, Bedfordshire LU7 7SY.

ZIMBABWE, CRICKET SOCIETY OF: J. B. Stockwell, 6 Howard Close, Mount Pleasant, Harare.

THE LAWS OF CRICKET

(2000 CODE)

World copyright of MCC and reprinted by permission of MCC. Copies of the "Laws of Cricket" are obtainable from Lord's Cricket Ground.

INDEX OF THE LAWS

THE PREAMBLE – THE SPIRIT OF CRICKET

Cricket is a game that owes much of its unique appeal to the fact that it should be played not only within its Laws, but also within the Spirit of the Game. Any action which is seen to abuse this spirit causes injury to the game itself. The major responsibility for ensuring the spirit of fair play rests with the captains.

1.   There are two Laws which place the responsibility for the team's conduct firmly on the captain.

Responsibility of captains

The captains are responsible at all times for ensuring that play is conducted within the Spirit of the Game as well as within the Laws.

Player's conduct

In the event of a player failing to comply with instructions by an umpire, or criticising by word or action the decisions of an umpire, or showing dissent, or generally behaving in a manner which might bring the game into disrepute, the umpire concerned shall in the first place report the matter to the other umpire and to the player's captain, and instruct the latter to take action.

2. Fair and unfair play

According to the Laws the umpires are the sole judges of fair and unfair play. The umpires may intervene at any time, and it is the responsibility of the captain to take action where required.

3. The umpires are authorised to intervene in cases of

- Time-wasting.
- Damaging the pitch.
- Dangerous or unfair bowling.
- Tampering with the ball.
- Any other action that they consider to be unfair.

4. The Spirit of the Game involves respect for

- Your opponents.
- Your own captain and team.
- The role of the umpires.
- The game's traditional values.

5. It is against the Spirit of the Game

- To dispute an umpire's decision by word, action or gesture.
- To direct abusive language towards an opponent or umpire.
- To indulge in cheating or any sharp practice, for instance:

   (a) To appeal knowing that the batsman is not out.

   (b) To advance towards an umpire in an aggressive manner when appealing.

   (c) To seek to distract an opponent either verbally or by harassment with persistent clapping or unnecessary noise under the guise of enthusiasm and motivation of one's own side.

6. Violence

There is no place for any act of violence on the field of play.

7. Players

Captains and umpires together set the tone for the conduct of a cricket match. Every player is expected to make an important contribution to this.

The players, umpires and scorers in a game of cricket may be of either gender and the Laws apply equally to both. The use, throughout the text, of pronouns indicating the male gender is purely for brevity. Except where specifically stated otherwise, every provision of the Laws is to be read as applying to women and girls equally as to men and boys.

LAW 1.   THE PLAYERS

1. Number of players

A match is played between two sides, each of 11 players, one of whom shall be captain. By agreement a match may be played between sides of more or less than 11 players, but not more than 11 players may field at any time.

2. Nomination of players

Each captain shall nominate his players in writing to one of the umpires before the toss. No player may be changed after the nomination without the consent of the opposing captain.

3. Captain

If at any time the captain is not available, a deputy shall act for him.

(a) If a captain is not available during the period in which the toss is to take place, then the deputy must be responsible for the nomination of the players, if this has not already been done, and for the toss. See 2 above and Law 12.4 (The toss).

(b) At any time after the toss, the deputy must be one of the nominated players.

4. Responsibility of captains

The captains are responsible at all times for ensuring that play is conducted within the spirit and traditions of the game as well as within the Laws. See The Preamble – The Spirit of Cricket and Law 42.1 (Fair and unfair play – responsibility of captains).

LAW 2. SUBSTITUTES AND RUNNERS; BATSMAN OR FIELDER LEAVING THE FIELD; BATSMAN RETIRING; BATSMAN COMMENCING INNINGS

1. Substitutes and runners

(a) If the umpires are satisfied that a player has been injured or become ill after the nomination of the players, they shall allow that player to have:

(i) A substitute acting instead of him in the field.

(ii) A runner when batting.

Any injury or illness that occurs at any time after the nomination of the players until the conclusion of the match shall be allowable, irrespective of whether play is in progress or not.

(b) The umpires shall have discretion, for other wholly acceptable reasons, to allow a substitute for a fielder, or a runner for a batsman, at the start of the match or at any subsequent time.

(c) A player wishing to change his shirt, boots, etc. must leave the field to do so. No substitute shall be allowed for him.

2. Objection to substitutes

The opposing captain shall have no right of objection to any player acting as a substitute on the field, nor as to where the substitute shall field. However, no substitute shall act as wicket-keeper. See 3 below.

3. Restrictions on the role of substitutes

A substitute shall not be allowed to bat or bowl nor to act as wicket-keeper or as captain on the field of play.

4. A player for whom a substitute has acted

A player is allowed to bat, bowl or field even though a substitute has previously acted for him.

5. Fielder absent or leaving the field

If a fielder fails to take the field with his side at the start of the match or at any later time, or leaves the field during a session of play:

(a) The umpire shall be informed of the reason for his absence.

(b) He shall not thereafter come on to the field during a session of play without the consent of the umpire. See 6 below. The umpire shall give such consent as soon as is practicable.

(c) If he is absent for 15 minutes or longer, he shall not be permitted to bowl thereafter, subject to (i), (ii) or (iii) below, until he has been on the field for at least that length of playing time for which he was absent.

   (i) Absence or penalty for time absent shall not be carried over into a new day's play.

   (ii) If, in the case of a follow-on or forfeiture, a side fields for two consecutive innings, this restriction shall, subject to (i) above, continue as necessary into the second innings but shall not otherwise be carried over into a new innings.

   (iii) The time lost for an unscheduled break in play shall be counted as time on the field for any fielder who comes on to the field at the resumption of play. See Law 15.1 (An interval).

6. Player returning without permission

If a player comes on to the field of play in contravention of 5(b) above and comes into contact with the ball while it is in play:

   (i) The ball shall immediately become dead and the umpire shall award five penalty runs to the batting side. See Law 42.17 (Penalty runs).

   (ii) The umpire shall inform the other umpire, the captain of the fielding side, the batsmen and, as soon as practicable, the captain of the batting side of the reason for this action.

   (iii) The umpires together shall report the occurrence as soon as possible to the executive of the fielding side and any governing body responsible for the match, who shall take such action as is considered appropriate against the captain and player concerned.

7. Runner

The player acting as a runner for a batsman shall be a member of the batting side and shall, if possible, have already batted in that innings. The runner shall wear external protective equipment equivalent to that worn by the batsman for whom he runs and shall carry a bat.

8. Transgression of the Laws by a batsman who has a runner

(a) A batsman's runner is subject to the Laws. He will be regarded as a batsman except where there are specific provisions for his role as a runner. See 7 above and Law 29.2 (Which is a batsman's ground).

(b) A batsman with a runner will suffer the penalty for any infringement of the Laws by his runner as though he had been himself responsible for the infringement. In particular he will be out if his runner is out under any of Laws 33 (Handled the ball), 37 (Obstructing the field) or 38 (Run out).

(c) When a batsman with a runner is striker he remains himself subject to the Laws and will be liable to the penalties that any infringement of them demands.

Additionally, if he is out of his ground when the wicket is put down at the wicket-keeper's end, he will be out in the circumstances of Law 38 (Run out) or Law 39 (Stumped) irrespective of the position of the non-striker or of the runner. If he is thus dismissed, runs completed by the runner and the other batsman before the dismissal shall not be scored. However, the penalty for a no-ball or a wide shall stand, together with any penalties to be awarded to either side when the ball is dead. See Law 42.17 (Penalty runs).

(d) When a batsman with a runner is not the striker:

   (i) He remains subject to Laws 33 (Handled the ball) and 37 (Obstructing the field) but is otherwise out of the game.

   (ii) He shall stand where directed by the striker's end umpire so as not to interfere with play.

   (iii) He will be liable, notwithstanding (i) above, to the penalty demanded by the Laws should he commit any act of unfair play.

9. Batsman leaving the field or retiring

A batsman may retire at any time during his innings. The umpires, before allowing play to proceed, shall be informed of the reason for a batsman retiring.

(a) If a batsman retires because of illness, injury or any other unavoidable cause, he is entitled to resume his innings subject to (c) below. If for any reason he does not do so, his innings is to be recorded as "Retired – not out".

(b) If a batsman retires for any reason other than as in (a) above, he may resume his innings only with the consent of the opposing captain. If for any reason he does not resume his innings it is to be recorded as "Retired – out".

(c) If after retiring a batsman resumes his innings, it shall be only at the fall of a wicket or the retirement of another batsman.

10. Commencement of a batsman's innings

Except at the start of a side's innings, a batsman shall be considered to have commenced his innings when he first steps on to the field of play, provided "Time" has not been called. The innings of the opening batsmen, and that of any new batsman at the resumption of play after a call of "Time", shall commence at the call of "Play".

LAW 3. THE UMPIRES

1. Appointment and attendance

Before the match, two umpires shall be appointed, one for each end to control the game as required by the Laws, with absolute impartiality. The umpires shall be present on the ground and report to the executive of the ground at least 45 minutes before the start of each day's play.

2. Change of umpire

An umpire shall not be changed during the match, other than in exceptional circumstances, unless he is injured or ill. If there has to be a change of umpire, the replacement shall act only as the striker's end umpire unless the captains agree that he should take full responsibility as an umpire.

3. Agreement with captains

Before the toss the umpires shall:

(a) Ascertain the hours of play and agree with the captains:

   (i) The balls to be used during the match. See Law 5 (The ball).

   (ii) Times and durations of intervals for meals and times for drinks intervals. See Law 15 (Intervals).

   (iii) The boundary of the field of play and allowances for boundaries. See Law 19 (Boundaries).

   (iv) Any special conditions of play affecting the conduct of the match.

(b) Inform the scorers of the agreements in (ii), (iii) and (iv) above.

4. To inform captains and scorers

Before the toss the umpires shall agree between themselves and inform both captains and both scorers:

   (i) Which clock or watch and back-up timepiece is to be used during the match.

   (ii) Whether or not any obstacle within the field of play is to be regarded as a boundary. See Law 19 (Boundaries).

5. The wickets, creases and boundaries

Before the toss and during the match, the umpires shall satisfy themselves that:

   (i) The wickets are properly pitched. See Law 8 (The wickets).

(ii) The creases are correctly marked. See Law 9 (The bowling, popping and return creases).

(iii) The boundary of the field of play complies with the requirements of Law 19.2 (Defining the boundary – boundary marking).

6. Conduct of the game, implements and equipment

Before the toss and during the match, the umpires shall satisfy themselves that:

(a) The conduct of the game is strictly in accordance with the Laws.

(b) The implements of the game conform to the requirements of Laws 5 (The ball) and 6 (The bat), together with either Laws 8.2 (Size of stumps) and 8.3 (The bails) or, if appropriate, Law 8.4 (Junior cricket).

(c)   (i) No player uses equipment other than that permitted.

(ii) The wicket-keeper's gloves comply with the requirements of Law 40.2 (Gloves).

7. Fair and unfair play

The umpires shall be the sole judges of fair and unfair play.

8. Fitness of ground, weather and light

The umpires shall be the final judges of the fitness of the ground, weather and light for play. See 9 below and Law 7.2 (Fitness of the pitch for play).

9. Suspension of play for adverse conditions of ground, weather or light

(a)   (i) All references to ground include the pitch. See Law 7.1 (Area of pitch).

(ii) For the purpose of this Law the batsmen at the wicket may deputise for their captain at any appropriate time.

(b) If at any time the umpires together agree that the condition of the ground, weather or light is not suitable for play, they shall inform the captains and, unless

(i) in unsuitable ground or weather conditions both captains agree to continue, or to commence, or to restart play, or

(ii) in unsuitable light the batting side wish to continue, or to commence, or to restart play,

they shall suspend play, or not allow play to commence or to restart.

(c)   (i) After agreeing to play in unsuitable ground or weather conditions, either captain may appeal against the conditions to the umpires before the next call of "Time". The umpires shall uphold the appeal only if, in their opinion, the factors taken into account when making their previous decision are the same or the conditions have further deteriorated.

(ii) After deciding to play in unsuitable light, the captain of the batting side may appeal against the light to the umpires before the next call of "Time". The umpires shall uphold the appeal only if, in their opinion, the factors taken into account when making their previous decision are the same or the condition of the light has further deteriorated.

(d) If at any time the umpires together agree that the conditions of ground, weather or light are so bad that there is obvious and foreseeable risk to the safety of any player or umpire, so that it would be unreasonable or dangerous for play to take place, then notwithstanding the provisions of 9(b)(i) and 9(b)(ii) above, they shall immediately suspend play, or not allow play to commence or to restart. The decision as to whether conditions are so bad as to warrant such action is one for the umpires alone to make.

Merely because the grass and the ball are wet and slippery does not warrant the ground conditions being regarded as unreasonable or dangerous. If the umpires consider the ground is so wet or slippery as to deprive the bowler of a reasonable foothold, the fielders of the power of free movement, or the batsmen of the ability to play their strokes or to run between the wickets, then these conditions shall be regarded as so bad that it would be unreasonable for play to take place.

(e) When there is a suspension of play it is the responsibility of the umpires to monitor the conditions. They shall make inspections as often as appropriate, unaccompanied by any of the players or officials. Immediately the umpires together agree that conditions are suitable for play they shall call upon the players to resume the game.

(f) If play is in progress up to the start of an agreed interval then it will resume after the interval unless the umpires together agree that conditions are or have become unsuitable or dangerous. If they do so agree, then they shall implement the procedure in (b) or (d) above, as appropriate, whether or not there had been any decision by the captains to continue, or any appeal against the conditions by either captain, prior to the commencement of the interval.

10. Exceptional circumstances

The umpires shall have the discretion to implement the procedures of 9 above for reasons other than ground, weather or light if they consider that exceptional circumstances warrant it.

11. Position of umpires

The umpires shall stand where they can best see any act upon which their decision may be required. Subject to this over-riding consideration the umpire at the bowler's end shall stand where he does not interfere with either the bowler's run-up or the striker's view.

The umpire at the striker's end may elect to stand on the off side instead of the on side of the pitch, provided he informs the captain of the fielding side, the striker and the other umpire of his intention to do so.

12. Umpires changing ends

The umpires shall change ends after each side has had one completed innings. See Law 14.2 (Forfeiture of an innings).

13. Consultation between umpires

All disputes shall be determined by the umpires. The umpires shall consult with each other whenever necessary. See also Law 27.6 (Consultation by umpires).

14. Signals

(a) The following code of signals shall be used by umpires.

(i) Signals made while the ball is in play:

Dead ball	— by crossing and re-crossing the wrists below the waist.
No-ball	— by extending one arm horizontally.
Out	— by raising the index finger above the head. (If not out the umpire shall call "Not out".)
Wide	— by extending both arms horizontally.

(ii) When the ball is dead, the signals above, with the exception of the signal for "Out", shall be repeated to the scorers. The signals listed below shall be made to the scorers only when the ball is dead.

Boundary 4	— by waving an arm from side to side finishing with the arm across the chest.
Boundary 6	— by raising both arms above the head.
Bye	— by raising an open hand above the head.
Commencement of last hour	— by pointing to a raised wrist with the other hand.
Five penalty runs awarded to the batting side	— by repeated tapping of one shoulder with the opposite hand.
Five penalty runs awarded to the fielding side	— by placing one hand on the opposite shoulder.
Leg-bye	— by touching a raised knee with the hand.
New ball	— by holding the ball above the head.
Revoke last signal	— by touching both shoulders, each with the opposite hand.

Short run   – by bending one arm upwards and touching the
                                              nearer shoulder with the tips of the fingers.

(b) The umpires shall wait until each signal to the scorers has been separately acknowledged
by a scorer before allowing play to proceed.

15. Correctness of scores

Consultation between umpires and scorers on doubtful points is essential. The umpires shall satisfy
themselves as to the correctness of the number of runs scored, the wickets that have fallen and,
where appropriate, the number of overs bowled. They shall agree these with the scorers at least
at every interval, other than a drinks interval, and at the conclusion of the match. See Laws 4.2
(Correctness of scores), 21.8 (Correctness of result) and 21.10 (Result not to be changed).

LAW 4.   THE SCORERS

1. Appointment of scorers

Two scorers shall be appointed to record all runs scored, all wickets taken and, where appropriate,
number of overs bowled.

2. Correctness of scores

The scorers shall frequently check to ensure that their records agree. They shall agree with the
umpires, at least at every interval, other than a drinks interval, and at the conclusion of the match,
the runs scored, the wickets that have fallen and, where appropriate, the number of overs bowled.
See Law 3.15 (Correctness of scores).

3. Acknowledging signals

The scorers shall accept all instructions and signals given to them by the umpires. They shall
immediately acknowledge each separate signal.

LAW 5.   THE BALL

1. Weight and size

The ball, when new, shall weigh not less than 5½oz/155.9g, nor more than 5¾oz/163g, and shall
measure not less than 8¹³/₁₆in/22.4cm, nor more than 9in/22.9cm in circumference.

2. Approval and control of balls

(a) All balls to be used in the match, having been approved by the umpires and captains,
shall be in the possession of the umpires before the toss and shall remain under their control
throughout the match.

(b) The umpire shall take possession of the ball in use at the fall of each wicket, at the start
of any interval and at any interruption of play.

3. New ball

Unless an agreement to the contrary has been made before the match, either captain may demand
a new ball at the start of each innings.

4. New ball in match of more than one day's duration

In a match of more than one day's duration, the captain of the fielding side may demand a new
ball after the prescribed number of overs has been bowled with the old one. The governing body
for cricket in the country concerned shall decide the number of overs applicable in that country,
which shall not be less than 75 overs.

The umpires shall indicate to the batsmen and the scorers whenever a new ball is taken into
play.

5. Ball lost or becoming unfit for play

If, during play, the ball cannot be found or recovered or the umpires agree that it has become unfit for play through normal use, the umpires shall replace it with a ball which has had wear comparable with that which the previous ball had received before the need for its replacement. When the ball is replaced the umpires shall inform the batsmen and the fielding captain.

6. Specifications

The specifications as described in 1 above shall apply to men's cricket only. The following specifications will apply to:

(i) *Women's cricket*
Weight   – from 4¹⁵⁄₁₆oz/140g to 5⁵⁄₁₆oz/151g.
Circumference – from 8¼in/21.0cm to 8⅞in/22.5cm.

(ii) *Junior cricket – Under-13*
Weight   – from 4¹¹⁄₁₆oz/133g to 5¹⁄₁₆oz/144g.
Circumference – from 8¹⁄₁₆in/20.5cm to 8¹¹⁄₁₆in/22.0cm.

LAW 6. THE BAT

1. Width and length

The bat overall shall not be more than 38in/96.5cm in length. The blade of the bat shall be made solely of wood and shall not exceed 4¼in/10.8cm at the widest part.

2. Covering the blade

The blade may be covered with material for protection, strengthening or repair. Such material shall not exceed ¹⁄₁₆in/1.56mm in thickness, and shall not be likely to cause unacceptable damage to the ball.

3. Hand or glove to count as part of bat

In these Laws,

(a) Reference to the bat shall imply that the bat is held by the batsman.

(b) Contact between the ball and either

(i) the striker's bat itself, or

(ii) the striker's hand holding the bat, or

(iii) any part of a glove worn on the striker's hand holding the bat

shall be regarded as the ball striking or touching the bat, or being struck by the bat.

LAW 7. THE PITCH

1. Area of pitch

The pitch is a rectangular area of the ground 22yds/20.12m in length and 10ft/3.05m in width. It is bounded at either end by the bowling creases and on either side by imaginary lines, one each side of the imaginary line joining the centres of the two middle stumps, each parallel to it and 5ft/1.52m from it. See Laws 8.1 (Width and pitching) and 9.2 (The bowling crease).

2. Fitness of the pitch for play

The umpires shall be the final judges of the fitness of the pitch for play. See Laws 3.8 (Fitness of ground, weather and light) and 3.9 (Suspension of play for adverse conditions of ground, weather or light).

3. Selection and preparation

Before the toss the ground authority shall be responsible for the selection and preparation of the pitch. During the match the umpires shall control its use and maintenance.

4. Changing the pitch

The pitch shall not be changed during the match unless the umpires decide that it is unreasonable or dangerous for play to continue on it and then only with the consent of both captains.

5. Non-turf pitches

In the event of a non-turf pitch being used, the artificial surface shall conform to the following measurements:

> Length – a minimum of 58ft/17.68m.
> Width – a minimum of 6ft/1.83m.

See Law 10.8 (Non-turf pitches).

LAW 8.   THE WICKETS

1. Width and pitching

Two sets of wickets shall be pitched opposite and parallel to each other at a distance of 22yds/20.12m between the centres of the two middle stumps. Each set shall be 9in/22.86cm wide and shall consist of three wooden stumps with two wooden bails on top.

2. Size of stumps

The tops of the stumps shall be 28in/71.1cm above the playing surface and shall be dome-shaped except for the bail grooves. The portion of a stump above the playing surface shall be cylindrical, apart from the domed top, with a circular section of diameter not less than $1^3/_8$in/3.49cm nor more than $1^1/_2$in/3.81cm.

3. The bails

    (a) The bails, when in position on the top of the stumps:

        (i) Shall not project more than $1/_2$in/1.27cm above them.

        (ii) Shall fit between the stumps without forcing them out of the vertical.

    (b) Each bail shall conform to the following specifications.

Overall length	– $4^5/_{16}$in/10.95cm.
Length of barrel	– $2^1/_8$in/5.40cm.
Longer spigot	– $1^3/_8$in/3.49cm.
Shorter spigot	– $^{13}/_{16}$in/2.06cm.

4. Junior cricket

In junior cricket, the same definitions of the wickets shall apply subject to the following measurements being used:

Width	– 8in/20.32cm.
Pitched for Under-13	– 21yds/19.20m.
Pitched for Under-11	– 20yds/18.29m.
Pitched for Under-9	– 18yds/16.46m.
Height above playing surface	– 27in/68.58cm.

Each stump

Diameter	– not less than $1^1/_4$in/3.18cm nor more than $1^3/_8$in/3.49cm.

Each bail

Overall	– $3^{13}/_{16}$in/9.68cm.
Barrel	– $1^{13}/_{16}$in/4.60cm.
Longer Spigot	– $1^1/_4$in/3.18cm.
Shorter Spigot	– $3/_4$in/1.91cm.

5. Dispensing with bails

The umpires may agree to dispense with the use of bails, if necessary. If they so agree then no bails shall be used at either end. The use of bails shall be resumed as soon as conditions permit. See Law 28.4 (Dispensing with bails).

LAW 9. THE BOWLING, POPPING AND RETURN CREASES

1. The creases

A bowling crease, a popping crease and two return creases shall be marked in white, as set out in 2, 3 and 4 below, at each end of the pitch.

2. The bowling crease

The bowling crease, which is the back edge of the crease marking, shall be the line through the centres of the three stumps at that end. It shall be 8ft 8in/2.64m in length, with the stumps in the centre.

3. The popping crease

The popping crease, which is the back edge of the crease marking, shall be in front of and parallel to the bowling crease and shall be 4ft/1.22m from it. The popping crease shall be marked to a minimum of 6ft/1.83m on either side of the imaginary line joining the centres of the middle stumps and shall be considered to be unlimited in length.

4. The return creases

The return creases, which are the inside edges of the crease markings, shall be at right angles to the popping crease at a distance of 4ft 4in/1.32m either side of the imaginary line joining the centres of the two middle stumps. Each return crease shall be marked from the popping crease to a minimum of 8ft/2.44m behind it and shall be considered to be unlimited in length.

LAW 10. PREPARATION AND MAINTENANCE OF THE PLAYING AREA

1. Rolling

The pitch shall not be rolled during the match except as permitted in (a) and (b) below.

(a) Frequency and duration of rolling
During the match the pitch may be rolled at the request of the captain of the batting side, for a period of not more than seven minutes, before the start of each innings, other than the first innings of the match, and before the start of each subsequent day's play. See (d) below.

(b) Rolling after a delayed start
In addition to the rolling permitted above, if, after the toss and before the first innings of the match, the start is delayed, the captain of the batting side may request to have the pitch rolled for not more than seven minutes. However, if the umpires together agree that the delay has had no significant effect on the state of the pitch, they shall refuse the request for the rolling of the pitch.

(c) Choice of rollers
If there is more than one roller available the captain of the batting side shall have the choice.

(d) Timing of permitted rolling
The rolling permitted (maximum seven minutes) before play begins on any day shall be started not more than 30 minutes before the time scheduled or rescheduled for play to begin. The captain of the batting side may, however, delay the start of such rolling until not less than ten minutes before the time scheduled or rescheduled for play to begin, should he so desire.

(e) Insufficient time to complete rolling
If a captain declares an innings closed, or forfeits an innings, or enforces the follow-on, and the other captain is prevented thereby from exercising his option of the rolling permitted (maximum seven minutes), or if he is so prevented for any other reason, the extra time required to complete the rolling shall be taken out of the normal playing time.

2. Sweeping

(a) If rolling is to take place the pitch shall first be swept to avoid any possible damage by rolling in debris. This sweeping shall be done so that the seven minutes allowed for rolling is not affected.

(b) The pitch shall be cleared of any debris at all intervals for meals, between innings and at the beginning of each day, not earlier than 30 minutes nor later than ten minutes before the time scheduled or rescheduled for play to begin. See Law 15.1 (An interval).

(c) Notwithstanding the provisions of (a) and (b) above, the umpires shall not allow sweeping to take place where they consider it may be detrimental to the surface of the pitch.

3. Mowing

(a) The pitch
The pitch shall be mown on each day of the match on which play is expected to take place, if ground and weather conditions allow.

(b) The outfield
In order to ensure that conditions are as similar as possible for both sides, the outfield shall be mown on each day of the match on which play is expected to take place, if ground and weather conditions allow.

If, for reasons other than ground and weather conditions, complete mowing of the outfield is not possible, the ground authority shall notify the captains and umpires of the procedure to be adopted for such mowing during the match.

(c) Responsibility for mowing
All mowings which are carried out before the match shall be the responsibility of the ground authority.

All subsequent mowings shall be carried out under the supervision of the umpires.

(d) Time of mowing
  (i) Mowing of the pitch on any day of the match shall be completed not later than 30 minutes before the time scheduled or rescheduled for play to begin on that day.

  (ii) Mowing of the outfield on any day of the match shall be completed not later than 15 minutes before the time scheduled or rescheduled for play to begin on that day.

4. Watering

The pitch shall not be watered during the match.

5. Re-marking creases

The creases shall be re-marked whenever either umpire considers it necessary.

6. Maintenance of footholes

The umpires shall ensure that the holes made by the bowlers and batsmen are cleaned out and dried whenever necessary to facilitate play. In matches of more than one day's duration, the umpires shall allow, if necessary, the re-turfing of footholes made by the bowler in his delivery stride, or the use of quick-setting fillings for the same purpose.

7. Securing of footholds and maintenance of pitch

During play, the umpires shall allow the players to secure their footholds by the use of sawdust provided that no damage to the pitch is caused and that Law 42 (Fair and unfair play) is not contravened.

8. Non-turf pitches

Wherever appropriate, the provisions set out in 1 to 7 above shall apply.

LAW 11. COVERING THE PITCH

1. Before the match

The use of covers before the match is the responsibility of the ground authority and may include full covering if required. However, the ground authority shall grant suitable facility to the captains to inspect the pitch before the nomination of their players and to the umpires to discharge their duties as laid down in Laws 3 (The umpires), 7 (The pitch), 8 (The wickets), 9 (The bowling, popping and return creases) and 10 (Preparation and maintenance of the playing area).

2. During the match

The pitch shall not be completely covered during the match unless provided otherwise by regulations or by agreement before the toss.

3. Covering bowlers' run-ups

Whenever possible, the bowlers' run-ups shall be covered in inclement weather, in order to keep them dry. Unless there is agreement for full covering under 2 above the covers so used shall not extend further than 5ft/1.52m in front of each popping crease.

4. Removal of covers

(a) If after the toss the pitch is covered overnight, the covers shall be removed in the morning at the earliest possible moment on each day that play is expected to take place.

(b) If covers are used during the day as protection from inclement weather, or if inclement weather delays the removal of overnight covers, they shall be removed promptly as soon as conditions allow.

LAW 12. INNINGS

1. Number of innings

(a) A match shall be one or two innings of each side according to agreement reached before the start of play.

(b) It may be agreed to limit any innings to a number of overs or by a period of time. If such an agreement is made then:

    (i) In a one-innings match it shall apply to both innings.

    (ii) In a two-innings match it shall apply to either
    the first innings of each side, or
    the second innings of each side, or
    both innings of each side.

2. Alternate innings

In a two-innings match each side shall take their innings alternately except in the cases provided for in Law 13 (The follow-on) or Law 14.2 (Forfeiture of an innings).

3. Completed innings

A side's innings is to be considered as completed if:

(a) The side is all out, or

(b) At the fall of a wicket, further balls remain to be bowled, but no further batsman is available to come in, or

(c) The captain declares the innings closed, or

(d) The captain forfeits the innings, or

(e) In the case of an agreement under 1(b) above, either

    (i) the prescribed number of overs has been bowled, or

    (ii) the prescribed time has expired.

4. The toss

The captains shall toss for the choice of innings on the field of play not earlier than 30 minutes, nor later than 15 minutes, before the scheduled or any rescheduled time for the match to start. Note, however, the provisions of Law 1.3 (Captain).

5. Decision to be notified

The captain of the side winning the toss shall notify the opposing captain of his decision to bat or to field, not later than ten minutes before the scheduled or any rescheduled time for the match to start. Once notified the decision may not be altered.

LAW 13.   THE FOLLOW-ON

1. Lead on first innings

(a) In a two-innings match of five days or more, the side which bats first and leads by at least 200 runs shall have the option of requiring the other side to follow their innings.

(b) The same option shall be available in two-innings matches of shorter duration with the minimum required leads as follows:

(i) 150 runs in a match of three or four days.

(ii) 100 runs in a two-day match.

(iii) 75 runs in a one-day match.

2. Notification

A captain shall notify the opposing captain and the umpires of his intention to take up this option. Law 10.1 (e) (Insufficient time to complete rolling) shall apply.

3. First day's play lost

If no play takes place on the first day of a match of more than one day's duration, 1 above shall apply in accordance with the number of days remaining from the actual start of the match. The day on which play first commences shall count as a whole day for this purpose, irrespective of the time at which play starts.

Play will have taken place as soon as, after the call of "Play", the first over has started. See Law 22.2 (Start of an over).

LAW 14.   DECLARATION AND FORFEITURE

1. Time of declaration

The captain of the batting side may declare an innings closed, when the ball is dead, at any time during a match.

2. Forfeiture of an innings

A captain may forfeit either of his side's innings. A forfeited innings shall be considered as a completed innings.

3. Notification

A captain shall notify the opposing captain and the umpires of his decision to declare or to forfeit an innings. Law 10.1 (e) (Insufficient time to complete rolling) shall apply.

LAW 15.   INTERVALS

1. An interval

The following shall be classed as intervals:

(i) The period between close of play on one day and the start of the next day's play.

(ii) Intervals between innings.

(iii) Intervals for meals.

(iv) Intervals for drinks.

(v) Any other agreed interval.

All these intervals shall be considered as scheduled breaks for the purposes of Law 2.5 (Fielder absent or leaving the field).

2. Agreement of intervals

(a) Before the toss:

(i) The hours of play shall be established.

(ii) Except as in (b) below, the timing and duration of intervals for meals shall be agreed.

(iii) The timing and duration of any other interval under 1(v) above shall be agreed.

(b) In a one-day match no specific time need be agreed for the tea interval. It may be agreed instead to take this interval between the innings.

(c) Intervals for drinks may not be taken during the last hour of the match, as defined in Law 16.6 (Last hour of match – number of overs). Subject to this limitation the captains and umpires shall agree the times for such intervals, if any, before the toss and on each subsequent day not later than ten minutes before play is scheduled to start. See also Law 3.3 (Agreement with captains).

3. Duration of intervals

(a) An interval for lunch or for tea shall be of the duration agreed under 2(a) above, taken from the call of "Time" before the interval until the call of "Play" on resumption after the interval.

(b) An interval between innings shall be ten minutes from the close of an innings to the call of "Play" for the start of the next innings, except as in 4, 6 and 7 below.

4. No allowance for interval between innings

In addition to the provisions of 6 and 7 below:

(a) If an innings ends when ten minutes or less remain before the time agreed for close of play on any day, there will be no further play on that day. No change will be made to the time for the start of play on the following day on account of the ten minutes between innings.

(b) If a captain declares an innings closed during an interruption in play of more than ten minutes duration, no adjustment shall be made to the time for resumption of play on account of the ten minutes between innings, which shall be considered as included in the interruption. Law 10.1(e) (Insufficient time to complete rolling) shall apply.

(c) If a captain declares an innings closed during any interval other than an interval for drinks, the interval shall be of the agreed duration and shall be considered to include the ten minutes between innings. Law 10.1(e) (Insufficient time to complete rolling) shall apply.

5. Changing agreed times for intervals

If for adverse conditions of ground, weather or light, or for any other reason, playing time is lost, the umpires and captains together may alter the time of the lunch interval or of the tea interval. See also 6, 7 and 9(c) below.

6. Changing agreed time for lunch interval

(a) If an innings ends when ten minutes or less remain before the agreed time for lunch, the interval shall be taken immediately. It shall be of the agreed length and shall be considered to include the ten minutes between innings.

(b) If, because of adverse conditions of ground, weather or light, or in exceptional circumstances, a stoppage occurs when ten minutes or less remain before the agreed time for lunch then, notwithstanding 5 above, the interval shall be taken immediately. It shall be of the agreed length. Play shall resume at the end of this interval or as soon after as conditions permit.

(c) If the players have occasion to leave the field for any reason when more than ten minutes remain before the agreed time for lunch then, unless the umpires and captains together agree to alter it, lunch will be taken at the agreed time.

7. Changing agreed time for tea interval

(a) (i) If an innings ends when 30 minutes or less remain before the agreed time for tea, then the interval shall be taken immediately. It shall be of the agreed length and shall be considered to include the ten minutes between innings.

(ii) If, when 30 minutes remain before the agreed time for tea, an interval between innings is already in progress, play will resume at the end of the ten-minute interval.

(b) (i) If, because of adverse conditions of ground, weather or light, or in exceptional circumstances, a stoppage occurs when 30 minutes or less remain before the agreed time for tea, then unless
   either there is an agreement to change the time for tea, as permitted in 5 above,
   or the captains agree to forgo the tea interval, as permitted in 10 below,
the interval shall be taken immediately. The interval shall be of the agreed length. Play shall resume at the end of this interval or as soon after as conditions permit.

(ii) If a stoppage is already in progress when 30 minutes remain before the time agreed for tea, 5 above will apply.

8. Tea interval – nine wickets down

If nine wickets are down at the end of the over in progress when the agreed time for the tea interval has been reached, then play shall continue for a period not exceeding 30 minutes, unless the players have cause to leave the field of play, or the innings is concluded earlier.

9. Intervals for drinks

(a) If on any day the captains agree that there shall be intervals for drinks, the option to take such intervals shall be available to either side. Each interval shall be kept as short as possible and in any case shall not exceed five minutes.

(b) (i) Unless both captains agree to forgo any drinks interval, it shall be taken at the end of the over in progress when the agreed time is reached. If, however, a wicket falls within five minutes of the agreed time then drinks shall be taken immediately. No other variation in the timing of drinks intervals shall be permitted except as provided for in (c) below.

(ii) For the purpose of (i) above and Law 3.9(a)(ii) (Suspension of play for adverse conditions of ground, weather or light) only, the batsmen at the wicket may deputise for their captain.

(c) If an innings ends or the players have to leave the field of play for any other reason within 30 minutes of the agreed time for a drinks interval, the umpires and captains together may rearrange the timing of drinks intervals in that session.

10. Agreement to forgo intervals

At any time during the match, the captains may agree to forgo the tea interval or any of the drinks intervals. The umpires shall be informed of the decision.

11. Scorers to be informed

The umpires shall ensure that the scorers are informed of all agreements about hours of play and intervals, and of any changes made thereto as permitted under this Law.

LAW 16.   START OF PLAY; CESSATION OF PLAY

1. Call of "Play"

The umpire at the bowler's end shall call "Play" at the start of the match and on the resumption of play after any interval or interruption.

2. Call of "Time"

The umpire at the bowler's end shall call "Time" on the cessation of play before any interval or interruption of play and at the conclusion of the match. See Law 27 (Appeals).

3. Removal of bails

After the call of "Time", the bails shall be removed from both wickets.

4. Starting a new over

Another over shall always be started at any time during the match, unless an interval is to be taken in the circumstances set out in 5 below, if the umpire, after walking at his normal pace, has arrived at his position behind the stumps at the bowler's end before the time agreed for the next interval, or for the close of play, has been reached.

5. Completion of an over

Other than at the end of the match:

> (a) If the agreed time for an interval is reached during an over, the over shall be completed before the interval is taken except as provided for in (b) below.

> (b) When less than two minutes remain before the time agreed for the next interval, the interval will be taken immediately if either

>> (i) a batsman is out or retires, or

>> (ii) the players have occasion to leave the field

> whether this occurs during an over or at the end of an over. Except at the end of an innings, if an over is thus interrupted it shall be completed on resumption of play.

6. Last hour of match – number of overs

When one hour of playing time of the match remains, according to the agreed hours of play, the over in progress shall be completed. The next over shall be the first of a minimum of 20 overs which must be bowled, provided that a result is not reached earlier and provided that there is no interval or interruption in play.

The umpire at the bowler's end shall indicate the commencement of this 20 overs to the players and the scorers. The period of play thereafter shall be referred to as the last hour, whatever its actual duration.

7. Last hour of match – interruptions of play

If there is an interruption in play during the last hour of the match, the minimum number of overs to be bowled shall be reduced from 20 as follows:

> (a) The time lost for an interruption is counted from the call of "Time" until the time for resumption of play as decided by the umpires.

> (b) One over shall be deducted for every complete three minutes of time lost.

> (c) In the case of more than one such interruption, the minutes lost shall not be aggregated; the calculation shall be made for each interruption separately.

> (d) If, when one hour of playing time remains, an interruption is already in progress:

>> (i) Only the time lost after this moment shall be counted in the calculation.

>> (ii) The over in progress at the start of the interruption shall be completed on resumption of play and shall not count as one of the minimum number of overs to be bowled.

> (e) If, after the start of the last hour, an interruption occurs during an over, the over shall be completed on resumption of play. The two part-overs shall between them count as one over of the minimum number to be bowled.

8. Last hour of match – intervals between innings

If an innings ends so that a new innings is to be started during the last hour of the match, the interval starts with the end of the innings and is to end ten minutes later.

(a) If this interval is already in progress at the start of the last hour, then to determine the number of overs to be bowled in the new innings, calculations are to be made as set out in 7 above.

(b) If the innings ends after the last hour has started, two calculations are to be made, as set out in (c) and (d) below. The greater of the numbers yielded by these two calculations is to be the minimum number of overs to be bowled in the new innings.

(c) Calculation based on overs remaining:

    (i) At the conclusion of the innings, the number of overs that remain to be bowled, of the minimum in the last hour, to be noted.

    (ii) If this is not a whole number it is to be rounded up to the next whole number.

    (iii) Three overs to be deducted from the result for the interval.

(d) Calculation based on time remaining:

    (i) At the conclusion of the innings, the time remaining until the agreed time for close of play to be noted.

    (ii) Ten minutes to be deducted from this time, for the interval, to determine the playing time remaining.

    (iii) A calculation to be made of one over for every complete three minutes of the playing time remaining, plus one more over for any further part of three minutes remaining.

9. Conclusion of match

The match is concluded:

(a) As soon as a result, as defined in sections 1, 2, 3 or 4 of Law 21 (The result), is reached.

(b) As soon as both

    (i) the minimum number of overs for the last hour are completed, and

    (ii) the agreed time for close of play is reached

unless a result has been reached earlier.

(c) If, without the match being concluded either as in (a) or in (b) above, the players leave the field, either for adverse conditions of ground, weather or light, or in exceptional circumstances, and no further play is possible thereafter.

10. Completion of last over of match

The over in progress at the close of play on the final day shall be completed unless either

    (i) a result has been reached, or

    (ii) the players have occasion to leave the field. In this case there shall be no resumption of play except in the circumstances of Law 21.9 (Mistakes in scoring), and the match shall be at an end.

11. Bowler unable to complete an over during last hour of match

If, for any reason, a bowler is unable to complete an over during the last hour, Law 22.8 (Bowler incapacitated or suspended during an over) shall apply.

LAW 17. PRACTICE ON THE FIELD

1. Practice on the field

(a) There shall be no bowling or batting practice on the pitch, or on the area parallel and immediately adjacent to the pitch, at any time on any day of the match.

(b) There shall be no bowling or batting practice on any other part of the square on any day of the match, except before the start of play or after the close of play on that day. Practice before the start of play:

(i) Must not continue later than 30 minutes before the scheduled time or any rescheduled time for play to start on that day.

(ii) Shall not be allowed if the umpires consider that, in the prevailing conditions of ground and weather, it will be detrimental to the surface of the square.

(c) There shall be no practice on the field of play between the call of "Play" and the call of "Time", if the umpire considers that it could result in a waste of time. See Law 42.9 (Time-wasting by the fielding side).

(d) If a player contravenes (a) or (b) above he shall not be allowed to bowl until at least five complete overs have been bowled by his side after the contravention. If an over is in progress at the contravention he shall not be allowed to complete that over nor shall the remaining part-over count towards the five overs above.

2. Trial run-up

No bowler shall have a trial run-up between the call of "Play" and the call of "Time" unless the umpire is satisfied that it will not cause any waste of time.

LAW 18.   SCORING RUNS

1. A run

The score shall be reckoned by runs. A run is scored:

(a) So often as the batsmen, at any time while the ball is in play, have crossed and made good their ground from end to end.

(b) When a boundary is scored. See Law 19 (Boundaries).

(c) When penalty runs are awarded. See 6 below.

(d) When "Lost ball" is called. See Law 20 (Lost ball).

2. Runs disallowed

Notwithstanding 1 above, or any other provisions elsewhere in the Laws, the scoring of runs or awarding of penalties will be subject to any disallowance of runs provided for within the Laws that may be applicable.

3. Short runs

(a) A run is short if a batsman fails to make good his ground on turning for a further run.

(b) Although a short run shortens the succeeding one, the latter if completed shall not be regarded as short. A striker taking stance in front of his popping crease may run from that point also without penalty.

4. Unintentional short runs

Except in the circumstances of 5 below:

(a) If either batsman runs a short run, unless a boundary is scored the umpire concerned shall call and signal "Short run" as soon as the ball becomes dead and that run shall not be scored.

(b) If, after either or both batsmen run short, a boundary is scored, the umpire concerned shall disregard the short running and shall not call or signal "Short run".

(c) If both batsmen run short in one and the same run, this shall be regarded as only one short run.

(d) If more than one run is short then, subject to (b) and (c) above, all runs so called shall not be scored.

If there has been more than one short run the umpire shall inform the scorers as to the number of runs scored.

5. Deliberate short runs

Notwithstanding 4 above, if either umpire considers that either or both batsmen deliberately runs short at his end, the following procedure shall be adopted:

(a) (i) The umpire concerned shall, when the ball is dead, warn the batsman or batsmen that the practice is unfair, indicate that this is a first and final warning and inform the other umpire of what has occurred.

(ii) The batsmen shall return to their original ends.

(iii) Whether a batsman is dismissed or not, the umpire at the bowler's end shall disallow all runs to the batting side from that delivery other than the penalty for a no-ball or wide, or penalties under Laws 42.5 (Deliberate distraction or obstruction of batsman) and 42.13 (Fielders damaging the pitch), if applicable.

(iv) The umpire at the bowler's end shall inform the scorers as to the number of runs scored.

(b) If there is any further instance of deliberate short running by either of the same batsmen in that innings, when the ball is dead the umpire concerned shall inform the other umpire of what has occurred and the procedure set out in (a)(ii) and (iii) above shall be repeated. Additionally, the umpire at the bowler's end shall:

(i) Award five penalty runs to the fielding side. See Law 42.17 (Penalty runs).

(ii) Inform the scorers as to the number of runs scored.

(iii) Inform the batsmen, the captain of the fielding side and, as soon as practicable, the captain of the batting side of the reason for this action.

(iv) Report the occurrence, with the other umpire, to the executive of the batting side and any governing body responsible for the match, who shall take such action as is considered appropriate against the captain and player or players concerned.

6. Runs scored for penalties

Runs shall be scored for penalties under 5 above and Laws 2.6 (Player returning without permission), 24 (No-ball), 25 (Wide ball), 41.2 (Fielding the ball), 41.3 (Protective helmets belonging to the fielding side) and 42 (Fair and unfair play).

7. Runs scored for boundaries

Runs shall be scored for boundary allowances under Law 19 (Boundaries).

8. Runs scored for lost ball

Runs shall be scored when "Lost ball" is called under Law 20 (Lost ball).

9. Batsman dismissed

When either batsman is dismissed:

(a) Any penalties to either side that may be applicable shall stand but no other runs shall be scored, except as stated in 10 below. Note, however, Law 42.17(b) (Penalty runs).

(b) 12(a) below will apply if the method of dismissal is caught, handled the ball or obstructing the field. 12(a) will also apply if a batsman is run out, except in the circumstances of Law 2.8 (Transgression of the Laws by a batsman who has a runner) where 12(b) below will apply.

(c) The not out batsman shall return to his original end except as stated in (b) above.

10. Runs scored when a batsman is dismissed

In addition to any penalties to either side that may be applicable, if a batsman is:

(a) Dismissed handled the ball, the batting side shall score the runs completed before the offence.

(b) Dismissed obstructing the field, the batting side shall score the runs completed before the offence.

If, however, the obstruction prevents a catch from being made, no runs other than penalties shall be scored.

(c) Dismissed run out, the batting side shall score the runs completed before the dismissal. If however, a striker with a runner is himself dismissed run out, no runs other than penalties shall be scored. See Law 2.8 (Transgression of the Laws by a batsman who has a runner).

11. Runs scored when ball becomes dead

(a) When the ball becomes dead on the fall of a wicket, runs shall be scored as laid down in 9 and 10 above.

(b) When the ball becomes dead for any reason other than the fall of a wicket, or is called dead by an umpire, unless there is specific provision otherwise in the Laws, the batting side shall be credited with:

   (i) All runs completed by the batsmen before the incident or call, and

   (ii) the run in progress if the batsmen have crossed at the instant of the incident or call. Note specifically, however, the provisions of Law 34.4(c) (Runs permitted from a ball lawfully struck more than once) and 42.5(b)(iii) (Deliberate distraction or obstruction of batsman), and

   (iii) any penalties that are applicable.

12. Batsman returning to wicket he has left

(a) If, while the ball is in play, the batsmen have crossed in running, neither shall return to the wicket he has left, except as in (b) below.

(b) The batsmen shall return to the wickets they originally left in the cases of, and only in the cases of:

   (i) A boundary.

   (ii) Disallowance of runs for any reason.

   (iii) The dismissal of a batsman, except as in 9(b) above.

LAW 19.   BOUNDARIES

1. The boundary of the field of play

(a) Before the toss, the umpires shall agree the boundary of the field of play with both captains. The boundary shall if possible be marked along its whole length.

(b) The boundary shall be agreed so that no part of any sightscreen is within the field of play.

(c) An obstacle or person within the field of play shall not be regarded as a boundary unless so decided by the umpires before the toss. See Law 3.4(ii) (To inform captains and scorers).

2. Defining the boundary – boundary marking

(a) Wherever practicable the boundary shall be marked by means of a white line or a rope laid along the ground.

(b) If the boundary is marked by a white line:

   (i) The inside edge of the line shall be the boundary edge.

   (ii) A flag, post or board used merely to highlight the position of a line marked on the ground must be placed outside the boundary edge and is not itself to be regarded as defining or marking the boundary. Note, however, the provisions of (c) below.

(c) If a solid object is used to mark the boundary, it must have an edge or a line to constitute the boundary edge.

   (i) For a rope, which includes any similar object of curved cross section lying on the ground, the boundary edge will be the line formed by the innermost points of the rope along its length.

   (ii) For a fence, which includes any similar object in contact with the ground, but with a flat surface projecting above the ground, the boundary edge will be the base line of the fence.

(d) If the boundary edge is not defined as in (b) or (c) above, the umpires and captains must agree, before the toss, what line will be the boundary edge. Where there is no physical marker for a section of boundary, the boundary edge shall be the imaginary straight line joining the two nearest marked points of the boundary edge.

(e) If a solid object used to mark the boundary is disturbed for any reason during play, then if possible it shall be restored to its original position as soon as the ball is dead. If this is not possible, then:

    (i) If some part of the fence or other marker has come within the field of play, that portion is to be removed from the field of play as soon as the ball is dead.

    (ii) The line where the base of the fence or marker originally stood shall define the boundary edge.

3. Scoring a boundary

(a) A boundary shall be scored and signalled by the umpire at the bowler's end whenever, while the ball is in play, in his opinion:

    (i) The ball touches the boundary, or is grounded beyond the boundary.

    (ii) A fielder, with some part of his person in contact with the ball, touches the boundary or has some part of his person grounded beyond the boundary.

(b) The phrases "touches the boundary" and "touching the boundary" shall mean contact with either

    (i) the boundary edge as defined in 2 above, or

    (ii) any person or obstacle within the field of play which has been designated a boundary by the umpires before the toss.

(c) The phrase "grounded beyond the boundary" shall mean contact with either

    (i) any part of a line or a solid object marking the boundary, except its boundary edge, or

    (ii) the ground outside the boundary edge, or

    (iii) any object in contact with the ground outside the boundary edge.

4. Runs allowed for boundaries

(a) Before the toss, the umpires shall agree with both captains the runs to be allowed for boundaries. In deciding the allowances, the umpires and captains shall be guided by the prevailing custom of the ground.

(b) Unless agreed differently under (a) above, the allowances for boundaries shall be six runs if the ball having been struck by the bat pitches beyond the boundary, but otherwise four runs. These allowances shall still apply even though the ball has previously touched a fielder. See also (c) below.

(c) The ball shall be regarded as pitching beyond the boundary and six runs shall be scored if a fielder:

    (i) Has any part of his person touching the boundary or grounded beyond the boundary when he catches the ball.

    (ii) Catches the ball and subsequently touches the boundary or grounds some part of his person beyond the boundary while carrying the ball but before completing the catch. See Law 32 (Caught).

5. Runs scored

When a boundary is scored:

(a) The penalty for a no-ball or a wide, if applicable, shall stand together with any penalties under any of Laws 2.6 (Player returning without permission), 18.5(b) (Deliberate short runs) or Law 42 (Fair and unfair play) that apply before the boundary is scored.

(b) The batting side, except in the circumstances of 6 below, shall additionally be awarded whichever is the greater of:

    (i) The allowance for the boundary.

    (ii) The runs completed by the batsmen, together with the run in progress if they have crossed at the instant the boundary is scored. When these runs exceed the boundary allowance, they shall replace the boundary for the purposes of Law 18.12 (Batsman returning to wicket he has left).

6. Overthrow or wilful act of fielder

If the boundary results either from an overthrow or from the wilful act of a fielder the runs scored shall be:

(i) The penalty for a no-ball or a wide, if applicable, and any penalties under Laws 2.6 (Player returning without permission), 18.5(b) (Deliberate short runs) or Law 42 (Fair and unfair play) that are applicable before the boundary is scored, and

(ii) the allowance for the boundary, and

(iii) the runs completed by the batsmen, together with the run in progress if they have crossed at the instant of the throw or act.

Law 18.12(a) (Batsman returning to the wicket he has left) shall apply as from the instant of the throw or act.

LAW 20.   LOST BALL

1. Fielder to call "Lost ball"

If a ball in play cannot be found or recovered, any fielder may call "Lost ball". The ball shall then become dead. See Law 23.1 (Ball is dead). Law 18.12(a) (Batsman returning to wicket he has left) shall apply as from the instant of the call.

2. Ball to be replaced

The umpires shall replace the ball with one which has had wear comparable with that which the previous ball had received before it was lost or became irrecoverable. See Law 5.5 (Ball lost or becoming unfit for play).

3. Runs scored

(a) The penalty for a no-ball or a wide, if applicable, shall stand, together with any penalties under any of Laws 2.6 (Player returning without permission), 18.5(b) (Deliberate short runs) or Law 42 (Fair and unfair play) that are applicable before the call of "Lost ball".

(b) The batting side shall additionally be awarded either

(i) the runs completed by the batsmen, together with the run in progress if they have crossed at the instant of the call, or

(ii) six runs,

whichever is the greater.

4. How scored

If there is a one-run penalty for a no-ball or for a wide, it shall be scored as a no-ball extra or as a wide as appropriate. See Laws 24.13 (Runs resulting from a no-ball – how scored) and 25.6 (Runs resulting from a wide – how scored). If any other penalties have been awarded to either side, they shall be scored as penalty extras. See Law 42.17 (Penalty runs).

Runs to the batting side in 3(b) above shall be credited to the striker if the ball has been struck by the bat, but otherwise to the total of byes, leg-byes, no-balls or wides as the case may be.

LAW 21.   THE RESULT

1. A win – two-innings match

The side which has scored a total of runs in excess of that scored in the two completed innings of the opposing side shall win the match. Note also 6 below.

A forfeited innings is to count as a completed innings. See Law 14 (Declaration and forfeiture).

2. A win – one-innings match

The side which has scored in its one innings a total of runs in excess of that scored by the opposing side in its one completed innings shall win the match. Note also 6 below.

3. Umpires awarding a match

(a) A match shall be lost by a side which either

(i) concedes defeat, or

(ii) in the opinion of the umpires, refuses to play

and the umpires shall award the match to the other side.

(b) If an umpire considers that an action by any player or players might constitute a refusal by either side to play then the umpires together shall ascertain the cause of the action. If they then decide together that this action does constitute a refusal to play by one side, they shall so inform the captain of that side. If the captain persists in the action the umpires shall award the match in accordance with (a)(ii) above.

(c) If action as in (b) above takes place after play has started and does not constitute a refusal to play:

    (i) Playing time lost shall be counted from the start of the action until play recommences, subject to Law 15.5 (Changing agreed times for intervals).

    (ii) The time for close of play on that day shall be extended by this length of time, subject to Law 3.9 (Suspension of play for adverse conditions of ground, weather or light).

    (iii) If applicable, no overs shall be deducted during the last hour of the match solely on account of this time.

4. A tie

The result of a match shall be a tie when the scores are equal at the conclusion of play, but only if the side batting last has completed its innings.

5. A draw

A match which is concluded, as defined in Law 16.9 (Conclusion of a match), without being determined in any of the ways stated in 1, 2, 3 or 4 above, shall count as a draw.

6. Winning hit or extras

(a) As soon as a result is reached, as defined in 1, 2, 3 or 4 above, the match is at an end. Nothing that happens thereafter shall be regarded as part of it. Note also 9 below.

(b) The side batting last will have scored enough runs to win only if its total of runs is sufficient without including any runs completed before the dismissal of the striker by the completion of a catch or by the obstruction of a catch.

(c) If a boundary is scored before the batsmen have completed sufficient runs to win the match, then the whole of the boundary allowance shall be credited to the side's total and, in the case of a hit by the bat, to the striker's score.

7. Statement of result

If the side batting last wins the match, the result shall be stated as a win by the number of wickets still then to fall. If the other side wins the match, the result shall be stated as a win by runs.

If the match is decided by one side conceding defeat or refusing to play, the result shall be stated as "Match conceded" or "Match awarded" as the case may be.

8. Correctness of result

Any decision as to the correctness of the scores shall be the responsibility of the umpires. See Law 3.15 (Correctness of scores).

9. Mistakes in scoring

If, after the umpires and players have left the field in the belief that the match has been concluded, the umpires discover that a mistake in scoring has occurred which affects the result, then, subject to 10 below, they shall adopt the following procedure.

(a) If, when the players leave the field, the side batting last has not completed its innings, and either

    (i) the number of overs to be bowled in the last hour has not been completed, or

    (ii) the agreed finishing time has not been reached,

then unless one side concedes defeat the umpires shall order play to resume.

If conditions permit, play will then continue until the prescribed number of overs has been completed and the time remaining has elapsed, unless a result is reached earlier. The number of overs and/or the time remaining shall be taken as they were when the players left the field; no account shall be taken of the time between that moment and the resumption of play.

(b) If, when the players leave the field, the overs have been completed and time has been reached, or if the side batting last has completed its innings, the umpires shall immediately inform both captains of the necessary corrections to the scores and to the result.

10. Result not to be changed

Once the umpires have agreed with the scorers the correctness of the scores at the conclusion of the match – see Laws 3.15 (Correctness of scores) and 4.2 (Correctness of scores) – the result cannot thereafter be changed.

LAW 22.   THE OVER

1. Number of balls

The ball shall be bowled from each wicket alternately in overs of six balls.

2. Start of an over

An over has started when the bowler starts his run-up or, if he has no run-up, his delivery action for the first delivery of that over.

3. Call of "Over"

When six balls have been bowled other than those which are not to count in the over and as the ball becomes dead – see Law 23 (Dead ball) – the umpire shall call "Over" before leaving the wicket.

4. Balls not to count in the over

(a) A ball shall not count as one of the six balls of the over unless it is delivered, even though a batsman may be dismissed or some other incident occurs before the ball is delivered.

(b) A ball which is delivered by the bowler shall not count as one of the six balls of the over:

   (i) If it is called dead, or is to be considered dead, before the striker has had an opportunity to play it. See Law 23 (Dead ball).

   (ii) If it is a no-ball. See Law 24 (No-ball).

   (iii) If it is a wide. See Law 25 (Wide ball).

   (iv) If it is called dead in the circumstances of either of Laws 23.3(b)(vi) (Umpire calling and signalling "Dead ball") or 42.4 (Deliberate attempt to distract striker).

5. Umpire miscounting

If an umpire miscounts the number of balls, the over as counted by the umpire shall stand.

6. Bowler changing ends

A bowler shall be allowed to change ends as often as desired, provided only that he does not bowl two overs, or parts thereof, consecutively in the same innings.

7. Finishing an over

(a) Other than at the end of an innings, a bowler shall finish an over in progress unless he is incapacitated, or he is suspended under any of Laws 17.1 (Practice on the field), 42.7 (Dangerous and unfair bowling – action by the umpire), 42.9 (Time-wasting by the fielding side), or 42.12 (Bowler running on the protected area after delivering the ball).

(b) If for any reason, other than the end of an innings, an over is left uncompleted at the start of an interval or interruption of play, it shall be completed on resumption of play.

8. Bowler incapacitated or suspended during an over

If for any reason a bowler is incapacitated while running up to bowl the first ball of an over, or is incapacitated or suspended during an over, the umpire shall call and signal "Dead ball". Another bowler shall complete the over from the same end, provided that he does not bowl two overs, or parts thereof, consecutively in one innings.

LAW 23.   DEAD BALL

1. Ball is dead

(a) The ball becomes dead when:

    (i) It is finally settled in the hands of the wicket-keeper or the bowler.

    (ii) A boundary is scored. See Law 19.3 (Scoring a boundary).

    (iii) A batsman is dismissed.

    (iv) Whether played or not it becomes trapped between the bat and person of a batsman or between items of his clothing or equipment.

    (v) Whether played or not it lodges in the clothing or equipment of a batsman or the clothing of an umpire.

    (vi) It lodges in a protective helmet worn by a member of the fielding side.

    (vii) There is a contravention of Law 41.2 (Fielding the ball) or Law 41.3 (Protective helmets belonging to the fielding side).

    (viii) This is an award of penalty runs under Law 2.6 (Player returning without permission).

    (ix) "Lost ball" is called. See Law 20 (Lost ball).

    (x) The umpire calls "Over" or "Time".

(b) The ball shall be considered to be dead when it is clear to the umpire at the bowler's end that the fielding side and both batsmen at the wicket have ceased to regard it as in play.

2. Ball finally settled

Whether the ball is finally settled or not is a matter for the umpire alone to decide.

3. Umpire calling and signalling "Dead ball"

(a) When the ball has become dead under 1 above, the bowler's end umpire may call "Dead ball", if it is necessary to inform the players.

(b) Either umpire shall call and signal "Dead ball" when:

    (i) He intervenes in a case of unfair play.

    (ii) A serious injury to a player or umpire occurs.

    (iii) He leaves his normal position for consultation.

    (iv) One or both bails fall from the striker's wicket before he has the opportunity of playing the ball.

    (v) He is satisfied that for an adequate reason the striker is not ready for the delivery of the ball and, if the ball is delivered, makes no attempt to play it.

    (vi) The striker is distracted by any noise or movement or in any other way while he is preparing to receive or receiving a delivery. This shall apply whether the source of the distraction is within the game or outside it. Note, however, the provisions of Law 42.4 (Deliberate attempt to distract the striker).
        The ball shall not count as one of the over.

    (vii) The bowler drops the ball accidentally before delivery.

    (viii) The ball does not leave the bowler's hand for any reason other than an attempt to run out the non-striker before entering his delivery stride. See Law 42.15 (Bowler attempting to run out non-striker before delivery).

    (ix) He is required to do so under any of the Laws.

4. Ball ceases to be dead

The ball ceases to be dead – that is, it comes into play – when the bowler starts his run-up or, if he has no run-up, his bowling action.

5. Action on call of "Dead ball"

(a) A ball is not to count as one of the over if it becomes dead or is to be considered dead before the striker has had an opportunity to play it.

(b) If the ball becomes dead or is to be considered dead after the striker has had an opportunity to play the ball, except in the circumstances of 3(b)(vi) above and Law 42.4 (Deliberate attempt to distract striker), no additional delivery shall be allowed unless "No-ball" or "Wide" has been called.

LAW 24.   NO-BALL

1. Mode of delivery

(a) The umpire shall ascertain whether the bowler intends to bowl right-handed or left-handed, and whether over or round the wicket, and shall so inform the striker.

It is unfair if the bowler fails to notify the umpire of a change in his mode of delivery. In this case the umpire shall call and signal "No-ball".

(b) Underarm bowling shall not be permitted except by special agreement before the match.

2. Fair delivery – the arm

For a delivery to be fair in respect of the arm the ball must not be thrown. See 3 below.

Although it is the primary responsibility of the striker's end umpire to ensure the fairness of a delivery in this respect, there is nothing in this Law to debar the bowler's end umpire from calling and signalling "No-ball" if he considers that the ball has been thrown.

(a) If, in the opinion of either umpire, the ball has been thrown, he shall:

    (i) Call and signal "No-ball".

    (ii) Caution the bowler, when the ball is dead. This caution shall apply throughout the innings.

    (iii) Inform the other umpire, the batsmen at the wicket, the captain of the fielding side and, as soon as practicable, the captain of the batting side of what has occurred.

(b) If either umpire considers that after such caution, a further delivery by the same bowler in that innings is thrown, the umpire concerned shall repeat the procedure set out in (a) above, indicating to the bowler that this is a final warning. This warning shall also apply throughout the innings.

(c) If either umpire considers that a further delivery by the same bowler in that innings is thrown.

    (i) The umpire concerned shall call and signal "No-ball". When the ball is dead he shall inform the other umpire, the batsmen at the wicket and, as soon as practicable, the captain of the batting side of what has occurred.

    (ii) The umpire at the bowler's end shall direct the captain of the fielding side to take the bowler off forthwith. The over shall be completed by another bowler, who shall neither have bowled the previous over nor be allowed to bowl the next over.

    The bowler thus taken off shall not bowl again in that innings.

    (iii) The umpires together shall report the occurrence as soon as possible to the executive of the fielding side and any governing body responsible for the match, who shall take such action as is considered appropriate against the captain and bowler concerned.

3. Definition of fair delivery – the arm

A ball is fairly delivered in respect of the arm if, once the bowler's arm has reached the level of the shoulder in the delivery swing, the elbow joint is not straightened partially or completely from that point until the ball has left the hand. This definition shall not debar a bowler from flexing or rotating the wrist in the delivery swing.

4. Bowler throwing towards striker's end before delivery

If the bowler throws the ball towards the striker's end before entering his delivery stride, either umpire shall instantly call and signal "No-ball". See Law 42.16 (Batsmen stealing a run). However, the procedure stated in 2 above of caution, informing, final warning, action against the bowler and reporting shall not apply.

5. Fair delivery – the feet

For a delivery to be fair in respect of the feet, in the delivery stride:

    (i) The bowler's back foot must land within and not touching the return crease.

    (ii) The bowler's front foot must land with some part of the foot, whether grounded or raised, behind the popping crease.

If the umpire at the bowler's end is not satisfied that both these conditions have been met, he shall call and signal "No-ball".

6. Ball bouncing more than twice or rolling along the ground

The umpire at the bowler's end shall call and signal "No-ball" if a ball which he considers to have been delivered, without having previously touched the bat or person of the striker, either

    (i) bounces more than twice, or

    (ii) rolls along the ground

before it reaches the popping crease.

7. Ball coming to rest in front of striker's wicket

If a ball delivered by the bowler comes to rest in front of the line of the striker's wicket, without having touched the bat or person of the striker, the umpire shall call and signal "No-ball" and immediately call and signal "Dead ball".

8. Call of "No-ball" for infringement of other Laws

In addition to the instances above, an umpire shall call and signal "No-ball" as required by the following Laws.

    Law 40.3   – Position of wicket-keeper.
    Law 41.5   – Limitation of on-side fielders.
    Law 41.6   – Fielders not to encroach on the pitch.
    Law 42.6   – Dangerous and unfair bowling.
    Law 42.7   – Dangerous and unfair bowling – action by the umpire.
    Law 42.8   – Deliberate bowling of high full-pitched balls.

9. Revoking a call of "No-ball"

An umpire shall revoke the call of "No-ball" if the ball does not leave the bowler's hand for any reason.

10. No-ball to over-ride wide

A call of "No-ball" shall over-ride the call of "Wide ball" at any time. See Law 25.1 (Judging a wide) and 25.3 (Call and signal of "Wide ball").

11. Ball not dead

The ball does not become dead on the call of "No-ball".

12. Penalty for a No-ball

A penalty of one run shall be awarded instantly on the call of "No-ball". Unless the call is revoked this penalty shall stand even if a batsman is dismissed. It shall be in addition to any other runs scored, any boundary allowance and any other penalties awarded.

13. Runs resulting from a no-ball – how scored

The one-run penalty for a no-ball shall be scored as a no-ball extra. If other penalty runs have been awarded to either side, these shall be scored as in Law 42.17 (Penalty runs). Any runs completed by the batsmen or a boundary allowance shall be credited to the striker if the ball has been struck by the bat; otherwise they also shall be scored as no-ball extras.

Apart from any award of a five-run penalty, all runs resulting from a no-ball, whether as no-ball extras or credited to the striker, shall be debited against the bowler.

14. No-ball not to count

A no-ball shall not count as one of the over. See Law 22.4 (Balls not to count in the over).

15. Out from a no-ball

When "No-ball" has been called, neither batsman shall be out under any of the Laws except Laws 33 (Handled the ball), 34 (Hit the ball twice), 37 (Obstructing the field) or 38 (Run out).

LAW 25.   WIDE BALL

1. Judging a wide

(a) If a bowler bowls a ball, not being a no-ball, the umpire shall adjudge it a wide if, according to the definition in (b) below, in his opinion the ball passes wide of the striker where he is standing and would also have passed wide of him in a normal guard position.

(b) The ball will be considered as passing wide of the striker unless it is sufficiently within his reach for him to be able to hit it with his bat by means of a normal cricket stroke.

2. Delivery not a wide

The umpire shall not adjudge a delivery as being a wide:

(a) If the striker, by moving, either

(i) causes the ball to pass wide of him, as defined in 1(b) above, or

(ii) brings the ball sufficiently within his reach to be able to hit it with his bat by means of a normal cricket stroke.

(b) If the ball touches the striker's bat or person.

3. Call and signal of "Wide ball"

(a) If the umpire adjudges a delivery to be a wide he shall call and signal "Wide ball" as soon as the ball passes the striker's wicket. It shall, however, be considered to have been a wide from the instant of delivery, even though it cannot be called wide until it passes the striker's wicket.

(b) The umpire shall revoke the call of "Wide ball" if there is then any contact between the ball and the striker's bat or person.

(c) The umpire shall revoke the call of "Wide ball" if a delivery is called a "No-ball". See Law 24.10 (No-ball to over-ride wide).

4. Ball not dead

The ball does not become dead on the call of "Wide ball".

5. Penalty for a wide

A penalty of one run shall be awarded instantly on the call of "Wide ball". Unless the call is revoked (see 3 above), this penalty shall stand even if a batsman is dismissed, and shall be in addition to any other runs scored, any boundary allowance and any other penalties awarded.

6. Runs resulting from a wide – how scored

All runs completed by the batsmen or a boundary allowance, together with the penalty for the wide, shall be scored as wide balls. Apart from any award of a five-run penalty, all runs resulting from a wide shall be debited against the bowler.

7. Wide not to count

A wide shall not count as one of the over. See Law 22.4 (Balls not to count in the over).

8. Out from a wide

When "Wide ball" has been called, neither batsman shall be out under any of the Laws except Laws 33 (Handled the ball), 35 (Hit wicket), 37 (Obstructing the field), 38 (Run out) or 39 (Stumped).

LAW 26.   BYE AND LEG-BYE

1. Byes

If the ball, not being a no-ball or a wide, passes the striker without touching his bat or person, any runs completed by the batsmen or a boundary allowance shall be credited as byes to the batting side.

2. Leg-byes

(a) If the ball, not having previously touched the striker's bat, strikes his person and the umpire is satisfied that the striker has either

(i) attempted to play the ball with his bat, or

(ii) tried to avoid being hit by the ball,

then any runs completed by the batsmen or a boundary allowance shall be credited to the batting side as leg-byes, unless "No-ball" has been called.

(b) If "No-ball" has been called, the runs in (a) above, together with the penalty for the no-ball, shall be scored as no-ball extras.

3. Leg-byes not to be awarded

If in the circumstances of 2(a) above the umpire considers that neither of the conditions (i) and (ii) therein has been met, then leg-byes will not be awarded. The batting side shall not be credited with any runs from that delivery apart from the one run penalty for a no-ball if applicable. Moreover, no other penalties shall be awarded to the batting side when the ball is dead. See Law 42.17 (Penalty runs). The following procedure shall be adopted.

(a) If no run is attempted but the ball reaches the boundary, the umpire shall call and signal "Dead ball", and disallow the boundary.

(b) If runs are attempted and if:

(i) Neither batsman is dismissed and the ball does not become dead for any other reason, the umpire shall call and signal "Dead ball" as soon as one run is completed or the ball reaches the boundary. The batsmen shall return to their original ends. The run or boundary shall be disallowed.

(ii) Before one run is completed or the ball reaches the boundary, a batsman is dismissed, or the ball becomes dead for any other reason, all the provisions of the Laws will apply, except that no runs and no penalties shall be credited to the batting side, other than the penalty for a no-ball if applicable.

LAW 27.   APPEALS

1. Umpire not to give batsman out without an appeal

Neither umpire shall give a batsman out, even though he may be out under the Laws, unless appealed to by the fielding side. This shall not debar a batsman who is out under any of the Laws from leaving his wicket without an appeal having been made. Note, however, the provisions of 7 below.

2. Batsman dismissed

A batsman is dismissed if either

(a) he is given out by an umpire, on appeal, or

(b) he is out under any of the Laws and leaves his wicket as in 1 above.

3. Timing of appeals

For an appeal to be valid it must be made before the bowler begins his run-up or, if he has no run-up, his bowling action to deliver the next ball, and before "Time" has been called.

The call of "Over" does not invalidate an appeal made prior to the start of the following over provided "Time" has not been called. See Laws 16.2 (Call of "Time") and 22.2 (Start of an over).

4. Appeal "How's that?"

An appeal "How's that?" covers all ways of being out.

5. Answering appeals

The umpire at the bowler's end shall answer all appeals except those arising out of any of Laws 35 (Hit wicket), 39 (Stumped) or 38 (Run out) when this occurs at the striker's wicket. A decision "Not out" by one umpire shall not prevent the other umpire from giving a decision, provided that each is considering only matters within his jurisdiction.

When a batsman has been given not out, either umpire may, within his jurisdiction, answer a further appeal provided that it is made in accordance with 3 above.

6. Consultation by umpires

Each umpire shall answer appeals on matters within his own jurisdiction. If an umpire is doubtful about any point that the other umpire may have been in a better position to see, he shall consult the latter on this point of fact and shall then give his decision. If, after consultation, there is still doubt remaining the decision shall be "Not out".

7. Batsman leaving his wicket under a misapprehension

An umpire shall intervene if satisfied that a batsman, not having been given out, has left his wicket under a misapprehension that he is out. The umpire intervening shall call and signal "Dead ball" to prevent any further action by the fielding side and shall recall the batsman.

8. Withdrawal of an appeal

The captain of the fielding side may withdraw an appeal only with the consent of the umpire within whose jurisdiction the appeal falls and before the outgoing batsman has left the field of play. If such consent is given the umpire concerned shall, if applicable, revoke his decision and recall the batsman.

9. Umpire's decision

An umpire may alter his decision provided that such alteration is made promptly. This apart, the umpire's decision, once made, is final.

LAW 28.   THE WICKET IS DOWN

1. Wicket put down

(a) The wicket is put down if a bail is completely removed from the top of the stumps, or a stump is struck out of the ground by:

    (i) The ball.

    (ii) The striker's bat, whether he is holding it or has let go of it.

    (iii) The striker's person or by any part of his clothing or equipment becoming detached from his person.

    (iv) A fielder, with his hand or arm, provided that the ball is held in the hand or hands so used, or in the hand of the arm so used.

        The wicket is also put down if a fielder pulls a stump out of the ground in the same manner.

(b) The disturbance of a bail, whether temporary or not, shall not constitute its complete removal from the top of the stumps, but if a bail in falling lodges between two of the stumps this shall be regarded as complete removal.

2. One bail off

If one bail is off, it shall be sufficient for the purpose of putting the wicket down to remove the remaining bail, or to strike or pull any of the three stumps out of the ground, in any of the ways stated in 1 above.

3. Remaking the wicket

If the wicket is broken or put down while the ball is in play, the umpire shall not remake the wicket until the ball is dead. See Law 23 (Dead ball). Any fielder, however, may:

(i) Replace a bail or bails on top of the stumps.

(ii) Put back one or more stumps into the ground where the wicket originally stood.

4. Dispensing with bails

If the umpires have agreed to dispense with bails, in accordance with Law 8.5 (Dispensing with bails), the decision as to whether the wicket has been put down is one for the umpire concerned to decide.

(a) After a decision to play without bails, the wicket has been put down if the umpire concerned is satisfied that the wicket has been struck by the ball, by the striker's bat, person, or items of his clothing or equipment separated from his person as described in 1(a)(ii) or 1(a)(iii) above, or by a fielder with the hand holding the ball or with the arm of the hand holding the ball.

(b) If the wicket has already been broken or put down, (a) above shall apply to any stump or stumps still in the ground. Any fielder may replace a stump or stumps, in accordance with 3 above, in order to have an opportunity of putting the wicket down.

LAW 29.   BATSMAN OUT OF HIS GROUND

1. When out of his ground

A batsman shall be considered to be out of his ground unless his bat or some part of his person is grounded behind the popping crease at that end.

2. Which is a batsman's ground?

(a) If only one batsman is within a ground:

(i) It is his ground.

(ii) It remains his ground even if he is later joined there by the other batsman.

(b) If both batsmen are in the same ground and one of them subsequently leaves it, (a)(i) above applies.

(c) If there is no batsman in either ground, then each ground belongs to whichever of the batsmen is nearer to it, or, if the batsmen are level, to whichever was nearer to it immediately prior to their drawing level.

(d) If a ground belongs to one batsman, then, unless there is a striker with a runner, the other ground belongs to the other batsman irrespective of his position.

(e) When a batsman with a runner is striker, his ground is always that at the wicket-keeper's end. However, (a), (b), (c) and (d) above will still apply, but only to the runner and the non-striker, so that that ground will also belong to either the non-striker or the runner, as the case may be.

3. Position of non-striker

The non-striker, when standing at the bowler's end, should be positioned on the opposite side of the wicket to that from which the ball is being delivered, unless a request to do otherwise is granted by the umpire.

LAW 30. BOWLED

1. Out Bowled

(a) The striker is out *Bowled* if his wicket is put down by a ball delivered by the bowler, not being a no-ball, even if it first touches his bat or person.

(b) Notwithstanding (a) above he shall not be out bowled if before striking the wicket the ball has been in contact with any other player or with an umpire. He will, however, be subject to Laws 33 (Handled the ball), 37 (Obstructing the field), 38 (Run out) and 39 (Stumped).

2. Bowled to take precedence

The striker is out bowled if his wicket is put down as in 1 above, even though a decision against him for any other method of dismissal would be justified.

LAW 31. TIMED OUT

1. Out Timed out

(a) Unless "Time" has been called, the incoming batsman must be in position to take guard or for his partner to be ready to receive the next ball within three minutes of the fall of the previous wicket. If this requirement is not met, the incoming batsman will be out, *Timed out*.

(b) In the event of protracted delay in which no batsman comes to the wicket, the umpires shall adopt the procedure of Law 21.3 (Umpires awarding a match). For the purposes of that Law the start of the action shall be taken as the expiry of the three minutes referred to above.

2. Bowler does not get credit

The bowler does not get credit for the wicket.

LAW 32. CAUGHT

1. Out Caught

The striker is out *Caught* if a ball delivered by the bowler, not being a no-ball, touches his bat without having previously been in contact with any member of the fielding side and is subsequently held by a fielder as a fair catch before it touches the ground.

2. Caught to take precedence

If the criteria of 1 above are met and the striker is not out bowled, then he is out caught even though a decision against either batsman for another method of dismissal would be justified. Runs completed by the batsmen before the completion of the catch will not be scored. Note also Laws 21.6 (Winning hit or extras) and 42.17(b) (Penalty runs).

3. A fair catch

A catch shall be considered to have been fairly made if:

(a) Throughout the act of making the catch:

(i) Any fielder in contact with the ball is within the field of play. See 4 below.

(ii) The ball is at no time in contact with any object grounded beyond the boundary.

The act of making the catch shall start from the time when a fielder first handles the ball and shall end when a fielder obtains complete control both over the ball and over his own movement.

(b) The ball is hugged to the body of the catcher or accidentally lodges in his clothing or, in the case of the wicket-keeper, in his pads. However, it is not a fair catch if the ball lodges in a protective helmet worn by a fielder. See Law 23 (Dead ball).

(c) The ball does not touch the ground, even though the hand holding it does so in effecting the catch.

(d) A fielder catches the ball after it has been lawfully struck more than once by the striker, but only if the ball has not touched the ground since first being struck.

(e) A fielder catches the ball after it has touched an umpire, another fielder or the other batsman. However, it is not a fair catch if the ball has touched a protective helmet worn by a fielder, although the ball remains in play.

(f) A fielder catches the ball in the air after it has crossed the boundary provided that:

(i) He has no part of his person touching, or grounded beyond, the boundary at any time when he is in contact with the ball.

(ii) The ball has not been grounded beyond the boundary.

See Law 19.3 (Scoring a boundary).

(g) The ball is caught off an obstruction within the boundary, provided it has not previously been decided to regard the obstruction as a boundary.

4. Fielder within the field of play

(a) A fielder is not within the field of play if he touches the boundary or has any part of his person grounded beyond the boundary. See Law 19.3 (Scoring a boundary).

(b) Six runs shall be scored if a fielder:

(i) Has any part of his person touching, or grounded beyond, the boundary when he catches the ball.

(ii) Catches the ball and subsequently touches the boundary or grounds some part of his person over the boundary while carrying the ball but before completing the catch.

See Laws 19.3 (Scoring a boundary) and 19.4 (Runs allowed for boundaries).

5. No runs to be scored

If the striker is dismissed caught, runs from that delivery completed by the batsmen before the completion of the catch shall not be scored, but any penalties awarded to either side when the ball is dead, if applicable, will stand. Law 18.12(a) (Batsman returning to wicket he has left) shall apply from the instant of the catch.

LAW 33.   HANDLED THE BALL

1. Out Handled the ball

Either batsman is out *Handled the ball* if he wilfully touches the ball while in play with a hand or hands not holding the bat unless he does so with the consent of the opposing side.

2. Not out Handled the ball

Notwithstanding 1 above, a batsman will not be out under this Law if:

(i) He handles the ball in order to avoid injury.

(ii) He uses his hand or hands to return the ball to any member of the fielding side without the consent of that side. Note, however, the provisions of Law 37.4 (Returning the ball to a member of the fielding side).

3. Runs scored

If either batsman is dismissed under this Law, any runs completed before the offence, together with any penalty extras and the penalty for a no-ball or wide, if applicable, shall be scored. See Laws 18.10 (Runs scored when a batsman is dismissed) and 42.17 (Penalty runs).

4. Bowler does not get credit

The bowler does not get credit for the wicket.

LAW 34.   HIT THE BALL TWICE

1. Out Hit the ball twice

(a) The striker is out *Hit the ball twice* if, while the ball is in play and it strikes any part of his person or is struck by his bat and, before the ball has been touched by a fielder, he wilfully strikes it again with his bat or person, other than a hand not holding the bat, except for the sole purpose of guarding his wicket. See 3 below and Laws 33 (Handled the ball) and 37 (Obstructing the field).

(b) For the purpose of this Law, "struck" or "strike" shall include contact with the person of the striker.

2. Not out Hit the ball twice

Notwithstanding 1(a) above, the striker will not be out under this Law if:

(i) He makes a second or subsequent stroke in order to return the ball to any member of the fielding side. Note, however, the provisions of Law 37.4 (Returning the ball to a member of the fielding side).

(ii) He wilfully strikes the ball after it has touched a fielder. Note, however, the provisions of Law 37.1 (Out obstructing the field).

3. Ball lawfully struck more than once

Solely in order to guard his wicket and before the ball has been touched by a fielder, the striker may lawfully strike the ball more than once with his bat or with any part of his person other than a hand not holding the bat.

Notwithstanding this provision, the striker may not prevent the ball from being caught by making more than one stroke in defence of his wicket. See Law 37.3 (Obstructing a ball from being caught).

4. Runs permitted from ball lawfully struck more than once

When the ball is lawfully struck more than once, as permitted in 3 above, only the first strike is to be considered in determining whether runs are to be allowed and how they are to be scored.

(a) If on the first strike the umpire is satisfied that either

(i) the ball first struck the bat, or

(ii) the striker attempted to play the ball with his bat, or

(iii) the striker tried to avoid being hit by the ball,

then any penalties to the batting side that are applicable shall be allowed.

(b) If the conditions in (a) above are met then, if they result from overthrows, and only if they result from overthrows, runs completed by the batsmen or a boundary will be allowed in addition to any penalties that are applicable. They shall be credited to the striker if the first strike was with the bat. If the first strike was on the person of the striker they shall be scored as leg-byes or no-ball extras, as appropriate. See Law 26.2 (Leg-byes).

(c) If the conditions of (a) above are met and there is no overthrow until after the batsmen have started to run, but before one run is completed:

(i) Only subsequent completed runs or a boundary shall be allowed. The first run shall count as a completed run for this purpose only if the batsmen have not crossed at the instant of the throw.

(ii) If in these circumstances the ball goes to the boundary from the throw then, notwithstanding the provisions of Law 19.6 (Overthrow or wilful act of fielder), only the boundary allowance shall be scored.

(iii) If the ball goes to the boundary as the result of a further overthrow, then runs completed by the batsmen after the first throw and before this final throw shall be added to the boundary allowance. The run in progress at the first throw will count only if they have not crossed at that moment; the run in progress at the final throw shall count only if they have crossed at that moment. Law 18.12 (Batsman returning to wicket he has left) shall apply as from the moment of the final throw.

(d) If, in the opinion of the umpire, none of the conditions in (a) above has been met then, whether there is an overthrow or not, the batting side shall not be credited with any runs from that delivery apart from the penalty for a no-ball if applicable. Moreover, no other penalties shall be awarded to the batting side when the ball is dead. See Law 42.17 (Penalty runs).

5. Ball lawfully struck more than once – action by the umpire

If no runs are to be allowed, either in the circumstances of 4(d) above, or because there has been no overthrow and:

(a) If no run is attempted but the ball reaches the boundary, the umpire shall call and signal "Dead ball" and disallow the boundary.

(b) If the batsmen run and:

(i) Neither batsman is dismissed and the ball does not become dead for any other reason, the umpire shall call and signal "Dead ball" as soon as one run is completed or the ball reaches the boundary. The batsmen shall return to their original ends. The run or boundary shall be disallowed.

(ii) A batsman is dismissed, or if for any other reason the ball becomes dead before one run is completed or the ball reaches the boundary, all the provisions of the Laws will apply except that the award of penalties to the batting side shall be as laid down in 4(a) or 4(d) above as appropriate.

6. Bowler does not get credit

The bowler does not get credit for the wicket.

LAW 35. HIT WICKET

1. Out Hit wicket

The striker is out *Hit wicket* if, while the ball is in play, his wicket is put down either by the striker's bat or person as described in Law 28.1(a)(ii) and (iii) (Wicket put down) either

(i) in the course of any action taken by him in preparing to receive or in receiving a delivery, or

(ii) in setting off for his first run immediately after playing, or playing at, the ball, or

(iii) if he makes no attempt to play the ball, in setting off for his first run, provided that in the opinion of the umpire this is immediately after he has had the opportunity of playing the ball, or

(iv) in lawfully making a second or further stroke for the purpose of guarding his wicket within the provisions of Law 34.3 (Ball lawfully struck more than once).

2. Not out Hit wicket

Notwithstanding 1 above, the batsman is not out under this Law should his wicket be put down in any of the ways referred to in 1 above if:

(a) It occurs after he has completed any action in receiving the delivery, other than as in 1(ii), (iii) or (iv) above.

(b) It occurs when he is in the act of running, other than in setting off immediately for his first run.

(c) It occurs when he is trying to avoid being run out or stumped.

(d) It occurs while he is trying to avoid a throw-in at any time.

(e) The bowler after starting his run-up, or his bowling action if he has no run-up, does not deliver the ball. In this case either umpire shall immediately call and signal "Dead ball". See Law 23.3 (Umpire calling and signalling "Dead ball").

(f) The delivery is a no-ball.

LAW 36.   LEG BEFORE WICKET

1. Out LBW

The striker is out *LBW* in the circumstances set out below.

(a) The bowler delivers a ball, not being a no-ball, and

(b) the ball, if it is not intercepted full pitch, pitches in line between wicket and wicket or on the off side of the striker's wicket, and

(c) the ball not having previously touched his bat, the striker intercepts the ball, either full pitch or after pitching, with any part of his person, and

(d) the point of impact, even if above the level of the bails, either

(i) is between wicket and wicket, or

(ii) is either between wicket and wicket or outside the line of the off stump, if the striker has made no genuine attempt to play the ball with his bat, and

(e) but for the interception, the ball would have hit the wicket.

2. Interception of the ball

(a) In assessing points (c), (d) and (e) in 1 above, only the first interception is to be considered.

(b) In assessing point (e) in 1 above, it is to be assumed that the path of the ball before interception would have continued after interception, irrespective of whether the ball might have pitched subsequently or not.

3. Off side of wicket

The off side of the striker's wicket shall be determined by the striker's stance at the moment the ball comes into play for that delivery.

LAW 37.   OBSTRUCTING THE FIELD

1. Out Obstructing the field

Either batsman is out *Obstructing the field* if he wilfully obstructs or distracts the opposing side by word or action. It shall be regarded as obstruction if either batsman wilfully, and without the consent of the fielding side, strikes the ball with his bat or person, other than a hand not holding the bat, after the ball has touched a fielder. See 4 below.

2. Accidental obstruction

It is for either umpire to decide whether any obstruction or distraction is wilful or not. He shall consult the other umpire if he has any doubt.

3. Obstructing a ball from being caught

The striker is out should wilful obstruction or distraction by either batsman prevent a catch being made.

This shall apply even though the striker causes the obstruction in lawfully guarding his wicket under the provisions of Law 34.3 (Ball lawfully struck more than once).

4. Returning the ball to a member of the fielding side

Either batsman is out under this Law if, without the consent of the fielding side and while the ball is in play, he uses his bat or person to return the ball to any member of that side.

5. Runs scored

If a batsman is dismissed under this Law, runs completed by the batsmen before the offence shall be scored, together with the penalty for a no-ball or a wide, if applicable. Other penalties that may be awarded to either side when the ball is dead shall also stand. See Law 42.17(b) (Penalty runs).

If, however, the obstruction prevents a catch from being made, runs completed by the batsmen before the offence shall not be scored, but other penalties that may be awarded to either side when the ball is dead shall stand. See Law 42.17(b) (Penalty runs).

6. Bowler does not get credit

The bowler does not get credit for the wicket.

LAW 38.   RUN OUT

1. Out Run out

(a) Either batsman is out *Run out*, except as in 2 below, if at any time while the ball is in play

(i) he is out of his ground and

(ii) his wicket is fairly put down by the opposing side.

(b) (a) above shall apply even though "No-ball" has been called and whether or not a run is being attempted, except in the circumstances of Law 39.3(b) (Not out Stumped).

2. Batsman not Run out

Notwithstanding 1 above, a batsman is not out run out if:

(a) He has been within his ground and has subsequently left it to avoid injury, when the wicket is put down.

(b) The ball has not subsequently been touched again by a fielder, after the bowler has entered his delivery stride, before the wicket is put down.

(c) The ball, having been played by the striker, or having come off his person, directly strikes a helmet worn by a fielder and without further contact with him or any other fielder rebounds directly on to the wicket. However, the ball remains in play and either batsman may be run out in the circumstances of 1 above if a wicket is subsequently put down.

(d) He is out stumped. See Law 39.1(b) (Out Stumped).

(e) He is out of his ground, not attempting a run and his wicket is fairly put down by the wicket-keeper without the intervention of another member of the fielding side, if "No-ball" has been called. See Law 39.3(b) (Not out Stumped).

3. Which batsman is out

The batsman out in the circumstances of 1 above is the one whose ground is at the end where the wicket is put down. See Laws 2.8 (Transgression of the Laws by a batsman who has a runner) and 29.2 (Which is a batsman's ground).

4. Runs scored

If a batsman is dismissed run out, the batting side shall score the runs completed before the dismissal together with the penalty for a no-ball or wide, if applicable. Other penalties to either side that may be awarded when the ball is dead shall also stand. See Law 42.17 (Penalty runs).

If, however, a striker with a runner is himself dismissed run out, runs completed by the runner and the other batsman before the dismissal shall not be scored. The penalty for a no-ball or a wide and any other penalties to either side that may be awarded when the ball is dead shall stand. See Laws 2.8 (Transgression of the Laws by a batsman who has a runner) and 42.17(b) (Penalty runs).

5. Bowler does not get credit

The bowler does not get credit for the wicket.

LAW 39.   STUMPED

1. Out Stumped

(a) The striker is out *Stumped* if

(i) he is out of his ground, and

(ii) he is receiving a ball which is not a no-ball, and

(iii) he is not attempting a run, and

(iv) his wicket is fairly put down by the wicket-keeper without the intervention of another member of the fielding side. Note Law 40.3 (Position of wicket-keeper).

(b) The striker is out stumped if all the conditions of (a) above are satisfied, even though a decision of run out would be justified.

2. Ball rebounding from wicket-keeper's person

(a) If the wicket is put down by the ball, it shall be regarded as having been put down by the wicket-keeper, if the ball

(i) rebounds on to the stumps from any part of his person, other than a protective helmet, or

(ii) has been kicked or thrown on to the stumps by the wicket-keeper.

(b) If the ball touches a helmet worn by the wicket-keeper, the ball is still in play but the striker shall not be out stumped. He will, however, be liable to be run out in these circumstances if there is subsequent contact between the ball and any member of the fielding side. Note, however, 3 below.

3. Not out Stumped

(a) If the striker is not out stumped, he is liable to be out run out if the conditions of Law 38 (Run out) apply, except as set out in (b) below.

(b) The striker shall not be out run out if he is out of his ground, not attempting a run, and his wicket is fairly put down by the wicket-keeper without the intervention of another member of the fielding side, if "No-ball" has been called.

LAW 40. THE WICKET-KEEPER

1. Protective equipment

The wicket-keeper is the only member of the fielding side permitted to wear gloves and external leg guards. If he does so, these are to be regarded as part of his person for the purposes of Law 41.2 (Fielding the ball). If by his actions and positioning it is apparent to the umpires that he will not be able to discharge his duties as a wicket-keeper, he shall forfeit this right and also the right to be recognised as a wicket-keeper for the purposes of Laws 32.3 (A fair catch), 39 (Stumped), 41.1 (Protective equipment), 41.5 (Limitation of on-side fielders) and 41.6 (Fielders not to encroach on the pitch).

2. Gloves

If the wicket-keeper wears gloves as permitted under 1 above, they shall have no webbing between fingers except that a single piece of flat non-stretch material may be inserted between index finger and thumb solely as a means of support. This insert shall not form a pouch when the hand is extended.

3. Position of wicket-keeper

The wicket-keeper shall remain wholly behind the wicket at the striker's end from the moment the ball comes into play until

(a) a ball delivered by the bowler either

(i) touches the bat or person of the striker, or

(ii) passes the wicket at the striker's end, or

(b) the striker attempts a run.

In the event of the wicket-keeper contravening this Law, the umpire at the striker's end shall call and signal "No-ball" as soon as possible after the delivery of the ball.

4. Movement by wicket-keeper

It is unfair if the wicket-keeper standing back makes a significant movement towards the wicket after the ball comes into play and before it reaches the striker. In the event of such unfair movement by the wicket-keeper, either umpire shall call and signal "Dead ball". It will not be considered a significant movement if the wicket-keeper moves a few paces forward for a slower delivery.

5. Restriction on actions of wicket-keeper

If the wicket-keeper interferes with the striker's right to play the ball and to guard his wicket, the striker shall not be out, except under Laws 33 (Handled the ball), 34 (Hit the ball twice), 37 (Obstructing the field) or 38 (Run out).

6. Interference with wicket-keeper by striker

If, in playing at the ball or in the legitimate defence of his wicket, the striker interferes with the wicket-keeper, he shall not be out, except as provided for in Law 37.3 (Obstructing a ball from being caught).

LAW 41.   THE FIELDER

1. Protective equipment

No member of the fielding side other than the wicket-keeper shall be permitted to wear gloves or external leg guards. In addition, protection for the hand or fingers may be worn only with the consent of the umpires.

2. Fielding the ball

A fielder may field the ball with any part of his person but if, while the ball is in play, he wilfully fields it otherwise:

    (a) The ball shall become dead and five penalty runs shall be awarded to the batting side. See Law 42.17 (Penalty runs).

    (b) The umpire shall inform the other umpire, the captain of the fielding side, the batsmen and, as soon as practicable, the captain of the batting side of what has occurred.

    (c) The umpires together shall report the occurrence as soon as possible to the executive of the fielding side and any governing body responsible for the match who shall take such action as is considered appropriate against the captain and player concerned.

3. Protective helmets belonging to the fielding side

Protective helmets, when not in use by fielders, shall only be placed, if above the surface, on the ground behind the wicket-keeper and in line with both sets of stumps. If a helmet belonging to the fielding side is on the ground within the field of play, and the ball while in play strikes it, the ball shall become dead. Five penalty runs shall then be awarded to the batting side. See Laws 18.11 (Runs scored when ball becomes dead) and 42.17 (Penalty runs).

4. Penalty runs not to be awarded

Notwithstanding 2 and 3 above, if from the delivery by the bowler the ball first struck the person of the striker and if, in the opinion of the umpire, the striker neither

    (i) attempted to play the ball with his bat, nor

    (ii) tried to avoid being hit by the ball,

then no award of five penalty runs shall be made and no other runs or penalties shall be credited to the batting side except the penalty for a no-ball if applicable. See Law 26.3 (Leg-byes not to be awarded).

5. Limitation of on-side fielders

At the instant of the bowler's delivery there shall not be more than two fielders, other than the wicket-keeper, behind the popping crease on the on side. A fielder will be considered to be behind the popping crease unless the whole of his person, whether grounded or in the air, is in front of this line.

In the event of infringement of this Law by the fielding side the umpire at the striker's end shall call and signal "No-ball".

6. Fielders not to encroach on the pitch

While the ball is in play and until the ball has made contact with the bat or person of the striker, or has passed the striker's bat, no fielder, other than the bowler, may have any part of his person grounded on or extended over the pitch.

In the event of infringement of this Law by any fielder other than the wicket-keeper, the umpire at the bowler's end shall call and signal "No-ball" as soon as possible after the delivery of the ball. Note, however, Law 40.3 (Position of wicket-keeper).

7. Movement by fielders

Any significant movement by any fielder after the ball comes into play and before the ball reaches the striker is unfair. In the event of such unfair movement, either umpire shall call and signal "Dead ball". Note also the provisions of Law 42.4 (Deliberate attempt to distract striker).

8. Definition of significant movement

(a) For close fielders anything other than minor adjustments to stance or position in relation to the striker is significant.

(b) In the outfield, fielders are permitted to move in towards the striker or striker's wicket, provided that 5 above is not contravened. Anything other than slight movement off line or away from the striker is to be considered significant.

(c) For restrictions on movement by the wicket-keeper see Law 40.4 (Movement by wicket-keeper).

LAW 42.   FAIR AND UNFAIR PLAY

1. Fair and unfair play – responsibility of captains

The responsibility lies with the captains for ensuring that play is conducted within the spirit and traditions of the game, as described in The Preamble – The Spirit of Cricket, as well as within the Laws.

2. Fair and unfair play – responsibility of umpires

The umpires shall be sole judges of fair and unfair play. If either umpire considers an action, not covered by the Laws, to be unfair, he shall intervene without appeal and, if the ball is in play, shall call and signal "Dead ball" and implement the procedure as set out in 18 below. Otherwise the umpires shall not interfere with the progress of play, except as required to do so by the Laws.

3. The match ball – changing its condition

(a) Any fielder may:

(i) Polish the ball provided that no artificial substance is used and that such polishing wastes no time.

(ii) Remove mud from the ball under the supervision of the umpire.

(iii) Dry a wet ball on a towel.

(b) It is unfair for anyone to rub the ball on the ground for any reason, interfere with any of the seams or the surface of the ball, use any implement, or take any other action whatsoever which is likely to alter the condition of the ball, except as permitted in (a) above.

(c) The umpires shall make frequent and irregular inspections of the ball.

(d) In the event of any fielder changing the condition of the ball unfairly, as set out in (b) above, the umpires after consultation shall:

(i) Change the ball forthwith. It shall be for the umpires to decide on the replacement ball, which shall, in their opinion, have had wear comparable with that which the previous ball had received immediately prior to the contravention.

(ii) Inform the batsmen that the ball has been changed.

(iii) Award five penalty runs to the batting side. See 17 below.

(iv) Inform the captain of the fielding side that the reason for the action was the unfair interference with the ball.

(v) Inform the captain of the batting side as soon as practicable of what has occurred.

(vi) Report the occurrence as soon as possible to the executive of the fielding side and any governing body responsible for the match, who shall take such action as is considered appropriate against the captain and team concerned.

(e) If there is any further instance of unfairly changing the condition of the ball in that innings, the umpires after consultation shall:

(i) Repeat the procedure in (d)(i), (ii) and (iii) above.

(ii) Inform the captain of the fielding side of the reason for the action taken and direct him to take off forthwith the bowler who delivered the immediately preceding ball. The bowler thus taken off shall not be allowed to bowl again in that innings.

(iii) Inform the captain of the batting side as soon as practicable of what has occurred.

(iv) Report the occurrence as soon as possible to the executive of the fielding side and any governing body responsible for the match, who shall take such action as is considered appropriate against the captain and team concerned.

4. Deliberate attempt to distract striker

It is unfair for any member of the fielding side deliberately to attempt to distract the striker while he is preparing to receive or receiving a delivery.

(a) If either umpire considers that any action by a member of the fielding side is such an attempt, at the first instance he shall:

(i) Immediately call and signal "Dead ball".

(ii) Warn the captain of the fielding side that the action is unfair and indicate that this is a first and final warning.

(iii) Inform the other umpire and the batsmen of what has occurred.

Neither batsman shall be dismissed from that delivery and the ball shall not count as one of the over.

(b) If there is any further such deliberate attempt in that innings, by any member of the fielding side, the procedures, other than warning, as set out in (a) above shall apply. Additionally, the umpire at the bowler's end shall:

(i) Award five penalty runs to the batting side. See 17 below.

(ii) Inform the captain of the fielding side of the reason for this action and, as soon as practicable, inform the captain of the batting side.

(iii) Report the occurrence, together with the other umpire, as soon as possible to the executive of the fielding side and any governing body responsible for the match, who shall take such action as is considered appropriate against the captain and player or players concerned.

5. Deliberate distraction or obstruction of batsman

In addition to 4 above, it is unfair for any member of the fielding side, by word or action, wilfully to attempt to distract or to obstruct either batsman after the striker has received the ball.

(a) It is for either one of the umpires to decide whether any distraction or obstruction is wilful or not.

(b) If either umpire considers that a member of the fielding side has wilfully caused or attempted to cause such a distraction or obstruction he shall:

(i) Immediately call and signal "Dead ball".

(ii) Inform the captain of the fielding side and the other umpire of the reason for the call.

Additionally:

(iii) Neither batsman shall be dismissed from that delivery.

(iv) Five penalty runs shall be awarded to the batting side. See 17 below. In this instance, the run in progress shall be scored, whether or not the batsmen had crossed at the instant of the call. See Law 18.11 (Runs scored when ball becomes dead).

(v) The umpire at the bowler's end shall inform the captain of the fielding side of the reason for this action and, as soon as practicable, inform the captain of the batting side.

(vi) The umpires shall report the occurrence as soon as possible to the executive of the fielding side and any governing body responsible for the match, who shall take such action as is considered appropriate against the captain and player or players concerned.

6. Dangerous and unfair bowling

(a) Bowling of fast short-pitched balls

(i) The bowling of fast short-pitched balls is dangerous and unfair if the umpire at the bowler's end considers that by their repetition and taking into account their length, height and direction they are likely to inflict physical injury on the striker, irrespective of the protective equipment he may be wearing. The relative skill of the striker shall be taken into consideration.

(ii) Any delivery which, after pitching, passes or would have passed over head height of the striker standing upright at the crease, although not threatening physical injury, is unfair and shall be considered as part of the repetition sequence in (i) above. The umpire shall call and signal "No-ball" for each such delivery.

(b) Bowling of high full-pitched balls

(i) Any delivery, other than a slow-paced one, which passes or would have passed on the full above waist height of the striker standing upright at the crease is to be deemed dangerous and unfair, whether or not it is likely to inflict physical injury on the striker.

(ii) A slow delivery which passes or would have passed on the full above shoulder height of the striker standing upright at the crease is to be deemed dangerous and unfair, whether or not it is likely to inflict physical injury on the striker.

7. Dangerous and unfair bowling – action by the umpire

(a) In the event of dangerous and/or unfair bowling, as defined in 6 above, by any bowler, except as in 8 below, at the first instance the umpire at the bowler's end shall call and signal "No-ball" and, when the ball is dead, caution the bowler, inform the other umpire, the captain of the fielding side and the batsmen of what has occurred. This caution shall continue to apply throughout the innings.

(b) If there is a second instance of such dangerous and/or unfair bowling by the same bowler in that innings, the umpire at the bowler's end shall repeat the above procedure and indicate to the bowler that this is a final warning.

Both the above caution and final warning shall continue to apply even though the bowler may later change ends.

(c) Should there be a further instance by the same bowler in that innings, the umpire shall:

(i) call and signal "No-ball".

(ii) Direct the captain, when the ball is dead, to take the bowler off forthwith. The over shall be completed by another bowler, who shall neither have bowled the previous over nor be allowed to bowl the next over.

The bowler thus taken off shall not be allowed to bowl again in that innings.

(iii) Report the occurrence to the other umpire, the batsmen and, as soon as practicable, the captain of the batting side.

(iv) Report the occurrence, with the other umpire, as soon as possible to the executive of the fielding side and to any governing body responsible for the match, who shall take such action as is considered appropriate against the captain and bowler concerned.

8. Deliberate bowling of high full-pitched balls

If the umpire considers that a high full pitch which is deemed to be dangerous and unfair, as defined in 6(b) above, was deliberately bowled, then the caution and warning prescribed in 7 above shall be dispensed with. The umpire shall:

(a) Call and signal "No-ball".

(b) Direct the captain, when the ball is dead, to take the bowler off forthwith.

(c) Implement the remainder of the procedure as laid down in 7(c) above.

9. Time-wasting by the fielding side

It is unfair for any member of the fielding side to waste time.

(a) If the captain of the fielding side wastes time, or allows any member of his side to waste time, or if the progress of an over is unnecessarily slow, at the first instance the umpire shall call and signal "Dead ball" if necessary and:

(i) Warn the captain, and indicate that this is a first and final warning.

(ii) Inform the other umpire and the batsmen of what has occurred.

(b) If there is any further waste of time in that innings, by any member of the fielding side, the umpire shall either

(i) if the waste of time is not during the course of an over, award five penalty runs to the batting side (See 17 below), or

(ii) if the waste of time is during the course of an over, when the ball is dead, direct the captain to take the bowler off forthwith. If applicable, the over shall be completed by another bowler, who shall neither have bowled the previous over nor be allowed to bowl the next over. The bowler thus taken off shall not be allowed to bowl again in that innings.

(iii) Inform the other umpire, the batsmen and, as soon as practicable, the captain of the batting side, of what has occurred.

(iv) Report the occurrence, with the other umpire, as soon as possible to the executive of the fielding side and to any governing body responsible for the match, who shall take such action as is considered appropriate against the captain and team concerned.

10. Batsman wasting time

It is unfair for a batsman to waste time. In normal circumstances the striker should always be ready to take strike when the bowler is ready to start his run-up.

(a) Should either batsman waste time by failing to meet this requirement, or in any other way, the following procedure shall be adopted. At the first instance, either before the bowler starts his run-up or when the ball is dead, as appropriate, the umpire shall:

(i) Warn the batsman and indicate that this is a first and final warning. This warning shall continue to apply throughout that innings. The umpire shall so inform each incoming batsman.

(ii) Inform the other umpire, the other batsman and the captain of the fielding side of what has occurred.

(iii) Inform the captain of the batting side as soon as practicable.

(b) If there is any further time-wasting by any batsman in that innings, the umpire shall, at the appropriate time while the ball is dead:

(i) Award five penalty runs to the fielding side. See 17 below.

(ii) Inform the other umpire, the other batsman, the captain of the fielding side and, as soon as practicable, the captain of the batting side, of what has occurred.

(iii) Report the occurrence, with the other umpire, as soon as possible to the executive of the batting side and to any governing body responsible for the match, who shall take such action as is considered appropriate against the captain and player or players, or, if appropriate, the team concerned.

11. Damaging the pitch – area to be protected

(a) It is incumbent on all players to avoid unnecessary damage to the pitch. It is unfair for any player to cause deliberate damage to the pitch.

(b) An area of the pitch, to be referred to as "the protected area", is defined as that area contained within a rectangle bounded at each end by imaginary lines parallel to the popping creases and 5ft/1.52m in front of each and on the sides by imaginary lines, one each side of the imaginary line joining the centres of the two middle stumps, each parallel to it and 1ft/30.48cm from it.

12. Bowler running on the protected area after delivering the ball

(a) If the bowler, after delivering the ball, runs on the protected area as defined in 11(b) above, the umpire shall at the first instance:

(i) Caution the bowler. This caution shall continue to apply throughout the innings.

(ii) Inform the other umpire, the captain of the fielding side and the batsmen of what has occurred.

(b) If, in that innings, the same bowler runs on the protected area again after delivering the ball, the umpire shall repeat the above procedure, indicating that this is a final warning.

(c) If, in that innings, the same bowler runs on the protected area a third time after delivering the ball, when the ball is dead the umpire shall:

(i) Direct the captain of the fielding side to take the bowler off forthwith. If applicable, the over shall be completed by another bowler, who shall neither have bowled the previous over nor be allowed to bowl the next over. The bowler thus taken off shall not be allowed to bowl again in that innings.

(ii) Inform the other umpire, the batsmen and, as soon as practicable, the captain of the batting side of what has occurred.

(iii) Report the occurrence, with the other umpire, as soon as possible to the executive of the fielding side and to any governing body responsible for the match, who shall take such action as is considered appropriate against the captain and bowler concerned.

13. Fielders damaging the pitch

(a) If any fielder causes avoidable damage to the pitch, other than as in 12(a) above, at the first instance the umpire shall, when the ball is dead:

(i) Caution the captain of the fielding side, indicating that this is a first and final warning. This caution shall continue to apply throughout the innings.

(ii) Inform the other umpire and the batsmen of what has occurred.

(b) If there is any further avoidable damage to the pitch by any fielder in that innings, the umpire shall, when the ball is dead:

(i) Award five penalty runs to the batting side. See 17 below.

(ii) Inform the other umpire, the batsmen, the captain of the fielding side and, as soon as practicable, the captain of the batting side of what has occurred.

(iii) Report the occurrence, with the other umpire, as soon as possible to the executive of the fielding side and any governing body responsible for the match, who shall take such action as is considered appropriate against the captain and player or players concerned.

14. Batsman damaging the pitch

(a) If either batsman causes avoidable damage to the pitch, at the first instance the umpire shall, when the ball is dead:

(i) Caution the batsman. This caution shall continue to apply throughout the innings. The umpire shall so inform each incoming batsman.

(ii) Inform the other umpire, the other batsman, the captain of the fielding side and, as soon as practicable, the captain of the batting side.

(b) If there is a second instance of avoidable damage to the pitch by any batsman in that innings:

(i) The umpire shall repeat the above procedure, indicating that this is a final warning.

(ii) Additionally he shall disallow all runs to the batting side from that delivery other than the penalty for a no-ball or a wide, if applicable. The batsmen shall return to their original ends.

(c) If there is any further avoidable damage to the pitch by any batsman in that innings, the umpire shall, when the ball is dead:

(i) Disallow all runs to the batting side from that delivery other than the penalty for a no-ball or a wide, if applicable.

(ii) Additionally award five penalty runs to the fielding side. See 17 below.

(iii) Inform the other umpire, the other batsman, the captain of the fielding side and, as soon as practicable, the captain of the batting side of what has occurred.

(iv) Report the occurrence, with the other umpire, as soon as possible to the executive of the batting side and any governing body responsible for the match, who shall take such action as is considered appropriate against the captain and player or players concerned.

15. Bowler attempting to run out non-striker before delivery

The bowler is permitted, before entering his delivery stride, to attempt to run out the non-striker. The ball shall not count in the over.

The umpire shall call and signal "Dead ball" as soon as possible if the bowler fails in the attempt to run out the non-striker.

16. Batsmen stealing a run

It is unfair for the batsmen to attempt to steal a run during the bowler's run-up. Unless the bowler attempts to run out either batsman – see 15 above and Law 24.4 (Bowler throwing towards striker's end before delivery) – the umpire shall:

(i) Call and signal "Dead ball" as soon as the batsmen cross in any such attempt.

(ii) Return the batsmen to their original ends.

(iii) Award five penalty runs to the fielding side. See 17 below.

(iv) Inform the other umpire, the other batsman, the captain of the fielding side and, as soon as practicable, the captain of the batting side of the reason for the action taken.

(v) Report the occurrence, with the other umpire, as soon as possible to the executive of the batting side and any governing body responsible for the match, who shall take such action as is considered appropriate against the captain and player or players concerned.

17. Penalty runs

(a) When penalty runs are awarded to either side, when the ball is dead the umpire shall signal the penalty runs to the scorers as laid down in Law 3.14 (Signals).

(b) Notwithstanding any provisions elsewhere in the Laws, penalty runs shall not be awarded once the match is concluded as defined in Law 16.9 (Conclusion of a match).

(c) When five penalty runs are awarded to the batting side, under either Law 2.6 (Player returning without permission) or Law 41 (The fielder) or under 3, 4, 5, 9 or 13 above, then:

(i) They shall be scored as penalty extras and shall be in addition to any other penalties.

(ii) They shall not be regarded as runs scored from either the immediately preceding delivery or the following delivery and shall be in addition to any runs from those deliveries.

(iii) The batsmen shall not change ends solely by reason of the five-run penalty.

(d) When five penalty runs are awarded to the fielding side, under Law 18.5(b) (Deliberate short runs), or under 10, 14 or 16 above, they shall be added as penalty extras to that side's total of runs in its most recently completed innings. If the fielding side has not completed an innings, the five penalty extras shall be added to its next innings.

18. Players' conduct

If there is any breach of the Spirit of the Game by a player failing to comply with the instructions of an umpire, or criticising his decisions by word or action, or showing dissent, or generally behaving in a manner which might bring the game into disrepute, the umpire concerned shall immediately report the matter to the other umpire.

The umpires together shall:

(i) Inform the player's captain of the occurrence, instructing the latter to take action.

(ii) Warn him of the gravity of the offence, and tell him that it will be reported to higher authority.

(iii) Report the occurrence as soon as possible to the executive of the player's team and any governing body responsible for the match, who shall take such action as is considered appropriate against the captain and player or players, and, if appropriate, the team concerned.

REGULATIONS OF THE INTERNATIONAL CRICKET COUNCIL

Extracts

1. Standard playing conditions

In 2000, the ICC Cricket Committee amended its standard playing conditions for all Tests and one-day internationals to include the new Laws of Cricket. The following playing conditions were to apply for one year from October 1, 2000:

Duration of Test Matches

Test matches shall be of five days' scheduled duration and of two innings per side. The two participating countries may:

(a) Provide for a rest day during the match, and/or a reserve day after the scheduled days of play.

(b) Play on any scheduled rest day, conditions and circumstances permitting, should a full day's play be lost on any day prior to the rest day.

(c) Play on any scheduled reserve day, conditions and circumstances permitting, should a full day's play be lost on any day. Play shall not take place on more than five days.

(d) Make up time lost in excess of five minutes in each day's play due to circumstances outside their control, other than acts of God.

Hours of Play and Minimum Overs in the Day in Test Matches

1. Start and cessation times shall be determined by the home board, subject to there being six hours scheduled for play per day (Pakistan a minimum of five and a half hours).

(a) Play shall continue on each day until the completion of a minimum number of overs or until the scheduled or rescheduled cessation time, whichever is the later. The minimum number of overs to be completed, unless an innings ends or an interruption occurs, shall be:

(i) on days other than the last day – a minimum of 90 overs (or a minimum of 15 overs per hour).

(ii) on the last day – a minimum of 75 overs (or 15 overs per hour) for playing time other than the last hour when a minimum of 15 overs shall be bowled. All calculations with regard to suspensions of play or the start of a new innings shall be based on one over for each full four minutes. (Fractions are to be ignored in all calculations except where there is a change of innings in a day's play, when the over in progress at the conclusion shall be rounded up.) If, however, at any time after 30 minutes of the last hour have elapsed both captains (the batsmen at the wicket may act for their captain) accept that there is no prospect of a result to the match, they may agree to cease play at that time.

(iii) Subject to weather and light, except in the last hour of the match, in the event of play being suspended for any reason other than normal intervals, the playing time on that day shall be extended by the amount of time lost up to a maximum of one hour. The minimum number of overs to be bowled shall be in accordance with the provisions of this clause (i.e. a minimum of 15 overs per hour) and the cessation time shall be rescheduled accordingly.

(iv) *Experimental Condition, subject to both Boards' agreement before the tour:* If any time is lost and cannot be made up under (a)(iii), additional time of up to a maximum of one hour per day shall be added to the scheduled playing hours for the next day, and subsequent day(s) as required. Of this additional time, the first 30 minutes (or less) shall be added before the scheduled start of the first session and the remainder to the last session. When additional time is added to subsequent day(s), no scheduled day's play shall exceed seven hours. The length of each session is subject to Law 15. Timings can be altered at any time on any day if time is lost, not necessarily on that day. The captains, umpires and referee can agree different timings under those circumstances before play starts on any day.

(b) When an innings ends, a minimum number of overs shall be bowled from the start of the new innings. The number of overs to be bowled shall be calculated at the rate of one over for each full four minutes to enable a minimum of 90 overs to be bowled in a day. The last hour of the match shall be excluded from this calculation (see (a) (ii)).

Where a change of innings occurs during a day's play, in the event of the team bowling second being unable to complete its overs by the scheduled cessation time, play shall continue until the required number of overs have been completed.

2. The umpires may decide to play 30 minutes (a minimum eight overs) extra time at the end of any day (other than the last day) if requested by either captain if, in the umpires' opinion, it would bring about a definite result on that day. If the umpires do not believe a result can be achieved, no extra time shall be allowed. If it is decided to play such extra time, the whole period shall be played out even though the possibility of finishing the match may have disappeared before the full period has expired. Only the actual amount of playing time up to the maximum 30 minutes' extra time by which play is extended on any day shall be deducted from the total number of hours of play remaining and the match shall end earlier on the final day by that amount of time.

Use of Lights: Experimental Condition for two years from August 1999, subject to both Boards' agreement before the tour

If, in the opinion of the umpires, natural light is deteriorating to an unfit level, they shall authorise the ground authorities to use the available artificial lighting so that the match can continue in acceptable conditions.

The lights are only to be used to enable a full day's play to be completed as provided for in Clause 1 above. In the event of power failure or lights malfunction, the existing provisions of Clause 1 shall apply.

Once the lights have been turned on, they must remain on for the remainder of the day's play.

Dangerous and Unfair Bowling: The Bowling of Fast, Short-Pitched Balls: Law 42.6

1. A bowler shall be limited to two fast, short-pitched deliveries per over.

2. A fast, short-pitched ball is defined as a ball which passes or would have passed above the shoulder height of the batsman standing upright at the crease.

3. In the event of a bowler bowling more than two fast, short-pitched deliveries in an over, either umpire shall call and signal "no-ball" on each occasion.

4. The umpire shall call and signal "no-ball" and then tap the head with the other hand.

If a bowler delivers a third fast, short-pitched ball in one over, not only must the umpire call no-ball, but he must invoke the procedures of caution, final warning, action against the bowler and reporting as set out in Law 42.7.

The above Regulation is not a substitute for Law 42.6 (as amended below), which umpires are able to apply at any time:

The bowling of fast, short-pitched balls is unfair if the umpire at the bowler's end considers that, by their repetition and taking into account their length, height and direction, they are likely to inflict physical injury on the striker, irrespective of the protective clothing and equipment he may be wearing. The relative skill of the striker shall also be taken into consideration.

The umpire at the bowler's end shall adopt the procedures of caution, final warning, action against the bowler and reporting as set out in Law 42.7.

New Ball: Law 5.4

The captain of the fielding side shall have the choice of taking a new ball any time after 80 overs have been bowled with the previous ball. The umpires shall indicate to the batsmen and the scorers whenever a new ball is taken into play.

Ball Lost or Becoming Unfit for Play: Law 5.5

The following shall apply in addition to Law 5.5

However, if the ball needs to be replaced after 110 overs for any of the reasons above, it shall be replaced by a new ball. If the ball is to be replaced, the umpires shall inform the batsmen.

Judging a Wide: Law 25.1

Law 25.1 will apply, but in addition

For bowlers whom umpires consider to be bowling down the leg side as a negative tactic, the one-day international wide interpretation will be applied. Any off-side or leg-side delivery which in the opinion of the umpire does not give the batsman a reasonable opportunity to score shall be called a wide. On the leg side, a ball landing clearly outside the leg stump going further away shall be called wide.

Practice on the Field: Law 17

At no time on any day of the match shall there be any bowling or batting practice on the pitch or the square, except in official netted practice pitch areas. In addition, there shall be no bowling or batting practice on any part of the square or the area immediately parallel to the match pitch after the commencement of play on any day. Any fielder contravening this Law may not bowl his next over.

No practice may take place on the field if, in the opinion of the umpires, it could result in a waste of time. In this circumstance, Law 42.9 shall apply.

Fieldsman Leaving the Field: Law 2.5

If a fielder fails to take the field with his side at the start of the match or at any later time, or leaves the field during a session of play, the umpire shall be informed of the reason for his absence, and he shall not thereafter come on to the field during a session without the consent of the umpire. The umpire shall give such consent as soon as practicable. If the player is absent from the field longer than eight minutes, he shall not be permitted to bowl in that innings after his return until he has been on the field for at least that length of playing time for which he was absent. In the event of a follow-on, this restriction will, if necessary, continue into the second innings. Nor shall he be permitted to bat unless or until, in the aggregate, he has returned to the field and/or his side's innings has been in progress for at least that length of playing time for which he has been absent or, if earlier, when his side has lost five wickets. The restrictions shall not apply if he has suffered an external blow (as opposed to an internal injury such as a pulled muscle) while participating earlier in the match and consequently been forced to leave the field, nor if he has been absent for exceptional and acceptable reasons (other than injury or illness) and consent for a substitute has been granted by the opposing captain.

2. Classification of first-class matches

1. Definitions

A match of three or more days' duration between two sides of 11 players played on natural turf pitches on international standard grounds and substantially conforming with standard playing conditions shall be regarded as a first-class fixture.

2. Rules

    (a) Full Members of the ICC shall decide the status of matches of three or more days' duration played in their countries.

(b) In matches of three or more days' duration played in countries which are not Full Members of the ICC, except Kenya (see 2.3 (l) below):

    (i) If the visiting team comes from a country which is a Full Member of the ICC, that country shall decide the status of matches.

    (ii) If the visiting team does not come from a country which is a Full Member of the ICC, or is a Commonwealth team composed of players from different countries, the ICC shall decide the status of matches.

Notes

(a) Governing bodies agree that the interest of first-class cricket will be served by ensuring that first-class status is not accorded to any match in which one or other of the teams taking part cannot on a strict interpretation of the definitions be adjudged first-class.

(b) In case of any disputes arising from these Rules, the Chief Executive of the ICC shall refer the matter for decision to the Council, failing unanimous agreement by postal communication being reached.

3. First-Class Status

The following matches shall be regarded as first-class, subject to the provisions of 2.1 (Definitions) being complied with:

(a) **In Great Britain and Ireland:** (i) County Championship matches. (ii) Official representative tourist matches from Full Member countries unless specifically excluded. (iii) MCC v any first-class county. (iv) Oxford, Cambridge and Durham University Centres of Excellence against first-class counties. (v) Oxford v Cambridge. (vi) Scotland v Ireland.

(b) **In Australia:** (i) Pura Milk Cup matches. (ii) Matches played by teams representing states of the Commonwealth of Australia between each other or against opponents adjudged first-class.

(c) **In Bangladesh:** (i) Matches between Bangladesh and a Full Member. (ii) Matches between Full Member teams adjudged first-class and Bangladesh. (iii) Matches between teams adjudged first-class and a Full Member. (iv) Matches between Bangladesh and Kenya. (v) Matches between teams adjudged first-class and Kenya. (vi) National League three-day matches between Biman Bangladesh Airlines, Dhaka Metropolis and the Divisions of Barisal, Chittagong, Dhaka, Khulna, Rajshahi and Sylhet.

(d) **In India:** (i) Ranji Trophy matches. (ii) Duleep Trophy matches. (iii) Irani Trophy matches. (iv) Matches played by teams representing state or regional associations affiliated to the Board of Control between each other or against opponents adjudged first-class. (v) All three-day matches played against representative visiting sides.

(e) **In New Zealand:** (i) Shell Trophy and Shell Conference matches. (ii) Matches played by teams representing major associations affiliated to New Zealand Cricket, between each other or against opponents adjudged first-class.

(f) **In Pakistan:** (i) Quaid-e-Azam Trophy (Grade 1) matches. (ii) Patron's Trophy (Grade 1) matches. (iii) Matches played by teams representing divisional associations affiliated to the Pakistan Cricket Board, between each other or against teams adjudged first-class.

(g) **In South Africa:** SuperSport Series four-day matches between Boland, Border, Eastern Province, Easterns, Free State, Gauteng, Griqualand West, KwaZulu-Natal, Northerns, North West, Western Province.

(h) **In Sri Lanka:** (i) Matches of three days or more against touring sides adjudged first-class. (ii) Inter-Club Division I tournament matches played over three or more days for the Premier Trophy.

(i) **In West Indies:** Matches played by teams representing Barbados, Guyana, Jamaica, the Leeward Islands, Trinidad & Tobago and the Windward Islands, either for the Busta Cup or against other opponents adjudged first-class.

(j) **In Zimbabwe:** (i) Matches of three days or more against touring sides adjudged first-class. (ii) Logan Cup competition three-day matches between Manicaland, Mashonaland, Mashonaland A, Matabeleland, Midlands and CFX Academy.

(k) **In all Full Member countries represented on the Council:** (i) Test matches and matches against teams adjudged first-class played by official touring teams. (ii) Official Test Trial matches. (iii) Special matches between teams adjudged first-class by the governing body or bodies concerned.

(l) **In Kenya:** (i) Matches between a Full Member and Kenya. (ii) Matches between teams adjudged first-class and Kenya.

3. Classification of one-day international matches

The following shall be classified as one-day internationals:

(a) All matches played in the official World Cup competition, including matches involving Associate Member countries.

(b) All matches played between the Full Member countries of the ICC as part of an official tour itinerary.

(c) All matches played as part of an official tournament between Full Member countries. These need not necessarily be held in a Full Member country.

(d) All matches between the Full Members and Kenya.

Note: Matches involving the A team of a Full Member country shall not be classified as one-day internationals.

4. Qualification rules for Test matches and one-day international matches

Qualification by Birth

A cricketer is qualified to play in Tests, one-day internationals or any other representative cricket match for the country of his birth provided he has not played in Tests, one-day internationals or, after October 1, 1994, in any other representative cricket match for any other Member country during the two immediately preceding years.

Qualification by Residence

A cricketer is qualified to play in Tests, one-day internationals or in any other representative cricket match for any Full or Associate Member country in which he has resided for at least 183 days in each of the four immediately preceding years provided that he has not played in Tests, one-day internationals or, after October 1, 1994, in any other representative cricket match for any other Member country during that period of four years.

Exceptional Circumstances

Should a player be deemed ineligible under the above qualifications and his Board believe that there are exceptional circumstances requiring consideration, a detailed written application shall be made to the Chief Executive of the ICC. The application will be referred to the Chairman of the Cricket Committee whose decision shall be final.

Notes: "Representative cricket match" means any cricket match in which a team representing a Member country at Under-19 level or above takes part, including Tests and one-day internationals.

The governing body for cricket of any Member country may impose more stringent qualification rules for that country.

ICC CODE OF CONDUCT

1. The captains are responsible at all times for ensuring that play is conducted within the spirit of the game as well as within the Laws.

2. Players and/or team officials shall at no time engage in conduct unbecoming to their status which could bring them or the game of cricket into disrepute.

3. Players and/or team officials must at all times accept the umpire's decision and not show dissent at the umpire's decision.

4. Players and/or team officials shall not verbally abuse, assault, intimidate or attempt to assault or intimidate any umpire, spectator, referee, player or team official. Nor shall any player or team official engage in any conduct towards or speak to any other player, umpire, spectator, referee or team official in a manner which offends, insults, humiliates, intimidates, disparages or vilifies the other person on the basis of that other person's race, religion, colour, descent or national or ethnic origin.

5. Players and/or team officials shall not use crude or abusive language nor make offensive gestures.

6. Players and/or team officials shall not disclose or comment publicly upon any alleged or actual breach of this Code, whether by themselves or any other person to whom the Code applies, or upon any hearing, report or decision arising from such an alleged or proven breach.

7. Players and/or team officials shall not at any time breach any ICC regulation which may be in force from time to time.

8. Players and/or team officials shall not make any public pronouncement or media comment which is detrimental either to the game of cricket in general; or to a particular tour whether or not they are personally involved with the tour; or to relations between the home boards of competing teams.

9. Players and/or team officials shall not bet on matches nor otherwise engage in conduct referred to in Appendix A of the ICC Code of Conduct Commission Terms of Reference.

10. Players shall be required to report to the captain and team manager any approach made to them by a bookmaker in conduct referred to in Appendix A.

11. Players and/or team officials shall not use or in any way be concerned in the use or distribution of illegal drugs.

APPENDIX A

Whether, at any time after July 1, 1993, any player of a cricket authority's team participating in any Test match, one-day international or representative cricket match, or any umpire, referee, team official or administrator of any such cricket authority representing or in any way related to the cricket authority of any such Member country

1. Has engaged in any of the following conduct:

    i. Bet on any match or series of matches, or on any connected event, in which such player, umpire, referee, team official or administrator took part or in which the Member country or any such individual was represented;

    ii. Induced or encouraged any other person to bet on any match or series of matches or on any connected event or to offer the facility for such bets to be placed;

    iii. Gambled or entered into any other form of financial speculation on any match or on any connected event;

    iv. Induced or encouraged any other person to gamble or enter into any other form of financial speculation on any match or any connected event;

    v. Was a party to contriving or attempting to contrive the result of any match or the occurrence of any connected event;

    vi. Failed to perform on his merits in any match owing to an arrangement relating to betting on the outcome of any match or on the occurrence of any connected event;

    vii. Induced or encouraged any other player not to perform on his merits in any match owing to any such arrangement;

    viii. Received from another person any money, benefit or other reward (whether financial or otherwise) for the provision of any information concerning the weather, the teams, the state of the ground, the status of, or the outcome of, any match or the occurrence of any connected event unless such information has been provided to a newspaper or other form of media in accordance with an obligation entered into in the normal course and disclosed in advance to the cricket authority of the relevant Member country;

    ix. Received any money, benefit or other reward (whether financial or otherwise) which could bring him or the game of cricket into disrepute;

    x. Provided any money, benefit or other reward (whether financial or otherwise) which could bring him or the game of cricket into disrepute;

    xi. Received any approaches from another person to engage in conduct such as that described above; or

2. Is aware that any other player or individual has engaged in conduct, or received approaches, such as described above; or

3. Has received or is aware that any other person has received threats of any nature which might induce him to engage in conduct, or acquiesce in any proposal made by an approach, such as described above.

4. Has engaged in any conduct which, in the opinion of the Executive Board, is prejudicial to the interests of the game of cricket.

CRIME AND PUNISHMENT

ICC Code of Conduct – Breaches and Penalties in 1999-2000

D. F. Whatmore
(Sri Lankan manager)   Sri Lanka v India, one-day international at Colombo (SSC).
Angry reaction after umpires showed him match balls. Reprimanded by C. W. Smith.

D. W. Fleming   Australia v Sri Lanka, 2nd Test at Galle.
Pushed dismissed batsman (Vaas). Fined 50 per cent of match fee by C. W. Smith.

Azhar Mahmood   Pakistan v Australia, 1st Test at Brisbane.
Failed to remove extra logo on back of helmet. Fined 20 per cent of match fee by J. R. Reid.

Mohammad Akram   Pakistan v Australia, 3rd Test at Perth.
Made avoidable body contact with running batsman. Severely reprimanded by J. R. Reid.

A. D. R. Campbell   Zimbabwe v Sri Lanka, 3rd Test at Harare.
Verbal abuse of Sri Lankan players. Fined 30 per cent of match fee, with ban for three one-day internationals suspended for six months, by J. L. Hendriks.

N. C. Johnson   Zimbabwe v Sri Lanka, 3rd Test at Harare.
Verbal abuse of Sri Lankan players. Fined 30 per cent of match fee, with ban for two one-day internationals suspended for three months, by J. L. Hendriks.

M. W. Goodwin   Zimbabwe v Sri Lanka, 3rd Test at Harare.
Verbal abuse of Sri Lankan players. Fined 30 per cent of match fee, with ban for one one-day international suspended for three months, by J. L. Hendriks.

B. K. V. Prasad   India v Australia, 2nd Test at Melbourne.
Gestured at dismissed batsman. Fined 35 per cent of match fee, with ban for one Test or two one-day internationals suspended for four months, by R. S. Madugalle.

D. S. Mohanty   India v Pakistan, one-day international at Adelaide.
Repeatedly stood outside fielding circle at moment of delivery. Asked to respect playing conditions by C. W. Smith.

L. Klusener   South Africa v Zimbabwe, one-day international at Port Elizabeth.
Verbal abuse of dismissed batsman (G. J. Whittall). Ban for two Tests and two one-day internationals suspended for three months by Hanumant Singh.

G. J. Whittall   Zimbabwe v South Africa, one-day international at Port Elizabeth.
Verbal abuse of bowler (Klusener). Fined 30 per cent of match fee, suspended for one month, by Hanumant Singh.

Inzamam-ul-Haq   Pakistan v Sri Lanka, 3rd Test at Karachi.
Public criticism of Sri Lankan players in newspaper article. Severely reprimanded and fined 25 per cent of match fee, suspended for six months, by B. F. Hastings.

G. W. Flower   Zimbabwe v West Indies, 1st Test at Port-of-Spain.
Hit stump out of ground when dismissed. Fined 40 per cent of match fee, with ban for one Test or two one-day internationals suspended for four months, by R. S. Madugalle.

Inzamam-ul-Haq   Pakistan v West Indies, 3rd Test at St John's.
Delayed departure when given out. Fined 50 per cent of match fee, plus 25 per cent of match fee for earlier breach in 3rd Test v Sri Lanka (see previous page), by P. J. Burge.

Arshad Khan   Pakistan v Sri Lanka, 2nd Test at Galle.
Dissent when lbw appeal turned down. Fined 30 per cent of match fee by J. R. Reid.

Waqar Younis   Pakistan v South Africa, one-day international at Colombo (RPS).
Changed condition of ball. Banned for one one-day international and fined 50 per cent of match fee by J. R. Reid.

Azhar Mahmood   Pakistan v South Africa, one-day international at Colombo (RPS).
Associated with changing condition of ball. Fined 30 per cent of match fee by J. R. Reid.

Moin Khan   Pakistan v South Africa, one-day international at Colombo (RPS).
Captain when Waqar Younis changed condition of ball. Severely reprimanded by J. R. Reid.

REGULATIONS FOR FIRST-CLASS MATCHES IN BRITAIN, 2000

Hours of play

Four-day matches:

1st, 2nd, 3rd days . . . 11.00 a.m. to 6.30 p.m.
4th day . . . . 11.00 a.m. to 6.00 p.m.

Three-day matches:

1st, 2nd days . . . . . . 11.30 a.m. to 6.30 p.m. (11.00 a.m. to 6.30 p.m. in tourist matches and Oxford v Cambridge)
3rd day . . . . 11.00 a.m. to 6.00 p.m.

Intervals

Lunch: 1.15 p.m. to 1.55 p.m. (1st, 2nd [3rd] days) in Championship and tourist matches and Oxford v Cambridge, 1.30 p.m. to 2.10 p.m. in others
1.00 p.m. to 1.40 p.m. (final day)
Where an innings concludes or there is a break in play within ten minutes of the scheduled lunch interval, the interval will commence at that time and be limited to 40 minutes.

Tea: (Championship matches) A tea interval of 20 minutes shall normally be taken at 4.10 p.m. (3.40 p.m. on final day), or at the conclusion of the over in progress at that time, provided 32 overs or less remain to be bowled (except on the final day). The over in progress shall be completed unless a batsman is out or retires either within two minutes of, or after, the scheduled time for the interval. In the event of more than 32 overs remaining, the tea interval will be delayed.

If an innings ends or there is a stoppage caused by weather within 30 minutes of the scheduled time, the tea interval shall be taken immediately. There will be no tea interval if the scheduled timing for the cessation of play is earlier than 5.30 p.m.

(Other matches) 4.10 p.m. to 4.30 p.m. (1st, 2nd [3rd] days), 3.40 p.m. to 4.00 p.m. (final day).

Note: The hours of play, including intervals, are brought forward by half an hour for matches scheduled to start in September.

(i) Play shall continue on each day until the completion of a minimum number of overs or until the scheduled cessation time, whichever is the later. The minimum number of overs, unless an innings ends or an interruption occurs, shall be 104 on days other than the last day, and 80 on the last day before the last hour.

(ii) Where there is a change of innings during a day's play (except during an interval or suspension of play or during the last hour of domestic matches), two overs will be deducted from the minimum number, plus any over in progress at the end of the completed innings (in domestic matches).

(iii) If interruptions for weather or light occur, other than in the last hour of the match, the minimum number of overs shall be reduced by one over for each full 3¾ minutes of the aggregate playing time lost.

(iv) On the last day, if any of the minimum of 80 overs, or as recalculated, have not been bowled when one hour of scheduled playing time remains, the last hour of the match shall be the hour immediately following the completion of those overs.

(v) Law 16.6, 16.7 and 16.8 will apply except that a minimum of 16 six-ball overs shall be bowled in the last hour, and *all* calculations with regard to suspensions of play or the start of a new innings shall be based on one over for each full 3¾ minutes. If, however, at 5.30 p.m. both captains accept that there is no prospect of a result or (in Championship games) of either side gaining any further first-innings bonus points, they may agree to cease play at that time or at any time after 5.30 p.m.

(vi) (Domestic matches). The captains may agree or, in the event of disagreement, the umpires may decide to play 30 minutes (a minimum eight overs) extra time at the end of any day other than the last day if, in their opinion, it would bring about a definite result on that day. The whole period shall be played out even though the possibility of finishing the match may have disappeared before the full period has expired. The time by which play is extended on any day shall be deducted from the total number of hours remaining, and the match shall end earlier on the last day by the amount of time by which play was extended.

(vii) Notwithstanding any other provision, there shall be no further play on any day, other than the last day, if a wicket falls or a batsman retires, or if the players leave the field during the last minimum over within two minutes of the scheduled cessation time or thereafter.

(viii) An over completed on resumption of a new day's play shall be disregarded in calculating minimum overs for that day.

(ix) The scoreboard shall show the total number of overs bowled with the ball in use and the minimum number remaining to be bowled in a day. In Championship matches, it shall show the number of overs up to 130 in each side's first innings and subsequently the number bowled with the current ball.

Substitutes

(Domestic matches only) Law 2.1 will apply, but in addition:

No substitute may take the field until the player for whom he is to substitute has been absent from the field for five consecutive complete overs, with the exception that if a fieldsman sustains an obvious, serious injury or is taken ill, a substitute shall be allowed immediately. In the event of any disagreement between the two sides as to the authenticity of an injury or illness, the umpires shall adjudicate. If a player leaves the field during an over, the remainder of that over shall not count in the calculation of the five complete overs.

A substitute shall be allowed by right immediately in the event of a cricketer currently playing in a Championship match being required to join the England team for a Test match (or one-day international). Such a substitute may be permitted to bat or bowl in that match, subject to the approval of the ECB. The cricketer who is substituted shall take no further part in the match, even though he may not be required by England. If batting at the time, he shall retire "not out" and his substitute may be permitted to bat later in that innings subject to the approval of the ECB.

Fieldsman leaving the field

No fieldsman shall leave the field or return during a session of play without the consent of the umpire at the bowler's end. The umpire's consent is also necessary if a substitute is required for a fieldsman at the start of play or when his side returns to the field after an interval. If a member of the fielding side does not take the field at the start of play, leaves the field or fails to return after an interval and is absent longer than eight minutes, ICC regulations apply (see page 1509) but, in domestic matches, there is no mention of the follow-on and it is explained that "external blow" should include, but not be restricted to, collisions with boundary boards, clashes of heads, heavy falls etc.

New ball

The captain of the fielding side shall have the choice of taking the new ball after 100 overs (80 in tourist matches) have been bowled with the old one.

Covering of pitches and surrounding areas

(Domestic matches) The whole pitch shall be covered:

    (a) The night before the match and, if necessary, until the first ball is bowled; and whenever necessary and possible at any time prior to that during the preparation of the pitch.

    (b) On each night of the match and, if necessary, throughout any rest days.

    (c) In the event of play being suspended on account of bad light or rain, during the specified hours of play.

The bowler's run-up shall be covered to a distance of at least ten yards, with a width of four yards, as will the areas 20 feet either side of the length of the pitch.

Declarations

Law 14 will apply, but, in addition, a captain may also forfeit his first innings, subject to the provisions set out in Law 14.2. If, due to weather conditions, play in a County Championship match has not started when less than eight hours' playing time remains, the first innings of each side shall automatically be forfeited and a one-innings match played.

MEETINGS AND DECISIONS IN 2000

ICC EXECUTIVE MEETING

The ICC's executive board, meeting in Singapore on February 9–10, announced the launch of the first ICC Cricket Week from April 2–9. This would include a one-day match between Asia and the Rest of the World, an Emerging Nations Tournament, worldwide events involving ICC cricket ambassadors, and extensive television coverage. Lord Griffiths delivered his report on the inquiries of the Australian and Indian boards into match-fixing allegations. The ICC also revoked the power of its bowling panel to suspend suspect bowlers; in future, it was to make recommendations to the players' national boards. The executive board approved Australia's plans for three indoor internationals in August, and agreed to the use of portable pitches for one-day internationals after a trial in New Zealand.

ECB SPONSORSHIP DEAL

The ECB announced on February 17 that the NatWest Group would sponsor the new annual, triangular one-day international series. A new grassroots programme, worth £450,000 over three years and to enhance practice facilities for young cricketers at clubs and schools, was also announced. However, NatWest would not be renewing its sponsorship of the NatWest Trophy, NatWest Development of Excellence programme and the England Under-19 team after 2000.

SPORT ENGLAND GRANT

On February 17, Sport England announced a grant of £982,000 to help fund development programmes devised by the ECB. This would enable the appointment of four regional women's club development officers along with three national coaches, as well as the setting up of a new groundsmanship advisers structure and a county board professional support programme.

ENGLAND SUMMER CONTRACTS

Twelve England players were awarded six-month ECB contracts on March 1, bringing them under the control of the England team management for the first time. The board set aside around £750,000 to cover the additional costs. The contracted players were: Nasser Hussain (*captain*), Mike Atherton, Andrew Caddick, Andrew Flintoff, Darren Gough, Dean Headley, Graeme Hick, Mark Ramprakash, Chris Schofield, Alec Stewart, Michael Vaughan and Craig White.

FIRST-CLASS FORUM

At a meeting of the First-Class Forum on March 7, a new, streamlined management structure was approved for a three-year trial, with the forum ceding key decision-making powers to its existing management board. This would now be responsible for the programme and playing conditions for first-class cricket, and for designating Test match grounds. The forum retained its powers to approve the budget, adopt discipline and registration regulations, and make decisions affecting the promotion and relegation format in the County Championship and National League. The international affairs sub-committee and the Second Eleven advisory group would be discontinued.

ECB BROADCASTING DEAL

On March 8, the ECB announced a new five-year agreement with BBC Radio for the ball-by-ball coverage on Radio 4 (long wave) of home Tests, one-day internationals and domestic one-day knockout competitions from the quarter-finals on, to come into effect from 2001.

ECB PITCH LIAISON OFFICERS

On April 6, the ECB named seven pitch liaison officers and match referees for the 2000 season. Mike Denness, Raman Subba Row, Alan Smith, Tony Brown, Peter Walker, Phil Sharpe and David Hughes were given the authority to attend any first-class fixture to monitor pitch preparation and performance, and to convene a panel which could penalise counties for substandard surfaces on a sliding scale of eight to 20 Championship points. They would be supported by three technical advisers, Chris Wood, Harry Brind and Tom Flintoft.

ICC EMERGENCY MEETING

The ICC held an emergency meeting at Lord's on May 2–3 to discuss match-fixing and betting on cricket matches. A code of unacceptable behaviour was drawn up, outlawing players, officials and administrators from: betting on any matches in which they are involved or over which they have influence; deliberately underperforming or encouraging any other player to underperform; and providing information to parties, other than the media, concerning the match, the teams or the state of the ground. All players, managers, referees, umpires, match officials and administrators would be required to provide a declaration stating whether or not they had been approached to become involved in corrupt conduct.

MCC ANNUAL GENERAL MEETING

The 213th AGM of the Marylebone Cricket Club was held on May 3, with the president, Tony Lewis, in the chair. The club approved resolutions regarding changes to its rules, the introduction of a new management and operational structure, and entrance and subscription increases for 2001. Membership of the club on December 31, 1999, was 19,735, made up of 17,035 members, 1,950 associate members, 595 honorary members and 116 senior members with 39 out-match members. There were 9,920 candidates awaiting election. In 1999, 442 vacancies arose.

Following the AGM, a special general meeting approved the 2000 Code of the Laws of Cricket, which includes, as a preamble, the Spirit of Cricket.

ICC ANNUAL CONFERENCE

At its annual conference, held in Paris and London on June 22–26, the ICC unanimously elected Bangladesh to full membership, so making them the tenth Test-playing country. The decision to grant Cayman Islands associate status was deferred for another year, but Cook Islands, Czech Republic, Finland, Norway, Oman, Philippines, Samoa and Tonga became Affiliates. It was confirmed that the 2003 World Cup, to be held in South Africa, would include the 11 countries holding one-day international status, along with the top three teams from the 2001 ICC Trophy. Sir Paul Condon was appointed director of the new Anti-Corruption Unit. In Paris, the executive board appointed World Sport Group and News Corporation to handle the sale of commercial rights to major cricket events for a period of seven years.

THE CRICKET FOUNDATION

On August 14, the Cricket Foundation announced development awards totalling £2.7 million for 2000-01. They were to go to the 38 County Boards, the Isle of Wight and the Channel Islands, and national cricket projects. A total of £1 million was designated for the employment of county development officers and support for volunteers, while £80,000 was made available for the improvement of the standard of pitches in club cricket.

ICC EXECUTIVE BOARD MEETING

On October 16–17, the ICC held an executive board meeting in Nairobi, Kenya, at which the Code of Conduct Commission's interim report on Justice Qayyum's inquiry was considered in detail, and Sir Paul Condon reported on the establishment of the Anti-Corruption Unit, its roles and responsibilities. The board confirmed that all players, umpires, referees, team officials, administrators, employees and groundsmen would be requested to complete declarations of any knowledge of corruption in cricket. The implementation of a ten-year programme of Test fixtures was considered, and approval in principle given to a three-stage process for dealing with players suspected of having an illegal bowling action.

ECB THROWING PANEL

After a meeting on November 7, the ECB throwing panel suspended Mark Wagh of Warwickshire from bowling in county cricket, and all other cricket directly under the auspices of the ECB, until further notice. The panel declared itself satisfied with the action of Sussex's James Kirtley, and allowed him to continue bowling.

CRICKET IN SCHOOLS

On November 17, the ECB and Channel 4 launched Howzat!, an initiative designed to promote cricket to children in schools. Two education resource packs had been produced: "Howzat! 1st Innings" for primary schools and "Howzat! 2nd Innings" for secondary schools. In all, 30,000 packs, containing suggested lesson plans and ideas, were produced for free distribution to schools in England and Wales.

ECB REGULATIONS FOR 2001

Changes affecting county cricket in 2001, announced on November 21, included the replacement of fines by points penalties (0.25 points per over) for slow over-rates in the Championship. The minimum rate remains 16 overs an hour for a match. In one-day games, the batting side will receive six runs for each complete over not bowled within the specified playing time; the full quota of overs will still be bowled in such instances. As a move to stop intimidatory appealing and premature celebrations after an appeal, all players not involved in fielding the ball must maintain their fielding positions until a decision is made. The ECB will source and distribute balls to the counties centrally, using designated makes for each competition (see Cricket Equipment, 2000). Matches between Durham UCCE and first-class counties were accorded first-class status and, subject to approval by the First-Class Forum, counties would be allowed to replace injured overseas players; it was expected that, from 2002, counties could replace overseas players on international duty.

ECB SPONSORSHIP DEAL

On December 11, the ECB announced that it was to extend its association with mobile telephone company Vodafone until the end of the 2005 English season. The new contract, worth a minimum of £12 million plus bonuses for success in Tests and one-day internationals, would come into effect on October 1, 2001. The agreement also included the sponsorship of the England A team, the England women's team and the Kwik Cricket programme.

FIRST-CLASS FORUM

The First-Class Forum approved the ECB budget for 2001 on December 14. The five per cent increase in payments to the first-class counties would give each county in the region of £1,275,000.

PART SEVEN: MISCELLANEOUS

CHRONICLE OF 2000

JANUARY

4 Australia beat India at Sydney, their seventh successive Test win. **8** ICC allow Shoaib Akhtar to play in one-day internationals, despite being banned for throwing. **11** West Indies end New Zealand tour after losing both Tests and five one-day internationals. **18** England beat South Africa at Centurion after both forfeit innings; first instance of forfeitures in Test cricket. **22** E. W. Swanton dies, aged 92. **28** India beat Sri Lanka in Under-19 World Cup final.

FEBRUARY

10 Saeed Anwar replaces Wasim Akram as Pakistan captain. **16** Geoff Miller joins England selectors. **20** Sachin Tendulkar announces he will stand down as India's captain after the home Test series against South Africa. **22** Roger Harper is appointed West Indies coach. England's women lose their fifth one-day international in New Zealand, following four defeats in Australia. In Dunedin, Australia extend their winning one-day international sequence to a record-equalling 11 (excluding a no-result). **24** Brian Lara resigns as West Indies captain. **26** Australia's one-day win in Christchurch gives them 12 in a row. Sourav Ganguly is appointed to lead India in the one-day series against South Africa.

MARCH

1 ECB announce central contracts for 12 England players. **3** Jimmy Adams is appointed West Indies captain; Lara says he will rest during the home Test series. In Auckland, New Zealand end Australia's unbeaten run of 14 one-day internationals (13 wins). **5** PCB announce that Javed Miandad will succeed Intikhab Alam as coach; Intikhab resigns in mid-Test. **6** India lose their first home Test series for 13 years, to South Africa. **8** Jamie Siddons, the highest run-scorer in Australian domestic first-class cricket, announces his retirement. The future of *Test Match Special* is guaranteed after ECB and BBC agree a five-year deal. **12** Moin Khan leads Pakistan in the absence of injured Saeed Anwar. **13** In Auckland, Shane Warne takes his 355th Test wicket to equal Dennis Lillee's Australian record, and Daniel Vettori becomes the youngest spinner to take 100 Test wickets. Anwar resigns as Pakistan captain; Moin remains in charge. **15** Warne overtakes Lillee as Australia equal their national record of eight successive wins. **20** West Indies, defending a target of 99, bowl out Zimbabwe for 63. **26** In Wellington, Steve Waugh becomes the first to make 150 or more against all eight other Test countries. **27** Australia win their ninth Test in a row. In his native Jamaica, Courtney Walsh beats Kapil Dev's world record of 434 Test wickets.

APRIL

2 ICC Cricket Week starts. In Hamilton, Adam Gilchrist becomes the first Australian wicket-keeper to make ten dismissals in a Test. **3** Australia win again; now one behind West Indies' record of 11 successive wins. **6** England's contracted players finally agree terms. **7** Delhi police charge South African captain Hansie Cronje and other team members with "cheating, fraud and criminal conspiracy related to match-fixing and betting". The earliest start to the English first-class season; Somerset's Michael Burns makes the first hundred. **9** Cronje denies "receiving any sum of money during the one-day international series in India", claiming he never spoke to any member of his team about throwing a game. Somerset beat Oxford Universities by 404 runs at Taunton. **10** South Africa's deputy foreign minister meets India's High Commissioner to discuss allegations of match-fixing and to request formally that India provide a copy of incriminating phone-taps. **11** Cronje admits to Bacher in a 3 a.m. phone call that he received $US10–15,000 in cash to provide "information and forecasts" on South Africa's one-day series in India, and is replaced as captain by Shaun Pollock. He denies involvement in match-fixing. **12** South Africa beat Australia by six wickets in Durban. South African board confirm that England's win at Centurion will form part of their inquiry. **13** South Africa's Sports Ministry promises an independent judicial inquiry. Cronje is now said to have received around 50,000 rand. Lord MacLaurin calls for a summit meeting of ICC Full Members. **14** Adam Gilchrist takes six catches, a world one-day international record, as Australia beat South Africa in Cape Town. **16** Chris Lewis claims in the *News of the World* that a bookmaker told him three England players accepted money. South Africa win one-day series against Australia 2–1. **17** Indian magazine *Outlook* alleges that Kapil Dev, Mohammad Azharuddin, Nayan Mongia and Ajay Jadeja were involved in illegal betting, quoting tape transcripts from the 1997 Titan Cup. **18** Lewis meets ECB representatives. Azharuddin and Kapil Dev deny charges. **20** Indian government release details of Justice Chandrachud's 1997 investigation into Manoj Prabhakar's allegation that he was offered money to play badly; the allegation "lacks substance and is unjustified". Dave Houghton resigns as Zimbabwe's coach to work for TV. **24** The rain relents: a full Benson and Hedges programme is played for the first time in the season. **26** All play is washed out on the opening day of the County Championship for the first time since 1966. **27** ECB reject Lewis's allegations. **29** Eddie Barlow, Bangladesh's coach, has a brain haemorrhage.

MAY

2 ICC begin two-day extraordinary meeting at Lord's to discuss allegations of match-fixing and betting. **3** MCC adopt the new code of Laws. **4** PCB receive Justice Qayyum's report into match-fixing. South Africa name Justice Edwin King to lead their inquiry into match-fixing. Durham end Surrey's 100 per cent record against them at the 18th attempt (nine Championship, nine one-day). **8** PCB chairman says Pakistan's judicial inquiry found "no planned match-fixing". Lara declares himself unavailable for West Indies' tour of England. **11** Lara declares himself available for tour of England. **13** England team announced on TV (Channel 4) for the first time. **18** In earliest English Test, England dismiss Zimbabwe for 83 at Lord's. **24** PCB release Qayyum Report: life bans recommended for Salim Malik and Ata-ur-Rehman. Prabhakar claims Kapil Dev offered him money to underperform against Pakistan in 1994-95; next day, Kapil denies the charge. **30** Sussex captain Adams fined £500 after altercation in Benson and Hedges game at Chelmsford. Shoaib Akhtar arrives at Trent Bridge as Nottinghamshire's overseas player.

JUNE

2 Wasim Akram leaves Channel 4's commentary team after criticism in Qayyum Report. Sri Lankan board's interim management committee resigns, complaining of an unhelpful attitude from the Sports Ministry. **4** Nottinghamshire openers Darren Bicknell and Guy Welton put on 406 in an unbroken partnership at Edgbaston. **6** Hampshire Second Eleven inaugurate the county's new venue at West End, playing Sussex Second Eleven on the nursery ground. **7** South Africa's King Commission on match-fixing opens; Pat Symcox says Cronje told him of an offer to throw a one-day game against Pakistan in January 1995, and told the team in December 1996 of a $US250,000 offer to lose a one-day game against India at Mumbai. **8** Gibbs admits agreeing to score less than

20 runs against India at Nagpur for $US15,000, but later reneged. **9** Gibbs is dropped from South Africa's tour of Sri Lanka. Strydom says Cronje offered him 70,000 rand, later doubled, to fix the First Test against India at Mumbai in February; Williams admits he agreed to concede 50 runs against India at Nagpur for $US15,000; he was injured in his second over. Shoaib Akhtar released by Nottinghamshire without playing a game because of a rib injury. Derbyshire are fined eight points for a substandard pitch. **10** Gloucestershire win their third successive Lord's final, beating Glamorgan in the Benson and Hedges Cup. Brian Statham dies, aged 69. Bacher alleges that two 1999 World Cup matches (Bangladesh v Pakistan, India v Pakistan) were fixed and that umpire Javed Akhtar was "on the payroll" of a bookmaker when he umpired England v South Africa at Headingley in 1998. **12** Lance Klusener and Mark Boucher testify that Cronje offered them 240,000 rand to lose the Bangalore Test against India in March; they treated it as a joke. **13** Jacques Kallis corroborates Klusener and Boucher's testimony; Dave Richardson supports Symcox's evidence. **14** Bacher denies allegations by Johannesburg lawyer Peter Soller that he was involved in arranging for the rebel West Indian side to lose a match in 1983; he says the money related to attendance bonuses. Nottinghamshire sign Paul Reiffel to replace Shoaib Akhtar. **15** Cronje admits accepting money from bookmakers but denies match-fixing; he admits the Centurion forfeitures were prompted and rewarded by Johannesburg bookmaker Marlon Aronstam. **16** In Colombo, Wasim Akram takes his 400th Test wicket, in Sri Lanka's 100th Test. **17** West Indies beat England in three days at Edgbaston. **19** Gloucestershire lose to the Zimbabweans by 524 runs, their heaviest defeat ever. **21** Cronje admits receiving money to provide information on the triangular series between South Africa, England and Zimbabwe. In Galle, Abdur Razzaq becomes the youngest bowler to take a Test hat-trick. Gloucestershire, beaten by Worcestershire in the NatWest third round, lose their first knockout game since 1998. **22** Cronje admits to smuggling money out of India and into South Africa. **23** Aronstam testifies that Cronje said he would throw a game for money. **24** Nasser Hussain breaks his thumb in National League game. **26** Bangladesh receive Test status. ICC appoint Sir Paul Condon to head Anti-Corruption Unit. Before adjourning, the King Commission is told of the first meeting between Cronje and bookmaker Sanjeev Chawla. **29** Marvan Atapattu and Sanath Jayasuriya reach 335 against Pakistan, the fifth-highest opening stand in Tests. **30** England and West Indies bowl each other out at Lord's on a day containing all four innings. Gloucestershire's NatWest defeat by Worcestershire is overturned; ECB order a replay.

JULY

1 England beat West Indies in three days at Lord's. Leanne Davis becomes the youngest England player at 15 years 66 days. **4** Gloucestershire win their NatWest replay. **6** First day/night international in England sees Zimbabwe beat West Indies. **9** Waqar Younis receives a one-match ban for ball-tampering in Sri Lanka. County champions Surrey top the table for the first time in 2000. **10** ICC advises ACB that Brett Lee's action will be scrutinised by the Illegal Deliveries panel. **12** Middlesex docked eight points for a substandard pitch at Southgate. **13** Alec Stewart equals the one-day international record of six catches. **15** England complete their first ten-wicket win in one-day internationals, against West Indies at Chester-le-Street. **19** Middlesex appeal successfully against their eight-point deduction. **20** Indian police and tax officials raid the homes of Indian cricketers and administrators in "Operation Gentleman". **21** Surrey's Martin Bicknell takes 16 for 119 against Leicestershire at Guildford, the best first-class match return in England since 1956. **22** England beat Zimbabwe in the NatWest Series final. **23** Sri Lanka beat South Africa in a Test for the first time – by an innings at Galle. **30** Sajjida Shah becomes the youngest international cricketer, aged 12 years 35 days, for Pakistan women in Ireland's inaugural Test.

AUGUST

2 Lee's action is cleared by ICC. **3** Atherton and Stewart begin their 100th Test. ECB decline an invitation to play Bangladesh in their inaugural Test. Andy Flower is replaced as Zimbabwe's captain by Heath Streak. **4** Shane Warne is replaced as Australia's vice-captain by Adam Gilchrist after revelations of obscene phone-calls. **5** Lala Amarnath dies, aged 88. **7** Umpire Alan Whitehead is rapped by the ECB for swearing at Warwickshire's Dougie Brown in July. **10** West Indies beat Pakistan in the Under-15 World Challenge final at Lord's. Arjuna Ranatunga retires from Test cricket. **11** King Commission submits its interim report to the South African government. **16** Australia beat South Africa in Melbourne's Colonial Stadium, the first official indoor one-day international. Surrey's Gary Butcher takes four wickets in four balls against Derbyshire. **17** At Headingley, Curtly Ambrose takes his 400th Test wicket. **18** England beat West Indies in two days; Andrew Caddick takes four wickets in one over. **19** Gibbs and Williams plead guilty to accepting bribes to underperform in India. Steve James reaches 309 not out, Glamorgan's highest individual score, out of 718 for three declared, the county's highest total, against Sussex at Colwyn Bay. **26** Somerset's Jason Kerr takes a hat-trick as they beat the West Indians by 269 runs. **27** Gloucestershire retain the NatWest Trophy by Duckworth/Lewis method on the reserve day of a rain-affected final against Warwickshire. **28** Gibbs and Williams are suspended from international cricket until January 2001. Surrey win Division Two of the National League. **29** Middlesex sack coaches Mike Gatting and Ian Gould. **31** Yorkshire fined eight points for a poor pitch at Scarborough.

SEPTEMBER

4 England beat West Indies at The Oval to win the Wisden Trophy for the first time since 1969; Ambrose retires from Test cricket. **5** Roy Fredericks dies, aged 57. **6** Gloucestershire win the National League to complete an unprecedented treble of one-day trophies. **9** Northamptonshire win Division Two of the County Championship. **12** Kapil Dev resigns as India's coach. **13** Surrey retain the County Championship. **16** In the Bulawayo Test against New Zealand, Zimbabwe's Grant Flower is no-balled for throwing by Darrell Hair. Hampshire incur an eight-point pitch penalty in the final first-class match at Northlands Road.

OCTOBER

4 Zimbabwe appoint Carl Rackemann as coach. **7** World Cup holders Australia go out to India in their first game of the ICC Knockout in Kenya. **9** Pakistan board ask government for judicial inquiry into the 1999 World Cup games against Bangladesh and India. **11** UCBSA agree a life ban from cricket for Cronje. **15** New Zealand beat India in ICC Knockout final. **16** England begin their first Test tour of Pakistan for 13 years. **27** Muttiah Muralitharan takes seven for 30 against India at Sharjah, a one-day international world record. **29** Sri Lanka bowl out India for 54 to win by a record 245 runs, in Sharjah final. **30** India's Central Bureau of Investigation (CBI) submit their match-fixing report to the government. Sponsors PPP Healthcare quit the County Championship.

NOVEMBER

1 Indian government publishes CBI report; Alec Stewart among 14 players named. He denies receiving money from a bookmaker and ECB say he will continue to play while investigations continue. **2** John Wright is appointed India's coach. **5** ECB confirm that 1991 Lancashire v Essex games are being investigated for match-fixing. **7** Sri Lanka set up an inquiry into match-fixing allegations in the CBI report against Ranatunga and Aravinda de Silva. Jimmy Hutchinson, longest-living first-class cricketer, dies aged 103. **8** Jonty Rhodes announces his retirement from Test cricket to concentrate on one-day cricket; Daryll Cullinan quits one-day cricket to concentrate on Test cricket. **10** Bangladesh's inaugural Test begins in Dhaka against India. **11** Aminul Islam hits a century for Bangladesh on Test debut. **13** India beat Bangladesh by nine wickets. **14** Sri Lankan board chief executive Dhammika Ranatunga, elder brother of Arjuna, is suspended. **15** India cancel their first Test tour to Pakistan in 11 years. **19** At Bloemfontein, Donald becomes the first South African to take 300 Test wickets. In Pakistan, Naved Latif scores 394 in a Quaid-e-Azam match for Sargodha against Gujranwala. **25** In Brisbane, Australia beat West Indies in three days for a record-equalling 11th successive Test win; Glenn McGrath has match figures of ten for 27. **27** BCCI find Azharuddin guilty of match-fixing; Kapil Dev and Mongia cleared. **29** In Faisalabad, Wasim Akram makes his 100th Test appearance. **30** England miss the deadline for international players to sign the ICC declaration regarding match-fixing and associations with bookmakers.

DECEMBER

1 In Perth, McGrath takes a hat-trick – including his 300th Test wicket – against West Indies. **3** Australia beat West Indies in three days, their 12th straight Test win. **4** Lord Cowdrey dies, aged 67. **5** Azharuddin and Ajay Sharma receive life bans for match-fixing; Prabhakar and Jadeja are banned for five years. **10** Test referee Barry Jarman stoned by crowd in Kanpur. **11** England beat Pakistan in Karachi, their first Test and series wins in Pakistan since 1961-62. **12** Jarman suspends Indian captain Ganguly for final one-day international against Zimbabwe for excessive appealing. Second interim King Commission report released, suggesting UCBSA should control cricket betting in South Africa. **13** Bookmaker Sanjeev Chawla arrested in London, but later released. **18** Documents from ICC offices handed to Anti-Corruption Unit. **19** Australia win at Adelaide; 13 in a row. **23** Hosts New Zealand beat Australia in the Women's World Cup final. **29** Australia beat West Indies at Melbourne; now it's 14. **30** At Durban, Muralitharan becomes the first Sri Lankan to take 300 Test wickets.

The following were also among items reported in the media during 2000

Gregson CC and the Pressbox's XI of Lancaster claimed to have played the last match of the old millennium in the UK after continuing under floodlights until 4.55 p.m. on December 31, 1999. Soup was served at teatime. (*Lancaster Guardian*, January 7)

A Muslim terrorist group, the Al-Umar Mujahideen, said it tried to kidnap the former Indian captain, Kapil Dev, in 1996 to try to secure the release of the group's leader from an Indian jail. "Our plans didn't work out," said a spokesman. (*The Hindu*, January 8)

Peter Lee, a 65-year-old retired sailor, lost the chance to become the first to win £1 million on the ITV quiz "Who Wants To Be A Millionaire?" when he declined to answer the question: "Which county cricket side is based at Chester-le-Street?" Having answered 14 previous questions correctly, he was given four options – Warwickshire, Durham, Northamptonshire or Leicestershire – but refused to try, and accepted £500,000 instead. "I don't follow cricket," he said. Durham later invited him as their guest for a day. (*Daily Mail*, January 19)

Relatives of Omar Kyam, the captain of the Sussex Under-18 team, went to Pakistan to search for him in terrorist training camps. Kyam, from Crawley, had been studying for his A-levels when he was recruited by a militant Islamic group. (*The Times*, January 22)

A fielder chasing a ball to the boundary in Lucknow, India, was killed by a 19-year-old youth having a driving lesson. Sanjay Misra, 22, was playing with six friends in the Begum Hazrat Mahal park when the accident happened. He was the owner of a small book store, and the breadwinner for his mother and younger brother. (*Times of India*, January 26)

A 12-year-old boy in the small Sri Lankan village of Kekanadura allegedly killed his ten-year-old brother with his bat during a dispute about the older boy's dismissal. Manjula Kumara died in hospital in Galle; his brother Sisara was sent to a children's home pending further investigations. (*The Island*, Colombo, January 29)

The former Test umpire, Dickie Bird, has been made a freeman of Barnsley, his home town. (*Daily Telegraph*, February 15)

An Indian man was killed by an opponent during a friendly match at Ras-al-Khaimah in the United Arab Emirates. After an argument about whether or not a run had been scored at a crucial stage of the match, Safi Qaffim allegedly picked up a bat and struck Labeed Mohammed on the head, knocking him unconscious. He died two hours later. The two men were said to be good friends. (*Asian Age*, February 20)

A Calcutta schoolteacher, Tejesh Adhikary, has invented a new game called "Reading Cricket" to help cricket-crazy students improve their literacy. Two teams are given separate unseen texts. The batting side has to read out a passage, and the fielding side appeals to an umpire if it feels a word is mispronounced or omitted. The batsman gets one run for reading a column correctly, and a boundary for pronouncing correctly any word in a foreign language. "This is a unique method for developing a flair for reading among school students," Mr Adhikary said. (*Asian Age*, February 28)

A new pub in Ashington, Northumberland, has been named the Rohan Kanhai, after the West Indian star who played three seasons for the local league club in the 1960s. (*The Journal*, Newcastle, March 31)

Paul McIntosh, a cricket-mad 11-year-old from Northampton, named his new pet rabbit "Hansie" after the South African captain, Hansie Cronje, three days before Cronje's downfall for his role in the match-fixing scandal. "We couldn't believe it," said Paul's mother, Elaine. "Our nine-year-old Lauren has been telling everybody that our rabbit has been arrested." (*Chronicle & Echo*, Northampton, April 10)

Sports scientists at John Moores University, Liverpool, endorsed Sir Donald Bradman's batting technique after subjecting it to "three-dimensional motion analysis". Professor Adrian Lees said their findings refuted suggestions that Bradman's wide, looping backlift made him a poor role model for young players. He said Bradman's unorthodoxy was "no worse" than the approved method. (*The Times*, April 26)

Brian Robinson, 74, an umpire in the North Lancashire and Cumbria League, claimed he was a victim of discrimination after being asked to resign because of his epilepsy. An umpires' federation official, Colin Bickerstaffe, said epilepsy was only one reason for the decision: "It is just that the committee felt he was no longer up to the rigours of umpiring." After a strongly worded letter from the British Epilepsy Association and a threat of legal action under disability discrimination laws, Robinson was reinstated. (*Westmorland Gazette*, April 28/June 9)

MCC has been selling an "official Lord's ball" stamped "made in England", which turned out to be almost entirely made in Pakistan. (*Sunday Telegraph*, April 30)

The Catholic school, Downside, has modified its practice of ringing the angelus bell at six o'clock every evening, even during cricket matches. The players were always obliged to stop the game and turn towards the Abbey, an act of piety regarded by some rival schools as "a sneaky Papist plot" that disrupted matches at crucial moments. Now the angelus can be put back to 6.40 p.m. – after close of play. (*Daily Telegraph*, May 1)

Adryan Winnan, an England Under-18 rugby player, was anxious to nurse a calf injury and not run too much in a Cornish League match for Penryn against Wendron. So his 300 not out included 15 sixes and 24 fours. (*The Guardian*, May 6)

A plaque has been unveiled to the 19th-century cricketer and historian, Arthur Haygarth, on the house where he was born in Hastings. Other former residents to be honoured by the town include Beatrix Potter and the frontiersman, Grey Owl. (*The Argus*, Brighton, May 8)

An evening's rabbit-shooting was among the prizes auctioned at the village cricket club's fundraising event in Allendale, Northumberland, along with bales of straw and a load of cow muck. (*The Guardian*, May 10)

Mick Nicholson picked up a cricket bat for the first time in eight months and, hitting 25 sixes and 14 fours, made 230 off 81 balls for Heaton against Northern Electric Blue Flames in the Northumberland League midweek division. (*The Journal*, Newcastle, May 13)

MIG-Khar openers Sahil Kukreja and Sushant Marathe both scored double-centuries and put on 459 together in a two-day Under-16 match against Kalyan-Ambernath in Mumbai. (*Asian Age*, May 14)

Film star Tom Cruise was taken to the Sydney Cricket Ground [on February 4] by director Sam Mendes to watch a one-day international. "He didn't know anything about cricket," said Mendes. "I told him about Warne and Tendulkar, how amazing Bradman was, and that Mark Taylor had declared when he was 334 not out, equal with Bradman's Australian Test record. Tom was so moved he was practically in tears. He enjoyed it so much he hired the box himself for a match the next day." (*Daily Telegraph*, May 27)

A pomeranian dog called Fred became a member of Chorley CC, Lancashire. His owners, Beryl and George Ritchie, paid the £25 subscription so Fred could go into the bar for his regular helping of beer. (*Daily Telegraph*, June 3)

Police investigated events at Alveston in Warwickshire after the Harvington wicket-keeper, Mark Barnard, was allegedly knocked out by batsman Nigel Crawford. The Alveston captain, Billy Dowling, said Crawford had been provoked in a match marked by "foul-mouthed and ugly" sledging. (*Daily Telegraph*, June 3)

Harry Barnes, a Manchester-based inventor, claimed to have solved the problems of contentious run-outs and stumpings in big matches after patenting a device called "Creasewatch". This involves using special electrical contacts between the stumps and bails. As soon as the bails are dislodged, video cameras would pick up the signal, removing the need for a third umpire to make a visual judgment. (*Sunday Telegraph*, June 4)

The Graces, Britain's first openly homosexual team, have applied to join the Surrey Cricket Board. The side includes former Yorkshire League and minor county players.

"People think we're just a load of old queens who think we look good in white, but actually we can and do play well," said captain Ian Crossland. "Sport is one of the last bastions of male homophobia." One of W.G.'s great-granddaughters, Rosemary Douglas, complained: "They are cashing in on the Grace name and it is unsuitable for this team to do so." (*Evening Standard*, June 7/*The Times*, June 9)

A village game between children in Pakistan escalated into a gunfight between their families which left five people dead. Three children, all cousins, were playing in the North-West Frontier village of Utmankhel Partas when a fight developed. One of the fathers, Shamsher Khan Bacha, reportedly saw his children being beaten up, took a gun to his uncle's house and opened fire on everyone inside. Shamsher, three of his cousins, and a mother of two died in the ensuing exchange. (Agence France-Presse, June 20)

The Russian chess grand master, Peter Svidler, has been nicknamed "Tendulkar" because he became a cricket fan after being introduced to the game by Nigel Short. (*Daily Telegraph*, June 21)

Ian Evans, the 49-year-old chairman of Ebbw Vale Cricket Club, collapsed and died while batting in a match at Pontypridd. He had only come into the team as a late replacement. Evans was a prolific try-scorer for the successful Ebbw Vale rugby team of the 1970s. (*Gwent Gazette*, June 22)

An 11-year-old girl, Bethany Brown, playing for Monk Bretton in a junior cup-tie in Yorkshire, stunned the all-male opposition of Elsecar by taking seven for nought in three overs. She took four in four balls in her last over. (*The Sun*, June 23)

Bats used and signed by many star cricketers were destroyed in a fire at the Gray-Nicolls factory in Robertsbridge, Sussex. Copies of *Wisden* and hundred-year-old catalogues were also destroyed in the blaze, the second major fire at the factory in eight years. Operating director Neil Gray said the damage was "catastrophic". (*Rye and Battle Observer*, June 23)

Lloyd Alley, grandson of former Somerset all-rounder and Test umpire Bill, took a hat-trick in a Taunton Under-11 club match. (*Daily Telegraph*, June 24)

A match played at Colchester Garrison had to be abandoned after the players were overwhelmed by parachutists. Marks Tey and Shalford, who compete in the Osborne League, were forced off the field by jumps being staged at a cocktail party for senior army officers and other dignitaries. The clubs had been warned in advance that there was a double-booking, but they could not be told what the other event was for security reasons. (*Evening Gazette*, Colchester, June 26)

Players from Scholes CC, near Holmfirth, Yorkshire, had an impromptu match stopped by police at 4.30 a.m. because they were "inappropriately dressed" – they were wearing only boots and socks. The team had been at a late-night party. (*The Sun*, June 29 – see also September 29)

Two clubs have been told they must bat at only one end of the ground at Littleover, Derbyshire. Littleover Centurions and St Augustine's were said to be hitting too many balls out of the ground into nearby properties. (*The Times*, July 4)

The RAM club of Crawley won a 45-over match in Division III of the West Sussex League by 400 runs. Tarun Patel scored 188 out of RAM's 428 for five against Billingshurst II, who were then bowled out for 28. All the RAM players were Indian and nearly all called Patel. (*Crawley Observer*, July 5)

A well-known South African Indian playwright, Aldrin Naidu, has announced plans to stage a play about Hansie Cronje's involvement in match-fixing under the title "Vak Hansie". *Vakansie* is an Afrikaans word meaning holiday, but could be misconstrued by its pronunciation as being dismissive of Cronje. *(Asian Age, July 10)*

Luen Man, 34, has been commuting from Switzerland to play village matches at Kirkby Overblow, Yorkshire. *(The Sun, July 12)*

MCC announced plans for a six-a-side corporate challenge that would allow 16 teams the right to play in a two-day competition on the hallowed turf for £5,500 each. During the competition, *Wisden* contributor Jonathan Rice scored an eight while batting with a runner: an all-run four and four overthrows. *(The Times, July 15/Daily Telegraph, September 12)*

Birstwith Cricket Club of the Nidderdale League in Yorkshire threatened to take the League to court after what it called a "draconian" decision to deduct six points for a breach of rules. Birstwith failed to lodge the appropriate forms when fast bowler Ian Bass rejoined the club. *(Daily Telegraph, July 29)*

The pub named after Geoffrey Boycott in Dewsbury, Yorkshire, returned to its old name of The Park after Boycott's conviction for assaulting a girlfriend. "From then on women just stopped coming in," said landlady Anne-Marie Higgins. There was also a "Boycott the Boycott" protest. The sign has now been burned, and the ashes kept behind the bar. *(News of the World, July 23)*

Lawyers acting for eight-year-old Benjamin Parker-Marshall have demanded a share of the profits of a high-profile memorial match staged in London for the West Indian fast bowler, Malcolm Marshall. Benjamin was Marshall's son by a care worker, Elizabeth Adegboyaga, but was excluded from his will and was not intended as a beneficiary from the match. Many top players turned out to raise an expected £100,000 for Marshall's widow and young son, Mali. *(The Guardian, July 24)*

Bob Furness, a policeman and captain of Bradford League team Lightcliffe II, was banned for a month after one of his batsmen allegedly received racial abuse from an Idle II player. Furness was protesting to the umpire about the incident. No action was taken against the opponent. *(The Guardian, July 26)*

Richard Stemp, the Nottinghamshire spin bowler, was suspended for the second time in a season while playing league cricket for Kimberley. He was banned for three matches for sledging a 15-year-old batsman, then banned for another four after being reported for dissent on his comeback against Radcliffe-on-Trent. *(The Times, July 29)*

The Hizbul, a militant anti-government group in Kashmir, played a friendly game against the Indian Army in the normally tense border area of Kupwara. A large crowd saw the Hizbul beat the Army by 25 runs. However, their commander left immediately the game was over for fear of being arrested by the soldiers. *(Gujarat Samachar, Ahmedabad, August 6)*

An umpire was beaten to death after giving a batsman run out during a softball cricket tournament in Ambalangoda, Sri Lanka. Three players attacked W. Kamal Ranjith de Silva with an iron bar. "There was rivalry between two families," said police. *(Daily Mirror (Colombo), August 10/The Sun, August 11)*

All 11 players in the Cuddalore women's team failed to score against Chennai B in India. However, the side scraped to six all out – in reply to 158 for one declared –

because of wides. One batswoman, Balasoundari, almost hit a four but the ball just failed to reach the boundary and she was unable to run because of cramp. (*CricInfo*, August 12)

Bengali film-maker Anjaan Chaudhury offered a film role to Donna Ganguly, wife of Indian captain Sourav, as a dancer in his forthcoming film, *Chandramallika*. When Ganguly would not allow his wife to act opposite any other male artiste, Chaudhury agreed to cast him as well. (*Gujarat Samachar*, Ahmedabad, August 20)

Sidath Wettimuny told Colombo police that he had been threatened with assault by another former Sri Lankan Test player, Hashan Tillekeratne. After the 1999 World Cup, Tillekeratne was dropped from the national team; Wettimuny was chairman of selectors at the time. The incident happened when Wettimuny went to pick up his son from a coaching session. Tillekeratne denied the allegation and said Wettimuny had wound down his car window and started insulting him. (*Daily News*, Colombo, August 23/ August 26)

The Kent batsman, David Fulton, has been hired to write an agony uncle column under the pseudonym "Dr Love" in *For You*, an Australian women's magazine. (*The Times*, August 26)

A no-ball cost Matthew Whiley of Nottinghamshire £5,000 in a competition at Lord's, run by Freeserve, to find Britain's fastest young bowler. Whiley recorded the fastest delivery – 86.5mph against 86.2 by Yorkshire's Matthew Hoggard – but overstepped by about half an inch. (*The Observer*, August 27)

Lambeth Council banned a performance by reggae star Beanie Man at one of the lunch intervals during the Oval Test – for fear of annoying residents. "It's incredibly petty," said a spokesman for Channel 4, under whose aegis Beanie Man was going to appear. (*Daily Telegraph*, August 30)

Raj Patel, a 40-year-old newsagent from Carshalton, Surrey, died from a blood clot two weeks after being hit on the shin while playing in a match. (*The Times*, August 30)

A black labrador has had a trophy named after him – the Sam Challenge Trophy – by Bridgend Cricket Club in South Wales. Sam has saved the club hundreds of pounds by finding lost balls in the undergrowth, with a record 27 in one season. "If some of our fielders could get to the ball as well as Sam, we would be league champions," said club chairman Jake Collier. (*Western Mail*, September 1)

Scientists believe missile-tracking technology could be used to remove the controversy from the lbw law. Researchers at Siemens are hoping to develop the Hawk-Eye technology, which predicts trajectories, to calculate whether a ball would have hit the stumps. Sunset + Vine, Channel 4's cricket producers, said they were interested; the England and Wales Cricket Board said they were not. (*Evening Standard*, September 6)

Sir Donald Bradman has failed in an attempt to scrap a plan to rename the road from Adelaide Airport to the city Sir Donald Bradman Drive. The move became controversial when a café-owner decided to rename her business Bradman's Café on the Drive, and then a sex shop applied to register the name Erotica on Bradman. The mayor of West Torrens municipality, John Trainer, said he believed the sex shop's move was "the final straw" for the 92-year-old Don, who made a personal appeal to the council. Later, the Australian prime minister, John Howard, added Bradman to a list of names – including those of the royal family – that cannot be exploited for commercial gain. (Reuters, September 7/*Sunday Times*, October 22)

Jason Phillips dismissed three members of the Dredge clan when he took a hat-trick for Knowle against Frome in a Somerset Cup tie. He dismissed the former Somerset county player, Colin Dredge – "the Demon of Frome" – then Colin's brother, Craig, and his nephew, Neil. (*Sunday Telegraph*, September 10)

A village cricketer in Pembrokeshire has been banned for 25 years by the county association for leading an obscene chant against two rival players. Willie Morris, 39, barracked the Lamphey openers, both Australians, while watching a cup final against Hook. His team, Llangwm, had been knocked out in an earlier round. "I must be the first cricketer to be banned for 25 years simply for speaking his mind," said Morris. However, he admitted that he had earlier been banned from cup finals for five years. "The man is a habitual troublemaker," said John Green, the Lamphey secretary. Brian James, secretary of Llangwm, said: "Lamphey's policy on importing cricketers is not popular." (*Daily Telegraph*, September 22)

Jack Hyams, 81, a retired pet shop owner from Hertfordshire, lost his chance to become the oldest cricketer to appear at Lord's when the match between Cross Arrows and the Royal Household was rained off. (*Sunday Telegraph*, September 24)

Players from Ben Rhydding CC, near Ilkley, Yorkshire, drew their largest crowd of the year – a dozen passing motorists – when they played a night fixture illuminated by car headlights. All the players were naked, although the umpire wore his white coat. Play lasted an hour until the police arrived after a complaint. Club captain Andrew Jennings insisted he was proud of his players. "It was the last night of the season and we'd had a few too many beers. We just thought: 'get 'em off and let's get on with it'. It was freezing. There were men of all shapes and sizes. It's what sport is all about." (*Telegraph & Argus*, Bradford, September 28)

Professor Peter Hennessey, author of *The Prime Minister*, said he was told by a civil servant that the greatest threat to Britain's national security occurred at the height of the Cold War, during the thrilling finish to the 1963 Lord's Test: "Every television screen in the Ballistic Early Warning System room was tuned to Lord's. The Russians could have taken us out at any time." (*Daily Telegraph*, October 17)

A horse chestnut that Geoff Boycott practised against as a schoolboy has been shortlisted for the title Greatest Tree in Yorkshire. (*Daily Telegraph*, October 27)

The actor and former Test match announcer, Alan Curtis, has been made an honorary member of MCC. "It's better than getting an Oscar," he said. "I think I must be the only actor ever to have been made an honorary member, and certainly the only socialist." (*Daily Telegraph*, November 13)

A new Australian film, *The Dish*, includes footage of a game of cricket played inside the radio telescope at Parkes, New South Wales. (*Inside Edge*, November)

Former Australian Test player Sam Loxton, 80, lost his wife and son in separate accidents on the same day. His wife, Joan, was found floating in the family swimming-pool at their Queensland home, having apparently fallen and hit her head. Their 47-year-old son, Michael, was killed by a shark while on holiday in Fiji. (*The Guardian*, December 15)

Good batsmen take their eye off the ball to play fast bowling, according to researchers who studied three players wearing head-mounted cameras. The study showed that, after looking steadfastly at the ball as it left a bowling machine, they glanced at the spot where they expected it to bounce before fixing on the ball again. (*Nature Neuroscience*, December)

CRICKET BOOKS, 2000

By GILLIAN REYNOLDS

For the last months of 2000 I lived on Planet Cricket, and it was a transformative experience. For many years I had observed this other world from afar. I knew it to be more martial than Mars. This is a place where battle odds are tough, victories sudden and defeats at the wicket more so (such defeats, my son the one-time pace bowler told me, are more like sudden deaths). I did not know until I read all these books how grievous are the injuries its warriors suffer – to fingers, hands, arms, legs, backs, eyes, jaws and parts distinctly more tender. Gallantries still occasionally mark its contests but, until book after book built up a fine collection of sledgings (given, taken and overheard), I had no real idea how brutal the conflicts have become.

The geology of Planet Cricket, I now see, has been marked this past half-century by four evolutionary stages: the Professional, the One-day, the Packer and the Fix. You can find many descriptions of their layers. The volcano that produced the last still rumbles on. History is a serious study here. Politics are murky. The equivalent of its North Star is *Wisden*.

The culture is rich and varied. I have written often about this strange world's epic poem, *Test Match Special*, that great unrolling radio tapestry which can, at its best, recall *Beowulf* and *The Battle of Maldon* (the clashes of blade, the blows upon helmet, the routs, triumphs and rejoicings in the mead halls). So ardent a public fan of *TMS* did I become that, one 1980s summer, I was accorded the rare privilege of being escorted through the Forbidden Zone of the Lord's Pavilion, up into the old commentary box above, to watch in silent wonder as Bill Frindall tallied the overs, to worship at the brown and white co-respondent shoe-clad feet of Brian Johnston.

Maybe it was a glimpse of Henry Blofeld picking his hangnails that made me realise there might be more to this game than *TMS*. Now, after the full immersion provided by the year's books, I have begun at last to get to grips with the real Planet Cricket: the passion, the politics, the psychology, the sex, the rifts, the nicknames, the statistics. Well, maybe not the statistics. For those of that mind, Frindall has brought his **Wisden Book of Test Cricket** as up to date as it can ever be. In its fifth edition, it now runs to three volumes and includes, for the first time, scores of all Women's Tests and appropriate records.

Quests are more my line. **Yakking around the world**, Simon Hughes's sequel to his bestselling prize-winner *A Lot of Hard Yakka*, actually bears the subtitle "a cricketer's quest for love and utopia". What rapidly became plain was the challenge to maintain a sympathetic interest in this particular quester, who was often to be found soliloquising about love and utopia when you would rather have known what was going on at the match, and vice versa. Hughes comes on like a cross between Jim Davidson and Jimmy Breslin, widening his verbal grin as he shows you his scars from the slings and arrows of not really very outrageous fortune. This book is about him learning to be a cricketer, a journalist, a grown-up. The first two he manages quite well.

"I've been playing away all my life," he begins, disclosing that cricket has taken him through five continents, 28 countries and 134 different towns. Quite a lot of girls, too. Sometimes he merely gazes, as at 19-year-old Venita gliding round her housemaid chores in Sri Lanka ("She barely spoke any English. Funny how that makes women seem sexier.") Sometimes he scores, as with tennis-playing Karen in South Africa ("It's funny how a ravishing woman can suddenly become quite unappealing when you discover she is desperate.") Finally he meets Tanya, who understands Fermat's Last Theorem, loves Prokofiev, Prince and prawn vindaloo and laughs at his jokes. Reader, he married her.

He keeps score at the end of each chapter. People, Beaches, Cricket, then multiplies them by Catches – of females, naturally – to make up his total. London tops his final score. Auckland and Sydney come joint second, Pretoria (Karen happened in Durban) lurks at the very bottom of the Hughes league. Cricket? He's more romantic about that, especially in his conclusions on how it is played in England. "We're canny, durable cricketers going stoically about our business. Like the British army, we're dependable, ballsy, good in a crisis; calmly confident of overcoming a superior force with an orderly, diligent approach and some courage." Well, sometimes.

John Harms is another quester. **Confessions of a thirteenth man** is about being an Australian, wanting to be a cricketer, settling for being a journalist. In 1998 he decides he will follow a complete Ashes tour right round Australia on a shoestring budget while driving a Camira, a car which once won a prize and was thought to herald a new era in Australian automobile design. It didn't. It's a difficult and demanding vehicle, demanding much care and some luck. Making it go becomes part of the quest.

Questing goes deep with Harms. He shifts stylistic gear to show where his epic journey begins. Writing about why he came to be potty about cricket, he employs the past tense. When he's on the actual tour, the central section of his narrative, he shifts to the historic present, ("I wake happy.") From then on we sup continuously from his full emotional cup. His account of the English fans, the Barmy Army, at the Gabba is tense, funny, vivid. He makes natural counterpoint of play and crowd reactions, captures the drama of a storm closing in. He's good at verbal ball-by-ball. Less convincingly, he also chases Grace, playing with the idea of being in love. Is the lady only in this plot so she can vanish? Did she ever really stand a chance against the combined charms of the Camira and the Waugh twins?

Waugh's Way, Roland Perry's biography of the Australian captain, would suggest not. This is no dispassionate historical assessment. Perry is a Steve Waugh fan, a staunch champion, but he is also gloriously readable, often memorable, always thoughtful. His account embraces all the major controversies, but there is never any question whose side he is on. He shows Waugh's evolution as cricketer and captain with solid admiration, but shrewdness too. If it's a herogram, at least he makes you understand why he's sending it. Even when it seems as if he's about to suspend the plot and describe the action, as in the account of the contrasting styles of Mark and Steve, putting on 153 together in the 1993 Fifth Test at Edgbaston, there's no doubt about his sympathies. "They batted freely and there was no trouble indentifying which twin was which. Mark was all style and flow... Steve, by contrast, made you gasp at his late flurry in strokemaking... Where Mark caressed the ball, Steve belted it. Fielders chased Mark's strokes; they gave up when Steve clobbered a delivery past them."

The Complete Shane Warne, by Ken Piesse, is the chronicle of a different hero: "every ball, every match – the whole story", as it promises on the cover, from 1990, when at 20 Warne first began to be noticed, to 2000, when he broke Dennis Lillee's Australian record of 355 Test wickets. This is the sort of handbook that could convert the dimmest statistophobe. In other words, I picked it up thinking the columns would dazzle about and make me feel even guiltier than usual, but I couldn't put it aside, such an invaluable guide it proved to other people's accounts of the same games. Spare but never lacking either in spirit or proportion, this is a gem. No floss, no gloss, just the essence. Piesse doesn't omit the injuries, the still-rumbling scandals over the attempted bribe in Pakistan, the significance of Cronje's disgrace, but neither does he forget to tell you the ways batsmen can take Warne on and win.

That Australia have not always been this invincible is the lesson Bob Woolmer drives home towards the end of **Woolmer on Cricket**, written with Ivo Tennant. Having coached South Africa to a level that astonished the world, and set more than the odd set of teeth grinding in England – where, for reasons he sets out with remarkable restraint, he decided the national coaching job was not for him – Woolmer saw victory in the semi-final of the 1999 World Cup vanish in the last over when Allan Donald was run out and the result, so memorably and historically, was a tie. It also happened to be his last day as South African coach. His description of how it felt, in the dressing-room, in his head, reading what the papers made of it afterwards, is gut-wrenchingly honest. But he is practical, too. He claims South Africa will be stronger for the defeat. He stresses that it took Australia ten years to turn their team around.

Much of the rest of the book is a carefully phrased account of why South Africa started from so far behind, and what it took to mould a new team in a new nation. He doesn't hold back on his judgments (one or two umpires come in for a roasting), he admits to quite a few mistakes of his own, but his concern is always to keep the game playable to the highest professional standards (which means looking after players' families, after the manner of Kerry Packer) and firmly out of the hands of the politicians and the old-boy network. His chapter analysing what went wrong with English cricket deserves reading and re-reading. The one on coaching is far-sighted, even if he seems totally in thrall to the idea of earpieces and pager messages between coach and on-field players. Leave aside this techno-fixation, here is a man who can tell any team how to improve. Would that our Secretary of State for Culture, Media and Sport could get together with his opposite number at the Department for Education and Employment to sort out some funding that would get cricket back into state schools – and then persuade Woolmer to run it.

David Lloyd's autobiography **Anything But Murder**, written with Alan Lee, makes a fascinating parallel. He stood down as England's coach after the 1999 World Cup, and I bet if Woolmer reads Lloyd's book he'll afford himself a grim smile at the way the ECB were yanking Lloyd's chain at the same time as they were giving him the runaround. Woolmer turns out to have been Lloyd's preferred successor, but I also bet that if Lloyd reads Woolmer's account of the ECB's shenanigans he'll get a touch of the *déjà vus*. It is hard not to like Lloyd, bouncy and optimistic and all. But then, as the song says, he has to go and spoil it all by saying something stupid, and at fairly regular intervals at that.

Geoffrey Boycott once remarked on this tendency. Lloyd found that "pretty offensive". They duly had a verbal shoot-out at the OK Corral, otherwise known as the press box at The Oval, which some might say was pretty routine Wars of the Roses stuff. But not the tabloid press or the ECB. The latter carpeted him for it – and, admittedly, for his rather more significant remarks about Muttiah Muralitharan's delivery – then issued a press statement which, while saying he had been "severely reprimanded" and "warned", concluded (rather in the manner of Mrs Thatcher describing Nigel Lawson as "unassailable" just before she sacked him) that Lloyd had their "full support". Good job Lloyd says he's a man who doesn't bear grudges.

Boycott has found an able advocate in Leo McKinstry, whose **Boycs: The True Story** maintains a sympathetic but level tone and manages to straighten more than one of the tilted pictures in Planet Cricket's Hall of Fame. Well, then, is Boycott "single-minded and purposeful" or "a self-centred bastard?" McKinstry uses both descriptions of his subject within a page of each other, contrasting verdicts from people who know him well. McKinstry's case is that cricket helped mould Boycott's character because he had to try so hard at it. Will, all-consuming dedication, ruthlessness to the point of giving almost everything else up for the game, disastrous selfishness as a team-mate, intolerable rudeness: is there no end to McKinstry's list of this man's qualities?

Well, yes, there is, and what is more there are quite good explanations for most of them. McKinstry doesn't offer excuses but does give convincing reasons for why he played as he did, setting each one down not sentimentally but sensitively. It certainly makes Boycott's battle with the French legal system, and the unflagging support of his real women friends, more comprehensible. Kelvin MacKenzie's finest radio hour was in signing Boycott to talkSPORT and, what's more, sticking to him when other patrons flaked away. This won't be the last book about Boycott, but it will take some doing to compose a better portrait.

Sir Vivian: The Definitive Autobiography, co-authored with Bob Harris, is a work of fire and passion. The first half of the opening chapter is a second-by-second account of Viv Richards going in to bat, dispassionate, controlled, focused. It would raise gooseflesh on a grapefruit. It should be required reading for anyone who wishes to succeed, in any profession. The rest of the book describes how he got to that point, ready for the finest innings of his life, through practice, determination and serious thought. Here he is as a very young man in Antigua, getting ready to go on tour with the Under-16s.

"… I would stand in front of a full-length mirror to practise my shots. I took the idea from the great boxer Muhammad Ali. I used to shadow-bat a lot, playing all the shots, tightening the defence, feeling the pick-up of the bat, how the grip felt." And he would get up in the night and do it all again. Not that he comes across as a saint. From putting stones in Joel Garner's soup pot – to disguise the fact that he and Ian Botham had scoffed the lot – to lessons in how to give and take a sledging, the book is ripe in incident. Yet, throughout, he is scathing about those whose determination and integrity do not match his own. The England selectors of 1988 come in for a right pasting. So do those Australian players, Glenn McGrath for one, who seem to him to bully then turn tail under attack. But he also brilliantly conveys how hard it is to be a captain, how it changes the psychological challenges and how his own routine – the nap before an innings, the total focus on his own game, even his batting style – had to alter in consequence. It won't be easy reading for West Indies fans, given the present state of their game. Other nations will quail at his unequivocal condemnation of match-fixing and of cricketers betting on games in which they are involved. "A kind of treason," he calls it.

To Richards, Kerry Packer is "a visionary who brought a great many changes to the game of cricket, most of them for the good". To Henry Blofeld, the writer and commentator, Packer is nothing of the kind. Blofeld's autobiography, **A Thirst for Life – with the Accent on Cricket**, is a view from the sidelines. Prevented by a road accident in 1957, when he was captain of cricket at Eton, from possibly pursuing a career at the crease, Blofeld's attachment to the game is sincere. But I wonder whether he really regrets not having had the long days on slow roads, getting from one match to another, the cold and dingy lodgings, the cracked back, the scraping of a winter living. Those who love his style will enjoy his alternative odyssey through press boxes, good vineyards and grand dinners. Those who don't will have every one of their prejudices richly confirmed.

John Reid: A Cricketing Life, by Joseph Romanos, is rich, useful and wise. Romanos intersperses his view of Reid with Reid's own views on players, past and present. Reid's career as player, captain, coach, Test selector, ICC referee and guru is glorious. It also neatly spans my four evolutionary ages of cricket. Reid made his first-class debut on New Year's Day 1948, playing for Wellington against Canterbury, aged 19. The next year he was the baby of the New Zealand team that toured England. It was the foundation of his game. "I learned about how to play cricket according to the rules, but also within the spirit of the game. I realised it was a game to be played hard, but to be enjoyed." Things have changed a lot since then. He deplores the loss of sporting spirit, of such elements of cricket etiquette as a team applauding an opponent, the way teams no longer even have a drink together after a day's play. The game is the poorer for it, he believes. This isn't crusty old nostalgia, by the way. It comes across as solid good sense to make the game universally playable, to keep alive its special spirit. Physical contact, swearing, spitting, charging up to the umpire, petulance, dissent will all incur his refereeing wrath. But there's a practical side to it, too. "A sponsor is hardly likely to be pleased to be paying money to a player who has been suspended for breaches of the Code of Conduct." As for throwing, he offers a definitive guide.

"Golden Age" is an expression I find tricky. What does it really mean? A memory with a marketing tag? A spigot for the nostalgia barrel? It almost put me off **Class of '59** by Chris Westcott. That would have been a pity, because this is a genuinely charming book. In 1996 Westcott was rummaging through his attic and came across a set of cricket cards he had collected as a boy, 48 portraits of county players produced by the American & British Chewing Gum Company in 1959. Then he had a bright idea. He would track down all the subjects and see what had become of them, to mark the 40th anniversary of the issue. It turned out to be a giant task. He's done it wonderfully. People talked to him freely and he has respected their confidence. When his subject is dead, he turns to the nearest source. This can make for unexpected insights. Mrs Enid Wooller on Wilf, Mrs Lee Tremlett on Maurice are a joy. Here's an example, a scene after a day's play in Bristol.

"We sat on the top deck of a bus and I asked Maurice, 'How did you do today?' He said 'All right', which was a typical answer he gave, he would not elaborate. I said 'How many runs did you score?' he said 'A few.'" Then she spies the headline in the newspaper the man in front is reading. Maurice had scored another century. "That was the kind of man he was."

Les Jackson (b 1921, Derbyshire and England) was a miner when he made his county debut in 1947 at the late age of 26. The next year he walked into the side and stayed there. When he retired in 1963, he held all the main records for a Derbyshire bowler. The colliery gave him a surface job every winter. When his cricket days were over, he went back to the NCB as a driver, became the director's chauffeur, retired for good in 1983. His proudest moment? Walking on to the pitch at Old Trafford for his first Test, against New Zealand in July 1949, playing with Compton, Edrich and Evans. Compare and contrast with Robin Marlar, Trevor Bailey, Ray Illingworth (this is a hot one) and Gamini Goonesena (b 1931, Ceylon, Nottinghamshire, Cambridge University and New South Wales) and the rest of the (oh all right then) Golden Agers. My only real complaint is that the cards are so badly reproduced; maybe smudgy black and white works better for memories.

Chris Westcott has been busy. His second book in the year is **The History of Cricket at the Saffrons, Eastbourne** to which E. W. Swanton wrote the foreword and the Duke of Devonshire furnished a preface. It is probably fair to say that this may not grip Liverpudlians as firmly as it will men of Eastbourne, but I must point out that it contains a powerful secret. Towards the end there's a chapter on the groundsmen. If you want to discover what magic ingredient was used to keep this wicket, as it is claimed, the best in the country – "a batsman's paradise" – all is revealed on page 242.

Cricket Lovely Cricket, by Vijay P. Kumar, is a 50th anniversary tribute to the summer which *Wisden* judged the one when West Indies cricket "firmly established itself" (with "those two little pals of mine, Ramadhin and Valentine" as the nation sang back in 1950). But this book is also a history going back to the 19th century, a scrapbook, an anthology of viewpoints, a detective story – what was the secret of Ramadhin's spin? – and an analysis of what that success has meant to West Indies cricket since. Not everyone will agree with Kumar's every judgment. Brian Lara "an unqualified genius"? Tell that to Bob Woolmer or John Reid. The picture research is excellent,

even if the quality of actual reproduction tends to the grainy. Kumar is an investment banker in New York. Even within those canyons of steel there is someone dreaming of how to bowl a leg-break with an off-break action.

Go back even further with Jeremy Malies and **Great Characters from Cricket's Golden Age**, the sort of book I would buy for my brother so that he would ever after bombard me with its glistening nuggets. For example, Henry Hyndman, b 7.3.1842, Paddington, London, d 22.11.1921, Hampstead, London. "Regarded by many as the founding father of British socialism, Henry Hyndman is a striking reminder that one man's loose cannon is another's freedom fighter." We are also reminded that Francis Thompson, who wrote "At Lord's" – the poem with the last line "O my Hornby and my Barlow long ago!" – was a junkie dropout before discovering that half of his heroic pair, Richard Gorton Barlow, was the son of a Bolton pharmacist's assistant, played for the Bolton senior club side at the age of 11, was one of only four professionals to tour Australia under the captaincy of the Hon. Ivo Bligh in 1883 (excelling at deck games *en route*), and turned out to be a canny businessman. On second thoughts, this is the sort of book I would buy for my brother and then keep.

His Own Enemy: The Rise and Fall of Edward Pooley, by Keith Booth, would make a cracking film. It's a portrait of a great professional cricketer of the second half of the 19th century, a wicket-keeper whose record for the number of dismissals in a first-class match stood for 128 years and was only broken by Wayne James in 1996. James writes the foreword. It is a most intriguing piece of scholarly sleuthing, Booth rooting about in old news-papers, parish records and reference books, checking his sources even though, Pooley having died in 1907, there is none alive who remembers him.

Why would he commit to this project? Because Pooley's name kept cropping up in the Surrey County Cricket Club minutes, usually for disciplinary or financial reasons. Booth's nose twitched but the trail was cold. Then, just as he was about to go to press, he had an almighty stroke of luck. Two Pooley great-grandchildren turned up and solved some of the mysteries. Booth's dogged research cracked a few more. Pooley was not a Surrey man by birth, as has been commonly assumed, and he tended to vary his age according to his circumstances. Booth gives his date of birth as February 13, 1842. He stood 5ft 6in, he drank, he gambled (once on a match in which he was an umpire), he had fist fights, he was hauled up before the magistrate for swearing at a reporter, and he came under suspicion of having thrown a match. His life as a husband and father was pretty irregular. He was once even more popular with the crowd than W. G. Grace, but ended his days in the workhouse. His grave is unknown. Now you see why, in his day, he was regarded both as "the best wicket-keeper in the world" (C. W. Alcock, 1872) and "his own enemy" (*Wisden*, 1908). And now you see why Booth wanted to uncover this story. He does it with flair. I read it in one go, cover to cover. One or two of the workhouses that sheltered Pooley are still in business.

How very different from **Arthur Haygarth: Cricketer, Historian and Old Harrovian**, 1825 to 1903, a collection of essays on whom has been assembled by Roger Heavens to mark the unveiling of a plaque at his birthplace in Hastings. Haygarth's own mighty work, *Scores and Biographies*, actually notes discrepancies in the reporting of Pooley's birth, a fact picked up by Booth, who naturally relies on Haygarth as a major, if not always completely reliable, source. Haygarth certainly saw Pooley play, recording his phenomenal 1867 season of 1,148 runs and 120 dismissals. Haygarth's accomplishments on and off the field are themselves amazing. For over 60 years he laboured away at his self-imposed task of *Scores and Biographies*, 14 volumes of which could claim every single line to have been penned by the author, and for love not money.

Does the ghost of Haygarth haunt Trevor Jones, author of **The Dream Fulfilled**? This is a chronicle of the summer of 1999, when Surrey won the County Championship and Jones followed them to every match, catching the players afterwards for their instant reactions, setting down his Man of the Day and Man of the Match, assembling press accounts of each day's play. As an interviewer, he is no Paxman. To Adam Hollioake: "Browny was absolutely awesome, wasn't he?" To Alistair Brown: "When I spoke to Butch about his 259 at Leicester and asked him if he had any early indications that he might be about to achieve something special he said that he did feel in extraordinarily good touch right from the start of his innings. Did you have any such feelings?" As a fan, he's in a class of his own.

Passport to Nowhere treads more troubled territory. This is a history of Aboriginal cricket from 1850 to 1939 by Bernard Whimpress, curator of the Adelaide Oval Museum. It shows the appalling effects of racism, colonial domination and Christian evangelism quite clearly, arguing that although individual Aboriginal cricketers succeeded, they were always barred from the highest level of participation. To this day, cricket as an Aboriginal team game has never been encouraged to take root or flourish.

There are portraits of some of the legends, of Jack Marsh who made a living as a runner and a cricketer, whose bowling was harshly judged by umpires whom Whimpress accuses of lack of integrity. Why was he excluded from the Test team? Whimpress suggests a clash between imperial ties and national loyalties, another dimension of the Gentlemen and Players divisions. His skill, he concludes, was not an issue. It was his colour. Eddie Gilbert bowled very fast, faster than anyone. He bowled Bradman. Did he chuck? Bradman said it was open to question: that from the pavilion his action looked fair, but from the batsman's angle he seemed to jerk the ball. He asks how could such a slight man get so much pace from such a short run-up? Whimpress can explain. His notes are meticulous. This is a stern read but a good one.

John Ireland has a new collection of **Cricket Characters**, his first big crop of caricatures since 1987, which volume, his publishers claim, is now a collector's item, changing hands at suitably enhanced prices. The message is buy now, while you can still afford this first edition for a modest £20. His style is vigorous and will make any reader laugh out loud at least once in every five pages. Jonathan Agnew has contributed the accompanying words and they are first-rate. It is harder by far to write short than long, and Agnew reveals a rich gift for combining the witty, the pithy, the judicious and the personal. Whoever brought the Ireland–Agnew team together was inspired. The complementarity of their respective styles is impressive. There are 12 batsmen, 17 bowlers, five all-rounders, three wicket-keepers, four umpires and commentators, and my copy of this handsome volume now falls open all by itself at Daniel Vettori (though I think Ireland paints him too old), Muttiah Muralitharan (too scary) and Shane Warne.

The Best of the Best, by Charles Davis, is a wondrous work. Davis is an Australian scientist and has come up with a formula. He takes statistics and reworks them, according to the bell curve method so beloved of management consultants and economists the world round, to determine patterns of change and scales of achievement. "The game may be variable and unpredictable but it is by no means random or chaotic. For the cricket statistician this is the essence of the game's fascination." Now is this man an alchemist, turning base figures into golden prophecy? Or is he just another conjurer? I would incline to the first, but then I am no good at the hard sums. His style is persuasive, even when he presents tables that will cause excited debate in any bar or parlour where sport is talked. Looking, for instance, at the effectiveness of sending in a night-watchman, he concludes that the tactic fails more than twice as often as it succeeds. Has Steve Waugh been reading Davis? He also claims that the popularity of the one-day game has peaked, or rather that Test cricket in Australia has achieved equilibrium with one-day. In India and Sri Lanka, however, the one-day game's popularity may be rising too fast to be sustainable, but he also wonders whether England wouldn't be better off playing more one-day internationals and sees the form as being the game's most likely international calling card in countries where it seeks to gain a toehold.

Boldly, he uses his method to determine the highest-scoring sportsmen ever in their respective fields: Bradman for cricket, Pelé for soccer, Ty Cobb for baseball, Jack Nicklaus for golf, Bjorn Borg for tennis and so on. When he comes to rating "rarity", a comparison with the standards of top-level players within the same sport, he admits to a complete boggle. Pelé's rarity rating is 1 in 14,000, Ty Cobb's is 1 in 6,000. Bradman's is 1 in 200,000. "It is Bradman who is anomalous," he says, "not the game of cricket itself."

Volume 3 of **The New Ball**, essays on cricket by divers hands, pursues the theme of Unlimited Overs in the breathless aftermath of the 1999 World Cup. I subscribe to *Granta* and to *Index on Censorship*, both of which this resembles in its softback format and editorial ambition, and also in their variability of must-read-now-put-the-answerphone-on qualities. I mean that as a compliment, by the way. The essay is a form to cherish and sustain. *The New Ball* does it admirably, but clearly believes it needs a bit of help. So it intersperses irritating double-page spreads within each contribution, featuring enlarged quotes, most words in grey but some words in black. The effect is like sitting next to a Tourette's syndrome sufferer. All is calm, or funny, or perceptive. Then suddenly you turn the page and something you've just read comes jumping out at you again, only bigger. It's like being hit over the head with a hammer or sitting through a loop of Fred Elliott's more memorable contributions to *Coronation Street*. "Meat is man's work, I say, MEAT IS MAN'S WORK."

That is my sole complaint. If I hadn't registered it you would now have been subjected to another flight of superlatives – for Paul Weaver's telling analysis of English performance, Mark Steel on class, crowds and the perils of the corporate box, Keith Booth, respected biographer of Ted Pooley, on being a scorer, Kevin Mitchell on gambling, scandals and the problems of reconciling rumour with fact. It is a total tonic to read about cricket as a living passion, not a museum piece, or a toff's province, or a rattling box of numbers, but a game with soul.

Like the orphan child, I have saved the best bit of this whole literary dinner for the last. David Underdown's **Start of Play: Cricket and Culture in Eighteenth-Century England** bubbles with scholarly glee. Underdown, a Somerset man, is Emeritus Professor of History at Yale. I should bear him a grudge for overturning my handy theory about cricket's four evolutionary stages, because his book shows that the roots of the professional game, the length of contests, the competitive rates of pay and the fixing of matches all happened long ago. So did the onset of bias towards London.

Early English cricket began in the Wealds and Downs of Kent, Surrey and Sussex. Underdown uncovers the reasons why. He shows how something that farm families played before and after harvest was taken up by their noble landlords, where gambling fitted in, how it gravitated naturally, if unfairly, towards the capital. His London bustles with pleasure gardens, explodes with fireworks, offers bear-baiting, cudgelling contests, races by women dressed only in drawers, cricket matches galore. In Kensington Gardens, Prince Frederick, the heir to the throne, captains his side vigorously, is hit on the head by a ball, dies of it. At the Artillery Ground, at Kennington Common, at the White Conduit public house in Islington, anywhere they could, people played cricket, watched it, bet on it. "When the London Club played Brompton on Chelsea Common in July 1731, two players came to blows after one of them tore the other's ruffles off his shirt... In 1738 Kent played London at the Artillery Ground in front of a huge crowd – 10,000 according to one estimate – and the match ended in confusion after an argument over 'whether one of the Londoners was fairly out.'"

To read Underdown is like taking a balloon flight over the past two and a half centuries, but this isn't just a joyride. What he has to say about the game chimes with the views of today's best players. How the teams turned into clubs and why clubs matter, now as then, is the bedrock of his argument. Cricket, he says, will only survive if it is rooted in its locality where people grow up playing it. His plea is for it to stay fun, to play as well as to watch. He is scathing about metropolitan bias, minatory about the distorting effects of too much money, very rude about the national media and scorching on the pernicious consequences of excess nationalism. He loves the game's democracy and preaches it with all his heart. Lucky Yale to have had him as a teacher. Lucky us to have this book.

Gillian Reynolds is the radio critic of the Daily Telegraph.

ADDITIONAL REVIEWS

Graeme Wright writes: Depending on the reader's frame of mind, Ted Corbett's **Great Cricket Betting Scandal** could be either a supplement or an antidote to Mihir Bose's commentary on match-fixing on pages 17–28. It is essentially the tour diary of B. L. M. Collinson, who took an MCC side to India in 1906-07 because "MCC were concerned that there was a conspiracy by players to change the result of matches at the behest of a gang of bookmakers," and were keen to flush out the miscreants. So it has to be fiction: cricket administrators weren't concerned about this in 1996, let alone 1906. Pity about Collinson, though. Turns out he was a cad and a cheat. A Surrey man, of course.

Corbett's publisher, the Manchester-based Parrs Wood Press, had a busy year. The three following biographies and a history of **The War of the Roses**, by Dean Hayes, came from the same stable. Hayes's book begins with a scorecard of the first fixture, at Whalley in 1867, but thereafter it's all potted scores and brief match reports through to 2000. Portraits and biographies of 48 Roses cricketers break up the pages. Yorkshire lead the series 77–51 apparently, Yorkshiremen have scored most runs, taken most wickets and catches, and effected most dismissals. For a Lancastrian, which Hayes appears to be, compiling such a history would have to be a labour of love.

Pat Symes's tribute to **"Maco"** is, as the author says, one that should not have been written for many years. Malcolm Marshall's death at 41 saddened the cricket world and, when West Indies cricket needs men of his stature as never before, left a great void. Mark Nicholas's fine funeral eulogy, reprinted here, reminds us how great. Much of the book appeared in 1987 as *Marshall Arts*; Symes, who ghosted Marshall's writings, has updated his story and woven in tributes, anecdotes and assessments from cricketers worldwide.

In **Ken Farnes: Diary of an Essex Master**, David Thurlow also tells of a fast bowler who died tragically young, only 30, in a flying accident during World War II. There is a story here trying to get out; it needed a judicious editor as midwife. The mass of material, including Farnes's autobiography, a tour diary and letters, needs more than mere organisation. Farnes's is a *Boy's Own* story: it should hum. A similar criticism applies to **A Somerset Hero Who Beat the Aussies: The Life and Times of J. C. 'Farmer' White**, with Basil Ashton Winkler throwing in his thoughts on more current times for good measure. Writing doesn't have to be a talent, it can be a craft, but it has to make the reader want to read on. Even enthusiasms should do that.

Ian Addis, Mick Dean and Brian Slough have a similar problem with too much material in **Brian Reynolds: The Times and Life of a Northamptonshire Sportsman** – to the extent that we learn the registration number of the Ford in which he courted his future wife. This is train-spotting gone mad. Yet somehow, with its snapshots, newspaper cuttings and assorted memorabilia, it just about works. In their enthusiasm for – let's be honest, their hero-worship of – the man who, on retiring, was his county's third-highest run-maker, they've caught not only the man himself but something of life in an age when community, in this instance Kettering, meant more

than commercialism. Brian Reynolds demonstrated shoe-making at the Festival of Britain in 1951; he might have been an England cricketer, and this would have been a different story. As it stands, it's a reminder of what is precious about cricket, and why some of us remain daft enough to watch a day's Championship cricket at Wantage Road, or some other intimate county ground, when instead we could be taking in reggae at Lord's or hamster-bubble races at Edgbaston. Nice to have the Marty Robbins reference, too.

More life and times, this time of "a Lancashire Cricket Legend", Ian Austin, in **Bully for You, Oscar**, with Andrew Collomosse. Like Austin's cricket, there are few frills; just down-to-earth prose, a few laughs and 100 per cent reliability. His views are worth reading, whether on fellow-players, captains, match-fixing, overseas players, England's man-management, or lack of it, or Lancashire's ups and downs. They don't come better than Ian Austin. Mike Atherton fans will enjoy this book as well.

Mike Coward's **Calypso Summer** came out to complement a TV documentary on the 1960-61 Australia–West Indies series that breathed life back into Test cricket and gave birth to the Frank Worrell Trophy. It was a magical tour well worth retelling in these troubled times. Coward does it admirably, backing up the story with photos, some unpublished until now, and comments from the participants. I followed this series, virtually ball by ball, on long-wave radio, yet I'd forgotten how gripping it was throughout. The Brisbane tied Test merely set it up. At Adelaide, for example, Ken Mackay and Lindsay Kline, Australia's last pair, hung on for 109 minutes to keep Australia in the series. Mackay, the "gum-chewing anti-hero", batted almost three and three-quarter hours for his unbeaten 62 and, rather than risk a catch off Wes Hall's final delivery, let it hit him in the ribs. On his return to the dressing-room, as Richie Benaud, his captain, tells it, "He went and sat down and obviously he was in a bit of pain. I said, 'Well done.' 'Thanks, mate,' he said. That was it."

Benaud has written the introduction to **Famous Cricketing Families**, by Kersi Meher-Homji, another illustrated Australian title which tells the stories of "great cricketing families that have not only produced some of the greatest players, but also added to the character of the game." The Benaud family is among them (more than 30 families are celebrated), and Richie also provides one of my favourite stories in David Rayvern Allen's **E. W. Swanton: A Celebration of his Life and Work**. It involves *Wisden's* Australian correspondent, John MacKinnon, and "one of the most incomprehensible captaincy decisions" EWS had ever seen. Richie was captaining Swanton's Arabs at the time. Some 270 pages of this title have appeared before as *Last Over*, which Rayvern Allen compiled with Swanton and which was reviewed in *Wisden* 1997; this leaves 150 or so more for Jim's own writing since then, plus affectionate and amusing memories from his friends and colleagues. Jim was an industrious journalist, but he shouldn't become an industry.

Rayvern Allen's own industry has also resulted in **Cricket Through the Pages**, a handsomely illustrated anthology spanning 200 years. Paintings, line-drawings, porcelain and other artefacts lend weight to the premise that cricket is more than a game, while the words, some from names famous in fields other than cricket, give a clue to how a love for cricket is fired and made to last. The editor admits that his anthology is pure indulgence, but we can all do with some of that.

Some of us can also do with help with the game itself. Derek Mark, coach at King William's College, Isle of Man, and Don Beard, a PE teacher, have crafted an interesting instructional book on **Batting** that analyses strokes in detail, illustrating and specifying how they should be played. It then shows, very usefully, the faults that occur and how they can be rectified. Bowling and fielding are to follow, apparently. Every school should have them.

Matthew Engel writes: Perhaps the most remarkable, if not the most marketable, cricket book of 2000 is the astonishing homage to the pioneer cricket photographer, G. W. Beldam. This massive work, **Great Cricketers: The Age of Grace & Trumper**, was compiled by Beldam's son, George. During the fraught production process, Beldam junior died, but his widow, with support from Boundary Books and MCC, managed to rescue the project. It is not a conventional biography, though that would be interesting enough on its own. (For brief information on Beldam, see Patrick Eagar's article in *Wisden* 2000, page 33.) Mostly, it is a jumble of his work, cricketing and otherwise: photographs, water-colours and the text he provided to go alongside Chevallier Tayler's famous 1905 illustrations of celebrated cricketers. There are 700 illustrations in all. Beldam was no mere snapper: his prime concern was for the technicalities of cricket. As his son wrote, he had "boundless enthusiasm for the minutiae of grip". The book is a mess, and desperately needed an editor who could give it coherence, but it is a glorious mess none the less.

BOOKS RECEIVED IN 2000

Note: The address for suppliers mentioned several times below are as follows:

Sportspages, 94–96 Charing Cross Road, London WC2H 0JG and Barton Square, St Ann's Square, Manchester M2 7HA.
Association of Cricket Statisticians (ACS)/Sport in Print, 3 Radcliffe Road, West Bridgford, Nottingham NG2 5FF.
Limlow Books, Blue Bell House, 2–4 Main Street, Scredington, Sleaford, Lincolnshire NG34 0AE.

GENERAL

Allen, David Rayvern ed. **E. W. Swanton** A Celebration of his Life and Work Foreword by John Major (Richard Cohen Books, £17.99)
Chalke, Stephen with Bryan "Bomber" Wells **One More Run** Gloucestershire versus Yorkshire, Cheltenham, August 1957 Illustrations by Ken Taylor and Susanna Kendall (Fairfield Books, 17 George's Road, Bath BA1 6EY, £8)
Coward, Mike **Calypso Summer** (ABC Books, GPO Box 9994, Sydney, NSW 2001, Australia, $A45)
Hargreaves, Peter S. **More Cricket Revelations** (Published by the author)
  Anecdotes and reminiscences from Wisden's *man in Denmark.*
Harms, John **Confessions of a thirteenth man** (Text Publishing, 171 La Trobe Street, Melbourne, Victoria 3000, Australia, no price given)
Hayes, Dean **The Wars of the Roses** A History of Lancashire v. Yorkshire Cricket Matches Foreword by Fred Trueman (Parrs Wood Press, £16.95)

Heavens, Roger **Essays on Arthur Haygarth** Cricketer, Historian and Old Harrovian (published by the author, 2 Lowfields, Little Eversden, Cambridgeshire CB3 7HU; limited edition of 208, no price given)

Hughes, Simon **yakking around the world** a cricketer's quest for love and utopia (Simon & Schuster, £12.99)

Jones, Trevor **The Dream Fulfilled** Surrey's 1999 County Championship Triumph Foreword by Micky Stewart (Sporting Declarations Books, PO Box 882, Sutton, Surrey SM2 5AW, £17.99 inc. p&p)

Kumar, Vijay P. **Cricket Lovely Cricket** West Indies vs. England 1950: 50th Anniversary Tribute Foreword by Sir Clyde Walcott and Appreciations by Brian Lara and Courtney Walsh (Fairfield Books, £16.95)

Malies, Jeremy **Great Characters from Cricket's Golden Age** (Robson Books, £16.95)

Meher-Homji, Kersi **Famous Cricketing Families** from Graces and Headleys to Chappells and Waughs Foreword by Richie Benaud (Kangaroo Press/Simon & Schuster Australia, $A29.95)

Porter, Clive **Kent Cricket Champions 1906** (Limlow Books, £9.95 + 50p p&p)

Underdown, David **Start of Play** Cricket and Culture in Eighteenth-Century England (Allen Lane, £20)

Westcott, Chris **Class of '59** From Bailey to Wooller: The Golden Age of County Cricket (Mainstream, £15.99)

Westcott, Chris **The History of Cricket at the Saffrons, Eastbourne** Foreword by E. W. Swanton, Preface by His Grace The Duke of Devonshire (Omnipress, £17.99)

Whimpress, Bernard **Passport to Nowhere** Aborigines in Australian Cricket 1850–1939 (Walla Walla Press, PO Box 717, Petersham, NSW 2049, Australia, no price given)

Woolmer, Bob with Ivo Tennant **Woolmer on Cricket** (Virgin Publishing, £16.99)

ANTHOLOGY

Allen, David Rayvern **Cricket Through the Pages** An Illustrated Anthology Spanning 200 Years of Cricket (André Deutsch, £17.99)

AUTOBIOGRAPHY

Austin, Ian with Andrew Collomosse **Bully For You, Oscar** The Life and Times of a Lancashire Cricket Legend Foreword by Michael Atherton (Mainstream, £15.99)

Blofeld, Henry **A Thirst for Life** with the Accent on Cricket (Hodder & Stoughton, £18.99)

Lloyd, David with Alan Lee **Anything But Murder** David Lloyd: the autobiography (Collins Willow, £16.99)

Richards, Viv with Bob Harris **Sir Vivian** The Definitive Autobiography (Michael Joseph, £16.99)

BIOGRAPHY

Addis, Ian with Mick Dean and Brian Slough **Brian Reynolds** The Times and Life of a Northamptonshire Sportsman (Diametric Publications, 45 Grosvenor Road, Kettering, Northants NN15 6TF, £17)

Booth, Keith **His Own Enemy** The Rise and Fall of Edward Pooley Foreword by Wayne James (Belmont Books, 6 Kingswood Drive, Sutton, Surrey SM2 5NB £12.50 + £1 p&p)

McKinstry, Leo **Boycs** The True Story (Partridge, £16.99)

Perry, Roland **Waugh's Way** The Steve Waugh story: learner, legend, leader (Random House Australia; in UK from Sportspages, £14.95 paperback)

Piesse, Ken **The Complete Shane Warne** (Viking; in UK from Sportspages, £14.95 paperback)

Romanos, Joseph **John Reid** A Cricketing Life Forewords by Lord Cowdrey of Tonbridge and Sir Wilson Whineray (Hodder Moa Beckett, 4 Whetu Place, Mairangi Bay, Auckland, New Zealand, $NZ34.95; in UK from Sportspages, £15.95)

Symes, Pat **"Maco"** The Malcolm Marshall Story (Parrs Wood Press, £9.95 paperback)

Thurlow, David **Ken Farnes** Diary of an Essex Master Foreword by Barry Norman (Parrs Wood Press, £16.95)

Tinkler, Basil Ashton **A Somerset Hero Who Beat the Aussies** The Life and Times of J. C. 'Farmer' White Foreword by Michael Hill (Parrs Wood Press, £16.95)

PICTORIAL

Beldam, George, jun. comp. **Great Cricketers: The Age of Grace & Trumper** Illustrated biography of G. W. Beldam (Boundary Books/MCC Cricket Library, £110. Limited edition of 500 copies. Telephone: 01477 533106)

Cricket Characters 2 The Cricket Caricatures of John Ireland Text by Jonathan Agnew (Queen Anne Press, £20)

Lord's The Home of Cricket Then and Now (Published by MCC Museum, Lord's, £3.50 + £1.50 p&p)

REFERENCE

Frindall, Bill **The Wisden Book of Test Cricket: Fifth Edition – Volume 1 1877–1970; Volume 2 1970–1996; Volume 3 1996–2000** inc. Test Match Records and Women's Tests Foreword by Sir Donald Bradman (Headline, £40 per volume)

Haigh, Gideon ed. **Wisden Cricketers' Almanack Australia 2000-01** Third edition (Hardie Grant, Melbourne, \$A39.95; in UK from Penguin Direct: see page 1532)

Kazi, Abid Ali ed. **First-Class Cricket in Pakistan: Volume III 1958-59 to 1962-63** (Pakistan Association of Cricket Statisticians and Scorers, 64/II, 20th Street, Khayaban-e-Badban, Phase 5, Defence Housing Authority, Karachi, Pakistan, Rs 300; in UK from Limlow Books, £25 inc. p&p)

Oslear, Don **Wisden The Laws of Cricket** The 2000 Code and its Interpretation (Ebury Press, £9.99 paperback)

Pervez, M. A. **A Dictionary of Cricket** Foreword by S. Venkataraghavan (Sangam Books; in UK from 57 London Fruit Exchange, Brushfield Street, London E1 6EP, £5.95)

STATISTICAL

Ambrose, Don comp. **1876: A Statistical Survey** (ACS, £6)

Bailey, Philip comp. **First-Class Cricket Matches 1904** (ACS, £14)

Bartlett, Kit **Laurence Barnard Fishlock** His Record Innings-by-Innings (ACS, £5)

Davis, Charles **The Best of the Best** A New Look at the Great Cricketers and Their Changing Times (ABC Books, GPO Box 9994, Sydney, NSW 2001, Australia, \$A29.95)

Hatton, Les **Don Kenyon** His Record Innings-by-Innings (ACS, £5.50)

Hudd, Gerald **Arthur Milton** His Record Innings-by-Innings (ACS, £5.50)

Hudd, Gerald **Reg Simpson** His Record Innings-by-Innings (ACS, £5.50)

Isaacs, Vic and Allen, Dave **Malcolm Marshall** His Record Innings-by-Innings (ACS, £9.50)

Isherwood, Robin and Bailey, Philip comp. **Northerns Cricketers (including Northern-Eastern Transvaal and Northern Transvaal) 1937/38–1999/00** (ACS, £2.50)

Lambert, Dennis **George Geary** His Record Innings-by-Innings (ACS, £9)

McKie, Dr Greg **W. M. Woodfull** His Record Innings-by-Innings (ACS, £5)

Sheen, Steven **Stan McCabe** His Record Innings-by-Innings (ACS, £5)

Wat, Charlie **The 1999 Test Year** (Cricket Stats Publications, PO Box 745 Moonee Ponds 3039 – not for sale)

TECHNICAL

Beard, Don and Mark, Derek **Batting** Techniques and Fault Finding Analysis (From D. Mark, 25 Scarlett Road, Castletown, Isle of Man IM9 1NS, £5.99 + £1.50 p&p)

Wildgoose, Dick and Fred **Cricket the Wildgoose Way** Development Coaching Foreword by David Gower (Cricket Federation for People with Disabilities, paperback)
Coaching for cricketers with mixed disabilities.

COUNTIES

Bailey, Philip comp. **Northamptonshire County Cricket Club First-Class Records 1905–1999** (Limlow Books, £9 + 50p p&p)

Miller, Douglas **Cricket Grounds of Gloucestershire** (ACS, £7.50)

FICTION

Corbett, Ted **The Great Cricket Betting Scandal** (Parrs Wood Press, £7.99)

FIRST-CLASS COUNTY YEARBOOKS, 2000

Derbyshire £5, Durham £6, Essex £7.50, Glamorgan £6, Gloucestershire £5, Hampshire £7.50, Kent £4.99, Lancashire £7, Leicestershire £7, Middlesex £8, Northamptonshire £9, Nottinghamshire £4.50, Somerset £7.50, Surrey £5, Sussex £7, Warwickshire £5, Worcestershire £6, Yorkshire £13. 2001 prices may change. Some counties may add charges for p&p.

OTHER HANDBOOKS AND ANNUALS

Agnew, Jonathan ed. **Benson and Hedges Cricket Year 2000** (Bloomsbury, £20)

Bailey, Philip comp. **ACS International Cricket Year Book 2000** (ACS, £9.95)

Berry, Mike ed. **2000 Minor Counties Annual** (from Mike Berry, Idsworth, 3 Fair Close, Frankton, Nr Rugby, Warwickshire CV23 9PL, £5 + £1 p&p)

Bryden, Colin ed. **Mutual & Federal South African Cricket Annual 2000** (UCBSA/Mutual & Federal, PO Box 1120, Johannesburg 2000, South Africa, no price given)

Club Cricket Conference **I'll Only Be Gone For A Few Days** (from CCC, 361 West Barnes Lane, Surrey KT3 6JF, £4.99 inc. p&p)

Il Cricket Italiano 2000 (from Federazione Cricket Italiana, Via S. Ignazio 9, 00186 Roma, Italy)

Fish, Stuart, ed. **League Cricket Annual Review** (Empire Publications, 1 Newton Street, Manchester M1 1HW, £6.99)

Frindall, Bill ed. **NatWest Playfair Cricket Annual 2000** (Headline, £5.99)

Hatton, Les comp. **First-Class Counties Second Eleven Annual 2000** (ACS, £4.95)

Irish Cricket Annual 2000 (from Dr E. M. Power, 5 Strangford Avenue, Belfast BT9 6PG, £4 inc. p&p)

Marshall, Chris ed. **The Cricketers' Who's Who 2000** (Lennard/Queen Anne Press, £12.99)

Maxwell, Jim ed. **ABC Cricket Book** (ABC Books, GPO Box 9994, Sydney, NSW 2001, Australia, $A6.95)

Miller, Allan ed. **Allan's Australian Cricket Annual 2000** (from Allan Miller, PO Box 974, Busselton, WA 6280, $A40; in UK from Sport in Print, £18.50)

Payne, Francis and Smith, Ian ed. **2000 New Zealand Cricket Almanack** (Hodder Moa Beckett, Auckland, New Zealand, no price given)

Ward, John ed. **Zimbabwe Cricket Year 1999** (Pangolin Press, Helena Close, Marlborough, Harare, Zimbabwe; in UK from Limlow Books, £15 inc. p&p)

REPRINTS AND UPDATES

Arthur Haygarth's/Marylebone Club Cricket Scores and Biographies Volumes VI (1858–1860), VII (1861–62) and VIII (1863–1864) A continuation of Frederick Lillywhite's Scores and Biographies from 1772 to 1854. (Facsimile edition, from Roger Heavens, 2 Lowfields, Little Eversden, Cambridgeshire CB3 7HJ; limited editions of 500, Vol VI £50; Vol VII and VIII £51 each, all + £4 p&p)

Botham, Ian with Peter Hayter **Botham: My Autobiography** Updated paperback (Collins Willow, £6.99)

Donald, Allan with Patrick Murphy **White Lightning** The Autobiography Revised and updated paperback (Collins Willow, £6.99)

Haigh, Gideon **Mystery Spinner** The Story of Jack Iverson UK edition (Aurum Press, £18.99)

Hill, Alan **Hedley Verity** Portrait of a Cricketer Foreword by Sir Donald Bradman (Mainstream, £14.99)

Hopps, David **A Century of Great Cricket Quotes** Updated paperback (Robson Books, £9.99)

Smith, Rick **Australian Test Cricketers** Foreword by Alan McGilvray (ABC Books, GPO Box 9994, Sydney, NSW 2001, Australia, $A32.95 paperback)

Stewart, Alec with Brian Murgatroyd **Alec Stewart's England Diary** (Collins Willow, £6.99) *Paperback of* A Captain's Diary *updated to include 1999-2000 tour.*

Tufnell, Phil with Peter Hayter **Phil Tufnell: What Now?** Updated paperback (Collins Willow, £6.99)

John Wisden's Cricketers' Almanack for 1908 and 1909 Facsimile editions (Willows Publishing, 17 The Willows, Stone, Staffordshire ST15 0DE, fax: 01785 615867, £50 inc. p&p for 1908 and £51 for 1909 in UK, £2 extra overseas postage; £5 extra for facsimile of original hard cloth cover)

Wisden Cricketers' Almanack for 1943, 1944 and 1945 Facsimile editions (Willows Publishing, £52 per volume inc. p&p in UK for facsimile of original hard cloth cover, £2 extra overseas postage; £48 inc. p&p for facsimile of original linen cover, £2 extra overseas)

PERIODICALS

The Cricketer International (monthly) ed. Peter Perchard (Beech Hanger, Ashurst, Tunbridge Wells, Kent TN3 9ST, £2.95)

The Cricketer Quarterly: Facts and Figures ed. Richard Lockwood (The Cricketer International, £3.25)

Cricket Lore (ten per volume, frequency variable) ed. Richard Hill (Cricket Lore, 22 Grazebrook Road, London N16 0HS, £35 per volume)

The Cricket Statistician (quarterly) ed. Philip Bailey (ACS, £2, free to ACS members)

The Journal of the Cricket Society (twice yearly) ed. Clive W. Porter (from P. Ellis, 63 Groveland Road, Beckenham, Kent BR3 3PX, £5 to non-members)

2001 Minor Counties News (up to ten per year) ed. Mike Berry (from Mike Berry, Idsworth, Fair Close, Frankton, Nr Rugby, Warwickshire CV23 9PL)

Red Stripe Caribbean Quarterly ed. Tony Cozier (The Nation Publishing Co, Fontabelle, St Michael, Barbados, annual subscription UK/Europe £14; US $US20; rest of the world $US28; in UK from Sportspages, £3.25 or £13 + £3.20 p&p for four issues)

The Scottish Cricketer (three per year) ed. Mike McLean (36 Marywood Square, Glasgow G41 2BJ, £2)

Wisden Cricket Monthly ed. Stephen Fay (The New Boathouse, 136–142 Bramley Road, London W10 6SR, £2.90. Subscriptions: 01795 414895, e-mail wisden@galleon.co.uk)

SELECTED LOCAL HISTORIES

Baxter, John **Have we got an Umpire?** Diary of Andover CC in 1999 (obtainable via e-mail info@andovercricketclub.co.uk, £4)

Gill, Tony **The Early Years** Jack Frost XI 1961–1999 History of a Wandering Club (Bards Original Publishing, Studio 1, 9 The Mount, Burtons' St Leonards, E. Sussex TN38 0HR, £4.99 + £1.50 p&p paperback)

Reyburn, Ross ed. **Life at the Graveyard** Moseley Ashfield Cricket Club 1900–2000 (from Slater Johnstone, 3 Temple Row West, Birmingham B2 5NY, £10 + £1 p&p paperback)

SOUVENIR BROCHURES

The Coca-Cola Trophy 2000 (Cricketers Benefit Fund Series, PO Box 88, Sharjah, UAE, no price given)

THE CRICKET SOCIETY LITERARY AWARD

The Cricket Society Literary Award has been presented since 1970 to the author of the cricket book judged as best of the year. The 2000 award, sponsored by PricewaterhouseCoopers, was won by Derek Birley for **A Social History of English Cricket**. The 2001 award was due to be presented in April; on the shortlist were George Beldam, junior, for **Great Cricketers: The Age of Grace & Trumper**; Gideon Haigh for **Mystery Spinner: The Story of Jack Iverson**; Leo McKinstry for **Boycs: The True Story**; Jeremy Malies for **Great Characters from Cricket's Golden Age**; and David Underdown for **Start of Play: Cricket and Culture in Eighteenth-Century England**.

CRICKET AND THE MEDIA, 2000

By SIMON HEFFER

It was as well Jim Swanton was back in the ultimate pavilion. He would not have enjoyed the uses to which the media were put in the service of cricket during 2000. Swanton disdained the school of cricket coverage that placed more emphasis on what happened off the field than what happened on it. Regrettably, thanks to the can of worms opened by Hansie Cronje, on-the-field had barely a look-in.

This was unfortunate, when one considers just how much there was to report. For the first time, the English game had a two-division County Championship, on the mixed effects of which the media expended relatively little effort. England won a Test series against West Indies for the first time in 31 years, and would go on, in the closing weeks of the year, to win a series in Pakistan for the first time in almost 39 years. But England's success was not so good a story as the match-fixers and the palm-greasers provided.

After Cronje was, as Michael Henderson phrased it in the *Daily Telegraph*, "fingered" by the New Delhi police on April 7, cricket's authorities strove (as Henderson also put it) to "clean up a game that is stewing in the juices of self-abasement". Their attempts to do so dominated the cricket pages from then on. The *Sunday Times* epitomised the excitement once the story broke: "Prison threat if Cronje is guilty", it said, printing in full the transcript of the taped conversation of March 14, 2000 between the fallen idol and Indian businessman Sanjeev Chawla. *The Times* printed a colour photograph of a man reading a South African newspaper on which the banner headline was "Shame" and, over a picture of Cronje, "the man who brought cricket and his country to its knees". (Before the year was out the photographs would depict another disgraced captain: effigies of India's Mohammad Azharuddin were burned after he was found guilty of match-fixing.)

The press then set about doing all they could to help the authorities. *News of the World* reporters posing as businessmen – do businessmen actually do any business these days, or do they just offer bribes? – secretly taped Salim Malik engaging in morally, and perhaps legally, unacceptable conduct. Imran Khan, in the *Telegraph*, argued that both David Richards of the ICC and South Africa's Ali Bacher had acted irresponsibly and complacently in the Warne/Waugh and Cronje scandals respectively, in not inquiring more actively into wrong-doing.

Scyld Berry of the *Sunday Telegraph* had a wider political point to make. Branding Cronje as "cowardly" – fair enough – he mocked the pose of Christian righteousness adopted by the former South African captain, who claimed he had been taken over by the devil. Berry reminded his readers that Afrikaners had quite easily lived with apartheid for more than 40 years while professing to be Christians, so a little match-fixing was quite straightforward. The *Daily Mail* pronounced that "greed and grudges spell the end for Cronje," and its veteran cricket writer, Peter Johnson, implored the ICC to "open its eyes" to the "gambling epidemic" killing the game. It also had an exclusive from Ray Illingworth on "the day the fixers tried to bribe me," detailing how the former England manager had been approached to throw a game in the 1996 World Cup.

By the autumn, when allegations were made that England's own Alec Stewart might be implicated, the matter was ripe for *The Times*' editorial columns. In a thoughtful leader entitled "Bribes before Wicket", the Thunderer thundered about the "shameful network of intrigue" at whose heart was Mohammad Azharuddin. It said that "every aspect of world cricket has been tarnished by this sad affair and fundamental reform is required to restore confidence". *The Times*' remedy, sensibly, included a curtailment of the constantly extending programme of "pointless" one-day matches on which the "criminal underworld" fed – a line set out in the paper six months earlier by the doyen of cricket writers, John Woodcock. At the time of writing, no such reform appears to be planned.

The Times' chief cricket correspondent, Christopher Martin-Jenkins, highlighted what he felt was another example of double standards in remarks by Lord MacLaurin that, unfortunately, overshadowed England's arrival in Pakistan in October. MacLaurin's demand that players under suspicion be suspended forthwith did not, Martin-Jenkins argued, match the English legal principle of innocent until proved guilty. The press rounded on MacLaurin when the Stewart allegations flared up, though the ECB chairman protested he had argued only for the suspension of those who refused to co-operate: and Stewart had not refused. The allegations against Stewart provoked another round of fevered speculation. "Who's next?" asked the *Mail*, noting that "Sleazebusters claim more Englishmen will be in the frame as the crisis grows".

Meanwhile, the field of play was inevitably eclipsed, although traditional themes had their annual airing. The day before England's stunning victory over West Indies in the Lord's Test, John Sadler in *The Sun* gave it to us straight about "the severe handicap of threadbare talent" under which England laboured. He applauded the reggae band that played during the lunch interval on the first day as a distraction from the "mediocrity", and was amused by the effect of this raciness on the "pensioners in panamas" in the Pavilion. England, though, were "flirting with sporting bankruptcy"; but there was less of that sort of thing as the summer wore on.

Another perennial theme was the up-and-down career of Graeme Hick. Michael Henderson, writing of the Worcestershire batsman's "customary recall", observed that "the axe that falls on Hick is as much a part of the summer as the picnic lawn at Glyndebourne". After the shocking hoick that got him out in the first innings of the Second Test against Pakistan, the press were once more calling for that axe: a contrast with the almost unanimous sympathy felt for Nasser Hussain, whose run-drought finally broke in December when England won in Karachi.

The broadcast media had less excuse to be sidetracked by scandal, their existence being mainly to cover live matches. An exception was Sky's increasingly excellent "World Cricket Centre", which provides the sort of televisual magazine coverage of which the game's followers have been starved for too long. In Channel 4's presentation of the Tests, one wondered whether

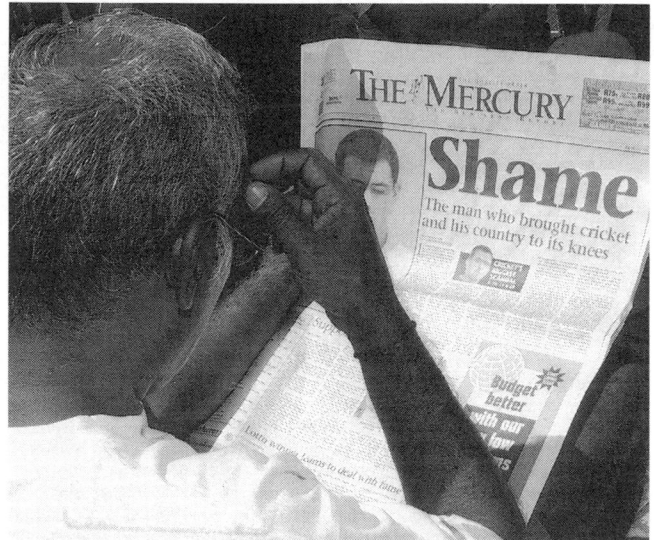

[*Juda Ngwenya, Popperfoto/Reuters*

the old days of the BBC would ever be lamented. Although at times the statistical technology could be a bit train-spotterish, and one occasionally felt subjected to one replay too many, the general approach was first-rate. It has much enhanced the viewer's enjoyment of the game. Sky's winter tour coverage remains a signal public service, under the benign and easy-going stewardship of David Gower. It suffers by comparison with Channel 4 only in what seems the greater intrusiveness of its advertising and promotional breaks.

That is true, too, of talkSPORT's winter radio coverage, on which Channel 4's Mark Nicholas is made to sound like a mid-Atlantic baseball presenter every time he gives us a "word from our sponsor". Talk set out from the beginning to take a different tone from *Test Match Special*, comprehensive rather than public school. After a while, that irritates; and for all Jack Bannister, one of their mainstays, knows about the game, his manner of delivery is unutterably dreary. Talk's coverage, while precise and accurate, is unappetisingly charm-free. Their attempt to secure the rights to home series failed, with *TMS* awarded the contract again in the spring of 2000. That, though, might not be a matter of unalloyed joy.

If the 2000 season was one of the best in recent times for the England team, it must rate as one of the worst for *TMS*. As part, one presumes, of the BBC-wide drive for political correctness, the number of ethnic and female voices was increased by a quantum, and not with any great improvement in quality. While Jonathan Agnew continues to be a consummate broadcaster, and CM-J provides expertise, understated humour and continuity, the rest of the team last season left something to be desired. Despite showing no loss of form nor scoring slowly, Henry Blofeld was rested for a couple of games. The charm factor of *TMS* – one of its greatest assets – plummeted accordingly.

Too often there were two West Indian voices on together, in Donna Symmonds with Sir Viv Richards as the analyst, which diluted the English flavour of the programme. A guest broadcaster has long been a feature of the *TMS* panel, and quite right too: but the other side are not supposed to take it over. By the end of the series Miss Symmonds had become rather tiresome, her precise and usually humourless tones being those of a prim and somewhat terrifying colonial schoolmistress. If the BBC must have a woman commentator – and it is still not compulsory – Eleanor Oldroyd, relegated far beneath her talent and sent to talk to people at the margins of the games during the intervals for rain, would be far more suitable. *TMS*, I suspect through no fault of its producer, Peter Baxter, appears to be losing its way. The Australian summer ahead gives it an ideal opportunity to redeem itself, but we could yet hear that Kylie Minogue has been brought in to do some ball-by-ball.

Finally, back to dear old Swanton, and dear old Hendo. The young whippersnapper found himself on the news pages of *The Times* in November for the "scathing attack" he made in *Wisden Cricket Monthly* on Swanton. Henderson described his *Telegraph* predecessor as a "boring" writer, a "frightful snob" with "no romance in his soul, no poetry in his veins". If, as must surely be the case, Jim has installed himself already as Eternal President of a celestial Cricket Writers' Club, I fear there is no point Hendo looking for a proposer and seconder.

Not that he was doing so well on earth, either. With immaculate timing, Hendo reserved the latest of his usually well-deserved nuclear assaults on the England establishment for the day before the famous victory at Karachi in December. In a gesture of solidarity, the *Telegraph* devoted its sports review front the following Saturday to letters of abuse directed against the great iconoclast. For a change, adjectives such as "disgraceful", "abominable", "inept", "depressing" and "bankrupt" were used to describe the cricket reporter, not the cricket.

Simon Heffer is a columnist on the Daily Mail.

CRICKET ON THE INTERNET, 2000

By ANDY OLDFIELD

Although the Internet is a new medium, it is old enough to have established some traditions. Change, however, is a constant. A prime example in 2000 was the Press Association's NewsCentre – traditionally a reliable site for cricket lovers in a hurry to get a no-nonsense overview of international and domestic matches and affairs. On April 19, 2000, new technology overtook it and it became Ananova (**ananova.com**). It was not so much a technological revolution as a digital face-lift, the most prominent face belonging to the eponymous Ananova, an animated virtual newscaster who looked like an amalgam of every "cyber-babe" ever to grace a computer game.

She was supposed to be programmed to act like a human newsreader, with emotional responses dictated by the story. On her launch she came across as a clunky cartoon, who took an age to read out headlines that most readers would take seconds to scan in text form. Text seemed to take second billing in Ananova's early days. Fortunately, things got back on track, and if you steered clear of the video reports button you could find cricket headlines, live scorecards and breaking news such as the South African match-fixing commission's suggestion that players' phone calls and e-mail be scanned in an effort to avoid future scandals.

Ananova, herself, failed to evolve over the year. Watching her read out Test news, the most striking things were her continuing scary facial mannerisms and verbal skills to disgrace a 1960s Dalek. Mike Atherton's name was a challenge she barely coped with. I didn't check how she handled Sri Lankans.

The comprehensive portal at the Lord's site ceased to be, at least in its usual format. Towards the end of June, the old address – lords.org – displayed a page offering links to two separate sites, one for information about MCC and Lord's, another for live scores, news, audio and video. The second link led to the CricInfo-powered ECB site. I had assumed its cumbersome address (**cricket.org/link_to_database/NATIONAL/ENG**) was temporary when I saw it in August, but it was still a fixture by the year end. An alternative is to use the proven CricInfo (**cricinfo.com**) site itself, and either choose England from the pull-down menu or click on the England flag – both on the front page. Whichever route you take, the site is worthwhile, as would be expected of anything bearing the CricInfo name. CricInfo was in expansive mood in 2000, valued at $150 million in June when India's largest Internet and e-commerce company, Satyam Infoway, invested $37.5 million in a 25 per cent stake.

The ECB site benefited from its CricInfo partnership, as in the first two months online it totalled 74.7 million page impressions. CricInfo itself broke the 100 million page-impression mark in October (its monthly average being around 60 million, with a previous record of 95 million), estimating that it reached more than 15 million fans in 180 countries. The ECB site provided detailed news and reports of domestic competitions throughout the year, as well as links to the women's game and internationals. It also specialised in live match commentary. Broadcasting in RealAudio proved a useful way of following tours. Series reviews and highlights were archived, and various players recorded online diaries while on tour. Sometimes filling the space seems to have been an effort. At other times, such as Alec Stewart's reflections on England's historic win at Karachi, the words flowed more easily.

Live Internet audio commentary has traditionally been beset by two problems. The first, the difficulty of obtaining broadcast rights, proved less of an obstacle in 2000. Besides the ECB coverage, CricInfo provided regular live commentary of overseas games. For instance, it won exclusive rights for the ICC Knockout in Kenya in October – the month that saw its page-impressions record. During Tests and one-day internationals, hunting through CricInfo was the easiest way of finding live audio feeds such as the Australian Nine Network commentary of Australia v West Indies, where Richie Benaud's voice was (fitfully) delivered in streaming Windows Media format. The second problem, quality of transmission, proved more persistent. Microsoft and RealNetworks both updated their player software several times, but the limiting factors of local telephone lines and the capacity of Internet service providers still meant that many broadcasts proved exercises in frustration, with lost connections and breaking-up sound.

While online multimedia is still fairly unreliable and slow, e-mail is un-surpassed for speedy news. CricInfo and Cricketline (**cricketline.com**) both ran e-mail newsletters (one concentrating on Indian cricket was also available from CricInfo) that summarised news and current matches, giving links to full details, if needed, on their respective web sites.

Statistics continued to be a draw, with many sites claiming to have the ultimate database of player and team performances. The Indian site, Khel (**khel.com**), Channel 4 (**cricket4.com**) and Sky (**sky.com**) all gave access to their databases via point-and-click browsing of lists and categories. CricInfo favoured its StatsGuru, a search-engine-style interface that let users type in names. Cricketline took advantage of the suitability of the web for statistics by setting up a timely special page, the Match Fixing Index, which highlighted matches where individuals and teams had performed below what form would suggest. Not that it gave proof of dodgy games, but it made for some interesting statistic-fuelled speculation.

Speculation was also the strong point of an Indian portal, Tehelka (**tehelka.com**), which published stories and e-mail discussions about match-fixing that would have horrified the lawyers of English and Australian sites. As well as breaking news online, Tehelka literally went multimedia by instigating the making and off-line screening of a documentary about the secret video made by Manoj Prabhakar. Transcripts of the video were published online, and latterly as a book, *Fallen Heroes: The Story That Shook The Nation*. Just as sensational in their own ways were the official reports into match-fixing by Justices Qayyum and King and by the Indian Central Bureau of Investigation (CBI): all three were posted in full on Internet sites, whereas traditional media were restricted by space to mere bites.

The Professional Cricketers' Association went online in May with the launch of **cricnet.com**. It offered all the features to be expected of a cricket portal, from live scoreboards, through halls of fame, cricket history sections, stats and player interviews. A welcome addition to the standard press agency news stories was the appearance of some longer features by analysts such as Tony Cozier. The coaching section provided insight into developments within youth cricket. For the 2001 season it has promised registered site members the option to get involved via promotions and competitions. If you sign up, there is also the facility to personalise the site's appearance. Answering questions about your interests results in tailored content, an increasingly common ploy used by portals to tempt users away from the competition.

Channel 4 joined the ranks of content providers when it expanded its sports coverage with Cricket4.com. Like CricInfo, cricnet, Cricketline, ECB and the rest, it has the usual mix of features, with coverage in standard web format or delivered by the Flash plug-in, which makes using its neat interactive maps a breeze. Planned for the Ashes summer is an online version of "The Analyst", with Simon Hughes writing about technical and historical aspects of the game.

Away from the larger commercial sites, fan-run pages proliferated. For an unofficial take on England, the Barmy Army site (**barmy-army.com**) maintained its presence for the third year as a forum for discussion via its message board. More than just a place to sound off, it also featured tour and ticket information, as well as lyric sheets for "teasing the Aussies, praising the English and pricking the balloon of one or two self-important journalists". A Barmy Army update was planned for when it joined the sports network **rivals.net**. This organisation came online in the second half of the year, based on the idea that fan sites can reach a wider audience if they're co-ordinated and given marketing help. Instead of using a search engine and relying on good luck, fans of many sports, including cricket, can just visit rivals.net and find a list of links to unofficial sites for county and international teams, as well as general cricket sites.

In a new medium like the Internet, three years can almost constitute an era, and November saw the end of one with the closure of Cricket Unlimited, the *Guardian* site that had been running in conjunction with **wisden.com** since June 1997. Wisden took the opportunity to go into hibernation for a major refurbishment, promising to return in time for the Ashes series carrying up-to-the-minute news, scores and statistics, as well as drawing on the treasure trove that is 138 years of *Wisden*. Sounds like a space to watch.

Andy Oldfield writes about the Internet for The Independent.

CRICKETANA IN 2000

By GORDON PHILLIPS

Despite cricket memorabilia becoming big business, it remains generally ignored or disdained by the mass media. However, two famous bats wielded by Sir Garfield Sobers broke down the indifference. Sold by Christie's (Melbourne) in October, the Slazenger he used to hit six successive sixes off Glamorgan's Malcolm Nash in 1968 sold for a world-record price of £52,500; coupled with the bat with which he made his then-record Test score of 365 not out against Pakistan in 1957-58, this pair realised £101,733. The Slazenger was purchased by a Washington businessman as a christening present for his son, to light a candle in a non-cricketing environment. He then set his sights on the ball that Sobers carted around and out of Swansea's St Helen's ground. Meanwhile, another American businessman may yet find a niche in the world of cricketana. Police have been investigating allegations against him of thefts totalling some £70,000.

Whereas Laurie Laumen's life-sized bronze of Victor Trumper sold for some £26,000 at Christie's in 1999, his larger than life-size bronze of W.G. remained unsold at its lower estimate of $A65,000 (£25,000). But a rare set of five bronze figures of romanticised youthful cricketers, made by Joseph Durham RA in 1863, found the right home for £16,000. Once seriously undervalued, Doulton Lambeth ware has become a banker and, because of competition from mainstream collectors, Staffordshire pieces have shot up in the last four years: the "Rifle Volunteers" in fine condition fetched £10,000, and a pair of figures after Caesar and Parr a world-record £4,200.

Occasionally seen water-colours of Victorian rural cricket still charm at modest prices, but demand for prints is slackening. The frequently auctioned Corbet Anderson lithographs appear tired, and, of the *Vanity Fair* prints, only E. W. Dillon, the final cricketer to appear in that magazine, is truly desirable at £2,200.

Signed photographs or *carte de visite* images of obscure Victorian players and tours are rapidly appreciating, a notable example being the self-compiled Charles Barnett coverage of an MCC tour to India, with off-duty and social photographs (£1,270). "Flicker books" featuring Clarrie Grimmett and Frank Woolley appear more numerous and less appealing.

It is alleged that the number of Australian collectors with full sets of *Wisden*, forever the Holy Grail, has risen from only 20 in the late 1970s to almost 100. This must include replica editions, for the 1864 edition alone is no mere bagatelle at £8,000, while the first three volumes bound in one and lacking the original wrappers still make £5,000. A set, 1864 to the present day, attracts £30,000.

Wisdens apart, the cornerstones of traditional collections – tour books, celebrity bats, ceramics, postcards – have widened markedly and are splendidly catered for in auctioneers' illustrated catalogues. A welcome newcomer in this field is Anthemion Auctions in Cardiff. The year's random selections could include John Arlott's typewriter, pub signs, pre-war London

Transport posters (averaging £500), clay pipes, cricketing golliwogs and "Bunnykins", Sir Jack Hobbs photographed in military uniform, Hambledon-crested china phone boxes, continental bisque and Parian figures, Lord's benches and Caribbean phonecards.

Good autograph material remains strong. A Spofforth letter doubled its estimate to reach £680, while other celebrity letter-writers included Daft, Hammond, the Lords Harris and Hawke, Hirst, Hobbs, Jessop, Kortright, Oldfield, Palairet, Ranji, Townsend and, inevitably, W.G. and Warner. But spontaneous signings on scraps of paper are almost a thing of the past, seen as diminishing the value of autographs.

The hunger for autographed material on the 1948 Australian "Invincibles" is unappeased, a team sheet reaching a staggering £1,020, while a secondary market is emerging for a modern limited-edition china plate, depicting the tourists, at prices well in advance of the initial sales, themselves over-subscribed. The same yearning applies to the Bodyline tour of 1932-33. Christmas cards signed by Maurice Tate (£600) or George Duckworth (£575) are matched by autographed tour sheets at £1,750. "Trumperana" still captivates: his bats can command £10,000, a signed sepia print up to £1,500, while a letter of 1913 outlining his philosophy of cricket was a snip at £1,840.

The last great unpublished work, George Beldam's *Great Cricketers: The Age of Grace & Trumper* finally and weightily reached discerning collectors' shelves in 2000. Classics such as *Boxall's Rules and Instructions* realised £7,400, Colman's *Noble Game* (£960), Daft's limited-edition *Kings of Cricket* (£1,320), with W.G.'s *Cricket* a reasonable £690.

Clothing featured stronger than ever. One eager purchaser spent £8,570 for the baggy green cap worn by Bert Oldfield when he was struck on the head by Harold Larwood during the Bodyline tour; other baggy greens – Lindsay Hassett (£4,000), Wally Grout (£2,400), Bobby Simpson (£2,300) and Mark Taylor (£1,600) – found counterparts in maroons worn by Sir Frank Worrell (£3,000) and Malcolm Marshall (£2,500). Among those wishing to disencumber themselves of attire and presentation pieces were Curtly Ambrose, Geoff Boycott, Hansie Cronje, Graham Dilley, Angus Fraser, Larry Gomes, Neil Hawke, Ray Illingworth, Paul Jarvis, Allan Lamb, Clive Lloyd, Derek Randall, Rt Rev. David Sheppard and C. K. Singh. Even Tom Moody's World Cup shirt brought in £700.

Noted commentators have coupled concern at the phenomenal output of modern memorabilia with anxiety that prices paid may never be recouped, let alone prove profitable investments. The admirable journal of the Cricket Memorabilia Society valiantly charts the deluge, while recalling that prices realised in the near-hysteria of the 1987 MCC Bicentenary auction have quintupled since then.

CRICKET EQUIPMENT IN 2000

By NORMAN HARRIS

The new Laws of Cricket introduced in 2000 concerned the way the game is, and should be, played. Equipment, by and large, escaped the attention of the revisionists, the notable exception being wicket-keeping gloves. Bob Taylor, the former England and Derbyshire keeper, was to the fore in advising the MCC's Laws committee to act on a modern trend towards webbing that provided a sizeable pouch between thumb and first finger. In his day, the glove's thumb and four fingers were unconnected. "An artificial aid had been introduced," Taylor explained. "With the Law as it was saying little about gloves, there would have been nothing to stop a keeper having a baseball glove hanging off the end of each hand." The Law is now more specific: there may be a firm strip between thumb and forefinger, to give support, but it cannot be elasticated or form a pouch.

The Law on stumps came in for modification as well. A minimum and maximum diameter is given, to allow for a stump to be thicker and hold a camera – though the distance between the outside edges of off and leg stumps must still be nine inches. The Law also states that the stumps must be cylindrical. They always have been, of course – at least in modern times – but there existed the possibility of stumps being square, triangular or any other shape. Perhaps sponsors missed a trick there.

Although bat and ball largely escaped the lawmakers' attention, the ball did not escape criticism elsewhere. It continued to be said of white balls that they swung too much, were too hard, went soft too suddenly, or became too discoloured. The main provider of the white ball in England, Dukes, robustly resisted these criticisms, but had to acknowledge an error when some of their red balls, used in the County Championship, were discovered to be light. This, it was argued, made them swing more; meanwhile, some Readers balls were found to be overweight. Dukes quickly identified the source of the problem, and rectified it, but the episode raised questions about the professionalism of county cricket.

It seemed to be part of the county game's lore that, at the start of the season, a small delegation from a county club – including a couple of bowlers – would visit a factory to choose their summer supply of balls. The lore, too, said that darker-coloured balls were favoured by these bowlers. Such balls might also be thought to fit better in the hand, and to "feel lighter". Of course, the ball-makers scoffed at this. But why *should* the bowlers, or indeed any player, choose the ball, an exercise they repeated before the start of every county match?

The boxes of balls would reach the counties with each ball in a uniquely numbered plastic bag so it could be traced if necessary. But such monitoring seldom happened because the balls were invariably taken out of their bags and mixed up by players anxious for a "feel test". As for balls failing the parameters of the Laws, it would seem that twice-yearly checks at factories by the British Standards Institution have been inadequate. Umpires can check for size with ring gauges. But they are unlikely to be able to measure the weight accurately, and certainly not the height of the seam.

By the end of the 2000 season the ECB finally decided to take action. If manufacturers were being encouraged to produce a ball that bowlers like, "It may well be that all balls for county cricket will have to come through our offices and be checked by us," acknowledged John Carr, the board's cricket operations director. Which is what will happen in 2001. The ECB will source and distribute balls to the counties, with particular makes nominated for the four competitions: Dukes for the Championship and the successor to the NatWest Trophy; Readers for the Norwich Union National League and Benson and Hedges Cup.

Just when innovation in bats seemed to have halted, word came from Australia of a model called the Angle Drive. Former state player Len Richardson accidentally made the discovery while playing in the back garden with his small son: when the bat handle broke, Richardson realised that the new angle of the blade was advantageous. Having the toe of the bat set back just an inch from the perpendicular, he argues, makes a considerable difference in keeping a driven ball on the ground. That inch converts to half a metre of elevation over 20 metres – the difference between the ball staying on the ground or being caught knee-high at mid-off.

Batsmen using the Angle Drive have set new records in Sydney grade cricket, with triple-hundreds being made even in junior games. But in England, where the Angle Drive has been a heavy scorer at a Kent club, established manufacturers queried whether the concept was as radical as is claimed. Leading players for whom bats are specially made sometimes ask for the blade to be "offset" a little. Richardson, however, insists that "If bat-makers or individuals insert a handle in a cricket bat greater than the 180-degree plane [i.e., backwards], they infringe my patent."

The biggest imminent development may well concern helmets. The ECB's insistence that all junior cricketers wear one was controversial, and caught suppliers unprepared. In July 2000, the board's Recreational Forum invited manufacturers to tender for a new, junior helmet that would be lighter (existing models being too heavy for young heads), better ventilated, accommodating of different-sized heads and, it is hoped, costing nearer £30 than £70.

It was a tall order, given existing manufacturing lead-times, and traditional suppliers were not optimistic. But, with the hunt on for new, high-tech materials, there was exciting talk of other industries and sports providing input – for example, motor-racing, canoeing and baseball. Maybe a radically new helmet might actually give cricket a growth spurt.

CRICKET GROUNDS IN 2000

Over the past two decades, new Test grounds have appeared at the rate of about one and a half every year: new countries have been granted Test status; big games have been shifted to secondary cities, previously thought unworthy of the honour; new stadiums have been built. Only one country has stood aside from this process. It is now almost a century since an English ground joined the club, when Bramall Lane, Sheffield (now, alas, given over to football) staged its one and only Test match in 1902. However, things are changing. The promotion of Bangladesh – whose cricket team is not yet a global crowd-puller – and the ICC's new fixture grid, which will require everyone to play everyone else in series of at least two matches, will force even England to be more inventive if Test cricket is to be profitable.

The new, controversial, pattern of the English season requires a fixture, possibly against an unattractive team, in mid-May, when the weather is often still wretched. There is thus scope for the addition of new Test centres that will regard such a game as an opportunity rather than a penance. There is reasonable hope and expectation in Durham that their county headquarters, the Riverside at Chester-le-Street, already staging one-day internationals, could make its debut with England v New Zealand in 2003. Durham believe they could extend their existing 15,000 capacity to 20,000, which would be more than adequate for such a fixture, especially if the wind were whipping off the North Sea. But a Test in the north-east would be enough of a novelty to attract attention at any time of year.

Australia are thinking along similar lines. There is little immediate hope of Bangladesh or Zimbabwe packing the Melbourne Cricket Ground. So there could be Tests in May up north there, too: possibly in Darwin, a city with no tradition of first-class cricket at all. Here, the climatic realities are rather different. Darwin is tropical, and too wet during the Australian summer to make cricket much fun. But May is perfect. Such a scheme would have the subsidiary benefit for the Australian Cricket Board of keeping their players occupied at a time when they are currently inclined to risk their fitness in the County Championship.

The optimism and ambition at Durham are not shared by many other counties. Yorkshire, forced to abandon their plans to move, have put their finances under strain just refurbishing Headingley. And Hampshire, whose cosy old ground at Northlands Road is becoming a housing estate, have been building their new stadium while staring at a £5 million hole in their finances. Teams like Sussex, who had grandiose ideas a year ago, have now suddenly discovered the virtues of home, sweet home.

Even the best loved of all county grounds had an alarming year in 2000. The autumnal floods at Worcester did not quite reach the record levels of 1947. But in those days the ground was deserted in the winter. Now, New Road is an all-year-round venue with a flourishing banqueting trade to help support the cricket. And when the River Severn spread out to cover much of the Midlands, Worcestershire were struggling to keep their heads above water in every sense.

The old belief is that regular floods are good for the wicket. "It's a myth," said secretary Mike Vockins. "These floods are really filthy. The silt is the worst. It's like brown talcum powder and if it gets wet it's like axle grease. It goes everywhere and we have to go round with a pressure hose to get rid of it. I really feel for the ground staff." Roy McLaren, the head groundsman, said: "I wish I was cleaning up for next season, but I bet I'm cleaning up for the next flood." Worcestershire used to be insured against flooding but, after five claims in 15 months, the insurance company cried for mercy. However, Vockins did go in for one bit of insurance. He invited Mike Denness from the ECB pitches committee down to see what McLaren is up against, just in case Worcestershire get into trouble this summer.

Certainly the ground was quite a sight. Only one banquet actually had to be cancelled; the luckier diners were enchanted to see the city's floodlit cathedral reflected in the great lake of water where cricket is supposedly played. If, as climatologists predict, the Severn is going to flood more frequently, this could be a regular occurrence. Beautiful, perhaps – but grass can take only so much; likewise the buildings. So will Worcestershire think about moving? "The first person to suggest it might as well jump off the bridge with a concrete block round their neck," says Vockins. "This ground means so much to Worcester."

CRICKET AND THE WEATHER, 2000

By PHILIP EDEN

As rain prevented play during last summer's NatWest final, Eleanor Oldroyd of the BBC and Roger Knight, secretary of MCC, were discussing the feasibility of turning Lord's into a covered stadium. A lack of engineering expertise meant that the discussion was never going to get seriously technical, but it was symptomatic of a growing desire to "fix" bad weather, rather than just grumbling about it. It was also a reflection of the indifferent weather of the 2000 season that the hundreds of hours of broadcast cricket needed so much chat to fill the lengthy voids between play.

I choose the word "indifferent" carefully. The weather of summer 2000 came in for a lot of flak, and not just in cricketing circles. It repeatedly made the headlines, often being described as "the worst in living memory" or "the worst since records began". The former I shall not comment on, save to say that "living memory" is a notoriously poor tool for making useful comparisons, but the worst since records began it manifestly was not. According to the *Wisden* summer index (see below), 57 of the previous 100 summers were better and 43 were worse. Quite why public and media opinion was so convinced that summer 2000 was unprecedentedly bad is perhaps better answered by a psychologist than a meteorologist.

The earliest start to the first-class season was blessed with three days of blue sky and warm sunshine, allowing Lancashire and Somerset to inflict crushing defeats on the Universities. Then the rains came, ruining most matches scheduled for the remainder of April. May comprised a dry, warm first half and a very wet second half, but the weather settled again in early June. Throughout the rest of the summer, rain fell regularly, though generally in small amounts; temperatures were variable; sunshine was in short supply. The three weeks from June 24 to July 14 were probably the most disappointing: averaged nationally, sunshine totalled just 40 hours compared with a normal amount of 150 hours. However, the third week of July was sunny (over 70 hours), and August was, according to the figures, a fairly good month.

Test cricket was played at an earlier date than ever before when the First Test against Zimbabwe opened at Lord's on May 18. Whatever the commercial reasons for scheduling seven Tests in a season, the meteorological implications of staging international matches in mid-May are clear. There is a higher risk of the ground being unfit for play, of the wicket being damp or wet, and of the weather itself being so inclement that playing and watching become a test of endurance. The mean midday temperature on May 18 ranges from 14 degrees centigrade in London to 12 degrees in Manchester; it is below ten degrees in ten per cent of years in London and 20 per cent of years in Manchester; afternoon maxima of just four or five degrees, although rare, are not unknown even in southern England at this stage of the season; and snow fell for several hours as far south as London overnight on May 17–18, 1955.

The meteorological statistics, averaged over England and Wales, for the 2000 season, were as follows:

	Average max temperature (°C)	Difference from normal for 1961-90	Total rainfall (mm)	% of normal	Total sunshine (hours)	% of normal
April (second half)...	14.3	+1.0	72	255	74	92
May	16.8	+0.9	80	124	198	95
June	19.6	+0.7	85	71	176	86
July..............	20.1	−0.6	60	86	158	85
August............	21.6	+1.2	66	77	194	109
September (first half) .	19.2	+0.8	52	127	60	80
2000 season	**19.0**	**+0.6**	**415**	**117**	**860**	**94**

Each summer has slightly different regional variations, although in most years northern and western counties are cooler, cloudier and damper than those in the east and south. The *Wisden* summer index allows us to compare the summer county by county. The index incorporates rainfall amount and frequency, sunshine and temperature in a single figure. The formula for the index is:

$$I = 20(Tx - 12) + \frac{(S - 400)}{3} + 2Rd + \frac{1}{3}(250 - R)$$

Tx is the mean maximum temperature, *S* is the total sunshine, *Rd* is the number of dry days, and *R* is the total rainfall, covering the period May 1 to August 31. The formula may look intimidating, but it is designed so that temperature, sunshine, rainfall frequency and rainfall amount each contribute roughly 25 per cent of the total. The final index ranges from zero for the theoretical worst possible summer to 1,000 for the theoretical best. The score for an average summer ranges from 510 at Chester-le-Street and 515 at Old Trafford to 645 at Hove and Lord's and 650 at The Oval. Broadly speaking, an index over 650 indicates a good summer, whereas one below 500 clearly describes a poor summer.

Values for each county for the summer of 2000 against the average value for the standard reference period 1961–90 are as follows:

	2000	Normal	Variation		2000	Normal	Variation
Derbyshire	545	565	−20	Middlesex	638	645	−7
Durham	464	510	−46	Northamptonshire	553	595	−42
Essex........	593	620	−27	Nottinghamshire .	560	575	−15
Glamorgan	535	540	−5	Somerset	588	605	−17
Gloucestershire .	577	575	+2	Surrey........	639	650	−11
Hampshire	648	625	+23	Sussex	628	645	−17
Kent	619	630	−11	Warwickshire ...	521	525	−4
Lancashire	491	515	−24	Worcestershire ..	599	595	+4
Leicestershire ..	550	570	−20	Yorkshire......	540	545	−5

All counties had lower scores in 2000 compared with 1999; however, Durham, Glamorgan, Lancashire and Yorkshire scored higher in 2000 than in 1998. Averaged nationally, though, last season's index of 556 was the lowest since 1992, and in the last 100 years it ranks 58th.

The *Wisden* weather index for the last ten years, together with the best and worst on record are as follows:

1991	538	1995	777	1999	637
1992	556	1996	663	2000	556
1993	573	1997	601		
1994	651	1998	565		

Highest: 812 in 1976.   **Lowest:** 309 in 1879.

A full list of summers between 1900 and 1999 can be found in *Wisden Cricketers' Almanack* 2000, pages 21–24. The best and worst individual cricket seasons of the 20th century were:

Best	Worst
812 (1976)	394 (1954)
799 (1989)	429 (1912)
777 (1995)	431 (1968)
770 (1911)	439 (1931)
746 (1990)	444 (1987)
741 (1949)	445 (1903)
737 (1921)	450 (1924)
726 (1959)	452 (1927)
718 (1947)	454 (1902)
712 (1975)	460 (1965)
710 (1933)	465 (1907)
707 (1901)	479 (1956)

Philip Eden is weather expert for BBC Radio Five Live, and the Daily *and* Sunday Telegraph.

CRICKET AND THE LAW, 2000

The captain of a cricket team was jailed for 12 months after being convicted of trying to seduce a 14-year-old girl who played for his club. Tony Brown, 46, was found guilty of four charges of indecent assault and of perverting the course of justice at Minshull Street Crown Court, Manchester on March 27. He had earlier been cleared of abducting the girl. Brown, of Stalybridge, near Manchester, was captain of the Denton Third Eleven when the girl joined his team. The court heard that Brown had been warned about his behaviour with the girl a year earlier. She had left the club but came back six months later, whereupon Brown turned his attentions to her once again.

Derek Kitto, the 63-year-old clerk of Penryn Town Council in Cornwall, was jailed for nine months after pleading guilty to siphoning off the council's funds to support his cricket team. Truro Crown Court heard on April 5 that Kitto, treasurer of St Gluvias Cricket Club, stole nearly £20,000, more than half of which he put in the club's kitty. This enabled St Gluvias to employ a Pakistani professional, Aziz Mohamed, even though the club had dropped a division and could no longer afford him. Ian Leadbetter, defending, said Kitto committed crime not to pay for personal extravagance: "It was done for a bizarre reason: quite simply to support this cricket club. As a result of that, he has lost almost everything."

A judge in Calcutta issued an order banning "reckless cricket matches" blocking city streets after a complaint from a resident of the Bagbazar district. Justice K. J. Sengupta ruled on June 27 that cricket should not disrupt the traffic between 4 p.m. and 11 p.m. The court heard that the games were not impromptu but sponsored floodlit tournaments, using loudspeakers to provide running commentary. The petitioner, Rajen Sen, complained that they blocked traffic and threatened life and property. He said they encouraged "rowdies" and "rampant gambling". Former Test cricketer Arun Lal declined to criticise the ruling, but added: "I feel sad for these boys as there are hardly any playgrounds in the city to cater for their needs."

Maria Grant, 45, was awarded £15,000 compensation for sex discrimination after failing to make the shortlist for the job of assistant secretary of the Lancashire Cricket Board. An employment tribunal in Manchester made the award on November 2 after hearing that Ms Grant, a former executive director of the Women's Cricket Association, had not even been called for an interview, although eight men were. When she asked for clarification, she was told she lacked knowledge of men's cricket. "There is no significant difference in how men and women play cricket, nor in the way it is administered," she told the tribunal.

The Australian Federal Police said on December 26 that 92-year-old Sir Donald Bradman had been tricked into providing his signature so it could be used on cricket memorabilia sold to the public. Earlier in the year, police had seized 26 bats and 29 wall plaques. "Sir Donald has to be Australia's greatest sporting icon," said Justice Minister Amanda Vanstone, "so this has to be the greatest rip-off." Investigations were continuing.

OBITUARY

AIBARA, EDULJI BUJORJI, who died on November 7, 2000, aged 86, was involved with the two Hyderabad teams that won the Ranji Trophy – 49 years apart. Eddie Aibara was a highly consistent batsman in the successful 1937-38 team, and coach when Hyderabad finally won the competition again in 1986-87. He averaged more than 40 in 45 Ranji Trophy matches over a 25-year period up to 1958-59, and was also notably successful against touring teams: he made 76 against MCC in 1951-52. *The Hindu* said he was one of the finest Indian players not to get a Test match, and he himself felt he was unlucky: "Maybe if I had been in Bombay, I would have played. It was the era of recommendations."

AMARNATH, NANIK BHARDWAJ, died on August 5, 2000, aged 88. "Lala" Amarnath scored India's first Test century and went on to become Indian cricket's patriarchal figure: as selector, manager, coach and broadcaster, as well as in a literal sense – his three sons became first-class cricketers and two played in Tests. Amarnath, a Punjabi, was also the first to kick against the stifling domination of Indian cricket by the local princes and their imperial backers. It severely damaged his career. Amarnath's figures in his 24 Tests are nothing special, but they do no justice to either his spasmodic brilliance or his enduring influence.

From a poor background in Lahore, when it was still part of India, he rose to prominence by scoring 109 ("a brilliant display" – *Wisden*) for Southern Punjab against MCC in 1933-34, and a few weeks later became a star with a century on his Test debut, India's first Test at home, at the genteel old Gymkhana ground in Bombay. With India facing an innings defeat, he took on the England attack and played, so he said later, "as if possessed by a mysterious power". He hit 83 in 78 minutes, hooking Nichols and Clark with confidence and going down the pitch to hit Hedley Verity. Slowing just a fraction, he reached his century in 117 minutes. According to Mihir Bose: "Amarnath was engulfed with spectators, garlanded and congratulated while the band played 'God Save the King'... As the day's play ended, women tore off their jewellery to present it to him, Maharajahs made gifts of money, and India hailed a hero." England's eventual easy win was almost forgotten in the hysteria.

Though he did little in the remaining two Tests of that series, Amarnath was by far the best player – with bat and ball – in the early stages of the unhappy Indian tour of 1936, captained by the Maharaj Kumar of Vizianagram ("Vizzy"). Furthermore, Amarnath knew he was the best player and, having waited, padded up, during an unusually big partnership in the match against Minor Counties at Lord's, he was infuriated to be told that other batsmen would be promoted ahead of him. He swore at the captain and tour treasurer, and was sensationally sent home. The team's subsequent failures, a commission of inquiry, and history as written by people with a more egalitarian world-view than Vizzy have all combined to exonerate him. But it meant a 12-year gap between his third Test and his fourth.

He remained a force in Indian cricket, however, scoring 241 for Hindus v The Rest in 1938-39. But when he visited England with the 1946 team, by then rehabilitated, his bowling was more potent than his batting, most dramatically in the first post-war Test, at Lord's, when he reduced England's first innings to 70 for four by dismissing Hutton, Washbrook, Compton and Hammond. "After a shuffling run of only three paces, he bowled off the wrong foot," said *Wisden* with slightly shocked admiration, "but he kept an almost impeccable length, moved his in-swingers probably more than any bowler in England, and mixed these with a cut leg-break of some venom."

The following year he was appointed India's captain for their first tour of Australia when Vijay Merchant withdrew. But with Bradman at his most merciless, India were understandably overwhelmed. Amarnath did little himself in the five Tests, averaging

[*Hulton Getty*

Waiting to bat, only to have other batsmen promoted ahead of him, provoked a spectacular outburst which led to "Lala" Amarnath being sent home from India's 1936 tour of England.

14 with the bat, and taking 13 wickets, although he was magnificent against state sides. His 228 against Victoria contained, Neil Harvey said, the best cover driving he ever saw. He remained captain against West Indies in 1948-49 and in Bombay narrowly failed to lead India to their first Test victory. Then cricket politics again turned against him. There were arguments about money and second-class treatment (the visitors were treated royally; Indian players were dumped in second-class hotels). Amarnath fell foul of the powerful board secretary, Anthony De Mello, who was furious with the man he had dragged "out of the gutter and made captain of India" and had him suspended for "continuous misbehaviour and breach of discipline".

Amarnath sought refuge in the Lancashire League. But he was buoyed by support from Bradman, who called him "a splendid ambassador", and by De Mello's subsequent fall from power. He was restored, though reduced to the ranks, in 1951-52 and took part when India at last won a Test, against England in Madras; passed over for the humiliating 1952 tour of England; and then given back the captaincy against Pakistan in 1952-53, apparently at the insistence of – of all people – Vizzy. Although India won their first series, Amarnath's contributions as a player were minor, and yet more internal machinations meant he left the job in anger. However, the wheel keeps spinning in Indian cricket and Amarnath's reputation grew with the years. He became chairman of selectors, most famously insisting on the inclusion of off-spinner Jasu Patel at Kanpur in 1959-60, which led to a historic win over Australia. Lala also supervised the development of his sons: Surinder, too, made a century on debut; Mohinder ("Jimmy") played 69 Tests. He was a well-informed and humorous commentator, and

Betty Archdale (*turning towards the camera*) with fellow members of the England team in October, 1934, shortly before they set sail for Australia.

in old age he acquired widespread affection as the nation's leading source of cricket anecdotes. But he never lost his habit of speaking his mind. "He was an impetuous man," said his contemporary, Mushtaq Ali, "quick to love and quick to fight." The Indian prime minister, A. B. Vajpayee, called him an icon.

ARCHDALE, HELEN ELIZABETH, MBE, who died on January 11, 2000, aged 92, was captain of the pioneering England women's team that toured Australia and New Zealand in 1934-35. The tour did much both to raise the status of women's cricket and to heal some of the damage done to Anglo-Australian cricket relations by Bodyline two years earlier. Betty Archdale herself earned much of the credit: "…her forthright yet engaging personality made her a popular figure to whom the sizable Australian crowds responded warmly," according to *Wisden Australia*. She was also a capable batsman, who twice made important 32s in a low-scoring series that England won. Instead of leading England again on the planned 1939-40 tour, she was commissioned in the WRNS and, after the war, emigrated to Australia. There she switched from a career in law to education, becoming principal of Sydney University Women's College and then head of Abbotsleigh Girls School, where she introduced sex education – and cricket. Betty Archdale also became a TV and radio personality, well-known for her witty and sensible approach to problems. In 1997 she was voted one of Australia's 100 Living Treasures and, in 1999, one of the first ten female honorary members of MCC. Her mother was a leading suffragette, imprisoned in 1912, and Betty was said to have collected stones for her to throw.

ARLIDGE, HAROLD JACK, died on October 27, 2000, aged 88. Jack Arlidge was the epitome of the locally based county cricket reporter, and the last of his generation. Originally from Wiltshire, he began covering Sussex just after the war and remained a fixture in the Hove press box for more than 50 years, first as correspondent of the Brighton *Evening Argus*, then as a freelance agency reporter, and finally as mentor to his son, Andy, who took over his work. He was *Wisden's* Sussex correspondent for many years. Jack's friendly welcome and mildly eccentric charm were a highlight of a trip to Hove for any visiting journalist ("Which phone can I use, Jack?" one might ask. "The one nearest Middlesbrough," he might reply). His delightful nature disguised the fact that for 40 years he had multiple sclerosis, which he never mentioned. He was also a popular local broadcaster, running a pioneering sports programme on BBC Radio Brighton, which he would invariably begin with the catchphrase: "Hello, sportsmen."

ARMSTRONG, THOMAS RILEY, died on February 6, 2000, aged 90. Tommy Armstrong was an orthodox slow left-armer who appeared for Derbyshire over a 22-year-span, from 1929 to 1950, but played only 58 matches. He was overshadowed by Tommy Mitchell and, after playing semi-regularly in the early 1930s, was rarely able to win a place. Armstrong took seven in an innings twice in 1933 and once more in 1937; in the season after the war, he topped the county averages with 28 wickets in five matches. He is best remembered, though, for his embarrassing role against Somerset at Wells on Derbyshire's most famous day: August 28, 1936. Arthur Wellard, dropped off Armstrong when one, hit him for five successive sixes and led Somerset to a stunning one-wicket win. However, results elsewhere meant Derbyshire still won their only Championship that evening.

ASPINALL, RONALD, died on August 16, 1999, aged 80. Ron Aspinall was a Yorkshire all-rounder whose career ended sadly, after he had been successful enough as a swing and seam bowler and lower-order run-getter in the late 1940s to be talked about as an England prospect. He opened the bowling with Alec Coxon so well in 1948 that *Wisden* noted the retirement of Bill Bowes "did not cause serious weakness". He made an even more brilliant start to 1949, taking 22 wickets for 140 in two Maytime fixtures against Somerset. But during a particularly niggardly opening spell (nine overs for 16) against Worcestershire in the next game, he damaged an Achilles tendon and missed the rest of the season. He still finished top of the national averages by a distance with 30 wickets at 9.63, but he never fully recovered and in 1950 was forced to retire. The injury allowed him to bowl occasionally and he became player, coach and groundsman with Durham, then a Minor County. In 1960, Aspinall joined the first-class umpire's list; he was unobtrusively efficient and lasted for 21 years before being dropped without much ceremony just short of his official retirement. In the winters, he worked as a joiner.

AUSTIN, HENRY WILFRED, died on August 26, 2000, his 94th birthday. "Bunny" Austin was the last British man to reach a Wimbledon singles final, in 1938, and a member of the Great Britain team that won the Davis Cup every year from 1933 to 1936. As a schoolboy, Austin opened the batting for Repton with the future England player Bryan Valentine, and was described as "sound and imperturbable" in *Wisden* 1926 (see Never a Famous Cricketer, p. 40).

BALDERSTONE, JOHN CHRISTOPHER, died suddenly at his home on March 6, 2000, aged 59; he had been suffering from cancer. Chris Balderstone – "Baldy" – was a formidably fit man who became a Test cricketer and an international umpire after a successful career in football. In the 1960s, he was a stylish inside-forward for Huddersfield Town and Carlisle United who played occasionally as an all-rounder for Yorkshire in the close season. However, when he passed 30, he was brought to Leicestershire by Ray Illingworth, and changed emphasis to become primarily a

[*Patrick Eagar*

Chris Balderstone during his first Test innings, against West Indies at Leeds in 1976.

cricketer. The move quickly paid dividends: his cool-headed 41 not out won Leicestershire the inaugural Benson and Hedges final, and Balderstone the Gold Award. Thereafter he flourished, averaging over 40 in the Championship in the next two years and, in 1974, also finishing top of the county bowling averages with his back-up left-arm spin. He still found time to play for Carlisle, and scored the penalty against Spurs that briefly put them top of the old First Division in September 1974.

However, his most famous day came a year later, and it was also Leicestershire's. On September 15, 1975, he was playing cricket at Chesterfield but had also committed himself to turn out for Doncaster Rovers against Brentford. This was the day

Leicestershire won their first-ever Championship, which they secured with bowling bonus points. Towards the close, Balderstone was still batting and the Doncaster manager, Stan Anderson, was pacing the Belle Vue ground with increasing agitation. With the Championship decided, Balderstone could easily have given his wicket away and headed off to football, but it was not in his nature. He stayed till stumps were drawn, had to change in the car, played his usual solid game of football, then came back to complete his century next morning.

His professionalism and courage earned him a place in the last two Tests against the fearsome 1976 West Indies, when he was already 35. It was a time when the selectors were struggling for candidates and, though starting respectably with 35 in the first innings at Headingley, he was twice blown away for nought by Michael Holding at The Oval, and left out of the winter tour party. He continued in county cricket for another ten years, and made his 32nd first-class century against Sussex when he was 45. This was a tribute to his fitness, though he was never fast: Martin Johnson once noted that his speed matched his initials – JCB. In 1988 he became a first-class umpire; he stood in two one-day internationals and made the historic decision, at Lord's in 1993, when Robin Smith was the first player given out by TV replay in an English Test. Genial and even-tempered, Baldy never attracted an unkind word on the circuit, which was a response to his own attitude. Barry Dudleston, a colleague as both player and umpire, said: "He only ever saw good in the game, both football and cricket."

BARKER, MAURICE PERCY, who died on September 6, 2000, aged 83, displayed considerable potential as a fast bowler for Warwickshire in 1946. Using his full 6ft 4in and keeping a good length, he took seven for 68 against Yorkshire at Edgbaston, and after five matches had taken 16 wickets at 23.62. However, Barker was already in the police force and opted out of county cricket. He was a stalwart of the local club in his home town of Leamington Spa.

BARRACLOUGH, ERIC SCOTT, who died in 1999, aged 77, was a professional for Bradford in the Bradford League for 15 seasons. He played twice for Yorkshire in 1949 and 1950, opening the bowling on his debut with Freddie Trueman – against Minor Counties at Lord's.

BEAR, MICHAEL JOHN, died on April 7, 2000, aged 66, after many years of heart trouble. Micky Bear was a pioneer of modern fielding techniques. He spent 15 seasons with Essex from 1954 to 1968 and, in an era when great athletes were still rare in English cricket, he was a stunningly good outfielder, able to move fast and throw flat, hard returns on the full from the furthest boundaries. He was also a gutsy and sometimes flamboyant – if not always fluent – left-handed opening batsman, who scored nine centuries in a career averaging 24.25.

BECHER, Major Sir WILLIAM FANE WRIXON, Bt, MC, died on January 6, 2000, aged 84. Billy Becher was a batsman who played three matches for Sussex before World War II. However, he was best-known in cricket as secretary of I Zingari, a post he held for 40 years. E. W. Swanton said: "He became the life and soul of the club, restoring its traditions both on the field and off." Becher won an immediate MC after leading a bayonet charge in North Africa in 1943.

BECK, JOHN EDWARD FRANCIS, who died on April 23, 2000, aged 65, played for New Zealand before appearing for his province, Wellington, and made his Test debut in dramatic circumstances. A left-handed bat and athletic fieldsman, he had been picked as a 19-year-old for the 1953-54 tour of South Africa on the basis of his schoolboy form and his raw promise. When Eric Dempster was unfit, he was drafted into the team for the Second Test at Ellis Park. Beck came out to bat for the first time on

Boxing Day with New Zealand 24 for three, two men retired hurt, and the dressing-room in shock because of news from home on Christmas Day that Bob Blair's fiancée was among the 151 killed in a rail accident. Though having to face Neil Adcock and Dave Ironside on a fiery pitch, he scored 16 in 52 minutes: eventually Bert Sutcliffe returned, with his head bandaged, to smash an unbeaten 80, helped by Blair, who heroically came in at No. 11. A week later, in more comfortable circumstances at Cape Town, Beck hit a six to take New Zealand to 500 in a Test innings for the first time, and was then run out for 99 by a direct hit. He scored 48 in the final Test at Port Elizabeth, and was thought to have a bright future.

However, Wellington did not pick him until the final match of the following season, and he was omitted from the next New Zealand tour. He finally consolidated his place for Wellington with a spectacular 149 against Canterbury in 1955-56, and was restored to the Test side against West Indies. He made New Zealand's top score of the Dunedin Test, 66 in just 81 minutes, and a further 55 at Wellington, and was still in the team at Eden Park when New Zealand finally won their first Test match, at the 45th attempt: his 38 was important in a low-scoring match. Thereafter, Beck drifted out of both the New Zealand and the Wellington team. He played only two matches in four seasons before making a Plunket Shield comeback in 1961-62 and, against Central Districts, hitting 103 not out, his second first-class century. His career was described by Don Neely as "one of the great mysteries in New Zealand cricket". And John Reid, his captain in 1955-56, said he was "crammed with natural ability". However, it is said he fell among the boozier elements of the team from the start, and never applied himself, especially to the failings in his defensive technique. He died just three days before a reunion of the team who took part in the maiden victory.

BOSCH, TERTIUS, died in hospital on February 13, 2000, aged 33. He had been suffering from the rare nervous disease, Guillain-Barré Syndrome. Bosch was one of the new generation of Afrikaner cricketers who emerged during the years of isolation, and at Bridgetown in 1991-92 he opened the bowling with Allan Donald in South Africa's first Test of their return to international cricket. His three victims included Brian Lara. Earlier, Bosch had played in two one-day internationals, including a game against New Zealand in the 1992 World Cup when his bowling was punished by Mark Greatbatch. A tall, strong, athletic man, he generated good pace from a short run-up, accompanied by a fearsome grunt: he grunted so loudly one day at Newlands that the crowd joined in. But the dressing-room view was that he could not switch off his personal amiability. "He seemed to lack the self-confidence and raw aggression which the great pace bowlers have," according to coach Bob Woolmer. "He had a mean bouncer," said team-mate Jonty Rhodes, "but used to apologise next ball for bowling it." A career in dentistry enabled him to adopt a more relaxed approach to his cricket. Bosch began playing at school in Vereeniging, and was spotted by Anton Ferreira while bowling in the nets at university. He joined Northern Transvaal, sharing the new ball with Fanie de Villiers, then later moved to Natal where, when Shaun Pollock and Lance Klusener were playing for South Africa in 1996-97, he shouldered much of the burden and helped the side to two trophies. He left a widow and two young children.

BOX-GRAINGER, CHRISTOPHER CHARLES WALTER, who died on November 20, 2000, aged 79, was chairman of the Cricket Society from 1967 to 1983 and a tireless enthusiast for the game. Before retiring from business, he was marketing director of a phone company.

BROOKE-TAYLOR, DAVID CHARLES KIRBY, who died on July 17, 2000, aged 80, was an amateur batsman who played 15 games for Derbyshire in the late 1940s. Against Northamptonshire at Rushden in 1947, he led his team to victory by hitting 61 not out with two sixes and ten fours.

BROWN, GEORGE RAINY REYNOLDS, who died on April 15, 2000, aged 94, was one of the last survivors of county cricket in the 1920s. He was one of only five players (like Jim Hutchinson, who also died in 2000) known to have lived more than 75 years after their Championship debut – which he made aged 18. Brown was a slow left-armer and useful batsman who played 23 times for Essex, twice for Cambridge and occasionally for the Europeans in India after he went there to work for ICI.

BURGESS, GORDON CHARLES, who died on September 2, 2000, aged 81, played seven matches for Auckland between 1941 and 1954. He later became a leading administrator, culminating in a term as president of the New Zealand Cricket Council. Burgess managed the team that ended New Zealand's 40-year wait for a win in a Test series, in Pakistan in 1969-70. Among the players was his son, Mark, who later captained the national team.

CAMERON, JOHN HEMSLEY, who died on February 13, 2000, aged 85, was vice-captain of the West Indian team to England in 1939, when his major triumph was bowling Harold Gimblett with his second ball in Test cricket. His cricketing peak had come eight years earlier, however: as an 17-year-old from Taunton School, playing for The Rest against the Lord's Schools, he took all ten wickets for 49 – plus the only two second innings wickets to fall. He bowled leg-breaks and an extremely cunning googly, and Sir Pelham Warner suggested that "no boy bowler of this type has ever excelled him". A year later, Cameron was in the Somerset team, but suddenly he lost the knack. "I wasn't what they call a wrist-spinner," he recalled years later, "I did it all with my fingers. Now I'd lost all control with them. I think the trouble was that they got too fat." He went up to Cambridge, where he won a Blue three times, and carried on playing for Somerset as an orthodox batsman who bowled fairly ordinary off-spin. He later taught, and unsuccessfully applied to be both Somerset's captain and secretary. As a black man, in an area where they were then rarities, Cameron was known in his early days as either "Monkey" or "Snowball". He was much-liked, but as David Foot wrote: "In private moments, he would confide his unhappy experiences at the wrong end of the colour bar."

CARRICK, PHILLIP, who died of leukaemia on January 11, 2000, aged 47, was captain of Yorkshire from 1987 to 1989. The highlight of his 24-year career with the club came when he led them to the Benson and Hedges Cup in 1987, perhaps Yorkshire's proudest day since they last won the County Championship 19 years earlier. "Fergie" Carrick was a slow left-arm bowler, all too acutely aware that neither he nor his team-mates could live up to the club's great traditions. In 1975, he took 79 wickets, including eight in an innings. But though he could turn the ball quite sharply then, he was forced to become more and more defensive in his bowling, and his arm got lower and lower. He was also a robust late-order hitter with a good eye, once smashing 105 on a terrible Headingley pitch in the 1978 Roses match. A man with a passion for cricket, and Yorkshire cricket in particular, he spent much of his time as captain frowning and doing the double teapot when things went wrong – but it was a mark of his commitment rather than of any ill-nature. Even on the worst days, he was always ready to stay behind, chatting and theorising about the game and its strategies. In 1989, with the team struggling again, he wrote to the committee calling for the abolition of the policy of picking only Yorkshire-born players. He was turned down, and the affair was a factor in his loss of the captaincy, but his attempt helped pave the way for the end of the tradition three years later. Carrick played on until 1993, and was desperately keen to become the fifth player to reach 10,000 runs and 1,000 wickets for Yorkshire: he failed by just six runs. A Surrey player even dropped a catch to help him in the final match, but play had to be abandoned. He went on to captain Pudsey Congs in the Bradford League and was still playing in August 1999 when he became ill. By this time, he had reached the first-class umpires' reserve list as a prelude to possible full-time

[*Patrick Eagar*

Yorkshire captain Phil Carrick holds the Benson and Hedges Cup after their 1987 victory over Northamptonshire.

umpiring, the perfect job for such an enthusiast. Carrick's premature death came only two years after that of his predecessor as Yorkshire captain, David Bairstow. His funeral, in a packed Bradford Cathedral, was attended by five England captains. One of them, Mike Gatting, said: "There was never anywhere too far for Phil to go to see a friend, and we all felt the same about him." The coach, Ralph Middlebrook, said Carrick had helped hundreds of young players: "He may not have been as good a bowler as Wilfred Rhodes, but in terms of acumen I would put him in the same bracket."

CHIDAMBARAM, MUTHIAH ANNAMALAI, who died on January 19, 2000, aged 81, was an Indian industrialist and cricket administrator. As president of the Indian Board of Control in the early 1960s, he introduced air travel for Test players, increased their match fees and started a fund for retired cricketers. He was the prime mover behind the new Test ground in Madras, opened in 1972 and named after him. As founder of Automobile Products of India, he introduced the motor scooter to the subcontinent.

CLARK, LEONARD STANLEY, who died on May 2, 2000, aged 86, was an amateur batsman who played 24 times for Essex in the first two seasons after the war, winning his cap in 1947. His highest score was 64 against Northamptonshire at Ilford.

CLARKE, BERNARD HENRY, who died on October 23, 2000, aged 86, was the Northamptonshire scorer from 1982 to 1989.

COSGROVE, ERNEST W., died on October 19, 2000, aged 51, after a long illness. A cheery, bear-like man, Ernie Cosgrove was one of the efficient band of enthusiasts who make Australian scoring the best in the world, and became the New South Wales scorer in 1985-86, doing the job in both state games and Sydney Tests. When his work as a schoolteacher took him to the outback town of Moree, he would commute hundreds of miles to games at the SCG.

COTTENHAM, Eighth Earl of, died on October 20, 2000, aged 51. He was reported to have been suffering from depression. As Viscount Crowhurst, "Charlie" Cottenham captained Eton against Harrow at Lord's in 1967. He was a fast bowler of some pace and ability and also turned out for Northamptonshire Second Eleven, appearing in the averages as C. Crowhurst and then as the Earl of Cottenham after he succeeded to the title on his father's death in 1968. Understandably, he had no wish to become a professional cricketer. Christened Kenelm Charles Everard Digby Pepys (pronounced Pepp-is), he was a well-known man-about-London in the 1970s, and later ran a successful chain of English-language schools while playing a good deal of cricket for such clubs as the Arabs and Eton Ramblers. He was also an international cross-country rider.

COWDREY of TONBRIDGE, Baron, died on December 4, 2000, aged 67, after suffering a stroke earlier in the year. Michael Colin Cowdrey was successively known to the world as Michael Cowdrey – when *Wisden* reported on him as a 13-year-old schoolboy prodigy – Colin Cowdrey, Sir Colin and finally Lord Cowdrey, when he became the first English cricketer to be given a peerage. In an era of outstanding English batsmen, he was the most durable, with a Test career spanning more than two decades. On his journey from teenage phenomenon to sporting statesman, he was at the heart of the game for half a century: Cowdrey was the first man to play 100 Tests, captained England 27 times and scored almost 43,000 first-class runs – 7,624 of them in Tests. In later years, he played a major role behind the scenes in marrying the traditions of international cricket with modern demands. Yet it was still possible, and only mildly unkind, for one of his contemporaries, Fred Trueman, to describe Cowdrey on his death as "a terrific talent who never fulfilled his potential". Amid the triumphs there was often a vague sense of unease: of unexpected failures, opportunities not taken. Despite everything, Cowdrey never achieved the greatest accolade English cricket can offer: he toured Australia six times, which equalled a record held by Johnny Briggs, but never once was he selected as captain; every time a more forceful figure shoved him out of the way when it mattered.

His entire early career, and most of the rest of it, was the stuff of male fantasy. His father, Ernest, a tea planter in India, was a first-class cricketer too, scoring 48 for the Europeans against MCC at Madras. Colin's parents met at a cricket club and, when he was born on Christmas Eve 1932, he was – famously – given the initials MCC, just in case anyone doubted his destiny. On the plantation Colin would play with an Indian boy eight years his senior, with occasional supervision from his father who initiated a rule, to encourage correct technique, that all leg-side shots would be given out. Colin was sent to a sporty prep school, Homefield, and apparently reached a century in his first proper match, only to give his wicket away and then discover that he had only 93. A modern thinker might be more conscious of the traumas rather than the triumphs. An only child – and not an insensitive one either – in the stern English schools of the 1940s, Colin did not see his parents for seven years owing to the twin tyrannies of distance and war. If, as countless spectators and writers later theorised, he had psychological flaws as a cricketer, who could be surprised? But skill at games is a great consolation to a boy, and Cowdrey was a natural: at golf, rackets and squash, as well as cricket. Within weeks of arriving at Tonbridge, he was in the First Eleven, though more for his leg-spin than his batting, and in the annual match against Clifton, then still played at Lord's, he scored 75 and 44, and took eight for 117. At 13, he was thought to be the youngest player ever at Lord's.

His leg-spin did not develop: Cowdrey later theorised that he could not grip a larger, adult, ball so well with his small hands, and that he lacked the necessary "bottle". But his batting began to flower gloriously: it was said that Maurice Tate, the last of his coaches at Tonbridge, would forget to signal while umpiring because he was so engrossed in Colin's strokeplay. As a 16-year-old he made an unbeaten 181 against the Buccaneers and was picked for Kent Second Eleven; at 17, he averaged 79 at school and, in August 1950, was eased into the county first team. At 18, just before he was due to go to Oxford, he scored 90 against Hampshire and 71 against the South Africans, became the youngest Kent player to be capped, and was picked for the Gentlemen at Scarborough against a Players side captained by Len Hutton. Cowdrey hit 106. At Oxford, his batting was impressive rather than earth-shattering. But he scored a century in the 1953 University Match, which prompted E. W. Swanton, in the *Daily Telegraph*, to compare him to Walter Hammond, the same thought that had struck Hutton two years earlier. He went close to 2,000 runs for Oxford and Kent that year but fell back in 1954 – he was astonished (more embarrassed than elated, according to one account) when he was chosen for the tour of Australia. He was 21. His parents saw him off at Tilbury; three weeks later, his father, aged 54, died of heart disease.

Only a few weeks after that, Cowdrey went out and attained cricketing manhood. Before he had even scored a Championship century, he made two hundreds in the match against a mighty New South Wales team. "He played throughout his two innings without a shadow of uncertainty," wrote Alan Ross, "the margin for error as negligible as in Hutton's own technique." The only question now was where, not whether, Cowdrey would bat in the Test match. In the end, England shied away from making him open – this time. He began with a crisp 40 in the defeat at Brisbane; at Sydney, in the Second Test, his partnership with Peter May turned the game; on New Year's Eve at Melbourne, he scored 102 out of 191 against Lindwall and Miller at their most incisive on a bad pitch: "a blend of leisurely driving and secure back play, of power and propriety," according to Ross. England won the game and, after he had made another 79 at Adelaide, the Ashes. A star was born.

But even in that glad, confident morning there were the first tiny clouds of criticism that would never go away. During his wonderful maiden century Cowdrey was becalmed on 56 for 40 minutes and, though it was now commonplace to compare him to Hammond, Hutton noted drily: "Wally was hungrier." When he came home, Cowdrey was conscripted into the RAF, then discharged after failing the medical because of damaged feet: he was attacked for this by MPs and anonymous letter-writers alike. An injured hand kept him out of all but one of the 1955 Tests. In the 1956 Ashes series he was obliged to open, which he never enjoyed, and South Africa that winter was a struggle. But by now Colin was married – to Penny, daughter of a Kent committee man (soon to be chairman), Stuart Chiesman, who ran a small chain of department stores in Kent. The son-in-law also rises and, though he was not a success in the drapery department at Lewisham, Cowdrey soon became a director of Chiesman's company. He was thus instantly freed from the cricket-or-business dilemma that had forced generations of amateurs out of the game prematurely, and which still haunted contemporaries such as May and Ted Dexter.

In 1957, he also became captain of Kent, a job he would hold for 15 seasons. But when West Indies toured that year, Cowdrey was not a certain selection for England. And when he went out to join May at 113 for three in the second innings of the opening Test at Edgbaston, England were still in thrall to Sonny Ramadhin and facing an innings defeat. It became one of the most famous Test match stands: 411 in eight hours 20 minutes. Not merely did they save the game, they transformed the relationship between the sides: Ramadhin was never a match-winner again. While May counter-attacked, Cowdrey stayed in his crease and played this most mysterious of bowlers as if he were an off-spinner, pushing forward and letting the leg-break go by. "Once Colin had committed himself to a policy of complete defence," said May later, "his technique was so good that he made no mistake in execution." Three weeks later, the other

Sir Donald Bradman and Colin Cowdrey at Adelaide Oval in 1974: both devoted their lives to promoting what is good in cricket.

Cowdrey reasserted himself and he smashed 152 at Lord's, followed by 55, 68 and two. England were now so dominant that he never needed to bat twice in any of the last four Tests. So, at last, his cricketing personality was starting to emerge fully. He would still be compared to Hammond, especially when he launched into his cover drive or pouched slip catches with absolute certainty. But still there was something of Hobbs: the lightness of touch both technically and spiritually – with a sense that he sympathised with a bowler a shade too much for the sternest tastes. And there was also something all his own: an introspection that, as at Edgbaston, could help him think through cricketing problems like a master detective, but at other times could exasperate even his closest admirers.

Cowdrey did not, between Tests, impose himself on county cricket: as with Hobbs, a hundred was enough, and he also found slow, constricting seamers rather tiresome (he would later name Barry Wood, the Lancashire dobber, as the bowler he hated facing most). He was arguably more impressive when the England ship sank in Australia in 1958-59 than against weak New Zealand the previous summer, and his century at Sydney saved England from a 5–0 whitewash. Soon, however, he was forced both to revert to opening and to take over as captain because May was ill. Ostensibly, both moves were successful: he continued to score steadily and England were unbeaten in his first ten Tests in charge, until Lord's 1961. For this game May was back in the side, and after it the selectors restored him to the captaincy for the rest of the Ashes series. Their friendship was solid – May's seniority was unquestioned and he was steadily fading out of the game – so Cowdrey still had every reason to assume he would return to the captaincy with the same certainty that characterised his rise to it.

But he chose not to go to India and Pakistan in 1961-62 (not an unusual decision at the time); Dexter took over, did well, and so began the saga that dominated English cricket throughout the 1960s. Should Cowdrey be captain? Or A.N. Other? With Walter Robins as chairman of selectors, the debate was widened before the 1962-63 Ashes tour to include the Rev. David Sheppard, who was encouraged away from his pastoral work in the East End by the possibility of captaincy. Dexter won the contest and Cowdrey was again No. 2, though he was the senior partner in the moment of glory, when he made 113 and 58 not out to secure victory at Melbourne. By now the politics were submerging the cricket. Dexter stayed as captain in 1963. This provided the single most compelling image of Cowdrey's career: the moment he walked out to bat at Lord's with a broken arm. In the event, he had to do nothing, but the injury initially kept him out of contention for the 1963-64 subcontinental tour when Dexter opted out. So M. J. K. Smith, an Oxonian protégé of Cowdrey, took over. For the next three years the captaincy switched between Dexter and Smith and, for the third time, Cowdrey went to Australia as faithful Achates, this time to Smith. He was now nearing his mid-thirties, and might have been edging towards retirement, as Dexter was, but when Smith was axed after England were hammered by West Indies at the start of the 1966 series, there seemed no one else.

The next three Tests also went badly, however, and, after a disaster at Headingley, Cowdrey was dropped from the side completely. With Brian Close as captain, England won at The Oval by an innings, and next year Close led England to five wins out of six against India and Pakistan. Cowdrey spent most of summer 1967 leading Kent to both the Gillette Cup and their most spirited challenge for the Championship since the 1920s, but he was brought back by England at a moment that ensured he missed Kent's crucial match against Yorkshire, which they lost. Close's reputation was sky-high, and every schoolboy (it was after all the 1960s) could assert that a tough-minded professional, raised in the hard northern tradition, was a better leader than an effete southerner like Cowdrey. The argument only intensified when Close was sacked after a time-wasting incident and a row with a spectator in county cricket. He was vetoed as captain for the West Indies tour, and Cowdrey was back, but very clearly as second choice.

Again he returned in triumph, having cashed in on Garry Sobers's much-reviled declaration in Port-of-Spain by scoring 71 himself ("Never has Cowdrey been more superb," said *The Guardian*). And though England yet again failed to win the Ashes in 1968, no one blamed him and there was much rejoicing when he made a hundred in his 100th Test. At the start of 1969, he was more firmly in the saddle than ever. Then an Achilles tendon snapped. His replacement, Ray Illingworth, was neither a regular Test player nor an experienced captain, but he proved a success and the following summer, before the Ashes tour, the selectors had to choose again. When he gave Cowdrey the news, Alec Bedser, the chairman, was most apologetic.

Cowdrey's fifth Ashes tour, his fourth as vice-captain, was a miserable one, even though the Ashes were won. He was ill for much of the following summer, and his career might have been drawing peacefully to its close. In 1970, he had led Kent to the Championship; having inherited a very weak side, he bequeathed Mike Denness a mighty one. But he did not let go, even after reaching his 100th hundred in 1973. Though he was sometimes left out of the Kent side, especially in one-day cricket, he was called up for his sixth Ashes tour in 1974-75 when an optimistic but ill-prepared England party suddenly ran into the hurricane-force of Lillee and Thomson.

England asked Cowdrey, then well into his 42nd year, if he would consider helping out; "I'd love to," he replied. Australian bewilderment was redoubled when, in the Second Test of that most virile of series, this rotund figure ambled towards the crease and introduced himself to Thomson: "I don't believe we've met. My name's Cowdrey". But he played him as well as anyone else. He retired the following summer, but not before scoring 151 to lead Kent to a stunning win against the Australians at Canterbury. A few days later he played his last game against the Aussies, for MCC at Lord's – and made a pair. "It was a vivid summarisation of his career," wrote Ivo Tennant, "of the way cricket took him to the very heights and back again." Though he played once in 1976, Colin was never able to take the field for Kent with his eldest son, Christopher, who was just about to break into the team, and later captained England once himself.

No one ever doubted Colin Cowdrey's cricketing ability. Fred Titmus has talked with awe about how, in dead county games, he would let John Murray behind the stumps nominate in advance the shot he would play: "Amazing talent, done without showing off." But there was always that enigmatic quality. Trevor Bailey said that he was too nice to demolish an attack truly, and that he worried too much. He certainly did worry. After his triumph at Melbourne in 1962-63, John Woodcock congratulated him and said he must be relieved it was all over, only to be told: "Yes, but now there's the next one to worry about." His character also caused some debate. Every cricket fan knew that Cowdrey walked when he thought he was out, and every prep school master thought this made him a hero. Professionals muttered darkly that he behaved differently on soft days in county cricket than at moments of crisis, banking on his reputation with umpires to get him through. "He was not generally liked by cricketers," said Illingworth. This had to be balanced against the thousands of people – high and low – who were charmed by his kindness and thoughtfulness. The unanimous judgment, though, was that he was indecisive, a captain incapable of inspiring his players and so much a ditherer that he even had to be persuaded to go for the runs at Port-of-Spain on that great day in 1967-68.

His later life shed unexpected light on all these speculations. In 1978, he left his wife and went to live with Lady Herries, a daughter of the Duke of Norfolk, causing temporary rifts with his children. They later married and she became famous in her own right as a racehorse trainer. In 1986, after some years pottering inconsequentially doing PR for Barclays, Cowdrey became president of MCC for the bicentenary year. He turned this Buggins' turn sinecure into an improbable platform for dynamic change. He forced out the long-serving secretary, Jack Bailey, to end an institutionalised feud with the Test and County Cricket Board, and meanwhile made the first moves to sever the umbilical cord between the MCC and ICC, remaining as ICC chairman after giving up the presidency. It was possible to have differing views of Cowdrey's actions – pro-Bailey members voted down the committee report and accounts – but dithery they were not. In the midst of it all, he was forced to have a heart by-pass operation and missed the bicentenary match and banquet. He remained ICC chairman until 1993, seeing through the change that made it a serious international body rather than an imperial relic, and continued active – given his new life in the Norfolk family – in helping run Arundel cricket and at Kent, where Christopher and his brother, Graham, ensured there was a Cowdrey on the books until 1998: a 48-year span.

In retirement, his involvement was thus more successful than all of the men preferred to him for on-field leadership: May, Dexter and Illingworth all failed as chairman of selectors, and Smith was an absurdly invisible tour manager. Cowdrey's reputation as a kindly elder statesman grew and grew: he was knighted in 1992 and in 1997 became a life peer, the second cricketer after Learie Constantine to be elevated to the House of Lords. He enjoyed himself there but never quite bestrode the Lords in the way he bestrode Lord's: there turned out not to be time, and perhaps his non-cricketing destiny should have been as an ambassador rather than any kind of politician. His last great service was to initiate "The Spirit of Cricket", the Preamble to the 2000 Code of Laws. Through his last years, he would often travel hundreds of miles to make beautifully crafted speeches to cricketing gatherings, expecting no money at all. "He loved to be loved," said a friend, and perhaps a man, however great, needs reassurance forever when he spends seven years of childhood apart from his parents. He was loved. And the memory of him in later years – portly, a fraction stooped, his fey voice ever-solicitous about all-comers – will remain, almost as indelibly as the memory of him in his pomp: fairly portly even then, caressing the best bowlers' finest efforts past cover as though it were the simplest trick in the world.

CROWE, DAVID WILLIAM, who died on May 11, 2000, aged 66, was a left-handed opener who played once for Wellington and twice for Canterbury in the 1950s. He was better known for fathering two New Zealand Test captains: Martin and Jeff. He followed their careers at close quarters, making friends everywhere thanks to his sound knowledge and rich humour.

DANIELL, NIGEL JOHN, who died on February 27, 2000, aged 85, was Somerset secretary in 1950. The job had previously been held by his father, John, a former club captain.

DAVEY, PHILIP JOHN, who died on December 8, 2000, aged 87, was an occasional amateur medium-pacer for Somerset from 1934 to 1937. Of his 22 wickets, the first was the one he cherished: Jack Hobbs, in his last season, caught by Arthur Wellard for 15. A month later, he induced an extraordinary Worcestershire collapse at Frome, finishing with figures of 9.2–3–9–6. Davey was a Taunton boy who went up to Cambridge, where he failed to get a first-class game. Teaching duties restricted his availability for the county.

DAVIS, MICHAEL JOHN, who died on October 13, 2000, aged 57, was a fast bowler signed by Northamptonshire after taking 46 wickets for Cheshire in 1961. He was inhibited by injuries and made only one first-class appearance in three seasons: against Oxford in 1963. He then returned to Cheshire.

DEARY, JOHN, MBE, who died on March 6, 2000, aged 72, was physiotherapist at The Oval from 1984 to 1996.

DEAS, KENNETH ROBIN, died on October 20, 2000, aged 73. Ken Deas was a fringe batsman and occasional slow left-armer for Auckland over a span of 14 seasons between 1947-48 and 1960-61. He also played for Scotland while working as a pharmacist in Edinburgh in the mid-1950s. Deas became best known as an administrator and selector for both Auckland and New Zealand, jobs in which he displayed astuteness and attention to detail but, above all, a sense of fun. Don Cameron, in the *New Zealand Herald*, said he saw "good humour, and good fellowship, as essential to the game he loved".

DE COURCY, JAMES HARRY, died on June 20, 2000, aged 73. Jimmy de Courcy was a stylish right-hand Australian batsman picked for the 1953 England tour, even though he played his club cricket in the Newcastle area of New South Wales and thus rarely faced the top-class bowling of the Sydney grades. But he had won acclaim for his daring strokeplay in an era when Australian cricket was becoming more cautious. He played in the last three Ashes Tests; Jack Fingleton called his 41 on debut, on a difficult pitch at Old Trafford, "a great innings, yes, a great one... much better than a few Test centuries under good conditions". He did little in the other two, but scored a scintillating 204 against a Combined Services attack led by Freddie Trueman at Kingston, and was thought likely to have a bright future. However, he was suddenly dropped from the New South Wales team 18 months later, picked only occasionally after that, and was not selected again for Australia. He remained a legend in Newcastle cricket for many years and also attained a kind of immortality when Tim Rice consciously picked the name Walter de Courcy as adviser to the American grand master, Trumper, in the musical *Chess*. Off the field he was notoriously taciturn, hence the nickname "Words". He lived and died in Newcastle, where he worked as a boilermaker.

DENNE, PETER HENRY, who died of cancer on May 24, 2000, aged 50, played ten times for Western Province in the early 1970s. He was a powerful middle-order batsman whose debut 55 against Transvaal remained his highest score.

DENNIS, FRANK, who died on November 21, 2000, aged 93, was a fast bowler for Yorkshire from 1928 to 1933. He had an extremely effective year in 1929 when he took 84 wickets, more than half his first-class total. *Wisden* praised his pace, though not his accuracy. With the attack in transition after the death of Roy Kilner and the retirement of Abe Waddington, Dennis had plenty of chances, but he was never as effective again. Bill Bowes and Hedley Verity soon became the bowling mainstays and Dennis faded into the Leagues and Minor Counties cricket with Cheshire. In 1948, he was persuaded to join a fruit farm scheme in New Zealand. The venture failed, but he stayed in the Christchurch area, never visited England again, and was a coach and selector for Canterbury. Len Hutton married Dennis's younger sister; he was thus uncle to Richard Hutton as well as Simon Dennis, who also played for Yorkshire.

DOWNES, OTHNIEL D'ARCY, died on April 25, 2000, aged 65. Despite his improbable nickname, "Hitler" Downes was a much-loved figure in Barbadian cricket. A whippy fast bowler, he was plucked from a poor area of Bridgetown to represent the island in 1957-58, although he had never played top-division league cricket, and took five for 24 on debut. He appeared in three more matches before quicker bowlers – including Wes Hall and Charlie Griffith – elbowed him from the team. In any case, he needed to make a living as a merchant seaman. Downes remained a passionate cricket-watcher and coach; among his protégés was Sherwin Campbell.

DYSON, JACK, who died on November 16, 2000, aged 66, was one of the leading all-round sportsmen of the 1950s. His career reached its apogee in 1956 when he won an FA Cup winner's medal with Manchester City, scoring the second goal in the 3–1 win mainly famous for the broken neck suffered by the City goalkeeper, Bert Trautmann. A few weeks later he was instrumental in Lancashire becoming the first team to win a first-class match without losing a wicket (Leicestershire 108 and 122; Lancashire 166 for nought declared and 66 for nought). Dyson shared unbroken opening stands with Alan Wharton; Lancashire declared their first innings to catch the opposition on a drying wicket. The heroes were rewarded with a crate of beer each by the committee. Dyson's briefly glorious football career faltered because of injuries, but as a cricketer he lasted longer. However, his only century in 150 first-class matches came against Scotland, and he had to cement his place with back-up off-breaks, taking seven for 83 at Taunton in 1960. Lancashire sacked him for insubordination later that year, but he returned in 1963 for two more seasons. In his days of stardom, Dyson married a beauty queen, but his later life was evidently blighted by poverty and unhappiness. When he died in an Oldham hospital, officials had to appeal for relatives to come forward.

EATON, PETER JOHN, who died suddenly on February 9, 2000, aged 57, was the Sussex head groundsman for 32 years, having been assistant to Len Creese for five years before that. He presided over his square with loving care and gruff good humour. For many years, Hove had some of the fastest pitches in the country, and Eaton won the Groundsman of the Year award three times. In recent years he was one of the ECB's deputy pitch consultants.

EDWARDS, PETER JOHN, who died on February 18, 2000, aged 63, was secretary/general manager of Essex from 1979 until his death. After working as manager of a brickworks, he took over the county (beating off 350 other applicants) in the year they finally began winning trophies, and matched the success on the field by bringing in modern marketing techniques that helped turn Essex grounds into huge encampments of sponsors' tents. Edwards loved Essex cricket, having been a member since he was ten, so his progressive leadership was matched by a rare empathy for the supporters' concerns. Though he stayed out of cricketing decisions, he kept a firm, even authoritarian, grip on everything else at the club: his finest hour was probably when he shooed the TV cameras off the players' balcony during a live interview after Yorkshire won the Sunday League at Chelmsford in 1983. As Essex made a financial success of the three-day game, Edwards bitterly opposed the move to four-day cricket, which he called "an absolute nonsense", and was often a lone opposition voice when he was elected to the ECB management board in 1997. He was painted by Lord's officials as a reactionary, which was an even bigger nonsense. His insistent voice was in favour of dynamic, popular Championship cricket as a spectator sport, and it will be much missed. "I work very, very long hours," he said in 1989, and predicted: "I shall die young because of the strains of it, but I still think it's a marvellous job to be in."

ELLIOTT, FRANK HENRY, who died on January 1, 2000, aged 66, was heavily involved in grassroots cricket, and was on the management committee of the National Cricket Association for 25 years. When the administration of the English game was restructured in 1997, he was elected to the management board of the new ECB.

FERNANDO, WIRANTHA, died on April 17, 2000, aged 40, after being attacked by a mob. Fernando was a minister in Sri Lanka's Western Provincial Council. A gifted batsman, he scored a hundred in each innings of a match for Prince of Wales College in 1975 and went on to represent Sri Lanka Under-19; he captained the team in a game in Pakistan when Ranjan Madugalle was injured. He also played for Moratuwa and Colombo Colts, and captained Colts to second place in Sri Lanka's Division One.

FERRALL, Sir RAYMOND ALFRED, CBE, died on June 1, 2000, aged 94. Ray Ferrall was an orthodox and skilful batsman who was a mainstay of the Tasmanian side in the 1930s when they played only occasional first-class matches. He made 67 on his debut against Victoria in 1933-34, and then a fine 84 in the return match at the MCG. Both times he shared big stands with Jack Badcock. He averaged 34.12 in his five matches. Ferrall was better known as a businessman: he developed his father's general store into a major food company, and held a string of directorships and public offices in Tasmania. At 91, he beat off a burglar – and was still writing a business column in the *Launceston Examiner*. He reached the final three in the voting for Tasmanian of the Century.

FORD, NEVILLE MONTAGUE, who died on June 15, 2000, aged 93, was acclaimed as "the new Jessop" after a succession of blazing innings at Oxford between 1928 and 1930. He came from a family of sportsmen – his grandfather played for MCC in 1839; his father (later headmaster of Harrow) and six uncles played for Repton, three of the uncles winning Cambridge Blues and one, F. G. J. Ford, playing for England. Neville Ford was a superb rackets and fives player, and as a batsman he was capable of sustaining his hard hitting. Four of his five first-class centuries were above 150, including 180 against Surrey in 1930, when he put on 276 in two hours 50 minutes with P. G. T. Kingsley. He also played 31 matches for Derbyshire and one for Middlesex without quite justifying the Jessopian description. He became a director of the paper-makers Wiggins Teape, and remained a popular figure in the grander wandering clubs.

[*Hulton Getty*

Roy Fredericks played his cricket with a true West Indian flavour, even if it brought his downfall: hooking Dennis Lillee early in the 1975 World Cup final, he trod on his wicket.

FREDERICKS, ROY CLIFTON, who died of cancer on September 5, 2000, aged 57, was one of the handful of batsmen who distinguished themselves by counter-attacking the great pace bowlers of the 1970s. He is remembered best for his blazing performance at Perth in 1975-76, when he raced to one of the most astonishing of all Test centuries. This series was eventually won 5–1 by Australia, with Lillee and Thomson at full pelt. But in the Second Test, on an incredibly fast WACA pitch, Fredericks took them on in amazing fashion. The harder they banged the ball in, the harder he cut and hooked. Into the second morning, he opened what might have been a diffident reply to Australia's 329: at lunch West Indies were 130 for one off 14 eight-ball overs; the 200 came up in the 22nd. Fredericks went on to reach a hundred from 71 balls and, though he grew tired, turned it into a match-winning 169. This was merely a distillation of his entire career. "There has," as Mike Selvey wrote, "probably never been a better or more willing exponent of the hook." His most famous single shot was a failure, however: right at the start of the first World Cup final, he hooked a ball from Lillee over long-leg – only to tread on his wicket in the process.

A small (about 5ft 6in) left-hander from Berbice, Fredericks made his debut for what was then British Guiana in 1963-64, and for nine years and 59 Tests – from 1968-69 until the World Series schism of 1977 – he provided half the answer to the conundrum of who should open for West Indies. This had been intractable even when Conrad Hunte was playing, and remained a source of constant change and argument until Gordon Greenidge emerged to join Fredericks in the mid-1970s. He preferred to tilt his cap back, rock on to his left foot and smash the ball hard, but he was capable of playing as a traditional opener. When West Indies first brought him in, for the 1968 Boxing Day Test at Melbourne after Clive Lloyd was injured, he batted throughout a slightly shortened, bitterly cold opening day while the rest of the batting collapsed around him. With 76 and 47, he emerged with distinction from a drab performance.

This was a period of steep but brief West Indies decline and, though it took him a while to perform as well again, Fredericks became an important brick in the rebuilding process. He scored three fifties in six innings when West Indies lost a series to England (for the last time until 2000) in 1969 but did not score a century until February 1972 against New Zealand at Sabina Park, when his 163 was overshadowed by the double-century from debutant Lawrence Rowe. They put on 269. At Edgbaston in 1973, he scored 150 in his patient mode – taking eight hours and surviving a crisis when he was completely bogged down against Ray Illingworth – and a cautious 138 to ensure the draw when West Indies were unexpectedly up against it in the Lord's Test of 1976. A month later at Headingley, he returned to the attack, scoring 79 before lunch and reaching 109 in 156 minutes. However, even then he was just doing an opener's job: on that day everyone else really cut loose and West Indies had 437 by the close. Though he scored eight Test hundreds in his 109 innings, this was a low ratio for a player who averaged above 40 – he preferred the blistering fifty.

Fredericks averaged 63.83 for Guyana. In his three years with Glamorgan (1971–73), he was less consistent but spasmodically magnificent and extremely popular – not least with his opening partner Alan Jones, even though Jones described his calling as "terrible" and suffered from his musical tastes when they roomed together. On an amazing day at Swansea, they put on 330 against Northamptonshire, at the time a record for any Glamorgan wicket; they still lost. Fredericks announced his retirement in 1978, while playing World Series, but five years later, aged 40, he made a comeback for Guyana, batted twice, and scored 103 against Trinidad & Tobago and 217 against Jamaica. It was an astonishing way to finish. By then, he was already a junior minister in Forbes Burnham's left-wing Guyanese government, responsible for youth and sport, and known as Comrade; earlier in his playing days he had generally endeared himself by calling everyone "old chap". He remained attached to the government, but later concentrated on coaching. By then, openers around the world were batting in anonymous helmets. Fredericks was one of the last players who not only relished facing the best bowlers but looked as though he did.

GABY, RICHARD THOMAS, died on June 27, 2000, aged 91. "Young Dick" Gaby followed his father at Lord's, working there from 1929 to 1973 in the tradition of stern but kindly Lord's retainers. He began as a telegraph boy, phoning through the members' bets (and turning in a profit by collecting their tuppences for the phone, then making a single call), and after the war became club superintendent. When Denis Compton and Bill Edrich joined the groundstaff in the 1930s, it was Gaby who handed them a broom and told them: "If you learn to use a broom properly, then you'll learn to use a bat properly." He was also secretary and historian of the Cross Arrows club. His father – "Old Dick" – was on the MCC staff for 63 years.

GADNEY, BERNARD CECIL, who died on November 14, 2000, aged 91, was a promising Minor Counties batsman for Oxfordshire in the early 1930s. Earlier, he had been in the Stowe Eleven with the actor David Niven. B. C. Gadney's cricket, however, was secondary to his rugby: he was England's scrum-half and captain, and began the move that led to Prince Obolensky's famous try against the All Blacks in 1936. Gadney later became headmaster of Malsis, a Yorkshire prep school.

GILL, JAMES RUPERT, who died on October 18, 2000, aged 89, played one first-class match: for Gentlemen of Ireland against MCC in 1948. Jimmy Gill opened the batting in both innings and scored both a century and a duck. No one is known to have a comparable first-class record. His 106 gave the Irish first-innings lead in a drawn match, even though Bob Wyatt scored a century for MCC.

GRAHAM, PETER ARTHUR ONSLOW, who died on March 2, 2000, aged 79, played six games for Somerset as an amateur fast bowler in 1948. Like Colin Cowdrey, he was born in India and educated at Tonbridge. On the first morning of his debut, he took three Glamorgan wickets in a first-class friendly at Newport, and made 33 late in the game in a vain effort to save it. However, his appearances were restricted because he had to work on his father's farm; later he became a tobacco farmer in Southern Rhodesia.

GRIEVE, Major CHARLES FREDERICK, who died in June 2000, aged 86, played only one first-class cricket match but was one of the most admired games players of the 1930s. He fitted a game for Oxford against Derbyshire in 1936 (in which he achieved little) into a busy sporting schedule. Grieve was already a rugby Blue and Scotland's fly-half; he later won a golf Blue and went on the 1938 Lions tour of South Africa, playing a crucial role in the test win at Newlands. He had a lengthy army career and played a lot of club cricket. Once, he was reputedly called from the wicket while on 99 to be told his wife had given birth to a son – Grieve was out next ball.

GUTTERIDGE, LESLIE EDWARD STEPHEN, who died on July 9, 2000, aged 86, was a pioneering cricket bookseller. While running Epworth Books, primarily an arm of the Methodist Church, he started a sideline in cricket books at their shop in North London and turned it into an unrivalled centre of cricketana in the two decades after World War II. His 1955 catalogue listed a complete run of *Wisdens* at £150, an investment which would have multiplied almost 200 times by now. Gutteridge was an enthusiastic cricket historian and wrote the well-researched history of *Wisden* in the 100th edition in 1963. He emigrated to Canada in 1967 and, having been born in Edmonton, London, died in Edmonton, Alberta.

HALLAM, MAURICE RAYMOND, who died on January 1, 2000, aged 68, was the fixed point at the top of the Leicestershire batting order throughout the 1950s and 1960s. Though he scored 24,488 runs, his average (28.84) does little justice to the quality of his play. He enjoyed taking on fast bowlers who gave him room to manoeuvre, and often failed against the most persistent attacks. At his best, however, he could be devastating, scoring quickly, gracefully and powerfully. Four of his 32 centuries were doubles, and twice he scored 200 and 100 in the same match, a feat surpassed only by Zaheer Abbas and matched by Neil Taylor of Kent. Hallam was a local boy, and first made his mark as captain of the Leicester football team that won the 1945-46 national schools trophy in front of a 35,000 full house at Filbert Street. He never had quite that much attention at Grace Road, though local judges insisted he had the ability to play for England. He had two stints as Leicestershire captain, before and after Tony Lock, and some team-mates recall his approach as a shade too gentlemanly for a fractious dressing-room. His popularity remained undimmed, however, and, after his retirement, he was closely associated with cricket in the area: as captain and coach of the second team, a member of the county management committee and coach at Uppingham School from 1975 to 1995, where his pupils included Jonathan Agnew and James Whitaker.

HANLEY, MARTIN ANDREW, who died on June 2, 2000, aged 81, was a South African off-spinner whose career coincided with that of two greats: Athol Rowan and Hugh Tayfield. His bowling was well-flighted and turned sharply, especially when he could make use of the breeze on his home ground at Newlands where, against England in 1948-49, he was given his only Test. His one wicket was the England captain, George Mann. Hanley remained a highly successful performer for Western Province, taking 49 wickets – and beating a 46-year-old provincial record – at 15.63 in 1952-53. His nephew, Rupert ("Spook"), was one of South Africa's leading bowlers of the 1980s.

HARVEY, ROBERT LYON, MBE, died on July 20, 2000, aged 88. Bob Harvey was a middle-order batsman for Natal (and later their captain) who made a brief entry into international cricket when South Africa's batsmen collectively lost form and confidence against the Australians in 1935-36. Having made a century against them for his province, he was picked for the Fourth and Fifth Tests, only to disappear amid the general clatter of South African wickets in a series dominated by Clarrie Grimmett. Between the two Tests he scored a second century against the touring team for Natal. Harvey also represented the province at rugby, and two of his sons were Natal cricketers.

HAWKE, NEIL JAMES NAPIER, died on Christmas Day, 2000, aged 61, having been ill for more than 20 years. "Hawkeye" was a mainstay of the Australian attack in the 1960s and took 91 wickets in 27 Tests. "He was a strapping medium-pacer," wrote Gideon Haigh, "with an un-aesthetic, asymmetrical action but a fine follow-through conducive to late movement." His stamina (built up by playing Australian Rules) and his uncomplaining good nature were vital to a team that, in his time, often had to scrap for any advantage. Hawke's best Test figures – seven for 105 – came at Sydney in 1965-66 when he bowled defiantly with the second new ball after England had touched 303 for one. Even so, he could not prevent an innings defeat. Nine months earlier, he had achieved match figures of ten for 115 in another losing cause at Georgetown. In England he is best remembered for yet another negative reason: as Fred Trueman's 300th Test victim at The Oval in 1964. However, Hawke had a more decisive role in that series. Batting at No. 9, he put on 105 with Peter Burge to transform the Headingley Test after Ted Dexter had controversially withdrawn the spinners and taken the new ball. Hawke had already collected five for 75 in the first innings, and Australia went on to win the only decided game of the series. He took 18 wickets in the five Tests, second only to Graham McKenzie, and 83 on the tour at 19.80. He was far less successful in 1968 and dropped after Lord's. Hawke remained a heroic figure in South Australia, where he was born – he also played briefly for Western Australia and Tasmania, and for seven years in the Lancashire League – and became an even greater icon after 1980, when he was infected following an operation and became so ill that he needed 30 operations in two years. For the rest of his life he suffered regular relapses, but his response was inspirational: as his wife, Beverley, put it, "He fought back from the brink of death time after time."

HEBDEN, GEOFFREY GEORGE LOCKWOOD, who died in April 2000, aged 81, was an all-rounder who appeared for Hampshire with insignificant success in six matches either side of World War II. He hit two hundreds in a match for Dorset against Cornwall at Penzance in 1952. His father, George, played for Middlesex.

[*Hulton Getty*

Neil Hawke's strength of character saw him through greater adversity than he ever met playing
Test cricket for Australia.

HERBERT, MORGAN URIAH, who died on June 15, 2000, aged 81, was a Western
Australian leg-spinner, using his fingers rather than his wrist, who came from up-
country to contend for a place in the Test team after taking seven for 45 for the state
against the Indians in their first-ever match in Australia in October 1947. However, he
played only once in the Sheffield Shield that year – when Western Australia won the
competition at their first attempt – and was hammered by the Harvey brothers of
Victoria: Neil and Merv. Two years later, Herbert had his revenge on Victoria when
he took eight wickets in the match and hit a rapid 46. He had little success otherwise
in his 18 first-class games, but was a dominant force in country cricket. As a golfer,
he holed in one six times.

HOWARD, JACK, who died on September 17, 1998, aged 80, was a left-handed
batsman and occasional wicket-keeper who played 41 games for Leicestershire with
modest success in the first three seasons after World War II. His father, Arthur, also
appeared for the county, and his brother, Alan, played for Glamorgan.

HUMPHRIES, NORMAN HAMPTON, who died on December 18, 2000, aged 83, was one of three brothers to play for Worcestershire. He had seven county matches in 1946 as an amateur batsman, but played most of his cricket for Kidderminster and Devon.

HURST, MICHAEL, who died on September 3, 2000, aged 70, was a Warwickshire Club and Ground player just after World War II but became better known as a cricketing businessman: he developed the Pluvius covers, now widely used on Test and county grounds. He was a member of the ECB pitches committee and a Warwickshire committee member for 20 years.

HUSSAIN, MUMTAZ, who died of cancer on May 5, 2000, aged 52, was a successful slow left-armer in the Ranji Trophy. He took 173 wickets for Hyderabad at an average of 19.18, and formed a potent combination with off-spinner Noshir Mehta. As a teenager, Hussain was in a 14-man squad for the Calcutta Test against West Indies in 1966-67, but Bishen Bedi was chosen instead and never looked back. Hussain had shot to prominence that season by taking a record 48 wickets in university cricket.

HUTCHINSON, JAMES METCALF, died on November 7, 2000, 22 days short of his 104th birthday and 80 years and 62 days after his county debut. A Derbyshire miner, Jim Hutchinson doubled up as a stalwart member of the county team in the 1920s. He was a gifted, if not always disciplined, batsman best known for his athleticism in the field; the Derbyshire history names him as the club's finest cover. He made five hundreds, including 143 against Leicestershire at Chesterfield in 1924. None of them, however, was as famous as his last: in 1996 he became only the eighth first-class cricketer known to have reached his 100th birthday, and in 1999 he overtook R. W. de Smidt of Western Province to become the longest-lived of all. He was an advertisement for the mining life even more than for cricket: he went down the pit aged 14, and after retiring from Derbyshire in 1931 became safety officer at a mine near Rotherham, playing for Thurnscoe until he was 66, driving a car until his late nineties and disobeying advice about avoiding fatty foods all along. Hutchinson ascribed his longevity to pork chops and onion rings. His memory, in extreme old age, was impressive, if selective, and he remained enthralled by recollections of Frank Woolley: "He was so tall, and every stroke looked perfect. His cover drive was a joy. My best shot was the cover drive, but I never knew if it was going in the air or along the ground."

INGMAN, KENNETH, died on February 20, 2000, aged 72. Ken Ingman was a PE teacher on the Wirral who devoted years of work to junior cricket, managing teams at every age group up to England Under-19. Of the England team that appeared at Centurion, in the last Test before his death, seven had played for him at various levels. Mike Atherton, who gave the address at his funeral, said that Ingman managed young players with tact and diplomacy, and imbued them with a sense of cricket tradition: "His cricket knowledge was sound but, more than that, he had seen generations of teenage cricketers come and go and he knew the problems and pitfalls."

JEFFREYS, KEITH STANLEY, who died on May 16, 2000, aged 79, was an outstanding schoolboy cricketer in Western Australia and made his first-class debut two months after his 17th birthday when he was picked for the state against an Australian XI in 1937-38. His finest hour came two years later, however, when he left his sickbed to make a match-saving 21 not out against South Australia. His opportunities were limited because Western Australia were not in the Sheffield Shield, but he scored heavily in grade cricket.

JONES, DAVID, who died in July 1998, aged 84, was a batsman on the fringes of the Nottinghamshire team in the late 1930s. He played 24 times, scoring 60 against Worcestershire at Trent Bridge in 1938.

JOWETT, DAVID COLIN PATRICK ROBERT, died on January 7, 2000, aged 68. "Jumbo" Jowett was a cheerful all-rounder who won a Blue at Oxford in each of his four years there, 1952 to 1955, and took seven for 132 with his off-spin against a mighty Surrey side at Guildford in 1954. In 50 first-class matches, he failed to appear on the winning side once, not quite beating the 57 by Cyril Perkins of Northamptonshire in the 1930s.

JOYNSON, WILLIAM REGINALD HAMBOROUGH, who died on December 4, 2000, aged 83, played two matches as a batsman for Oxford in 1939.

LANCE, ALFRED ARTHUR, who died on September 11, 1999, aged 82, was curator of the Adelaide Oval from 1953 to 1980. He prepared his first Test pitch in 1954-55 and successfully remade the square in 1956 with layers of black soil, loam and cinders: 12 of the 17 Tests on pitches under his control produced results. Lance had to work with little help and with ancient equipment, but he loved the pitch and the ground, and died in his cottage at the Oval's southern end.

LANDER, CHRISTOPHER, died of cancer on May 5, 2000, aged 59. Chris "Crash" Lander was a tabloid cricket writer for almost three decades, for the *Daily Mirror* and, briefly, *The Sun*, capable of turning in contentious – even outrageous – copy that caused offence rarely and lasting offence never. On the contrary, in an era of declining press–player relations, Lander bridged the divide thanks to his charm, good nature and sense of fun. He had a unique relationship with Ian Botham in which they became almost blood-brothers. This reached its peak on Botham's first charity walk through Britain in 1985. The official ghostwriter from *The Sun* dropped out a few miles from John o'Groats; Lander, from the rival *Mirror*, was still there at Land's End. After this, he was briefly persuaded to change papers, but soon moved back, though in later years dim-witted *Mirror* executives badly under-appreciated his contacts and his con-scientiousness. Sometimes, this was hard to spot beneath an adventurous personal life and a unique status as the press corps' lord of misrule. Very occasionally, the paper's craziness and his joined in happy harmony, as when he was ordered to report a day's Test cricket from the sponsors' swimming-pool on the boundary at Queen's Park Oval. There he stood, to general delight, surrounded by girls in bikinis as if he were Hugh Hefner. Botham described him as "a sensational human being".

LAWRENCE, DOUGLAS ROSYTH, who died on July 8, 2000, aged 70, played seven times for Scotland in the late 1950s. He was a fast bowler whose best first-class figures, four for 56, came at Aberdeen in 1957 against an MCC side led by Freddie Brown. Three weeks later, against Ireland, he came in at 49 for nine, with all the wickets having fallen to off-spinner Frank Fee; after sharing a stand of 33, he ruined Fee's chance of lasting fame in *Wisden* by getting bowled at the other end. Lawrence was later a keen coach, and in 1990 president of the Scottish Cricket Union.

LEWIS, GERALD, who was killed in a road accident on January 26, 2000, aged 62, was a fanatical walker. His obsession bewildered and entranced spectators at Queen's Park Oval, Port-of-Spain. At a ferocious pace, he would march round the boundary before play, afterwards and during the intervals, proudly carrying the Trinidad & Tobago flag ahead of him. He repeated this at other major sporting events and constituted a minor national institution. Lewis was killed on his way home from a cricket match at Pointe-à-Pierre when a taxi hit his bicycle.

LOBB, BRYAN, who died suddenly on May 3, 2000, aged 69, was a popular Somerset player whose name belied the pace and bounce of his bowling. He moved west after one game for Warwickshire in 1953 and four years later became the first post-war Somerset fast bowler to take 100 wickets. His action was unorthodox, even uncoordinated.

"His fielding could be mesmerically bad," wrote David Foot. "And so, at times, was his judgment of a run, reinforced by his natural sense of jovial self-deprecation: 'I once got run out by deep mid-on, who overtook me as I unwisely strolled to the other end.'" Lobb took 370 wickets in 116 matches up to 1969, when he became geography and games teacher at Edgarley Hall, the prep school for Millfield. He was still bowling for Glastonbury in his mid-sixties.

LOXTON, COLIN CAMERON, who died on September 2, 2000, aged 86, was an Australian all-rounder. He played once for Cambridge University against The Army in 1935, and four matches for Queensland in 1937-38. His son, John, was a Queensland regular in the 1960s.

LUBBOCK, CHRISTOPHER WILLIAM STUART, died on May 16, 2000, aged 80. Bill Lubbock was an amateur all-rounder who played six games for Northamptonshire before World War II. Fresh from Charterhouse, he made 69 on his first-class debut against Warwickshire in 1938. He was also capable of bowling at considerable pace and, with the help of three appearances for Oxford, came second in the first-class averages in 1939 with 19 wickets at 14.26, sandwiched between Hedley Verity and Bill Bowes. Lubbock missed his Blue, however, and the war ensured he never got another chance. He joined the Navy (reverting to the name Christopher) and served as flag lieutenant to various admirals, a job he compared to being a butler. In 1947, he was called to the Bar and became a Master in the Queen's Bench Division. "His mannerisms often seemed better suited to the Edwardian era than to modern times," said the *Daily Telegraph*. "He drove his car so slowly that he claimed to have once been overtaken by a combine harvester." After June 1 each year, he wore a straw boater with an I Zingari ribbon.

McCARTHY, CUAN NEIL, who died on August 14, 2000, aged 71, was a top-class pace bowler from Natal, but his reputation was blighted by allegations of throwing. McCarthy was one of the fastest bowlers of his era, with a fearsome nip-backer, and made a sensational entry into Test cricket as a 19-year-old in the unforgettable Durban Test of 1948-49: he took six for 43 in the second innings before England sneaked to a famous two-wicket win. Although he played in South Africa's next 14 Tests, he was never quite as successful again. He took 21 wickets in that series "with that appalling long stride of his... stretching further than you think a man could stretch," as John Arlott said in one of his commentaries. But his success-rate fell away in Australia a year later and on the England tour of 1951. *Wisden* blamed him – and especially his reliance on the bouncer – for South Africa's failure to win at Old Trafford: "If only he had tried to hit the stumps England could scarcely have survived on such treacherous turf." Mainly, though, it was not his stride or his bouncer that damaged his career but his action. There were murmurings that he threw in 1951, and he was finally called after he went up to Cambridge in 1952 – by umpire Paddy Corrall while McCarthy was playing for the university at Worcester. He was apparently unnerved both by this and by the consequences of his bowling. Robin Marlar recalled that, when he hit the Oxford tailender, Alan Coxon, in the University Match, the ball flew from his head and struck the sightscreen first bounce. He also put Jim Langridge in hospital with a bouncer at Hove; Langridge was apparently never the same again. McCarthy himself disappeared from first-class cricket, though he turned out a little for Dorset, and farmed for a while in South Africa. Off the field, he was a gentle man, much liked by his university contemporaries.

MACDONALD, THOMAS JOHN, died on March 23, 1998, aged 89, although his death was not reported at the time. Tom Macdonald was an opening batsman who played mainly for Ireland and Lincolnshire, but appeared once for Cambridge, against Somerset in 1930. He was the last survivor of the Irish team that beat the West Indies at Dublin in 1928.

MAJOLA, KHAYA, who died of cancer on August 28, 2000, aged 47, was one of the unsung heroes of South African cricket's transition from apartheid. Majola was the director of amateur cricket at the United Cricket Board from its foundation in 1991 until his death, supervising the board's widely praised development programme. He had been a gifted cricketer himself and was chosen to play in England for Derrick Robins's XI under Clive Rice, after he had impressed them as an opponent in South Africa. However, on his return, he refused to have anything to do with the white-dominated cricket bodies, still floundering under apartheid, and returned to the matting wickets and parched, rutted outfields of the Eastern Province townships. In 17 years, he played in 85 interprovincial matches organised by the black-led cricket authorities, scoring 2,735 runs and taking 214 wickets with his left-arm spin. Only two other players completed the 2,000 runs–200 wickets double in these matches, which have been given retrospective first-class status by the UCB. Majola was appointed captain of the South African Cricket Board national team in the 1980s, but unity came too late for him to have any chance of testing his skills in international cricket. Instead, he smoothed the path for others on the field and off it. His younger brother, Gerald, is chief executive of the UCB.

MARKHAM, LAWRENCE ANDERSON, died on August 5, 2000, aged 75. "Fish" Markham was a leg-spinner and competent tail-end batsman from Natal who was brought into the South African team for the Ellis Park Test against England in 1948-49. He had been suffering from jaundice, was confronted by an unfavourable pitch and had just 13 overs in the two innings, costing 72 runs. He did, however, bowl Denis Compton, who apparently failed to spot the googly. Markham had been devastating in the previous year's Currie Cup, when his 32 wickets cost only 12.87 each; against Orange Free State that season he scored 134, sharing an eighth-wicket stand of 174 with Ossie Dawson that remains a provincial record.

MARKHAM, NEVILLE EVELYN, who died on April 26, 2000, aged 74, was an all-rounder for Natal in the 1950s. He was the younger brother of "Fish" Markham.

MARSHALL, JOHN MAURICE ALEX, died on March 19, 2000, aged 83. Jack Marshall was a Warwickshire amateur leg-spinner who made an immediate impression in county cricket by taking five for 65 on his debut, against Worcestershire at Dudley in 1946. He was the county's second-leading wicket-taker that season with 43 – way behind Eric Hollies – but was never as effective again. However, he was a competent-enough batsman at around No. 7 and continued to play occasionally before concentrating on teaching. He was reputed to have bowled an 11-ball over in his debut innings, after he took a wicket with the sixth ball and the umpire became confused. However, a study of the scorebook failed to authenticate this.

MERRYWEATHER, JAMES HERBERT, died on February 19, 2000, aged 71. Jim Merryweather was an off-spinner who took 714 wickets for Wiltshire between 1954 and 1979. Though well past 40, he played in all four matches for the outclassed Minor Counties (South) team in the inaugural year of the Benson and Hedges Cup, 1972, and took nine wickets.

MEYER, MICHAEL LEVERSON, who died on August 3, 2000, aged 79, was the most famous translator into English of the Scandinavian dramatists, Ibsen and Strindberg. He was also a cricket fanatic and edited *Summer Days*, a 1983 anthology by writers not normally associated with the game.

MILLER, FRANK JOSEPH, who died on January 3, 2000, aged 83, kept wicket for Ireland in seven first-class matches between 1949 and 1953. He habitually stood up to the stumps, no matter how fast the bowler.

MOIR, ALEXANDER McKENZIE, died on June 17, 2000, aged 80. Alex Moir made the Otago first-team squad as a batsman in 1937 but did not play a first-class match for another 13 years, by which time he had watched the great Bill O'Reilly and decided to turn himself into a leg-spinner. He did this well enough to win rapid promotion to the 1950-51 New Zealand team against England, and had an epic bowl on his Test debut on a dreary pitch at Christchurch, taking six for 155 in 56.3 overs. As he had only a fraction of O'Reilly's pace through the air and not quite enough spin, he never did as well again against top-class players in his 16 subsequent Tests, though he took five for 62 against England at Auckland four years later, immediately before New Zealand were infamously bowled out for 26. Moir had a talent for being in the action. In the Second Test of the 1950-51 series, at Wellington, he had become the first player since Warwick Armstrong in 1921 to deliver two consecutive overs in a Test: he bowled both the last over before tea and the first afterwards without the umpires realising. The following year, in the Auckland Test against West Indies, he refused to run out Allan Rae when he slipped and fell after being sent back by his partner. Rae, then on ten, went on to 99. This was in keeping with Moir's light-hearted approach to the game: he clapped when Auckland's Ken Hough hit him for four sixes at Dunedin in 1959-60 and bought him a beer afterwards. He was not altogether guileless – batsmen thought they could pick his googly because he clicked his fingers, so he got first slip to do some extra clicking – but he always enjoyed his cricket.

MONTGOMERY, STANLEY WILLIAM, who died on October 6, 2000, aged 80, was a Glamorgan middle-order batsman. A Londoner who was briefly on the Essex staff, he moved to Wales and played 29 times between 1949 and 1953. He never captured a regular place despite a blazing start: in his second match he scored 117 against Hampshire, sharing a stand of 264 with Maurice Robinson, still the club's fifth-wicket record. He played in the half-back line for several Football League clubs and later coached at Bradfield College.

MORRISON, ARCHIBALD JOHN, who died on April 12, 2000, aged 92, was for many years county cricket's most recognisable – and audible – spectator. Known universally as "Loppylugs", John Morrison was a Worcestershire member for more than 70 years, and for many of them he celebrated every wicket, boundary and landmark with a blast on an antique hunting horn. This era lasted until Worcestershire reached a Gillette Cup final at Lord's and, amid the excitement (and perhaps the port-and-brandy in his hip flask), he began blasting for both sides. Folklore records that the horn was knocked from his hands, trampled and then buried in the Lord's rose garden. Unfortunately for some Worcester spectators, Loppy simply began hallooing, just as loudly, instead. Warwickshire, always a more cheerless club, banned him. Mike Vockins, the Worcestershire secretary, handled him with a mixture of affection and exasperation, and eventually rationed the halloos, which were always a close second to the ladies' toilets on the official log of members' complaints. "Some thought this only encouraged him to try to win top place," said Vockins. Even when silent, Loppylugs was instantly recognisable with his white hair, Dickensian beard and headgear that ranged from a straw boater with floral decoration to an Akubra hat, complete with corks, to a Worcestershire baseball cap. The love of hunting was genuine, even obsessive. He was also, astonishingly enough, a successful chartered accountant – and a very generous donor to players' benefit funds.

MORTON, GEOFFREY DALGLEISH, who died on January 28, 2000, aged 77, was a fast-medium bowler who played twice for Middlesex in 1950. He was later coach at Malvern College.

NIELSEN, EIGIL, who died on September 7, 2000, aged 81, was the only man to represent Denmark at both football and cricket. One of their best batsmen, he scored more than 8,000 runs, averaging almost 35, including 17 centuries. At the 1948 Olympics, he was goalkeeper in the side that won the bronze medal, and he was still regularly playing in veterans' kickarounds until he died.

PARKHOUSE, WILLIAM GILBERT ANTHONY, died on August 10, 2000, aged 74. Gilbert Parkhouse was a batsman of class and style, unlucky to play in the 1950s when England had an unusual abundance of such men. He played in seven Tests, with an eight-year gap between the first five and the last two. Most of his life was bound up with Wales and Scotland, rather than England. He was a Welsh hero: having been brought up close to the ground at St Helen's, he became arguably the greatest batsman Glamorgan have produced; then, after retirement, he spent 20 years coaching both cricket and rugby in Edinburgh, where he made an unusually deep impression.

Parkhouse's entry into county cricket was delayed by war and his own national service (he was wounded in Palestine). But in 1948, after making his debut at No. 3 in a friendly, he played throughout Glamorgan's Championship season. By July he was scoring centuries. Two years later, he was in the Test team against West Indies at Lord's, where his second-innings 48 gave England temporary hope of averting a famous defeat. "He read Ramadhin with both conviction and elegance," said John Arlott. Parkhouse made a further 69 at Trent Bridge, and cut Ramadhin to pieces to score 88 in front of a massive Bank Holiday crowd at Swansea: "To old men's eyes it was a film of yesteryear," wrote J. R. Jones in *The Cricketer*, "with Grimmett on the retreat before the brave and chivalrous lance of Cyril Walters." He was selected for the 1950-51 Australasian tour, but it was there that his rise, which the 1951 *Wisden* called "meteoric," began to lose momentum. The 1952 Almanack was less enthusiastic: "For all the polish of some of his off-side play, Parkhouse did not impress against fast bowlers and he was susceptible to the short bouncer." He struggled with injury and illness and, though he played in two Ashes Tests plus one in New Zealand, did little. Some critics blamed him for being too ready to try to square-cut.

The perception that he had been found wanting at the highest level turned selectors against him. Glamorgan's return to mediocrity did not help; nor did their pitches, designed for spinners rather than strokeplay. Parkhouse's figures were rarely outstanding: in a 17-year career, he made 32 centuries and averaged 31.68. But his cricket was always more a matter of quality rather than quantity. Certainly, there were no obvious flaws in technique: he was orthodox, and happy to get on the back foot against both the quicks – he was a skilled hooker – and the slows: "You bloody Laplander," cried Tom Goddard, after being tickled to leg yet again. It was his effortless cover driving, though, that is best remembered (some contemporaries compared him to Colin Cowdrey) and he could on-drive beautifully. He was also a superb slip, comparable to Cowdrey in that as well, and a marvellous runner between the wickets.

In 1953, Parkhouse switched to opening, and thereafter his partnerships with Emrys Davies and then Bernard Hedges were the basis of the Glamorgan batting order. In the hot summer of 1959, both he and his county returned to top form, and at Headingley Parkhouse was recalled to form a new opening partnership with Geoff Pullar. They put on 146, a first-wicket record against India, with Parkhouse making 78, and he scored a further 49 at Old Trafford. Then he was replaced by Raman Subba Row and never picked again. He played on in county cricket until 1964, after which he began his new life at Stewart's Melville College in Edinburgh, where his protégés included Scottish rugby's Calder twins, Jim and Finlay.

Parkhouse himself had played rugby for Swansea, and high-class hockey and badminton. But he never looked robust, and in later years he did become afflicted by a combination of ailments, including the effects of two early hip operations. He was a quiet, gentle man with little hint of a Welsh accent. Like Charlie Barnett, he went to Wycliffe College, a minor public school, and fitted uneasily into the rigidities of the cricketing class system. "He preferred a steak and a bottle of red to a pint and a sing-song," remembered one team-mate. But he was regarded with widespread affection

Gilbert Parkhouse was one of the most stylish batsmen to wear a Glamorgan cap, and unlucky
not to wear an England one more than seven times.

for his kindness and his dignity. Once, according to a possibly apocryphal story, when
the team was being berated by Wilf Wooller, he listened for a while, then replied: "I'll
have you know, Mr Wooller, that I've played for England."

PENBERTHY, GERALD, who died on May 25, 2000, aged 66, both played and umpired
in a village final at Lord's. He played for Troon when they won in 1973, and was
umpire 18 years later when St Fagan's beat Harome. His son, Tony, is vice-captain of
Northamptonshire.

POPE, HAROLD, who died on June 20, 2000, aged 81, was the youngest of Derbyshire's three-man papal brotherhood. A leg-spinning all-rounder, he played ten matches for them before and after World War II and later became a coach at Repton School.

PRASHAD, MARTIN JOEL, who died on October 26, 2000, aged 42, was a Guyanese-born batsman who emigrated to Canada in 1979 and became captain of the national team. He played in three ICC Trophy competitions. In 1984, he scored 104 against Jamaica.

RAJAN, SUNDER, who died on February 20, 2000, aged 63, was one of India's leading cricket writers and became sports editor of the *Times of India*. He wrote three books in the 1970s on Indian tours.

READ, HOLCOMBE DOUGLAS, died on January 5, 2000, aged 89. "Hopper" Read was briefly regarded as the fastest bowler in England and was picked to play against South Africa at The Oval in 1935, when he took six wickets – all important ones – on a shirt-front pitch. However, after wintering in Australasia with the non-Test-playing team captained by E. R. T. Holmes, he returned to an ultimatum from his employers: chartered accountancy or cricket. Like so many of his generation, he felt obliged to opt for business, and never played serious cricket again. Read had appeared for Surrey against both universities in 1933 without showing much – he had failed to make the First Eleven at Winchester – and the county raised no objection when Essex (for whom his father, A. H. Read, had played) asked if he might be available. In the second match of the astounding inaugural Brentwood Festival of 1934 – immediately after the game in which Kent had declared at 803 for four – Jack Hobbs, then 51, made one of his increasingly rare appearances, reputedly in response to reports about the pitch. Read, in his opening over, first dislodged his cap, then bowled him. He went on to take seven for 35, and Surrey were all out in 90 minutes. Read handed out similar treatment to several other counties later in the season, and finished with 69 wickets. A year later, having missed most of the early games, he travelled with Essex to face unbeaten Yorkshire at Huddersfield. Bowling uphill, he took six for 11 as Yorkshire were dismissed for 31. The figures, said J. M. Kilburn in the *Yorkshire Post*, "cannot do full justice to the life and fire of the attack". Read took ten wickets in the next match, against Worcestershire, and two weeks later won his England cap. He finished the season with 97 wickets, but after that most of his cricket was played for Englefield Green and the Butterflies. His career wickets (219) comfortably exceeded his runs (158); he once made eight successive ducks.

ROBERTS, ALDWYN, who died on February 11, 2000, aged 77, was better known as the calypsonian, Lord Kitchener. His calypsos, often with cricketing themes, dominated the Trinidad carnival for many years. He was filmed leading the pitch invasion at Lord's when West Indies achieved their historic win in 1950.

ROE, RONALD, died in August 2000, aged 80. Ron Roe was an administrative stalwart of the old Test and County Cricket Board in the days when it employed a handful of staff. From the board's foundation in 1968 until he retired in 1985, Roe was the promotions officer, editing the annual tour guide and other publications. He was an enthusiastic weekend player for Hatch End.

RUNCIE of CUDDESDON, The Rt Rev. Baron, MC, PC, who died on July 11, 2000, aged 78, was Archbishop of Canterbury from 1980 to 1991. Robert Runcie was a useful schoolboy cricketer at Merchant Taylors', Crosby, where he was opening bat and captain. He also played for his Oxford college, Brasenose, and remained a lifelong lover of the game. After retiring from Canterbury, he became one of the best of all

"Hopper" Read's tearaway fast bowling won him an England cap and an MCC tour in 1935 –
but after that his profession took precedence over first-class cricket.

[*North News*

For all that Mark Saxelby disliked Sunday cricket, his unbeaten League hundred for Nottingham-shire at Chester-le-Street in 1993 encouraged Durham to sign him the following season. The move provided a successful interlude in a tragic career.

cricketing speakers, crafting witty, erudite and self-deprecating speeches with loving care. He spoke beautifully at the 1997 Wisden Dinner and then, though he was already very ill, delivered a masterful eulogy at E. W. Swanton's funeral in February 2000. His father-in-law, J. C. W. Turner, played for Worcestershire.

RUNDLE, DESMOND JOHN, AO, who died on November 18, 1999, aged 69, managed the 1993 Australian team in England. Des Rundle was treasurer of the South Australian Cricket Association for 24 years and finance director of the Australian Cricket Board for 14. He was a successful bowler in Adelaide grade cricket in the 1950s.

SAXELBY, MARK, died on October 12, 2000, aged 31, having apparently committed suicide by drinking weedkiller. It emerged that he had been suffering from chronic clinical depression almost throughout his cricketing career, and the baffled comments of team-mates about his inability to match achievement to promise could be seen in a new and poignant light. In dressing-rooms, he was thought to be likable but withdrawn, and his cricketing ups and downs were often attributed to his back problems. A tall, gifted left-handed batsman, he followed his older brother, Kevin, on to the Nottingham-shire staff, with limited success, then suddenly blossomed after moving to Durham in 1994. On his Championship debut for them, he scored a brilliant 181 against Derbyshire at Chesterfield and followed with 63 and 131 at Stockton-on-Tees on his home debut. Though his form inevitably dwindled, he still scored more than 1,000 Championship runs that season, and things only started to go seriously wrong after the arrival of Mike Roseberry the following year. This forced Saxelby to drop down the order, which he disliked, and he was released. He began playing league cricket for Heanor Town, to such effect that in 2000 Derbyshire hurriedly registered him for their home Championship match against Lancashire. Kevin Saxelby said his brother disliked Sunday cricket because there were often large crowds; he also felt uncomfortable if someone praised his batting. "It came as a terrible, terrible shock," he said, "but we knew he'd been through torment."

SCHANSCHIEFF, BRIAN ALEXANDER, who died on September 27, 2000, aged 94, was successively treasurer, chairman and president of Northamptonshire. His 17 years as treasurer from 1954 to 1971 were notable for a hefty improvement in the club's financial stability. His son, Simon, is the current chairman.

SENANYAKE, PRADEEP, was killed on May 8, 2000, when his car was hit by a train. Senanyake was a batsman and leg-spinner who represented Kalutara PCC in Sri Lanka's Division One.

SHACKLETON, LEONARD FRANCIS, died on November 28, 2000, aged 78. Len Shackleton, who played Minor Counties cricket for Northumberland and Durham after World War II, was better known as a brilliant and controversial footballer – "the Clown Prince of Soccer" – for Newcastle, Sunderland and England. However, his popularity spread into his cricket: he once delighted a substantial crowd at Jesmond by running out a batsman from cover with a perfect kick on to the stumps. He said that one of his proudest moments in sport was his 117 not out and eight for 35 with his seamers for Benwell against Benwell Hill in the Northumberland League.

SHARPE, PETER SAMUEL, QPM, died of a brain tumour on December 1, 2000, aged 56. Sharpe was a batsman on the Sussex staff in the early 1960s before concentrating on a career in the police. He was chief constable of Hertfordshire from 1994 until forced to retire through illness in 2000. In 1973 he helped found the British Police Cricket Section and later became chairman.

SMITH, ALFRED ERNEST DAVID, died on January 20, 2000, aged 85. David Smith was a prominent umpire for many years, and a football referee, and was said to be the first official to take charge of games at both Wembley and Lord's. He was on the Minor Counties umpires' list between 1949 and 1975, but in several of those seasons was promoted to the first-class panel. He stood with Syd Buller in the semi-final between Northamptonshire and Sussex in the inaugural year of the Gillette Cup (1963). A founder of the Association of Cricket Umpires, and a leading light for many years, he ran Smith's Bureau of Cricket Umpires, which provided officials for a number of competitions.

STAINTON, ROBERT GEORGE, died on August 15, 2000, aged 90. Bob Stainton won an Oxford Blue in 1933 after making a rapid 89 against the West Indians, also gained a Blue for football, and, in the old inter-war manner, went on to play for Sussex whenever his schoolmastering permitted. He scored steadily, his fielding, said *Wisden*, was "brilliant", and in 1938 he captained the team when A. J. Holmes was away, insisting on leading out the amateurs and professionals together. After service as an RAF navigator, he became a prep school head of unusual sensitivity who would sometimes tell his class to sit in silence and watch the sunset. He retired early to become an artist.

STATHAM, JOHN BRIAN, CBE, died from leukaemia on June 10, 2000, aged 69. Brian Statham was one of the best of all English fast bowlers, and beyond question the best-liked. A gentle man who had to be persuaded to bowl a bouncer, he was a mainstay of the England team in its vintage period between 1951 and 1963: he took 252 wickets in 70 Tests. His name will be forever coupled with that of Freddie Trueman, though they actually played together in only half his Tests. Statham's name always came second because he was the foil to Trueman's sabre – and the more reticent man. In cricketing folklore he is remembered primarily for his accuracy: "If they miss, I hit," he would say. This diminishes his astonishing skill. He was indeed accurate; so are many fast-medium bowlers. Statham kept his line and length at a very high pace indeed, comparable with all but the very fastest of Test match bowlers. A batsman hit by Statham – even on the foot, which was more likely than the head – knew all about it. In Statham's case the area around off stump was more a corridor of certainty than uncertainty, but if the ball hit the seam it jagged back in very sharply. The results were always formidable, and occasionally devastating.

Statham came from Gorton, in Manchester. There was no silver spoon, but there was cricket in his background: three of his brothers appeared in local leagues. He played for Denton West and then Stockport, but Lancashire never noticed him. His corporal during national service in the RAF – a southerner – recommended him to MCC, however. He was told to write to Old Trafford, and Statham was offered a trial. In May 1950 he was on the ground staff; a month after reporting to the coach, Harry Makepeace, he was in the first team. It was his 20th birthday: "He was a youngster who carried his flannels in a canvas bag," said *Wisden*, "and his boots in a brown paper parcel." His reputation grew quietly until the Roses match at Old Trafford in August, when he shocked a huge and expectant crowd by immediately falling over in his run-up. He picked himself up, dusted himself down and later that over ripped out Frank Lowson's middle stump. In the same spell he also dismissed Ted Lester and Willie Watson; all three got ducks and *Wisden* said his bowling "bordered on the sensational". Five months later, along with his county colleague, Roy Tattersall, he was flown out to Australia to join Freddie Brown's injury-stricken party. Both Cyril Washbrook and Len Hutton, who had seen him at close quarters in the Roses match, argued for him, though many in the party had never seen him. Coming straight from a hard English winter, Statham played his first first-class game for MCC on a day of extreme midsummer heat at Adelaide. It might have broken some young players but, with his easy-going, beer-and-fags style, Statham was soon just "George" to everyone and fitted in beautifully. It was the New Zealand leg of the tour before he made his mark on the field, with figures of four for 17 in more Mancunian conditions against Otago. Then in Christchurch, ten months after his arrival at Old Trafford, he became a Test cricketer.

It took a while for him to make the impact in Tests that he had in county cricket, and he made only occasional appearances for England over the next three seasons. None the less, he continued to improve – 97 wickets at just 15.11 in 1951, 110 at 18.08 in 1952, 101 at 16.33 in 1953. Even more significantly, he quickened up to the point of being a genuine fast bowler rather than a sharp fast-medium, and on the difficult West Indies tour of 1953-54 he came into his own. At Sabina Park, he opened the bowling with Trueman for the first time for England and, in the Third Test at Georgetown, turned the series with a devastating new-ball spell, sending back Worrell, Stollmeyer and Walcott for ten runs. Alex Bannister of the *Daily Mail* reported that Stollmeyer had received the best fast ball bowled for England since Alec Bedser bowled Bradman for a duck at Adelaide seven years earlier.

Statham was England's leading wicket-taker in Tests in the West Indies, and the following winter he reached his peak. The name in the headlines was Frank Tyson, whose ferocious bursts at Sydney and Melbourne gave England the Ashes. But the quiet man made it possible: while Tyson raced with the wind at Sydney, Statham battled into it; he took five for 60 to restrict Australia's lead in the first innings at Melbourne, and gave the batsmen no respite in the second, when Tyson took seven for 27. By now, with Bedser fading, Statham was England's most reliable bowler. And sometimes he was more than that. At Lord's in 1955, he bowled unchanged in the second innings as South Africa were dismissed for 111 to lose a match they had been dominating. His figures were 29–12–39–7: it was a feat of endurance even allowing for a lunch break extended to two hours by bad light.

Brian Statham's searing pace and unforgiving accuracy lay at the heart of England's glory days in the 1950s.

All this time, he was – year after year – Lancashire's leading bowler. And lacking anyone to give him the support he himself provided so unstintingly for England, until the emergence of Ken Higgs in 1958, he sometimes had to do all the work himself. At Coventry in 1957, he bowled Lancashire to an innings win with match figures of 15 for 89. Though he dipped in and out of the England team, through injuries and the whims of selection, his form remained remarkably constant, whether or not it was reflected in the statistics. A half-volley remained a major event. On the unhappy Ashes tour of 1958-59, he took seven for 57 on the way to defeat at Melbourne, and reports suggested he often bowled just as well for less reward. He had a few final hurrahs for England in the early 1960s, but on his fourth Ashes tour, in 1962-63, his pace had declined; the following summer he appeared to fade out of Test cricket. Yet he was recalled two years later and, together with Higgs, bowled out South Africa for 208 at The Oval. He was 35 but still took 137 wickets that season at 12.52 and could apparently have gone on a fifth Ashes tour had he wanted. By now, he was Lancashire captain, a job he held for three years. His performances never wavered and Lancashire's were reasonable, although by the end, *Wisden* said, his decisions "often puzzled". It was a happy ship, though: "Fewer jollier bands have ever laughed and sung their way through the shires," said Derek Hodgson, who travelled with them for the *Daily Express*. In 1967 Statham passed Johnny Briggs to become Lancashire's leading wicket-taker, and he added 69 more in his last season, 1968. In all first-class cricket, he took 2,260 wickets, putting him 19th on the all-time list. But his average of 16.37 is the best of the top 20 wicket-takers and beaten only by Briggs – who bowled on the primitive pitches of the 19th century – among the top 30.

His methods remain a matter of some debate. His action was certainly too chest-on to be accepted as classical. He swung the ball only rarely, and perhaps never by design. Part of the secret seems to have been that Statham was not merely supple but double-jointed. "He could put his right arm round his face and touch his right ear and do the same with his left arm and his left ear at the same time," said an admiring Geoff Pullar. He was certainly an impressive athlete: a beautiful outfielder and an occasionally effective left-handed tailender. His bowling quality was never in dispute. Nor was his character: he had an enchantingly easy-going temperament. "I only saw him lose his rag twice," said Pullar, his Lancashire and England team-mate. "Both times he was certain they had gloved a catch. One was Easton McMorris in the West Indies – he hit him on the chest and made him spit blood. The other was 'Pom-Pom' Fellows-Smith, and he knocked his cap off." Even the accuracy seems to have been a reflection of his temperament: "I'm not going to run in 30 yards and watch a batsman shoulder arms," Statham once said. "It's a waste of energy."

Despite his huge popularity, his life after cricket was a difficult one. He was employed by Guinness to go round pubs and clubs – more celebrity PR than selling. But after the company was taken over, a stern new management tried to force timetables and paperwork on him, and Statham's life was made intolerable. He became ill and in 1989 his financial plight was such that his friend Trueman organised some benefit dinners for him. More than 1,000 turned up at the Grosvenor House in London. He was a cricketer who engendered admiration and affection from both those who saw him from a distance, and those who knew him best. "I knew him for 50 years and we never had a wrong word," said Trueman.

SUMMERS, DOUGLAS WALTER LEVI, died on January 1, 2000, aged 88. Doug Summers was a slow left-arm bowler who played one match for Worcestershire, as an 18-year-old, against Warwickshire at Dudley in 1930. His father, F. T. Summers, kept wicket for the county in the 1920s.

SWANTON, ERNEST WILLIAM, CBE, who died on January 22, 2000, aged 92, was the most influential and most durable cricket writer of the 20th century. In the columns of the *Daily Telegraph*, he was always E. W. Swanton; to his friends and enemies alike, he was "Jim". There were plenty of enemies and he was called many other names besides over the years, but he was never ignored. In the 30 years after World War II, as the *Telegraph* cricket correspondent, he carried an authority both in print and in person that perhaps no writer can have surpassed in any sport. And the glory never faded. In a quarter-century of nominal retirement, he continued to write columns that were read with eagerness and some trepidation in the game's committee-rooms. In an unusual moment of self-deprecation, Swanton cheerfully referred to himself as a dinosaur. In fact, he was the reverse: he hated many of the changes in cricket, but he adapted to them, and retained the ability to comment on them confidently, relevantly and pertinently without ever losing sight of cricket's eternal values – hence his enduring importance.

"He became a supreme journalist with very strong views. He always tried to do his best for the highest principles of the game."

Lord Cowdrey

"They've elected Swanton pope."

Jack Fingleton, seeing white smoke billowing from a chimney near Lord's

"Jim perhaps deserved to have his leg pulled, but this must never be allowed to take anything away from his skill as a writer and a broadcaster, and nor does it in any way detract from his kindness all through his life to budding journalists and the young in and around the game of cricket."

Henry Blofeld

"He was a boring writer and his overbearing manner appalled people close to him."

Michael Henderson, current Daily Telegraph *cricket correspondent*

"He had the sort of humour and wit that put life in proportion. I remember on one of my first, nervous visits to Canterbury Cricket Week, I knocked over a bottle of wine at lunch and it spilt on the dresses of two lady guests. We all jumped up; only Jim quietly murmured: 'This is a moment to think of eternity.'"

Lord Runcie

"No one born and bred outside the Caribbean wrote with such affection for, and understanding of, West Indies cricket."

Caribbean Cricket Quarterly

Swanton was a walking database, encompassing almost the whole of 20th-century cricket. He believed he had been taken in his pram to see W. G. Grace batting for London County, and vividly recalled having watched Surrey v Yorkshire in the two-day Championship season of 1919, and the Oval Test of 1921. At his school, Cranleigh, he played just once for the First Eleven. Then – having decided not to follow his father on to the Stock Exchange – he went straight into journalism, aged 17, and graduated from a menial job at the Amalgamated Press to the *Evening Standard* in 1927. He soon found himself as the rugby correspondent, but wrote regularly on cricket and began reporting Tests in 1930. In May 1932, Swanton was told he would be sent on the Ashes tour the following winter, a brave and novel idea for any newspaper as the norm had been to rely on news agency reports. Before then, however, he was sent to Leyton, and was there when Holmes and Sutcliffe scored 555 and broke the world record for an opening stand. Unfortunately, so were the rival London papers: the *Evening News* and *The Star*. Their correspondents got ahead of him in the queue for the only telephone; his story missed an edition – the ultimate humiliation for a journalist – and the *Standard* began to think that if this youngster could not report the news on time

[*Hulton Getty*

Gubby, later Sir George, Allen and Jim Swanton arrive at Westminster Abbey in April 1967 to attend the Memorial Service for Sir Frank Worrell.

from Essex, he would hardly manage it from Australia. They sent their tennis writer, Bruce Harris, instead.

It turned out to be the most controversial tour of all time, but hindsight and history suggest that, if the British public had understood better what was going on, England's bodyline strategy could have been stopped. That would have required the presence of a knowledgeable and fearless correspondent: Swanton, for instance. It is true that much of that hindsight has been provided by Swanton himself, but it is none the less plausible. This was his only major journalistic setback. By now, he was becoming a well-known sporting man-about-town and, as social climbing was not the least of his gifts, he made all kinds of useful connections, both off the cricket field and on it. He went on tour to North America with Sir Julien Cahn and founded his own touring club, the Arabs, still going strong, which claimed in 1935 to be the first cricket team to travel by air: to Jersey. As a competent, even inventive batsman, if a rather unathletic one, he was invited to play for Middlesex: his first game for the Second Eleven was Denis Compton's last before his promotion to higher things, and they put on 100 together. In 1937 and 1938 he played three first-team games, all against the universities, with a highest score of 26. H. S. Altham asked him to collaborate on his second edition of *A History of Cricket*, and Swanton was also starting to broadcast: a modest contract from the BBC enabled him to go on the 1938-39 tour of South Africa.

When war came, he joined the Bedfordshire Yeomanry. He was sent to Singapore, wounded and was in hospital when the Japanese overran the colony. Swanton was a captive for more than three years, carrying with him a battered 1939 *Wisden* (marked "Not subversive" by a Japanese censor). His weight went down from 15 stone to just over ten and he was left with a withered left shoulder and upper arm from an attack of polio ("It hasn't improved a golf-swing which was hardly a thing of beauty in the first place," he wrote later) and a deepened faith, which led him to spend the first six years after the war living in Pusey House, Oxford, a major centre of Anglo-Catholicism. He might have turned to the priesthood, but worldly success intervened. After a disastrous experiment with an amiable golfer called Sir Guy Campbell, the *Telegraph* needed a new cricket correspondent, and Swanton was appointed in time for the second post-war Test, against India at Old Trafford. A few weeks later he was on board ship en route for the 1946-47 Ashes tour.

And so Swanton's grand reign began. Cricket was higher in public affection than ever before. With the *Morning Post* closed, *The Times* sale still tiny and *The Guardian* based in Manchester, the *Telegraph* was the paper of choice for the cricket-reading classes of Middle England, and its correspondent was bound to be a power in the game. Furthermore, Swanton was a regular broadcaster whose close-of-play summaries are still widely held to be the best there have been. In print and on air, he reported the facts with little colour or embellishment, which distinguished him from Neville Cardus in print and John Arlott on air. His literary style was basic – "halfway between the Ten Commandments and Enid Blyton", as J. J. Warr famously put it. But that suited the *Telegraph*, which disapproved of Cardusian fancy. Just before he died, Swanton recited his writing method: "First, briefly, the basic facts – what happened. Next, a critical view – why it happened." Finally, came the chronological detail, which grew in length once newsprint came off the ration. The significant part was the critical view, which was always delivered magisterially, if not pontifically. Part of its power came from Swanton's own sonorous voice and air of grandeur. But he could not have carried off the act if he had not had a profound – and ultimately matchless – knowledge of cricket and cricketers.

Though he was imbued with the values of cricket's establishment, he was often a voice for change. He welcomed overseas players in the County Championship, and one-day cricket. ("This 'instant cricket' is very far from being a gimmick," he wrote after the first Gillette Cup final in 1963, "and there is a place in it for all the arts of cricket.") Swanton was appalled when Gloucestershire sacked Tom Graveney as their captain in 1960 in favour of the Old Etonian, Tom Pugh, and was an early convert to the idea of boycotting South Africa over apartheid. He had become uneasy on the 1956-57 tour, and his strong connection with the West Indies – he led two private tours there and had a holiday home on Barbados – helped propel him into the progressive camp. He abhorred sledging, coloured clothing and the four-day Championship.

It was his personal style that brought him the most detractors, and he did not always treat social inferiors graciously. The historian Rowland Bowen rechristened him Pomponius Ego. Ray Illingworth remarked that he was too snobbish to travel in the same car as his chauffeur. Swanton reported only rarely from the more down-market county grounds: he is believed to have visited Leicester and Northampton only once each, and these occasions had to be treated like state visits, with elaborate preparations so that both he and his amanuensis would not have to endure routine privations. He expected a gin and tonic on cue. Once, when told the bar had run out of ice, he responded irritably, "Didn't you tell them who it was for?" This is a well-sourced story. The *Telegraph* sub-editors were not allowed to change a solitary comma of his copy, and they waited gleefully for his mistakes. These were, however, infrequent. His excesses were softened by both his belated marriage, in 1958 – to Ann Carbutt, a widow and an accomplished pianist and golfer – and the passing years. He was a much nicer man in old age. As Lord Runcie said at his funeral: "The solemnity, prickliness and, yes, arrogance that were part of the serious perfectionist gave way to the gentle self-mockery and kindly wisdom which never seemed to fail us."

After retirement from the *Telegraph* in 1975, he still seemed ubiquitous. He wrote regularly in the paper and for *The Cricketer*, where he was editorial director from 1967 to 1988, and eventually acquired the unlikely magazine title of president. He became president of Kent in 1981. He chaired the MCC committee that helped build the indoor school at Lord's, and was chairman of the arts and libraries committee, taking an abiding interest in the treasures of Lord's. Only the presidency of MCC and a knighthood eluded him, and he probably thought wistfully about both. His autobiography, *Sort of A Cricket Person*, was published in 1972, and was perhaps the last such book to include, without irony, a chapter called "The Gay Thirties". Its closing chapter was "Last Over", but his longevity meant there was time for an anthology of his clippings, *As I Said at the Time*, a book actually called *Last Over* and eventually a collection of his obituaries, *Cricketers of My Time*. It contained appreciations of 83 players, and he had known every one of them except George Hirst. He was still writing columns all through 1999, and though his initial-filled paragraphs about Oxbridge and Eton v Harrow seemed dated, his comments on the game remained astonishingly fresh.

His first nationally published article, in *All Sports Weekly* (under the byline Ernest Swanton, which he never used again), was an appreciation of Frank Woolley. He voted for Woolley – along with Constantine, Bradman, Sobers and Worrell – when asked to name his Five Cricketers of the Century for *Wisden* 2000, making the point that Woolley had scored his runs at 50 an hour. He applauded good, joyous, sporting cricket and, excluding only the very greatest of players, did more than anyone in the 20th century to ensure that good cricket prevailed.

A tribute by John Woodcock appears in Wisden *2000, pp 84–86.*

SWART, PETER DOUGLAS, died on March 13, 2000, aged 53, from a suspected heart attack. A gifted South African all-rounder who came to the fore just after the country was isolated, he would have been a certainty to play one-day internationals, at least: he could force the pace with the bat, bowl at a sharp fast-medium and field athletically. Born in Rhodesia, he moved south to play for Western Province, and then Boland, under Eddie Barlow, while spending northern summers in the Lancashire League. In 1978 and 1979, he was an overseas player for Glamorgan but had limited success. He later became the Boland groundsman and relaid three of the pitches on the difficult Paarl wicket. His approach to life – as well as cricket – was robust.

SYMONDS, CRAWFORD, who died on July 20, 2000, aged 85, was a wicket-keeper and left-hand bat, called into the South Australian team in 1945-46. He failed to live up to his batting reputation in his four matches, but let through only five byes in a Victorian innings of 697.

TAYLOR, ALFRED McDONALD, died on May 11, 2000, aged 82. "Charlie" Taylor was a fast-scoring batsman who hit four centuries for Barbados in only 16 first-class matches, as well as being an athletic fielder and occasional wicket-keeper. He made his debut for the island in 1941-42 but did not reappear for another five years: this time he made an unbeaten 110 out of 601, batting at No. 9, and was promoted to open. He made 161 against MCC in 1947-48, and in the Test that followed fielded substitute for both sides. Against Trinidad a year later, Taylor scored 168, putting on 278 for the first wicket with Roy Marshall. His son, Alfred, also played for Barbados.

TAYLOR, CHRISTOPHER, who died on January 27, 2000, aged 79, was head steward of Kent for 31 years and also the club's curator. He wrote a history of the Canterbury Festival and co-authored a photographic history of Kent with E. W. Swanton.

THORNE, Major-General Sir DAVID CALTHROP, KBE, CVO, died of cancer on April 23, 2000, aged 66. As Major Thorne, he played first-class matches for Combined Services against both Oxford and Cambridge in 1964, scoring 59 to save them from a two-day defeat in the Oxford match. He also played for Norfolk with his twin brother, Michael. As the army's youngest major-general, he was vice-quartermaster in the Falklands War and took over command of forces there when the conflict ended. He was later director-general of the Royal Commonwealth Society.

TODD, ERIC DUNSTER, who died on December 10, aged 90, was a northern cricket writer in the best *Guardian* tradition. He joined the paper in 1958 from the *Manchester Evening Chronicle* to cover both cricket and football after the death of Donny Davies in the Munich air crash, bringing in evening-paper speed and professionalism and the craftsmanship of a born writer. He lasted 17 years before retirement and lived on for a further quarter-century, though both stays seemed improbable: in Frank Keating's words, "his hobbies were stoic hypochondria and writing unposted letters of resignation to the editor". Both on the page and in person, Todd had a mordant, lugubrious style, ideal for capturing such occasions as the last day of cricket on the old ground at Sheffield: "During the depths of winter, the ghosts of cricketers long since dead no doubt will haunt Bramall Lane, and from time to time if they listen carefully enough, football spectators may hear an occasional 'owzat' or 'gerra move on, Lancasheer'."

WALSH, Judge BRIAN, QC, who died on September 23, 2000, aged 65, was chairman of Yorkshire from 1986 to 1991, the period immediately after the huge schism caused by the club's original attempt to sack Geoff Boycott. "His charm and diplomacy did much to heal the rifts at a difficult time," said the *Daily Telegraph*. As a barrister, Walsh was involved in many high-profile cases: he defended Jon Venables, one of the ten-year-old boys who murdered the Liverpool toddler, James Bulger.

WESTBROOK, JOAN HILDA, who died on January 25, 2000, aged 76, opened the batting and kept wicket for England women in three Tests against New Zealand in 1954.

WHITE, CRAWFORD, who died on November 29, 2000, aged 90, was a Fleet Street cricket correspondent for 28 years. His distinguished-sounding byline appeared first in the *News Chronicle* after the war; when the paper closed in 1960 he switched briefly to the *Daily Mail* before settling on the *Daily Express* until he retired in 1975. In the

Crawford White (*centre*) debates the future of cricket at the *Daily Express* in 1966. With him are (*from left*) Brian Close, Doug Insole, Ted Dexter and Colin Cowdrey.

1930s, White had been a fast bowler who generated too much pace and bounce for many Lancashire League batsmen, and he was a member of the Lancashire Second Eleven in 1934, when both the first and second team won their Championships. However, he turned down the idea of a county career and kept his day job – on the *Darwen News* – while playing as a professional for St Annes and Royton. His greatest day on the field was taking ten for 34 for Darwen against Leyland Motors in 1945, although he was almost picked for MCC in British Guiana during an injury crisis in 1947-48 and did play in an unofficial one-day fixture. He was a crisp, able writer (and, in the early days, a broadcaster) without many literary pretensions. But he earned respect for his obvious knowledge of the game, his kindly manner and his military bearing (he was an intelligence officer in wartime Bomber Command). In retirement, he remained a familiar press box figure as a PR for the Test match sponsors, Cornhill. He would pour journalists their lunchtime wine with a gentle reminder: "Remember the magic word," i.e., mention Cornhill in your copy. John Arlott was once refused a final top-up, and next day *The Guardian* referred to the Prudential Test. However, White's good nature was a major factor in establishing the general principle of identifying sponsors.

WHITEHEAD, JOHN PARKIN, who died on August 15, 2000, aged 74, was a quick bowler remembered for one outstanding spell when, after achieving little in six seasons (interrupted by national service) at Yorkshire, he made his debut for Worcestershire in the traditional tour-opener against the 1953 Australians. Whitehead sent back McDonald,

Morris and Hassett to make the score 28 for three, and had Keith Miller dropped off a hard chance to the wicket-keeper first ball. Miller went on to make an unbeaten 220. Whitehead finished with five for 89, figures he never matched in three seasons at New Road before fading out of county cricket. He had impressed the county six years earlier by taking five for ten against them for Combined Services at Hereford. Four of his victims were bowled for ducks and Worcestershire, 30 for seven at one stage, recovered only to 84.

WIMALARATNE, B. WILSON, died in September 2000, aged 61. Willie Wimalaratne came to prominence in 1952 by scoring a century in one of Sri Lanka's biggest schools matches: St Joseph's v St Peter's. He later played for Colombo Colts and Nondescripts and in the 1960s became a leading umpire.

YATAWARA, SONNY, died on September 2, 2000, aged 62. "Yata" was one of Sri Lanka's top fast bowlers in the years before the country attained Test status. He bowled with disconcerting pace and bounce on matting wickets and as a schoolboy at Ananda College injured three St Peter's batsmen, leading to a suspension of fixtures between the teams. His moment of glory came when he bowled Garry Sobers in an exhibition match as the West Indians were on their way home from the 1960-61 Australian tour. "His demise," reported the Sri Lankan correspondent of *The Cricketer*, "was mainly due to his over-indulgence in spiritous pursuits."

CAREER FIGURES OF TEST CRICKETERS

	Tests				First-class			
	Runs	Avge	Wkts	Avge	Runs	Avge	Wkts	Avge
Amarnath, L.	878	24.38	45	32.91	10,426	41.37	463	22.98
Balderstone, J. C. . .	39	9.75	1	80.00	19,034	34.11	310	26.32
Beck, J. E. F.	394	26.26	—	—	1,508	23.93	0	—
Bosch, T.	5	—	3	34.66	372	8.08	210	27.56
Cameron, J. H.	6	2.00	3	29.33	2,772	18.23	184	30.77
Cowdrey, M. C. . . .	7,624	44.06	0	—	42,719	42.89	65	51.21
De Courcy, J. H. . .	81	16.20	—	—	3,778	37.03	0	—
Fredericks, R. C. . .	4,334	42.49	7	78.28	16,384	45.89	75	37.94
Hanley, M. A.	0	0.00	1	88.00	308	9.62	182	21.69
Harvey, R. L.	51	12.75	—	—	1,298	38.17	37	26.10
Hawke, N. J. N. . . .	365	16.59	91	29.41	3,383	23.99	458	26.39
McCarthy, C. N. . . .	28	3.11	36	41.94	141	4.27	176	25.85
Markham, I. A	20	20.00	1	72.00	268	15.76	53	16.84
Moir, A. M.	327	14.86	28	50.64	2,102	16.42	368	24.56
Parkhouse, W. G. A.	373	28.69	—	—	23,508	31.68	2	62.50
Read, H. D.	—	—	6	33.33	158	3.67	219	22.93
Statham, J. B.	675	11.44	252	24.84	5,424	10.80	2,260	16.37

DIRECTORY OF BOOKSELLERS AND AUCTIONEERS

BOOKSELLERS

AARDVARK BOOKS, Copperfield, High Street, Harmston, Lincoln LN5 9SN. Tel/fax: 01522 722671. Peter Taylor specialises in *Wisdens*. Send SAE for list. Restoration service available for *Wisdens* and other books. *Wisdens* also purchased.

ACUMEN BOOKS, Nantwich Road, Audley, Staffordshire ST7 8DL. Tel: 01782 720753; fax: 01782 720798; e-mail: wca@acumenbooks.co.uk; website: www.acumenbooks.co.uk. Everything for umpires, scorers, coaches and others, including standard text-books, all for worldwide import or export.

TIM BEDDOW, 66 Oak Road, Oldbury, West Midlands B68 0BD. Tel: 0121 421 7117; fax: 0121 422 0077; e-mail: timbeddowsports@btinternet.com; website: www.btinternet.com/~timbeddowsports. Large stock of cricket/football books, programmes and signed material. Items purchased. Send SAE for catalogue. Stall at Thwaite Gate, Edgbaston, every first-team match.

BODYLINE BOOKS, 150a Harbord Street, London SW6 6PH. Tel: 020 7385 2176; fax: 020 7610 3314; e-mail: cricket@dircon.co.uk. Specialists in *Wisdens*, signed books, postcards, prints and all other cricket ephemera. All major credit cards accepted. Private premises.

CRICKET BOOKS DIRECT, 3 Luke Street, London EC2A 4PX. Tel: 020 7739 7173; fax: 020 7729 2305; website: www.sportsbooksdirect.co.uk. A comprehensive selection of the latest and best new cricket books, especially imports from Australia. Regular catalogues issued.

IAN DYER CRICKET BOOKS, 29 High Street, Gilling West, Richmond, North Yorkshire DL10 5JG. Tel/fax: 01748 822786; e-mail: iandyer@cricketbooks.co.uk; website: www.cricketbooks.co.uk. Specialist in antiquarian books and *Wisdens*. Full e-commerce facilities on the website.

K. FAULKNER, 65 Brookside, Wokingham, Berkshire RG41 2ST. Tel: 0118 978 5255; e-mail: kfaulkner@bowmore.demon.co.uk; website: www.bowmore.demon.co.uk. Cricket books, *Wisdens*, memorabilia bought and sold. Catalogues issued. Also at Gloucestershire CCC shop, Nevil Road, Bristol BS7 9EJ.

JUST CRICKET BOOKS, 16 Wordsworth Drive, Kenilworth CV8 2TB. Tel: 01926 850389; e-mail: jshaw50691@aol.com. Extensive range of modern and antiquarian cricket books – send details of requirements or for abbreviated listing.

E. O. KIRWAN, 3 Pine Tree Garden, Oadby, Leicestershire LE2 5UT. Tel: 0116 271 4267 (evenings and weekends only). Second-hand and antiquarian cricket books, *Wisdens*, autograph material and cricket ephemera of all kinds.

*J. W. McKENZIE, 12 Stoneleigh Park Road, Ewell, Epsom, Surrey KT19 0QT. Tel: 020 8393 7700; fax: 020 8393 1694; e-mail: jwmck@netcomuk.co.uk; website: www.mckenzie-cricket.co.uk. Specialists in antiquarian second-hand cricket books, particularly *Wisdens*, and memorabilia. Established 1969. Catalogues sent on request. Publishers of cricket books. Shop premises open regular business hours.

ROGER PAGE, 10 Ekari Court, Yallambie, Victoria 3085, Australia. Tel: (03) 9435 6332; fax: (03) 9432 2050. Dealer in new and second-hand cricket books. Distributor of overseas cricket annuals and magazines. Agent for Cricket Statisticians and Cricket Memorabilia Society.

THE PARRS WOOD PRESS, Freepost, Manchester M15 9PW. Tel: 0161 226 4466; email: sport@parrswoodpress.com; website: www.parrswoodpress.com. The Parrs Wood Press is a publisher of quality new cricket books. Contact us for a free catalogue.

*PENGUIN DIRECT. Tel: 020 8757 4036. New *Wisdens* for 1996–2000 and the first three editions of *Wisden Australia* available from Wisden's mail-order supplier. Prices from £12.50, including p&p.

RED ROSE BOOKS, 196 Belmont Road, Bolton BL1 7AR. Tel: 01204 596118; fax: 01204 597070; e-mail: redrosebooks@btinternet.com; website: www.redrosebooks.co.uk. Specialist dealer in second-hand and antiquarian cricket books. Catalogue sent on request.

WILLIAM H. ROBERTS, The Crease, 113 Hill Grove, Salendine Nook, Huddersfield, West Yorkshire HD3 3TL. Tel/fax: 01484 654463; e-mail: william.roberts2@virgin.net; website: www.williamroberts-cricket.com. Second-hand/antiquarian cricket books, *Wisdens*, autograph material and memorabilia bought and sold. Catalogues sent on request.

ST MARY'S BOOKS & PRINTS, 9 St Mary's Hill, Stamford, Lincs PE9 2DP. Tel: 01780 763033; e-mail: st.marys.books@freeuk.com; website: www.st-marys-books.co.uk. Dealers in *Wisdens* and second-hand cricket books and *Vanity Fair* prints.

CHRISTOPHER SAUNDERS, Orchard Books, Kingston House, High Street, Newnham on Severn, Gloucestershire GL14 1BB. Tel: 01594 516030; fax: 01594 517273; e-mail: chrisbooks@aol.com. Office/bookroom by appointment. Second-hand/antiquarian cricket books and memorabilia bought and sold. Regular catalogues issued containing selections from over 10,000 items in stock.

SPORT-IN-PRINT, 3 Radcliffe Road, West Bridgford, Nottingham NG2 5FF. Tel/fax: 0115 945 5407. All in-print ACS publications; also new and second-hand cricket and soccer books.

*SPORTSPAGES, Caxton Walk, 94–96 Charing Cross Road, London WC2H 0JG. Tel: 020 7240 9604; fax: 020 7836 0104. Barton Square, St Ann's Square, Manchester M2 7HA. Tel: 0161 832 8530; fax: 0161 832 9391; website: www.sportspages.co.uk. New cricket books, audio and video tapes, including imports, especially from Australasia; retail and mail-order service.

STUART TOPPS, 40 Boundary Avenue, Wheatley Hills, Doncaster, South Yorkshire DN2 5QU. Tel: 01302 366044. Our 120-page plus catalogue of cricket books, *Wisdens*, booklets, brochures and county yearbooks is always available.

*WILLOWS PUBLISHING CO., 17 The Willows, Stone, Staffordshire ST15 0DE. Tel: 01785 814700. *Wisden* reprints 1885, 1900–1910, 1916–1919 and 1941–1945. Send SAE for prices.

WISTERIA BOOKS, Wisteria Cottage, Birt Street, Birtsmorton, Malvern, Worcestershire WR13 6AW. Tel/fax: 01684 833578. Visit our family run stall at county grounds for new, second-hand, antiquarian cricket books and ephemera, or contact Grenville Simons at the address above. Send SAE for catalogue.

MARTIN WOOD CRICKET BOOKS, 1c Wickenden Road, Sevenoaks, Kent TN13 3PJ. Tel/fax: 01732 457205. Send first-class stamp for annual catalogue listing by subject: *Wisdens*, Annuals, Biographies, Tours, Histories, Counties, Fiction and also Autographs. Established 1970.

AUCTIONEERS

*CHRISTIE'S, 85 Old Brompton Road, South Kensington, London SW7 3LD. Tel: 020 7321 3402; e-mail: cnewbon@Christies.com. In 2000, South Kensington restructured its Sporting Memorabilia Department. Cricket sales have been held on a regular basis since the inaugural MCC Bicentenary Sale in 1987, and enquiries should now be directed to Clair Newbon.

MULLOCK MADELEY, The Old Shippon, Wall under Heywood, Church Stretton, Shropshire. Tel: 01694 771771; website: www.mullockmadeley.co.uk. Mullock Madeley hold specialist sporting memorabilia auctions. For details, please visit either our website or our offices.

*T. VENNETT-SMITH, 11 Nottingham Road, Gotham, Nottinghamshire NG11 0HE. Tel: 0115 983 0541. Auctioneers and valuers. Twice-yearly auctions of cricket and sports memorabilia. The cricket auction is run by cricketers for cricket-lovers worldwide.

*DOMINIC WINTER, Specialist Book Auctioneers & Valuers, The Old School, Maxwell Street, Swindon, Wiltshire SN1 5DR. Tel: 01793 611340; fax: 01793 491727; e-mail: info@dominic-winter.co.uk; website: www.dominic-winter.co.uk. Twice-yearly auction sales of sports books and memorabilia, including *Wisdens*.

Asterisks indicate businesses that have display advertisements elsewhere in the Almanack. See Index of Advertisements for details.

DIRECTORY OF CRICKET SUPPLIERS

COMPUTER DATABASES

FBSS LTD, Windsor, Little Stambridge Hall Lane, Rochford SS4 1EN. Tel: 01702 530060; fax: 01702 542988; e-mail: accounts@fbss.co.uk; website: www.fbss.co.uk. Cricket Organiser™ for Windows™. The software package for all cricket clubs and schools.

GORDON VINCE, 5 Chaucer Grove, Camberley, Surrey, GU15 2XZ. E-mail: gordon@gvince.demon.co.uk. The Cricket Statistics System is used worldwide to produce the widest range of averages and statistics, from Test to village level. Also available with an extensive range of up-to-date databases of matches from around the world.

CRICKET EQUIPMENT

DUKE SPORTSWEAR, Unit 4, Magdalene Road, Torquay, Devon TQ1 4AF. Tel/fax: 01803 292012. Test-standard sweaters to order in your club colours, using the finest yarns.

DUNCAN FEARNLEY, Mill Race Lane, Stourbridge, West Midlands DY8 1JN, England. Tel: 01384 370898; fax: 01384 444969, Email: fearnley@arcsports.co.uk; website: www.fearnleycricket.com. Manufacturers and suppliers of the finest cricket bats, equipment, clothing, footwear, flicx pitches and bowling machines.

FORDHAM SPORTS, 81 Robin Hood Way, Kingston Vale, London SW15 3PW. Tel: 020 8974 5654; e-mail: fordham@fordhamsports.co.uk; website: www.fordhamsports.co.uk. Cricket equipment specialist with largest range of branded stock in London at discount prices. Mail order worldwide. Free catalogue.

GUNN & MOORE, 119/121 Stanstead Road, Forest Hill, London SE23 1HJ. Tel: 020 8291 3344; fax: 020 8699 4008. Gunn & Moore, established in 1885, are the world's most comprehensive provider of cricket bats, equipment, footwear and clothing.

LUKE EYRES, Freepost, Denny Industrial Estate, Pembroke Avenue, Waterbeach, Cambridge CB5 8BR. Tel: 01353 863125. 100% wool, cotton or acrylic sweaters as supplied to major county clubs, international cricket teams and schools.

NOMAD BOX CO. LTD, Rockingham Road, Market Harborough, Leicestershire LE16 7QE. Tel: 01858 464878. Nomad manufacture "coffins" for Test, county and club players, with designs to suit every pocket. Wide range available, from flight-case coffins to standard, umpire and junior models.

STUART & WILLIAMS (BOLA), 6 Brookfield Road, Cotham, Bristol BS6 5PQ. E-mail: info@bola.co.uk; website: www.bola.co.uk. Manufacturer of bowling machines and ball-throwing machines for all sports. Machines for recreational and commercial application for sale to the UK and overseas.

CRICKET TOURS (OVERSEAS)

ALL WAYS SPORTS TRAVEL, 7 Whielden Street, Old Amersham, Buckinghamshire HP7 0HT. Tel: 01494 432747; fax: 01494 432767; e-mail: sales@all-ways.co.uk; website: www.all-ways.co.uk. Specialist tour operators to the South Pacific. Cricket supporters' tours to Australia and New Zealand.

BLADE, 34 Barton Gate, Barton-under-Needwood, Staffordshire, DE13 8AG. Tel: 01283 711111; fax: 01283 711700; e-mail: enquiries@blade.uk.com; website www.blade.uk.com. Specialists in tailor-made travel. Supporters tours to all major sporting events worldwide. Annual Pro-Am Cricket Festival in Barbados. PCA official travel company.

SUN LIVING, 10 Milton Court, Ravenshead, Nottingham, NG15 9BD. Tel: 01623 795365; fax: 01623 797421. Worldwide specialists in cricket tours for all levels and ages, plus our ever-popular supporters' tours. ABTA and ATOL bonded.

TRAVEL PORTFOLIO, 18/19 Guildhall Street, Bury St Edmunds, Suffolk IP33 1QD. Tel: 01284 762255. Specialists in cricket supporters' tours to Australia, New Zealand and destinations worldwide. We tailor-make tours for independent travellers wishing to experience the country while following cricket.

CRICKET TOURS (UK & IRELAND)

BESTWESTERN LIVERMEAD CLIFF HOTEL, Sea Front, Torquay, Devon TQ2 6RQ. Tel: 01803 299666. Torquay's only three-star water's edge hotel at sea level. Widely supported by touring sides and cricket personalities.

PENGWERN SPORTS TOURS, The Halfway House Inn, Cleobury Road, Eardington, Bridgnorth, Shropshire WV16 5LS. Tel: 01746 762670; fax: 01746 768063; e-mail: pete@pengwernsportstours.com; website: www.pengwernsportstours.com. Midweek cricket tours with golf days in the Heart of England. Over 300 tours hosted in the past 12 years.

RADBROOK HALL HOTEL, Shrewsbury, SY3 9BQ. Tel: 01743 236676; e-mail: tours@awmsport.co.uk; website: www.awmsport.co.uk. Midweek and weekend cricket tours, including fixtures and golf breaks with booked tee times. Facilities include gymnasium, squash, sauna and jacuzzi.

RED HOUSE HOTEL, 2 Whipton Village Road, Exeter. Tel: 01392 256104. Centrally situated for cricket tours. Family-run hotel, rooms en-suite with satellite TV. Licensed bar, carvery and restaurant. Late bar (and food) available. Fixtures can be arranged. Car park.

SHIRE SPORTS, *The Sports Tour Specialists*, PO Box 142, Nantwich, Cheshire, CW5 8JF. Tel: 0870 7458200; fax: 0870 7458654; e-mail: tours@shiresports.co.uk; website: www.shiresports.co.uk. Club cricket tours fully arranged to all venues throughout the UK and Ireland. Over 100 tours arranged each year. Established 1993.

GIFTS, MEMORABILIA AND LIMITED-EDITION PRINTS

DD DESIGNS, 62 St Catherine's Grove, Lincoln, Lincolnshire LN5 8NA. E-mail: ddprints@aol.com. Specialists in signed limited-edition prints. Official producer of *Wisden's* "Cricketers of the Year" sets, and other art portfolios.

JOCELYN GALSWORTHY, 237 Chelsea Cloisters, Sloane Avenue, London SW3 3DT. Tel: 020 7591 0698. Limited-edition prints signed and numbered by the artist. Original cricket paintings for sale. Free brochure.

NICK POTTER LTD, 34 Sackville Street, London W1S 3ED. Tel: 020 7439 4029; fax: 020 7439 4027; email: art@nickpotter.com; website: www.nickpotter.com. Specialists in fine cricket pictures, prints and memorabilia dating from the 19th century to the present day. Large stock held in our London gallery.

TONY SHELDON COLLECTIBLES PROMOTIONS, 29 Highclere Road, Higher Crumpsall, Manchester M8 4WH. Tel/fax: 0161 740 3714. Sets of trade (cigarette) cards designed, produced and supplied to your specifications.

SPORTING-GIFTS.COM LTD, 6 Arundel Close, Chippenham, Wiltshire SN14 0PR. Tel: 01249 464975; website: www.sporting-gifts.com. For a wide selection of cricket and sports gifts, figures, photographs, prints, games, books and videos.

PAVILION AND GROUND EQUIPMENT

AUTOGUIDE EQUIPMENT LTD, Station Works, Tisbury, Wiltshire SP3 6QZ. Tel: 01747 870711; fax: 01747 871171; e-mail: colinpearson@autoguide.co.uk. Manufacturers of the world-famous Auto-Roller cricket wicket roller.

E. A. COMBS LTD, Pulteney Works, London E18 1PS. Tel: 020 8530 4216. Pavilion clocks for permanent and temporary siting. Wide choice of sizes and styles to suit any ground.

EUROPEAN TIMING SYSTEMS, Oldbury-on-Severn, Bristol BS35 1PL. Tel: 01454 413606; fax: 01454 415139. ETS manufacture electronic scoreboards using high-visibility 9″/12″/18″ displays. Types available to suit small clubs up to county standard. Recent installations at Old Trafford and Glamorgan.

FSL SCOREBOARDS, Sandholes Road, Cookstown, Co. Tyrone, N. Ireland, BT80 9AR. Tel: 028 8676 6131; fax: 028 8676 2414; website: www.fsl.ltd.uk. Complete range of electronic scoreboards including: portable, indoor, stand-alone, and kits for modifying manual scoreboards.

JMS CRICKET LTD, Bobbin Mill Close, Steeton, West Yorkshire BD20 6PZ. Tel: 01535 654520/0113 2590444; e-mail: admin@jmscricket.com. Buy direct from the manufacturer. Mobile and flat covers, sightscreens and practice frames.

RADFORD EZYNET, tel: 01386 861029; email: enquiries@radfordezynet.co.uk; website: www.radfordezynet.co.uk. World-leading demountable and portable cricket nets, providing flexibility, security and long life.

STADIA SPORTS INTERNATIONAL LTD, 19/20 Lancaster Way Business Park, Ely, Cambridgeshire CB6 3NW. Tel: 01353 668688; fax: 01353 669444; e-mail: sales@stadia-sports.co.uk. Quality sightscreens, scoreboards/boxes, net cages, synthetic wickets and wicket covers.

STUART CANVAS PRODUCTS, Warren Works, Hardwick Grange, Warrington, Cheshire WA1 4RF. Tel: 01925 814525; fax: 01925 831709. Designers, manufacturers and suppliers of flat sheets, mobiles, roller & hover covers – sold throughout the world, including Test and county grounds.

TILDENET LTD, Hartcliffe Way, Bristol BS3 5RJ. Tel: 0117 966 9684; fax: 0117 923 1251. Tildenet offer a wide range of cricket equipment, including cricket practice nets, sightscreens and perimeter fencing. For details, contact Lawrence Green.

PITCHES (TURF AND NON-TURF)

C. H. BINDER LTD, Moreton, Ongar, Essex CM5 0HY. Tel: 01277 890246; fax: 01277 890105; website: www.binderloams.co.uk; email: sales@binderloams.co.uk. Sole producers of Ongar Loam™ top-dressing for cricket pitches, grass seed, fertilisers etc. Catalogues and quotations on request. Collections available.

CLUB SURFACES LIMITED, The Barn, Bisham Grange, Marlow, Buckinghamshire SL7 1RS. Tel: 01628 485969; fax: 01628 471944. ClubTurf, world-leading non-turf pitch since 1978 with over 5,000 installations. Unique in-house manufacture and installation – proved best in independent Sports Council tests. Contact Derek Underwood for an information pack.

MALCOLM DORMAN LTD, Westcott Venture Park, Ashenden Road, Westcott, Buckinghamshire HP18 0XB. Tel: 01296 658255; fax: 01296 655636; e-mail: sales@sportslawn.com. New design of non-turf pitch. Factory-made and assembled in one day. Consistent and low-cost.

DURA-SPORT LTD, Unit 12, Cornwall Business Centre, Cornwall Road, South Wigston, Leicestershire LE18 4XH. Tel: 0116 2770899; fax: 0116 2770433; e-mail: durasport@compuserve.com. Full range of synthetic surfaces for cricket, including the world-renowned Notts Sport® non-turf cricket pitches.

NOTTS SPORT®, Premier House, 18 Mandervell Road, Oadby, Leicester LE2 5LQ. Tel: 0116 272 0222; fax: 0116 272 0617; e-mail: info@nottssport.com; website: www.nottssport.com. World-renowned pitch systems. Clients include ICC, MCC, ECB and many national and regional bodies.

PEAK SPORTS, Unit 4, Ford Street, Brinksway, Stockport SK3 0BT. Tel: 0161 480 2502; fax: 0161 480 1652. Agents for Wimbledon Unreal Grass pitches. Simply glue to concrete, nail to tarmac or roll out on the gym floor. Guaranteed ten years. Write for a brochure. Installed at Radley, Winchester, Manchester GS, Ipswich, Wellington, Merchiston Castle, etc.

J. M. SMITH, Bobbin Mill Close, Steeton, West Yorkshire BD20 6PZ. Tel: 01535 654520; e-mail: admin@jmscricket.com. Top-quality artificial match and practice facilities individually designed. Also ECB consultant for turf pitches.

SOCIETIES

CRICKET MEMORABILIA SOCIETY, Hon. Secretary, Tony Sheldon, 29 Highclere Road, Crumpsall, Manchester M8 4WH. Tel/fax: 0161 740 3714. For collectors worldwide – meetings, speakers, auctions, magazines, directory, merchandise, and – most of all – friendship.

TROPHIES & AWARDS

COLBORNE TROPHIES LTD, tel: 01225 764101; fax: 01225 762009; email: sales@awards.org.uk. Long-established and reliable suppliers of trophies and awards. Fast mail-order service and discounts available. Free catalogue.

TEST MATCHES, 2000-01

Full details of these Tests, and others too late for inclusion, will appear in the 2002 edition of *Wisden*.

ZIMBABWE v NEW ZEALAND

First Test: At Bulawayo, September 12, 13, 14, 15, 16. New Zealand won by seven wickets. Toss: Zimbabwe. Zimbabwe 350 (G. J. Rennie 36, S. V. Carlisle 38, A. D. R. Campbell 88, H. H. Streak 51, M. L. Nkala 30 not out; P. J. Wiseman five for 90) and 119 (A. D. R. Campbell 45; C. L. Cairns five for 31, P. J. Wiseman three for 54); New Zealand 338 (M. J. Horne 110, C. D. McMillan 58, C. L. Cairns 33, A. C. Parore 32 not out, D. L. Vettori 49; P. A. Strang eight for 109) and 132 for three (M. S. Sinclair 43 not out, C. D. McMillan 31 not out).

Cairns pulled ahead of Danny Morrison (160 Test wickets) to become New Zealand's second-leading wicket-taker after Sir Richard Hadlee (431). Strang became the first Zimbabwean to take eight wickets in a Test innings, and only the second to take ten in a Test. In New Zealand's second innings, Grant Flower was called three times for throwing by Darrell Hair.

Second Test: At Harare, September 19, 20, 21, 22, 23. New Zealand won by eight wickets. Toss: New Zealand. New Zealand 465 (M. H. Richardson 99, M. S. Sinclair 44, N. J. Astle 86, C. L. Cairns 124, D. J. Nash 62; H. K. Olonga three for 115) and 74 for two (M. S. Sinclair 35 not out); Zimbabwe 166 (G. W. Flower 49, S. V. Carlisle 31, A. Flower 48; S. B. O'Connor three for 43) and 370 (A. Flower 65, G. J. Whittall 188 not out, H. H. Streak 54; S. B. O'Connor four for 73).

New Zealand took the series 2–0; Stephen Fleming became their most successful Test captain, his 12 wins in 29 Tests beating Geoff Howarth's 11 in 30. Cairns and Nash added 144 in their first innings, a New Zealand eighth-wicket Test record. Andy Flower became the first to score 3,000 Test runs for Zimbabwe, in his 45th match.

BANGLADESH v INDIA

Inaugural Test: At Dhaka, November 10, 11, 12, 13. India won by nine wickets. Toss: Bangladesh. Bangladesh 400 (Habibul Bashar 71, Aminul Islam 145, Akram Khan 35, Khaled Masud 32; S. B. Joshi five for 142) and 91 (Habibul Bashar 30; J. Srinath three for 19, S. B. Joshi three for 27); India 429 (S. Ramesh 58, M. Kartik 43, S. C. Ganguly 84, S. B. Joshi 92, A. B. Agarkar 34; Naimur Rahman six for 132, Mohammad Rafiq three for 117) and 64 for one (R. Dravid 41 not out).

Aminul Islam became the third player to score a century in his country's maiden Test, after Charles Bannerman for Australia in 1876-77 and Dave Houghton for Zimbabwe in 1992-93; Naimur Rahman returned the best bowling figures in such a Test since Tom Kendall's seven for 55, also for Australia in 1876-77. Only Zimbabwe (456 v India in 1992-93) had scored more in their maiden Test than Bangladesh's first-innings 400, and only South Africa (84 v England in 1888-89) had scored less than their second-innings 91. India won an overseas Test for the first time since August 1993 (Sri Lanka).

PAKISTAN v ENGLAND

First Test Match

At Lahore, November 15, 16, 17, 18, 19. Drawn. Toss: England.

England

M. A. Atherton c Yousuf Youhana b Saqlain Mushtaq .	73	– lbw b Mushtaq Ahmed	20
M. E. Trescothick c Salim Elahi b Saqlain Mushtaq .	71	– lbw b Wasim Akram	1
G. P. Thorpe c and b Saqlain Mushtaq	118	– (4) c Abdur Razzaq b Saqlain Mushtaq .	5
†A. J. Stewart lbw b Saqlain Mushtaq	3	– (5) not out.	27
*N. Hussain c Wasim Akram b Saqlain Mushtaq	7	– (3) retired hurt.	0
G. A. Hick b Saqlain Mushtaq	16	– b Shahid Afridi	14
C. White c Yousuf Youhana b Saqlain Mushtaq .	93		
I. D. K. Salisbury lbw b Saqlain Mushtaq.	31		
A. F. Giles not out	37		
A. R. Caddick not out.	5		
B 3, l-b 13, n-b 10	26	L-b 7, n-b 3	10

1/134 2/169 3/173 4/183   (8 wkts dec.) 480   1/4 2/29 3/39 4/77   (4 wkts dec.) 77
5/225 6/391 7/398 8/468

D. Gough did not bat.

In the second innings, N. Hussain retired hurt at 13.

Bowling: *First Innings*—Wasim Akram 22–8–40–0; Abdur Razzaq 22–6–55–0; Saqlain Mushtaq 74–20–164–8; Mushtaq Ahmed 44–6–132–0; Shahid Afridi 18–6–38–0; Qaiser Abbas 16–3–35–0. *Second Innings*—Wasim Akram 6–5–1–1; Abdur Razzaq 7–0–21–0; Saqlain Mushtaq 10–2–14–1; Mushtaq Ahmed 8–0–32–1; Shahid Afridi 1.1–0–2–1.

Pakistan

Saeed Anwar lbw b Hick	40	Wasim Akram c White b Giles	1
Shahid Afridi c Gough b Giles	52	Saqlain Mushtaq not out	32
Salim Elahi b White	44	Mushtaq Ahmed c and b White.	0
Inzamam-ul-Haq b Giles	63	B 3, l-b 5, n-b 8	16
Yousuf Youhana c Stewart b Giles	124		
Qaiser Abbas c Hick b White	2	1/63 2/101 3/199 4/203	401
*†Moin Khan lbw b Caddick	17	5/210 6/236 7/272	
Abdur Razzaq lbw b White	10	8/273 9/400 10/401	

Bowling: Gough 17–6–45–0; Caddick 24–4–68–1; Giles 59–20–113–4; Salisbury 31–5–71–0; Hick 8–0–42–1; White 24.3–5–54–4.

Umpires: D. B. Hair (Australia) and Riazuddin.
Referee: R. S. Madugalle (Sri Lanka).

Atherton was the sixth Englishman to reach 7,000 runs, in his 103rd Test. Thorpe's 118 contained only two fours. Saqlain Mushtaq returned figures of 74–20–164–8, then added 127 with Yousuf Youhana for Pakistan's ninth wicket.

PAKISTAN v ENGLAND

Second Test Match

At Faisalabad, November 29, 30, December 1, 2, 3. Drawn. Toss: Pakistan.

Pakistan

Saeed Anwar c Thorpe b Giles	53		
Shahid Afridi c Thorpe b Gough	10	– c Giles b Gough	10
Salim Elahi c Atherton b Giles	41	– (1) c Stewart b Giles	72
Inzamam-ul-Haq b Giles	0	– c Hick b Salisbury	71
Yousuf Youhana c Thorpe b Gough	74		
Abdur Razzaq b White	9	– (3) not out	100
*†Moin Khan c Hussain b Giles	65		
Wasim Akram st Stewart b Giles	1	– (5) not out	4
Saqlain Mushtaq c Trescothick b Gough	34		
Arshad Khan c Thorpe b White	2		
Danish Kaneria not out	8		
B 1, l-b 12, n-b 6	19	B 6, l-b 5, n-b 1	12
	316	(3 wkts dec.)	269

1/33 2/96 3/96 4/130 5/151
6/271 7/271 8/276 9/283 10/316

1/13 2/111 3/259

Bowling: *First Innings*—Gough 23.1–2–79–3; Caddick 15–3–49–0; White 25–6–71–2; Giles 35–13–75–5; Salisbury 10–0–29–0. *Second Innings*—Gough 10.2–1–32–1; Caddick 18–1–49–0; Giles 26–3–90–1; White 19–3–55–0; Salisbury 7–0–32–1.

England

M. A. Atherton c Yousuf Youhana b Saqlain Mushtaq	32	– not out	65
M. E. Trescothick st Moin Khan b Danish Kaneria	30	– b Saqlain Mushtaq	10
*N. Hussain lbw b Saqlain Mushtaq	23	– c Moin Khan b Arshad Khan	5
I. D. K. Salisbury c Yousuf Youhana b Arshad Khan	33		
G. P. Thorpe lbw b Wasim Akram	79	– (4) b Arshad Khan	0
†A. J. Stewart c Abdur Razzaq b Danish Kaneria	13	– (5) c Yousuf Youhana b Shahid Afridi	22
G. A. Hick c Yousuf Youhana b Abdur Razzaq	17	– (6) b Shahid Afridi	0
C. White b Saqlain Mushtaq	41	– (7) not out	9
A. F. Giles c Shahid Afridi b Abdur Razzaq	0		
A. R. Caddick c Moin Khan b Abdur Razzaq	5		
D. Gough not out	19		
B 4, l-b 14, n-b 32	50	L-b 4, n-b 10	14
	342	(5 wkts)	125

1/49 2/105 3/106 4/203 5/235
6/274 7/274 8/275 9/295 10/342

1/44 2/57 3/57
4/108 5/110

Bowling: *First Innings*—Wasim Akram 26–6–69–1; Abdur Razzaq 20–0–74–3; Danish Kaneria 34–9–89–2; Saqlain Mushtaq 30.4–8–62–3; Arshad Khan 25–12–29–1; Shahid Afridi 1–0–1–0. *Second Innings*—Wasim Akram 5–1–13–0; Abdur Razzaq 1–1–0–0; Saqlain Mushtaq 19–4–26–1; Danish Kaneria 7–0–30–0; Arshad Khan 13–4–31–2; Shahid Afridi 12–3–21–2.

Umpires: S. A. Bucknor (West Indies) and Mian Mohammad Aslam.
Referee: R. S. Madugalle (Sri Lanka).

This was Wasim Akram's 100th Test. Gough drew level with Angus Fraser, on 177 Test wickets, as England's joint tenth-leading wicket-taker. Abdur Razzaq reached his maiden Test hundred the day after his 21st birthday.

PAKISTAN v ENGLAND

Third Test Match

At Karachi, December 7, 8, 9, 10, 11. England won by six wickets. Toss: Pakistan.

Pakistan

Saeed Anwar lbw b Gough	8	– c Thorpe b Caddick	21
Imran Nazir c Giles b Trescothick	20	– c Stewart b Gough	4
Salim Elahi b Caddick	28	– c Thorpe b Giles	37
Inzamam-ul-Haq c Trescothick b White	142	– b Giles	27
Yousuf Youhana c and b Giles	117	– (6) c Stewart b White	24
Abdur Razzaq c Hussain b Giles	21	– (7) c Atherton b Giles	1
*†Moin Khan c Hick b Giles	13	– (8) c Hussain b White	14
Shahid Afridi b Giles	10	– (9) not out	15
Saqlain Mushtaq b Gough	16	– (5) lbw b Gough	4
Waqar Younis b Gough	17	– run out	0
Danish Kaneria not out	0	– lbw b Gough	0
B 3, l-b 3, n-b 7	13	B 3, l-b 5, n-b 3	11

1/8 2/44 3/64 4/323 5/325   405   1/24 2/26 3/71 4/78 5/128   158
6/340 7/359 8/374 9/402 10/405   6/128 7/139 8/143 9/149 10/158

Bowling: *First Innings*—Gough 27.4–5–82–3; Caddick 23–1–76–1; Trescothick 14–1–34–1; White 22–3–64–1; Salisbury 18–3–49–0; Giles 35–7–94–4. *Second Innings*—Gough 13–4–30–3; Caddick 15–2–40–1; Giles 27–12–38–3; Salisbury 3–0–12–0; White 12–4–30–2.

England

M. A. Atherton c Moin Khan b Abdur Razzaq	125	– c Saeed Anwar b Saqlain Mushtaq	26
M. E. Trescothick c Imran Nazir b Waqar Younis	13	– c Inzamam-ul-Haq b Saqlain Mushtaq	24
*N. Hussain c Inzamam-ul-Haq b Shahid Afridi	51	– (6) not out	6
G. P. Thorpe lbw b Waqar Younis	18	– not out	64
†A. J. Stewart c Yousuf Youhana b Saqlain Mushtaq	29	– (3) c Moin Khan b Saqlain Mushtaq	5
G. A. Hick c Shahid Afridi b Waqar Younis	12	– (5) b Waqar Younis	40
C. White st Moin Khan b Danish Kaneria	35		
A. F. Giles b Waqar Younis	19		
I. D. K. Salisbury not out	20		
A. R. Caddick c Moin Khan b Danish Kaneria	3		
D. Gough c Yousuf Youhana b Saqlain Mushtaq	18		
B 12, l-b 9, n-b 24	45	B 8, l-b 2, w 1	11

1/29 2/163 3/195 4/256 5/278   388   1/38 2/51 3/65 4/156   (4 wkts) 176
6/309 7/339 8/345 9/349 10/388

Bowling: *First Innings*—Waqar Younis 36–5–88–4; Abdur Razzaq 28–7–64–1; Shahid Afridi 16–3–34–1; Saqlain Mushtaq 52.1–17–101–2; Danish Kaneria 47–17–80–2. *Second Innings*—Waqar Younis 6–0–27–1; Abdur Razzaq 4–0–17–0; Saqlain Mushtaq 17.3–1–64–3; Danish Kaneria 3–0–18–0; Shahid Afridi 11–1–40–0.

Umpires: S. A. Bucknor (West Indies) and Mohammad Nazir.
Referee: R. S. Madugalle (Sri Lanka).

In near-darkness on the final evening, England won a Test in Pakistan for the first time since 1961-62, and took the series 1–0. They had fielded an unchanged eleven throughout. It was the first time Pakistan had lost a Test in Karachi in 35 games (34 at the National Stadium). Inzamam-ul-Haq reached 1,000 Test runs for 2000. Atherton batted more than nine and a half hours and overtook Wally Hammond (7,249) as England's fifth-highest run-scorer. Giles took 17 wickets in the series, a record for England in Pakistan.

SOUTH AFRICA v NEW ZEALAND

First Test: At Bloemfontein, November 17, 18, 19, 20, 21. South Africa won by five wickets. Toss: South Africa. South Africa 471 for nine dec. (G. Kirsten 31, J. H. Kallis 160, N. D. McKenzie 55, M. V. Boucher 76, N. Boje 43; S. B. O'Connor three for 87, C. S. Martin three for 89) and 103 for five (D. R. Tuffey three for 38); New Zealand 229 (S. P. Fleming 57, N. J. Astle 37; A. A. Donald three for 69, S. M. Pollock four for 37) and 342 (M. H. Richardson 77, S. P. Fleming 99, C. D. McMillan 78; A. A. Donald three for 43, M. Ntini six for 66).

Donald became the first South African to take 300 Test wickets, in his 63rd Test.

Second Test: At Port Elizabeth, November 30, December 1, 2, 3, 4. South Africa won by seven wickets. Toss: South Africa. New Zealand 298 (M. S. Sinclair 150, C. D. McMillan 39; A. A. Donald four for 69, S. M. Pollock four for 64) and 148 (M. H. Richardson 60; L. Klusener three for eight); South Africa 361 (G. Kirsten 49, H. H. Dippenaar 35, D. J. Cullinan 33, S. M. Pollock 33, N. D. McKenzie 120, N. Boje 51; C. S. Martin four for 104) and 89 for three (G. Kirsten 47 not out).

Sinclair's 150 was the highest Test score for New Zealand against South Africa.

Third Test: At Johannesburg, December 8, 9, 10, 11, 12. Drawn. Toss: South Africa. New Zealand 200 (M. H. Richardson 46, H. J. H. Marshall 40 not out; M. Ntini three for 29); South Africa 261 for three dec. (H. H. Dippenaar 100, J. H. Kallis 79 not out, D. J. Cullinan 31 not out).

The first, third and fourth days were washed out. The match award was given to groundsman Chris Scott and his staff. South Africa took the series 2–0.

INDIA v ZIMBABWE

First Test: At Delhi, November 18, 19, 20, 21, 22. India won by seven wickets. Toss: Zimbabwe. Zimbabwe 422 for nine dec. (S. V. Carlisle 58, A. D. R. Campbell 70, A. Flower 183 not out; J. Srinath four for 81) and 225 (S. V. Carlisle 32, A. Flower 70; J. Srinath five for 60); India 458 for four dec. (S. S. Das 58, R. Dravid 200 not out, S. R. Tendulkar 122) and 190 for three (R. Dravid 70 not out, S. R. Tendulkar 39, S. C. Ganguly 65 not out).

Flower and Henry Olonga (11 not out) shared an unbroken stand of 97, a Zimbabwean last-wicket record, in the first innings. Dravid replied with his maiden Test double-hundred.

Second Test: At Nagpur, November 25, 26, 27, 28, 29. Drawn. Toss: India. India 609 for six dec. (S. S. Das 110, S. Ramesh 48, R. Dravid 162, S. R. Tendulkar 201 not out, S. C. Ganguly 30); Zimbabwe 382 (G. J. Whittall 84, S. V. Carlisle 51, A. Flower 55, G. W. Flower 106 not out; J. Srinath three for 81) and 503 for six (G. J. Rennie 37, A. D. R. Campbell 102, A. Flower 232 not out, D. P. Viljoen 38, Extras 30; Sarandeep Singh four for 136).

Zimbabwe were 166 behind when they lost their third second-innings wicket; Campbell scored his maiden hundred in his 47th Test, while Flower's 232 not out was the highest by a wicket-keeper in Tests; in the two-match series, he scored 540 at 270.00. India, for whom Dravid totalled 432 for once out, took the series 1–0.

AUSTRALIA v WEST INDIES

First Test: At Brisbane, November 23, 24, 25. Australia won by an innings and 126 runs. Toss: Australia. West Indies 82 (G. D. McGrath six for 17) and 124 (S. Chanderpaul 62 not out; G. D. McGrath four for ten, B. Lee three for 40); Australia 332 (M. J. Slater 54, M. L. Hayden 44, S. R. Waugh 41, A. C. Gilchrist 48, B. Lee 62 not out; M. I. Black four for 83, M. Dillon three for 79).

Australia equalled West Indies' record of 11 consecutive Test wins in 1984. Only Chanderpaul passed 20 in either West Indies innings; on the opening day they were dismissed in double figures for the fifth time in 17 Tests since March 1999. McGrath's match analysis was 33–21–27–10; he overtook Craig McDermott (291) to become Australia's third-leading Test wicket-taker.

Second Test: At Perth, December 1, 2, 3. Australia won by an innings and 27 runs. Toss: Australia. West Indies 196 (W. W. Hinds 50, R. D. Jacobs 96 not out; G. D. McGrath three for 48, J. N. Gillespie three for 46) and 173 (W. W. Hinds 41, J. C. Adams 40 not out; B. Lee five for 61); Australia 396 for eight dec. (M. L. Hayden 69, M. E. Waugh 119, A. C. Gilchrist 50, B. Lee 41 not out).

Australia won a record 12th successive Test. McGrath took a hat-trick in the game's ninth over, which included his 300th wicket in his 64th Test.

Third Test: At Adelaide, December 15, 16, 17, 18, 19. Australia won by five wickets. Toss: West Indies. West Indies 391 (B. C. Lara 182, J. C. Adams 49, M. N. Samuels 35; J. N. Gillespie five for 89, C. R. Miller five for 81) and 141 (D. Ganga 32, B. C. Lara 39; G. D. McGrath three for 27, C. R. Miller five for 32); Australia 403 (M. J. Slater 83, M. L. Hayden 58, M. E. Waugh 63, R. T. Ponting 92, D. R. Martyn 46 not out, Extras 34; M. Dillon three for 84) and 130 for five (J. L. Langer 48, D. R. Martyn 34 not out; M. Dillon three for 42).

Gilchrist captained Australia after Steve Waugh was injured at Perth. In West Indies' first innings, the ball hit a fielder's helmet; though originally signalled as five byes, this was officially amended to five penalty runs under Law 41.3, the first instance of penalties in Test cricket. Miller took five wickets for eight runs in 52 balls on his way to ten for 113 as West Indies' second innings collapsed from 87 for two.

Fourth Test: At Melbourne, December 26, 27, 28, 29. Australia won by 352 runs. Toss: West Indies. Australia 364 (M. J. Slater 30, J. L. Langer 31, S. R. Waugh 121 not out, A. C. Gilchrist 37; M. Dillon four for 76) and 262 for five dec. (M. L. Hayden 30, J. L. Langer 80, M. E. Waugh 78 not out); West Indies 165 (M. N. Samuels 60 not out, R. D. Jacobs 42; J. N. Gillespie three for 48, A. J. Bichel five for 60) and 109 (M. N. Samuels 46; J. N. Gillespie six for 40, C. R. Miller three for 40).

Jacobs took seven catches in Australia's first innings, equalling the Test record. Waugh returned and became Test cricket's fifth-highest scorer, overtaking Javed Miandad (8,540). In their second innings, West Indies collapsed to 23 for six (all to Gillespie). Glenn McGrath failed to take a wicket for the first time in 32 Tests since missing the Indian tour in 1997-98.

Fifth Test: At Sydney, January 2, 3, 4, 5, 6. Australia won by six wickets. Toss: West Indies. West Indies 272 (S. L. Campbell 79, W. W. Hinds 70, B. C. Lara 35; S. C. G. MacGill seven for 104) and 352 (S. L. Campbell 54, W. W. Hinds 46, R. R. Sarwan 51, R. D. Jacobs 62, M. V. Nagamootoo 68; G. D. McGrath three for 80, C. R. Miller four for 102); Australia 452 (M. J. Slater 96, S. R. Waugh 103, R. T. Ponting 51, A. C. Gilchrist 87, C. R. Miller 37 not out; M. V. Nagamootoo three for 119) and 174 for four (M. J. Slater 86 not out, S. R. Waugh 38).

Australia completed a 5-0 whitewash to take their run of Test wins to 15. Miller dyed his hair blue in honour of the Australian Federation's centenary. Slater equalled Steve Waugh's record of nine Test scores in the nineties. Walsh ended the series on 494 Test wickets.

NEW ZEALAND v ZIMBABWE

Only Test: At Wellington, December 26, 27, 28, 29, 30. Drawn. Toss: New Zealand. New Zealand 487 for seven dec. (M. H. Richardson 75, N. J. Astle 141, C. D. McMillan 142, A. C. Parore 50 not out; B. C. Strang three for 116) and 153 for four dec. (S. P. Fleming 55, N. J. Astle 51 not out); Zimbabwe 340 for six dec. (G. J. Rennie 93, A. Flower 79, T. N. Madondo 74 not out; C. S. Martin five for 71) and 60 for two (G. J. Rennie 37).

Astle and McMillan added 222 in the first innings, a New Zealand fifth-wicket record. Flower completed his sixth consecutive Test fifty and became only the second batsman to reach 1,000 Test runs in 2000.

SOUTH AFRICA v SRI LANKA

First Test: At Durban, December 26, 27, 28, 29, 30. Drawn. Toss: South Africa. South Africa 420 (G. Kirsten 180, D. J. Cullinan 59, L. Klusener 50, N. Boje 32, Extras 31; C. R. D. Fernando five for 98, M. Muralitharan five for 122) and 140 for seven dec. (G. Kirsten 34; M. Muralitharan six for 39); Sri Lanka 216 (K. Sangakkara 74, D. P. M. D. Jayawardene 98; S. M. Pollock three for 40) and 149 for six (R. P. Arnold 30).

Pollock became the second South African to take 200 wickets, in his 49th Test, while Muralitharan's 11 for 161 made him the first Sri Lankan to take 300, in his 58th. Pollock had claimed five or more in an innings eight times in nine Tests against Sri Lanka.

Second Test: At Cape Town, January 2, 3, 4. South Africa won by an innings and 229 runs. Toss: Sri Lanka. Sri Lanka 95 (K. Sangakkara 32; S. M. Pollock six for 30, M. Ngam three for 26) and 180 (D. P. M. D. Jayawardene 45, W. P. U. J. C. Vaas 38; M. Ngam three for 36, N. Boje four for 28); South Africa 504 for seven dec. (G. Kirsten 52, J. H. Kallis 49, D. J. Cullinan 112, N. D. McKenzie 47, M. V. Boucher 92, L. Klusener 97, N. Boje 31 not out; R. P. Arnold three for 76).

Pollock reduced Sri Lanka to 13 for four on the opening morning. Herschelle Gibbs, returning after a six-month suspension for his role in the Cronje affair, made a two-ball duck, but Cullinan scored his 12th Test hundred, a South African record, and his fourth in succession at Cape Town. South Africa's win was their biggest in Tests.

Third Test: At Centurion, January 20, 21, 22. South Africa won by an innings and seven runs. Toss: Sri Lanka. South Africa 378 (D. J. Cullinan 48, N. D. McKenzie 103, M. V. Boucher 38, S. M. Pollock 111; D. N. T. Zoysa four for 76); Sri Lanka 119 (R. S. Kaluwitharana 32; M. Ntini four for 39) and 252 (K. Sangakkara 98, R. P. Arnold 71; J. M. Kemp three for 33).

Pollock reached his maiden Test hundred, in his 51st Test, in 95 balls. South Africa took the series 2–0 when Sangakkara was last out, two short of a maiden hundred in his sixth Test.

THE WISDEN WORLD CHAMPIONSHIP

On February 11, 2001, almost six years after Wisden began campaigning for the introduction of a World Test Championship, the International Cricket Council announced that it planned to introduce an official Championship starting this May, and based on the Wisden formula.

The decision came at an executive board meeting in Melbourne which also decided to introduce a fixture grid. This obliges each Test-playing country to play the other nine, both home and away, over a five-year timescale in series of at least two Tests. One-off Tests have been abolished.

Details of how the system would work in practice were still being finalised. But the ICC said it wanted to take over the existing Wisden table and make it official, which is what we have been advocating since our own, unofficial Championship began in 1996. Wisden have also suggested that there should be a trophy – perhaps the Bradman Cup – to be held by the leading team in the world and then handed over as soon as it is superseded.

The grid will eventually remove the main difficulty of the current table, which needs averages to operate because not every team has played everyone else. The last gap among the first nine countries should be removed in 2003, when Australia are scheduled to host Zimbabwe. Bangladesh will continue to be a special case until they have played a reasonable number of fixtures.

Australia completed their fourth consecutive year unchallenged at the top of the Wisden table early in 2001. South Africa remained close behind with West Indies – thanks to an unbeaten record in recent home series – still third despite their abysmal away form. This emphasises the point that the Championship is a league table based on results, not a ranking system based on subjective interpretation of form.

The Championship works by counting the most recent series, both home and away, between each pair of countries. Teams receive two points for winning a series, and one for drawing. For now, a one-off Test counts as a series. Series not renewed after seven years are excluded from the table, recalculation taking place each September. The current table includes series played since September 1993.

THE WISDEN WORLD CHAMPIONSHIP TABLE

(as at February 11, 2001)

		Series played	Won	Lost	Drawn	Points	Average
1.	Australia	15	12	2	1	25	1.67
2.	South Africa	15	10	3	2	22	1.47
3.	West Indies	14	6	5	3	15	1.071
4.	Sri Lanka	15	6	5	4	16	1.067
5.	Pakistan	15	6	7	2	14	0.933
6.	England	14	6	7	1	13	0.929
7.	New Zealand	16	5	9	2	12	0.75
8.	India	15	4	8	3	11	0.73
9.	Zimbabwe	14	2	10	2	6	0.43
	Bangladesh	1	0	1	0	—	—

Previous leaders: October 13–December 12, 1996 South Africa; December 17–January 28, 1997 Australia, South Africa and West Indies (joint); Australia have led since January 28, 1997.

Matches between the Asian countries in 1998-99, including the Asian Championship final in Dhaka, are treated as three series: India v Pakistan; Sri Lanka v India; Pakistan v Sri Lanka.

The standings are updated regularly in *Wisden Cricket Monthly* and on Wisden's website, www.wisden.com.

INTERNATIONAL SCHEDULE, 2001–2006

At an executive board meeting in Melbourne, in February 2001, the International Cricket Council unveiled a ten-year schedule of Tests and one-day internationals. The schedule initially runs from May 2001 to April 2011; all of the ICC's ten Test-playing members are to play each other in home and away Test series (with a minimum of two matches to a series) during each five-year period.

The programme is based around Test matches, but in most cases there will be associated one-day internationals. Countries may revise dates as long as they do not disrupt other series. The following table shows the schedule from May 2001 to April 2006.

	Australia	Bangladesh	England	India	New Zealand	Pakistan	South Africa	Sri Lanka	West Indies	Zimbabwe
Australia	—	9/05	11/02	12/03	11/01	12/04	12/01 12/05	12/02	11/04	11/03
Bangladesh	10/03	—	12/03	4/04	10/04	1/02	4/03	11/04	12/02	10/01
England	7/01 6/05	5/05	—	7/02	5/04	5/01	7/03	5/02	7/04	5/03
India	9/04	4/05	12/01 2/06	—	10/03	2/04 1/06	11/04	11/05	10/02	2/02
New Zealand	2/05	12/01	2/02	12/02	—	12/03	2/04	12/04	12/05	2/06
Pakistan	9/02	9/03	11/05	4/03 2/05	9/01	—	10/03	3/05	2/02	10/04
South Africa	2/02 2/06	4/02	12/04	10/01	10/05	12/02	—	10/02	12/03	2/05
Sri Lanka	2/04	7/02	11/03	7/01	6/01 5/03	3/06	8/04	—	7/05	12/01
West Indies	4/03	5/04	2/04	4/02	6/02	5/05	3/05	7/03	—	4/06
Zimbabwe	4/02	1/04	11/04	6/01 10/05	9/05	11/02	9/01	4/04	7/01 10/03	—

Home teams listed on left, away teams across top.

ENGLAND'S INTERNATIONAL SCHEDULE, 2001–2006

Home

2001   Tests and ODIs v Pakistan and Australia
2002   Tests and ODIs v Sri Lanka and India
2003   Tests and ODIs v Zimbabwe and South Africa
2004   Tests and ODIs v New Zealand and West Indies
2005   Tests and ODIs v Bangladesh and Australia

Away

2001-02   Tests and ODIs v India and New Zealand
2002-03   Tests and ODIs v Australia WORLD CUP in South Africa
2003-04   Tests and ODIs v Sri Lanka, Bangladesh and West Indies
2004-05   Tests and ODIs v Zimbabwe and South Africa
2005-06   Tests and ODIs v Pakistan and India

All tours subject to confirmation.

FIXTURES, 2001

All County Championship matches are of four days' duration; tourist matches are four days unless stated; University Centres of Cricketing Excellence matches are of three days; and other first-class matches are three days unless stated. † *Not first-class.*

Monday, April 16

Cambridge	Cambridge UCCE v Kent
Derby	†Derbys v Bradford/ Leeds UCCE
Chester-le-Street	Durham v Durham UCCE
Leicester	†Leics v Loughborough UCCE
Taunton	†Somerset v Cardiff UCCE
Oxford	Oxford UCCE v Middx

Friday, April 20

County Championship, Division One

Leicester	Leics v Essex
Northampton	Northants v Glam
Taunton	Somerset v Lancs
The Oval	Surrey v Kent

County Championship, Division Two

Chester-le-Street	Durham v Glos
Lord's	Middx v Worcs
Birmingham	Warwicks v Hants
Nottingham	†Notts v Loughborough UCCE

Wednesday, April 25

County Championship, Division One

Chelmsford	Essex v Northants
Cardiff	Glam v Somerset
Canterbury	Kent v Yorks
Manchester	Lancs v Surrey

County Championship, Division Two

Derby	Derbys v Middx
Nottingham	Notts v Durham
Worcester	Worcs v Sussex
Abergavenny	†Cardiff UCCE v Glos
Oxford	Oxford UCCE v Hants

Sunday, April 29

†Norwich Union League Division One (1 day)

Canterbury	Kent v Warwicks
Leicester	Leics v Glos

Division Two (1 day)

Derby	Derbys v Glam
Manchester	Lancs v Hants
Lord's	Middx v Durham
Worcester	Worcs v Sussex

Monday, April 30

†Benson and Hedges Cup (1 day)

Nottingham	Notts v Leics
Worcester	Worcs v Northants
Leeds	Yorks v Derbys

Tuesday, May 1

†Benson and Hedges Cup (1 day)

Cardiff	Glam v Somerset
Canterbury	Kent v Hants
Liverpool	Lancs v Durham
The Oval	Surrey v Middx
Hove	Sussex v Essex
Birmingham	Warwicks v Glos

†The Trophy – First Round (1 day)
(see page 1638)

Wednesday, May 2

†Benson and Hedges Cup (1 day)

Derby	Derbys v Durham
Cardiff	Glam v Worcs
Bristol	Glos v Northants
Southampton	Hants v Essex
Leicester	Leics v Lancs
Taunton	Somerset v Warwicks
The Oval	Surrey v Sussex
Leeds	Yorks v Notts

Thursday, May 3

†Benson and Hedges Cup (1 day)

Leicester	Leics v Yorks
Lord's	Middx v Kent

Friday, May 4

Nottingham	British Universities v Pakistanis (3 days)

†**Benson and Hedges Cup** (1 day)

Chester-le-Street	Durham v Notts
Chelmsford	Essex v Kent
Bristol	Glos v Glam
Southampton	Hants v Surrey
Liverpool	Lancs v Derbys
Northampton	Northants v Warwicks
Hove	Sussex v Middx
Worcester	Worcs v Somerset

Saturday, May 5

†**Benson and Hedges Cup** (1 day)

Chester-le-Street	Durham v Leics
Northampton	Northants v Somerset
The Oval	Surrey v Essex
Birmingham	Warwicks v Glam

Sunday, May 6

†**Benson and Hedges Cup** (1 day)

Derby	Derbys v Notts
Bristol	Glos v Worcs
Liverpool	Lancs v Yorks
Lord's	Middx v Hants
Hastings	Sussex v Kent

Monday, May 7

†**Benson and Hedges Cup** (1 day)

Chelmsford	Essex v Middx
Cardiff	Glam v Northants
Southampton	Hants v Sussex
Canterbury	Kent v Surrey
Leicester	Leics v Derbys
Nottingham	Notts v Lancs
Taunton	Somerset v Glos
Worcester	Worcs v Warwicks
Leeds	Yorks v Durham

Tuesday, May 8

Derby	Derbys v Pakistanis (3 days)

Wednesday, May 9

County Championship, Division One

Leicester	Leics v Lancs
Northampton	Northants v Surrey
Leeds	Yorks v Somerset

County Championship, Division Two

Bristol	Glos v Middx
Southampton	Hants v Worcs
Hove	Sussex v Notts
Birmingham	Warwicks v Durham

Cambridge	Cambridge UCCE v Essex

Saturday, May 12

Canterbury	Kent v Pakistanis (3 days)

Sunday, May 13

†**Norwich Union League Division One** (1 day)

Northampton	Northants v Glos
The Oval	Surrey v Notts
Leeds	Yorks v Somerset

Division Two (1 day)

Derby	Derbys v Essex
Southampton	Hants v Worcs

Tuesday, May 15

†**The Trophy – Second Round** (1 day)
(see page 1638)

Wednesday, May 16

County Championship, Division One

Chelmsford	Essex v Yorks
Manchester	Lancs v Glam
Taunton	Somerset v Kent
The Oval	Surrey v Leics

County Championship, Division Two

Chester-le-Street	Durham v Middx
Southampton	Hants v Glos
Nottingham	Notts v Warwicks
Worcester	Worcs v Derbys
Cambridge	Cambridge UCCE v Sussex

Thursday, May 17

Lord's	ENGLAND v PAKISTAN (1st npower Test, 5 days)
Northampton	†Northants v Bradford/ Leeds UCCE

Sunday, May 20

†**Norwich Union League Division One** (1 day)

Bristol	Glos v Yorks
Nottingham	Notts v Warwicks

Taunton	Somerset v Kent
The Oval	Surrey v Leics

Division Two (1 day)

Chester-le-Street	Durham v Middx
Chelmsford	Essex v Sussex
Manchester	Lancs v Glam
Worcester	Worcs v Derbys

Tuesday, May 22

†Benson and Hedges Cup – Quarter-final
(1 day)

Wednesday, May 23

†Benson and Hedges Cup – Quarter-finals
(1 day)

Nottingham or	†Notts or Leics or
Leicester or	Derbys or Yorks v
Derby or Leeds	Pakistanis (1 day)

Subject to involvement in B&H Cup quarter-finals.

Thursday, May 24 or Friday, May 25

Leicester	Leics v Pakistanis
	(3 or 4 days)

Friday, May 25

County Championship, Division One

Swansea	Glam v Kent
The Oval	Surrey v Essex
Leeds	Yorks v Northants

County Championship, Division Two

Derby	Derbys v Hants
Bristol	Glos v Worcs
Lord's	Middx v Notts
Hove	Sussex v Warwicks

Sunday, May 27

†Norwich Union League
Division Two (1 day)

Chester-le-Street	Durham v Lancs

Tuesday, May 29

†Norwich Union League
Division One (1 day)

Birmingham	Warwicks v Glos
	(day/night)

Wednesday, May 30

County Championship, Division One

Swansea	Glam v Yorks
Tunbridge Wells	Kent v Essex
Leicester	Leics v Somerset
Northampton	Northants v Lancs

County Championship, Division Two

Chester-le-Street	Durham v Notts
Southampton	Hants v Sussex
Southgate	Middx v Derbys
The Oval	†Surrey v
	Loughborough UCCE

Thursday, May 31

Manchester	ENGLAND v
	PAKISTAN (2nd
	npower Test, 5 days)

County Championship, Division Two

Birmingham	Warwicks v Glos

Friday, June 1

Worcester	Worcs v Australians
	(3 days)

Sunday, June 3

†Norwich Union League
Division One (1 day)

Tunbridge Wells	Kent v Somerset
Oakham School	Leics v Notts
Northampton	Northants v Surrey

Division Two (1 day)

Swansea	Glam v Sussex
Southampton	Hants v Essex
Southgate	Middx v Derbys

Tuesday, June 5

Lord's (tbc)	†Middx v Australians
	(1 day)

Wednesday, June 6

County Championship, Division One

Chelmsford	Essex v Glam
Manchester	Lancs v Leics
The Oval	Surrey v Somerset
Leeds	Yorks v Kent

County Championship, Division Two

Derby	Derbys v Durham
Nottingham	Notts v Glos
Horsham	Sussex v Worcs
Oxford	Oxford UCCE v Warwicks

Thursday, June 7

Birmingham	†ENGLAND v PAKISTAN (NatWest Series, 1 day, day/night)
Northampton	Northants v Australians

Saturday, June 9

Cardiff	†PAKISTAN v AUSTRALIA (NatWest Series, 1 day)

Sunday, June 10

Bristol	†ENGLAND v AUSTRALIA (NatWest Series, 1 day)

†Norwich Union League
Division One (1 day)

Northampton	Northants v Warwicks
Nottingham	Notts v Glos
The Oval	Surrey v Somerset
Leeds	Yorks v Kent

Division Two (1 day)

Derby	Derbys v Durham
Chelmsford	Essex v Glam
Manchester	Lancs v Middx
Horsham	Sussex v Worcs

Tuesday, June 12

Lord's	†ENGLAND v PAKISTAN (NatWest Series, 1 day)

Wednesday, June 13

County Championship, Division One

Ilford	Essex v Surrey
Maidstone	Kent v Glam
Leicester	Leics v Northants
Bath	Somerset v Yorks

County Championship, Division Two

Gloucester	Glos v Durham

Southgate	Middx v Hants
Arundel	Sussex v Derbys
Worcester	Worcs v Warwicks
Chester-le-Street	Durham UCCE v Lancs

Thursday, June 14

Manchester	†ENGLAND v AUSTRALIA (NatWest Series, 1 day, day/night)

Saturday, June 16

Chester-le-Street	†PAKISTAN v AUSTRALIA (NatWest Series, 1 day)

Sunday, June 17

Leeds	†ENGLAND v PAKISTAN (NatWest Series, 1 day)

†Norwich Union League
Division One (1 day)

Gloucester	Glos v Warwicks
Maidstone	Kent v Notts
Leicester	Leics v Northants
Bath	Somerset v Yorks

Division Two (1 day)

Ilford	Essex v Durham
Southgate	Middx v Hants
Arundel	Sussex v Derbys
Worcester	Worcs v Lancs

Tuesday, June 19

Nottingham	†PAKISTAN v AUSTRALIA (NatWest Series, 1 day, day/night)

County Championship, Division One

Manchester	Lancs v Essex

Wednesday, June 20

County Championship, Division One

Canterbury	Kent v Leics
Northampton	Northants v Somerset

County Championship, Division Two

Derby	Derbys v Glos

Southampton	Hants v Durham
Nottingham	Notts v Sussex
Birmingham	Warwicks v Middx
Bradford	†Bradford/Leeds UCCE
	v Yorks
Cardiff	†Glam v Cardiff UCCE
Worcester	Worcs v Durham UCCE

Thursday, June 21

The Oval	†ENGLAND v AUSTRALIA (NatWest Series, 1 day)

Saturday, June 23

Lord's	†NATWEST SERIES FINAL (1 day)

†Norwich Union League
Division Two (1 day)

Manchester	Lancs v Essex (day/night)

Sunday, June 24

†Norwich Union League
Division One (1 day)

Nottingham	Notts v Somerset
The Oval	Surrey v Kent
Birmingham	Warwicks v Leics
Leeds	Yorks v Northants

Division Two (1 day)

Derby	Derbys v Middx
Cardiff	Glam v Worcs
Southampton	Hants v Durham

Monday, June 25

†Benson and Hedges Cup – Semi-finals
(1 day)

Arundel	MCC v Australians (3 days)

Wednesday, June 27

†The Trophy – Third Round (1 day)
(see page 1638)

Lord's	†UCCE FINAL (1 day)

Thursday, June 28

Lord's	†Oxford U. v Cambridge U. (1 day)

Friday, June 29

Chelmsford	Essex v Australians (3 days)

County Championship, Division One

Cardiff	Glam v Northants
The Oval	Surrey v Lancs
Leeds	Yorks v Leics

County Championship, Division Two

Chester-le-Street	Durham v Warwicks
Southampton	Hants v Derbys
Lord's	Middx v Sussex
Worcester	Worcs v Notts

Saturday, June 30

Cambridge	Cambridge U. v Oxford U. (4 days)
Nottingham	†Sir Garfield Sobers Invitation XI v Sir Richard Hadlee Invitation XI (1 day)

Sunday, July 1

†Norwich Union League
Division One (1 day)

Taunton	Somerset v Glos
Nottingham	†England Masters v Australia Masters (1 day)

Tuesday, July 3

†Norwich Union League
Division Two (1 day)

Derby	Derbys v Worcs (day/night)

Wednesday, July 4

County Championship, Division One

Canterbury	Kent v Lancs
Leicester	Leics v Surrey
Northampton	Northants v Yorks
Taunton	Somerset v Essex

County Championship, Division Two

Bristol	Glos v Warwicks
Nottingham	Notts v Middx

†Norwich Union League
Division Two (1 day)

| Southampton | Hants v Sussex |
| | (day/night) |

Thursday, July 5

Birmingham	ENGLAND v
	AUSTRALIA
	(1st npower Test,
	5 days)

County Championship, Division Two

| Derby | Derbys v Worcs |

Friday, July 6

County Championship, Division Two

| Hove | Sussex v Hants |

Sunday, July 8

†Norwich Union League
Division One (1 day)

Canterbury	Kent v Glos
Leicester	Leics v Surrey
Northampton	Northants v Yorks
Taunton	Somerset v Notts

Division Two (1 day)

| Chester-le-Street | Durham v Glam |
| Southgate | Middx v Essex |

Wednesday, July 11

†The Trophy – Fourth Round (1 day)
(see page 1638)

Friday, July 13

Taunton or	Somerset or Glam or
Cardiff or Bristol	Glos v Australians
	(4 days)

Saturday, July 14

Lord's	†BENSON AND
	HEDGES CUP
	FINAL (1 day)

Sunday, July 15

†Norwich Union League
Division One (1 day)

Nottingham	Notts v Kent
Birmingham	Warwicks v Northants
Scarborough	Yorks v Leics

Division Two (1 day)

Southampton	Hants v Derbys
Manchester	Lancs v Durham
Worcester	Worcs v Middx

Monday, July 16

†Norwich Union League
Division Two (1 day)

| Hove | Sussex v Essex |
| | (day/night) |

Tuesday, July 17

†Norwich Union League
Division One (1 day)

| Bristol | Glos v Somerset |
| | (day/night) |

Wednesday, July 18

County Championship, Division One

Southend	Essex v Kent
Cardiff	Glam v Leics
Guildford	Surrey v Northants

County Championship, Division Two

Chester-le-Street	Durham v Sussex
Southampton	Hants v Notts
Birmingham	Warwicks v Derbys

†Norwich Union League
Division Two (1 day)

| Manchester | Lancs v Worcs |
| | (day/night) |

Thursday, July 19

Lord's	ENGLAND v
	AUSTRALIA
	(2nd npower Test,
	5 days)

County Championship, Division One

| Manchester | Lancs v Somerset |

Friday, July 20

County Championship, Division Two

| Worcester | Worcs v Glos |

Sunday, July 22

†Norwich Union League
Division One (1 day)

| Leicester | Leics v Kent |
| Guildford | Surrey v Northants |

Division Two (1 day)

Chester-le-Street	Durham v Sussex
Southend	Essex v Hants
Cardiff	Glam v Derbys

Monday, July 23

†Norwich Union League
Division One (1 day)

Leeds	Yorks v Warwicks (day/night)

Tuesday, July 24

†The Trophy – Quarter-final (1 day)

Wednesday, July 25

†The Trophy – Quarter-finals (1 day)

Friday, July 27

County Championship, Division One

Leicester	Leics v Kent
Northampton	Northants v Essex
Taunton	Somerset v Glam
Leeds	Yorks v Lancs

County Championship, Division Two

Derby	Derbys v Notts
Cheltenham	Glos v Sussex
Lord's	Middx v Durham
Hove	†England Under-19 v West Indies Under-19 (1st 1-day, day/night)

Saturday, July 28

Southampton	Hants v Australians (3 days)

Sunday, July 29

†Norwich Union League
Division One (1 day)

Birmingham	Warwicks v Surrey
Chelmsford	†England Under-19 v West Indies Under-19 (2nd 1-day)

Monday, July 30

Chelmsford	†England Under-19 v West Indies Under-19 (3rd 1-day)

Tuesday, July 31

†Norwich Union League
Division One (1 day)

Cheltenham	Glos v Notts

Division Two (1 day)

Worcester	Worcs v Durham (day/night)

Wednesday, August 1

County Championship, Division One

Chelmsford	Essex v Leics
Colwyn Bay	Glam v Lancs
Canterbury	Kent v Somerset
Leeds	Yorks v Surrey

County Championship, Division Two

Cheltenham	Glos v Hants

†Norwich Union League
Division Two (1 day)

Hove	Sussex v Middx (day/night)

Thursday, August 2

Nottingham	ENGLAND v AUSTRALIA (3rd npower Test, 5 days)

County Championship, Division Two

Hove	Sussex v Middx
Kidderminster	Worcs v Durham

†Norwich Union League
Division One (1 day)

Birmingham	Warwicks v Notts (day/night)

Friday, August 3

County Championship, Division Two

Birmingham	Warwicks v Notts

Sunday, August 5

†Norwich Union League
Division One (1 day)

Cheltenham	Glos v Northants
Canterbury	Kent v Leics
Leeds	Yorks v Surrey

Division Two (1 day)

Derby	Derbys v Hants
Colwyn Bay	Glam v Lancs

Monday, August 6

Leicester	†England Under-19 v West Indies Under-19 (1st Test, 4 days)

Tuesday, August 7

County Championship, Division One

Manchester	Lancs v Yorks

Wednesday, August 8

Hove	Sussex v Australians (3 days)

County Championship, Division One

Northampton	Northants v Kent
Taunton	Somerset v Leics
The Oval	Surrey v Glam

County Championship, Division Two

Chester-le-Street	Durham v Derbys
Southampton	Hants v Warwicks
Lord's	Middx v Glos
Nottingham	Notts v Worcs

Saturday, August 11

†The Trophy – 1st Semi-final (1 day)

Sunday, August 12

†The Trophy – 2nd Semi-final (1 day)

†Norwich Union League Division One (1 day)

Northampton	Northants v Kent
Taunton	Somerset v Leics
The Oval	Surrey v Glos

Division Two (1 day)

Chester-le-Street	Durham v Derbys
Chelmsford	Essex v Worcs
Southampton	Hants v Glam
Lord's	Middx v Lancs
Belfast	†Ireland v Australians (1 day)

Monday, August 13

†Norwich Union League Division One (1 day)

Nottingham	Notts v Yorks (day/night)

Tuesday, August 14

†Norwich Union League Division One (1 day)

Canterbury	Kent v Surrey (day/night)

†Triple Crown Tournament (1 day)

Arundel	England Board XI v Scotland
Horsham	Ireland v Wales

Wednesday, August 15

County Championship, Division One

Cardiff	Glam v Essex
Manchester	Lancs v Northants
Leicester	Leics v Yorks

County Championship, Division Two

Derby	Derbys v Sussex
Bristol	Glos v Notts
Birmingham	Warwicks v Worcs

†Norwich Union League Division Two (1 day)

Chester-le-Street	Durham v Hants (day/night)
Nottingham	†England Under-19 v West Indies Under-19 (2nd Test, 4 days)

†Triple Crown Tournament (1 day)

Stirlands	England Board XI v Ireland
Worthing	Scotland v Wales

Thursday, August 16

Leeds	ENGLAND v AUSTRALIA (4th npower Test, 5 days)

County Championship, Division One

Canterbury	Kent v Surrey

†Triple Crown Tournament (1 day)

East Grinstead	Scotland v Ireland
Brighton College	England Board XI v Wales

Friday, August 17

County Championship, Division Two

Chester-le-Street	Durham v Hants

Sunday, August 19

†Norwich Union League
Division One (1 day)

Leicester	Leics v Yorks
Nottingham	Notts v Northants
Birmingham	Warwicks v Somerset

Division Two (1 day)

Cardiff	Glam v Essex
Lord's	Middx v Worcs

Monday, August 20

†Norwich Union League
Division Two (1 day)

Manchester	Lancs v Sussex
	(day/night)
Scarborough	†Combined Services v
	MCC (1 day)

Tuesday, August 21

County Championship, Division One

Scarborough	Yorks v Glam

†Norwich Union League
Division One (1 day)

Taunton	Somerset v Surrey
	(day/night)

Wednesday, August 22

County Championship, Division One

Colchester	Essex v Lancs

County Championship, Division Two

Lord's	Middx v Warwicks
Nottingham	Notts v Derbys
Hove	Sussex v Durham
Worcester	Worcs v Hants

†Norwich Union League
Division One (1 day)

Northampton	Northants v Leics
	(day/night)

Thursday, August 23

The Oval	ENGLAND v
	AUSTRALIA
	(5th npower Test,
	5 days)

County Championship, Division One

Northampton	Northants v Leics
Taunton	Somerset v Surrey

Sunday, August 26

†Norwich Union League
Division One (1 day)

Scarborough	Yorks v Notts

Division Two (1 day)

Colchester	Essex v Lancs
Lord's	Middx v Glam
Hove	Sussex v Durham
Worcester	Worcs v Hants

Monday, August 27

†Norwich Union League
Division One (1 day)

Bristol	Glos v Kent
Leicester	Leics v Somerset
Birmingham	Warwicks v Yorks

Division Two (1 day)

Derby	Derbys v Sussex
Cardiff	Glam v Durham
Southampton	Hants v Lancs

Tuesday, August 28

†Norwich Union League
Division Two (1 day)

Colchester	Essex v Middx
	(day/night)
Chester-le-Street	†England Under-19 v
	West Indies Under-19
	(3rd Test, 4 days)

Wednesday, August 29

†Norwich Union League
Division One (1 day)

Beckenham (tbc)	Kent v Yorks

Division Two (1 day)

Cardiff	Glam v Hants
	(day/night)

†The Trophy, 2002 – First Round (1 day)
(see page 1639)

Thursday, August 30

†Norwich Union League
Division One (1 day)

Northampton	Northants v Somerset
Whitgift School	Surrey v Warwicks

Division Two (1 day)

Hove	Sussex v Lancs (day/night)

Saturday, September 1

Lord's	†THE TROPHY FINAL (1 day)

Sunday, September 2

**†Norwich Union League
Division One** (1 day)

Bristol	Glos v Leics
Northampton	Northants v Notts
Taunton	Somerset v Warwicks

Division Two (1 day)

Chester-le-Street	Durham v Essex
Richmond	Middx v Sussex
Worcester	Worcs v Glam

Monday, September 3

**†Norwich Union League
Division One** (1 day)

The Oval	Surrey v Yorks (day/night)

Division Two (1 day)

Manchester	Lancs v Derbys (day/night)

Tuesday, September 4

**†Norwich Union League
Division Two** (1 day)

Hove	Sussex v Glam (day/night)
Lord's	†ECB 38-County Final (1 day)

Wednesday, September 5

County Championship, Division One

Chelmsford	Essex v Somerset
Canterbury	Kent v Northants
The Oval	Surrey v Yorks

County Championship, Division Two

Chester-le-Street	Durham v Worcs
Bristol	Glos v Derbys
Southampton	Hants v Middx

**†Norwich Union League
Division One** (1 day)

Leicester	Leics v Warwicks (day/night)

Thursday, September 6

Lord's	†National Club Championship Final (1 day)

Friday, September 7

County Championship, Division One

Leicester	Leics v Glam

County Championship, Division Two

Birmingham	Warwicks v Sussex

Sunday, September 9

**†Norwich Union League
Division One** (1 day)

Canterbury	Kent v Northants
Nottingham	Notts v Surrey

Division Two (1 day)

Chester-le-Street	Durham v Worcs
Chelmsford	Essex v Derbys
Southampton	Hants v Middx
Lord's	†National Village Championship Final (1 day)

Monday, September 10

**†Norwich Union League
Division One** (1 day)

Scarborough	Yorks v Glos

Wednesday, September 12

County Championship, Division One

Cardiff	Glam v Surrey
Manchester	Lancs v Kent
Taunton	Somerset v Northants
Scarborough	Yorks v Essex

County Championship, Division Two

Derby	Derbys v Warwicks
Nottingham	Notts v Hants
Hove	Sussex v Glos
Worcester	Worcs v Middx

Thursday, September 13

†**The Trophy, 2002 – Second Round** (1 day)
(see page 1639)

Sunday, September 16	Birmingham Warwicks v Kent
†Norwich Union League **Division One** (1 day)	**Division Two** (1 day)
	Derby Derbys v Lancs
Bristol Glos v Surrey	Cardiff Glam v Middx
Nottingham Notts v Leics	Hove Sussex v Hants
Taunton Somerset v Northants	Worcester Worcs v Essex

†THE TROPHY, 2001

All matches are of one day's duration.

First Round – Tuesday, May 1

1	Chippenham	Wilts v Derbys Board XI
2	Challow & Childrey	Oxon v Hunts Board XI
3	Shrewsbury	Salop v Devon
4	Sleaford	Lincs v Suffolk
5	North Perrott	Somerset Board XI v Wales
6	Maidstone	Kent Board XI v Hants Board XI
7	Southgate	Middx Board XI v Northumberland
8	Luton	Beds v Notts Board XI
9	Porthill Park	Staffs v Worcs Board XI
10	Nelson	Lancs Board XI v Yorks Board XI

Second Round – Tuesday, May 15

11	March	Cambs v Match 1 winner
12	Cheam	Surrey Board XI v Match 2 winner
13	Hastings	Sussex Board XI v Match 3 winner
14	Lincoln Lindum or Mildenhall	Match 4 winner v Essex Board XI
15	Manor Park	Norfolk v Match 5 winner
16	Maidstone or Southampton	Match 6 winner v Bucks
17	Richmond or Jesmond	Match 7 winner v Berks
18	Bournemouth	Dorset v Match 8 winner
19	Cannock or Kidderminster	Match 9 winner v Cumberland
20	Northampton	Northants Board XI v Match 10 winner
21	Brockhampton	Herefordshire v Glos Board XI
22	Coventry & NW	Warwicks Board XI v Leics Board XI
23	Truro	Cornwall v Cheshire
24	Welwyn Garden City	Herts v Durham Board XI

Third Round – Wednesday, June 27

25	Match 11 winner v Somerset	33	Match 19 winner v Kent
26	Match 12 winner v Surrey	34	Match 20 winner v Northants
27	Match 13 winner v Glos	35	Match 21 winner v Middx
28	Match 14 winner v Notts	36	Match 22 winner v Lancs
29	Match 15 winner v Leics	37	Match 23 winner v Sussex
30	Match 16 winner v Warwicks	38	Match 24 winner v Worcs
31	Match 17 winner v Essex	39	Glam v Derbys
32	Match 18 winner v Yorks	40	Durham v Hants

Fourth Round – Wednesday, July 11

41	Match 38 winner v Match 35 winner	45	Match 27 winner v Match 40 winner
42	Match 25 winner v Match 39 winner	46	Match 27 winner v Match 40 winner
43	Match 32 winner v Match 26 winner	47	Match 30 winner v Match 31 winner
44	Match 33 winner v Match 34 winner	48	Match 28 winner v Match 29 winner

Quarter-finals to be played on Tuesday, July 24, and Wednesday, July 25.

1st Semi-final to be played on Saturday, August 11.
2nd Semi-final to be played on Sunday, August 12.

Final to be played on Saturday, September 1, at Lord's.

†THE TROPHY, 2002

All matches are of one day's duration.

First Round – Wednesday, August 29, 2001

1	Welwyn Garden City	Herts v Staffs
2	Chelmsford	Essex Board XI v Sussex Board XI
3	Boughton Hall, Chester	Cheshire v Lancs Board XI
4	Dunstable	Beds v Derbys Board XI
5	Southgate	Middx Board XI v Scotland
6	Manor Park	Norfolk v Holland
7	Christ Church, Oxford	Oxon v Notts Board XI
8	South Wilts	Wilts v Ireland
9	tba	Leics Board XI v Northants Board XI
10	Millom	Cumberland v Warwicks Board XI
11	Copdock	Suffolk v Denmark
12	Godmanchester	Hunts Board XI v Glos Board XI
13	Dinton	Bucks v Worcs Board XI
14	Lincoln Lindum	Lincs v Berks

Second Round – Thursday, September 13, 2001

15	Jesmond	Northumberland v Match 1 winner
16	Chelmsford or Hastings	Match 2 winner v Wales
17	Oxton or Northern	Match 3 winner v Cornwall
18	Exmouth	Devon v Match 4 winner
19	Shenley Park or Linlithgow	Match 5 winner v Dorset
20	Manor Park or Amsterdam	Match 6 winner v Somerset Board XI
21	Shifnal	Salop v Match 7 winner
22	Southampton	Hants Board XI v Match 8 winner
23	Hinckley or Northampton	Match 9 winner v Kent Board XI
24	March	Cambs v Match 10 winner
25	Bury St Edmunds or Colwall	Match 11 winner v Herefordshire
26	Ramsey or Bristol	Match 12 winner v Yorks Board XI
27	Beaconsfield or Kidderminster	Match 13 winner v Durham Board XI
28	Bourne or Finchampstead	Match 14 winner v Surrey Board XI

†MINOR COUNTIES CHAMPIONSHIP, 2001

Unless otherwise indicated, all matches are of three days' duration.

MAY

20–Northumberland v Herts (Jesmond).

27–Cambs v Herts (March); Devon v Wilts (Bovey Tracey); Dorset v Herefordshire (Bournemouth); Lincs v Beds (Grantham); Oxon v Salop (Thame).

JUNE

10–Cambs v Norfolk (Saffron Walden); Northumberland v Beds (Jesmond); Salop v Berks (Wellington); Staffs v Lincs (Leek).

11–Cumberland v Suffolk (Carlisle).

17–Berks v Wales (Falkland CC); Herefordshire v Wilts (Colwall); Oxon v Cheshire (Challow & Childrey).

18–Salop v Cornwall (Bridgnorth).

JULY

1–Beds v Bucks (Bedford Town); Cornwall v Dorset (St Austell); Herts v Staffs (Hertford); Lincs v Suffolk (Grantham); Wales v Oxon (Swansea).

8–Bucks v Northumberland (High Wycombe); Cornwall v Oxon (Truro); Suffolk v Staffs (Bury St Edmunds); Wales v Devon (Cardiff).

9–Cumberland v Norfolk (Barrow).

15–Beds v Staffs (Flitwick); Bucks v Cumberland (Beaconsfield); Cheshire v Wilts (Cheadle Hulme); Cornwall v Berks (Penzance); Dorset v Wales (Bournemouth); Herts v Lincs (Long Marston); Suffolk v Cambs (Mildenhall).

22–Herefordshire v Berks (Kington); Herts v Bucks (Bishop's Stortford); Salop v Dorset (Whitchurch); Suffolk v Northumberland (Ransomes, Ipswich); Wilts v Cornwall (South Wilts CC).

23–Cheshire v Devon (Alderley Edge); Cumberland v Cambs (Netherfield).

24–Norfolk v Lincs (Manor Park, Norwich).

29–Cambs v Beds (Cambridge); Devon v Oxon (Mount Wise, Plymouth); Dorset v Cheshire (Bournemouth); Norfolk v Bucks (Manor Park, Norwich); Staffs v Cumberland (Stone); Wales v Herefordshire (Abergavenny).

AUGUST

5–Berks v Cheshire (Reading CC); Herefordshire v Devon (Luctonions CC); Norfolk v Northumberland (Manor Park, Norwich); Wilts v Salop (Corsham).

19–Beds v Herts (Luton); Berks v Dorset (Finchampstead); Bucks v Suffolk (Marlow); Cheshire v Salop (Bowdon); Devon v Cornwall (Exmouth); Lincs v Cumberland (Grantham); Northumberland v Cambs (Jesmond); Oxon v Herefordshire (Banbury); Staffs v Norfolk (Walsall); Wilts v Wales (Westbury).

SEPTEMBER

9–Final.

†ECB 38-COUNTY CUP, 2001

All matches are of one day's duration.

Teams are County Board XIs and do not include first-class counties.

MAY

13–Somerset v Devon (Taunton).

20–Beds v Cambs (Bedford Town); Dorset v Berks (Bournemouth); Hants v Sussex (Hursley Park); Kent v Bucks (Ashford); Lincs v Notts (Bourne); Northants v Norfolk (Raunds); Salop v Warwicks (Oswestry); Staffs v Derbys (Tamworth); Suffolk v Essex (Woodbridge School); Wales v Herefordshire (Pontarddulais); Wilts v Cornwall (Warminster).

22–Lancs v Cumberland (Blackpool).

27–Berks v Sussex (Hurst); Bucks v Kent (Ascott Park); Channel Islands v Hants (St Saviour, Jersey); Cornwall v Somerset (St Just); Hunts v Essex (Godmanchester); Leics v Northants (Hinckley Town); Northumberland v Lancs (Benwell Hill);

Notts v Derbys (Boots, Nottingham); Staffs v Cheshire (Longton); Worcs v Wales (Kidderminster).

28–Middx v Suffolk (Shenley Park).

30–Cheshire v Notts (New Brighton).

31–Durham v Lancs (Gateshead Fell); Yorks v Cumberland (Harrogate).

JUNE

3–Cambs v Leics (March); Cumberland v Northumberland (Keswick); Glos v Devon (Bristol University); Herts v Middx (Harpenden); Hunts v Suffolk (Papworth); Lincs v Staffs (Cleethorpes); Northants v Beds (Old Northamptonians); Oxon v Kent (Christ Church, Oxford); Salop v Wales (Wem); Sussex v Dorset (Hastings Park); Warwicks v Worcs (Stratford-upon-Avon).

7–Lancs v Yorks (Haslingden); Surrey v Oxon (Imber Court).

10–Cornwall v Glos (Cambourne); Devon v Wilts (Torquay); Essex v Herts (tba); Oxon v Surrey (Christ Church, Oxford); Warwicks v Herefordshire (Stratford-upon-Avon).

12–Durham v Yorks (Chester-le-Street).

13–Middx v Hunts (Enfield).

14–Surrey v Bucks (Imber Court).

17–Beds v Norfolk (Southill Park); Cambs v Northants (Wisbech); Cumberland v Durham (Askam); Derbys v Lincs (Derby); Hants v Dorset (Southampton); Somerset v Glos (North Perrott); Suffolk v Herts (Exning); Sussex v Channel Islands (Horsham).

19–Yorks v Northumberland (Osbaldwick).

20–Derbys v Cheshire (Heanor Town).

24–Berks v Hants (Thatcham); Bucks v Oxon (Wormsley); Devon v Cornwall (Torquay); Dorset v Channel Islands (Bournemouth SC); Essex v Middx (Chelmsford); Herefordshire v Salop (Kington); Herts v Hunts (West Herts); Kent v Surrey (Ashford); Leics v Beds (Hinckley Town); Norfolk v Cambs (Manor Park); Northumberland v Durham (Longhirst); Notts v Staffs (Boots, Nottingham); Wales v Warwicks (Pontarddulais); Wilts v Somerset (Swindon).

JULY

1–Channel Islands v Berks (St Saviour, Jersey); Norfolk v Leics (Manor Park).

8–Glos v Wilts (Bristol); Worcs v Salop (Kidderminster).

10–Cheshire v Lincs (Nantwich).

Quarter-finals to be played on July 19.

Semi-finals to be played on August 9.

Final to be played on September 4 at Lord's.

SECOND ELEVEN CHAMPIONSHIP, 2001

Unless otherwise stated, all matches are of three days' duration.

APRIL

24–Durham v Notts (Chester-le-Street; 4 days); Warwicks v Sussex (tba; 4 days).

MAY

1–Middx v Surrey (Vine Lane, Uxbridge; 4 days); Warwicks v Yorks (tba; 4 days).

2–Derbys v Worcs (Heanor); Lancs v Leics (Blackpool).

7–Durham v Leics (Chester-le-Street; 4 days).

8–Glam v Hants (Panteg; 4 days); Surrey v Kent (The Oval; 4 days).

9–Northants v Notts (Milton Keynes); Somerset v Warwicks (Taunton).

14–Surrey v Northants (Sutton).

15–Derbys v Leics (Derby; 4 days); Sussex v Hants (Hove; 4 days); Yorks v Durham (Middlesbrough; 4 days).

16–Glos v Notts (Bristol); Lancs v Glam (Crosby); Middx v Somerset (Ealing).

23–Essex v Northants (Saffron Walden); Glam v Glos (Pontarddulais); Kent v Derbys (Maidstone); Yorks v Worcs (Scarborough).

29–Notts v Warwicks (Nottingham; 4 days); Worcs v Northants (Kidderminster); Yorks v Middx (Todmorden).

30–Glos v Lancs (Cheltenham College); Somerset v Surrey (Taunton); Sussex v Leics (Hastings).

JUNE

4–Durham v Warwicks (Chester-le-Street).

5–Hants v Essex (Southampton; 4 days); Kent v Glos (Canterbury; 4 days); Lancs v Yorks (tba; 4 days); Notts v Middx (Boots, Nottingham); Sussex v Surrey (Hove; 4 days).

6–Leics v Derbys (Hinckley); Somerset v Northants (Taunton).

12–Glam v Worcs (Abergavenny; 4 days); Hants v Kent (Southampton; 4 days).

13–Derbys v Durham (Dunstall); Northants v Leics (Stowe School); Yorks v Notts (Rotherham).

19–Essex v Middx (Chelmsford; 4 days); Hants v Notts (Finchampstead; 4 days); Lancs v Derbys (Middleton; 4 days); Somerset v Glos (Taunton; 4 days).

JULY

10–Essex v Derbys (Coggeshall); Hants v Somerset (Southampton; 4 days); Leics v Yorks (Hinckley; 4 days); Northants v Sussex (Northampton; 4 days); Worcs v Glos (Kidderminster; 4 days).

16–Durham v Essex (Stockton); Surrey v Hants (The Oval; 4 days).

17–Kent v Middx (Canterbury; 4 days); Northants v Yorks (Northampton; 4 days); Notts v Lancs (Nottingham HS; 4 days); Somerset v Worcs (Taunton; 4 days).

18–Leics v Glam (Oakham School); Warwicks v Glos (tba).

23–Durham v Glos (Chester-le-Street CC).

24–Notts v Northants (Worksop College); Sussex v Somerset (Hastings; 4 days); Warwicks v Lancs (Stratford-upon-Avon; 4 days).

25–Glam v Middx (Usk); Leics v Kent (Hinckley).

31–Derbys v Yorks (Chesterfield; 4 days); Glos v Hants (Bristol; 4 days); Leics v Notts (Hinckley; 4 days); Northants v Durham (Milton Keynes; 4 days); Surrey v Glam (Whitgift School; 4 days); Sussex v Essex (Horsham; 4 days); Worcs v Warwicks (Barnt Green; 4 days).

AUGUST

8–Essex v Notts (Halstead); Glos v Surrey (Cheltenham College tbc; 4 days); Middx v Hants (Harrow); Warwicks v Derbys (tba); Worcs v Lancs (Halesowen tbc); Yorks v Kent (Harrogate).

14–Essex v Kent (Chelmsford; 4 days); Middx v Northants (Vine Lane, Uxbridge; 4 days); Warwicks v Glam (tba; 4 days); Worcs v Sussex (Worcester; 4 days).

15–Surrey v Notts (Banstead).

21–Derbys v Northants (Derby; 4 days); Glam v Somerset (Panteg; 4 days); Glos v Yorks (Hatherley & Reddings CC; 4 days); Hants v Worcs (Southampton; 4 days); Kent v Sussex (Canterbury; 4 days); Lancs v Durham (Manchester; 4 days).

22–Notts v Leics (Boots, Nottingham); Surrey v Middx (Wimbledon).

28–Glos v Glam (Bristol; 4 days); Kent v Northants (Maidstone; 4 days); Notts v Derbys (Unity Casuals CC; 4 days); Yorks v Lancs (Stamford Bridge; 4 days).

29–Leics v Somerset (Hinckley); Surrey v Essex (Guildford); Warwicks v Middx (Kenilworth); Worcs v Durham (Worcester).

SEPTEMBER

4–Northants v Surrey (Northampton; 4 days).

5–Durham v Yorks (Darlington); Glam v Derbys (Cardiff); Hants v Warwicks (Bournemouth SC); Lancs v Essex (Manchester); Middx v Glos (Ealing); Notts v Kent (Nottingham).

11–Middx v Sussex (Southgate; 4 days).

†SECOND ELEVEN TROPHY, 2001

All matches are of one day's duration.

MAY

21–Glos v Somerset (Bristol); Hants v Glam (Southampton).

24–Middx v Minor Counties (Richmond)

29–Glam v Hants (Pontarddulais).

JUNE

1–Derbys v Yorks (Glossop); MCC Young Professionals v Essex (Shenley Park).

12–Northants v Middx (Northampton); Surrey v Essex (The Oval); Yorks v Notts (York).

14–Minor Counties v Middx (Finchampstead).

15–Minor Counties v Warwicks (Finchampstead).

18–Essex v MCC Young Professionals (Old Brentwoods); Lancs v Derbys (Nelson); Worcs v Somerset (Worcester).

20–Kent v MCC Young Professionals (Tonbridge School); Warwicks v Leics (tba).

21–Minor Counties v Northants (High Wycombe).

22–Minor Counties v Leics (Marlow); Sussex v Kent (Hastings).

25–Durham v Lancs (Seaton Carew); Glam v Somerset (Newport); Hants v Worcs (Southampton); Middx v Warwicks (Ealing); Notts v Derbys (Welbeck Colliery); Sussex v Surrey (Hove).

26–Lancs v Durham (Manchester); Notts v Yorks (Unity Casuals CC); Sussex v Essex (Hove).

27–Derbys v Notts (Derby); Hants v Somerset (Southampton); Leics v Warwicks (Leicester); MCC Young Professionals v Surrey (Wormsley); Worcs v Glam (Worcester).

28–Kent v Sussex (Maidstone); Leics v Middx (Leicester); Worcs v Glos (Ombersley tbc); Yorks v Durham (Bingley).

29–Derbys v Durham (Chesterfield); Glos v Hants (Bristol); Kent v Surrey (Canterbury); Lancs v Yorks (Manchester); Northants v Leics (Northampton); Somerset v Glam (Taunton); Sussex v MCC Young Professionals (Stirlands).

JULY

1–Glos v Worcs (Bristol).

2–Kent v Essex (Folkestone); Leics v Northants (Oakham School); Notts v Durham (Nottingham); Somerset v Hants (North Perrott); Surrey v MCC Young Professionals (Banstead); Yorks v Derbys (Castleford).

3–Glam v Worcs (Neath); Lancs v Notts (Radcliffe); Middx v Northants (Ealing); Somerset v Glos (Weston-super-Mare).

4–Durham v Notts (Sunderland); Essex v Sussex (Wickford); Glam v Glos (Ebbw Vale); MCC Young Professionals v Kent (Shenley Park); Worcs v Hants (Worcester); Yorks v Lancs (Elland).

5–Durham v Derbys (South Shields); MCC Young Professionals v Sussex (Shenley Park); Middx v Leics (Finchley); Northants v Minor Counties (Stowe School).

6–Derbys v Lancs (Denby); Durham v Yorks (Darlington); Essex v Kent (Billericay); Hants v Glos (Southampton); Leics v Minor Counties (Oakham School); Surrey v Sussex (The Oval); Warwicks v Northants (tba).

9–Glos v Glam (Old Bristolians); Northants v Warwicks (Northampton); Somerset v Worcs (Clevedon); Surrey v Kent (The Oval).

10–Notts v Lancs (Caythorpe); Warwicks v Middx (West Bromwich Dartmouth).

12–Warwicks v Minor Counties (tba).

13–Essex v Surrey (Coggeshall).

Semi-finals to be played on August 6 and 7.

Final to be played on September 3 (reserve day September 4).

†WOMEN'S CRICKET, 2001

APRIL

28–tba   National Club Knockout Plate final (postponed from 2000)

JUNE

18–Southgate   MCC Invitation XI v Australians

19–Southgate   ECB Development XI v Australians

21–Radlett   ECB Development XI v Australians

24–Shenley Park   ENGLAND v AUSTRALIA (1st Test, 4 days)

29–Derby   ENGLAND v AUSTRALIA (1st one-day)

JULY

2–Northampton   ENGLAND v AUSTRALIA (2nd one-day)

3–Lord's   ENGLAND v AUSTRALIA (3rd one-day)

6–Leeds   ENGLAND v AUSTRALIA (2nd Test, 4 days)

28–Cambridge   County Championship (5 days)

AUGUST

12–Malvern   Cricket Week (6 days)

SEPTEMBER

1–Milton Keynes   Premier League final

8–tba   National Club Knockout Plate and Cup finals

INDEX OF TEST MATCHES

INDEX OF FILLERS AND INSERTS

INDEX OF ADVERTISEMENTS

Roman numerals refer to the colour section between pages 48 and 49.

INDEX OF UNUSUAL OCCURRENCES